Neu

Preiswert

Zuverlässig

Dieses neue Taschenbuch ist ein ganz außergewöhnliches Wörterbuch. Sein Inhalt basiert auf den zweisprachigen Wörterbüchern des Verlages Langenscheidt — des bedeutendsten Verlages auf diesem Gebiet. Es enthält über 40 000 Stichwörter, gibt die Aussprache in beiden Teilen in Internationaler Lautschrift und besitzt besondere Anhänge für Eigennamen, Abkürzungen und Maße und Gewichte.

Neu und einzigartig ist die Fülle der grammatischen Informationen: Mehr als 15 000 deutsche Substantive und Verben haben Angaben zur Deklination und Konjugation. Über die unregelmäßigen Verben in beiden Sprachen gibt der Hauptteil und der Anhang zuverlässig Auskunft.

Dieses Wörterbuch ist somit ein modernes und handliches Nachschlagewerk für jeden, der in seinem Beruf, beim Lernen oder Lehren mit der englischen und deutsc...

D0949073

LANGENSCHEIDTS

DEUTSCH-ENGLISCHES
ENGLISCH-DEUTSCHES
WÖRTERBUCH

Beide Teile in einem Band

Bearbeitet und herausgegeben

von der

LANGENSCHEIDT-REDAKTION

PUBLISHED BY POCKET BOOKS NEW YORK

LANGENSCHEIDT'S

GERMAN-ENGLISH
ENGLISH-GERMAN
DICTIONARY

Two Volumes in One

Edited by
THE LANGENSCHEIDT
EDITORIAL STAFF

PUBLISHED BY POCKET BOOKS NEW YORK

LANGENSCHEIDT'S GERMAN-ENGLISH ENGLISH-GERMAN DICTIONARY

POCKET BOOK edition published March, 1953

New Revised and Enlarged Edition published March, 1970

8th printing.........................August, 1974

Langenscheidt's German-English English-German Dictionary was formerly published under the imprint of Washington Square Press, a division of Simon & Schuster, Inc.

This POCKET BOOK edition may not be sold in Germany, Switzerland and Austria.

This revised and enlarged original POCKET BOOK edition is printed from brand-new plates made from newly set, clear, easy-to-read type. POCKET BOOK editions are published by POCKET BOOKS, a division of Simon & Schuster, Inc., 630 Fifth Avenue, New York, N.Y. 10020. Trademarks registered in the United States and other countries.

L

Preface

For over 100 years Langenscheidt's bilingual dictionaries have been an essential tool of the language student. For several decades Langenscheidt's German-English dictionaries have been used in all walks of life as well as in schools.

However, languages are in a constant process of change. To bring you abreast of these changes Langenscheidt has compiled this entirely new dictionary. Many new words which have entered the German and English languages in the last few years have been included in the vocabulary: e.g., Mondfähre, Mehrwertsteuer, Einwegflasche, Antirakete; lunar probe, heart transplant, non-violence.

Langenscheidt's German-English Dictionary contains another new and long desired feature for the English-speaking user: it provides clear answers to questions of declension and conjugation in over 15,000 German noun and verb entries (see pp. 7 to 8).

The phonetic transcription of the German and English headwords follows the principles laid down by the International Phonetic Association (IPA).

In addition to the vocabulary this Dictionary contains special quick-reference sections of proper names — up-to-date with names like Wankel, Mössbauer, Henze —, abbreviations and weights and measures.

Designed for the widest possible variety of uses, this Dictionary, with its more than 40,000 entries in all, will be of great value to students, teachers, and tourists as well as in home and office libraries.

Contents

Arrangement of the Dictionary and Guide for the User

1. Arrangement. Strict alphabetical order has been maintained throughout this Dictionary. The irregular plural forms of English nouns as well as the principal parts (infinitive, preterite, and past participle) of the irregular English and German verbs have also been given in their proper alphabetical order; e.g. *man - men; bite - bit - bitten; beißen - biß - gebissen*.

2. Pronunciation. Pronunciation is given in square brackets by means of the symbols of the International Phonetic Association. No transcription of compounds is given if the parts appear as separate headwords. The German suffixes as given on page 12 are not transcribed unless they are parts of catchwords.

3. Explanatory additions have been printed in italics; e.g. *abstract Inhalt* kurz zs.-fassen; *Abbau pulling down (of structure); abbauen pull down (structure); durchsichtig glass,* etc.: transparent.

4. Subject Labels. The field of knowledge from which a headword or some of its meanings are taken is, where possible, indicated by figurative or abbreviated labels or by other labels written out in full. A figurative or abbreviated label placed immediately after a headword applies to all translations. Any label preceding an individual translation refers to this only. In Part I, any abbreviated label with a colon applies to all following translations. An F placed before a German illustrative phrase or its English equivalent indicates that the phrase in question is colloquial usage. An F: placed before a German phrase applies to that phrase and its translation(s). Figurative labels have always, other labels sometimes, been placed between illustrative phrases and their translations.

5. Translations of similar meanings have been subdivided by **commas**, the various senses by **semicolons**.

6. American spelling has been given in the following ways: *theat|re, Am. -er, defen|ce, Am. -se; council(l)or, hono(u)r, judg(e)ment; plough, Am. plow.*

7. Grammatical References in Part I. Parts of speech (adjective, verb, etc.) have been indicated throughout. Entries have been subdivided by Arabic numerals to distinguish the various parts of speech.

I. Nouns. The inflectional forms *(genitive singular / nominative plural)* follow immediately after the indication of gender. No forms are given for compounds if the parts appear as separate headwords.

The horizontal stroke replaces that part of the word which remains unchanged in the inflexion: *Affe m (-n/-n); Affäre f (-/-n).*

The sign ⸗ indicates that an Umlaut appears in the inflected form in question: *Blatt n (-[e]s/⸗er).*

II. Verbs. Verbs have been treated in the following ways:

a) *bändigen* v/t. *(ge-, h):* The past participle of this verb is formed by means of the prefix *ge-* and the auxiliary verb *haben: er hat gebändigt.*

b) *abfassen* v/t. *(sep., -ge-, h):* In conjugation the prefix *ab* must be separated from the primary verb *fassen: er faßt ab; er hat abgefaßt.*

c) *verderben* v/i. *(irr., no -ge-, sein): irr.* following the verb refers the reader to the list of irregular German verbs in the appendix (p. 573) for the principal parts of this particular verb: *es verdarb; es ist verdorben.*

d) *abfallen* v/i. *(irr. fallen, sep., -ge-, sein):* A reference such as *irr. fallen* indicates that the compound verb *abfallen* is conjugated exactly like the primary verb *fallen* as given in the list of irregular verbs: *er fiel ab; er ist abgefallen.*

e) *sieden* v/t. and v/i. *([irr.,] ge-, h):* The square brackets indicate that *sieden* can be treated as a regular or irregular verb: *er siedete or er sott; er hat gesiedet or er hat gesotten.*

III. Prepositions. Prepositions governing a headword are given in both languages. The grammatical construction following a German preposition is indicated only if the preposition governs two different cases. If a German preposition applies to all translations it is given only with the first whereas its English equivalents are given after each translation: *schützen* ... protect (*gegen, vor dat.* against, from), defend (against, from), guard (against, from); shelter (from).

IV. Subdivision. Entries have been subdivided by Arabic numerals

a) to distinguish the various parts of speech: *laut 1. adj.* ...; *2. adv.* ...; *3. prp.* ...; *4. ♀ m* ...;

b) to distinguish between the transitive and intransitive meanings of a verb if these differ in their translations;

c) to show that in case of change of meaning a noun or verb may be differently inflected or conjugated: *Bau m* 1. (-[e]s/*no pl.*)...; 2. (-[e]s/-ten) ...; 3. (-[e]s/-e) ...; *schwimmen v/i.* (*irr.*, ge-) 1. (*sein*) ...; 2. (*h*) ...

If grammatical indications come before the subdivision they refer to all translations following: *Alte* (-*n*/-*n*) 1. *m* ...; 2. *f* ...; *humpeln v/i.* (ge-) 1. (*sein*) ...; 2. (*h*) ...

8. Grammatical References in Part II. Parts of speech (adjective, verb, etc.) have been indicated only in cases of doubt. Entries have been subdivided by Arabic numerals to distinguish the various parts of speech.

a) (~*ally*) after an English adjective means that the adverb is formed by affixing ...ally: *automatic* (~*ally*) = *automatically*.

b) *irr.* following a verb refers the reader to the list of irregular English verbs in the appendix (p. 575) for the principal parts of this particular verb. A reference such as *irr. fall* indicates that the compound verb, e.g. *befall*, is conjugated exactly like the primary verb *fall*.

Symbols and Abbreviations Used in This Dictionary

1. Symbols

The swung dash or tilde (~ ♀, ~ ♀) serves as a mark of repetition within an entry. The tilde in bold type (~) represents either the complete word at the beginning of the entry or the unchanged part of that word which is followed by a vertical line (|). The simple tilde (~) represents: a) the headword immediately preceding, which itself may contain a tilde in bold type; b) in phonetic transcription, any part of the preceding transcription that remains unchanged.

When the initial letter changes from small to capital or vice versa, the usual tilde is replaced by ♀ or ♀.

Examples: *abandon* [ə'bændən], ~*ment* [~nmənt = ə'bændənmənt]; *certi|ficate*, ~*fication*, ~*fy*, ~*tude*. *Drama*, ~*tiker*, ♀*tisch*; *Haus|flur*, ~*frau*; *fassen: sich kurz* ~.

☐ after an English adjective means that an adverb may be formed regularly from it by adding ...*ly*, or by changing ...*le* into ...*ly*, or ...*y* into ...*ily*; e.g.: *rich* ☐ = *richly*; *acceptable* ☐ = *acceptably*; *happy* ☐ = *happily*.

F   *familiar*, familiär; *colloquial usage*, Umgangssprache.

P   *low colloquialism*, populär, Sprache des Volkes.

V   *vulgar*, vulgär.

†   *archaic*, veraltet.

⚒   *rare, little used*, selten.

🕮   *scientific term*, wissenschaftlich.

♣   *botany*, Botanik.

⊕   *engineering*, Technik; *handicraft*, Handwerk.

⚒   *mining*, Bergbau.

⚔   *military term*, militärisch.

⚓   *nautical term*, Schiffahrt.

†   *commercial term*, Handelswesen.

🚂   *railway, railroad*, Eisenbahn.

✈   *aviation*, Flugwesen.

✉   *postal affairs*, Postwesen.

♪ *musical term*, Musik.

△ *architecture*, Architektur.

⚡ *electrical engineering*, Elektrotechnik.

⚖ *legal term*, Rechtswissenschaft.

♈ *mathematics* Mathematik.

⚵ *farming*, Landwirtschaft.

♎ *chemistry*, Chemie.

♐ *medicine*, Medizin.

2. Abbreviations

a.   *also*, auch.

abbr.   *abbreviation*, Abkürzung.

acc.   *accusative (case)*, Akkusativ.

adj.   *adjective*, Adjektiv.

adv.   *adverb*, Adverb.

allg.   *commonly*, allgemein.

Am.   *American English*, amerikanisches Englisch.

anat.   *anatomy*, Anatomie.

appr.   *approximately*, etwa.

art.   *article*, Artikel.

ast.   *astronomy*, Astronomie.

attr.   *attributively*, attributiv.

biol.   *biology*, Biologie.

Brt.   *British English*, britisches Englisch.

b.s.   *bad sense*, in schlechtem Sinne.

bsd.   *especially*, besonders.

cj.   *conjunction*, Konjunktion.

co.   *comic(al)*, scherzhaft.

coll.   *collectively*, als Sammelwort.

comp.   *comparative*, Komparativ.

contp.   *contemptuously*, verächtlich.

dat.   *dative (case)*, Dativ.

dem.   *demonstrative*, Demonstrativ...

ea.   *one another, each other*, einander.

eccl.   *ecclesiastical*, kirchlich.

e-e, e-e, e-e a(n), eine.

e-m, e-m, e-m to a(n), einem.

e-n, e-n, e-n a(n), einen.

engS.   *more strictly taken*, in engerem Sinne.

e-r, e-r, e-r of a(n), to a(n), einer.

e-s, e-s, e-s of a(n), eines.

esp.   *especially*, besonders.

et., et., et. something, etwas.

etc.   *et cetera, and so on*, und so weiter.

f   *feminine*, weiblich.

fig.   *figuratively*, bildlich.

frz.   *French*, französisch.

gen.   *genitive (case)*. Genitiv.

geogr.   *geography*, Geographie.

geol.   *geology*, Geologie.

geom.   *geometry*, Geometrie.

ger.   *gerund*, Gerundium.

Ggs.   *antonym*, Gegensatz.

gr.   *grammar*, Grammatik.

h   *have*, haben.

hist.   *history*, Geschichte.

hunt.   *hunting*, Jagdwesen.

ichth.   *ichthyology*, Ichthyologie.

impers.   *impersonal*, unpersönlich.

indef.   *indefinite*, Indefinit...

inf.   *infinitive (mood)*, Infinitiv.

int.   *interjection*, Interjektion.

interr.   *interrogative*, Interrogativ...

iro.   *ironically*, ironisch.

irr.   *irregular*, unregelmäßig.

j., j., j. someone, jemand.

j-m, j-m, j-m to s.o. jemandem.

j-n, j-n, j-n someone, jemanden.

j-s, j-s, j-s, someone's, jemandes.

konkr.   *concretely*, konkret.

ling.   *linguistics*, Linguistik.

lit.   *literary*, nur in der Schriftsprache vorkommend.

m   *masculine*, männlich.

m-e, m-e, m-e my, meine.

m-r   *of my, to my*, meiner.

metall.   *metallurgy*, Metallurgie.

meteor.   *meteorology*, Meteorologie.

min.   *mineralogy*, Mineralogie.

mot.   *motoring*, Kraftfahrwesen.

mount.   *mountaineering*, Bergsteigerei.

mst   *mostly, usually*, meistens.

myth.   *mythology*, Mythologie.

n   *neuter*, sächlich.

nom.   *nominative (case)*, Nominativ.

npr.   *proper name*, Eigenname.

od.   *or*, oder.

opt.   *optics*, Optik.

orn.	*ornithology*, Ornithologie.
o.s.	*oneself*, sich.
P.,	*person*, Person.
p.	*person*, Person.
paint.	*painting*, Malerei.
parl.	*parliamentary term*, parlamentarischer Ausdruck.
pass.	*passive voice*, Passiv.
pers.	*personal*, Personal...
pharm.	*pharmacy*, Pharmazie.
phls.	*philosophy*, Philosophie.
phot.	*photography*, Photographie.
phys.	*physics*, Physik.
physiol.	*physiology*, Physiologie.
pl.	*plural*, Plural.
poet.	*poetry*, Dichtung.
pol.	*politics*, Politik.
poss.	*possessive*, Possessiv...
p.p.	*past participle*, Partizip Perfekt.
p.pr.	*present participle*, Partizip Präsens.
pred.	*predicative*, prädikativ.
pres.	*present*, Präsens.
pret.	*preterit(e)*, Präteritum.
pron.	*pronoun*, Pronomen.
prov.	*provincialism*, Provinzialismus.
prp.	*preposition*, Präposition.
psych.	*psychology*, Psychologie.
refl.	*reflexive*, reflexiv.
rel.	*relative*, Relativ...
rhet.	*rhetoric*, Rhetorik.
S., S.	*thing*, Sache.
s.	*see, refer to*, siehe.
schott.	*Scotch*, schottisch.
s-e, s-e,	*s-e his*, one's, seine.
sep.	*separable*, abtrennbar.
sg.	*singular*, Singular.

sl.	*slang*, Slang.
s-m, s-m,	*s-m to his, to one's*, seinem.
s-n, s-n,	*s-n his, one's*, seinen.
s.o., s.o.,	*s.o. someone*, jemand(en).
s-r, s-r,	*s-r of his, of one's, to his, to one's*, seiner.
s-s, s-s,	*s-s of his, of one's*, seines.
s.th., s.th.,	*s.th. something*, etwas.
subj.	*subjunctive (mood)*, Konjunktiv.
sup.	*superlative*, Superlativ.
surv.	*surveying*, Landvermessung.
tel.	*telegraphy*, Telegraphie.
teleph.	*telephony*, Fernsprechwesen.
thea.	*theat|re, Am. -er*, Theater.
typ.	*typography*, Typographie.
u., u.	*and*, und.
univ.	*university*, Hochschulwesen, Studentensprache.
v/aux.	*auxiliary verb*, Hilfsverb.
vb.	*verb*, Verb.
vet.	*veterinary medicine*, Veterinärmedizin.
vgl.	*confer*, vergleiche.
v/i.	*verb intransitive*, intransitives Verb.
v/refl.	*verb reflexive*, reflexives Verb.
v/t.	*verb transitive*, transitives Verb.
weitS.	*more widely taken*, in weiterem Sinne.
z.B.	*for example*, zum Beispiel.
zo.	*zoology*, Zoologie.
zs.	*together*, zusammen.
Zssg(n).	*compound word(s)*, Zusammensetzung(en).

Guide to Pronunciation
for the German-English Part

The length of vowels is indicated by [:] following the vowel symbol, the stress by ['] preceding the stressed syllable. The glottal stop [ʔ] is the forced stop between one word or syllable and a following one beginning with a vowel, as in *unentbehrlich* [unʔɛnt'be:rliç].

A. Vowels

[a] as in French *carte*: Mann [man].

[ɑ:] as in *father*: Wagen ['vɑ:gən].

[e] as in *bed*: Edikt [e'dikt].

[e:] resembles the sound in *day*: Weg [ve:k].

[ə] unstressed e as in *ago*: Bitte ['bitə].

[ɛ] as in *fair*: männlich ['mɛnliç], Geld [gɛlt].

[ɛ:] same sound but long: zählen ['tsɛ:lən].

[i] as in *it*: Wind [vint].

[i:] as in *meet*: hier [hi:r].

[ɔ] as in *long*: Ort [ɔrt].

[ɔ:] same sound but long as in *draw*: Komfort [kɔm'fɔ:r].

[o] as in *molest*: Moral [mo'rɑ:l].

[o:] resembles the English sound in *go* [gou] but without the [u]: Boot [bo:t].

[ø:] as in French *feu*. The sound may be acquired by saying [e] through closely rounded lips: schön [ʃø:n].

[ø] same sound but short: Ökonomie [økono'mi:].

[œ] as in French *neuf*. The sound resembles the English vowel in *her*. Lips, however, must be well rounded as for [ɔ]: öffnen ['œfnən].

[u] as in *book*: Mutter ['mutər].

[u:] as in *boot*: Uhr [u:r].

[y] almost like the French u as in *sur*. It may be acquired by saying [i] through fairly closely rounded lips: Glück [glyk].

[y:] same sound but long: führen ['fy:rən].

B. Diphthongs

[aɪ] as in *like*: Mai [maɪ].
[aʊ] as in *mouse*: Maus [maʊs].

[ɔʏ] as in *boy*: Beute ['bɔʏtə], Läufer ['lɔʏfər].

C. Consonants

[b] as in *better*: besser ['bɛsər].

[d] as in *dance*: du [du:].

[f] as in *find*: finden ['findən], Vater ['fɑ:tər], Philosoph [filo'zo:f].

[g] as in *gold*: Gold [gɔlt], Geld [gɛlt].

[ʒ] as in *measure*: Genie [ʒe'ni:], Journalist [ʒurna'list].

[h] as in *house* but not aspirated: Haus [haʊs].

[ç] an approximation to this sound may be acquired by assuming the mouth-configuration for [i] and emitting a strong current of breath: Licht [liçt], Mönch [mœnç], lustig ['lustiç].

[x] as in Scotch *loch*. Whereas [ç] is pronounced at the front of the mouth, [x] is pronounced in the throat: Loch [lɔx].

[j] as in *year*: ja [jɑ:].

[k] as in *kick*: keck [kɛk], Tag [tɑ:k], Chronist [kro'nist], Café [ka'fe:].

[l] as in *lump*. Pronounced like English initial "clear l": lassen ['lasən].

[m] as in *mouse*: Maus [maʊs].

[n] as in *not*: nein [naɪn].

[ŋ] as in *sing*, *drink*: singen ['ziŋən], trinken ['triŋkən].

[p] as in *pass*: Paß [pas], Weib [vaɪp], obgleich [ɔp'glaɪç].

[r] as in *rot*. There are two pronunciations: the frontal or lingual r and the uvular r (the latter unknown in England): *rot* [roːt].

[s] as in *miss*. Unvoiced when final, doubled, or next a voiceless consonant: *Glas* [glɑːs], *Masse* ['masə], *Mast* [mast], *naß* [nas].

[z] as in *zero*. S voiced when initial in a word or syllable: *Sohn* [zoːn], *Rose* ['roːzə].

[ʃ] as in *ship*: *Schiff* [ʃif], *Charme* [ʃarm], *Spiel* [ʃpiːl], *Stein* [ʃtaɪn].

[t] as in *tea*: *Tee* [teː], *Thron* [troːn], *Stadt* [ʃtat], *Bad* [baːt], *Findling* ['fintliŋ], *Wind* [vint].

[v] as in *vast*: *Vase* ['vɑːzə], *Winter* ['vintər].

[ă, ĕ, ŏ] are nasalized vowels. Examples: *Ensemble* [ă'sãːbəl], *Terrain* [tɛ'rɛ̃ː], *Bonbon* [bŏ'bŏː].

List of Suffixes

often given without phonetic transcription

-bar	[-bɑːr]	-ist	[-ist]
-chen	[-çən]	-keit	[-kaɪt]
-d	[-t]	-lich	[-liç]
-de	[-də]	-ling	[-liŋ]
-ei	[-aɪ]	-losigkeit	[-loːziçkaɪt]
-en	[-ən]	-nis	[-nis]
-end	[-ənt]	-sal	[-zɑːl]
-er	[-ər]	-sam	[-zɑːm]
-haft	[-haft]	-schaft	[-ʃaft]
-heit	[-haɪt]	-sieren	[-ziːrən]
-ie	[-iː]	-ste	[-stə]
-ieren	[-iːrən]	-tät	[-tɛːt]
-ig	[-iç]	-tum	[-tuːm]
-ik	[-ik]	-ung	[-uŋ]
-in	[-in]	-ungs-	[-uŋs-]
-isch	[-iʃ]		

Erläuterung der phonetischen Umschrift im englisch-deutschen Teil

A. Vokale und Diphthonge

[ɑː] reines langes a, wie in Vater, kam, Schwan: *far* [fɑː], *father* ['fɑːðə].

[ʌ] kommt im Deutschen nicht vor. Kurzes dunkles a, bei dem die Lippen nicht gerundet sind. Vorn und offen gebildet: *butter* ['bʌtə], *come* [kʌm], *colour* ['kʌlə], *blood* [blʌd], *flourish* ['flʌriʃ], *twopence* ['tʌpəns].

[æ] heller, ziemlich offener, nicht zu kurzer Laut. Raum zwischen Zunge und Gaumen noch größer als bei ä in Ähre: *fat* [fæt], *man* [mæn].

[ɛə] nicht zu offenes halblanges ä; im Englischen nur vor r, das als ein dem ä nachhallendes ə erscheint: *bare* [bɛə], *pair* [pɛə], *there* [ðɛə].

[ai] Bestandteile: helles, zwischen ɑː und æ liegendes a und schwächeres offenes i. Die Zunge hebt sich halbwegs zur i-Stellung: *I* [ai], *lie* [lai], *dry* [drai].

[au] Bestandteile: helles, zwischen ɑː und æ liegendes a und schwächeres offenes u: *house* [haus], *now* [nau].

[ei] halboffenes e, nach i auslautend, indem die Zunge sich halbwegs zur i-Stellung hebt: *date* [deit], *play* [plei], *obey* [əˈbei].

[e] halboffenes kurzes e, etwas geschlossener als das e in Bett: *bed* [bed], *less* [les].

[ə] flüchtiger Gleitlaut, ähnlich dem deutschen flüchtig gesprochenen e in Gelage: *about* [əˈbaut], *butter* ['bʌtə], *nation* ['neiʃən], *connect* [kəˈnekt].

[iː] langes i wie in lieb, Bibel, aber etwas offener einsetzend als im Deutschen; wird in Südengland doppellautig gesprochen, indem sich die Zunge allmählich zur i-Stellung hebt: *scene* [siːn], *sea* [siː], *feet* [fiːt], *ceiling* ['siːliŋ].

[i] kurzes offenes i wie in bin, mit: *big* [big], *city* ['siti].

[iə] halboffenes halblanges i mit nachhallendem ə: *here* [hiə], *hear* [hiə], *inferior* [inˈfiəriə].

[ou] halboffenes langes o, in schwaches u auslautend; keine Rundung der Lippen, kein Heben der Zunge: *note* [nout], *boat* [bout], *below* [biˈlou].

[ɔː] offener langer, zwischen a und o schwebender Laut: *fall* [fɔːl], *nought* [nɔːt], *or* [ɔː], *before* [biˈfɔː].

[ɔ] offener kurzer, zwischen a und o schwebender Laut, offener als das o in Motto: *god* [gɔd], *not* [nɔt], *wash* [wɔʃ], *hobby* ['hɔbi].

[əː] im Deutschen fehlender Laut; offenes langes ö, etwa wie gedehnt gesprochenes ö in öffnen, Mörder; kein Vorstülpen oder Runden der Lippen, kein Heben der Zunge: *word* [wəːd], *girl* [gəːl], *learn* [ləːn], *murmur* ['məːmə].

[ɔi] Bestandteile: offenes o und schwächeres offenes i. Die Zunge hebt sich halbwegs zur i-Stellung: *voice* [vɔis], *boy* [bɔi], *annoy* [əˈnɔi].

[uː] langes u wie in Buch, doch ohne Lippenrundung; vielfach diphthongisch als halboffenes langes u mit nachhallendem geschlossenen u: *fool* [fuːl], *shoe* [ʃuː], *you* [juː], *rule* [ruːl], *canoe* [kəˈnuː].

[uə] halboffenes halblanges u mit nachhallendem ə: *poor* [puə], *sure* [ʃuə], *allure* [əˈljuə].

[u] flüchtiges u: *put* [put], *look* [luk], *full* [ful].

Die **Länge eines Vokals** wird durch [ː] bezeichnet, z.B. *ask* [ɑːsk], *astir* [əˈstəː].

Vereinzelt werden auch die folgenden französischen Nasallaute gebraucht: [ã] wie in frz. *blanc*, [ɔ̃] wie in frz. *bonbon* und [ɛ̃] wie in frz. *vin*.

B. Konsonanten

[r] nur vor Vokalen gesprochen. Völlig verschieden vom deutschen Zungenspitzen- oder Zäpfchen-r. Die Zungenspitze bildet mit der oberen Zahnwulst eine Enge, durch die der Ausatmungsstrom mit Stimmton hindurchgetrieben wird, ohne den Laut zu rollen. Am Ende eines Wortes wird r nur bei Bindung mit dem Anlautvokal des folgenden Wortes gesprochen: *rose* [rouz], *pride* [praid], *there is* [ðɛərˈiz].

[ʒ] stimmhaftes sch, wie g in Genie, j in Journal: *azure* [ˈæʒə], *jazz* [dʒæz], *jeep* [dʒi:p], *large* [lɑ:dʒ].

[ʃ] stimmloses sch, wie im Deutschen Schnee, rasch: *shake* [ʃeik], *washing* [ˈwɔʃiŋ], *lash* [læʃ].

[θ] im Deutschen nicht vorhandener stimmloser Lispellaut; durch Anlegen der Zunge an die oberen Schneidezähne hervorgebracht: *thin* [θin], *path* [pɑ:θ], *method* [ˈmeθəd].

[ð] derselbe Laut wie θ, nur stimmhaft, d.h. mit Stimmton: *there* [ðɛə], *breathe* [bri:ð], *father* [ˈfɑ:ðə].

[s] stimmloser Zischlaut, entsprechend dem deutschen ß in Spaß, reißen: *see* [si:], *hats* [hæts], *decide* [diˈsaid].

[z] stimmhafter Zischlaut wie im Deutschen sausen: *zeal* [zi:l], *rise* [raiz], *horizon* [həˈraizn].

[ŋ] wird wie der deutsche Nasenlaut in fangen, singen gebildet: *ring* [riŋ], *singer* [ˈsiŋə].

[ŋk] derselbe Laut mit nachfolgendem k wie im Deutschen senken, Wink: *ink* [iŋk], *tinker* [ˈtiŋkə].

[w] flüchtiges, mit Lippe an Lippe gesprochenes w, aus der Mundstellung für u: gebildet: *will* [wil], *swear* [swɛə], *queen* [kwi:n].

[f] stimmloser Lippenlaut wie im Deutschen flott, Pfeife: *fat* [fæt], *tough* [tʌf], *effort* [ˈefət].

[v] stimmhafter Lippenlaut wie im Deutschen Vase, Ventil: *vein* [vein], *velvet* [ˈvelvit].

[j] flüchtiger zwischen j und i schwebender Laut: *onion* [ˈʌnjən], *yes* [jes], *filial* [ˈfiljəl].

Die Betonung der englischen Wörter wird durch das Zeichen [ˈ] vor der zu betonenden Silbe angegeben, z.B. *onion* [ˈʌnjən]. Sind zwei Silben eines Wortes mit Tonzeichen versehen, so sind beide gleichmäßig zu betonen, z.B. *unsound* [ˈʌnˈsaund].

Um Raum zu sparen, werden die Endung -ed* und das Plural-s** der englischen Stichwörter hier im Vorwort einmal mit Lautschrift gegeben, erscheinen dann aber im Wörterverzeichnis ohne Lautschrift, sofern keine Ausnahmen vorliegen.

* [-d] nach Vokalen und stimmhaften Konsonanten; [-t] nach stimmlosen Konsonanten; [-id] nach auslautendem d und t.

** [-z] nach Vokalen und stimmhaften Konsonanten; [-s] nach stimmlosen Konsonanten.

Numerals

Cardinal Numbers

0 null *nought, zero, cipher*	51 einundfünfzig *fifty-one*
1 eins *one*	60 sechzig *sixty*
2 zwei *two*	61 einundsechzig *sixty-one*
3 drei *three*	70 siebzig *seventy*
4 vier *four*	71 einundsiebzig *seventy-one*
5 fünf *five*	80 achtzig *eighty*
6 sechs *six*	81 einundachtzig *eighty-one*
7 sieben *seven*	90 neunzig *ninety*
8 acht *eight*	91 einundneunzig *ninety-one*
9 neun *nine*	100 hundert *a or one hundred*
10 zehn *ten*	101 hundert(und)eins *a hundred and one*
11 elf *eleven*	200 zweihundert *two hundred*
12 zwölf *twelve*	300 dreihundert *three hundred*
13 dreizehn *thirteen*	572 fünfhundert(und)zweiund-siebzig *five hundred and seventy-two*
14 vierzehn *fourteen*	1000 tausend *a or one thousand*
15 fünfzehn *fifteen*	1972 neunzehnhundertzweiund-siebzig *nineteen hundred and seventy-two*
16 sechzehn *sixteen*	
17 siebzehn *seventeen*	
18 achtzehn *eighteen*	
19 neunzehn *nineteen*	500 000 fünfhunderttausend *five hundred thousand*
20 zwanzig *twenty*	1 000 000 eine Million *a or one million*
21 einundzwanzig *twenty-one*	
22 zweiundzwanzig *twenty-two*	2 000 000 zwei Millionen *two million*
23 dreiundzwanzig *twenty-three*	
30 dreißig *thirty*	1 000 000 000 eine Milliarde *a or one milliard (Am. billion)*
31 einunddreißig *thirty-one*	
40 vierzig *forty*	
41 einundvierzig *forty-one*	
50 fünfzig *fifty*	

Ordinal Numbers

1. erste *first (1st)*	16. sechzehnte *sixteenth*
2. zweite *second (2nd)*	17. siebzehnte *seventeenth*
3. dritte *third (3rd)*	18. achtzehnte *eighteenth*
4. vierte *fourth (4th)*	19. neunzehnte *nineteenth*
5. fünfte *fifth (5th), etc.*	20. zwanzigste *twentieth*
6. sechste *sixth*	21. einundzwanzigste *twenty-first*
7. siebente *seventh*	22. zweiundzwanzigste *twenty-second*
8. achte *eighth*	
9. neunte *ninth*	23. dreiundzwanzigste *twenty-third*
10. zehnte *tenth*	
11. elfte *eleventh*	30. dreißigste *thirtieth*
12. zwölfte *twelfth*	31. einunddreißigste *thirty-first*
13. dreizehnte *thirteenth*	40. vierzigste *fortieth*
14. vierzehnte *fourteenth*	41. einundvierzigste *forty-first*
15. fünfzehnte *fifteenth*	50. fünfzigste *fiftieth*

51. einundfünfzigste *fifty-first*
60. sechzigste *sixtieth*
61. einundsechzigste *sixty-first*
70. siebzigste *seventieth*
71. einundsiebzigste *seventy-first*
80. achtzigste *eightieth*
81. einundachtzigste *eighty-first*
90. neunzigste *ninetieth*
100. hundertste (*one*) *hundredth*
101. hundert(und)erste (*one*) *hundred and first*
200. zweihundertste *two hundredth*

300. dreihundertste *three hundredth*
572. fünfhundert(und)zweiund-siebzigste *five hundred and seventy-second*
1000. tausendste (*one*) *thousandth*
1970. neunzehnhundert(und)sieb-zigste *nineteen hundred and seventieth*
500000. fünfhunderttausendste *five hundred thousandth*
1000000. millionste (*one*) *millionth*
2000000. zweimillionste *two millionth*

Fractional Numbers and other Numerical Values

$1/2$ halb *one* or *a half*
$1/2$ eine halbe Meile *half a mile*
$1 1/2$ anderthalb or eineinhalb *one and a half*
$2 1/2$ zweieinhalb *two and a half*
$1/3$ ein Drittel *one* or *a third*
$2/3$ zwei Drittel *two thirds*
$1/4$ ein Viertel *one fourth, one* or *a quarter*
$3/4$ drei Viertel *three fourths, three quarters*
$1 1/4$ ein und eine viertel Stunde *one hour and a quarter*
$1/5$ ein Fünftel *one* or *a fifth*
$3 4/5$ drei vier Fünftel *three and four fifths*
0,4 null Komma vier *point four (.4)*
2,5 zwei Komma fünf *two point five (2.5)*

einfach *single*
  zweifach *double, twofold*
  dreifach *threefold, treble, triple*
  vierfach *fourfold, quadruple*
  fünffach *fivefold, quintuple*

einmal *once*
  zweimal *twice*
  drei-, vier-, fünfmal *three* or *four* or *five times*
  zweimal soviel(e) *twice as much* or *many*

erstens, zweitens, drittens *first(ly), secondly, thirdly; in the first* or *second* or *third place*

$2 \times 3 = 6$ zwei mal drei ist sechs, zwei multipliziert mit drei ist sechs *twice three are* or *make six, two multiplied by three are* or *make six*

$7 + 8 = 15$ sieben plus acht ist fünfzehn *seven plus eight are fifteen*

$10 - 3 = 7$ zehn minus drei ist sieben *ten minus three are seven*

$20 : 5 = 4$ zwanzig (dividiert) durch fünf ist vier *twenty divided by five make four*

PART I

GERMAN-ENGLISH
DICTIONARY

A

Aal *ichth.* [a:l] *m* (-[e]s/-e) eel; '~-
'glatt *adj.* (as) slippery as an eel.
Aas [a:s] *n* **1.** (-es/~x-e) carrion,
carcass; **2.** *fig.* (-es/Äser) beast;
'~geier *orn.* *m* vulture.
ab [ap] **1.** *prp. (dat.):* ~ Brüssel from
Brussels onwards; ~ Fabrik, Lager
etc. ✝ ex works, warehouse, *etc.*;
2. *prp. (dat.,* F *acc.):* ~ erstem *or*
ersten März from March 1st, on
and after March 1st; **3.** ✝ *prp. (gen.)*
less; ~ Unkosten less charges; **4.** *adv.*
time: von jetzt ~ from now on, in
future; ~ und zu from time to time,
now and then; von da ~ from that
time forward; *space: thea.* exit, *pl.*
exeunt; von da ~ from there
(on).
abänder|n ['ap⁹-] *v/t. (sep., -ge-, h)*
alter, modify; *parl.* amend; '2ung
f alteration, modification; *parl.*
amendment *(to bill, etc.);* '2ungs-
antrag *parl. m* amendment.
abarbeiten ['ap⁹-] *v/t. (sep., -ge-, h)*
work off *(debt);* sich ~ drudge, toil.
Abart ['ap⁹-] *f* variety.
'**Abbau** *m* **1.** (-[e]s/no *pl.)* pulling
down, demolition *(of structure);*
dismantling *(of machine, etc.);* dismissal, discharge *(of personnel);*
reduction *(of staff, prices, etc.);*
cut *(of prices, etc.);* **2.** ⚒ (-[e]s/-e)
working, exploitation; '2en *v/t.*
(sep., -ge-, h) pull *or* take down,
demolish *(structure);* dismantle
(machine, etc.); dismiss, discharge
(personnel); reduce *(staff, prices,
etc.);* cut *(prices, etc.);* ⚒ work,
exploit.
'**ab|beißen** *v/t. (irr. beißen, sep.,
-ge-, h)* bite off; '~bekommen *v/t.*
(irr. kommen, sep., no -ge-, h) get
off; s-n Teil *or* s. ~ get one's share;
et. ~ be hurt, get hurt.
abberuf|en *v/t. (irr. rufen, sep., no
-ge-, h)* recall; '2ung *f* recall.
'**ab|bestellen** *v/t. (sep., no -ge-, h)*
countermand, cancel one's order
for *(goods, etc.);* cancel one's subscription to, discontinue *(newspaper, etc.);* '~biegen *v/i. (irr. biegen, sep., -ge-, sein)* p. turn off;
road: turn off, bend; *nach beides
(links)* ~ turn right (left); von e-r
Straße ~ turn off a road.
'**Abbild** *n* likeness; image; 2en
['~don] *v/t. (sep., -ge-, h)* figure,
represent; sie ist auf der ersten
Seite abgebildet her picture is on
the front page; ~ung ['~duŋ] *f*
picture, illustration.
'**abbinden** *v/t. (irr. binden, sep.,*

-ge-, h) untie, unbind, remove; ⚕
ligate, tie up.
'**Abbitte** *f* apology; ~ leisten *or* tun
make one's apology *(bei j-m wegen
et.* to s.o. for s.th.); '2n *v/t. (irr.
bitten, sep., -ge-, h):* j-m et. ~
apologize to s.o. for s.th.
'**ab|blasen** *v/t. (irr. blasen, sep.,
-ge-, h)* blow off *(dust, etc.);* call
off *(strike, etc.),* cancel; ✗ break
off *(attack);* '~blättern *v/i. (sep.,
-ge-, sein)* paint, *etc.:* scale, peel
(off); ⚕ *skin:* desquamate; ⚘ shed
the leaves; '~blenden *(sep., -ge-, h)*
1. *v/t.* screen *(light);* mot. dim, dip
(headlights); **2.** *v/i.* mot. dim *or* dip
the headlights; *phot.* stop down;
'~blitzen F *v/i. (sep., -ge-, sein)*
meet with a rebuff; ~ lassen snub;
'~brausen *(sep., -ge-)* **1.** *v/refl.* (h)
have a shower-(bath), douche; **2.** F
v/i. (sein) rush off; '~brechen *(irr.
brechen, sep., -ge-)* **1.** *v/t.* (h) break
off *(a. fig.);* pull down, demolish
(building, etc.); strike *(tent);* *fig.*
stop; das Lager ~ break up camp,
strike tents; **2.** *v/i. (sein)* break off;
3. *fig. v/i.* (h) stop; '~bremsen *v/t.*
and *v/i. (sep., -ge-, h)* slow down;
brake; '~brennen *(irr. brennen,
sep., -ge-)* **1.** *v/t.* (h) burn down
(building, etc.); let *or* set off *(firework);* **2.** *v/i. (sein)* burn away *or*
down; s. abgebrannt; '~bringen
v/t. (irr. bringen, sep., -ge-, h) get
off; j-n ~ von argue s.o. out of;
dissuade s.o. from; '~bröckeln *v/i.
(sep., -ge-, sein)* crumble *(a.* ✝).
'**Abbruch** *m* pulling down, demolition *(of building, etc.);* rupture *(of
relations);* breaking off *(of negotia-
tions, etc.);* *fig.* damage, injury; j-m
~ tun damage s.o.
'**ab|brühen** *v/t. (sep., -ge-, h)*
scald; s. abgebrüht; '~bürsten *v/t.
(sep., -ge-, h)* brush off *(dirt, etc.);*
brush *(coat, etc.);* '~büßen *v/t.
(sep., -ge-, h)* expiate, atone for
(sin, etc.); serve *(sentence).* [bet.⟩
Abc [a:be'tse:] *n* (-/-) ABC, alpha-⟩
'**abdank|en** *v/i. (sep., -ge-, h)* re-
sign; *ruler:* abdicate; '2ung *f* (-/-en)
resignation; abdication.
'**ab|decken** *v/t. (sep., -ge-, h)* un-
cover; untile *(roof);* unroof *(building);* clear *(table);* cover; '~dichten
v/t. (sep., -ge-, h) make tight; seal
up *(window, etc.);* ⊕ pack *(gland,
etc.);* '~dienen *v/t. (sep., -ge-, h):*
s-e Zeit ~ ✗ serve one's time;
'~drängen *v/t. (sep., -ge-, h)* push
aside; '~drehen *(sep., -ge-, h)*

2*

1. v/t. twist off (wire); turn off (water, gas, etc.); ⚡ switch off (light); **2.** ⚓, 🚗 v/i. change one's course; '**.drosseln** mot. v/t. (sep., -ge-, h) throttle.

'**Abdruck** m (-[e]s/⁼e) impression, print, mark; cast; '**2en** v/t. (sep., -ge-, h) print; publish (article).

'**abdrücken** (sep., -ge-, h) **1.** v/t. fire (gun, etc.); F hug or squeeze affectionately; sich ~ leave an impression or a mark; **2.** v/i. pull the trigger.

Abend ['a:bənt] m (-s/-e) evening; am ~ in the evening, at night; heute abend tonight; morgen (gestern) abend tomorrow (last) night; s. essen; '**.anzug** m evening dress; '**.blatt** n evening paper; '**.brot** n supper, dinner; '**.dämmerung** f (evening) twilight, dusk; '**.essen** n s. Abendbrot; '**.gesellschaft** f evening party; '**.kasse** thea. f box-office; '**.kleid** n evening dress or gown; '**.land** n (-[e]s/no pl.) the Occident; **2ländisch** adj. ['..lɛndiʃ] western, occidental; '**.mahl** eccl. n (-[e]s/-e) the (Holy) Communion, the Lord's Supper; '**.rot** n evening or sunset glow.   [evening.\

abends adv. ['a:bənts] in the]
'**Abend|schule** f evening school, night-school; '**.sonne** f setting sun; '**.toilette** f evening dress; '**.wind** m evening breeze; '**.zeitung** f evening paper.

Abenteu|er ['a:bəntɔʏər] n (-s/-) adventure; **2erlich** adj. adventurous; fig.: strange; wild, fantastic; **.rer** ['..rər] m (-s/-) adventurer.

aber ['a:bər] **1.** adv. again; Tausende und ~ Tausende thousands upon thousands; **2.** cj. but; oder ~ otherwise, (or) else; **3.** int.: ~! now then!; ~, ~! come, come!; ~ nein! no!, on the contrary!; **4.** 2 n (-s/-) but.

'**Aber|glaube** m superstition; 2-**gläubisch** adj. ['..glɔʏbiʃ] superstitious.

aberkenn|en ['ap?-] v/t. (irr. kennen, sep., no -ge-, h): j-m et. ~ deprive s.o. of s.th. (a. ⚖); dispossess s.o. of s.th.; '**2ung** f (-/-en) deprivation (a. ⚖); dispossession.

aber|malig adj. ['a:bərma:liç] repeated; **.mals** adv. ['..s] again, once more.

ab|ernten ['ap?-] v/t. (sep., -ge-, h) reap, harvest; **.essen** ['ap?-] (irr. essen, sep., -ge-, h) **1.** v/t. clear (plate); **2.** v/i. finish eating; '**.fahren** (irr. fahren, sep., -ge-) **1.** v/i. (sein) leave (nach for), depart (for), start (for); set out or off (for); **2.** v/t. (h) carry or cart away (load).

'**Abfahrt** f departure (nach for), start (for); setting out or off (for); skiing: downhill run; '**.bahnsteig** m departure platform; '**.slauf** m skiing: downhill race; '**.ssignal** n starting-signal; '**.szeit** f time of departure; ⚓ a. time of sailing.

'**Abfall** m defection (von from), falling away (from); esp. pol. secession (from); eccl. apostasy (from); often Abfälle pl. waste, refuse, rubbish, Am. a. garbage; ⊕ clippings pl., shavings pl.; at butcher's: offal; '**.eimer** m dust-bin, Am. ash can; '**2en** v/i. (irr. fallen, sep., -ge-, sein) leaves, etc.: fall (off); ground, etc.: slope (down); fig. fall away (von from); esp. pol. secede (from); eccl. apostatize (from); ~ gegen come off badly by comparison with, be inferior to; '**.erzeugnis** n waste product; by-product.

'**abfällig** adj. judgement, etc.: adverse, unfavo(u)rable; remark: disparaging, depreciatory.

'**Abfallprodukt** n by-product; waste product.

'**ab|fangen** v/t. (irr. fangen, sep., -ge-, h) catch; snatch (ball, etc.); intercept (letter, etc.); ⚓, 🏹 prop; ✗ check (attack); 🎣 flatten out; mot., 🚗 right; '**.färben** v/i. (sep., -ge-, h): der Pullover färbt ab the colo(u)r of the pull-over runs (auf acc. on); ~ auf (acc.) influence, affect.

'**abfass|en** v/t. (sep., -ge-, h) compose, write, pen; catch (thief, etc.); '**2ung** f composition; wording.

'**ab|faulen** v/i. (sep., -ge-, sein) rot off; '**.fegen** v/t. (sep., -ge-, h) sweep off; '**.feilen** v/t. (sep., -ge-, h) file off.

abfertig|en ['apfɛrtigən] v/t. (sep., -ge-, h) dispatch (a. 🚂); customs: clear; serve, attend to (customer); j-n kurz ~ snub s.o.; '**2ung** f (-/-en) dispatch; customs: clearance; schroffe ~ snub.   [(off), discharge.\

'**abfeuern** v/t. (sep., -ge-, h) fire]

'**abfind|en** v/t. (irr. finden, sep., -ge-, h) satisfy, pay off (creditor); compensate; sich mit et. ~ resign o.s. to s.th.; put up with s.th.; '**2ung** f (-/-en) settlement; satisfaction; compensation; '**2ung(summe)** f indemnity; compensation.

'**ab|flachen** v/t. and v/refl. (sep., -ge-, h) flatten; '**.flauen** v/i. (sep., -ge-, sein) wind, etc.: abate; interest, etc.: flag; ♥ business: slacken; '**.fliegen** v/i. (irr. fliegen, sep., -ge-, sein) leave by plane; 🛫 take off, start; '**.fließen** v/i. (irr. fließen, sep., -ge-, sein) drain or flow off or away.   [parture.\

'**Abflug** 🛫 m take-off, start, de-]
'**Abfluß** m flowing or draining off or away; discharge (a. ✗); drain (a. fig.); sink; outlet (of lake, etc.).

'**abfordern** v/t. (sep., -ge-, h): j-m et. ~ demand s.th. of or from s.o.

Abfuhr ['apfu:r] *f* (-/-en) removal; *fig.* rebuff.

'abführ|en (*sep.*, *-ge-*, *h*) **1.** *v/t.* lead off *or* away; march (*prisoner*) off; pay over (*money*) (*an acc.* to); **2.** ♂ *v/i.* purge (the bowels), loosen the bowels; **'~end** ♂ *adj.* purgative, aperient, laxative; **'2mittel** ♂ *n* purgative, aperient, laxative.

'abfüllen *v/t.* (*sep.*, *-ge-*, *h*) decant; *in Flaschen ~* bottle; *Bier in Fässer ~* rack casks with beer.

'Abgabe *f sports*: pass; casting (*of one's vote*); sale (*of shares, etc.*); *mst ~n pl.* taxes *pl.*; rates *pl.*, *Am.* local taxes *pl.*; duties *pl.*; **'2frei** *adj.* tax-free; duty-free; **'2npflichtig** *adj.* taxable; dutiable; liable to tax *or* duty.

'Abgang *m* departure; start; *thea.* exit (*a. fig.*); retirement (*from a job*); loss, wastage; deficiency (*in weight, etc.*); ♂ discharge; ♂ miscarriage; *nach ~ von der Schule* after leaving school.

'abgängig *adj.* missing.

'Abgangszeugnis *n* (school-)leaving certificate, *Am. a.* diploma.

'Abgas *n* waste gas; *esp. mot.* exhaust gas. [toil-worn, worn-out.)

abgearbeitet *adj.* ['apgə'arbaitət]]

'abgeben *v/t.* (*irr. geben, sep., -ge-*, *h*) leave (*bei, an dat.* at); hand in (*paper, etc.*); deposit, leave (*luggage*); cast (*one's vote*); *sports*: pass (*ball, etc.*); sell, dispose of (*goods*); give off (*heat, etc.*); *e-e Erklärung ~* make a statement; *s-e Meinung ~* express one's opinion (*über acc.* on); *j-m et. ~* von et. give s.o. some of s.th.; *e-n guten Gelehrten ~* make a good scholar; *sich ~ mit* occupy o.s. with *s.th.*; *sie gibt sich gern mit Kindern ab* she loves to be among children.

'abge|brannt *adj.* burnt down; *F fig.* hard up, *sl.* broke; **'~brüht** *fig. adj.* ['~bry:t] hardened, callous; **'~droschen** *adj.* trite, hackneyed; **'~feimt** *adj.* ['~faimt] cunning, crafty; **'~griffen** *adj.* worn; *book*: well-thumbed; **'~härtet** *adj.* ['~hertet] hardened (*gegen* to), inured (to); **'~härmt** *adj.* ['~hermt] careworn.

'abgehen (*irr. gehen, sep., -ge-*) **1.** *v/i.* (*sein*) go off *or* away; leave, start, depart; *letter, etc.*: be dispatched; *post*: go; *thea.* make one's exit; *side-road*: branch off; *goods*: sell; *button, etc.*: come off; *stain, etc.*: come out; ♂ be discharged; (*von e-m Amt*) ~ give up a post; retire; *von der Schule ~* leave school; *~ von* digress from (*main subject*); deviate from (*rule*); alter, change (*one's opinion*); relinquish (*plan, etc.*); *diese Eigenschaft geht ihm ab* he lacks this quality; *gut ~* end well, pass off well; *hiervon geht or gehen*

... *ab* ♱ less, minus; **2.** *v/t.* (*h*) measure by steps; patrol.

abge|hetzt *adj.* ['apgəhetst] harassed; exhausted; run down; breathless; **~kartet** F *adj.* ['~kartət]: *~e Sache* prearranged affair, put-up job; **'~legen** *adj.* remote, distant; secluded; out-of-the-way; **~macht** *adj.* ['~maxt]: *~!* it's a bargain *or* deal!; **~magert** *adj.* ['~ma:gərt] emaciated; **~neigt** *adj.* ['~naikt] disinclined (*dat.* for *s.th.*; *zu tun* to do), averse (*to*; from doing), unwilling (*zu tun* to do); ~ **nutzt** *adj.* ['~nutst] worn-out.

Abgeordnete ['apgə'ɔrdnətə] *m, f* (-*n*/-*n*) deputy, delegate; *in Germany*: member of the Bundestag *or* Landtag; *Brt.* Member of Parliament, *Am.* Representative.

'abgerissen *fig. adj.* ragged; shabby; *style, speech*: abrupt, broken.

'Abgesandte *m, f* (-*n*/-*n*) envoy; emissary; ambassador.

'abgeschieden *fig. adj.* isolated, secluded, retired; **'2heit** *f* (-/-en) seclusion; retirement.

'abgeschlossen *adj. flat*: self-contained; *training, etc.*: complete.

abgeschmackt *adj.* ['apgəʃmakt] tasteless; tactless; **'2heit** *f* (-/-en) tastelessness; tactlessness.

'abgesehen *adj.*: ~ *von* apart from, *Am. a.* aside from.

abge|spannt *fig. adj.* ['apgəʃpant] exhausted, tired, run down; **'~standen** *adj.* stale, flat; **'~storben** *adj.* numb; dead; **~stumpft** *adj.* ['~ʃtumpft] blunt(ed); *fig.* indifferent (*gegen* to); **'~tragen** *adj.* worn-out; threadbare, shabby.

'abgewöhnen *v/t.* (*sep., -ge-*, *h*): *j-m et. ~* break *or* cure s.o. of s.th.; *sich das Rauchen ~* give up smoking.

abgezehrt *adj.* ['apgətse:rt] emaciated, wasted.

'abgießen *v/t.* (*irr. gießen, sep., -ge-*, *h*) pour off; ♂ decant; ⊕ cast.

'Abglanz *m* reflection (*a. fig.*).

'abgleiten *v/i.* (*irr. gleiten, sep., -ge-*, *sein*) slip off; slide off; glide)

'Abgott *m* idol. [off.)

abgöttisch *adv.* ['apgœtiʃ]: *j-n ~ lieben* idolize *or* worship s.o.; dote (up)on s.o.

'ab|grasen *v/t.* (*sep., -ge-*, *h*) graze; *fig.* scour; **'~grenzen** *v/t.* (*sep., -ge-*, *h*) mark off, delimit, demarcate (*a. fig.*); *fig.* define.

'Abgrund *m* abyss; precipice; chasm, gulf; *am Rande des ~s* on the brink of disaster.

'Abguß *m* cast.

'ab|hacken *v/t.* (*sep., -ge-*, *h*) chop *or* cut off; **'~haken** *fig. v/t.* (*sep., -ge-*, *h*) tick *or* check off; **'~halten** *v/t.* (*irr. halten, sep., -ge-*, *h*) hold (*meeting, examination, etc.*); keep out (*rain*); *j-n von der Arbeit ~* keep

s.o. from his work; *j-n davon* ~
et. zu tun keep *or* restrain s.o. from
doing s.th.; *et. von j-m* ~ keep s.th.
away from s.o.; '~handeln *v/t.*
(*sep.*, *-ge-*, *h*) discuss, treat; *j-m
et.* ~ bargain s.th. out of s.o.
abhanden *adv.* [ap'handən]: ~ kommen get lost.
'**Abhandlung** *f* treatise (*über acc.*
[up]on), dissertation ([up]on, concerning); essay.
'**Abhang** *m* slope, incline; declivity.
'**abhängen 1.** *v/t.* (*sep.*, *-ge-*, *h*) take
down (*picture, etc.*); 🕮 uncouple;
2. *v/i.* (*irr.* hängen, *sep.*, *-ge-*, *h*):
~ *von* depend (up)on.
abhängig *adj.* ['aphεŋiç]: ~ *von* dependent (up)on; '2keit *f* (*-/no pl.*)
dependence (*von* [up]on).
ab|härmen ['aphεrmən] *v/refl.*
(*sep.*, *-ge-*, *h*) pine away (*über acc.*
at); '~härten *v/t.* (*sep.*, *-ge-*, *h*)
harden (*gegen* to), inure (to); *sich*
~ harden o.s. (*gegen* to), inure o.s.
(to); '~hauen (*irr.* hauen, *sep.*,
-ge-) **1.** *v/t.* (*h*) cut *or* chop off;
2. F *v/i.* (*sein*) be off; *hau ab! sl.*
beat it!, scram!; '~häuten *v/t.*
(*sep.*, *-ge-*, *h*) skin, flay; '~heben
(*irr.* heben, *sep.*, *-ge-*, *h*) **1.** *v/t.* lift
or take off; *teleph.* lift (*receiver*);
(*with*)draw (*money*); *sich* ~ *von*
stand out against; *fig. a.* contrast
with; **2.** *v/i.* cut (the cards); *teleph.*
lift the receiver; '~heilen *v/i.* (*sep.*,
-ge-, *sein*) heal (up); '~helfen *v/i.*
(*irr.* helfen, *sep.*, *-ge-*, *h*): *e-m Übel*
~ cure *or* redress an evil; *dem ist
nicht abzuhelfen* there is nothing to
be done about it; '~hetzen *v/refl.*
(*sep.*, *-ge-*, *h*) tire o.s. out; rush,
hurry.
'**Abhilfe** *f* remedy, redress, relief;
~ *schaffen* take remedial measures.
'**abhobeln** *v/t.* (*sep.*, *-ge-*, *h*) plane
(away, down).
abhold *adj.* ['apholt] averse (*dat.*
to *s.th.*); ill-disposed (*towards
s.o.*).
'**ab|holen** *v/t.* (*sep.*, *-ge-*, *h*) fetch;
call for, come for; *j-n von der Bahn*
~ go to meet s.o. at the station;
'~holzen *v/t.* (*sep.*, *-ge-*, *h*) fell,
cut down (*trees*); deforest; '~hor-
chen 🗲 *v/t.* (*sep.*, *-ge-*, *h*) aus-
cultate, sound; '~hören *v/t.* (*sep.*,
-ge-, *h*) listen in to, intercept (*telephone conversation*); *e-n Schüler* ~
hear a pupil's lesson.
Abitur [abi'tuːr] *n* (*-s/🗲-e*) school-
leaving examination (*qualifying for
university entrance*).
'**ab|jagen** *v/t.* (*sep.*, *-ge-*, *h*) *j-m et.*
~ recover s.th. from s.o.; '~kanzeln
F *v/t.* (*sep.*, *-ge-*, *h*) reprimand, F
tell *s.o.* off; '~kaufen *v/t.* (*sep.*,
-ge-, *h*): *j-m et.* ~ buy *or* purchase
s.th. from s.o.

Abkehr *fig.* ['apkeːr] *f* (*-/no pl.*)
estrangement (*von* from); withdrawal (from); '2en *v/t.* (*sep.*, *-ge-*,
h) sweep off; *sich* ~ *von* turn away
from; *fig.*: take no further interest
in; become estranged from; withdraw from.
'**ab|klingen** *v/i.* (*irr.* klingen, *sep.*,
-ge-, *sein*) fade away; *pain, etc.*: die
down; *pain, illness*: ease off; '~klop-
fen (*sep.*, *-ge-*, *h*) **1.** *v/t.* knock (*dust,
etc.*) off; dust (*coat, etc.*); 🎵 sound,
percuss; **2.** *v/i. conductor*: stop the
orchestra; '~knicken *v/t.* (*sep.*,
-ge-, *h*) snap *or* break off; bend
off; '~knöpfen *v/t.* (*sep.*, *-ge-*, *h*)
unbutton; F *j-m Geld* ~ get money
out of s.o.; '~kochen (*sep.*, *-ge-*, *h*)
1. *v/t.* boil; scald (*milk*); **2.** *v/i.*
cook in the open air (*a.* 🗲); '~kom-
mandieren 🗲 *v/t.* (*sep.*, *no -ge-*, *h*)
detach, detail; second (*officer*).
Abkomme ['apkɔmə] *m* (*-n/-n*)
descendant.
'**abkommen** **1.** *v/i.* (*irr.* kommen,
sep., *-ge-*, *sein*) come away, get
away *or* off; *von e-r Ansicht* ~ change
one's opinion; *von e-m Thema* ~
digress from a topic; *vom Wege* ~
lose one's way; **2.** 2 *n* (*-s/-*) agreement.
abkömm|lich *adj.* ['apkœmliç] dis-
pensable; available; *er ist nicht* ~
he cannot be spared; '2ling ['~liŋ]
m (*-s/-e*) descendant.
'**ab|koppeln** *v/t.* (*sep.*, *-ge-*, *h*) un-
couple; '~kratzen (*sep.*, *-ge-*) **1.** *v/t.*
(*h*) scrape off; **2.** *sl. v/i.* (*sein*) kick
the bucket; '~kühlen *v/t.* (*sep.*,
-ge-, *h*) cool; refrigerate; *sich* ~ cool
down (*a. fig.*).
Abkunft ['apkunft] *f* (*-/🗲-e*) descent; origin, extraction; birth.
'**abkürz|en** *v/t.* (*sep.*, *-ge-*, *h*)
shorten; abbreviate (*word, story,
etc.*); *den Weg* ~ take a short cut;
'2ung *f* (*-/-en*) abridgement; abbreviation; short cut.
'**abladen** *v/t.* (*irr.* laden, *sep.*, *-ge-*, *h*)
unload; dump (*rubbish, etc.*).
'**Ablage** *f* place of deposit; filing
tray; files *pl.*; cloak-room.
'**ab|lagern** (*sep.*, *-ge-*) **1.** *v/t.* (*h*)
season (*wood, wine*); age (*wine*);
sich ~ settle; be deposited; **2.** *v/i.*
(*sein*) *wood, wine*: season; *wine*: age;
'~lassen (*irr.* lassen, *sep.*, *-ge-*, *h*)
1. *v/t.* let (*liquid*) run off; let
off (*steam*); drain (*pond, etc.*);
2. *v/i.* leave off (*von et.* [doing]
s.th.).
'**Ablauf** *m* running off; outlet, drain;
sports: start; *fig.* expiration; end;
nach ~ *von* at the end of; '2en (*irr.*
laufen, *sep.*, *-ge-*) **1.** *v/i.* (*sein*) run
off; drain off; *period of time*: expire; ✝ *bill of exchange*: fall due;
clock, etc.: run down; *thread, film*:
unwind; *spool*: run out; *gut* ~ end

well; 2. v/t. (h) wear out (shoes); scour (region, etc.); sich die Beine ~ run one's legs off; s. Rang.

'**Ableben** n (-s/ no pl.) death, decease (esp. ⚔️), ⚔️ demise.

'**ab|lecken** v/t. (sep., -ge-, h) lick (off); '~**legen** (sep., -ge-, h) 1. v/t. take off (garments); leave off (garments); give up, break o.s. of (habit); file (documents, letters, etc.); make (confession, vow); take (oath, examination); Zeugnis ~ bear witness (für to; von of); s. Rechenschaft; 2. v/i. take off one's (hat and) coat.

'**Ableger** ⚘ m (-s/-) layer, shoot.

'**ablehn|en** (sep., -ge-, h) 1. v/t. decline, refuse; reject (doctrine, candidate, etc.); turn down (proposal, etc.); 2. v/i. decline; dankend ~ decline with thanks; '~**end** adj. negative; '**2ung** f (-/-en) refusal; rejection.

ableit|en v/t. (sep., -ge-, h) divert (river, etc.); drain off or away (water, etc.); gr., Ⓐ, fig. derive (aus, von from); fig. infer (from); '**2ung** f diversion; drainage; gr., Ⓐ derivation (a. fig.).

'**ab|lenken** v/t. (sep., -ge-, h) turn aside; divert (suspicion, etc.) (von from); phys., etc.: deflect (rays, etc.); j-n von der Arbeit ~ distract s.o. from his work; '~**lesen** v/t. (irr. lesen, sep., -ge-, h) read (speech, etc.); read (off) (values from instruments); '~**leugnen** v/t. (sep., -ge-, h) deny, disavow, disown.

'**ab|liefer|n** v/t. (sep., -ge-, h) deliver; hand over; surrender; '**2ung** f delivery.

'**ablöschen** v/t. (sep., -ge-, h) blot (up) (ink); ⊕ temper (steel).

'**ablös|en** v/t. (sep., -ge-, h) detach; take off; ✕, etc.: relieve; supersede (predecessor in office); discharge (debt); redeem (obligation); sich ~ come off; fig. alternate, take turns; '**2ung** f detachment; ✕, etc.: relief; fig. supersession; discharge; redemption.

'**abmach|en** v/t. (sep., -ge-, h) remove, detach; fig. settle, arrange (business, etc.); agree (up)on (price, etc.); '**2ung** f (-/-en) arrangement, settlement; agreement.

'**abmager|n** v/i. (sep., -ge-, sein) lose flesh; grow lean or thin; '**2ung** f (-/-en) emaciation.

'**ab|mähen** v/t. (sep., -ge-, h) mow (off); '~**malen** v/t. (sep., -ge-, h) copy.

'**Abmarsch** m start; ✕ marching off; '**2ieren** v/i. (sep., no -ge-, sein) start; ✕ march off.

'**abmeld|en** v/t. (sep., -ge-, h): j-n von der Schule ~ give notice of the withdrawal of a pupil (from school); sich polizeilich ~ give notice to the police of one's departure (from

town, etc.); '**2ung** f notice of withdrawal; notice of departure.

'**abmess|en** v/t. (irr. messen, sep., -ge-, h) measure; '**2ung** f (-/-en) measurement.

'**ab|montieren** v/t. (sep., no -ge-, h) disassemble; dismantle, strip (machinery); remove (tyre, etc.); '~**mühen** v/refl. (sep., -ge-, h) drudge, toil; '~**nagen** v/t. (sep., -ge-, h) gnaw off; pick (bone).

Abnahme ['apna:mǝ] f (-/♦-n) taking off; removal; ⚔️ amputation; ✝ taking delivery; ✝ purchase; ✝ sale; ⊕ acceptance (of machine, etc.); administering (of oath); decrease, diminution; loss (of weight).

'**abnehm|en** (irr. nehmen, sep., -ge-, h) 1. v/t. take off; remove; teleph. lift (receiver); ⚔️ amputate; gather (fruit); ⊕ accept (machine, etc.); j-m et. ~ take s.th. from s.o.; ✝ a. buy or purchase s.th. from s.o.; j-m zuviel ~ overcharge s.o.; 2. v/i. decrease, diminish; decline; lose weight; moon: wane; storm: abate; days: grow shorter; '**2er** ✝ m (-s/-) buyer; customer; consumer.

'**Abneigung** f aversion (gegen to); disinclination (to); dislike (to, of, for); antipathy (against, to).

abnorm adj. [ap'nɔrm] abnormal; anomalous; exceptional; **2i'tät** f (-/-en) abnormality; anomaly.

'**abnötigen** v/t. (sep., -ge-, h): j-m et. ~ extort s.th. from s.o.

'**ab|nutzen** v/t. and v/refl. (sep., -ge-, h), '~**nützen** v/t. and v/refl. (sep.,-ge-, h) wear out; '**2nutzung** f, '**2nützung** f (-/-en) wear (and tear).

Abonn|ement [abɔn(ǝ)'mã:] n (-s/ -s) subscription (auf acc. to); ~**ent** [~'nɛnt] m (-en/-en) subscriber; **2ieren** [~'ni:rǝn] v/t. (no -ge-, h) subscribe to (newspaper) **2iert** adj. [~'ni:rt]: ~ sein auf (acc.) take in (newspaper, etc.).

abordn|en ['ap'?-] v/t. (sep., -ge-, h) depute, delegate, Am. a. deputize; '**2ung** f delegation, deputation.

Abort [a'bɔrt] m (-[e]s-e) lavatory, toilet.

'**ab|passen** v/t. (sep., -ge-, h) fit, adjust; watch for, wait for (s.o., opportunity); waylay s.o.; '~**pflükken** v/t. (sep., -ge-, h) pick, pluck (off), gather; '~**plagen** v/refl. (sep., -ge-, h) toil; '~**platzen** v/i. (sep., -ge-, sein) burst off; fly off; '~**prallen** v/i. (sep., -ge-, sein) rebound, bounce (off); ricochet; '~**putzen** v/t. (sep., -ge-, h) clean (off, up); wipe off; polish; '~**raten** v/i. (irr. raten, sep., -ge-, h): j-m ~ von dissuade s.o. from, advise s.o. against; '~**räumen** v/t. (sep., -ge-, h) clear (away); '~**reagieren** v/t. (sep., no -ge-, h) work off (one's anger, etc.); sich ~ F a. let off steam.

'abrechn|en (sep., -ge-, h) 1. v/t. deduct; settle (account); 2. v/i.: mit j-m ~ settle with s.o.; fig. settle (accounts) with s.o., F get even with s.o.; 'Qung f settlement (of accounts); deduction, discount.

'Abrede f: in ~ stellen deny or question s.th.

'abreib|en v/t. (irr. reiben, sep., -ge-, h) ℘ub off; rub down (body); polish; 'Qung f rub-down; F fig. beating.

'Abreise f departure (nach for); 'Qn v/i. (sep., -ge-, sein) depart (nach for), leave (for), start (for), set out (for).

'abreiß|en (irr. reißen, sep., -ge-) 1. v/t. (h) tear or pull off; pull down (building); s. abgerissen; 2. v/i. (sein) break off; button, etc.: come off; 'Qkalender m tear-off calendar.

'ab|richten v/t. (sep., -ge-, h) train (animal), break (horse) (in); '~riegeln v/t. (sep., -ge-, h) bolt, bar (door); block (road).

'Abriß m draft; summary, abstract; (brief) outlines pl.; brief survey.

'ab|rollen (sep., -ge-) v/t. (h) and v/i. (sein) unroll; uncoil; unwind, unreel; roll off; '~rücken (sep., -ge-) 1. v/t. (h) move off or away (von from), remove; 2. ℀ v/i. (sein) march off, withdraw.

'Abruf m call; recall; auf ~ ♰ on call; 'Qen v/t. (irr. rufen, sep., -ge-, h) call off (a. ♰), call away; recall; ☰ call out.

'ab|runden v/t. (sep., -ge-, h) round (off); '~rupfen v/t. (sep., -ge-, h) pluck off.

abrupt adj. [ap'rupt] abrupt.

'abrüst|en ℀ v/i. (sep., -ge-, h) disarm; 'Qung ℀ f disarmament.

'abrutschen v/i. (sep., -ge-, sein) slip off, glide down; ℀ skid.

'Absage f cancellation; refusal; 'Qn (sep., -ge-, h) 1. v/t. cancel, call off; refuse; recall (invitation); 2. v/i. guest: decline; j-m ~ cancel one's appointment with s.o.

'absägen v/t. (sep., -ge-, h) saw off; F fig. sack s.o.

'Absatz m stop, pause; typ. paragraph; ♰ sale; heel (of shoe); landing (of stairs); 'Qfähig ♰ adj. saleable, marketable; '~markt ♰ m market, outlet; '~möglichkeit ♰ f opening, outlet.

'abschaben v/t. (sep., -ge-, h) scrape off.

'abschaff|en v/t. (sep., -ge-, h) abolish; abrogate (law); dismiss (servants); 'Qung f (-/-en) abolition; abrogation; dismissal.

'ab|schälen v/t. (sep., -ge-, h) peel (off), pare; bark (tree); '~schalten v/t. (sep., -ge-, h) switch off, turn off or out; ∉ disconnect.

'abschätz|en v/t. (sep., -ge-, h) esti-

mate; value; assess; 'Qung f valuation; estimate; assessment.

'Abschaum m (-[e]s/no pl.) scum; fig. a. dregs pl.

'Abscheu m (-[e]s/no pl.) horror (vor dat. of), abhorrence (of); loathing (of); disgust (for).

'abscheuern v/t. (sep., -ge-, h) scour (off); wear out; chafe, abrade.

abscheulich adj. [ap'ʃɔɪlɪç] abominable, detestable, horrid; 2keit f (-/-en) detestableness; atrocity.

'ab|schicken v/t. (sep., -ge-, h) send off, dispatch; ℀ post, esp. Am. mail; '~schieben v/t. (irr. schieben, sep., -ge-, h) push or shove off.

Abschied ['apʃiːt] m (-[e]s/♱-e) departure; parting; leave-taking; farewell; dismissal, ℀ discharge; ~ nehmen take leave (von of), bid farewell (to); j-m den ~ geben dismiss s.o., ℀ discharge s.o.; s-n ~ nehmen resign, retire; '~sfeier f farewell party; '~sgesuch n resignation.

'ab|schießen v/t. (irr. schießen, sep., -ge-, h) shoot off; shoot, discharge, fire (off) (fire-arm); launch (rocket); kill, shoot; (shoot or bring) down (aircraft); s. Vogel; '~schinden v/refl. (irr. schinden, sep., -ge-, h) toil and moil, slave, drudge; '~schirmen v/t. (sep., -ge-, h) shield (gegen from); screen (from), screen off (from); '~schlachten v/t. (sep., -ge-, h) slaughter, butcher.

'Abschlag ♰ m reduction (in price); auf ~ on account; 2en ['apʃlɑːgən] v/t. (irr. schlagen, sep., -ge-, h) knock off, beat off, strike off; cut off (head); refuse (request); repel (attack).

abschlägig adj. ['apʃlɛːgɪç] negative; ~e Antwort refusal, denial.

'Abschlagszahlung f payment on account; instal(l)ment.

'abschleifen v/t. (irr. schleifen, sep., -ge-, h) grind off; fig. refine, polish.

'Abschlepp|dienst mot. m towing service, Am. a. wrecking service; 'Qen v/t. (sep., -ge-, h) drag off; mot. tow off.

'abschließen (irr. schließen, sep., -ge-, h) 1. v/t. lock (up); ⊕ seal (up); conclude (letter, etc.); settle (account); balance (the books); effect (insurance); contract (loan); fig. seclude, isolate; s-n Handel ~ strike a bargain; sich ~ seclude o.s.; 2. v/i. conclude; '~d 1. adj. concluding; final; 2. adv. in conclusion.

'Abschluß m settlement; conclusion; ⊕ seal; '~prüfung f final examination, finals pl., Am. a. graduation; '~zeugnis n leaving certificate; diploma.

'ab|schmeicheln v/t. (sep., -ge-, h): j-m et. ~ coax s.th. out of s.o.; '~schmelzen (irr. schmelzen, sep.,

abschmieren -ge-) v/t. (h) and v/i. (sein) melt (off); ⊕ fuse; '~**schmieren** ⊕ v/t. (sep., -ge-, h) lubricate, grease; '~**schnallen** v/t. (sep., -ge-, h) unbuckle; take off (ski, etc.); '~**schneiden** (irr. schneiden, sep., -ge-, h) 1. v/t. cut (off); slice off; den Weg ~ take a short cut; j-m das Wort ~ cut s.o. short; 2. v/i.: gut ~ come out or off well.

'**Abschnitt** m ⚭ segment; ✝ coupon; typ. section, paragraph; counterfoil, Am. a. stub (of cheque, etc.); stage (of journey); phase (of development); period (of time).

'**ab|schöpfen** v/t. (sep., -ge-, h) skim (off); '~**schrauben** v/t. (sep., -ge-, h) unscrew, screw off.

'**abschrecken** v/t. (sep., -ge-, h) deter (von from); scare away; '~**d** adj. deterrent; repulsive, forbidding.

'**abschreib|en** (irr. schreiben, sep., -ge-, h) 1. v/t. copy; write off (debt, etc.); plagiarize; in school: crib; 2. v/i. send a refusal; '2er m copyist; plagiarist; '2ung ✝ f (-/-en) depreciation.

'**abschreiten** v/t. (irr. schreiten, sep., -ge-, h) pace (off); e-e Ehrenwache ~ inspect a guard of hono(u)r.

'**Abschrift** f copy, duplicate.

'**abschürf|en** v/t. (sep., -ge-, h) graze, abrade (skin); '2ung f (-/-en) abrasion.

'**Abschuß** m discharge (of fire-arm); launching (of rocket); hunt. shooting; shooting down, downing (of aircraft); '~**rampe** f launching platform.

abschüssig adj. ['apʃysiç] sloping; steep.

'**ab|schütteln** v/t. (sep., -ge-, h) shake off (a. fig.); fig. get rid of; '~**schwächen** v/t. (sep., -ge-, h) weaken, lessen, diminish; '~**schweifen** v/i. (sep., -ge-, sein) deviate; fig. digress; '~**schwenken** v/i. (sep., -ge-, sein) swerve; ⚔ wheel; '~**schwören** v/i. (irr. schwören, sep., -ge-, h) abjure; forswear; '~**segeln** v/i. (sep., -ge-, sein) set sail, sail away.

abseh|bar adj. ['apze:baːr]: in ~er Zeit in the not-too-distant future; '~**en** (irr. sehen, sep., -ge-, h) 1. v/t. (fore)see; j-m et. ~ learn s.th. by observing s.o.; es abgesehen haben auf (acc.) have an eye on, be aiming at; 2. v/i.: ~ von refrain from; disregard.

abseits ['apzaɪts] 1. adv. aside, apart; football, etc.: off side; 2. prp. (gen.) aside from; off (the road).

'**absend|en** v/t. (irr. senden,] sep., -ge-, h) send off, dispatch; ✉ post, esp. Am. mail; '2er ✉ m sender.

'**absengen** v/t. (sep., -ge-, h) singe off.

'**Absenker** ⚭ m (-s/-) layer, shoot.

'**absetz|en** (sep., -ge-, h) 1. v/t. set or put down, deposit; deduct (sum); take off (hat); remove, dismiss (official); depose, dethrone (king); drop, put down (passenger); ✝ sell (goods); typ. set up (in type); thea.: ein Stück ~ take off a play; 2. v/i. break off, stop, pause; '2ung f (-/-en) deposition; removal, dismissal.

'**Absicht** f (-/-en) intention, purpose, design; '2lich 1. adj. intentional; 2. adv. on purpose.

'**absitzen** (irr. sitzen, sep., -ge-) 1. v/i. (sein) rider: dismount; 2. v/t. (h) serve (sentence), F do (time).

absolut adj. [apzoˈluːt] absolute.

absolvieren [apzɔlˈviːrən] v/t. (no -ge-, h) absolve; complete (studies); get through, graduate from (school).

'**absonder|n** v/t. (sep., -ge-, h) separate; 🔬 secrete; sich ~ withdraw; '2ung f (-/-en) separation; 🔬 secretion.

ab|sorbieren [apzɔrˈbiːrən] v/t. (no -ge-, h) absorb; '~**speisen** fig. v/t. (sep., -ge-, h) put s.o. off.

abspenstig adj. ['apʃpɛnstiç]: ~ machen entice away (von from).

'**absperr|en** v/t. (sep., -ge-, h) lock; shut off; bar (way); block (road); turn off (gas, etc.); '2hahn m stopcock.

'**ab|spielen** v/t. (sep., -ge-, h) play (record, etc.); play back (tape recording); sich ~ happen, take place; '~**sprechen** v/t. (irr. sprechen, sep., -ge-, h) deny; arrange, agree; '~**springen** v/i. (irr. springen, sep., -ge-, sein) jump down or off; ⚙ jump, bale out, (Am. only) bail out; rebound.

'**Absprung** m jump; sports: takeoff.

'**abspülen** v/t. (sep., -ge-, h) wash up; rinse.

'**abstamm|en** v/i. (sep., -ge-, sein) be descended; gr. be derived (both: von from); '2ung f (-/-en) descent; gr. derivation.

'**Abstand** m distance; interval; ✝ compensation, indemnification; ~ nehmen von desist from.

ab|statten ['apʃtatən] v/t. (sep., -ge-, h): e-n Besuch ~ pay a visit; Dank ~ return or render thanks; '~**stauben** v/t. (sep., -ge-, h) dust.

'**abstech|en** (irr. stechen, sep., -ge-, h) 1. v/t. cut (sods); stick (pig, sheep, etc.); stab (animal); 2. v/i. contrast (von with); '2er m (-s/-) excursion, trip; detour.

'**ab|stecken** v/t. (sep., -ge-, h) unpin, undo; fit, pin (dress); surv. mark out; '~**stehen** v/i. (irr. stehen, sep., -ge-, h) stand off; stick out, protrude; s. abgestanden; '~**steigen** v/i. (irr. steigen, sep., -ge-, sein) descend; alight (von from) (carriage); get off, dismount (from) (horse); put up (in dat. at) (hotel); **.stellen** v/t. (sep., -ge-, h) put down; stop, turn off (gas, etc.); park (car); fig. put an end to s.th.; **.stempeln** v/t. (sep., -ge-, h) stamp; **.sterben** v/i. (irr. sterben, sep., -ge-, sein) die off; limb: mortify.

Abstieg ['apʃtiːk] m (-[e]s/-e) descent; fig. decline.

'**abstimm|en** (sep., -ge-, h) 1. v/i. vote; 2. v/t. tune in (radio); fig.: harmonize; time; ✝ balance (books); **'Qung** f voting; vote; tuning.

Abstinenzler [apstiˈnɛntslər] m (-s/-) teetotal(l)er.

'**abstoppen** (sep., -ge-, h) 1. v/t. stop; slow down; sports: clock, time; 2. v/i. stop.

'**abstoßen** v/t. (irr. stoßen, sep., -ge-, h) knock off; push off; clear off (goods); fig. repel; sich die Hörner ~ sow one's wild oats; '**.d** fig. adj. repulsive.

abstrakt adj. [apˈʃtrakt] abstract.

'**ab|streichen** v/t. (irr. streichen, sep., -ge-, h) take or wipe off; **.streifen** v/t. (sep., -ge-, h) strip off; take or pull off (glove, etc.); slip off (dress); wipe (shoes); '**.streiten** v/t. (irr. streiten, sep., -ge-, h) contest, dispute; deny.

'**Abstrich** m deduction, cut; ⚕ swab.

'**ab|stufen** v/t. (sep., -ge-, h) graduate; gradate; '**.stumpfen** (sep., -ge-) 1. v/t. (h) blunt; fig. dull (mind); 2. fig. v/i. (sein) become dull.

'**Absturz** m fall; ✈ crash.

'**ab|stürzen** v/i. (sep., -ge-, sein) fall down; ✈ crash; '**.suchen** v/t. (sep., -ge-, h) search (nach for); scour or comb (area) (for).

absurd adj. [apˈzurt] absurd, preposterous.

Abszeß 🕯 [apsˈtsɛs] m (Abszesses/ Abszesse) abscess.

Abt [apt] m (-[e]s/ᵘe) abbot.

'**abtakeln** ⚓ v/t. (sep., -ge-, h) unrig, dismantle, strip.

Abtei [apˈtai] f (-/-en) abbey.

Ab|'teil 🚃 n compartment; '**Qteilen** v/t. (sep., -ge-, h) divide; △ partition off; '**.teilung** f division; **.teilung** f department; ward (of hospital); compartment; ✕ detachment; **.teilungsleiter** m head of a department.

'**abtelegraphieren** v/i. (sep., no -ge-, h) cancel a visit, etc. by telegram.

Äbtissin [ɛpˈtisin] f (-/-nen) abbess.

'**ab|töten** v/t. (sep., -ge-, h) destroy, kill (bacteria, etc.); '**.tragen** v/t. (irr. tragen, sep., -ge-, h) carry off; pull down (building); wear out (garment); pay (debt).

abträglich adj. ['aptrɛːkliç] injurious, detrimental.

'**abtreib|en** (irr. treiben, sep., -ge-) 1. v/t. (h) drive away or off; ein Kind ~ procure abortion; 2. ⚓, ✕ v/i. (sein) drift off; '**Qung** f (-/-en) abortion.

'**abtrennen** v/t. (sep., -ge-, h) detach; separate; sever (limbs, etc.); take (trimmings) off (dress).

'**abtret|en** (irr. treten, sep., -ge-) 1. v/t. (h) wear down (heels); wear out (steps, etc.); fig. cede, transfer; 2. v/i. (sein) retire, withdraw; resign; thea. make one's exit; '**Qer** m (-s/-) doormat; '**Qung** f (-/-en) cession, transfer.

'**ab|trocknen** (sep., -ge-) 1. v/t. (h) dry (up); wipe (dry); sich ~ dry oneself, rub oneself down; 2. v/i. (sein) dry up, become dry; '**.tropfen** v/i. (sep., -ge-, sein) liquid: drip; dishes, vegetables: drain.

abtrünnig adj. ['aptrʏniç] unfaithful, disloyal; eccl. apostate; **Qe** ['**.gə**] m (-n/-n) deserter; eccl. apostate.

'**ab|tun** v/t. (irr. tun, sep., -ge-, h) take off; settle (matter); fig.: dispose of; dismiss; **.urteilen** ['apᵊ-] v/t. (sep., -ge-, h) pass sentence on s.o.; '**.wägen** v/t. ([irr. wägen,] sep., -ge-, h) weigh (out); fig. consider carefully; '**.wälzen** v/t. (sep., -ge-, h) roll away; fig. shift; '**.wandeln** v/t. (sep., -ge-, h) vary, modify; '**.wandern** v/i. (sep., -ge-, sein) wander away; migrate (von from).

'**Abwandlung** f modification, variation.

'**abwarten** (sep., -ge-, h) 1. v/t. wait for, await; s-e Zeit ~ bide one's time; 2. v/i. wait.

abwärts adv. ['apvɛrts] down, downward(s).

'**abwaschen** v/t. (irr. waschen, sep., -ge-, h) wash (off, away); bathe; sponge off; wash up (dishes, etc.).

'**abwechseln** (sep., -ge-, h) 1. v/t. vary; alternate; 2. v/i. vary; alternate; mit j-m ~ take turns; '**.d** adj. alternate.

'**Abwechs(e)lung** f (-/-en) change; alternation; variation; diversion; zur ~ for a change.

'**Abweg** m: auf ~e geraten go astray; **Qig** adj. ['**.giç**] erroneous, wrong.

'**Abwehr** f defen|ce, Am. -se; warding off (of thrust, etc.); '**.dienst** ✕ m counter-espionage service; '**Qen** v/t. (sep., -ge-, h) ward off; avert; repulse, repel; ward off (attack, enemy).

'**abweich|en** v/i. (irr. weichen, sep., -ge-, sein) deviate (von from), swerve (from); differ (from); compass-needle: deviate; '**Qung** f (-/-en) deviation; difference; deflexion, (Am. only) deflection.

'**abweiden** v/t. (sep., -ge-, h) graze.

'**abweis|en** v/t. (irr. weisen, sep., -ge-, h) refuse, reject; repel (a. ✕);

rebuff; '~end *adj.* unfriendly, cool; '2ung *f* refusal, rejection; repulse (*a.* ✕); rebuff.

'ab|wenden *v/t.* ([*irr.* wenden,] *sep.*, -ge-, *h*) turn away; avert (*disaster, etc.*); parry (*thrust*); sich ~ turn away (von from); '~werfen *v/t.* (*irr.* werfen, *sep.*, -ge-, *h*) throw off; ✕ drop (*bombs*); shed, cast (*skin, etc.*); shed (*leaves*); yield (*profit*).

'abwert|en *v/t.* (*sep.*, -ge-, *h*) devaluate; '2ung *f* devaluation.

abwesen|d *adj.* ['apve:zənt] absent; '2heit *f* (-/'~ -en) absence.

'ab|wickeln *v/t.* (*sep.*, -ge-, *h*) unwind, unreel, wind off; transact (*business*); '~wiegen *v/t.* (*irr.* wiegen, *sep.*, -ge-, *h*) weigh (out) (*goods*); '~wischen *v/t.* (*sep.*, -ge-, *h*) wipe (off); '~würgen *v/t.* (*sep.*, -ge-, *h*) strangle, throttle, choke; *mot.* stall; '~zahlen *v/t.* (*sep.*, -ge-, *h*) pay off; pay by instal(l)ments; '~zählen *v/t.* (*sep.*, -ge-, *h*) count (out, over).

'Abzahlung *f* instal(l)ment, payment on account; '~sgeschäft *n* hire-purchase.

'abzapfen *v/t.* (*sep.*, -ge-, *h*) tap, draw off.

'Abzehrung *f* (-/-en) wasting away, emaciation; 🐾 consumption.

'Abzeichen *n* badge; ✕ marking.

'ab|zeichnen *v/t.* (*sep.*, -ge-, *h*) copy, draw; mark off; initial; tick off; sich ~ gegen stand out against; '~ziehen (*irr.* ziehen, *sep.*, -ge-) 1. *v/t.* (*h*) take off, remove; Å subtract; strip (*bed*); bottle (*wine*); *phot.* print (*film*); *typ.* pull (*proof*); take out (*key*); das Fell ~ skin (*animal*); 2. *v/i.* (sein) go away; ✕ march off; *smoke*: escape; *thunderstorm, clouds*: move on.

'Abzug *m* departure; ✕ withdrawal, retreat; ⊕ drain; outlet; deduction (*of sum*); *phot.* print; *typ.* proof (-sheet).

abzüglich *prp.* (*gen.*) ['aptsy:kliç] less, minus, deducting.

'Abzugsrohr *n* waste-pipe.

abzweig|en ['aptsvaɪgən] (*sep.*, -ge-) 1. *v/t.* (*h*) branch; divert (*money*); sich ~ branch off; 2. *v/i.* (sein) branch off; '2ung *f* (-/-en) branch; road-junction.

ach *int.* [ax] oh!, ah!, alas!; ~ so! oh, I see!

Achse ['aksə] *f* (-/-n) axis; ⊕: axle; shaft; axle(-tree) (*of carriage*); auf der ~ on the move.

Achsel ['aksəl] *f* (-/-n) shoulder; die ~n zucken shrug one's shoulders; '~höhle *f* armpit.

acht[1] [axt] 1. *adj.* eight; in ~ Tagen today week, this day week; vor ~ Tagen a week ago; 2. 2 *f* (-/-en) (figure) eight.

Acht[2] [~] *f* (-/*no pl.*) ban, outlawry; attention; außer acht lassen dis-

regard; sich in acht nehmen be careful; be on one's guard (*vor j-m or et.* against s.o. *or* s.th.); look out (*for* s.o. *or* s.th.).

'achtbar *adj.* respectable.

'achte *adj.* eighth; 2l ['~əl] *n* (-s/-) eighth (part).

'achten (ge-, *h*) 1. *v/t.* respect, esteem; regard; 2. *v/i.*: ~ auf (*acc.*) pay attention to; achte auf meine Worte mark *or* mind my words; darauf ~, daß see to it that, take care that.

ächten ['eçtən] *v/t.* (ge-, *h*) outlaw, proscribe; ban.

'Achter *m* (-s/-) *rowing*: eight.

achtfach *adj.* ['axtfax] eightfold.

'achtgeben *v/i.* (*irr.* geben, *sep.*, -ge-, *h*) be careful; pay attention (auf *acc.* to); take care (of); gib acht! look *or* watch out!, be careful!

'achtlos *adj.* inattentive, careless, heedless.

Acht'stundentag *m* eight-hour day.

'Achtung *f* (-/*no pl.*) attention; respect, esteem, regard; ~! look out!, ✕ attention!; ~ Stufe! mind the step!; 2svoll *adj.* respectful.

'achtzehn *adj.* eighteen; ~te *adj.* ['~tə] eighteenth.

achtzig *adj.* ['axtsiç] eighty; '~ste *adj.* eightieth.

ächzen ['eçtsən] *v/i.* (ge-, *h*) groan, moan.

Acker ['akər] *m* (-s/ⁿ) field; '~bau *m* agriculture; farming; '2bautreibend *adj.* agricultural, farming; '~geräte *n/pl.* farm implements *pl.*; '~land *n* arable land; '2n *v/t. and v/i.* (ge-, *h*) plough, till, *Am.* plow.

addi|eren [a'di:rən] *v/t.* (*no* -ge-, *h*) add (up); 2tion [adi'tsjo:n] *f* (-/-en) addition, adding up.

Adel ['a:dəl] *m* (-s/*no pl.*) nobility, aristocracy; '2ig *adj.* noble; '2n *v/t.* (ge-, *h*) ennoble (*a. fig.*); *Brt.* knight, raise to the peerage; '~stand *m* nobility; aristocracy; *Brt.* peerage.

Ader ['a:dər] *f* (-/-n) ✕, wood, *etc.*: vein; *anat.*: vein; artery; zur ~ lassen bleed.

adieu *int.* [a'djø:] good-bye, farewell, adieu, F cheerio.

Adjektiv *gr.* ['atjekti:f] *n* (-s/-e) adjective.

Adler *orn.* ['a:dlər] *m* (-s/-) eagle; '~nase *f* aquiline nose.

adlig *adj.* ['a:dliç] noble; 2e ['~gə] *m* (-n/-n) nobleman, peer.

Admiral ⚓ [atmi'ra:l] *m* (-s/-e, ⁿe) admiral.

adopt|ieren [adɔp'ti:rən] *v/t.* (*no* -ge-, *h*) adopt; 2ivkind [~'ti:f-] *n* adopted child.

Adressat [adrɛ'sa:t] *m* (-en/-en) addressee; consignee (*of goods*).

Adreßbuch [a'drɛs-] *n* directory.

Adress|e [a'drɛsə] f (-/-n) address; direction; per ~ care of (abbr. c/o); **2ieren** [ʌ'siːrən] v/t. (no -ge-, h) address, direct; † consign; falsch ~ misdirect.

adrett adj. [a'drɛt] smart, neat.

Adverb gr. [at'vɛrp] n (-s/-ien) adverb.

Affäre [a'fɛːrə] f (-/-n) (love) affair; matter, business, incident.

Affe zo. ['afə] m (-n/-n) ape; monkey.

Affekt [a'fɛkt] m (-[e]s/-e) emotion; passion; **2iert** adj. [ʌ'tiːrt] affected; 'affig f adj. foppish; affected; silly.

Afrikan|er [afri'kaːnər] m (-s/-) African; **2isch** adj. African.

After anat. ['aftər] m (-s/-) anus.

Agent [a'gɛnt] m (-en/-en) agent; broker; pol. (secret) agent; ~ur [ʌ'tuːr] f (-/-en) agency.

aggressiv adj. [agrɛ'siːf] aggressive.

Agio † ['aːʒio] n (-s/no pl.) agio, premium.

Agitator [agi'taːtər] m (-s/-) agitator. [brooch.\

Agraffe [a'grafə] f (-/-n) clasp;\

agrarisch adj. [a'graːriʃ] agrarian.

Ägypt|er [ɛː'gyptər] m (-s/-) Egyptian; **2isch** adj. Egyptian.

ah int. [aː] ah!

aha int. [a'ha] aha!, I see!

Ahle ['aːlə] f (-/-n) awl, pricker; punch.

Ahn [aːn] m (-[e]s, -en/-en) ancestor; ~en pl. a. forefathers pl.

ähneln ['ɛːnəln] v/i. (ge-, h) be like, resemble.

ahnen ['aːnən] v/t. (ge-, h) have a presentiment of or that; suspect; divine.

ähnlich adj. ['ɛːnliç] like, resembling; similar (dat. to); iro.: das sieht ihm ~ that's just like him; **2keit** f (-/-en) likeness, resemblance; similarity.

Ahnung ['aːnuŋ] f (-/-en) presentiment; foreboding; notion, idea; **2slos** adj. unsuspecting; **2svoll** adj. full of misgivings.

Ahorn ♀ ['aːhɔrn] m (-s/-e) maple (-tree).

Ähre ♀ ['ɛːrə] f (-/-n) ear, head; spike; ~n lesen glean.

Akademi|e [akadɛ'miː] f (-/-n) academy, society; ~ker [ʌ'deːmikər] m (-s/-) university man, esp. Am. university graduate; **2sch** adj. [ʌ'deːmiʃ] academic.

Akazie ♀ [a'kaːtsjə] f (-/-n) acacia.

akklimatisieren [aklimati'ziːrən] v/t. and v/refl. (no -ge-, h) acclimatize, Am. acclimate.

Akkord [a'kɔrt] m (-[e]s/-e) ♪ chord; † contract; agreement; composition; im ~ † by the piece or job; ~arbeit f piece-work; ~arbeiter m piece-worker; ~lohn m piece-wages pl.

akkredit|ieren [akredi'tiːrən] v/t. (no -ge-, h) accredit (bei to); **2iv** [ʌ'tiːf] n (-s/-e) credentials pl.; † letter of credit.

Akku F ⊕ ['aku] m (-s/-s), ~mulator ⊕ [ʌmu'laːtər] m (-s/-en) accumulator, (storage-)battery.

Akkusativ gr. ['akuzatiːf] m (-s/-e) accusative (case). [acrobat.\

Akrobat [akro'baːt] m (-en/-en)\

Akt [akt] m (-[e]s/-e) act(ion), deed; thea. act; paint. nude.

Akte ['aktə] f (-/-n) document, deed; file; ~n pl. records pl., papers pl.; deeds pl., documents pl.; files pl.; zu den ~n to be filed; zu den ~n legen file; '~ndeckel m folder; '~nmappe f, '~ntasche f portfolio; briefcase; '~nzeichen n reference or file number.

Aktie † ['aktsjə] f (-/-n) share, Am. stock; ~n besitzen hold shares, Am. hold stock; '~nbesitz m shareholdings pl., Am. stockholdings pl.; '~ngesellschaft f appr. joint-stock company, Am. (stock) corporation; '~nkapital n share-capital, Am. capital stock.

Aktion [ak'tsjoːn] f (-/-en) action; activity; pol., etc.: campaign, drive; ⚔ operation; ~är [ʌ'nɛːr] m (-s/-e) shareholder, Am. stockholder.

aktiv adj. [ak'tiːf] active.

Aktiv|a † [ak'tiːva] n/pl. assets pl.; ~posten [ʌ'tiːf-] m asset (a. fig.).

aktuell adj. [aktu'ɛl] current, present-day, up-to-date, topical.

Akust|ik [a'kustik] f (-/no pl.) acoustics sg., pl.; **2isch** adj. acoustic.

akut adj. [a'kuːt] acute.

Akzent [ak'tsɛnt] m (-[e]s/-e) accent; stress; **2uieren** [ʌu'iːrən] v/t. (no -ge-, h) accent(uate); stress.

Akzept † [ak'tsɛpt] n (-[e]s/-e) acceptance; ~ant [ʌ'tant] m (-en/-en) acceptor; **2ieren** [ʌ'tiːrən] v/t. (no -ge-, h) accept.

Alarm [a'larm] m (-[e]s/-e) alarm; ~ blasen or schlagen ⚔ sound or give the alarm; ~bereitschaft f: in ~ sein stand by; **2ieren** [ʌ'miːrən] v/t. (no -ge-, h) alarm.

Alaun 🜄 [a'laun] m (-[e]s/-e) alum.

albern adj. ['albərn] silly, foolish.

Album ['album] n (-s/Alben) album.

Alge ♀ ['algə] f (-/-n) alga, seaweed.

Algebra ♙ ['algebra] f (-/no pl.) algebra.

Alibi 🜨 ['aːlibi] n (-s/-s) alibi.

Alimente 🜨 [ali'mɛntə] pl. alimony.

Alkohol ['alkohol] m (-s/-e) alcohol; **2frei** adj. non-alcoholic, esp. Am. soft; ~es Restaurant temperance restaurant; ~iker [ʌ'hoːlikər] m (-s/-) alcoholic; **2isch** adj. [ʌ'hoːliʃ] alcoholic; '~schmuggler m liquor-smuggler, Am. bootlegger; '~verbot n prohibition; '~vergiftung f alcoholic poisoning.

all¹ [al] 1. *pron.* all; ~e everybody; ~es in ~em on the whole; vor ~em first of all; 2. *adj.* all; every, each; any; ~e beide both of them; auf ~e Fälle in any case, at all events; ~e Tage every day; ~e zwei Minuten every two minutes.

All² [~] *n* (-s/no pl.) the universe.

'**alle** F *adj.* all gone; ~ werden come to an end; supplies, etc.: run out.

Allee [a'le:] *f* (-/-n) avenue; (tree-lined) walk.

allein [a'laɪn] 1. *adj.* alone; single; unassisted; 2. *adv.* alone; only; 3. *cj.* yet, only, but, however; 2be-rechtigung *f* exclusive right; 2be-sitz *m* exclusive possession; 2herr-scher *m* absolute monarch, autocrat; dictator; ~ig *adj.* only, exclusive, sole; 2sein *n* loneliness, solitariness, solitude; ~stehend *adj. p.*: alone in the world; single; building, etc.: isolated, detached; 2verkauf *m* exclusive sale; monopoly; 2vertreter *m* sole representative or agent; 2vertrieb *m* sole distributors pl.

allemal *adv.* ['alə'ma:l] always; ein für ~ once (and) for all.

'**allen|falls** *adv.* if need be; possibly, perhaps; at best.

allenthalben † *adv.* ['alənt'halbən] everywhere.

aller|'best *adj.* best ... of all, very best; ~dings *adv.* ['~dɪŋs] indeed; to be sure; ~! certainly!, Am. F sure!; '~erst 1. *adj.* first ... of all, very first; foremost; 2. *adv.*: zu ~ first of all.

Allergie ℱ [aler'gi:] *f* (-/-n) allergy.

'**aller|'hand** *adj.* of all kinds or sorts; F das ist ja ~! F I say!; sl. that's the limit!; '2'heiligen *n* (-/no pl.) All Saints' Day; ~lei *adj.* ['~laɪ] of all kinds or sorts; '2'lei *n* (-s/-s) medley; '~'letzt 1. *adj.* last of all, very last; latest (news, fashion, etc.); 2. *adv.*: zu ~ last of all; '~'liebst 1. *adj.* dearest of all; (most) lovely; 2. *adv.*: am ~en best of all; '~'meist 1. *adj.* most; 2. *adv.*: am ~en mostly; chiefly; '~'nächst *adj.* very next; '~'neu(e)st *adj.* the very latest; '2'seelen *n* (-/no pl.) All Souls' Day; '~'seits *adv.* on ~il sides; universally; '~'wenigst *adv.*: am ~en least of all.

'**alle|'samt** *adv.* one and all, all together; '~'zeit *adv.* always, at all times, for ever.

'**all|'gegenwärtig** *adj.* omnipresent, ubiquitous; '~ge'mein 1. *adj.* general; common; universal; 2. *adv.*: im ~en in general, generally; '2ge'meinheit *f* (-/no pl.) generality; universality; general public; '2'heilmittel *n* panacea, cure-all (both a. fig.).

Allianz [ali'ants] *f* (-/-en) alliance.

alli'ier|en *v/refl.* (no -ge-, h) ally o.s. (mit to, with); 2te *m* (-n/-n) ally.

'**all|'jährlich** 1. *adj.* annual; 2. *adv.* annually, every year; '2macht *f* (-/no pl.) omnipotence; '~'mächtig *adj.* omnipotent, almighty; ~mäh-lich [~'mɛ:lɪç] 1. *adj.* gradual; 2. *adv.* gradually, by degrees.

Allopathie ℱ [alopa'ti:] allopathy.

all|seitig *adj.* ['alzartɪç] universal; all-round; '2strom ⚡ *m* (-[e]s/no pl.) alternating current/direct current (abbr. A.C./D.C.); '2tag *m* workday; week-day; fig. everyday life, daily routine; '~'täglich *adj.* daily; fig. common, trivial; '2tags-leben *n* (-s/no pl.) everyday life; '~'wissend *adj.* omniscient; '2'wissenheit *f* (-/no pl.) omniscience; '~'wöchentlich *adj.* weekly; '~zu *adv.* (much) too; '~zu'viel *adv.* too much.

Alm [alm] *f* (-/-en) Alpine pasture, alp.

Almosen ['almo:zən] *n* (-s/-) alms; ~ pl. alms pl., charity.

Alp|druck ['alp-] *m* (-[e]s/⁓e), '~drücken *n* (-s/no pl.) nightmare.

Alpen ['alpən] pl. Alps pl.

Alphabet [alfa'be:t] *n* (-[e]s/-e) alphabet; 2isch *adj.* alphabetic(al).

'**Alptraum** *m* nightmare.

als *cj.* [als] than; as, like; (in one's capacity) as; but, except; temporal: after, when; as; ~ ob as if, as though; so viel ~ as much as; er ist zu dumm, ~ daß er es verstehen könnte he is too stupid to understand it; '~'bald *adv.* immediately; '~'dann *adv.* then.

also ['alzo:] 1. *adv.* thus, so; 2. *cj.* therefore, so, consequently; na ~! there you are!

alt¹ *adj.* [alt] old; aged; ancient, antique; stale; second-hand.

Alt² ♪ [~] *m* (-s/-e) alto, contralto.

Altar [al'ta:r] *m* (-[e]s/⁓e) altar.

Alteisen ['alt°-] *n* scrap-iron.

'**Alte** (-n/-n) 1. *m* old man; F: der ~ the governor; hist.: die ~n pl. the ancients pl.; 2. *f* old woman.

'**Alter** *n* (-s/-) age; old age; seniority; er ist in meinem ~ he is my age; von mittlerem ~ middle-aged.

älter *adj.* ['ɛltər] older; senior; der ~e Bruder the elder brother.

altern ['altərn] *v/i.* (ge-, h, sein) grow old, age.

Alternative [alterna'ti:və] *f* (-/-n) alternative; keine ~ haben have no choice.

'**Alters|grenze** *f* age-limit; retirement age; '~heim *n* old people's home; '~rente *f* old-age pension; '2schwach *adj.* decrepit; senile; '~schwäche *f* decrepitude; '~ver-sorgung *f* old-age pension.

Altertum ['altərtuːm] n 1. (-s/no pl.) antiquity; 2. (-s/ᵘer) mst Altertümer pl. antiquities pl.

altertümlich adj. ['altərtyːmliç] ancient, antique, archaic.

'**Altertums|forscher** m arch(a)eologist; **᷍kunde** f arch(a)eology.

ältest adj. ['ɛltəst] oldest; eldest (sister, etc.); earliest (recollections); '**᷍e** m (-n/-n) elder; senior; mein ᷍r my eldest (son).

Altistin ♪ [al'tistin] f (-/-nen) altosinger, contralto-singer.

'**altklug** adj. precocious, forward.

ältlich adj. ['ɛltliç] elderly, oldish.

'**Alt|material** n junk, scrap; salvage; **᷍meister** m doyen, dean, F Grand Old Man (a. sports); sports: ex-champion; '᷍**modisch** adj. old-fashioned; **᷍papier** n waste paper; '**᷍philologe** m classical philologist or scholar; **᷍stadt** f old town or city; '**᷍warenhändler** m second-hand dealer; ᷍'**weibersommer** m Indian summer; gossamer.

Aluminium 🜚 [alu'miːnjum] n (-s/no pl.) aluminium, Am. aluminum.

am prp. [am] = an dem.

Amateur [ama'tøːr] m (-s/-e) amateur.

Amboß ['ambɔs] m (Ambosses/Ambosse) anvil.

ambulan|t ⚕ adj. [ambu'lant]: ᷍ Behandelter out-patient; ⚕z [᷍ts] f (-/-en) ambulance.

Ameise zo. ['aːmaizə] f (-/-n) ant; '**᷍nhaufen** m ant-hill.

Amerikan|er [ameri'kaːnər] m (-s/-), **᷍erin** f (-/-nen) American; **⚕isch** adj. American.

Amme ['amə] f (-/-n) (wet-)nurse.

Amnestie [amnɛs'tiː] f (-/-n) amnesty, general pardon.

Amor ['aːmɔr] m (-s/no pl.) Cupid.

Amortis|ation [amɔrtiza'tsjoːn] f (-/-en) amortization, redemption; **⚕ieren** [᷍'ziːrən] v/t. (no -ge-, h) amortize, redeem; pay off.

Ampel ['ampəl] f (-/-n) hanging lamp; traffic light.

Amphibie zo. [am'fiːbjə] f (-/-n) amphibian.

Ampulle [am'pulə] f (-/-n) ampoule.

Amput|ation [amputa'tsjoːn] f (-/-en) amputation; **⚕ieren** ⚕ [᷍'tiːrən] v/t. (no -ge-. h) amputate; **᷍ierte** m (-n/-n) amputee.

Amsel orn. ['amzəl] f (-/-n) blackbird.

Amt [amt] n (-[e]s/ᵘer) office; post; charge; office, board; official duty; function; (telephone) exchange; **⚕ieren** [᷍'tiːrən] v/i. (no -ge-, h) hold office; officiate; '**⚕lich** adj. official; '**᷍mann** m district administrator; hist. bailiff.

'**Amts|arzt** m medical officer of

health; '**᷍befugnis** f competence, authority; '**᷍bereich** m, '**᷍bezirk** m jurisdiction; '**᷍blatt** n gazette; '**᷍eid** m oath of office; '**᷍einführung** f inauguration; '**᷍führung** f administration; '**᷍geheimnis** n official secret; '**᷍gericht** n appr. district court; '**᷍geschäfte** n/pl. official duties pl.; '**᷍gewalt** f (official) authority; '**᷍handlung** f official act; '**᷍niederlegung** f (-/ᵛ-en) resignation; '**᷍richter** m appr. district court judge; '**᷍siegel** n official seal; '**᷍vorsteher** m head official.

Amulett [amu'lɛt] n (-[e]s/-e) amulet, charm.

amüs|ant adj. [amy'zant] amusing, entertaining; **᷍ieren** [᷍'ziːrən] v/t. (no -ge-, h) amuse, entertain; sich ᷍ amuse or enjoy o.s., have a good time.

an [an] 1. prp. (dat.) at; on, upon; in; against; to; by, near, close to; ᷍ der Themse on the Thames; ᷍ der Wand on or against the wall; es ist ᷍ dir zu inf. it is up to you to inf.; am Leben alive; am 1. März on March 1st; am Morgen in the morning; 2. prp. (acc.) to; on; on to; at; against; about; bis ᷍ as far as, up to; 3. adv. on; von heute ᷍ from this day forth, from today; von nun or jetzt ᷍ from now on.

analog adj. [ana'loːk] analogous (dat. or zu to, with).

Analphabet [an(ᵛ)alfa'beːt] m (-en/-en) illiterate (person).

Analys|e [ana'lyːzə] f (-/-n) analysis; **⚕ieren** [᷍'ziːrən] v/t. (no -ge-, h) analy|se, Am. -ze.

Anämie ⚕ [anɛ'miː] f (-/-n) an(a)emia.

Ananas ['ananas] f (-/-, -se) pineapple.

Anarchie [anar'çiː] f (-/-n) anarchy.

Anatom|ie [anato'miː] f (-/no pl.) anatomy; **⚕isch** adj. [᷍'toːmiʃ] anatomical.

'**anbahnen** v/t. (sep., -ge-, h) pave the way for, initiate; open up; sich ᷍ be opening up.

'**Anbau** m 1. ✿ (-[e]s/no pl.) cultivation; 2. 🏠 (-[e]s/-ten) outbuilding, annex, extension, addition; '**⚕en** v/t. (sep., -ge-, h) ✿ cultivate, grow; 🏠 add (an acc. to); '**᷍fläche** ✿ f arable land.

'**anbehalten** v/t. (irr. halten, sep., no -ge-, h) keep (garment, etc.) on.

an'bei ✝ adv. enclosed.

'**an|beißen** (irr. beißen, sep., -ge-, h) 1. v/t. bite into; 2. v/i. fish: bite; '**᷍bellen** v/t. (sep., -ge-, h) bark at; **᷍beraumen** ['᷍bəraumən] v/t. (sep., no -ge-, h) appoint, fix; '**᷍beten** v/t. (sep., -ge-, h) adore, worship.

'**Anbetracht** m: in ᷍ considering, in consideration of.

'anbetteln v/t. (sep., -ge-, h) beg from, solicit alms of.

'Anbetung f (-/%-en) worship, adoration; '2swürdig adj. adorable.

'an|bieten v/t. (irr. bieten, sep., -ge-, h) offer; '~binden v/t. (irr. binden, sep., -ge-, h) bind, tie (up); ~ an (dat., acc.) tie to; s. angebunden; '~blasen v/t. (irr. blasen, sep., -ge-, h) blow at or (up)on.

'Anblick m look; view; sight, aspect; '2en v/t. (sep., -ge-, h) look at; glance at; view; eye.

'an|blinzeln v/t. (sep., -ge-, h) wink at; '~brechen (irr. brechen, sep., -ge-) 1. v/t. (h) break into (provisions, etc.); open (bottle, etc.); 2. v/i. (sein) begin; day: break, dawn; '~brennen (irr. brennen, sep., -ge-) 1. v/t. (h) set on fire; light (cigar, etc.); 2. v/i. (sein) catch fire; burn; '~bringen v/t. (irr. bringen, sep., -ge-, h) bring; fix (an dat. to), attach (to); place; † dispose of (goods); lodge (complaint); s. angebracht.

'Anbruch m (-[e]s/no pl.) beginning; break (of day).

'anbrüllen v/t. (sep., -ge-, h) roar at.

Andacht ['andaxt] f (-/-en) devotion(s pl.); prayers pl.

andächtig ['andɛçtiç] devout.

'andauern v/i. (sep., -ge-, h) last, continue, go on.

'Andenken n (-s/-) memory, remembrance; keepsake, souvenir; zum ~ an (acc.) in memory of.

ander adj. ['andər] other; different; next; opposite; am ~en Tag (on) the next day; e-n Tag um den ~en every other day; ein ~er Freund another friend; nichts ~es nothing else.

andererseits adv. ['andərər'zaits] on the other hand.

ändern ['ɛndərn] v/t. (ge-, h) alter; change; ich kann es nicht ~ I can't help it; sich ~ alter; change.

'andern|falls adv. otherwise, else.

anders adv. ['andərs] otherwise; differently (als from); else; j. ~ somebody else; ich kann nicht ~, ich muß weinen I cannot help crying; ~ werden change.

'ander'seits adv. s. andererseits.

'anders'wo adv. elsewhere.

anderthalb adj. ['andərt'halp] one and a half.

'Änderung f (-/-en) change, alteration.

ander|wärts adv. ['andər'verts] elsewhere; '~weitig 1. adj. other; 2. adv. otherwise.

'andeut|en v/t. (sep., -ge-, h) indicate; hint; intimate; imply; suggest; '2ung f intimation; hint; suggestion.

'Andrang m rush; ⚕ congestion.

andre adj. ['andrə] s. andere.

'andrehen v/t. (sep., -ge-, h) turn on (gas, etc.); ≠ switch on (light).

'androh|en v/t. (sep., -ge-, h): j-m et. ~ threaten s.o. with s.th.; '2ung f threat.

aneignen ['an?-] v/refl. (sep., -ge-, h) appropriate; acquire; adopt; seize; usurp.

aneinander adv. [an?aɪ'nandər] together; ~geraten v/i. (irr. raten, sep., no -ge-, sein) clash (mit with).

anekeln ['an?-] v/t. (sep., -ge-, h) disgust, sicken.

Anerbieten ['an?-] n (-s/-) offer.

anerkannt adj. ['an?-] acknowledged, recognized.

anerkenn|en ['an?-] v/t. (irr. kennen, sep., no -ge-, h) acknowledge (als as), recognize; appreciate; own (child); hono(u)r (bill); '2ung f (-/-en) acknowledgement; recognition; appreciation.

'anfahr|en (irr. fahren, sep., -ge-) 1. v/i. (sein) start; ↘ descend; angefahren kommen drive up; 2. v/t. (h) run into; carry, convey; j-n ~ let fly at s.o.; '2t f approach; drive.

'Anfall ⚕ m fit, attack; '2en (irr. fallen, sep., -ge-) 1. v/t. (h) attack; assail; 2. v/i. (sein) accumulate; money: accrue.

anfällig adj. ['anfɛliç] susceptible (für to); prone to (diseases, etc.).

'Anfang m beginning, start, commencement; ~ Mai at the beginning of May, early in May; '2en v/t. and v/i. (irr. fangen, sep., -ge-, h) begin, start, commence.

Anfäng|er ['anfɛŋər] m (-s/-) beginner; '2lich 1. adj. initial; 2. adv. in the beginning.

anfangs adv. ['anfaŋs] in the beginning; '2buchstabe m initial (letter); großer ~ capital letter; 2gründe ['~gryndə] m/pl. elements pl.

'anfassen (sep., -ge-, h) 1. v/t. seize; touch; handle; 2. v/i. lend a hand.

anfecht|bar adj. ['anfɛçtba:r] contestable; '~en v/t. (irr. fechten, sep., -ge-, h) contest, dispute; ⚖ avoid (contract); '2ung f (-/-en) contestation; ⚖ avoidance; fig. temptation.

an|fertigen ['anfɛrtigən] v/t. (sep., -ge-, h) make, manufacture; '~feuchten v/t. (sep., -ge-, h) moisten, wet, damp; '~feuern v/t. (sep., -ge-, h) fire, heat; sports: cheer; fig. encourage; '~flehen v/t. (sep., -ge-, h) implore; '~fliegen ✈ v/t. (irr. fliegen, sep., -ge-, h) approach, head for (airport, etc.); '2flug m ✈ approach (flight); fig. touch, tinge.

'anforder|n v/t. (sep., -ge-, h) demand; request; claim; '2ung f demand; request; claim.

'Anfrage f inquiry; '2n v/i. (sep., -ge-, h) ask (bei j-m s.o.); inquire (bei j-m nach et. of s.o. about s.th.).

an|freunden ['anfrɔyndən] v/refl.
(sep., -ge-, h): sich ~ mit make
friends with; '~frieren v/i. (irr.
frieren, sep., -ge-, sein) freeze on
(an dat. or acc. to); '~fügen v/t.
(sep., -ge-, h) join, attach (an acc.
to); '~fühlen v/t. (sep., -ge-, h)
feel, touch; sich ~ feel.

Anfuhr ['anfuːr] f (-/-en) conveyance, carriage.

'anführ|en v/t. (sep., -ge-, h) lead;
allege; ✗ command; quote, cite
(authority, passage, etc.); dupe, fool,
trick; '2er m (ring)leader; '2ungs-
zeichen n/pl. quotation marks pl.,
inverted commas pl.

'Angabe f declaration; statement;
instruction; F fig. bragging, show-
ing off.

'angeb|en (irr. geben, sep., -ge-, h)
1. v/t. declare; state; specify; allege;
give (name, reason); ✝ quote (prices);
denounce, inform against; 2.
v/i. cards: deal first; F fig. brag,
show off, Am. blow; '2er m (-s/-)
informer; F braggart, Am. blow-
hard; ~lich adj. ['~pliç] supposed;
pretended, alleged.

'angeboren adj. innate, inborn; ✗
congenital.

'Angebot n offer (a. ✝); at auction
sale: bid; ✝ supply.

'ange|bracht adj. appropriate, suit-
able; well-timed; '~bunden adj.:
kurz ~ sein be short (gegen with).

'angehen (irr. gehen, sep., -ge-)
1. v/i. (sein) begin; meat, etc.: go
bad, go off; es geht an it will do;
2. v/t. (h): j-n ~ concern s.o.; das
geht dich nichts an that is no business of yours.

'angehör|en v/i. (sep., no -ge-, h)
belong to; '2ige ['~igə] m, f (-n/-n):
seine ~n pl. his relations pl.; die
nächsten ~n pl. the next of kin.

Angeklagte ⚖ ['angəklɑːktə] m, f
(-n/-n) the accused; prisoner (at the
bar); defendant.

Angel ['aŋəl] f (-/-n) hinge; fishing-
tackle, fishing-rod.

'angelegen adj.: sich et. ~ sein lassen make s.th. one's business; '2-
heit f business, concern, affair,
matter.

'Angel|gerät n fishing-tackle; '2n
(ge-, h) 1. v/i. fish (nach for), angle
(for) (both a. fig.); ~ in fish (river,
etc.); 2. v/t. fish (trout); '~punkt
fig. m pivot.

'Angel|sachse m Anglo-Saxon; '2-
sächsisch adj. Anglo-Saxon.

'Angelschnur f fishing-line.

'ange|messen adj. suitable, appro-
priate; reasonable; adequate; '~-
nehm adj. pleasant, agreeable,
pleasing; sehr ~! glad or pleased to
meet you; ~regt adj. ['~reːkt] stim-
ulated; discussion: animated, lively;
'~sehen adj. respected, esteemed.

'Angesicht n (-[e]s/-er, -e) face,
countenance; von ~ zu ~ face to
face; '2s prp. (gen.) in view of.

angestammt adj. ['angəʃtamt] hereditary, innate.

Angestellte ['angəʃtɛltə] m, f (-n/-n)
employee; die ~n pl. the staff.

'ange|trunken adj. tipsy; ~wandt
adj. ['~vant] applied; '~wiesen
adj.: ~ sein auf (acc.) be dependent
or thrown (up)on.

'angewöhnen v/t. (sep., -ge-, h):
j-m et. ~ accustom s.o. to s.th.; sich
et. ~ get into the habit of s.th.;
take to (smoking).

'Angewohnheit f custom, habit.

Angina ✗ [aŋ'giːna] f (-/Anginen)
angina; tonsillitis.

'angleichen v/t. (irr. gleichen, sep.,
-ge-, h) assimilate (an acc. to, with),
adjust (to); sich ~ an (acc.) assimilate to or with, adjust or adapt o.s.
to.

Angler ['aŋlər] m (-s/-) angler.

'angliedern v/t. (sep., -ge-, h) join;
annex; affiliate.

Anglist [aŋ'glist] m (-en/-en) professor or student of English, An-
gli(ci)st.

'angreif|en v/t. (irr. greifen, sep.,
-ge-, h) touch; draw upon (capital,
provisions); attack; affect (health,
material); 🜚 corrode; exhaust;
'2er m (-s/-) aggressor, assailant.

'angrenzend adj. adjacent; adjoining.

'Angriff m attack, assault; in ~ nehmen set about; '~skrieg m offensive
war; '2slustig adj. aggressive.

Angst [aŋst] f (-/ɛe) fear; anxiety;
anguish; ich habe ~ I am afraid (vor
dat. of); '~hase m coward.

ängstigen ['ɛŋstigən] v/t. (ge-, h)
frighten, alarm; sich ~ be afraid
(vor dat. of); be alarmed (um about).

ängstlich adj. ['ɛŋstliç] uneasy,
nervous; anxious; afraid; scrupulous; timid; '2keit f (-/no pl.) anxiety; scrupulousness; timidity.

'an|haben v/t. (irr. haben, sep., -ge-,
h) have (garment) on; das kann mir
nichts ~ that can't do me any harm;
'~haften v/i. (sep., -ge-, h) stick,
adhere (dat. to); '~haken v/t. (sep.,
-ge-, h) hook on; tick (off), Am.
check (off) (name, item).

'anhalten (irr. halten, sep., -ge-, h)
1. v/t. stop; j-n ~ zu et. keep s.o. to
s.th.; den Atem ~ hold one's breath;
2. v/i. continue, last; stop; um ein
Mädchen ~ propose to a girl; '~d
adj. continuous; persevering.

'Anhaltspunkt m clue.

'Anhang m appendix, supplement
(to book, etc.); followers pl., adher-
ents pl.

'anhäng|en (sep., -ge-, h) 1. v/t.
hang on; affix, attach, join; add;
couple (on) (coach, vehicle); 2. v/i.

(*irr.* hängen) adhere to; '**2er** *m* (*-s/-*) adherent, follower; pendant (*of necklace, etc.*); label, tag; trailer (*behind car, etc.*).

anhänglich *adj.* ['anhɛnliç] devoted, attached; '**2keit** *f* (*-/no pl.*) devotion, attachment.

Anhängsel ['anhɛnzəl] *n* (*-s/-*) appendage.

'**anhauchen** *v/t.* (*sep.*, *-ge-*, *h*) breathe on; blow (*fingers*).

'**anhäuf|en** *v/t. and v/refl.* (*sep.*, *-ge-*, *h*) pile up, accumulate; '**2ung** *f* accumulation.

'**an|heben** *v/t.* (*irr.* heben, *sep.*, *-ge-*, *h*) lift, raise; '**_heften** *v/t.* (*sep.*, *-ge-*, *h*) fasten (*an acc.* to); stitch (to).

an'heim|fallen *v/i.* (*irr.* fallen, *sep.*, *-ge-*, *sein*): *j-m* ~ fall to s.o.; **_stellen** *v/t.* (*sep.*, *-ge-*, *h*): *j-m et.* ~ leave s.th. to s.o.

'**Anhieb** *m*: *auf* ~ at the first go.

'**Anhöhe** *f* rise, elevation, hill.

'**anhören** *v/t.* (*sep.*, *-ge-*, *h*) listen to; *sich* ~ sound.

Anilin ⚗ [ani'li:n] *n* (*-s/no pl.*) anilin(e).

'**ankämpfen** *v/i.* (*sep.*, *-ge-*, *h*): ~ *gegen* struggle against.

'**Ankauf** *m* purchase.

Anker ⚓ ['aŋkər] *m* (*-s/-*) anchor; *vor* ~ *gehen* cast anchor; '**_kette** ⚓ *f* cable; '**2n** ⚓ *v/t. and v/i.* (*ge-*, *h*) anchor; '**_uhr** *f* lever watch.

'**anketten** *v/t.* (*sep.*, *-ge-*, *h*) chain (*an dat. or acc.* to).

'**Anklage** *f* accusation, charge; ⚖ *a.* indictment; '**2n** *v/t.* (*sep.*, *-ge-*, *h*) accuse (*gen. or wegen of*), charge (*with*); ⚖ *a.* indict (for).

'**Ankläger** *m* accuser; *öffentlicher* ~ ⚖ public prosecutor, *Am.* district attorney.

'**anklammern** *v/t.* (*sep.*, *-ge-*, *h*) clip *s.th.* on; *sich* ~ cling (*an dat. or acc.* to).

'**Anklang** *m*: ~ *an* (*acc.*) suggestion of; ~ *finden* meet with approval.

'**an|kleben** *v/t.* (*sep.*, *-ge-*, *h*) stick on (*an dat. or acc.* to); glue on (to); paste on (to); gum on (to); '**_kleiden** *v/t.* (*sep.*, *-ge-*, *h*) dress; *sich* ~ dress (o.s.); '**_klopfen** *v/i.* (*sep.*, *-ge-*, *h*) knock (*an acc.* at); '**_knipsen** ⚡ *v/t.* (*sep.*, *-ge-*, *h*) turn or switch on; '**_knüpfen** (*sep.*, *-ge-*, *h*) 1. *v/t.* tie (*an dat. or acc.* to); *fig.* begin; *Verbindungen* ~ form connexions or (*Am. only*) connections; 2. *v/i.* refer (*an acc.* to); '**_kommen** *v/i.* (*irr.* kommen, *sep.*, *-ge-*, *sein*) arrive; ~ *auf* (*acc.*) depend (up)on; *es darauf* ~ *lassen* run the risk, risk it; *darauf kommt es an* that is the point; *es kommt nicht darauf an* it does not matter.

Ankömmling ['ankœmliŋ] *m* (*-s/-e*) new-comer, new arrival.

'**ankündig|en** *v/t.* (*sep.*, *-ge-*, *h*) announce; advertise; '**2ung** *f* announcement; advertisement.

Ankunft ['ankunft] *f* (*-/no pl.*) arrival.

'**an|kurbeln** *v/t.* (*sep.*, *-ge-*, *h*) *mot.* crank up; *die Wirtschaft* ~ F boost the economy; '**_lächeln** *v/t.* (*sep.*, *-ge-*, *h*), '**_lachen** *v/t.* (*sep.*, *-ge-*, *h*) smile at.

'**Anlage** *f* construction; installation; ⊕ plant; grounds *pl.*, park; plan, arrangement, layout; enclosure (*to letter*); ↑ investment; talent; predisposition, tendency; *öffentliche* ~*n pl.* public gardens *pl.*; '**_kapital** ↑ *n* invested capital.

'**anlangen** (*sep.*, *-ge-*) 1. *v/i.* (*sein*) arrive at; 2. *v/t.* (*h*) F touch; concern; *was mich anlangt* as far as I am concerned, (speaking) for myself.

Anlaß ['anlas] *m* (*Anlasses/Anlässe*) occasion; *ohne allen* ~ without any reason.

'**anlass|en** *v/t.* (*irr.* lassen, *sep.*, *-ge-*, *h*) F leave or keep (*garment, etc.*) on; leave (*light, etc.*) on; ⊕ start, set going; *sich gut* ~ promise well; '**2er** *mot. m* (*-s/-*) starter.

anläßlich *prp.* (*gen.*) ['anlɛsliç] on the occasion of.

'**Anlauf** *m* start, run; '**2en** (*irr.* laufen, *sep.*, *-ge-*) 1. *v/i.* (*sein*) run up; start; tarnish, (grow) dim; ~ *gegen* run against; 2. ⚓ *v/t.* (*h*) call or touch at (*port*).

'**an|legen** (*sep.*, *-ge-*, *h*) 1. *v/t.* put (*an acc.* to, against); lay out (*garden*); invest (*money*); level (*gun*); put on (*garment*); found (*town*); ⚗ apply (*dressing*); lay in (*provisions*); *Feuer* ~ *an* (*acc.*) set fire to; 2. *v/i.* ⚓: land; moor; ~ *auf* (*acc.*) aim at; '**_lehnen** *v/t.* (*sep.*, *-ge-*, *h*) lean (*an acc.* against); leave or set (*door*) ajar; *sich* ~ *an* (*acc.*) lean against or on.

Anleihe ['anlaɪə] *f* (*-/-n*) loan.

'**anleit|en** *v/t.* (*sep.*, *-ge-*, *h*) guide (*zu* to); instruct (*in dat.* in); '**2ung** *f* guidance, instruction; guide.

'**Anliegen** *n* (*-s/-*) desire, request.

'**an|locken** *v/t.* (*sep.*, *-ge-*, *h*) allure, entice; decoy; '**_machen** *v/t.* (*sep.*, *-ge-*, *h*) fasten (*an acc.* to), fix (to); make, light (*fire*); ⚡ switch on (*light*); dress (*salad*); '**_malen** *v/t.* (*sep.*, *-ge-*, *h*) paint.

'**Anmarsch** *m* approach.

anmaß|en ['anma:sən] *v/refl.* (*sep.*, *-ge-*, *h*) arrogate *s.th.* to o.s.; assume (*right*); presume; '**_end** *adj.* arrogant; '**2ung** *f* (*-/-en*) arrogance, presumption.

'**anmeld|en** *v/t.* (*sep.*, *-ge-*, *h*) announce, notify; *sich* ~ *bei* make an appointment with; '**2ung** *f* announcement, notification.

'anmerk|en v/t. (sep., -ge-, h) mark; note down; j-m et. ~ observe or perceive s.th. in s.o.; '2ung f (-/-en) remark; note; annotation; comment.

'anmessen v/t. (irr. messen, sep., -ge-, h): j-m e-n Anzug ~ measure s.o. for a suit; s. angemessen.

'Anmut f (-/no pl.) grace, charm, loveliness; '2ig adj. charming, graceful, lovely.

'an|nageln v/t. (sep., -ge-, h) nail on (an acc. to); '~nähen v/t. (sep., -ge-, h) sew on (an acc. to).

annäher|nd adj. ['annɛ:ornt] approximate; '2ung f (-/-en) approach.

Annahme ['anna:mə] f (-/-n) acceptance; receiving-office; fig. assumption, supposition.

'annehm|bar adj. acceptable; price: reasonable; '~en (irr. nehmen, sep., -ge-, h) 1. v/t. accept, take; fig.: suppose, take it, Am. guess; assume; contract (habit); adopt (child); parl. pass (bill); sich (gen.) ~ attend to s.th.; befriend s.o.; 2. v/i. accept; '2lichkeit f (-/-en) amenity, agreeableness.

Annexion [anɛk'sjo:n] f (-/-en) annexation.

Annonce [a'nõ:sə] f (-/-n) advertisement.   [mous.]

anonym adj. [ano'ny:m] anony-)

anordn|en ['an⁹-] v/t. (sep., -ge-, h) order; arrange; direct; '2ung f arrangement; direction; order.

anpacken v/t. (sep., -ge-, h) seize, grasp; fig. tackle.

'anpass|en v/t. (sep., -ge-, h) fit, adapt, suit; adjust; try or fit (garment) on; sich ~ adapt to o.s. (dat. to); '2ung f (-/-en) adaptation; '~ungsfähig adj. adaptable.

'anpflanz|en v/t. (sep., -ge-, h) cultivate, plant; '2ung f cultivation; plantation.

Anprall ['anpral] m (-[e]s/%-e) impact; '2en v/i. (sep., -ge-, sein) strike (an acc. against).

'anpreisen v/t. (irr. preisen, sep., -ge-, h) commend, praise; boost, push.

'Anprobe f try-on, fitting.

'an|probieren v/t. (sep., no -ge-, h) try or fit on; '~raten v/t. (irr. raten, sep., -ge-, h) advise; '~rechnen v/t. (sep., -ge-, h) charge; hoch ~ value highly.

'Anrecht n right, title, claim (auf acc. to).

'Anrede f address; '2n v/t. (sep., -ge-, h) address, speak to.

'anreg|en v/t. (sep., -ge-, h) stimulate; suggest; '~end adj. stimulative, stimulating; suggestive; '2ung f stimulation; suggestion.

'Anreiz m incentive; '2en v/t. (sep., -ge-, h) stimulate; incite.

'an|rennen v/i. (irr. rennen, sep., -ge-, sein): ~ gegen run against; angerannt kommen come running; '~richten v/t. (sep., -ge-, h) prepare, dress (food, salad); cause, do (damage).

anrüchig adj. ['anryçiç] disreputable.

'anrücken v/i. (sep., -ge-, sein) approach.

'Anruf m call (a. teleph.); '2en v/t. (irr. rufen, sep., -ge-, h) call (zum Zeugen to witness); teleph. ring up, F phone, Am. call up; hail (ship); invoke (God, etc.); appeal to (s.o.'s help).

'anrühren v/t. (sep., -ge-, h) touch; mix.

'Ansage f announcement; '2n v/t. (sep., -ge-, h) announce; '~r m (-s/-) announcer; compère, Am. master of ceremonies.

'ansammeln v/t. (sep., -ge-, h) collect, gather; accumulate, amass; sich ~ collect, gather; accumulate.

ansässig adj. ['anzɛsiç] resident.

'Ansatz m start.

'an|schaffen v/t. (sep., -ge-, h) procure, provide; purchase; sich et. ~ provide or supply o.s. with s.th.; '~schalten ∫ v/t. (sep., -ge-, h) connect; switch on (light).

'anschau|en v/t. (sep., -ge-, h) look at, view; '~lich adj. clear, vivid; graphic.

'Anschauung f (-/-en) view; perception; conception; intuition; contemplation; '~smaterial n illustrative material; '~sunterricht ['an-ʃauuŋs⁹-] m visual instruction, object-lessons pl.; '~svermögen n intuitive faculty.

'Anschein m (-[e]s/no pl.) appearance; '2end adj. apparent, seeming.

'an|schicken v/refl. (sep., -ge-, h): sich ~, et. zu tun get ready for s.th.; prepare for s.th.; set about doing s.th.; ~schirren ['~ʃirən] v/t. (sep., -ge-, h) harness.

'Anschlag m ⊕ stop, catch; ♪ touch; notice; placard, poster, bill; estimate; calculation; plot; e-n ~ auf j-n verüben make an attempt on s.o.'s life; ~brett ['~k-] n noticeboard, Am. bulletin board; 2en ['~gən] (irr. schlagen, sep., -ge-, h) 1. v/t. strike (an dat. or acc. against), knock (against); post up (bill); ♪ touch; level (gun); estimate, rate; 2. v/i. strike (an acc. against), knock (against); dog: bark; ♂ take (effect); food: agree (bei with); ~säule ['~k-] f advertising pillar; ~zettel ['~k-] m notice; placard, poster, bill.

'anschließen v/t. (irr. schließen, sep., -ge-, h) fix with a lock; join, attach, annex; ⊕, ∮ connect; sich j-m ~ join s.o.; sich e-r Meinung ~

follow an opinion; '**∼d** adj. adjacent (an acc. to); subsequent (to).

'**Anschluß** m joining; 🚲, ⚡, teleph., gas, etc.: connexion, (Am. only) connection; **∼ haben** an (acc.) 🚲, boat: connect with; 🚂 run in connexion with; teleph.: **∼ finden** make friends (an acc. with), F pal up (with); teleph.: **∼ bekommen** get through; '**∼dose** ⚡ f (wall) socket; '**∼zug** 🚂 m connecting train, connexion.

'**an|schmiegen** v/refl. (sep., -ge-, h): **sich ∼** an (acc.) nestle to; '**∼schmieren** v/t. (sep., -ge-, h) (be)smear, grease; F fig. cheat; '**∼schnallen** v/t. (sep., -ge-, h) buckle on; bitte **∼!** ✈ fasten seat-belts, please!; '**∼schnauzen** F v/t. (sep., -ge-, h) snap at, blow s.o. up, Am. a. bawl s.o. out; '**∼schneiden** v/t. (irr. schneiden, sep., -ge-, h) cut; broach (subject).

'**Anschnitt** m first cut or slice.

'**an|schrauben** v/t. (sep., -ge-, h) screw on (an dat. or acc. to); '**∼schreiben** v/t. (irr. schreiben, sep., -ge-, h) write down; sports, games: score; et. **∼ lassen** have s.th. charged to one's account; buy s.th. on credit; '**∼schreien** v/t. (irr. schreien, sep., -ge-, h) shout at.

'**Anschrift** f address.

an|schuldigen ['anʃuldigən] v/t. (sep., -ge-, h) accuse, incriminate; '**∼schwärzen** v/t. (sep., -ge-, h) blacken; fig. a. defame.

'**anschwell|en** (irr. schwellen, sep., -ge-) 1. v/i. (sein) swell; increase, rise; 2. v/t. (h) swell; '**2ung** f swelling.

anschwemm|en ['anʃvɛmən] v/t. (sep., -ge-, h) wash ashore; geol. deposit (alluvium); '**2ung** f (-/-en) wash; geol. alluvial deposits pl., alluvium.

'**ansehen** 1. v/t. (irr. sehen, sep., -ge-, h) (take a) look at; view; regard, consider (als as); et. mit **∼** witness s.th.; '**∼ für** take for; man sieht ihm sein Alter nicht an he does not look his age; 2. **2 n** (-s/no pl.) authority, prestige; respect; F appearance, aspect.

ansehnlich adj. ['anze:nlɪç] considerable; good-looking.

'**an|seilen** mount. v/t. and v/refl. (sep., -ge-, h) rope; '**∼sengen** v/t. (sep., -ge-, h) singe; '**∼setzen** (sep., -ge-, h) 1. v/t. put (an acc. to); add (to); fix, appoint (date); rate; fix, quote (prices); charge; put forth (leaves, etc.); put on (flesh); put (food) on (to boil); Rost **∼** rust; 2. v/i. try; start; get ready.

'**Ansicht** f (-/-en) sight, view; fig. view, opinion; meiner **∼** nach in my opinion; zur **∼** ✝ on approval; '**∼-(post)karte** f picture postcard; '**∼ssache** f matter of opinion.

3*

'**ansied|eln** v/t. and v/refl. (sep., -ge-, h) settle; '**2ler** m settler; '**2lung** f settlement.

'**Ansinnen** n (-s/-) request, demand.

'**anspann|en** v/t. (sep., -ge-, h) stretch; put or harness (horses, etc.) to the carriage, etc.; fig. strain, exert; '**2ung** f fig. f strain, exertion.

'**anspeien** v/t. (irr. speien, sep., -ge-, h) spit (up)on or at.

'**anspiel|en** v/i. (sep., -ge-, h) cards: lead; sports: lead off; football: kick off; **∼ auf** (acc.) allude to, hint at; '**2ung** f (-/-en) allusion, hint.

'**anspitzen** v/t. (sep., -ge-, h) point, sharpen.

'**Ansporn** m (-[e]s/⚓ -e) spur; '**2en** v/t. (sep., -ge-, h) spur s.o. on.

'**Ansprache** f address, speech; e-e **∼ halten** deliver an address.

'**ansprechen** v/t. (irr. sprechen, sep., -ge-, h) speak to, address; appeal to; '**∼d** adj. appealing.

'**an|springen** (irr. springen, sep., -ge-) 1. v/i. (sein) engine: start; 2. v/t. (h) jump (up)on, leap at; '**∼spritzen** v/t. (sep., -ge-, h) splash (j-n mit et. s.th. on s.o.); (be-) sprinkle.

'**Anspruch** m claim (a. ⚖) (auf acc. to), pretension (to); ⚖ title (to); **∼ haben auf** (acc.) be entitled to; in **∼ nehmen** claim s.th.; Zeit in **∼** nehmen take up time; '**2slos** adj. unpretentious; unassuming; '**2svoll** adj. pretentious.

'**an|spülen** v/t. (sep., -ge-, h) s. anschwemmen; '**∼stacheln** v/t. (sep., -ge-, h) goad (on).

Anstalt ['anʃtalt] f (-/-en) establishment, institution; **∼en treffen zu** make arrangements for.

'**Anstand** m 1. (-[e]s/⚓e) hunt. stand; objection; 2. (-[e]s/⚓ ⚓e) good manners pl.; decency, propriety.

anständig adj. ['anʃtɛndɪç] decent; respectable; price: fair, handsome; '**2keit** f (-/⚓-en) decency.

'**Anstands|gefühl** n sense of propriety; tact; '**2los** adv. unhesitatingly.

'**anstarren** v/t. (sep., -ge-, h) stare or gaze at.

anstatt prp. (gen.) and cj. [an'ʃtat] instead of.

'**anstaunen** v/t. (sep., -ge-, h) gaze at s.o. or s.th. in wonder.

'**ansteck|en** v/t. (sep., -ge-, h) pin on; put on (ring); 🌡 infect; set on fire; kindle (fire); light (candle, etc.); '**∼end** adj. infectious; contagious; fig. a. catching; '**2ung** ⚕ f (-/-en) infection; contagion.

'**an|stehen** v/i. (irr. stehen, sep., -ge-, h) queue up (nach for), Am. stand in line (for); '**∼steigen** v/i. (irr. steigen, sep., -ge-, sein) ground: rise, ascend; fig. increase.

'**anstell|en** v/t. (sep., -ge-, h) engage, employ, hire; make (ex-

periments); draw (*comparison*); turn on (*light, etc.*); manage; *sich* ~ queue up (*nach* for), *Am.* line up (for); *sich dumm* ~ set about *s.th.* stupidly; '~ig *adj.* handy, skil(l)ful; 'ℒung *f* place, position, job; employment.

Anstieg ['anʃtiːk] *m* (-[e]s/-e) ascent.

'**anstift|en** *v/t.* (*sep., -ge-, h*) instigate; 'ℒer *m* instigator; 'ℒung *f* instigation.

'**anstimmen** *v/t.* (*sep., -ge-, h*) strike up (*tune*).

'**Anstoß** *m* football: kick-off; *fig.* impulse; offen|ce, *Am.* -se; ~ erregen give offence (*bei* to); ~ nehmen an (*dat.*) take offence at; ~ geben zu et. start s.th., initiate s.th.; 'ℒen (*irr. stoßen, sep., -ge-*) 1. *v/t.* (h) push, knock (*acc. or an* against); nudge; 2. *v/i.* (sein) knock (*an acc.* against); border (*on,* upon); adjoin; 3. *v/i.* (h): mit der Zunge ~ lisp; *auf j-s Gesundheit* ~ drink (to) s.o.'s health; 'ℒend *adj.* adjoining.

anstößig *adj.* ['anʃtøːsiç] shocking.

'**an|strahlen** *v/t.* (*sep., -ge-, h*) illuminate; floodlight (*building, etc.*); *fig.* beam at *s.o.;* '~streben *v/t.* (*sep., -ge-, h*) aim at, aspire to, strive for.

'**anstreich|en** *v/t.* (*irr. streichen, sep., -ge-, h*) paint; whitewash; mark; underline (*mistake*); 'ℒer *m* (-s/-) house-painter; decorator.

anstreng|en ['anʃtrɛŋən] *v/t.* (*sep., -ge-, h*) exert; try (*eyes*); fatigue; Prozeß ~ bring an action (*gegen j-n* against s.o.); *sich* ~ exert o.s.; '~end *adj.* strenuous; trying (*für* to); 'ℒung *f* (-/-en) exertion, strain, effort.

'**Anstrich** *m* paint, colo(u)r; coat (-ing); *fig.:* tinge; air.

'**Ansturm** *m* assault; onset; ~ *auf* (*acc.*) rush for; † run on (*bank*).

'**anstürmen** *v/i.* (*sep., -ge-, sein*) storm, rush.

'**Anteil** *m* share, portion; ~ nehmen an (*dat.*) take an interest in; sympathize with; ~**nahme** ['~naː-mə] *f* (-/no pl.) sympathy; interest; '~schein † *m* share-certificate.

Antenne [an'tɛnə] *f* (-/-n) aerial.

Antialkoholiker [anti'alko'hoːlikər, '~] *m* (-s/-) teetotaller.

antik *adj.* [an'tiːk] antique.

Antilope *zo.* [anti'loːpə] *f* (-/-n) antelope.

Antipathie [antipa'tiː] *f* (-/-n) antipathy.

'**antippen** F *v/t.* (*sep., -ge-, h*) tap.

Antiquar [anti'kvaːr] *m* (-s/-e) second-hand bookseller; ~iat [~ar-'jaːt] *n* (-[e]s/-e) second-hand bookshop; ℒisch *adj. and adv.* [~'kvaːriʃ] second-hand.

Antiquitäten [antikvi'tɛːtən] *f/pl.* antiques *pl.*

'**Anti-Rakete** *f* anti-ballistic missile.

antiseptisch ✗ *adj.* [anti'zɛptiʃ] antiseptic.

Antlitz ['antlits] *n* (-es/✎ -e) face, countenance.

Antrag ['antraːk] *m* (-[e]s/⸚e) offer, proposal; application, request; *parl.* motion; ~ stellen auf (*acc.*) make an application for; *parl.* put a motion for; '~steller *m* (-s/-) applicant; *parl.* mover; ⚖ petitioner.

'**an|treffen** *v/t.* (*irr. treffen, sep., -ge-, h*) meet with, find; '~treiben (*irr. treiben, sep., -ge-*) 1. *v/i.* (sein) drift ashore; 2. *v/t.* (h) drive (on); *fig.* impel; '~treten (*irr. treten, sep., -ge-*) 1. *v/t.* (h) enter upon (*office*); take up (*position*); set out on (*journey*); enter upon take possession of (*inheritance*); 2. *v/i.* (sein) take one's place; ✗ fall in.

'**Antrieb** *m* motive, impulse; ⊕ drive, propulsion.

'**Antritt** *m* (-[e]s/✎ -e) entrance (*into office*); taking up (*of position*); setting out (*on journey*); entering into possession (*of inheritance*).

'**antun** *v/t.* (*irr. tun, sep., -ge-, h*): j-m et. ~ do s.th. to s.o.; *sich et.* ~ lay hands on o.s.

'**Antwort** *f* (-/-en) answer, reply (*auf acc.* to); 'ℒen (*irr. ge-, h*) 1. *v/i.* answer (j-m s.o.), reply (*j-m* to s.o.; *both:* auf acc. to); 2. *v/t.* answer (*auf acc.* to), reply (to); '~schein *m* (international) reply coupon.

'**an|vertrauen** *v/t.* (*sep., no -ge-, h*): j-m et. ~ (en)trust s.o. with s.th., entrust s.th. to s.o.; confide s.th. to s.o.; '~wachsen *v/i.* (*irr. wachsen, sep., -ge-, sein*) take root; *fig.* increase; ~ an (*acc.*) grow on to.

Anwalt ['anvalt] *m* (-[e]s/⸚e) lawyer; solicitor, *Am.* attorney; counsel; barrister, *Am.* counsel(l)or; *fig.* advocate.

'**Anwandlung** *f* fit; impulse.

'**Anwärter** *m* candidate, aspirant; expectant.

Anwartschaft ['anvartʃaft] *f* (-/-en) expectancy; candidacy; prospect (*auf acc.* of).

'**anweis|en** *v/t.* (*irr. weisen, sep., -ge-, h*) assign; instruct; direct; *s.* angewiesen; 'ℒung *f* assignment; instruction; direction; † cheque, *Am.* check; draft; *s.* Postanweisung.

'**anwend|en** *v/t.* (*irr. wenden, sep., -ge-, h*) employ, use; apply (*auf acc.* to); *s.* angewandt; 'ℒung *f* application.

'**anwerben** *v/t.* (*irr. werben, sep., -ge-, h*) ✗ enlist, enrol(l); engage.

'**Anwesen** *n* estate; property.

'**anwesen|d** *adj.* present; 'ℒheit *f* (-/no pl.) presence.

'**Anzahl** *f* (-/no pl.) number; quantity.

'**anzahl|en** v/t. (sep., -ge-, h) pay on account; pay a deposit; '**2ung** f (first) instal(l)ment; deposit.

'**anzapfen** v/t. (sep., -ge-, h) tap.

'**Anzeichen** n symptom; sign.

Anzeige ['antsaɪgə] f (-/-n) notice, announcement; ✝ advice; advertisement; ⚏ information; '**2n** v/t. (sep., -ge-, h) announce, notify; ✝ advise; advertise; indicate; ⊕ instrument: indicate, show; thermometer: read (degrees); j-n ~ denounce s.o., inform against s.o.

'**anziehen** (irr. ziehen, sep., -ge-, h) **1.** v/t. draw, pull; draw (rein); tighten (screw); put on (garment); dress; fig. attract; **2.** v/i. draw; prices: rise; '**~d** adj. attractive, interesting.

'**Anziehung** f attraction; '**~skraft** f attractive power; attraction.

'**Anzug** m **1.** (-[e]s/⁼e) dress; suit; **2.** (-[e]s/no pl.): im ~ sein storm: be gathering; danger: be impending.

anzüglich adj. ['antsy:klɪç] personal; '**2keit** f (-/-en) personality.

'**anzünden** v/t. (sep., -ge-, h) light, kindle; strike (match); set (building) on fire.

apathisch adj. [a'pɑ:tɪʃ] apathetic.

Apfel ['apfəl] m (-s/⁼) apple; '**~mus** n apple-sauce; **~sine** [~'zi:nə] f (-/-n) orange; '**~wein** m cider.

Apostel [a'pɔstəl] m (-s/-) apostle.

Apostroph [apo'stro:f] m (-s/-e) apostrophe.

Apotheke [apo'te:kə] f (-/-n) chemist's shop, pharmacy, Am. drugstore; **~r** m (-s/-) chemist, Am. druggist, pharmacist.

Apparat [apa'rɑ:t] m (-[e]s/-e) apparatus; device; teleph.: am ~! speaking!; teleph.: am ~ bleiben hold the line.

Appell [a'pɛl] m (-s/-e) ✕: roll-call; inspection; parade; fig. appeal (an acc. to); **2ieren** [~'li:rən] v/i. (no -ge-, h) appeal (an acc. to).

Appetit [ape'ti:t] m (-[e]s/-e) appetite; **2lich** adj. appetizing, savo(u)ry, dainty.

Applaus [a'plaus] m (-es/✞ -e) applause.

Aprikose [apri'ko:zə] f (-/-n) apricot.

April [a'pril] m (-[s]/-e) April.

Aquarell [akva'rɛl] n (-s/-e) watercolo(u)r (painting), aquarelle.

Aquarium [a'kvɑ:rium] n (-s/ Aquarien) aquarium.

Äquator [ɛ'kvɑ:tɔr] m (-s/✞ -en) equator.

Ära ['ɛ:ra] f (-/✞ Ären) era.

Arab|er ['arabər] m (-s/-) Arab; **2isch** adj. [a'rɑ:bɪʃ] Arabian, Arab(ic).

Arbeit ['arbaɪt] f (-/-en) work; labo(u)r, toil; employment, job;

task; paper; workmanship; bei der ~ at work; sich an die ~ machen, an die ~ gehen set to work; (keine) ~ haben be in (out of) work; die ~ niederlegen stop work, down tools; '**2en** (ge-, h) **1.** v/i. work; labo(u)r, toil; **2.** v/t. work; make.

'**Arbeiter** m (-s/-) worker; workman, labo(u)rer, hand; '**~in** f (-/-nen) female worker; working woman, workwoman; '**~klasse** f working class(es pl.); '**~partei** f Labo(u)r Party; '**~schaft** f (-/-en), '**~stand** m working class(es pl.), labo(u)r.

'**Arbeit|geber** m (-s/-), '**~geberin** f (-/-nen) employer; '**~nehmer** m (-s/-), '**~nehmerin** f (-/-nen) employee.

'**arbeitsam** adj. industrious.

'**Arbeits|amt** n labo(u)r exchange; '**~anzug** m overall; '**~beschaffung** f (-/-en) provision of work; '**~bescheinigung** f certificate of employment; '**~einkommen** n earned income; '**2fähig** adj. able to work; '**~gericht** n labo(u)r or industrial court; '**~kleidung** f working clothes pl.; '**~kraft** f working power; worker, hand; Arbeitskräfte pl. a. labo(u)r; '**~leistung** f efficiency; power (of engine); output (of factory); '**~lohn** m wages pl., pay; '**2los** adj. out of work, unemployed; '**~lose** m (-n/-n): die ~n pl. the unemployed pl.; '**~losenunterstützung** f unemployment benefit; ~ beziehen F be on the dole; '**~losigkeit** f (-/no pl.) unemployment; '**~markt** m labo(u)r market; '**~minister** m Minister of Labour, Am. Secretary of Labor; '**~nachweis(stelle** f) m employment registry office, Am. labor registry office; '**~niederlegung** f (-/-en) strike, Am. F a. walkout; '**~pause** f break, intermission; '**~platz** m place of work; job; '**~raum** m workroom; '**2scheu** adj. work-shy; '**~scheu** f aversion to work; '**~schutzgesetz** n protective labo(u)r law; '**~tag** m working day, workday; '**2unfähig** adj. incapable of working; disabled; '**~weise** f practice, method of working; '**~willige** m (-n/-n) non-striker; '**~zeit** f working time; working hours pl.; '**~zeug** n tools pl.; '**~zimmer** n workroom; study.

Archäo|loge [arçeo'lo:gə] m (-n/-n) arch(a)eologist; **~logie** [~o'gi:] f (-/no pl.) arch(a)eology.

Arche ['arçə] f (-/-n) ark.

Architekt [arçi'tɛkt] m (-en/-en) architect; **~ur** [~'tu:r] f (-/-en) architecture.

Archiv [ar'çi:f] n (-s/-e) archives pl.; record office.

Areal [are'ɑ:l] n (-s/-e) area.

Arena [a'reːna] *f* (-/Arenen) arena; bullring; (circus-)ring.

arg *adj.* [ark] bad; wicked; gross.

Ärger ['ɛrgər] *m* (-s/*no pl.*) vexation, annoyance; anger; **2lich** *adj.* vexed, F mad, angry (*auf, über acc.* at *s.th.*, with *s.o.*); annoying, vexatious; '2n *v/t.* (ge-, h) annoy, vex, irritate, fret; bother; *sich ~* feel angry *or* vexed (*über acc.* at, about *s.th.*; with *s.o.*); '**~nis** *n* (-ses/-se) scandal, offen[ce, *Am.* -se.

'Arg|list *f* (-/*no pl.*) cunning, craft (-iness); **2listig** *adj.* crafty, cunning; **2los** *adj.* guileless; artless, unsuspecting; **~wohn** ['~voːn] *m* (-[e]s/*no pl.*) suspicion; **2wöhnen** ['~vøːnən] *v/t.* (ge-, h) suspect; **2wöhnisch** *adj.* suspicious.

Arie ♪ ['aːrjə] *f* (-/-n) aria.

Aristokrat [aristo'kraːt] *m* (-en/-en), **~in** *f* (-/-nen) aristocrat; **~ie** [~kra-'tiː] *f* (-/-n) aristocracy.

Arkade [ar'kaːdə] *f* (-/-n) arcade.

arm¹ *adj.* [arm] poor.

Arm² [~] *m* (-[e]s/-e) arm; branch (*of river, etc.*); F: *j-n auf den ~ nehmen* pull *s.o.*'s leg.

Armaturenbrett [arma'tuːrənbrɛt] *n* instrument board, dash-board.

'Arm|band *n* bracelet; **~banduhr** ['armbantʔ-] *f* wrist watch; '**~bruch** *m* fracture of the arm.

Armee [ar'meː] *f* (-/-n) army.

Ärmel ['ɛrməl] *m* (-s/-) sleeve; '**~kanal** *m the* (English) Channel.

'Armen|haus *n* alms-house, *Brt. a.* workhouse; '**~pflege** *f* poor relief; '**~pfleger** *m* guardian of the poor; welfare officer; '**~unterstützung** *f* poor relief.

ärmlich *adj.* ['ɛrmlɪç] *s. armselig.*

'armselig *adj.* poor; wretched; miserable; shabby; paltry.

Armut ['armuːt] *f* (-/*no pl.*) poverty.

Aroma [a'roːma] *n* (-s/Aromen, Aromata, -s) aroma, flavo(u)r; fragrance.

Arrest [a'rɛst] *m* (-es/-e) arrest; confinement; seizure (*of goods*); detention (*of pupil, etc.*); *~ bekommen* be kept in.

Art [aːrt] *f* (-/-en) kind, sort; ♀, *zo.* species; manner, way; nature; manners *pl.*; breed, race (*of animals*); *auf die(se) ~* in this way; '2en *v/i.* (ge-, sein): *~ nach* take after. [artery.\
Arterie *anat.* [ar'teːrjə] *f* (-/-n)|

artig *adj.* ['aːrtɪç] good, well-behaved; civil, polite; '2keit *f* (-/-en) good behavio(u)r; politeness; civility, *a.* civilities *pl.*

Artikel [ar'tiːkəl] *m* (-s/-) article; commodity.

Artillerie [artilə'riː] *f* (-/-n) artillery.

Artist [ar'tist] *m* (-en/-en), **~in** *f* (-/-nen) circus performer.

Arznei [arts'naɪ] *f* (-/-en) medicine, F physic; **2kunde** *f* (-/*no pl.*) pharmaceutics; **~mittel** *n* medicine, drug.

Arzt [aːrtst] *m* (-es/*≈*e) doctor, medical man; physician.

Ärztin ['ɛːrtstin] *f* (-/-nen) woman *or* lady doctor.

ärztlich *adj.* ['ɛːrtstlɪç] medical.

As [as] *n* (-ses/-se) ace.

Asche ['aʃə] *f* (-/-n) ash(es *pl.*); '**~n-bahn** *f sports:* cinder-track, *mot.* dirt-track; '**~nbecher** *m* ash-tray; **~nbrödel** ['~nbrøːdəl] *n* (-s/*no pl.*), **~nputtel** ['~nputəl] *n* **1.** (-s/*no pl.*) Cinderella; **2.** (-s/-) drudge.

Ascher'mittwoch *m* Ash Wednesday.

'asch'grau *adj.* ash-grey, ashy, *Am.* ash-gray.

äsen *hunt.* ['ɛːzən] *v/i.* (ge-, h) graze, browse.

Asiat [az'jaːt] *m* (-en/-en), **~in** *f* (-/-nen) Asiatic, Asian; **2isch** *adj.* Asiatic, Asian.

Asket [as'keːt] *m* (-en/-en) ascetic.

Asphalt [as'falt] *m* (-[e]s/-e) asphalt; **2ieren** [~'tiːrən] *v/t.* (*no* -ge-, h) asphalt.

aß [aːs] *pret. of essen.*

Assistent [asis'tɛnt] *m* (-en/-en), **~in** *f* (-/-nen) assistant.

Ast [ast] *m* (-es/*≈*e) branch, bough; knot (*in timber*); '**~loch** *n* knot-hole.

Astro|naut [astro'naut] *m* (-en/-en) astronaut; **~nom** [~'noːm] *m* (-en/-en) astronomer.

Asyl [a'zyːl] *n* (-s/-e) asylum; *fig.* sanctuary.

Atelier [atə'lje:] *n* (-s/-s) studio.

Atem ['aːtəm] *m* (-s/*no pl.*) breath; *außer ~* out of breath; **2los** *adj.* breathless; '**~not** ♫ *f* difficulty in breathing; '**~pause** *f* breathing-space; '**~zug** *m* breath, respiration.

Äther ['ɛːtər] *m* **1.** (-s/*no pl.*) *the* ether; **2.** ♫ (-s/-) ether; **2isch** *adj.* [ɛ'teːriʃ] ethereal, etheric.

Athlet [at'leːt] *m* (-en/-en), **~in** *f* (-/-nen) athlete; **~ik** *f* (-/*no pl.*) athletics *mst sg.*; **2isch** *adj.* athletic.

atlantisch *adj.* [at'lantiʃ] Atlantic.

Atlas ['atlas] *m* **1.** *geogr.* (-/*no pl.*) Atlas; **2.** (-, -ses/-se, Atlanten) *maps:* atlas; **3.** (-, -ses/-se) *textiles:* satin.

atmen ['aːtmən] *v/i. and v/t.* (ge-, h) breathe.

Atmosphär|e [atmo'sfɛːrə] *f* (-/-n) atmosphere; **2isch** *adj.* atmospheric.

'Atmung *f* (-/-en) breathing, respiration.

Atom [a'toːm] *n* (-s/-e) atom; **2ar** *adj.* [ato'maːr] atomic; **~bombe** *f* atomic bomb, atom-bomb, A-bomb; **~energie** *f* atomic *or* nuclear energy; **~forschung** *f* atomic *or* nuclear research; **~kern** *m* atomic nucleus; **~kraftwerk** *n* nuclear power station; **~meiler** *m* atomic pile, nuclear reactor; **~physiker** *m* atomic physicist; **~reaktor** *m* nuclear reactor, atomic pile; **~versuch** *m* atomic test; **~waffe** *f* atomic *or* nuclear weapon; **~wissenschaftler** *m* atomic scientist; **~zeitalter** *n* atomic age.

Attent|at [atɛn'tɑːt] *n* (-[e]s/-e) (attempted) assassination; *fig.* outrage; **~äter** [‿ɛːtər] *m* (-s/-) assailant, assassin.

Attest [a'tɛst] *n* (-es/-e) certificate; **2ieren** [‿'tiːrən] *v/t.* (*no* -ge-, *h*) attest, certify.

Attraktion [atrak'tsjoːn] *f* (-/-en) attraction.

Attrappe [a'trapə] *f* (-/-n) dummy.

Attribut [atri'buːt] *n* (-[e]s/-e) attribute; *gr.* attributive.

ätz|en ['ɛtsən] *v/t.* (ge-, *h*) corrode; ⚗ cauterize; etch (*metal plate*); **~end** *adj.* corrosive; caustic (*a. fig.*); **2ung** *f* (-/-en) corrosion; ⚗ cauterization; etching.

au *int.* [au] oh!; ouch!

auch *cj.* [aux] also, too, likewise; even; ~ *nicht* neither, nor; *wo* ~ (*immer*) wher(eso)ever; *ist es* ~ *wahr?* is it really true?

Audienz [audi'ɛnts] *f* (-/-en) audience, hearing.

auf [auf] 1. *prp.* (*dat.*) (up)on; in; at; of; by; ~ *dem Tisch* (up)on the table; ~ *dem Markt* in the market; ~ *der Universität* at the university; ~ *e-m Ball* at a ball; 2. *prp.* (*acc.*) on; in; at; to; towards (*a.* ~ ... *zu*); up; ~ *deutsch* in German; ~ *e-e Entfernung von* at a range of; ~ *die Post etc. gehen* go to the post-office, *etc.*; ~ *ein Pfund gehen 20 Schilling* 20 shillings go to a pound; *es geht* ~ *neun* it is getting on to nine; ~ ... *hin* on the strength of; 3. *adv.* up(wards); ~ *und ab gehen* walk up and down *or* to and fro; 4. *cj.*: ~ *daß* (in order) that; ~ *daß nicht* that not, lest; 5. *int.*: ~*!* up!

auf|arbeiten ['auf‿-] *v/t.* (*sep.*, -ge-, *h*) work off (*arrears of work*); furbish up; F do up (*garments*); **~atmen** *fig.* ['auf‿-] *v/i.* (*sep.*, -ge-, *h*) breathe again.

'Aufbau *m* (-[e]s/*no pl.*) building up; construction (*of play, etc.*); F *esp. Am.* setup (*of organization*); *mot.* body (*of car, etc.*); **2en** *v/t.* (*sep.*, -ge-, *h*) erect, build up; construct.

'auf|bauschen *v/t.* (*sep.*, -ge-, *h*) puff out; *fig.* exaggerate; **~beißen** *v/t.* (*irr.* beißen, *sep.*, -ge-, *h*) crack; **~bekommen** *v/t.* (*irr.* kommen, *sep.*, *no* -ge-, *h*) get open (*door*); be given (*a task*); **~bessern** *v/t.* (*sep.*, -ge-, *h*) raise (*salary*); **~bewahren** *v/t.* (*sep.*, *no* -ge-, *h*) keep; preserve;

'~bieten *v/t.* (*irr.* bieten, *sep.*, -ge-, *h*) summon; exert; ✗ raise; **'~binden** *v/t.* (*irr.* binden, *sep.*, -ge-, *h*) untie; **'~bleiben** *v/i.* (*irr.* bleiben, *sep.*, -ge-, *sein*) sit up; *door, etc.*: remain open; **'~blenden** (*sep.*, -ge-, *h*) 1. *mot. v/i.* turn up the headlights; 2. *v/t.* fade in (*scene*); **'~blicken** *v/i.* (*sep.*, -ge-, *h*) look up; raise one's eyes; **'~blitzen** *v/i.* (*sep.*, -ge-, *h*, *sein*) flash (up); **'~blühen** *v/i.* (*sep.*, -ge-, *sein*) bloom; flourish.

'aufbrausen *fig. v/i.* (*sep.*, -ge-, *sein*) fly into a passion; **'~d** *adj.* hot-tempered.

'auf|brechen (*irr.* brechen, *sep.*, -ge-) 1. *v/t.* (*h*) break open; force open; 2. *v/i.* (*sein*) burst open; set out (*nach for*); **'~bringen** *v/t.* (*irr.* bringen, *sep.*, -ge-, *h*) raise (*money, troops*); capture (*ship*); rouse *or* irritate *s.o.*

'Aufbruch *m* departure, start.

'auf|bügeln *v/t.* (*sep.*, -ge-, *h*) iron; **'~bürden** *v/t.* (*sep.*, -ge-, *h*): *j-m et.* ~ impose s.th. on s.o.; **'~decken** *v/t.* (*sep.*, -ge-, *h*) uncover; spread (*cloth*); *fig.* disclose; **'~drängen** *v/t.* (*sep.*, -ge-, *h*) force, obtrude (*j-m* [*up*]*on s.o.*); **'~drehen** *v/t.* (*sep.*, -ge-, *h*) turn on (*gas, etc.*).

'aufdringlich *adj.* obtrusive.

'Aufdruck *m* (-[e]s/-e) imprint; surcharge.

'aufdrücken *v/t.* (*sep.*, -ge-, *h*) impress.

aufeinander *adv.* [auf⁹ai'nandər] one after *or* upon another; **2folge** *f* succession; **~folgend** *adj.* successive.

Aufenthalt ['aufɛnthalt] *m* (-[e]s/-e) stay; residence; delay; 🚆 stop; **'~sgenehmigung** *f* residence permit.

auferlegen ['auf⁹ɛrleːgən] *v/t.* (*sep.*, *no* -ge-, *h*) impose (*j-m on s.o.*).

aufersteh|en ['auf⁹ɛrʃteːən] *v/i.* (*irr.* stehen, *sep.*, *no* -ge-, *sein*) rise (from the dead); **2ung** *f* (-/-en) resurrection.

auf|essen ['auf⁹-] *v/t.* (*irr.* essen, *sep.*, -ge-, *h*) eat up; **'~fahren** *v/i.* (*irr.* fahren, *sep.*, -ge-, *sein*) ascend; start up; *fig.* fly out; ⚓ run aground; *mot.* drive *or* run (*auf acc.* against, into).

'Auffahrt *f* ascent; driving up; approach; drive, *Am.* driveway; **'~srampe** *f* ramp.

'auf|fallen *v/i.* (*irr.* fallen, *sep.*, -ge-, *sein*) be conspicuous; *j-m* ~ strike s.o.; **'~fallend** *adj.*, **'~fällig** *adj.* striking; conspicuous; flashy.

'auffangen *v/t.* (*irr.* fangen, *sep.*, -ge-, *h*) catch (up); parry (*thrust*).

'auffass|en *v/t.* (*sep.*, -ge-, *h*) conceive; comprehend; interpret; **'2ung** *f* conception; interpretation; grasp.

'auffinden *v/t.* (*irr.* finden, *sep.*, -ge-, *h*) find, trace, discover, locate.

'aufforder|n *v/t.* (*sep.*, -ge-, *h*) ask, invite; call (up)on; *esp.* ⚤ summon; '2ung *f* invitation; *esp.* ⚤ summons.

'auffrischen (*sep.*, -ge-) 1. *v/t.* (*h*) freshen up, touch up; brush up (*knowledge*); revive; 2. *v/i.* (*sein*) *wind:* freshen.

'aufführ|en *v/t.* (*sep.*, -ge-, *h*) *thea.* represent, perform, act; enumerate; enter (*in list*); einzeln ~ specify, *Am.* itemize; *sich* ~ behave; '2ung *f thea.* performance; enumeration; entry; specification; conduct.

'Aufgabe *f* task; problem; *school:* homework; posting, *Am.* mailing (*of letter*); booking (*of luggage*), *Am.* checking (*of baggage*); resignation (*from office*); abandonment; giving up (*business*); es sich zur ~ machen make it one's business.

'Aufgang *m* ascent; *ast.* rising; staircase.

'aufgeben (*irr.* geben, *sep.*, -ge-, *h*) 1. *v/t.* give up, abandon; resign from (*office*); insert (*advertisement*); post, *Am.* mail (*letter*); book (*luggage*), *Am.* check (*baggage*); hand in, send (*telegram*); ✝ give (*order*); set, *Am.* assign (*homework*); set (*riddle*); 2. *v/i.* give up *or* in.

'Aufgebot *n* public notice; ⚔ levy; *fig.* array; banns *pl.* (*of marriage*).

'aufgehen *v/i.* (*irr.* gehen, *sep.*, -ge-, *sein*) open; ♉ leave no remainder; *sewing:* come apart; *paste, star, curtain:* rise; *seed:* come up; ~ in (*dat.*) be merged in; *fig.* be devoted to (*work*); in Flammen ~ go up in flames.

aufgeklärt *adj.* ['aufgəkle:rt] enlightened; '2heit *f* (-/no *pl.*) enlightenment.

'Aufgeld ✝ *n* agio, premium.

aufge|legt *adj.* ['aufgəle:kt] disposed (zu for); in the mood (zu *inf.* for *ger.*, to *inf.*); gut (schlecht) ~ in a good (bad) humo(u)r; '~schlossen *fig. adj.* open-minded; '~weckt *fig. adj.* ['~vekt] bright.

'auf|gießen *v/t.* (*irr.* gießen, *sep.*, -ge-, *h*) pour (on); make (*tea*); '~greifen *v/t.* (*irr.* greifen, *sep.*, -ge-, *h*) snatch up, *fig.* take up;

'Aufguß *m* infusion. [seize.]

'auf|haben (*irr.* haben, *sep.*, -ge-, *h*) 1. *v/t.* have on (*hat*); have open (*door*); have to do (*task*); 2. *F v/i.*: das Geschäft hat auf the shop is open; '~haken *v/t.* (*sep.*, -ge-, *h*) unhook; '~halten *v/t.* (*irr.* halten, *sep.*, -ge-, *h*) keep *or* stop, detain, delay; hold up (*traffic*); ~ stay; sich ~ bei dwell on; sich ~ mit spend one's time on; '~hängen *v/t.* (*irr.* hängen, *sep.*, -ge-, *h*) hang (up); ⊕ suspend.

'aufheb|en *v/t.* (*irr.* heben, *sep.*, -ge-, *h*) lift (up), raise; pick up; raise (*siege*); keep, preserve; cancel, annul, abolish; break off (*engagement*); break up (*meeting*); sich ~ neutralize; die Tafel ~ rise from the table; gut aufgehoben sein be well looked after; viel Aufhebens machen make a fuss (von about); '2ung *f* (-/-en) raising; abolition; annulment; breaking up.

'auf|heitern *v/t.* (*sep.*, -ge-, *h*) cheer up; sich ~ *weather:* clear up; *face:* brighten; '~hellen *v/t. and v/refl.* (*sep.*, -ge-, *h*) brighten.

'aufhetzen *v/t.* (*sep.*, -ge-, *h*) incite, instigate *s.o.*; '2ung *f* (-/-en) instigation, incitement.

'auf|holen (*sep.*, -ge-, *h*) 1. *v/t.* make up (for); ♒ haul up; 2. *v/i.* gain (gegen on); pull up (to); '~hören *v/i.* (*sep.*, -ge-, *h*) cease, stop; *Am.* quit (*all:* zu tun doing); F: da hört (sich) doch alles auf! that's the limit!, *Am.* that beats everything!; '~kaufen *v/t.* (*sep.*, -ge-, *h*) buy up.

'aufklär|en *v/t.* (*sep.*, -ge-, *h*) clear up; enlighten (über *acc.* on); ⚔ reconnoit|re, *Am.* -er; sich ~ clear up; '2ung *f* enlightenment; ⚔ reconnaissance.

'auf|kleben *v/t.* (*sep.*, -ge-, *h*) paste on, stick on, affix on; '~klinken *v/t.* (*sep.*, -ge-, *h*) unlatch; '~knöpfen *v/t.* (*sep.*, -ge-, *h*) unbutton.

'aufkommen 1. *v/i.* (*irr.* kommen, *sep.*, -ge-, *sein*) rise; recover (*from illness*); come up; come into fashion or use; *thought:* arise; ~ für et. answer for s.th.; ~ gegen prevail against *s.o.*; 2. 2 *n* (-s/no *pl.*) rise; recovery.

'auf|krempeln *v/t.* (*sep.*, -ge-, *h*) turn up, roll up; tuck up; '~lachen *v/i.* (*sep.*, -ge-, *h*) burst out laughing; '~laden *v/t.* (*irr.* laden, *sep.*, -ge-, *h*) load; ⚡ charge.

'Auflage *f* edition (*of book*); circulation (*of newspaper*); ⊕ support.

'auf|lassen *v/t.* (*irr.* lassen, *sep.*, -ge-, *h*) F leave open (*door*, etc.); F keep on (*hat*); ⚤ cede; '~lauern *v/i.* (*sep.*, -ge-, *h*): j-m ~ lie in wait for s.o.

'Auflauf *m* concourse; riot; *dish:* soufflé; '2en *v/i.* (*irr.* laufen, *sep.*, -ge-, *sein*) *interest:* accrue; ♒ run aground.

'auflegen (*sep.*, -ge-, *h*) 1. *v/t.* put on, lay on; apply (auf *acc.* to); print, publish (*book*); *teleph.* hang up; 2. *teleph. v/i.* ring off.

'auflehn|en *v/t.* (*sep.*, -ge-, *h*) lean (on); sich ~ lean (on); *fig.* rebel, revolt (gegen against); '2ung *f* (-/-en) rebellion.

'**auf|lesen** v/t. (irr. lesen, sep., -ge-, h) gather, pick up; '**~leuchten** v/i. (sep., -ge-, h) flash (up); '**~liegen** v/i. (irr. liegen, sep., -ge-, h) lie (auf dat. on).

'**auflös|bar** adj. (dis)soluble; '**~en** v/t. (sep., -ge-, h) undo (knot); break up (meeting); dissolve (salt, etc.; marriage, business, Parliament, etc.); solve (⚗, riddle); disintegrate; fig. aufgelöst upset; '**2ung** f (dis-) solution; disintegration.

'**aufmach|en** v/t. (sep., -ge-, h) open; undo (dress, parcel); put up (umbrella); make up, get up; sich ~ wind: rise; set out (nach acc. for); make for; die Tür ~ answer the door; '**2ung** f (-/-en) make-up, get-up.

'**aufmarschieren** v/i. (sep., no -ge-, sein) form into line; ~ lassen ✗ deploy.

'**aufmerksam** adj. attentive (gegen to); j-n ~ machen auf (acc.) call s.o.'s attention to; '**2keit** f (-/-en) attention; token.

'**aufmuntern** v/t. (sep., -ge-, h) rouse; encourage; cheer up.

Aufnahme ['aufna:mə] f (-/-n) taking up (of work); reception; admission; phot.: taking; photograph, shot; shooting (of a film); '**2fähig** adj. capable of absorbing; mind: receptive (für of); '**~gebühr** f admission fee; '**~gerät** n phot. camera; recorder; '**~prüfung** f entrance examination.

'**aufnehmen** v/t. (irr. nehmen, sep., -ge-, h) take up; pick up; take s.o. in; take down (dictation, etc.); take s.th. in (mentally); receive (guests); admit; raise, borrow (money); draw up, record; shoot (film); phot. take (picture); gut (übel) ~ take well (ill); es ~ mit be a match for.

aufopfer|n ['auf⁹-] v/t. (sep., -ge-, h) sacrifice; '**2ung** f sacrifice.

'**auf|passen** v/i. (sep., -ge-, h) attend (auf acc. to); watch; at school: be attentive; look out; ~ auf (acc.) take care of; '**~platzen** v/i. (sep., -ge-, sein) burst (open); '**~polieren** v/t. (sep., no -ge-, h) polish up; '**~prallen** v/i. (sep., -ge-, sein): auf den Boden ~ strike the ground; '**~pumpen** v/t. (sep., -ge-, h) blow up (tyre, etc.); '**~raffen** v/t. (sep., -ge-, h) snatch up; sich ~ rouse o.s. (zu for); muster up one's energy; '**~räumen** (sep., -ge-, h) 1. v/t. put in order; tidy (up), Am. straighten up; clear away; 2. v/i. tidy up; ~ mit do away with.

'**aufrecht** adj. and adv. upright (a. fig.), erect; '**~erhalten** v/t. (irr. halten, sep., no -ge-, h) maintain, uphold; '**2erhaltung** f (-/no pl.) maintenance.

'**aufreg|en** v/t. (sep., -ge-, h) stir up,

excite; sich ~ get excited or upset (über acc. about); aufgeregt excited; upset; '**2ung** f excitement, agitation.

'**auf|reiben** v/t. (irr. reiben, sep., -ge-, h) chafe (skin, etc.); fig.: destroy; exhaust, wear s.o. out; '**~reißen** (irr. reißen, sep., -ge-) 1. v/t. (h) rip or tear up or open; fling open (door); open (eyes) wide; 2. v/i. (sein) split open, burst.

'**aufreiz|en** v/t. (sep., -ge-, h) incite, stir up; '**~end** adj. provocative; '**2ung** f instigation.

'**aufrichten** v/t. (sep., -ge-, h) set up, erect; sich ~ stand up; straighten; sit up (in bed).

'**aufrichtig** adj. sincere, candid; '**2keit** f sincerity, cando(u)r.

'**aufriegeln** v/t. (sep., -ge-, h) unbolt.

'**Aufriß** △ m elevation.

'**aufrollen** v/t. and v/refl. (sep., -ge-, h) roll up; unroll.

'**Aufruf** m call, summons; '**2en** v/t. (irr. rufen, sep., -ge-, h) call up; call on s.o.

Aufruhr ['aufru:r] m (-[e]s/-e) uproar, tumult; riot, rebellion.

'**aufrühr|en** v/t. (sep., -ge-, h) stir up; revive; fig. rake up; '**2er** m (-s/-) rebel; '**~erisch** adj. rebellious.

'**Aufrüstung** ✗ f (re)armament.

'**auf|rütteln** v/t. (sep., -ge-, h) shake up; rouse; '**~sagen** v/t. (sep., -ge-, h) say, repeat; recite.

aufsässig adj. ['aufzɛsiç] rebellious.

'**Aufsatz** m essay; composition; ⊕ top.

'**auf|saugen** v/t. (sep., -ge-, h) suck up; 🜊 absorb; '**~scheuchen** v/t. (sep., -ge-, h) scare (away); disturb; rouse; '**~scheuern** v/t. (sep., -ge-, h) scour; 🜊 chafe; '**~schichten** v/t. (sep., -ge-, h) pile up; '**~schieben** v/t. (irr. schieben, sep., -ge-, h) slide open; fig.: put off; defer, postpone; adjourn.

'**Aufschlag** m striking; impact; additional or extra charge; facing (on coat), lapel (of coat); cuff (on sleeve); turn-up (on trousers); tennis: service; '**2en** ['-gən] (irr. schlagen, sep., -ge-) 1. v/t. (h) open; turn up (sleeve, etc.); take up (abode); pitch (tent); raise (prices); cut (one's knee) open; 2. v/i. (sein) strike, hit; ✝ rise, go up (in price); tennis: serve.

'**auf|schließen** v/t. (irr. schließen, sep., -ge-, h) unlock, open; '**~schlitzen** v/t. (sep., -ge-, h) slit or rip open.

'**Aufschluß** fig. m information.

'**auf|schnallen** v/t. (sep., -ge-, h) unbuckle; '**~schnappen** (sep., -ge-) 1. v/t. (h) snatch; fig. pick up; 2. v/i. (sein) snap open; '**~schnei-**

den (*irr.* schneiden, *sep.*, -ge-, h)
1. *v/t.* cut open; cut up (*meat*);
2. *fig. v/i.* brag, boast.

'**Aufschnitt** *m* (slices *pl.* of) cold
meat, *Am.* cold cuts *pl.*

'**auf**|**schnüren** *v/t.* (*sep.*, -ge-, h)
untie; unlace; '**~schrauben** *v/t.*
(*sep.*, -ge-, h) screw (*part acc.* on);
unscrew; '**~schrecken** (*sep.*, -ge-)
1. *v/t.* (h) startle; **2.** *v/i.* (*irr.*
schrecken, sein) start (up).

'**Aufschrei** *m* shriek, scream; *fig.*
outcry.

'**auf**|**schreiben** *v/t.* (*irr.* schreiben,
sep., -ge-, h) write down; '**~**
schreien *v/i.* (*irr.* schreien, *sep.*,
-ge-, h) cry out, scream.

'**Aufschrift** *f* inscription; address,
direction (*on letter*); label.

'**Aufschub** *m* deferment; delay;
adjournment; respite.

'**auf**|**schürfen** *v/t.* (*sep.*, -ge-, h)
graze (*skin*); '**~schwingen** *v/refl.*
(*irr.* schwingen, *sep.*, -ge-, h) soar,
rise; *sich zu et. ~* bring o.s. to do
s.th.

'**Aufschwung** *m fig.* rise, *Am.* up-
swing; ✝ boom.

'**aufsehen 1.** *v/i.* (*irr.* sehen, *sep.*,
-ge-, h) look up; **2.** ⚲ *n* (-s/*no pl.*)
sensation; *~ erregen* cause a sensation; '**~erregend** *adj.* sensational.

'**Aufseher** *m* overseer; inspector.

'**aufsetzen** (*sep.*, -ge-, h) **1.** *v/t.* set
up; put on (*hat, countenance*); draw
up (*document*); *sich ~* sit up; **2.** ⚲
v/i. touch down.

'**Aufsicht** *f* (-/-en) inspection, supervision; *store*: shopwalker, *Am.* floor-
walker; '**~sbehörde** *f* board of control; '**~srat** *m* board of directors.

'**auf**|**sitzen** *v/i.* (*irr.* sitzen, *sep.*,
-ge-, h) *rider*: mount; '**~spannen**
v/t. (*sep.*, -ge-, h) stretch; put up
(*umbrella*); spread (*sails*); '**~sparen**
v/t. (*sep.*, -ge-, h) save; *fig.* reserve;
'**~speichern** *v/t.* (*sep.*, -ge-, h)
store up; '**~sperren** *v/t.* (*sep.*, -ge-,
h) open wide; '**~spielen** (*sep.*, -ge-,
h) **1.** *v/t. and v/i.* strike up; **2.** *v/refl.*
show off; *sich ~ als* set up for; '**~**
spießen *v/t.* (*sep.*, -ge-, h) pierce;
with horns: gore; run through,
spear; '**~springen** *v/i.* (*irr.* springen, *sep.*, -ge-, sein) jump up; *door*:
fly open; crack; *skin*: chap; '**~spü-**
ren *v/t.* (*sep.*, -ge-, h) hunt up;
track down; '**~stacheln** *fig. v/t.*
(*sep.*, -ge-, h) goad; incite, instigate;
'**~stampfen** *v/i.* (*sep.*, -ge-, h)
stamp (one's foot).

'**Aufstand** *m* insurrection; rebellion;
uprising, revolt.

aufständisch *adj.* ['aufʃtɛndiʃ] rebellious; '**⚲e** *m* (-n/-n) insurgent,
rebel.

'**auf**|**stapeln** *v/t.* (*sep.*, -ge-, h) pile
up; ✝ store (up); '**~stechen** *v/t.*
(*irr.* stechen, *sep.*, -ge-, h) puncture,

prick open; ⚔ lance; '**~stecken** *v/t.*
(*sep.*, -ge-, h) pin up; put up (*hair*);
'**~stehen** *v/i.* (*irr.* stehen, *sep.*, -ge-)
1. (sein) stand up; rise, get up; revolt; **2.** F (h) stand open; '**~steigen**
v/i. (*irr.* steigen, *sep.*, -ge-, sein) rise,
ascend; ⚵ take off; *rider*: mount.

'**aufstell**|**en** *v/t.* (*sep.*, -ge-, h) set
up, put up; ⚙ draw up; post (*sen-
tries*); make (*assertion*); set (*example*); erect (*column*); set (*trap*);
nominate (*candidate*); draw up
(*bill*); lay down (*rule*); make out
(*list*); set up, establish (*record*);
'**⚲ung** *f* putting up; drawing up;
erection; nomination; ✝ statement;
list.

Aufstieg ['aufʃtiːk] *m* (-[e]s/-e)
ascent, *Am. a.* ascension; *fig.* rise.

'**auf**|**stöbern** *fig. v/t.* (*sep.*, -ge-, h)
hunt up; '**~stoßen** (*irr.* stoßen, *sep.*,
-ge-) **1.** *v/t.* (h) push open; *~ auf*
(*acc.*) knock against; **2.** *v/i.* (h, sein)
of food: rise, repeat; belch; '**~strei-**
chen *v/t.* (*irr.* streichen, *sep.*, -ge-,
h) spread (*butter*).

'**Aufstrich** *m* spread (*for bread*).

'**auf**|**stützen** *v/t.* (*sep.*, -ge-, h) prop
up, support s.th.; *sich ~ auf* (*acc.*)
lean on; '**~suchen** *v/t.* (*sep.*, -ge-, h)
visit (*places*); go to see *s.o.*, look
s.o. up.

'**Auftakt** *m* ♪ upbeat; *fig.* prelude,
preliminaries *pl.*

'**auf**|**tauchen** *v/i.* (*sep.*, -ge-, sein)
emerge, appear, turn up; '**~tauen**
(*sep.*, -ge-) **1.** *v/t.* (h) thaw; **2.** *v/i.*
(sein) thaw (*a. fig.*); '**~teilen** *v/t.*
(*sep.*, -ge-, h) divide (up), share.

Auftrag ['auftraːk] *m* (-[e]s/⸗e)
commission; instruction; mission;
⚓ mandate; ✝ order; ⚲**en** ['**~**ɡən]
v/t. (*irr.* tragen, *sep.*, -ge-, h) serve
(up) (*meal*); lay on (*paint*); wear
out (*dress*); *j-m et. ~* charge s.o.
with s.th.; '**~geber** ['**~**k-] *m* (-s/-)
employer; customer; principal; '**~s-**
erteilung ['**~**ksʔɛrtailuŋ] *f* (-/-en)
placing of an order.

'**auf**|**treffen** *v/i.* (*irr.* treffen, *sep.*,
-ge-, sein) strike, hit; '**~treiben** *v/t.*
(*irr.* treiben, *sep.*, -ge-, h) hunt up;
raise (*money*); '**~trennen** *v/t.* (*sep.*,
-ge-, h) rip; unstitch (*seam*).

'**auftreten** **1.** *v/i.* (*irr.* treten, *sep.*,
-ge-, sein) tread; *thea., witness, etc.*:
appear (*als* as); behave, act; (*difficulties*: arise; **2.** ⚲ *n* (-s/*no pl.*) appearance; occurrence (*of events*);
behavio(u)r.

'**Auftrieb** *m phys. and fig.* buoyancy; ⚵ lift; *fig.* impetus.

'**Auftritt** *m thea.* scene (*a. fig.*);
appearance (*of actor*).

'**auf**|**trumpfen** *fig. v/i.* (*sep.*, -ge-, h)
put one's foot down; '**~tun** *v/t.* (*irr.*
tun, *sep.*, -ge-, h) open; *sich ~* open;
chasm: yawn; *society*: form; '**~tür-**
men *v/t.* (*sep.*, -ge-, h) pile *or* heap

up; *sich* ~ tower up; pile up; *difficulties*: accumulate; '~**wachen** *v/i.* (*sep.*, *-ge-*, *sein*) awake, wake up; '~**wachsen** *v/i.* (*irr.* wachsen, *sep.*, *-ge-*, *sein*) grow up.

'**Aufwallung** *f* ebullition, surge.

Aufwand ['aufvant] *m* (-[e]s/*no pl.*) expense, expenditure (*an dat.* of); pomp; splendid *or* great display (*of words*, *etc.*).

'**aufwärmen** *v/t.* (*sep.*, *-ge-*, *h*) warm up.

'**Aufwarte|frau** *f* charwoman, *Am. a.* cleaning woman; '~**n** *v/i.* (*sep.*, *-ge-*, *h*) wait (up)on *s.o.*, attend on *s.o.*; wait (at table).

aufwärts *adv.* ['aufverts] upward(s).

'**Aufwartung** *f* attendance; visit; *j-m s-e* ~ *machen* pay one's respects to *s.o.*, call on *s.o.*

'**aufwasch|en** *v/t.* (*irr.* waschen, *sep.*, *-ge-*, *h*) wash up; '2**wasser** *n* dish-water.

'**auf|wecken** *v/t.* (*sep.*, *-ge-*, *h*) awake(n), wake (up); '~**weichen** (*sep.*, *-ge-*) 1. *v/t.* (*h*) soften; soak; 2. *v/i.* (*sein*) soften, become soft; '~**weisen** *v/t.* (*irr.* weisen, *sep.*, *-ge-*, *h*) show, exhibit; produce; '~**wenden** *v/t.* ([*irr.* wenden,] *sep.*, *-ge-*, *h*) spend; *Mühe* ~ take pains; '~**werfen** *v/t.* (*irr.* werfen, *sep.*, *-ge-*, *h*) raise (*a.* question).

'**aufwert|en** *v/t.* (*sep.*, *-ge-*, *h*) revalorize; revalue; '2**ung** *f* revalorization; revaluation.

'**aufwickeln** *v/t. and v/refl.* (*sep.*, *-ge-*, *h*) wind up, roll up.

aufwiegel|n ['aufvi:gəln] *v/t.* (*sep.*, *-ge-*, *h*) stir up, incite, instigate; '2**ung** *f* (-/-en) instigation.

'**aufwiegen** *fig. v/t.* (*irr.* wiegen, *sep.*, *-ge-*, *h*) make up for.

Aufwiegler ['aufvi:glər] *m* (-s/-) agitator; instigator.

'**aufwirbeln** (*sep.*, *-ge-*) 1. *v/t.* (*h*) whirl up; raise (*dust*); *fig.* viel Staub ~ create a sensation; 2. *v/i.* (*sein*) whirl up.

'**aufwisch|en** *v/t.* (*sep.*, *-ge-*, *h*) wipe up; '2**lappen** *m* floor-cloth.

'**aufwühlen** *v/t.* (*sep.*, *-ge-*, *h*) turn up; *fig.* stir.

'**aufzähl|en** *v/t.* (*sep.*, *-ge-*, *h*) count up; *fig.* enumerate, *Am. a.* call off; specify, *Am.* itemize; '2**ung** *f* (-/-en) enumeration; specification.

'**auf|zäumen** *v/t.* (*sep.*, *-ge-*, *h*) bridle; '~**zehren** *v/t.* (*sep.*, *-ge-*, *h*) consume.

'**aufzeichn|en** *v/t.* (*sep.*, *-ge-*, *h*) draw; note down; record; '2**ung** *f* note; record.

'**auf|zeigen** *v/t.* (*sep.*, *-ge-*, *h*) show; demonstrate; point out (*mistakes*, *etc.*); disclose; '~**ziehen** (*irr.* ziehen, *sep.*, *-ge-*) 1. *v/t.* (*h*) draw *or* pull up; (*pull*) open; hoist (*flag*); bring up (*child*); mount (*picture*);

wind (up) (*clock*, *etc.*); *j-n* ~ tease *s.o.*, pull *s.o.'s* leg; *Saiten auf e-e Violine* ~ string a violin; 2. *v/i.* (*sein*) ✗ draw up; *storm*: approach.

'**Aufzucht** *f* rearing, breeding.

'**Aufzug** *m* ⊕ hoist; lift, *Am.* elevator; *thea.* act; attire; show.

'**aufzwingen** *v/t.* (*irr.* zwingen, *sep.*, *-ge-*, *h*): *j-m et.* ~ force *s.th.* upon *s.o.*

Augapfel ['auk'-] *m* eyeball.

Auge ['augə] *n* (-s/-n) eye; sight; ⚘ bud; *in meinen* ~n in my view; *im* ~ *behalten* keep an eye on; keep in mind; *aus den* ~n *verlieren* lose sight of; *ein* ~ *zudrücken* turn a blind eye (*bei* to); *ins* ~ *fallen* strike the eye; *große* ~n *machen* open one's eyes wide; *unter vier* ~n face to face, privately; *kein* ~ *zutun* not to get a wink of sleep.

'**Augen|arzt** *m* oculist, eye-doctor; '~**blick** *m* moment, instant; '2~**blicklich** 1. *adj.* instantaneous; momentary; present; 2. *adv.* instant(aneous)ly; at present; '~**braue** *f* eyebrow; '~**entzündung** ⚕ *f* inflammation of the eye; '~**heilkunde** *f* ophthalmology; '~**klinik** *f* ophthalmic hospital; '~**leiden** ⚕ *n* eye-complaint; '~**licht** *n* eyesight; '~**lid** *n* eyelid; '~**maß** *n*: *ein gutes* ~ a sure eye; *nach dem* ~ by eye; '~**merk** ['~merk] *n* (-[e]s/*no pl.*): *sein* ~ *richten auf* (*acc.*) turn one's attention to; have *s.th.* in view; '~**schein** *m* appearance; *in* ~ *nehmen* examine, view, inspect; '2~**scheinlich** *adj.* evident; '~**wasser** *n* eyewash, eye-lotion; '~**wimper** *f* eyelash; '~**zeuge** *m* eyewitness.

August [au'gust] *m* (-[e]s, - /-e) August.

Auktion [auk'tsjo:n] *f* (-/-en) auction; *a.* sale; '~**ator** [~o'na:tɔr] *m* (-s/-en) auctioneer.

Aula ['aula] *f* (-/-Aulen, -s) (assembly) hall, *Am.* auditorium.

aus [aus] 1. *prp.* (*dat.*) out of; from; of; by; for; in; ~ *Achtung* out of respect; ~ *London kommen* come from London; ~ *diesem Grunde* for this reason; ~ *Ihrem Brief ersehe ich* I see from your letter; 2. *adv.* out; over; *die Schule ist* ~ school is over; *F: von mir* ~ for all I care; *auf et.* ~ *sein* be keen on *s.th.*; *es ist* ~ *mit ihm* it is all over with him; *das Spiel ist* ~! the game is up!; *er weiß weder ein noch* ~ he is at his wit's end; *on instruments*, *etc.*: *an* — ~ *on* — *off*.

ausarbeit|en ['aus'-] *v/t.* (*sep.*, *-ge-*, *h*) work out; elaborate; '2**ung** *f* (-/-en) working-out; elaboration; composition.

aus|arten ['aus'-] *v/i.* (*sep.*, *-ge-*, *sein*) degenerate; get out of hand; ~**atmen** ['aus'-] (*sep.*, *-ge-*, *h*)

1. v/i. breathe out; **2.** v/t. breathe out; exhale (*vapour, etc.*); '~**baggern** v/t. (*sep., -ge-, h*) dredge (*river, etc.*); excavate (*ground*).

'**Ausbau** m (-[e]s/-ten) extension; completion; development; '**Qen** v/t. (*sep., -ge-, h*) develop; extend; finish, complete; ⊕ dismantle (*engine*).

'**ausbedingen** v/t. (*irr. bedingen, sep., no -ge-, h*) stipulate.

'**ausbesser|n** v/t. (*sep., -ge-, h*) mend, repair, *Am.* F *a.* fix; '**Qung** f repair, mending.

'**Ausbeut|e** f (-/-%-n) gain, profit; yield; ✕ output; '**Qen** v/t. (*sep., -ge-, h*) exploit; sweat (*workers*); '~**ung** f (-/-en) exploitation.

'**ausbild|en** v/t. (*sep., -ge-, h*) form, develop; train; instruct, educate; ✕ drill; '**Qung** f development; training; instruction; education; ✕ drill.

'**ausbitten** v/t. (*irr. bitten, sep., -ge-, h*): sich et. ~ request s.th.; insist on s.th.

'**ausbleiben 1.** v/i. (*irr. bleiben, sep., -ge-, sein*) stay away, fail to appear; **2.** ⌀ n (-s/no pl.) non-arrival, non-appearance; absence.

'**Ausblick** m outlook (*auf acc.* over, on), view (of), prospect (of); *fig.* outlook (on).

'**aus|bohren** v/t. (*sep., -ge-, h*) bore, drill; '~**brechen** (*irr. brechen, sep., -ge-*) **1.** v/t. (h) break out; vomit; **2.** v/i. (sein) break out; *fig.* burst out (*laughing, etc.*).

'**ausbreit|en** v/t. (*sep., -ge-, h*) spread (out); stretch (out) (*arms, wings*); display; sich ~ spread; '**Qung** f (-/-%-en) spreading.

'**ausbrennen** (*irr. brennen, sep., -ge-*) **1.** v/t. (h) burn out; ⚕ cauterize; **2.** v/i. (sein) burn out.

'**Ausbruch** m outbreak; eruption (*of volcano*); escape (*from prison*); outburst (*of emotion*).

'**aus|brüten** v/t. (*sep., -ge-, h*) hatch (*a. fig.*); '~**bürgern** v/t. (*sep., -ge-, h*) denationalize, expatriate.

'**Ausdauer** f perseverance; '**Qnd** adj. persevering; ♧ perennial.

'**ausdehn|en** v/t. and v/refl. (*sep., -ge-, h*) extend (*auf acc.* to); expand; stretch; '**Qung** f expansion; extension; extent.

'**aus|denken** v/t. (*irr. denken, sep., -ge-, h*) think s.th. out, *Am. a.* think s.th. up, contrive, devise, invent; imagine; '~**dörren** v/t. (*sep., -ge-, h*) dry up; parch; '~**drehen** v/t. (*sep., -ge-, h*) turn off (*radio, gas*); ✦ turn out, switch off (*light*).

'**Ausdruck** m **1.** (-[e]s/no pl.) expression; **2.** (-[e]s/=e) expression; term.

'**ausdrück|en** v/t. (*sep., -ge-, h*) press, squeeze (out); stub out (*cig-

arette*); *fig.* express; '~**lich** adj. express, explicit.

'**ausdrucks|los** adj. inexpressive, expressionless; blank; '~**voll** adj. expressive; '**Qweise** f mode of expression; style.

'**Ausdünstung** f (-/-en) exhalation; perspiration; odo(u)r, smell.

auseinander adv. [aus'ar'nandər] asunder, apart; separate(d); ~**bringen** v/t. (*irr. bringen, sep., -ge-, h*) separate, sever; ~**gehen** v/i. (*irr. gehen, sep., -ge-, sein*) meeting, crowd: break up; opinions: differ; friends: part; crowd: disperse; roads: diverge; ~**nehmen** v/t. (*irr. nehmen, sep., -ge-, h*) take apart or to pieces; ⊕ disassemble, dismantle; ~**setzen** *fig.* v/t. (*sep., -ge-, h*) explain; sich mit j-m ~ ✦ compound with s.o.; argue with s.o.; have it out with s.o.; sich mit e-m Problem ~ get down to a problem; come to grips with a problem; **Qsetzung** f (-/-en) explanation; discussion; settlement (*with creditors, etc.*); kriegerische ~ armed conflict.

auserlesen adj. ['aus'-] exquisite, choice; select(ed).

auserwählen ['aus'-] v/t. (*sep., no -ge-, h*) select, choose.

'**ausfahr|en** (*irr. fahren, sep., -ge-*) **1.** v/i. (sein) drive out, go for a drive; ⚓ leave (*port*); **2.** v/t. (h) take (*baby*) out (*in pram*); take s.o. for a drive; rut (*road*); ✈ lower (*undercarriage*); '**Qt** f drive; excursion; way out, exit (*of garage, etc.*); gateway; departure.

'**Ausfall** m falling out; ✦: loss; deficit; '**Qen** v/i. (*irr. fallen, sep., -ge-, sein*) fall out; not to take place; turn out, prove; ~ lassen drop; cancel; die Schule fällt aus there is no school; '**Qend** adj. offensive, insulting.

'**aus|fasern** v/i. (*sep., -ge-, sein*) ravel out, fray; '~**fegen** v/t. (*sep., -ge-, h*) sweep (out).

ausfertig|en ['ausfertigən] v/t. (*sep., -ge-, h*) draw up (*document*); make out (*bill, etc.*); issue (*passport*); '**Qung** f (-/-en) drawing up; issue; draft; copy; in doppelter ~ in duplicate. [*chen find out*; discover.]

ausfindig adj. ['ausfindiç]: ~ ma-]

'**Ausflucht** f (-/-e) excuse, evasion, shift, subterfuge.

'**Ausflug** m trip, excursion, outing.

Ausflügler ['ausfly:klər] m (-s/-) excursionist, tripper, tourist.

'**Ausfluß** m flowing out; discharge (*a. ⚕*); outlet, outfall.

'**aus|fragen** v/t. (*sep., -ge-, h*) interrogate, *Am. a.* quiz; sound; '~**fransen** v/i. (*sep., -ge-, sein*) fray.

Ausfuhr ✦ ['ausfu:r] f (-/-en) export(ation); '~**artikel** ✦ m export (article).

'ausführ|bar adj. practicable; ✝ exportable; '~en v/t. (sep., -ge-, h) execute, carry out, perform, Am. a. fill; ✝ export; explain; j-n ~ take s.o. out.

'Ausfuhr|genehmigung f export permit; '~handel m export trade.

'ausführlich 1. adj. detailed; comprehensive; circumstantial; 2. adv. in detail, at (some) length; '2keit f (-/no pl.) minuteness of detail; particularity; comprehensiveness; copiousness.

'Ausführung f execution, performance; workmanship; type, make; explanation; '~sbestimmungen ✝ f/pl. export regulations pl.

'Ausfuhr|verbot n embargo on exports; '~waren f/pl. exports pl.; '~zoll m export duty.

'ausfüllen v/t. (sep., -ge-, h) fill out or up; fill in, complete (form); Am. fill out (blank).

'Ausgabe f distribution; edition (of book); expense, expenditure; issue (of shares, etc.); issuing office.

'Ausgang m going out; exit; way out; outlet; end; result; '~skapital ✝ n original capital; '~spunkt m starting-point; '~sstellung f starting-position.

'ausgeben v/t. (irr. geben, sep., -ge-, h) give out; spend (money); issue (shares, etc.); sich ~ für pass o.s. off for, pretend to be.

ausge|beult adj. ['ausgəbɔylt] baggy; ~bombt adj. ['~bɔmpt] bombed out; ~dehnt adj. ['~de:nt] expansive, vast, extensive; ~dient adj. ['~di:nt] worn out; superannuated; retired, pensioned off; ~er Soldat ex-serviceman, veteran; '~fallen fig. adj. odd, queer, unusual.

'ausgehen v/i. (irr. gehen, sep., -ge-, sein) go out; take a walk; end; colour: fade; hair: fall out; money, provisions: run out; uns gehen die Vorräte aus we run out of provisions; darauf ~ aim at; gut etc. ~ turn out well, etc.; leer ~ come away empty-handed; von et. ~ start from s.th.

'ausge|lassen fig. adj. frolicsome, boisterous; '~nommen prp. 1. (acc.) except (for); 2. (nom.): Anwesende ~ present company excepted; '~prägt adj. ['~prɛ:kt] marked, pronounced; ~rechnet fig. adv. ['~rɛçnət] just; ~ er he of all people; ~ heute today of all days; '~schlossen fig. adj. impossible.

'ausgestalten v/t. (sep., no -ge-, h) arrange (celebration); et. zu et. ~ develop or turn s.th. into s.th.

ausge|sucht fig. adj. ['ausgəzu:xt] exquisite, choice; '~wachsen adj. full-grown; ~zeichnet fig. adj. ['~tsaiçnət] excellent.

ausgiebig adj. ['ausgi:biç] abundant, plentiful; meal: substantial.

'ausgießen v/t. (irr. gießen, sep., -ge-, h) pour out.

Ausgleich ['ausglaiç] m (-[e]s/-e) compromise; compensation; ✝ settlement; sports: equalization (of score); tennis: deuce (score of 40 all); '2en v/t. (irr. gleichen, sep., -ge-, h) equalize; compensate (loss); ✝ balance.

'aus|gleiten v/i. (irr. gleiten, sep., -ge-, sein) slip, slide; '~graben v/t. (irr. graben, sep., -ge-, h) dig out or up (a. fig.); excavate; exhume (body).

Ausguck ⚓ ['ausguk] m (-[e]s/-e) look-out.

'Ausguß m sink; '~eimer m slop-pail.

'aus|haken v/t. (sep., -ge-, h) unhook; '~halten (irr. halten, sep., -ge-, h) 1. v/t. endure, bear, stand; ♪ sustain (note); 2. v/i. hold out; last; '~händigen ['~hɛndigən] v/t. (sep., -ge-, h) deliver up, hand over, surrender.

'Aushang m notice, placard, poster.

'aushänge|n 1. v/t. (sep., -ge-, h) hang or put out; unhinge (door); 2. v/i. (irr. hängen, sep., -ge-, h) have been hung or put out; '2~schild n signboard.

aus|harren ['ausharən] v/i. (sep., -ge-, h) persevere; hold out; '~hauchen v/t. (sep., -ge-, h) breathe out, exhale; '~heben v/t. (irr. heben, sep., -ge-, h) dig (trench); unhinge (door); recruit, levy (soldiers); excavate (earth); rob (nest); clean out, raid (nest of criminals); '~helfen v/i. (irr. helfen, sep., -ge-, h) help out.

'Aushilf|e f (temporary) help or assistance; sie hat e-e ~ she has s.o. to help out; '2sweise adv. as a makeshift; temporarily.

'aushöhl|en v/t. (sep., -ge-, h) hollow out; '2ung f hollow.

'aus|holen (sep., -ge-, h) 1. v/i. raise one's hand (as if to strike); weit ~ go far back (in narrating s.th.); 2. v/t. sound, pump s.o.; '~horchen v/t. (sep., -ge-, h) sound, pump s.o.; '~hungern v/t. (sep., -ge-, h) starve (out); '~husten v/t. (sep., -ge-, h) cough up; '~kennen v/refl. (irr. kennen, sep., -ge-, h) know one's way (about place); be well versed, be at home (in subject); er kennt sich aus he knows what's what; '~kleiden v/t. (sep., -ge-, h) undress; ⊕ line, coat; sich ~ undress; '~klopfen v/t. (sep., -ge-, h) beat (out); dust (garment); knock out (pipe); '~klügeln ['~kly:gəln] v/t. (sep., -ge-, h) work s.th. out; contrive; puzzle s.th. out.

'auskommen 1. v/i. (irr. kommen, sep., -ge-, sein) get out; escape; ~

mit manage with *s.th.*; get on with *s.o.*; ~ *ohne* do without; *mit dem Geld* ~ make both ends meet; 2. ♀ *n* (-*s*/*no pl.*) competence, competency.

'**auskundschaften** *v/t.* (*sep.*, -*ge*-, *h*) explore; ✗ reconnoit|re, *Am.* -er, scout.

Auskunft ['auskunft] *f* (-/⸚e) information; inquiry office, inquiries *pl.*, *Am.* information desk; '**~stelle** *f* inquiry office, inquiries *pl.*, *Am.* information bureau.

'**aus|lachen** *v/t.* (*sep.*, -*ge*-, *h*) laugh at, deride; '**~laden** *v/t.* (*irr. laden*, *sep.*, -*ge*-, *h*) unload; discharge (*cargo from ship*); cancel *s.o.'s* invitation, put off (*guest*).

'**Auslage** *f* display, show (*of goods*); *in der* ~ in the (shop) window; ~*n pl.* expenses *pl.*

'**Ausland** *n* (-[e]*s*/*no pl.*): *das* ~ foreign countries *pl.*; *ins* ~, *im* ~ abroad.

Ausländ|er ['auslɛndər] *m* (-*s*/-), '**~erin** *f* (-/-*nen*) foreigner; alien; '♀**isch** *adj.* foreign; ♀, *zo.* exotic.

'**Auslandskorrespondent** *m* foreign correspondent.

'**auslass|en** *v/t.* (*irr. lassen*, *sep.*, -*ge*-, *h*) let out (*water*); melt (down) (*butter*); render down (*fat*); let out (*garment*); let down (*hem*); leave out, omit (*word*); cut *s.th.* out; miss or cut out (*meal*); miss (*dance*); *s-n Zorn an j-m* ~ vent one's anger on *s.o.*; *sich* ~ *über* (*acc.*) say *s.th.* about; express one's opinion about; '♀**ung** *f* (-/-*en*) omission; remark, utterance; '♀**ungszeichen** *gr. n* apostrophe.

'**aus|laufen** *v/i.* (*irr. laufen*, *sep.*, -*ge*-, *sein*) run or leak out (*aus et. of s.th.*); leak; end (*in s.th.*); *machine:* run down; ⚓ (set) sail; '**~leeren** *v/t.* (*sep.*, -*ge*-, *h*) empty; 🕭 evacuate (*bowels*).

'**ausleg|en** *v/t.* (*sep.*, -*ge*-, *h*) lay out; display (*goods*); explain, interpret; advance (*money*); '♀**ung** *f* (-/-*en*) explanation, interpretation.

'**aus|leihen** *v/t.* (*irr. leihen*, *sep.*, -*ge*-, *h*) lend (out), *esp. Am.* loan; '**~lernen** *v/i.* (*sep.*, -*ge*-, *h*) finish one's apprenticeship; *man lernt nie aus* we live and learn.

'**Auslese** *f* choice, selection; *fig.* pick; '♀**n** *v/t.* (*irr. lesen*, *sep.*, -*ge*-, *h*) pick out, select; finish reading (*book*).

'**ausliefer|n** *v/t.* (*sep.*, -*ge*-, *h*) hand or turn over, deliver (up); extradite (*criminal*); *ausgeliefert sein* (*dat.*) be at the mercy of; '♀**ung** *f* delivery; extradition.

'**aus|liegen** *v/i.* (*irr. liegen*, *sep.*, -*ge*-, *h*) be displayed, be on show; '**~löschen** *v/t.* (*sep.*, -*ge*-, *h*) put out, switch off (*light*); extinguish (*fire*) (*a. fig.*); efface (*word*); wipe

out, erase; '**~losen** *v/t.* (*sep.*, -*ge*-, *h*) draw (lots) for.

'**auslös|en** *v/t.* (*sep.*, -*ge*-, *h*) ⊕ release; redeem, ransom (*prisoner*); redeem (*from pawn*); *fig.* cause, start; arouse (*applause*); '♀**er** *m* (-*s*/-) ⊕ release, *esp. phot.* trigger.

'**aus|lüften** *v/t.* (*sep.*, -*ge*-, *h*) air, ventilate; '**~machen** *v/t.* (*sep.*, -*ge*-, *h*) make out, sight, spot; *sum:* amount to; constitute, make up; put out (*fire*); ⚡ turn out, switch off (*light*); agree on, arrange; settle; *es macht nichts aus* it does not matter; *würde es Ihnen et.* ~ *, wenn ...?* would you mind (*ger.*) ...?; '**~malen** *v/t.* (*sep.*, -*ge*-, *h*) paint; *sich et.* ~ picture *s.th.* to o.s., imagine *s.th.*

'**Ausmaß** *n* dimension(s *pl.*), measurement(s *pl.*); *fig.* extent.

'**aus|mergeln** ['ausmɛrgəln] *v/t.* (*sep.*, -*ge*-, *h*) emaciate; exhaust; '**~merzen** ['~mɛrtsən] *v/t.* (*sep.*, -*ge*-, *h*) eliminate; eradicate; '**~messen** *v/t.* (*irr. messen*, *sep.*, -*ge*-, *h*) measure.

Ausnahm|e ['ausnɑːmə] *f* (-/-*n*) exception; '♀**sweise** *adv.* by way of exception; exceptionally.

'**ausnehmen** *v/t.* (*irr. nehmen*, *sep.*, -*ge*-, *h*) take out; draw (*fowl*); F fleece *s.o.*; *fig.* except, exempt; '**~d** 1. *adj.* exceptional; 2. *adv.* exceedingly.

'**aus|nutzen** *v/t.* (*sep.*, -*ge*-, *h*) utilize; take advantage of; *esp.* 🔨, ✗ exploit; '**~packen** (*sep.*, -*ge*-, *h*) 1. *v/t.* unpack; 2. F *fig. v/i.* speak one's mind; '**~pfeifen** *thea. v/t.* (*irr. pfeifen*, *sep.*, -*ge*-, *h*) hiss; '**~plaudern** *v/t.* (*sep.*, -*ge*-, *h*) blab or let out; '**~polstern** *v/t.* (*sep.*, -*ge*-, *h*) stuff, pad; wad; '**~probieren** *v/t.* (*sep., no* -*ge*-, *h*) try, test.

Auspuff *mot.* ['auspuf] *m* (-[e]*s*/-*e*) exhaust; '**~gas** *mot. n* exhaust gas; '**~rohr** *mot. n* exhaust-pipe; '**~topf** *mot. m* silencer, *Am.* muffler.

'**aus|putzen** *v/t.* (*sep.*, -*ge*-, *h*) clean; '**~quartieren** *v/t.* (*sep., no* -*ge*-, *h*) dislodge; ✗ billet out; '**~radieren** *v/t.* (*sep., no* -*ge*-, *h*) erase; '**~rangieren** *v/t.* (*sep., no* -*ge*-, *h*) discard; '**~rauben** *v/t.* (*sep.*, -*ge*-, *h*) rob; ransack; '**~räumen** *v/t.* (*sep.*, -*ge*-, *h*) empty, clear (out); remove (*furniture*); '**~rechnen** *v/t.* (*sep.*, -*ge*-, *h*) calculate, compute; reckon (out), *Am.* figure out or up (*all a. fig.*).

'**Ausrede** *f* excuse, evasion, subterfuge; '♀**n** (*sep.*, -*ge*-, *h*) 1. *v/i.* finish speaking; ~ *lassen* hear *s.o.* out; 2. *v/t.*: *j-m et.* ~ dissuade *s.o.* from *s.th.*

'**ausreichen** *v/i.* (*sep.*, -*ge*-, *h*) suffice; '**~d** *adj.* sufficient.

'**Ausreise** *f* departure; ⚓ voyage out.

'ausreiß|en (*irr.* reißen, sep., -ge-) 1. *v/t.* (h) pull *or* tear out; 2. *v/i.* (sein) run away; 'Qer *m* runaway.

aus|renken ['ausreŋkən] *v/t.* (sep., -ge-, h) dislocate; '⁓richten *v/t.* (sep., -ge-, h) straighten; ✗ dress; adjust; deliver (*message*); do, effect; accomplish; obtain; arrange (*feast*); richte ihr e-n Gruß von mir aus! remember me to her!; ⁓rotten ['⁓rotən] *v/t.* (sep., -ge-, h) root out; *fig.* extirpate, exterminate.

'Ausruf *m* cry; exclamation; 'Qen (*irr.* rufen, sep., -ge-,h) 1. *v/i.* cry out, exclaim; 2. *v/t.* proclaim; '⁓e-zeichen *n* exclamation mark, *Am. a.* exclamation point; '⁓ung *f* (-/-en) proclamation; '⁓ungszeichen *n s.* Ausrufezeichen. [-ge-, h) rest.)

'ausruhen *v/i., v/t. and v/refl.* (sep.,)
'ausrüst|en *v/t.* (sep., -ge-, h) fit out; equip; 'Qung *f* outfit, equipment, fittings *pl.* [disseminate.)

'aussäen *v/t.* (sep., -ge-, h) sow; *fig.*)
'Aussage *f* statement; declaration; ₁⅔ evidence; *gr.* predicate; 'Qn (sep., -ge-, h) 1. *v/t.* state, declare; ₁⅔ depose; 2. ₁⅔ *v/i.* give evidence.

'Aussatz ⚕ *m* (-es/no *pl.*) leprosy.
'aus|saugen *v/t.* (sep., -ge-, h) suck (out); *fig.* exhaust (*land*); '⁓schal-ten *v/t.* (sep., -ge-, h) eliminate; ⚡ cut out, switch off, turn off *or* out (*light*).

Ausschank ['ausʃaŋk] *m* (-[e]s/⁼e) retail (*of alcoholic drinks*); public house, F pub.

'Ausschau *f* (-/no *pl.*): ⁓ halten nach be on the look-out for, watch for.
'ausscheid|en (*irr.* scheiden, sep., -ge-) 1. *v/t.* (h) separate; ⚗, ⚕, *physiol.* eliminate; ⚕ secrete; 2. *v/i.* (sein) retire; withdraw; *sports:* drop out; 'Qung *f* separa-tion; elimination (*a. sports*); ⚕ secretion.

'aus|schiffen *v/t. and v/refl.* (sep., -ge-, h) disembark; '⁓schimpfen *v/t.* (sep., -ge-, h) scold, tell *s.o.* off, berate; ⁓schirren ['⁓ʃirən] *v/t.* (sep.,-ge-,h) unharness; '⁓schlach-ten *v/t.* (sep., -ge-, h) cut up; can-nibalize (*car, etc.*); *fig.* exploit, make the most of; '⁓schlafen (*irr.* schlafen, sep., -ge-, h) 1. *v/i.* sleep one's fill; 2. *v/t.* sleep off (*effects of drink, etc.*).

'Ausschlag *m* ⚕ eruption, rash; deflexion (*of pointer*); den ⁓ geben settle it; Qen ['⁓gən] (*irr.* schlagen, sep., -ge-) 1. *v/t.* (h) knock *or* beat out; line; refuse, decline; 2. *v/i.* (h) *horse:* kick; *pointer:* deflect; 3. *v/i.* (h, sein) bud; Qgebend *adj.* ['⁓k-] decisive.

'ausschließ|en *v/t.* (*irr.* schließen, sep., -ge-, h) shut *or* lock out; *fig.:* exclude; expel; *sports:* disqualify; '⁓lich *adj.* exclusive.

'Ausschluß *m* exclusion; expulsion; *sports:* disqualification.

'ausschmücken *v/t.* (sep., -ge-, h) adorn, decorate; *fig.* embellish.

'Ausschnitt *m* cut; décolleté, (low) neck (*of dress*); cutting, *Am.* clip-ping (*from newspaper*); *fig.* part, section.

'ausschreib|en *v/t.* (*irr.* schreiben, sep., -ge-, h) write out; copy; write out (*word*) in full; make out (*in-voice*); announce; advertise; 'Qung *f* (-/-en) announcement; advertise-ment.

'ausschreit|en (*irr.* schreiten, sep., -ge-) 1. *v/i.* (sein) step out, take long strides; 2. *v/t.* (h) pace (*room*), measure by steps; 'Qung *f* (-/-en) excess; ⁓en *pl.* riots *pl.*

'Ausschuß *m* refuse, waste, rub-bish; committee, board.

'aus|schütteln *v/t.* (sep., -ge-, h) shake out; '⁓schütten *v/t.* (sep., -ge-, h) pour out; spill; † distrib-ute (*dividend*); j-m sein Herz ⁓ pour out one's heart to s.o.; '⁓schwär-men *v/i.* (sep., -ge-, sein) swarm out; ⁓ (lassen) ✗ extend, deploy.

'ausschweif|end *adj.* dissolute; 'Qung *f* (-/-en) debauchery, excess.
'ausschwitzen *v/t.* (sep., -ge-, h) exude.

'aussehen 1. *v/i.* (*irr.* sehen, sep., -ge-, h) look; wie sieht er aus? what does he look like?; es sieht nach Regen aus it looks like rain; 2. Q *n* (-s/ no *pl.*) look(s *pl.*), ap-pearance.

außen *adv.* ['ausən] (on the) out-side; von ⁓ her from (the) outside; nach ⁓ (hin) outward(s); 'Qauf-nahme *f* film: outdoor shot; 'Qbordmotor *m* outboard motor.

'aussenden *v/t.* (*irr.* senden,] sep., -ge-, h) send out.

'Außen|hafen *m* outport; '⁓handel *m* foreign trade; '⁓minister *m* foreign minister; Foreign Secretary, *Am.* Secretary of State; '⁓ministe-rium *n* foreign ministry; Foreign Office, *Am.* State Department; '⁓politik *f* foreign policy; 'Qpoli-tisch *adj.* of *or* referring to foreign affairs; '⁓seite *f* outside; surface; '⁓seiter *m* (-s/-) outsider; ⁓stände † ['⁓ʃtɛndə] *pl.* outstanding debts *pl., Am.* accounts *pl.* receivable; '⁓welt *f* outer *or* outside world.

außer ['ausər] 1. *prp.* (*dat.*) out of; beside(s), *Am.* aside from; except; ⁓ sich sein be beside o.s. (vor Freude with joy); 2. *cj.:* ⁓ daß except that; ⁓ wenn unless; '⁓dem *cj.* besides, moreover.

äußere ['ɔysərə] 1. *adj.* exterior, outer, external, outward; 2. Q *n* (Äußer[e]n/no *pl.*) exterior, outside, outward appearance.

'außer|gewöhnlich *adj.* extra-

ordinary; exceptional; '_halb
1. *prp.* (*gen.*) outside, out of; beyond; 2. *adv.* on the outside.
äußerlich *adj.* ['ɔysərliç] external,
outward; '2keit *f* (-/-en) super-
ficiality; formality.
äußern ['ɔysərn] *v/t.* (ge-, h) utter,
express; advance; *sich ~ matter*:
manifest itself; *p.* express o.s.
'**außer'ordentlich** *adj.* extraordinary.
äußerst ['ɔysərst] 1. *adj.* outermost;
fig. utmost, extreme; 2. *adv.* extremely, highly.
außerstande *adj.* [ausər'ʃtandə]
unable, not in a position.
'**Äußerung** *f* (-/-en) utterance,
remark.
'**aussetz|en** (*sep.*, -ge-, h) 1. *v/t.* set
or put out; lower (*boat*); promise
(*reward*); settle (*pension*); bequeath;
expose (*child*); expose (*dat.* to);
et. ~ an (*dat.*) find fault with;
2. *v/i.* intermit; fail; *activity*: stop;
suspend; *mot.* misfire; '2ung *f*
(-/-en) exposure (*of child, to weather, etc.*) (*a.* ♃).
'**Aussicht** *f* (-/-en) view (*auf acc.*
of); *fig.* prospect (of), chance (of);
in ~ haben have in prospect; '2slos
adj. hopeless, desperate; '2sreich
adj. promising, full of promise.
aussöhn|en ['ausze:nən] *v/t.* (*sep.*,
-ge-, h) reconcile *s.o.* (*mit* to *s.th.*,
with *s.o.*); *sich ~* reconcile o.s. (to
s.th., with *s.o.*); '2ung *f* (-/-en)
reconciliation.
'**aussondern** *v/t.* (*sep.*, -ge-, h)
single out; separate.
'**aus|spannen** (*sep.*, -ge-, h) 1. *v/t.*
stretch, extend; F *fig.* steal (*s.o.'s
girl friend*); unharness (*draught
animal*); 2. *fig. v/i.* (take a) rest,
relax; '_speien *v/t. and v/i.* (*irr.
speien, sep.*, -ge-, h) spit out.
'**aussperr|en** *v/t.* (*sep.*, -ge-, h)
shut out; lock out (*workmen*); '2ung
f (-/-en) lock-out.
'**aus|spielen** (*sep.*, -ge-, h) 1. *v/t.*
play (*card*); 2. *v/i. at cards*: lead; *er
hat ausgespielt* he is done for;
'_spionieren *v/t.* (*sep.*, *no* -ge-, h)
spy out.   [cent; discussion.\
'**Aussprache** *f* pronunciation, ac-/
'**aussprechen** (*irr. sprechen, sep.*,
-ge-, h) 1. *v/t.* pronounce, express;
sich ~ für (*gegen*) declare o.s. for
(against); 2. *v/i.* finish speaking.
'**Ausspruch** *m* utterance; saying;
remark.
'**aus|spucken** *v/i. and v/t.* (*sep.*,
-ge-, h) spit out; '_spülen *v/t.* (*sep.*,
-ge-, h) rinse.
'**Ausstand** *m* strike, *Am.* F *a.* walkout; *in den ~ treten* go on strike,
Am. F *a.* walk out.
'**ausstatt|en** ['ausʃtatən] *v/t.* (*sep.*,
-ge-, h) fit out, equip; furnish;
supply (*mit* with); give a dowry to

(*daughter*); get up (*book*); '2ung *f*
(-/-en) outfit, equipment; furniture; supply; dowry; get-up (*of
book*).
'**aus|stechen** *v/t.* (*irr. stechen, sep.*,
-ge-, h) cut out (*a. fig.*); put out
(*eye*); '_stehen (*irr. stehen, sep.*,
-ge-, h) 1. *v/t. payments*: be out-
standing; 2. *v/t.* endure, bear;
'_steigen *v/i.* (*irr. steigen, sep.*,
-ge-, *sein*) get out *or* off, alight.
'**ausstell|en** *v/t.* (*sep.*, -ge-, h) ex-
hibit; make out (*invoice*); issue
(*document*); draw (*bill*); '2er *m* (-s/-)
exhibitor; drawer; '2ung *f* exhibition; show; '2ungsraum *m*
show-room.
'**aussterben** *v/i.* (*irr. sterben, sep.*,
-ge-, *sein*) die out; become extinct.
'**Aussteuer** *f* trousseau, dowry.
'**ausstopfen** *v/t.* (*sep.*, -ge-, h) stuff;
wad, pad.
'**ausstoß|en** *v/t.* (*irr. stoßen, sep.*,
-ge-, h) thrust out, eject; expel;
utter (*cry*); heave (*sigh*); ♃ cashier;
'2ung *f* (-/-en) expulsion.
'**aus|strahlen** *v/t. and v/i.* (*sep.*,
-ge-, h) radiate; '_strecken *v/t.*
(*sep.*, -ge-, h) stretch (out); '_strei-
chen *v/t.* (*irr. streichen, sep.*, -ge-, h)
strike out; smooth (down); '_
streuen *v/t.* (*sep.*, -ge-, h) scatter;
spread (*rumours*); '_strömen (*sep.*,
-ge-) 1. *v/i.* (sein) stream out; *gas,
light*: emanate; *gas, steam*: escape;
2. *v/t.* (h) pour (out); '_suchen *v/t.*
(*sep.*, -ge-, h) choose, select.
'**Austausch** *m* exchange; '2bar *adj.*
exchangeable; '2en *v/t.* (*sep.*, -ge-,
h) exchange.
'**austeil|en** *v/t.* (*sep.*, -ge-, h) dis-
tribute; deal out (*blows*); '2ung *f*
distribution.
Auster *zo.* ['austər] *f* (-/-n) oyster.
'**austragen** *v/t.* (*irr. tragen, sep.*,
-ge-, h) deliver (*letters, etc.*); hold
(*contest*).
Austral|ier [au'stra:liər] *m* (-s/-)
Australian; 2**isch** *adj.* Australian.
'**austreib|en** *v/t.* (*irr. treiben, sep.*,
-ge-, h) drive out; expel; '2ung *f*
(-/-en) expulsion.
'**aus|treten** (*irr. treten, sep.*, -ge-)
1. *v/t.* (h) tread *or* stamp out; wear
out (*shoes*); wear down (*steps*);
2. *v/i.* (sein) emerge, come out;
river: overflow its banks; retire
(*aus* from); F ease o.s.; *~ aus*
leave (*society, etc.*); '_trinken (*irr.
trinken, sep.*, -ge-, h) 1. *v/t.* drink
up; empty, drain; 2. *v/i.* finish
drinking; '2tritt *m* leaving; retirement; '_trocknen (*sep.*, -ge-) 1. *v/t.*
(h) dry up; drain (*land*); parch
(*throat, earth*); 2. *v/i.* (sein) dry up.
ausüb|en ['aus?-] *v/t.* (*sep.*, -ge-, h)
exercise; practi|se, *Am.* -ce (*profes-
sion*); exert (*influence*); '2ung *f*
practice; exercise.

'Ausverkauf ✝ *m* selling off *or* out (*of stock*); sale; '2t ✝, *thea. adj.* sold out; *theatre notice*: 'full house'.

'Auswahl *f* choice; selection; ✝ assortment. [choose, select.\
'auswählen *v/t.* (*sep.*, -ge-, *h*)\
'Auswander|er *m* emigrant; '2n *v/i.* (*sep.*, -ge-, *sein*) emigrate; '~ung *f* emigration.

auswärt|ig *adj.* ['ausvertiç] out-of-town; non-resident; foreign; *das Auswärtige Amt s. Außenministerium*; ~s *adv.* ['~s] outward(s); out of doors; out of town; abroad; ~ essen dine out.

'auswechseln 1. *v/t.* (*sep.*, -ge-, *h*) exchange; change; replace; **2.** 2 *n* (-s/*no pl.*) exchange; replacement.

'Ausweg *m* way out (*a. fig.*); outlet; *fig.* expedient.

'ausweichen *v/i.* (*irr.* weichen, *sep.*, -ge-, *sein*) make way (for); *fig.* evade, avoid; '~d *adj.* evasive.

Ausweis ['ausvais] *m* (-es/-e) (bank) return; identity card, *Am.* identification (card); 2en ['~zən] *v/t.* (*irr.* weisen, *sep.*, -ge-, *h*) turn out, expel; evict; deport; show, prove; *sich* ~ prove one's identity; '~papiere *n/pl.* identity papers *pl.*; ~ung ['~zuŋ] *f* expulsion; '~ungsbefehl *m* expulsion order.

'ausweiten *v/t. and v/refl.* (*sep.*, -ge-, *h*) widen, stretch, expand.

'auswendig 1. *adj.* outward, outside; **2.** *adv.* outwardly, outside; *fig.* by heart.

'aus|werfen *v/t.* (*irr.* werfen, *sep.*, -ge-, *h*) throw out, cast; eject; 🎇 expectorate; allow (*sum of money*); '~werten *v/t.* (*sep.*, -ge-, *h*) evaluate; analyze, interpret; utilize, exploit; '~wickeln *v/t.* (*sep.*, -ge-, *h*) unwrap; '~wiegen *v/t.* (*irr.* wiegen, *sep.*, -ge-, *h*) weigh out; '~wirken *v/refl.* (*sep.*, -ge-, *h*) take effect, operate; *sich* ~ *auf* (*acc.*) affect; '2wirkung *f* effect; '~wischen *v/t.* (*sep.*, -ge-, *h*) wipe out, efface; '~wringen *v/t.* (*irr.* wringen, *sep.*, -ge-, *h*) wring out.

'Auswuchs *m* excrescence, outgrowth (*a. fig.*), protuberance.

'Auswurf *m* 🎇 expectoration; *fig.* refuse, dregs *pl.*

'aus|zahlen *v/t.* (*sep.*, -ge-, *h*) pay out; pay *s.o.* off; '~zählen *v/t.* (*sep.*, -ge-, *h*) count out.

'Auszahlung *f* payment.

'Auszehrung *f* (-/-en) consumption.

'auszeichn|en *v/t.* (*sep.*, -ge-, *h*) mark (out); *fig.* distinguish (*sich o.s.*); '2ung *f* marking; distinction; hono(u)r; decoration.

'auszieh|en (*irr.* ziehen, *sep.*, -ge-) **1.** *v/t.* (*h*) draw out, extract; take off (*garment*); *sich* ~ undress; **2.** *v/i.* (*sein*) set out; move (out), remove, move house; '2platte *f* leaf (*of table*).

'Auszug *m* departure; ⚒ marching out; removal; extract, excerpt (*from book*); summary; ✝ statement (of account). [tic, genuine.\
authentisch *adj.* [au'tentiʃ] authen-\
Auto ['auto] *n* (-s/-s) (motor-)car, *Am. a.* automobile; ~ *fahren* drive, motor; '~bahn *f* motorway, autobahn; ~biogra'phie *f* autobiography; ~bus ['~bus] *m* (-ses/-se) (motor-)bus; (motor) coach; '~bushaltestelle *f* bus stop; ~didakt [~di'dakt] *m* (-en/-en) autodidact, self-taught person; '~droschke *f* taxi(-cab), *Am.* cab; '~fahrer *m* motorist; ~gramm *n* autograph; ~'grammjäger *m* autograph hunter; '~händler *m* car dealer; ~kino *n* drive-in cinema; ~krat [~'kra:t] *m* (-en/-en) autocrat; ~kratie [~a-'ti:] *f* (-/-n) autocracy; ~mat [~'ma:t] *m* (-en/-en) automaton; slot-machine, vending machine; ~'matenrestaurant *n* self-service restaurant, *Am.* automat; ~mation ⊕ [~ma'tsjo:n] *f* (-/*no pl.*) automation; 2'matisch *adj.* automatic; '~mechaniker *m* car mechanic; ~mobil [~mo'bi:l] *n* (-s/-e) *s. Auto*; 2nom *adj.* [~'no:m] autonomous; ~nomie [~o'mi:] *f* (-/-n) autonomy.

Autor ['auto:r] *m* (-s/-en) author.

'Autoreparaturwerkstatt *f* car repair shop, garage. [thor(ess).\
Autorin [au'to:rin] *f* (-/-nen) au-\
autori|sieren [autori'zi:rən] *v/t.* (*no* -ge-, *h*) authorize; ~tär *adj.* [~'tɛ:r] authoritarian; 2'tät *f* (-/-en) authority.

'Auto|straße *f* motor-road; '~vermietung *f* (-/-en) car hire service.

avisieren ✝ [avi'zi:rən] *v/t.* (*no* -ge-, *h*) advise.

Axt [akst] *f* (-/⁀e) ax(e).

Azetylen 🜛 [atsety'le:n] *n* (-s/*no pl.*) acetylene. [2n *adj.* azure.\
Azur [a'tsu:r] *m* (-s/*no pl.*) azure;\

B

Bach [bax] *m* (-[e]s/⁀e) brook, *Am. a.* run. [port.\
Backbord ⚓ ['bak-] *n* (-[e]s/-e)\
Backe ['bakə] *f* (-/-n) cheek.\
backen ['bakən] (*irr.*, ge-, *h*) **1.** *v/t.* bake; fry; dry (*fruit*); **2.** *v/i.* bake; fry.

'Backen|bart *m* (side-)whiskers *pl.*, *Am. a.* sideburns *pl.*; '~zahn *m* molar (tooth), grinder.

Bäcker ['bɛkər] *m* (-*s*/-) baker; **~ei** [~'raɪ] *f* (-/-*en*) baker's (shop), bakery.
'**Back|fisch** *m* fried fish; *fig.* girl in her teens, teenager, *Am. a.* bobby soxer; '**~obst** *n* dried fruit; '**~ofen** *m* oven; '**~pflaume** *f* prune; '**~pulver** *n* baking-powder; '**~stein** *m* brick; '**~ware** *f* baker's ware.
Bad [ba:t] *n* (-[e]*s*/⸗*er*) bath; *in river, etc.*: *a.* bathe; *s. Badeort*; *ein ~ nehmen* take *or* have a bath.
Bade|anstalt ['ba:dəˀ-] *f* (public swimming) baths *pl.*; '**~anzug** *m* bathing-costume, bathing-suit; '**~hose** *f* bathing-drawers *pl.*, (bathing) trunks *pl.*; '**~kappe** *f* bathing-cap; '**~kur** *f* spa treatment; '**~mantel** *m* bathing-gown, *Am.* bathrobe; '**~meister** *m* bath attendant; swimming-instructor; '**2n** (ge-, *h*) **1.** *v/t.* bath (*baby, etc.*); bathe (*eyes, etc.*); **2.** *v/i.* bath, tub; have *or* take a bath; *in river, etc.*: bathe; *~ gehen* go swimming; '**~ofen** *m* geyser, boiler, *Am. a.* water heater; '**~ort** *m* watering-place; spa; seaside resort; '**~salz** *n* bath-salt; '**~strand** *m* bathing-beach; '**~tuch** *n* bath-towel; '**~wanne** *f* bath-tub; '**~zimmer** *n* bathroom.
Bagatell|e [baga'tɛlə] *f* (-/-*n*) trifle, trifling matter, bagatelle; **2i'sieren** *v/t.* (*no* -*ge*-, *h*) minimize (the importance of), *Am. a.* play down.
Bagger ['bagər] *m* (-*s*/-) excavator; dredge(r); '**2n** *v/i. and v/t.* (ge-, *h*) excavate; dredge.
Bahn [ba:n] *f* (-/-*en*) course; path; 🚂 railway, *Am.* railroad; *mot.* lane; trajectory (*of bullet, etc.*); *ast.* orbit; *sports*: track, course, lane; *skating*: rink; *bowling*: alley; '**2brechend** *adj.* pioneer(ing), epoch-making; *art*: avant-gardist; '**~damm** *m* railway embankment, *Am.* railroad embankment; '**2en** *v/t.* (ge-, *h*) clear, open (up) (*way*); *den Weg ~* prepare *or* pave the way (*dat.* for); *sich e-n Weg ~* force *or* work *or* elbow one's way; '**~hof** *m* (railway-) station, *Am.* (railroad-)station; '**~linie** *f* railway-line, *Am.* railroad line; '**~steig** *m* platform; '**~steigkarte** *f* platform ticket; '**~übergang** *m* level crossing, *Am.* grade crossing.
Bahre ['ba:rə] *f* (-/-*n*) stretcher, litter; bier.
Bai [baɪ] *f* (-/-*en*) bay; creek.
Baisse ✝ ['bɛ:s(ə)] *f* (-/-*n*) depression (on the market); fall (in prices); *auf ~ spekulieren* ✝ bear, speculate for a fall, *Am.* sell short; '**~spekulant** *m* bear.
Bajonett ⚔ [bajo'nɛt] *n* (-[e]*s*/-e) bayonet; *das ~ aufpflanzen* fix the bayonet.
Bake ['ba:kə] *f* (-/-*n*) ⚓ beacon; 🚂 warning-sign.
Bakterie [bak'te:rjə] *f* (-/-*n*) bacterium, microbe, germ.
bald *adv.* [balt] soon; shortly; before long; F almost, nearly; early; *so ~ als möglich* as soon as possible; *~ hier, ~ dort* now here, now there; **~ig** *adj.* ['~diç] speedy; *~e Antwort* ✝ early reply.
Baldrian ['baldria:n] *m* (-*s*/-e) valerian.
Balg [balk] **1.** *m* (-[e]*s*/⸗e) skin; body (*of doll*); bellows *pl.*; **2.** F *m, n* (-[e]*s*/⸗*er*) brat, urchin; **2en** ['balgən] *v/refl.* (ge-, *h*) scuffle (*um* for), wrestle (for).
Balken ['balkən] *m* (-*s*/-) beam; rafter.
Balkon [bal'kõ:; ~'ko:n] *m* (-*s*/-*s*; -*s*/-e) balcony; *thea.* dress circle, *Am.* balcony; **~tür** *f* French window.
Ball [bal] *m* (-[e]*s*/⸗e) ball; *geogr., ast. a.* globe; ball, dance; *auf dem ~* at the ball.
Ballade [ba'la:də] *f* (-/-*n*) ballad.
Ballast ['balast] *m* (-*es*/⚒-e) ballast; *fig.* burden, impediment; dead weight.
'**ballen**[1] *v/t.* (ge-, *h*) (form into a) ball; clench (*fist*); *sich ~* (form into a) ball; cluster.
'**Ballen**[2] *m* (-*s*/-) bale; *anat.* ball; *~ Papier* ten reams *pl.*
Ballett [ba'lɛt] *n* (-[e]*s*/-e) ballet; **~änzer** [ba'lɛttɛntsər] *m* (-*s*/-) ballet-dancer.
ball|förmig *adj.* ['balfœrmiç] ball-shaped, globular; '**2kleid** *n* ball-dress.
Ballon [ba'lõ:; ~o:n] *m* (-*s*/-*s*; -*s*/-*s*, -e) balloon.
'**Ball|saal** *m* ball-room; '**~spiel** *n* ball-game, game of ball.
Balsam ['balza:m] *m* (-*s*/-e) balsam, balm (*a. fig.*); **2ieren** [~a'mi:rən] *v/t.* (*no* -*ge*-, *h*) embalm.
Balz [balts] *f* (-/-*en*) mating season; display (*by cock-bird*).
Bambus ['bambus] *m* (-*ses*/-*se*) bamboo; '**~rohr** *n* bamboo, cane.
banal *adj.* [ba'na:l] commonplace, banal, trite; trivial; **2ität** [~ali'tɛ:t] *f* (-/-*en*) banality; commonplace; triviality.
Banane [ba'na:nə] *f* (-/-*n*) banana; **~nstecker** ⚡ *m* banana plug.
Band [bant] **1.** *m* (-[e]*s*/⸗e) volume; **2.** *n* (-[e]*s*/⸗*er*) band; ribbon; tape; *anat.* ligament; **3.** *fig. n* (-[e]*s*/-e) bond, tie; **4.** 2 *pret. of binden.*
Bandag|e [ban'da:ʒə] *f* (-/-*n*) bandage; **2ieren** [~a'ʒi:rən] *v/t.* (*no* -*ge*-, *h*) (apply a) bandage.
Bande ['bandə] *f* (-/-*n*) *billiards*: cushion; *fig.* gang, band.
bändigen ['bɛndigən] *v/t.* (ge-, *h*)

tame; break in (*horse*); subdue (*a. fig.*); *fig.* restrain. master.

Bandit [ban'di:t] *m* (-en/-en) bandit.

'**Band**|**maß** *n* tape measure; '~säge *f* band-saw; '~scheibe *anat. f* intervertebral disc; '~wurm *zo. m* tapeworm.

bang *adj.* [baŋ], ~e *adj.* ['~ə] anxious (um about), uneasy (about), concerned (for); *mir ist* ~ I am afraid (*vor dat.* of); *j-m* **bange machen** frighten *or* scare s.o.; '~en *v/i.* (ge-, h) be anxious *or* worried (um about).

Bank [baŋk] *f* 1. (-/-̈e) bench; *school:* desk; F *durch die* ~ without exception, all through; *auf die lange* ~ **schieben** put off, postpone; **shelve**; 2. † (-/-en) bank; *Geld auf der* ~ money in the bank; '~anweisung *f* cheque, *Am.* check; '~ausweis *m* bank return *or* statement; '~beamte *m* bank clerk *or* official; '~einlage *f* deposit.

Bankett [baŋ'kɛt] *n* (-[e]s/-e) banquet.

'**Bank**|**geheimnis** *n* banker's duty of secrecy; '~geschäft † *n* bank (-ing) transaction, banking operation; '~haus *n* bank(ing-house).

Bankier [baŋk'je:] *m* (-s/-s) banker.

'**Bank**|**konto** *n* bank(ing) account; '~note *f* (bank) note, *Am.* (bank) bill.

bankrott [baŋ'krɔt] 1. *adj.* bankrupt; 2. ℒ *m* (-[e]s/-e) bankruptcy, insolvency, failure; ~ **machen** fail, go *or* become bankrupt.

'**Bankwesen** *n* banking.

Bann [ban] *m* (-[e]s/-e) ban; *fig.* spell; *eccl.* excommunication; 'ℒen *v/t.* (ge-, h) banish (*a. fig.*); exorcize (*devil*); avert (*danger*); *eccl.* excommunicate; spellbind.

Banner ['banər] *n* (-s/-) banner (*a. fig.*); standard; '~träger *m* standard-bearer.

'**Bann**|**fluch** *m* anathema; '~meile *f* precincts *pl.*; ⚥ area around government buildings within which processions and meetings are prohibited.

bar¹ [ba:r] 1. *adj.*: *e-r Sache* ~ destitute *or* devoid of s.th.; ~*es Geld* ready money, cash; ~*er Unsinn* sheer nonsense; 2. *adv.*: ~ **bezahlen** pay in cash, pay money down.

Bar² [~] *f* (-/-s) bar; night-club.

Bär [bɛ:r] *m* (-en/-en) bear; *j-m e-n* ~*en aufbinden* hoax s.o.

Baracke [ba'rakə] *f* (-/-n) barrack; ~**nlager** *n* hutment.

Barbar [bar'ba:r] *m* (-en/-en) barbarian; ~**ei** [~a'rai] *f* (-/-en) barbarism; barbarity; ℒ**isch** [~'ba:rif] *adj.* barbarian; barbarous; *art*, *taste:* barbaric.

'**Bar**|**bestand** *m* cash in hand; '~betrag *m* amount in cash.

'**Bärenzwinger** *m* bear-pit.

barfuß *adj. and adv.* ['ba:r-], ~**füßig** *adj. and adv.* ['~fy:siç] barefoot.

barg [bark] *pret. of* bergen.

'**Bar**|**geld** *n* cash, ready money; 'ℒ**geldlos** *adj.* cashless; ~*er Zahlungsverkehr* cashless money transfers *pl.*; ℒ**häuptig** *adj. and adv.* ['~hɔyptiç] bare-headed, uncovered.

Bariton ♩ ['ba:ritɔn] *m* (-s/-e) baritone. [launch.)

Barkasse ⚓ [bar'kasə] *f* (-/-n)|

barmherzig *adj.* [barm'hɛrtsiç] merciful, charitable; *der* ~*e Samariter* the good Samaritan; ℒ**e Schwester** Sister of Mercy *or* Charity; ℒ**keit** *f* (-/-en) mercy, charity.

Barometer [baro'-] *n* barometer.

Baron [ba'ro:n] *m* (-s/-e) baron; ~**in** *f* (-/-nen) baroness.

Barre ['barə] *f* (-/-n) bar.

Barren ['barən] *m* (-s/-) *metall.* bar, ingot, bullion; *gymnastics:* parallel bars *pl.*

Barriere [bar'jɛ:rə] *f* (-/-n) barrier.

Barrikade [bari'ka:də] *f* (-/-n) barricade; ~**n errichten** raise barricades.

barsch *adj.* [barʃ] rude, gruff, rough.

'**Bar**|**schaft** *f* (-/-en) ready money, cash; '~scheck † *m* open cheque, *Am.* open check.

barst [barst] *pret. of* bersten.

Bart [ba:rt] *m* (-[e]s/-̈e) beard; bit (*of key*); *sich e-n* ~ **wachsen lassen** grow a beard.

bärtig *adj.* ['bɛ:rtiç] bearded.

'**bartlos** *adj.* beardless.

'**Barzahlung** *f* cash payment; *nur gegen* ~ † terms strictly cash.

Basis ['ba:zis] *f* (-/*Basen*) base; *fig.* basis.

Baß ♩ [bas] *m* (*Basses/Bässe*) bass; '~geige *f* bass-viol.

Bassist [ba'sist] *m* (-en/-en) bass (singer).

Bast [bast] *m* (-es/-e) bast; velvet (*on antlers*).

Bastard ['bastart] *m* (-[e]s/-e) bastard; half-breed; *zo.*, ⚘ hybrid.

bast|**eln** ['bastəln] (ge-, h) 1. *v/t.* build, F rig up; 2. *v/i.* build; 'ℒ**ler** *m* (-s/-) amateur craftsman, do-it-yourself man.

bat [ba:t] *pret. of* bitten.

Bataillon [batal'jo:n] *n* (-s/-e) battalion.

Batist [ba'tist] *m* (-[e]s/-e) cambric.

Batterie ✕, ⚡ [bata'ri:] *f* (-/-n) battery.

Bau [bau] *m* 1. (-[e]s/*no pl.*) building, construction; build, frame; 2. (-[e]s/-ten) building, edifice; 3. (-[e]s/-e) burrow, den (*a. fig.*), earth.

'**Bau**|**arbeiter** *m* workman in the building trade; '~art *f* architecture, style; method of construction; *mot.* type, model.

Bauch [baʊx] m (-[e]s/ᵘe) anat. abdomen, belly; paunch; ship: bottom; '⁀ig adj. big-bellied, bulgy; '⁀landung f belly landing; '⁀redner m ventriloquist; '⁀schmerzen m/pl., '⁀weh n (-s/no pl.) belly-ache, stomach-ache.

bauen ['baʊən] (ge-, h) 1. v/t. build, construct; erect, raise; build, make (nest); make (violin, etc.); 2. v/i. build; ~ auf (acc.) trust (in); rely or count or depend on.

Bauer ['baʊər] 1. m (-n, -s/-n) farmer; peasant, countryman; chess: pawn; 2. n, m (-s/-) (bird-)cage.

Bäuerin ['bɔʏərɪn] f (-/-nen) farmer's wife; peasant woman.

Bauerlaubnis ['baʊʔ-] f building permit.

bäuerlich adj. ['bɔʏərlɪç] rural, rustic.

Bauern|fänger contp. ['baʊərn-fɛŋər] m (-s/-) trickster, confidence man; '⁀haus n farm-house; '⁀hof m farm.

'**bau|fällig** adj. out of repair, dilapidated; '⁀gerüst n scaffold(-ing); '⁀handwerker m craftsman in the building trade; '⁀herr m owner; '⁀holz n timber, Am. lumber; '⁀jahr n year of construction; ~ 1969 1969 model or make; '⁀kasten m box of bricks; '⁀kunst f architecture.

'**baulich** adj. architectural, structural; in gutem ⁀en Zustand in good repair.

Baum [baʊm] m (-[e]s/ᵘe) tree.

'**Baumeister** m architect.

baumeln ['baʊməln] v/i. (ge-, h) dangle, swing; mit den Beinen ~ dangle or swing one's legs.

'**Baum|schere** f (eine a pair of) pruning-shears pl.; '⁀schule f nursery (of young trees); '⁀stamm m trunk; '⁀wolle f cotton; '⁀wollen adj. (made of) cotton.

'**Bau|plan** m architect's or building plan; '⁀platz m building plot or site, Am. location; '⁀polizei f Board of Surveyors.

Bausch [baʊʃ] m (-es/-e, ᵘe) pad; bolster; wad; in ~ und Bogen altogether, wholesale, in the lump; '⁀en v/t. (ge-, h) swell; sich ~ bulge, swell out, billow (out).

'**Bau|stein** m brick, building stone; building block; fig. element; '⁀stelle f building site; '⁀stil m (architectural) style; '⁀stoff m building material; '⁀unternehmer m building contractor; '⁀zaun m hoarding.

Bay|er ['baɪər] m (-n/-n) Bavarian; '⁀(e)risch adj. Bavarian.

Bazill|enträger ❡ [ba'tsɪlən-] m (germ-)carrier; ⁀us [⁀us] m (-/Bazillen) bacillus, germ.

beabsichtigen [bə'apzɪçtɪgən] v/t.

(no -ge-, h) intend, mean, propose (zu tun to do, doing).

be'acht|en v/t. (no -ge-, h) pay attention to; notice; observe; ⁀ens-wert adj. noteworthy, remarkable; ⁀lich adj. remarkable; considerable; ⁀ung f attention; consideration; notice; observance.

Beamte [bə'amtə] m (-n/-n) official, officer, Am. a. officeholder; functionary; Civil Servant.

be'ängstigend adj. alarming, disquieting.

beanspruch|en [bə'anʃpruxən] v/t. (no -ge-, h) claim, demand; require (efforts, time, space, etc.); ⊕ stress; ⁀ung f (-/-en) claim; demand (gen. on); ⊕ stress, strain.

beanstand|en [bə'anʃtandən] v/t. (no -ge-, h) object to; ⁀ung f (-/-en) objection (gen. to).

beantragen [bə'antraːgən] v/t. (no -ge-, h) apply for; ᵗᵗ, parl. move, make a motion; propose.

be'antwort|en v/t. (no -ge-, h) answer (a. fig.), reply to; ⁀ung f (-/-en) answer, reply; in ~ (gen.) in answer or reply to.

be'arbeit|en v/t. (no -ge-, h) work; ✗ till; dress (leather); hew (stone); process; ⁀ treat; ᵗᵗ be in charge of (case); edit, revise (book); adapt (nach from); esp. ♪ arrange; j-n ~ work on s.o.; batter s.o.; ⁀ung f (-/-en) working; revision (of book); thea. adaptation; esp. ♪ arrangement; processing; ⁀ treatment.

be'argwöhnen v/t. (no -ge-, h) suspect, be suspicious of.

beaufsichtig|en [bə'aʊfzɪçtɪgən] v/t. (no -ge-, h) inspect, superintend, supervise, control; look after (child); ⁀ung f (-/-en) inspection, supervision, control.

be'auftrag|en v/t. (no -ge-, h) commission (zu inf. to inf.), charge (mit with); ⁀te [⁀ktə] m (-n/-n) commissioner; representative; deputy; proxy.

be'bauen v/t. (no -ge-, h) ⚠ build on; ✗ cultivate.

beben ['beːbən] v/i. (ge-, h) shake (vor dat. with), tremble (with); shiver (with); earth: quake.

Becher ['bɛçər] m (-s/-) cup (a. fig.).

Becken ['bɛkən] n (-s/-) basin, Am. a. bowl; ♪ cymbal(s pl.); anat. pelvis.

bedacht adj. [bə'daxt]: ~ sein auf (acc.) look after, be concerned about, be careful or mindful of; darauf ~ sein zu inf. be anxious to inf.

bedächtig adj. [bə'dɛçtɪç] deliberate.

bedang [bə'daŋ] pret. of bedingen.

be'danken v/refl. (no -ge-, h): sich bei j-m für et. ~ thank s.o. for s.th.

Bedarf [bə'darf] *m* (-[e]s/*no pl.*) need (*an dat.* of), want (of); ✝ demand (for); **~sartikel** [bə'darfs²-] *m/pl.* necessaries *pl.*, requisites *pl.*

bedauerlich *adj.* [bə'dauərlïç] regrettable, deplorable.

be'dauer|n 1. *v/t.* (*no -ge-, h*) feel or be sorry for *s.o.*; pity *s.o.*; regret, deplore *s.th.*; **2.** **2** *n* (-s/*no pl.*) regret; pity; **~swert** *adj.* pitiable, deplorable.

be'deck|en *v/t.* (*no -ge-, h*) cover; ✗ escort; ⚓ convoy; **~t** *adj.* sky: overcast; **2ung** *f* cover(ing); ✗ escort; ⚓ convoy.

be'denken 1. *v/t.* (*irr.* denken, *no -ge-, h*) consider; think *s.th.* over; *j-n in s-m Testament* ~ remember s.o. in one's will; **2.** **2** *n* (-s/-) consideration; objection; hesitation; scruple; **~los** *adj.* unscrupulous.

be'denklich *adj.* doubtful; *character: a.* dubious; *situation, etc.:* dangerous, critical; delicate; risky.

Be'denkzeit *f* time for reflection; *ich gebe dir e-e Stunde* ~ I give you one hour to think it over.

be'deut|en *v/t.* (*no -ge-, h*) mean, signify; stand for; **~end** *adj.* important, prominent; *sum, etc.* considerable; **~sam** *adj.* significant.

Be'deutung *f* meaning, significance; importance; **2slos** *adj.* insignificant; meaningless; **2svoll** *adj.* significant; **~swandel** *ling.* *m* semantic change.

be'dien|en (*no -ge-, h*) **1.** *v/t.* serve; wait on; ⊕ operate, work (*machine*); ✗ serve (*gun*); answer (*telephone*); *sich* ~ *at table:* help o.s.; **2.** *v/i.* serve; wait (at table); *cards:* follow suit; **2ung** *f* (-/-en) service, *esp.* ✝ attendance; *in restaurant, etc.:* service; waiter, waitress; shop assistant(s *pl.*).

beding|en [bə'dïŋən] *v/t.* ([*irr.*,] *no -ge-, h*) condition; stipulate; require; cause; imply; **~t** *adj.* conditional (*durch on*); restricted; ~ *sein durch* be conditioned by; **2ung** *f* (-/-en) condition; stipulation; *~en pl.* ✝ terms *pl.*; **~ungslos** *adj.* unconditional.

be'dräng|en *v/t.* (*no -ge-, h*) press hard, beset; **2nis** *f* (-/-se) distress.

be'droh|en *v/t.* (*no -ge-, h*) threaten; menace; **~lich** *adj.* threatening; **2ung** *f* threat, menace (*gen.* to).

be'drück|en *v/t.* (*no -ge-, h*) oppress; depress; deject; **2ung** *f* (-/-en) oppression; depression; dejection.

bedungen [bə'duŋən] *p.p.* of bedingen.

be'dürf|en *v/i.* (*irr.* dürfen, *no -ge-, h*): *e-r Sache* ~ need or want or require s.th.; **2nis** *n* (-ses/-se) need, want, requirement; *sein* ~ *verrichten* relieve o.s. or nature; **2nisan-**

stalt [bə'dyrfnïs²-] *f* public convenience, *Am.* comfort station; **~tig** *adj.* needy, poor, indigent.

be'ehren *v/t.* (*no -ge-, h*) hono(u)r, favo(u)r; *ich beehre mich zu inf.* I have the hono(u)r to *inf.*

be'eilen *v/refl.* (*no -ge-, h*) hasten, hurry, make haste, *Am.* F *a.* hustle.

beeindrucken [bə'aïndrukən] *v/t.* (*no -ge-, h*) impress, make an impression on.

beeinfluss|en [bə'aïnflusən] *v/t.* (*no -ge-, h*) influence; affect; *parl.* lobby; **2ung** *f* (-/-en) influence; *parl.* lobbying.

beeinträchtig|en [bə'aïntrεçtïgən] *v/t.* (*no -ge-, h*) impair, injure, affect (*adversely*); **2ung** *f* (-/-en) impairment (*gen.* of); injury (to).

be'end|en *v/t.* (*no -ge-, h*), **~igen** [~ïgən] *v/t.* (*no -ge-, h*) (bring to an) end, finish, terminate; **2igung** [~ïguŋ] *f* (-/-en) ending, termination.

beengt *adj.* [bə'εŋkt] *space:* narrow, confined, cramped; *sich* ~ *fühlen* feel cramped (for room); feel oppressed or uneasy.

be'erben *v/t.* (*no -ge-, h*): *j-n* ~ be s.o.'s heir.

beerdig|en [bə'e:rdïgən] *v/t.* (*no -ge-, h*) bury; **2ung** *f* (-/-en) burial, funeral.

Beere ['be:rə] *f* (-/-n) berry.

Beet ✗ [be:t] *n* (-[e]s/-e) bed.

befähig|en [bə'fε:ïgən] *v/t.* (*no -ge-, h*) enable (*zu inf.* to *inf.*); qualify (*für, zu* for); **~t** *adj.* [~çt] (cap)able; **2ung** *f* (-/-en) qualification; capacity.

befahl [bə'fa:l] *pret.* of befehlen.

befahr|bar *adj.* [bə'fa:rba:r] passable, practicable, trafficable; ⚓ navigable; **~en** *v/t.* (*irr.* fahren, *no -ge-, h*) drive or travel on; ⚓ navigate (*river*).

be'fallen *v/t.* (*irr.* fallen, *no -ge-, h*) attack; befall; *disease: a.* strike; *fear:* seize.

be'fangen *adj.* embarrassed; self-conscious; prejudiced (*a.* ₴₴); ₴₴ bias(s)ed; **2heit** *f* (-/-en) embarrassment; self-consciousness; ₴₴ bias, prejudice.

be'fassen *v/refl.* (*no -ge-, h*): *sich* ~ *mit* occupy o.s. with; engage in; attend to; deal with.

Befehl [bə'fe:l] *m* (-[e]s/-e) command (*über acc.* of); order; **2en** (*irr., no -ge-, h*) **1.** *v/t.* command; order; **2.** *v/i.* command; **2igen** ✗ [~ïgən] *v/t.* (*no -ge-. h*) command.

Be'fehlshaber *m* (-s/-) commander(-in-chief); **2isch** *adj.* imperious.

be'festig|en *v/t.* (*no -ge-, h*) fasten (*an dat.* to), fix (to), attach (to); ✗ fortify; *fig.* strengthen; **2ung** *f* (-/-en) fixing, fastening; ✗ fortification; *fig.* strengthening.

be'feuchten v/t. (no -ge-, h) moisten, damp; wet.

be'finden 1. v/refl. (irr. finden, no -ge-, h) be; **2.** 2 n (-s/no pl.) (state of) health.

be'flaggen v/t. (no -ge-, h) flag.

be'flecken v/t. (no -ge-, h) spot, stain (a. fig.); fig. sully.

beflissen adj. [bə'flisən] studious; 2heit f (-/no pl.) studiousness, assiduity.

befohlen [bə'fo:lən] p.p. of befehlen.

be'folg|en v/t. (no -ge-, h) follow, take (advice); obey (rule); adhere to (principle); 2ung f (-/-%-en) observance (of); adherence (to).

be'förder|n v/t. (no -ge-, h) convey, carry; haul (goods); transport; forward; ✝ ship (a. ♣); promote (to be) (a. ✕); 2ung f conveyance, transport(ation), forwarding; promotion; 2ungsmittel n (means of) transport, Am. (means of) transportation.

be'fragen v/t. (no -ge-, h) question, interview; interrogate.

be'frei|en v/t. (no -ge-, h) (set) free (von from); liberate (nation, mind, etc.) (from); rescue (captive) (from); exempt s.o. (from); deliver s.o. (aus, von from); 2er m liberator; 2ung f (-/-en) liberation, deliverance; exemption.

Befremden [bə'frɛmdən] n (-s/ no pl.) surprise.

befreund|en [bə'frɔyndən] v/refl. (no -ge-, h): sich mit j-m ~ make friends with s.o.; sich mit et. ~ get used to s.th., reconcile o.s. to s.th.; ~et adj. friendly; on friendly terms; ~ sein be friends.

befriedig|en [bə'fri:digən] v/t. (no -ge-, h) satisfy; appease (hunger); meet (expectations, demand); pay off (creditor); ~end adj. satisfactory; 2ung f (-/-en) satisfaction.

be'fristen v/t. (no -ge-, h) set a time-limit.

be'frucht|en v/t. (no -ge-, h) fertilize; fructify; fecundate; impregnate; 2ung f (-/-en) fertilization; fructification; fecundation; impregnation.

Befug|nis [bə'fu:knis] f (-/-se) authority, warrant; esp. 🕮 competence; 2t adj. authorized; competent.

be'fühlen v/t. (no -ge-, h) feel; touch, handle, finger.

Be'fund m (-[e]s/-e) result; finding(s pl.) 🕮 diagnosis.

be'fürchten v/t. (no -ge-, h) fear, apprehend; suspect; 2ung f (-/-en) fear, apprehension, suspicion.

befürworten [bə'fy:rvɔrtən] v/t. (no -ge-, h) plead for, advocate.

begab|t adj. [bə'gɑ:pt] gifted, talented; 2ung [~buŋ] f (-/-en) gift, talent(s pl.).

begann [bə'gan] pret. of beginnen.

be'geben v/t. (irr. geben, no -ge-, h) ✝ negotiate (bill of exchange); sich ~ happen; sich ~ nach go to, make for; sich in Gefahr ~ expose o.s. to danger.

begegn|en [bə'ge:gnən] v/i. (no -ge-, sein) meet s.o. or s.th., meet with; incident: happen to; anticipate, prevent; 2ung f (-/-en) meeting.

be'gehen v/t. (irr. gehen, no -ge-, h) walk (on); inspect; celebrate (birthday, etc.); commit (crime); make (mistake); ein Unrecht ~ do wrong.

begehr|en [bə'ge:rən] v/t. (no -ge-, h) demand, require; desire, crave (for); long for; ~lich adj. desirous, covetous.

begeister|n [bə'gaɪstərn] v/t. (no -ge-, h) inspire, fill with enthusiasm; sich ~ für feel enthusiastic about; 2ung f (-/no pl.) enthusiasm, inspiration.

Be'gier f, ~de [~də] f (-/-n) desire (nach for), appetite (for); concupiscence; 2ig adj. eager (nach for, auf acc. for; zu inf. to inf.), desirous (nach of; zu inf. to inf.), anxious (zu inf. to inf.).

be'gießen v/t. (irr. gießen, no -ge-, h) water; baste (roasting meat); F wet (bargain).

Beginn [bə'gin] m (-[e]s/no pl.) beginning, start, commencement; origin; 2en v/t. and v/i. (irr. no -ge-, h) begin, start, commence.

beglaubig|en [bə'glaubigən] v/t. (no -ge-, h) attest, certify; legalize, authenticate; 2ung f (-/-en) attestation, certification; legalization; 2ungsschreiben n credentials pl.

be'gleichen ✝ v/t. (irr. gleichen, no -ge-, h) pay, settle (bill, debt).

be'gleit|en v/t. (no -ge-, h) accompany (a. ♪ auf dat. on), escort; attend (a. fig.); see (s.o. home, etc.); 2er m (-s/-) companion, attendant; escort; ♪ accompanist; 2erscheinung f attendant symptom; 2-schreiben n covering letter; 2ung f (-/-en) company; attendants pl., retinue (of sovereign, etc.); esp. ✕ escort; ♣, ✕ convoy; ♪ accompaniment.

be'glückwünschen v/t. (no -ge-, h) congratulate (zu on).

begnadig|en [bə'gna:digən] v/t. (no -ge-, h) pardon; pol. amnesty; 2ung f (-/-en) pardon; pol. amnesty.

begnügen [bə'gny:gən] v/refl. (no -ge-, h): sich ~ mit content o.s. with, be satisfied with.

begonnen [bə'gɔnən] p.p. of beginnen.

be'graben v/t. (irr. graben, no -ge-, h) bury (a. fig.); inter.

Begräbnis [bə'grɛ:pnis] n (-ses/-se) burial; funeral, obsequies pl.

begradigen [bə'grɑːdigən] *v/t.* (*no -ge-, h*) straighten (*road, frontier, etc.*).

be'greif|en *v/t.* (*irr. greifen, no -ge-, h*) comprehend, understand; **~lich** *adj.* comprehensible.

be'grenz|en *v/t.* (*no -ge-, h*) bound, border; *fig.* limit; **2theit** *f* (*-/-en*) limitation (*of knowledge*); narrowness (*of mind*); **2ung** *f* (*-/-en*) boundary; bound, limit; limitation.

Be'griff *m* idea, notion, conception; comprehension; *im ~ sein zu inf.* be about *or* going to *inf.*

be'gründ|en *v/t.* (*no -ge-, h*) establish, found; give reasons for, substantiate (*claim charge*); **2ung** *f* establishment, foundation; *fig.* substantiation (*of claim or charge*); reason.

be'grüß|en *v/t.* (*no -ge-, h*) greet, welcome; salute; **2ung** *f* (*-/-en*) greeting, welcome; salutation.

begünstig|en [bə'gynstigən] *v/t.* (*no -ge-, h*) favo(u)r; encourage; patronize; **2ung** *f* (*-/-en*) favo(u)r; encouragement; patronage.

begutachten [bə'guːt⁹-] *v/t.* (*no -ge-, h*) give an opinion on; examine; *~ lassen* obtain expert opinion on, submit *s.th.* to an expert.

begütert *adj.* [bə'gyːtərt] wealthy, well-to-do.

be'haart *adj.* hairy.

behäbig *adj.* [bə'hɛːbiç] phlegmatic, comfort-loving; *figure:* portly.

be'haftet *adj.* afflicted (*with disease, etc.*).

behag|en [bə'hɑːgən] **1.** *v/i.* (*no -ge-, h*) please *or* suit *s.o.*; **2.** *2 n* (*-s/no pl.*) comfort, ease; **~lich** *adj.* [~k-] comfortable; cosy, snug.

be'halten *v/t.* (*irr. halten, no -ge-, h*) re¹tain; keep (*für sich* to o.s.); remember.

Behälter [bə'hɛltər] *m* (*-s/-*) container, receptacle; box; *for liquid:* reservoir; *for oil, etc.:* tank.

be'hand|eln *v/t.* (*no -ge-, h*) treat; deal with (*a. subject*); ⊕ process; ♣ treat; dress (*wound*); **2lung** *f* treatment; handling; ⊕ processing.

be'hängen *v/t.* (*no -ge-, h*) hang, drape (*mit with*); *sich ~ mit* cover *or* load o.s. with (*jewellery*).

beharr|en [bə'harən] *v/i.* (*no -ge-, h*) persist (*auf dat.* in); **~lich** *adj.* persistent; **2lichkeit** *f* (*-/no pl.*) persistence.

be'hauen *v/t.* (*no -ge-, h*) hew; trim (*wood*).

behaupt|en [bə'hauptən] *v/t.* (*no -ge-, h*) assert; maintain; **2ung** *f* (*-/-en*) assertion; statement.

Behausung [bə'hauzuŋ] *f* (*-/-en*) habitation; lodging.

Be'helf *m* (*-[e]s/-e*) expedient, (make)shift; *s. Notbehelf*; **2en** *v/refl.* (*irr. helfen, no -ge-, h*): *sich*

~ mit make shift with; *sich ~ ohne* do without; **~sheim** *n* temporary home.

behend *adj.* [bə'hɛnt], **~e** *adj.* [~də] nimble, agile; smart; **2igkeit** [~d-] *f* (*-/no pl.*) nimbleness, agility; smartness. [lodge, shelter.)

be'herbergen *v/t.* (*no -ge-, h*))

be'herrsch|en *v/t.* (*no -ge-, h*) rule (over), govern; command (*situation, etc.*); have command of (*language*); *sich ~* control o.s.; **2er** *m* ruler (*gen. over, of*); **2ung** *f* (*-/-en*) command, control.

beherzigen [bə'hɛrtsigən] *v/t.* (*no -ge-, h*) take to heart, (bear in) mind.

be'hexen *v/t.* (*no -ge-, h*) bewitch.

be'hilflich *adj.*: *j-m ~ sein* help s.o. (*bei* in).

be'hindern *v/t.* (*no -ge-, h*) hinder, hamper, impede; handicap; obstruct (*a. traffic, etc.*).

Behörde [bə'høːrdə] *f* (*-/-n*) authority, *mst* authorities *pl.*; board; council.

be'hüten *v/t.* (*no -ge-, h*) guard, preserve (*vor dat.* from).

behutsam *adj.* [bə'huːtzaːm] cautious, careful; **2keit** *f* (*-/no pl.*) caution.

bei *prp.* (*dat.*) *by;* **~** *Schmidt* care of (*abbr.* c/o) Schmidt; **~m** *Buchhändler* at the bookseller's; *~ uns* with us; *~ der Hand nehmen* take by the hand; *ich habe kein Geld ~ mir* I have no money about *or* on me; *~ der Kirche* near the church; *~ guter Gesundheit* in good health; *wie es ~ Schiller heißt* as Schiller says; *die Schlacht ~ Waterloo* the Battle of Waterloo; *~ e-m Glase Wein* over a glass of wine; *~ alledem* for all that; *Stunden nehmen ~* take lessons from *or* with; *~ günstigem Wetter* weather permitting.

'beibehalten *v/t.* (*irr. halten, sep., no -ge-, h*) keep up, retain.

'Beiblatt *n* supplement (*zu* to).

'beibringen *v/t.* (*irr. bringen, sep., -ge-, h*) bring forward; produce (*witness, etc.*); *j-m et. ~* impart (*news, etc.*) to s.o.; teach s.o. *s.th.*; inflict (*defeat, wound, etc.*) on s.o.

Beichte ['baiçtə] *f* (*-/-n*) confession; **2n** *v/t. and v/i.* (*ge-, h*) confess.

beide *adj.* ['baidə] both; *nur wir ~* just the two of us; *in ~n Fällen* in either case.

beider|lei *adj.* ['baidərlai] of both kinds; *~ Geschlechts* of either sex; **'~seitig 1.** *adj.* on both sides; mutual; **2.** *adv.* mutually; **'~seits 1.** *prp.* on both sides (*gen.* of); **2.** *adv.* mutually.

'Beifahrer *m* (*-s/-*) (front-seat) passenger; assistant driver; *motor racing:* co-driver.

'Beifall *m* (-[e]s/*no pl.*) approbation; applause; cheers *pl.*

'beifällig *adj.* approving; favo(u)rable.

'Beifallsruf *m* acclaim; ~e *pl.* cheers *pl.*

'beifügen *v/t.* (*sep.*, -ge-, h) add; enclose.

'Beigeschmack *m* (-[e]s/*no pl.*) slight flavo(u)r; smack (of) (*a. fig.*).

'Beihilfe *f* aid; allowance; *for study:* grant; *for project:* subsidy; ⚖ aiding and abetting; *j-m* ~ *leisten* ⚖ aid and abet s.o.

'beikommen *v/i.* (*irr.* kommen, *sep.*, -ge-, sein) get at.

Beil [baɪl] *n* (-[e]s/-e) hatchet; chopper; cleaver; ax(e).

'Beilage *f* supplement (*to newspaper*); F trimming. *pl.* (*of meal*); vegetables *pl.*

beiläufig *adj.* ['baɪlɔyfɪç] casual; incidental.

'beileg|en *v/t.* (*sep.*, -ge-, h) add (*dat.* to); enclose; settle (*dispute*); '2ung *f* (-/-en) settlement.

Beileid ['baɪlaɪt] *n* condolence; *j-m sein* ~ *bezeigen* condole with s.o. (*zu* on, upon).

'beiliegen *v/i.* (*irr.* liegen, *sep.*, -ge-, h) be enclosed (*dat.* with).

'beimessen *v/t.* (*irr.* messen, *sep.*, -ge-, h) attribute (*dat.* to), ascribe (to); attach (*importance*) (to).

'beimisch|en *v/t.* (*sep.*, -ge-, h): *e-r Sache b.* ~ mix s.th. with s.th.; '2ung *f* admixture.

Bein [baɪn] *n* (-[e]s/-e) leg; bone.

'beinah(e) *adv.* almost, nearly.

'Beiname *m* appellation; nickname.

'Beinbruch *m* fracture of the leg.

beiordnen ['baɪ?-] *v/t.* (*sep.*, -ge-, h) adjoin; co-ordinate (*a. gr.*).

'beipflichten *v/i.* (*sep.*, -ge-, h) agree with s.o.; assent to s.th.

'Beirat *m* (-[e]s/⸚e) adviser, counsel(l)or; advisory board.

be'irren *v/t.* (*no -ge-*, h) confuse.

beisammen *adv.* [baɪˈzamən] together.

'Beisein *n* presence; *im* ~ (*gen.*) *or von in the presence of s.o.*, *in s.o.'s presence.*

bei'seite *adv.* aside, apart; *Spaß ~! joking apart!*

'beisetz|en *v/t.* (*sep.*, -ge-, h) bury, inter; '2ung *f* (-/-en) burial, funeral.

'Beisitzer ⚖ *m* (-s/-) assessor; associate judge; member (*of committee*).

'Beispiel *n* example, instance; *zum* ~ for example *or* instance; '2haft *adj.* exemplary; '2los *adj.* unprecedented, unparalleled; singular.

beißen ['baɪsən] (*irr.*, ge-, h) **1.** *v/t.* bite; *fleas*, *etc.:* bite, sting; **2.** *v/i.* bite (*auf acc.* on; *in acc.* into); *fleas*, *etc.:* bite, sting; *smoke:* bite, burn (*in dat.* in); *pepper*, *etc.:* bite,

burn (*auf dat.* on); '~d *adj.* biting, pungent (*both a. fig.*); *pepper*, *etc.:* hot.

'Beistand *m* assistance.

'beistehen *v/i.* (*irr.* stehen, *sep.*, -ge-, h): *j-m* ~ stand by *or* assist *or* help s.o.

'beisteuern *v/t. and v/i.* (*sep.*, -ge-, h) contribute (*zu* to).

Beitrag ['baɪtraːk] *m* (-[e]s/⸚e) contribution; share; subscription, *Am.* dues *pl.*; article (*in newspaper*, *etc.*).

'bei|treten *v/i.* (*irr.* treten, *sep.*, -ge-, sein) join (*political party*, *etc.*); '2tritt *m* joining.

'Beiwagen *m* side-car (*of motorcycle*); trailer (*of tram*).

'Beiwerk *n* accessories *pl.*

'beiwohnen *v/i.* (*sep.*, -ge-, h) assist *or* be present at, attend.

bei'zeiten *adv.* early; in good time.

beizen ['baɪtsən] *v/t.* (ge-, h) corrode; *metall.* pickle; bate (*hides*); stain (*wood*); ✗ cauterize; *hunt.* hawk.

bejahen [bəˈjaːən] *v/t.* (*no -ge-*, h) answer in the affirmative, affirm; ~d *adj.* affirmative.

be'jahrt *adj.* aged.

Bejahung *f* (-/-en) affirmation, affirmative answer; *fig.* acceptance.

be'jammern *s. beklagen.*

be'kämpfen *v/t.* (*no -ge-*, h) fight (against), combat; *fig.* oppose.

bekannt [bəˈkant] known (*dat.* to); *j-n mit j-m* ~ *machen* introduce s.o. to s.o.; *j-m* ~ *m* (-n/-n) acquaintance, *mst* friend; '~lich *adv.* as you know; ~machen *v/t.* (*sep.*, -ge-, h) make known; '2machung *f* (-/-en) publication; public notice; 2schaft *f* (-/-en) acquaintance.

be'kehr|en *v/t.* (*no -ge-*, h) convert; 2te *m, f* (-n/-n) convert; 2ung *f* (-/-en) conversion (*zu* to).

be'kenn|en *v/t.* (*irr.* kennen, *no -ge-*, h) admit; confess; *sich schuldig* ~ ⚖ plead guilty; *sich* ~ *zu* declare o.s. for; profess *s.th.*; 2tnis *n* (-ses/-se) confession; creed.

be'klagen *v/t.* (*no -ge-*, h) lament, deplore; *sich* ~ complain (*über acc.* of, about); ~swert *adj.* deplorable, pitiable.

Beklagte [bəˈklaːktə] *m, f* (-n/-n) *civil case:* defendant, *the* accused.

be'klatschen *v/t.* (*no -ge-*, h) applaud, clap.

be'kleben *v/t.* (*no -ge-*, h) glue *or* stick *s.th.* on *s.th.*; *mit Etiketten* ~ label *s.th.*; *mit Papier* ~ paste *s.th.* up with paper; *e-e Mauer mit Plakaten* ~ paste (up) posters on a wall.

bekleckern F [bəˈklɛkərn] *v/t.* (*no -ge-*, h) stain (*garment*); *sich* ~ soil one's clothes.

be'klecksen *v/t.* (*no -ge-*, h) stain, daub; blot.

be'kleid|en v/t. (no -ge-, h) clothe, dress; hold, fill (office, etc.); ~ mit invest with; £ung f clothing, clothes pl.

be'klemm|en v/t. (no -ge-, h) oppress; £ung f (-/-en) oppression; anguish, anxiety.

be'kommen (irr. kommen, no -ge-) 1. v/t. (h) get, receive; obtain; get, catch (illness); have (baby); catch (train, etc.); Zähne ~ teethe, cut one's teeth; 2. v/i. (sein): j-m (gut) ~ agree with s.o.; j-m nicht or schlecht ~ disagree with s.o.

bekömmlich adj. (bə'kœmliç) wholesome (dat. to).

beköstig|en [bə'kœstigən] v/t. (no -ge-, h) board, feed; £ung f (-/₣ -en) board(ing).

be'kräftig|en v/t. (no -ge-, h) confirm; £ung f (-/-en) confirmation.

be'kränzen v/t. (no -ge-, h) wreathe; festoon.

be'kritteln v/t. (no -ge-, h) carp at, criticize.

be'kümmern v/t. (no -ge-, h) afflict, grieve; trouble; s. kümmern.

be'laden v/t. (irr. laden, no -ge-, h) load; fig. burden.

Belag [bə'la:k] m (-[e]s/⁺e) covering; ⊕ coat(ing); surface (of road); foil (of mirror); ⚔ fur (on tongue); (slices of) ham, etc. (on bread); filling (of roll).

Belager|er [bə'la:gərər] m (-s/-) besieger; £n v/t. (no -ge-, h) besiege, beleaguer; ~ung f siege.

Belang [bə'laŋ] m (-[e]s/-e) importance; ~e pl. interests pl.; £en v/t. (no -ge-, h) concern; ₳₳ sue; £los adj. unimportant; ~losigkeit f (-/-en) insignificance.

be'lasten v/t. (no -ge-, h) load; fig. burden; ₳₳ incriminate; mortgage (estate, etc.); j-s Konto (mit e-r Summe) ~ ✝ charge or debit s.o.'s account (with a sum).

belästig|en [bə'lɛstigən] v/t. (no -ge-, h) molest; trouble, bother; £ung f molestation; trouble.

Be'lastung f (-/-en) load (a. ⚡, ⊕); fig. burden; ✝ debit; encumbrance; ₳₳ incrimination; erbliche ~ hereditary taint; ~szeuge ₳₳ m witness for the prosecution.

be'laufen v/refl. (irr. laufen, no -ge-, h): sich ~ auf (acc.) amount to.

be'lauschen v/t. (no -ge-, h) overhear, eavesdrop on s.o.

be'leb|en fig. v/t. (no -ge-, h) enliven, animate; stimulate; ~t adj. street: busy, crowded; stock exchange: brisk; conversation: lively, animated.

Beleg [bə'le:k] m (-[e]s/-e) proof; ₳₳ (supporting) evidence; document; voucher; £en [¸gən] v/t. (no -ge-, h) cover; reserve (seat, etc.); prove, verify; univ. enrol(l) or register for,

Am. a. sign up for (course of lectures, term); ein Brötchen mit et. ~ put s.th. on a roll, fill a roll with s.th.; ~schaft f (-/-en) personnel, staff; labo(u)r force; ~stelle f reference; £t adj. engaged, occupied; hotel, etc.: full; voice: thick, husky; tongue: coated, furred; ~es Brot (open) sandwich.

be'lehr|en v/t. (no -ge-, h) instruct, inform; sich ~ lassen take advice; ~end adj. instructive; £ung f (-/-en) instruction; information; advice.

beleibt adj. [bə'laipt] corpulent, stout, bulky, portly.

beleidig|en [bə'laidigən] v/t. (no -ge-, h) offend (s.o.; ear, eye, etc.); insult; ~end adj. offensive, insulting; £ung f (-/-en) offen|ce, Am. -se; insult.

be'lesen adj. well-read.

be'leucht|en v/t. (no -ge-, h) light (up), illuminate (a. fig.); fig. shed or throw light on; £ung f (-/-en) light(ing); illumination; £ungskörper m lighting appliance.

be'licht|en phot. v/t. (no -ge-, h) expose; £ung phot. f exposure.

Be'lieb|en n (-s/no pl.) will, choice; nach ~ at will; es steht in Ihrem ~ I leave it to you to; £ig 1. adj. any; jeder ~e anyone; 2. adv. at pleasure; ~ viele as many as you like; £t adj. [~pt] popular (bei with); ~theit f (-/no pl.) popularity.

be'liefer|n v/t. (no -ge-, h) supply, furnish (mit with); £ung f (-/no pl.) supply.

bellen ['bɛlən] v/i. (ge-, h) bark.

belobigen [bə'lo:bigən] v/t. (no -ge-, h) commend, praise.

be'lohn|en v/t. (no -ge-, h) reward; recompense; £ung f (-/-en) reward; recompense.

be'lügen v/t. (irr. lügen, no -ge-, h): j-n ~ lie to s.o.

belustig|en [bə'lustigən] v/t. (no -ge-, h) amuse, entertain; sich ~ amuse o.s.; £ung f (-/-en) amusement, entertainment.

bemächtigen [bə'mɛçtigən] v/refl. (no -ge-, h): sich e-r Sache ~ take hold of s.th., seize s.th.; sich e-r Person ~ lay hands on s.o., seize s.o.

be'malen v/t. (no -ge-, h) cover with paint; paint; daub.

bemängeln [bə'mɛŋəln] v/t. (no -ge-, h) find fault with, cavil at.

be'mannen v/t. (no -ge-, h) man.

be'merk|bar adj. perceptible; ~en v/t. (no -ge-, h) notice, perceive; remark, mention; ~enswert adj. remarkable (wegen for); £ung f (-/-en) remark.

bemitleiden [bə'mitlaidən] v/t. (no -ge-, h) pity, commiserate (with); ~swert adj. pitiable.

be'müh|en v/t. (no -ge-, h) trouble (j-n in or wegen et. s.o. about s.th.);

sich ~ trouble o.s.; endeavo(u)r; *sich um e-e Stelle* ~ apply for a position; ₂ung *f* (-/-en) trouble; endeavo(u)r, effort.

be'nachbart *adj.* neighbo(u)ring; adjoining, adjacent (to).

benachrichtig|en [bə'naːxriçtigən] *v/t.* (*no -ge-, h*) inform, notify; † advise; ₂ung *f* (-/-en) information; notification; † advice.

benachteilig|en [bə'naːxtaɪligən] *v/t.* (*no -ge-, h*) place *s.o.* at a disadvantage, discriminate against *s.o.*; handicap; *sich benachteiligt fühlen* feel handicapped *or* at a disadvantage; ₂ung *f* (-/-en) disadvantage; discrimination; handicap.

be'nehmen 1. *v/refl.* (*irr. nehmen, no -ge-, h*) behave (o.s.); 2. ⚥ *n* (-s/no pl.) behavio(u)r, conduct.

be'neiden *v/t.* (*no -ge-, h*) envy (*j-n um et. s.o. s.th.*); ~swert *adj.* enviable.

be'nennen *v/t.* (*irr. nennen, no -ge-, h*) name. [rascal; urchin.]

Bengel ['bɛŋəl] *m* (-s/-) (little)

benommen *adj.* [bə'nɔmən] bemused, dazed, stunned; ~ *sein* be in a daze.

be'nötigen *v/t.* (*no -ge-, h*) need, require, want.

be'nutz|en *v/t.* (*no -ge-, h*) use (*a. patent, etc.*); make use of; avail o.s. of (*opportunity*); take (*tram, etc.*); ₂ung *f* use.

Benzin [bɛn'tsiːn] *n* (-s/-e) 🜊 benzine; *mot.* petrol, F juice, *Am.* gasoline, F gas; ~motor *m* petrol engine, *Am.* gasoline engine; *s.* Tank.

beobacht|en [bə'oːbaxtən] *v/t.* (*no -ge-, h*) observe; watch; *police:* shadow; ₂er *m* (-s/-) observer; ₂ung *f* (-/-en) observation.

beordern [bə'ɔrdərn] *v/t.* (*no -ge-, h*) order, command.

be'packen *v/t.* (*no -ge-, h*) load (*mit* with). [(*mit* with).]

be'pflanzen *v/t.* (*no -ge-, h*) plant]

bequem *adj.* [bə'kveːm] convenient; comfortable; *p.:* easy-going; lazy; ~en *v/refl.* (*no -ge-, h*): *sich* ~ *zu* condescend to; consent to; ₂lichkeit *f* (-/-en) convenience; comfort, ease; indolence.

be'rat|en (*irr. raten, no -ge-, h*) 1. *v/t.* advise *s.o.*; consider, debate, discuss *s.th.*; *sich* ~ confer (*mit j-m* with s.o.; *über et.* on *or* about s.th.); 2. *v/i.* confer; *über et.* ~ consider, debate, discuss s.th., confer on *or* about s.th.; ₂er *m* (-s/-) adviser, counsel(l)or; consultant; ~schlagen (*no -ge-, h*) 1. *v/i. s.* beraten 2; 2. *v/refl.* confer (*mit j-m* with s.o.; *über et.* on *or* about s.th.); ₂ung *f* (-/-en) advice; debate; consultation; conference; ₂ungsstelle *f* advisory bureau.

be'raub|en *v/t.* (*no -ge-, h*) rob, deprive (*gen.* of); ₂ung *f* (-/-en) robbery, deprivation.

be'rauschen *v/t.* (*no -ge-, h*) intoxicate (*a. fig.*).

be'rechn|en *v/t.* (*no -ge-, h*) calculate; † charge (*zu* at); ~end *adj.* calculating, selfish; ₂ung *f* calculation.

berechtig|en [bə'rɛçtigən] *v/t.* (*no -ge-, h*) *j-n* ~ *zu* entitle s.o. to; authorize s.o. to; ~t *adj.* [~çt] entitled (*zu* to); qualified (to); *claim:* legitimate; ₂ung *f* (-/-en) title (*zu* to); authorization.

be'red|en *v/t.* (*no -ge-, h*) talk *s.th.* over; persuade *s.o.*; gossip about *s.o.*; ₂samkeit [~tzaːmkart] *f* (-/no pl.) eloquence; ~t *adj.* [~t] eloquent (*a. fig.*).

Be'reich *m, n* (-[e]s/-e) area; reach; *fig.* scope, sphere; *science, etc.:* field, province; ₂ern *v/t.* (*no -ge-, h*) enrich; *sich* ~ enrich o.s.; ~erung *f* (-/-en) enrichment.

be'reif|en *v/t.* (*no -ge-, h*) hoop (*barrel*); tyre, (*Am. only*) tire (*wheel*); ₂ung *f* (-/-en) (set of) tyres *pl.*, (*Am. only*) (set of) tires *pl.*

be'reisen *v/t.* (*no -ge-, h*) tour (in), travel (over); *commercial traveller:* cover (*district*).

bereit *adj.* [bə'rart] ready, prepared; ~en *v/t.* (*no -ge-, h*) prepare; give (*joy, trouble, etc.*); ~s *adv.* already; ₂schaft *f* (-/-en) readiness; *police:* squad; ~stellen *v/t.* (*sep., -ge-, h*) place *s.th.* ready; provide; ₂ung *f* (-/-en) preparation; ~willig *adj.* ready, willing; ₂willigkeit *f* (-/no pl.) readiness, willingness.

be'reuen *v/t.* (*no -ge-, h*) repent (of); regret, rue.

Berg [bɛrk] *m* (-[e]s/-e) mountain; hill; ~e *pl. von* F heaps *pl.* of, piles *pl.* of; *über den* ~ *sein* be out of the wood, *Am.* be out of the woods; *über alle* ~e off and away; *die Haare standen ihm zu* ~e his hair stood on end; ⚥'ab *adv.* downhill (*a. fig.*); ⚥'an *adv. s.* bergauf; '~arbeiter *m* miner; ⚥'auf *adv.* uphill (*a. fig.*); '~bahn 🚠 *f* mountain railway; '~bau *m* (-[e]s/*pl.*) mining.

bergen ['bɛrgən] *v/t.* (*irr., ge-, h*) save; rescue *s.o.*; ⚓ salvage, salve.

bergig *adj.* ['bɛrgiç] mountainous, hilly.

'Berg|kette *f* mountain chain *or* range; '~mann ⚒ *m* (-[e]s/Bergleute) miner; '~predigt *f* (-/no pl.) *the* Sermon on the Mount; '~recht *n* mining laws *pl.*; '~rennen *mot. n* mountain race; '~rücken *m* ridge; '~rutsch *m* landslide, landslip; '~spitze *f* mountain peak; '~steiger *m* (-s/-) mountaineer; '~sturz *m s.* Bergrutsch.

'Bergung f (-/-en) ⚓ salvage; rescue; ⚓arbeiten ['berguŋs⁹-] f/pl. salvage operations pl.; rescue work.

'Bergwerk n mine; ⚓saktien ['berkverks⁹-] f/pl. mining shares pl.

Bericht [bə'riçt] m (-[e]s/-e) report (über acc. on); account (of); ⚓en (no -ge-, h) 1. v/t. report; j-m et. ⚓ inform s.o. of s.th.; tell s.o. about s.th.; 2. v/i. report (über acc. on); journalist: a. cover (über et. s.th.); ⚓erstatter m (-s/-) reporter; correspondent; ⚓erstattung f reporting; report(s pl.).

berichtig|en [bə'riçtigən] v/t. (no -ge-, h) correct (s.o.; error, mistake, etc.); put right (mistake); emend (corrupt text); ✝ settle (claim, debt, etc.); 2ung f (-/-en) correction; emendation; settlement.

be'riechen v/t. (irr. riechen, no -ge-, h) smell or sniff at.

Berliner [ber'li:nər] 1. m (-s/-) Berliner; 2. adj. (of) Berlin.

Bernstein ['bernʃtaɪn] m amber; schwarzer ⚓ jet.

bersten ['berstən] v/i. (irr., ge-, sein) burst (fig. vor dat. with).

berüchtigt adj. [bə'ryçtiçt] notorious (wegen for), ill-famed.

berücksichtig|en [bə'rykziçtigən] v/t. (no -ge-, h) take s.th. into consideration, pay regard to s.th.; consider s.o.; 2ung f (-/-en) consideration; regard.

Beruf [bə'ru:f] m (-[e]s/-e) calling; profession; vocation; trade; occupation; 2en 1. v/t. (irr. rufen, no -ge-, h): j-n zu e-m Amt ⚓ appoint s.o. to an office; sich auf j-n ⚓ refer to s.o.; 2. adj. competent; qualified; 2lich adj. professional; vocational.

Be'rufs|ausbildung f vocational or professional training; ⚓beratung f vocational guidance; ⚓kleidung f work clothes pl.; ⚓krankheit f occupational disease; ⚓schule f vocational school; ⚓spieler m sports: professional (player); 2tätig adj. working; ⚓tätige [⚓gə] pl. working people pl.

Be'rufung f (-/-en) appointment (zu to); ✝ appeal (bei dat. to); reference (auf acc. to); ⚓sgericht n court of appeal.

be'ruhen v/i. (no -ge-, h): ⚓ auf (dat.) rest or be based on; et. auf sich ⚓ lassen let a matter rest.

beruhig|en [bə'ru:igən] v/t. (no -ge- h) quiet, calm; soothe; sich ⚓ calm down; 2ung f (-/-en) calming (down); soothing; comfort; 2ungsmittel ⚕ n sedative.

berühmt adj. [bə'ry:mt] famous (wegen for); celebrated; 2heit f (-/-en) fame, renown; famous or celebrated person, celebrity; person of note.

be'rühr|en v/t. (no -ge-, h) touch (a. fig.); touch (up)on (subject); 2ung f (-/-en) contact; touch; in ⚓ kommen mit come into contact with.

be'sag|en v/t. (no -ge-, h) say; mean, signify; ⚓t adj. [⚓kt] (afore-) said; above(-mentioned).

besänftigen [bə'zɛnftigən] v/t. (no -ge-, h) appease, calm, soothe.

Be'satz m (-es/⚓e) trimming; braid.

Be'satzung f ⚔ occupation troops pl.; ⚓ garrison; ⚓, ⚓ crew; ⚓macht ⚔ f occupying power.

be'schädig|en v/t. (no -ge-, h) damage, injure; 2ung f damage, injury (gen. to).

be'schaffen 1. v/t. (no -ge-, h) procure; provide; raise (money); 2. adj.: gut (schlecht) ⚓ sein be in good (bad) condition or state; 2heit f (-/-en) state, condition; properties pl.

beschäftig|en [bə'ʃɛftigən] v/t. (no -ge-, h) employ, occupy; keep busy; sich ⚓ occupy or busy o.s.; 2ung f (-/-en) employment; occupation.

be'schäm|en v/t. (no -ge-, h) (put to) shame, make s.o. feel ashamed; ⚓end adj. shameful; humiliating; ⚓t adj. ashamed (über acc. of); 2ung f (-/-en) shame; humiliation.

beschatten [bə'ʃatən] v/t. (no -ge-, h) shade; fig. shadow s.o., Am. sl. tail s.o.

be'schau|en v/t. (no -ge-, h) look at, view; examine, inspect (goods, etc.); ⚓lich adj. contemplative, meditative.

Bescheid [bə'ʃaɪt] m (-[e]s/-e) answer; ✝ decision; information (über acc. on, about); ⚓ geben let s.o. know; ⚓ bekommen be informed or notified; ⚓ hinterlassen leave word (bei with, at); ⚓ wissen be informed, know, F be in the know.

bescheiden adj. [bə'ʃaɪdən] modest, unassuming; 2heit f (-/no pl.) modesty.

bescheinig|en [bə'ʃaɪnigən] v/i. (no -ge-, h) certify, attest; den Empfang ⚓ acknowledge receipt; es wird hiermit bescheinigt, daß this is to certify that; 2ung f (-/-en) certification, attestation; certificate; receipt; acknowledgement.

be'schenken v/t. (no -ge-, h): j-n ⚓ make s.o. a present; j-n mit et. ⚓ present s.o. with s.th.; j-n reichlich ⚓ shower s.o. with gifts.

be'scher|en v/t. (no -ge-, h): j-n ⚓ give s.o. presents (esp. for Christmas); 2ung f (-/-en) presentation of gifts; F fig. mess.

be'schieß|en v/t. (irr. schießen, no -ge-, h) fire or shoot at or on; bombard (a. phys.), shell; 2ung f (-/-en) bombardment.

be'schimpf|en v/t. (no -ge-, h) abuse, insult; call s.o. names; 2ung f (-/-en) abuse; insult, affront.

be'schirmen v/t. (no -ge-, h) shelter, shield, guard, protect (vor dat. from); defend (against).

be'schlafen v/t. (irr. schlafen, no -ge-, h): et. ~ sleep on a matter, take counsel of one's pillow.

Be'schlag m ⊕ metal fitting(s pl.); furnishing(s pl.) (of door, etc.); shoe (of wheel, etc.); (horse)shoe; ⚖ seizure, confiscation; in ~ nehmen, mit ~ belegen seize; ⚖ seize, attach (real estate, salary, etc.); confiscate (goods, etc.); monopolize s.o.'s attention.

be'schlagen 1. v/t. (irr. schlagen, no -ge-, h) cover (mit with); ⊕ fit, mount; shoe (horse); hobnail (shoe); **2.** v/i. (irr. schlagen, no -ge-, h) window, wall, etc.: steam up; mirror, etc.: cloud or film over; **3.** adj. windows, etc.: steamed-up; fig. well versed (auf, in dat. in).

Beschlagnahme [bə'ʃlaːknaːmə] f (-/-n) seizure; confiscation (of contraband goods, etc.); ⚖ sequestration, distraint (of property); ⚔ requisition (of houses etc.); embargo, detention (of ship); **2n** v/t. (no -ge-, h) seize; attach (real estate); confiscate; ⚖ sequestrate, distrain upon (property); ⚔ requisition; ⚓ embargo.

beschleunig|en [bə'ʃlɔynɪɡən] v/t. (no -ge-, h) mot. accelerate; hasten, speed up; s-e Schritte ~ quicken one's steps; **2ung** f (-/-en) acceleration.

be'schließen v/t. (irr. schließen, no -ge-, h) end, close, wind up; resolve, decide.

Be'schluß m decision, resolution, Am. a. resolve; ⚖ decree; **2fähig** adj.: ~ sein form or have a quorum; **~fassung** f (passing of a) resolution.

be'schmieren v/t. (no -ge-, h) (be)smear (with grease, etc.).

be'schmutzen v/t. (no -ge-, h) soil (a. fig.), dirty; bespatter.

be'schneiden v/t. (irr. schneiden, no -ge-, h) clip, cut; lop (tree); trim, clip (hair, hedge, etc.); dress (vinestock, etc.); fig. cut down, curtail, F slash.

beschönig|en [bə'ʃøːnɪɡən] v/t. (no -ge-, h) gloss over, palliate; **2ung** f (-/-en) gloss, palliation.

beschränk|en [bə'ʃrɛŋkən] v/t. (no -ge-, h) confine, limit, restrict, Am. a. curb; sich ~ auf (acc.) confine o.s. to; **~t** fig. adj. of limited intelligence; **2ung** f (-/-en) limitation, restriction.

be'schreib|en v/t. (irr. schreiben, no -ge-, h) write on (piece of paper, etc.), cover with writing; describe, give a description of; **2ung** f (-/-en) description; account.

be'schrift|en v/t. (no -ge-, h) in-scribe; letter; **2ung** f (-/-en) inscription; lettering.

beschuldig|en [bə'ʃʊldɪɡən] v/t. (no -ge-, h) accuse (gen. of [doing] s.th.), esp. ⚖ charge (with); **2te** [~ktə] m, f (-n/-n) the accused; **2ung** f (-/-en) accusation, charge.

Be'schuß m (Beschusses/no pl.) bombardment.

be'schütz|en v/t. (no -ge-, h) protect, shelter, guard (vor dat. from); **2er** m (-s/-) protector; **2ung** f (-/-en) protection.

be'schwatzen v/t. (no -ge-, h) talk s.o. into (doing) s.th., coax s.o. into (doing s.th.).

Beschwerde [bə'ʃveːrdə] f (-/-n) trouble; ⚕ complaint; complaint (über acc. about); ⚖ objection (gegen to); **~buch** n complaints book.

beschwer|en [bə'ʃveːrən] v/t. (no -ge-, h) burden (a. fig.); weight (loose sheets, etc.); lie heavy on (stomach); weigh on (mind, etc.); sich ~ complain (über acc. about, of; bei to); **~lich** adj. troublesome.

beschwichtigen [bə'ʃvɪçtɪɡən] v/t. (no -ge-, h) appease, calm (down), soothe.

be'schwindeln v/t. (no -ge-, h) tell a fib or lie; cheat, F diddle (um out of).

be'schwipst F adj. tipsy.

be'schwör|en v/t. (irr. schwören, no -ge-, h) take an oath on s.th.; implore or entreat s.o.; conjure (up), invoke (spirit); **2ung** f (-/-en) conjuration.

be'seelen v/t. (no -ge-, h) animate, inspire.

be'sehen v/t. (irr. sehen, no -ge-, h) look at; inspect; sich et. ~ look at s.th.; inspect s.th.

beseitig|en [bə'zaɪtɪɡən] v/t. (no -ge-, h) remove, do away with; **2ung** f (-/-en) removal.

Besen ['beːzən] m (-s/-) broom; **~stiel** m broomstick.

besessen adj. [bə'zɛsən] obsessed, possessed (von by, with); wie ~ like mad; **2e** m, f (-n/-n) demoniac.

be'setz|en v/t. (no -ge-, h) occupy (seat, table, etc.); fill (post, etc.); man (orchestra); thea. cast (play); ⚔ occupy; trim (dress, etc.); set (crown with jewels, etc.); **~t** adj. engaged, occupied; seat: taken; F bus, etc.: full up; hotel: full; teleph. engaged, Am. busy; **2ung** f (-/-en) thea. cast; ⚔ occupation.

besichtig|en [bə'zɪçtɪɡən] v/t. (no -ge-, h) view, look over; inspect (a. ⚔); visit; **2ung** f (-/-en) sightseeing; visit (gen. to); inspection (a. ⚔).

be'sied|eln v/t. (no -ge-, h) colonize, settle; populate; **2lung** f (-/-en) colonization, settlement.

be'siegeln v/t. (no -ge-, h) seal (a. fig.).

be'siegen v/t. (no -ge-, h) conquer; defeat, beat (a. sports).

be'sinn|en v/refl. (irr. sinnen, no -ge-, h) reflect, consider; sich ~ auf (acc.) remember, think of; **~lich** adj. reflective, contemplative.

Be'sinnung f (-/no pl.) reflection; consideration; consciousness; (wieder) zur ~ kommen recover consciousness; fig. come to one's senses; **2slos** adj. unconscious.

Be'sitz m possession; in ~ nehmen, ~ ergreifen von take possession of; **2anzeigend** gr. adj. possessive; **2en** v/t. (irr. sitzen, no -ge-, h) possess; **~er** m (-s/-) possessor, owner, proprietor; den ~ wechseln change hands; **~ergreifung** f taking possession (von of), occupation; **~tum** n (-s/#er), **~ung** f (-/-en) possession; property; estate.

be'sohlen v/t. (no -ge-, h) sole.

besold|en [bə'zɔldən] v/t. (no -ge-, h) pay a salary to (civil servant, etc.); pay (soldier); **2ung** f (-/-en) pay; salary.

besonder adj. [bə'zɔndər] particular, special; peculiar; separate; **2heit** f (-/-en) particularity; peculiarity; **~s** adv. especially, particularly; chiefly, mainly; separately.

besonnen adj. [bə'zɔnən] sensible, considerate, level-headed; prudent; discreet; **2heit** f (-/no pl.) considerateness; prudence; discretion; presence of mind.

be'sorg|en v/t. (no -ge-, h) get (j-m et. s.o. s.th.), procure (s.th. for s.o.); do, manage; **2nis** [~knis] f (-/-se) apprehension, fear, anxiety, concern (über acc. about, at); **~niserregend** adj. alarming; **~t** adj. [~kt] uneasy (um about); worried (about), concerned (about); anxious (um for, about); **2ung** f (-/-en) procurement; management; errand; **~en machen** go shopping.

be'sprech|en v/t. (irr. sprechen, no -ge-, h) discuss, talk s.th. over; arrange; review (book, etc.); sich ~ mit confer with (über acc. about); **2ung** f (-/-en) discussion; review; conference.

be'spritzen v/t. (no -ge-, h) splash, (be)spatter.

besser ['bɛsər] **1.** adj. better; superior; **2.** adv. better; '**~n** v/t. (ge-, h) (make) better, improve; reform; sich ~ get or become better, improve, change for the better; mend one's ways; '**2ung** f (-/-en) improvement; change for the better; reform (of character); **$** improvement, recovery; gute ~! I wish you a speedy recovery!

best [bɛst] **1.** adj. best; der erste ~e (just) anybody; ~en Dank thank

you very much; sich von s-r ~en Seite zeigen be on one's best behavio(u)r; **2.** adv. best; am ~en best; aufs ~e, ~ens in the best way possible; zum ~en geben recite (poem), tell (story), oblige with (song); j-n zum ~en haben or halten make fun of s.o., F pull s.o.'s leg; ich danke ~ens! thank you very much!

Be'stand m (continued) existence; continuance; stock; † stock-intrade; † cash in hand; ~ haben be lasting, last.

be'ständig adj. constant, steady; lasting; continual; weather: settled; **2keit** f (-/-en) constancy, steadiness; continuance.

Bestand|saufnahme † [bə-'ʃtants⁹-] f stock-taking, Am. inventory; **~teil** m component, constituent; elemen., ingredient; part.

be'stärken v/t. (no -ge-, h) confirm, strengthen, encourage (in dat. in).

bestätig|en [bə'ʃtɛːtigən] v/t. confirm (a. ŧ verdict, † order); attest; verify (statement, etc.); ratify (law, treaty); † acknowledge (receipt); **2ung** f (-/-en) confirmation; attestation; verification; ratification; acknowledgement.

bestatt|en [bə'ʃtatən] v/t. (no -ge-, h) bury, inter; **2ung** f (-/-en) burial, interment; funeral; **2ungsinstitut** [bə'ʃtatuŋs⁹-] n undertakers pl.

'Beste 1. n (-n/no pl.) the best (thing); zu deinem ~n in your interest; zum ~n der Armen for the benefit of the poor; das ~ daraus machen make the best of it; **2.** m, f (-n/-n): er ist der ~ in s-r Klasse he is the best in his class.

Besteck [bə'ʃtɛk] n (-[e]s/-e) **$** (case or set of) surgical instruments pl.; (single set of) knife, fork and spoon; (complete set of) cutlery, Am. a. flatware.

be'stehen 1. v/t. (irr. stehen, no -ge-, h) come off victorious in (combat, etc.); have (adventure); stand, undergo (well) (test, trial); pass (test, examination); **2.** v/i. (irr. stehen, no -ge-, h) be, exist; continue, last; ~ auf (dat.) in.sist (up)on; ~ aus consist of; **3.** 2 n (-s/no pl.) existence; continuance; passing.

be'stehlen v/t. (irr. stehlen, no -ge-, h) steal from, rob.

be'steig|en v/t. (irr. steigen, no -ge-, h) climb (up) (mountain, tree, etc.); mount (horse, bicycle, etc.); ascend (throne); get into or on, board (bus, train, plane); **2ung** f ascent; accession (to throne).

be'stell|en v/t. (no -ge-, h) order; † a. place an order for; subscribe to (newspaper, etc.); book, reserve (room, seat, etc.); make an appointment with s.o.; send for (taxi, etc.); cultivate, till (soil, etc.); give (mes-

sage, greetings); *j-n zu sich* ~ send for s.o.; **Qung** *f* order; subscription (to); booking, *esp. Am.* reservation; ♪ cultivation; message.

'**besten'falls** *adv.* at (the) best.

be'steuer|n *v/t. (no -ge-, h)* tax; **Qung** *f* taxation.

besti|alisch *adj.* [bɛst'jɑːlɪʃ] bestial; brutal; inhuman; *weather, etc.*: F beastly; **Qe** ['~jə] *f (-/-n)* beast; *fig.* brute, beast, inhuman person.

be'stimmen *(no -ge-, h)* **1.** *v/t.* determine, decide; fix *(date, place, price, etc.)*; appoint *(date, time, place, etc.)*; prescribe; define *(species, word, etc.)*; *j-n für or zu et.* ~ designate *or* intend s.o. for s.th.; **2.** *v/i.*: ~ *über (acc.)* dispose of.

be'stimmt 1. *adj. voice, manner, etc.*: decided, determined, firm; *time, etc.*: appointed, fixed; *point, number, etc.*: certain; *answer, etc.*: positive; *tone, answer, intention, idea*: definite *(a. gr.)*; ~ *nach* ♉ ♃ bound for; **2.** *adv.* certainly, surely; **Qheit** *f (-/-en)* determination, firmness; certainty.

Be'stimmung *f* determination; destination *(of s.o. for the church, etc.)*; designation, appointment *(of s.o. as successor, etc.)*; definition; ♊ provision *(in document)*; *(amtliche)* ~en *pl.* (official) regulations *pl.*; ~**sort** [bə'ʃtimuŋs²-] *m* destination.

be'straf|en *v/t. (no -ge-, h)* punish *(wegen, für* for; *mit* with); **Qung** *f (-/-en)* punishment.

be'strahl|en *v/t. (no -ge-, h)* irradiate *(a. ⚕)*; **Qung** *f* irradiation; ⚕ ray treatment, radiotherapy.

Be'streb|en *n (-s/no pl.)*, ~**ung** *f (-/-en)* effort, endeavo(u)r.

be'streichen *v/t. (irr. streichen, no -ge-, h)* coat, cover; spread; *mit Butter* ~ butter.

be'streiten *v/t. (irr. streiten, no -ge-, h)* contest, dispute, challenge *(point, right, etc.)*; deny *(facts, guilt, etc.)*; defray *(expenses, etc.)*; fill *(programme)*.

be'streuen *v/t. (no -ge-, h)* strew, sprinkle *(mit* with); *mit Mehl* ~ flour; *mit Zucker* ~ sugar.

be'stürmen *v/t. (no -ge-, h)* storm, assail *(a. fig.)*; pester, plague *(s.o. with questions, etc.)*.

be'stürz|t *adj.* dismayed, struck with consternation *(über acc.* at); **Qung** *f (-/-en)* consternation, dismay.

Besuch [bə'zuːx] *m (-[e]s/-e)* visit *(gen., bei, in dat.* to); call *(bei* on; *in dat.* at); attendance *(gen.* at) *(lecture, church, etc.)*; visitor(s *pl.*), company; **Qen** *v/t. (no -ge-. h)* visit; call on, go to see; attend *(school, etc.)*; frequent; ~**er** *m* visitor, caller; ~**szeit** *f* visiting hours *pl.*

be'tasten *v/t. (no -ge-, h)* touch, feel, finger; ⚕ palpate.

betätigen [bə'tɛːtigən] *v/t. (no -ge-, h)* ⊕ operate *(machine, etc.)*; put on, apply *(brake)*; *sich* ~ als act *or* work as; *sich politisch* ~ dabble in politics.

betäub|en [bə'tɔybən] *v/t. (no -ge-, h)* stun *(a. fig.)*, daze *(by blow, noise, etc.)*; deafen *(by noise, etc.)*; slaughtering: stun *(animal)*; ⚕ an(a)esthetize; **Qung** *f (-/-en)* ⚕ an(a)esthetization; ⚕ an(a)esthesia; *fig.* stupefaction; **Qungsmittel** ⚕ *n* narcotic, an(a)esthetic.

beteilig|en [bə'tailigən] *v/t. (no -ge-, h)*: *j-n* ~ give s.o. a share *(an dat.* in); *sich* ~ take part *(an dat., bei* in), participate *(a. ♊) (in)*; **Qte** [~çtə] *m, f (-n/-n)* person *or* party concerned; **Qung** *f (-/-en)* participation *(a. ♊, ♃)*, partnership; share, interest *(a. ♃)*.

beten ['beːtən] *v/i.* *(ge-, h)* pray *(um* for), say one's prayers; *at table*: say grace

be'teuer|n *v/t. (no -ge- h)* protest *(one's innocence)*; swear (to *s.th.* that); **Qung** *f* protestation; solemn declaration.

be'titeln *v/t. (no -ge-, h)* entitle *(book, etc.)*; style *(s.o. 'baron', etc.)*.

Beton ⊕ [be'tõː; be'tɔːn] *m (-s/-s; -s/-e)* concrete.

be'tonen *v/t. (no -ge-, h)* stress; *fig. a.* emphasize.

betonieren [beto'niːrən] *v/t. (no -ge-, h)* concrete.

Be'tonung *f (-/-en)* stress; emphasis.

betör|en [bə'tøːrən] *v/t. (no -ge-, h)* dazzle, infatuate, bewitch; **Qung** *f (-/-en)* infatuation.

Betracht [bə'traxt] *m (-[e]s/no pl.)*: *in* ~ *ziehen* take into consideration; *(nicht) in* ~ *kommen* (not to) come into question; **Qen** *v/t. (no -ge-, h)* view; contemplate; *fig. a.* consider.

beträchtlich *adj.* [bə'trɛçtlɪç] considerable.

Be'trachtung *f (-/-en)* view; contemplation; consideration.

Betrag [bə'traːk] *m (-[e]s/⸚e)* amount, sum; **Qen** [~gən] **1.** *v/t. (irr. tragen, no -ge-, h)* amount to; **2.** *v/refl. (irr. tragen, no -ge-, h)* behave (o.s.); **3.** **Q** *n (-s/no pl.)* behavio(u)r, conduct.

be'trauen *v/t. (no -ge-, h)*: *j-n mit et.* ~ entrust *or* charge s.o. with s.th.

be'trauern *v/t. (no -ge-, h)* mourn (for, over).

Betreff [bə'trɛf] *m (-[e]s/-e)* at head of *letter*: reference; **Qen** *v/t. (irr. treffen, no -ge-, h)* befall; refer to; concern; *was ... betrifft* as for, as to; **Qend** *adj.* concerning; *das* ~*e Geschäft* the business referred to *or* in question; **Qs** *prp. (gen.)* concerning; as to.

be'treiben 1. v/t. (irr. treiben, no -ge-, h) carry on (business, etc.); pursue (one's studies); operate (railway line, etc.); **2.** ⚲ n (-s/no pl.): auf ~ von at or by s.o.'s instigation.

be'treten 1. v/t. (irr. treten, no -ge-, h) step on; enter (room, etc.); **2.** adj. embarrassed, abashed.

betreu|en [bə'trɔyən] v/t. (no -ge-, h) look after; attend to; care for; **2ung** f (-/no pl.) care (gen. of, for).

Betrieb [bə'tri:p] m (-[e]s/-e) working, running, esp. Am. operation; business, firm, enterprise; plant, works sg.; workshop, Am. a. shop; fig. bustle; in ~ working; **2sam** adj. active; industrious.

Be'triebs|anleitung f operating instructions pl.; **~ausflug** m firm's outing; **~ferien** f (works) holiday; **~führer** m s. Betriebsleiter; **~kapital** n working capital; **~kosten** pl. working expenses pl., Am. operating costs pl. **~leiter** m (works) manager, superintendent; **~leitung** f management; **~material** n working materials pl.; 🚂 rolling stock; **~rat** m works council; **2sicher** adj. safe to operate; foolproof; **~störung** f breakdown; **~unfall** m industrial accident, accident while at work.

be'trinken v/refl. (irr. trinken, no -ge-, h) get drunk.

betroffen adj. [bə'trɔfən] afflicted (von by), stricken (with); fig. disconcerted.

be'trüben v/t. (no -ge-, h) grieve, afflict.

Be'trug m cheat(ing); fraud (a. ⚖️); deceit.

be'trüg|en v/t. (irr. trügen, no -ge-, h) deceive; cheat (a. at games); defraud; F skin; **2er** m (-s/-) cheat, deceiver, impostor, confidence man, swindler, trickster; **~erisch** adj. deceitful, fraudulent.

be'trunken adj. drunken; pred. drunk; **2e** m (-n/-n) drunk(en man).

Bett [bɛt] n (-[e]s/-en) bed; **~bezug** m plumeau case; **~decke** f blanket; bedspread, coverlet.

Bettel|brief ['bɛtəl-] m begging letter; **~ei** [~'lai] f (-/-en) begging, mendicancy; **2n** v/i. (ge-, h) beg (um for); ~ gehen go begging; **~stab** m: an den ~ bringen reduce to beggary.

'Bett|gestell n bedstead; **2lägerig** adj. ['~lɛ:gəriç] bedridden, confined to bed, Am. a. bedfast; **~laken** n sheet.

Bettler ['bɛtlər] m (-s/-) beggar, Am. sl. panhandler.

'Bett|überzug m plumeau case; **~uch** ['bɛttu:x] n sheet; **'~vorleger** m bedside rug; **'~wäsche** f bedlinen; **'~zeug** n bedding.

be'tupfen v/t. (no -ge-, h) dab.

beug|en ['bɔygən] v/t. (ge-, h) bend, bow; fig. humble, break (pride); gr. inflect (word), decline (noun, adjective); sich ~ bend (vor dat. to), bow (to); **'2ung** f (-/-en) bending; gr. inflection, declension.

Beule ['bɔylə] f (-/-n) bump, swelling; boil; on metal, etc.: dent.

beunruhig|en [bə'unru:igən] v/t. (no -ge-, h) disturb, trouble, disquiet, alarm; sich ~ über (acc.) be uneasy about, worry about; **2ung** f (-/no pl.) disturbance; alarm; uneasiness.

beurkund|en [bə'u:rkundən] v/t. (no -ge-, h) attest, certify, authenticate; **2ung** f (-/-en) attestation, certification, authentication.

beurlaub|en [bə'u:rlaubən] v/t. (no -ge-, h) give or grant s.o. leave (of absence); give s.o. time off; suspend (civil servant, etc.); **2ung** f (-/-en) leave (of absence); suspension.

beurteil|en [bə'urtailən] v/t. (no -ge-, h) judge (nach by); **2ung** f (-/-en) judg(e)ment.

Beute ['bɔytə] f (-/no pl.) booty, spoil(s pl.); loot; prey; hunt. bag; fig. prey, victim (gen. to).

Beutel ['bɔytəl] m (-s/-) bag; purse; pouch.

'Beutezug m plundering expedition.

bevölker|n [bə'fœlkərn] v/t. (no -ge-, h) people, populate; **2ung** f (-/-en) population.

bevollmächtig|en [bə'fɔlmɛçtigən] v/t. (no -ge-, h) authorize, empower; **2te** [~çtə] m, f (-n/-n) authorized person or agent, deputy; pol. plenipotentiary; **2ung** f (-/-en) authorization.

be'vor cj. before.

bevormund|en fig. [bə'fo:rmundən] v/t. (no -ge-, h) patronize, keep in tutelage; **2ung** fig. f (-/-en) patronizing, tutelage.

be'vorstehen v/i. (irr. stehen, sep., -ge-, h) be approaching, be near; crisis, etc.: be imminent; j-m ~ be in store for s.o., await s.o.; **~d** adj. approaching; imminent.

bevorzug|en [bə'fo:rtsu:gən] v/t. (no -ge-, h) prefer; favo(u)r; ⚖️ privilege; **2ung** f (-/-en) preference.

be'wach|en v/t. (no -ge-, h) guard, watch; **2ung** f (-/-en) guard; escort.

bewaffn|en [bə'vafnən] v/t. (no -ge-, h) arm; **2ung** f (-/-en) armament; arms pl.

be'wahren v/t. (no -ge-, h) keep, preserve (mst fig.: secret, silence, etc.).

be'währen v/refl. (no -ge-, h) stand the test, prove a success; sich ~ als prove o.s. (as) (a good teacher, etc.); sich ~ in prove o.s. efficient in (one's profession, etc.); sich nicht ~ prove a failure.

be'wahrheiten v/refl. (no -ge-, h) prove (to be) true; prophecy, etc.: come true.

be'währt adj. friend, etc.: tried; solicitor, etc.: experienced; friendship, etc.: long-standing; remedy, etc.: proved, proven.

Be'währung f 夜 probation; in Zeiten der ~ in times of trial; s. bewähren; **~sfrist** 夜 f probation.

bewaldet adj. [bə'valdət] wooded, woody, Am. a. timbered.

bewältigen [bə'vɛltigən] v/t. (no -ge-, h) overcome (obstacle); master (difficulty); accomplish (task).

be'wandert adj. (well) versed (in dat. in), proficient (in); in e-m Fach gut ~ sein have a thorough knowledge of a subject.

be'wässer|n v/t. (no -ge-, h) water (garden, lawn, etc.); irrigate (land, etc.); **2ung** f (-/-en) watering; irrigation.

bewegen¹ [bə've:gən] v/t. (irr., no -ge-, h): j-n ~ zu induce or get s.o. to.

beweg|en² [~] v/t. and v/refl. (no -ge-, h) move, stir; **2grund** [~k-] m motive (gen., für for); **~lich** [~k-] movable; p., mind, etc.: agile, versatile; active; **2lichkeit** [~k-] f (-/no pl.) mobility; agility; versatility; **~t** adj. [~kt] sea: rough, heavy; fig. moved, touched; voice: choked, trembling; life: eventful; times, etc.: stirring, stormy; **2ung** f (-/-en) movement; motion (a. phys.); fig. emotion; in ~ setzen set going or in motion; **~ungslos** adj. motionless, immobile.

be'weinen v/t. (no -ge-, h) weep or cry over; lament (for, over).

Beweis [bə'vais] m (-es/-e) proof (für of); **~e** (a pl.) evidence (esp. 夜); **2en** [~zən] v/t. (irr. weisen, no -ge-, h) prove; show (interest, etc.); **~führung** f argumentation; **~grund** m argument; **~material** n evidence; **~stück** n (piece of) evidence; 夜 exhibit.   [leave it at that.]

be'wenden vb.: es dabei ~ lassen]

be'werb|en v/refl. (irr. werben, no -ge-, h): sich ~ um apply for, Am. run for; stand for; compete for (prize); court (woman); **2er** m (-s/-) applicant (um for); candidate; competitor; suitor; **2ung** f application; candidature; competition; courtship; **2ungsschreiben** n (letter of) application.

bewerkstelligen [bə'vɛrkʃtɛligən] v/t. (no -ge-, h) manage, effect, bring about.

be'wert|en v/t. (no -ge-, h) value (auf acc. at; nach by); **2ung** f valuation.

bewillig|en [bə'viligən] v/t. (no -ge-, h) grant, allow; **2ung** f (-/-en) grant, allowance.

be'wirken v/t. (no -ge-, h) cause; bring about, effect.

be'wirt|en v/t. (no -ge-, h) entertain; **~schaften** v/t. (no -ge-, h) farm (land); ⚔ cultivate (field); manage (farm, etc.); ration (food, etc.); control (foreign exchange, etc.); **2ung** f (-/-en) entertainment; hospitality.

bewog [bə'vo:k] pret. of bewegen¹; **~en** [bə'vo:gən] p.p. of bewegen¹.

be'wohn|en v/t. (no -ge-, h) inhabit, live in; occupy; **2er** m (-s/-) inhabitant; occupant.

bewölk|en [bə'vœlkən] v/refl. (no -ge-, h) sky: cloud up or over; brow: cloud over, darken; **~t** adj. sky: clouded, cloudy, overcast; brow: clouded, darkened; **2ung** f (-/no pl.) clouds pl.

be'wunder|n v/t. (no -ge-, h) admire (wegen for); **~nswert** adj. admirable; **2ung** f (-/-en) admiration.

bewußt adj. [bə'vust] deliberate, intentional; sich e-r Sache ~ sein be conscious or aware of s.th.; die ~e Sache the matter in question; **~los** adj. unconscious; **2sein** n (-s/no pl.) consciousness.

be'zahl|en (no -ge-, h) **1.** v/t. pay; pay for (s.th. purchased); pay off, settle (debt); **2.** v/i. pay (für for); **2ung** f payment; settlement.

be'zähmen v/t. (no -ge-, h) tame (animal); restrain (one's anger, etc.); sich ~ control or restrain o.s.

be'zauber|n v/t. (no -ge-, h) bewitch, enchant (a. fig.); fig. charm, fascinate; **2ung** f (-/-en) enchantment, spell; fascination.

be'zeichn|en v/t. (no -ge-, h) mark; describe (als as), call; **~end** adj. characteristic, typical (für of); **2ung** f indication (of direction, etc.); mark, sign, symbol; name, designation, denomination.

be'zeugen v/t. (no -ge-, h) 夜 testify to, bear witness to (both a. fig.); attest.

be'zieh|en v/t. (irr. ziehen, no -ge-, h) cover (upholstered furniture, etc.); put cover on (cushion, etc.); move into (flat, etc.); enter (university); draw (salary, pension, etc.); get, be supplied with (goods); take in (newspaper, etc.); sich ~ sky: cloud over; sich ~ auf (acc.) refer to; **2er** m (-s/-) subscriber (gen. to).

Be'ziehung f relation (zu et. to s.th.; zu j-m with s.o.); connexion, (Am. only) connection (zu with); in dieser ~ in this respect; **2sweise** adv. respectively; or rather.

Bezirk [bə'tsirk] m (-[e]s/-e) district, Am. a. precinct; s. Wahlbezirk.

Bezogene ✝ [bə'tso:gənə] m (-n/-n) drawee.

Bezug [bə'tsu:k] m cover(ing), case; purchase (of goods); subscription (*to newspaper*); *in* ~ *auf* (*acc.*) with regard *or* reference to, as to; ~ *nehmen auf* (*acc.*) refer to, make reference to.

bezüglich [bə'tsy:kliç] 1. *adj.* relative, relating (*both: auf acc.* to); 2. *prp.* (*gen.*) regarding, concerning.

Be'zugsbedingungen † *f/pl.* terms *pl.* of delivery.

be'zwecken *v/t.* (*no* -ge-, *h*) aim at; ~ *mit* intend by.

be'zweifeln *v/t.* (*no* -ge-, *h*) doubt, question.

be'zwing|en *v/t.* (*irr.* zwingen, *no* -ge-, *h*) conquer (*fortress, mountain, etc.*); overcome, master (*feeling, difficulty, etc.*); *sich* ~ keep o.s. under control, restrain o.s.; **2ung** *f* (-/-en) conquest; mastering.

Bibel ['bi:bəl] *f* (-/-n) Bible.

Biber *zo.* ['bi:bər] *m* (-s/-) beaver.

Bibliothek [biblio'te:k] *f* (-/-en) library; ~**ar** [~e'ka:r] *m* (-s/-e) librarian.

biblisch *adj.* ['bi:bliʃ] biblical, scriptural; ~e *Geschichte* Scripture.

bieder *adj.* ['bi:dər] honest, upright, worthy (*a. iro.*); simple-minded; **2keit** *f* (-/*no pl.*) honesty, uprightness; simple-mindedness.

bieg|en ['bi:gən] (*irr.*, ge-) 1. *v/t.* (*h*) bend; 2. *v/refl.* (*h*) bend; *sich vor Lachen* ~ double up with laughter; 3. *v/i.* (*sein*): *um e-e Ecke* ~ turn (round) a corner; ~**sam** *adj.* ['bi:kza:m] wire, *etc.*: flexible; *body.* lithe, supple; pliant (*a. fig.*); **2samkeit** *f* (-/*no pl.*) flexibility; suppleness; pliability; **2ung** *f* (-/-en) bend, wind (*of road, river*); curve (*of road, arch*).

Biene *zo.* ['bi:nə] *f* (-/-n) bee; ~**nkönigin** *f* queen bee; ~**nkorb** *m* (bee)hive; ~**nschwarm** *m* swarm of bees; ~**nstock** *m* (bee)hive; ~**nzucht** *f* bee-keeping; ~**nzüchter** *m* bee-keeper.

Bier [bi:r] *n* (-[e]s/-e) beer; *helles* ~ pale beer, ale; *dunkles* ~ dark beer; stout, porter; ~ *vom Faß* beer on draught; '~**brauer** *m* brewer; '~**brauerei** *f* brewery; '~**garten** *m* beer-garden; '~**krug** *m* beer-mug, *Am.* stein.

Biest [bi:st] *n* (-es/-er) beast, brute.

bieten ['bi:tən] (*irr.*, ge-, *h*) 1. *v/t.* offer; † *at auction sale*: bid; *sich* ~ *opportunity, etc.*: offer itself, arise, occur; 2. † *v/i. at auction sale*: bid.

Bigamie [biga'mi:] *f* (-/-n) bigamy.

Bilanz [bi'lants] *f* (-/-en) balance; balance-sheet, *Am. a.* statement; *fig.* result, outcome; *die* ~ *ziehen* strike a balance; *fig.* take stock (*of one's life, etc.*).

Bild [bilt] *n* (-[e]s/-er) picture; image; illustration; portrait; *fig.* idea, notion; '~**bericht** *m press:* picture story.

bilden ['bildən] *v/t.* (ge-, *h*) form; shape; *fig.*: educate, train (*s.o., mind, etc.*); develop (*mind, etc.*); form, be, constitute (*obstacle, etc.*); *sich* ~ form; *fig.* educate o.s., improve one's mind; *sich e-e Meinung* ~ form an opinion.

Bilder|buch ['bildər-] *n* picture-book; '~**galerie** *f* picture-gallery; '~**rätsel** *n* rebus.

'**Bild|fläche** *f*: F *auf der* ~ *erscheinen* appear on the scene; F *von der* ~ *verschwinden* disappear (from the scene); '~**funk** *m* radio picture transmission; television; '~**hauer** *m* (-s/-) sculptor; ~**hauerei** [~'rai] *f* (-/-en) sculpture; '**2lich** *adj.* pictorial; *word, etc.*: figurative; '~**nis** *n* (-ses/-se) portrait; '~**röhre** *f* picture *or* television tube; '~**säule** *f* statue; '~**schirm** *m* (television) screen; '**2schön** *adj.* most beautiful; '~**seite** *f* face, head (*of coin*); '~**streifen** *m* picture *or* film strip; '~**telegraphie** *f* (-/*no pl.*) phototelegraphy.

'**Bildung** *f* (-/-en) forming, formation (*both a. gr.*: *of plural, etc.*); constitution (*of committee, etc.*); education; culture; (good) breeding.

Billard ['biljart] *n* (-s/-e) billiards; ~**en** (-s/-e) billiard-table.

billig *adj.* ['biliç] just, equitable; fair; *price:* reasonable, moderate; *goods:* cheap, inexpensive; *recht und* ~ right and proper; ~**en** [~gən] *v/t.* (ge-, *h*) approve of, *Am. a.* approbate; '**2keit** *f* (-/*no pl.*) justness, equity; fairness; reasonableness, moderateness; **2ung** ['~guŋ] *f* (-/~-en) approval, sanction.

Binde ['bində] *f* (-/-n) band; tie; ♣ bandage; (arm-)sling; *s. Damenbinde*; '~**gewebe** *anat. n* connective tissue; '~**glied** *n* connecting link; '~**haut** *anat. f* conjunctiva; '~**hautentzündung** ♣ *f* conjunctivitis; '**2n** (*irr.*, ge-, *h*) 1. *v/t.* bind, tie (*an acc.* to); bind (*book, etc.*); make (*broom, wreath, etc.*); knot (*tie*); *sich* ~ bind *or* commit *or* engage o.s.; 2. *v/i.* bind; unite; ⊕ cement, *etc.*: set, harden; '~**strich** *m* hyphen; '~**wort** *gr. n* (-[e]s/=er) conjunction.

Bindfaden ['bint-] *m* string; pack-thread.

'**Bindung** *f* (-/-en) binding (*a. of ski*); ♪ slur, tie, ligature; *fig.* commitment (*a. pol.*); engagement; ~**en** *pl.* bonds *pl.*, ties *pl.*

binnen *prp.* (*dat., a. gen.*) ['binən] within; ~ *kurzem* before long.

'**Binnen|gewässer** *n* inland water; '~**hafen** *m* close port; '~**handel** *m* domestic *or* home trade, *Am.* domestic commerce; '~**land** *n* inland, interior; '~**verkehr** *m* inland traffic *or* transport.

Binse ♀ ['bɪnzə] f (-/-n) rush; F: *in die ~n gehen* go to pot; '~**nwahrheit** f, '~**nweisheit** f truism.

Biochemie [bioçe'miː] f (-/no pl.) biochemistry.

Biograph|ie [biogra'fiː] f (-/-n) biography; **2isch** adj. [~'grafɪʃ] biographic(al).

Biolog|ie [biolo'giː] f (-/no pl.) biology; **2isch** adj. [~'loːgɪʃ] biological.

Birke ♀ ['bɪrkə] f (-/-n) birch(-tree).

Birne ['bɪrnə] f (-/-n) ♀ pear; ⚡ (electric) bulb; *fig. sl.* nob, *Am.* bean.

bis [bɪs] 1. *prp.* (*acc.*) *space:* to, as far as; *time:* till, until, by; *zwei ~ drei* two or three, two to three; *~ auf weiteres* until further orders, for the meantime; *~ vier zählen* count up to four; *alle ~ auf drei* all but *or* except three; 2. *cj.* till, until.

Bisamratte *zo.* ['biːzam-] f muskrat.

Bischof ['bɪʃɔf] m (-s/-e) bishop.

bischöflich adj. ['bɪʃøːflɪç] episcopal.

bisher adv. [bɪs'heːr] hitherto, up to now, so far; '~**ig** adj. until now; hitherto existing; former.

Biß [bɪs] 1. m (*Bisses/Bisse*) bite; 2. **2** *pret. of* beißen.

bißchen ['bɪsçən] 1. adj.: *ein ~ a little*, a (little) bit of; 2. *adv.:* *ein ~ a little* (bit).

Bissen ['bɪsən] m (-s/-) mouthful; morsel; bite.

'**bissig** adj. biting (a. fig.); remark: cutting; *Achtung, ~er Hund!* beware of the dog!

Bistum ['bɪstuːm] n (-s/-er) bishopric, diocese.

bisweilen adv. [bɪs'vaɪlən] sometimes, at times, now and then.

Bitte ['bɪtə] f (-/-n) request (*um* for); entreaty; *auf j-s ~* (*hin*) at s.o.'s request.

'**bitten** (*irr.*, ge-, h) 1. v/t.: *j-n um et. ~* ask *or* beg s.o. for s.th.; *j-n um Entschuldigung ~* beg s.o.'s pardon; *dürfte ich Sie um Feuer ~?* may I trouble you for a light?; *bitte* please; (*wie*) *bitte?* (I beg your) pardon?; *bitte!* offering s.th.: (please,) help yourself, (please,) do take some *or* one; *danke (schön)* — *bitte (sehr)!* thank you — not at all, you're welcome, don't mention it, F that's all right; 2. v/i.: *um et. ~* ask *or* beg for s.th.

bitter adj. ['bɪtər] bitter (a. fig.); *frost:* sharp; **2keit** f (-/-en) bitterness; *fig. a.* acrimony; '~**lich** adv. bitterly.

'**Bitt|gang** *eccl.* m procession; '~**schrift** f petition; '~**steller** m (-s/-) petitioner.

bläh|en ['blɛːən] (ge-, h) 1. v/t. inflate, distend, swell out; belly (out),

swell out (*sails*); *sich ~ sails:* belly (out), swell out; *skirt:* balloon out; 2. ✿ v/i. cause flatulence; '~**end** ✿ adj. flatulent; '2**ung** ✿ f (-/-en) flatulence, F wind.

Blam|age [bla'maːʒə] f (-/-n) disgrace, shame; **2ieren** [~'miːrən] v/t. (*no -ge-*, h) make a fool of s.o., disgrace; *sich ~* make a fool of o.s.

blank adj. [blaŋk] shining, shiny, bright; polished; F fig. broke.

blanko † ['blaŋko] 1. adj. form, etc.: blank, not filled in; *in* blank; 2. adv.: *~ verkaufen stock exchange:* sell short; '2**scheck** m blank cheque, *Am.* blank check; '2**unterschrift** f blank signature; '2**vollmacht** f full power of attorney, carte blanche.

Bläschen ✿ ['blɛːsçən] n (-s/-) vesicle, small blister.

Blase ['blaːzə] f (-/-n) bubble; blister (a. ✿); *anat.* bladder; bleb (*in glass*); ⊕ flaw; '~**balg** m (*ein a pair of*) bellows pl.; '2**n** (*irr.*, ge-, h) 1. v/t. blow; blow, sound; play (*wind-instrument*); 2. v/i. blow.

Blas|instrument ♪ ['blaːs-] n wind-instrument; '~**kapelle** f brass band.

blaß adj. [blas] pale (*vor dat.* with); *~ werden* turn pale; *keine blasse Ahnung* not the faintest idea.

Blässe ['blɛsə] f (-/no pl.) paleness.

Blatt [blat] n (-[e]s/-er) leaf (*of book*, ✿); petal (*of flower*); leaf, sheet (*of paper*); ♪ sheet; blade (*of oar, saw, airscrew, etc.*); sheet (*of metal*); *cards:* hand; (news)paper.

Blattern ✿ ['blatərn] pl. smallpox.

blättern ['blɛtərn] v/i. (ge-, h): *in e-m Buch ~* leaf through a book, thumb a book.

'**Blatternarbe** f pock-mark; '2**ig** adj. pock-marked.

'**Blätterteig** m puff paste.

'**Blatt|gold** n gold-leaf, gold-foil; '~**laus** *zo.* f plant-louse; '~**pflanze** f foliage plant.

blau [blau] 1. adj. blue; F fig. drunk, tight, boozy; *~er Fleck* bruise; *~es Auge* black eye; *mit e-m ~en Auge davonkommen* get off cheaply; 2. **2** n (-s/no pl.) blue (colo[u]r); *Fahrt ins ~e* mystery tour. [blue.]

bläuen ['blɔɪən] v/t. (ge-, h) (dye)]

'**blau|grau** adj. bluish grey; '2**jacke** ♣ f bluejacket, sailor.

'**bläulich** adj. bluish.

'**Blausäure** ✿ f (-/no pl.) hydrocyanic *or* prussic acid.

Blech [blɛç] n (-[e]s/-e) sheet metal; metal sheet, plate; F fig. balderdash, rubbish, *Am. sl. a.* baloney; '~**büchse** f tin, *Am.* can; '2**ern** adj. (of tin; *sound:* brassy; *sound, voice:* tinny; '~**musik** f brass-band music; '~**waren** f/pl. tinware.

Blei [blaɪ] n (-[e]s/-e) 1. n lead; 2. F n, m (lead) pencil.

bleiben ['blaɪbən] v/i. (irr., ge-, sein) remain, stay; be left; ruhig ~ keep calm; ~ bei keep to s.th., stick to s.th.; bitte bleiben Sie am Apparat teleph. hold the line, please; '~d adj. lasting, permanent; '~lassen v/t. (irr. lassen, sep., no -ge-, h) leave s.th. alone; laß das bleiben! don't do it!; leave it alone!; stop that (noise, etc.).

bleich adj. [blaɪç] pale (vor dat. with); '~en (ge-) 1. v/t. (h) make pale; bleach; blanch; 2. v/i. (irr., sein) bleach; lose colo(u)r, fade; '~süchtig ♯ adj. chlorotic, greensick.

bleiern adj. (of) lead, leaden (a. fig.). 'Blei|rohr n lead pipe; '~soldat m tin soldier; '~stift m (lead) pencil; '~stifthülse f pencil cap; '~stiftspitzer m (-s/-) pencil-sharpener; '~vergiftung ♯ f lead-poisoning.

Blend|e ['blɛndə] f (-/-n) phot. diaphragm, stop; ⚠ blind or sham window; '2en (ge-, h) 1. v/t. blind; dazzle (both a. fig.); 2. v/i. light: dazzle the eyes; '~laterne ['blɛnt-] f dark lantern.

blich [bliç] pret. of bleichen 2.

Blick [blik] m (-[e]s/-e) glance, look; view (auf acc. of); auf den ersten ~ at first sight; ein böser ~ an evil or angry look; '2en v/i. (ge-, h) look, glance (auf acc., nach at); '~fang m eye-catcher.

blieb [bli:p] pret. of bleiben.

blies [bli:s] pret. of blasen.

blind adj. [blint] blind (a. fig.: gegen, für to; vor dat. with); metal: dull, tarnished; window: opaque (with age, dirt); mirror: clouded, dull; cartridge: blank; ~er Alarm false alarm; ~er Passagier stowaway; auf e-m Auge ~ blind in one eye.

'**Blinddarm** anat. m blind gut; appendix; '~entzündung ♯ f appendicitis.

Blinde ['blɪndə] (-n/-n) 1. m blind man; 2. f blind woman; ~nanstalt ['blɪndən?-] f institute for the blind; '~nheim n home for the blind; '~nhund m guide dog, Am. a. seeing-eye dog; '~nschrift f braille.

'**blind|fliegen** ✈ (irr. fliegen, sep., -ge-) v/t. (h) and v/i. (sein) fly blind or on instruments; '2flug ✈ m blind flying or flight; '2gänger m ✗ blind shell, dud; F fig. washout; '2heit f (-/no pl.) blindness; '~lings adv. ['~lɪŋs] blindly; at random; '2schleiche zo. f (-/-n) slow-worm, blind-worm; '~schreiben v/t. and v/i. (irr. schreiben, sep., -ge-, h) touch-type.

blink|en ['blɪŋkən] v/i. (ge-, h) star, light: twinkle; metal, leather, glass, etc.: shine; signal (with lamps),

flash; '2er mot. m (-s/-) flashing indicator; '2feuer n flashing light.

blinzeln ['blɪntsəln] v/i. (ge-, h) blink (at light, etc.); wink.

Blitz [blits] m (-es/-e) lightning; '~ableiter m (-s/-) lightning-conductor; '2en v/i. (ge-, h) flash; es blitzt it is lightening; '~gespräch teleph. n special priority call; '~licht phot. n flash-light; '2!schnell adv. with lightning speed; '~strahl m flash of lightning.

Block [blɔk] m 1. (-[e]s/=e) block; slab (of cooking chocolate); block, log (of wood); ingot (of metal); parl., pol., ♜ bloc; 2. (-[e]s/=e, -s) block (of houses); pad, block (of paper); '~ade ✗, ⚓ ['~'ka:də] f (-/-n) blockade; '~adebrecher m (-s/-) blockade-runner; '~haus n log cabin; 2ieren ['~'ki:rən] (no -ge-, h) 1. v/t. block (up); lock (wheel); 2. v/i. brakes, etc.: jam.

blöd adj. [bløːt], ~e adj. ['~də] imbecile, stupid, dull; silly; '2heit f (-/-en) imbecility; stupidity, dullness; silliness; '2sinn m imbecility; rubbish, nonsense; '~sinnig adj. imbecile; idiotic, stupid, foolish.

blöken ['bløːkən] v/i. (ge-, h) sheep, calf: bleat.

blond adj. [blɔnt] blond, fair (-haired).

bloß [bloːs] 1. adj. bare, naked; mere; ~e Worte mere words; mit dem ~en Auge wahrnehmbar visible to the naked eye; 2. adv. only, merely, simply, just.

Blöße ['bløːsə] f (-/-n) bareness, nakedness; fig. weak point or spot; sich e-e ~ geben give o.s. away; lay o.s. open to attack; keine ~ bieten be invulnerable.

'**bloß|legen** v/t. (sep., -ge-, h) lay bare, expose; '~stellen v/t. (sep., -ge-, h) expose, compromise, unmask; sich ~ compromise o.s.

blühen ['blyːən] v/i. (ge-, h) blossom, flower, bloom; fig. flourish, thrive, prosper; ♜ boom.

Blume ['bluːmə] f (-/-n) flower; wine: bouquet; beer: froth.

'**Blumen|beet** n flower-bed; '~blatt n petal; '~händler m florist; '~strauß m bouquet or bunch of flowers; '~topf m flowerpot; '~zucht f floriculture.

Bluse ['bluːzə] f (-/-n) blouse.

Blut [bluːt] n (-[e]s/no pl.) blood; ~ vergießen shed blood; böses ~ machen breed bad blood; '~andrang ♯ m congestion; '2arm adj. bloodless; ♯ an(a)emic; '~armut ♯ f an(a)emia; '~bad n carnage, massacre; '~bank ♯ f blood bank; '~blase f blood blister; '~druck m blood pressure; 2dürstig adj. ['~dyrstiç] bloodthirsty.

Blüte ['blyːtə] f (-/-n) blossom,

5*

bloom, flower; *esp. fig.* flower; prime, heyday (*of life*).

Blutegel ['blu:t⁹e:gəl] *m* (-s/-) leech.

'bluten *v/i.* (ge-, *h*) bleed (*aus from*); *aus der Nase* ~ bleed at the nose.

Bluterguß ♂ ['blu:t⁹-] *m* effusion of blood.

'Blütezeit *f* flowering period *or* time; *fig. a.* prime, heyday.

'Blut|gefäß *anat. n* blood-vessel; **~gerinnsel** ♂ ['~gərinzəl] *n* (-s/-) clot of blood; **'~gruppe** *f* blood group; **'~hund** *zo. m* bloodhound.

'blutig *adj.* bloody, blood-stained; *es ist mein ~er Ernst* I am dead serious; *~er Anfänger* mere beginner, F greenhorn.

Blut|körperchen ['blu:tkœrpərçən] *n* (-s/-) blood corpuscle; **'~kreislauf** *m* (blood) circulation; **'~lache** *f* pool of blood; **'~leer** *adj.*, **'~los** *adj.* bloodless; **'~probe** *f* blood test; **'~rache** *f* blood feud *or* revenge *or* vengeance, vendetta; **'~rot** *adj.* blood-red; crimson; **'~rünstig** *adj.* ['~rynstiç] bloodthirsty; bloody; **'~schande** *f* incest; **'~spender** *m* blood-donor; **'~stillend** *adj.* blood-sta(u)nching; **'~sturz** *m* h(a)emorrhage; **'~sverwandt** *adj.* related by blood (*mit* to); **'~sverwandtschaft** *f* blood-relationship, consanguinity; **'~übertragung** *f* blood-transfusion; **'~ung** *f* (-/-en) bleeding, h(a)emorrhage; **'~unterlaufen** *adj. eye:* bloodshot; **'~vergießen** *n* bloodshed; **'~vergiftung** *f* blood-poisoning.

Bö [bø] *f* (-/-en) gust, squall.

Bock [bɔk] *m* (-[e]s/=e) *deer, hare, rabbit:* buck; *he-goat,* F billy-goat; *sheep:* ram; *gymnastics:* buck; *e-n ~ schießen* commit a blunder, *sl.* commit a bloomer; *den ~ zum Gärtner machen* set the fox to keep the geese; **'~en** *v/i.* (ge-, *h*) *horse:* buck; *child:* sulk; *p.* be obstinate *or* refractory; *mot.* move jerkily, *Am.* F *a.* buck; **'~ig** *adj.* stubborn, obstinate, pigheaded; **'~sprung** *m* leap-frog; *gymnastics:* vault over the buck; *Bocksprünge machen* caper, cut capers.

Boden ['bo:dən] *m* (-s/=) ground; ♂ soil; bottom; floor; loft; **'~kammer** *f* garret, attic; **'~los** *adj.* bottomless; *fig.* enormous; unheard-of; **'~personal** ✈ *n* ground personnel *or* staff, *Am.* ground crew; **'~reform** *f* land reform; **'~satz** *m* grounds *pl.*, sediment; **'~schätze** ['~fetsə] *m/pl.* mineral resources *pl.*; **'~ständig** *adj.* native, indigenous.

bog [bo:k] *pret. of biegen.*

Bogen ['bo:gən] *m* (-s/-, =) bow, bend, curve; & arc; △ arch; *skiing:* turn; *skating:* curve; sheet (*of paper*); **'~förmig** *adj.* arched; **'~gang** △ *m* arcade; **'~lampe** ∉ *f* arc-lamp; **'~schütze** *m* archer, bowman.

Bohle ['bo:lə] *f* (-/-n) thick plank, board.

Bohne ['bo:nə] *f* (-/-n) bean; *grüne ~n pl.* French beans *pl., Am.* string beans *pl.*; *weiße ~n pl.* haricot beans *pl.*; F *blaue ~n pl.* bullets *pl.*; **'~stange** *f* beanpole (*a.* F *fig.*).

bohnern ['bo:nərn] *v/t.* (ge-, *h*) polish (*floor, etc.*), (bees)wax (*floor*).

bohr|en ['bo:rən] (ge-, *h*) **1.** *v/t.* bore, drill (*hole*); sink, bore (*well, shaft*); bore, cut, drive (*tunnel, etc.*); **2.** *v/i.* drill (*a. dentistry*); bore; **'2er** ⊕ *m* (-s/-) borer, drill.

'böig *adj.* squally, gusty; ✈ bumpy.

Boje ['bo:jə] *f* (-/-n) buoy.

Bollwerk ✗ ['bɔlvɛrk] *n* bastion, bulwark (*a. fig.*).

Bolzen ⊕ ['bɔltsən] *m* (-s/-) bolt.

Bombard|ement [bɔmbardə'mã:] *n* (-s/-s) bombardment; bombing; shelling; **2ieren** [~'di:rən] *v/t.* (no -ge-, *h*) bomb; shell; bombard (*a. fig.*).

Bombe ['bɔmbə] *f* (-/-n) bomb; *fig.* bomb-shell; **'2nsicher** *adj.* bombproof; F *fig.* dead sure; **'~nschaden** *m* bomb damage; **'~r** ✗ ✈ *m* (-s/-) bomber.

Bon ✝ [bõ:] *m* (-s/-s) coupon; voucher; credit note.

Bonbon [bõ'bõ:] *m, n* (-s/-s) sweet (-meat), bon-bon, F goody, *Am.* candy.

Bonze F ['bɔntsə] *m* (-n/-n) bigwig, *Am. a.* big shot.

Boot [bo:t] *n* (-[e]s/-e) boat; **'~shaus** *n* boat-house; **'~smann** *m* (-[e]s/ *Bootsleute*) boatswain.

Bord [bɔrt] *m* (-[e]s/-e) **1.** *m* shelf; **2.** ⊕, ✈ *m*: *an ~* on board, aboard (*ship, aircraft, etc.*); *über ~* overboard; *von ~ gehen* go ashore; **'~funker** ⊕, ✈ *m* wireless *or* radio operator; **'~stein** *m* kerb, *Am.* curb.

borgen ['bɔrgən] *v/t.* (ge-, *h*) borrow (*von, bei* from, of); lend, *Am. a.* loan (*j-m et. s.th.* to s.o.).

Borke ['bɔrkə] *f* (-/-n) bark (*of tree*).

borniert *adj.* [bɔr'ni:rt] narrow-minded, of restricted intelligence.

Borsalbe ['bo:r-] *f* boracic ointment.

Börse ['bœrzə] *f* (-/-n) purse; ✝ stock exchange; stock-market; money-market; **'~nbericht** *m* market report; **'2nfähig** *adj. stock:* negotiable on the stock exchange; **'~nkurs** *m* quotation; **'~nmakler** *m* stock-broker; **'~nnotierung** *f* (official, stock exchange) quotation; **'~npapiere** *n/pl.* listed securities *pl.*; **'~nspekulant** *m* stockjobber; **'~nzeitung** *f* financial newspaper.

Borst|e ['bɔrstə] *f* (-/-n) bristle (*of hog or brush, etc.*); **2ig** *adj.* bristly.

Borte ['bɔrtə] *f* (-/-n) border (*of carpet, etc.*); braid, lace.

'bösartig *adj.* malicious, vicious; **♂** malignant; **2keit** *f* (-/-en) viciousness; **♂** malignity.

Böschung ['bœʃuŋ] *f* (-/-en) slope; embankment (*of railway*); bank (*of river*).

böse ['bøːzə] **1.** *adj.* bad, evil, wicked; malevolent, spiteful; angry (*über acc.* at, about; *auf j-n* with s.o.); *er meint es nicht ~* he means no harm; **2.** ♀ *n* (-n/no *pl.*) evil; **2wicht** ['~vɪçt] *m* (-[e]s/-er, -e) villain, rascal.

bos|haft *adj.* ['boːshaft] wicked; spiteful; malicious; **'2heit** *f* (-/-en) wickedness; malice; spite.

'böswillig *adj.* malevolent; *~e Absicht* **♂** malice prepense; *~es Verlassen* **♂** wilful desertion; **'2keit** *f* (-/-en) malevolence.

bot [boːt] *pret. of bieten.*

Botan|ik [bo'taːnik] *f* (-/no *pl.*) botany; **2iker** *m* (-s/-) botanist; **2isch** *adj.* botanical.

Bote ['boːtə] *m* (-n/-n) messenger; **'~ngang** *m* errand; *Botengänge machen* run errands.

'Botschaft *f* (-/-en) message; *pol.* embassy; **'~er** *m* (-s/-) ambassador; *in British Commonwealth countries:* High Commissioner.

Bottich ['bɔtɪç] *m* (-[e]s/-e) tub; wash-tub; *brewing:* tun. vat.

Bouillon [bu'ljõː] *f* (-/-s) beef tea.

Bowle ['boːlə] *f* (-/-n) vessel: bowl; *cold drink consisting of fruit, hock and champagne or soda-water: appr.* punch.

box|en ['bɔksən] **1.** *v/i.* (ge-, h) box; **2.** *v/t.* (ge-, h) punch *s.o.*; **3.** ♀ *n* (-s/no *pl.*) boxing; pugilism; **'2er** *m* (-s/-) boxer; pugilist; **'2handschuh** *m* boxing-glove; **'2kampf** *m* boxing-match, bout, fight; **'2sport** *m* boxing.

Boykott [bɔy'kɔt] *m* (-[e]s/-e) boycott; **2ieren** [~'tiːrən] *v/t.* (no -ge-, h) boycott.

brach [braːx] **1.** *pret. of brechen.* **2.** *adv.* fallow; uncultivated (*both a. fig.*).

brachte ['braxtə] *pret. of bringen.*

Branche † ['brãːʃə] *f* (-/-n) line (*of business*), trade; branch.

Brand [brant] *m* (-[e]s/♯e) burning, fire, blaze; **♂** gangrene; **♀, ♂** blight, smut, mildew; **'~blase** *f* blister; **'~bombe** *f* incendiary bomb; **2en** ['~dən] *v/i.* (ge-, h) surge (*a. fig.*), break (*an acc.*, gegen against); **'~fleck** *m* burn; **2ig** *adj.* ['~dɪç] **♀, ♂** blighted, smutted; **♂** gangrenous; **'~mal** *n* brand; *fig.* stigma, blemish; **'2marken** *v/t.* (ge-, h) brand (*animal*); *fig.* brand

or stigmatize *s.o.*; **'~mauer** *f* fire (-proof) wall; **'~schaden** *m* damage caused by *or* loss suffered by fire; **'2schatzen** *v/t.* (ge-, h) lay (*town*) under contribution; sack, pillage; **'~stätte** *f,* **'~stelle** *f* scene of fire; **'~stifter** *m* incendiary, *Am.* F *a.* firebug; **'~stiftung** *f* arson; **~ung** ['~duŋ] *f* (-/-en) surf, surge, breakers *pl.*; **'~wache** *f* fire-watch; **'~wunde** *f* burn; scald; **'~zeichen** *n* brand.

brannte ['brantə] *pret. of brennen.*

Branntwein ['brantvaın] *m* brandy, spirits *pl.*; whisk(e)y; gin; **'~brennerei** *f* distillery.

braten ['braːtən] **1.** *v/t.* (*irr.*, ge-, h) *in oven:* roast; grill; *in frying-pan:* fry; bake (*apple*); *am Spieß ~* roast on a spit, barbecue; **2.** *v/i.* (*irr.*, ge-, h) roast; grill; fry; *in der Sonne ~ p.* roast *or* grill in the sun; **3.** ♀ *m* (-s/-) roast (meat); joint; **'2fett** *n* dripping; **'2soße** *f* gravy.

'Brat|fisch *m* fried fish; **'~hering** *m* grilled herring; **'~huhn** *n* roast chicken; **'~kartoffeln** *pl.* fried potatoes *pl.*; whisk(e)y; **'~ofen** *m* (kitchen) oven; **'~pfanne** *f* frying-pan, *Am. a.* skillet; **'~röhre** *f s. Bratofen.*

Brauch [braux] *m* (-[e]s/♯e) custom, usage; use, habit; practice; **2bar** *adj. p.,* thing: useful; *p.* capable, able; thing: serviceable; **'2en** (h) **1.** *v/t.* (ge-) need, want; require; take (*time*); use; **2.** *v/aux.* (no -ge-): *du brauchst es nur zu sagen* you only have to say so; *er hätte nicht zu kommen ~* he need not have come; **'~tum** *n* (-[e]s/♯er) custom; tradition; folklore.

Braue ['brauə] *f* (-/-n) eyebrow.

brau|en ['brauən] *v/t.* (ge-, h) brew; **'2er** *m* (-s/-) brewer; **2erei** [~'raı] *f* (-/-en) brewery; **'2haus** *n* brewery.

braun *adj.* [braun] brown; *horse:* bay; *~ werden* get a tan (*on one's skin*).

Bräune ['brɔynə] *f* (-/no *pl.*) brown colo(u)r; (sun) tan; **'2n** (ge-, h) **1.** *v/t.* make *or* dye brown; *sun:* tan; **2.** *v/i.* tan.

'Braunkohle *f* brown coal, lignite.

'bräunlich *adj.* brownish.

Brause ['brauzə] *f* (-/-n) rose, sprinkling-nozzle (*of watering can*); *s. Brausebad; s. Brauselimonade;* **'~bad** *n* shower(-bath); **'~limonade** *f* fizzy lemonade; **'2n** *v/i.* (ge-, h) wind, water, etc.: roar; rush; have a shower(-bath); **'~pulver** *n* effervescent powder.

Braut [braut] *f* (-/♯e) fiancée; *on wedding-day:* bride; **'~führer** *m* best man.

Bräutigam ['brɔytigam] *m* (-s/-e) fiancé; *on wedding-day:* bridegroom, *Am. a.* groom.

'Braut|jungfer *f* bridesmaid; **'~**

kleid n wedding-dress; '**~kranz** m bridal wreath; '~**leute** pl., '~**paar** n engaged couple; on wedding-day: bride and bridegroom; '~**schleier** m bridal veil.

brav adj. [bra:f] honest, upright; good, well-behaved; brave.

bravo int. ['bra:vo] bravo!, well done!

Bravour [bra'vu:r] f (-/no pl.) bravery, courage; brilliance.

Brecheisen ['brɛç?-] n crowbar; (burglar's) jemmy, Am. a. jimmy.

'**brechen** (irr., ge-) 1. v/t. (h) break; pluck (flower); refract (ray, etc.); fold (sheet of paper); quarry (stone); vomit; die Ehe ~ commit adultery; sich ~ break (one's leg, etc.); opt. be refracted; 2. v/i. (h) break; vomit; mit j-m ~ break with s.o.; 3. v/i. (sein) break, get broken; bones: break, fracture.

'**Brech|mittel** ♫ n emetic; F fig. sickener; '~**reiz** m nausea; '~**stange** f crowbar, Am. a. pry; '~**ung** opt. f (-/-en) refraction.

Brei [braɪ] m (-[e]s/-e) paste; pulp; mash; pap (for babies); made of oatmeal: porridge; (rice, etc.) pudding; '2**ig** adj. pasty; pulpy; pappy.

breit adj. [braɪt] broad, wide; zehn Meter ~ ten metres wide; ~e Schichten der Bevölkerung large sections of or the bulk of the population; '~**beinig** 1. adj. with legs wide apart; 2. adv.: ~ gehen straddle.

Breite ['braɪtə] f (-/-n) breadth, width; ast., geogr. latitude; '2n v/t. (ge-, h) spread; '~**ngrad** m degree of latitude; '~**nkreis** m parallel (of latitude).

'**breit|machen** v/refl. (sep., -ge-, h) spread o.s.; take up room; '~**schlagen** v/t. (irr. schlagen, sep., -ge-, h): F j-n ~ persuade s.o.; F j-n zu et. ~ talk s.o. into (doing) s.th.; '2**seite** ⚓ f broadside.

Bremse ['brɛmzə] f (-/-n) zo. gadfly; horse-fly; ⊕ brake; '2n (ge-, h) v/i. brake, put on the brakes; slow down; 2. v/t. brake, put on the brakes to; slow down; fig. curb.

'**Brems|klotz** m brake-block; ⚙ wheel chock; '~**pedal** n brake pedal; '~**vorrichtung** f brake-mechanism; '~**weg** m braking distance.

brenn|bar adj. ['brɛnbaːr] combustible, burnable; '2**dauer** f burning time; '~**en** (irr., ge-, h) 1. v/t. burn; distil(l) (brandy); roast (coffee); bake (brick, etc.); 2. v/i. burn; be ablaze, be on fire; wound, eye: smart, burn; nettle: sting; vor Ungeduld ~ burn with impatience; F darauf ~ zu inf. be burning to inf.; es brennt! fire!

'**Brenn|er** m (-s/-) p. distiller; fixture: burner; '~**essel** ['brɛnnɛsəl] f

stinging nettle; '~**glas** n burning glass; '~**holz** n firewood; '~**material** n fuel; '~**öl** n lamp-oil; fuel-oil; '~**punkt** m focus, focal point; in den ~ rücken bring into focus (a. fig.); im ~ des Interesses stehen be the focus of interest; '~**schere** f curling-tongs pl.; '~**spiritus** m methylated spirit; '~**stoff** m combustible; mot. fuel.

brenzlig ['brɛntsliç] 1. adj. burnt; matter: dangerous; situation: precarious; ~er Geruch burnt smell, smell of burning; 2. adv.: es riecht ~ it smells of burning.

Bresche ['brɛʃə] f (-/-n) breach (a. fig.), gap; in die ~ springen help s.o. out of a dilemma.

Brett [brɛt] n (-[e]s/-er) board; plank; shelf; spring-board; '~**spiel** n game played on a board.

Brezel ['breːtsəl] f (-/-n) pretzel.

Brief [briːf] m (-[e]s/-e) letter; '~**aufschrift** f address (on a letter); '~**beschwerer** m (-s/-) paperweight; '~**bogen** m sheet of notepaper; '~**geheimnis** n secrecy of correspondence; '~**karte** f correspondence card (with envelope); '~**kasten** m letter-box; pillar-box, Am. mailbox; '2**lich** adj. and adv. by letter, in writing; '~**marke** f (postage) stamp; '~**markensammlung** f stamp-collection; '~**öffner** m letter-opener; '~**ordner** m letter-file; '~**papier** n notepaper; '~**porto** n postage; '~**post** f mail, post; '~**tasche** f wallet, Am. a. billfold; '~**taube** f carrier pigeon, homing pigeon, homer; '~**träger** m postman, Am. mailman; '~**umschlag** m envelope; '~**waage** f letterbalance; '~**wechsel** m correspondence; '~**zensur** f postal censorship.

briet [briːt] pret. of braten.

Brikett [bri'kɛt] n (-[e]s/-s) briquet (-te).

Brillant [bril'jant] 1. m (-en/-en) brilliant, cut diamond; 2. ♀ adj. brilliant; '~**ring** m diamond ring.

Brille ['brilə] f (-/-n) (eine a pair of) glasses pl. or spectacles pl.; goggles pl.; lavatory seat; '~**nfutteral** n spectacle-case; '~**nträger** m person who wears glasses.

bringen ['brɪŋən] v/t. (irr., ge-, h) bring; take; see (s.o. home, etc.); put (in order); make (sacrifice); yield (interest); an den Mann ~ dispose of, get rid of; j-n dazu ~ et. zu tun make or get s.o. to do s.th.; et. mit sich ~ involve s.th.; j-n um et. ~ deprive s.o. of s.th.; j-n zum Lachen ~ make s.o. laugh.

Brise ['briːzə] f (-/-n) breeze.

Brit|e ['britə] m (-n/-n) Briton, Am. a. Britisher; die ~n pl. the British pl.; '2**isch** adj. British.

bröckeln ['brœkəln] v/i. (ge-, h) crumble; become brittle.

Brocken ['brɔkən] **1.** m (-s/-) piece; lump (of earth or stone, etc.); morsel (of food); F ein harter ~ a hard nut; **2.** 2 v/t. (ge-, h): Brot in die Suppe ~ break bread into soup.

brodeln ['bro:dəln] v/i. (ge-, h) bubble, simmer.

Brombeer|e ['brɔm-] f blackberry; '~strauch m blackberry bush.

Bronch|ialkatarrh ♀ [brɔnçi'a:lkatar] m bronchial catarrh; '~ien anat. f/pl. bronchi(a) pl.; ~itis ♀ [~'çi:tis] f (-/Bronchitiden) bronchitis.

Bronze ['brõ:sə] f (-/-n) bronze; '~medaille f bronze medal.

Brosche ['brɔʃə] f (-/-n) brooch.

broschier|en [brɔ'ʃi:rən] v/i. (no -ge-, h) sew, stitch (book); ~t adj. book: paper-backed, paper-bound; fabric: figured.

Broschüre [brɔ'ʃy:rə] f (-/-n) booklet; brochure; pamphlet.

Brot [bro:t] n (-[e]s/-e) bread; loaf; sein ~ verdienen earn one's living; '~aufstrich m spread.

Brötchen ['brø:tçən] n (-s/-) roll.

'**Brot|korb** m: j-m den ~ höher hängen put s.o. on short allowance; '2los fig. adj. unemployed; unprofitable; '~rinde f crust; '~schneidemaschine f bread-cutter; '~schnitte f slice of bread; '~studium n utilitarian study; '~teig m bread dough.

Bruch [brux] (-[e]s/=e) break(ing); breach; ♀ fracture (of bones); ♀ hernia; crack; fold (in paper); crease (in cloth); split (in silk); ᴀ fraction; breach (of promise); violation (of oath, etc.); violation, infringement (of law, etc.); '~band ♀ n truss.

brüchig adj. ['bryçiç] fragile; brittle; voice: cracked.

'**Bruch|landung** ✈ f crash-landing; '~rechnung f fractional arithmetic, F fractions pl.; '~strich ᴀ m fraction bar; '~stück n fragment (a. fig.); '~teil m fraction; im ~ e-r Sekunde in a split second; '~zahl f fraction(al) number.

Brücke ['brykə] f (-/-n) bridge; carpet: rug; sports: bridge; e-e ~ schlagen über (acc.) build or throw a bridge across, bridge (river); '~nkopf ✕ m bridge-head; '~npfeiler m pier (of bridge).

Bruder ['bru:dər] m (-s/=) brother; eccl. (lay) brother, friar; '~krieg m fratricidal or civil war; '~kuß m fraternal kiss.

brüderlich ['bry:dərliç] **1.** adj. brotherly, fraternal; **2.** adv.: ~ teilen share and share alike; '2keit f (-/no pl.) brotherliness, fraternity.

Brühe ['bry:ə] f (-/-n) broth; stock;

beef tea; F dirty water; drink: F dishwater; '2heiß adj. scalding hot; '~würfel m beef cube.

brüllen ['brylən] v/i. (ge-, h) roar; bellow; cattle: low; bull: bellow; vor Lachen ~ roar with laughter; ~des Gelächter roar of laughter.

brumm|en ['brumən] v/i. (ge-, h) p. speak in a deep voice, mumble; growl (a. fig.); insect: buzz; engine: buzz, boom; fig. grumble, Am. F grouch; mir brummt der Schädel my head is buzzing; '2bär fig. m grumbler, growler, Am. F grouch; '2er m (-s/-) bluebottle; dung-beetle; '~ig adj. grumbling, Am. F grouchy.

brünett adj. [bry'nɛt] woman: brunette.

Brunft hunt. [brunft] f (-/=e) rut; '~zeit f rutting season.

Brunnen ['brunən] m (-s/-) well; spring; fountain (a. fig.); e-n ~ graben sink a well; '~wasser n pump-water, well-water.

Brunst [brunst] f (-/=e) zo. rut (of male animal), heat (of female animal); lust, sexual desire.

brünstig adj. ['brynstiç] zo. rutting, in heat; lustful.

Brust [brust] f (-/=e) chest, anat. thorax; breast; (woman's) breast(s pl.), bosom; aus voller ~ at the top of one's voice, lustily; '~bild n half-length portrait.

brüsten ['brystən] v/refl. (ge-, h) boast, brag.

'**Brust|fell** anat. n pleura; '~fell-entzündung ♀ f pleurisy; '~kasten m, '~korb m chest, anat. thorax; '~schwimmen n (-s/no pl.) breast-stroke.

Brüstung ['brystuŋ] f (-/-en) balustrade, parapet.

'**Brustwarze** anat. f nipple.

Brut [bru:t] f (-/-en) brooding, sitting; brood; hatch; fry, spawn (of fish); fig. F brood, (bad) lot.

brutal adj. [bru'ta:l] brutal; 2ität [~ali'tɛ:t] f (-/-en) brutality.

Brutapparat zo. ['bru:t?-] m incubator.

brüten ['bry:tən] v/i. (ge-, h) brood, sit (on egg); incubate; ~ über (dat.) brood over.

'**Brutkasten** ♀ m incubator.

brutto ✝ adv. ['bruto] gross; '2gewicht n gross weight; '2register-tonne f gross register ton; '2verdienst m gross earnings pl.

Bube ['bu:bə] m (-n/-n) boy, lad; knave, rogue; cards: knave, jack; '~nstreich m, '~nstück n boyish prank; knavish trick.

Buch [bu:x] n (-[e]s/=er) book; volume; '~binder m (book-)binder; '~drucker m printer; ~druckerei [~'rai] f printing; printing-office, Am. print shop.

Buche ♀ ['buːxə] *f* (-/-n) beech.

buchen ['buːxən] *v/t.* (ge-, h) book, reserve (*passage, flight, etc.*); *book-keeping*: book (*item, sum*), enter (*transaction*) in the books; et. *als Erfolg ~* count s.th. as a success.

Bücher|abschluß ✝ ['byːçər-] *m* closing *or* balancing of books; **'~brett** *n* bookshelf; **~ei** [~'raɪ] *f* (-/-en) library; **'~freund** *m* book-lover, bibliophil(e); **'~revisor** ✝ *m* (-s/-en) auditor; accountant; **'~schrank** *m* bookcase; **'~wurm** *m* bookworm.

'Buch|fink *orn. m* chaffinch; **'~halter** *m* (-s/-) book-keeper; **'~haltung** *f* book-keeping; **'~handel** *m* book-trade; **'~händler** *m* book-seller; **'~handlung** *f* bookshop, *Am.* bookstore.

Büchse ['byksə] *f* (-/-n) box, case; tin, *Am.* can; rifle; **'~nfleisch** *n* tinned meat, *Am.* canned meat; **'~nöffner** ['byksən?-] *m* tin-opener, *Am.* can opener.

Buchstab|e ['buːxʃtaːbə] *m* (-n/-n) letter, character; *typ.* type; ♀ieren [~a'biːrən] *v/t.* (*no* -ge-, h) spell.

buchstäblich ['buːxʃteːpliç] **1.** *adj.* literal; **2.** *adv.* literally; word for word.

Bucht [buxt] *f* (-/-en) bay; bight; creek, inlet.

'Buchung *f* (-/-en) booking, reservation; *book-keeping*: entry.

Buckel ['bukəl] **1.** *m* (-s/-) hump, hunch; humpback, hunchback; boss, stud, knob; **2.** *f* (-/-n) boss, stud, knob.

'buckelig *adj. s.* bucklig.

bücken ['bykən] *v/refl.* (ge-, h) bend (down), stoop.

bucklig *adj.* ['buklɪç] humpbacked, hunchbacked.

Bückling ['byklɪŋ] *m* (-s/-e) bloater, red herring; *fig.* bow.

Bude ['buːdə] *f* (-/-n) stall, booth; hut, cabin, *Am.* shack; F: place; den; (student's, *etc.*) digs *pl.*

Budget [by'dʒeː] *n* (-s/-s) budget.

Büfett [by'feː; by'fet] *n* (-[e]s/-s; -[e]s/-e) sideboard, buffet; buffet, bar, *Am. a.* counter; *kaltes ~* buffet supper *or* lunch.

Büffel ['byfəl] *m* (-s/-) *zo.* buffalo; F *fig.* lout, blockhead.

Bug [buːk] *m* (-[e]s/-e) ♣ bow; ✕ nose; fold; (sharp) crease.

Bügel ['byːgəl] *m* (-s/-) bow (*of spectacles, etc.*); handle (*of handbag, etc.*); coat-hanger; stirrup; **'~brett** *n* ironing-board; **'~eisen** *n* (flat-)iron; **'~falte** *f* crease; **'2n** *v/t.* (ge-, h) iron (*shirt, etc.*), press (*suit, skirt, etc.*).

Bühne ['byːnə] *f* (-/-n) platform (*a.* ⊕); scaffold; *thea.* stage; *fig.*: *die ~* the stage; *die politische ~* the political scene; **~nanweisungen** ['byː-** nən?-] *f/pl.* stage directions *pl.*; **'~nbild** *n* scene(ry); décor; stage design; **'~ndichter** *m* playwright, dramatist; **'~nlaufbahn** *f* stage career; **'~nstück** *n* stage play.

buk [buːk] *pret. of* backen.

Bull|auge ♣ ['bul-] *n* porthole, bull's eye; **'~dogge** *zo. f* bulldog.

Bulle ['bulə] **1.** *zo. m* (-n/-n) bull; **2.** *eccl. f* (-/-n) bull.

Bummel ['bumal] *m* (-s/-) stroll, spree, pub-crawl, *sl.* binge; **~ei** [~'laɪ] *f* (-/-en) dawdling; negligence; **'2n** *v/i.* (ge-) **1.** (*sein*) stroll, saunter; pub-crawl; **2.** (*h*) dawdle (*on way, at work*), waste time; **'~streik** *m* go-slow (strike), *Am.* slowdown; **'~zug** *m* slow train, *Am.* way train.

Bummler ['bumlər] *m* (-s/-) saunterer, stroller; loafer, *Am.* F *a.* bum; dawdler.

Bund [bunt] **1.** *m* (-[e]s/¤e) *pol.* union, federation, confederacy; (waist-, neck-, wrist)band; **2.** *n* (-[e]s/-e) bundle (*of faggots*); bundle, truss (*of hay or straw*); bunch (*of radishes, etc.*).

Bündel ['byndəl] *n* (-s/-) bundle, bunch; **'2n** *v/t.* (ge-, h) make into a bundle, bundle up.

Bundes|bahn ['bundəs-] *f* Federal Railway(s *pl.*); **'~bank** *f* Federal Bank; **'~genosse** *m* ally; **'~gerichtshof** *m* Federal Supreme Court; **'~kanzler** *m* Federal Chancellor; **'~ministerium** *n* Federal Ministry; **'~post** *f* Federal Postal Administration; **'~präsident** *m* President of the Federal Republic; **'~rat** *m* Bundesrat, Upper House of German Parliament; **'~republik** *f* Federal Republic; **'~staat** *m* federal state; confederation; **'~tag** *m* Bundestag, Lower House of German Parliament.

bündig *adj.* ['byndɪç] *style, speech*: concise, to the point, terse.

Bündnis ['byntnɪs] *n* (-ses/-se) alliance; agreement.

Bunker ['buŋkər] *m* (-s/-) ✕, coal, fuel, *etc.*: bunker; bin; air-raid shelter; ✕ bunker, pill-box; ♣ (submarine) pen.

bunt *adj.* [bunt] (multi-)colo(u)red, colo(u)rful; motley; *bird, flower, etc.*: variegated; bright, gay; *fig.* mixed, motley; full of variety; **'2druck** *m* colo(u)r-print(ing); **'2stift** *m* colo(u)red pencil, crayon.

Bürde ['byrdə] *f* (-/-n) burden (*a. fig.*: *für j-n* to s.o.), load.

Burg [burk] *f* (-/-en) castle; fortress, citadel (*a. fig.*).

Bürge ♂ ['byrgə] *m* (-n/-n) guarantor, security, surety, bailsman; sponsor; **'2n** *v/i.* (ge-, h): *für j-n ~* stand guarantee *or* surety *or* security for s.o., *Am. a.* bond s.o.; stand bail for s.o.; vouch *or* answer for s.o.; sponsor s.o.; *für et.* ~ stand security for s.th. guarantee s.th.; vouch *or* answer for s.th.

Bürger ['byrgər] *m* (-s/-) citizen; townsman; '~krieg *m* civil war.

'**bürgerlich** *adj.* civic, civil; ~e Küche plain cooking; *Verlust der* ~en Ehrenrechte loss of civil rights; *Bürgerliches Gesetzbuch* German Civil Code; '2e *m* (-n/-n) commoner.

'**Bürger|meister** *m* mayor; *in Germany: a.* burgomaster; *in Scotland:* provost; '~recht *n* civic rights *pl.*; citizenship; '~schaft *f* (-/-en) citizens *pl.*; '~steig *m* pavement, *Am.* sidewalk; '~wehr *f* militia.

Bürgschaft ['byrkʃaft] *f* (-/-en) security; bail; guarantee.

Büro [by'ro:] *n* (-s/-s) office; ~angestellte *m, f* (-n/-n) clerk; ~arbeit *f* office-work; ~klammer *f* paper-clip; ~krat [~o'kra:t] *m* (-en/-en) bureaucrat; ~kratie [~o-kra'ti:] *f* (-/-n) bureaucracy; red tape; 2kratisch *adj.* [~o'kra:tiʃ] bureaucratic; ~stunden *f/pl.* office hours *pl.*; ~vorsteher *m* head *or* senior clerk.

Bursch [burʃ] *m* (-en/-en), ~e ['~ə] *m* (-n/-n) boy, lad, youth; F chap, *Am. a.* guy; *ein übler* ~ a bad lot, F a bad egg.

burschikos *adj.* [burʃi'ko:s] free and easy; *esp. girl:* boyish, unaffected, hearty.

Bürste ['byrstə] *f* (-/-n) brush; '2n *v/t.* (ge-, h) brush.

Busch [buʃ] *m* (-es/ⁿe) bush, shrub.

Büschel ['byʃəl] *n* (-s/-) bunch;

tuft, handful (*of hair*); wisp (*of straw or hair*).

'**Busch|holz** *n* brushwood, underwood; '2ig *adj.* hair, eyebrows, *etc.*: bushy, shaggy; covered with bushes or scrub, bushy; '~messer *n* bushknife; machete; '~neger *m* maroon; '~werk *n* bushes *pl.*, shrubbery, *Am. a.* brush.

Busen ['bu:zən] *m* (-s/-) bosom, breast (*esp. of woman*); *fig.* bosom, heart; *geog.* bay, gulf; '~freund *m* bosom friend.

Bussard *orn.* ['busart] *m* (-[e]s/-e) buzzard.

Buße ['bu:sə] *f* (-/-n) atonement (*for sins*), penance; repentance; satisfaction; fine; ~ *tun* do penance.

büßen ['by:sən] (ge-, h) 1. *v/t.* expiate, atone for (*sin, crime*); *er mußte es mit s-m Leben* ~ he paid for it with his life; *das sollst du mir* ~! you'll pay for that!; 2. *v/i.* atone, pay (*für* for).

'**Büßer** *m* (-s/-) penitent.

'**buß|fertig** *adj.* penitent, repentant, contrite; '2fertigkeit *f* (-/*no pl.*) repentance, contrition; '2tag *m* day of repentance; *Buß- und Bettag* day of prayer and repentance.

Büste ['bystə] *f* (-/-n) bust; '~n-halter *m* (-s/-) brassière, F bra.

Büttenpapier ['bytən-] *n* handmade paper.

Butter ['butər] *f* (-/*no pl.*) butter; '~blume ⚫ *f* buttercup; '~brot *n* (slice *or* piece of) bread and butter; F: *für ein* ~ for a song; '~brotpapier *n* greaseproof paper; '~dose *f* butter-dish; '~faß *n* butter-churn; '~milch *f* buttermilk; '2n *v/i.* (ge-, h) churn.

C

Café [ka'fe:] *n* (-s/-s) café, coffee-house.

Cape [ke:p] *n* (-s/-s) cape.

Cell|ist ♪ [tʃe'list] *m* (-en/-en) violoncellist, (')cellist; ~o ♪ ['~o] *n* (-s/-s, Celli) violoncello, (')cello.

Celsius ['tsɛlzius]: 5 *Grad* ~ (*abbr. 5° C*) five degrees centigrade.

Chaiselongue [ʃɛz(ə)'lõ:] *f* (-/-n, -s) chaise longue, lounge, couch.

Champagner [ʃam'panjər] *m* (-s/-) champagne.

Champignon ⚫ ['ʃampinjõ] *m* (-s/-s) champignon, (common) mushroom.

Chance ['ʃã:sə] *f* (-/-n) chance; *keine* ~ *haben* not to stand a chance; *sich eine* ~ *entgehen lassen* miss a chance *or* an opportunity; *die* ~n *sind gleich* the chances *or* odds are even.

Chaos ['ka:ɔs] *n* (-/*no pl.*) chaos.

Charakter [ka'raktər] *m* (-s/-e) character; nature; *a bild n* character (sketch); ~darsteller *thea. m* character actor; ~fehler *m* fault in s.o.'s character; 2fest *adj.* of firm *or* strong character; 2i'sieren *v/t.* (*no -ge-, h*) characterize, describe (*als acc.* as); ~i'sierung *f* (-/-en), ~istik [~'ristik] *f* (-/-en) characterization; 2istisch *adj.* [~'ristiʃ] characteristic *or* typical (*für* of); 2lich *adj.* of *or* concerning (the) character; 2los *adj.* characterless, without (strength of) character, spineless; ~rolle *thea. f* character role; ~zug *m* characteristic, feature, trait.

charm|ant *adj.* [ʃar'mant] charming, winning; 2e [ʃarm] *m* (-s/*no pl.*) charm, grace.

Chassis [ʃa'siː] n (-/-) mot., radio: frame, chassis.

Chauffeur [ʃɔ'føːr] m (-s/-e) chauffeur, driver.

Chaussee [ʃo'seː] f (-/-n) highway, (high) road.

Chauvinismus [ʃovi'nismus] m (-/ no pl.) jingoism; chauvinism.

Chef [ʃɛf] m (-s/-s) head, chief; ✝ principal, F boss; senior partner.

Chemi|**e** [çe'miː] f (-/no pl.) chemistry; **~iefaser** f chemical fib|re, Am. -er; **~ikalien** [ʃi'kaːljən] f/pl. chemicals pl.; **~iker** ['çeːmikər] m (-s/-) (analytical) chemist; **2isch** adj. ['çeːmiʃ] chemical.

Chiffr|**e** ['ʃifər] f (-/-n) number; cipher; in advertisement: box number; **2ieren** [ʃi'friːrən] v/t. (no -ge-, h) cipher, code (message, etc.); write in code or cipher.

Chines|**e** [çi'neːzə] m (-n/-n) Chinese, contp. Chinaman; **2isch** adj. Chinese.

Chinin 🜛 [çi'niːn] n (-s/no pl.) quinine.

Chirurg [çi'rurk] m (-en/-en) surgeon; **~ie** [~'giː] f (-/-n) surgery; **2isch** adj. [~giʃ] surgical.

Chlor 🜛 [kloːr] n (-s/no pl.) chlorine; **2en** v/t. (ge-, h) chlorinate (water); **~kalk** 🜛 m chloride of lime.

Chloroform 🜛 [kloro'fɔrm] n (-/no pl.) chloroform; **2ieren** 🜪 [~'miːrən] v/t. (no -ge-, h) chloroform.

Cholera 🜪 ['koːlərа] f (-/no pl.) cholera.

cholerisch adj. [ko'leːriʃ] choleric, irascible.

Chor [koːr] m 1. 🜊 a. n (-[e]s/-e, ⁓e) chancel, choir; ♪ (organ-)loft; 2. (-[e]s/⁓e) in drama: chorus; singers: choir, chorus; piece of music: chorus; **~al** [ko'raːl] m (-s/⁓e) cho-

ral(e); hymn; **~gesang** m choral singing, chorus; **~sänger** m member of a choir; chorister.

Christ [krist] m (-en/-en) Christian; **~baum** m Christmas-tree; **~enheit** f (-/no pl.): die ~ Christendom; **~entum** n (-s/no pl.) Christianity; **~kind** n (-[e]s/no pl.) Christ-child, Infant Jesus; **2lich** adj. Christian.

Chrom [kroːm] n (-s/no pl.) metal: chromium; pigment: chrome.

chromatisch ♪, opt. adj. [kro'maːtiʃ] chromatic.

Chronik ['kroːnik] f (-/-en) chronicle.

chronisch adj. ['kroːniʃ] disease: chronic (a. fig.).

Chronist [kro'nist] m (-en/-en) chronicler.

chronologisch adj. [krono'loːgiʃ] chronological.

circa adv. ['tsirka] about, approximately.

Clique ['klikə] f (-/-n) clique, set, group, coterie; **~nwirtschaft** f (-/no pl.) cliquism.

Conférencier [kõferã'sjeː] m (-s/-s) compère, Am. master of ceremonies.

Couch [kautʃ] f (-/-es) couch.

Coupé [ku'peː] n (-s/-s) mot. coupé; 🜪 🚪 compartment.

Couplet [ku'pleː] n (-s/-s) comic or music-hall song.

Coupon [ku'põː] m (-s/-s) coupon; dividend-warrant; counterfoil.

Courtage ✝ [kur'taːʒə] f (-/-n) brokerage.

Cousin [ku'zɛ̃] m (-s/-s), **~e** [~'iːnə] f (-/-n) cousin.

Creme [kreːm, krɛm] f (-/-s) cream (a. fig.: only sg.).

Cut [kœt, kat] m (-s/-s), **~away** ['kœtəveː, 'katəveː] m (-s/-s) cutaway (coat), morning coat.

D

da [daː] **1.** adv. space: there; ~ wo where; hier und ~ here and there; ~ bin ich here I am; ~ haben wir's! there we are!; von ~ an from there; time: ~ erst only then, not till then; von ~ an from that time (on), since then; hier und ~ now and then or again; **2.** cj. time: as, when, while; nun, ~ du es einmal gesagt hast now (that) you have mentioned it; causal: as, since, because; ~ ich krank war, konnte ich nicht kommen as or since I was ill I couldn't come.

dabei adv. [da'baɪ, when emphatic: 'daːbaɪ] near (at hand), by; about, going (zu inf. to inf.), on the point

(of ger.); besides; nevertheless, yet, for all that; was ist schon ~? what does it matter?; lassen wir es ~ let's leave it at that; ~ bleiben stick to one's point, persist in it. **da'bei**|**bleiben** v/i. (irr. bleiben, sep., -ge-, sein) stay with it or them; **~sein** v/i. (irr. sein, sep., -ge-, sein) be present or there; **~stehen** v/i. (irr. stehen, sep., -ge-, h) stand by or near.

'dableiben v/i. (irr. bleiben, sep., -ge-, sein) stay, remain.

da capo adv. [da'kaːpo] at opera, etc.: encore.

Dach [dax] n (-[e]s/⁓er) roof; fig. shelter; **~antenne** f roof aerial;

'**∼decker** m (-s/-) roofer; tiler; slater; '**∼fenster** n skylight; dormer window; '**∼garten** m roofgarden; '**∼gesellschaft †** f holding company; '**∼kammer** f attic, garret; '**∼pappe** f roofing felt; '**∼rinne** f gutter, eaves pl.

dachte ['daxtə] pret. of denken.

Dachs zo. [daks] m (-es/-e) badger; '**∼bau** m (-[e]s/-e) badger's earth.

'**Dach|sparren** m rafter; '**∼stube** f attic, garret; '**∼stuhl** m roof framework; '**∼ziegel** m (roofing) tile.

dadurch [da'durç, when emphatic: 'da:durç] 1. adv. for this reason, in this manner or way, thus; by it or that; 2. cj.: ∼, daß owing to (the fact that), because; by ger.

dafür adv. [da'fy:r, when emphatic: 'da:fy:r] for it or that; instead (of it); in return (for it), in exchange; ∼ sein be in favo(u)r of it; ∼ sein zu inf. be for ger., be in favo(u)r of ger.; er kann nichts ∼ it is not his fault; ∼ sorgen, daß see to it that.

Da'fürhalten n (-s/no pl.): nach meinem ∼ in my opinion.

dagegen [da'ge:gən, when emphatic: 'da:ge:gən] 1. adv. against it or that; in comparison with it, compared to it; ∼ sein be against it, be opposed to it; ich habe nichts ∼ I have no objection (to it); 2. cj. on the other hand, however.

daheim adv. [da'haim] at home.

daher [da'he:r, when emphatic: 'da:he:r] 1. adv. from there; prefixed to verbs of motion: along; fig. from this, hence; ∼ kam es, daß thus it happened that; 2. cj. therefore; that is (the reason) why.

dahin adv. [da'hin, when emphatic: 'da:hin] there, to that place; gone, past; prefixed to verbs of motion: along; j-n ∼ bringen, daß induce s.o. to inf.; m-e Meinung geht ∼, daß my opinion is that.

da'hingestellt adj.: es ∼ sein lassen (,ob) leave it undecided (whether).

dahinter adv. [da'hintər, when emphatic: 'da:hintər] behind it or that, at the back of it; es steckt nichts ∼ there is nothing in it.

da'hinterkommen v/i. (irr. kommen, sep., -ge-, sein) find out about it.

damalig adj. ['da:ma:liç] then, of that time; der ∼e Besitzer the then owner; '**∼s** adv. then, at that time.

Damast [da'mast] m (-es/-e) damask.

Dame ['da:mə] f (-/-n) lady; dancing, etc.: partner; cards, chess: queen; s. Damespiel; '**∼brett** n draught-board, Am. checkerboard.

'**Damen|binde** f (woman's) sanitary towel, Am. sanitary napkin; '**∼doppel** n tennis: women's doubles pl.; '**∼einzel** n tennis: women's singles pl.; '**∼haft** adj. ladylike; '**∼konfektion** f ladies' ready-made clothes pl.; '**∼mannschaft** f sports: women's team; '**∼schneider** m ladies' tailor, dressmaker.

'**Damespiel** n (game of) draughts pl., Am. (game of) checkers pl.

damit 1. adv. [da'mit, when emphatic: 'da:mit] with it or that, therewith, herewith; by it or that; was will er ∼ sagen? what does he mean by it?; wie steht es ∼? how about it?; ∼ einverstanden sein agree to it; 2. cj. (in order) that, in order to inf.; so (that); ∼ nicht lest, (so as) to avoid that; for fear that (all with subjunctive).

dämlich F adj. ['dɛ:mliç] silly, asinine.

Damm [dam] m (-[e]s/∼e) dam; dike, dyke; ⚓ embankment; embankment, Am. levee (of river); roadway; fig. barrier; '**∼bruch** m bursting of a dam or dike.

dämmer|ig adj. ['dɛməriç] dusky; '**2licht** n twilight; '**∼n** v/i. (ge-, h) dawn (a. fig.: F j-m on s.o.); grow dark or dusky; '**2ung** f (-/-en) twilight, dusk; in the morning: dawn.

Dämon ['dɛ:mɔn] m (-s/-en) demon; **2isch** adj. [dɛ'mo:niʃ] demoniac(al).

Dampf [dampf] m (-[e]s/∼e) steam; vapo(u)r; '**∼bad** n vapo(u)r-bath; '**∼boot** n steamboat; '**2en** v/i. (ge-, h) steam.

dämpfen ['dɛmpfən] v/t. (ge-, h) deaden (pain, noise, force of blow); muffle (bell, drum, oar); damp (sound, oscillation, fig. enthusiasm); ♪ mute (stringed instrument); soften (colour, light); attenuate (wave); steam (cloth, food); stew (meat, fruit); fig. suppress, curb (emotion).

'**Dampfer** m (-s/-) steamer, steamship.

'**Dämpfer** m (-s/-) damper (a. ♪ of piano); ♪ mute (for violin, etc.).

'**Dampf|heizung** f steam-heating; '**∼kessel** m (steam-)boiler; '**∼maschine** f steam-engine; '**∼schiff** n steamer, steamship; '**∼walze** f steam-roller.

danach adv. [da'na:x, when emphatic: 'da:na:x] after it or that; afterwards; subsequently; accordingly; ich fragte ihn ∼ I asked him about it; iro. er sieht ganz ∼ aus he looks very much like it.

Däne ['dɛ:nə] m (-n/-n) Dane.

daneben adv. [da'ne:bən, when emphatic: 'da:ne:bən] next to it or that, beside it or that; besides, moreover; beside the mark.

da'nebengehen F v/i. (irr. gehen, sep., -ge-, sein) bullet, etc.: miss the target or mark; remark, etc.: miss one's effect, F misfire.

daniederliegen [da'ni:dər-] v/i.

(irr. liegen, sep., -ge-, h) be laid up *(an dat.* with*); trade:* be depressed.

dänisch *adj.* ['dɛːniʃ] Danish.

Dank [daŋk] **1.** *m* (-[e]s/*no pl.*) thanks *pl.,* gratitude; reward; *j-m* ~ *sagen* thank s.o.; *Gott sei* ~*!* thank God!; **2.** ℒ *prp. (dat.)* owing *or* thanks to; '℥**bar** *adj.* thankful, grateful *(j-m* to s.o.; *für* for); profitable; '℥**barkeit** *f* (-/*no pl.*) gratitude; '℥**en** *v/i.* (ge-, h) thank *(j-m für et.* s.o. for s.th.); *danke (schön)!* thank you (very much)!; *danke* thank you; *nein, danke* no, thank you; *nichts zu* ~ don't mention it; '℥**enswert** *adj. thing:* one can be grateful for; *efforts, etc.:* kind; *task, etc.:* rewarding, worth-while; '~**gebet** *n* thanksgiving (prayer); '~**schreiben** *n* letter of thanks.

dann *adv.* [dan] then; ~ *und wann* (every) now and then.

daran *adv.* [da'ran, *when emphatic:* 'dɑːran] at *(or* by, in, on, to) it *or* that; *sich* ~ *festhalten* hold on tight to it; ~ *festhalten* stick to it; *nahe* ~ *sein zu inf.* be on the point *or* verge of *ger.*

da'rangehen *v/i. (irr. gehen, sep., -ge-, sein)* set to work; set about *ger.*

darauf *adv.* [da'rauf, *when emphatic:* 'dɑːrauf] *space:* on (top of) it *or* that; *time:* thereupon, after it *or* that; *am Tage* ~ the day after, the next *or* following day; *zwei Jahre* ~ two years later; ~ *kommt es an* that's what matters; ~**hin** *adv.* [darauf'hin, *when emphatic:* 'dɑːraufhin] thereupon.

daraus *adv.* [da'raus, *when emphatic:* 'dɑːraus] out of it *or* that, from it *or* that; ~ *folgt* hence it follows; *was ist* ~ *geworden?* what has become of it?; *ich mache mir nichts* ~ I don't care *or* mind (about it).

darben ['darbən] *v/i.* (ge-, h) suffer want; starve.

darbiet|en ['dɑːr-] *v/t. (irr. bieten, sep., -ge-, h)* offer, present; perform; '℥**ung** *f* (-/-en) *thea., etc.:* performance.

'darbringen *v/t. (irr. bringen, sep., -ge-, h)* offer; make *(sacrifice).*

darein *adv.* [da'rain, *when emphatic:* 'dɑːrain] into it *or* that, therein.

da'rein|finden *v/refl. (irr. finden, sep., -ge-, h)* put up with it; ~**mischen** *v/refl. (sep., -ge-, h)* interfere (with it); ~**reden** *v/i. (sep., -ge-, h)* interrupt; *fig.* interfere.

darin *adv.* [da'rin, *when emphatic:* 'dɑːrin] in it *or* that; therein; *es war nichts* ~ there was nothing in it *or* them.

darleg|en ['dɑːr-] *v/t. (sep., -ge-, h)* lay open, expose, disclose; show; explain; demonstrate; point out; '℥**ung** *f* (-/-en) exposition; explanation; statement.

Darlehen ['dɑːrleːən] *n* (-s/-) loan.

Darm [darm] *m* (-[e]s/℥e) gut, *anat.* intestine; (sausage-)skin; *Därme pl.* intestines *pl.,* bowels *pl.*

'darstell|en *v/t. (sep., -ge-, h)* represent; show; depict; delineate; describe; *actor:* interpret *(character, part),* represent *(character); graphic arts:* graph, plot *(curve, etc.);* '℥**er** *thea. m* (-s/-) interpreter *(of a part);* actor; '℥**ung** *f* representation; *thea.* performance.

'dartun *v/t. (irr. tun, sep., -ge-, h)* prove; demonstrate; set forth.

darüber *adv.* [da'ryːbər, *when emphatic:* 'dɑːryːbər] over it *or* that; across it; in the meantime; ~ *werden Jahre vergehen* it will take years; *wir sind* ~ *hinweg* we got over it; *ein Buch* ~ *schreiben* write a book about it.

darum [da'rum, *when emphatic:* 'dɑːrum] **1.** *adv.* around it *or* that; *er kümmert sich nicht* ~ he does not care; *es handelt sich* ~ *zu inf.* the point is to *inf.;* **2.** *cj.* therefore, for that reason; ~ *ist er nicht gekommen* that's (the reason) why he hasn't come.

darunter *adv.* [da'runtər, *when emphatic:* 'dɑːruntər] under it *or* that; beneath it; among them; less; *zwei Jahre und* ~ two years and under; *was verstehst du* ~? what do you understand by it?

das [das] *s. der.*

dasein ['dɑː-] **1.** *v/i. (irr. sein, sep., -ge-, sein)* be there *or* present; exist; **2.** ℒ *n* (-s/*no pl.*) existence; life; being.

daß *cj.* [das] that; ~ *nicht* less; *es sei denn,* ~ unless; *ohne* ~ without *ger.; nicht* ~ *ich wüßte* not that I know of.

'dastehen *v/i. (irr. stehen, sep., -ge-, h)* stand (there).

Daten ['dɑːtən] *pl.* data *pl.* (a. ⊕), facts *pl.;* particulars *pl.;* '~**verarbeitung** *f* (-/-en) data processing.

datieren [da'tiːrən] *v/t. and v/i. (no -ge-, h)* date.   [(case).]

Dativ *gr.* ['dɑːtiːf] *m* (-s/-e) dative*/*

Dattel ['datəl] *f* (-/-n) date.

Datum ['dɑːtum] *n* (-s/Daten) date.

Dauer ['dauər] *f* (-/*no pl.*) length, duration; continuance; *auf die* ~ in the long run; *für die* ~ *von* for a period *or* term of; *von* ~ *sein* last well; '℥**haft** *adj.* peace, *etc.:* lasting; *material, etc.:* durable; *colour, dye:* fast; '~**karte** *f* season ticket, *Am.* commutation ticket; '~**lauf** *m* jog-trot; endurance-run; '℥**n** *v/i.* (ge-, h) continue, last; take *(time);* '~**welle** *f* permanent wave, F perm.

Daumen ['daumən] m (-s/-) thumb; j-m den ~ halten keep one's fingers crossed (for s.o.); '~abdruck m (-[e]s/-e) thumb-print.

Daune ['daunə] f (-/-n): ~(n pl.) down; '~ndecke f eiderdown (quilt).

davon adv. [da'fɔn, when emphatic: 'da:fɔn] of it or that; thereof; from it or that; off, away; was habe ich ~? what do I get from it?; das kommt ~! it serves you right!

da'von|kommen v/i. (irr. kommen, sep., -ge-, sein) escape, get off; ~laufen v/i. (irr. laufen, sep., -ge-, sein) run away.

davor adv. [da'fo:r, when emphatic: 'da:fo:r] space: before it or that, in front of it or that; er fürchtet sich ~ he is afraid of it.

dazu adv. [da'tsu:, when emphatic: 'da:tsu:] to it or that; for it or that; for that purpose; in addition to that; noch ~ at that; ~ gehört Zeit it requires time.

da'zu|gehörig adj. belonging to it; ~kommen v/i. (irr. kommen, sep., -ge-, sein) appear (on the scene); find time.

dazwischen adv. [da'tsvɪʃən] between (them), in between; ~kommen v/i. (irr. kommen, sep., -ge-, sein) thing: intervene, happen.

Debatt|e [de'batə] f (-/-n) debate; ℒieren [~'ti:rən] (no -ge-, h) 1. v/t. discuss; debate; 2. v/i. debate (über acc. on).

Debüt [de'by:] n (-s/-s) first appearance, début.

dechiffrieren [deʃi'fri:rən] v/t. (no -ge-, h) decipher, decode.

Deck ⚓ [dek] n (-[e]s/-s, ⚓-e) deck; '~adresse f cover (address); '~bett n feather bed.

Decke ['dekə] f (-/-n) cover(ing); blanket; (travel[l]ing) rug; ceiling; '~l m (-s/-) lid, cover (of box or pot, etc.); lid (of piano); (book-)cover; ℒn (ge-, h) 1. v/t. cover; den Tisch ~ lay the table; 2. v/i. paint: cover.

'Deck|mantel m cloak, mask, disguise; '~name m assumed name, pseudonym; '~ung f (-/-en) cover; security.

defekt [de'fekt] 1. adj. defective, faulty; 2. ℒ m (-[e]s/-e) defect, fault.

defin|ieren [defi'ni:rən] v/t. (no -ge-, h) define; ℒition [~i'tsjo:n] f (-/-en) definition; ~itiv [~i'ti:f] definite; definitive.

Defizit † ['de:fitsit] n (-s/-e) deficit, deficiency.

Degen ['de:gən] m (-s/-) sword; fencing: épée.

degradieren [degra'di:rən] v/t. (no -ge-, h) degrade, Am. a. demote.

dehn|bar adj. ['de:nba:r] extensible; elastic; metal: ductile; notion,

etc.: vague; '~en v/t. (ge-, h) extend; stretch; 'ℒung f (-/-en) extension; stretch(ing).

Deich [daɪç] m (-[e]s/-e) dike, dyke.

Deichsel ['daɪksəl] f (-/-n) pole, shaft.

dein poss. pron. [daɪn] your; der (die, das) ~e yours; ich bin ~ I am yours; die Deinen pl. your family; ~erseits adv. ['~ər'zaɪts] for or on your part; '~esgleichen pron. your like, your (own) kind, F the like(s) of you.

Dekan eccl. and univ. [de'ka:n] m (-s/-e) dean.

Deklam|ation [deklama'tsjo:n] f (-/-en) declamation; reciting; ℒieren [~'mi:rən] v/t. and v/i. (no -ge-, h) recite; declaim.

Deklin|ation gr. [deklina'tsjo:n] f (-/-en) declension; ℒieren gr. [~'ni:rən] v/t. (no -ge-, h) decline.

Dekor|ateur [dekora'tø:r] m (-s/-e) decorator; window-dresser; thea. scene-painter; ~ation [~'tsjo:n] f (-/-en) decoration; (window-)dressing; thea. scenery; ℒieren [~'ri:rən] v/t. (no -ge-, h) decorate; dress (window).

Dekret [de'kre:t] n (-[e]s/-e) decree.

delikat adj. [deli'ka:t] delicate (a. fig.); delicious; fig. ticklish; ℒesse [~a'tesə] f (-/-n) delicacy; dainty.

Delphin zo. [del'fi:n] m (-s/-e) dolphin.

Dement|i [de'menti] n (-s/-s) (formal) denial; ℒieren [~'ti:rən] v/t. (no -ge-, h) deny, give a (formal) denial of.

'dem|entsprechend adv., '~gemäß adv. correspondingly, accordingly; '~nach adv. therefore, hence; accordingly; '~nächst adv. soon, shortly, before long.

demobili'sier|en (no -ge-, h) 1. v/t. demobilize; disarm; 2. v/i. disarm; ℒung f (-/-en) demobilization.

Demokrat [demo'kra:t] m (-en/-en) democrat; ~ie [~a'ti:] f (-/-n) democracy; ℒisch adj. [~'kra:tiʃ] democratic.

demolieren [demo'li:rən] v/t. (no -ge-, h) demolish.

Demonstr|ation [demɔnstra'tsjo:n] f (-/-en) demonstration; ℒieren [~'stri:rən] v/t. and v/i. (no -ge-, h) demonstrate.

Demont|age [demɔn'ta:ʒə] f (-/-n) disassembly; dismantling; ℒieren [~'ti:rən] v/t. (no -ge-, h) disassemble; dismantle.

Demut ['de:mu:t] f (-/no pl.) humility, humbleness.

demütig adj. ['de:my:tiç] humble; ~en ['~gən] v/t. (ge-, h) humble, humiliate.

denk|bar ['deŋkba:r] 1. adj. conceivable; thinkable, imaginable; 2. adv.: ~ einfach most simple;

'**₂en** *(irr., ge-,* h*)* 1. *v/i.* think; ~ *an (acc.)* think of; remember; ~ *über (acc.)* think about; *j-m zu* ~ *geben* set s.o. thinking; 2. *v/t.* think; *sich et.* ~ imagine *or* fancy s.th.; *das habe ich mir gedacht* I thought as much; '₂mal *n* monument; memorial; '₂schrift *f* memorandum; memoir; '₂stein *m* memorial stone; '~würdig *adj.* memorable; '₂zettel *fig. m* lesson.

denn [dɛn] 1. *cj.* for; *mehr* ~ *je* more than ever; 2. *adv.* then; *es sei* ~, *daß* unless, except; *wieso* ~? how so.

dennoch *cj.* ['dɛnnɔx] yet, still, nevertheless; though.

Denunz|iant [denun'tsjant] *m* (-en/ -en) informer; ~**iation** [~'tsjoːn] *f* (-/-en) denunciation; ₂**ieren** [~'tsiː- rən] *v/t.* *(no -ge-,* h*)* inform against, denounce.

Depesche [de'pɛʃə] *f* (-/-n) dispatch; telegram, F wire; wireless.

deponieren [depo'niːrən] *v/t.* *(no -ge-,* h*)* deposit.

Depositen † [depo'ziːtən] *pl.* deposits *pl.*; ~**bank** *f* deposit bank.

der [deːr], **die** [diː], **das** [das] 1. *art.* the; 2. *dem. pron.* that, this; he, she, it; *die pl.* these, those, they, them; 3. *rel. pron.* who, which, that.

'**der'artig** *adj.* such, of such a kind of this *or* that kind.

derb *adj.* [dɛrp] *cloth:* coarse, rough; *shoes, etc.:* stout, strong; *ore, etc.:* massive; *p.:* sturdy; rough; *food:* coarse; *p., manners:* rough, coarse; *way of speaking:* blunt, unrefined; *joke:* crude; *humour:* broad.

der'gleichen *adj.* such, of that kind; *used as a noun:* the like, such a thing; *und* ~ and the like; *nichts* ~ nothing of the kind.

der- ['deːrjeːnigə], '**die-** ['diː- nigə] *dem. pron.* he *who,* she *who,* that *which;* diejenigen *pl.* those *who,* those *which.*

der- [deːr'zɛlbə], **die-,** '**das'selbe** *dem. pron.* the same; he, she, it.

Desert|eur [dezɛr'tøːr] *m* (-s/-e) deserter; ₂**ieren** [~'tiːrən] *v/i.* *(no -ge-,* sein*)* desert.

desgleichen [dɛs'glaiçən] 1. *dem. pron.* such a thing; 2. *cj.* likewise.

deshalb ['dɛshalp] 1. *cj.* for this *or* that reason; therefore; 2. *adv.:* *ich tat es nur* ~, *weil* I did it only because.

desinfizieren [dɛs?infi'tsiːrən] *v/t.* *(no -ge-,* h*)* disinfect.

Despot [dɛs'poːt] *m* (-en/-en) despot; ₂**isch** *adj.* despotic.

destillieren [dɛsti'liːrən] *v/t.* *(no -ge-,* h*)* distil.

desto *adv.* ['dɛsto] (all, so much) the; ~ *besser* all the better; ~ *erstaunter* (all) the more astonished.

deswegen *cj. and adv.* ['dɛs've:gən] *s. deshalb.*

Detail [de'tai] *n* (-s/-s) detail.

Detektiv [detɛk'tiːf] *m* (-s/-e) detective.

deuten ['dɔytən] *(ge-,* h*)* 1. *v/t.* interpret; read *(stars, dream, etc.);* 2. *v/i.:* ~ *auf (acc.)* point at.

'**deutlich** *adj.* clear, distinct, plain.

deutsch *adj.* [dɔytʃ] German; '₂e *m, f* (-n/-n) German.

'**Deutung** *f* (-/-en) interpretation, explanation.

Devise [de'viːzə] *f* (-/-n) motto; ~n *pl.* † foreign exchange *or* currency.

Dezember [de'tsɛmbər] *m* (-[s]/-) December.

dezent *adj.* [de'tsɛnt] *attire, etc.:* decent, modest; *literature, etc.:* decent; *behaviour:* decent, proper; *music, colour:* soft, restrained; *lighting, etc.:* subdued.

Dezernat [detsɛr'naːt] *n* (-[e]s/-e) (administrative) department.

dezimal *adj.* [detsi'maːl] decimal; ₂**bruch** *m* decimal fraction; ₂**stelle** *f* decimal place.

dezi'mieren *v/t.* *(no -ge-,* h*)* decimate; *fig. a.* reduce (drastically).

Diadem [dia'deːm] *n* (-s/-e) diadem.

Diagnose [dia'gnoːzə] *f* (-/-n) diagnosis.

diagonal *adj.* [diago'naːl] diagonal; ₂**e** *f* (-/-n) diagonal.

Dialekt [dia'lɛkt] *m* (-[e]s/-e) dialect; ₂**isch** *adj.* dialectal.

Dialog [dia'loːk] *m* (-[e]s/-e) dialogue, *Am. a.* dialog.

Diamant [dia'mant] *m* (-en/-en) diamond.

Diät [di'ɛːt] *f* (-/*no pl.*) diet; *diät leben* live on a diet;   [yourself.]

dich *pers. pron.* [diç] you; ~ *(selbst)]*

dicht [diçt] 1. *adj. fog, rain, etc.:* dense; *fog, forest, hair:* thick; *eyebrows:* bushy, thick; *crowd:* thick, dense; *shoe, etc.:* (water)tight; 2. *adv.:* ~ *an (dat.) or bei* close to.

'**dichten**[1] *v/t.* *(ge-,* h*)* make tight.

'**dicht|en**[2] *(ge-,* h*)* 1. *v/t.* compose, write; 2. *v/i.* compose *or* write poetry; '₂**er** *m* (-s/-) poet; author; ~**erisch** *adj.* poetic(al); '₂**kunst** *f* poetry.

'**Dichtung**[1] ⊕ *f* (-/-en) seal(ing).

'**Dichtung**[2] *f* (-/-en) poetry; fiction; poem, poetic work.

dick *adj.* [dik] *wall, material, etc.:* thick; *book:* thick, bulky; *p.* fat, stout; '₂**e** *f* (-/-n) thickness; bulkiness; *p.* fatness, stoutness; '~**fellig** *adj. p.* thick-skinned; '~**flüssig** *adj.* thick; viscid, viscous, syrupy; ₂**icht** ['~içt] *n* (-[e]s/-e) thicket; '₂**kopf** *m* stubborn person, F pig-headed person; ~**leibig** *adj.* ['~laibiç] corpulent; *fig.* bulky.

die [diː] *s. der.*

Dieb [diːp] *m* (-[e]s/-e) thief, *Am.* F *a.* crook; ~**erei** [diːbə'rai] *f* (-/-en) thieving, thievery.

Diebes|bande ['diːbəs-] *f* band of thieves; '**~gut** *n* stolen goods *pl.*

dieb|isch *adj.* ['diːbiʃ] thievish; *fig.* malicious; **2stahl** ['diːp-] *m* (-[e]s/ ~e) theft, 🏛 *mst* larceny.

Diele ['diːlə] *f* (-/-n) board, plank; hall, *Am. a.* hallway.

dienen ['diːnən] *v/i.* (ge-, h) serve (*j-m* s.o.; *als* as; *zu* for; *dazu, zu inf.* to *inf.*); *womit kann ich ~?* what can I do for you?

'**Diener** *m* (-s/-) (man-, domestic) servant; *fig.* bow (*vor dat.* to); '**~in** *f* (-/-nen) (woman-)servant, maid; '**~schaft** *f* (-/-en) servants *pl.*

'**dienlich** *adj.* useful, convenient; expedient, suitable.

Dienst [diːnst] *m* (-es/-e) service; duty; employment; ~ *haben* be on duty; *im (außer)* ~ on (off) duty.

Dienstag ['diːnstaːk] *m* (-[e]s/-e) Tuesday.

'**Dienst|alter** *n* seniority, length of service; '**2bar** *adj.* subject (*j-m* to s.o.); subservient (to); '**~bote** *m* domestic (servant), *Am.* help; '**2eifrig** *adj.* (over-)eager (in one's duty); '**2frei** *adj.* off duty; **~er Tag** day off; '**~herr** *m* master; employer; '**~leistung** *f* service; '**2lich** *adj.* official; '**~mädchen** *n* maid, *Am.* help; '**~mann** *m* (street-)porter; '**~stunden** *f/pl.* office hours *pl.*; '**2tauglich** *adj.* fit for service or duty; **2tuend** *adj.* ['~tuːənt] on duty; '**2untauglich** *adj.* unfit for service or duty; '**~weg** *m* official channels *pl.*; '**~wohnung** *f* official residence.

dies [diːs], **~er** ['diːzər], **~e** ['diːzə], **~es** ['diːzəs] *adj. and dem. pron.* this; *diese pl.* these; *dieser Tage* one of these days; *used as a noun:* this one; he, she, it; *diese pl.* they.

Dieselmotor ['diːzəl-] *m* Diesel engine.

dies|jährig *adj.* ['diːsjɛːriç] of this year, this year's; '**~mal** *adv.* this time; for (this) once; '**~seits** ['~zaits] 1. *adv.* on this side; 2. *prp.* (*gen.*) on this side of.

Dietrich ['diːtriç] *m* (-s/-e) skeleton key; picklock.

Differenz [difə'rɛnts] *f* (-/-en) difference; disagreement.

Diktat [dik'taːt] *n* (-[e]s/-e) dictation; *nach* ~ at or from dictation; **~or** [~ɔr] *m* (-s/-en) dictator; **2o-risch** *adj.* [~a'toːriʃ] dictatorial; **~ur** [~a'tuːr] *f* (-/-en) dictatorship.

dik'tieren *v/t. and v/i.* (no -ge-, h) dictate.

Dilettant [dile'tant] *m* (-en/-en) dilettante, dabbler; amateur.

Ding [diŋ] *n* (-[e]s/-e) thing; *guter* ~e in good spirits; *vor allen* ~en first of all, above all.

Diphtherie 🩺 [difte'riː] *f* (-/-n) diphtheria.

Diplom [di'ploːm] *n* (-[e]s/-e) diploma, certificate.

Diplomat [diplo'maːt] *m* (-en/-en) diplomat; diplomatist; **~ie** [~a'tiː] *f* (-/no *pl.*) diplomacy; **2isch** *adj.* [~'maːtiʃ] diplomatic (*a. fig.*).

dir *pers. pron.* [diːr] (to) you.

direkt [di'rɛkt] 1. *adj.* direct; **~er Wagen** 🚂 through carriage, *Am.* through car; 2. *adv.* direct(ly); **2ion** [~'tsjoːn] *f* (-/-en) direction; management; board of directors; **2or** [di'rɛktɔr] *m* (-s/-en) director; manager; headmaster, *Am.* principal; **2orin** [~'toːrin] *f* (-/-nen) headmistress, *Am.* principal; **2rice** [~'triːs(ə)] *f* (-/-n) directress; manageress.

Dirigent ♪ [diri'gɛnt] *m* (-en/-en) conductor; **2ieren** ♪ [~'giːrən] *v/t. and v/i.* (no -ge-, h) conduct.

Dirne ['dirnə] *f* (-/-n) prostitute.

Disharmon|ie ♪ [disharmo'niː] *f* (-/-n) disharmony, dissonance (*both a. fig.*); **2isch** *adj.* [~'moːniʃ] discordant, dissonant.

Diskont 🏛 [dis'kɔnt] *m* (-s/-e) discount; **2ieren** [~'tiːrən] *v/t.* (no -ge-, h) discount.

diskret *adj.* [dis'kreːt] discreet; **2ion** [~e'tsjoːn] *f* (-/no *pl.*) discretion.

Disku|ssion [disku'sjoːn] *f* (-/-en) discussion, debate; **2'tieren** (no -ge-, h) 1. *v/t.* discuss, debate; 2. *v/i.:* ~ *über* (*acc.*) have a discussion about, debate (up)on.

dispo|nieren [dispo'niːrən] *v/i.* (no -ge-, h) make arrangements; plan ahead; dispose (*über acc.* of); **2si-tion** [~zi'tsjoːn] *f* (-/-en) disposition; arrangement; disposal.

Distanz [di'stants] *f* (-/-en) distance (*a. fig.*); **2ieren** [~'tsiːrən] *v/refl.* (no -ge-, h): *sich* ~ *von* dis(as)sociate o.s. from.

Distel 🌿 ['distəl] *f* (-/-n) thistle.

Distrikt [di'strikt] *m* (-[e]s/-e) district; region; area.

Disziplin [distsi'pliːn] *f* (-/-en) discipline.

Divid|ende 🏛 [divi'dɛndə] *f* (-/-n) dividend; **2ieren** [~'diːrən] *v/t.* (no -ge-, h) divide (*durch* by).

Diwan ['diːvaːn] *m* (-s/-e) divan.

doch [dɔx] 1. *cj.* but, though; however, yet; 2. *adv. in answer to negative question:* yes; *bist du noch nicht fertig? — ~! aren't you ready yet? — yes, I am; also ~! I knew it!, I was right after all!; komm herein! do come in!; nicht ~! I don't!*

Docht [dɔxt] *m* (-[e]s/-e) wick.

Dock ⚓ [dɔk] *n* (-[e]s/-s) dock.

Dogge 🐕 ['dɔgə] *f* (-/-n) Great Dane.

Dohle *orn.* ['doːlə] *f* (-/-n) (jack)daw.

Doktor ['dɔktɔr] *m* (-s/-en) doctor.

Dokument [doku'mɛnt] *n* (-[e]s/-e)

document; ⚜ instrument; **~arfilm** [,'ta:r-] m documentary (film).

Dolch [dɔlç] m (-[e]s/-e) dagger; poniard; **'~stoß** m dagger-thrust.

Dollar ['dɔlar] m (-s/-s) dollar.

dolmetsch|en ['dɔlmɛtʃən] v/i. and v/t. (ge-, h) interpret; **'2er** m (-s/-) interpreter.

Dom [do:m] m (-[e]s/-e) cathedral.

Domäne [do'mɛ:nə] f (-/-n) domain (a. fig.); province.

Domino ['do:mino] (-s/-s) **1.** m domino; **2.** n (game of) dominoes pl.

Donner ['dɔnər] m (-s/-) thunder; **'2n** v/i. (ge-, h) thunder (a. fig.); **'~schlag** m thunderclap (a. fig.); **'~stag** m Thursday; **'~wetter** n thunderstorm; F fig. telling off; F: **~!** my word!, by Jove!; F zum **~!** F confound it!, sl. damn it.

Doppel ['dɔpəl] n (-s/-) duplicate; tennis, etc.: double, Am. doubles pl.; **'~bett** n double bed; **'~decker** m (-s/-) 🛩 biplane; double-decker (bus); **'~ehe** f bigamy; **~gänger** ['~gɛŋər] m (-s/-) double; **'~punkt** m colon; **'~sinn** m double meaning, ambiguity; **'2sinnig** adj. ambiguous, equivocal; **'~stecker** ⚡ m two-way adapter; **'2t 1.** adj. double; **2.** adv. doubly; twice; **'~zentner** m quintal; **2züngig** adj. ['~tsyŋiç] two-faced.

Dorf [dɔrf] n (-[e]s/=er) village; **'~bewohner** m villager.

Dorn [dɔrn] m **1.** (-[e]s/-en) thorn (a. fig.), prickle, spine; j-m ein ~ im Auge sein to be a thorn in s.o.'s flesh or side; **2.** (-[e]s/-e) tongue (of buckle); spike (of running-shoe, etc.); ⊕ punch; **'2ig** adj. thorny (a. fig.).

dörr|en ['dœrən] v/t. (ge-, h) dry; **'2fleisch** n dried meat; **'2gemüse** n dried vegetables pl.; **'2obst** n dried fruit.

Dorsch ichth. [dɔrʃ] m (-es/-e) cod(fish).

dort adv. [dɔrt] there; over there; **'~her** adv. from there; **'~hin** adv. there, to that place; **'~ig** adj. there, in or of that place.

Dose ['do:zə] f (-/-n) box; tin, Am. can; **~nöffner** ['do:zən-] m (-s/-) tin-opener, Am. can opener.

Dosis ['do:zis] f (-/Dosen) dose (a. fig.).

dotieren [do'ti:rən] v/t. (no -ge-, h) endow.

Dotter ['dɔtər] m, n (-s/-) yolk.

Dozent [do'tsɛnt] m (-en/-en) (university) lecturer, Am. assistant professor.

Drache ['draxə] m (-n/-n) dragon; **'~n** m (-s/-) kite; fig. termagant, shrew, battle-axe.

Dragoner [dra'go:nər] m (-s/-) ✗ dragoon (a. fig.).

Draht [dra:t] m (-[e]s/=e) wire; **'2en** v/t. (ge-, h) telegraph, wire; **'~geflecht** n (-[e]s/-e) wire netting; **'~hindernis** ✗ n wire entanglement; **'2ig** adj. p. wiry; **'2los** adj. wireless; **'~seilbahn** f funicular (railway); **'~stift** m wire tack; **'~zieher** F fig. m (-s/-) wire-puller.

drall adj. [dral] girl, legs, etc.: plump; woman: buxom.

Drama ['dra:ma] n (-s/Dramen) drama; **~tiker** [dra'ma:tikər] m (-s/-) dramatist; **2tisch** adj. [dra-'ma:tiʃ] dramatic.

dran F adv. [dran] s. daran; er ist gut (übel) ~ he's well (badly) off; ich bin ~ it's my turn.

Drang [draŋ] **1.** m (-[e]s/⸜e) pressure, rush; fig. urge; **2.** 2 pret. of dringen.

drängen ['drɛŋən] (ge-, h) **1.** v/t. press (a. fig.), push; fig. urge; creditor: dun; sich ~ crowd, throng; **2.** v/i. press, be pressing or urgent.

drangsalieren [dranza'li:rən] v/t. (no -ge-, h) harass, vex, plague.

drastisch adj. ['drastiʃ] drastic.

drauf F adv. [drauf] s. darauf; ~ und dran sein zu inf. be on the point of ger.; **2gänger** ['~gɛŋər] m (-s/-) dare-devil, Am. sl. a. go-getter.

draus F adv. [draus] s. daraus.

draußen adv. ['drausən] outside; out of doors; abroad; out at sea.

drechs|ein ['drɛksəln] v/t. (ge-, h) turn (wood, etc.); **2ler** ['~slər] m (-s/-) turner.

Dreck F [drɛk] m (-[e]s/no pl.) dirt; mud; filth (a. fig.); F fig. trash; F ~ am Stecken haben not to have a clean slate; F das geht dich einen ~ an that's none of your business; **'2ig** adj. dirty; filthy.

Dreh|bank ['dre:-] f (-/=e) (turning-)lathe; **'2bar** adj. revolving, rotating; **'~bleistift** m propelling pencil; **'~buch** n scenario; script; **'~bühne** thea. f revolving stage; **'2en** v/t. (ge-, h) turn; shoot (film); roll (cigarette); es dreht sich darum zu inf. it is a matter of ger.; sich ~ turn; **'~kreuz** n turnstile; **'~orgel** f barrel-organ; **'~punkt** m ⊕ centre of rotation, Am. center of rotation, pivot (a. fig.); **'~strom** ⚡ m three-phase current; **'~stuhl** m swivel-chair; **'~tür** f revolving door; **'~ung** f (-/-en) turn; rotation.

drei adj. [drai] three; **'~beinig** adj. three-legged; **'2eck** n triangle; **'~eckig** adj. triangular; **~erlei** adj. ['~ər'lai] of three kinds or sorts; **'~fach** adj. ['~fax] threefold, treble, triple; **'~farbig** adj. three-col-o(u)r(ed); **'2fuß** m tripod; **~jährig** adj. ['~jɛ:riç] three-year-old; triennial; **'~mal** adv. three times; **'~malig** adj. done or repeated three times; three; **2'meilenzone** ⚓, ⚜ f three-mile limit; **'2rad** n tricycle;

'**„seitig** adj. three-sided; trilateral; '**„silbig** adj. trisyllabic.
dreißig adj. ['draisiç] thirty; '**„ste** adj. thirtieth.
dreist adj. [draist] bold, audacious; cheeky, saucy; '**2igkeit** f (-/-en) boldness, audacity; cheek, sauciness.
'**drei|stimmig** ♩ adj. for or in three voices; **„tägig** adj. ['„tɛːgiç] three-day; '**„teilig** adj. in three parts, tripartite; '**„zehn(te)** adj. thirteen(th).
dresch|en ['drɛʃən] v/t. and v/i. (irr., ge-, h) thresh; thrash; '**2flegel** m flail; '**2maschine** f threshing-machine.
dressieren [drɛˈsiːrən] v/t. (no -ge-, h) train; break in (horse).
drillen ✂, ✈ ['drilən] v/t. (ge-, h) drill.
Drillinge ['driliŋə] m/pl. triplets pl.
drin F adv. [drin] s. darin.
dringen ['driŋən] v/i. (irr., ge-) **1.** (sein): ~ durch force one's way through s.th., penetrate or pierce s.th.; ~ aus break forth from s.th.; noise: come from; ~ in (acc.) penetrate into; in j-n ~ urge or press s.o.; an die Öffentlichkeit ~ get abroad; **2.** (h): ~ auf (acc.) insist on, press for; '**„d** adj. urgent, pressing; suspicion: strong.
'**dringlich** adj. urgent, pressing; '**2keit** f (/no pl.) urgency.
drinnen adv. ['drinən] inside; indoors.
dritt|e adj. ['dritə] third; '**2el** n (-s/-) third; '**„ens** adv. thirdly; '**„letzt** adj. last but two.
Drog|e f ['droːgə] f (-/-n) drug; **„erie** [droːgəˈriː] f (-/-n) chemist's (shop), Am. drugstore; **„ist** [droˈgist] m (-en/-en) (retail pharmaceutical) chemist.
drohen ['droːən] v/i. (ge-, h) threaten, menace.
Drohne ['droːnə] f (-/-n) zo. drone (a. fig.).
dröhnen ['drøːnən] v/i. (ge-, h) voice, etc.: resound; cannon, drum, etc.: roar; voice, cannon: boom.
Drohung ['droːuŋ] f (-/-en) threat, menace.
drollig adj. ['drɔliç] amusing, quaint, comical.
Dromedar zo. [droməˈdaːr] n (-s/-e) dromedary.
drosch [drɔʃ] pret. of dreschen.
Droschke ['drɔʃkə] f (-/-n) taxi (-cab), Am. a. cab, hack; '**„nkutscher** m cabman, driver, Am. a. hackman.
Drossel orn. ['drɔsəl] f (-/-n) thrush; '**2n** ⊕ v/t. (ge-, h) throttle.
drüben adv. ['dryːbən] over there, yonder.
drüber F adv. ['dryːbər] s. darüber.
Druck [druk] m **1.** (-[e]s/=e) pres-

sure; squeeze (of hand, etc.); **2.** typ. (-[e]s/-e) print(ing); '**„bogen** m printed sheet; '**„buchstabe** m block letter.
drucken ['drukən] v/t. (ge-, h) print; ~ lassen have s.th. printed, publish.
drücken ['drykən] (ge-, h) **1.** v/t. press; squeeze (hand, etc.); force down (prices, wages, etc.); lower (record); press, push (button, etc.). F sich ~ vor (dat.) or von shirk (work, etc.); **2.** v/i. shoe: pinch.
'**Drucker** m (-s/-) printer.
'**Drücker** m (-s/-) door-handle; trigger.
Drucker|ei [drukəˈrai] f (-/-en) printing office, Am. printery, print shop; '**„schwärze** f printer's or printing-ink.
'**Druck|fehler** m misprint; '**„fehlerverzeichnis** n errata pl.; '**2fertig** adj. ready for press; '**„kammer** f pressurized cabin; '**„knopf** m patent fastener, snap-fastener; ∮ push-button; '**„luft** f compressed air; '**„pumpe** f pressure pump; '**„sache(n** pl.) ✉ f printed matter, Am. a. second-class or third-class matter; '**„schrift** f block letters; publication; '**„taste** f press key.
drum F adv., cj. [drum] s. darum.
drunter F adv. ['druntər] s. darunter.
Drüse anat. ['dryːzə] f (-/-n) gland.
du pers. pron. [duː] you.
Dublette [duˈblɛtə] f (-/-n) duplicate.
ducken ['dukən] v/refl. (ge-, h) duck, crouch; fig. cringe (vor dat. to, before).
Dudelsack ♩ ['duːdəl-] m bagpipes pl.
Duell [duˈɛl] n (-s/-e) duel; **2ieren** [duˈɛˈliːrən] v/refl. (no -ge-, h) (fight a) duel (mit with).
Duett ♩ [duˈɛt] n (-[e]s/-e) duet.
Duft [duft] m (-[e]s/=e) scent, fragrance, perfume; '**2en** v/i. (ge-, h) smell, have a scent, be fragrant; '**2end** adj. fragrant; '**2ig** adj. dainty, fragrant.
duld|en ['duldən] (ge-, h) **1.** v/t. bear, stand, endure, suffer (pain, grief, etc.); tolerate, put up with; **2.** v/i. suffer; **„sam** adj. ['„t-] tolerant; '**2samkeit** f (/no pl.) tolerance; **2ung** ['„duŋ] f (-/⸓-en) toleration; sufferance.
dumm adj. [dum] stupid, dull, Am. F dumb; '**2heit** f (-/-en) stupidity, dullness; stupid or foolish action; '**2kopf** m fool, blockhead, Am. sl. a. dumbbell.
dumpf adj. [dumpf] smell, air, etc.: musty, fusty; atmosphere: stuffy, heavy; sound, sensation, etc.: dull; '**„ig** adj. cellar, etc.: damp, musty.
Düne ['dyːnə] f (-/-n) dune, sand-hill.

Dung [duŋ] *m* (-[e]s/*no pl.*) dung, manure.

düngen ['dyŋən] *v/t.* (ge-, h) dung, manure; fertilize; **'2r** *m* (-s/-) *s.* *Dung;* fertilizer.

dunkel ['duŋkəl] **1.** *adj.* dark; dim; *fig.* obscure; *idea, etc.:* dim, faint, vague; **2.** **2** *n* (-s/*no pl.*) *s.* *Dunkelheit.*

Dünkel ['dyŋkəl] *m* (-s/*no pl.*) conceit, arrogance; **'2haft** *adj.* conceited, arrogant.

'Dunkel|heit *f* (-/*no pl.*) darkness (*a. fig.*); *fig.* obscurity; **'~kammer** *phot. f* dark-room; **'2n** *v/i.* (ge-, h) grow dark, darken.

dünn *adj.* [dyn] *paper, material, voice, etc.:* thin; *hair, population, etc.:* thin, sparse; *liquid:* thin, watery; *air:* rare(fied).

Dunst [dunst] *m* (-es/*≈e) vapo(u)r; haze, mist; fume.

dünsten ['dynstən] (ge-, h) **1.** *v/t.* steam (*fish, etc.*); stew (*fruit, etc.*); **2.** *v/i.* steam.

'dunstig *adj.* vaporous; hazy.

Duplikat [dupli'ka:t] *n* (-[e]s/-e) duplicate.

Dur ♪ [du:r] *n* (-/-) major.

durch [durç] **1.** *prp.* (*acc.*) through; **2.** *adv.:* *die ganze Nacht* ~ all night long; ~ *und* ~ through and through; thoroughly.

durcharbeiten [durç²-] (*sep.*, -ge-, h) **1.** *v/t.* study thoroughly; *sich* ~ *durch* work through (*book, etc.*); **2.** *v/i.* work without a break.

durch'aus *adv.* through and through; thoroughly; by all means; absolutely; quite; ~ *nicht* not at all, by no means.

'durch|biegen *v/t.* (*irr.* biegen, *sep.*, -ge-, h) bend; deflect (*beam, etc.*); *sich* ~ *beam, etc.:* deflect, sag; **'~blättern** *v/t.* (*sep.*, -ge-, h) glance or skim through (*book, etc.*), *Am.* thumb through, skim; **'2blick** *m:* ~ *auf* (*acc.*) view through to, vista over, view of; **'~blicken** *v/i.* (*sep.*, -ge-, h) look through; ~ *lassen, daß* give to understand that.

durch'|bluten *v/t.* (*no* -ge-, h) supply with blood; **~'bohren** *v/t.* (*no* -ge-, h) pierce, perforate; *mit Blicken* ~ look daggers at *s.o.*

'durch|braten *v/t.* (*irr.* braten, *sep.*, -ge-, h) roast thoroughly; **~brechen** (*irr.* brechen) **1.** ['~'brɛçən] *v/t.* (*sep.*, -ge-, sein) break through or apart; **2.** [~'] *v/t.* (*sep.*, -ge-, h) break apart or in two; **3.** [~'brɛçən] *v/t.* (*no* -ge-, h) break through, breach; run (*blockade*); crash (*sound barrier*); **'~brennen** *v/i.* (*irr.* brennen, *sep.*, -ge-, sein) ⚡ *fuse:* blow; F *fig.* run away; *woman:* elope; **'~bringen** *v/t.* (*irr.* bringen, *sep.*, -ge-, h) bring or get through; dissipate, squander (*money*); **'2bruch** *m* ⚔ break-

through; rupture; breach; *fig.* ultimate success.

durch'denken *v/t.* (*irr.* denken, *no* -ge-, h) think *s.th.* over thoroughly.

'durch|drängen *v/refl.* (*sep.*, -ge-, h) force or push one's way through; **~dringen** (*irr.* dringen) **1.** ['~'drɪŋən] *v/i.* (*sep.*, -ge-, sein) penetrate (through); win acceptance (*mit* for) (*proposal*); **2.** [~'drɪŋən] *v/t.* (*no* -ge-, h) penetrate, pierce; *water, smell, etc.:* permeate.

durcheinander [durç²aı'nandər] **1.** *adv.* in confusion or disorder; pell-mell; **2.** **2** *n* (-s/-) muddle, mess, confusion; **~bringen** *v/t.* (*irr.* bringen, *sep.*, -ge-, h) confuse *s.o.*; *fig.* mix (*things*) up; **~werfen** *v/t.* (*irr.* werfen, *sep.*, -ge-, h) throw into disorder; *fig.* mix up.

durchfahr|en (*irr.* fahren) **1.** ['~'fa:rən] *v/i.* (*sep.*, -ge-, sein) pass or pass or drive through; **2.** [~'fa:rən] *v/t.* (*no* -ge-, h) go or pass or travel or drive through; traverse (*tract of country, etc.*); **'2t** *f* passage (through); gate(way); **~verboten!** no thoroughfare!

'Durchfall *m* ⚕ diarrh(o)ea; F *fig.* failure, *Am. a.* flunk; **2en** (*irr.* fallen) **1.** ['~falən] *v/i.* (*sep.*, -ge-, sein) fall through; fail, F get ploughed (*in examination*); *thea.* be a failure, *sl.* be a flop; ~ *lassen* reject, F plough; **2.** [~'falən] *v/t.* (*no* -ge-, h) fall or drop through (*space*).

'durch|fechten *v/t.* (*irr.* fechten, *sep.*, -ge-, h) fight or see *s.th.* through; **~finden** *v/refl.* (*irr.* finden, *sep.*, -ge-, h) find one's way (through).

durch'|flechten *v/t.* (*irr.* flechten, *no* -ge-, h) interweave, intertwine; **~forschen** *v/t.* (*no* -ge-, h) search through, investigate; explore (*region, etc.*).

'Durchfuhr ✝ *f* (-/-en) transit.

durchführ|bar *adj.* ['durçfy:rba:r] practicable, feasible, workable; **~en** *v/t.* (*sep.*, -ge-, h) lead or take through or across; *fig.* carry out or through; realize; **'2ungsbestimmung** *f* (implementing) regulation.

'Durchgang *m* passage; ✝ transit; *sports:* run; **'~sverkehr** *m* through traffic; ✝ transit traffic; **'~szoll** *m* transit duty.

'durchgebraten *adj.* well done.

'durchgehen (*irr.* gehen, *sep.*, -ge-) **1.** *v/i.* (sein) go or walk through; *bill:* pass, be carried; run away or off; abscond; *woman:* elope; *horse:* bolt; **2.** *v/i.* (sein) go through (*street, etc.*); **3.** *v/t.* (h, sein) go or look or read through (*work, book, etc.*); **'~d 1.** *adj.* continuous (*a.*); **~er** *Zug* through train; **2.** *adv.* generally; throughout.

durch'geistigt *adj.* spiritual.

'durch|greifen *v/i.* (*irr.* greifen,

sep., -ge-, *h*) put one's hand through; *fig.* take drastic measures or steps; '**greifend** *adj.* drastic; radical, sweeping; '**halten** (*irr. halten, sep.*, -ge-, *h*) 1. *v/t.* keep up (*pace, etc.*); 2. *v/i.* hold out; '**hauen** *v/t.* (*irr. hauen, sep.*, -ge-, *h*) cut *or* chop through; *fig.* give *s.o.* a good hiding; '**helfen** *v/i.* (*irr. helfen, sep.*, -ge-, *h*) help through (*a. fig.*); '**kämpfen** *v/t.* (*sep.*, -ge-, *h*) fight out; *sich* ~ fight one's way through; '**kneten** *v/t.* (*sep.*, -ge-, *h*) knead *or* work thoroughly; '**kommen** *v/i.* (*irr. kommen, sep.*, -ge-, *sein*) come *or* get *or* pass through; *sick person:* pull through; *in examination:* pass.

durch'**kreuzen** *v/t.* (*no* -ge-, *h*) cross, foil, thwart (*plan, etc.*). **Durch**|**laß** ['durçlas] *m* (*Durchlasses/Durchlässe*) passage; '**2lassen** *v/t.* (*irr. lassen, sep.*, -ge-, *h*) let pass, allow to pass, let through; *Wasser* ~ leak; '**2lässig** *adj.* pervious (to), permeable (to); leaky.

durch**laufen** (*irr. laufen*) 1. ['~lauf<ə>n] *v/i.* (*sep.*, -ge-, *sein*) run *or* pass through; 2. ['~] *v/t.* (*sep.*, -ge-, *h*) wear out (*shoes, etc.*); 3. [~'laufən] *v/t.* (*no* -ge-, *h*) pass through (*stages, departments, etc.*); *sports:* cover (*distance*).

durch'**leben** *v/t.* (*no* -ge-, *h*) go or live through.

'durch**lesen** *v/t.* (*irr. lesen, sep.*, -ge-, *h*) read through.

durch**leuchten** (*h*) 1. ['~lɔyçtən] *v/i.* (*sep.*, -ge-) shine through; 2. [~'lɔyçtən] *v/t.* (*no*-ge-) ⚕ X-ray; *fig.* investigate.

durch**löchern** [durç'lœçərn] *v/t.* (*no* -ge-, *h*) perforate, make holes into *s.th.*

'durch**machen** *v/t.* (*sep.*, -ge-, *h*) go through (*difficult times, etc.*); undergo (*suffering*).

'**Durchmarsch** *m* march(ing) through.

'**Durchmesser** *m* (*-s/-*) diameter.

durch'**nässen** *v/t.* (*no* -ge-, *h*) wet through, soak, drench.

'durch|**nehmen** *v/t.* (*irr. nehmen, sep.*, -ge-, *h*) go through *or* over (*subject*); '**pausen** *v/t.* (*sep.*, -ge-, *h*) trace, calk (*design, etc.*).

durch**queren** [durç'kve:rən] *v/t.* (*no* -ge-, *h*) cross, traverse.

'durch|**rechnen** *v/t.* (*sep.*, -ge-, *h*) (re)calculate, check; '**2reise** *f* journey *or* way through; '**reisen** 1. ['~raizən] *v/i.* (*sep.*, -ge-, *sein*) travel *or* pass through; 2. [~'raizən] *v/t.* (*no* -ge-, *h*) travel over *or* through *or* across; '**2reisende** *m, f* (*-n/-n*) person travel(l)ing through, *Am. a.* transient; ~ through passenger; '**reißen** (*irr. reißen, sep.*, -ge-) 1. *v/i.* (*sein*) tear, break; 2. *v/t.* (*h*) tear

6*

asunder, tear in two; ~**schauen** (*h*) 1. ['~ʃauən] *v/i.* and *v/t.* (*sep.*, -ge-) look through; 2. *fig.* [~'ʃauən] *v/t.* (*no* -ge-) see through.

'durch**scheinen** *v/i.* (*irr. scheinen, sep.*, -ge-, *h*) shine through; '~**d** *adj.* translucent; transparent.

'durch**scheuern** *v/t.* (*sep.*, -ge-, *h*) rub through; ~**schießen** (*irr. schießen*) 1. ['~ʃi:sən] *v/t.* (*sep.*, -ge-, *h*) shoot through; 2. ['~] *v/i.* (*sep.*, -ge-, *sein*) *water:* shoot *or* race through; 3. [~'ʃi:sən] *v/t.* (*no*-ge-, *h*) shoot *s.th.* through; *typ.:* space out (*lines*); interleave (*book*).

'**Durchschlag** *m* colander, strainer; carbon copy; **2en** (*irr. schlagen*) 1. ['~ʃla:gən] *v/t.* (*sep.*, -ge-, *h*) break *or* pass through; strain (*peas, etc.*); *sich* ~ get along, make one's way; 2. ['~] *v/i.* (*sep.*, -ge-, *h*) *typ.* come through; take *or* have effect; 3. [~'ʃla:gən] *v/t.* (*no* -ge-, *h*) pierce; *bullet:* penetrate; '**2end** *adj.* effective, telling; ~**papier** ['~k-] *n* copying paper.

durch**schneiden** *v/t.* (*irr. schneiden, h*) 1. ['~ʃnaidən] (*sep.*, -ge-) cut through; 2. [~'ʃnaidən] (*no* -ge-) cut through, cut in two.

'**Durchschnitt** *m* cutting through; ⊕ section, profile; ⊼ intersection; *fig.* average; *im* ~ on an average; '**2lich** 1. *adj.* average; normal; 2. *adv.* on an average; normally; ~**swert** *m* average value.

'durch|**sehen** (*irr. sehen, sep.*, -ge-, *h*) 1. *v/i.* see *or* look through; 2. *v/t.* see *or* look through *s.th.*; look *s.th.* over, go over *s.th.*; '**seihen** (*sep.*, -ge-, *h*) filter, strain; ~**setzen** *v/t.* (*h*) 1. ['~zetsən] (*sep.*, -ge-) put (*plan, etc.*) through; force through; *seinen Kopf* ~ have one's way; *sich* ~ *opinion, etc.:* gain acceptance; 2. [~'zetsən] (*no* -ge-) intersperse.

'**Durchsicht** *f* looking through *or* over; examination; correction; *typ.* reading; '**2ig** *adj.* glass, water, *etc.*: transparent; *fig.* clear, lucid; '**igkeit** *f* (*-/no pl.*) transparency; *fig.* clarity, lucidity.

'durch|**sickern** *v/i.* (*sep.*, -ge-, *sein*) seep *or* ooze through; *news, etc.:* leak out; ~**sieben** *v/t.* (*h*) 1. ['~zi:bən] (*sep.*, -ge-) sieve, sift; bolt (*flour*); 2. [~'zi:bən] (*no*-ge-) riddle (*with bullets*); '**sprechen** *v/t.* (*irr. sprechen, sep.*, -ge-, *h*) discuss, talk over; ~**stechen** *v/t.* (*irr. stechen, h*) 1. ['~ʃteçən] (*sep.*, -ge-) stick (*needle, etc.*) through *s.th.*; stick through *s.th.*; 2. [~'ʃteçən] (*no*-ge-) pierce; cut through (*dike, etc.*); '**stecken** *v/t.* (*sep.*, -ge-, *h*) pass *or* stick through.

'**Durchstich** *m* cut(ting).

durch'**stöbern** *v/t.* (*no* -ge-, *h*) ransack (*room, pockets, etc.*); rummage through (*drawers*, *papers*, *etc.*).

'durchstreichen v/t. (*irr. streichen*, *sep.*, *-ge-*, *h*) strike *or* cross out, cancel.

durch'streifen v/t. (*no -ge-*, *h*) roam *or* wander through *or* over *or* across.

durch'such|en v/t. (*no -ge-*, *h*) search (*a.* $\frac{r}{r}$); **2ung** f (*-/-en*) search.

durchtrieben adj. [durç'triːbən] cunning, artful; **2heit** f (*-/no pl.*) cunning, artfulness.

durch'wachen v/t. (*no -ge-*, *h*) pass (*the night*) waking.

durch'wachsen adj. bacon: streaky.

durchwandern 1. ['₂vandərn] v/i. (*sep.*, *-ge-*, *sein*) walk *or* pass through; 2. [₂'vandərn] v/t. (*no -ge-*, *h*) walk *or* pass through (*place*, *area*, *etc.*).

durch'weben v/t. (*no -ge-*, *h*) interweave; *fig.* a. intersperse.

durchweg adv. ['durçvɛk] throughout, without exception.

durch|weichen 1. ['₂vaiçən] v/i. (*sep.*, *-ge-*, *sein*) soak; 2. [₂'vaiçən] v/t. (*no -ge-*, *h*) soak, drench; '**₂winden** v/refl. (*irr. winden*, *sep.*, *-ge-*, *h*) worm *or* thread one's way through; **₂wühlen** (*h*) 1. *fig.* ['₂vyːlən] v/refl. (*sep.*, *-ge-*, *h*) work one's way through; 2. [₂'vyːlən] v/t. (*no -ge-*) rummage; '**₂zählen** v/t. (*sep.*, *-ge-*, *h*) count; **₂ziehen** (*irr. ziehen*) 1. ['₂tsiːən] v/i. (*sep.*, *-ge-*, *sein*) pass *or* go *or* come *or* march through; 2. ['₂] v/t. (*sep.*, *-ge-*, *h*) pull (*thread*, *etc.*) through; 3. [₂'tsiːən] v/t. (*no -ge-*, *h*) go *or* travel through; *scent*, *etc.*: fill, pervade (*room*, *etc.*).

durch'zucken v/t. (*no -ge-*, *h*) flash through.

'Durchzug m passage through; draught, *Am.* draft.

'durchzwängen v/refl. (*sep.*, *-ge-*, *h*) squeeze o.s. through.

dürfen ['dyrfən] (*irr.*, *h*) 1. v/i. (*ge-*): ich darf (nicht) I am (not) allowed to; 2. v/aux. (*no -ge-*): ich darf inf. I am permitted *or* allowed to inf.; I may inf.; du darfst nicht inf. you must not inf.; iro.: wenn ich bitten darf if you please.

durfte ['durftə] pret. of dürfen.

dürftig adj. ['dyrftiç] poor; scanty.

dürr adj. [dyr] wood, leaves, etc.: dry; land: barren, arid; p. gaunt, lean, skinny; '**2e** f (*-/-n*) dryness; barrenness; leanness.

Durst [durst] m (*-es/no pl.*) thirst (nach for); ₂ haben be thirsty.

dürsten ['dyrstən] v/i. (*ge-*, *h*): ₂ nach thirst for.

'durstig adj. thirsty (nach for).

Dusche ['duʃə] f (*-/-n*) shower (-bath); '**2n** v/refl. and v/i. (*ge-*, *h*) have a shower(-bath).

Düse ['dyːzə] f (*-/-n*) ⊕ nozzle; ✈ jet; **₂nantrieb** ['₂n⁹-] m jet propulsion; mit ₂ jet-propelled; '**₂nflugzeug** n jet(-propelled) aircraft, F jet; '**₂njäger** ✈ m jet fighter.

düster adj. ['dyːstər] dark, gloomy (*both a. fig.*); light: dim; fig.: sad; depressing; '**2heit** f (*-/no pl.*), '**2keit** f (*-/no pl.*) gloom(iness).

Dutzend ['dutsənt] n (*-s/-e*) dozen; ein ₂ Eier a dozen eggs; ₂e von Leuten dozens of people; '**2weise** adv. by the dozen, in dozens.

Dynam|ik [dy'naːmik] f (*-/no pl.*) dynamics; **2isch** adj. dynamic(al).

Dynamit [dyna'miːt] n (*-s/no pl.*) dynamite.

Dynamo [dy'naːmo] m (*-s/-s*), **₂maschine** f dynamo, generator.

D-Zug ['deːtsuːk] m express train.

E

Ebbe ['ɛbə] f (*-/-n*) ebb(-tide); low tide; '**2n** v/i. (*ge-*, *sein*) ebb.

eben ['eːbən] 1. adj. even; plain, level; ⅍ plane; zu ₂er Erde on the ground floor, *Am.* on the first floor; 2. adv. exactly; just; ₂ erst just now; '**2bild** n image, likeness; **₂bürtig** adj. ['₂byrtiç] of equal birth; j-m ₂ sein be a match for s.o., be s.o.'s equal; '**₂da** adv., '**₂daselbst** adv. at the very (same) place, just there; quoting books: ibidem (*abbr.* ib., ibid.); '**₂'der**, '**₂'die**, '**₂'das** dem. pron. = '**₂der'selbe**, '**₂die'selbe**, '**₂das'selbe** dem. pron. the very (same); '**₂**

des'wegen adv. for that very reason.

Ebene ['eːbənə] f (*-/-n*) plain; ⅍ plane; fig. level.

'eben|erdig adj. and adv. at street level; on the ground floor, *Am.* on the first floor; '**₂falls** adv. likewise; '**2holz** n ebony; '**₂maß** n symmetry; harmony; regularity (*of features*); '**₂mäßig** adj. symmetrical; harmonious; regular; '**₂so** adv. just so; just as ...; likewise; '**₂sosehr** adv., '**₂soviel** adv. just as much; '**₂sowenig** adv. just as little *or* few (*pl.*), no more.

Eber zo. ['e:bər] m (-s/-) boar; '~esche ♀ f mountain-ash.

ebnen ['e:bnən] v/t. (ge-, h) level; fig. smooth.

Echo ['ɛço] n (-s/-s) echo.

echt adj. [ɛçt] genuine; true; pure; real; colour: fast; document: authentic; '2heit f (-/no pl.) genuineness; purity; reality; fastness; authenticity.

Eck [ɛk] n (-[e]s/-e) s. Ecke; '~ball m sports: corner-kick; '~e f (-/-n) corner; edge; '2ig adj. angular; fig. awkward; '~platz m corner-seat; '~stein m corner-stone; '~zahn m canine tooth.

edel adj. ['e:dəl] noble; min. precious; organs of the body: vital; '~denkend adj. noble-minded; '2-mann m nobleman; '2mut m generosity; '~mütig adj. ['~my:tiç] noble-minded, generous; '2stein m precious stone; gem.

Edikt [e'dikt] n (-[e]s/-e) edict.

Efeu ♀ ['e:fɔy] m (-s/no pl.) ivy.

Effekt [ɛ'fɛkt] m (-[e]s/-e) effect; '~en pl. effects pl.; ✝: securities pl.; stocks pl.; '~enhandel m dealing in stocks; '~hascherei [~haʃə'raɪ] f (-/-en) claptrap; 2iv adj. [~'ti:v] effective; 2uieren [~u'i:rən] v/t. (no -ge-, h) effect; execute, Am. a. fill; '2voll adj. effective, striking.

egal adj. [e'ga:l] equal; F all the same.

Egge ['ɛgə] f (-/-n) harrow; '2n v/t. (ge-, h) harrow.

Egois|mus [ego'ismus] m (-/Egoismen) ego(t)ism; ~t m (-en/-en) ego-(t)ist; 2tisch adj. selfish, ego(t)istic(al).

ehe[1] cj. ['e:ə] before.

Ehe[2] [~]f(-/-n) marriage; matrimony; '~anbahnung f (-/-en) matrimonial agency; '~brecher m (-s/-) adulterer; '~brecherin f (-/-nen) adulteress; '2brecherisch adj. adulterous; '~bruch m adultery; '~frau f wife; '~gatte m, '~gattin f spouse; '~leute pl. married people pl.; '2lich adj. conjugal; child: legitimate; '~losigkeit f (-/no pl.) celibacy; single life.

ehemal|ig adj. ['e:əma:liç] former, ex-...; old; '~s adv. formerly.

'**Ehe|mann** m husband; '~paar n married couple.

'**eher** adv. sooner; rather; more likely; je ~, desto besser the sooner the better.

'**Ehering** m wedding ring.

ehern adj. ['e:ərn] brazen, of brass.

'**Ehe|scheidung** f divorce; '~schließung f (-/-en) (contraction of) marriage; '~stand m (-[e]s/no pl.) married state, matrimony; '~stifter m, '~stifterin f (-/-nen) matchmaker; '~vermittlung f s. Eheanbahnung; '~versprechen n promise of mar-

riage; '~vertrag m marriage contract.

Ehrabschneider ['e:r⁹apʃnaɪdər] m (-s/-) slanderer.

'**ehrbar** adj. hono(u)rable, respectable; modest; '2keit f (-/no pl.) respectability; modesty.

Ehre ['e:rə] f (-/-n) hono(u)r; zu ~n (gen.) in hono(u)r of; '2n v/t. (ge-, h) hono(u)r; esteem.

'**ehren|amtlich** adj. honorary; '2-bürger m honorary citizen; '2dok-tor m honorary doctor; '2erklä-rung f (full) apology; '2gast m guest of hono(u)r; '2gericht n court of hono(u)r; '~haft adj. hon-o(u)rable; '2kodex m code of hon-o(u)r; '2legion ['~legio:n] f (-/no pl.) Legion of Hono(u)r; '2mann m man of hono(u)r; '2mitglied n honorary member; '2platz m place of hono(u)r; '2recht n: bürgerliche ~e pl. civil rights pl.; '2rettung f rehabilitation; '~rührig adj. defamatory; '2sache f affair of hono(u)r; point of hono(u)r; '~voll adj. hon-o(u)rable; '~wert adj. hono(u)rable; '2wort n (-[e]s/-e) word of hono(u)r.

ehr|erbietig adj. ['e:r⁹ɛrbi:tiç] respectful; '2erbietung f (-/-en) reverence; '2furcht f (-/~-en) respect; awe; '~furchtgebietend adj. awe-inspiring, awesome; '~fürchtig adj. ['~fyrçtiç] respectful; '2gefühl n (-[e]s/no pl.) sense of hono(u)r; '2geiz m ambition; '~geizig adj. ambitious.

'**ehrlich** adj. honest; commerce, game: fair; opinion: candid; ~ während am längsten honesty is the best policy; '2keit f (-/no pl.) honesty; fairness.

'**ehrlos** adj. dishono(u)rable, infamous; '2igkeit f (-/no pl.) dishonesty, infamy.

'**ehr|sam** adj. s. ehrbar; '2ung f (-/-en) hono(u)r (conferred on s.o.); '~vergessen adj. dishono(u)rable, infamous; '2verlust ₤ₜ m (-es/no pl.) loss of civil rights; '~würdig adj. venerable, reverend.

ei[1] int. [aɪ] ah!, indeed!

Ei[2] [~] n (-[e]s/-er) egg; physiol. ovum.

Eibe ♀ ['aɪbə] f (-/-n) yew(-tree).

Eiche ♀ ['aɪçə] f (-/-n) oak(-tree); '~l ['~l] f (-/-n) ♀ acorn; cards: club; '~lhäher orn. ['~he:ər] m (-s/-) jay.

eichen[1] ['aɪçən] v/t. (ge-, h) ga(u)ge.

eichen[2] adj. [~] oaken, of oak.

Eich|hörnchen zo. ['aɪçhœrnçən] n (-s/-) squirrel; '~maß n standard.

Eid [aɪt] m (-es/-e) oath; '2brüchig adj.: ~ werden break one's oath.

Eidechse zo. ['aɪdɛksə] f (-/-n) lizard.

eidesstattlich ₤ₜ adj. ['aɪdəs-] in lieu of (an) oath; ~e Erklärung statutory declaration.

'eidlich 1. *adj.* sworn; 2. *adv.* on oath.

'Eidotter *m, n* yolk.

'Eier|kuchen *m* omelet(te), pancake; '⁓schale *f* egg-shell; '⁓stock *anat. m* ovary; '⁓uhr *f* egg-timer.

Eifer ['aɪfər] *m* (-s/*no pl.*) zeal; eagerness; ardo(u)r; '⁓er *m* (-s/-) zealot; '⁓sucht *f* (-/*no pl.*) jealousy; '2süchtig *adj.* jealous (auf *acc.* of).

eifrig *adj.* ['aɪfrɪç] zealous, eager; ardent.

eigen *adj.* ['aɪgən] own; particular; strange, odd; *in compounds:* ...⁓owned; peculiar (dat. to); '2art *f* peculiarity; '⁓artig *adj.* peculiar; singular; 2brötler ['⁓brø:tlər] *m* (-s/-) odd *or* eccentric person, crank; '2gewicht *n* dead weight; ⁓händig *adj. and adv.* ['⁓hendɪç] with one's own hands; '2heim *n* house of one's own; homestead; '2heit *f* (-/-en) peculiarity; oddity; *of language:* idiom; '2liebe *f* self-love; '2lob *n* self-praise; '⁓mächtig *adj.* arbitrary; '2name *m* proper name; ⁓nützig *adj.* ['⁓nytsɪç] self-interested, selfish; '⁓s *adv.* expressly, specially; on purpose.

'Eigenschaft *f* (-/-en) quality (of s.o.); property (of s.th.); in s-r ⁓ als in his capacity as; '⁓swort *gr. n* (-[e]s/⁓er) adjective.

'Eigensinn *m* (-[e]s/*no pl.*) obstinacy; '2ig *adj.* wil(l)ful, obstinate.

'eigentlich 1. *adj.* proper; actual; true, real; 2. *adv.* properly (speaking).

'Eigentum *n* (-s/⁓er) property.

Eigentüm|er ['aɪgənty:mər] *m* (-s/-) owner, proprietor; '2lich *adj.* peculiar; odd; '⁓lichkeit *f* (-/-en) peculiarity.

'Eigentums|recht *n* ownership; copyright; '⁓wohnung *f* freehold flat.

'eigenwillig *adj.* self-willed; *fig.* individual.

eign|en ['aɪgnən] *v/refl.* (ge-, h): sich ⁓ für be suited for; '2ung *f* (-/-en) aptitude, suitability.

'Eil|bote 2 *m* express messenger; durch ⁓n by special delivery; '⁓brief 2 *m* express letter, *Am.* special delivery letter.

Eile ['aɪlə] *f* (-/*no pl.*) haste, speed; hurry; '2n *v/i.* (ge-, sein) hasten, make haste; hurry; *letter, affair:* be urgent; 2nds *adv.* ['⁓ts] quickly, speedily.

'Eil|fracht *f*, '⁓gut *n* express goods *pl., Am.* fast freight; '2ig *adj.* hasty, speedy; urgent; es ⁓ haben be in a hurry.

Eimer ['aɪmər] *m* (-s/-) bucket, pail.

ein [aɪn] 1. *adj.* one; 2. *indef. art.* a, an.

einander *adv.* [aɪ'nandər] one another; each other.

ein|arbeiten ['aɪn⁓-] *v/t.* (sep., -ge-, h): j-n ⁓ in (acc.) make s.o. acquainted with; ⁓armig *adj.* ['aɪn⁓-] one-armed; ⁓äschern ['aɪn⁹eʃərn] *v/t.* (sep., -ge-, h) burn to ashes; cremate (dead body); '2äscherung *f* (-/-en) cremation; ⁓atmen ['aɪn⁹-] *v/t.* (sep., -ge-, h) breathe, inhale; ⁓äuglig *adj.* ['aɪn⁹ɔyglɪç] one-eyed.

'Einbahnstraße *f* one-way street.

'einbalsamieren *v/t.* (sep., no -ge-, h) embalm.

'Einband *m* (-[e]s/⁓e) binding; cover.

'ein|bauen *v/t.* (sep., -ge-, h) build in; install (engine, etc.); '⁓behalten *v/t.* (irr. halten, sep., no -ge-, h) detain; '⁓berufen *v/t.* (irr. rufen, sep., no -ge-, h) convene; ✗ call up, *Am.* induct.

'einbett|en *v/t.* (sep., -ge-, h) embed; '2zimmer *n* single(-bedded) room.

'einbild|en *v/refl.* (sep., -ge-, h) fancy, imagine; '2ung *f* imagination, fancy; conceit.

'einbinden *v/t.* (irr. binden, sep., -ge-, h) bind (books).

'Einblick *m* insight (in acc. into).

'einbrechen (irr. brechen, sep., -ge-) 1. *v/t.* (h) break open; 2. *v/i.* (sein) break in; of night, etc.: set in; ⁓ in (acc.) break into (house).

'Einbrecher *m* at night: burglar; by day: housebreaker.

'Einbruch *m* ✗ invasion; housebreaking, burglary; bei ⁓ der Nacht at nightfall; '⁓(s)diebstahl *m* house-breaking, burglary.

einbürger|n ['aɪnbyrgərn] *v/t.* (sep., -ge-, h) naturalize; '2ung *f* (-/-en) naturalization.

'Ein|buße *f* loss; '2büßen *v/t.* (sep., -ge-, h) lose, forfeit.

ein|dämmen ['aɪndɛmən] *v/t.* (sep., -ge-, h) dam (up); embank (river); *fig.* check; '⁓deutig *adj.* unequivocal; clear, plain.

'eindring|en *v/i.* (irr. dringen, sep., -ge-, sein) enter; penetrate; intrude; ⁓ in (acc.) penetrate (into); force one's way into; invade (country); '⁓lich *adj.* urgent; '2ling ['⁓lɪŋ] *m* (-s/-e) intruder; invader.

'Eindruck *m* (-[e]s/⁓e) impression.

'ein|drücken *v/t.* (sep., -ge-, h) press in; crush (in) (hat); break (pane); '⁓drucksvoll *adj.* impressive; ⁓engen ['aɪn⁹-] *v/t.* (sep., -ge-, h) narrow; *fig.* limit.

ein|er¹ ['aɪnər], '⁓e, '⁓(e)s *indef. pron.* one.

Einer² [⁓] *m* (-s/-) ✗ unit, digit; *rowing:* single sculler, skiff.

einerlei ['aɪnər'laɪ] 1. *adj.* of the same kind; immaterial; es ist mir ⁓ it is all the same to me; 2. 2 *n* (-s/*no pl.*) sameness; monotony; humdrum (of one's existence).

einerseits *adv.* ['aɪnər'zaɪts] on the one hand.

einfach *adj.* ['aɪnfax] simple; single; plain; *meal:* frugal; *ticket:* single, *Am.* one-way; **'2heit** *f* (-/*no pl.*) simplicity.

einfädeln ['aɪnfɛːdəln] *v/t.* (*sep.*, -ge-, *h*) thread; *fig.* start, set on foot; contrive.

'Einfahrt *f* entrance, entry.

'Einfall *m* ✕ invasion; idea, inspiration; **'2en** *v/i.* (*irr.* fallen, *sep.*, -ge-, sein) fall in, collapse; break in (*on a conversation*), interrupt, cut short; chime in; ♪ join in; invade; *j-m* ~ occur to s.o.

Ein|falt ['aɪnfalt] *f* (-/*no pl.*) simplicity; silliness; **2fältig** *adj.* ['~fɛltɪç] simple; silly; **'~faltspinsel** *m* simpleton, *Am.* F sucker.

'ein|farbig *adj.* one-colo(u)red, uni-colo(u)red; plain; **'~fassen** *v/t.* (*sep.*, -ge-, *h*) border; set (*precious stone*); **'2fassung** *f* border; setting; **'~fetten** *v/t.* (*sep.*, -ge-, *h*) grease; oil; **'~finden** *v/refl.* (*irr.* finden, *sep.*, -ge-, *h*) appear; arrive; **'~flechten** *fig. v/t.* (*irr.* flechten, *sep.*, -ge-, *h*) put in, insert; **'~fließen** *v/i.* (*irr.* fließen, *sep.*, -ge-, sein) flow in; ~ *in* (*acc.*) flow into; ~ *lassen* mention in passing; **'~flößen** *v/t.* (*sep.*, -ge-, *h*) infuse.

'Einfluß *m* influx; *fig.* influence; **'2reich** *adj.* influential.

ein|förmig *adj.* ['aɪnfœrmɪç] uniform; monotonous; **~frieden** ['~friːdən] *v/t.* (*sep.*, -ge-, *h*) fence, enclose; **'2friedung** *f* (-/-en) enclosure; **'~frieren** (*irr.* frieren, *sep.*, -ge-) 1. *v/i.* (sein) freeze (in); 2. *v/t.* (*h*) freeze (*food*); **'~fügen** *v/t.* (*sep.*, -ge-, *h*) put in; *fig.* insert; *sich* ~ fit in.

Einfuhr ✝ ['aɪnfuːr] *f* (-/-en) import(ation); **'~bestimmungen** *f/pl.* import regulations *pl.*

'einführen *v/t.* (*sep.*, -ge-, *h*) ✝ import; introduce (*s.o.*, *custom*); insert; initiate; install (*s.o. in an office*).

'Einfuhrwaren ✝ *f/pl.* imports *pl.*

'Eingabe *f* petition; application.

'Eingang *m* entrance; entry; arrival (*of goods*); *nach* ~ on receipt; **'~s-buch** ✝ *n* book of entries.

'eingeben *v/t.* (*irr.* geben, *sep.*, -ge-, *h*) give, administer (*medicine*) (*dat.* to); prompt, suggest (to).

'einge|bildet *adj.* imaginary; conceited (*auf acc.* of); **'~boren** *adj.* native; **'2borene** *m, f* (-*n*/-*n*) native.

Eingebung ['aɪngeːbʊŋ] *f* (-/-en) suggestion; inspiration.

einge|denk *adj.* ['aɪngədɛŋk] mindful (*gen.* of); **'~fallen** *adj.* eyes, cheeks: sunken, hollow; emaciated; **~fleischt** *fig. adj.* ['~gəflaɪʃt] in-veterate; confirmed; **~er** *Junggeselle* confirmed bachelor.

'eingehen (*irr.* gehen, *sep.*, -ge-) 1. *v/i.* (sein) *mail, goods:* come in, arrive; ♀, *animal:* die; cease (to exist); *material:* shrink; ~ *auf* (*acc.*) agree to; enter into; 2. *v/t.* (*h*, sein) enter into (*relationship*); contract (*marriage*); *ein Risiko* ~ run a risk, *esp. Am.* take a chance; ~ *in Vergleich* ~ come to terms; *Verbindlichkeiten* ~ incur liabilities; *e-e Wette* ~ make a bet; *eingegangene Gelder* *n/pl.* receipts *pl.*; **'~d** *adj.* detailed; thorough; *examination:* close.

Eingemachte ['aɪngəmaxtə] *n* (-*n*/ *no pl.*) preserves *pl.*; pickles *pl.*

'eingemeinden *v/t.* (*sep.*, *no* -ge-, *h*) incorporate (*dat.* into).

'einge|nommen *adj.* partial (*für* to); prejudiced (*gegen* against); *von sich* ~ conceited; **'2sandt** ⚲ *n* (-*s*/-*s*) letter to the editor; **~schnappt** F *fig. adj.* ['~gəʃnapt] offended, touchy; **'~sessen** *adj.* long-established; **'2ständnis** *n* confession, avowal; **'~stehen** *v/t.* (*irr.* stehen, *sep.*, *no* -ge-, *h*) confess, avow.

Eingeweide *anat.* ['aɪngəvaɪdə] *pl.* viscera *pl.*; intestines *pl.*; bowels *pl.*; *esp. of animals:* entrails *pl.*

'einge|wöhnen *v/refl.* (*sep.*, *no* -ge-, *h*) accustom o.s. (*in acc.* to); acclimatize o.s., *Am.* acclimate o.s. (to); get used (to).

eingewurzelt *adj.* ['~gəvʊrtsəlt] deep-rooted, inveterate.

'eingießen *v/t.* (*irr.* gießen, *sep.*, -ge-, *h*) pour in *or* out.

eingleisig *adj.* ['aɪnglaɪzɪç] single-track.

'ein|graben *v/t.* (*irr.* graben, *sep.*, -ge-, *h*) dig in; bury; engrave; *sich* ~ ✕ dig o.s. in, entrench o.s.; *fig.* engrave itself (*on one's memory*); **'~gravieren** *v/t.* (*sep.*, *no* -ge-, *h*) engrave.

'eingreifen 1. *v/i.* (*irr.* greifen, *sep.*, -ge-, *h*) intervene; ~ *in* (*acc.*) interfere with; encroach on (*s.o.'s rights*); *in die Debatte* ~ join in the debate; 2. ⚙ *n* (-*s*/*no pl.*) intervention.

'Eingriff *m* *fig.* encroachment; ⚕ operation.

'einhaken *v/t.* (*sep.*, -ge-, *h*) fasten; *sich bei j-m* ~ take s.o.'s arm.

'Einhalt *m* (-[e]*s*/*no pl.*): ~ *gebieten* (*dat.*) put a stop to; **'2en** *fig.* (*irr.* halten, *sep.*, -ge-, *h*) 1. *v/t.* observe, keep; 2. *v/i.* stop, leave off (*zu tun* doing).

'ein|hängen ([*irr.* hängen,] *sep.*, -ge-, *h*) 1. *v/t.* hang in; hang up, replace (*receiver*); *sich bei j-m* ~ take s.o.'s arm, link arms with s.o.; 2. *teleph. v/i.* hang up; **'~heften** *v/t.* (*sep.*, -ge-, *h*) sew *or* stitch in.

'einheimisch *adj.* native (*in dat.*

to), indigenous (to) (*a.* ♃); ♪ endemic; *product*: home-grown; '2e *m, f* (*-n/-n*) native; resident.

'**Einheit** *f* (*-/-en*) unity; oneness; ♃, *phys.*, ✕ unit; '2lich *adj.* uniform; '~spreis *m* standard price.

'**einheizen** (*sep.*, *-ge-*, *h*) **1.** *v/i.* make a fire; **2.** *v/t.* heat (*stove*).

einhellig *adj.* ['ainhɛliç] unanimous.

'**einholen** (*sep.*, *-ge-*, *h*) **1.** *v/t.* catch up with, overtake; make up for (*lost time*); make (*inquiries*); take (*order*); seek (*advice*); ask for (*permission*); buy; **2.** *v/i.*: ~ gehen go shopping.

'**Einhorn** *zo. n* unicorn.

'**einhüllen** *v/t.* (*sep.*, *-ge-*, *h*) wrap (up *or* in); envelop.

einig *adj.* ['ainiç] united; ~ *sein* agree; *nicht* ~ *sein* differ (*über acc.* about); ~e *indef. pron.* ['~gə] several; some; ~en ['~igən] *v/t.* (*ge-*, *h*) unite; *sich* ~ come to terms; ~er-maßen *adv.* ['~gər'ma:sən] in some measure; somewhat; ~es *indef. pron.* ['~gəs] some(thing); '2-keit *f* (*-/no pl.*) unity; concord; 2ung ['~g-] *f* (*-/-en*) union; agreement.

ein|impfen ['ain?-] *v/t.* (*sep.*, *-ge-*, *h*) ♪ inoculate (*a. fig.*); '~jagen *v/t.* (*sep.*, *-ge-*, *h*): *j-m Furcht* ~ scare s.o.

einjährig *adj.* ['ainjɛ:riç] one-year-old; *esp.* ♃ annual; *animal*: yearling.

'**ein|kalkulieren** *v/t.* (*sep.*, *no -ge-*, *h*) take into account, allow for; '~kassieren *v/t.* (*sep.*, *no -ge-*, *h*) cash; collect.

'**Einkauf** *m* purchase; *Einkäufe machen s.* einkaufen 2; '2en (*sep.*, *-ge-*, *h*) **1.** *v/t.* buy, purchase; **2.** *v/i.* make purchases, go shopping.

'**Einkäufer** *m* buyer.

'**Einkaufs|netz** *n* string bag; '~preis † *m* purchase price; '~tasche *f* shopping-bag.

'**ein|kehren** *v/i.* (*sep.*, *-ge-*, *sein*) put up *or* stop (*at an inn*); '~kerben *v/t.* (*sep.*, *-ge-*, *h*) notch; '~kerkern *v/t.* (*sep.*, *-ge-*, *h*) imprison; '~klagen *v/t.* (*sep.*, *-ge-*, *h*) sue for; '~klammern *v/t.* (*sep.*, *-ge-*, *h*) *typ.* bracket; put in brackets.

'**Einklang** *m* unison; harmony.

'**ein|kleiden** *v/t.* (*sep.*, *-ge-*, *h*) clothe; fit out; '~klemmen *v/t.* (*sep.*, *-ge-*, *h*) squeeze (in); jam; '~klinken (*sep.*, *-ge-*) **1.** *v/t.* (*h*) latch; **2.** *v/i.* (*sein*) latch; engage; '~knicken (*sep.*, *-ge-*) *v/t.* (*h*) *and v/i.* (*sein*) bend in, break; '~kochen (*sep.*, *-ge-*) **1.** *v/t.* (*h*) preserve; **2.** *v/i.* (*sein*) boil down *or* away.

'**Einkommen** *n* (*-s/-*) income, revenue; '~steuer *f* income-tax.

'**einkreisen** *v/t.* (*sep.*, *-ge-*, *h*) encircle.

Einkünfte ['ainkynftə] *pl.* income, revenue.

'**einlad|en** *v/t.* (*irr.* laden, *sep.*, *-ge-*, *h*) load (in) (*goods*); *fig.* invite; '2ung *f* invitation.

'**Einlage** *f* enclosure (*in letter*); † investment; deposit (*of money*); *gambling*: stake; inserted piece; ♪ arch-support; temporary filling (*of tooth*); '2rn † *v/t.* (*sep.*, *-ge-*, *h*) store (up).

Einlaß ['ainlas] *m* (*Einlasses/Einlässe*) admission, admittance.

'**einlassen** *v/t.* (*irr.* lassen, *sep.*, *-ge-*, *h*) let in, admit; ~ in (*acc.*) ♁ imbed in; *sich* ~ in *or auf* (*both acc.*) engage in, enter into.

'**ein|laufen** *v/i.* (*irr.* laufen, *sep.*, *-ge-*, *sein*) come in, arrive; *ship*: enter; *material*: shrink; '~leben *v/refl.* (*sep.*, *-ge-*, *h*) accustom o.s. (*in acc.* to).

'**einlege|n** *v/t.* (*sep.*, *-ge-*, *h*) lay *or* put in; insert; ⊕ inlay; deposit (*money*); pickle; preserve (*fruit*); *Berufung* ~ lodge an appeal (*bei* to); *Ehre* ~ mit gain hono(u)r *or* credit by; '2sohle *f* insole, sock.

'**einleit|en** *v/t.* (*sep.*, *-ge-*, *h*) start; introduce; '~end *adj.* introductory; '2ung *f* introduction.

'**ein|lenken** *fig.* *v/i.* (*sep.*, *-ge-*, *h*) come round; '~leuchten *v/i.* (*sep.*, *-ge-*, *h*) be evident *or* obvious; '~liefern *v/t.* (*sep.*, *-ge-*, *h*) deliver (up); *in ein Krankenhaus* ~ take to a hospital, *Am.* hospitalize; '~lösen *v/t.* (*sep.*, *-ge-*, *h*) ransom (*prisoner*); redeem (*pledge*); † hono(u)r (*bill*); cash (*cheque*); † meet (*bill*); '~machen *v/t.* (*sep.*, *-ge-*, *h*) preserve (*fruit*); tin, *Am.* can.

'**einmal** *adv.* once; one day; *auf* ~ all at once; *es war* ~ once (upon a time) there was; *nicht* ~ not even; '2eins *n* (*-/-*) multiplication table; '~ig *adj.* single; unique.

'**Einmarsch** *m* marching in, entry; '2ieren *v/i.* (*sep.*, *no -ge-*, *sein*) march in, enter.

'**ein|mengen** *v/refl.* (*sep.*, *-ge-*, *h*), '~mischen *v/refl.* (*sep.*, *-ge-*, *h*) meddle, interfere (*in acc.* with), *esp. Am. sl.* butt in.

'**Einmündung** *f* junction (*of roads*); mouth (*of river*).

einmütig *adj.* ['ainmy:tiç] unanimous; '2keit *f* (*-/no pl.*) unanimity.

Einnahme ['ainna:mə] *f* (*-/-n*) ✕ taking, capture; *mst* ~n *pl.* takings *pl.*, receipts *pl.*

'**einnehmen** *v/t.* (*irr.* nehmen, *sep.*, *-ge-*, *h*) take (*meal, position, ✕*); † take (*money*); † earn, make (*money*); take up, occupy (*room*); *fig.* captivate; '~d *adj.* taking, engaging, captivating.

'**einnicken** *v/i.* (*sep.*, *-ge-*, *sein*) doze *or* drop off.

Einöde ['aɪnˀ-] f desert, solitude.
ein|ordnen ['aɪnˀ-] v/t. (sep., -ge-, h) arrange in proper order; classify; file (letters, etc.); **'~packen** v/t. (sep., -ge-, h) pack up; wrap up; **'~pferchen** v/t. (sep., -ge-, h) pen in; fig. crowd, cram; **'~pflanzen** v/t. (sep., -ge-, h) plant; fig. implant; **'~pökeln** v/t. (sep., -ge-, h) pickle, salt; **'~prägen** v/t. (sep., -ge-, h) imprint; impress; sich ~ imprint itself; commit s.th. to one's memory; **'~quartieren** v/t. (sep., no -ge-, h) quarter, billet; **'~rahmen** v/t. (sep., -ge-, h) frame; **'~räumen** fig. v/t. (sep., -ge-, h) grant, concede; **'~rechnen** v/t. (sep., -ge-, h) comprise, include; **'~reden** (sep., -ge-, h) 1. v/t.: j-m ~ persuade or talk s.o. into (doing) s.th.; 2. v/i.: auf j-n ~ talk insistently to s.o.; **'~reichen** v/t. (sep., -ge-, h) hand in, send in, present; **'~reihen** v/t. (sep., -ge-, h) insert (unter acc. in); class (with); place (among); sich ~ take one's place.
einreihig adj. ['aɪnraɪç] jacket: single-breasted.
'Einreise f entry; **'~erlaubnis** f, **'~genehmigung** f entry permit.
'ein|reißen (irr. reißen, sep., -ge-) 1. v/t. (h) tear; pull down (building); 2. v/i. (sein) tear; abuse, etc.: spread; **~renken** ['~rɛŋkən] v/t. (sep., -ge-, h) ✗ set; fig. set right.
'einricht|en v/t. (sep., -ge-, h) establish; equip; arrange; set up (shop); furnish (flat); es ~ manage; sich ~ establish o.s., settle down; economize; sich ~ auf (acc.) prepare for; **'~ung** f establishment; arrangement, esp. Am. setup; equipment; furniture; fittings pl. (of shop); institution.
'ein|rollen v/t. (sep., -ge-, h) roll up or in; sich ~ roll up; curl up; **'~rosten** v/i. (sep., -ge-, sein) rust; screw, etc.: rust in; **'~rücken** (sep., -ge-) 1. v/i. (sein) enter, march in; ✗ join the army; 2. v/t. (h) insert (advertisement in a paper); typ. indent (line, word, etc.); **'~rühren** v/t. (sep., -ge-, h) stir (in).
eins adj. [aɪns] one.
einsam adj. lonely, solitary; **'2keit** f (-/✗ -en) loneliness, solitude.
'einsammeln v/t. (sep., -ge-, h) gather; collect.
'Einsatz m inset; insertion (of piece of material); gambling: stake, pool; ♪ striking in, entry; employment; engagement (a. ✗); ✗ action, operation; unter ~ s-s Lebens at the risk of one's life.
'ein|saugen v/t. (sep., -ge-, h) suck in; fig. imbibe; **'~schalten** v/t. (sep., -ge-, h) insert; ⚡ switch or turn on; den ersten Gang ~ mot. go into first or bottom gear; sich ~

intervene; **'~schärfen** v/t. (sep., -ge-, h) inculcate (dat. upon); **'~schätzen** v/t. (sep., -ge-, h) assess, appraise, estimate (auf acc. at); value (a. fig.); **'~schenken** v/t. (sep., -ge-, h) pour in or out; **'~schicken** v/t. (sep., -ge-, h) send in; **'~schieben** v/t. (irr. schieben, sep., -ge-, h) insert; **'~schiffen** v/t. and v/refl. (sep., -ge-, h) embark; **'2schiffung** f (-/-en) embarkation; **'~schlafen** v/i. (irr. schlafen, sep., -ge-, sein) fall asleep; **~schläfern** ['~ʃlɛːfərn] v/t. (sep., -ge-, h) lull to sleep; ⚘ narcotize.
'Einschlag m striking (of lightning); impact (of missile); fig. touch; **'2en** (irr. schlagen, sep., -ge-, h) 1. v/t. drive in (nail); break (in); smash (in); wrap up; take (road); tuck in (hem, etc.); enter upon (career); 2. v/i. shake hands; lightning, missile: strike; fig. be a success; nicht ~ fail; (wie e-e Bombe) ~ cause a sensation; auf j-n ~ belabour s.o.
einschlägig adj. ['aɪnʃlɛːgɪç] relevant, pertinent.
'Einschlagpapier n wrapping-paper.
'ein|schleichen v/refl. (irr. schleichen, sep., -ge-, h) creep or sneak in; **'~schleppen** v/t. (sep., -ge-, h) ⚓ tow in; import (disease); **'~schleusen** fig. v/t. (sep., -ge-, h) channel or let in; **'~schließen** v/t. (irr. schließen, sep., -ge-, h) lock in or up; enclose; ✗ surround, encircle; fig. include; **'~schließlich** prp. (gen.) inclusive of; including, comprising; **'~schmeicheln** v/refl. (sep., -ge-, h) ingratiate o.s. (bei with); **'~schmeichelnd** adj. insinuating; **'~schmuggeln** v/t. (sep., -ge-, h) smuggle in; **'~schnappen** v/i. (sep., -ge-, sein) catch; fig. s. eingeschnappt; **'~schneidend** fig. adj. incisive, drastic.
'Einschnitt m cut, incision; notch.
'ein|schnüren v/t. (irr. schreien, sep., -ge-, h) lace (up); **~schränken** ['~ʃrɛŋkən] v/t. (sep., -ge-, h) restrict, confine; reduce (expenses); sich ~ economize; **'2schränkung** f (-/-en) restriction; reduction.
'Einschreibe|brief m registered letter; **'2n** v/t. (irr. schreiben, sep., -ge-, h) enter; book; enrol(l); ✗ enlist, enrol(l); ✆ register; ~ lassen have registered; sich ~ enter one's name.
'einschreiten 1. fig. v/i. (irr. schreiten, sep., -ge-, sein) step in, interpose, intervene; take action (gegen against); 2. 2 n (-s/no pl.) intervention.
'ein|schrumpfen v/i. (sep., -ge-, sein) shrink; **'~schüchtern** v/t. (sep., -ge-, h) intimidate; bully; **'2schüchterung** f (-/-en) intim-

idation; '~schulen v/t. (sep., -ge-, h) put to school.

'Einschuß m bullet-hole; ✝ invested capital.

'ein|segnen v/t. (sep., -ge-, h) consecrate; confirm (children); '2segnung f consecration; confirmation.

'einsehen 1. v/t. (irr. sehen, sep., -ge-, h) look into; fig.: see, comprehend; realize; 2. 2 n (-s/no pl.): ein ~ haben show consideration.

'einseifen v/t. (sep., -ge-, h) soap; lather (beard); F fig. humbug (s.o.).

einseitig adj. ['aınzaıtıç] one-sided; ✗, pol., ⚹ unilateral.

'einsend|en v/t. (irr. senden), sep., -ge-, h) send in; '2er m (-s/-) sender; contributor (to a paper).

'einsetz|en (sep., -ge-, h) 1. v/t. set or put in; stake (money); insert; institute; instal(l), appoint (s.o.); fig. use, employ; risk (one's life); sich ~ für stand up for; 2. v/i. fever, flood, weather: set in; ♪ strike in; '2ung f (-/-en) insertion; appointment, installation.

'Einsicht f (-/-en) inspection; fig. insight, understanding; judiciousness; '2ig adj. judicious; sensible.

'einsickern v/i. (sep., -ge-, sein) soak in; infiltrate.

'Einsiedler m hermit.

einsilbig adj. ['aınzılbıç] monosyllabic; fig. taciturn; '2keit f (-/no pl.) taciturnity.

'einsinken v/i. (irr. sinken, sep., -ge-, sein) sink (in).

Einspänn|er ['aınʃpɛnər] m (-s/-) one-horse carriage; '2ig adj. one-horse.

'ein|sparen v/t. (sep., -ge-, h) save, economize; '~sperren v/t. (sep., -ge-, h) imprison; lock up, confine; '~springen v/i. (irr. springen, sep., -ge-, sein) ⊕ catch; fig. step in, help out; für j-n ~ substitute for s.o.; '~spritzen v/t. (sep., -ge-, h) inject; '2spritzung f (-/-en) injection.

'Einspruch m objection, protest, veto; appeal; '~srecht n veto.

'einspurig adj. single-track.

einst adv. [aınst] once; one or some day.

'Einstand m entry; tennis: deuce.

'ein|stecken v/t. (sep., -ge-, h) put in; pocket; plug in; '~steigen v/i. (irr. steigen, sep., -ge-, sein) get in; ~! 🚂 take your seats!, Am. all aboard!

'einstell|en v/t. (sep., -ge-, h) put in; ✗ enrol(l), enlist, Am. muster in; engage, employ, Am. a. hire; give up; stop, cease, Am. a. quit (payment, etc.); adjust (mechanism) (auf acc. to); tune in (radio) (on), opt., focus (on) (a. fig.); die Arbeit ~ cease working; strike, Am. a. walk out; sich ~ appear; sich ~ auf (acc.) be

prepared for; adapt o.s. to; '2ung f ✗ enlistment; engagement; adjustment; focus; (mental) attitude, mentality.

'einstimm|en ♪ v/i. (sep., -ge-, h) join in; '~ig adj. unanimous; '2igkeit f (-/no pl.) unanimity.

einstöckig adj. ['aınʃtœkıç] one-storied.

'ein|streuen fig. v/t. (sep., -ge-, h) intersperse; '~studieren v/t. (sep., no -ge-, h) study; thea. rehearse; '~stürmen v/i. (sep., -ge-, sein): auf j-n ~ rush at s.o.; '2sturz m falling in, collapse; '~stürzen v/i. (sep., -ge-, sein) fall in, collapse.

einst|weilen adv. ['aınst'vaılən] for the present; in the meantime; '~weilig adj. temporary.

'ein|tauschen v/t. (sep., -ge-, h) exchange (gegen for); '~teilen v/t. (sep., -ge-, h) divide (in acc. into); classify; '~teilig adj. one-piece; '2teilung f division; classification.

eintönig adj. ['aıntø:nıç] monotonous; '2keit f (-/<sup> -en) monotony.

'Eintopf(gericht n) m hot-pot; stew.

'Eintracht f (-/no pl.) harmony, concord.

einträchtig adj. ['aıntrɛçtıç] harmonious.

'eintragen v/t. (irr. tragen, sep., -ge-, h) enter; register; bring in, yield (profit); sich ~ in (acc.) sign.

einträglich adj. ['aıntrɛ:klıç] profitable.

'Eintragung f (-/-en) entry; registration.

'ein|treffen v/i. (irr. treffen, sep., -ge-, sein) arrive; happen; come true; '~treiben v/t. (irr. treiben, sep., -ge-, h) drive in or home; collect (debts, taxes); '~treten (irr. treten, sep.,-ge-, h) 1. v/i. (sein) enter; occur, happen, take place; ~ für stand up for; ~ in (acc.) enter into (rights); enter upon (possession); enter (room); join (the army, etc.); 2. v/t. (h) kick in (door); sich et. ~ run s.th. into one's foot.

'Eintritt m entry, entrance; admittance; beginning, setting-in (of winter, etc.); ~ frei! admission free!; ~ verboten! no admittance!; '~sgeld n entrance or admission fee; sports: gate money; '~skarte f admission ticket.

'ein|trocknen v/i. (sep., -ge-, sein) dry (up); '~trüben v/refl. (sep., -ge-, h) become cloudy or overcast; '~üben ['aın°-] v/t. (sep., -ge-, h) practi|se, Am. -ce s.th.; train s.o.

einver|leiben ['aınfɛrlaıbən] v/t. ([sep.,] no -ge-, h) incorporate (dat. in); annex (to); F sich et. ~ eat or drink s.th.; '2nehmen n (-s/no pl.) agreement, understanding; in gutem ~ on friendly terms; '~standen *adj.*: ~ *sein* agree; 'Q̶**ständnis** *n* agreement.

'**Einwand** *m* (-[e]s/₌e) objection (*gegen* to).

'**Einwander|er** *m* immigrant; 'Q̶**n** *v/i.* (*sep.*, -ge-, *sein*) immigrate; '**~ung** *f* immigration.

'**einwandfrei** *adj.* unobjectionable; perfect; faultless; *alibi*: sound.

einwärts *adv.* ['aɪnvɛrts] inward(s).

'**Einwegflasche** *f* one-way bottle, non-return bottle.

'**einweih|en** *v/t.* (*sep.*, -ge-, *h*) *eccl.* consecrate; inaugurate; ~ *in* (*acc.*) initiate *s.o.* into; '**~ung** *f* (-/-en) consecration; inauguration; initiation.

'**einwend|en** *v/t.* ([*irr. wenden,*] *sep.*, -ge-, *h*) object; 'Q̶**ung** *f* objection.

'**einwerfen** (*irr. werfen, sep.*, -ge-, *h*) **1.** *v/t.* throw in (*a. fig.*); smash, break (*window-pane*); post, *Am.* mail (*letter*); interject (*remark*); **2.** *v/i.* football: throw in.

'**einwickel|n** *v/t.* (*sep.*, -ge-, *h*) wrap (up), envelop; 'Q̶**papier** *n* wrapping-paper.

einwillig|en ['aɪnvɪligən] *v/i.* (*sep.*, -ge-, *h*) consent, agree (*in acc.* to); 'Q̶**ung** *f* (-/-en) consent, agreement.

'**einwirk|en** *v/i.* (*sep.*, -ge-, *h*): ~ *auf* (*acc.*) act (up)on; influence; effect; 'Q̶**ung** *f* influence; effect.

Einwohner ['aɪnvoːnər] *m* (-s/-), '**~in** *f* (-/-nen) inhabitant, resident.

'**Einwurf** *m* throwing in; *football*: throw-in; *fig.* objection; slit (*for letters, etc.*); slot (*for coins*).

'**Einzahl** *gr.* (-/⅓-en) singular (number); 'Q̶**en** *v/t.* (*sep.*, -ge-, *h*) pay in; '**~ung** *f* payment; deposit (*at bank*).

einzäunen ['aɪntsɔynən] *v/t.* (*sep.*, -ge-, *h*) fence in.

Einzel ['aɪntsəl] *n* (-s/-) *tennis*: single, *Am.* singles *pl.*; **~gänger** ['**~**gɛnər] *m* (-s/-) outsider; F lone wolf; '**~handel** ✝ *m* retail trade; '**~händler** ✝ *m* retailer, retail dealer; '**~heit** *f* (-/-en) detail, item; **~en** *pl.* particulars *pl.*, details *pl.*; 'Q̶**n 1.** *adj.* single; particular; individual; separate; *of shoes, etc.*: odd; *im* **~en** in detail; **2.** *adv.*: ~ *angeben* or *aufführen* specify, *esp. Am.* itemize; '**~ne** *m* (-n/-n) the individual; '**~verkauf** *m* retail sale; '**~wesen** *n* individual.

'**einziehen** (*irr. ziehen, sep.*, -ge-) **1.** *v/t.* (*h*) draw in; *esp.* ⊕ retract; ✗ call up, *Am.* draft; induct; ⚖ seize, confiscate; make (*inquiries*) (*über acc.* on, about); **2.** *v/i.* (*sein*) enter; move in; *liquid*: soak in; ~ *in* (*acc.*) move into (*flat, etc.*).

einzig *adj.* ['aɪntsɪç] only; single; sole; unique; '**~artig** *adj.* unique, singular.

'**Einzug** *m* entry, entrance; moving in.

'**einzwängen** *v/t.* (*sep.*, -ge-, *h*) squeeze, jam.

Eis [aɪs] *n* (-es/*no pl.*) ice; ice-cream; '**~bahn** *f* skating-rink; '**~bär** *zo. m* polar bear; '**~bein** *n* pickled pork shank; '**~berg** *m* iceberg; '**~decke** *f* sheet of ice; '**~diele** *f* ice-cream parlo(u)r.

Eisen ['aɪzən] *n* (-s/-) iron.

'**Eisenbahn** *f* railway, *Am.* railroad; *mit der* ~ by rail, by train; '**~er** *m* (-s/-) railwayman; '**~fahrt** *f* railway journey; '**~knotenpunkt** *m* (railway) junction; '**~unglück** *n* railway accident; '**~wagen** *m* railway carriage, *Am.* railroad car; coach.

'**Eisen|blech** *n* sheet-iron; '**~erz** *n* iron-ore; '**~gießerei** *f* iron-foundry; 'Q̶**haltig** *adj.* ferruginous; '**~hütte** *f* ironworks *sg., pl.*; '**~waren** *f/pl.* ironmongery, *esp. Am.* hardware; '**~warenhändler** *m* ironmonger, *esp. Am.* hardware dealer.

eisern *adj.* ['aɪzərn] iron, of iron.

'**Eis|gang** *m* breaking up of the ice; ice-drift; Q̶**gekühlt** *adj.* ['**~**gəkyːlt] iced; 'Q̶**grau** *adj.* hoary; '**~hockey** *n* ice-hockey; Q̶**ig** *adj.* ['aɪzɪç] icy; 'Q̶**kalt** *adj.* icy (cold); '**~kunstlauf** *m* figure-skating; '**~lauf** *m*, '**~laufen** *n* (-s/*no pl.*) skating; skate; '**~läufer** *m* skater; '**~meer** *n* polar sea; '**~schnellauf** *m* speed-skating; '**~scholle** *f* ice-floe; '**~schrank** *m s. Kühlschrank*; '**~vogel** *orn. m* kingfisher; '**~zapfen** *m* icicle; '**~zeit** *f geol. f* ice-age.

eitel *adj.* ['aɪtəl] vain (*auf acc.* of); conceited; mere; 'Q̶**keit** *f* (-/-en) vanity.

Eiter ⚕ ['aɪtər] *m* (-s/*no pl.*) matter, pus; '**~beule** ⚕ *f* abscess; 'Q̶**ig** *adj.* purulent; 'Q̶**n** ⚕ *v/i.* (ge-, *h*) fester, suppurate; '**~ung** ⚕ *f* (-/-en) suppuration.

eitrig ⚕ *adj.* ['aɪtrɪç] purulent.

'**Eiweiß** *n* (-es/-e) white of egg; 🦴 albumen; Q̶**haltig** 🦴 *adj.* albuminous.

'**Eizelle** *f* egg-cell, ovum.

Ekel 1. ['eːkəl] *m* (-s/*no pl.*) disgust (*vor dat.* at), loathing; aversion; ⚕ nausea; **2.** F *n* (-s/-) nasty person; 'Q̶**erregend** *adj.* nauseating, sickening; 'Q̶**haft** *adj.*, Q̶**ig** *adj.* revolting; *fig.* disgusting; 'Q̶**n** *v/refl.* (ge-, *h*): *sich* ~ be nauseated (*vor dat.* at); *fig.* be or feel disgusted (at).

eklig *adj.* ['eːklɪç] *s. ekelhaft.*

elasti|sch *adj.* [e'lastɪʃ] elastic; Q̶**zität** [**~**tsi'tɛːt] *f* (-/*no pl.*) elasticity.

Elch *zo.* [ɛlç] *m* (-[e]s/-e) elk; moose.

Elefant *zo.* [ele'fant] *m* (-en/-en) elephant.

elegan|t adj. [ele'gant] elegant; smart; **2z** [..ts] f (-/no pl.) elegance.
elektrifizier|en [elektrifi'tsi:rən] v/t. (no -ge-, h) electrify; **2ung** f (-/-en) electrification.
Elektri|ker [e'lɛktrikər] m (-s/-) electrician; **2sch** adj. electric(al); **2sieren** [..'zi:rən] v/t. (no -ge-, h) electrify.
Elektrizität [elɛktritsi'tɛ:t] f (-/no pl.) electricity; **..sgesellschaft** f electricity supply company; **..s-werk** n (electric) power station, power-house, Am. power plant.
Elektrode [elɛk'tro:də] f (-/-n) electrode.
Elektro|gerät [e'lɛktro-] n electric appliance; **..lyse** [..'ly:zə] f (-/-n) electrolysis.
Elektron ⚡ [e'lɛktrɔn] n (-s/-en) electron; **..engehirn** [..'tro:nən-] n electronic brain; **..ik** [..'tro:nik] f (-/no pl.) electronics sg.
Elektro'technik f electrical engineering; **..er** m electrical engineer.
Element [ele'mɛnt] n (-[e]s/-e) element.
elementar adj. [elemɛn'ta:r] elementary; **2schule** elementary or primary school, Am. grade school.
Elend ['e:lɛnt] 1. n (-[e]s/no pl.) misery; need, distress; 2. ⚓ adj. miserable, wretched; needy, distressed; **'..sviertel** n slums pl.
elf¹ [ɛlf] 1. adj. eleven; 2. ⚓ f (-/-en) eleven (a. sports).
Elf² [..] m (-en/-en), **..e** ['ɛlfə] f (-/-n) elf, fairy.
'Elfenbein n (-[e]s/⚓-e) ivory; **'2ern** adj. ivory.
Elf'meter m football: penalty kick; **..marke** f penalty spot.
'elfte adj. eleventh.
Elite [e'li:tə] f (-/-n) élite.
'Ellbogen anat. m (-s/-) elbow.
Elle ['ɛlə] f (-/-n) yard; anat. ulna.
Elster orn. ['ɛlstər] f (-/-n) magpie.
elter|lich adj. ['ɛltərliç] parental; **'2n** pl. parents pl.; **..nlos** adj. parentless, orphaned; **'2nteil** m parent.   [(-/-n) enamel.]
Email [e'ma:j] n (-s/-s), **..le** [..ə] f)
Emanzipation [emantsipa'tsjo:n] f (-/-en) emancipation.
Embargo [ɛm'bargo] n (-s/-s) embargo.
Embolie ⚕ [ɛmbo'li:] f (-/-n) embolism.
Embryo biol. ['ɛmbryo] m (-s/-s, -nen) embryo.
Emigrant [emi'grant] m (-en/-en) emigrant.
empfahl [ɛm'pfa:l] pret. of empfehlen.
Empfang [ɛm'pfaŋ] m (-[e]s/⚓e) reception (a. radio); receipt (of s.th.); nach or bei ~ on receipt; **'2en** v/t. (irr. fangen, no -ge-, h) receive; welcome; conceive (child).

Empfänger [ɛm'pfɛŋər] m (-s/-) receiver, recipient; payee (of money); addressee (of letter); ✝ consignee (of goods).
em'pfänglich adj. susceptible (für to); **2keit** f (-/no pl.) susceptibility.
Em'pfangs|dame f receptionist; **..gerät** n receiver, receiving set; **..schein** m receipt; **..zimmer** n reception-room.
empfehl|en [ɛm'pfe:lən] v/t. (irr., no -ge-, h) recommend; commend; ~ Sie mich (dat.) please remember me to; **..enswert** adj. (re)commendable; **2ung** f (-/-en) recommendation; compliments pl.
empfinden [ɛm'pfindən] v/t. (irr. finden, no -ge-, h) feel; perceive.
empfindlich adj. [ɛm'pfintliç] sensitive (a. phot., ⚗) (für, gegen to); pred. a. susceptible (gegen to); delicate; tender; p.: touchy, sensitive; cold: severe; pain, loss, etc.: grievous; pain: acute; **2keit** f (-/-en) sensitivity; sensibility; touchiness; delicacy.
empfindsam adj. [ɛm'pfintza:m] sensitive; sentimental; **2keit** f (-/-en) sensitiveness; sentimentality.
Empfindung [ɛm'pfindun] f (-/-en) perception; sensation; sentiment; **2slos** adj. insensible; esp. fig. unfeeling; **..svermögen** n faculty of perception.
empfohlen [ɛm'pfo:lən] p.p. of empfehlen.
empor adv. [ɛm'po:r] up, upwards.
empören [ɛm'pø:rən] v/t. (no -ge-, h) incense; shock; sich ~ revolt (a. fig.), rebel; grow furious (über acc. at); empört indignant, shocked (both: über acc. at).
em'por|kommen v/i. (irr. kommen, sep., -ge-, sein) rise (in the world); **2kömmling** [..kœmliŋ] m (-s/-e) upstart; **..ragen** v/i. (sep., -ge-, h) tower, rise; **..steigen** v/i. (irr. steigen, sep., -ge-, sein) rise, ascend.
Em'pörung f (-/-en) rebellion, revolt; indignation.
emsig adj. ['ɛmziç] busy, industrious, diligent; **2keit** f (-/no pl.) busyness, industry, diligence.
Ende ['ɛndə] n (-s/-n) end; am ~ at or in the end; after all; eventually; zu ~ gehen end; expire; run short; **'2n** v/i. (ge-, h) end; cease, finish.
end|gültig adj. ['ɛntgyltiç] final, definitive; **'..lich** adv. finally, at last; **..los** adj. ['..lo:s] endless; **'2punkt** m final point; **'2runde** f sports: final; **'2station** ⚓ f terminus, Am. terminal; **'2summe** f (sum) total.
Endung ling. ['ɛndun] f (-/-en) ending, termination.
Endzweck ['ɛnt-] m ultimate object.

Energie [enɛr'gi:] *f* (-/-n) energy;
Ωlos *adj.* lacking (in) energy.
e'nergisch *adj.* vigorous; energetic.
eng *adj.* [ɛŋ] narrow; *clothes*: tight;
close; intimate; *im ˷eren Sinne*
strictly speaking.
engagieren [ãga'ʒi:rən] *v/t.* (*no*
-ge-, h) engage, *Am. a.* hire.
Enge ['ɛŋə] *f* (-/-n) narrowness; *fig.*
straits *pl.*
Engel ['ɛŋəl] *m* (-s/-) angel.
'engherzig *adj.* ungenerous, petty.
Engländer ['ɛŋlɛndər] *m* (-s/-)
Englishman; *die ˷ pl.* the English
pl.; '˷**in** *f* (-/-nen) Englishwoman.
englisch *adj.* ['ɛŋliʃ] English;
British.
'Engpaß *m* defile, narrow pass, *Am.*
a. notch; *fig.* bottle-neck.
en gros † *adv.* [ã'gro:] wholesale.
En'groshandel † *m* wholesale
trade.
'engstirnig *adj.* narrow-minded.
Enkel ['ɛŋkəl] *m* (-s/-) grandchild;
grandson; ˷**in** *f* (-/-nen) grand-
daughter.
enorm *adj.* [e'nɔrm] enormous; F
fig. tremendous.
Ensemble *thea.*, ♩ [ã'sã:bəl] *n*
(-s/-s) ensemble; company.
entart|en [ɛnt'a:rtən] *v/i.* (*no -ge-,*
sein) degenerate; **Ωung** *f* (-/-en)
degeneration.
entbehr|en [ɛnt'be:rən] *v/t.* (*no*
-ge-, h) lack; miss, want; do without; ˷**lich** *adj.* dispensable; superfluous; **Ωung** *f* (-/-en) want, privation.
ent'bind|en (*irr. binden, no -ge-, h*)
1. *v/t.* dispense, release (*von* from);
deliver (*of a child*); **2.** *v/i.* be confined; **Ωung** *f* dispensation, release;
delivery; **Ωungsheim** *n* maternity
hospital.
ent'blöß|en *v/t.* (*no -ge-, h*) bare,
strip; uncover (*head*); ˷**t** *adj.* bare.
ent'deck|en *v/t.* (*no -ge-, h*) dis-
cover; detect; disclose; ˷**er** *m* (-s/-)
discoverer; **Ωung** *f* discovery.
Ente ['ɛntə] *f* (-/-n) *orn.* duck; *false*
report: F canard, hoax.
ent'ehr|en *v/t.* (*no -ge-, h*) dis-
hono(u)r; **Ωung** *f* degradation; rape.
ent'eign|en *v/t.* (*no -ge-, h*) ex-
propriate; dispossess; **Ωung** *f* ex-
propriation; dispossession.
ent'erben *v/t.* (*no -ge-, h*) disinherit.
entern ['ɛntərn] *v/t.* (*ge-, h*) board,
grapple (*ship*).
ent|'fachen *v/t.* (*no -ge-, h*) kindle;
fig. a. rouse (*passions*); ˷**'fallen** *v/i.*
(*irr. fallen, no -ge-, sein*): *j-m ˷*
escape s.o.; *fig.* slip s.o.'s memory;
auf j-n ˷ fall to s.o.'s share; *s. weg-*
fallen; ˷**'falten** *v/t.* (*no -ge-, h*)
unfold; *fig.*: develop; display; *sich ˷*
unfold; *fig.* develop (*zu* into).
ent'fern|en *v/t.* (*no -ge-, h*) remove;
sich ˷ withdraw; ˷**t** *adj.* distant,

remote (*both a. fig.*); **Ωung** *f* (-/-en)
removal; distance; range; **Ωungs-**
messer *phot. m* (-s/-) range-finder.
ent'flammen (*no -ge-*) *v/t.* (*h*) *and*
v/i. (*sein*) inflame; ˷**'fliehen** *v/i.*
(*irr. fliehen, no -ge-, sein*) flee,
escape (*aus or dat.* from); ˷**'frem-**
den *v/t.* (*no -ge-, h*) estrange,
alienate (*j-m* from s.o.).
ent'führ|en *v/t.* (*no -ge-, h*) abduct,
kidnap; run away with; **Ωer** *m*
abductor, kidnap(p)er; **Ωung** *f* ab-
duction, kidnap(p)ing.
ent'gegen 1. *prp.* (*dat.*) in opposition
to, contrary to; against; **2.** *adv.*
towards; ˷**gehen** *v/i.* (*irr. gehen,*
sep., -ge-, sein) go to meet; ˷**ge-**
setzt *adj.* opposite; *fig.* contrary;
˷**halten** *v/t.* (*irr. halten, sep., -ge-,*
h) hold out; *fig.* object; ˷**kommen**
v/i. (*irr. kommen, sep., -ge-, sein*)
come to meet; *fig.* meet s.o.('s
wishes) halfway; **Ωkommen** *n*
(-s/*no pl.*) obligingness; ˷**kommend**
adj. obliging; ˷**nehmen** *v/t.* (*irr.*
nehmen, sep., -ge-, h) accept,
receive; ˷**sehen** *v/i.* (*dat.*) (*irr.*
sehen, sep., -ge-, h) await; look forward to; ˷**setzen** *v/t.* (*sep., -ge-, h*)
oppose; ˷**stehen** *v/i.* (*irr. stehen,*
sep., -ge-, h) be opposed (*dat.* to);
˷**strecken** *v/t.* (*sep., -ge-, h*) hold
or stretch out (*dat.* to); ˷**treten** *v/i.*
(*dat.*) (*irr. treten, sep., -ge-, sein*)
step up to s.o.; oppose; face (*danger*).
entgegn|en [ɛnt'ge:gnən] *v/i.* (*no*
-ge-, h) reply; return; retort; **Ωung**
f (-/-en) reply; retort.
ent'gehen *v/i.* (*irr. gehen, no -ge-,*
sein) escape.
entgeistert *adj.* [ɛnt'gaistərt] a-
ghast, thunderstruck, flabbergasted.
Entgelt [ɛnt'gɛlt] *n* (-[e]s/*no pl.*)
recompense; **Ωen** *v/t.* (*irr. gelten,*
no -ge-, h) atone *or* suffer *or* pay for.
entgleis|en [ɛnt'glaizən] *v/i.* (*no*
-ge-, sein) run off the rails, be
derailed; *fig.* (make a) slip; **Ωung** *f*
(-/-en) derailment; *fig.* slip.
ent'gleiten *v/i.* (*irr. gleiten, no -ge-,*
sein) slip (*dat.* from).
ent'halt|en *v/t.* (*irr. halten, no*
-ge-, h) contain, hold, include;
sich ˷ (*gen.*) abstain *or* refrain from;
˷**sam** *adj.* abstinent; **Ωsamkeit** *f*
(-/*no pl.*) abstinence; **Ωung** *f*
abstention.
ent'haupten *v/t.* (*no -ge-, h*) behead,
decapitate.
ent'hüll|en *v/t.* (*no -ge-, h*) un-
cover; unveil; *fig.* reveal, disclose;
Ωung *f* (-/-en) uncovering; unveil-
ing; *fig.* revelation, disclosure.
Enthusias|mus [ɛntuzi'asmus] *m*
(-/*no pl.*) enthusiasm; ˷**t** *m* (-en/-en)
enthusiast; *film, sports*: F fan;
Ωtisch *adj.* enthusiastic.
ent'kleiden *v/t. and v/refl.* (*no -ge-,*
h) undress.

ent'kommen 1. v/i. (irr. kommen, no -ge-, sein) escape (j-m s.o.; aus from), get away or off; 2. 2 n (-s/no pl.) escape.

entkräft|en [ɛnt'krɛftən] v/t. (no -ge-, h) weaken, debilitate; fig. refute; 2ung f (-/-en) weakening; debility; fig. refutation.

ent'lad|en v/t. (irr. laden, no -ge-, h) unload; esp. ⚡ discharge; explode; sich ~ esp. ⚡ discharge; gun: go off; anger: vent itself; 2ung f unloading; esp. ⚡ discharge; explosion.

ent'lang 1. prp. (dat.; acc.) along; 2. adv. along; er geht die Straße ~ he goes along the street.

ent'larven v/t. (no -ge-, h) unmask; fig. a. expose.

ent'lass|en v/t. (irr. lassen, no -ge-, h) dismiss, discharge; F give s.o. the sack, Am. a. fire; 2ung f (-/-en) dismissal, discharge; 2ungsgesuch n resignation.

ent'last|en v/t. (no -ge-, h) unburden; ⚖ᵗᵍ exonerate, clear (from suspicion).

Ent'lastung f (-/-en) relief; discharge; exoneration; ~straße f by-pass (road); ~szeuge m witness for the defen|ce, Am. -se.

ent|'laufen v/i. (irr. laufen, no -ge-, sein) run away (dat. from); ~ledigen [~'le:digən] v/refl. (gen.) (no -ge-, h): rid o.s. of s.th., get rid of s.th.; acquit o.s. of (duty); execute (orders); ~'leeren v/t. (no -ge-, h) empty. [of-the-way.\

ent'legen adj. remote, distant, out-]

ent|'lehnen v/t. (no -ge-, h) borrow (dat. or aus from); ~'locken v/t. (no -ge-, h) draw, elicit (dat. from); ~'lohnen v/t. (no -ge-, h) pay (off); ~'lüften v/t. (no -ge-, h) ventilate; ~militarisieren [~militari'zi:rən] v/t. (no -ge-, h) demilitarize; ~mutigen [~'mu:tigən] v/t. (no -ge-, h) discourage; ~nehmen v/t. (irr. nehmen, no -ge- h) take (dat. from); ~ aus (with)draw from; fig. gather or learn from; ~'rätseln v/t. (no -ge-, h) unriddle; ~'reißen v/t. (irr. reißen, no -ge-, h) snatch away (dat. from); ~'richten v/t. (no -ge-, h) pay; ~'rinnen v/i. (irr. rinnen, no -ge-, sein) escape (dat. from); ~'rollen v/t. (no -ge-, h) unroll; ~'rücken v/t. (no -ge-, h) remove (dat. from), carry off or away; ~'rückt adj. entranced; lost in thought.

ent'rüst|en v/t. (no -ge-, h) fill with indignation; sich ~ become angry or indignant (über acc. at s.th., with s.o.); ~et adj. indignant (über acc. at s.th., with s.o.); 2ung f indignation.

ent'sag|en v/i. (no -ge-, h) renounce, resign; 2ung f (-/-en) renunciation, resignation.

ent'schädig|en v/t. (no -ge-, h) indemnify, compensate; 2ung f indemnification, indemnity; compensation.

ent'scheid|en (irr. scheiden, no -ge-, h) 1. v/t. decide; sich ~ question, etc.: be decided; p.: decide (für for; gegen against; über acc. on); come to a decision; 2. v/i. decide; ~end adj. decisive; crucial; 2ung f decision.

entschieden adj. [ɛnt'ʃi:dən] decided; determined, resolute; 2heit f (-/no pl.) determination.

ent'schließen v/refl. (irr. schließen, no -ge-, h) decide, determine, determine (zu on s.th.; zu inf. to inf.), make up one's mind (zu inf. to inf.).

ent'schlossen adj. resolute, determined; 2heit f (-/no pl.) resoluteness.

ent'schlüpfen v/i. (no -ge-, sein) escape, slip (dat. from).

Ent'schluß m resolution, resolve, decision, determination.

entschuldig|en [ɛnt'ʃuldigən] v/t. (no -ge-, h) excuse; sich ~ apologize (bei to; für for); sich ~ lassen beg to be excused; 2ung f (-/-en) excuse; apology; ich bitte (Sie) um ~ I beg your pardon.

ent'senden v/t. (irr. senden, no -ge-, h) send off, dispatch; delegate, depute.

ent'setz|en 1. v/t. (no -ge-, h) dismiss (from a position); ✗ relieve; frighten; sich ~ be terrified or shocked (über acc. at); 2. 2 n (-/no pl.) horror, fright; ~lich adj. horrible, dreadful, terrible, shocking.

ent'sinnen v/refl. (gen.) (irr. sinnen, no -ge-, h) remember or recall s.o., s.th.

ent'spann|en v/t. (no -ge-, h) relax; unbend; sich ~ relax; political situation: ease; 2ung f relaxation; pol. détente.

ent'sprech|en v/i. (irr. sprechen, no -ge-, h) answer (description, etc.); correspond to; meet (demand); ~end adj. corresponding; appropriate; 2ung f (-/-en) equivalent.

ent'springen v/i. (irr. springen, no -ge-, sein) escape (dat. from); river: rise, Am. head; s. entstehen.

ent'stammen v/i. (no -ge-, sein) be descended from; come from or of, originate from.

ent'steh|en v/i. (irr. stehen, no -ge-, sein) arise, originate (both: aus from); 2ung f (-/-en) origin.

ent'stell|en v/t. (no -ge-, h) disfigure; deface, deform; distort; 2ung f disfigurement; distortion, misrepresentation.

ent'täusch|en v/t. (no -ge-, h) disappoint; 2ung f disappointment.

ent'thronen v/t. (no -ge-, h) dethrone.

entvölker|n [ɛnt'fœlkərn] v/t. (no

-ge-, h) depopulate; **2ung** f (-/-en) depopulation.

ent'**wachsen** v/i. (irr. wachsen, no -ge-, sein) outgrow.

entwaffn|en [ent'vafnən] v/t. (no -ge-, h) disarm; **2ung** f (-/-en) disarmament.

ent'**warnen** v/i. (no -ge-, h) civil defence: sound the all-clear (signal).

ent'**wässer|n** v/t. (no -ge-, h) drain; **2ung** f (-/-en) drainage; ☌ dehydration.

ent'**weder** cj.: ~ ... oder either ... or.

ent|'**weichen** v/i. (irr. weichen, no -ge-, sein) escape (aus from); ~'**weihen** v/t. (no -ge-, h) desecrate, profane; ~'**wenden** v/t. (no -ge-, h) pilfer, purloin (j-m et. s.th. from s.o.); ~'**werfen** v/t. (irr. werfen, no -ge-, h) draft, draw up (document); design; sketch, trace out, outline; plan.

ent'**wert|en** v/t. (no -ge-, h) depreciate, devaluate; cancel (stamp); **2ung** f depreciation, devaluation; cancellation.

ent'**wickeln** v/t. (no -ge-, h) develop (a. phot.); evolve; sich ~ develop.

Entwicklung [ent'viklun] f (-/-en) development; evolution; ~**shilfe** f development aid.

ent|'**wirren** v/t. (no -ge-, h) disentangle, unravel; ~'**wischen** v/i. (no -ge-, sein) slip away, escape (j-m [from] s.o.; aus from); j-m ~ give s.o. the slip; ~**wöhnen** [~'vø:nən] v/t. (no -ge-, h) wean.

Ent'wurf m sketch; design; plan; draft.

ent|'**wurzeln** v/t. (no -ge-, h) uproot; ~'**ziehen** v/t. (irr. ziehen, no -ge-, h) deprive (j-m et. s.o. of s.th.); withdraw (dat. from); sich ~ avoid, elude; evade (responsibility); ~'**ziffern** v/t. (no -ge-, h) decipher, make out; tel. decode.

ent'**zücken** 1. v/t. (no -ge-, h) charm, delight; 2. **2** n (-s/no pl.) delight, rapture(s pl.), transport(s pl.).

ent'**zückend** adj. delightful; charming.

Ent'zug m (-[e]s/no pl.) withdrawal; cancellation (of licence); deprivation.

entzünd|bar adj. [ɛnt'tsʏntbaːr] (in)flammable; ~**en** v/t. (no -ge-, h) inflame (a. ☌), kindle; sich ~ catch fire; ☌ become inflamed; **2ung** ☌ f inflammation.

ent'**zwei** adv. asunder, in two, to pieces; ~**en** v/t. (no -ge-, h) disunite, set at variance; sich ~ quarrel, fall out (both: mit with); ~**gehen** v/i. (irr. gehen, sep., -ge-, sein) break, go to pieces; **2ung** f (-/-en) disunion.

Enzian ♀ ['ɛntsjaːn] m (-s/-e) gentian.

Enzyklopädie [ɛntsyklope'diː] f (-/-n) (en)cyclop(a)edia.

Epidemie ☌ [epide'miː] f (-/-n) epidemic (disease).

Epilog [epi'loːk] m (-s/-e) epilog(ue).

episch adj. ['eːpiʃ] epic.

Episode [epi'zoːdə] f (-/-n) episode.

Epoche [e'pɔxə] f (-/-n) epoch.

Epos ['eːpɔs] n (-/Epen) epic (poem).

er pers. pron. [eːr] he.

erachten [ɛr'-] 1.v/t. (no -ge-, h) consider, think, deem; 2. **2** n (-s/no pl.) opinion; m-s ~s in my opinion.

erbarmen [ɛr'barmən] 1. v/refl. (gen.) (no -ge-, h) pity or commiserate s.o.; 2. **2** n (-s/no pl.) pity, compassion, commiseration; mercy; ~**swert** adj. pitiable.

erbärmlich adj. [ɛr'bɛrmliç] pitiful, pitiable; miserable; behaviour: mean.

er'**barmungslos** adj. pitiless, merciless, relentless.

er'**bau|en** v/t. (no -ge-, h) build (up), construct, raise; fig. edify; **2er** m (-s/-) builder; constructor; ~**lich** adj. edifying; **2ung** fig. f (-/-en) edification, Am. uplift.

Erbe ['ɛrbə] 1. m (-n/-n) heir; 2. n (-s/no pl.) inheritance, heritage.

er'**beben** v/i. (no -ge-, sein) tremble, shake, quake.

'**erben** v/t. (ge-, h) inherit.

er'**beuten** v/t. (no -ge-, h) capture.

er'**bieten** v/refl. (irr. bieten, no -ge-, h) offer, volunteer.

'**Erbin** f (-/-nen) heiress.

er'**bitten** v/t. (irr. bitten, no -ge-, h) beg or ask for, request, solicit.

er'**bitter|n** v/t. (no -ge-, h) embitter, exasperate; **2ung** f (-/~ -en) bitterness, exasperation.

Erbkrankheit ☌ ['ɛrp-] f hereditary disease.

erblassen [ɛr'blasən] v/i. (no -ge-, sein) grow or turn pale, lose colo(u)r.

Erblasser ⚖ ['ɛrplasər] m (-s/-) testator; '~**in** f (-/-nen) testatrix.

er'**bleichen** v/i. (no -ge-, sein) s. erblassen.

erblich adj. ['ɛrpliç] hereditary; '**2keit** physiol. f (-/no pl.) heredity.

er'**blicken** v/t. (no -ge-, h) perceive, see; catch sight of.

erblind|en [ɛr'blindən] v/i. (no -ge-, sein) grow blind; **2ung** f (-/-en) loss of sight.

er'**brechen** 1. v/t. (irr. brechen, no -ge-, h) break or force open; vomit; sich ~ ☌ vomit; 2. **2** n (-s/no pl.) vomiting.

Erbschaft ['ɛrpʃaft] f (-/-en) inheritance, heritage.

Erbse ♀ ['ɛrpsə] f (-/-n) pea; '~**n-brei** m pease-pudding, Am. pea purée; '~**nsuppe** f pea-soup.

Erb|stück ['ɛrp-] n heirloom; '~**sünde** f original sin; '~**teil** n (portion of) an) inheritance.

Erd|arbeiter ['eːrt-] m digger, navvy; '∼ball m globe; '∼beben n (-s/-) earthquake; '∼beere ♀ ♀ strawberry; '∼boden m earth; ground, soil; ∼e ['eːrdə] f (-/♀ -n) earth; ground; soil; world; '♀en ♂ v/t. (ge-, h) earth, ground.

er'denklich adj. imaginable.

Erdgeschoß ['eːrt-] n ground-floor, Am. first floor.

er'dicht|en v/t. (no -ge-, h) invent, feign; ∼et adj. fictitious.

erdig adj. ['eːrdiç] earthy.

Erd|karte ['eːrt-] f map of the earth; '∼kreis m earth, world; '∼kugel f globe; '∼kunde f geography; '∼leitung ♂ ♀ earth-connexion, earth-wire, Am. ground wire; '∼nuß f peanut; '∼öl n mineral oil, petroleum.

er'dolchen v/t. (no -ge-, h) stab (with a dagger).

Erdreich ['eːrt-] n ground, earth.

er'dreisten v/refl. (no -ge-, h) dare, presume.

er'drosseln v/t. (no -ge-, h) strangle, throttle.

er'drücken v/t. (no -ge-, h) squeeze or crush to death; ∼d fig. adj. overwhelming.

Erd|rutsch ['eːrt-] m landslip; landslide (a. pol.); '∼schicht f layer of earth, stratum; '∼teil m part of the world; geogr. continent.

er'dulden v/t. (no -ge-, h) suffer, endure.

er'eifern v/refl. (no -ge-, h) get excited, fly into a passion.

er'eignen v/refl. (no -ge-, h) happen, come to pass, occur.

Ereignis [er'aiknis] n (-ses/-se) event, occurrence; ♀reich adj. eventful.

Eremit [ere'miːt] m (-en/-en) hermit, anchorite.

ererbt adj. [er'erpt] inherited.

er'fahr|en 1. v/t. (irr. fahren, no -ge-, h) learn; hear; experience; 2. adj. experienced, expert, skil(l)ful; ♀ung f (-/-en) experience; practice; skill.

er'fassen v/t. (no -ge-, h) grasp (a. fig.), seize, catch; cover; register, record.

er'find|en v/t. (irr. finden, no -ge-, h) invent; ♀er m inventor; ∼erisch adj. inventive; ♀ung f (-/-en) invention.

Erfolg [er'fɔlk] m (-[e]s/-e) success; result; ♀en [∼gən] v/i. (no -ge-, sein) ensue follow; happen; ♀los adj. [∼k-] unsuccessful; vain; ♀reich adj. [∼k-] successful.

er'forder|lich adj. necessary; required; ∼n v/t. (no -ge-, h) require, demand; ♀nis n (-ses/-se) requirement, demand, exigence, exigency.

er'forsch|en v/t. (no -ge-, h) inquire into, investigate; explore (country); ♀er m investigator; explorer; ♀ung f investigation; exploration.

er'freu|en v/t. (no -ge-, h) please; delight; gratify; rejoice; sich e-r Sache ∼ enjoy s.th.; ∼lich adj. delightful, pleasing, pleasant, gratifying.

er'frier|en v/i. (irr. frieren, no -ge-, sein) freeze to death; ♀ung f (-/-en) frost-bite.

er'frisch|en v/t. (no -ge-, h) refresh; ♀ung f (-/-en) refreshment.

erfroren adj. limb: frost-bitten.

er'füll|en v/t. (no -ge-, h) fill; fig. fulfil(l); perform (mission); comply with (s.o.'s wishes); meet (requirements); ♀ung f fulfil(l)ment; performance; compliance; ♀ungsort †, ♂♂ [er'fyluŋs⁹-] m place of performance (of contract).

ergänz|en [er'gɛntsən] v/t. (no -ge-, h) complete, complement; supplement; replenish (stores, etc.); ∼end adj. complementary, supplementary; ♀ung f (-/-en) completion; supplement; replenishment; gr. complement; ♀ungsband m (-[e]s/∼e) supplementary volume.

er'geben 1. v/t. (irr. geben, no -ge-, h) yield, give; prove; sich ∼ surrender; difficulties: arise; devote o.s. to s.th.; sich ∼ aus result from; sich ∼ in (acc.) resign o.s. to; 2. adj. devoted (dat. to); ∼st adv. respectfully; ♀heit f (-/no pl.) devotion.

Ergeb|nis [er'geːpnis] n (-ses/-se) result, outcome; sports: score; ∼ung [∼buŋ] f (-/-en) resignation; ✗ surrender.

er'gehen v/i. (irr. gehen, no -ge-, sein) be issued; ∼ lassen issue, publish; über sich ∼ lassen suffer, submit to; wie ist es ihm ergangen? how did he come off?; sich ∼ in (dat.) indulge in.

ergiebig adj. [er'giːbiç] productive, rich.

er'gießen v/refl. (irr. gießen, no -ge-, h) flow (in acc. into; über acc. over).

er'götz|en 1. v/t. (no -ge-, h) delight; sich ∼ an (dat.) delight in; 2. ♀ n (-s/no pl.) delight; ∼lich adj. delightful.

er'greif|en v/t. (irr. greifen, no -ge-, h) seize; grasp; take (possession, s.o.'s part, measures, etc.); take to (flight); take up (profession, pen, arms); fig. move, affect, touch; ♀ung f (-/♀ -en) seizure.

Er'griffenheit f (-/no pl.) emotion.

er'gründen v/t. (no -ge-, h) fathom; fig. penetrate, get to the bottom of.

Er'guß m outpouring; effusion.

er'haben adj. elevated; fig. exalted, sublime; ∼ sein über (acc.) be above; ♀heit f (-/♀ -en) elevation; fig. sublimity.

er'halt|en 1. v/t. (irr. halten, no -ge-, h) get; obtain; receive; preserve, keep; support, maintain; sich ~ von subsist on; 2. adj.: gut ~ in good repair or condition; 2ung f preservation; maintenance.
erhältlich adj. [ɛr'hɛltlɪç] obtainable.
er|'hängen v/t. (no -ge-, h) hang; ~'härten v/t. (no -ge-, h) harden; fig. confirm; ~'haschen v/t. (no -ge-, h) snatch, catch.
er'heb|en v/t. (irr. heben, no -ge-, h) lift, raise; elevate; exalt; levy, raise, collect (taxes, etc.); Klage ~ bring an action; sich ~ rise; question, etc.: arise; ~end fig. adj. elevating; ~lich adj. [~p-] considerable; 2ung [~buŋ] f (-/-en) elevation; levy (of taxes); revolt; rising ground.
er|'heitern v/t. (no -ge-, h) cheer up, amuse; ~'hellen v/t. (no -ge-, h) light up; fig. clear up; ~'hitzen v/t. (no -ge-, h) heat; sich ~ get or grow hot; ~'hoffen v/t. (no -ge-, h) hope for.
er'höh|en v/t. (no -ge-, h) raise; increase; 2ung f (-/-en) elevation; rise (in prices, wages); advance (in prices); increase.
er'hol|en v/refl. (no -ge-, h) recover; (take a) rest, relax; 2ung f (-/-en) recovery; recreation; relaxation; 2ungsurlaub [ɛr'ho:luŋs°-] m holiday, Am. vacation; recreation leave; ⚕ convalescent leave, sick-leave. [(request).\]
er'hören v/t. (no-ge-, h) hear; grant|
erinner|n [ɛr'ɪnɔrn] v/t. (no -ge-, h): j-n ~ an (acc.) remind s.o. of; sich ~ (gen.), sich ~ an (acc.) remember s.o. or s.th., recollect s.th.; 2ung f (-/-en) remembrance; recollection; reminder; ~en pl. reminiscences pl.
er'kalten v/i. (no -ge-, sein) cool down (a. fig.), get cold.
erkält|en [ɛr'kɛltən] v/refl. (no -ge-, h): sich (sehr) ~ catch (a bad) cold; 2ung f (-/-en) cold.
er'kennen v/t. (irr. kennen, no -ge-, h) recognize (an dat. by); perceive, discern; realize.
er'kenntlich adj. perceptible; sich ~ zeigen show one's appreciation; 2keit f (-/-en) gratitude; appreciation.
Er'kenntnis 1. f perception; realization; 2. ⚖ n (-ses/-se) decision, sentence, finding.
Erker ['ɛrkɔr] m (-s/-) bay; '~fenster n bay-window.
er'klär|en v/t. (no -ge-, h) explain; account for; declare, state; sich ~ declare (für for; gegen against); ~lich adj. explainable, explicable; ~t adj. professed, declared; 2ung f (-/-en) explanation; declaration.
er'klingen v/i. (irr. klingen, no -ge-, sein) (re)sound, ring (out).

erkoren adj. [ɛr'ko:rən] (s)elect, chosen.
er'krank|en v/i. (no -ge-, sein) fall ill, be taken ill (an dat. of, with); become affected; 2ung f (-/-en) illness, sickness, falling ill.
er|'kühnen v/refl. (no -ge-, h) venture, presume, make bold (zu inf. to inf.); ~'kunden v/t. (no -ge-, h) explore; ✕ reconnoit|re, Am. -er.
erkundig|en [ɛr'kundɪgən] v/refl. (no -ge-, h) inquire (über acc. after; nach after or for s.o.; about s.th.); 2ung f (-/-en) inquiry.
er|'lahmen fig. v/i. (no -ge-, sein) grow weary, tire; slacken; interest: wane, flag; ~'langen v/t. (no -ge-, h) obtain, get.
Er'laß [ɛr'las] m (Erlasses/Erlasse) dispensation, exemption; remission (of debt, penalty, etc.); edict, decree; 2'lassen v/t. (irr. lassen, no -ge-, h) remit (debt, penalty, etc.); dispense (j-m et. s.o. from s.th.); issue (decree); enact (law).
erlauben [ɛr'laubən] v/t. (no -ge-, h) allow, permit; sich et. ~ indulge in s.th.; sich ~ zu inf. ✝ beg to inf.
Erlaubnis [ɛr'laupnɪs] f (-/no pl.) permission; authority; ~schein m permit.
er'läuter|n v/t. (no -ge-, h) explain, illustrate; comment (up)on; 2ung f explanation, illustration; comment.
Erle ⚘ ['ɛrlə] f (-/-n) alder.
er'leb|en v/t. (no -ge-, h) (live to) see; experience; go through; 2nis [~pnɪs] n (-ses/-se) experience; adventure.
erledig|en [ɛr'le:dɪgən] v/t. (no -ge-, h) dispatch; execute; settle (matter); ~t adj. [~çt] finished, settled; fig.: played out; F done for; F: du bist für mich ~ I am through with you; 2ung [~guŋ] f (-/⚓ -en) dispatch; settlement.
er'leichter|n v/t. (no -ge-, h) lighten (burden); fig.: make easy, facilitate; relieve; 2ung f (-/-en) ease; relief; facilitation; ~en pl. facilities pl.
er|'leiden v/t. (irr. leiden, no -ge-, h) suffer, endure; sustain (damage, loss); ~'lernen v/t. (no -ge-, h) learn, acquire.
er'leucht|en v/t. (no -ge-, h) illuminate; fig. enlighten; 2ung f (-/-en) illumination; fig. enlightenment.
er'liegen v/i. (irr. liegen, no -ge-, sein) succumb (dat. to).
erlogen adj. [ɛr'lo:gən] false, untrue.
Erlös [ɛr'lø:s] m (-es/-e) proceeds pl.
erlosch [ɛr'lɔʃ] pret. of erlöschen; ~en 1. p.p. of erlöschen; 2. adj. extinct.
er'löschen v/i. (irr., no -ge-, sein) go out; fig. become extinct; contract: expire.
er'lös|en v/t. (no -ge-, h) redeem;

deliver; 2er *m* (-s/-) redeemer, de-
liverer; *eccl.* Redeemer, Saviour;
2ung *f* redemption; deliverance.
er**mächtig**|en [ɛr'mɛçtigən] *v/t.* (*no*
-ge-, *h*) authorize; 2ung *f* (-/-en)
authorization; authority; warrant.
er'**mahn**|en *v/t.* (*no* -ge-, *h*) ad-
monish; 2ung *f* admonition.
er'**mangel**|n *v/i.* (*no* -ge-, *h*) be
wanting (*gen.* in); 2ung *f* (-/*no pl.*):
in ~ (*gen.*) in default of, for want of,
failing.
er'**mäßig**|en *v/t.* (*no* -ge-, *h*) abate,
reduce, cut (down); 2ung *f* (-/-en)
abatement, reduction.
er'**matt**|en (*no* -ge-) 1. *v/t.* (*h*) fa-
tigue, tire, exhaust; 2. *v/i.* (*sein*)
tire, grow weary; *fig.* slacken; 2ung
f (-/-en) fatigue, exhaustion.
er'**messen** 1. *v/t.* (*irr.* messen, *no*
-ge-, *h*) judge; 2. 2 *n* (-s/*no pl.*)
judg(e)ment; discretion.
er'**mittel**|n *v/t.* (*no* -ge-, *h*) ascer-
tain, find out; ⅌ investigate; 2(e)-
lung [-(ə)luŋ] *f* (-/-en) ascertainment; inquiry; ⅌ investigation.
er'**möglichen** *v/t.* (*no* -ge-, *h*) render *or* make possible.
er'**mord**|en *v/t.* (*no* -ge-, *h*) murder;
assassinate; 2ung *f* (-/-en) murder;
assassination.
er'**müd**|en (*no* -ge-) 1. *v/t.* (*h*) tire,
fatigue; 2. *v/i.* (*sein*) tire, get tired
or fatigued; 2ung *f* (-/✗-en)
fatigue, tiredness.
er'**munter**|n *v/t.* (*no* -ge-, *h*) rouse,
encourage; animate; 2ung *f* (-/-en)
encouragement, animation.
er**mutig**|en [ɛr'muːtigən] *v/t.* (*no*
-ge-, *h*) encourage; 2ung *f* (-/-en)
encouragement.
er'**nähr**|en *v/t.* (*no* -ge-, *h*) nourish,
feed; support; 2er *m* (-s/-) bread-
winner, supporter; 2ung *f* (-/✗-en)
nourishment; support; *physiol.*
nutrition.
er'**nenn**|en *v/t.* (*irr.* nennen, *no* -ge-,
h) nominate, appoint; 2ung *f*
nomination, appointment.
er'**neu**|ern *v/t.* (*no* -ge-, *h*) renew,
renovate; revive; 2erung *f* renew-
al, renovation; revival; ✗t *adv.* once
more.
er**niedrig**|en [ɛr'niːdrigən] *v/t.* (*no*
-ge-, *h*) degrade; humiliate, humble;
2ung *f* (-/-en) degradation; humiliation.
Ernst [ɛrnst] 1. *m* (-es/*no pl.*)
seriousness; earnest(ness); gravity;
im ~ in earnest; 2. 2 *adj.* = '2**haft**
adj., '2**lich** *adj.* serious, earnest;
grave.
Ernte ['ɛrntə] *f* (-/-n) harvest; crop;
✗'**dankfest** *n* harvest festival; '2n
v/t. (ge-, *h*) harvest, gather (in),
reap (*a. fig.*).
er'**nüchter**|n *v/t.* (*no* -ge-, *h*) (make)
sober; *fig.* disillusion; 2ung *f* (-/-en)
sobering; *fig.* disillusionment.

Er'**ober**|er *m* (-s/-) conqueror; 2n
v/t. (*no* -ge-, *h*) conquer; ✗ung *f*
(-/-en) conquest.
er'**öffn**|en *v/t.* (*no* -ge-, *h*) open;
inaugurate; disclose (*j-m et.* s.th.
to s.o.); notify; 2ung *f* opening;
inauguration; disclosure.
er**örter**|n [ɛr'œrtərn] *v/t.* (*no* -ge-, *h*)
discuss; 2ung *f* (-/-en) discussion.
Erpel *orn.* ['ɛrpəl] *m* (-s/-) drake.
er**picht** *adj.* [ɛr'piçt]: ~ auf (*acc.*)
bent *or* intent *or* set *or* keen on.
er'**press**|en *v/t.* (*no* -ge-, *h*) extort
(*von* from); blackmail; 2er *m* (-s/-),
2erin *f* (-/-nen) extort(ion)er;
blackmailer; 2ung *f* (-/-en) ex-
tortion; blackmail.
er'**proben** *v/t.* (*no* -ge-, *h*) try, test.
er**quick**|en [ɛr'kvikən] *v/t.* (*no* -ge-,
h) refresh; 2ung *f* (-/-en) refreshment.
er|'**raten** *v/t.* (*irr.* raten, *no* -ge-, *h*)
guess, find out; ✗'**rechnen** *v/t.* (*no*
-ge-, *h*) calculate, compute, work
out.
er**reg**|**bar** *adj.* [ɛr'reːkbaːr] ex-
citable; ✗en [✗gən] *v/t.* (*no* -ge-, *h*)
excite; cause; 2er [✗gər] *m* (-s/-)
exciter (*a. ⚡*); ✗ germ, virus; 2ung
[✗guŋ] *f* excitation; excitement.
er'**reich**|**bar** *adj.* attainable; within
reach *or* call; ✗en *v/t.* (*no* -ge-, *h*)
reach; *fig.* achieve, attain; catch
(*train*); come up to (*certain standard*).
er'**rett**|en *v/t.* (*no* -ge-, *h*) rescue;
2ung *f* rescue.
er'**richt**|en *v/t.* (*no* -ge-, *h*) set up,
erect; establish; 2ung *f* erection;
establishment.
er|'**ringen** *v/t.* (*irr.* ringen, *no* -ge-,
h) gain, obtain; achieve (*success*);
✗'**röten** *v/i.* (*no* -ge-, *sein*) blush.
Errungenschaft [ɛr'ruŋənʃaft] *f*
(-/-en) acquisition; achievement.
Er'satz *m* (-es/*no pl.*) replacement;
substitute; compensation; amends
sg., damages *pl.*; indemnification;
s. Ersatzmann, Ersatzmittel; ✗ **leisten** make amends; ✗**mann** *m* substitute; ✗**mine** *f* refill (*for pencil*);
✗**mittel** *n* substitute, surrogate;
✗**reifen** *mot. m* spare tyre, (*Am.
only*) spare tire; ✗**teil** ⊕ *n, m* spare
(part).
er'**schaff**|en *v/t.* (*irr.* schaffen, *no*
-ge-, *h*) create; 2ung *f* (-/*no pl.*)
creation.
er'**schallen** *v/i.* ([*irr.* schallen,] *no*
-ge-, *sein*) (re)sound; ring.
er'**schein**|en 1. *v/i.* (*irr.* scheinen,
no -ge-, *sein*) appear; 2. 2 *n* (-s/*no
pl.*) appearance; 2ung *f* (-/-en) appearance; apparition; vision.
er|'**schießen** *v/t.* (*irr.* schießen, *no*
-ge-, *h*) shoot (dead); ✗'**schlaffen**
v/i. (*no* -ge-, *sein*) tire; relax; *fig.*
languish, slacken; ✗'**schlagen** *v/t.*
(*irr.* schlagen, *no* -ge-, *h*) kill, slay;

~'schließen v/t. (irr. schließen, no -ge-, h) open; open up (new market); develop (district).

er'schöpf|en v/t. (no -ge-, h) exhaust; 2ung f exhaustion.

erschrak [ɛrˈʃraːk] pret. of erschrecken 2.

er'schrecken 1. v/t. (no -ge-, h) frighten, scare; 2. v/i. (irr., no -ge-, sein) be frightened (über acc. at); ~d adj. alarming, startling.

erschrocken [ɛrˈʃrɔkn] 1. p.p. of erschrecken 2. 2. adj. frightened, terrified.

erschütter|n [ɛrˈʃytɐn] v/t. (no -ge-, h) shake; fig. shock, move; 2ung f (-/-en) shock; fig. emotion; ✗ concussion; ⊕ percussion.

er'schweren v/t. (no -ge-, h) make more difficult; aggravate.

er'schwing|en v/t. (irr. schwingen, no -ge-, h) afford; ~lich adj. within s.o.'s means: prices: reasonable.

er|'sehen v/t. (irr. sehen, no -ge-, h) see, learn, gather (all: aus from); ~'sehnen v/t. (no -ge-, h) long for; ~'setzen v/t. (no -ge-, h) repair; make up for, compensate (for); replace; refund.

er'sichtlich adj. evident, obvious.

er'sinnen v/t. (irr. sinnen, no -ge-, h) contrive, devise.

er'spar|en v/t. (no -ge-, h) save; j-m et. ~ spare s.o. s.th.; 2nis f (-/-se) saving.

er'sprießlich adj. useful, beneficial.

erst [eːrst] 1. adj.: der (die, das) ~e the first; 2. adv. first; at first; only; not ... till or until.

er'starr|en v/i. (no -ge-, sein) stiffen; solidify; congeal; set; grow numb; fig. blood: run cold; ~t adj. benumbed; 2ung f (-/-en) numbness; solidification; congealment; setting.

erstatt|en [ɛrˈʃtatn] v/t. (no -ge-, h) restore; s. ersetzen; Bericht ~ (make a) report; 2ung f (-/-en) restitution.

'Erstaufführung f thea. first night or performance, premiere; film: a. first run.

er'staun|en 1. v/i. (no -ge-, sein) be astonished (über acc. at); 2. v/t. (no -ge-, h) astonish; 3. 2 n astonishment; in ~ setzen astonish; ~lich adj. astonishing, amazing.

er'stechen v/t. (irr. stechen, no -ge-, h) stab.

er'steig|en v/t. (irr. steigen, no -ge-, h) ascend, climb; 2ung f ascent.

erstens adv. ['eːrstəns] first, firstly.

er'stick|en (no -ge-) v/t. (h) and v/i. (sein) choke, suffocate; stifle; 2ung f (-/-en) suffocation. [rate, F A 1.]

'erstklassig adj. first-class, first-]

er'streben v/t. (no -ge-, h) strive after or for; ~swert adj. desirable.

er'strecken v/refl. (no -ge-, h) extend; sich ~ über (acc.) cover.

er'suchen 1. v/t. (no -ge-, h) request; 2. 2 n (-s/-) request.

er|'tappen v/t. (no -ge-, h) catch, surprise; s. frisch; ~'tönen v/i. (no -ge-, sein) (re)sound.

Ertrag [ɛrˈtraːk] m (-[e]s/=e) produce, yield; proceeds pl., returns pl.; ✗ output; 2en [~gən] v/t. (irr. tragen, no -ge-, h) bear, endure; suffer; stand.

erträglich adj. [ɛrˈtrɛːkliç] tolerable.

er|'tränken v/t. (no -ge-, h) drown; ~'trinken v/i. (irr. trinken, no -ge-, sein) be drowned, drown; ~übrigen [ɛrˈyːbrigən] v/t. (no -ge-, h) save; spare (time); sich ~ be unnecessary; ~'wachen v/i. (no -ge-, sein) awake, wake up.

er'wachsen 1. v/i. (irr. wachsen, no -ge-, sein) arise (aus from); 2. adj. grown-up, adult; 2e m, f (-n/-n) grown-up, adult.

er'wäg|en v/t. (irr. wägen, no -ge-, h) consider, think s.th. over; 2ung f (-/-en) consideration.

er'wählen v/t. (no -ge-, h) choose, elect.

er'wähn|en v/t. (no -ge-, h) mention; 2ung f (-/-en) mention.

er'wärmen v/t. (no -ge-, h) warm, heat; sich ~ warm (up).

er'wart|en v/t. (no -ge-, h) await, wait for; fig. expect; 2ung f expectation.

er|'wecken v/t. (no -ge-, h) wake, rouse; fig. awake; cause (fear); arouse (suspicion); ~'wehren v/refl. (gen.) (no -ge-, h) keep or ward off; ~'weichen v/t. (no -ge-, h) soften; fig. move; ~'weisen v/t. (irr. weisen, no -ge-, h) prove; show (respect); render (service); do, pay (honour); do (favour).

er'weiter|n v/t. and v/refl. (no -ge-, h) expand, enlarge, extend, widen; 2ung f (-/-en) expansion, enlargement, extension.

Erwerb [ɛrˈvɛrp] m (-[e]s/-e) acquisition; living; earnings pl.; business; 2en [~bən] v/t. (irr. werben, no -ge-, h) acquire; gain; earn.

erwerbs|los adj. [ɛrˈvɛrpsloːs] unemployed; ~tätig adj. (gainfully) employed; ~unfähig adj. [ɛr-ˈvɛrpsˀ-] incapable of earning one's living; 2zweig m line of business.

Erwerbung [ɛrˈvɛrbuŋ] f acquisition.

er'wider|n [ɛrˈviːdərn] v/t. (no -ge-, h) return; answer, reply; retort; 2ung f (-/-en) return; answer, reply.

er'wischen v/t. (no -ge-, h) catch, trap, get hold of.

er'wünscht adj. desired; desirable; welcome.

er'würgen v/t. (no -ge-, h) strangle, throttle.

Erz ⚔ [e:rts] n (-es/-e) ore; poet. brass.

er'zähl|en v/t. (no -ge-, h) tell; relate; narrate; 2er m, 2erin f (-/-nen) narrator; writer; 2ung f narration; (short) story, narrative.

'Erz|bischof eccl. m archbishop; '~bistum eccl. n archbishopric; '~engel eccl. m archangel.

er'zeug|en v/t. (no -ge-, h) beget; produce; make, manufacture; 2er m (-s/-) father (of child); ✝ producer; 2nis n produce; production; ⊕ product; 2ung f production.

'Erz|feind m arch-enemy; '~herzog m archduke; '~herzogin f archduchess; '~herzogtum n archduchy.

er'ziehe|n v/t. (irr. ziehen, no -ge-, h) bring up, rear, raise; educate; 2r m (-s/-) educator; teacher, tutor; 2rin f (-/-nen) teacher; governess; ~risch adj. educational, pedagogic (-al).

Er'ziehung f (-/~, -en) upbringing; breeding; education; ~sanstalt [er'tsi:uŋs?-] f reformatory, approved school; ~swesen n (-s/no pl.) educational matters pl. or system.

er|'zielen v/t. (no -ge-, h) obtain; realize (price); achieve (success); sports: score (points, goal); ~'zürnen v/t. (no -ge-, h) make angry, irritate, enrage; ~'zwingen v/t. (irr. zwingen, no -ge-, h) (en)force; compel; extort (von from).

es pers. pron. [es] 1. pers.: it, he, she; wo ist das Buch? — ~ ist auf dem Tisch where is the book? — it is on the table; das Mädchen blieb stehen, als ~ seine Mutter sah the girl stopped when she saw her mother; 2. impers.: it; ~ gibt there is, there are; ~ ist kalt it is cold; ~ klopft there is a knock at the door.

Esche ♀ ['ɛʃə] f (-/-n) ash(-tree).

Esel zo. ['e:zəl] m (-s/-) donkey; esp. fig. ass; ~ei [~'laɪ] f (-/-en) stupidity, stupid thing, folly; '~s-brücke f at school: crib, Am. pony; ~sohr ['e:zəls?-] n dog's ear (of book).

Eskorte [ɛs'kɔrtə] f (-/-n) ⚔ escort; ♨ convoy.

Espe ♀ ['ɛspə] f (-/-n) asp(en).

'eßbar adj. eatable, edible.

Esse ['ɛsə] f (-/-n) chimney.

essen ['ɛsən] 1. v/i. (irr., ge-, h) eat; zu Mittag ~ (have) lunch; dine, have dinner; zu Abend ~ dine, have dinner; esp. late at night: sup, have supper; auswärts ~ eat or dine out; 2. v/t. (irr., ge-, h) eat; et. zu Mittag etc. ~ have s.th. for lunch, etc.; 3. 2 n (-s/-) eating; food; meal; dish; midday meal: lunch, dinner; evening meal: dinner; last meal of the day: supper; '2szeit f lunch-time; dinner-time; supper-time.

Essenz [ɛ'sɛnts] f (-/-en) essence.

Essig ['ɛsɪç] m (-s/-e) vinegar; '~gurke f pickled cucumber, gherkin.

'Eß|löffel m soup-spoon; '~nische f dining alcove, Am. dinette; '~tisch m dining-table; '~waren f/pl. eatables pl., victuals pl., food; '~zimmer n dining-room.

etablieren [eta'bli:rən] v/t. (no -ge-, h) establish, set up.

Etage [e'ta:ʒə] f (-/-n) floor, stor(e)y; ~nwohnung f flat, Am. a. apartment.

Etappe [e'tapə] f (-/-n) ⚔ base; fig. stage, leg.

Etat [e'ta:] m (-s/-s) budget, parl. the Estimates pl.; ~sjahr n fiscal year. [or sg.]

Ethik ['e:tik] f (-/~, -en) ethics pl.]

Etikett [eti'kɛt] n (-[e]s/-e, -s) label; ticket; tag; gummed: Am. a. sticker; ~e f (-/-n) etiquette; 2ieren [~'ti:-rən] v/t. (no -ge-, h) label.

etliche indef. pron. ['ɛtlɪçə] some, several.

Etui [e'tvi:] n (-s/-s) case.

etwa adv. ['ɛtva] perhaps, by chance; about, Am. a. around; ~ig adj. ['~?ɪç] possible, eventual.

etwas ['ɛtvas] 1. indef. pron. something; anything; 2. adj. some; any; 3. adv. somewhat; 4. 2 n (-/-): das gewisse ~ that certain something.

euch pers. pron. [ɔʏç] you; ~ (selbst) yourselves.

euer poss. pron. ['ɔʏər] your; der (die, das) eu(e)re yours.

Eule orn. ['ɔʏlə] f (-/-n) owl; ~n nach Athen tragen carry coals to Newcastle.

euresgleichen pron. ['ɔʏrəs'glaɪçən] people like you, F the likes of you.

Europä|er [ɔʏro'pɛ:ər] m (-s/-) European; 2isch adj. European.

Euter ['ɔʏtər] n (-s/-) udder.

evakuieren [evaku'i:rən] v/t. (no -ge-, h) evacuate.

evangeli|sch adj. [evaŋ'ge:lɪʃ] evangelic(al); Protestant; Lutheran; 2um [~jum] n (-s/Evangelien) gospel.

eventuell [eventu'ɛl] 1. adj. possible; 2. adv. possibly, perhaps.

ewig adj. ['e:vɪç] eternal; everlasting; perpetual; auf ~ for ever; '2keit f (-/-en) eternity; F: seit e-r ~ for ages.

exakt adj. [ɛ'ksakt] exact; 2heit f (-/-en) exactitude, exactness; accuracy.

Exam|en [ɛ'ksa:mən] n (-s/-, Examina) examination, F exam; 2inieren [~ami'ni:rən] v/t. (no -ge-, h) examine.

Exekutive [ɛksəku'ti:və] f (-/no pl.) executive power.

Exempel [ɛ'ksɛmpəl] n (-s/-) example, instance.

Exemplar [ɛksɛm'plɑːr] *n* (-s/-e) specimen; copy (*of book*).

exerzier|en ✕ [ɛksɛr'tsiːrən] *v/i. and v/t.* (*no -ge-, h*) drill; **Splatz** ✕ *m* drill-ground, parade-ground.

Exil [ɛ'ksiːl] *n* (-s/-e) exile.

Existenz [ɛksis'tɛnts] *f* (-/-en) existence; living, livelihood; **minimum** *n* subsistence minimum.

exis'tieren *v/i.* (*no -ge-, h*) exist; subsist.

exotisch *adj.* [ɛ'ksoːtiʃ] exotic.

exped|ieren [ɛkspe'diːrən] *v/t.* (*no -ge-, h*) dispatch; **Sition** [ʌi'tsjoːn] *f* (-/-en) dispatch, forwarding; expedition; ✝ dispatch *or* forwarding office.

Experiment [ɛksperi'mɛnt] *n* (-[e]s/-e) experiment; **Sieren** [ʌ'tiːrən] *v/i.* (*no -ge-, h*) experiment.

explo|dieren [ɛksploʹdiːrən] *v/i.* (*no -ge-, sein*) explode, burst; **Ssion** [ʌ'zjoːn] *f* (-/-en) explosion; **siv** *adj.* [ʌ'ziːf] explosive.

Export [ɛks'pɔrt] *m* (-[e]s/-e) export(ation); **Sieren** [ʌ'tiːrən] *v/t.* (*no -ge-, h*) export.

extra *adj.* ['ɛkstra] extra; special; **Sblatt** *n* extra edition (*of newspaper*), *Am.* extra.

Extrakt [ɛks'trakt] *m* (-[e]s/-e) extract.

Extrem [ɛks'treːm] **1.** *n* (-s/-e) extreme; **2. 2** *adj.* extreme.

Exzellenz [ɛkstsɛ'lɛnts] *f* (-/-en) Excellency.

exzentrisch *adj.* [ɛks'tsɛntriʃ] eccentric.

Exzeß [ɛks'tsɛs] *m* (Exzesses/Exzesse) excess.

F

Fabel ['fɑːbəl] *f* (-/-n) fable (*a. fig.*); plot (*of story, book, etc.*); **Shaft** *adj.* fabulous; marvellous; **Sn** *v/i.* (*ge-, h*) tell (tall) stories.

Fabrik [fa'briːk] *f* (-/-en) factory, works *sg., pl.*, mill; **ant** [ʌi'kant] *m* (-en/-en) factory-owner, mill-owner; manufacturer; **arbeit** *f* factory work; *s.* Fabrikware; **arbeiter** *m* factory worker *or* hand; **at** [ʌi'kɑːt] *n* (-[e]s/-e) make; product; **ationsfehler** [ʌa'tsjoːns-] *m* flaw; **besitzer** *m* factory-owner; **marke** *f* trade mark; **stadt** *f* factory *or* industrial town; **ware** *f* manufactured article; **zeichen** *n s.* Fabrikmarke.

Fach [fax] *n* (-[e]s/=er) section, compartment, shelf (*of bookcase, cupboard, etc.*); pigeon-hole (*in desk*); drawer; *fig.* subject; *s.* Fachgebiet; '**arbeiter** *m* skilled worker; **arzt** *m* specialist (*für* in); '**ausbildung** *f* professional training; '**ausdruck** *m* technical term.

fächeln ['fɛçəln] *v/t.* (*ge-, h*) fan *s.o.*

Fächer ['fɛçər] *m* (-s/-) fan; **Sförmig** *adj.* ['ʌfœrmiç] fan-shaped.

'**Fach|gebiet** *n* branch, field, province; '**kenntnisse** *f/pl.* specialized knowledge; '**kreis** *m*: *in* en among experts; '**Skundig** *adj.* competent, expert; '**literatur** *f* specialized literature; '**mann** *m* expert; **Smännisch** *adj.* ['ʌmeniʃ] expert; '**schule** *f* technical school; '**werk** △ *n* framework.

Fackel ['fakəl] *f* (-/-n) torch; '**Sn** F *v/i.* (*ge-, h*) hesitate, F shilly-shally; '**zug** *m* torchlight procession.

fad *adj.* [fɑːt], **e** *adj.* ['fɑːdə] food: insipid, tasteless; stale; *p.* dull, boring.

Faden ['fɑːdən] *m* (-s/=) thread (*a. fig.*); *fig.*: an e-m hängen hang by a thread; '**nudeln** *f/pl.* vermicelli *pl.*; **Sscheinig** *adj.* ['ʌʃainiç] threadbare: *excuse, etc.*: flimsy, thin.

fähig *adj.* ['fɛːiç] capable (*zu inf.* of *ger.; gen.* of); able (to *inf.*); **Skeit** *f* (-/-en) (cap)ability; talent, faculty.

fahl *adj.* [fɑːl] pale, pallid; *colour*: faded; *complexion*: leaden, livid.

fahnd|en ['fɑːndən] *v/i.* (*ge-, h*): *nach j-m* search for s.o.; **Sung** *f* (-/-en) search.

Fahne ['fɑːnə] *f* (-/-n) flag; standard; banner; ♐, ✕ *fig.* colo(u)rs *pl.*; *typ.* galley-proof.

'**Fahnen|eid** *m* oath of allegiance; '**flucht** *f* desertion; **Sflüchtig** *adj.*: *werden* desert (the colo[u]rs); '**stange** *f* flagstaff, *Am. a.* flagpole.

'**Fahr|bahn** *f*, '**damm** *m* roadway.

Fähre ['fɛːrə] *f* (-/-n) ferry(-boat).

fahren ['fɑːrən] (*irr., ge-*) **1.** *v/i.* (*sein*) driver, vehicle, etc.: drive, go, travel; *cyclist*: ride, cycle; ♐ sail; *mot.* motor; mit der Eisenbahn go by train *or* rail; *spazieren* go for *or* take a drive; mit der Hand über (*acc.*) pass one's hand over; lassen let go *or* slip; gut (schlecht) bei do *or* fare well (badly) at *or* with; er ist gut dabei gefahren he did very well out of it; **2.** *v/t.* (*h*) carry, convey; drive (*car, train, etc.*); ride (*bicycle, etc.*).

'**Fahrer** *m* (-s/-) driver; '**flucht** *f* (-/*no pl.*) hit-and-run offence, *Am.* hit-and-run offense.

'**Fahr**|**gast** *m* passenger; *in taxi:* fare; '**~geld** *n* fare; '**~gelegenheit** *f* transport facilities *pl.*; '**~gestell** *n mot.* chassis; ⚙ undercarriage, landing gear; '**~karte** *f* ticket; '**~kartenschalter** *m* booking-office, *Am.* ticket office; '**2lässig** *adj.* careless, negligent; '**~lässigkeit** *f* (-/~-en) carelessness, negligence; '**~lehrer** *mot. m* driving instructor; '**~plan** *m* timetable, *Am. a.* schedule; '**2planmäßig 1.** *adj.* regular, *Am.* scheduled; **2.** *adv.* on time, *Am. a.* on schedule; '**~preis** *m* fare; '**~rad** *n* bicycle, F bike; '**~schein** *m* ticket; '**~schule** *mot. f* driving school, school of motoring; '**~stuhl** *m* lift, *Am.* elevator; '**~stuhlführer** *m* lift-boy, lift-man, *Am.* elevator operator; '**~stunde** *mot. f* driving lesson.

Fahrt [faːrt] *f* (-/-en) ride, drive; journey, voyage, passage; trip; *~ ins Blaue* mystery tour; *in voller ~* (at) full speed.

Fährte ['fɛːrtə] *f* (-/-n) track (*a. fig.*); *auf der falschen ~ sein* be on the wrong track.

'**Fahr**|**vorschrift** *f* rule of the road; '**~wasser** *n* ⚓ navigable water; *fig.* track; '**~weg** *m* roadway; '**~zeug** *n* vehicle; ⚓ vessel.

Fakt|**or** ['faktɔr] *m* (-s/-en) factor; **~otum** [~'toːtum] *n* (-s/-s, Faktoten) factotum; **~ur** ✝ [~'tuːr] *f* (-/-en), **~ura** ✝ [~'tuːra] *f* (-/Fakturen) invoice.

Fakultät *univ.* [fakul'tɛːt] *f* (-/-en) faculty.

Falke *orn.* ['falkə] *m* (-n/-n) hawk, falcon.

Fall [fal] *m* (-[e]s/~e) fall (*of body, stronghold, city, etc.*); *gr.,* ɡ̊s, ɡ̊͟ case; *gesetzt den ~* suppose; *auf alle Fälle* at all events; *auf jeden ~* in any case, at any rate; *auf keinen ~* on no account, in no case.

Falle ['falə] *f* (-/-n) trap (*a. fig.*); pitfall (*a. fig.*); *e-e ~ stellen* set a trap (*j-m* for s.o.).

fallen ['falən] **1.** *v/i.* (*irr.,* ge-, sein) fall, drop; ⚔ be killed in action; *shot:* be heard; *flood water:* subside; *auf j-n ~ suspicion, etc.:* fall on s.o.; *~ lassen* drop (*plate, etc.*); **2.** **2** *n* (-s/no pl.) fall(ing).

fällen ['fɛlən] *v/t.* (ge-, h) fell, cut down (*tree*); ⚔ lower (*bayonet*); ɡ̊s pass (*judgement*); give (*decision*).

'**fallenlassen** *v/t.* (*irr. lassen, sep., no -ge-,* h) drop (*plan, claim, etc.*).

fällig *adj.* ['fɛliç] due; payable; '**2keit** *f* (-/~-en) maturity; '**2keitstermin** *m* date of maturity.

'**Fall**|**obst** *n* windfall; **~reep** ⚓ [~reːp] *n* (-[e]s/-e) gangway.

falls *cj.* [fals] if; in the event of *ger.*; in case.

'**Fall**|**schirm** *m* parachute; '**~**

'**schirmspringer** *m* parachutist; '**~strick** *m* snare; '**~tür** *f* trap door.

falsch [falʃ] **1.** *adj.* false; wrong; *bank-note, etc.:* counterfeit; *money:* base; *bill of exchange, etc.:* forged; *p.* deceitful; **2.** *adv.:* *~ gehen watch:* go wrong; *~ verbunden!* *teleph.* sorry, wrong number.

fälsch|**en** ['fɛlʃən] *v/t.* (ge-, h) falsify; forge, fake (*document, etc.*); counterfeit (*bank-note, coin, etc.*); fake (*calculations, etc.*); tamper with (*financial account*); adulterate (*food, wine*); '**2er** *m* (-s/-) forger, faker; adulterator.

'**Falsch**|**geld** *n* counterfeit or bad or base money; '**~heit** *f* (-/-en) falseness, falsity; duplicity, deceitfulness; '**~meldung** *f* false report; '**~münzer** *m* (-s/-) coiner; '**~münzerwerkstatt** *f* coiner's den; '**2spielen** *v/i.* (*sep., -ge-,* h) cheat (at cards); '**~spieler** *m* cardsharper.

'**Fälschung** *f* (-/-en) forgery; falsification; fake; adulteration.

Falt|**boot** ['falt-] *n* folding canoe, *Am.* foldboat, faltboat; **~e** ['~ə] *f* (-/-n) fold; pleat (*in skirt, etc.*); crease (*in trousers*); wrinkle (*on face*); '**2en** *v/t.* (ge-, h) fold; clasp or join (*one's hands*); '**2ig** *adj.* folded; pleated; wrinkled.

Falz [falts] *m* (-es/-e) fold; rabbet (*for woodworking, etc.*); bookbinding: guard; '**2en** *v/t.* (ge-, h) fold; rabbet.

familiär *adj.* [famil'jɛːr] familiar; informal.

Familie [fa'miːljə] *f* (-/-n) family (*a. zo.,* ⚘).

Fa'milien|**angelegenheit** *f* family affair; **~anschluß** *m*: *~ haben* live as one of the family; **~nachrichten** *f/pl. in newspaper:* birth, marriage and death announcements *pl.*; **~name** *m* family name, surname, *Am. a.* last name; **~stand** *m* marital status.

Fanati|**ker** [fa'naːtikər] *m* (-s/-) fanatic; **2sch** *adj.* fanatic(al).

Fanatismus [fana'tismus] *m* (-/no pl.) fanaticism.

fand [fant] *pret. of finden.*

Fanfare [fan'faːrə] *f* (-/-n) fanfare, flourish (of trumpets).

Fang [faŋ] *m* (-[e]s/~e) capture, catch(ing); *hunt.* bag; '**2en** *v/t.* (*irr.* ge-, h) catch (*animal, ball, thief, etc.*); '**~zahn** *m* fang (*of dog, wolf, etc.*); tusk (*of boar*).

Farb|**band** ['farp-] *n* (typewriter) ribbon; **~e** ['~bə] *f* (-/-n) colo(u)r; paint; dye; complexion; *cards:* suit; **2echt** *adj.* ['farpˀ-] colo(u)rfast.

färben ['fɛrbən] *v/t.* (ge-, h) colo(u)r (*glass, food, etc.*); dye (*material, hair, Easter eggs, etc.*); tint (*hair,*

paper, glass); stain (*wood, fabrics, glass, etc.*); sich ~ take on or assume a colo(u)r; sich rot ~ turn or go red.
'**farben|blind** adj. colo(u)r-blind; '2**druck** m (-[e]s/-e) colo(u)r print; '**~prächtig** adj. splendidly colo(u)rful.

Färber ['fɛrbər] m (-s/-) dyer.

Farb|fernsehen ['farp-] n colo(u)r television; '**~film** m colo(u)r film; 2**ig** adj. ['~biç] colo(u)red; glass: tinted, stained; fig. colo(u)rful; 2**los** adj. ['~p-] colo(u)rless; '**~photographie** f colo(u)r photography; '**~stift** m colo(u)red pencil; '**~stoff** m colo(u)ring matter; '**~ton** m tone; shade, tint.

Färbung ['fɛrbuŋ] f (-/-en) colo(u)ring (a. fig.); shade (a. fig.).

Farnkraut ♀ ['farnkraut] n fern.

Fasan orn. [fa'zaːn] m (-[e]s/-e[n]) pheasant.

Fasching ['faʃiŋ] m (-s/-e, -s) carnival.

Fasel|ei [faːzə'lai] f (-/-en) drivelling, waffling; twaddle; '2**n** v/i. (ge-, h) blather; F waffle.

Faser ['faːzər] f (-/-en) anat., ♀, fig. fib|re, Am. -er; cotton, wool, etc.: staple; '2**ig** adj. fibrous; '2**n** v/i. (ge-, h) wool: shed fine hairs.

Faß [fas] n (Fasses/Fässer) cask, barrel; tub; vat; '**~bier** n draught beer.

Fassade ⚠ [fa'saːdə] f (-/-n) façade, front (a. fig.); '**~nkletterer** m (-s/-) cat burglar.

fassen ['fasən] (ge-, h) 1. v/t. seize, take hold of; catch, apprehend (criminal); hold; s. einfassen; fig. grasp, understand, believe; pluck up (courage); form (plan); make (decision); sich ~ compose o.s.; sich kurz ~ be brief; 2. v/i.: ~ nach reach for. [ceivable.]
'**faßlich** adj. comprehensible, con-
'**Fassung** f (-/-en) setting (of jewels); ⚡ socket; fig.: composure; draft (-ing); wording, version; die ~ verlieren lose one's self-control; aus der ~ bringen disconcert; '**~skraft** f (powers of) comprehension, mental capacity; '**~svermögen** n (holding) capacity; fig. s. Fassungskraft.

fast adv. [fast] almost, nearly; ~ nichts next to nothing; ~ nie hardly ever.

fasten ['fastən] v/i. (ge-, h) fast; abstain from food and drink; '2**zeit** f Lent.
'**Fast|nacht** f (-/no pl.) Shrovetide; carnival; '**~tag** m fast-day.

fatal adj. [fa'taːl] situation, etc.: awkward; business, etc.: unfortunate; mistake, etc.: fatal.

fauchen ['fauxən] v/i. (ge-, h) cat, etc.: spit; F p. spit (with anger); locomotive, etc.: hiss.

faul adj. [faul] fruit, etc.: rotten, bad; fish, meat: putrid, bad; fig. lazy, indolent, idle; fishy; ~e Ausrede lame excuse; '**~en** v/i. (ge-, h) rot, go bad, putrefy.

faulenze|n ['faulentsən] v/i. (ge-, h) idle; laze, loaf; '2**r** m (-s/-) idler, sluggard, F lazy-bones.
'**Faul|heit** f (-/no pl.) idleness, laziness; 2**ig** adj. putrid.

Fäulnis ['fɔylnis] f (-/no pl.) rottenness; putrefaction; decay.
'**Faul|pelz** m s. Faulenzer; '**~tier** n zo. sloth (a. fig.).

Faust [faust] f (-/-e) fist; auf eigene ~ on one's own initiative; '**~handschuh** m mitt(en); '**~schlag** m blow with the fist, punch, Am. F a. slug.

Favorit [favo'riːt] m (-en/-en) favo(u)rite.

Faxe ['faksə] f (-/-n): ~n machen (play the) fool; ~n schneiden pull or make faces.

Fazit ['faːtsit] n (-s/-e, -s) result, upshot; total; das ~ ziehen sum or total up.

Februar ['feːbruaːr] m (-[s]/-e) February.

fecht|en ['fɛçtən] v/i. (irr., ge-, h) fight; fenc. fence; '2**er** m (-s/-) fencer.

Feder ['feːdər] f (-/-n) feather; (ornamental) plume; pen; ⊕ spring; '**~bett** n feather bed; '**~busch** m tuft of feathers; plume; '**~gewicht** n boxing, etc.: featherweight; '**~halter** m (-s/-) penholder; '**~kiel** m quill; '**~kraft** f elasticity, resilience; '**~krieg** m paper war; literary controversy; '2**leicht** adj. (as) light as a feather; '**~lesen** n (-s/no pl.): nicht viel ~s machen mit make short work of; '**~messer** n penknife; '2**n** v/i. (ge-, h) be elastic; '2**nd** adj. springy, elastic; '**~strich** m stroke of the pen; '**~vieh** n poultry; '**~zeichnung** f pen-and-ink drawing.

Fee [feː] f (-/-n) fairy.

Fegefeuer ['feːgə-] n purgatory.

fegen ['feːgən] v/t. (ge-, h) sweep; clean.

Fehde ['feːdə] f (-/-n) feud; private war; in ~ liegen be at feud; F be at daggers drawn.

Fehl [feːl] m: ohne ~ without fault or blemish; '**~betrag** m deficit, deficiency.

fehlen ['feːlən] v/i. (ge-, h) be absent; be missing or lacking; do wrong; es fehlt ihm an (dat.) he lacks; was fehlt Ihnen? what is the matter with you?; weit gefehlt! far off the mark!

Fehler ['feːlər] m (-s/-) mistake, error, F slip; fault; ⊕ defect, flaw; '2**frei** adj., '2**los** adj. faultless, perfect; ⊕ flawless; '2**haft** adj. faulty; defective; incorrect.
'**Fehl|geburt** f miscarriage, abor-

tion; '2gehen v/i. (irr. gehen, sep., -ge-, sein) go wrong; '~griff fig. m mistake, blunder; '~schlag fig. m failure; '2schlagen fig. v/i. (irr. schlagen, sep., -ge-, sein) fail, miscarry; '~schuß m miss; '2treten v/i. (irr. treten, sep., -ge- sein) make a false step; '~tritt m false step; slip; fig. slip, fault; '~urteil ⚖ n error of judg(e)ment; '~zündung mot. f misfire, backfire.

Feier ['faɪər] f (-/-n) ceremony; celebration; festival; festivity; '~abend m finishing or closing time; ~ machen finish, F knock off; '2lich adj. promise, oath, etc.: solemn; act: ceremonial; '~lichkeit f (-/-en) solemnity; ceremony; '2n (ge-, h) 1. v/t. hold (celebration); celebrate, observe (feast, etc.); 2. v/i. celebrate; rest (from work), make holiday; '~tag m holiday; festive day.

feig adj. [faɪk] cowardly.

feige[1] adj. ['faɪgə] cowardly.

Feige[2] [,] f (-/-n) fig; '~nbaum ♀ m fig-tree; '~nblatt n fig-leaf.

Feig|heit ['faɪkhaɪt] f (-/no pl.) cowardice, cowardliness; '~ling ['~klɪŋ] m (-s/-e) coward.

feil adj. [faɪl] for sale, to be sold; fig. venal; '~bieten v/t. (irr. bieten, sep., -ge-, h) offer for sale.

Feile ['faɪlə] f (-/-n) file; '2n (ge-, h) 1. v/t. file (a. fig.); fig. polish; 2. v/i. ~ an (dat.) file (at); fig. polish (up).

feilschen ['faɪlʃən] v/i. (ge-, h) bargain (um for), haggle (for, about), Am. a. dicker (about).

fein adj. [faɪn] fine; material, etc.: high-grade; wine, etc.: choice; fabric, etc.: delicate, dainty; manners: polished; p. polite; distinction: subtle.

Feind [faɪnt] m (-[e]s/-e) enemy (a. ✕); '2lich adj. hostile, inimical; '~schaft f (-/-en) enmity, animosity, hostility; '2selig adj. hostile (gegen to); '~seligkeit f (-/-en) hostility; malevolence.

'fein|fühlend adj., '~fühlig adj. sensitive; '2gefühl n sensitiveness; delicacy; '2gehalt m (monetary) standard; '2heit f (-/-en) fineness, delicacy, daintiness; politeness; elegance; '2kost f high-class groceries pl., Am. delicatessen; '2mechanik f precision mechanics; '2schmecker m (-s/-) gourmet, epicure; '~sinnig adj. subtle.

feist adj. [faɪst] fat, stout.

Feld [fɛlt] n (-[e]s/-er) field (a. ✕, ⚛, sports); ground, soil; plain; chess: square; △, ⊕ panel, compartment; ins ~ ziehen take the field; '~arbeit f agricultural work; '~bett n camp-bed; '~blume f wild flower; '~dienst ✕ m field service; '~flasche f water-bottle;

'~frucht f fruit of the field; '~geschrei n war-cry, battle-cry; '~herr m general; '~kessel m camp-kettle; '~lazarett ✕ n field-hospital; '~lerche orn. f skylark; '~marschall m Field Marshal; '2marschmäßig ✕ adj. in full marching order; '~maus zo. f field-mouse; '~messer m (land) surveyor; '~post ✕ f army postal service; '~schlacht ✕ f battle; '~stecher m (-s/-) (ein a pair of) field-glasses pl.; '~stuhl m camp-stool; '~webel ['~ve:bəl] m (-s/-) sergeant; '~weg m (field) path; '~zeichen ✕ n standard; '~zug m ✕ campaign (a. fig.), (military) expedition; Am. fig. a. drive.

Felge ['fɛlgə] f (-/-n) felloe (of cart-wheel); rim (of car wheel, etc.).

Fell [fɛl] n (-[e]s/-e) skin, pelt, fur (of dead animal); coat (of cat, etc.); fleece (of sheep).

Fels [fɛls] m (-en/-en), ~en ['~zən] m (-s/-) rock; ~block ['fɛls-] m rock; boulder; 2ig adj. ['~zɪç] rocky.

Fenchel ♀ ['fɛnçəl] m (-s/no pl.) fennel.

Fenster ['fɛnstər] n (-s/-) window; '~brett n window-sill; '~flügel m casement (of casement window); sash (of sash window); '~kreuz n cross-bar(s pl.); '~laden m shutter; '~rahmen m window-frame; '~riegel m window-fastener; '~scheibe f (window-)pane; '~sims m, n window-sill.

Ferien ['fe:rjən] pl. holiday(s pl.), esp. Am. vacation; leave, Am. a. furlough; parl. recess; ⚖ vacation, recess; '~kolonie f children's holiday camp.

Ferkel ['fɛrkəl] n (-s/-) young pig; contp. p. pig.

fern [fɛrn] 1. adj. far (off), distant; remote; 2. adv. far (away); von ~ from a distance.

'Fernamt teleph. n trunk exchange, Am. long-distance exchange.

'fernbleiben 1. v/i. (irr. bleiben, sep., -ge-, sein) remain or stay away (dat. from); 2. 2 n (-s/no pl.) absence (from school, etc.); absenteeism (from work).

Fern|e ['fɛrnə] f (-/-n) distance; remoteness; aus der ~ from or at a distance; '2er 1. adj. farther; fig.: further; future; 2. adv. further (-more), in addition, also; ~ liefen ... also ran ...; '~flug ✈ m long-distance flight; 2gelenkt adj. ['~gəlɛŋkt] missile: guided; aircraft, etc.: remote-control(l)ed; '~gespräch teleph. n trunk call, Am. long-distance call; 2gesteuert adj. s. ferngelenkt; '~glas n binoculars pl.; 2halten v/t. and v/refl. (irr. halten, sep., -ge-, h) keep away (von from); '~heizung f district heating; '~la-

ster F *mot. m* long-distance lorry, *Am.* long haul truck; '**.lenkung** f (-/-en) remote control; '**.liegen** *v/i.* (*irr.* liegen, *sep.*, -ge-, h): es liegt mir fern zu *inf.* I am far from *ger.*; '**.rohr** *n* telescope; '**.schreiber** *m* teleprinter, *Am.* teletypewriter; '**.sehen 1.** *n* (-s/*no pl.*) television; 2. ♀ *v/i.* (*irr.* sehen, *sep.*, -ge-, h) watch television; '**.seher** *m* television set; *p.* television viewer, televiewer; '**.sehsendung** f television broadcast, telecast; '**.sicht** f visual range.

'**Fernsprech|amt** *n* telephone exchange, *Am. a.* central; '**.anschluß** *m* telephone connection; '**.er** *m* telephone; '**.leitung** f telephone line; '**.zelle** f telephone box.

'**fern|stehen** *v/i.* (*irr.* stehen, *sep.*, -ge-, h) have no real (point of) contact (*dat.* with); '**♀steuerung** f *s. Fernlenkung;* '**♀unterricht** *m* correspondence course *or* tuition; '**♀verkehr** *m* long-distance traffic.

Ferse ['fɛrzə] f (-/-n) heel.

fertig *adj.* ['fɛrtiç] ready; *article, etc.*: finished; *clothing*: ready-made; **mit et. ~ werden** get s.th. finished; **mit et. ~ sein** have finished s.th.; '**.bringen** *v/t.* (*irr.* bringen, *sep.*, -ge-, h) bring about; manage; '**♀keit** f (-/-en) dexterity; skill; fluency (*in the spoken language*); '**.machen** *v/t.* (*sep.*, -ge-, h) finish, complete; get s.th. ready; *fig.* finish, settle *s.o.'s* hash; *sich* ~ get ready; '**♀stellung** f completion; '**♀waren** *f/pl.* finished goods *pl.* or products *pl.*

fesch F *adj.* [fɛʃ] hat, dress, *etc.*: smart, stylish, chic; dashing.

Fessel ['fɛsəl] f (-/-n) chain, fetter, shackle; *vet.* fetlock; *fig.* bond, fetter, tie; '**.ballon** *m* captive balloon; '**♀n** *v/t.* (ge-, h) chain, fetter, shackle; *j-n* ~ hold *or* arrest *s.o.'s* attention; fascinate s.o.

fest [fɛst] **1.** *adj.* firm; solid; fixed; fast; *principle*: firm, strong; *sleep*: sound; *fabric*: close; **2.** ♀ *n* (-es/-e) festival, celebration; holiday, *eccl.* feast; '**.binden** *v/t.* (*irr.* binden, *sep.*, -ge-, h) fasten, tie (*an dat.* to); '**♀essen** *n* banquet, feast; '**.fahren** *v/refl.* (*irr.* fahren, *sep.*, -ge-, h) get stuck; *fig.* reach a deadlock; '**♀halle** f (festival) hall; '**.halten** (*irr.* halten, *sep.*, -ge-, h) **1.** *v/i.* hold fast *or* tight; ~ *an* (*dat.*) adhere *or* keep to; **2.** *v/t.* hold on to; hold tight; *sich ~ an* (*dat.*) hold on to; '**.igen** ['..igən] *v/t.* (ge-, h) consolidate (*one's position, etc.*); strengthen (*friendship, etc.*); stabilize (*currency*); '**♀igkeit** ['..ç-] f (-/*no pl.*) firmness; solidity; '**♀land** *n* mainland, continent; '**.legen** *v/t.* (*sep.*, -ge-, h) fix, set; *sich auf et.* ~

commit *o.s.* to s.th.; '**.lich** *adj. meal, day, etc.*: festive; *reception etc.*: ceremonial; '**♀lichkeit** f (-/-en) festivity; festive character; '**.machen** (*sep.*, -ge-, h) **1.** *v/t.* fix, fasten, attach (*an dat.* to); ♣ moor; **2.** ♣ *v/i.* moor; put ashore; '**♀mahl** *n* banquet, feast; '**♀nahme** ['..nɑːmə] f (-/-n) arrest; '**.nehmen** *v/t.* (*irr.* nehmen, *sep.*, -ge-, h) arrest, take into custody; '**♀rede** f speech of the day; '**.setzen** *v/t.* (*sep.*, -ge-, h) fix, set; *sich* ~ *dust, etc.*: become ingrained; *p.* settle (down); '**♀spiel** *n* festival; '**.stehen** *v/i.* (*irr.* stehen, *sep.*, -ge-, h) stand firm; *fact*: be certain; '**.stehend** *adj.* fixed, stationary; *fact*: established; '**.stellen** *v/t.* (*sep.*, -ge-, h) establish (*fact, identity, etc.*); ascertain, find out (*fact, s.o.'s whereabouts, etc.*); state; see, perceive (*fact, etc.*); '**♀stellung** f establishment; ascertainment; statement; '**♀tag** *m* festive day; festival, holiday; *eccl.* feast; '**♀ung** ⚔ f (-/-en) fortress; '**♀zug** *m* festive procession.

fett [fɛt] **1.** *adj.* fat; fleshy; *voice*: oily; *land, etc.*: rich; **2.** ♀ *n* (-[e]s/-e) fat; grease (*a.* ⊕); '**♀druck** *typ. m* bold type; '**♀fleck** *m* grease-spot; '**.ig** *adj.* hair, skin, *etc.*: greasy, oily; *fingers, etc.*: greasy; *substance*: fatty.

Fetzen ['fɛtsən] *m* (-s/-) shred; rag, *Am. a.* frazzle; scrap (*of paper*); *in* ~ in rags.

feucht *adj.* [fɔyçt] climate, air, *etc.*: damp, moist; *air, zone, etc.*: humid; '**♀igkeit** f (-/*no pl.*) moisture (*of substance*); dampness (*of place, etc.*); humidity (*of atmosphere, etc.*).

Feuer ['fɔyər] *n* (-s/-) fire; light; *fig.* ardo(u)r; ~ **fangen** catch fire; *fig.* fall for (*girl*); '**.alarm** *m* fire alarm; '**♀beständig** *adj.* fire-proof, fire-resistant; '**.bestattung** f cremation; '**.eifer** *m* ardo(u)r; '**♀fest** *adj. s.* feuerbeständig; '**♀gefährlich** *adj.* inflammable; '**.haken** *m* poker; '**.löscher** *m* (-s/-) fire extinguisher; '**.melder** *m* (-s/-) fire-alarm; '**♀n** (ge-, h) **1.** ✗ *v/i.* shoot, fire (*auf acc.* at, on); **2.** F *fig. v/t.* hurl; '**.probe** *fig.* f crucial test; '**♀rot** *adj.* fiery (red), (as) red as fire; '**.sbrunst** f conflagration; '**.schiff** ♣ *n* lightship; '**.schutz** *m* fire prevention; ✗ covering fire; '**.sgefahr** f danger *or* risk of fire; '**♀speiend** *adj.*: ~*er Berg* volcano; '**.spritze** f fire engine; '**.stein** *m* flint; '**.versicherung** f fire insurance (company); '**.wache** f fire station, *Am. a.* firehouse; '**.wehr** f fire-brigade, *Am. a.* fire department; '**.wehrmann** *m* fireman; '**.werk** *n* (display of) fireworks *pl.*; '**.werkskörper** *m* firework; '**.~**

zange f (e-e a pair of) firetongs pl.; '␣zeug n lighter.

feurig adj. ['fɔyriç] fiery (a. fig.); fig. ardent.

Fiasko [fi'asko] n (-s/-s) (complete) failure, fiasco; sl. flop.

Fibel ['fi:bəl] f (-/-n) spelling-book, primer.

Fichte ♀ ['fiçtə] f (-/-n) spruce; '␣nnadel f pine-needle.

fidel adj. [fi'de:l] cheerful, merry, jolly, Am. F a. chipper.

Fieber ['fi:bər] n (-s/-) temperature, fever; ~ haben have or run a temperature; '␣anfall m attack or bout of fever; '2haft adj. feverish (a. fig.); febrile; '2krank adj. ill with fever; '␣mittel n febrifuge; '2n v/i. (ge-, h) have or run a temperature; ~ nach crave or long for; '␣schauer m chill, shivers pl.; '␣tabelle f temperature-chart; '␣thermometer n clinical thermometer.

fiel [fi:l] pret. of fallen.

Figur [fi'gu:r] f (-/-en) figure; chess: chessman, piece.

figürlich adj. [fi'gy:rliç] meaning, etc.: figurative.

Filet [fi'le:] n (-s/-s) fillet (of beef, pork, etc.).

Filiale [fi'jɑːlə] f (-/-n) branch.

Filigran(arbeit f) [fili'grɑːn(⁹-)] n (-s/-e) filigree.

Film [film] m (-[e]s/-e) film, thin coating (of oil, wax, etc.); phot. film; film, (moving) picture, Am. a. motion picture, F movie; e-n ~ einlegen phot. load a camera; '␣atelier n film studio; '␣aufnahme f filming, shooting (of a film); film (of sporting event, etc.); '2en (ge-, h) 1. v/t. film, shoot (scene, etc.); 2. v/i. film; make a film; '␣gesellschaft f film company, Am. motion-picture company; '␣kamera f film camera, Am. motion-picture camera; '␣regisseur m film director; '␣reklame f screen advertising; '␣schauspieler m film or screen actor, Am. F movie actor; '␣spule f (film) reel; '␣streifen m film strip; '␣theater n cinema, Am. motion-picture or F movie theater; '␣verleih m (-[e]s/-e) film distributors pl.; '␣vorführer m projectionist; '␣vorstellung f cinema performance, Am. F movie performance.

Filter ['filtər] (-s/-) 1. m (coffee-, etc.) filter; 2. ⊕ n filter; '2n v/t. (ge-, h) filter (water, air, etc.); filtrate (water, impurities, etc.); strain (liquid); '␣zigarette f filter-tipped cigarette.

Filz [filts] m (-es/-e) felt; fig. F skinflint; '2ig adj. felt-like; of felt; fig. F niggardly, stingy; '␣laus f crab louse.

Finanz|amt [fi'nants⁹amt] n (inland) revenue office, office of the Inspector of Taxes; '␣en f/pl. finances pl.; 2iell adj. [␣'tsjel] financial; 2ieren [␣'tsi:rən] v/t. (no -ge-, h) finance (scheme, etc.); sponsor (radio programme, etc.); '␣lage f financial position; '␣mann m financier; '␣minister m minister of finance; Chancellor of the Exchequer, Am. Secretary of the Treasury; '␣ministerium n ministry of finance; Exchequer, Am. Treasury Department; '␣wesen n (-s/no pl.) finances pl.; financial matters pl.

Findelkind ['findəl-] n foundling.

finden ['findən] (irr., ge-, h) 1. v/t. find; discover, come across; find, think, consider; wie ~ Sie ...? how do you like ...?; sich ~ thing: be found; 2. v/i.: ~ zu find one's way to.

'Finder m (-s/-) finder; '␣lohn m finder's reward.

'findig adj. resourceful, ingenious.

Findling ['fintliŋ] m (-s/-e) foundling; geol. erratic block, boulder.

fing [fiŋ] pret. of fangen.

Finger ['fiŋər] m (-s/-) finger; sich die ~ verbrennen burn one's fingers; er rührte keinen ~ he lifted no finger; '␣abdruck m fingerprint; '␣fertigkeit f manual skill; '␣hut m thimble; ♀ foxglove; '2n v/i. (ge-, h): ~ nach fumble for; '␣spitze f finger-tip; '␣spitzengefühl fig. n sure instinct; '␣übung f f finger exercise; '␣zeig ['␣tsaik] m (-[e]s/-e) hint, F pointer.

Fink orn. [fiŋk] m (-en/-en) finch.

finster adj. ['finstər] night, etc.: dark; shadows, wood, etc.: sombre; night, room, etc.: gloomy, murky; person, nature: sullen; thought, etc.: sinister, sombre, gloomy; '2nis f (-/no pl.) darkness, gloom.

Finte ['fintə] f (-/-n) feint; fig. a. ruse, trick.

Firma ✝ ['firma] f (-/Firmen) firm, business, company.

firmen eccl. ['firmən] v/t. (ge-, h) confirm.

'Firmen|inhaber m owner of a firm; '␣wert m goodwill.

Firn [firn] m (-[e]s/-e) firn, névé.

First ⚠ [first] m (-es/-e) ridge; '␣ziegel m ridge tile.

Fisch [fiʃ] m (-es/-e) fish; '␣dampfer m trawler; '2en v/t. and v/i. (ge-, h) fish; '␣er m (-s/-) fisherman; '␣erboot n fishing-boat; '␣erdorf n fishing-village; '␣erei ['␣'rai] f (-/-en) fishery; fishing; '␣fang m fishing; '␣geruch m fishy smell; '␣gräte f fish-bone; '␣grätenmuster n herring-bone pattern; '␣händler m fishmonger, Am. fish dealer; '2ig adj. fishy; '␣laich m spawn; '␣leim m fish-glue; '␣mehl n fish-meal; '␣schuppe f scale; '␣tran m train-oil; '␣vergiftung

$\mathbb{Z}$ *f* fish-poisoning; '*zucht* *f* pisciculture, fish-hatching; '*zug* *m* catch, haul, draught (of fish).

fiskalisch *adj.* ['fis'kɑːliʃ] fiscal, governmental.

Fiskus ['fiskus] *m* (-/$\mathbb{Z}$, -se, Fisken) Exchequer, *esp. Am.* Treasury; government.

Fistel $\mathbb{Z}$ ['fistəl] *f* (-/-n) fistula; '*stimme* *f* falsetto.

Fittich ['fitiç] *m* (-[e]s/-e) *poet.* wing; *j-n unter s-e* $\sim e$ *nehmen* take s.o. under one's wing.

fix *adj.* [fiks] *salary, price, etc.*: fixed; quick, clever, smart; *e-e* $\sim e$ *Idee* an obsession; *ein* $\sim er$ *Junge* a smart fellow; '**2ierbad** *phot.* [fi-'ksiːrbɑːt] *n* fixing bath; *ieren* [fi'ksiːrən] *v/t.* (*no -ge-, h*) fix (*a. phot.*); fix one's eyes (up)on, stare at s.o.; '**2stern** *ast.* *m* fixed star; '**2um** *n* (-s/Fixa) fixed *or* basic salary.

flach *adj.* [flax] *roof, etc.*: flat; *ground, etc.*: flat, level, even; *water, plate, fig.*: shallow; $\mathbb{A}$ plane.

Fläche ['flɛçə] *f* (-/-n) surface, $\mathbb{A}$ *a.* plane; sheet (*of water, snow, etc.*); *geom.* area; tract, expanse (*of land, etc.*); '*ninhalt a* $\mathbb{A}$ ['flɛçnʔ-] *m* (surface) area; '*nmaß* *n* square *or* surface measure.

'**Flach|land** *n* plain, flat country; '*rennen* *n* *turf:* flat race.

Flachs $\mathbb{Z}$ [flaks] *m* (-es/*no pl.*) flax.

flackern ['flakərn] *v/i.* (*ge-, h*) *light, flame, eyes, etc.*: flicker, wave; *voice:* quaver, shake.

Flagge $\mathbb{Z}$ ['flagə] *f* (-/-n) flag, colo(u)rs *pl.*; '**2n** *v/i.* (*ge-, h*) fly *or* hoist a flag; signal (with flags).

Flak $\mathbb{Z}$ [flak] *f* (-/-, -s) anti-aircraft gun; anti-aircraft artillery.

Flamme ['flamə] *f* (-/-n) flame; blaze; '*nmeer* *n* sea of flames; '*nwerfer* $\mathbb{Z}$ *m* (-s/-) flamethrower.

Flanell [fla'nɛl] *m* (-s/-e) flannel; *anzug* *m* flannel suit; *hose* *f* flannel trousers *pl.*, flannels *pl.*

Flank|e ['flaŋkə] *f* (-/-n) flank (*a.* $\triangle$, $\oplus$, $\mathbb{Z}$, *mount.*); side; **2ieren** [*.*'kiːrən] *v/t.* (*no -ge-, h*) flank.

Flasche ['flaʃə] *f* (-/-n) bottle; flask.

'**Flaschen|bier** *n* bottled beer; '*hals* *m* neck of a bottle; '*öffner* *m* (-s/-) bottle-opener; '*zug* $\oplus$ *m* block and tackle.

flatter|haft *adj.* ['flatərhaft] *girl, etc.*: fickle, flighty; *mind:* fickle, volatile; '*n* *v/i.* (*ge-*) **1.** (*h, sein*) *bird, butterfly, etc.*: flutter (about); *bird, bat, etc.*: flit (about); **2.** (*h*) *hair, flag, garment, etc.*: stream, fly; *mot. wheel:* shimmy, wobble; *car steering:* judder; **3.** (*sein*): *auf den Boden* $\sim$ flutter to the ground.

flau *adj.* [flau] weak, feeble, faint; *sentiment, reaction, etc.*: lukewarm;

drink: stale; *colour:* pale, dull; $\mathbb{Z}$ *market, business, etc.*: dull, slack; $\sim e$ *Zeit* slack period.

Flaum [flaum] *m* (-[e]s/*no pl.*) down, fluff; fuzz.

Flau|s [flaus] *m* (-es/-e), *sch* [*.*ʃ] *m* (-es/-e) tuft (*of wool, etc.*); napped coating.

Flausen F ['flauzən] *f/pl.* whims *pl.*, fancies *pl.*, (funny) ideas *pl.*; F fibs *pl.*; *j-m* $\sim$ *in den Kopf setzen* put funny ideas into s.o.'s head; *j-m* $\sim$ *vormachen* tell s.o. fibs.

Flaute ['flautə] *f* (-/-n) $\mathbb{Z}$ dead calm; *esp.* $\dagger$ dullness, slack period.

Flecht|e ['flɛçtə] *f* (-/-n) braid, plait (*of hair*); $\mathbb{Q}$ lichen; $\mathbb{Z}$ herpes; '**2en** *v/t.* (*irr.*, *ge-*, *h*) braid, plait (*hair, ribbon, etc.*); weave (*basket, wreath, etc.*); wreath (*flowers*); twist (*rope, etc.*); '*werk* *n* wickerwork.

Fleck [flɛk] *m* (-[e]s/-e, -en) **1.** mark (*of dirt, grease, etc.*; *zo.*); spot (*of grease, paint, etc.*); smear (*of oil, blood, etc.*); stain (*of wine, coffee, etc.*); blot (*of ink*); place, spot; *fig.* blemish, spot, stain; **2.** patch (*of material*); *bootmaking:* heel-piece; '*en* *m* (-s/-) *s.* Fleck 1; small (market-)town, townlet; '*enwasser* *n* spot *or* stain remover; '*fieber* $\mathbb{Z}$ *n* (epidemic) typhus; '**2ig** *adj.* spotted; stained.

Fledermaus *zo.* ['fleːdər-] *f* bat.

Flegel ['fleːgəl] *m* (-s/-) flail; *fig.* lout, boor; '*ei* [*.*'lai] *f* (-/-en) rudeness; loutishness; '*haft* *adj.* rude-ill-mannered; loutish; '*jahre* *pl.* awkward age.

flehen ['fleːən] **1.** *v/i.* (*ge-*, *h*) entreat, implore (*zu j-m* s.o.; *um et.* s.th.); **2.** $\mathbb{Q}$ *n* (-s/*no pl.*) supplication, imploration, entreaty.

Fleisch [flaiʃ] *n* (-es/*no pl.*) flesh; meat; $\mathbb{Q}$ pulp; '*brühe* *f* meat-broth; beef tea; '*er* *m* (-s/-) butcher; '*erei* [*.*'rai] *f* (-/-en) butcher's (shop), *Am.* butcher shop; '*extrakt* *m* meat extract; '**2fressend** *adj.* carnivorous; '*hackmaschine* *f* mincing machine, mincer, *Am.* meat grinder; '**2ig** *adj.* fleshy; $\mathbb{Q}$ pulpy; '*konserven* *f/pl.* tinned *or* potted meat, *Am.* canned meat; '*kost* *f* meat (food); '**2lich** *adj.* *desires, etc.*: carnal, fleshly; '**2los** *adj.* meatless; '*pastete* *f* meat pie, *Am. a.* potpie; '*speise* *f* meat dish; '*vergiftung* *f* meat *or* ptomaine poisoning; '*ware* *f* meat (product); '*wolf* *m* *s.* Fleisch'hackmaschine.

Fleiß [flais] *m* (-es/*no pl.*) diligence, industry; '**2ig** *adj.* diligent, industrious, hard-working.

fletschen ['flɛtʃən] *v/t.* (*ge-*, *h*): *die Zähne* $\sim$ *animal:* bare its teeth; *p.* bare one's teeth.

Flicken ['flikən] **1.** *m* (-s/-) patch;

2. ♀ v/t. (ge-, h) patch (*dress, tyre, etc.*); repair (*shoe, roof, etc.*); cobble (*shoe*).

'Flick|schneider *m* jobbing tailor; '~schuster *m* cobbler; '~werk *n* (-[e]s/*no pl.*) patchwork.

Flieder ♀ ['fliːdər] *m* (-s/-) lilac.

Fliege ['fliːgə] *f* (-/-n) *zo.* fly; bow-tie.

'fliegen 1. v/i. (*irr.*, ge-, sein) fly; go by air; 2. v/t. (*irr.*, ge-, h) fly, pilot (*aircraft, etc.*); convey (*goods, etc.*) by air; 3. ♀ *n* (-s/*no pl.*) flying; ✕ *a.* aviation.

Fliegen|fänger ['fliːgənfɛŋər] *m* (-s/-) fly-paper; '~fenster *n* fly-screen; '~gewicht *n* boxing. *etc.*: flyweight; '~klappe *f* fly-flap, *Am.* fly swatter; '~pilz ♀ *m* fly agaric.

'Flieger *m* (-s/-) flyer; ✕ airman, aviator; pilot; F plane, bomber; *cycling*: sprinter; '~abwehr ✕ *f* anti-aircraft defen|ce, *Am.* -se; '~alarm ✕ *m* air-raid alarm *or* warning; '~bombe ✕ *f* aircraft bomb; '~offizier ✕ *m* air-force officer.

flieh|en ['fliːən] (*irr.*, ge-) 1. v/i. (sein) flee (*vor dat.* from), run away; 2. v/t. (h) flee, avoid, keep away from; '2kraft *phys.* *f* centrifugal force. [(floor-)tile.)

Fliese ['fliːzə] *f* (-/-n) (wall-)tile;)

Fließ|band ['fliːs-] *n* (-[e]s/*=er*) conveyor-belt; assembly-line; '2en v/i. (*irr.*, ge-, sein) river, traffic, *etc.*: flow; *tap-water, etc.*: run; '2end 1. *adj.* water: running; *traffic*: moving; *speech, etc.*: fluent; 2. *adv.*: ~ lesen (*sprechen*) read (speak) fluently; '~papier *n* blotting-paper.

Flimmer ['flimər] *m* (-s/-) glimmer, glitter; '2n v/i. (ge-, h) glimmer, glitter; *television, film*: flicker; es flimmert mir vor den Augen everything is dancing in front of my eyes.

flink *adj.* (fliŋk] quick, nimble, brisk.

Flinte ['flintə] *f* (-/-n) shotgun; *die* ~ ins Korn werfen throw up the sponge.

Flirt [flœrt] *m* (-es/-s) flirtation; '2en v/i. (ge-, h) flirt (*mit* with).

Flitter ['flitər] *m* (-s/-) tinsel (*a.fig.*), spangle; '~kram *m* cheap finery; '~wochen *pl.* honeymoon.

flitzen F ['flitsən] v/i. (ge-, sein) whisk, scamper; dash (off, *etc.*).

flocht [flɔxt] *pret.* of flechten.

Flock|e ['flɔkə] *f* (-/-n) flake (*of snow, soap, etc.*), flock (*of wool*); '2ig *adj.* fluffy, flaky.

flog [floːk] *pret.* of fliegen.

floh[1] [floː] *pret.* of fliehen.

Floh[2] *zo.* [~] *m* (-[e]s/*=e*) flea.

Flor [floːr] *m* (-s/-e) bloom, blossom; *fig.* bloom, prime; gauze; crêpe, crape.

Florett *fenc.* [flo'rɛt] *n* (-[e]s/-e) foil.

florieren [flo'riːrən] v/i. (*no* -ge-, h)

---

business, *etc.*: flourish, prosper, thrive.

Floskel ['flɔskəl] *f* (-/-n) flourish; empty phrase.

floß[1] [flɔs] *pret.* of fließen.

Floß[2] [floːs] *n* (-es/*=e*) raft, float.

Flosse ['flɔsə] *f* (-/-n) fin; flipper (*of penguin, etc.*).

flöß|en ['fløːsən] v/t. (ge-, h) raft, float (*timber, etc.*); '2er *m* (-s/-) rafter, raftsman.

Flöte ♪ ['fløːtə] *f* (-/-n) flute; '2n (ge-, h) 1. v/i. (play the) flute; 2. v/t. play on the flute.

flott *adj.* [flɔt] ♧ floating, afloat; *pace, etc.*: quick, brisk; *music, etc.*: gay, lively; *dress, etc.*: smart, stylish; *car, etc.*: sporty, racy; *dancer, etc.*: excellent.

Flotte ['flɔtə] *f* (-/-n) ♧ fleet; ✕ navy; '~nstützpunkt ✕ *m* naval base.

Flotille ♧ [flɔ'tiljə] *f* (-/-n) flotilla.

Flöz *geol.*, ✕ [fløːts] *n* (-es/-e) seam; layer, stratum.

Fluch [fluːx] *m* (-[e]s/*=e*) curse, malediction; *eccl.* anathema; curse, swear-word; '2en v/i. (ge-, h) swear, curse.

Flucht [fluxt] *f* (-/-en) flight (*vor dat.* from); escape (*aus dat.* from); line (*of windows, etc.*); suite (*of rooms*); flight (*of stairs*).

flücht|en ['flyçtən] (ge-) v/i. (sein) and v/refl. (h) flee (*nach, zu* to); run away; escape; '~ig *adj.* fugitive (*a. fig.*); thought, *etc.*: fleeting; fame, *etc.*: transient; *p.* careless, superficial; ♧ volatile; '2ling ['~liŋ] *m* (-s/-e) fugitive; *pol.* refugee; '2lingslager *n* refugee camp.

Flug [fluːk] *m* (-[e]s/*=e*) flight; *im* ~(e) rapidly; quickly; '~abwehrrakete *f* anti-aircraft missile; '~bahn *f* trajectory (*of rocket, etc.*);✕ flight path; '~ball *m* tennis, *etc.*: volley; '~blatt *n* handbill, leaflet, *Am.* a. flier; '~boot ✕ *n* flying-boat; '~dienst ✕ *m* air service.

Flügel ['flyːgəl] *m* (-s/-) wing (*a.* △, ✕, ✕); blade, vane (*of propeller, etc.*); *s.* Fensterflügel, Türflügel, Lungenflügel; sail (*of windmill, etc.*); ♪ grand piano; '~fenster △ *n* casement-window; '2lahm *adj.* broken-winged; '~mann ✕ *m* marker; flank man; '~tür △ *f* folding door.

Fluggast ['fluːk-] *m* (air) passenger.

flügge *adj.* ['flyːgə] fledged; ~ werden fledge; *fig.* begin to stand on one's own feet.

'Flug|hafen *m* airport; '~linie *f* ✕ air route; airline; '~platz *m* airfield, aerodrome, *Am. a.* airdrome; airport; '~sand *geol.* *m* wind-blown sand; '~schrift *f* pamphlet; '~sicherung *f* air traffic control; '~sport *m* sporting aviation; '~wesen *n* aviation, aeronautics.

'Flugzeug n aircraft, aeroplane, F plane, *Am. a.* airplane; '~bau m aircraft construction; '~führer m pilot; '~halle f hangar; '~rumpf m fuselage, body; '~träger m aircraft carrier, *Am. sl.* flattop; '~unglück n air crash *or* disaster.

Flunder *ichth.* ['flundər] f (-/-n) flounder.

Flunker|ei F ['fluŋkə'raɪ] f (-/-en) petty lying, F fib(bing); '~n v/i. (ge-, h) F fib, tell fibs.

fluoreszieren [fluores'tsiːrən] v/i. (no -ge-, h) fluoresce.

Flur [fluːr] **1.** f (-/-en) field, meadow; *poet.* lea; **2.** m (-[e]s/-e) (entrance-)hall.

Fluß [flus] m (Flusses/Flüsse) river, stream; flow(ing); *fig.* fluency, flux; 2'abwärts *adv.* downriver, downstream; 2'aufwärts *adv.* upriver, upstream; '~bett n river bed.

flüssig *adj.* ['flysiç] fluid, liquid; *metal*: molten, melted; ✝ *money, capital, etc.*: available, in hand; *style*: fluent, flowing; '2keit f (-/-en) fluid, liquid; fluidity, liquidity; availability; fluency.

'Fluß|lauf m course of a river; '~mündung f mouth of a river; '~pferd *zo.* n hippopotamus; '~schiffahrt f river navigation *or* traffic.

flüstern ['flystərn] v/i. and v/t. (ge-, h) whisper.

Flut [fluːt] f (-/-en) flood; high tide, (flood-)tide; *fig.* flood, torrent, deluge; '2en (ge-) **1.** v/i. (sein) water, crowd, *etc.*: flood, surge (*über acc.* over); **2.** v/t. (h) flood (dock, *etc.*); '~welle f tidal wave.

focht [fɔxt] *pret. of* fechten.

Fohlen *zo.* ['foːlən] **1.** n (-s/-) foal; *male*: colt; *female*: filly; **2.** 2 v/i. (ge-, h) foal.

Folge ['fɔlgə] f (-/-n) sequence, succession (*of events*); instalment, part (*of radio series, etc.*); consequence, result; series; set, suit; future; ~n pl. aftermath.

'folgen v/i. (dat.) (ge-, sein) follow; succeed (*j-m s.o.*; *auf acc. to*); follow, ensue (*aus* from); obey (*j-m s.o.*); ~dermaßen *adv.* ['~dərmaːsən] as follows; '~schwer *adj.* of grave consequence, grave.

'folgerichtig *adj.* logical; consistent.

folger|n ['fɔlgərn] v/t. (ge-, h) infer, conclude, deduce (*aus* from); '2ung f (-/-en) inference, conclusion, deduction.

'folgewidrig *adj.* illogical; inconsistent.

folglich *cj.* ['fɔlkliç] therefore, consequently.

folgsam *adj.* ['fɔlkzaːm] obedient; '2keit f (-/no pl.) obedience.

Folie ['foːljə] f (-/-n) foil.

Folter ['fɔltər] f (-/-n) torture; *auf die* ~ *spannen* put to the rack; *fig.* F a. keep on tenterhooks; '2n v/t. (ge-, h) torture, torment; '~qual f torture, *fig. a.* torment.

Fonds ✝ [fõː] m (-/-) fund (*a. fig.*); funds pl.

Fontäne [fɔn'tɛːnə] f (-/-n) fountain.

foppen ['fɔpən] v/t. (ge-, h) tease, F pull s.o.'s leg; hoax, fool.

forcieren [fɔr'siːrən] v/t. (no -ge-, h) force (up).

'Förder|band n (-[e]s/-er) conveyor-belt; '2lich *adj.* conducive (*dat.* to), promotive (*of*); '~korb ☆ m cage.

fordern ['fɔrdərn] v/t. (ge-, h) demand; claim (*compensation, etc.*); ask (*price, etc.*); challenge (*to duel*).

fördern ['fœrdərn] v/t. (ge-, h) further, advance, promote; ☆ haul, raise (*coal, etc.*); *zutage* ~ reveal, bring to light.

'Forderung f (-/-en) demand; claim; charge; challenge.

'Förderung f (-/-en) furtherance, advancement, promotion; ☆ haulage; output.   [trout.]

Forelle *ichth.* [fo'rɛlə] f (-/-n)│

Form [fɔrm] f (-/-en) form; figure, shape; model; ⊕ mo(u)ld; *sports*: form, condition; 2al *adj.* [~'maːl] formal; ~alität [~ali'tɛːt] f (-/-en) formality; ~at [~'maːt] n (-[e]s/-e) size; *von* ~ of distinction; ~el ['~əl] f (-/-n) formula; 2ell *adj.* [~'mɛl] formal; 2en v/t. (ge-, h) form (*object, character, etc.*); shape, fashion (*wood, metal, etc.*); mo(u)ld (*clay, character, etc.*); '~enlehre *gr.* f accidence; '~fehler m informality; ✝ flaw; 2ieren [~'miːrən] v/t. (no -ge-, h) form; draw up, line up; *sich* ~ line up.

förmlich *adj.* ['fœrmliç] formal; ceremonious; '2keit f (-/-en) formality; ceremoniousness.

'formlos *adj.* formless, shapeless; *fig.* informal.

Formular [fɔrmu'laːr] n (-s/-e) form, *Am. a.* blank.

formu'lieren v/t. (no -ge-, h) formulate (*question, etc.*); word, phrase (*question, contract, etc.*).

forsch *adj.* [fɔrʃ] vigorous, energetic; smart, dashing.

forsch|en ['fɔrʃən] v/i. (ge-, h): ~ *nach* (dat.) search for *or* after; ~ *in* (dat.) search (through); '2er m (-s/-) researcher, research worker.

'Forschung f (-/-en) research (work); '~sreise f (exploring) expedition; '~sreisende m explorer.

Forst [fɔrst] m (-es/-e[n]) forest; '~aufseher m (forest-)keeper, gamekeeper.

Förster ['fœrstər] m (-s/-) forester; ranger.

'**Forst|haus** n forester's house; '~**revier** n forest district; '~**wesen** n, '~**wirtschaft** f forestry.

Fort¹ ✠ [fo:r] n (-s/-s) fort.

fort² adv. [fort] away, gone; on; gone, lost; in e-m ~ continuously; und so ~ and so on or forth; s. a. weg.

'**fort|bestehen** v/i. (irr. stehen, sep., no -ge-, h) continue, persist; '~**bewegen** v/t. (sep., no -ge-, h) move (on, away); sich ~ move, walk; '2**dauer** f continuance; '~**dauern** v/i. (sep., -ge-, h) continue, last; '~**fahren** v/i. (irr. fahren, sep., -ge-) 1. (sein) depart, leave; drive off; 2. (h) continue, keep on (et. zu tun doing s.th.); '~**führen** v/t. (sep., -ge-, h) continue, carry on; '2**gang** m departure, leaving; continuance; '~**gehen** v/i. (irr. gehen, sep., -ge- sein) go (away); leave; '~**geschritten** adj. advanced; '2**kommen** n (-s/no pl.) progress; '~**laufend** adj. consecutive, continuous; '~**pflanzen** v/t. (sep., -ge-, h) propagate; sich ~ biol. propagate, reproduce; phys., disease, rumour: be propagated; '2**pflanzung** f propagation; reproduction; '~**reißen** v/t. (irr. reißen, sep., -ge-, h) avalanche, etc.: sweep or carry away; '~**schaffen** v/t. (sep., -ge-, h) get or take away, remove; '~**schreiten** v/i. (irr. schreiten, sep., -ge-, sein) advance, proceed, progress; '~**schreitend** adj. progressive; '2**schritt** m progress; '~**schrittlich** adj. progressive; '~**setzen** v/t. (sep., -ge-, h) continue, pursue; '2**setzung** f (-/-en) continuation, pursuit; ~ folgt to be continued; '~**während** 1. adj. continual, continuous; perpetual; 2. adv. constantly, always.

Forum ['fo:rum] n (-s/Foren, Fora and -s) forum.

Foto... ['fo:to-] s. Photo...

Foyer [foa'je:] n (-s/-s) thea. foyer, Am. and parl. lobby; hotel: foyer, lounge.

Fracht [fraxt] f (-/-en) goods pl.; 🚂 carriage, freight, ⚓, 🗲 freight (-age), cargo; '~**brief** m 🚂 consignment note, Am., ⚓ bill of lading; '~**dampfer** m cargo steamer, freighter; '~**er** m (-s/-) freighter; '2**frei** adj. carriage or freight paid; '~**führer** m carrier, Am. a. teamster; '~**geld** n carriage charges pl., 🗲, ⚓, Am. freight; '~**gut** n goods pl., freight; '~**stück** n package.

Frack [frak] m (-[e]s/=e, -s) dress coat, tail-coat, F tails; '~**anzug** m dress-suit.

Frage ['fra:gə] f (-/-n) question; gr., rhet. interrogation; problem, point; e-e ~ stellen ask a question; in ~ stellen question; '~**bogen** m questionnaire; form; '2**en** (ge-, h)

1. v/t. ask; question; es fragt sich, ob it is doubtful whether; 2. v/i. ask; question; '~**er** m (-s/-) questioner; '~**wort** gr. n (-[e]s/=er) interrogative; '~**zeichen** n question-mark, point of interrogation, Am. mst interrogation point; 2**lich** adj. ['fra:k-] doubtful, uncertain; in question; 2**los** adv. ['fra:k-] undoubtedly, unquestionably.

Fragment [frag'ment] n (-[e]s/-e) fragment.

fragwürdig adj. ['fra:k-] doubtful, dubious, questionable.

Fraktion [frak'tsjo:n] f (-/-en) (parliamentary) group.

frank|ieren [fraŋ'ki:rən] v/t. (no -ge-, h) prepay, stamp; ~**o** adv. ['~o] free; post(age) paid; parcel: carriage paid.

Franse ['franzə] f (-/-n) fringe.

Franz|ose [fran'tso:zə] m (-n/-n) Frenchman; die ~n pl. the French pl.; ~**ösin** [~'ø:zin] f (-/-nen) Frenchwoman; 2**ösisch** [~'ø:ziʃ] French.

fräs|en ⊕ ['frɛ:zən] v/t. (ge-, h) mill; 2**maschine** ['frɛ:s-] f milling-machine.

Fraß [fra:s] 1. F m (-es/-e) sl. grub; 2. 2 pret. of fressen.

Fratze ['fratsə] f (-/-n) grimace, F face; ~n schneiden make grimaces.

Frau [frau] f (-/-en) woman; lady; wife; ~ X Mrs X.

'**Frauen|arzt** m gyn(a)ecologist; '~**klinik** f hospital for women; '~**rechte** n/pl. women's rights pl.; '~**stimmrecht** pol. n women's suffrage; '~**zimmer** mst contp. n female, woman.

Fräulein ['frɔylain] n (-s/-, F -s) young lady; teacher; shop-assistant; waitress; ~ X Miss X.

'**fraulich** adj. womanly.

frech adj. [freç] impudent, insolent, F saucy, cheeky, Am. F a. sassy, sl. fresh; lie, etc.: brazen; thief, etc.: bold, daring; '2**heit** f (-/-en) impudence, insolence; F sauciness; cheek; boldness.

frei adj. [frai] free (von from, of); position: vacant; field: open; parcel: carriage-paid; journalist, etc.: freelance; liberal; candid, frank; licentious; ~ Haus ✝ franco domicile; ~**er Tag** day off; im Freien in the open air.

'**Frei|bad** n open-air bath; ~**beuter** ['~bɔytər] m (-s/-) freebooter; '2**bleibend** ✝ adj. price, etc.: subject to alteration; offer: conditional; '~**brief** m charter; fig. warrant; '~**denker** m (-s/-) freethinker.

Freier ['fraiər] m (-s/-) suitor.

'**Frei|exemplar** n free or presentation copy; '~**frau** f baroness; '~**gabe** f release; 2**geben** (irr. geben, sep., -ge-, h) 1. v/t. release; give *(s.o. an hour, etc.)* off; **2.** *v/i.*: j-m ~ give s.o. time off; **'2gebig** *adj.* generous, liberal; **'~gebigkeit** *f* (-/-en) generosity, liberality; **'~gepäck** *n* free luggage; **'2haben** *v/i.* (*irr. haben, sep., -ge-, h*) have a holiday; have a day off; **'~hafen** *m* free port; **'2halten** *v/t.* (*irr. halten, sep., -ge-, h*) keep free *or* clear; *in restaurant, etc.*: treat; **'~handel** *m* free trade.

'Freiheit *f* (-/-en) liberty; freedom; *dichterische* ~ poetic licence, *Am.* poetic license.

'Frei|herr *m* baron; **'~karte** *f* free (*thea. a.* complimentary) ticket; **'2lassen** *v/t.* (*irr. lassen, sep., -ge-, h*) release, set free *or* at liberty; *gegen Kaution* ~ ⚖ release on bail; **'~lassung** *f* (-/-en) release; **'~lauf** *m* free-wheel.

'freilich *adv.* indeed, certainly, of course; admittedly.

'Frei|lichtbühne *f* open-air stage *or* theat|re, *Am.* -er; **'2machen** *v/t.* (*sep.*, -ge-, *h*) ✉ prepay, stamp (*letter, etc.*); *sich* ~ undress, take one's clothes off; **'~marke** *f* stamp; **'~maurer** *m* freemason; **~maurerei** [~'raɪ] *f* (-/no pl.) freemasonry; **'~mut** *m* frankness; **2mütig** *adj.* [ˈ~myːtɪç] frank; **'2schaffend** *adj.*: ~er Künstler free-lance artist; **'~schärler** ✕ [ˈ~ʃɛːrlər] *m* (-s/-) volunteer, irregular; **'~schein** *m* licen|ce, *Am.* -se; **'2sinnig** *adj.* liberal; **'2sprechen** *v/t.* (*irr. sprechen, sep., -ge-, h*) *esp. eccl.* absolve (von from); ⚖ acquit (of); release (*apprentice*) from his articles; **'~sprechung** *f* (-/-en) *esp. eccl.* absolution; release from articles; = **'~spruch** ⚖ *m* acquittal; **'2staat** *pol. m* free state; **'2stehen** *v/i.* (*irr. stehen, sep., -ge-, h*) house, *etc.*: stand empty; *es steht Ihnen frei zu inf.* you are free *or* at liberty to *inf.*; **'2stellen** *v/t.* (*sep.*, -ge-, *h*): j-n ~ exempt s.o. (von from) (*a.* ✕); j-m et. ~ leave s.th. open to s.o.; **'~stoß** *m* football: free kick; **'~tag** *m* Friday; **'~tod** *m* suicide; **'2tragend** △ *adj.* cantilever; **'~treppe** *f* outdoor staircase; **'2willig 1.** *adj.* voluntary; **2.** *adv. a.* of one's own free will; **'~willige** [ˈ~vɪligə] *m* (-n/-n) volunteer; **'~zeit** *f* free *or* spare *or* leisure time; **2zügig** *adj.* [ˈ~tsyːgɪç] free to move; **'~zügigkeit** *f* (-/no pl.) freedom of movement.

fremd *adj.* [frɛmt] strange; foreign; alien; extraneous; **'~artig** *adj.* strange; exotic.

Fremde [ˈfrɛmdə] **1.** *f* (-/no pl.) distant *or* foreign parts; *in der* ~ far away from home, abroad; **2.** *m, f* (-n/-n) stranger; foreigner; **'~buch** *n* visitors' book; **'~nführer** *m* guide, cicerone; **'~nheim** *n* boarding house; **'~nindustrie** [ˈfrɛmdən⁹-] *f* tourist industry; **'~nlegion** ✕ *f* Foreign Legion; **'~nverkehr** *m* tourism, tourist traffic; **'~nzimmer** *n* spare (bed-) room; *tourism*: room.

'Fremd|herrschaft *f* fofeign rule; **'~körper** ⚕ *m* foreign body; **2ländisch** *adj.* [ˈ~lɛndɪʃ] foreign, exotic; **'~sprache** *f* foreign language; **2sprachig** *adj.*, **2sprachlich** *adj.* foreign-language; **'~wort** *n* (-[e]s/~er) foreign word.

Frequenz *phys.* [freˈkvɛnts] *f* (-/-en) frequency.

fressen [ˈfrɛsən] **1.** *v/t.* (*irr.*, ge-, *h*) eat; *beast of prey*: devour; F *p.* devour, gorge; **2.** *v/i.* (*irr.*, ge-, *h*) eat; F *p.* gorge; **3.** ♀ *n* (-s/no pl.) feed, food.

'Freß|gier *f* voracity, gluttony; **'~napf** *m* feeding dish.

Freude [ˈfrɔʏdə] *f* (-/-n) joy, gladness; delight; pleasure; ~ haben an (*dat.*) find *or* take pleasure in.

'Freuden|botschaft *f* glad tidings *pl.*; **'~fest** *n* happy occasion; **'~feuer** *n* bonfire; **'~geschrei** *n* shouts *pl.* of joy; **'~tag** *m* day of rejoicing, red-letter day; **'~taumel** *m* transports *pl.* of joy.

'freud|estrahlend *adj.* radiant with joy; **'2ig** *adj.* joyful; happy; ~es Ereignis happy event; **'~los** *adj.* [ˈfrɔʏtloːs] joyless, cheerless.

freuen [ˈfrɔʏən] *v/t.* (ge-, *h*): es freut mich, daß I am glad *or* pleased (that); *sich* ~ über (*acc.*) be pleased about *or* with, be glad about; *sich* ~ auf (*acc.*) look forward to.

Freund [frɔʏnt] *m* (-es/-e) (boy-) friend; **~in** [ˈ~dɪn] *f* (-/-nen) (girl-) friend; **'2lich** *adj.* friendly, kind, nice; cheerful, bright; *climate*: mild; **'~lichkeit** *f* (-/-en) friendliness, kindness; **'~schaft** *f* (-/-en) friendship; ~ schließen make friends (mit with); **'2schaftlich** *adj.* friendly.

Frevel [ˈfreːfəl] *m* (-s/-) outrage (an *dat.*, gegen on), crime (against); **'2haft** *adj.* wicked, outrageous; impious; **'2n** *v/i.* (ge-, *h*) commit a crime *or* outrage (gegen against).

Frevler [ˈfreːflər] *m* (-s/-) evil-doer, offender; blasphemer.

Friede(n) [ˈfriːdə(n)] *m* (Friedens/ Frieden) peace; *im Frieden* in peace-time; *laß mich in Frieden!* leave me alone!

'Friedens|bruch *m* violation of (the) peace; **'~stifter** *m* peacemaker; **'~störer** *m* (-s/-) disturber of the peace; **'~verhandlungen** *f/pl.* peace negotiations *pl.*; **'~vertrag** *m* peace treaty.

fried|fertig *adj.* [ˈfriːt-] peaceable, peace-loving; **'2hof** *m* cemetery, graveyard; churchyard; **'~lich** *adj.*

s. friedfertig; peaceful; '**~liebend** *adj.* peace-loving.

frieren ['fri:rən] *v/i.* (*irr.*, ge-) **1.** (*sein*) *liquid*: freeze, become frozen; *river, etc.*: freeze (over, up); *window-pane, etc.*: freeze over; **2.** (*h*) be *or* feel cold; *mich friert or ich friere an den Füßen* my feet are cold.

Fries △ [fri:s] *m* (-es/-e) frieze.

frisch [friʃ] **1.** *adj. food, flowers, etc.*: fresh; *egg*: new-laid; *linen, etc.*: clean; *auf ~er Tat ertappen* catch red-handed; **2.** *adv.*: *~ gestrichen!* wet paint!, *Am.* fresh paint!; **ᘔe** ['~ə] *f* (-/*no pl.*) freshness.

Friseu|r [fri'zø:r] *m* (-s/-e) hairdresser; (*men's*) barber; **~se** [~zə] *f* (-/-n) (woman) hairdresser.

fri'sier|en *v/t.* (*no* -ge-, *h*): *j-n ~* do *or* dress s.o.'s hair; F: *einen Wagen ~ mot.* tune up *or* soup up *or* hot up a car; *sich ~* do one's hair; **ᘔkommode** *f* dressing-table; **ᘔsalon** *m* hairdressing saloon; **ᘔtisch** *m s. Frisierkommode.*

Frist [frist] *f* (-/-en) (fixed *or* limited) period of time; time allowed; term; ⚖ prescribed time; ⚖, ✝ respite, grace; '**ᘔen** *v/t.* (ge-, *h*): *sein Dasein ~* scrape along, scrape a living.

Frisur [fri'zu:r] *f* (-/-en) hair-style, hair-do, coiffure.

frivol *adj.* [fri'vo:l] frivolous, flippant; **ᘔität** [~oli'tɛ:t] *f* (-/-en) frivolity, flippancy.

froh *adj.* [fro:] joyful, glad; cheerful; happy; gay (*a. colour*).

fröhlich *adj.* ['frø:liç] gay, merry, cheerful, happy, *Am.* F *a.* chipper; '**ᘔkeit** *f* (-/⸗ -en) gaiety, cheerfulness; merriment.

froh|'locken *v/i.* (*no* -ge-, *h*) shout for joy, be jubilant; exult (*über acc.* at, in); gloat (over); '**ᘔsinn** *m* (-[e]s/*no pl.*) gaiety, cheerfulness.

fromm *adj.* [frɔm] *p.* pious, religious; *life, etc.*: godly; *prayer, etc.*: devout; *horse, etc.*: docile; *~e Lüge* white lie; *~er Wunsch* wishful thinking, idle wish.

Frömmelei [frœmə'laɪ] *f* (-/-en) affected piety, bigotry.

'**Frömmigkeit** *f* (-/-en) piety, religiousness; godliness; devoutness.

Fron [fro:n] *f* (-/-en), '**~arbeit** *f*, '**~dienst** *hist. m* forced *or* compulsory labo(u)r *or* service; *fig.* drudgery.

frönen ['frø:nən] *v/i.* (*dat.*) (ge-, *h*) indulge in; be a slave to.

Front [frɔnt] *f* (-/-en) △ front, façade, face; ⚔ front (line), line; *pol.*, ✝, *etc.*: front.

fror [fro:r] *pret. of frieren.*

Frosch *zo.* [frɔʃ] *m* (-es/⸚e) frog; '**~perspektive** *f* worm's-eye view.

Frost [frɔst] *m* (-es/⸚e) frost; chill; '**~beule** *f* chilblain.

frösteln ['frœstəln] *v/i.* (ge-, *h*) feel chilly, shiver (with cold).

'**frostig** *adj.* frosty (*a. fig.*); *fig.* cold, frigid, icy.

'**Frost|salbe** ⚕ *f* chilblain ointment; '**~schaden** *m* frost damage; '**~schutzmittel** *mot. n* anti-freezing mixture; '**~wetter** *n* frosty weather.

frottier|en [frɔ'ti:rən] *v/t.* (*no* -ge-, *h*) rub; **ᘔ(hand)tuch** *n* Turkish towel.

Frucht [fruxt] *f* (-/⸚e) ♀ fruit (*a. fig.*); corn; crop; *fig.* reward, result; '**ᘔbar** *adj.* fruitful (*esp. fig.*); fertile (*a. biol.*); '**~barkeit** *f* (-/*no pl.*) fruitfulness; fertility; '**ᘔbringend** *adj.* fruit-bearing; *fig.* fruitful; '**ᘔen** *fig. v/i.* (ge-, *h*) be of use; '**~knoten** ♀ *m* ovary; '**ᘔlos** *adj.* fruitless; *fig. a.* ineffective.

früh [fry:] **1.** *adj.* early; *am ~en Morgen* in the early morning; *~es Aufstehen* early rising; *~e Anzeichen* early symptoms; *~er* former; **2.** *adv.* in the morning; *~ aufstehen* rise early; *heute ~* this morning; *morgen ~* tomorrow morning; *~er* earlier; formerly, in former times; *~estens* at the earliest; '**ᘔaufsteher** *m* (-s/-) early riser, F early bird; '**ᘔe** *f* (-/*no pl.*): *in aller ~* very early in the morning; '**ᘔgeburt** *f* premature birth; premature baby *or* animal; '**ᘔgottesdienst** *m* early service; '**ᘔjahr** *n*, **ᘔling** ['~liŋ] *m* (-s/-e) spring; **~'morgens** *adv.* early in the morning; '**~reif** *fig. adj.* precocious; '**ᘔsport** *m* early morning exercises; '**ᘔstück** *n* breakfast; '**~stücken** (ge-, *h*) **1.** *v/i.* (have) breakfast; **2.** *v/t.* have *s.th.* for breakfast; '**ᘔzug** 🚂 *m* early train.

Fuchs [fuks] *m* (-es/⸚e) *zo.* fox (*a. fig.*); *horse*: sorrel.

Füchsin *zo.* ['fyksin] *f* (-/-nen) she-fox, vixen.

'**Fuchs|jagd** *f* fox-hunt(ing); '**~pelz** *m* fox-fur; '**ᘔ'rot** *adj.* foxy-red, sorrel; '**~schwanz** *m* foxtail; ⊕ pad-saw; ♀ amarant(h); '**ᘔ'teufels'wild** F *adj.* mad with rage, F hopping mad.

fuchteln ['fuxtəln] *v/i.* (ge-, *h*): *~ mit* (*dat.*) wave (*one's hands*) about.

Fuder ['fu:dər] *n* (-s/-) cart-load; tun (*of wine*).

Fuge ['fu:gə] *f* (-/-n) ⊕ joint; seam; ♪ fugue.

füg|en ['fy:gən] *v/refl.* (ge-, *h*) submit, give in, yield (*dat.*, *in acc.* to); comply (with); **~sam** *adj.* ['fy:k-] (com)pliant; manageable.

fühl|bar *adj.* ['fy:lba:r] tangible, palpable; *fig.* sensible, noticeable; '**~en** (ge-, *h*) **1.** *v/t.* feel; be aware of; *sich glücklich ~* feel happy; **2.** *v/i.*: *mit j-m ~* feel for *or* sympathize with s.o.; '**ᘔer** *m* (-s/-) feeler

(a. fig.); '²ung f (-/-en) touch, contact (a. ⚡); ~ haben be in touch (mit with); ~ verlieren lose touch.

fuhr [fu:r] pret. of fahren.

Fuhre ['fu:rə] f (-/-n) cart-load.

führen ['fy:rən] (ge-, h) 1. v/t. lead, guide (blind person, etc.); show (zu dat. to); wield (paint-brush, etc.); ✕ command (regiment, etc.); have, bear (title, etc.); carry on (conversation, etc.); conduct (campaign, etc.); ✝ run (shop, etc.); deal in (goods); lead (life); keep (diary, etc.); ⚐ try (case); wage (war) (mit, gegen against); ~ durch show round; sich ~ conduct o.s., behave (o.s.); 2. v/i. path, etc.: lead, run, go (nach, zu to); sports, etc.: (hold the) lead, be ahead; ~ zu lead to, result in; '~d adj. leading, prominent, Am. a. banner.

'Führer m (-s/-) leader (a. pol., sports); guide(-book); '~raum ✈ m cockpit; '~schein mot. m driving licence, Am. driver's license; '~sitz m mot. driver's seat, ✈ pilot's seat; '~stand ⚒ m (driver's) cab.

'Fuhr|geld n, '~lohn m cartage, carriage; '~mann m (-[e]s/~er, Fuhrleute) carter, carrier, wag(g)oner; driver; '~park m fleet (of lorries), Am. fleet (of trucks).

'Führung f (-/-en) leadership; conduct, management; guidance; conduct, behavio(u)r; sports, etc.: lead; '~szeugnis n certificate of good conduct.

'Fuhr|unternehmer m carrier, haulage contractor, Am. a. trucker, teamster; '~werk n (horse-drawn) vehicle; cart, wag(g)on.

Fülle ['fylə] f (-/no pl.) fullness (a. fig.); corpulence, plumpness, stoutness; fig. wealth, abundance, profusion.

füllen[1] ['fylən] v/t. (ge-, h) fill (a. tooth); stuff (cushion, poultry, etc.).

Füllen[2] zo. [~] n (-s/-) foal; male: colt; female: filly.

'Füll|er F m (-s/-), '~feder(halter m) f fountain-pen; '~horn n horn of plenty; '~ung f (-/-en) filling; panel (of door, etc.).

Fund [funt] m (-[e]s/-e) finding, discovery; find.

Fundament [funda'ment] n(-[e]s/-e) ⚛ foundation; fig. basis.

'Fund|büro n lost-property office; '~gegenstand m object found; '~grube fig. f rich source, mine.

fünf adj. [fynf] five; '²eck n pentagon; '~fach adj. ['~fax] fivefold, quintuple; '²kampf m sports: pentathlon; '²linge ['~liŋə] m/pl. quintuplets pl.; '~te adj. fifth; '²tel n (-s/-) fifth; '~tens adv. fifthly, in the fifth place; '~zehn(te) adj. fifteen(th); ~zig adj. ['~tsiç] fifty; '~zigste adj. fiftieth.

fungieren [fuŋ'gi:rən] v/i. (no -ge-, h): ~ als officiate or act as.

Funk [fuŋk] m (-s/no pl.) radio, wireless; '~anlage f radio or wireless installation or equipment; '~bastler m do-it-yourself radio ham; '~bild n photo-radiogram.

Funke ['fuŋkə] m (-ns/-n) spark; fig. a. glimmer.

'funkeln v/i. (ge-, h) sparkle, glitter; star: twinkle, sparkle.

'Funken[1] esp. fig. m (-s/-) s. Funke.

'funken[2] v/t. (ge-, h) radio, wireless, broadcast.

'Funk|er m (-s/-) radio or wireless operator; '~gerät n radio (communication) set; '~spruch m radio or wireless message; '~station f radio or wireless station; '~stille f radio or wireless silence; '~streifenwagen m radio patrol car.

Funktion [fuŋk'tsjo:n] f (-/-en) function; '~är [~tsjo'nɛ:r] m (-s/-e) functionary, official; ²ieren [~o-'ni:rən] v/i. (no -ge-, h) function, work.

'Funk|turm m radio or wireless tower; '~verkehr m radio or wireless communication; '~wagen m radio car; '~wesen n (-s/no pl.) radio communication.

für prp. (acc.) [fy:r] for; in exchange or return for; in favo(u)r of; in s.o.'s place; Schritt ~ Schritt step by step; Tag ~ Tag day after day; ich ~ meine Person ... as for me, I ...; das Für und Wider the pros and cons pl.

'Fürbitte f intercession.

Furche ['furçə] f (-/-n) furrow (a. in face); rut; ⊕ groove; '²n v/t. (ge-, h) furrow (a. face); ⊕ groove.

Furcht [furçt] f (-/no pl.) fear, dread; aus ~ vor for fear of; '²bar adj. awful, terrible, dreadful.

fürchten ['fyrçtən] (ge-, h) 1. v/t. fear, dread; sich ~ vor (dat.) be afraid or scared of; 2. v/i.: ~ um fear for.

'fürchterlich adj. s. furchtbar.

'furcht|los adj. fearless; '²losigkeit f (-/no pl.) fearlessness; '~sam adj. timid, timorous; '²samkeit f (-/no pl.) timidity.

Furie fig. ['fu:rjə] f (-/-n) fury.

Furnier ⊕ [fur'ni:r] n (-s/-e) veneer; ²en v/t. (no -ge-, h) veneer.

'Für|sorge f care; öffentliche ~ public welfare work; '~sorgeamt n welfare department; '~sorgeerziehung f corrective training for juvenile delinquents; '~sorger m (-s/-) social or welfare worker; '²sorglich adj. considerate, thoughtful, solicitous; '~sprache f intercession (für for, bei with); '~sprecher m intercessor.

Fürst [fyrst] m (-en/-en) prince; sovereign; '~enhaus n dynasty;

'**enstand** m prince's rank; '**entum** n (-s/ᵘer) principality; '**2lich 1.** adj. princely (a. fig.), royal; fig. magnificent, sumptuous; **2.** adv.: ~ leben live like a lord or king; '**lichkeiten** f/pl. royalties pl.

Furt [furt] f (-/-en) ford.

Furunkel ✆ [fuˈrunkəl] m (-s/-) boil, furuncle.

'**Fürwort** gr. n (-[e]s/ᵘer) pronoun.

Fusel F [ˈfuːzəl] m (-s/-) low-quality spirits, F rotgut.

Fusion ✝ [fuˈzjoːn] f (-/-en) merger, amalgamation.

Fuß [fuːs] m (-es/ᵘe) foot; ~ fassen find a foothold; fig. become established; auf gutem (schlechtem) ~ stehen mit be on good (bad) terms with; zu ~ on foot; zu ~ gehen walk; gut zu ~ sein be a good walker; '**abstreifer** m (-s/-) door-scraper, door-mat; '**angel** f mantrap; '**ball** m (association) football, F and Am. soccer; '**ballspieler** m football player, footballer; '**bank** f footstool; '**bekleidung** f footwear, footgear; '**boden** m floor (-ing); '**bodenbelag** m floor covering; '**bremse** mot. f foot-brake;

'**2en** v/i. (ge-, h): ~ auf (dat.) be based or founded on; '**gänger** [ˈgɛnər] m (-s/-) pedestrian; '**gelenk** anat. n ankle joint; '**note** f footnote; '**pfad** m footpath; '**sack** m foot-muff; '**sohle** anat. f sole of the foot; '**soldat** ✗ m footsoldier, infantryman; '**spur** f footprint; track; '**stapfe** [ˈʃtapfə] f (-/-n) footprint, fig. a. footstep; '**steig** m footpath; '**tritt** m kick; '**wanderung** f walking tour, hike; '**weg** m footpath.

Futter [ˈfutər] n **1.** (-s/no pl.) food, sl. grub, Am. F a. chow; feed, fodder; **2.** (-s/-) lining; ⚠ casing.

Futteral [futəˈraːl] n (-s/-e) case (for spectacles, etc.); cover (of umbrella); sheath (of knife).

'**Futtermittel** n feeding stuff.

füttern [ˈfytərn] v/t. (ge-, h) feed; line (dress, etc.); ⚠ case.

'**Futter|napf** m feeding bowl or dish; '**neid** fig. m (professional) jealousy; '**stoff** m lining (material).

'**Fütterung** f (-/-en) feeding; lining; ⚠ casing.

Futur gr. [fuˈtuːr] n (-s/-e) future (tense).

G

gab [gaːp] pret. of geben.

Gabe [ˈgaːbə] f (-/-n) gift, present; alms; donation; ⚕ dose; talent.

Gabel [ˈgaːbəl] f (-/-n) fork; '**2n** v/refl. (ge-, h) fork, bifurcate; '**ung** f (-/-en) bifurcation.

gackern [ˈgakərn] v/i. (ge-, h) cackle.

gaffen [ˈgafən] v/i. (ge-, h) gape; stare.

Gage [ˈgaːʒə] f (-/-n) salary, pay.

gähnen [ˈgɛːnən] **1.** v/i. (ge-, h) yawn; **2.** 2 n (-s/no pl.) yawning.

Gala [ˈgala] f (-/no pl.) gala; in ~ in full dress.

galant adj. [gaˈlant] gallant; courteous; 2**erie** [~ˈriː] f (-/-n) gallantry; courtesy.

Galeere ⚓ [gaˈleːrə] f (-/-n) galley.

Galerie [galəˈriː] f (-/-n) gallery.

Galgen [ˈgalgən] m (-s/-) gallows, gibbet; '**frist** f respite; '**gesicht** n gallows-look, hangdog look; '**humor** m grim humo(u)r; '**strick** m, '**vogel** m gallows-bird, hangdog.

Galle anat. [ˈgalə] f (-/-n) bile (of person); gall (of animal) (a. fig.); '**nblase** anat. f gall-bladder; '**nleiden** n bilious complaint; '**nstein** ✆ m gall-stone, bile-stone.

Gallert [ˈgalərt] n (-[e]s/-e), ~**e** [gaˈlɛrtə] f (-/-n) gelatine, jelly.

'**gallig** fig. adj. bilious.

Galopp [gaˈlɔp] m (-s/-s, -e) gallop; canter; 2**ieren** [~ˈpiːrən] v/i. (no -ge-, sein) gal¹op; canter.

galt [galt] pret. of gelten.

galvani|sch adj. [galˈvaːniʃ] galvanic; ~**ieren** [~aniˈ-] v/t. (no -ge-, h) galvanize.

Gang¹ [gaŋ] m (-[e]s/ᵘe) walk; s. Gangart; fig. motion; running, working (of machine); errand; way; course (of events, of a meal, etc.); passage(-way); alley; corridor, gallery; in vehicle, between seats: gangway, esp. Am. aisle; 🚆 corridor, Am. aisle; fencing: pass; anat. duct; mot. gear; erster (zweiter, dritter, vierter) ~ low or bottom (second, third, top) gear; in ~ bringen or setzen set going or in motion, Am. operate; in ~ kommen get going, get started; im ~ sein be in motion; ⊕ be working or running; fig. be in progress; in vollem ~ in full swing.

gang² adj. [~]: ~ und gäbe customary, traditional.

'**Gang|art** f gait, walk (of person); pace (of horse); 2**bar** [~baːr] adj. road: practicable, passable; money: current; ✝ goods: marketable; s. gängig.

Gängelband [ˈgɛŋəl-] n leading-strings *pl.*; *am* ~ *führen* keep in leading-strings, lead by the nose.

gängig *adj.* ['gɛŋiç] *money*: current; ✝ *goods*: marketable; ~er *Ausdruck* current word *or* phrase.

Gans *orn.* [gans] *f* (-/ᵘe) goose.

Gänse|blümchen ⚘ ['gɛnzəbly·mçən] *n* (-s/-) daisy; '~**braten** *m* roast goose; '~**feder** *f* goose-quill; '~**füßchen** ['·fy·sçən] *n/pl.* quotation marks *pl.*, inverted commas *pl.*; '~**haut** *f* goose-skin; *fig. a.* goose-flesh, *Am. a.* goose pimples *pl.*; '~**klein** *n* (-s/*no pl.*) (goose-)giblets *pl.*; '~**marsch** *m* single *or* Indian file; ~**rich** *orn.* ['·riç] *m* (-s/-e) gander; '~**schmalz** *n* goose-grease.

ganz [gants] **1.** *adj.* all; entire, whole; complete, total, full; *den* ~*en Tag* all day (long); **2.** *adv.* quite; entirely, *etc.* (*s.* **1.**); very; ~ *Auge* (*Ohr*) all eyes (ears); ~ *und gar* wholly, totally; ~ *und gar nicht* not at all; *im* ~*en* on the whole, generally; in all; ✝ in the lump; '♀e *n* (-*n/no pl.*) whole; totality; *aufs* ~ *gehen* go all out, *esp. Am. sl.* go the whole hog.

gänzlich *adj.* ['gɛntsliç] complete, total, entire.

'**Ganztagsbeschäftigung** *f* full-time job *or* employment.

gar [gɑ·r] **1.** *adj. food*: done; **2.** *adv.* quite, very; even; ~ *nicht* not at all.

Garage [ga'rɑ·ʒə] *f* (-/-n) garage.

Garantie [garan'ti·] *f* (-/-n) guarantee, warranty, ✝⅔ guaranty; ♀**ren** *v/t.* (*no* -ge-, *h*) guarantee, warrant.

Garbe ['garbə] *f* (-/-n) sheaf.

Garde ['gardə] *f* (-/-n) guard.

Garderobe [gardə'ro·bə] *f* (-/-n) wardrobe; cloakroom, *Am.* check-room; *thea.* dressing-room; ~**nfrau** *f* cloak-room attendant, *Am.* hat-check girl; ~**nmarke** *f* check; ~**nschrank** *m* wardrobe; ~**nständer** *m* coat-stand, hat-stand, hall-stand.

Garderobiere [gardəro'bjɛ·rə] *f* (-/-n) *s. Garderobenfrau; thea.* wardrobe mistress.

Gardine [gar'di·nə] *f* (-/-n) curtain.

gär|en ['gɛ·rən] *v/i.* (*irr.*, ge-, *h, sein*) ferment; ♀**mittel** *n* ferment.

Garn [garn] *n* (-[e]s-e) yarn; thread; cotton; net; *j-m ins* ~ *gehen* fall into s.o.'s snare.

Garnele *zo.* [gar'ne·lə] *f* (-/-n) shrimp.

garnieren [gar'ni·rən] *v/t.* (*no* -ge-, *h*) trim; garnish (*esp. a dish*).

Garnison ✕ [garni'zo·n] *f* (-/-en) garrison, post.

Garnitur [garni'tu·r] *f* (-/-en) trimming; ⊕ fittings *pl.*; set.

garstig *adj.* ['garstiç] nasty, bad; ugly.

'**Gärstoff** *m* ferment.

Garten ['gartən] *m* (-s/ᵘ) garden; '~**anlage** *f* gardens *pl.*, park; '~**ar-**

8*

---

beit *f* gardening; '~**bau** *m* horti-culture; ~**erde** *f* (garden-)mo(u)ld; '~**fest** *n* garden-party, *Am. a.* lawn party; '~**geräte** *n/pl.* gardening-tools *pl.*; '~**stadt** *f* garden city.

Gärtner ['gɛrtnər] *m* (-s/-) gardener; ~**ei** ['·raɪ] *f* (-/-en) gardening, horti-culture; nursery; '~**in** *f* (-/-nen) gardener.

Gärung ['gɛ·ruŋ] *f* (-/-en) fermen-tation.

Gas [gɑ·s] *n* (-es/-e) gas; ~ *geben mot.* open the throttle, *Am.* step on the gas; '~**anstalt** *f* gas-works, *Am. a.* gas plant; '~**behälter** *m* gasometer, *Am.* gas tank *or* con-tainer; '~**beleuchtung** *f* gaslight; '~**brenner** *m* gas-burner; ♀**förmig** *adj.* ['·fœrmiç] gaseous; '~**hahn** *m* gas-tap; '~**herd** *m* gas-stove, *Am.* gas range; '~**leitung** *f* gas-mains *pl.*; '~**messer** *m* (-s/-) gas-meter; '~**ofen** *m* gas-oven; '~**pedal** *mot. n* accelerator (pedal), *Am.* gas pedal.

Gasse ['gasə] *f* (-/-n) lane, by-street, alley(-way); '~**nhauer** *m* (-s/-) street ballad, popular song; '~**n-junge** *m* street arab.

Gast [gast] *m* (-es/ᵘe) guest; visitor; customer (*of public house, etc.*); *thea.*: guest (artist); guest star; '~**arbeiter** *m* foreign worker; '~**bett** *n* spare bed.

Gäste|buch ['gɛstə-] *n* visitors' book; '~**zimmer** *n* guest-room; spare (bed)room; *s. Gaststube.*

'**gast|freundlich** *adj.* hospitable; ♀**freundschaft** *f* hospitality; ♀**ge-ber** *m* (-s/-) host; ♀**geberin** *f* (-/-nen) hostess; '♀**haus** *n*, '♀**hof** *m* restaurant; inn, hotel; ♀**hörer** *univ. m* guest student, *Am. a.* auditor.

gastieren *thea.* [gas'ti·rən] *v/i.* (*no* -ge-, *h*) appear as a guest.

'**gast|lich** *adj.* hospitable; '♀**mahl** *n* feast, banquet; '♀**recht** *n* right of *or* to hospitality; '♀**rolle** *thea. f* guest part; starring part *or* role; '♀**spiel** *thea. n* guest appearance *or* performance; starring (perform-ance); '♀**stätte** *f* restaurant; '♀**stube** *f* taproom; restaurant; '♀**wirt** *m* innkeeper, landlord; '♀**wirtin** *f* innkeeper, landlady; '♀**wirtschaft** *f* inn, public house, restaurant; '♀**zimmer** *n s. Gästezimmer.*

'**Gas|uhr** *f* gas-meter; '~**werk** *n s. Gasanstalt.*

Gatte ['gatə] *m* (-n/-n) husband; spouse, consort.

Gatter ['gatər] *n* (-s/-) lattice; rail-ing, grating.

'**Gattin** *f* (-/-nen) wife; spouse, con-sort.

Gattung ['gatuŋ] *f* (-/-en) kind; sort; type; species; genus.

gaukeln ['gaʊkəln] *v/i.* (ge-, *h*) juggle; *birds, etc.*: flutter.

Gaul [gaʊl] *m* (-[e]s/⁼e) (old) nag.

Gaumen *anat.* ['gaʊmən] *m* (-s/-) palate.

Gauner ['gaʊnər] *m* (-s/-) scoundrel, swindler, sharper, *sl.* crook; **~ei** [~'raɪ] *f* (-/-en) swindling, cheating, trickery.

Gaze ['gaːzə] *f* (-/-n) gauze.

Gazelle *zo.* [ga'tsɛlə] *f* (-/-n) gazelle.

Geächtete [gə'ɛçtətə] *m, f* (-n/-n) outlaw.

Gebäck [gə'bɛk] *n* (-[e]s/-e) baker's goods *pl.*; pastry; fancy cakes *pl.*

ge'backen *p.p.* of backen.

Gebälk [gə'bɛlk] *n* (-[e]s/no *pl.*) framework, timber-work; beams *pl.*

gebar [gə'baːr] *pret.* of gebären.

Gebärde [gə'bɛːrdə] *f* (-/-n) gesture; **2n** *v/refl.* (no -ge-, h) conduct o.s., behave; **~nspiel** *n* (-[e]s/no *pl.*) gesticulation; dumb show, pantomime; **~nsprache** *f* language of gestures.

Gebaren [gə'baːrən] *n* (-s/no *pl.*) conduct, deportment, behavio(u)r.

gebären [gə'bɛːrən] *v/t.* (irr., no -ge-, h) bear, bring forth (*a. fig.*); give birth to.

Ge|bäude [gə'bɔrdə] *n* (-s/-) building, edifice, structure; **~bell** [~'bɛl] *n* (-[e]s/no *pl.*) barking.

geben ['geːbən] *v/t.* (irr., ge-, h) give (*j-m* et. s.o. s.th.); present (s.o. with s.th.); put; yield *s.th.*; deal (*cards*); pledge (*one's word*); *von sich* ~ emit; utter (*words*); bring up, vomit (*food*); et. (*nichts*) ~ auf (*acc.*) set (no) great store by; *sich geschlagen* ~ give in; *sich zufrieden* ~ content o.s. (*mit* with); *sich zu erkennen* ~ make o.s. known; *es gibt* there is, there are; *was gibt es?* what is the matter?; *thea.*: gegeben werden be on.

Gebet [gə'beːt] *n* (-[e]s/-e) prayer.

ge'beten *p.p.* of bitten.

Gebiet [gə'biːt] *n* (-[e]s/-e) territory; district; region; area; *fig.*: field; province; sphere.

ge'biet|en (irr. bieten, no -ge-, h) 1. *v/t.* order, command; 2. *v/i.* rule; **2er** *m* (-s/-) master, lord, governor; **2erin** *f* (-/-nen) mistress; **~erisch** *adj.* imperious; commanding.

Gebilde [gə'bildə] *n* (-s/-) form, shape; structure; **2t** *adj.* educated; cultured, cultivated.

Gebirg|e [gə'birgə] *n* (-s/-) mountains *pl.*; mountain chain *or* range; **2ig** *adj.* mountainous; **~sbewohner** *m* mountaineer; **~szug** *m* mountain range.

Ge'biß *n* (Gebisses/Gebisse) (set of) teeth; (set of) artificial *or* false teeth, denture; *harness*: bit.

ge|'bissen *p.p.* of beißen; **~'blasen** *p.p.* of blasen; **~'blichen** *p.p.* of bleichen 2; **~blieben** [~'bliːbən] *p.p.* of bleiben; **~blümt** *adj.*

[~'blyːmt] *pattern, design*: flowered; *material*: sprigged; **~'bogen** 1. *p.p.* of biegen; 2. *adj.* bent, curved; **~boren** [~'boːrən] 1. *p.p.* of gebären; 2. *adj.* born; *ein ~er Deutscher* German by birth; *~e Schmidt* née Smith.

ge'borgen 1. *p.p.* of bergen; 2. *adj.* safe, sheltered; **2heit** *f* (-/no *pl.*) safety, security.

geborsten [gə'bɔrstən] *p.p.* of bersten.

Ge'bot *n* (-[e]s/-e) order; command; bid(ding), offer; *eccl.*: *die Zehn ~e pl.* the Ten Commandments *pl.*; **2en** *p.p.* of bieten.

ge|bracht [gə'braxt] *p.p.* of bringen; **~brannt** [~'brant] *p.p.* of brennen; **~'braten** *p.p.* of braten.

Ge'brauch *m* 1. (-[e]s/no *pl.*) use; ⚕ application; 2. (-[e]s/⁼e) usage, practice; custom; **2en** *v/t.* (no -ge-, h) use, employ; **2t** *adj.* clothes, *etc.*: second-hand.

gebräuchlich [gə'brɔyçlɪç] in use; usual, customary.

Ge'brauchs|anweisung *f* directions *pl.* or instructions *pl.* for use; **~artikel** *m* commodity, necessary, requisite; personal article; **2fertig** *adj.* ready for use; *coffee, etc.*: instant; **~muster** ✝ *n* sample; registered design.

Ge'braucht|wagen *mot. m* used car; **~waren** *f/pl.* second-hand articles *pl.*

Ge'brechen *n* (-s/-) defect, infirmity; affliction.

ge'brechlich *adj.* fragile; *p.*: frail, weak; infirm; **2keit** *f* (-/-en) fragility; infirmity.

gebrochen [gə'brɔxən] *p.p.* of brechen.

Ge|brüder [gə'bryːdər] *pl.* brothers *pl.*; **~brüll** [~'bryl] *n* (-[e]s/no *pl.*) roaring; lowing (*of cattle*).

Gebühr [gə'byːr] *f* (-/-en) due; duty; charge; rate; fee; **~en** *pl.* fee(s *pl.*), dues *pl.*; **2en** *v/i.* (no -ge-, h) be due (*dat.* to); *sich* ~ be proper *or* fitting; **2end** *adj.* due; becoming; proper; **2enfrei** *adj.* free of charge; **2enpflichtig** *adj.* liable to charges, chargeable.

gebunden [gə'bundən] 1. *p.p.* of binden; 2. *adj.* bound.

Geburt [gə'buːrt] *f* (-/-en) birth; **~enkontrolle** *f*, **~enregelung** *f* birth-control; **~enziffer** *f* birthrate.

gebürtig *adj.* [gə'byrtɪç]: ~ aus a native of.

Ge'burts|anzeige *f* announcement of birth; **~fehler** *m* congenital defect; **~helfer** *m* obstetrician; **~hilfe** *f* obstetrics, midwifery; **~jahr** *n* year of birth; **~land** *n* native country; **~ort** *m* birth-place; **~schein** *m* birth certificate; **~tag** *m* birthday; **~urkunde** f birth certificate.

Gebüsch [gə'byʃ] n (-es/-e) bushes pl., undergrowth, thicket.

gedacht [gə'daxt] p.p. of denken.

Gedächtnis [gə'dɛçtnis] n (-ses/-se) memory; remembrance, recollection; im ~ behalten keep in mind; zum ~ (gen.) in memory of; **~feier** f commemoration.

Gedanke [gə'daŋkə] m (-ns/-n) thought; idea; in **~n** (versunken or verloren) absorbed in thought; sich **~n machen über** (acc.) worry about. **Ge'danken|gang** m train of thought; **~leser** m, **~leserin** f (-/-nen) thought-reader; **2los** adj. thoughtless; **~strich** m dash; **2voll** adj. thoughtful, pensive.

Ge|därm [gə'dɛrm] n (-[e]s/-e) mst pl. entrails pl., bowels pl., intestines pl.; **~deck** [~'dɛk] n (-[e]s/-e) cover; menu; ein ~ auflegen lay a place.

gedeihen [gə'daiən] 1. v/i. (irr., no -ge-, sein) thrive, prosper; 2. 2 n (-s/no pl.) thriving, prosperity.

ge'denken 1. v/i. (gen.) (irr. denken, no -ge-, h) think of; remember, recollect; commemorate; mention; ~ zu inf. intend to inf.; 2. 2 n (-s/no pl.) memory, remembrance (an acc. of).

Ge'denk|feier f commemoration; **~stein** m memorial stone; **~tafel** f commemorative or memorial tablet.

Ge'dicht n (-[e]s/-e) poem.

gediegen adj. [gə'di:gən] solid; pure; **2heit** f (-/no pl.) solidity; purity.

gedieh [gə'di:] pret. of gedeihen; **~en** p.p. of gedeihen.

Gedräng|e [gə'drɛŋə] n (-s/no pl.) crowd, throng; **2t** adj. crowded, packed, crammed; style: concise.

ge|droschen [gə'drɔʃən] p.p. of dreschen; **~'drückt** fig. adj. depressed; **~drungen** [~'druŋən] 1. p.p. of dringen; 2. adj. compact; squat, stocky, thickset.

Geduld [gə'dult] f (-/no pl.) patience; **2en** [~dən] v/refl. (no -ge-, h) have patience; **2ig** [~diç] adj. patient.

ge|dunsen adj. [gə'dunzən] bloated; **~durft** [~'durft] p.p. of dürfen 1; **~ehrt** adj. [~'eːrt] hono(u)red; correspondence: Sehr **~er** Herr N.! Dear Sir, Dear Mr N.; **~eignet** adj. [~'aignət] fit (für, zu, als for s.th.); suitable (to, for); qualified (for).

Gefahr [gə'fɑːr] f (-/-en) danger, peril; risk; auf eigene ~ at one's own risk; ~ laufen zu inf. run the risk of ger.

gefährden [gə'fɛːrdən] v/t. (no -ge-, h) endanger; risk.

ge'fahren p.p. of fahren.

gefährlich adj. [gə'fɛːrliç] dangerous.

ge'fahrlos adj. without risk, safe.

Gefährt|e [gə'fɛːrtə] m (-en/-en), **~in** f (-/-nen) companion, fellow.

Gefälle [gə'fɛlə] n (-s/-) fall, slope, incline, descent, gradient, esp. Am. a. grade; fall (of river, etc.).

Ge'fallen 1. m (-s/-) favo(u)r; 2. n (-s/no pl.): ~ finden an (dat.) take (a) pleasure in, take a fancy to or for; 3. 2 v/i. (irr. fallen, no -ge-, h) please (j-m s.o.); er gefällt mir I like him; sich et. ~ lassen put up with s.th.; 4. 2 p.p. of fallen.

gefällig adj. [gə'fɛliç] pleasing, agreeable; p.: complaisant, obliging; kind; **2keit** f (-/~-en) complaisance, kindness; favo(u)r; **~st** adv. (if you) please.

ge'fangen 1. p.p. of fangen; 2. adj. captive, imprisoned; **2e** m (-n/-n), f (-n/-n) prisoner, captive; **2enlager** n prison(ers') camp; **2nahme** f (-/no pl.) capture; seizure, arrest; **~nehmen** v/t. (irr. nehmen, sep., -ge-, h) take prisoner; fig. captivate; **2schaft** f (-/no pl.) captivity, imprisonment; **~setzen** v/t. (sep., -ge-, h) put in prison.

Gefängnis [gə'fɛŋnis] n (-ses/-se) prison, jail, gaol, Am. a. penitentiary; **~direktor** m governor, warden; **~strafe** f (sentence or term of) imprisonment; **~wärter** m warder, gaoler, jailer, (prison) guard.

Gefäß [gə'fɛːs] n (-es/-e) vessel.

gefaßt adj. [gə'fast] composed; ~ auf (acc.) prepared for.

Ge|fecht [gə'fɛçt] n (-[e]s/-e) engagement; combat, fight; action; **~fieder** [~'fiːdər] n (-s/-) plumage, feathers pl.

ge|'fleckt adj. spotted; **~flochten** [~'flɔxtən] p.p. of flechten; **~flogen** [~'floːgən] p.p. of fliegen; **~flohen** [~'floːən] p.p. of fliehen; **~flossen** [~'flɔsən] p.p. of fließen.

Ge|'flügel n (-s/no pl.) fowl; poultry; **~flüster** [~'flystər] n (-s/no pl.) whisper(ing).

gefochten [gə'fɔxtən] p.p. of fechten.

Ge'folg|e n (-s/no pl.) retinue, train, followers pl.; attendants pl.; **~schaft** f (-/-en) followers pl.

gefräßig adj. [gə'frɛːsiç] greedy, voracious; **2keit** f (-/no pl.) greediness, gluttony, voracity.

ge'fressen p.p. of fressen.

ge'frier|en v/i. (irr. frieren, no -ge-, sein) congeal, freeze; **2fleisch** n frozen meat; **2punkt** m freezing-point; **2schutz(mittel** n) m antifreeze.

gefroren [gə'froːrən] p.p. of frieren; **2e** [~ə] n (-n/no pl.) ice-cream.

Gefüge [gə'fyːgə] n (-s/-) structure; texture.

ge'**fügig** *adj.* pliant; 2**keit** *f* (-/*no pl.*) pliancy.

Gefühl [gə'fy:l] *n* (-[e]s/-e) feeling; touch; sense (*für* of); sensation; 2**los** *adj.* unfeeling, insensible (*gegen* to); 2**sbetont** *adj.* emotional; 2**voll** *adj.* (full of) feeling; tender; sentimental.

ge|**funden** [gə'fundən] *p.p. of* finden; ~**gangen** [~'gaŋən] *p.p. of* gehen.

ge'**geben** *p.p. of* geben; ~**enfalls** *adv.* in that case; if necessary.

gegen *prp.* (*acc.*) ['ge:gən] *space, time:* towards; against, 🏛 versus; about, *Am.* around; by; compared with; (in exchange) for; *remedy:* for; *freundlich sein* ~ be kind to (-wards); ~ *bar* for cash.

'**Gegen**|**angriff** *m* counter-attack; '~**antrag** *m* counter-motion; '~**antwort** *f* rejoinder; '~**befehl** *m* counter-order; '~**beschuldigung** *f* countercharge; '~**besuch** *m* return visit; '~**bewegung** *f* counter-movement; '~**beweis** *m* counter-evidence.

Gegend ['ge:gənt] *f* (-/-en) region; area.

'**Gegen**|**dienst** *m* return service, service in return; '~**druck** *m* counter-pressure; *fig.* reaction; 2**ei'nander** *adv.* against one another *or* each other; '~**erklärung** *f* counter-statement; '~**forderung** *f* counter-claim; '~**frage** *f* counter-question; '~**geschenk** *n* return present; '~**gewicht** *n* counterbalance, counterpoise; '~**gift** ⚕ *n* antidote; '~**kandidat** *m* rival candidate; '~**klage** *f* countercharge; '~**leistung** *f* return (service), equivalent; '~**lichtaufnahme** *phot.* ['ge:gənlıçt?-] *f* back-lighted shot; '~**liebe** *f* requited love; *keine* ~ *finden* meet with no sympathy *or* enthusiasm; '~**maßnahme** *f* counter-measure; '~**mittel** *n* remedy (*gegen* for), antidote (against, for); '~**partei** *f* opposite party; '~**probe** *f* check-test; '~**satz** *m* contrast; opposition; *im* ~ *zu* in contrast to *or* with, in opposition to; 2**sätzlich** *adj.* ['~zetslıç] contrary, opposite; '~**seite** *f* opposite side; 2**seitig** *adj.* mutual, reciprocal; '~**seitigkeit** *f* (-/*no pl.*): *auf* ~ *assurance:* mutual; *auf* ~ *beruhen* be mutual; '~**spieler** *m* games, *sports:* opponent; antagonist; '~**spionage** *f* counter-espionage; '~**stand** *m* object; subject, topic; '~**strömung** *f* counter-current; '~**stück** *n* counterpart; match; '~**teil** *n* contrary, reverse; *im* ~ *on* the contrary; 2**teilig** *adj.* contrary, opposite; 2'**über 1.** *adv.* opposite; **2.** *prp.* (*dat.*) opposite (to); to (-wards); as against; face to face with; ~'**über** *n* (-s/-) vis-à-vis;

2'**überstehen** *v/i.* (*irr.* stehen, *sep.,* -ge-, *h*) (*dat.*) be faced with; face; ~'**überstellung** *esp.* 🏛 *f* confrontation; '~**vorschlag** *m* counter-proposal; ~**wart** ['~vart] *f* (-/*no pl.*) presence; present time; *gr.* present tense; 2**wärtig** ['~vertıç] **1.** *adj.* present; actual; **2.** *adv.* at present; '~**wehr** *f* defen|ce, *Am.* -se; resistance; '~**wert** *m* equivalent; '~**wind** *m* contrary wind, head wind; '~**wirkung** *f* counter-effect; reaction; 2**zeichnen** *v/t.* (*sep.,* -ge-, *h*) countersign; '~**zug** *m* counter-move (*a. fig.*); 🚂 corresponding train.

ge|**gessen** [gə'gesən] *p.p. of* essen; ~**glichen** [~'glıçən] *p.p. of* gleichen; ~**gliedert** *adj.* articulate, jointed; ~**glitten** [~'glıtən] *p.p. of* gleiten; ~**glommen** [~'glɔmən] *p.p. of* glimmen.

Gegner ['ge:gnər] *m* (-s/-) adversary, opponent; ~**schaft** *f* (-/-en) opposition.

ge|**golten** [gə'gɔltən] *p.p. of* gelten; ~**goren** [~'go:rən] *p.p. of* gären; ~**gossen** [~'gɔsən] *p.p. of* gießen; ~**graben** *p.p. of* graben; ~**griffen** [~'grıfən] *p.p. of* greifen; ~**habt** [~'ha:pt] *p.p. of* haben.

Gehalt [gə'halt] **1.** *m* (-[e]s/-e) contents *pl.*; capacity; merit; **2.** *n* (-[e]s/~er) salary; 2**en** *p.p. of* halten; 2**los** [~lo:s] *adj.* empty; ~**sempfänger** [gə'halts?-] *m* salaried employee *or* worker; ~**serhöhung** [gə'halts?-] *f* rise (in salary), *Am.* raise; 2**voll** *adj.* rich; substantial; *wine:* racy.

gehangen [gə'haŋən] *p.p. of* hängen 1.

gehässig *adj.* [gə'hesıç] malicious, spiteful; 2**keit** *f* (-/-en) malice, spitefulness.

ge'**hauen** *p.p. of* hauen.

Ge|**häuse** [gə'hɔyzə] *n* (-s/-) case, box; cabinet; shell; core (*of apple, etc.*); ~**hege** [~'he:gə] *n* (-s/-) enclosure.

geheim *adj.* [gə'haım] secret; 2**dienst** *m* secret service.

Ge'**heimnis** *n* (-ses/-se) secret; mystery; ~**krämer** *m* mystery-monger; 2**voll** *adj.* mysterious.

Ge'**heim**|**polizei** *f* secret police; ~**polizist** *m* detective; plain-clothes man; ~**schrift** *f* cipher; *tel.* code.

ge'**heißen** *p.p. of* heißen.

gehen ['ge:ən] *v/i.* (*irr.,* ge-, sein) go; walk; leave; *machine:* go, work; *clock, watch:* go; *merchandise:* sell; *wind:* blow; *paste:* rise; *wie geht es Ihnen?* how are you (getting on)?; *das geht nicht* that won't do; *in sich* ~ repent; *wieviel Pfennige auf e-e Mark?* how many pfennigs go to a mark?; *das Fenster geht nach Norden* the window faces *or* looks north; *es geht nichts über* (acc.) there is nothing like; **wenn es nach mir ginge** if I had my way.

Geheul [gə'hɔyl] n (-[e]s/no pl.) howling.

Ge'hilf|e m (-n/-n), **_in** f (-/-nen) assistant; fig. helpmate.

Ge'hirn n (-[e]s/-e) brain(s pl.); **_erschütterung** f concussion (of the brain); **_schlag** m cerebral apoplexy.

gehoben [gə'ho:bən] **1.** p.p. of **heben**; **2.** adj. speech, style: elevated; **_e Stimmung** elated mood.

Gehöft [gə'hø:ft] n (-[e]s/-e) farm (-stead).

geholfen [gə'hɔlfən] p.p. of **helfen**.

Gehölz [gə'hœlts] n (-es/-e) wood, coppice, copse.

Gehör [gə'hø:r] n (-[e]s/no pl.) hearing; ear; **nach dem _** by ear; **j-m _ schenken** lend an ear to s.o.; **sich _ verschaffen** make o.s. heard.

ge'horchen v/i. (no -ge-, h) obey (j-m s.o.).

ge'hör|en v/i. (no -ge-, h) belong (dat. or zu to); **es gehört sich** it is proper or fit or right or suitable; **das gehört nicht hierher** that's not to the point; **_ig 1.** adj. belonging (dat. or zu to); fit, proper, right; due; F good; **2.** adv. duly; F thoroughly.

gehorsam [gə'ho:rza:m] **1.** adj. obedient; **2.** ♀ m (-s/no pl.) obedience.

'Geh|steig m, **_weg** m pavement, Am. sidewalk; **_werk** ⊕ n clockwork, works pl.

Geier orn. ['gaɪər] m (-s/-) vulture.

Geige ♪ ['gaɪgə] f (-/-n) violin, F fiddle; (auf der) _ spielen play (on) the violin; **_nbogen** ♪ m (violin-) bow; **_nkasten** ♪ m violin-case; **'_r** ♪ m (-s/-), **'_rin** ♪ f (-/-nen) violinist.

'Geigerzähler phys. m Geiger counter.

geil adj. [gaɪl] lascivious, wanton; luxuriant.

Geisel ['gaɪzəl] f (-/-n) hostage.

Geiß zo. [gaɪs] f (-/-en) (she-, nanny-)goat; **'_blatt** ♦ n (-[e]s/no pl.) honeysuckle, woodbine; **'_bock** zo. m he-goat, billy-goat.

Geißel ['gaɪsəl] f (-/-n) whip, lash; fig. scourge; **'♀n** v/t. (ge-, h) whip, lash; fig. castigate.

Geist [gaɪst] m (-es/-er) spirit; mind, intellect; wit; ghost; sprite; **'Geister|erscheinung** f apparition; **'♀haft** adj. ghostly.

'geistes|abwesend adj. absent-minded; **'♀arbeiter** m brain-worker, white-collar worker; **'_blitz** m brain-wave, flash of genius; **'♀gabe** f talent; **'♀gegenwärtig** presence of mind; **'_gegenwärtig** adj. alert; quick-witted; **'_gestört** adj. mentally disturbed; **'_krank**

adj. insane, mentally ill; **'♀krankheit** f insanity, mental illness; **'_schwach** adj. feeble-minded, imbecile; **'_verwandt** adj. congenial; **'♀wissenschaften** f/pl. the Arts pl., the Humanities pl.; **'♀zustand** m state of mind.

'geistig adj. intellectual, mental; spiritual; **_e Getränke** n/pl. spirits pl.

'geistlich adj. spiritual; clerical; sacred; **'♀e** m (-n/-n) clergyman; minister; **'♀keit** f (-/no pl.) clergy.

'geist|los adj. spiritless; dull; stupid; **'_reich** adj., **'_voll** adj. ingenious, spirited.

Geiz [gaɪts] m (-es/no pl.) avarice; **'_hals** m miser, niggard; **'♀ig** adj. avaricious, stingy, mean.

Gejammer [gə'jamər] n (-s/no pl.) lamentation(s pl.), wailing.

gekannt [gə'kant] p.p. of **kennen**.

Geklapper [gə'klapər] n (-s/no pl.) rattling.

Geklirr [gə'klir] n (-[e]s/no pl.), **_e** [_ə] n (-s/no pl.) clashing, clanking.

ge|klungen [_'kluŋən] p.p. of **klingen**; **_'kniffen** p.p. of **kneifen**; **_'kommen** p.p. of **kommen**; **_konnt** [_'kɔnt] p.p. of **können** 1, 2.

Ge|kreisch [gə'kraɪʃ] n (-es/no pl.) screaming, screams pl.; shrieking; **_kritzel** [_'kritsəl] n (-s/no pl.) scrawl(ing), scribbling, scribble.

ge|krochen [gə'krɔxən] p.p. of **kriechen**; **_künstelt** adj. [_'kynstəlt] affected.

Gelächter [gə'lɛçtər] n (-s/-) laughter.

ge'laden p.p. of **laden**.

Ge'lage n (-s/-) feast; drinking-bout.

Gelände [gə'lɛndə] n (-s/-) ground; terrain; country; area; **♀gängig** mot. adj. cross-country; **_lauf** m sports: cross-country race or run.

Geländer [gə'lɛndər] n (-s/-) railing, balustrade; banisters pl.

ge'lang pret. of **gelingen**.

ge'langen v/i. (no -ge-, sein): **_ an** (acc.) or in (acc.) arrive at, get or come to; **_ zu** attain (to), gain.

ge'lassen 1. p.p. of **lassen**; **2.** adj. calm, composed.

Gelatine [ʒela'ti:nə] f (-/no pl.) gelatin(e).

ge'laufen p.p. of **laufen**; **_läufig** adj. [_'lɔyfiç] current; fluent, easy; tongue: voluble; familiar; **_laut** adj. [_'laʊt] in a (good, etc.) humo(u)r or Am. mood.

Geläut [gə'lɔyt] n (-[e]s/-e), **_e** [_ə] n (-s/-) ringing (of bells); chimes pl. (of church bells).

gelb adj. [gɛlp] yellow; **'_lich** adj. yellowish; **'♀sucht** ♀ f (-/no pl.) jaundice.

Geld [gɛlt] n (-[e]s/-er) money; **im**

~ *schwimmen* be rolling in money; *zu* ~ *machen* turn into cash; '~**angelegenheit** f money-matter; '~**anlage** f investment; '~**ausgabe** f expense; '~**beutel** m purse; '~**entwertung** f devaluation of the currency; '~**erwerb** m money-making; '~**geber** m (-s/-) financial backer, investor; '~**geschäfte** n/pl. money transactions pl.; 2**gierig** adj. greedy for money, avaricious; '~**mittel** n/pl. funds pl., resources pl.; '~**schein** m bank-note, Am. bill; '~**schrank** m strong-box, safe; '~**sendung** f remittance; '~**strafe** f fine; '~**stück** n coin; '~**tasche** f money-bag; notecase, Am. billfold; '~**überhang** m surplus money; '~**umlauf** m circulation of money; '~**umsatz** m turnover (of money); '~**verlegenheit** f pecuniary embarrassment; '~**wechsel** m exchange of money; '~**wert** m (-[e]s/no pl.) value of money, money value.

Gelee [ʒəˈleː] n, m (-s/-s) jelly.

ge'legen 1. p.p. of liegen; 2. adj. situated, Am. a. located; convenient, opportune; 2**heit** f (-/-en) occasion; opportunity; chance; facility; bei ~ on occasion.

Ge'legenheits|arbeit f casual or odd job, Am. a. chore; ~**arbeiter** m casual labo(u)rer, odd-job man; ~**kauf** m bargain.

ge'legentlich 1. adj. occasional; 2. prp. (gen.) on the occasion of.

ge'lehr|ig adj. docile; 2**igkeit** f (-/no pl.) docility; 2**samkeit** f (-/no pl.) learning; ~**t** adj. [~t] learned; 2**te** [~ə] m (-n/-n) learned man, scholar.

Geleise [gəˈlaɪzə] n (-s/-) rut, track; 🚂 rails pl., line, esp. Am. tracks pl.

Geleit [gəˈlaɪt] n (-[e]s/-e) escort; attendance; j-m das ~ geben accompany s.o.; 2**en** v/t. (no -ge-, h) accompany, conduct; escort; ~**zug** 🚢 m convoy.

Gelenk anat., ⊕, ⚙ [gəˈlɛŋk] n (-[e]s/-e) joint; 2**ig** adj. pliable, supple.

ge'lernt adj. worker: skilled; trained; ~**lesen** p.p. of lesen.

Geliebte [gəˈliːptə] (-n/-n) 1. m lover; 2. f mistress, sweetheart.

geliehen [gəˈliːən] p.p. of leihen.

ge'linde 1. adj. soft, smooth, gentle; 2. adv.: gelinde gesagt to put it mildly, to say the least.

gelingen [gəˈlɪŋən] 1. v/i. (irr., no -ge-, sein) succeed; es gelingt mir zu inf. I succeed in ger.; 2. 2 n (-s/no pl.) success.

ge'litten p.p. of leiden.

gellen [ˈgɛlən] (ge-, h) 1. v/i. shrill; yell; of ears: ring, tingle; 2. v/t. shrill; yell; '~**d** adj. shrill, piercing.

ge'loben v/t. (no -ge-, h) vow, promise.

Gelöbnis [gəˈløːpnɪs] n (-ses/-se) promise, pledge; vow.

ge'logen p.p. of lügen.

gelt|en [ˈgɛltən] (irr., ge-, h) 1. v/t. be worth; 2. v/i. be of value; be valid; go; count; money: be current; maxim, etc.: hold (good or true); et. ~ have credit or influence; j-m ~ concern s.o.; ~ für or als pass for, be reputed or thought or supposed to be; ~ lassen let pass, allow; ~d machen maintain, assert; s-n Einfluß bei j-m ~d machen bring one's influence to bear on s.o.; das gilt nicht that is not fair; that does not count; es galt unser Leben our life was at stake; 2**ung** f (-/~ -en) validity; value; currency; authority (of person); zur ~ kommen tell; take effect; show; 2**ungsbedürfnis** n desire to show off. [ise; vow.\]

Gelübde [gəˈlʏpdə] n (-s/-) prom-\

gelungen [gəˈlʊŋən] 1. p.p. of gelingen; 2. adj. successful; amusing, funny; F: das ist ja ~! that beats everything!

gemächlich adj. [gəˈmɛːçlɪç] comfortable, easy; 2**keit** f (-/no pl.) ease, comfort.

Gemahl [gəˈmaːl] m (-[e]s/-e) consort; husband.

ge'mahlen p.p. of mahlen.

Gemälde [gəˈmɛːldə] n (-s/-) painting, picture; ~**galerie** f picture-gallery.

gemäß prp. (dat.) [gəˈmɛːs] according to; 2**igt** adj. moderate; temperate (a. geogr.).

gemein adj. [gəˈmaɪn] common; general; low, vulgar, mean, coarse; et. ~ haben mit have s.th. in common with.

Gemeinde [gəˈmaɪndə] f (-/-n) community; parish; municipality; eccl. congregation; ~**bezirk** m district; municipality; ~**rat** m municipal council; ~**steuer** f rate, Am. local tax; ~**vorstand** m district council.

ge'mein|gefährlich adj. dangerous to the public; ~**er Mensch** public danger, Am. public enemy; 2**heit** f (-/-en) vulgarity; meanness; mean trick; 2**nützig** adj. of public utility; 2**platz** m commonplace; ~**sam** adj. common; joint; mutual; 2**schaft** f (-/-en) community; intercourse; ~**schaftlich** adj. s. gemeinsam; 2**schaftsarbeit** [gəˈmaɪnʃafts-] f team-work; 2**sinn** m (-[e]s/no pl.) public spirit; ~**verständlich** adj. popular; 2**wesen** n community; 2**wohl** n public welfare.

Ge'menge n (-s/-) mixture.

ge'messen 1. p.p. of messen; 2. adj. measured; formal; grave.

Gemetzel [gəˈmɛtsəl] n (-s/-) slaughter, massacre.

gemieden [gə'mi:dən] *p.p. of mei-den.*

Gemisch [gə'miʃ] *n* (-es/-e) mixture; ⚗ compound, composition.

ge|mocht [gə'mɔxt] *p.p. of mögen;* **~molken** [gə'mɔlkən] *p.p. of melken.*

Gemse *zo.* ['gɛmzə] *f* (-/-n) chamois.

Gemurmel [gə'murməl] *n* (-s/no *pl.*) murmur(ing).

Gemüse [gə'my:zə] *n* (-s/-) vegetable(s *pl.*); greens *pl.*; **~anbau** *m* vegetable gardening, *Am.* truck farming; **~garten** *m* kitchen garden; **~händler** *m* greengrocer.

gemußt [gə'must] *p.p. of müssen* 1.

Gemüt [gə'my:t] *n* (-[e]s/-er) mind; feeling; soul; heart; disposition; temper; **2lich** *adj.* good-natured; genial; comfortable, snug, cosy, cozy; **~lichkeit** *f* (-/no *pl.*) snugness, cosiness; easy-going; genial temper.

Ge'müts|art *f* disposition, nature, temper, character; **~bewegung** *f* emotion; **2krank** *adj.* emotionally disturbed; melancholic; depressed; **~krankheit** *f* mental disorder; melancholy; **~ruhe** *f* composure; **~verfassung** *f*, **~zustand** *m* state of mind, humo(u)r.

ge'mütvoll *adj.* emotional; full of feeling.

genannt [gə'nant] *p.p. of nennen.*

genas [gə'nɑ:s] *pret. of genesen.*

genau *adj.* [gə'nau] exact, accurate; precise; strict; es ~ nehmen (mit) be particular (about); **2eres** full particulars *pl.*; **2igkeit** *f* (-/-en) accuracy, exactness; precision; strictness.

genehm *adj.* [gə'ne:m] agreeable, convenient; **~igen** [~igən] *v/t.* (no -ge-, h) grant; approve (of); **2igung** *f* (-/-en) grant; approval; licen|ce, *Am.* -se; permit; permission; consent.

geneigt *adj.* [gə'naikt] well disposed (*j-m* towards s.o.); inclined (*zu* to).

General ⚔ [genə'rɑ:l] *m* (-s/-e, **~e**) general; **~bevollmächtigte** *m* chief representative *or* agent; **~direktor** *m* general manager, managing director; **~feldmarschall** ⚔ *m* field-marshal; **~intendant** *thea.* m (artistic) director; **~konsul** *m* consul-general; **~konsulat** *n* consulate-general; **~leutnant** ⚔ *m* lieutenant-general; **~major** ⚔ *m* major-general; **~probe** *thea.* f dress rehearsal; **~stab** ⚔ *m* general staff; **~stabskarte** ⚔ *f* ordnance (survey) map, *Am.* strategic map; **~streik** *m* general strike; **~versammlung** *f* general meeting; **~vertreter** *m* general agent; **~vollmacht** *f* full power of attorney.

Generation [genəra'tsjo:n] *f* (-/-en) generation.

generell *adj.* [genə'rɛl] general.

genes|en [gə'ne:zən] 1. *v/i.* (irr., no -ge-, sein) recover (*von* from); 2. *p.p. of* 1; **2ende** *m, f* (-n/-n) convalescent; **2ung** *f* (-/~, -en) recovery.

genial *adj.* [gen'jɑ:l] highly gifted, ingenious; **2ität** [~ali'te:t] *f* (-/no *pl.*) genius.

Genick [gə'nik] *n* (-[e]s/-e) nape (of the neck), (back of the) neck.

Genie [ʒe'ni:] *n* (-s/-s) genius.

ge'nieren *v/t.* (no -ge-, h) trouble, bother; *sich* ~ feel *or* be embarrassed *or* shy; be self-conscious.

genießen [gə'ni:sən] *v/t.* (irr., no -ge-, h) enjoy; eat; drink; et. ~ take some food *or* refreshments; *j-s* Vertrauen ~ be in s.o.'s confidence.

Genitiv *gr.* ['ge:niti:f] *m* (-s/-e) genitive (case); possessive (case).

ge|nommen [gə'nɔmən] *p.p. of nehmen;* **~normt** *adj.* standardized; **~noß** [~'nɔs] *pret. of genießen.*

Genoss|e [gə'nɔsə] *m* (-n/-n) companion, mate; comrade (*a. pol.*); **2en** *p.p. of genießen;* **~enschaft** *f* (-/-en) company, association; co(-)operative (society); **~in** *f* (-/-nen) (female) companion; comrade (*a. pol.*).

genug *adj.* [gə'nu:k] enough, sufficient.

Genüg|e [gə'ny:gə] *f* (-/no *pl.*): *zur* ~ enough, sufficiently; **2en** *v/i.* (no -ge-, h) be enough, suffice; *das* genügt that will do; *j-m* ~ satisfy s.o.; **2end** *adj.* sufficient; **2sam** *adj.* [~k-] easily satisfied; frugal; **~samkeit** [~k-] *f* (-/no *pl.*) modesty; frugality.

Genugtuung [gə'nu:ktu:uŋ] *f*(-/-en) satisfaction.
[gender.]

Genus *gr.* ['ge:nus] *n* (-/Genera)]

Genuß [gə'nus] *m* (Genusses/Genüsse) enjoyment; pleasure; use; consumption; taking (of *food*); *fig.* treat; **~mittel** *n* semi-luxury; **~sucht** *f* (-/no *pl.*) thirst for pleasure; **2süchtig** *adj.* pleasure-seeking.

Geo|graph [geo'grɑ:f] *m* (-en/-en) geographer; **~graphie** [~a'fi:] *f* (-/no *pl.*) geography; **2graphisch** *adj.* [~'grɑ:fiʃ] geographic(al); **~loge** [~'lo:gə] *m* (-n/-n) geologist; **~logie** [~lo'gi:] *f* (-/no *pl.*) geology; **2logisch** *adj.* [~'lo:giʃ] geologic(al); **~metrie** [~me'tri:] *f* (-/-n) geometry; **2metrisch** *adj.* [~'me:triʃ] geometric(al).

Gepäck [gə'pɛk] *n* (-[e]s/no *pl.*) luggage, ⚔ *or Am.* baggage; **~annahme** *f* luggage (registration) counter, *Am.* baggage (registration) counter; **~aufbewahrung** *f* (-/-en) left-luggage office, *Am.* checkroom; **~ausgabe** *f* luggage delivery office, *Am.* baggage room; **~netz** *n* luggage-rack, *Am.* baggage rack; **~schein** *m* luggage-ticket, *Am.* baggage check; **~träger** *m* porter, *Am. a.* redcap; *on bicycle:* carrier; **~wagen** *m* luggage van, *Am.* baggage car.

ge|pfiffen [gə'pfifən] *p.p. of* pfeifen; **~pflegt** *adj.* [~'pfle:kt] *appearance:* well-groomed; *hands, garden, etc.:* well cared-for; *garden, etc.:* well-kept.

Gepflogenheit [gə'pflo:gənhart] *f* (-/-en) habit; custom; usage.

Ge|plapper [gə'plapər] *n* (-s/*no pl.*) babbling, chattering; **~plauder** [~-'plaudər] *n* (-s/*no pl.*) chatting, small talk; **~polter** [~'pɔltər] *n* (-s/*no pl.*) rumble; **~präge** [~'prɛ:gə] *n* (-s/-) impression; stamp (*a. fig.*).

ge|priesen [gə'pri:zən] *p.p. of* preisen; **~quollen** [~'kvɔlən] *p.p. of* quellen.

gerade [gə'ra:də] **1.** *adj.* straight (*a. fig.*); *number, etc.:* even; direct; *bearing:* upright, erect; **2.** *adv.* just; *er schrieb* ~ he was (just) writing; *nun* ~ now more than ever; ~ *an dem Tage* on that very day; **3.** 2 *f* (-/-n) & straight line; straight(*of race-course*); *linke(rechte)* ~ *boxing:* straight left (right); ~ *'aus* *adv.* straight on *or* ahead; **~he'raus** *adv.* frankly; **~nwegs** *adv.* [~nve:ks] directly; **~stehen** *v/i.* (*irr. stehen, sep.,* -ge-, *h*) stand erect; ~ *für* answer for *s.th.*; **~wegs** *adv.* [~ve:ks] straight, directly; **~zu** *adv.* straight; almost; downright.

ge'rannt *p.p. of* rennen.

Gerassel [gə'rasəl] *n* (-s/*no pl.*) clanking; rattling.

Gerät [gə'rɛ:t] *n* (-[e]s/-e) tool, implement, utensil; ⊕ gear; *teleph., radio:* set; apparatus; equipment; *elektrisches* ~ electric(al) appliance.

ge'raten 1. *v/i.* (*irr. raten, no* -ge-, *sein*) come *or* fall *or* get (*an acc.* by, upon; *auf acc.* on, upon; *in acc.* in, into); (*gut*) ~ succeed, turn out well; *in Brand* ~ catch fire; *ins Stocken* ~ come to a standstill; *in Vergessenheit* ~ fall *or* sink into oblivion; *in Zorn* ~ fly into a passion; **2.** *p.p. of* raten.

Gerate'wohl *n*: *aufs* ~ at random.

geräumig *adj.* [gə'rɔʏmiç] spacious.

Geräusch [gə'rɔʏʃ] *n* (-es/-e) noise; **2los** *adj.* noiseless; **2voll** *adj.* noisy.

gerb|en ['gɛrbən] *v/t.* (ge-, *h*) tan; **'2er** *m* (-s/-) tanner; **2erei** [~'rar] *f* (-/-en) tannery.

ge'recht *adj.* just; righteous; ~ *werden* (*dat.*) do justice to; be fair to; meet; please *s.o.*; fulfil (*requirements*); **2igkeit** *f* (-/*no pl.*) justice; righteousness; *j-m* ~ *widerfahren lassen* do *s.o.* justice.

Ge'rede *n* (-s/*no pl.*) talk; gossip; rumo(u)r.

ge'reizt *adj.* irritable, irritated; **2heit** *f* (-/*no pl.*) irritation.

ge'reuen *v/t.* (*no* -ge-, *h*): *es gereut mich* I repent (of) it, I am sorry for it.

Gericht [gə'riçt] *n* (-[e]s/-e) dish; course; *s.* Gerichtshof; *mst rhet. and fig.* tribunal; **2lich** *adj.* judicial, legal.

Ge'richts|barkeit *f* (-/-en) jurisdiction; **~bezirk** *m* jurisdiction; **~diener** *m* (court) usher; **~gebäude** *n* court-house; **~hof** *m* lawcourt, court of justice; **~kosten** *pl.* (law-)costs *pl.*; **~saal** *m* courtroom; **~schreiber** *m* clerk (of the court); **~stand** *m* (legal) domicile; venue; **~tag** *m* court-day; **~verfahren** *n* legal proceedings *pl.*, lawsuit; **~verhandlung** *f* (court) hearing; trial; **~vollzieher** *m* (-s/-) (court-)bailiff.

gerieben [gə'ri:bən] *p.p. of* reiben.

gering *adj.* [gə'riŋ] little, small; trifling, slight; mean, low; poor; inferior; **~achten** *v/t.* (*sep.,* -ge-, *h*) think little of; disregard; **~er** *adj.* inferior. less, minor; **~fügig** *adj.* insignificant, trifling, slight; ~ **schätzen** *v/t.* (*sep.,* -ge-, *h*) *s.* geringachten; **~schätzig** *adj.* disdainful, contemptuous, slighting; **2schätzung** *f* (-/*no pl.*) disdain; disregard; **~st** *adj.* least; *nicht im* ~*en* not in the least.

ge'rinnen *v/i.* (*irr. rinnen, no* -ge-, *sein*) curdle (*a. fig.*); congeal; coagulate, clot.

Ge'rippe *n* (-s/-) skeleton (*a. fig.*); ⊕ framework.

ge|rissen [gə'risən] **1.** *p.p. of* reißen; **2.** *fig. adj.* cunning, crafty, smart; **~ritten** [~'ritən] *p.p. of* reiten.

germanis|ch *adj.* [gɛr'ma:niʃ] Germanic, Teutonic; **2t** [~ɐ'nist] *m* (-en/-en) Germanist, German scholar; student of German.

gern(e) *adv.* ['gɛrn(ə)] willingly, gladly; ~ *haben or mögen* be fond of, like; *er singt* ~ he is fond of singing, he likes to sing.

ge'rochen *p.p. of* riechen.

Geröll [gə'rœl] *n* (-[e]s/-e) boulders *pl.*

geronnen [gə'rɔnən] *p.p. of* rinnen.

Gerste & ['gɛrstə] *f* (-/-n) barley; **'~nkorn** *n* barleycorn; & sty(e).

Gerte ['gɛrtə] *f* (-/-n) switch, twig.

Geruch [gə'rux] *m* (-[e]s/-e) smell, odo(u)r; scent; *fig.* reputation; **2los** *adj.* odo(u)rless, scentless; **~ssinn** *m* (-[e]s/ *no pl.*) sense of smell.

Gerücht [gə'rʏçt] *n* (-[e]s/-e) rumo(u)r.

ge'ruchtilgend *adj.*: ~*es Mittel* deodorant.

ge'rufen *p.p. of* rufen.

ge'ruhen *v/i.* (*no* -ge-, *h*) deign, condescend, be pleased.

Gerümpel [gə'rrympəl] n (-s/no pl.) lumber, junk.

Gerundium gr. [gə'rundjum] n (-s/Gerundien) gerund.

gerungen [gə'ruŋən] p.p. of ringen.

Gerüst [gə'ryst] n (-[e]s/-e) scaffold(ing); stage; trestle.

ge'salzen p.p. of salzen.

gesamt adj. [gə'zamt] whole, entire, total, all; ~ausgabe f complete edition; ~betrag m sum total; ~deutsch adj. all-German.

gesandt [gə'zant] p.p. of senden; 2e [~ə] m (-n/-n) envoy; 2schaft f (-/-en) legation.

Ge'sang m (-[e]s/ⁿe) singing; song; ~buch eccl. n hymn-book; ~slehrer m singing-teacher; ~verein m choral society, Am. glee club.

Gesäß anat. [gə'zɛːs] n (-es/-e) seat, buttocks pl., posterior, F bottom, behind.

ge'schaffen p.p. of schaffen 1.

Geschäft [gə'ʃɛft] n (-[e]s/-e) business; transaction; affair; occupation; shop, Am. store; 2ig adj. busy, active; ~igkeit f (-/no pl.) activity; 2lich 1. adj. business ...; commercial; 2. adv. on business.

Ge'schäfts|bericht m business report; ~brief m business letter; ~frau f business woman; ~freund m business friend, correspondent; ~führer m manager; ~haus n business firm; office building; ~inhaber m owner or holder of a business; shopkeeper; ~jahr n financial or business year, Am. fiscal year; ~lage f business situation; ~leute pl. businessmen pl.; ~mann m businessman; 2mäßig adj. business-like; ~ordnung f standing orders pl.; rules pl. (of procedure); ~papiere n/pl. commercial papers pl.; ~partner m (business) partner; ~räume m/pl. business premises pl.; ~reise f business trip; ~reisende m commercial travel(l)er, Am. travel(l)ing salesman; ~schluß m closing-time; nach ~ a. after business hours; ~stelle f office; ~träger m pol. chargé d'affaires; † agent, representative; 2tüchtig adj. efficient, smart; ~unternehmen n business enterprise; ~verbindung f business connexion or connection; ~viertel n business cent|re, Am. -er; Am. downtown; shopping cent|re, Am. -er; ~zeit f office hours pl., business hours pl.; ~zimmer n office, bureau; ~zweig m branch (of business), line (of business).

geschah [gə'ʃaː] pret. of geschehen.

geschehen [gə'ʃeːən] 1. v/i. (irr., no -ge-, sein) happen, occur, take place; be done; es geschieht ihm recht it serves him right; 2. p.p. of

1; 3. 2 n (-s/-) events pl., happenings pl.

gescheit adj. [gə'ʃaɪt] clever, intelligent, bright.

Geschenk [gə'ʃɛŋk] n (-[e]s/-e) present, gift; ~packung f gift-box.

Geschicht|e [gə'ʃiçtə] f 1. (-/-n) story; tale; fig. affair; 2. (-/no pl.) history; 2lich adj. historical; ~forscher m, ~sschreiber m historian.

Ge'schick n 1. (-[e]s/-e) fate; destiny; 2. (-[e]s/no pl.) = ~lichkeit f (-/-en) skill; dexterity; aptitude; 2t adj. skil(l)ful; dexterous; apt; clever.

ge|schieden [gə'ʃiːdən] p.p. of scheiden; ~schienen ['ʃiːnən] p.p. of scheinen.

Geschirr [gə'ʃir] n (-[e]s/-e) vessel; dishes pl.; china; earthenware, crockery; service; horse: harness.

ge'schlafen p.p. of schlafen; ~'schlagen p.p. of schlagen.

Ge'schlecht n (-[e]s/-er) sex; kind, species; race; family; generation; gr. gender; 2lich adj. sexual.

Ge'schlechts|krankheit ♀ f venereal disease; ~reife f puberty; ~teile anat. n/pl. genitals pl.; ~trieb m sexual instinct or urge; ~verkehr m (-[e]s/no pl.) sexual intercourse; ~wort gr. n (-[e]s/ⁿer) article.

ge|schlichen [gə'ʃliçən] p.p. of schleichen; ~schliffen [~'ʃlifən] 1. p.p. of schleifen; 2. adj. jewel: cut; fig. polished; ~schlossen [~'ʃlɔsən] 1. p.p. of schließen; 2. adj. formation: close; collective; ~ Gesellschaft private party; ~schlungen [~'ʃluŋən] p.p. of schlingen.

Geschmack [gə'ʃmak] m (-[e]s/ⁿe, co. ~e) taste (a. fig.); flavo(u)r; ~ finden an (dat.) take a fancy to; 2los adj. tasteless; pred. fig. in bad taste; ~(s)sache f matter of taste; 2voll adj. tasteful; pred. fig. in good taste.

ge|schmeidig adj. [gə'ʃmaɪdiç] supple, pliant; ~schmissen [~'ʃmisən] p.p. of schmeißen; ~schmolzen [~'ʃmɔltsən] p.p. of schmelzen.

Geschnatter [gə'ʃnatər] n (-s/no pl.) cackling (of geese); chatter(ing) (of girls, etc.).

ge|schnitten [gə'ʃnitən] p.p. of schneiden; ~schoben [~'ʃoːbən] p.p. of schieben; ~scholten [~'ʃɔltən] p.p. of schelten.

Geschöpf [gə'ʃœpf] n (-[e]s/-e) creature.

ge'schoren p.p. of scheren.

Geschoß [gə'ʃɔs] n (Geschosses/Geschosse) projectile; missile; stor(e)y, floor.

geschossen [gə'ʃɔsən] p.p. of schießen.

Ge'schrei n (-[e]s/no pl.) cries pl.; shouting; fig. noise, fuss.

ge|schrieben [gə'ʃriːbən] p.p. of schreiben; **schrie(e)n** [**'**ʃriː(ə)n] p.p. of schreien; **schritten** [**'**ʃritən] p.p. of schreiten; **schunden** [**'**ʃundən] p.p. of schinden.

Geschütz ✗ [gə'ʃyts] n (-es/-e) gun, cannon; ordnance.

Geschwader ✗ [gə'ʃvaːdər] n (-s/-) ⚓ squadron; ✈ wing, Am. group.

Geschwätz [gə'ʃvɛts] n (-es/no pl.) idle talk; gossip; **2ig** adj. talkative.

geschweige cj. [gə'ʃvaigə]: ~ (denn) not to mention; let alone, much less.

geschwiegen [gə'ʃviːgən] p.p. of schweigen.

geschwind adj. [gə'ʃvint] fast, quick, swift; **2igkeit** [**'**diçkait] f (-/-en) quickness; speed; pace; phys. velocity; rate; mit e-r ~ von ... at the rate of ...; **2igkeitsbegrenzung** f speed limit.

Geschwister [gə'ʃvistər] n (-s/-): ~ pl. brother(s pl.) and sister(s pl.).

ge|schwollen [gə'ʃvolən] 1. p.p. of schwellen; 2. adj. language: bombastic, pompous; **schwommen** [**'**ʃvomən] p.p. of schwimmen.

geschworen [gə'ʃvoːrən] p.p. of schwören; **2e** [**'**ə] m, f (-n/-n) juror; die**n** pl. the jury; **2engericht** n jury.

Geschwulst ⚕ [gə'ʃvulst] f (-/ᵘe) swelling; tumo(u)r.

ge|schwunden [gə'ʃvundən] p.p. of schwinden; **schwungen** [**'**ʃvuŋən] p.p. of schwingen.

Geschwür ⚕ [gə'ʃvyːr] n (-[e]s/-e) abscess, ulcer.

ge'sehen p.p. of sehen.

Gesell ✎ [gə'zɛl] m (-en/-en), **e** [**'**ə] m (-n/-n) companion, fellow; ⊕ journeyman; **2en** v/refl. (no -ge-, h) associate, come together; sich zu j-m ~ join s.o.; **2ig** adj. social; sociable.

Ge'sellschaft f (-/-en) society; company (a. ✝); party; j-m ~ leisten keep s.o. company; **er** m (-s/-) companion; ✝ partner; **erin** f (-/-nen) (lady) companion; ✝ partner; **2lich** adj. social.

Ge'sellschafts|dame f (lady) companion; **reise** f party tour; **spiel** n party or round game; **tanz** m ball-room dance.

gesessen [gə'zesən] p.p. of sitzen.

Gesetz [gə'zets] n (-es/-e) law; statute; **buch** n code; statute-book; **entwurf** m bill; **eskraft** f legal force; **essammlung** f code; **2gebend** adj. legislative; **geber** m (-s/-) legislator; **gebung** f (-/-en) legislation; **2lich** 1. adj. lawful, legal; 2. adv.: ~ geschützt patented, registered; **2los** adj. lawless; **2mäßig** adj. legal; lawful.

ge'setzt 1 adj. sedate, staid; sober;

mature; 2. cj.: ~ den Fall, (daß) ... suppose or supposing (that) ...

ge'setzwidrig adj. unlawful, illegal.

Ge'sicht n (-[e]s/-er) face; countenance; fig. character; zu ~ bekommen catch sight or a glimpse of; set eyes on.

Ge'sichts|ausdruck m (facial) expression; **farbe** f complexion; **kreis** m horizon; **punkt** m point of view, viewpoint, aspect, esp. Am. angle; **zug** m mst Gesichtszüge pl. feature(s pl.), lineament(s pl.).

Ge'sims n ledge.

Gesinde [gə'zində] n (-s/-) (domestic) servants pl.; **l** [**'**l] n (-s/no pl.) rabble, mob.

ge'sinn|t adj. in compounds: ...-minded; wohl ~ well disposed (j-m towards s.o.); **2ung** f (-/-en) mind; conviction; sentiment(s pl.); opinions pl.

gesinnungs|los adj. [gə'zinuŋsloːs] unprincipled; **treu** adj. loyal; **2wechsel** m change of opinion; esp. pol. volte-face.

ge|sittet adj. [gə'zitət] civilized; well-bred, well-mannered; **'soffen** p.p. of saufen; **sogen** [**'**zoːgən] p.p. of saugen; **sonnen** [**'**zonən] 1. p.p. of sinnen; 2. adj. minded, disposed; **sotten** [**'**zotən] p.p. of sieden; **'spalten** p.p. of spalten.

Ge'spann ✎ n (-[e]s/-e) team, Am. a. span; oxen: yoke; fig. pair, couple.

ge'spannt adj. tense (a. fig.); rope: tight, taut; fig. intent; attention: close; relations: strained; ~ sein auf (acc.) be anxious for; auf ~em Fuß on bad terms; **2heit** f (-/no pl.) tenseness, tension.

Gespenst [gə'ʃpɛnst] n (-es/-er) ghost, spect|re, Am. -er; **2isch** adj. ghostly.

Ge'spiel|e m (-n/-n), **in** f (-/-nen) playmate.

gespien [gə'ʃpiːn] p.p. of speien.

Gespinst [gə'ʃpinst] n (-es/-e) web, tissue (both a. fig.); spun yarn.

gesponnen [gə'ʃponən] p.p. of spinnen.

Gespött [gə'ʃpœt] n (-[e]s/no pl.) mockery, derision, ridicule; zum ~ der Leute werden become a laughing-stock.

Gespräch [gə'ʃprɛːç] n (-[e]s/-e) talk; conversation; teleph. call; dialogue; **2ig** adj. talkative.

ge|sprochen [gə'ʃprɔxən] p.p. of sprechen; **'sprossen** p.p. of sprießen; **sprungen** [**'**ʃpruŋən] p.p. of springen.

Gestalt [gə'ʃtalt] f (-/-en) form, figure, shape; stature; **2en** v/t. and v/refl. (no -ge-, h) form, shape; **ung** f (-/-en) formation; arrangement, organization.

gestanden [gə'ʃtandən] p.p. of stehen.

ge'ständ|ig *adj.*: ~ *sein* confess; ~nis [~t-] *n* (-ses/-se) confession.

Ge'stank *m* (-[e]s/*no pl.*) stench.

gestatten [gə'ʃtatən] *v/t.* (*no* -ge-, h) allow, permit.

Geste ['gɛstə] *f* (-/-n) gesture.

ge'stehen (*irr. stehen, no* -ge-, h) 1. *v/t.* confess, avow; 2. *v/i.* confess.

Ge'|stein *n* (-[e]s/-e) rock, stone; ~stell [~'ʃtɛl] *n* (-[e]s/-e) stand, rack, shelf; frame; trestle, horse.

gestern *adv.* ['gɛstərn] yesterday; ~ *abend* last night.

gestiegen [gə'ʃtiːgən] *p.p. of steigen.*

Ge'stirn *n* (-[e]s/-e) star; *astr.* constellation; 2t *adj.* starry.

ge|stoben [gə'ʃtoːbən] *p.p. of stieben*; ~stochen [~'ʃtɔxən] *p.p. of stechen*; ~stohlen [~'ʃtoːlən] *p.p. of stehlen*; ~storben [~'ʃtɔrbən] *p.p. of sterben*; ~stoßen *p.p. of stoßen*; ~strichen [~'ʃtriçən] *p.p. of streichen.*

gestrig *adj.* ['gɛstriç] of yesterday, yesterday's ...

ge'stritten *p.p. of streiten.*

Ge'strüpp [gə'ʃtryp] *n* (-[e]s/-e) brushwood; undergrowth.

gestunken [gə'ʃtuŋkən] *p.p. of stinken.*

Ge'stüt [gə'ʃtyːt] *n* (-[e]s/-e) stud farm; *horses kept for breeding, etc.*: stud.

Ge'such [gə'zuːx] *n* (-[e]s/-e) application, request; petition; 2t *adj.* wanted; sought-after; *politeness:* studied.

gesund *adj.* [gə'zunt] sound, healthy; salubrious; wholesome (*a. fig.*); ~er *Menschenverstand* common sense; ~en [~dən] *v/i.* (*no* -ge-, sein) recover.

Ge'sundheit *f* (-/*no pl.*) health (-iness); wholesomeness (*a. fig.*); *auf j-s ~ trinken* drink (to) s.o.'s health; 2lich *adj.* sanitary; ~ *geht es ihm gut* he is in good health.

Ge'sundheits|amt *n* Public Health Department; ~pflege *f* hygiene; public health service; 2schädlich *adj.* injurious to health, unhealthy, unwholesome; ~wesen *n* Public Health; ~zustand *m* state of health, physical condition.

ge|sungen [gə'zuŋən] *p.p. of singen*; ~sunken [~'zuŋkən] *p.p. of sinken*; ~tan [~'taːn] *p.p. of tun.*

Getöse [gə'tøːzə] *n* (-s/*no pl.*) din, noise.

ge'tragen 1. *p.p. of tragen*; 2. *adj.* solemn.

Getränk [gə'trɛŋk] *n* (-[e]s/-e) drink, beverage.

ge'trauen *v/refl.* (*no* -ge-, h) dare, venture.

Getreide [gə'traɪdə] *n* (-s/-) corn, *esp. Am.* grain; cereals *pl.*; ~(an)bau *m* corn-growing, *esp. Am.* grain growing; ~pflanze *f* cereal plant;

~speicher *m* granary, grain silo, *Am.* elevator.

ge'treten *p.p. of treten.*

ge'treu(lich) *adj.* faithful, loyal; true.

Getriebe [gə'triːbə] *n* (-s/-) bustle; ⊕ gear(ing); ⊕ drive.

ge|trieben [gə'triːbən] *p.p. of treiben*; ~troffen [~'trɔfən] *p.p. of treffen*; ~trogen [~'troːgən] *p.p. of trügen.*

ge'trost *adv.* confidently.

ge'trunken *p.p. of trinken.*

Ge|tue [gə'tuːə] *n* (-s/*no pl.*) fuss; ~tümmel [~'tyməl] *n* (-s/-) turmoil; ~viert [~'fiːrt] *n* (-[e]s/-e) square.

Gewächs [gə'vɛks] *n* (-es/-e) growth (*a. ♀*); plant; vintage; ~haus *n* greenhouse, hothouse, conservatory.

ge|'wachsen 1. *p.p. of wachsen*; 2. *adj.*: *j-m ~ sein* be a match for s.o.; *e-r Sache ~ sein* be equal to s.th.; *sich der Lage ~ zeigen* rise to the occasion; ~wagt *adj.* [~'vaːkt] risky; bold; ~wählt *adj.* [~'vɛːlt] *style:* refined; ~'wahr *adj.*: ~ *werden* (*acc. or gen.*) perceive *s.th.*; become aware of *s.th.*; ~ *werden, daß* become aware that.

Gewähr [gə'vɛːr] *f* (-/*no pl.*) guarantee, warrant, security; 2en *v/t.* (*no* -ge-, h) grant, allow; give, yield, afford; *j-n ~ lassen* let s.o. have his way; leave s.o. alone; 2leisten *v/t.* (*no* -ge-, h) guarantee.

Ge'wahrsam *m* (-s/-e) custody, safe keeping.

Ge'währsmann *m* informant, source.

Gewalt [gə'valt] *f* (-/-en) power; authority; control; force, violence; *höhere ~* act of God; *mit ~* by force; ~herrschaft *f* despotism, tyranny; 2ig *adj.* powerful, mighty; vehement; vast; ~maßnahme *f* violent measure; 2sam 1. *adj.* violent; 2. *adv. a.* forcibly; ~ *öffnen* force open; open by force; ~tat *f* act of violence; 2tätig *adj.* violent.

Gewand [gə'vant] *n* (-[e]s/⁀er) garment; robe; *esp. eccl.* vestment.

ge'wandt 1. *p.p. of wenden* 2; 2. *adj.* agile, nimble, dexterous, adroit; clever; 2heit *f* (-/*no pl.*) agility, nimbleness; adroitness, dexterity; cleverness.

ge'wann *pret. of gewinnen.*

Gewäsch F [gə'vɛʃ] *n* (-es/*no pl.*) twaddle, nonsense.

ge'waschen *p.p. of waschen.*

Gewässer [gə'vɛsər] *n* (-s/-) water(s *pl.*).

Gewebe [gə'veːbə] *n* (-s/-) tissue (*a. anat. and fig.*); fabric, web; texture.

Ge'wehr *n* gun; rifle; ~kolben *m* (rifle-)butt; ~lauf *m* (rifle-, gun-) barrel.

Geweih [gə'vaɪ] n (-[e]s/-e) horns pl., head, antlers pl.

Gewerbe [gə'vɛrbə] n (-s/-) trade, business; industry; **~freiheit** f freedom of trade; **~schein** m trade licen|ce, Am. -se; **~schule** f technical school; **~steuer** f trade tax; **2treibend** adj. carrying on a business, engaged in trade; **~treibende** m (-n/-n) tradesman.

gewerb|lich adj. [gə'vɛrplɪç] commercial, industrial; **~smäßig** adj. professional.

Ge'werkschaft f (-/-en) trade(s) union, Am. labor union; **~ler** m (-s/-) trade(s)-unionist; **2lich** adj. trade-union; **~sbund** m Trade Union Congress, Am. Federation of Labor.

ge|wesen [gə'veːzən] p.p. of sein; **~wichen** [~'vɪçən] p.p. of weichen.

Gewicht [gə'vɪçt] n (-[e]s/-e) weight, Am. F a. heft; **e-r Sache ~ beimessen** attach importance to s.th.; **~ haben** carry weight (bei dat. with); **~ legen auf et.** lay stress on s.th.; **ins ~ fallen** be of great weight, count, matter; **2ig** adj. weighty (a. fig.).

ge|wiesen [gə'viːzən] p.p. of weisen; **~willt** adj. [~'vɪlt] willing.

Ge|wimmel [gə'vɪməl] n (-s/no pl.) swarm; throng; **~winde** ⊕ [~'vɪndə] n (-s/-) thread.

Gewinn [gə'vɪn] m (-[e]s/-e) gain; † gains pl.; profit; lottery ticket: prize; game: winnings pl.; **~anteil** m dividend; **~beteiligung** f profit-sharing; **2bringend** adj. profitable; **2en** (irr., no -ge-, h) **1.** v/t. win; gain; get; **2.** v/i. win; gain; fig. improve; **2end** adj. manner, smile: winning, engaging; **~er** m (-s/-) winner.

Ge'wirr n (-[e]s/-e) tangle, entanglement; streets: maze; voices: confusion.

gewiß [gə'vɪs] **1.** adj. certain; ein gewisser Herr N. a certain Mr. N., one Mr. N.; **2.** adv.: **~!** certainly!, to be sure!, Am. sure!

Ge'wissen n (-s/-) conscience; **2haft** adj. conscientious; **2los** adj. unscrupulous; **~sbisse** m/pl. remorse, pangs pl. of conscience; **~sfrage** f question of conscience.

gewissermaßen [gəvɪsər-'maːsən] adv. to a certain extent.

Ge'wißheit f (-/-en) certainty; certitude.

Gewitter [gə'vɪtər] n (-s/-) (thunder)storm; **2n** v/i. (no -ge-, h): es gewittert there is a thunderstorm; **~regen** m thunder-shower; **~wolke** f thundercloud.

ge|woben [gə'voːbən] p.p. of weben; **~wogen 1.** p.p. of wägen and wiegen¹; **2.** adj. (dat.) well or kindly disposed towards, favo(u)rably inclined towards.

gewöhnen [gə'vøːnən] v/t. (no -ge-, h) accustom, get used (an acc. to).

Gewohnheit [gə'voːnhaɪt] f (-/-en) habit; custom; **2smäßig** adj. habitual.

ge'wöhnlich adj. common; ordinary; usual, customary; habitual; common, vulgar.

ge'wohnt adj. customary, habitual; (es) **~ sein zu** inf. be accustomed or used to inf.

Gewölbe [gə'vœlbə] n (-s/-) vault.

ge|wonnen [gə'vɔnən] p.p. of gewinnen; **~worben** [~'vɔrbən] p.p. of werben; **~worden** [~'vɔrdən] p.p. of werden; **~worfen** [~'vɔrfən] p.p. of werfen; **~wrungen** [~'vrʊŋən] p.p. of wringen.

Gewühl [gə'vyːl] n (-[e]s/no pl.) bustle; milling crowd.

gewunden [gə'vʊndən] **1.** p.p. of winden; **2.** adj. twisted; winding.

Gewürz [gə'vyrts] n (-es/-e) spice; condiment; **~nelke** ♀ f clove.

ge'wußt p.p. of wissen.

Ge|'zeit f: mst **~en** pl. tide(s pl.); **~'zeter** n (-s/no pl.) (shrill) clamo(u)r.

ge|'ziert adj. affected; **~zogen** [~'tsoːgən] p.p. of ziehen.

Gezwitscher [gə'tsvɪtʃər] n (-s/no pl.) chirping, twitter(ing).

gezwungen [gə'tsvʊŋən] **1.** p.p. of zwingen; **2.** adj. forced, constrained.

Gicht ♀ [gɪçt] f (-/no pl.) gout; **2isch** ♀ adj. gouty; **~knoten** ♀ m gouty knot.

Giebel ['giːbəl] m (-s/-) gable(-end).

Gier [giːr] f (-/no pl.) greed(iness) (nach for); **2ig** adj. greedy (nach for, of).

'Gießbach m torrent.

gieß|en ['giːsən] (irr., ge-, h) **1.** v/t. pour; ⊕ cast, found; water (flowers); **2.** v/i.: es gießt it is pouring (with rain); **2er** m (-s/-) founder; **2erei** [~'raɪ] f (-/-en) foundry; **2kanne** f watering-can or -pot.

Gift [gɪft] n (-[e]s/-e) poison; venom (esp. of snakes) (a. fig.); malice, spite; **2ig** adj. poisonous; venomous; malicious, spiteful; **'~schlange** f venomous or poisonous snake; **'~zahn** m poison-fang.

Gigant [gi'gant] m (-en/-en) giant.

Gimpel orn. ['gɪmpəl] m (-s/-) bullfinch.

ging [gɪŋ] pret. of gehen.

Gipfel ['gɪpfəl] m (-s/-) summit; top; peak; **'~konferenz** pol. f summit meeting or conference; **'2n** v/i. (ge-, h) culminate.

Gips [gɪps] m (-es/-e) min. gypsum; ⊕ plaster (of Paris); **'~abdruck** m, **'~abguß** m plaster cast; **'2en** v/t. (ge-, h) plaster; **'~verband** ♀ m plaster (of Paris) dressing.

Giraffe zo. [gi'rafə] f (-/-n) giraffe.

girieren † [ʒi'riːrən] v/t. (no -ge-, h) endorse, indorse (bill of exchange).

Girlande [gir'landə] f (-/-n) garland.

Giro † ['ʒiːro] n (-s/-s) endorsement, indorsement; '~bank f clearing-bank; '~konto n current account.

girren ['girən] v/i. (ge-, h) coo.

Gischt [gɪʃt] m (-es/⅃ -e) and f (-/⅃ -en) foam, froth; spray; spindrift.

Gitarre ♪ [gi'tarə] f (-/-n) guitar.

Gitter ['gitər] n (-s/-) grating; lattice; trellis; railing; '~bett n crib; '~fenster n lattice-window.

Glacéhandschuh [gla'seː-] m kid glove.

Glanz [glants] m (-es/no pl.) brightness; lust|re, Am. -er; brilliancy; splendo(u)r.

glänzen ['glɛntsən] v/i. (ge-, h) glitter, shine; '~d adj. bright, brilliant; fig. splendid.

'Glanz|leistung f brilliant achievement or performance; '~papier n glazed paper; '~punkt m highlight; '~zeit f golden age, heyday.

Glas [glaːs] n (-es/⅃er) glass; ~er ['⅃zər] m (-s/-) glazier.

gläsern adj. ['glɛːzərn] of glass; fig. glassy.

'Glas|glocke f (glass) shade or cover; globe; bell-glass; '~hütte f glass-works sg., pl.

glasieren [gla'ziːrən] v/t. (no -ge-, h) glaze; ice, frost (cake).

glasig adj. ['glaːziç] glassy, vitreous.

'Glasscheibe f pane of glass.

Glasur [gla'zuːr] f (-/-en) glaze, glazing; enamel; icing, frosting (on cakes).

glatt [glat] 1. adj. smooth (a. fig.); even; lie, etc.: flat, downright; road, etc.: slippery; 2. adv. smoothly, evenly; ~ anliegen fit closely or tightly; ~ rasiert clean-shaven; et. ~ ableugnen deny s.th. flatly.

Glätte ['glɛtə] f (-/-n) smoothness; road, etc.: slipperiness.

'Glatteis n glazed frost, icy glaze, Am. glaze; F: j-n aufs ~ führen lead s.o. up the garden path.

'glätten v/t. (ge-, h) smooth.

Glatze ['glatsə] f (-/-n) bald head.

Glaube ['glaubə] m (-ns/⅃-n) faith, belief (an acc. in); '2n (ge-, h) 1. v/t. believe; think, suppose, Am. a. guess; 2. v/i. believe (j-m s.o.; an acc. in).

'Glaubens|bekenntnis n creed, profession or confession of faith; '~lehre f, '~satz m dogma, doctrine.

glaubhaft adj. ['glaup-] credible; plausible; authentic.

gläubig adj. ['glɔybiç] believing, faithful; 2e n (-n/-n) m, f (-n/-n)

believer; 2er † ['⅃gər] m (-s/-) creditor.

glaubwürdig adj. ['glaup-] credible.

gleich [glaiç] 1. adj. equal (an dat. in); the same; like; even, level; in ~er Weise likewise; zur ~en Zeit at the same time; es ist mir ~ it's all the same to me; das ~e the same; as much; er ist nicht (mehr) der ~e he is not the same man; 2. adv. alike, equally; immediately, presently, directly, at once; just; es ist ~ acht (Uhr) it is close on or nearly eight (o'clock); ~altrig adj. ['⅃altriç] (of) the same age; '~artig adj. homogeneous; similar; uniform; '~bedeutend adj. synonymous; equivalent (to); tantamount (mit to); '~berechtigt adj. having equal rights; '~bleibend adj. constant, steady; ~en v/i. (irr., ge-, h) equal; resemble.

'gleich|falls adv. also, likewise; '~förmig adj. ['⅃fœrmiç] uniform; '~gesinnt adj. like-minded; '2gewicht n balance (a. fig.); equilibrium, equipoise; pol.: ~ der Kräfte balance of power; '~gültig adj. indifferent (gegen to); es ist mir ~ I don't care; ~, was du tust no matter what you do; '2gültigkeit f indifference; '2heit f (-/-en) equality; likeness; '2klang m unison, consonance, harmony; '~kommen v/i. (irr. kommen, sep., -ge-, sein): e-r Sache ~ amount to s.th.; j-m ~ equal s.o.; '~laufend adj. parallel; '~lautend adj. consonant; identical; '~machen v/t. (sep., -ge-, h) make equal (dat. to), equalize (to or with); '2maß n regularity; evenness; fig. equilibrium; '~mäßig adj. equal; regular; constant; even; '2mut m equanimity; '~mütig adj. even-tempered; calm; '~namig adj. ['⅃naːmiç] of the same name; '2nis n (-ses/-se) parable; rhet. simile; '~sam adv. as it were, so to speak; '~schalten v/t. (sep., -ge-, h) ⊕ synchronize; pol. co-ordinate, unify; '~seitig adj. equilateral; '~setzen v/t. (sep., -ge-, h) equate (dat. or mit with); '~stehen v/i. (irr. stehen, sep., -ge-, h) be equal; '~stellen v/t. (sep., -ge-, h) equalize, equate (dat. with); put s.o. on an equal footing (with); '2stellung f equalization, equation; '2strom ⅃ m direct current; '2ung ⅃ f (-/-en) equation; '~wertig adj. equivalent, of the same value, of equal value; '~zeitig adj. simultaneous; synchronous; contemporary.

Gleis [glais] n (-es/-e) s. Geleise.

gleiten ['glaitən] v/i. (irr., ge-, sein) glide, slide.

'Gleit|flug m gliding flight, glide, ✈ volplane; '~schutzreifen m non-skid tyre, (*Am. only*) non-skid tire; '᷉schutz(vorrichtung *f*) *m* anti-skid device.

Gletscher ['glɛtʃər] *m* (-s/-) glacier; '᷉spalte *f* crevasse.

glich [gliç] *pret. of gleichen*.

Glied [gliːt] *n* (-[e]s/-er) *anat.* limb; member (*a. anat.*); link; ⚔ rank, file; ᷉ern ['᷉dərn] *v/t.* (ge-, *h*) joint, articulate; arrange; divide (*in acc.* into); '᷉erung *f* (-/-en) articulation; arrangement; division; formation; '᷉maßen ['᷉tmaːsən] *pl.* limbs *pl.*, extremities *pl.*

glimmen ['glimən] *v/i.* ([*irr.,*] ge-, *h*) *fire:* smo(u)lder (*a. fig.*); glimmer; glow.

glimpflich ['glimpfliç] 1. *adj.* lenient, mild; 2. *adv.:* ᷉ davonkommen get off lightly.

glitschig *adj.* ['glitʃiç] slippery.

glitt [glit] *pret. of gleiten*.

glitzern ['glitsərn] *v/i.* (ge-, *h*) glitter, glisten.

Globus ['gloːbus] *m* (-, -ses/Globen, Globusse) globe.

Glocke ['glɔkə] *f* (-/-n) bell; shade; (glass) cover.

'**Glocken|schlag** *m* stroke of the clock; '᷉spiel *n* chime(s *pl.*); '᷉stuhl *m* bell-cage; '᷉turm *m* bell tower, belfry.

Glöckner ['glœknər] *m* (-s/-) bell-ringer.

glomm [glɔm] *pret. of glimmen*.

Glorie ['gloːrjə] *f* (-/-n) glory; '᷉nschein *fig. m* halo, aureola.

glorreich *adj.* ['gloːr-] glorious.

glotzen F ['glɔtsən] *v/i.* (ge-, *h*) stare.

Glück [glyk] *n* (-[e]s/*no pl.*) fortune; good luck; happiness, bliss, felicity; prosperity; *auf gut* ᷉ on the off chance; ᷉ *haben* be lucky, succeed; *das* ᷉ *haben zu inf.* have the good fortune to *inf.*; *j-m* ᷉ *wünschen* congratulate s.o. (*zu* on); *viel* ᷉*l* good luck!; *zum* ᷉ fortunately; '2bringend *adj.* lucky.

Glucke *orn.* ['glukə] *f* (-/-n) sitting hen.   [gen.]

'**glücken** *v/i.* (ge-, sein) *s. gelin-*

gluckern ['glukərn] *v/i.* (ge-, *h*) *water, etc.:* gurgle.

'**glücklich** *adj.* fortunate; happy; lucky; '᷉er|weise *adv.* fortunately.

'**Glücksbringer** *m* (-s/-) mascot.

glück|selig *adj.* blissful, blessed, happy.

glucksen ['gluksən] *v/i.* (ge-, *h*) gurgle.

'**Glücks|fall** *m* lucky chance, stroke of (good) luck; '᷉göttin *f* Fortune; '᷉kind *n* lucky person; '᷉pfennig *m* lucky penny; '᷉pilz *m* lucky person; '᷉spiel *n* game of chance; *fig.* gamble; '᷉stern *m* lucky star; '᷉tag *m* happy *or* lucky day, red-letter day.

'**glück|strahlend** *adj.* radiant(ly happy); '2wunsch *m* congratulation, good wishes *pl.*; compliments *pl.*; ᷉ *zum Geburtstag* many happy returns (of the day).

Glüh|birne ⚡ ['glyː-] *f* (electric-light) bulb; '2en *v/i.* (ge-, *h*) glow; '2end *adj.* glowing; *iron:* red-hot; *coal:* live; *fig.* ardent, fervid; '2(end)'heiß *adj.* burning hot; '᷉lampe *f* incandescent lamp; '᷉wein *m* mulled wine; ᷉würmchen *zo.* ['᷉vyrmçən] *n* (-s/-) glow-worm.

Glut [gluːt] *f* (-/-en) heat, glow (*a. fig.*); glowing fire, embers *pl.*; *fig.* ardo(u)r.

Gnade ['gnaːdə] *f* (-/-n) grace; favo(u)r; mercy; clemency; pardon; ⚔ quarter.

'**Gnaden|akt** *m* act of grace; '᷉brot *n* (-[e]s/*no pl.*) bread of charity; '᷉frist *f* reprieve; '᷉gesuch *n* petition for mercy.

gnädig *adj.* ['gnɛːdiç] gracious; merciful; *address:* 2e Frau Madam.

Gnom [gnoːm] *m* (-en/-en) gnome, goblin.

Gobelin [gobə'lɛ̃ː] *m* (-s/-s) Gobelin tapestry.

Gold [gɔlt] *n* (-[e]s/*no pl.*) gold; '᷉barren *m* gold bar, gold ingot, bullion; '᷉borte *f* gold lace; 2en *adj.* ['᷉dən] gold; *fig.* golden; '᷉feder *f* gold nib; '᷉fisch *m* goldfish; '2gelb *adj.* golden-(yellow); '᷉gräber ['᷉grɛːbər] *m* (-s/-) gold-digger; '᷉grube *f* gold-mine; '2haltig *adj.* gold-bearing, containing gold; 2ig *fig. adj.* ['᷉diç] sweet, lovely, *Am.* F *a.* cute; '᷉mine *f* gold-mine; '᷉münze *f* gold coin; '᷉schmied *m* goldsmith; '᷉schnitt *m* gilt edge; *mit* ᷉ gilt-edged; '᷉stück *n* gold coin; '᷉waage *f* gold-balance; '᷉währung *f* gold standard.

Golf[1] *geogr.* [gɔlf] *m* (-[e]s/-e) gulf.

Golf[2] [᷉] *n* (-s/*no pl.*) golf; '᷉platz *m* golf-course, (golf-)links *pl.*; '᷉schläger *m* golf-club; '᷉spiel *n* golf; '᷉spieler *m* golfer.

Gondel ['gɔndəl] *f* (-/-n) gondola; ⚔ *mst* car.

gönnen ['gœnən] *v/t.* (ge-, *h*): *j-m et.* ᷉ allow *or* grant *or* not to grudge s.o. s.th.

'**Gönner** *m* (-s/-) patron; *Am. a.* sponsor; '2haft *adj.* patronizing.

gor [goːr] *pret. of gären*.

Gorilla *zo.* [go'rila] *m* (-s/-s) gorilla.

goß [gɔs] *pret. of gießen*.

Gosse ['gɔsə] *f* (-/-n) gutter (*a. fig.*).

Gott [gɔt] *m* (-es, ⚔ -s/⚔er) God; god, deity; '2ergeben *adj.* resigned (to the will of God).

'**Gottes|dienst** *eccl. m* (divine) service; '2fürchtig *adj.* godfearing; '᷉haus *n* church, chapel; '᷉läste-

rer *m* (-s/-) blasphemer; **~läste-rung** *f* blasphemy.

'**Gottheit** *f* (-/-en) deity, divinity.

Göttin ['gœtin] *f* (-/-nen) goddess.

göttlich *adj.* ['gœtliç] divine.

gott|'lob *int.* thank God *or* goodness!; **~los** *adj.* godless; impious; F *fig. deed:* unholy, wicked; **'2ver-trauen** *n* trust in God.

Götze ['gœtsə] *m* (-n/-n) idol; **~nbild** *n* idol; **~ndienst** *m* idolatry.

Gouvern|ante [guvɛr'nantə] *f* (-/-n) governess; **~eur** [~'nø:r] *m* (-s/-e) governor.

Grab [gra:p] *n* (-[e]s/ᵘer) grave, tomb, sepulch|re, *Am.* -er.

Graben ['gra:bən] 1. *m* (-s/ᵘ) ditch; ✕ trench; 2. ♀ *v/t.* (*irr.*, ge-, *h*) dig; *animal:* burrow.

Grab|gewölbe ['gra:p-] *n* vault, tomb; **~mal** *n* monument; tomb, sepulch|re, *Am.* -er; **~rede** *f* funeral sermon; funeral oration *or* address; **~schrift** *f* epitaph; **~stätte** *f* burial-place; grave, tomb; **~stein** *m* tombstone; gravestone.

Grad [gra:t] *m* (-[e]s/-e) degree; grade, rank; 15 *Kälte* 15 degrees below zero; **~einteilung** *f* graduation; **~messer** *m* (-s/-) graduated scale, graduator; *fig.* criterion; **~netz** *n* map: grid.

Graf [gra:f] *m* (-en/-en) *in Britain:* earl; count.

Gräfin ['grɛ:fin] *f* (-/-nen) countess.

'**Grafschaft** *f* (-/-en) county.

Gram [gra:m] 1. *m* (-[e]s/*no pl.*) grief, sorrow; 2. ♀ *adj.: j-m ~ sein* bear s.o. ill will *or* a grudge.

grämen ['grɛ:mən] *v/t.* (ge-, *h*) grieve; *sich ~* grieve (*über acc.* at, for, over).

Gramm [gram] *n* (-s/-e) gramme, *Am.* gram.

Grammati|k [gra'matik] *f* (-/-en) grammar; **2sch** *adj.* grammatical.

Granat *m.n.* [gra'na:t] *m* ᵗ-[e]s/-e) garnet; ᵁᵉ ✕ *f* (-/-n) shell; grᵉnade; **~splitter** ✕ *m* shell-splinter; **~trichter** ✕ *m* shell-crater; **~wer-fer** ✕ *m* (-s/-) mortar.

Granit *m.n.* [gra'ni:t] *m* (-s/-e) granite.

Granne ♀ ['granə] *f* (-/-n) awn, beard.

Graphi|k ['gra:fik] *f* (-/-en) graphic arts *pl.*; **2sch** *adj.* graphic(al).

Graphit *m.n.* [gra'fi:t] *m* (-s/-e) graphite.

Gras ♀ [gra:s] *n* (-es/ᵘer) grass; **2bewachsen** *adj.* ['~bəvaksən] grass-grown, grassy; **2en** ['~zən] *v/i.* (ge-, *h*) graze; **~halm** *m* blade of grass; **~narbe** *f* turf, sod; **~platz** *m* grass-plot, green.

grassieren [gra'si:rən] *v/i.* (*no -ge-*, *h*) rage, prevail.

gräßlich *adj.* ['grɛsliç] horrible; hideous, atrocious.

Grassteppe ['gra:s-] *f* prairie, savanna(h).

Grat [gra:t] *m* (-[e]s/-e) edge, ridge.

Gräte ['grɛ:tə] *f* (-/-n) (fish-)bone.

Gratifikation [gratifika'tsjo:n] *f* (-/-en) gratuity, bonus.

gratis *adv.* ['gra:tis] gratis, free of charge.

Gratul|ant [gratu'lant] *m* (-en/-en) congratulator; **~ation** [~'tsjo:n] *f* (-/-en) congratulation; **2ieren** [~-'li:rən] *v/i.* (*no -ge-*, *h*) congratulate (*j-m zu et. s.o. on s.th.*); *j-m zum Geburtstag ~* wish s.o. many happy returns (of the day).

grau *adj.* [grau] grey, *esp. Am.* gray.

grauen[1] *v/i.* (ge-, *h*): *day:* dawn.

'**grauen**[2] 1. *v/i.* (ge-, *h*): *mir graut vor* (*dat.*) I shudder at, I dread; 2. **2** *n* (-s/*no pl.*) horror (*vor dat.* of); **~erregend** *adj.*, **~haft** *adj.*, **~voll** *adj.* horrible, dreadful.

gräulich *adj.* ['grɔyliç] greyish, *esp. Am.* grayish.

Graupe ['graupə] *f* (-/-n) (peeled) barley, pot-barley; **'~ln** 1. *f/pl.* sleet; 2. **2** *v/i.* (ge-, *h*) sleet.

'**grausam** *adj.* cruel; **2keit** *f* (-/-en) cruelty.

grausen ['grauzən] 1. *v/i.* (ge-, *h*) *s. grauen*[2] 1; 2. **2** *n* (-s/*no pl.*) horror (*vor dat.* of).

'**grausig** *adj.* horrible. [graver.\]

Graveur [gra'vø:r] *m* (-s/-e) en-\]

gravieren [gra'vi:rən] *v/t.* (*no -ge-*, *h*) engrave; **~d** *fig. adj.* aggravating.

gravitätisch [gravi'tɛ:tiʃ] *adj.* grave; dignified; solemn; stately.

Grazie ['gra:tsjə] *f* (-/-n) grace(fulness).

graziös *adj.* [gra'tsjø:s] graceful.

greifen ['graifən] (*irr.*, ge-, *h*) 1. *v/t.* seize, grasp, catch hold of; ♪ touch (*string*); *et. an den Hut ~* touch one's hat; *~ nach* grasp *or* snatch at; *um sich ~* spread; *j-m unter die Arme ~* give s.o. a helping hand; *zu strengen Mitteln ~* resort to severe measures; *zu den Waffen ~* take up arms.

Greis [grais] *m* (-es/-e) old man; **2enhaft** *adj.* ['~zən-] senile (*a. ✏*); **~in** ['~zin] *f* (-/-nen) old woman.

grell *adj.* [grɛl] *light:* glaring; *colour:* loud; *sound:* shrill.

Grenze ['grɛntsə] *f* (-/-n) limit; *territory:* boundary; *state:* frontier, borders *pl.*; *e-e ~ ziehen* draw the line; **'2n** *v/i.* (ge-, *h*): *~ an* (*acc.*) border on (*a. fig.*); *fig.* verge on; **'2nlos** *adj.* boundless.

'**Grenz|fall** *m* border-line case; **'~land** *n* borderland; '**~linie** *f* boundary *or* border line; **'~schutz** *m* frontier *or* border protection; frontier *or* border guard; '**~stein** *m* boundary stone; **'~übergang** *m* frontier *or* border crossing(-point).

Greuel ['grɔyəl] *m* (-s/-) horror;

abomination; atrocity; '~tat f atrocity.

Griech|e ['griːçə] m (-n/-n) Greek; '2isch adj. Greek; △, features: Grecian.

griesgrämig adj. ['griːsgrɛːmiç] morose, sullen.

Grieß [griːs] m (-es/-e) gravel (a. ℱ), grit; semolina; '~brei m semolina pudding.

Griff [grif] 1. m (-[e]s/-e) grip, grasp, hold; ♪ touch; handle (of knife, etc.); hilt (of sword); 2. 2 pret. of greifen.

Grille ['grilə] f (-/-n) zo. cricket; fig. whim, fancy; '2nhaft adj. whimsical.

Grimasse [gri'masə] f (-/-n) grimace; ~n schneiden pull faces.

Grimm [grim] m (-[e]s/no pl.) fury, rage; '2ig adj. furious, fierce, grim.

Grind [grint] m (-[e]s/-e) scab, scurf.

grinsen ['grinzən] 1. v/i. (ge-, h) grin (über acc. at); sneer (at); 2. 2 n (-s/no pl.) grin; sneer.

Grippe ℱ ['gripə] f (-/-n) influenza, F flu(e), grippe.

grob adj. [grɔp] coarse; gross; rude; work, skin: rough; '2heit f (-/-en) coarseness; grossness; rudeness; ~en pl. rude things pl.

grölen F ['grøːlən] v/t. and v/i. (ge-, h) bawl.

Groll [grɔl] m (-[e]s/no pl.) grudge, ill will; '2en v/i. (ge-, h) thunder: rumble; j-m ~ bear s.o. ill will or a grudge.

Gros[1] [groːs] n (-ses/-se) gross.

Gros[2] [groː] n (-/-) main body.

Groschen ['grɔʃən] m (-s/-) penny.

groß adj. [groːs] great; large; big; figure: tall; huge; fig. great, grand; heat: intense; cold: severe; loss: heavy; die 2en pl. the grown-ups pl.; im ~en wholesale, on a large scale; im ~en (und) ganzen on the whole; ~er Buchstabe capital (letter); das ~e Los the first prize; ich bin kein ~er Tänzer I am not much of a dancer; '~artig adj. great, grand, sublime; first-rate; '2aufnahme f film: close-up.

Größe ['grøːsə] f (-/-n) size; largeness; height, tallness; quantity (esp. ℞); importance: greatness; p. celebrity; thea. star.

'Großeltern pl. grandparents pl.

'großenteils adv. to a large or great extent, largely.

'Größenwahn m megalomania.

'Groß|grundbesitz m large landed property; '~handel ✝ m wholesale trade; '~handelspreis ✝ m wholesale price; '~händler ✝ m wholesale dealer, wholesaler; '~handlung ✝ f wholesale business; '~herzog m grand duke; '~industrielle m big industrialist.

Grossist [grɔ'sist] m (-en/-en) s. Großhändler.

groß|jährig adj. ['groːsjɛːriç] of age; ~ werden come of age; '2jährigkeit f (-/no pl.) majority, full (legal) age; '2kaufmann m wholesale merchant; '2kraftwerk ℱ n superpower station; '2macht f great power; '2maul n braggart; '2mut f (-/no pl.) generosity; ~mütig adj. ['~myːtiç] magnanimous, generous; '2mutter f grandmother; '2neffe m great-nephew, grandnephew; '2nichte f great-niece, grand-niece; '2onkel m great-uncle, grand-uncle; '2schreibung f (-/-en) use of capital letters; capitalization; '~sprecherisch adj. boastful; '~spurig adj. arrogant; '2stadt f large town or city; '~städtisch adj. of or in a large town or city; '2tante f great-aunt, grand-aunt.

größtenteils adv. ['grøːstəntaɪls] mostly, chiefly, mainly.

'groß|tun v/i. (irr. tun, sep., -ge-, h) swagger, boast; sich mit et. ~ boast or brag of or about s.th.; '2vater m grandfather; '2verdiener m (-s/-) big earner; '2wild n big game; '~ziehen v/t. (irr. ziehen, sep., -ge-, h) bring up (child); rear, raise (child, animal); ~zügig adj. ['~tsyːgiç] liberal; generous; broad-minded; planning: a. on a large scale.

grotesk adj. [gro'tesk] grotesque.

Grotte ['grɔtə] f (-/-n) grotto.

grub [gruːp] pret. of graben.

Grübchen ['gryːpçən] n (-s/-) dimple.

Grube ['gruːbə] f (-/-n) pit; ℞ mine, pit.

Grübel|ei [gryːbə'laɪ] f (-/-en) brooding, musing, meditation; 2n ['~ln] v/i. (ge-, h) muse, meditate, ponder (all: über acc. on, over), Am. F a. mull (over).

'Gruben|arbeiter ℞ m miner; '~gas ℞ n fire-damp; '~lampe ℞ f miner's lamp.

Gruft [gruft] f (-/-e) tomb, vault.

grün [gryːn] 1. adj. green; ~er Hering fresh herring; ~er Junge greenhorn; ~ und blau schlagen beat s.o. black and blue; vom ~en Tisch aus armchair (strategy, etc.); 2. 2 n (-s/no pl.) green; verdure.

Grund [grunt] m (-[e]s/-e) ground; soil; bottom (a. fig.); land, estate; foundation; fig.: motive; reason; argument; von ~ auf thoroughly, fundamentally; '~ausbildung f basic instruction; ℞ basic (military) training; '~bedeutung f basic or original meaning; '~bedingung f basic or fundamental condition; '~begriff m fundamental or basic idea; ~e pl. principles pl.; rudiments pl.; '~besitz m land(ed property); '~besitzer m landowner; '~buch n land register.

gründ|en ['gryndən] v/t. (ge-, h) establish; † promote; sich ~ auf (acc.) be based or founded on; '2er m (-s/-) founder; † promoter.

'grund|'falsch adj. fundamentally wrong; '2farbe f ground-colo(u)r; opt. primary colo(u)r; '2fläche f base; area (of room, etc.); '2gebühr f basic rate or fee; flat rate; '2gedanke m basic or fundamental idea; '2gesetz n fundamental law; ½ appr. constitution; '2kapital † n capital (fund); '2lage f foundation, basis; '~legend adj. fundamental, basic.

gründlich adj. ['gryntliç] thorough; knowledge: profound.

'Grund|linie f base-line; '2los adj. bottomless; fig.: groundless; unfounded; '~mauer f foundation-wall. [Thursday.)

Grün'donnerstag eccl. m Maundy)

'Grund|regel f fundamental rule; '~riß m △ ground-plan; outline; compendium; '~satz m principle; '2sätzlich ['~zɛtsliç] 1. adj. fundamental; 2. adv. in principle; on principle; '~schule f elementary or primary school; '~stein m △ foundation-stone; fig. corner-stone; '~steuer f land-tax; '~stock m basis, foundation; '~stoff m element; '~strich m down-stroke; '~stück n plot (of land); ½ (real) estate; premises pl.; '~stücksmakler m real estate agent, Am. realtor; '~ton m ♪ keynote; ground shade.

'Gründung f (-/-en) foundation, establishment.

'grund|ver'schieden adj. entirely different; '2wasser geol. n (under-)ground water; '2zahl gr. f cardinal number; '2zug m main feature, characteristic.

'grünlich adj. greenish.

'Grün|schnabel fig. m greenhorn; whipper-snapper; '~span m (-[e]s/no pl.) verdigris.

grunzen ['gruntsən] v/i. and v/t. (ge-, h) grunt.

Gruppe ['grupə] f (-/-n) group; ✕ section, Am. squad; 2ieren [~'pi:rən] v/t. (no -ge-, h) group, arrange in groups; sich ~ form groups.

Gruselgeschichte ['gru:zəl-] f tale of horror, spine-chilling story or tale, F creepy story or tale.

Gruß [gru:s] m (-es/=e) salutation; greeting; esp. ✕, ⚓ salute; mst Grüße pl. regards pl.; respects pl., compliments pl.

grüßen ['gry:sən] v/t. (ge-, h) greet, esp. ✕ salute; hail; ~ Sie ihn von mir remember me to him; j-n ~ lassen send one's compliments or regards to s.o.

Grütze ['grytsə] f (-/-n) grits pl., groats pl.

guck|en ['gukən] v/i. (ge-, h) look; peep, peer; '2loch n peep- or spy-hole.

Guerilla ✕ [ge'ril(j)a] f (-/-s) guer(r)illa war.

gültig adj. ['gyltiç] valid; effective, in force; legal; coin: current; ticket: available; '2keit f (-/no pl.) validity; currency (of money); availability (of ticket).

Gummi ['gumi] n, m (-s/-s) gum; (india-)rubber; '~ball m rubber ball; '~band n elastic (band); rubber band; '~baum ♀ m gum-tree; (india-)rubber tree.

gum'mieren v/t. (no -ge-, h) gum.

'Gummi|handschuh m rubber glove; '~knüppel m truncheon, Am. club; '~schuhe m/pl. rubber shoes pl., Am. rubbers pl.; '~sohle f rubber sole; '~stiefel m wellington (boot), Am. rubber boot; '~zug m elastic; elastic webbing.

Gunst [gunst] f (-/no pl.) favo(u)r, goodwill; zu ~en (gen.) in favo(u)r of.

günst|ig adj. ['gynstiç] favo(u)rable; omen: propitious; im ~sten Fall at best; zu ~en Bedingungen † on easy terms; 2ling ['~liŋ] m (-s/-e) favo(u)rite.

Gurgel ['gurgəl] f (-/-n): j-m an die ~ springen leap or fly at s.o.'s throat; '2n v/i. (ge-, h) ✼ gargle; gurgle.

Gurke ['gurkə] f (-/-n) cucumber; pickled: gherkin.

gurren ['gurən] v/i. (ge-, h) coo.

Gurt [gurt] m (-[e]s/-e) girdle; harness: girth; strap; belt.

Gürtel ['gyrtəl] m (-s/-) belt; girdle; geogr. zone.

Guß [gus] m (Gusses/Güsse) ⊕ founding, casting; typ. fount, Am. font; rain: downpour, shower; '~eisen n cast iron; '2eisern adj. cast-iron; '~stahl m cast steel.

gut[1] [gu:t] 1. adj. good; ~e Worte fair words; ~es Wetter fine weather; ~er Dinge or ~en Mutes sein be of good cheer; ~e Miene zum bösen Spiel machen grin and bear it; ~ so! good!, well done!; ~ werden get well, heal; fig. turn out well; ganz ~ not bad; schon ~! never mind!, all right!; sei so ~ und ... (will you) be so kind as to inf.; auf ~ deutsch in plain German; j-m ~ sein love or like s.o.; 2. adv. well; ein ~ gehendes Geschäft a flourishing business; du hast ~ lachen it's easy or very well for you to laugh; es ~ haben be lucky; be well off.

Gut[2] [~] n (-[e]s/=er) possession, property; (landed) estate; † goods pl.

'Gut|achten n (-s/-) (expert) opinion; 'achter m (-s/-) expert; consultant; 'artig adj. good-natured; ∦ benign; dünken ['dyŋkən] n (-s/no pl.): nach at discretion or pleasure.

Gute 1. n (-n/no pl.) the good; s tun do good; 2. m, f (-n/-n): die n pl. the good pl.

Güte ['gy:tə] f (-/no pl.) goodness, kindness; † class, quality; in amicably; F: meine l good gracious!; haben Sie die zu inf. be so kind as to inf.

'Güter|abfertigung f dispatch of goods; = 'annahme f goods office, Am. freight office; 'bahnhof m goods station, Am. freight depot or yard; 'gemeinschaft ½ f community of property; 'trennung ½ f separation of property; 'verkehr m goods traffic, Am. freight traffic; 'wagen m (goods) wag(g)on, Am. freight car; offener (goods) truck; geschlossener (goods) van, Am. boxcar; 'zug m goods train, Am. freight train.

'gut|gelaunt adj. good-humo(u)red; 'gläubig adj. acting or done in good faith; s. leichtgläubig; 'haben v/t. (irr. haben, sep., -ge-, h) have credit for (sum of money); '2haben † n credit (balance); 'heißen v/t. (irr. heißen, sep., -ge-, h)

approve (of); 'herzig adj. good-natured, kind-hearted.

'gütig adj. good, kind(ly).

'gütlich adv.: sich einigen settle s.th. amicably; sich tun an (dat.) regale o.s. on.

'gut|machen v/t. (sep., -ge-, h) make up for, compensate, repair; 'mütig adj. ['my:tiç] good-natured; '2mütigkeit f (-/ -en) good nature.

'Gutsbesitzer m landowner; owner of an estate.

'Gut|schein m credit note, coupon; voucher; '2schreiben v/t. (irr. schreiben, sep., -ge-, h): j-m e-n Betrag put a sum to s.o.'s credit; 'schrift † f credit(ing).

'Guts|haus n farm-house; manor house; 'herr m lord of the manor; landowner; 'hof m farmyard; estate, farm; 'verwalter m (landlord's) manager or steward.

'gutwillig adj. willing; obliging.

Gymnasi|albildung [gymna'zja:l-] f classical education; ast [ast] m (-en/-en) appr. grammar-school boy; um ['na:zjum] n (-s/Gymnasien) appr. grammar-school.

Gymnasti|k [gym'nastik] f (-/no pl.) gymnastics pl.; '2sch adj. gymnastic.

Gynäkologe ∦ [gyne:ko'lo:gə] m (-n/-n) gyn(a)ecologist.

H

Haar [ha:r] n (-[e]s/-e) hair; sich die e kämmen comb one's hair; sich die e schneiden lassen have one's hair cut; aufs to a hair; um ein by a hair's breadth; 'ausfall m loss of hair; 'bürste f hairbrush; '2en v/i. and v/refl. (ge-, h) lose or shed one's hairs; 'esbreite f: um by a hair's breadth; '2'fein adj. (as) fine as a hair; fig. subtle; 'gefäß anat. n capillary (vessel); '2ge'nau adj. exact to a hair; '2ig adj. hairy; in compounds: ...-haired; '2'klein adv. to the last detail; 'klemme f hair grip, Am. bobby pin; 'nadel f hairpin; 'nadelkurve f hairpin bend; 'netz n hair-net; 'öl n hair-oil; '2'scharf 1. adj. very sharp; fig. very precise; 2. adv. by a hair's breadth; 'schneidemaschine f (e-e a pair of) (hair) clippers pl.; 'schneider m barber, (men's) hairdresser; 'schnitt m haircut; 'schwund m loss of hair; 'spalte'rei f (-/-en) hair-splitting; '2sträubend adj. hair-raising, horrifying; 'tracht f hair-style, coiffure; 'wäsche f hair-wash,

shampoo; 'wasser n hair-lotion; 'wuchs m growth of the hair; 'wuchsmittel n hair-restorer.

Habe ['ha:bə] f (-/no pl.) property; belongings pl.

haben ['ha:bən] 1. v/t. (irr., ge-, h) have; F fig.: sich (make a) fuss; etwas (nichts) auf sich be of (no) consequence; unter sich be in control of, command; zu † goods: obtainable, to be had; da wir's there we are!; 2. 2 † n (-s/-) credit (side).

Habgier ['ha:p-] f avarice, covetousness; '2ig adj. avaricious, covetous.

habhaft adj. ['ha:phaft]: werden (gen.) get hold of; catch, apprehend.

Habicht orn. ['ha:biçt] m (-[e]s/-e) (gos)hawk.

Hab|seligkeiten ['ha:p-] f/pl. property, belongings pl.; 'sucht f s. Habgier; '2süchtig adj. s. habgierig.

Hacke ['hakə] f (-/-n) ⚒ hoe, mattock; (pick)axe; heel.

Hacken ['hakən] 1. m (-s/-) heel; die zusammenschlagen ✗ click one's heels; 2. 2 v/t. (ge-, h) ⚒

hack (*soil*); mince (*meat*); chop (*wood*).

'**Hackfleisch** *n* minced meat, *Am.* ground meat.

Häcksel ['hɛksəl] *n, m* (-s/*no pl.*) chaff, chopped straw.

Hader ['haːdər] *m* (-s/*no pl.*) dispute, quarrel; discord; '2**n** *v/i.* (ge-, h) quarrel (*mit* with).

Hafen ['haːfən] *m* (-s/=) harbo(u)r; port; '~**anlagen** *f/pl.* docks *pl.*; '~**arbeiter** *m* docker, *Am. a.* longshoreman; '~**damm** *m* jetty; pier; '~**stadt** *f* seaport.

Hafer ['haːfər] *m* (-s/-) oats *pl.*; '~**brei** *m* (oatmeal) porridge; '~**flocken** *f/pl.* porridge oats *pl.*; '~**grütze** *f* groats *pl.*, grits *pl.*; '~**schleim** *m* gruel.

Haft 🕮 [haft] *f* (-/*no pl.*) custody, detention, confinement; '2**bar** *adj.* responsible, 🕮 liable (*für* for); '~**befehl** *m* warrant of arrest; '2**en** *v/i.* (ge-, h) stick, adhere (*an dat.* to); ~ *für* 🕮 answer for, be liable for.

Häftling ['heftliŋ] *m* (-s/-e) prisoner.

'**Haftpflicht** 🕮 *f* liability; '2**ig** *adj.* liable (*für* for); '~**versicherung** *f* third-party insurance.

'**Haftung** *f* (-/-en) responsibility, 🕮 liability; *mit beschränkter* ~ limited.

Hagel ['haːgəl] *m* (-s/-) hail; *fig. a.* shower, volley; '~**korn** *n* hailstone; '2**n** *v/i.* (ge-, h) hail (*a. fig.*); '~**schauer** *m* shower of hail, (brief) hailstorm.

hager *adj.* ['haːgər] lean, gaunt, scraggy, lank.

Hahn [haːn] *m* 1. *orn.* (-[e]s/=e) cock; rooster; 2. ⊕ (-[e]s/=e, -en) (stop)cock, tap, *Am. a.* faucet; '~**enkampf** *m* cock-fight; '~**enschrei** *m* cock-crow.

Hai *ichth.* [hai] *m* (-[e]s/-e), '~**fisch** *m* shark.

Hain *poet.* [hain] *m* (-[e]s/-e) grove; wood.

häkel|n ['heːkəln] *v/t. and v/i.* (ge-, h) crochet; '2**nadel** *f* crochet needle or hook.

Haken ['haːkən] *m* 1. *m* (-s/-) hook (*a. boxing*); peg; *fig.* snag, catch; 2. 2 *v/i.* (ge-, h) get stuck, jam.

'**hakig** *adj.* hooked.

halb [halp] 1. *adj.* half; *eine* ~*e Stunde* half an hour, a half-hour; *eine* ~*e Flasche Wein* a half-bottle of wine; *ein* ~*es Jahr* half a year; ~*e Note J* minim, *Am. a.* half note; ~*er Ton J* semitone, *Am. a.* half tone; 2. *adv.* half; ~ *voll* half full; ~ *soviel* half as much; *es schlug* ~ it struck the half-hour.

'**halb|amtlich** *adj.* semi-official; '2**bruder** *m* half-brother; '2**dunkel** *n* semi-darkness; dusk, twilight; ~**er** *prp.* (*gen.*) ['halbər] on account of; for the sake of; '2**fabri-**

kat ⊕ *n* semi-finished product; '~**gar** *adj.* underdone, *Am. a.* rare; '2**gott** *m* demigod; '2**heit** *f* (-/-en) half-measure.

halbieren [hal'biːrən] *v/t.* (*no* -ge-, h) halve, divide in half; *A* bisect.

'**Halb|insel** *f* peninsula; '~**jahr** *n* half-year, six months *pl.*; 2**jährig** *adj.* ['~jeːriç] half-year, of six months; '2**jährlich** 1. *adj.* half-yearly; 2. *adv. a.* twice a year; '~**kreis** *m* semicircle; '~**kugel** *f* hemisphere; '2**laut** 1. *adj.* low, subdued; 2. *adv.* in an undertone; '2**mast** *adv.* (at) half-mast, *Am. a.* (at) half-staff; '~**messer** *A m* (-s/-) radius; '~**mond** *m* half-moon, crescent; '2**part** *adv.*: ~ *machen* go halves, F go fifty-fifty; '~**schuh** *m* (low) shoe; '~**schwester** *f* half-sister; '~**tagsbeschäftigung** *f* part-time job *or* employment; '2**tot** *adj.* half-dead; 2**wegs** *adv.* ['~'veːks] half-way; *fig.* to some extent, tolerably; '~**welt** *f* demi-monde; 2**wüchsig** *adj.* ['~vyːksiç] adolescent, *Am. a.* teen-age; '~**zeit** *f* *sports*: half(-time).

Halde ['haldə] *f* (-/-n) slope; 🗙 dump.

half [half] *pret. of* helfen.

Hälfte ['helftə] *f* (-/-n) half, 🕮 moiety; *die* ~ *von* half of.

Halfter ['halftər] *m, n* (-s/-) halter.

Halle ['halə] *f* (-/-n) hall; *hotel*: lounge; *tennis*: covered court; ✈ hangar.

hallen ['halən] *v/i.* (ge-, h) (re)sound, ring, (re-)echo.

'**Hallen|bad** *n* indoor swimming-bath, *Am. a.* natatorium; '~**sport** *m* indoor sports *pl.*

hallo [ha'loː] 1. *int.* hallo!, hello!, hullo!; 2. 2 *fig. n* (-s/-s) hullabaloo.

Halm ♦ [halm] *m* (-[e]s/-e) blade; stem, stalk; straw.

Hals [hals] *m* (-es/=e) neck; throat; ~ *über Kopf* head over heels; *auf dem* ~*e haben* have on one's back, be saddled with; *sich den* ~ *verrenken* crane one's neck; '~**abschneider** *fig. m* extortioner, F shark; '~**band** *n* necklace; collar (*for dog, etc.*); '~**entzündung** *&* *f* sore throat; '~**kette** *f* necklace; string; chain; '~**kragen** *m* collar; '~**schmerzen** *m/pl.*: ~ *haben* have a sore throat; '2**starrig** *adj.* stubborn, obstinate; '~**tuch** *n* neckerchief; scarf; '~**weite** *f* neck size.

Halt [halt] *m* (-[e]s/-e) hold; foothold, handhold; support (*a. fig.*); *fig.*: stability; security; mainstay.

halt 1. *int.* stop!; 🗙 halt!; 2. F *adv.* just; *das ist* ~ *so* that's the way it is.

'**haltbar** *adj. material, etc.*: durable, lasting; *colour*: fast; *fig. theory, etc.*: tenable.

'**halten** (*irr.,* ge-, h) 1. *v/t.* hold (*fort,*

position, water, etc.); maintain (*position, level, etc.*); keep (*promise, order, animal, etc.*); make, deliver (*speech*); give, deliver (*lecture*); take in (*newspaper*); ~ für regard as, take to be; take for; es ~ mit side with; be fond of; kurz~ keep *s.o.* short; viel (wenig) ~ von think highly (little) of; sich ~ hold out; last; *food*: keep; sich gerade ~ hold *o.s.* straight; sich gut ~ in examination, etc.: do well; *p.* be well preserved; sich ~ an (*acc.*) adhere or keep to; **2.** *v/i.* stop, halt; *ice*: bear; *rope, etc.*: stand the strain; ~ zu stick to or by; ~ auf (*acc.*) set store by, value; auf sich ~ pay attention to one's appearance; have self-respect.

'**Halte|punkt** *m* 📷, *etc.*: wayside stop, halt; *shooting*: point of aim; *phys.* critical point; '~r *m* (-s/-) keeper; *a.* owner; *devices*: ... holder; '~stelle f stop; 📷 station, stop; '~signal 📷 *n* stop signal.

halt|los *adj.* ['haltlo:s] *p.* unsteady, unstable; *theory, etc.*: baseless, without foundation; '~machen *v/i.* (*sep., -ge-, h*) stop, halt; vor nichts ~ stick or stop; at nothing; '2ung f (-/-en) deportment, carriage; pose; *fig.* attitude (*gegenüber* towards); self-control; *stock exchange*: tone.

hämisch *adj.* ['hɛ:miʃ] spiteful, malicious.

Hammel ['haməl] *m* (-s/-, ") wether; '~fleisch *n* mutton; '~keule f leg of mutton; '~rippchen *n* (-s/-) mutton chop.

Hammer ['hamər] *m* (-s/") hammer; (*auctioneer's*) gavel; unter den ~ kommen come under the hammer.

hämmern ['hɛmərn] (*ge-, h*) **1.** *v/t.* hammer; **2.** *v/i.* hammer (*a. an dat.* at *door, etc.*); hammer away (*auf dat.* at *piano*); *heart, etc.*: throb (violently), pound.

Hämorrhoiden 🖋 [hɛ:mɔro'i:dən] *f/pl.* h(a)emorrhoids *pl.*, piles *pl.*

Hampelmann ['hampəlman] *m* jumping-jack; *fig.* (mere) puppet.

Hamster zo. ['hamstər] *m* (-s/-) hamster; '2n *v/t. and v/i.* (*ge-, h*) hoard.

Hand [hant] f (-/-"e) hand; j-m die ~ geben shake hands with *s.o.*; an ~ (*gen.*) or von with the help or aid of; aus erster ~ first-hand, at first hand; bei der ~, zur ~ at hand; ~ und Fuß haben be sound, hold water; seine ~ im Spiele haben have a finger in the pie; '~arbeit f manual labo(u)r or work; (handi)craft; needlework, '~arbeiter *m* manual labo(u)rer; '~bibliothek f reference library; '~breit **1.** f (-/-) hand's breadth; **2.** 2 *adj.* a hand's breadth across; '~bremse *mot.* f hand-brake; '~buch *n* manual, handbook.

Hände|druck ['hɛndə-] *m* (-[e]s/-"e)

handshake; '~klatschen *n* (-s/no *pl.*) (hand-)clapping; applause.

Handel ['handəl] *m* **1.** (-s/no *pl.*) commerce; trade; business; market; traffic; transaction, deal, bargain; **2.** (-s/=): Händel *pl.* quarrels *pl.*, contention; '2n *v/i.* (*ge-, h*) act, take action; † trade (mit with *s.o.*, in goods), deal (in goods); bargain (um for), haggle (over); ~ von treat of, deal with; es handelt sich um it concerns, it is a matter of.

'**Handels|abkommen** *n* trade agreement; '~bank f commercial bank; '2einig *adj.*: ~ werden come to terms; '~genossenschaft f traders' co-operative association; '~gericht *n* commercial court; '~gesellschaft f (trading) company; '~haus *n* business house, firm; '~kammer f Chamber of Commerce; '~marine f mercantile marine; '~minister *m* minister of commerce; President of the Board of Trade, *Am.* Secretary of Commerce; '~ministerium *n* ministry of commerce; Board of Trade, *Am.* Department of Commerce; '~reisende *m* commercial traveller, *Am.* traveling salesman, F drummer; '~schiff *n* merchantman; '~schiffahrt f merchant shipping; '~schule f commercial school; '~stadt f commercial town; '2üblich *adj.* customary in trade; '~vertrag *m* commercial treaty, trade agreement.

'**handeltreibend** *adj.* trading.

'**Hand|feger** *m* (-s/-) hand-brush; '~fertigkeit f manual skill; '2fest *adj.* sturdy, strong; *fig.* well-founded, sound; '~feuerwaffen f/pl. small arms *pl.*; '~fläche f flat of the hand, palm; '2gearbeitet *adj.* hand-made; '~geld *n* earnest money; ⚔ bounty; '~gelenk *anat.* *n* wrist; '~gemenge *n* scuffle, mêlée; '~gepäck *n* hand luggage, *Am.* hand baggage; '~granate ⚔ f hand-grenade; '2greiflich *adj.* violent; *fig.* tangible, palpable; ~ werden turn violent, *Am. a.* get tough; '~griff *m* grasp; handle, grip; *fig.* manipulation; '~habe *fig.* f handle; '2haben *v/t.* (*ge-, h*) handle, manage; operate (*machine, etc.*); administer (*law*); '~karren *m* hand-cart; '~koffer *m* suitcase, *Am. a.* valise; '~kuß *m* kiss on the hand; '~langer *m* (-s/-) hodman, handy man; *fig.* dog's-body, henchman.

Händler ['hɛndlər] *m* (-s/-) dealer, trader.

'**handlich** *adj.* handy; manageable.

Handlung ['handluŋ] f (-/-en) act, action; deed; *thea.* action, plot; † shop, *Am.* store.

'**Handlungs|bevollmächtigte** *m* proxy; '~gehilfe *m* clerk; shop-assistant, *Am.* salesclerk; '~reisen-de *m s.* Handelsreisende; '~weise *f* conduct; way of acting.

'**Hand|rücken** *m* back of the hand; '~schelle *f* handcuff, manacle; '~schlag *m* handshake; '~schrei-ben *n* autograph letter; '~schrift *f* handwriting; manuscript; '2~schriftlich 1. *adj.* hand-written; 2. *adv.* in one's own handwriting; '~schuh *m* glove; '~streich ✕ *m* surprise attack, coup de main; *im ~ nehmen* take by surprise; '~tasche *f* handbag, *Am. a.* purse; '~tuch *n* towel; '~voll *f* (-/-) handful; '~wa-gen *m* hand-cart; '~werk *n* (handi)craft, trade; '~werker *m* (-s/-) (handi)craftsman, artisan; workman; '~werkzeug *n* (kit of) tools *pl.*; '~wurzel *anat. f* wrist; '~zeichnung *f* drawing.

Hanf ♀ [hanf] *m* (-[e]s/*no pl.*) hemp.

Hang [haŋ] *m* (-[e]s/⸚e) slope, incline, declivity; hillside; *fig.* inclination, propensity (*zu* for; *zu inf.* to *inf.*); tendency (to).

Hänge|boden ['hɛŋə-] *m* hanging-loft; '~brücke △ *f* suspension bridge; '~lampe *f* hanging lamp; '~matte *f* hammock.

hängen ['hɛŋən] 1. *v/i.* (*irr.*, ge-, h) hang, be suspended; adhere, stick, cling (*an dat.* to); ~ *an* (*dat.*) be attached *or* devoted to; 2. *v/t.* (ge-, h) hang, suspend; '~bleiben *v/i.* (*irr.* bleiben, *sep.*, -ge-, sein) get caught (up) (*an dat.* on, in); *fig.* stick (in the memory).

hänseln ['hɛnzəln] *v/t.* (ge-, h) tease (*wegen* about), F rag.

Hansestadt ['hanzə-] *f* Hanseatic town.

Hanswurst [hans'-] *m* (-es/-e, F ⸚e) merry andrew; Punch; *fig. contp.* clown, buffoon.

Hantel ['hantəl] *f* (-/-n) dumb-bell.

hantieren [han'ti:rən] *v/i.* (*no* -ge-, h) be busy (*mit* with); work (*an dat.* on).

Happen ['hapən] *m* (-s/-) morsel, mouthful, bite; snack.

Harfe ♪ ['harfə] *f* (-/-n) harp.

Harke ✗ ['harkə] *f* (-/-n) rake; '2n *v/t. and v/i.* (ge-, h) rake.

harmlos *adj.* ['harmlo:s] harmless, innocuous; inoffensive.

Harmon|ie [harmo'ni:] *f* (-/-n) harmony (*a.* ♪); 2ieren *v/i.* (*no* -ge-, h) harmonize (*mit* with); *fig. a.* be in tune (with); ~ika ♪ [~'mo:-nika] *f* (-/-s, Harmoniken) accordion; mouth-organ; 2isch *adj.* [~'mo:niʃ] harmonious.

Harn [harn] *m* (-[e]s/-e) urine; '~blase *anat. f* (urinary) bladder; '2en *v/i.* (ge-, h) pass water, urinate.

Harnisch ['harniʃ] *m* (-es/-e) armo(u)r; *in ~ geraten* be up in arms (*über acc.* about).

'**Harnröhre** *anat. f* urethra.

Harpun|e [har'pu:nə] *f* (-/-n) harpoon; 2ieren [~u'ni:rən] *v/t.* (*no* -ge-, h) harpoon.

hart [hart] 1. *adj.* hard; *fig. a.* harsh; heavy, severe; 2. *adv.* hard; ~ *arbeiten* work hard.

Härte ['hɛrtə] *f* (-/-n) hardness; *fig. a.* hardship; severity; '2n (ge-, h) 1. *v/t.* harden (*metal*); temper (*steel*); case-harden (*iron, steel*); 2. *v/i. and v/refl.* harden, become *or* grow hard; *steel:* temper.

'**Hart|geld** *n* coin(s *pl.*), specie; '~gummi *n* hard rubber; ✝ ebon-ite, vulcanite; '2herzig *adj.* hard-hearted; 2köpfig *adj.* ['~kœpfiç] stubborn, headstrong; 2näckig *adj.* ['~nɛkiç] *p.* obstinate, obdurate; *effort* dogged, tenacious; ✗ *ail-ment:* refractory.

Harz [ha:rts] *n* (-es/-e) resin; ♪ rosin; *mot.* gum; '2ig *adj.* resinous.

Hasardspiel [ha'zart-] *n* game of chance; *fig.* gamble.

haschen ['haʃən] (ge-, h) 1. *v/t.* catch (hold of), snatch; *sich ~ children:* play tag; 2. *v/i.: ~ nach* snatch at; *fig.* strain after (*effect*), fish for (*compliments*).

Hase ['ha:zə] *m* (-n/-n) zo. hare; *ein alter ~* an old hand, an old-timer.

Haselnuß ♀ ['ha:zəlnus] *f* hazel-nut.

'**Hasen|braten** *m* roast hare; '~fuß F *fig. m* coward, F funk; '~panier F *n: das ~ ergreifen* take to one's heels; '~scharte ✗ *f* hare-lip.

Haß [has] *m* (Hasses/*no pl.*) hatred.

'**hassen** *v/t.* (ge-, h) hate.

häßlich *adj.* ['hɛsliç] ugly; *fig. a.* nasty, unpleasant.

Hast [hast] *f* (-/*no pl.*) hurry, haste; rush; *in wilder ~* in frantic haste; '2en *v/i.* (ge-, sein) hurry, hasten; rush; '2ig *adj.* hasty, hurried.

hätscheln ['hɛ:tʃəln] *v/t.* (ge-, h) caress, fondle, pet; pamper, coddle.

hatte ['hatə] *pret. of* haben.

Haube ['haubə] *f* (-/-n) bonnet (*a.* ⊕, *mot.*); cap; *orn.* crest, tuft; *mot. Am. a.* hood.

Haubitze ✕ [hau'bitsə] *f* (-/-n) howitzer.

Hauch [haux] *m* (-[e]s/✗ -e) breath; *fig.:* waft, whiff (*of perfume, etc.*); touch, tinge (*of irony, etc.*); '2en (ge-, h) 1. *v/i.* breathe; 2. *v/t.* breathe, whisper; *gr.* aspirate.

Haue ['hauə] *f* (-/-n) ✗ hoe, mat-tock; pick; F hiding, spanking; '2n (*irr.*, ge-, h) 1. *v/t.* hew (coal, stone); cut up (*meat*); chop (*wood*); cut (hole, steps, etc.); beat (*child*); *sich ~* (have a) fight; 2. *v/i.: ~ nach* cut at, strike out at.

Haufen ['haufən] *m* (-s/-) heap, pile (*both* F *a. fig.*); *fig.* crowd.

häufen ['hɔyfən] *v/t.* (ge-, h) heap

(up), pile (up); accumulate; *sich ~* pile up, accumulate; *fig.* become more frequent, increase.

'**häufig** *adj.* frequent; '**2keit** *f* (-/*no pl.*) frequency.

'**Häufung** *fig. f* (-/-en) increase, *fig.* accumulation.

Haupt [haupt] *n* (-[e]s/*⸚*er) head; *fig.* chief, head, leader; '**~altar** *m* high altar; '**~anschluß** *teleph. m* subscriber's main station; '**~bahnhof** 🚉 *m* main *or* central station; '**~beruf** *m* full-time occupation; '**~buch** † *n* ledger; '**~darsteller** *thea. m* leading actor; '**~fach** *univ. n* main *or* principal subject, *Am. a.* major; '**~film** *m* feature (film); '**~geschäft** *n* main transaction; main shop; '**~geschäftsstelle** *f* head *or* central office; '**~gewinn** *m* first prize; '**~grund** *m* main reason; **~handelsartikel** † ['haupthandəls²-] *m* staple.

Häuptling ['hɔyptliŋ] *m* (-s/-e) chief(tain).

'**Haupt|linie** 🚉 *f* main *or* trunk line; '**~mann** ⚔ *m* (-[e]s/*Hauptleute*) captain; '**~merkmal** *n* characteristic feature; '**~postamt** *n* general post office, *Am.* main post office; '**~punkt** *m* main *or* cardinal point; '**~quartier** *n* headquarters *sg. or pl.*; '**~rolle** *thea. f* lead(ing part); '**~sache** *f* main thing *or* point; '**2sächlich** *adj.* main, chief, principal; '**~satz** *gr. m* main clause; '**~stadt** *f* capital; '**2städtisch** *adj.* metropolitan; '**~straße** *f* main street; major road; '**~treffer** *m* first prize, jackpot; '**~verkehrsstraße** *f* main road; arterial road; '**~verkehrsstunden** *f/pl.*, '**~verkehrszeit** *f* rush hour(s *pl.*), peak hour(s *pl.*); '**~versammlung** *f* general meeting; '**~wort** *gr. n* (-[e]s/*⸚*er) substantive, noun.

Haus [haus] *n* (-es/*⸚*er) house; building; home, family, household; dynasty; † (business) house, firm; *parl.* House; *nach ~e* home; *zu ~e* at home, F in; '**~angestellte** *f* (-n/-n) (house-)maid; '**~apotheke** *f* (household) medicine-chest; '**~arbeit** *f* housework; '**~arrest** *m* house arrest; '**~arzt** *m* family doctor; '**~aufgaben** *f/pl.* homework, F prep; '**2backen** *fig. adj.* homely; '**~bar** *f* cocktail cabinet; '**~bedarf** *m* household requirements *pl.*; '**~besitzer** *m* house-owner; '**~diener** *m* (man-)servant; *hotel:* porter, boots *sg.*

hausen ['hauzən] *v/i.* (ge-, h) live; play *or* work havoc (*in a place*).

'**Haus|flur** *m* (entrance-)hall, *esp. Am.* hallway; '**~frau** *f* housewife; '**~halt** *m* household; '**2halten** *v/i.* (*irr. halten, sep.,* -ge-, h) be economical (*mit* with), economize (on);

'**~hälterin** ['~heltərin] *f* (-/-nen) housekeeper; '**~halt(s)plan** *parl. m* budget; '**~haltung** *f* housekeeping; household, family; '**~haltwaren** *f/pl.* household articles *pl.*; '**~herr** *m* master of the family; landlord.

hausier|en [hau'ziːrən] *v/i.* (*no -ge-,* h) hawk, peddle (*mit et. s.th.*); *~ gehen* be a hawker *or* pedlar; **2er** *m* (-s/-) hawker, pedlar.

'**Haus|kleid** *n* house dress; '**~knecht** *m* boots; '**~lehrer** *m* private tutor.

häuslich ['hɔyslɪç] *adj.* domestic; domesticated; '**2keit** *f* (-/*no pl.*) domesticity; family life; home.

'**Haus|mädchen** *n* (house-)maid; '**~mannskost** *f* plain fare; '**~meister** *m* caretaker; janitor; '**~mittel** *n* popular medicine; '**~ordnung** *f* rules *pl.* of the house; '**~rat** *m* household effects *pl.*; '**~recht** *n* domestic authority; '**~sammlung** *f* house-to-house collection; '**~schlüssel** *m* latchkey; front-door key; '**~schuh** *m* slipper.

Hauss|e † ['hoːs(ə)] *f* (-/-n) rise, boom; **~ier** [hos'jeː] *m* (-s/-s) speculator for a rise, bull.

'**Haus|stand** *m* household; *e-n ~ gründen* set up house; '**~suchung** ⚖ *f* house search, domiciliary visit, *Am. a.* house check; '**~tier** *n* domestic animal; '**~tür** *f* front door; '**~verwalter** *m* steward; '**~wirt** *m* landlord; '**~wirtin** *f* (-/-nen) landlady.

Haut [haut] *f* (-/*⸚*e) skin; hide; film; *bis auf die ~* to the skin; *aus der ~ fahren* jump out of one's skin; F *e-e ehrliche ~* an honest soul; '**~abschürfung** 🩹 *f* skin abrasion; '**~arzt** *m* dermatologist; '**~ausschlag** 🩹 *m* rash; '**2eng** *adj.* garment: skin-tight; '**~farbe** *f* complexion.

Hautgout [o'gu] *m* (-s/*no pl.*) high taste.

häutig *adj.* ['hɔytiç] membranous; covered with skin.

'**Haut|krankheit** *f* skin disease; '**~pflege** *f* care of the skin; '**~schere** *f* (e-e a pair of) cuticle scissors *pl.*

Havarie ⚓ [hava'riː] *f* (-/-n) average.

H-Bombe ⚔ ['haː-] *f* H-bomb.

he *int.* [heː] hi!, hi there!; I say!

Hebamme ['heːp²amə] *f* midwife.

Hebe|baum ['heːbə-] *m* lever (*for raising heavy objects*); '**~bühne** *mot. f* lifting ramp; '**~eisen** *n* crowbar; '**~kran** *m* lifting crane.

Hebel ⚙ ['heːbəl] *m* (-s/-) lever; '**~arm** *m* lever arm.

heben ['heːbən] *v/t.* (*irr.,* ge-, h) lift (*a. sports*), raise (*a. fig.*); heave (*heavy load*); hoist; recover (*treas-*

ure); raise (*sunken ship*); *fig.* promote, improve, increase; *sich ~* rise, go up.

Hecht *ichth.* [hɛçt] *m* (-[e]s/-e) pike.

Heck [hɛk] *n* (-[e]s/-e, -s) ⚓ stern; *mot.* rear; ✠ tail.

Hecke ['hɛkə] *f* (-/-n) ⚔ hedge; *zo.* brood, hatch; '**2n** *v/t. and v/i.* (ge-, h) breed, hatch; '**~nrose** ⚔ *f* dog-rose. [hallo!]

heda *int.* ['he:dɑ:] hi (there)!,]

Heer [he:r] *n* (-[e]s/-e) ✠ army; *fig. a.* host; '**~esdienst** *m* military service; '**~esmacht** *f* military force(s *pl.*); '**~eszug** *m* military expedition; '**~führer** *m* general; '**~lager** *n* (army) camp; '**~schar** *f* army, host; '**~straße** *f* military road; highway; '**~zug** *m s. Heereszug.*

Hefe ['he:fə] *f* (-/-n) yeast; barm.

Heft [hɛft] *n* (-[e]s/-e) dagger, *etc.*: haft; *knife:* handle; *fig.* reins *pl.*; exercise book; *periodical*, *etc.*: issue, number.

'**heft|en** *v/t.* (ge-, h) fasten, fix (*an acc.* on to); affix, attach (to); pin on (to); tack, baste (*seam*, *etc.*); stitch, sew (*book*); '**~faden** *m* basting thread.

'**heftig** *adj. storm, anger, quarrel, etc.:* violent, fierce; *rain, etc.:* heavy; *pain, etc.:* severe; *speech, desire, etc.:* vehement, passionate; *p.* irascible; '**2keit** *f* (-/~-en) violence, fierceness; severity; vehemence; irascibility.

'**Heft|klammer** *f* paper-clip; '**~pflaster** *n* sticking plaster.

hegen ['he:gən] *v/t.* (ge-, h) preserve (*game*); nurse, tend (*plants*); have, entertain (*feelings*); harbo(u)r (*fears, suspicions, etc.*).

Hehler ⚖ ['he:lər] *m* (-s/-) receiver (of stolen goods); '**~ei** [~'raɪ] *f* (-/-en) receiving (of stolen goods).

Heide ['haɪdə] 1. *m* (-n/-n) heathen; 2. *f* (-/-n) heath(-land); = '**~kraut** ⚔ *n* heather; '**~land** *n* heath(-land).

'**Heiden|geld** F *n* pots *pl.* of money; '**~lärm** F *m* hullabaloo; '**~spaß** F *m* capital fun; '**~tum** *n* (-s/no *pl.*) heathenism. [(-ish).]

heidnisch *adj.* ['haɪdnɪʃ] heathen]

heikel *adj.* ['haɪkəl] *p.* fastidious, particular; *problem*, *etc.*: delicate, awkward.

heil [haɪl] 1. *adj. p.* safe, unhurt; whole, sound; 2. ⚙ *n* (-[e]s/no *pl.*) welfare, benefit; *eccl.* salvation; 3. *int.* hail!

Heiland *eccl.* ['haɪlant] *m* (-[e]s/-e) Saviour, Redeemer.

'**Heil|anstalt** *f* sanatorium, *Am. a.* sanitarium; spa; '**~bad** *n* medicinal bath; spa; '**~bar** *adj.* curable; '**2en** (ge-) 1. *v/t.* (h) cure, heal; *~ von* cure *s.o.* of; 2. *v/i.* (sein) heal (up); '**~gehilfe** *m* male nurse.

heilig *adj.* ['haɪliç] holy; sacred; solemn; **2er Abend** Christmas Eve; **2e** ['~gə] *m*, *f* (-n/-n) saint; '**~en** ['~gən] *v/t.* (ge-, h) sanctify (*a. fig.*), hallow; '**2keit** *f* (-/no *pl.*) holiness; sacredness, sanctity; '**~sprechen** *v/t.* (*irr. sprechen*, *sep.*, -ge-, h) canonize; '**2sprechung** *f* (-/-en) canonization; '**2tum** *n* (-[e]s/=er) sanctuary; sacred relic; **2ung** ['~guŋ] *f* (-/-en) sanctification (*a. fig.*), hallowing.

'**Heil|kraft** *f* healing *or* curative power; '**2kräftig** *adj.* healing, curative; '**~kunde** *f* medical science; '**2los** *fig. adj.* confusion: utter, great; '**~mittel** *n* remedy, medicament; '**~praktiker** *m* non-medical practitioner; '**~quelle** *f* medicinal spring; '**2sam** *adj.* curative; *fig.* salutary. [Army.]

Heilsarmee ['haɪls?-] *f* Salvation]

'**Heil|ung** *f* (-/-en) cure, healing, successful treatment; '**~verfahren** *n* therapy.

heim [haɪm] 1. *adv.* home; 2. ⚙ *n* (-[e]s/-e) home; hostel; '**2arbeit** *f* homework, outwork.

Heimat ['haɪmɑːt] *f* (-/✠ -en) home; own country; native land; '**~land** *n* own country, native land; '**2lich** *adj.* native; '**2los** *adj.* homeless; '**~ort** *m* home town *or* village; '**~vertriebene** *m* expellee.

Heimchen *zo.* ['haɪmçən] *n* (-s/-) cricket.

'**heimisch** *adj. trade, industry, etc.*: home, local, domestic; ⚙, *zo.*, *etc.*: native, indigenous; *~ werden* settle down; become established; *sich ~ fühlen* feel at home.

Heim|kehr ['haɪmke:r] *f* (-/no *pl.*) return (home), homecoming; '**2kehren** *v/i.* (*sep.*, -ge-, sein), '**2kommen** *v/i.* (*irr. kommen*, *sep.*, -ge-, sein) return home.

'**heimlich** *adj. plan, feeling, etc.*: secret; *meeting, organization, etc.*: clandestine; *glance, movement, etc.*: stealthy, furtive.

'**Heim|reise** *f* homeward journey; '**2suchen** *v/t.* (*sep.*, -ge-, h) disaster, *etc.*: afflict, strike; *ghost:* haunt; *God:* visit, punish; '**~tücke** *f* underhand malice, treachery; '**2tückisch** *adj.* malicious, treacherous, insidious; **2wärts** *adv.* ['~verts] homeward(s); '**~weg** *m* way home; '**~weh** *n* homesickness, nostalgia; *~ haben* be homesick.

Heirat ['haɪrɑːt] *f* (-/-en) marriage; '**2en** (ge-, h) 1. *v/t.* marry; 2. *v/i.* marry, get married.

'**Heirats|antrag** *m* offer *or* proposal of marriage; '**2fähig** *adj.* marriageable; '**~kandidat** *m* possible marriage partner; '**~schwindler** *m* marriage impostor; '**~vermittler** *m* matrimonial agent.

heiser adj. ['haɪzər] hoarse; husky; **ℒkeit** f (-/no pl.) hoarseness; huskiness.

heiß adj. [haɪs] hot; fig. a. passionate, ardent; mir ist ~ I am or feel hot.

heißen ['haɪsən] (irr., ge-, h) 1. v/t.: e-n Lügner ~ call s.o. a liar; willkommen ~ welcome; 2. v/i. be called; mean; wie ~ Sie? what is your name?; was heißt das auf englisch? what's that in English?

heiter adj. ['haɪtər] day, weather: bright; sky: bright, clear; p., etc.: cheerful, gay; serene; **ℒkeit** f (-/no pl.) brightness; cheerfulness, gaiety; serenity.

heiz|en ['haɪtsən] (ge-, h) 1. v/t. heat (room, etc.); light (stove); fire (boiler); 2. v/i. stove, etc.: give out heat; turn on the heating; mit Kohlen ~ burn coal; **ℒer** m (-s/-) stoker, fireman; **ℒkissen** n electric heating pad; **ℒkörper** m central heating: radiator; ℊ heating element; **ℒmaterial** n fuel; **ℒung** f (-/-en) heating.

Held [hɛlt] m (-en/-en) hero.

Helden|gedicht n epic (poem); **ℒhaft** adj. heroic, valiant; '~mut m heroism, valo(u)r; **ℒmütig** adj. ['~my:tiç] heroic; '~tat f heroic or valiant deed; '~tod m hero's death; '~tum n (-[e]s/no pl.) heroism.

helfen ['hɛlfən] v/i. (dat.) (irr., ge-, h) help, assist, aid; ~ gegen be good for; sich nicht zu ~ wissen be helpless.

Helfer m (-s/-) helper, assistant; '~shelfer m accomplice.

hell adj. [hɛl] sound, voice, light, etc.: clear; light, flame, etc.: bright; hair: fair; colour: light; ale: pale; '~blau adj. light-blue; '~blond adj. very fair; '~hörig adj. p.: quick of hearing; fig. perceptive; ⌂ poorly sound-proofed; **ℒseher** m clairvoyant.

Helm [hɛlm] m (-[e]s/-e) ⚔ helmet; ⌂ dome, cupola; ⚓ helm; '~busch m plume.

Hemd [hɛmt] n (-[e]s/-en) shirt; vest; '~bluse f shirt-blouse, Am. shirtwaist.

Hemisphäre [he:mi'sfɛ:rə] f (-/-n) hemisphere.

hemm|en ['hɛmən] v/t. (ge-, h) check, stop (movement, etc.); stem (stream, flow of liquid); hamper (free movement, activity); be a hindrance to; psych.: gehemmt sein be inhibited; **ℒnis** n (-ses/-se) hindrance, impediment; **ℒschuh** m slipper; fig. hindrance, F drag (für acc. on); **ℒung** f (-/-en) stoppage, check; psych.: inhibition.

Hengst zo. [hɛŋst] m (-es/-e) stallion.

Henkel ['hɛŋkəl] m (-s/-) handle, ear.

Henker ['hɛŋkər] m (-s/-) hangman, executioner; F: zum ~! hang it (all)!

Henne zo. ['hɛnə] f (-/-n) hen.

her adv. [he:r] here; hither; es ist schon ein Jahr ~, daß ... or seit ... it is a year since ...; wie lange ist es ~, seit ... how long is it since ...; hinter (dat.) ~ sein be after; ~ damit! out with it!

herab adv. [hɛ'rap] down, downward; **~lassen** v/t. (irr. lassen, sep., -ge-, h) let down, lower; fig. sich ~ condescend; **~lassend** adj. condescending; **~setzen** v/t. (sep., -ge-, h) take down; fig. belittle, disparage s.o.; ⫫ reduce, lower, cut (price, etc.); **ℒsetzung** fig. f (-/-en) reduction; disparagement; **~steigen** v/i. (irr. steigen, sep., -ge-, sein) climb down, descend; **~würdigen** v/t. (sep., -ge-, h) degrade, belittle, abase.

heran adv. [hɛ'ran] close, near; up; nur ~! come on!; **~bilden** v/t. (sep., -ge-, h) train, educate (zu as s.th., to be s.th.); **~kommen** v/i. (irr. kommen, sep., -ge-, sein) come or draw near; approach; ~ an (acc.) come up to s.o.; measure up to; **~wachsen** v/i. (irr. wachsen, sep., -ge-, sein) grow (up) (zu into).

herauf adv. [hɛ'rauf] up(wards), up here; upstairs; **~beschwören** v/t. (irr. schwören, sep., no -ge-, h) evoke, call up, conjure up (spirit, etc.); fig. a. bring about, provoke, give rise to (war, etc.); **~steigen** v/i. (irr. steigen, sep., -ge-, sein) climb up (here), ascend; **~ziehen** (irr. ziehen, sep.) 1. v/t. (h) pull or hitch up (trousers, etc.); 2. v/i. (sein) cloud, etc.: come up.

heraus adv. [hɛ'raus] out, out here; zum Fenster ~ out of the window; ~ mit der Sprache! speak out!; **~bekommen** v/t. (irr. kommen, sep., no -ge-, h) get out; get (money) back; fig. find out; **~bringen** v/t. (irr. bringen, sep., -ge-, h) bring or get out; thea. stage; **~finden** v/t. (irr. finden, sep., -ge-, h) find out; fig. a. discover; **~forderer** m (-s/-) challenger; **~fordern** v/t. (sep., -ge-, h) challenge (zu to a fight); provoke; **ℒforderung** f (-/-en) challenge; provocation; **~geben** (irr. geben, sep., -ge-, h) 1. v/t. surrender; hand over; restore; edit (periodical, etc.); publish (book, etc.); issue (regulations, etc.); 2. v/i. give change (auf acc. for); **ℒgeber** m (-s/-) editor; publisher; **~kommen** v/i. (irr. kommen, sep., -ge-, sein) come out; fig. a. appear, be published; **~nehmen** v/t. (irr. nehmen, sep., -ge-, h) take out; sich viel ~ take liberties; **~putzen** v/t. (sep., -ge-, h) dress up; sich ~ dress (o.s.)

up; ~reden v/refl. (sep., -ge-, h) talk one's way out; ~stellen v/t. (sep., -ge-, h) put out; fig. emphasize, set forth; sich ~ emerge, turn out; ~strecken v/t. (sep., -ge-, h) stretch out; put out; ~streichen v/t. (irr. streichen, sep., -ge-, h) cross out, delete (word, etc.); fig. extol, praise; ~winden fig. v/refl. (irr. winden, sep., -ge-, h) extricate o.s. (aus from).

herb adj. [herp] fruit, flavour, etc.: tart; wine, etc.: dry; features, etc.: austere; criticism, etc.: harsh; disappointment, etc.: bitter.

herbei adv. [her'bai] here; ~l come here!; ~eilen [her'bai°-] v/i. (sep., -ge-, sein) come hurrying; ~führen fig. v/t. (sep., -ge-, h) cause, bring about, give rise to; ~schaffen v/t. (sep., -ge-, h) bring along; procure.

Herberge ['herbergə] f (-/-n) shelter, lodging; inn.

'Herbheit f (-/no pl.) tartness; dryness; fig.: austerity; harshness, bitterness.

Herbst [herpst] m (-[e]s/-e) autumn, Am. a. fall.

Herd [he:rt] m (-[e]s/-e) hearth, fireplace; stove; fig. seat, focus.

Herde ['he:rdə] f (-/-n) herd (of cattle, pigs, etc.) (contp. a. fig.); flock (of sheep, geese, etc.).

herein adv. [he'rain] in (here); ~l come in!; ~brechen fig. v/i. (irr. brechen, sep., -ge-, sein) night: fall; ~ über (acc.) misfortune, etc.: befall; ~fallen fig. v/i. (irr. fallen, sep., -ge-, sein) be taken in.

'her|fallen v/i. (irr. fallen, sep., -ge-, sein): ~ über (acc.) attack (a. fig.), fall upon; F fig. pull to pieces; '2gang m course of events, details pl.; ~geben v/t. (irr. geben, sep., -ge-, h) give up, part with, return; yield; sich ~ zu lend o.s. to; '~gebracht fig. adj. traditional; customary; '~halten (irr. halten, sep., -ge-, h) 1. v/t. hold out; 2. v/i.: ~ müssen be the one to pay or suffer (für for).

Hering ichth. ['he:rin] m (-s/-e) herring.

'her|kommen v/i. (irr. kommen, sep., -ge-, sein) come or get here; come or draw near; ~ von come from; fig. a. be due to, be caused by; ~kömmlich adj. ['~kœmlic] traditional; customary; 2kunft ['~kunft] f (-/no pl.) origin; birth, descent; '~leiten v/t. (sep., -ge-, h) lead here; fig. derive (von from); '2leitung fig. f derivation.

Herold ['he:rolt] m (-[e]s/-e) herald.

Herr [her] m (-n, ⚓-en/-en) lord, master; eccl. the Lord; gentleman; ~ Maier Mr Maier; mein ~ Sir; m-e ~en gentlemen; ~ der Situation master of the situation.

'Herren|bekleidung f men's cloth-

ing; '~einzel n tennis: men's singles pl.; '~haus n manor-house; 2-los adj. ['~lo:s] ownerless; '~reiter m sports: gentleman-jockey; '~schneider m men's tailor; '~zimmer n study; smoking-room.

herrichten ['he:r-] v/t. (sep., -ge-, h) arrange, prepare.

'herrisch adj. imperious, overbearing; voice, etc.: commanding, peremptory.

'herrlich adj. excellent, glorious, magnificent, splendid; '2keit f (-/-en) glory, splendo(u)r.

'Herrschaft f (-/-en) rule, dominion (über acc. of); fig. mastery; master and mistress; m-e ~en ladies and gentlemen!; '2lich adj. belonging to a master or landlord; fig. high-class, elegant.

herrsch|en ['herʃən] v/i. (ge-, h) rule (über acc. over); monarch: reign (over); govern; fig. prevail, be; '2er m (-s/-) ruler; sovereign, monarch; '2sucht f thirst for power; '~süchtig adj. thirsting for power; imperious.

'her|rühren v/i. (sep., -ge-, h): ~ von come from, originate with; '~sagen v/t. (sep., -ge-, h) recite; say (prayer); '~stammen v/i. (sep., -ge-, h): ~ von or aus be descended from; come from; be derived from; '~stellen v/t. (sep., -ge-, h) place here; ✝ make, manufacture, produce; '2stellung f (-/-en) manufacture, production.

herüber adv. [hɛ'ry:bər] over (here), across.

herum adv. [hɛ'rum] (a)round; about; ~führen v/t. (sep., -ge-, h) show (a)round; ~ in (dat.) show over; ~lungern v/i. (sep., -ge-, h) loaf or loiter or hang about; ~reichen v/t. (sep., -ge-, h) pass or hand round; ~sprechen v/refl. (irr. sprechen, sep., -ge-, h) get about, spread; ~treiben v/refl. (irr. treiben, sep., -ge-, h) F gad or knock about.

herunter adv. [hɛ'runtər] down (here); downstairs; von oben ~ down from above; ~bringen v/t. (irr. bringen, sep., -ge-, h) bring down; fig. a. lower, reduce; ~kommen v/i. (irr. kommen, sep., -ge-, sein) come down(stairs); fig.: come down in the world; deteriorate; ~machen v/t. (sep., -ge-, h) take down; turn (collar, etc.) down; fig. give s.o. a dressing-down; fig. pull to pieces; ~reißen v/t. (irr. reißen, sep., -ge-, h) pull or tear down; fig. pull to pieces; ~sein F fig. v/i. (irr. sein, sep., -ge-, sein) be low in health; ~wirtschaften v/t. (sep., -ge-, h) run down.

hervor adv. [hɛr'fo:r] forth, out; ~bringen v/t. (irr. bringen, sep.,

-ge-, h) bring out, produce (a. fig.); yield (fruit); fig. utter (word); ~**gehen** v/i. (irr. gehen, sep., -ge-, sein) p. come (aus from); come off (victorious) (from); fact, etc.: emerge (from); be clear or apparent (from); ~**heben** fig. v/t. (irr. heben, sep., -ge-, h) stress, emphasize; give prominence to; ~**holen** v/t. (sep., -ge-, h) produce; ~**ragen** v/i. (sep., -ge-, h) project (über acc. over); fig. tower (above); ~**ragend** adj. projecting, prominent; fig. outstanding, excellent; ~**rufen** v/t. (irr. rufen, sep., -ge-, h) thea. call for; fig. arouse, evoke; ~**stechend** fig. adj. outstanding; striking; conspicuous.

Herz [herts] n (-ens/-en) anat. heart (a. fig.); cards: hearts pl.; fig. courage, spirit; sich ein ~ fassen take heart; mit ganzem ~en whole-heartedly; sich et. zu ~en nehmen take s.th. to heart; es nicht übers ~ bringen zu inf. not to have the heart to inf.; '~**anfall** m heart attack.

'**Herzens|brecher** m (-s/-) lady-killer; ~**lust** f: nach ~ to one's heart's content; ~**wunsch** m heart's desire.

'**herz|ergreifend** fig. adj. heart-moving; '**2fehler** ✠ m cardiac defect; '**2gegend** anat. f cardiac region; '~**haft** adj. hearty, good; '~**ig** adj. lovely, Am. a. cute; **2infarkt** ✠ ['~⁹infarkt] m (-[e]s/-e) cardiac infarction; '**2klopfen** ✠ n (-s/no pl.) palpitation; '~**krank** adj. having heart trouble; '~**lich** 1. adj. heartfelt; cordial, hearty; ~es Beileid sincere sympathy; 2. adv.: ~ gern with pleasure; '~**los** adj. heartless; unfeeling.

Herzog ['hertso:k] m (-[e]s/~e, -e) duke; ~**in** f (-/-nen) duchess; ~**tum** n (-[e]s/~er) dukedom; duchy.

'**Herz|schlag** m heartbeat; ✠ heart failure; '~**schwäche** ✠ f cardiac insufficiency; '~**verpflanzung** ✠ f heart transplant; '**2zerreißend** adj. heart-rending.

Hetz|e ['hetsə] f (-/-n) hurry, rush; instigation (gegen acc. against); baiting (of); '**2en** (ge-) 1. v/t. (h) course (hare); bait (bear, etc.); hound: hunt, chase (animal); fig. hurry, rush; sich ~ hurry, rush; e-n Hund auf j-n ~ set a dog at s.o.; 2. v/i. (h) fig.: cause discord; agitate (gegen against); 3. fig. v/i. (sein) hurry, rush; '~**er** fig. m (-s/-) instigator; agitator; '**2erisch** adj. virulent, inflammatory; '~**jagd** f hunt(ing); fig.: virulent campaign; rush, hurry; '~**presse** f yellow press.

Heu [hɔy] n (-[e]s/no pl.) hay; '~**boden** m hayloft.

Heuchel|ei [hɔyçə'laɪ] f (-/-en) hypocrisy; '**2n** (ge-, h) 1. v/t. simulate, feign, affect; 2. v/i. feign, dissemble; play the hypocrite.

'**Heuchler** m (-s/-) hypocrite; '**2isch** adj. hypocritical.

heuer ['hɔyər] 1. adv. this year; 2. ♀ ⚓ f (-/-n) pay, wages pl.; '~**n** v/t. (ge-, h) hire; ⚓ engage, sign on (crew), charter (ship).

heulen ['hɔylən] v/i. (ge-, h) wind, etc.: howl; storm, wind, etc.: roar; siren: wail; F p. howl, cry.

'**Heu|schnupfen** ✠ m hay-fever; ~**schrecke** zo. ['~ʃrɛkə] f (-/-n) grasshopper, locust.

heut|e adv. ['hɔytə] today; ~ abend this evening, tonight; ~ früh, ~ morgen this morning; ~ in acht Tagen today or this day week; ~ vor acht Tagen a week ago today; '~**ig** adj. this day's, today's; present; ~**zutage** adv. ['hɔyttsuta:gə] nowadays, these days.

Hexe ['hɛksə] f (-/-n) witch, sorceress; fig.: hell-cat; hag; '**2n** v/i. (ge-, h) practice witchcraft; F fig. work miracles; '~**nkessel** fig. m inferno; '~**nmeister** m wizard, sorcerer; '~**nschuß** ✠ m lumbago; ~**rei** ['~'raɪ] f (-/-en) witchcraft, sorcery, magic.

Hieb [hi:p] 1. m (-[e]s/-e) blow, stroke; lash, cut (of whip, etc.); a. punch (with fist); fenc. cut; ~e pl. hiding, thrashing; 2. ♀ pret. of hauen.

hielt [hi:lt] pret. of halten.

hier adv. [hi:r] here; in this place; ~! present!; ~ entlang! this way!

hier|an adv. ['hi:'ran, when emphatic 'hi:ran] at or by or in or on or to it or this; ~**auf** adv. ['hi:'rauf, when emphatic 'hi:rauf] on it or this; after this or that, then; ~**aus** adv. ['hi:'raus, when emphatic 'hi:raus] from or out of it or this; ~**bei** adv. ['hi:r'baɪ, when emphatic 'hi:rbaɪ] here; in this case, in connection with this; ~**durch** adv. ['hi:r'durç, when emphatic 'hi:rdurç] through here; by this, hereby; ~**für** adv. ['hi:r'fy:r, when emphatic 'hi:rfy:r] for it or this; ~**her** adv. ['hi:r'he:r, when emphatic 'hi:rhe:r] here, hither; bis ~ as far as here; ~**in** adv. ['hi:'rin, when emphatic 'hi:rin] in it or this; in here; ~**mit** adv. ['hi:r'mit, when emphatic 'hi:rmit] with it or this, herewith; ~**nach** adv. ['hi:r'na:x, when emphatic 'hi:rna:x] after it or this; according to this; ~**über** adv. ['hi:'ry:bər, when emphatic 'hi:ry:bər] over it or this; over here; on this (subject); ~**unter** adv. ['hi:'runtər, when emphatic 'hi:runtər] under it or this; among these; by this or that; ~**von** adv. ['hi:r'fɔn, when emphatic 'hi:rfɔn] of or from it or this; ~**zu** adv. ['hi:r'tsu:, when emphatic 'hi:rtsu:]

with it or this; (in addition) to this.

hiesig adj. ['hi:ziç] of or in this place or town, local.

hieß [hi:s] pret. of heißen.

Hilfe ['hilfə] f (-/-n) help; aid, assistance; succour; relief (für to); ~l help!; mit ~ von with the help or aid of; '~ruf m shout or cry for help.

'**hilf|los** adj. helpless; '~reich adj. helpful.

'**Hilfs|aktion** f relief measures pl.; '~arbeiter m unskilled worker or labo(u)rer; '2bedürftig adj. needy, indigent; '~lehrer m assistant teacher; '~mittel n aid; device; remedy; expedient; '~motor m: Fahrrad mit ~ motor-assisted bicycle; '~quelle f resource; '~schule f elementary school for backward children; '~werk n relief organization.

Himbeere ♀ ['himbe:rə] f rasp-|
[berry.|

Himmel ['himəl] m (-s/-) sky, heavens pl.; eccl., fig. heaven; '~bett n tester-bed; '2blau adj. sky-blue; '~fahrt eccl. f ascension (of Christ); Ascension-day; '2schreiend adj. crying.

'**Himmels|gegend** f region of the sky; cardinal point; '~körper m celestial body; '~richtung f point of the compass, cardinal point; direction; '~strich m region, climate zone.

'**himmlisch** adj. celestial, heavenly.

hin adv. [hin] there; gone, lost; ~ und her to and fro, Am. back and forth; ~ und wieder now and again or then; ~ und zurück there and back.

hinab adv. [hi'nap] down; ~steigen v/i. (irr. steigen, sep., -ge-, sein) climb down, descend.

hinarbeiten ['hin?-] v/i. (sep., -ge-, h): ~ auf (acc.) work for or towards.

hinauf adv. [hi'nauf] up (there); upstairs; ~gehen v/i. (irr. gehen, sep., -ge-, sein) go up(stairs); prices, wages, etc.: go up, rise; ~steigen v/i. (irr. steigen, sep., -ge-, sein) climb up, ascend.

hinaus adv. [hi'naus] out; ~ mit euch! out with you!; auf (viele) Jahre ~ for (many) years (to come); ~gehen v/i. (irr. gehen, sep., -ge-, sein) go or walk out; ~ über (acc.) go beyond, exceed; ~ auf (acc.) window, etc.: look out on, overlook; intention, etc.: drive or aim at; ~laufen v/i. (irr. laufen, sep., -ge-, sein) run or rush out; ~ auf (acc.) come or amount to; ~schieben fig. v/t. (irr. schieben, sep., -ge-, h) put off, postpone, defer; ~werfen v/t. (irr. werfen, sep., -ge-, h) throw out (aus of); turn or throw or F chuck s.o. out.

'**Hin|blick** m: im ~ auf (acc.) in view of, with regard to; '2bringen v/t. (irr. bringen, sep., -ge-, h) take there; while away, pass (time).

hinder|lich adj. ['hindərliç] hindering, impeding; j-m ~ sein be in s.o.'s way; '~n v/t. (ge-, h) hinder, hamper (bei, in dat. in); ~ an (dat.) prevent from; '2nis n (-ses/-se) hindrance; sports: obstacle; turf, etc.: fence; '2nisrennen n obstacle-race.

hin'durch adv. through; all through, throughout; across.

hinein adv. [hi'nam] in; ~ mit dir! in you go!; ~gehen v/i. (irr. gehen, sep., -ge-, sein) go in; ~ in (acc.) go into; in den Topf gehen ... hinein the pot holds or takes ...

'**Hin|fahrt** f journey or way there; '2fallen v/i. (irr. fallen, sep., -ge-, sein) fall (down); '2fällig adj. p. frail; regulation, etc.: invalid; ~ machen invalidate, render invalid.

hing [hiŋ] pret. of hängen 1.

'**Hin|gabe** f devotion (an acc. to); '2geben v/t. (irr. geben, sep., -ge-); give up or away; sich ~ (dat.) give o.s. to; devote o.s. to; '~gebung f (-/-en) devotion; '2gehen v/i. (irr. gehen, sep., -ge-, sein) go or walk there; go (zu to); path, etc.: lead there; lead (zu to a place); '2halten v/t. (irr. halten, sep., -ge-, h) hold out (object, etc.); put s.o. off.

hinken ['hiŋkən] v/i. (ge-) 1. (h) limp (auf dem rechten Fuß with one's right leg), have a limp; 2. (sein) limp (along).

'**hin|länglich** adj. sufficient, adequate; '~legen v/t. (sep., -ge-, h) lay or put down; sich ~ lie down; '~nehmen v/t. (irr. nehmen, sep., -ge-, h) accept, take; put up with; '~raffen v/t. (sep., -ge-, h) death, etc.: snatch s.o. away, carry s.o. off; '~reichen (sep., -ge-) 1. v/t. reach or stretch or hold out (dat. to); 2. v/i. suffice; ~reißen fig. v/t. (irr. reißen, sep., -ge-, h) carry away; enrapture, ravish; '~reißend adj. ravishing, captivating; '~richten v/t. (sep., -ge-, h) execute, put to death; '2richtung f execution; '~setzen v/t. (sep., -ge-, h) set or put down; sich ~ sit down; '2sicht f regard, respect; in ~ auf (acc.) = ~sichtlich prp. (gen.) with regard to, as to, concerning; '~stellen v/t. (sep., -ge-, h) place; put; put down; et. ~ als represent s.th. as; make s.th. appear (as).

hintan|setzen [hint'an-] v/t. (sep., -ge-, h) set aside; 2setzung f (-/-en) setting aside; ~stellen v/t. (sep., -ge-, h) set aside; 2stellung f (-/-en) setting aside.

hinten adv. ['hintən] behind, at the

back; in the background; in the rear.

hinter *prp.* ['hintər] **1.** (*dat.*) behind, *Am. a.* back of; ~ *sich lassen* out-distance; **2.** (*acc.*) behind; '**2bein** *n* hind leg; **2bliebenen** *pl.* [.'bli:bə-nən] *the* bereaved *pl.*; surviving dependants *pl.*; .'**bringen** *v/t.* (*irr.* bringen, *no* -ge-, h): j-m et. ~ inform s.o. of s.th. (secretly); **ei'nander** *adv.* one after the other; in succession; '**2gedanke** *m* ulterior motive; .'**gehen** *v/t.* (*irr.* gehen, *no* -ge-, h) deceive, F double-cross; **2'gehung** *f* (-/-en) deception; '**2grund** *m* background (*a. fig.*); '**2halt** *m* ambush; .**hältig** *adj.* ['.hɛltiç] insidious; underhand; '**2haus** *n* back *or* rear building; .'**her** *adv.* behind; afterwards; '**2hof** *m* backyard; **2'kopf** *m* back of the head; .'**lassen** *v/t.* (*irr.* lassen, *no* -ge-, h) leave (behind); **2'lassenschaft** *f* (-/-en) property (left), estate; .'**legen** *v/t.* (*no* -ge-, h) deposit, lodge (*bei* with); **2'legung** *f* (-/-en) deposit(ion); '**2list** *f* deceit; craftiness; insidiousness; '**listig** *adj.* deceitful; crafty; insidious; '**2mann** *m* ✗ rear-rank man; *fig.*: † subsequent endorser; *pol.* backer; wire-puller; instigator; '**2n** F *m* (-s/-) backside, behind, bottom; '**2rad** *n* rear wheel; '**rücks** *adv.* [.ryks] from behind; *fig.* behind his, *etc.* back; '**2seite** *f* back; '**2teil** *n* back (part); rear (part); F *s. Hintern*; .'**treiben** *v/t.* (*irr.* treiben, *no* -ge-, h) thwart, frustrate; '**2treppe** *f* backstairs *pl.*; '**2tür** *f* back door; .'**ziehen** ⚖ *v/t.* (*irr.* ziehen, *no* -ge-, h) evade (*tax, duty, etc.*); **2'ziehung** *f* evasion.

hinüber *adv.* [hi'ny:bər] over (there); across.

Hin- und 'Rückfahrt *f* journey there and back, *Am.* round trip.

hinunter *adv.* [hi'nuntər] down (there); downstairs; .**schlucken** *v/t.* (*sep.*, -ge-, h) swallow (down); *fig.* swallow.

'**Hinweg**[1] *m* way there *or* out.

hinweg[2] *adv.* [hin'vɛk] away, off; .**gehen** *v/i.* (*irr.* gehen, *sep.*, -ge-sein): ~ *über* (*acc.*) go *or* walk over *or* across; *fig.* pass over, ignore; .**kommen** *v/i.* (*irr.* kommen, *sep.*, -ge-, sein): ~ *über* (*acc.*) get over (*a. fig.*); .**sehen** *v/i.* (*irr.* sehen, *sep.*, -ge-, h): ~ *über* (*acc.*) see *or* look over; *fig.* overlook, shut one's eyes to; .**setzen** *v/refl.* (*sep.*, -ge-, h): sich ~ *über* (*acc.*) ignore, disregard, make light of.

Hin|weis ['hinvais] *m* (-es/-e) reference (*auf acc.* to); hint (at); indication (of); '**2weisen** (*irr.* weisen, *sep.*, -ge-, h) **1.** *v/t.*: j-n ~ *auf* (*acc.*) draw *or* call s.o.'s attention to; **2.** *v/i.*: ~

auf (*acc.*) point at *or* to, indicate (*a. fig.*); *fig.*: point out; hint at; '**2werfen** *v/t.* (*irr.* werfen, *sep.*, -ge-, h) throw down; *fig.*: dash off (*sketch, etc.*); say *s.th.* casually; '**2wirken** *v/i.* (*sep.*, -ge-, h): ~ *auf* (*acc.*) work towards; use one's influence to; '**2ziehen** (*irr.* ziehen, *sep.*, -ge-) **1.** *fig. v/t.* (h) attract *or* draw there; with ~ *space*: extend (*bis zu* to), stretch (*to*); *time*: drag on; **2.** *v/i.* (sein) go *or* move there; '**2zielen** *fig. v/i.* (*sep.*, -ge-, h): ~ *auf* (*acc.*) aim *or* drive at.

hin'zu *adv.* there; near; in addition; .**fügen** *v/t.* (*sep.*, -ge-, h) add (zu to) (*a. fig.*); **2fügung** *f* (-/-en) addition; .**kommen** *v/i.* (*irr.* kommen, *sep.*, -ge-, sein) come up (zu to); supervene; be added; *es kommt (noch) hinzu, daß* add to this that, (and) moreover; .**rechnen** *v/t.* (*sep.*, -ge-, h) add (zu to), include (in, among); .**setzen** *v/t.* (*sep.*, -ge-, h) s. *hinzufügen*; .**treten** *v/i.* (*irr.* treten, *sep.*, -ge-, sein) s. *hinzukommen*; join; .**ziehen** *v/t.* (*irr.* ziehen, *sep.*, -ge-, h) call in (*doctor, etc.*).

Hirn [hirn] *n* (-[e]s/-e) *anat.* brain; *fig.* brains *pl.*; mind; '**gespinst** *n* figment of the mind, chimera; '**2los** *fig. adj.* brainless, senseless; '.**schale** *anat.* f brain-pan, cranium; '.**schlag** 💀 *m* apoplexy; '**2verbrannt** *adj.* crazy, F crack-brained, cracky.

Hirsch *zo.* [hirʃ] *m* (-es/-e) *species:* deer; stag, hart; '.**geweih** *n* (stag's) antlers *pl.*; '.**kuh** *f* hind; '.**leder** *n* buckskin, deerskin.

Hirse ♀ ['hirzə] *f* (-/-n) millet.

Hirt [hirt] *m* (-en/-en), .**e** ['.ə] *m* (-n/-n) herdsman; shepherd.

hissen ['hisən] *v/t.* (*sep.*, -ge-, h) hoist, raise (*flag*); 🕆 *a.* trice up (*sail*).

Histori|ker [hi'sto:rikər] *m* (-s/-) historian; **2sch** *adj.* historic(al).

Hitz|e ['hitsə] *f* (-/*no pl.*) heat; '**2ebeständig** *adj.* heat-resistant, heat-proof; '.**ewelle** *f* heat-wave, hot spell; '**2ig** *adj. p.* hot-tempered, hot-headed; *discussion:* heated; '.**kopf** *m* hothead; '.**schlag** 💀 *m* heat-stroke.

hob [ho:p] *pret. of* heben.

Hobel ⊕ ['ho:bəl] *m* (-s/-) plane; '.**bank** *f* carpenter's bench; '**2n** *v/t.* (ge-, h) plane.

hoch [ho:x] **1.** *adj.* high; *church spire, tree, etc.:* tall; *position, etc.:* high, important; *guest, etc.:* distinguished; *punishment, etc.:* heavy, severe; *age:* great, old; *hohe See* open sea, high seas *pl.*; **2.** *adv.:* ~ *lebe ...l* long live ...l **3.** **2** *n* (-s/-s) cheer; toast; *meteorology:* high (-pressure area).

'**hoch|achten** *v/t.* (*sep.*, -ge-, h) esteem highly; '**2achtung** *f* high

esteem or respect; '~achtungsvoll
1. adj. (most) respectful; 2. adv.
correspondence: yours faithfully or
sincerely, esp. Am. yours truly;
'2adel m greater or higher nobility;
'2amt eccl. n high mass; '2antenne
f overhead aerial; '2bahn f elevated
or overhead railway, Am. elevated
railroad; '2betrieb m intense activity, rush; '2burg fig. f stronghold; '~deutsch adj. High or standard German; '2druck m high pressure (a. fig.); mit ~ arbeiten work at
high pressure; '2ebene f plateau,
tableland; '~fahrend adj. high-
handed, arrogant; '~fein adj.
superfine; '2form f: in ~ in top
form; '2frequenz ≠ f high frequency; '2gebirge n high mountains pl.; '2genuß m great enjoyment; '2glanz m high polish;
'2haus n multi-stor(e)y building,
skyscraper; '~herzig adj. noble-
minded; generous; '2herzigkeit f
(-/-en) noble-mindedness; generosity; '2konjunktur ≠ f boom,
business prosperity; '2land n
upland(s pl.), highlands pl.; '2mut
m arrogance, haughtiness; ~mütig
adj. ['~my:tiç] arrogant, haughty;
~näsig F adj. ['~nɛ:ziç] stuck-up;
'2ofen ⊕ m blast-furnace; '~rot
adj. bright red; '2saison f peak
season, height of the season;
'~schätzen v/t. (sep., -ge-, h) esteem
highly; '2schule f university, academy; '2seefischerei f deep-sea
fishing; '2sommer m midsummer;
'2spannung ≠ f high tension or
voltage; '2sprung m sports: high
jump.

höchst [hø:çst] 1. adj. highest; fig.
a.: supreme; extreme; 2. adv.
highly, most, extremely.

Hochstap|elei [ho:xʃtɑ:pə'laɪ] f
(-/-en) swindling; '~ler m (-s/-)
confidence man, swindler.

höchstens adv. ['hø:çstəns] at (the)
most, at best.

'Höchst|form f sports: top form;
'~geschwindigkeit f maximum
speed; speed limit; '~leistung f
sports: record (performance); ⊕
maximum output (of machine, etc.);
'~lohn m maximum wages pl.;
'~maß n maximum; '~preis m
maximum price.

'hoch|trabend fig. adj. high-flown;
pompous; 2verrat m high treason;
'2wald m high forest; '2wasser n
high tide or water; flood; '~wertig
adj. high-grade, high-class; '2wild
n big game; '2wohlgeboren m
(-s/-) Right Hono(u)rable.

Hochzeit ['hɔxtsaɪt] f (-/-en) wedding; marriage; 2lich adj. bridal,
nuptial; '~sgeschenk n wedding
present; '~sreise f honeymoon
(trip).

Hocke ['hɔkə] f (-/-n) gymnastics:
squat-vault; skiing: crouch; '2n
v/i. (ge-, h) squat, crouch; '~r m
(-s/-) stool.

Höcker ['hœkər] m (-s/-) surface,
etc.: bump; camel, etc.: hump; p.
hump, hunch; '2ig adj. animal:
humped; p. humpbacked, hunchbacked; surface, etc.: bumpy, rough,
uneven.

Hode anat. ['ho:də] m (-n/-n), f
(-/-n), '~n anat. m (-s/-) testicle.

Hof [ho:f] m (-[e]s/⁼e) court(yard);
farm; king, etc.: court; ast. halo;
j-m den ~ machen court s.o.; '~da-
me f lady-in-waiting; '2fähig adj.
presentable at court.

Hoffart ['hɔfart] f (-/no pl.) arrogance, haughtiness; pride.

hoffen ['hɔfən] (ge-, h) 1. v/i. hope
(auf acc. for); trust (in); 2. v/t.:
das Beste ~ hope for the best; '~t-
lich adv. it is to be hoped that,
I hope, let's hope.

Hoffnung ['hɔfnʊŋ] f (-/-en) hope
(auf acc. for, of); in der ~ zu inf.
in the hope of ger., hoping to inf.;
s-e ~ setzen auf (acc.) pin one's
hopes on; '2slos adj. hopeless;
'2svoll adj. hopeful; promising.

'Hofhund m watch-dog.

höfisch adj. ['hø:fiʃ] courtly.

höflich adj. ['hø:fliç] polite, civil,
courteous (gegen to); '2keit f (-/-en)
politeness, civility, courtesy.

'Hofstaat m royal or princely household; suite, retinue.

Höhe ['hø:ə] f (-/-n) height; ✈, ♈,
ast., geogr. altitude; hill; peak;
amount (of bill, etc.); size (of sum,
fine, etc.); level (of price, etc.);
severity (of punishment, etc.); ♪
pitch; in gleicher ~ mit on a level
with; auf der ~ sein be up to the
mark; in die ~ up(wards).

Hoheit ['ho:haɪt] f (-/-en) pol.
sovereignty; title: Highness; '~s-
gebiet n (sovereign) territory; '~s-
gewässer n/pl. territorial waters
pl.; '~szeichen n national emblem.

'Höhen|kurort m high-altitude
health resort; '~luft f mountain
air; '~sonne f mountain sun; ☀
ultra-violet lamp; '~steuer ✈ n
elevator; '~zug m mountain range.

'Höhepunkt m highest point; ast.,
fig. culmination, zenith; fig. a.:
climax; summit, peak.

hohl adj. [ho:l] hollow (a. fig.);
cheeks, etc.: sunken; hand: cupped;
sound hollow, dull.

Höhle ['hø:lə] f (-/-n) cave, cavern;
den, lair (of bear, lion, etc.) (both a.
fig.); hole, burrow (of fox, rabbit,
etc.); hollow; cavity.

'Hohl|maß n dry measure; '~raum
m hollow, cavity; '~spiegel m
concave mirror.

Höhlung ['hø:luŋ] f (-/-en) excavation; hollow, cavity.

'Hohlweg m defile.

Hohn [ho:n] m (-[e]s/no pl.) scorn, disdain; derision.

höhnen ['hø:nən] v/i. (ge-, h) sneer, jeer, mock, scoff (über acc. at).

'Hohngelächter n scornful or derisive laughter.

'höhnisch adj. scornful; sneering, derisive.

Höker ['hø:kər] m (-s/-) hawker, huckster; **'2n** v/i. (ge-, h) huckster, hawk about.

holen ['ho:lən] v/t. (ge-, h) fetch; go for; a. ~ lassen send for; draw (breath); sich e-e Krankheit ~ catch a disease; sich bei j-m Rat ~ seek s.o.'s advice.

Holländer ['hɔləndər] m (-s/-) Dutchman.

Hölle ['hœlə] f (-/✶-n) hell.

'Höllen|angst fig. f: e-e ~ haben be in a mortal fright or F blue funk; **'~lärm** F fig. m infernal noise; **'~maschine** f infernal machine, time bomb; **'~pein** F fig. f torment of hell.

'höllisch adj. hellish, infernal (both a. fig.).

holper|ig adj. ['hɔlpəriç] surface, road, etc.: bumpy, rough, uneven; vehicle, etc.: jolty, jerky; verse, style, etc.: rough, jerky; **'~n** (ge-) 1. v/i. (sein) vehicle: jolt, bump; 2. v/i. (h) vehicle: jolt, bump; be jolty or bumpy.

Holunder ♀ [ho'lundər] m (-s/-) elder.

Holz [hɔlts] n (-es/⁻er) wood; timber, Am. lumber; **'~bau** ⌂ m wooden structure; **'~bildhauer** m woodcarver; **'~blasinstrument** ♪ n woodwind instrument; **'~boden** m wood(en) floor; wood-loft.

hölzern adj. ['hœltsərn] wooden; fig. a. clumsy, awkward.

'Holz|fäller m (-s/-) woodcutter, woodman, Am. a. lumberjack, logger; **'~hacker** m (-s/-) woodchopper, woodcutter, Am. lumberjack; **'~händler** m wood or timber merchant, Am. lumberman; **'~haus** n wooden house, Am. frame house; **'2ig** adj. woody; **'~kohle** f charcoal; **'~platz** m wood or timber yard, Am. lumberyard; **'~schnitt** m woodcut, wood-engraving; **'~schnitzer** m wood-carver; **'~schuh** m wooden shoe, clog; **'~stoß** m pile or stack of wood; stake; **'~weg** fig. m: auf dem ~ sein be on the wrong track; **'~wolle** f wood-wool; fine wood shavings pl., Am. a. excelsior.

Homöopath ⚕ [homøo'pa:t] m (-en/-en) hom(o)eopath(ist); **~ie** [~'ti:] f (-/no pl.) hom(o)eopathy; **2isch** adj. [~'pa:tiʃ] hom(o)eopathic.

Honig ['ho:niç] m (-s/-e) honey;

'~kuchen m honey-cake; gingerbread; **'2süß** adj. honey-sweet, honeyed (a. fig.); **'~wabe** f honeycomb.

Honor|ar [hono'ra:r] n (-s/-e) fee; royalties pl.; salary; **~atioren** [~a-'tsjo:rən] pl. notabilities pl.; **2ieren** [~'ri:rən] v/t. (no -ge-, h) fee, pay a fee to; ✝ hono(u)r, meet (bill of exchange).

Hopfen ['hɔpfən] m (-s/-) ♀ hop; brewing: hops pl.

hops|a int. ['hɔpsa] (wh)oops!; upsadaisy!; **'~en** F v/i. (ge-, sein) hop, jump.

hörbar adj. ['hø:rba:r] audible.

horch|en ['hɔrçən] v/i. (ge-, h) listen (auf acc. to); eavesdrop; **'2er** m (-s/-) eavesdropper.

Horde ['hɔrdə] f (-/-n) horde, gang.

hör|en ['hø:rən] (ge-, h) 1. v/t. hear; listen (in) to (radio); attend (lecture, etc.); hear, learn; 2. v/i. hear (von dat. from); listen; ~ auf (acc.) listen to; schwer ~ be hard of hearing; ~ Sie mal! look here!; I say!; **'2er** m (-s/-) hearer; radio: listener(-in); univ. student; teleph. receiver; **'2erschaft** f (-/-en) audience; **'2gerät** n hearing aid; **'~ig** adj.: j-m ~ sein be enslaved to s.o.; **'2igkeit** f (-/no pl.) subjection.

Horizont [hori'tsɔnt] m (-[e]s/-e) horizon; skyline; s-n ~ erweitern broaden one's mind; das geht über meinen ~ that's beyond me; **2al** adj. [~'ta:l] horizontal.

Hormon [hɔr'mo:n] n (-s/-e) hormone.

Horn [hɔrn] n 1. (-[e]s/⁻er) horn (of bull); ♪, mot., etc.: horn; ✗ bugle; peak; 2. (-[e]s/-e) horn, horny matter; **'~haut** f horny skin; anat. cornea (on eye).

Hornisse zo. [hɔr'nisə] f (-/-n) hornet.

Hornist ♪ [hɔr'nist] m (-en/-en) horn-player; ✗ bugler.

Horoskop [horo'sko:p] n (-s/-e) horoscope; j-m das ~ stellen cast s.o.'s horoscope.

'Hör|rohr n ear-trumpet; ✍ stethoscope; **'~saal** m lecture-hall; **'~spiel** n radio play; **'~weite** f: in ~ within earshot.

Hose ['ho:zə] f (-/-n) (e-e a pair of) trousers pl. or Am. pants pl.; slacks pl.

'Hosen|klappe f flap; **~latz** ['~lats] m (-es/⁻e) flap; fly; **'~tasche** f trouser-pocket; **'~träger** m: (ein Paar) ~ pl. (a pair of) braces pl. or Am. suspenders pl.

Hospital [hɔspi'ta:l] n (-s/-e, ⁻er) hospital.

Hostie eccl. ['hɔstjə] f (-/-n) host, consecrated or holy wafer.

Hotel [ho'tɛl] n (-s/-s) hotel; **~besitzer** m hotel owner or proprietor;

~gewerbe n hotel industry; **~ier** [ˌˈjeː] m (-s/-s) hotel-keeper.

Hub ⊕ [huːp] m (-[e]s/ⁱe) mot. stroke (of piston); lift (of valve, etc.); **~raum** mot. m capacity.

hübsch adj. [hypʃ] pretty, nice; good-looking, handsome; attractive.

'Hubschrauber ✈ m (-s/-) helicopter.

Huf [huːf] m (-[e]s/-e) hoof; **~eisen** n horseshoe; **~schlag** m hoof-beat; (horse's) kick; **~schmied** m farrier.

Hüft|e anat. ['hyftə] f (-/-n) hip; esp. zo. haunch; **~gelenk** n hipjoint; **~gürtel** m girdle; suspender belt, Am. garter belt.

Hügel ['hyːgəl] m (-s/-) hill(ock); **2ig** adj. hilly.

Huhn orn. [huːn] n (-[e]s/ⁱer) fowl, chicken; hen; junges ~ chicken.

Hühnchen ['hyːnçən] n (-s/-) chicken; ein ~ zu rupfen haben have a bone to pick (mit with).

Hühner|auge ['hyːnər-] n corn; **~ei** n hen's egg; **~hof** m poultry-yard, Am. chicken yard; **~hund** zo. m pointer, setter; **~leiter** f chicken-ladder.

Huld [hult] f (-/no pl.) grace, favo(u)r; **2igen** ['ˌdɪgən] v/i. (dat.) (ge-, h) pay homage to (sovereign, lady, etc.); indulge in (vice, etc.); **~igung** f (-/-en) homage; **2reich** adj., **2voll** adj. gracious.

Hülle ['hylə] f (-/-n) cover(ing), wrapper; letter, balloon, etc.: envelope; book, etc.: jacket; umbrella, etc.: sheath; **2n** v/t. (ge-, h) wrap, cover, envelope (a. fig.); sich in Schweigen ~ wrap o.s. in silence.

Hülse ['hylzə] f (-/-n) legume, pod (of leguminous plant); husk, hull (of rice, etc.); skin (of pea, etc.); ✗ case; **~nfrucht** f legume(n); leguminous plant; **~nfrüchte** f/pl. pulse.

human adj. [hu'maːn] humane; **2ität** [ˌaniˈtɛːt] f (-/no pl.) humanity.

Hummel zo. ['huməl] f (-/-n) bumble-bee.

Hummer zo. ['humər] m (-s/-) lobster.

Humor [hu'moːr] m (-s/✗,-e) humo(u)r; **~ist** [ˌoˈrist] m (-en/-en) humorist; **2istisch** adj. [ˌoˈristiʃ] humorous.

humpeln ['humpəln] v/i. (ge-) 1. (sein) hobble (along), limp (along); 2. (h) (have a) limp, walk with a limp.

Hund [hunt] m (-[e]s/-e) zo. dog; ✗ tub; ast. dog, canis; auf den ~ kommen go to the dogs.

'Hunde|hütte f dog-kennel, Am. a. doghouse; **~kuchen** m dog-biscuit; **~leine** f (dog-)lead or leash; **~peitsche** f dog-whip.

hundert ['hundərt] 1. adj. a or one

hundred; 2. **2** n (-s/-e) hundred; fünf vom ~ five per cent; zu ~en by hundreds; **~fach** adj., **~fältig** adj. hundredfold; **2'jahrfeier** f centenary, Am. a. centennial; **~jährig** adj. ['ˌjɛːrɪç] centenary, a hundred years old; **~st** adj. hundredth.

'Hunde|sperre f muzzling-order; **~steuer** f dog tax.

Hündi|n zo. ['hyndɪn] f (-/-nen) bitch, she-dog; **2sch** adj. doggish; fig. servile, cringing.

'hunds|ge'mein F adj. dirty, mean, scurvy; **~mise'rabel** F adj. rotten, wretched, lousy; **2tage** m/pl. dog-days pl.

Hüne ['hyːnə] m (-n/-n) giant.

Hunger ['huŋər] m (-s/no pl.) hunger (fig. nach for); ~ bekommen get hungry; ~ haben be or feel hungry; **~kur** f starvation cure; **~leider** F m (-s/-) starveling, poor devil; **~lohn** m starvation wages pl.; **2n** v/i. (ge-, h) hunger (fig. nach after, for); go without food; ~ lassen starve s.o.; **~snot** f famine; **~streik** m hunger-strike; **~tod** m death from starvation; **~tuch** fig. n: am ~ nagen have nothing to bite.

'hungrig adj. hungry (fig. nach for).

Hupe mot. ['huːpə] f (-/-n) horn, hooter; klaxon; **2n** v/i. (ge-, h) sound one's horn, hoot.

hüpfen ['hypfən] v/i. (ge-, sein) hip, skip; gambol, frisk (about).

Hürde ['hyrdə] f (-/-n) hurdle; fold, pen; **~nrennen** n hurdle-race.

Hure ['huːrə] f (-/-n) whore, prostitute.

hurtig adj. quick, swift; agile, nimble.

Husar ✗ [hu'zaːr] m (-en/-en) hussar.

husch int. [huʃ] in or like a flash; shoo!; **~en** v/i. (ge-, sein) slip, dart; small animal: scurry, scamper; bat, etc.: flit.

hüsteln ['hyːstəln] 1. v/i. (ge-, h) cough slightly; 2. **2** n (-s/no pl.) slight cough.

husten ['huːstən] 1. v/i. (ge-, h) cough; 2. **2** m (-s/✗,-) cough.

Hut [huːt] 1. m (-[e]s/ⁱe) hat; den ~ abnehmen take off one's hat; ~ ab vor (dat.)! hats off to ...!; 2. f (-/no pl.) care, charge; guard; auf der ~ sein be on one's guard (vor dat. against).

hüte|n ['hyːtən] v/t. (ge-, h) guard, protect, keep watch over; keep (secret); tend (sheep, etc.); das Bett ~ be confined to (one's) bed; sich ~ vor (dat.) beware of; **2r** m (-s/-) keeper, guardian; herdsman.

'Hut|futter n hat-lining; **~krempe** f hat-brim; **~macher** m (-s/-) hatter; **~nadel** f hat-pin.

Hütte ['hytə] f (-/-n) hut; cottage, cabin; ⊕ metallurgical plant; mount.

refuge; **~nwesen** ⊕ *n* metallurgy, metallurgical engineering.
Hyäne *zo.* [hy'ɛ:nə] *f* (-/-n) hy(a)ena.
Hyazinthe ♀ [hya'tsɪntə] *f* (-/-n) hyacinth. [hydrant.\
Hydrant [hy'drant] *m* (-en/-en)\
Hydrauli|k *phys.* [hy'draulik] *f* (-/*no pl.*) hydraulics *pl.*; **2sch** *adj.* hydraulic.
Hygien|e [hy'gje:nə] *f* (-/*no pl.*) hygiene; **2isch** *adj.* hygienic(al).
Hymne ['hymnə] *f* (-/-n) hymn.
Hypno|se [hyp'no:zə] *f* (-/-n) hypnosis; **2tisieren** [~oti'zi:rən] *v/t. and v/i.* (*no* -ge-, *h*) hypnotize.

Hypochond|er [hypo'xɔndər] *m* (-s/-) hypochondriac; **2risch** *adj.* hypochondriac.
Hypotenuse ⅃ [hypote'nu:zə] *f* (-/-n) hypotenuse.
Hypothek [hypo'te:k] *f* (-/-en) mortgage; e-e ~ *aufnehmen* raise a mortgage; **2arisch** *adj.* [~e'ka:rɪʃ]: *~e Belastung* mortgage.
Hypothe|se [hypo'te:zə] *f* (-/-n) hypothesis; **2tisch** *adj.* hypothetical.
Hyster|ie *psych.* [hyste'ri:] *f* (-/-n) hysteria; **2isch** *psych. adj.* [~'te:rɪʃ] hysterical.

I

ich [iç] **1.** *pers. pron.* I; **2.** ♀ *n* (-[s]/ -[s]) *psych. the* ego.
Ideal [ide'a:l] **1.** *n* (-s/-e) ideal; **2.** ♀ *adj.* ideal; **2isieren** [~ali'zi:rən] *v/t.* (*no* -ge-, *h*) idealize; **~ismus** [~a'lismus] *m* (-/*Idealismen*) idealism; **~ist** [~a'list] *m* (-en/-en) idealist.
Idee [i'de:] *f* (-/-n) idea, notion.
identi|fizieren [identifi'tsi:rən] *v/t.* (*no* -ge-, *h*) identify; *sich ~* identify *o.s.*; **~sch** *adj.* [i'dɛntɪʃ] identical; **2tät** [~'te:t] *f* (-/*no pl.*) identity.
Ideolog|ie [ideolo'gi:] *f* (-/-n) ideology; **2isch** *adj.* [~'lo:gɪʃ] ideological.
Idiot [idi'o:t] *m* (-en/-en) idiot; **~ie** [~o'ti:] *f* (-/-n) idiocy; **2isch** *adj.* [~'o:tɪʃ] idiotic.
Idol [i'do:l] *n* (-s/-e) idol.
Igel *zo.* ['i:gəl] *m* (-s/-) hedgehog.
Ignor|ant [igno'rant] *m* (-en/-en) ignorant person, ignoramus; **~anz** [~ts] *f* (-/*no pl.*) ignorance; **2ieren** *v/t.* (*no* -ge-, *h*) ignore, take no notice of.
ihm *pers. pron.* [i:m] *p.* (to) him; *thing:* (to) it.
ihn *pers. pron.* [i:n] *p.* him; *thing:* it.
Ihnen *pers. pron.* (to) them; *Ihnen sg. and pl.* (to) you.
ihr [i:r] **1.** *pers. pron.*: (*2nd pl. nom.*) you; (*3rd sg. dat.*) (to) her; **2.** *poss. pron.*: her; their; *Ihr sg. and pl.* your; *der (die, das)* ~*e* hers; theirs; *der (die, das) Ihre sg. and pl.* yours; **~erseits** ['~ɔr'zaɪts] *adv.* on her part; on their part; *Ihrerseits sg. and pl.* on your part; **'~esgleichen** *pron.* (of) her *or* their kind, her *or* their equal; *Ihresgleichen sg.* (of) your kind, your equal; *pl.* (of) your kind, your equals; **'~et'wegen** *adv.* for her *or* their sake, on her *or* their account; *Ihretwegen sg. or pl.* for your sake, on your account; **'~et-willen** *adv.*: *um* ~ *s. ihretwegen;*

~ige *poss. pron.* ['~igə]: *der (die, das)* ~ hers; theirs; *der (die, das) Ihrige* yours.
illegitim *adj.* [ilegi'ti:m] illegitimate.
illusorisch *adj.* [ilu'zo:rɪʃ] illusory, deceptive.
illustrieren [ilu'stri:rən] *v/t.* (*no* -ge-, *h*) illustrate.
Iltis *zo.* ['iltis] *m* (-ses/-se) fitchew, polecat.
im *prp.* [im] = *in dem.*
imaginär *adj.* [imagi'nɛ:r] imaginary.
'Imbiß *m* light meal, snack; **'~stube** *f* snack bar.
Imker ['imkər] *m* (-s/-) bee-master, bee-keeper.
immatrikulieren [imatriku'li:rən] *v/t.* (*no* -ge-, *h*) matriculate, enrol(l); *sich ~ lassen* matriculate, enrol(l).
immer *adv.* ['imər] always; ~ *mehr* more and more; ~ *wieder* again *or* time and again; *für* ~ for ever, for good; **'2grün** ♀ *n* (-s/-e) evergreen; **'~hin** *adv.* still; yet; **'~zu** *adv.* always, continually.
Immobilien [imo'bi:ljən] *pl.* immovables *pl.*, real estate; **~händler** *m s. Grundstücksmakler.*
immun *adj.* [i'mu:n] immune (*gegen* against; *from*); **2ität** [~uni'tε:t] *f* (-/*no pl.*) immunity.
Imperativ *gr.* ['imperati:f] *m* (-s/-e) imperative (mood).
Imperfekt *gr.* ['imperfekt] *n* (-s/-e) imperfect (tense), past tense.
Imperialis|mus [imperia'lismus] *m* (-/*no pl.*) imperialism; **~t** *m* (-en/-en) imperialist; **2tisch** *adj.* imperialistic.
impertinent *adj.* [imperti'nεnt] impertinent, insolent.
impf|en ⚕ ['impfən] *v/t.* (ge-, *h*) vaccinate; inoculate; **'2schein** *m* certificate of vaccination *or* inoculation; **'2stoff** ⚕ *m* vaccine;

serum; **²ung** f (-/-en) vaccination; inoculation.

imponieren [impo'niːrən] v/i. (no -ge-, h): j-m ~ impress s.o.

Import † [im'pɔrt] m (-[e]s/-e) import(ation); **~eur** † [ˌ'tøːr] m (-s/-e) importer; **²ieren** [ˌ'tiːrən] v/t. (no -ge-, h) import.

imposant adj. [impo'zant] imposing, impressive.

imprägnieren [imprɛ'gniːrən] v/t. (no -ge-, h) impregnate; (water-) proof (raincoat, etc.).

improvisieren [improvi'ziːrən] v/t. and v/i. (no -ge-, h) improvise.

Im'puls m (-es/-e) impuls; **²iv** adj. [ˌ'ziːf] impulsive.　　　　[be able.\

imstande adj. [im'ʃtandə]: ~ sein]

in prp. (dat.; acc.) [in] **1.** place: in, at; within; into, in; with names of important towns: in, ²½ at; with names of villages and less important towns: at; im Hause in the house, indoors, in; im ersten Stock on the first floor; ~ der Schule (im Theater) at school (the theat|re, Am. -er); ~ die Schule (~s Theater) to school (the theat|re, Am. -er); ~ England in England; waren Sie schon einmal in England? have you ever been to England? **2.** time: in, at, during; within; ~ drei Tagen (with)in three days; heute ~ vierzehn Tagen today fortnight; im Jahre 1960 in 1960; im Februar in February; im Frühling in (the) spring; ~ der Nacht at night; ~ letzter Zeit lately, of late, recently; **3.** mode: ~ großer Eile in great haste; ~ Frieden leben live at peace; ~ Reichweite within reach; **4.** condition, state: im Alter von fünfzehn Jahren at (the age of) fifteen; ~ Behandlung under treatment.

'Inbegriff m (quint)essence; embodiment, incarnation; paragon; **²en** adj. included, inclusive (of).

'Inbrunst f (-/no pl.) ardo(u)r, fervo(u)r.

'inbrünstig adj. ardent, fervent.

in'dem cj. whilst, while; by (ger.); ~ er mich ansah, sagte er looking at me he said.

Inder ['indər] m (-s/-) Indian.

in'des(sen) 1. adv. meanwhile; **2.** cj. while; however.

Indianer [in'djaːnər] m (-s/-) (American or Red) Indian.

Indikativ gr. ['indikatiːf] m (-s/-e) indicative (mood).

indirekt adj. indirect.

indisch adj. ['indiʃ] Indian.

'indiskret adj. indiscreet; **²ion** [ˌe'tsjoːn] f (-/-en) indiscretion.

indiskutabel adj. ['indiskuta:bəl] out of the question.

individu|ell adj. [individu'ɛl] individual; **²um** [ˌ'viːduum] n (-s/ Individuen) individual.

Indizienbeweis ⁀½ [in'diːtsjən-] m circumstantial evidence.

Indoss|ament † [indɔsa'ment] n (-s/-e) endorsement, indorsement; **²ieren** † [ˌ'siːrən] v/t. (no -ge-, h) indorse, endorse.

Industrialisierung [industriali'ziːruŋ] f (-/-en) industrialization.

Industrie [indus'triː] f (-/-n) industry; **~anlage** f industrial plant; **~arbeiter** m industrial worker; **~ausstellung** f industrial exhibition; **~erzeugnis** n industrial product; **~gebiet** n industrial district or area; **²ll** adj. [ˌ'ɛl] industrial; **~lle** [ˌ'ɛlə] m (-n/-n) industrialist; **~staat** m industrial country.

ineinander adv. [in'ʔaɪ'nandər] into one another; **~greifen** ⊕ v/i. (irr. greifen, sep., -ge-, h) gear into one another, interlock.

infam adj. [in'faːm] infamous.

Infanter|ie ✗ [infantə'riː] f (-/-n) infantry; **~ist** ✗ m (-en/-en) infantryman.

Infektion ⚕ [infɛk'tsjoːn] f (-/-en) infection; **~skrankheit** ⚕ f infectious disease.

Infinitiv gr. ['infinitiːf] m (-s/-e) infinitive (mood).

infizieren [infi'tsiːrən] v/t. (no -ge-, h) infect.　　　　　　[flation.\

Inflation [infla'tsjoːn] f (-/-en) in-]

Inform|ation [informa'tsjoːn] f (-/-en) information; **²ieren** [ˌ'miːrən] v/t. (no -ge-, h) inform; falsch ~ misinform.

Ingenieur [inʒe'njøːr] m (-s/-e) engineer.

Ingwer ['iŋvər] m (-s/no pl.) ginger.

Inhaber ['inhaːbər] m (-s/-) owner, proprietor (of business or shop); occupant (of flat); keeper (of shop); holder (of office, share, etc.); bearer (of cheque, etc.).

'Inhalt m (-[e]s/-e) contents pl. (of bottle, book, etc.); tenor (of speech); geom. volume; capacity (of vessel).

'Inhalts|angabe f summary; **²los** adj. empty, devoid of substance; **²reich** adj. full of meaning; life: rich, full; **~verzeichnis** n on parcel: list of contents; in book: table of contents.

Initiative [initsja'tiːvə] f (-/no pl.) initiative; die ~ ergreifen take the initiative.

Inkasso † [in'kaso] n (-s/-s, Inkassi) collection.

'inkonsequen|t adj. inconsistent; **²z** ['ˌts] f (-/-en) inconsistency.

In'krafttreten n (-s/no pl.) coming into force, taking effect (of new law, etc.).

'Inland n (-[e]s/no pl.) home (country); inland.

inländisch adj. ['inlɛndiʃ] native; inland; home; domestic; product: home-made.

Inlett ['inlɛt] n (-[e]s/-e) bedtick.

in'mitten prp. (gen.) in the midst of, amid(st).

'inne|haben v/t. (irr. haben, sep., -ge-, h) possess, hold (office, record, etc.); occupy (flat); **'~halten** v/i. (irr. halten, sep., -ge-, h) stop, pause.

innen adv. ['inən] inside, within; indoors; nach ~ inwards.

'Innen|architekt m interior decorator; **'~ausstattung** f interior decoration, fittings pl., furnishing; **'~minister** m minister of the interior; Home Secretary, Am. Secretary of the Interior; **'~ministerium** n ministry of the interior; Home Office, Am. Department of the Interior; **'~politik** f domestic policy; **'~seite** f inner side, inside; **'~stadt** f city, Am. downtown.

inner adj. ['inər] interior; inner; 𝄢, pol. internal; '𝔞e n (-n/no pl.) interior; Minister(ium) des Innern s. Innenminister(ium); 𝔞eien [~'raiən] f/pl. offal(s pl.); '~halb 1. prp. (gen.) within; 2. adv. within, inside; **~lich** adv. inwardly; esp. 𝄢 internally.

innig adj. ['iniç] intimate, close; affectionate.

Innung ['inuŋ] f (-/-en) guild, corporation.

inoffiziell adj. ['in⁹-] unofficial.

ins prp. [ins] = in das.

Insasse ['inzasə] m (-n/-n) inmate; occupant, passenger (of car).

'Inschrift f inscription; legend (on coin, etc.).

Insekt zo. [in'zɛkt] n (-[e]s/-en) insect.

Insel ['inzəl] f (-/-n) island; '~bewohner m islander.

Inser|at [inza'raːt] n (-[e]s/-e) advertisement, F ad; 𝔞ieren [~'riːrən] v/t. and v/i. (no -ge-, h) advertise.

insge|'heim adv. secretly; **~'samt** adv. altogether.

in'sofern cj. so far; ~ als in so far as.

insolvent † adj. ['inzɔlvɛnt] insolvent.

Inspekt|ion [inspɛk'tsjoːn] f (-/-en) inspection; **~or** [in'spɛktɔr] m (-s/-en) inspector; surveyor; overseer.

inspirieren [inspi'riːrən] v/t. (no -ge-, h) inspire.

inspizieren [inspi'tsiːrən] v/t. (no -ge-, h) inspect (troops, etc.); examine (goods); survey (buildings).

Install|ateur [instala'tøːr] m (-s/-e) plumber; (gas- or electrical) fitter; 𝔞ieren [~'liːrən] v/t. (no -ge-, h) install.

instand adv. [in'ʃtant]: ~ halten keep in good order; keep up; ⊕

maintain; ~ setzen repair; 𝔞**haltung** f maintenance; upkeep.

'inständig adv.: j-n ~ bitten implore or beseech s.o.

Instanz [in'ʃtants] f (-/-en) authority; 𝔯𝔯 instance; **~enweg** 𝔯𝔯 m stages of appeal; auf dem ~ through the prescribed channels.

Instinkt [in'ʃtiŋkt] m (-[e]s/-e) instinct; 𝔞iv adv. [~'tiːf] instinctively.

Institut [insti'tuːt] n (-[e]s/-e) institute.

Instrument [instru'mɛnt] n (-[e]s/-e) instrument.

inszenier|en esp. thea. [instse'niːrən] v/t. (no -ge-, h) (put on the) stage; 𝔞ung thea. f (-/-en) staging, production.

Integr|ation [integra'tsjoːn] f (-/-en) integration; 𝔞ieren [~'griːrən] v/t. (no -ge-, h) integrate.

intellektuell adj. [intelɛktu'ɛl] intellectual, highbrow; 𝔞e m (-n/-n) intellectual, highbrow.

intelligen|t adj. [inteli'gɛnt] intelligent; 𝔞z [~ts] f (-/-en) intelligence.

Intendant thea. [inten'dant] m (-en/-en) director.

intensiv adj. [inten'ziːf] intensive; intense.

interess|ant adj. [intere'sant] interesting; 𝔞e [~'resə] n (-s/-n) interest (an dat., für in); 𝔞engebiet [~'resən-] n field of interest; 𝔞engemeinschaft [~'resən-] f community of interests; combine, pool, trust; 𝔞ent [~'sɛnt] m (-en/-en) interested person or party; † prospective buyer, esp. Am. prospect; **~ieren** [~'siːrən] v/t. (no -ge-, h) interest (für in); sich ~ für take an interest in.

intern adj. [in'tɛrn] internal; 𝔞at [~'naːt] n (-[e]s/-e) boarding-school.

international adj. [internatsjo'naːl] international.

inter|'nieren v/t. (no -ge-, h) intern; 𝔞'nierung f (-/-en) internment; 𝔞'nist 𝄢 m (-en/-en) internal specialist, Am. internist.

inter|pretieren [interpre'tiːrən] v/t. (no -ge-, h) interpret; 𝔞punktion [~puŋk'tsjoːn] f (-/-en) punctuation; 𝔞vall [~'val] n (-s/-e) interval; **~venieren** [~ve'niːrən] v/i. (no -ge-, h) intervene; 𝔞'zonenhandel m interzonal trade; 𝔞'zonenverkehr m interzonal traffic.

intim adj. [in'tiːm] intimate (mit with); 𝔞ität [~imi'tɛːt] f (-/-en) intimacy.

'intoleran|t adj. intolerant; 𝔞z ['~ts] f (-/-en) intolerance.

intransitiv gr. adj. ['intranzitiːf] intransitive.

I:ntrig|e [in'triːgə] f (-/-n) intrigue, scheme, plot; 𝔞ieren [~i'giːrən] v/i. (no -ge-, h) intrigue, scheme, plot.

Invalid|e [inva'li:də] *m* (-n/-n) invalid; disabled person; **~enrente** *f* disability pension; **~ität** [~idi-'tε:t] *f* (-/*no pl.*) disablement, disability.

Inventar [invεn'tɑːr] *n* (-s/-e) inventory, stock.

Inventur † [invεn'tuːr] *f* (-/-en) stock-taking; **~ machen** take stock.

invest|ieren † [invεs'tiːrən] *v/t.* (*no* -ge-, *h*) invest; **2ition** † [~i'tsjoːn] *f* (-/-en) investment.

inwie|'fern *cj.* to what extent; in what way *or* respect; **~'weit** *cj.* how far, to what extent.

in'zwischen *adv.* in the meantime, meanwhile.

Ion *phys.* [i'oːn] *n* (-s/-en) ion.

ird|en *adj.* ['irdən] earthen; **~isch** *adj.* earthly; worldly; mortal.

Ire ['iːrə] *m* (-n/-n) Irishman; **die ~n** *pl.* the Irish *pl.*

irgend *adv.* ['irgənt] *in compounds*: some; any (*a. negative and in questions*); *wenn ich ~ kann* if I possibly can; **~'ein(e)** *indef. pron. and adj.* some(one); any(one); **~'einer** *indef. pron. s. irgend jemand*; **~'ein(e)s** *indef. pron.* some; any; **~etwas** *indef. pron.* something; anything; **~ jemand** *indef. pron.* someone; anyone; **~'wann** *adv.* some time (*or* other); **~'wie** *adv.* somehow; anyhow; **~'wo** *adv.* somewhere; anywhere; **~'wo'her** *adv.* from somewhere; from anywhere; **~'wo'hin** *adv.* somewhere; anywhere.

'irisch *adj.* Irish.

Iron|ie [iro'niː] *f* (-/-n) irony; **2isch** *adj.* [i'roːniʃ] ironic(al).

irre ['irə] 1. *adj.* confused; *fig.* insane; mad; 2. **2** *f* (-/*no pl.*): *in die ~ gehen* go astray; 3. **2** *m*, *f* (-n/-n) lunatic; mental patient; *wie ein ~* like a madman; **'~führen** *v/t.* (*sep.*, -ge-, *h*) mislead; *fig.* mislead; **'~gehen** *v/i.* (*irr. gehen, sep.*, -ge-, *sein*) go astray, stray; lose one's way; **'~machen** *v/t.* (*sep.*, -ge-, *h*) puzzle, bewilder; perplex; confuse;

~n 1. *v/i.* (ge-, *h*) err; wander; 2. *v/refl.* (ge-, *h*) be mistaken (*in dat.* in *s.o.*, about *s.th.*); be wrong.

'Irren|anstalt **✛** *f* lunatic asylum, mental home *or* hospital; **'~arzt** **✛** *m* alienist, mental specialist; **'~haus** **✛** *n s.* Irrenanstalt.

'irrereden *v/i.* (*sep.*, -ge-, *h*) rave.

'Irr|fahrt *f* wandering; Odyssey; **'~garten** *m* labyrinth, maze; **'~glaube** *m* erroneous belief; false doctrine, heterodoxy; heresy; **'2-gläubig** *adj.* heterodox; heretical; **'2ig** *adj.* erroneous, mistaken, false, wrong.

irritieren [iri'tiːrən] *v/t.* (*no* -ge-, *h*) irritate, annoy; confuse.

'Irr|lehre *f* false doctrine, heterodoxy; heresy; **'~licht** *n* will-o'-the-wisp, jack-o'-lantern; **'~sinn** *m* insanity; madness; **'2sinnig** *adj.* insane; mad; *fig.*: fantastic; terrible; **'~sinnige** *m*, *f* (-n/-n) *s. irre* 3; **'~tum** *m* (-s/**~**er) error, mistake; *im ~ sein* be mistaken; **2tümlich** ['~tyːmliç] 1. *adj.* erroneous; 2. *adv.* = **2tümlicherweise** *adv.* by mistake; mistakenly, erroneously; **'~wisch** *m s.* Irrlicht; *p.* flibbertigibbet.

Ischias **✛** ['iʃias] *f*, F *a.*: *n*, *m* (-/*no pl.*) sciatica.

Islam ['islam, is'lɑːm] *m* (-s/*no pl.*) Islam.

Isländ|er ['iːslεndər] *m* (-s/-) Icelander; **'2isch** *adj.* Icelandic.

Isolator **ϟ** [izo'lɑːtɔr] *m* (-s/-en) insulator.

Isolier|band **ϟ** [izo'liːr-] *n* insulating tape; **2en** *v/t.* (*no* -ge-, *h*) isolate; **~masse** **ϟ** *f* insulating compound; **~schicht** **ϟ** *f* insulating layer; **~ung** *f* (-/-en) isolation (*a.* **ϟ**); **ϟ** quarantine; **ϟ** insulation.

Isotop **🜊**, *phys.* [izo'toːp] *n* (-s/-e) isotope.

Israeli [isra'eːli] *m* (-s/-s) Israeli.

Italien|er [ital'jeːnər] *m* (-s/-) Italian; **2isch** *adj.* Italian.

I-Tüpfelchen *fig.* ['iːtypfəlçən] *n* (-s/-): *bis aufs ~* to a T.

J

ja [jɑː] 1. *adv.* yes; **⚓**, *parl.* aye, *Am. parl. a.* yea; **~ doch**, **~ freilich** yes, indeed; to be sure; *da ist er ~!* well, there he is!; *ich sagte es Ihnen* — I told you so; *tut es ~ nicht!* don't you dare do it!; *vergessen Sie es ~ nicht!* be sure not to forget it!; 2. *cj.*: **~ sogar**, **~ selbst** nay (even); *wenn* — *ja* if so; *er ist* — *mein Freund* why, he is my friend; 3. *int.*: **~**, *weißt du*

denn nicht, daß why, don't you know that.

Jacht **⚓** [jaxt] *f* (-/-en) yacht; **'~klub** *m* yacht-club.

Jacke ['jakə] *f* (-/-n) jacket.

Jackett [ʒa'kεt] *n* (-s/-e, -s) jacket.

Jagd [jɑːkt] *f* (-/-en) hunt(ing); *with a gun*: shoot(ing); chase; *s. Jagdrevier*; *auf (die)* **~** *gehen* go hunting *or* shooting, *Am. a.* be gunning; **~ machen auf** (*acc.*) hunt after *or* for;

'∼aufseher *m* gamekeeper, *Am.* game warden; '∼bomber ✕ *m* (-s/-) fighter-bomber; '∼büchse *f* sporting rifle; '∼flinte *f* sporting gun; fowling-piece; '∼flugzeug ✕ *n* fighter (aircraft); '∼geschwader ✕ *n* fighter wing, *Am.* fighter group; '∼gesellschaft *f* hunting *or* shooting party; '∼haus *n* shooting-box *or* -lodge, hunting-box *or* -lodge; '∼hund *m* hound; '∼hütte *f* shooting-box, hunting-box; '∼pächter *m* game-tenant; '∼rennen *n* steeplechase; '∼revier *n* hunting-ground, shoot; '∼schein *m* shooting licen|ce, *Am.* -se; '∼schloß *n* hunting seat; '∼tasche *f* game-bag.

jagen ['ja:gən] (ge-, h) 1. *v/i.* go hunting *or* shooting, hunt; shoot; rush, dash; 2. *v/t.* hunt; chase; *aus dem Hause* ∼ turn *s.o.* out (of doors).

Jäger ['je:gər] *m* (-s/-) hunter, huntsman, sportsman; ✕ rifleman; '∼latein F *fig. n* huntsmen's yarn, tall stories *pl.* [(jaguar.\]

Jaguar *zo.* ['ja:gua:r] *m* (-s/-e)/

jäh *adj.* [je:] sudden, abrupt; precipitous, steep.

Jahr [ja:r] *n* (-[e]s/-e) year; *ein halbes* ∼ half a year, six months *pl.*; *einmal im* ∼ once a year; *im* ∼*e 1900* in 1900; *mit 18* ∼*en, im Alter von 18* ∼*en* at (the age of) eighteen; *letztes* ∼ last year; *das ganze* ∼ *hindurch or über* all the year round; ♀'aus *adv.*: ∼, jahrein year in, year out; year after year; '∼buch *n* year-book, annual; ∼ *ein adv. s. jahraus.*

'Jahrelang 1. *adv.* for years; 2. *adj.*: ∼*e Erfahrung* (many) years of experience.

jähren ['je:rən] *v/refl.* (ge-, h): *es jährt sich heute, daß* ... it is a year ago today that ..., it is a year today since ...

'Jahres|abonnement *n* annual subscription (*to magazine, etc.*); *thea.* yearly season ticket; '∼abschluß *m* annual statement of accounts; '∼anfang *m* beginning of the year; *zum* ∼ *die besten Wünsche!* best wishes for the New Year; '∼bericht *m* annual report; '∼einkommen *n* annual *or* yearly income; '∼ende *n* end of the year; '∼gehalt *n* annual salary; '∼tag *m* anniversary; '∼wechsel *m* turn of the year; '∼zahl *f* date, year; '∼zeit *f* season, time of the year.

'Jahrgang *m* volume, year (*of periodical, etc.*); *p.* age-group; *univ., school:* year, class; *wine:* vintage.

Jahr'hundert *n* (-s/-e) century; ∼feier *f* centenary, *Am.* centennial; ∼wende *f* turn of the century.

jährig *adj.* ['je:riç] one-year-old.

jährlich ['je:rliç] 1. *adj.* annual, yearly; 2. *adv.* every year; yearly, once a year.

'Jahr|markt *m* fair; ∼'tausend *n* (-s/-e) millennium; ∼'tausendfeier *f* millenary; ∼'zehnt *n* (-[e]s/-e) decade.

'Jähzorn *m* violent (fit of) temper; irascibility; '2ig *adj.* hot-tempered; irascible.

Jalousie [ʒalu'zi:] *f* (-/-n) (Venetian) blind, *Am. a.* window shade.

Jammer ['jamər] *m* (-s/no pl.) lamentation; misery; *es ist ein* ∼ it is a pity.

jämmerlich *adj.* ['jemərliç] miserable, wretched; piteous; pitiable (*esp. contp.*).

jammer|n ['jamərn] *v/i.* (ge-, h) lament (*nach, um* for; *über acc.* over); moan; wail, whine; '∼schade *adj.*: *es ist* ∼ it is a thousand pities, it is a great shame.

Januar ['janua:r] *m* (-[s]/-e) January.

Japan|er [ja'pa:nər] *m* (-s/-) Japanese; *die* ∼ *pl.* the Japanese *pl.*; 2isch *adj.* Japanese.

Jargon [ʒar'gõ] *m* (-s/-s) jargon, cant, slang.

Jasmin ♣ [jas'mi:n] *m* (-s/-e) jasmin(e), jessamin(e).

'Jastimme *parl. f* aye, *Am. a.* yea.

jäten ['je:tən] *v/t.* (ge-, h) weed.

Jauche ['jauxə] *f* (-/-n) ♪ liquid manure; sewage.

jauchzen ['jauxtsən] *v/i.* (ge-, h) exult, rejoice, cheer; *vor Freude* ∼ shout for joy.

jawohl *adv.* [ja'vo:l] yes; yes, indeed; yes, certainly; that's right; ✕, *etc.*: yes, Sir!

'Jawort *n* consent; *j-m das* ∼ *geben* accept *s.o.*'s proposal (of marriage).

je [je:] 1. *adv.* ever, at any time; always; *ohne ihn* ∼ *gesehen zu haben* without ever having seen him; *seit eh und* ∼ since time immemorial, always; *distributive with numerals:* ∼ *zwei* two at a time, two each, two by two, by *or* in twos; *sie bekamen* ∼ *zwei Äpfel* they received two apples each; *für* ∼ *zehn Wörter* for every ten words; *in Schachteln mit or zu* ∼ *zehn Stück verpackt* packed in boxes of ten; 2. *cj.*: ∼ *nach Größe* according to *or* depending on size; ∼ *nachdem* it depends; ∼ *nachdem, was er für richtig hält* according as he thinks fit; ∼ *nachdem, wie er sich fühlt* depending on how he feels; ∼ *mehr, desto besser* the more the better; ∼ *länger,* ∼ *lieber* the longer the better; 3. *prp.*: *die Birnen kosten e-e Mark* ∼ *Pfund* the pears cost one mark a pound; *s. pro.*

jede|(r, -s) *indef. pron.* ['je:də(r, -s)] every; any; *of a group:* each; *of two persons:* either; *jeder, der* whoever; *jeden zweiten Tag* every other day; '∼n'falls *adv.* at all events, in any case; '~rmann *indef. pron.* everyone, everybody; '~r'zeit *adv.* always, at any time; '~s'mal *adv.* each *or* every time; ~ *wenn* whenever.

jedoch *cj.* [je'dɔx] however, yet, nevertheless.

'jeher *adv.*: *von or seit* ~ at all times, always, from time immemorial.

jemals *adv.* ['je:maːls] ever, at any time.

jemand *indef. pron.* ['je:mant] someone, somebody; *with questions and negations:* anyone, anybody.

jene(r, -s) *dem. pron.* ['je:nə(r, -s)] that (one); jene *pl.* those (one).

jenseitig *adj.* ['jenzaitiç] opposite.

jenseits 1. *prp.* (*gen.*) on the other side of, beyond, across; 2. *adv.* on the other side, beyond; 3. ♀ *n* (-/*no pl.*) *the* other *or* next world, *the* world to come, *the* beyond.

jetzig *adj.* ['jetsiç] present, existing; *prices, etc.:* current.

jetzt *adv.* [jetst] now, at present; *bis* ~ until now; so far; *eben* ~ just now; *erst* ~ only now; *für* ~ for the present; *gleich* ~ at once, right away; *noch* ~ even now; *von* ~ *an* from now on.

jeweil|ig *adj.* ['je:vailiç] respective; ~s *adv.* ['~s] respectively, at a time; from time to time (*esp.* ♄).

Joch [jɔx] *n* (-[e]s/-e) yoke; *in mountains:* col, pass, saddle, ⚠ bay; '~bein *anat. n* cheek-bone.

Jockei ['dʒɔki] *m* (-s/-s) jockey.

Jod ♎ [jo:t] *n* (-[e]s/*no pl.*) iodine.

jodeln ['jo:dəln] *v/i.* (ge-, h) yodel.

Johanni [jo'hani] *n* (-/*no pl.*), ~s [~s] *n* (-/*no pl.*) Midsummer day; ~s-beere *f* currant; *rote* ~ red currant; ~stag *m eccl.* St John's day; Midsummer day.

johlen ['jo:lən] *v/i.* (ge-, h) bawl, yell, howl.

Jolle ⚓ ['jɔlə] *f* (-/-n) jolly-boat, yawl, dinghy.

Jongl|eur [ʒõ'glø:r] *m* (-s/-e) juggler; ~ieren *v/t. and v/i.* (*no -ge-, h*) juggle.

Journal [ʒur'naːl] *n* (-s/-e) journal; newspaper; magazine; diary; ⚓ log-book; ~ist [~a'list] *m* (-en/-en) journalist, *Am.* a. newspaperman.

Jubel ['ju:bəl] *m* (-s/*no pl.*) jubilation, exultation, rejoicing; cheering; '♀n *v/i.* (ge-, h) jubilate; exult, rejoice (*über acc.* at).

Jubil|ar [jubi'laːr] *m* (-s/-e) person celebrating his jubilee, *etc.*; ~äum [~ɛ:um] *n* (-s/ *Jubiläen*) jubilee.

Juchten ['juxtən] *m, n* (-s/*no pl.*), '~leder *n* Russia (leather).

jucken ['jukən] (ge-, h) 1. *v/i.* itch; 2. *v/t.* irritate, (make) itch; F *sich* ~ scratch (o.s.).

Jude ['ju:də] *m* (-n/-n) Jew; '♀n-feindlich *adj.* anti-Semitic; '~n-

tum *n* (-s/*no pl.*) Judaism; '~nver-folgung *f* persecution of Jews, Jew-baiting; pogrom.

Jüd|in ['jy:din] *f* (-/-nen) Jewess; '♀isch *adj.* Jewish.

Jugend ['ju:gənt] *f* (-/*no pl.*) youth; '~amt *n* youth welfare department; '~buch *n* book for the young; '~freund *m* friend of one's youth; school-friend; '~fürsorge *f* youth welfare; '~gericht *n* juvenile court; '~herberge *f* youth hostel; '~jahre *n/pl.* early years, youth; '~krimi-nalität *f* juvenile delinquency; '♀lich *adj.* youthful, juvenile, young; '~liche *m, f* (-n/-n) young person; juvenile; young man, youth; young girl; teen-ager; '~liebe *f* early *or* first love, calf-love, *Am.* a. puppy love; old sweetheart *or* flame; '~schriften *f/pl.* books for the young; '~schutz *m* protection of children and young people; '~streich *m* youthful prank; '~werk *n* early work (*of author*); '~e *pl.* a. juvenilia *pl.*; '~zeit *f* (time *or* days of) youth.

Jugoslav|e [ju:go'slaːvə] *m* (-en/-en) Jugoslav, Yugoslav; ♀isch *adj.* Jugoslav, Yugoslav.

Juli ['ju:li] *m* (-[s]/-s) July.

jung *adj.* [juŋ] young; youthful; *peas:* green; *beer, wine:* new; ~es *Gemüse* young *or* early vegetables *pl.*; F *fig.* young people, small fry.

Junge 1. *m* (-n/-n) boy, youngster; lad; fellow, chap, *Am.* guy; *cards:* knave, jack; 2. *n* (-n/-n) young; puppy (*of dog*); kitten (*of cat*); calf (*of cow, elephant, etc.*); cub (*of beast of prey*); ~ *werfen* bring forth young; *ein* ~s a young one; '♀nhaft *adj.* boyish; '~nstreich *m* boyish prank *or* trick.

jünger ['jyŋər] 1. *adj.* younger, junior; *er ist drei Jahre* ~ *als ich* he is my junior by three years, he is three years younger than I; 2. ♀ *m* (-s/-) disciple.

Jungfer ['juŋfər] *f* (-/-n): *alte* ~ old maid *or* spinster.

'Jungfern|fahrt ⚓ *f* maiden voyage *or* trip; '~flug ✈ *m* maiden flight; '~rede *f* maiden speech.

'Jung|frau *f* maid(en), virgin; ♀-fräulich *adj.* ['~frɔ:yliç] virginal; *fig.* virgin; '~fräulichkeit *f* (-/*no pl.*) virginity, maidenhood; '~ge-selle *m* bachelor; '~gesellenstand *m* bachelorhood; '~gesellin *f* (-/-nen) bachelor girl.

Jüngling ['jyŋliŋ] *m* (-s/-e) youth, young man.

jüngst [jyŋst] 1. *adj.* youngest; *time:* (most) recent, latest; *das* ♀e *Ge-richt, der* ♀e *Tag* Last Judg(e)ment, Day of Judg(e)ment; 2. *adv.* recently, lately.

'jungverheiratet *adj.* newly married; '♀en *pl. the* newlyweds *pl.*

Juni ['juːni] *m* (-[s]/-s) June; '**käfer** *zo. m* cockchafer, June-bug.

junior ['juːnjɔr] 1. *adj.* junior; 2. ♀ *m* (-s/-en) junior (*a. sports*).

Jura ['juːra] *n/pl.*: ~ studieren read or study law.

Jurist [ju'rist] *m* (-en/-en) lawyer; law-student; ♀isch *adj.* legal.

Jury [ʒy'riː] *f* (-/-s) jury.

justier|en ⊕ [jus'tiːrən] *v/t.* (*no* -ge-, *h*) adjust; ♀ung ⊕ *f* (-/-en) adjustment.

Justiz [jus'tiːts] *f* (-/*no pl.*) (administration of) justice; **~beamte** *m*

judicial officer; **~gebäude** *n* courthouse; **~inspektor** *m* judicial officer; **~irrtum** *m* judicial error; **~minister** *m* minister of justice; Lord Chancellor, *Am.* Attorney General; **~ministerium** *n* ministry of justice; *Am.* Department of Justice; **~mord** *m* judicial murder.

Juwel [ju'veːl] *m, n* (-s/-en) jewel, gem; **~en** *pl.* jewel(le)ry; **~ier** [~e-'liːr] *m* (-s/-e) jewel(l)er.

Jux F [juks] *m* (-es/-e) (practical) joke, fun, spree, lark; prank.

K

(Compare also C and Z)

Kabel ['kaːbəl] *n* (-s/-) cable.

Kabeljau *ichth.* ['kaːbəljau] *m* (-s/-e, -s) cod(fish).

'kabeln *v/t. and v/i.* (ge-, *h*) cable.

Kabine [ka'biːnə] *f* (-/-n) cabin; *at hairdresser's, etc.*: cubicle; cage (*of lift*).

Kabinett *pol.* [kabi'nɛt] *n* (-s/-e) cabinet, government.

Kabriolett [kabrio'lɛt] *n* (-s/-e) cabriolet, convertible.

Kachel ['kaxəl] *f* (-/-n) (Dutch *or* glazed) tile; '**~ofen** *m* tiled stove.

Kadaver [ka'daːvər] *m* (-s/-) carcass.

Kadett [ka'dɛt] *m* (-en/-en) cadet.

Käfer *zo.* ['kɛːfər] *m* (-s/-) beetle, chafer.

Kaffee ['kafe, ka'feː] *m* (-s/-s) coffee; (')**~bohne** ♀ *f* coffee-bean; (')**~kanne** *f* coffee-pot; (')**~mühle** *f* coffee-mill *or* -grinder; (')**~satz** *m* coffee-grounds *pl.*; (')**~tasse** *f* coffee-cup.

Käfig ['kɛːfiç] *m* (-s/-e) cage (*a. fig.*).

kahl *adj.* [kaːl] *p.* bald; *tree, etc.*: bare; *landscape, etc.*: barren, bleak; *rock, etc.*: naked; '♀kopf *m* baldhead, baldpate; '**~köpfig** *adj.* ['~kœpfiç] bald(-headed).

Kahn [kaːn] *m* (-[e]s/⁼e) boat; riverbarge; ~ fahren go boating; '**~fahren** *n* (-s/*no pl.*) boating.

Kai [kai] *m* (-s/-e, -s) quay, wharf.

Kaiser ['kaizər] *m* (-s/-) emperor; '**~krone** *f* imperial crown; ♀lich *adj.* imperial; '**~reich** *n*, '**~tum** *n* (-[e]s/⁼er) empire; '**~würde** *f* imperial status.

Kajüte ⊕ [ka'jyːtə] *f* (-/-n) cabin.

Kakao [ka'kaːo] *m* (-s/-s) cocoa; ♀ *a.* cacao.

Kakt|ee ♀ [kak'teː(ə)] *f* (-/-n), **~us** ♀ ['~us] *m* (-/Kakteen, F Kaktusse) cactus.

Kalauer ['kaːlauər] *m* (-s/-) stale joke; pun.

Kalb *zo.* [kalp] *n* (-[e]s/⁼er) calf; ♀en ['~bən] *v/i.* (ge-, *h*) calve; '**~fell** *n* calfskin; '**~fleisch** *n* veal; '**~leder** *n* calf(-leather).

'Kalbs|braten *m* roast veal; '**~keule** *f* leg of veal; '**~leder** *n s.* Kalbleder; '**~nierenbraten** *m* loin of veal.

Kalender [ka'lɛndər] *m* (-s/-) calendar; almanac; **~block** *m* dateblock; **~jahr** *n* calendar year; **~uhr** *f* calendar watch *or* clock.

Kali ♀ ['kaːli] *n* (-s/-s) potash.

Kaliber [ka'liːbər] *n* (-s/-) calib|re, *Am.* -er (*a. fig.*), bore (*of firearm*).

Kalk [kalk] *m* (-[e]s/-e) lime; *geol.* limestone; '**~brenner** *m* limeburner; '♀en *v/t.* (ge-, *h*) whitewash (*wall, etc.*); ♂ lime (*field*); '♀ig *adj.* limy; '**~ofen** *m* limekiln; '**~stein** *m* limestone; '**~steinbruch** *m* limestone quarry.

Kalorie [kalo'riː] *f* (-/-n) calorie.

kalt *adj.* [kalt] *climate, meal, sweat, etc.*: cold; *p., manner, etc.*: cold, chilly, frigid; mir ist ~ I am cold; **~e** Küche cold dishes *pl. or* meat, *etc.*; j-m die ~e Schulter zeigen give s.o. the cold shoulder; **~blütig** *adj.* ['~blyːtiç] cold-blooded (*a. fig.*).

Kälte ['kɛltə] *f* (-/*no pl.*) cold; chill; coldness, chilliness (*both a. fig.*); vor ~ zittern shiver with cold; fünf Grad ~ five degrees below zero; '**~grad** *m* degree below zero; '**~welle** *f* cold spell.

'kalt|stellen *fig. v/t.* (sep., -ge-, *h*) shelve, reduce to impotence; '♀welle *f* cold wave.

kam [kaːm] *pret. of* kommen.

Kamel *zo.* [ka'meːl] *n* (-[e]s/-e) camel; **~haar** *n textiles*: camel hair.

Kamera *phot.* ['kaməra] *f* (-/-s) camera.

Kamerad [kamə'rɑːt] *m* (-en/-en) comrade; companion; mate, F pal, chum; **~schaft** *f* (-/-en) comradeship, companionship; **2schaftlich** *adj.* comradely, companionable.

Kamille ♀ [ka'milə] *f* (-/-n) camomile; **~ntee** *m* camomile tea.

Kamin [ka'miːn] *m* (-s/-e) chimney (*a. mount.*); fireplace, fireside; **~sims** *m*, *n* mantelpiece; **~vorleger** *m* hearth-rug; **~vorsetzer** *m* (-s/-) fender.

Kamm [kam] *m* (-[e]s/≈e) comb; crest (*of bird or wave*); crest, ridge (*of mountain*).

kämmen ['kɛmən] *v/t.* (ge-, *h*) comb; *sich (die Haare)* ~ comb one's hair.

Kammer ['kamər] *f* (-/-n) (small) room; closet; *pol.* chamber; board; ₰₰ division (*of court*); '**~diener** *m* valet; '**~frau** *f* lady's maid; '**~gericht** ₰₰ *n* supreme court; '**~herr** *m* chamberlain; '**~jäger** *m* vermin exterminator; '**~musik** *f* chamber music; '**~zofe** *f* chambermaid.

'**Kamm|garn** *n* worsted (yarn); '**~rad** ⊕ *n* cogwheel.

Kampagne [kam'panjə] *f* (-/-n) campaign.

Kampf [kampf] *m* (-[e]s/≈e) combat, fight (*a. fig.*); struggle (*a. fig.*); battle (*a. fig.*); *fig.* conflict; *sports:* contest, match; *boxing:* fight, bout; '**~bahn** *f* *sports:* stadium, arena; '**2bereit** *adj.* ready for battle.

kämpfen ['kɛmpfən] *v/i.* (ge-, *h*) fight (*gegen* against; *mit* with; *um* for) (*a. fig.*); struggle (*a. fig.*); *fig.* contend, wrestle (*mit* with).

Kampfer ['kampfər] *m* (-s/no pl.) camphor.

Kämpfer ['kɛmpfər] *m* (-s/-) fighter (*a. fig.*); ✕ combatant, warrior.

'**Kampf|flugzeug** *n* tactical aircraft; '**~geist** *m* fighting spirit; '**~platz** *m* battlefield; *fig.*, *sports:* arena; '**~preis** *m* *sports:* prize; † cut-throat price; '**~richter** *m* referee, judge, umpire; '**2unfähig** *adj.* disabled.

kampieren [kam'piːrən] *v/i.* (no -ge-, *h*) camp.

Kanal [ka'nɑːl] *m* (-s/≈e) canal; channel (*a.* ⊕, *fig.*); *geogr.* the Channel; sewer, drain; **~isation** [~aliza'tsjoːn] *f* (-/-en) *river:* canalization; *town, etc.:* sewerage; drainage; **2isieren** [~ali'ziːrən] *v/t.* (no -ge-, *h*) canalize; sewer.

Kanarienvogel *orn.* [ka'nɑːrjən-] *m* canary(-bird).

Kandare [kan'dɑːrə] *f* (-/-n) curb (-bit).

Kandid|at [kandi'dɑːt] *m* (-en/-en) candidate; applicant; **~atur** [~a'tuːr] *f* (-/-en) candidature, candidacy; **2ieren** [~'diːrən] *v/i.* (no -ge-, *h*) be a candidate (*für* for);

~ **für** apply for, stand for, *Am.* run for (*office, etc.*).

Känguruh *zo.* ['kɛŋguruː] *n* (-s/-s) kangaroo.

Kaninchen *zo.* [ka'niːnçən] *n* (-s/-) rabbit; **~bau** *m* rabbit-burrow.

Kanister [ka'nistər] *m* (-s/-) can.

Kanne ['kanə] *f* (-/-n) milk, *etc.*: jug; *coffee, tea:* pot; *oil, milk:* can; '**~gießer** F *fig. m* political wiseacre.

Kannibal|e [kani'bɑːlə] *m* (-n/-n) cannibal; **2isch** *adj.* cannibal.

kannte ['kantə] *pret. of* kennen.

Kanon ♪ ['kɑːnɔn] *m* (-s/-s) canon.

Kanon|ade ✕ [kano'nɑːdə] *f* (-/-n) cannonade; **~e** [~'noːnə] *f* (-/-n) ✕ cannon, gun; F *fig.:* big shot; *esp. sports:* ace, crack.

Ka'nonen|boot ✕ *n* gunboat; **~donner** *m* boom of cannon; **~futter** *fig. n* cannon-fodder; **~kugel** *f* cannon-ball; **~rohr** *n* gun barrel.

Kanonier ✕ [kano'niːr] *m* (-s/-e) gunner.

Kant|e ['kantə] *f* (-/-n) edge; brim; '**~en** *m* (-s/-) end of loaf; '**2en** *v/t.* (ge-, *h*) square (*stone, etc.*); set on edge; tilt; edge (*skis*); '**2ig** *adj.* angular, edged; square(d).

Kantine [kan'tiːnə] *f* (-/-n) canteen.

Kanu ['kɑːnu] *n* (-s/-s) canoe.

Kanüle ⚕ [ka'nyːlə] *f* (-/-n) tubule, cannula.

Kanzel ['kantsəl] *f* (-/-n) *eccl.* pulpit; ✈ cockpit; ✕ (gun-)turret.; '**~redner** *m* preacher.

Kanzlei [kants'laɪ] *f* (-/-en) office.

'**Kanzler** *m* (-s/-) chancellor.

Kap *geogr.* [kap] *n* (-s/-s) headland.

Kapazität [kapatsi'tɛːt] *f* (-/-en) capacity; *fig.* authority.

Kapell|e [ka'pɛlə] *f* (-/-n) *eccl.* chapel; ♪ band; **~meister** *m* bandleader, conductor.

kaper|n ⚓ ['kɑːpərn] *v/t.* (ge-, *h*) capture, seize; '**2schiff** *n* privateer.

kapieren F [ka'piːrən] *v/t.* (no -ge-, *h*) grasp, get.

Kapital [kapi'tɑːl] 1. *n* (-s/-e, -ien) capital, stock, funds *pl.*; ~ *und Zinsen* principal and interest; 2. 2 *adj.* capital; **~anlage** *f* investment; **~flucht** *f* flight of capital; **~gesellschaft** *f* joint-stock company; **2isieren** [~ali'ziːrən] *v/t.* (no -ge-, *h*) capitalize; **~ismus** [~a'lismus] *m* (-/no pl.) capitalism; **~ist** [~a'list] *m* (-en/-en) capitalist; **~markt** [~'tɑːl-] *m* capital market; **~verbrechen** *n* capital crime.

Kapitän [kapi'tɛːn] *m* (-s/-e) captain; ~ *zur See* naval captain; **~leutnant** *m* (senior) lieutenant.

Kapitel [ka'pitəl] *n* (-s/-) chapter (*a. fig.*).

Kapitul|ation ✕ [kapitula'tsjoːn] *f* (-/-en) capitulation, surrender; **2ieren** [~'liːrən] *v/i.* (no -ge-, *h*) capitulate, surrender.

Kaplan *eccl.* [ka'plɑ:n] *m* (-s/⸗e) chaplain.

Kappe ['kapə] *f* (-/-n) cap; hood (*a.* ⊕); bonnet; '⸗n *v/t.* (ge-, *h*) cut (*cable*); lop, top (*tree*).

Kapriole [kapri'o:lə] *f* (-/-n) equitation: capriole; *fig.*: caper; prank.

Kapsel ['kapsəl] *f* (-/-n) case, box; ⚕, ⚙, *anat.*, *etc.*: capsule.

kaputt *adj.* [ka'put] broken; *elevator, etc.*: out of order; *fruit, etc.*: spoilt; *p.*: ruined; tired out, F fagged out; **⸗gehen** *v/i.* (*irr.* gehen, *sep.*, -ge-, sein) break, go to pieces; spoil.

Kapuze [ka'pu:tsə] *f* (-/-n) hood; *eccl.* cowl.

Karabiner [kara'bi:nər] *m* (-s/-) carbine.

Karaffe [ka'rafə] *f* (-/-n) carafe (*for wine or water*); decanter (*for liqueur, etc.*).

Karambol|age [karambo'lɑ:ʒə] *f* (-/-n) collision, crash; *billiards*: cannon, *Am. a.* carom; ⸗ieren *v/i.* (*no* -ge-, sein) cannon, *Am. a.* carom; F *fig.* collide.

Karat [ka'rɑ:t] *n* (-[e]s/-e) carat.

Karawane [kara'vɑ:nə] *f* (-/-n) caravan.

Karbid [kar'bi:t] *n* (-[e]s/-e) carbide.

Kardinal *eccl.* [kardi'nɑ:l] *m* (-s/⸗e) cardinal.

Karfreitag *eccl.* [kɑ:r'-] *m* Good Friday.

karg *adj.* [kark] *soil*: meagre; *vegetation*: scant, sparse; *meal*: scanty, meagre, frugal; **⸗en** [' ⸗gən] *v/i.* (ge-, *h*): ⸗ *mit* be sparing of.

kärglich *adj.* ['kerkliç] scanty, meagre; poor.

kariert *adj.* [ka'ri:rt] check(ed), chequered, *Am.* checkered.

Karik|atur [karika'tu:r] *f* (-/-en) caricature, cartoon; ⸗ieren [‿'ki:rən] *v/t.* (*no* -ge-, *h*) caricature, cartoon.

karmesin *adj.* [karme'zi:n] crimson.

Karneval ['karnəval] *m* (-s/-e, -s) Shrovetide, carnival.

Karo ['kɑ:ro] *n* (-s/-s) square, check; *cards*: diamonds *pl.*

Karosserie *mot.* [karɔsə'ri:] *f* (-/-n) body.

Karotte ⚘ [ka'rɔtə] *f* (-/-n) carrot.

Karpfen *ichth.* ['karpfən] *m* (-s/-) carp.

Karre ['karə] *f* (-/-n) cart; wheelbarrow.

Karriere [kar'je:rə] *f* (-/-n) (successful) career.

Karte ['kartə] *f* (-/-n) card; postcard; map; chart; ticket; menu, bill of fare; list.

Kartei [kar'tai] *f* (-/-en) card-index; **⸗karte** *f* index-card, filing-card; **⸗schrank** *m* filing cabinet.

Kartell ⚓ [kar'tel] *n* (-s/-e) cartel.

'Karten|brief *m* letter-card; **'⸗haus**

n ⚓ chart-house; *fig.* house of cards; '⸗legerin *f* (-/-nen) fortune-teller from the cards; '⸗spiel *n* card-playing; card-game.

Kartoffel [kar'tɔfəl] *f* (-/-n) potato, F spud; **⸗brei** *m* mashed potatoes *pl.*; **⸗käfer** *m* Colorado *or* potato beetle, *Am. a.* potato bug; **⸗schalen** *f/pl.* potato peelings *pl.*

Karton [kar'tõ:, kar'to:n] *m* (-s/-s, -e) cardboard, pasteboard; cardboard box, carton.   [*Kartei.*]

Kartothek [karto'te:k] *f* (-/-en) s.|

Karussell [karu'sel] *n* (-s/-s, -e) roundabout, merry-go-round, *Am. a.* car(r)ousel.

Karwoche *eccl.* ['kɑ:r-] *f* Holy *or* Passion Week.

Käse ['kɛ:zə] *m* (-s/-) cheese.

Kasern|e ⚔ [ka'zɛrnə] *f* (-/-n) barracks *pl.*; **⸗enhof** *m* barrack-yard *or* -square; ⸗ieren [‿'ni:rən] *v/t.* (*no* -ge-, *h*) quarter in barracks, barrack.

'käsig *adj.* cheesy; *complexion*: pale, pasty.

Kasino [ka'zi:no] *n* (-s/-s) casino, club(-house); (*officers'*) mess.

Kasperle ['kasperlə] *n*, *m* (-s/-) Punch; **'⸗theater** *n* Punch and Judy show.

Kasse ['kasə] *f* (-/-n) cash-box; till (*in shop, etc.*); cash-desk, pay-desk (*in bank, etc.*); pay-office (*in firm*); *thea., etc.*: box-office, booking-office; cash; *bei* ⸗ in cash.

'Kassen|abschluß ✝ *m* balancing of the cash (accounts); '⸗anweisung *f* disbursement voucher; '⸗bestand *m* cash in hand; '⸗bote *m* bank messenger; '⸗buch *n* cash book; '⸗erfolg *m* *thea., etc.*: box-office success; '⸗patient ✱ *m* panel patient; '⸗schalter *m* bank, *etc.*: teller's counter.

Kasserolle [kasə'rɔlə] *f* (-/-n) stewpan, casserole.

Kassette [ka'setə] *f* (-/-n) box (*for money, etc.*); casket (*for jewels, etc.*); slip-case (*for books*); *phot.* plateholder.

kassiere|n [ka'si:rən] (*no* -ge-, *h*) **1.** *v/i.* waiter, *etc.*: take the money (*für* for); **2.** *v/t.* take (*sum of money*); collect (*contributions, etc.*); annul; ⚖ quash (*verdict*); ⸗r *m* (-s/-) cashier; *bank*: *a.* teller; collector.

Kastanie ⚘ [ka'stɑ:njə] *f* (-/-n) chestnut.

Kasten ['kastən] *m* (-s/⸗, ⚒ -) box; chest (*for tools, etc.*); case (*for violin, etc.*); bin (*for bread, etc.*).

Kasus *gr.* ['kɑ:sus] *m* (-/-) case.

Katalog [kata'lo:k] *m* (-[e]s/-e) catalogue, *Am. a.* catalog; ⸗isieren [‿ogi'zi:rən] *v/t.* (*no* -ge-, *h*) catalogue, *Am. a.* catalog.

Katarrh ✱ [ka'tar] *m* (-s/-e) (common) cold, catarrh.

katastroph|al *adj.* [katastro'fɑːl] catastrophic, disastrous; **⁲e** [~'stroːfə] *f* (-/-n) catastrophe, disaster.
Katechismus *eccl.* [kate'çismus] *m* (-/*Katechismen*) catechism.
Katego|rie [katego'riː] *f* (-/-n) category; **⁲risch** *adj.* [~'goːriʃ] categorical.
Kater ['kɑːtər] *m* (-s/-) *zo.* male cat, tom-cat; *fig. s. Katzenjammer.*
Katheder [ka'teːdər] *n, m* (-s/-) lecturing-desk.
Kathedrale [kate'drɑːlə] *f* (-/-n) cathedral.
Katholi|k [kato'liːk] *m* (-en/-en) (Roman) Catholic; **⁲sch** *adj.* [~'toːliʃ] (Roman) Catholic.
Kattun [ka'tuːn] *m* (-s/-e) calico; cotton cloth *or* fabric; chintz.
Katze *zo.* ['katsə] *f* (-/-n) cat; '**~njammer** F *fig. m* hangover, morning-after feeling.
Kauderwelsch ['kaudərvɛlʃ] *n* (-[s]/*no pl.*) gibberish, F double Dutch; '**⁲en** *v/i.* (ge-, *h*) gibber, F talk double Dutch.
kauen ['kauən] *v/t. and v/i.* (ge-, *h*) chew.
kauern ['kauərn] (ge-, *h*) **1.** *v/i.* crouch; squat; **2.** *v/refl.* crouch (down); squat (down); duck (down).
Kauf [kauf] *m* (-[e]s/⸗e) purchase; bargain, F good buy; acquisition; purchasing, buying; '**~brief** *m* deed of purchase; '**⁲en** *v/t.* (ge-, *h*) buy, purchase; acquire (by purchase); *sich et.* ~ buy o.s. s.th., buy s.th. for o.s.
Käufer ['kɔʏfər] *m* (-s/-) buyer, purchaser; customer.
'**Kauf|haus** *n* department store; '**~laden** *m* shop, *Am. a.* store.
käuflich ['kɔʏfliç] **1.** *adj.* for sale; purchasable; *fig.* open to bribery, bribable; venal; **2.** *adv.*: ~ *erwerben* (acquire by) purchase; ~ *überlassen* transfer by way of sale.
'**Kauf|mann** *m* (-[e]s/*Kaufleute*) businessman; merchant; trader, dealer, shopkeeper; *Am. a.* storekeeper; **⁲männisch** *adj.* ['~mɛniʃ] commercial, mercantile; '**~vertrag** *m* contract of sale.
'**Kaugummi** *m* chewing-gum.
kaum *adv.* [kaum] hardly, scarcely, barely; ~ *glaublich* hard to believe.
'**Kautabak** *m* chewing-tobacco.
Kaution [kau'tsjoːn] *f* (-/-en) security, surety; ⚖ *mst* bail.
Kautschuk ['kautʃuk] *m* (-s/-e) caoutchouc, pure rubber.
Kavalier [kava'liːr] *m* (-s/-e) gentleman; beau, admirer.
Kavallerie ⚔ [kavalə'riː] *f* (-/-n) cavalry, horse.
Kaviar ['kɑːviar] *m* (-s/-e) caviar(e).
keck *adj.* [kɛk] bold; impudent, saucy, cheeky; '**⁲heit** *f* (-/-en) boldness; impudence, sauciness, cheekiness.
Kegel ['keːgəl] *m* (-s/-) *games*: skittle, pin; *esp.* ⅍, ⊕ cone; ~ *schieben s. kegeln*; '**~bahn** *f* skittle, alley, *Am.* bowling alley; **⁲förmig** *adj.* ['~fœrmiç] conic(al), coniform; tapering; '**⁲n** *v/i.* (ge-, *h*) play (at) skittles *or* ninepins, *Am.* bowl.
Kegler ['keːglər] *m* (-s/-) skittle-player, *Am.* bowler.
Kehl|e ['keːlə] *f* (-/-n) throat; '**~kopf** *anat. m* larynx.
Kehre ['keːrə] *f* (-/-n) (sharp) bend, turn; '**⁲n** *v/t.* (ge-, *h*) sweep, brush; turn (*nach oben* upwards); *j-m den Rücken* ~ turn one's back on s.o.
Kehricht ['keːriçt] *m, n* (-[e]s/*no pl.*) sweepings *pl.*, rubbish.
'**Kehrseite** *f* wrong side, reverse; *esp. fig.* seamy side.
'**kehrtmachen** *v/i.* (*sep.*, -ge-, *h*) turn on one's heel; ⚔ turn *or* face about.
keifen ['kaɪfən] *v/i.* (ge-, *h*) scold, chide.
Keil [kaɪl] *m* (-[e]s/-e) wedge; gore, gusset; '**~e** F *f* (-/*no pl.*) thrashing, hiding; '**~er** *zo. m* (-s/-) wild-boar; **~erei** F [~'raɪ] *f* (-/-en) row, scrap; **⁲förmig** *adj.* ['~fœrmiç] wedge-shaped, cuneiform; '**~kissen** *n* wedge-shaped bolster; '**~schrift** *f* cuneiform characters *pl.*
Keim [kaɪm] *m* (-[e]s/-e) ⚘, *biol.* germ; ⚘: seed-plant; shoot; sprout; *fig.* seeds *pl.*, germ, bud; '**⁲en** *v/i.* (ge-, *h*) *seeds, etc.*: germinate; *seeds, plants, potatoes, etc.*: sprout; *fig.* b(o)urgeon; '**⁲frei** *adj.* sterilized, sterile; '**~träger** ⚕ *m* (germ-)carrier; '**~zelle** *f* germ-cell.
kein *indef. pron.* [kaɪn] *as adj.*: ~(e) no, not any; ~ *anderer als* none other but; *as noun*: ~er, ~e, ~(e)s none, no one, nobody; ~*er von beiden* neither (of the two); ~*er von uns* none of us; '**~es'falls** *adv.*, **~eswegs** *adv.* ['~'veːks] by no means, not at all; '**~mal** *adv.* not once, not a single time.
Keks [keːks] *m, n* (-, -es/-, -e) biscuit, *Am.* cookie; cracker.
Kelch [kɛlç] *m* (-[e]s/-e) cup, goblet; *eccl.* chalice, communion-cup; ⚘ calyx.
Kelle ['kɛlə] *f* (-/-n) scoop; ladle; *tool*: trowel.
Keller ['kɛlər] *m* (-s/-) cellar; basement; **~ei** [~'raɪ] *f* (-/-en) wine-vault; '**~geschoß** *n* basement; '**~meister** *m* cellarman.
Kellner ['kɛlnər] *m* (-s/-) waiter; '**~in** *f* (-/-nen) waitress.
Kelter ['kɛltər] *f* (-/-n) winepress; '**⁲n** *v/t.* (ge-, *h*) press.
kenn|en ['kɛnən] *v/t.* (*irr.*, ge-, *h*) know, be acquainted with; have knowledge of *s.th.*; '**~enlernen** *v/t.* (*sep.*, -ge-, *h*) get *or* come to know;

make *s.o.*'s acquaintance, meet *s.o.*; '2er *m* (-s/-) expert; connoisseur; '‚tlich *adj.* recognizable (*an dat.* by); ‚ machen mark; label; '2tnis *f* (-/-se) knowledge; ‚ nehmen von take not(ic)e of; '2zeichen *n* mark, sign; *mot.* registration (number), *Am.* license number; *fig.* hallmark, criterion; '‚zeichnen *v/t.* (ge-, h) mark, characterize.

kentern ♣ ['kɛntərn] *v/i.* (ge-, sein) capsize, keel over, turn turtle.

Kerbe ['kɛrbə] *f* (-/-n) notch, nick; slot; '2n *v/t.* (ge-, h) notch, nick, indent.

Kerker ['kɛrkər] *m* (-s/-) gaol, jail, prison; '‚meister *m* gaoler, jailer.

Kerl F [kɛrl] *m* (-s, ⚔ -es/-e, F -s) man; fellow, F chap, bloke, *esp. Am.* guy.

Kern [kɛrn] *m* (-[e]s/-e) kernel (*of nut, etc.*); stone, *Am.* pit (*of cherry, etc.*); pip (*of orange, apple, etc.*); core (*of the earth*); *phys.* nucleus; *fig.* core, heart, crux; Kern... *s. a.* Atom...; '‚energie *f* nuclear energy; '‚forschung *f* nuclear research; '‚gehäuse *n* core; '2ge'sund *adj.* thoroughly healthy, F as sound as a bell; '2ig *adj.* full of pips; *fig.*: pithy; solid; '‚punkt *m* central *or* crucial point; '‚spaltung *f* nuclear fission.

Kerze ['kɛrtsə] *f* (-/-n) candle; '‚n-licht *n* candle-light; '‚nstärke *f* candle-power.

keß F *adj.* [kɛs] pert, jaunty; smart.

Kessel ['kɛsəl] *m* (-s/-) kettle; cauldron; boiler; hollow.

Kette ['kɛtə] *f* (-/-n) chain; range (*of mountains, etc.*); necklace; '2n *v/t.* (ge-, h) chain (*an acc.* to).

'Ketten|hund *m* watch-dog; '‚raucher *m* chain-smoker; '‚reaktion *f* chain reaction.

Ketzer ['kɛtsər] *m* (-s/-) heretic; ‚ei [‚'raɪ] *f* (-/-en) heresy; '2isch *adj.* heretical.

keuch|en ['kɔʏçən] *v/i.* (ge-, h) pant, gasp; '2husten ⚕ *m* (w)hooping cough.

Keule ['kɔʏlə] *f* (-/-n) club; leg (*of mutton, pork, etc.*).

keusch *adj.* [kɔʏʃ] chaste, pure; '2heit *f* (-/no *pl.*) chastity, purity.

kichern ['kiçərn] *v/i.* (ge-, h) giggle, titter.

Kiebitz ['ki:bits] *m* (-es/-e) *orn.* pe(e)wit; F *fig.* kibitzer; '2en F *fig. v/i.* (ge-, h) kibitz.

Kiefer ['ki:fər] **1.** *anat. m* (-s/-) jaw(-bone); **2.** ♣ *f* (-/-n) pine.

Kiel [ki:l] *m* (-[e]s/-e) ♣ keel; quill; '‚raum *m* bilge, hold; '‚wasser *n* wake (*a. fig.*).

Kieme *zo.* ['ki:mə] *f* (-/-n) gill.

Kies [ki:s] *m* (-es/-e) gravel; *sl. fig.* dough; ‚el ['‚zəl] *m* (-s/-) pebble, flint; '‚weg *m* gravel-walk.

Kilo ['ki:lo] *n* (-s/-[s]), ‚gramm [kilo'gram] *n* kilogram(me); ‚hertz [‚'hɛrts] *n* (-/no *pl.*) kilocycle per second; ‚'meter *m* kilomet|re, *Am.* -er; ‚'watt *n* kilowatt.

Kimme ['kimə] *f* (-/-n) notch.

Kind [kint] *n* (-[e]s/-er) child; baby. 'Kinder|arzt *m* p(a)ediatrician; ‚ei [‚'raɪ] *f* (-/-en) childishness; childish trick; trifle; '‚frau *f* nurse; '‚fräulein *n* governess; '‚funk *m* children's program(me); '‚garten *m* kindergarten, nursery school; '‚lähmung ⚕ *f* infantile paralysis, polio(myelitis); '2'leicht *adj.* very easy *or* simple, F as easy as winking *or* as ABC; '‚lied *n* children's song; '2los *adj.* childless; '‚mädchen *n* nurse(maid); '‚spiel *n* children's game; *ein ‚ s. kinderleicht*; '‚stube *f* nursery; *fig.* manners *pl.*, upbringing; '‚wagen *m* perambulator, F pram, *Am.* baby carriage; '‚zeit *f* childhood; '‚zimmer *n* children's room.

'Kindes|alter *n* childhood, infancy; '‚beine *n/pl.*: *von ‚n an* from childhood, from a very early age; '‚kind *n* grandchild.

'Kind|heit *f* (-/no *pl.*) childhood; 2isch *adj.* ['‚dɪʃ] childish; '2lich *adj.* childlike.

Kinn *anat.* [kin] *n* (-[e]s/-e) chin; '‚backe *f*, '‚backen *m* (-s/-) jaw(-bone); '‚haken *m boxing*: hook to the chin; uppercut; '‚lade *f* jaw(-bone).

Kino ['ki:no] *n* (-s/-s) cinema, F *the* pictures *pl.*, *Am.* motion-picture theater, F *the* movies *pl.*; *ins ‚ gehen* go to the cinema *or* F pictures, *Am.* F go to the movies; '‚besucher *m* cinema-goer, *Am.* F moviegoer; '‚vorstellung *f* cinema-show, *Am.* motion-picture show.

Kippe F ['kipə] *f* (-/-n) stub, fag-end, *Am. a.* butt; *auf der ‚ stehen or sein* hang in the balance; '2n (ge-) **1.** *v/i.* (sein) tip (over), topple (over), tilt (over); **2.** *v/t.* (h) tilt, tip over *or* up.

Kirche ['kirçə] *f* (-/-n) church.

'Kirchen|älteste *m* (-n/-n) churchwarden, elder; '‚buch *n* parochial register; '‚diener *m* sacristan, sexton; '‚gemeinde *f* parish; '‚jahr *n* ecclesiastical year; '‚lied *n* hymn; '‚musik *f* sacred music; '‚schiff ⚖ *n* nave; '‚steuer *f* church-rate; '‚stuhl *m* pew; '‚vorsteher *m* churchwarden.

'Kirch|gang *m* church-going; ‚gänger ['‚gɛŋər] *m* (-s/-) churchgoer; '‚hof *m* churchyard; '2lich *adj.* ecclesiastical; '‚spiel *n* parish; '‚turm *m* steeple; ‚weih ['‚vaɪ] *f* (-/-en) parish fair.

Kirsche ['kirʃə] *f* (-/-n) cherry.

Kissen ['kisən] n (-s/-) cushion; pillow; bolster, pad.

Kiste ['kistə] f (-/-n) box, chest; crate.

Kitsch [kitʃ] m (-es/no pl.) trash, rubbish; 'ꞥig adj. shoddy, trashy.

Kitt [kit] m (-[e]s/-e) cement; putty.

Kittel ['kitəl] m (-s/-) overall; smock, frock.

'**kitten** v/t. (ge-, h) cement; putt.

kitz|eln ['kitsəln] (ge-, h) 1. v/t. tickle; 2. v/i.: meine Nase kitzelt my nose is tickling; '**ꞥig** adj. ticklish (a. fig.).

Kladde ['kladə] f (-/-n) rough note-book, waste-book.

klaffen ['klafən] v/i. (ge-, h) gape, yawn.

kläffen ['klɛfən] v/i. (ge-, h) yap, yelp.

klagbar 🇿🇿 adj. ['klɑːkbɑːr] matter, etc.: actionable; debt, etc.: suable.

Klage ['klɑːgə] f (-/-n) complaint; lament; 🇿🇿 action, suit; '**ꞥn** (ge-, h) 1. v/i. complain (über acc. of, about; bei to); lament; 🇿🇿 take legal action (gegen against); 2. v/t.: j-m et. ꞥ complain to s.o. of or about s.th.

Kläger 🇿🇿 ['klɛːgər] m (-s/-) plaintiff; complainant.

kläglich adj. ['klɛːkliç] pitiful, piteous, pitiable; cries, etc.: plaintive; condition: wretched, lamentable; performance, result, etc.: miserable, poor; failure, etc.: lamentable, miserable.

klamm [klam] 1. adj. hands, etc.: numb or stiff with cold, clammy; 2. 🇿🇿 f (-/-en) ravine, gorge, canyon.

Klammer ['klamər] f (-/-n) ⊕ clamp, cramp; (paper-)clip; gr., typ., A bracket, parenthesis; '**ꞥn** (ge-, h) 1. v/t. clip together; sich ꞥ close (wound) with clips; sich ꞥ an (acc.) cling to (a. fig.); 2. v/i. boxing: clinch.

Klang [klaŋ] 1. m (-[e]s/ꞥe) sound, tone (of voice, instrument, etc.); tone (of radio, etc.); clink (of glasses, etc.); ringing (of bells, etc.); timbre; 2. 🇿🇿 pret. of klingen; '**ꞥfülle** ♪ f sonority; 'ꞥlos adj. toneless; 'ꞥvoll adj. sonorous.

Klappe ['klapə] f (-/-n) flap, flap, drop leaf (of table, etc.); shoulder strap (of uniform, etc.); tailboard (of lorry, etc.); ⊕, ♫, anat. valve; ♪ key; F fig.: bed; trap; '**ꞥn** (ge-, h) 1. v/t.: nach oben ꞥ tip up; nach unten ꞥ lower, put down; 2. v/i. clap, flap; fig. come off well, work out fine, Am. sl. a. click.

Klapper ['klapər] f (-/-n) rattle; 'ꞥig adj. vehicle, etc.: rattly, ramshackle; furniture: rickety; person, horse, etc.: decrepit; '**ꞥkasten** F m wretched piano; rattletrap; '**ꞥn** (ge-, h) clatter, rattle (mit et. s.th.); er klapperte vor Kälte mit den Zäh-

nen his teeth were chattering with cold; '**ꞥschlange** zo. f rattlesnake, Am. a. rattler.

'**Klapp|kamera** phot. f folding camera; '**ꞥmesser** n clasp-knife, jack-knife; '**ꞥsitz** m tip-up or flap seat; '**ꞥstuhl** m folding chair; '**ꞥtisch** m folding table, Am. a. gate-leg(ged) table; '**ꞥult** ['klappult] n folding desk.

Klaps [klaps] m (-es/-e) smack, slap; '**ꞥen** v/t. (ge-, h) smack, slap.

klar adj. [klɑːr] clear; bright; transparent, limpid; pure; fig.: clear, distinct; plain; evident, obvious; sich ꞥ sein über (acc.) be clear about; ꞥen Kopf bewahren keep a clear head.

klären ['klɛːrən] v/t. (ge-, h) clarify; fig. clarify, clear up, elucidate.

'**klar|legen** v/t. (sep., -ge-, h), '**ꞥstellen** v/t. (sep., -ge-, h) clear up.

'**Klärung** f (-/-en) clarification; fig. a. elucidation.

Klasse ['klasə] f (-/-n) class, category; school: class, form, Am. a. grade; (social) class.

'**Klassen|arbeit** f (test) paper; 'ꞥbewußt adj. class-conscious; '**ꞥbewußtsein** n class-consciousness; '**ꞥbuch** n class-book; '**ꞥhaß** m class-hatred; '**ꞥkamerad** m classmate; '**ꞥkampf** m class-war(fare); '**ꞥzimmer** n classroom, schoolroom.

klassifizier|en [klasifi'tsiːrən] v/t. (no -ge-, h) classify; **ꞥung** f (-/-en) classification.

Klass|iker ['klasikər] m (-s/-) classic; 'ꞥisch adj. classic(al).

klatsch [klatʃ] 1. int. smack!, slap!; 2. 🇿🇿 m (-es/-e) smack, slap; F fig.: gossip; scandal; 'ꞥbase f ['ꞥbɑːzə] f (-/-n) gossip; 'ꞥe f (-/-n) fly-flap; '**ꞥen** (ge-, h) 1. v/t. fling, hurl; Beifall ꞥ clap, applaud (j-m s.o.) 2. v/i. splash; applaud, clap; F fig. gossip; '**ꞥhaft** adj. gossiping, gossipy; 'ꞥmaul F n s. Klatschbase; 'ꞥꞥnaß F adj. soaking wet.

Klaue ['klauə] f (-/-n) claw; paw; fig. clutch.

Klause ['klauzə] f (-/-n) hermitage; cell.

Klausel 🇿🇿 ['klauzəl] f (-/-n) clause; proviso; stipulation.

Klaviatur ♪ [klavja'tuːr] f (-/-en) keyboard, keys pl.

Klavier ♪ [kla'viːr] n (-s/-e) piano (-forte); '**ꞥkonzert** n piano concert or recital; '**ꞥlehrer** m piano teacher; '**ꞥsessel** m music-stool; '**ꞥstimmer** m (-s/-) piano-tuner; '**ꞥstunde** f piano-lesson.

kleb|en ['kleːbən] (ge-, h) 1. v/t. glue, paste, stick; 2. v/i. stick, adhere (an dat. to); '**ꞥend** adj. adhesive; 'ꞥepflaster n adhesive or sticking plaster; '**ꞥrig** adj. adhesive, sticky; 'ꞥstoff m adhesive; glue.

Klecks [klɛks] m (-es/-e) blot (of ink); mark (of dirt, grease, paint, etc.); spot (of grease, paint, etc.); stain (of wine, coffee, etc.); '2en (ge-) 1. v/i. (h) make a mark or spot or stain; 2. v/i. (sein) ink, etc.: drip (down); 3. v/t. (h): et. auf et. ~ splash or spill s.th. on s.th.

Klee ♣ [kle:] m (-s/no pl.) clover, trefoil.

Kleid [klart] n (-[e]s/-er) garment; dress, frock; gown; ~er pl. clothes pl.; 2en ['~dən] v/t. (ge-, h) dress, clothe; sich ~ dress (o.s.); j-n gut ~ suit or become s.o.

Kleider|ablage ['klaɪdər-] f cloak-room, Am. a. checkroom; '~bügel m coat-hanger; '~bürste f clothes-brush; '~haken m clothes-peg; '~schrank m wardrobe; '~ständer m hat and coat stand; '~stoff m dress material.

'**kleidsam** adj. becoming.

Kleidung ['klaɪduŋ] f (-/-en) clothes pl., clothing; dress; '~sstück n piece or article of clothing; garment.

Kleie ['klaɪə] f (-/-n) bran.

klein [klaɪn] 1. adj. little (only attr.), small; fig. a. trifling, petty; 2. adv.: ~ schreiben write with a small (initial) letter; ~ anfangen start in a small or modest way; 3. noun: von ~ auf from an early age; '2auto n baby or small car; '2bahn f narrow-ga(u)ge railway; '2bildkamera f miniature camera; '2geld n (small) change; '~gläubig adj. of little faith; '2handel ✝ m retail trade; '2händler m retailer; '2heit f (-/no pl.) smallness, small size; '2holz n firewood, matchwood, kindling.

'**Kleinigkeit** f (-/-en) trifle, triviality; '~skrämer m pettifogger.

'**Klein|kind** n infant; '2laut adj. subdued; '2lich adj. paltry, pedantic, fussy; '~mut m pusillanimity; despondency; 2mütig adj. ['~my-tic] pusillanimous; despondent; '2schneiden v/t. (irr. schneiden, sep., -ge-, h) cut into small pieces; '~staat m small or minor state; '~stadt f small town; '~städter m small-town dweller, Am. a. small-towner; '2städtisch adj. small-town, provincial; '~vieh n small livestock.

Kleister ['klaɪstər] m (-s/-) paste; '2n v/t. (ge-, h) paste.

Klemm|e ['klɛmə] f (-/-n) ⊕ clamp; ⚡ terminal; F in der ~ sitzen be in a cleft stick, F be in a jam; '2en v/t. (ge-, h) jam, squeeze, pinch; '~er m (-s/-) pince-nez; '~schraube ⊕ f set screw.

Klempner ['klɛmpnər] m (-s/-) tin-man, tin-smith, Am. a. tinner; plumber.

Klerus ['kle:rus] m (-/no pl.) clergy.

Klette ['klɛtə] f (-/-n) ♣ bur(r); fig. a. leech.

Kletter|er ['klɛtərər] m (-s/-) climber; '2n v/i. (ge-, sein) climb, clamber (auf e-n Baum [up] a tree); '~pflanze f climber, creeper.

Klient [kli'ɛnt] m (-en/-en) client.

Klima ['kli:ma] n (-s/-s, -te) climate; fig. a. atmosphere; '~anlage f air-conditioning plant; 2tisch adj. [~'mɑːtɪʃ] climatic.

klimpern ['klɪmpərn] v/i. (ge-, h) jingle, chink (mit et. s.th.); F strum or tinkle away (auf acc. on, at piano, guitar).

Klinge ['klɪŋə] f (-/-n) blade.

Klingel ['klɪŋəl] f (-/-n) bell, hand-bell; '~knopf m bell-push; '2n v/i. (ge-, h) ring (the bell); doorbell, etc.: ring; es klingelt the doorbell is ringing; '~zug m bell-pull.

klingen ['klɪŋən] v/i. (irr., ge-, h) sound; bell, metal, etc.: ring; glasses, etc.: clink; musical instrument: speak.

Klini|k ['kli:nik] f (-/-en) nursing home; private hospital; clinic(al hospital); '2sch adj. clinical.

Klinke ['klɪŋkə] f (-/-n) latch; (door-) handle.

Klippe ['klɪpə] f (-/-n) cliff; reef; crag; rock; fig. rock, hurdle.

klirren ['klɪrən] v/i. (ge-, h) window-pane, chain, etc.: rattle; chain, swords, etc.: clank, jangle; keys, spurs, etc.: jingle; glasses, etc.: clink, chink; pots, etc.: clatter; ~ mit rattle; jingle.

Klistier ✝ [kli'sti:r] n (-s/-e) enema.

Kloake [klo'ɑːkə] f (-/-n) sewer, cesspool (a. fig.).

Klob|en ['klo:bən] m (-s/-) ⊕ pulley, block; log; '2ig adj. clumsy (a. fig.).

klopfen ['klɔpfən] (ge-, h) 1. v/i. heart, pulse: beat, throb; knock (at door, etc.); tap (on shoulder); pat (on cheek); es klopft there's a knock at the door; 2. v/t. knock, drive (nail, etc.).

Klöppel ['klœpəl] m (-s/-) clapper (of bell); lacemaking: bobbin; beetle; '~spitze f pillow-lace, bone-lace.

Klops [klɔps] m (-es/-e) meat ball.

Klosett [klo'zɛt] n (-s/-e, -s) lavatory, (water-)closet, W.C., toilet; ~papier n toilet-paper.

Kloß [klo:s] m (-es/╪e) earth, clay, etc.: clod, lump; cookery: dumpling.

Kloster ['klo:stər] n (-s/╪) cloister; monastery; convent, nunnery; '~bruder m friar; '~frau f nun; '~gelübde n monastic vow.

Klotz [klɔts] m (-es/╪e) block, log (a. fig.).

Klub [klup] m (-s/-s) club; '~kamerad m clubmate; '~sessel m lounge-chair.

Kluft [kluft] f 1. (-/╪e) gap (a. fig.),

crack; cleft; gulf, chasm (both a. fig.); 2. F (-/-en) outfit, F togs pl.; uniform.

klug adj. [klu:k] clever; wise, intelligent, sensible; prudent; shrewd; cunning; '2heit f (-/no pl.) cleverness; intelligence; prudence; shrewdness; good sense.

Klump|en ['klumpən] m (-s/-) lump (of earth, dough, etc.); clod (of earth, etc.); nugget (of gold, etc.); heap; '_fuß m club-foot; '2ig adj. lumpy; cloddish.

knabbern ['knabərn] (ge-, h) 1. v/t. nibble, gnaw; 2. v/i. nibble, gnaw (an dat. at).

Knabe ['kna:bə] m (-n/-n) boy; lad; F alter _ F old chap.

'Knaben|alter n boyhood; '_chor m boys' choir; '2haft adj. boyish.

Knack [knak] m (-[e]s/-e) crack, snap, click; '2en (ge-, h) 1. v/i. wood: crack; fire: crackle; click; 2. v/t. crack (nut, etc.); F crack open (safe); e-e harte Nuß zu _ haben have a hard nut to crack; _s [-s] m (-es/-e) s. Knack; F fig. defect; '2sen v/i. (ge-, h) s. knacken 1.

Knall [knal] m (-[e]s/-e) crack, bang (of shot); bang (of explosion); crack (of rifle or whip); report (of gun); detonation, explosion, report; '_bonbon m, n cracker; '_effekt fig. m sensation; '2en v/i. (ge-, h) rifle, whip: crack; fireworks, door, etc.: bang; gun: fire; cork, etc.: pop; explosive, etc.: detonate.

knapp adj. [knap] clothes: tight, close-fitting; rations, etc.: scanty, scarce; style, etc.: concise; lead, victory, etc.: narrow; majority, etc.: bare; mit _er Not entrinnen have a narrow escape; _ werden run short; '2e ⚔ m (-n/-n) miner; '_halten v/t. (irr. halten, sep., -ge-, h) keep s.o. short; '2heit f (-/no pl.) scarcity, shortage; conciseness; '_schaft ⚔ f (-/-en) miners' society.

Knarre ['knarə] f (-/-n) rattle; F rifle, gun; '2n v/i. (ge-, h) creak; voice: grate.

knattern ['knatərn] v/i. (ge-, h) crackle; machine-gun, etc.: rattle; mot. roar.

Knäuel ['knɔyəl] m, n (-s/-) clew, ball; fig. bunch, cluster.

Knauf [knauf] m (-[e]s/⸗e) knob; pommel (of sword).

Knauser ['knauzər] m (-s/-) niggard, miser, skinflint; _ei [_'rai] f (-/-en) niggardliness, miserliness; '2ig adj. niggardly, stingy; '2n v/i. (ge-, h) be stingy.

Knebel ['kne:bəl] m (-s/-) gag; '2n v/t. (ge-, h) gag; fig. muzzle (press).

Knecht [knɛçt] m (-[e]s/-e) servant; farm-labo(u)rer, farm-hand; slave; '2en v/t. (ge-, h) enslave; tyrannize;

subjugate; '_schaft f (-/no pl.) servitude, slavery.

kneif|en ['knaifən] (irr., ge-, h) 1. v/t. pinch, nip; 2. v/i. pinch; F fig. back out, Am. F a. crawfish; '2er m (-s/-) pince-nez; '2zange f (e-e a pair of) pincers pl. or nippers pl.

Kneipe ['knaipə] f (-/-n) public house, tavern, F pub, Am. a. saloon; '2n v/i. (ge-, h) carouse, tipple, F booze; '_rei f (-/-en) drinking-bout, carousal.

kneten ['kne:tən] v/t. (ge-, h) knead (dough, etc.); ⚕ a. massage (limb, etc.).

Knick [knik] m (-[e]s/-e) wall, etc.: crack; paper, etc.: fold, crease; path, etc.: bend; '2en v/t. (ge-, h) fold, crease; bend; break.

Knicker F ['knikər] m (-s/-) s. Knauser.

Knicks [kniks] m (-es/-e) curts(e)y; e-n _ machen ⸗ '2en v/i. (ge-, h) (drop a) curts(e)y (vor dat. to).

Knie [kni:] n (-s/-) knee; '2fällig adv. on one's knees; '_kehle anat. f hollow of the knee; '2n v/i. (ge-, h) kneel, be on one's knees; '_scheibe anat. f knee-cap, knee-pan; '_strumpf m knee-length sock.

Kniff [knif] 1. m (-[e]s/-e) crease, fold; fig. trick, knack; 2. 2 pret. of kneifen; '2(e)lig adj. ['_(ə)liç] tricky; intricate.

knipsen ['knipsən] (ge-, h) 1. v/t. clip, punch (ticket, etc.); F phot. take a snapshot of, snap; 2. F phot. v/i. take snapshots.

Knirps [knirps] m (-es/-e) little man; little chap, F nipper; '2ig adj. very small.

knirschen ['knirʃən] v/i. (ge-, h) gravel, snow, etc.: crunch, grind; teeth, etc.: grate; mit den Zähnen _ grind or gnash one's teeth.

knistern ['knistərn] v/i. (ge-, h) woodfire, etc.: crackle; dry leaves, silk, etc.: rustle.

knitter|frei adj. ['knitər-] crease-resistant; '2n v/t. and v/i. (ge-, h) crease, wrinkle.

Knoblauch ♣ ['kno:plaux] m (-[e]s/no pl.) garlic.

Knöchel anat. ['knϭçəl] m (-s/-) knuckle; ankle.

Knoch|en anat. ['knϭxən] m (-s/-) bone; '_enbruch ⚕ m fracture (of a bone); '2ig adj. bony.

Knödel ['knø:dəl] m (-s/-) dumpling.

Knolle ♣ ['knɔlə] f (-/-n) tuber; bulb.

Knopf [knϭpf] m (-[e]s/⸗e) button.

knöpfen ['knœpfən] v/t. (ge-, h) button.

'Knopfloch n buttonhole.

Knorpel ['knϭrpəl] m (-s/-) cartilage, gristle.

Knorr|en ['knϭrən] m (-s/-) knot,

knag, gnarl; '♀ig *adj.* gnarled, knotty.

Knospe ♀ ['knɔspə] *f* (-/-n) bud; '♀n *v/i.* (ge-, h) (be in) bud.

Knot|en ['kno:tən] 1. *m* (-s/-) knot (*a. fig.*, ♣.); 2. ♀ *v/t.* (ge-, h) knot; '✲enpunkt *m* ⚕ junction; intersection; '♀ig *adj.* knotty.

Knuff F [knuf] *m* (-[e]s/ᵘe) poke, cuff, nudge; '♀en F *v/t.* (ge-, h) poke, cuff, nudge.

knülle|n ['knylən] *v/t. and v/i.* (ge-, h) crease, crumple; '♀r F *m* (-s/-) hit.

knüpfen ['knypfən] *v/t.* (ge-, h) make, tie (*knot, etc.*); make (*net*); knot (*carpet, etc.*); tie (*shoe-lace, etc.*); strike up (*friendship, etc.*); attach (*condition, etc.*) (*an acc.* to).

Knüppel ['knypəl] *m* (-s/-) cudgel.

knurren ['knurən] *v/i.* (ge-, h) growl, snarl; *fig.* grumble (*über acc.* at, over about); *stomach:* rumble.

knusp(e)rig *adj.* ['knusp(ə)riç] crisp, crunchy.

Knute ['knu:tə] *f* (-/-n) knout.

Knüttel ['knytəl] *m* (-s/-) cudgel.

Kobold ['ko:bɔlt] *m* (-[e]s/-e) (hob-) goblin, imp.

Koch [kɔx] *m* (-[e]s/ᵘe) cook; '✲buch *n* cookery-book, *Am.* cookbook; '♀en (ge-, h) 1. *v/t.* boil (*water, egg, fish, etc.*); cook (*meat, vegetables, etc.*) (*by boiling*); make (*coffee, tea, etc.*); 2. *v/i.* water, *etc.*: boil (*a. fig.*); do the cooking; be a (*good, etc.*) cook; '✲er *m* (-s/-) cooker.

Köcher ['kœçər] *m* (-s/-) quiver.

'**Koch|kiste** *f* haybox; '✲löffel *m* wooden spoon; '✲nische *f* kitchenette; '✲salz *n* common salt; '✲topf *m* pot, saucepan.

Köder ['kø:dər] *m* (-s/-) bait (*a. fig.*); lure (*a. fig.*); '♀n *v/t.* (ge-, h) bait; lure; *fig. a.* decoy.

Kodex ['ko:dɛks] *m* (-es, -/-e, Kodizes) code.

Koffer ['kɔfər] *m* (-s/-) (suit)case; trunk; '✲radio *n* portable radio (set).

Kognak ['kɔnjak] *m* (-s/-s, ✲-e) French brandy, cognac.

Kohl ♀ [ko:l] *m* (-[e]s/-e) cabbage.

Kohle ['ko:lə] *f* (-/-n) coal; charcoal; ⚡ carbon; *wie auf (glühenden)* ✲n *sitzen* be on tenterhooks.

'**Kohlen|bergwerk** *n* coal-mine, coal-pit, colliery; '✲eimer *m* coalscuttle; '✲händler *m* coal-merchant; '✲kasten *m* coal-box; '✲revier ⚒ *n* coal-district; '✲säure 🜨 *f* carbonic acid; '✲stoff 🜨 *m* carbon.

'**Kohle|papier** *n* carbon paper; '✲zeichnung *f* charcoal-drawing.

'**Kohl|kopf** ♀ *m* (head of) cabbage; '✲rübe ♀ *f* Swedish turnip.

Koje ♣ ['ko:jə] *f* (-/-n) berth, bunk.

Kokain [koka'i:n] *n* (-s/no *pl.*) cocaine, *sl.* coke, snow.

kokett *adj.* [ko'kɛt] coquettish; ♀erie [✲ə'ri:] *f* (-/-n) coquetry, coquettishness; ✲ieren [✲'ti:rən] *v/i.* (no -ge-, h) coquet, flirt (*mit* with; *a. fig.*).

Kokosnuß ♀ ['ko:kɔs-] *f* coconut.

Koks [ko:ks] *m* (-es/-e) coke.

Kolben ['kɔlbən] *m* (-s/-) butt (*of rifle*); ⊕ piston; '✲stange *f* piston-rod.

Kolchose [kɔl'ço:zə] *f* (-/-n) collective farm, kolkhoz.

Kolleg *univ.* [kɔ'le:k] *n* (-s/-s, -ien) course of lectures; ✲e [✲gə] *m* (-n/-n) colleague; ✲ium [✲gjum] *n* (-s/*Kollegien*) council, board; teaching staff.

Kollekt|e *eccl.* [kɔ'lɛktə] *f* (-/-n) collection; ✲ion ✝ [✲'tsjo:n] *f* (-/-en) collection, range.

Koller ['kɔlər] *m* (-s/-) *vet.* staggers *pl.*; F *fig.* rage, tantrum; '♀n *v/i.* 1. (*h*) turkey-cock: gobble; pigeon: coo; *bowels:* rumble; *vet.* have the staggers; 2. (*sein*) ball, tears, *etc.*: roll.

kolli|dieren [kɔli'di:rən] *v/i.* (no -ge-, sein) collide; *fig.* clash; ✲sion [✲'zjo:n] *f* (-/-en) collision; *fig.* clash, conflict.

Kölnischwasser ['kœlniʃ-] *n* eau-de-Cologne.

Kolonialwaren [kolo'nja:l-] *f/pl.* groceries *pl.*; ✲händler *m* grocer; ✲handlung *f* grocer's (shop), *Am.* grocery.

Kolon|ie [kolo'ni:] *f* (-/-n) colony; ✲isieren [✲i'zi:rən] *v/t.* (no -ge-, h) colonize.

Kolonne [ko'lɔnə] *f* (-/-n) column; convoy; gang (*of workers, etc.*).

kolorieren [kolo'ri:rən] *v/t.* (no -ge-, h) colo(u)r.

Kolo|ß [ko'lɔs] *m* (*Kolosses/Kolosse*) colossus; ✲ssal *adj.* [✲'sa:l] colossal, huge (*both a. fig.*).

Kombin|ation [kɔmbina'tsjo:n] *f* (-/-en) combination; overall; ✈ flying-suit; *football, etc.*: combined attack; ✲ieren [✲'ni:rən] (no -ge-, h) 1. *v/t.* combine; 2. *v/i.* reason, deduce; *football, etc.*: combine, move.

Kombüse ♣ [kɔm'by:zə] *f* (-/-n) galley, caboose.

Komet *ast.* [ko'me:t] *m* (-en/-en) comet.

Komfort [kɔm'fo:r] *m* (-s/no *pl.*) comfort; ♀abel *adj.* [✲r'ta:bəl] comfortable.

Komik ['ko:mik] *f* (-/no *pl.*) humo(u)r, fun(niness); '✲er *m* (-s/-) comic actor, comedian.

komisch *adj.* ['ko:miʃ] comic(al), funny; *fig.* funny, odd, queer.

Komitee [komi'te:] *n* (-s/-s) committee.

Kommand|ant ✗ [kɔman'dant] m (-en/-en), ~eur ✗ [ˌˈdøːr] m (-s/-e) commander, commanding officer; 2ieren [ˌˈdiːrən] (no -ge-, h) 1. v/i. order, command, be in command; 2. v/t. ✗ command, be in command of; order; ~itgesellschaft ✝ [~ˈdiːt-] f limited partnership; ~o [ˌˈmando] n (-s/-s) ✗ command, order; order(s pl.), directive(s pl.); ✗ detachment; ~obrücke ⚓ f navigating bridge.

kommen ['kɔmən] v/i. (irr., ge-, sein) come; arrive; ~ lassen send for s.o., order s.th.; et. ~ sehen foresee; an die Reihe ~ it is one's turn; ~ auf (acc.) think of, hit upon; remember; zu dem Schluß ~, daß decide that; hinter et. ~ find s.th. out; um et. ~ lose s.th.; zu et. ~ come by s.th.; wieder zu sich ~ come round or to; wie ~ Sie dazu! how dare you!

Komment|ar [kɔmɛn'taːr] m (-s/-e) commentary, comment; ~ator [~ˈtɔr] m (-s/-en) commentator; 2ieren [ˌˈtiːrən] v/t. (no -ge-, h) comment on.

Kommissar [kɔmiˈsaːr] m (-s/-e) commissioner; superintendent; pol. commissar.

Kommißbrot F [kɔˈmis-] n army or ration bread, Am. a. G.I. bread.

Kommission [kɔmiˈsjoːn] f (-/-en) commission (a. ✝); committee; ~är ✝ [ˌoˈnɛːr] m (-s/-e) commission agent.

Kommode [kɔˈmoːdə] f (-/-n) chest of drawers, Am. bureau.

Kommunis|mus pol. [kɔmuˈnismus] m (-/no pl.) communism; ~t m (-en/-en) communist; 2tisch adj. communist(ic).

Komöd|iant [kɔmøˈdjant] m (-en/-en) comedian; fig. play-actor; ~ie [ˌˈmøːdjə] f (-/-n) comedy; ~ spielen play-act.

Kompagnon ✝ [kɔmpanˈjõ] m (-s/-s) (business-)partner, associate.

Kompanie ✗ [kɔmpaˈniː] f (-/-n) company.

Kompaß ['kɔmpas] m (Kompasses/ Kompasse) compass.

kompetent adj. [kɔmpeˈtɛnt] competent.

komplett adj. [kɔmˈplɛt] complete.

Komplex [kɔmˈplɛks] m (-es/-e) complex (a. psych.); block (of houses).

Kompliment [kɔmpliˈmɛnt] n (-[e]s/-e) compliment.

Komplize [kɔmˈpliːtsə] m (-n/-n) accomplice.

komplizier|en [kɔmpliˈtsiːrən] v/t. (no -ge-, h) complicate; ~t adj. machine, etc.: complicated; argument, situation, etc.: complex; ~er Bruch ✀ compound fracture.

Komplott [kɔmˈplɔt] n (-[e]s/-e) plot, conspiracy.

11 SW E II

kompo|nieren ♪ [kɔmpoˈniːrən] v/t. and v/i. (no -ge-, h) compose; 2nist m (-en/-en) composer; 2sition [ˌziˈtsjoːn] f (-/-en) composition.

Kompott [kɔmˈpɔt] n (-[e]s/-e) compote, stewed fruit, Am. a. sauce.

komprimieren [kɔmpriˈmiːrən] v/t. (no -ge-, h) compress.

Kompromi|ß [kɔmproˈmis] m (Kompromisses/Kompromisse) compromise; 2ßlos adj. uncompromising; 2ttieren [ˌˈtiːrən] v/t. (no -ge-, h) compromise.

Kondens|ator [kɔndɛnˈzaːtɔr] m (-s/-en) ⚡ capacitor, condenser (a. ♻); 2ieren [ˌˈziːrən] v/t. (no -ge-, h) condense.

Kondens|milch [kɔnˈdɛns-] f evaporated milk; ~streifen ✈ m condensation or vapo(u)r trail; ~wasser n water of condensation.

Konditor [kɔnˈdiːtɔr] m (-s/-en) confectioner, pastry-cook; ~ei [ˌˈiˈtoˈraɪ] f (-/-en) confectionery, confectioner's (shop); ~eiwaren f/pl. confectionery.

Konfekt [kɔnˈfɛkt] n (-[e]s/-e) sweets pl., sweetmeat, Am. a. soft candy; chocolates pl.

Konfektion [kɔnfɛkˈtsjoːn] f (-/-en) (manufacture of) ready-made clothing; ~sanzug [kɔnfɛkˈtsjoːns?-] m ready-made suit; ~sgeschäft n ready-made clothes shop.

Konfer|enz [kɔnfeˈrɛnts] f (-/-en) conference; 2ieren [ˌˈriːrən] v/i. (no -ge-, h) confer (über acc. on).

Konfession [kɔnfɛˈsjoːn] f (-/-en) confession, creed; denomination; 2ell adj. [ˌoˈnɛl] confessional, denominational; ~sschule [ˌˈsjoːns-] f denominational school.

Konfirm|and eccl. [kɔnfirˈmant] m (-en/-en) candidate for confirmation, confirmee; ~ation [ˌˈatsjoːn] f (-/-en) confirmation; 2ieren [ˌˈmiːrən] v/t. (no -ge-, h) confirm.

konfiszieren ⚖ [kɔnfisˈtsiːrən] v/t. (no -ge-, h) confiscate, seize.

Konfitüre [kɔnfiˈtyːrə] f (-/-n) preserve(s pl.), (whole-fruit) jam.

Konflikt [kɔnˈflikt] m (-[e]s/-e) conflict.

konform adv. [kɔnˈfɔrm]: ~ gehen mit agree or concur with.

konfrontieren [kɔnfrɔnˈtiːrən] v/t. (no -ge-, h) confront (mit with).

konfus adj. [kɔnˈfuːs] p., a. ideas: muddled; p. muddle-headed.

Kongreß [kɔnˈgrɛs] m (Kongresses/ Kongresse) congress; Am. parl. Congress; ~halle f congress hall.

König ['køːnɪç] m (-s/-e) king; 2lich adj. ['ˌk-] royal; regal; ~reich ['ˌk-] n kingdom; ~swürde ['ˌks-] f royal dignity, kingship; ~tum n (-s/ᵘer) monarchy; kingship.

Konjug|ation gr. [kɔnjugaˈtsjoːn] f

(-/-en); **2ieren** [~'giːrən] v/t. (no -ge-, h) conjugate.

Konjunkt|iv gr. ['kɔnjuŋktiːf] m (-s/-e) subjunctive (mood); **~ur †** [~'tuːr] f (-/-en) trade or business cycle; economic or business situation.

konkret adj. [kɔn'kreːt] concrete.

Konkurrent [konku'rɛnt] m (-en/-en) competitor, rival.

Konkurrenz [konku'rɛnts] f (-/-en) competition; competitors pl., rivals pl.; sports: event; **2fähig** adj. able to compete; competitive; **~geschäft** n rival business or firm; **~kampf** m competition.

konkur'rieren v/i. (no -ge-, h) compete (mit with; um for).

Konkurs †, ṣ½ [kɔn'kurs] m (-es/-e) bankruptcy, insolvency, failure; **~ anmelden** file a petition in bankruptcy; in **~** gehen or geraten become insolvent, go bankrupt; **~er-klärung** ṣ½ f declaration of insolvency; **~masse** ṣ½ f bankrupt's estate; **~verfahren** ṣ½ n bankruptcy proceedings pl.; **~verwalter** ṣ½ m trustee in bankruptcy; liquidator.

können ['kœnən] **1.** v/i. (irr., ge-, h): ich kann nicht I can't, I am not able to; **2.** v/t. (irr., ge-, h) know, understand; e-e Sprache **~** know a language, have command of a language; **3.** v/aux. (irr., no -ge-, h) be able to inf., be capable of ger.; be allowed or permitted to inf.; es kann sein it may be; du kannst hingehen you may go there; er kann schwimmen he can swim, he knows how to swim; **4.** 2 n (-s/no pl.) ability; skill; proficiency.

Konnossement † [kɔnəsə'mɛnt] n (-[e]s/-e) bill of lading.

konnte ['kɔntə] pret. of können.

konsequen|t adj. [kɔnze'kvɛnt] consistent; **2z** [~ts] f (-/-en) consistency; consequence; die **~en** ziehen do the only thing one can.

konservativ adj. [kɔnzerva'tiːf] conservative.

Konserven [kɔn'zɛrvən] f/pl. tinned or Am. canned foods pl.; **~büchse** f, **~dose** f tin, Am. can; **~fabrik** f tinning factory, esp. Am. cannery.

konservieren [kɔnzɛr'viːrən] v/t. (no -ge-, h) preserve.

Konsonant gr. [kɔnzo'nant] m (-en/-en) consonant.

Konsortium † [kɔn'zɔrtsjum] n (-s/Konsortien) syndicate.

konstruieren [kɔnstru'iːrən] v/t. (no -ge-, h) gr. construe; ⊕: construct; design.

Konstruk|teur ⊕ [kɔnstruk'tøːr] m (-s/-e) designer; **~tion** ⊕ [~'tsjoːn] f (-/-en) construction; **~tionsfehler** ⊕ m constructional defect.

Konsul pol. ['kɔnzul] m (-s/-n) consul; **~at** pol. [~'laːt] n (-[e]s/-e) consulate; **2tieren** v/t. (no -ge-, h) consult, seek s.o.'s advice.

Konsum [kɔn'zuːm] m **1.** (-s/no pl.) consumption; **2.** (-s/-s) co-operative shop, Am. co-operative store, F co-op; **3.** (-s/no pl.) consumers' co-operative society, F co-op; **~ent** [~u'mɛnt] m (-en/-en) consumer; **2ieren** [~u'miːrən] v/t. (no -ge-, h) consume; **~verein** m s. Konsum 3.

Kontakt [kɔn'takt] m (-[e]s/-e) contact (a. f); in **~** stehen mit be in contact or touch with.

Kontinent ['kɔntinɛnt] m (-[e]s/-e) continent.

Kontingent [kɔntiŋ'gɛnt] n (-[e]s/-e) ✕ contingent, quota (a. †).

Konto † ['kɔnto] n (-s/Konten, Kontos, Konti) account; **~auszug †** m statement of account; **~korrent-konto †** [~ko'rɛnt-] n current account.

Kontor [kɔn'toːr] n (-s/-e) office; **~ist** [~o'rist] m (-en/-en) clerk.

Kontrast [kɔn'trast] m (-[e]s/-e) contrast.

Kontroll|e [kɔn'trɔlə] f (-/-n) control; supervision; check; **2ieren** [~'liːrən] v/t. (no -ge-, h) control; supervise; check.

Kontroverse [kɔntro'vɛrzə] f (-/-n) controversy.

konventionell adj. [kɔnvɛntsjo'nɛl] conventional.

Konversation [kɔnverza'tsjoːn] f (-/-en) conversation; **~slexikon** n encyclop(a)edia.

Konzentr|ation [kɔntsentra'tsjoːn] f (-/-en) concentration; **2ieren** [~'triːrən] v/t. (no -ge-, h) concentrate, focus (attention, etc.) (auf acc. on); sich **~** concentrate (auf acc. on).

Konzern † [kɔn'tsɛrn] m (-s/-e) combine, group.

Konzert ♪ [kɔn'tsɛrt] n (-[e]s/-e) concert; recital; concerto; **~saal** ♪ m concert-hall.

Konzession [kɔntse'sjoːn] f (-/-en) concession; licen|ce, Am. -se; **2ieren** [~o'niːrən] v/t. (no -ge-, h) license.

Kopf [kɔpf] m (-[e]s/ⁿe) head; top; brains pl.; pipe: bowl; ein fähiger **~** a clever fellow; **~** hoch! chin up!; j-m über den **~** wachsen outgrow s.o.; fig. get beyond s.o.; **~arbeit** f brain-work; **'~bahnhof** 🚂 m terminus, Am. terminal; **'~bedeckung** f headgear, headwear.

köpfen ['kœpfən] v/t. (ge-, h) behead, decapitate; football: head (ball).

'Kopf|ende n head; **'~hörer** m headphone, headset; **'~kissen** n pillow; **2los** adj. headless; fig. confused; **'~nicken** n (-s/no pl.) nod; **'~rechnen** n (-s/no pl.) mental arithmetic; **'~salat** m cabbage-lettuce;

'**~schmerzen** m/pl. headache; '**~sprung** m header; '**~tuch** n scarf; 2**~über** adv. head first, headlong; '**~weh** n (-[e]s/-e) s. *Kopfschmerzen*; '**~zerbrechen** n (-s/no pl.): j-m ~ machen puzzle s.o.

Kopie [ko'pi:] f(-/-n) copy; duplicate; *phot.*, *film*: print; **~rstift** m indelible pencil.

Koppel ['kɔpəl] **1.** f (-/-n) hounds: couple; horses: string; paddock; **2.** ⚔ n (-s/-) belt; 2**n** v/t. (ge-, h) couple (a. ⊕, ♂).

Koralle [ko'ralə] f (-/-n) coral, **~fischer** m coral-fisher.

Korb [kɔrp] m (-[e]s/⸚e) basket; *fig.* refusal; Hahn im ~ cock of the walk; '**~möbel** n/pl. wicker furniture.

Kordel ['kɔrdəl] f (-/-n) string, twine; cord.

Korinthe [ko'rintə] f (-/-n) currant.

Kork [kɔrk] m (-[e]s/-e), '**~en** m (-s/-) cork; '**~(en)zieher** m (-s/-) corkscrew.

Korn [kɔrn] **1.** n (-[e]s/⸚er) seed; grain, **2.** n (-[e]s/-e) corn, cereals pl.; **3.** n (-[e]s/⸚-e) front sight; **4.** F m (-[e]s/-) (German) corn whisky.

körnig adj. ['kœrniç] granular; in compounds: ...-grained.

Körper ['kœrpər] m (-s/-) body (a. phys., ⚗); ♂ solid; '**~bau** m build, physique; 2**behindert** adj. ['~bəhindərt] (physically) disabled, handicapped; '**~beschaffenheit** f constitution, physique; '**~fülle** f corpulence; '**~geruch** m body-odo(u)r; '**~größe** f stature; '**~kraft** f physical strength; 2**lich** adj. physical; corporal; bodily; '**~pflege** f care of the body, hygiene; '**~schaft** f (-/-en) body (corporate), corporation; '**~verletzung** ⚖ f bodily harm, physical injury.

korrekt adj. [kɔ'rekt] correct; 2**or** [~ɔr] m (-s/-en) (proof-)reader; 2**ur** [~'tu:r] f (-/-en) correction; 2**urbogen** m proof-sheet.

Korrespond|ent [kɔrɛspɔn'dɛnt] m (-en/-en) correspondent; **~enz** [~ts] f (-/-en) correspondence; 2**ieren** [~'di:rən] v/i. (no -ge-, h) correspond (mit with).

korrigieren [kɔri'gi:rən] v/t. (no -ge-, h) correct.

Korsett [kɔr'zet] n (-[e]s/-e, -s) corset, stays pl.

Kosename ['ko:zə-] m pet name.

Kosmetik [kɔs'me:tik] f (-/no pl.) beauty culture; **~erin** f (-/-nen) beautician, cosmetician.

Kost [kɔst] f (-/no pl.) food, fare; board; diet; '2**bar** adj. present, etc.: costly, expensive; health, time, etc.: valuable; mineral, etc.: precious.

'**kosten**[1] v/t. (ge-, h) taste, try, sample.

'**Kosten**[2] **1.** pl. cost(s pl.); expense(s pl.), charges pl.; auf ~ (gen.) at the expense of; **2.** 2 v/t. (ge-, h) cost; take, require (time, etc.); '**~anschlag** m estimate, tender; '2**frei** **1.** adj. free; **2.** adv. free of charge; '2**los** s. kostenfrei.

köstlich adj. ['kœstliç] delicious.

'**Kost|probe** f taste, sample (a. fig.); 2**spielig** adj. ['~ʃpi:liç] expensive, costly.

Kostüm [kɔs'ty:m] n (-s/-e) costume, dress; suit; **~fest** n fancy-dress ball.

Kot [ko:t] m (-[e]s/no pl.) mud, mire; excrement.

Kotelett [kot(ə)'let] n (-[e]s/-s, ⚞-e) pork, veal, lamb: cutlet; pork, veal, mutton: chop; **~en** pl. sidewhiskers pl., Am. a. sideburns pl.

'**Kot|flügel** mot. m mudguard, Am. a. fender; '2**ig** adj. muddy, miry.

Krabbe zo. ['krabə] f (-/-n) shrimp; crab.

krabbeln ['krabəln] v/i. (ge-, sein) crawl.

Krach [krax] m (-[e]s/-e, -s) crack, crash (a. ✝); quarrel, sl. bust-up; F row; ~ machen kick up a row; '2**en** v/i. (ge-) **1.** (h) thunder: crash; cannon: roar, thunder; **2.** (sein) crash (a. ✝), smash.

krächzen ['krɛçtsən] v/t. and v/i. (ge-, h) croak.

Kraft [kraft] f (-/⸚e) strength; force (a. ⚔); power (a. ♀, ⊕); energy; vigo(u)r; efficacy; in ~ sein (setzen, treten) be in (put into, come into) operation or force; außer ~ setzen repeal, abolish (law); **2.** 2 prp. (gen.) by virtue of; '**~anlage** ♂ f power plant; '**~brühe** f beef tea; '**~fahrer** m driver, motorist; '**~fahrzeug** n motor vehicle.

kräftig adj. ['krɛftiç] strong (a. fig.), powerful; fig. nutritious, rich; **~en** ['~gən] (ge-, h) **1.** v/t. strengthen; **2.** v/i. give strength.

'**kraft|los** adj. powerless; feeble; weak; '2**probe** f trial of strength; '2**rad** n motor cycle; '2**stoff** mot. m fuel; '2**voll** adj. powerful (a. fig.); '2**wagen** m motor vehicle; '2**werk** ♂ n power station.

Kragen ['kra:gən] m (-s/-) collar; '**~knopf** m collar-stud, Am. collar button.

Krähe orn. ['krɛ:ə] f (-/-n) crow; '2**n** v/i. (ge-, h) crow.

Kralle ['kralə] f (-/-n) claw (a. fig.); talon, clutch.

Kram [kra:m] m (-[e]s/no pl.) stuff, odds and ends pl.; fig. affairs pl., business.

Krämer ['krɛ:mər] m (-s/-) shopkeeper.

Krampf [krampf] *m* (-[e]s/ᵘe) cramp; spasm, convulsion; '**~ader** *f* varicose vein; '**2haft** *adj.* spasmodic, convulsive; *laugh*: forced.

Kran ⊕ [krɑːn] *m* (-[e]s/ᵘe, -e) crane.

krank *adj.* [kraŋk] sick; *organ, etc.*: diseased; ~ *sein p.* be ill, *esp. Am.* be sick; *animal*: be sick or ill; ~ *werden p.* fall ill *or esp. Am.* sick; *animal*: fall sick; '2e *m, f* (-n/-n) sick person, patient, invalid.

kränkeln ['krɛŋkəln] *v/i.* (ge-, h) be sickly, be in poor health.

'kranken *fig. v/i.* (ge-, h) suffer (*an dat.* from).

kränken ['krɛŋkən] *v/t.* (ge-, h) offend, injure; wound *or* hurt *s.o.'s* feelings; *sich* ~ feel hurt (*über acc.* at, about).

'Kranken|bett *n* sick-bed; '**~geld** *n* sick-benefit; '**~haus** *n* hospital; '**~kasse** *f* health insurance (fund); '**~kost** *f* invalid diet; '**~lager** *n s. Krankenbett*; '**~pflege** *f* nursing; '**~pfleger** *m* male nurse; '**~schein** *m* medical certificate; '**~schwester** *f* (sick-)nurse; '**~versicherung** *f* health *or* sickness insurance; '**~wagen** *m* ambulance; '**~zimmer** *n* sick-room.

'krank|haft *adj.* morbid, pathological; '**2heit** *f* (-/-en) illness, sickness; disease.

'Krankheits|erreger 𝄞 *m* pathogenic agent; '**~erscheinung** *f* symptom (*a. fig.*).

'kränklich *adj.* sickly, ailing.

'Kränkung *f* (-/-en) insult, offen|ce, *Am.* -se.

Kranz [krants] *m* (-es/ᵘe) wreath; garland.

Kränzchen *fig.* ['krɛntsçən] *n* (-s/-) tea-party, F hen-party.

kraß *adj.* [kras] crass, gross.

kratzen ['kratsən] (ge-, h) **1.** *v/i.* scratch; **2.** *v/t.* scratch; *sich* ~ scratch (o.s.).

kraulen ['kraulən] (ge-) **1.** *v/t.* (h) scratch gently; **2.** *v/i.* (sein) *sports*: crawl.

kraus *adj.* [kraus] curly, curled; crisp; frizzy; *die Stirn* ~ *ziehen* knit one's brow; '2e *f* (-/-n) ruff(le), frill.

kräuseln ['krɔyzəln] *v/t.* (ge-, h) curl, crimp 〈*hair, etc.*〉; pucker 〈*lips*〉; *sich* ~ *hair*: curl; *waves, etc.*: ruffle; *smoke*: curl *or* wreath up.

Kraut 🌿 [kraut] *n* **1.** (-[e]s/ᵘer) plant; herb; **2.** (-[e]s/*no pl.*) tops *pl.*; cabbage; weed.

Krawall [kra'val] *m* (-[e]s/-e) riot; shindy, F row, *sl.* rumpus.

Krawatte [kra'vatə] *f* (-/-n) (neck-)tie.

Kreatur [krea'tuːr] *f* (-/-en) creature.

Krebs [kreːps] *m* (-es/-e) *zo.* crayfish, *Am. a.* crawfish; *ast.* Cancer, Crab; 𝄞 cancer; ~e *pl.* † returns *pl.*

Kredit † [kre'diːt] *m* (-[e]s/-e) credit; *auf* ~ on credit; **2fähig** † *adj.* credit-worthy.

Kreide ['kraɪdə] *f* (-/-n) chalk; *paint.* crayon.

Kreis [kraɪs] *m* (-es/-e) circle (*a. fig.*); *ast.* orbit; 𝄞 circuit; district, *Am.* county; *fig.*: sphere, field; range.

kreischen ['kraɪʃən] (ge-, h) **1.** *v/i.* screech, scream; squeal, shriek; *circular saw, etc.*: grate (on the ear); **2.** *v/t.* shriek, screech (*insult, etc.*).

Kreisel ['kraɪzəl] *m* (-s/-) (whipping-)top; '**~kompaß** *m* gyro-compass.

kreisen ['kraɪzən] *v/i.* (ge-, h) (move in a) circle; revolve, rotate; 𝄞 *bird*: circle; *bird*: wheel; *blood, money*: circulate.

kreis|förmig *adj.* ['kraɪsfœrmiç] circular; '**2lauf** *m physiol., money, etc.*: circulation; *business, trade*: cycle; '**2laufstörungen** 𝄞 *f/pl.* circulatory trouble; '**~rund** *adj.* circular; '**2säge** ⊕ *f* circular saw, *Am. a.* buzz saw; '**2verkehr** *m* roundabout (traffic).

Krempe ['krɛmpə] *f* (-/-n) brim (*of hat*).

Krempel F ['krɛmpəl] *m* (-s/*no pl.*) rubbish, stuff, lumber.

krepieren [kre'piːrən] *v/i.* (*no* -ge-, sein) *shell*: burst, explode; *sl.* kick the bucket, peg *or* snuff out; *animal*: die, perish.

Krepp [krɛp] *m* (-s/-s, -e) crêpe; crape; '**~apier** ['krɛppapiːr] *n* crêpe paper; '**~sohle** *f* crêpe(-rubber) sole.

Kreuz [krɔyts] **1.** *n* (-es/-e) cross (*a. fig.*); crucifix; *anat.* small of the back; 𝄞 sacral region; *cards*: club(s *pl.*); ♪ sharp; *zu* ~e *kriechen* eat humble pie; **2.** **2** *adv.*: ~ *und quer* in all directions; criss-cross.

'kreuzen (ge-, h) **1.** *v/t.* cross, fold 〈*arms, etc.*〉; ♀, *zo.* cross(-breed), hybridize; *sich* ~ *roads*: cross, intersect; *plans, etc.*: clash; **2.** ⚓ *v/i.* cruise.

'Kreuzer ⚓ *m* (-s/-) cruiser.

'Kreuz|fahrer *hist. m* crusader; '**~fahrt** *f hist.* crusade; ⚓ cruise; '**~feuer** *n* ⚔ cross-fire (*a. fig.*); **2igen** ['~igən] *v/t.* (ge-, h) crucify; **~igung** ['~iguŋ] *f* (-/-en) crucifixion; '**~otter** *zo. f* common viper; '**~ritter** *hist. m* knight of the Cross; '**~schmerzen** *m/pl.* back ache; '**~spinne** *zo. f* garden- *or* cross-spider; '**~ung** *f* (-/-en) 🐞, roads, *etc.*: crossing, intersection; *roads*: crossroads; ♀, *zo.* cross-breeding, hybridization; '**~verhör** 🏛 *n* cross-examination; *ins* ~ *nehmen* cross-examine; '2weise *adv.* crosswise, crossways; '**wortträtsel** *n* crossword (puzzle); '**zug** *hist. m* crusade.

kriech|en ['kri:çən] *v/i.* (*irr.*, *ge-*, *sein*) creep, crawl; *fig.* cringe (*vor dat.* to, before); '2**er** *contp. m* (*-s/-*) toady; 2**erei** *contp.* ['raɪ] *f* (*-/-en*) toadyism.

Krieg [kri:k] *m* (*-[e]s/-e*) war; *im* at war; *s.* **führen.**

kriegen F ['kri:gən] *v/t.* (*ge-*, *h*) catch, seize; get.

Krieg|er ['kri:gər] *m* (*-s/-*) warrior; '**erdenkmal** *n* war memorial; '2**erisch** *adj.* warlike; militant; '2**führend** *adj.* belligerent; '**führung** *f* warfare.

'**Kriegs|beil** *fig. n*: *das* *begraben* bury the hatchet; 2**beschädigt** *adj.* ['bəʃɛ:diçt] war-disabled; '**beschädigte** *m* (*-n/-n*) disabled ex-serviceman; '**dienst** ✗ *m* war service; '**dienstverweigerer** ✗ *m* (*-s/-*) conscientious objector; '**erklärung** *f* declaration of war; '**flotte** *f* naval force; '**gefangene** *m* prisoner of war; '**gefangenschaft** ✗ *f* captivity; '**gericht** 🕮 *n* court martial; '**gewinnler** ['gəvinlər] *m* (*-s/-*) war profiteer; '**hafen** *m* naval port; '**kamerad** *m* wartime comrade; '**list** *f* stratagem; '**macht** *f* military forces *pl.*; '**minister** *hist. m* minister of war; Secretary of State for War, *Am.* Secretary of War; '**ministerium** *hist. n* ministry of war; War Office, *Am.* War Department; '**rat** *m* council of war; '**schauplatz** ✗ *m* theat|re *or Am.* -er of war; '**schiff** *n* warship; '**schule** *f* military academy; '**teilnehmer** *m* combatant; ex-serviceman, *Am.* veteran; '**treiber** *m* (*-s/-*) warmonger; '**verbrecher** *m* war criminal; '**zug** *m* (military) expedition, campaign.

Kriminal|beamte [krimi'na:l-] *m* criminal investigator, *Am.* plainclothes man; '**film** *n* crime film; thriller; '**polizei** *f* criminal investigation department; '**roman** *m* detective *or* crime novel, thriller, *sl.* whodun(n)it.

kriminell *adj.* [krimi'nɛl] criminal; 2**e** *m* (*-n/-n*) criminal.

Krippe ['kripə] *f* (*-/-n*) crib, manger; crèche.

Krise ['kri:zə] *f* (*-/-n*) crisis.

Kristall [kris'tal] **1.** *m* (*-s/-e*) crystal; **2.** *n* (*-s/no pl.*) crystal(-glass); 2**isieren** [i'zi:rən] *v/i.* and *v/refl.* (*no -ge-*, *h*) crystallize.

Kriti|k [kri'ti:k] *f* (*-/-en*) criticism; ♪, *thea.*, *etc.*: review, criticism; F *unter aller* beneath contempt; *üben an* (*dat.*) *s.* **kritisieren;** **ker** ['kri:tikər] *m* (*-s/-*) critic; *books:* reviewer; 2**sch** *adj.* ['kri:tiʃ] critical (*gegenüber of*); 2**sieren** [kriti'zi:rən] *v/t.* (*no -ge-*, *h*) criticize; review (*book*).

kritt|eln ['kritəln] *v/t.* (*ge-*, *h*) find fault (*an dat.* with), cavil (at); 2**ler** ['lər] *m* (*-s/-*) fault-finder, caviller.

Kritzel|ei [kritsə'laɪ] *f* (*-/-en*) scrawl(ing), scribble, scribbling; '2**n** *v/t.* and *v/i.* (*ge-*, *h*) scrawl, scribble.

kroch [krɔx] *pret. of* **kriechen.**

Krokodil *zo.* [kroko'di:l] *n* (*-s/-e*) crocodile.

Krone ['kro:nə] *f* (*-/-n*) crown; coronet (*of duke, earl, etc.*).

krönen ['krø:nən] *v/t.* (*ge-*, *h*) crown (*zum König king*) (*a. fig.*).

'**Kron|leuchter** *m* chandelier; lust|re, *Am.* -er; electrolier; '**prinz** *m* crown prince; '**prinzessin** *f* crown princess.

'**Krönung** *f* (*-/-en*) coronation, crowning; *fig.* climax, culmination.

'**Kronzeuge** 🕮 *m* chief witness; King's evidence, *Am.* State's evidence.

Kropf 𝓢 [krɔpf] goit|re, *Am.* -er.

Kröte *zo.* ['krø:tə] *f* (*-/-n*) toad.

Krücke ['krykə] *f* (*-/-n*) crutch.

Krug [kru:k] *m* (*-[e]s/-e*) jug, pitcher; jar; mug; tankard.

Krume ['kru:mə] *f* (*-/-n*) crumb; ♪ topsoil.

Krümel ['kry:məl] *m* (*-s/-*) small crumb; '2**n** *v/t.* and *v/i.* (*ge-*, *h*) crumble.

krumm *adj.* [krum] *p.* bent, stooping; *limb, nose, etc.*: crooked; *spine*: curved; *deal, business, etc.*: crooked; '**beinig** *adj.* bandy- *or* bow-legged.

krümmen ['krymən] *v/t.* (*ge-*, *h*) bend (*arm, back, etc.*); crook (*finger, etc.*); curve (*metal sheet, etc.*); *sich* *person, snake, etc.*: writhe; *worm, etc.*: wriggle; *sich vor Schmerzen* writhe with pain; *sich vor Lachen* be convulsed with laughter.

'**Krümmung** *f* (*-/-en*) *road, etc.*: bend; *arch, road, etc.*: curve; *river, path, etc.*: turn, wind, meander; *earth's surface, spine, etc.*: curvature.

Krüppel ['krypəl] *m* (*-s/-*) cripple.

Kruste ['krustə] *f* (*-/-n*) crust.

Kübel ['ky:bəl] *m* (*-s/-*) tub; pail, bucket.

Kubik|meter [ku'bi:k-] *n*, *m* cubic met|re, *Am.* -er; **wurzel** 𝒜 *f* cube root.

Küche ['kyçə] *f* (*-/-n*) kitchen; cuisine, cookery; *s.* **kalt.**

Kuchen ['ku:xən] *m* (*-s/-*) cake, flan; pastry.

'**Küchen|gerät** *n*, '**geschirr** *n* kitchen utensils *pl.*; '**herd** *m* (kitchen-)range; cooker, stove; '**schrank** *m* kitchen cupboard *or* cabinet; '∼zettel *m* bill of fare, menu.

Kuckuck *orn.* ['kukuk] *m* (-s/-e) cuckoo.

Kufe ['ku:fə] *f* (-/-n) 🛷 skid; *sleigh, etc.*: runner.

Küfer ['ky:fər] *m* (-s/-) cooper; cellarman.

Kugel ['ku:gəl] *f* (-/-n) ball; ✕ bullet; 𝔸, *geogr.* sphere; *sports*: shot, weight; 2**förmig** *adj.* ['∼fœrmiç] spherical, ball-shaped, globular; '∼**gelenk** ⊕, *anat. n* ball-and-socket joint; '∼**lager** ⊕ *n* ball-bearing; '2**n** (ge-) **1.** *v/i.* (sein) *ball, etc.*: roll; **2.** *v/t.* (h) roll (*ball, etc.*); *sich* ∼ *children, etc.*: roll about; F double up (vor with *laughter*); '∼**schreiber** *m* ball(-point)-pen; '∼**stoßen** *n* (-s/no *pl.*) *sports*: putting the shot *or* weight.

Kuh *zo.* [ku:] *f* (-/∺e) cow.

kühl *adj.* [ky:l] cool (*a. fig.*); '2**anlage** *f* cold-storage plant; '2**e** *f* (-/*no pl.*) cool(ness); '∼**en** *v/t.* (ge-, h) cool (*wine, wound, etc.*); chill (*wine, etc.*); '2**er** *mot. m* (-s/-) radiator; '2**raum** *m* cold-storage chamber; '2**schrank** *m* refrigerator, F fridge.

kühn *adj.* [ky:n] bold (*a. fig.*), daring; audacious.

'**Kuhstall** *m* cow-house, byre, *Am. a.* cow barn.

Küken *orn.* ['ky:kən] *n* (-s/-) chick.

kulant † *adj.* [ku'lant] *firm, etc.*: accommodating, obliging; *price, terms, etc.*: fair, easy.

Kulisse [ku'lisə] *f* (-/-n) *thea.* wing, side-scene; *fig.* front; ∼*n pl. a.* scenery; *hinter den* ∼*n* behind the scenes.

Kult [kult] *m* (-[e]s/-e) cult, worship.

kultivieren [kulti'vi:rən] *v/t.* (*no* -ge-, h) cultivate (*a. fig.*).

Kultur [kul'tu:r] *f* (-/-en) 🌱 cultivation; *fig.*: culture; civilization; 2**ell** *adj.* [∼u'rel] cultural; ∼**film** [∼'tu:r-] *m* educational film; ∼**geschichte** *f* history of civilization; ∼**volk** *n* civilized people.

Kultus ['kultus] *m* (-/*Kulte*) *s.* Kult; '∼**minister** *m* minister of education and cultural affairs; '∼**ministerium** *n* ministry of education and cultural affairs.

Kummer ['kumər] *m* (-s/*no pl.*) grief, sorrow; trouble, worry.

kümmer|lich *adj.* ['kymərliç] *life, etc.*: miserable, wretched; *conditions, etc.*: pitiful, pitiable; *result, etc.*: poor; *resources*: scanty; '∼**n** *v/t.* (ge-, h): *es kümmert mich* I bother, I worry; *sich* ∼ *um* look after, take care of; see to; meddle with.

'**kummervoll** *adj.* sorrowful.

Kump|an F [kum'pɑ:n] *m* (-s/-e) companion; F mate, chum, *Am.* F *a.*

buddy; ∼**el** ['∼pəl] *m* (-s/-, F -s) 🛠 pitman, collier; F work-mate; F *s. Kumpan.*

Kunde ['kundə] **1.** *m* (-n/-n) customer, client; **2.** *f* (-/-n) knowledge.

Kundgebung ['kunt-] *f* (-/-en) manifestation; *pol.* rally.

kündig|en ['kyndigən] (ge-, h) **1.** *v/i.*: *j-m* ∼ give s.o. notice; **2.** *v/t.* † call in (*capital*); ⚖️ cancel (*contract*); *pol.* denounce (*treaty*); '2**ung** *f* (-/-en) notice; † calling in; ⚖️ cancellation; *pol.* denunciation.

'**Kundschaft** *f* (-/-en) customers *pl.*, clients *pl.*; custom, clientele; ✕ *m* (-s/-) scout; spy.

künftig ['kynftiç] **1.** *adj.* *event, years, etc.*: future; *event, programme, etc.*: coming; *life, world, etc.*: next; **2.** *adv.* in future, from now on.

Kunst [kunst] *f* (-/∺e) art; skill; '∼**akademie** *f* academy of arts; '∼**ausstellung** *f* art exhibition; '∼**druck** *m* art print(ing); '∼**dünger** *m* artificial manure, fertilizer; 2**fertig** *adj.* skilful, skilled; '∼**fertigkeit** *f* artistic skill; '∼**gegenstand** *m* objet d'art; 2**gerecht** *adj.* skilful; professional; expert; '∼**geschichte** *f* history of art; '∼**gewerbe** *n* arts and crafts *pl.*; applied arts *pl.*; '∼**glied** *n* artificial limb; '∼**griff** *m* trick, dodge; artifice, knack; '∼**händler** *m* art-dealer; '∼**kenner** *m* connoisseur of *or* in art; '∼**leder** *n* imitation *or* artificial leather.

Künstler ['kynstlər] *m* (-s/-) artist; ♪, *thea.* performer; '2**isch** *adj.* artistic.

künstlich *adj.* ['kynstliç] *eye, flower, light, etc.*: artificial; *teeth, hair, etc.*: false; *fibres, dyes, etc.*: synthetic.

'**Kunst|liebhaber** *m* art-lover; '∼**maler** *m* artist, painter; '∼**reiter** *m* equestrian; circus-rider; ∼**schätze** ['∼ʃetsə] *m/pl.* art treasures *pl.*; '∼**seide** *f* artificial silk, rayon; '∼**stück** *n* feat, trick, F stunt; '∼**tischler** *m* cabinet-maker; '∼**verlag** *m* art publishers *pl.*; '2**voll** *adj.* artistic, elaborate; '∼**werk** *n* work of art.

kunterbunt F *fig. adj.* ['kuntər-] higgledy-piggledy.

Kupfer ['kupfər] *n* (-s/*no pl.*) copper; '∼**geld** *n* copper coins *pl.*, F coppers *pl.*; '2**n** *adj.* (of) copper; '2**rot** *adj.* copper-colo(u)red; '∼**stich** *m* copper-plate engraving.

Kupon [ku'põ:] *m* (-s/-s) *s.* Coupon.

Kuppe ['kupə] *f* (-/-n) rounded hilltop; *nail*: head.

Kuppel 🔺 ['kupəl] *f* (-/-n) dome, cupola; ∼**ei** ⚖️ [∼'lai] *f* (-/-en) procuring; '2**n** (ge-, h) **1.** *v/t. s.* koppeln; **2.** *mot. v/i.* declutch.

Kuppl|er ['kuplər] *m* (-s/-) pimp, procurer; '∼**ung** *f* (-/-en) ⊕ coupling (*a.* 🚂); *mot.* clutch.

Kur [kuːr] *f* (-/-en) course of treatment, cure.

Kür [kyːr] *f* (-/-en) *sports*: s. *Kürlauf*; voluntary exercise.

Kuratorium [kura'toːrium] *n* (-s/ *Kuratorien*) board of trustees.

Kurbel ⊕ ['kurbəl] *f* (-/-n) crank, winch, handle; '**2n** *v/t.* (ge-, h) **1.** *v/t.* shoot (*film*); *in die Höhe* ~ winch up (*load*, *etc.*); wind up (*car window*, *etc.*); **2.** *v/i.* crank.

Kürbis ♀ ['kyrbis] *m* (-ses/-se) pumpkin.

'**Kur|gast** *m* visitor to *or* patient at a health resort *or* spa; '**~haus** *n* spa hotel.

Kurier [ku'riːr] *m* (-s/-e) courier, express (messenger).

kurieren ♣ [ku'riːrən] *v/t.* (no -ge-, h) cure.

kurios *adj.* [kur'joːs] curious, odd, strange, queer.   [skating.\

'**Kürlauf** *m sports*: free (roller)

'**Kur|ort** *m* health resort; spa; '**~pfuscher** *m* quack (doctor); '**~pfusche'rei** *f* (-/-en) quackery.

Kurs [kurs] *m* (-es/-e) ✝ currency; ✝ rate, price; ⚓ *and fig.* course; course, class; '**~bericht** ✝ *m* market-report; '**~buch** 🕮 *n* railway guide, *Am.* railroad guide.

Kürschner ['kyrʃnər] *m* (-s/-) furrier.

kursieren [kur'ziːrən] *v/i.* (no -ge-, h) *money*, *etc.*: circulate, be in circulation; *rumour*, *etc.*: circulate, be afloat, go about.

Kursivschrift *typ.* [kur'ziːf-] *f* italics *pl.*

Kursus ['kurzus] *m* (-/Kurse) course, class.

'**Kurs|verlust** ✝ *m* loss on the stock exchange; '**~wert** ✝ *m* market value; '**~zettel** ✝ *m* stock exchange list.

Kurve ['kurvə] *f* (-/-n) curve; *road*, *etc.*: *a.* bend, turn.

kurz [kurts] **1.** *adj. space*: short; *time*, *etc.*: short, brief; ~ *und bündig* brief, concise; ~*e Hose* shorts *pl.*; *mit* ~*en Worten* with a few words; *den kürzeren ziehen* get the worst of it; **2.** *adv.* in short; ~ *angebunden sein* be curt *or* sharp; ~ *und gut* in short, in a word; ~ *vor London* short of London; *sich* ~ *fassen* be brief *or* concise; *in* ~*em* before long, shortly; *vor* ~*em* a short time ago; *zu* ~ *kommen* come off badly, get a raw deal; *um es* ~ *zu sagen* to cut a long story short; '**2arbeit** ✝ *f* short-

time work; '**2arbeiter** ✝ *m* short-time worker; **~atmig** *adj.* ['~⁹aːtmiç] short-winded.

Kürze ['kyrtsə] *f* (-/no pl.) shortness; brevity; *in* ~ shortly, before long; '**2n** *v/t.* (ge-, h) shorten (*dress*, *etc.*) (*um by*); abridge, condense (*book*, *etc.*); cut, reduce (*expenses*, *etc.*).

'**kurz|er'hand** *adv.* without hesitation; on the spot; '**2film** *m* short (film); '**2form** *f* shortened form; '**~fristig** *adj.* short-term; ✝ *bill*, *etc.*: short-dated; '**2geschichte** *f* (short) short story; '**~lebig** *adj.* ['~leːbiç] short-lived; '**2nachrichten** *f/pl.* news summary.

kürzlich *adv.* ['kyrtsliç] lately, recently, not long ago.

'**Kurz|schluß** ⚡ *m* short circuit, F short; '**~schrift** *f* shorthand, stenography; '**2sichtig** *adj.* short-sighted, near-sighted; **2'um** *adv.* in short, in a word.

'**Kürzung** *f* (-/-en) shortening (*of dress*, *etc.*); abridg(e)ment, condensation (*of book*, *etc.*); cut, reduction (*of expenses*, *etc.*).

'**Kurz|waren** *f/pl.* haberdashery, *Am.* dry goods *pl.*, notions *pl.*; '**~weil** *f* (-/no pl.) amusement, entertainment; '**2weilig** *adj.* amusing, entertaining; '**~welle** ⚡ *f* short wave; *radio*: short-wave band.

Kusine [ku'ziːnə] *f* (-/-n) s. *Cousine*.

Kuß [kus] *m* (Kusses/Küsse) kiss; '**2echt** *adj.* kiss-proof.

küssen ['kysən] *v/t. and v/i.* (ge-, h) kiss.

'**kußfest** *adj.* s. *kußecht*.

Küste ['kystə] *f* (-/-n) coast; shore.

'**Küsten|bewohner** *m* inhabitant of a coastal region; '**~fischerei** *f* inshore fishery *or* fishing; '**~gebiet** *n* coastal area *or* region; '**~schiffahrt** *f* coastal shipping.

Küster *eccl.* ['kystər] *m* (-s/-) verger, sexton, sacristan.

Kutsch|bock ['kutʃ-] *m* coach-box; '**~e** *f* (-/-n) carriage, coach; '**~enschlag** *m* carriage-door, coach-door; '**~er** *m* (-s/-) coachman; **2ieren** [~'tʃiːrən] (no -ge-) **1.** *v/t.* (h) drive *s.o.* in a coach; **2.** *v/i.* (h) (drive a) coach; **3.** *v/i.* (sein) (drive *or* ride in a) coach.

Kutte ['kutə] *f* (-/-n) cowl.

Kutter ⚓ ['kutər] *m* (-s/-) cutter.

Kuvert [ku'vert; ku'veːr] *n* (-[e]s/-e; -s/-s) envelope; *at table*: cover.

Kux ⚒ [kuks] *m* (-es/-e) mining share.

L

Lab zo. [lɑːp] n (-[e]s/-e) rennet.
labil adj. [la'biːl] unstable (a. ⊕, 📚); phys., 🔬 labile.
Labor [la'boːr] n (-s/-s, -e) s. Laboratorium; **~ant** [labo'rant] m (-en/-en) laboratory assistant; **~atorium** [labora'toːrjum] n (-s/ Laboratorien) laboratory; **2ieren** [ˌoˈriːrən] v/i. (no -ge-, h): ~ an (dat.) labo(u)r under, suffer from.
Labyrinth [laby'rint] n (-[e]s/-e) labyrinth, maze.
Lache ['laxə] f (-/-n) pool, puddle.
lächeln ['lɛçəln] 1. v/i. (ge-, h) smile (über acc. at); höhnisch ~ sneer (über acc. at); 2. 2 n (-s/no pl.) smile; höhnisches ~ sneer.
lachen ['laxən] 1. v/i. (ge-, h) laugh (über acc. at); 2. 2 n (-s/no pl.) laugh(ter).
lächerlich adj. ['lɛçərlɪç] ridiculous, laughable, ludicrous; absurd; derisory, scoffing; ~ machen ridicule; sich ~ machen make a fool of o.s.
Lachs ichth. [laks] m (-es/-e) salmon.
Lack [lak] m (-[e]s/-e) (gum-)lac; varnish; lacquer, enamel; 2ieren [la'kiːrən] v/t. (no -ge-, h) lacquer, varnish, enamel; **~leder** n patent leather; **~schuhe** m/pl. patent leather shoes pl., F patents pl.
Lade|fähigkeit ['lɑːdə-] f loading capacity; **~fläche** f loading area; **~hemmung** ✗ f jam, stoppage; **~linie** ⚓ f load-line.
laden¹ ['lɑːdən] v/t. (irr., ge-, h) load; load (gun), charge (a. 🔌); freight, ship; 🏛️ cite, summon; invite, ask (guest).
Laden² [ˌ] m (-s/≈) shop, Am. store; shutter; **~besitzer** m s. Ladeninhaber; **~dieb** m shop-lifter; **~diebstahl** m shop-lifting; **~hüter** m drug on the market; **~inhaber** m shopkeeper, Am. storekeeper; **~kasse** f till; **~preis** m selling-price, retail price; **~schild** n shopsign; **~schluß** m closing time; nach ~ after hours; **~tisch** m counter.
Lade|platz m loading-place; **~rampe** f loading platform or ramp; **~raum** m loading space; ⚓ hold; **~schein** ⚓ m bill of lading.
Ladung f (-/-en) loading; load, freight; ⚓ cargo; 🔌 charge (a. of gun); 🏛️ summons.
lag [lɑːk] pret. of liegen.
Lage ['lɑːgə] f (-/-n) situation, position; site, location (of building); state, condition; attitude; geol. layer, stratum; round (of beer, etc.); in der ~ sein zu inf. be able to inf., be in a position to inf.; versetzen

Sie sich in meine ~ put yourself in my place.
Lager ['lɑːgər] n (-s/-) couch, bed; den, lair (of wild animals); geol. deposit; ⊕ bearing; warehouse, storehouse, depot; store, stock (✝ pl. a. Läger); ✗, etc.: camp, encampment; auf ~ ✝ on hand, in stock; **~buch** n stock-book; **~feuer** n camp-fire; **~geld** n storage; **~haus** n warehouse; 2n (ge-, h) 1. v/i. lie down, rest; ✗ (en)camp; ✝ be stored; 2. v/t. lay down; ✗ (en)camp; ✝ store, warehouse; sich ~ lie down, rest; **~platz** m ✝ depot; resting-place; ✗, etc.: camp-site; **~raum** m store-room; **~ung** f (-/-en) storage (of goods).
Lagune [la'guːnə] f (-/-n) lagoon.
lahm adj. [lɑːm] lame; **~en** v/i. (ge-, h) be lame.
lähmen ['lɛːmən] v/t. (ge-, h) (make) lame; paraly|se, Am. -ze (a. fig.).
lahmlegen v/t. (sep., -ge-, h) paraly|se, Am. -ze; obstruct.
Lähmung 🩺 f (-/-en) paralysis.
Laib [laɪp] m (-[e]s/-e) loaf.
Laich [laɪç] m (-[e]s/-e) spawn; 2en v/i. (ge-, h) spawn.
Laie ['laɪə] m (-n/-n) layman; amateur; **~nbühne** f amateur theat|re, Am. -er.
Lakai [la'kaɪ] m (-en/-en) lackey (a. fig.), footman.
Lake ['lɑːkə] f (-/-n) brine, pickle.
Laken ['lɑːkən] n (-s/-) sheet.
lallen ['lalən] v/i. and v/t. (ge-, h) stammer; babble.
Lamelle [la'mɛlə] f (-/-n) lamella, lamina; ♦ gill (of mushrooms).
lamentieren [lamɛn'tiːrən] v/i. (no -ge-, h) lament (um for; über acc. over).
Lamm zo. [lam] n (-[e]s/ⁿer) lamb; **~fell** n lambskin; 2fromm adj. (as) gentle or (as) meek as a lamb.
Lampe ['lampə] f (-/-n) lamp.
Lampen|fieber n stage fright; **~licht** n lamplight; **~schirm** m lamp-shade.
Lampion [lãˈpjõː] m, n (-s/-s) Chinese lantern.
Land [lant] n (-[e]s/ⁿer, poet. -e) land; country; territory; ground, soil; an ~ gehen go ashore; auf dem ~e in the country; aufs ~ gehen go into the country; außer ~es gehen go abroad; zu ~e by land; **~arbeiter** m farm-hand; **~besitz** m landed property; 🏛️ real estate; **~besitzer** m landowner, landed proprietor; **~bevölkerung** f rural population.
Lande|bahn 🛬 ['landə-] f runway; **~deck** 🛬 n flight-deck.

land'einwärts adv. upcountry, inland.

landen ['landən] (ge-) **1.** v/i. (sein) land; **2.** v/t. (h) ♨ disembark (troups); ✈ land, set down (troups).

'Landenge f neck of land, isthmus.

Landeplatz ✈ ['landə-] m landing-field.

Ländereien [lendə'raiən] pl. landed property, lands pl., estates pl.

Länderspiel ['lendər-] n sports: international match.

Landes|grenze ['landəs-] f frontier, boundary; '**~innere** n interior, inland, upcountry; '**~kirche** f national church; Brt. Established Church; '**~regierung** f government; in Germany: Land government; '**~sprache** f native language, vernacular; **2üblich** adj. customary; '**~verrat** m treason; '**~verräter** m traitor to his country; '**~verteidigung** f national defen|ce, Am. -se.

'Land|flucht f rural exodus; '**~friedensbruch** ꞃ♎ m breach of the public peace; '**~gericht** n appr. district court; '**~gewinnung** f (-/-en) reclamation of land; '**~gut** n country-seat, estate; '**~haus** n country-house, cottage; '**~karte** f map; '**~kreis** m rural district; **2läufig** adj. ['~ɔyfiç] customary, current, common.

ländlich adj. ['lentliç] rural, rustic.

'Land|maschinen f/pl. agricultural or farm equipment; '**~partie** f picnic, outing, excursion into the country; '**~plage** iro. f nuisance; '**~rat** m (-[e]s/⁓e) appr. district president; '**~ratte** ♨ f landlubber; '**~recht** n common law; '**~regen** m persistent rain.

'Landschaft f (-/-en) province, district, region; countryside, scenery; esp. paint. landscape; **2lich** adj. provincial; scenic (beauty, etc.).

'Landsmann m (-[e]s/Landsleute) (fellow-)countryman, compatriot; was sind Sie für ein ~? what's your native country?

'Land|straße f highway, high road; '**~streicher** m (-s/-) vagabond, tramp, Am. sl. hobo; '**~streitkräfte** f/pl. land forces pl., the Army; ground forces pl.; '**~strich** m tract of land, region; '**~tag** m Landtag, Land parliament.

Landung ['landuŋ] f (-/-en) ♨, ✈ landing; disembarkation; arrival; '**~sbrücke** ♨ f floating: landing-stage; pier; '**~ssteg** ♨ m gangway, gang-plank.

'Land|vermesser m (-s/-) surveyor; '**~vermessung** f land-surveying; **2wärts** adv. ['~verts] landward(s); '**~weg** m: auf dem ~e by land; '**~wirt** m farmer, agriculturist; '**~wirtschaft** f agriculture, farming; **2wirtschaftlich** adj. agri-

cultural; **~e** Maschinen f/pl. s. Landmaschinen; '**~zunge** f spit.

lang [laŋ] **1.** adj. long; p. tall; er machte ein ~es Gesicht his face fell; **2.** adv. long; e-e Woche ~ for a week; über kurz oder ~ sooner or later; **~**(e) anhaltend continuous; **~**(e) entbehrt long-missed; **~**(e) ersehnt long-wished-for; das ist schon **~**(e) her that was a long time ago; **~** und breit at (full or great) length; noch **~**(e) nicht not for a long time yet; far from ger.; wie **~e** lernen Sie schon Englisch? how long have you been learning English?; **~atmig** adj. ['~ɑːtmiç] long-winded; '**~e** adv. s. lang 2.

Länge ['leŋə] f (-/-n) length; tallness; geogr., ast. longitude; der ~ nach (at) full length, lengthwise.

langen ['laŋən] v/i. (ge-, h) suffice, be enough; ~ nach reach for.

'Längen|grad m degree of longitude; '**~maß** n linear measure.

'länger 1. adj. longer; **~e** Zeit (for) some time; **2.** adv. longer; ich kann es nicht ~ ertragen I cannot bear it any longer; je ~, je lieber the longer the better.

'Langeweile ['(-, Langenweile/no pl.) boredom, tediousness, ennui.

'lang|fristig adj. long-term; '**~jährig** adj. of long standing; **~e** Erfahrung (many) years of experience; **2lauf** m skiing: cross-country run or race.

'länglich adj. longish, oblong.

'Langmut f (-/no pl.) patience, forbearance.

längs [leŋs] **1.** prp. (gen., dat.) along(side of); ~ der Küste fahren ♨ (sail along the) coast; **2.** adv. lengthwise; '**2achse** f longitudinal axis.

'lang|sam adj. slow; **2schläfer** ['~ʃɛːfər] m (-s/-) late riser, lie-abed; '**2spielplatte** f long-playing record.

längst adv. [leŋst] long ago or since; ich weiß es ~ I have known it for a long time; '**~ens** adv. at the longest; at the latest; at the most.

'lang|stielig adj. long-handled; '**2-streckenlauf** m long-distance run or race; **2weile** f (-, Langenweile/no pl.) s. Langeweile; '**~weilen** v/t. (ge-, h) bore; sich ~ be bored; '**~weilig** adj. tedious, boring, dull; **~e** Person bore; '**2welle** f ♉ long wave; radio: long wave band; **~wierig** adj. ['~viːriç] protracted, lengthy; ♙ lingering.

Lanze ['lantsə] f (-/-n) spear, lance.

Lappalie [la'paːljə] f (-/-n) trifle.

Lapp|en ['lapən] m (-s/-) patch; rag; duster; (dish- or floor-)cloth; anat., ♉ lobe; **2ig** adj. flabby.

läppisch adj. ['lepiʃ] foolish, silly.

Lärche ♀ ['lɛrçə] f (-/-n) larch.

Lärm [lɛrm] m (-[e]s/no pl.) noise; din; ~ schlagen give the alarm; '2en v/i. (ge-, h) make a noise; '2end adj. noisy.

Larve ['larfə] f (-/-n) mask; face (often iro.); zo. larva, grub.

las [lɑːs] pret. of lesen.

lasch F adj. [laʃ] limp, lax.

Lasche ['laʃə] f (-/-n) strap; tongue (of shoe).

lassen ['lasən] (irr., h) 1. v/t. (ge-) let; leave; laß das! don't!; laß das Weinen! stop crying!; ich kann es nicht ~ I cannot help (doing) it; sein Leben ~ für sacrifice one's life for; 2. v/i. (ge-): von et. ~ desist from s.th., renounce s.th.; do without s.th.; 3. v/aux. (no -ge-) allow, permit, let; make, cause; drucken ~ have s.th. printed; gehen ~ let s.o. go; ich habe ihn dieses Buch lesen ~ I have made him read this book; von sich hören ~ send word; er läßt sich nichts sagen he won't take advice; es läßt sich nicht leugnen there is no denying (the fact).

lässig adj. ['lɛsiç] indolent, idle; sluggish; careless.

Last [last] f (-/-en) load; burden; weight; cargo, freight; fig. weight, charge, trouble; zu ~en von ✝ to the debit of; j-m zur ~ fallen be a burden to s.o.; j-m et. zur ~ legen lay s.th. at s.o.'s door or to s.o.'s charge; '~auto n s. Lastkraftwagen.

'lasten v/i. (ge-, h): ~ auf (dat.) weigh or press (up)on; '2aufzug m goods lift, Am. freight elevator.

Laster ['lastər] n (-s/-) vice.

Lästerer ['lɛstərər] m (-s/-) slanderer, backbiter.

'lasterhaft adj. vicious; corrupt.

Läster|maul ['lɛstər-] n s. Lästerer; '2n v/i. (ge-, h) slander, calumniate, defame; abuse; '~ung f (-/-en) slander, calumny.

lästig adj. ['lɛstiç] troublesome; annoying; uncomfortable, inconvenient.

'Last|kahn m barge, lighter; '~kraftwagen m lorry, Am. truck; '~schrift ✝ f debit; '~tier n pack animal; '~wagen m s. Lastkraftwagen.

Latein [la'taɪn] n (-s/no pl.) Latin; 2isch adj. Latin.

Laterne [la'tɛrnə] f (-/-n) lantern; street-lamp; '~npfahl m lamp-post.

latschen F ['lɑːtʃən] v/i. (ge-, sein) shuffle (along).

Latte ['latə] f (-/-n) pale; lath; sports: bar; '~nkiste f crate; '~nverschlag m latticed partition; '~nzaun m paling, Am. picket fence.

Lätzchen ['lɛtsçən] n (-s/-) bib, feeder.

lau adj. [laʊ] tepid, lukewarm (a. fig.).

Laub [laʊp] n (-[e]s/no pl.) foliage, leaves pl.; '~baum m deciduous tree.

Laube ['laʊbə] f (-/-n) arbo(u)r, bower; '~ngang m arcade.

'Laub|frosch zo. m tree-frog; '~säge f fret-saw.

Lauch ♀ [laʊx] m (-[e]s/-e) leek.

Lauer ['laʊər] f (-/no pl.): auf der ~ liegen or sein lie in wait or ambush, be on the look-out; '2n v/i. (ge-, h) lurk (auf acc. for); ~ auf (acc.) watch for; '2nd adj. louring, lowering.

Lauf [laʊf] m (-[e]s/⸗e) run(ning); sports: a. run, heat; race; current (of water); course; barrel (of gun); ♪ run; im ~e der Zeit in (the) course of time; '~bahn f career; '~bursche m errand-boy, office-boy; '~disziplin f sports: running event.

'laufen (irr., ge-) 1. v/i. (sein) run; walk; flow; time: pass, go by, elapse; leak; die Dinge ~ lassen let things slide; j-n ~ lassen let s.o. go; 2. v/t. (sein, h) run; walk; '~d adj. running; current; regular; ~en Monats ✝ instant; auf dem ~en sein be up to date, be fully informed.

Läufer ['lɔyfər] m (-s/-) runner (a. carpet); chess: bishop; football: half-back.

'Lauf|masche f ladder, Am. a. run; '~paß F m sack, sl. walking papers pl.; '~planke ♣ f gang-board, gang-plank; '~schritt m: im ~ running; '~steg m footbridge; ♣ gangway.

Lauge ['laʊgə] f (-/-n) lye.

Laun|e ['laʊnə] f (-/-n) humo(u)r; mood; temper; caprice, fancy, whim; guter ~ in (high) spirits; '2enhaft adj. capricious; '2isch adj. moody; wayward.

Laus zo. [laʊs] f (-/⸗e) louse; '~bub ['~buːp] m (-en/-en) young scamp, F young devil, rascal.

lausch|en ['laʊʃən] v/i. (ge-, h) listen; eavesdrop; '~ig adj. snug, cosy; peaceful.

laut [laʊt] 1. adj. loud (a. fig.); noisy; 2. adv. aloud, loud(ly); (sprechen Sie) ~er! speak up!, Am. louder!; 3. prp. (gen., dat.) according to; ✝ as per; 4. 2 m (-[e]s/-e) sound; '2e ♪ f (-/-n) lute; '~en v/i. (ge-, h) sound; words, etc.: run; read; ~ auf (acc.) passport, etc.: be issued to.

läuten ['lɔytən] (ge-, h) 1. v/i. ring; toll; es läutet the bell is ringing; 2. v/t. ring; toll.

'lauter adj. pure; clear; genuine; sincere; mere, nothing but, only.

läuter|n ['lɔytərn] v/t. (ge-, h) purify; ⊕ cleanse; refine; '2ung f (-/-en) purification; refining.

'**laut|los** *adj.* noiseless; mute; silent; *silence*: hushed; '2**schrift** *f* phonetic transcription; '2**sprecher** *m* loud-speaker; '2**stärke** *f* sound intensity; *radio*: (sound-)volume; 2**stärkeregler** ['ˌrɛːɡlər] *m* (-s/-) volume control.

'**lauwarm** *adj.* tepid, lukewarm.

Lava *geol.* ['laːva] *f* (-/Laven) lava.

Lavendel ♀ [la'vɛndəl] *m* (-s/-) lavender.

lavieren [la'viːrən] *v/i.* (*no* -ge-, *h*, *sein*) ♣ tack (*a. fig.*).

Lawine [la'viːnə] *f* (-/-n) avalanche.

lax *adj.* [laks] lax, loose; *morals*: a. easy.

Lazarett [latsa'rɛt] *n* (-[e]s/-e) (military) hospital.

leben[1] ['leːbən] (ge-, *h*) 1. *v/i.* live; be alive; ~ *Sie wohl!* good-bye!, farewell!; *j-n hochleben lassen* cheer s.o.; *at table*: drink s.o.'s health; *von et.* ~ live on s.th.; *hier lebt es sich gut* it is pleasant living here; 2. *v/t.* live (*one's life*).

Leben[2] [~] *n* (-s/-) life; stir, animation, bustle; *am* ~ *bleiben* remain alive, survive; *am* ~ *erhalten* keep alive; *ein neues* ~ *beginnen* turn over a new leaf; *ins* ~ *rufen* call into being; *sein* ~ *aufs Spiel setzen* risk one's life; *sein* ~ *lang* all one's life; *ums* ~ *kommen* lose one's life; perish.

lebendig *adj.* [le'bɛndiç] living; *pred.*: alive; quick; lively.

'**Lebens|alter** *n* age; '~**anschauung** *f* outlook on life; '~**art** *f* manners *pl.*, behavio(u)r; '~**auffassung** *f* philosophy of life; '~**bedingungen** *f/pl.* living conditions *pl.*; '~**beschreibung** *f* life, biography; '~**dauer** *f* span of life; ⊕ durability; '2**echt** *adj.* true to life; '~**erfahrung** *f* experience of life; '2**fähig** *adj.* ♀ *and fig.* viable; '~**gefahr** *f* danger of life; ~**l** danger (of death)!; *unter* ~ *at the risk of one's life*; '2**gefährlich** *adj.* dangerous (to life), perilous; '~**gefährte** *m* life's companion; '~**größe** *f* life-size; *in* ~ at full length; '~**kraft** *f* vital power, vigo(u)r, vitality; '2**länglich** *adj.* for life, lifelong; '~**lauf** *m* course of life; personal record, curriculum vitae; '2**lustig** *adj.* gay, merry; '~**mittel** *pl.* food (-stuffs *pl.*), provisions *pl.*, groceries *pl.*; '2**müde** *adj.* weary *or* tired of life; '2**notwendig** *adj.* vital, essential; '~**retter** *m* life-saver, rescuer; '~**standard** *m* standard of living; '~**unterhalt** *m* livelihood; *s-n* ~ *verdienen* earn one's living; '~**versicherung** *f* life-insurance; '~**wandel** *m* life, (moral) conduct; '~**weise** *f* mode of living, habits *pl.*; *gesunde* ~ regimen; '~**weisheit** *f* worldly wisdom; '2**wichtig** *adj.* vital, essential; ~*e Organe pl.* vitals

pl.; '~**zeichen** *n* sign of life; '~**zeit** *f* lifetime; *auf* ~ for life.

Leber *anat.* ['leːbər] *f* (-/-n) liver; '~**fleck** *m* mole; '2**krank** *adj.*, '2**leidend** *adj.* suffering from a liver-complaint; '~**tran** *m* cod-liver oil; '~**wurst** *f* liver-sausage, *Am.* liverwurst.

'**Lebewesen** *n* living being, creature.

Lebe'wohl *n* (-[e]s/-e, -s) farewell.

leb|haft *adj.* ['leːphaft] lively; vivid; spirited; *interest*: keen; *traffic*: busy; '2**kuchen** *m* gingerbread; '~**los** *adj.* lifeless; '2**zeiten** *pl.*: *zu s-n* ~ in his lifetime.

lechzen ['lɛçtsən] *v/i.* (ge-, *h*): ~ *nach* languish *or* yearn *or* pant for.

Leck [lɛk] *n* (-[e]s/-s) leak; 2. ♀ *adj.* leaky; ~ *werden* ♣ spring a leak.

lecken ['lɛkən] (ge-, *h*) 1. *v/t.* lick; 2. *v/i.* lick; leak.

lecker *adj.* ['lɛkər] dainty; delicious; '2**bissen** *m* dainty, delicacy.

Leder ['leːdər] *n* (-s/-) leather; *in* ~ *gebunden* leather-bound; '2**n** *adj.* leathern, of leather.

ledig *adj.* ['leːdiç] single, unmarried; *child*: illegitimate; ~**lich** *adv.* ['~k-] solely, merely.

Lee ♣ [leː] *f* (-/*no pl.*) lee (side).

leer [leːr] 1. *adj.* empty; vacant; void; vain; blank; 2. *adv.*: ~ *laufen* ⊕ idle; '2**e** *f* (-/*no pl.*) emptiness, void (*a. fig.*); *phys.* vacuum; '~**en** *v/t.* (ge-, *h*) empty; clear (out); pour out; '2**gut** † *n* empties *pl.*; '2**lauf** *m* ⊕ idling; *mot.* neutral gear; *fig.* waste of energy; '~**stehend** *adj.* flat: empty, unoccupied, vacant.

legal *adj.* [le'gaːl] legal, lawful.

Legat [le'gaːt] 1. *m* (-en/-en) legate; 2. ‡ *n* (-[e]s/-e) legacy.

legen ['leːgən] (ge-, *h*) 1. *v/t.* lay; place; put; *sich* ~ *wind, etc.*: calm down, abate; cease; *Wert* ~ *auf* (*acc.*) attach importance to; 2. *v/i. hen*: lay.

Legende [le'gɛndə] *f* (-/-n) legend.

legieren [le'giːrən] *v/t.* (*no* -ge-, *h*) ⊕ alloy; *cookery*: thicken (*mit* with).

Legislative [leːgisla'tiːvə] *f* (-/-n) legislative body *or* power.

legitim *adj.* [legi'tiːm] legitimate; ~**ieren** [ˌi'miːrən] *v/t.* (*no* -ge-, *h*) legitimate; authorize; *sich* ~ prove one's identity.

Lehm [leːm] *m* (-[e]s/-e) loam; mud; '2**ig** *adj.* loamy.

Lehn|e [leːnə] *f* (-/-n) support; arm, back (*of chair*); '2**en** (ge-, *h*) 1. *v/i.* lean (*an dat.* against); 2. *v/t.* lean, rest (*an acc.*, *gegen* against); *sich* ~ *an* (*acc.*) lean against; *sich* ~ *auf* (*acc.*) rest *or* support o.s. (up-) on; *sich aus dem Fenster* ~ lean out of the window; '~**sessel** *m*, '~**stuhl** *m* armchair, easy chair.

Lehrbuch ['le:r-] n textbook.
Lehre ['le:rə] f (-/-n) rule, precept; doctrine; system; science; theory; lesson, warning; moral (of fable); instruction, tuition; ⊕ ga(u)ge; ⊕ pattern; in der ~ sein be apprenticed (bei to); in die ~ geben apprentice, article (both: bei, zu to); '2n v/t. (ge-. h) teach, instruct; show.
'Lehrer m (-s/-) teacher; master, instructor; '~in f (-/-nen) (lady) teacher; (school)mistress; '~kollegium n staff (of teachers).
'Lehr|fach n subject; '~film m instructional film; '~gang m course (of instruction); '~geld n premium; '~herr m master, sl. boss; '~jahre n/pl. (years pl. of) apprenticeship; '~junge m s. Lehrling; '~körper m univ. professoriate, faculty; '~kraft f teacher; professor; '~ling m (-s/-e) apprentice; '~mädchen n girl apprentice; '~meister m master; '~methode f method of teaching; '~plan m curriculum, syllabus; '2reich adj. instructive; '~satz m↯ theorem; doctrine; eccl. dogma; '~stoff m subject-matter, subject(s pl.); '~stuhl m professorship; '~vertrag m articles pl. of apprenticeship, indenture(s pl.); '~zeit f apprenticeship.
Leib [laip] m (-[e]s/-er) body; belly, anat. abdomen; womb; bei lebendigem ~e alive; mit ~ und Seele body and soul; sich j-n vom ~e halten keep s.o. at arm's length; '~arzt m physician in ordinary, personal physician; '~chen n (-s/-) bodice.
Leibeigen|e ['laip⁹aigənə] m (-n/-n) bond(s)man, serf; '~schaft f (-/no pl.) bondage, serfdom.
Leibes|erziehung ['laibəs-] f physical training; '~frucht f f(o)etus; '~kraft f: aus Leibeskräften pl. with all one's might; '~übung f bodily or physical exercise.
'Leib|garde f body-guard; '~gericht n favo(u)rite dish; 2haftig adj. [~'haftiç]: der ~e Teufel the devil incarnate; '2lich adj. bodily, corpor(e)al; '~rente f life-annuity; '~schmerzen m/pl. stomach-ache, belly-ache, ⅀ colic; '~wache f body-guard; '~wäsche f underwear.
Leiche ['laiçə] f (-/-n) (dead) body, corpse.
Leichen|beschauer ⅀ ['laiçənbəʃauər] m (-s/-) appr. coroner; '~bestatter m (-s/-) undertaker, Am. a. mortician; '~bittermiene F f woebegone look or countenance; '2blaß adj. deadly pale; '~halle f mortuary; '~schau ⅀ f appr. (coroner's) inquest; '~schauhaus n morgue; '~tuch n (-[e]s/=er) shroud; '~verbrennung f cremation; '~wagen m hearse.

Leichnam ['laiçna:m] m (-[e]s/-e) s. Leiche.
leicht [laiçt] 1. adj. light; easy; slight; tobacco: mild; 2. adv.: es ~ nehmen take it easy; '~athlet m athlete; '2athletik f athletics pl., Am. track and field events pl.; '~fertig adj. light(-minded); careless, frivolous, flippant; '2fertigkeit f levity; carelessness, frivolity, flippancy; '2gewicht n boxing: lightweight; '~gläubig adj. credulous; '~hin adv. lightly, casually; 2igkeit ['~iç-] f (-/-en) lightness; ease, facility; '~lebig adj. easy-going; '2metall n light metal; '2sinn m (-[e]s/no pl.) frivolity, levity; carelessness; '~sinnig adj. light-minded, frivolous; careless; '~verdaulich adj. easy to digest; '~verständlich adj. easy to understand.
leid [lait] 1. adv.: es tut mir ~ I am sorry (um for), I regret; 2. 2 n (-[e]s/no pl.) injury, harm; wrong; grief, sorrow; ~en [~dən] (ir., ge-, h) 1. v/i. suffer (an dat. from); 2. v/t.: (nicht) ~ können (dis)like; 2en ['~dən] n (-s/-) suffering; complaint; ~end ⅀ adj. ['~dənt] ailing.
'Leidenschaft f (-/-en) passion; '2lich adj. passionate; ardent; vehement; '2slos adj. dispassionate.
'Leidens|gefährte m, '~gefährtin f fellow-sufferer.
leid|er adv. ['laidər] unfortunately; int. alas!; ~ muß ich inf. I'm (so) sorry to inf.; ich muß ~ gehen I am afraid I have to go; '~ig adj. disagreeable; ~lich adj. ['lait-] tolerable; fairly well; 2tragende ['lait-] m, f (-n/-n) mourner; er ist der ~ dabei he is the one who suffers for it; 2wesen ['lait-] n (-s/no pl.): zu meinem ~ to my regret.
Leier ♪ ['laiər] f (-/-n) lyre; '~kasten m barrel-organ; '~kastenmann m organ-grinder.
Leih|bibliothek ['lai-] f, '~bücherei f lending or circulating library, Am. a. rental library; '2en v/t. (irr., ge-, h) lend; borrow (von from); '~gebühr f lending fee(s pl.); '~haus n pawnshop, Am. a. loan office; '2weise adv. as a loan.
Leim [laim] m (-[e]s/-e) glue; F aus dem ~ gehen get out of joint; F: auf den ~ gehen fall for it, fall into the trap; '2en v/t. (ge-, h) glue; size.
Lein ♀ [lain] m (-[e]s/-e) flax.
Leine ['lainə] f (-/-n) line, cord; (dog-)lead, leash.
leinen ['lainən] 1. adj. (of) linen; 2. 2 n (-s/-) linen; in ~ gebunden cloth-bound; '2schuh m canvas shoe.
'Lein|öl n linseed-oil; '~samen m linseed; '~wand f (-/no pl.) linen (cloth); paint. canvas; film: screen.

leise adj. ['laızə] low, soft; gentle; slight, faint; ~r stellen turn down (radio).

Leiste ['laıstə] f (-/-n) border, ledge; ♠ fillet; anat. groin.

leisten ['laıstən] 1. v/t. (ge-, h) do; perform; fulfil(l); take (oath); render (service); ich kann mir das ~ I can afford it; 2. ♀ ⊕ m (-s/-) last; boot-tree, Am. a. shoetree; '♀-bruch ♂ m inguinal hernia.

'Leistung f (-/-en) performance; achievement; work(manship); result(s pl.); ⊕ capacity; output (of factory); benefit (of insurance company); '♀sfähig adj. productive; efficient, ⊕ a. powerful; '♀sfähigkeit f efficiency; ⊕ productivity; ⊕ capacity, producing-power.

Leit|artikel ['laıt-] m leading article, leader, editorial; '♀bild n image; example.

leiten ['laıtən] v/t. (ge-, h) lead, guide; conduct (a. phys., ♪); fig. direct, run, manage, operate; preside over (meeting); '~d adj. leading; phys. conductive; ~e Stellung key position.

'Leiter 1. m (-s/-) leader; conductor (a. phys., ♪); guide; manager; 2. f (-/-n) ladder; '~in f (-/-nen) leader; conductress, guide; manageress; '~wagen m rack-wag(g)on.

'Leit|faden m manual, textbook, guide; '~motiv ♪ n leit-motiv; '~spruch m motto; '~tier n leader; '~ung f (-/-en) lead(ing), conducting, guidance; management, direction, administration, Am. a. operation; phys. conduction; ♪ lead; circuit; tel. line; mains pl. (for gas, water, etc.); pipeline; die ~ ist besetzt teleph. the line is engaged or Am. busy.

'Leitungs|draht m conducting wire, conductor; '~rohr n conduit(-pipe); main (for gas, water, etc.); '~wasser n (-s/=) tap water.

'Leitwerk ♐ n tail unit or group, empennage.

Lekt|ion [lɛk'tsjo:n] f (-/-en) lesson; ~or ['lɛktɔr] m (-s/-en) lecturer; reader; ~üre [~'ty:rə] f 1. (-/no pl.) reading; 2. (-/-n) books pl.

Lende anat. ['lɛndə] f (-/-n) loin(s pl.).

lenk|bar adj. ['lɛŋkba:r] guidable, manageable, tractable; docile; ⊕ steerable, dirigible; '~en v/t. (ge-, h) direct, guide; turn; rule; govern; drive (car); ♣ steer; Aufmerksamkeit ~ auf (acc.) draw attention to; '♀rad mot. n steering wheel; '♀-säule mot. f steering column; '♀-stange f handle-bar (of bicycle); '♀ung mot. f (-/-en) steering-gear.

Lenz [lɛnts] m (-es/-e) spring.

Leopard zo. [leo'part] m (-en/-en)

Lepra ♂ ['le:pra] f (-/no pl.) leprosy.

Lerche orn. ['lɛrçə] f (-/-n) lark.

lern|begierig adj. ['lɛrn-] eager to learn, studious; '~en v/t. and v/i. (ge-, h) learn; study.

Lese ['le:zə] f (-/-n) gathering; s. Weinlese; '~buch n reader; '~lampe f reading-lamp.

lesen ['le:zən] (irr., ge-, h) 1. v/t. read; ♪ gather; Messe ~ eccl. say mass; 2. v/i. read; univ. (give a) lecture (über acc. on); '~swert adj. worth reading.

'Leser m (-s/-), '~in f (-/-nen) reader; ♪ gatherer; vintager; '♀lich adj. legible; '~zuschrift f letter to the editor.

'Lesezeichen n book-mark.

'Lesung parl. f (-/-en) reading.

letzt adj. [lɛtst] last; final; ultimate; ~e Nachrichten pl. latest news pl.; ~e Hand anlegen put the finishing touches (an acc. to); das ~e the last thing; der ~ere the latter; der (die, das) Letzte the last (one); zu guter Letzt last but not least; finally; '~ens adv., '~hin adv. lately, of late; '♀lich adv. s. letztens; finally; ultimately.|

Leucht|e ['lɔʏçtə] f (-/-n) (fig. shining) light, lamp (a. fig.), luminary (a. fig., esp. p.); '♀en v/i. (ge-, h) (give) light, shine (forth); beam, gleam; '~en n (-s/no pl.) shining, light, luminosity; '♀end adj. shining, bright; luminous; brilliant (a. fig.); '~er m (-s/-) candlestick; s. Kronleuchter; '~feuer n ♣, ♐, etc.: beacon(-light), flare (light); '~käfer zo. m glow-worm; '~kugel ♐ f Very light; flare; '~turm m lighthouse; '~ziffer f luminous figure.

leugnen ['lɔʏgnən] v/t. (ge-, h) deny; disavow; contest.

Leukämie ♂ [lɔʏkɛ'mi:] f (-/-n) leuk(a)emia.

Leumund ['lɔʏmunt] m (-[e]s/no pl.) reputation, repute; character; '~szeugnis ♐ n character reference.

Leute ['lɔʏtə] pl. people pl.; persons pl.; ⚥, pol. men pl.; workers: hands pl.; F folks pl.; domestics pl., servants pl.

Leutnant ⚔ ['lɔʏtnant] m (-s/-s, ♐ -e) second lieutenant.

leutselig adj. ['lɔʏtze:lɪç] affable.

Lexikon ['lɛksikɔn] n (-s/Lexika, Lexiken) dictionary; encyclop(a)edia.

Libelle zo. [li'bɛlə] f (-/-n) dragonfly.

liberal adj. [libe'ra:l] liberal.

Licht [lɪçt] 1. n (-[e]s/-er) light; brightness; lamp; candle; hunt. eye; ~ machen ♪ switch or turn on the light (pl.); das ~ der Welt erblicken see the light, be born; 2. ♀ adj. light, bright; clear; ~er Augenblick ♂ lucid interval; '~anlage f

lighting plant; **'~bild** n photo
(-graph); **'~bildervortrag** m slide
lecture; **'~blick** fig. m bright spot;
'~bogen ⚡ m arc; **'2durchlässig**
adj. translucent; **'2echt** adj. fast
(to light), unfading; **'2empfind-**
lich adj. sensitive to light, phot.
sensitive; **~ machen** sensitize.

'lichten v/t. (ge-, h) clear (forest);
den Anker **~ ⚓** weigh anchor; sich **~**
hair, crowd: thin.

lichterloh adv. ['liçtər'lo:] blazing,
in full blaze.

'Licht|geschwindigkeit f speed of
light; **'~hof** m glass-roofed court;
patio; halo (a. phot.); **'~leitung** f
lighting mains pl.; **'~maschine**
mot. f dynamo, generator; **'~pause**
f blueprint; **'~quelle** f light source,
source of light; **'~reklame** f neon
sign; **'~schacht** m well; **'~schalter**
m (light) switch; **'~schein** m gleam
of light; **'2scheu** adj. shunning the
light; **'~signal** n light or luminous
signal; **'~spieltheater** n s. Film-
theater, Kino; **'~strahl** m ray or
beam of light (a. fig.); **'2undurch-**
lässig adj. opaque.

'Lichtung f (-/-en) clearing, opening, glade.

'Lichtzelle f s. Photozelle.

Lid [li:t] n (-[e]s/-er) eyelid.

lieb adj. [li:p] dear; nice, kind;
child: good; in letters: **~er Herr N.**
dear Mr N.; **~er Himmel!** good
Heavens!, dear me!; es ist mir **~**,
daß I am glad that; **'2chen** n (-s/-)
sweetheart.

Liebe ['li:bə] f (-/no pl.) love (zu of,
for); aus **~** for love; aus **~** zu for the
love of; **'2n** (ge-, h) **1.** v/t. love; be
in love with; be fond of, like; **2.** v/i.
(be in) love; **'~nde** m, f (-n/-n): die
~n pl. the lovers pl.

'liebens|wert adj. lovable, charm-
ing; **'~würdig** adj. lovable, amiable; das ist sehr **~** von Ihnen that is
very kind of you; **'2würdigkeit** f
(-/-en) amiability, kindness.

'lieber 1. adj. dearer; **2.** adv. rather,
sooner; **~ haben** prefer, like better.

'Liebes|brief m love-letter; **'~**
dienst m favo(u)r, kindness; good
turn; **'~erklärung** f: e-e **~** machen
declare one's love; **'~heirat** f love-
match; **'~kummer** m lover's grief;
'~paar n (courting) couple, lovers
pl.; **'~verhältnis** n love-affair.

'liebevoll adj. loving, affectionate.

lieb|gewinnen ['li:p-] v/t. (irr. ge-
winnen, sep., no -ge-, h) get or grow
fond of; **'~haben** v/t. (irr. haben,
sep., -ge-, h) love, be fond of; **'2ha-**
ber m (-s/-) lover; beau; fig. amateur;
2haberei fig. [~'raɪ] f (-/-en) hobby;
'2haberpreis m fancy price; **'2ha-**
berwert m sentimental value;
'~kosen v/t. (no -ge-, h) caress,
fondle; **'2kosung** f (-/-en) caress;

'~lich adj. lovely, charming,
delightful.

Liebling ['li:plɪŋ] m (-s/-e) darling,
favo(u)rite; esp. animals: pet; esp.
form of address: darling, esp. Am.
honey; **'~sbeschäftigung** f fa-
vo(u)rite occupation, hobby.

lieb|los adj. ['li:p-] unkind; careless;
'2schaft f (-/-en) (love-)affair;
'2ste m, f (-n/-n) sweetheart; darling.

Lied [li:t] n (-[e]s/-er) song; tune.

liederlich adj. ['li:dərlɪç] slovenly,
disorderly; careless; loose, dissolute.

lief [li:f] pret. of laufen.

Lieferant [li:fə'rant] m (-en/-en)
supplier, purveyor; caterer.

Liefer|auto ['li:fər-] n s. Liefer-
wagen; **'2bar** adj. to be delivered;
available; **'~bedingungen** f/pl.;
terms pl. of delivery; **'~frist** f term
of delivery; **'2n** v/t. (ge-, h) deliver;
j-m et. **~** furnish or supply s.o. with
s.th.; **'~schein** m delivery note;
'~ung f (-/-en) delivery; supply;
consignment; instal(l)ment (of book);
'~ungsbedingungen; **'~wagen** m delivery-
van, Am. delivery wagon.

Liege ['li:gə] f (-/-n) couch; bed-
chair.

liegen ['li:gən] v/i. (irr., ge-, h) lie;
house, etc.: be (situated); room:
face; an wem liegt es? whose fault
is it? es liegt an or bei ihm zu inf.
it is for him to inf.; es liegt daran,
daß the reason for it is that; es liegt
mir daran zu inf. I am anxious to
inf.; es liegt mir nichts daran it does
not matter or it is of no consequence
to me; **'~bleiben** v/i. (irr. bleiben,
sep., -ge-, sein) stay in bed; break
down (on the road, a. mot., etc.);
work, etc.: stand over; fall behind;
✝ goods: remain on hand; **'~lassen**
v/t. (irr. lassen, sep., [-ge-,] h) leave;
leave behind; leave alone; leave off
(work); j-n links **~** ignore s.o., give
s.o. the cold shoulder; **'2schaften**
f/pl. real estate.

'Liege|stuhl m deck-chair; **'~wagen**
🚃 m couchette coach.

lieh [li:] pret. of leihen.

ließ [li:s] pret. of lassen.

Lift [lɪft] m (-[e]s/-e, -s) lift, Am.
elevator.

Liga ['li:ga] f (-/Ligen) league.

Likör [li'kø:r] m (-s/-e) liqueur,
cordial.

lila adj. ['li:la] lilac.

Lilie ['li:ljə] f (-/-n) lily.

Limonade [limo'na:də] f (-/-n) soft
drink, fruit-juice; lemonade.

Limousine mot. [limu'zi:nə] f (-/-n)
limousine, saloon car, Am. sedan.

lind adj. [lɪnt] soft, gentle; mild.

Linde 🌳 ['lɪndə] f (-/-n) lime(-tree),
linden(-tree).

linder|n ['lindərn] v/t. (ge-, h) soften; mitigate; alleviate, soothe; allay, ease (pain); '₂ung f (-/-₂-en) softening; mitigation; alleviation; easing.

Lineal [line'a:l] n (-s/-e) ruler.

Linie ['li:njə] f (-/-n) line; '₂npapier n ruled paper; '₂nrichter m sports: linesman; '₂ntreu pol. adj.: ~ sein follow the party line.

lin(i)ieren [li'ni:rən; lini'i:rən] v/t. (no -ge-, h) rule, line.

link adj. [liŋk] left; ~e Seite left (-hand) side, left; of cloth: wrong side; '₂e f (-n/-n) the left (hand); pol. the Left (Wing); boxing: the left; '₂isch adj. awkward, clumsy.

links adv. on or to the left; '₂händer ['₂hendər] m (-s/-) left-hander, Am. a. southpaw.

Linse ['linzə] f (-/-n) ♀ lentil; opt. lens.

Lippe ['lipə] f (-/-n) lip; '₂nstift m lipstick.

liquidieren [likvi'di:rən] v/t. (no -ge-, h) liquidate (a. pol.); wind up (business company); charge (fee).

lispeln ['lispəln] v/i. and v/t. (ge-, h) lisp; whisper.

List [list] f (-/-en) cunning, craft; artifice, ruse, trick; stratagem.

Liste ['listə] f (-/-n) list, roll.

listig adj. cunning, crafty, sly.

Liter ['li:tər] n, m (-s/-) lit|re, Am. -er.

literarisch adj. [lite'ra:riʃ] literary.

Literatur [litera'tu:r] f (-/-en) literature; '₂beilage f literary supplement (in newspaper); ₂geschichte f history of literature; ₂verzeichnis n bibliography.

litt [lit] pret. of leiden.

Litze ['litsə] f (-/-n) lace, cord, braid; ✠ strand(ed wire).

Livree [li'vre:] f (-/-n) livery.

Lizenz [li'tsents] f (-/-en) licen|ce, Am. -se; '₂inhaber m licensee.

Lob [lo:p] n (-[e]s/no pl.) praise; commendation; '₂en ['lo:bən] v/t. (ge-, h) praise; '₂enswert adj. ['lo:bəns-] praise-worthy, laudable; ₂gesang ['lo:p-] m hymn, song of praise; ₂hudelei [lo:phu:də'lai] f (-/-en) adulation, base flattery.

löblich adj. ['lø:pliç] s. lobenswert.

Lobrede ['lo:p-] f eulogy, panegyric.

Loch [lɔx] n (-[e]s/-er) hole; '₂en v/t. (ge-, h) perforate, pierce; punch (ticket, etc.); '₂er m (-s/-) punch, perforator; '₂karte f punch(ed) card.

Locke ['lɔkə] f (-/-n) curl, ringlet.

'locken[1] v/t. and v/refl. (ge-, h) curl.

'locken[2] v/t. (ge-, h) hunt.: bait; decoy (a. fig.); fig. allure, entice.

'Locken|kopf m curly head; ₂wickler ['₂viklər] m (-s/-) curler, roller.

locker adj. ['lɔkər] loose; slack; '₂n v/t. (ge-, h) loosen; slacken; relax (grip); break up (soil); sich ~ loosen, (be)come loose; give way; fig. relax.

'lockig adj. curly.

'Lock|mittel n s. Köder; '₂vogel m decoy (a. fig.); Am. a. stool pigeon (a. fig.).

lodern ['lo:dərn] v/i. (ge-, h) flare, blaze.

Löffel ['lœfəl] m (-s/-) spoon; ladle; '₂n v/t. (ge-, h) spoon up; ladle out; '₂voll m (-/-) spoonful.

log [lo:k] pret. of lügen.

Loge ['lo:ʒə] f (-/-n) thea. box; freemasonry: lodge; '₂nschließer thea. m (-s/-) box-keeper.

logieren [lo'ʒi:rən] v/i. (no -ge-, h) lodge, stay, Am. a. room (all: bei with; in dat. at).

logisch adj. ['lo:giʃ] logical; '₂erweise adv. logically.

Lohn [lo:n] m (-[e]s/-e) wages pl., pay(ment); hire; fig. reward; '₂büro n pay-office; '₂empfänger m wage-earner; '₂en v/t. (ge-, h) compensate, reward; sich ~ pay; es lohnt sich zu inf. it is worth while ger., it pays to inf.; '₂end adj. paying; advantageous; fig. rewarding; '₂erhöhung f increase in wages, rise, Am. raise; '₂forderung f demand for higher wages; '₂steuer f tax on wages or salary; '₂stopp m (-s/no pl.) wage freeze; '₂tarif m wage rate; '₂tüte f pay envelope.

lokal [lo'ka:l] 1. adj. local; 2. ₂ n (-[e]s/-e) locality, place; restaurant; public house, F pub, F local, Am. saloon.

Lokomotiv|e [lokomo'ti:və] f (-/-n) (railway) engine, locomotive; ₂führer [~'ti:f-] m engine-driver, Am. engineer.

Lorbeer ♀ ['lɔrbeːr] m (-s/-en) laurel, bay.

Lore ['lo:rə] f (-/-n) lorry, truck.

Los[1] [lo:s] n (-es/-e) lot; lottery ticket; fig. fate, destiny, lot; das Große ~ ziehen win the first prize, Am. sl. hit the jackpot; durchs ~ entscheiden decide by lot.

los[2] [~] 1. pred. adj. loose; free; was ist ~? what is the matter?, F what's up?, Am. F what's cooking?; ~ sein be rid of; 2. int.: ~! go (on or ahead)!

losarbeiten ['lo:s-] v/i. (sep., -ge-, h) start work(ing).

lösbar adj. ['lø:sba:r] soluble, ♣ a. solvable.

'los|binden v/t. (irr. binden, sep., -ge-, h) untie, loosen; '₂brechen (irr. brechen, sep., -ge-) 1. v/t. (h) break off; 2. v/i. (sein) break or burst out.

Lösch|blatt ['lœʃ-] n blotting-paper; '₂en v/t. (ge-, h) extinguish, put out (fire, light); blot out (writing);

erase (*tape recording*); cancel (*debt*); quench (*thirst*); slake (*lime*); ⚓ unload; '**∼er** m (-s/-) blotter; '**∼papier** n blotting-paper.

lose adj. ['loːzə] loose.

Lösegeld n ransom.

losen ['loːzən] v/i. (ge-, h) cast or draw lots (um for).

lösen ['løːzən] v/t. (ge-, h) loosen, untie; buy, book (*ticket*); solve (*task, doubt, etc.*); break off (*engagement*); annul (*agreement, etc.*); 🜍 dissolve; *ein Schuß löste sich* the gun went off.

'**los|fahren** v/i. (*irr.* fahren, sep., -ge-, sein) depart, drive off; '**∼gehen** v/i. (*irr.* gehen, sep., -ge-, sein) go or be off; come off, get loose; gun: go off; begin, start; F *auf j-n* ∼ fly at s.o.; '**∼haken** v/t. (sep., -ge-, h) unhook; '**∼kaufen** v/t. (sep., -ge-, h) ransom, redeem; '**∼ketten** v/t. (sep., -ge-, h) unchain; '**∼kommen** v/i. (*irr.* kommen, sep., -ge-, sein) get loose or free; '**∼lachen** v/i. (sep., -ge-, h) laugh out; '**∼lassen** v/t. (*irr.* lassen, sep., -ge-, h) let go; release.

löslich 🜍 adj. ['løːsliç] soluble.

'**los|lösen** v/t. (sep., -ge-, h) loosen, detach; sever; '**∼machen** v/t. (sep., -ge-, h) unfasten, loosen; *sich* ∼ disengage (o.s.) (*von* from); '**∼reißen** v/t. (*irr.* reißen, sep., -ge-, h) tear off; *sich* ∼ break away, *esp. fig.* tear o.s. away (*both: von* from); '**∼sagen** v/refl. (sep., -ge-, h): *sich* ∼ *von* renounce; '**∼schlagen** (*irr.* schlagen, sep., -ge-, h) 1. v/t. knock off; 2. v/i. open the attack; *auf j-n* ∼ attack s.o.; '**∼schnallen** v/t. (sep., -ge-, h) unbuckle; '**∼schrauben** v/t. (sep., -ge-, h) unscrew, screw off; '**∼sprechen** v/t. (*irr.* sprechen, sep., -ge-, h) absolve (*von* of, from); acquit (of); free (from, of); '**∼stürzen** v/i. (sep., -ge-, sein): ∼ *auf* (*acc.*) rush at.

Losung ['loːzuŋ] f 1. (-/-en) ⚔ password, watchword; *fig.* slogan; 2. *hunt.* (-/no pl.) droppings pl., dung.

Lösung ['løːzuŋ] f (-/-en) solution; '**∼smittel** n solvent.

'**los|werden** v/t. (*irr.* werden, sep., -ge-, sein) get rid of, dispose of; '**∼ziehen** v/i. (*irr.* ziehen, sep., -ge-, sein) set out, take off, march away.

Lot [loːt] n (-[e]s/-e) plumb(-line), plummet.

löten ['løːtən] v/t. (ge-, h) solder.

Lotse ⚓ ['loːtsə] m (-n/-n) pilot; '**2n** v/t. (ge-, h) ⚓ pilot (a. *fig.*).

Lotterie [lɔtə'riː] f (-/-n) lottery; '**∼gewinn** m prize; '**∼los** n lottery ticket.

Lotto ['lɔto] n (-s/-s) numbers pool, lotto.

Löwe zo. ['løːvə] m (-n/-n) lion.

'**Löwen|anteil** F m lion's share; '**∼maul** ♀ n (-[e]s/no pl.) snapdragon; '**∼zahn** ♀ m (-[e]s/no pl.) dandelion.

'**Löwin** zo. f (-/-nen) lioness.

loyal adj. [loa'jaːl] loyal.

Luchs zo. [luks] m (-es/-e) lynx.

Lücke ['lykə] f (-/-n) gap; blank, void (a. *fig.*); '**∼nbüßer** m stopgap; '**2nhaft** adj. full of gaps; *fig.* defective, incomplete; '**2nlos** adj. without a gap; *fig.*: unbroken; complete; *∼er Beweis* close argument.

lud [luːt] pret. of laden.

Luft [luft] f (-/∼e) air; breeze; breath; *frische* ∼ *schöpfen* take the air; *an die* ∼ *gehen* go for an airing; *aus der* ∼ *gegriffen* (totally) unfounded, fantastic; *es liegt et. in der* ∼ there is s.th. in the wind; *in die* ∼ *fliegen* be blown up, explode; *in die* ∼ *gehen* explode, *sl.* blow one's top; *in die* ∼ *sprengen* blow up; F *j-n an die* ∼ *setzen* turn s.o. out, *Am. sl.* give s.o. the air; *sich or s-n Gefühlen* ∼ *machen* give vent to one's feelings.

'**Luft|alarm** m air-raid alarm; '**∼angriff** m air raid; '**∼aufnahme** f aerial photograph; '**∼ballon** m (air-)balloon; '**∼bild** n aerial photograph, airview; '**∼blase** f air-bubble; '**∼brücke** f air-bridge; *for supplies, etc.*: air-lift.

Lüftchen ['lyftçən] n (-s/-) gentle breeze.

'**luft|dicht** adj. air-tight; '**2druck** *phys.* m (-[e]s/no pl.) atmospheric or air pressure; '**2druckbremse** ⊕ f air-brake; '**∼durchlässig** adj. permeable to air.

lüften ['lyftən] (ge-, h) 1. v/i. air; 2. v/t. air; raise (*hat*); lift (*veil*); disclose (*secret*).

'**Luft|fahrt** f aviation, aeronautics; '**∼feuchtigkeit** f atmospheric humidity; '**2gekühlt** ⊕ adj. air-cooled; '**∼hoheit** f air sovereignty; '**2ig** adj. airy; breezy; flimsy; '**∼kissen** n air-cushion; '**∼klappe** f air-valve; '**∼korridor** m air corridor; '**∼krankheit** f airsickness; '**∼krieg** m aerial warfare; '**∼kurort** m climatic health resort; '**∼landetruppen** f/pl. airborne troops pl.; '**2leer** adj. void of air, evacuated; *∼er Raum* vacuum; '**∼linie** f air line, bee-line; '**∼loch** n ⫸ air-pocket; vent(-hole); '**∼post** f air mail; '**∼pumpe** f air-pump; '**∼raum** m airspace; '**∼röhre** *anat.* f windpipe, trachea; '**∼schacht** m air-shaft; '**∼schaukel** f swing-boat; '**∼schiff** n airship; '**∼schloß** n castle in the air or in Spain; '**∼schutz** m air-raid protection; '**∼schutzkeller** m air-raid shelter; '**∼sprünge** ['∼ʃprYŋə] m/pl.: ∼ *machen* cut capers pl.; gambol; '**∼stützpunkt** ⚔ m air base.

'**Lüftung** f (-/-en) airing; ventilation.

'**Luft|veränderung** f change of air; '**~verkehr** m air-traffic; '**~verkehrsgesellschaft** f air transport company, airway, Am. airline; '**~verteidigung** ✕ f air defen|ce, Am. -se; '**~waffe** ✕ f air force; '**~weg** m airway; auf dem ~ by air; '**~zug** m draught, Am. draft.

Lüge ['ly:gə] f (-/-n) lie, falsehood; j-n ~n strafen give the lie to s.o.

'**lügen** v/i. (irr., ge-, h) (tell a) lie; '**~haft** adj. lying, mendacious; untrue, false.

Lügner ['ly:gnər] m (-s/-), '**~in** f (-/-nen) liar; '**Qisch** adj. s. lügenhaft.

Luke ['lu:kə] f (-/-n) dormer- or garret-window; hatch.

Lümmel ['lyməl] m (-s/-) lout, boor; saucy fellow; '**Qn** v/refl. (ge-, h) loll, lounge, sprawl.

Lump [lump] m (-en/-en) ragamuffin, beggar; cad, Am. sl. rat, heel; scoundrel.

'**Lumpen 1.** m (-s/-) rag; **2.** ♀ vb.: sich nicht ~ lassen come down handsomely; '**~pack** n rabble, riffraff; '**~sammler** m rag-picker.

'**lumpig** adj. ragged; fig.: shabby, paltry; mean.

Lunge ['luŋə] f (-/-n) anat. lungs pl.; of animals: a. lights pl.

'**Lungen|entzündung** ♬ f pneumonia; '**~flügel** anat. m lung; '**Qkrank** ♬ adj. suffering from consumption, consumptive; '**~kranke** ♬ m, f consumptive (patient); '**~krankheit** ♬ f lung-disease; '**~schwindsucht** ♬ f (pulmonary) consumption.

lungern ['luŋərn] v/i. (ge-, h) s. herumlungern.

Lupe ['lu:pə] f (-/-n) magnifying-glass; unter die ~ nehmen scrutinize, take a good look at.

Lust [lust] f (-/=e) pleasure, delight; desire; lust; ~ haben zu inf. have a mind to inf., feel like ger.; haben Sie ~ auszugehen? would you like to go out?

lüstern adj. ['lystərn] desirous (nach of), greedy (of, for); lewd, lascivious, lecherous.

'**lustig** adj. merry, gay; jolly, cheerful; amusing, funny; sich ~ machen über (acc.) make fun of; '**Qkeit** f (-/no pl.) gaiety, mirth; jollity, cheerfulness; fun.

Lüstling ['lystliŋ] m (-s/-e) voluptuary, libertine.

'**lust|los** adj. dull, spiritless; ✝ flat; '**Qmord** m rape and murder; '**Qspiel** n comedy.

lutschen ['lutʃən] v/i. and v/t. (ge-, h) suck.

Luv ⚓ [lu:f] f (-/no pl.) luff, windward.

luxuriös adj. [luksu'rjø:s] luxurious.

Luxus ['luksus] m (-/no pl.) luxury (a. fig.); '**~artikel** m luxury; '**~ausgabe** f de luxe edition (of books); '**~ware** f luxury (article); fancy goods pl.

Lymph|drüse anat. ['lymf-] f lymphatic gland; '**~e** f (-/-n) lymph; ♬ vaccine; '**~gefäß** anat. n lymphatic vessel.

lynchen ['lynçən] v/t. (ge-, h) lynch.

Lyrik ['ly:rik] f (-/no pl.) lyric verses pl., lyrics pl.; '**~er** m (-s/-) lyric poet.

'**lyrisch** adj. lyric; lyrical (a. fig.).

M

Maat ⚓ [mɑːt] m (-[e]s/-e[n]) (ship's) mate.

Mache F ['maxə] f (-/no pl.) make-believe, window-dressing, sl. eye-wash; et. in der ~ haben have s.th. in hand.

machen ['maxən] (ge-, h) **1.** v/t. make; do; produce, manufacture; give (appetite, etc.); sit for, undergo (examination); come or amount to; make (happy, etc.); was macht das (aus)? what does that matter?; das macht nichts! never mind!, that's (quite) all right!; da(gegen) kann man nichts ~ that cannot be helped; ich mache mir nichts daraus I don't care about it; mach, daß du fortkommst! off with you!; j-n ~ lassen, was er will let s.o. do as he pleases; sich ~ an (acc.) go or set

about; sich et. ~ lassen have s.th. made; **2.** F v/i.: na, mach schon! hurry up!; '**Qschaften** f/pl. machinations pl.

Macht [maxt] f (-/=e) power; might; authority; control (über acc. of); an der ~ pol. in power; '**~befugnis** f authority, power; '**~haber** pol. m (-s/-) ruler.

mächtig adj. ['meçtiç] powerful (a. fig.); mighty; immense, huge; ~ sein (gen.) be master of s.th.; have command of (language).

'**Macht|kampf** m struggle for power; '**Qlos** adj. powerless; '**~politik** f power politics sg., pl.; policy of the strong hand; '**~spruch** m authoritative decision; '**Qvoll** adj. powerful (a. fig.); '**~vollkommenheit** f authority; '**~wort** n (-[e]s/-e) word of command; *ein ~ sprechen* put one's foot down.

'**Machwerk** *n* concoction, F put-up job; *elendes ~* bungling work.

Mädchen ['mɛːtçən] *n* (-s/-) girl; maid(-servant); *~ für alles* maid of all work; *fig. a.* jack of all trades; '**◯haft** *adj.* girlish; '**~name** *m* girl's name; maiden name; '**~schule** *f* girls' school.

Made *zo.* ['maːdə] *f* (-/-n) maggot, mite; *fruit:* worm.

Mädel ['mɛːdəl] *n* (-s/-, F -s) girl, lass(ie).

madig *adj.* ['maːdiç] maggoty, full of mites; *fruit:* wormeaten.

Magazin [maga'tsiːn] *n* (-s/-e) store, warehouse; ✕, *in rifle, periodical:* magazine.

Magd [maːkt] *f* (-/ᵉe) maid(-servant).

Magen ['maːgən] *m* (-s/ᵘ, *a.* -) stomach, F tummy; *animals:* maw; '**~beschwerden** *f/pl.* stomach *or* gastric trouble, indigestion; '**~bit-ter** *m* (-s/-) bitters *pl.*; '**~geschwür** ⚕ *n* gastric ulcer; '**~krampf** *m* stomach cramp; '**~krebs** ⚕ *m* stomach cancer; '**~leiden** *n* gastric complaint; '**~säure** *f* gastric acid.

mager *adj.* ['maːgər] meag|re, *Am.* -er (*a. fig.*); *p.*, *animal, meat:* lean, *Am. a.* scrawny; '**◯milch** *f* skim milk.

Magie [ma'giː] *f* (-/*no pl.*) magic; **~r** ['maːgjər] *m* (-s/-) magician.

magisch *adj.* ['maːgiʃ] magic(al).

Magistrat [magis'traːt] *m* (-[e]s/-e) municipal *or* town council.

Magnet [ma'gneːt] *m* (-[e]s, -en/ -e[n]) magnet (*a. fig.*); lodestone; **◯isch** *adj.* magnetic; **◯isieren** [~eti'ziːrən] *v/t.* (*no -ge-, h*) magnetize; '**~nadel** [~'gneːt-] *f* magnetic needle.

Mahagoni [maha'goːni] *n* (-s/*no pl.*) mahogany (wood).

mähen ['mɛːən] *v/t.* (ge-, h) cut, mow, reap.

Mahl [maːl] *n* (-[e]s/ᵘer, -e) meal, repast.

'**mahlen** (*irr.*, ge-, h) 1. *v/t.* grind, mill; 2. *v/i. tyres:* spin.

'**Mahlzeit** *f s.* Mahl; F feed.

Mähne ['mɛːnə] *f* (-/-n) mane.

mahn|en ['maːnən] *v/t.* (ge-, h) remind, admonish (*both: an acc.* of); *j-n wegen e-r Schuld ~* press s.o. for payment, dun s.o.; '**◯mal** *n* (-[e]s/-e) memorial; '**◯ung** *f* (-/-en) admonition; ✝ reminder, dunning; '**◯zet-tel** *m* reminder.

Mai [maɪ] *m* (-[e]s, -/-e) May; '**~baum** *m* maypole; **~glöckchen** ⚘ ['~glœkçən] *n* (-s/-) lily of the valley; '**~käfer** *zo. m* cockchafer, may-beetle, may-bug.

Mais ⚘ [maɪs] *m* (-es/-e) maize, Indian corn, *Am.* corn.

Majestät [majɛ'stɛːt] *f* (-/-en) majesty; **◯isch** *adj.* majestic; **~s-beleidigung** *f* lese-majesty.

Major ✕ [ma'joːr] *m* (-s/-e) major.

Makel ['maːkəl] *m* (-s/-) stain, spot; *fig. a.* blemish, fault; '**◯los** *adj.* stainless, spotless; *fig. a.* unblemished, faultless, immaculate.

mäkeln F ['mɛːkəln] *v/i.* (ge-, h) find fault (*an dat.* with), carp (at), F pick (at).

Makler ✝ ['maːklər] *m* (-s/-) broker; '**~gebühr** ✝ *f* brokerage.

Makulatur ⊕ [makula'tuːr] *f* (-/-en) waste paper.

Mal¹ [maːl] *n* (-[e]s/-e, ᵘer) mark, sign; *sports:* start(ing-point), goal; spot, stain; mole.

Mal² [~] 1. *n* (-[e]s/-e) time; *für dieses ~* this time; *zum ersten ~e* for the first time; *mit e-m ~e* all at once, all of a sudden; 2. ⚲ *adv.* times, multiplied by; *drei ~ fünf ist fünfzehn* three times five is *or* are fifteen; F *s. einmal.*

'**malen** *v/t.* (ge-, h) paint; portray.

'**Maler** *m* (-s/-) painter; artist; **~ei** [~'raɪ] *f* (-/-en) painting; '**◯isch** *adj.* pictorial, painting; *fig.* picturesque.

'**Malkasten** *m* paint-box.

'**malnehmen** ⚲ *v/t.* (*irr.* nehmen, sep., -ge-, h) multiply (mit by).

Malz [malts] *n* (-es/*no pl.*) malt; '**~bier** *n* malt beer.

Mama [ma'maː, F 'mama] *f* (-/-s) mamma, mammy, F ma, *Am.* F a. mummy, mom.

man *indef. pron.* [man] one, you, we; they, people; *~ sagte mir* I was told. [manager.]

Manager ['mɛnidʒər] *m* (-s/-)|

manch [manç], '**~er**, '**~e**, '**~es** *adj. and indef. pron.* many a; **~e** *pl.* some, several; **~erlei** *adj.* ['~ər'laɪ] diverse, different; all sorts of, ... of several sorts; *auf ~ Art* in various ways; *used as a noun:* many *or* various things; '**~mal** *adv.* sometimes, at times.

Mandant ⚖ [man'dant] *m* (-en/-en) client.

Mandarine ⚘ [manda'riːnə] *f* (-/-n) tangerine.

Mandat [man'daːt] *n* (-[e]s/-e) authorization; ⚖ brief; *pol.* mandate; *parl.* seat.

Mandel ['mandəl] *f* (-/-n) ⚘ almond; *anat.* tonsil; '**~baum** ⚘ *m* almond-tree; '**~entzündung** ⚕ *f* tonsillitis.

Manege [ma'neːʒə] *f* (-/-n) (circus-)ring, manège.

Mangel¹ ['maŋəl] *m* 1. (-s/*no pl.*) want, lack, deficiency; shortage; penury; *aus ~ an* for want of; *~ leiden an* (*dat.*) be in want of; 2. (-s/ᵘ) defect, shortcoming.

Mangel² [~] *f* (-/-n) mangle; calender.

'mangelhaft adj. defective; deficient; unsatisfactory; '2igkeit f (-/no pl.) defectiveness; deficiency.

'mangeln¹ v/i. (ge-, h): es mangelt an Brot there is a lack or shortage of bread, bread is lacking or wanting; es mangelt ihm an (dat.) he is in need of or short of or wanting in, he wants or lacks.

'mangeln² v/t. (ge-, h) mangle (clothes, etc.); ⊕ calender (cloth, paper).

'mangels prp. (gen.) for lack or want of; esp. ⚖ in default of.

'Mangelware † f scarce commodity; goods pl. in short supply.

Manie [ma'ni:] f (-/-n) mania.

Manier [ma'ni:r] f (-/-en) manner; 2lich adj. well-behaved; polite, mannerly.   [manifesto.\

Manifest [mani'fɛst] n (-es/-e))

Mann [man] m (-[e]s/⸚er) man; husband.

'mannbar adj. marriageable; '2-keit f (-/no pl.) puberty, manhood.

Männchen ['mɛnçən] n (-s/-) little man; zo. male; birds: cock.

'Mannes|alter n virile age, manhood; '⸚kraft f virility.

mannig|fach adj. ['maniç-], '⸚faltig adj. manifold, various, diverse; '2faltigkeit f (-/no pl.) manifoldness, variety, diversity.

männlich adj. ['mɛnliç] male; gr. masculine; fig. manly; '2keit f (-/no pl.) manhood, virility.

'Mannschaft f (-/-en) (body of) men; ♣ crew; sports: team, side; '⸚sführer m sports: captain; '⸚s-geist m (-es/no pl.) sports: team spirit.

Manöv|er [ma'nø:vər] n (-s/-) manœuvre, Am. maneuver; 2rieren [⸚'vri:rən] v/i. (no -ge-, h) manœuvre, Am. maneuver.

Mansarde [man'zardə] f (-/-n) attic, garret; ⸚nfenster n dormer-window.

mansche|n F ['manʃən] (ge-, h) 1. v/t. mix, work; 2. v/i. dabble (in dat. in); 2'rei F f (-/-en) mixing, F mess; dabbling.

Manschette [man'ʃɛtə] f (-/-n) cuff; ⸚nknopf m cuff-link.

Mantel ['mantəl] m (-s/⸚) coat; overcoat, greatcoat; cloak, mantle (both a. fig.); ⊕ case, jacket; (outer) cover (of tyre).

Manuskript [manu'skript] n (-[e]s/-e) manuscript; typ. copy.

Mappe ['mapə] f (-/-n) portfolio, brief-case; folder; s. a. Schreibmappe, Schulmappe.

Märchen ['mɛːrçən] n (-s/-) fairy-tale; fig. (cock-and-bull) story, fib; '⸚buch n book of fairy-tales; '2haft adj. fabulous (a. fig.).

Marder zo. ['mardər] m (-s/-) marten.

12*

Marine [ma'ri:nə] f (-/-n) marine; ⚔ navy, naval forces pl.; ⸚minister m minister of naval affairs; First Lord of the Admiralty, Am. Secretary of the Navy; ⸚ministerium n ministry of naval affairs; the Admiralty, Am. Department of the Navy.

marinieren [mari'ni:rən] v/t. (no -ge-, h) pickle, marinade.

Marionette [mario'nɛtə] f (-/-n) puppet, marionette; ⸚ntheater n puppet-show.

Mark [mark] 1. f (-/-) coin: mark; 2. n (-[e]s/no pl.) anat. marrow; ⚜ pith; fig. core.

markant adj. [mar'kant] characteristic; striking; (well-)marked.

Marke ['markə] f (-/-n) mark, sign, token; ⚜, etc.: stamp; † brand, trade-mark; coupon; '⸚nartikel † m branded or proprietary article.

mar'kier|en (no -ge-, h) 1. v/t. mark (a. sports); brand (cattle, goods, etc.); 2. F fig. v/i. put it on; 2ung f (-/-en) mark(ing).

'markig adj. marrowy; fig. pithy.

Markise [mar'ki:zə] f (-/-n) blind, (window-)awning.

'Markstein m boundary-stone, landmark (a. fig.).

Markt [markt] m (-[e]s/⸚e) † market; s. Marktplatz; fair; auf den bringen † put on the market; '⸚flecken m small market-town; '⸚platz m market-place; '⸚schreier m (-s/-) quack; puffer.

Marmelade [marmə'la:də] f (-/-) jam; marmalade (made of oranges).

Marmor ['marmor] m (-s/-e) marble; 2ieren [⸚o'ri:rən] v/t. (no -ge-, h) marble, vein, grain; 2n adj. [⸚.ɔrn] (of) marble.   [whim, caprice.\

Marotte [ma'rɔtə] f (-/-n) fancy,)

Marsch [marʃ] 1. m (-es/⸚e) march (a. ♪); 2. f (-/-en) marsh, fen.

Marschall ['marʃal] m (-s/⸚e) marshal.

'Marsch|befehl ⚔ m marching orders pl.; 2ieren [⸚'ʃi:rən] v/i. (no -ge-, sein) march; '⸚land n marshy land.

Marter ['martər] f (-/-n) torment, torture; '2n v/t. (ge-, h) torment, torture; '⸚pfahl m stake.

Märtyrer ['mɛrtyrər] m (-s/-) martyr; '⸚tod m martyr's death; '⸚tum n (-s/no pl.) martyrdom.

Marxis|mus pol. [mar'ksismus] m (-/no pl.) Marxism; ⸚t pol. m (-en/-en) Marxian, Marxist; 2tisch pol. adj. Marxian, Marxist.

März [mɛrts] m (-[e]s/-e) March.

Marzipan [martsi'pa:n] n, ⚘ m (-s/-e) marzipan, marchpane.

Masche ['maʃə] f (-/-n) mesh; knitting: stitch; F fig. trick, line; '2n-fest adj. ladder-proof, Am. runproof.

Maschine [ma'ʃiːnə] f (-/-n) machine; engine.
maschinell adj. [maʃi'nɛl] mechanical; ~e Bearbeitung machining.
Ma'schinen|bau ⊕ m (-[e]s/no pl.) mechanical engineering; ~gewehr ✕ n machine-gun; ℒmäßig adj. mechanical; automatic; ~pistole ✕ f sub-machine-gun; ~schaden m engine trouble; ~schlosser m (engine) fitter; ~schreiberin f (-/-nen) typist; ~schrift f typescript.
Maschin|erie [maʃinə'riː] f (-/-n) machinery; ~ist [~'nist] m (-en/-en) machinist.
Masern ❀ ['maːzərn] pl. measles pl.
Mask|e ['maskə] f (-/-n) mask (a. fig.); ~enball m fancy-dress or masked ball; ~erade [~'raːdə] f (-/-n) masquerade; ℒieren [~'kiːrən] v/t. (no -ge-, h) mask; sich ~ put on a mask; dress o.s. up (als as).
Maß [maːs] 1. n (-es/-e) measure; proportion; fig. moderation; ~e pl. und Gewichte pl. weights and measures pl.; ~e pl. room, etc.: measurements pl.; 2. f (-/-[e]) appr. quart (of beer); 3. ℒ pret. of messen.
Massage [ma'saːʒə] f (-/-n) massage.
'Maßanzug m tailor-made or bespoke suit, Am. a. custom(-made) suit.
Masse ['masə] f (-/-n) mass; bulk; substance; multitude; crowd; ⚖ assets pl., estate; die breite ~ the rank and file; F e-e ~ a lot of, F lots pl. or heaps pl. of.
'Maßeinheit f measuring unit.
'Massen|flucht f stampede; ~grab n common grave; ~güter † [~'gyː-tər] n/pl. bulk goods pl.; ℒhaft adj. abundant; ~produktion † f mass production; ~versammlung f mass meeting, Am. a. rally; 'ℒ-weise adv. in masses, in large numbers.
Masseu|r [ma'søːr] m (-s/-e) masseur; ~se [~zə] f (-/-n) masseuse.
'maß|gebend adj. standard; authoritative, decisive; board: competent; circles: influential, leading; '~halten v/i. (irr. halten, sep., -ge-, h) keep within limits, be moderate.
mas'sieren v/t. (no -ge-, h) massage, knead.
'massig adj. massy, bulky; solid.
mäßig adj. ['mɛːsiç] moderate; food, etc.: frugal; † price: moderate, reasonable; result, etc.: poor; ~en ['~gən] v/t. (ge-, h) moderate; sich ~ moderate or restrain o.s.; 'ℒung f (-/-en) moderation; restraint.
massiv [ma'siːf] 1. adj. massive, solid; 2. ℒ geol. n (-s/-e) massif.
'Maß|krug m beer-mug, Am. a. stein; 'ℒlos adj. immoderate; boundless; exorbitant, excessive;

extravagant; ~nahme ['~naːmə] f (-/-n) measure, step, action; 'ℒregeln v/t. (ge-, h) reprimand; inflict disciplinary punishment on; '~schneider m bespoke or Am. custom tailor; '~stab m measure, rule(r); maps, etc.: scale; fig. yardstick, standard; 'ℒvoll adj. moderate.
Mast¹ ⚓ [mast] m (-es/-e[n]) mast.
Mast² ❀ [~] f (-/-en) fattening; mast, food; ~darm anat. m rectum.
mästen ['mɛstən] v/t. (ge-, h) fatten, feed; stuff (geese, etc.).
'Mastkorb ⚓ m mast-head, crows-nest.
Material [mater'jaːl] n (-s/-ien) material; substance; stock, stores pl.; fig.: material, information; evidence; ~ismus phls. [~a'lismus] m (-/no pl.) materialism; ~ist [~a'list] m (-en/-en) materialist; ℒistisch adj. [~a'listiʃ] materialistic.
Materie [ma'teːrjə] f (-/-n) matter (a. fig.), stuff; fig. subject; ℒll adj. [~er'jɛl] material.
Mathemati|k [matema'tiːk] f (-/no pl.) mathematics sg.; ~ker [~'maːtikər] m (-s/-) mathematician; ℒsch adj. [~'maːtiʃ] mathematical.
Matinee thea. [mati'neː] f (-/-s) morning performance.
Matratze [ma'tratsə] f (-/-n) mattress.
Matrone [ma'troːnə] f (-/-n) matron; ℒnhaft adj. matronly.
Matrose [ma'troːzə] m (-n/-n) sailor, seaman.
Matsch [matʃ] m (-es/no pl.), ~e F ['~ə] f (-/no pl.) pulp, squash; mud, slush; 'ℒig adj. pulpy, squashy; muddy, slushy.
matt adj. [mat] faint, feeble; voice, etc.: faint; eye, colour, etc.: dim; colour, light, † stock exchange, style, etc.: dull; metal: tarnished; gold, etc.: dead, dull; chess: mated; ⚡ bulb: non-glare; glass: ground, frosted, matted; ~ setzen at chess: (check)mate s.o.
Matte ['matə] f (-/-n) mat.
'Mattigkeit f (-/no pl.) exhaustion, feebleness; faintness.
'Mattscheibe f phot. focus(s)ing screen; television: screen.
Mauer ['mauər] f (-/-n) wall; ~blümchen fig. ['~blyːmçən] n (-s/-) wall-flower; 'ℒn (-/-n) 1. v/i. make a wall, lay bricks; 2. v/t. build (in stone or brick); '~stein m brick; '~werk n masonry, brickwork.
Maul [maul] n (-[e]s/ℒer) mouth; sl.: halt's ~! shut up!; 'ℒen F v/i. (ge-, h) sulk, pout; '~esel zo. m mule, hinny; '~held F m braggart; '~korb m muzzle; ~schelle F f box on the ear; '~tier zo. n mule;

'**~wurf** zo. m mole; '**~wurfshügel** m molehill.

Maurer ['maurər] m (-s/-) brick-layer, mason; '**~meister** m master mason; '**~polier** m bricklayers' foreman.

Maus zo. [maus] f (-/"e) mouse; **~efalle** ['~zə-] f mousetrap; 2en ['~zən] (ge-, h) 1. v/i. catch mice; 2. F v/t. pinch, pilfer, F swipe.

Mauser ['mauzər] f (-/no pl.) mo(u)lt(ing); in der ~ sein be mo(u)lting; '2n v/refl. (ge-, h) mo(u)lt.

Maximum ['maksimum] n (-s/Maxima) maximum.

Mayonnaise [majo'nɛːzə] f (-/-n) mayonnaise.

Mechani|k [me'ça:nik] f 1. (-/no pl.) mechanics mst sg.; 2. ⊕ (-/-en) mechanism; **~ker** m (-s/-) mechanic; 2sch adj. mechanical; 2sieren [~ani'zi:rən] v/t. (no -ge-, h) mechanize; '~smus ⊕ [~a'nismus] m (-/Mechanismen) mechanism; clock, watch, etc.: works pl.

meckern ['mɛkərn] v/i. (ge-, h) bleat; fig. grumble (über acc. over, at, about), carp (at); nag (at); sl. grouse, Am. sl. gripe.

Medaill|e [me'daljə] f (-/-n) medal; **~on** [~'jõː] n (-s/-s) medallion; locket.

Medikament [medika'mɛnt] n (-[e]s/-e) medicament, medicine.

Medizin [medi'tsiːn] f 1. (-/no pl.) (science of) medicine; 2. (-/-en) medicine, F physic; **~er** m (-s/-) medical man; medical student; 2isch adj. medical; medicinal.

Meer [meːr] n (-[e]s/-e) sea (a. fig.), ocean; '**~busen** m gulf, bay; '**~enge** f strait(s pl.); '**~esspiegel** m sea level; '**~rettich** ♣ m horse-radish; '**~schweinchen** zo. n guinea-pig.

Mehl [meːl] n (-[e]s/-e) flour; meal; '**~brei** m pap; '2ig adj. floury, mealy; farinaceous; '**~speise** f sweet dish, pudding; '**~suppe** f gruel.

mehr [meːr] 1. adj. more; er hat ~ Geld als ich he has (got) more money than I; 2. adv. more; nicht ~ no more, no longer, not any longer; ich habe nichts ~ I have nothing left; '2arbeit f additional work; overtime; '2ausgaben f/pl. additional expenditure; '2betrag m surplus; '**~deutig** adj. ambiguous; '2einnahme(n pl.) f additional receipts pl.; '**~en** v/t. (ge-, h) augment, increase; sich ~ multiply, grow; '**~ere** adj. and indef. pron. several, some; '**~fach** 1. adj. manifold, repeated; 2. adv. repeatedly, several times; '2gebot n higher bid; '2heit f (-/-en) majority, plurality; '2kosten pl. additional expense; '**~malig** adj. repeated, reiterated;

~mals adv. ['~maːls] several times, repeatedly; '**~sprachig** adj. polyglot; '**~stimmig** ♪ adj.: ~er Gesang part-song; '2verbrauch m excess consumption; '2wertsteuer ✝ f (-/no pl.) value-added tax; '2zahl f majority; gr. plural (form); die ~ (gen.) most of.

meiden ['maɪdən] v/t. (irr., ge-, h) avoid, shun, keep away from.

Meile ['maɪlə] f (-/-n) mile; '**~n-stein** m milestone.

mein poss. pron. [maɪn] my; der (die, das) ~e my; die 2en pl. my family, F my people or folks pl.; ich habe das ~e getan I have done all I can; '~e Damen und Herren! Ladies and Gentlemen!

Meineid ♣ ['maɪn?-] m perjury; '2ig adj. perjured.

meinen ['maɪnən] v/t. (ge-, h) think, believe, be of (the) opinion, Am. a. reckon, guess; say; mean; wie ~ Sie das? what do you mean by that?; ~ Sie das ernst? do you (really) mean it?; es gut ~ mean well.

meinetwegen adv. ['maɪnət'-] for my sake; on my behalf; because of me, on my account; for all I care; I don't mind or care.

'**Meinung** f (-/-en) opinion (über acc., von about, of); die öffentliche ~ (the) public opinion; meiner ~ nach in my opinion, to my mind; j-m (gehörig) die ~ sagen give s.o. a piece of one's mind; '~saustausch ['maɪnuŋs?-] m exchange of views (über acc. on); '~sverschiedenheit f difference of opinion (über acc. on); disagreement.

Meise orn. ['maɪzə] f (-/-n) titmouse.

Meißel ['maɪsəl] m (-s/-) chisel; '2n v/t. and v/i. (ge-, h) chisel; carve.

meist [maɪst] 1. adj. most; die ~en Leute most people; die ~e Zeit most of one's time; 2. adv.: s. meistens; am ~en most (of all); 2bietende ['~biːtəndə] m (-n/-n) highest bidder; '~ens adv. ['~əns], '~enteils adv. mostly, in most cases; usually.

Meister ['maɪstər] m (-s/-) master, sl. boss; sports: champion; '2haft 1. adj. masterly; 2. a. adv. in a masterly manner or way; '2n v/t. (ge-, h) master; '2schaft f 1. (-/no pl.) mastery; 2. (-/-en) sports: championship, title; '~stück n, '~werk n masterpiece.

'**Meistgebot** n highest bid, best offer.

Melanchol|ie [melaŋko'liː] f (-/-n) melancholy; 2isch adj. [~'ko:liʃ] melancholy; ~ sein F have the blues.

Melde|amt ['mɛldə-] n registration office; '~liste f sports: list of entries; '2n v/t. (ge-, h) announce; j-m et. ~ inform s.o. of s.th.; officially: notify s.th. to s.o.; j-n ~

enter s.o.'s name *(für, zu* for); *sich* ~ report o.s. *(bei* to); *school, etc.*: put up one's hand; answer the telephone; enter (one's name) *(für, zu* for *examination, etc.*); *sich* ~ *zu* apply for; *sich auf ein Inserat* ~ answer an advertisement.

'**Meldung** f (-/-en) information, advice; announcement; report; registration; application; *sports:* entry.

melke|n ['mɛlkən] *v/t.* ([*irr.*,] ge-, h) milk; '**2r** m (-s/-) milker.

Melod|ie ♪ [melo'di:] f (-/-n) melody; tune, air; **2isch** *adj.* [~'lo:diʃ] melodious, tuneful.

Melone [me'lo:nə] f (-/-n) ♀ melon; F bowler(-hat), *Am.* derby.

Membran [mem'bra:n] f (-/-en), ~e f (-/-n) membrane; *teleph. a.* diaphragm.

Memme F ['mɛmə] f (-/-n) coward; poltroon.

Memoiren [memo'a:rən] *pl.* memoirs *pl.*

Menagerie [menaʒə'ri:] f (-/-n) menagerie.

Menge ['mɛŋə] f (-/-n) quantity; amount; multitude; crowd; *in großer* ~ in abundance; *persons, animals:* in crowds; e-e ~ *Geld* plenty of money, F lots *pl.* of money; e-e ~ *Bücher* a great many books; '**2n** *v/t.* (ge-, h) mix, blend; *sich* ~ mix (*unter acc.* with), mingle (with); *sich* ~ *in* (*acc.*) meddle *or* interfere with.

Mensch [mɛnʃ] m (-en/-en) human being; man; person, individual; *die* ~*en pl.* people *pl.*, the world, mankind; *kein* ~ nobody.

'**Menschen|affe** *zo.* m anthropoid ape; '~**alter** n generation, age; '~**feind** m misanthropist; '**2feindlich** *adj.* misanthropic; '~**fresser** m (-s/-) cannibal, man-eater; '~**freund** m philanthropist; '**2-freundlich** *adj.* philanthropic; '~**gedenken** n (-s/*no pl.*): *seit* ~ from time immemorial, within the memory of man; '~**geschlecht** n human race, mankind; '~**haß** m misanthropy; '~**kenner** m judge of men *or* human nature; '~**kenntnis** f knowledge of human nature; '~**leben** n human life; '**2leer** *adj.* deserted; '~**liebe** f philanthropy; '~**menge** f crowd (of people), throng; '**2möglich** *adj.* humanly possible; '~**raub** m kidnap(p)ing; '~**rechte** n/pl. human rights *pl.*; '**2scheu** *adj.* unsociable, shy; '~**seele** f: *keine* ~ not a living soul; '~**verstand** m human understanding; *gesunder* ~ common sense, F horse sense; '~**würde** f dignity of man.

'**Menschheit** f (-/*no pl.*) human race, mankind.

'**menschlich** *adj.* human; *fig.* hu-

mane; '**2keit** f (-/*no pl.*) human nature; humanity, humaneness.

Mentalität [mɛntali'tɛ:t] f (-/-en) mentality.

merk|bar *adj.* ['mɛrkba:r] s. merklich; '**2blatt** n leaflet, instructional pamphlet; '**2buch** n notebook; '~**en** (ge-, h) 1. *v/t.*: ~ *auf* (*acc.*) pay attention to, listen to; 2. *v/t.* notice, perceive; find out, discover; *sich et.* ~ remember s.th.; bear s.th. in mind; '~**lich** *adj.* noticeable, perceptible; '**2mal** n (-[e]s/-e) mark, sign; characteristic, feature.

'**merkwürdig** *adj.* noteworthy, remarkable; strange, odd, curious; ~**erweise** *adv.* ['~gər'-] strange to say, strangely enough; '**2keit** f (-/-en) remarkableness; curiosity; peculiarity.

meßbar *adj.* ['mɛsba:r] measurable.

Messe ['mɛsə] f (-/-n) ✝ fair; *eccl.* mass; ⚓ mess.

messen ['mɛsən] *v/t.* (irr., ge-, h) measure; ⚓ sound; *sich mit j-m* ~ compete with s.o.; *sich nicht mit j-m* ~ *können* be no match for s.o.; *gemessen an* (*dat.*) measured against, compared with.

Messer ['mɛsər] n (-s/-) knife; ⚕ scalpel; *bis aufs* ~ to the knife; *auf des* ~*s Schneide* on a razor-edge *or* razor's edge; '~**griff** m knife-handle; '~**held** m stabber; '~**klinge** f knife-blade; '~**schmied** m cutler; '~**schneide** f knife-edge; '~**stecher** m (-s/-) stabber; '~**stecherei** [~ʃtɛça'raɪ] f (-/-en) knifing, knife-battle; '~**stich** m stab with a knife.

Messing ['mɛsiŋ] n (-s/*no pl.*) brass; '~**blech** n sheet-brass.

'**Meß|instrument** n measuring instrument; '~**latte** f surveyor's rod; '~**tisch** m surveyor's *or* plane table.

Metall [me'tal] n (-s/-e) metal; ~**arbeiter** m metal worker; **2en** *adj.* (of) metal, metallic; ~**geld** n coin(s *pl.*), specie; ~**glanz** m metallic lust|re, *Am.* -er; **2haltig** *adj.* metalliferous; ~**industrie** f metallurgical industry; ~**waren** f/pl. hardware.

Meteor *ast.* [mete'o:r] m (-s/-e) meteor; ~**ologe** [~oro'lo:gə] m (-n/-n) meteorologist; ~**ologie** [~orolo'gi:] f (-/*no pl.*) meteorology.

Meter ['me:tər] n, m (-s/-) met|re, *Am.* -er; '~**maß** n tape-measure.

Method|e [me'to:də] f (-/-n) method; ⊕ *a.* technique; **2isch** *adj.* methodical. [metropolis.\

Metropole [metro'po:lə] f (-/-n)\
Metzel|ei [mɛtsə'laɪ] f (-/-en) slaughter, massacre; '**2n** *v/t.* (ge-, h) butcher, slaughter, massacre.

Metzger ['mɛtsgər] m (-s/-) butcher; ~**ei** [~'raɪ] f (-/-en) butcher's (shop).

Meuchel|mord ['mɔʏçəl-] m assassination; '~**mörder** m assassin.

Meute ['mɔytə] f (-/-n) pack of hounds; fig. gang; '~rei [~'raɪ] f (-/-en) mutiny; '~rer m (-s/-) mutineer; '2risch adj. mutinous; '2rn v/i. (ge-, h) mutiny (gegen against).

mich pers. pron. [miç] me; ~ (selbst) myself.

mied [miːt] pret. of meiden.

Mieder ['miːdər] n (-s/-) bodice; corset; '~waren f/pl. corsetry.

Miene ['miːnə] f (-/-n) countenance, air; feature; gute ~ zum bösen Spiel machen grin and bear it; ~ machen zu inf. offer or threaten to inf.

mies F adj. [miːs] miserable, poor; out of sorts, seedy.

Miet|e ['miːtə] f (-/-n) rent; hire; zur ~ wohnen live in lodgings, be a tenant; '2en v/t. (ge-, h) rent (land, building, etc.); hire (horse, etc.); (take on) lease (land, etc.); ⚓, ✕ charter; '~er m (-s/-) tenant; lodger, Am. a. roomer; ♈ lessee; '2frei adj. rent-free; '~shaus n block of flats, Am. apartment house; '~vertrag m tenancy agreement; lease; '~wohnung f lodgings pl., flat, Am. apartment.

Migräne ♈ [mi'grɛːnə] f (-/-n) migraine, megrim; sick headache.

Mikrophon [mikro'foːn] n (-s/-e) microphone, F mike.

Mikroskop [mikro'skoːp] n (-s/-e) microscope, 2isch adj. microscopic(al).

Milbe zo. ['milbə] f (-/-n) mite.

Milch [milç] f (-/no pl.) milk; milt, soft roe (of fish); '~bar f milk-bar; '~bart fig. m stripling; '~brötchen n (French) roll; '~gesicht n baby face; '~glas n frosted glass; '2ig adj. milky; '~kanne f milk-can; '~kuh f milk cow (a. fig.); '~mädchen F n milkmaid, dairymaid; '~mann F m milkman, dairyman; '~pulver n milk-powder; '~reis m rice-milk; '~straße ast. f Milky Way, Galaxy; '~wirtschaft f dairy-farm(ing); '~zahn m milktooth.

mild [milt] 1. adj. weather, punishment, etc.: mild; air, weather, light, etc.: soft; wine, etc.: mellow, smooth; reprimand, etc.: gentle; 2. adv.: et. ~ beurteilen take a lenient view of s. th.

milde ['mildə] 1. adj. s. mild 1; 2. adv.: ~ gesagt to put it mildly; 3. 2 f (-/no pl.) mildness; softness; smoothness; gentleness.

milder|n ['mildərn] v/t. (ge-, h) soften, mitigate; soothe, alleviate (pain, etc.); ~de Umstände ♈ extenuating circumstances; '2ung f (-/-en) softening, mitigation; alleviation.

'**mild|herzig** adj. charitable; '2herzigkeit f (-/no pl.) charitableness;

'~tätig adj. charitable; '2tätigkeit f charity.

Milieu [mil'jøː] n (-s/-s) surroundings pl., environment; class, circles pl.; local colo(u)r.

Militär [mili'tɛːr] 1. n (-s/no pl.) military, armed forces pl.; army; 2. m (-s/-s) military man, soldier; ~attaché [~ataʃeː] m (-s/-s) military attaché; ~dienst m military service; 2isch adj. military; ~musik f military music; ~regierung f military government; ~zeit f (-/no pl.) term of military service.

Miliz ✕ [mi'liːts] f (-/-en) militia; ~soldat ✕ m militiaman.

Milliarde [mil'jardə] f (-/-n) thousand millions, milliard, Am. billion.

Millimeter [mili'-] n, m millimet|re, Am. -er.

Million [mil'joːn] f (-/-en) million; ~är [~o'nɛːr] m (-s/-e) millionaire.

Milz anat. [milts] f (-/-en) spleen, milt.

minder ['mindər] 1. adv. less; nicht ~ no less, likewise; 2. adj. less(er); smaller; minor; inferior; ~begabt adj. less gifted; ~bemittelt adj. ['~bəmitəlt] of moderate means; '2betrag m deficit, shortage; '2einnahme f shortfall in receipts; '2gewicht n short weight; '2heit f (-/-en) minority; ~jährig adj. ['~jɛːriç] under age, minor; '2jährigkeit f (-/no pl.) minority; '~n v/t. and v/refl. (ge-, h) diminish, lessen, decrease; '2ung f (-/-en) decrease, diminution; ~wertig adj. inferior, of inferior quality; '2wertigkeit f (-/no pl.) inferiority; ✝ inferior quality; '2wertigkeitskomplex m inferiority complex.

mindest adj. ['mindəst] least; slightest; minimum; nicht die ~e Aussicht not the slightest chance; nicht im ~en not in the least, by no means; zum ~en at least; '2alter n minimum age; '2anforderungen f/pl. minumum requirements pl.; '2betrag m lowest amount; '2einkommen n minimum income; '~ens adv. at least; '2gebot n lowest bid; '2lohn m minimum wage; '2maß n minimum; auf ein ~ herabsetzen minimize; '2preis m minimum price.

Mine ['miːnə] f (-/-n) ✕, ✕, ⚓ mine; pencil: lead; ball-point-pen: refill.

Mineral [mina'raːl] n (-s/-e, -ien) mineral, 2isch adj. mineral; ~ogie [~alo'giː] f (-/-no pl.) mineralogy; ~wasser n (-s/⁼) mineral water.

Miniatur [minia'tuːr] f (-/-en) miniature; ~gemälde n miniature.

Minirock ['mini-] m miniskirt.

Minister [mi'nistər] m (-s/-) minister; Secretary (of State), Am. Secretary; **~ium** [~'te:rjum] *n* (-s/Ministerien) ministry; Office, *Am.* Department; **~präsident** *m* prime minister, premier; *in Germany, etc.*: minister president; **~rat** *m* (-[e]s/≠e) cabinet council.

minus *adv.* ['mi:nus] minus, less, deducting.

Minute [mi'nu:tə] *f* (-/-n) minute; **~nzeiger** *m* minute-hand.

mir *pers. pron.* [mi:r] (to) me.

Misch|ehe ['miʃ'-] *f* mixed marriage; intermarriage; **'2en** *v/t.* (ge-, h) mix, mingle; blend (*coffee, tobacco, etc.*); alloy (*metal*); shuffle (*cards*); sich ~ in (*acc.*) interfere in; join in (*conversation*); sich ~ unter (*acc.*) mix or mingle with (*the crowd*); **~ling** ['~liŋ] *m* (-s/-e) halfbreed, half-caste; ♀, *zo.* hybrid; **~masch** F ['~maʃ] *m* (-es/-e) hotchpotch, jumble; **'~ung** *f* (-/-en) mixture; blend; alloy.

miß|achten [mis'-] *v/t.* (no -ge-, h) disregard, ignore, neglect; slight, despise; **'2achtung** *f* disregard, neglect; **'~behagen 1.** *v/i.* (no -ge-, h) displease; **2.** ♀ *n* discomfort, uneasiness; **'2bildung** *f* malformation, deformity; **~'billigen** *v/t.* (no -ge-, h) disapprove (of); **2'billigung** *f* disapproval; **'2brauch** *m* abuse; misuse; **'~brauchen** *v/t.* (no -ge-, h) abuse; misuse; **~bräuchlich** *adj.* ['~brɔyçliç] abusive; improper; **~'deuten** *v/t.* (no -ge-, h) misinterpret; **2deutung** *f* misinterpretation.

missen ['misən] *v/t.* (ge-, h) miss; do without, dispense with.

'Miß|erfolg *m* failure; fiasco; **'~ernte** *f* bad harvest, crop failure.

Misse|tat ['misə-] *f* misdeed; crime; **'~täter** *m* evil-doer, offender; criminal.

miß|'fallen *v/i.* (irr. fallen, no -ge-, h): j-m ~ displease s.o.; **'2fallen** *n* (-s/no pl.) displeasure, dislike; **'~fällig 1.** *adj.* displeasing; shocking; disparaging; **2.** *adv.*: sich ~ äußern über (*acc.*) speak ill of; **'2geburt** *f* monster, freak (of nature), deformity; **'2geschick** *n* bad luck, misfortune; mishap; **~gestimmt** *fig. adj.* ['~gəʃtimt] *s.* mißmutig; **'~glücken** *v/i.* (no -ge-, sein) fail; **~gönnen** *v/t.* (no -ge-, h): j-m et. ~ envy or grudge s.o. s.th.; **2griff** *m* mistake, blunder; **2gunst** *f* envy, jealousy; **'~günstig** *adj.* envious, jealous; **~'handeln** *v/t.* (no -ge-, h) ill-treat; maul, sl. manhandle; **2'handlung** *f* ill-treatment; mauling, sl. manhandling; ⚖ assault and battery; **'2heirat** *f* misalliance; **'~hellig** *adj.* dissonant, dissentient; **'2helligkeit** *f* (-/-en) dissonance, dissension; discord.

Mission [mis'jo:n] *f* (-/-en) mission

(*a. pol. and fig.*); **~ar** [~o'na:r] *m* (-s/-e) missionary.

'Miß|klang *m* dissonance, discord (*both a. fig.*); **'~kredit** *fig. m* (-[e]s/no pl.) discredit; in ~ bringen bring discredit upon s.o.

miß|'lang *pret.* of mißlingen; **'~lich** *adj.* awkward; unpleasant; **~liebig** *adj.* ['~li:biç] unpopular; **~lingen** [~'liŋən] *v/i.* (irr., no -ge-, sein) fail; **2lingen** *n* (-s/no pl.) failure; **2mut** *m* ill humo(u)r; discontent; **'~mutig** *adj.* ill-humo(u)red; discontented; **~'raten 1.** *v/i.* (irr. raten, no -ge-, sein) fail; turn out badly; **2.** *adj.* wayward; ill-bred; **2stand** *m* nuisance; grievance; **'2stimmung** *f* ill humo(u)r; **2ton** *m* (-[e]s/≠e) dissonance, discord (*both a. fig.*); **~'trauen** *v/i.* (no -ge-, h): j-m ~ distrust or mistrust s.o.; **2trauen** *n* (-s/no pl.) distrust, mistrust; suspicion; **~trauisch** ['~trauiʃ] *adj.* distrustful; suspicious; **2vergnügen** *n* (-s/no pl.) displeasure; **~vergnügt** *adj.* displeased; discontented; **2verhältnis** *n* disproportion; incongruity; **2verständnis** *n* misunderstanding; dissension; **'~verstehen** *v/t.* (irr. stehen, no -ge-, h) misunderstand, mistake (*intention, etc.*); **2wirtschaft** *f* maladministration, mismanagement.

Mist [mist] *m* (-es/-e) dung, manure; dirt; F *fig.* trash, rubbish; **'~beet** *n* hotbed.

Mistel ♀ ['mistəl] *f* (-/-n) mistletoe.

'Mist|gabel *f* dung-fork; **'~haufen** *m* dung-hill.

mit [mit] **1.** *prp.* (*dat.*) with; ~ 20 Jahren at (the age of) twenty; ~ e-m Schlage at a blow; ~ Gewalt by force; ~ der Bahn by train; **2.** *adv.* also, too; ~ dabeisein be there too, be (one) of the party.

Mit|arbeiter ['mit'-] *m* co-worker; writing, art, *etc.*: collaborator; colleague; *newspaper, etc.*: contributor (*an dat.* to); **'2benutzen** *v/t.* (*sep.,* no -ge-, h) use jointly or in common; **'~besitzer** *m* joint owner; **'~bestimmungsrecht** *n* right of co-determination; **'~bewerber** *m* competitor; **'~bewohner** *m* co-inhabitant, fellow-lodger; **'~bringen** *v/t.* (irr. bringen, *sep.,* -ge-, h) bring along (with one); **~bringsel** ['~briŋzəl] *n* (-s/-) little present; **'~bürger** *m* fellow-citizen; **~einander** *adv.* [mit'ai'nandər] together, jointly; with each other, with one another; **~empfinden** ['mit'-] *n* (-s/no pl.) sympathy; **~erbe** ['mit'-] *m* co-heir; **~esser** ♀ ['mit'-] *m* (-s/-) blackhead; **'2fahren** *v/i.* (irr. fahren, *sep.,* -ge-, sein): mit j-m ~ drive or go with s.o.; j-n ~ lassen give s.o. a lift; **'2fühlen**

v/i. (*sep.*, *-ge-*, *h*) sympathize (*mit* with); '♀**geben** *v/t.* (*irr. geben*, *sep.*, *-ge-*, *h*) give along (*dat.* with); '♀**gefühl** *n* sympathy; '♀**gehen** *v/i.* (*irr. gehen*, *sep.*, *-ge-*, *sein*): *mit j-m* ~ go with s.o.; '♀**gift** *f* (*-/-en*) dowry, marriage portion.

'**Mitglied** *n* member; '♀**erversammlung** *f* general meeting; '♀**erzahl** *f* membership; '♀**sbeitrag** *m* subscription; '♀**schaft** *f* (*-/no pl.*) membership.

mit|'**hin** *adv.* consequently, therefore; ♀**inhaber** ['mit♀-] *m* copartner; '♀**kämpfer** *m* fellowcombatant; '♀**kommen** *v/i.* (*irr. kommen*, *sep.*, *-ge-*, *sein*) come along (*mit* with); *fig.* be able to follow; '♀**läufer** *pol. m* nominal member; *contp.* trimmer.

'**Mitleid** *n* (*-[e]s/no pl.*) compassion, pity; sympathy; *aus* ~ out of pity; ~ *haben mit* have or take pity on; '♀**enschaft** *f* (*-/no pl.*): *in* ~ *ziehen* affect; implicate, involve; damage; '♀**ig** *adj.* compassionate, pitiful; ♀(s)**los** *adj.* ['♀-t-] pitiless, merciless; ♀(s)**voll** *adj.* ['♀-t-] pitiful, compassionate.

'**mit**|'**machen** (*sep.*, *-ge-*, *h*) 1. *v/i.* make one of the party; 2. *v/t.* take part in, participate in; follow, go with (*fashion*); go through (*hardships*); '♀**mensch** *m* fellow creature; '♀**nehmen** *v/t.* (*irr. nehmen*, *sep.*, *-ge-*, *h*) take along (with one); *fig.* exhaust, wear out; *j-n* (*im Auto*) ~ give s.o. a lift; **~nichten** *adv.* [♀-'niçtən] by no means, not at all; '♀**rechnen** *v/t.* (*sep.*, *-ge-*, *h*) include (in the account); *nicht* ~ leave out of account; *nicht mitgerechnet* not counting; '♀**reden** (*sep.*, *-ge-*, *h*) 1. *v/i.* join in the conversation; 2. *v/t.*: *ein Wort or Wörtchen mitzureden haben* have a say (*bei* in); '♀**reißen** *v/t.* (*irr. reißen*, *sep.*, *-ge-*, *h*) tear or drag along; *fig.* sweep along.

'**Mitschuld** *f* complicity (*an dat.* in); '♀**ig** *adj.* accessary (*an dat.* to *crime*); '♀**ige** *m* accessary, accomplice.

'**Mitschüler** *m* schoolfellow.

'**mitspiel**|**en** (*sep.*, *-ge-*, *h*) 1. *v/i.* play (*bei* with); *sports*: be on the team; *thea.* appear, star (*in a play*); join in a game; *matter*: be involved; *j-m arg or übel* ~ play s.o. a nasty trick; 2. *fig. v/t.* join in (*game*); '♀**er** *m* partner.

'**Mittag** *m* midday, noon; *heute* ♀ at noon today; *zu* ~ *essen* lunch, dine; **~essen** *n* lunch(eon), dinner; '♀**s** *adv.* at noon.

'**Mittags**|**pause** *f* lunch hour; '**~ruhe** *f* midday rest; '**~schlaf** *m*, '**~schläfchen** *n* after-dinner nap, siesta; '**~stunde** *f* noon; '**~tisch**

fig. m lunch, dinner; '**~zeit** *f* noontide; lunch-time, dinner-time.

Mitte ['mitə] *f* (*-/-n*) middle; cent|re, *Am.* -er; *die goldene* ~ the golden or happy mean; *aus unserer* ~ from among us; ~ *Juli* in the middle of July; ~ *Dreißig* in the middle of one's thirties.

'**mitteil**|**en** *v/t.* (*sep.*, *-ge-*, *h*): *j-m et.* ~ communicate s.th. to s.o.; impart s.th. to s.o.; inform s.o. of s.th.; make s.th. known to s.o.; '**~sam** *adj.* communicative; '♀**ung** *f* (*-/-en*) communication; information; communiqué.

Mittel ['mitəl] *n* (*-s/-*) means *sg.*, way; remedy (*gegen* for); average; ♀ mean; *phys.* medium; ~ *pl. a.* means *pl.*, funds *pl.*, money; ~ *pl. und Wege* ways and means *pl.*; '**~alter** *n* Middle Ages *pl.*; '♀**alterlich** *adj.* medi(a)eval; '♀**bar** *adj.* mediate, indirect; '♀**ding** *n*: *ein* ~ *zwischen ... und ...* something between ... and ...; '**~finger** *m* middle finger; '**~gebirge** *n* highlands *pl.*; '♀**groß** *adj.* of medium height; medium-sized; '**~läufer** *m sports*: centre half back, *Am.* center half back; '♀**los** *adj.* without means, destitute; '♀**mäßig** *adj.* middling; mediocre; '**~mäßigkeit** *f* (*-/no pl.*) mediocrity; '**~punkt** *m* cent|re, *Am.* -er; *fig. a.* focus; '♀**s** *prp.* (*gen.*) by (means of), through; '**~schule** *f* intermediate school, *Am.* high school; '**~smann** *m* (*-[e]s/*"er, *Mittelsleute*) mediator, go-between; '**~stand** *m* middle classes *pl.*; '**~stürmer** *m sports*: centre forward, *Am.* center forward; '**~weg** *fig. m* middle course; '**~wort** *gr. n* (*-[e]s/*"er) participle.

mitten *adv.* ['mitən]: ~ *in or an or auf or unter* (*acc.*; *dat.*) in the midst or middle of; ~ *entzwei* right in two; ~ *im Winter* in the depth of winter; ~ *in der Nacht* in the middle or dead of night; ~ *ins Herz* right into the heart; **~'drin** F *adv.* right in the middle; **~'durch** F *adv.* right through or across.

Mitter|**nacht** ['mitər-] *f* midnight; *um* ~ at midnight; ♀**nächtig** *adj.* ['**~**nɛçtiç], '♀**nächtlich** *adj.* midnight.

Mittler ['mitlər] 1. *m* (*-s/-*) mediator, intercessor; 2. ♀ *adj.* middle, central; average, medium; '♀'**weile** *adv.* meanwhile, (in the) meantime.

Mittwoch ['mitvɔx] *m* (*-[e]s/-e*) Wednesday; '♀**s** *adv.* on Wednesday(s), every Wednesday.

mit|'**unter** *adv.* now and then, sometimes; '**~verantwortlich** *adj.* jointly responsible; '**~welt** *f* (*-/no pl.*): *die* ~ our, *etc.* contemporaries *pl.*

'mitwirk|en *v/i.* (*sep.*, -ge-, *h*) co-operate (*bei* in), contribute (to), take part (in); '2ende *m* (-*n*/-*n*) *thea.* performer, actor, player (*a. ♪*); die ~*n pl.* the cast; '2ung *f* (-/no *pl.*) co(-)operation, contribution.

'Mitwisser *m* (-*s*/-) confidant; ⁿᵗᵗᶻ accessary.   [*rechnen.*]

'mitzählen *v/t.* (*sep.*, -ge-, *h*) *s.* mit-|

Mix|becher ['miks-] *m* (cocktail-shaker; '2en *v/t.* (ge-, *h*) mix; ~tur [~'tu:r] *f* (-/-en) mixture.

Möbel ['mø:bəl] *n* (-*s*/-) piece of furniture; ~ *pl.* furniture; '~händler *m* furniture-dealer; '~spediteur *m* furniture-remover; '~stück *n* piece of furniture; '~tischler *m* cabinet-maker; '~wagen *m* pan-technicon, *Am.* furniture truck.

mobil *adj.* ['mo'bi:l] ⚔ mobile; *F* active, nimble; ~ machen ⚔ mobilize; 2iar [~il'ja:r] *n* (-*s*/-*e*) furniture; movables *pl.*; ~isieren [~ili-'zi:rən] *v/t.* (no -ge-, *h*) ⚔ mobilize; ✝ realize (*property*, *etc.*); 2machung ⚔ [mo'bi:lmaxuŋ] *f* (-/-en) mobilization.

möblieren [mø'bli:rən] *v/t.* (no -ge-, *h*) furnish; möbliertes Zimmer furnished room, *F* bed-sitter.

mochte ['mɔxtə] *pret.* of mögen.

Mode ['mo:də] *f* (-/-n) fashion, vogue; use, custom; die neueste ~ the latest fashion; *in* ~ in fashion *or* vogue; *aus der* ~ kommen grow *or* go out of fashion; die ~ bestimmen set the fashion; '~artikel *m/pl.* fancy goods *pl.*, novelties *pl.*; '~far-be *f* fashionable colo(u)r.

Modell [mo'dɛl] *n* (-*s*/-*e*) ⊕, *fashion*, *paint.*: model; pattern, design; ⊕ mo(u)ld; *j-m* ~ stehen *paint.* pose for s.o.; ~eisenbahn *f* model railway; 2ieren [~'li:rən] *v/t.* (no -ge-, *h*) model, mo(u)ld, fashion.

'Moden|schau *f* dress parade, fashion-show; '~zeitung *f* fashion magazine.

Moder ['mo:dər] *m* (-*s*/no *pl.*) must, putrefaction; '~geruch *m* musty smell; '2ig *adj.* musty, putrid.

modern¹ ['mo:dərn] *v/i.* (ge-, *h*) putrefy, rot, decay.

modern² *adj.* [mo'dɛrn] modern; progressive; up-to-date; fashionable; ~isieren [~i'zi:rən] *v/t.* (no -ge-, *h*) modernize, bring up to date.

'Mode|salon *m* fashion house; '~schmuck *m* costume jewel(le)ry; '~waren *f/pl.* fancy goods *pl.*; '~zeichner *m* fashion-designer.

modifizieren [modifi'tsi:rən] *v/t.* (no -ge-, *h*) modify.

modisch *adj.* ['mo:diʃ] fashionable, stylish.   [liner.]

Modistin [mo'distin] *f* (-/-nen) mil-|

Mogel|ei F [mo:gə'laɪ] *f* (-/-en) cheat; '2n F *v/i.* (ge-, *h*) cheat.

mögen ['mø:gən] (*irr.*, *h*) **1.** *v/i.* (ge-) be willing; ich mag nicht I don't like to; **2.** *v/t.* (ge-) want, wish; like, be fond of; nicht ~ dislike; not to be keen on (*food*, *etc.*); lieber ~ like better, prefer; **3.** *v/aux.* (no -ge-) may, might; ich möchte wissen I should like to know; ich möchte lieber gehen I would rather go; das mag (wohl) sein that's (well) possible; wo er auch sein mag wherever he may be; mag er sagen, was er will let him say what he likes.

möglich ['mø:kliç] **1.** *adj.* possible; practicable, feasible; *market*, *criminal*, *etc.*: potential; alle ~en all sorts of; alles ~e all sorts of things; sein ~stes tun do one's utmost *or* level best; nicht ~! you don't say (so)!; so bald *etc.* wie ~ = **2.** *adv.*: ~st bald *etc.* as soon, *etc.*, as possible; '~er'weise *adv.* possibly, if possible; perhaps; '2keit *f* (-/-en) possibility; chance; nach ~ if possible.

Mohammedan|er [mohame'da:-nər] *m* (-*s*/-) Muslim, Moslem, Mohammedan; 2isch *adj.* Muslim, Moslem, Mohammedan.

Mohn ⚘ [mo:n] *m* (-[*e*]*s*/-*e*) poppy.

Möhre ⚘ ['mø:rə] *f* (-/-*n*) carrot.

Mohrrübe ⚘ ['mo:r-] *f* carrot.

Molch *zo.* [mɔlç] *m* (-[*e*]*s*/-*e*) salamander; newt.

Mole ⚓ ['mo:lə] *f* (-/-*n*) mole, jetty.

molk [mɔlk] *pret.* of melken.

Molkerei [mɔlkə'raɪ] *f* (-/-en) dairy; ~produkte *n/pl.* dairy products *pl.*

Moll ♪ [mɔl] *n* (-/-) minor (key).

mollig F *adj.* ['mɔliç] snug, cosy, plump, rounded.

Moment [mo'mɛnt] (-[*e*]*s*/-*e*) **1.** *m* moment, instant; im ~ at the moment; **2.** *n* motive; fact(or); ⊕ momentum; ⊕ impulse (*a. fig.*); 2an [~'ta:n] **1.** *adj.* momentary; **2.** *adv.* at the moment, for the time being; ~aufnahme *phot. f* snapshot, instantaneous photograph.

Monarch [mo'narç] *m* (-*en*/-*en*) monarch; ~ie [~'çi:] *f* (-/-*n*) monarchy.

Monat ['mo:nat] *m* (-[*e*]*s*/-*e*) month; 2elang **1.** *adj.* lasting for months; **2.** *adv.* for months; '2lich **1.** *adj.* monthly; **2.** *adv.* monthly, a month.

Mönch [mœnç] *m* (-[*e*]*s*/-*e*) monk, friar.

'Mönchs|kloster *n* monastery; '~kutte *f* (monk's) frock; '~leben *n* monastic life; '~orden *m* monastic order; '~zelle *f* monk's cell.

Mond [mo:nt] *m* (-[*e*]*s*/-*e*) moon; hinter dem ~ leben be behind the times; '~fähre *f* lunar module; '~finsternis *f* lunar eclipse; '2hell *adj.* moonlit; '~schein *m* (-[*e*]*s*/no *pl.*) moonlight; '~sichel *f* crescent; '2süchtig *adj.* moonstruck.

Mono|log [mono'lo:k] *m* (-*s*/-*e*)

monologue, *Am. a.* monolog; soliloquy; ᶜ**pol** ✝ *n* (-s/-e) monopoly; ⱻ**polisieren** [‿oli'ziːrən] *v/t.* (no -ge-, h) monopolize; ⱻ**'ton** *adj.* monotonous; ‿**tonie** [‿to'niː] *f* (-/-n) monotony.

Monstrum ['mɔnstrum] *n* (-s/*Monstren, Monstra*) monster.

Montag ['moːn-] *m* Monday; ⱻ**s** *adv.* on Monday(s), every Monday.

Montage ⊕ [mɔn'taːʒə] *f* (-/-n) mounting, fitting; setting up; assemblage, assembly.

Montan|industrie [mɔn'taːn-] *f* coal and steel industries *pl.*; ‿**union** *f* European Coal and Steel Community.

Mont|eur [mɔn'tøːr] *m* (-s/-e) ⊕ fitter, assembler; *esp. mot.,* ⚡ mechanic; ‿**euranzug** *m* overall; ⱻ**ieren** [‿'tiːrən] *v/t.* (no -ge-, h) mount, fit; set up; assemble; ‿**ur** ✕ [‿'tuːr] *f* (-/-en) regimentals *pl.*

Moor [moːr] *n* (-[e]s/-e) bog; swamp; '‿**bad** *n* mud-bath; ⱻ**ig** *adj.* boggy, marshy.

Moos ⚡ [moːs] *n* (-es/-e) moss; ⱻ**ig** *adj.* mossy.

Moped *mot.* ['moːpet] *n* (-s/-s) moped.

Mops *zo.* [mɔps] *m* (-es/*e) pug; ⱻ**en** *v/t.* (ge-, h) F pilfer, pinch; *sl.*: *sich* ~ be bored stiff.

Moral [mo'raːl] *f* (-/*⚡-en) morality; morals *pl.*; moral; ✕, *etc.*: morale; ⱻ**isch** *adj.* moral; ⱻ**isieren** [‿ali'ziːrən] *v/i.* (no -ge-, h) moralize.

Morast [mo'rast] *m* (-es/-e, *e) slough, morass; *s. Moor*; mire, mud; ⱻ**ig** *adj.* marshy; muddy, miry.

Mord [mɔrt] *m* (-[e]s/-e) murder (*an dat.* of); e-n ~ *begehen* commit murder; '‿**anschlag** *m* murderous assault; ⱻ**en** ['‿dən] *v/i.* (ge-, h) commit murder(s).

Mörder ['mœrdər] *m* (-s/-) murderer; ⱻ**isch** *adj.* murderous; *climate, etc.:* deadly; ✝ *competition*: cut-throat.

'**Mord|gier** *f* lust of murder, bloodthirstiness; ⱻ**gierig** *adj.* bloodthirsty; '‿**kommission** *f* homicide squad; '‿**prozeß** ⚖ *m* murder trial.

'**Mords|angst** F *f* blue funk, *sl.* mortal fear; '‿**glück** F *n* stupendous luck; '‿**kerl** F *m* devil of a fellow; '‿**spek'takel** F *m* hullabaloo.

Morgen ['mɔrgən] 1. *m* (-s/-) morning; *measure*: acre; *am* ~ *s.* morgens; 2. ⱻ *adv.* tomorrow; ~ *früh (abend)* tomorrow morning (evening *or* night); ~ *in acht Tagen* tomorrow week; '‿**ausgabe** *f* morning edition; '‿**blatt** *n* morning paper; '‿**dämmerung** *f* dawn, daybreak; '‿**gebet** *n* morning prayer; '‿**gymnastik** *f* morning exercises *pl.*; '‿**land** *n* (-[e]s/*no pl.*) Orient, East;

'‿**rock** *m* peignoir, dressing-gown, wrapper (*for woman*); '‿**röte** *f* dawn; ⱻ**s** *adv.* in the morning; '‿**zeitung** *f* morning paper.

'**morgig** *adj.* of tomorrow.

Morphium *pharm.* ['mɔrfium] *n* (-s/*no pl.*) morphia, morphine.

morsch *adj.* [mɔrʃ] rotten, decayed; brittle.

Mörser ['mœrzər] *m* (-s/-) mortar (*a.* ✕).

Mörtel ['mœrtəl] *m* (-s/-) mortar.

Mosaik [moza'iːk] *n* (-s/-en) mosaic; ‿**fußboden** *m* mosaic *or* tessellated pavement.

Moschee [mɔ'ʃeː] *f* (-/-n) mosque.

Moschus ['mɔʃus] *m* (-/*no pl.*) musk.

Moskito *zo.* [mɔs'kiːto] *m* (-s/-s) mosquito; ‿**netz** *n* mosquito-net.

Moslem ['mɔslem] *m* (-s/-s) Muslim, Moslem.

Most [mɔst] *m* (-es/-e) must, grape-juice; *of apples*: cider; *of pears*: perry.

Mostrich ['mɔstriç] *m* (-[e]s/*no pl.*) mustard.

Motiv [mo'tiːf] *n* (-s/-e) motive, reason; *paint.,* ♪ motif; ⱻ**ieren** [‿i'viːrən] *v/t.* (no -ge-, h) motivate.

Motor ['moːtɔr] *m* (-s/-e) engine, *esp.* ⚡ motor; ✎ motor boat; '‿**defekt** *m* engine *or* ⚡ motor trouble; '‿**haube** *f* bonnet, *Am.* hood; ⱻ**isieren** [motori'ziːrən] *v/t.* (no -ge-, h) motorize; ‿**isierung** [motori'ziːruŋ] *f* (-/*no pl.*) motorization; '‿**rad** *n* motor (bi)cycle; '‿**radfahrer** *m* motor cyclist; '‿**roller** *m* (motor) scooter; '‿**sport** *m* motoring.

Motte *zo.* ['mɔtə] *f* (-/-n) moth.

'**Motten|kugel** *f* moth-ball; ⱻ**sicher** *adj.* mothproof; ⱻ**zerfressen** *adj.* moth-eaten.

Motto ['mɔto] *n* (-s/-s) motto.

Möwe *orn.* ['møːvə] *f* (-/-n) sea-gull, (sea-)mew.

Mücke *zo.* ['mykə] *f* (-/-n) midge, gnat, mosquito; *aus e-r* ~ *e-n Elefanten machen* make a mountain out of a molehill; '‿**nstich** *m* gnat-bite.

Mucker ['mukər] *m* (-s/-) bigot, hypocrite.

müd|e *adj.* ['myːdə] tired, weary; *e-r Sache* ~ *sein* be weary *or* tired of s.th.; ⱻ**igkeit** *f* (-/*no pl.*) tiredness, weariness.

Muff [muf] *m* **1.** (-[e]s/-e) muff; **2.** (-[e]s/*no pl.*) mo(u)ldy *or* musty smell; '‿**e** ⊕ *f* (-/-n) sleeve, socket; ⱻ**eln** F *v/i.* (ge-, h) munch; mumble; ⱻ**ig** *adj.* smell, *etc.*: musty, fusty; *air*: close; *fig.* sulky, sullen.

Mühe ['myːə] *f* (-/-n) trouble, pains *pl.*; *(nicht) der* ~ *wert* (not) worth while; *j-m* ~ *machen* give s.o. trouble; *sich* ~ *geben* take pains (*mit* over, *with* s.th.); ⱻ**los** *adj.*

effortless, easy; '⏾n v/refl. (ge-, h) take pains, work hard; '⏾voll adj. troublesome, hard; laborious.
Mühle ['my:lə] f (-/-n) mill.
'Müh|sal f (-/-e) toil, trouble; hardship; '⏾sam, '⏾selig 1. adj. toilsome, troublesome; difficult; 2. adv. laboriously; with difficulty.
Mulatte [mu'latə] m (-n/-n) mulatto.
Mulde ['muldə] f (-/-n) trough; depression, hollow.
Mull [mul] m (-[e]s/-e) mull.
Müll [myl] m (-[e]s/no pl.) dust, rubbish, refuse, Am. a. garbage; '⏾abfuhr f removal of refuse; '⏾eimer m dust-bin, Am. garbage can.
Müller ['mylər] m (-s/-) miller.
'Müll|fahrer m dust-man, Am. garbage collector; '⏾haufen m dust-heap; '⏾kasten m s. Mülleimer; '⏾kutscher m s. Müllfahrer; '⏾wagen m dust-cart, Am. garbage cart.
Multipli|kation ⚔ [multiplika-'tsjo:n] f (-/-en) multiplication; ⏾zieren ⚔ [~'tsi:rən] v/t. (no -ge-, h) multiply (mit by).
Mumie ['mu:mjə] f (-/-n) mummy.
Mumps ⚔ [mumps] m, F f (-/no pl.) mumps.
Mund [munt] m (-[e]s/⏞er) mouth; den ~ halten hold one's tongue; den ~ voll nehmen talk big; sich den ~ verbrennen put one's foot in it; nicht auf den ~ gefallen sein have a ready or glib tongue; j-m über den ~ fahren cut s.o. short; '⏾art f dialect; '⏾artlich adj. dialectal.
Mündel ['myndəl] m, n (-s/-), girl: a. f (-/-n) ward, pupil; '⏾sicher adj.: ⏾e Papiere n/pl. 🌱 gilt-edged securities pl.
münden ['myndən] v/i. (ge-, h): ~ in (acc.) river, etc.: fall or flow into; street, etc.: run into.
'mund|faul adj. too lazy to speak; '⏾gerecht adj. palatable (a. fig.); '⏾harmonika f f mouth-organ; '⏾höhle anat. f oral cavity.
mündig ⚖ adj. ['myndiç] of age; ~ werden come of age; '⏾keit f (-/no pl.) majority.
mündlich ['myntliç] 1. adj. oral, verbal; 2. adv. a. by word of mouth.
'Mund|pflege f oral hygiene; '⏾raub ⚖ m theft of comestibles; '⏾stück n mouthpiece (of musical instrument, etc.); tip (of cigarette); 'otot adj.: ~ machen silence or gag s.o.
'Mündung f (-/-en) mouth; a. estuary (of river); muzzle (of fire-arms).
'Mund|vorrat m provisions pl., victuals pl.; '⏾wasser n (-s/⏞) mouth-wash, gargle; '⏾werk F fig. n: ein gutes ~ haben have the gift of the gab.
Munition [muni'tsjo:n] f (-/-en) ammunition.

munkeln F ['muŋkəln] (ge-, h) 1. v/i. whisper; 2. v/t. whisper, rumo(u)r; man munkelt there is a rumo(u)r afloat. [lively; merry.)
munter adj. ['muntər] awake; fig.⏜
Münz|e ['myntsə] f (-/-n) coin; (small) change; medal; mint; für bare ~ nehmen take at face value; j-m et. mit gleicher ~ heimzahlen pay s.o. back in his own coin; '⏾einheit f (monetary) unit, standard of currency; '⏾en v/t. (ge-, h) coin, mint; gemünzt sein auf (acc.) be meant for, be aimed at; '⏾fernsprecher teleph. m coin-box telephone; '⏾fuß m standard (of coinage); '⏾wesen n monetary system.
mürbe adj. ['myrbə] tender; pastry, etc.: crisp, short; meat: well-cooked; material: brittle; F fig. worn-out, demoralized; F j-n ~ machen break s.o.'s resistance; F ~ werden give in.
Murmel ['murməl] f (-/-n) marble; '⏾n v/t. and v/i. (ge-, h) mumble, murmur; '⏾tier zo. n marmot.
murren ['murən] v/i. (ge-, h) grumble, F grouch (both: über acc. at, over, about).
mürrisch adj. ['myriʃ] surly, sullen.
Mus [mu:s] n (-es/-e) pap; stewed fruit.
Muschel ['muʃəl] f (-/-n) zo.: mussel; shell, conch; teleph. ear-piece.
Museum [mu'ze:um] n (-s/Museen) museum.
Musik [mu'zi:k] f (-/no pl.) music; '⏾alienhandlung [~i'ka:ljən-] f music-shop; ⏾alisch adj. [~i'ka:liʃ] musical; ~ant [~i'kant] m (-en/-en) musician; ~automat m juke-box; ~er ['mu:zikər] m (-s/-) musician; bandsman; ~instrument n musical instrument; ~lehrer m music-master; ~stunde f music-lesson; ~truhe f radiogram(ophone), Am. radio-phonograph.
musizieren [muzi'tsi:rən] v/i. (no -ge-, h) make or have music.
Muskat ⚘ [mus'ka:t] m (-[e]s/-e) nutmeg; ~nuß ⚘ f nutmeg.
Muskel ['muskəl] m (-s/-n) muscle; '⏾kater F m stiffness and soreness, Am. a. charley horse; '⏾kraft f muscular strength; '⏾zerrung ⚕ f pulled muscle.
Muskul|atur [muskula'tu:r] f (-/-en) muscular system, muscles pl.; ⏾ös adj. [~'lø:s] muscular, brawny.
Muß [mus] n (-/no pl.) necessity; es ist ein ~ it is a must.
Muße ['mu:sə] f (-/no pl.) leisure; spare time; mit ~ at one's leisure.
Musselin [musə'li:n] m (-s/-e) muslin.
müssen ['mysən] (irr., h) 1. v/i. (ge-): ich muß I must; 2. v/aux. (no -ge-): ich muß I must, I have to;

I am obliged or compelled or forced to; I am bound to; *ich habe gehen ~* I had to go; *ich müßte (eigentlich) wissen* I ought to know.

müßig *adj.* ['myːsiç] idle; superfluous; useless; '2gang *m* idleness, laziness; '2gänger ['~gɛŋər] *m* (-s/-) idler, loafer; lazy-bones.

mußte ['mustə] *pret. of müssen.*

Muster ['mustər] *n* (-s/-) model; example, paragon; design, pattern; specimen; sample; '~betrieb *m* model factory or ~ farm; '~gatte *m* model husband; '2gültig, '2haft **1.** *adj.* model, exemplary, perfect; **2.** *adv.*: *sich ~ benehmen* be on one's best behavio(u)r; '~kollektion ✝ *f* range of samples; '2n *v/t.* (ge-, h) examine; eye; ✕ inspect, review; figure, pattern (*fabric, etc.*); '~schutz *m* protection of patterns and designs; '~ung *f* (-/-en) examination; ✕ review; pattern (*of fabric, etc.*); '~werk *n* standard work.

Mut [muːt] *m* (-[e]s/*no pl.*) courage; spirit; pluck; ~ *fassen* pluck up courage, summon one's courage; *den ~ sinken lassen* lose courage or heart; *guten ~(e)s sein* be of good cheer; '2ig *adj.* courageous, plucky; '2los *adj.* discouraged; despondent; '~losigkeit *f* (-/*no pl.*) discouragement; despondency; 2maßen ['~maːsən] *v/t.* (ge-, h) suppose, guess, surmise; '2maßlich *adj.* presumable; supposed; *heir:* presumptive; '~maßung *f* (-/-en) supposition, surmise; *bloße ~en pl.* guesswork.

Mutter ['mutər] *f* **1.** (-/Ꞌ) mother; **2.** ⊕ (-/-n) nut; '~brust *f* mother's breast; '~leib *m* womb.

mütterlich *adj.* ['mytərliç] motherly; maternal; **~erseits** *adv.* ['~ər-'zarts] on or from one's mother's side; *uncle, etc.*: maternal.

'**Mutter**|**liebe** *f* motherly love; '2los *adj.* motherless; '~mal *n* birth-mark, mole; '~milch *f* mother's milk; '~schaft *f* (-/*no pl.*) maternity, motherhood; '2seelen-al'lein *adj.* all or utterly alone; ~söhnchen ['~zøːnçən] *n* (-s/-) milksop, *sl.* sissy; '~sprache *f* mother tongue; '~witz *m* (-es/*no pl.*) mother wit.

'**Mutwill**|**e** *m* wantonness; mischievousness; '2ig *adj.* wanton; mischievous; wilful.

Mütze ['mytsə] *f* (-/-n) cap.

Myrrhe ['myrə] *f* (-/-n) myrrh.

Myrte ♀ ['myrtə] *f* (-/-n) myrtle.

mysteri|**ös** *adj.* [myster'jøːs] mysterious; 2um [~'teːrjum] *n* (-s/ *Mysterien*) mystery.

Mystifi|**kation** [mystifika'tsjoːn] *f* (-/-en) mystification; 2zieren [~'tsiːrən] *v/t.* (*no* -ge-, h) mystify.

Mysti|**k** ['mystik] *f* (-/*no pl.*) mysticism; '2sch *adj.* mystic(al).

Myth|**e** ['myːtə] *f* (-/-n) myth; '2isch *adj.* mythic; *esp. fig.* mythical; ~ologie [mytolo'giː] *f* (-/-n) mythology; 2ologisch *adj.* [myto-'loːgiʃ] mythological; ~os ['~ɔs] *m* (-/*Mythen*), ~us ['~us] *m* (-/*Mythen*) myth.

N

na *int.* [na] now!, then!, well!, *Am. a.* hey!

Nabe ['naːbə] *f* (-/-n) hub.

Nabel *anat.* ['naːbəl] *m* (-s/-) navel.

nach [naːx] **1.** *prp.* (*dat.*) *direction, striving:* after; to(wards), for (*a. ~ ... hin or zu*); *succession:* after; *time:* after, past; *manner, measure, example:* according to; ~ *Gewicht* by weight; ~ *deutschem Geld* in German money; *e-r ~ dem andern* one by one; *fünf Minuten ~ eins* five minutes past one; **2.** *adv.* after; ~ *und ~* little by little, gradually; ~ *wie vor* now as before, still.

nachahm|**en** ['naːxʔaːmən] *v/t.* (sep., -ge-, h) imitate, copy; counterfeit; '~enswert *adj.* worthy of imitation, exemplary; '2er *m* (-s/-) imitator; '2ung *f* (-/-en) imitation; copy; counterfeit, fake.

Nachbar ['naxbaːr] *m* (-n, -s/-n), '~in *f* (-/-nen) neighbo(u)r; '~

schaft *f* (-/-en) neighbo(u)rhood, vicinity.

'**Nachbehandlung** ✚ *f* after-treatment.

'**nachbestell**|**en** *v/t.* (sep., *no* -ge-, h) repeat one's order for *s.th.*; '2ung *f* repeat (order).

'**nachbeten** *v/t.* (sep., -ge-, h) echo.

'**Nachbildung** *f* copy, imitation; replica; dummy.

'**nachblicken** *v/i.* (sep., -ge-, h) look after.

nachdem *cj.* [naːx'deːm] after, when; *je ~* according as.

'**nachdenk**|**en** *v/i.* (*irr.* denken, sep., -ge-, h) think (*über acc.* over, about); reflect, meditate (*über acc.* on); '2en *n* (-s/*no pl.*) reflection, meditation; musing; '~lich *adj.* meditative, reflecting; pensive.

'**Nachdichtung** *f* free version.

'**Nachdruck** *m* **1.** (-[e]s/*no pl.*) stress, emphasis; **2.** *typ.* (-[e]s/-e) reprint; *unlawfully*: piracy, pirated edition; '2en *v/t.* (*sep.*, -ge-, *h*) reprint; *unlawfully*: pirate.

nachdrücklich ['nɑːxdryklɪç] 1. *adj.* emphatic, energetic; forcible; positive; 2. *adv.*: ~ betonen emphasize.

nacheifern ['nɑːxʔ-] *v/i.* (*sep.*, -ge-, *h*) emulate *s.o.*

nacheinander *adv.* [nɑːxʔaɪˈnandər] one after another, successively; by *or* in turns.

nachempfinden ['nɑːxʔ-] *v/t.* (*irr.* empfinden, *sep.*, *no* -ge-, *h*) *s.* nachfühlen.

nacherzähl|en ['nɑːxʔ-] *v/t.* (*sep.*, *no* -ge-, *h*) repeat; retell; dem Englischen nacherzählt adapted from the English; 2ung ['nɑːxʔ-] *f* repetition; story retold, reproduction.

'Nachfolge *f* succession; '2n *v/i.* (*sep.*, -ge-, sein) follow *s.o.*; j-m im Amt ~ succeed *s.o.* in his office; '~r *m* (-s/-) follower; successor.

'nachforsch|en *v/i.* (*sep.*, -ge-, *h*) investigate; search for; '2ung *f* investigation, inquiry, search.

'Nachfrage *f* inquiry; † demand; '2n *v/i.* (*sep.*, -ge-, *h*) inquire (nach after).

'nach|fühlen *v/t.* (*sep.*, -ge-, *h*): es j-m ~ feel *or* sympathize with *s.o.*; '~füllen *v/t.* (*sep.*, -ge-, *h*) fill up, refill; '~geben *v/i.* (*irr.* geben, *sep.*, -ge-, *h*) give way (dat. to); *fig.* give in, yield (to); '2gebühr ✉ *f* surcharge; '~gehen *v/i.* (*irr.* gehen, *sep.*, -ge-, sein) follow (*s.o.*, business, trade, etc.); pursue (pleasure); attend to (business); investigate *s.th.*; *watch*: be slow; '2geschmack *m* (-[e]s/*no pl.*) after-taste.

nachgiebig *adj.* ['nɑːxgiːbɪç] elastic, flexible; *fig. a.* yielding, compliant; '2keit *f* (-/-en) flexibility; compliance.

'nachgrübeln *v/i.* (*sep.*, -ge-, *h*) ponder, brood (both: über acc. over), muse (on).

nachhaltig *adj.* ['nɑːxhaltɪç] lasting, enduring.

nach'her *adv.* afterwards; then; bis ~! see you later!, so long!

'Nachhilfe *f* help, assistance; '~lehrer *m* coach, private tutor; '~unterricht *m* private lesson(s *pl.*), coaching.

'nach|holen *v/t.* (*sep.*, -ge-, *h*) make up for, make good; '2hut ✗ *f* (-/-en) rear(-guard); die ~ bilden bring up the rear (a. fig.); '~jagen *v/i.* (*sep.*, -ge-, sein) chase *or* pursue *s.o.*; '~klingen *v/i.* (*irr.* klingen, *sep.*, -ge-, *h*) resound, echo.

'Nachkomme *m* (-n/-n) descendant; ~n *pl. esp.* ⁂ issue; '2n *v/i.* (*irr.* kommen, *sep.*, -ge-, sein) follow; come later; obey (order); meet (liabilities); '~nschaft *f* (-/-en) descendants *pl., esp.* ⁂ issue.

'Nachkriegs... post-war.

Nachlaß ['nɑːxlas] *m* (Nachlasses/ Nachlasse, Nachlässe) † reduction, discount; assets *pl.*, estate, inheritance (of deceased).

'nachlassen (*irr.* lassen, *sep.*, -ge-, *h*) 1. *v/t.* reduce (price); 2. *v/i.* deteriorate; slacken, relax; diminish; *pain, rain, etc.*: abate; *storm*: calm down; *strength*: wane; *interest*: flag.

'nachlässig *adj.* careless, negligent.

'nach|laufen *v/i.* (*irr.* laufen, *sep.*, -ge-, sein) run (dat. after); '~lesen *v/t.* (*irr.* lesen, *sep.*, -ge-, *h*) in book: look up; 🌾 glean; '~liefern *v/t.* (*sep.*, -ge-, *h*) deliver subsequently; repeat delivery of; '~lösen *v/t.* (*sep.*, -ge-, *h*): e-e Fahrkarte ~ take a supplementary ticket; buy a ticket en route; '~machen *v/t.* (*sep.*, -ge-, *h*) imitate (j-m et. *s.o.* in *s.th.*); copy; counterfeit, forge; '~messen *v/t.* (*irr.* messen, *sep.*, -ge-, *h*) measure again.

'Nachmittag *m* afternoon; '2s *adv.* in the afternoon; '~svorstellung *thea. f* matinée.

Nach|nahme ['nɑːxnaːmə] *f* (-/-n) cash on delivery, *Am.* collect on delivery; per ~ schicken send C.O.D.; '~name *m* surname, last name; '~porto ✉ *n* surcharge.

'nach|prüfen *v/t.* (*sep.*, -ge-, *h*) verify; check; '~rechnen *v/t.* (*sep.*, -ge-, *h*) reckon over again; check (bill).

'Nachrede *f*: üble ~ ⁂ defamation (of character); *oral*: slander, *written*: libel; '2n *v/t.* (*sep.*, -ge-, *h*): j-m Übles ~ slander *s.o.*

Nachricht ['nɑːxrɪçt] *f* (-/-en) news; message; report; information, notice; ~ geben s. benachrichtigen; '~enagentur *f* news agency; '~endienst *m* news service; ✗ intelligence service; '~ensprecher *m* newscaster; '~enwesen *n* (-s/*no pl.*) communications *pl.*

'nachrücken *v/i.* (*sep.*, -ge-, sein) move along.

'Nach|ruf *m* obituary (notice); '~ruhm *m* posthumous fame.

'nachsagen *v/t.* (*sep.*, -ge-, *h*) repeat; man sagt ihm nach, daß he is said to *inf.*

'Nachsaison *f* dead *or* off season.

'nachschicken *v/t.* (*sep.*, -ge-, *h*) *s.* nachsenden.

'nachschlage|n *v/t.* (*irr.* schlagen, *sep.*, -ge-, *h*) consult (book); look up (word); '2werk *n* reference-book.

'Nach|schlüssel *m* skeleton key; '~schrift *f* in letter: postscript; '~schub *esp.* ✗ *m* supplies *pl.*; '~schubweg ✗ *m* supply line.

'nach|sehen (*irr.* sehen, *sep.*, -ge-, *h*) 1. *v/i.* look after; ~, ob (go and) see whether; 2. *v/t.* look after; examine, inspect; check; overhaul (*machine*); *s. nachschlagen*; *j-m et.* ~ indulge s.o. in s.th.; '~senden v/t. ([irr. senden,] *sep., -ge-, h*) send after; send on, forward (*letter*) (*j-m to s.o.*).

'Nachsicht *f* indulgence; '~ig *adj.*, '~voll *adj.* indulgent, forbearing.

'Nachsilbe *gr. f* suffix.

'nach|sinnen v/i. (*irr. sinnen, sep., -ge-, h*) muse, meditate (*über acc.* [up]on); '~sitzen v/i. (*irr. sitzen, sep., -ge-, h*) *pupil*: be kept in.

'Nach|sommer *m* St. Martin's summer, *esp. Am.* Indian summer; '~speise *f* dessert; '~spiel *fig. n* sequel.

'nach|spionieren v/i. (*sep., no -ge-, h*) spy (*dat.* on); '~sprechen v/i. *and* v/t. (*irr. sprechen, sep., -ge-, h*) repeat; '~spülen v/t. (*sep., -ge-, h*) rinse; '~spüren v/i. (*sep., -ge-, h*) (*dat.*) track, trace.

nächst [nɛːçst] **1.** *adj.* succession, time: next; distance, relation: nearest; **2.** *prp.* (*dat.*) next to, next after; '2'beste *m, f, n* (*-n/-n*): der (die) ~ anyone; das ~ anything; er fragte den ~n he asked the next person he met.

'nachstehen v/i. (*irr. stehen, sep., -ge-, h*): *j-m in nichts* ~ be in no way inferior to s.o.

'nachstell|en (*sep., -ge-, h*) **1.** v/t. place behind; put back (*watch*); ⊕ adjust (*screw, etc.*); **2.** v/i.: *j-m* ~ be after s.o.; '2ung *fig. f* persecution.

'Nächstenliebe *f* charity.

'nächstens *adv.* shortly, (very) soon, before long.

'nach|streben v/i. (*sep., -ge-, h*) *s. nacheifern*; '~suchen v/i. (*sep., -ge-, h*): ~ um apply for, seek.

Nacht [naxt] *f* (*-/=e*) night; *bei* ~, *des* ~s *s. nachts*; '~arbeit *f* night-work; '~asyl *n* night-shelter; '~ausgabe *f* night edition (*of newspaper*); '~dienst *m* night-duty.

'Nachteil *m* disadvantage, drawback; *im* ~ *sein* be at a disadvantage; '2ig *adj.* disadvantageous.

'Nacht|essen *n* supper; '~falter *zo. m* (*-s/-*) moth; '~gebet *n* evening prayer; '~geschirr *n* chamberpot; '~hemd *n* night-gown, *Am. a.* night robe; *for men*: nightshirt.

Nachtigall *orn.* ['naxtigal] *f* (*-/-en*) nightingale.

'Nachtisch *m* (*-es/no pl.*) sweet, dessert.

'Nachtlager *n* (*a*) lodging for the night; bed.

nächtlich *adj.* ['nɛçtliç] nightly, nocturnal.

'Nacht|lokal *n* night-club; '~mahl *n* supper; '~portier *m* night-porter; '~quartier *n* night-quarters *pl.*

Nachtrag ['naːxtraːk] *m* (*-[e]s/=e*) supplement; '2en v/t. (*irr. tragen, sep., -ge-, h*) carry (*j-m et.* s.th. after s.o.); add; ✝ post up (*ledger*); *j-m et.* ~ bear s.o. a grudge; '2end *adj.* unforgiving, resentful.

nachträglich *adj.* ['naːxtrɛːkliç] additional; subsequent.

nachts *adv.* [naxts] at *or* by night.

'Nacht|schicht *f* night-shift; '2-schlafend *adj.*: *zu* ~er Zeit in the middle of the night; '~schwärmer *fig. m* night-reveller; '~tisch *m* bedside table; '~topf *m* chamberpot; '~vorstellung *thea. f* night performance; '~wache *f* nightwatch; '~wächter *m* (night-)watchman; '~wandler [~vandlər] *m* (*-s/-*) sleep-walker; '~zeug *n* night-things *pl.*

'nachwachsen v/i. (*irr. wachsen, sep., -ge-, sein*) grow again.

'Nachwahl *parl. f* by-election.

Nachweis ['naːxvaɪs] *m* (*-es/-e*) proof, evidence; '2bar *adj.* demonstrable; traceable; 2en [~zən] v/t. (*irr. weisen, sep., -ge-, h*) point out, show; trace; prove; '2lich *adj. s. nachweisbar*.

'Nach|welt *f* posterity; '~wirkung *f* after-effect; consequences *pl.*; aftermath; '~wort *n* (*-[e]s/-e*) epilog(ue); '~wuchs *m* (*-[e]s/no pl.*) rising generation.

'nach|zahlen v/t. (*sep., -ge-, h*) pay in addition; '~zählen v/t. (*sep., -ge-, h*) count over (again), check; '2zahlung *f* additional payment.

Nachzügler ['naːxtsyːklər] *m* (*-s/-*) straggler, late-comer.

Nacken ['nakən] *m* (*-s/-*) nape (of the neck), neck.

nackt *adj.* [nakt] naked, nude; bare (*a. fig.*); *young birds*: unfledged; *truth*: plain.

Nadel ['naːdəl] *f* (*-/-n*) needle; pin; brooch; '~arbeit *f* needlework; '~baum ♣ *m* conifer(ous tree); '~stich *m* prick; stitch; *fig.* pinprick.

Nagel ['naːgəl] *m* (*-s/=*) *anat.*, ⊕ nail; *of wood*: peg; spike; stud; *die Arbeit brennt mir auf den Nägeln* it's a rush job; '~haut *f* cuticle; '~lack *m* nail varnish; '2n v/t. (*ge-, h*) nail (*an or auf acc.* to); ~necessaire [~nɛsɛːr] *n* (*-s/-s*) manicure-case; '2'neu F *adj.* bran(d)-new; '~pflege *f* manicure.

nage|n ['naːgən] (*ge-, h*) **1.** v/i. gnaw; ~ an (*dat.*) gnaw at; pick (*bone*); **2.** v/t. gnaw; '2tier *zo. n* rodent, gnawer.

nah *adj.* [naː] near, close (*bei* to); nearby; *danger*: imminent.

Näharbeit ['nɛː?-] *f* needlework, sewing.

'Nahaufnahme *f film*: close-up.

nahe *adj.* ['naːə] *s. nah*.

Nähe ['nɛːə] f (-/no pl.) nearness, proximity, vicinity; *in der ~* close by.

'nahe|gehen v/i. (irr. gehen, sep., -ge-, sein) (dat.) affect, grieve; **'~kommen** v/i. (irr. kommen, sep., -ge-, sein) (dat.) approach; get at (truth); **'~legen** v/t. (sep., -ge-, h) suggest; **'~liegen** v/i. (irr. liegen, sep., -ge-, h) suggest itself, be obvious.

nahen ['nɑːən] **1.** v/i. (ge-, sein) approach; **2.** v/refl. (ge-, h) approach (j-m s.o.).

nähen ['nɛːən] v/t. and v/i. (ge-, h) sew, stitch.

näher adj. ['nɛːər] nearer, closer; road: shorter; *das Nähere* (further) particulars pl. or details pl.

'Näherin f (-/-nen) seamstress.

'nähern v/t. (ge-, h) approach (dat. to); *sich ~* approach (j-m s.o.).

'nahe'zu adv. nearly, almost.

'Nähgarn n (sewing-)cotton.

'Nahkampf ✗ m close combat.

nahm [nɑːm] pret. of nehmen.

'Näh|maschine f sewing-machine; **'~nadel** f (sewing-)needle.

nähren ['nɛːrən] v/t. (ge-, h) nourish (a. fig.), feed; nurse (child); *sich ~* von live or feed on.

nahrhaft adj. ['nɑːrhaft] nutritious, nourishing.

Nahrung f (-/no pl.) food, nourishment, nutriment.

'Nahrungs|aufnahme f intake of food; **~mittel** n/pl. food(-stuff), victuals pl.

'Nährwert m nutritive value.

Naht [nɑːt] f (-/ːe) seam; ✗ suture.

'Nahverkehr m local traffic.

'Nähzeug n sewing-kit.

naiv adj. [na'iːf] naïve, naive, simple; **ℒität** [naivi'tɛːt] f (-/no pl.) naïveté, naivety, simplicity.

Name ['nɑːmə] m (-ns/-n) name; *im ~n* (gen.) on behalf of; *dem ~n nach* nominal(ly), in name only; *dem ~n nach kennen* know by name; *die Dinge beim rechten ~n nennen* call a spade a spade; *darf ich um Ihren ~n bitten?* may I ask your name?

'namen|los adj. nameless, anonymous; fig. unutterable; **'~s 1.** adv. named, by the name of, called; **2.** prp. (gen.) in the name of.

'Namens|tag m name-day; **'~vetter** m namesake; **'~zug** m signature.

namentlich ['nɑːməntlɪç] **1.** adj. nominal; **2.** adv. by name; especially, in particular.

'namhaft adj. notable; considerable; *~ machen* name.

nämlich ['nɛːmlɪç] **1.** adj. the same; **2.** adv. namely, that is (to say).

nannte ['nantə] pret. of nennen.

Napf [napf] m (-[e]s/ːe) bowl, basin.

Narb|e ['narbə] f (-/-n) scar; **'ℒig** adj. scarred; leather: grained.

Narko|se ✗ [nar'koːzə] f (-/-n) narcosis; **ℒtisieren** [ˌoti'ziːrən] v/t. (no -ge-, h) narcotize.

Narr [nar] m (-en/-en) fool; jester; *zum ~en halten* = **'ℒen** v/t. (ge-, h) make a fool of, fool.

'Narren|haus F n madhouse; **'~kappe** f fool's-cap; **'ℒsicher** adj. foolproof.

'Narrheit f (-/-en) folly.

Närrin ['nɛrin] f (-/-nen) fool, foolish woman.

'närrisch adj. foolish, silly; odd.

Narzisse ♀ [nar'tsisə] f (-/-n) narcissus; gelbe ~ daffodil.

nasal adj. [na'zɑːl] nasal; *~e Sprechweise* twang.

nasch|en ['naʃən] (ge-, h) **1.** v/i. nibble (an dat. at); gern ~ have a sweet tooth; **2.** v/t. nibble; eat s.th. on the sly; **ℒereien** [ˌ'raɪən] f/pl. dainties pl., sweets pl.; **'~haft** adj. fond of dainties or sweets.

Nase ['nɑːzə] f (-/-n) nose; *die ~ rümpfen* turn up one's nose (über acc. at).

näseln ['nɛːzəln] v/i. (ge-, h) speak through the nose, nasalize; snuffle.

'Nasen|bluten n (-s/no pl.) nosebleeding; **'~loch** n nostril; **'~spitze** f tip of the nose.

naseweis adj. ['nɑːzəvaɪs] pert, saucy.

nasführen ['nɑːs-] v/t. (ge-, h) fool, dupe.

Nashorn zo. ['nɑːs-] n rhinoceros.

naß adj. [nas] wet; damp, moist.

Nässe ['nɛsə] f (-/no pl.) wet(ness); moisture; ⚗ humidity; **'ℒn** (ge-, h) **1.** v/t. wet; moisten; **2.** ✗ v/i. discharge.

'naßkalt adj. damp and cold, raw.

Nation [na'tsjoːn] f (-/-en) nation.

national adj. [natsjo'nɑːl] national; **ℒhymne** f national anthem; **ℒismus** [ˌa'lismus] m (-/Nationalismen) nationalism; **ℒität** [ˌali'tɛːt] f (-/-en) nationality; **ℒmannschaft** f national team.

Natter ['natər] f (-/-n) zo. adder, viper; fig. serpent.

Natur [na'tuːr] f **1.** (-/no pl.) nature; **2.** (-/-en) constitution; temper(ament), disposition, nature; *von ~* by nature.

Naturalien [natu'rɑːljən] pl. natural produce sg.; *in ~* in kind.

naturalisieren [naturali'ziːrən] v/t. (no -ge-, h) naturalize.

Naturalismus [natura'lismus] m (-/no pl.) naturalism.

Naturanlage [na'tuːrˀ-] f (natural) disposition.

Naturell [natu'rɛl] n (-s/-e) natural disposition, nature, temper.

Na'tur|ereignis n, **~erscheinung** f phenomenon; **~forscher** m naturalist, scientist; ℓ**gemäß** adj. natural; **~geschichte** f natural history; **~gesetz** n law of nature, natural law; ℓ**getreu** adj. true to nature; life-like; **~kunde** f (natural) science.

na**türlich** [na'ty:rliç] **1.** adj. natural; genuine; innate; unaffected; **2.** adv. naturally, of course.

Na'tur|produkte n/pl. natural products pl. or produce sg.; **~schutz** m wild-life conservation; **~schutzgebiet** n, **~schutzpark** m national park, wild-life (p)reserve; **~trieb** m instinct; **~wissenschaft** f (natural) science; **~wissenschaftler** m (natural) scientist.

Nebel ['ne:bəl] m (-s/-) fog; mist; haze; smoke; ℓ**haft** fig. adj. nebulous, hazy, dim; **~horn** n fog-horn.

neben prp. (dat.; acc.) ['ne:bən] beside, by (the side of); near to; against, compared with; apart or Am. a. aside from, besides.

neben|'an adv. next door; close by; ℓ**anschluß** teleph. ['ne:bən?-] m extension (line); ℓ**arbeit** ['ne:bən?-] f extra work; ℓ**ausgaben** ['ne:bən?-] f/pl. incidental expenses pl., extras pl.; ℓ**ausgang** ['ne:bən?-] m side-exit, side-door; ℓ**bedeutung** f secondary meaning, connotation; **~bei** adv. by the way; besides; ℓ**beruf** m side-line; **'~beruflich** adv. as a side-line; in one's spare time; ℓ**beschäftigung** f s. Nebenberuf; ℓ**buhler** ['~bu:lər] m rival; **~ei'nander** adv. side by side; **~ bestehen** co-exist; ℓ**eingang** ['ne:bən?-] m side-entrance; ℓ**einkünfte** ['ne:bən?-] pl., ℓ**einnahmen** ['ne:bən?-] f/pl. casual emoluments pl., extra income; ℓ**erscheinung** ['ne:bən?-] f accompaniment; ℓ**fach** n subsidiary subject, Am. minor (subject); ℓ**fluß** m tributary (river); ℓ**gebäude** n annex(e); outhouse; ℓ**geräusch** n radio: atmospherics pl., interference, jamming; ℓ**gleis** & n siding, side-track; ℓ**handlung** thea. f underplot; ℓ**haus** n adjoining house; **~'her** adv., **~'hin** adv. by his or her side; s. nebenbei; ℓ**kläger** ½ m co-plaintiff; ℓ**kosten** pl. extras pl.; ℓ**mann** m person next to one; ℓ**produkt** n by-product; ℓ**rolle** f minor part (a. thea.); ℓ**sache** f minor matter, side issue; **'~sächlich** adj. subordinate, incidental; unimportant; ℓ**satz** gr. m subordinate clause; ℓ**stehend** adj. in the margin; ℓ**stelle** f branch; agency; teleph. extension; ℓ**straße** f by-street, by-road; ℓ**strecke** & f branch line; ℓ**tisch** m next table; ℓ**tür** f side-door; ℓ**verdienst** m incidental or extra earnings pl.; ℓ**zimmer** n adjoining room.

'**neblig** adj. foggy, misty, hazy.

nebst prp. (dat.) [ne:pst] together with, besides; including.

neck|en ['nɛkən] v/t. (ge-, h) tease, banter, sl. kid; ℓ**erei** [~'raɪ] f (-/-en) teasing, banter; **'~isch** adj. playful; droll, funny.

Neffe ['nɛfə] m (-n/-n) nephew.

negativ [nega'ti:f] **1.** adj. negative; **2.** ℓ n (-s/-e) negative.

Neger ['ne:gər] m (-s/-) negro; **'~in** f (-/-nen) negress.

nehmen ['ne:mən] v/t. (irr., ge-, h) take; receive; charge (money); zu sich ~ take, have (meal); j-m et. ~ take s.th. from s.o.; ein Ende ~ come to an end; es sich nicht ~ lassen zu inf. insist upon ger.; streng genommen strictly speaking.

Neid [naɪt] m (-[e]s/no pl.) envy; ℓ**en** ['naɪdən] v/t. (ge-, h) j-m et. ~ envy s.o. s.th.; **~er** ['~dər] m (-s/-) envious person; **~hammel** F ['naɪt-] m dog in the manger; ℓ**isch** adj. ['~dɪʃ] envious (auf acc. of); ℓ**los** adj. ['naɪt-] ungrudging.

Neige ['naɪgə] f (-/-n) decline; barrel: dregs pl.; glass: heeltap; zur ~ gehen (be on the) decline; esp. ♥ run short; ℓ**n** (ge-, h) **1.** v/t. and v/refl. bend, incline; **2.** v/i.: er neigt zu Übertreibungen he is given to exaggeration.

'**Neigung** f (-/-en) inclination (a. fig.); slope, incline.

nein adv. [naɪn] no.

Nektar ['nɛkta:r] m (-s/no pl.) nectar.

Nelke ♀ ['nɛlkə] f (-/-n) carnation, pink; spice: clove.

nennen ['nɛnən] v/t. (irr., ge-, h) name; call; term; mention; nominate (candidate); sports: enter (für for); sich ... ~ be called ...; ℓ**swert** adj. worth mentioning.

'**Nenn|er** ♫ m (-s/-) denominator; **'~ung** f (-/-en) naming; mentioning; nomination (of candidates); sports: entry; **'~wert** m nominal or face value; zum ~ ♥ at par.

Neon ♚ ['ne:ɔn] n (-s/no pl.) neon; **~röhre** f neon tube.

Nerv [nɛrf] m (-s/-en) nerve; j-m auf die ~en fallen or gehen get on s.o.'s nerves.

'**Nerven|arzt** m neurologist; ℓ**aufreibend** adj. trying; **~heilanstalt** f mental hospital; **~kitzel** m (-s/no pl.) thrill, sensation; ℓ**krank** adj. neurotic; ℓ**leidend** adj. neuropathic, neurotic; **~schwäche** f nervous debility; ℓ**stärkend** adj. tonic; **~system** n nervous system; **~zusammenbruch** m nervous breakdown.

nerv|ig adj. ['nɛrviç] sinewy; **~ös** adj. [~'vø:s] nervous; ℓ**osität** [~ozi'tɛ:t] f (-/no pl.) nervousness.

Nerz zo. [nɛrts] m (-es/-e) mink.

Nessel ⚘ ['nɛsəl] *f* (-/-n) nettle.
Nest [nɛst] *n* (-es/-er) nest; F *fig.* bed; F *fig.* hick *or* one-horse town.
nett *adj.* [nɛt] nice; neat, pretty, *Am. a.* cute; pleasant; kind.
netto ✝ *adv.* ['nɛto] net, clear.
Netz [nɛts] *n* (-es/-e) net; *fig.* network; **'~anschluß** ⚡ *m* mains connection, power supply; **'~haut** *anat. f* retina; **'~spannung** ⚡ *f* mains voltage.

neu *adj.* [nɔY] new; fresh; recent; modern; **~ere** *Sprachen* modern languages; **~este** *Nachrichten* latest news; *von* **~em** anew, afresh; *ein* **~es** *Leben beginnen* turn over a new leaf; *was gibt es Neues?* what is the news?, *Am.* what is new?

'Neu|anschaffung *f* (-/-en) recent acquisition; **'2artig** *adj.* novel; **'~auflage** *typ. f*, **'~ausgabe** *typ. f* new edition; reprint; **'~bau** *m* (-[e]s/-ten) new building; **'2bearbeitet** *adj.* revised; **'~e** *m* (-n/-n) new man; new-comer; novice; **'2entdeckt** *adj.* recently discovered.

neuer|dings *adv.* ['nɔYər'diŋs] of late, recently; **'2er** *m* (-s/-) innovator.

Neuerscheinung ['nɔY⁹-] *f* new book *or* publication.

'Neuerung *f* (-/-en) innovation.

'neu|geboren *adj.* new-born; **'~gestalten** *v/t.* (*sep.*, *-ge-*, *h*) reorganize; **'2gestaltung** *f* reorganization; **'2gier** *f*, **'2gierde** ['~də] *f* (-/*no pl.*) curiosity, inquisitiveness; **'~gierig** *adj.* curious (*auf acc.* about, of), inquisitive, *sl.* nos(e)y; *ich bin* **~**, *ob* I wonder whether *or* if; **'2heit** *f* (-/-en) newness, freshness, novelty.

'Neuigkeit *f* (-/-en) (e-e a piece of) news.

'Neu|jahr *n* New Year('s Day); **'~land** *n* (-[e]s/*no pl.*): **~** *erschließen* break fresh ground (*a. fig.*); **'2lich** *adv.* the other day, recently; **'~ling** *m* (-s/-e) novice; *contp.* greenhorn; **'2modisch** *adj.* fashionable; **'~mond** *m* (-[e]s/*no pl.*) new moon.

neun *adj.* [nɔYn] nine; **'~te** *adj.* ninth; **'2tel** *n* (-s/-) ninth part; **'~tens** *adv.* ninthly; **'~zehn** *adj.* nineteen; **'~zehnte** *adj.* nineteenth; **'~zig** *adj.* ['~tsiç] ninety; **'~zigste** *adj.* ninetieth.

'Neu|philologe *m* student *or* teacher of modern languages; **'~regelung** *f* reorganization, rearrangement.

neutr|al *adj.* [nɔY'trɑːl] neutral; **2alität** [~ali'tɛːt] *f* (-/*no pl.*) neutrality; **2um** *gr.* ['nɔYtrum] *n* (-s/*Neutra*, *Neutren*) neuter.

'neu|vermählt *adj.* newly married; *die* **2en** *pl.* the newly-weds *pl.*; **'2wahl** *parl. f* new election; **'~wertig** *adj.* as good as new; **'2zeit** *f* (-/*no pl.*) modern times *pl.*

nicht *adv.* [niçt] not; *auch* **~** nor; **~** *anziehend* unattractive; **~** *besser* no better; **~** *bevollmächtigt* non-commissioned; **~** *einlösbar* ✝ inconvertible; **~** *erscheinen* fail to attend.

'Nicht|achtung *f* disregard; **'2amtlich** *adj.* unofficial; **'~angriffspakt** *pol. m* non-aggression pact; **'~annahme** *f* non-acceptance; **'~befolgung** *f* non-observance.

Nichte ['niçtə] *f* (-/-n) niece.

'nichtig *adj.* null, void; invalid; vain, futile; *für* **~** *erklären* declare null and void, annul; **'2keit** *f* (-/-en) 🔒 nullity; vanity, futility.

'Nichtraucher *m* non-smoker.

nichts [niçts] **1.** *indef. pron.* nothing, naught, not anything; **2.** 2 *n* (-/*no pl.*) nothing(ness); *fig.*: nonentity; void; **'~ahnend** *adv.* unsuspecting; **'~destoweniger** *adv.* nevertheless; **'~nutzig** *adj.* ['~nutsiç] good-for-nothing, worthless; **'~sagend** *adj.* insignificant; **2tuer** ['~tuːər] *m* (-s/-) idler; **'~würdig** *adj.* vile, base, infamous.

'Nicht|vorhandensein *n* absence; lack; **'~wissen** *n* ignorance.

nick|en ['nikən] *v/i.* (ge-, *h*) nod; bow; **'2erchen** F *n* (-s/-): *ein* **~** *machen* take a nap, have one's forty winks.

nie *adv.* [niː] never, at no time.

nieder ['niːdər] **1.** *adj.* low; base, mean, vulgar; *value*, *rank*: inferior; **2.** *adv.* down.

'Nieder|gang *m* decline; **'2gedrückt** *adj.* dejected, downcast; **'2gehen** *v/i.* (*irr. gehen*, *sep.*, *-ge-*, *sein*) go down; 🜨 descend; *storm*: break; **'2geschlagen** *adj.* dejected, downcast; **'2hauen** *v/t.* (*irr. hauen*, *sep.*, *-ge-*, *h*) cut down; **'2kommen** *v/i.* (*irr. kommen*, *sep.*, *-ge-*, *sein*) be confined; be delivered (*mit of*); **'~kunft** ['~kunft] *f* (-/*~e*) confinement, delivery; **'~lage** *f* defeat; ✝ warehouse; branch; **'2lassen** *v/t.* (*irr. lassen*, *sep.*, *-ge-*, *h*) let down; *sich* **~** settle (down); *bird*: alight; sit down; establish o.s.; settle (*in dat.* at); **'~lassung** *f* (-/-en) establishment; settlement; branch, agency; **'2legen** *v/t.* (*sep.*, *-ge-*, *h*) lay *or* put down; resign (*position*); retire from (*business*); abdicate; *die Arbeit* **~** (go on) strike, down tools, *Am.* F a. walk out; *sich* **~** lie down, go to bed; **'2machen** *v/t.* (*sep.*, *-ge-*, *h*) cut down; massacre; **'~schlag** *m* 🜪 precipitate; sediment; precipitation (*of rain*, *etc.*); *radioactive*: fall-out; *boxing*: knock-down, knock-out; **'2schlagen** *v/t.* (*irr. schlagen*, *sep.*, *-ge-*, *h*) knock down; *boxing*: a. floor; cast down (*eyes*); suppress; put down, crush (*rebellion*); 🔒 quash; *sich* **~**

$\curvearrowright$ precipitate; '2schmettern *fig.*
v/t. (*sep.*, -ge-, h) crush; '2setzen
v/t. (*sep.*, -ge-, h) set *or* put down;
sich ~ sit down; *birds:* perch, alight;
'2strecken *v/t.* (*sep.*, -ge-, h) lay
low, strike to the ground, floor;
'2trächtig *adj.* base, mean; F
beastly; '~ung *f* (-/-en) lowlands *pl.*

niedlich *adj.* ['niːtliç] neat, nice,
pretty, *Am. a.* cute.

Niednagel ['niːt-] *m* agnail, hang-
nail.

niedrig *adj.* ['niːdriç] low (*a. fig.*);
moderate; *fig.* mean, base.

niemals *adv.* ['niːmaːls] never, at
no time.

niemand *indef. pron.* ['niːmant]
nobody, no one, none; '2sland *n*
(-[e]s/*no pl.*) no man's land.

Niere ['niːrə] *f* (-/-n) kidney; '~n-
braten *m* loin of veal.

niesel|**n** F ['niːzəln] *v/i.* (ge-, h)
drizzle; '2regen F *m* drizzle.

niesen ['niːzən] *v/i.* (ge-, h) sneeze.

Niet ⊕ [niːt] *m* (-[e]s/-e) rivet; '~e *f*
(-/-n) lottery: blank; F *fig.* wash-
out; '2en ⊕ *v/t.* (ge-, h) rivet.

Nilpferd *zo.* ['niːl-] *n* hippopotamus.

Nimbus ['nimbus] *m* (-/-se) halo (*a.
fig.*), nimbus.

nimmer *adv.* ['nimər] never; '~
mehr *adv.* nevermore; '2satt *m*
(-, -[e]s/-e) glutton; 2'wiedersehen F *n:* auf ~ never to meet
again; *er verschwand auf* ~ he left
for good. [*dat.* at).\
nippen ['nipən] *v/i.* (ge-, h) sip (*an*)\
Nipp|**es** ['nipəs] *pl.*, '~sachen *pl.*
(k)nick-(k)nacks *pl.*

nirgend|**s** *adv.* ['nirgənts], '~(s)'wo
adv. nowhere.

Nische ['niːʃə] *f* (-/-n) niche, recess.

nisten ['nistən] *v/i.* (ge-, h) nest.

Niveau [ni'voː] *n* (-s/-s) level; *fig. a.*
standard.

nivellieren [nive'liːrən] *v/t.* (*no*
-ge-, h) level, grade.

Nixe ['niksə] *f* (-/-n) water-nymph,
mermaid.

noch [nɔx] **1.** *adv.* still; yet; ~ *ein*
another, one more; ~ *einmal* once
more *or* again; ~ *etwas* something
more; ~ *etwas?* anything else?; ~
heute this very day; ~ *immer* still;
~ *nicht* not yet; ~ *nie* never before;
~ *so* ever so; ~ *im 19. Jahrhundert*
as late as the 19th century; *es wird*
~ *2 Jahre dauern* it will take two
more *or* another two years; **2.** *cj.:*
s. weder; ~**malig** *adj.* ['~maːliç]
repeated; ~**mals** *adv.* ['~maːls]
once more *or* again.

Nomad|**e** [no'maːdə] *m* (-n/-n)
nomad; 2isch *adj.* nomadic.

Nominativ *gr.* ['noːminatiːf] *m*
(-s/-e) nominative (case).

nominieren [nomi'niːrən] *v/t.* (*no*
-ge-, h) nominate.

Nonne ['nɔnə] *f* (-/-n) nun; '~n-
kloster *n* nunnery, convent.

Nord *geogr.* [nɔrt], ~en ['~dən] *m*
(-s/*no pl.*) north; 2isch *adj.* ['~diʃ]
northern.

nördlich *adj.* ['nœrtliç] northern,
northerly.

'**Nord**|**licht** *n* northern lights *pl.*;
~'ost(en *m*) north-east; '~pol *m*
North Pole; 2wärts *adv.* ['~vɛrts]
northward(s), north; ~'west(en *m*)
north-west.

nörg|**eln** ['nœrgəln] *v/i.* (ge-, h)
nag, carp (*an dat.* at); grumble;
2ler ['~lər] *m* (-s/-) faultfinder,
grumbler.

Norm [nɔrm] *f* (-/-en) standard;
rule; norm.

normal *adj.* [nɔr'maːl] normal;
regular; *measure, weight, time:*
standard; ~isieren [~ali'ziːrən]
v/refl. (*no* -ge-, h) return to normal.

'**norm**|**en** *v/t.* (ge-, h), ~**ieren**
[~'miːrən] *v/t.* (*no* -ge-, h) standardize.

Not [noːt] *f* (-/~e) need, want; necessity; difficulty, trouble; misery;
danger, emergency, distress (*a.* ⚓);
~ *leiden* suffer privations; *in* ~ *geraten* become destitute, get into
trouble; *in* ~ *sein* be in trouble; *zur*
~ at a pinch; *es tut not, daß* it is necessary that.

Notar [no'taːr] *m* (-s/-e) (public)
notary.

'**Not**|**ausgang** *m* emergency exit;
'~behelf *m* makeshift, expedient,
stopgap; '~bremse *f* emergency
brake; '~brücke *f* temporary
bridge; ~durft ['~durft] *f* (-/*no pl.*):
s-e ~ *verrichten* relieve o.s.; 2dürf-
tig *adj.* scanty, poor; temporary.

Note ['noːtə] *f* (-/-n) note (*a.* ♪);
pol. note, memorandum; *school:*
mark.

'**Noten**|**bank** † *f* bank of issue; '~
schlüssel ♪ *m* clef; '~system ♪ *n*
staff.

'**Not**|**fall** *m* case of need, emergency;
'2falls *adv.* if necessary; '2gedrun-
gen *adv.* of necessity, needs.

notier|**en** [no'tiːrən] *v/t.* (*no* -ge-, h)
make a note of, note (down); †
quote; 2ung *f* (-/-en) quotation.

nötig *adj.* ['nøːtiç] necessary; ~ *haben need;* ~**en** ['~gən] *v/t.* (ge-, h)
force, oblige, compel; press, urge
(*guest*); '~en'falls *adv.* if necessary;
2ung *f* (-/-en) compulsion; pressing; ♰ intimidation.

Notiz [no'tiːts] *f* (-/-en) notice; note,
memorandum; ~ *nehmen von* take
notice of; pay attention to; *keine* ~
nehmen von ignore; *sich* ~ *machen* take notes; ~**block** *m* pad,
Am. a. scratch pad; ~**buch** *n* note-
book.

'**Not**|**lage** *f* distress; emergency;
'2landen ✈ *v/i.* (ge-, sein) make

13*

a forced *or* emergency landing; '~landung f forced *or* emergency landing; '2leidend *adj.* needy, destitute; distressed; '~lösung f expedient; '~lüge f white lie.

notorisch *adj.* [no'to:riʃ] notorious.

'Not|ruf *teleph. m* emergency call; '~signal *n* emergency *or* distress signal; '~sitz *mot. m* dick(e)y(-seat), *Am. a.* rumble seat; '~stand *m* emergency; '~standsarbeiten *f/pl.* relief works *pl.*; '~standsgebiet *n* distressed area; '~standsgesetze *n/pl.* emergency laws *pl.*; '~verband *m* first-aid dressing; '~verordnung f emergency decree; '~wehr f self-defen|ce, *Am.* -se; '2wendig *adj.* necessary; '~wendigkeit f (-/-en) necessity; '~zucht f (-/*no pl.*) rape.

Novelle [no'vɛlə] f (-/-n) short story, novella; *parl.* amendment.

November [no'vɛmbər] *m* (-[s]/-) November.

Nu [nu:] *m* (-/*no pl.*): im ~ in no time.

Nuance [ny'ã:sə] f (-/-n) shade.

nüchtern *adj.* ['nʏçtərn] empty, fasting; sober (*a. fig.*); matter-of-fact; *writings:* jejune; prosaic; cool; plain; '2heit f (-/*no pl.*) sobriety; *fig.* soberness.

Nudel ['nu:dəl] f (-/-n) noodle.

null [nul] 1. *adj.* null; nil; *tennis:* love; ~ und nichtig null and void; 2. 2 f (-/-en) nought, cipher (*a. fig.*); zero; '2punkt *m* zero.

numerieren [numə'ri:rən] *v/t.* (*no* -ge-, h) number; *numerierter Platz* reserved seat.

Nummer ['numər] f (-/-n) number

(*a. newspaper, thea.*); size (*of shoes, etc.*); *thea.* turn; *sports:* event; '~nschild *mot. n* number-plate.

nun [nu:n] 1. *adv.* now, at present; then; ~? well?; ~ *also* well then; 2. *int.* now then!; '~mehr *adv.* now.

nur *adv.* [nu:r] only; (nothing) but; merely; ~ noch only.

Nuß [nus] f (-/Nüsse) nut; '~kern *m* kernel; '~knacker *m* (-s/-) nutcracker; '~schale f nutshell.

Nüstern ['ny:stərn] *f/pl.* nostrils *pl.*

nutz *adj.* [nuts] *s.* nütze; 2anwendung f practical application; '~bar *adj.* useful; '~bringend *adj.* profitable.

nütze *adj.* ['nʏtsə] useful; zu nichts ~ sein be of no use, be good for nothing.

Nutzen ['nutsən] 1. *m* (-s/-) use; profit, gain; advantage; utility; 2. 2 *v/i.* and *v/t.* (ge-, h) *s.* nützen.

nützen ['nʏtsən] (ge-, h) 1. *v/i.:* zu et. ~ be of use *or* useful for s.th.; j-m ~ serve s.o.; es nützt nichts zu *inf.* it is no use *ger.*; 2. *v/t.* use, make use of; put to account; avail o.s. of, seize (*opportunity*).

'Nutz|holz *n* timber; '~leistung f capacity.

nützlich *adj.* ['nʏtsliç] useful, of use; advantageous.

'nutz|los *adj.* useless; 2nießer ['~ni:sər] *m* (-s/-) usufructuary; '2nießung f (-/-en) usufruct.

'Nutzung f (-/-en) using; utilization.

Nylon ['naɪlon] *n* (-s/*no pl.*) nylon; ~strümpfe ['~ʃtrʏmpfə] *m/pl.* nylons *pl.*, nylon stockings *pl.*

Nymphe ['nʏmfə] f (-/-n) nymph.

O

o *int.* [o:] oh!, ah!; ~ weh! alas!, oh dear (me)!

Oase [o'a:zə] f (-/-n) oasis.

ob *cj.* [ɔp] whether, if; als ~ as if, as though.

Obacht ['o:baxt] f (-/*no pl.*): ~ geben auf (*acc.*) pay attention to, take care of, heed.

Obdach ['ɔpdax] *n* (-[e]s/*no pl.*) shelter, lodging; '2los *adj.* unsheltered, homeless; '~lose *m*, f (-n/-n) homeless person; '~losenasyl *n* casual ward.

Obdu|ktion f [ɔpduk'tsjo:n] f (-/-en) post-mortem (examination), autopsy; 2zieren *v/t.* [~'tsi:rən] *v/t.* (*no* -ge-, h) perform an autopsy on.

oben *adv.* ['o:bən] above; *mountain:* at the top; *house:* upstairs; on the surface; von ~ from above; von ~ bis unten from top to bottom;

von ~ herab behandeln treat haughtily; '~an *adv.* at the top; '~auf *adv.* on the top; on the surface; ~drein *adv.* ['~'draɪn] into the bargain, at that; ~erwähnt *adj.* ['o:bən?ɛrvɛ:nt], '~genannt *adj.* above-mentioned, aforesaid; '~hin *adv.* superficially, perfunctorily.

ober ['o:bər] 1. *adj.* upper, higher; *fig. a.* superior; 2. 2 *m* (-s/-) (head) waiter; *German cards:* queen.

Ober|arm ['o:bər?-] *m* upper arm; ~arzt ['o:bər?-] *m* head physician; ~aufseher ['o:bər?-] *m* superintendent; ~aufsicht ['o:bər?-] f superintendence; '~befehl ⚔ *m* supreme command; '~befehlshaber ⚔ *m* commander-in-chief; '~bekleidung f outer garments *pl.*, outer wear; '~bürgermeister *m* chief burgomaster; Lord Mayor;

'~deck ♣ n upper deck; '~fläche f surface; ²flächlich adj. ['~fleçliç] superficial; fig. a. shallow; '²halb prp. (gen.) above; '~hand fig. f: die ~ gewinnen über (acc.) get the upper hand of; '~haupt n head, chief; '~haus Brt. parl. n House of Lords; '~hemd n shirt; ~herrschaft f supremacy.

'Oberin f (-/-nen) eccl. Mother Superior; at hospital: matron.

ober|irdisch adj. ['o:bər⁹-] over-ground, above ground; ✈ overhead; '²kellner m head waiter; '²kiefer anat. m upper jaw; '²körper m upper part of the body; '²land n upland; '²lauf m upper course (of river); '²leder n upper; '²leitung f chief management; ✈ overhead wires pl.; '²leutnant ✗ m (Am. first) lieutenant; '²licht n skylight; '²lippe f upper lip; '²schenkel m thigh; '²schule f secondary school, Am. a. high school.

'oberst 1. adj. uppermost, topmost, top; highest (a. fig.); fig. chief, principal; rank, etc.: supreme; 2. ♀ ✗ m (-en, -s/-en, -e) colonel. 'Ober|staatsanwalt ♊ m chief public prosecutor; '~stimme ♪ f treble, soprano.

'Oberst|leutnant ✗ m lieutenant-colonel.

'Ober|tasse f cup; '~wasser fig. n: ~ bekommen get the upper hand.

obgleich cj. [ɔp'glaɪç] (al)though.

'Obhut f (-/no pl.) care, guard; protection; custody; in (seine) ~ nehmen take care or charge of.

obig adj. ['o:biç] above(-mentioned), aforesaid.

Objekt [ɔp'jɛkt] n (-[e]s/-e) object (a. gr.); project; ♦ a. transaction. objektiv [ɔpjɛk'ti:f] 1. adj. objective; impartial, detached; actual, practical; 2. ♀ n (-s/-e) object-glass, objective; phot. lens; ²ität [~ivi-'te:t] f (-/no pl.) objectivity; impartiality.

obligat adj. [obli'ga:t] obligatory; indispensable; inevitable; ²ion ♦ [~a'tsjo:n] f (-/-en) bond, debenture; ~orisch adj. [~a'to:riʃ] obligatory (für on), compulsory, mandatory.

'Obmann m chairman; ♊ foreman (of jury); umpire; ♦ shop-steward, spokesman.

Oboe ♪ [o'bo:ə] f (-/-n) oboe, haut-boy.

Obrigkeit ['o:briçkaɪt] f (-/-en) the authorities pl.; government; '²lich adj. magisterial, official; '~sstaat m authoritarian state.

ob'schon cj. (al)though.

Observatorium ast. [ɔpzɛrva'to:r-jum] n (-s/Observatorien) observatory.

Obst [o:pst] n (-es/no pl.) fruit;

'~bau m fruit-culture, fruit-grow-ing; '~baum m fruit-tree; '~ernte f fruit-gathering; fruit-crop; '~gar-ten m orchard; '~händler m fruiterer, Am. fruitseller; '~züch-ter m fruiter, fruit-grower.

obszön adj. [ɔps'tsø:n] obscene, filthy.

ob'wohl cj. (al)though.

Ochse zo. ['ɔksə] m (-n/-n) ox; bullock; '~nfleisch n beef.

öde ['ø:də] 1. adj. deserted, desolate; waste; fig. dull, tedious; 2. ♀ f (-/-n) desert, solitude; fig. dullness, tedium.

oder cj. ['o:dər] or.

Ofen ['o:fən] m (-s/¨) stove; oven; kiln; furnace; '~heizung f heating by stove; '~rohr n stove-pipe.

offen adj. ['ɔfən] open (a. fig.); position: vacant; hostility: overt; fig. frank, outspoken.

'offen'bar 1. adj. obvious, evident; apparent; 2. adv. a. it seems that; ~en [ɔfən'-] v/t. (no -ge-, h) reveal, disclose; manifest; sich j-m ~ open one's heart to s.o.; ²ung [ɔfən'-] f (-/-en) manifestation; revelation; ²ungseid ♊ [ɔfən'ba:ruŋs⁹-] m oath of manifestation.

'Offenheit fig. f (-/no pl.) openness, frankness.

'offen|herzig adj. open-hearted, sincere; frank; '~kundig adj. public; notorious; '~sichtlich adj. mani-fest, evident, obvious.

offensiv adj. [ɔfɛn'zi:f] offensive; ²e [~və] f (-/-n) offensive.

'offenstehen v/i. (irr. stehen, sep., -ge-, h) stand open; ♦ bill: be out-standing; fig. be open (j-m to s.o.); es steht ihm offen zu inf. he is free or at liberty to inf.

öffentlich ['œfəntliç] 1. adj. public; ~es Ärgernis public nuisance; ~er Dienst Civil Service; 2. adv. pub-licly, in public; ~ auftreten make a public appearance; '²keit f (-/no pl.) publicity; the public; in aller ~ in public.

offerieren [ɔfə'ri:rən] v/t. (no -ge-, h) offer.

Offerte [ɔ'fɛrtə] f (-/-n) offer; tender.

offiziell adj. [ɔfi'tsjɛl] official.

Offizier ✗ [ɔfi'tsi:r] m (-s/-e) (com-missioned) officer; ~skorps ✗ [~sko:r] n (-/-) body of officers, the officers pl.; ~smesse ♀ ✗ officers' mess; ♀ a. wardroom.

offiziös adj. [ɔfi'tsjø:s] officious, semi-official.

öffn|en ['œfnən] v/t. (ge-, h) open; a. uncork (bottle); ♂ dissect (body); sich ~ open (a. ⚘) (m -s/-) opener; '²ung f (-/-en) opening, aperture; '²ungszeiten f/pl. hours pl. of opening, business hours pl.

oft adv. [ɔft] often, frequently.

öfters adv. ['œftərs] s. oft.

'oftmal|ig adj. frequent, repeated; '~s adv. s. oft.

oh int. [o:] o(h)!

ohne ['o:nə] 1. prp. (acc.) without; 2. cj.: ~ daß, ~ zu inf. without ger.; ~'dies adv. anyhow, anyway; ~'glei-chen adv. unequal(l)ed, matchless; ~'hin adv. s. ohnedies.

'Ohn|macht f (-/-en) powerlessness; impotence; ℁ faint, unconscious-ness; in ~ fallen faint, swoon; ~machtsanfall ℁ ['o:nmaxts?-] m fainting fit, swoon; 'ℨmächtig adj. powerless; impotent; ℁ uncon-scious; ~ werden faint, swoon.

Ohr [o:r] n (-[e]s/-en) ear; fig. a. hearing; ein ~ haben für have an ear for; ganz ~ sein be all ears; F j-n übers ~ hauen cheat s.o., sl. do s.o. (in the eye); bis über die ~en up to the ears or eyes.

Öhr [ø:r] n (-[e]s/-e) eye (of needle).

'Ohren|arzt m aurist, ear specialist; 'ℨbetäubend adj. deafening; '~lei-den n ear-complaint; '~schmalz n ear-wax; '~schmaus m treat for the ears; '~schmerzen m/pl. ear-ache; '~zeuge m ear-witness.

'Ohr|feige f box on the ear(s), slap in the face (a. fig.); 'ℨfeigen v/t. (ge-, h) j-n ~ box s.o.'s ear(s), slap s.o.'s face; ~läppchen ['~lɛpçən] n (-s/-) lobe of ear; '~ring m ear-ring.

Ökonom|ie [økono'mi:] f (-/-n) economy; ℨisch adj. [~'no:miʃ] economical.

Oktav [ɔk'ta:f] n (-s/-e) octavo; ~e ♪ [~və] f (-/-n) octave.

Oktober [ɔk'to:bər] m (-[s]/-) October.

Okul|ar opt. [oku'la:r] n (-s/-e) eye-piece, ocular; ℨieren ♂ v/t. (no -ge-, h) inoculate, graft.

Öl [ø:l] n (-[e]s/-e) oil; ~ ins Feuer gießen add fuel to the flames; ~ auf die Wogen gießen pour oil on the (troubled) waters; '~baum ♀ m olive-tree; '~berg eccl. m (-[e]s/no pl.) Mount of Olives; 'ℨen v/t. (ge-, h) oil; ⊕ a. lubricate; '~farbe f oil-colo(u)r, oil-paint; '~gemälde n oil-painting; '~heizung f oil heating; 'ℨig adj. oily (a. fig.).

Oliv|e ♀ [o'li:və] f (-/-n) olive; ~enbaum ♀ m olive-tree; ℨgrün adj. olive(-green).

Öl|male'rei f oil-painting; '~quelle f oil-spring, gusher; oil-well; '~ung f (-/-en) oiling; ⊕ a. lubrication; Letzte ~ eccl. extreme unction.

Olympi|ade [olymp'ja:də] f (-/-n) Olympiad; a. Olympic Games pl.; ℨsch adj. [o'lympiʃ] Olympic; Olym-pische Spiele pl. Olympic Games pl.

'Ölzweig m olive-branch.

Omelett [ɔm(ə)'lɛt] n (-[e]s/-e, -s), ~e [~'lɛt] f (-/-n) omelet(te).

Om|en ['o:mən] n (-s/-, Omina) omen, augury; ℨinös adj. [omi'nø:s] ominous.

Omnibus ['ɔmnibus] m (-ses/-se) (omni)bus; (motor-)coach; '~halte-stelle f bus-stop.

Onkel ['ɔŋkəl] m (-s/-, F -s) uncle.

Oper ['o:pər] f (-/-n) ♪ opera; opera-house.

Operat|eur [opəra'tø:r] m (-s/-e) operator; ℁ surgeon; ~ion ℁, ✕ [~'tsjo:n] f (-/-en) operation; ~ions-saal ℁ m operating room, Am. surgery; ℨiv ℁ adj. [~'ti:f] operative.

Operette ♪ [opə'rɛtə] f (-/-n) operetta.

operieren [opə'ri:rən] (no -ge-, h) 1. v/t.: j-n ~ ℁ operate (up)on s.o. (wegen for); 2. ℁, ✕ v/i. operate; sich ~ lassen ℁ undergo an opera-tion.

'Opern|glas n, ~gucker F ['~gukər] m (-s/-) opera-glass(es pl.); '~haus n opera-house; '~sänger m opera-singer, operatic singer; '~text m libretto, book (of an opera).

Opfer ['ɔpfər] n (-s/-) sacrifice; offering; victim (a. fig.); ein ~ brin-gen make a sacrifice; j-m zum ~ fallen be victimized by s.o.; '~gabe f offering; 'ℨn (ge-, h) 1. v/t. sacri-fice; immolate; sich für et. ~ sacri-fice o.s. for s.th.; 2. v/i. (make a) sacrifice (dat. to); '~stätte f place of sacrifice; '~tod m sacrifice of one's life; '~ung f (-/-en) sacrificing, sacrifice; immolation.

Opium ['o:pjum] n (-s/no pl.) opium.

opponieren [ɔpo'ni:rən] v/i. (no -ge-, h) be opposed (gegen to), resist.

Opposition [ɔpozi'tsjo:n] f (-/-en) opposition (a. parl.); ~sführer parl. m opposition leader; ~spartei parl. f opposition party.

Optik ['ɔptik] f (-/-, ~-en) optics; phot. lens system; fig. aspect; '~er m (-s/-) optician.

Optim|ismus [ɔpti'mismus] m (-/no pl.) optimism; ~ist m (-en/-en) optimist; ℨistisch adj. optimis-tic.

'optisch adj. optic(al); ~e Täu-schung optical illusion.

Orakel [o'ra:kəl] n (-s/-) oracle; ℨhaft adj. oracular; ℨn v/i. (no -ge-, h) speak oracularly; '~spruch m oracle.

Orange [o'rã:ʒə] f (-/-n) orange; ℨfarben adj. orange(-colo[u]red); ~nbaum ♀ m orange-tree.

Oratorium ♪ [ora'to:rjum] n (-s/ Oratorien) oratorio.

Orchester [ɔr'kɛstər] n (-s/-) orchestra.

Orchidee ♀ [ɔrçi'de:ə] f (-/-n) orchid.

Orden ['ɔrdən] *m* (-s/-) order (*a. eccl.*); order, medal, decoration.

'Ordens|band *n* ribbon (of an order); **'~bruder** *eccl. m* brother, friar; **'~gelübde** *eccl. n* monastic vow; **'~schwester** *eccl. f* sister, nun; **'~verleihung** *f* conferring (of) an order.

ordentlich *adj.* ['ɔrdəntliç] tidy; orderly; proper; regular; respectable; good, sound; *~er Professor univ.* professor in ordinary.

ordinär *adj.* [ɔrdi'nɛːr] common, vulgar, low.

ordn|en ['ɔrdnən] *v/t.* (ge-, h) put in order; arrange, fix (up); settle (*a. ✝ liabilities*); **'~er** *m* (-s/-) at festival, *etc.*: steward; *for papers, etc.*: file.

'Ordnung *f* (-/-en) order; arrangement; system; rules *pl.*, regulations *pl.*; class; *in ~ bringen* put in order.

'ordnungs|gemäß, '~mäßig 1. *adj.* orderly, regular; **2.** *adv.* duly; **'~ruf** *parl. m* call to order; **'2strafe** *f* disciplinary penalty; fine; **'~widrig** *adj.* contrary to order, irregular; **'2zahl** *f* ordinal number.

Ordonnanz ✗ [ɔrdɔ'nants] *f* (-/-en) orderly.

Organ [ɔr'gaːn] *n* (-s/-e) organ.

Organisat|ion [ɔrganiza'tsjoːn] *f* (-/-en) organization; **~ionstalent** *n* organizing ability; **~or** [~'zaːtɔr] *m* (-s/-en) organizer; **2orisch** *adj.* [~a'toːriʃ] organizational, organizing.

or'ganisch *adj.* organic.

organi'sieren *v/t.* (*no* -ge-, h) organize; *sl.* scrounge; (*nicht*) *organisiert(er Arbeiter)* (non-)unionist.

Organismus [ɔrga'nismus] *m* (-/Organismen) organism; ✗ *a.* system.

Organist ♪ [ɔrga'nist] *m* (-en/-en) organist.

Orgel ♪ ['ɔrgəl] *f* (-/-n) organ, *Am. a.* pipe organ; **'~bauer** *m* organ-builder; **'~pfeife** *f* organ-pipe; **'~spieler** ♪ *m* organist.

Orgie ['ɔrgjə] *f* (-/-n) orgy.

Oriental|e [orien'taːlə] *m* (-n/-n) oriental; **2isch** *adj.* oriental.

orientier|en [orien'tiːrən] *v/t.* (*no* -ge-, h) inform, instruct; *sich ~ orient(ate) o.s.* (*a. fig.*); inform o.s. (*über acc.* of); *gut orientiert sein über* (*acc.*) be well informed about, be familiar with; **2ung** *f* (-/-en) orientation; *fig. a.* information; *die ~ verlieren* lose one's bearings.

Origin|al [origi'naːl] **1.** *n* (-s/-e) original; **2.** ♀ *adj.* original; **~alität** [~ali'tɛːt] *f* (-/-en) originality; **2ell** *adj.* [~'nɛl] original; *design, etc.*: ingenious.

Orkan [ɔr'kaːn] *m* (-[e]s/-e) hurricane; typhoon; **2artig** *adj. storm:* violent; *applause:* thunderous, frenzied.

Ornat [ɔr'naːt] *m* (-[e]s/-e) robe(s *pl.*), vestment.

Ort [ɔrt] *m* (-[e]s/-e) place; site; spot, point; locality; place, village, town; *~ der Handlung thea.* scene (of action); *an ~ und Stelle* on the spot; *höher(e)n ~(e)s* at higher quarters; **'2en** *v/t.* (ge-, h) locate.

ortho|dox *adj.* [ɔrto'dɔks] orthodox; **2graphie** [~gra'fiː] *f* (-/-n) orthography; **~graphisch** *adj.* [~'graːfiʃ] orthographic(al); **2päde** ✗ [~'pɛːdə] *m* (-n/-n) orthop(a)edist; **2pädie** [~pɛ'diː] *f* (-/*no pl.*) orthop(a)edics, orthop(a)edy; **~pädisch** *adj.* [~'pɛːdiʃ] orthop(a)edic.

örtlich *adj.* ['œrtliç] local; ✗ *a.* topical; **2keit** *f* (-/-en) locality.

'Orts|angabe *f* statement of place; **2ansässig** *adj.* resident, local; **~ansässige** ['~gə] *m* (-n/-n) resident; **~beschreibung** *f* topography; **~besichtigung** *f* local inspection.

'Ortschaft *f* (-/-en) place, village.

'Orts|gespräch *teleph. n* local call; **'~kenntnis** *f* knowledge of a place; **2kundig** *adj.* familiar with the locality; **'~name** *m* place-name; **'~verkehr** *m* local traffic; **'~zeit** *f* local time.

Öse ['øːzə] *f* (-/-n) eye, loop; eyelet (*of shoe*).

Ost *geogr.* [ɔst] east; **'~en** *m* (-s/*no pl.*) east; *the* East; *der Ferne* (*Nahe*) *~* the Far (Near) East.

ostentativ *adj.* [ɔstenta'tiːf] ostentatious.

Oster|ei ['oːstərʔ-] *n* Easter egg; **'~fest** *n* Easter; **'~hase** *m* Easter bunny *or* rabbit; **'~lamm** *n* paschal lamb; **'~n** *n* (-/-) Easter.

Österreich|er ['øːstəraiçər] *m* (-s/-) Austrian; **2isch** *adj.* Austrian.

östlich ['œstliç] **1.** *adj.* eastern; *wind, etc.*: easterly; **2.** *adv.*: *~ von* east of.

ost'wärts *adv.* ['ɔstvɛrts] eastward(s); **2wind** *m* east(erly) wind.

Otter *zo.* ['ɔtər] **1.** *m* (-s/-) otter; **2.** *f* (-/-n) adder, viper.

Ouvertüre ♪ [uver'tyːrə] *f* (-/-n) overture.

oval [o'vaːl] **1.** *adj.* oval; **2.** ♀ *n* (-s/-e) oval.

Ovation [ova'tsjoːn] *f* (-/-en) ovation; *j-m ~en bereiten* give s.o. ovations.

Oxyd ✗ [ɔ'ksyːt] *n* (-[e]s/-e) oxide; **2ieren** [~y'diːrən] (*no* -ge-) **1.** *v/t.* (h) oxidize; **2.** *v/i.* (sein) oxidize.

Ozean ['oːtseaːn] *m* (-s/-e) ocean.

P

Paar [pɑ:r] **1.** *n* (-[e]s/-e) pair; couple; **2.** ⌢ *adj.*: ein ⌢ a few, some; *j-m* ein ⌢ Zeilen schreiben drop s.o. a few lines; '⌢en *v/t.* (ge-, h) pair, couple; mate (*animals*); sich ⌢ (form a) pair; *animals*: mate; *fig.* join, unite; '⌢lauf *m sports*: pair-skating; '⌢läufer *m sports*: pair-skater; '⌢mal *adv.*: ein ⌢ several *or* a few times; '⌢ung *f* (-/-en) coupling; mating, copulation; *fig.* union; '⌢weise *adv.* in pairs *or* couples, by twos.

Pacht [paxt] *f* (-/-en) lease, tenure, tenancy; *money payment*: rent; '⌢en *v/t.* (ge-, h) (take on) lease; rent.

Pächter ['pɛçtər] *m* (-s/-), '⌢in *f* (-/-nen) lessee, lease-holder; tenant.

'**Pacht|ertrag** *m* rental; '⌢geld *n* rent; '⌢gut *n* farm; '⌢vertrag *m* lease; '⌢weise *adv.* on lease.

Pack [pak] **1.** *m* (-[e]s/-e, ⸚e) *s.* Packen²; **2.** *n* (-[e]s/no *pl.*) rabble.

Päckchen ['pɛkçən] *n* (-s/-) small parcel, *Am. a.* package; ein ⌢ Zigaretten a pack(et) of cigarettes.

packen¹ ['pakən] (ge-, h) **1.** *v/t.* pack (up); seize, grip, grasp, clutch; collar; *fig.* grip, thrill; *F* pack dich! F clear out!, *sl.* beat it!; **2.** *v/i.* pack (up); **3.** ⌢ *n* (-s/no *pl.*) packing.

Packen² [⌢] *m* (-s/-) pack(et), parcel, bale.

'**Packer** *m* (-s/-) packer; '⌢ei [⌢'raɪ] *f* **1.** (-/-en) packing-room; **2.** (-/no *pl.*) packing.

'**Pack|esel** *fig. m* drudge; '⌢material *n* packing materials *pl.*; '⌢papier *n* packing-paper, brown paper; '⌢pferd *n* pack-horse; '⌢ung *f* (-/-en) pack(age), packet; ⌢ pack; e-e ⌢ Zigaretten a pack(et) of cigarettes; '⌢wagen *m s.* Gepäck-wagen.

Pädagog|e [pɛda'go:gə] *m* (-n/-n) pedagog(ue), education(al)ist; ⌢ik *f* (-/no *pl.*) pedagogics, pedagogy; ⌢isch *adj.* pedagogic(al).

Paddel ['padəl] *n* (-s/-) paddle; '⌢boot *n* canoe; '⌢n *v/i.* (ge-, h, sein) paddle, canoe.

Page ['pa:ʒə] *m* (-n/-n) page.

pah *int.* [pa:] pah!, pooh!, pshaw!

Paket [pa'ke:t] *n* (-[e]s/-e) parcel, packet, package; ⌢annahme ⚒ *f* parcel counter; ⌢karte ⚒ *f* dispatch-note; ⌢post *f* parcel post; ⌢zustellung ⚒ *f* parcel delivery.

Pakt [pakt] *m* (-[e]s/-e) pact; agreement; treaty.

Palast [pa'last] *m* (-es/⸚e) palace.

Palm|e ⚒ ['palmə] *f* (-/-n) palm (-tree); '⌢öl *n* palm-oil; ⌢'sonntag *eccl. m* Palm Sunday.

panieren [pa'ni:rən] *v/t.* (no -ge-, h) crumb.

Pani|k ['pa:nik] *f* (-/-en) panic; stampede; '⌢sch *adj.* panic; von ⌢em Schrecken erfaßt panic-stricken.

Panne ['panə] *f* (-/-n) breakdown, *mot. a.* engine trouble; *tyres*: puncture; *fig.* blunder.

panschen ['panʃən] (ge-, h) **1.** *v/i.* splash (about); **2.** *v/t.* adulterate (*wine, etc.*).

Panther *zo.* ['pantər] *m* (-s/-) panther.

Pantine [pan'ti:nə] *f* (-/-n) clog.

Pantoffel [pan'tɔfəl] *m* (-s/-n, F -) slipper; unter dem ⌢ stehen be henpecked; ⌢held F *m* henpecked husband.

pantschen ['pantʃən] *v/i. and v/t.* (ge-, h) *s.* panschen.

Panzer ['pantsər] *m* (-s/-) armo(u)r; ✕ tank; *zo.* shell; '⌢abwehr ✕ *f* anti-tank defen|ce, *Am.* -se; '⌢glas *n* bullet-proof glass; '⌢hemd *n* coat of mail; '⌢kreuzer ✕ *m* armo(u)red cruiser; '⌢n *v/t.* (ge-, h) armo(u)r; '⌢platte *f* armo(u)r-plate; '⌢schiff ✕ *n* ironclad; '⌢schrank *m* safe; '⌢ung *f* (-/-en) armo(u)r-plating; '⌢wagen *m* armo(u)red car; ✕ tank.

Papa [pa'pa:, F 'papa] *m* (-s/-s) papa, F pa, dad(dy), *Am. a.* pop.

Papagei *orn.* [papa'gaɪ] *m* (-[e]s, -en/-e[n]) parrot.

Papier [pa'pi:r] *n* (-s/-e) paper; ⌢e *pl.* papers *pl.*, documents *pl.*; papers *pl.*, identity card; ein Bogen ⌢ a sheet of paper; ⌢en *adj.* (of) paper; *fig.* dull; ⌢fabrik *f* paper-mill; ⌢geld *n* (-[e]s/no *pl.*) paper-money; banknotes *pl.*, *Am.* bills *pl.*; ⌢korb *m* waste-paper-basket; ⌢schnitzel *f n or m/pl.* scraps *pl.* of paper; ⌢tüte *f* paper-bag; ⌢waren *f/pl.* stationery.

'**Papp|band** *m* (-[e]s/⸚e) paperback; '⌢deckel *n* pasteboard, cardboard.

Pappe ['papə] *f* (-/-n) pasteboard, cardboard.

Pappel ⚒ ['papəl] *f* (-/-n) poplar.

päppeln F ['pɛpəln] *v/t.* (ge-, h) feed (with pap).

papp|en F ['papən] (ge-, h) **1.** *v/t.* paste; **2.** *v/i.* stick; '⌢ig *adj.* sticky; '⌢karton *m* (-s/-e) *and* '⌢schachtel *f* cardboard box, carton.

Papst [pa:pst] *m* (-es/⸚e) pope.

päpstlich *adj.* ['pɛ:pstliç] papal.

'**Papsttum** *n* (-s/no *pl.*) papacy.

Parade [pa'ra:də] *f* (-/-n) parade; ✕ review; *fencing*: parry.

Paradies [para'di:s] *n* (-es/-e) paradise; ⌢isch *fig. adj.* [⌢'di:ziʃ] heavenly, delightful.

paradox *adj.* [para'dɔks] paradoxical.

Paragraph [para'grɑːf] m (-en, -s/-en) article, section; paragraph; section-mark.

parallel adj. [para'leːl] parallel; 2e f (-/-n) parallel.

Paralys|e [para'lyːzə] f (-/-n) paralysis; 2ieren ⚕ [‿y'ziːrən] v/t. (no -ge-, h) paralyse.

Parasit [para'ziːt] m (-en/-en) parasite.

Parenthese [paren'teːzə] f (-/-n) parenthesis.

Parforcejagd [par'fɔrs-] f hunt (-ing) on horseback (with hounds), after hares: coursing.

Parfüm [par'fyːm] n (-s/-e, -s) perfume, scent; ‿erie [‿ymə'riː] f (-/-n) perfumery; 2ieren [‿y'miːrən] v/t. (no -ge-, h) perfume, scent.

pari † adv. ['paːri] par; al ‿ at par.

parieren [pa'riːrən] (no -ge-, h) 1. v/t. fencing: parry (a. fig.); pull up (horse); 2. v/i. obey (j-m s.o.).

Park [park] m (-s/-s, -e) park; '‿anlage f park; '‿aufseher m park-keeper; '2en (ge-, h) 1. v/i. park; ‿ verboten! no parking!; 2. v/t. park.

Parkett [par'ket] n (-[e]s/-e) parquet; thea. (orchestra) stalls pl., esp. Am. orchestra or parquet.

'Park|gebühr f parking-fee; '‿licht n parking light; '‿platz m (car-) park, parking lot; '‿uhr mot. f parking meter.

Parlament [parla'ment] n (-[e]s/-e) parliament; 2arisch adj. [‿'taːrif] parliamentary.

Parodie [paro'diː] f (-/-n) parody; 2ren v/t. (no -ge-, h) parody.

Parole [pa'roːlə] f (-/-n) ⚔ password, watchword; fig. slogan.

Partei [par'tai] f (-/-en) party (a. pol.); j-s ‿ ergreifen take s.o.'s part, side with s.o.; ‿apparat pol. m party machinery; ‿gänger [‿genər] m (-s/-) partisan; 2isch adj., 2lich adj. partial (für to); prejudiced (gegen against); 2los pol. adj. independent; ‿mitglied pol. n party member; ‿programm pol. n platform; ‿tag pol. m convention; ‿zugehörigkeit pol. f party membership.

Parterre [par'ter] n (-s/-s) ground floor, Am. first floor; thea.: pit, Am. parterre, Am. parquet circle.

Partie [par'tiː] f (-/-n) † parcel, lot; outing, excursion; cards, etc.: game; ♪ part; marriage: match.

Partitur ♪ [parti'tuːr] f (-/-en) score.

Partizip gr. [parti'tsiːp] n (-s/-ien) participle.

Partner ['partnər] m (-s/-), '‿in f (-/-nen) partner; film: a. co-star; '‿schaft f (-/-en) partnership.

Parzelle [par'tselə] f (-/-n) plot, lot, allotment.

Paß [pas] m (Passes/Pässe) pass;

passage; football, etc.: pass; passport.

Passage [pa'saːʒə] f (-/-n) passage; arcade.

Passagier [pasa'ʒiːr] m (-s/-e) passenger, in taxis: a. fare; ‿flugzeug n air liner.

Passah ['pasa] n (-s/no pl.), '‿fest n Passover.

Passant [pa'sant] m (-en/-en), ‿in f (-/-nen) passer-by.

'Paßbild n passport photo(graph).

passen ['pasən] (ge-, h) 1. v/i. fit (j-m s.o.; auf acc. or für or zu et. s.th.); suit (j-m s.o.), be convenient; cards, football: pass; ‿ zu go with, match (with); 2. v/refl. be fit or proper; '‿d adj. fit, suitable; convenient (für for).

passier|bar adj. [pa'siːrbaːr] passable, practicable; ‿en (no -ge-) 1. v/i. (sein) happen; 2. v/t. (h) pass (over or through); 2schein m pass, permit.

Passion [pa'sjoːn] f (-/-en) passion; hobby; eccl. Passion.

passiv ['pasiːf] 1. adj. passive; 2. 2 gr. n (-s/‿e) passive (voice); 2a † [pa'siːva] pl. liabilities pl.

Paste ['pastə] f (-/-n) paste.

Pastell [pa'stel] n (-[e]s/-e) pastel.

Pastete [pa'steːtə] f (-/-n) pie; ‿nbäcker m pastry-cook.

Pate ['paːtə] 1. m (-n/-n) godfather; godchild; 2. f (-/-n) godmother; '‿nkind n godchild; '‿nschaft f (-/-en) sponsorship.

Patent [pa'tent] n (-[e]s/-e) patent; ✕ commission; ein ‿ anmelden apply for a patent; ‿amt n Patent Office; ‿anwalt m patent agent; 2ieren [‿'tiːrən] v/t. (no -ge-, h) patent; et. ‿ lassen take out a patent for s.th.; ‿inhaber m patentee; ‿urkunde f letters patent.

Patient [pa'tsjent] m (-en/-en), ‿in f (-/-nen) patient.

Patin ['paːtin] f (-/-nen) godmother.

Patriot [patri'oːt] m (-en/-en), ‿in f (-/-nen) patriot.

Patron [pa'troːn] m (-s/-e) patron, protector; contp. fellow, bloke, customer; ‿at [‿o'naːt] n (-[e]s/-e) patronage; ‿e [pa'troːnə] f (-/-n) cartridge, Am. a. shell.

Patrouill|e ✕ [pa'truljə] f (-/-n) patrol; 2ieren ✕ [‿'jiːrən] v/i. (no -ge-, h) patrol.

Patsch|e F fig. ['patʃə] f (-/no pl.): in der ‿ sitzen be in a fix or scrape; '2en F (ge-) 1. v/i. (h, sein) splash; 2. v/t. (h) slap; '2'naß adj. dripping wet, drenched.

patzig F adj. ['patsiç] snappish.

Pauke ♪ ['paukə] f (-/-n) kettledrum; '2n F v/i. and v/t. (ge-, h) school: cram.

Pauschal|e [pau'ʃaːlə] f (-/-n), ‿summe f lump sum.

Pause ['pauzə] f (-/-n) pause, stop, interval; *school:* break, *Am.* recess; *thea.* interval, *Am.* intermission; ♪ rest; *drawing:* tracing; '2n v/t. (ge-, h) trace; '2nlos adj. uninterrupted, incessant; '~nzeichen n *wireless:* interval signal.

pau'sieren v/i. (*no* -ge-, h) pause.

Pavian zo. ['pa:viɑ:n] m (-s/-e) baboon.

Pavillon ['paviljõ] m (-s/-s) pavilion.

Pazifist [patsi'fist] m (-en/-en) pacif(ic)ist.

Pech [peç] n 1. (-[e]s /-e) pitch; 2. F *fig.* (-[e]s/*no pl.*) bad luck; '~strähne F f run of bad luck; '~vogel F m unlucky fellow.

pedantisch adj. [pe'dantiʃ] pedantic; punctilious, meticulous.

Pegel ['pe:gəl] m (-s/-) water-ga(u)ge.

peilen ['pailən] v/t. (ge-, h) sound (*depth*); take the bearings of (*coast*).

Pein [pain] f (-/*no pl.*) torment, torture, anguish; 2igen ['.igən] v/t. (ge-, h) torment; ~iger ['.igər] m (-s/-) tormentor.

'peinlich adj. painful, embarrassing; particular, scrupulous, meticulous.

Peitsche ['paitʃə] f (-/-n) whip; '2n v/t. (ge-, h) whip; '~nhieb m lash.

Pelikan orn. ['pe:likɑ:n] m (-s/-e) pelican.

Pelle ['pɛlə] f (-/-n) skin, peel; '2en v/t. (ge-, h) skin, peel; '~kartoffeln f/pl. potatoes pl. (boiled) in their jackets or skins.

Pelz [pelts] m (-es/-e) fur; *garment:* mst furs pl.; '2gefüttert adj. fur-lined; '~händler m furrier; '~handschuh m furred glove; '2ig adj. furry; ♂ *tongue:* furred; '~mantel m fur coat; '~stiefel m fur-lined boot; '~tiere n/pl. fur-covered animals pl.

Pendel ['pendəl] n (-s/-) pendulum; '2n v/i. (ge-, h) oscillate, swing; 🚃 shuttle, *Am.* commute; '~tür f swing-door; '~verkehr 🚃 m shuttle service.

Pension [pã'sjõ:, pɑŋ'zjo:n] f (-/-en) (old-age) pension, retired pay; board; boarding-house; ~är [~o-'nɛ:r] m (-s/-e) (old-age) pensioner; boarder; ~at [.o'nɑ:t] n (-[e]s/-e) boarding-school; 2ieren [.o'ni:rən] v/t. (*no* -ge-, h) pension (off); sich ~ lassen retire; ~sgast m boarder.

Pensum ['penzum] n (-s/Pensen, Pensa) task, lesson.

perfekt 1. adj. [per'fɛkt] perfect; *agreement:* settled; 2. 2 gr. ['~] n (-[e]s/-e) perfect (tense).

Pergament [perga'ment] n (-[e]s/-e) parchment.

Periode [per'jo:də] f (-/-n) period; ♂ periods pl.; 2isch adj. periodic (-al).

Peripherie [perife'ri:] f (-/-n)

circumference; outskirts pl. (*of town*).

Perle ['perlə] f (-/-n) pearl; *of glass:* bead; '2n v/i. (ge-, h) sparkle; '~nkette f pearl necklace; '~nschnur f string of pearls or beads.

'Perl|muschel zo. f pearl-oyster; ~mutt ['.mut] n (-s/*no pl.*), ~'mutter f (-/*no pl.*) mother-of-pearl.

Person [per'zo:n] f (-/-en) person; *thea.* character.

Personal [perzo'nɑ:l] n (-s/*no pl.*) staff, personnel; ~abteilung f personnel office; ~angaben f/pl. personal data pl.; ~ausweis m identity card; ~chef m personnel officer or manager or director; ~ien [.jən] pl. particulars pl., personal data pl.; ~pronomen gr. n personal pronoun.

Per'sonen|verzeichnis n list of persons; *thea.* dramatis personae pl.; ~wagen m 🚃 (passenger-)carriage or *Am.* car, coach; *mot.* (motor-)car; ~zug 🚃 m passenger train.

personifizieren [perzonifi'tsi:rən] v/t. (*no* -ge-, h) personify.

persönlich adj. [per'zø:nliç] personal; *opinion, letter:* a. private; 2keit f (-/-en) personality; personage.

Perücke [pe'rykə] f (-/-n) wig.

Pest ♂ [pest] f (-/*no pl.*) plague.

Petersilie ♀ [petər'zi:ljə] f (-/-n) parsley.

Petroleum [pe'tro:leum] n (-s/*no pl.*) petroleum; *for lighting, etc.:* paraffin, *esp. Am.* kerosene.

Pfad [pfɑ:t] m (-[e]s/-e) path, track; '~finder m boy scout; '~finderin f (-/-nen) girl guide, *Am.* girl scout.

Pfahl [pfɑ:l] m (-[e]s/≈e) stake, pale, pile.

Pfand [pfant] n (-[e]s/≈er) pledge; ♰ deposit, security; *real estate:* mortgage; *game:* forfeit; '~brief ♰ m debenture (bond).

pfänden ♯ ['pfɛndən] v/t. (ge-, h) seize s.th.; distrain upon s.o. or s.th.

'Pfand|haus n s. Leihhaus; '~leiher m (-s/-) pawnbroker; '~schein m pawn-ticket.

'Pfändung ♯ f (-/-en) seizure; distraint.

Pfanne ['pfanə] f (-/-n) pan; '~kuchen m pancake.

Pfarr|bezirk ['pfar-] m parish; '~er m (-s/-) parson; *Church of England:* rector, vicar; *dissenters:* minister; '~gemeinde f parish; '~haus n parsonage; *Church of England:* rectory, vicarage; '~kirche f parish church; '~stelle f (church) living.

Pfau orn. [pfau] m (-[e]s/-en) peacock.

Pfeffer ['pfefər] m (-s/-) pepper; '~gurke f gherkin; '2ig adj. peppery; '~kuchen m gingerbread;

~minze ♀ ['~mintsə] f (-/no pl.) peppermint; '~minzplätzchen n peppermint; '2n v/t. (ge-, h) pepper; '~streuer m (-s/-) pepperbox, pepper-castor, pepper-caster.

Pfeife ['pfaifə] f (-/-n) whistle; ✕ fife; pipe (of organ, etc.); (tobacco-) pipe; '2n (irr., ge-, h) 1. v/i. whistle (dat. to, for); radio: howl; pipe; 2. v/t. whistle; pipe; '~nkopf m pipe-bowl.

Pfeil [pfail] m (-[e]s/-e) arrow.

Pfeiler ['pfailər] m (-s/-) pillar (a. fig.); pier (of bridge, etc.).

'pfeil'schnell adj. (as) swift as an arrow; '2spitze f arrow-head.

Pfennig ['pfeniç] m (-[e]s/-e) coin: pfennig; fig. penny, farthing.

Pferch [pferç] m (-[e]s/-e) fold, pen; '2en v/t. (ge-, h) fold, pen; fig. cram.

Pferd zo. [pfe:rt] n (-[e]s/-e) horse; zu ~e on horseback.

Pferde|geschirr ['pfe:rdə-] n harness; '~koppel f (-/-n) paddock, Am. a. corral; '~rennen n horse-race; '~schwanz m horse's tail; hair-style: pony-tail; '~stall m stable; '~stärke ⊕ f horsepower.

pfiff[1] [pfif] pret. of pfeifen.

Pfiff[2] m (-[e]s/-e) whistle; fig. trick; '2ig adj. cunning, artful.

Pfingst|en eccl. ['pfiŋstən] n (-/-), '~fest eccl. n Whitsun(tide); '~montag eccl. m Whit Monday; '~rose ♀ f peony; '~sonntag eccl. m Whit Sunday.

Pfirsich ['pfirziç] m (-[e]s/-e) peach.

Pflanz|e ['pflantsə] f (-/-n) plant; '2en v/t. (ge-, h) plant, set; pot; '~enfaser f vegetable fib|re, Am. -er; '~enfett n vegetable fat; '2enfressend adj. herbivorous; '~er m (-s/-) planter; '~ung f (-/-en) plantation.

Pflaster ['pflastər] n (-s/-) ✗ plaster; road: pavement; '~er m (-s/-) paver, pavio(u)r; '2n v/t. (ge-, h) plaster; pave (road); '~stein m paving-stone; cobble.

Pflaume ['pflaumə] f (-/-n) plum; dried: prune.

Pflege ['pfle:gə] f (-/-n) care; ✗ nursing; cultivation (of art, garden, etc.); ⊕ maintenance; in ~ geben put out (child) to nurse; in ~ nehmen take charge of; '2bedürftig adj. needing care; '~befohlene ['~bəfo:lənə] m, f (-n/-n) charge; '~eltern pl. foster-parents pl.; '~heim ✗ n nursing home; '~kind n foster-child; '2n (ge-, h) 1. v/t. take care of; attend (to); foster (child); ✗ nurse; maintain; cultivate (art, garden); 2. v/i.: ~ zu inf. be accustomed or used or wont to inf., be in the habit of ger.; sie pflegte zu sagen she used to say; '~r m (-s/-) fosterer; ✗ male nurse;

trustee; ✗ guardian, curator; '~rin f (-/-nen) nurse.

Pflicht [pfliçt] f (-/-en) duty (gegen to); obligation; '2bewußt adj. conscious of one's duty; '2eifrig adj.zealous; '~erfüllung f performance of one's duty; '~fach n school, univ.: compulsory subject; '~gefühl n sense of duty; '2gemäß adj. dutiful; '2getreu adj. dutiful, loyal; '2schuldig adj. in duty bound; '2vergessen adj. undutiful, disloyal; '~verteidiger ✗ m assigned counsel.

Pflock [pflɔk] m (-[e]s/✗e) plug, peg.

pflücken ['pflykən] v/t. (ge-, h) pick, gather, pluck.

Pflug [pflu:k] m (-[e]s/✗e) plough, Am. plow.

pflügen ['pfly:gən] v/t. and v/i. (ge-, h) plough, Am. plow.

Pforte ['pfɔrtə] f (-/-n) gate, door.

Pförtner ['pfœrtnər] m (-s/-) gate-keeper, door-keeper, porter, janitor.

Pfosten ['pfɔstən] m (-s/-) post.

Pfote ['pfo:tə] f (-/-n) paw.

Pfropf [pfrɔpf] m (-[e]s/-e) s. Pfropfen.

'Pfropfen 1. m (-s/-) stopper; cork; plug; ✗ clot (of blood); 2. ♀ v/t. (ge-, h) stopper; cork; fig. cram; ✗ graft.

Pfründe eccl. ['pfryndə] f (-/-n) prebend; benefice, (church) living.

Pfuhl [pfu:l] m (-[e]s/-e) pool, puddle; fig. sink, slough.

pfui int. [pfui] fie!, for shame!

Pfund [pfunt] n (-[e]s/-e) pound; 2ig F adj. '~diç] great, Am. swell; '2weise adv. by the pound.

pfusch|en F ['pfuʃən] (ge-, h) 1. v/i. bungle; 2. v/t. bungle, botch; 2erei F ['~rai] f (-/-en) bungle, botch.

Pfütze ['pfytsə] f (-/-n) puddle, pool.

Phänomen [fɛno'me:n] n (-s/-e) phenomenon; 2al adj. ['~e'na:l] phenomenal.

Phantasie [fanta'zi:] f (-/-n) imagination, fancy; vision; ♪ fantasia; 2ren (no -ge-, h) 1. v/i. dream; ramble; ✗ be delirious or raving; ♪ improvise; 2. v/t. dream; ♪ improvise.

Phantast [fan'tast] m (-en/-en) visionary, dreamer; 2isch adj. fantastic; F great, terrific.

Phase ['fɑ:zə] f (-/-n) phase (a. ⚡), stage.

Philanthrop [filan'tro:p] m (-en/-en) philanthropist.

Philolog|e [filo'lo:gə] m (-n/-n), '~in f (-/-nen) philologist; '~ie [~o'gi:] f (-/-n) philology.

Philosoph [filo'zo:f] m (-en/-en) philosopher; '~ie [~o'fi:] f (-/-n) philosophy; 2ieren [~o'fi:rən] v/i. (no -ge-, h) philosophize (über acc. on); 2isch adj. [~'zo:fiʃ] philosophical.

Phlegma ['flɛgma] *n* (-s/no *pl.*) phlegm; **2tisch** *adj.* [~'maːtiʃ] phlegmatic.

phonetisch *adj.* [fo'neːtiʃ] phonetic.

Phosphor ⚗ ['fɔsfɔr] *m* (-s/no *pl.*) phosphorus.

Photo F ['foːto] **1.** *n* (-s/-s) photo; **2.** *m* (-s/-s) = '~apparat *m* camera.

Photograph [foto'graːf] *m* (-en/-en) photographer; ~ie [~a'fiː] *f* **1.** (-/-n) photograph, photo, picture; **2.** (-/no *pl.*) as an *art*: photography; **2ieren** [~a'fiːrən] (no -ge-, h) **1.** *v/t.* photograph; take a picture of; *sich* ~ *lassen* have one's photo(graph) taken; **2.** *v/i.* photograph; **2isch** *adj.* [~'graːfiʃ] photographic.

Photo|ko'pie *f* photostat; **~ko'piergerät** *n* photostat; **'~zelle** *f* photo-electric cell.

Phrase ['fraːzə] *f* (-/-n) phrase.

Physik [fy'ziːk] *f* (-/no *pl.*) physics *sg.*; **2alisch** *adj.* [~i'kaːliʃ] physical; **~er** ['fyːzikər] *m* (-s/-) physicist.

physisch *adj.* ['fyːziʃ] physical.

Pian|ist [pia'nist] *m* (-en/-en) pianist; **~o** [pi'aːno] *n* (-s/-s) piano.

Picke ⊕ ['pikə] *f* (-/-n) pick(axe).

Pickel ['pikəl] *m* (-s/-) ⚕ pimple; ⊕ pick(axe); ice-pick; **'2ig** *adj.* pimpled, pimply.

picken ['pikən] *v/i. and v/t.* (ge-, h) pick, peck.

picklig *adj.* ['pikliç] *s.* pickelig.

Picknick ['piknik] *n* (-s/-e, -s) picnic.

piekfein F *adj.* ['piːk'-] smart, tip-top, slap-up.

piep(s)en ['piːp(s)ən] *v/i.* (ge-, h) cheep, chirp, peep; squeak.

Pietät [pie'tɛːt] *f* (-/no *pl.*) reverence; piety; **2los** *adj.* irreverent; **2voll** *adj.* reverent.

Pik [piːk] **1.** *m* (-s/-e, -s) peak; **2.** F *m* (-s/-e): e-n ~ *auf j-n haben* bear s.o. a grudge; **3.** *n* (-s/-s) *cards*: spade(s *pl.*).

pikant *adj.* [pi'kant] piquant, spicy (*both a. fig.*); *das Pikante* the piquancy.

Pike ['piːkə] *f* (-/-n) pike; *von der* ~ *auf dienen* rise from the ranks.

Pilger ['pilgər] *m* (-s/-) pilgrim; **'~fahrt** *f* pilgrimage; **2n** *v/i.* (ge-, sein) go on *or* make a pilgrimage; wander.

Pille ['pilə] *f* (-/-n) pill.

Pilot [pi'loːt] *m* (-en/-en) pilot.

Pilz ♣ [pilts] *m* (-es/-e) fungus, *edible*: mushroom, *inedible*: toad-stool.

pimp(e)lig F *adj.* ['pimp(ə)liç] sickly; effeminate.

Pinguin *orn.* ['piŋguiːn] *m* (-s/-e) penguin.

Pinsel ['pinzəl] *m* (-s/-) brush; F *fig.* simpleton; **'2n** *v/t. and v/i.* (ge-, h) paint; daub; **'~strich** *m* stroke of the brush.

Pinzette [pin'tsɛtə] *f* (-/-n) (e-e a pair of) tweezers *pl.*

Pionier [pio'niːr] *m* (-s/-e) pioneer, *Am. a.* trail blazer; ✂ engineer.

Pirat [pi'raːt] *m* (-en/-en) pirate.

Pirsch *hunt.* [pirʃ] *f* (-/no *pl.*) deer-stalking, *Am. a.* still hunt.

Piste ['pistə] *f* (-/-n) *skiing, etc.*: course; ✈ runway.

Pistole [pis'toːlə] *f* (-/-n) pistol, *Am.* F *a.* gun, rod; **~ntasche** *f* holster.

placieren [pla'siːrən] *v/t.* (no -ge-, h) place; *sich* ~ *sports*: be placed (*second, etc.*).

Plackerei F [plakə'raɪ] *f* (-/-en) drudgery.

plädieren [plɛ'diːrən] *v/i.* (no -ge-, h) plead (*für* for).

Plädoyer 🏛 [plɛdoa'jeː] *n* (-s/-s) pleading.

Plage ['plaːgə] *f* (-/-n) trouble, nuisance, A plague; torment; **'2n** *v/t.* (ge-, h) torment; trouble, bother; F plague; *sich* ~ toil, drudge.

Plagiat [plag'jaːt] *n* (-[e]s/-e) plagiarism; *ein* ~ *begehen* plagia-rize.

Plakat [pla'kaːt] *n* (-[e]s/-e) poster, placard, bill; **~säule** *f* advertisement pillar.

Plakette [pla'kɛtə] *f* (-/-n) plaque.

Plan [plaːn] *m* (-[e]s/~e) plan; design, intention; scheme.

Plane ['plaːnə] *f* (-/-n) awning, tilt.

'planen *v/t.* (ge-, h) plan; scheme.

Planet [pla'neːt] *m* (-en/-en) planet.

planieren ⊕ [pla'niːrən] *v/t.* (no -ge-, h) level.

Planke ['plaŋkə] *f* (-/-n) plank, board.

plänkeln ['plɛŋkəln] *v/i.* (ge-, h) skirmish (*a. fig.*).

'plan|los 1. *adj.* planless, aimless, desultory; **2.** *adv.* at random; **'~mäßig 1.** *adj.* systematic, planned; **2.** *adv.* as planned.

planschen ['planʃən] *v/i.* (ge-, h) splash, paddle.

Plantage [plan'taːʒə] *f* (-/-n) plantation.

Plapper|maul F ['plapər-] *n* chatterbox; **'2n** F *v/i.* (ge-, h) chatter, prattle, babble.

plärren ['plɛrən] *v/i. and v/t.* (ge-, h) blubber; bawl.

Plasti|k [plastik] **1.** *f* (-/no *pl.*) plastic art; **2.** *f* (-/-en) sculpture; ✂ plastic; **3.** ⊕ *n* (-s/-s) plastic; **'2sch** *adj.* plastic; three-dimensional.

Platin [pla'tiːn] *n* (-s/no *pl.*) platinum.

plätschern ['plɛtʃərn] *v/i.* (ge-, h) dabble, splash; *water*: ripple, murmur.

platt *adj.* [plat] flat, level, even; *fig.* trivial, commonplace, trite; F *fig.* flabbergasted.

Plättbrett ['plɛt-] *n* ironing-board.

Platte ['platǝ] *f* (-/-n) plate; dish; sheet (*of metal, etc.*); flag, slab (*of stone*); *mountain*: ledge; top (*of table*); tray, salver; disc, record; F *fig.* bald pate; *kalte* ~ cold meat.

plätten ['plɛtǝn] *v/t.* (ge-, *h*) iron.

'Platten|spieler *m* record-player; **'~teller** *m* turn-table.

'Platt|form *f* platform; **'~fuß** *m* flat-foot; F *mot.* flat; **'~heit** *fig. f* (-/-en) triviality; commonplace, platitude, *Am. sl. a.* bromide.

Platz [plats] *m* (-es/-e) place; spot, *Am. a.* point; room, space; site; seat; square; *round*: circus; *sports*: ground; *tennis*: court; ~ *behalten* remain seated; ~ *machen* make way or room (*dat.* for); ~ *nehmen* take a seat, sit down, *Am. a.* have a seat; *ist hier noch* ~? is this seat taken or engaged or occupied?; *den dritten* ~ *belegen sports*: be placed third, come in third; **'~anweiserin** *f* (-/-nen) usherette.

Plätzchen ['plɛtsçǝn] *n* (-s/-) snug place; spot; biscuit, *Am.* cookie.

'platzen *v/i.* (ge-, *sein*) burst; explode; crack, split.

'Platz|patrone *f* blank cartridge; **'~regen** *m* downpour.

Plauder|ei [plaudǝ'raɪ] *f* (-/-en) chat; talk; small talk; **'2n** (ge-, *h*) (have a) chat (*mit* with), talk (to); chatter.

plauz *int.* [plauts] bang!

Pleite F ['plaɪtǝ] **1.** *f* (-/-n) smash; *fig.* failure; **2. 2** F *adj.* (dead) broke, *Am. sl.* bust.

Plissee [pli'se:] *n* (-s/-s) pleating; **~rock** *m* pleated skirt.

Plomb|e ['plɔmbǝ] *f* (-/-n) (lead) seal; stopping, filling (*of tooth*); **2ieren** [~'bi:rǝn] *v/t.* (*no* -ge-, *h*) seal; stop, fill (*tooth*).

plötzlich *adj.* ['plœtsliç] sudden.

plump *adj.* [plump] clumsy; **~s** *int.* plump, plop; **'~sen** *v/i.* (ge-, *sein*) plump, plop, flop.

Plunder F ['plundǝr] *m* (-s/*no pl.*) lumber, rubbish, junk.

plündern ['plyndǝrn] (ge-, *h*) **1.** *v/t.* plunder, pillage, loot, sack; **2.** *v/i.* plunder, loot.

Plural *gr.* ['plu:ra:l] *m* (-s/-e) plural (number).

plus *adv.* [plus] plus.

Plusquamperfekt *gr.* ['pluskvamperfɛkt] *n* (-s/-e) pluperfect (tense), past perfect.

Pöbel ['pø:bǝl] *m* (-s/*no pl.*) mob, rabble; **2haft** *adj.* low, vulgar.

pochen ['pɔxǝn] *v/i.* (ge-, *h*) knock, rap, tap; *heart*: beat, throb, thump; *auf sein Recht* ~ stand on one's rights.

Pocke ['pɔkǝ] *f* (-/-n) pock; **'~n** *m pl.* smallpox; **'2nnarbig** *adj.* pock-marked.

Podest [po'dɛst] *n, m* (-es/-e) pedestal (*a. fig.*).

Podium ['po:dium] *n* (-s/Podien) podium, platform, stage.

Poesie [poe'zi:] *f* (-/-n) poetry.

Poet [po'e:t] *m* (-en/-en) poet; **2isch** *adj.* poetic(al).

Pointe [po'ɛ̃:tǝ] *f* (-/-n) point.

Pokal [po'ka:l] *m* (-s/-e) goblet; *sports*: cup; **~endspiel** *n sports*: cup final; **~spiel** *n football*: cup-tie.

Pökel|fleisch ['pø:kǝl-] *n* salted meat; **'2n** *v/t.* (ge-, *h*) pickle, salt.

Pol [po:l] *m* (-s/-e) pole; *ɇ a.* terminal; **2ar** *adj.* [po'la:r] polar (*a. ɇ*).

Pole ['po:lǝ] *m* (-n/-n) Pole.

Polemi|k [po'le:mik] *f* (-/-en) polemic(s *pl.*); **2sch** *adj.* polemic (-al); **2sieren** [~emi'zi:rǝn] *v/i.* (*no* -ge-, *h*) polemize.

Police [po'li:s(ǝ)] *f* (-/-n) policy.

Polier ⊕ [po'li:r] *m* (-s/-e) foreman; **2en** *v/t.* (*no* -ge-, *h*) polish, burnish; furbish.

Politi|k [poli'ti:k] *f* (-/% -en) policy; politics *sg., pl.*; **~ker** [po'li:tikǝr] *m* (-s/-) politician; statesman; **2sch** *adj.* [po'li:tiʃ] political; **2sieren** [~iti'zi:rǝn] *v/i.* (*no* -ge-, *h*) talk politics.

Politur [poli'tu:r] *f* (-/-en) polish; lust|re, *Am.* -er, finish.

Polizei [poli'tsaɪ] *f* (-/% -en) police; **~beamte** *m* police officer; **~knüppel** *m* truncheon, *Am.* club; **~kommissar** *m* inspector; **2lich** *adj.* (of or by the) police); **~präsident** *m* president of police; *Brt.* Chief Constable, *Am.* Chief of Police; **~präsidium** *n* police headquarters *pl.*; **~revier** *n* police-station; police precinct; **~schutz** *m*: *unter* ~ under police guard; **~streife** *f* police patrol; police squad; **~stunde** *f* (-/*no pl.*) closing-time; **~verordnung** *f* police regulation(s *pl.*); **~wache** *f* police-station.

Polizist [poli'tsist] *m* (-en/-en) policeman, constable, *sl.* bobby, cop; **~in** *f* (-/-nen) policewoman.

polnisch *adj.* ['pɔlniʃ] Polish.

Polster ['pɔlstǝr] *n* (-s/-) pad; cushion; bolster; *s. Polsterung*; **'~möbel** *n/pl.* upholstered furniture; upholstery; **'2n** *v/t.* (ge-, *h*) upholster, stuff; pad, wad; **'~sessel** *m*, **'~stuhl** *m* upholstered chair; **'~ung** *f* (-/-en) padding, stuffing; upholstery.

poltern ['pɔltǝrn] *v/i.* (ge-, *h*) make a row; rumble; *p.* bluster.

Polytechnikum [poly'tɛçnikum] *n* (-s/Polytechnika, Polytechniken) polytechnic (school).

Pommes frites [pɔm'frit] *pl.* chips *pl., Am.* French fried potatoes *pl.*

Pomp [pɔmp] *m* (-[e]s/*no pl.*) pomp, splendo(u)r; **2haft** *adj.*, **2ös** *adj.* [~'pø:s] pompous, splendid.

Pony ['pɔni] 1. *zo. n* (-s/-s) pony;
2. *m* (-s/-s) *hairstyle:* bang, fringe.
popul|är *adj.* [popu'lɛ:r] popular;
2arität [‿ari'tɛ:t] *f* (-/*no pl.*)
popularity.
Por|e ['po:rə] *f* (-/-n) pore; **2ös** *adj.*
[po'rø:s] porous; permeable.
Portemonnaie [portmɔ'nɛ:] *n* (-s/-s)
purse.
Portier [pɔr'tje:] *m* (-s/-s) *s.* Pförtner.
Portion [pɔr'tsjo:n] *f* (-/-en) portion, share; ✗ ration; helping, serving; *zwei* ‿en Kaffee coffee for two.
Porto ['porto] *n* (-s/-s, Porti) postage; **2frei** *adj.* post-free; prepaid,
esp. Am. postpaid; **2pflichtig** *adj.*
subject to postage.
Porträt [pɔr'trɛ:; ‿t] *n* (-s/-s;
-[e]s/-e) portrait, likeness; **2ieren**
[‿ɛ'ti:rən] *v/t.* (*no* -ge-, *h*) portray.
Portugies|e [portu'gi:zə] *m* (-n/-n)
Portuguese; *die* ‿*n pl.* the Portuguese *pl.*; **2isch** *adj.* Portuguese.
Porzellan [pɔrtsɛ'la:n] *n* (-s/-e)
porcelain, china.
Posaune [po'zaunə] *f* (-/-n) ♪
trombone; *fig.* trumpet.
Pose ['po:zə] *f* (-/-n) pose, attitude;
fig. a. air.
Position [pozi'tsjo:n] *f* (-/-en)
position; social standing; ⚓ station.
positiv *adj.* ['po:ziti:f] positive.
Positur [pozi'tu:r] *f* (-/-en) posture;
sich in ~ *setzen* strike an attitude.
Posse *thea.* ['pɔsə] *f* (-/-n) farce.
'Possen *m* (-s/-) trick, prank; **2haft**
adj. farcical, comical; **'‿reißer** *m*
(-s/-) buffoon, clown.
possessiv *gr. adj.* ['pɔsɛsi:f] possessive.
pos'sierlich *adj.* droll, funny.
Post [pɔst] *f* (-/-en) post, *Am.* mail;
mail, letters *pl.*; post office; *mit
der ersten* ~ by the first delivery;
'‿amt *n* post office; **'‿anschrift** *f*
mailing address; **'‿anweisung** *f*
postal order; **'‿beamte** *m* post-
office clerk; **'‿bote** *m* postman,
Am. mailman; **'‿dampfer** *m*
packet-boat.
Posten ['pɔstən] *m* (-s/-) post, place,
station; job; ✗ sentry, sentinel;
item; entry; *goods:* lot, parcel.
'Postfach *n* post-office box.
pos'tieren *v/t.* (*no* -ge-, *h*) post,
station, place; *sich* ~ station o.s.
'Post|karte *f* postcard, *with printed
postage stamp: Am. a.* postal card;
'‿kutsche *f* stage-coach; **'2lagernd**
adj. to be (kept until) called for,
poste restante, *Am.* (in care of)
general delivery; **'‿leitzahl** *f* post-
code; **'‿minister** *m* minister of
post; *Brt. a. Am.* Postmaster
General; **'‿paket** *n* postal parcel;
'‿schalter *m* (post-office) window;
'‿scheck *m* postal cheque, *Am.*
postal check; **'‿schließfach** *n*

post-office box; **'‿sparbuch** *n*
post-office savings-book; **'‿stem-
pel** *m* postmark; **2wendend** *adv.*
by return of post; **'‿wertzeichen**
n (postage) stamp; **'‿zug** 🚂 *m*
mail-train.
Pracht [praxt] *f* (-/✦, -en, ✦e) splen-
do(u)r, magnificence; luxury.
prächtig *adj.* ['prɛçtiç] splendid,
magnificent; gorgeous; grand.
'prachtvoll *adj. s.* prächtig.
Prädikat [predi'ka:t] *n* (-[e]s/-e) *gr.*
predicate; *school, etc.:* mark.
prägen ['prɛ:gən] *v/t.* (ge-, *h*)
stamp; coin (*word, coin*).
prahlen ['pra:lən] *v/i.* (ge-, *h*) brag,
boast (*mit* of); ~ *mit* show off *s.th.*
'Prahler *m* (-s/-) boaster, braggart;
‿ei [‿'rai] *f* (-/-en) boasting,
bragging; **2isch** *adj.* boastful;
ostentatious.
Prakti|kant [prakti'kant] *m* (-en/-en)
probationer; **'‿ker** *m* (-s/-) practical man; expert; **‿kum** ['‿kum] *n*
(-s/Praktika, Praktiken) practical
course; **2sch** *adj.* practical; useful,
handy; **‿er Arzt** general practitioner;
2zieren ✦, ✦ [‿'tsi:rən] *v/i.* (*no*
-ge-, *h*) practi|se, *Am.* -ce medicine
or the law.   [prelate.]
Prälat *eccl.* [prɛ'la:t] *m* (-en/-en)
Praline [pra'li:nə] *f* (-/-n): ~*n pl.*
chocolates *pl.*
prall *adj.* [pral] tight; plump; *sun:*
blazing; **'‿en** *v/i.* (ge-, *sein*) bounce
or bound (*auf acc., gegen* against).
Prämi|e ['prɛ:mjə] *f* (-/-n) ✦
premium; prize; bonus; **2(i)eren**
[prɛ'mi:rən, prɛmi'i:rən] *v/t.* (*no*
-ge-, *h*) award a prize to.
prang|en ['praŋən] *v/i.* (ge-, *h*)
shine, make a show; **'2er** *m* (-s/-)
pillory.
Pranke ['praŋkə] *f* (-/-n) paw.
pränumerando *adv.* [prɛ:numə-
'rando] beforehand, in advance.
Präpa|rat [prɛpa'ra:t] *n* (-[e]s/-e)
preparation; *microscopy:* slide;
2'rieren *v/t.* (*no* -ge-, *h*) prepare.
Präposition *gr.* [prepozi'tsjo:n] *f*
(-/-en) preposition.
Prärie [prɛ'ri:] *f* (-/-n) prairie.
Präsens *gr.* ['prɛ:zɛns] *n* (-/Präsen-
tia, Präsenzien) present (tense).
Präsi|dent [prɛzi'dɛnt] *m* (-en/-en)
president; chairman; **2'dieren** *v/i.*
(*no* -ge-, *h*) preside (*über acc.* over);
be in the chair; **‿dium** ['‿'zi:djum]
n (-s/Präsidien) presidency, chair.
prasseln ['prasəln] *v/i.* (ge-, *h*)
fire: crackle; *rain:* patter.
prassen ['prasən] *v/i.* (ge-, *h*) feast,
carouse.
Präteritum *gr.* [prɛ'te:ritum] *n*
(-s/Präterita) preterite (tense); past
tense.
Praxis ['praksis] *f* 1. (-/*no pl.*)
practice; 2. (-/Praxen) practice (*of
doctor or lawyer*).

Präzedenzfall [prɛtseˈdɛnts-] m precedent; ǵᵗᶻ a. case-law.

präzis adj. [preˈtsiːs], ~e adj. [~zə] precise.

predig|en [ˈpreːdigən] v/i. and v/t. (ge-, h) preach; '2er m (-s/-) preacher; clergyman; 2t [ˈ~diçt] f (-/-en) sermon (a. fig.); fig. lecture.

Preis [praɪs] m (-es/-e) price; cost; competition: prize; award; reward; praise; um jeden ~ at any price or cost; '~ausschreiben n (-s/-) competition.

preisen [ˈpraɪzən] v/t. (irr., ge-, h) praise.

'Preis|erhöhung f rise or increase in price(s); '~gabe f abandonment; revelation (of secret); '2geben v/t. (irr. geben, sep., -ge-, h) abandon; reveal, give away (secret); disclose, expose; '2gekrönt adj. prize-winning, prize (novel, etc.); '~gericht n jury; '~lage f range of prices; '~liste f price-list; '~nachlaß m price cut; discount; '~richter m judge, umpire; '~schießen n (-s/-) shooting competition; '~stopp m (-s/no pl.) price freeze; '~träger m prize-winner; '2wert adj.: ~ sein be a bargain.

prell|en [ˈprɛlən] v/t. (ge-, h) fig. cheat, defraud (um of); sich et. ~ ⚡ contuse or bruise s.th.; '2ung ⚡ f (-/-en) contusion.

Premier|e thea. [prəmˈjɛːrə] f (-/-n) première, first night; ~minister [~ˈjeː-] m prime minister.

Presse [ˈprɛsə] f 1. (-/-n) ⊕, typ. press; squeezer; 2. (-/no pl.) newspapers generally: the press; '~amt n public relations office; '~freiheit f freedom of the press; '~meldung f news item; '2n v/t. (ge-, h) press; squeeze; '~photograph m press-photographer; '~vertreter m reporter; public relations officer.

Preßluft [ˈprɛs-] f (-/no pl.) compressed air.

Prestige [prɛsˈtiːʒə] n (-s/no pl.) prestige; ~ verlieren a. lose face.

Preuß|e [ˈprɔʏsə] m (-n/-n) Prussian; '2isch adj. Prussian.

prickeln [ˈprɪkəln] v/i. (ge-, h) prick(le), tickle; itch; fingers: tingle.

Priem [priːm] m (-[e]s/-e) quid.

pries [priːs] pret. of preisen.

Priester [ˈpriːstər] m (-s/-) priest; '~in f (-/-nen) priestess; '2lich adj. priestly, sacerdotal; '~rock m cassock.

prim|a F adj. [ˈpriːma] first-rate, F A 1; ✝ a. prime; F swell; ~är adj. [priˈmɛːr] primary.

Primel ⚘ [ˈpriːməl] f (-/-n) primrose.

Prinz [prɪnts] m (-en/-en) prince; ~essin [~ˈtsɛsin] f (-/-nen) princess; '~gemahl m prince consort.

Prinzip [prɪnˈtsiːp] n (-s/-ien)

principle; aus ~ on principle; im ~ in principle, basically.

Priorität [prioriˈtɛːt] f 1. (-/-en) priority; 2. (-/no pl.) time: priority.

Prise [ˈpriːzə] f (-/-n) ⚓ prize; e-e ~ a pinch of (salt, snuff).

Prisma [ˈprɪsma] n (-s/Prismen) prism.

Pritsche [ˈprɪtʃə] f (-/-n) bat; plank-bed.

privat adj. [priˈvaːt] private; 2adresse f home address; 2mann m (-[e]s/Privatmänner, Privatleute) private person or gentleman; 2patient ⚕ m paying patient; 2person f private person; 2schule f private school.

Privileg [priviˈleːk] n (-[e]s/-ien, -e) privilege.

pro prp. [proː] per; ~ Jahr per annum; ~ Kopf per head; ~ Stück a piece.

Probe [ˈproːbə] f (-/-n) experiment; trial, test; metall. assay; sample; specimen; proof; probation; check; thea. rehearsal; audition; auf ~ on probation, on trial; auf die ~ stellen (put to the) test; '~abzug typ., phot. m proof; '~exemplar n specimen copy; '~fahrt f ⚓ trial trip; mot. trial run; '~flug m test or trial flight; '2n v/t. (ge-, h) exercise; thea. rehearse; '~nummer f specimen copy or number; '~seite typ. f specimen page; '~sendung f goods on approval; '2weise adv. on trial; p. a. on probation; '~zeit f time of probation.

probieren [proˈbiːrən] v/t. (no -ge-, h) try, test; taste (food.)

Problem [proˈbleːm] n (-s/-e) problem; 2atisch adj. [~eˈmaːtiʃ] problematic(al).

Produkt [proˈdukt] n (-[e]s/-e) product (a. ⚶); ✗ produce; result; ~ion [~ˈtsjoːn] f (-/-en) production; output; 2iv adj. [~ˈtiːf] productive.

Produz|ent [produˈtsɛnt] m (-en/-en) producer; 2ieren [~ˈtsiːrən] v/t. (no -ge-, h) produce; sich ~ perform; contp. show off.

professionell adj. [profesioˈnɛl] professional, by trade.

Profess|or [proˈfɛsɔr] m (-s/-en) professor; ~ur [~ˈsuːr] f (-/-en) professorship, chair.

Profi [ˈproːfi] m (-s/-s) sports: professional, F pro.   [on tyre: tread.\

Profil [proˈfiːl] n (-s/-e) profile;\

Profit [proˈfiːt] m (-[e]s/-e) profit; 2ieren [~iˈtiːrən] v/i. (no -ge-, h) profit (von by).

Prognose [proˈgnoːzə] f (-/-n) ✗ prognosis; meteor. forecast.

Programm [proˈgram] n (-s/-e) program(me); politisches ~ political program(me), Am. platform.

Projektion [projɛkˈtsjoːn] f (-/-en) projection; ~sapparat [projɛkˈtsjoːnˀ-] m projector.

proklamieren [prokla'mi:rən] *v/t.* (*no -ge-, h*) proclaim.

Prokur|a † [pro'ku:ra] *f* (-/*Prokuren*) procuration; **~ist** [~ku'rɪst] *m* (-*en*/-*en*) confidential clerk.

Proletarl|er [prole'ta:rjər] *m* (-*s*/-) proletarian; **Ssch** *adj.* proletarian.

Prolog [pro'lo:k] *m* (-[*e*]*s*/-*e*) prolog(ue).

prominen|t *adj.* [promi'nɛnt] prominent; **Sz** [~ts] *f* (-/*no pl.*) notables *pl.*, celebrities *pl.*; high society.

Promo|tion *univ.* [promo'tsjo:n] *f* (-/-*en*) graduation; **Svieren** [~'vi:rən] *v/i.* (*no -ge-, h*) graduate (*an dat.* from), take one's degree.

Pronomen *gr.* [pro'no:mɛn] *n* (-*s*/-, *Pronomina*) pronoun.

Propeller [pro'pɛlər] *m* (-*s*/-) ⏚, ✈ (screw-)propeller, screw; ✈ airscrew.

Prophe|t [pro'fe:t] *m* (-*en*/-*en*) prophet; **Stisch** *adj.* prophetic; **Szeien** [~e'tsaɪən] *v/t.* (*no -ge-, h*) prophesy; predict, foretell; **~'zeiung** *f* (-/-*en*) prophecy; prediction.

Proportion [propor'tsjo:n] *f* (-/-*en*) proportion.

Prosa ['pro:za] *f* (-/*no pl.*) prose.

prosit *int.* ['pro:zɪt] your health!, here's to you!, cheers!

Prospekt [pro'spɛkt] *m* (-[*e*]*s*/-*e*) prospectus; brochure, leaflet, folder.

prost *int.* [pro:st] *s.* prosit.

Prostituierte [prostitu'i:rtə] *f* (-*n*/-*n*) prostitute.

Protest [pro'tɛst] *m* (-*es*/-*e*) protest; **~ einlegen** *or* **erheben gegen** (enter a) protest against.

Protestant *eccl.* [protes'tant] *m* (-*en*/-*en*) Protestant; **Sisch** *adj.* Protestant.

protes'tieren *v/i.* (*no -ge-, h*): **gegen et. ~** protest against s.th., object to s.th.

Prothese ⚕ [pro'te:zə] *f* (-/-*n*) pro(s)thesis; *dentistry:* a. denture; artificial limb.

Protokoll [proto'kɔl] *n* (-*s*/-*e*) record, minutes *pl.* (*of meeting*); *diplomacy:* protocol; **das ~ aufnehmen** take down the minutes; **das ~ führen** keep the minutes; **zu ~ geben** depose, state in evidence; **zu ~ nehmen** take down, record; **Sieren** [~'li:rən] (*no -ge-, h*) **1.** *v/t.* record, take down (on record); **2.** *v/i.* keep the minutes.

Protz *contp.* [prɔts] *m* (-*en*, -*es*/-*e*[*n*]) braggart, F show-off; **Sen** *v/i.* (*ge-, h*) show off (*mit dat.* with); **Sig** *adj.* ostentatious, showy.

Proviant [pro'vjant] *m* (-*s*/✍-*e*) provisions *pl.*, victuals *pl.*

Provinz [pro'vɪnts] *f* (-/-*en*) province; *fig.* the provinces *pl.*; **Sial** *adj.* [~'tsja:l], **Siell** *adj.* [~'tsjel] provincial.

Provis|ion † [provi'zjo:n] *f* (-/-*en*) commission; **Sorisch** *adj.* [~'zo:rɪʃ] provisional, temporary.

provozieren [provo'tsi:rən] *v/t.* (*no -ge-, h*) provoke.

Prozent [pro'tsɛnt] *n* (-[*e*]*s*/-*e*) per cent; **~satz** *m* percentage; proportion; **Sual** *adj.* [~u'a:l] percental; **~er Anteil** percentage.

Prozeß [pro'tsɛs] *m* (*Prozesses*/*Prozesse*) process; ⚖: action, lawsuit; trial; (legal) proceedings *pl.*; **e-n ~ gewinnen** win one's case; **e-n ~ gegen j-n anstrengen** bring an action against s.o., sue s.o.; **j-m den ~ machen** try s.o., put s.o. on trial; **kurzen ~ machen mit** make short work of.

prozessieren [protse'si:rən] *v/i.* (*no -ge-, h*): **mit j-m ~** go to law against s.o., have the law of s.o.

Prozession [protse'sjo:n] *f* (-/-*en*) procession.

prüde *adj.* ['pry:də] prudish.

prüf|en ['pry:fən] *v/t.* (*ge-, h*) examine; try, test; quiz; check, verify; **~end** *adj. look:* searching, scrutinizing; **Ser** *m* (-*s*/-) examiner; **Sling** *m* (-*s*/-*e*) examinee; **Sstein** *fig. m* touchstone; **Sung** *f* (-/-*en*) examination; *school, etc.:* a. F exam; test; quiz; verification, checking, check-up; **e-e ~ machen** go in for *or* sit for *or* take an examination.

'Prüfungs|arbeit *f*, **'~aufgabe** *f* examination-paper; **'~ausschuß** *m*, **'~kommission** *f* board of examiners.

Prügel ['pry:gəl] **1.** *m* (-*s*/-) cudgel, club, stick; **2.** F *fig. pl.* beating, thrashing; **~ei** [~'laɪ] *f* (-/-*en*) fight, row; **'~knabe** *m* scapegoat; **Sn** F *v/t.* (*ge-, h*) cudgel, flog; beat (up), thrash; **sich ~** (have a) fight.

Prunk [prʊŋk] *m* (-[*e*]*s*/*no pl.*) splendo(u)r; pomp, show; **Sen** *v/i.* (*ge-, h*) make a show (*mit et.* of), show off (*mit et.* s.th.); **Svoll** *adj.* splendid, gorgeous.

Psalm *eccl.* [psalm] *m* (-*s*/-*en*) psalm.

Pseudonym [psɔydo'ny:m] *n* (-*s*/-*e*) pseudonym.

pst *int.* [pst] hush!

Psychi|ater [psyçi'a:tər] *m* (-*s*/-) psychiatrist, alienist; **Ssch** *adj.* ['psy:çiʃ] psychic(al).

Psycho|analyse [psyço?ana'ly:zə] *f* (-/*no pl.*) psychoanalysis; **~analytiker** [~tikər] *m* (-*s*/-) psychoanalist; **~loge** [~'lo:gə] *m* (-*n*/-*n*) psychologist; **se** [~'ço:zə] *f* (-/-*n*) psychosis; panic.

Pubertät [puber'tɛ:t] *f* (-/*no pl.*) puberty.

Publikum ['pu:blikum] *n* (-*s*/*no pl.*) the public; audience; spectators *pl.*, crowd; readers *pl.*

publiz|ieren [publi'tsi:rən] *v/t.* (*no*

-ge-, h) publish; 2ist m (-en/-en) publicist; journalist.

Pudding ['pudiŋ] m (-s/-e, -s) cream.

Pudel zo. ['pu:dəl] m (-s/-) poodle; '2'naß F adj. dripping wet, drenched.

Puder ['pu:dər] m (-s/-) powder; '⸲dose f powder-box; compact; '2n v/t. (ge-, h) powder; sich ⸲ powder o.s. or one's face; '⸲quaste f powder-puff; '⸲zucker m powdered sugar.

Puff F [puf] m (-[e]s/⸲e, -e) poke, nudge; '2en (ge-, h) 1. F v/t. nudge; 2. v/i. pop; '⸲er 🔧 m (-s/-) buffer.

Pullover [pu'lo:vər] m (-s/-) pull-over, sweater.

Puls [puls] m (-es/-e) pulse; '⸲ader anat. f artery; 2ieren [⸲'zi:rən] v/i. (no -ge-, h) pulsate, throb; '⸲schlag 🔧 m pulsation.

Pult [pult] n (-[e]s/-e) desk.

Pulv|er ['pulfər] n (-s/-) powder; gunpowder; F fig. cash, sl. brass, dough; '2erig adj. powdery; 2eri-sieren [⸲vəri'zi:rən] v/t. (no -ge-, h) pulverize; 2rig adj. ['⸲friç] powdery.

Pump F [pump] m (-[e]s/-e): auf ⸲ on tick; '⸲e f (-/-n) pump; '2en (ge-, h) 1. v/i. pump; 2. v/t. pump; F fig.: give s.th. on tick; borrow (et. von j-m s.th. from s.o.).

Punkt [puŋkt] m (-[e]s/-e) point (a. fig.); dot; typ., gr. full stop, period; spot, place; fig. item; article, clause (of agreement); der springende ⸲ the point; toter ⸲ deadlock, dead end; wunder ⸲ tender subject, sore point; ⸲ zehn Uhr on the stroke of ten, at 10 (o'clock) sharp; in vielen ⸲en on many points, in many respects; nach ⸲en siegen sports: win on points; 2ieren [⸲'ti:rən] v/t. (no -ge-, h) dot, point; 🔧 puncture, tap; drawing, painting: stipple.

pünktlich adj. ['pyŋktliç] punctual; ⸲ sein on time; '2keit f (-/no pl.) punctuality.

Punsch [punʃ] m (-es/-e) punch.

Pupille anat. [pu'pilə] f (-/-n) pupil.

Puppe ['pupə] f (-/-n) doll (a. fig.); puppet (a. fig.); tailoring: dummy; zo. chrysalis, pupa; '⸲nspiel n puppet-show; '⸲nstube f doll's room; '⸲nwagen m doll's pram, Am. doll carriage or buggy.

pur adj. [pu:r] pure, sheer.

Püree [py're:] n (-s/-s) purée, mash.

Purpur ['purpur] m (-s/no pl.) purple; '2farben adj., '2n adj., '2rot adj. purple.

Purzel|baum ['purtsəl-] m somersault; e-n ⸲ schlagen turn a somersault; '2n v/i. (ge-, sein) tumble.

Puste F ['pu:stə] f (-/no pl.) breath; ihm ging die ⸲ aus he got out of breath.

Pustel 🔧 ['pustəl] f (-/-n) pustule, pimple.

pusten ['pu:stən] v/i. (ge-, h) puff, pant; blow.

Pute orn. ['pu:tə] f (-/-n) turkey (-hen); '⸲r orn. m (-s/-) turkey (-cock); '2r'rot adj. (as) red as a turkey-cock.

Putsch [putʃ] m (-es/-e) putsch, insurrection; riot; '2en v/i. (ge-, h) revolt, riot.

Putz [puts] m (-es/-e) on garments: finery; ornaments pl.; trimming; 🏛 roughcast, plaster; '2en v/t. (ge-, h) clean, cleanse; polish, wipe; adorn; snuff (candle); polish, Am. shine (shoes); sich ⸲ smarten or dress o.s. up; sich die Nase ⸲ blow or wipe one's nose; sich die Zähne ⸲ brush one's teeth; '⸲frau f char-woman, Am. a. scrubwoman, '2ig adj. droll, funny; '⸲lappen m cleaning rag; '⸲zeug n cleaning utensils pl.

Pyjama [pi'dʒa:ma] m (-s/-s) (ein a suit of) pyjamas pl. or Am. a. pajamas pl.

Pyramide [pyra'mi:də] f (-/-n) pyramid (a. 🏛); ✕ stack (of rifles); 2nförmig adj. [⸲nfœrmiç] pyram-idal.

Q

Quacksalber ['kvakzalbər] m (-s/-) quack (doctor); ⸲ei F [⸲'raɪ] f (-/-en) quackery; '2n v/i. (ge-, h) (play the) quack.

Quadrat [kva'dra:t] n (-[e]s/-e) square; 2 Fuß im ⸲ 2 feet square; ins ⸲ erheben square; 2isch adj. square; Å equation: quadratic; ⸲meile f square mile; ⸲meter n, m square met|re, Am. -er; ⸲wurzel Å f square root; ⸲zahl Å f square number.

quaken ['kva:kən] v/i. (ge-, h) duck: quack; frog: croak.

quäken ['kvɛ:kən] v/i. (ge-, h) squeak.

Quäker ['kvɛ:kər] m (-s/-) Quaker, member of the Society of Friends.

Qual [kva:l] f (-/-en) pain; torment; agony.

quälen ['kvɛ:lən] v/t. (ge-, h) tor-ment (a. fig.); torture; ago-nize; fig. bother, pester; sich ⸲ toil, drudge.

Qualifikation [kvalifika'tsjoːn] *f* (-/-en) qualification.

qualifizieren [kvalifi'tsiːrən] *v/t. and v/refl.* (*no* -ge-, *h*) qualify (*zu* for).

Qualit|ät [kvali'tɛːt] *f* (-/-en) quality; **2ativ** [ˌkvaliˈtiːf] 1. *adj.* qualitative; 2. *adv.* as to quality. **Quali'täts|arbeit** *f* work of high quality; **~stahl** *m* high-grade steel; **~ware** *f* high-grade *or* quality goods *pl.*

Qualm [kvalm] *m* (-[e]s/*no pl.*) dense smoke; fumes *pl.*; vapo(u)r, steam; **2en** (ge-, *h*) 1. *v/i.* smoke, give out vapo(u)r *or* fumes; *F p.* smoke heavily; 2. *F v/t.* puff (away) at (*cigar, pipe, etc.*); **2ig** *adj.* smoky.

'qualvoll *adj.* very painful; *pain:* excruciating; *fig.* agonizing, harrowing.

Quantit|ät [kvanti'tɛːt] *f* (-/-en) quantity; **2ativ** [ˌkvaliˈtiːf] 1. *adj.* quantitative; 2. *adv.* as to quantity. **Quantum** ['kvantum] *n* (-s/Quanten) quantity, amount; quantum (*a. phys.*).

Quarantäne [karan'tɛːnə] *f* (-/-n) quarantine; *in ~ legen* (put in) quarantine. [curd(s *pl.*).\]

Quark [kvark] *m* (-[e]s/*no pl.*)\

Quartal [kvar'taːl] *n* (-s/-e) quarter (of a year); *univ.* term.

Quartett [kvar'tɛt] *n* (-[e]s/-e) ♪ quartet(te); *cards:* four.

Quartier [kvar'tiːr] *n* (-s/-e) accommodation; ✕ quarters *pl.*, billet.

Quaste ['kvastə] *f* (-/-n) tassel; (powder-)puff.

Quatsch F [kvatʃ] *m* (-es/*no pl.*) nonsense, fudge, *sl.* bosh, rot, *Am. sl. a.* baloney; **2en** F *v/i.* (ge-, *h*) twaddle, blether, *sl.* talk rot; (have a) chat; **~kopf** F *m* twaddler.

Quecksilber ['kvɛk-] *n* mercury, quicksilver.

Quelle ['kvɛlə] *f* (-/-n) spring, source (*a. fig.*); *oil:* well; *fig.* fountain, origin; **2n** *v/i.* (irr., ge-, sein) gush, well; **~nangabe** ['kvɛlən⁹-] *f*

mention of sources used; **~nforschung** *f* original research.

Quengel|ei F [kvɛŋə'laɪ] *f* (-/-en) grumbling, whining; nagging; **2n** F *v/i.* (ge-, *h*) grumble, whine; nag.

quer *adv.* [kveːr] crossways, crosswise; F *fig.* wrong; F *~ gehen go* wrong; *~ über* (*acc.*) across.

'Quer|e *f* (-/*no pl.*): *der ~ nach* crossways, crosswise; F *j-m in die ~ kommen* cross s.o.'s path; *fig.* thwart s.o.'s plans; **~frage** *f* crossquestion; **~kopf** *fig. m* wrongheaded fellow; **2schießen** F *v/i.* (irr. schießen, sep., -ge-, *h*) try to foil s.o.'s plans; **~schiff** ⚠ *n* transept; **~schläger** ✕ *m* ricochet; **~schnitt** *m* cross-section (*a. fig.*); **~straße** *f* cross-road; *zweite ~ rechts* second turning to the right; **~treiber** *m* (-s/-) schemer; **~treibe'rei** *f* (-/-en) intriguing, machination.

Querulant [kveru'lant] *m* (-en/-en) querulous person, grumbler, *Am. sl. a.* griper.

quetsch|en ['kvɛtʃən] *v/t.* (ge-, *h*) squeeze; ✂ bruise, contuse; *sich den Finger ~* jam one's finger; **2ung** ✂ *f* (-/-en), **2wunde** ✂ *f* bruise, contusion.

quick *adj.* [kvik] lively, brisk.

quieken ['kviːkən] *v/i.* (ge-, *h*) squeak, squeal.

quietsch|en ['kviːtʃən] *v/i.* (ge-, *h*) squeak, squeal; *door-hinge, etc.:* creak, squeak; *brakes, etc.:* screech; **'~ver'gnügt** F *adj.* (as) jolly as a sandboy.

Quirl [kvirl] *m* (-[e]s/-e) twirlingstick; **2en** *v/t.* (ge-, *h*) twirl.

quitt *adj.* [kvit]: *~ sein mit j-m* be quits *or* even with s.o.; *jetzt sind wir ~* that leaves us even; **~ieren** [ˌkvi'tiːrən] *v/t.* (*no* -ge-, *h*) receipt (*bill, etc.*); quit, abandon (*post, etc.*); **2ung** *f* (-/-en) receipt; *fig.* answer; *gegen ~* against receipt.

quoll [kvɔl] *pret. of quellen.*

Quot|e ['kvoːtə] *f* (-/-n) quota; share, portion; **~ient** ⅍ [kvo'tsjɛnt] *m* (-en/-en) quotient.

R

Rabatt ✝ [ra'bat] *m* (-[e]s/-e) discount, rebate.

Rabe *orn.* ['raːbə] *m* (-n/-n) raven; **2n'schwarz** F *adj.* raven, jet-black.

rabiat *adj.* [ra'bjaːt] rabid, violent.

Rache ['raxə] *f* (-/*no pl.*) revenge, vengeance; retaliation.

Rachen *anat.* ['raxən] *m* (-s/-) throat, pharynx; jaws *pl.*

rächen ['rɛçən] *v/t.* (ge-, *h*) avenge,

revenge; *sich ~ an* (*dat.*) revenge o.s. *or* be revenged on.

'Rachen|höhle *anat. f* pharynx; **~katarrh** ✂ *m* cold in the throat.

'rach|gierig *adj.*, **'~süchtig** *adj.* revengeful, vindictive.

Rad [raːt] *n* (-[e]s/ᵘer) wheel; (bi)cycle, F bike; (*ein*) *~ schlagen peacock:* spread its tail; *sports:* turn cart-wheels; *unter die Räder*

kommen go to the dogs; '**~achse** f
axle(-tree).

Radar ['rɑːdɑːr, raˈdɑːr] m, n (-s/-s)
radar.

Radau F [raˈdaʊ] m (-s/no pl.) row,
racket, hubbub.

radebrechen ['rɑːdə-] v/t. (ge-, h)
speak (language) badly, murder
(language).

radeln ['rɑːdəln] v/i. (ge-, sein)
cycle, pedal, F bike.

Rädelsführer ['rɛːdəls-] m ring-
leader.

Räderwerk ⊕ ['rɛːdər-] n gearing.

'**rad|fahren** v/i. (irr. fahren, sep.,
-ge-, sein) cycle, (ride a) bicycle,
pedal, F bike; '**2fahrer** m cyclist,
Am. a. cycler or wheelman.

radier|en [raˈdiːrən] v/t. (no -ge-, h)
rub out, erase; art: etch; 2**gummi**
m (india-)rubber, esp. Am. eraser;
2**messer** n eraser; 2**ung** f (-/-en)
etching.

Radieschen ♀ [raˈdiːsçən] n (-s/-)
(red) radish.

radikal adj. [radiˈkɑːl] radical.

Radio ['rɑːdjo] n (-s/-s) radio, wireless; im ~ on the radio, on the air;
2**aktiv** phys. adj. [radjoakˈtiːf]
radio(-)active; ~**er Niederschlag**
fall-out; '**~apparat** m radio or
wireless (set).

Radium ⚛ ['rɑːdjum] n (-s/no pl.)
radium.

Radius ⚛ ['rɑːdjus] m (-/Radien)
radius.

'**Rad|kappe** f hub cap; '**~kranz** m
rim; '**~rennbahn** f cycling track;
'**~rennen** n cycle race; '**~sport** m
cycling; '**~spur** f rut, track.

raffen ['rafən] v/t. (ge-, h) snatch
up; gather (dress).

raffiniert adj. [rafiˈniːrt] refined;
fig. clever, cunning.

ragen ['rɑːgən] v/i. (ge-, h) tower,
loom.

Ragout [raˈguː] n (-s/-s) ragout,
stew, hash.

Rahe ⚓ ['rɑːə] f (-/-n) yard.

Rahm [rɑːm] m (-[e]s/no pl.) cream.

Rahmen ['rɑːmən] 1. m (-s/-) frame;
fig.: frame, background, setting;
scope; aus dem ~ fallen be out of
place; 2. ♀ v/t. (ge-, h) frame.

Rakete [raˈkeːtə] f (-/-n) rocket;
e-e ~ abfeuern or starten launch a
rocket; dreistufige ~ three-stage
rocket; ~**nantrieb** [raˈkeːtən?-] m
rocket propulsion; mit ~ rocket-
propelled; ~**nflugzeug** n rocket
(-propelled) plane; ~**ntriebwerk**
n propulsion unit.

Ramm|bär ⊕ ['ram-] m, '**~bock** m,
'**~e** f (-/-n) ram(mer); '2**en** v/t.
(ge-, h) ram.

Rampe ['rampə] f (-/-n) ramp,
ascent; '**~nlicht** n footlights pl.;
fig. limelight.

Ramsch [ramʃ] m (-es/⚓ -e) junk,

trash; im ~ kaufen buy in the lump;
'**~verkauf** m jumble-sale; '**~ware**
f job lot.

Rand [rant] m (-[e]s/~er) edge, brink
(a. fig.); fig. verge; border; brim
(of hat, cup, etc.); rim (of plate,
etc.); margin (of book, etc.); lip (of
wound); Ränder pl. under the eyes:
rings pl., circles pl.; vor Freude
außer ~ und Band geraten be beside
o.s. with joy; er kommt damit nicht
zu ~e he can't manage it; '**~be-
merkung** f marginal note; fig.
comment.

rang[1] [raŋ] pret. of ringen.

Rang[2] [~] m (-[e]s/~e) rank, order; ⚔
rank; position; thea. tier; erster ~
thea. dress-circle, Am. first balcony;
zweiter ~ thea. upper circle, Am.
second balcony; ersten ~es first-
class, first-rate; j-m den ~ ablaufen
get the start or better of s.o.

Range ['raŋə] m (-n/-n), f (-/-n)
rascal; romp.

rangieren [rãˈʒiːrən] (no -ge-, h)
1. 🚂 v/t. shunt, Am. a. switch;
2. fig. v/i. rank.

'**Rang|liste** f sports, etc.: ranking
list; ⚔ army-list, navy or air-force
list; '**~ordnung** f order of precedence.

Ranke ♀ ['raŋkə] f (-/-n) tendril;
runner.

Ränke ['rɛŋkə] m/pl. intrigues pl.

'**ranken** v/refl. (ge-, h) creep, climb.

rann [ran] pret. of rinnen.

rannte ['rantə] pret. of rennen.

Ranzen ['rantsən] m (-s/-) knapsack; satchel.

ranzig adj. ['rantsiç] rancid, rank.

Rappe zo. ['rapə] m (-n/-n) black
horse.

rar adj. [rɑːr] rare, scarce.

Rarität [rariˈtɛːt] f (-/-en) rarity;
curiosity, curio.

rasch adj. [raʃ] quick, swift, brisk;
hasty; prompt.

rascheln ['raʃəln] v/i. (ge-, h) rustle.

rasen[1] ['rɑːzən] v/i. (ge-) 1. (h)
rage, storm; rave; 2. (sein) race,
speed; '2**d** adj. raving; frenzied;
speed: tearing; pains: agonizing;
headache: splitting; j-n ~ machen
drive s.o. mad.

Rasen[2] [~] m (-s/-) grass; lawn;
turf; '**~platz** m lawn, grass-plot.

Raserei F [rɑːzəˈraɪ] f (-/-en) rage,
fury; frenzy, madness; F mot.
scorching; j-n zur ~ bringen drive
s.o. mad.

Rasier|apparat [raˈziːr-] m (safety)
razor; 2**en** v/t. (no -ge-, h) shave;
sich ~ (lassen get a) shave; ~**klinge**
f razor-blade; ~**messer** n razor;
~**pinsel** m shaving-brush; ~**seife** f
shaving-soap; ~**wasser** n after-
shave lotion; ~**zeug** n shaving kit.

Rasse ['rasə] f (-/-n) race; zo. breed.

rasseln ['rasəln] v/i. (ge-, h) rattle.

'Rassen|frage f (-/no pl.) racial issue; '~kampf m race conflict; '~problem n racial issue; '~schranke f colo(u)r bar; '~trennung f (-/no pl.) racial segregation; '~unruhen f/pl. race riots pl.

'rasserein adj. thoroughbred, pure-bred.

'rassig adj. thoroughbred; fig. racy.

Rast [rast] f (-/-en) rest, repose; break, pause; '2en v/i. (ge-, h) rest, repose; '2los adj. restless; '~platz m resting-place; mot. picnic area.

Rat [raːt] m 1. (-[e]s/no pl.) advice, counsel; suggestion; fig. way out; zu ~e ziehen consult; j-n um ~ fragen ask s.o.'s advice; 2. (-[e]s/~e) council, board; council(l)or, alderman.

Rate ['raːtə] f (-/-n) instal(l)ment (a. ✝); auf ~n ✝ on hire-purchase.

'raten (irr., ge-, h) 1. v/t. advise, counsel (j-m zu inf. s.o. to inf.); 2. v/t. guess, divine.

'raten|weise adv. by instal(l)ments; '2zahlung ✝ f payment by instal(l)ments.

'Rat|geber m (-s/-) adviser, counsel(l)or; '~haus n town hall, Am. a. city hall.

ratifizieren [ratifi'tsiːrən] v/t. (no -ge-, h) ratify.

Ration [ra'tsjoːn] f (-/-en) ration, allowance; 2ell adj. [~o'nel] rational; efficient; economical; 2ieren [~o'niːrən] v/t. (no -ge-, h) ration.

'rat|los adj. puzzled, perplexed, at a loss; '~sam adj. advisable; expedient; '2schlag m (piece of) advice, counsel.

Rätsel ['rɛːtsəl] n (-s/-) riddle, puzzle; enigma, mystery; '2haft adj. puzzling; enigmatic(al), mysterious.

Ratte zo. ['ratə] f (-/-n) rat.

rattern ['ratərn] v/i. (ge-, h, sein) rattle, clatter.

Raub [raup] m (-[e]s/no pl.) robbery; kidnap(p)ing; piracy (of intellectual property); booty, spoils pl.; '~bau m (-[e]s/no pl.): ~ treiben ✗ exhaust the land; ✗ rob a mine; ~ treiben mit undermine (one's health); 2en ['~bən] v/t. (ge-, h) rob, take by force, steal; kidnap; j-m et. ~ rob or deprive s.o. of s.th.

Räuber ['rɔybər] m (-s/-) robber; '~bande f gang of robbers; '2isch adj. rapacious, predatory.

'Raub|fisch ichth. m fish of prey; '~gier f rapacity; '2gierig adj. rapacious; '~mord m murder with robbery; '~mörder m murderer and robber; '~tier zo. n beast of prey; '~überfall m hold-up, armed robbery; '~vogel orn. m bird of prey; '~zug m raid.

Rauch [raux] m (-[e]s/no pl.) smoke; fume; '2en (ge-, h) 1. v/i. smoke;

fume; p. (have a) smoke; 2. v/t. smoke (cigarette); '~er m (-s/-) smoker; s. Raucherabteil.

Räucheraal ['rɔyçər?-] m smoked eel.

Raucherabteil 🚂 ['rauxər?-] n smoking-car(riage), smoking-compartment, smoker.

'Räucher|hering m red or smoked herring, kipper; '2n (ge-, h) 1. v/t. smoke, cure (meat, fish); 2. v/i. burn incense.

'Rauch|fahne f trail of smoke; '~fang m chimney, flue; '~fleisch n smoked meat; '2ig adj. smoky; '~tabak m tobacco; '~waren f/pl. tobacco products pl.; furs pl.; '~zimmer n smoking-room.

Räud|e ['rɔydə] f (-/-n) mange, scab; '2ig adj. mangy, scabby.

Rauf|bold contp. ['raufbolt] m (-[e]s/-e) brawler, rowdy, Am. sl. tough; '2en (ge-, h) 1. v/t. pluck, pull; sich die Haare ~ tear one's hair; 2. v/i. fight, scuffle; ~erei [~ə'raɪ] f (-/-en) fight, scuffle.

rauh adj. [rau] rough; rugged; weather: inclement, raw; voice: hoarse; fig.: harsh; coarse, rude; in ~en Mengen galore; 2reif m (-[e]s/no pl.) hoar-frost, poet. rime.

Raum [raum] m (-[e]s/~e) room, space; expanse; area; room; premises pl.; '~anzug m space suit.

räumen ['rɔymən] v/t. (ge-, h) remove, clear (away); leave, give up, esp. ✗ evacuate; vacate (flat).

'Raum|fahrt f astronautics; '~flug m space flight; '~inhalt m volume, capacity; '~kapsel f capsule.

räumlich adj. ['rɔymliç] relating to space, of space, spatial.

'Raum|meter n, m cubic met|re, Am. -er; '~schiff n space craft or ship; '~sonde f space probe; '~station f space station.

'Räumung f (-/-en) clearing, removal; esp. ✝ clearance; vacating (of flat), by force: eviction; ✗ evacuation (of town); '~sverkauf ✝ m clearance sale.

raunen ['raunən] (ge-, h) 1. v/i. whisper, murmur; 2. v/t. whisper, murmur; man raunt rumo(u)r has it.

Raupe zo. ['raupə] f (-/-n) caterpillar; '~nschlepper ⊕ m caterpillar tractor.

raus int. [raus] get out!, sl. beat it!, scram!

Rausch [rauʃ] m (-es/~e) intoxication, drunkenness; fig. frenzy, transport(s pl.); e-n ~ haben be drunk; '2en v/i. (ge-) 1. (h) leaves, rain, silk: rustle; water, wind: rush; surf: roar; applause: thunder; 2. (sein) movement: sweep; '~gift n narcotic (drug), F dope.

räuspern ['rɔyspərn] v/refl. (ge-, h) clear one's throat.

Razzia ['ratsja] f (-/Razzien) raid, round-up.

reagieren [rea'gi:rən] v/i. (no -ge-, h) react (auf acc. [up]on; to); fig. and ⊕ a. respond (to).

Reaktion [reak'tsjo:n] f (-/-en) reaction (a. pol.); fig. a. response (auf acc. to); ~är [~'nɛːr] 1. m (-s/-e) reactionary; 2. ℒ adj. reactionary.

Reaktor phys. [re'aktɔr] m (-s/-en) (nuclear) reactor, atomic pile.

real adj. [re'aːl] real; concrete; ~isieren [reali'ziːrən] v/t. (no -ge-, h) realize; ℒismus [rea'lismus] m (-/no pl.) realism; ~istisch adj. [rea'listiʃ] realistic; ℒität [reali'tɛːt] f (-/-en) reality; ℒschule f non-classical secondary school.

Rebe ♀ ['reːbə] f (-/-n) vine.

Rebell [re'bɛl] m (-en/-en) rebel; ℒieren [~'liːrən] v/i. (no -ge-, h) rebel, revolt, rise; ℒisch adj. rebellious.

Reb|huhn orn. ['reːp-] n partridge; ~laus zo. ['reːp-] f vine-fretter, phylloxera; ~stock ♀ ['reːp-] m vine.

Rechen ['rɛçən] m (-s/-) rake; grid.

Rechen|aufgabe ['rɛçən-] f sum, (arithmetical) problem; ~fehler m arithmetical error, miscalculation; ~maschine f calculating-machine; ~schaft f (-/no pl.): ~ ablegen give or render an account (über acc. of), account or answer (for); zur ~ ziehen call to account (wegen for); ~schieber m ✶ slide-rule.

rechne|n ['rɛçnən] (ge-, h) 1. v/t. reckon, calculate; estimate, value; charge; ~ zu rank with or among(st); 2. v/i. count; ~ auf (acc.) or mit count or reckon on or rely (up)on; ~risch adj. arithmetical.

'Rechnung f (-/-en) calculation, sum, reckoning; account, bill; invoice (of goods); in restaurant: bill, Am. check; score; auf ~ on account; ~ legen render an account (über acc. of); e-r Sache ~ tragen make allowance for s.th.; es geht auf meine ~ in restaurants: it is my treat, Am. F this is on me; '~sprüfer m auditor.

recht¹ [rɛçt] 1. adj. right; real; legitimate; right, correct; zur ~en Zeit in due time, at the right moment; ein ~er Narr a regular fool; mir ist es ~ I don't mind; ~ haben be right; j-m ~ geben agree with s.o.; 2. adv. right(ly), well; very; rather; really; correctly; ganz ~! quite (so)!; es geschieht ihm ~ it serves him right; ~ gern gladly, with pleasure; ~ gut quite good or well; ich weiß nicht ~ I wonder.

Recht² [~] n (-[e]s/-e) right (auf

acc. to), title (to), claim (on), interest (in); privilege; power, authority; ⚖ law; justice; ~ sprechen administer justice; mit ~ justly.

'Rechte f (-n/-n) right hand; boxing: right; pol. the Right.

Rechteck ['rɛçt?-] n (-[e]s/-e) rectangle; 'ℒig adj. rectangular.

recht|fertigen ['rɛçtfɛrtigən] v/t. (ge-, h) justify; defend, vindicate; 'ℒfertigung f (-/-en) justification; vindication, defen|ce, Am. -se; '~gläubig adj. orthodox; ~haberisch adj. ['~haːbəriʃ] dogmatic; '~lich adj. legal, lawful, legitimate; honest, righteous; '~los adj. without rights; outlawed; 'ℒlosigkeit f (-/no pl.) outlawry; '~mäßig adj. legal, lawful, legitimate; 'ℒmäßigkeit f (-/no pl.) legality, legitimacy.

rechts adv. [rɛçts] on or to the right (hand).

'Rechts|anspruch m legal right or claim (auf acc. on, to), title (to); '~anwalt m lawyer, solicitor; barrister, Am. attorney (at law); '~außen m (-/-) football: outside right; '~beistand m legal adviser, counsel.

'recht|schaffen 1. adj. honest, righteous; 2. adv. thoroughly, downright, F awfully; 'ℒschreibung f (-/-en) orthography, spelling.

'Rechts|fall m case, cause; '~frage f question of law; issue of law; '~gelehrte m jurist, lawyer; 'ℒgültig adj. s. rechtskräftig; '~kraft f (-/no pl.) legal force or validity; 'ℒkräftig adj. valid, legal; judgement: final; '~kurve f right-hand bend; '~lage f legal position or status; '~mittel n legal remedy; '~nachfolger m assign, assignee; '~person f legal personality; '~pflege f administration of justice, judicature.

'Rechtsprechung f (-/-en) jurisdiction.

'Rechts|schutz m legal protection; '~spruch m legal decision; judg(e)ment; sentence; verdict (of jury); '~steuerung mot. f (-/-en) right-hand drive; '~streit m action, lawsuit; '~verfahren n (legal) proceedings pl.; '~verkehr mot. m right-hand traffic; '~verletzung f infringement; '~vertreter m s. Rechtsbeistand; '~weg m: den ~ beschreiten take legal action, go to law; unter Ausschluß des ~es eliminating legal proceedings; 'ℒwidrig adj. illegal, unlawful; '~wissenschaft f jurisprudence.

'recht|wink(e)lig adj. right-angled; '~zeitig 1. adj. punctual; opportune; 2. adv. in (due) time, punctually, Am. on time.

Reck [rɛk] n (-[e]s/-e) sports: horizontal bar.

recken ['rɛkən] v/t. (ge-, h) stretch; sich ~ stretch o.s.

Redakt|eur [redak'tøːr] m (-s/-e) editor; **~ion** [~'tsjoːn] f (-/-en) editorship; editing, wording; editorial staff, editors pl.; editor's or editorial office; **2ionell** adj. [~tsjo'nɛl] editorial.

Rede ['reːdə] f (-/-n) speech; oration; language; talk, conversation; discourse; direkte ~ gr. direct speech; indirekte ~ gr. reported or indirect speech; e-e ~ halten make or deliver a speech; zur ~ stellen call to account (wegen for); davon ist nicht die ~ that is not the point; davon kann keine ~ sein that's out of the question; es ist nicht der ~ wert it is not worth speaking of; **2gewandt** adj. eloquent; **'~kunst** f rhetoric; **2n** (ge-, h) 1. v/t. speak; talk; 2. v/i. speak (mit to); talk (to), chat (with); discuss (über et. s.th.); sie läßt nicht mit sich ~ she won't listen to reason.

Redensart ['reːdənsʔ-] f phrase, expression; idiom; proverb, saying.

redigieren [redi'giːrən] v/t. (no -ge-, h) edit; revise.

redlich ['reːtlɪç] 1. adj. honest, upright; sincere; 2. adv.: sich ~ bemühen take great pains.

Redner ['reːdnər] m (-s/-) speaker; orator; **'~bühne** f platform; **2isch** adj. oratorical, rhetorical; **'~pult** n speaker's desk.

redselig adj. ['reːtzeːlɪç] talkative.

reduzieren [redu'tsiːrən] v/t. (no -ge-, h) reduce (auf acc. to).

Reede ⚓ ['reːdə] f (-/-n) roads pl., roadstead; **'~r** m (-s/-) shipowner; **~'rei** f (-/-en) shipping company or firm.

reell [re'ɛl] 1. adj. respectable, honest; business firm: solid; goods: good; offer: real; 2. adv.: ~ bedient werden get good value for one's money.

Refer|at [refe'raːt] n (-[e]s/-e) report; lecture; paper; ein ~ halten esp. univ. read a paper; **~endar** [~ɛn'daːr] m (-s/-e) ⚖ junior lawyer; at school: junior teacher; **~ent** [~'rɛnt] m (-en/-en) reporter, speaker; **~enz** [~'rɛnts] f (-/-en) reference; **2ieren** [~'riːrən] v/i. (no -ge-, h) report (über acc. [up]on); (give a) lecture (on); esp. univ. read a paper (on).

reflektieren [reflɛk'tiːrən] (no -ge-, h) 1. phys. v/t. reflect; 2. v/i. reflect (über acc. [up]on); ~ auf (acc.) ~ think of buying; be interested in.

Reflex [re'flɛks] m (-es/-e) phys. reflection or reflexion; ⚕ reflex (action); **2iv** gr. adj. [~'ksiːf] reflexive.

Reform [re'fɔrm] f (-/-en) reform; **~er** m (-s/-) reformer; **2ieren** [~'miːrən] v/t. (no -ge-, h) reform.

Refrain [rə'frɛː] m (-s/-s) refrain, chorus, burden.

Regal [re'gaːl] n (-s/-e) shelf.

rege adj. ['reːgə] active, brisk, lively; busy.

Regel ['reːgəl] f (-/-n) rule; regulation; standard; physiol. menstruation, menses pl.; in der ~ as a rule; **'2los** adj. irregular; disorderly; **'2mäßig** adj. regular; **'2n** v/t. (ge-, h) regulate, control; arrange, settle; put in order; **'2recht** adj. regular; **'~ung** f (-/-en) regulation, control; arrangement, settlement; **'2widrig** adj. contrary to the rules, irregular; abnormal; sports: foul.

regen¹ ['reːgən] v/t. and v/refl. (ge-, h) move, stir.

Regen² [~] m (-s/-) rain; vom ~ in die Traufe kommen jump out of the frying-pan into the fire, get from bad to worse; **'2arm** adj. dry; **'~bogen** m rainbow; **'~bogenhaut** anat. f iris; **'2dicht** adj. rain-proof; **'~guß** m downpour; **'~mantel** m waterproof, raincoat, mac(k)intosh, F mac; **'2reich** adj. rainy; **'~schauer** m shower (of rain); **'~schirm** m umbrella; **'~tag** m rainy day; **'~tropfen** m raindrop; **'~wasser** n rain-water; **'~wetter** n rainy weather; **'~wolke** f rain-cloud; **'~wurm** zo. m earthworm, Am. a. angleworm; **'~zeit** f rainy season.

Regie [re'ʒiː] f (-/-n) management; thea., film: direction; unter der ~ von directed by.

regier|en [re'giːrən] (no -ge-, h) 1. v/i. reign; 2. v/t. govern (a. gr.), rule; **2ung** f (-/-en) government, Am. administration; reign.

Re'gierungs|antritt m accession (to the throne); **~beamte** m government official; Brt. Civil Servant; **~bezirk** m administrative district; **~gebäude** n government offices pl.

Regiment [regi'mɛnt] n 1. (-[e]s/-e) government, rule; 2. ✕ (-[e]s/-er) regiment.

Regisseur [reʒi'søːr] m (-s/-e) thea. stage manager, director; film: director.

Regist|er [re'gɪstər] n (-s/-) register (a. ♪), record; index; **~ratur** [~ra-'tuːr] f (-/-en) registry; registration.

registrier|en [regɪs'triːrən] v/t. (no -ge-, h) register, record; **2kasse** f cash register.

reglos adj. ['reːkloːs] motionless.

regne|n ['reːgnən] v/i. (ge-, h) rain; es regnet in Strömen it is pouring with rain; **'~risch** adj. rainy.

Regreß ⚖, † [re'grɛs] m (Regresses/Regresse) recourse; **2pflichtig** ⚖, † adj. liable to recourse.

regulär adj. [regu'lɛːr] regular.

regulier|bar *adj.* [regu'li:rbaːr] adjustable, controllable; **~en** *v/t.* (*no -ge-, h*) regulate, adjust; control.

Regung ['reːguŋ] *f* (-/-en) movement, motion; emotion; impulse; **'2slos** *adj.* motionless.

Reh *zo.* [reː] *n* (-[e]s/-e) deer, roe; *female:* doe.

rehabilitieren [rehabili'tiːrən] *v/t.* (*no -ge-, h*) rehabilitate.

'Reh|bock *zo. m* roebuck; **'2braun** *adj.*, '2farben *adj.* fawn-colo(u)red; **'~geiß** *zo. f* doe; '~kalb *zo. n*, **~kitz** *zo.* ['~kits] *n* (-es/-e) fawn.

Reib|e ['raɪbə] *f* (-/-n), **~eisen** ['raɪp⁹-] *n* grater.

reib|en ['raɪbən] (*irr.*, ge-, h) **1.** *v/i.* rub (*an dat.* [up]on); **2.** *v/t.* rub, grate; pulverize; *wund* ~ chafe, gall; **2erei** F *fig.* [~'raɪ] *f* (-/-en) (constant) friction; '2ung *f* (-/-en) friction; '~ungslos *adj.* frictionless; *fig.* smooth.

reich¹ *adj.* [raɪç] rich (*an dat.* in); wealthy; ample, abundant, copious.

Reich² [~] *n* (-es/-e) empire; kingdom (*of animals, vegetables, minerals*); *poet.*, *rhet.*, *fig.* realm.

reichen ['raɪçən] (ge-, h) **1.** *v/t.* offer; serve (*food*); *j-m et.* ~ hand *or* pass s.th. to s.o.; *sich die Hände* ~ join hands; **2.** *v/i.* reach; extend; suffice; *das reicht!* that will do!

reich|haltig *adj.* ['raɪçhaltɪç] rich; abundant, copious; '~lich **1.** *adj.* ample, abundant, copious, plentiful; ~ *Zeit* plenty of time; **2.** F *adv.* rather, fairly, F pretty, plenty; '2tum *m* (-s/⁓er) riches *pl.*; wealth (*an dat.* of).

'Reichweite *f* reach; ✕ range; *in* ~ within reach, near at hand.

reif¹ *adj.* [raɪf] ripe, mature.

Reif² [~] *m* (-[e]s/*no pl.*) white *or* hoar-frost, *poet.* rime.

'Reife *f* (-/*no pl.*) ripeness, maturity.

'reifen¹ *v/i.* (ge-) **1.** (sein) ripen, mature; **2.** (h): *es hat gereift* there is a white *or* hoar-frost.

'Reifen² *m* (-s/-) hoop; ring; tyre, (*Am. only*) tire; *as ornament:* circlet; ~ *wechseln mot.* change tyres; '~panne *mot. f* puncture, *Am. a.* blowout.

'Reife|prüfung *f s. Abitur;* '~zeugnis *n s. Abschlußzeugnis.*

'reiflich *adj.* mature, careful.

Reihe ['raɪə] *f* (-/-n) row; line; rank; series; number; *thea.* row, tier; *der* ~ *nach* by turns; *ich bin an der* ~ *it* is my turn.

'Reihen|folge *f* succession, sequence; *alphabetische* ~ alphabetical order; '~haus *n* terrace-house, *Am.* row house; '2weise *adv.* in rows.

Reiher *orn.* ['raɪər] *m* (-s/-) heron.

Reim [raɪm] *m* (-[e]s/-e) rhyme; '2en (-, ge-, h) **1.** *v/i.* rhyme; **2.** *v/t. and v/refl.* rhyme (*auf acc.* with).

rein *adj.* [raɪn] pure; clean; clear; ~*e Wahrheit* plain truth; '2ertrag *m* net proceeds *pl.*; '2fall f *m* letdown; '2gewicht *n* net weight; '2gewinn *m* net profit; '2heit *f* (-/*no pl.*) purity; cleanness.

'reinig|en *v/t.* (ge-, h) clean(se); *fig.* purify; '2ung *f* (-/-en) clean(s)ing; *fig.* purification; cleaners *pl.*; *chemische* ~ dry cleaning; '2ungsmittel *n* detergent, cleanser.

'rein|lich *adj.* clean; cleanly; neat, tidy; '2machefrau *f* charwoman; **~rassig** *adj.* pedigree, thoroughbred, *esp. Am.* purebred; '2schrift *f* fair copy.

Reis¹ ♀ [raɪs] *m* (-es/-e) rice.

Reis² ♀ [~] *n* (-es/-er) twig, sprig.

Reise ['raɪzə] *f* (-/-n) journey, ⚓, ✈ voyage; travel; tour; trip; passage; '~büro *n* travel agency *or* bureau; '~decke *f* travel(l)ing-rug; '2fertig *adj.* ready to start; '~führer *m* guide(-book); '~gepäck *n* luggage, *Am.* baggage; '~gesellschaft *f* tourist party; '~kosten *pl.* travel(l)ing-expenses *pl.*; '~leiter *m* courier; '2n *v/i.* (ge-, sein) travel, journey; ~ *nach* go to; *ins Ausland* ~ go abroad; '~nde *m*, *f* (-n/-n) († commercial) travel(l)er; *in trains:* passenger; *for pleasure:* tourist; **~necessaire** ['~nesɛ:r] *n* (-s/-s) dressing-case; '~paß *m* passport; '~scheck *m* traveller's cheque, *Am.* traveler's check; '~schreibmaschine *f* portable typewriter; '~tasche *f* travel(l)ing-bag, *Am.* grip(sack).

Reisig ['raɪzɪç] *n* (-s/*no pl.*) brushwood.

Reißbrett ['raɪs-] *n* drawing-board.

reißen ['raɪsən] **1.** *v/t.* (*irr.*, ge-, h) tear; pull; *an sich* ~ seize; *sich* ~ scratch o.s. (*an dat.* with); *sich* ~ *um* scramble for; **2.** *v/i.* (*irr.*, ge-, sein) break; burst; split; tear; *mir riß die Geduld* I lost (all) patience; **3.** 2 F *m* (-s/*no pl.*) rheumatism; '~d *adj.* rapid; *animal:* rapacious; *pain:* acute; **~en** *Absatz finden* sell like hot cakes.

'Reiß|er F *m* (-s/-) draw, box-office success; thriller; '~feder *f* drawing-pen; '~leine *f* ✈ rip-cord; '~nagel *m s. Reißzwecke;* '~schiene *f* (T-)square; '~verschluß *m* zipfastener, zipper, *Am. a.* slide fastener; '~zeug *n* drawing instruments *pl.*; '~zwecke *f* drawing-pin, *Am.* thumbtack.

Reit|anzug ['raɪt-] *m* riding-dress; '~bahn *f* riding-school, manège; riding-track; '2en (*irr.*, ge-) **1.** *v/i.* (sein) ride, go on horseback; **2.** *v/t.* (h) ride; '~er *m* (-s/-) rider, horseman; ✕, *police:* trooper; *filing:* tab; ~e'rei *f* (-/-en) cavalry; '~erin *f* (-/-nen) horsewoman; '~gerte *f* riding-whip; '⸜hose f (riding-) breeches pl.; '⸜knecht m groom; '⸜kunst f horsemanship; '⸜lehrer m riding master; '⸜peitsche f riding-whip; '⸜pferd zo. n riding-horse, saddle-horse; '⸜schule f riding-school; '⸜stiefel m/pl. riding-boots pl.; '⸜weg m bridle-path.

Reiz [raits] m (-es/-e) irritation; charm, attraction; allurement; '2-bar adj. sensitive; irritable, excitable, Am. sore; '2en (ge-, h) 1. v/t. irritate (a. ⚕); excite; provoke; nettle; stimulate, rouse; entice, (al)lure, tempt, charm, attract; 2. v/i. cards: bid; '2end adj. charming, attractive; Am. cute; lovely; '2los adj. unattractive; '⸜mittel n stimulus; ⚕ stimulant; '⸜ung f (-/-en) irritation; provocation; '2-voll adj. charming, attractive.

rekeln F ['re:kəln] v/refl. (ge-, h) loll, lounge, sprawl.

Reklamation [reklama'tsjo:n] f (-/-en) claim; complaint, protest.

Reklame [re'kla:mə] f (-/-n) advertising; advertisement, F ad; publicity; ~ machen advertise; ~ machen für et. advertise s.th.

rekla'mieren (no -ge-, h) 1. v/t. (re)claim; 2. v/i. complain (wegen about).

Rekonvaleszen|t [rekɔnvales'tsɛnt] m (-en/-en), '⸜tin f (-/-nen) convalescent; ⸜z [⸜ts] f (-/no pl.) convalescence.

Rekord [re'kɔrt] m (-[e]s/-e) sports, etc.: record.

Rekrut ✗ [re'kru:t] m (-en/-en) recruit; 2ieren ✗ [⸜u'ti:rən] v/t. (no -ge-, h) recruit.

Rektor ['rɛktɔr] m (-s/-en) headmaster, rector, Am. principal; univ. chancellor, rector, Am. president.

relativ adj. [rela'ti:f] relative.

Relief [rel'jɛf] n (-s/-s, -e) relief.

Religi|on [reli'gjo:n] f (-/-en) religion; 2ös adj. [⸜ø:s] religious; pious, devout; ⸜osität [⸜ozi'tɛ:t] f (-/no pl.) religiousness; piety.

Reling ⚓ ['re:lɪŋ] f (-/-s, -e) rail.

Reliquie [re'li:kviə] f (-/-n) relic.

Ren zo. [rɛn; re:n] n (-s/-s; -s/-e) reindeer.

Renn|bahn ['rɛn-] f racecourse, Am. race track, horse-racing: a. the turf; mot. speedway; '⸜boot n racing boat, racer.

rennen ['rɛnən] 1. v/i. (irr., ge-, sein) run; race; 2. v/t. (irr., ge-, h): j-n zu Boden ⸜ run s.o. down; 3. 2 n (-s/-) run(ning); race; heat.

'Renn|fahrer m mot. racing driver, racer; racing cyclist; '⸜läufer m ski racer; '⸜mannschaft f race-crew; '⸜pferd zo. n racehorse, racer; '⸜rad n racing bicycle, racer; '⸜sport m racing; horse-racing: a. the turf; '⸜stall m racing stable;

'⸜strecke f racecourse, Am. race track; mot. speedway; distance (to be run); '⸜wagen m racing car, racer.

renommiert adj. [renɔ'mi:rt] famous, noted (wegen for).

renovieren [reno'vi:rən] v/t. (no -ge-, h) renovate, repair; redecorate (interior of house).

rent|abel adj. [rɛn'ta:bəl] profitable, paying; '2e f (-/-n) income, revenue; annuity; (old-age) pension; rent; 2enempfänger ['rɛn-tən⁹-] m s. Rentner; rentier.

Rentier zo. ['rɛn-] n s. Ren.

rentieren [rɛn'ti:rən] v/refl. (no -ge-, h) pay.

Rentner ['rɛntnər] m (-s/-) (old-age) pensioner.

Reparatur [repara'tu:r] f (-/-en) repair; ⸜werkstatt f repair-shop; mot. a. garage, service station.

repa'rieren v/t. (no -ge-, h) repair, Am. F fix.

Report|age [repɔr'ta:ʒə] f (-/-n) reporting, commentary, coverage; ⸜er [re'pɔrtər] m (-s/-) reporter.

Repräsent|ant [reprezɛn'tant] m (-en/-en) representative; ⸜anten-haus Am. parl. n House of Representatives; 2ieren (no -ge-, h) 1. v/t. represent; 2. v/i. cut a fine figure.

Repressalie [reprɛ'sa:ljə] f (-/-n) reprisal.

reproduzieren [reprodu'tsi:rən] v/t. (no -ge-, h) reproduce.

Reptil zo. [rɛp'ti:l] n (-s/-ien, ⚕-s) reptile.

Republik [repu'bli:k] f (-/-en) republic; ⸜aner pol. [⸜i'ka:nər] m (-s/-) republican; 2anisch adj. [⸜i'ka:nɪʃ] republican.

Reserve [re'zɛrvə] f (-/-n) reserve; ⸜rad mot. n spare wheel.

reser'vier|en v/t. (no -ge-, h) reserve; ~ lassen book (seat, etc.); ⸜t adj. reserved (a. fig.).

Resid|enz [rezi'dɛnts] f (-/-en) residence; 2ieren v/i. (no -ge-, h) reside.

resignieren [rezi'gni:rən] v/i. (no -ge-, h) resign.

Respekt [re'spɛkt] m (-[e]s/no pl.) respect; 2ieren [⸜'ti:rən] v/t. (no -ge-, h) respect; 2los adj. irreverent; disrespectful; 2voll adj. respectful.

Ressort [rɛ'sɔ:r] n (-s/-s) department; province.

Rest [rɛst] m (-es/-e, ⚕ -er) rest, remainder; residue (a. 🜍); esp. 🜂 remnant (of cloth); leftover (of food); das gab ihm den ~ that finished him (off).

Restaurant [rɛsto'rã:] n (-s/-s) restaurant.

'Rest|bestand m remnant; '⸜be-trag m remainder, balance; '2lich adj. remaining; '2los adv. com-pletely; entirely; '**~zahlung** f payment of balance; final payment.

Resultat [rezul'ta:t] n (-[e]s/-e) result, outcome; *sports*: score.

retten ['rɛtən] v/t. (ge-, h) save; deliver, rescue.

Rettich ♀ ['rɛtiç] m (-s/-e) radish.

'**Rettung** f (-/-en) rescue; deliverance; escape.

'**Rettungs|boot** n lifeboat; '**~gürtel** m lifebelt; '**2los** adj. irretrievable, past help or hope, beyond recovery; '**~mannschaft** f rescue party; **~ring** m life-buoy.

Reu|e ['rɔyə] f (-/no pl.) repentance (über acc. of), remorse (at); '**2en** v/t. (ge-, h): et. reut mich I repent (of) s.th.; '**2evoll** adj. repentant; **2(müt)ig** adj. ['.~(my:t)iç] repentant.

Revanche [re'vã:ʃ(ə)] f (-/-n) revenge; **~spiel** n return match.

revan'chieren v/refl. (no -ge-, h) take or have one's revenge (an dat. on); return (für et. s.th.).

Revers 1. [re've:r] n, m (-/-) lapel (of coat); 2. [re'vɛrs] m (-es/-e) declaration; ⚖ bond.

revidieren [revi'di:rən] v/t. (no -ge-, h) revise; check; ✝ audit.

Revier [re'vi:r] n (-s/-e) district, quarter; s. Jagdrevier.

Revision [revi'zjo:n] f (-/-en) revision (a. typ.); ✝ audit; ⚖ appeal; ~ einlegen ⚖ lodge an appeal.

Revolt|e [re'vɔltə] f (-/-n) revolt, uprising; **2ieren** [.~'ti:rən] v/i. (no -ge-, h) revolt, rise (in revolt).

Revolution [revolu'tsjo:n] f (-/-en) revolution; **~är** [.~o'nɛ:r] 1. m (-s/-e) revolutionary; 2. ♀ adj. revolutionary.

Revolver [re'vɔlvər] m (-s/-) revolver, Am. F a. gun.

Revue [rə'vy:] f (-/-n) review; thea. revue, (musical) show; ~ passieren lassen pass in review.

Rezens|ent [retsɛn'zɛnt] m (-en/-en) critic, reviewer; **2ieren** v/t. (no -ge-, h) review, criticize; **~ion** [.~'zjo:n] f (-/-en) review, critique.

Rezept [re'tsɛpt] n (-[e]s/-e) ♀ prescription; cooking: recipe (a. fig.).

Rhabarber ♀ [ra'barbər] m (-s/no pl.) rhubarb.

rhetorisch adj. [re'to:riʃ] rhetorical.

rheumati|sch ♀ adj. [rɔy'ma:tiʃ] rheumatic; **2smus** ♀ [.~a'tismus] m (-/Rheumatismen) rheumatism.

rhythm|isch adj. ['rytmiʃ] rhythmic(al); **2us** ['.~us] m (-/Rhythmen) rhythm.

richten ['riçtən] v/t. (ge-, h) set right, arrange, adjust; level, point (gun) (auf acc. at); direct (gegen at); ⚖ judge; execute; zugrunde ~ ruin, destroy; in die Höhe ~ raise, lift up; sich ~ nach conform to, act according to; take one's bearings from;

gr. agree with; depend on; price: be determined by; ich richte mich nach Ihnen I leave it to you.

'**Richter** m (-s/-) judge; '**2lich** adj. judicial; '**~spruch** m judg(e)ment, sentence.

'**richtig** 1. adj. right, correct, accurate; proper; true; just; ein ~er Londoner a regular cockney; 2. adv.: ~ gehen clock: go right; '**2keit** f (-/no pl.) correctness; accuracy; justness; '**~stellen** v/t. (sep., -ge-, h) put or set right, rectify.

'**Richt|linien** f/pl. (general) directions pl., rules pl.; '**~preis** ✝ m standard price; '**~schnur** f ⊕ plumb-line; fig. rule (of conduct); guiding principle.

'**Richtung** f (-/-en) direction; course, way; fig. line; **~anzeiger** mot. ['riçtuŋs?-] m (-s/-) flashing indicator, trafficator; '**2weisend** adj. directive, leading, guiding.

'**Richtwaage** ⊕ f level.

rieb [ri:p] pret. of reiben.

riechen ['ri:çən] (irr., ge-, h) 1. v/i. smell (nach of; an dat. at); sniff (an dat. at); 2. v/t. smell; sniff.

rief [ri:f] pret. of rufen.

riefeln ⊕ ['ri:fəln] v/t. (ge-, h) flute, groove.

Riegel ['ri:gəl] m (-s/-) bar, bolt; bar, cake (of soap); bar (of chocolate).

Riemen ['ri:mən] m (-s/-) strap, thong; belt; ⚓ oar.

Ries [ri:s] n (-es/-e) ream.

Riese ['ri:zə] m (-n/-n) giant.

rieseln ['ri:zəln] v/i. (ge-) 1. (sein) small stream: purl, ripple; trickle; 2. (h): es rieselt it drizzles.

ries|engroß adj. ['ri:zən'-], '**~enhaft** adj., '.~ig adj. gigantic, huge; '**2in** f (-/-nen) giantess.

riet [ri:t] pret. of raten.

Riff [rif] n (-[e]s/-e) reef.

Rille ['rilə] f (-/-n) groove; ⊕ a. flute.

Rimesse ✝ [ri'mɛsə] f (-/-n) remittance.

Rind zo. [rint] n (-[e]s/-er) ox; cow; neat; ~er pl. (horned) cattle pl.; zwanzig ~er twenty head of cattle.

Rinde ['rində] f (-/-n) ♀ bark; rind (of fruit, bacon, cheese); crust (of bread).

'**Rinder|braten** m roast beef; '**~herde** f herd of cattle; '**~hirt** m cowherd, Am. cowboy.

'**Rind|fleisch** n beef; '.~(s)leder n neat's-leather, cow-hide; '.~vieh n (horned) cattle pl., neat pl.

Ring [riŋ] m (-[e]s/-e) ring; circle; link (of chain); ✝ ring, pool, trust, Am. F combine; '**~bahn** f circular railway.

ringel|n ['riŋəln] v/refl. (ge-, h) curl, coil; '**2natter** zo. f ring-snake.

ring|en ['riŋən] (irr., ge-, h) 1. v/i. wrestle; struggle (um for); nach Atem ~ gasp (for breath); 2. v/t. wring (hands, washing); '2er m (-s/-) wrestler.

ring|förmig adj. ['riŋfœrmiç] annular, ring-like; '2kampf m sports: wrestling(-match); '2richter m boxing: referee.

rings adv. [riŋs] around; '_he'rum adv., '_'um adv., '_um'her adv. round about, all (a)round.

Rinn|e ['rinə] f (-/-n) groove, channel; gutter (of roof or street); gully; '2en v/i. (irr., ge-, sein) run, flow; drip; leak; '_sal ['_za:l] n (-[e]s/-e) watercourse, streamlet; '_stein n gutter; sink (of kitchen unit).

Rippe ['ripə] f (-/-n) rib; ⚓ groin; bar (of chocolate); '2n v/t. (ge-, h) rib; '_nfell anat. n pleura; '_nfellentzündung ♂ f pleurisy; '_nstoß m dig in the ribs; nudge.

Risiko ['ri:ziko] n (-s/-s, Risiken) risk; ein ~ eingehen take a risk.

risk|ant adj. [ris'kant] risky; _ieren v/t. (no -ge-, h) risk.

Riß [ris] 1. m (Risses/Risse) rent, tear; split (a. fig.); crack; in skin: chap; scratch; ⊕ draft, plan; fig. rupture; 2. 2 pret. of reißen.

rissig adj. ['risiç] full of rents; skin, etc.: chappy; ~ werden crack.

Rist [rist] m (-es/-e) instep; back of the hand; wrist.

Ritt [rit] 1. m (-[e]s/-e) ride; 2. 2 pret. of reiten.

'Ritter m (-s/-) knight; zum ~ schlagen knight; '_gut n manor; '2lich adj. knightly, chivalrous; '_lichkeit f (-/-en) gallantry, chivalry.

rittlings adv. ['ritliŋs] astride (auf e-m Pferd a horse).

Ritz [rits] m (-es/-e) crack, chink; scratch; '_e f (-/-n) crack, chink; fissure; '2en v/t. (ge-, h) scratch; cut.

Rival|e [ri'va:lə] m (-n/-n), _in f (-/-nen) rival; 2isieren [_ali'zi:rən] v/i. (no -ge-, h) rival (mit j-m s.o.); _ität [_ali'tɛ:t] f (-/-en) rivalry.

Rizinusöl ['ri:tsinus?-] n (-[e]s/no pl.) castor oil.

Robbe zo. ['rɔbə] f (-/-n) seal.
Robe ['ro:bə] f (-/-n) gown; robe.
Roboter ['rɔbɔtər] m (-s/-) robot.
robust adj. [ro'bust] robust, sturdy, vigorous.

roch [rɔx] pret. of riechen.
röcheln ['rœçəln] (ge-, h) 1. v/i. rattle; 2. v/t. gasp out (words).

Rock [rɔk] m (-[e]s/"e) skirt; coat, jacket; '_schoß m coat-tail.

Rodel|bahn ['ro:dəl-] f tobogganrun; '2n v/i. (ge-, h, sein) toboggan, Am. a. coast; '_schlitten m sled(ge), toboggan.

roden ['ro:dən] v/t. (ge-, h) clear (land); root up, stub (roots).

Rogen ichth. ['ro:gən] m (-s/-) roe, spawn.

Roggen ♉ ['rɔgən] m (-s/-) rye.

roh adj. [ro:] raw; fig.: rough, rude; cruel, brutal; oil, metal: crude; '2bau m (-[e]s/-ten) rough brickwork; '2eisen n pig-iron.

Roheit ['ro:hart] f (-/-en) rawness; roughness (a. fig.); fig.: rudeness; brutality.

'Roh|ling m (-s/-e) brute, ruffian; '_material n raw material; '_produkt n raw product.

Rohr [ro:r] n (-[e]s/-e) tube, pipe; duct; ♉: reed; cane.

Röhre ['rø:rə] f (-/-n) tube, pipe; duct; radio: valve, Am. (electron) tube.

'Rohr|leger m (-s/-) pipe fitter, plumber; '_leitung f plumbing; pipeline; '_post f pneumatic dispatch or tube; '_stock m cane; '_zucker m cane-sugar.

'Rohstoff m raw material.

Rolladen ['rɔlla:dən] m (-s/", -) rolling shutter.

'Rollbahn ⚹ f taxiway, taxi-strip.

Rolle ['rɔlə] f (-/-n) roll; roller; coil (of rope, etc.); pulley; beneath furniture: cast|or, -er; mangle; thea. part, role; fig. figure; ~ Garn reel of cotton, Am. spool of thread; das spielt keine ~ that doesn't matter, it makes no difference; Geld spielt keine ~ money (is) no object; aus der ~ fallen forget o.s.

'rollen (ge-) 1. v/t. (sein) roll; ⚹ taxi; 2. v/t. (h) roll; wheel; mangle (laundry).

'Rollenbesetzung thea. f cast.

'Roller m (-s/-) children's toy: scooter; mot. (motor) scooter.

'Roll|feld n manœuvring area, Am. maneuvering area; '_film phot. m roll film; '_kragen m turtle neck; '_schrank m rollfronted cabinet; '_schuh m roller-skate; '_schuhbahn f roller-skating rink; '_stuhl m wheel chair; '_treppe f escalator; '_wagen m lorry, truck.

Roman [ro'ma:n] m (-s/-e) novel, (work of) fiction; novel of adventure and fig.: romance; _ist [_a'nist] m (-en/-en) Romance scholar or student; _schriftsteller m novelist.

Romanti|k [ro'mantik] f (-/no pl.) romanticism; 2sch adj. romantic.
Röm|er ['rø:mər] m (-s/-) Roman; '2isch adj. Roman.

röntgen ['rœntgən] v/t. (ge-, h) X-ray; '2aufnahme f, '2bild n X-ray; '2strahlen m/pl. X-rays pl.

rosa adj. ['ro:za] pink.

Rose ['ro:zə] f (-/-n) ♉ rose; ♂ erysipelas.

'Rosen|kohl ♉ m Brussels sprouts pl.; '_kranz eccl. m rosary; '2rot *adj.* rose-colo(u)red, rosy; '**\sstock** & *m* (-[e]s/\se) rose-bush.

'**rosig** *adj.* rosy (*a. fig.*), rose-colo(u)red, roseate.

Rosine [ro'zi:nə] *f* (-/-n) raisin.

Roß *zo.* [rɔs] *n* (Rosses/*Rosse*, F *Rösser*) horse, *poet.* steed; '**\shaar** *n* horsehair.

Rost [rɔst] *m* **1.** (-es/*no pl.*) rust; **2.** (-es/-e) grate; gridiron; grill; '**\sbraten** *m* roast joint.

'**rosten** *v/i.* (ge-, h, sein) rust.

rösten ['rø:stən] *v/t.* (ge-, h) roast, grill; toast (*bread*); fry (*potatoes*).

'**Rost|fleck** *m* rust-stain; *in cloth:* iron-mo(u)ld; '**2frei** *adj.* rustless, rustproof; *esp. steel:* stainless; '**2ig** *adj.* rusty, corroded.

rot [ro:t] **1.** *adj.* red; **2.** 2 *n* (-s/-, F -s) red.

Rotationsmaschine *typ.* [rota-'tsjo:ns-] *f* rotary printing machine.

'**rot|backig** *adj.* ruddy; '**\sblond** *adj.* sandy.

Röte ['rø:tə] *f* (-/*no pl.*) redness, red (colo[u]r); blush; '**2n** *v/t.* (ge-, h) redden; paint *or* dye red; *sich* \s redden; flush, blush.

'**rot|gelb** *adj.* reddish yellow; '**\sglühend** *adj.* red-hot; '**2haut** *f* red-skin.

rotieren [ro'ti:rən] *v/i.* (*no* -ge-, h) rotate, revolve.

Rot|käppchen ['ro:tkɛpçən] *n* (-s/-) Little Red Riding Hood; '**\skehlchen** *orn.* *n* (-s/-) robin (redbreast).

rötlich *adj.* ['rø:tliç] reddish.

'**Rot|stift** *m* red crayon *or* pencil; '**\stanne** & *f* spruce (fir).

Rotte ['rɔtə] *f* (-/-n) band, gang.

'**Rot|wein** *m* red wine; claret; '**\swild** *zo.* *n* red deer.

Rouleau [ru'lo:] *n* (-s/-s) *s.* Rollladen; *Brit., Am.* (window) shade.

Route ['ru:tə] *f* (-/-n) route.

Routine [ru'ti:nə] *f* (-/*no pl.*) routine, practice.

Rübe & ['ry:bə] *f* (-/-n) beet; weiße \s (Swedish) turnip, *Am. a.* rutabaga; *rote* \s red beet, beet(root); *gelbe* \s carrot.

Rubin [ru'bi:n] *m* (-s/-e) ruby.

ruch|bar *adj.* ['ru:xba:r]: \s *werden* become known, get about *or* abroad; '**\slos** *adj.* wicked, profligate.

Ruck [ruk] *m* (-[e]s/-e) jerk, *Am.* F yank; jolt (*of vehicle*).

Rück|antwort ['ryk\?-] *f* reply; *Postkarte mit* \s reply postcard; *mit bezahlter* \s *telegram:* reply paid; '**2bezüglich** *gr. adj.* reflexive; '**\sblick** *m* retrospect(ive view) (*auf acc.* at); reminiscences *pl.*

rücken[1] ['rykən] (ge-) **1.** *v/t.* (h) move, shift; **2.** *v/i.* (sein) move; *näher* \s near, approach.

Rücken[2] [\s] *m* (-s/-) back; ridge (*of mountain*); '**\sdeckung** *fig. f* backing, support; '**\slehne** *f* back

(*of chair, etc.*); '**\smark** *anat. n* spinal cord; '**\sschmerzen** *m/pl.* pain in the back, back ache; '**\sschwimmen** *n* (-s/*no pl.*) back-stroke swimming; '**\swind** *m* following *or* tail wind; '**\swirbel** *anat. m* dorsal vertebra.

Rück|erstattung ['ryk\?-] *f* restitution; refund (*of money*), reimbursement (*of expenses*); '**\sfahrkarte** *f* return (ticket), *Am. a.* round-trip ticket; '**\sfahrt** *f* return journey *or* voyage; *auf der* \s *on the* way back; '**\sfall** *m* relapse; '**2fällig** *adj.*: \s *werden* relapse; '**\sflug** *m* return flight; '**\sfrage** *f* further inquiry; '**\sgabe** *f* return, restitution; '**\sgang** *fig. m* retrogression; † recession, decline; '**2gängig** *adj.* retrograde; \s *machen* cancel; '**\sgrat** *anat. n* (-[e]s/-e) spine, backbone (*both a. fig.*); '**\shalt** *m* support; '**2haltlos** *adj.* unreserved, frank; '**\shand** *f* (-/*no pl.*) *tennis:* backhand (stroke); '**\skauf** *m* repurchase; '**\skehr** ['\ske:r] *f* (-/*no pl.*) return; '**\skopp(e)lung** & *f* (-/-en) feed-back; '**\slage** *f* reserve(s *pl.*); savings *pl.*; 2läufig *fig. adj.* ['\slɔyfiç] retrograde; '**\slicht** *mot. n* tail-light, tail-lamp, rear-light; '**2lings** *adv.* backwards; from behind; '**\smarsch** *m* march back *or* home; retreat; '**\sporto** & *n* return postage; '**\sreise** *f* return journey, journey back *or* home.

'**Rucksack** *m* knapsack, rucksack.

'**Rück|schlag** *m* backstroke; *fig.* setback; '**\sschluß** *m* conclusion, inference; '**\sschritt** *fig. m* retrogression, set-back; *pol.* reaction; '**\sseite** *f* back, reverse; *a.* tail (*of coin*); '**\ssendung** *f* return; '**\ssicht** *f* respect, regard, consideration (*auf j-n* for s.o.); '**2sichtslos** *adj.* inconsiderate (*gegen of*), regardless (of); ruthless; reckless; \s*es Fahren mot.* reckless driving; '**2sichtsvoll** *adj.* regardful (*gegen of*); considerate, thoughtful; '**\ssitz** *mot. m* back-seat; '**\sspiegel** *mot. m* rear-view mirror; '**\sspiel** *n sports:* return match; '**\ssprache** *f* consultation; \s *nehmen mit* consult (*lawyer*), consult with (*fellow workers*); *nach* \s *mit* on consultation with; '**\sstand** *m* arrears *pl.*; backlog; & residue; *im* \s *sein mit* be in arrears *or* behind with; '**2ständig** *fig. adj.* old-fashioned, backward; \s*e Miete* arrears of rent; '**\sstoß** *m* recoil; kick (*of gun*); '**\sstrahler** *m* (-s/-) rear reflector, cat's eye; '**\stritt** *m* withdrawal, retreat; resignation; '**\strittbremse** *f* back-pedal brake, *Am.* coaster brake; '**\sversicherung** *f* reinsurance; 2wärts *adv.* ['\sverts] back, backward(s); '**\swärtsgang** *mot. m* reverse (gear); '⁓**weg** *m* way back, return.

'**ruckweise** *adv.* by jerks.

'**rück|wirkend** *adj.* reacting; ⅖, *etc.*: retroactive, retrospective; '⁓**wirkung** *f* reaction; '2**zahlung** *f* repayment; '2**zug** *m* retreat.

Rüde ['ry:də] 1. *zo. m* (-*n*/-*n*) male dog *or* fox *or* wolf; large hound; 2. 2 *adj.* rude, coarse, brutal.

Rudel ['ru:dəl] *n* (-*s*/-) troop; pack (*of wolves*); herd (*of deer*).

Ruder ['ru:dər] *n* (-*s*/-) oar; rudder (*a.* 🎇); helm; '⁓**boot** *n* row(ing)-boat; '⁓**er** *m* (-*s*/-) rower, oarsman; '⁓**fahrt** *f* row; '2**n** (*ge*-) 1. *v/i.* (*h, sein*) row; 2. *v/t.* (*h*) row; '⁓**regatta** ['⁓regata] *f* (-/*Ruderregatten*) boat race, regatta; '⁓**sport** *m* rowing.

Ruf [ru:f] *m* (-[*e*]*s*/-*e*) call; cry, shout; summons; *univ.* call; reputation, repute; fame; standing, credit; '2**en** (*irr., ge*-, *h*) 1. *v/i.* call; cry, shout; 2. *v/t.* call; ⁓ *lassen* send for.

'**Ruf|name** *m* Christian *or* first name; '⁓**nummer** *f* telephone number; '⁓**weite** *f* (-/*no pl.*): *in* ⁓ within call *or* earshot.

Rüge ['ry:gə] *f* (-/-*n*) rebuke, censure, reprimand; '2**n** *v/t.* (*ge*-, *h*) rebuke, censure, blame.

Ruhe ['ru:ə] *f* (-/*no pl.*) rest, repose; sleep; quiet, calm; tranquillity; silence; peace; composure; *sich zur* ⁓ *setzen* retire; '⁓*!* quiet!, silence!; *immer mit der* ⁓*!* take it easy!; *lassen Sie mich in* ⁓*!* let me alone!; '2**bedürftig** *adj.*: ⁓ *sein* want *or* need rest; '⁓**gehalt** *n* pension; '2**los** *adj.* restless; '2**n** *v/i.* (*ge*-, *h*) rest, repose; sleep; *laß die Vergangenheit* ⁓*!* let bygones be bygones!; '⁓**pause** *f* pause; lull; '⁓**platz** *m* resting-place; '⁓**stand** *m* (-[*e*]*s*/*no pl.*) retirement; *im* ⁓ retired; *in den* ⁓ *treten* retire; *in den* ⁓ *versetzen* superannuate, pension off, retire; '⁓**stätte** *f*: *letzte* ⁓ last resting-place; '⁓**störer** *m* (-*s*/-) disturber of the peace, peacebreaker; '⁓**störung** *f* disturbance (of the peace), disorderly behavio(u)r, riot.

'**ruhig** *adj.* quiet; *mind, water:* tranquil, calm; silent; ⊕ smooth.

Ruhm [ru:m] *m* (-[*e*]*s*/*no pl.*) glory; fame, renown.

rühm|en ['ry:mən] *v/t.* (*ge*-, *h*) praise, glorify; *sich e-r Sache* ⁓ boast of s.th.; '⁓**lich** *adj.* glorious, laudable.

'**ruhm|los** *adj.* inglorious; '⁓**reich** *adj.* glorious.

Ruhr 🎇 [ru:r] *f* (-/*no pl.*) dysentery.

Rühr|ei ['ry:r?-] *n* scrambled egg; '2**en** (*ge*-, *h*) 1. *v/t.* stir, move; *fig.* touch, move, affect; *sich* ⁓ stir, move, bustle; 2. *v/i.*: *an et.* ⁓ touch s.th.; *wir wollen nicht daran* ⁓ let sleeping dogs lie; '2**end**

adj. touching, moving; '2**ig** *adj.* active, busy; enterprising; nimble; '2**selig** *adj.* sentimental; '⁓**ung** *f* (-/*no pl.*) emotion, feeling.

Ruin [ru'i:n] *m* (-*s*/*no pl.*) ruin; decay; ⁓**e** *f* (-/-*n*) ruin(s *pl.*); *fig.* ruin, wreck; 2**ieren** [rui'ni:rən] *v/t.* (*no* -*ge*-, *h*) ruin; destroy, wreck; spoil; *sich* ⁓ ruin o.s.

rülpsen ['rylpsən] *v/i.* (*ge*-, *h*) belch.

Rumän|e [ru'mɛ:nə] *m* (-*n*/-*n*) Ro(u)manian; '2**isch** *adj.* Ro(u)manian.

Rummel F ['ruməl] *m* (-*s*/*no pl.*) hurly-burly, row; bustle; revel; *in publicity:* F ballyhoo; '⁓**platz** *m* fun fair, amusement park.

rumoren [ru'mo:rən] *v/i.* (*no* -*ge*-, *h*) make a noise *or* row; *bowels:* rumble.

Rumpel|kammer F ['rumpəl-] *f* lumber-room; '2**n** F *v/i.* (*ge*-, *h, sein*) rumble.

Rumpf [rumpf] *m* (-[*e*]*s*/⁓*e*) *anat.* trunk, body; torso (*of statue*); 🚢 hull, frame, body; 🎇 fuselage, body.

rümpfen ['rympfən] *v/t.* (*ge*-, *h*): *die Nase* ⁓ turn up one's nose, sniff (*über acc.* at).

rund [runt] 1. *adj.* round (*a. fig.*); circular; 2. *adv.* about; '2**blick** *m* panorama, view all (a)round; 2**e** ['rundə] *f* (-/-*n*) round; *sports:* lap; *boxing:* round; round, patrol; beat (*of policeman*); *in der or die* ⁓ (a)round; ⁓**en** ['⁓dən] *v/refl.* (*ge*-, *h*) (grow) round; '2**fahrt** *f* drive round (*town, etc.*); *s. Rundreise*; '2**flug** *m* circuit (*über* of); '2**frage** *f* inquiry, poll.

'**Rundfunk** *m* broadcast(ing); broadcasting service; broadcasting company; radio, wireless; *im* ⁓ over the wireless, on the radio *or* air; '⁓**anstalt** *f* broadcasting company; '⁓**ansager** *m* (radio) announcer; '⁓**gerät** *n* radio *or* wireless set; '⁓**gesellschaft** *f* broadcasting company; '⁓**hörer** *m* listener(-in); ⁓ *pl. a.* (radio) audience; '⁓**programm** *n* broadcast *or* radio program(me); '⁓**sender** *m* broadcast transmitter; broadcasting *or* radio station; '⁓**sendung** *f* broadcast; '⁓**sprecher** *m* broadcaster, broadcast speaker, (radio) announcer; '⁓**station** *f* broadcasting *or* radio station; '⁓**übertragung** *f* radio transmission, broadcast(ing); broadcast (*of programme*).

'**Rund|gang** *m* tour, round, circuit; '⁓**gesang** *m* glee, catch; '2**he'raus** *adv.* in plain words, frankly, plainly; '2**he'rum** *adv.* round about, all (a)round; '2**lich** *adj.* round(ish); rotund, plump; '⁓**reise** *f* circular tour *or* trip, sight-seeing trip, *Am. a.* round trip; '⁓**schau** *f* panorama;

newspaper: review; '~schreiben *n* circular (letter); '²'weg *adv.* flatly, plainly.

Runz|el ['runtsəl] *f* (-/-n) wrinkle; '²elig *adj.* wrinkled; '²eln *v/t.* (ge-, *h*) wrinkle; *die Stirn ~* knit one's brows, frown; '²lig *adj.* wrinkled.

Rüpel ['ry:pəl] *m* (-s/-) boor, lout; '²haft *adj.* coarse, boorish, rude.

rupfen ['rupfən] *v/t.* (ge-, *h*) pull up *or* out, pick; pluck (*fowl*) (*a. fig.*).

ruppig *adj.* ['rupiç] ragged, shabby; *fig.* rude.

Rüsche ['ry:ʃə] *f* (-/-n) ruffle, frill.

Ruß [ru:s] *m* (-es/*no pl.*) soot.

Russe ['rusə] *m* (-n/-n) Russian.

Rüssel ['rysəl] *m* (-s/-) trunk (*of elefant*); snout (*of pig*).

'ruß|en *v/i.* (ge-, *h*) smoke; '~ig *adj.* sooty.

'russisch *adj.* Russian.

rüsten ['rystən] (ge-, *h*) 1. *v/t. and v/refl.* prepare, get ready (*zu* for); 2. *esp.* ✕ *v/i.* arm.

rüstig *adj.* ['rystiç] vigorous, strong; '²keit *f* (-/*no pl.*) vigo(u)r.

'Rüstung *f* (-/-en) preparations *pl.*; ✕ arming, armament; armo(u)r; ~sindustrie ['rystuŋs?-] *f* armament industry.

'Rüstzeug *n* (set of) tools *pl.*, implements *pl.*; *fig.* equipment.

Rute ['ru:tə] *f* (-/-n) rod; switch; *fox's tail*: brush.

Rutsch [rutʃ] *m* (-es/-e) (land)slide; F short trip; '~bahn *f*, '~e *f* (-/-n) slide, chute; '²en *v/i.* (ge-, *sein*) glide, slide; slip; *vehicle*: skid; '²ig *adj.* slippery.

rütteln ['rytəln] (ge-, *h*) 1. *v/t.* shake, jog; jolt; 2. *v/i.* shake, jog; *car*: jolt; *an der Tür ~* rattle at the door; *daran ist nicht zu ~* that's a fact.

S

Saal [za:l] *m* (-[e]s/*Säle*) hall.

Saat [za:t] *f* (-/-en) sowing; standing *or* growing crops *pl.*; seed (*a. fig.*); '~feld *n* corn-field; '~gut *n* (-[e]s/*no pl.*) seeds *pl.*; '~kartoffel *f* seed-potato.

Sabbat ['zabat] *m* (-s/-e) Sabbath.

sabbern F ['zabərn] *v/i.* (ge-, *h*) slaver, slobber, *Am. a.* drool; twaddle, *Am. sl. a.* drool.

Säbel ['zɛ:bəl] *m* (-s/-) sab|re, *Am.* -er; *mit dem ~ rasseln pol.* rattle the sabre; '~beine *n/pl.* bandy legs *pl.*; '²beinig *adj.* bandy-legged; '~hieb *m* sabre-cut; '²n F *fig. v/t.* (ge-, *h*) hack.

Sabot|age [zabo'ta:ʒə] *f* (-/-n) sabotage, ~eur [.ø:r] *m* (-s/-e) saboteur; ²ieren *v/t.* (*no* -ge-, *h*) sabotage.

Sach|bearbeiter ['zax-] *m* (-s/-) official in charge; *social work*: case worker; '~beschädigung *f* damage to property; '²dienlich *adj.* relevant, pertinent; useful, helpful.

'Sache *f* (-/-n) thing; affair, matter, concern; ᵗᵗᵗ case; point; issue; ~*n pl.* things *pl.*; *beschlossene ~* foregone conclusion; *e-e ~ für sich a* matter apart; (*nicht*) *zur ~ gehörig* (ir)relevant, *pred. a.* to (off) the point; *bei der ~ bleiben* stick to the point; *gemeinsame ~ machen mit* make common cause with.

'sach|gemäß *adj.* appropriate, proper; '²kenntnis *f* expert knowledge; '~kundig *adj. s.* sachverständig; '²lage *f* state of affairs, situation; '~lich 1. *adj.* relevant, pertinent, *pred. a.* to the point; matter-of-fact, business-like; unbias(s)ed; objective; 2. *adv.*: ~ *einwandfrei od. richtig* factually correct.

sächlich *gr. adj.* ['zɛçliç] neuter.

'Sachlichkeit *f* (-/*no pl.*) objectivity; impartiality; matter-of-factness.

'Sach|register *n* (subject) index; '~schaden *m* damage to property.

Sachse ['zaksə] *m* (-n/-n) Saxon.

sächsisch *adj.* ['zɛksiʃ] Saxon.

sacht *adj.* [zaxt] soft, gentle; slow.

Sach|verhalt *m* ['zaxfɛrhalt] *m* (-[e]s/-e) facts *pl.* (of the case); '²verständig *adj.* expert; '~verständige *m* (-n/-n) expert, authority; ᵗᵗᵗ expert witness; '~wert *m* real value.

Sack [zak] *m* (-[e]s/ᵘe) sack; bag; *mit ~ und Pack* with bag and baggage; '~gasse *f* blind alley, cul-de-sac, impasse (*a. fig.*), *Am. a.* dead end (*a. fig.*); *fig.* deadlock; '~leinwand *f* sackcloth.

Sadis|mus [za'dismus] *m* (-/*no pl.*) sadism; ~t *m* (-en/-en) sadist; ²tisch *adj.* sadistic.

säen ['zɛ:ən] *v/t. and v/i.* (ge-, *h*) sow (*a. fig.*).

Saffian ['zafja:n] *m* (-s/*no pl.*) morocco.

Saft [zaft] *m* (-[e]s/ᵘe) juice (*of vegetables or fruits*); sap (*of plants*) (*a. fig.*); '²ig *adj.* fruits, *etc.*: juicy; *meadow, etc.*: lush; *plants*: sappy (*a. fig.*); *joke, etc.*: spicy, coarse; '²los *adj.* juiceless; sapless (*a. fig.*).

Sage ['za:gə] *f* (-/-n) legend, myth; *die ~ geht* the story goes.

Säge ['zɛ:gə] f (-/-n) saw; '~blatt n saw-blade; '~bock m saw-horse, Am. a. sawbuck; '~fisch *ichth. m* sawfish; '~mehl n sawdust.

sagen ['za:gən] (ge-, h) **1.** v/t. say; j-m et. ~ tell s.o. s.th., say s.th. to s.o.; j-m ~ lassen, daß send s.o. word that; er läßt sich nichts ~ he will not listen to reason; das hat nichts zu ~ that doesn't matter; j-m gute Nacht ~ bid s.o. good night; **2.** v/i. say; es ist nicht zu ~ it is incredible or fantastic; wenn ich so ~ darf if I may express myself in these terms; sage und schreibe believe it or not; no less than, as much as.

'**sägen** v/t. and v/i. (ge-, h) saw.

'**sagenhaft** adj. legendary, mythical; F fig. fabulous, incredible.

Säge|**späne** ['zɛ:gəʃpɛ:nə] m/pl. sawdust; '~werk n sawmill.

sah [za:] pret. of sehen.

Sahne ['za:nə] f (-/no pl.) cream.

Saison [zɛ'zõ:] f (-/-s) season; ℒbe-dingt adj. seasonal.

Saite ['zaitə] f (-/-n) string, chord (a. fig.); ~ninstrument ['zaitən?-] n stringed instrument.

Sakko ['zako] m, n (-s/-s) lounge coat; '~anzug m lounge suit.

Sakristei [zakris'tai] f (-/-en) sacristy, vestry.

Salat [za'la:t] m (-[e]s/-e) salad; ♀ lettuce.

Salb|**e** ['zalbə] f (-/-n) ointment; 'ℒen v/t. (ge-, h) rub with ointment; anoint; '~ung f (-/-en) anointing, unction (a. fig.); 'ℒungsvoll fig. adj. unctuous.

saldieren † [zal'di:rən] v/t. (no -ge-, h) balance, settle.

Saldo † ['zaldo] m (-s/Salden, Saldos, Saldi) balance; den ~ ziehen strike the balance; '~vortrag † m balance carried down.

Saline [za'li:nə] f (-/-n) salt-pit, salt-works.

Salmiak ℛ [zal'mjak] m, n (-s/no pl.) sal-ammoniac, ammonium chloride; ~geist m (-es/no pl.) liquid ammonia.

Salon [za'lõ:] m (-s/-s) drawing-room, Am. a. parlor; ♣ saloon; ℒfähig adj. presentable; ~löwe fig. m lady's man, carpet-knight; ~wagen 🚃 m salooncar, saloon carriage, Am. parlor car.

Salpeter ℛ [zal'pe:tər] m (-s/no pl.) saltpet|re Am. -er; nit|re, Am. -er.

Salto ['zalto] m (-s/-s, Salti) somersault; ~ mortale break-neck leap; e-n ~ schlagen turn a somersault.

Salut [za'lu:t] m (-[e]s/-e) salute; ~ schießen fire a salute; ℒieren [~u'ti:rən] v/i. (no -ge-, h) (stand at the) salute.

Salve ['zalvə] f (-/-n) volley; ♣ broadside; salute.

Salz [zalts] n (-es/-e) salt; '~berg-werk n salt-mine; '~en v/t. ([irr.,] ge-, h) salt; '~faß n, ~fäßchen ['~fɛsçən] n (-s/-) salt-cellar; '~gurke f pickled cucumber; 'ℒhal-tig adj. saline, saliferous; '~hering m pickled herring; 'ℒig adj. salt(y); s. salzhaltig; '~säure ℛ f hydro-chloric or muriatic acid; '~wasser n (-s/⸚) salt water, brine; '~werk n salt-works, saltern.

Same ['za:mə] m (-ns/-n), '~n m (-s/-) ♀ seed (a. fig.); biol. sperm, semen; '~nkorn ♀ n grain of seed.

Sammel|**büchse** ['zaməl-] f col-lecting-box; '~lager n collecting point; refugees, etc.: assembly camp; 'ℒn (ge-, h) **1.** v/t. gather; collect (stamps, etc.); sich ~ gather; fig.: concentrate; compose o.s.; **2.** v/i. collect money (für for); '~platz m meeting-place, place of appointment; 💥, ♣ rendezvous.

Samml|**er** ['zamlər] m (-s/-) col-lector; '~ung f **1.** (-/-en) collection; **2.** fig. (-/no pl.) composure; con-centration.

Samstag ['zams-] m Saturday.

samt¹ [zamt] **1.** adv.: ~ und sonders one and all; **2.** prp. (dat.) together or along with.

Samt² [~] m (-[e]s/-e) velvet.

sämtlich ['zɛmtliç] **1.** adj. all (to-gether); complete; **2.** adv. all (to-gether or of them).

Sanatorium [zana'to:rjum] n (-s/Sanatorien) sanatorium, Am. a. sanitarium.

Sand [zant] m (-[e]s/-e) sand; j-m ~ in die Augen streuen throw dust into s.o.'s eyes; im ~e verlaufen end in smoke, come to nothing.

Sandale [zan'da:lə] f (-/-n) sandal.

'**Sand**|**bahn** f sports: dirt-track; '~bank f sandbank; '~boden m sandy soil; '~grube f sand-pit; ℒig adj. ['~diç] sandy; '~korn n grain of sand; '~mann fig. m (-[e]s/no pl.) sandman, dustman; '~papier n sandpaper; '~sack m sand-bag; '~stein m sandstone.

sandte ['zantə] pret. of senden.

'**Sand**|**torte** f Madeira cake; '~uhr f sand-glass; '~wüste f sandy desert.

sanft adj. [zanft] soft; gentle; mild; smooth; slope, death, etc.: easy; ~er Zwang non-violent coercion; mit ~er Stimme softly, gently; ~mütig adj. ['~my:tiç] gentle, mild; meek.

sang [zaŋ] pret. of singen.

Sänger ['zɛŋər] m (-s/-) singer.

Sanguini|**ker** [zaŋgu'i:nikər] m (-s/-) sanguine person; ℒsch adj. sanguine.

sanier|**en** [za'ni:rən] v/t. (no -ge-, h) improve the sanitary conditions of; esp. †: reorganize; readjust; 'ℒung f (-/-en) sanitation; esp. †: reorgani-zation; readjustment.

sanitär *adj.* [zaniˈtɛːr] sanitary.
Sanität|er [zaniˈtɛːtər] *m* (-s/-) ambulance man; ✕ medical orderly.
sank [zaŋk] *pret. of* sinken.
Sankt [zaŋkt] Saint, St.
sann [zan] *pret. of* sinnen.
Sard|elle *ichth.* [zarˈdɛlə] *f* (-/-n) anchovy; ⁓ine *ichth.* [ˌ⁓iːnə] *f* (-/-n) sardine.
Sarg [zark] *m* (-[e]s/⁼e) coffin, *Am. a.* casket; '⁓deckel *m* coffin-lid.
Sarkas|mus [zarˈkasmus] *m* (-/⁂ Sarkasmen) sarcasm; ⁑tisch *adj.* [ˌ⁓tiʃ] sarcastic.
saß [zaːs] *pret. of* sitzen.
Satan [ˈzɑːtan] *m* (-s/-e) Satan; *fig.* devil; ⁑isch *fig. adj.* [zaˈtɑːniʃ] satanic.
Satellit *ast., pol.* [zateˈliːt] *m* (-en/-en) satellite; ⁓enstaat *pol. m* satellite state.
Satin [saˈtɛ̃ː] *m* (-s/-s) satin; sateen.
Satir|e [zaˈtiːrə] *f* (-/-n) satire; ⁓iker [ˌ⁓ikər] *m* (-s/-) satirist; ⁑isch *adj.* satiric(al).
satt *adj.* [zat] satisfied, satiated, full; *colour:* deep, rich; *sich* ⁓ *essen* eat one's fill; *ich bin* ⁓ I have had enough; F *et.* ⁓ *haben* be tired *or* sick of s.th., *sl.* be fed up with s.th.
Sattel [ˈzatəl] *m* (-s/⁼) saddle; '⁓gurt *m* girth; '⁑n *v/t.* (ge-, h) saddle.
'Sattheit *f* (-/*no pl.*) satiety, fullness; richness, intensity (*of colours*).
sättig|en [ˈzɛtigən] (ge-, h) 1. *v/t.* satisfy, satiate; ⁂, *phys.* saturate; 2. *v/i. food:* be substantial; '⁑ung *f* (-/-en) satiation; ⁂, *fig.* saturation.
Sattler [ˈzatlər] *m* (-s/-) saddler; ⁓ei [ˌ⁓ˈrai] *f* (-/-en) saddlery.
'sattsam *adv.* sufficiently.
Satz [zats] *m* (-es/⁼e) *gr.* sentence, clause; *phls.* maxim; ♃ proposition, theorem; ♪ movement; *tennis, etc.:* set; *typ.* setting, composition; sediment, dregs *pl.*, grounds *pl.*; rate (*of prices, etc.*); set (*of stamps, tools, etc.*); leap, bound.
'Satzung *f* (-/-en) statute, by-law; '⁑sgemäß *adj.* statutory.
'Satzzeichen *gr.* *n* punctuation mark.
Sau [zau] *f* 1. (-/⁼e) *zo.* sow; *fig. contp.* filthy swine; 2. *hunt.* (-/-en) wild sow.
sauber *adj.* [ˈzaubər] clean; neat (*a. fig.*), tidy; attitude: decent; *iro.* fine, nice; '⁑keit *f* (-/*no pl.*) clean(li)ness; tidiness, neatness; decency (*of attitude*).
säuber|n [ˈzɔybərn] *v/t.* (ge-, h) clean(se); tidy, clean up (*room, etc.*); clear (*von* of); purge (*of, from*) (*a. fig., pol.*); '⁑ungsaktion *pol. f* purge.
sauer [ˈzauər] 1. *adj.* sour (*a. fig.*), acid (*a.* ⁂); *cucumber:* pickled; *task, etc.:* hard, painful; *fig.* morose,

surly; 2. *adv.:* ⁓ *reagieren auf et.* take s.th. in bad part.
säuer|lich *adj.* [ˈzɔyərliç] sourish, acidulous; '⁑n *v/t.* (ge-, h) (make) sour, acidify (*a.* ⁂); leaven (*dough*).
'Sauer|stoff ⁂ *m* (-[e]s/*no pl.*) oxygen; '⁑teig *m* leaven.
saufen [ˈzaufən] *v/t. and v/i.* (*irr.*, ge-, h) *animals:* drink; F *p. sl.* soak, lush.
Säufer F [ˈzɔyfər] *m* (-s/-) sot, *sl.* soak.
saugen [ˈzaugən] ([*irr.*,] ge-, h) 1. *v/i.* suck (*an et.* s.th.); 2. *v/t.* suck.
säuge|n [ˈzɔygən] *v/t.* (ge-, h) suckle, nurse; '⁑tier *n* mammal.
Säugling [ˈzɔyklɪŋ] *m* (-s/-e) baby, suckling; '⁓sheim *n* baby-farm, baby-nursery.
'Saug|papier *n* absorbent paper; '⁓pumpe *f* suction-pump; '⁓wirkung *f* suction-effect.
Säule [ˈzɔylə] *f* (-/-n) 🏛, *anat.* column (*a.* of smoke, mercury, *etc.*); pillar, support (*both a. fig.*); '⁓ngang *m* colonnade; '⁓nhalle *f* pillared hall; portico.
Saum [zaum] *m* (-[e]s/⁼e) seam, hem; border, edge.
säum|en [ˈzɔymən] *v/t.* (ge-, h) hem; border, edge; *die Straßen* ⁓ line the streets; '⁓ig *adj.* payer: dilatory.
'Saum|pfad *m* mule-track; '⁓tier *n* sumpter-mule.
Säure [ˈzɔyrə] *f* (-/-n) sourness; acidity (*a.* 💊 of stomach); ⁂ acid.
Saure'gurkenzeit *f* silly *or* slack season.
säuseln [ˈzɔyzəln] (ge-, h) 1. *v/i. leaves, wind:* rustle, whisper; 2. *v/t. p.* say airily, purr.
sausen [ˈzauzən] *v/i.* (ge-) 1. (*sein*) F rush, dash; *bullet, etc.:* whiz(z), whistle; 2. (h) *wind:* whistle, sough.
'Saustall *m* pigsty; F *fig. a.* horrid mess.
Saxophon ♪ [zaksoˈfoːn] *n* (-s/-e) saxophone.
Schab|e [ˈʃɑːbə] *f* (-/-n) *zo.* cockroach; ⊕ *s.* Schabeisen; '⁓efleisch *n* scraped meat; '⁓eisen ⊕ *n* scraper, shaving-tool; '⁓emesser ⊕ *n* scraping-knife; '⁑en *v/t.* (ge-, h) scrape (*a.* ⊕); grate, rasp; scratch; '⁓er ⊕ *m* (-s/-) scraper.
Schabernack [ˈʃɑːbərnak] *m* (-[e]s/-e) practical joke, hoax, prank.
schäbig *adj.* [ˈʃɛːbiç] shabby (*a. fig.*), F seedy, *Am.* F *a.* dowdy, tacky; *fig.* mean.
Schablone [ʃaˈbloːnə] *f* (-/-n) model, pattern; stencil; *fig.:* routine; cliché; ⁑nhaft *adj.*, ⁑nmäßig *adj.* according to pattern; *fig.:* mechanical; *attr. a.* routine.
Schach [ʃax] *n* (-s/-s) chess; ⁓! check!; ⁓ *und matt!* checkmate!;

in or im ~ *halten* keep s.o. in check; '~brett *n* chessboard.

schachern ['ʃaxərn] *v/i.* (ge-, h) haggle (*um* about, over), chaffer (about, over), Am. a. dicker; ~ *mit* barter (away).

'Schach|feld *n* square; '~figur *f* chess-man, piece; *fig.* pawn; '2-'matt *adj.* (check)mated; *fig.* tired out, worn out; '~spiel *n* game of chess. [a. pit.]

Schacht [ʃaxt] *m* (-[e]s/=e) shaft; ⚒)

Schachtel ['ʃaxtəl] *f* (-/-n) box; F *alte* ~ old frump.

'Schachzug *m* move (at chess); *geschickter* ~ clever move (a. fig.).

schade *pred. adj.* ['ʃaːdə]: *es ist* ~ it is a pity; *wie* ~*!* what a pity!; *zu* ~ *für* too good for.

Schädel ['ʃɛːdəl] *m* (-s/-) skull, cranium; '~bruch 𝒔 *m* fracture of the skull.

schaden ['ʃaːdən] 1. *v/i.* (ge-, h) damage, injure, harm, hurt (*j-m* s.o.); be detrimental (to s.o.); *das schadet nichts* it does not matter, never mind; 2. 2 *m* (-s/=) damage (*an dat.* to); injury, harm; infirmity; hurt; loss; '2ersatz *m* indemnification, compensation; damages *pl.*; ~ *verlangen* claim damages; ~ *leisten* pay damages; *auf* ~ *(ver)klagen* 𝑔𝑡𝑠 sue for damages; '2freude *f* malicious enjoyment of others' misfortunes, schadenfreude; '~froh *adj.* rejoicing over others' misfortunes.

schadhaft *adj.* ['ʃaːthaft] damaged; defective, faulty; *building, etc.*: dilapidated; *pipe, etc.*: leaking; *tooth, etc.*: decayed.

schädig|en ['ʃɛːdigən] *v/t.* (ge-, h) damage, impair, wrong, harm; '2ung *f* (-/-en) damage (*gen.* to), impairment (of); prejudice (to).

schädli|ch *adj.* ['ʃɛːtliç] harmful, injurious; noxious; detrimental; prejudicial; 2ng ['~ŋ] *m* (-s/-e) zo. pest; ♣ destructive weed; noxious person; ~*e pl.* 𝒔 *a.* vermin.

schadlos *adj.* ['ʃaːtloːs]: *sich* ~ *halten* recoup *or* idemnify o.s. (*für* for).

Schaf [ʃaːf] *n* (-[e]s/-e) zo. sheep; *fig.* simpleton; '~bock zo. *m* ram.

Schäfer ['ʃɛːfər] *m* (-s/-) shepherd; '~hund *m* sheep-dog; Alsatian (wolf-hound).

Schaffell ['ʃaːf²-] *n* sheepskin.

schaffen ['ʃafən] 1. *v/t.* (*irr.*, ge-, h) create, produce; 2. *v/t.* (ge-, h) convey, carry, move; take, bring; cope with, manage; 3. *v/i.* (ge-, h) be busy, work.

Schaffner ['ʃafnər] *m* (-s/-) 🚃 guard, Am. conductor; *tram, bus*: conductor.

'Schafhirt *m* shepherd.

Schafott [ʃa'fɔt] *n* (-[e]s/-e) scaffold.

'Schaf|pelz *m* sheepskin coat; '~stall *m* fold.

Schaft [ʃaft] *m* (-[e]s/=e) shaft (*of lance, column, etc.*); stick (*of flag*); stock (*of rifle*); shank (*of tool, key, etc.*); leg (*of boot*); '~stiefel *m* high boot; ~ *pl. a.* Wellingtons *pl.*

'Schaf|wolle *f* sheep's wool; '~zucht *f* sheep-breeding, sheep-farming.

schäkern ['ʃɛːkərn] *v/i.* (ge-, h) jest, joke; flirt.

schal[1] *adj.* [ʃaːl] insipid; stale; *fig. a.* flat.

Schal[2] [~] *m* (-s/-e, -s) scarf, muffler; comforter.

Schale ['ʃaːlə] *f* (-/-n) bowl; ⊕ scale (*of scales*); shell (*of eggs, nuts, etc.*); peel, skin (*of fruit*); shell, crust (*of tortoise*); paring, peeling; F: *sich in* ~ *werfen* doll o.s. up.

schälen ['ʃɛːlən] *v/t.* (ge-, h) remove the peel *or* skin from; pare, peel (*fruit, potatoes, etc.*); *sich* ~ *skin*: peel *or* come off.

Schalk [ʃalk] *m* (-[e]s/-e, =e) rogue, wag; '2haft *adj.* roguish, waggish.

Schall [ʃal] *m* (-[e]s/⸜-e, =e) sound; '~dämpfer *m* sound absorber; *mot.* silencer, Am. muffler; silencer (*on fire-arms*); '2dicht *adj.* soundproof; '2en *v/i.* ([irr.,] ge-, h) sound; ring, peal; '2end *adj.*: ~*es Gelächter* roars *pl.* or a peal of laughter; '~mauer *f* sound barrier; '~platte *f* record, disc, disk; '~welle *f* sound-wave.

schalt [ʃalt] *pret. of* schelten.

'Schaltbrett ⚡ *n* switchboard.

schalten ['ʃaltən] (ge-, h) 1. *v/i.* ⚡ switch; *mot.* change or shift gears; direct, rule; 2. *v/t.* ⊕ actuate; operate, control.

'Schalter *m* (-s/-) 🎭, *theatre, etc.*: booking-office; ✉, *bank, etc.*: counter; ⚡ switch; ⊕, *mot.* controller.

'Schalt|hebel *m mot.* gear lever; ⊕, ⚡ control lever; ⚡ switch lever; '~jahr *n* leap-year; '~tafel ⚡ *f* switchboard, control panel; '~tag *m* intercalary day.

Scham [ʃaːm] *f* (-/*no pl.*) shame; bashfulness, modesty; *anat.* privy parts *pl.*, genitals *pl.*

schämen ['ʃɛːmən] *v/refl.* (ge-, h) be *or* feel ashamed (*gen. or wegen* of).

'Scham|gefühl *n* sense of shame; '2haft *adj.* bashful, modest; '~haftigkeit *f* (-/*no pl.*) bashfulness, modesty; '2los *adj.* shameless; impudent; '~losigkeit *f* (-/-en) shamelessness; impudence; '2rot *adj.* blushing; ~ *werden* blush; '~röte *f* blush; '~teile *anat. m/pl.* privy parts *pl.*, genitals *pl.*

Schande ['ʃandə] *f* (-/⸜-n) shame, disgrace.

schänden ['ʃɛndən] *v/t.* (ge-, h)

dishono(u)r, disgrace; desecrate, profane; rape, violate; disfigure.
Schandfleck *fig.* ['ʃant-] *m* blot, stain; eyesore.
schändlich *adj.* ['ʃɛntliç] shameful, disgraceful, infamous; '**⁀keit** *f* (-/-en) infamy.
'**Schandtat** *f* infamous act(ion).
'**Schändung** *f* (-/-en) dishono(u)ring; profanation, desecration; rape, violation; disfigurement.
Schanze ['ʃantsə] *f* (-/-n) ⚔ entrenchment; ⚓ quarter-deck; *sports*: ski-jump; '**⁀n** *v/i.* (ge-, *h*) throw up entrenchments, entrench.
Schar [ʃa:r] *f* (-/-en) troop, band; *geese, etc.*: flock; ploughshare, *Am.* plowshare; '**⁀en** *v/t.* (ge-, *h*) assemble, collect; *sich* ~ *a.* flock (*um* round).
scharf [ʃarf] **1.** *adj.* sharp; *edge*: keen; *voice, sound*: piercing, shrill; *smell, taste*: pungent; *pepper, etc.*: hot; *sight, hearing, intelligence, etc.*: keen; *answer, etc.*: cutting; ⚔ *ammunition*: live; ~ *sein auf* (*acc.*) be very keen on; **2.** *adv.*: ~ *ansehen* look sharply at; ~ *reiten* ride hard; '**⁀blick** *fig. m* (-[e]s/*no pl.*) clear-sightedness.
Schärfe ['ʃɛrfə] *f* (-/-n) sharpness; keenness; pungency; '**⁀n** *v/t.* (ge-, *h*) put an edge on, sharpen; strengthen (*memory*); sharpen (*sight, hearing, etc.*).
'**Scharf|macher** *fig. m* (-s/-) firebrand, agitator; '**~richter** *m* executioner; '**~schütze** ⚔ *m* sharpshooter, sniper; '**⁀sichtig** *adj.* sharp-sighted; *fig.* clear-sighted; '**~sinn** *m* (-[e]s/*no pl.*) sagacity; acumen; '**⁀sinnig** *adj.* sharp-witted, shrewd; sagacious.
Scharlach ['ʃarlax] *m* **1.** (-s/-e) scarlet; **2.** ⚕ (-s/*no pl.*) scarlet fever; '**⁀rot** *adj.* scarlet.
Scharlatan ['ʃarlatan] *m* (-s/-e) charlatan, quack (doctor); mountebank.
Scharmützel [ʃar'mytsəl] *n* (-s/-) skirmish.
Scharnier ⊕ [ʃar'ni:r] *n* (-s/-e) hinge, joint.
Schärpe ['ʃɛrpə] *f* (-/-n) sash.
scharren ['ʃarən] (ge-, *h*) **1.** *v/i.* scrape (*mit den Füßen* one's feet); *hen, etc.*: scratch; *horse*: paw; **2.** *v/t.* *horse*: paw (*ground*).
Schart|e ['ʃartə] *f* (-/-n) notch, nick; *mountains*: gap, *Am.* notch; e-e ~ *auswetzen* repair a fault; wipe out a disgrace; '**⁀ig** *adj.* jagged, notchy.
Schatten ['ʃatən] *m* (-s/-) shadow (*a. fig.*); shade (*a. paint.*); '**~bild** *n* silhouette; '**⁀haft** *adj.* shadowy; '**~kabinett** *pol. n* shadow cabinet; '**~riß** *m* silhouette; '**~seite** *f* shady side; *fig.* seamy side.

schattier|en [ʃa'ti:rən] *v/t.* (*no* -ge-, *h*) shade, tint; **⁀ung** *f* (-/-en) shading; shade (*a. fig.*), tint.
'**schattig** *adj.* shady.
Schatz [ʃats] *m* (-es/⸚e) treasure; *fig.* sweetheart, darling; '**~amt** ✝ *n* Exchequer, *Am.* Treasury (Department); '**~anweisung** ✝ *f* Treasury Bond, *Am. a.* Treasury Note.
schätzen ['ʃɛtsən] *v/t.* (ge-, *h*) estimate; value (*auf acc.* at); price (at); rate; appreciate; esteem; *sich glücklich* ~ *zu inf.* be delighted to *inf.*; '**~swert** *adj.* estimable.
'**Schatz|kammer** *f* treasury; '**~meister** *m* treasurer.
'**Schätzung** *f* **1.** (-/-en) estimate, valuation; rating; **2.** (-/*no pl.*) appreciation, estimation; esteem.
'**Schatzwechsel** ✝ *m* Treasury Bill.
Schau [ʃaʊ] *f* (-/-en) inspection; show, exhibition; *zur* ~ *stellen* exhibit, display.
Schauder ['ʃaʊdər] *m* (-s/-) shudder(ing), shiver, tremor; *fig.* horror, terror; '**⁀haft** *adj.* horrible, dreadful; F *fig. a.* awful; '**⁀n** *v/i.* (ge-, *h*) shudder, shiver (*both*: *vor dat.* at).
schauen ['ʃaʊən] *v/i.* (ge-, *h*) look (*auf acc.* at).
Schauer ['ʃaʊər] *m* (-s/-) *rain, etc.*: shower (*a. fig.*); shudder(ing), shiver; attack, fit; thrill; '**⁀lich** *adj.* dreadful, horrible; '**⁀n** *v/i.* (ge-, *h*) *s. schaudern*; '**~roman** *m* penny dreadful, thriller.
Schaufel ['ʃaʊfəl] *f* (-/-n) shovel; dust-pan; '**⁀n** *v/t. and v/i.* (ge-, *h*) shovel.
'**Schaufenster** *n* shop window, *Am. a.* show-window; '**~bummel** *m*: e-n ~ *machen* go window-shopping; '**~dekoration** *f* window-dressing; '**~einbruch** *m* smash-and-grab raid.
Schaukel ['ʃaʊkəl] *f* (-/-n) swing; '**⁀n** (ge-, *h*) **1.** *v/i.* swing; *ship, etc.*: rock; **2.** *v/t.* rock (*baby, etc.*); '**~pferd** *n* rocking-horse; '**~stuhl** *m* rocking-chair, *Am. a.* rocker.
Schaum [ʃaʊm] *m* (-[e]s/⸚e) foam; *beer, etc.*: froth, head; *soap*: lather; '**~bad** *n* bubble bath.
schäumen ['ʃɔʏmən] *v/i.* (ge-, *h*) foam, froth; lather; *wine, etc.*: sparkle.
'**Schaum|gummi** *n, m* foam rubber; **⁀ig** *adj.* foamy, frothy; '**~wein** *m* sparkling wine.
'**Schau|platz** *m* scene (of action), theat|re, *Am.* -er; '**~prozeß** ⚖ *m* show trial.
schaurig *adj.* ['ʃaʊriç] horrible, horrid.
'**Schau|spiel** *n* spectacle; *thea.* play; '**~spieler** *m* actor, player; '**~spielhaus** *n* playhouse, theat|re, *Am.* -er; '**~spielkunst** *f* (-/*no pl.*) dra-

matic art, *the* drama; '**~steller** *m* (-s/-) showman.

Scheck ✛ [ʃɛk] *m* (-s/-s) cheque, *Am.* check; '**~buch** *n*, '**~heft** *n* cheque-book, *Am.* checkbook.

'**scheckig** *adj.* spotted; *horse:* piebald.

scheel [ʃeːl] **1.** *adj.* squint-eyed, cross-eyed; *fig.* jealous, envious; **2.** *adv.:* j-n ~ ansehen look askance at s.o.

Scheffel ['ʃɛfəl] *m* (-s/-) bushel; '**2n** *v/t.* (ge-, h) amass (*money, etc.*).

Scheibe ['ʃaɪbə] *f* (-/-n) disk, disc (*a. of sun, moon*); *esp. ast.* orb; slice (*of bread, etc.*); pane (*of window*); *shooting:* target; '**~nhonig** *m* honey in combs; '**~nwischer** *mot. m* (-s/-) wind-screen wiper, *Am.* windshield wiper.

Scheide ['ʃaɪdə] *f* (-/-n) sword, *etc.*: sheath, scabbard; border, boundary; '**~münze** *f* small coin; '**2n** (*irr.,* ge-) **1.** *v/t.* (h) separate; $\frac{n}{m}$ analyse; *sich* ~ *lassen von* $\frac{v}{12}$ divorce (*one's husband or wife*); **2.** *v/i.* (sein) depart; part (*von* with); *aus dem Dienst* ~ retire from service; *aus dem Leben* ~ depart from this life; '**~wand** *f* partition; '**~weg** *fig. m* cross-roads *sg.*

'**Scheidung** *f* (-/-en) separation; $\frac{v}{12}$ divorce; '**~sgrund** $\frac{v}{12}$ *m* ground for divorce; '**~sklage** $\frac{v}{12}$ *f* divorce-suit; *die* ~ *einreichen* file a petition for divorce.

Schein [ʃaɪn] *m* **1.** (-[e]s/no *pl.*) shine; *sun, lamp, etc.*: light; *fire:* blaze; *fig.* appearance. **2.** (-[e]s/-e) certificate; receipt; bill; (bank-) note; '**2bar** *adj.* seeming, apparent; '**2en** *v/i.* (*irr.,* ge-, h) shine; *fig.* seem, appear, look; '**~grund** *m* pretext, preten|ce, *Am.* -se; '**2heilig** *adj.* sanctimonious, hypocritical; '**~tod** ⚕ *m* suspended animation; '**2tot** *adj.* in a state of suspended animation; '**~werfer** *m* (-s/-) reflector, projector; ✕, ⚓, searchlight; *mot.* headlight; *thea.* spotlight.

Scheit [ʃaɪt] *n* (-[e]s/-e) log, billet.

Scheitel ['ʃaɪtəl] *m* (-s/-) crown *or* top of the head; *hair:* parting; summit, peak; *esp.* Å vertex; '**2n** *v/t.* (ge-, h) part (*hair*).

Scheiterhaufen ['ʃaɪtər-] *m* (funeral) pile; stake.

'**scheitern** *v/i.* (ge-, sein) ⚓ run aground, be wrecked; *fig.* fail, miscarry. [box on the ear.]

Schelle ['ʃɛlə] *f* (-/-n) (little) bell;

'**Schellfisch** *ichth. m* haddock.

Schelm [ʃɛlm] *m* (-[e]s/-e) rogue; '**~enstreich** *m* roguish trick; '**2isch** *adj.* roguish, arch.

Schelte ['ʃɛltə] *f* (-/-n) scolding; '**2n** (*irr.,* ge-, h) **1.** *v/t.* scold, rebuke; **2.** *v/i.* scold.

Schema ['ʃeːma] *n* (-s/-s, -ta, Sche-men) scheme; model, pattern; arrangement; **2tisch** *adj.* [ʃeˈmɑːtiʃ] schematic.

Schemel ['ʃeːməl] *m* (-s/-) stool.

Schemen ['ʃeːmən] *m* (-s/-) phantom, shadow; '**2haft** *adj.* shadowy.

Schenke ['ʃɛŋkə] *f* (-/-n) public house, F pub; tavern, inn.

Schenkel ['ʃɛŋkəl] *m* (-s/-) *anat.* thigh; *anat.* shank; *triangle, etc.*: leg; Å *angle:* side.

schenken ['ʃɛŋkən] *v/t.* (ge-, h) give; remit (*penalty, etc.*); j-m et. ~ give s.o. s.th., present s.o. with s.th., make s.o. a present of s.th.

'**Schenkung** $\frac{v}{12}$ *f* (-/-en) donation; '**~surkunde** $\frac{v}{12}$ ['ʃɛŋkuŋsʔ-] *f* deed of gift.

Scherbe ['ʃɛrbə] *f* (-/-n), '**~n** *m* (-s/-) (broken) piece, fragment.

Schere ['ʃeːrə] *f* (-/-n) (e-e a pair of) scissors *pl.*; *zo. crab, etc.*: claw; '**2n** *v/t.* **1.** (*irr.,* ge-, h) shear (*a. sheep*); clip; shave (*beard*); cut (*hair*); clip, prune (*hedge*); **2.** (ge-, h): *sich um* et. ~ trouble about s.th.; '**~nschleifer** *m* (-s/-) knife-grinder; '**~rei** [~ˈraɪ] *f* (-/-en) trouble, bother.

Scherz [ʃɛrts] *m* (-es/-e) jest, joke; ~ *beiseite* joking apart; *im* ~, *zum* ~ in jest *or* joke; ~ *treiben mit* make fun of; '**2en** *v/i.* (ge-, h) jest, joke; '**2haft** *adj.* joking, sportive.

scheu [ʃɔy] **1.** *adj.* shy, bashful, timid; *horse:* skittish; ~ *machen* frighten; **2.** ♀ *f* (-/no *pl.*) shyness; timidity; aversion (*vor dat.* to).

scheuchen ['ʃɔyçən] *v/t.* (ge-, h) scare, frighten (away).

'**scheuen** (ge-, h) **1.** *v/i.* shy (*vor dat.* at), take fright (at); **2.** *v/t.* shun, avoid; fear; *sich* ~ *vor* (*dat.*) shy at, be afraid of.

Scheuer|lappen ['ʃɔyər-] *m* scouring-cloth, floor-cloth; '**~leiste** *f* skirting-board; '**2n** (ge-, h) **1.** *v/t.* scour, scrub; chafe; **2.** *v/i.* chafe.

'**Scheuklappe** *f* blinker, *Am. a.* blinder.

Scheune ['ʃɔynə] *f* (-/-n) barn.

Scheusal ['ʃɔyzaːl] *n* (-[e]s/-e) monster.

scheußlich ['ʃɔysliç] hideous, atrocious (F *a. fig.*), abominable (F *a. fig.*); '**2keit** *f* **1.** (-/no *pl.*) hideousness; **2.** (-/-en) abomination; atrocity.

Schi [ʃiː] *m* (-s/-er) *etc. s.* Ski, *etc.*

Schicht [ʃɪçt] *f* (-/-en) layer; *geol.* stratum (*a. fig.*); *at work:* shift; (social) class, rank, walk of life; '**2en** *v/t.* (ge-, h) arrange *or* put in layers, pile up; classify; '**2weise** *adv.* in layers; *work:* in shifts.

Schick [ʃɪk] **1.** *m* (-[e]s/no *pl.*) chic, elegance, style; **2.** ♀ *adj.* chic, stylish, fashionable.

schicken ['ʃɪkən] *v/t.* (ge-, h) send

(nach, zu to); remit (money); nach j-m ~ send for s.o.; sich ~ für become, suit, befit s.o.; sich ~ in put up with, resign o.s. to s.th.

'schicklich adj. becoming, proper, seemly; '2keit f (-/no pl.) propriety, seemliness.

'Schicksal n (-[e]s/-e) fate, destiny.

Schiebe|dach mot. ['ʃiːbə-] n sliding roof; '~fenster n sash-window; '2n (irr., ge-, h) 1. v/t. push, shove; shift (blame) (auf acc. on to); F fig. sell on the black market; 2. F fig. v/i. profiteer; '~r m (-s/-) bolt (of door); ⊕ slide; fig. profiteer, black marketeer, sl. spiv; '~tür f sliding door.

'Schiebung fig. f (-/-en) black marketeering, profiteering; put-up job.

schied [ʃiːt] pret. of scheiden.

Schieds|gericht ['ʃiːts-] n court of arbitration, arbitration committee; '~richter m arbitrator; tennis, etc.: umpire; football, etc.: referee; '2richterlich adj. arbitral; '~spruch m award, arbitration.

schief [ʃiːf] 1. adj. sloping, slanting; oblique; face, mouth: wry; fig. false, wrong; ~e Ebene ⚡ inclined plane; 2. adv.: j-n ~ ansehen look askance at s.o.

Schiefer ['ʃiːfər] m (-s/-) slate; splinter; '~stift m slate-pencil; '~tafel f slate.

'schiefgehen v/i. (irr. gehen, sep., -ge-, sein) go wrong or awry.

schielen ['ʃiːlən] v/i. (ge-, h) squint, be cross-eyed; ~ auf (acc.) squint at; leer at.

schien [ʃiːn] pret. of scheinen.

Schienbein ['ʃiːn-] n shin(-bone), tibia.

Schiene ['ʃiːnə] f (-/-n) 🚊, etc.: rail; 🗲 splint; '2n 🗲 v/t. (ge-, h) splint.

schießen ['ʃiːsən] (irr., ge-) 1. v/t. (h) shoot; tot ~ shoot dead; ein Tor ~ score (a goal); Salut ~ fire a salute; 2. v/i. (h): auf j-n ~ shoot or fire at; gut ~ be a good shot; 3. v/i. (sein) shoot, dart, rush.

'Schieß|pulver n gunpowder; '~scharte 🗲 f loop-hole, embrasure; '~scheibe f target; '~stand m shooting-gallery or -range.

Schiff [ʃif] n (-[e]s/-e) ⚓ ship, vessel; △ church: nave.

Schiffahrt ['ʃiffaːrt] f (-/-en) navigation.

'schiff|bar adj. navigable; '2bau m shipbuilding; '2bauer m (-s/-) shipbuilder; '2bruch m shipwreck (a. fig.); ~ erleiden be shipwrecked; fig. make or suffer shipwreck; '~brüchig adj. shipwrecked; '2brücke f pontoon-bridge; '~en v/i. (ge-, sein) navigate, sail; '2er

m (-s/-) sailor; boatman; navigator; skipper.

'Schiffs|junge m cabin-boy; '~kapitän m (sea-)captain; '~ladung f shipload; cargo; '~makler m shipbroker; '~mannschaft f crew; '~raum m hold; tonnage; '~werft f shipyard, esp. ⚓ dockyard, Am. a. navy yard.

Schikan|e [ʃiˈkaːnə] f (-/-n) vexation, nasty trick; 2ieren [~kaˈniːrən] v/t. (no -ge-, h) vex, ride.

Schild [ʃilt] 1. 🗲 m (-[e]s/-e) shield, buckler; 2. n (-[e]s/-er) shop, etc.: sign(board), facia; name-plate; traffic: signpost; label; cap: peak; '~drüse anat. f thyroid gland.

'Schilder|haus n 🗲 sentry-box; '~maler m sign-painter; '2n v/t. (ge-, h) describe, delineate; '~ung f (-/-en) description, delineation.

'Schild|kröte zo. f tortoise; turtle; '~wache 🗲 f sentinel, sentry.

Schilf ⚘ [ʃilf] n (-[e]s/-e) reed; '2ig adj. reedy; '~rohr n reed.

schillern ['ʃilərn] v/i. (ge-, h) show changing colo(u)rs; be iridescent.

Schimmel ['ʃiməl] m 1. zo. (-s/-) white horse; 2. ⚘ (-s/no pl.) mo(u)ld, mildew; '2ig adj. mo(u)ldy, musty; '2n v/i. (ge-, h) become mo(u)ldy, Am. a. mo(u)ld.

Schimmer ['ʃimər] m (-s/no pl.) glimmer, gleam (a. fig.); '2n v/i. (ge-, h) glimmer, gleam.

Schimpanse zo. [ʃimˈpanzə] m (-n/-n) chimpanzee.

Schimpf [ʃimpf] m (-[e]s/-e) insult; disgrace; mit ~ und Schande ignominiously; '2en (ge-, h) 1. v/i. rail (über acc., auf acc. at, against); 2. v/t. scold; j-n e-n Lügner ~ call s.o. a liar; '2lich adj. disgraceful (für to), ignominious (to); '~name m abusive name; '~wort n term of abuse; ~e pl. a. invectives pl.

Schindel ['ʃindəl] f (-/-n) shingle.

schinden ['ʃindən] v/t. (irr., ge-, h) flay, skin (rabbit, etc.); sweat (worker); sich ~ drudge, slave, sweat.

'Schinder m (-s/-) knacker; fig. sweater, slave-driver; ~ei fig. [~'rai] f (-/-en) sweating; drudgery, grind.

Schinken ['ʃinkən] m (-s/-) ham.

Schippe ['ʃipə] f (-/-n) shovel; '2n v/t. (ge-, h) shovel.

Schirm [ʃirm] m (-[e]s/-e) umbrella; parasol, sunshade; wind, television, etc.: screen; lamp: shade; cap: peak, visor; '~futteral n umbrella-case; '~herr m protector; patron; '~herrschaft f protectorate; patronage; unter der ~ von event: under the auspices of; '~mütze f peaked cap; '~ständer m umbrella-stand.

Schlacht 🗲 [ʃlaxt] f (-/-en) battle (bei of); '~bank f shambles; '2en v/t. (ge-, h) slaughter, butcher.

15*

Schlächter ['ʃlɛçtər] *m* (-s/-) butcher.

'**Schlacht|feld** ✗ *n* battle-field; '**‿haus** *n,* '**‿hof** *m* slaughter-house, abattoir; '**‿kreuzer** ⚓ *m* battle-cruiser; '**‿plan** *m* ✗ plan of action (*a. fig.*); '**‿schiff** ⚓ *n* battleship; '**‿vieh** *n* slaughter cattle.

Schlack|e ['ʃlakə] *f* (-/-n) *wood, coal:* cinder; *metall.* dross (*a. fig.*), slag; *geol.* scoria; '**2ig** *adj.* drossy, slaggy; F *weather:* slushy.

Schlaf [ʃlaːf] *m* (-[e]s/no *pl.*) sleep; *im* ‿(e) in one's sleep; *e-n leichten (festen)* ‿ *haben* be a light (sound) sleeper; *in tiefem ‿e liegen* be fast asleep; '**‿abteil** 🚂 *n* sleeping-compartment; '**‿anzug** *m* (*ein a* pair of) pyjamas *pl. or Am.* pajamas *pl.*

Schläfchen ['ʃleːfçən] *n* (-s/-) doze, nap, F forty winks *pl.*; *ein* ‿ *machen* take a nap, F have one's forty winks.

'**Schlafdecke** *f* blanket.

Schläfe ['ʃleːfə] *f* (-/-n) temple.

'**schlafen** *v/i.* (*irr.,* ge-, h) sleep; ‿ *gehen, sich* ‿ *legen* go to bed.

schlaff *adj.* [ʃlaf] slack, loose; *muscles, etc.:* flabby, flaccid; *plant, etc.:* limp; *discipline, morals, etc.:* lax; '**2heit** *f* (-/no *pl.*) slackness; flabbiness; limpness; *fig.* laxity.

'**Schlaf|gelegenheit** *f* sleeping accommodation; '**‿kammer** *f* bedroom; '**‿krankheit** 🐛 *f* sleeping-sickness; '**‿lied** *n* lullaby; '**2los** *adj.* sleepless; '**‿losigkeit** *f* (-/no *pl.*) sleeplessness, 🐛 insomnia; '**‿mittel** 🐛 *n* soporific; '**‿mütze** *f* nightcap; *fig.* sleepyhead.

schläfrig *adj.* ['ʃleːfriç] sleepy, drowsy; '**2keit** *f* (-/no *pl.*) sleepiness, drowsiness.

'**Schlaf|rock** *m* dressing-gown, Am. *a.* robe; '**‿saal** *m* dormitory; '**‿sack** *m* sleeping-bag; '**‿stelle** *f* sleeping-place; night's lodging; '**‿tablette** 🐛 *f* sleeping-tablet; '**2trunken** *adj.* very drowsy; '**‿wagen** 🚂 *m* sleeping-car(riage), Am. *a.* sleeper; '**‿wandler** ['‿vandlər] *m* (-s/-) sleep-walker, somnambulist; '**‿zimmer** *n* bedroom.

Schlag [ʃlaːk] *m* (-[e]s/ʷe) blow (*a. fig.*); stroke (*of clock, piston*) (*a. tennis, etc.*); slap (*with palm of hand*); punch (*with fist*); kick (*of horse's hoof*); 🔌 shock; beat (*of heart or pulse*); clap (*of thunder*); warbling (*of bird*); door (*of carriage*); 🐛 apoplexy; *fig.* race, kind, sort; breed (*esp. of animals*); *Schläge bekommen* get a beating; ‿ *sechs Uhr* on the stroke of six; '**‿ader** *anat.* *f* artery; '**‿anfall** 🐛 *m* (stroke of) apoplexy, stroke; '**2artig 1.** *adj.* sudden, abrupt; **2.** *adv.* all of a sudden; '**‿baum** *m* turnpike.

schlagen ['ʃlaːgən] (*irr.,* ge-, h) **1.** *v/t.* strike, beat, hit; punch; slap; beat, defeat; fell (*trees*); fight (*battle*); *Alarm* ‿ sound the alarm; *zu Boden* ‿ knock down; *in den Wind* ‿ cast *or* fling to the winds; *sich* ‿ (have a) fight; *sich et. aus dem Kopf or Sinn* ‿ put s.th. out of one's mind, dismiss s.th. from one's mind; **2.** *v/i.* strike, beat; *heart, pulse:* beat, throb; *clock:* strike; *bird:* warble; *das schlägt nicht in mein Fach* that is not in my line; *um sich* ‿ lay about one; '**‿d** *fig. adj.* striking.

Schlager ['ʃlaːgər] *m* (-s/-) ♪ song hit; *thea.* hit, draw, box-office success; *book:* best seller.

Schläger ['ʃleːgər] *m* (-s/-) rowdy, hooligan; *cricket, etc.:* batsman; *horse:* kicker; *cricket, etc.:* bat; *golf:* club; *tennis, etc.:* racket; *hockey, etc.:* stick; **‿ei** [‿'raɪ] *f* (-/-en) tussle, fight.

'**schlag|fertig** *fig. adj.* quick at repartee; **‿e** *Antwort* repartee; '**2fertigkeit** *fig. f* (-/no *pl.*) quickness at repartee; '**2instrument** ♪ *n* percussion instrument; '**2kraft** *f* (-/no *pl.*) striking power (*a.* ✗); '**2loch** *n* pot-hole; '**2mann** *m rowing:* stroke; '**2ring** *m* knuckle-duster, Am. *a.* brass knuckles *pl.*; '**2sahne** *f* whipped cream; '**2schatten** *m* cast shadow; '**2seite** ⚓ *f* list; ‿ *haben* ⚓ f List; F *fig.* be half-seas-over; '**2uhr** *f* striking clock; '**2werk** *n clock:* striking mechanism; '**2wort** *n* catchword, slogan; '**2zeile** *f* headline; banner headline, Am. banner; '**2zeug** ♪ *n in orchestra:* percussion instruments *pl.*; *in band:* drums *pl.,* percussion; '**2zeuger** ♪ *m* (-s/-) *in orchestra:* percussionist; *in band:* drummer.

schlaksig *adj.* ['ʃlaːksiç] gawky.

Schlamm [ʃlam] *m* (-[e]s/ʷ-e, ʷe) mud, mire; '**‿bad** *n* mud-bath; '**2ig** *adj.* muddy, miry.

Schlämmkreide ['ʃlɛm-] *f* (-/no *pl.*) whit(en)ing.

Schlamp|e ['ʃlampə] *f* (-/-n) slut, slattern; '**2ig** *adj.* slovenly, slipshod.

schlang [ʃlaŋ] *pret. of* schlingen.

Schlange ['ʃlaŋə] *f* (-/-n) *zo.* snake, *rhet.* serpent (*a. fig.*); *fig.*: snake in the grass; queue, Am. *a.* line; ‿ *stehen* queue up (*um for*), Am. line up (for).

schlängeln ['ʃlɛŋəln] *v/refl.* (ge-, h): *sich* ‿ *durch person:* worm one's way *or* o.s. through; *path, river, etc.*: wind (one's way) through, meander through.

'**Schlangenlinie** *f* serpentine line.

schlank *adj.* [ʃlaŋk] slender, slim; '**2heit** *f* (-/no *pl.*) slenderness, slimness; '**2heitskur** *f*: *e-e* ‿ *machen* slim.

schlapp F *adj.* [ʃlap] tired, exhausted,

worn out; '₂e F f (-/-n) reverse, set-back; defeat; '₄machen F v/i. (sep., -ge-, h) break down, faint.

schlau adj. [ʃlaʊ] sly, cunning; crafty, clever, F cute.

Schlauch [ʃlaʊx] m (-[e]s/₄e) tube; hose; car, etc.: inner tube; '₄boot n rubber dinghy, pneumatic boat.

Schlaufe ['ʃlaʊfə] f (-/-n) loop.

schlecht [ʃlɛçt] 1. adj. bad; wicked; poor; temper: ill; quality: inferior; ₄e Laune haben be in a bad temper; ₄e Aussichten poor prospects; ₄e Zeiten hard times; mir ist ₄ I feel sick; 2. adv. badly, ill; ₄erdings adv. ['₄ɔːr'dɪŋs] absolutely, down-right, utterly; ₄gelaunt adj. ['₄gə-laʊnt] ill-humo(u)red, in a bad temper; '₄hin adv. plainly, simply; '₂igkeit f (-/-en) badness; wicked-ness; ₄en pl. base acts pl., mean tricks pl.; '₄machen v/t. (sep., -ge-, h) run down, backbite; ₄weg adv. ['₄vɛk] plainly, simply.

schleich|en ['ʃlaɪçən] v/i. (irr., ge-, sein) creep (a. fig.); sneak, steal; '₂er m (-s/-) creeper; fig. sneak; '₂handel m illicit trade; smuggling, contraband; '₂händler m smuggler, contrabandist; black marketeer; '₂weg m secret path.

Schleier ['ʃlaɪər] m (-s/-) veil (a. fig.); mist: a. haze; den ₄ nehmen take the veil; '₂haft fig. adj. mys-terious, inexplicable.

Schleife ['ʃlaɪfə] f (-/-n) loop (a. ⚡); slip-knot; bow; wreath: streamer; loop, horse-shoe bend.

'**schleif|en 1.** v/t. (irr., ge-, h) whet (knife, etc.); cut (glass, precious stones); polish (a. fig.); 2. v/t. (ge-, h) ₂ slur; drag, trail; ✗ raze (for-tress, etc.); 3. v/i. (ge-, h) drag, trail; '₂stein m grindstone, whet-stone.

Schleim [ʃlaɪm] m (-[e]s/-e) slime; 🌿 mucus, phlegm; '₄haut anat. f mucous membrane; '₂ig adj. slimy (a. fig.); mucous.

schlemm|en ['ʃlɛmən] v/i. (ge-, h) feast, gormandize; '₂er m (-s/-) glutton, gormandizer; ₂erei [₄'raɪ] f (-/-en) feasting, gluttony.

schlen|dern ['ʃlɛndərn] v/i. (ge-, sein) stroll, saunter; ₂drian ['₄driaːn] m (-[e]s/no pl.) jogtrot; beaten track.

schlenkern ['ʃlɛŋkərn] (ge-, h) 1. v/t. dangle, swing; 2. v/i.: mit den Armen ₄ swing one's arms.

Schlepp|dampfer ['ʃlɛp-] m steam tug, tug(boat); '₄e f (-/-n) train (of woman's dress); '₂en (ge-, h) 1. v/t. carry with difficulty, haul, Am. F a. tote; ⚓, ⚡, mot. tow, haul; ⚓ tug; ✝ tout (customers); sich ₄ drag o.s.; 2. v/i. dress: drag, trail; '₂end fig. speech: drawling; gait: shuffling; style: heavy; con-

versation, etc.: tedious; '₄er ⚓ m (-s/-) steam tug, tug(boat); '₄tau n tow(ing)-rope; ins ₄ nehmen take in or on tow (a. fig.).

Schleuder ['ʃlɔʏdər] f (-/-n) sling, catapult (a. ⚡), Am. a. slingshot; spin drier; '₂n (ge-, h) 1. v/t. fling, hurl (a. fig.); sling, catapult (a. ⚡); spin-dry (washing); 2. mot. v/i. skid; '₄preis ✝ m ruinous or give-away price; zu ₄en dirt-cheap.

schleunig adj. ['ʃlɔʏnɪç] prompt, speedy, quick.

Schleuse ['ʃlɔʏzə] f (-/-n) lock, sluice; '₂n v/t. (ge-, h) lock (boat) (up or down); fig. manœuvre, Am. maneuver.

schlich [ʃlɪç] pret. of schleichen.

schlicht adj. [ʃlɪçt] plain, simple; modest, unpretentious; hair: smooth, sleek; '₄en fig. v/t. (ge-, h) settle, adjust; settle by arbitration; '₂er fig. m (-s/-) mediator; arbitra-tor.

schlief [ʃliːf] pret. of schlafen.

schließ|en ['ʃliːsən] (irr., ge-, h) 1. v/t. shut, close; shut down (factory, etc.); shut up (shop); con-tract (marriage); conclude (treaty, speech, etc.); parl. close (debate); in die Arme ₄ clasp in one's arms; in sich ₄ comprise, include; Freund-schaft ₄ make friends (mit with); 2. v/i. shut, close; school: break up; aus et. ₄ auf (acc.) infer or conclude s.th. from s.th.; '₂fach ⚙ n post-office box; '₄lich adv. finally, eventually; at last; after all.

Schliff [ʃlɪf] 1. m (-[e]s/-e) polish (a. fig.); precious stones, glass: cut; 2. ② pret. of schleifen 1.

schlimm [ʃlɪm] 1. adj. bad; evil, wicked, nasty; serious; F 🌿 bad, sore; ₄er worse; am ₄sten, das ②ste the worst; es wird immer ₄er things are going from bad to worse; 2. adv.: ₄ daran sein be badly off; '₄sten'falls adv. at (the) worst.

Schling|e ['ʃlɪŋə] f (-/-n) loop, sling (a. 🌿); noose; coil (of wire or rope); hunt. snare (a. fig.); den Kopf in die ₄ stecken put one's head in the noose; '₄el m (-s/-) rascal, naughty boy; '₂en v/t. (irr., ge-, h) wind, twist; plait; die Arme ₄ um (acc.) fling one's arms round; sich um et. ₄ wind round; '₄pflanze ⚘ f creeper, climber.

Schlips [ʃlɪps] m (-es/-e) (neck)tie.

Schlitten ['ʃlɪtən] m (-s/-) sled(ge); sleigh; sports: toboggan.

'**Schlittschuh** m skate; ₄ laufen skate; '₄läufer m skater.

Schlitz [ʃlɪts] m (-es/-e) slit, slash; slot; '₂en v/t. (ge-, h) slit, slash.

Schloß [ʃlɔs] 1. n (Schlosses/Schlös-ser) lock (of door, gun, etc.); castle; palace; ins ₄ fallen door: snap to;

hinter ~ *und Riegel* behind prison bars; **2.** ♀ *pret. of* schließen.

Schlosser ['ʃlɔsər] *m* (-s/-) locksmith; mechanic, fitter.

Schlot [ʃloːt] *m* (-[e]s/-e, ⁼e) chimney; flue; ♄, ⚓ funnel; '~feger *m* (-s/-) chimney-sweep(er).

schlotter|ig *adj.* ['ʃlɔtəriç] shaky, tottery; loose; '~n *v/i.* (ge-, h) *garment*: hang loosely; *p.* shake, tremble (*both*: *vor dat.* with).

Schlucht [ʃluxt] *f* (-/-en) gorge, mountain cleft; ravine, *Am. a.* gulch.

schluchzen ['ʃluxtsən] *v/i.* (ge-, h) sob.

Schluck [ʃluk] *m* (-[e]s/-e, ⁼e) draught, swallow; mouthful, sip; '~auf *m* (-s/*no pl.*) hiccup(s *pl.*).

'schlucken 1. *v/t. and v/i.* swallow (*a. fig.*); **2.** ♀ *m* (-s/*no pl.*) hiccup(s *pl.*).

schlug [ʃluːk] *pret. of* schlagen.

Schlummer ['ʃlumər] *m* (-s/*no pl.*) slumber; '~n *v/i.* (ge-, h) slumber.

Schlund [ʃlunt] *m* (-[e]s/⁼e) *anat.* pharynx; *fig.* abyss, chasm, gulf.

schlüpf|en ['ʃlypfən] *v/i.* (ge-, sein) slip, slide; *in die Kleider* ~ slip on one's clothes; *aus den Kleidern* ~ slip out of *or* slip off one's clothes; '₂er *m* (-s/-) (*ein a pair of*) knickers *pl. or* drawers *pl. or* F panties *pl.*; briefs *pl.*

Schlupfloch ['ʃlupf-] *n* loop-hole.

'schlüpfrig *adj.* slippery; *fig.* lascivious.

'Schlupfwinkel *m* hiding-place.

schlurfen ['ʃlurfən] *v/i.* (ge-, sein) shuffle, drag one's feet.

schlürfen ['ʃlyrfən] *v/t. and v/i.* (ge-, h) drink *or* eat noisily; sip.

Schluß [ʃlus] *m* (Schlusses/Schlüsse) close, end; conclusion; *parl.* closing (*of debate*).

Schlüssel ['ʃlysəl] *m* (-s/-) key (zu of; *fig.* to); ♪ clef; *fig.*: code; quota; '~bart *m* key-bit; '~bein *anat. n* collar-bone, clavicle; '~bund *m, n* (-[e]s/-e) bunch of keys; '~industrie *fig. f* key industry; '~loch *n* keyhole; '~ring *m* key-ring.

'Schluß|folgerung *f* conclusion, inference; '~formel *f in letter*: complimentary close.

schlüssig *adj.* ['ʃlysiç] *evidence*: conclusive; *sich* ~ *werden* make up one's mind (*über acc.* about).

'Schluß|licht *n* ⚓, *mot., etc.*: taillight; *sports*: last runner; bottom club; '~runde *f sports*: final; '~schein ♰ *m* contract-note.

Schmach [ʃmaːx] *f* (-/*no pl.*) disgrace; insult; humiliation.

schmachten ['ʃmaxtən] *v/i.* (ge-, h) languish (*nach for*), pine (for).

schmächtig *adj.* ['ʃmɛçtiç] slender, slim; *ein* ~*er Junge* a (mere) slip of a boy.

'schmachvoll *adj.* disgraceful; humiliating.

schmackhaft *adj.* ['ʃmakhaft] palatable, savo(u)ry.

schmäh|en ['ʃmɛːən] *v/t.* (ge-, h) abuse, revile; decry, disparage; slander, defame; '~lich *adj.* ignominious, disgraceful; '₂schrift *f* libel, lampoon; '₂ung *f* (-/-en) abuse; slander, defamation.

schmal *adj.* [ʃmaːl] narrow; *figure*: slender, slim; *face*: thin; *fig.* poor, scanty.

schmäler|n ['ʃmɛːlərn] *v/t.* (ge-, h) curtail; impair; belittle; '₂ung *f* (-/-en) curtailment; impairment; detraction.

'Schmal|film *phot. m* substandard film; '~spur ⚓ *f* narrow ga(u)ge; '~spurbahn ⚓ *f* narrow-ga(u)ge railway; '₂spurig ⚓ *adj.* narrow-ga(u)ge.

Schmalz [ʃmalts] *n* (-es/-e) grease; lard; '₂ig *adj.* greasy; lardy; F *fig.* soppy, sentimental.

schmarotz|en [ʃma'rɔtsən] *v/i.* (*no* -e-, h) sponge (*bei on*); ₂er *m* (-s/-) ⚕, *zo.* parasite; *fig. a.* sponge.

Schmarre F ['ʃmarə] *f* (-/-n) slash, cut; scar.

Schmatz [ʃmats] *m* (-es/-e) smack, loud kiss; '₂en *v/i.* (ge-, h) smack (*mit den Lippen* one's lips); eat noisily.

Schmaus [ʃmaus] *m* (-es/⁼e) feast, banquet; *fig.* treat; ₂en *v/i.* ['~zən] (ge-, h) feast, banquet.

schmecken ['ʃmɛkən] (ge-, h) **1.** *v/t.* taste, sample; **2.** *v/i.*: ~ *nach* taste *or* smack of (*both a. fig.*); *dieser Wein schmeckt mir* I like *or* enjoy this wine.

Schmeichel|ei [ʃmaiçə'lai] *f* (-/-en) flattery; cajolery; '₂haft *adj.* flattering; '₂n *v/i.* (ge-, h): *j-m* ~ flatter s.o.; cajole s.o.

Schmeichler ['ʃmaiçlər] *m* (-s/-) flatterer; '₂isch *adj.* flattering; cajoling.

schmeiß|en F ['ʃmaisən] (*irr.*, ge-, h) **1.** *v/t.* throw, fling, hurl; slam, bang (*door*); **2.** *v/i.*: *mit Geld um sich* ~ squander one's money; '₂fliege *zo. f* blowfly, bluebottle.

Schmelz [ʃmɛlts] *m* **1.** (-es/-e) enamel; *fig.* (-es/*no pl.*) bloom; ♪ sweetness, mellowness; '₂en (*irr.*, ge-) **1.** *v/i.* (sein) melt (*a. fig.*); liquefy; *fig.* melt away, dwindle; **2.** *v/t.* (h) melt, smelt, fuse (*ore, etc.*); liquefy; '~erei [~'rai] *f* (-/-en), '~hütte *f* foundry; '~ofen *m* smelting furnace; '~tiegel *m* melting-pot, crucible.

Schmerbauch ['ʃmeːr-] *m* paunch, pot-belly, F corporation, *Am. sl. a.* bay window.

Schmerz [ʃmerts] *m* (-es/-en) pain (*a. fig.*); ache; *fig.* grief, sorrow;

'2en (ge-, h) 1. v/i. pain (a. fig.), hurt; ache; 2. v/t. pain (a. fig.); hurt; fig. grieve, afflict; '2haft adj. painful; '2lich adj. painful, grievous; '2lindernd adj. soothing; '2los adj. painless.

Schmetter|ling zo. ['ʃmɛtərliŋ] m (-s/-e) butterfly; '2n (ge-, h) 1. v/t. dash (zu Boden to the ground); in Stücke to pieces); 2. v/i. crash; trumpet, etc.: bray, blare; bird: warble.

Schmied [ʃmiːt] m (-[e]s/-e) (black)smith; ~e ['~də] f (-/-n) forge, smithy; ~eisen ['~də?-] n wrought iron; '~ehammer m sledge(-hammer); '2en ['~dən] v/t. (ge-, h) forge; make, devise, hatch (plans).

schmiegen ['ʃmiːgən] v/refl. (ge-, h) nestle (an acc. to).

schmiegsam adj. ['ʃmiːkzaːm] pliant, flexible; supple (a. fig.); '2keit f (-/no pl.) pliancy, flexibility; suppleness (a. fig.).

Schmier|e ['ʃmiːrə] f (-/-n) grease; thea. contr. troop of strolling players, sl. penny gaff; '2en v/t. (ge-, h) smear; ⊕ grease, oil, lubricate; butter (bread); spread (butter, etc.); scrawl, scribble; painter: daub; ~enkomödiant ['~kɔmødjant] m (-en/-en) strolling actor, barnstormer, sl. ham [~erei [~'raɪ] f (-/-en) scrawl; paint. daub; '2ig adj. greasy; dirty; fig.: filthy; F smarmy; '~mittel ⊕ n lubricant.

Schminke ['ʃmiŋkə] f (-/-n) make-up (a. thea.), paint; rouge; thea. grease-paint; '2n v/t. and v/refl. (ge-, h) paint, make up; rouge (o.s.); put on lipstick.

Schmirgel ['ʃmirgəl] m (-s/no pl.) emery; '2n v/t. (ge-, h) (rub with) emery; '~papier n emery-paper.

Schmiß [ʃmis] 1. m (Schmisses/ Schmisse) gash, cut; (duelling-) scar; 2. F m (Schmisses/no pl.) verve, go, Am. sl. a. pep; 3. 2 pret. of schmeißen.

schmoll|en ['ʃmɔlən] v/i. (ge-, h) sulk, pout; '2winkel m sulking-corner.

schmolz [ʃmɔlts] pret. of schmelzen.

Schmor|braten ['ʃmoːr-] m stewed meat; '2en v/t. and v/i. (ge-, h) stew (a. fig.).

Schmuck [ʃmuk] 1. m (-[e]s/✻ -e) ornament; decoration; jewel(le)ry, jewels pl.; 2. 2 adj. neat, smart, spruce, trim.

schmücken ['ʃmykən] v/t. (ge-, h) adorn, trim; decorate.

'schmuck|los adj. unadorned; plain; '2sachen f/pl. jewel(le)ry, jewels pl.

Schmuggel [ʃmugəl] m (-s/no pl.), ~ei [~'laɪ] f (-/-en) smuggling; '2n v/t. and v/i. (ge-, h) smuggle; '~ware f contraband, smuggled goods pl.

Schmuggler ['ʃmuglər] m (-s/-) smuggler.

schmunzeln ['ʃmuntsəln] v/i. (ge-, h) smile amusedly.

Schmutz [ʃmuts] m (-es/no pl.) dirt; filth; fig. a. smut; '2en v/i. (ge-, h) soil, get dirty; '~fink fig. m mudlark; '~fleck m smudge, stain; fig. blemish; '2ig adj. dirty; filthy; fig. a. mean, shabby.

Schnabel ['ʃnaːbəl] m (-s/ᵘ) bill, esp. bird of prey: beak.

Schnalle ['ʃnalə] f (-/-n) buckle; '2n v/t. (ge-, h) buckle; strap.

schnalzen ['ʃnaltsən] v/i. (ge-, h): mit den Fingern ~ snap one's fingers; mit der Zunge ~ click one's tongue.

schnappen ['ʃnapən] (ge-, h) 1. v/i. lid, spring, etc.: snap; lock: catch; nach et. ~ snap or snatch at; nach Luft ~ gasp for breath; 2. F v/t. catch, sl. nab (criminal).

'Schnapp|messer n flick-knife; '~schloß n spring-lock; '~schuß phot. m snapshot.

Schnaps [ʃnaps] m (-es/ᵘe) strong liquor, Am. hard liquor; brandy; ein (Glas) ~ a dram.

schnarch|en ['ʃnarçən] v/i. (ge-, h) snore; '2er m (-s/-) snorer.

schnarren ['ʃnarən] v/i. (ge-, h) rattle; jar.

schnattern ['ʃnatərn] v/i. (ge-, h) cackle; fig. a. chatter, gabble.

schnauben ['ʃnaubən] (ge-, h) 1. v/i. snort; vor Wut ~ foam with rage; 2. v/t.: sich die Nase ~ blow one's nose.

schnaufen ['ʃnaufən] v/i. (ge-, h) pant, puff, blow; wheeze.

Schnauz|bart ['ʃnauts-] m m(o)ustache; '~e f (-/-n) snout, muzzle; ⊕ nozzle; teapot, etc.: spout; sl. fig. potato-trap; '2en F v/i. (ge-, h) jaw.

Schnecke zo. ['ʃnɛkə] f (-/-n) snail; slug; '~nhaus n snail's shell; '~ntempo n: im ~ at a snail's pace.

Schnee [ʃneː] m (-s/no pl.) snow; '~ball m snowball; '~ballschlacht f pelting-match with snowballs; 2bedeckt adj. ['~bədɛkt] snow-covered, mountain-top: snow-capped; '2blind adj. snow-blind; '~blindheit f snow-blindness; '~brille f (e-e a pair of) snow-goggles pl.; '~fall m snow-fall; '~flocke f snow-flake; '~gestöber n (-s/-) snow-storm; '~glöckchen ♀ ['~glœkçən] n (-s/-) snowdrop; '~grenze f snow-line; '~mann m snow man; '~pflug m snow-plough, Am. snowplow; '~schuh m snowshoe; '~sturm m snow-storm, blizzard; '~wehe f (-/-n) snow-drift; '2weiß adj. snow-white.

Schneid F [ʃnaɪt] m (-[e]s/no pl.) pluck, dash, sl. guts pl.

Schneide ['ʃnaɪdə] f (-/-n) edge; '~mühle f sawmill; '2n (irr., ge-, h)

1. v/t. cut; carve (*meat*); pare, clip (*finger-nails, etc.*); 2. v/i. cut.

'**Schneider** m (-s/-) tailor; **~ei** [~'raɪ] f 1. (-/*no pl.*) tailoring; dressmaking; 2. (-/-en) tailor's shop; dressmaker's shop; '**~in** f (-/-nen) dressmaker; '**~meister** m master tailor; '**2n** (ge-, h) 1. v/i. tailor; do tailoring; do dressmaking; 2. v/t. make, tailor.

'**Schneidezahn** m incisor.

'**schneidig** *fig. adj.* plucky; dashing, keen; smart, *Am. sl. a.* nifty.

schneien ['ʃnaɪən] v/i. (ge-, h) snow.

schnell [ʃnɛl] 1. *adj.* quick, fast; rapid; swift, speedy; *reply, etc.*: prompt; sudden; 2. *adv.*: ~ fahren drive fast; ~ handeln act promptly or without delay; (*mach*) ~! be quick!, hurry up!

Schnelläufer ['ʃnɛlɔøfər] m sprinter; speed skater.

'**schnell|en** (ge-) v/t. (h) and v/i. (sein) jerk; '**2feuer** ✕ n rapid fire; '**2hefter** m (-s/-) folder.

'**Schnelligkeit** f (-/*no pl.*) quickness, fastness; rapidity; swiftness; promptness; speed, velocity.

'**Schnell|imbiß** m snack (bar); '**~imbißstube** f snack bar; '**~kraft** f (-/*no pl.*) elasticity; '**~verfahren** n ⅌ summary proceeding; ⊕ highspeed process; '**~zug** ⦿ m fast train, express (train).

schneuzen ['ʃnɔʏtsən] v/refl. (ge-, h) blow one's nose.

schniegeln ['ʃniːgəln] v/refl. (ge-, h) dress or smarten or spruce (o.s.) up.

Schnipp|chen ['ʃnɪpçən] n: F j-m ein ~ schlagen outwit or overreach s.o.; '**2isch** *adj.* pert, snappish, *Am. F a.* snippy.

Schnitt [ʃnɪt] 1. m (-[e]s/-e) cut; dress, *etc.*: cut, make, style; pattern; *book*: edge; ⅍ (inter)section; *fig.*: average; F profit; 2. ♀ *pret. of* schneiden; '**2blumen** f/pl. cut flowers pl.; '**~e** f (-/-n) slice; '**~er** m (-s/-) reaper, mower; '**~fläche** ⅍ f section(al plane); '**2ig** *adj.* streamline(d); '**~muster** n pattern; '**~punkt** m (point of) intersection; '**~wunde** f cut, gash.

Schnitzel ['ʃnɪtsəl] 1. n (-s/-) schnitzel; 2. F n, m (-s/-) chip; *paper*: scrap; ~ pl. ⊕ parings pl., shavings pl.; *paper*: a. clippings pl.; '**2n** v/t. (ge-, h) chip, shred; whittle.

schnitzen ['ʃnɪtsən] v/t. (ge-, h) carve, cut (in wood).

'**Schnitzer** m (-s/-) carver; F *fig.* blunder, *Am. sl. a.* boner; **~ei** [~'raɪ] f 1. (-/-en) carving, carved work; 2. (-/*no pl.*) carving.

schnöde *adj.* ['ʃnøːdə] contemptuous; disgraceful; base, vile; **~r** *Mammon* filthy lucre.

Schnörkel ['ʃnœrkəl] m (-s/-) flourish (*a. fig.*), scroll (*a.* 𝄐).

schnorr|en F ['ʃnɔrən] v/t. and v/i. (ge-, h) cadge; '**2er** m (-s/-) cadger.

schnüff|eln ['ʃnʏfəln] v/i. (ge-, h) sniff, nose (*both: an dat. at*); *fig.* nose about, *Am.* F *a.* snoop around; '**2ler** *fig.* m (-s/-) spy, *Am.* F *a.* snoop; F sleuth(-hound).

Schnuller ['ʃnulər] m (-s/-) dummy, comforter.

Schnulze F ['ʃnultsə] f (-/-n) sentimental song or film or play, F tearjerker.

Schnupf|en ['ʃnupfən] 1. m (-s/-) cold, catarrh; 2. ♀ v/i. (ge-, h) take snuff; '**~er** m (-s/-) snuff-taker; '**~tabak** m snuff.

schnuppe F *adj.* ['ʃnupə]: *das ist mir* ~ I don't care (F a damn); '**~rn** v/i. (ge-, h) sniff, nose (*both: an dat.* at).

Schnur [ʃnuːr] f (-/-̈e) cord; string, twine; line; ≠ flex.

Schnür|band ['ʃnyːr-] n lace; **~chen** ['~çən] n (-s/-): *wie am* ~ like clockwork; '**2en** v/t. (ge-, h) lace (up); (bind with) cord, tie up.

'**schnurgerade** *adj.* dead straight.

Schnurr|bart ['ʃnur-] m m(o)ustache; '**2en** (ge-, h) 1. v/i. wheel, *etc.*: whirr(r); *cat*: purr (*a. fig.*); F *fig.* cadge; 2. F *fig.* v/t. cadge.

Schnür|senkel ['ʃnyːrzɛŋkəl] m (-s/-) shoe-lace, shoe-string; '**~stiefel** m lace-boot.

schnurstracks *adv.* ['ʃnuːrˈʃtraks] direct, straight; on the spot, at once, *sl.* straight away.

schob [ʃoːp] *pret. of* schieben.

Schober ['ʃoːbər] m (-s/-) rick, stack.

Schock [ʃɔk] 1. n (-[e]s/-e) threescore; 2. ♀ m (-[e]s/-s, ⚓-e) shock; **2ieren** [~'kiːrən] v/t. (*no -ge-, h) shock, scandalize.

Schokolade [ʃokoˈlaːdə] f (-/-n) chocolate.

scholl [ʃɔl] *pret. of* schallen.

Scholle ['ʃɔlə] f (-/-n) clod (*of earth*), *poet.* glebe; floe (*of ice*); *ichth.* plaice.

schon *adv.* [ʃoːn] already; ~ *lange* for a long time; ~ *gut!* all right!; ~ *der Gedanke* the very idea; ~ *der Name* the bare name; *hast du* ~ *einmal* ...? have you ever ...?; *mußt du* ~ *gehen?* need you go yet?; ~ *um 8 Uhr* as early as 8 o'clock.

schön [ʃøːn] 1. *adj.* beautiful; *man*: handsome (*a. fig.*); *weather*: fair, fine (*a. iro.*); *das* ~ *Geschlecht* the fair sex; *die* ~ *en Künste* the fine arts; ~ *e Literatur* belles-lettres pl.; 2. *adv.*: ~ *warm* nice and warm; *du hast mich* ~ *erschreckt* you gave me quite a start.

schonen ['ʃoːnən] v/t. (ge-, h) spare (*j-n* s.o.); *j-s Leben* s.o.'s life); take care of; husband (*strength, etc.*); sich ~ take care of o.s., look after o.s.

'**Schönheit** f 1. (-/no pl.) beauty; of woman: a. pulchritude; 2. (-/-en) beauty; beautiful woman, belle; '**~spflege** f beauty treatment.

'**schöntun** v/i. (irr. tun, sep., -ge-, h) flatter (j-m s.o.); flirt (*dat.* with).

'**Schonung** f 1. (-/no pl.) mercy; sparing, forbearance; careful treatment; 2. (-/-en) tree-nursery; '**2slos** adj. unsparing, merciless, relentless.

Schopf [ʃɔpf] m (-[e]s/⁼e) tuft; orn. a. crest.

schöpfen ['ʃœpfən] v/t. (ge-, h) scoop, ladle; draw (*water at well*); draw, take (*breath*); take (*courage*); neue Hoffnung ~ gather fresh hope; Verdacht ~ become suspicious.

'**Schöpf|er** m (-s/-) creator; '**2erisch** adj. creative; '**~ung** f (-/-en) creation.

schor [ʃoːr] pret. of scheren.

Schorf [ʃɔrf] m (-[e]s/-e) scurf; scab, crust; '**2ig** adj. scurfy; scabby.

Schornstein ['ʃɔrn-] m chimney; ♣, a. funnel; '**~feger** m (-s/-) chimney-sweep(er).

Schoß 1. [ʃoːs] m (-es/⁼e) lap; womb; coat: tail; 2. 2 [ʃɔs] pret. of schießen.

Schote ['ʃoːtə] f (-/-n) pod, husk.

Schott|e ['ʃɔtə] m (-n/-n) Scot, Scotchman, Scotsman; die ~n pl. the Scotch pl.; '**~er** m (-s/-) gravel; (road-)metal; '**2isch** adj. Scotch, Scottish.

schräg [ʃrɛːk] 1. adj. oblique, slanting; sloping; 2. adv.: ~ gegenüber diagonally across (von from).

schrak [ʃraːk] pret. of schrecken 2.

Schramme ['ʃramə] f (-/-n) scratch; skin: a. abrasion; '**2n** v/t. (ge-, h) scratch; graze, abrade (*skin*).

Schrank [ʃraŋk] m (-[e]s/⁼e) cupboard, esp. Am. closet; wardrobe.

'**Schranke** f (-/-n) barrier (a. fig.); ⬛ a. (railway-)gate; ⚖ bar; ~n pl. fig. bounds pl., limits pl.; '**2nlos** fig. adj. boundless; unbridled; '**~nwärter** ⬛ m gate-keeper.

'**Schrankkoffer** m wardrobe trunk.

Schraube ['ʃraubə] f (-/-n) ⊕ screw; ♣ screw(-propeller); '**2n** v/t. (ge-, h) screw.

'**Schrauben|dampfer** ♣ m screw (steamer); '**~mutter** ⊕ f nut; '**~schlüssel** ⊕ m spanner, wrench; '**~zieher** ⊕ m screwdriver.

Schraubstock ⊕ ['ʃraup-] m vice, Am. vise.

Schrebergarten ['ʃreːbər-] m allotment garden.

Schreck [ʃrɛk] m (-[e]s/-e) fright, terror; consternation; '**~bild** n bugbear; '**~en** m (-s/-) fright, terror; consternation; '**2en** (ge-) 1. v/t. (h) frighten, scare; 2. v/i. (irr., sein):

only in compounds; '**~ensbotschaft** f alarming or terrible news; '**~ensherrschaft** f reign of terror; '**2haft** adj. fearful, timid; '**2lich** adj. terrible, dreadful (both a. F fig.); '**~schuß** m scare shot; fig. warning shot.

Schrei [ʃrai] m (-[e]s/-e) cry; shout; scream.

schreiben ['ʃraibən] 1. v/t. and v/i. (irr., ge-), h) write (j-m to s.o.; über acc. on); mit der Maschine ~ type(write); 2. v/t. (irr., ge-, h) spell; 3. 2 n (-s/-) letter.

'**Schreiber** m (-s/-) writer; secretary, clerk.

schreib|faul adj. ['ʃraip-] lazy in writing; '**2feder** f pen; '**2fehler** m mistake in writing or spelling, slip of the pen; '**2heft** n exercise-book; '**2mappe** f writing-case; '**2maschine** f typewriter; (mit der) ~ schreiben type(write); '**2material** n writing-materials pl., stationery; '**2papier** n writing-paper; '**2schrift** typ. f script; '**2tisch** m (writing-)desk; '**2ung** f (-/-en) spelling; '**2unterlage** f desk pad; '**2waren** f/pl. writing-materials pl., stationery; '**2warenhändler** m stationer; '**2zeug** n writing-materials pl.

'**schreien** (irr., ge-, h) 1. v/t. shout; scream; 2. v/i. cry (out) (vor dat. with pain, etc.; nach for bread, etc.); shout (vor with); scream (with); '**~d** adj. colour: loud; injustice: flagrant.

schreiten ['ʃraitən] v/i. (irr., ge-, sein) step, stride (über acc. across); fig. proceed (zu to).

schrie [ʃriː] pret. of schreien.

schrieb [ʃriːp] pret. of schreiben.

Schrift [ʃrift] f (-/-en) (hand-)writing, hand; typ. type; character, letter; writing; publication; die Heilige ~ the (Holy) Scriptures pl.; '**~art** f type; '**2deutsch** adj. literary German; '**~führer** m secretary; '**~leiter** m editor; '**2lich** 1. adj. written, in writing; 2. adv. in writing; '**~satz** m ⚖ pleadings pl.; typ. composition, type-setting; '**~setzer** m compositor, type-setter; '**~sprache** f literary language; '**~steller** m (-s/-) author, writer; '**~stück** n piece of writing, paper, document; '**~tum** n (-s/no pl.) literature; '**~wechsel** m exchange of letters, correspondence; '**~zeichen** n character, letter.

schrill adj. [ʃril] shrill, piercing.

Schritt [ʃrit] 1. m (-[e]s/-e) step (a. fig.); pace (a. fig.); ~e unternehmen take steps; 2. 2 pret. of schreiten; '**~macher** m (-s/-) sports: pace-maker; '**2weise** 1. adj. gradual; 2. adv. a. step by step.

schroff adj. [ʃrɔf] rugged, jagged;

steep, precipitous; *fig.* harsh, gruff;
~er Widerspruch glaring contradiction.

schröpfen ['ʃrœpfən] *v/t.* (ge-, h) 🙰
cup; *fig.* milk, fleece.

Schrot [ʃroːt] *m, n* (-[e]s/-e) crushed
grain; small shot; '~brot *n* wholemeal bread; '~flinte *f* shotgun.

Schrott [ʃrɔt] *m* (-[e]s/-e) scrap
(-iron *or* -metal).

schrubben ['ʃrubən] *v/t.* (ge-, h)
scrub.

Schrulle ['ʃrulə] *f* (-/-n) whim, fad.

schrumpf|en ['ʃrumpfən] *v/i.* (ge-,
sein) shrink (*a.* ⊕, 🙰, *fig.*); '2ung *f*
(-/-en) shrinking; shrinkage.

Schub [ʃuːp] *m* (-[e]s/⸚e) push,
shove; *phys.*, ⊕ thrust; *bread,
people, etc.*: batch; '~fach *n* drawer;
'~karren *m* wheelbarrow; '~kasten
m drawer; '~kraft *phys.*, ⊕ *f* thrust;
'~lade *f* (-/-n) drawer.

Schubs F [ʃups] *m* (-es/-e) push;
'2en F *v/t.* (ge-, h) push.

schüchtern *adj.* ['ʃʏçtərn] shy,
bashful, timid; *girl*: coy; '2heit *f*
(-/no *pl.*) shyness, bashfulness,
timidity; coyness (*of girl*).

schuf [ʃuːf] *pret. of schaffen 1.*

Schuft [ʃuft] *m* (-[e]s/-e) scoundrel,
rascal; cad; '2en F *v/i.* (ge-, h)
drudge, slave, plod; '2ig *adj.*
scoundrelly, rascally; caddish.

Schuh [ʃuː] *m* (-[e]s/-e) shoe; *j-m
et. in die ~e schieben* put the blame
for s.th. on s.o.; *wissen, wo der ~
drückt* know where the shoe pinches;
'~anzieher *m* (-s/-) shoehorn;
'~band *n* shoe-lace *or* -string;
'~creme *f* shoe-cream, shoe-polish; '~geschäft *n* shoe-shop;
'~löffel *m* shoehorn; '~macher
m (-s/-) shoemaker; '~putzer *m*
(-s/-) shoeblack, *Am. a.* shoeshine;
'~sohle *f* sole; '~spanner *m* (-s/-)
shoetree; '~werk *n*, '~zeug F *n*
foot-wear, boots and shoes *pl.*

'**Schul|amt** *n* school-board; '~arbeit *f* homework; '~bank *f* (school-)
desk; '~beispiel *n* test-case, typical
example; '~besuch *m* (-[e]s/no *pl.*)
attendance at school; '~bildung *f*
education; *höhere ~* secondary education; '~buch *n* school-book.

Schuld [ʃult] *f* 1. (-/no *pl.*) guilt;
fault, blame; *es ist s-e ~* it is his
fault, he is to blame for it; 2. ~
debt; *~en machen* contract *or* incur
debts; '2bewußt *adj.* conscious of
one's guilt; '2en ['~dən] *v/t.* (ge-, h):
j-m et. ~ owe s.o. s.th.; *j-m Dank ~*
be indebted to s.o. (*für* for); 2haft
adj. ['~thaft] culpable.

'**Schuldiener** *m* school attendant *or*
porter.

schuldig *adj.* ['ʃuldɪç] guilty (*e-r
Sache* of s.th.); *respect, etc.*: due;
j-m et. ~ sein owe s.o. s.th.; *Dank
~ sein* be indebted *to* s.o. (*für* for);

für ~ befinden 🙰🙰 find guilty; 2e
['~gə] *m, f* (-n/-n) guilty person;
culprit; '2keit *f* (-/no *pl.*) duty,
obligation.

'**Schuldirektor** *m* headmaster, *Am.
a.* principal.

'**schuld|los** *adj.* guiltless, innocent;
'2losigkeit *f* (-/no *pl.*) guiltlessness,
innocence; '2ner ['~dnər] *m* (-s/-)
debtor; '2schein *m* evidence of
debt, certificate of indebtedness,
IOU (= I owe you); '2verschreibung *f* bond, debt certificate.

Schule ['ʃuːlə] *f* (-/-n) school;
höhere ~ secondary school, *Am. a.*
high school; *auf or in der ~* at
school; *in die ~ gehen* go to school;
'2n *v/t.* (ge-, h) train, school; *pol.*
indoctrinate.

Schüler ['ʃyːlər] *m* (-s/-) schoolboy,
pupil; *phls., etc.*: disciple; '~austausch *m* exchange of pupils; '~in
f (-/-nen) schoolgirl.

'**Schul|ferien** *pl.* holidays *pl.*, vacation; '~fernsehen *n* educational
TV; '~funk *m* educational broadcast; '~gebäude *n* school(house);
'~geld *n* school fee(s *pl.*), tuition;
'~hof *m* playground, *Am. a.* schoolyard; '~kamerad *m* schoolfellow;
'~lehrer *m* schoolmaster, teacher;
'~mappe *f* satchel; '2meistern
v/t. (ge-, h) censure pedantically;
'~ordnung *f* school regulations *pl.*;
'2pflichtig *adj.* schoolable; '~rat
m supervisor of schools, school
inspector; '~schiff *n* training-ship;
'~schluß *m* end of school; end of
term; '~schwänzer *m* (-s/-) truant;
'~stunde *f* lesson.

Schulter ['ʃultər] *f* (-/-n) shoulder;
'~blatt *anat. n* shoulder-blade; '2n
v/t. (ge-, h) shoulder.

'**Schul|unterricht** *m* school, lessons *pl.*; school instruction; '~versäumnis *f* (-/no *pl.*) absence from
school; '~wesen *n* educational system; '~zeugnis *n* report.

schummeln F ['ʃuməln] *v/i.* (ge-, h)
cheat, *Am.* F a. chisel.

Schund [ʃunt] 1. *m* (-[e]s/no *pl.*)
trash, rubbish (both *a. fig.*); 2. 2
pret. of schinden; '~literatur *f*
trashy literature; '~roman *m*
trashy novel, *Am. a.* dime novel.

Schuppe ['ʃupə] *f* (-/-n) scale; ~n
pl. on head: dandruff; '2en 1. *m*
(-s/-) shed; *mot.* garage; ✈ hangar;
2. 2 *v/t.* (ge-, h) scale (*fish*); *sich ~
skin*: scale off; '2ig *adj.* scaly.

Schür|eisen ['ʃyːrʔ~] *n* poker; '2en
v/t. (ge-, h) poke; stoke; *fig.* fan,
foment.

schürfen ['ʃyrfən] (ge-, h) 1. ⚒ *v/i.*
prospect (*nach* for); 2. *v/t.* ⚒
prospect for; *sich den Arm ~* graze
one's arm.

Schurk|e ['ʃurkə] *m* (-n/-n) scoundrel, knave; ~erei [~'raɪ] *f* (-/-en) rascality, knavish trick; '2isch adj. scoundrelly, knavish.

Schürze ['ʃyrtsə] f (-/-n) apron; children: pinafore; '2n v/t. (ge-, h) tuck up (skirt); tie (knot); purse (lips); '~njäger m skirt-chaser, Am. sl. wolf.

Schuß [ʃus] m (Schusses/Schüsse) shot (a. sports); ammunition: round; sound: report; charge; wine, etc.: dash (a. fig.); in ~ sein be in full swing, be in full working order.

Schüssel ['ʃysəl] f (-/-n) basin (for water, etc.); bowl, dish, tureen (for soup, vegetables, etc.).

'**Schuß|waffe** f fire-arm; '~weite f range; '~wunde f gunshot wound.

Schuster ['ʃuːstər] m (-s/-) shoemaker; '2n fig. v/i. (ge-, h) s. pfuschen.

Schutt [ʃut] m (-[e]s/no pl.) rubbish, refuse; rubble, debris.

Schüttel|frost ⚕ ['ʃytəl-] m shivering-fit; '2n v/t. (ge-, h) shake; den Kopf ~ shake one's head; j-m die Hand ~ shake hands with s.o.

schütten ['ʃytən] (ge-, h) 1. v/t. pour; spill (auf acc. on); 2. v/i.: es schüttet it is pouring with rain.

Schutz [ʃuts] m (-es/no pl.) protection (gegen, vor dat. against), defen|ce, Am. -se (against, from); shelter (from); safeguard; cover; '~brille f (e-e a pair of) goggles pl.

Schütze ['ʃytsə] m (-n/-n) marksman, shot; ⚔ rifleman; '2n v/t. (ge-, h) protect (gegen, vor dat. against, from), defend (against, from), guard (against, from); shelter (from); safeguard (rights, etc.).

Schutzengel ['ʃutsˀ-] m guardian angel.

'**Schützen|graben** ⚔ m trench; '~könig m champion shot.

'**Schutz|haft** ⚖ f protective custody; '~heilige m patron saint; '~herr m patron, protector; '~impfung ⚕ f protective inoculation; smallpox: vaccination.

Schützling ['ʃytslɪŋ] m (-s/-e) protégé, female: protégée.

'**schutz|los** adj. unprotected; defen|celess, Am. -seless; '2mann m (-[e]s/=er, Schutzleute) policeman, (police) constable, sl. bobby, sl. cop; '2marke f trade mark, brand; '2-mittel n preservative; ⚕ prophylactic; '2patron m patron saint; '2umschlag m (dust-)jacket, wrapper; '~zoll m protective duty.

Schwabe ['ʃvaːbə] m (-n/-n) Swabian.

schwäbisch adj. ['ʃvɛːbiʃ] Swabian.

schwach adj. [ʃvax] resistance, team, knees (a. fig.), eyes, heart, voice, character, tea, gr. verb, ✝ demand, etc.: weak; person, etc.: infirm; person, recollection, etc.: feeble; sound, light, hope, idea, etc.: faint;

consolation, attendance, etc.: poor; light, recollection, etc.: dim; resemblance: remote; das ~e Geschlecht the weaker sex; ~e Seite weak point or side.

Schwäche ['ʃvɛçə] f (-/-n) weakness (a. fig.); infirmity; fig. foible; e-e ~ haben für have a weakness for; '2n v/t. (ge-, h) weaken (a. fig.); impair (health).

'**Schwach|heit** f (-/-en) weakness; fig. a. frailty; '~kopf m simpleton, soft(y), Am. ⵏ a. sap(head); 2köpfig adj. ['~kœpfiç] weak-headed, soft, Am. sl. a. sappy.

schwäch|lich adj. ['ʃvɛçliç] weakly, feeble; delicate, frail; '2ling m (-s/-e) weakling (a. fig.).

'**schwach|sinnig** adj. weak- or feeble-minded; '2strom ⚡ m (-[e]s/no pl.) weak current.

Schwadron ⚔ [ʃvaˈdroːn] f (-/-en) squadron; 2ieren [~oˈniːrən] v/t. (no -ge-, h) swagger, vapo(u)r.

Schwager ['ʃvaːgər] m (-s/=) brother-in-law.

Schwägerin ['ʃvɛːgərin] f (-/-nen) sister-in-law.   [swallow.\]

Schwalbe orn. ['ʃvalbə] f (-/-n)\}

Schwall [ʃval] m (-[e]s/-e) swell, flood; words: torrent.

Schwamm [ʃvam] 1. m (-[e]s/=e) sponge; ⚕ fungus; ⚕ dry-rot; 2. ⚲ pret. of schwimmen; '2ig adj. spongy; face, etc.: bloated.

Schwan orn. [ʃvaːn] m (-[e]s/=e) swan.

schwand [ʃvant] pret. of schwinden.

schwang [ʃvaŋ] pret. of schwingen.

schwanger adj. ['ʃvaŋər] pregnant, with child, in the family way.

schwängern ['ʃvɛŋərn] v/t. (ge-, h) get with child, impregnate (a. fig.).

'**Schwangerschaft** f (-/-en) pregnancy.

schwanken ['ʃvaŋkən] v/i. (ge-) 1. (h) earth, etc.: shake, rock; ✝ prices: fluctuate; branches, etc.: sway; fig. waver, oscillate, vacillate; 2. (sein) stagger, totter.

Schwanz [ʃvants] m (-es/=e) tail (a. ⚞, ast.); fig. train.

schwänz|eln ['ʃvɛntsəln] v/i. (ge-, h) wag one's tail; fig. fawn (um [up]on); '~en v/t. (ge-, h) cut (lecture, etc.); die Schule ~ play truant, Am. a. play hooky.

Schwarm [ʃvarm] m (-[e]s/=e) bees, etc.: swarm; birds: a. flight, flock; fish: school, shoal; birds, girls, etc.: bevy; ⵏ fig. fancy, craze; p.: idol, hero; flame.

schwärmen ['ʃvɛrmən] v/i. (ge-, h) bees, etc.: swarm; fig.: revel; rave (von about, of), gush (over); ~ für be wild about, adore s.o.

'**Schwärmer** m (-s/-) enthusiast; esp. eccl. fanatic; visionary; fireworks: cracker, squib; zo. hawkmoth; ~ei [~'raɪ] f (-/-en) enthusiasm (für for); idolization; ecstasy; *esp. eccl.* fanaticism; '2isch *adj.* enthusiastic; gushing, raving; adoring; *esp. eccl.* fanatic(al).

Schwarte ['ʃvartə] f (-/-n) bacon: rind; F *fig.* old book.

schwarz *adj.* [ʃvarts] black (*a. fig.*); dark; dirty; ~es Brett notice-board, *Am.* bulletin board; ~es Brot brown bread; ~er Mann bog(e)y; ~er Markt black market; ~ auf weiß in black and white; *auf die* ~e Liste setzen blacklist; '2arbeit f illicit work; '2brot *n* brown bread; '2e *m, f* (*-n/-n*) black.

Schwärze ['ʃvertsə] f (-/no *pl.*) blackness (*a. fig.*); darkness; '2n *v/t.* (ge-, h) blacken.

'schwarz|fahren F *v/i.* (*irr. fahren, sep., -ge-, sein*) travel without a ticket; *mot.* drive without a licence; '2fahrer *m* fare-dodger; *mot.* person driving without a licence; '2fahrt f ride without a ticket; *mot.* drive without a licence; '2handel *m* illicit trade, black marketeering; '2händler *m* black marketeer; '2hörer *m* listener without a licence.

'schwärzlich *adj.* blackish.

'Schwarz|markt *m* black market; '~seher *m* pessimist; *TV:* viewer without a licence; '~sender *m* pirate broadcasting station; ~'weißfilm *m* black-and-white film.

schwatzen ['ʃvatsən] *v/i.* (ge-, h) chat; chatter, tattle.

schwätz|en ['ʃvetsən] *v/i.* (ge-, h) *s. schwatzen;* '2er *m* (*-s/-*) chatterbox; tattler, prattler; gossip.

'schwatzhaft *adj.* talkative, garrulous.

Schwebe *fig.* ['ʃve:bə] f (-/no *pl.*): *in der* ~ *sein* be in suspense; *law, rule, etc.:* be in abeyance; '~bahn f aerial railway *or* ropeway; '2n *v/i.* (ge-, h) be suspended; *bird:* hover (*a. fig.*); glide; *fig.* be pending (*a.* ⁂); *in Gefahr* ~ be in danger.

Schwed|e ['ʃve:də] *m* (*-n/-n*) Swede; '2isch *adj.* Swedish.

Schwefel ⁂ ['ʃve:fəl] *m* (*-s/no pl.*) sulphur, *Am. a.* sulfur; '~säure ⁂ f (-/no *pl.*) sulphuric acid, *Am. a.* sulfuric acid.

Schweif [ʃvaɪf] *m* (-[e]s/-e) tail (*a. ast.*); *fig.* train; '2en (ge-) 1. *v/i.* (sein) rove, ramble; 2. ⊕ *v/t.* (h) curve; scallop.

schweigen ['ʃvaɪɡən] 1. *v/i.* (*irr., ge-, h*) be silent; 2. 2 *n* (*-s/no pl.*) silence; '~d *adj.* silent.

schweigsam ['ʃvaɪkza:m] *adj.* taciturn; '2keit f (-/no *pl.*) taciturnity.

Schwein [ʃvaɪn] *n* 1. (-[e]s/-e) zo. pig, hog, swine (*all a. contp. fig.*); 2. F (-[e]s/no *pl.*): ~ *haben* be lucky.

'Schweine|braten *m* roast pork;

'~fleisch *n* pork; '~hund F *contp. m* swine; '~rei [~'raɪ] f (-/-en) mess; dirty trick; smut(ty story); '~stall *m* pigsty (*a. fig.*).

'schweinisch *fig. adj.* swinish; smutty.

'Schweinsleder *n* pigskin.

Schweiß [ʃvaɪs] *m* (-es/-e) sweat, perspiration; '2en ⊕ *v/t.* (ge-, h) weld; '~er ⊕ *m* (-s/-) welder; '~fuß *m* perspiring foot; '2ig *adj.* sweaty, damp with sweat.

Schweizer ['ʃvaɪtsər] *m* (-s/-) Swiss; *on farm:* dairyman.

schwelen ['ʃve:lən] *v/i.* (ge-, h) smo(u)lder (*a. fig.*).

schwelg|en ['ʃvelɡən] *v/i.* (ge-, h) lead a luxurious life; revel; *fig.* revel (*in dat.* in); '2er *m* (-s/-) revel(l)er; epicure; 2erei [~'raɪ] f (-/-en) revel(ry), feasting; '~erisch *adj.* luxurious; revel(l)ing.

Schwell|e ['ʃve:lə] f (-/-n) sill, threshold (*a. fig.*); ⚏ sleeper, *Am.* tie; '2en 1. *v/i.* (*irr., ge-, sein*) swell (out); 2. *v/t.* (ge-, h) swell; '~ung f (-/-en) swelling.

Schwemme ['ʃvemə] f (-/-n) watering-place; horse-pond; *at tavern, etc.:* taproom; ⚓ glut (*of fruit, etc.*).

Schwengel ['ʃveŋəl] *m* (-s/-) clapper (*of bell*); handle (*of pump*).

schwenk|en ['ʃveŋkən] (ge-) 1. *v/t.* (h) swing; wave (*hat, etc.*); brandish (*stick, etc.*); rinse (*washing*); 2. *v/i.* (sein) turn, wheel; '2ung f (-/-en) turn; *fig.* change of mind.

schwer [ʃve:r] 1. *adj.* heavy; *problem, etc.:* hard, difficult; *illness, mistake, etc.:* serious; *punishment, etc.:* severe; *fault, etc.:* grave; *wine, cigar, etc.:* strong; ~e Zeiten hard times; 2 Pfund ~ sein weigh two pounds; 2. *adv.:* ~ arbeiten work hard; ~ hören be hard of hearing; '2e f (-/no *pl.*) heaviness; *phys.* gravity (*a. fig.*); severity; '~fällig *adj.* heavy, slow; clumsy; '2gewicht *n sports:* heavy-weight; *fig.* main emphasis; '2gewichtler *m* (-s/-) *sports:* heavy-weight; '~hörig *adj.* hard of hearing; '2industrie f heavy industry; '2kraft *phys.* f (-/no *pl.*) gravity; '2lich *adv.* hardly, scarcely; '2mut f (-/no *pl.*) melancholy; ~mütig *adj.* ['~my:tiç] melancholy; '2punkt *m* centre of gravity, *Am.* center of gravity; *fig.:* crucial point; emphasis.

Schwert [ʃve:rt] *n* (-[e]s/-er) sword.

'Schwer|verbrecher *m* felon; '2verdaulich *adj.* indigestible, heavy; '2verständlich *adj.* difficult *or* hard to understand; '2verwundet *adj.* seriously wounded; '2wiegend *fig. adj.* weighty, momentous.

Schwester ['ʃvɛstər] f (-/-n) sister; nurse.

schwieg [ʃviːk] pret. of schweigen.

Schwieger|eltern ['ʃviːgər-] pl. parents-in-law pl.; '~mutter f mother-in-law; '~sohn m son-in-law; '~tochter f daughter-in-law; '~vater m father-in-law.

Schwiel|e ['ʃviːlə] f (-/-n) callosity; '2ig adj. callous.

schwierig adj. ['ʃviːriç] difficult, hard; '2keit f (-/-en) difficulty, trouble.

Schwimm|bad ['ʃvim-] n swimming-bath, Am. swimming pool; '2en v/i. (irr., ge-) 1. (sein) swim; thing: float; ich bin über den Fluß geschwommen I swam across the river; in Geld ~ be rolling in money; 2. (h) swim; ich habe lange unter Wasser geschwommen I swam under water for a long time; '~gürtel m swimming-belt; lifebelt; '~haut f web; '~lehrer m swimming-instructor; '~weste f life-jacket.

Schwindel ['ʃvindəl] m (-s/no pl.) ✆ vertigo, giddiness, dizziness; F fig.: swindle, humbug; sl. eyewash; cheat, fraud; '~anfall ✆ m fit of dizziness; '2erregend adj. dizzy (a. fig.); '~firma ✝ f long firm, Am. wildcat firm; '2n v/i. (ge-, h) cheat, humbug, swindle.

schwinden ['ʃvindən] v/i. (irr., ge-, sein) dwindle, grow less; strength, colour, etc.: fade.

'Schwindl|er m (-s/-) swindler, cheat, humbug; liar; '2ig ✆ adj. giddy, dizzy.

Schwind|sucht ✆ ['ʃvint-] f (-/no pl.) consumption; '2süchtig ✆ adj. consumptive.

Schwing|e ['ʃviŋə] f (-/-n) wing, poet. pinion; swingle; '2en (irr., ge-, h) 1. v/t. swing; brandish (weapon); swingle (flax); 2. v/i. swing; ⊕ oscillate; sound, etc.: vibrate; '~ung f (-/-en) oscillation; vibration.

Schwips F [ʃvips] m (-es/-e): e-n ~ haben be tipsy, have had a drop too much.

schwirren ['ʃvirən] v/i. (ge-) 1. (sein) whir(r); arrow, etc.: whiz(z); insects: buzz; rumours, etc.: buzz, circulate; 2. (h): mir schwirrt der Kopf my head is buzzing.

'Schwitz|bad n sweating-bath, hot-air bath, vapo(u)r bath; '2en (ge-, h) 1. v/i. sweat, perspire; 2. f fig. v/t.: Blut und Wasser ~ be in great anxiety.

schwoll [ʃvɔl] pret. of schwellen.

schwor [ʃvoːr] pret. of schwören.

schwören ['ʃvøːrən] (irr., ge-, h) 1. v/t. swear; e-n Meineid ~ commit perjury; j-m Rache ~ vow vengeance against s.o.; 2. v/i. swear (bei by);

~ auf (acc.) have great belief in, F swear by.

schwül adj. [ʃvyːl] sultry, oppressively hot; '2e f (-/no pl.) sultriness.

Schwulst [ʃvulst] m (-es/⁓e) bombast.

schwülstig adj. ['ʃvylstiç] bombastic, turgid.

Schwund [ʃvunt] m (-[e]s/no pl.) dwindling; wireless, etc.: fading; ✆ atrophy.

Schwung [ʃvuŋ] m (-[e]s/⁓e) swing; fig. verve, go; flight (of imagination); buoyancy; '2haft ✝ adj. flourishing, brisk; '~rad ⊕ n flywheel; watch, clock: balance-wheel; '2voll adj. full of energy or verve; attack, translation, etc.: spirited; style, etc.: racy.

Schwur [ʃvuːr] m (-[e]s/⁓e) oath; '~gericht ⚖ n England, Wales: appr. court of assize.

sechs [zɛks] 1. adj. six; 2. 2 f (-/-en) six; '2eck n (-[e]s/-e) hexagon; '~eckig adj. hexagonal; '~fach adj. sixfold, sextuple; '~mal adv. six times; '~monatig adj. lasting or of six months, six-months ...; '~monatlich 1. adj. six-monthly; 2. adv. every six months; '~stündig adj. ['~ʃtyndiç] lasting or of six hours, six-hour ...; '2tagerennen n cycling: six-day race; '~tägig adj. ['~tɛːgiç] lasting or of six days.

sechs|te adj. ['zɛkstə] sixth; '2tel n (-s/-) sixth (part); '~tens adv. sixthly, in the sixth place.

sech|zehn(te) adj.['zɛç-] sixteen(th); '~zig adj. ['~tsiç] sixty; '~zigste adj. sixtieth.

See [zeː] 1. m (-s/-n) lake; 2. f (-/no pl.) sea; an die ~ gehen go to the seaside; in ~ gehen or stechen put to sea; auf ~ at sea; auf hoher ~ on the high seas; zur ~ gehen go to sea; 3. f (-/-n) sea, billow; '~bad n seaside resort; '~fahrer m sailor, navigator; '~fahrt f navigation; voyage; '2fest adj. seaworthy; ~ sein be a good sailor; '~gang m (motion of the) sea; '~hafen m seaport; '~handel ✝ m maritime trade; '~herrschaft f naval supremacy; '~hund zo. m seal; '2krank adj. seasick; '~krankheit f (-/no pl.) seasickness; '~krieg m naval war(fare).

Seele ['zeːlə] f (-/-n) soul (a. fig.); mit or von ganzer ~ with all one's heart.

'Seelen|größe f (-/no pl.) greatness of soul or mind; '~heil n salvation, spiritual welfare; '2los adj. soulless; '~qual f anguish of mind, (mental) agony; '~ruhe f peace of mind; coolness.

'seelisch adj. psychic(al), mental.

'Seelsorge f (-/no pl.) cure of souls;

ministerial work; '~r m (-s/-) pastor, minister.

'See|macht f naval power; '~mann m (-[e]s/Seeleute) seaman, sailor; '~meile f nautical mile; '~not f (-/no pl.) distress (at sea); '~räuber m pirate; ~räuberei [~'raɪ] f (-/-en) piracy; '~recht n maritime law; '~reise f voyage; '~schiff n sea-going ship; '~schlacht f naval battle; '~schlange f sea serpent; '~sieg m naval victory; '~stadt f seaside town; '~streitkräfte f/pl. naval forces pl.; 'Qtüchtig adj. seaworthy; ~warte f naval observatory; '~weg m sea-route; auf dem ~ by sea; '~wesen n (-s/no pl.) maritime or naval affairs pl.

Segel ['ze:gəl] n (-s/-) sail; unter ~ gehen set sail '~boot n sailing-boat, Am. sailboat; sports: yacht; '~fliegen n (-s/no pl.) gliding, soaring; '~flug m gliding flight, glide; '~flugzeug n glider; 'Qn (ge-) 1. v/i. (h, sein) sail; sports: yacht; 2. v/t. (h) sail; '~schiff n sailing-ship, sailing-vessel; '~sport m yachting; '~tuch n (-[e]s/-e) sailcloth, canvas.

Segen ['ze:gən] m (-s/-) blessing (a. fig.), esp. eccl. benediction; 'Qs-reich adj. blessed.

Segler ['ze:glər] m (-s/-) sailing-vessel, sailing-ship; fast, good, etc. sailer; yachtsman.

segn|en ['ze:gnən] v/t. (ge-, h) bless; 'Qung f (-/-en) s. Segen.

sehen ['ze:ən] (irr., ge-, h) 1. v/i. see; gut ~ have good eyes; ~ auf (acc.) look at; be particular about; ~ nach look for; look after; 2. v/t. see; notice; watch, observe; '~swert adj. worth seeing; 'Qswürdigkeit f (-/-en) object of interest, curiosity; ~en pl. sights pl. (of a place).

Seher ['ze:ər] m (-s/-) seer, prophet; '~blick m (-[e]s/no pl.) prophetic vision; '~gabe f (-/no pl.) gift of prophecy.

'Seh|fehler m visual defect; '~kraft f vision, eyesight.

Sehne ['ze:nə] f (-/-n) anat. sinew, tendon; string (of bow); ♪ chord.

'sehnen v/refl. (ge-, h) long (nach for), yearn (for, after); sich danach ~ zu inf. be longing to inf.

'Sehnerv anat. m visual or optic nerve.

'sehnig adj. sinewy (a. fig.), stringy.

'sehn|lich adj. longing; ardent; passionate; 'Qsucht f longing, yearning; '~süchtig adj., '~suchtsvoll adj. longing, yearning; eyes, etc.: a. wistful.

sehr adv. [ze:r] before adj. and adv.: very, most; with vb.: (very) much, greatly.

'Seh|rohr ♆ n periscope; '~weite f

range of sight, visual range; in ~ within eyeshot or sight.

seicht adj. [zaɪçt] shallow; fig. a. superficial.

Seide ['zaɪdə] f (-/-n) silk.

'seiden adj. silk, silken (a. fig.); 'Qflor m silk gauze; 'Qglanz m silky lust|re, Am. -er; 'Qhändler m mercer; Qpapier n tissue(-paper); Qraupe zo. f silkworm; Qspinnerei f silk-spinning mill; Qstoff m silk cloth or fabric.

'seidig adj. silky.

Seife ['zaɪfə] f (-/-n) soap.

'Seifen|blase f soap-bubble; '~kistenrennen n soap-box derby; '~lauge f (soap-)suds pl.; '~pulver n soap-powder; '~schale f soap-dish; '~schaum m lather.

'seifig adj. soapy.

seih|en ['zaɪən] v/t. (ge-, h) strain, filter; 'Qer m (-s/-) strainer, colander.

Seil [zaɪl] n (-[e]s/-e) rope; '~bahn f funicular or cable railway; '~er m (-s/-) rope-maker; '~tänzer m rope-dancer.

sein¹ [zaɪn] 1. v/i. (irr., ge-, sein) be; exist; 2. Q n (-s/no pl.) being; existence.

sein² poss. pron. [~] his, her, its (in accordance with gender of possessor); der (die, das) ~e his, hers, its; ~ Glück machen make one's fortune; die Seinen pl. his family or people.

'seiner|seits adv. for his part; '~zeit adv. then, at that time; in those days.

'seines|gleichen pron. his equal(s pl.); j-n wie ~ behandeln treat s.o. as one's equal; er hat nicht ~ he has no equal; there is no one like him.

seit [zaɪt] 1. prp. (dat.): ~ 1945 since 1945; ~ drei Wochen for three weeks; 2. cj. since; es ist ein Jahr her, ~ ... it is a year now since ...; '~dem [~'de:m] 1. adv. since or from that time, ever since; 2. cj. since.

Seite ['zaɪtə] f (-/-n) side (a. fig.); flank (a. ×, △); page (of book).

'Seiten|ansicht f profile, side-view; '~blick m side-glance; '~flügel △ m wing; '~hieb fig. m innuendo, sarcastic remark; 'Qs prp. (gen.) on the part of; by; '~schiff △ n church: aisle; '~sprung fig. m extra-marital adventure; '~straße f bystreet; '~stück fig. n counterpart (zu of); '~weg m by-way.

seit'her adv. since (then, that time).

'seit|lich adj. lateral; '~wärts adv. ['~vɛrts] sideways; aside.

Sekret|är [zekre'tɛ:r] m (-s/-e) secretary; bureau; ~ariat [~ari'a:t] n (-[e]s/-e) secretary's office; secretariat(e); ~ärin f (-/-nen) secretary.

Sekt [zɛkt] *m* (-[e]s/-e) champagne.

Sekt|e ['zɛktə] *f* (-/-n) sect; **~ierer** [~'tiːrər] *m* (-s/-) sectarian.

Sektor ['zɛktɔr] *m* (-s/-en) Ⓐ, ✂, *pol.* sector; *fig.* field, branch.

Sekunde [zeˈkundə] *f* (-/-n) second; **~nbruchteil** *m* split second; **~nzeiger** *m* second-hand.

selb adj. [zɛlp] same; **~er** F *pron.* ['~bər] *s.* selbst 1.

selbst [zɛlpst] **1.** *pron.* self; personally; *ich ~* I myself; *von ~ p.* of one's own accord; *thing:* by itself, automatically; **2.** *adv.* even; **3.** Ⓢ *n* (-/no pl.) (one's own) self; ego.

selbständig adj. ['zɛlpʃtɛndiç] independent; *sich ~ machen* set up for o.s.; **Ⓢkeit** *f* (-/no pl.) independence.

'Selbst|anlasser *mot. m* self-starter; **'~anschluß** *teleph. m* automatic connection; **'~bedienungsladen** *m* self-service shop; **'~beherrschung** *f* self-command, self-control; **'~bestimmung** *f* self-determination; **'~betrug** *m* self-deception; **'Ⓢbewußt** adj. self-confident, self-reliant; **'~bewußtsein** *n* self-confidence, self-reliance; **'~binder** *m* (-s/-) tie; **'~erhaltung** *f* self-preservation; **'~erkenntnis** *f* self-knowledge; **'~erniedrigung** *f* self-abasement; **'Ⓢgefällig** adj. (self-)complacent; **'~gefälligkeit** *f* (-/no pl.) (self-)complacency; **'~gefühl** *n* (-[e]s/no pl.) self-reliance; **Ⓢgemacht** adj. ['~gəmaxt] home-made; **'Ⓢgerecht** adj. self-righteous; **'~gespräch** *n* soliloquy, monolog(ue); **'Ⓢherrlich 1.** adj. high-handed, autocratic(al); **2.** adv. with a high hand; **'~hilfe** *f* self-help; **'~kostenpreis** ✝ *m* cost price; **'~laut** gr. *m* vowel; **'Ⓢlos** adj. unselfish, disinterested; **'~mord** *m* suicide; **'~mörder** *m* suicide; **'Ⓢmörderisch** adj. suicidal; **'Ⓢsicher** adj. self-confident, self-assured; **'~sucht** *f* (-/no pl.) selfishness, ego(t)ism; **'Ⓢsüchtig** adj. selfish, ego(t)istic(al); **'Ⓢtätig** ⊕ adj. self-acting, automatic; **'~täuschung** *f* self-deception; **'~überwindung** *f* (-/no pl.) self-conquest; **'~unterricht** *m* self-instruction; **'~verleugnung** *f* self-denial; **'~versorger** *m* (-s/-) self-supporter; **'Ⓢverständlich 1.** adj. self-evident, obvious; **2.** adv. of course, naturally; **~! a.** by all means!; **'~verständlichkeit** *f* **1.** (-/-en) matter of course; **2.** (-/no pl.) matter-of-factness; **'~verteidigung** *f* self-defen|ce, Am. -se; **'~vertrauen** *n* self-confidence, self-reliance; **'~verwaltung** *f* self-government, autonomy; **'Ⓢzufrieden** adj. self-satisfied; **'~zufriedenheit** *f* self-

satisfaction; **'~zweck** *m* (-[e]s/no pl.) end in itself.

selig adj. ['zeːliç] *eccl.* blessed; late, deceased; *fig.* blissful, overjoyed; **'Ⓢkeit** *fig. f* (-/-en) bliss, very great joy.

Sellerie ⚘ ['zɛləri:] *m* (-s/-[s]), *f* (-/-) celery.

selten ['zɛltən] **1.** adj. rare; scarce; **2.** adv. rarely, seldom; **'Ⓢheit** *f* (-/-en) rarity, scarcity; rarity, curio(sity); **'Ⓢheitswert** *m* (-[e]s/no pl.) scarcity value.

Selterswasser ['zɛltərs-] *n* (-s/ᵘ) seltzer (water), soda-water.

seltsam ['zɛltzaːm] strange, odd.

Semester univ. [zeˈmɛstər] *n* (-s/-) term.

Semikolon gr. [zemiˈkoːlɔn] *n* (-s/-s, Semikola) semicolon.

Seminar [zemiˈnaːr] *n* (-s/-e) univ. seminar; seminary (for priests).

Senat [zeˈnaːt] *m* (-[e]s/-e) senate; parl. Senate.

send|en ['zɛndən] v/t. **1.** [irr.,] ge-h) send; forward; **2.** (ge-, h) transmit; broadcast, Am. a. radio(broadcast); telecast; **'Ⓢer** *m* (-s/-) transmitter; broadcasting station.

'Sende|raum *m* (broadcasting) studio; **'~zeichen** *n* interval signal.

'Sendung *f* (-/-en) ✝ consignment, shipment; broadcast; telecast; *fig.* mission. (⚘.)

Senf [zɛnf] *m* (-[e]s/-e) mustard (a.)

sengen ['zɛŋən] v/t. (ge-, h) singe, scorch; '~d adj. heat: parching.

senil adj. [zeˈniːl] senile; **Ⓢität** [~iliˈtɛːt] *f* (-/no pl.) senility.

senior adj. ['zeːniɔr] senior.

Senk|blei ['zɛŋk-] *n* ♠ plumb, plummet; ⚓ a. sounding-lead; **'Ⓢe** geogr. *f* (-/-n) depression, hollow; **'Ⓢen** v/t. (ge-, h) lower; sink (a. voice); let down; bow (head); cut (prices, etc.); sich ~ land, buildings, etc.: sink, subside; ceiling, etc.: sag; **'~fuß** ꭚ *m* flat-foot; **'~fußeinlage** *f* arch support; **'~grube** *f* cesspool; **'Ⓢrecht** adj. vertical, esp. Ⓐ perpendicular; **'~ung** *f* (-/-en) geogr. depression, hollow; lowering, reduction (of prices); ꭞ sedimentation.

Sensation [zɛnzaˈtsjoːn] *f* (-/-en) sensation; **Ⓢell** adj. [~'nɛl] sensational; **~slust** *f* (-/no pl.) sensationalism; **~spresse** *f* yellow press.

Sense ['zɛnzə] *f* (-/-n) scythe.

sensi|bel adj. [zɛnˈziːbəl] sensitive; **Ⓢbilität** [~ibiliˈtɛːt] *f* (-/no pl.) sensitiveness.

sentimental adj. [zɛntimɛnˈtaːl] sentimental; **Ⓢität** [~aliˈtɛːt] *f* (-/-en) sentimentality.

September [zɛpˈtɛmbər] *m* (-[s]/-) September.

Serenade ♪ [zere'nɑ:də] f (-/-n)
serenade.

Serie ['ze:rjə] f (-/-n) series; set;
billiards: break; '2nmäßig **1.** adj.
standard; **2.** adv.: ~ herstellen
produce in mass; '~nproduktion f
mass production.

seriös adj. [ze'rjø:s] serious; trustworthy, reliable.

Serum ['ze:rum] n (-s/Seren, Sera)
serum.

Service[1] [zer'vi:s] n (-s/-) service,
set.

Service[2] ['zø:rvis] m, n (-/-s)
service.

servier|en [zer'vi:rən] v/t. (no -ge-,
h) serve; 2wagen m trolley(-table).

Serviette [zer'vjetə] f (-/-n) (table-)
napkin.

Sessel ['zɛsəl] m (-s/-) armchair,
easy chair; '~lift m chair-lift.

seßhaft adj. ['zɛshaft] settled, established; resident.

Setzei ['zɛtsʔ-] n fried egg.

'**setzen** (ge-) **1.** v/t. (h) set, place,
put; *typ.* compose; ✗ plant; erect,
raise (*monument*); stake (*money*)
(*auf acc.* on); *sich* ‥ sit down, take
a seat; *bird:* perch; *foundations of
house, sediment, etc.* settle; **2.** v/i.
(h): ~ auf (acc.) back (*horse, etc.*);
3. v/i. (sein): ~ über (acc.) leap
(*wall, etc.*); clear (*hurdle, etc.*); take
(*ditch, etc.*).

'**Setzer** *typ.* m (-s/-) compositor,
type-setter; ~ei *typ.* [~'raɪ] f (-/-en)
composing-room.

Seuche ['zɔyçə] f (-/-n) epidemic
(disease).

seufz|en ['zɔyftsən] v/i. (ge-, h)
sigh; '2er m (-s/-) sigh.

sexuell adj. [zɛksu'ɛl] sexual.

sezieren [ze'tsi:rən] v/t. (no -ge-, h)
dissect (a. fig.).

sich refl. pron. [ziç] oneself; sg.
himself, herself, itself; pl. themselves; sg. yourself, pl. yourselves;
each other, one another; sie blickte
~ um she looked about her.

Sichel ['ziçəl] f (-/-n) sickle; s.
Mondsichel.

sicher ['ziçər] **1.** adj. secure (vor dat.
from), safe (from), proof (against);
hand: steady; certain, sure; positive; aus ~er Quelle from a reliable
source; er ~ Sache ~ sein to be sure of
s.th.; **2.** adv. s. sicherlich; um ~ zu
gehen to be on the safe side, to
make sure.

'**Sicherheit** f (-/-en) security;
safety; surety, certainty; positive-
ness; assurance (of manner); in ~
bringen place in safety; ~snadel f
safety-pin; ~sschloß n safety-lock.

'**sicher|lich** adv. surely, certainly;
undoubtedly; er wird ~ kommen he
is sure to come; '~n v/t. (ge-, h)
secure (a. ✗, ⊕); guarantee (a. ✝);
protect, safeguard; sich et. ~ secure

(*prize, seat, etc.*); '~stellen v/t.
(sep., -ge-, h) secure; '2ung f
(-/-en) securing; safeguard(ing); ⊕
security, guaranty; ⊕ safety device;
∮ fuse.

Sicht [ziçt] f (-/no pl.) visibility;
view; in ~ kommen come in(to) view
or sight; auf lange ~ in the long run;
auf or bei ~ ✝ at sight; '2bar adj.
visible; '2en v/t. (ge-, h) ⊕ sight;
fig. sift; '2lich adv. visibly; '~ver-
merk m visé, visa (on passport).

sickern ['zikərn] v/i. (ge-, sein)
trickle, ooze, seep.

sie pers. pron. [zi:] nom.: sg. she,
pl. they; acc.: sg. her, pl. them; Sie
nom. and acc.: sg. and pl. you.

Sieb [zi:p] n (-[e]s/-e) sieve; riddle
(for soil, gravel, etc.).

sieben[1] ['zi:bən] v/t. (ge-, h) sieve,
sift; riddle.

sieben[2] [~] **1.** adj. seven; **2.** ♀ f (-/-)
(number) seven; böse ~ shrew,
vixen; '~fach adj. sevenfold; '~mal
adj. seven times; '2sachen F f/pl.
belongings pl., F traps pl.; '~te adj.
seventh; '2tel n (-s/-) seventh
(part); '~tens adv. seventhly, in the
seventh place.

sieb|zehn(te) adj. ['zi:p-] seven-
teen(th); ~zig adj. ['~tsiç] seventy;
'~zigste adj. seventieth.

siech adj. [zi:ç] sickly; '2tum n
(-s/no pl.) sickliness, lingering illness.

Siedehitze ['zi:də-] f boiling-heat.

siedeln ['zi:dəln] v/i. (ge-, h) settle;
Am. a. homestead.

siede|n ['zi:dən] v/t. and v/i. ([irr.,]
ge-, h) boil, simmer; '2punkt m
boiling-point (a. fig.).

Siedler ['zi:dlər] m (-s/-) settler;
Am. a. homesteader; '~stelle f
settler's holding; Am. a. homestead.

'**Siedlung** f (-/-en) settlement; housing estate.

Sieg [zi:k] m (-[e]s/-e) victory (über
acc. over); sports: a. win; den ~
davontragen win the day, be victorious.

Siegel ['zi:gəl] n (-s/-) seal (a. fig.);
signet; '~lack m sealing-wax; '2n
v/t. (ge-, h) seal; '~ring m signet-
ring.

sieg|en ['zi:gən] v/i. (ge-, h) be vic-
torious (über acc. over), conquer
s.o.; sports: win; '2er m (-s/-) con-
queror, rhet. victor; sports: winner.

Siegeszeichen ['zi:gəs-] n trophy.

'**siegreich** adj. victorious, triumphant.

Signal [zɪ'gnɑ:l] n (-s/-e) signal;
2isieren [~ali'zi:rən] v/t. (no -ge-, h)
signal.

Silbe ['zilbə] f (-/-n) syllable; '~n-
trennung f syllabi(fi)cation.

Silber ['zilbər] n (-s/no pl.) silver;
s. Tafelsilber; '2n adj. (of) silver;

'**~zeug** F *n* silver plate, *Am. a.* silverware.

Silhouette [zilu'ɛtə] *f* (-/-n) silhouette; skyline.

Silvester [zil'vɛstər] *n* (-s/-), **~abend** *m* new-year's eve.

simpel ['zimpəl] **1.** *adj.* plain, simple; stupid, silly; **2.** 2 *m* (-s/-) simpleton.

Sims [zims] *m, n* (-es/-e) ledge; sill (*of window*); mantelshelf (*of fireplace*); shelf; △ cornice.

Simul|ant [zimu'lant] *m* (-en/-en) *esp.* ✕, ♣ malingerer; **2ieren** (*no -ge-, h*) **1.** *v/t.* sham, feign, simulate (*illness, etc.*); **2.** *v/i.* sham, feign; *esp.* ✕, ♣ malinger.

Sinfonie ♪ [zinfo'ni:] *f* (-/-n) symphony.

sing|en ['ziŋən] *v/t. and v/i.* (*irr., ge-, h*) sing; *vom Blatt* ~ sing at sight; *nach Noten* ~ sing from music; **2sang** F *m* (-[e]s/*no pl.*) singsong; **2spiel** *n* musical comedy; **2stimme** ♪ *f* vocal part.

Singular *gr.* ['ziŋgulɑːr] *m* (-s/-e) singular (number).

'**Singvogel** *m* song-bird, songster.

sinken ['ziŋkən] *v/i.* (*irr., ge-, sein*) sink; *ship: a.* founder, go down; ✝ *prices:* fall, drop, go down; *den Mut* ~ *lassen* lose courage.

Sinn [zin] *m* (-[e]s/-e) sense; taste (*für* for); tendency; sense, meaning; *von* ~*en sein* be out of one's senses; *im* ~ *haben* have in mind; *in gewissem* ~*e* in a sense; '**~bild** *n* symbol, emblem; '**2bildlich** *adj.* symbolic(al), emblematic; **2en** *v/i.* (*irr., ge-, h*): *auf Rache* ~ meditate revenge.

'**Sinnen|lust** *f* sensuality; '**~mensch** *m* sensualist; '**~rausch** *m* intoxication of the senses.

sinnentstellend *adj.* ['zin²-] garbling, distorting. [world.]

'**Sinnenwelt** *f* (-/*no pl.*) material]

'**Sinnes|änderung** *f* change of mind; '**~art** *f* disposition, mentality; '**~organ** *n* sense-organ; '**~täuschung** *f* illusion, hallucination.

'**sinn|lich** *adj.* sensual; material; '**2lichkeit** *f* (-/*no pl.*) sensuality; '**~los** *adj.* senseless; futile, useless; '**2losigkeit** *f* (-/-en) senselessness; futility, uselessness; '**~reich** *adj.* ingenious; '**~verwandt** *adj.* synonymous.

Sipp|e ['zipə] *f* (-/-n) tribe; (blood-) relations *pl.*; family; '**~schaft** *contp. f* (-/-en) relations *pl.*; *fig.* clan, clique; *die ganze* ~ the whole lot.

Sirene [zi're:nə] *f* (-/-n) siren.

Sirup ['zi:rup] *m* (-s/-e) syrup, *Am.* sirup; treacle, molasses *sg.*

Sitte ['zitə] *f* (-/-n) custom; habit; usage; ~*n pl.* morals *pl.*; manners *pl.*

'**Sitten|bild** *n*, '**~gemälde** *n* genre (-painting); *fig.* picture of manners and morals; '**~gesetz** *n* moral law; '**~lehre** *f* ethics *pl.*; '**2los** *adj.* immoral; '**2losigkeit** *f* (-/-en) immorality; '**~polizei** *f* *appr.* vice squad; '**~prediger** *m* moralizer; '**~richter** *fig. m* censor, moralizer; '**2streng** *adj.* puritanic(al).

'**sittlich** *adj.* moral; '**2keit** *f* (-/*no pl.*) morality; '**2keitsverbrechen** *n* sexual crime.

'**sittsam** *adj.* modest; '**2keit** *f* (-/*no pl.*) modesty.

Situation [zitua'tsjoːn] *f* (-/-en) situation.

Sitz [zits] *m* (-es/-e) seat (*a. fig.*); fit (*of dress, etc.*).

'**sitzen** *v/i.* (*irr., ge-, h*) sit, be seated; *dress, etc.:* fit; blow, etc.: tell; F *fig.* do time; ~ *bleiben* remain seated, keep one's seat; '**~bleiben** *v/i.* (*irr. bleiben, sep., -ge-, sein*) *girl at dance:* F be a wallflower; *girl:* be left on the shelf; *at school:* not to get one's remove; ~ *auf* (*dat.*) be left with (*goods*) on one's hands; '**~d** *adj.* ~*e Tätigkeit* sedentary work; '**~lassen** *v/t.* (*irr. lassen, sep., [no] -ge-, h*) leave *s.o.* in the lurch, let *s.o.* down; *girl:* jilt (*lover*); leave (*girl*) high and dry; *auf sich* ~ pocket (*insult, etc.*).

'**Sitz|gelegenheit** *f* seating accommodation, seat(s *pl.*); ~ *bieten für* seat; '**~platz** *m* seat; '**~streik** *m* sit-down or stay-in strike.

'**Sitzung** *f* (-/-en) sitting (*a. parl., paint.*); meeting, conference; '**~speriode** *f* session.

Skala ['skaːla] *f* (-/Skalen, Skalas) scale (*a. ♪*); dial (*of radio set*); *fig.* gamut; *gleitende* ~ sliding scale.

Skandal [skan'daːl] *m* (-s/-e) scandal; row, riot; **2ös** *adj.* [~a'løːs] scandalous.

Skelett [ske'lɛt] *n* (-[e]s/-e) skeleton.

Skep|sis ['skɛpsis] *f* (-/*no pl.*) scepticism, *Am. a.* skepticism; **~tiker** ['~tikər] *m* (-s/-) sceptic, *Am. a.* skeptic; '**2tisch** *adj.* sceptical, *Am. a.* skeptical.

Ski [ʃiː] *m* (-s/-er, ✎, -) ski; ~ *laufen or fahren* ski; '**~fahrer** *m*, '**~läufer** *m* skier; '**~lift** *m* ski-lift; '**~sport** *m* (-[e]s/*no pl.*) skiing.

Skizz|e ['skitsə] *f* (-/-n) sketch (*a. fig.*); **2ieren** [~'tsiːrən] *v/t.* (*no -ge-, h*) sketch, outline (*both a. fig.*).

Sklav|e ['sklaːvə] *m* (-n/-n) slave (*a. fig.*); '**~enhandel** *m* slave-trade; '**~enhändler** *m* slave-trader; **~e'rei** *f* (-/-en) slavery; '**2isch** *adj.* slavish.

Skonto ✝ ['skɔnto] *m, n* (-s/-s, ✎ Skonti) discount.

Skrupel ['skruːpəl] *m* (-s/-) scruple; '**2los** *adj.* unscrupulous.

Skulptur [skulp'tuːr] *f* (-/-en) sculpture.

Slalom ['slɑ:lɔm] *m* (-s/-s) skiing, *etc.*: slalom.

Slaw|e ['slɑ:və] *m* (-n/-n) Slav; **'2isch** *adj.* Slav(onic).

Smaragd [sma'rakt] *m* (-[e]s/-e) emerald; **2grün** *adj.* emerald.

Smoking ['smo:kiŋ] *m* (-s/-s) dinner-jacket, *Am. a.* tuxedo, F tux.

so [zo:] **1.** *adv.* so, thus; like this *or* that; as; ~ *ein* such a; ~ ... *wie* as ... as; *nicht* ~ ... *wie* not so ... as; *oder* ~ by hook or by crook; **2.** *cj.* so, therefore, consequently; ~ *daß* so that; **~bald** *cj.* [zo'-]: ~ (*als*) as soon as.

Socke ['zɔkə] *f* (-/-n) sock; **'~l** *m* (-s/-) ⌂ pedestal, socle; socket (*of lamp*); **'~n** *m* (-s/-) sock; **'~nhalter** *m/pl.* suspenders *pl.*, *Am.* garters *pl.*

Sodawasser ['zo:da-] *n* (-s/⁼) soda(-water).

Sodbrennen ꝭ ['zo:t-] *n* (-s/*no pl.*) heartburn.

soeben *adv.* [zo'-] just (now).

Sofa ['zo:fa] *n* (-s/-s) sofa.

sofern *cj.* [zo'-] if, provided that; ~ *nicht* unless.

soff [zɔf] *pret. of* saufen.

sofort *adv.* [zo'-] at once, immediately, directly, right *or* straight away; **~ig** *adj.* immediate, prompt.

Sog [zo:k] **1.** *m* (-[e]s/-e) suction; ⊕ wake (*a. fig.*), undertow; **2.** ♀ *pret. of* saugen.

so|gar *adv.* [zo'-] even; **~genannt** *adj.* [zo:-] so-called; **~gleich** *adv.* [zo'-] *s.* sofort.

Sohle ['zo:lə] *f* (-/-n) sole; bottom (*of valley, etc.*); ꝭ floor.

Sohn [zo:n] *m* (-[e]s/⁼e) son.

solange *cj.* [zo'-]: ~ (*als*) so *or* as long as. [such.]

solch *pron.* [zɔlç] such; *als* ~ e(*r*) as)

Sold ꭗ [zɔlt] *m* (-[e]s/-e) pay.

Soldat [zɔl'dɑ:t] *m* (-en/-en) soldier; *der unbekannte* ~ the Unknown Warrior *or* Soldier.

Söldner ['zœldnər] *m* (-s/-) mercenary.

Sole ['zo:lə] *f* (-/-n) brine, salt water.

solid *adj.* [zo'li:t] solid (*a. fig.*); *basis, etc.*: sound; ♱ firm, *etc.*: sound, solvent; *prices*: reasonable, fair; *p.* steady, staid, respectable.

solidarisch *adj.* [zoli'dɑ:riʃ]: *sich* ~ *erklären mit* declare one's solidarity with.

solide *adj.* [zo'li:də] *s.* solid.

Solist [zo'list] *m* (-en/-en) soloist.

Soll ♱ [zɔl] *n* (-[s]/-[s]) debit; (output) target.

'sollen (*h*) **1.** *v/i.* (ge-): *ich sollte* (*eigentlich*) I ought to; **2.** *v/aux.* (*irr.*, *no* -ge-): *er soll* he shall; he is to; he is said to; *ich sollte* I should; *er sollte* (*eigentlich*) *zu Hause sein* he ought to be at home; *er sollte seinen Vater niemals wiedersehen* he was never to see his father again.

Solo ['zo:lo] *n* (-s/-s, *Soli*) solo.

somit *cj.* [zo'-] thus; consequently.

Sommer ['zɔmər] *m* (-s/-) summer; **'~frische** *f* (-/-n) summer-holidays *pl.*; summer-resort; **'2lich** *adj.* summer-like, summer(l)y; **'~sprosse** *f* freckle; **'2sprossig** *adj.* freckled; **'~wohnung** *f* summer residence, *Am.* cottage, summer house; **'~zeit** *f* **1.** (-/-en) *season*: summertime; **2.** (-/*no pl.*) summer time, *Am.* daylight-saving time.

Sonate ♪ [zo'nɑ:tə] *f* (-/-n) sonata.

Sonde ['zɔndə] *f* (-/-n) probe.

Sonder|angebot ['zɔndər-] *n* special offer; **'~ausgabe** *f* special (edition); **'2bar** *adj.* strange, odd; **'~beilage** *f* inset, supplement (*of newspaper*); **'~berichterstatter** *m* special correspondent; **'2lich 1.** *adj.* special, peculiar; **2.** *adv.*: *nicht* ~ not particularly; **'~ling** *m* (-s/-e) crank, odd person; **'2n 1.** *cj.* but; *nicht nur*, ~ *auch* not only, but (also); **2.** *v/t.* (ge-, *h*): *die Spreu vom Weizen* ~ sift the chaff from the wheat; **'~recht** *n* privilege; **'~zug** ꭗ *m* special (train).

sondieren [zɔn'di:rən] (*no* -ge-, *h*) **1.** *v/t.* ꝭ probe (*a. fig.*); **2.** *fig.* *v/i.* make tentative inquiries.

Sonn|abend ['zɔn⁹-] *m* (-s/-e) Saturday; **'~e** *f* (-/-n) sun; **'2en** *v/t.* (ge-, *h*) (expose to the) sun; *sich* ~ sun o.s. (*a. fig. in dat.* in), bask in the sun.

'Sonnen|aufgang *m* sunrise; **'~bad** *n* sun-bath; **'~brand** *m* sunburn; **'~bräune** *f* sunburn, tan, *Am.* (sun) tan; **'~brille** *f* (e-e a pair of) sunglasses *pl.*; **'~finsternis** *f* solar eclipse; **'~fleck** *m* sun-spot; **'2klar** *fig. adj.* (as) clear as daylight; **'~licht** *n* (-[e]s/*no pl.*) sunlight; **'~schein** *m* (-[e]s/*no pl.*) sunshine; **'~schirm** *m* sunshade, parasol; **'~segel** *n* awning; **'~seite** *f* sunny side (*a. fig.*); **'~stich** ꝭ *m* sunstroke; **'~strahl** *m* sunbeam; **'~uhr** *f* sun-dial; **'~untergang** *m* sunset, sundown; **'2verbrannt** *adj.* sunburnt, tanned; **'~wende** *f* solstice.

'sonnig *adj.* sunny (*a. fig.*).

'Sonntag *m* Sunday.

'Sonntags|anzug *m* Sunday suit *or* best; **'~fahrer** *mot. contp. m* Sunday driver; **'~kind** *n* person born on a Sunday; *fig.* person born under a lucky star; **'~rückfahrkarte** ꭗ *f* week-end ticket; **'~ruhe** *f* Sunday rest; **'~staat** F *co. m* (-[e]s/*no pl.*) Sunday go-to-meeting clothes *pl.*

sonor *adj.* [zo'no:r] sonorous.

sonst [zɔnst] **1.** *adv.* otherwise, *with pron.* else; usually, normally; *wer* ~? who else?; *wie* ~ as usual; ~ *nichts* nothing else; **2.** *cj.* otherwise, or else; **'~ig** *adj.* other; **'~wie** *adv.*

in some other way; '**~wo** *adv.* elsewhere, somewhere else.

Sopran ♪ [zo'praːn] *m (-s/-e)* soprano; sopranist; **~istin** ♪ [~a'nistin] *f (-/-nen)* soprano, sopranist.

Sorge ['zɔrgə] *f (-/-n)* care; sorrow; uneasiness, anxiety; **~** *tragen für* take care of; *sich ~n machen um* be anxious *or* worried about; *mach dir keine ~n* don't worry.

'**sorgen** *(ge-, h)* **1.** *v/i.*: **~** *für* care for, provide for; take care of, attend to; *dafür ~, daß* take care that; **2.** *v/refl.*: *sich ~ um* be anxious *or* worried about; '**~frei** *adj.*, '**~los** *adj.* carefree, free from care; '**~voll** *adj.* full of cares; *face*: worried, troubled.

Sorg|falt ['zɔrkfalt] *f (-/no pl.)* care(fulness); **2fältig** *adj.* ['~fɛltiç] careful; '**2lich** *adj.* careful, anxious; '**2los** *adj.* carefree; thoughtless; negligent; careless; '**2sam** *adj.* careful.

Sort|e ['zɔrtə] *f (-/-n)* sort, kind, species, *Am. a.* stripe; **2ieren** [~'tiːrən] *v/t. (no -ge-, h)* (as)sort; arrange; **~iment** [~i'mɛnt] *n (-[e]s/-e)* assortment.

Soße ['zoːsə] *f (-/-n)* sauce; gravy.

sott [zɔt] *pret. of sieden.*

Souffl|eurkasten *thea.* [su'flœːr-] *m* prompt-box, prompter's box; **~euse** *thea.* [~zə] *f (-/-n)* prompter; **2ieren** *thea. (no -ge-, h)* **1.** *v/i.* prompt *(j-m s.o.)*; **2.** *v/t.* prompt.

Souverän [suvə'rɛːn] **1.** *m (-s/-e)* sovereign; **2.** ② *adj.* sovereign; *fig.* superior; **~ität** [~ɛni'tɛːt] *f (-/no pl.)* sovereignty.

so|viel [zo'-] **1.** *cj.* so *or* as far as; *~ ich weiß* so far as I know; **2.** *adv.*: *doppelt ~* twice as much; **~'weit 1.** *cj.*: **~** *es mich betrifft* in so far as it concerns me, so far as I am concerned; **2.** *adv.*: **~** *ganz gut* not bad (for a start); **~wieso** *adv.* [zovi'zoː] in any case, anyhow, anyway.

Sowjet [zɔ'vjɛt] *m (-s/-s)* Soviet; **2isch** *adj.* Soviet.

sowohl *cj.* [zo'-]: **~** *... als (auch)* ... both ... and ..., ... as well as ...

sozial *adj.* [zo'tsjaːl] social; **2demokrat** *m* social democrat; **~isieren** [~ali'ziːrən] *v/t. (no -ge-, h)* socialize; **2isierung** [~ali'ziːruŋ] *f (-/-en)* socialization; **2ist** [~a'list] *m (-en/-en)* socialist; **~istisch** *adj.* [~a'listiʃ] socialist.

Sozius ['zoːtsjus] *m (-/-se)* ✝ partner; *mot.* pillion-rider; '**~sitz** *mot. m* pillion.

sozusagen *adv.* [zotsu'zaːgən] so to speak, as it were.

Spachtel ['ʃpaxtəl] *m (-s/-)*, *f (-/-n)* spatula.

spähe|n ['ʃpɛːən] *v/i. (ge-, h)* look

16*

---

out *(nach* for); peer; '**2r** *m (-s/-)* look-out; ✗ scout.

Spalier [ʃpa'liːr] *n (-s/-e)* trellis, espalier; *fig.* lane; **~** *bilden* form a lane.

Spalt [ʃpalt] *m (-[e]s/-e)* crack, split, rift, crevice, fissure; '**~e** *f (-/-n) s. Spalt; typ.* column; **2en** *v/t. (irr.]* ge-, h) split *(a. fig.* hairs), cleave *(block of wood, etc.)*; *sich ~* split (up); '**~ung** *f (-/-en)* splitting, cleavage; *fig.* split; *eccl.* schism.

Span [ʃpaːn] *m (-[e]s/~e)* chip, shaving, splinter.

Spange ['ʃpaŋə] *f (-/-n)* clasp; buckle; clip; slide *(in hair)*; strap *(of shoes)*; bracelet.

Span|ier ['ʃpaːnjər] *m (-s/-)* Spaniard; **2isch** *adj.* Spanish.

Spann [ʃpan] **1.** *m (-[e]s/-e)* instep; **2.** ② *pret. of* spinnen; '**~e** *f (-/-n)* span; ✗, *orn.* spread *(of wings)*; ✝ margin; '**2en** *(ge-, h)* **1.** *v/t.* stretch *(rope, muscles, etc.)*; cock *(rifle)*; bend *(bow, etc.)*; tighten *(spring, etc.)*; *vor den Wagen* **~** harness to the carriage; *s. gespannt;* **2.** *v/i.* be (too) tight; '**2end** *adj.* exciting, thrilling, gripping; '**~kraft** *f (-/no pl.)* elasticity; *fig.* energy; '**~ung** *f (-/-en)* tension *(a. fig.)*; ⚡ voltage; ⊕ strain, stress; ⚠ span; *fig.* close attention.

Spar|büchse ['ʃpaːr-] *f* money-box; '**2en** *(ge-, h)* **1.** *v/t.* save *(money, strength, etc.)*; put by; **2.** *v/i.* save; economize, cut down expenses; **~** *mit* be chary of *(praise, etc.)*; '**~er** *m (-s/-)* saver.

Spargel ♀ ['ʃpargəl] *m (-s/-)* asparagus.

'**Spar|kasse** *f* savings-bank; '**~konto** *n* savings-account.

spärlich *adj.* ['ʃpɛːrliç] *crop, dress, etc.*: scanty; *population, etc.*: sparse; *hair*: thin.

Sparren ['ʃparən] *m (-s/-)* rafter, spar.

'**sparsam 1.** *adj.* saving, economical *(mit* of); **2.** *adv.*: **~** *leben* lead a frugal life, economize; **~** *umgehen mit* use sparingly, be frugal of; '**2keit** *f (-/no pl.*) economy, frugality.

Spaß [ʃpaːs] *m (-es/~e)* joke, jest; fun, lark; amusement; *aus* *or* *im or zum* **~** in fun; **~** *beiseite* joking apart; *er hat nur ~ gemacht* he was only joking; '**2en** *v/i. (ge-, h)* joke, jest, make fun; *damit ist nicht zu ~* that is no joking matter; '**2haft** *adj.*, '**2ig** *adj.* facetious, waggish; funny; '**~macher** *m (-s/-)*, '**~vogel** *m* wag, joker.

spät [ʃpɛːt] **1.** *adj.* late; advanced; *zu ~* too late; *am ~en Nachmittag* late in the afternoon; *wie ~ ist es?* what time is it?; **2.** *adv.* late; *er kommt 5 Minuten zu ~* he is five minutes late (zu for); ~ in der Nacht late at night.

Spaten ['ʃpɑːtən] m (-s/-) spade.

'späte|r 1. adj. later; **2.** adv. later on; afterward(s); früher oder ~ sooner or later; **~stens** adv. ['~stəns] at the latest.

Spatz orn. [ʃpats] m (-en, -es/-en) sparrow.

spazieren [ʃpa'tsiːrən] v/i. (no -ge-, sein) walk, stroll; **~fahren** (irr. fahren, sep., -ge-) **1.** v/i. (sein) go for a drive; **2.** v/t. (h) take for a drive; take (baby) out (in pram); **~gehen** v/i. (irr. gehen, sep., -ge-, sein) go for a walk.

Spa'zier|fahrt f drive, ride; **~gang** m walk, stroll; e-n ~ machen go for a walk; **~gänger** [~gɛŋər] m (-s/-) walker, stroller; **~weg** m walk.

Speck [ʃpɛk] m (-[e]s/-e) bacon.

Spedi|teur [ʃpedi'tøːr] m (-s/-e) forwarding agent; (furniture) remover; **~tion** [~'tsjoːn] f (-/-en) forwarding agent or agency.

Speer [ʃpeːr] m (-[e]s/-e) spear; sports: javelin; **~werfen** n (-s/no pl.) javelin-throw(ing); **~werfer** m (-s/-) javelin-thrower.

Speiche ['ʃpaɪçə] f (-/-n) spoke.

Speichel ['ʃpaɪçəl] m (-s/no pl.) spit(tle), saliva; **~lecker** fig. m (-s/-) lickspittle, toady.

Speicher ['ʃpaɪçər] m (-s/-) granary; warehouse; garret, attic.

speien ['ʃpaɪən] (irr., ge-, h) **1.** v/t. spit out (blood, etc.); volcano, etc.: belch (fire, etc.); **2.** v/i. spit; vomit, be sick.

Speise ['ʃpaɪzə] f (-/-n) food, nourishment; meal; dish; **~eis** n ice-cream; **~kammer** f larder, pantry; **~karte** f bill of fare, menu; **'2n** (ge-, h) **1.** v/i. s. essen **1.** at restaurants: take one's meals; **2.** v/t. feed; ⊕, ⚡ a. supply (mit with); **~nfolge** f menu; **~röhre** anat. f gullet, (o)esophagus; **~saal** m dining-hall; **~schrank** m (meat-)safe; **~wagen** 🚃 m dining-car, diner; **~zimmer** n dining-room.

Spektakel F [ʃpɛk'tɑːkəl] m (-s/-) noise, din.

Spekul|ant [ʃpeku'lant] m (-en/-en) speculator; **~ation** [~a'tsjoːn] f (-/-en) speculation; ✝ a. venture; **2ieren** [~'liːrən] v/i. (no -ge-, h) speculate (auf acc. on).

Spelunke [ʃpe'luŋkə] f (-/-n) den; drinking-den, Am. F a. dive.

Spende ['ʃpɛndə] f (-/-n) gift; alms pl.; contribution; **'2n** v/t. (ge-, h) give; donate (money to charity, blood, etc.); eccl. administer (sacraments); bestow (praise) (dat. on); **'~r** m (-s/-) giver; donor.

spen'dieren v/t. (no -ge-, h): j-m et. ~ treat s.o. to s.th., stand s.o. s.th.

Sperling orn. ['ʃpɛrlɪŋ] m (-s/-e) sparrow.

Sperr|e ['ʃpɛrə] f (-/-n) barrier; 🚃 barrier, Am. gate; toll-bar; ⊕ lock(ing device), detent; barricade; ✝, ⚓ embargo; ✕ blockade; sports: suspension; **'2en** (ge-, h) **1.** v/t. close; ✝, ⚓ embargo; cut off (gas supply, electricity, etc.); stop (cheque, etc.); sports: suspend; **2.** v/i. jam, be stuck; **~holz** n plywood; **~konto** ✝ n blocked account; **~kreis** ⚡ m wave-trap; **~sitz** thea. m stalls pl., Am. orchestra; **~ung** f (-/-en) closing; stoppage (of cheque, etc.); ✝, ⚓ embargo; ✕ blockade; **~zone** f prohibited area.

Spesen ['ʃpeːzən] pl. expenses pl., charges pl.

Spezial|ausbildung [ʃpe'tsjaːl?-] f special training; **~fach** n special(i)ty; **~geschäft** ✝ n one-line shop, Am. specialty store; **2isieren** [~ali'ziːrən] v/refl. (no -ge-, h) specialize (auf acc. in); **~ist** [~a'lɪst] m (-en/-en) specialist; **~ität** [~ali-'tɛːt] f (-/-en) special(i)ty.

speziell adj. [ʃpe'tsjɛl] specific, special, particular.

spezifisch adj. [ʃpe'tsiːfɪʃ]: ~es Gewicht specific gravity.

Sphäre ['ʃfɛːrə] f (-/-n) sphere (a. fig.).

Spick|aal ['ʃpɪk-] m smoked eel; **'2en** (ge-, h) **1.** v/t. lard; fig. (inter-)lard (mit with); F: j-n ~ grease s.o.'s palm; **2.** F fig. v/i. crib.

spie [ʃpiː] pret. of speien.

Spiegel ['ʃpiːgəl] m (-s/-) mirror (a. fig.), looking-glass; **~bild** n reflected image; **'2bildlich** adj. mirror-like; **~ei** ['ʃpiːgəl?-] n fried egg; **'2glatt** adj. water: glassy, unrippled; road, etc.: very slippery; **'2n** (ge-, h) **1.** v/i. shine; **2.** v/refl. be reflected; **~schrift** f mirror-writing.

Spieg(e)lung ['ʃpiːg(ə)luŋ] f (-/-en) reflection, reflexion; mirage.

Spiel [ʃpiːl] n (-[e]s/-e) play (a. fig.); game (a. fig.); match; ♪ playing; ein ~ Karten a pack of playing-cards, Am. a. a deck; auf dem ~ stehen be at stake; aufs ~ setzen jeopardize, stake; **~art** ♀, zo. f variety; **~ball** m tennis: game ball; billiards: red ball; fig. plaything, sport; **~bank** f (-/-en) gaming-house; **'2en** (ge-, h) **1.** v/i. play; gamble; ~ mit play with; fig. a. toy with; **2.** v/t. play (tennis, violin, etc.); thea. act, play (part); mit j-m Schach ~ play s.o. at chess; den Höflichen ~ do the polite; **'2end** fig. adv. easily; **~er** m (-s/-) player; gambler; **~erei** f (-/-en) pastime; child's amusement; **~ergebnis** n sports: result, score; **~feld** n sports: (playing-)field; pitch; **'~film** m feature film or picture; '~gefährte m playfellow, playmate; '~karte f playing-card; '~leiter m thea. stage manager; cinematography: director; sports: referee; '~marke f counter, sl. chip; '~plan m thea., etc.: program(me); repertory; '~platz m playground; '~raum fig. m play, scope; '~regel f rule (of the game); '~sachen f/pl. playthings pl., toys pl.; '~schuld f gambling-debt; '~schule f infant-school, kindergarten; '~tisch m card-table; gambling-table; '~uhr f musical box, Am. music box; '~verderber m (-s/-) spoil-sport, killjoy, wet blanket; '~waren f/pl. playthings pl., toys pl.; '~zeit f thea. season; sports: time of play; '~zeug n toy(s pl.), plaything(s pl.).

Spieß [ʃpiːs] m (-es/-e) spear, pike; spit; den ~ umdrehen turn the tables; '~bürger m bourgeois, Philistine, Am. a. Babbit; '2bürgerlich adj. bourgeois, Philistine; '~er m (-s/-) s. Spießbürger; '~geselle m accomplice; '~ruten f/pl.: ~ laufen run the gauntlet (a. fig.).

spinal adj. [ʃpiˈnaːl]: ~e Kinderlähmung 💊 infantile paralysis, poliomyelitis, F polio.

Spinat 🌿 [ʃpiˈnaːt] m (-[e]s/-e) spinach.

Spind [ʃpint] n, m (-[e]s/-e) wardrobe, cupboard; ⚔, sports, etc.: locker.

Spindel [ˈʃpindəl] f (-/-n) spindle; '2dürr adj. (as) thin as a lath.

Spinn|e zo. [ˈʃpinə] f (-/-n) spider; '2en (irr., ge-, h) 1. v/t. spin (a. fig.); ~ hatch (plot, etc.); 2. v/i. cat: purr; F fig. be crazy, sl. be nuts; ~engewebe n cobweb; '~er m (-s/-) spinner; F fig. silly; ~eˈrei f (-/-en) spinning; spinning-mill; ~maschine f spinning-machine; '~webe f (-/-n) cobweb.

Spion [ʃpiˈoːn] m (-s/-e) spy, intelligencer; fig. judas; ~age [~oˈnaːʒə] f (-/no pl.) espionage; 2ieren [~oˈniːrən] v/i. (no -ge-, h) (play the) spy.

Spiral|e [ʃpiˈraːlə] f (-/-n) spiral (a. ⚙), helix; 2förmig adj. [~fœrmiç] spiral, helical.

Spirituosen [ʃpirituˈoːzən] pl. spirits pl.

Spiritus [ˈʃpiːritus] m (-/-se) spirit, alcohol; '~kocher m (-s/-) spirit stove.

Spital [ʃpiˈtaːl] n (-s/⁓er) hospital; alms-house; home for the aged.

spitz [ʃpits] 1. adj. pointed (a. fig.); 🜨 angle: acute; fig. poignant; ~e Zunge sharp tongue; 2. adv.: ~ zulaufen taper (off); '2bube m thief; rogue, rascal (both a. co.); 2büberei [~byːbəˈraɪ] f (-/-en) roguery, ras-

cality (both a. co.); ~bübisch adj. [ˈ~byːbiʃ] eyes, smile, etc.: roguish.

'Spitz|e f (-/-n) point (of pencil, weapon, jaw, etc.); tip (of nose, finger, etc.); nib (of tool, etc.); spire; head (of enterprise, etc.); lace; an der ~ liegen sports: be in the lead; j-m die ~ bieten make head against s.o.; auf die ~ treiben carry to an extreme; '~el m (-s/-) (common) informer; 2en v/t. (ge-, h) point, sharpen; den Mund ~ purse (up) one's lips; die Ohren ~ prick up one's ears (a. fig.).

'Spitzen|leistung f top performance; ⊕ maximum capacity; '~lohn m top wages pl.

'spitz|findig adj. subtle, captious; '2findigkeit f (-/-en) subtlety, captiousness; '2hacke f pickax(e), pick; '~ig adj. pointed; fig. a. poignant; '2marke typ. f head(ing); '2name m nickname.

Splitter [ˈʃplitər] m (-s/-) splinter, shiver; chip; '2frei adj. glass: shatterproof; '2ig adj. splintery; '2n v/i. (ge-, h, sein) splinter, shiver; '2ˈnackt F adj. stark naked, Am. a. mother-naked'; '~partei pol. f splinter party.

spontan adj. [ʃpɔnˈtaːn] spontaneous.

sporadisch adj. [ʃpoˈraːdiʃ] sporadic.

Sporn [ʃpɔrn] m (-[e]s/Sporen) spur; die Sporen geben put or set spurs to (horse); sich die Sporen verdienen win one's spurs; '2en v/t. (ge-, h) spur.

Sport [ʃpɔrt] m (-[e]s/🏹 -e) sport; fig. hobby; ~ treiben go in for sports; '~ausrüstung f sports equipment; '~geschäft n sporting-goods shop; '~kleidung f sport clothes pl., sportswear; '~lehrer m games-master; '2lich adj. sporting, sportsmanlike; figure: athletic; '~nachrichten f/pl. sports news sg., pl.; '~platz m sports field; stadium.

Spott [ʃpɔt] m (-[e]s/no pl.) mockery; derision; scorn; (s-n) ~ treiben mit make sport of; '2billig F adj. dirt-cheap.

Spötte|lei [ʃpœtəˈlaɪ] f (-/-en) raillery, sneer, jeer; '2ln v/i. (ge-, h) sneer (über acc. at), jeer (at).

'spotten v/i. (ge-, h) mock (über acc. at); jeer (at); jeder Beschreibung ~ beggar description.

Spötter [ˈʃpœtər] m (-s/-) mocker, scoffer; ~ei [~ˈraɪ] f (-/-en) mockery.

'spöttisch adj. mocking; sneering; ironical.

'Spott|name m nickname; '~preis m ridiculous price; für e-n ~ for a mere song; '~schrift f lampoon, satire.

sprach [ʃpraːx] pret. of sprechen.

'Sprache f (-/-n) speech; language

(a. fig.); diction; zur ~ bringen bring up, broach; zur ~ kommen come up (for discussion); **'Sprach|eigentümlichkeit** f idiom; **'~fehler** ⚥ m impediment (in one's speech); **'~führer** m language guide; **'~gebrauch** m usage; **'~gefühl** n (-[e]s/no pl.) linguistic instinct; **2kundig** adj. [-kundiç] versed in languages; **'~lehre** f grammar; **'~lehrer** m teacher of languages; **'~lich** adj. linguistic, grammatical; **'2los** adj. speechless; **'~rohr** n speaking-trumpet, megaphone; fig.: mouthpiece; organ; **'~schatz** m vocabulary; **'~störung** f impediment (in one's speech); **'~wissenschaft** f philology, science of language; linguistics pl.; **'~wissenschaftler** m philologist; linguist; **2wissenschaftlich** adj. philological; linguistic.

sprang [ʃpraŋ] pret. of springen.

Sprech|chor ['ʃprɛç-] m speaking chorus; **'2en** (irr., ge-, h) 1. v/t. speak (language, truth, etc.); ꝛꞇ pronounce (judgement); say (prayer); j-n zu ~ wünschen wish to see s.o.; j-n schuldig ~ ꝛꞇ pronounce s.o. guilty; F Bände ~ speak volumes (für for); 2. v/i. speak; talk (both: mit to, with; über acc., von of, about); er ist nicht zu ~ you cannot see him; **'~er** m (-s/-) speaker; radio: announcer; spokesman; **'~fehler** m slip of the tongue; **'~stunde** f consulting-hours pl.; **'~übung** f exercise in speaking; **'~zimmer** n consulting-room, surgery.

spreizen ['ʃpraɪtsən] v/t. (ge-, h) spread (out); a. straddle (legs); sich ~ pretend to be unwilling.

Spreng|bombe ✕ ['ʃprɛŋ-] f high-explosive bomb, demolition bomb; **'~el** eccl. m (-s/-) diocese, see; parish; **'2en** (ge-) 1. v/t. (h) sprinkle, water (road, lawn, etc.); blow up, blast (bridge, rocks, etc.); burst open (door, etc.); spring (mine, etc.); gambling: break (bank); break up (meeting, etc.); 2. v/i. (sein) gallop; **'~stoff** m explosive; **'~ung** f (-/-en) blowing-up, blasting; explosion; **'~wagen** m water(ing)-cart.

Sprenkel ['ʃprɛŋkəl] m (-s/-) speckle, spot; **'2n** v/t. (ge-, h) speckle, spot.

Spreu [ʃprɔy] f (-/no pl.) chaff; s. sondern 2.

Sprich|wort ['ʃpriç-] n (-[e]s/-wer) proverb, adage; **'2wörtlich** adj. proverbial (a. fig.).

sprießen ['ʃpriːsən] v/i. (irr., ge-, sein) sprout; germinate.

Spring|brunnen ['ʃprɪŋ-] m fountain; **'2en** v/i. (irr., ge-, sein) jump, leap; ball, etc.: bounce; swimming: dive; burst, crack, break; in die Augen ~ strike the eye; ~ über (acc.)

jump (over), leap, clear; **'~er** m (-s/-) jumper; swimming: diver; chess: knight; **'~flut** f spring tide.

Sprit [ʃprit] m (-[e]s/-e) spirit, alcohol; F mot. fuel, petrol, sl. juice, Am. gasoline, F gas.

Spritz|e ['ʃprɪtsə] f (-/-n) syringe (a. ✗), squirt; ⊕ fire-engine; j-m e-e ~ geben ✗ give s.o. an injection; **'2en** (ge-) 1. v/t. (h) sprinkle, water (road, lawn, etc.); splash (water, etc.) (über acc. on, over); 2. v/i. (h) splash; pen: splutter; 3. v/i. (sein) F fig. dash, flit; ~ aus (blood, etc.: spurt or spout from (wound, etc.); **'~er** m (-s/-) splash; **'~tour** F f: e-e ~ machen go for a spin.

spröde adj. ['ʃprøːdə] glass, etc.: brittle; skin: chapped, chappy; esp. girl: prudish, prim, coy.

Sproß [ʃprɔs] 1. m (Sprosses/Sprosse) ♀ shoot, sprout, scion (a. fig.); fig.: offspring; 2. 2 pret. of sprießen.

Sprosse ['ʃprɔsə] f (-/-n) rung, round, step.

Sprößling ['ʃprœslɪŋ] m (-s/-e) ♀ s. Sproß 1.; co. son.

Spruch [ʃprux] m (-[e]s/-e) saying; dictum; ꝛꞇ sentence; ꝛꞇ verdict; **'~band** n banner; **'2reif** adj. ripe for decision.

Sprudel ['ʃpruːdəl] m (-s/-) mineral water; **'2n** v/i. (ge-) 1. (h) bubble, effervesce; 2. (sein): ~ aus or von gush from.

sprüh|en ['ʃpryːən] (ge-) 1. v/t. spray, sprinkle (liquid); throw off (sparks); Feuer ~ eyes: flash fire; 2. v/i. (h): ~ vor sparkle with (wit, etc.); es sprüht it is drizzling; 3. v/i. (sein) sparks: fly; **'2regen** m drizzle.

Sprung [ʃpruŋ] m (-[e]s/-e) jump, leap, bound; swimming: dive; crack, fissure; **'~brett** n sports: spring-board; fig. stepping-stone; **'~feder** f spiral spring.

Spuck|e F ['ʃpukə] f (-/no pl.) spit(tle); **'2en** (ge-, h) 1. v/t. spit (out) (blood, etc.); 2. v/i. spit; engine: splutter; **'~napf** m spittoon, Am. a. cuspidor.

Spuk [ʃpuːk] m (-[e]s/-e) apparition, ghost, co. spook; F fig. noise; **'2en** v/i. (ge-, h): ~ in (dat.) haunt (a place); hier spukt es this place is haunted.

Spule ['ʃpuːlə] f (-/-n) spool, reel; bobbin; ⚡ coil; **'2n** v/t. (ge-, h) spool, reel.

spülen ['ʃpyːlən] (ge-, h) 1. v/t. rinse (clothes, mouth, cup, etc.); wash up (dishes, etc.); an Land ~ wash ashore; 2. v/i. flush the toilet.

Spund [ʃpunt] m (-[e]s/-e) bung; plug; **'~loch** n bunghole.

Spur [ʃpuːr] f (-/-en) trace (a. fig.); track (a. fig.); print (a. fig.); rut (of wheels); j-m auf der ~ sein be on s.o.'s track.

spür|en ['ʃpy:rən] *v/t.* (ge-, *h*) feel; sense; perceive; **'⸚sinn** *m* (-[e]s/*no pl.*) scent; *fig. a.* flair (**für** for).

Spurweite 🚂 *f* ga(u)ge.

sputen ['ʃpu:tən] *v/refl.* (ge-, *h*) make haste, hurry up.

Staat [ʃtaːt] *m* **1.** F (-[e]s/*no pl.*) pomp, state; finery; **~ machen mit** make a parade of; **2.** (-[e]s/-en) state; government; **'⸚enbund** *m* (-[e]s/⸚e) confederacy, confederation; **'⸚enlos** *adj.* stateless; **'⸚lich** *adj.* state; national; political; public.

'Staats|angehörige *m, f* (-n/-n) national, citizen, *esp. Brt.* subject; **'⸚angehörigkeit** *f* (-/*no pl.*) nationality, citizenship; **'⸚anwalt** ⚖ *m* public prosecutor, *Am.* prosecuting attorney; **'⸚beamte** *m* Civil Servant, *Am. a.* public servant; **'⸚begräbnis** *n* state *or* national funeral; **'⸚besuch** *m* official *or* state visit; **'⸚bürger** *m* citizen; **'⸚bürgerkunde** *f* (-/*no pl.*) civics *sg.*; **'⸚bürgerschaft** *f* (-/-en) citizenship; **'⸚dienst** *m* Civil Service; **'⸚eigen** *adj.* state-owned; **'⸚feind** *m* public enemy; **'⸚feindlich** *adj.* subversive; **'⸚gewalt** *f* (-/*no pl.*) supreme power; **'⸚haushalt** *m* budget; **'⸚hoheit** *f* (-/*no pl.*) sovereignty; **'⸚kasse** *f* treasury, *Brt.* exchequer; **'⸚klugheit** *f* political wisdom; **'⸚kunst** *f* (-/*no pl.*) statesmanship; **'⸚mann** *m* statesman; **'⸚männisch** *adj.* ['⸚meniʃ] statesmanlike; **'⸚oberhaupt** *n* head of (the) state; **'⸚papiere** *n/pl.* Government securities *pl.*; **'⸚rat** *m* Privy Council; **'⸚recht** *n* public law; **'⸚schatz** *m s.* Staatskasse; **'⸚schulden** *f/pl.* national debt; **'⸚sekretär** *m* under-secretary of state; **'⸚streich** *m* coup d'état; **'⸚trauer** *f* national mourning; **'⸚vertrag** *m* treaty; **'⸚wesen** *n* polity; **'⸚wirtschaft** *f* public sector of the economy; **'⸚wissenschaft** *f* political science; **'⸚wohl** *n* public weal.

Stab [ʃtaːp] *m* (-[e]s/⸚e) staff (*a. fig.*); bar (*of metal, wood*); crosier, staff (*of bishop*); wand (*of magician*); relay-race, 🎵 *conducting*: baton; *pole-vaulting*: pole.

stabil *adj.* [ʃtaˈbiːl] stable (*a.* ✝); *health*: robust.

stabilisier|en [ʃtabiliˈziːrən] *v/t.* (*no* -ge-, *h*) stabilize (*a.* ✝); **⸚ung** *f* (-/-en) stabilization (*a.* ✝).

stach [ʃtaːx] *pret. of* stechen.

Stachel ['ʃtaxəl] *m* (-s/-n) prickle (*of plant, hedgehog, etc.*); sting (*of bee, etc.*); tongue (*of buckle*); spike (*of sports shoe*); *fig.*: sting; goad; **'⸚beere** 🌿 *f* gooseberry; **'⸚draht** *m* barbed wire; **'⸚ig** *adj.* prickly, thorny.

'stachlig *adj. s.* stachelig.

Stadi|on ['ʃtaːdjɔn] *n* (-s/Stadien) stadium; **⸚um** ['⸚um] *n* (-s/Stadien) stage, phase.

Stadt [ʃtat] *f* (-/⸚e) town; city.

Städt|chen ['ʃtɛːtçən] *n* (-s/-) small town; **'⸚ebau** *m* (-[e]s/*no pl.*) town-planning; **'⸚er** *m* (-s/-) townsman; **~** *pl.* townspeople *pl.*

'Stadt|gebiet *n* urban area; **'⸚gespräch** *n teleph.* local call; *fig.* town talk, talk of the town; **'⸚haus** *n* town house.

städtisch *adj.* ['ʃtɛːtiʃ] municipal.

'Stadt|plan *m* city map; plan (**of a** town); **'⸚planung** *f* town-planning; **'⸚rand** *m* outskirts *pl.* (of a town); **'⸚rat** *m* (-[e]s/⸚e) town council; town council(l)or; **'⸚teil** *m,* **'⸚viertel** *n* quarter.

Staffel ['ʃtafəl] *f* (-/-n) relay; relay-race; ⸚**ei** *paint.* [⸚'laɪ] *f* (-/-en) easel; **'⸚lauf** *m* relay-race; **'⸚n** *v/t.* (ge-, *h*) graduate (*taxes, etc.*); stagger (*hours of work, etc.*).

Stahl¹ [ʃtaːl] *m* (-[e]s/⸚e, -e) steel.

stahl² *pret. of* stehlen.

stählen ['ʃtɛːlən] *v/t.* (ge-, *h*) ⊕ harden (*a. fig.*); temper.

'Stahl|feder *f* steel pen; steel spring; **'⸚kammer** *f* strong-room; **'⸚stich** *m* steel engraving.

stak [ʃtaːk] *pret. of* stecken 2.

Stall [ʃtal] *m* (-[e]s/⸚e) stable (*a. fig.*); cow-house, cowshed; pigsty, *Am. a.* pigpen; shed; **'⸚knecht** *m* stableman; **'⸚ung** *f* (-/-en) stabling; **⸚en** *pl.* stables *pl.*

Stamm [ʃtam] *m* (-[e]s/⸚e) 🌿 stem (*a. gr.*), trunk; *fig.*: race; stock; family; tribe; **'⸚aktie** ✝ *f* ordinary share, *Am.* common stock; **'⸚baum** *m* family *or* genealogical tree, pedigree (*a. zo.*); *fig.* album; book that contains the births, deaths, and marriages in a family; *zo.* studbook; **'⸚eln** [⸚lən] *v/i.* **1.** *v/t.* stammer (out); **2.** *v/i.* stammer; **'⸚eltern** *pl.* ancestors *pl.*, first parents *pl.*; **'⸚en** *v/i.* (ge-, sein): **~ von** *or* **aus** come from (*town, etc.*), *Am. a.* hail from; date from (*certain time*); *gr.* be derived from; **aus gutem Haus ~** be of good family; **'⸚gast** *m* regular customer *or* guest, F regular.

stämmig *adj.* ['ʃtɛmiç] stocky; thickset, squat(ty).

'Stamm|kapital ✝ *n* share capital, *Am.* capital stock; **'⸚kneipe** F *f* one's favo(u)rite pub, local; **'⸚kunde** *m* regular customer, patron; **'⸚tisch** *m* table reserved for regular guests; **'⸚utter** ['ʃtammutər] *f* (-/⸚) ancestress; **'⸚vater** *m* ancestor; **⸚verwandt** *adj.* cognate, kindred; *pred.* of the same race.

stampfen ['ʃtampfən] (ge-) **1.** *v/t.* (*h*) mash (*potatoes, etc.*); **aus dem Boden ~** conjure up; **2.** *v/i.* (*h*) stamp (one's foot); *horse:* paw;

3. v/i. (sein): ~ durch .plod through; ⚓ pitch through.

Stand [ʃtant] **1.** m (-[e]s/≈e) stand (-ing), standing or upright position; footing, foothold; s. Standplatz; stall; fig.: level; state; station, rank, status; class; profession; reading (of thermometer, etc.); ast. position; sports: score; auf den neuesten ~ bringen bring up to date; e-n schweren ~ haben have a hard time (of it); **2.** ♀ pret. of stehen.

Standarte [ʃtanˈdartə] f (-/-n) standard, banner.

'Standbild n statue.

Ständchen ['ʃtɛntçən] n (-s/-) serenade; j-m ein ~ bringen serenade s.o.

Ständer ['ʃtɛndər] m (-s/-) stand; post, pillar, standard.

'Standes|amt n registry (office), register office; **'2amtlich** adj.: ~e Trauung civil marriage; **'~beamte** m registrar; **'~dünkel** m pride of place; **'2gemäß** adj., **'2mäßig** adj. in accordance with one's rank; **'~person** f person of rank or position; **'~unterschied** m social difference.

'standhaft adj. steadfast; firm; constant; ~ bleiben stand pat; resist temptation; **'2igkeit** f (-/no pl.) steadfastness; firmness.

'standhalten v/i. (irr. halten, sep., -ge-, h) hold one's ground; j-m or e-r Sache ~ resist s.o. or s.th.

ständig adj. ['ʃtɛndiç] permanent; constant; income, etc.: fixed.

'Stand|ort m position (of ship, etc.); ✗ garrison, post; **'~platz** m stand; **'~punkt** fig. m point of view, standpoint, angle, Am. a. slant; **'~quartier** ✗ n fixed quarters pl.; **'~recht** ✗ n martial law; **'~uhr** f grandfather's clock.

Stange ['ʃtaŋə] f (-/-n) pole; rod, bar (of iron, etc.); staff (of flag); Anzug or Kleid von der ~ sl. reach-me-down, Am. ↑ hand-me-down.

stank [ʃtaŋk] pret. of stinken.

Stänker|(er) contp. ['ʃtɛŋkər(ər)] m (-s/-) mischief-maker, quarrel(l)er; **'2n** F v/i. (ge-, h) make mischief.

Stanniol [ʃtaˈnjoːl] n (-s/-e) tin foil.

Stanze ['ʃtantsə] f (-/-n) stanza; ⊕ punch, stamp, die; **'2n** ⊕ v/t. (ge-, h) punch, stamp.

Stapel ['ʃtaːpəl] m (-s/-) pile, stack; ⚓ stocks pl.; vom or von ~ lassen ⚓ launch; vom or von ~ laufen ⚓ be launched; **'~lauf** ⚓ m launch; **'2n** v/t. (ge-, h) pile (up), stack; **'~platz** m dump; emporium.

stapfen ['ʃtapfən] v/i. (ge-, sein) plod (durch through).

Star 1. [ʃtaːr] m (-[e]s/-e) orn. starling; ✗ cataract; j-m den ~ stechen open s.o.'s eyes; **2.** [staːr] m (-s/-s) thea., etc.: star.

starb [ʃtarp] pret. of sterben.

stark [ʃtark] **1.** adj. strong (a. fig.); stout, corpulent; fig.: intense; large; ~e Erkältung bad cold; ~er Raucher heavy smoker; ~e Seite strong point, forte; **2.** adv. very much; ~ erkältet sein have a bad cold; ~ übertrieben grossly exaggerated.

Stärke ['ʃtɛrkə] f (-/-n) strength (a. fig.); stoutness, corpulence; fig.: intensity; largeness; strong point, forte; 🧪 starch; **'2n** v/t. (ge-, h) strengthen (a. fig.); starch (linen, etc.); sich ~ take some refreshment(s).

'Starkstrom ⚡ m heavy current.

'Stärkung f (-/-en) strengthening; fig. a. refreshment; **'~smittel** n restorative; ✗ a. tonic.

starr [ʃtar] **1.** adj. rigid (a. fig.), stiff; gaze: fixed; ~ vor (dat.) numb with (cold, etc.); transfixed with (horror, etc.); dumbfounded with (amazement, etc.); **2.** adv.: j-n ~ ansehen stare at s.o.; **'~en** v/i. (ge-, h) stare (auf acc. at); vor Schmutz ~ be covered with dirt; **'2heit** f (-/no pl.) rigidity (a. fig.), stiffness; **'2kopf** m stubborn or obstinate fellow; **'~köpfig** adj. ['~kœpfiç] stubborn, obstinate; **'2krampf** ✗ m (-[e]s/no pl.) tetanus; **'2sinn** m (-[e]s/no pl.) stubbornness, obstinacy; **'~sinnig** adj. stubborn, obstinate.

Start [ʃtart] m (-[e]s/-s, ✈ -e) start (a. fig.); ✈ take-off; **'~bahn** ✈ f runway; **'2bereit** adj. ready to start; ✈ ready to take off; **'2en** (ge-) **1.** v/i. (sein) start; ✈ take off; **2.** v/t. (h) start; fig. a. launch; **'~er** m (-s/-) sports: starter; **'~platz** m starting-place.

Station [ʃtaˈtsjoːn] f (-/-en) station; ward (of hospital); (gegen) freie ~ board and lodging (found); ~ machen break one's journey; **~svorsteher** 🚂 m station-master, Am. a. station agent.

Statist [ʃtaˈtist] m (-en/-en) thea. supernumerary (actor), F super; film: extra; **~ik** f (-/-en) statistics pl., sg.; **~iker** m (-s/-) statistician; **2isch** adj. statistic(al).

Stativ [ʃtaˈtiːf] n (-s/-e) tripod.

Statt [ʃtat] **1.** f (-/no pl.): an Eides ~ in lieu of an oath; an Kindes ~ annehmen adopt; **2.** ♀ prp. (gen.) instead of; ~ zu inf. instead of ger.; ~ meiner in my place.

Stätte ['ʃtɛtə] f (-/-n) place, spot; scene (of events).

'statt|finden v/i. (irr. finden, sep., -ge-, h) take place, happen; **'~haft** adj. admissible, allowable; legal.

'Statthalter m (-s/-) governor.

'stattlich adj. stately; impressive; sum of money, etc.: considerable.

Statue ['ʃtaːtuə] f (-/-n) statue.

statuieren [ʃtatuˈiːrən] v/t. (no -ge-,

h): ein Exempel ~ make an example (an dat. of).

Statur [ʃtaˈtuːr] f (-/-en) stature, size.

Statut [ʃtaˈtuːt] n (-[e]s/-en) statute; ~en pl. regulations pl.; ✝ articles pl. of association.

Staub [ʃtaup] m (-[e]s/⊕ -e, ~e) dust; powder.

Staubecken [ˈʃtauゥ-] n reservoir.

stauben [ˈʃtaubən] v/i. (ge-, h) give off dust, make or raise a dust.

stäuben [ˈʃtɔybən] (ge-, h) 1. v/t. dust; 2. v/i. spray.

'Staub|faden ⚥ m filament; **'2ig** adj. [ˈ~biç] dusty; **~sauger** [ˈ~] m (-s/-) vacuum cleaner; **~tuch** [ˈ~ɒ-] n (-[e]s/~er) duster.

stauchen ⊕ [ˈʃtauxən] v/t. (ge-, h) upset, jolt.

'Staudamm m dam.

Staude ⚥ [ˈʃtaudə] f (-/-n) perennial (plant); head (of lettuce).

stau|en [ˈʃtauən] v/t. (ge-, h) dam (up) (river, etc.); ⚓ stow; sich ~ waters, etc.: be dammed (up); vehicles: be jammed; **'2er** ⚓ m (-s/-) stevedore.

staunen [ˈʃtaunən] 1. v/i. (ge-, h) be astonished (über acc. at); 2. ⚥ n (-s/no pl.) astonishment; **'~swert** adj. astonishing. [temper.]

Staupe vet. [ˈʃtaupə] f (-/-n) dis-]

'Stau|see m reservoir; **'~ung** f (-/-en) damming (up) (of water); stoppage; ✿ congestion (a. of traffic); jam; ⚓ stowage.

stechen [ˈʃtɛçən] (irr., ge-, h) 1. v/t. prick; insect, etc.: sting; flea, mosquito, etc.: bite; card: take, trump (other card); ⊕ engrave (in or auf acc. on); cut (lawn, etc.); sich in den Finger ~ prick one's finger; 2. v/i. prick; stab (nach at); insect, etc.: sting; flea, mosquito, etc.: bite; sun: burn; j-m in die Augen ~ strike s.o.'s eye; '~d adj. pain, look, etc.: piercing; pain: stabbing.

Steck|brief 🕮 [ˈʃtɛk-] m warrant of apprehension; **'2brieflich** 🕮 adv.: er wird ~ gesucht a warrant is out against him; **'~dose** ⚡ f (wall) socket; **'2en 1.** v/t. (ge-, h) put; esp. ⊕ insert (in acc. into); ✿ stick; pin (an acc. to, on); ☙ set, plant; 2. v/i. ([irr.,] ge-, h) be; stick, be stuck; tief in Schulden ~ be deeply in debt; **'~en** m (-s/-) stick; **'2en-bleiben** v/i. (irr. bleiben, sep., -ge-, sein) get stuck; speaker, etc.: break down; **'~enpferd** n hobby-horse; fig. hobby; **'~er** ⚡ m (-s/-) plug; **'~kontakt** ⚡ m s. Steckdose; **'~nadel** f pin.

Steg [ʃteːk] m (-[e]s/-e) foot-bridge; ⚓ landing-stage; **'~reif** m (-[e]s/-e): aus dem ~ extempore, offhand (both a. attr.); aus dem ~ sprechen extemporize, F ad-lib.

stehen [ˈʃteːən] v/i. (irr., ge-, h) stand; be; be written; dress: suit, become (j-m s.o.); ~ vor be faced with; ~ gut ~ mit be on good terms with; es kam ihm or ihn teuer zu ~ it cost him dearly; wie steht's mit ...? what about ...?; wie steht das Spiel? what's the score?; ~ bleiben remain standing; **'~bleiben** v/i. (irr. bleiben, sep., -ge-, sein) stand (still), stop; leave off reading, etc.; **'~lassen** v/t. (irr. lassen, sep., [no] -ge-, h) turn one's back (up)on; leave (meal) untouched; leave (behind), forget; leave alone.

'Steher m (-s/-) sports: stayer.

'Steh|kragen m stand-up collar; **'~lampe** f standard lamp; **'~leiter** f (e-e a pair of) steps pl., step-ladder.

stehlen [ˈʃteːlən] (irr., ge-, h) 1. v/t. steal; j-m Geld ~ steal s.o.'s money; 2. v/i. steal.

'Stehplatz m standing-room; **'~in-haber** m Am. F standee; in bus, etc.: straphanger.

steif adj. [ʃtaif] stiff (a. fig.); numb (vor Kälte with cold); **'~halten** v/t. (irr. halten, sep. -ge-, h): F die Ohren ~ keep a stiff upper lip.

Steig [ʃtaik] m (-[e]s/-e) steep path; **'~bügel** m stirrup.

steigen [ˈʃtaigən] 1. v/i. (irr., ge-, sein) flood, barometer, spirits, prices, etc.: rise; mists, etc.: ascend; blood, tension, etc.: mount; prices, etc.: increase; auf e-n Baum ~ climb a tree; 2. ⚥ n (-s/no pl.) rise; fig. a. increase.

steigern [ˈʃtaigərn] v/t. (ge-, h) raise; increase; enhance; gr. compare.

'Steigerung f (-/-en) raising; increase; enhancement; gr. comparison; **'~sstufe** gr. f degree of comparison.

Steigung [ˈʃtaiguŋ] f (-/-en) rise, gradient, ascent, grade.

steil adj. [ʃtail] steep; precipitous.

Stein [ʃtain] m (-[e]s/-e) stone (a. ⚥, ⚕), Am. F a. rock; s. Edel⚥; **'2alt** F adj. (as) old as the hills; **'~bruch** m quarry; **'~druck** m (-[e]s/no pl.) lithography; 2. (-[e]s/-e) lithograph; **'~drucker** m lithographer; **'2ern** adj. stone-..., of stone; fig. stony; **'~gut** n (-[e]s/-e) crockery, stoneware, earthenware; **'2ig** adj. stony; **'2igen** [ˈ~gən] v/t. (ge-, h) stone; **~igung** [ˈ~guŋ] f (-/-en) stoning; **'~kohle** f mineral coal; pit-coal; **~metz** [ˈ~mɛts] m (-en/-en) stonemason; **'~obst** n stone-fruit; **'2reich** F adj. immensely rich; **'~salz** n (-es/no pl.) rock-salt; **'~setzer** m (-s/-) pavio(u)r; **'~wurf** m throwing of a stone; fig. stone's throw; **'~zeit** f (-/no pl.) stone age.

Steiß [ʃtais] m (-es/-e) buttocks pl., rump; **'~bein** anat. n coccyx.

Stelldichein co. ['ʃtɛldiçʔaɪn] n (-[s]/-[s]) meeting, appointment, rendezvous, Am. F a. date.

Stelle ['ʃtɛlə] f (-/-n) place; spot; point; employment, situation, post, place, F job; agency, authority; passage (of book, etc.); freie ~ vacancy; an deiner ~ in your place, if I were you; auf der ~ on the spot; zur ~ sein be present.

'**stellen** v/t. (ge-, h) put, place, set, stand; regulate (watch, etc.); set (watch, trap, task, etc.); stop (thief, etc.); hunt down (criminal); furnish, supply, provide; Bedingungen ~ make conditions; e-e Falle ~ a. lay a snare; sich ~ give o.s. up (to the police); stand, place o.s. (somewhere); sich krank ~ feign or pretend to be ill.

'**Stellen|angebot** n position offered, vacancy; '~gesuch n application for a post; '2weise adv. here and there, sporadically.

'**Stellung** f (-/-en) position, posture; position, situation, (place of) employment; position, rank, status; arrangement (a. gr.); ⚔ position; ~ nehmen give one's opinion (zu on), comment (upon); ~nahme ['~na:-mə] f (-/-n) attitude (zu to[wards]); opinion (on); comment (on); 2slos adj. unemployed.

'**stellvertret|end** adj. vicarious, representative; acting, deputy; ~er Vorsitzender vice-chairman, deputy chairman; '2er m representative; deputy; proxy; '2ung f representation; substitution; proxy.

Stelz|bein contp. ['ʃtɛlts-] n wooden leg; '~e f (-/-n) stilt; '2en mst iro. v/i. (ge-, sein) stalk.

stemmen ['ʃtɛmən] v/t. (ge-, h) lift (weight); sich ~ press (gegen against); fig. resist or oppose s.th.

Stempel ['ʃtɛmpəl] m (-s/-) stamp; ⊕ piston; ♀ pistil; '~geld F n the dole; '~kissen n ink-pad; '2n (ge-, h) 1. v/t. stamp; hallmark (gold, silver); 2. v/i. F: ~ gehen be on the dole.

Stengel ♀ ['ʃtɛŋəl] m (-s/-) stalk, stem.

Steno F ['ʃtenoˌ] f (-/no pl.) s. Stenographie; ~'gramm n (-s/-e) stenograph; ~graph [~'gra:f] m (-en/-en) stenographer; ~graphie [~a'fi:] f (-/-n) stenography, shorthand; 2graphieren [~a'fi:rən] (no -ge-, h) 1. v/t. take down in shorthand; 2. v/i. know shorthand; 2graphisch [~'gra:fiʃ] 1. adj. shorthand, stenographic; 2. adv. in shorthand; ~typistin [~ty'pistin] f (-/-nen) shorthand-typist.

Stepp|decke ['ʃtɛp-] f quilt, Am. a. comforter; '2en 1. v/t. quilt; stitch; 2. v/i. tap-dance.

Sterbe|bett ['ʃtɛrbə-] n deathbed; '~fall m (case of) death; '~kasse f burial-fund.

'**sterben** 1. v/i. (irr., ge-, sein) die (a. fig.) (an dat. of); esp. ⚖ decease; 2. ⚲ n (-s/no pl.): im ~ liegen be dying.

sterblich ['ʃtɛrpliç] 1. adj. mortal; 2. adv.: ~ verliebt sein be desperately in love (in acc. with); '2keit f (-/no pl.) mortality; '2keitsziffer f death-rate.

stereotyp adj. [stereoˈtyːp] typ. stereotyped (a. fig.); ~ieren [~y'pi:rən] v/t. (no -ge-, h) stereotype.

steril adj. [teˈriːl] sterile; ~isieren [~ili'zi:rən] v/t. (no -ge-, h) sterilize.

Stern [ʃtɛrn] m (-[e]s/-e) star (a. fig.); '~bild ast. n constellation; '~deuter m (-s/-) astrologer; '~deutung f astrology; '~enbanner n Star-Spangled Banner, Stars and Stripes pl., Old Glory; '~fahrt mot. f motor rally; '~gucker F m (-s/-) star-gazer; '2hell adj. starry, starlit; '~himmel m (-s/no pl.) starry sky; '~kunde f (-/no pl.) astronomy; '~schnuppe f (-/-n) shooting star; '~warte f observatory.

stet adj. [ʃteːt], '~ig adj. continual, constant; steady; '2igkeit f (-/no pl.) constancy, continuity; steadiness; ~s adv. always; constantly.

Steuer ['ʃtɔʏər] 1. n (-s/-) ⊕ helm, rudder; steering-wheel; 2. f (-/-n) tax; duty; rate, local tax; '~amt n s. Finanzamt; '~beamte m revenue officer; '~berater m (-s/-) tax adviser; '~bord ♣ n (-[e]s/-e) starboard; '~erhebung f levy of taxes; '~erklärung f tax-return; '~ermäßigung f tax allowance; '2frei adj. tax-free; goods: duty-free; '~freiheit f (-/no pl.) exemption from taxes; '~hinterziehung f tax-evasion; '~jahr n fiscal year; '~klasse f tax-bracket; '~knüppel ✈ m control lever or stick; '~mann m (-[e]s/~er, Steuerleute) ♣ helmsman, steersman, Am. a. wheelsman; coxwain (a. rowing); '2n (ge-) 1. v/t. (h) ♣, ✈ steer, navigate, pilot; ⊕ control; fig. direct, control; 2. v/i. (h) check s.th.; 3. v/i. (sein): ~ in (acc.) ♣ enter (harbour, etc.); ~ nach ♣ be bound for; '2pflichtig adj. taxable; goods: dutiable; '~rad n steering-wheel; '~ruder ♣ n helm; rudder; '~satz m rate of assessment; '~ung f (-/-en) ♣, ✈ steering; ⊕, ♂ control (a. fig.); ✈ controls pl.; '~veranlagung f tax assessment; '~zahler m (-s/-) taxpayer; ratepayer.

Steven ♣ ['ʃteːvən] m (-s/-) stem; stern-post.

Stich [ʃtiç] m (-[e]s/-e) prick (of needle, etc.); sting (of insect, etc.);

stab (*of knife, etc.*); sewing: stitch; cards: trick; ⊕ engraving; ✗ stab; ~ halten hold water; im ~ lassen abandon, desert, forsake.

Stichel|ei *fig.* ['ʃtiçə'laɪ] *f* (-/-en) gibe, jeer; '*Qn fig. v/i.* (ge-, h) gibe (gegen at), jeer (at).

'**Stich|flamme** *f* flash; '**Qhaltig** *adj.* valid, sound; ~ sein hold water; '**~probe** *f* random test *or* sample, *Am. a.* spot check; '**~tag** *m* fixed day; '**~wahl** *f* second ballot; '**~wort** *n* **1.** *typ.* (-[e]s/*~er*) headword; **2.** *thea.* (-[e]s/-e) cue; '**~wunde** *f* stab.

sticken ['ʃtɪkən] *v/t. and v/i.* (ge-, h) embroider.

'**Stick|garn** *n* embroidery floss; '**~husten** ✗ *m* (w)hooping cough; '**Qig** *adj.* stuffy, close; '**~stoff** ✗ *m* (-[e]s/*no pl.*) nitrogen.

stieben ['ʃtiːbən] *v/i.* ([irr.,] ge-, h, sein) sparks, etc.: fly about.

Stief... ['ʃtiːf-] step...

Stiefel ['ʃtiːfəl] *m* (-s/-) boot; '**~knecht** *m* bootjack; '**~schaft** *m* leg of a boot.

'**Stief|mutter** *f* (-/*~*) stepmother; '**~mütterchen** ♀ ['~mʏtərçən] *n* (-s/-) pansy; '**~vater** *m* stepfather.

stieg [ʃtiːk] *pret. of steigen.*

Stiel [ʃtiːl] *m* (-[e]s/-e) handle; helve (*of weapon, tool*); haft (*of axe*); stick (*of broom*); ♀ stalk.

Stier [ʃtiːr] **1.** *zo. m* (-[e]s/-e) bull; **2.** ♀ *adj.* staring; '**Qen** *v/i.* (ge-, h) stare (*auf acc.* at); '**~kampf** *m* bullfight.

stieß [ʃtiːs] *pret. of stoßen.*

Stift [ʃtɪft] **1.** *m* (-[e]s/-e) pin; peg; tack; pencil, crayon; F *fig.*: youngster; apprentice; **2.** *n* (-[e]s/-e, -er) charitable institution; '**Qen** *v/t.* (ge-, h) endow, give, *Am. a.* donate; found; *fig.* cause; make (*mischief, peace*); '**~er** *m* (-s/-) donor; founder; *fig.* author; '**~ung** *f* (-/-en) (charitable) endowment, donation; foundation.

Stil [ʃtiːl] *m* (-[e]s/-e) style (*a. fig.*); '**Qgerecht** *adj.* stylish; **Qisieren** [ʃtili'ziːrən] *v/t.* (*no* -ge-, h) stylize; **Qistisch** *adj.* [ʃti'listiʃ] stylistic.

still *adj.* [ʃtɪl] still, quiet; silent; ✝ dull, slack; secret; ~! silence!; im ~en secretly; ~er Gesellschafter sleeping *or* silent partner; der Qe Ozean the Pacific (Ocean); 'Qe *f* (-/*no pl.*) stillness, quiet(ness); silence; in aller ~ quietly, silently; privately; Qeben *paint.* ['ʃtɪlleːbən] *n* (-s/-) still life; '**~egen** ['ʃtɪlleːgən] *v/t.* (sep., -ge-, h) shut down (*factory, etc.*); stop (*traffic*); '**~en** *v/t.* (ge-, h) soothe (*pain*); appease (*appetite*); quench (*thirst*); sta(u)nch (*blood*); nurse (*baby*); '**~halten** *v/i.* (*irr.* halten, sep., -ge-, h) keep still; '**Qiegen** ['ʃtɪlliːgən] *v/i.*

(*irr.* liegen, sep., -ge-, h) *factory, etc.*: be shut down; *traffic*: be suspended; *machines, etc.*: be idle.

stillos *adj.* ['ʃtiːllɔːs] without style.

'**stillschweigen 1.** *v/i.* (*irr.* schweigen, sep., -ge-, h) be silent; ~ zu et. ignore s.th.; **2.** ♀ *n* (-s/*no pl.*) silence; secrecy; ~ bewahren observe secrecy; et. mit ~ übergehen pass s.th. over in silence; '**~d** *adj.* silent; agreement, etc.: tacit.

'**Still|stand** *m* (-[e]s/*no pl.*) standstill; *fig.*: stagnation (*a.* ✝); deadlock; **Qstehen** *v/i.* (*irr.* stehen, sep., -ge-, h) stop; be at a standstill; *still-gestanden!* ✗ attention!

'**Stil|möbel** *n/pl.* period furniture; '**Qvoll** *adj.* stylish.

Stimm|band *anat.* ['ʃtɪm-] *n* (-[e]s/*~er*) vocal c(h)ord; '**Qberechtigt** *adj.* entitled to vote; '**~e** *f* (-/-n) voice (*a.* ♪, *fig.*); vote; comment; ♪ part; '**Qen** (ge-, h) **1.** *v/t.* tune (*piano, etc.*); *j-n fröhlich* ~ put s.o. in a merry mood; **2.** *v/i.* be true *or* right; *sum, etc.*: be correct; ~ für vote for; '**~enmehrheit** *f* majority *or* plurality of votes; '**~enthaltung** *f* abstention; '**~enzählung** *f* counting of votes; '**~gabel** ♪ *f* tuning-fork; '**~recht** *n* right to vote; *pol.* franchise; '**~ung** *f* (-/-en) ♪ tune; *fig.* mood, humo(u)r; '**Qungsvoll** *adj.* impressive; '**~zettel** *m* ballot, voting-paper.

stinken ['ʃtɪŋkən] *v/i.* (*irr.*, ge-, h) stink (*nach* of); F *fig.* be fishy.

Stipendium *univ.* [ʃti'pɛndjʊm] *n* (-s/*Stipendien*) scholarship; exhibition.

stipp|en ['ʃtɪpən] *v/t.* (ge-, h) dip, steep; '**Qvisite** F *f* flying visit.

Stirn [ʃtɪrn] *f* (-/-en) forehead, brow; *fig.* face, cheek; *j-m die* ~ bieten make head against s.o.; *s.* runzeln; '**~runzeln** *n* (-s/*no pl.*) frown(ing).

stob [ʃtoːp] *pret. of stieben.*

stöbern F ['ʃtøːbərn] *v/i.* (ge-, h) rummage (about) (*in dat.* in).

stochern ['ʃtɔxərn] *v/i.* (ge-, h): ~ in (*dat.*) poke (*fire*); pick (*teeth*).

Stock [ʃtɔk] *m* **1.** (-[e]s/*~e*) stick; cane; ♪ baton; beehive; ♀ stock; **2.** (-[e]s/-) stor(e)y, floor; *im ersten* ~ on the first floor, *Am.* on the second floor; '**Qbe'trunken** F *adj.* dead drunk; '**Qblind** F *adj.* stone-blind; '**Qdunkel** F *adj.* pitch-dark.

Stöckelschuh ['ʃtœkəl-] *m* high-heeled shoe.

'**stocken** *v/i.* (ge-, h) stop; *liquid*: stagnate (*a. fig.*); *speaker*: break down; *voice*: falter; *traffic*: be blocked; *ihm stockte das Blut* his blood curdled.

'**Stock|engländer** F *m* thorough *or* true-born Englishman; '**Qfinster** F *adj.* pitch-dark; '**~fleck** *m* spot of mildew; '❷**(fleck)ig** *adj.* foxy, mildewy; '❷'**nüchtern** F *adj.* (as) sober as a judge; '**schnupfen** ❖ *m* chronic rhinitis; '❷'**taub** F *adj.* stone-deaf; '**ung** *f* (-/-en) stop (-page); stagnation (*of liquid*) (*a. fig.*); block (*of traffic*); '**werk** *n* stor(e)y, floor.

Stoff [ʃtɔf] *m* (-[e]s/-e) matter, substance; material, fabric, textile; material, stuff; *fig.*: subject(-matter); food; '❷**lich** *adj.* material.

stöhnen ['ʃtøːnən] *v/i.* (ge-, h) groan, moan.

Stolle ['ʃtɔlə] *f* (-/-n) loaf-shaped *Christmas cake*; '**n** *m* (-s/-) ❖: *Stolle*: ⚒ tunnel, gallery (*a.* ✕).

stolpern ['ʃtɔlpərn] *v/i.* (ge-, sein) stumble (*über acc.* over), trip (over) (*both a. fig.*).

stolz [ʃtɔlts] 1. *adj.* proud (*auf acc.* of) (*a. fig.*); haughty; 2. ♀ *m* (-es/*no pl.*) pride (*auf acc.* in); haughtiness; **ieren** [~'tsiːrən] *v/i.* (*no* -ge-, sein) strut, flaunt.

stopfen ['ʃtɔpfən] (ge-) 1. *v/t.* stuff; fill (*pipe*); cram (*poultry, etc.*); darn (*sock, etc.*); *j-m den Mund* ~ stop s.o.'s mouth; 2. ❖ *v/i.* cause constipation.

'**Stopf|garn** *n* darning-yarn; '**nadel** *f* darning-needle.

Stoppel ['ʃtɔpəl] *f* (-/-n) stubble; '**bart** F *m* stubbly beard; '❷**ig** *adj.* stubbly.

stopp|en ['ʃtɔpən] (ge-, h) 1. *v/t.* stop; time, F clock; 2. *v/i.* stop; '❷**licht** *mot. n* stop-light; '❷**uhr** *f* stop-watch.

Stöpsel ['ʃtœpsəl] *m* (-s/-) stopper, cork; plug (*a.* ⚡); F *fig.* whipper-snapper; '❷**n** *v/t.* (ge-, h) stopper, cork; plug (up).

Storch *orn.* [ʃtɔrç] *m* (-[e]s/⸚e) stork.

stören ['ʃtøːrən] (ge-, h) 1. *v/t.* disturb; trouble; radio: jam (*reception*); *lassen Sie sich nicht* ~! I don't let me disturb you!; *darf ich Sie kurz* ~? may I trouble you for a minute?; 2. *v/i.* be intruding; be in the way; ❷**fried** ['~friːt] *m* (-[e]s/-e) troublemaker; intruder.

störr|ig *adj.* ['ʃtœːrıç], '**isch** *adj.* stubborn, obstinate; *a. horse*: restive.

'**Störung** *f* (-/-en) disturbance; trouble (*a.* ⊕); breakdown; *radio*: jamming, interference.

Stoß [ʃtoːs] *m* (-es/⸚e) push, shove; thrust (*a. fencing*); kick; butt; shock; knock, strike; blow; *swimming, billiards*: stroke; jolt (*of car, etc.*); pile, stock, heap; '**dämpfer** *mot. m* shock-absorber; '❷**en** (*irr.*, ge-) 1. *v/t.* (h) push, shove; thrust (*weapon, etc.*); kick; butt; knock, strike; pound (*pepper, etc.*); *sich* ~ *an* (*dat.*) strike *or* knock against; *fig.* take offence at; 2. *v/i.* (h) thrust

(*nach at*); kick (at); butt (at); *goat, etc.*: butt; *car*: jolt; ~ *an* (*acc.*) adjoin, border on; 3. *v/i.* (sein): F ~ *auf* (*acc.*) come across; meet with (*opposition, etc.*); ~ *gegen or an* (*acc.*) knock *or* strike against.

'**Stoß|seufzer** *m* ejaculation; '**stange** *mot. f* bumper; '❷**weise** *adv.* by jerks; by fits and starts; '**zahn** *m* tusk.

stottern ['ʃtɔtərn] (ge-, h) 1. *v/t.* stutter (out); stammer; 2. *v/i.* stutter; stammer; F *mot.* conk (out).

Straf|anstalt ['ʃtraːf?-] *f* penal institution; prison; *Am.* penitentiary; '**arbeit** *f* imposition, F impo(t); '❷**bar** *adj.* punishable, penal; '**e** *f* (-/-n) punishment; ⚖, ✝, *sports, fig.* penalty; fine; *bei* ~ *von* on *or* under pain of; *zur* ~ as a punishment; '❷**en** *v/t.* (ge-, h) punish.

straff [ʃtraf] *adj.* tight; *rope: a.* taut; *fig.* strict, rigid.

'**straf|fällig** *adj.* liable to prosecution; '❷**gesetz** *n* penal law; '❷**gesetzbuch** *n* penal code.

sträf|lich *adj.* ['ʃtrɛːflıç] culpable; reprehensible; inexcusable; ❷**ling** ['~lıŋ] *m* (-s/-e) convict, *Am. sl. a.* lag.

'**straf|los** *adj.* unpunished; '❷**losigkeit** *f* (-/*no pl.*) impunity; '❷**porto** *n* surcharge; '❷**predigt** *f* severe lecture; *j-m e-e* ~ *halten* lecture s.o. severely; '❷**prozeß** *m* criminal action; '❷**raum** *m football*: penalty area; '❷**stoß** *m football*: penalty kick; '❷**verfahren** *n* criminal proceedings *pl.*

Strahl [ʃtraːl] *m* (-[e]s/-en) ray (*a. fig.*); beam; flash (*of lightning, etc.*); jet (*of water, etc.*); '❷**en** *v/i.* (ge-, h) radiate; shine (*vor dat.* with); *fig.* beam (*vor dat.* with), shine (with); '**ung** *f* (-/-en) radiation, rays *pl.*

Strähne ['ʃtrɛːnə] *f* (-/-n) lock, strand (*of hair*); skein, hank (*of yarn*); *fig.* stretch.

stramm *adj.* [ʃtram] tight; *rope: a.* taut; stalwart; *soldier*: smart.

strampeln ['ʃtrampəln] *v/i.* (ge-, h) kick.

Strand [ʃtrant] *m* (-[e]s/⸍-e, ⸚e) beach; '**anzug** *m* beach-suit; ❷**en** ['~dən] *v/i.* (ge-, sein) ⚓ strand, run ashore; *fig.* fail, founder; '**gut** *n* stranded goods *pl.*; *fig.* wreckage; '**korb** *m* roofed wicker chair for use on the beach; **promenade** ['~promənaːdə] *f* (-/-n) promenade, *Am.* boardwalk.

Strang [ʃtraŋ] *m* (-[e]s/⸚e) cord (*a. anat.*); rope; halter (*for hanging s.o.*); trace (*of harness*); 🚉 track; *über die Stränge schlagen* kick over the traces.

Strapaz|e [ʃtraˈpaːtsə] *f* (-/-n) fatigue; toil; ❷**ieren** [~aˈtsiːrən] *v/t.*

(no -ge-, h) fatigue, strain *(a. fig.)*; wear out *(fabric, etc.)*; **2ierfähig** *adj.* [~a'tsi:r-] long-lasting; **2lös** *adj.* [~a'tsjø:s] fatiguing.

Straße ['ʃtra:sə] *f (-/-n)* road, highway; street *(of town, etc.)*; strait; *auf der* ~ on the road; in the street.

'Straßen|anzug *m* lounge-suit, *Am.* business suit; **'~bahn** *f* tram(way), tram-line, *Am.* street railway; streetcar line; *s. Straßenbahnwagen;* **'~bahnhaltestelle** *f* tram stop, *Am.* streetcar stop; **'~bahnwagen** *m* tram(-car), *Am.* streetcar; **'~beleuchtung** *f* street lighting; **'~damm** *m* roadway; **'~händler** *m* hawker; **'~junge** *m* street arab, *Am.* street Arab; **'~kehrer** *m (-s/-)* scavenger, street orderly; **'~kreuzung** *f* crossing, cross roads; **'~reinigung** *f* street-cleaning, scavenging; **'~rennen** *n* road-race.

strategisch *adj.* [ʃtra'te:giʃ] strategic(al).

sträuben ['ʃtrɔybən] *v/t. (ge-, h)* ruffle up *(its feathers, etc.)*; *sich* ~ *hair:* stand on end; *sich* ~ *gegen* kick against *or* at.

Strauch [ʃtraux] *m (-[e]s/~er)* shrub; bush.

straucheln ['ʃtrauxəln] *v/i. (ge-, sein)* stumble *(über acc.* over, at), trip *(over) (both a. fig.)*.

Strauß [ʃtraus] *m* **1.** *orn. (-es/-e)* ostrich; **2.** *(-es/~e)* bunch *(of flowers)*; bouquet; *strife*, combat.

Strebe ['ʃtre:bə] *f (-/-n)* strut, support, brace.

'streben 1. *v/i. (ge-, h):* ~ *nach* strive for *or* after, aspire to *or* after; **2.** *2 n (-s/no pl.)* striving *(nach* for, after), aspiration *(for, after)*; effort, endeavo(u)r.

'Streber *m (-s/-)* pusher, careerist; *at school: sl.* swot.

strebsam *adj.* ['ʃtre:pza:m] assiduous; ambitious; **'2keit** *f (-/no pl.)* assiduity; ambition.

Strecke ['ʃtrekə] *f (-/-n)* stretch; route; tract, extent; distance *(a. sports)*; course; 🐎, *etc.:* section, line; *hunt.* bag; *zur* ~ *bringen hunt.* bag, hunt down *(a. fig.)*; **'2n** *v/t. (ge-, h)* stretch, extend; dilute *(fluid)*; *sich* ~ stretch *(o.s.)*; *die Waffen* ~ lay down one's arms; *fig. a.* give in.

Streich [ʃtraiç] *m (-[e]s/-e)* stroke; blow; *fig.* trick, prank; *j-m e-n* ~ *spielen* play a trick on s.o.; **2eln** ['~əln] *v/t. (ge-, h)* stroke; caress; pat; **'2en** *(irr., ge-) 1. v/t. (h)* rub; spread *(butter, etc.)*; paint; strike out, delete, cancel *(a. fig.)*; strike, lower *(flag, sail)*; **2.** *v/i. (sein)* prowl *(um round)*; **3.** *v/i. (h):* mit der Hand über et. ~ pass one's hand over s.th.; **'~holz** *n* match; **'~instrument** ♪ *n* stringed instrument;

'~orchester *n* string band; **'~riemen** *m* strop.

Streif [ʃtraif] *m (-[e]s/-e)* *s. Streifen;* **'~band** *n (-[e]s/~er)* wrapper; **~e** *f (-/-n)* patrol; patrolman; raid.

'streifen (ge-) 1. *v/t. (h)* stripe, streak; graze, touch lightly in passing, brush; touch (up)on *(subject)*; **2.** *v/i. (sein):* ~ *durch* rove, wander through; **3.** *v/i. (h):* ~ an *(acc.)* graze, brush; *fig.* border *or* verge on; **4.** **2** *m (-s/-)* strip; stripe; streak.

'streif|ig *adj.* striped; **'2licht** *n* sidelight; **'2schuß** 🗡 *m* grazing shot; **'2zug** *m* ramble; 🗡 raid.

Streik [ʃtraik] *m (-[e]s/-s)* strike, *Am. F a.* walkout; *in den* ~ *treten* go on strike, *Am. F a.* walk out; **'~brecher** *m (-s/-)* strike-breaker, blackleg, scab; **'2en** *v/i. (ge-, h)* (be on) strike; go on strike, *Am. F a.* walk out; **~ende** ['~əndə] *m, f (-n/-n)* striker; **'~posten** *m* picket.

Streit [ʃtrait] *m (-[e]s/-e)* quarrel; dispute; conflict; 🏛 litigation; **'2bar** *adj.* pugnacious; **'2en** *v/i. and v/refl. (irr., ge-, h)* quarrel *(mit* with; *wegen* for; *über acc.* about); **'~frage** *f* controversy, (point of) issue; **'2ig** *adj.* debatable, controversial; *j-m et.* ~ *machen* dispute s.o.'s right to s.th.; **'~igkeiten** *f/pl.* quarrels *pl.*; disputes *pl.*; **'~kräfte** 🗡 ['~kreftə] *f/pl.* (military *or* armed) forces *pl.*; **'2lustig** *adj.* pugnacious, aggressive; **'2süchtig** *adj.* quarrelsome; pugnacious.

streng [ʃtreŋ] **1.** *adj.* severe; stern; strict; austere; *discipline, etc.:* rigorous; *weather, climate:* inclement; *examination:* stiff; **2.** *adv.:* ~ *vertraulich* in strict confidence; **'2e** *f (-/no pl.)* s. streng 1: severity; sternness; strictness; austerity; rigo(u)r; inclemency; stiffness; **'~genommen** *adv.* strictly speaking; **'~gläubig** *adj.* orthodox.

Streu [ʃtrɔy] *f (-/-en)* litter; **'2en** *v/t. (ge-, h)* strew, scatter; **'~zucker** *m* castor sugar.

Strich [ʃtriç] **1.** *m (-[e]s/-e)* stroke; line; dash; tract *(of land)*; *j-m e-n* ~ *durch die Rechnung machen* queer s.o.'s pitch; **2.** **2** *pret. of streichen;* **'~regen** *m* local shower; **'2weise** *adv.* here and there.

Strick [ʃtrik] *m (-[e]s/-e)* cord; rope; halter, rope *(for hanging s.o.)*; *F fig.* (young) rascal; **'2en** *v/t. and v/i. (ge-, h)* knit; **'~garn** *n* knitting-yarn; **'~jacke** *f* cardigan, jersey; **'~leiter** *f* rope-ladder; **'~nadel** *f* knitting-needle; **'~waren** *f/pl.* knitwear; **'~zeug** *n* knitting(-things *pl.*).

Striemen ['ʃtri:mən] *m (-s/-)* weal, wale.

Strippe F ['ʃtripə] *f (-/-n)* band; string; shoe-lace; *an der* ~ *hängen* be on the phone.

stritt [ʃtrit] *pret. of* streiten; '**~ig** *adj.* debatable, controversial; **~er** Punkt (point of) issue.

Stroh [ʃtro:] *n* (-[e]s/*no pl.*) straw; thatch; '**~dach** *n* thatch(ed roof); '**~halm** *m* straw; *nach e-m ~ greifen* catch at a straw; '**~hut** *m* straw hat; '**~mann** *m* man of straw; scarecrow; *fig.* dummy; '**~sack** *m* straw mattress; '**~witwe** F *f* grass widow.

Strolch [ʃtrɔlç] *m* (-[e]s/-e) scamp, F vagabond; '**2en** *v/i.* (ge-, sein): ~ *durch* rove.

Strom [ʃtro:m] *m* (-[e]s/"e) stream (*a. fig.*); (large) river; *é* current (*a. fig.*); *es regnet in Strömen* it is pouring with rain; **2'ab(wärts)** *adv.* down-stream; **2'auf(wärts)** *adv.* up-stream.

strömen ['ʃtrø:mən] *v/i.* (ge-, sein) stream; flow, run; *rain:* pour; *people:* stream, pour (*aus* out of; *in acc.* into).

'**Strom|kreis** *é m* circuit; '**~linienform** *f* (-/*no pl.*) streamline shape; '**2linienförmig** *adj.* streamline(d); '**~schnelle** *f* (-/-n) rapid, *Am. a.* riffle; '**~sperre** *é f* stoppage of current.

'**Strömung** *f* (-/-en) current; *fig. a.* trend, tendency.

'**Stromzähler** *é m* electric meter.

Strophe ['ʃtro:fə] *f* (-/-n) stanza, verse.

strotzen ['ʃtrɔtsən] *v/i.* (ge-, h): ~ *von* abound in; teem with (*blunders, etc.*); burst with (*health, etc.*).

Strudel ['ʃtru:dəl] *m* (-s/-) eddy, whirlpool; *fig.* whirl; '**2n** *v/i.* (ge-, h) swirl, whirl. [ture.\

Struktur [ʃtruk'tu:r] *f* (-/-en) struc-\

Strumpf [ʃtrumpf] *m* (-[e]s/"e) stocking; '**~band** *n* (-[e]s/"er) garter; '**~halter** *m* (-s/-) suspender, *Am.* garter; '**~waren** *f/pl.* hosiery.

struppig *adj.* ['ʃtrupiç] *hair:* rough, shaggy; *dog, etc.:* shaggy.

Stube ['ʃtu:bə] *f* (-/-n) room.

'**Stuben|hocker** *fig. m* (-s/-) stay-at-home; '**~mädchen** *n* chambermaid; '**2rein** *adj.* house-trained.

Stück [ʃtyk] *n* (-[e]s/-e) piece (*a. ♪*); fragment; head (*of cattle*); lump (*of sugar*); *thea.* play; *aus freien ~en* of one's own accord; *in ~e gehen or schlagen* break to pieces; '**~arbeit** *f* piece-work; '**2weise** *adv.* piece by piece; (by) piecemeal; † by the piece; '**~werk** *fig. n* patchwork.

Student [ʃtu'dɛnt] *m* (-en/-en), **~in** *f* (-/-nen) student, undergraduate.

Studie ['ʃtu:djə] *f* (-/-n) study (*über acc., zu* of, in) (*a. art, literature*); paint, etc.: sketch; '**~nrat** *m* (-[e]s/"e) appr. secondary-school teacher; '**~nreise** *f* study trip.

studier|en [ʃtu'di:rən] (*no* -ge-, h) **1.** *v/t.* study, read (*law, etc.*); **2.** *v/i.*

study; be a student; **2zimmer** *n* study.

Studium ['ʃtu:djum] *n* (-s/Studien) study (*a. fig.*); studies *pl.*

Stufe ['ʃtu:fə] *f* (-/-n) step; *fig.:* degree; grade; stage.

'**Stufen|folge** *fig. f* gradation; '**~leiter** *f* step-ladder; *fig.* scale; '**2weise 1.** *adj.* gradual; **2.** *adv.* gradually, by degrees.

Stuhl [ʃtu:l] *m* (-[e]s/"e) chair, seat; *in a church:* pew; *weaving:* loom; *♞ s.* Stuhlgang; *fig.* lose leg of a chair; '**~gang** *♞ m* (-[e]s/*no pl.*) stool; motion; '**~lehne** *f* back of a chair.

stülpen ['ʃtylpən] *v/t.* (ge-, h) put (*über acc.* over); clap (*hat*) (*auf acc.* on).

stumm *adj.* [ʃtum] dumb, mute; *fig. a.* silent; *gr.* silent, mute.

Stummel ['ʃtuməl] *m* (-s/-) stump; stub.

'**Stummfilm** *m* silent film.

Stümper F ['ʃtympər] *m* (-s/-) bungler; **~ei** F [~'rai] *f* (-/-en) bungling; bungle; '**2haft** *adj.* bungling; '**2n** F *v/i.* (ge-, h) bungle, botch.

stumpf [ʃtumpf] **1.** *adj.* blunt; *A angle:* obtuse; *senses:* dull, obtuse; apathetic; **2.** ♀ *m* (-[e]s/"e) stump, stub; *mit ~ und Stiel* root and branch; '**2sinn** *m* (-[e]s/*no pl.*) stupidity, dul(l)ness; '**~sinnig** *adj.* stupid, dull.

Stunde ['ʃtundə] *f* (-/-n) hour; lesson, *Am. a.* period; '**2n** *v/t.* (ge-, h) grant respite for.

'**Stunden|kilometer** *m* kilometre per hour, *Am.* kilometer per hour; '**2lang 1.** *adj.: nach ~em Warten* after hours of waiting; **2.** *adv.* for hours (and hours); '**~lohn** *m* hourly wage; '**~plan** *m* timetable, *Am.* schedule; '**2weise 1.** *adj.: ~ Beschäftigung* part-time employment; **2.** *adv.* by the hour; '**~zeiger** *m* hour-hand.

stündlich ['ʃtyntliç] **1.** *adj.* hourly; **2.** *adv.* hourly, every hour; at any hour.

'**Stundung** *f* (-/-en) respite.

stur F *adj.* [ʃtu:r] *gaze:* fixed, staring; *p.* pigheaded, mulish.

Sturm [ʃturm] *m* (-[e]s/"e) storm (*a. fig.*); ⚓ gale.

stürm|en ['ʃtyrmən] (ge-) **1.** *v/t.* (h) ✕ storm (*a. fig.*); **2.** *v/i.* (h) *wind:* storm, rage; *es stürmt* it is stormy weather; **3.** *v/i.* (sein) rush; '**2er** *m* (-s/-) *football, etc.:* forward; '**~isch** *adj.* stormy; *fig.:* impetuous; tumultuous.

'**Sturm|schritt** ✕ *m* double-quick step; '**~trupp** ✕ *m* storming-party; '**~wind** *m* storm-wind.

Sturz [ʃturts] *m* (-es/"e) fall, tumble; overthrow (*of government, etc.*);

fig. ruin; † slump; '**∼bach** *m* torrent.

stürzen ['ʃtyrtsən] (ge-) **1.** *v/i.* (sein) (have a) fall, tumble; *fig.* rush, plunge (*in acc.* into); **2.** *v/t.* (h) throw; overthrow(*government, etc.*); *fig.* plunge (*in acc.* into), precipitate (into); *j-n ins Unglück ∼* ruin s.o.; *sich in Schulden ∼* plunge into debt.

'**Sturz|flug** 🛬 *m* (nose)dive; '**∼helm** *m* crash-helmet.

Stute *zo.* ['ʃtuːtə] *f* (-/-n) mare.

Stütze ['ʃtytsə] *f* (-/-n) support, prop, stay (*all a. fig.*).

stutzen ['ʃtutsən] (ge-, h) **1.** *v/t.* cut (*hedge*); crop (*ears, tail, hair*); clip (*hedge, wing*); trim (*hair, beard, hedge*); dock (*tail*); lop (*tree*); **2.** *v/i.* start (*bei* at); stop dead *or* short.

'**stützen** *v/t.* (ge-, h) support, prop, stay (*all a. fig.*); *∼ auf* (*acc.*) base *or* found on; *sich ∼ auf* (*acc.*) lean on; *fig.* rely (up)on; *argument, etc.*: be based on.

'**Stutz|er** *m* (-s/-) dandy, fop, *Am. a.* dude; '**Ωig** *adj.* suspicious; *∼ machen* make suspicious.

'**Stütz|pfeiler** 🏛 *m* abutment; '**∼punkt** *m* *phys.* fulcrum; ✕ base.

Subjekt [zup'jɛkt] *n* (-[e]s/-e) *gr.* subject; *contp.* individual; **Ωiv** *adj.* [∼'tiːf] subjective; **∼ivität** [∼ivi'tɛːt] *f* (-/*no pl.*) subjectivity.

Substantiv *gr.* ['zupstantiːf] *n* (-s/-e) noun, substantive; **Ωisch** *gr. adj.* ['∼viʃ] substantival.

Substanz [zup'stants] *f* (-/-en) substance (*a. fig.*).

subtra|hieren ➗ [zuptra'hiːrən] *v/t.* (no -ge-, h) subtract; **Ωktion** ➗ [∼k'tsjoːn] *f* (-/-en) subtraction.

Such|dienst ['zuːx-] *m* tracing service; '**∼e** *f* (-/*no pl.*) search (*nach* for); *auf der ∼ nach* in search of; '**Ωen** (ge-, h) **1.** *v/t.* seek (*advice, etc.*); search for; look for; *Sie haben hier nichts zu ∼* you have no business to be here; **2.** *v/i.*: *∼ nach* seek for *or* after; search for; look for; '**∼er** *phot. m* (-s/-) view-finder.

Sucht [zuxt] *f* (-/⁀e) mania (*nach* for), rage (for), addiction (to).

süchtig *adj.* ['zyçtiç] having a mania (*nach* for); *∼ sein* be a drug addict; **Ωe** ['∼gə] *m, f* (-n/-n) drug addict *or* fiend.

Süd *geogr.* [zyːt], **∼en** ['∼dən] *m* (-s/*no pl.*) south; **∼früchte** ['zyːt-fryçtə] *f/pl.* fruits from the south; '**Ωlich 1.** *adj.* south(ern); southerly **2.** *adv.*: *∼ von* (to the) south of; **∼'ost** *geogr. m* (-s/*no pl.*) south-east; **Ω'östlich** *adj.* south-east(ern); '**∼pol** *geogr. m* (-s/*no pl.*) South Pole; **Ωwärts** *adv.* ['∼verts] southward(s); **∼'west** *geogr.*, **∼'westen** *m* (-s/*no pl.*) south-west;

Ω'westlich *adj.* south-west(ern); '**∼wind** *m* south wind.

süffig F *adj.* ['zyfiç] palatable, tasty.

suggerieren [zuge'riːrən] *v/t.* (no -ge-, h) suggest.

suggestiv *adj.* [zuges'tiːf] suggestive.

Sühne ['zyːnə] *f* (-/-n) expiation, atonement; '**Ωn** *v/t.* (ge-, h) expiate, atone for.

Sülze ['zyltsə] *f* (-/-n) jellied meat.

summ|arisch *adj.* [zu'maːriʃ] summary (*a.* ⁀); '**Ωe** *f* (-/-n) sum (*a. fig.*); (sum) total; amount.

'**summen** (ge-, h) **1.** *v/i.* bees, *etc.*: buzz, hum; **2.** *v/t.* hum (*song, etc.*).

sum'mieren *v/t.* (no -ge-, h) sum *or* add up; *sich ∼* run up.

Sumpf [zumpf] *m* (-[e]s/⁀e) swamp, bog, marsh; '**Ωig** *adj.* swampy, boggy, marshy.

Sünd|e ['zyndə] *f* (-/-n) sin (*a. fig.*); '**∼enbock** F *m* scapegoat; '**∼er** *m* (-s/-) sinner; **Ωhaft** ['∼t-] **1.** *adj.* sinful; **2.** *adv.*: F *∼ teuer* awfully expensive; **Ωig** ['∼diç] *adj.* sinful; **Ωigen** ['∼digən] *v/i.* (ge-, h) (commit a) sin.

Superlativ ['zuːpɛrlatiːf] *m* (-s/-e) *gr.* superlative degree; *in ∼en sprechen* speak in superlatives.

Suppe ['zupə] *f* (-/-n) soup; broth. '**Suppen|löffel** *m* soup-spoon; '**∼schöpfer** *m* soup ladle; '**∼schüssel** *f* tureen; '**∼teller** *m* soup-plate.

surren ['zurən] *v/i.* (ge-, h) whir(r); *insects:* buzz.

Surrogat [zuro'gaːt] *n* (-[e]s/-e) substitute.

suspendieren [zuspɛn'diːrən] *v/t.* (no -ge-, h) suspend.

süß *adj.* [zyːs] sweet (*a. fig.*); '**Ωe** *f* (-/*no pl.*) sweetness; '**∼en** *v/t.* (ge-, h) sweeten; '**Ωigkeiten** *pl.* sweets *pl.*, sweetmeats *pl.*, *Am. a.* candy; '**∼lich** *adj.* sweetish; mawkish (*a. fig.*); '**Ωstoff** *m* saccharin(e); '**Ω-wasser** *n* (-s/-) fresh water.

Symbol [zym'boːl] *n* (-s/-e) symbol; **∼ik** *f* (-/*no pl.*) symbolism; **Ωisch** *adj.* symbolic(al).

Symmetr|ie [zyme'triː] *f* (-/-n) symmetry; **Ωisch** *adj.* [∼'meːtriʃ] symmetric(al).

Sympath|ie [zympa'tiː] *f* (-/-n) liking; **Ωisch** *adj.* [∼'paːtiʃ] likable; *er ist mir ∼* I like him; **Ωisieren** [∼i'ziːrən] *v/i.* (no -ge-, h) sympathize (*mit* with).

Symphonie ♪ [zymfo'niː] *f* (-/-n) symphony; **∼orchester** *n* symphony orchestra.

Symptom [zymp'toːm] *n* (-s/-e) symptom; **Ωatisch** *adj.* [∼o'maːtiʃ] symptomatic (*für* of).

Synagoge [zyna'goːgə] *f* (-/-n) synagogue.

synchronisieren [zynkroni'ziːrən] *v/t.* (no -ge-, h) synchronize; dub.

Syndik|at [zyndi'ka:t] *n* (-[e]s/-e) syndicate; **~us** ['zyndikus] *m* (-/-se, *Syndizi*) syndic.

Synkope ♪ [zyn'ko:pǝ] *f* (-/-n) syncope.

synonym [zyno'ny:m] **1.** *adj.* synonymous; **2.** ♀ *n* (-s/-e) synonym.

Syntax *gr.* ['zyntaks] *f* (-/-en) syntax.

synthetisch *adj.* [zyn'te:tiʃ] synthetic.

System [zys'te:m] *n* (-s/-e) system; scheme; **~atisch** *adj.* [~e'ma:tiʃ] systematic(al), methodic(al).

Szene ['stse:nǝ] *f* (-/-n) scene (*a. fig.*); in ~ setzen stage; **~rie** [stsenǝ-'ri:] *f* (-/-n) scenery.

T

Tabak ['ta:bak, 'tabak, ta'bak] *m* (-s/-e) tobacco; (')**~händler** *m* tobacconist; (')**~sbeutel** *m* tobacco-pouch; (')**~sdose** *f* snuff-box; (')**~waren** *pl.* tobacco products *pl.*, F smokes *pl.*

tabellarisch [tabe'la:riʃ] **1.** *adj.* tabular; **2.** *adv.* in tabular form. **Tabelle** [ta'belǝ] *f* (-/-n) table; schedule.

Tablett [ta'blɛt] *n* (-[e]s/-e, -s) tray; *of metal:* salver; **~e** *pharm. f* (-/-n) tablet; lozenge.

Tachometer [taxo'-] *n*, *m* (-s/-) ⊕ tachometer; *mot. a.* speedometer.

Tadel ['ta:dǝl] *m* (-s/-) blame; censure; reprimand, rebuke, reproof; reproach; *at school:* bad mark; '**~los** *adj.* faultless, blameless; excellent, splendid; '**~n** *v/t.* (ge-, h) blame (*wegen* for); censure; reprimand, rebuke, reprove; scold; find fault with.

Tafel ['ta:fǝl] *f* (-/-n) table; plate (*a. book illustration*); slab; *on houses, etc.:* tablet, plaque; slate; blackboard; signboard, notice-board, *Am.* billboard; cake, bar (*of chocolate, etc.*); dinner-table; dinner; **~förmig** *adj.* ['~fœrmiç] tabular; '**~geschirr** *n* dinner-service, dinner-set; '**~land** *n* tableland, plateau; '**~n** *v/i.* (ge-, h) dine; feast, banquet; '**~service** *n s. Tafelgeschirr*; '**~silber** *n* silver plate, *Am.* silverware.

Täf(e)lung ['tɛ:f(ǝ)luŋ] *f* (-/-en) wainscot, panelling.

Taft [taft] *m* (-[e]s/-e) taffeta.

Tag [ta:k] *m* (-[e]s/-e) day; *officially:* date; *am* or *bei* ~e by day; *e-s* ~es one day; *den ganzen* ~ all day long; ~ *für* ~ day by day; *über* ~e ⚒ aboveground; *unter* ~e ⚒ underground; *heute vor acht* ~en a week ago; *heute in acht* (*vierzehn*) ~en today *or* this day week (fortnight), a week (fortnight) today; *denkwürdiger* or *freudiger* ~ red-letter day; *freier* ~ day off; *guten* ~! how do you do?; good morning!; good afternoon!; F hallo!, hullo!, *Am.* hello!; *am hellichten* ~e in broad daylight; *es wird* ~ it dawns; *an den*

~ *bringen* (*kommen*) bring (come) to light; *bis auf den heutigen* ~ to this day; ♀ *aus* *adv.*: ~, *tagein* day in, day out.

Tage|blatt ['ta:gǝ-] *n* daily (paper); '**~buch** *n* journal, diary.

tagein *adv.* [ta:k'aɪn] *s. tagaus.*

tage|lang *adv.* ['ta:gǝ-] day after day, for days together; '♀lohn *m* day's *or* daily wages *pl.*; ♀löhner ['~lø:nǝr] *m* (-s/-) day-labo(u)rer; '**~n** *v/i.* (ge-, h) dawn; hold a meeting, meet, sit; ⚖ be in session; '♀reise *f* day's journey.

Tages|anbruch ['ta:gǝs⁹-] *m* daybreak, dawn; *bei* ~ at daybreak *or* dawn; '**~befehl** ⚔ *m* order of the day; '**~bericht** *m* daily report, bulletin; '**~einnahme** † *f* receipts *pl.* or takings *pl.* of the day; '**~gespräch** *n* topic of the day; '**~kasse** *f* thea. box-office, booking-office; *s. Tageseinnahme*; '**~kurs** † *m* current rate; *stock exchange:* quotation of the day; '**~licht** *n* daylight; '**~ordnung** *f* order of the day, agenda; *das ist an der* ~ that is the order of the day, that is quite common; '**~presse** *f* daily press; '**~zeit** *f* time of day; daytime; *zu jeder* ~ at any hour, at any time of the day; '**~zeitung** *f* daily (paper).

tage|weise *adv.* ['ta:gǝ-] by the day; '♀werk *n* day's work; man-day.

täglich *adj.* ['tɛ:kliç] daily.

tags *adv.* [ta:ks]: ~ *darauf* the following day, the day after; ~ *zuvor* (on) the previous day, the day before.

'**Tagschicht** *f* day shift.

tagsüber *adv.* ['ta:ks⁹-] during the day, in the day-time.

Tagung ['ta:guŋ] *f* (-/-en) meeting.

Taille ['taljǝ] *f* (-/-n) waist; bodice (*of dress*).

Takel ⚓ ['ta:kǝl] *n* (-s/-) tackle; **~age** ⚓ [taka'la:ʒǝ] *f* (-/-n) rigging, tackle; '♀n ⚓ *v/t.* (ge-, h) rig (*ship*); '**~werk** ⚓ *n s. Takelage.*

Takt [takt] *m* **1.** (-[e]s/-e) ♪ time, measure; bar; *mot.* stroke; *den* ~ *halten* ♪ keep time; *den* ~ *schlagen* ♪ beat time; **2.** (-[e]s/*no pl.*) tact; '♀fest *adj.* steady in keeping time;

fig. firm; '~ik ✗ *f* (-/-en) tactics *pl.* and *sg.* (*a. fig.*); '~iker *m* (-s/-) tactician; '2isch *adj.* tactical; '2los *adj.* tactless; '~stock *m* baton; '~strich ♪ *m* bar; '2voll *adj.* tactful.

Tal [ta:l] *n* (-[e]s/=er) valley, *poet. a.* dale; *enges ~* glen.

Talar [ta'la:r] *m* (-s/-e) 🕮, *eccl., univ.* gown; 🕮 robe.

Talent [ta'lɛnt] *n* (-[e]s/-e) talent, gift, aptitude, ability; 2iert *adj.* [~'ti:rt] talented, gifted.

'**Talfahrt** *f* downhill journey; ⚓ passage downstream.

Talg [talk] *m* (-[e]s/-e) suet; *melted:* tallow; '~drüse *anat. f* sebaceous gland; 2ig *adj.* ['~giç] suety; tallowish, tallowy; '~licht *n* tallow candle.

Talisman ['ta:lisman] *m* (-s/-e) talisman, (good-luck) charm.

'**Talsperre** *f* barrage, dam.

Tampon ⚕ [tɑ̃'põː, 'tampɔn] *m* (-s/-s) tampon, plug.

Tang ♀ [taŋ] *m* (-[e]s/-e) seaweed.

Tank [taŋk] *m* (-[e]s/-s, -e) tank; '2en *v/i.* (ge-, 'h) get (some) petrol, *Am.* get (some) gasoline; '~er ⚓ *m* (-s/-) tanker; '~stelle *f* petrol station, *Am.* gas *or* filling station; '~wagen *m mot.* tank truck, *Am. a.* gasoline truck, tank trailer; 🚂 tank-car; '~wart ['~vart] *m* (-[e]s/-e) pump attendant.

Tanne ♀ ['tanə] *f* (-/-n) fir(-tree).

'**Tannen|baum** *m* fir-tree; '~nadel *f* fir-needle; '~zapfen *m* fir-cone.

Tante ['tantə] *f* (-/-n) aunt.

Tantieme [tɑ̃'tjeːmə] *f* (-/-n) royalty, percentage, share in profits.

Tanz [tants] *m* (-es/=e) dance.

tänzeln ['tɛntsəln] *v/i.* (ge-, h, sein) dance, trip, frisk.

'**tanzen** *v/i.* (h, sein) *and v/t.* (h) dance.

Tänzer ['tɛntsər] *m* (-s/-), '~in *f* (-/-nen) dancer; *thea.* ballet-dancer; partner.

'**Tanz|lehrer** *m* dancing-master; '~musik *f* dance-music; '~saal *m* dancing-room, ball-room, dance-hall; '~schule *f* dancing-school; '~stunde *f* dancing-lesson.

Tapete [ta'pe:tə] *f* (-/-n) wallpaper, paper-hangings *pl.*

tapezier|en [tape'tsi:rən] *v/t.* (no -ge-, h) paper; 2er *m* (-s/-) paperhanger; upholsterer.

tapfer *adj.* ['tapfər] brave; valiant, heroic; courageous; '2keit *f* (-/no *pl.*) bravery, valo(u)r; heroism; courage.

tappen ['tapən] *v/i.* (ge-, sein) grope (about), fumble. [awkward.)

täppisch *adj.* ['tɛpiʃ] clumsy,]

tapsen F ['tapsən] *v/i.* (ge-, sein) walk clumsily.

Tara ✝ ['ta:ra] *f* (-/Taren) tare.

Tarif [ta'ri:f] *m* (-s/-e) tariff, (table of) rates *pl.*, price-list; 2lich *adv.* according to tariff; ~lohn *m* standard wage(s *pl.*); ~vertrag *m* collective *or* wage agreement.

tarn|en ['tarnən] *v/t.* (ge-, h) camouflage; *esp. fig.* disguise; '2ung *f* (-/-en) camouflage.

Tasche ['taʃə] *f* (-/-n) pocket (*of garment*); (hand)bag; pouch; *s.* Aktentasche, Schultasche.

'**Taschen|buch** *n* pocket-book; '~dieb *m* pickpocket, *Am. sl.* dip; '~geld *n* pocket-money; *monthly:* allowance; '~lampe *f* (electric) torch, *esp. Am.* flashlight; '~messer *n* pocket-knife; '~spielerei *f* juggle(ry); '~tuch *n* (pocket) handkerchief; '~uhr *f* (pocket-)watch; '~wörterbuch *n* pocket dictionary.

Tasse ['tasə] *f* (-/-n) cup.

Tastatur [tasta'tu:r] *f* (-/-en) keyboard, keys *pl.*

Tast|e ['tastə] *f* (-/-n) key; '2en (ge-, h) 1. *v/i.* touch; grope (*nach* for, after), fumble (for); 2. *v/t.* touch, feel; *sich ~* feel *or* grope one's way; '~sinn *m* (-[e]s/no *pl.*) sense of touch.

Tat [ta:t] 1. *f* (-/-en) action, act, deed; offen|ce, *Am.* -se, crime; *in der ~* indeed, in fact, as a matter of fact, really; *auf frischer ~ ertappen* catch *s.o.* red-handed; *zur ~ schreiten* proceed to action; *in die ~ umsetzen* implement, carry into effect; 2. 2 *pret. of* tun; '~bestand 🕮 *m* facts *pl.* of the case; '2enlos *adj.* inactive, idle.

Täter ['tɛ:tər] *m* (-s/-) perpetrator; offender, culprit.

tätig *adj.* ['tɛ:tiç] active; busy; *~ sein bei* work at; be employed with; ~en ✝ ['~gən] *v/t.* (ge-, h) effect, transact; conclude; '2keit *f* (-/-en) activity; occupation, business, job; profession.

'**Tat|kraft** *f* (-/no *pl.*) energy; enterprise; '2kräftig *adj.* energetic, active.

tätlich *adj.* ['tɛ:tliç] violent; *~ werden gegen* assault; '2keiten *f/pl.* (acts *pl.* of) violence; 🕮 assault (and battery).

Tatort 🕮 ['ta:t°-] *m* (-[e]s/-e) place *or* scene of a crime.

tätowieren [tɛto'vi:rən] *v/t.* (no -ge-, h) tattoo.

'**Tat|sache** *f* (matter of) fact; '~sachenbericht *m* factual *or* documentary report, matter-of-fact account; '2sächlich *adj.* actual, real. [pat.)

tätscheln ['tɛtʃəln] *v/t.* (ge-, h) pet,]

Tatze ['tatsə] *f* (-/-n) paw, claw.

Tau¹ [tau] *n* (-[e]s/-e) rope, cable.

Tau² [~] *m* (-[e]s/no *pl.*) dew.

taub *adj.* [taup] deaf (*fig.: gegen* to); *fingers, etc.:* benumbed, numb; *nut:*

deaf, empty; *rock:* dead; ‿es Ei
addle egg; *auf e-m Ohr* ‿ *sein* be
deaf of or in one ear.

Taube *orn.* ['taubə] *f* (-/-n) pigeon;
'‿nschlag *m* pigeon-house.

'**Taub|heit** *f* (-/*no pl.*) deafness;
numbness; '2stumm *adj.* deaf and
dumb; '‿stumme *m, f* (-n/-n) deaf
mute.

tauch|en ['tauxən] (ge-) **1.** *v/t.*
(*h*) dip, plunge; **2.** *v/i.* (*h, sein*) dive,
plunge; dip; *submarine:* submerge;
'2er *m* (-s/-) diver; '2sieder *m* (-s/-)
immersion heater.

tauen ['tauən] *v/i.* (ge-) **1.** (*h, sein*):
der Schnee or es taut the snow *or*
it is thawing; *der Schnee ist von
den Dächern getaut* the snow has
melted off the roofs; **2.** (*h*): *es taut*
dew is falling.

Taufe ['taufə] *f* (-/-n) baptism,
christening; '2n *v/t.* (ge-, *h*) baptize,
christen.

Täufling ['tɔyfliŋ] *m* (-s/-e) child *or*
person to be baptized.

'**Tauf|name** *m* Christian name, *Am.
a.* given name; '‿pate **1.** *m* godfather; **2.** *f* godmother; '‿patin *f*
godmother; '‿schein *m* certificate
of baptism.

taug|en ['taugən] *v/i.* (ge-, *h*) be
good, be fit, be of use (*all: zu* for);
(*zu*) *nichts* ‿ be good for nothing,
be no good, be of no use; '2enichts
m (-, -es/-e) good-for-nothing, *Am.
sl.* dead beat; '‿lich *adj.* ['tauk-]
good, fit, useful (*all: für, zu* for, to
inf.); able; ⚓, ⚔ able-bodied.

Taumel ['tauməl] *m* (-s/*no pl.*)
giddiness; rapture, ecstasy; '2ig
adj. reeling; giddy; '2n *v/i.* (ge-,
sein) reel, stagger; be giddy.

Tausch [tauʃ] *m* (-es/-e) exchange;
barter; '2en *v/t.* (ge-, *h*) exchange;
barter (*gegen* for).

täuschen ['tɔyʃən] *v/t.* (ge-, *h*)
deceive, delude, mislead (on purpose); cheat; *sich* ‿ deceive o.s.; be
mistaken; *sich* ‿ *lassen* let o.s. be
deceived; '‿d *adj.* deceptive, delu-
sive; *resemblance:* striking.

'**Tauschhandel** *m* barter.

'**Täuschung** *f* (-/-en) deception,
delusion.

tausend *adj.* ['tauzənt] a thousand;
'‿fach *adj.* thousandfold; '2fuß *zo.
m,* 2füß(l)er *zo.* ['-fy:s(l)ər] *m*
(-s/-) mill‿pede, milliped(e), *Am. a.*
wireworm; '‿st *adj.* thousandth;
'2stel *n* (-s/-) thousandth (part).

'**Tau|tropfen** *m* dew-drop; '‿wetter
n thaw.

Taxameter [taksa'-] *m* taximeter.

Taxe ['taksə] *f* (-/-n) rate; fee;
estimate; *s.* Taxi.

Taxi ['taksi] *n* (-[s]/-[s]) taxi(-cab),
cab, *Am. a.* hack.

ta'xieren *v/t.* (*no* ge-, *h*) rate,
estimate; *officially:* value, appraise.

'**Taxistand** *m* cabstand.

Technik ['tɛçnik] *f* **1.** (-/*no pl.*)
technology; engineering; **2.** (-/-en)
skill, workmanship; technique,
practice; ♪ execution; '‿er *m* (-s/-)
(technical) engineer; technician;
‿um ['‿um] *n* (-s/Technika, Tech-
niken) technical school.

'**technisch** *adj.* technical; ‿e *Hochschule* school of technology.

Tee [te:] *m* (-s/-s) tea; '‿büchse *f*
tea-caddy; '‿gebäck *n* scones *pl.*,
biscuits *pl., Am. a.* cookies *pl.*;
'‿kanne *f* teapot; '‿kessel *m* tea-
kettle; '‿löffel *m* tea-spoon.

Teer [te:r] *m* (-[e]s/-e) tar; '2en *v/t.*
(ge-, *h*) tar.

'**Tee|rose** ♀ *f* tea-rose; '‿sieb *n*
tea-strainer; '‿tasse *f* teacup;
'‿wärmer *m* (-s/-) tea-cosy.

Teich [taiç] *m* (-[e]s/-e) pool,
pond.

Teig [taik] *m* (-[e]s/-e) dough, paste;
2ig *adj.* ['‿giç] doughy, pasty;
'‿waren *f/pl.* farinaceous food;
noodles *pl.*

Teil [tail] *m, n* (-[e]s/-e) part; portion, share; component; ⅓ party;
zum ‿ partly, in part; *ich für mein
‿ ... for my part I ...; '2bar *adj.*
divisible; '‿chen *n* (-s/-) particle;
'2en *v/t.* (ge-, *h*) divide; *fig.* share;
'2haben *v/i.* (*irr.* haben, *sep.*, -ge-,
h) participate, (have a) share (*both:
an dat.* in); '‿haber ✝ *m* (-s/-)
partner; '‿nahme ['‿na:mə] *f* (-/*no
pl.*) participation (*an dat.* in); *fig.:*
interest (in); sympathy (with);
2nahmslos *adj.* ['‿na:mslo:s] indifferent, unconcerned; passive;
apathetic; '‿nahmslosigkeit *f*
(-/*no pl.*) indifference; passiveness;
apathy; '2nehmen *v/i.* (*irr.* nehmen,
sep., -ge-, *h*): ‿ *an* (*dat.*) take part *or*
participate in; join in; be present
at, attend at; *fig.* sympathize with;
'‿nehmer *m* (-s/-) participant;
member; *univ., etc.*: student; con-
testant; *sports:* competitor; *teleph.*
subscriber; 2s *adv.* [‿s] partly;
'‿strecke *f* section; stage, leg; ⛟
fare stage; '‿ung *f* (-/-en) division;
'2weise *adv.* partly, partially, in
part; '‿zahlung *f* (payment by)
instal(l)ments.

Teint [tɛ̃:] *m* (-s/-s) complexion.

Tele|fon [tele'fo:n] *n* (-s/-e) *etc. s.*
Telephon, etc.; ‿graf [‿'gra:f] *m*
(-en/-en) *etc. s. Telegraph, etc.*;
‿gramm [‿'gram] *n* (-s/-e) telegram, wire; *overseas:* cable(gram).

Telegraph [tele'gra:f] *m* (-en/-en)
telegraph; ‿enamt [‿ən'ʔ-] *n* telegraph office; 2ieren [‿a'fi:rən] *v/t.
and v/i.* (*no* -ge-, *h*) telegraph, wire;
overseas: cable; 2isch [‿'gra:fiʃ]
1. *adj.* telegraphic; **2.** *adv.* by telegram, by wire; by cable; ‿ist
[‿a'fist] *m* (-en/-en), ‿istin *f* (-/-nen)

telegraph operator, telegrapher, telegraphist.

Teleobjektiv *phot.* ['teːleˑ-] *n* telephoto lens.

Telephon [teleˈfoːn] *n* (-s/-e) telephone, F phone; *am ~ on the* (tele)phone; *ans ~ gehen* answer the (tele)phone; *~ haben* be on the (tele)phone; *~anschluß* *m* telephone connexion *or* connection; *~buch* *n* telephone directory; *~gespräch* *n* (tele)phone call; conversation *or* chat over the (tele-) phone; *~hörer* *m* (telephone) receiver, handset; **2ieren** [ˌˑoˈniːrən] *v/i.* (*no -ge-, h*) telephone, F phone; *mit j-m ~ ring s.o. up, Am.* call s.o. up; **2isch** *adv.* [ˌˑˈfoːnɪʃ] *by* (tele)phone, over the (tele)phone; *~ist* [ˌˑoˈnɪst] *m* (-en/-en), *~istin* *f* (-/-nen) (telephone) operator, telephonist; *~vermittlung* *f s. Telephonzentrale;* *~zelle* *f* telephone kiosk *or* box, call-box, *Am.* telephone booth; *~zentrale* *f* (telephone) exchange.

Teleskop *opt.* [teleˈskoːp] *n* (-s/-e) telescope.

Teller ['tɛlər] *m* (-s/-) plate.

Tempel ['tɛmpəl] *m* (-s/-) temple.

Temperament [tɛmpəraˈmɛnt] *n* (-[e]s/-e) temper(ament); *fig.* spirit(s *pl.*); **2los** *adj.* spiritless; **2voll** *adj.* (high-)spirited.

Temperatur [tɛmpəraˈtuːr] *f* (-/-en) temperature; *j-s ~ messen* take s.o.'s temperature.

Tempo ['tɛmpo] *n* (-s/-s, Tempi) time; pace; speed; rate.

Tendenz [tɛnˈdɛnts] *f* (-/-en) tendency; trend; **2iös** *adj.* [ˌˑtsjøːs] tendentious.

Tennis ['tɛnis] *n* (-/*no pl.*) (lawn) tennis; '*~ball* *m* tennis-ball; '*~platz* *m* tennis-court; '*~schläger* *m* (tennis-)racket; '*~spieler* *m* tennis player; '*~turnier* *n* tennis tournament.

Tenor ♩ [teˈnoːr] *m* (-s/=e) tenor.

Teppich ['tɛpiç] *m* (-s/-e) carpet; '*~kehrmaschine* *f* carpet-sweeper.

Termin [tɛrˈmiːn] *m* (-s/-e) appointed time *or* day; 🕳, ✝ date, term; *sports:* fixture; *äußerster ~* final date, dead(-)line; *~geschäfte* ✝ *n/pl.* futures *pl.;* *~kalender* *m* appointment book *or* pad; 🕳 causelist, *Am.* calendar; *~liste* 🕳 *f* causelist, *Am.* calendar.

Terpentin [tɛrpɛnˈtiːn] *n* (-s/-e) turpentine.

Terrain [tɛˈrɛ̃ː] *n* (-s/-s) ground; plot; building site.

Terrasse [tɛˈrasə] *f* (-/-n) terrace; **2nförmig** *adj.* [ˌˑnfœrmiç] terraced, in terraces.

Terrine [tɛˈriːnə] *f* (-/-n) tureen.

Territorium [tɛriˈtoːrjum] *n* (-s/ Territorien) territory.

Terror ['tɛrɔr] *m* (-s/*no pl.*) terror; **2isieren** [ˌˑoriˈziːrən] *v/t.* (*no -ge-, h*) terrorize.

Terz ♩ [tɛrts] *f* (-/-en) third; *~ett* ♩ [ˌˑtsɛt] *n* (-[e]s/-e) trio.

Testament [tɛstaˈmɛnt] *n* (-[e]s/-e) (last) will, (*often:* last will and) testament; *eccl.* Testament; **2arisch** [ˌˑtaˈriːʃ] 1. *adj.* testamentary; 2. *adv.* by will; *~svollstrecker* *m* (-s/-) executor; *officially:* administrator.

testen ['tɛstən] *v/t.* (ge-, h) test.

teuer *adj.* ['tɔʏər] dear (*a. fig.*), expensive; *wie ~ ist es?* how much is it?

Teufel ['tɔʏfəl] *m* (-s/-) devil; *der ~* the Devil, Satan; *zum ~!* F dickens!, hang it!; *wer zum ~?* F who the devil *or* deuce?; *der ~ ist los* the fat's in the fire; *scher dich zum ~!* F go to hell!, go to blazes!; *~ei* [ˌˑˈlaɪ] *f* (-/-en) devilment, mischief, devilry, *Am.* deviltry; '*~skerl* F *m* devil of a fellow.

'**teuflisch** *adj.* devilish, diabolic(al).

Text [tɛkst] *m* (-es/-e) text; words *pl.* (*of song*); book, libretto (*of opera*); '*~buch* *n* book; libretto.

Textil|ien [tɛksˈtiːljən] *pl.,* *~waren* *pl.* textile fabrics *pl.,* textiles *pl.*

'**textlich** *adv.* concerning the text.

Theater [teˈaːtər] *n* 1. (-s/-) theat|re, *Am.* -er; stage; 2. F (-s/*no pl.*) play-acting; *~besucher* *m* playgoer; *~karte* *f* theatre ticket; *~kasse* *f* box-office; *~stück* *n* play; *~vorstellung* *f* theatrical performance; *~zettel* *m* playbill.

theatralisch *adj.* [teaˈtraːliʃ] theatrical, stagy.

Theke ['teːkə] *f* (-/-n) *at inn:* bar, *Am. a.* counter; *at shop:* counter.

Thema ['teːma] *n* (-s/Themen, Themata) theme, subject; topic (*of discussion*).

Theolog|e [teoˈloːgə] *m* (-n/-n) theologian, divine; *~ie* [ˌˑoˈgiː] *f* (-/-n) theology.

Theoret|iker [teoˈreːtikər] *m* (-s/-) theorist; **2isch** *adj.* theoretic(al).

Theorie [teoˈriː] *f* (-/-n) theory.

Therapie 🔬 [teraˈpiː] *f* (-/-n) therapy. [spa.]

Thermalbad [tɛrˈmaːl-] *n* thermal)

Thermometer [tɛrmoˈ-] *n* (-s/-) thermometer; *~stand* *m* (thermometer) reading.

Thermosflasche ['tɛrmɔs-] *f* vacuum bottle *or* flask, thermos (flask).

These ['teːzə] *f* (-/-n) thesis.

Thrombose 🔬 [trɔmˈboːzə] *f* (-/-n) thrombosis.

Thron [troːn] *m* (-[e]s/-e) throne; '*~besteigung* *f* accession to the throne; '*~erbe* *m* heir to the throne, heir apparent; '*~folge* *f* succession to the throne; '*~folger* *m* (-s/-) successor to the throne; '*~rede* *parl.* *f* Queen's *or* King's Speech.

17*

Thunfisch *ichth.* ['tu:n-] *m* tunny, tuna.

Tick F [tik] *m* (-[e]s/-s, -e) crotchet, fancy, kink; e-n ~ haben have a bee in one's bonnet.

ticken ['tikən] *v/i.* (ge-, h) tick.

tief [ti:f] **1.** *adj.* deep (a. *fig.*); *fig.*: profound; low; *im* ~*sten Winter* in the dead or depth of winter; **2.** *adv.*: *bis* ~ *in die Nacht* far into the night; *das läßt* ~ *blicken* that speaks volumes; *zu* ~ *singen* sing flat; **3.** 2 *meteor.* *n* (-[e]s/-s) depression, low(-pressure area); '2bau *m* civil or underground engineering; '2druckgebiet *meteor. n s. Tief*; '2e *f* (-/-n) depth (a. *fig.*); *fig.* profundity; '2ebene *f* low plain, lowland; '2enschärfe *phot. f* depth of focus; '2flug *m* low-level flight; '2gang ⚓ *m* draught, *Am.* draft; ~gebeugt *fig. adj.* ['.gəbɔʏkt] deeply afflicted, bowed down; '~gekühlt *adj.* deep-frozen; '~greifend *adj.* fundamental, radical; '2land *n* lowland(s *pl.*); '~liegend *adj. eyes*: sunken; *fig.* deep-seated; '2schlag *m boxing*: low hit; '~schürfend *fig. adj.* profound; thorough; '2see *f* deep sea; '~sinnig *adj.* thoughtful, pensive; F *adj.* melancholy; '2stand *m* (-[e]s/no *pl.*) low level.

Tiegel ['ti:gəl] *m* (-s/-) saucepan, stew-pan; ⊕ crucible.

Tier [ti:r] *n* (-[e]s/-e) animal; beast; brute; *großes* ~ *fig. sl.* bigwig, big bug, *Am.* big shot; '~arzt *m* veterinary (surgeon), F vet, *Am. a.* veterinarian; '~garten *m* zoological gardens *pl.*, zoo; '~heilkunde *f* veterinary medicine; '2isch *adj.* animal; *fig.* bestial, brutish, savage; '~kreis *ast. m* zodiac; ~quälerei [.kvɛːlə'raɪ] *f* (-/-en) cruelty to animals; '~reich *n* (-[e]s/no *pl.*) animal kingdom; '~schutzverein *m* Society for the Prevention of Cruelty to Animals.

Tiger *zo.* ['ti:gər] *m* (-s/-) tiger; '~in *zo. f* (-/-nen) tigress.

tilg|en ['tilgən] *v/t.* (ge-, h) extinguish; efface; wipe or blot out, erase; *fig.* obliterate; annul, cancel; discharge, pay (*debt*); redeem (*mortgage, etc.*); '2ung *f* (-/-en) extinction; extermination; cancel(l)ing; discharge, payment; redemption.

Tinktur [tiŋk'tu:r] *f* (-/-en) tincture. [*sitzen* F be in a scrape.\]

Tinte ['tintə] *f* (-/-n) ink; *in der* ~\]

'Tinten|faß *n* ink-pot, *desk*: inkwell; '~fisch *ichth. m* cuttle-fish; '~fleck *m*, '~klecks *m* (ink-)blot; '~stift *m* indelible pencil.

Tip [tip] *m* (-s/-s) hint, tip; '2pen (ge-, h) **1.** *v/i.* F type; *fig.* guess; *j-m auf die Schulter* ~ tap s.o. on his shoulder; **2.** *v/t.* tip; foretell, predict; F type.

Tiroler [ti'ro:lər] **1.** *m* (-s/-) Tyrolese; **2.** *adj.* Tyrolese.

Tisch [tiʃ] *m* (-es/-e) table; *bei* ~ at table; *den* ~ *decken* lay the table or cloth, set the table; *reinen* ~ *machen* make a clean sweep (*damit of it*); *zu* ~ *bitten* invite or ask to dinner or supper; *bitte zu* ~! dinner is ready!; '~decke *f* table-cloth; '2fertig *adj. food*: ready-prepared; '~gast *m* guest; '~gebet *n*: *das* ~ *sprechen* say grace; '~gesellschaft *f* dinner-party; '~gespräch *n* table-talk; '~lampe *f* table-lamp; desk lamp.

Tischler ['tiʃlər] *m* (-s/-) joiner; carpenter; cabinet-maker; ~ei [.'raɪ] *f* (-/-en) joinery; joiner's workshop.

'Tisch|platte *f* top (of a table), table top; leaf (*of extending table*); '~rede *f* toast, after-dinner speech; '~tennis *n* table tennis, ping-pong; '~tuch *n* table-cloth; '~zeit *f* dinner-time.

Titan [ti'ta:n] *m* (-en/-en) Titan; 2isch *adj.* titanic.

Titel ['ti:təl] *m* (-s/-) title; e-n ~ (*inne*)haben *sports*: hold a title; '~bild *n* frontispiece; cover picture (*of magazine, etc.*); '~blatt *n* title-page; cover (*of magazine*); '~halter *m* (-s/-) *sports*: title-holder; '~kampf *m boxing*: title fight; '~rolle *thea. f* title-role.

titulieren [titu'li:rən] *v/t.* (no -ge-, h) style, call, address as.

Toast [to:st] *m* (-es/-e, -s) toast (a. *fig.*).

tob|en ['to:bən] *v/i.* (ge-, h) rage, rave, storm, bluster; *children*: romp; 2sucht 🟊 ['to:p-] *f* (-/no *pl.*) raving madness, frenzy; ~süchtig *adj.* ['to:p-] raving mad, frantic.

Tochter ['tɔxtər] *f* (-/⸚) daughter; '~gesellschaft † *f* subsidiary company.

Tod [to:t] *m* (-[e]s/⸜ -e) death; ⚰ decease.

Todes|angst ['to:dəs⸜-] *f* mortal agony; *fig.* mortal fear; *Todesängste ausstehen* be scared to death, be frightened out of one's wits; '~anzeige *f* obituary (notice); '~fall *m* (case of) death; *Todesfälle pl.* deaths *pl.*, ⚔ casualties *pl.*; '~kampf *m* death throes *pl.*, mortal agony; '~strafe *f* capital punishment, death penalty; *bei* ~ *verboten* forbidden on or under pain or penalty of death; '~ursache *f* cause of death; '~urteil *n* death or capital sentence, death-warrant.

'Tod|feind *m* deadly or mortal enemy; '2krank *adj.* dangerously ill.

tödlich ['tø:tliç] deadly; fatal; *wound*: a. mortal.

'tod|'müde *adj.* dead tired; '~

'schick F *adj.* dashing, gorgeous; '√sicher F *adj.* cock-sure; '2sünde *f* deadly *or* mortal sin.

Toilette [toaˈlɛtə] *f* (-/-n) dress(ing): toilet; lavatory, gentlemen's *or* ladies' room, *esp. Am.* toilet.

Toi'letten|artikel *m/pl.* toilet articles *pl.*, *Am. a.* toiletry; √papier *n* toilet-paper; √tisch *m* toilet (-table), dressing-table, *Am. a.* dresser.

toleran|t *adj.* [toleˈrant] tolerant (gegen of); 2z [√ts] *f* 1. (-/no pl.) tolerance, toleration (*esp. eccl.*); 2. ⊕ (-/-en) tolerance, allowance.

toll [tɔl] 1. *adj.* (raving) mad, frantic; mad, crazy, wild (*all a. fig.*); fantastic; *noise, etc.*: frightful, F awful; *das ist ja* ~ F that's (just) great; 2. *adv.*: es ~ treiben carry on like mad; es zu ~ treiben go too far; '√en *v/i.* (ge-, h, sein) *children*: romp; '2haus *fig. n* bedlam; '2heit *f* (-/-en) madness; mad trick; '√kühn *adj.* foolhardy, rash; '2wut *vet. f* rabies.

Tolpatsch F ['tɔlpatʃ] *m* (-es/-e) awkward *or* clumsy fellow; '2ig F *adj.* awkward, clumsy.

Tölpel F ['tœlpəl] *m* (-s/-) awkward *or* clumsy fellow; boob(y).

Tomate [toˈmaːtə] *f* (-/-n) tomato.

Ton¹ [toːn] *m* (-[e]s/-e) clay.

Ton² [√] *m* (-[e]s/√e) sound; ♪ tone (*a. of language*); ♪ *single*: note; accent, stress; *fig.* tone; *paint.* tone, tint, shade; *guter* ~ good form; *den* ~ *angeben* set the fashion; *zum guten* ~ *gehören* be the fashion; *große Töne reden or* F *spucken* F talk big, boast; '√abnehmer *m* pick-up; '2angebend *adj.* setting the fashion, leading; '√arm *m* pick-up arm (*of record-player*); '√art ♪ *f* key; '√band *n* recording tape; '√bandgerät *n* tape recorder.

tönen ['tøːnən] (ge-, h) 1. *v/i.* sound, ring; 2. *v/t.* tint, tone, shade.

tönern *adj.* ['tøːnərn] (of) clay, earthen.

'Ton|fall *m in speaking:* intonation, accent; '√film *m* sound film; '√lage *f* pitch; '√leiter ♪ *f* scale, gamut; '2los *adj.* soundless; *fig.* toneless; '√meister *m* sound engineer.

Tonne ['tɔnə] *f* (-/-n) *large:* tun; *smaller:* barrel, cask; ♣ measure of weight: ton.

Tonsilbe *gr. f* accented syllable.

Tonsur [tɔnˈzuːr] *f* (-/-en) tonsure.

'Tönung *paint. f* (-/-en) tint, tinge, shade.

'Tonwaren *f/pl. s.* Töpferware.

Topf [tɔpf] *m* (-[e]s/√e) pot.

Töpfer ['tœpfər] *m* (-s/-) potter; stove-fitter; √ei [√'ae] *f* (-/-en) pottery; '√ware *f* pottery, earthenware, crockery.

topp¹ *int.* [tɔp] done!, agreed!

Topp² ♣ [√] *m* (-s/-e, -s) top, masthead.

Tor¹ [toːr] *n* (-[e]s/-e) gate; gateway (*a. fig.*); *football:* goal; *skiing:* gate.

Tor² [√] *m* (-en/-en) fool.

Torf [tɔrf] *m* (-[e]s/no pl.) peat.

Torheit ['toːrhaet] *f* (-/-en) folly.

'Torhüter *m* gate-keeper; *sports:* goalkeeper.

töricht *adj.* ['tøːriçt] foolish, silly.

Törin ['tøːrin] *f* (-/-nen) fool(ish woman).

torkeln ['tɔrkəln] *v/i.* (ge-, h, sein) reel, stagger, totter.

'Tor|latte *f sports:* cross-bar; '√lauf *m skiing:* slalom; '√linie *f sports:* goal-line.

Tornister [tɔrˈnistər] *m* (-s/-) knapsack; satchel.

torpedieren [tɔrpeˈdiːrən] *v/t.* (no -ge-, h) torpedo (*a. fig.*).

Torpedo [tɔrˈpeːdo] *m* (-s/-s) torpedo; √boot *n* torpedo-boat.

'Tor|pfosten *m* gate-post; *sports:* goal-post; '√schuß *m* shot at the goal; '√schütze *m sports:* scorer.

Torte ['tɔrtə] *f* (-/-n) fancy cake, *Am.* layer cake; tart, *Am.* pie.

Tortur [tɔrˈtuːr] *f* (-/-en) torture; *fig.* ordeal.

'Tor|wart ['toːrvart] *m* (-[e]s/-e) *sports:* goalkeeper; '√weg *m* gateway.

tosen ['toːzən] *v/i.* (ge-, h, sein) roar, rage; '√d *adj. applause:* thunderous.

tot *adj.* [toːt] dead (*a. fig.*); deceased; √er Punkt ⊕ dead cent|re, *Am.* -er; *fig.:* deadlock; fatigue; √es Rennen *sports:* dead heat.

total *adj.* [toˈtaːl] total, complete.

'tot|arbeiten *v/refl.* (sep., -ge-, h) work o.s. to death; '2e (-n/-n) 1. *m* dead man; (dead) body, corpse; *die* √n *pl.* the dead *pl.*, the deceased *pl. or* departed *pl.*; ✗ casualties *pl.*; 2. *f* dead woman.

'Toten|bett *n* deathbed; '2blaß *adj.* deadly *or* deathly pale; '√blässe *f* deadly paleness *or* pallor; '2'bleich *adj. s.* totenblaß; √gräber ['√grɛːbər] *m* (-s/-) grave-digger (*a. zo.*); '√hemd *n* shroud; '√kopf *m* death's-head (*a. zo.*); *emblem of death:* a. skull and cross-bones; '√liste *f* death-roll (*a.* ✗), *esp.* ✗ casualty list; '√maske *f* death-mask; '√messe *eccl. f* mass for the dead, requiem; '√schädel *m* death's-head, skull; '√schein *m* death certificate; '2'still *adj.* (as) still as the grave; '√stille *f* dead(ly) silence, deathly stillness.

'tot|geboren *adj.* still-born; '2geburt *f* still birth; '√lachen *v/refl.* (sep., -ge-, h) die of laughing.

Toto ['to:to] m, F a. n (-s/-s) football pools pl.
'tot|schießen v/t. (irr. schießen, sep., -ge-, h) shoot dead, kill; '♀schlag ₐ̸ₜ m manslaughter, homicide; '↗schlagen v/t. (irr. schlagen, sep., -ge-, h) kill (a. time), slay; '↗schweigen v/t. (irr. schweigen, sep., -ge-, h) hush up; '↗ste-chen v/t. (irr. stechen, sep., -ge-, h) stab to death; '↗stellen v/refl. (sep., -ge-, h) feign death.
'Tötung f (-/-en) killing, slaying; ₐ̸ₜ homicide; fahrlässige ~ ₐ̸ₜ man-slaughter.
Tour [tu:r] f (-/-en) tour; excursion, trip; ⊕ turn, revolution; auf ↗en kommen mot. pick up speed; '↗en-wagen mot. m touring car.
Tourist [tu'rist] m (-en/-en), ↗in f (-/-nen) tourist.
Tournee [tur'ne:] f (-/-s, -n) tour.
Trab [tra:p] m (-[e]s/no pl.) trot.
Trabant [tra'bant] m (-en/-en) satellite.
trab|en ['tra:bən] v/i. (ge-, h, sein) trot; ♀rennen ['tra:p-] n trotting race.
Tracht [traxt] f (-/-en) dress, cos-tume; uniform; fashion; load; e-e (gehörige) ~ Prügel a (sound) thrash-ing; '♀en v/i. (ge-, h): ~ nach et. strive for; j-m nach dem Leben ~ seek s.o.'s life.
trächtig adj. ['trɛçtiç] (big) with young, pregnant.   [tradition.]
Tradition [tradi'tsjo:n] f (-/-en)
traf [tra:f] pret. of treffen.
Trag|bahre ['tra:k-] f stretcher, litter; '♀bar adj. portable; dress: wearable; fig.: bearable; reason-able; ↗e ['↗gə] f (-/-n) hand-barrow; s. Tragbahre.
träge adj. ['trɛ:gə] lazy, indolent; phys. inert (a. fig.).
tragen ['tra:gən] (irr., ge-, h) 1. v/t. carry; bear (costs, arms, respon-sibility, etc.); bear, endure; support; bear, yield (fruit, ⁎ interest, etc.); wear (dress, etc.); bei sich ~ have about one; sich gut ~ material: wear well; zur Schau ~ show off; 2. v/i. tree: bear, yield; gun, voice: carry; ice: bear.
Träger ['trɛ:gər] m (-s/-) carrier; porter (of luggage); holder, bearer (of name, licence, etc.); wearer (of dress); (shoulder-)strap (of slip, etc.); ⊕ support; Δ girder.
Trag|fähigkeit ['tra:k-] f carrying or load capacity; ⚓ tonnage; '↗flä-che f, '↗flügel ⁎ m wing, plane.
Trägheit ['trɛ:khart] f (-/no pl.) laziness, indolence; phys. inertia (a. fig.).
tragisch adj. ['tra:giʃ] tragic (a. fig.); fig. tragical.
Tragödie [tra'gø:djə] f (-/-n) trag-edy.

Trag|riemen ['tra:k-] m (carrying) strap; sling (of gun); '↗tier n pack animal; '↗tüte f carrier-bag; '↗weite f range; fig. import(ance), consequences pl.; von großer ~ of great moment.
Train|er ['trɛ:nər] m (-s/-) trainer; coach; ♀ieren [↗'ni:rən] (no -ge-, h) 1. v/t. train; coach; 2. v/i. train; ↗ing ['↗iŋ] n (-s/-s) training; '↗ings-anzug m sports: track suit.
traktieren [trak'ti:rən] v/t. (no -ge-, h) treat (badly).
Traktor ⊕ ['traktɔr] m (-s/-en) tractor.
trällern ['trɛlərn] v/t. and v/i. (ge-, h) troll.
trampel|n ['trampəln] v/i. (ge-, h) trample, stamp; '♀pfad m beaten track.
Tran [tra:n] m (-[e]s/-e) train-oil, whale-oil.
Träne ['trɛ:nə] f (-/-n) tear; in ↗n ausbrechen burst into tears; '♀n v/i. (ge-, h) water; '↗ngas n tear-gas.
Trank [traŋk] 1. m (-[e]s/⁎e) drink, beverage; ⁎ potion; 2. ♀ pret. of trinken.
Tränke ['trɛŋkə] f (-/-n) watering-place; '♀n v/t. (ge-, h) water (animals); soak, impregnate (mate-rial).
Trans|formator ⚡ [transfɔr'ma:-tɔr] m (-s/-en) transformer; ↗fu-sion ⚕ [↗u'zjo:n] f (-/-en) trans-fusion.
Transistorradio [tran'zistɔr-] n transistor radio or set.
transitiv gr. adj. ['tranziti:f] transi-tive.
transparent [transpa'rɛnt] 1. adj. transparent; 2. ♀ n (-[e]s/-e) trans-parency; in political processions, etc.: banner.
transpirieren [transpi'ri:rən] v/i. (no -ge-, h) perspire.
Transplantation ⚕ [transplanta-'tsjo:n] f transplant (operation).
Transport [trans'pɔrt] m (-[e]s/-e) transport(ation), conveyance, car-riage; ♀abel adj. [↗'ta:bəl] (trans-) portable; ↗er m (-s/-) ⚓, ⁎ (troop-)transport; '♀fähig adj. transportable, sick person: a. trans-ferable; ♀ieren [↗'ti:rən] v/t. (no -ge-, h) transport, convey, carry; ↗unternehmen n transport (operation).
Trapez [tra'pe:ts] n (-es/-e) ⚚ trapezium, Am. trapezoid; gym-nastics: trapeze.
trappeln ['trapəln] v/i. (ge-, sein) horse: clatter; children, etc.: patter.
Trass|ant ✝ [tra'sant] m (-en/-en) drawer; ↗at ✝ [↗'sa:t] m (-en/-en) drawee; ↗e ⊕ f (-/-n) line; ♀ieren [↗'si:rən] v/t. (no -ge-, h) ⊕ lay or trace out; ~ auf (acc.) ✝ draw on.

trat [tra:t] *pret. of* treten.

Tratte ✝ ['tratə] *f* (-/-n) draft.

Traube ['traubə] *f* (-/-n) bunch of grapes; grape; cluster; '**∼nsaft** *m* grape-juice; '**∼nzucker** *m* grape-sugar, glucose.

trauen ['trauən] (ge-, h) 1. *v/t.* marry; *sich* ∼ *lassen* get married; 2. *v/i.* trust (*j-m s.o.*), confide (*dat.* in); *ich traute meinen Ohren nicht* I could not believe my ears.

Trauer ['trauər] *f* (-/*no pl.*) sorrow, affliction; *for dead person:* mourning; '**∼botschaft** *f* sad news; '**∼fall** *m* death; '**∼feier** *f* funeral ceremonies *pl.*, obsequies *pl.*; '**∼flor** *m* mourning-crape; '**∼geleit** *n* funeral procession; '**∼gottesdienst** *m* funeral service; '**∼kleid** *n* mourning (-dress); '**∼marsch** *m* funeral march; '**∼n** *v/i.* (ge-, h) mourn (*um* for); be in mourning; '**∼spiel** *n* tragedy; '**∼weide** ♀ *f* weeping willow; '**∼zug** *m* funeral procession.

Traufe ['traufə] *f* (-/-n) eaves *pl.*; gutter; *s. Regen²*.

träufeln ['trɔyfəln] *v/t.* (ge-, h) drop, drip, trickle. [cosy, snug.\

traulich *adj.* ['trauliç] intimate;\

Traum [traum] *m* (-[e]s/*∼e*) dream (*a. fig.*); reverie; *das fällt mir nicht im* ∼ *ein!* I would not dream of (doing) it!; '**∼bild** *n* vision; '**∼deuter** *m* (-s/-) dream-reader.

träumen ['trɔymən] *v/i. and v/t.* (ge-, h) dream; '**2er** *m* (-s/-) dreamer (*a. fig.*); 2erei [∼'rai] *f* (-/-en) dreaming; *fig. a.* reverie (*a. ♪*), day-dream, musing; '**∼erisch** *adj.* dreamy; musing.

traurig *adj.* ['trauriç] sad (*über acc.* at), *Am.* F blue; wretched.

'Trau|ring *m* wedding-ring; '**∼schein** *m* marriage certificate *or* lines *pl.*; '**∼ung** *f* (-/-en) marriage, wedding; '**∼zeuge** *m* witness to a marriage.

Trecker ⊕ ['trɛkər] *m* (-s/-) tractor.

Treff [trɛf] *n* (-s/-s) *cards:* club(s *pl.*).

treffen¹ ['trɛfən] (*irr.*, ge-) 1. *v/t.* (h) hit (*a. fig.*), strike; concern; *disadvantageously:* affect; meet; *nicht* ∼ miss; *e-e Entscheidung* ∼ come to a decision; *Maßnahmen* ∼ take measures *or* steps; *Vorkehrungen* ∼ take precautions *or* measures; *sich* ∼ happen; meet; gather, assemble; *a.* have an appointment (*mit* with), F have a date (with); *das trifft sich gut!* that's lucky!, how fortunate!; *sich getroffen fühlen* feel hurt; *wen trifft die Schuld?* who is to blame?; *das Los traf ihn* the lot fell on him; *du bist gut getroffen* paint., *phot.* this is a good likeness of you; *vom Blitz getroffen* struck by lightning; 2. *v/i.* (h) hit; 3. *v/i.* (sein): ∼ *auf* (*acc.*) meet with; encounter (*a.* ✕).

Treffen² [∼] *n* (-s/-) meeting; rally; gathering; ✕ encounter; '**2d** *adj.* remark: appropriate, to the point.

'Treff|er *m* (-s/-) hit (*a. fig.*); prize; '**∼punkt** *m* meeting-place.

Treibeis ['traip?-] *n* drift-ice.

treiben¹ ['traibən] (*irr.*, ge-) 1. *v/t.* (h) drive; ⊕ put in motion, propel; drift (*smoke, snow*); put forth (*leaves*); force (*plants*); *fig.* impel, urge, press (*j-n zu inf. s.o.* to *inf.*); carry on (*business, trade*); *Musik* (*Sport*) ∼ go in for music (sports); *Sprachen* ∼ study languages; *es zu weit* ∼ go too far; *wenn er es weiterhin so treibt* if he carries *or* goes on like that; *was treibst du da?* what are you doing there?; 2. *v/i.* (sein) drive; float, drift; 3. *v/i.* (h) ∼ shoot; *dough:* ferment, work.

Treiben² [∼] *n* (-s/*no pl.*) driving; doings *pl.*, goings-on *pl.*; *geschäftiges* ∼ bustle; '**2d** *adj.:* ∼*e Kraft* driving force.

Treib|haus ['traip-] *n* hothouse; '**∼holz** *n* drift-wood; '**∼jagd** *f* battue; '**∼riemen** *m* driving-belt; '**∼stoff** *m* fuel; propell|ant, -ent (*of rocket*).

trenn|en ['trɛnən] *v/t.* (ge-, h) separate, sever; rip (*seam*); *teleph.*, ∉ cut off, disconnect; isolate, segregate; *sich* ∼ separate (*von* from), part (*from or with s.o.*; *with s.th.*); '**2schärfe** *f radio:* selectivity; '**2ung** *f* (-/-en) separation; disconne|xion, -ction; segregation (*of races, etc.*); '**2(ungs)wand** *f* partition (wall). [(-bit).\

Trense ['trɛnzə] *f* (-/-n) snaffle

Treppe ['trɛpə] *f* (-/-n) staircase, stairway, (*e-e a* flight *or* pair of) stairs *pl.*; *zwei* ∼*n hoch* on the second floor, *Am.* on the third floor.

'Treppen|absatz *m* landing; '**∼geländer** *n* banisters *pl.*; '**∼haus** *n* staircase; '**∼stufe** *f* stair, step.

Tresor [tre'zo:r] *m* (-s/-e) safe; *bank:* strong-room, vault.

treten ['tre:tən] (*irr.*, ge-) 1. *v/i.* (h) tread, step (*j-n or j-m auf die Zehen* on *s.o.'s* toes); 2. *v/i.* (sein) tread, step (*j-m auf die Zehen* on *s.o.'s* toes); walk; *ins Haus* ∼ enter the house; *j-m unter die Augen* ∼ appear before *s.o.*, face *s.o.*; *j-m zu nahe* ∼ offend *s.o.*; *zu j-m* ∼ step *or* walk up to *s.o.*; *über die Ufer* ∼ overflow its banks; 3. *v/t.* (h) tread; kick; *mit Füßen* ∼ trample upon.

treu *adj.* [trɔy] faithful, loyal; '**2bruch** *m* breach of faith, perfidy; '**2e** *f* (-/*no pl.*) fidelity, faith(fulness), loyalty; **2händer** ['∼hɛndər] *m* (-s/-) trustee; '**∼herzig** *adj.* guileless; ingenuous, simpleminded; '**∼los** *adj.* faithless (*gegen* to), disloyal (to); perfidious.

Tribüne [tri'by:nə] *f* (-/-n) platform; *sports, etc.*: (grand) stand.

Tribut [tri'bu:t] *m* (-[e]s/-e) tribute.

Trichter ['triçtər] *m* (-s/-) funnel; *made by bomb, shell, etc.*: crater; horn (*of wind instruments, etc.*).

Trick [trik] *m* (-s/-e, -s) trick; '~film *m* animation, animated cartoon.

Trieb [tri:p] 1. *m* (-[e]s/-e) ♀ sprout, (new) shoot; driving force; impulse; instinct; (sexual) urge; desire; 2. ♀ *pret.* of treiben; '~feder *f* main-spring; *fig.* driving force, motive; '~kraft *f* motive power; *fig.* driving force, motive; '~wagen 🚃 *m* rail-car, rail-motor; '~werk ⊕ *n* gear (drive), (driving) mechanism, transmission; engine.

triefen ['tri:fən] *v/i.* ([irr.,] ge-, h) drip (*von* with); *eye*: run.

triftig *adj.* ['triftiç] valid.

Trigonometrie ⚗ [trigonome'tri:] *f* (-/no pl.) trigonometry.

Trikot [tri'ko:] (-s/-s) 1. *m* stockinet; 2. *n* tights *pl.*; vest; ~agen [~o'ta:-ʒən] *f/pl.* hosiery.

Triller ♪ ['trilər] *m* (-s/-) trill, shake, quaver; '♀n ♪ *v/i.* and *v/t.* (ge-, h) trill, shake, quaver; *bird*: a. warble.

trink|bar *adj.* ['triŋkbɑ:r] drinkable; '♀becher *m* drinking-cup; '~en (*irr.*, ge-, h) 1. *v/t.* drink; take, have (tea, *etc.*); 2. *v/i.* drink; ~ auf (acc.) drink to, toast; '♀er *m* (-s/-) drinker; drunkard; '♀gelage *n* drinking-bout; '♀geld *n* tip, gratuity; *j-m e-e Mark ~ geben* tip s.o. one mark; '♀glas *n* drinking-glass; '♀halle *f* at spa: pump-room; '♀kur *f*: e-e ~ machen drink the waters; '♀spruch *m* toast; '♀wasser *n* (-s/no pl.) drinking-water.

Trio ['tri:o] *n* (-s/-s) trio (a. ♪).

trippeln ['tripəln] *v/i.* (ge-, sein) trip.

Tritt [trit] *m* (-[e]s/-e) tread, step; footprint; *noise*: footfall, (foot)step; kick; ⊕ treadle; *s.* Trittbrett, Trittleiter; *im (falschen) ~ in* (out of) step; ~ halten keep step; '~brett *n* step, footboard; *mot.* running-board; '~leiter *f* stepladder, (e-e a pair *or* set of) steps *pl.*

Triumph [tri'umf] *m* (-[e]s/-e) triumph; ♀al *adj.* [~'fa:l] triumphant; '~bogen *m* triumphal arch; ♀ieren [~'fi:rən] *v/i.* (no -ge-, h) triumph (*über* acc. over).

trocken *adj.* ['trɔkən] dry (a. *fig.*); *soil, land*: arid; '♀dock ⚓ *n* dry dock; '♀haube *f* (hood of) hairdrier; '♀heit *f* (-/no pl.) dryness; drought, aridity; '~legen *v/t.* (sep., -ge-, h) dry up; drain (*land*); change the napkins of, *Am.* change the diapers of (*baby*); '♀obst *n* dried fruit.

trocknen ['trɔknən] (ge-) 1. *v/i.* (sein) dry; 2. *v/t.* (h) dry.

Troddel ['trɔdəl] *f* (-/-n) tassel.

Trödel F ['trø:dəl] *m* (-s/no pl.) second-hand articles *pl.*; lumber, *Am.* junk; rubbish; '♀n F *fig. v/i.* (ge-, h) dawdle, loiter.

Trödler ['trø:dlər] *m* (-s/-) second-hand dealer, *Am.* junk dealer, junkman; *fig.* dawdler, loiterer.

troff [trɔf] *pret.* of triefen.

Trog¹ [tro:k] *m* (-[e]s/-e) trough.

trog² [~] *pret.* of trügen.

Trommel ['trɔməl] *f* (-/-n) drum; ⊕ *a.* cylinder, barrel; '~fell *n* drumskin; *anat.* ear-drum; '♀n *v/i.* and *v/t.* (ge-, h) drum.

Trommler ['trɔmlər] *m* (-s/-) drummer.

Trompete [trɔm'pe:tə] *f* (-/-n) trumpet; ♀n *v/i.* and *v/t.* (no -ge-, h) trumpet; ~r *m* (-s/-) trumpeter.

Tropen ['tro:pən]: *die* ~ *pl.* the tropics *pl.*

Tropf F [trɔpf] *m* (-[e]s/-e) simpleton; *armer* ~ poor wretch.

tröpfeln ['trœpfəln] (ge-) 1. *v/i.* (h) drop, drip, trickle; *tap*: a. leak; *es tröpfelt rain*: a few drops are falling; 2. *v/i.* (sein): ... *aus or von* trickle *or* drip from; 3. *v/t.* (h) drop, drip.

tropfen¹ ['trɔpfən] (ge-) 1. *v/i.* (h) drop, drip, trickle; *tap*: a. leak; *candle*: gutter; 2. *v/i.* (sein): ~ *aus or von* trickle *or* drip from; 3. *v/t.* (h) drop, drip.

Tropfen² [~] *m* (-s/-) drop; *ein ~ auf den heißen Stein* a drop in the ocean *or* bucket; ♀förmig *adj.* ['~fœrmiç] drop-shaped; '♀weise *adv.* drop by drop, by drops.

Trophäe [tro'fɛ:ə] *f* (-/-n) trophy.

tropisch *adj.* ['tro:piʃ] tropical.

Trosse ['trɔsə] *f* (-/-n) cable; ⚓ *a.* hawser.

Trost [tro:st] *m* (-es/no pl.) comfort, consolation; *das ist ein schlechter* ~ that is cold comfort; *du bist wohl nicht (recht) bei* ~! F you must be out of your mind!

tröst|en ['trø:stən] *v/t.* (ge-, h) console, comfort; *sich* ~ console o.s. (*mit* with); ~ *Sie sich!* be of good comfort!, cheer up!; '~lich *adj.* comforting.

'**trost|los** *adj.* disconsolate, inconsolable; *land, etc.*: desolate; *fig.* wretched; '♀losigkeit *f* (-/no pl.) desolation; *fig.* wretchedness; '♀-preis *m* consolation prize, booby prize; '~reich *adj.* consolatory, comforting.

Trott [trɔt] *m* (-[e]s/-e) trot; F *fig.* jogtrot, routine; '~el F *m* (-s/-) idiot, fool, ninny; '♀en *v/i.* (ge-, sein) trot.

trotz [trɔts] 1. *prp.* (gen.) in spite of, despite; ~ *alledem* for all that; 2. ♀ *m* (-es/no pl.) defiance; obstinacy; ~dem cj. ['~de:m] nevertheless; (al)though; '~en v/i. (ge-, h) (dat.) defy, dare; brave (danger); be obstinate; sulk; '~ig adj. defiant; obstinate; sulky.

trüb adj. [try:p], ~e adj. ['~bə] liquid: muddy, turbid, thick; mind, thinking: confused, muddy, turbid; eyes, etc.: dim, dull; weather: dull, cloudy, dreary (all a. fig.); experiences: sad.

Trubel ['tru:bəl] m (-s/no pl.) bustle.

trüben ['try:bən] v/t. (ge-, h) make thick or turbid or muddy; dim; darken; spoil (pleasures, etc.); blur (view); dull (mind); sich ~ liquid: become thick or turbid or muddy; dim, darken; relations: become strained.

Trüb|sal ['try:pza:l] f (-/~-e): ~ blasen mope, F be in the dumps, have the blues; '2selig adj. sad, gloomy, melancholy, wretched, miserable; dreary; '~sinn m (-e)s/ no pl.) melancholy, sadness, gloom; '2sinnig adj. melancholy, gloomy, sad; ~ung ['~buŋ] f (-/-en) liquid: muddiness, turbidity (both a. fig.); dimming, darkening.

Trüffel ♦ ['tryfəl] f (-/-n), F m (-s/-) truffle.

Trug¹ [tru:k] m (-[e]s/no pl.) deceit, fraud; delusion (of senses).

trug² [~] pret. of tragen.

'Trugbild n phantom; illusion.

trüg|en ['try:gən] (irr., ge-, h) 1. v/t. deceive; 2. v/i. be deceptive; '~e-risch adj. deceptive, delusive; treacherous.

'Trugschluß m fallacy, false conclusion.

Truhe ['tru:ə] f (-/-n) chest, trunk; radio, etc.: cabinet, console.

Trümmer ['trymər] pl. ruins pl.; rubble, debris, ♦, ☞ wreckage; '~haufen m heap of ruins or rubble.

Trumpf [trumpf] m (-[e]s/~e) cards: trump (card) (a. fig.); s-n ~ ausspielen play one's trump card.

Trunk [truŋk] m (-[e]s/~e) drink; draught; drinking; '2en adj. drunken; pred. drunk (a. fig. von, vor with); intoxicated; '~enbold contp. ['~bɔlt] m (-[e]s/-e) drunkard, sot; '~enheit f (-/no pl.) drunkenness, intoxication; ~ am Steuer ♣₅ drunken driving, drunkenness at the wheel; '~sucht f alcoholism, dipsomania; '2süchtig adj. addicted to drink, given to drinking.

Trupp [trup] m (-s/-s) troop, band, gang; ☒ detachment.

'Truppe f (-/-n) ☒ troop, body; ☒ unit; thea. company, troupe; ~n pl. ☒ troops, forces pl.; die ~n pl. ☒ the (fighting) services pl., the armed forces pl.

'Truppen|gattung f arm, branch, division; '~schau f military review;

'~transporter ♣, ☒ m (troop-) transport; '~übungsplatz m training area.

Truthahn orn. ['tru:t-] m turkey (-cock).

Tschech|e ['tʃɛçə] m (-n/-n), '~in f (-/-nen) Czech; 2isch adj. Czech.

Tube ['tu:bə] f (-/-n) tube.

tuberkul|ös ✠ adj. [tuberku'lø:s] tuberculous, tubercular; 2ose ✠ [~o:zə] f (-/-n) tuberculosis.

Tuch [tu:x] n 1. (-[e]s/-e) cloth; fabric; 2. (-[e]s/~er) head covering: kerchief; shawl, scarf; round neck: neckerchief; duster; rag; '~füh-lung f (-/no pl.) close touch.

tüchtig ['tyçtiç] 1. adj. able, fit; clever; proficient; efficient; excellent; good; thorough; 2. adv. vigorously; thoroughly; F awfully; 2keit f (-/no pl.) ability, fitness; cleverness; proficiency; efficiency; excellency.

'Tuchwaren f/pl. drapery, cloths pl.

Tück|e ['tykə] f (-/-n) malice, spite; 2isch adj. malicious, spiteful; treacherous.

tüfteln F ['tyftəln] v/i. (ge-, h) puzzle (an dat. over).

Tugend ['tu:gənt] f (-/-en) virtue; ~bold ['~bɔlt] m (-[e]s/-e) paragon of virtue; 2haft adj. virtuous.

Tüll [tyl] m (-s/-e) tulle.

Tulpe ♦ ['tulpə] f (-/-n) tulip.

tummel|n ['tuməln] v/refl. (ge-, h) children: romp; hurry; bestir o.s.; '2platz m playground; fig. arena.

Tümmler ['tymlər] m (-s/-) orn. tumbler; zo. porpoise.

Tumor ♪ ['tu:mɔr] m (-s/-en) tumo(u)r.

Tümpel ['tympəl] m (-s/-) pool.

Tumult [tu'mult] m (-[e]s/-e) tumult; riot, turmoil, uproar; row.

tun [tu:n] 1. v/t. (irr., ge-, h) do; make; put (to school, into the bag, etc.); dazu ~ add to it; contribute; ich kann nichts dazu ~ I cannot help it; es ist mir darum zu ~ I am anxious about (it); zu ~ haben have to do; be busy; es tut nichts it doesn't matter; 2. v/i. (irr., ge-, h) do; make; so ~ als ob make as if; pretend to inf.; das tut gut! that is a comfort!; that's good!; 3. 2 n (-s/no pl.) doings pl.; proceedings pl.; action; ~ und Treiben ways and doings pl.

Tünche ['tynçə] f (-/-n) whitewash (a. fig.); '2n v/t. (ge-, h) whitewash.

Tunichtgut ['tu:niçtgu:t] m (-, -[e]s/-e) ne'er-do-well, good-for-nothing.

Tunke ['tuŋkə] f (-/-n) sauce; '2n v/t. (ge-, h) dip, steep.

tunlichst adv. ['tu:nliçst] if possible.

Tunnel ['tunəl] m (-s/-, -s) tunnel; subway.

Tüpfel ['typfəl] *m, n* (-s/-) dot, spot; '**2n** *v/t.* (ge-, h) dot, spot.

tupfen ['tupfən] **1.** *v/t.* (ge-, h) dab; dot, spot; **2.** **2** *m* (-s/-) dot, spot.

Tür [ty:r] *f* (-/-en) door; *mit der ~ ins Haus fallen* blurt (things) out; *j-n vor die ~ setzen* turn s.o. out; *vor der ~ stehen* be near *or* close at hand; *zwischen ~ und Angel* in passing; '**~angel** *f* (door-)hinge.

Turbine ⊕ [tur'bi:nə] *f* (-/-n) turbine; **~flugzeug** *n* turbo-jet.

Turbo-Prop-Flugzeug ['turbo-'prɔp-] *n* turbo-prop.

'**Tür|flügel** *m* leaf (of a door); '**~füllung** *f* (door-)panel; '**~griff** *m* door-handle.

Türk|e ['tyrkə] *m* (-n/-n) Turk; '**~in** *f* (-/-nen) Turk(ish woman); **~is** *min.* [~'ki:s] *m* (-es/-e) turquoise; '**2isch** *adj.* Turkish.

'**Türklinke** *f* door-handle; latch.

Turm [turm] *m* (-[e]s/-e) tower; *a.* steeple (*of church*); *chess:* castle, rook.

Türm|chen ['tyrmçən] *n* (-s/-) turret; '**2en** (ge-) **1.** *v/t.* (h) pile up; *sich ~* tower; **2.** F *v/i.* (sein) bolt, F skedaddle, *Am. sl. a.* skiddoo.

'**turm|hoch** *adv.: j-m ~ überlegen sein* stand head and shoulders above s.o.; '**2spitze** *f* spire; '**2-springen** *n* (-s/no *pl.*) *swimming:* high diving; '**2uhr** *f* tower-clock, church-clock.

turnen ['turnən] **1.** *v/i.* (ge-, h) do gymnastics; **2.** **2** *n* (-s/no *pl.*) gymnastics *pl.*

'**Turn|er** *m* (-s/-), '**~erin** *f* (-/-nen) gymnast; '**~gerät** *n* gymnastic apparatus; '**~halle** *f* gym(nasium); '**~hemd** *n* (gym-)shirt; '**~hose** *f* shorts *pl.*

Turnier [tur'ni:r] *n* (-s/-e) tournament.

'**Turn|lehrer** *m* gym master; '**~lehrerin** *f* gym mistress; '**~schuh** *m* gym-shoe; '**~stunde** *f* gym lesson; '**~unterricht** *m* instruction in gymnastics; '**~verein** *m* gymnastic *or* athletic club.

'**Tür|pfosten** *m* door-post; '**~rahmen** *m* door-case, door-frame; '**~schild** *n* door-plate.

Tusche ['tuʃə] *f* (-/-n) India(n) *or* Chinese ink; '**2n** *v/i.* (ge-, h) whisper; '**2n** *v/t.* (ge-, h) draw in India(n) ink.

Tüte ['ty:tə] *f* (-/-n) paper-bag.

tuten ['tu:tən] *v/i.* (ge-, h) toot(le); *mot.* honk, blow one's horn.

Typ [ty:p] *m* (-s/-en) type; ⊕ *a.* model; **~e** *f* (-/-n) *typ.* type; F *fig.* (queer) character.

Typhus ♨ ['ty:fus] *m* (-/no *pl.*) typhoid (fever).

'**typisch** *adj.* typical (*für* of).

Tyrann [ty'ran] *m* (-en/-en) tyrant; **~ei** [~'nai] *f* (-/-en) tyranny; **2isch** *adj.* [ty'ranɪʃ] tyrannical; **2isieren** [~i'zi:rən] *v/t.* (no -ge-, h) tyrannize (over) *s.o.*, oppress, bully.

U

U-Bahn ['u:-] *f s.* Untergrundbahn.

übel ['y:bəl] **1.** *adj.* evil, bad; *nicht ~* not bad, pretty good; *mir ist ~* I am *or* feel sick; **2.** *adv.* ill; *~ gelaunt sein* be in a bad mood; *es gefällt mir nicht ~* I rather like it; **3.** **2** *n* (-s/-) evil; *s. Übelstand; das kleinere ~ wählen* choose the lesser evil; '**~gelaunt** *adj.* ill-humo(u)red; '**2keit** *f* (-/-en) sickness, nausea; '**~nehmen** *v/t.* (*irr.* nehmen, *sep.*, -ge-, h) take *s.th.* ill *or* amiss; '**2-stand** *m* grievance; '**2täter** *m* evil-doer, wrongdoer.

'**übelwollen 1.** *v/i.* (*sep.*, -ge-, h): *j-m ~* wish s.o. ill; be ill-disposed towards s.o.; **2.** **2** *n* (-s/no *pl.*) ill will, malevolence; '**~d** *adj.* malevolent.

üben ['y:bən] (ge-, h) **1.** *v/t.* exercise; practi|se, *Am. a.* -ce; *Geduld ~* exercise patience; *Klavier ~* practise the piano; **2.** *v/i.* exercise; practi|se, *Am. a.* -ce.

über ['y:bər] **1.** *prp.* (dat.; acc.) over, above; across (*river, etc.*); via, by way of (*Munich, etc.*); *sprechen ~* (acc.) talk about *or* of; *~ Politik sprechen* talk politics; *nachdenken ~* (acc.) think about *or* of; *ein Buch schreiben ~* (acc.) write a book on; *~ Nacht bleiben bei* stay overnight at; *~ s-e Verhältnisse leben* live beyond one's income; *~ kurz oder lang* sooner *or* later; **2.** *adv.: die ganze Zeit ~* all along; *j-m in et. ~ sein* excel s.o. in s.th.

über'all *adv.* everywhere, anywhere, *Am. a.* all over.

über|'anstrengen *v/t.* (no -ge-, h) overstrain; *sich ~* overstrain o.s.; **~'arbeiten** *v/t.* (no -ge-, h) retouch (*painting, etc.*); revise (*book, etc.*); *sich ~* overwork o.s.

überaus *adv.* ['y:bər?-] exceedingly, extremely.

'**überbelichten** *phot. v/t.* (no -ge-, h) over-expose.

über'bieten *v/t.* (*irr.* bieten, *no* -ge-, h) *at auction:* outbid; *fig.:* beat; surpass.

Überbleibsel ['y:bərblaipsəl] *n*

(-s/-) remnant, *Am.* F *a.* holdover; ~ *pl. a.* remains *pl.*

'Überblick *m* survey, general view (*both*: über acc. of).

über|'blicken *v/t.* (*no* -ge-, *h*) overlook; *fig.* survey, have a general view of; ~'bringen *v/t.* (*irr.* bringen, *no* -ge-, *h*) deliver; 2'bringer *m* (-s/-) bearer; ~'brücken *v/t.* (*no* -ge-, *h*) bridge; *fig.* bridge over *s.th.*; ~'dachen *v/t.* (*no* -ge-, *h*) roof over; ~'dauern *v/t.* (*no* -ge-, *h*) outlast, outlive; ~'denken *v/t.* (*irr.* denken, *no* -ge-, *h*) think *s.th.* over.

über'dies *adv.* besides, moreover.

über'drehen *v/t.* (*no* -ge-, *h*) overwind (*watch, etc.*); strip (*screw*).

'Überdruck *m* 1. (-[e]s/-e) overprint; ✻ *a.* surcharge; 2. ⊕ (-[e]s/~e) overpressure.

Über|druß ['y:bərdrus] *m* (Überdrusses/no pl.) satiety; bis zum ~ to satiety; 2drüssig *adj.* (gen.) ['~y-siç] disgusted with, weary *or* sick of.

Übereif|er ['y:bər?-] *m* over-zeal; 2rig *adj.* ['y:bər?-] over-zealous.

über'eil|en *v/t.* (*no* -ge-, *h*) precipitate, rush; sich ~ hurry too much; ~t *adj.* precipitate, rash.

übereinander *adv.* [y:bər?ar'nan-dər] one upon the other; ~schlagen *v/t.* (*irr.* schlagen, sep., -ge-, *h*) cross (one's legs).

über'ein|kommen *v/i.* (*irr.* kommen, sep., -ge-, sein) agree; 2kommen *n* (-s/-), 2kunft [~kunft] *f* (-/~e) agreement; ~stimmen *v/i.* (sep., -ge-, *h*) *p.* agree (mit with); *thing*: correspond (with, to); 2stimmung *f* agreement; correspondence; in ~ mit in agreement *or* accordance with.

über|fahren 1. ['~fɑ:rən] *v/i.* (*irr.* fahren, sep., -ge-, sein) cross; 2. [~'fɑ:rən] *v/t.* (*irr.* fahren, *no* -ge-, *h*) run over; disregard (*traffic sign, etc.*); 2fahrt *f* passage; crossing.

'Überfall *m* ✻ surprise; ✻ invasion (auf acc. of); ✻ raid; hold-up; assault ([up]on).

über'fallen *v/t.* (*irr.* fallen, *no* -ge-, *h*) ✻ surprise; ✻ invade; ✻ raid; hold up; assault.

'über|fällig *adj.* overdue; 2fallkommando *n* flying squad, *Am.* riot squad.

über'fliegen *v/t.* (*irr.* fliegen, *no* -ge-, *h*) fly over *or* across; *fig.* glance over, skim (through); den Atlantik ~ fly (across) the Atlantic.

'überfließen *v/i.* (*irr.* fließen, sep., -ge-, sein) overflow.

über'flügeln *v/t.* (*no* -ge-, *h*) ✻ outflank; *fig.* outstrip, surpass.

'Über|fluß *m* (Überflusses/no pl.) abundance (an dat. of); superfluity (of); ~ haben an (dat.) abound in;

'2flüssig *adj.* superfluous; redundant.

über'fluten *v/t.* (*no* -ge-, *h*) overflow, flood (a. *fig.*).

'Überfracht *f* excess freight.

über|führen *v/t.* 1. ['~fy:rən] (sep., -ge-, *h*) convey (*dead body*); 2. [~'fy:rən] (*no* -ge-, *h*) s. 1; ✻✻ convict (gen. of); 2führung *f* (-/-en) conveyance (of *dead body*); bridge, *Am.* overpass; ✻✻ conviction (gen. of). [*dat.* of).\]

'Überfülle *f* superabundance (an)

über|'füllen *v/t.* (*no* -ge-, *h*) overfill; cram; overcrowd; sich den Magen ~ glut o.s.; ~'füttern *v/t.* (*no* -ge-, *h*) overfeed.

'Übergabe *f* delivery; handing over; surrender (a. ✻).

'Übergang *m* bridge; ⊞ crossing; *fig.* transition (a. ♪); *esp.* ✻✻ devolution; '~sstadium *n* transition stage.

über|'geben *v/t.* (*irr.* geben, *no* -ge-, *h*) deliver up; hand over; surrender (a. ✻); sich ~ vomit, be sick; ~gehen 1. ['~ge:ən] *v/i.* (*irr.* gehen, sep., -ge-, sein) pass over; *work, duties*: devolve (auf acc. [up]on); ~ in (acc.) pass into; ~ zu et. proceed to s.th.; 2. [~'ge:ən] *v/t.* (*irr.* gehen, *no* -ge-, *h*) pass over, ignore.

'Übergewicht *n* (-[e]s/no pl.) overweight; *fig. a.* preponderance (über acc. over).

über'gießen *v/t.* (*irr.* gießen, *no* -ge-, *h*): mit Wasser ~ pour water over *s.th.*; mit Fett ~ baste (*roasting meat*).

'über|greifen *v/i.* (*irr.* greifen, sep., -ge-, *h*): ~ auf (acc.) encroach (up-) on (s.o.'s rights); *fire, epidemic, etc.*: spread to; 2griff *m* encroachment (auf acc. [up]on), inroad (on); '~haben F *v/t.* (*irr.* haben, sep., -ge-, *h*) have (*coat, etc.*) on; *fig.* have enough of, *sl.* be fed up with.

über'handnehmen *v/i.* (*irr.* nehmen, sep., -ge-, *h*) be rampant, grow *or* wax rife.

'überhängen 1. *v/i.* (*irr.* hängen, sep., -ge-, *h*) overhang; 2. *v/t.* (sep., -ge-, *h*) put (*coat, etc.*) round one's shoulders; sling (*rifle*) over one's shoulder.

über'häufen *v/t.* (*no* -ge-, *h*): ~ mit swamp with (*letters, work, etc.*); overwhelm with (*inquiries, etc.*).

über'haupt *adv.*: wer will denn ~, daß er kommt? who wants him to come anyhow?; wenn ~ if at all; ~ nicht not at all; ~ kein no ... whatever.

überheblich *adj.* [y:bər'he:pliç] presumptuous, arrogant; 2keit *f* (-/~-en) presumption, arrogance.

über|'hitzen *v/t.* (*no* -ge-, *h*) overheat (a. ⚕); ⊕ superheat; ~'holen *v/t.* (*no* -ge-, *h*) overtake (a. mot.);

esp. sports: outstrip (*a. fig.*); over-haul, *esp. Am. a.* service; **~'holt** *adj.* outmoded; *pred. a.* out of date; **~'hören** *v/t.* (*no -ge-, h*) fail to hear, miss; ignore.

'überirdisch *adj.* supernatural; un-earthly.

'überkippen *v/i.* (*sep., -ge-, sein*) *p.* overbalance, lose one's balance.

über'kleben *v/t.* (*no -ge-, h*) paste over.

'Überkleidung *f* outer garments *pl.*

'überklug *adj.* would-be wise, sapient.

'überkochen *v/i.* (*sep., -ge-, sein*) boil over; F *leicht ~* be very irri-table.

über'kommen *v/t.* (*irr. kommen, no -ge-, h*): *Furcht überkam ihn* he was seized with fear; **~'laden** *v/t.* (*irr. laden, no -ge-, h*) overload; overcharge (*battery, picture, etc.*).

'Überland|flug *m* cross-country flight; **'~zentrale** *& f* long-distance power-station.

über'lassen *v/t.* (*irr. lassen, no -ge-, h*): *j-m et. ~* let s.o. have s.th.; *fig.* leave s.th. to s.o.; *j-n sich selbst ~ leave* s.o. to himself; *j-n s-m Schicksal ~* leave *or* abandon s.o. to his fate; **~'lasten** *v/t.* (*no -ge-, h*) overload; *fig.* overburden.

über'laufen 1. [**'~lauf**ən] *v/i.* (*irr. laufen, sep., -ge-, sein*) run over; boil over; ⚔ desert (*zu* to); **2.** [**~'lauf**ən] *v/t.* (*irr. laufen, no -ge-, h*): *es überlief mich kalt* a shudder passed over me; *überlaufen werden von doctor, etc.:* be besieged by (*patients, etc.*); **3.** *adj.* [**~'lauf**ən] *place, profession, etc.:* overcrowded; **'Qläufer** *m* ⚔ deserter; *pol.* rene-gade, turncoat.

'überlaut *adj.* too loud.

über'leben (*no -ge-, h*) **1.** *v/t.* survive, outlive; **2.** *v/i.* survive; **Qde** *m, f* (*-/-n*) survivor.

'überlebensgroß *adj.* bigger than life-size(d).

überlebt *adj.* [y:bər'le:pt] outmod-ed, disused, out of date.

'überlegen[1] F *v/t.* (*sep., -ge-, h*) give (*child*) a spanking.

über'leg|en[2] 1. *v/t. and v/refl.* (*no -ge-, h*) consider, reflect upon, think about; *ich will es mir ~* I will think it over; *es sich anders ~* change one's mind; **2.** *v/i.* (*no -ge-, h*): *er überlegt noch* he hasn't made up his mind yet; **3.** *adj.* superior (*dat.* to; *an dat.* in); **Qenheit** *f* (*-/no pl.*) superiority; preponderance; **~t** *adj.* [**~kt**] deliberate; prudent; **Qung** [**~guŋ**] *f* (*-/-en*) consideration, reflection; *nach reiflicher ~* after mature deliberation.

über'lesen *v/t.* (*irr. lesen, no -ge-, h*) read *s.th.* through quickly, run over *s.th.*; overlook.

über'liefer|n *v/t.* (*no -ge-, h*) hand down *or* on (*dat.* to); **Qung** *f* tradi-tion.

über'listen *v/t.* (*no -ge-, h*) outwit, F outsmart.

'Über|macht *f* (*-/no pl.*) superiority; *esp.* ⚔ superior forces *pl.*; *in der ~ sein* be superior in numbers; **'Qmächtig** *adj.* superior.

über'malen *v/t.* (*no -ge-, h*) paint out; **~'mannen** *v/t.* (*no -ge-, h*) overpower, overcome, overwhelm (*all. a. fig.*).

'Über|maß *n* (*-es/no pl.*) excess (*an dat.* of); **'Qmäßig 1.** *adj.* excessive; immoderate; **2.** *adv.* excessively, *Am. a.* overly; *~ trinken* drink to excess.

'Übermensch *m* superman; **'Qlich** *adj.* superhuman.

über'mitt|eln *v/t.* (*no -ge-, h*) trans-mit; convey; **Qung** *f* (*-/-en*) trans-mission; conveyance.

'übermorgen *adv.* the day after tomorrow.

über'müd|et *adj.* overtired; **Qung** *f* (*-/⚔-en*) overfatigue.

'Über|mut *m* wantonness; frolic-someness; **Qmütig** *adj.* [**'~my:tiç**] wanton; frolicsome.

'übernächst *adj. the* next but one; *~e Woche* the week after next.

über'nacht|en *v/i.* (*no -ge-, h*) stay overnight (*bei* at *a friend's* [*house*], with *friends*), spend the night (at, with); **Qung** *f* (*-/-en*) spending the night; *~ und Frühstück* bed and breakfast.

Übernahme ['y:bɑrnɑ:mə] *f* (*-/-n*) field of application s. übernehmen **1:** taking over; undertaking; assump-tion; adoption.

'übernatürlich *adj.* supernatural.

übernehmen *v/t.* **1.** [**~'ne:mən**] (*irr. nehmen, no -ge-, h*) take over (*busi-ness, etc.*); undertake (*responsibility, etc.*); take (*lead, risk, etc.*); assume (*direction of business, office, etc.*); adopt (*idea, custom, etc.*); *sich ~* overreach o.s.; **2.** ⚔ [**'~ne:mən**] (*irr. nehmen, sep., -ge-, h*) slope, shoul-der (*arms*).

'über|ordnen *v/t.* (*sep., -ge-, h*): *j-n j-m ~* set s.o. over s.o.; **'~par-teilich** *adj.* non-partisan; **'Qpro-duktion** *f* over-production.

über'prüf|en *v/t.* (*no -ge-, h*) reconsider; verify; check; review; screen *s.o.*; **Qung** *f* reconsideration; checking; review.

über'queren *v/t.* (*no -ge-, h*) cross; **'ragen** *v/t.* (*no -ge-, h*) tower above (*a. fig.*), overtop; *fig.* sur-pass.

überrasch|en [y:bər'raʃən] *v/t.* (*no -ge-, h*) surprise; catch (*bei* at, in); **Qung** *f* (*-/-en*) surprise.

über'red|en *v/t.* (*no -ge-, h*) per-suade (*zu inf.* to *inf.*, into *ger.*);

talk (into *ger.*); 2ung *f* (-/♀-en) persuasion.

über'reich|en *v/t.* (*no* -ge-, h) present; 2ung *f* (-/♀-en) presentation.

über|'reizen *v/t.* (*no* -ge-, h) overexcite; ~'reizt *adj.* overstrung; ~'rennen *v/t.* (*irr.* rennen, *no* -ge-, h) overrun.

'Überrest *m* remainder; ~e *pl.* remains *pl.*; sterbliche ~e *pl.* mortal remains *pl.*

über'rump|eln *v/t.* (*no* -ge-, h) (take by) surprise; 2(e)lung *f* (-/♀-en) surprise.

über'rund|en *v/t.* (*no* -ge-, h) *sports:* lap; *fig.* surpass; 2ung *f* (-/-en) lapping.

übersät *adj.* [y:bər'zɛ:t] studded, dotted.

über'sättig|en *v/t.* (*no* -ge-, h) surfeit (*a. fig.*); ♏ supersaturate; 2ung *f* (-/-en) surfeit (*a. fig.*); ♏ supersaturation.

'Überschallgeschwindigkeit *f* supersonic speed.

über|'schatten *v/t.* (*no* -ge-, h) overshadow (*a. fig.*); ~'schätzen *v/t.* (*no* -ge-, h) overrate, overestimate.

'Überschlag *m* gymnastics: somersault; ✈ loop; ⚡ flashover; *fig.* estimate, approximate calculation; 2en (*irr.* schlagen) 1. ['~ʃla:gən] *v/t.* (*sep.*, -ge-, h) cross (*one's legs*); 2. ['~ʃla:gən] *v/i.* (*sep.*, -ge-, sein) *voice:* become high-pitched; 3. [~'ʃla:gən] *v/t.* (*no* -ge-, h) skip (*page, etc.*); make a rough estimate of (*cost, etc.*); sich ~ fall head over heels; *car, etc.*: (be) turn(ed) over; ✈ loop the loop; *voice:* become high-pitched; sich ~ vor (*dat.*) outdo (*one's friendliness, etc.*); 4. *adj.* [~'ʃla:gən] lukewarm, tepid.

'überschnappen *v/i.* (*sep.*, -ge-, sein) *voice:* become high-pitched; F *p.* go mad, turn crazy.

über|'schneiden *v/refl.* (*irr.* schneiden, *no* -ge-, h) overlap; intersect; ~'schreiben *v/t.* (*irr.* schreiben, *no* -ge-, h) superscribe; entitle; make *s.th.* over (*dat.* to); ~'schreiten *v/t.* (*irr.* schreiten, *no* -ge-, h) cross; transgress (*limit, bound*); infringe (*rule, etc.*); exceed (*speed limit, one's instructions, etc.*); sie hat die 40 bereits überschritten she is on the wrong side of 40.

'Über|schrift *f* heading, title; headline; '~schuh *m* overshoe.

'Über|schuß *m* surplus, excess; profit; 2schüssig *adj.* ['~ʃysiç] surplus, excess.

über'schütten *v/t.* (*no* -ge-, h): ~ mit pour (*water, etc.*) on; *fig.*: overwhelm with (*inquiries, etc.*); shower (*gifts, etc.*) upon.

überschwemm|en [y:bər'ʃvemən]

v/t. (*no* -ge-, h) inundate, flood (*both a. fig.*); 2ung *f* (-/-en) inundation, flood(ing).

überschwenglich *adj.* ['y:bər-ʃveŋliç] effusive, gushy.

'Übersee: nach ~ gehen go overseas; '~dampfer ♇ *m* transoceanic steamer; '~handel *m* (-s/*no pl.*) oversea(s) trade.

über|'sehen *v/t.* (*irr.* sehen, *no* -ge-, h) survey; overlook (*printer's error, etc.*); *fig.* ignore, disregard.

über|'send|en *v/t.* (*irr.* senden,) *no* -ge-, h) send, transmit; consign; 2ung *f* sending, transmission; ✝ consignment.

'übersetzen[1] (*sep.*, -ge-) 1. *v/i.* (*sein*) cross; 2. *v/t.* (h) ferry.

über|'setz|en[2] *v/t.* (*no* -ge-, h) translate (*in acc. into*), render (*into*); ⊕ gear; 2er *m* (-s/-) translator; 2ung *f* (-/-en) translation (*aus from; in acc. into*); rendering; ⊕ gear(ing), transmission.

'Übersicht *f* (-/-en) survey (*über acc.* of); summary; 2lich *adj.* clear(ly arranged).

über|'siedeln ['y:bərzi:dəln] *v/i.* (*sep.*, -ge-, sein) and [~'zi:dəln] *v/i.* (*no* -ge-, sein) remove (*nach* to); 2siedelung [~'zi:dəluŋ] *f* (-/-en), 2siedlung [~'zi:dluŋ, ~'zi:dluŋ] *f* (-/-en) removal (*nach* to).

'übersinnlich *adj.* transcendental; *forces:* psychic.

über|'spann|en *v/t.* (*no* -ge-, h) cover (*mit* with); den Bogen ~ go too far; ~t *adj.* extravagant; *p.* eccentric; *claims, etc.*: exaggerated; 2theit *f* (-/♀-en) extravagance; eccentricity.

über'spitzt *adj.* oversubtle; exaggerated.

über|springen 1. ['~ʃpriŋən] *v/i.* (*irr.* springen, *sep.*, -ge-, sein) ⚡ spark; jump; *in a speech, etc.*: ~ von … zu … jump or skip from (*one subject*) to (*another*); 2. [~'ʃpriŋən] *v/t.* (*irr.* springen, *no* -ge-, h) jump, clear; skip (*page, etc.*); jump (*class*).

über|stehen (*irr.* stehen) 1. ['~ʃte:ən] *v/i.* (*sep.*, -ge-, h) jut (*out or forth*), project; 2. [~'ʃte:ən] *v/t.* (*no* -ge-, h) survive (*misfortune, etc.*); weather (*crisis*); get over (*illness*).

über|'steigen *v/t.* (*irr.* steigen, *no* -ge-, h) climb over; *fig.* exceed; ~'stimmen *v/t.* (*no* -ge-, h) outvote, vote down.

'überstreifen *v/t.* (*sep.*, -ge-, h) slip *s.th.* over.

überströmen 1. ['~ʃtrø:mən] *v/i.* (*sep.*, -ge-, sein) overflow (*vor dat.* with); 2. [~'ʃtrø:mən] *v/t.* (*no* -ge-, h) flood, inundate.

'Überstunden *f/pl.* overtime; ~ machen work overtime.

über'stürz|en *v/t.* (*no* -ge-, h) rush, hurry (up *or* on); sich ~ act rashly; *events*: follow in rapid succession; ‿*t adj.* precipitate, rash; Qung *f* (-/‿-en) precipitancy.

über'|teuern *v/t. (no -ge-, h)* overcharge; ‿'**tölpeln** *v/t. (no -ge-, h)* dupe, take in; ‿'**tönen** *v/t. (no -ge-, h)* drown.

Übertrag † ['y:bərtra:k] *m* (-[e]s/ ‿e) carrying forward; sum carried forward.

über'trag|bar *adj.* transferable; † negotiable; ♫ communicable; ‿en [‿gən] **1.** *v/t. (irr. tragen, no -ge-, h)* † carry forward; make over (*property*) (*auf acc.* to); ♫ transfuse (*blood*); delegate (*rights, etc.*) (*dat.* to); render (*book, etc.*) (*in acc.* into); transcribe (*s.th. written in short-hand*); ♫, ⊕, *phys., radio*: transmit; *radio*: a. broadcast; *im Fernsehen* ‿ televise; *ihm wurde eine wichtige Mission* ‿ he was charged with an important mission; **2.** *adj.* figurative; Qung [‿guŋ] *f* (-/-en) *field of application s.* übertragen **1**: carrying forward; making over; transfusion; delegation; rendering; free translation; transcription; transmission; broadcast; ‿ *im Fernsehen* telecast.

über'treffen *v/t. (irr. treffen, no -ge-, h)* excel *s.o.* (*an dat.* in; *in dat.* in, at); surpass (in), exceed (in).

über'treib|en *(irr. treiben, no -ge-, h)* **1.** *v/t.* overdo; exaggerate, overstate; **2.** *v/i.* exaggerate, draw the long bow; Qung *f* (-/-en) exaggeration, overstatement.

'übertreten[1] *v/i. (irr. treten, sep., -ge-, sein) sports*: cross the take-off line; *fig.* go over (*zu* to); *zum Katholizismus* ‿ turn Roman Catholic.

über'tret|en[2] *v/t. (irr. treten, no -ge-, h)* transgress, violate, infringe (*law, etc.*); *sich den Fuß* ‿ sprain one's ankle; Qung *f* (-/-en) transgression, violation, infringement.

'Übertritt *m* going over (*zu* to); *eccl.* conversion (to).

übervölker|n [y:bər'fœlkərn] *v/t. (no -ge-, h)* over-populate; Qung *f* (-/‿-en) over-population.

über'vorteilen *v/t. (no -ge-, h)* overreach, F do.

über'wach|en *v/t. (no -ge-, h)* supervise, superintend; control; *police*: keep under surveillance, shadow; Qung *f* (-/‿-en) supervision, superintendence; control; surveillance.

überwältigen [y:bər'vɛltigən] *v/t. (no -ge-, h)* overcome, overpower, overwhelm (*all a. fig.*); ‿d *fig. adj.* overwhelming.

über'weis|en *v/t. (irr. weisen, no -ge-, h)* remit (*money*) (*dat.* or an *acc.* to); (*zur Entscheidung etc.*) ‿ refer (to); Qung *f* (-/-en) remittance;

reference (*an acc.* to); *parl.* devolution.

überwerfen *(irr. werfen)* **1.** ['‿ver-fən] *v/t. (sep., -ge-, h)* slip (*coat*) on; **2.** [‿'verfən] *v/refl. (no -ge-, h)* fall out (*mit* with).

über'wieg|en *(irr. wiegen, no -ge-, h)* **1.** *v/t.* outweigh; **2.** *v/i.* preponderate; predominate; ‿'**wiegend** *adj.* preponderant; predominant; ‿ 'winden *v/t. (irr. winden, no -ge-, h)* overcome (*a. fig.*), subdue; *sich* ‿ *zu inf.* bring o.s. to *inf.*; ‿'**wintern** *v/i. (no -ge-, h)* (pass the) winter.

'Über|wurf *m* wrap; ‿'**zahl** *f* (-/‿-en) numerical superiority; *in der* ‿ superior in numbers; Qzählig *adj.* ['‿tse:liç] supernumerary; surplus.

über'zeug|en *v/t. (no -ge-, h)* convince (*von* of); satisfy (of); Qung *f* (-/-en) conviction.

überziehe|n *v/t. (irr. ziehen)* **1.** ['‿tsi:ən] *(sep., -ge-, h)* put on; **2.** [‿'tsi:ən] *(no -ge-, h)* cover; put clean sheets on (*bed*); † overdraw (*account*); *sich* ‿ *sky*: become overcast; 'Qr *m* (-s/-) overcoat, topcoat. **'Überzug** *m* cover; case, tick; ⊕ coat(ing). [ary; normal.‿

üblich *adj.* ['y:pliç] usual, customary‿

U-Boot ⚓, ✕ ['u:-] *n* submarine, *in Germany: a.* U-boat.

übrig *adj.* ['y:briç] left, remaining; *die* ‿e *Welt* the rest of the world; *die* ‿en *pl.* the others *pl.*, the rest; *im* ‿en for the rest; by the way; ‿ *haben* have *s.th.* left; *keine Zeit* ‿ *haben* have no time to spare; *etwas* ‿ *haben für* care for, have a soft spot for; *ein* ‿es *tun* go out of one's way; ‿**bleiben** *v/i. (irr. bleiben, sep., -ge-, sein)* be left; remain; *es blieb ihm nichts anderes übrig* he had no (other) alternative (*als* but); ‿ens *adv.* ['‿gəns] by the way; ‿**lassen** ['‿la-] *v/t. (irr. lassen, sep., -ge-, h)* leave; *viel zu wünschen* ‿ leave much to be desired.

'Übung *f* (-/-en) exercise; practice; drill; '‿shang *m* skiing: nursery slope.

Ufer ['u:fər] *n* (-s/-) shore (*of sea, lake*); bank (*of river, etc.*).

Uhr [u:r] *f* (-/-en) clock; watch; *um vier* ‿ at four o'clock; '‿armband *n* (-[e]s/‿er) watch-strap; '‿feder *f* watch-spring; '‿macher *m* (-s/-) watch-maker; '‿werk *n* clockwork; watch-work; '‿zeiger *m* hand (*of clock or watch*); '‿zeigersinn *m* (-[e]s/no pl.): *im* ‿ clockwise; *entgegen dem* ‿ counter-clockwise.

Uhu *orn.* ['u:hu:] *m* (-s/-s) eagle-owl.

Ulk [ulk] *m* (-[e]s/-e) fun, lark; 'Qen *v/i. (ge-, h)* (sky)lark, joke; Qig *adj.* funny.

Ulme ♣ ['ulmə] *f* (-/-n) elm.

Ultimatum [ulti'ma:tum] *n* (-s/-s *Ul-*

Ultimo — 271 — umhauen

timaten, -s) ultimatum; j-m ein ~
stellen deliver an ultimatum to s.o.
Ultimo † ['ultimo] m (-s/-s) last
day of the month.
Ultrakurzwelle phys. [ultra'-] f
ultra-short wave, very-high-fre-
quency wave.
um [um] **1.** prp. (acc.) round, about;
~ vier Uhr at four o'clock; ~ sein Leben laufen run for one's life; et. ~
einen Meter verfehlen miss s.th. by
a metre; et. ~ zwei Mark verkaufen
sell s.th. at two marks; **2.** prp. (gen.):
~ seinetwillen for his sake; **3.** cj.: ~
so besser all the better, so much the
better; ~ so mehr (weniger) all the
more (less); ~ zu (in order) to; **4.**
adv.: er drehte sich ~ he turned
round.
um|ändern ['um?-] v/t. (sep., -ge-,
h) change, alter; **~arbeiten** ['um?-]
v/t. (sep., -ge-, h) make over (coat,
etc.); revise (book, etc.); ~ zu make
into.
um'arm|en v/t. (no -ge-, h) hug,
embrace; sich ~ embrace; **2ung** f
(-/-en) embrace, hug.
'Umbau m (-[e]s/-e, -ten) rebuilding; reconstruction; **2en** v/t. (sep.,
-ge-, h) rebuild; reconstruct.
'umbiegen v/t. (irr. biegen, sep.,
-ge-, h) bend; turn up or down.
'umbild|en v/t. (sep., -ge-, h)
remodel, reconstruct; reorganize,
reform; reshuffle (cabinet); **2ung** f
(-/-en) remodel(l)ing, reconstruction; reorganization, pol. reshuffle.
'um|binden v/t. (irr. binden, sep.,
-ge-, h) put on (apron, etc.); **~blät-
tern** (sep., -ge-, h) **1.** v/t. turn over;
2. v/i. turn over the page; **~brechen**
v/t. (irr. brechen) **1.** ~ ['~breçən]
(sep., -ge-, h) dig, break up (ground);
2. typ. [~'breçən] (no -ge-, h) make
up; **~bringen** v/t. (irr. bringen,
sep., -ge-, h) kill; sich ~ kill o.s.;
'2bruch m typ. make-up; fig.:
upheaval; radical change; **~bu-
chen** v/t. (sep., -ge-, h) † transfer
or switch to another account; book
for another date; **~disponieren**
v/i. (sep., no -ge-, h) change one's
plans.
'umdreh|en v/t. (sep., -ge-, h) turn;
s. Spieß; sich ~ turn round; **2ung**
[um'-] f (-/-en) turn; phys., ⊕ rotation, revolution.
um|fahren (irr. fahren) **1.** ['~fa:rən]
v/t. (sep., -ge-, h) run down; **2.**
[~'fa:rən] v/i. (sep., -ge-, sein)
go a roundabout way; **3.** [~'fa:rən]
v/t. (no -ge-, h) drive round; ⊕
sail round; ⊕ double (cape);
~fallen v/i. (irr. fallen, sep., -ge-,
sein) fall; collapse; tot ~ drop dead.
'Umfang m (-[e]s/no pl.) circumference, circuit; perimeter; girth
(of body, tree, etc.); fig.: extent;
volume; in großem ~ on a large

scale; **'2reich** adj. extensive;
voluminous; spacious.
um'fassen v/t. (no -ge-, h) clasp;
embrace (a. fig.); ✗ envelop; fig.
comprise, cover, comprehend; **~d**
adj. comprehensive, extensive;
sweeping, drastic.
'umform|en v/t. (sep., -ge-, h)
remodel, recast, transform (a. fig.);
∮ convert; **'2er** ∮ m (-s/-) trans-
former; converter.
'Umfrage f poll; öffentliche ~
public opinion poll.
'Umgang m **1.** (-[e]s/=e) △ gallery,
ambulatory; eccl. procession (round
the fields, etc.); **2.** (-[e]s/no pl.) intercourse (mit with); company; ~ ha-
ben mit associate with.
umgänglich adj. ['umgɛnlɪç] sociable, companionable, affable.
'Umgangs|formen f/pl. manners
pl.; **~sprache** f colloquial usage;
in der deutschen ~ in colloquial
German.
um'garnen v/t. (no -ge-, h) ensnare.
um'geb|en **1.** v/t. (irr. geben, no
-ge-, h) surround; mit e-r Mauer ~
wall in; **2.** surrounded (von
with, by) (a. fig.); **2ung** f (-/-en)
environs pl. (of town, etc.); surroundings pl., environment (of
place, person, etc.).
umgeh|en (irr. gehen) **1.** ['~ge:ən]
v/i. (sep., -ge-, sein) make a detour;
rumour, etc.: go about, be afloat;
ghost: walk; ~ mit use s.th.; deal
with s.o.; keep company with; ein
Gespenst soll im Schlosse ~ the
castle is said to be haunted;
2. [~'ge:ən] v/t. (no -ge-, h) go
round; ✗ flank; bypass (town, etc.);
fig. avoid, evade; circumvent, elude
(law, etc.); **~end** adj. immediate;
2ungsstraße [um'ge:uns-] f bypass.
umgekehrt ['umgəke:rt] **1.** adj.
reverse; inverse, inverted; in ~er
Reihenfolge in reverse order; im ~en
Verhältnis zu in inverse proportion
to; **2.** adv. vice versa.
'umgraben v/t. (irr. graben, sep.
-ge-, h) dig (up).
um'grenzen v/t. (no -ge-, h) encircle; enclose; fig. circumscribe,
limit.
'umgruppier|en v/t. (sep., no -ge-,
h) regroup; **'2ung** f (-/-en) regroup-
ing.
'um|haben F v/t. (irr. haben, sep.,
-ge-, h) have (coat, etc.) on; **'2hang**
m wrap; cape; **'~hängen** v/t. (sep.,
-ge-, h) rehang (pictures); sling
(rifle) over one's shoulder; sich den
Mantel ~ put one's coat round
one's shoulders; **'~hauen** v/t. (irr.
hauen, sep., -ge-, h) fell, cut down;
F: die Nachricht hat mich umge-
hauen I was bowled over by the
news.

um'her|blicken v/i. (sep., -ge-, h) look about (one); **~streifen** v/i. (sep., -ge-, sein) rove.

um'hinkönnen v/i. (irr. können, sep., -ge-, h): ich kann nicht umhin, zu sagen I cannot help saying.

um'hüll|en v/t. (no -ge-, h) wrap up (mit in), envelop (in); 2**ung** f (-/-en) wrapping, wrapper, envelopment.

Umkehr ['umke:r] f (-/no pl.) return; 2**en** (sep., -ge-) 1. v/i. (sein) return, turn back; 2. v/t. (h) turn out (one's pocket, etc.); invert (a. ♪); reverse (a. ⚡, ♫); '**~ung** f (-/-en) reversal; inversion.

'**umkippen** (sep., -ge-) 1. v/t. (h) upset, tilt; 2. v/i. (sein) upset, tilt (over); F faint.

um'klammer|n v/t. (no -ge-, h) clasp; boxing: clinch; 2**ung** f (-/-en) clasp; boxing: clinch.

'**umkleid|en** v/refl. (sep., -ge-, h) change (one's clothes); 2**eraum** m dressing-room.

'**umkommen** v/i. (irr. kommen, sep., -ge-, sein) be killed (bei in), die (in), perish (in); vor Langeweile ~ die of boredom.

'**Umkreis** m (-es/no pl.) & circumscribed circle; im ~ von within a radius of.   [round.\
um'kreisen v/t. (no -ge-, h) circle\
'**um|krempeln** v/t. (sep., -ge-, h) tuck up (shirt-sleeves, etc.); change (plan, etc.); (völlig) ~ turn s.th. inside out; '**~laden** v/t. (irr. laden, sep., -ge-, h) reload; ⚓, ⚒ tranship.

'**Umlauf** m circulation; phys., ⊕ rotation; circular (letter); in ~ setzen or bringen circulate, put into circulation; im ~ sein circulate, be in circulation; rumours: a. be afloat; außer ~ setzen withdraw from circulation; '**~bahn** f orbit; 2**en** (irr. laufen) 1. ['~laufən] v/t. (sep., -ge-, h) knock over; 2. ['~laufən] v/i. (sep., -ge-, sein) circulate; make a detour; 3. [~'laufən] v/t. (no -ge-, h) run round.

'**Umlege|kragen** m turn-down collar; 2**n** v/t. (sep., -ge-, h) lay down; ⊕ throw (lever); storm, etc.: beat down (wheat, etc.); re-lay (cable, etc.); put (coat, etc.) round one's shoulders; apportion (costs, etc.); fig. sl. do s.o. in.

'**umleit|en** v/t. (sep., -ge-, h) divert; 2**ung** f diversion, detour.

'**umliegend** adj. surrounding; circumjacent.

um'nacht|et adj.: geistig ~ mentally deranged; 2**ung** f (-/~-en): geistige ~ mental derangement.

'**um|packen** v/t. (sep., -ge-, h) repack; **~pflanzen** v/t. 1. ['~pflantsən] (sep., -ge-, h) transplant; 2. [~'pflantsən] (no -ge-, h): ~ mit plant s.th. round with; **~pflügen** v/t. (sep., -ge-, h) plough, Am. plow.

um'rahmen v/t. (no -ge-, h) frame; musikalisch ~ put into a musical setting.

umrand|en [um'randən] v/t. (no -ge-, h) edge, border; 2**ung** f (-/-en) edge, border.

um'ranken v/t. (no -ge-, h) twine (mit with).

'**umrechn|en** v/t. (sep., -ge-, h) convert (in acc. into); 2**ung** f (-/no pl.) conversion; 2**ungskurs** m rate of exchange.

umreißen v/t. (irr. reißen) 1. ['~raisən] (sep., -ge-, h) pull down; knock s.o. over; 2. [~'raisən] (no -ge-, h) outline.   [round (a. fig.).\
um'ringen v/t. (no -ge-, h) sur-\
'**Um|riß** m outline (a. fig.), contour; 2**rühren** v/t. (sep., -ge-, h) stir; 2**satteln** (sep., -ge-, h) 1. v/t. resaddle; 2. F fig. v/i. change one's studies or occupation; ~ von ... auf (acc.) change from ... to ...; '**~satz** ⚹ m turnover; sales pl.; return(s pl.); stock exchange: business done.

'**umschalt|en** (sep., -ge-, h) 1. v/t. ⊕ change over; ⚡ commutate; ⚡, ⊕ switch; 2. ⚡, ⊕ v/i. switch over; '2**er** m ⊕ change-over switch; ⚡ commutator; 2**ung** f (-/-en) ⊕ change-over; ⚡ commutation.

'**Umschau** f (-/no pl.): ~ halten nach look out for, be on the look-out for; 2**en** v/refl. (sep., -ge-, h) look round (nach for); look about (for) (a. fig.), look about one.

'**umschicht|en** v/t. (sep., -ge-, h) pile afresh; fig. regroup (a. ⚹); '**~ig** adv. by or in turns; '2**ung** f (-/-en) regrouping; soziale ~en pl. social upheavals pl.

um'schiff|en v/t. (no -ge-, h) circumnavigate; double (cape); 2**ung** f (-/⚹-en) circumnavigation; doubling.

'**Umschlag** m envelope; cover, wrapper; jacket; turn-up, Am. cuff (of trousers); ⚕ compress; ⚕ poultice; trans-shipment (of goods); fig. change, turn; 2**en** (irr. schlagen, sep., -ge-, h) 1. v/t. (h) knock s.o. down; cut down, fell (tree); turn (leaf); turn up (sleeves, etc.); turn down (collar); trans-ship (goods); 2. v/i. (sein) turn over, upset; ⚓ capsize, upset; wine, etc.: turn sour; fig. turn (in acc. into); '**~hafen** m port of trans-shipment.

um'|schließen v/t. (irr. schließen, no -ge-, h) embrace, surround (a. ⚔), enclose; ⚹ invest; **~schlingen** v/t. (irr. schlingen, no -ge-, h) embrace.

'**um'schmeißen** F v/t. (irr. schmeißen, sep., -ge-, h) s. umstoßen; '**~**

schnallen v/t. (sep., -ge-, h) buckle on.

umschreib|en v/t. (irr. schreiben) 1. ['ˌʃraɪbən] (sep., -ge-, h) rewrite; transfer (property, etc.) (auf acc. to); 2. [ˌˈʃraɪbən] (no -ge-, h) ♣ circumscribe; paraphrase; 2ung f (-/-en) 1. ['ˌʃraɪbʊŋ] rewriting; transfer (auf acc. to); 2. [ˌˈʃraɪbʊŋ] ♣ circumscription; paraphrase.

'Umschrift f circumscription; phonetics: transcription.

'umschütten v/t. (sep., -ge-, h) pour into another vessel; spill.

'Um|schweife pl.: ~ machen beat about the bush; ohne ~ pointblank; '2schwenken fig. v/i. (sep., -ge-, sein) veer or turn round; '~schwung fig. m revolution; revulsion (of public feeling, etc.); change (in the weather, etc.); reversal (of opinion, etc.).

um'seg|eln v/t. (no -ge-, h) sail round; double (cape); circumnavigate (globe, world); 2(e)lung f (-/-en) sailing round (world, etc.); doubling; circumnavigation.

'um|sehen v/refl. (irr. sehen, sep., -ge-, h) look round (nach for); look about (for) (a. fig.), look about one; '~sein F v/i. (irr. sein, sep., -ge-, sein) time: be up; holidays, etc.: be over; '~setzen v/t. (sep., -ge-, h) transpose (a. ♪); ♂ transplant; ✝ turn over; spend (money) (in acc. on books, etc.); in die Tat ~ realize, convert into fact.

'Umsicht f (-/no pl.) circumspection; '2ig adj. circumspect.

'umsied|eln (sep., -ge-) 1. v/t. (h) resettle; 2. v/i. (sein) (re)move (nach, in acc. to); '2lung f(-/♣-en) resettlement; evacuation; removal.

um'sonst adv. gratis, free of charge; in vain; to no purpose; nicht ~ not without good reason.

umspann|en v/t. 1. ['ˌʃpanən] (sep., -ge-, h) change (horses); ✝ transform; 2. [ˌˈʃpanən] (no -ge-, h) span; fig. a. embrace; '2er ✝ m (-s/-) transformer.

'umspringen v/i. (irr. springen, sep., -ge-, sein) shift, veer (round); ~ mit treat badly, etc.

'Umstand m circumstance; fact, detail; unter diesen Umständen in or under the circumstances; unter keinen Umständen in or under no circumstances, on no account; unter Umständen possibly; ohne Umstände without ceremony; in anderen Umständen sein be in the family way.

umständlich adj. ['umʃtɛntlɪç] story, etc.: long-winded; method, etc.: roundabout; p. fussy; das ist (mir) viel zu ~ that is far too much trouble (for me); '2keit f (-/♣-en) long-windedness; fussiness.

'Umstands|kleid n maternity robe; '~wort gr. n (-[e]s/ˌer) adverb.

'umstehend 1. adj.: auf der ~en Seite overleaf; 2. adv. overleaf; 2en ['ˌdən] pl. the bystanders pl.

'Umsteige|karte f transfer; '2n v/i. (irr. steigen, sep., -ge-, sein) change (nach for); ☷ a. change trains (for).

Umsteigkarte ['umʃtaɪk-] f s. Umsteigekarte.

umstell|en v/t. 1. ['ˌʃtɛlən] (sep., -ge-, h) transpose (a. gr.); shift (furniture) about or round; convert (currency, production) (auf acc. to); sich ~ change one's attitude; accommodate o.s. to new conditions; adapt o.s. (auf acc. to); 2. [ˌˈʃtɛlən] (no -ge-, h) surround; 2ung ['ˌʃtɛlʊŋ] f transposition; fig.: conversion; adaptation; change.

'um|stimmen v/t. (sep., -ge-, h) ♪ tune to another pitch; j-n ~ change s.o.'s mind, bring s.o. round; '~stoßen v/t. (irr. stoßen, sep., -ge-, h) knock over; upset; fig. annul; ♣ overrule, reverse; upset (plan).

um|'stricken fig. v/t. (no -ge-, h) ensnare; ~stritten adj. [ˌˈʃtrɪtən] disputed, contested; controversial.

'Um|sturz m subversion, overturn; '2stürzen (sep., -ge-) 1. v/t. (h) upset, overturn (a. fig.); fig. subvert; 2. v/i. (sein) upset, overturn; fall down; 2stürzlerisch adj. ['ˌlɔrɪʃ] subversive.

'Umtausch m (-es/♣-e) exchange; ✝ conversion (of currency, etc.); '2en v/t. (sep., -ge-, h) exchange (gegen for); ✝ convert.

'umtun F v/t. (irr. tun, sep., -ge-, h) put (coat, etc.) round one's shoulders; sich ~ nach look about for.

'umwälz|en v/t. (sep., -ge-, h) roll round; fig. revolutionize; '~end adj. revolutionary; '2ung fig. f (-/-en) revolution, upheaval.

'umwand|eln v/t. (sep., -ge-, h) transform (in acc. into); ✝, ✝ convert (into); ♣ commute (into); '2lung f transformation; ✝, ✝ conversion; ♣ commutation.

'um|wechseln v/t. (sep., -ge-, h) change; '2weg m roundabout way or route; detour; auf ~en in a roundabout way; '~wehen v/t. (sep., -ge-, h) blow down or over; '2welt f (-/♣-en) environment; '~wenden 1. v/t. (sep., -ge-, h) turn over; 2. v/refl. (irr. wenden,] sep., -ge-, h) look round (nach for).

um'werben v/t. (irr. werben, no -ge-, h) court, woo.

'umwerfen v/t. (irr. werfen, sep., -ge-, h) upset (a. fig.), overturn; sich e-n Mantel ~ throw a coat round one's shoulders.

um|'wickeln v/t. (no -ge-, h): et. mit Draht ~ wind wire round s.th.;

~wölken [~'vœlkən] *v/refl.* (*no* -ge-, *h*) cloud over (*a. fig.*); **~zäunen** [~'tsɔynən] *v/t.* (*no* -ge-, *h*) fence (in).

umziehen (*irr. ziehen*) **1.** ['~tsiːən] *v/i.* (*sep.*, -ge-, *sein*) (re)move (*nach* to); move house; **2.** ['~tsiːən] *v/refl.* (*sep.*, -ge-, *h*) change (one's clothes); **3.** [~'tsiːən] *v/refl.* (*no* -ge-, *h*) cloud over.

umzingeln [um'tsiŋəln] *v/t.* (*no* -ge-, *h*) surround, encircle.

'Umzug *m* procession; move (*nach* to), removal (to); change of residence.

unab|änderlich *adj.* [un⁹ap'ɛndərliç] unalterable; **~hängig** ['~hɛŋiç] **1.** *adj.* independent (*von* of); **2.** *adv.*: ~ *von* irrespective of; **'2hängigkeit** *f* (-/*no pl.*) independence (*von* of); **~kömmlich** *adj.* ['~kœmliç]: er ist im Moment ~ we cannot spare him at the moment, we cannot do without him at the moment; **~'lässig** *adj.* incessant, unremitting; **~sehbar** *adj.* [~'zeːbaːr] incalculable; *in* ~er *Ferne* in a distant future; **~'sichtlich** *adj.* unintentional; inadvertent; **~wendbar** *adj.* [~'vɛntbaːr] inevitable, inescapable.

unachtsam *adj.* ['un⁹-] careless, heedless; **'2keit** *f* (-/⸴-en) carelessness, heedlessness.

unähnlich *adj.* ['un⁹-] unlike, dissimilar (*dat.* to).

unan|fechtbar *adj.* [un⁹an'-] unimpeachable, unchallengeable, incontestable; **~gebracht** *adj.* inappropriate; *pred. a.* out of place; **'~gefochten 1.** *adj.* undisputed; unchallenged; **2.** *adv.* without any hindrance; **~gemessen** *adj.* unsuitable; improper; inadequate; **~genehm** *adj.* disagreeable, unpleasant; awkward; troublesome; **~'nehmbar** *adj.* unacceptable (*für* to); **'2nehmlichkeit** *f* (-/-en) unpleasantness; awkwardness; troublesomeness; **~en** *pl.* trouble, inconvenience; **'~sehnlich** *adj.* unsightly; plain; **'~ständig** *adj.* indecent; obscene; **'2ständigkeit** *f* (-/-en) indecency; obscenity; **~'tastbar** *adj.* unimpeachable; inviolable.

unarpetitlich *adj.* ['un⁹-] *food, etc.*: unappetizing; *sight, etc.*: distasteful, ugly.

Unart ['un⁹-] **1.** *f* bad habit; **2.** *m* (-[e]s/-e) naughty child; **'2ig** *adj.* naughty; **'~igkeit** *f* (-/-en) naughty behavio(u)r, naughtiness.

unauf|dringlich *adj.* ['un⁹auf-] unobtrusive; unostentatious; **'~fällig** *adj.* inconspicuous; unobtrusive; **~findbar** *adj.* [~'fɪntbaːr] undiscoverable, untraceable; **~gefordert** ['~gəfɔrdərt] **1.** *adj.* un-

asked; **2.** *adv.* without being asked, of one's own accord; **~'hörlich** *adj.* incessant, continuous, uninterrupted; **'~merksam** *adj.* inattentive; **'2merksamkeit** *f* (-/-en) inattention, inattentiveness; **'~richtig** *adj.* insincere; **'2richtigkeit** *f* (-/-en) insincerity; **~schiebbar** *adj.* [~'ʃiːpbaːr] urgent; ~ *sein* brook no delay.

unaus|bleiblich *adj.* [un⁹aus'blaɪp-liç] inevitable; *das war* ~ that was bound to happen; **~'führbar** *adj.* impracticable; **~geglichen** *adj.* ['~gəgliçən] unbalanced (*a.* ✝); **~'löschlich** *adj.* indelible; *fig. a.* inextinguishable; **~'sprechlich** *adj.* unutterable; unspeakable; inexpressible; **~'stehlich** *adj.* unbearable, insupportable.

'unbarmherzig *adj.* merciless, unmerciful; **'2keit** *f* (-/*no pl.*) mercilessness, unmercifulness.

unbe|absichtigt *adj.* ['unbə⁹apziçtiçt] unintentional, undesigned; **'~achtet** *adj.* unnoticed; **~anstandet** *adj.* ['unbə⁹-] unopposed, not objected to; **'~baut** *adj.* ✗ untilled; *land:* undeveloped; **'~dacht** *adj.* inconsiderate; imprudent; **~denklich 1.** *adj.* unobjectionable; **2.** *adv.* without hesitation; **~'deutend** *adj.* insignificant; slight; **~'dingt 1.** *adj.* unconditional; *obedience, etc.*: implicit; **2.** *adv.* by all means; under any circumstances; **~'fahrbar** *adj.* impracticable, impassable; **'~fangen** *adj.* unprejudiced, unbias(s)ed; ingenuous; unembarrassed; **~'friedigend** *adj.* unsatisfactory; **~friedigt** *adj.* ['~çt] dissatisfied; disappointed; **'~fugt** *adj.* unauthorized; incompetent; **'2fugte** *m* (-n/-n) unauthorized person; **~n** *ist der Zutritt verboten!* no trespassing!; **~'gabt** *adj.* untalented; **~'greiflich** *adj.* inconceivable, incomprehensible; **'~grenzt** *adj.* unlimited; boundless; **'~gründet** *adj.* unfounded; **'2hagen** *n* uneasiness; discomfort; **'~haglich** *adj.* uneasy; uncomfortable; **~'helligt** *adj.* [~'hɛliçt] unmolested; **'~herrscht** *adj.* lacking self-control; **'2herrschtheit** *f* (-/*no pl.*) lack of self-control; **'~hindert** *adj.* unhindered, free; **~holfen** *adj.* ['~bə-hɔlfən] clumsy, awkward; **'2holfenheit** *f* (-/*no pl.*) clumsiness, awkwardness; **~'irrt** *adj.* unswerving; **'~kannt** *adj.* unknown; ~e *Größe* ⅍ unknown quantity (*a. fig.*); **~'kümmert** *adj.* unconcerned (*um, wegen* about), careless (*of, about*); **'~lebt** *adj.* inanimate; *street, etc.*: unfrequented; **~'lehrbar** *adj.*: ~ *sein* take no advice; **'~liebt** *adj.* unpopular; *sich* ~ *machen* get o.s. disliked; **'~mannt** *adj.* unmanned;

'~merkt adj. unnoticed; '~mittelt adj. impecunious, without means; ~nommen adj. [~'nɔmən]: es bleibt ihm ~ zu inf. he is at liberty to inf.; '~nutzt adj. unused; '~quem adj. uncomfortable; inconvenient; '2quemlichkeit f lack of comfort; inconvenience; '~rechtigt adj. unauthorized; unjustified; ~schadet prp. (gen.) [~'ʃɑ:dət] without prejudice to; ~schädigt adj. ['~çt] uninjured, undamaged; '~scheiden adj. immodest; ~scholten adj. ['~ʃɔltən] blameless, irreproachable; '~schränkt adj. unrestricted; absolute; ~schreiblich adj. [~'ʃrɑɪpliç] indescribable; ~'sehen adv. unseen; without inspection; '~setzt adj. unoccupied; vacant; ~siegbar adj. [~'zi:kbɑ:r] invincible; ~sonnen adj. thoughtless, imprudent; rash; '2sonnenheit f (-/-en) thoughtlessness; rashness; '~ständig adj. inconstant; unsteady; weather: changeable, unsettled (a. †); p. erratic; '2ständigkeit f (-/no pl.) inconstancy; changeability; ~stätigt adj. ['~çt] unconfirmed; letter, etc.: unacknowledged; ~'stechlich adj. incorruptible, unbribable; 2'stechlichkeit f (-/no pl.) incorruptibility; '~stimmt adj. indeterminate (a. ♁); indefinite (a. gr.); uncertain; feeling, etc.: vague; '2stimmtheit f (-/no pl.) indeterminateness, indetermination; indefiniteness; uncertainty; vagueness; ~'streitbar adj. incontestable; indisputable; '~stritten adj. uncontested, undisputed; '~teiligt adj. unconcerned (an dat. in); indifferent; ~'trächtlich adj. inconsiderable, insignificant. [flexible.\
unbeugsam adj. [un'bɔʏkzɑ:m] in-/
'**unbe|wacht** adj. unwatched, unguarded (a. fig.); '~waffnet adj. unarmed; eye: naked; '~weglich adj. immovable; motionless; '~wiesen adj. unproven; '~wohnt adj. uninhabited; unoccupied, vacant; '~wußt adj. unconscious; ~'zähmbar adj. indomitable.
'**Un|bilden** pl.: ~ der Witterung inclemency of the weather; '~bildung f lack of education.
'**un|billig** adj. unfair; '~blutig 1. adj. bloodless; 2. adv. without bloodshed.
unbotmäßig adj. ['unbo:t-] insubordinate; '2keit f (-/-en) insubordination.
'**un|brauchbar** adj. useless; '~christlich adj. unchristian.
und cj. [unt] and; F: na ~? so what?
'**Undank** m ingratitude; '2bar adj. ungrateful (gegen to); task, etc.: thankless; '~barkeit f ingratitude, ungratefulness; fig. thanklessness.

un|'denkbar adj. unthinkable; inconceivable; ~'denklich adj.: seit ~en Zeiten from time immemorial; '~deutlich adj. indistinct; speech: a. inarticulate; fig. vague, indistinct; '~deutsch adj. un-German; '~dicht adj. leaky; '2ding n: es wäre ein ~, zu behaupten, daß ... it would be absurd to claim that ... '**unduldsam** adj. intolerant; '2keit f intolerance.
undurch|'dringlich adj. impenetrable; countenance: impassive; ~'führbar adj. impracticable; '~lässig adj. impervious, impermeable; '~sichtig adj. opaque; fig. mysterious.
uneben adj. ['un?-] ground: uneven, broken; way, etc.: bumpy; '2heit f 1. (-/no pl.) unevenness; 2. (-/-en) bump.
un|echt adj. ['un?-] jewellery, etc.: imitation; hair, teeth, etc.: false; money, jewellery, etc.: counterfeit; picture, etc.: fake; ♁ fraction: improper; '~ehelich adj. illegitimate.
Unehr|e ['un?-] f dishono(u)r; j-m ~ machen discredit s.o.; '2enhaft adj. dishono(u)rable; '2lich adj. dishonest; '~lichkeit f dishonesty.
uneigennützig adj. ['un?-] disinterested, unselfish.
uneinig adj. ['un?-]: ~ sein be at variance (mit with); disagree (über acc. on); '2keit f variance, disagreement.
un|ein'nehmbar adj. impregnable; '~empfänglich adj. insusceptible (für of, to).
unempfindlich adj. ['un?-] insensitive (gegen to); '2keit f insensitiveness (gegen to).
un|'endlich 1. adj. endless, infinite (both a. fig.); 2. adv. infinitely (a. fig.); ~ lang endless; ~ viel no end of (money, etc.); 2keit f (-/no pl.) endlessness, infinitude, infinity (all a. fig.).
unent|behrlich adj. ['un?ent'be:rliç] indispensable; '~geltlich adj. gratuitous, gratis; 2. adv. gratis, free of charge; ~'rinnbar adj. ineluctable; '~schieden 1. adj. undecided; ~ enden game: end in a draw or tie; 2. ♁ n (-s/-) draw, tie; '~schlossen adj. irresolute; '2schlossenheit f irresoluteness, irresolution; ~schuldbar adj. [~'ʃultbɑ:r] inexcusable; ~wegt adv. [~'ve:kt] untiringly; continuously; ~'wirrbar adj. inextricable.
uner|'bittlich adj. [un?er'bitliç] inexorable; fact: stubborn; '~fahren adj. inexperienced; ~findlich adj. [~'fintliç] incomprehensible; ~'forschlich adj. inscrutable; '~freulich adj. unpleasant; ~'füllbar adj. unrealizable; '~giebig adj. unproductive (an dat. of); '~heb-

lich adj. irrelevant (für to); inconsiderable; **~hört** adj. **1.** ['~hø:rt] unheard; **2.** [~'hø:rt] unheard-of; outrageous; **~kannt** adj. unrecognized; **~'klärlich** adj. inexplicable; **~läßlich** adj. [~'lɛsliç] indispensable (für to, for); **~laubt** adj. ['~laupt] unauthorized; illegal, illicit; **~e** Handlung s̷̷t̷ tort; **~ledigt** adj. ['~le:diçt] unsettled (a. ✝); **~meßlich** adj. [~'mɛsliç] immeasurable, immense; **~müdlich** adj. [~'my:tliç] p. indefatigable, untiring; efforts, etc.: untiring, unremitting; **~quicklich** adj. unpleasant, unedifying; **~'reichbar** adj. inattainable; inaccessible; pred. a. above or beyond or out of reach; **~'reicht** adj. unrival(l)ed, unequal(l)ed; **~sättlich** adj. [~'zɛtliç] insatiable, insatiate; **~'schöpflich** adj. inexhaustible.

unerschrocken adj. ['un⁹-] intrepid, fearless; **2heit** f (-/no pl.) intrepidity, fearlessness.

uner|schütterlich adj. [un⁹ɛr'ʃytərliç] unshakable; **~'schwinglich** adj. price: prohibitive; pred. a. above or beyond or out of reach (für of); **~'setzlich** adj. irreplaceable; loss, etc.: irreparable; **~'träglich** adj. intolerable, unbearable; **~wartet** adj. unexpected; **~wünscht** adj. undesirable, undesired.

'unfähig adj. incapable (zu inf. of ger.); unable (to inf.); inefficient; **2keit** f incapability (zu inf. of ger.); inability (to inf.); inefficiency.

'Unfall m accident; e-n ~ haben meet with or have an accident; **~station** f emergency ward; **~versicherung** f accident insurance.

un'faßlich adj. incomprehensible, inconceivable; das ist mir ~ that is beyond me.

un'fehlbar 1. adj. infallible (a. eccl.); decision, etc.: unimpeachable; instinct, etc.: unfailing; **2.** adv. without fail; inevitably; **2keit** f (-/no pl.) infallibility.

'un|fein adj. indelicate; pred. a. lacking in refinement; **'~fern** prp. (gen. or von) not far from; **'~fertig** adj. unfinished; fig. a. half-baked; **'~flätig** adj. ['~flɛ:tiç] dirty, filthy.

'unfolgsam adj. disobedient; **'2keit** f disobedience.

un|förmig adj. ['unfœrmiç] misshapen; shapeless; **'~frankiert** adj. unstamped; **'~frei** adj. not free; ✎ unstamped; **'~freiwillig** adj. involuntary; humour: unconscious; **'~freundlich** adj. unfriendly (zu with), unkind (to); climate, weather: inclement; room, day: cheerless; **'2friede(n)** m discord.

'unfruchtbar adj. unfruitful; sterile; **'2keit** f (-/no pl.) unfruitfulness; sterility.

Unfug ['unfu:k] m (-[e]s/no pl.) mischief.

Ungar ['ungar] m (-n/-n) Hungarian; **'2isch** adj. Hungarian.

'ungastlich adj. inhospitable.

unge|achtet prp. (gen.) ['ungə⁹axtət] regardless of; despite; **~ahnt** adj. ['ungə⁹-] undreamt-of; unexpected; **~'bärdig** adj. ['~bɛ:rdiç] unruly; **'~beten** adj. uninvited, unasked; **~er** Gast intruder, sl. gatecrasher; **'~bildet** adj. uneducated; **'~bräuchlich** adj. unusual; **'~braucht** adj. unused; **'~bührlich** adj. improper, undue, unseemly; **'~bunden** adj. book: unbound; fig.: free; single; **'~deckt** adj. table: unlaid; sports, ✗: ✝: uncovered; paper currency: fiduciary.

'Ungeduld f impatience; **'2ig** adj. impatient.

'ungeeignet adj. unfit (für for s.th., to do s.th.); p. a. unqualified; moment: inopportune.

ungefähr ['ungəfɛ:r] **1.** adj. approximate, rough; **2.** adv. approximately, roughly, about, Am. F a. around; von ~ by chance; **'~det** adj. unendangered; safe; **'~lich** adj. harmless; pred. a. not dangerous.

'unge|fällig adj. disobliging; **'~halten** adj. displeased (über acc. at); **'~hemmt 1.** adj. unchecked; **2.** adv. without restraint; **'~heuchelt** adj. unfeigned.

ungeheuer ['ungəhɔyər] **1.** adj. vast, huge, enormous; **2.** 2 n (-s/-) monster; **~lich** adj. [~'hɔyərliç] monstrous.

'ungehobelt adj. not planed; fig. uncouth, rough.

'ungehörig adj. undue, improper; **'2keit** f (-/◌̸-en) impropriety.

'ungehorsam 1. adj. disobedient; **2.** 2 m disobedience.

'unge|künstelt adj. unaffected; **'~kürzt** adj. unabridged.

'ungelegen adj. inconvenient, inopportune; **'2heiten** f/pl. inconvenience; trouble; j-m ~ machen put s.o. to inconvenience.

'unge|lehrig adj. indocile; **'~lenk** adj. awkward, clumsy; **'~lernt** adj. unskilled; **'~mütlich** adj. uncomfortable; room: a. cheerless; p. nasty; **'~nannt** adj. unnamed; p. anonymous.

'ungenau adj. inaccurate, inexact; **'2igkeit** f inaccuracy, inexactness.

'ungeniert adj. free and easy, unceremonious; undisturbed.

'unge|nießbar adj. ['ungəni:sba:r] uneatable; undrinkable; F p. unbearable, pred. a. in a bad humo(u)r; **'~nügend** adj. insufficient; **'~pflegt** adj. unkempt; **'~rade** adj. odd; **'~raten** adj. spoilt, undutiful.

'ungerecht adj. unjust (gegen to); **'Ɂigkeit** f (-/-en) injustice.

'un|gern adv. unwillingly, grudgingly; reluctantly; **'˷geschehen** adj.: ˷ machen undo s.th.

'Ungeschick n (-[e]s/no pl.), **'˷lichkeit** f awkwardness, clumsiness, maladroitness; **'Ɂt** adj. awkward, clumsy, maladroit.

unge|schlacht adj. ['ungəʃlaxt] hulking; uncouth; **'˷schliffen** adj. unpolished, rough (both a. fig.); **'˷schminkt** adj. not made up; fig. unvarnished.

'ungesetzlich adj. illegal, unlawful, illicit; **'Ɂkeit** f (-/-en) illegality, unlawfulness.

'unge|sittet adj. uncivilized; unmannerly; **'˷stört** adj. undisturbed, uninterrupted; **'˷straft 1.** adj. unpunished; **2.** adv. with impunity; ˷ davonkommen get off or escape scot-free.

ungestüm ['ungəʃtyːm] **1.** adj. impetuous; violent; **2.** Ɂ n (-[e]s/no pl.) impetuosity; violence.

'unge|sund adj. climate: unhealthy; appearance: a. unwholesome; food: unwholesome; **'˷teilt** adj. undivided (a. fig.); **˷trübt** adj. ['˷tryːpt] untroubled; unmixed; **Ɂtüm** ['˷tyːm] n (-[e]s/-e) monster; **˷übt** adj. ['˷ʔyːpt] untrained; inexperienced; **'˷waschen** adj. unwashed.

'ungewiß adj. uncertain; j-n im ungewissen lassen keep s.o. in suspense; **'Ɂheit** f (-/˷-en) uncertainty; suspense.

'unge|wöhnlich adj. unusual, uncommon; **'˷wohnt** adj. unaccustomed; unusual; **'˷zählt** adj. numberless, countless; **Ɂziefer** ['˷tsiːfər] n (-s/-) vermin; **'˷ziemend** adj. improper, unseemly; **'˷zogen** adj. ill-bred, rude, uncivil; child: naughty; **'˷zügelt** adj. unbridled.

'ungezwungen adj. unaffected, easy; **'Ɂheit** f (-/˷-en) unaffectedness, ease, easiness.

'Unglaube(n) m unbelief, disbelief.

'ungläubig adj. incredulous, unbelieving (a. eccl.); infidel; **'Ɂe** m, f unbeliever; infidel.

unglaub|lich adj. [un'glauplɪç] incredible; **'˷würdig** adj. p. untrustworthy; thing: incredible; **˷e** Geschichte cock-and-bull story.

'ungleich 1. adj. unequal, different; uneven; unlike; **2.** adv. (by) far, much; **'˷artig** adj. heterogeneous; **'Ɂheit** f difference, inequality; unevenness; unlikeness; **'˷mäßig** adj. uneven; irregular.

'Unglück n (-[e]s/˷-e) misfortune; bad or ill luck; accident; calamity, disaster; misery; **'Ɂlich** adj. unfortunate, unlucky; unhappy; **Ɂ˷licher'weise** adv. unfortunately,

unluckily; **'Ɂselig** adj. unfortunate; disastrous.

'Unglücks|fall m misadventure; accident; **'˷rabe** F m unlucky fellow.

'Un|gnade f (-/no pl.) disgrace, disfavo(u)r; in ˷ fallen fall into disgrace with, incur s.o.'s disfavo(u)r; **'Ɂgnädig** adj. ungracious, unkind.

'ungültig adj. invalid; ticket: not available; money: not current; ᵗᵗᵗ (null and) void; **'Ɂkeit** f invalidity; ᵗᵗᵗ a. voidness.

'Un|gunst f disfavo(u)r; inclemency (of weather); zu meinen ˷en to my disadvantage; **'Ɂgünstig** adj. unfavo(u)rable; disadvantageous.

'un|gut adj.: ˷es Gefühl misgiving; nichts für ˷l no offen|ce, Am. -se!; **'˷haltbar** adj. shot: unstoppable; theory, etc.: untenable; **'˷handlich** adj. unwieldy, bulky.

'Unheil n mischief; disaster, calamity; **'Ɂbar** adj. incurable; **'Ɂvoll** adj. sinister, ominous.

'unheimlich 1. adj. uncanny (a. fig.), weird; sinister; F fig. tremendous, terrific; **2.** F fig. adv.: ˷ viel heaps of, an awful lot of.

'unhöflich adj. impolite, uncivil; **'Ɂkeit** f impoliteness, incivility.

Unhold ['unhɔlt] m (-[e]s/-e) fiend.

'un|hörbar adj. inaudible; **'˷hygienisch** adj. unsanitary, insanitary.

Uni ['uni] f (-/-s) F varsity.

Uniform [uni'fɔrm] f (-/-en) uniform.

Unikum ['uːnikum] n (-s/Unika, -s) unique (thing); queer fellow.

uninteress|ant adj. ['unʔ-] uninteresting, boring; **'˷iert** adj. uninterested (an dat. in).

Universität [univerzi'tɛːt] f (-/-en) university.

Universum [uni'vɛrzum] n (-s/no pl.) universe.

Unke ['uŋkə] f (-/-n) zo. fire-bellied toad; F fig. croaker; **'Ɂn** F v/i. (ge-, h) croak.

'unkennt|lich adj. unrecognizable; **'Ɂlichkeit** f (-/no pl.): bis zur ˷ past all recognition; **'Ɂnis** f (-/no pl.) ignorance.

'unklar adj. not clear; meaning, etc.: obscure; answer, etc.: vague; im ˷en sein be in the dark (über acc. about); **'Ɂheit** f want of clearness; vagueness; obscurity.

'unklug adj. imprudent, unwise.

'Unkosten pl. cost(s pl.), expenses pl.; sich in (große) ˷ stürzen go to great expense.

'Unkraut n weed.

un|kündbar adj. ['unkyntbaːr] loan, etc.: irredeemable; employment: permanent; **˷kundig** adj. ['˷kundiç] ignorant (gen. of); **'˷längst**

adv. lately, recently, the other day; **'.lauter** *adj. competition:* unfair; **'.leidlich** *adj.* intolerable, insufferable; **'.leserlich** *adj.* illegible; **.leugbar** *adj.* ['.lɔykbaːr] undeniable; **'.logisch** *adj.* illogical; **'.~lösbar** *adj.* unsolvable, insoluble.

'Unlust *f* (*-/no pl.*) reluctance (*zu inf.* to *inf.*); **'2ig** *adj.* reluctant.

'un|manierlich *adj.* unmannerly; **'.männlich** *adj.* unmanly; **.maßgeblich** *adj.* ['.~geːplɪç]: *nach m-r .en Meinung* in my humble opinion; **'.mäßig** *adj.* immoderate; intemperate; **'2menge** *f* enormous *or* vast quantity *or* number.

'Unmensch *m* monster, brute; **'2-lich** *adj.* inhuman, brutal; **'.lichkeit** *f* inhumanity, brutality.

'un|mißverständlich *adj.* unmistakable; **'.mittelbar** *adj.* immediate, direct; **'.möbliert** *adj.* unfurnished; **'.modern** *adj.* unfashionable, outmoded.

'unmöglich *adj.* impossible; **'2keit** *f* impossibility.

'Unmoral *f* immorality; **'2isch** *adj.* immoral.

'unmündig *adj.* under age.

'un|musikalisch *adj.* unmusical; **'2mut** *m* (*-[e]s/no pl.*) displeasure (*über acc.* at, over); **'.nachahmlich** *adj.* inimitable; **'.nachgiebig** *adj.* unyielding; **'.nachsichtig** *adj.* strict, severe; inexorable; **'.~'nahbar** *adj.* inaccessible, unapproachable; **'.natürlich** *adj.* unnatural; affected; **'.nötig** *adj.* unnecessary, needless; **'.nütz** *adj.* useless; **.~ordentlich** *adj.* ['unᵑ-] untidy; *room, etc.:* a. disorderly; **2ordnung** ['unᵑ-] *f* disorder, mess.

'unpartei|isch *adj.* impartial, unbias(s)ed; **'2ische** *m* (*-n/-n*) referee; umpire; **'2lichkeit** *f* impartiality.

'un|passend *adj.* unsuitable; improper; inappropriate; **'.passierbar** *adj.* impassable.

unpäßlich *adj.* ['unpɛslɪç] indisposed, unwell; **'2keit** *f* (*-/-en*) indisposition.

'un|persönlich *adj.* impersonal (*a. gr.*); **'.politisch** *adj.* unpolitical; **'.praktisch** *adj.* unpractical, *Am. a.* impractical; **'2rat** *m* (*-[e]s/no pl.*) filth; rubbish; *~ wittern* smell a rat.

'unrecht 1. *adj.* wrong; *~ haben* be wrong; *j-m ~ tun* wrong s.o.; **2.** **2** *n* (*-[e]s/no pl.*): *mit or zu ~* wrongly; *ihm ist ~ geschehen* he has been wronged; **'.mäßig** *adj.* unlawful; **'2mäßigkeit** *f* unlawfulness.

'unreell *adj.* dishonest; unfair.

'unregelmäßig *adj.* irregular (*a. gr.*); **'2keit** *f* (*-/-en*) irregularity.

'unreif *adj.* unripe, immature (*both a. fig.*); **'2e** *f* unripeness, immaturity (*both a. fig.*).

'un|rein *adj.* impure (*a. eccl.*); unclean (*a. fig.*); **'.reinlich** *adj.* uncleanly; **.'rettbar** *adv.*: *~ verloren* irretrievably lost; **'.richtig** *adj.* incorrect, wrong.

Unruh ['unruː] *f* (*-/-en*) balance (-wheel); **'.e** *f* (*-/-n*) restlessness, unrest (*a. pol.*); uneasiness; disquiet(ude); flurry; alarm; *~n pl.* disturbances *pl.*, riots *pl.*; **'2ig** *adj.* restless; uneasy; *sea:* rough, choppy.

'unrühmlich *adj.* inglorious.

uns *pers. pron.* [uns] us; *dat.:* a. to us; *~* (*selbst*) ourselves, *after prp.*: us; *ein Freund von ~* a friend of ours.

'un|sachgemäß *adj.* inexpert; **'.~sachlich** *adj.* not objective; personal; **.säglich** *adj.* [.'zeːklɪç] unspeakable; untold; **'.sanft** *adj.* ungentle; **'.sauber** *adj.* dirty; *fig. a.* unfair (*a. sports*); **'.schädlich** *adj.* innocuous, harmless; **'.scharf** *adj.* blurred; *pred. a.* out of focus; **.'schätzbar** *adj.* inestimable, invaluable; **'.scheinbar** *adj.* plain, *Am. a.* homely.

'unschicklich *adj.* improper, indecent; **'2keit** *f* (*-/-en*) impropriety, indecency.

unschlüssig *adj.* ['unʃlysɪç] irresolute; **'2keit** *f* (*-/no pl.*) irresoluteness, irresolution.

'un|schmackhaft *adj.* insipid; unpalatable, unsavo(u)ry; **'.schön** *adj.* unlovely, unsightly; *fig. a.* unpleasant.

'Unschuld *f* (*-/no pl.*) innocence; **'2ig** *adj.* innocent (*an dat.* of).

'unselbständig *adj.* dependent (on others); **'2keit** *f* (lack of in)dependence.

unser ['unzər] **1.** *poss. pron.* our; *der* (*die, das*) *~e* ours; *die ~en pl.* our relations *pl.*; **2.** *pers. pron.* of us; *wir waren ~ drei* there were three of us.

'unsicher *adj.* unsteady; unsafe, insecure; uncertain; **'2heit** *f* unsteadiness; insecurity, unsafeness; uncertainty.

'unsichtbar *adj.* invisible.

'Unsinn *m* (*-[e]s/no pl.*) nonsense; **'2ig** *adj.* nonsensical.

'Unsitt|e *f* bad habit; abuse; **'2lich** *adj.* immoral; indecent (*a. ⚥⚥*); **'.~lichkeit** *f* (*-/-en*) immorality.

'un|solid(e) *adj. p.* easy-going; *life:* dissipated; *✝* unreliable; **'.sozial** *adj.* unsocial, antisocial; **'.sportlich** *adj.* unsportsmanlike; unfair (*gegenüber* to).

'unstatthaft *adj.* inadmissible.

'unsterblich *adj.* immortal.

Un'sterblichkeit *f* immortality.

'un|stet *adj.* unsteady; *character, life:* unsettled; **'2stimmigkeit** ['.~ʃtɪmɪçkaɪt] *f* (*-/-en*) discrepancy; dissension; **'.sträflich** *adj.* blameless; **'**streitig *adj.* incontestable; **'**sympathisch *adj.* disagreeable; er ist mir ~ I don't like him; **'**tätig *adj.* inactive; idle.

'untauglich *adj.* unfit (*a.* ✗); unsuitable; **'**keit *f* (*-/no pl.*) unfitness (*a.* ✗).

un'teilbar *adj.* indivisible.

unten *adv.* ['untən] below; downstairs; von oben bis ~ from top to bottom.

unter ['untər] **1.** *prp.* (*dat.*; *acc.*) below, under; among; ~ anderem among other things; ~ zehn Mark (for) less than ten marks; ~ Null below zero; ~ aller Kritik beneath contempt; ~ diesem Gesichtspunkt from this point of view; **2.** *adj.* lower; inferior; die ~en Räume the downstair(s) rooms.

Unter|abteilung ['untər?-] *f* subdivision; ~arm ['untər?-] *m* forearm; **'**bau *m* (*-[e]s/-ten*) 🏛 substructure (*a.* 🏭), foundation.

unter|'bieten *v/t.* (*irr.* bieten, no -ge-, h) underbid; ✝ undercut, undersell (*competitor*); lower (*record*); ~'binden *v/t.* (*irr.* binden, no -ge-, h) 🩺 ligature; *fig.* stop; ~'bleiben *v/i.* (*irr.* bleiben, no -ge-, sein) remain undone; not to take place.

unter'brech|en *v/t.* (*irr.* brechen, no -ge-, h) interrupt (*a.* 🎵); break, *Am. a.* stop over; ⚡ break (*circuit*); **'**ung *f* (*-/-en*) interruption; break, *Am. a.* stopover.   [mit.)

unter'breiten *v/t.* (*no -ge-, h*) sub-)

'unterbring|en *v/t.* (*irr.* bringen, sep., -ge-, h) place (*a.* ✝); accommodate, lodge; **'**ung *f* (*-/-en*) accommodation; ✝ placement.

unterdessen *adv.* [untər'dɛsən] (in the) meantime, meanwhile.

unter'drück|en *v/t.* (*no -ge-, h*) oppress (*subjects, etc.*); repress (*revolt, sneeze, etc.*); suppress (*rising, truth, yawn, etc.*); put down (*rebellion, etc.*); **'**ung *f* (*-/-en*) oppression; repression; suppression; putting down.

unterernähr|t *adj.* ['untər?-] underfed, undernourished; **'**ung *f* (*-/no pl.*) underfeeding, malnutrition.

Unter'führung *f* subway, *Am.* underpass.

'Untergang *m* (*-[e]s/✗-e*) *ast.* setting; ⚓ sinking; *fig.* ruin.

Unter'gebene *m* (*-n/-n*) inferior, subordinate; *contp.* underling.

'untergehen *v/i.* (*irr.* gehen, sep., -ge-, sein) *ast.* set; ⚓ sink, founder; *fig.* be ruined.

untergeordnet *adj.* ['untərgə?ɔrdnət] subordinate; *importance:* secondary.

'Untergewicht *n* (*-[e]s/no pl.*) underweight.

unter'graben *fig. v/t.* (*irr.* graben, no -ge-, h) undermine.

'Untergrund *m* (*-[e]s/no pl.*) subsoil; **'**bahn *f* underground (railway), in London: tube; *Am.* subway; **'**bewegung *f* underground movement.

'unterhalb *prp.* (*gen.*) below, underneath.

'Unterhalt *m* (*-[e]s/no pl.*) support, subsistence, livelihood; maintenance.

unter'halt|en *v/t.* (*irr.* halten, no -ge-, h) maintain; support; entertain, amuse; sich ~ converse (*mit* with; über acc. on, about), talk (with; on, about); sich gut ~ enjoy o.s.; **'**ung *f* maintenance, upkeep; conversation, talk; entertainment.

'Unterhändler *m* negotiator; ✗ Parlementaire.

'Unter|haus *parl. n* (*-es/no pl.*) House of Commons; **'**hemd *n* vest, undershirt; **'**holz *n* (*-es/no pl.*) underwood, brushwood; **'**hose *f* (e-e a pair of) drawers *pl.*, pants *pl.*; **'**irdisch *adj.* subterranean, underground (*both a. fig.*).

unter'joch|en *v/t.* (*no -ge-, h*) subjugate, subdue; **'**ung *f* (*-/-en*) subjugation.

'Unter|kiefer *m* lower jaw; **'**kleid *n* slip; **'**kleidung *f* underclothes *pl.*, underclothing, underwear.

unter'kommen **1.** *v/i.* (*irr.* kommen, sep., -ge-, sein) find accommodation; find employment; **2.** 2 *n* (*-s/✗-*) accommodation; employment, situation.

'unter|kriegen F *v/t.* (*sep., -ge-, h*) bring to heel; sich nicht ~ lassen not to knuckle down or under; **'**kunft ['~kunft] *f* (*-/✗-e*) accommodation, lodging; ✗ quarters *pl.*; **'**lage *f* base; pad; *fig.*: voucher; ~n *pl.* documents *pl.*; data *pl.*

unter'lass|en *v/t.* (*irr.* lassen, no -ge-, h) omit (zu tun doing, to do); neglect (to do, doing); fail (to do); **'**ung *f* (*-/-en*) omission; neglect; failure; **'**ungssünde *f* sin of omission.

'unterlegen[1] *v/t.* (*sep., -ge-, h*) lay or put under; give (*another meaning*).

unter'legen[2] *adj.* inferior (*dat.* to); 2e *m* (*-n/-n*) loser; underdog; **'**heit *f* (*-/no pl.*) inferiority.

'Unterleib *m* abdomen, belly.

unter'liegen *v/i.* (*irr.* liegen, no -ge-, sein) be overcome (*dat.* by); be defeated (by), *sports: a.* lose (to); *fig.:* be subject to; be liable to; es unterliegt keinem Zweifel, daß ... there is no doubt that ...

'Unter|lippe *f* lower lip; **'**mieter *m* subtenant, lodger, *Am. a.* roomer.

unter'nehmen **1.** *v/t.* (*irr.* nehmen, no -ge-, h) undertake; take (*steps*);

2. ♀ *n* (*-s/-*) enterprise; ♀ *a.* business; ♀ operation.

unter'nehm|end *adj.* enterprising; **♀er** ♀ *m* (*-s/-*) entrepreneur; contractor; employer; **♀ung** *f* (*-/-en*) enterprise, undertaking; ♀ operation; **~ungslustig** *adj.* enterprising.

'Unter|offizier ♀ *m* non-commissioned officer; **'♀ordnen** *v/t.* (*sep., -ge-, h*) subordinate (*dat.* to); **sich ~** submit (to).

Unter'redung *f* (*-/-en*) conversation, conference.

Unterricht ['untərriçt] *m* (*-[e]s/♀ -e*) instruction, lessons *pl.*

unter'richten *v/t.* (*no -ge-, h*): **~ in** (*dat.*) instruct in, teach (*English, etc.*); **~ von** inform *s.o.* of.

'Unterrichts|ministerium *n* ministry of education; **'~stunde** *f* lesson, (teaching) period; **'~wesen** *n* (*-s/no pl.*) education; teaching.

'Unterrock *m* slip.

unter'sagen *v/t.* (*no -ge-, h*) forbid (*j-m et. s.o.* to do s.th.).

'Untersatz *m* stand; saucer.

unter'schätzen *v/t.* (*no -ge-, h*) undervalue; underestimate, underrate.

unter'scheid|en *v/t. and v/i.* (*irr. scheiden, no -ge-, h*) distinguish (*zwischen* between; *von* from); **sich ~** differ (*von* from); **♀ung** *f* distinction.

'Unterschenkel *m* shank.

'unterschieb|en *v/t.* (*irr. schieben, sep., -ge-, h*) push under; *fig.:* attribute (*dat.* to); substitute (*statt* for); **'♀ung** *f* substitution.

Unterschied ['untərʃi:t] *m* (*-[e]s/-e*) difference; distinction; **zum ~ von** in distinction from *or* to; **'♀lich** *adj.* different; differential; variable, varying; **'♀slos** *adj.* indiscriminate; undiscriminating.

unter'schlag|en *v/t.* (*irr. schlagen, no -ge-, h*) embezzle; suppress (*truth, etc.*); **♀ung** *f* (*-/-en*) embezzlement; suppression.

'Unterschlupf *m* (*-[e]s/⸚e, -e*) shelter, refuge.

unter'schreiben *v/t. and v/i.* (*irr. schreiben, no -ge-, h*) sign.

'Unterschrift *f* signature.

'Untersee|boot ♀, ♀ *n s. U-Boot*; **'~kabel** *n* submarine cable.

unter'setzt *adj.* thick-set, squat.

unterst *adj.* ['untərst] lowest, undermost.

'Unterstand ♀ *m* shelter, dug-out.

unter'stehen (*irr. stehen, no -ge-, h*) **1.** *v/i.* (*dat.*) be subordinate to; be subject to (*law, etc.*); **2.** *v/refl.* dare; *untersteh dich!* don't you dare!; **~stellen** *v/t.* **1.** ['~ʃtelən] (*sep., -ge-, h*) put *or* place under; garage (*car*); **sich ~** take shelter (*vor dat.* from); **2.** [~'ʃtelən] (*no -ge-, h*) (pre)suppose, assume; impute (*dat.*

to); *j-m ~* ♀ put (*troops, etc.*) under s.o.'s command; **♀'stellung** *f* (*-/-en*) assumption, supposition; imputation; **~'streichen** *v/t.* (*irr. streichen, no -ge-, h*) underline, underscore (*both a. fig.*).

unter'stütz|en *v/t.* (*no -ge-, h*) support; back up; **♀ung** *f* (*-/-en*) support (*a.* ♀); assistance, aid; relief.

unter'such|en *v/t.* (*no -ge-, h*) examine (*a.* ♀); inquire into, investigate (*a.* ♀); explore; ♀ try; analy|se, *Am.* -ze (*a.* ♀); **♀ung** *f* (*-/-en*) examination (*a.* ♀); inquiry (*gen.* into), investigation (*a.* ♀); exploration; analysis (*a.* ♀).

Unter'suchungs|gefangene *m* prisoner on remand; **~gefängnis** *n* remand prison; **~haft** *f* detention on remand; **~richter** *m* investigating judge.

Untertan ['untərta:n] *m* (*-s, -en/ -en*) subject.

untertänig *adj.* ['untərtɛːniç] submissive.

'Unter|tasse *f* saucer; **'♀tauchen** (*sep., -ge-*) **1.** *v/i.* (*sein*) dive, dip; duck; *fig.* disappear; **2.** *v/t.* (*h*) duck.

'Unterteil *n, m* lower part.

unter'teil|en *v/t.* (*no -ge-, h*) subdivide; **♀ung** *f* subdivision.

'Unter|titel *m* subheading; subtitle; *a.* caption (*of film*); **'~ton** *m* undertone; **'♀vermieten** *v/t.* (*no -ge-, h*) sublet.

unter'wander|n *pol. v/t.* (*no -ge-, h*) infiltrate; **♀ung** *pol. f* infiltration.

'Unterwäsche *f s. Unterkleidung.*

unterwegs *adv.* [untər've:ks] on the *or* one's way.

unter'weis|en *v/t.* (*irr. weisen, no -ge-, h*) instruct (*in dat.* in); **♀ung** *f* instruction.

'Unterwelt *f* underworld (*a. fig.*).

unter'werf|en *v/t.* (*irr. werfen, no -ge-, h*) subdue (*dat.* to), subjugate (to); subject (to); submit (to); *sich ~* submit (to); **♀ung** *f* (*-/-en*) subjugation, subjection; submission (*unter acc.* to).

unterworfen *adj.* [untər'vorfən] subject (*dat.* to).

unterwürfig *adj.* [untər'vyrfiç] submissive; subservient; **♀keit** *f* (*-/no pl.*) submissiveness; subservience.

unter'zeichn|en *v/t.* (*no -ge-, h*) sign; **♀er** *m* signer, *the* undersigned; subscriber (*gen.* to); signatory (*gen.* to *treaty*); **♀erstaat** *m* signatory state; **♀ete** *m, f* (*-n/-n*) *the* undersigned; **♀ung** *f* signature, signing.

unterziehen *v/t.* (*irr. ziehen*) **1.** ['~tsi:ən] (*sep., -ge-, h*) put on underneath; **2.** [~'tsi:ən] (*no -ge-, h*) subject (*dat.* to); *sich e-r Operation ~* undergo an operation; *sich e-r Prüfung ~* go in *or* sit for an examination; *sich der Mühe ~ zu inf.* take the trouble to *inf.*

'**Untiefe** f shallow, shoal.
'**Untier** n monster (a. fig.).
un|tilgbar adj. [un'tilkba:r] indelible; † government annuities: irredeemable; ~'**tragbar** adj. unbearable, intolerable; costs: prohibitive; ~'**trennbar** adj. inseparable.

'**untreu** adj. untrue (dat. to), disloyal (to); husband, wife: unfaithful (to); '~e f disloyalty; unfaithfulness, infidelity.

un|'tröstlich adj. inconsolable, disconsolate; ~**trüglich** adj. [~'try:kliç] infallible, unerring.

'**Untugend** f vice, bad habit.
unüber|legt adj. ['un⁹y:bər-] inconsiderate, thoughtless; '~**sichtlich** adj. badly arranged; difficult to survey; involved; mot. corner: blind; ~'**trefflich** adj. unsurpassable; ~**windlich** adj. [~'vintliç] invincible; fortress: impregnable; obstacle, etc.: insurmountable; difficulties, etc.: insuperable.

unum|gänglich adj. [un⁹um'geŋliç] absolutely necessary; ~**schränkt** adj. [~'frɛŋkt] absolute; ~**stößlich** adj. [~'ftø:sliç] irrefutable; incontestable; irrevocable; ~**wunden** adj. [~vundən] frank, plain.

ununterbrochen adj. ['un⁹untər-brɔxən] uninterrupted; incessant.
unver|'änderlich adj. unchangeable; invariable; ~'**antwortlich** adj. irresponsible; inexcusable; ~'**besserlich** adj. incorrigible; '~**bindlich** adj. not binding or obligatory; answer, etc.: non-committal; ~**blümt** adj. [~'bly:mt] plain, blunt; ~**bürgt** adj. [~'byrkt] unwarranted; news: unconfirmed; '~**dächtig** adj. unsuspected; '~**daulich** adj. indigestible (a. fig.); '~**dient** adj. undeserved; '~**dorben** adj. unspoiled, unspoilt; fig.: uncorrupted; pure, innocent; '~**drossen** adj. indefatigable, unflagging; '~**dünnt** adj. undiluted, Am. a. straight; ~'**einbar** adj. incompatible; '~**fälscht** adj. unadulterated; fig. genuine; ~**fänglich** adj. ['~fɛŋliç] not captious; ~**froren** adj. ['~fro:rən] unabashed, impudent; '**²frorenheit** f (-/-en) impudence, F cheek; '~**gänglich** adj. imperishable; ~**geßlich** adj. unforgettable; ~'**gleichlich** adj. incomparable; '~**hältnismäßig** adj. disproportionate; '~**heiratet** adj. unmarried, single; '~**hofft** adj. unhoped-for, unexpected; '~**hohlen** adj. unconcealed; '~**käuflich** adj. unsal(e)able; not for sale; ~'**kennbar** adj. unmistakable; ~'**letzbar** adj. invulnerable; fig. a. inviolable; ~**meidlich** adj. [~'martliç] inevitable; '~**mindert** adj. undiminished; ~**mittelt** adj. abrupt.

'**Unvermögen** n (-s/no pl.) inability; impotence; '²**d** adj. impecunious, without means.
'**unvermutet** adj. unexpected.
'**Unver|nunft** f unreasonableness, absurdity; '²**nünftig** adj. unreasonable, absurd; '²**richteterdinge** adv. without having achieved one's object.

'**unverschämt** adj. impudent, impertinent; '²**heit** f (-/-en) impudence, impertinence.

'**unver|schuldet** adj. not in debt; through no fault of mine, etc.; '~**sehens** adv. unawares, suddenly, all of a sudden; ~**sehrt** adj. ['~ze:rt] uninjured; '~**söhnlich** adj. implacable, irreconcilable; '~**sorgt** adj. unprovided for; '²**stand** m injudiciousness; folly, stupidity; '~**ständig** adj. injudicious; foolish; ~**ständlich** adj. unintelligible; incomprehensible; das ist mir ~ that is beyond me; '~**sucht** adj.: nichts ~ lassen leave nothing undone; ~**träglich** adj. unsociable; quarrelsome; '~**wandt** adj. steadfast; ~**wundbar** adj. [~'vuntba:r] invulnerable; ~**wüstlich** adj. [~'vy:stliç] indestructible; fig. irrepressible; ~**zagt** adj. ['~tsa:kt] intrepid, undaunted; ~**zeihlich** adj. unpardonable; ~'**zinslich** adj. bearing no interest; non-interest-bearing; ~**züglich** adj. [~'tsy:kliç] immediate, instant.

'**unvollendet** adj. unfinished.
'**unvollkommen** adj. imperfect; '²**heit** f imperfection.
'**unvollständig** adj. incomplete; '²**keit** f (-/no pl.) incompleteness.
'**unvorbereitet** adj. unprepared; extempore.
'**unvoreingenommen** adj. unbias(s)ed, unprejudiced; '²**heit** f freedom from prejudice.
'**unvor|hergesehen** adj. unforeseen; ~**schriftsmäßig** adj. irregular.
'**unvorsichtig** adj. incautious; imprudent; '²**keit** f incautiousness; imprudence.
'**unvor|'stellbar** adj. unimaginable; '~**teilhaft** adj. unprofitable; dress, etc.: unbecoming.
'**unwahr** adj. untrue; '²**heit** f untruth.
'**unwahrscheinlich** adj. improbable, unlikely; '²**keit** f (-/-en) improbability, unlikelihood.
'**un|wegsam** adj. pathless, impassable; '~**weit** prp. (gen. or von) not far from; '~**wesen** n (-s/no pl.) nuisance; sein ~ treiben be up to one's tricks; '~**wesentlich** adj. unessential, immaterial (für to); '²**wetter** n thunderstorm; '~**wichtig** adj. unimportant, insignificant.

unwider|legbar adj. [unvi:dər'le:kbaːr] irrefutable; ~'ruflich *adj.* irrevocable (*a.* ✝).

unwider'stehlich *adj.* irresistible; 2keit *f* (*-/no pl.*) irresistibility.

unwieder'bringlich *adj.* irretrievable.

'Unwill|e *m* (*-ns/no pl.*), '~en *m* (*-s/no pl.*) indignation (*über acc.* at), displeasure (at, over); 2ig *adj.* indignant (*über acc.* at), displeased (at, with); unwilling; '2kürlich *adj.* involuntary.

'unwirklich *adj.* unreal.

'unwirksam *adj.* ineffective, inefficient; *laws, rules, etc.*: inoperative; ♃ inactive; '2keit *f* (*-/no pl.*) ineffectiveness, inefficiency; ♃ inactivity.

unwirsch *adj.* ['unvirʃ] testy.

unwirt|lich *adj.* inhospitable, desolate; '~schaftlich *adj.* uneconomic(al).

'unwissen|d *adj.* ignorant; 2heit *f* (*-/no pl.*) ignorance; '~tlich *adj.* unwitting, unknowing.

'unwohl *adj.* unwell, indisposed; '2sein *n* (*-s/no pl.*) indisposition.

'unwürdig *adj.* unworthy (*gen.* of).

un|zählig *adj.* [un'tsɛːliç] innumerable; '2zart *adj.* indelicate.

Unze ['untsə] *f* (*-/-n*) ounce.

'Unzeit *f*: zur ~ inopportunely; '2gemäß *adj.* old-fashioned; inopportune; '2ig *adj.* untimely; unseasonable; *fruit*: unripe.

unzer'brechlich *adj.* unbreakable; ~'reißbar *adj.* untearable; ~'störbar *adj.* indestructible; ~'trennlich *adj.* inseparable.

'un|ziemlich *adj.* unseemly; '2zucht *f* (*-/no pl.*) lewdness; ⅔ sexual offen|ce, *Am.* -se; '~züchtig *adj.* lewd; obscene.

'unzufrieden *adj.* discontented (*mit* with), dissatisfied (with, at); '2heit *f* discontent, dissatisfaction.

'unzugänglich *adj.* inaccessible.

unzulänglich *adj.* ['untsulɛŋliç] insufficient; '2keit *f* (*-/-en*) insufficiency; shortcoming.

'unzulässig *adj.* inadmissible; *esp.* ⅔ *influence*: undue.

'unzurechnungsfähig *adj.* irresponsible; '2keit *f* irresponsibility.

'unzu|reichend *adj.* insufficient; '~sammenhängend *adj.* incoherent; '~träglich *adj.* unwholesome; '~treffend *adj.* incorrect; inapplicable (*auf acc.* to).

'unzuverlässig *adj.* unreliable, untrustworthy; *friend: a.* uncertain; '2keit *f* unreliability, untrustworthiness.

'unzweckmäßig *adj.* inexpedient; '2keit *f* inexpediency.

'un|zweideutig *adj.* unequivocal; unambiguous; '~zweifelhaft 1. *adj.* undoubted, undubitable; 2. *adv.* doubtless.

üppig *adj.* ['ypiç] 𝕻 luxuriant, exuberant, opulent; *food:* luxurious, opulent; *figure:* voluptuous; '2keit *f* (*-/♃-en*) luxuriance, luxuriancy, exuberance; voluptuousness.

ur|alt *adj.* ['uːrʔalt] very old; (as) old as the hills; 2aufführung ['uːrʔ-] *f* world première.

Uran [u'raːn] *n* (*-s/no pl.*) uranium.

urbar *adj.* ['uːrbaːr] arable, cultivable; ~ *machen* reclaim; '2machung *f* (*-/-en*) reclamation.

'Ur|bevölkerung *f* aborigines *pl.*; '~bild *n* original, prototype; 2eigen *adj.* one's very own; '~enkel *m* great-grandson; '~großeltern *pl.* great-grandparents *pl.*; '~großmutter *f* great-grandmother; '~großvater *m* great-grandfather.

'Urheber *m* (*-s/-*) author; '~recht *n* copyright (*an dat.* in); '~schaft *f* (*-/no pl.*) authorship.

Urin [u'riːn] *m* (*-s/-e*) urine; 2ieren [~i'niːrən] *v/i.* (*no -ge-, h*) urinate.

'Urkund|e *f* document; deed; '~enfälschung *f* forgery of documents; 2lich *adj.* ['~tliç] documentary.

Urlaub ['uːrlaup] *m* (*-[e]s/-e*) leave (of absence) (×); holiday(s *pl.*), *esp. Am.* vacation; '~er [~bər] *m* (*-s/-*) holiday-maker, *esp. Am.* vacationist, vacationer.

Urne ['urnə] *f* (*-/-n*) urn; ballot-box.

'ur|plötzlich 1. *adj.* very sudden, abrupt; 2. *adv.* all of a sudden; '2sache *f* cause; reason; *keine ~l* don't mention it, *Am. a.* you are welcome; '~sächlich *adj.* causal; '2schrift *f* original (text); '2sprung *m* origin; source; ~sprünglich *adj.* ['~ʃprʏŋliç] original; '2stoff *m* primary matter.

Urteil ['urtaɪl] *n* (*-s/-e*) judg(e)ment; ⅔ *a.* sentence; *meinem ~ nach* in my judg(e)ment; *sich ein ~ bilden* form a judg(e)ment (*über acc.* of, on); '2en *v/i.* (*ge-, h*) judge (*über acc.* of; *nach* by, from); '~skraft *f* (*-/♃-e*) discernment.

'Ur|text *m* original (text); '~wald *m* primeval *or* virgin forest; 2wüchsig *adj.* ['~vyːksiç] original; *fig.*: natural; rough; '~zeit *f* primitive times *pl.*

Utensilien [uten'ziːljən] *pl.* utensils *pl.*

Utop|ie [uto'piː] *f* (*-/-n*) Utopia; 2isch *adj.* [u'toːpiʃ] Utopian, utopian.

V

Vagabund [vaga'bunt] m (-en/-en) vagabond, vagrant, tramp, Am. hobo, F bum.

Vakuum ['va:kuⁱum] n (-s/Vakua, Vakuen) vacuum.

Valuta ✝ [va'lu:ta] f (-/Valuten) value; currency.

Vanille [va'niljə] f (-/no pl.) vanilla.

variabel adj. [vari'a:bəl] variable.

Varia|nte [vari'antə] f (-/-n) variant; ~tion [~'tsjo:n] f (-/-en) variation.

Varieté [varie'te:] n (-s/-s), ~theater n variety theatre, music-hall, Am. vaudeville theater.

variieren [vari'i:rən] v/i. and v/t. (no -ge-, h) vary.

Vase ['va:zə] f (-/-n) vase.

Vater ['fa:tər] m (-s/⁼) father; '~land n native country or land, mother country; '~landsliebe f patriotism.

väterlich adj. ['fɛ:tərliç] fatherly, paternal.

'Vater|schaft f (-/no pl.) paternity, fatherhood; '~unser eccl. n (-s/-) Lord's Prayer.

Vati ['fa:ti] m (-s/-s) dad(dy).

Veget|arier [vege'ta:rjər] m (-s/-) vegetarian; ~arisch adj. vegetarian; ~ation [~a'tsjo:n] f (-/-en) vegetation; Sieren [~'ti:rən] v/i. (no -ge-, h) vegetate.

Veilchen ❀ ['failçən] n (-s/-) violet.

Vene anat. ['ve:nə] f (-/-n) vein.

Ventil [vɛn'ti:l] n (-s/-e) valve (a. ♪); ♪ stop (of organ); fig. vent, outlet; ~ation [~ila'tsjo:n] f (-/-en) ventilation; ~ator [~i'la:tər] m (-s/-en) ventilator, fan.

verab|folgen [fɛr'ap-] v/t. (no -ge-, h) deliver; give; ♣ administer (medicine); ~reden v/t. (no -ge-, h) agree upon, arrange; appoint, fix (time, place); sich ~ make an appointment, Am. F (have a) date; Sredung f (-/-en) agreement; arrangement; appointment, Am. F date; ~reichen v/t. (no -ge-, h) s. verabfolgen; ~scheuen v/t. (no -ge-, h) abhor, detest, loathe; ~schieden [~ʃi:dən] v/t. (no -ge-, h) dismiss; retire (officer); ✕ discharge (troops); parl. pass (bill); sich ~ take leave (von of), say goodbye (to); Sschiedung f (-/-en) dismissal; discharge; passing.

ver|'achten v/t. (no -ge-, h) despise; ~ächtlich adj. [~'ɛçtliç] contemptuous; contemptible; S'achtung f contempt; ~allgemeinern [~ʔalgə'mainərn] v/t. (no -ge-, h) generalize; ~altet adj. antiquated, obsolete, out of date.

Veranda [ve'randa] f (-/Veranden) veranda(h), Am. a. porch.

veränder|lich adj. [fɛr'endərliç] changeable; variable (a. ♈, gr.); ~n v/t. and v/refl. (no -ge-, h) alter, change; vary; Sung f change, alteration (in dat. in; an dat. to); variation.

verängstigt adj. [fɛr'ɛŋstiçt] intimidated, scared.

ver'anlag|en v/t. (no -ge-, h) of taxation: assess; ~t adj. [~kt] talented; Sung [~guŋ] f (-/-en) assessment; fig. talent(s pl.); ♣ predisposition.

ver'anlass|en v/t. (no -ge-, h) cause, occasion; arrange; Sung f (-/-en) occasion, cause; auf m-e ~ at my request or suggestion.

ver|'anschaulichen v/t. (no -ge-, h) illustrate; ~'anschlagen v/t. (no -ge-, h) rate, value, estimate (all: auf acc. at).

ver'anstalt|en v/t. (no -ge-, h) arrange, organize; give (concert, ball, etc.); Sung f (-/-en) arrangement; event; sports: event, meeting, Am. meet.

ver'antwort|en v/t. (no -ge-, h) take the responsibility for; account for; ~lich adj. responsible; j-n ~ machen für hold s.o. responsible for.

Ver'antwortung f (-/-en) responsibility; die ~ tragen be responsible; zur ~ ziehen call to account; Sslos adj. irresponsible.

ver|'arbeiten v/t. (no -ge-, h) work up; ⊕ process, manufacture (both: zu into); digest (food) (a. fig.); ~'ärgern v/t. (no -ge-, h) vex, annoy.

ver'arm|en v/i. (no -ge-, sein) become poor; ~t adj. impoverished.

ver|'ausgaben v/t. (no -ge-, h) spend (money); sich ~ run short of money; fig. spend o.s.; ~'äußern v/t. (no -ge-, h) sell; alienate.

Verb gr. [vɛrp] n (-s/-en) verb.

Ver'band m (-[e]s/⁼e) ♣ dressing, bandage; association, union; ✕ formation, unit; ~(s)kasten m first-aid box; ~(s)zeug n dressing (material).

ver'bann|en v/t. (no -ge-, h) banish (a. fig.), exile; Sung f (-/-en) banishment, exile.

ver|barrikadieren [fɛrbarika'di:-rən] v/t. (no -ge-, h) barricade; block (street, etc.); ~'bergen v/t. (irr. bergen, no -ge-, h) conceal, hide.

ver'besser|n v/t. (no -ge-, h) improve; correct; Sung f improvement; correction.

ver'beug|en v/refl. (no -ge-, h) bow (vor dat. to); Sung f bow.

ver|'biegen v/t. (irr. biegen, no

-ge-, *h*) bend, twist, distort; ~
'**bieten** *v/t.* (*irr.* bieten, *no* -ge-, *h*)
forbid, prohibit; ~'**billigen** *v/t.*
(*no* -ge-, *h*) reduce in price,
cheapen.

ver'bind|en *v/t.* (*irr.* binden, *no*
-ge-, *h*) ✗ dress; tie (together);
bind (up); link (*mit* to); join, unite,
combine; connect (*a. teleph.*);
teleph. put *s.o.* through (*mit* to);
j-m die Augen ~ blindfold *s.o.*; *sich*
~ join, unite, combine (*a. ♊*); *ich
bin Ihnen sehr verbunden* I am
greatly obliged to you; *falsch verbunden!* wrong number!;
~**lich** *adj.* [~tlıç] obligatory; obliging; 2**lichkeit** *f* (-/-en) obligation,
liability; obligingness, civility.

Ver'bindung *f* union; alliance;
combination; association (*of ideas*);
connexion, (*Am. only*) connection
(*a. teleph.*, 🚂, ⚓, ⊕); relation;
communication (*a. teleph.*); 🜋
compound; *geschäftliche* ~ business relations *pl.*; *teleph.*: ~ *bekommen* (*haben*) get (be) through;
die ~ *verlieren mit* lose touch with;
in ~ *bleiben* (*treten*) keep (get) in
touch (*mit* with); *sich in* ~ *setzen
mit* communicate with, *esp. Am.*
contact *s.o.*; ~**sstraße** *f* communication road, feeder road; ~**stür** *f*
communication door.

ver'bissen [fer'bisən] dogged;
crabbed; ~'**bitten** *v/refl.* (*irr.* bitten,
no -ge-, *h*): *das verbitte ich mir!*
I won't suffer *or* stand that!

ver'bitter|n *v/t.* (*no* -ge-, *h*) em-
bitter; 2**ung** *f* (-/~-en) bitterness
(of heart).

verblassen [fer'blasən] *v/i.* (*no*
-ge-, *sein*) fade (*a. fig.*).

Verbleib [fer'blaip] *m* (-[e]s/*no pl.*)
whereabouts *sg.*, *pl.*; 2**en** [~bən] *v/i.*
(*irr.* bleiben, *no* -ge-, *sein*) be left,
remain.

ver'blend|en *v/t.* (*no* -ge-, *h*) 🏛
face (*wall, etc.*); *fig.* blind, delude;
2**ung** *f* (-/~-en) 🏛 facing; *fig.*
blindness, delusion.   [faded.]

verblichen *adj.* [fer'blıçən] colour:)

verblüff|en [fer'blyfən] *v/t.* (*no*
-ge-, *h*) amaze; perplex; puzzle;
dumbfound; 2**ung** *f* (-/~-en)
amazement, perplexity.

ver'|blühen *v/i.* (*no* -ge-, *sein*) fade,
wither; ~'**bluten** *v/i.* (*no* -ge-, *sein*)
bleed to death.

ver'borgen *adj.* hidden; secret;
2**heit** *f* (-/*no pl.*) concealment;
secrecy.

Verbot [fer'bo:t] *n* (-[e]s/-e) prohibition; 2**en** *adj.* forbidden, pro-
hibited; *Rauchen* ~ no smoking.

Ver'brauch *m* (-[e]s/~ ~e) consumption (*an dat.* of); 2**en** *v/t.* (*no*
-ge-, *h*) consume, use up; wear out;
~**er** *m* (-s/-) consumer; 2**t** *adj.* air:
stale; *p.* worn out.

ver'brechen 1. *v/t.* (*irr.* brechen,
no -ge-, *h*) commit; *was hat er ver-
brochen?* what is his offen|ce, *Am.*
-se?, what has he done?; **2.** 2 *n*
(-s/-) crime, offen|ce, *Am.* -se.

Ver'brecher *m* (-s/-) criminal;
2**isch** *adj.* criminal; ~**tum** *n* (-s/*no
pl.*) criminality.

ver'breit|en *v/t.* (*no* -ge-, *h*) spread,
diffuse; shed (*light, warmth, happiness*); *sich* ~ spread; *sich* ~ *über*
(*acc.*) enlarge (up)on (*theme*); ~**ern**
v/t. and v/refl. (*no* -ge-, *h*) widen,
broaden; 2**ung** *f* (-/~-en) spread
(-ing), diffusion.

ver'brenn|en (*irr.* brennen, *no* -ge-)
1. *v/i.* (*sein*) burn; **2.** *v/t.* (*h*) burn
(up); cremate (*corpse*); 2**ung** *f*
(-/-en) burning, combustion;
cremation (*of corpse*); *wound*: burn.

ver'bringen *v/t.* (*irr.* bringen, *no*
-ge-, *h*) spend, pass.

verbrüder|n [fer'bry:dərn] *v/refl.*
(*no* -ge-, *h*) fraternize; 2**ung** *f*
(-/-en) fraternization.

ver'|brühen *v/t.* (*no* -ge-, *h*) scald;
sich ~ scald *o.s.*; ~'**buchen** *v/t.*
(*no* -ge-, *h*) book.

Verbum *gr.* ['vɛrbum] *n* (-s/*Verba*)
verb.

verbünden [fer'byndən] *v/refl.* (*no*
-ge-, *h*) ally o.s. (*mit* to, with).

Verbundenheit [fer'bundənhait] *f*
(-/*no pl.*) bonds *pl.*, ties *pl.*; solidarity; affection.

Ver'bündete *m, f* (-n/-n) ally, con-
federate; *die* ~*n pl.* the allies *pl.*

ver'|bürgen *v/t.* (*no* -ge-, *h*) guar-
antee, warrant; *sich* ~ *für* answer
or vouch for; ~'**büßen** *v/t.* (*no* -ge-,
h): *e-e Strafe* ~ serve a sentence,
serve (one's) time.

Verdacht [fer'daxt] *m* (-[e]s/*no pl.*)
suspicion; *in* ~ *haben* suspect.

verdächtig *adj.* [fer'dɛçtɪç] sus-
pected (*gen.* of); *pred.* suspect;
suspicious; ~**en** [~gən] *v/t.* (*no*
-ge-, *h*) suspect *s.o.* (*gen.* of); cast
suspicion on; 2**ung** *f* (-/-en)
suspicion; insinuation.

verdamm|en [fer'damən] *v/t.* (*no*
-ge-, *h*) condemn, damn (*a. eccl.*);
2**nis** *f* (-/*no pl.*) damnation; ~**t
1.** *adj.* damned; F: ~! damn (it)!,
confound it!; **2.** F *adv.*: ~ *kalt*
beastly cold; 2**ung** *f* (-/~-en) condemnation, damnation.

ver'|dampfen (*no* -ge-) *v/t.* (*h*) *and
v/i.* (*sein*) evaporate; ~'**danken** *v/t.*
(*no* -ge-, *h*): *j-m et.* ~ owe s.th. to
s.o.

verdarb [fer'darp] *pret. of* verderben.

verdau|en [fer'dauən] *v/t.* (*no* -ge-,
h) digest; ~**lich** *adj.* digestible;
leicht ~ easy to digest, light; 2**ung**
f (-/*no pl.*) digestion; 2**ungsstö-
rung** *f* indigestion.

Ver'deck *n* (-[e]s/-e) ⚓ deck;

hood (*of carriage, car, etc.*); top (*of vehicle*); 2en *v/t.* (*no -ge-, h*) cover; conceal, hide.

ver'denken *v/t.* (*irr.* denken, *no -ge-, h*): ich kann es ihm nicht ~, daß I cannot blame him for *ger.*

Verderb [fɛr'dɛrp] *m* (-[e]s/*no pl.*) ruin; 2en [~bən] 1. *v/i.* (*irr., no -ge-, sein*) spoil (*a. fig.*); rot; *meat, etc.*: go bad; *fig.* perish; 2. *v/t.* (*irr., no -ge-, h*) spoil; *fig. a.*: corrupt; ruin; er will es mit niemandem ~ he tries to please everybody; sich den Magen ~ upset one's stomach; ~en [~bən] *n* (-s/*no pl.*) ruin; 2lich *adj.* [~pliç] pernicious; *food*: perishable; ~nis [~pnis] *f* (-/~-se) corruption; depravity; 2t *adj.* [~pt] corrupted, depraved.

ver|'deutlichen *v/t.* (*no -ge-, h*) make plain *or* clear; ~'dichten *v/t.* (*no -ge-, h*) condense; sich ~ condense; *suspicion*: grow stronger; ~'dicken *v/t. and v/refl.* (*no -ge-, h*) thicken; ~'dienen *v/t.* (*no -ge-, h*) merit, deserve; earn (*money*).

Ver'dienst (-es/-e) 1. *m* gain, profit; earnings *pl.*; 2. *n* merit; es ist sein ~, daß it is owing to him that; 2voll *adj.* meritorious, deserving; ~spanne † *f* profit margin.

ver|'dient *adj. p.* of merit; (well-) deserved; sich ~ gemacht haben um deserve well of; ~'dolmetschen *v/t.* (*no -ge-, h*) interpret (*a. fig.*); ~'doppeln *v/t. and v/refl.* (*no -ge-, h*) double.

verdorben [fɛr'dɔrbən] 1. *p.p.* of verderben; 2. *adj. meat*: tainted; *stomach*: disordered, upset; *fig.* corrupt, depraved.

ver|'dorren [fɛr'dɔrən] *v/i.* (*no -ge-, sein*) wither (up); ~'drängen *v/t.* (*no -ge-, h*) push away, thrust aside; *fig.* displace; *psych.* repress; ~'drehen *v/t.* (*no -ge-, h*) distort, twist (*both a. fig.*); roll (*eyes*); *fig.* pervert; j-m den Kopf ~ turn s.o.'s head; ~'dreht F *fig. adj.* crazy; ~'dreifachen *v/t. and v/refl.* (*no -ge-, h*) triple.

verdrieß|en [fɛr'dri:sən] *v/t.* (*irr., no -ge-, h*) vex, annoy; ~lich *adj.* vexed, annoyed; sulky; *thing*: annoying.

ver|droß [fɛr'drɔs] *pret.* of verdrießen; ~drossen [~'drɔsən] 1. *p.p.* of verdrießen; 2. *adj.* sulky; listless.

ver'drucken *typ. v/t.* (*no -ge-, h*) misprint.

Verdruß [fɛr'drus] *m* (Verdrusses/~ Verdrusse) vexation, annoyance.

ver'dummen (*no -ge-*) 1. *v/t.* (*h*) make stupid. 2. *v/i.* (*sein*) become stupid.

ver'dunk|eln *v/t.* (*no -ge-, h*) darken, obscure (*both a. fig.*); black out (*window*); sich ~ darken;

2(e)lung *f* (-/~-en) darkening; obscuration; black-out; ᵍᵗᵍ collusion.

ver|'dünnen *v/t.* (*no -ge-, h*) thin; dilute (*liquid*); ~'dunsten *v/i.* (*no -ge-, sein*) volatilize, evaporate; ~'dursten *v/i.* (*no -ge-, sein*) die of thirst; ~dutzt *adj.* [~'dutst] nonplussed.

ver'ed|eln *v/t.* (*no -ge-, h*) ennoble; refine; improve; ᵩ graft; process (*raw materials*); 2(e)lung *f* (-/~-en) refinement; improvement; processing.

ver'ehr|en *v/t.* (*no -ge-, h*) revere, venerate; worship; admire, adore; 2er *m* (-s/-) worship(p)er; admirer, adorer; 2ung *f* (-/~-en) reverence, veneration; worship; adoration.

vereidigen [fɛr'aidigən] *v/t.* (*no -ge-, h*) swear (*witness*); at entrance into office: swear s.o. in.

Verein [fɛr'ain] *m* (-[e]s/-e) union; society, association; club.

ver'einbar *adj.* compatible (*mit* with), consistent (with); ~en *v/t.* (*no -ge-, h*) agree upon; arrange; 2ung *f* (-/-en) agreement, arrangement.

ver'einen *v/t.* (*no -ge-, h*) s. vereinigen.

ver'einfach|en *v/t.* (*no -ge-, h*) simplify; 2ung *f* (-/-en) simplification.

ver'einheitlichen *v/t.* (*no -ge-, h*) unify, standardize.

ver'einig|en *v/t.* (*no -ge-, h*) unite, join; associate; sich ~ unite, join; associate o.s.; 2ung *f* 1. (-/~-en) union; 2. (-/-en) union; society, association.

ver'ein|samen *v/i.* (*no -ge-, sein*) grow lonely *or* solitary; ~zelt *adj.* isolated; sporadic.

ver|'eiteln *v/t.* (*no -ge-, h*) frustrate; ~'ekeln *v/t.* (*no -ge-, h*): er hat mir das Essen verekelt he spoilt my appetite; ~'enden *v/i.* (*no -ge-, sein*) *animals*: die, perish; ~enge(r)n [~'ɛŋə(r)n] *v/t. and v/refl.* (*no -ge-, h*) narrow.

ver'erb|en *v/t.* (*no -ge-, h*) leave, bequeath; *biol.* transmit; sich ~ be hereditary; sich ~ auf (*acc.*) descend (up)on; 2ung *f* (-/~-en) *biol.* transmission; *physiol.* heredity; 2ungslehre *f* genetics.

verewig|en [fɛr'e:vigən] *v/t.* (*no -ge-, h*) perpetuate; ~t *adj.* [~çt] deceased, late.

ver'fahren 1. *v/i.* (*irr.* fahren, *no -ge-, sein*) proceed; ~ mit deal with; 2. *v/t.* (*irr.* fahren, *no -ge-, h*) mismanage, muddle, bungle; sich ~ miss one's way; 3. 2 *n* (-s/-) procedure; proceeding(s *pl.* ᵗᵗᵍ); ⊕ process.

Ver'fall *m* (-[e]s/*no pl.*) decay, decline; dilapidation (*of house, etc.*);

$\frac{z^t}{r}$ forfeiture; expiration; maturity (*of bill of exchange*); 2en 1. *v/i.* (*irr.* fallen, *no* -ge-, sein) decay; *house*: dilapidate; *document, etc.*: expire; *pawn*: become forfeited; *right*: lapse; *bill of exchange*: fall due; *sick person*: waste away; ~ auf (*acc.*) hit upon (*idea, etc.*); ~ in (*acc.*) fall into; j-m ~ become s.o.'s slave; 2. *adj.* ruinous; addicted (*dat.* to drugs, etc.); ~erscheinung [fɛr'fals⁹-] *f* symptom of decline; ~tag *m* day of payment.

ver|'fälschen *v/t.* (*no* -ge-, h) falsify; adulterate (*wine, etc.*); ~fänglich *adj.* [~'fɛnliç] *question*: captious, insidious; risky; embarrassing; ~'färben *v/refl.* (*no* -ge-, h) change colo(u)r.

ver'fass|en *v/t.* (*no* -ge-, h) compose, write; 2er *m* (-s/-) author.

Ver'fassung *f* state, condition; *pol.* constitution; disposition (*of mind*); 2smäßig *adj.* constitutional; 2swidrig *adj.* unconstitutional.

ver|'faulen *v/i.* (*no* -ge-, sein) rot, decay; ~'fechten *v/t.* (*irr.* fechten, *no* -ge-, h) defend, advocate.

ver'fehl|en *v/t.* (*no* -ge-, h) miss; 2ung *f* (-/-en) offen|ce, *Am.* -se.

ver'feind|en [fɛr'faɪndən] *v/t.* (*no* -ge-, h) make enemies of; sich ~ mit make an enemy of; ~feinern [~'faɪnərn] *v/t. and v/refl.* (*no* -ge-, h) refine; ~fertigen [~'fɛrtigən] *v/t.* (*no* -ge-, h) make, manufacture, compose.

ver'film|en *v/t.* (*no* -ge-, h) film, screen; 2ung *f* (-/-en) filmversion.

ver|'finstern *v/t.* (*no* -ge-, h) darken, obscure; sich ~ darken; ~'flachen (*no* -ge-) *v/i.* (sein) and *v/refl.* (h) (become) shallow (*a. fig.*); ~'flechten *v/t.* (*irr.* flechten, *no* -ge-, h) interlace; *fig.* involve; ~'fliegen (*irr.* fliegen, *no* -ge-) 1. *v/i.* (sein) evaporate; *time*: fly; *fig.* vanish; 2. *v/refl.* (h) *bird*: stray; ✈ lose one's bearings, get lost; ~'fließen *v/i.* (*irr.* fließen, *no* -ge-, sein) *colours*: blend; *time*: elapse; ~flossen [~'flɔsən] *time*: past; F ein ~er Freund a late friend, an ex-friend.

ver'fluch|en *v/t.* (*no* -ge-, h) curse, *Am.* F cuss; ~t *adj.* damned; ~! damn (it)!, confound it!

ver|'flüchtigen [fɛr'flyçtigən] *v/t.* (*no* -ge-, h) volatilize; sich ~ evaporate (*a. fig.*); F *fig.* vanish; ~flüssigen [~'flysigən] *v/t. and v/refl.* (*no* -ge-, h) liquefy.

ver'folg|en *v/t.* (*no* -ge-, h) pursue, persecute; follow (*tracks*); trace; *thoughts, dream*: haunt; gerichtlich ~ prosecute; 2er *m* (-s/-) pursuer; persecutor; 2ung *f* (-/-en) pursuit; persecution; pursuance; gericht-

liche ~ prosecution; 2ungswahn ♀ *m* persecution mania.

ver|frachten [fɛr'fraxtən] *v/t.* (*no* -ge-, h) freight, *Am. a.* ship (*goods*); ⚓ ship; F j-n ~ in (*acc.*) bundle s.o. in(to) (*train, etc.*); ~froren *adj.* chilled through; ~früht *adj.* premature.

verfüg|bar *adj.* [fɛr'fy:kbaːr] available; ~en [~gən] (*no* -ge-, h) 1. *v/t.* decree, order; 2. *v/i.*: ~ über (*acc.*) have at one's disposal; dispose of; 2ung [~guŋ] *f* (-/-en) decree, order; disposal; j-m zur ~ stehen (stellen) be (place) at s.o.'s disposal.

ver'führ|en *v/t.* (*no* -ge-, h) seduce; 2er *m* (-s/-) seducer; ~erisch *adj.* seductive; enticing, tempting; 2ung *f* seduction.

vergangen *adj.* [fɛr'gaŋən] gone, past; im ~en Jahr last year; 2heit *f* (-/-en) past; *gr.* past tense.

vergänglich *adj.* [fɛr'gɛnliç] transient, transitory.

vergas|en [fɛr'gaːzən] *v/t.* (*no* -ge-, h) gasify; gas *s.o.*; 2er *mot.* *m* (-s/-) carburet(t)or.

vergaß [fɛr'gaːs] *pret.* of vergessen.

ver'geb|en *v/t.* (*irr.* geben, *no* -ge-, h) give away (*an j-n* to s.o.); confer (on), bestow (on); place (*order*); forgive; sich et. ~ compromise one's dignity; ~ens *adv.* [~s] in vain; ~lich [~pliç] 1. *adj.* vain; 2. *adv.* in vain; 2ung [~buŋ] *f* (-/✎-en) bestowal, conferment (*both*: an *acc.* on); forgiveness, pardon.

vergegenwärtigen [fɛrgeːgənˈvɛrtigən] *v/t.* (*no* -ge-, h) represent; sich et. ~ visualize s.th.

ver'gehen 1. *v/i.* (*irr.* gehen, *no* -ge-, sein) pass (away); fade (away); ~ vor (*dat.*) die of; 2. *v/refl.* (*irr.* gehen, *no* -ge-, h): sich an j-m ~ assault s.o.; violate s.o.; sich gegen das Gesetz ~ offend against or violate the law; 3. 2 *n* (-s/-) offen|ce, *Am.* -se.

ver'gelt|en *v/t.* (*irr.* gelten, *no* -ge-, h) repay, requite; reward; retaliate; 2ung *f* (-/-en) requital; retaliation, retribution.

vergessen [fɛr'gɛsən] 1. *v/t.* (*irr.*, *no* -ge-, h) forget; leave; 2. *p.p.* of 1; 2heit *f* (-/*no pl.*): in ~ geraten sink or fall into oblivion.

vergeßlich *adj.* [fɛr'gɛsliç] forgetful.

vergeud|en [fɛr'gɔydən] *v/t.* (*no* -ge-, h) dissipate, squander, waste (*time, money*); 2ung *f* (-/✎-en) waste.

vergewaltig|en [fɛrgə'valtigən] *v/t.* (*no* -ge-, h) violate; rape; 2ung *f* (-/-en) violation; rape.

ver|gewissern [fɛrgə'wisərn] *v/refl.* (*no* -ge-, h) make sure (e-r Sache of s.th.); ~'gießen v/t. (irr. gießen, no -ge-, h) shed (tears, blood); spill (liquid).

ver'gift|en v/t. (no -ge-, h) poison (a. fig.); sich ~ take poison; 2ung f (-/-en) poisoning.

Vergißmeinnicht ♀ [fɛr'gɪsmaɪn-nɪçt] n (-[e]s/-[e]) forget-me-not.

vergittern [fɛr'gɪtərn] v/t. (no -ge-, h) grate.

Vergleich [fɛr'glaɪç] m (-[e]s/-e) comparison; ♐♐: agreement; compromise, composition; 2bar adj. comparable (mit to); 2en v/t. (irr. gleichen, no -ge-, h) compare (mit with, to); sich ~ mit ♐♐ come to terms with; verglichen mit as against, compared to; 2sweise adv. comparatively.

vergnügen [fɛr'gny:gən] 1. v/t. (no -ge-, h) amuse; sich ~ enjoy o.s.; 2. 2 n (-s/-) pleasure, enjoyment; entertainment; ~ finden an (dat.) take pleasure in; viel ~! have a good time! [gay.]
vergnügt adj. [fɛr'gny:kt] merry,)
Ver'gnügung f (-/-en) pleasure, amusement, entertainment; ~sreise f pleasure-trip, tour; 2ssüchtig adj. pleasure-seeking.

ver'golden [fɛr'gɔldən] v/t. (no -ge-, h) gild; ~göttern fig. [~'gœtərn] v/t. (no -ge-, h) idolize, adore; ~graben v/t. (irr. graben, no -ge-, h) bury (a. fig.); sich ~ bury o.s.; ~greifen v/refl. (irr. greifen, no -ge-, h) sprain (one's hand, etc.); sich ~ an (dat.) lay (violent) hands on, attack, assault; embezzle (money); encroach upon (s.o.'s property); ~griffen adj. [~'grɪfən] goods: sold out; book: out of print.

vergrößer|n [fɛr'grø:sərn] v/t. (no -ge-, h) enlarge (a. phot.); opt. magnify; sich ~ enlarge; 2ung f 1. (-/-en) phot. enlargement; opt. magnification; 2. (-/♐-en) enlargement; increase; extension; 2ungsglas n magnifying glass.

Vergünstigung [fɛr'gynstɪgʊŋ] f (-/-en) privilege.

vergüt|en [fɛr'gy:tən] v/t. (no -ge-, h) compensate (j-m et. s.o. for s.th.); reimburse (money spent); 2ung f (-/-en) compensation; reimbursement.

ver'haft|en v/t. (no -ge-, h) arrest; 2ung f (-/-en) arrest.

ver'halten 1. v/t. (irr. halten, no -ge-, h) keep back; catch or hold (one's breath); suppress, check; sich ~ thing: be; p. behave; sich ruhig ~ keep quiet; 2. 2 n (-s/no pl.) behavio(u)r, conduct.

Verhältnis [fɛr'hɛltnɪs] n (-ses/-se) proportion, rate; relation(s pl.) (zu with); F liaison, love-affair; F mistress; ~se pl. conditions pl., circumstances pl.; means pl.; 2mäßig

adv. in proportion; comparatively; ~wort gr. n (-[e]s/♐er) preposition.

Ver'haltungsmaßregeln f/pl. instructions pl.

ver'hand|eln (no -ge-, h) 1. v/i. negotiate, treat (über acc., wegen for); ♐♐ try (über et. s.th.); 2. v/t. discuss; 2lung f negotiation; discussion; ♐♐ trial, proceedings pl.

ver'häng|en v/t. (no -ge-, h) cover (over), hang; inflict (punishment) (über acc. upon); 2nis n (-ses/-se) fate; ~nisvoll adj. fatal; disastrous.

ver'härmt adj. [fɛr'hɛrmt] careworn; ~harren [~'harən] v/i. (no -ge-, h, sein) persist (auf dat., bei, in dat. in), stick (to); ~'härten v/t. and v/refl. (no -ge-, h) harden; ~haßt adj. [~'hast] hated; hateful, odious; ~'hätscheln v/t. (no -ge-, h) coddle, pamper, spoil; ~'hauen v/t. (irr. hauen, no -ge-, h) thrash.

verheer|en [fɛr'he:rən] v/t. (no -ge-, h) devastate, ravage, lay waste; ~end fig. adj. disastrous; 2ung f (-/-en) devastation.

ver'hehlen [fɛr'he:lən] v/t. (no -ge-, h) s. verheimlichen; ~'heilen v/i. (no -ge-, sein) heal (up).

ver'heimlich|en v/t. (no -ge-, h) hide, conceal; 2ung f (-/♐-en) concealment.

ver'heirat|en v/t. (no -ge-, h) marry (mit to); sich ~ marry; 2ung f (-/♐-en) marriage.

ver'heiß|en v/t. (irr. heißen, no -ge-, h) promise; 2ung f (-/-en) promise; ~ungsvoll adj. promising.

ver'helfen v/t. (irr. helfen, no -ge-, h): j-m zu et. ~ help s.o. to s.th.

ver'herrlich|en v/t. (no -ge-, h) glorify; 2ung f (-/♐-en) glorification.

ver'hetzen v/t. (no -ge-, h) instigate; ~'hexen v/t. (no -ge-, h) bewitch.

ver'hinder|n v/t. (no -ge-, h) prevent; 2ung f (-/♐-en) prevention.

ver'höhn|en v/t. (no -ge-, h) deride, mock (at), taunt; 2ung f (-/-en) derision, mockery.

Verhör ♐♐ [fɛr'hø:r] n (-[e]s/-e) interrogation, questioning (of prisoners, etc.); examination; 2en v/t. (no -ge-, h) examine, hear; interrogate; sich ~ hear it wrong.

ver'hüllen v/t. (no -ge-, h) cover, veil; ~'hungern v/i. (no -ge-, sein) starve; ~'hüten v/t. (no -ge-, h) prevent.

ver'irr|en v/refl. (no -ge-, h) go astray, lose one's way; ~t adj.: ~es Schaf stray sheep; 2ung fig. f (-/-en) aberration; error.

ver'jagen v/t. (no -ge-, h) drive away.

verjähr|en ♐♐ [fɛr'jɛ:rən] v/i. (no -ge-, sein) become prescriptive;

2ung f (-/-en) limitation, (negative) prescription.

verjüngen [fɛr'jyŋən] v/t. (no -ge-, h) make young again, rejuvenate; reduce (scale); sich ~ grow young again, rejuvenate; taper off.

Ver'kauf m sale; 2en v/t. (no -ge-, h) sell; zu ~ for sale; sich gut ~ sell well.

Ver'käuf|er m seller; vendor; shop-assistant, salesman, Am. a. (sales-) clerk; ~erin f (-/-nen) seller; vendor; shop-assistant, saleswoman, shop girl, Am. a. (sales)clerk; 2lich adj. sal(e)able; for sale.

Ver'kaufs|automat m slot-machine, vending machine; ~schlager m best seller.

Verkehr [fɛr'ke:r] m (-[e]s/⚹-e) traffic; transport(ation); communication; correspondence; ⚓, ✈, ✕, etc.: service; commerce, trade; intercourse (a. sexually); aus dem ~ ziehen withdraw from service; withdraw (money) from circulation; 2en (no -ge-, h) 1. v/t. convert (in acc. into), turn (into); 2. v/i. ship, bus, etc.: run, ply (zwischen dat. between); bei j-m ~ go to or visit s.o.'s house; ~ in (dat.) frequent (public house, etc.); ~ mit associate or mix with; have (sexual) intercourse with.

Ver'kehrs|ader f arterial road; ~ampel f traffic lights pl., traffic signal; ~büro n tourist bureau; ~flugzeug n air liner; ~insel f refuge, island; ~minister m minister of transport; ~mittel n (means of) conveyance or transport, Am. transportation; ~polizist m traffic policeman or constable, sl. traffic cop; 2reich adj. congested with traffic, busy; ~schild n traffic sign; ~schutzmann m s. Verkehrspolizist; ~stauung f, ~stockung f traffic block, traffic jam; ~störung f interruption of traffic; ⚹, etc.: breakdown; ~straße f thoroughfare; ~teilnehmer m road user; ~unfall m traffic accident; ~verein m tourist agency; ~verhältnisse pl. traffic conditions pl.; ~vorschrift f traffic regulation; ~wesen n (-s/no pl.) traffic; ~zeichen n traffic sign.

ver'kehrt adj. inverted, upside down; fig. wrong; ~kennen v/t. (irr. kennen, no -ge-, h) mistake; misunderstand; misjudge.

Ver'kettung f (-/-en) concatenation (a. fig.).

ver'|klagen ⚖ v/t. (no -ge-, h) sue (auf acc., wegen for); bring an action against s.o.; ~'kleben v/t. (no -ge-, h) paste s.th. up.

ver'kleid|en v/t. (no -ge-, h) disguise; ⊕: line; face; wainscot; encase; sich ~ disguise o.s.; 2ung f (-/-en) disguise; ⊕: lining; facing; panel(l)ing, wainscot(t)ing.

verkleiner|n [fɛr'klaınərn] v/t. (no -ge-, h) make smaller, reduce, diminish; fig. belittle, derogate; 2ung f (-/-en) reduction, diminution; fig. derogation.

ver'|klingen v/i. (irr. klingen, no -ge-, sein) die away; ~knöchern [~'knœçərn] (no -ge-) 1. v/t. (h) ossify; 2. v/i. (sein) ossify; fig. a. fossilize; ~'knoten v/t. (no -ge-, h) knot; ~'knüpfen v/t. (no -ge-, h) knot or tie (together); fig. connect, combine; ~'kohlen (no -ge-) 1. v/t. (h) carbonize; char; F: j-n ~ pull s.o.'s leg; 2. v/i. (sein) char; ~'kommen 1. v/i. (irr. kommen, no -ge-, sein) decay; p.: go downhill or to the dogs; become demoralized; 2. adj. decayed; depraved; corrupt; ~'korken v/t. (no -ge-, h) cork (up).

ver'körper|n v/t. (no -ge-, h) personify, embody; represent; esp. thea. impersonate; 2ung f (-/-en) personification, embodiment; impersonation.

ver'|krachen F v/refl. (no -ge-, h) fall out (mit with); ~'krampft adj. cramped; ~'kriechen v/refl. (irr. kriechen, no -ge-, h) hide; ~'krümmt adj. crooked; ~'krüppelt adj. [~'krypəlt] crippled; stunted; ~krustet adj. [~'krustət] (en)crusted; caked; ~'kühlen v/refl. (no -ge-, h) catch (a) cold.

ver'kümmer|n v/i. (no -ge-, sein) ♀, ⚹ become stunted; ⚹ atrophy; fig. waste away; ~t adj. stunted; atrophied; rudimentary (a. biol.).

verkünd|en [fɛr'kyndən] v/t. (no -ge-, h), ~igen v/t. (no -ge-, h) announce; publish, proclaim; pronounce (judgement); 2igung f, 2ung f (-/-en) announcement; proclamation; pronouncement.

ver'|kuppeln v/t. (no -ge-, h) ⊕ couple; fig. pander; ~'kürzen v/t. (no -ge-, h) shorten; abridge; beguile (time, etc.); ~'lachen v/t. (no -ge-, h) laugh at; ~'laden v/t. (irr. laden, no -ge-, h) load, ship; ⚑ entrain (esp. troops).

Verlag [fɛr'la:k] m (-[e]s/-e) publishing house, the publishers pl.; im ~ von published by.

ver'lagern v/t. (no -ge-, h) displace, shift; sich ~ shift.

Ver'lags|buchhändler m publisher; ~buchhandlung f publishing house; ~recht n copyright.

ver'langen 1. v/t. (no -ge-, h) demand; require; desire; 2. v/i. (no -ge-, h): ~ nach ask for; long for; 3. 2 n (-s/⚹ -) desire; longing (nach for); demand, request; auf ~ by request, † on demand; auf ~ von at the request of, at s.o.'s request.

verläger|n [fɛr'lɛŋərn] v/t. (no

-ge-, h) lengthen; prolong, extend; 2ung f (-/-en) lengthening; prolongation, extension.

ver'langsamen v/t. (no -ge-, h) slacken, slow down.

ver'lassen v/t. (irr. lassen, no -ge-, h) leave; forsake, abandon, desert; sich ~ auf (acc.) rely on; 2heit f (-/no pl.) abandonment; loneliness.

verläßlich adj. [fer'lesliç] reliable.

Ver'lauf m lapse, course (of time); progress. development (of matter); course (of disease, etc.); im ~ (gen.) or von in the course of; e-n schlimmen ~ nehmen take a bad turn; 2en (irr. laufen, no -ge-) 1. v/i. (sein) time: pass, elapse; matter: take its course; turn out, develop; road, etc.: run, extend; 2. v/refl. (h) lose one's way, go astray; crowd: disperse; water: subside.

ver'lauten v/i. (no -ge-, sein): ~ lassen give to understand, hint; wie verlautet as reported.

ver'leb|en v/t. (no -ge-, h) spend, pass; ~t adj. [~pt] worn out.

ver'leg|en 1. v/t. (no -ge-, h) mislay; transfer, shift, remove; ⊕ lay (cable, etc.); bar (road); put off, postpone; publish (book); sich ~ auf (acc.) apply o.s. to; 2. adj. embarrassed; at a loss (um for answer, etc.); 2enheit f (-/~-en) embarrassment; difficulty; predicament; 2er m (-s/-) publisher; 2ung (-/-en) transfer, removal; ⊕ laying; time: postponement.

ver'leiden v/t. (no -ge-, h) s. verekeln.

ver'leih|en v/t. (irr. leihen, no -ge-, h) lend, Am. a. loan; hire or let out; bestow (right, etc.) (j-m on s.o.); award (price); 2ung f (-/-en) lending, loan; bestowal.

ver|'leiten v/t. (no -ge-, h) mislead; induce; seduce; ꝗꝗ suborn; ~'lernen v/t. (no -ge-, h) unlearn, forget; ~'lesen v/t. (irr. lesen, no -ge-, h) read out; call (names) over; pick (vegetables, etc.); sich ~ read wrong.

verletz|en [fer'letsən] v/t. (no -ge-, h) hurt, injure; fig. a.: offend; violate; ~end adj. offensive; 2te [~tə] m, f (-n/-n) injured person; die ~n pl. the injured pl.; 2ung f (-/-en) hurt, injury, wound; fig. violation.

ver'leugn|en v/t. (no -ge-, h) deny; disown; renounce (belief, principle, etc.); sich ~ lassen have o.s. denied (vor j-m to s.o.); 2ung f (-/-en) denial; renunciation.

verleumd|en [fer'lɔymdən] v/t. (no -ge-, h) slander, defame; ~erisch adj. slanderous; 2ung f (-/-en) slander, defamation, in writing: libel.

ver'lieb|en v/refl. (no -ge-, h): sich ~ in (acc.) fall in love with; ~t adj.

19 SW E II

[~pt] in love (in acc. with); amorous; 2theit f (-/~-en) amorousness.

verlieren [fer'li:rən] (irr., no -ge-, h) 1. v/t. lose; shed (leaves, etc.); sich ~ lose o.s.; disappear; 2. v/i. lose.

ver'lob|en v/t. (no -ge-, h) engage (mit to); sich ~ become engaged; 2te [~ptə] (-n/-n) 1. m fiancé; die ~n pl. the engaged couple sg.; 2. f fiancée; 2ung [~buŋ] f (-/-en) engagement.

ver'lock|en v/t. (no -ge-, h) allure, entice; tempt; ~end adj. tempting; 2ung f (-/-en) allurement, enticement.

verlogen adj. [fer'lo:gən] mendacious; 2heit f (-/~-en) mendacity.

verlor [fer'lo:r] pret. of verlieren; ~en 1. p.p. of verlieren; 2. adj. lost; fig. forlorn; ~e Eier poached eggs; ~engehen v/i. (irr. gehen, sep., -ge-, sein) be lost.

ver'los|en v/t. (no -ge-, h) raffle; 2ung f (-/-en) lottery, raffle.

ver'löten v/t. (no -ge-, h) solder.

Verlust [fer'lust] m (-es/-e) loss; ~e pl. ꝗꝗ casualties pl.

ver'machen v/t. (no -ge-, h) bequeath, leave s.th. (dat. to).

Vermächtnis [fer'meçtnis] n (-ses/-se) will; legacy, bequest.

vermähl|en [fer'me:lən] v/t. (no -ge-, h) marry (mit to); sich ~ (mit) marry (s.o.); 2ung f (-/-en) wedding, marriage.

ver'mehr|en v/t. (no -ge-, h) increase (um by), augment; multiply; add to; durch Zucht ~ propagate; breed; sich ~ increase, augment; multiply (a. biol.); propagate (itself), zo. breed; 2ung f (-/~-en) increase; addition (gen. to); propagation.

ver'meid|en v/t. (irr. meiden, no -ge-, h) avoid; 2ung f (-/~-en) avoidance.

ver|meintlich adj. [fer'maintliç] supposed; ~'mengen v/t. (no -ge-, h) mix, mingle, blend.

Vermerk [fer'merk] m (-[e]s/-e) note, entry; 2en v/t. (no -ge-, h) note down, record.

ver'mess|en 1. v/t. (irr. messen, no -ge-, h) measure; survey (land); 2. adj. presumptuous; 2enheit f (-/~-en) presumption; 2ung f (-/-en) measurement; survey (of land).

ver'miete|n v/t. (no -ge-, h) let, esp. Am. rent; hire (out); ꝗꝗ lease; zu ~ on or for hire; Haus zu ~ house to (be) let; 2r m landlord, ꝗꝗ lessor; letter, hirer.

ver'mindern v/t. (no -ge-, h) diminish, lessen; reduce, cut.

ver'misch|en v/t. (no -ge-, h) mix, mingle, blend; ~t adj. mixed; news, *etc.*: miscellaneous; 2ung *f* (-/⚹ -en) mixture.

ver'mis|sen *v/t.* (*no* -ge-, *h*) miss; ̇ßt *adj.* [̇'mist] missing; 2ßte *m, f* (-*n*/-*n*) missing person; die ̃*n pl.* the missing *pl.*

vermitt|eln [fɛr'mitəln] (*no* -ge-, *h*) 1. *v/t.* mediate (*settlement, peace*); procure, get; give (*impression, etc.*); impart (*knowledge*) (*j-m* to s.o.); 2. *v/i.* mediate (*zwischen dat.* between); intercede (*bei* with, *für* for), intervene; 2ler *m* mediator; go-between; ✝ agent; 2lung *f* (-/-en) mediation; intercession, intervention; *teleph.* (telephone) exchange.

ver'modern *v/i.* (*no* -ge-, *sein*) mo(u)lder, decay, rot.

ver'mögen 1. *v/t.* (*irr.* mögen, *no* -ge-, *h*) ~ *zu inf.* be able to *inf.*; et. ~ *bei j-m* have influence with s.o.; 2. 2 *n* (-*s*/-) ability, power; property; fortune; means *pl.*; ☆ assets *pl.*; ̃d *adj.* wealthy; *pred.* well off; 2sverhältnisse *pl.* pecuniary circumstances *pl.*

vermut|en [fɛr'muːtən] *v/t.* (*no* -ge-, *h*) suppose, presume, *Am. a.* guess; conjecture, surmise; ̇lich 1. *adj.* presumable; 2. *adv.* presumably; I suppose; 2ung *f* (-/-en) supposition, presumption; conjecture, surmise.

vernachlässig|en [fɛr'naːxlɛsigən] *v/t.* (*no* -ge-, *h*) neglect; 2ung *f* (-/⚹ -en) neglect(ing).

ver'narben *v/i.* (*no* -ge-, *sein*) cicatrize, scar over. [with.⟩

ver'narrt *adj.*: ̃ *in* (*acc.*) infatuated⟩

ver'nehm|en *v/t.* (*irr.* nehmen, *no* -ge-, *h*) hear, learn; examine, interrogate; ̇lich *adj.* audible, distinct; 2ung ☆ *f* (-/-en) interrogation, questioning; examination.

ver'neig|en *v/refl.* (*no* -ge-, *h*) bow (*vor dat.* to); 2ung *f* bow.

verein|en [fɛr'naɪnən] (*no* -ge-, *h*) 1. *v/t.* answer in the negative; deny; 2. *v/i.* answer in the negative; ̃end *adj.* negative; 2ung *f* (-/-en) negation; denial; *gr.* negative.

vernicht|en [fɛr'nɪçtən] *v/t.* (*no* -ge-, *h*) annihilate; destroy; dash (*hopes*); ̃end *adj.* destructive (*a. fig.*); *look*: withering; *criticism*: scathing; *defeat, reply*: crushing; 2ung *f* (-/⚹ -en) annihilation; destruction.

ver|nickeln [fɛr'nɪkəln] *v/t.* (*no* -ge-, *h*) nickel(-plate); ̃'nieten *v/t.* (*no* -ge-, *h*) rivet.

Vernunft [fɛr'nʊnft] *f* (-/*no pl.*) reason; ~ *annehmen* listen to *or* hear reason; *j-n zur* ~ *bringen* bring s.o. to reason *or* to his senses.

vernünftig *adj.* [fɛr'nʏnftɪç] rational; reasonable; sensible.

ver'öden (*no* -ge-) 1. *v/t.* (*h*) make

desolate; 2. *v/i.* (*sein*) become desolate.

ver'öffentlich|en *v/t.* (*no* -ge-, *h*) publish; 2ung *f* (-/-en) publication.

ver'ordn|en *v/t.* (*no* -ge-, *h*) decree; order (*a.* ☆); ✝ prescribe (*j-m* to *or* for s.o.); 2ung *f* decree, order; ☆ prescription.

ver'pachten *v/t.* (*no* -ge-, *h*) rent, ☆ lease (*building, land*).

Ver'pächter *m* landlord, ☆ lessor.

ver'pack|en *v/t.* (*no* -ge-, *h*) pack (up); wrap up; 2ung *f* packing (material); wrapping.

ver|'passen *v/t.* (*no* -ge-, *h*) miss (*train, opportunity, etc.*); ̃'patzen F [̃'patsən] *v/t.* (*no* -ge-, *h*) *s.* verpfuschen; ̃'pesten *v/t.* (*no* -ge-, *h*) *fumes*: contaminate (*the air*); ̃'pfänden *v/t.* (*no* -ge-, *h*) pawn, pledge (*a. fig.*); mortgage.

ver'pflanz|en *v/t.* (*no* -ge-, *h*) transplant (*a.* ☆); 2ung *f* transplantation; ☆ *a.* transplant.

ver'pfleg|en *v/t.* (*no* -ge-, *h*) board; supply with food, victual; 2ung *f* (-/⚹ -en) board; food-supply; provisions *pl.*

ver'pflicht|en *v/t.* (*no* -ge-, *h*) oblige; engage; 2ung *f* (-/-en) obligation; duty; ✝, ☆ liability; engagement, commitment.

ver'pfusch|en F *v/t.* (*no* -ge-, *h*) bungle, botch; make a mess of; ̃t *adj. life*: ruined, wrecked.

ver|'pönt *adj.* [fɛr'pøːnt] taboo; ̃'prügeln F *v/t.* (*no* -ge-, *h*) thrash, flog, F wallop; ̃'puffen *fig. v/i.* (*no* -ge-, *sein*) fizzle out.

Ver'putz *m* △ *m* (-es/⚹ -e) plaster; 2en △ *v/t.* (*no* -ge-, *h*) plaster.

ver|'quicken [fɛr'kvikən] *v/t.* (*no* -ge-, *h*) mix up; ̃'quollen *adj. wood*: warped; *face*: bloated; *eyes*: swollen; ̃'rammeln [̃'raməln] *v/t.* (*no* -ge-, *h*) bar(ricade).

Verrat [fɛr'raːt] *m* (-[e]s/*no pl.*) betrayal (*an dat.* of); treachery (to); ☆ treason (to); 2en *v/t.* (*irr.* raten, *no* -ge-, *h*) betray, give s.o. away; give away (*secret*); *sich* ~ betray o.s., give o.s. away.

Ver'räter [fɛr'rɛːtər] *m* (-*s*/-) traitor (*an dat.* to); 2isch *adj.* treacherous; *fig.* telltale.

ver'rechn|en *v/t.* (*no* -ge-, *h*) reckon up; charge; settle; set off (*mit* against); account for; ~ *mit* offset against; *sich* ~ miscalculate, make a mistake (*a. fig.*); *fig.* be mistaken; *sich um e-e Mark* ~ be one mark out; 2ung *f* settlement; clearing; booking *or* charging (*to account*); 2ungsscheck *m* collection-only cheque *or* Am. check.

ver'regnet *adj.* rainy, rain-spoilt.

ver'reis|en *v/i.* (*no* -ge-, *sein*) go on a journey; ̃t *adj.* out of town; (*geschäftlich*) ~ away (on business).

verrenk|en [fɛrˈrɛŋkən] *v/t.* (*no -ge-, h*) 🠶: wrench; dislocate, luxate; *sich et.* ~ 🠶 dislocate *or* luxate s.th.; *sich den Hals* ~ crane one's neck; ⸰ung 🠶 *f* (-/-en) dislocation, luxation.

ver|'richten *v/t.* (*no -ge-, h*) do, perform; execute; *sein Gebet* ~ say one's prayer(s); ~'**riegeln** *v/t.* (*no -ge-, h*) bolt, bar.

verringer|n [fɛrˈrɪŋərn] *v/t.* (*no -ge-, h*) diminish, lessen; reduce, cut; *sich* ~ diminish, lessen; ⸰ung *f* (-/-en) diminution; reduction, cut.

ver|'rosten *v/i.* (*no -ge-, sein*) rust; ~**rotten** [~ˈrɔtən] *v/i.* (*no -ge-, sein*) rot.

ver|'rück|en *v/t.* (*no -ge-, h*) displace, (re)move, shift; ~**t** *adj.* mad, crazy (*both a. fig.:* nach about); *wie* ~ like mad; *j-n* ~ machen drive s.o. mad; ⸰te (-n/-n) **1.** *m* lunatic, madman; **2.** *f* lunatic, madwoman; ⸰theit *f* (-/-en) madness; foolish action; craze.

Ver|'ruf *m* (-[e]s/*no pl.*): *in* ~ bringen bring discredit (up)on; *in* ~ kommen get into discredit; ⸰en *adj.* ill-reputed, ill-famed.

ver|'rutsch|en *v/i.* (*no -ge-, sein*) slip; ~**t** *adj.* not straight.

Vers [fɛrs] *m* (-es/-e) verse.

ver|'sagen 1. *v/t.* (*no -ge-, h*) refuse, deny (*j-m et.* s.o. s.th.); *sich et.* ~ deny o.s. s.th.; **2.** *v/i.* (*no -ge-, h*) fail, break down; *gun:* misfire; **3.** ⸰n *n* (-s/*no pl.*) failure.   [ure.\

Ver|'sager *m* (-s/-) misfire; *p.* fail-\

ver|'salzen *v/t.* [*irr.* salzen,] *no -ge-, h*) oversalt; F *fig.* spoil.

ver|'samm|eln *v/t.* (*no -ge-, h*) assemble; *sich* ~ assemble, meet; ⸰lung *f* assembly, meeting.

Versand [fɛrˈzant] *m* (-[e]s/*no pl.*) dispatch, Am. *a.* shipment; mailing; ~ *ins Ausland a.* export(ation); ~**abteilung** *f* forwarding department; ~**geschäft** *n*, ~**haus** *n* mailorder business *or* firm *or* house.

ver|'säum|en *v/t.* (*no -ge-, h*) neglect (*one's duty, etc.*); miss (*opportunity, etc.*); lose (*time*); ~ *zu inf.* fail *or* omit to *inf.*; ⸰nis *n* (-ses/-se) neglect, omission, failure.

ver|'schachern F *v/t.* (*no -ge-, h*) barter (away); ~'**schaffen** *v/t.* (*no -ge-, h*) procure, get; *sich* ~ obtain, get; raise (*money*); *sich Respekt* ~ make o.s. respected; ~'**schämt** *adj.* bashful; ~'**schanzen** *v/refl.* (*no -ge-, h*) entrench o.s.; *sich* ~ hinter (*dat.*) (take) shelter behind; ~'**schärfen** *v/t.* (*no -ge-, h*) heighten, intensify; aggravate; *sich* ~ get worse; ~'**scheiden** *v/i.* (*irr.* scheiden, *no -ge-, sein*) pass away; ~'**schenken** *v/t.* (*no -ge-, h*) give *s.th.* away; make a present of; ~'**scherzen** *v/t. and v/refl.* (*no*

-ge-, h) forfeit; ~'**scheuchen** *v/t.* (*no -ge-, h*) frighten *or* scare away; *fig.* banish; ~'**schicken** *v/t.* (*no -ge-, h*) send (away), dispatch, forward.

ver|'schieb|en *v/t.* (*irr.* schieben, *no -ge-, h*) displace, shift, (re)move; 🚂 shunt; put off, postpone; F *fig.* 🠶 sell underhand; *sich* ~ shift; ⸰ung *f* shift(ing); postponement.

verschieden *adj.* [fɛrˈʃiːdən] different (*von* from); dissimilar, unlike; *aus* ~en Gründen for various *or* several reasons; Verschiedenes various things *pl.*, *esp.* 🠶 sundries *pl.*; ~**artig** *adj.* of a different kind, various; ⸰heit *f* (-/-en) difference; diversity, variety; ~**tlich** *adv.* repeatedly; at times.

ver|'schiff|en *v/t.* (*no -ge-, h*) ship; ⸰ung *f* (-/-🠶-en) shipment.

ver|'schimmeln *v/i.* (*no -ge-, sein*) get mo(u)ldy, Am. mo(u)ld; ~'**schlafen 1.** *v/t.* (*irr.* schlafen, *no -ge-, h*) miss by sleeping; sleep (*afternoon, etc.*) away; sleep off (*headache, etc.*); **2.** *v/i.* (*irr.* schlafen, *no -ge-, h*) oversleep (o.s.); **3.** *adj.* sleepy, drowsy.

Ver|'schlag *m* shed; box; crate; ⸰en [~ɡən] **1.** *v/t.* (*irr.* schlagen, *no -ge-, h*) board up; nail up; es verschlug ihm die Sprache it made him dumb(-)founded him; **2.** *adj.* cunning; *eyes:* a. shifty; ~**enheit** *f* (-/*no pl.*) cunning.

verschlechter|n [fɛrˈʃlɛçtərn] *v/t.* (*no -ge-, h*) deteriorate, make worse; *sich* ~ deteriorate, get worse; ⸰ung *f* (-/-🠶-en) deterioration; change for the worse.

ver|'schleiern *v/t.* (*no -ge-, h*) veil (*a. fig.*).

Verschleiß [fɛrˈʃlaɪs] *m* (-es/🠶-e) wear (and tear); ⸰en *v/t.* [(irr.,) *no -ge-, h*) wear out.

ver|'schleppen *v/t.* (*no -ge-, h*) carry off; *pol.* displace (*person*); abduct, kidnap; delay, protract; neglect (*disease*); ~'**schleudern** *v/t.* (*no -ge-, h*) dissipate, waste; 🠶 sell at a loss, sell dirt-cheap; ~'**schließen** *v/t.* (*irr.* schließen, *no -ge-, h*) shut, close; lock (*door*); lock up (*house*).

verschlimmern [fɛrˈʃlɪmərn] *v/t.* (*no -ge-, h*) make worse, aggravate; • *sich* ~ get worse.

ver|'schlingen *v/t.* (*irr.* schlingen, *no -ge-, h*) devour; wolf (down) (*one's food*); intertwine, entwine, interlace); *sich* ~ intertwine, entwine, interlace.

verschli|ß [fɛrˈʃlɪs] *pret.* of verschleißen; ~**ssen** [~sən] *p.p.* of verschleißen.

verschlossen *adj.* [fɛrˈʃlɔsən] closed, shut; *fig.* reserved; ⸰heit *f* (-/*no pl.*) reserve.

ver'schlucken v/t. (no -ge-, h) swallow (up); sich ~ swallow the wrong way.

Ver'schluß m lock; clasp; lid; plug; stopper (of bottle); seal; fastener, fastening; phot. shutter; unter ~ under lock and key.

ver|'schmachten v/i. (no -ge-, sein) languish, pine away; vor Durst ~ die or be dying of thirst, be parched with thirst; ~'schmähen v/t. (no -ge-, h) disdain, scorn.

ver'schmelz|en (irr. schmelzen, no -ge-) v/t. (h) and v/i. (sein) melt, fuse (a. fig.); blend; fig.: amalgamate; merge (mit in, into); 2ung f (-/~-en) fusion; ♥ merger; fig. amalgamation.

ver|'schmerzen v/t. (no -ge-, h) get over (the loss of); ~'schmieren v/t. (no -ge-, h) smear (over); blur; ~schmitzt adj. [~'ʃmɪtst] cunning; roguish; arch; ~'schmutzen (no -ge-) 1. v/t. (h) soil, dirty; pollute (water); 2. v/i. (sein) get dirty; ~'schnaufen F v/i. and v/refl. (no -ge-, h) stop for breath; ~'schneiden v/t. (irr. schneiden, no -ge-, h) cut badly; blend (wine, etc.); geld, castrate; ~'schneit adj. covered with snow; mountains: a. snow-capped; roofs: a. snow-covered.

Ver'schnitt m (-[e]s/no pl.) blend.

ver'schnupf|en F fig. v/t. (no -ge-, h) nettle, pique; ~t ⊹ adj.: ~ sein have a cold.

ver|'schnüren v/t. (no -ge-, h) tie up, cord; ~schollen adj. [~'ʃɔlən] not heard of again; missing; ⊹⊹ presumed dead; ~'schonen v/t. (no -ge-, h) spare; j-n mit et. ~ spare s.o. s.th.

verschöne(r)n [fɛr'ʃøːnə(r)n] v/t. (no -ge-, h) embellish, beautify; 2ung f (-/-en) embellishment.

ver|schossen adj. [fɛr'ʃɔsən] colour: faded; F ~ sein in (acc.) be madly in love with; ~schränken [~'ʃrɛŋkən] v/t. (no -ge-, h) cross, fold (one's arms).

ver'schreib|en v/t. (irr. schreiben, no -ge-, h) use up (in writing); ⊹ prescribe (j-m for s.o.); ⊹⊹ assign (j-m to s.o.); sich ~ make a slip of the pen; sich e-r Sache ~ devote o.s. to s.th.; 2ung f (-/-en) assignment; prescription.

ver|schroben adj. [fɛr'ʃroːbən] eccentric, queer, odd; ~'schrotten v/t. (no -ge-, h) scrap; ~schüchtert adj. [~'ʃʏçtərt] intimidated.

ver'schulden 1. v/t. (no -ge-, h) be guilty of; be the cause of; 2. 2 n (-s/no pl.) fault.

ver|'schuldet adj. indebted, in debt; ~'schütten v/t. (no -ge-, h) spill (liquid); block (up) (road); bury s.o. alive; ~schwägert adj. [~'ʃvɛːgərt] related by marriage;

~'schweigen v/t. (irr. schweigen, no -ge-, h) conceal (j-m et. s.th. from s.o.).

verschwend|en [fɛr'ʃvɛndən] v/t. (no -ge-, h) waste, squander (an acc. on); lavish (on); 2er m (-s/-) spendthrift, prodigal; ~erisch adj. prodigal, lavish (both: mit of); wasteful; 2ung f (-/~-en) waste; extravagance.

verschwiegen adj. [fɛr'ʃviːgən] discreet; place: secret, secluded; 2heit f (-/no pl.) discretion, secrecy.

ver|'schwimmen v/i. (irr. schwimmen, no -ge-, sein) become indistinct or blurred; ~'schwinden v/i. (irr. schwinden, no -ge-, sein) disappear, vanish; F verschwinde! go away!, sl. beat it!; 2'schwinden n (-s/no pl.) disappearance; ~schwommen adj. [~'ʃvɔmən] vague (a. fig.); blurred; fig. woolly.

ver'schwör|en v/refl. (irr. schwören, no -ge-, h) conspire; 2er m (-s/-) conspirator; 2ung f (-/-en) conspiracy, plot.

ver'seh|en 1. v/t. (irr. sehen, no -ge-, h) fill (an office); look after (house, etc.); mit et. ~ furnish or supply with; sich ~ make a mistake; ehe man sich's versieht all of a sudden; 2. 2 n (-s/-) oversight, mistake, slip; aus ~ = ~tlich adv. by mistake; inadvertently.

Versehrte [fɛr'zeːrtə] m (-n/-n) disabled person.

ver'send|en v/t. ([irr. senden,] no -ge-, h) send, dispatch, forward, Am. ship; by water: ship; ins Ausland ~ a. export; 2ung f (-/~-en) dispatch, shipment, forwarding.

ver|'sengen v/t. (no -ge-, h) singe, scorch; ~'senken v/t. (no -ge-, h) sink; sich ~ in (acc.) immerse o.s. in; ~sessen adj. [~'zɛsən]: ~ auf (acc.) bent on, mad after.

ver'setz|en v/t. (no -ge-, h) displace, remove; transfer (officer); at school: remove, move up, Am. promote; transplant (tree, etc.); pawn, pledge; F fig. stand (lover, etc.) up; ~ in (acc.) put or place into (situation, condition); j-m e-n Schlag ~ give or deal s.o. a blow; in Angst ~ frighten or terrify s.o.; in den Ruhestand ~ pension s.o. off, retire s.o.; versetzt werden be transferred; at school: go up; ~ Sie sich in m-e Lage put or place yourself in my position; Wein mit Wasser ~ mix wine with water, add water to wine; et. ~ reply s.th.; 2ung f (-/-en) removal; transfer; at school: remove, Am. promotion.

ver'seuch|en v/t. (no -ge-, h) infect; contaminate; 2ung f (-/~-en) infection; contamination.

ver'sicher|n v/t. (no -ge-, h) assure

(*a. one's life*); protest, affirm; insure (*one's property or life*); **sich ~** insure *or* assure o.s.; **sich ~ (, daß)** make sure (that); **2te** *m, f* (*-n/-n*) **insurant,** the insured *or* assured, policy-holder; **2ung** *f* assurance, affirmation; insurance; (life-)assurance; insurance company.

Ver'sicherungs|gesellschaft *f* insurance company; **~police** *f,* **~schein** *m* policy of assurance, insurance policy.

ver'|sickern *v/i.* (*no -ge-, sein*) trickle away; **~'siegeln** *v/t.* (*no -ge-, h*) seal (up); **~'siegen** *v/i.* (*no -ge-, sein*) dry up, run dry; **~'silbern** *v/t.* (*no -ge-, h*) silver; F *fig.* realize, convert into cash; **~-'sinken** *v/i.* (*irr. sinken, no -ge-, sein*) sink; *s. versunken;* **~'sinnbildlichen** *v/t.* (*no -ge-, h*) symbolize.

Version [vɛr'zjoːn] *f* (*-/-en*) version.
'Versmaß *n* met|re, *Am.* -er.

versöhn|en [fɛr'zøːnən] *v/t.* (*no -ge-, h*) reconcile (*mit* to, with); **sich** (*wieder*) **~** become reconciled; **~lich** *adj.* conciliatory; **2ung** *f* (*-/-en*) reconciliation.

ver'sorg|en *v/t.* (*no -ge-, h*) provide (*mit* with), supply (with); take care of, look after; **~t** *adj.* [**~kt**] provided for; **2ung** [**~gun**] *f* (*-/-en*) providing (*mit* with), supplying (with); supply, provision.

ver'spät|en *v/refl.* (*no -ge-, h*) be late; **~et** *adj.* belated, late, *Am.* tardy; **2ung** *f* (*-/-en*) lateness, *Am.* tardiness; **~ haben** be late; **mit 2 Stunden ~** two hours behind schedule.

ver'|speisen *v/t.* (*no -ge-, h*) eat (up); **~'sperren** *v/t.* (*no -ge-, h*) lock (up); bar, block (up), obstruct (*a. view*); **~'spielen** *v/t.* (*no -ge-, h*) at cards, *etc.*: lose (*money*); **~'spielt** *adj.* playful; **~'spotten** *v/t.* (*no -ge-, h*) scoff at, mock (at), deride, ridicule; **~'sprechen** *v/t.* (*irr. sprechen, no -ge-, h*) promise; **sich ~** make a mistake in speaking; **sich viel ~ von** expect much of; **2'sprechen** *n* (*-s/% -*) promise; **~'sprühen** *v/t.* (*no -ge-, h*) spray; **~'spüren** *v/t.* (*no -ge-, h*) feel, perceive, be conscious of.

ver'staatlich|en *v/t.* (*no -ge-, h*) nationalize; **2ung** *f* (*-/% -en*) nationalization.

Verstand [fɛr'ʃtant] *m* (*-[e]s/no pl.*) understanding; intelligence, intellect, brains *pl.*; mind, wits *pl.*; reason; (common) sense.

Verstandes|kraft [fɛr'ʃtandəs-] *f* intellectual power *or* faculty; **2-mäßig** *adj.* rational; intellectual; **~mensch** *m* matter-of-fact person.

verständ|ig *adj.* [fɛr'ʃtɛndɪç] intelligent; reasonable, sensible; judi-

cious; **~igen** [**~gən**] *v/t.* (*no -ge-, h*) inform (*von* of), notify (of); **sich mit j-m ~** make o.s. understood to s.o.; come to an understanding with s.o.; **2igung** [**~gun**] *f* (*-/% -en*) information; understanding, agreement; *teleph.* communication; **~lich** *adj.* [**~tlɪç**] intelligible; understandable; *j-m et.* **~ machen** make s.th. clear to s.o.; **sich ~ machen** make o.s. understood.

Verständnis [fɛr'ʃtɛntnɪs] *n* (*-ses/% -se*) comprehension, understanding; insight; appreciation (*für* of); **~ haben für** appreciate; **2los** *adj.* uncomprehending; *look, etc.*: blank; unappreciative; **2voll** *adj.* understanding; appreciative; sympathetic; *look:* knowing.

ver'stärk|en *v/t.* (*no -ge-, h*) strengthen, reinforce (*a.* ⊕, ✂); amplify (*radio signals, etc.*); intensify; **2er** *m* (*-s/-*) *in radio, etc.*: amplifier; **2ung** *f* (*-/% -en*) strengthening, reinforcement (*a.* ✂); amplification; intensification.

ver'staub|en *v/i.* (*no -ge-, sein*) get dusty; **~t** *adj.* [**~pt**] dusty.

ver'stauch|en ✗ *v/t.* (*no -ge-, h*) sprain; **sich den Fuß ~** sprain one's foot; **2ung** ✗ *f* (*-/-en*) sprain.

ver'stauen *v/t.* (*no -ge-, h*) stow away.

Versteck [fɛr'ʃtɛk] *n* (*-[e]s/-e*) hiding-place; *for gangsters, etc.: Am.* F *a.* hide-out; **~ spielen** play at hide-and-seek; **2en** *v/t.* (*no -ge-, h*) hide, conceal; **sich ~** hide.

ver'stehen *v/t.* (*irr. stehen, no -ge-, h*) understand, see, F grasp; comprehend; realize; know (*language*); **es ~ zu** *inf.* know how to *inf.*; **Spaß ~** take a joke; **zu ~ geben** intimate; **~ Sie?** do you see?; **ich ~!** I see!; **verstanden?** (do you) understand?, F (do you) get me?; **falsch ~** misunderstand; **~ Sie mich recht!** don't misunderstand me!; **was ~ Sie unter** (*dat.*)**?** what do you mean *or* understand by ...?; **er versteht et. davon** he knows a thing or two about it; **sich ~ understand** one another; **sich ~ auf** (*acc.*) know well, be an expert at *or* in; **sich mit j-m gut ~** get on well with s.o.; **es versteht sich von selbst** it goes without saying.

ver'steifen *v/t.* (*no -ge-, h*) ⊕ strut, brace; stiffen; **sich ~** stiffen; **sich ~ auf** (*acc.*) make a point of, insist on.

ver'steiger|n *v/t.* (*no -ge-, h*) (sell by *or Am.* at) auction; **2ung** *f* (sale by *or Am.* at) auction, auction-sale.

ver'steinern (*no -ge-*) *v/t.* (*h*) *and* *v/i.* (*sein*) turn into stone, petrify (*both a. fig.*).

ver'stell|bar *adj.* adjustable; **~en** *v/t.* (*no -ge-, h*) shift; adjust; disarrange; bar, block (up), obstruct; disguise (voice, etc.); sich ~ play or act a part; dissemble, feign; 2ung f (-/%-en) disguise; dissimulation.

ver'|steuern v/t. (no -ge-, h) pay duty or tax on; ~stiegen fig. adj. [~'ſti:gən] eccentric.

ver'stimm|en v/t. (no -ge-, h) put out of tune; fig. put out of humo(u)r; ~t adj. out of tune; fig. out of humo(u)r, F cross; 2ung f ill humo(u)r; disagreement; ill feeling.

ver'stockt adj. stubborn, obdurate; 2heit f (-/no pl.) obduracy.

verstohlen adj. [fɛr'ſto:lən] furtive.

ver'stopf|en v/t. (no -ge-, h) stop (up); clog, block (up), obstruct; jam, block (passage, street); ♂ constipate; 2ung ♂ f (-/%-en) constipation.

verstorben adj. [fɛr'ſtɔrbən] late, deceased; 2e m, f (-n/-n) the deceased, Am. ⅔ a. decedent; die ~n pl. the deceased pl., the departed pl.

ver'stört adj. scared; distracted, bewildered; 2heit f (-/no pl.) distraction, bewilderment.

Ver'stoß m offen|ce, Am. -se; contravention (gegen of law); infringement (on trade name, etc.); blunder; 2en (irr. stoßen, no -ge-, h) 1. v/t. expel (aus from); repudiate, disown (wife, child, etc.); 2. v/i.: ~ gegen offend against; contravene (law); infringe (rule, etc.).

ver'|streichen (irr. streichen, no -ge-) 1. v/i. (sein) time: pass, elapse; expire; 2. v/t. (h) spread (butter, etc.); ~'streuen v/t. (no -ge-, h) scatter.

verstümmel|n [fɛr'ſtyməln] v/t. (no -ge-, h) mutilate; garble (text, etc.); 2ung f (-/-en) mutilation.

ver'stummen v/i. (no -ge-, sein) grow silent or dumb.

Verstümmlung [fɛr'ſtymluŋ] f (-/-en) mutilation.

Versuch [fɛr'zu:x] m (-[e]s/-e) attempt, trial; phys., etc.: experiment; e-n ~ machen mit give s.o. or s.th. a trial; try one's hand at s.th., have a go at s.th.; 2en v/t. (no -ge-, h) try, attempt; taste; j-n ~ tempt s.o.; es ~ mit give s.o. or s.th. a trial.

Ver'suchs|anstalt f research institute; ~kaninchen fig. n guinea-pig; 2weise adv. by way of trial or (an) experiment; on trial; ~zweck m: zu ~en pl. for experimental purposes pl.

Ver'suchung f (-/-en) temptation; j-n in ~ bringen tempt s.o.; in ~ sein be tempted.

ver'|sündigen v/refl. (no -ge-, h) sin (an dat. against); ~sunken fig. adj. [~'zuŋkən]: ~ in (acc.) absorbed

or lost in; ~'süßen v/t. (no -ge-, h) sweeten.

ver'tag|en v/t. (no -ge-, h) adjourn; parl. prorogue; sich ~ adjourn, Am. a. recess; 2ung f adjournment; parl. prorogation.

ver'tauschen v/t. (no -ge-, h) exchange (mit for).

verteidig|en [fɛr'taɪdɪgən] v/t. (no -ge-, h) defend; sich ~ defend o.s.; 2er m (-s/-) defender; ⅔ fig. advocate; ⅔ counsel for the defen|ce, Am. -se, Am. attorney for the defendant or defense; football: fullback; 2ung f (-/%-en) defen|ce, Am. -se.

Ver'teidigungs|bündnis n defensive alliance; ~minister m minister of defence; Brt. Minister of Defence, Am. Secretary of Defense; ~ministerium n ministry of defence; Brt. Ministry of Defence, Am. Department of Defense.

ver'teil|en v/t. (no -ge-, h) distribute; spread (colour, etc.); 2er m (-s/-) distributor; 2ung f (-/%-en) distribution.

ver'teuern v/t. (no -ge-, h) raise or increase the price of.

ver'tief|en v/t. (no -ge-, h) deepen (a. fig.); sich ~ deepen; sich ~ in (acc.) plunge in(to); become absorbed in; 2ung f (-/-en) hollow, cavity; recess.

vertikal adj. [vɛrti'ka:l] vertical.

ver'tilg|en v/t. (no -ge-, h) exterminate; F consume, eat (up) (food); 2ung f (-/%-en) extermination.

ver'tonen ♪ v/t. (no -ge-, h) set to music.

Vertrag [fɛr'tra:k] m (-[e]s/-⁼e) agreement, contract; pol. treaty; 2en [~gən] v/t. (irr. tragen, no -ge-, h) endure, bear, stand; diese Speise kann ich nicht ~ this food does not agree with me; sich ~ things: be compatible or consistent; colours: harmonize; p.: agree; get on with one another; sich wieder ~ be reconciled, make it up; 2lich [~kliç] 1. adj. contractual, stipulated; 2. adv. as stipulated; ~ verpflichtet sein be bound by contract; sich ~ verpflichten contract (zu for s.th.; zu inf. to inf.).

verträglich adj. [fɛr'trɛ:kliç] sociable.

Ver'trags|bruch m breach of contract; 2brüchig adj.: ~ werden commit a breach of contract; ~entwurf m draft agreement; ~partner m party to a contract.

ver'trauen 1. v/i. (no -ge-, h) trust (j-m s.o.); ~ auf (acc.) trust or confide in; 2. 2 n (-s/no pl.) confidence, trust; im ~ confidentially, between you and me; ~erweckend adj. inspiring confidence; promising.

Ver'trauens|bruch m breach or

betrayal of trust; **~frage** *parl. f:* die **~ stellen** put the question of confidence; **~mann** *m* (-[e]s/⁼er, Vertrauensleute) spokesman; shop-steward; confidential agent; **~sache** *f: das ist ~* that is a matter of confidence; **~stellung** *f* position of trust; **2voll** *adj.* trustful, trusting; **~votum** *parl. n* vote of confidence; **2würdig** *adj.* trustworthy, reliable.

ver'traulich *adj.* confidential, in confidence; intimate, familiar; **2keit** *f* (-/-en) confidence; intimacy, familiarity.

ver'traut *adj.* intimate, familiar; **2e** (-n/-n) **1.** *m* confidant, intimate friend; **2.** *f* confidante, intimate friend; **2heit** *f* (-/⁑-en) familiarity.

ver'treib|en *v/t.* (irr. treiben, no -ge-, h) drive away; expel (*aus from*); turn out; ✝ sell, distribute (*goods*); *sich die Zeit ~* pass one's time, kill time; **2ung** *f* (-/⁑-en) expulsion.

ver'tret|en *v/t.* (irr. treten, no -ge-, h) represent (*s.o., firm, etc.*); substitute for *s.o.*; attend to, look after (*s.o.'s interests*); hold (*view*); *parl.* sit for (*borough*); answer for *s.th.*; *j-s Sache ~* ⁛⁛ plead s.o.'s case *or* cause; *sich den Fuß ~* sprain one's foot; *F sich die Beine ~* stretch one's legs; **2er** *m* (-s/-) representative; ✝ *a.* agent; proxy, agent; substitute, deputy; exponent; (sales) representative; door-to-door salesman; commercial travel(l)er, *esp. Am.* travel(l)ing salesman; **2ung** *f* (-/-en) representation (*a. pol.*); ✝ agency; *in office:* substitution; *in ~ by proxy; in ~:* acting for.

Vertrieb ✝ [fer'tri:p] *m* (-[e]s/-e) sale; distribution; **~ene** [~bənə] *m,f* (-n/-n) expellee.

ver'trocknen *v/i.* (no -ge-, sein) dry up; **~'trödeln** F *v/t.* (no -ge-, h) dawdle away, waste (*time*); **~'trösten** *v/t.* (no -ge-, h) put off; **~'tuschen** F *v/t.* (no -ge-, h) hush up; **~'übeln** *v/t.* (no -ge-, h) take *s.th.* amiss; **~'üben** *v/t.* (no -ge-, h) commit, perpetrate.

ver'unglück|en *v/i.* (no -ge-, sein) meet with *or* have an accident; F *fig.* fail, go wrong; *tödlich ~* be killed in an accident; **2te** *m,f* (-n/-n) casualty.

verun|reinigen [fer'unrainigən] *v/t.* (no -ge-, h) soil, dirty; defile; contaminate (*air*); pollute (*water*); **~stalten** [~ʃtaltən] *v/t.* (no -ge-, h) disfigure.

ver'untreu|en *v/t.* (no -ge-, h) embezzle; **2ung** *f* (-/-en) embezzlement.

ver'ursachen *v/t.* (no -ge-, h) cause.

ver'urteil|en *v/t.* (no -ge-, h) condemn (*zu* to) (*a. fig.*), sentence (to);

convict (*wegen* of); **2te** *m, f* (-n/-n) convict; **2ung** *f* (-/-en) condemnation (*a. fig.*), conviction.

ver|vielfältigen [fer'fi:lfɛltigən] *v/t.* (no -ge-, h) manifold; **~vollkommnen** [~'fɔlkɔmnən] *v/t.* (no -ge-, h) perfect; *sich ~* perfect o.s.

vervollständig|en [fer'fɔlʃtɛndigən] *v/t.* (no -ge-, h) complete; **2ung** *f* (-/⁑-en) completion.

ver|'wachsen **1.** *v/i.* (irr. wachsen, no -ge-, sein): *miteinander ~* grow together; **2.** *adj.* deformed; ✠ humpbacked, hunchbacked; **~'wackeln** *phot.* *v/t.* (no -ge-, h) blur.

ver'wahr|en *v/t.* (no -ge-, h) keep; *sich ~ gegen* protest against; **~lost** *adj.* [~lo:st] child, garden, *etc.*: uncared-for, neglected; degenerate; **2ung** *f* keeping; charge; custody; *fig.* protest; *j-m et. in ~ geben* give s.th. into s.o.'s charge; *in ~ nehmen* take charge of.

verwaist *adj.* [fer'vaist] orphan(ed); *fig.* deserted.

ver'walt|en *v/t.* (no -ge-, h) administer, manage; **2er** *m* (-s/-) administrator, manager; steward (*of estate*); **2ung** *f* (-/-en) administration; management.

ver'wand|eln *v/t.* (no -ge-, h) change, turn, transform; *sich ~* change (*all: in acc.* into); **2lung** *f* (-/-en) change; transformation.

verwandt *adj.* [fer'vant] related (*mit* to); languages, tribes, *etc.*: kindred; languages, sciences: cognate (with); *pred.* akin (to) (*a. fig.*); **2e** *m, f* (-n/-n) relative, relation; **2schaft** *f* (-/-en) relationship; relations *pl.*; *geistige ~* congeniality.

ver'warn|en *v/t.* (no -ge-, h) caution; **2ung** *f* caution.

ver'wässern *v/t.* (no -ge-, h) water (down), dilute; *fig.* water down, dilute.

ver'wechs|eln *v/t.* (no -ge-, h) mistake (*mit* for); confound, mix up, confuse (*all: mit* with); **2(e)lung** *f* (-/-en) mistake; confusion.

verwegen *adj.* [fer've:gən] daring, bold, audacious; **2heit** *f* (-/⁑-en) boldness, audacity, daring.

ver|'wehren *v/t.* (no -ge-, h): *j-m et. ~* (de)bar s.o. from (doing) s.th.; *den Zutritt ~* deny *or* refuse admittance (*zu* to); **~'weichlicht** *adj.* effeminate, soft.

ver'weiger|n *v/t.* (no -ge-, h) deny, refuse; disobey (*order*); **2ung** *f* denial, refusal.

ver'weilen *v/i.* (no -ge-, h) stay, linger; *bei et. ~* dwell (up)on s.th.

Verweis [fer'vais] *m* (-es/-e) reprimand; rebuke, reproof; reference (*auf acc.* to); **2en** [~zən] *v/t.* (irr. weisen, no -ge-, h): *j-n des Landes ~* expel s.o. from Germany, *etc.*;

j-m et. ~ reprimand s.o. for s.th.;
j-n ~ *auf (acc.)* or *an (acc.)* refer s.o.
to.

ver'welken *v/i. (no -ge-, sein)* fade,
wither (up).

ver'wend|en *v/t.* ([*irr.* wenden,] *no*
-ge-, h) employ, use; apply *(für*
for); spend *(time, etc.) (auf acc.*
on); *sich bei j-m ~ für* intercede
with s.o. for; 2ung *f (-/~-en)* use,
employment; application; *keine ~*
haben für have no use for.

ver'werf|en *v/t. (irr.* werfen, *no*
-ge-, h) reject; ⅜ quash *(verdict)*;
~lich *adj.* abominable.

ver'werten *v/t. (no -ge-, h)* turn to
account, utilize.

verwes|en *[fɛr'veːzən] v/i. (no -ge-,*
sein) rot, decay; 2ung *f (-/~-en)*
decay.

ver'wick|eln *v/t. (no -ge-, h)* entan-
gle *(in acc.* in); *sich ~* entangle o.s.
(in) *(a. fig.);* ~elt *fig. adj.* complicated; 2(e)lung *f (-/-en)* entanglement; *fig. a.* complication.

ver'wilder|n *v/i. (no -ge-, sein)* run
wild; ~t *adj. garden, etc.:* uncculti-
vated, weed-grown; *fig.* wild, unruly.

ver'winden *v/t. (irr.* winden, *no*
-ge-, h) get over *s.th.*

ver'wirklich|en *v/t. (no -ge-, h)*
realize; *sich ~* be realized, *esp. Am.*
materialize; come true; 2ung *f*
(-/~-en) realization.

ver'wirr|en *v/t. (no -ge-, h)* entan-
gle; *j-n ~* confuse s.o.; embarrass
s.o.; ~t *fig. adj.* confused; embarrassed; 2ung *fig. f (-/-en)* confusion.

ver'wischen *v/t. (no -ge-, h)* wipe or
blot out; efface *(a. fig.);* blur,
obscure; cover up *(one's tracks).*

ver'witter|n *geol. v/i. (no -ge-, sein)*
weather; ~t *adj. geol.* weathered;
weather-beaten *(a. fig.).*

ver'witwet *adj.* widowed.

verwöhn|en *[fɛr'vøːnən] v/t. (no*
-ge-, h) spoil; ~t *adj.* fastidious,
particular.

verworren *adj. [fɛr'vɔrən] ideas,*
etc.: confused; *situation, plot:* intricate.

verwund|bar *adj. [fɛr'vʊntbaːr]*
vulnerable *(a. fig.);* ~en *[~dən] v/t.*
(no -ge-, h) wound.

ver'wunder|lich *adj.* astonishing;
2ung *f (-/~-en)* astonishment.

Ver'wund|ete ⚔ *m (-n/-n)* wounded
(soldier), casualty; ~ung *f (-/-en)*
wound, injury.

ver'wünsch|en *v/t. (no -ge-, h)*
curse; 2ung *f (-/-en)* curse.

ver'wüst|en *v/t. (no -ge-, h)* lay
waste, devastate, ravage *(a. fig.);*
2ung *f (-/-en)* devastation, ravage.

verzag|en *[fɛr'tsaːgən] v/i. (no -ge-,*
h) despond *(an dat.* of); ~t *adj. [~kt]*
despondent; 2theit *[~kt-] f (-/no*
pl.) despondenc|e, -cy.

ver|'zählen *v/refl. (no -ge-, h)*
miscount; ~zärteln *[~'tsɛːrtəln]*
v/t. (no -ge-, h) coddle, pamper;
~'zaubern *v/t. (no -ge-, h)* bewitch,
enchant, charm; ~'zehren *v/t. (no*
-ge-, h) consume *(a. fig.).*

ver'zeichn|en *v/t. (no -ge-, h)* note
down; record; list; *fig.* distort; ~
können, zu ~ haben score *(success,*
etc.); ~et *paint. adj.* out of drawing;
2is *n (-ses/-se)* list, catalog(ue);
register; inventory; index *(of book)*;
table, schedule.

verzeih|en *[fɛr'tsaɪən] (irr., no -ge-,*
h) 1. *v/t.* pardon, forgive; ~ *Sie!*
I beg your pardon!; excuse me!;
sorry!; 2. *v/t.* pardon, forgive *(j-m*
et. s.o. s.th.); ~lich *adj.* pardonable;
2ung *f (-/no pl.)* pardon; ~! I beg
your pardon!, sorry!

ver'zerr|en *v/t. (no -ge-, h)* distort;
sich ~ become distorted; 2ung *f*
distortion.

ver'zetteln *v/t. (no -ge-, h)* enter on
cards; *sich ~* fritter away one's
energies.

Verzicht *[fɛr'tsɪçt] m (-[e]s/-e)*
renunciation *(auf acc.* of); 2en *v/i.*
(no -ge-, h) renounce *(auf et. s.th.)*;
do without *(s.th.).*

verzieh *[fɛr'tsiː] pret. of* verzeihen.

ver'ziehen[1] *(irr.* ziehen, *no -ge-)*
1. *v/i. (sein)* (re)move *(nach* to);
2. *v/t. (h)* spoil *(child);* distort; *das*
Gesicht ~ make a wry face, screw
up one's face, grimace; *ohne e-e*
Miene zu ~ without betraying the
least emotion; *sich ~ wood:* warp;
crowd, clouds: disperse; *storm,*
clouds: blow over; F disappear.

ver'ziehen[2] *p.p. of* verzeihen.

ver'zier|en *v/t. (no -ge-, h)* adorn,
decorate; 2ung *f (-/-en)* decoration;
ornament.

verzins|en *[fɛr'tsɪnzən] v/t. (no*
-ge-, h) pay interest on; *sich ~* yield
interest; 2ung *f (-/~-en)* interest.

ver'zöger|n *v/t. (no -ge-, h)* delay,
retard; *sich ~* be delayed; 2ung *f*
(-/-en) delay, retardation.

ver'zollen *v/t. (no -ge-, h)* pay duty
on; *haben Sie et. zu ~?* have you
anything to declare?

verzück|t *adj. [fɛr'tsʏkt]* ecstatic,
enraptured; 2ung *f (-/~-en)*
ecstasy, rapture; *in ~ geraten* go
into ecstasies *(wegen* over).

Ver'zug *m (-[e]s/no pl.)* delay; ✝
default; *in ~ geraten* ✝ come in
default; *im ~ sein* (be in) default.

ver'zweif|eln *v/i. (no -ge-, h, sein)*
despair *(an dat.* of); *es ist zum* Verzweifeln it is enough to drive one
mad; ~elt *adj.* hopeless; desperate;
2lung *f [~luŋ] f (-/no pl.)* despair;
j-n zur ~ bringen drive s.o. to despair.

verzweig|en *v/refl.*
(no -ge-, h) ramify; *trees:* branch
(out); *road:* branch; *business firm,*

etc.: branch out; **2ung** *f* (*-/-en*) ramification; branching.

verzwickt *adj.* [fɛr'tsvikt] intricate, complicated.

Veteran [vete'rɑ:n] *m* (*-en/-en*) ✕ veteran (*a. fig.*), ex-serviceman.

Veterinär [veteri'nɛ:r] *m* (*-s/-e*) veterinary (surgeon), F vet.

Veto ['ve:to] *n* (*-s/-s*) veto; *ein ~ einlegen gegen* put a veto on, veto *s.th.*

Vetter ['fɛtər] *m* (*-s/-n*) cousin; **'~nwirtschaft** *f* (*-/no pl.*) nepotism.

vibrieren [vi'bri:rən] *v/i.* (*no -ge-, h*) vibrate.

Vieh [fi:] *n* (*-[e]s/no pl.*) livestock, cattle; animal, brute, beast; F *fig.* brute, beast; **'~bestand** *m* livestock; **'~händler** *m* cattle-dealer; **'~hof** *m* stockyard; **2isch** *adj.* bestial, beastly, brutal; **'~wagen** 🚃 *m* stock-car; **'~weide** *f* pasture; **'~zucht** *f* stock-farming, cattle-breeding; **'~züchter** *m* stock-breeder, stock-farmer, cattle-breeder, *Am. a.* rancher.

viel [fi:l] **1.** *adj.* much; *~e pl.* many; a lot (*of*), lots of; plenty of (*cake, money, room, time, etc.*); *das ~e Geld* all that money; *seine ~en Geschäfte pl.* his numerous affairs *pl.*; *sehr ~e pl.* a great many *pl.*; *ziemlich ~* a good deal of; *ziemlich ~e pl.* a good many *pl.*; *zuviel* far too much; *sehr ~* a great *or* good deal; **2.** *adv.* much; *~ besser* much *or* a good deal *or* a lot better; *et. ~ lieber tun* prefer to do *s.th.*

viel|beschäftigt *adj.* ['fi:lbəʃɛftiçt] very busy; **'~deutig** *adj.* ambiguous; **~erlei** *adj.* ['~ər'laɪ] of many kinds, many kinds of; multifarious; **~fach** ['~fax] **1.** *adj.* multiple; **2.** *adv.* in many cases, frequently; **~fältig** *adj.* ['~fɛltiç] multiple, manifold, multifarious; **'~leicht** *adv.* perhaps, maybe; **~mals** *adv.* ['~ma:ls] *ich danke Ihnen ~* many thanks, thank you very much; *sie läßt (dich) ~ grüßen* she sends you her kind regards; *ich bitte ~ um Entschuldigung* I am very sorry, I do beg your pardon; **~'mehr** *cj.* rather; **'~sagend** *adj.* significant, suggestive; **~seitig** *adj.* ['~zaɪtiç] many-sided, versatile; **'~versprechend** *adj.* (very) promising.

vier [fi:r] four; *zu ~t* four of us *or* them; *auf allen ~en* on all fours; *unter ~ Augen* confidentially, privately; *um halb ~* at half past three; **'~beinig** *adj.* four-legged; **'2eck** *n* square, quadrangle; **'~eckig** *adj.* square, quadrangular; **~erlei** *adj.* ['~ər'laɪ] of four different kinds, four kinds of; **'~fach** *adj.* ['~fax] fourfold; **~e Ausfertigung** four copies; **2füßer** *zo.* ['~fy:sər] *m* (*-s/-*) quadruped; **~füßig** *adj.* ['~fy:siç]

four-footed; *zo.* quadruped; **2füßler** *zo.* ['~fy:slər] *m* (*-s/-*) quadruped; **~händig** ♪ *adv.* ['~hɛndiç]: *~ spielen* play a duet; **~jährig** *adj.* ['~jɛ:riç] four-year-old, of four; **2linge** ['~liŋə] *m/pl.* quadruplets *pl.*, F quads *pl.*; **'~mal** *adv.* four times; **~schrötig** *adj.* ['~ʃrø:tiç] square-built, thickset; **~seitig** *adj.* ['~zaɪtiç] four-sided; A quadrilateral; **'2sitzer** *esp. mot. m* (*-s/-*) four-seater; **~stöckig** *adj.* ['~ʃtœkiç] four-storeyed, four-storied; **2takt-motor** *mot. m* four-stroke engine; **'~te** *adj.* fourth; **'~teilen** *v/t.* (*ge-, h*) quarter.

Viertel ['firtəl] *n* (*-s/-*) fourth (part); quarter; *~ fünf, (ein) ~ nach vier* a quarter past four; *drei ~ vier* a quarter to four; **'~jahr** *n* three months *pl.*, quarter (of a year); **'2jährlich, 2'jährlich 1.** *adj.* quarterly; **2.** *adv.* every three months, quarterly; **'~note** ♪ *f* crotchet, *Am. a.* quarter note; **'~pfund** *n*, **~'pfund** *n* quarter of a pound; **~'stunde** *f* quarter of an hour, *Am.* quarter hour.

vier|tens *adv.* ['fi:rtəns] fourthly; **2'vierteltakt** ♪ *m* common time.

vierzehn *adj.* ['fi:rtse:n] fourteen; *~ Tage pl.* a fortnight, *Am.* two weeks *pl.*; **'~te** *adj.* fourteenth.

vierzig *adj.* ['fi:rtsiç] forty; **'~ste** *adj.* fortieth.

Vikar *eccl.* [vi'kɑ:r] *m* (*-s/-e*) curate; vicar.

Villa ['vila] *f* (*-/Villen*) villa.

violett *adj.* [vio'lɛt] violet.

Violine ♪ [vio'li:nə] *f* (*-/-n*) violin.

Viper *zo.* ['vi:pər] *f* (*-/-n*) viper.

virtuos *adj.* [virtu'o:s] masterly; **2e** [~zə] *m* (*-n/-n*), **2in** [~zin] *f* (*-/-nen*) virtuoso; **2ität** [~ozi'tɛ:t] *f* (*-/no pl.*) virtuosity.

Virus 🜊 ['vi:rus] *n, m* (*-/Viren*) virus.

Vision [vi'zjo:n] *f* (*-/-en*) vision.

Visitation [vizita'tsjo:n] *f* (*-/-en*) search; inspection.

Visite 🜊 [vi'zi:tə] *f* (*-/-n*) visit; **~nkarte** *f* visiting-card, *Am.* calling card.

Visum ['vi:zum] *n* (*-s/Visa, Visen*) visa, visé.

Vitalität [vitali'tɛ:t] *f* (*-/no pl.*) vitality. [min.]

Vitamin [vita'mi:n] *n* (*-s/-e*) vita-]

Vize|kanzler ['fi:tsə~] *m* vice-chancellor; **'~könig** *m* viceroy; **'~konsul** *m* vice-consul; **'~präsident** *m* vice-president.

Vogel ['fo:gəl] *m* (*-s/⁔*) bird; F *e-n ~ haben* have a bee in one's bonnet, *sl.* have bats in the belfry; *den ~ abschießen* carry off the prize, *Am. sl.* take the cake; *schräger ~* (*-s/-*) bird-cage; **'~flinte** *f* fowling-piece; **'2frei** *adj.* outlawed; **'~futter** *n* food for birds, bird-seed; **'~kunde**

f (*-/no pl.*) ornithology; '**~lieb-haber** *m* bird-fancier; '**~nest** *n* bird's nest, bird-nest; '**~perspektive** *f* (*-/no pl.*), '**~schau** *f* (*-/no pl.*) bird's-eye view; '**~scheuche** *f* (*-/-n*) scarecrow (*a. fig.*); **~'Strauß-Politik** *f* ostrich policy; **~** *betreiben* hide one's head in the sand (like an ostrich); '**~warte** *f* ornithological station; '**~zug** *m* passage *or* migration of birds.

Vokab|el [vo'ka:bəl] *f* (*-/-n*) word; **~ular** [~abu'la:r] *n* (*-s/-e*) vocabulary.

Vokal *ling.* [vo'ka:l] *m* (*-s/-e*) vowel.

Volk [fɔlk] *n* **1.** (*-[e]s/~er*) people; nation; swarm (*of bees*); covey (*of partridges*); **2.** (*-[e]s/no pl.*) populace, the common people; *contp.* the common *or* vulgar herd; *der Mann aus dem ~e* the man in the street *or Am.* on the street.

Völker|bund ['fœlkɐr-] *m* (*-[e]s/no pl.*) League of Nations; '**~kunde** *f* (*-/no pl.*) ethnology; '**~recht** *n* (*-[e]s/no pl.*) international law, law of nations; '**~wanderung** *f* age of national migrations.

'**Volks|abstimmung** *pol.* *f* plebiscite; '**~ausgabe** *f* popular edition (*of book*); '**~bücherei** *f* free *or* public library; '**~charakter** *m* national character; '**~dichter** *m* popular *or* national poet; '**~entscheid** *pol.* ['~ɛntʃaɪt] *m* (*-[e]s/-e*) referendum; plebiscite; '**~fest** *n* fun fair, amusement park *or* grounds *pl.*; public merry-making; national festival; '**~gunst** *f* popularity; '**~herrschaft** *f* democracy; '**~hochschule** *f* adult education (courses *pl.*); '**~lied** *n* folk-song; '**~menge** *f* crowd (of people), multitude; '**~partei** *f* people's party; '**~republik** *f* people's republic; '**~schule** *f* elementary *or* primary school, *Am. a.* grade school; '**~schullehrer** *m* elementary *or* primary teacher, *Am.* grade teacher; '**~sprache** *f* vernacular; '**~stamm** *m* tribe; race; '**~stück** *thea. n* folk-play; '**~tanz** *m* folk-dance; '**~tracht** *f* national costume; **²tümlich** *adj.* ['~ty:mliç] national; popular; '**~versammlung** *f* public meeting; '**~vertreter** *parl. m* deputy, representative, member of parliament; *Brt.* Member of Parliament, *Am.* Representative; '**~vertretung** *parl. f* representation of the people; parliament; '**~wirt** *m* (political) economist; '**~wirtschaft** *f* economics, political economy; **~wirtschaftler** ['~tlɐr] *m* (*-s/-*) *s.* Volkswirt; '**~zählung** *f* census.

voll [fɔl] **1.** *adj.* full; filled; whole, complete, entire; *figure, face:* full, round; *figure:* buxom; *~er Knospen* full of buds; *aus ~em Halse* at the top of one's voice; *aus ~em Herzen* from the bottom of one's heart; *in ~er Blüte* in full blossom; *in ~er Fahrt* at full speed; *mit ~en Händen* lavishly, liberally; *mit ~em Recht* with perfect right; *um das Unglück ~zumachen* to make things worse; **2.** *adv.* fully, in full; *~ und ganz* fully, entirely; *j-n nicht für ~ ansehen or nehmen* have a poor opinion of s.o., think little of s.o.

'**voll|auf** *adv.*, ~'**auf** *adv.* abundantly, amply, F plenty; '**~automatisch** *adj.* fully automatic; '**²bad** *n* bath; '**²bart** *m* beard; '**²beschäftigung** *f* full employment; '**²besitz** *m* full possession; '**²blut(pferd)** *zo. n* thoroughbred (horse); '**~bringen** *v/t.* (*irr.* bringen, *no* -ge-, h) accomplish, achieve; perform; '**²dampf** *m* full steam; F: *mit ~ at or in full blast; ~en* (*no* -ge-, h) finish, complete; '**~endet** *adj.* perfect; **~ends** *adv.* ['~ɛnts] entirely, wholly, altogether; **²endung** *f* (*-/~ -en*) finishing, completion; *fig.* perfection.

Völlerei [fœlə'raɪ] *f* (*-/~ -en*) gluttony.

voll|'führen *v/t.* (*no* -ge-, h) execute, carry out; '**~füllen** *v/t.* (*sep.*, -ge-, h) fill (up); '**²gas** *mot. n: ~ geben* open the throttle; *mit ~* with the throttle full open; at full speed; '**~gepfropft** *adj.* ['~gəpfrɔpft] crammed, packed; '**~gießen** *v/t.* (*irr.* gießen, *sep.*, -ge-, h) fill (up); '**²gummi** *n, m* solid rubber.

völlig *adj.* ['fœliç] entire, complete; *silence, calm, etc.*: dead.

voll|jährig *adj.* ['fɔljɛ:riç]: *~ sein* be of age; *~ werden* come of age; '**²jährigkeit** *f* (*-/no pl.*) majority; '**~kommen** *adj.* perfect; **²'kommenheit** *f* (*-/~ -en*) perfection; '**²kornbrot** *n* whole-meal bread; '**~machen** *v/t.* (*sep.*, -ge-, h) fill (up) F soil, dirty; *um das Unglück vollzumachen* to make things worse; '**²macht** *f* (*-/-en*) full power, authority; **²** power of attorney; ~ *haben* be authorized; '**²matrose** ♧ *m* able-bodied seaman; '**²milch** *f* whole milk; '**²mond** *m* full moon; '**~packen** *v/t.* (*sep.*, -ge-, h) stuff, cram; '**²pension** *f* (*-/-en*) full board; '**~schenken** *v/t.* (*sep.*, -ge-, h) fill (up); '**~schlank** *adj.* stout, corpulent; '**~ständig** *adj.* complete; '**~stopfen** *v/t.* (*sep.*, -ge-, h) stuff, cram; *sich ~* stuff o.s.; *sich die Taschen ~* stuff one's pockets; '**~strecken** *v/t.* (*no* -ge-, h) execute; **²'streckung** *f* (*-/-en*) execution; '**~tönend** *adj.* sonorous; rich; '**²treffer** *m* direct hit; '**²versammlung** *f* plenary meeting *or* assembly; General Assembly (*of the United Nations*); '**~wertig** *adj.* equivalent, equal in value; full; '~zählig adj. complete; ~'ziehen v/t. (irr. ziehen, no -ge-, h) execute; consummate (marriage); sich ~ take place; ℒ'ziehung f (-/~-en), ℒ'zug m (-[e]s/no pl.) execution.

Volontär [volɔn'tɛːr] m (-s/-e) unpaid assistant.

Volt ∮ [vɔlt] n (-, -[e]s/-) volt.

Volumen [vo'luːmən] n (-s/-, Volumina) volume.

vom prp. [fɔm] = von dem

von prp. (dat.) [fɔn] space, time: from; instead of gen.: of; passive: by; ~ Hamburg from Hamburg; ~ nun an from now on; ~ morgen an from tomorrow (on), beginning tomorrow; ein Freund ~ mir a friend of mine; die Einrichtung ~ Schulen the erection of schools; ~ dem or vom Apfel essen eat (some) of the apple; der Herzog ~ Edinburgh the Duke of Edinburgh; ein Gedicht ~ Schiller a poem by Schiller; ~ selbst by itself; ~ selbst, ~ sich aus by oneself; ~ drei Meter Länge three metres long; ein Betrag ~ 300 Mark a sum of 300 marks; e-e Stadt ~ 10 000 Einwohnern a town of 10,000 inhabitants; reden ~ talk of or about s.th.; speak on (scientific subject); ~ mir aus as far as I am concerned; I don't mind, for all I care; das ist nett ~ ihm that is nice of him; ich habe ~ ihm gehört I have heard of him; ~statten adv. [~'ʃtatn]: gut ~ gehen go well.

vor prp. (dat.; acc.) [foːr] space: in front of, before; time: before; ~ langer Zeit a long time ago; ~ einigen Tagen a few days ago; (heute) ~ acht Tage a week ago (today); am Tage ~ (on) the day before, on the eve of; 5 Minuten ~ 12 five minutes to twelve; Am. five minutes of twelve; fig. at the eleventh hour; ~ der Tür stehen be imminent, be close at hand; ~ e-m Hintergrund against a background; ~ Zeugen in the presence of witnesses; ~ allen Dingen above all; (dicht) ~ dem Untergang stehen be on the brink or verge of ruin; ~ Hunger sterben die of hunger; ~ Kälte zittern tremble with cold; schützen (verstecken) ~ protect (hide) from or against; ~ sich gehen take place, pass off; ~ sich hin lächeln smile to o.s.; sich fürchten ~ be afraid of, fear.

Vor|abend ['foːrʔ-] m eve; '~ahnung f presentiment, foreboding.

voran adv. [fo'ran] at the head (dat. of), in front (of), before; Kopf ~ head first; ~gehen v/i. (irr. gehen, sep., -ge-, sein) lead the way; precede; ~kommen v/i. (irr. kommen, sep., -ge-, sein) make progress; fig. get on (in life).

Voran|schlag ['foːrʔan-] m (rough)

estimate; '~zeige f advance notice; film: trailer.

vorarbeite|n ['foːrʔ-] v/t. and v/i. (sep., -ge-, h) work in advance; 'ℒr m foreman.

voraus adv. [fo'raus] in front (dat. of), ahead (of); im ~ in advance, beforehand; ~bestellen v/t. (sep., no -ge-, h) s. vorbestellen; ~bezahlen v/t. (sep., no -ge-, h) pay in advance, prepay; ~gehen v/i. (irr. gehen, sep., -ge-, sein) go on before; s. vorangehen; ℒsage f prediction; prophecy; forecast (of weather); ~sagen v/t. (sep., -ge-, h) foretell, predict; prophesy; forecast (weather, etc.); ~schicken v/t. (sep., -ge-, h) send on in advance; fig. mention beforehand, premise; ~sehen v/t. (irr. sehen, sep., -ge-, h) foresee; ~setzen v/t. (sep., -ge-, h) (pre)suppose, presume, assume; vorausgesetzt, daß provided that; ℒsetzung f (-/-en) (pre)supposition, assumption; prerequisite; ℒsicht f foresight; aller ~ nach in all probability; ~sichtlich adj. presumable, probable, likely; ℒzahlung f advance payment or instal(l)ment.

'Vor|bedacht 1. m (-[e]s/no pl.): mit ~ deliberately, on purpose; 2. ℒ adj. premeditated; '~bedeutung f foreboding, omen, portent; '~bedingung f prerequisite.

Vorbehalt ['foːrbəhalt] m (-[e]s/-e) reservation, reserve; 'ℒen 1. v/t. (irr. halten, sep., no -ge-, h): sich ~ reserve (right, etc.); 2. adj.: Änderungen ~ subject to change (without notice); 'ℒlos adj. unreserved, unconditional.

vorbei adv. [foːr'baɪ] space: along, by, past (all: an dat. s.o., s.th.); time: over, gone; 3 Uhr ~ past three (o'clock); ~fahren v/i. (irr. fahren, sep., -ge-, sein) drive past; ~gehen v/i. (irr. gehen, sep., -ge-, sein) pass, go by; pain: pass (off); storm: blow over; ~ an (dat.) pass; im Vorbeigehen in passing; ~kommen v/i. (irr. kommen, sep., -ge-, sein) pass by; F drop in; F ~ an (dat.) get past (obstacle, etc.); ~lassen v/t. (irr. lassen, sep., -ge-, h) let pass.

'Vorbemerkung f preliminary remark or note.

'vorbereit|en v/t. (sep., no -ge-, h) prepare (für, auf acc. for); 'ℒung f preparation (für, auf acc. for).

'Vorbesprechung f preliminary discussion or talk.

'vor|bestellen v/t. (sep., no -ge-, h) order in advance; book (room, etc.); '~bestraft adj. previously convicted.

'vorbeug|en (sep., -ge-, h) 1. v/i. prevent (e-r Sache s.th.); 2. v/t. and v/refl. bend forward; '~end *adj.* preventive; ⚕ *a.* prophylactic; '2ung *f* prevention.

'Vorbild *n* model; pattern; example; prototype; '2lich *adj.* exemplary; ~ung ['fo:r-duŋ] *f* preparatory training.

'vor|bringen *v/t.* (*irr.* bringen, *sep.*, -ge-, h) bring forward, produce; advance (*opinion*); 🕱 prefer (*charge*); utter, say, state; '~datieren *v/t.* (*sep.*, *no* -ge-, *h*) post-date.

vorder *adj.* ['fɔrdər] front, fore.

'Vorder|achse *f* front axle; '~ansicht *f* front view; '~bein *n* foreleg; '~fuß *m* forefoot; '~grund *m* foreground (*a. fig.*); '~haus *n* front building; '~mann *m* man in front (*of s.o.*); '~rad *n* front wheel; ~radantrieb *mot.* ['fɔrdəra:t?-] *m* front-wheel drive; '~seite *f* front (side); obverse (*of coin*); '~sitz *m* front seat; '2st *adj.* foremost; '~teil *n, m* front (part); '~tür *f* front door; '~zahn *m* front tooth; '~zimmer *n* front room.

'vordrängen *v/refl.* (*sep.*, -ge-, *h*) press *or* push forward.

'vordring|en *v/i.* (*irr.* dringen, *sep.*, -ge-, sein) advance; '~lich *adj.* urgent. [blank.)

'Vordruck *m* (-[e]s/-e) form, *Am. a.*)

voreilig *adj.* ['fo:r?-] hasty, rash, precipitate; ~e *Schlüsse ziehen* jump to conclusions.

voreingenommen *adj.* ['fo:r?-] prejudiced, bias(s)ed; '2heit *f* (-/*no pl.*) prejudice, bias.

vor|enthalten ['fo:r?-] *v/t.* (*irr.* halten, *sep.*, *no* -ge-, *h*) keep back, withhold (*j-m et. s.th.* from *s.o.*); 2entscheidung ['fo:r?-] *f* preliminary decision; ~erst *adv.* ['fo:r?-] for the present, for the time being.

Vorfahr ['fo:rfa:r] *m* (-en/-en) ancestor.

'vorfahr|en *v/i.* (*irr.* fahren, *sep.*, -ge-, sein) drive up; pass; den Wagen ~ *lassen* order the car; '2t(srecht *n*) *f* right of way, priority.

'Vorfall *m* incident, occurrence, event; '2en *v/i.* (*irr.* fallen, *sep.*, -ge-, sein) happen, occur.

'vorfinden *v/t.* (*irr.* finden, *sep.*, -ge-, *h*) find.

'Vorfreude *f* anticipated joy.

'vorführ|en *v/t.* (*sep.*, -ge-, *h*) bring forward, produce; bring (*dat.* before); show, display, exhibit; demonstrate (*use of s.th.*); show, present (*film*); '2er *m* projectionist (*in cinema theatre*); '2ung *f* presentation, showing; ⊕ demonstration; 🕱 production (*of prisoner*); *thea., film:* performance.

'Vor|gabe *f* *sports:* handicap; *athletics:* stagger; *golf, etc.:* odds *pl.*; '~gang *m* incident, occurrence, event; facts *pl.*; file, record(s *pl.*); *biol.*, ⊕ process; ~gänger ['~gɛŋər]

m (-s/-), '~gängerin *f* (-/-nen) predecessor; '~garten *m* front garden.

'vorgeben *v/t.* (*irr.* geben, *sep.*, -ge-, *h*) *sports:* give (*j-m s.o.*); *fig.* pretend, allege.

'Vor|gebirge *n* promontory, cape, headland; foot-hills *pl.*; '~gefühl *n* presentiment, foreboding.

'vorgehen 1. *v/i.* (*irr.* gehen, *sep.*, -ge-, sein) ⚔ advance; F lead the way; go on before; *watch, clock:* be fast, gain (*fünf Minuten* five minutes); take precedence (*dat.* of, over), be more important (*than*); take action, act; proceed (*a.* 🕱; gegen against); go on, happen, take place; 2. 2 *n* (-s/*no pl.*) action, proceeding.

'Vor|geschmack *m* (-[e]s/*no pl.*) foretaste, ~gesetzte ['~gəzɛtstə] *m* (-n/-n) superior; *esp. Am.* F boss; '2gestern *adv.* the day before yesterday; '2greifen *v/i.* (*irr.* greifen, *sep.*, -ge-, *h*) anticipate (*j-m or e-r Sache s.o. or s.th.*).

'vorhaben 1. *v/t.* (*irr.* haben, *sep.*, -ge-, *h*) intend, mean; be going to do *s.th.*; *nichts* ~ be at a loose end; haben Sie heute abend et. vor? have you anything on tonight?; was hat er jetzt wieder vor? what is he up to now?; was hast du mit ihm vor? what are you going to do with him?; 2. 2 *n* (-s/-) intention, purpose, 🕱 intent; plan; project.

'Vorhalle *f* vestibule, (entrance-) hall; lobby; porch.

'vorhalt|en (*irr.* halten, *sep.*, -ge-, *h*) 1. *v/t.:* j-m et. ~ hold *s.th.* before *s.o.*; *fig.* reproach *s.o.* with *s.th.*; 2. *v/i.* last; '2ung *f* remonstrance; j-m ~en machen remonstrate with *s.o.* (wegen on).

vorhanden *adj.* [for'handən] at hand, present; available (*a.* ✝); ✝ on hand, in stock; ~ sein exist; 2sein *n* presence, existence.

'Vor|hang *m* curtain; '~hängeschloß *n* padlock.

'vorher *adv.* before, previously; in advance, beforehand.

vor'her|bestellen *v/t.* (*sep.*, *no* -ge-, *h*) *s.* vorbestellen; ~bestimmen *v/t.* (*sep.*, *no* -ge-, *h*) determine beforehand, predetermine; ~gehen *v/i.* (*irr.* gehen, *sep.*, -ge-, sein) precede; ~ig *adj.* preceding, previous.

'Vorherr|schaft *f* predominance; '2schen *v/i.* (*sep.*, -ge-, *h*) predominate, prevail; '2schend *adj.* predominant, prevailing.

Vor'her|sage *f s.* Voraussage; 2sagen *v/t.* (*sep.*, -ge-, *h*) *s.* voraussagen; 2sehen *v/t.* (*irr.* sehen, *sep.*, -ge-, *h*) foresee; 2wissen *v/t.* (*irr.* wissen, *sep.*, -ge-, *h*) know beforehand, foreknow.

'vor|hin *adv.*, ~'hin *adv.* a short while ago, just now.

'Vor|hof *m* outer court, forecourt; *anat.* auricle (*of heart*); ~hut ⚔ *f* vanguard.

'vor|ig *adj.* last; ~jährig *adj.* ['~je:riç] of last year, last year's.

'Vor|kämpfer *m* champion, pioneer; '~kehrung *f* (-/-en) precaution; ~en treffen take precautions; '~kenntnisse *f/pl.* preliminary or basic knowledge (*in dat.* of); *mit guten* ~n *in* (*dat.*) well grounded in.

'vorkommen *v/i.* (*irr. kommen, sep.*, -ge-, *sein*) be found; occur, happen; *es kommt mir vor* it seems to me; 2. 2 *n* (-s/-) occurrence.

'Vor|kommnis *n* (-ses/-se) occurrence; event; '~kriegszeit *f* pre-war times *pl.*

'vorlad|en *v/t.* (*irr. laden, sep.*, -ge-, *h*) summon; '2ung ⚖ *f* summons.

'Vorlage *f* copy; pattern; *parl.* bill; presentation; production (*of document*); *football:* pass.

'vorlassen *v/t.* (*irr. lassen, sep.*, -ge-, *h*) let *s.o.* pass, allow *s.o.* to pass; admit.

'Vorläuf|er *m*, '~erin *f* (-/-nen) forerunner; '2ig 1. *adj.* provisional, temporary; 2. *adv.* provisionally, temporarily; for the present, for the time being.

'vorlaut *adj.* forward, pert.

'Vorleben *n* past (life), antecedents *pl.*

'vorlege|n *v/t.* (*sep.*, -ge-, *h*) put (*lock*) on; produce (*document*); submit (*plans, etc. for discussion, etc.*); propose (*plan, etc.*); present (*bill, etc.*); *j-m et.* ~ lay or place or put *s.th.* before *s.o.*; show *s.o. s.th.*; *at table:* help *s.o.* to *s.th.*; *j-m e-e Frage* ~ put a question to *s.o.*; *sich* ~ lean forward; '2r *m* (-s/-) rug.

'vorles|en *v/t.* (*irr. lesen, sep.*, -ge-, *h*) read aloud; *j-m et.* ~ read (out) *s.th.* to *s.o.*; '2ung *f* lecture (*über acc.* on; *vor dat.* to); *e-e* ~ *halten* (give a) lecture.

'vorletzt *adj.* last but one; ~e *Nacht* the night before last.

'Vorlieb|e *f* (-/*no pl.*) predilection, preference; 2nehmen [~'li:p-] *v/i.* (*irr. nehmen, sep.*, -ge-, *h*) be satisfied (*mit* with); ~ *mit dem, was da ist at meals:* take pot luck.

'vorlieg|en *v/i.* (*irr. liegen, sep.*, -ge-, *h*) lie before *s.o.*; be there, exist; *da muß ein Irrtum* ~ there must be a mistake; *was liegt gegen ihn vor?* what is the charge against him?; '~d *adj.* present, in question.

'vor|lügen *v/t.* (*irr. lügen, sep.*, -ge-, *h*): *j-m et.* ~ tell *s.o.* lies; '~machen *v/t.* (*sep.*, -ge-, *h*): *j-m et.* ~ show *s.o.* how to do *s.th.*; *fig.* impose upon *s.o.*; *sich* (*selbst*) *et.* ~ fool o.s.

'Vormacht *f* (-/~e), '~stellung *f* predominance; supremacy; hegemony.

'Vormarsch ⚔ *m* advance.

'vormerken *v/t.* (*sep.*, -ge-, *h*) note down, make a note of; reserve; *sich* ~ *lassen für* put one's name down for.

'Vormittag *m* morning, forenoon; '2s *adv.* in the morning.

'Vormund *m* (-[e]s/-e, ~er) guardian; '~schaft *f* (-/-en) guardianship.

vorn *adv.* [fɔrn] in front; *nach* ~ forward; *von* ~ from the front; *ich sah sie von* ~ I saw her face; *von* ~ *anfangen* begin at the beginning; *noch einmal von* ~ *anfangen* begin anew, make a new start.

'Vorname *m* Christian name, first name, *Am. a.* given name.

vornehm ['fo:rne:m] 1. *adj.* of (superior) rank, distinguished; aristocratic; noble; fashionable; ~e *Gesinnung* high character; 2. *adv.*: ~ *tun* give o.s. airs; '2en *v/t.* (*irr. nehmen, sep.*, -ge-, *h*) take *s.th.* in hand; deal with; make (*changes, etc.*); take up (*book*); F *sich j-n* ~ take *s.o.* to task (*wegen* for, about); *sich* ~ resolve (up)on *s.th.*; resolve (*zu inf.* to *inf.*), make up one's mind (*to inf.*); *sich vorgenommen haben a.* be determined (*zu inf.* to *inf.*); '2heit *f* (-/*no pl.*) refinement; elegance; high-mindedness.

'vorn|herein *adv.*, ~he'rein *adv.*: *von* ~ from the first or start or beginning.

Vorort ['fo:r9-] *m* (-[e]s/-e) suburb; '~(s)verkehr *m* suburban traffic; '~(s)zug *m* local (train).

'Vor|posten *m* outpost (*a.* ⚔); '~rang *m* (-[e]s/*no pl.*) precedence (*vor dat.* of, over), priority (over); '~rat *m* store, stock (*an dat.* of); *Vorräte pl. a.* provisions *pl.*, supplies *pl.*; 2rätig *adj.* ['~rɛ:tiç] available; ✝ *a.* on hand, in stock; '2rechnen *v/t.* (*sep.*, -ge-, *h*) reckon up (*j-m* to *s.o.*); '~recht *n* privilege; '~rede *f* preface, introduction; '~redner *m* previous speaker; '~richtung ⊕ *f* contrivance, device; '2rücken (*sep.*, -ge-) 1. *v/t.* (*h*) move (*chair, etc.*) forward; 2. *v/i.* (*sein*) advance; '~runde *f* *sports:* preliminary round; '2sagen *v/i.* (*sep.*, -ge-, *h*): *j-m* ~ prompt *s.o.*; '~saison *f* off or dead season; '~satz *m* intention, purpose, design; 2sätzlich *adj.* ['~zetsliç] intentional, deliberate; ~er *Mord* ⅔ wil(l)ful murder; '~schein *m*: *zum* ~ *bringen* bring forward, produce; *zum* ~ *kommen* appear, turn up; '2schieben *v/t.* (*irr. schieben, sep.*, -ge-, *h*) push *s.th.* forward; slip (*bolt*); *s. vorschützen*; '2schießen *v/t.* (*irr.* schießen, *sep.*, -ge-, h) advance (*money*).

'**Vorschlag** *m* proposition, proposal; suggestion; offer; **2en** ['~gən] *v/t.* (*irr.* schlagen, *sep.*, -ge-, h) propose; suggest; offer.

'**Vor|schlußrunde** *f* sports: semifinal; '**2schnell** *adj.* hasty, rash; '**2schreiben** *v/t.* (*irr.* schreiben, *sep.*, -ge-, h): j-m et. ~ write s.th. out for s.o.; *fig.* prescribe.

'**Vorschrift** *f* direction, instruction; prescription (*esp.* ♗); order (*a.* ♗); regulation(s *pl.*); '**2smäßig** *adj.* according to regulations; ~e Kleidung regulation dress; '**2swidrig** *adj. and adv.* contrary to regulations.

'**Vor|schub** *m*: ~ leisten (*dat.*) countenance (*fraud, etc.*); further, encourage; ♗♗ aid and abet; '~**schule** *f* preparatory school; '~**schuß** *m* advance; *for barrister*: retaining fee, retainer; '**2schützen** *v/t.* (*sep.*, -ge-, h) pretend, plead (*sickness, etc. as excuse*); '**2schweben** *v/i.* (*sep.*, -ge-, h): mir schwebt et. vor I have s.th. in mind.

'**vorseh|en** *v/t.* (*irr.* sehen, *sep.*, -ge-, h) plan; design; ♗♗ provide; sich ~ take care, be careful; sich ~ vor (*dat.*) guard against; '**2ung** *f* (-/♗-en) providence.

'**vorsetzen** *v/t.* (*sep.*, -ge-, h) put forward; place *or* put *or* set before, offer.

'**Vorsicht** *f* caution; care; ~! caution!, danger!; look out!, be careful!; ~, Glas! Glass, with care!; ~, Stufe! mind the step!; '**2ig** *adj.* cautious; careful; ~! F steady!

'**vorsichts|halber** *adv.* as a precaution; '**2maßnahme** *f*, '**2maßregel** *f* precaution(ary measure); ~n treffen take precautions.

'**Vorsilbe** *gr. f* prefix.

'**vorsingen** *v/t.* (*irr.* singen, *sep.*, -ge-, h): j-m et. ~ sing s.th. to s.o.

'**Vorsitz** *m* (-es/no *pl.*) chair, presidency; den ~ führen *or* haben be in the chair, preside (*bei over*; *at*); den ~ übernehmen take the chair; ~**ende** ['~əndə] (-n/-n) **1.** *m* chairman, president; **2.** *f* chairwoman.

'**Vorsorg|e** *f* (-/no *pl.*) provision; providence; precaution; ~ treffen make provision; '**2en** *v/i.* (*sep.*, -ge-, h) provide; **2lich** ['~klіç] **1.** *adj.* precautionary; **2.** *adv.* as a precaution.

'**Vorspeise** *f* appetizer, hors d'œuvre.

'**vorspiegeln** *v/t.* (*sep.*, -ge-, h) pretend; j-m et. ~ delude s.o. (with false hopes, *etc.*); '**2(e)lung** *f* pretence, Am. -se.

'**Vorspiel** *n* prelude; '**2en** *v/t.* (*sep.*, -ge-, h): j-m et. ~ play s.th. to s.o.

'**vor|sprechen** (*irr.* sprechen, *sep.*, -ge-, h) **1.** *v/t.* pronounce (j-m et.

s.th. to *or* for s.o.); **2.** *v/i.* call (*bei* on *s.o.*; *at an office*); *thea.* audition; '~**springen** *v/i.* (*irr.* springen, *sep.*, -ge-, sein) jump forward; project; '**2sprung** *m* ⚔ projection; sports: lead; *fig.* start, advantage (*vor dat.* of); '**2stadt** *f* suburb; '~**städtisch** *adj.* suburban; '**2stand** *m* board of directors, managing directors *pl.*

'**vorsteh|en** *v/i.* (*irr.* stehen, *sep.*, -ge-, h) project, protrude; *fig.*: direct; manage (*both*: e-r Sache s.th.); '**2er** *m* director, manager; head, chief.

'**vorstell|en** *v/t.* (*sep.*, -ge-, h) put forward; put (*clock*) on; introduce (j-n j-m s.o. to s.o.); mean, stand for; represent; sich ~ bei have an interview with; sich et. ~ imagine or fancy s.th.; '**2ung** *f* introduction, presentation; interview (*of applicant for post*); *thea.* performance; *fig.*: remonstrance; idea, conception; imagination; **2ungsvermögen** *n* imagination.

'**Vor|stoß** ⚔ *m* thrust, advance; '~**strafe** *f* previous conviction; '**2strecken** *v/t.* (*sep.*, -ge-, h) thrust out, stretch forward; advance (*money*); '~**stufe** *f* first step *or* stage; '**2täuschen** *v/t.* (*sep.*, -ge-, h) feign, pretend.

Vorteil ['fɔrtaɪl] *m* advantage (*a.* sports); profit; *tennis:* (ad)vantage; '**2haft** *adj.* advantageous (*für* to), profitable (to).

Vortrag ['foːrtraːk] *m* (-[e]s/⁼e) performance; execution (*esp.* ♪); recitation (*of poem*); ♪ recital; lecture; report; ♱ balance carried forward; e-n ~ halten (give a) lecture (*über acc.* on); **2en** ['~gən] *v/t.* (*irr.* tragen. *sep.*, -ge-, h) ♱ carry forward; report on; recite (*poem*); perform, *esp.* ♪ execute; lecture on; state, express (*opinion*); ~**ende** ['~gəndə] *m* (-n/-n) performer; lecturer; speaker.

vor|trefflich *adj.* [foːrˈtrɛflіç] excellent; '~**treten** *v/i.* (*irr.* treten, *sep.*, -ge-, sein) step forward; *fig.* project, protrude, stick out; '**2tritt** *m* (-[e]s/no *pl.*) precedence.

vorüber *adv.* [foˈryːbər] *space:* by, past; *time:* gone by, over; ~**gehen** *v/i.* (*irr.* gehen, *sep.*, -ge-, sein) pass, go by; ~**gehend** *adj.* passing; temporary; **2gehende** [~də] *m* (-n/-n) passer-by; ~**ziehen** *v/i.* (*irr.* ziehen, *sep.*, -ge-, sein) march past, pass by; *storm:* blow over.

Vor|übung ['foːrʔ-] *f* preliminary practice; ~**untersuchung** ♗♗ ['foːrʔ-] *f* preliminary inquiry.

Vorurteil ['foːrʔ-] *n* prejudice; '**2s-los** *adj.* unprejudiced, unbias(s)ed.

'**Vor|verkauf** *thea. m* booking in advance; im ~ bookable (*bei* at);

'**Qverlegen** v/t. (sep., no -ge-, h) advance; '**.wand** m (-[e]s/=e) pretext, preten|ce, Am. -se.

vorwärts adv. ['fo:rvɛrts] forward, onward, on; ~! go ahead!; '**.kommen** v/i. (irr. kommen, sep., -ge-, sein) (make) progress; fig. make one's way, get on (in life).

vorweg adv. [for'vɛk] beforehand; **.nehmen** v/t. (irr. nehmen, sep., -ge-, h) anticipate.

vor|weisen v/t. (irr. weisen, sep., -ge-, h) produce, show; '**.werfen** v/t. (irr. werfen, sep., -ge-, h) throw or cast before; j-m et. ~ reproach s.o. with s.th.; '**.wiegend** 1. adj. predominant, preponderant; 2. adv. predominantly, chiefly, mainly, mostly; '**.witzig** adj. forward, pert; inquisitive.

'**Vorwort** n (-[e]s/-e) preface (by author); foreword.

'**Vorwurf** m reproach; subject (of drama, etc.); j-m e-n ~ or Vorwürfe machen reproach s.o. (wegen with); '**Qsvoll** adj. reproachful.

'**vor|zählen** v/t. (sep., -ge-, h) enumerate, count out (both: j-m to s.o.); '**Qzeichen** n omen; '**.zeichnen** v/t. (sep., -ge-, h): j-m et. ~ draw or sketch s.th. for s.o.; show s.o. how to draw s.th.; fig. mark out, destine; '**.zeigen** v/t. (sep., -ge-, h) produce, show.

'**Vorzeit** f antiquity; in literature often: times of old, days of yore; '**Qig** adj. premature.

'**vor|ziehen** v/t. (irr. ziehen, sep., -ge-, h) draw forth; draw (curtains); fig. prefer; '**Qzimmer** n antechamber, anteroom; waiting-room; '**Qzug** fig. m preference; advantage; merit; priority; '**.züglich** adj. [~'tsy:kliç] excellent, superior, exquisite.

'**Vorzugs|aktie** f preference share or stock, Am. preferred stock; '**.preis** m special price; '**Qweise** adv. preferably; chiefly.

Votum ['vo:tum] n (-s/Voten, Vota) vote.

vulgär adj. [vul'gɛ:r] vulgar.

Vulkan [vul'ka:n] m (-s/-e) volcano; **Qisch** adj. volcanic.

W

Waag|e ['va:gə] f (-/-n) balance, (e-e a pair of) scales pl.; die ~ halten (dat.) counterbalance; '**Qerecht** adj., **Qrecht** adj. ['va:k-] horizontal, level; '**.schale** ['va:k-] f scale.

Wabe ['va:bə] f (-/-n) honeycomb.

wach adj. [vax] awake; hell~ wide awake; ~ werden awake, wake up; '**Qe** f (-/-n) watch; guard; guardhouse, guardroom; police-station; sentry, sentinel; ~ haben be on guard; ~ halten keep watch; '**.en** v/i. (ge-, h) (keep) watch (über acc. over); sit up (bei with); '**Qhund** m watch-dog.

Wacholder ♀ [va'xɔldər] m (-s/-) juniper.

'**wach|rufen** v/t. (irr. rufen, sep., -ge-, h) rouse, evoke; '**.rütteln** v/t. (sep., -ge-, h) rouse (up); fig. rouse, shake up.

Wachs [vaks] n (-es/-e) wax.

'**wachsam** adj. watchful, vigilant; '**Qkeit** f (-/no pl.) watchfulness, vigilance.

wachsen[1] ['vaksən] v/i. (irr., ge-, sein) grow; fig. increase.

wachsen[2] [~] v/t. (ge-, h) wax.

wächsern adj. ['vɛksərn] wax; fig. waxen, waxy.

'**Wachs|kerze** f, '**.licht** n wax candle; '**.tuch** n waxcloth, oilcloth.

Wachstum ['vakstu:m] n (-s/no pl.) growth; fig. increase.

Wächte mount. ['vɛçtə] f (-/-n) cornice.

Wachtel orn. ['vaxtəl] f (-/-n) quail.

Wächter ['vɛçtər] m (-s/-) watcher, guard(ian); watchman.

'**Wacht|meister** m sergeant; '**.turm** m watch-tower.

wackel|ig adj. ['vakəliç] shaky (a. fig.), tottery (furniture, etc.): rickety; tooth, etc.: loose; '**Qkontakt** ≠ m loose connexion or (Am. only) connection; '**.n** v/i. (ge-, h) shake; table, etc.: wobble; tooth, etc.: be loose; tail, etc.: wag; ~ mit wag s.th.

wacker adj. ['vakər] honest, upright; brave, gallant.

wacklig adj. ['vakliç] s. wackelig.

Wade ['va:də] f (-/-n) calf; '**.nbein** anat. n fibula.

Waffe ['vafə] f (-/-n) weapon (a. fig.); ~n pl. a. arms pl.

Waffel ['vafəl] f (-/-n) waffle; wafer.

'**Waffen|fabrik** f armaments factory, Am. a. armory; '**.gattung** f arm; '**.gewalt** f (-/no pl.): mit ~ by force of arms; '**Qlos** adj. weaponless, unarmed; '**.schein** m firearm certificate, Am. gun license; '**.stillstand** m armistice (a. fig.), truce.

Wage|hals ['va:gəhals] m daredevil; '**Qhalsig** adj. daring, foolhardy; attr. a. daredevil; '**.mut** m daring

wagen[1] ['va:gən] *v/t.* (ge-, h) venture; risk, dare; *sich ~* venture (*an acc.* [up]on).

Wagen[2] [~] *m* (-s/-, ▪) carriage (*a.* 🚂); *Am.* 🚂 car; 🚂 coach; **wag(g)on**; cart; car; lorry, truck; van.

wägen ['vɛ:gən] *v/t.* ([*irr.*,] ge-, h) weigh (*a. fig.*).

'**Wagen|heber** *m* (-s/-) (lifting) jack; '~**park** *m* (-[e]s/*no pl.*) fleet of vehicles; '~**schmiere** *f* grease; '~**spur** *f* rut.

Waggon 🚂 [va'gõ:] *m* (-s/-s) (railway) carriage, *Am.* (railroad) car.

wag|halsig *adj.* ['va:khalsiç] *s.* **wagehalsig**; '**2nis** *n* (-ses/-se) venture, risk.

Wahl [va:l] *f* (-/-en) choice; alternative; selection; *pol.* election; e-e *~ treffen* make a choice; *s-e ~ treffen* take one's choice; *ich hatte keine (andere) ~* I had no choice.

wählbar *adj.* ['vɛ:lba:r] eligible; '**2keit** *f* (-/*no pl.*) eligibility.

wahl|berechtigt *adj.* ['va:lbərɛçtiçt] entitled to vote; '**2beteiligung** *f* percentage of voting, F turn-out; '**2bezirk** *m* constituency.

'**wählen** (ge-, h) 1. *v/t.* choose; *pol.* elect; *teleph.* dial; 2. *v/i.* choose, take one's choice; *teleph.* dial (the number).

'**Wahlergebnis** *n* election return.

'**Wähler** *m* (-s/-) elector, voter; '**2isch** *adj.* particular (*in dat.* in, about, as to); nice (about), fastidious, F choosy; '~**schaft** *f* (-/-en) constituency, electorate.

'**Wahl|fach** *n* optional subject, *Am. a.* elective; '**2fähig** *adj.* having a vote; eligible; '~**gang** *m* ballot; '~**kampf** *m* election campaign; '~**kreis** *m* constituency; '~**lokal** *n* polling station; '**2los** *adj.* indiscriminate; '~**recht** *n* (-[e]s/*no pl.*) franchise; '~**rede** *f* electoral speech.

'**Wählscheibe** *teleph. f* dial.

'**Wahl|spruch** *m* device, motto; '~**stimme** *f* vote; '~**urne** *f* ballotbox; '~**versammlung** *f* electoral rally; '~**zelle** *f* polling-booth; '~**zettel** *m* ballot, voting-paper.

Wahn [va:n] *m* (-[e]s/*no pl.*) delusion, illusion; mania; '~**sinn** *m* (-[e]s/*no pl.*) insanity, madness (*both a. fig.*); '**2sinnig** *adj.* insane, mad (*vor dat.* with) (*both a. fig.*); ~**sinnige** ['~gə] *m* (-n/-n) madman, lunatic; '~**vorstellung** *f* delusion, hallucination; '~**witz** *m* (-es/*no pl.*) madness, insanity; '**2witzig** *adj.* mad, insane.

wahr *adj.* [va:r] true; real; genuine; '~**en** *v/t.* (ge-, h) safeguard (*interests, etc.*); maintain (*one's dignity*); *den Schein ~* keep up *or* save appearances.

währen ['vɛ:rən] *v/i.* (ge-, h) last, continue.

'**während** 1. *prp.* (*gen.*) during; pending; 2. *cj.* while, whilst; while, whereas.

'**wahrhaft** *adv.* really, truly, indeed; ~**ig** ['~'haftiç] 1. *adj.* truthful, veracious; 2. *adv.* really, truly, indeed.

'**Wahrheit** *f* (-/-en) truth; *in ~* in truth; *j-m die ~ sagen* give s.o. a piece of one's mind; '**2getreu** *adj.* true, faithful; '~**sliebe** *f* (-/*no pl.*) truthfulness, veracity; '**2sliebend** *adj.* truthful, veracious.

'**wahr|lich** *adv.* truly, really; '~**nehmbar** *adj.* perceivable, perceptible; '~**nehmen** *v/t.* (*irr. nehmen, sep., -ge-, h*) perceive, notice; avail o.s. of (*opportunity*); safeguard (*interests*); '**2nehmung** *f* (-/-en) perception, observation; '~**sagen** *v/i.* (*sep., -ge-, h*) tell *or* read fortunes; *sich ~ lassen* have one's fortune told; '**2sagerin** *f* (-/-nen) fortuneteller; ~'**scheinlich** 1. *adj.* probable; likely; 2. *adv.*: *ich werde ~ gehen* I am likely to go; 2'**scheinlichkeit** *f* (-/⅌-en) probability, likelihood; *aller ~ nach* in all probability *or* likelihood.

'**Wahrung** *f* (-/*no pl.*) maintenance; safeguarding.

'**Währung** *f* (-/-en) currency; standard; '~**sreform** *f* currency *or* monetary reform.

'**Wahrzeichen** *n* landmark.

Waise ['vaizə] *f* (-/-n) orphan; '~**nhaus** *n* orphanage.

Wal *zo.* [va:l] *m* (-[e]s/-e) whale.

Wald [valt] *m* (-[e]s/ᵘer) wood, forest; '~**brand** *m* forest fire; **2ig** *adj.* ['~diç] wooded, woody; **2reich** *adj.* ['~t-] rich in forests; ~**ung** ['~duŋ] *f* (-/-en) forest.

Walfänger ['va:lfɛŋər] *m* (-s/-) whaler.

walken ['valkən] *v/t.* (ge-, h) full (*cloth*); mill (*cloth, leather*).

Wall [val] *m* (-[e]s/ᵘe) ✕ rampart (*a. fig.*); dam; mound.

Wallach ['valax] *m* (-[e]s/-e) gelding.

wallen ['valən] *v/i.* (ge-, h, sein) hair, articles of dress, *etc.*: flow; simmer; boil (*a. fig.*).

wall|fahren ['valfa:rən] *v/i.* (ge-, sein) (go on a) pilgrimage; '**2fahrer** *m* pilgrim; '**2fahrt** *f* pilgrimage; '~**fahrten** *v/i.* (ge-, sein) (go on a) pilgrimage.

'**Wallung** *f* (-/-en) ebullition; 🔥 congestion; *(Blut) in ~ bringen* make *s.o.'s* blood boil, enrage.

Walnuß ['val-] *f* walnut; '~**baum** 🌳 *m* walnut(-tree).

Walroß *zo.* ['val-] *n* walrus.

walten ['valtən] *v/i.* (ge-, h): *s-s Amtes ~* attend to one's duties; *Gnade ~ lassen* show mercy.

Walze ['valtsə] *f* (-/-n) roller, cylin-

der; ⊕ *a.* roll; ⊕, ♪ barrel; '**2n** *v/t.* (ge-, *h*) roll (*a.* ⊕).
wälzen ['vɛltsən] *v/t.* (ge-, *h*) roll; roll (*problem*) round in one's mind; shift (*blame*) (*auf acc.* [up]on); *sich* ~ roll; wallow (*in mud, etc.*); welter (*in blood, etc.*).
Walzer ♪ ['valtsər] *m* (-*s*/-) waltz.
Wand [vant] **1.** *f* (-/⁼e) wall; partition; **2.** 2 *pret. of winden.*
Wandel ['vandəl] *m* (-*s*/*no pl.*) change; '**2bar** *adj.* changeable; variable; '**~gang** *m*, '**~halle** *f* lobby; '**2n** (ge-) **1.** *v/i.* (*sein*) walk; **2.** *v/refl.* (*h*) change.
Wander|er ['vandərər] *m* (-*s*/-) wanderer; hiker; '**~leben** *n* (-*s*/*no pl.*) vagrant life; '**2n** *v/i.* (ge-, *sein*) wander; hike; '**~niere** ⚕ *f* floating kidney; '**~prediger** *m* itinerant preacher; '**~preis** *m* challenge trophy; '**~schaft** *f* (-/*no pl.*) wanderings *pl.*; *auf* (*der*) ~ on the tramp; '**~ung** *f* (-/-*en*) walking-tour; hike.
'**Wand|gemälde** *n* mural (painting); '**~kalender** *m* wall-calendar; '**~karte** *f* wall-map.
Wandlung ['vandluŋ] *f* (-/-*en*) change, transformation; *eccl.* transubstantiation; ⚖ redhibition.
'**Wand|schirm** *m* folding-screen; '**~schrank** *m* wall-cupboard; '**~spiegel** *m* wall-mirror; '**~tafel** *f* blackboard; '**~teppich** *m* tapestry; '**~uhr** *f* wall-clock.
wandte ['vantə] *pret. of wenden* 2.
Wange ['vaŋə] *f* (-/-*n*) cheek.
Wankel|mut ['vaŋkəlmu:t] *m* fickleness, inconstancy; **2mütig** *adj.* ['~my:tiç] fickle, inconstant.
wanken ['vaŋkən] *v/i.* (ge-, *h*, *sein*) totter, stagger (*a. fig.*); *house, etc.*: rock; *fig.* waver.
wann *adv.* [van] when; *s. dann*; *seit* ~? how long?, since when?
Wanne ['vanə] *f* (-/-*n*) tub; bath (-tub), F tub; '**~nbad** *n* bath, F tub.
Wanze *zo.* ['vantsə] *f* (-/-*n*) bug, *Am. a.* bedbug.
Wappen ['vapən] *n* (-*s*/-) (coat of) arms *pl.*; '**~kunde** *f* (-/*no pl.*) heraldry; '**~schild** *m*, *n* escutcheon; '**~tier** *n* heraldic animal.
wappnen *fig.* ['vapnən] *v/refl.* (ge-, *h*): *sich* ~ *gegen* be prepared for; *sich mit Geduld* ~ have patience.
war [vɑ:r] *pret. of sein*[1].
warb [varp] *pret. of werben.*
Ware ['vɑ:rə] *f* (-/-*n*) commodity, article of trade; ~*n pl. a.* goods *pl.*, merchandise, wares *pl.*
'**Waren|aufzug** *m* hoist; '**~bestand** *m* stock (on hand); '**~haus** *n* department store; '**~lager** *n* stock; warehouse, *Am. a.* stock room; '**~probe** *f* sample; '**~zeichen** *n* trade mark.
warf [varf] *pret. of werfen.*

warm *adj.* [varm] warm (*a. fig.*); *meal*: hot; *schön* ~ nice and warm.
Wärme ['vɛrmə] *f* (-/⚒-*n*) warmth; *phys.* heat; '**~grad** *m* degree of heat; '**2n** *v/t.* (ge-, *h*) warm; *sich die Füße* ~ warm one's feet.
'**Wärmflasche** *f* hot-water bottle.
'**warmherzig** *adj.* warm-hearted.
Warm'wasser|heizung *f* hot-water heating; **~versorgung** *f* hot-water supply.
warn|en ['varnən] *v/t.* (ge-, *h*) warn (*vor dat.* of, against), caution (against); '**2signal** *n* danger-signal (*a. fig.*); '**2streik** *m* token strike; '**2ung** *f* (-/-*en*) warning, caution; **2ungstafel** ['varnuŋs-] *f* notice-board.
Warte *fig.* ['vartə] *f* (-/-*n*) point of view.
warten ['vartən] *v/i.* (ge-, *h*) wait (*auf acc.* for); be in store (for *s.o.*); *j-n* ~ *lassen* keep s.o. waiting.
Wärter ['vɛrtər] *m* (-*s*/-) attendant; keeper; (male) nurse.
'**Warte|saal** *m*, '**~zimmer** *n* waiting-room.
Wartung ⊕ ['vartuŋ] *f* (-/⚒-*en*) maintenance.
warum *adv.* [va'rum] why.
Warze ['vartsə] *f* (-/-*n*) wart; nipple.
was [vas] **1.** *interr. pron.* what; ~ *kostet das Buch?* how much is this book?; F ~ *rennst du denn so* (*schnell*)? why are you running like this?; ~ *für* (*ein*) ...! what a(n) ...!; ~ *für ein* ...? what ...?; **2.** *rel. pron.* what; ~ (*auch immer*), *alles* ~ what(so)ever; ..., ~ *ihn völlig kalt ließ* ... which left him quite cold; **3.** F *indef. pron.* something; *ich will dir mal* ~ *sagen* I'll tell you what.
wasch|bar *adj.* ['vaʃbɑ:r] washable; '**2becken** *n* wash-basin, *Am.* wash-bowl.
Wäsche ['vɛʃə] *f* (-/-*n*) wash(ing); laundry; linen (*a. fig.*); underwear; *in der* ~ *sein* be at the wash; *sie hat heute große* ~ she has a large wash today.
waschecht *adj.* ['vaʃ⁹-] washable; *colour*: *a.* fast; *fig.* dyed-in-the-wool.
'**Wäsche|klammer** *f* clothes-peg, clothes-pin; '**~leine** *f* clothes-line.
'**waschen** *v/t.* (*irr.*, ge-, *h*) wash; *sich* ~ (have a) wash; *sich das Haar or den Kopf* ~ wash *or* shampoo one's hair *or* head; *sich gut* ~ (*lassen*) wash well.
Wäscher|ei [vɛʃə'raɪ] *f* (-/-*en*) laundry; '**~in** *f* (-/-*nen*) washer-woman, laundress.
'**Wäscheschrank** *m* linen closet.
'**Wasch|frau** *f s. Wäscherin*; '**~haus** *n* wash-house; '**~kessel** *m* copper; '**~korb** *m* clothes-basket;

'₋küche f wash-house; '₋lappen m face-cloth, Am. washrag, wash-cloth; '₋maschine f washing machine, washer; '₋pulver n washing powder; '₋raum m lavatory, Am. a. washroom; '₋schüssel f wash-basin; '₋tag m wash(ing)-day; '₋ung f (-/-en) ⚓ wash; ablution; '₋weib contp. n gossip; '₋wanne f wash-tub.

Wasser ['vasər] n (-s/-, ≈) water; ~ lassen make water; zu ~ und zu Land(e) by sea and land; '₋ball m 1. beach-ball; water-polo ball; 2. (-[e]s/no pl.) water-polo; '₋ballspiel n 1. (-[e]s/no pl.) water-polo; 2. water-polo match; '₋behälter m reservoir, water-tank; '₋blase f water-blister; '₋dampf m steam; 'Ꝟdicht adj. waterproof; water-tight; '₋eimer m water-pail, bucket; '₋fall m waterfall, cascade; cataract; '₋farbe f water-colo(u)r; '₋flugzeug n waterplane, seaplane; '₋glas n 1. tumbler; 2. 🜊 (-s/no pl.) water-glass; '₋graben m ditch; '₋hahn m tap, Am. a. faucet; '₋hose f waterspout.

wässerig adj. ['vesəriç] watery; washy (a. fig.); j-m den Mund ~ machen make s.o.'s mouth water.

'Wasser|kanne f water-jug, ewer; '₋kessel m kettle; '₋klosett n water-closet, W.C.; '₋kraft f water-power; '₋kraftwerk n hydroelectric power station or plant, water-power station; '₋krug m water-jug, ewer; '₋kur f water-cure, hydropathy; '₋lauf m water-course; '₋leitung f water-supply; '₋leitungsrohr n water-pipe; '₋mangel m shortage of water; 'Ꝟn v/i. (ge-, h) alight on water; splash down. [(salted herring, etc.).]

wässern ['vesərn] v/t. (ge-, h) soak}
'Wasser|pflanze f aquatic plant; '₋rinne f gutter; '₋rohr n water-pipe; '₋schaden m damage caused by water; '₋scheide f watershed, Am. a. divide; '₋scheu adj. afraid of water; '₋schlauch m water-hose; '₋spiegel m water-level; '₋sport m aquatic sports pl.; '₋spülung f (-/-en) flushing (system); '₋stand m water-level; '₋standsanzeiger ['vasərtants?~] m water-gauge; '₋stiefel m/pl. waders pl.; '₋stoff 🜊 m (-[e]s/no pl.) hydrogen; '₋stoffbombe f hydrogen bomb, H-bomb; '₋strahl m jet of water; '₋straße f waterway; '₋tier n aquatic animal; '₋verdrängung f (-/-en) displacement; '₋versorgung f water-supply; '₋waage f spirit-level, water-level; '₋weg m waterway; auf dem ~ by water; '₋welle f water-wave; '₋werk n waterworks sg., pl.; '₋zeichen n watermark.

wäßrig adj. ['vesriç] s. wässerig.

waten ['vɑːtən] v/i. (ge-, sein) wade.

watscheln ['vɑːtʃəln] v/i. (ge-, sein, h) waddle.

Watt ⚡ [vat] n (-s/-) watt.

Watt|e ['vatə] f (-/-n) cotton-wool; surgical cotton; wadding; '₋ebausch m wad; 2ieren [~'tiːrən] v/t. wad, pad.

weben ['veːbən] v/t. and v/i. ([irr.,] ge-, h) weave.

'Weber m (-s/-) weaver; ₋ei [~'rai] f 1. (-/no pl.) weaving; 2. (-/-en) weaving-mill.

Webstuhl ['veːpʃtuːl] m loom.

Wechsel ['veksəl] m (-s/-) change; allowance; † bill (of exchange); hunt. runway; eigener ~ † promissory note; '₋beziehung f correlation; '₋fälle ['~fɛlə] pl. vicissitudes pl.; '₋fieber ꝵ n (-s/no pl.) intermittent fever; malaria; '₋frist † f usance; '₋geld n change; '₋kurs m rate of exchange; '₋makler † m bill-broker; 'Ꝟn (ge-, h) 1. v/t. change; vary; exchange (words, etc.); den Besitzer ~ change hands; die Kleider ~ change (one's clothes); 2. v/i. change; vary; alternate; '₋nehmer † m (-s/-) payee; '₋seitig adj. ['~zaitiç] mutual, reciprocal; '₋strom ⚡ m alternating current; '₋stube f exchange office; 'Ꝟweise adv. alternately, by or in turns; '₋wirkung f interaction.

wecke|n ['vekən] v/t. (ge-, h) wake (up), waken; arouse (a. fig.); 'Ꝟr m (-s/-) alarm-clock.

wedeln ['veːdəln] v/i. (ge-, h): ~ mit wag (tail).

weder cj. ['veːdər]: ~ ... noch neither ... nor.

Weg¹ [veːk] m (-[e]s/-e) way (a.fig.); road (a. fig.); path; route; walk; auf halbem ~ half-way; am ~e by the roadside; aus dem ~e gehen steer clear of; aus dem ~e räumen remove (a. fig.); in die ~e leiten set on foot, initiate.

weg² adv. [vek] away, off; gone; geh ~! be off (with you)!; ~ mit ihm! off with him!; Hände ~! hands off!; F ich muß ~ I must be off; F ganz ~ sein be quite beside o.s.; '₋bleiben F v/i. (irr. bleiben, sep., -ge-, sein) stay away; be omitted; '₋bringen v/t. (irr. bringen, sep., -ge-, h) take away; a. remove (things).

wegen prp. (gen.) ['veːgən] because of, on account of, owing to.

weg|fahren ['vek-] (irr. fahren, sep., -ge-) 1. v/t. (h) remove; cart away; 2. v/i. (sein) leave; '₋fallen v/i. (irr. fallen, sep., -ge-, sein) be omitted; be abolished; 'Ꝟgang m (-[e]s/no pl.) going away, departure; '₋gehen v/i. (irr. gehen, sep., -ge-, sein) go away or off; merchandise:

sell; '~haben F v/t. (irr. haben, sep., -ge-, h): e-n ~ be tight; have a screw loose; er hat noch nicht weg, wie man es machen muß he hasn't got the knack of it yet; '~jagen v/t. (sep., -ge-, h) drive away; '~kommen F v/i. (irr. kommen, sep., -ge-, sein) get away; be missing; gut (schlecht) ~ come off well (badly); mach, daß du wegkommst! be off (with you)!; '~lassen v/t. (irr. lassen, sep., -ge-, h) let s.o. go; leave out, omit; '~laufen v/i. (irr. laufen, sep., -ge-, sein) run away; '~legen v/t. (sep., -ge-, h) put away; '~machen F v/t. (sep., -ge-, h) remove; a. take out (stains); '~müssen F v/i. (irr. müssen 1, sep., -ge-, h): ich muß weg I must be off; 2nahme f (-/-n) taking (away); '~nehmen v/t. (irr. nehmen, sep., -ge-, h) take up, occupy (time, space); j-m et. ~ take s.th. away from s.o.; '~raffen fig. v/t. (sep., -ge-, h) carry off.

Wegrand ['ve:k-] m wayside.

weg|räumen ['vek-] v/t. (sep., -ge-, h) clear away, remove; '~schaffen v/t. (sep., -ge-, h) remove; '~schikken v/t. (sep., -ge-, h) send away or off; '~sehen v/i. (irr. sehen, sep., -ge-, h) look away; ~ über (acc.) overlook, shut one's eyes to; '~setzen v/t. (sep., -ge-, h) put away; sich ~ über (acc.) disregard, ignore; '~streichen v/t. (irr. streichen, sep., -ge-, h) strike off or out; '~tun v/t. (irr. tun, sep., -ge-, h) put away or aside.

Wegweiser ['ve:kvaɪzər] m (-s/-) signpost, finger-post; fig. guide.

weg|wenden ['vek-] v/t. ([irr. wenden,] sep., -ge-, h) turn away, avert (one's eyes); sich ~ turn away; '~werfen v/t. (irr. werfen, sep., -ge-, h) throw away; '~werfend adj. disparaging; '~wischen v/t. (sep., -ge-, h) wipe off; '~ziehen (irr. ziehen, sep., -ge-) 1. v/t. (h) pull or draw away; 2. v/i. (sein) (re)move.

weh [ve:] 1. adj. sore; 2. adv.: ~ tun ache, hurt; j-m ~ tun pain or hurt s.o.; fig. a. grieve s.o.; sich ~ tun hurt o.s.; mir tut der Finger ~ my finger hurts.

Wehen¹ ['ve:ən] f/pl. labo(u)r, travail.

wehen² [~] (ge-, h) 1. v/t. blow; 2. v/i. blow; es weht ein starker Wind it is blowing hard.

weh|klagen v/i. (ge-, h) lament (um for, over); '~leidig adj. snivel(l)ing; voice: plaintive; '~mut f (-/no pl.) wistfulness; ~mütig adj. ['~my:-tiç] wistful.

Wehr [ve:r] 1. f (-/-en): sich zur ~ setzen offer resistance (gegen to); show fight; 2. n (-[e]s/-e) weir;

~dienst ✗ m military service; '2en v/refl. (ge-, h) defend o.s.; offer resistance (gegen to); '2fähig ✗ adj. able-bodied; '2los adj. defenceless, Am. defenseless; '~pflicht ✗ f (-/no pl.) compulsory military service, conscription; '2pflichtig ✗ adj. liable to military service.

Weib [vaɪp] n (-[e]s/-er) woman; wife; '~chen zo. n (-s/-) female.

Weiber|feind ['vaɪbər-] m womanhater; '~held contp. m ladies' man; '~volk F n (-[e]s/no pl.) womenfolk.

weib|isch adj. ['vaɪbiʃ] womanish, effeminate; '~lich adj. ['~p-] female; gr. feminine; womanly, feminine.

weich adj. [vaɪç] soft (a. fig.); meat, etc.: tender; egg: soft-boiled; ~ werden soften; fig. relent.

Weiche¹ ☒ ['vaɪçə] f (-/-n) switch; ~n pl. points pl.

Weiche² anat. [~] f (-/-n) flank, side.

weichen¹ ['vaɪçən] v/i. (irr., ge-, sein) give way, yield (dat. to); nicht von der Stelle ~ not to budge an inch; j-m nicht von der Seite ~ stick to s.o.

weichen² [~] v/i. (ge-, h, sein) soak.

'Weichensteller ☒ m (-s/-) points-man, switch-man.

'weich|herzig adj. soft-hearted, tender-hearted; '~lich adj. somewhat soft; fig. effeminate; 2ling ['~lɪŋ] m (-s/-e) weakling, milksop, molly(-coddle), sl. sissy; '2tier n mollusc.

Weide¹ ♀ ['vaɪdə] f (-/-n) willow.

Weide² ✏ [~] f (-/-n) pasture; auf der ~ out at grass; '~land n pasture(-land); '2n (ge-, h) 1. v/t. feed, pasture, graze; sich ~ an (dat.) gloat over; feast on; 2. v/i. pasture, graze.

'Weiden|korb m wicker basket, osier basket; '~rute f osier switch.

weidmännisch hunt. adj. ['vaɪt-meniʃ] sportsmanlike.

weiger|n ['vaɪgərn] v/refl. (ge-, h) refuse, decline; '2ung f (-/-en) refusal.

Weihe eccl. ['vaɪə] f (-/-n) consecration; ordination; '2n eccl. v/t. (ge-, h) consecrate; j-n zum Priester ~ ordain s.o. priest.

Weiher ['vaɪər] m (-s/-) pond.

'weihevoll adj. solemn.

Weihnachten ['vaɪnaxtən] n (-s/no pl.) Christmas, Xmas.

'Weihnachts|abend m Christmas eve; '~baum m Christmas-tree; '~ferien pl. Christmas holidays pl.; '~fest n Christmas; '~geschenk n Christmas present; '~gratifikation f Christmas bonus; '~karte f Christmas card; '~lied n carol, Christmas hymn; '~mann m Father Christmas, Santa Claus; '~markt m Christmas fair; '~zeit f

(-/no pl.) Christmas(-tide) (in Germany beginning on the first Advent Sunday).

'Weih|rauch eccl. m incense; '~wasser eccl. n (-s/no pl.) holy water.

weil cj. [vaɪl] because, since, as.

Weil|chen ['vaɪlçən] n (-s/-): ein ~ a little while, a spell; '~e f (-/no pl.): e-e ~ a while.

Wein [vaɪn] m (-[e]s/-e) wine; ♀ vine; wilder ~ ♀ Virginia creeper; '~bau m (-[e]s/no pl.) vine-growing, viticulture; '~beere f grape; '~berg m vineyard; '~blatt n vine-leaf.

wein|en ['vaɪnən] v/i. (ge-, h) weep (um, vor dat. for), cry (vor dat. for joy, etc., with hunger, etc.); '~erlich adj. tearful, lachrymose; whining.

'Wein|ernte f vintage; '~essig m vinegar; '~faß n wine-cask; '~flasche f wine-bottle; '~geist m (-[e]s/-e) spirit(s pl.) of wine; '~glas n wineglass; '~handlung f wine-merchant's shop; '~karte f wine-list; '~keller m wine-vault; '~kelter f winepress; '~kenner m connoisseur of or in wines.

'Weinkrampf ⚕ m paroxysm of weeping.

'Wein|kühler m wine-cooler; '~lese f vintage; '~presse f winepress; '~ranke f vine-tendril; '~rebe f vine; '2rot adj. claret-colo(u)red; '~stock m vine; '~traube f grape, bunch of grapes.

weise¹ ['vaɪzə] 1. adj. wise; sage; 2. ⚥ m (-n/-n) wise man, sage.

Weise² [~] f (-/-n) ♪ melody, tune; fig. manner, way; auf diese ~ in this way.

weisen ['vaɪzən] (irr., ge-, h) 1. v/t.: j-m die Tür ~ show s.o. the door; von der Schule ~ expel from school; von sich ~ reject (idea, etc.); deny (charge, etc.); 2. v/i.: ~ auf (acc.) point at or to.

Weis|heit ['vaɪshaɪt] f (-/⚥-en) wisdom; am Ende s-r ~ sein be at one's wit's end; '~heitszahn m wisdom-tooth; '2machen v/t. (sep., -ge-, h): j-m et. ~ make s.o. believe s.th.

weiß adj. [vaɪs] white; '2blech n tin(-plate); '2brot n white bread; '2e m (-n/-n) white (man); '~en v/t. (ge-, h) whitewash; '~glühend adj. white-hot, incandescent; '2kohl m white cabbage; '~lich adj. whitish; '2waren pl. linen goods pl.; '2wein m white wine.

Weisung ['vaɪzʊŋ] f (-/-en) direction, directive.

weit [vaɪt] 1. adj. distant (von from); world, garment: wide; area, etc.: vast; garment: loose; journey, way: long; conscience: elastic; 2. adv.: ~ entfernt far away; ~ entfernt von a. a long distance from; fig. far from;

~ und breit far and wide; ~ über sechzig (Jahre alt) well over sixty; bei ~em (by) far; von ~em from a distance.

weit|ab adv. ['vaɪt'-] far away (von from); '~aus adv. (by) far, much; '2blick m (-[e]s/no pl.) far-sightedness; '~blickend adj. far-sighted, far-seeing; '~en v/t. and v/refl. (ge-, h) widen.

'weiter 1. adj. particulars, etc.: further; charges, etc.: additional, extra; ~e fünf Wochen another five weeks; bis auf ~es until further notice; ohne ~es without any hesitation; off-hand; 2. adv. furthermore, moreover; ~! go on!; nichts ~ nothing more; und so ~ and so on; bis hierher und nicht ~ so far and no farther; '2e n (-n/no pl.) the rest; further details pl.

'weiter|befördern v/t. (sep., no -ge-, h) forward; '~bestehen v/i. (irr. stehen, sep., no -ge-, h) continue to exist, survive; '~bilden v/t. (sep., -ge-, h) give s.o. further education; sich ~ improve one's knowledge; continue one's education; '~geben v/t. (irr. geben, sep., -ge-, h) pass (dat., an acc. to); '~gehen v/i. (irr. gehen, sep., -ge-, sein) pass or move on, walk along; fig. continue, go on; '~hin adv. in (the) future; furthermore; et. ~ tun continue doing or to do s.th.; '~kommen v/i. (irr. kommen, sep., -ge-, sein) get on; '~können v/i. (irr. können, sep., -ge-, h) be able to go on; '~leben v/i. (sep., -ge-, h) live on, survive (a. fig.); '~machen v/t. and v/i. (sep., -ge-, h) carry on.

'weit|gehend adj. powers: large; support: generous; '~gereist adj. travel(l)ed; '~greifend adj. far-reaching; '~herzig adj. broad-minded; '~hin adv. far off; ~läufig ['~lɔyfiç] 1. adj. house, etc.: spacious; story, etc.: detailed; relative: distant; 2. adv.: ~ erzählen (tell in) detail; er ist ~ verwandt mit mir he is a distant relative of mine; '~reichend adj. far-reaching; '~schweifig adj. diffuse, prolix; '~sichtig adj. ⚕ far-sighted; fig. a. far-seeing; '2sichtigkeit ⚕ f (-/⚥-en) far-sightedness; '2sprung m (-[e]s/no pl.) long jump, Am. broad jump; '~tragend adj. ✕ long-range; fig. far-reaching; '~verbreitet adj. widespread.

Weizen ♀ ['vaɪtsən] m (-s/-) wheat; '~brot n wheaten bread; '~mehl n wheaten flour.

welch [vɛlç] 1. interr. pron. what; which; ~er? which one?; ~er von beiden? which of the two?; 2. rel. pron. who, that; which, that; 3. F indef. pron.: es gibt ~e, die sagen, daß ... there are some who say that ...; *es sollen viele Ausländer hier sein, hast du schon ~e gesehen?* many foreigners are said to be here, have you seen any yet?

welk *adj.* [vɛlk] faded, withered; *skin:* flabby, flaccid; '**~en** *v/i.* (ge-, sein) fade, wither.

Wellblech ['vɛlblɛç] *n* corrugated iron.

Welle ['vɛlə] *f* (-/-n) wave (*a. fig.*); ⊕ shaft.

'**wellen** *v/t. and v/refl.* (ge-, h) wave; '**2bereich** ≠ *m* wave-range; **~förmig** *adj.* ['~fœrmiç] undulating, undulatory; '**2länge** ≠ *f* wavelength; '**2linie** *f* wavy line; '**2reiten** *n* (-s/*no pl.*) surf-riding.

'**wellig** *adj.* wavy.

'**Wellpappe** *f* corrugated cardboard *or* paper.

Welt [vɛlt] *f* (-/-en) world; *die ganze ~* the whole world, all the world; *auf der ~* in the world, *auf der ganzen ~* all over the world; *zur ~ bringen* give birth to, bring into the world.

'**Welt|all** *n* universe, cosmos; '**~anschauung** *f* Weltanschauung; '**~ausstellung** *f* world fair; '**2bekannt** *adj.* known all over the world; '**2berühmt** *adj.* world-famous; '**~bürger** *m* cosmopolite; '**2erschütternd** *adj.* world-shaking; '**2fremd** *adj.* wordly innocent; '**~friede(n)** *m* universal peace; '**~geschichte** *f* (-/*no pl.*) universal history; '**2gewandt** *adj.* knowing the ways of the world; '**~handel** ✝ *m* (-s/*no pl.*) world trade; '**~karte** *f* map of the world; '**2klug** *adj.* wordly-wise; '**~krieg** *m* world war; *der zweite ~* World War II; '**~lage** *f* international situation; '**~lauf** *m* course of the world; '**2lich** 1. *adj.* wordly; secular, temporal; 2. *adv.*: *~ gesinnt* wordly-minded; '**~literatur** *f* world literature; '**~macht** *f* world-power; '**2männisch** *adj.* ['~mɛniʃ] man-of-the-world; '**~markt** *m* (-[e]s/*no pl.*) world market; '**~meer** *n* ocean; '**~meister** *m* world champion; '**~meisterschaft** *f* world championship; '**~raum** *m* (-[e]s/*no pl.*) (outer) space; '**~reich** *n* universal empire; *das Britische ~* the British Empire; '**~reise** *f* journey round the world; '**~rekord** *m* world record; '**~ruf** *m* (-[e]s/*no pl.*) world-wide reputation; '**~schmerz** *m* Weltschmerz; '**~sprache** *f* world *or* universal language; '**~stadt** *f* metropolis; '**2weit** *adj.* world-wide; '**~wunder** *n* wonder of the world.

Wende ['vɛndə] *f* (-/-n) turn (*a. swimming*); *fig. a.* turning-point; '**~kreis** *m geogr.* tropic; *mot.* turning-circle.

Wendeltreppe ['vɛndəl-] *f* winding

staircase, (e-e a flight of) winding stairs *pl.*, spiral staircase.

'**Wende|marke** *f sports*: turning-point; '**2n** 1. *v/t.* (ge-, h) turn (*coat, etc.*); turn (*hay*) about; 2. *v/refl.* (*irr.*) ge-, h): *sich ~ an* (*acc.*) turn to; address o.s. to; apply to (*wegen* for); 3. *v/i.* (ge-, h) ⊕, *mot.* turn; *bitte ~!* please turn over!; '**~punkt** *m* turning-point.

'**wend|ig** *adj.* nimble, agile (*both a. fig.*); *mot.*, ⊕ easily steerable; *mot.* flexible; '**2ung** *f* (-/-en) turn (*a. fig.*); ✕ facing; *fig.*: change; expression; idiom.

wenig ['ve:niç] 1. *adj.* little; *~e pl.* few *pl.*; *~er* less; *~er pl.* fewer; *ein klein ~* Geduld a little bit of patience; *das ~e* the little; 2. *adv.* little; *~er* less; ᵈ *a.* minus; *am ~sten* least (of all); '**2keit** *f* (-/-en): *meine ~* my humble self; **~stens** *adv.* ['~stəns] at least.

wenn *cj.* [vɛn] when; if; *~ ... nicht* if ... not, unless; *~ auch* (al)though, even though; *~ auch noch so* however; *und ~ nun ...?* what if ...?; *wie wäre es, ~ wir jetzt heimgingen?* what about going home now?

wer [ve:r] 1. *interr. pron.* who; which; *~ von euch?* which of you?; 2. *rel. pron.* who; *~ auch* (*immer*) who(so)ever; 3. *indef. pron.* somebody; anybody; *ist schon ~ gekommen?* has anybody come yet?

Werbe|abteilung ['vɛrbə-] *f* advertising *or* publicity department; '**~film** *m* advertising film.

'**werb|en** (*irr.*, ge-, h) 1. *v/t.* canvass (*votes, subscribers, etc.*); ✕ recruit, enlist; 2. *v/i.*: *~ für* advertise, *Am. a.* advertize; make propaganda for; canvass for; '**2ung** *f* (-/-en) advertising, publicity, *Am. a.* advertizing; propaganda; canvassing; ✕ enlistment, recruiting.

Werdegang ['ve:rdə-] *m* career; ⊕ process of manufacture.

'werden 1. *v/i.* (*irr.*, ge-, sein) become, get; grow; turn (*pale, sour, etc.*); *was ist aus ihm geworden?* what has become of him?; *was will er (einmal) ~?* what is he going to be?; 2. ᵠ *n* (-s/*no pl.*): *noch im ~ sein* be in embryo.

werfen ['vɛrfən] (*irr.*, ge-, h) 1. *v/t.* throw (*nach at*); *zo.* throw (*young*); cast (*shadow, glance, etc.*); *Falten ~* fall in folds; set badly; 2. *v/i.* throw; *zo.* litter; *~ mit* throw (*auf acc.*, *nach at*).

Werft ⚓ [vɛrft] *f* (-/-en) shipyard, dockyard.

Werk [vɛrk] *n* (-[e]s/-e) work; act; ⊕ works *pl.*; works *sg.*, *pl.*, factory; *das ~ e-s Augenblicks* the work of a moment; *zu ~e gehen* proceed; '**~bank** ⊕ *f* work-bench; '**~meister** *m* foreman; **~statt** ['~ʃtat] *f*

(-/ʷen) workshop; '**tag** m workday; '**2tätig** adj. working; '**zeug** n tool; implement; instrument.

Wermut ['veːrmuːt] m (-[e]s/no pl.) ♀ wormwood; verm(o)uth.

wert [veːrt] **1.** adj. worth; worthy (gen. of); ~, getan zu werden worth doing; **2.** ♀ m (-[e]s/-e) value (a. ♣, ♠, phys., fig.); worth (a. fig.); Briefmarken im ~ von 2 Schilling 2 shillings' worth of stamps; großen ~ legen auf (acc.) set a high value (up)on.

'**Wert|brief** m money-letter; '**2en** v/t. (ge-, h) value; appraise; '**gegenstand** m article of value; '**2los** adj. worthless, valueless; '**papiere** n/pl. securities pl.; '**sachen** pl. valuables pl.; '**ung** f (-/-en) valuation; appraisal; sports: score; '**2voll** adj. valuable, precious.

Wesen ['veːzən] n **1.** (-s/no pl.) entity, essence; nature, character; viel ~s machen um make a fuss of; **2.** (-s/-) being, creature; '**2los** adj. unreal; '**2tlich** adj. essential, substantial.

weshalb [vɛs'halp] **1.** interr. pron. why; **2.** cj. that's why.

Wespe zo. ['vɛspə] f (-/-n) wasp.

West geogr. [vɛst] west; '**en** m (-s/no pl.) west; the West.

Weste ['vɛstə] f (-/-n) waistcoat, ✝ and Am. vest; e-e reine ~ haben have a clean slate.

'**west|lich** adj. west; westerly; western; '**2wind** m west(erly) wind.

Wett|bewerb ['vɛtbəverp] m (-[e]s/-e) competition (a. ✝); '**büro** n betting office; '**e** f (-/-n) wager, bet; e-e ~ eingehen lay or make a bet; '**eifer** m emulation, rivalry; '**2eifern** v/i. (ge-, h) vie (mit with; in dat. in; um for); '**2en** (ge-, h) **1.** v/t. wager, bet; **2.** v/i.: mit j-m um et. ~ wager or bet s.o. s.th.; ~ auf (acc.) wager or bet on, back.

Wetter[1] ['vɛtər] n (-s/-) weather.

Wetter[2] [~] m (-s/-) better.

'**Wetter|bericht** m weather-forecast; '**2fest** adj. weather-proof; '**karte** f weather-chart; '**lage** f weather-conditions pl.; '**leuchten** n (-s/no pl.) sheet-lightning; '**vorhersage** f (-/-n) weather-forecast; '**warte** f weather-station.

'**Wett|kampf** m contest, competition; '**kämpfer** m contestant; '**lauf** m race; '**läufer** m racer, runner; '**2machen** v/t. (sep., -ge-, h) make up for; '**rennen** n race; '**rüsten** n (-s/no pl.) armament race; '**spiel** n match, game; '**streit** m contest. [sharpen.]

wetzen ['vɛtsən] v/t. (ge-, h) whet, }

wich [viç] pret. of weichen[1].

Wichse ['viksə] f **1.** (-/-n) blacking; polish; **2.** F fig. (-/no pl.) thrashing; '**2n** v/t. (ge-, h) black; polish.

wichtig adj. ['viçtiç] important; sich ~ machen show off; '**2keit** f (-/♣-en) importance; '**2tuer** ['~tuːər] m (-s/-) pompous fellow; '**tuerisch** adj. pompous.

Wickel ['vikəl] m (-s/-) roll(er); ♣: compress; packing; '**2n** v/t. (ge-, h) wind; swaddle (baby); wrap.

Widder zo. ['vidər] m (-s/-) ram.

wider prp. (acc.) ['viːdər] against, contrary to; '**borstig** adj. crossgrained; '**fahren** v/i. (irr. fahren, no -ge-, sein) happen (dat. to); '**2haken** m barb; '**2hall** ['~hal] m (-[e]s/-e) echo, reverberation; fig. response; '**hallen** v/i. (sep., -ge-, h) (re-)echo (von with), resound (with); '**legen** v/t. (no -ge-, h) refute, disprove; '**lich** adj. repugnant, repulsive; disgusting; '**natürlich** adj. unnatural; '**rechtlich** adj. illegal, unlawful; '**2rede** f contradiction; '**2ruf** m ♣♣ revocation; retraction; '**rufen** v/t. (irr. rufen, no -ge-, h) revoke; retract (a. ♣♣); '**ruflich** adj. revocable; '**2sacher** ['~zaxər] m (-s/-) adversary; '**2schein** m reflection; '**setzen** v/refl. (no -ge-, h): sich e-r Sache ~ oppose or resist s.th.; '**2setzlich** adj. refractory; insubordinate; '**sinnig** adj. absurd; '**spenstig** adj. ['~ʃpɛnstiç] refractory; '**2spenstigkeit** f (-/♣-en) refractoriness; '**spiegeln** v/t. (sep., -ge-, h) reflect (a. fig.); sich ~ in (dat.) be reflected in; '**sprechen** v/i. (irr. sprechen, no -ge-, h): j-m ~ contradict s.o.; '**2spruch** m contradiction; opposition; im ~ zu in contradiction to; '**sprüchlich** adj. ['~ʃpryːçliç] contradictory; '**spruchslos 1.** adj. uncontradicted; **2.** adv. without contradiction; '**2stand** m resistance (a. ♂); opposition; ~ leisten offer resistance (dat. to); auf heftigen ~ stoßen meet with stiff opposition; '**standsfähig** adj. resistant (a. ⊕); '**stehen** v/i. (irr. stehen, no -ge-, h) resist (e-r Sache s.th.); '**streben** v/i. (no -ge-, h): es widerstrebt mir, dies zu tun I hate doing or to do that, I am reluctant to do that; '**strebend** adv. reluctantly; '**2streit** m (-[e]s/♣-e) antagonism; fig. conflict; '**wärtig** adj. ['~vɛrtiç] unpleasant, disagreeable; disgusting; '**2wille** m aversion (gegen to, for, from); dislike (to, of, for); disgust (at, for); reluctance, unwillingness; '**willig** adj. reluctant, unwilling.

widm|en ['vitmən] v/t. (ge-, h) dedicate; '**2ung** f (-/-en) dedication.

widrig adj. ['viːdriç] adverse; **enfalls** adv. ['~gən'-] failing which, in default of which.

wie [vi:] **1.** *adv.* how; ~ *alt ist er?* what is his age?; ~ *spät ist es?* what is the time?; **2.** *cj.:* *ein Mann ~ er* a man such as he, a man like him; ~ *er dies hörte* hearing this; *ich hörte,* ~ *er es sagte* I heard him saying so.

wieder *adv.* ['vi:dər] again, anew; *immer ~* again and again; 2'**aufbau** *m* (-[e]s/*no pl.*) reconstruction; rebuilding; ~'**aufbauen** *v/t.* (*sep.,* -ge-, h) reconstruct; ~'**aufleben** *v/i.* (*sep.,* -ge-, sein) revive; 2'**aufleben** *n* (-s/*no pl.*) revival; 2'**aufnahme** *f* resumption; ~'**aufnehmen** *v/t.* (*irr.* nehmen, *sep.,* -ge-, h) resume; 2**beginn** *m* recommencement; re-opening; '~**bekommen** *v/t.* (*irr.* kommen, *sep.,* no -ge-, h) get back; '~**beleben** *v/t.* (*sep.,* no -ge-, h) resurrect; 2**belebung** *f* (-/-en) revival; *fig. a.* resurrection; 2'**belebungsversuch** *m* attempt at resuscitation; '~**bringen** *v/t.* (*irr.* bringen, *sep.,* -ge-, h) bring back; restore, give back; ~'**einsetzen** *v/t.* (*sep.,* -ge-, h) restore; ~'**einstellen** *v/t.* (*sep.,* -ge-, h) re-engage; 2**ergreifung** *f* reseizure; '~**erkennen** *v/t.* (*irr.* kennen, *sep.,* no -ge-, h) recognize (*an dat.* by); ~**erstatten** *v/t.* (*sep.,* no -ge-, h) restore; reimburse, refund (*money*); '~**geben** *v/t.* (*irr.* geben, *sep.,* -ge-, h) give back, return; render, reproduce; ~'**gutmachen** *v/t.* (*sep.,* -ge-, h) make up for; 2'**gutmachung** *f* (-/-en) reparation; ~'**herstellen** *v/t.* (*sep.,* -ge-, h) restore; ~**holen** *v/t.* (h) **1.** [~'ho:lən] (*no* -ge-) repeat; **2.** ['~ho:lən] (*sep.,* -ge-) fetch back; 2'**holung** *f* (-/-en) repetition; '~**käuen** ['~kɔʏən] (*sep.,* -ge-, h) **1.** *v/t.* ruminate, chew the cud; **2.** F *fig. v/t.* repeat over and over; 2**kehr** ['~ke:r] *f* (-/*no pl.*) return; recurrence; '~**kehren** *v/i.* (*sep.,* -ge-, sein) return; recur; '~**kommen** *v/i.* (*irr.* kommen, *sep.,* -ge-, sein) come back, return; '~**sehen** *v/t. and v/refl.* (*irr.* sehen, *sep.,* -ge-, h) see or meet again; 2**sehen** *n* (-s/*no pl.*) meeting again; *auf* ~*!* good-bye!; '~**tun** *v/t.* (*irr.* tun, *sep.,* -ge-, h) do again, repeat; '~**um** *adv.* again, anew; '~**vereinigen** *v/t.* (*sep.,* no -ge-, h) reunite; 2**vereinigung** *f* reunion; *pol.* reunification; 2'**verheiratung** *f* remarriage; 2**verkäufer** *m* reseller; retailer; 2**wahl** *f* re-election; '~**wählen** *v/t.* (*sep.,* -ge-, h) re-elect; 2'**zulassung** *f* readmission.

Wiege ['vi:gə] *f* (-/-n) cradle.

wiegen¹ ['vi:gən] *v/t. and v/i.* (*irr.,* ge-, h) weigh.

wiegen² [~] *v/t.* (ge-, h) rock; *in Sicherheit* ~ rock in security, lull into (a false sense of) security.

'Wiegenlied *n* lullaby.

wiehern ['vi:ərn] *v/i.* (ge-, h) neigh.

Wiener ['vi:nər] *m* (-s/-) Viennese; 2**isch** *adj.* Viennese.

wies [vi:s] *pret. of* weisen.

Wiese ['vi:zə] *f* (-/-n) meadow.

wie'so *interr. pron.* why; why so.

wie'viel *adv.* how much; ~ *pl.* how many *pl.*; ~**te** *adv.* [~tə]: *den ~ten haben wir heute?* what's the date today?

wild [vilt] **1.** *adj.* wild; savage; ~**es** *Fleisch* 🖉 proud flesh; ~**e** *Ehe* concubinage; ~**er** *Streik* ✝ wildcat strike; **2.** 2 *n* (-[e]s/*no pl.*) game; venison. '**Wild|bach** *m* torrent; '~**bret** ['~bret] *n* (-s/*no pl.*) game; venison.

Wilde ['vildə] *m* (-n/-n) savage.

Wilder|er ['vildərər] *m* (-s/-) poacher; 2**n** *v/i.* (ge-, h) poach.

'**Wild|fleisch** *n s.* Wildbret; 2**fremd** F *adj.* quite strange; '~**hüter** *m* gamekeeper; '~**leder** *n* buckskin; 2**ledern** *adj.* buckskin; doeskin; '~**nis** *f* (-/-se) wilderness, wild (*a. fig.*); '~**schwein** *n* wildboar.

Wille ['vilə] *m* (-ns/✶ -n) will; *s-n ~n durchsetzen* have one's way; *gegen s-n ~n* against one's will; *j-m s-n ~n lassen* let s.o. have his (own) way; 2**nlos** *adj.* lacking will-power. '**Willens|freiheit** *f* (-/*no pl.*) freedom of (the) will; '~**kraft** *f* (-/*no pl.*) will-power; '~**schwäche** *f* (-/*no pl.*) weak will; 2**stark** *adj.* strong-willed; '~**stärke** *f* (-/*no pl.*) strong will, will-power.

'**will|ig** *adj.* willing, ready; '~**kommen** *adj.* welcome; 2**kür** [~ky:r] *f* (-/*no pl.*) arbitrariness; '~**kürlich** *adj.* arbitrary.

wimmeln ['viməln] *v/i.* (ge-, h) swarm (*von* with), teem (with).

wimmern ['vimərn] *v/i.* (ge-, h) whimper, whine.

Wimpel ['vimpəl] *m* (-s/-) pennant, pennon, streamer.

Wimper ['vimpər] *f* (-/-n) eyelash.

Wind [vint] *m* (-[e]s/-e) wind; '~**beutel** *m* cream-puff; F *fig.* windbag.

Winde ['vində] *f* (-/-n) windlass, reel.

Windel ['vindəl] *f* (-/-n) diaper, (baby's) napkin; ~**n** *pl. a.* swaddling-clothes *pl.*

'**winden** *v/t.* (*irr.,* ge-, h) wind; twist, twirl; make, bind (*wreath*); *sich* ~ *vor* (*dat.*) writhe with.

'**Wind|hose** *f* whirlwind, tornado; '~**hund** *m* greyhound; 2**ig** *adj.* ['~diç] windy; F *fig.* excuse: thin, lame; '~**mühle** *f* windmill; '~**pocken** 🖉 *pl.* chicken-pox; '~**richtung** *f* direction of the wind; '~**rose** ⚓ *f* compass card; '~**schutzscheibe** *f* wind-screen, *Am.* windshield; '~**stärke** *f* wind velocity; 'Qstill *adj.* calm; '₋stille *f* calm; '₋stoß *m* blast of wind, gust.

'Windung *f* (-/-en) winding, turn; bend (*of way, etc.*); coil (*of snake, etc.*).

Wink [viŋk] *m* (-[e]s/-e) sign; wave; wink; *fig.*: hint; tip.

Winkel ['viŋkəl] *m* (-s/-) Å angle; corner, nook; '₋ig *adj.* angular; *street*: crooked; '₋zug *m* subterfuge, trick, shift.

'winken *v/i.* (ge-, h) make a sign; beckon; *mit dem Taschentuch* ~ wave one's handkerchief.

winklig *adj.* ['viŋkliç] *s.* winkelig.

winseln ['vinzəln] *v/i.* (ge-, h) whimper, whine.

Winter ['vintər] *m* (-s/-) winter; *im* ~ *in winter*; 'Qlich *adj.* wintry; '₋schlaf *m* hibernation; '₋sport *m* winter sports *pl.*

Winzer ['vintsər] *m* (-s/-) vine-dresser; vine-grower; vintager.

winzig *adj.* ['vintsiç] tiny, diminutive.

Wipfel ['vipfəl] *m* (-s/-) top.

Wippe ['vipə] *f* (-/-n) seesaw; 'Qn *v/i.* (ge-, h) seesaw.

wir *pers. pron.* [viːr] we; ~ *drei* the three of us.

Wirbel ['virbəl] *m* (-s/-) whirl, swirl; eddy; flurry (*of blows, etc.*); *anat.* vertebra; 'Qig *adj.* giddy, vertiginous; wild; 'Qn *v/i.* (ge-, h) whirl; *drums*: roll; '₋säule *anat. f* spinal *or* vertebral column; '₋sturm *m* cyclone, tornado, *Am. a.* twister; '₋tier *n* vertebrate; '₋wind *m* whirlwind (*a. fig.*).

wirk|en ['virkən] (ge-, h) 1. *v/t.* knit, weave; work (*wonders*); 2. *v/i.*: ~ *als* act *or* function as; ~ *auf* (*acc.*) produce an impression on; *beruhigend* ~ have a soothing effect; '₋lich *adj.* real, actual; true, genuine; 'Qlichkeit *f* (-/-en) reality; *in* ~ in reality; '₋sam *adj.* effective, efficacious; 'Qsamkeit *f* (-/⸗-en) effectiveness, efficacy; 'Qung *f* (-/-en) effect.

'Wirkungs|kreis *m* sphere *or* field of activity; 'Qlos *adj.* ineffective, inefficacious; '₋losigkeit *f* (-/no *pl.*) ineffectiveness, inefficacy; 'Qvoll *adj. s.* wirksam.

wirr *adj.* [vir] confused; *speech*: incoherent; *hair*: dishevel(l)ed; 'Qen *pl.* disorders *pl.*; troubles *pl.*; Qwarr ['₋var] *m* (-s/no *pl.*) confusion, muddle.

Wirsingkohl ['virziŋ-] *m* (-[e]s/no *pl.*) savoy.

Wirt [virt] *m* (-[e]s/-e) host; landlord; innkeeper.

'Wirtschaft *f* (-/-en) housekeeping; economy; trade and industry; economics *pl.*; *s.* Wirtshaus; F mess; 'Qen *v/i.* (ge-, h) keep house; economize; F bustle (about); '₋erin

f (-/-nen) housekeeper; 'Qlich *adj.* economic; economical.

'Wirtschafts|geld *n* housekeeping money; '₋jahr *n* financial year; '₋krise *f* economic crisis; '₋politik *f* economic policy; '₋prüfer *m* (-s/-) chartered accountant, *Am.* certified public accountant.

'Wirtshaus *n* public house, F pub.

Wisch [viʃ] *m* (-es/-e) wisp (*of straw, etc.*); *contp.* scrap of paper; 'Qen *v/t.* (ge-, h) wipe.

wispern ['vispərn] *v/t. and v/i.* (ge-, h) whisper.

Wiß|begierde ['vis-] *f* (-/no *pl.*) thirst for knowledge; 'Qbegierig *adj.* eager for knowledge.

wissen ['visən] 1. *v/t.* (*irr.*, ge-, h) know; *man kann nie* ~ you never know, you never can tell; 2. Q *n* (-s/no *pl.*) knowledge; *meines* ~*s* to my knowledge, as far as I know.

'Wissenschaft *f* (-/-en) science; knowledge; '₋ler *m* (-s/-) scholar; scientist; researcher; 'Qlich *adj.* scientific.

'Wissens|drang *m* (-[e]s/no *pl.*) urge *or* thirst for knowledge; 'Q-wert *adj.* worth knowing.

'wissentlich *adj.* knowing, conscious.

wittern ['vitərn] *v/t.* (ge-, h) scent, smell; *fig. a.* suspect.

'Witterung *f* (-/⸗-en) weather; *hunt.* scent; '₋sverhältnisse ['₋sfer-hɛltnisə] *pl.* meteorological conditions *pl.* [*m* (-s/-) widower.]

Witwe ['vitvə] *f* (-/-n) widow; '₋r}

Witz [vits] *m* 1. (-es/no *pl.*) wit; 2. (-es/-e) joke; ~*e reißen* crack jokes; '₋blatt *n* comic paper; 'Qig *adj.* witty; funny.

wo [voː] 1. *adv.* where?; 2. *cj.*: F *ach* ~! nonsense!

wob [voːp] *pret. of* weben.

wo'bei *adv.* at what?; at which; in doing so.

Woche ['vɔxə] *f* (-/-n) week; *heute in e-r* ~ today week.

'Wochen|bett *n* childbed; '₋blatt *n* weekly (paper); '₋ende *n* weekend; 'Qlang 1. *adj.*: *nach* ~*em Warten* after (many) weeks of waiting; 2. *adv.* for weeks; '₋lohn *m* weekly pay *or* wages *pl.*; '₋markt *m* weekly market; '₋schau *f* news-reel; '₋tag *m* week-day.

wöchentlich ['vœçəntliç] 1. *adj.* weekly; 2. *adv.* weekly, every week; *einmal* ~ once a week.

'Wöchnerin ['vœçnərin] *f* (-/-nen) woman in childbed.

wo|'durch *adv.* by what?, how?; by which, whereby; ~'für *adv.* for what?, what ... for?; (in return) for which. [gen[1].]

wog [voːk] *pret. of* wägen *and* wie-}

Woge ['voːgə] *f* (-/-n) wave (*a. fig.*), billow; *die* ~*n glätten* pour oil on troubled waters; '_n v/i. (ge-, h) surge (a. fig.), billow; wheat: a. wave; heave.

wo|'her adv. from where?, where ... from?; ~ wissen Sie das? how do you (come to) know that?; _'hin adv. where (... to)?

wohl [vo:l] 1. adv. well; sich nicht ~ fühlen be unwell; ~ oder übel willy-nilly; leben Sie ~! farewell!; er wird ~ reich sein he is rich, I suppose; 2. ♀ n (-[e]s/no pl.): ~ und Wehe weal and woe; auf Ihr ~! your health!, here is to you!

'Wohl|befinden n well-being; good health; '_behagen n comfort, ease; '♀behalten adv. safe; '♀bekannt adj. well-known; '_ergehen n (-s/no pl.) welfare, prosperity; ♀erzogen adj. ['_♀ertso·gən] well-bred, well-behaved; '_fahrt f (-/no pl.) welfare; public assistance; '_gefallen n (-s/no pl.) pleasure; sein ~ haben an (dat.) take delight in; '♀gemeint adj. well-meant, well-intentioned; ♀gemut adj. ['_gə-mu:t] cheerful; '♀genährt adj. well-fed; '_geruch m scent, perfume; '♀gesinnt adj. well-disposed (j-m towards s.o.); '♀habend adj. well-to-do; '♀ig adj. comfortable; cosy, snug; '_klang m (-[e]s/no pl.) melodious sound, harmony; '♀klingend adj. melodious, harmonious; '_laut m s. Wohlklang; '_leben n (-s/no pl.) luxury; ♀riechend adj. fragrant; '♀schmeckend savo(u)ry; '_sein n well-being; good health; '_stand m (-[e]s/no pl.) prosperity, wealth; '_tat f kindness, charity; fig. comfort, treat; '_täter m benefactor; '♀tätig adj. charitable, beneficient; '_tätigkeit f charity; '♀tuend adj. ['_tu:-ənt] pleasant, comfortable; '♀tun v/i. (irr. tun, sep., -ge-, h) do good; '♀verdient adj. well-deserved; p. of great merit; '_wollen n (-s/no pl.) goodwill; benevolence; favo(u)r; '♀wollen v/i. (sep., -ge-, h) be well-disposed (j-m towards s.o)

wohn|en ['vo:nən] v/i. (ge-, h) live (in dat. in, at; bei j-m with s.o.); reside (in, at; with); '♀haus n dwelling-house; block of flats, Am. apartment house; '_haft adj. resident, living; '_lich adj. comfortable; cosy, snug; '♀ort m dwelling-place, residence; esp. ⅛ domicile; '♀sitz m residence; mit ~ in resident in or at; ohne festen ~ without fixed abode; '♀ung f (-/-en) dwelling, habitation; flat, Am. apartment.

'Wohnungs|amt n housing office; '_not f housing shortage; '_problem n housing problem.

'Wohn|wagen m caravan, trailer; '_zimmer n sitting-room, esp. Am. living room.

wölb|en ['vœlbən] v/t. (ge-, h) vault; arch; sich ~ arch; '♀ung f (-/-en) vault, arch; curvature.

Wolf zo. [vɔlf] m (-[e]s/‌ᵉe) wolf.

Wolke ['vɔlkə] f (-/-n) cloud.

'Wolken|bruch m cloud-burst; '_kratzer m (-s/-) skyscraper; '♀los adj. cloudless.

'wolkig adj. cloudy, clouded.

Woll|decke ['vɔl-] f blanket; '_e f (-/-n) wool.

wollen¹ ['vɔlən] (h) 1. v/t. (ge-) wish, desire; want; lieber ~ prefer; nicht ~ refuse; er weiß, was er will he knows his mind; 2. v/i. (ge-): ich will schon, aber ... I want to, but...; 3. v/aux. (no -ge-) be willing; intend, be going to; be about to; lieber ~ prefer; nicht ~ refuse; er hat nicht gehen ~ he refused to go.

woll|en² adj. [~] wool(l)en; '_ig adj. wool(l)y; '♀stoff m wool(l)en.

Wol|lust ['vɔlust] f (-/‌ᵉe) voluptuousness; ♀lüstig adj. ['_lystiç] voluptuous.

'Wollwaren pl. wool(l)en goods pl.

wo|'mit adv. with what?, what ... with?; with which; _'möglich adv. perhaps, maybe.

Wonn|e ['vɔnə] f (-/-n) delight, bliss; '♀ig adj. delightful, blissful.

wo|ran adv. [vo:'ran]: ~ denkst du? what are you thinking of?; ich weiß nicht, ~ ich mit ihm bin I don't know what to make of him; ~ liegt es, daß ...? how is it that ...?; _'rauf adv. on what?, what ... on?; whereupon, after which; _ wartest du? what are you waiting for?; _'raus adv. from what?; what ... of?; from which; _'rin adv. [_'rin] in what?; in which.

Wort [vɔrt] n 1. (-[e]s/‌ᵉer) word; er kann seine Wörter noch nicht he hasn't learnt his words yet; 2. (-[e]s/-e) word; term, expression; ums ~ bitten ask permission to speak; das ~ ergreifen begin to speak; parl. rise to speak, address the House, esp. Am. take the floor; das ~ führen be the spokesman; ~ halten keep one's word; '♀brüchig adj.: er ist ~ geworden he has broken his word.

Wörter|buch ['vœrtər-] n dictionary; '_verzeichnis n vocabulary, list of words.

'Wort|führer m spokesman; '♀getreu adj. literal; '♀karg adj. taciturn; _klauberei [_klaubə'rai] f (-/-en) word-splitting; '_laut m (-[e]s/no pl.) wording; text. [eral.]

wörtlich adj. ['vœrtliç] verbal, lit-]

'Wort|schatz m (-es/no pl.) vocabulary; '_schwall m (-[e]s/no pl.) verbiage; '_spiel n pun (über acc., mit [up]on), play upon words; '_stellung gr. f word order, order of words; '_stamm ling. m stem; '_streit m, '_wechsel m dispute.

wo|rüber adv. [vo:'ry:bər] over or upon what?, what ... over or about or on?; over or upon which, about which; **.rum** adv. [.'rum] about what?, what ... about?; about or for which; ~ handelt es sich? what is it about?; **.runter** adv. [.'runtər] under or among what?, what ... under?; under or among which; **.'von** adv. of or from what?, what ... from or of?; about what?, what ... about?; of or from which; **.'vor** adv. of what?, what ... of?; of which; **.'zu** adv. for what?, what ... for?; for which.

Wrack [vrak] n (-[e]s/-e, -s) ⚓ wreck (a. fig.).

wrang [vraŋ] pret. of wringen.

wring|en ['vriŋən] v/t. (irr., ge-, h) wring; **'.maschine** f wringing-machine.

Wucher ['vu:xər] m (-s/no pl.) usury; ~ treiben practise usury; **'.er** m (-s/-) usurer; **'.gewinn** m excess profit; **'.isch** adj. usurious; **'.n** v/i. (ge-, h) grow exuberantly; **'.ung** f (-/-en) ⚕ exuberant growth; ⚘ growth; **'.zinsen** m/pl. usurious interest.

Wuchs [vu:ks] 1. m (-es/-e) growth; figure, shape; stature; 2. ② pret. of wachsen.

Wucht [vuxt] f (-/⚓-en) weight; force; **'2ig** adj. heavy.

Wühl|arbeit ['vy:l-] f insidious agitation, subversive activity; **'2en** v/i. (ge-, h) dig; pig: root; fig. agitate; ~ in (dat.) rummage (about) in; **'.er** m (-s/-) agitator.

Wulst [vulst] m (-es/⚓e), f (-/⚓e) pad; bulge; △ roll(-mo[u]lding); ⊕ bead; **'2ig** adj. lips: thick.

wund adj. [vunt] sore; ~e Stelle sore; ~er Punkt tender spot; **2e** ['.də] f (-/-n) wound; alte ~n wieder auf-reißen reopen old sores.

Wunder ['vundər] n (-s/-) miracle; fig. a. wonder, marvel; ~ wirken pills, etc.: work marvels; kein ~, wenn man bedenkt ... no wonder, considering ...; **'2bar** adj. miraculous; fig. a. wonderful, marvel-(l)ous; **'.kind** n infant prodigy; **'2lich** adj. queer, odd; **'2n** v/t. (ge-, h) surprise, astonish; sich ~ be surprised or astonished (über acc. at); **'2schön** adj. very beautiful; **'.tat** f wonder, miracle; **'.täter** m won-der-worker; **'2tätig** adj. wonder-working; **'2voll** adj. wonderful; **'.werk** n marvel, wonder.

'Wund|fieber ⚕ n wound-fever; **'.starrkrampf** ⚕ m tetanus.

Wunsch [vunʃ] m (-es/⚓e) wish, de-sire; request; auf ~ by or on re-quest; if desired; nach ~ as desired; mit den besten Wünschen zum Fest with the compliments of the season.

Wünschelrute ['vynʃəl-] f divin-ing-rod, dowsing-rod; **.ngänger** ['.gɛŋər] m (-s/-) diviner, dowser.

wünschen ['vynʃən] v/t. (ge-, h) wish, desire; wie Sie ~ as you wish; was ~ Sie? what can I do for you?; **'.swert** adj. desirable.

'wunsch|gemäß adv. as requested or desired, according to one's wishes; **'2zettel** m list of wishes.

wurde ['vurdə] pret. of werden.

Würde ['vyrdə] f (-/-n) dignity; unter seiner ~ beneath one's dig-nity; **'2los** adj. undignified; **'.n-träger** m dignitary; **'2voll** adj. dignified; grave.

'würdig adj. worthy (gen. of); dig-nified; grave; **.en** ['.gən] v/t. (ge-, h) appreciate, value; mention hono(u)rably; laud, praise; j-n keines Blickes ~ ignore s.o. com-pletely; **2ung** ['.guŋ] f (-/-en) ap-preciation, valuation.

Wurf [vurf] m (-[e]s/⚓e) throw, cast; zo. litter.

Würfel ['vyrfəl] m (-s/-) die; cube (a. ⚠); **'.becher** m dice-box; **'2n** v/i. (ge-, h) (play) dice; **'.spiel** n game of dice; **'.zucker** m lump sugar. [tile.]

'Wurfgeschoß n missile, projec-]

würgen ['vyrgən] (ge-, h) 1. v/t. choke, strangle; 2. v/i. choke; retch.

Wurm zo. [vurm] m (-[e]s/⚓er) worm; **'2en** F v/t. (ge-, h) vex; rankle (j-n in s.o.'s mind); **'2-stichig** adj. worm-eaten.

Wurst [vurst] f (-/⚓e) sausage; F das ist mir ganz ~ I don't care a rap.

Würstchen ['vyrstçən] n (-s/-) sau-sage; heißes ~ hot sausage, Am. hot dog.

Würze ['vyrtsə] f (-/-n) seasoning, flavo(u)r; spice, condiment; fig. salt.

Wurzel ['vurtsəl] f (-/-n) root (a. gr., ⚠); ~ schlagen strike or take root (a. fig.); **'2n** v/i. (ge-, h) (strike or take) root; ~ in (dat.) take one's root in, be rooted in.

'würz|en v/t. (ge-, h) spice, season, flavo(u)r; **'.ig** adj. spicy, well-seasoned, aromatic.

wusch [vu:ʃ] pret. of waschen.

wußte ['vustə] pret. of wissen.

Wust F [vu:st] m (-es/no pl.) tangled mass; rubbish; mess.

wüst adj. [vy:st] desert, waste; con-fused; wild, dissolute; rude; **'2e** f (-/-n) desert, wast ·; **2ling** ['.liŋ] m (-s/-e) debauche ·, libertine, rake.

Wut [vu:t] f (-/no pl.) rage, fury; in ~ in a rage; **'.anfall** m fit of rage.

wüten ['vy:tən] v/i. (ge-, h) rage (a. fig.); **'.d** adj. furious, enraged (über acc. at; auf acc. with), esp. Am. F a. mad (über acc., auf acc. at).

Wüterich ['vy:tə·iç] m (-[e]s/-e) berserker; bloodthirsty man.

'wutschnaubend adj. foaming with rage.

X, Y

X-Beine ['iks-] *n/pl.* knock-knees *pl.*; '**X-beinig** *adj.* knock-kneed.
x-beliebig *adj.* [iksbə'li:biç] any (... you please); jede(r, -s) ~e ... any ...
x-mal *adv.* ['iks-] many times, *sl.* umpteen times.

X-Strahlen ['iks-] *m/pl.* X-rays *pl.*
x-te *adj.* ['ikstə]: zum ~n Male for the umpteenth time.
Xylophon ♪ [ksylo'fo:n] *n* (-s/-e) xylophone.
Yacht ⚓ [jaxt] *f* (-/-en) yacht.

Z

Zacke ['tsakə] *f* (-/-n) s. Zacken.
'**Zacken 1.** *m* (-s/-) (sharp) point; prong; tooth (of comb, saw, rake); jag (of rock); **2.** ♀ *v/t.* (ge-, h) indent, notch; jag.
'**zackig** *adj.* indented, notched; rock: jagged; pointed; ✗ F *fig.* smart.
zaghaft *adj.* ['tsa:khaft] timid; '**2igkeit** *f* (-/no pl.) timidity.
zäh *adj.* [tse:] tough, tenacious (both a. fig.); liquid: viscid, viscous; fig. dogged; '**flüssig** *adj.* viscid, viscous, sticky; '**2igkeit** *f* (-/no pl.) toughness, tenacity (both a. fig.); viscosity; fig. doggedness.
Zahl [tsa:l] *f* (-/-en) number; figure, cipher; '**2bar** *adj.* payable.
'**zählbar** *adj.* countable.
zahlen ['tsa:lən] (ge-, h) **1.** *v/i.* pay; at restaurant: ~ (, bitte)! the bill, please!, Am. the check, please!; **2.** *v/t.* pay.
zählen ['tse:lən] (ge-, h) **1.** *v/t.* count, number; ~ zu count or number among; **2.** *v/i.* count; ~ auf (acc.) count (up)on, rely (up)on.
'**Zahlen|lotto** *n* s. Lotto; '**2mäßig 1.** *adj.* numerical; **2.** *adv.*: j-m ~ überlegen sein outnumber s.o.
'**Zähler** *m* (-s/-) counter; ⅍ numerator; for gas, etc.: meter.
'**Zahl|karte** *f* money-order form (for paying direct into the postal cheque account); '**2los** *adj.* numberless, innumerable, countless; '**meister** ✗ *m* paymaster; '**2reich 1.** *adj.* numerous; **2.** *adv.* in great number; '**tag** *m* pay-day; '**ung** *f* (-/-en) payment.
'**Zählung** *f* (-/-en) counting.
'**Zahlungs|anweisung** *f* order to pay; '**aufforderung** *f* request for payment; '**bedingungen** *f/pl.* terms pl. of payment; '**befehl** *m* order to pay; '**einstellung** *f* suspension of payment; '**2fähig** *adj.* solvent; '**fähigkeit** *f* solvency; '**frist** *f* term for payment; '**mittel** *n* currency; gesetzliches ~ legal tender; '**schwierigkeiten** *f/pl.* financial or pecuniary difficulties

pl.; '**termin** *m* date of payment; '**2unfähig** *adj.* insolvent; '**unfähigkeit** *f* insolvency.
'**Zahlwort** *gr.* *n* (-[e]s/⁓er) numeral.
zahm *adj.* [tsa:m] tame (a. fig.), domestic(ated).
zähm|en ['tse:mən] *v/t.* (ge-, h) tame (a. fig.), domesticate; '**2ung** *f* (-/⁓-en) taming (a. fig.), domestication.
Zahn [tsa:n] *m* (-[e]s/⁓e) tooth; ⊕ tooth, cog; Zähne bekommen cut one's teeth; '**arzt** *m* dentist, dental surgeon; '**bürste** *f* tooth-brush; '**creme** *f* tooth-paste; '**2en** *v/i.* (ge-, h) teethe, cut one's teeth; '**ersatz** *m* denture; '**fäule** 🦷 ['⁓fɔylə] *f* (-/no pl.) dental caries; '**fleisch** *n* gums pl.; '**füllung** *f* filling, stopping; '**geschwür** 🦷 *n* gumboil; '**heilkunde** *f* dentistry; '**2los** *adj.* toothless; '**lücke** *f* gap between the teeth; '**pasta** ['⁓pasta] *f* (-/Zahnpasten), '**paste** *f* tooth-paste; '**rad** ⊕ *n* cog-wheel; '**radbahn** /rack-railway; '**schmerzen** *m/pl.* toothache; '**stocher** *m* (-s/-) toothpick.
Zange ['tsaŋə] *f* (-/-n) (e-e a pair of) tongs pl. or pliers pl. or pincers pl.; 🦷, zo. forceps sg., pl.
Zank [tsaŋk] *m* (-[e]s/no pl.) quarrel, F row; '**apfel** *m* bone of contention; '**2en** (ge-, h) **1.** *v/i.* scold (mit j-m s.o.); **2.** *v/refl.* quarrel, wrangle.
zänkisch *adj.* ['tseŋkiʃ] quarrelsome.
Zäpfchen ['tsepfçən] *n* (-s/-) small peg; anat. uvula.
Zapfen ['tsapfən] **1.** *m* (-s/-) plug; peg, pin; bung (of barrel); pivot; ♀ cone; **2.** ♀ *v/t.* (ge-, h) tap; '**streich** ✗ *m* tattoo, retreat, Am. a. taps pl.
'**Zapf|hahn** *m*, Am. faucet; '**säule** mot. *f* petrol pump.
zappel|ig *adj.* ['tsapəliç] fidgety; '**n** *v/i.* (ge-, h) struggle; fidget.
zart *adj.* [tsa:rt] tender; soft; gentle; delicate; '**fühlend** *adj.* delicate; '**2gefühl** *n* (-[e]s/no pl.) delicacy (of feeling).

zärtlich adj. ['tsɛːrtliç] tender; fond, loving; **2keit** f 1. (-/no pl.) tenderness; fondness; 2. (-/-en) caress.

Zauber ['tsaubər] m (-s/-) spell, charm, magic (all a. fig.); fig.: enchantment; glamo(u)r; **~ei** [~'raɪ] f (-/-en) magic, sorcery; witchcraft; conjuring; **'~er** m (-s/-) sorcerer, magician; conjurer; **'~flöte** f magic flute; **'~formel** f spell; **'2-haft** adj. magic(al); fig. enchanting; **'~in** f (-/-nen) sorceress, witch; fig. enchantress; **'~kraft** f magic power; **'~kunststück** n conjuring trick; **'2n** (ge-, h) 1. v/i. practise magic or witchcraft; do conjuring tricks; 2. v/t. conjure; **'~spruch** m spell; **'~stab** m (magic) wand; **'~wort** n (-[e]s/-e) magic word, spell.

zaudern ['tsaudərn] v/i. (ge-, h) hesitate; linger, delay.

Zaum [tsaum] m (-[e]s/-e) bridle; im ~ halten keep in check.

zäumen ['tsɔymən] v/t. (ge-, h) bridle.

'Zaumzeug n bridle.

Zaun [tsaun] m (-[e]s/-e) fence; **'~gast** m deadhead; **'~könig** orn. m wren; **'~pfahl** m pale.

Zebra zo. ['tse:bra] n (-s/-s) zebra; **'~streifen** m zebra crossing.

Zech|e ['tsɛçə] f (-/-n) score, reckoning, bill; ⚒ mine; coal-pit, colliery; f die ~ bezahlen foot the bill, F stand treat; **'2en** v/i. (ge-, h) carouse, tipple; **'~gelage** n carousal, carouse; **'~preller** m (-s/-) bilk(er).

Zeh [tse:] m (-[e]s/-en), **~e** f (-/-n) toe; **'~enspitze** f point or tip of the toe; auf ~n on tiptoe.

zehn [tse:n] ten; **'2er** m (-s/-) ten; coin: F ten-pfennig piece; **~fach** adj. ['~fax] tenfold; **'~jährig** adj. ['~jɛːriç] ten-year-old, of ten (years); **'2kampf** m sports: decathlon; **'~mal** adv. ten times; **'~te** ['~tə] 1. adj. tenth; 2. ⚺ † m (-n/-n) tithe; **2tel** ['~təl] n (-s/-) tenth (part); **~tens** adv. ['~təns] tenthly.

zehren ['tse:rən] v/i. (ge-, h) make thin; ~ von live on s.th.; fig. live off (the capital); ~ an prey (up)on (one's mind); undermine (one's health).

Zeichen ['tsaɪçən] n (-s/-) sign; token; mark; indication, symptom; signal; zum ~ (gen.) in sign of, as a sign of; **'~block** m drawing-block; **'~brett** n drawing-board; **'~lehrer** m drawing-master; **'~papier** n drawing-paper; **'~setzung** gr. f (-/no pl.) punctuation; **'~sprache** f sign-language; **'~stift** m pencil, crayon; **'~trickfilm** m animation, animated cartoon; **'~unterricht** m drawing-lessons pl.

zeichn|en ['tsaɪçnən] (ge-, h) 1. v/t.

draw (plan, etc.); design (pattern); mark; sign; subscribe (sum of money) (zu to); subscribe for (shares); 2. v/i. draw; sie zeichnet gut she draws well; **'2er** m (-s/-) draftsman, draughtsman; designer; subscriber (gen. for shares); **'2ung** f (-/-en) drawing; design; illustration; zo. marking (of skin, etc.); subscription.

Zeige|finger ['tsaɪɡə-] m forefinger, index (finger); **'2n** (ge-, h) 1. v/t. show; point out; indicate; demonstrate; sich ~ appear; 2. v/i.: ~ auf (acc.) point at; ~ nach point to; **'~r** m (-s/-) hand (of clock, etc.); pointer (of dial, etc.); **'~stock** m pointer.

Zeile ['tsaɪlə] f (-/-n) line; row; j-m ein paar ~n schreiben drop s.o. a line or a few lines. [siskin.]

Zeisig orn. ['tsaɪziç] m (-[e]s/-e)⏎

Zeit [tsaɪt] f (-/-en) time; epoch, era, age; period, space (of time); term; freie ~ spare time; mit der ~ in the course of time; von ~ zu ~ from time to time; vor langer ~ long ago, a long time ago; zur ~ (gen.) in the time of; at (the) present; zu meiner ~ in my time; zu s-r ~ in due course (of time); das hat ~ there is plenty of time for that; es ist höchste ~ it is high time; j-m ~ lassen give s.o. time; laß dir ~! take your time!; sich die ~ vertreiben pass the time, kill time.

'Zeit|abschnitt m epoch, period; **'~alter** n age; **'~angabe** f exact date and hour; date; **'~aufnahme** phot. f time-exposure; **'~dauer** f length of time, period (of time); **'~enfolge** gr. f sequence of tenses; **'~geist** m (-es/no pl.) spirit of the time(s), zeitgeist; **'2gemäß** adj. modern, up-to-date; **'~genosse** m contemporary; **'2genössisch** adj. ['~ɡənœsiʃ] contemporary; **'~geschichte** f contemporary history; **'~gewinn** m gain of time; **'2ig** 1. adj. early; 2. adv. on time; **'~karte** f season-ticket, Am. commutation ticket; **'~lang** f: e-e ~ for some time, for a while; **'~lebens** adv. for life, all one's life; **'2lich** 1. adj. temporal; 2. adv. as to time; ~ zusammenfallen coincide; **'2los** adj. timeless; **'~lupe** phot. f slow motion; **'~lupenaufnahme** phot. f slow-motion picture; **'2nah** adj. current, up-to-date; **'~ordnung** f chronological order; **'~punkt** m moment; time; date; **'~rafferaufnahme** phot. f time-lapse photography; **'2raubend** adj. time-consuming; pred. a. taking up much time; **'~raum** m space (of time), period; **'~rechnung** f chronology; era; **'~schrift** f journal, periodical, magazine; review; **'~tafel** f chronological table.

'Zeitung f (-/-en) (news)paper, journal.

'Zeitungs|abonnement n subscription to a paper; '~artikel m newspaper article; '~ausschnitt m (press or newspaper) cutting, (Am. only) (newspaper) clipping; ~kiosk ['~kiosk] m (-[e]s/-e) news-stand; '~notiz f press item; '~papier n newsprint; '~verkäufer m newsvendor; news-boy, news-man; '~wesen n journalism, the press.

'Zeit|verlust m loss of time; '~verschwendung f waste of time; ~vertreib ['~fɛrtraɪp] m (-[e]s/-e) pastime; zum ~ to pass the time; 2weilig adj. ['~vaɪlɪç] temporary; 2weise adv. for a time; at times, occasionally; '~wort gr. n (-[e]s/-er) verb; '~zeichen n time-signal.

Zell|e ['tsɛlə] f (-/-n) cell; '~stoff m, ~ulose ⊕ [~u'loːzə] f (-/-n) cellulose.

Zelt [tsɛlt] n (-[e]s/-e) tent; '2en v/i. (ge-, h) camp; '~leinwand f canvas; '~platz m camping-ground.

Zement [tse'mɛnt] m (-[e]s/-e) cement; 2ieren [~'tiːrən] v/t. (no -ge-, h) cement.

Zenit [tse'niːt] m (-[e]s/no pl.) zenith (a. fig.).

zens|ieren [tsɛn'ziːrən] v/t. (no -ge-, h) censor (book, etc.); at school: mark, Am. a. grade; 2or ['~ɔr] m (-s/-en) censor; 2ur [~'zuːr] f 1. (-/no pl.) censorship; 2. (-/-en) at school: mark, Am. a. grade; (school) report, Am. report card.

Zentimeter [tsɛnti'-] n, m centimet|re, Am. -er.

Zentner ['tsɛntnər] m (-s/-) (Brt. appr.) hundredweight.

zentral adj. [tsɛn'traːl] central; 2ef (-/-n) central office; teleph. (telephone) exchange, Am. a. central; 2heizung f central heating.

Zentrum ['tsɛntrʊm] n (-s/Zentren) cent|re, Am. -er.   [Am. -er.]

Zepter ['tsɛptər] n (-s/-) scept|re,

zer'beiß|en [tsɛr'-] v/t. (irr. beißen, no -ge-, h) bite to pieces; ~'bersten v/i. (irr. bersten, no -ge-, sein) burst asunder.

zer'brech|en (irr. brechen, no -ge-) 1. v/t. (h) break (to pieces); sich den Kopf ~ rack one's brains; 2. v/i. (sein) break; ~lich adj. breakable, fragile.

zer|'bröckeln v/t. (h) and v/i. (sein) (no -ge-) crumble; ~'drücken v/t. (no -ge-, h) crush; crease (dress).

Zeremon|ie [tseremo'niː, ~'moːnjə] f (-/-n) ceremony; 2iell adj. [~o'njɛl] ceremonial; ~iell [~o'njɛl] n (-s/-e) ceremonial.

zer'fahren adj. road: rutted; p.: flighty, giddy; scatter-brained; absent-minded.

Zer'fall m (-[e]s/no pl.) ruin, decay;

disintegration; 2en v/i. (irr. fallen, no -ge-, sein) fall to pieces, decay; disintegrate; in mehrere Teile ~ fall into several parts.

zer'|fetzen v/t. (no -ge-, h) tear in or to pieces; ~'fleischen v/t. (no -ge-, h) mangle; lacerate; ~'fließen v/i. (irr. fließen, no -ge-, sein) melt (away); ink, etc.: run; ~'fressen v/t. (irr. fressen, no -ge-, h) eat away; 🜚 corrode; ~'gehen v/i. (irr. gehen, no -ge-, sein) melt, dissolve; ~'gliedern v/t. (no -ge-, h) dismember; anat. dissect; fig. analy|se, Am. -ze; ~'hacken v/t. (no -ge-, h) cut (in)to pieces; mince; chop (up) (wood, meat); ~'kauen v/t. (no -ge-, h) chew; ~'kleinern v/t. (no -ge-, h) mince (meat); chop up (wood); grind.

zer'knirsch|t adj. contrite; 2ung f (-/-en) contrition.

zer'|knittern v/t. (no -ge-, h) (c)rumple, wrinkle, crease; ~'knüllen v/t. (no -ge-, h) crumple up (sheet of paper); ~'kratzen v/t. (no -ge-, h) scratch; ~'krümeln v/t. (no -ge-, h) crumble; ~'lassen v/t. (irr. lassen, no -ge-, h) melt; ~'legen v/t. (no -ge-, h) take apart or to pieces; carve (joint); 🜚, gr., fig. analy|se, Am. -ze; ~'lumpt adj. ragged, tattered; ~'mahlen v/t. (irr. mahlen, no -ge-, h) grind; ~malmen [~'malmən] v/t. (no -ge-, h) crush; crunch; ~'mürben v/t. (no -ge-, h) wear down or out; ~'platzen v/i. (no -ge-, sein) burst; explode; ~'quetschen v/t. (no -ge-, h) crush, squash; mash (esp. potatoes).

Zerrbild ['tsɛr-] n caricature.

zer'|reiben v/t. (irr. reiben, no -ge-, h) rub to powder, grind down, pulverize; ~'reißen (irr. reißen, no -ge-) 1. v/t. (h) tear, rip up; in Stücke ~ tear to pieces; 2. v/i. (sein) tear; rope, string: break.

zerren ['tsɛrən] (ge-, h) 1. v/t. tug, pull; drag; 🞂 strain; 2. v/i.: ~ an (dat.) pull at.

zer'rinnen v/i. (irr. rinnen, no -ge-, sein) melt away; fig. vanish.

'Zerrung 🞂 f (-/-en) strain.

zer|'rütten [tsɛr'rytən] v/t. (no -ge-, h) derange, unsettle; disorganize; ruin, shatter (one's health or nerves); wreck (marriage); ~'sägen v/t. (no -ge-, h) saw up; ~schellen [~'ʃɛlən] v/i. (no -ge-, sein) be dashed or smashed; 🜚 be wrecked; 🞂 crash; ~'schlagen 1. v/t. (irr. schlagen, no -ge-, h) break or smash (to pieces); sich ~ come to nothing; 2. adj. battered; fig. knocked up; ~'schmettern v/t. (no -ge-, h) smash, dash, shatter; ~'schneiden v/t. (irr. schneiden, no -ge-, h) cut in two; cut up, cut to pieces.

zer'setz|en v/t. and v/refl. (no -ge-, h) decompose; **2ung** f (-/⚮-en) decomposition.

zer|'spalten v/t. ([irr. spalten,] no -ge-, h) cleave, split; **~'splittern** (no -ge-) 1. v/t. (h) split (up), splinter; fritter away (one's energy, etc.); 2. v/i. (sein) split (up), splinter; **~'sprengen** v/t. (no -ge-, h) burst (asunder); disperse (crowd); **~'springen** v/i. (irr. springen, no -ge-, sein) burst; glass: crack; mein Kopf zerspringt mir I've got a splitting headache; **~'stampfen** v/t. (no -ge-, h) crush; pound.

zer'stäub|en v/t. (no -ge-, h) spray; **2er** m (-s/-) sprayer, atomizer.

zer'stör|en v/t. (no -ge-, h) destroy; **2er** m (-s/-) destroyer (a. ⚓); **2ung** f destruction.

zer'streu|en v/t. (no -ge-, h) disperse, scatter; dissipate (doubt, etc.); fig. divert; sich ~ disperse, scatter; fig. amuse o.s.; **~t** fig. adj. absent(-minded); **2theit** f (-/⚮-en) absent-mindedness; **2ung** f 1. (-/-en) dispersion; diversion, amusement; 2. phys. (-/no pl.) dispersion (of light).

zerstückeln [tser'ʃtykəln] v/t. (no -ge-, h) cut up, cut (in)to pieces; dismember (body, etc.).

zer|'teilen v/t. and v/refl. (no -ge-, h) divide (in acc. into); **~'trennen** v/t. (no -ge-, h) rip (up) (dress); **~'treten** v/t. (irr. treten, no -ge-, h) tread down; crush; tread or stamp out (fire); **~'trümmern** v/t. (no -ge-, h) smash.

Zerwürfnis [tser'vyrfnis] n (-ses/-se) dissension, discord.

Zettel ['tsetəl] m (-s/-) slip (of paper), scrap of paper; note; ticket; label, sticker; tag; s. Anschlagzettel; s. Theaterzettel; **~kartei** f, **'~kasten** m card index.

Zeug [tsɔyk] n (-[e]s/-e) stuff (a. fig. contp.), material; cloth; tools pl.; things pl.

Zeuge ['tsɔygə] m (-n/-n) witness; **'2n** (ge-, h) 1. v/i. witness; ⚖ give evidence; für (gegen, von) et. ~ testify for (against, of) s.th.; ~ von be evidence of, bespeak (courage, etc.); 2. v/t. beget.

'Zeugen|aussage ⚖ f testimony, evidence; **'~bank** f (-/-e) witness-box, Am. witness stand.

Zeugin ['tsɔygin] f (-/-nen) (female) witness.

Zeugnis ['tsɔyknis] n (-ses/-se) ⚖ testimony, evidence; certificate; (school) report, Am. report card.

Zeugung ['tsɔyguŋ] f (-/-en) procreation; **'2sfähig** adj. capable of begetting; **'~skraft** f generative power; **'2sunfähig** adj. ['tsɔyguŋs?-] impotent.

Zick|lein zo. ['tsiklain] n (-s/-) kid;

~zack ['~tsak] m (-[e]s/-e) zigzag; im ~ fahren etc. zigzag.

Ziege zo. ['tsi:gə] f (-/-n) (she-)goat, nanny(-goat).

Ziegel ['tsi:gəl] m (-s/-) brick; tile (of roof); **'~dach** n tiled roof; **~ei** [~'lai] f (-/-en) brickworks sg., pl., brickyard; **'~stein** m brick.

'Ziegen|bock zo. m he-goat; **'~fell** n goatskin; **'~hirt** m goatherd; **'~leder** n kid(-leather); **'~peter** ⚕ m (-s/-) mumps.

Ziehbrunnen ['tsi:-] m draw-well.

ziehen ['tsi:ən] (irr., ge-) 1. v/t. pull, draw; draw (line, weapon, lots, conclusion, etc.); drag; 🌱 cultivate; zo. breed; take off (hat); dig (ditch); draw, extract (tooth); 🝙 extract (root of number); Blasen ~ raise blisters; e-n Vergleich ~ draw or make a comparison; j-n ins Vertrauen ~ take s.o. into one's confidence; in Erwägung ~ take into consideration; in die Länge ~ draw out; fig. protract; Nutzen ~ aus derive profit or benefit from; an sich ~ draw to one; Aufmerksamkeit etc. auf sich ~ attract attention, etc.; et. nach sich ~ entail or involve s.th.; 2. v/i. (h) pull (an dat. at); chimney, cigar, etc.: draw; puff (an e-r Zigarre at a cigar); tea: infuse, draw; play: draw (large audiences); F 🝙 goods: draw (customers), take; es zieht there is a draught, Am. there is a draft; 3. v/i. (sein) move, go; march; (re)move (nach to); birds: migrate; 4. v/refl. (h) extend, stretch, run; wood: warp; sich in die Länge ~ drag on.

'Zieh|harmonika ♪ f accordion; **'~ung** f (-/-en) drawing (of lots).

Ziel [tsi:l] n (-[e]s/-e) aim (a. fig.); mark; sports: winning-post, goal (a. fig.); target; 🝙 objective; destination (of voyage); fig. end, purpose, target, object(ive); term; sein ~ erreichen gain one's end(s pl.); über das ~ hinausschießen overshoot the mark; zum ~e führen succeed, be successful; sich zum ~ setzen zu inf. aim at ger., Am. aim to inf.; **'~band** n sports: tape; **'2bewußt** adj. purposeful; **'2en** v/i. (ge-, h) (take) aim (auf acc. at); **'~fernrohr** n telescopic sight; **'2los** adj. aimless, purposeless; **'~scheibe** f target, butt; ~ des Spottes butt or target (of derision); **'2strebig** adj. purposive.

ziemlich ['tsi:mliç] 1. adj. fair, tolerable; considerable; 2. adv. pretty, fairly, tolerably; rather; about.

Zier [tsi:r] f (-/no pl.), **~de** ['~də] f (-/-n) ornament; fig. a. hono(u)r (für to); **'2en** v/t. (ge-, h) ornament, adorn; decorate; sich ~ be affected; esp. of woman: be prudish; refuse; '≗lich adj. delicate; neat; graceful, elegant; '⸏lichkeit f (-/≗-en) delicacy; neatness; gracefulness, elegance; '⸏pflanze f ornamental plant.

Ziffer ['tsifər] f (-/-n) figure, digit; '⸏blatt n dial(-plate), face.

Zigarette [tsiga'rɛtə] f (-/-n) cigaret(te); ⸏automat [⸏⸏ʔ-] m cigarette slot-machine; ⸏netui [⸏ⁿʔ-] n cigarette-case; ⸏nspitze f cigarette-holder; ⸏nstummel m stub, Am. a. butt.

Zigarre [tsi'garə] f (-/-n) cigar.

Zigeuner [tsi'gɔynər] m (-s/-), ⸏inf (-/-nen) gipsy, gypsy.

Zimmer ['tsimər] n (-s/-) room; apartment; '⸏antenne f radio, etc.: indoor aerial, Am. a. indoor antenna; '⸏einrichtung f furniture; '⸏flucht f suite (of rooms); '⸏mädchen n chamber-maid; '⸏mann m (-[e]s/Zimmerleute) carpenter; '≗n (ge-, h) 1. v/t. carpenter; fig. frame; 2. v/i. carpenter; '⸏pflanze f indoor plant; '⸏vermieterin f (-/-nen) landlady.

zimperlich adj. ['tsimpərliç] prim; prudish; affected.

Zimt [tsimt] m (-[e]s/-e) cinnamon.

Zink ⚗ [tsiŋk] n (-[e]s/no pl.) zinc; '⸏blech n sheet zinc.

Zinke ['tsiŋkə] f (-/-n) prong; tooth (of comb or fork); '⸏n m (-s/-) s. Zinke.

Zinn ⚗ [tsin] n (-[e]s/no pl.) tin.

Zinne ['tsinə] f (-/-n) ▲ pinnacle; ⚔ battlement.

Zinnober [tsi'no:bər] m (-s/-) cinnabar; ≗rot adj. vermilion.

Zins [tsins] m (-es/-en) rent; tribute; mst ⸏en pl. interest; ⸏en tragen yield or bear interest; '≗bringend adj. bearing interest; ⸏eszins ['⸏zəs-] m compound interest; '≗frei adj. rent-free; free of interest; '⸏fuß m, '⸏satz m rate of interest.

Zipf|el ['tsipfəl] m (-s/-) tip, point, end; corner (of handkerchief, etc.); lappet (of garment); '≗elig adj. having points or ends; '⸏elmütze f jelly-bag cap; nightcap.

Zirkel ['tsirkəl] m (-s/-) circle (a. fig.); ⸹ (ein a pair of) compasses pl. or dividers pl.

zirkulieren [tsirku'li:rən] v/i. (no -ge-, h) circulate.

Zirkus ['tsirkus] m (-/-se) circus.

zirpen ['tsirpən] v/i. (ge-, h) chirp, cheep.

zisch|eln ['tsiʃəln] v/t. and v/i. (ge-, h) whisper; '⸏en v/i. (ge-, h) hiss; whiz(z).

ziselieren [tsize'li:rən] v/t. (no -ge-, h) chase.

Zit|at [tsi'ta:t] n (-[e]s/-e) quotation; ≗ieren [⸏'ti:rən] v/t. (no -ge-, h) summon; quote.

Zitrone [tsi'tro:nə] f (-/-n) lemon;

⸏nlimonade f lemonade; lemon squash; ⸏npresse f lemon-squeezer; ⸏nsaft m lemon juice.

zittern ['tsitərn] v/i. (ge-, h) tremble, shake (vor dat. with).

zivil [tsi'vi:l] 1. adj. civil; civilian; price: reasonable; 2. ♀ n (-s/no pl.) civilians pl.; s. Zivilkleidung; ≗bevölkerung f civilian population, civilians pl.; ≗isation [⸏iliza'tsjo:n] f (-/≗-en) civilization; ⸏isieren [⸏ili'zi:rən] v/t. (no -ge-, h) civilize; ≗ist [⸏i'list] m (-en/-en) civilian; ≗kleidung f civilian or plain clothes pl.

Zofe ['tso:fə] f (-/-n) lady's maid.

zog [tso:k] pret. of ziehen.

zögern ['tsø:gərn] 1. v/i. (ge-, h) hesitate; linger; delay; 2. ♀ n (-s/no pl.) hesitation; delay.

Zögling ['tsø:kliŋ] m (-s/-e) pupil.

Zoll [tsɔl] m 1. (-[e]s/-) inch; 2. (-[e]s/⸏e) customs pl., duty; the Customs pl.; '⸏abfertigung f customs clearance; '⸏amt n customhouse; '⸏beamte m customs officer; '⸏behörde f the Customs pl.; '⸏erklärung f customs declaration; '≗frei adj. duty-free; '⸏kontrolle f customs examination; '≗pflichtig adj. liable to duty; '⸏stock m footrule; '⸏tarif m tariff.

Zone ['tso:nə] f (-/-n) zone.

Zoo [tso:] m (-[s]/-s) zoo.

Zoolog|e [tso⁹o'lo:gə] m (-n/-n) zoologist; ⸏ie [⸏o'gi:] f (-/no pl.) zoology; ≗isch adj. [⸏'lo:giʃ] zoological.

Zopf [tsɔpf] m (-[e]s/⸏e) plait, tress; pigtail; alter ⸏ antiquated ways pl. or custom.

Zorn [tsɔrn] m (-[e]s/no pl.) anger; '≗ig adj. angry (auf j-n with s.o.; auf et. at s.th.).

Zote ['tso:tə] f (-/-n) filthy or smutty joke, obscenity.

Zott|el ['tsɔtəl] f (-/-n) tuft (of hair); tassel; '≗(e)lig adj. shaggy.

zu [tsu:] 1. prp. (dat.) direction: to, towards, up to; at, in; on; in addition to, along with; purpose: for; ⸏ Beginn at the beginning or outset; ⸏ Weihnachten at Christmas; zum ersten Mal for the first time; ⸏ e-m ... Preise at a ... price; ⸏ meinem Erstaunen to my surprise; ⸏ Tausenden by thousands; ⸏ Wasser by water; ⸏ zweien by twos; zum Beispiel for example; 2. adv. too; direction: towards, to; F closed, shut; with inf.: to; ich habe ⸏ arbeiten I have to work.

'zubauen v/t. (sep., -ge-, h) build up or in; block.

Zubehör ['tsu:bəhø:r] n, m (-[e]s/-e) appurtenances pl., fittings pl., Am. F fixings pl.; esp. ⊕ accessories pl.

'zubereit|en v/t. (sep., no -ge-, h) prepare; ≗ung f preparation.

'zu|billigen v/t. (sep., -ge-, h) grant; ~binden v/t. (irr. binden, sep., -ge-, h) tie up; ~blinzeln v/i. (sep., -ge-, h) wink at s.o.; ~brin-gen v/t. (irr. bringen, sep., -ge-, h) pass, spend (time).

Zucht [tsuxt] f 1. (-/no pl.) disci-pline; breeding, rearing; rearing of bees, etc.: culture; ♀ cultivation; 2. (-/-en) breed, race; ~bulle zo. m bull (for breeding).

zücht|en ['tsʏçtən] v/t. (ge-, h) breed (animals); grow, cultivate (plants); 'Ꝗer m (-s/-) breeder (of animals); grower (of plants).

'Zucht|haus n penitentiary; punish-ment: penal servitude; ~häusler ['~hɔʏslər] m (-s/-) convict; '~hengst zo. m stud-horse, stallion.

züchtig adj. ['tsʏçtiç] chaste, mod-est; ~en ['~gən] v/t. (ge-, h) flog.

'zucht|los adj. undisciplined; 'Ꝗlo-sigkeit f (-/~-en) want of discipline; 'Ꝗstute zo. f brood-mare.

zucken ['tsukən] v/i. (ge-, h) jerk; move convulsively, twitch (all: mit et. s.th.); with pain: wince; lightning: flash.

zücken ['tsʏkən] v/t. (ge-, h) draw (sword); F pull out (purse, pencil).

Zucker ['tsukər] m (-s/no pl.) sugar; '~dose f sugar-basin, Am. sugar bowl; '~erbse ♀ f green pea; '~guß m icing, frosting; '~hut m sugar-loaf; 'Ꝗig adj. sugary; 'Ꝗkrank adj. diabetic; 'Ꝗn v/t. (ge-, h) sugar; '~rohr ♀ n sugar-cane; '~rübe ♀ f sugar-beet; 'Ꝗsüß adj. (as) sweet as sugar; '~wasser n sugared water; '~zange f (e-e a pair of) sugar-tongs pl.

zuckrig adj. ['tsukriç] sugary.

'Zuckung ♀ f (-/-en) convulsion.

'zudecken v/t. (sep., -ge-, h) cover (up).

zudem adv. [tsu'de:m] besides, moreover.

'zu|drehen v/t. (sep., -ge-, h) turn off (tap); j-m den Rücken ~ turn one's back on s.o.; '~dringlich adj. importunate, obtrusive; '~drücken v/t. (sep., -ge-, h) close, shut; '~erkennen v/t. (irr. kennen, sep., no -ge-, h) award (a. ﬆ); adjudge (dat. to) (a. ﬆ).

zuerst adv. [tsu'-] first (of all); at first; er kam ~ an he was the first to arrive.

'zufahr|en v/i. (irr. fahren, sep., -ge-, sein) drive on; ~ auf (acc.) drive to (-wards); fig. rush at s.o.; 'Ꝗt f ap-proach; drive, Am. driveway; 'Ꝗtsstraße f approach (road).

'Zufall m chance, accident; durch ~ by chance, by accident; 'Ꝗen v/i. (irr. fallen, sep., -ge-, sein) eyes: be closing (with sleep); door: shut (of itself); j-m ~ fall to s.o.('s share).

'zufällig 1. adj. accidental; attr.

chance; casual; 2. adv. accidentally, by chance.

'zufassen v/i. (sep., -ge-, h) seize (hold of) s.th.; (mit) ~ lend or give a hand.

'Zuflucht f (-/❀-̈e) refuge, shelter, resort; s-e ~ nehmen zu have re-course to s.th., take refuge in s.th.

'Zufluß m afflux; influx (a. ✝); affluent, tributary (of river); ✝ supply.

'zuflüstern v/t. (sep., -ge-, h): j-m et. ~ whisper s.th. to s.o.

zufolge prp. (gen.; dat.) [tsu'fɔlgə] according to.

zufrieden adj. [tsu'-] content(ed), satisfied; Ꝗheit f (-/no pl.) content-ment, satisfaction; ~lassen v/t. (irr. lassen, sep., -ge-, h) let s.o. alone; ~stellen v/t. (sep., -ge-, h) satisfy; ~stellend adj. satisfactory.

'zu|frieren v/i. (irr. frieren, sep., -ge-, sein) freeze up or over; '~fügen v/t. (sep., -ge-, h) add; do, cause; inflict (wound, etc.) (j-m [up]on s.o.); Ꝗfuhr f ['~fu:r] f (-/-en) supply; supplies pl.; influx; '~füh-ren v/t. (sep., -ge-, h) carry, lead, bring; ⊕ feed; supply (a. ⊕).

Zug [tsu:k] m (-[e]s/❀-̈e) draw(ing), pull(ing); ⊕ traction; ⚒ expedi-tion, campaign; procession; migra-tion (of birds); drift (of clouds); range (of mountains); ⊕ train; feature; trait (of character); bent, tendency, trend; draught, Am. draft (of air); at chess: move; drink-ing: draught, Am. draft; at cigarette, etc.: puff.

'Zu|gabe f addition; extra; thea. encore; '~gang m entrance; access; approach; Ꝗgänglich adj. ['~gɛn-liç] accessible (für to); 'Ꝗgeben v/t. (irr. geben, sep., -ge-, h) add; fig.: allow; confess; admit.

zugegen adj. [tsu'-] present (bei at.).

'zugehen v/i. (irr. gehen, sep., -ge-, sein) door, etc.: close, shut; p. move on, walk faster; happen; auf j-n ~ go up to s.o., move or walk towards s.o.

'Zugehörigkeit f (-/no pl.) member-ship (zu to) (society, etc.); belong-ing (to).

Zügel ['tsy:gəl] m (-s/-) rein; bridle (a. fig.); 'Ꝗlos adj. unbridled; fig.: unrestrained; licentious; 'Ꝗn v/t. (ge-, h) rein (in); fig. bridle, check.

'Zuge|ständnis n concession; 'Ꝗ-stehen v/t. (irr. stehen, sep., -ge-, h) concede.

'zugetan adj. attached (dat. to).

'Zugführer 🚋 m guard, Am. con-ductor. [-ge-, h) add.]

'zugießen v/t. (sep., -ge-, h) add.

zug|ig adj. ['tsu:giç] draughty, Am. drafty; Ꝗkraft f ['~k-] f ⊕ traction; fig. attraction, draw, appeal; ~kräf-tig adj. ['~k-]: ~ sein be a draw.

zugleich adv. [tsu'-] at the same time; together.

'**Zug|luft** f (-/no pl.) draught, Am. draft; '~maschine f traction-engine, tractor; '~pflaster 🐛 n blister.

'**zu|greifen** v/i. (irr. greifen, sep., -ge-, h) grasp or grab at s.th.; at table: help o.s.; lend a hand; '2griff m grip, clutch.

zugrunde adv. [tsu'grundə]: ~ gehen perish; ~ richten ruin.

'**Zugtier** n draught animal, Am. draft animal.

zu|gunsten prp. (gen.) [tsu'gunstən] in favo(u)r of; ~'gute adv.: j-m et. ~ halten give s.o. credit for s.th.; ~ kommen be for the benefit (dat. of).

'**Zugvogel** m bird of passage.

'**zuhalten** v/t. (irr. halten, sep.,-ge-, h) hold (door) to; sich die Ohren ~ stop one's ears.   [home.]

Zuhause [tsu'hauzə] n (-/no pl.)

'**zu|heilen** v/i. (sep., -ge-, sein) heal up, skin over; '~hören v/i. (sep., -ge-, h) listen (dat. to).

'**Zuhörer** m hearer, listener; ~ pl. audience; '~schaft f (-/~-en) audience.

'**zu|jubeln** v/i. (sep., -ge-, h) cheer; '~kleben v/t. (sep., -ge-, h) paste or glue up; gum (letter) down; '~knallen v/t. (sep., -ge-, h) bang, slam (door, etc.); '~knöpfen v/t. (sep., -ge-, h) button (up); '~kommen v/i. (irr. kommen, sep., -ge-, sein): auf j-n ~ come up to s.o.; j-m ~ be due to s.o.; j-m et. ~ lassen let s.o. have s.th.; send s.o. s.th.; '~korken v/t. (sep., -ge-, h) cork (up).

Zu|kunft [tsu:kunft] f (-/no pl.) future; gr. future (tense); '2künftig 1. adj. future; ~er Vater father-to-be; 2. adv. in future.

'**zu|lächeln** v/i. (sep., -ge-, h) smile at or (up)on; '2lage f extra pay, increase; rise, Am. raise (in salary or wages); '~langen v/i. (sep., -ge-, h) at table: help o.s.; '~lassen v/t. (irr. lassen, sep., -ge-, h) leave (door) shut; keep closed; fig.: admit s.o.; license; allow, suffer; admit of (only one interpretation, etc.); '~lässig adj. admissible, allowable; '2lassung f (-/-en) admission; permission; licen|ce, Am. -se.

'**zulegen** v/t. (sep., -ge-, h) add; F sich et. ~ get o.s. s.th.

zuleide adv. [tsu'laɪdə]: j-m et. ~ tun do s.o. harm, harm or hurt s.o.

'**zuleiten** v/t. (sep., -ge-, h) let in (water, etc.); conduct to; pass on to s.o.

zu|letzt adv. [tsu'-] finally, at last; er kam ~ an he was the last to arrive; ~'liebe adv.: j-m ~ for s.o.'s sake.

zum prp. [tsum] = zu dem.

'**zumachen** v/t. (sep., -ge-, h) close, shut; button (up) (coat); fasten.

zumal cj. [tsu'-] especially, particularly.   [up.)

'**zumauern** v/t. (sep., -ge-, h) wall

zumut|en [tsu'mu:tən] v/t. (sep., -ge-, h): j-m et. ~ expect s.th. of s.o.; sich zuviel ~ overtake o.s., overtax one's strength, etc.; '2ung f (-/-en) exacting demand, exaction; fig. impudence.

zunächst [tsu'-] 1. prp. (dat.) next to; 2. adv. first of all; for the present.

'**zu|nageln** v/t. (sep., -ge-, h) nail up; '~nähen v/t. (sep., -ge-, h) sew up; 2nahme ['~nɑːmə] f (-/-n) increase, growth; '2name m surname.

zünden ['tsyndən] v/i. (ge-, h) kindle; esp. mot. ignite; fig. arouse enthusiasm.

Zünd|holz ['tsynt-] n match; '~kerze mot. f spark(ing)-plug, Am. spark plug; '~schlüssel mot. m ignition key; '~schnur f fuse; '~stoff fig. m fuel; ~ung mot. ['~duŋ] f (-/-en) ignition.

'**zunehmen** v/i. (irr. nehmen, sep., -ge-, h) increase (an dat. in); grow; put on weight; moon: wax; days: grow longer.

'**zuneig|en** (sep., -ge-, h) 1. v/i. incline to(wards). 2. v/refl. incline to(wards); sich dem Ende ~ draw to a close; '2ung f (-/~-en) affection.

Zunft [tsunft] f (-/⸗e) guild, corporation.

Zunge ['tsuŋə] f (-/-n) tongue.

züngeln ['tsyŋəln] v/i. (ge-, h) play with its tongue; flame: lick.

'**zungen|fertig** adj. voluble; '2fertigkeit f (-/no pl.) volubility; '2spitze f tip of the tongue.

zunichte adv. [tsu'niçtə]: ~ machen or werden bring or come to nothing.

'**zunicken** v/i. (sep., -ge-, h) nod to.

zu|nutze adv. [tsu'nutsə]: sich et. ~ machen turn s.th. to account, utilize s.th.; ~'oberst adv. at the top, uppermost.

zupfen ['tsupfən] (ge-, h) 1. v/t. pull, tug, twitch; 2. v/i. pull, tug, twitch (all: an dat. at).

zur prp. [tsu:r] = zu der.

'**zurechnungsfähig** adj. of sound mind; 🛄 responsible; '2keit 🛄 f (-/no pl.) responsibility.

zurecht|finden [tsu'-] v/refl. (irr. finden, sep., -ge-, h) find one's way; ~kommen v/i. (irr. kommen, sep., -ge-, sein) arrive in time; ~ (mit) get on (well) (with); manage s.th.; ~legen v/t. (sep., -ge-, h) arrange; sich e-e Sache ~ think s.th. out; ~machen F v/t. (sep., -ge-, h) get ready, prepare, Am. F iix; adapt (für to, for purpose); sich ~ of *woman*: make (o.s.) up; **~weisen** *v/t.* (*irr. weisen, sep., -ge-, h*) reprimand(s); **2weisung** *f* reprimand.

'zu|reden *v/i.* (*sep., -ge-, h*): j-m ~ try to persuade s.o.; encourage s.o.; **'~reiten** *v/t.* (*irr. reiten, sep., -ge-, h*) break in; **'~riegeln** *v/t.* (*sep., -ge-, h*) bolt (up).

zürnen ['tsyrnən] *v/i.* (*ge-, h*) be angry (*j-m* with s.o.).

zurück *adv.* [tsu'ryk] back; backward(s); behind; **~behalten** *v/t.* (*irr. halten, sep., -ge-, h*) keep back, retain; **~bekommen** *v/t.* (*irr. kommen, no -ge-, h*) get back; **~bleiben** *v/i.* (*irr. bleiben, sep., -ge-, sein*) remain *or* stay behind; fall behind, lag; **~blicken** *v/i.* (*sep., -ge-, h*) look back; **~bringen** *v/t.* (*irr. bringen, sep., -ge-, h*) bring back; **~datieren** *v/t.* (*sep., no -ge-, h*) date back, antedate; **~drängen** *v/t.* (*sep., -ge-, h*) push back; *fig.* repress; **~erobern** *v/t.* (*sep., no -ge-, h*) reconquer; **~erstatten** *v/t.* (*sep., no -ge-, h*) restore, return; refund (*expenses*); **~fahren** (*irr. fahren, sep., -ge-*) 1. *v/i.* (*sein*) drive back; *fig.* start; 2. *v/t.* (*h*) drive back; **~fordern** *v/t.* (*sep., -ge-, h*) reclaim; **~führen** *v/t.* (*sep., -ge-, h*) lead back; ~ *auf* (*acc.*) reduce to (*rule, etc.*); refer to (*cause, etc.*); **~geben** *v/t.* (*irr. geben, sep., -ge-, h*) give back, return, restore; **~gehen** *v/i.* (*irr. gehen, sep., -ge-, sein*) go back; return; **~gezogen** *adj.* retired; **~greifen** *fig. v/i.* (*irr. greifen, sep., -ge-, h*): ~ *auf* (*acc.*) fall back (up)on; **~halten** (*irr. halten, sep., -ge-, h*) 1. *v/t.* hold back; 2. *v/i.*: ~ *mit* keep back; **~haltend** *adj.* reserved; **~haltung** *f* (*-/[•]-en*) reserve; **~kehren** *v/i.* (*sep., -ge-, sein*) return; **~kommen** *v/i.* (*irr. kommen, sep., -ge-, sein*) come back; return (*fig. auf acc.* to); **~lassen** *v/t.* (*irr. lassen, sep., -ge-, h*) leave (behind); **~legen** *v/t.* (*sep., -ge-, h*) lay aside; cover (*distance, way*); **~nehmen** *v/t.* (*irr. nehmen, sep., -ge-, h*) take back; withdraw, retract (*words, etc.*); **~prallen** *v/i.* (*sep., -ge-, sein*) rebound; start; **~rufen** *v/t.* (*irr. rufen, sep., -ge-, h*) call back; *sich ins Gedächtnis ~* recall; **~schicken** *v/t.* (*sep., -ge-, h*) send back; **~schlagen** (*irr. schlagen, sep., -ge-, h*) 1. *v/t.* drive (*ball*) back; repel (*enemy*); turn down (*blanket*); 2. *v/i.* strike back; **~schrecken** *v/i.* (*sep., -ge-, sein*) 1. (*irr. schrecken*) shrink back (*vor dat.* from *etc.*); 2. shrink (*vor dat.* from *work, etc.*); **~setzen** *v/t.* (*sep., -ge-, h*) put back; *fig.* slight, neglect; **~stellen** *v/t.* (*sep., -ge-, h*) put back (*a. clock*); *fig.* defer, postpone; **~strahlen** *v/t.* (*sep., -ge-, h*) reflect;

~streifen *v/t.* (*sep., -ge-, h*) turn *or* tuck up (*sleeve*); **~treten** *v/i.* (*irr. treten, sep., -ge-, sein*) step *or* stand back; *fig.*: recede; resign; withdraw; **~weichen** *v/i.* (*irr. weichen, sep., -ge-, sein*) fall back; recede (*a. fig.*); **~weisen** *v/t.* (*irr. weisen, sep., -ge-, h*) decline, reject; repel (*attack*); **~zahlen** *v/t.* (*sep., -ge-, h*) pay back (*a. fig.*); **~ziehen** (*irr. ziehen, sep., -ge-*) 1. *v/t.* (*h*) draw back; *fig.* withdraw; *sich ~* retire, withdraw; **✕** retreat; 2. *v/i.* (*sein*) move *or* march back.

'Zuruf *m* call; **'2en** *v/t.* (*irr. rufen, sep., -ge-, h*) call (out), shout (*j-m et. s.th.* to s.o.).

'Zusage *f* promise; assent; **'2n** (*sep., -ge-, h*) 1. *v/t.* promise; 2. *v/i.* promise to come; *j-m ~ food, etc.*: agree with s.o.; accept s.o.'s invitation; suit s.o.

zusammen *adv.* [tsu'zamən] together; at the same time; *alles ~* (all) in all; ~ *betragen* amount to, total (up to); **2arbeit** *f* (*-/no pl.*) co-operation; team-work; **~arbeiten** *v/i.* (*sep., -ge-, h*) work together; co-operate; **~beißen** *v/t.* (*sep., -ge-, h*): *die Zähne ~* set one's teeth; **~brechen** *v/i.* (*irr. brechen, sep., -ge-, sein*) break down; collapse; **2bruch** *m* breakdown; collapse; **~drücken** *v/t.* (*sep., -ge-, h*) compress, press together; **~fahren** *fig. v/i.* (*irr. fahren, sep., -ge-, sein*) start (*bei* at; *vor dat.* with); **~fallen** *v/i.* (*irr. fallen, sep., -ge-, sein*) fall in, collapse; coincide; **~falten** *v/t.* (*sep., -ge-, h*) fold up; **~fassen** *v/t.* (*sep., -ge-, h*) summarize, sum up; **2fassung** *f* (*-/-en*) summary; **~fügen** *v/t.* (*sep., -ge-, h*) join (together); **~halten** (*irr. halten, sep., -ge-, h*) 1. *v/t.* hold together; 2. *v/i.* hold together; *friends*: F stick together; **2hang** *m* coherence, coherency, connection; context; **~hängen** (*sep., -ge-, h*) 1. *v/i.* (*irr. hängen*) cohere; *fig.* be connected; 2. *v/t.* hang together; **~klappen** *v/t.* (*sep., -ge-, h*) fold up; close (*clasp-knife*); **~kommen** *v/i.* (*irr. kommen, sep., -ge-, sein*) meet; **2kunft** [~kunft] *f* (*-/=e*) meeting; **~laufen** *v/i.* (*irr. laufen, sep., -ge-, sein*) run *or* crowd together; **✕** converge; *milk*: curdle; **~legen** *v/t.* (*sep., -ge-, h*) lay together; fold up; club (*money*) (together); **~nehmen** *fig. v/t.* (*irr. nehmen, sep., -ge-, h*) collect (*one's wits*); *sich ~* be on one's good behavio(u)r; pull o.s. together; **~packen** *v/t.* (*sep., -ge-, h*) pack up; **~passen** *v/i.* (*sep., -ge-, h*) match, harmonize; **~rechnen** *v/t.* (*sep., -ge-, h*) add up; **~reißen** F *v/refl.* (*irr. reißen, sep., -ge-, h*) pull o.s. together; **~rollen**

v/t. and v/refl. (sep., -ge-, h) coil (up); **~rotten** *v/refl. (sep., -ge-, h)* band together; **~rücken** *(sep., -ge-)* **1.** *v/t. (h)* move together; **2.** *v/i. (sein)* close up; **~schlagen** *(irr. schlagen, sep., -ge-)* **1.** *v/t. (h)* clap *(hands)* (together); F smash to pieces; beat *s.o.* up; **2.** *v/i. (sein):* ~ *über (dat.)* close over; **~schließen** *v/refl. (irr. schließen, sep., -ge-, h)* join; unite; **2schluß** *m* union; **~schrumpfen** *v/i. (sep., -ge-, sein)* shrivel (up), shrink; **~setzen** *v/t. (sep., -ge-, h)* put together; compose; compound *(a. ♫, word);* ⊕ assemble; *sich ~ aus* consist of; **2setzung** *f (-/-en)* composition; compound; ⊕ assembly; **~stellen** *v/t. (sep., -ge-, h)* put together; compile; combine; **2stoß** *m* collision *(a. fig.);* ✗ encounter; *fig.* clash; **~stoßen** *v/i. (irr. stoßen, sep., -ge-, sein)* collide *(a. fig.);* adjoin; *fig.* clash; ~ *mit* knock *(heads, etc.)* together; **~stürzen** *v/i. (sep., -ge-, sein)* collapse; *house, etc.:* fall in; **~tragen** *v/t. (irr. tragen, sep., -ge-, h)* collect; compile *(notes);* **~treffen** *v/i. (irr. treffen, sep., -ge-, sein)* meet; coincide; **2treffen** *n (-s/no pl.)* meeting; encounter *(of enemies);* coincidence; **~treten** *v/i. (irr. treten, sep., -ge-, sein)* meet; *parl. a.* convene; **~wirken** *v/i. (sep., -ge-, h)* co-operate; **2wirken** *n (-s/no pl.)* co-operation; **~zählen** *v/t. (sep., -ge-, h)* add up, count up; **~ziehen** *v/t. (irr. ziehen, sep., -ge-, h)* draw together; contract; concentrate *(troops); sich ~* contract.

'Zusatz *m* addition; admixture, *metall.* alloy; supplement.

zusätzlich *adj.* ['tsu:zetsliç] additional.

'zuschau|en *v/i. (sep., -ge-, h)* look on *(e-r Sache* at s.th.*); j-m ~* watch s.o. *(bei et.* doing s.th.*);* **2er** *m (-s/-)* spectator, looker-on, onlooker; **'2erraum** *thea. m* auditorium.

'zuschicken *v/t. (sep., -ge-, h)* send *(dat.* to*);* mail; consign *(goods).*

'Zuschlag *m* addition; extra charge; excess fare; ✆ surcharge; *at auction:* knocking down; **2en** ['~gən] *(irr. schlagen, sep., -ge-)* **1.** *v/i. (h)* strike; **2.** *v/i. (sein) door:* slam (to); **3.** *v/t. (h)* bang, slam *(door)* (to); *at auction:* knock down *(dat.* to*).*

'zu|schließen *v/t. (irr. schließen, sep., -ge-, h)* lock (up); **'~schnallen** *v/t. (sep., -ge-, h)* buckle (up); **'~schnappen** *(sep., -ge-)* **1.** *v/i. (h) dog:* snap; **2.** *v/i. (sein) door:* snap to; **'~schneiden** *v/t. (irr. schneiden, sep., -ge-, h)* cut up; cut *(suit)* (to size); **2schnitt** *m (-[e]s/✎-e)* cut; style; **'~schnüren** *v/t. (sep., -ge-, h)* lace up; cord up; **'~schrauben** *v/t.*

(sep., -ge-, h) screw up or tight; **'~schreiben** *v/t. (irr. schreiben, sep., -ge-, h): j-m et. ~* ascribe or attribute s.th. to s.o.; **'2schrift** *f* letter.

zuschulden *adv.* ['tsu¹-]: *sich et. ~ kommen lassen* make o.s. guilty of s.th.

'Zu|schuß *m* allowance; subsidy, grant *(of government);* **'2schütten** *v/t. (sep., -ge-, h)* fill up *(ditch);* F add; **'2sehen** *v/i. (irr. sehen, sep., -ge-, h) s. zuschauen; ~, daß* see (to it) that; **2sehends** *adv.* ['~ts] visibly; **'2senden** *v/t. [(irr. senden,] sep., -ge-, h) s. zuschicken;* **'2setzen** *(sep., -ge-, h)* **1.** *v/t.* add; lose *(money);* **2.** *v/i.* lose money; *j-m ~* press s.o. hard.

'zusicher|n *v/t. (sep., -ge-, h): j-m et. ~* assure s.o. of s.th.; promise s.o. s.th.; **2ung** *f* promise, assurance.

'zu|spielen *v/t. (sep., -ge-, h) sports:* pass *(ball) (dat.* to*);* **'~spitzen** *v/t. (sep., -ge-, h)* point; *sich ~* taper (off); *fig.* come to a crisis; **'2spruch** *m (-[e]s/no pl.)* encouragement; consolation; ♰ custom; **'2stand** *m* condition, state; *in gutem ~ house:* in good repair.

zustande *adv.* [tsu'ʃtandə]: ~ *bringen* bring about; ~ *kommen* come about; *nicht ~ kommen* not to come off.

'zuständig *adj.* competent; **2keit** *f (-/-en)* competence.

zustatten *adv.* [tsu'ʃtatən]: *j-m ~ kommen* be useful to s.o.

'zustehen *v/i. (irr. stehen, sep., -ge-, h)* be due *(dat.* to*).*

'zustell|en *v/t. (sep., -ge-, h)* deliver *(a. ✍); ﬆﬔ* serve *(j-m* on s.o.*);* **'2ung** *f* delivery; *ﬆﬔ* service.

'zustimm|en *v/i. (sep., -ge-, h)* agree *(dat.:* to s.th.*; with s.o.);* consent *(to s.th.);* **'2ung** *f* consent.

'zustoßen *fig. v/i. (irr. stoßen, sep., -ge-, sein): j-m ~* happen to s.o.

zutage *adv.* [tsu'ta:gə]: ~ *treten* come to light.

Zutaten ['tsu:ta:tən] *f/pl.* ingredients *pl. (of food);* trimmings *pl. (of dress).*   [fall to s.o.'s share.\

zuteil *adv.* [tsu'taɪl]: *j-m ~ werden*
'zuteil|en *v/t. (sep., -ge-, h)* allot, apportion; **'2ung** *f* allotment, apportionment; ration.

'zutragen *v/refl. (irr. tragen, sep., -ge-, h)* happen.

'zutrauen 1. *v/t. (sep., -ge-, h): j-m et. ~* credit s.o. with s.th.; *sich zuviel ~* overrate o.s.; **2.** *2 n (-s/no pl.)* confidence *(zu* in*).*

'zutraulich *adj.* confiding, trustful, trusting; *animal:* friendly, tame.

'zutreffen *v/i. (irr. treffen, sep., -ge-, h)* be right, be true; ~ *auf (acc.)* be true of; **'~d** *adj.* right, correct; applicable.

'zutrinken v/i. (irr. trinken, sep., -ge-, h): j-m ~ drink to s.o.

'Zutritt m (-[e]s/no pl.) access; admission; ~ verboten! no admittance! [bottom.]

zuunterst adv. [tsu'-] right at the

zuverlässig adj. ['tsu:ferlɛsiç] reliable; certain; 2keit f (-/no pl.) reliability; certainty.

Zuversicht ['tsu:ferziçt] f (-/no pl.) confidence; 2lich adj. confident.

zuviel adv. [tsu'-] too much; e-r ~ one too many.

zuvor adv. [tsu'-] before, previously; first; ~kommen v/i. (irr. kommen, sep., -ge-, sein): j-m ~ anticipate s.o.; e-r Sache ~ anticipate or prevent s.th.; ~kommend adj. obliging; courteous.

Zuwachs ['tsu:vaks] m (-es/no pl.) increase; 2en v/i. (irr. wachsen, sep., -ge-, sein) become overgrown; wound: close.

zu|wege adv. [tsu've:gǝ]: ~ bringen bring about; ~'weilen adv. sometimes.

'zu|weisen v/t. (irr. weisen, sep., -ge-, h) assign; '~wenden v/t. (irr. wenden, sep., -ge-, h) (dat.) turn to(wards); fig.: give; bestow on; sich ~ (dat.) turn to(wards).

zuwenig adv. [tsu'-] too little.

'zuwerfen v/t. (irr. werfen, sep., -ge-, h) fill up (pit); slam (door) (to); j-m ~ throw (ball, etc.) to s.o.; cast (look) at s.o.

zuwider prp. (dat.) [tsu'-] contrary to, against; repugnant, distasteful; ~handeln v/i. (sep., -ge-, h) (dat.) act contrary or in opposition to; esp. ✠ contravene; 2handlung ✠ f contravention.

'zu|winken v/i. (sep., -ge-, h) (dat.) wave to; beckon to; '~zahlen v/t. (sep., -ge-, h) pay extra; '~zählen v/t. (sep., -ge-, h) add; '~ziehen (irr. ziehen, sep., -ge-) 1. v/t. (h) draw together; draw (curtains); consult (doctor, etc.); sich ~ incur (s.o.'s displeasure, etc.); ✠ catch (disease); 2. v/i. (sein) move in; ~züglich prp. (gen.) ['tsy:k-] plus.

Zwang [tsvaŋ] 1. m (-[e]s/¨-e) compulsion, coercion; constraint; ✠ duress(e); force; sich ~ antun check or restrain o.s.; 2. 2 pret. of zwingen.

zwängen ['tsvɛŋǝn] v/t. (ge-, h) press, force.

'zwanglos fig. adj. free and easy, informal; 2igkeit f (-/-en) ease, informality.

'Zwangs|arbeit f hard labo(u)r; '~jacke f strait waistcoat or jacket; '~lage f embarrassing situation; 2läufig fig. adj. ['~lɔyf-] necessary; '~maßnahme f coercive measure; '~vollstreckung ✠ f distraint, execution; '~vorstellung ✠ f

obsession, hallucination; '2weise adv. by force; '~wirtschaft f (-/¨-en) controlled economy.

zwanzig adj. ['tsvantsiç] twenty; ~ste adj. ['~stǝ] twentieth.

zwar cj. [tsva:r] indeed, it is true; und ~ and that, that is.

Zweck [tsvɛk] m (-[e]s/-e) aim, end, object, purpose; design; keinen ~ haben be of no use; s-n ~ erfüllen answer its purpose; zu dem ~ (gen.) for the purpose of; 2dienlich adj. serviceable, useful, expedient.

Zwecke ['tsvɛkǝ] f (-/-n) tack; drawing-pin, Am. thumbtack.

'zweck|los adj. aimless, purposeless, useless; '~mäßig adj. expedient, suitable; '2mäßigkeit f (-/no pl.) expediency.

zwei adj. [tsvai] two; '~beinig adj. two-legged; 2bettzimmer n double (bedroom); ~deutig adj. ['~dɔy-tiç] ambiguous; suggestive; ~erlei adj. ['~ǝr'lai] of two kinds, two kinds of; ~fach adj. ['~fax] double, twofold.

Zweifel ['tsvaifǝl] m (-s/-) doubt; 2haft adj. doubtful, dubious; 2los adj. doubtless; 2n v/i. (ge-, h) doubt (an e-r Sache s.th.; an j-m s.o.).

Zweig [tsvaik] m (-[e]s/-e) branch (a. fig.); kleiner ~ twig; '~geschäft n, '~niederlassung f, '~stelle f branch.

zwei|jährig adj. ['tsvaijɛ:riç] two-year-old, of two (years); '2kampf m duel, single combat; '~mal adv. twice; '~malig adj. (twice) repeated; ~motorig adj. ['~moto:riç] two- or twin-engined; '~reihig adj. having two rows; suit: double-breasted; '~schneidig adj. double-or two-edged (both a. fig.); '~seitig adj. two-sided; contract, etc.: bilateral; fabric: reversible, 2sitzer esp. mot. m (-s/-) two-seater; '~sprachig adj. bilingual; '~stimmig adj. for two voices; ~stöckig adj. ['~ʃtœkiç] two-stor|eyed, -ied; '~stufig ⊕ adj. two-stage; ~stündig adj. of ['~ʃtyndiç] of or lasting two hours, two-hour.

zweit adj. [tsvait] second; ein ~er another; aus ~er Hand second-hand; zu ~ by twos; wir sind zu ~ there are two of us. [engine.]

'Zweitaktmotor mot. m two-stroke]

'zweit'best adj. second-best.

'zweiteilig adj. garment: two-piece.

zweitens adv. ['tsvaitǝns] secondly.

'zweitklassig adj. second-class, second-rate.

Zwerchfell anat. ['tsvɛrç-] n diaphragm.

Zwerg [tsvɛrk] m (-[e]s/-e) dwarf; 2enhaft adj. ['~gǝn-] dwarfish.

Zwetsch(g)e ['tsvɛtʃ(g)ǝ] f (-/-n) plum.

Zwick|el ['tsvikəl] m (-s/-) sewing: gusset; '2en v/t. and v/i. (ge-, h) pinch, nip; '~er m (-s/-) (ein a pair of) eye-glasses pl., pince-nez; '~mühle fig. f dilemma, quandary, fix.

Zwieback ['tsvi:bak] m (-[e]s/=e, -e) rusk, zwieback.

Zwiebel ['tsvi:bəl] f (-/-n) onion; bulb (of flowers, etc.).

Zwie|gespräch ['tsvi:-] n dialog(ue); '~licht n (-[e]s/no pl.) twilight; '~spalt m (-[e]s/-e, =e) disunion; conflict; 2spältig adj. ['~ʃpɛltiç] disunited; emotions: conflicting; '~tracht f (-/no pl.) discord.

Zwilling|e ['tsviliŋə] m/pl. twins pl.; '~sbruder m twin brother; '~sschwester f twin sister.

Zwinge ['tsviŋə] f (-/-n) ferrule (of stick, etc.); ⊕ clamp; '2n v/t. (irr., ge-, h) compel, constrain; force; '2nd adj. forcible; arguments: cogent, compelling; imperative; '~r m (-s/-) outer court; kennel(s pl.); bear-pit.

zwinkern ['tsviŋkərn] v/i. (ge-, h) wink, blink.

Zwirn [tsvirn] m (-[e]s/-e) thread, cotton; '~sfaden m thread.

zwischen prp. (dat.; acc.) ['tsviʃən] between (two); among (several); '2bilanz ✝ f interim balance; '2deck ⚓ n steerage; ~'durch F adv. in between; for a change; '2ergebnis n provisional result; '2fall m incident; '2händler ✝ m middleman; '2landung ✈ f intermediate landing, stop, Am. a. stop-over; (Flug) ohne ~ non-stop (flight);

'2pause f interval, intermission; '2prüfung f intermediate examination; '2raum m space, interval; '2ruf m (loud) interruption; '2spiel n interlude; '~staatlich adj. international; Am. between States: interstate; '2station f intermediate station; '2stecker ⚡ m adapter; '2stück n intermediate piece, connexion, (Am. only) connection; '2stufe f intermediate stage; '2wand f partition (wall); '2zeit f interval; in der ~ in the meantime.

Zwist [tsvist] m (-es/-e), '~igkeit f (-/-en) discord; disunion; quarrel.

zwitschern ['tsvitʃərn] v/i. (ge-, h) twitter, chirp.

Zwitter ['tsvitər] m (-s/-) hermaphrodite.

zwölf adj. [tsvœlf] twelve; um ~ (Uhr) at twelve (o'clock); (um) ~ Uhr mittags (at) noon; (um) ~ Uhr nachts (at) midnight; 2'fingerdarm anat. m duodenum; ~te adj. ['~tə] twelfth.

Zyankali [tsyan'kɑ:li] n (-s/no pl.) potassium cyanide.

Zyklus ['tsy:klus, 'tsyk-] m (-/Zyklen) cycle; course, set (of lectures, etc.).

Zylind|er [tsi'lindər, tsy'-] m (-s/-) ⚙, ⊕ cylinder; chimney (of lamp); top hat; 2risch adj. [~driʃ] cylindrical.

Zyni|ker ['tsy:nikər] m (-s/-) cynic; '2sch adj. cynical; ~smus [tsy-'nismus] m (-/Zynismen) cynicism.

Zypresse ⚘ [tsy'presə] f (-/-n) cypress.

Zyste 🝳 ['tsystə] f (-/-n) cyst.

PART II

ENGLISH-GERMAN
DICTIONARY

A

a [ei, ə] *Artikel*: ein(e); per, pro, je; *all of a size* alle gleich groß; *twice a week* zweimal wöchentlich.

A 1 F [ei'wʌn] Ia, prima.

aback [ə'bæk] rückwärts; ~ *fig.* überrascht, verblüfft, bestürzt.

abandon [ə'bændən] auf-, preisgeben; verlassen; überlassen; ~ed verworfen; ~ment [ʌnmənt] Auf-, Preisgabe *f*; Unbeherrschtheit *f*.

abase [ə'beis] erniedrigen, demütigen; ~ment [ʌsmənt] Erniedrigung *f*.

abash [ə'bæʃ] beschämen, verlegen machen; ~ment [ʌʃmənt] Verlegenheit *f*.

abate [ə'beit] *v/t.* verringern; *Mißstand* abstellen; *v/i.* abnehmen, nachlassen; ~ment [ʌtmənt] Verminderung *f*; Abschaffung *f*.

abattoir ['æbətwɑː] Schlachthaus *n*.

abb|ess ['æbis] Äbtissin *f*; ~ey ['æbi] Abtei *f*; ~ot ['æbət] Abt *m*.

abbreviat|e [ə'briːvieit] (ab)kürzen; ~ion [əbriːvi'eiʃən] Abkürzung *f*.

ABC ['eibiː'siː] Abc *n*, Alphabet *n*.

ABC weapons *pl.* ABC-Waffen *f/pl.*

abdicat|e ['æbdikeit] entsagen (*dat.*); abdanken; ~ion [æbdi-'keiʃən] Verzicht *m*; Abdankung *f*.

abdomen ['æbdəmen] Unterleib *m*, Bauch *m*.

abduct [æb'dʌkt] entführen.

aberration [æbə'reiʃən] Abweichung *f*; *fig.* Verirrung *f*.

abet [ə'bet] aufhetzen; anstiften; unterstützen; ~tor [ʌtə] Anstifter *m*; (Helfers)Helfer *m*.

abeyance [ə'beiəns] Unentschiedenheit *f*; *in* ~ ɡ⁷ in der Schwebe.

abhor [əb'hɔː] verabscheuen; ~rence [əb'hɔrəns] Abscheu *m* (*of* vor *dat.*); ~rent □ [ʌnt] zuwider (*to dat.*); abstoßend.

abide [ə'baid] [*irr.*] *v/i.* bleiben (*by* bei); *v/t.* erwarten; (v)ertragen.

ability [ə'biliti] Fähigkeit *f*.

abject □ ['æbdʒekt] verächtlich, gemein.

abjure [əb'dʒuə] abschwören; entsagen (*dat.*).

able □ ['eibl] fähig, geschickt; *be* ~ imstande sein, können; ~-bodied kräftig.

abnegat|e ['æbnigeit] ableugnen; verzichten auf (*acc.*); ~ion [æbni-'geiʃən] Ableugnung *f*; Verzicht *m*.

abnormal □ [æb'nɔːməl] abnorm.

aboard [ə'bɔːd] ⚓ an Bord (*gen.*); *all* ~! *Am.* 🚂 etc. einsteigen!

abode [ə'boud] **1.** *pret. u. p.p. von abide*; **2.** Aufenthalt *m*; Wohnung *f*.

aboli|sh [ə'bɔliʃ] abschaffen, aufheben; ~tion [æbə'liʃən] Abschaffung *f*, Aufhebung *f*; ~tionist [ʌnist] Gegner *m* der Sklaverei.

A-bomb ['eibɔm] = *atomic bomb.*

abomina|ble □ [ə'bɔminəbl] abscheulich; ~te [ʌneit] verabscheuen; ~tion [əbɔmi'neiʃən] Abscheu *m*.

aboriginal □ [æbə'ridʒənl] einheimisch; Ur...

abortion ɡ⁷ [ə'bɔːʃən] Fehlgeburt *f*; Abtreibung *f*.

abortive □ [ə'bɔːtiv] vorzeitig; erfolglos, fehlgeschlagen; verkümmert.

abound [ə'baund] reichlich vorhanden sein; Überfluß haben (*in an dat.*).

about [ə'baut] **1.** *prp.* um (...herum); bei; im Begriff; über (*acc.*); *I had no money* ~ me ich hatte kein Geld bei mir; *what are you* ~? was macht ihr da?; **2.** *adv.* herum, umher; in der Nähe; etwa; ungefähr um, gegen; *bring* ~ zustande bringen.

above [ə'bʌv] **1.** *prp.* über; *fig.* erhaben über; ~ *all* vor allem; ~ *ground fig.* am Leben; **2.** *adv.* oben; darüber; **3.** *adj.* obig.

abreact [æbri'ækt] abreagieren.

abreast [ə'brest] nebeneinander.

abridg|e [ə'bridʒ] (ver)kürzen; ~(e)ment [ʌdʒmənt] (Ver)Kürzung *f*; Auszug *m*.

abroad [ə'brɔːd] im (ins) Ausland; überall(hin); *there is a report* ~ es geht das Gerücht; *all* ~ ganz im Irrtum.

abrogate ['æbrougeit] aufheben.

abrupt □ [ə'brʌpt] jäh; zs.-hanglos; schroff.

abscess ɡ⁷ ['æbsis] Geschwür *n*.

abscond [əb'skɔnd] sich davonmachen.

absence ['æbsəns] Abwesenheit *f*; Mangel *m*; ~ *of mind* Zerstreutheit *f*.

absent 1. □ ['æbsənt] abwesend; nicht vorhanden; **2.** [æb'sent]: ~ *o.s.* fernbleiben; ~-minded □ ['æbsənt'maindid] zerstreut, geistesabwesend.

absolut|e □ ['æbsəluːt] absolut; unumschränkt; vollkommen; unvermischt; unbedingt; ~ion [æbsə-'luːʃən] Lossprechung *f*.

absolve [əb'zɔlv] frei-, lossprechen.

absorb [əb'sɔːb] aufsaugen; *fig.* ganz in Anspruch nehmen.

absorption [əb'sɔːpʃən] Aufsaugung *f*; *fig.* Vertieftsein *n*.

abstain [əb'stein] sich enthalten.

abstemious □ [æb'sti:mjəs] enthaltsam; mäßig.

abstention [æb'stenʃən] Enthaltung f.

abstinen|ce ['æbstinəns] Enthaltsamkeit f; ~t □ [~nt] enthaltsam.

abstract 1. □ ['æbstrækt] abstrakt; 2. [~] Auszug m; gr. Abstraktum n; 3. [æb'strækt] abstrahieren; ablenken; entwenden; Inhalt kurz zs.-fassen; ~ed □ zerstreut; ~ion [~kʃən] Abstraktion f; (abstrakter) Begriff.

abstruse □ [æb'stru:s] fig. dunkel, schwer verständlich; tiefgründig.

absurd [əb'sə:d] absurd, sinnwidrig; lächerlich.

abundan|ce [ə'bʌndəns] Überfluß m; Fülle f; Überschwang m; ~t □ [~nt] reich(lich).

abus|e 1. [ə'bju:s] Mißbrauch m; Beschimpfung f; 2. [~u:z] mißbrauchen; beschimpfen; ~ive □ [~u:siv] schimpfend; Schimpf...

abut [ə'bʌt] (an)grenzen (upon an).

abyss [ə'bis] Abgrund m.

academic|(al □) [ækə'demik(əl)] akademisch; ~ian [ækædə'miʃən] Akademiemitglied n.

academy [ə'kædəmi] Akademie f.

accede [æk'si:d] ~ to beitreten (dat.); Amt antreten; Thron besteigen.

accelerat|e [æk'seləreit] beschleunigen; fig. ankurbeln; ~or [æk'seləreitə] Gaspedal n.

accent 1. ['æksənt] Akzent m (a. gr.); 2. [æk'sent] v/t. akzentuieren, betonen; ~uate [~tjueit] akzentuieren, betonen.

accept [ək'sept] annehmen; † akzeptieren; hinnehmen; ~able □ [~təbl] annehmbar; ~ance [~əns] Annahme f; † Akzept n.

access ['ækses] Zugang m; ⚕ Anfall m; easy of ~ zugänglich; ~ road Zufahrtstraße f; ~ary [æk'sesəri] Mitwisser(in), Mitschuldige(r m) f; = accessory 2; ~ible □ [~səbl] zugänglich; give ~ to Antritt m (to gen.); Eintritt m (to in acc.); ~ to the throne Thronbesteigung f.

accessory [æk'sesəri] 1. □ zusätzlich; 2. Zubehörteil n.

accident ['æksidənt] Zufall m; Un(glücks)fall m; ~al □ [æksi'dentl] zufällig; nebensächlich.

acclaim [ə'kleim] j-m zujubeln.

acclamation [æklə'meiʃən] Zuruf m.

acclimatize [ə'klaimətaiz] akklimatisieren, eingewöhnen.

acclivity [ə'kliviti] Steigung f; Böschung f.

accommodat|e [ə'kɔmədeit] anpassen; unterbringen; Streit schlichten; versorgen; j-m aushelfen (with mit Geld); ~ion [əkɔmə'deiʃən] Anpassung f; Aushilfe f; Bequemlichkeit f; Unterkunft f; Beilegung f; seating ~ Sitzgelegenheit f; ~ train Am. Personenzug m.

accompan|iment [ə'kʌmpənimənt] Begleitung f; ~y [ə'kʌmpəni] begleiten; accompanied with verbunden mit.

accomplice [ə'kɔmplis] Komplice m.

accomplish [ə'kɔmpliʃ] vollenden; ausführen; ~ed vollendet, perfekt; ~ment [~ʃmənt] Vollendung f; Ausführung f; Tat f, Leistung f; Talent n.

accord [ə'kɔ:d] 1. Übereinstimmung f; with one ~ einstimmig; 2. v/i. übereinstimmen; v/t. gewähren; ~ance [~dəns] Übereinstimmung f; ~ant □ [~nt] übereinstimmend; ~ing [~diŋ]: ~ to gemäß (dat.); ~ingly [~ŋli] demgemäß.

accost [ə'kɔst] j-n bsd. auf der Straße ansprechen.

account [ə'kaunt] 1. Rechnung f; Berechnung f; † Konto n; Rechenschaft f; Bericht m; of no ~ ohne Bedeutung; on no ~ auf keinen Fall; on ~ of wegen; take into ~ take ~ of in Betracht ziehen, berücksichtigen; turn to ~ ausnutzen; keep ~s die Bücher führen; call to ~ zur Rechenschaft ziehen; give a good ~ of o.s. sich bewähren; make ~ of Wert auf et. (acc.) legen; 2. v/i.: ~ for Rechenschaft über et. (acc.) ablegen; (sich) erklären; be much ~ed of hoch geachtet sein; v/t. ansehen als; ~able □ [~təbl] verantwortlich; erklärlich; ~ant [~ənt] Buchhalter m; chartered ~, Am. certified public ~ vereidigter Bücherrevisor; ~ing [~tiŋ] Buchführung f.

accredit [ə'kredit] beglaubigen.

accrue [ə'kru:] erwachsen (from aus).

accumulat|e [ə'kju:mjuleit] (sich) (an)häufen; ansammeln; ~ion [əkju:mju'leiʃən] Anhäufung f.

accura|cy [ə'ækjurasi] Genauigkeit f; ~te □ [~rit] genau; richtig.

accurs|ed [ə'kə:sid], ~t [~st] verflucht, verwünscht.

accus|ation [ækju(:)'zeiʃən] Anklage f, Beschuldigung f; ~ative gr. [ə'kju:zətiv] a. ~ case Akkusativ m; ~e [ə'kju:z] anklagen, beschuldigen; ~er [~zə] Kläger(in).

accustom [ə'kʌstəm] gewöhnen (to an acc.); ~ed gewohnt, üblich; gewöhnt (to an acc., zu inf.).

ace [eis] As n (a. fig.); ~ in the hole Am. F fig. Trumpf m in Reserve; within an ~ um ein Haar.

acerbity [ə'sə:biti] Herbheit f.

acet|ic [ə'si:tik] essigsauer; ~ify [ə'setifai] säuern.

ache [eik] 1. schmerzen; sich sehnen (for nach; to do zu tun); 2. anhaltende Schmerzen m/pl.

achieve [ə'tʃi:v] ausführen; erreichen; ~ment [~vmənt] Ausführung f; Leistung f.

acid ['æsid] 1. sauer; 2. Säure f; ~ity [ə'siditi] Säure f.

acknowledg|e [ək'nɔlidʒ] anerkennen; zugeben; † bestätigen; ~e/~ment [~dʒmənt] Anerkennung f; Bestätigung f; Eingeständnis n.

acme ['ækmi] Gipfel m; ✺ Krisis f.

acorn ♀ ['eikɔ:n] Eichel f.

acoustics [ə'ku:stiks] pl. Akustik f.

acquaint [ə'kweint] bekannt machen; j-m mitteilen; be ~ed with kennen; ~ance [~təns] Bekanntschaft f; Bekannte(r m) f.

acquiesce [ækwi'es] (in) hinnehmen (acc.); einwilligen (in acc.).

acquire [ə'kwaiə] erwerben; ~ment [~əmənt] Fertigkeit f.

acquisition [ækwi'ziʃən] Erwerbung f; Errungenschaft f.

acquit [ə'kwit] freisprechen; ~ o.s. of Pflicht erfüllen; ~ o.s. well s-e Sache gut machen; ~tal [~tl] Freisprechung f, Freispruch m; ~tance [~təns] Tilgung f.

acre ['eikə] Morgen m (4047 qm).

acrid ['ækrid] scharf, beißend.

across [ə'krɔs] 1. adv. hin-, herüber; (quer) durch; drüben; überkreuz; 2. prp. (quer) über (acc.); jenseits (gen.), über (dat.); come ~, run ~ stoßen auf (acc.).

act [ækt] 1. v/i. handeln; sich benehmen; wirken; funktionieren; thea. spielen; v/t. thea. spielen; 2. Handlung f, Tat f; thea. Akt m; Gesetz n; Beschluß m; Urkunde f, Vertrag m; ~ing ['æktiŋ] 1. Handeln n; thea. Spiel(en) n; 2. tätig, amtierend.

action ['ækʃən] Handlung f (a. thea.); Tätigkeit f; Tat f; Wirkung f; Klage f, Prozeß m; Gang m (Pferd etc.); Gefecht n; Mechanismus m; take ~ Schritte unternehmen.

activ|e □ ['æktiv] aktiv; tätig; rührig, wirksam; † lebhaft; ~ity [æk'tiviti] Tätigkeit f; Betriebsamkeit f; bsd. † Lebhaftigkeit f.

act|or ['æktə] Schauspieler m; ~ress ['æktris] Schauspielerin f.

actual □ ['æktjuəl] wirklich, tatsächlich, eigentlich.

actuate ['æktjueit] in Gang bringen.

acute □ [ə'kju:t] spitz; scharf(sinnig); brennend (Frage); ✺ akut.

ad F [æd] = advertisement.

adamant fig. ['ædəmənt] unerbittlich.

adapt [ə'dæpt] anpassen (to, for dat.); Text bearbeiten (from nach); zurechtmachen; ~ation [ædæp'teiʃən] Anpassung f, Bearbeitung f.

add [æd] v/t. hinzufügen; addieren; v/i.: ~ to vermehren; hinzukommen zu.

addict ['ædikt] Süchtige(r m) f; ~ed [ə'diktid] ergeben (to dat.); ~ to e-m Laster verfallen.

addition [ə'diʃən] Hinzufügen n; Zusatz m; An-, Ausbau m; Addition f; in ~ außerdem; in ~ to außer, zu; ~al □ [~nl] zusätzlich.

address [ə'dres] 1. Worte richten (to an acc.); sprechen zu; 2. Adresse f; Ansprache f; Anstand m, Manieren f/pl.; pay one's ~es to a lady e-r Dame den Hof machen; ~ee [ædre'si:] Adressat m, Empfänger m.

adept ['ædept] 1. erfahren; geschickt; 2. Eingeweihte(r m) f; Kenner m.

adequa|cy ['ædikwəsi] Angemessenheit f; ~te □ [~kwit] angemessen.

adhere [əd'hiə] (to) haften (an dat.); fig. festhalten (an dat.); ~nce [~ərəns] Anhaften n, Festhalten n; ~nt [~nt] Anhänger(in).

adhesion [əd'hi:ʒən] = adherence; fig. Einwilligung f.

adhesive [əd'hi:siv] 1. □ klebend; ~ plaster, ~ tape Heftpflaster n; 2. Klebstoff m.

adjacent □ [ə'dʒeisənt] (to) anliegend (dat.); anstoßend (an acc.); benachbart.

adjective gr. ['ædʒiktiv] Adjektiv n, Eigenschaftswort n.

adjoin [ə'dʒɔin] angrenzen an (acc.).

adjourn [ə'dʒə:n] aufschieben; (v/i. sich) vertagen; ~ment [~nmənt] Aufschub m; Vertagung f.

adjudge [ə'dʒʌdʒ] zuerkennen; verurteilen.

adjust [ə'dʒʌst] in Ordnung bringen; anpassen; Streit schlichten; Mechanismus u. fig. einstellen (to auf acc.); ~ment [~tmənt] Anordnung f; Einstellung f; Schlichtung f.

administ|er [əd'ministə] verwalten; spenden; ✺ verabfolgen; ~ justice Recht sprechen; ~ration [ədminis-'treiʃən] Verwaltung f; Regierung f; bsd. Am. Amtsperiode f e-s Präsidenten; ~rative [əd'ministrətiv] Verwaltungs...; ~rator [~reitə] Verwalter m.

admir|able □ ['ædmərəbl] bewundernswert; (vor)trefflich; ~ation [ædmə'reiʃən] Bewunderung f; ~e [əd'maiə] bewundern; verehren.

admiss|ible □ [əd'misəbl] zulässig; ~ion [~iʃən] Zulassung f; F Eintritt(sgeld n) m; Eingeständnis n.

admit [əd'mit] v/t. (her)einlassen (to, into in acc.), eintreten lassen; zulassen (to zu); zugeben; ~tance [~təns] Einlaß m, Zutritt m.

admixture [əd'mikstʃə] Beimischung f, Zusatz m.

admon|ish [əd'mɔniʃ] ermahnen; warnen (of, against vor dat.); ~ition [ædmə'niʃən] Ermahnung f; Warnung f.

ado [ə'du:] Getue *n*; Lärm *m*; Mühe *f*.

adolescen|ce [ædou'lesns] Adoleszenz *f*, Reifezeit *f*; ~t [~nt] **1.** jugendlich, heranwachsend; **2.** Jugendliche(r *m*) *f*.

adopt [ə'dɔpt] adoptieren; sich aneignen; ~ion [~pʃən] Annahme *f*.

ador|able □ [ə'dɔ:rəbl] verehrungswürdig; ~ation [ædɔ:'reiʃən] Anbetung *f*; ~e [ə'dɔ:] anbeten.

adorn [ə'dɔ:n] schmücken, zieren; ~ment [~nmənt] Schmuck *m*.

adroit □ [ə'drɔit] gewandt.

adult ['ædʌlt] **1.** erwachsen; **2.** Erwachsene(r *m*) *f*.

adulter|ate [ə'dʌltəreit] (ver)fälschen; ~er [~rə] Ehebrecher *m*; ~ess [~ris] Ehebrecherin *f*; ~ous □ [~rəs] ehebrecherisch; ~y [~ri] Ehebruch *m*.

advance [əd'vɑːns] **1.** *v/i.* vorrücken, vorgehen; steigen; Fortschritte machen; *v/t.* vorrücken, vorbringen; vorausbezahlen; vorschießen; (be)fördern; *Preis* erhöhen; beschleunigen; **2.** Vorrücken *n*; Fortschritt *m*; Angebot *n*; Vorschuß *m*; Erhöhung *f*; *in* ~ *im* voraus; ~d vor-, fortgeschritten; ~ *in years* in vorgerücktem Alter; ~ment [~smənt] Förderung *f*; Fortschritt *m*.

advantage [əd'vɑːntidʒ] Vorteil *m*; Überlegenheit *f*; Gewinn *m*; *take* ~ *of* ausnutzen; ~ous □ [ædvən'teidʒəs] vorteilhaft.

adventur|e [əd'ventʃə] Abenteuer *n*, Wagnis *n*; Spekulation *f*; ~er [~rə] Abenteurer *m*; Spekulant *m*; ~ous □ [~rəs] abenteuerlich; wagemutig.

adverb *gr.* ['ædvə:b] Adverb *n*, Umstandswort *n*.

advers|ary ['ædvəsəri] Gegner *m*, Feind *m*; ~e □ ['ædvə:s] widrig; feindlich; ungünstig, nachteilig (*to* für); ~ity [əd'və:siti] Unglück *n*.

advertise [ˈædvətaiz] ankündigen; inserieren; Reklame machen (für); ~ment [əd'və:tismənt] Ankündigung *f*, Inserat *n*; Reklame *f*; ~ing ['ædvətaizin] Reklame *f*, Werbung *f*; ~ *agency* Annoncenbüro *n*; ~ *designer* Reklamezeichner *m*; ~ *film* Reklamefilm *m*; *screen* ~ Filmreklame *f*.

advice [əd'vais] Rat(schlag) *m*; (*mst pl.*) Nachricht *f*, Meldung *f*; *take medical* ~ e-n Arzt zu Rate ziehen.

advis|able □ [əd'vaizəbl] ratsam; ~e [əd'vaiz] *v/t.* j-n beraten; j-m raten; † benachrichtigen, avisieren; *v/i.* (sich) beraten; ~er [~zə] Ratgeber(in).

advocate 1. ['ædvəkit] Anwalt *m*; Fürsprecher *m*; **2.** [~keit] verteidigen, befürworten.

aerial ['ɛəriəl] **1.** □ luftig; Luft...;

~view Luftaufnahme *f*; **2.** *Radio, Fernsehen*: Antenne *f*.

aero|... ['ɛərou] Luft...; ~cab *Am.* F ['ɛərəkæb] Lufttaxi *n* (*Hubschrauber als Zubringer*); ~drome [~ədroum] Flugplatz *m*; ~naut [~nɔ:t] Luftschiffer *m*; ~nautics [ɛərə'nɔ:tiks] *pl.* Luftfahrt *f*; ~plane ['ɛərəplein] Flugzeug *n*; ~stat ['ɛəroustæt] Luftballon *m*.

aesthetic [iːs'θetik] ästhetisch; ~s *sg.* Ästhetik *f*.

afar [ə'fɑː] fern, weit (weg).

affable □ ['æfəbl] leutselig.

affair [ə'fɛə] Geschäft *n*; Angelegenheit *f*; Sache *f*; F Ding *n*; Liebschaft *f*.

affect [ə'fekt] (ein- *od.* sich aus-) wirken auf (*acc.*); (be)rühren; *Gesundheit* angreifen; gern mögen; vortäuschen, nachahmen; ~ation [æfek'teiʃən] Vorliebe *f*; Ziererei *f*; Verstellung *f*; ~ed □ gerührt; befallen (*von Krankheit*); angegriffen (*Augen etc.*); geziert, affektiert; ~ion [~kʃən] Gemütszustand *m*; (Zu)Neigung *f*; Erkrankung *f*; ~ionate □ [~ʃnit] liebevoll.

affidavit [æfi'deivit] *schriftliche* beeidigte Erklärung.

affiliate [ə'filieit] *als Mitglied* aufnehmen; angliedern; ~d *company* Tochtergesellschaft *f*.

affinity [ə'finiti] *fig.* (geistige) Verwandtschaft; ⚗ Affinität *f*.

affirm [ə'fə:m] bejahen; behaupten; bestätigen; ~ation [æfə:'meiʃən] Behauptung *f*; Bestätigung *f*; ~ative [ə'fə:mətiv] **1.** □ bejahend; **2.:** *answer in the* ~ bejahen.

affix [ə'fiks] (*to*) anheften (an *acc.*); befestigen (an *dat.*); *Siegel* aufdrücken (*dat.*); bei-, zufügen (*dat.*).

afflict [ə'flikt] betrüben; plagen; ~ion [~kʃən] Betrübnis *f*; Leiden *n*.

affluen|ce ['æfluəns] Überfluß *m*; Wohlstand *m*; ~t [~nt] **1.** □ reich (-lich); ~ *society* Wohlstandsgesellschaft *f*; **2.** Nebenfluß *m*.

afford [ə'fɔ:d] liefern; erschwingen; *I can* ~ *it* ich kann es mir leisten.

affront [ə'frʌnt] **1.** beleidigen; trotzen (*dat.*); **2.** Beleidigung *f*.

afield [ə'fiːld] im Felde; (weit) weg.

afloat [ə'flout] ⏚ *u. fig.* flott; schwimmend; auf See; umlaufend; *set* ~ flottmachen; *fig.* in Umlauf setzen.

afraid [ə'freid] bange; *be* ~ *of* sich fürchten *od.* Angst haben vor (*dat.*).

afresh [ə'freʃ] von neuem.

African ['æfrikən] **1.** afrikanisch; **2.** Afrikaner(in); *Am. a.* Neger(in).

after ['ɑːftə] **1.** *adv.* hinterher; nachher; **2.** *prp.* nach; hinter (... her); ~ *all* schließlich (doch); **3.** *cj.* nachdem; **4.** *adj.* später; Nach...; ~crop Nachernte *f*; ~glow Abendrot *n*; ~math [~mæθ]

Nachwirkung(en *pl.*) *f*, Folgen *f*/*pl.*; **~noon** [‚~'nu:n] Nachmittag *m*; **~season** Nachsaison *f*; **~taste** Nachgeschmack *m*; **~-thought** nachträglicher Einfall; **~wards** [‚~wədz] nachher; später.

again [ə'gen] wieder(um); ferner; dagegen; *~ and ~*, *time and ~* immer wieder; *as much ~* noch einmal soviel.

against [ə'genst] gegen; *räumlich:* gegen; an, vor (*dat. od. acc.*); *fig.* in Erwartung (*gen.*), für; *as ~* verglichen mit.

age [eidʒ] **1.** (Lebens)Alter *n*; Zeit (-alter *n*) *f*; Menschenalter *n*; (*old*) **~** Greisenalter *n*; *of ~* mündig; *over ~* zu alt; *under ~* unmündig; *wait for ~s* F e-e Ewigkeit warten; **2.** alt werden *od.* machen; **~d** ['eidʒid] alt; [eidʒd]: *~ twenty* 20 Jahre alt.

agency ['eidʒənsi] Tätigkeit *f*; Vermittlung *f*; Agentur *f*, Büro *n*.

agenda [ə'dʒendə] Tagesordnung *f*.

agent ['eidʒənt] Handelnde(r *m*) *f*; Agent *m*; wirkende Kraft, Agens *n*.

age-worn ['eidʒwɔ:n] altersschwach.

agglomerate [ə'glɔməreit] (sich) zs.-ballen; (sich) (an)häufen.

agglutinate [ə'glu:tineit] zs.-, an-, verkleben.

aggrandize [ə'grændaiz] vergrößern; erhöhen.

aggravate ['ægrəveit] erschweren; verschlimmern; F ärgern.

aggregate **1.** ['ægrigeit] (sich) anhäufen; vereinigen (to with); sich belaufen auf (*acc.*); **2.** □ [‚~git] gehäuft; gesamt; **3.** [‚~] Anhäufung *f*; Aggregat *n*.

aggress|ion [ə'greʃən] Angriff *m*; **~or** [‚~esə] Angreifer *m*.

aggrieve [ə'gri:v] kränken; schädigen. [setzt.|

aghast [ə'gɑ:st] entgeistert, ent-|

agil|e □ ['ædʒail] flink, behend; **~ity** [ə'dʒiliti] Behendigkeit *f*.

agitat|e ['ædʒiteit] *v/t.* bewegen, schütteln; *fig.* erregen; erörtern; *v/i.* agitieren; **~ion** [ædʒi'teiʃən] Bewegung *f*, Erschütterung *f*; Aufregung *f*; Agitation *f*; **~or** ['ædʒiteitə] Agitator *m*, Aufwiegler *m*.

ago [ə'gou]: *a year ~* vor e-m Jahr.

agonize ['ægənaiz] (sich) quälen.

agony ['ægəni] Qual *f*, Pein *f*; Ringen *n*; Todeskampf *m*.

agree [ə'gri:] *v/i.* übereinstimmen; sich vertragen; einig werden (*on*, *upon* über *acc.*); übereinkommen; *~ to* zustimmen (*dat.*); einverstanden sein mit; **~able** □ [ə'griəbl] (to) angenehm (für); übereinstimmend (mit); **~ment** [ə'gri:mənt] Übereinstimmung *f*; Vereinbarung *f*, Abkommen *n*; Vertrag *m*.

agricultur|al [ægri'kʌltʃərəl] land-

wirtschaftlich; **~e** ['ægrikʌltʃə] Landwirtschaft *f*; **~ist** [ægri'kʌltʃərist] Landwirt *m*.

aground ⚓ [ə'graund] gestrandet; *run ~* stranden, auflaufen.

ague 🞮 ['eigju:] Wechselfieber *n*; Schüttelfrost *m*.

ahead [ə'hed] vorwärts; voraus; vorn; *straight ~* geradeaus.

aid [eid] **1.** helfen (*dat.*; *in* bei *et.*); fördern; **2.** Hilfe *f*, Unterstützung *f*.

ail [eil] *v/i.* kränkeln; *v/t.* schmerzen, weh(e) tun (*dat.*); *what ~s him?* was fehlt ihm?; **~ing** ['eiliŋ] leidend; **~ment** ['eilmənt] Leiden *n*.

aim [eim] **1.** *v/i.* zielen (*at* auf *acc.*); *~ at* *fig.* streben nach; *~ to do* bsd. *Am.* beabsichtigen *od.* versuchen zu tun, tun wollen; *v/t. ~ at* Waffe etc. richten auf *od.* gegen (*acc.*); **2.** Ziel *n*; Absicht *f*; **~less** □ ['eimlis] ziellos.

air¹ [ɛə] **1.** Luft *f*; Luftzug *m*; *by ~* auf dem Luftwege; *in the open ~* im Freien; *be in the ~* *fig.* in der Luft liegen; ungewiß sein; *on the ~* im Rundfunk (*senden*); *be on (off) the ~* in (außer) Betrieb sein (*Sender*); *put on the ~* im Rundfunk senden; **2.** (aus)lüften; *fig.* an die Öffentlichkeit bringen; erörtern.

air² [‚~] Miene *f*; Aussehen *n*; *give o.s. ~s* vornehm tun.

air³ ♩ [‚~] Arie *f*, Weise *f*, Melodie *f*.

air|-base 🞮 ['ɛəbeis] Luftstützpunkt *m*; **~bed** Luftmatratze *f*; **~borne** 🞮 in der Luft (*Flugzeug*) 🞮 Luftlande...; **~brake** Druckluftbremse *f*; **~-conditioned** mit Klimaanlage; **~craft** Flugzeug (-e *pl.*) *n*; **~field** 🞮 Flugplatz *m*; **~ force** 🞮 Luftwaffe *f*; **~ hostess** 🞮 Stewardess *f*; **~jacket** Schwimmweste *f*; **~lift** Luftbrücke *f*; **~liner** 🞮 Verkehrsflugzeug *n*; **~ mail** Luftpost *f*; **~man** 🞮 ['ɛəmæn] Flieger *m*; **~plane** *Am.* Flugzeug *n*; **~pocket** 🞮 Luftloch *n*; **~port** 🞮 Flughafen *m*; **~raid** 🞮 Luftangriff *m*; **~-raid precautions** *pl.* Luftschutz *m*; **~-raid shelter** Luftschutzraum *m*; **~ route** 🞮 Luftweg *m*; **~-tight** luftdicht; *~ case* sl. todsicherer Fall; **~-tube** Luftschlauch *m*; **~ umbrella** 🞮 Luftsicherung *f*; **~way** 🞮 Luftverkehrslinie *f*.

airy □ ['ɛəri] luftig; leicht(fertig).

aisle ⌂ [ail] Seitenschiff *n*; Gang *m*.

ajar [ə'dʒa:] halb offen, angelehnt.

akin [ə'kin] verwandt (*to* mit).

alacrity [ə'lækriti] Munterkeit *f*; Bereitwilligkeit *f*, Eifer *m*.

alarm [ə'lɑ:m] **1.** Alarm(zeichen *n*) *m*; Angst *f*; **2.** alarmieren; beunruhigen; **~-clock** Wecker *m*.

albuminous [æl'bju:minəs] eiweißartig, -haltig.

alcohol ['ælkəhɔl] Alkohol *m*; **~ic**

[ælkə'hɔlik] alkoholisch; **~ism** ['æl-kəhɔlizəm] Alkoholvergiftung f.

alcove ['ælkouv] Nische f; Laube f.

alderman ['ɔ:ldəmən] Stadtrat m.

ale [eil] Ale n (Art engl. Bier).

alert [ə'lə:t] 1. □ wachsam; munter; 2. Alarm(bereitschaft f) m; on the **~** auf der Hut; in Alarmbereitschaft.

alibi ['ælibai] Alibi n; Am. F Entschuldigung f; Ausrede f.

alien ['eiljən] 1. fremd, ausländisch; 2. Ausländer(in); **~able** [**~**nəbl] veräußerlich; **~ate** [**~**neit] veräußern; fig. entfremden (from dat.); **~ist** [**~**nist] Irrenarzt m, Psychiater m.

alight [ə'lait] 1. brennend; erhellt; 2. ab-, aussteigen; ⚡ niedergehen, landen; sich niederlassen.

align [ə'lain] (sich) ausrichten (with nach); surv. abstecken; **~ o.s. with** sich anschließen an (acc.).

alike [ə'laik] 1. adj. gleich, ähnlich; 2. adv. gleich; ebenso.

aliment ['ælimənt] Nahrung f; **~ary** [æli'mentəri] nahrhaft; **~ canal** Verdauungskanal m.

alimony ⚥ ['æliməni] Unterhalt m.

alive [ə'laiv] lebendig; in Kraft, gültig; empfänglich (to für); lebhaft; belebt (with von).

all [ɔ:l] 1. adj. all; ganz; jede(r, -s); **for ~ that** dessenungeachtet, trotzdem; 2. pron. alles; alle pl.; **at ~** gar, überhaupt; **not at ~** durchaus nicht; **for ~ (that) I care** meinetwegen; **for ~ I know** soviel ich weiß; 3. adv. ganz, völlig; **~ at once** auf einmal; **~ the better** desto besser; **~ but** beinahe, fast; **~ in** Am. F fertig, ganz erledigt; **~ right** (alles) in Ordnung.

all-American [ɔ:lə'merikən] rein amerikanisch; die ganzen USA vertretend.

allay [ə'lei] beruhigen; lindern.

alleg|ation [æle'geiʃən] unerwiesene Behauptung; **~e** [ə'ledʒ] behaupten; **~ed** angeblich.

allegiance [ə'li:dʒəns] Lehnspflicht f; (Untertanen)Treue f.

alleviate [ə'li:vieit] erleichtern, lindern.

alley ['æli] Allee f; Gäßchen n; Gang m; bsd. Am. schmale Zufahrtsstraße.

alliance [ə'laiəns] Bündnis n.

allocat|e ['æləkeit] zuteilen, anweisen; **~ion** [ælə'keiʃən] Zuteilung f.

allot [ə'lɔt] zuweisen; **~ment** [**~**t-mənt] Zuteilung f; Los n; Parzelle f.

allow [ə'lau] erlauben; bewilligen, gewähren; zugeben; ab-, anrechnen; vergüten; **~ for** berücksichtigen; **~able** □ [ə'lauəbl] erlaubt, zulässig; **~ance** [**~**əns] Erlaubnis f; Bewilligung f; Taschengeld n; Zuschuß m; Vergütung f; Nachsicht f;

---

make ~ for s.th. et. in Betracht ziehen.

alloy 1. ['ælɔi] Legierung f; 2. [ə'lɔi] legieren; fig. verunedeln.

all-red ['ɔ:l'red] rein britisch.

all-round ['ɔ:l'raund] zu allem brauchbar; vielseitig.

all-star Am. ['ɔ:l'sta:] Sport u. thea.: aus den besten (Schau)Spielern bestehend.

allude [ə'lu:d] anspielen (to auf acc.).

allure [ə'ljuə] (an-, ver)locken; **~ment** [**~**mənt] Verlockung f.

allusion [ə'lu:ʒən] Anspielung f.

ally 1. [ə'lai] (sich) vereinigen, verbünden (to, with mit); 2. ['ælai] Verbündete(r m) f, Bundesgenosse m; **the Allies** pl. die Alliierten pl.

almanac ['ɔ:lmənæk] Almanach m.

almighty [ɔ:l'maiti] 1. □ allmächtig; 2 ♀ Allmächtige(r) m.

almond ♀ ['a:mənd] Mandel f.

almoner ['a:mənə] Krankenhausfürsorger(in).

almost ['ɔ:lmoust] fast, beinahe.

alms [a:mz] sg. u. pl. Almosen n; **~-house** ['a:mzhaus] Armenhaus n.

aloft [ə'lɔft] (hoch) (dr)oben.

alone [ə'loun] allein; **let od. leave ~** in Ruhe od. bleiben lassen; **let ~ ...** abgesehen von ...

along [ə'lɔŋ] 1. adv. weiter, vorwärts, her; mit, bei (sich); **all ~** die ganze Zeit; **~ with** zs. mit; **get ~ with you!** F scher dich weg!; 2. prp. entlang, längs; **~side** [**~**ŋ'said] Seite an Seite; neben.

aloof [ə'lu:f] fern; weitab; **stand ~** abseits stehen.

aloud [ə'laud] laut; hörbar.

alp [ælp] Alp(e) f; ⚭s pl. Alpen pl.

already [ɔ:l'redi] bereits, schon.

also ['ɔ:lsou] auch; ferner.

altar ['ɔ:ltə] Altar m.

alter ['ɔ:ltə] (sich) (ver)ändern; ab-umändern; **~ation** [ɔ:ltə'reiʃən] Änderung f (to an dat.).

alternat|e 1. ['ɔ:ltə:neit] abwechseln (lassen); **alternating current ⚡** Wechselstrom m; 2. □ [ɔ:l'tə:nit] abwechselnd; 3. [**~**] Am. Stellvertreter m; **~ion** [ɔ:ltə:'neiʃən] Abwechslung f; Wechsel m; **~ive** [ɔ:l'tə:nətiv] 1. □ nur eine Wahl zwischen zwei Möglichkeiten lassend; 2. Alternative f; Wahl f; Möglichkeit f.

although [ɔ:l'ðou] obgleich.

altitude ['æltitju:d] Höhe f.

altogether [ɔ:ltə'geðə] im ganzen (genommen), alles in allem; gänzlich.

aluminium [ælju'minjəm] Aluminium n.

aluminum Am. [ə'lu:minəm] = aluminium.

always ['ɔ:lwəz] immer, stets.

am [æm; im Satz əm] 1. sg. pres. von be.

amalgamate [ə'mælgəmeit] amalgamieren; (sich) verschmelzen.

amass [ə'mæs] (an-, auf)häufen.

amateur ['æmətə:] Amateur m; Liebhaber m; Dilettant m.

amaz|e [ə'meiz] in Staunen setzen, verblüffen; ~ement [ʌzmənt] Staunen n, Verblüffung f; ~ing □ [~ziŋ] erstaunlich, verblüffend.

ambassador [æm'bæsədə] Botschafter m, Gesandte(r) m.

amber ['æmbə] Bernstein m.

ambigu|ity [æmbi'gju(:)iti] Zwei-, Vieldeutigkeit f; ~ous □ [æm-'bigjuəs] zwei-, vieldeutig; doppelsinnig.

ambitio|n [æm'biʃən] Ehrgeiz m; Streben n (of nach); ~us □ [~ʃəs] ehrgeizig; begierig (of, for nach).

amble ['æmbl] 1. Paßgang m; 2. im Paßgang gehen od. reiten; schlendern.

ambulance ['æmbjuləns] Feldlazarett n; Krankenwagen m; ~ station Sanitätswache f, Unfallstation f.

ambus|cade [æmbəs'keid], ~h ['æmbuʃ] 1. Hinterhalt m; be od. lie in ambush for s.o. j-m auflauern; 2. auflauern (dat.); überfallen.

ameliorate [ə'mi:ljəreit] v/t. verbessern; v/i. besser werden.

amend [ə'mend] (sich) (ver)bessern; berichtigen; Gesetz (ab)ändern; ~ment [~dmənt] Besserung f; ₤'ₜ Berichtigung f; parl. Änderungsantrag m; Am. Zusatzartikel m zur Verfassung der USA; ~s sg. (Schaden)Ersatz m.

amenity [ə'mi:niti] Annehmlichkeit f; Anmut f; amenities pl. angenehmes Wesen.

American [ə'merikən] 1. amerikanisch; ~ cloth Wachstuch n; ~ plan Hotelzimmervermietung mit voller Verpflegung; 2. Amerikaner(in); ~ism [~nizəm] Amerikanismus m; ~ize [~naiz] (sich) amerikanisieren.

amiable □ ['eimjəbl] liebenswürdig, freundlich.

amicable □ ['æmikəbl] freundschaftlich; gütlich.

amid(st) [ə'mid(st)] inmitten (gen.); (mitten) unter; mitten in (dat.).

amiss [ə'mis] verkehrt; übel; ungelegen; take ~ übelnehmen.

amity ['æmiti] Freundschaft f.

ammonia [ə'mounjə] Ammoniak n.

ammunition [æmju'niʃən] Munition f.

amnesty ['æmnesti] 1. Amnestie f (Straferlaß); 2. begnadigen.

among(st) [ə'mʌŋ(st)] (mitten) unter, zwischen; [in acc.).

amorous □ ['æmərəs] verliebt (of)

amount [ə'maunt] 1. (to) sich belaufen (auf acc.); hinauslaufen (auf acc.); 2. Betrag m, (Gesamt-)

Summe f; Menge f; Bedeutung f, Wert m.

amour [ə'muə] Liebschaft f; ~-propre Selbstachtung f; Eitelkeit f.

ample □ ['æmpl] weit, groß; geräumig; reichlich.

ampli|fication [æmplifi'keiʃən] Erweiterung f; rhet. weitere Ausführung f; phys. Verstärkung f; ~fier ['æmplifaiə] Radio: Verstärker m; ~fy [~fai] erweitern; verstärken; weiter ausführen; ~tude [~itju:d] Umfang m, Weite f, Fülle f.

amputate ['æmpjuteit] amputieren.

amuse [ə'mju:z] amüsieren; unterhalten; belustigen; ~ment [~zmənt] Unterhaltung f; Zeitvertreib m.

an [æn, ən] Artikel: ein(e).

an(a)emia [ə'ni:mjə] Blutarmut f.

an(a)esthetic [ænis'θetik] 1. betäubend, Narkose...; 2. Betäubungsmittel n.

analog|ous □ [ə'næləgəs] analog, ähnlich; ~y [~ədʒi] Ähnlichkeit f, Analogie f.

analys|e ['ænəlaiz] analysieren; zerlegen; ~is [ə'næləsis] Analyse f.

anarchy ['ænəki] Anarchie f, Gesetzlosigkeit f; Zügellosigkeit f.

anatom|ize [ə'nætəmaiz] zergliedern; ~y [~mi] Anatomie f; Zergliederung f, Analyse f.

ancest|or ['ænsistə] Vorfahr m, Ahn m; ~ral [æn'sestrəl] angestammt; ~ress ['ænsistris] Ahne f; ~ry [~ri] Abstammung f; Ahnen m/pl.

anchor ['æŋkə] 1. Anker m; at ~ vor Anker; 2. (ver)ankern; ~age [~əridʒ] Ankerplatz m.

anchovy ['æntʃəvi] Sardelle f.

ancient ['einʃənt] 1. alt, antik; uralt; 2. the ~s pl. hist. die Alten, die antiken Klassiker.

and [ænd, ənd] und.

anew [ə'nju:] von neuem.

angel ['eindʒəl] Engel m; ~ic(al □) [æn'dʒelik(əl)] engelgleich.

anger ['æŋgə] 1. Zorn m, Ärger m (at über acc.); 2. erzürnen, ärgern.

angina [æn'dʒainə] Angina f, Halsentzündung f.

angle ['æŋgl] 1. Winkel m; fig. Standpunkt m; 2. angeln (for nach).

Anglican ['æŋglikən] 1. anglikanisch; Am. a. englisch; 2. Anglikaner(in).

Anglo-Saxon ['æŋglou'sæksən] 1. Angelsachse m; 2. angelsächsisch.

angry ['æŋgri] zornig, böse (a. ₰) (with s.o., at s.th. über, auf acc.).

anguish ['æŋgwiʃ] Pein f, (Seelen-) Qual f, Schmerz m.

angular □ ['æŋgjulə] winkelig; Winkel...; fig. eckig.

animadver|sion [ænimæd'və:ʃən]

Verweis *m*, Tadel *m*; ~t [~ə:t] tadeln, kritisieren.

animal ['æniməl] **1.** Tier *n*; **2.** tierisch.

animat|e ['ænimeit] beleben; beseelen; aufmuntern; ~ion [æni-'mei∫ən] Leben *n* (und Treiben *n*), Lebhaftigkeit *f*, Munterkeit *f*.

animosity [æni'mɔsiti] Feindseligkeit *f*.

ankle ['æŋkl] Fußknöchel *m*.

annals ['ænlz] *pl.* Jahrbücher *n/pl.*

annex 1. [ə'neks] anhängen; annektieren; **2.** ['æneks] Anhang *m*; Anbau *m*; ~ation [ænek'sei∫ən] Annexion *f*, Aneignung *f*; Einverleibung *f*.

annihilate [ə'naiəleit] vernichten; = *annul*.

anniversary [æni'və:səri] Jahrestag *m*; Jahresfeier *f*.

annotat|e ['ænouteit] mit Anmerkungen versehen; kommentieren; ~ion [ænou'tei∫ən] Kommentieren *n*; Anmerkung *f*.

announce [ə'nauns] ankündigen; ansagen; ~ment [~smənt] Ankündigung *f*; Ansage *f*; *Radio:* Durchsage *f*; Anzeige *f*; ~r [~sə] *Radio:* Ansager *m*.

annoy [ə'nɔi] ärgern; belästigen; ~ance [ə'nɔiəns] Störung *f*; Plage *f*; Ärgernis *n*.

annual ['ænjuəl] **1.** □ jährlich; Jahres...; **2.** einjährige Pflanze; Jahrbuch *n*. [Rente *f*.)

annuity [ə'nju(:)iti] (Jahres-)|

annul [ə'nʌl] für ungültig erklären, annullieren; ~ment [~lmənt] Aufhebung *f*.

anodyne ⚕ ['ænoudain] **1.** schmerzstillend; **2.** schmerzstillendes Mittel.

anoint [ə'nɔint] salben.

anomalous □ [ə'nɔmələs] anomal, unregelmäßig, regelwidrig.

anonymous □ [ə'nɔniməs] anonym, ungenannt.

another [ə'nʌðə] ein anderer; ein zweiter; noch ein.

answer ['ɑ:nsə] **1.** *v/t. et.* beantworten; *j-m* antworten; entsprechen (*dat.*); *Zweck* erfüllen; *dem Steuer* gehorchen; *e-r Vorladung* Folge leisten; ~ *the bell od. door* (die Haustür) aufmachen; *v/i.* antworten (*to s.o.* j-m; *to a question* auf e-e Frage); entsprechen (*to dat.*); Erfolg haben; sich lohnen; ~ *for* einstehen für; bürgen für; **2.** Antwort *f* (*to* auf *acc.*); ~able □ [~ərəbl] verantwortlich.

ant [ænt] Ameise *f*.

antagonis|m [æn'tægənizəm] Widerstreit *m*; Widerstand *m*; Feindschaft *f*; ~t [~ist] Gegner(in).

antagonize [æn'tægənaiz] ankämpfen gegen; sich *j-n* zum Feind machen.

antecedent [ænti'si:dənt] **1.** □ vor-

hergehend; früher (*to* als); **2.** Vorhergehende(s) *n*.

anterior [æn'tiəriə] vorhergehend; früher (*to* als); vorder.

ante-room ['æntirum] Vorzimmer *n*.

anthem ['ænθəm] Hymne *f*.

anti|... ['ænti] Gegen...; gegen ... eingestellt *od.* wirkend; ~aircraft Fliegerabwehr...; ~biotic [~bai-'ɔtik] Antibiotikum *n*.

antic ['æntik] Posse *f*; ~s *pl.* Mätzchen *n/pl.*; (tolle) Sprünge *m/pl.*

anticipat|e [æn'tisipeit] vorwegnehmen; zuvorkommen (*dat.*); voraussehen, ahnen; erwarten; ~ion [æntisi'pei∫ən] Vorwegnahme *f*; Zuvorkommen *n*; Voraussicht *f*; Erwartung *f*; *in* ~ im voraus.

antidote ['æntidout] Gegengift *n*.

antipathy [æn'tipəθi] Abneigung *f*.

antiqua|ry ['æntikwəri] Altertumsforscher *m*; Antiquitätensammler *m*, -händler *m*; ~ted [~kweitid] veraltet, überlebt.

antiqu|e [æn'ti:k] **1.** □ antik, alt (-modisch); **2.** alter Kunstgegenstand; ~ity [æn'tikwiti] Altertum *n*; Vorzeit *f*.

antiseptic [ænti'septik] **1.** antiseptisch; **2.** antiseptisches Mittel.

antlers ['æntləz] *pl.* Geweih *n*.

anvil ['ænvil] Amboß *m*.

anxiety [æŋ'zaiəti] Angst *f*; *fig.* Sorge *f* (*for* um); ⚕ Beklemmung *f*.

anxious □ ['æŋk∫əs] ängstlich, besorgt (*about* um, wegen); begierig, gespannt (*for* auf *acc.*); bemüht (*for* um).

any ['eni] **1.** *pron.* (irgend)einer; einige *pl.*; (irgend)welcher; (irgend) etwas; jeder (beliebige); *not* ~ keiner; **2.** *adv.* irgend(wie); ~body (irgend) jemand; jeder; ~how irgendwie; jedenfalls; ~one = anybody; ~thing (irgend) etwas, alles; ~ *but* alles andere als; ~way = anyhow; ohnehin; ~where irgendwo(hin); überall.

apart [ə'pɑ:t] einzeln; getrennt; für sich; beiseite; ~ *from* abgesehen von.

apartheid [ə'pɑ:theit] Apartheid *f*, Rassentrennung(spolitik) *f*.

apartment [ə'pɑ:tmənt] Zimmer *n*, *Am. a.* Wohnung *f*; ~ *house Am.* Mietshaus *n*.

apathetic [æpə'θetik] apathisch, gleichgültig.

ape [eip] **1.** Affe *m*; **2.** nachäffen.

aperient [ə'piəriənt] Abführmittel *n*.

aperture ['æpətjuə] Öffnung *f*.

apiary ['eipjəri] Bienenhaus *n*.

apiculture ['eipikʌlt∫ə] Bienenzucht *f*.

apiece [ə'pi:s] (für) das Stück; je.

apish □ ['eipi∫] affig; äffisch.

apolog|etic [əpɔlə'dʒetik] (~ally) verteidigend; rechtfertigend; entschuldigend; ~ize [ə'pɔlədʒaiz] sich entschuldigen (*for* wegen; *to* bei); ~y [~d3i] Entschuldigung *f*; Rechtfertigung *f*; F Notbehelf *m*.

apoplexy ['æpəpleksi] Schlag(anfall) *m*.

apostate [ə'pɔstit] Abtrünnige(r*m*)*f*.

apostle [ə'pɔsl] Apostel *m*.

apostroph|e [ə'pɔstrəfi] Anrede *f*; Apostroph *m*; ~ize [~faiz] anreden, sich wenden an (*acc.*).

appal [ə'pɔ:l] erschrecken.

apparatus [æpə'reitəs] Apparat *m*, Vorrichtung *f*, Gerät *n*.

apparel [ə'pærəl] **1.** Kleidung *f*; **2.** (be)kleiden.

appar|ent [ə'pærənt] anscheinend; offenbar; ~ition [æpə'riʃən] Erscheinung *f*; Gespenst *n*.

appeal [ə'pi:l] **1.** (*to*) ₜ̸ₜ appellieren (an *acc.*); sich berufen (auf *e-n Zeugen*); sich wenden (an *acc.*); wirken (auf *acc.*); Anklang finden (bei); ~ *to the country parl.* Neuwahlen ausschreiben; **2.** ₜ̸ₜ Revision *f*, Berufung(sklage) *f*; ₜ̸ₜ Rechtsmittel *n*; *fig.* Appell *m* (*to an acc.*); Wirkung *f*, Reiz *m*; ~ *for mercy* ₜ̸ₜ Gnadengesuch *n*; ~ing □ [~liŋ] flehend; ansprechend.

appear [ə'piə] (er)scheinen; sich zeigen; *öffentlich* auftreten; ~ance [~ərəns] Erscheinen *n*, Auftreten *n*; Äußere(s) *n*, Erscheinung *f*; Anschein *m*; ~s *pl.* äußerer Schein; *to od. by all* ~s allem Anschein nach.

appease [ə'pi:z] beruhigen; beschwichtigen; stillen; mildern; beilegen.

appellant [ə'pelənt] **1.** appellierend; **2.** Appellant(in), Berufungskläger (-in).

append [ə'pend] anhängen; hinzu-, beifügen; ~age [~did3] Anhang *m*; Anhängsel *n*; Zubehör *n*, *m*; ~icitis [əpendi'saitis] Blinddarmentzündung *f*; ~ix [ə'pendiks] Anhang *m*; *a. vermiform* ~ ℰ Wurmfortsatz *m*, Blinddarm *m*.

appertain [æpə'tein] gehören (*to* zu).

appetite ['æpitait] (*for*) Appetit *m* (auf *acc.*); *fig.* Verlangen *n* (nach).

appetizing ['æpitaiziŋ] appetitanregend.

applaud [ə'plɔ:d] applaudieren, Beifall spenden; loben.

applause [ə'plɔ:z] Applaus *m*, Beifall *m*.

apple ['æpl] Apfel *m*; ~-cart Apfelkarren *m*; *upset s.o.'s* ~ F j-s Pläne über den Haufen werfen; ~pie gedeckter Apfelkuchen; *in* ~ *order* F in schönster Ordnung; ~sauce Apfelmus *n*; *Am. sl.* Schmus *m*, Quatsch *m*.

appliance [ə'plaiəns] Vorrichtung *f*; Gerät *n*; Mittel *n*.

applica|ble ['æplikəbl] anwendbar

(*to auf acc.*); ~nt [~ənt] Bittsteller (-in); Bewerber(in) (*for* um); ~tion [æpli'keiʃən] (*to*) Auf-, Anlegung *f* (auf *acc.*); Anwendung *f* (auf *acc.*); Bedeutung *f* (für); Gesuch *n* (*for* um); Bewerbung *f*.

apply [ə'plai] *v/t.* (*to*) (auf)legen (auf *acc.*); anwenden (auf *acc.*); verwenden (für); ~ *o.s. to* sich widmen(*dat.*); *v/i.* (*to*) passen, sich anwenden lassen (auf *acc.*); gelten (für); sich wenden (an *acc.*); (*for*) sich bewerben (um); nachsuchen (um).

appoint [ə'pɔint] bestimmen; festsetzen; verabreden; ernennen (*s.o. governor* j-n zum ...); berufen (*to* auf *e-n Posten*); *well* ~ed gut eingerichtet; ~ment [~tmənt] Bestimmung *f*; Stelldichein *n*; Verabredung *f*; Ernennung *f*, Berufung *f*; Stelle *f*; ~s *pl.* Ausstattung *f*, Einrichtung *f*.

apportion [ə'pɔ:ʃən] ver-, zuteilen; ~ment [~nmənt] Verteilung *f*.

apprais|al [ə'preizəl] Abschätzung *f*; ~e [ə'preiz] abschätzen, taxieren.

apprecia|ble □ [ə'pri:ʃəbl] (ab-) schätzbar; merkbar; ~te [~ʃieit] *v/t.* schätzen; würdigen; dankbar sein für; *v/i.* im Werte steigen; ~tion [əpri:ʃi'eiʃən] Schätzung *f*, Würdigung *f*; Verständnis *n* (*of* für); Einsicht *f*; Dankbarkeit *f*; Aufwertung *f*.

apprehen|d [æpri'hend] ergreifen; fassen, begreifen; befürchten; ~sion [~nʃən] Ergreifung *f*, Festnahme *f*; Fassungskraft *f*, Auffassung *f*; Besorgnis *f*; ~sive □ [~nsiv] schnell begreifend (*of acc.*); ängstlich; besorgt (*of*, *for* um, wegen; *that* daß).

apprentice [ə'prentis] **1.** Lehrling *m*; **2.** in die Lehre geben (*to dat.*); ~ship [~iʃip] Lehrzeit *f*; Lehre *f*.

approach [ə'prəutʃ] **1.** *v/i.* näherkommen, sich nähern; *v/t.* sich nähern (*dat.*), herangehen *od.* herantreten an (*acc.*); **2.** Annäherung *f*; *fig.* Herangehen *n*; Methode *f*; Zutritt *m*; Auffahrt *f*.

approbation [æprə'beiʃən] Billigung *f*, Beifall *m*.

appropriat|e 1. [ə'prouprieit] sich aneignen; verwenden; *parl.* bewilligen; **2.** □ [~iit] (*to*) angemessen (*dat.*); passend (für); eigen (*dat.*); ~ion [əproupri'eiʃən] Aneignung *f*; Verwendung *f*.

approv|al [ə'pru:vəl] Billigung *f*, Beifall *m*; ~e [~u:v] billigen, anerkennen; (~ *o.s.* sich) erweisen als; ~ed □ bewährt.

approximate 1. [ə'prɔksimeit] sich nähern; **2.** □ [~mit] annähernd; ungefähr; nahe.

apricot ['eiprikɔt] Aprikose *f*.

April ['eiprəl] April *m*.

apron ['eiprən] Schürze f; **~-string**
Schürzenband n; *be tied to one's*
wife's (mother's) **~s** *fig.* unterm
Pantoffel stehen (der Mutter am
Rockzipfel hängen).

apt □ [æpt] geeignet, passend; begabt; ~ *to* geneigt zu; **~itude** ['æp-
titju:d], **~ness** ['æptnis] Neigung f
(*to* zu); Befähigung f.

aquatic [ə'kwætik] Wasserpflanze f;
~s pl. Wassersport m.

aque|duct ['ækwidʌkt] Aquädukt m,
Wasserleitung f; **~ous** □ ['eikwiəs]
wässerig.

aquiline ['ækwilain] Adler...; gebogen; **~** *nose* Adlernase f.

Arab ['ærəb] Araber(in); **~ic** [~bik]
1. arabisch; 2. Arabisch n.

arable ['ærəbl] pflügbar; Acker...

arbit|er ['a:bitə] Schiedsrichter m;
fig. Gebieter m; **~rariness** [~trəri-
nis] Willkür f; **~rary** □ [~trəri]
willkürlich; eigenmächtig; **~rate**
[~reit] entscheiden, schlichten;
~ration [a:bi'treiʃən] Schieds-
spruch m; Entscheidung f; **~rator**
ʤ̃ʒ ['a:bitreitə] Schiedsrichter m.

arbo(u)r ['a:bə] Laube f.

arc *ast.*, ʆ *etc.* [a:k] (ʆ Licht-)
Bogen m; **~ade** [a:'keid] Arkade f;
Bogen-, Laubengang m.

arch¹ [a:tʃ] 1. Bogen m; Gewölbe n;
2. (sich) wölben; überwölben.

arch² [~] erst; schlimmst; Haupt...;
Erz...

arch³ □ [~] schelmisch.

archaic [a:'keiik] (~ally) veraltet.

archangel ['a:keindʒəl] Erzengel m.

archbishop ['a:tʃ'biʃəp] Erzbischof
m.

archer ['a:tʃə] Bogenschütze m; **~y**
[~əri] Bogenschießen n.

architect ['a:kitekt] Architekt m;
Urheber(in), Schöpfer(in); **~onic**
[a:kitek'tonik] (~ally) architekto-
nisch; *fig.* aufbauend; **~ure** ['a:ki-
tektʃə] Architektur f, Baukunst f.

archives ['a:kaivz] pl. Archiv n.

archway ['a:tʃwei] Bogengang m.

arc|-lamp ['a:klæmp], **~-light** ʆ
Bogenlampe f.

arctic ['a:ktik] 1. arktisch, nördlich;
Nord..., Polar...; 2. *Am.* wasser-
dichter Überschuh.

arden|cy ['a:dənsi] Hitze f, Glut f;
Innigkeit f; **~t** □ [~nt] *mst fig.* heiß,
glühend; *fig.* feurig; eifrig.

ardo(u)r ['a:də] *fig.* Glut f; Eifer m.

arduous □ ['a:djuəs] mühsam; zäh.

are [a:; *im Satz* ə] *pres. pl. u. 2. sg.*
von be.

area ['ɛəriə] Areal n; (Boden-)
Fläche f; Flächenraum m; Gegend f;
Gebiet n; Bereich m.

Argentine ['a:dʒəntain] 1. argen-
tinisch; 2. Argentinier(in); *the* **~**
Argentinien n.

argue ['a:gju:] v/t. erörtern; beweisen; begründen; einwenden; **~**

s.o. into j-n zu *et.* bereden; v/i.
streiten; Einwendungen machen.

argument ['a:gjumənt] Beweis
(-grund) m; Streit(frage f) m; Erörterung f; Thema n; **~ation**
[a:gjumen'teiʃən] Beweisführung f

arid ['ærid] dürr, trocken (*a. fig.*).

arise [ə'raiz] [*irr.*] sich erheben (*a.*
fig.); ent-, erstehen (*from* aus); **~n**
[ə'rizn] *p.p von* arise.

aristocra|cy [æris'tokrəsi] Aristo-
kratie f (*a. fig.*), Adel m; **~t** ['æris-
təkræt] Aristokrat(in); **~tic(al** □)
[æristə'krætik(əl)] aristokratisch.

arithmetic [ə'riθmətik] Rechnen n.

ark [a:k] Arche f.

arm¹ [a:m] Arm m; Armlehne f;
keep s.o. at **~**'s *length* sich j-n vom
Leibe halten; *infant in* **~s** Säugling
m.

arm² [~] 1. Waffe f (*mst pl.*); Waf-
fengattung f; *be* (*all*) *up in* **~s** in
vollem Aufruhr sein; *in Harnisch*
geraten; 2. (sich) (be)waffnen;
(aus)rüsten; ⊕ armieren.

armada [a:'ma:də] Kriegsflotte f.

arma|ment ['a:məmənt] (Kriegs-
aus)Rüstung f; Kriegsmacht f; **~**
race Wettrüsten n; **~ture** ['a:mə-
tjuə] Rüstung f; ⚡, *phys.* Armatur f.

armchair ['a:m'tʃɛə] Lehnstuhl m,
Sessel m.

armistice ['a:mistis] Waffenstillstand m (*a. fig.*).

armo(u)r ['a:mə] 1. ⚔ Rüstung f,
Panzer m (*a. fig.*, *zo.*); 2. panzern;
~ed *car* Panzerwagen m; **~y** ['a:-
məri] Rüstkammer f (*a. fig.*); *Am.*
Rüstungsbetrieb m, Waffenfabrik f.

armpit ['a:mpit] Achselhöhle f.

army ['a:mi] Heer n, Armee f; *fig.*
Menge f; **~** *chaplain* Militärgeist-
liche(r) m.

arose [ə'rouz] *pret. von* arise.

around [ə'raund] 1. *adv.* rund-
(her)um; *Am.* F hier herum; 2. *prp.*
um ... her(um); *bsd. Am.* F ungefähr, etwa (*bei Zahlenangaben*).

arouse [ə'rauz] aufwecken; *fig.* aufrütteln; erregen.

arraign [ə'rein] *vor* Gericht stellen,
anklagen; *fig.* rügen.

arrange [ə'reindʒ] (an)ordnen, *bsd.*
♪ einrichten; festsetzen; *Streit*
schlichten; vereinbaren; erledigen;
~ment [~dʒmənt] Anordnung f;
Disposition f; Übereinkommen n;
Vorkehrung f; ♪ Arrangement n.

array [ə'rei] 1. (Schlacht)Ordnung
f; *fig.* Aufgebot n; 2. ordnen, aufstellen; aufbieten; kleiden, putzen.

arrear [ə'riə] *mst pl.* Rückstand m,
bsd. Schulden f/pl.

arrest [ə'rest] 1. Verhaftung f;
Haft f; Beschlagnahme f; 2. verhaften; beschlagnahmen; anhalten,
hemmen.

arriv|al [ə'raivəl] Ankunft f; Auf-
treten n; Ankömmling m; **~s** *pl.* an-

gekommene Personen f/pl., Züge m/pl., Schiffe n/pl.; ~e [ə'raiv] (an-)kommen, eintreffen; erscheinen; eintreten (Ereignis); ~ at erreichen (acc.).

arroga|nce ['ærəgəns] Anmaßung f; Überheblichkeit f; ~nt □ [~nt] anmaßend; überheblich; ~te ['ærougeit] sich er. anmaßen.

arrow ['ærou] Pfeil m; ~-head Pfeilspitze f; ~y ['æroui] pfeilartig.

arsenal ['a:sinl] Zeughaus n.

arsenic ['a:snik] Arsen(ik) n.

arson ['a:sn] Brandstiftung f.

art [a:t] Kunst f; fig. List f; Kniff m; ~s pl. Geisteswissenschaften f/pl.; Faculty of ~s philosophische Fakultät f.

arter|ial [a:'tiəriəl] Pulsader...; ~ road Hauptstraße f; ~y ['a:təri] Arterie f, Pulsader f; fig. Verkehrsader f.   [schmitzt.]

artful □ ['a:tful] schlau, ver-]

article ['a:tikl] Artikel m; fig. Punkt m; ~d to in der Lehre bei.

articulat|e 1. [a:'tikjuleit] deutlich (aus)sprechen; Knochen zs.-fügen; **2.** □ [~lit] deutlich; gegliedert; ~ion [a:tikju'leiʃən] deutliche Aussprache; anat. Gelenkfügung f.

artific|e ['a:tifis] Kunstgriff m; List f; ~ial □ [a:ti'fiʃəl] künstlich; Kunst...; ~ person ⚖ juristische Person.

artillery [a:'tiləri] Artillerie f; ~man Artillerist m.

artisan [a:ti'zæn] Handwerker m.

artist ['a:tist] Künstler(in); ~e [a:'ti:st] Artist(in); ~ic(al) [a:'tistik(əl)] künstlerisch; Kunst...

artless □ ['a:tlis] ungekünstelt, schlicht; arglos.

as [æz, əz] **1.** adv. so; (ebenso wie) (in der Eigenschaft) als; ~ big ~ so groß wie; ~ well ebensogut; auch; ~ well ~ sowohl ... als auch; **2.** cj. (so) wie; ebenso; (zu der Zeit) als, während; da, weil, indem; sofern; ~ it were sozusagen; such ~ to derart, daß; ~ for, ~ to was (an)betrifft; ~ from von ... an.

ascend [ə'send] v/i. (auf-, empor-, hinauf)steigen; zeitlich: zurückgehen (to bis zu); v/t. be-, ersteigen; hinaufsteigen; Fluß etc. hinauffahren; ~ancy, ~ency [~dənsi] Überlegenheit f, Einfluß m; Herrschaft f.

ascension [ə'senʃən] Aufsteigen n (bsd. ast.); Am. a. Aufstieg m (e-s Ballons or.); 2 (Day) Himmelfahrt(stag m) f.

ascent [ə'sent] Aufstieg m; Besteigung f; Steigung f; Aufgang m.

ascertain [æsə'tein] ermitteln.

ascetic [ə'setik] (~ally) asketisch.

ascribe [əs'kraib] zuschreiben.

aseptic ⚕ [æ'septik] **1.** aseptisch; **2.** aseptisches Mittel.

ash¹ [æʃ] ♀ Esche f; Eschenholz n.

ash² (~), mst. pl. ~es ['æʃiz] Asche f; Ash Wednesday Aschermittwoch m.

ashamed [ə'ʃeimd] beschämt; be ~ of sich e-r Sache od. j-s schämen.

ash can Am. ['æʃkæn] = dust-bin.

ashen ['æʃn] Aschen...; aschfahl.

ashore [ə'ʃɔ:] am od. ans Ufer od. Land; run ~, be driven ~ stranden.

ash|-pan ['æʃpæn] Asch(en)kasten m; ~-tray Asch(en)becher m.

ashy ['æʃi] aschig; aschgrau.

Asiatic [eiʃi'ætik] **1.** asiatisch; **2.** Asiat(in).

aside [ə'said] **1.** beiseite (a. thea.); abseits; seitwärts; ~ from Am. abgesehen von; **2.** thea. Aparte n.

ask [a:sk] v/t. fragen (s.th. nach et.); verlangen (of, from s.o. von j-m); bitten (s.o. [for] s.th. j. um et.; that darum, daß); erbitten; ~ (s.o.) a question (j-m) e-e Frage stellen; v/i.: ~ for bitten um, fragen nach; he ~ed for it od. for trouble er wollte es ja so haben; to be had for the ~ing umsonst zu haben.

askance [əs'kæns], **askew** [əs'kju:] von der Seite, seitwärts; schief.

asleep [ə'sli:p] schlafend; in den Schlaf; eingeschlafen, be ~ schlafen; fall ~ einschlafen.

asparagus ♀ [əs'pærəgəs] Spargel m.

aspect ['æspekt] Äußere n; Aussicht f, Lage f; Aspekt m, Seite f, Gesichtspunkt m.

asperity [æs'periti] Rauheit f; Unebenheit f; fig. Schroffheit f.

asphalt ['æsfælt] **1.** Asphalt m; **2.** asphaltieren.

aspic ['æspik] Aspik m, Sülze f.

aspir|ant [əs'paiərənt] Bewerber (-in); ~ate ling. ['æspəreit] aspirieren; ~ation [æspə'reiʃən] Aspiration f; Bestrebung f; ~e [əs'paiə] streben, trachten (to, after, at nach).

ass [æs] Esel m.

assail [ə'seil] angreifen, überfallen (a. fig.); befallen (Zweifel etc.); ~ant [~lənt] Angreifer(in).

assassin [ə'sæsin] (Meuchel)Mörder(in); ~ate [~neit] (meuchlings) ermorden; ~ation [əsæsi'neiʃən] Meuchelmord m.

assault [ə'sɔ:lt] **1.** Angriff m (a. fig.); **2.** anfallen; ⚖ tätlich angreifen od. beleidigen; ✕ bestürmen (a. fig.).

assay [ə'sei] **1.** (Erz-, Metall-)Probe f; **2.** v/t. untersuchen; v/i. Am. Edelmetall enthalten.

assembl|age [ə'semblidʒ] (An-) Sammlung f; ⊕ Montage f; ~e [ə'sembl] (sich) versammeln; zs.-, berufen; ⊕ montieren; ~y [~li] Versammlung f; Gesellschaft f; ⊕ Montage f; ~ line ⊕ Fließband n; ~ man pol. Abgeordnete(r) m.

assent [ə'sent] **1.** Zustimmung *f*; **2.** (*to*) zustimmen (*dat.*); billigen.

assert [ə'sə:t] (sich) behaupten; **~ion** [ə'sə:ʃən] Behauptung *f*; Erklärung *f*; Geltendmachung *f*.

assess [ə'ses] besteuern; zur Steuer veranlagen (*at* mit); **~able** □ [.~əbl] steuerpflichtig; **~ment** [.~smənt] (Steuer)Veranlagung *f*; Steuer *f*.

asset ['æset] ✝ Aktivposten *m*; *fig.* Gut *n*, Gewinn *m*; **~s** *pl.* Vermögen *n*; ✝ Aktiva *pl.*; ⚖ Konkursmasse *f*.

asseverate [ə'sevəreit] beteuern.

assiduous □ [ə'sidjuəs] emsig, fleißig; aufmerksam.

assign [ə'sain] an-, zuweisen; bestimmen; zuschreiben; **~ation** [æsig'neiʃən] Verabredung *f*, Stelldichein *n*; = **~ment** [ə'sainmənt] An-, Zuweisung *f*; *bsd. Am.* Auftrag *m*; ⚖ Übertragung *f*.

assimilat|e [ə'simileit] (sich) angleichen (*to*, *with dat.*); **~ion** [əsimi'leiʃən] Assimilation *f*, Angleichung *f*.

assist [ə'sist] *j-m* beistehen, helfen; unterstützen; **~ance** [.~təns] Beistand *m*; Hilfe *f*; **~ant** [.~nt] **1.** behilflich; **2.** Assistent(in).

assize ⚖ [ə'saiz] (Schwur)Gerichtssitzung *f*; **~s** *pl. periodisches* Geschworenengericht.

associa|te 1. [ə'souʃieit] (sich) zugesellen (*with dat.*), (sich) vereinigen; Umgang haben (*with* mit); **2.** [.~ʃiit] verbunden; **3.** [.~] (Amts)Genosse *m*; Teilhaber *m*; **~tion** [əsousi'eiʃən] Vereinigung *f*, Verbindung *f*; *Handels- etc.* Gesellschaft *f*; Genossenschaft *f*; Verein *m*.

assort [ə'sɔ:t] *v/t.* sortieren, zs.-stellen; *v/i.* passen (*with* zu); **~ment** [.~tmənt] Sortieren *n*; ✝ Sortiment *n*, Auswahl *f*.

assum|e [ə'sju:m] annehmen; vorgeben; übernehmen; **~ption** [ə'sʌmpʃən] Annahme *f*; Übernahme *f*; *eccl.* ⚹ (*Day*) Mariä Himmelfahrt *f*.

assur|ance [ə'ʃuərəns] Zu-, Versicherung *f*; Zuversicht *f*; Sicherheit *f*, Gewißheit *f*; Selbstsicherheit *f*; Dreistigkeit *f*; **~e** [ə'ʃuə] (*Leben* ver)sichern; sicherstellen; **~ed 1.** (*adv.* **~edly** [.~ridli]) sicher; dreist; **2.** Versicherte(r *m*) *f*.

asthma ['æsmə] Asthma *n*.

astir [ə'stə:] auf (den Beinen); in Bewegung, rege.

astonish [əs'tɔniʃ] in Erstaunen setzen; verwundern; befremden; *be ~ed* erstaunt sein (*at* über *acc.*); **~ing** □ [.~ʃiŋ] erstaunlich; **~ment** [.~ʃmənt] (Er)Staunen *n*; Verwunderung *f*.

astound [əs'taund] verblüffen.

astray [əs'trei] vom (rechten) Wege ab (*a. fig.*); irre; *go ~* sich verlaufen, fehlgehen.

astride [əs'traid] mit gespreizten Beinen; rittlings (*of* auf *dat.*).

astringent ⚕ [əs'trindʒənt] **1.** □ zs.-ziehend; **2.** zs.-ziehendes Mittel.

astro|logy [əs'trɔlədʒi] Astrologie *f*; **~naut** ['æstrənɔːt] Astronaut *m*, Raumfahrer *m*; **~nomer** [əs'trɔnəmə] Astronom *m*; **~nomy** [.~mi] Astronomie *f*.

astute □ [əs'tju:t] scharfsinnig; schlau; **~ness** [.~tnis] Scharfsinn *m*.

asunder [ə'sʌndə] auseinander; entzwei.

asylum [ə'sailəm] Asyl *n*.

at [æt; *unbetont* ət] *prp.* an; auf; aus; bei; für; in; mit; nach; über; um; von; vor; zu; ~ *school* in der Schule; ~ *the age of* im Alter von.

ate [et] *pret. von* eat 1.

atheism ['eiθiizəm] Atheismus *m*.

athlet|e ['æθliːt] (*bsd.* Leicht-) Athlet *m*; **~ic(al** □) [æθ'letik(əl)] athletisch; **~ics** *pl.* (*bsd.* Leicht-) Athletik *f*.

Atlantic [ət'læntik] **1.** atlantisch; **2.** *a.* ~ *Ocean* Atlantik *m*.

atmospher|e ['ætməsfiə] Atmosphäre *f* (*a. fig.*); **~ic(al** □) [ætməs'ferik(əl)] atmosphärisch.

atom ⚛ ['ætəm] Atom *n* (*a. fig.*); **~ic** [ə'tɔmik] atomartig, Atom...; atomistisch; ~ *age* Atomzeitalter *n*; ~ (*a. atom*) *bomb* Atombombe *f*; ~ *pile* Atomreaktor *m*; **~ic-powered** durch Atomkraft betrieben; **~ize** ['ætəmaiz] in Atome auflösen; atomisieren; **~izer** [.~zə] Zerstäuber *m*.

atone [ə'toun]: ~ *for* büßen für *et.*; **~ment** [.~mənt] Buße *f*; Sühne *f*.

atroci|ous □ [ə'trouʃəs] scheußlich, gräßlich; grausam; **~ty** [ə'trɔsiti] Scheußlichkeit *f*, Gräßlichkeit *f*; Grausamkeit *f*.

attach [ə'tætʃ] *v/t.* (*to*) anheften (an, *acc.*), befestigen (an *dat.*); *Wert, Wichtigkeit etc.* beilegen (*dat.*); ⚖ *j-n* verhaften; *et.* beschlagnahmen; ~ *o.s. to* sich anschließen an (*acc.*); **~ed:** ~ *to* gehörig zu; *j-m* zugetan, ergeben; **~ment** [.~mənt] Befestigung *f*; Bindung *f* (*to*, for an *acc.*); Anhänglichkeit *f* (an *acc.*), Neigung *f* (zu); Anhängsel *n* (*to gen.*); ⚖ Verhaftung *f*; Beschlagnahme *f*.

attack [ə'tæk] **1.** angreifen (*a. fig.*); befallen (*Krankheit*); *Arbeit* in Angriff nehmen; **2.** Angriff *m*; ✗ Anfall *m*; Inangriffnahme *f*.

attain [ə'tein] *v/t. Ziel* erreichen; *v/i.* ~ *to* gelangen zu; **~ment** [.~nmənt] Erreichung *f*; *fig.* Aneignung *f*; **~s** *pl.* Kenntnisse *f/pl.*; Fertigkeiten *f/pl.*

attempt [ə'tempt] **1.** versuchen; **2.** Versuch *m*; Attentat *n*.

attend [ə'tend] *v/t.* begleiten; bedienen; pflegen; ✻ behandeln; *j-m* aufwarten; beiwohnen (*dat.*); *Vorlesung etc.* besuchen; *v/i.* achten, hören (*to auf acc.*); anwesend sein (*at bei*); ~ to erledigen; ~ance [~dəns] Begleitung *f;* Aufwartung *f;* Pflege *f;* ✻ Behandlung *f;* Gefolge *n;* Anwesenheit *f* (*at bei*); Besuch *m* (*der Schule etc.*); Besucher(zahl *f*) *m/pl.;* Publikum *n; be in* ~ zu Diensten stehen; ~ant [~nt] **1.** begleitend (*on, upon acc.*); anwesend (*at bei*); **2.** Diener(in); Begleiter(in); Wärter(in); Besucher(in) (*at gen.*); ⊕ Bedienungsmann *m;* ~*s pl.* Dienerschaft *f.*

attent|ion [ə'tenʃən] Aufmerksamkeit *f* (*a. fig.*); ~! ✗ Achtung!; ~ive □ [~ntiv] aufmerksam.

attest [ə'test] bezeugen; beglaubigen; *bsd.* ✗ vereidigen.

attic ['ætik] Dachstube *f.* [dung *f.*\ **attire** [ə'taiə] **1.** kleiden; **2.** Klei-\ **attitude** ['ætitju:d] (Ein)Stellung *f;* Haltung *f; fig.* Stellungnahme *f.*

attorney [ə'tɔ:ni] Bevollmächtigte(r) *m; Am.* Rechtsanwalt *m; power of* ~ Vollmacht *f;* ♀ *General* Generalstaats- *od.* Kronanwalt *m, Am.* Justizminister *m.*

attract [ə'trækt] anziehen, *Aufmerksamkeit* erregen; *fig.* reizen; ~ion [~kʃən] Anziehung(skraft) *f; fig.* Reiz *m;* Zugartikel *m; thea.* Zugstück *n;* ~ive [~ktiv] anziehend; reizvoll; zugkräftig; ~iveness [~vnis] Reiz *m.*

attribute 1. [ə'tribju:t] beimessen, zuschreiben; zurückführen (*to auf acc.*); **2.** ['ætribju:t] Attribut *n* (*a. gr.*), Eigenschaft *f,* Merkmal *n.*

attune [ə'tju:n] (ab)stimmen.

auburn ['ɔ:bən] kastanienbraun.

auction ['ɔ:kʃən] **1.** Auktion *f; sell by* ~, *put up for* ~ versteigern; **2.** *mst* ~ *off* versteigern; ~eer [ɔ:kʃə'niə] Auktionator *m.*

audaci|ous □ [ɔ:'deiʃəs] kühn; unverschämt; ~ty [ɔ:'dæsiti] Kühnheit *f;* Unverschämtheit *f.*

audible □ ['ɔ:dəbl] hörbar; Hör...

audience ['ɔ:djəns] Publikum *n,* Zuhörerschaft *f;* Leserkreis *m;* Audienz *f;* Gehör *n; give* ~ *to* Gehör schenken (*dat.*).

audit ['ɔ:dit] **1.** Rechnungsprüfung *f;* **2.** *Rechnungen* prüfen; ~or [~tə] Hörer *m;* Rechnungs-, Buchprüfer *m;* ~orium [ɔ:di'tɔ:riəm] Hörsaal *m; Am.* Vortrags-, Konzertsaal *m.*

auger ⊕ ['ɔ:gə] *großer* Bohrer.

aught [ɔ:t] (irgend) etwas; *for* ~ *I care* meinetwegen; *for* ~ *I know* soviel ich weiß.

augment [ɔ:g'ment] vergrößern; ~ation [ɔ:gmen'teiʃən] Vermehrung *f,* Vergrößerung *f;* Zusatz *m.*

augur ['ɔ:gə] **1.** Augur *m;* **2.** weissagen, voraussagen (*well Gutes, ill*

Übles); ~y ['ɔ:gjuri] Prophezeiung *f;* An-, Vorzeichen *n;* Vorahnung *f.*

August[1] ['ɔ:gəst] *Monat* August *m.* **august**[2] □ [ɔ:'gʌst] erhaben.

aunt [ɑ:nt] Tante *f.*

auspic|e ['ɔ:spis] Vorzeichen *n;* ~s *pl.* Auspizien *pl.;* Schirmherrschaft *f;* ~ious □ [ɔ:s'piʃəs] günstig.

auster|e □ [ɔs'tiə] streng; herb; hart; einfach; ~ity [ɔs'teriti] Strenge *f;* Härte *f;* Einfachheit *f.*

Australian [ɔs'treiljən] **1.** australisch; **2.** Australier(in).

Austrian ['ɔstriən] **1.** österreichisch; **2.** Österreicher(in).

authentic [ɔ:'θentik] (~ally) authentisch; zuverlässig; echt.

author ['ɔ:θə] Urheber(in); Autor (-in); Verfasser(in); ~itative □ [ɔ:'θɔritətiv] maßgebend; gebieterisch; zuverlässig; ~ity [ɔ:'θɔriti] Autorität *f;* (Amts)Gewalt *f,* Vollmacht *f;* Einfluß *m* (*over auf acc.*); Ansehen *n;* Glaubwürdigkeit *f;* Quelle *f;* Fachmann *m;* Behörde *f* (*mst pl.*); *on the* ~ *of* auf *j-s* Zeugnis hin; ~ize ['ɔ:θəraiz] *j-n* autorisieren, bevollmächtigen; *et.* gutheißen; ~ship ['ɔ:θəʃip] Urheberschaft *f.*

autocar ['ɔ:touka:] Kraftwagen *m.* **autocra|cy** [ɔ:'tɔkrəsi] Autokratie *f;* ~tic(al □) [ɔ:tə'krætik(əl)] autokratisch, despotisch.

autogiro 🛪 ['ɔ:tou'dʒaiərou] Autogiro *n,* Tragschrauber *m.*

autograph ['ɔ:təgra:f] Autogramm *n.* [Restaurant *n.*\ **automat** ['ɔ:təmæt] Automaten-\ **automat|ic** [ɔ:tə'mætik] (~ally) **1.** automatisch; ~ *machine* (Verkaufs)Automat *m;* **2.** *Am.* Selbstladepistole *f,* -gewehr *n;* ~ion [~'meiʃən] Automation *f;* ~on *fig.* [ɔ:'tɔmətən] Roboter *m.*

automobile *bsd. Am.* ['ɔ:təməbi:l] Automobil *n.*

autonomy [ɔ:'tɔnəmi] Autonomie *f.* **autumn** ['ɔ:təm] Herbst *m;* ~al □ [ɔ:'tʌmnəl] herbstlich; Herbst...

auxiliary [ɔ:g'ziljəri] helfend; Hilfs...

avail [ə'veil] **1.** nützen, helfen; ~ *o.s. of* sich *e-r S.* bedienen; **2.** Nutzen *m; of no* ~ nutzlos; ~able □ [~əbl] benutzbar; verfügbar; *pred.* erhältlich, vorhanden; gültig.

avalanche ['ævəla:nʃ] Lawine *f.*

avaric|e ['ævəris] Geiz *m;* Habsucht *f;* ~ious □ [ævə'riʃəs] geizig; habgierig.

avenge [ə'vendʒ] rächen, *et.* ahnden; ~r [~dʒə] Rächer(in).

avenue ['ævinju:] Allee *f;* Prachtstraße *f; fig.* Weg *m,* Straße *f.*

aver [ə'və:] behaupten.

average ['ævəridʒ] **1.** Durchschnitt *m;* ⚓ Havarie *f;* **2.** □ durchschnittlich; Durchschnitts...; **3.** durchschnittlich schätzen (*at* auf *acc.*); durchschnittlich betragen *od.* arbeiten *etc.*

avers|e □ [ə'və:s] abgeneigt (*to, from dat.*); widerwillig; **~ion** [ə'və:ʃən] Widerwille *m.*

avert [ə'və:t] abwenden (*a. fig.*).

aviat|ion ℀ [eivi'eiʃən] Fliegen *n*; Flugwesen *n*; Luftfahrt *f*; **~or** ['eivieitə] Flieger *m.*

avid □ ['ævid] gierig (*of* nach; *for* auf *acc.*).

avoid [ə'vɔid] (ver)meiden; *j-m* ausweichen; *t²₂* anfechten; ungültig machen; **~ance** [~dəns] Vermeidung *f.*

avouch [ə'vautʃ] verbürgen, bestätigen; = *avow.*

avow [ə'vau] bekennen, (ein)gestehen; anerkennen; **~al** [ə'vauəl] Bekenntnis *n*, (Ein)Geständnis *n*; **~edly** [ə'vauidli] eingestandenermaßen.

await [ə'weit] erwarten (*a. fig.*).

awake [ə'weik] **1.** wach, munter; *be* ~ *to* sich *.e-r S.* bewußt sein; **2.** [*irr.*] *v/t.* (*mst* **~n** [~kən]) (er)wecken; *v/i.* erwachen; gewahr werden *to s.th. et.*).

award [ə'wɔ:d] **1.** Urteil *n*, Spruch

m; Belohnung *f*; Preis *m*; **2.** zuerkennen, *Orden etc.* verleihen.

aware [ə'wɛə]: *be* ~ wissen (*of* von *od. acc.*), sich bewußt sein (*of gen.*); *become* ~ *of et.* gewahr werden, merken.

away [ə'wei] (hin)weg; fort; immer weiter, darauflos; ~ *back Am.* F (schon) damals, weit zurück.

awe [ɔ:] **1.** Ehrfurcht *f*, Scheu *f* (*of* vor *dat.*); **2.** (Ehr)Furcht einflößen (*dat.*).

awful □ ['ɔ:ful] ehrfurchtgebietend; furchtbar; F *fig.* schrecklich.

awhile [ə'wail] e-e Weile.

awkward □ ['ɔ:kwəd] ungeschickt, unbeholfen; linkisch; unangenehm; dumm, ungünstig, unpraktisch.

awl [ɔ:l] Ahle *f*, Pfriem *m.*

awning ['ɔ:niŋ] Plane *f*; Markise *f.*

awoke [ə'wouk] *pret. u. p.p. von* awake 2.

awry [ə'rai] schief; *fig.* verkehrt.

ax(e) [æks] Axt *f*, Beil *n.*

axis ['æksis], *pl.* **axes** ['æksi:z] Achse *f.*

axle ⊕ ['æksl] *a.* **~-tree** (Rad-) Achse *f*, Welle *f.*

ay(e) [ai] Ja *n*; *parl.* Jastimme *f*; *the ~s have it* die Mehrheit ist dafür.

azure ['æʒə] azurn, azurblau.

B

babble ['bæbl] **1.** stammeln; (nach-) plappern; schwatzen; plätschern (*Bach*); **2.** Geplapper *n*; Geschwätz *n.*

baboon *zo.* [bə'bu:n] Pavian *m.*

baby ['beibi] **1.** Säugling *m*, kleines Kind, Baby *n*; *Am. sl.* Süße *f* (*Mädchen*); **2.** Baby...; Kinder...; klein; **~hood** [~ihud] frühe Kindheit.

bachelor ['bætʃələ] Junggeselle *m*; *univ.* Bakkalaureus *m* (*Grad*).

back [bæk] **1.** Rücken *m*; Rückseite *f*; Rücklehne *f*; Hinterende *n*; *Fußball:* Verteidiger *m*; **2.** *adj.* Hinter..., Rück...; hinter; hinterwärtig; entlegen; rückläufig; rückständig; **3.** *adv.* zurück; **4.** *v/t.* mit e-m Rücken versehen; unterstützen; hinten anstoßen an (*acc.*); zurückbewegen; wetten *od.* setzen auf (*acc.*); ✝ indossieren; *v/i.* sich rückwärts bewegen, zurückgehen *od.* zurückfahren; ~ *alley Am.* finstere Seitengasse; **~bite** ['bækbait] [*irr.* (*bite*)] verleumden; **~bone** Rückgrat *n*; **~er** ['bækə] Unterstützer (-in); ✝ Indossierer *m*; Wetter(in); **~-fire** *mot.* Frühzündung *f*; **~ground** Hintergrund *m*; **~number** alte Nummer (*e-r Zeitung*); **~**

pedal rückwärtstreten (*Radfahren*); **~ling** *brake* Rücktrittbremse *f*; **~side** Hinter-, Rückseite *f*; **~slapper** *Am.* [~slæpə] plump vertraulicher Mensch; **~slide** [*irr.* (*slide*)] rückfällig werden; **~stairs** Hintertreppe *f*; **~stop** *Am. Baseball:* Gitter *n hinter dem Fänger*; *Schießstand:* Kugelfang *m*; **~stroke** Rückenschwimmen *n*; **~talk** *Am.* freche Antworten; **~track** *Am.* F *fig.* e-n Rückzieher machen; **~ward** ['bækwəd] **1.** *adj.* Rück(wärts)...; langsam; zurückgeblieben, rückständig; zurückhaltend; **2.** *adv.* (*a.* **~wards** [~dz]) rückwärts, zurück; **~water** Stauwasser *n*; abgelegene Waldgebiete; *fig.* Provinz *f*; **~woodsman** Hinterwäldler *m.*

bacon ['beikən] Speck *m.*

bacteri|ologist [bæktiəri'ɔlədʒist] Bakteriologe *m*; **~um** [bæk'tiəriəm], *pl.* **~a** [~iə] Bakterie *f.*

bad □ [bæd] schlecht, böse, schlimm; falsch (*Münze*); faul (*Schuld*); *he is ~ly off* er ist übel dran; *~ly wounded* schwerverwundet; *want ~ly* F dringend brauchen; *be in ~ with Am.* F in Ungnade bei.

bade [beid] *pret. von* bid 1.

badge [bædʒ] Ab-, Kennzeichen *n.*
badger ['bædʒə] **1.** *zo.* Dachs *m*; **2.** hetzen, plagen, quälen.
badlands *Am.* ['bædlændz] *pl.* Ödland *n.*
badness ['bædnis] schlechte Beschaffenheit; Schlechtigkeit *f.*
baffle ['bæfl] *j-n* verwirren; *Plan etc.* vereiteln, durchkreuzen.
bag [bæg] **1.** Beutel *m*, Sack *m*; Tüte *f*; Tasche *f*; ~ *and baggage* mit Sack und Pack; **2.** in e-n Beutel *etc.* tun, einsacken; *hunt.* zur Strecke bringen; (sich) bauschen.
baggage *Am.* ['bægidʒ] (Reise-) Gepäck *n*; ~ **car** *Am.* ⑤ Gepäckwagen *m*; ~ **check** *Am.* Gepäckschein *m.*
bagpipe ['bægpaip] Dudelsack *m.*
bail [beil] **1.** Bürge *m*; Bürgschaft *f*; Kaution *f*; *admit to* ~ ⚖ gegen Bürgschaft freilassen; **2.** bürgen für; ~ *out j-n* freibürgen; ✈ mit dem Fallschirm abspringen.
bailiff ['beilif] Gerichtsdiener *m*; (Guts)Verwalter *m*; Amtmann *m.*
bait [beit] **1.** Köder *m*; *fig.* Lockung *f*; **2.** *v/t.* *Falle etc.* beködern; *hunt.* hetzen; *fig.* quälen; reizen; *v/i.* rasten; einkehren.
bak|e [beik] **1.** backen; braten; *Ziegel* brennen; (aus)dörren; **2.** *Am.* gesellige Zusammenkunft; ~**er** ['beikə] Bäcker *m*; ~**ery** [~əri] Bäckerei *f*; ~**ing-powder** [~kiŋpaudə] Backpulver *n.*
balance ['bæləns] **1.** Waage *f*; Gleichgewicht *n* (*a. fig.*); Harmonie *f*; ✝ Bilanz *f*, Saldo *m*, Überschuß *m*; Restbetrag *m*; F Rest *m*; *a.* ~ *wheel* Unruh(e) *f der Uhr*; ~ *of power pol.* Kräftegleichgewicht *n*; ~ *of trade* (Außen-) Handelsbilanz *f*; **2.** *v/t.* (ab-, er)wägen; im Gleichgewicht halten; ausgleichen; ✝ bilanzieren; saldieren; *v/i.* balancieren; sich ausgleichen.
balcony ['bælkəni] Balkon *m.*
bald [bɔːld] kahl; *fig.* nackt; dürftig.
bale ✝ [beil] Ballen *m.*
baleful □ ['beilful] verderblich; unheilvoll.
balk [bɔːk] **1.** (Furchen)Rain *m*; Balken *m*; Hemmnis *n*; **2.** *v/t.* (ver-) hindern; enttäuschen; vereiteln; *v/i.* stutzen, scheuen.
ball¹ [bɔːl] **1.** Ball *m*; Kugel *f*; (Hand-, Fuß)Ballen *m*; Knäuel *m*, *n*; Kloß *m*; *Sport:* Wurf *m*; *keep the* ~ *rolling* das Gespräch in Gang halten; *play* ~ *Am.* F mitmachen; **2.** (sich) (zs.-)ballen.
ball² [~] Ball *m*, Tanzgesellschaft *f.*
ballad ['bæləd] Ballade *f*; Lied *n.*
ballast ['bæləst] **1.** Ballast *m*; ⑤ Schotter *m*, Bettung *f*; **2.** mit

Ballast beladen; ⑤ beschottern, betten.
ball-bearing(s *pl.*) ⊕ ['bɔːl-'beəriŋ(z)] Kugellager *n.*
ballet ['bælei] Ballett *n.*
balloon [bə'luːn] **1.** Ballon *m*; **2.** im Ballon aufsteigen; sich blähen; ~**ist** [~nist] Ballonfahrer *m.*
ballot ['bælət] **1.** Wahlzettel *m*; (geheime) Wahl; **2.** (geheim) abstimmen; ~ *for losen um*; ~**-box** Wahlurne *f.*
ball(-point) pen ['bɔːl(pɔint)pen] Kugelschreiber *m.*
ball-room ['bɔːlrum] Ballsaal *m.*
balm [bɑːm] Balsam *m*; *fig.* Trost *m.*
balmy □ ['bɑːmi] balsamisch (*a. fig.*).
baloney *Am. sl.* [bə'louni] Quatsch *m.*
balsam ['bɔːlsəm] Balsam *m.*
balustrade [bæləs'treid] Balustrade *f*, Brüstung *f*; Geländer *n.*
bamboo [bæm'buː] Bambus *m.*
bamboozle F [bæm'buːzl] beschwindeln.
ban [bæn] **1.** Bann *m*; Acht *f*; (amtliches) Verbot; **2.** verbieten.
banal [bə'nɑːl] banal, abgedroschen.
banana [bə'nɑːnə] Banane *f.*
band [bænd] **1.** Band *n*; Streifen *m*; Schar *f*; ♪ Kapelle *f*; **2.** zs.-binden; ~ *o.s.* sich zs.-tun *od.* zs.-rotten.
bandage ['bændidʒ] **1.** Binde *f*, Verband *m*; **2.** bandagieren; verbinden.
bandbox ['bændbɔks] Hutschachtel *f.*
bandit ['bændit] Bandit *m.*
band|-master ['bændmɑːstə] Kapellmeister *m*; ~**stand** Musikpavillon *m*; ~ **wagon** *Am.* Wagen *m* mit Musikkapelle; *jump on the* ~ sich der erfolgsprechenden Sache anschließen.
bandy ['bændi] *Worte etc.* wechseln; ~**-legged** säbelbeinig.
bane [bein] Ruin *m*; ~**ful** □ ['beinful] verderblich.
bang [bæŋ] **1.** Knall *m*; Ponyfrisur *f*; **2.** dröhnend (zu)schlagen; ~**-up** *Am. sl.* ['bæŋ'ʌp] Klasse, prima.
banish ['bæniʃ] verbannen; ~**ment** [~ʃmənt] Verbannung *f.*
banisters ['bænistəz] *pl.* Treppengeländer *n.*
bank [bæŋk] **1.** Damm *m*; Ufer *n*; (Spiel-, Sand-, Wolken- *etc.*)Bank *f*; ~ *of issue* Notenbank *f*; **2.** *v/t.* eindämmen; ✝ Geld auf die Bank legen; ✈ in die Kurve bringen; *v/i.* Bankgeschäfte machen; ein Bankkonto haben; ✈ in die Kurve gehen; ~ *on* sich verlassen auf (*acc.*); ~**-bill** ['bæŋkbil] Bankwechsel *m*; *Am. s.* banknote; ~**er** [~kə] Bankier *m*; [~kiŋ] Bankgeschäft *n*; Bankwesen *n*; *attr.* Bank...; ~**-note** Banknote *f*; Kassenschein *m*; ~

rate Diskontsatz m; **~rupt** [~krəpt]
1. Bankrotteur m; 2. bankrott;
3. bankrott machen; **~ruptcy**
[~tsi] Bankrott m, Konkurs m.
banner ['bænə] Banner n; Fahne f.
banns [bænz] pl. Aufgebot n.
banquet ['bæŋkwit] 1. Festmahl n;
2. v/t. festlich bewirten; v/i. tafeln.
banter ['bæntə] necken, hänseln.
baptism ['bæptizəm] Taufe f.
baptist ['bæptist] Täufer m.
baptize [bæp'taiz] taufen.
bar [baː] 1. Stange f; Stab m;
Barren m; Riegel m; Schranke f;
Sandbank f; fig. Hindernis n; ✗
Spange f; ♪ Takt(strich) m; (Gerichts)Schranke f; fig. Urteil n;
Anwaltschaft f; Bar f im Hotel etc.;
2. verriegeln; (ver-, ab)sperren;
verwehren; einsperren; (ver)hin-
dern; ausschließen.
barb [baːb] Widerhaken m; **~ed**
wire Stacheldraht m.
barbar|ian [baː'bɛəriɛn] 1. bar-
barisch; 2. Barbar(in); **~ous** □
['baːbərəs] barbarisch; roh; grausam.
barbecue ['baːbikjuː] 1. großer
Bratrost; Am. Essen n (im Freien),
bei dem die Tiere ganz gebraten
werden; 2. im ganzen braten.
barber ['baːbə] (Herren)Friseur m.
bare [bɛə] 1. nackt, bloß; kahl; bar,
leer; arm, entblößt; 2. entblößen;
~faced □ ['bɛəfeist] frech; **~foot,**
~footed barfuß; **~headed** bar-
häuptig; **~ly** ['bɛəli] kaum.
bargain ['baːgin] 1. Geschäft n;
Handel m, Kauf m; vorteilhafter
Kauf; a (dead) ~ spottbillig; it's a ~!
F abgemacht!; into the ~ obendrein;
2. handeln, übereinkommen.
barge [baːdʒ] Flußboot n, Lastkahn
m; Hausboot n; **~man** ['baːdʒmən]
Kahnführer m.
bark[1] [baːk] 1. Borke f, Rinde f;
2. abrinden; Haut abschürfen.
bark[2] [~] 1. bellen; 2. Bellen n.
bar-keeper ['baːkiːpə] Barbesitzer
m; Barkellner m.
barley ['baːli] Gerste f; Graupe f.
barn [baːn] Scheune f; bsd. Am.
(Vieh)Stall m; **~storm** Am. pol.
['baːnstɔːm] herumreisen u. (Wahl-)
Reden halten.
barometer [bə'rɔmitə] Barometer n.
baron ['bærən] Baron m, Freiherr
m; **~ess** [~nis] Baronin f.
barrack(s pl.) ['bærək(s)] (Miets-)
Kaserne f.
barrage ['bæraːʒ] Staudamm m.
barrel ['bærəl] 1. Faß n, Tonne f;
Gewehr- etc. Lauf m; ⊕ Trommel
f; Walze f; 2. in Fässer füllen;
~organ ♪ Drehorgel f.
barren □ ['bærən] unfruchtbar;
dürr, trocken; tot (Kapital).
barricade [bæri'keid] 1. Barrikade
f; 2. verbarrikadieren; sperren.

barrier ['bæriə] Schranke f (a. fig.);
Barriere f, Sperre f; Hindernis
n.
barrister ['bæristə] (plädierender)
Rechtsanwalt, Barrister m.
barrow[1] ['bærou] Trage f; Karre f.
barrow[2] [~] Hügelgrab n, Tumulus
m.
barter ['baːtə] 1. Tausch(handel)
m; 2. tauschen (for gegen); F
schachern.
base[1] □ [beis] gemein; unecht.
base[2] [~] 1. Basis f; Grundlage f;
Fundament n; Fuß m; ⚗ Base f;
Stützpunkt m; 2. gründen, stützen.
base|ball ['beisbɔːl] Baseball m;
~born von niedriger Abkunft;
unehelich; **~less** ['beislis] grundlos;
~ment ['beismənt] Fundament n;
Kellergeschoß n.
baseness ['beisnis] Gemeinheit f.
bashful □ ['bæʃful] schüchtern.
basic ['beisik] (**~ally**) grundlegend;
Grund...; ⚗ basisch.
basin ['beisn] Becken n; Schüssel f;
Tal-, Wasser-, Hafenbecken n.
bas|is ['beisis], pl. **~es** ['beisiːz]
Basis f; Grundlage f; ✗, ⚓ Stützpunkt m.
bask [baːsk] sich sonnen (a. fig.).
basket ['baːskit] Korb m; **~ball**
Korbball(spiel n) m; **~ dinner, ~**
supper Am. Picknick n.
bass ♪ [beis] Baß m.
basso ♪ ['bæsou] Baß(sänger) m.
bastard ['bæstəd] 1. □ unehelich;
unecht; Bastard...; 2. Bastard m.
baste[1] [beist] Braten begießen;
durchprügeln.
baste[2] [~] lose nähen, (an)heften.
bat[1] [bæt] Fledermaus f; as blind
as a ~ stockblind.
bat[2] [~] Sport: 1. Schlagholz n;
Schläger m; 2. den Ball schlagen.
batch [bætʃ] Schub m Brote (a. fig.);
Stoß m Briefe etc. (a. fig.).
bate [beit] verringern; vermahlen.
bath [baːθ] 1. Bad n; ♿ chair Rollstuhl m; 2. baden.
bathe [beið] baden.
bathing ['beiðiŋ] Baden n, Bad n;
attr. Bade...; **~suit** Badeanzug m.
bath|robe Am. ['baːθroub] Bade-
mantel m; **~room** Badezimmer n;
~sheet Badelaken n; **~towel**
Badetuch n; **~tub** Badewanne f.
batiste ♰ [bæ'tiːst] Batist m.
baton ['bætən] Stab m; Taktstock
m.
battalion ✗ [bə'tæljən] Bataillon n.
batten ['bætn] 1. Latte f; 2. sich
mästen.
batter ['bætə] 1. Sport: Schläger m;
2. Rührteig m; 2. heftig schlagen;
verbeulen; **~ down** od. in Tür einschlagen; **~y** [~əri] Schlägerei f;
Batterie f; ⚡ Akku m; fig. Satz m;
assault and **~** ⚖ tätlicher Angriff.
battle ['bætl] 1. Schlacht f (of bei);

2. streiten, kämpfen; **~ax(e)** Streitaxt f; F Xanthippe f; **~field** Schlachtfeld n; **~ments** [ˌlmənts] pl. Zinnen f/pl.; **~plane** ✕ Kriegsflugzeug n; **~ship** ✕ Schlachtschiff n.

Bavarian [bəˈvɛəriən] **1.** bay(e)-risch; **2.** Bayer(in).

bawdy [ˈbɔːdi] unzüchtig.

bawl [bɔːl] brüllen; johlen, grölen; **~ out** auf-, losbrüllen.

bay[1] [bei] **1.** rotbraun; **2.** Braune(r) m (Pferd).

bay[2] [~] Bai f, Bucht f; Erker m.

bay[3] [~] Lorbeer m.

bay[4] [~] **1.** bellen, anschlagen; **2.** stand at **~** sich verzweifelt wehren; bring to **~** Wild etc. stellen.

bayonet ✕ [ˈbeiənit] **1.** Bajonett n; **2.** mit dem Bajonett niederstoßen.

bayou Am. [ˈbaiuː] sumpfiger Nebenarm.

bay window [ˈbeiˈwindou] Erkerfenster n; Am. sl. Vorbau m (Bauch).

baza(a)r [bəˈzɑː] Basar m.

be [biː, bi] [irr.] **1.** v/i. sein; there is od. are es gibt; here you are again! da haben wir's wieder!; **~** about beschäftigt sein mit; **~** at s.th. et. vorhaben; **~** off aus sein; sich fortmachen; **2.** v/aux.: **~** reading beim Lesen sein, gerade lesen; I am to inform you ich soll Ihnen mitteilen; **3.** v/aux. mit p.p. zur Bildung des Passivs: werden.

beach [biːtʃ] **1.** Strand m; **2.** ⚓ auf den Strand setzen od. ziehen; **~comber** [ˈbiːtʃkoumə] fig. Nichtstuer m.

beacon [ˈbiːkən] Blinklicht n; Leuchtfeuer n, Leuchtturm m.

bead [biːd] Perle f; Tropfen m; Visier-Korn n; **~s** pl. a. Rosenkranz m.

beak [biːk] Schnabel m; Tülle f.

beaker [ˈbiːkə] Becher(glas n) m.

beam [biːm] **1.** Balken m; Waagebalken m; Strahl m; Glanz m; Radio: Richtstrahl m; **2.** (aus-) strahlen.

bean [biːn] Bohne f; Am. sl. Birne f (Kopf); full of **~s** F lebensprühend.

bear[1] [bɛə] Bär m; ✝ sl. Baissier m.

bear[2] [~] [irr.] v/t. tragen; hervorbringen, gebären; Liebe etc. hegen; ertragen; **~** down überwältigen; **~** out unterstützen, bestätigen; v/i. tragen; fruchtbar od. trächtig sein; leiden, dulden; **~** up standhalten, fest bleiben; **~** (up)on einwirken auf (acc.); bring to **~** zur Anwendung bringen, einwirken lassen, Druck etc. ausüben.

beard [biəd] **1.** Bart m; ♀ Granne f; **2.** v/t. j-m entgegentreten, trotzen.

bearer [ˈbɛərə] Träger(in); Überbringer(in), Wechsel-Inhaber(in).

bearing [ˈbɛəriŋ] (Er)Tragen n;

Betragen n; Beziehung f; Richtung f.

beast [biːst] Vieh n, Tier n; Bestie f; **~ly** [ˈbiːstli] viehisch; scheußlich.

beat [biːt] **1.** [irr.] v/t. schlagen; prügeln; besiegen, Am. F j-m zuvorkommen; übertreffen; Am. F betrügen; **~** it! Am. sl. hau ab!; **~** the band Am. F wichtig od. großartig sein; **~** a retreat den Rückzug antreten; **~** one's way Am. F sich durchschlagen; **~** up auftreiben; v/i. schlagen; **~** about the bush wie die Katze um den heißen Brei herumgehen; **2.** Schlag m; ♪ Takt(schlag) m; Pulsschlag m; Runde f, Revier n e-s Schutzmannes etc.; Am. sensationelle Erstmeldung e-r Zeitung; **3.** F baff, verblüfft; **~en** [ˈbiːtn] p.p. von beat 1; (aus)getreten (Weg).

beatitude [biˈ(ː)ætitjuːd] (Glück-) Seligkeit f.

beatnik [ˈbiːtnik] Beatnik m, junger Antikonformist und Bohemien.

beau [bou] Stutzer m; Anbeter m.

beautiful □ [ˈbjuːtəful] schön.

beautify [ˈbjuːtifai] verschönern.

beauty [ˈbjuːti] Schönheit f; Sleeping ♀ Dornrös-chen n; **~** parlo(u)r, **~** shop Schönheitssalon m.

beaver [ˈbiːvə] Biber m; Biberpelz m.

becalm [biˈkɑːm] beruhigen.

became [biˈkeim] pret. von become.

because [biˈkɔz] weil; **~** of wegen.

beckon [ˈbekən] (j-m zu)winken.

become [biˈkʌm] [irr.] v/i. werden (of aus); v/t. anstehen, ziemen (dat.); sich schicken für; kleiden (Hut etc.); **~ing** □ [ˌmiŋ] passend; schicklich; kleidsam.

bed [bed] **1.** Bett n; Lager n e-s Tieres; ♂ Beet n; Unterlage f; **2.** betten.

bed-clothes [ˈbedklouðz] pl. Bettwäsche f.

bedding [ˈbediŋ] Bettzeug n; Streu f.

bedevil [biˈdevl] behexen; quälen.

bedlam [ˈbedləm] Tollhaus n.

bed|rid(den) [ˈbedrid(n)] bettlägerig; **~room** Schlafzimmer n; **~spread** Bett-, Tagesdecke f; **~stead** Bettstelle f; **~time** Schlafenszeit f.

bee [biː] zo. Biene f; Am. nachbarliches Treffen; Wettbewerb m; have a **~** in one's bonnet F e-e fixe Idee haben.

beech ♀ [biːtʃ] Buche f; **~nut** Bucheicker f.

beef [biːf] **1.** Rindfleisch n; **2.** Am. F nörgeln; **~** tea Fleischbrühe f; **~y** [ˈbiːfi] fleischig; kräftig.

bee|hive [ˈbiːhaiv] Bienenkorb m, -stock m; **~keeper** Bienenzüchter m; **~line** kürzester Weg; make a **~** for Am. schnurstracks losgehen auf (acc.).

been [bi:n, bin] *p.p. von* be.

beer [biə] Bier *n*; *small* ~ Dünnbier *n*. [Bete *f*.\

beet ♀ [bi:t] (Runkel)Rübe *f*,\

beetle[1] ['bi:tl] Käfer *m*.

beetle[2] [~] **1.** überhängend; buschig (*Brauen*); **2.** *v/i*. überhängen.

beetroot ['bi:tru:t] rote Rübe.

befall [bi'fɔ:l] [*irr.* (*fall*)] *v/t.* zustoßen (*dat.*); *v/i.* sich ereignen.

befit [bi'fit] sich schicken für.

before [bi'fɔ:] **1.** *adv. Raum:* vorn; voran; *Zeit:* vorher, früher; schon (*früher*); **2.** *cj.* bevor, ehe, bis; **3.** *prp.* vor; ~hand vorher, zuvor; voraus (*with dat.*).

befriend [bi'frend] sich j-m freundlich erweisen.

beg [beg] *v/t. et.* erbetteln; erbitten (*of von*); *j-n* bitten; ~ *the question* um den Kern der Frage herumgehen; *v/i.* betteln; bitten; betteln gehen; sich gestatten.

began [bi'gæn] *pret. von* begin.

beget [bi'get] [*irr.* (*get*)] (er)zeugen.

beggar ['begə] **1.** Bettler(in); F Kerl *m*; **2.** zum Bettler machen; *fig.* übertreffen; *it* ~*s all description* es spottet jeder Beschreibung.

begin [bi'gin] [*irr.*] beginnen (*at* bei, mit); ~**ner** [~nə] Anfänger(in); ~**ning** [~niŋ] Beginn *m*, Anfang *m*.

begone [bi'gɔn] fort!, F pack dich!

begot [bi'gɔt] *pret. von* beget; ~**ten** [~tn] **1.** *p.p. von* beget; **2.** *adj.* erzeugt.

begrudge [bi'grʌdʒ] mißgönnen.

beguile [bi'gail] täuschen; betrügen (*of, out of* um); *Zeit* vertreiben.

begun [bi'gʌn] *p.p. von* begin.

behalf [bi'hɑ:f]: *on od. in* ~ *of* im Namen von; um ... (*gen.*) willen.

behav|e [bi'heiv] sich benehmen; ~**io(u)r** [~vjə] Benehmen *n*, Betragen *n*.

behead [bi'hed] enthaupten.

behind [bi'haind] **1.** *adv.* hinten; dahinter; zurück; **2.** *prp.* hinter; ~**hand** zurück, im Rückstand.

behold [bi'hould] [*irr.* (*hold*)] **1.** erblicken; **2.** siehe (da)!; ~**en** [~dən] verpflichtet, verbunden.

behoof [bi'hu:f]: *to* (*for, on*) (*the*) ~ *of* in *j-s* Interesse, um *j-s* willen.

behoove *Am.* [bi'hu:v] = behove.

behove [bi'houv]: *it* ~*s s.o. to inf.* es ist j-s Pflicht, zu *inf.*

being [bi:iŋ] (Da)Sein *n*; Wesen *n*; *in* ~ lebend; wirklich (vorhanden).

belabo(u)r [bi'leibə] verbleuen.

belated [bi'leitid] verspätet.

belch [beltʃ] **1.** rülpsen; ausspeien; **2.** Rülpsen *n*; Ausbruch *m*.

beleaguer [bi'li:gə] belagern.

belfry ['belfri] Glockenturm *m*, -stuhl *m*. [**2.** Belgier(in).\

Belgian ['beldʒən] **1.** belgisch;\

belie [bi'lai] Lügen strafen.

belief [bi'li:f] Glaube *m* (*in an acc.*).

believable [bi'li:vəbl] glaubhaft.

believe [bi'li:v] glauben (*in an acc.*); ~**r** [~və] Gläubige(r *m*) *f*.

belittle *fig.* [bi'litl] verkleinern.

bell [bel] Glocke *f*; Klingel *f*; ~**boy** *Am.* ['belbɔi] Hotelpage *m*.

belle [bel] Schöne *f*, Schönheit *f*.

belles-lettres ['bel'letr] *pl.* Belletristik *f*, schöne Literatur.

bellhop *Am. sl.* ['belhɔp] Hotelpage *m*.

bellied ['belid] bauchig.

belligerent [bi'lidʒərənt] **1.** kriegführend; **2.** kriegführendes Land.

bellow ['belou] **1.** brüllen; **2.** Gebrüll *n*; ~**s** *pl.* Blasebalg *m*.

belly ['beli] **1.** Bauch *m*; **2.** (sich) bauchen; (an)schwellen.

belong [bi'lɔŋ] (an)gehören; ~ *to* gehören *dat. od.* zu; sich gehören für; *j-m* gebühren; ~**ings** [~ŋiŋz] *pl.* Habseligkeiten *f/pl.*

beloved [bi'lʌvd] **1.** geliebt; **2.** Geliebte(r *m*) *f*.

below [bi'lou] **1.** *adv.* unten; **2.** *prp.* unter.

belt [belt] **1.** Gürtel *m*; ✗ Koppel *n*; Zone *f*, Bezirk *m*; ⊕ Treibriemen *m*; **2.** umgürten; ~ *out Am.* F herausschmettern, loslegen (*singen*).

bemoan [bi'moun] betrauern, beklagen.

bench [bentʃ] Bank *f*; Richterbank *f*; Gerichtshof *m*; Arbeitstisch *m*.

bend [bend] **1.** Biegung *f*, Kurve *f*; ♎ Seemannsknoten *m*; **2.** [*irr.*] (sich) biegen; *Geist etc.* richten (*to, on* auf *acc.*); (sich) beugen; sich neigen (*to* vor *dat.*).

beneath [bi'ni:θ] = below.

benediction [beni'dikʃən] Segen *m*.

benefact|ion [beni'fækʃən] Wohltat *f*; ~**or** ['benifæktə] Wohltäter *m*.

beneficen|ce [bi'nefisəns] Wohltätigkeit *f*; ~**t** □ [~nt] wohltätig.

beneficial □ [beni'fiʃəl] wohltuend; zuträglich; nützlich.

benefit ['benifit] **1.** Wohltat *f*; Nutzen *m*, Vorteil *m*; Wohltätigkeitsveranstaltung *f*; (Wohlfahrts-)Unterstützung *f*; **2.** nützen; begünstigen; Nutzen ziehen.

benevolen|ce [bi'nevələns] Wohlwollen *n*; ~**t** □ [~nt] wohlwollend; gütig, mildherzig.

benign □ [bi'nain] freundlich, gütig; zuträglich; ✗ gutartig.

bent [bent] **1.** *pret. u. p.p. von* bend **2**; ~ *on* versessen auf (*acc.*); **2.** Hang *m*; Neigung *f*.

benzene 🜍 ['benzi:n] Benzol *n*.

benzine 🜍 ['benzi:n] Benzin *n*.

bequeath [bi'kwi:ð] vermachen.

bequest [bi'kwest] Vermächtnis *n*.

bereave [bi'ri:v] [*irr.*] berauben.

bereft [bi'reft] *pret. u. p.p. von* bereave.

beret ['berei] Baskenmütze *f*.

berry ['beri] Beere *f.*

berth [bə:θ] 1. ⚓ Ankergrund *m*; Koje *f*; *fig.* (gute) Stelle; 2. vor Anker gehen.

beseech [bi'si:tʃ] [*irr.*] ersuchen; bitten; um *et.* bitten; flehen.

beset [bi'set] [*irr.* (set)] umgeben; bedrängen; verfolgen.

beside *prp.* [bi'said] neben; weitab von; ~ o.s. außer sich (with vor); ~ the point, ~ the question nicht zur Sache gehörig; ~s [~dz] 1. *adv.* außerdem; 2. *prp.* abgesehen von, außer.

besiege [bi'si:dʒ] belagern.

besmear [bi'smiə] beschmieren.

besom ['bi:zəm] (Reisig)Besen *m.*

besought [bi'sɔ:t] *pret. u. p.p.* von *beseech.*

bespatter [bi'spætə] (be)spritzen.

bespeak [bi'spi:k] [*irr.* (speak)] vorbestellen; verraten, (an)zeigen; *bespoke tailor* Maßschneider *m.*

best [best] 1. *adj.* best; höchst; größt, meist; ~ *man* Brautführer *m*; 2. *adv.* am besten, aufs beste; 3. Beste(r *m*, ~s *n*) *f*, Besten *pl.*; to the ~ of ... nach bestem ...; *make the ~ of* tun, was man kann, mit; *at* ~ im besten Falle.

bestial ☐ ['bestjəl] tierisch, viehisch.

bestow [bi'stou] geben, schenken, verleihen (on, upon *dat.*).

bet [bet] 1. Wette *f*; 2. [*irr.*] wetten; *you* ~ F sicherlich.

betake [bi'teik] [*irr.* (take)]: ~ o.s. to sich begeben nach; *fig.* s-e Zuflucht nehmen zu.

bethink [bi'θiŋk] [*irr.* (think)]: ~ o.s. sich besinnen (of auf *acc.*); ~ o.s. to *inf.* sich in den Kopf setzen zu *inf.*

betimes [bi'taimz] beizeiten.

betray [bi'trei] verraten (*a. fig.*); verleiten; ~er [~eiə] Verräter(in).

betrothal [bi'trouðəl] Verlobung *f.*

better ['betə] 1. *adj.* besser; *he is* ~ es geht ihm besser; 2. Bessere(s) *n*; ~s *pl.* Höherstehenden *pl.*, Vorgesetzten *pl.*; *get the* ~ *of* die Oberhand gewinnen über (*acc.*); überwinden; 3. *adv.* besser; mehr; *so much the* ~ desto besser; *you had* ~ *go* es wäre besser, wenn du gingest; 4. *v/t.* (ver)bessern; *v/i.* sich bessern; ~ment [~əmənt] Verbesserung *f.*

between [bi'twi:n] (*a.* **betwixt** [bi'twikst]) 1. *adv.* dazwischen; 2. *prp.* zwischen, unter.

bevel ['bevəl] schräg, schief.

beverage ['bevəridʒ] Getränk *n.*

bevy ['bevi] Schwarm *m*; Schar *f.*

bewail [bi'weil] be-, wehklagen.

beware [bi'weə] sich hüten (of vor).

bewilder [bi'wildə] irremachen; verwirren; bestürzt machen; ~ment [~əmənt] Verwirrung *f*; Bestürzung *f.*

bewitch [bi'witʃ] bezaubern, behexen.

beyond [bi'jɔnd] 1. *adv.* darüber hinaus; 2. *prp.* jenseits, über (... hinaus); mehr als; außer.

bi... [bai] zwei ...

bias ['baiəs] 1. *adj. u. adv.* schief, schräg; 2. Neigung *f*; Vorurteil *n*; 3. beeinflussen; ~sed befangen.

bib [bib] (Sabber)Lätzchen *n.*

Bible ['baibl] Bibel *f.*

biblical ☐ ['biblikəl] biblisch; Bibel...

bibliography [bibli'ɔgrəfi] Bibliographie *f.*

bicarbonate 🜄 [bai'ka:bənit] doppeltkohlensaures Natron.

biceps ['baiseps] Bizeps *m.*

bicker ['bikə] (sich) zanken; flakkern; plätschern; prasseln.

bicycle ['baisikl] 1. Fahrrad *n*; 2. radfahren, radeln.

bid [bid] 1. [*irr.*] gebieten, befehlen; (ent)bieten; *Karten*: reizen; ~ *fair* versprechen; ~ *farewell* Lebewohl sagen; 2. Gebot *n*, Angebot *n*; ~den ['bidn] *p.p.* von *bid* 1.

bide [baid] [*irr.*]: ~ *one's time* den rechten Augenblick abwarten.

biennial [bai'eniəl] zweijährig.

bier [biə] (Toten)Bahre *f.*

big [big] groß; erwachsen; schwanger; F wichtig(tuerisch); ~ *business* Großunternehmertum *n*; ~ *shot* F hohes Tier; ~ *stick* Am. Macht (-entfaltung) *f*; *talk* ~ den Mund vollnehmen.

bigamy ['bigəmi] Doppelehe *f.*

bigot ['bigət] Frömmler(in); blinder Anhänger; ~ry [~tri] Frömmelei *f.*

bigwig F ['bigwig] hohes Tier (*P.*).

bike F [baik] (Fahr)Rad *n.*

bilateral ☐ [bai'lætərəl] zweiseitig.

bile [bail] Galle *f* (*a. fig.*).

bilious ☐ ['biljəs] gallig (*a. fig.*).

bill[1] [bil] Schnabel *m*; Spitze *f.*

bill[2] F [bil] 1. Gesetzentwurf *m*; Klage-, Rechtsschrift *f*; *a.* ~ *of exchange* Wechsel *m*; Zettel *m*; *Am.* Banknote *f*; ~ *of fare* Speisekarte *f*; ~ *of lading* Seefrachtbrief *m*, Konnossement *n*; ~ *of sale* Kaufvertrag *m*; ♀ *of Rights englische* Freiheitsurkunde (1689); *Am.* die ersten 10 Zusatzartikel zur Verfassung der USA; 2. (durch Anschlag) ankündigen.

billboard *Am.* ['bil'bɔ:d] Anschlagbrett *n.*

billfold *Am.* ['bilfould] Brieftasche *f* für Papiergeld.

billiards ['biljədz] *pl. od. sg.* Billiard(spiel) *n.*

billion ['biljən] Billion *f*; *Am.* Milliarde *f.*

billow ['bilou] 1. Woge *f* (*a. fig.*); 2. wogen; ~y [~oui] wogend.

billy *Am.* ['bili] (Gummi)Knüppel *m.*

bin [bin] Kasten *m*, Behälter *m*.
bind [baind] [*irr.*] *v/t.* (an-, ein-, um-, auf-, fest-, ver)binden; verpflichten; *Handel* abschließen; *Saum* einfassen; *v/i.* binden; ~**er** ['baində] Binder *m*; Binde *f*; ~**ing** [~diŋ] 1. bindend; 2. Binden *n*; Einband *m*; Einfassung *f*.
binocular [bi'nɔkjulə] *mst* ~**s** *pl.* Feldstecher *m*, Fern-, Opernglas *n*.
biography [bai'ɔgrəfi] Biographie *f*.
biology [bai'ɔlədʒi] Biologie *f*.
biped *zo.* ['baiped] Zweifüßer *m*.
birch [bəːtʃ] 1. ♀ Birke *f*; (Birken-) Rute *f*; 2. mit der Rute züchtigen.
bird [bəːd] Vogel *m*; ~**'s-eye** ['bəːdzai]: ~ view Vogelperspektive *f*.
birth [bəːθ] Geburt *f*; Ursprung *m*; Entstehung *f*; Herkunft *f*; *bring to* ~ entstehen lassen, veranlassen; *give* ~ *to* gebären, zur Welt bringen; ~ **control** Geburtenregelung *f*; ~**day** ['bəːθdei] Geburtstag *m*; ~**place** Geburtsort *m*.
biscuit ['biskit] Zwieback *m*; Keks *m*, *n*; Biskuit *n* (*Porzellan*).
bishop ['biʃəp] Bischof *m*; Läufer *m* *im Schach*; ~**ric** [~prik] Bistum *n*.
bison *zo.* ['baisn] Wisent *m*.
bit [bit] 1. Bißchen *n*, Stückchen *n*; Gebiß *n am Zaum*; *Schlüssel*-Bart *m*; *a (little)* ~ ein (kleines) bißchen *n*; 2. zäumen; zügeln; 3. *pret. von* bite 2.
bitch [bitʃ] Hündin *f*; V Hure *f*.
bite [bait] 1. Beißen *n*; Biß *m*; Bissen *m*; ⊕ Fassen *n*; 2. [*irr.*] (an)beißen; brennen (*Pfeffer*); schneiden (*Kälte*); ⊕ fassen; *fig.* verletzen.
bitten ['bitn] *p.p. von* bite 2.
bitter ['bitə] 1. ⬜ bitter; streng; *fig.* verbittert; 2. ~**s** *pl.* Magenbitter *m*.
biz F [biz] Geschäft *n*.
blab F [blæb] (aus)schwatzen.
black [blæk] 1. ⬜ schwarz; dunkel; finster; ~ eye blaues Auge; 2. schwärzen; wichsen; ~ out verdunkeln; 3. Schwarz *n*; Schwärze *f*; Schwarze(r *m*) *f* (*Neger*); ~**amoor** ['blækəmuə] Neger *m*; ~**berry** Brombeere *f*; ~**bird** Amsel *f*; ~**board** Wandtafel *f*; ~**en** [~kən] *v/t.* schwärzen; *fig.* anschwärzen; *v/i.* schwarz werden; ~**guard** ['blægaːd] 1. Lump *m*, Schuft *m*; 2. ⬜ schuftig; ~**head** ✿ Mitesser *m*; ~**ing** [~kiŋ] Schuhwichse *f*; ~**ish** [~iʃ] schwärzlich; ~**jack** 1. *bsd. Am.* Totschläger *m* (*Instrument*); 2. niederknüppeln; ~**leg** Betrüger *m*; ~**letter** *typ.* Fraktur *f*; ~**mail** 1. Erpressung *f*; 2. *j-n* erpressen; ~ **market** schwarzer Markt; ~**ness** [~knis] Schwärze *f*; ~**out** Verdunkelung *f*; ~ **pudding** Blutwurst *f*; ~**smith** Grobschmied *m*.

bladder *anat.* ['blædə] Blase *f*.
blade [bleid] Blatt *n*, ♀ Halm *m*; *Säge-*, *Schulter-* *etc.* Blatt *n*; Propellerflügel *m*; Klinge *f*.
blame [bleim] 1. Tadel *m*; Schuld *f*; 2. tadeln; *be to* ~ *for* schuld sein an (*dat.*); ~**ful** ['bleimful] tadelnswert; ~**less** ⬜ [~mlis] tadellos.
blanch [blaːntʃ] bleichen; erbleichen (lassen); ~ over beschönigen.
bland ⬜ [blænd] mild, sanft.
blank [blæŋk] 1. ⬜ blank; leer; unausgefüllt; unbeschrieben; ✝ Blanko...; verdutzt; ~ cartridge ✕ Platzpatrone *f*; 2. Weiße *n*; Leere *f*; leerer Raum; Lücke *f*; unbeschriebenes Blatt, Formular *n*; Niete *f*.
blanket ['blæŋkit] 1. Wolldecke *f*; wet ~ *fig.* Dämpfer *m*; Spielverderber *m*; 2. (mit e-r Wolldecke) zudecken; 3. *Am.* umfassend, Gesamt...
blare *zo.* [blɛə] schmettern; grölen.
blasphem|e [blæs'fiːm] lästern (*against* über *acc.*); ~**y** ['blæsfimi] Gotteslästerung *f*.
blast [blaːst] 1. Windstoß *m*; Ton *m e-s Blasinstruments*; ⊕ Gebläse (-luft *f*) *n*; Luftdruck *m e-r Explosion*; ♀ Meltau *m*; 2. (in die Luft) sprengen; zerstören (*a. fig.*); ~ (*it*)*!* verdammt; ~**-furnace** ⊕ ['blaːst'fəːnis] Hochofen *m*.
blatant ⬜ ['bleitənt] lärmend.
blather *Am.* ['blæðə] schwätzen.
blaze [bleiz] 1. Flamme(n *pl.*) *f*; Feuer *n*; ~**s** *pl. sl.* Teufel *m*, Hölle *f*; heller Schein; *fig.* Ausbruch *m*; *go to* ~**s!** zum Teufel mit dir!; 2. *v/i.* brennen, flammen, lodern; leuchten; ~ abroad ausposaunen; *v/t.* ['bleizə] Blazer *m*.
blazon ['bleizn] Wappen(kunde *f*)*n*.
bleach [bliːtʃ] bleichen; ~**er** ['bliːtʃə] Bleicher(in); *mst* ~**s** *pl. Am.* nichtüberdachte Zuschauerplätze.
bleak ⬜ [bliːk] öde, kahl; rauh; *fig.* trüb, freudlos, finster.
blear [bliə] 1. trüb; 2. trüben; ~**-eyed** ['bliəraid] triefäugig.
bleat [bliːt] 1. Blöken *n*; 2. blöken.
bleb [bleb] Bläs-chen *n*, Pustel *f*.
bled [bled] *pret. u. p.p. von* bleed.
bleed [bliːd] [*irr.*] *v/i.* bluten; *v/t.* zur Ader lassen; *fig.* schröpfen; ~**ing** ['bliːdiŋ] 1. Bluten *n*; Aderlaß *m*; 2. *sl.* verflixt.
blemish ['blemiʃ] 1. Fehler *m*; Makel *m*, Schande *f*; 2. verunstalten; brandmarken.
blench [blentʃ] *v/i.* zurückschrecken; *v/t.* die Augen schließen vor.
blend [blend] 1. [*irr.*] (sich) (ver)mischen; *Wein etc.* verschneiden; 2. Mischung *f*; ✝ Verschnitt *m*.
blent [blent] *pret. u. p.p. von* blend 1.
bless [bles] segnen; preisen; be-

glücken; ~ me! herrje!; ~ed □ [pret. u. p.p. blest; adj. 'blesid] glückselig; gesegnet; ~ing [~siŋ] Segen m.

blew [blu:] pret. von blow² u. blow³1.

blight [blait] 1. ♀ Mehltau m; fig. Gifthauch m; 2. vernichten.

blind □ [blaind] 1. blind (fig. to gegen); geheim; nicht erkennbar; ~ alley Sackgasse f; ~ly fig. blindlings; 2. Blende f; Fenster-Vorhang m, Jalousie f; Am. Versteck n; Vorwand m; 3. blenden; verblenden (to gegen); abblenden; ~fold ['blaindfould] 1. blindlings; 2. j-m die Augen verbinden; ~worm Blindschleiche f.

blink [bliŋk] 1. Blinzeln n; Schimmer m; 2. v/i. blinzeln; blinken; schimmern; v/t. absichtlich übersehen; ~er ['bliŋkə] Scheuklappe f.

bliss [blis] Seligkeit f, Wonne f.

blister ['blistə] 1. Blase f (auf der Haut, im Lack); Zugpflaster n; 2. Blasen bekommen od. ziehen (auf dat.).

blithe □ mst poet. [blaið] lustig.

blizzard ['blizəd] Schneesturm m.

bloat [blout] aufblasen; aufschwellen; ~er ['bloutə] Bückling m.

block [blɔk] 1. (Häuser-, Schreib-etc.)Block m; Klotz m; Druckstock m; Verstopfung f, Stockung f; 2. formen; verhindern; ~ in entwerfen, skizzieren; mst ~ up (ab-, ver-) sperren; blockieren.

blockade [blɔ'keid] 1. Blockade f; 2. blockieren.

block|head ['blɔkhed] Dummkopf m; ~ letters Druckschrift f.

blond(e f) [blɔnd] 1. blond; 2. Blondine f.

blood [blʌd] Blut n; fig. Blut n; Abstammung f; in cold ~ kalten Blutes, kaltblütig; ~-curdling ['blʌdkə:dliŋ] haarsträubend; ~horse Vollblutpferd n; ~shed Blutvergießen n; ~shot blutunterlaufen; ~thirsty blutdürstig; ~vessel Blutgefäß n; ~y □ ['blʌdi] blutig; blutdürstig.

bloom [blu:m] 1. Blüte f; Reif m auf Früchten; fig. Schmelz m; 2. (er-) blühen (a. fig.).

blossom ['blɔsəm] 1. Blüte f; 2. blühen.

blot [blɔt] 1. Klecks m; fig. Makel m; 2. v/t. beklecksen, beflecken; (ab-) löschen; ausstreichen; v/i. klecksen.

blotch [blɔtʃ] Pustel f; Fleck m.

blotter ['blɔtə] Löscher m; Am. Protokollbuch n. [Löschpapier n.]

blotting-paper ['blɔtiŋpeipə]}

blouse [blauz] Bluse f.

blow¹ [~] Schlag m, Stoß m.

blow² [~] irr.] blühen.

blow³ [~] irr.] 1. v/i. blasen; wehen; schnaufen; ~ up in die Luft fliegen; v/t. (weg- etc.)blasen; wehen; ♪

durchbrennen; ~ one's nose sich die Nase putzen; ~ up sprengen; 2. Blasen n, Wehen n; ~er ['blouə] Bläser m.

blown [bloun] p.p. von blow² und blow³ 1.

blow|-out mot. ['blouaut] Reifenpanne f; ~pipe Gebläsebrenner m.

bludgeon ['blʌdʒən] Knüppel m.

blue [blu:] 1. □ blau; F trüb, schwermütig; 2. Blau n; 3. blau färben; blauen; ~bird ['blu:bə:d] amerikanische Singdrossel; ~ laws Am. strenge (puritanische) Gesetze; ~s [blu:z] pl. Trübsinn f; ♪ Blues m.

bluff [blʌf] 1. □ schroff; steil; derb; 2. Steilufer n; Irreführung f; 3. bluffen, irreführen.

bluish ['blu(:)iʃ] bläulich.

blunder ['blʌndə] 1. Fehler m, Schnitzer m; 2. e-n Fehler machen; stolpern; stümpern; verpfuschen.

blunt [blʌnt] 1. □ stumpf (a. fig.); plump, grob, derb; 2. abstumpfen.

blur [blə:] 1. Fleck(en) m; fig. Verschwommenheit f; 2. v/t. beflecken; verwischen; Sinn trüben.

blush [blʌʃ] 1. Schamröte f; Erröten n; flüchtiger Blick; 2. erröten; (sich) röten.

bluster ['blʌstə] 1. Brausen n, Getöse n; Prahlerei f; 2. brausen; prahlen.

boar [bɔ:] Eber m; hunt. Keiler m.

board [bɔ:d] 1. (Anschlag)Brett n; Konferenztisch m; Ausschuß m; Gremium n; Behörde f; Verpflegung f; Pappe f; on a train Am. in e-m Zug; ♀ of Trade Handelsministerium n; 2. v/t. dielen, verschalen; beköstigen; an Bord gehen; ♣ entern; bsd. Am. einsteigen in (ein Fahr- od. Flugzeug); v/i. in Kost sein; ~er ['bɔ:də] Kostgänger(in); Internatsschüler(in); ~ing-house ['bɔ:diŋhaus] Pension f; ~ing-school ['bɔ:diŋsku:l] Internatsschule f; ~walk bsd. Am. Strandpromenade f.

boast [boust] 1. Prahlerei f; 2. (of, about) sich rühmen (gen.), prahlen (mit); ~ful □ ['boustful] prahlerisch.

boat [bout] Boot n; Schiff n; ~ing ['boutiŋ] Bootfahrt f.

bob [bɔb] 1. Quaste f; Ruck m; Knicks m; Schopf m; sl. Schilling m; 2. v/t. Haar stutzen; ~bed hair Bubikopf m; v/i. springen, tanzen; knicksen.

bobbin ['bɔbin] Spule f (a. ♀).

bobble Am. F ['bɔbl] Fehler m.

bobby sl. ['bɔbi] Schupo m, Polizist m.

bobsleigh ['bɔbslei] Bob(sleigh) m (Rennschlitten).

bode¹ [boud] prophezeien.

bode² [~] pret. von bide.

bodice ['bɔdis] Mieder n; Taille f.

bodily ['bɔdili] körperlich.

body ['bɔdi] Körper m, Leib m; Leichnam m; Körperschaft f; Hauptteil m; mot. Karosserie f; ✕ Truppenkörper m; **~guard** Leibwache f.

Boer ['bouə] Bure m; attr. Buren...

bog [bɔg] 1. Sumpf m, Moor n; 2. im Schlamm versenken.

boggle ['bɔgl] stutzen; pfuschen.

bogus ['bougəs] falsch; Schwindel...

boil [bɔil] 1. kochen, sieden; (sich) kondensieren; 2. Sieden n; Beule f, Geschwür n; **~er** ['bɔilə] (Dampf-) Kessel m.

boisterous □ ['bɔistərəs] ungestüm; heftig, laut; lärmend.

bold □ [bould] kühn; keck, dreist; steil; typ. fett; make ~ sich erkühnen; **~ness** ['bouldnis] Kühnheit f; Keckheit f, Dreistigkeit f.

bolster ['boulstə] 1. Kopfkeil m; Unterlage f; 2. polstern; (unter-) stützen.

bolt [boult] 1. Bolzen m; Riegel m; Blitz(strahl) m; Ausreißen n; 2. adv. ~ upright kerzengerade; 3. v/t. verriegeln; F hinunterschlingen, sieben; v/i. eilen; durchgehen (Pferd); Am. pol. abtrünnig werden; **~er** ['boultə] Ausreißer(in).

bomb [bɔm] 1. Bombe f; 2. mit Bomben belegen.

bombard [bɔm'baːd] bombardieren.

bombastic [bɔm'bæstik] schwülstig.

bomb-proof ['bɔmpruːf] bombensicher.

bond [bɔnd] Band n; Fessel f; Bündnis n; Schuldschein m; ✝ Obligation f; in ~ ✝ unter Zollverschluß; **~age** ['bɔndidʒ] Hörigkeit f; Knechtschaft f; **~(s)man** [~d(z)mən] Leibeigene(r) m.

bone [boun] 1. Knochen m; Gräte f; ~s pl. a. Gebeine n/pl.; ~ of contention Zankapfel m; make no ~s about F nicht lange fackeln mit; 2. die Knochen auslösen (aus); aus-, entgräten.

bonfire ['bɔnfaiə] Freudenfeuer n.

bonnet ['bɔnit] Haube f, Schute(nhut m) f; ⊕ (Motor)Haube f.

bonus ✝ ['bounəs] Prämie f; Gratifikation f; Zulage f.

bony ['bouni] knöchern; knochig.

boob Am. [buːb] Dummkopf m.

booby ['buːbi] Tölpel m.

book [buk] 1. Buch n; Heft n; Liste f; Block m; 2. buchen; eintragen; Fahrkarte etc. lösen; e-n Platz etc. bestellen; Gepäck aufgeben; **~burner** Am. F ['bukbəːnə] intoleranter Mensch; **~case** Bücherschrank m; **~ing-clerk** ['bukiŋklaːk] Schalterbeamte(r) m, -in f; **~ing-office** ['bukiŋɔfis] Fahrkartenausgabe f, -schalter m; thea.

Kasse f; **~ish** □ [~iʃ] gelehrt; **~keeping** Buchführung f; **~let** ['buklit] Büchlein n; Broschüre f; **~seller** Buchhändler m.

boom¹ [buːm] 1. ✝ Aufschwung m, Hochkonjunktur f, Hausse f; Reklamerummel m; 2. in die Höhe treiben od. gehen; für et. Reklame machen.

boom² [~] brummen; dröhnen.

boon¹ [buːn] Segen m, Wohltat f.

boon² [~] freundlich, munter.

boor fig. [buə] Bauer m, Lümmel m; **~ish** □ ['buəriʃ] bäuerisch, lümmel-, flegelhaft.

boost [buːst] heben; verstärken (a. ⚡); Reklame machen.

boot¹ [buːt]: to ~ obendrein.

boot² [~] Stiefel m; Kofferraum m; **~black** Am. ['buːtblæk] = shoeblack; **~ee** ['buːtiː] Damen-Halbstiefel m.

booth [buːð] (Markt- etc.)Bude f; Wahlzelle f; Am. Fernsprechzelle f.

boot|lace ['buːtleis] Schnürsenkel m; **~legger** Am. [~legə] Alkoholschmuggler m.

booty ['buːti] Beute f, Raub m.

border ['bɔːdə] 1. Rand m, Saum m; Grenze f; Einfassung f; Rabatte f; 2. einfassen; grenzen (upon an acc.).

bore¹ [bɔː] 1. Bohrloch n; Kaliber n; fig. langweiliger Mensch; Plage f; 2. bohren; langweilen; belästigen.

bore² [~] pret. von bear².

born [bɔːn] p.p. von bear² gebären.

borne [bɔːn] p.p. von bear² tragen.

borough ['bʌrə] Stadt(teil m) f; Am. a. Wahlbezirk m von New York City; municipal ~ Stadtgemeinde f.

borrow ['bɔrou] borgen, entleihen.

bosom ['buzəm] Busen m; fig. Schoß m.

boss F [bɔs] 1. Boss m, Chef m; bsd. Am. pol. (Partei)Bonze m; 2. leiten; **~y** Am. F ['bɔsi] tyrannisch, herrisch.

botany ['bɔtəni] Botanik f.

botch [bɔtʃ] 1. Flicken m; Flickwerk n; 2. flicken; verpfuschen.

both [bouθ] beide(s); ~ ... and sowohl ... als (auch).

bother F ['bɔðə] 1. Plage f; 2. (sich) plagen, (sich) quälen.

bottle ['bɔtl] 1. Flasche f; 2. auf Flaschen ziehen.

bottom ['bɔtəm] 1. Boden m, Grund m; Grundfläche f, Fuß m, Sohle f; F Hintern m; fig. Wesen n, Kern m; at the ~ ganz unten; fig. im Grunde; 2. grundlegend, Grund...

bough [bau] Ast m, Zweig m.

bought [bɔːt] pret. u. p.p von buy.

boulder ['bouldə] Geröllblock m.

bounce [bauns] 1. Sprung m, Rückprall m; F Aufschneiderei f; Auftrieb m; 2. (hoch)springen; aufschneiden; **~r** ['baunsə] F Mordskerl m; Am. sl. Rausschmeißer m.

bound[1] [baund] 1. *pret. u. p.p von* *bind*; 2. *adj.* verpflichtet; bestimmt, unterwegs (for nach).
bound[2] [~] 1. Grenze *f*, Schranke *f*; 2. begrenzen; beschränken.
bound[3] [~] 1. Sprung *m*; 2. (hoch-)springen; an-, abprallen.
boundary ['baundəri] Grenze *f*.
boundless □ ['baundlis] grenzenlos.
bount|eous □ ['bauntiəs], **~iful** □ [~iful] freigebig; reichlich.
bounty ['baunti] Freigebigkeit *f*; Spende *f*; † Prämie *f*.
bouquet ['bukei] Bukett *n*, Strauß *m*; Blume *f des Weines*.
bout [baut] *Fecht*-Gang *m*; *Tanz*-Tour *f*; ✗ Anfall *m*; Kraftprobe *f*.
bow[1] [bau] 1. Verbeugung *f*; 2. *v/i.* sich (ver)beugen; *v/t.* biegen; beugen.
bow[2] ⚓ [~] Bug *m*.
bow[3] [bou] 1. Bogen *m*; Schleife *f*; 2. geigen.
bowdlerize ['baudləraiz] *Text* von anstößigen Stellen reinigen.
bowels ['bauəlz] *pl.* Eingeweide *n*; *das Innere*; *fig.* Herz *n*.
bower ['bauə] Laube *f*.
bowl[1] [boul] Schale *f*, Schüssel *f*; *Pfeifen*-Kopf *m*.
bowl[2] [~] 1. Kugel *f*, ~s *pl.* Bowling *n*; 2. *v/t.* Ball *etc.* werfen; *v/i.* rollen; kegeln.
box[1] [bɔks] Buchsbaum *m*; Büchse *f*, Schachtel *f*, Kasten *m*; Koffer *m*; ⊕ Gehäuse *n*; *thea.* Loge *f*; Abteilung *f*; 2. in Kästen *etc.* tun.
box[2] [~] 1. boxen; 2.: ~ on the ear Ohrfeige *f*.
Boxing-Day ['bɔksiŋdei] zweiter Weihnachtsfeiertag.
box|-keeper ['bɔkski:pə] Logenschließer(in); **~office** Theaterkasse *f*.
boy [bɔi] Junge *m*, junger Mann; Bursche *m* (a. *Diener*); **~friend** Freund *m*; ~ scout Pfadfinder *m*; **~hood** ['bɔihud] Knabenalter *n*; **~ish** □ ['bɔiiʃ] knabenhaft; kindisch.
brace [breis] 1. ⊕ Strebe *f*; Stützbalken *m*; Klammer *f*; Paar *n* (*Wild, Geflügel*); ~s *pl.* Hosenträger *m/pl.*; 2. absteifen; verankern; (an)spannen; *fig.* stärken.
bracelet ['breislit] Armband *n*.
bracket ['brækit] 1. ⚔ Konsole *f*; Winkelstütze *f*; typ. Klammer *f*; *Leuchter*-Arm *m*; *lower income* ~ niedrige Einkommensstufe; 2. einklammern; *fig.* gleichstellen.
brackish ['brækiʃ] brackig, salzig.
brag [bræg] 1. Prahlerei *f*; 2. prahlen.   [2. □ prahlerisch.)
braggart ['brægət] 1. Prahler *m*; (
braid [breid] 1. *Haar*-Flechte *f*; Borte *f*; Tresse *f*; 2. flechten; mit Borte besetzen.
brain [brein] 1. Gehirn *n*; Kopf *m*

(*fig. mst* ~s = *Verstand*); 2. *j-m* den Schädel einschlagen; **~pan** ['brein-pæn] Hirnschale *f*; **~(s) trust** *Am.* [~n(z)trʌst] Expertenrat *m* (*mst pol.*); **~wave** F Geistesblitz *m*.
brake [breik] 1. ⊕ Bremse *f*; 2. bremsen; **~(s)man** 🚂 ['breik(s)-mən] Bremser *m*; *Am.* Schaffner *m*.
bramble ['bræmbl] Brombeerstrauch *m*.
bran [bræn] Kleie *f*.
branch [brɑ:ntʃ] 1. Zweig *m*; Fach *n*; Linie *f des Stammbaumes*; Zweigstelle *f*; 2. sich ver-, abzweigen.
brand [brænd] 1. (*Feuer*)Brand *m*; Brandmal *n*; Marke *f*; Sorte *f*; 2. einbrennen; brandmarken.
brandish ['brændiʃ] schwingen.
bran(d)-new ['bræn(d)'nju:] nagelneu.
brandy ['brændi] Kognak *m*; Weinbrand *m*.
brass [brɑ:s] Messing *n*; F Unverschämtheit *f*; ~ *band* Blechblaskapelle *f*; ~ *knuckles pl. Am.* Schlagring *m*.
brassière ['bræsiə] Büstenhalter *m*.
brave [breiv] 1. tapfer; prächtig; 2. trotzen; mutig begegnen (*dat.*); **~ry** ['breivəri] Tapferkeit *f*; Pracht *f*.
brawl [brɔ:l] 1. Krakeel *m*, Krawall *m*; 2. krakeelen, Krawall machen.
brawny ['brɔ:ni] muskulös.
bray[1] [brei] 1. Eselsschrei *m*; 2. schreien; schmettern; dröhnen.
bray[2] [~] (zer)stoßen, zerreiben.
brazen □ ['breizn] bronzen; metallisch; *a.* **~faced** unverschämt.
Brazilian [brə'ziljən] 1. brasilianisch; 2. Brasilianer(in).
breach [bri:tʃ] 1. Bruch *m*; *fig.* Verletzung *f*; ✗ Bresche *f*; 2. e-e Bresche schlagen in (*acc.*).
bread [bred] Brot *n*; *know which side one's ~ is buttered* s-n Vorteil (er)kennen.
breadth [bredθ] Breite *f*, Weite *f*, Größe *f des Geistes*; *Tuch*-Bahn *f*.
break [breik] 1. Bruch *m*; Lücke *f*; Pause *f*; Absatz *m*; † *Am.* (Preis-)Rückgang *m*; *Tages*-Anbruch *m*; *a bad* ~ F e-e Dummheit; Pech *n*; *a lucky* ~ Glück *n*; 2. [*irr.*] *v/t.* (zer)brechen; unterbrechen; übertreten; *Tier* abrichten; *Bank* sprengen; *Brief* erbrechen; *Tür* aufbrechen; abbrechen; *Vorrat* anbrechen; *Nachricht* schonend mitteilen; ruinieren; ~ *up* zerbrechen; auflösen; *v/i.* (zer)brechen; aus-, los-, an-, auf-, hervorbrechen; umschlagen (*Wetter*); ~ *away* sich losreißen; ~ *down* zs.-brechen; steckenbleiben; versagen; **~able** ['breikəbl] zerbrechlich; **~age** [~kidʒ] (*a.* † *Waren*)Bruch *m*; **~down** Zs.-bruch *m*; Maschinen-

schaden *m*; *mot.* Panne *f*; **~fast** ['brekfəst] 1. Frühstück *n*; 2. frühstücken; **~-up** ['breik'ʌp] Verfall *m*; Auflösung *f*; Schulschluß *m*; **~water** ['~kwɔːtə] Wellenbrecher *m*.

breast [brest] Brust *f*; Busen *m*; Herz *n*; *make a clean ~ of s.th.* et. offen gestehen; **~-stroke** ['breststrouk] Brustschwimmen *n*.

breath [breθ] Atem(zug) *m*; Hauch *m*; *waste one's ~* s-e Worte verschwenden; **~e** [briːð] *v/i.* atmen; *fig.* leben; *v/t.* (aus-, ein)atmen; hauchen; flüstern; **~less** □ ['breθlis] atemlos.

bred [bred] *pret. u. p.p. von* breed 2.

breeches ['britʃiz] *pl.* Knie-, Reithosen *f/pl.*

breed [briːd] 1. Zucht *f*; Rasse *f*; Herkunft *f*; *Am.* Mischling *m bsd. weiß-indianisch*; 2. [*irr.*] *v/t.* erzeugen; auf-, erziehen; züchten; *v/i.* sich fortpflanzen; **~er** ['briːdə] Erzeuger(in); Züchter(in); **~ing** [~diŋ] Erziehung *f*; Bildung *f*; (Tier-) Zucht *f*.

breez|e [briːz] Brise *f*; **~y** ['briːzi] windig, luftig; frisch, flott.

brethren ['breðrin] *pl.* Brüder *m/pl.*

brevity ['breviti] Kürze *f*.

brew [bruː] 1. *v/t. u. v/i.* brauen; zubereiten; *fig.* anzetteln; 2. Gebräu *n*; **~ery** ['bruəri] Brauerei *f*.

briar ['braiə] = brier.

brib|e [braib] 1. Bestechung(sgeld *n*, -sgeschenk *n*) *f*; 2. bestechen; **~ery** ['braibəri] Bestechung *f*.

brick [brik] 1. Ziegel(stein) *m*; *drop a ~ sl.* ins Fettnäpfchen treten; 2. mauern; **~layer** ['brikleiə] Maurer *m*; **~works** *sg.* Ziegelei *f*.

bridal □ ['braidl] bräutlich; Braut-…; **~** *procession* Brautzug *m*.

bride [braid] Braut *f*, Neuvermählte *f*; **~groom** ['braidgrum] Bräutigam *m*, Neuvermählte(r) *m*; **~smaid** [~dzmeid] Brautjungfer *f*.

bridge [bridʒ] 1. Brücke *f*; 2. e-e Brücke schlagen über (*acc.*); *fig.* überbrücken.

bridle ['braidl] 1. Zaum *m*; Zügel *m*; 2. *v/t.* (auf)zäumen; zügeln; *v/i. a. ~ up* den Kopf zurückwerfen; **~-path**, **~-road** Reitweg *m*.

brief [briːf] 1. □ kurz, bündig; 2. ⚖ schriftliche Instruktion; *hold a ~ for* einstehen für; **~-case** ['briːfkeis] Aktenmappe *f*.

brier ♣ ['braiə] Dorn-, Hagebuttenstrauch *m*, wilde Rose.

brigade ✕ [bri'geid] Brigade *f*.

bright □ [brait] hell, glänzend, klar; lebhaft; gescheit; **~en** ['braitn] *v/t.* auf-, erhellen; polieren; aufheitern; *v/i.* sich aufhellen; **~ness** [~nis] Helligkeit *f*; Glanz *m*; Klarheit *f*; Heiterkeit *f*; Aufgeweckheit *f*.

brillian|ce, **~cy** ['briljəns, ~si] Glanz *m*; **~t** [~nt] 1. □ glänzend; prächtig; 2. Brillant *m*.

brim [brim] 1. Rand *m*; Krempe *f*; 2. bis zum Rande füllen *od.* voll sein; **~full**, **~-ful** ['brim'ful] ganz voll; **~stone** † ['brimstən] Schwefel *m*.

brindle(d) ['brindl(d)] scheckig.

brine [brain] Salzwasser *n*, Sole *f*.

bring [briŋ] [*irr.*] bringen; *j.* veranlassen; *Klage* erheben; *Grund etc.* vorbringen; **~** *about*, **~** *to pass* zustande bringen; **~** *down Preis* herabsetzen; **~** *forth* hervorbringen; gebären; **~** *home to j.* überzeugen; **~** *round* wieder zu sich bringen; **~** *up* auf-, erziehen.

brink [briŋk] Rand *m*.

brisk □ [brisk] lebhaft, munter; frisch; flink; belebend.

bristl|e ['brisl] 1. Borste *f*; 2. (sich) sträuben; hochfahren, zornig werden; **~** *with fig.* starren von; **~ed**, **~y** [~li] gesträubt; struppig.

British ['britiʃ] britisch; *the ~ pl. die* Briten *pl.*; **~er** *bsd. Am.* [~ʃə] Einwohner(in) Großbritanniens.

brittle ['britl] zerbrechlich, spröde.

broach [broutʃ] *Faß* anzapfen; vorbringen; *Thema* anschneiden.

broad □ [brɔːd] breit; weit; hell (*Tag*); deutlich (*Wink etc.*); derb (*Witz*); allgemein; weitherzig, liberal; **~cast** ['brɔːdkɑːst] 1. weitverbreitet; 2. [*irr.* (cast)] weit verbreiten; *Radio:* senden; 3. Rundfunk (-sendung *f*) *m*; **~cloth** feiner Wollstoff; **~-minded** großzügig.

brocade † [brə'keid] Brokat *m*.

broil [brɔil] 1. Lärm *m*, Streit *m*; 2. auf dem Rost braten; *fig.* schmoren.

broke [brouk] 1. *pret. von* break 2; 2. *sl.* pleite, ohne e-n Pfennig; **~n** ['broukən] 1. *p.p. von* break 2; 2.: **~** *health* zerrüttete Gesundheit.

broker ['broukə] Altwarenhändler *m*; Zwangsversteigerer *m*; Makler *m*.

bronc(h)o *Am.* ['brɔŋkou] (halb-) wildes Pferd; **~-buster** [~oubʌstə] Zureiter *m*.

bronze [brɔnz] 1. Bronze *f*; 2. bronzen, Bronze…; 3. bronzieren.

brooch [broutʃ] Brosche *f*, Spange *f*.

brood [bruːd] 1. Brut *f*; *attr.* Zucht…; 2. brüten (*a. fig.*); **~er** *Am.* ['bruːdə] Brutkasten *m*.

brook [bruk] Bach *m*.

broom [brum] Besen *m*; **~stick** ['brumstik] Besenstiel *m*.

broth [brɔθ] Fleischbrühe *f*.

brothel ['brɔθl] Bordell *n*.

brother ['brʌðə] Bruder *m*; **~(s)** *and sister(s)* Geschwister *pl.*; **~hood** [~əhud] Bruderschaft *f*; **~-in-law** [~ərinlɔː] Schwager *m*; **~ly** [~əli] brüderlich.

brought [brɔːt] *pret. u. p.p. von* bring.

brow [brau] (Augen)Braue *f*; Stirn *f*; Rand *m* e-s *Steilhanges*; ⁓**beat** ['braubiːt] [*irr.* (*beat*)] einschüchtern; tyrannisieren.

brown [braun] 1. braun; 2. Braun *n*; 3. (sich) bräunen.

browse [brauz] 1. Grasen *n*; *fig.* Schmökern *n*; 2. grasen, weiden; *fig.* schmökern.

bruise [bruːz] 1. Quetschung *f*; 2. (zer)quetschen.

brunt [brʌnt] Hauptstoß *m*, (volle) Wucht; *das* Schwerste.

brush [brʌʃ] 1. Bürste *f*; Pinsel *m*; *Fuchs-Rute f*; Scharmützel *n*; Unterholz *n*; 2. *v/t.* (ab-, aus)bürsten; streifen; *j.* abbürsten; ⁓ *up* wieder aufbürsten, *fig.* auffrischen; *v/i.* bürsten; (davon)stürzen; ⁓ *against* s.o. *j.* streifen; ⁓**wood** ['brʌʃwud] Gestrüpp *n*, Unterholz *n*.

brusque □ [brusk] brüsk, barsch.

Brussels sprouts ♀ ['brʌsl'sprauts] *pl.* Rosenkohl *m*.

brut|al □ ['bruːtl] viehisch; roh, gemein; ⁓**ality** [bruːˈtæliti] Brutalität *f*, Roheit *f*; ⁓**e** [bruːt] 1. tierisch; unvernünftig; gefühllos; 2. Vieh *n*; □ Untier *n*, Scheusal *n*.

bubble ['bʌbl] 1. Blase *f*; Schwindel *m*; 2. sieden; sprudeln.

buccaneer [bʌkəˈniə] Seeräuber *m*.

buck [bʌk] 1. *zo.* Bock *m*; Stutzer *m*; *Am. sl.* Dollar *m*; 2. *v/i.* bocken; ⁓ *for Am.* sich bemühen um; ⁓ *up* F sich zs.-reißen; *v/t. Am.* F sich stemmen gegen; *Am.* F die Oberhand gewinnen wollen über *et.*

bucket ['bʌkit] Eimer *m*, Kübel *m*.

buckle ['bʌkl] 1. Schnalle *f*; 2. *v/t.* (an-, auf-, um-, zu)schnallen; *v/i.* ⊕ sich (ver)biegen; ⁓ *to a task* sich ernsthaft an eine Aufgabe machen.

buck|shot *hunt.* ['bʌkʃɔt] Rehposten *m*; ⁓**skin** Wildleder *n*.

bud [bʌd] 1. Knospe *f*; *fig.* Keim *m*; 2. *v/t.* ✗ veredeln; *v/i.* knospen.

buddy *Am.* F ['bʌdi] Kamerad *m*.

budge [bʌdʒ] (sich) bewegen.

budget ['bʌdʒit] Vorrat *m*; Staatshaushalt *m*; *draft* ⁓ Haushaltsplan *m*.

buff [bʌf] 1. Ochsenleder *n*; Lederfarbe *f*; 2. lederfarben.

buffalo *zo.* ['bʌfələu] Büffel *m*.

buffer ⚙ ['bʌfə] Puffer *m*; Prellbock *m*.

buffet[1] ['bʌfit] 1. Puff *m*, Stoß *m*, Schlag *m*; 2. puffen, schlagen; kämpfen.

buffet[2] [⁓] Büfett *n*; Anrichte *f*.

buffet[3] ['bufei] Büfett *n*, Theke *f*; Tisch *m* mit Speisen u. Getränken; Erfrischungsraum *m*.

buffoon [bʌˈfuːn] Possenreißer *m*.

bug [bʌg] Wanze *f*; *Am.* Insekt *n*, Käfer *m*; *Am. sl.* Defekt *m*, Fehler *m*; *big* ⁓ *sl.* hohes Tier.

bugle ['bjuːgl] Wald-, Signalhorn *n*.

build [bild] 1. [*irr.*] bauen; errichten; 2. Bauart *f*; Schnitt *m*; ⁓**er** ['bildə] Erbauer *m*, Baumeister *m*; ⁓**ing** [⁓diŋ] Erbauen *n*; Bau *m*, Gebäude *n*; *attr.* Bau...

built [bilt] *pret. u. p.p. von* build 1.

bulb [bʌlb] ♀ Zwiebel *f*, Knolle *f*; (Glüh)Birne *f*.

bulge [bʌldʒ] 1. (Aus)Bauchung *f*; Anschwellung *f*; 2. sich (aus)bauchen; (an)schwellen; hervorquellen.

bulk [bʌlk] Umfang *m*; Masse *f*; Hauptteil *m*; ⚓ Ladung *f*; *in* ⁓ *lose*; *in großer Menge*; ⁓**y** ['bʌlki] umfangreich; unhandlich; ⚓ sperrig.

bull[1] [bul] 1. Bulle *m*, Stier *m*; ✝ *sl.* Haussier *m*; 2. ✝ *die Kurse* treiben.

bull[2] [⁓] päpstliche Bulle.

bulldog ['buldɔg] Bulldogge *f*.

bulldoze *Am.* F ['buldouz] terrorisieren; ⁓**r** ⊕ [⁓zə] Bulldozer *m*, Planierraupe *f*.

bullet ['bulit] Kugel *f*, Geschoß *n*.

bulletin ['bulitin] Tagesbericht *m*; ⁓ *board Am.* Schwarzes Brett.

bullion ['buljən] Gold-, Silberbarren *m*; Gold-, Silberlitze *f*.

bully ['buli] 1. Maulheld *m*; Tyrann *m*; 2. prahlerisch; *Am.* F prima; 3. einschüchtern; tyrannisieren.

bulwark *mst fig.* ['bulwək] Bollwerk *n*.

bum *Am.* F [bʌm] 1. Nichtstuer *m*, Vagabund *m*; 2. *v/t.* nassauern.

bumble-bee ['bʌmblbiː] Hummel *f*.

bump [bʌmp] 1. Schlag *m*; Beule *f*; *fig.* Sinn *m* (of *für*); 2. (zs.-)stoßen; holpern; *Rudern:* überholen.

bumper ['bʌmpə] volles Glas (*Wein*); F *et. Riesiges; mot. Stoßstange f; ⁓ crop Rekorderntef; ⁓ house thea.* volles Haus.

bun [bʌn] 1. Rosinenbrötchen *n*; *Haar-Knoten m*.

bunch [bʌntʃ] 1. Bund *n*; Büschel *n*; Haufen *m*; ⁓ *of grapes* Weintraube *f*; 2. (zs.-)bündeln; bauschen.

bundle ['bʌndl] 1. Bündel *n*, Bund *n*; 2. *v/t. a.* ⁓ *up* (zs.-)bündeln.

bung [bʌŋ] Spund *m*.

bungalow ['bʌŋgəlou] Bungalow *m* (*einstöckiges Haus*).

bungle ['bʌŋgl] 1. Pfuscherei *f*; 2. (ver)pfuschen.

bunion ✗ ['bʌnjən] entzündeter Fußballen.

bunk[1] *Am. sl.* [bʌŋk] Quatsch *m*.

bunk[2] [⁓] Schlafkoje *f*.

bunny ['bʌni] Kaninchen *n*.

buoy ⚓ [bɔi] 1. Boje *f*; 2. *Fahrwasser betonnen; mst* ⁓ *up fig.* aufrechterhalten; ⁓**ant** □ ['bɔiənt] schwimmfähig; hebend; spannkräftig; *fig.* heiter.

burden ['bəːdn] 1. Last *f*; Bürde *f*; ⚓ Ladung *f*; ⚓ Tragfähigkeit *f*;

2. beladen; belasten; **~some** [~n-səm] lästig; drückend.

bureau [bjuə'rou] Büro *n*, Geschäftszimmer *n*; Schreibpult *n*; *Am.* Kommode *f*; **~cracy** [~'rɔ-krəsi] Bürokratie *f*.

burg *Am.* F [bə:g] Stadt *f*.

burgess ['bə:dʒis] Bürger *m*.

burglar ['bə:glə] Einbrecher *m*; **~y** [~əri] Einbruch(sdiebstahl) *m*.

burial ['beriəl] Begräbnis *n*.

burlesque [bə:'lesk] **1.** possenhaft; **2.** Burleske *f*, Posse *f*; **3.** parodieren.

burly ['bə:li] stämmig, kräftig.

burn [bə:n] **1.** Brandwunde *f*; Brandmal *n*; **2.** [*irr.*] (ver-, an-) brennen; **~er** [bə:nə] Brenner *m*.

burnish ['bə:niʃ] polieren, glätten.

burnt [bə:nt] *pret. u. p.p. von* burn **2.**

burrow ['bʌrou] **1.** Höhle *f*, Bau *m*; **2.** (sich ein-, ver)graben.

burst [bə:st] **1.** Bersten *n*; Krach *m*; Riß *m*; Ausbruch *m*; **2.** [*irr.*] *v/i.* bersten, platzen; zerspringen; explodieren; ~ *from* sich losreißen von; ~ *forth*, ~ *out* hervorbrechen; ~ *into tears* in Tränen ausbrechen; *v/t.* (zer)sprengen.

bury ['beri] be-, vergraben; beerdigen; verbergen.

bus F [bʌs] (Omni)Bus *m*; ~ *boy Am.* Kellnergehilfe *m*.

bush [buʃ] Busch *m*; Gebüsch *n*.

bushel ['buʃl] Scheffel *m* (*36,37 Liter*).

bushy ['buʃi] buschig.

business ['biznis] Geschäft *n*; Beschäftigung *f*; Beruf *m*; Angelegenheit *f*; Aufgabe *f*; ✝ Handel *m*; ~ *of the day* Tagesordnung *f*; on ~ geschäftlich; *have no* ~ *to inf.* nicht befugt sein zu *inf.*; *mind one's own* ~ sich um s-e eigenen Angelegenheiten kümmern; **~ hours** *pl.* Geschäftszeit *f*; **~like** geschäftsmäßig; sachlich; **~man** Geschäftsmann *m*; **~ tour**, **~ trip** Geschäftsreise *f*.

bust[1] [bʌst] Büste *f*.

bust[2] *Am.* F [~] Bankrott *m*.

bustle ['bʌsl] **1.** Geschäftigkeit *f*; geschäftiges Treiben *n*; **2.** *v/i.* (umher)wirtschaften; hasten; *v/t.* hetzen, jagen.

busy □ ['bizi] **1.** beschäftigt; geschäftig; fleißig (*at* bei, an dat.); lebhaft; *Am. teleph.* besetzt; **2.** (*mst* ~ *o.s.* sich) beschäftigen (*with, in, at, about, ger.* mit).

but [bʌt, bət] **1.** *cj.* aber, jedoch, sondern; *a.* ~ *that* wenn nicht; indessen; **2.** *prp.* außer; *the last* ~ *one* der vorletzte; *the next* ~ *one* der übernächste; ~ *for* wenn nicht ... gewesen wäre; ohne; **3.** *nach Negation:* der (die *od.* das) nicht; *there is*

no one ~ *knows* es gibt niemand, der nicht wüßte; **4.** *adv.* nur; ~ *just* soeben, eben erst; ~ *now* erst jetzt; *all* ~ fast, nahe daran; *nothing* ~ nur; *I cannot* ~ *inf.* ich kann nur *inf.*

butcher ['butʃə] **1.** Schlächter *m*, Fleischer *m*, Metzger *m*; *fig.* Mörder *m*; **2.** (*fig.* ab-, hin)schlachten; **~y** [~əri] Schlächterei *f*; Schlachthaus *n*.

butler ['bʌtlə] Butler *m*; Kellermeister *m*.

butt [bʌt] **1.** Stoß *m*; *a.* ~ *end* (dickes) Ende *e-s Baumes etc.*; Stummel *m*, Kippe *f*; *Gewehr*-Kolben *m*; Schießstand *m*; (End)Ziel *n*; *fig.* Zielscheibe *f*; **2.** (mit dem Kopf) stoßen.

butter ['bʌtə] **1.** Butter *f*; F Schmeichelei *f*; **2.** mit Butter bestreichen; **~cup** Butterblume *f*; **~fingered** tolpatschig; **~fly** Schmetterling *m*; **~y** [~əri] **1.** butter(art)ig; Butter...; **2.** Speisekammer *f*.

buttocks ['bʌtəks] *pl.* Gesäß *n*.

button ['bʌtn] **1.** Knopf *m*; Knospe *f*; **2.** an-, zuknöpfen.

buttress ['bʌtris] **1.** Strebepfeiler *m*; *fig.* Stütze *f*; **2.** (unter)stützen.

buxom ['bʌksəm] drall, stramm.

buy [bai] [*irr.*] *v/t.* (an-, ein)kaufen (*from* bei); **~er** ['baiə] (Ein)Käufer (-in).

buzz [bʌz] **1.** Gesumm *n*; Geflüster *n*; ~ *saw Am.* Kreissäge *f*; **2.** *v/i.* summen; surren; ~ *about* herumschwirren, herumeilen.

buzzard ['bʌzəd] Bussard *m*.

by [bai] **1.** *prp. Raum:* bei; an, neben; *Richtung:* durch, über; an (*dat.*) entlang *od.* vorüber; *Zeit:* an, bei; spätestens bis, bis zu; *Urheber, Ursache:* von, durch (*bsd. beim pass.*); *Mittel, Werkzeug:* durch, mit; *Art u. Weise:* bei; *Schwur:* bei; *Maß:* um, bei; *Richtschnur:* gemäß, bei; ~ *the dozen* dutzendweise; ~ *o.s.* allein; ~ *land* zu Lande; ~ *rail* per Bahn; *day* ~ *day* Tag für Tag; ~ *twos* zu zweien; **2.** *adv.* dabei; vorbei; beiseite; ~ *and* ~ nächstens, bald; nach und nach; ~ *the* ~ nebenbei bemerkt; ~ *and large Am.* im großen und ganzen; **3.** *adj.* Neben...; Seiten...; **~-election** ['baiilekʃən] Nachwahl *f*; **~gone** vergangen; **~-law** Ortsstatut *n*; **~s** *pl.* Satzung *f*, Statuten *n/pl.*; **~-line** *Am.* Verfasserangabe *f zu e-m Artikel*; **~-name** Bei-, Spitzname *m*; **~-pass** Umgehungsstraße *f*; **~-path** Seitenpfad *m*; **~-product** Nebenprodukt *n*; **~-road** Seitenweg *m*; **~stander** Zuschauer *m*; **~street** Neben-, Seitenstraße *f*; **~way** Seitenweg *m*; **~-word** Sprichwort *n*; Inbegriff *m*; *be a* ~ *for* sprichwörtlich bekannt sein wegen.

C

cab [kæb] Droschke f, Mietwagen m, Taxi n; ⚓ Führerstand m.

cabbage ♀ ['kæbidʒ] Kohl m.

cabin ['kæbin] **1.** Hütte f; ✈ Kabine f, Kajüte f; Kammer f; **2.** einpferchen; **~boy** Schiffsjunge m; **~ cruiser** ⚓ Kabinenkreuzer m.

cabinet ['kæbinit] Kabinett n, Ministerrat m; Schrank m, Vitrine f; (Radio)Gehäuse n; **~ council** Kabinettssitzung f; **~-maker** Kunsttischler m.

cable ['keibl] **1.** Kabel n; ⚓ Ankertau n; **2.** tel. kabeln; **~-car** Kabine f, Gondel f; Drahtseilbahn f; **~gram** [‿lgræm] Kabeltelegramm n.

cabman ['kæbmən] Droschkenkutscher m, Taxifahrer m.

caboose [kə'buːs] ⚓ Kombüse f; Am. ⚒ Eisenbahnerwagen m am Güterzug.

cab-stand ['kæbstænd] Taxi-, Droschkenstand m.

cacao [kə'kɑːou] Kakaobaum m, -bohne f.

cackle ['kækl] **1.** Gegacker n, Geschnatter n; **2.** gackern, schnattern.

cad F [kæd] Prolet m; Kerl m.

cadaverous □ [kə'dævərəs] leichenhaft; leichenblaß.

cadence ♪ ['keidəns] Kadenz f; Tonfall m; Rhythmus m.

cadet [kə'det] Kadett m.

café ['kæfei] Café n.

cafeteria bsd. Am. [kæfi'tiəriə] Restaurant n mit Selbstbedienung.

cage [keidʒ] **1.** Käfig m; Kriegsgefangenenlager n; ✕ Förderkorb m; **2.** einsperren.

cagey □ bsd. Am. F ['keidʒi] gerissen, raffiniert.

cajole [kə'dʒoul] j-m schmeicheln; j-n beschwatzen.

cake [keik] **1.** Kuchen m; Tafel f Schokolade, Riegel m Seife etc.; **2.** zs.-backen.

calami|tous □ [kə'læmitəs] elend; katastrophal; **~ty** [‿ti] Elend n, Unglück n; Katastrophe f.

calcify ['kælsifai] (sich) verkalken.

calculat|e ['kælkjuleit] v/t. kalkulieren; be-, aus-, errechnen; v/i. rechnen (on, upon auf acc.); Am. F vermuten; **~ion** [kælkju'leiʃən] Kalkulation f, Berechnung f; Voranschlag m; Überlegung f.

caldron ['kɔːldrən] Kessel m.

calendar ['kælində] **1.** Kalender m; Liste f; **2.** registrieren.

calf [kɑːf], pl. **calves** [kɑːvz] Kalb n; Wade f; a. **~-leather** ['kɑːfleðə] Kalbleder n; **~-skin** Kalbfell n.

calibre ['kælibə] Kaliber n.

calico ✝ ['kælikou] Kaliko m.

call [kɔːl] **1.** Ruf m; teleph. Anruf m,

Gespräch n; fig. Berufung f (to in ein Amt; auf e-n Lehrstuhl); Aufruf m; Aufforderung f; Signal n; Forderung f; Besuch m; Nachfrage f (for nach); Kündigung f v. Geldern; on ~ ✝ auf Abruf; **2.** v/t. (herbei-) rufen; (an)rufen; (ein)berufen; Am. Baseball: Spiel abbrechen; fig. berufen (to in ein Amt); nennen; wecken; Aufmerksamkeit lenken (to auf acc.); be **~ed** heißen; **~** s.o. names j. beschimpfen, beleidigen; **~** down bsd. Am. F anpfeifen; **~** in Geld kündigen; **~** over Namen verlesen; **~** up aufrufen; teleph. anrufen; v/i. rufen; teleph. anrufen; vorsprechen (at an e-m Ort; on s.o. bei j-m); **~** at a port e-n Hafen anlaufen; **~** for rufen nach; et. fordern; abholen; to be (left till) **~ed** for postlagernd; **~** on sich an j. wenden (for wegen); j. berufen, auffordern (to inf. zu); **~box** ['kɔːlbɔks] Fernsprechzelle f; **~er** ['kɔːlə] teleph. Anrufer(in); Besucher(in).

calling ['kɔːliŋ] Rufen n; Berufung f; Beruf m; **~ card** Am. Visitenkarte f.

call-office ['kɔːlɔfis] Fernsprechstelle f.

callous □ ['kæləs] schwielig; fig. dickfellig; herzlos.

callow ['kælou] nackt (ungefiedert); fig. unerfahren.

calm [kɑːm] **1.** □ still, ruhig; **2.** (Wind)Stille f, Ruhe f; **3.** (~ down sich) beruhigen; besänftigen.

calori|c phys. [kə'lɔrik] Wärme f; **~e** phys. ['kæləri] Wärmeeinheit f.

column|iate [kə'lʌmnieit] verleumden; **~iation** [kəlʌmni'eiʃən], **~y** ['kæləmni] Verleumdung f.

calve [kɑːv] kalben; **~s** [kɑːvz] pl. von calf.

cambric ✝ ['keimbrik] Batist m.

came [keim] pret. von come.

camel zo., ⚓ ['kæməl] Kamel n.

camera ['kæmərə] Kamera f; in zᵈ unter Ausschluß der Öffentlichkeit.

camomile ♀ ['kæməmail] Kamille f.

camouflage ✕ ['kæmuflɑːʒ] **1.** Tarnung f; **2.** tarnen.

camp [kæmp] **1.** Lager n; ✕ Feldlager n; **~ bed** Feldbett n; **2.** lagern; **~** out zelten.

campaign [kæm'pein] **1.** Feldzug m; **2.** e-n Feldzug mitmachen od. führen.

camphor ['kæmfə] Kampfer m.

campus Am. ['kæmpəs] Universitätsgelände n.

can¹ [kæn] [irr.] v/aux. können, fähig sein zu; dürfen.

can² [‿] **1.** Kanne f; Am. Büchse f; **2.** Am. in Büchsen konservieren.

Canadian [kə'neidjən] 1. kanadisch; 2. Kanadier(in).

canal [kə'næl] Kanal m (a. ☸).

canard [kæ'nɑːd] (Zeitungs)Ente f.

canary [kə'nɛəri] Kanarienvogel m.

cancel ['kænsəl] (durch)streichen; entwerten; absagen; a. ~ out fig. aufheben; be ~led ausfallen.

cancer ast., ☸ ['kænsə] Krebs m; ~ous [~rəs] krebsartig.

candid □ ['kændid] aufrichtig; offen.

candidate ['kændidit] Kandidat m (for für), Bewerber m (for um).

candied ['kændid] kandiert.

candle ['kændl] Licht n, Kerze f; burn the ~ at both ends mit s-n Kräften Raubbau treiben; ~stick Leuchter m.

cando(u)r ['kændə] Aufrichtigkeit f.

candy ['kændi] 1. Kandis(zucker) m; Am. Süßigkeiten f/pl.; 2. v/t. kandieren.

cane [kein] 1. ♀ Rohr n; (Rohr-)Stock m; 2. prügeln.

canine ['keinain] Hunde...

canker ['kæŋkə] ☸ Mundkrebs m; ♀ Brand m.

canned Am. [kænd] Büchsen...

cannery Am. ['kænəri] Konservenfabrik f.

cannibal ['kænibal] Kannibale m.

cannon ['kænən] Kanone f.

cannot ['kænɔt] nicht können etc.; s. can¹.

canoe [kə'nuː] Kanu n; Paddelboot n.

canon ['kænən] Kanon m; Regel f; Richtschnur f; ~ize [~naiz] heiligsprechen.

canopy ['kænəpi] Baldachin m; fig. Dach n; ∆ Überdachung f.

cant¹ [kænt] 1. Schrägung f; Stoß m; 2. kippen; kanten.

cant² [~] 1. Zunftsprache f; Gewäsch n; scheinheiliges Gerede; 2. zunftmäßig od. scheinheilig reden.

can't F [kɑːnt] = cannot.

cantankerous F □ [kən'tæŋkərəs] zänkisch, mürrisch.

canteen [kæn'tiːn] ✕ Feldflasche f; Kantine f; ✕ Kochgeschirr n; Besteckkasten m.

canton 1. ['kæntən] Bezirk m; 2. ✕ [kən'tuːn] (sich) einquartieren.

canvas ['kænvəs] Segeltuch n; Zelt (-e pl.) n; Zeltbahn f; Segel n/pl.; paint. Leinwand f; Gemälde n.

canvass [~] 1. (Stimmen)Werbung f; Am. a. Wahlnachprüfung f; 2. v/t. erörtern; v/i. (Stimmen, a. Kunden) werben.

caoutchouc ['kautʃuk] Kautschuk m.

cap [kæp] 1. Kappe f; Mütze f; Haube f; ⊕ Aufsatz m; Zündhütchen n; set one's ~ at sich e-n Mann

angeln (Frau); 2. mit e-r Kappe etc. bedecken; fig. krönen; F übertreffen; die Mütze abnehmen.

capab|ility [keipə'biliti] Fähigkeit f; ~le □ ['keipəbl] fähig (of zu).

capaci|ous □ [kə'peiʃəs] geräumig; ~ty [kə'pæsiti] Inhalt m; Aufnahmefähigkeit f; geistige (od. ⊕ Leistungs)Fähigkeit f (for ger. zu inf.); Stellung f; in my ~ as in meiner Eigenschaft als.

cape¹ [keip] Kap n, Vorgebirge n.

cape² [~] Cape n, Umhang m.

caper ['keipə] 1. Kapriole f, Luftsprung m; cut ~s = 2. Kapriolen od. Sprünge machen.

capital ['kæpitl] 1. □ Kapital...; todeswürdig, Todes...; hauptsächlich, Haupt...; vortrefflich; ~ crime Kapitalverbrechen n; ~ punishment Todesstrafe f; 2. Hauptstadt f; Kapital n; mst ~ letter Großbuchstabe m; ~ism [~təlizəm] Kapitalismus m; ~ize [kə'pitəlaiz] kapitalisieren.

capitulate [kə'pitjuleit] kapitulieren (to vor dat.).

capric|e [kə'priːs] Laune f; ~ious □ [~iʃəs] kapriziös, launisch.

Capricorn ast. ['kæprikɔːn] Steinbock m.

capsize [kæp'saiz] v/i. kentern; v/t. zum Kentern bringen.

capsule ['kæpsjuːl] Kapsel f.

captain ['kæptin] Führer m; Feldherr m; ⚓ Kapitän m; ✕ Hauptmann m.

caption ['kæpʃən] 1. Überschrift f; Titel m; Film: Untertitel m; 2. v/t. Am. mit Überschrift etc. versehen.

captious □ ['kæpʃəs] spitzfindig.

captiv|ate ['kæptiveit] fig. gefangennehmen, fesseln; ~e ['kæptiv] 1. gefangen, gefesselt; 2. Gefangene(r m) f; ~ity [kæp'tiviti] Gefangenschaft f.

capture ['kæptʃə] 1. Eroberung f; Gefangennahme f; 2. (ein)fangen; erobern; erbeuten; ⚓ kapern.

car [kɑː] Auto n; (Eisenbahn-, Straßenbahn-)Wagen m; Ballonkorb m; Luftschiff-Gondel f; Kabine f e-s Aufzugs.

caramel ['kærəmel] Karamel m; Karamelle f.

caravan ['kærəvæn] Karawane f; Wohnwagen m.

caraway ♀ ['kærəwei] Kümmel m.

carbine ['kɑːbain] Karabiner m.

carbohydrate ↑ ['kɑːbou'haidreit] Kohle(n)hydrat n.

carbon ['kɑːbən] ↑ Kohlenstoff m; ~ copy Brief-Durchschlag m; ~ paper Kohlepapier n.

carburet(t)or mot. ['kɑːbjuretə] Vergaser m.

car|case, mst ~cass ['kɑːkəs] (Tier-)Kadaver m; Fleischerei: Rumpf m.

card [kɑːd] Karte f; have a ~ up

one's sleeve et. in petto haben; **~board** ['kɑ:dbɔ:d] Kartonpapier *n*; Pappe *f*; ~ *box* Pappkarton *m*.

cardigan ['kɑ:digən] Wolljacke *f*.

cardinal □ ['kɑ:dinl] 1. Haupt...; hochrot; ~ *number* Grundzahl *f*; 2. Kardinal *m*.

card-index ['kɑ:dindeks] Kartei *f*.

card-sharper ['kɑ:dʃɑ:pə] Falschspieler *m*.

care [kɛə] 1. Sorge *f*; Sorgfalt *f*, Obhut *f*, Pflege *f*; *medical* ~ ärztliche Behandlung; ~ *of* (*abbr.* c/o) ... per Adresse, bei ...; *take* ~ *of* acht(geb)en auf (*acc.*); *with* ~*!* Vorsicht!; 2. Lust haben (*to inf.* zu); ~ *for* sorgen für; sich kümmern um; sich etwas machen aus; *I don't* ~ *!* F meinetwegen!; *I couldn't* ~ *less* F es ist mir völlig egal; *well* ~*d-for* gepflegt. [bahn *f*; 2. rasen.\

career [kə'riə] 1. Karriere *f*; Lauf-⌐

carefree ['kɛəfri:] sorgenfrei.

careful □ ['kɛəful] besorgt (*for* um), achtsam (*of* auf *acc.*); vorsichtig; sorgfältig; ~**ness** [~lnis] Sorgsamkeit *f*; Vorsicht *f*; Sorgfalt *f*.

careless □ ['kɛəlis] sorglos; nachlässig; unachtsam; leichtsinnig; ~**ness** [~snis] Sorglosigkeit *f*; Nachlässigkeit *f*.

caress [kə'res] 1. Liebkosung *f*; 2. liebkosen; *fig.* schmeicheln.

caretaker ['kɛəteikə] Wärter(in); (Haus)Verwalter(in).

care-worn ['kɛəwɔ:n] abgehärmt.

carfare *Am.* ['kɑ:fɛə] Fahrgeld *n*.

cargo ⚓ ['kɑ:gou] Ladung *f*.

caricature [kærikə'tjuə] 1. Karikatur *f*; 2. karikieren.

carmine ['kɑ:main] Karmin(rot) *n*.

carn|al □ ['kɑ:nl] fleischlich; sinnlich; ~**ation** [kɑ:'neiʃən] 1. Fleischton *m*; ♀ Nelke *f*; 2. blaßrot.

carnival ['kɑ:nivəl] Karneval *m*.

carnivorous [kɑ:'nivərəs] fleischfressend.

carol ['kærəl] 1. Weihnachtslied *n*; 2. Weihnachtslieder singen.

carous|e [kə'rauz] 1. *a.* ~**al** [~ʒəl] (Trink)Gelage *n*; 2. zechen.

carp [kɑ:p] Karpfen *m*.

carpent|er ['kɑ:pintə] Zimmermann *m*; ~**ry** [~tri] Zimmerhandwerk *n*; Zimmermannsarbeit *f*.

carpet ['kɑ:pit] 1. Teppich *m*; *bring on the* ~ aufs Tapet bringen; 2. mit e-m Teppich belegen; ~**bag** Reisetasche *f*; ~**bagger** [~tbægə] politischer Abenteurer.

carriage ['kæridʒ] Beförderung *f*, Transport *m*; Fracht *f*; Wagen *m*; Fuhr-, Frachtlohn *m*; Haltung *f*; Benehmen *n*; ~**drive** Anfahrt *f* (*vor e-m Hause*); ~**free**, ~**paid** frachtfrei; ~**way** Fahrbahn *f*.

carrier ['kæriə] Fuhrmann *m*; Spediteur *m*; Träger *m*; Gepäckträger *m*; ~**pigeon** Brieftaube *f*.

carrion ['kæriən] Aas *n*; *attr.* Aas...

carrot ['kærət] Mohrrübe *f*.

carry ['kæri] 1. *v/t. wohin* bringen, führen, tragen (*a. v/i.*), fahren, befördern; (*bei sich*) haben; *Ansicht* durchsetzen; *Gewinn, Preis* davontragen; *Zahlen* übertragen; *Ernte, Zinsen* tragen; *Mauer* etc. weiterführen; *Benehmen* fortsetzen; *Antrag, Kandidaten* durchbringen; ✗ erobern; *be carried* angenommen werden (*Antrag*); durchkommen (*Kandidat*); ~ *the day* den Sieg davontragen; ~ *forward od. over* ⤵ übertragen; ~ *on* fortsetzen, weiterführen; *Geschäft etc.* betreiben; ~ *out od. through* durchführen; 2. *Trag-, Schußweite *f*.

cart [kɑ:t] 1. Karren *m*; Wagen *m*; *put the* ~ *before the horse fig.* das Pferd beim Schwanz aufzäumen; 2. karren, fahren; ~**age** ['kɑ:tidʒ] Fahren *n*; Fuhrlohn *m*.

carter ['kɑ:tə] Fuhrmann *m*.

cartilage ['kɑ:tilidʒ] Knorpel *m*.

carton ['kɑ:tən] Karton *m*.

cartoon [kɑ:'tu:n] *paint.* Karton *m*; ⊕ Musterzeichnung *f*; Karikatur *f*; Zeichentrickfilm *m*; ~**ist** [~nist] Karikaturist *m*.

cartridge ['kɑ:tridʒ] Patrone *f*; ~**paper** Zeichenpapier *n*.

cart-wheel [kɑ:'twi:l] Wagenrad *n*; *Am.* Silberdollar *m*; *turn* ~s radschlagen.

carve [kɑ:v] *Fleisch* vorschneiden, zerlegen; schnitzen; meißeln; ~**r** ['kɑ:və] (Bild)Schnitzer *m*; Vorschneider *m*; Vorlegemesser *n*.

carving ['kɑ:viŋ] Schnitzerei *f*.

cascade [kæs'keid] Wasserfall *m*.

case¹ [keis] *m* Behälter *m*; Kiste *f*; Etui *n*; Gehäuse *n*; Schachtel *f*; Fach *n*; *typ.* Setzkasten *m*; 2. (ein-) stecken; ver-, umkleiden.

case² [~] *Fall m* (*a. gr.*, ✘, ⚕); *gr.* Kasus *m*; ✘ *a. Kranke(r) m f*; *Am.* F komischer Kauz; ⚕ Schriftsatz *m*; Hauptargument *n*; Sache *f*, Angelegenheit *f*.

case-harden ⊕ ['keishɑ:dn] hartgießen; ~*ed fig.* hartgesotten.

case-history ['keishistəri] Vorgeschichte *f*; Krankengeschichte *f*.

casement ['keismənt] Fensterflügel *m*; ~ *window* Flügelfenster *n*.

cash [kæʃ] 1. Bargeld *n*, Kasse *f*; ~ *down, for* ~ gegen bar; ~ *on delivery* Lieferung *f* gegen bar; (per) Nachnahme *f*; ~ *register* Registrierkasse *f*; 2. einkassieren, einlösen; ~**book** ['kæʃbuk] Kassabuch *n*; ~**ier** [kæ'ʃiə] Kassierer(in).

casing ['keisiŋ] Überzug *m*, Gehäuse *n*, Futteral *m*; ⚓ Verkleidung *f*.

cask [kɑ:sk] Faß *n*.

casket ['kɑ:skit] Kassette *f*; *Am.* Sarg *m*.

casserole ['kæsəroul] Kasserolle f.
cassock eccl. ['kæsək] Soutane f.
cast [ka:st] **1.** Wurf m; ⊕ Guß
(-form f) m; Abguß m, Abdruck m;
Schattierung f, Anflug m; Form f,
Art f; ♣ Auswerfen n von Senkblei
etc.; thea. (Rollen)Besetzung f;
2. [irr.] v/t. (ab-, aus-, hin-, um-,
weg)werfen; zo. Haut etc. abwerfen; Zähne etc. verlieren; verwerfen; gestalten; ⊕ gießen; a.
~ up aus-, zs.-rechnen; thea. Rolle
besetzen; Rolle übertragen (to
dat.); be ~ in a lawsuit ⚖ e-n
Prozeß verlieren; ~ lots losen (for
um); ~ in one's lot with s.o. j-s Los
teilen; be ~ down niedergeschlagen
sein; v/i. sich gießen lassen; ⊕
sich (ver)werfen; ~ about for sinnen
auf (acc.); sich et. überlegen.
castanet [kæstə'net] Kastagnette f.
castaway ['ka:stəwei] **1.** verworfen,
♣ schiffbrüchig; **2.** Verworfene(r
m) f; Schiffbrüchige(r m) f.
caste [ka:st] Kaste f (a. fig.).
castigate ['kæstigeit] züchtigen;
fig. geißeln.
cast iron ['ka:st'aiən] Gußeisen n;
cast-iron gußeisern.
castle ['ka:sl] Burg f, Schloß n;
Schach: Turm m.
castor[1] ['ka:stə]: ~ oil Rizinusöl n.
castor[2] [..] Laufrolle f unter Möbeln;
(Salz-, Zucker- etc.) Streuer m.
castrate [kæs'treit] kastrieren.
cast steel ['ka:ststi:l] Gußstahl m;
cast-steel aus Gußstahl.
casual ☐ ['kæʒjuəl] zufällig; gelegentlich; F lässig; ~ty [..lti] Unfall m; ⚔ Verlust m.
cat [kæt] Katze f; ~ burglar Fas-
sadenkletterer m.
catalo|gue, Am. ~g ['kætəlɔg] **1.** Ka-
talog m; Am. univ. Vorlesungs-
verzeichnis n; **2.** katalogisieren.
catapult ['kætəpʌlt] Schleuder f;
⚔ Katapult m, n.
cataract ['kætərækt] Katarakt m,
Wasserfall m; ⚕ grauer Star.
catarrh [kə'ta:] Katarrh m; Schnupfen m.
catastrophe [kə'tæstrəfi] Kata-
strophe f.
catch [kætʃ] **1.** Fang m; Beute f,
fig. Vorteil m; ♪ Rundgesang m;
Kniff m; ⊕ Haken m, Griff m,
Klinke f; **2.** [irr.] v/t. fassen, fest-
kriegen; fangen, ergreifen; ertappen; Blick etc. auffangen; Zug
etc. erreichen; bekommen; sich
Krankheit zuziehen, holen; fig. erfassen; ~ (a) cold sich erkälten; ~
s.o.'s eye j-m ins Auge fallen; ~ up
auffangen; F j. unterbrechen; einholen; **3.** v/i. sich verfangen, hängenbleiben; fassen, einschnappen
(Schloß etc.); ~ on F Anklang
finden; Am. F kapieren; ~ up with
⁖. einholen; ~all ['kætʃɔ:l] Am.

Platz m od. Behälter m für alles
mögliche (a. fig. u. attr.); ~er [..ʃə]
Fänger(in); ~ing [..ʃiŋ] packend; ⚕
ansteckend; ~line Schlagzeile f;
~word Schlagwort n; Stichwort n.
catechism ['kætikizəm] Katechismus m.
categor|ical ☐ [kæti'gɔrikəl] kate-
gorisch; ~y ['kætigəri] Kategorie f.
cater ['keitə]: ~ for Lebensmittel
liefern für; fig. sorgen für; ~ing
[..əriŋ] Verpflegung f.
caterpillar ['kætəpilə] zo. Raupe f;
⊕ Raupe(nschlepper m) f.
catgut ['kætgʌt] Darmsaite f.
cathedral [kə'θi:drəl] Dom m,
Kathedrale f.
Catholic ['kæθəlik] **1.** katholisch;
2. Katholik(in).
catkin ♀ ['kætkin] Kätzchen n.
cattish fig. ['kætiʃ] falsch.
cattle ['kætl] Vieh n; ~-breeding
Viehzucht f; ~-plague vet. Rinder-
pest f.   [catch 2.]
caught [kɔ:t] pret. u. p.p. von]
ca(u)ldron ['kɔ:ldrən] Kessel m.
cauliflower ♀ ['kɔliflauə] Blumen-
kohl m.
caulk ♣ [kɔ:k] kalfatern (abdichten).
caus|al ☐ ['kɔ:zəl] ursächlich; ~e
[kɔ:z] **1.** Ursache f, Grund m; ⚖
Klage(grund m) f; Prozeß m; Angelegenheit f, Sache f; **2.** verursachen, veranlassen; ~eless ☐
['kɔ:zlis] grundlos.
causeway ['kɔ:zwei] Damm m.
caustic ⚕ ['kɔ:stik] (~ally) ätzend;
fig. beißend, scharf.
caution ['kɔ:ʃən] **1.** Vorsicht f;
Warnung f; Verwarnung f; ~
money Kaution f; **2.** warnen; verwarnen.
cautious ☐ ['kɔ:ʃəs] behutsam, vorsichtig; ~ness [..snis] Behutsam-
keit f, Vorsicht f.
cavalry ⚔ ['kævəlri] Reiterei f.
cave [keiv] **1.** Höhle f; **2.** v/i. ~ in
einstürzen; klein beigeben.
cavern ['kævən] Höhle f; ~ous fig.
[..nəs] hohl.
cavil ['kævil] **1.** Krittelei f; **2.** kritteln (at, about an dat.).
cavity ['kæviti] Höhle f; Loch n.
cavort Am. F [kə'vɔ:t] sich auf-
bäumen, umherspringen.
caw [kɔ:] **1.** krächzen; **2.** Krächzen n.
cayuse Am. F ['kaiju:s] kleines
(Indianer)Pferd.
cease [si:s] v/i. (from) aufhören
(mit), ablassen (von); v/t. aufhören
mit; ~less ☐ ['si:slis] unaufhörlich.
cede [si:d] abtreten, überlassen.
ceiling ['si:liŋ] Zimmer-Decke f;
Höchstgrenze f; ~ price Höchst-
preis m.
celebrat|e ['selibreit] feiern; ~ed
gefeiert, berühmt (for wegen);
~ion [seli'breiʃən] Feier f.

celebrity [si'lebriti] Berühmtheit f.
celerity [si'leriti] Geschwindigkeit f.
celery ⚘ ['seləri] Sellerie m, f.
celestial □ [si'lestjəl] himmlisch.
celibacy ['selibəsi] Ehelosigkeit f.
cell [sel] allg. Zelle f; ⚡ Element n.
cellar ['selə] Keller m.
cement [si'ment] 1. Zement m;
Kitt m; 2. zementieren; (ver)kitten.
cemetery ['semitri] Friedhof m.
censor ['sensə] 1. Zensor m; 2. zen-
sieren; ~ious □ [sen'sɔ:riəs] kritisch; kritt(e)lig; ~ship ['sensəʃip]
Zensur f; Zensoramt n.
censure ['senʃə] 1. Tadel m; Verweis m; 2. tadeln.
census ['sensəs] Volkszählung f.
cent [sent] Hundert n; Am. Cent m
= ¹/₁₀₀ Dollar; per ~ Prozent n.
centenary [sen'ti:nəri] Hundert-
jahrfeier f.
centennial [sen'tenjəl] 1. hundert-
jährig; 2. hundertjähriges Jubi-
läum.
centi|grade ['sentigreid]: 10 degrees
~ 10 Grad Celsius; ~metre, Am.
~meter Zentimeter n, m; ~pede zo.
[~ipi:d] Hundertfüßer m.
central □ ['sentrəl] zentral; ~
heating Zentralheizung f; ~ office,
⚡ ~ station Zentrale f; ~ize [~laiz]
zentralisieren.
cent|re, Am. ~er ['sentə] 1. Zen-
trum n, Mittelpunkt m; 2. zentral;
3. (sich) konzentrieren; zentralisieren; zentrieren.
century ['sentʃuri] Jahrhundert n.
cereal ['siəriəl] 1. Getreide...;
2. Getreide(pflanze f) n; Hafer-,
Weizenflocken f/pl.; Corn-flakes pl.
cerebral anat. ['seribrəl] Gehirn...
ceremon|ial [seri'mounjəl] 1. □
a. ~ious □ [~jəs] zeremoniell;
förmlich; 2. Zeremoniell n; ~y
['serimэni] Zeremonie f; Feierlichkeit f; Förmlichkeit(en pl.) f.
certain □ ['sə:tn] sicher, gewiß;
zuverlässig; bestimmt; gewisse(r, -s);
~ty [~nti] Sicherheit f, Gewißheit
f; Zuverlässigkeit f.
certi|ficate 1. [sə'tifikit] Zeugnis n,
Schein m; ~ of birth Geburts-
urkunde f; medical ~ ärztliches
Attest; 2. [~keit] bescheinigen;
~fication [sə:tifi'keiʃən] Bescheini-
gung f; ~fy ['sə:tifai] et. bescheinigen; bezeugen; ~tude [~itju:d]
Gewißheit f.
cessation [se'seiʃən] Aufhören n.
cession ['seʃən] Abtretung f.
cesspool ['sespu:l] Senkgrube f.
chafe [tʃeif] v/t. reiben; wundreiben; erzürnen; v/i. sich scheuern;
sich wundreiben; toben.
chaff [tʃɑ:f] 1. Spreu f; Häcksel n;
F Neckerei f; 2. zu Häcksel schneiden; F necken.
chaffer ['tʃæfə] feilschen.

chaffinch ['tʃæfintʃ] Buchfink m.
chagrin ['ʃægrin] 1. Ärger m;
2. ärgern.
chain [tʃein] 1. Kette f; fig. Fessel f;
~ store bsd. Am. Kettenladen m,
Zweiggeschäft n; 2. (an)ketten; fig.
fesseln.
chair [tʃeə] Stuhl m; Lehrstuhl m;
Vorsitz m; be in the ~ den Vorsitz
führen; ~man ['tʃeəmən] Vor-
sitzende(r) m; Präsident m.
chalice ['tʃælis] Kelch m.
chalk [tʃɔ:k] 1. Kreide f; 2. mit
Kreide (be)zeichnen; mst ~ up an-
kreiden; ~ out entwerfen.
challenge ['tʃælindʒ] 1. Heraus-
forderung f; ✗ Anruf m; bsd. ᵗᵗ
Ablehnung f; 2. herausfordern; anrufen; ablehnen; anzweifeln.
chamber ['tʃeimbə] parl., zo., ⚘, ⊕,
Am. Kammer f; ~s pl. Geschäfts-
räume m/pl.; ~-maid Zimmer-
mädchen n.
chamois ['ʃæmwɑ:] 1. Gemse f; a.
~-leather [oft a. 'ʃæmiledə] Wildleder n; 2. chamois (gelbbraun).
champagne [ʃæm'pein] Champagner m.
champion ['tʃæmpjən] 1. Vor-
kämpfer m, Verfechter m; Verteidiger m; Sport: Meister m;
2. verteidigen; kämpfen für; fig.
stützen; 3. großartig; ~ship Meisterschaft f.
chance [tʃɑ:ns] 1. Zufall m; Schicksal n; Glück(sfall m) n; Chance f;
Aussicht f (of auf acc.); (günstige)
Gelegenheit; Möglichkeit f; by ~
zufällig; take a ~, take one's ~ es
darauf ankommen lassen; 2. zufällig; gelegentlich; 3. v/i. geschehen; sich ereignen; ~ upon
stoßen auf (acc.); v/t. F wagen.
chancellor ['tʃɑ:nsələ] Kanzler m.
chancery ['tʃɑ:nsəri] Kanzleigericht
n; fig. in ~ in der Klemme.
chandelier [ʃændi'liə] Lüster m.
chandler ['tʃɑ:ndlə] Krämer m.
change [tʃeindʒ] 1. Veränderung f,
Wechsel m, Abwechs(e)lung f;
Tausch m; Wechselgeld n; Kleingeld n; 2. v/t. (ver)ändern; (aus-)
wechseln, (aus-, ver)tauschen (for
gegen); ~ trains umsteigen; v/i. sich
ändern, wechseln; sich umziehen;
~able □ ['tʃeindʒəbl] veränderlich;
~less □ [~dʒlis] unveränderlich;
~ling [~liŋ] Wechselbalg m; ~
over Umstellung f.
channel ['tʃænl] 1. Kanal m; Fluß-
bett n; Rinne f; fig. Weg m; 2. furchen; aushöhlen.
chant [tʃɑ:nt] 1. (Kirchen)Gesang
m; fig. Singsang m; 2. singen.
chaos ['keiɔs] Chaos n.
chap¹ [tʃæp] 1. Riß m, Sprung m;
2. rissig machen od. werden.
chap² [~] Bursche m, Kerl m,
Junge m.

chap[3] [ˌ] Kinnbacken *m*; ˌs *pl.* Maul *n*; ⊕ Backen *f/pl.*

chapel ['tʃæpəl] Kapelle *f*; Gottesdienst *m.*

chaplain ['tʃæplin] Kaplan *m.*

chapter ['tʃæptə] Kapitel *n*; *Am.* Orts-, Untergruppe *f* e-r *Vereinigung.*

char [tʃɑː] verkohlen.

character ['kæriktə] Charakter *m*; Merkmal *n*; Schrift(zeichen *n*) *f*; Sinnesart *f*; Persönlichkeit *f*; Original *n*; *thea.*, *Roman* Person *f*; Rang *m*, Würde *f*; (*bsd.* guter) Ruf; Zeugnis *n*; **ˌistic** [kæriktə'ristik] **1.** (ˌally) charakteristisch (*of* für); **2.** Kennzeichen *n*; **ˌize** ['kæriktəraiz] charakterisieren.

charcoal ['tʃɑːkoul] Holzkohle *f.*

charge [tʃɑːdʒ] **1.** Ladung *f*; *fig.* Last *f* (*on* für); Verwahrung *f*, Obhut *f*; Schützling *m*; Mündel *m*, *f*, *n*; Amt *n*, Stelle *f*; Auftrag *m*, Befehl *m*; Angriff *m*; Ermahnung *f*; Beschuldigung *f*, Anklage *f*; Preis *m*, Forderung *f*; ˌs *pl.* ✝ Kosten *pl.*; be in ˌ *of* et. in Verwahrung haben; mit *et.* beauftragt sein; für *et.* sorgen; **2.** *v/t* laden; beladen, belasten; beauftragen; j-m *et.* einschärfen, befehlen; ermahnen; beschuldigen, anklagen (*with gen.*); zuschreiben (*on, upon dat.*); fordern, verlangen; an-, berechnen, in Rechnung stellen (*to dat.*); angreifen (*a. v/i.*); behaupten.

chariot *poet. od. hist.* ['tʃæriət] Streit-, Triumphwagen *m.*

charitable ☐ ['tʃæritəbl] mild(tätig), wohltätig.

charity ['tʃæriti] Nächstenliebe *f*; Wohltätigkeit *f*; Güte *f*; Nachsicht *f*; milde Gabe.

charlatan ['ʃɑːlətən] Marktschreier *m.*

charm [tʃɑːm] **1.** Zauber *m*; *fig.* Reiz *m*; **2.** bezaubern; *fig.* entzücken; **ˌing** ☐ ['tʃɑːmiŋ] bezaubernd.

chart [tʃɑːt] **1.** ⚓ Seekarte *f*; Tabelle *f*; **2.** auf e-r Karte einzeichnen.

charter ['tʃɑːtə] **1.** Urkunde *f*; Freibrief *m*; Patent *n*; Frachtvertrag *m*; **2.** privilegieren; ⚓, ✈ chartern, mieten.

charwoman ['tʃɑːwumən] Putz-, Reinemachefrau *f.*

chary ['tʃɛəri] vorsichtig.

chase [tʃeis] **1.** Jagd *f*; Verfolgung *f*; gejagtes Wild; **2.** jagen, hetzen; Jagd machen auf (*acc.*).

chasm ['kæzəm] Kluft *f* (*a. fig.*); Lücke *f.*

chaste ☐ [tʃeist] rein, keusch, unschuldig; schlicht (*Stil.*).

chastise [tʃæs'taiz] züchtigen.

chastity ['tʃæstiti] Keuschheit *f.*

chat [tʃæt] **1.** Geplauder *n*, Plauderei *f*; **2.** plaudern.

chattels ['tʃætlz] *pl. mst goods and* ˌ Hab *n* und Gut *n*; Vermögen *n.*

chatter ['tʃætə] **1.** plappern; schnattern; klappern; **2.** Geplapper *n*; **ˌbox** F Plaudertasche *f*; **ˌer** [ˌərə] Schwätzer(in).

chatty ['tʃæti] gesprächig.

chauffeur ['ʃoufə] Chauffeur *m.*

chaw *sl.* [tʃɔː] kauen; ˌ *up Am. mst fig.* fix und fertig machen.

cheap ☐ [tʃiːp] billig; *fig.* gemein; **ˌen** ['tʃiːpən] (sich) verbilligen; *fig.* herabsetzen.

cheat [tʃiːt] **1.** Betrug *m*, Schwindel *m*; Betrüger(in); **2.** betrügen.

check [tʃek] **1.** Schach(stellung *f*) *n*; Hemmnis *n* (*on* für); Zwang *m*, Aufsicht *f*; Kontrolle *f* (*on gen.*); Kontrollmarke *f*; *Am.* (Gepäck-) Schein *m*; *Am.* ✝ = cheque; *Am.* Rechnung *f im Restaurant*, karierter Stoff; **2.** *v/i.* an-, innehalten; *Am.* e-n Scheck ausstellen; ˌ *in Am.* (in e-m Hotel) absteigen; ˌ *out Am.* das Hotel (*nach Bezahlung der Rechnung*) verlassen; *v/t.* hemmen; kontrollieren; nachprüfen; *Kleider* in der Garderobe abgeben; *Am.* *Gepäck* aufgeben; **ˌer** ['tʃekə] Aufsichtsbeamte(r) *m*; ˌs *pl. Am.* Damespiel *n*; **ˌing-room** [ˌkiŋrum] *Am.* Gepäckaufbewahrung *f*; **ˌmate 1.** Schachmatt *n*; **2.** matt setzen; **ˌup** *Am.* scharfe Kontrolle.

cheek [tʃiːk] Backe *f*, Wange *f*; F Unverschämtheit *f*; **cheeky** ☐ ['tʃiːki] frech.

cheer [tʃiə] **1.** Stimmung *f*, Fröhlichkeit *f*; Hoch(ruf *m*) *n*; Beifall(sruf) *m*; Speisen *f/pl.*, Mahl *n*; three ˌs! dreimal hoch!; **2.** *v/t. a.* ˌ *up* aufheitern; mit Beifall begrüßen; *a.* ˌ *on* anspornen; *v/i.* hoch rufen; jauchzen; *a.* ˌ *up* Mut fassen; **ˌful** ☐ ['tʃiəful] heiter; **ˌio** F [ˌəri'ou] *Am.* mach's gut!, tschüs!; prosit!; **ˌless** ☐ [ˌəlis] freudlos; **ˌy** ☐ [ˌəri] heiter, froh.

cheese [tʃiːz] Käse *m.*

chef [ʃef] Küchenchef *m.*

chemical ['kemikəl] **1.** ☐ chemisch; **2.** ˌs *pl.* Chemikalien *pl.*

chemise [ʃi'miːz] (Frauen)Hemd *n.*

chemist ['kemist] Chemiker(in); Apotheker *m*; Drogist *m*; **ˌry** [ˌtri] Chemie *f.*

cheque ✝ [tʃek] Scheck *m*; crossed ˌ Verrechnungsscheck *m.*

chequer ['tʃekə] **1.** *mst* ˌs *pl.* Karomuster *n*; **2.** karieren; **ˌed** gewürfelt; *fig.* bunt.

cherish ['tʃeriʃ] hegen, pflegen.

cherry ['tʃeri] Kirsche *f.*

chess [tʃes] Schach(spiel) *n*; **ˌboard** ['tʃesbɔːd] Schachbrett *n*; **ˌman** Schachfigur *f.*

chest [tʃest] Kiste *f*, Lade *f*; *anat.* Brustkasten *m*; ˌ *of drawers* Kommode *f.*

chestnut ['tʃesnʌt] 1. ♀ Kastanie f; F alter Witz; 2. kastanienbraun.

chevy F ['tʃevi] 1. Hetzjagd f; Barlaufspiel n; 2. hetzen, jagen.

chew [tʃu:] kauen; sinnen; ~ the fact od. rag Am. sl. die Sache durchkauen; **~ing-gum** ['tʃu(:)iŋgʌm] Kaugummi m.

chicane [ʃi'kein] 1. Schikane f; 2. schikanieren.

chicken ['tʃikin] Hühnchen n, Küken n; **~hearted** furchtsam, feige; **~pox** ♂ [~npɔks] Windpocken f/pl.

chid [tʃid] pret. u. p.p. von chide; **~den** ['tʃidn] p.p. von chide.

chide lit. [tʃaid] [irr.] schelten.

chief [tʃi:f] 1. □ oberst; Ober...; Haupt...; hauptsächlich; ~ clerk Bürovorsteher m; 2. Oberhaupt n, Chef m; Häuptling m; ...-in-~ Ober...; **~tain** ['tʃi:ftən] Häuptling m.

chilblain ['tʃilblein] Frostbeule f.

child [tʃaild] Kind n; from a ~ von Kindheit an; with ~ schwanger; **~birth** ['tʃaildbə:θ] Niederkunft f; **~hood** [~dhud] Kindheit f; **~ish** □ [~diʃ] kindlich; kindisch; **~like** kindlich; **~ren** ['tʃildrən] pl. v. child.

chill [tʃil] 1. eisig, frostig; 2. Frost m, Kälte f; ♂ Fieberfrost m; Erkältung f; 3. v/t. erkalten lassen; abkühlen; v/i. erkalten; erstarren; **~y** ['tʃili] kalt, frostig.

chime [tʃaim] 1. Glockenspiel n; Geläut n; fig. Einklang m; 2. läuten; fig. harmonieren, übereinstimmen.

chimney ['tʃimni] Schornstein m; Rauchfang m; Lampen-Zylinder m; **~sweep(er)** Schornsteinfeger m.

chin [tʃin] 1. Kinn n; take it on the ~ Am. F es standhaft ertragen; 2.: ~ o.s. Am. e-n Klimmzug machen.

china ['tʃainə] Porzellan n.

Chinese ['tʃai'niːz] 1. chinesisch; 2. Chinese(n pl.) m, Chinesin f.

chink [tʃiŋk] Ritz m, Spalt m.

chip [tʃip] 1. Schnitzel n, Stückchen n; Span m; Glas- etc. Splitter m; Spielmarke f; have a ~ on one's shoulder Am. F aggressiv sein; ~s pl. Pommes frites pl.; 2. v/t. schnitzeln; an-, abschlagen; v/i. abbröckeln; **~muck** ['tʃipmʌk], **~munk** [~ʌŋk] nordamerikanisches gestreiftes Eichhörnchen.

chirp [tʃə:p] 1. zirpen; zwitschern; 2. Gezirp n.

chisel ['tʃizl] 1. Meißel m; 2. meißeln; sl. (be)mogeln.

chit-chat ['tʃittʃæt] Geplauder n.

chivalr|ous □ ['ʃivəlrəs] ritterlich; **~y** [~ri] Ritterschaft f, Rittertum n; Ritterlichkeit f.

chive ♀ [tʃaiv] Schnittlauch m.

chlor|ine ['klɔ:ri:n] Chlor n; **~oform** ['klɔrəfɔ:m] 1. Chloroform n; 2. chloroformieren.

chocolate ['tʃɔkəlit] Schokolade f.

choice [tʃɔis] 1. Wahl f; Auswahl f; 2. □ auserlesen, vorzüglich.

choir ['kwaiə] Chor m.

choke [tʃouk] 1. v/t. (er)würgen, (a. v/i.) ersticken; ♂ (ab)drosseln; (ver)stopfen; mst ~ down hinunterwürgen; 2. Erstickungsanfall m; ⊕ Würgung f; mot. Choke m, Starterklappe f.

choose [tʃu:z] [irr.] (aus)wählen; ~ to inf. vorziehen zu inf.

chop [tʃɔp] 1. Hieb m; Kotelett n; **~s** pl. Maul n, Rachen m; ⊕ Backen f/pl.; 2. v/t. hauen, hacken; zerhacken; austauschen; v/i. wechseln; **~per** ['tʃɔpə] Hackmesser n; **~py** [~pi] unstet; unruhig (See); böig (Wind).

choral □ ['kɔ:rəl] chormäßig; Chor...; **~(e)** ♪ [kɔ'rɑ:l] Choral m.

chord [kɔ:d] Saite f; Akkord m.

chore Am. [tʃɔ:] Hausarbeit f (mst pl.).

chorus ['kɔrəs] 1. Chor m; Kehrreim m; 2. im Chor singen od. sprechen.

chose [tʃouz] pret. von choose; **~n** ['tʃouzn] p.p. von choose.

chow Am. sl. [tʃau] Essen n.

Christ [kraist] Christus m.

christen ['krisn] taufen; **~ing** [~niŋ] Taufe f; attr. Tauf...

Christian ['kristjən] 1. □ christlich; ~ name Vor-, Taufname m; 2. Christ(in); **~ity** [kristi'æniti] Christentum n.

Christmas ['krisməs] Weihnachten n.

chromium ['kroumjəm] Chrom n (Metall); **~plated** verchromt.

chronic ['krɔnik] (~ally) chronisch (mst ♂), dauernd; sl. ekelhaft; **~le** [~kl] 1. Chronik f; 2. aufzeichnen.

chronolog|ical □ [krɔnə'lɔdʒikəl] chronologisch; **~y** [krə'nɔlədʒi] Zeitrechnung f; Zeitfolge f.

chubby F ['tʃʌbi] rundlich; pausbäckig; plump (a. fig.).

chuck¹ [tʃʌk] 1. Glucken n; my ~! mein Täubchen!; 2. glucken.

chuck² F [~] 1. schmeißen; 2. (Hinaus)Wurf m.

chuckle ['tʃʌkl] kichern, glucksen.

chum F [tʃʌm] 1. (Stuben)Kamerad m; 2. zs.-wohnen.

chump F [tʃʌmp] Holzklotz m.

chunk F [tʃʌŋk] Klotz m.

church [tʃə:tʃ] Kirche f; attr. Kirch(en)...; ~ service Gottesdienst m; **~warden** ['tʃə:tʃ'wɔ:dn] Kirchenvorsteher m; **~yard** Kirchhof m.

churl [tʃə:l] Grobian m; Flegel m; **~ish** □ ['tʃə:liʃ] grob, flegelhaft.

churn [tʃə:n] 1. Butterfaß n; 2. buttern; aufwühlen.

chute [ʃu:t] Stromschnelle f; Gleit-, Rutschbahn f; Fallschirm m.

cider ['saidə] Apfelmost *m*.

cigar [si'gɑ:] Zigarre *f*.

cigarette [sigə'ret] Zigarette *f*; **~-case** Zigarettenetui *n*.

cigar-holder [si'gɑ:houldə] Zigarrenspitze *f*.

cilia ['siliə] *pl*. (Augen)Wimpern *f/pl*.

cinch *Am. sl*. [sintʃ] sichere Sache.

cincture ['siŋktʃə] Gürtel *m*, Gurt *m*.

cinder ['sində] Schlacke *f*; **~s** *pl*. Asche *f*; **~ella** [sində'relə] Aschenbrödel *n*; **~-path** *Sport*: Aschenbahn *f*.

cine-camera ['sini'kæmərə] Filmkamera *f*.

cinema ['sinəmə] Kino *n*; Film *m*.

cinnamon ['sinəmən] Zimt *m*.

cipher ['saifə] **1.** Ziffer *f*; Null *f* (*a. fig.*); Geheimschrift *f*, Chiffre *f*; **2.** chiffrieren; (aus)rechnen.

circle ['sə:kl] **1.** Kreis *m*; *Bekannten- etc.* Kreis *m*; Kreislauf *m*; *thea.* Rang *m*; Ring *m*; **2.** (um)kreisen.

circuit ['sə:kit] Kreislauf *m*; ⚡ Stromkreis *m*; Rundreise *f*; Gerichtsbezirk *m*; ✈ Rundflug *m*; **short ~** ⚡ Kurzschluß *m*; **~ous** □ [sə(:)'kju(:)itəs] weitschweifig; Um...

circular ['sə:kjulə] **1.** □ kreisförmig; Kreis...; **~ letter** Rundschreiben *n*; **~ note** ✝ Kreditbrief *m*; **2.** Rundschreiben *n*; Laufzettel *m*.

circulat|e ['sə:kjuleit] *v/i.* umlaufen, zirkulieren; *v/t.* in Umlauf setzen; **~ing** [~tiŋ]: **~ library** Leihbücherei *f*; **~ion** [sə:kju'leiʃən] Zirkulation *f*, Kreislauf *m*; *fig.* Umlauf *m*; Verbreitung *f*; *Zeitungs-*Auflage *f*.

circum|... ['sə:kəm] (her)um; **~ference** [se'kʌmfərəns] (Kreis-)Umfang *m*, Peripherie *f*; **~jacent** [sə:kəm'dʒeisənt] umliegend; **~locution** [~mlə'kju:ʃən] Umständlichkeit *f*; Weitschweifigkeit *f*; **~navigate** [~m'nævigeit] umschiffen; **~scribe** ['sə:kəmskraib] ⊛ umschreiben; *fig.* begrenzen; **~spect** □ [~spekt] um-, vorsichtig; **~stance** [~stəns] Umstand *m* (**~s** *pl. a.* Verhältnisse *n/pl.*); Einzelheit *f*; Umständlichkeit *f*; **~stantial** □ [~m'stænʃəl] umständlich; **~ evidence** ⚖ Indizienbeweis *m*; **~vent** [~m'vent] überlisten; vereiteln.

circus ['sə:kəs] Zirkus *m*; (runder) Platz.

cistern ['sistən] Wasserbehälter *m*.

cit|ation [sai'teiʃən] Vorladung *f*; Anführung *f*, Zitat *n*; *Am. öffentliche* Ehrung; **~e** [sait] ⚖ vorladen; anführen; zitieren.

citizen ['sitizn] (Staats)Bürger(in); Städter(in); **~ship** [~nʃip] Bürgerrecht *n*, Staatsangehörigkeit *f*.

citron ['sitrən] Zitrone *f*.

city ['siti] **1.** Stadt *f*; *the* ⚖ die City, das Geschäftsviertel; **2.** städtisch, Stadt...; ⚖ *article* Börsen-, Handelsbericht *m*; **~ editor** *Am.* Lokalredakteur *m*; **~ hall** *Am.* Rathaus *n*; **~ manager** *Am.* Oberstadtdirektor *m*.

civic ['sivik] (staats)bürgerlich; städtisch; **~s** *sg.* Staatsbürgerkunde *f*.

civil □ ['sivl] bürgerlich, Bürger...; zivil; ⚖ zivilrechtlich; höflich; ⚖ *Servant* Verwaltungsbeamt|e(r) *m*, **-in** *f*; ⚖ *Service* Staatsdienst *m*; **~ian** ✕ [si'viljən] Zivilist *m*; **~ity** [~liti] Höflichkeit *f*; **~ization** [sivilai'zeiʃən] Zivilisation *f*, Kultur *f*; **~ize** ['sivilaiz] zivilisieren.

clad [klæd] **1.** *pret. u. p.p. von clothe*; **2.** *adj.* gekleidet.

claim [kleim] **1.** Anspruch *m*; Anrecht *n* (*to auf acc.*); Forderung *f*; *Am.* Parzelle *f*; **2.** beanspruchen; fordern; sich berufen auf (*acc.*); **~ to be** sich ausgeben für; **~ant** ['kleimənt] Beanspruchende(r *m*) *f*; ⚖ Kläger *m*.

clairvoyant(e) [kleə'vɔiənt] Hellseher(in).

clamber ['klæmbə] klettern.

clammy □ ['klæmi] feuchtkalt, klamm.

clamo(u)r ['klæmə] **1.** Geschrei *n*, Lärm *m*; **2.** schreien (*for nach*).

clamp ⊕ [klæmp] **1.** Klammer *f*; **2.** verklammern; befestigen.

clan [klæn] Clan *m*, Sippe *f* (*a. fig.*).

clandestine □ [klæn'destin] heimlich; Geheim...

clang [klæŋ] **1.** Klang *m*, Geklirr *n*; **2.** schallen; klirren lassen.

clank [klæŋk] **1.** Gerassel *n*, Geklirr *n*; **2.** rasseln, klirren (mit).

clap [klæp] **1.** Klatschen *n*; Schlag *m*, Klaps *m*; **2.** schlagen (mit) klatschen; **~board** *Am.* ['klæpbɔ:d] Schaltbrett *n*; **~trap** Effekthascherei *f*.

claret ['klærət] roter Bordeaux; *allg.* Rotwein *m*; Weinrot *n*; *sl.* Blut *n*.

clarify ['klærifai] *v/t.* (ab)klären; *fig.* klären; *v/i.* sich klären.

clarity ['klæriti] Klarheit *f*.

clash [klæʃ] **1.** Geklirr *n*; Zs.-stoß *m*; Widerstreit *m*; **2.** klirren (mit); zs.-stoßen.

clasp [klɑ:sp] **1.** Haken *m*, Klammer *f*; Schnalle *f*; Spange *f*; *fig.* Umklammerung *f*; Umarmung *f*; **2.** *v/t.* an-, zuhaken; *fig.* umklammern; umfassen; *v/i.* festhalten; **~-knife** ['klɑ:sp'naif] Taschenmesser *n*.

class [klɑ:s] **1.** Klasse *f*; Stand *m*; (Unterrichts)Stunde *f*; Kurs *m*; *Am. univ.* Jahrgang *m*; **2.** (in Klassen) einteilen, einordnen.

classic ['klæsik] Klassiker *m*; **~s**

pl. die alten Sprachen; ~(al □)
[~k(əl)] klassisch.

classi|fication [klæsifi'keiʃən] Klassifizierung *f*, Einteilung *f*; ~**fy**
['klæsifai] klassifizieren, einstufen.

clatter ['klætə] **1.** Geklapper *n*;
2. klappern (mit); *fig.* schwatzen.

clause [klɔːz] Klausel *f*, Bestimmung
f; *gr.* (Neben)Satz *m*.

claw [klɔː] **1.** Klaue *f*, Kralle *f*,
Pfote *f*; *Krebs*-Schere *f*; **2.** (zer-)
kratzen; (um)krallen.

clay [klei] Ton *m*; *fig.* Erde *f*.

clean [kliːn] **1.** *adj.* □ rein; sauber;
2. *adv.* rein, völlig; **3.** reinigen (*of*
von); sich waschen lassen (*Stoff
etc.*); ~ *up* aufräumen; ~**er** ['kliːnə]
Reiniger *m*; *mst* ~**s** *pl.* (chemische)
Reinigung; ~**ing** [~niŋ] Reinigung
f; ~**liness** ['klenlinis] Reinlichkeit
f; ~**ly 1.** *adv.* ['kliːnli] rein; sauber;
2. *adj.* ['klenli] reinlich; ~**se** [klenz]
reinigen; säubern.

clear [kliə] **1.** □ klar; hell, rein;
fig. rein (*from* von); frei (*of* von);
ganz, voll; † rein, netto; **2.** *v/t.*
er-, aufhellen; (auf)klären; reinigen (*of, from* von); *Wald* lichten,
roden; wegräumen (*a.* ~ *away of.
off*); *Hindernis* nehmen; *Rechnung*
bezahlen; † (aus)klarieren, verzollen; ⁂ freisprechen; befreien;
rechtfertigen (*from* von); *v/i. a.* ~
up sich aufhellen; sich verziehen;
~**ance** [~kliərəns] Aufklärung *f*;
Freilegung *f*; Räumung *f*; † Abrechnung *f*; ⚓, † Verzollung *f*;
~**ing** [~riŋ] Aufklärung *f*; Lichtung
f, Rodung *f*; † Ab-, Verrechnung
f; ⚲ *House* Ab-, Verrechnungsstelle *f*.

cleave[1] [kliːv] [*irr.*] (sich) spalten;
Wasser, Luft (zer)teilen.

cleave[2] [~] *fig.* festhalten (*to an dat.*);
treu bleiben (*dat.*).

cleaver ['kliːvə] Hackmesser *n*.

clef ♪ [klef] Schlüssel *m*.

cleft [kleft] **1.** Spalte *f*; Sprung *m*,
Riß *m*; **2.** *pret. u. p.p. von* cleave[1].

clemen|cy ['klemənsi] Milde *f*; ~**t**
□ [~nt] mild.

clench [klentʃ] *Lippen etc.* fest zs.-
pressen; *Zähne* zs.-beißen; *Faust*
ballen; festhalten.

clergy ['klɔːdʒi] Geistlichkeit *f*;
~**man** Geistliche(r) *m*.

clerical ['klerikəl] **1.** □ geistlich;
Schreib(er)...; **2.** Geistliche(r) *m*.

clerk [klɑːk] Schreiber(in); Büroangestellte(r *m*) *f*; Sekretär(in); †
kaufmännische(r) Angestellte(r);
Am. Verkäufer(in); Küster *m*.

clever □ ['klevə] gescheit; geschickt.

clew [kluː] Knäuel *m, n*; = clue.

click [klik] **1.** Knacken *n*; ⊕ Sperrhaken *m*, -klinke *f*; **2.** knacken; zu-,
einschnappen; klappen.

client ['klaiənt] Klient(in); Kund|e

m, -in *f*; ~**èle** [kliːɑ̃ːn'teil] Kundschaft *f*.

cliff [klif] Klippe *f*; Felsen *m*.

climate ['klaimit] Klima *n*.

climax ['klaimæks] **1.** *rhet.* Steigerung *f*; Gipfel *m*, Höhepunkt *m*;
2. (sich) steigern.

climb [klaim] (er)klettern, (er-)
klimmen, (er)steigen; ~**er** ['klaimə]
Kletterer *m*, Bergsteiger(in); *fig.*
Streber(in); ⚘ Kletterpflanze *f*;
~**ing** [~miŋ] Klettern *n*; *attr.*
Kletter...

clinch [klintʃ] **1.** ⊕ Vernietung *f*;
Festhalten *n*; *Boxen:* Umklammerung *f*; **2.** *v/t.* vernieten; festmachen; *s. clench*; *v/i.* festhalten.

cling [kliŋ] [*irr.*] (*to*) festhalten (an
dat.), sich klammern (an *acc.*);
sich (an)schmiegen (an *acc.*); *j-m*
anhängen.

clinic ['klinik] Klinik *f*; klinisches
Praktikum; ~**al** □ [~kəl] klinisch.

clink [kliŋk] **1.** Geklirr *n*; **2.** klingen,
klirren (lassen); klimpern mit; ~**er**
['kliŋkə] Klinker(stein) *m*.

clip[1] [klip] **1.** Schur *f*; *at one* ~ *Am.*
F auf einmal; **2.** ab-, aus-, beschneiden; *Schafe etc.* scheren.

clip[2] [~] Klammer *f*; Spange *f*.

clipp|er ['klipə]: (*a. pair of*) ~**s** *pl.*
Haarschneide-, Schermaschine *f*;
Klipper *m*; ⚓ Schnellsegler *m*; ✈
Verkehrsflugzeug *n*; ~**ings** [~piŋz]
pl. Abfälle *m/pl.*; Zeitungs- *etc.*
Ausschnitte *m/pl.*

cloak [klouk] **1.** Mantel *m*; **2.** *fig.* bemänteln, verhüllen; ~**-room**
['kloukrum] Garderobe(nraum *m*) *f*;
Toilette *f*; ⚓ Gepäckabgabe *f*.

clock [klɔk] *Schlag-, Wand-*Uhr *f*;
~**wise** ['klɔkwaiz] im Uhrzeigersinn; ~**work** Uhrwerk *n*; *like* ~
wie am Schnürchen.

clod [klɔd] Erdklumpen *m*; *a.* ~
hopper (Bauern)Tölpel *m*.

clog [klɔg] **1.** Klotz *m*; Holzschuh *m*,
Pantine *f*; **2.** belasten; hemmen;
(sich) verstopfen.

cloister ['klɔistə] Kreuzgang *m*;
Kloster *n*.

close 1. □ [klous] geschlossen; verborgen; verschwiegen; knapp, eng;
begrenzt; nah, eng; bündig; dicht;
gedrängt; schwül; knickerig; genau; fest (*Griff*); ~ *by*, ~ *to* dicht
bei; ~ *fight*, ~ *quarters pl.* Handgemenge *n*, Nahkampf *m*; ~(*ed*)
season, ~ *time hunt.* Schonzeit *f*;
sail ~ *to the wind fig.* sich hart an der
Grenze des Erlaubten bewegen;
2. [klouz] Schluß *m*; Abschluß *m*;
[klous] Einfriedung *f*; Hof *m*; **3.**
[klouz] *v/t.* (ab-, ein-, ver-, zu-)
schließen; beschließen; *v/i.* (sich)
schließen; abschließen; handgemein werden; ~ *in* hereinbrechen
(*Nacht*); kürzer werden (*Tage*); ~
on (*prp.*) sich schließen um, um-

fassen; ~ness ['klousnis] Genauigkeit *f*, Geschlossenheit *f*.

closet ['kləzit] 1. Kabinett *n*; (Wand)Schrank *m*; = water-~; 2.: be ~ed with mit *j-m* e-e geheime Beratung haben. [nahme *f*.\

close-up ['klousʌp] *Film*: Großauf-\

closure ['klouʒə] Verschluß *m*; *parl.* (Antrag *m* auf) Schluß *m* e-r *Debatte*.

clot [klət] 1. Klümpchen *n*; 2. zu Klümpchen gerinnen (lassen).

cloth [kləθ] Stoff *m*, Tuch *n*; Tischtuch *n*; Kleidung *f*, *Amts*-Tracht *f*; *the* ~ F der geistliche Stand; *lay the* ~ den Tisch decken; ~binding Leineneinband *m*; ~bound in Leinen gebunden.

clothe [klouð] [*irr.*] (an-, be)kleiden; einkleiden.

clothes [klouðz] *pl.* Kleider *n/pl.*; Kleidung *f*; Anzug *m*; Wäsche *f*; ~basket ['klouðzbɑːskit] Waschkorb *m*; ~line Wäscheleine *f*; ~peg Kleiderhaken *m*; Wäscheklammer *f*; ~pin *bsd. Am.* Wäscheklammer *f*; ~press Kleider-, Wäscheschrank *m*.

clothier ['klouðiə] Tuch-, Kleiderhändler *m*.

clothing ['klouðiŋ] Kleidung *f*.

cloud [klaud] 1. Wolke *f* (*a. fig.*); Trübung *f*; Schatten *m*; 2. (sich) be-, umwölken (*a. fig.*); ~burst ['klaudbəːst] Wolkenbruch *m*; ~less □ [~dlis] wolkenlos; ~y □ [~di] wolkig; Wolken...; trüb; unklar.

clout [klaut] Lappen *m*; F Kopfnuß *f*.

clove¹ [klouv] (Gewürz)Nelke *f*.

clove² [~] *pret. von* cleave¹; ~n ['klouvn] 1. *p.p. von* cleave¹; 2. *adj.* gespalten.

clover ♣ ['klouvə] Klee *m*.

clown [klaun] Hanswurst *m*; Tölpel *m*; ~ish □ ['klauniʃ] bäurisch; plump; clownhaft.

cloy [klɔi] übersättigen, überladen.

club [klʌb] 1. Keule *f*; (Gummi-)Knüppel *m*; Klub *m*; ~s *pl. Karten*: Kreuz *n*; 2. *v/t.* mit e-r Keule schlagen; *v/i.* sich zs.-tun; ~foot ['klʌbfut] Klumpfuß *m*.

clue [kluː] Anhaltspunkt *m*, Fingerzeig *m*.

clump [klʌmp] 1. Klumpen *m*; *Baum*-Gruppe *f*; 2. trampeln; zs.-drängen.

clumsy □ ['klʌmzi] unbeholfen, ungeschickt; plump.

clung [klʌŋ] *pret. u. p.p. von* cling.

cluster ['klʌstə] 1. Traube *f*; Büschel *n*; Haufen *m*; 2. büschelweise wachsen; (sich) zs.-drängen.

clutch [klʌtʃ] 1. Griff *m*; ⊕ Kupplung *f*; Klaue *f*; 2. (er)greifen.

clutter ['klʌtə] 1. Wirrwarr *m*; 2. durch-ea.-rennen; durch-ea.-bringen.

coach [koutʃ] 1. Kutsche *f*; ⚏ Wagen *m*; Reisebus *m*; Einpauker *m*; Trainer *m*; 2. in e-r Kutsche fahren; (ein)pauken; trainieren; ~man ['koutʃmən] Kutscher *m*.

coagulate [kou'ægjuleit] gerinnen (lassen).

coal [koul] 1. (Stein)Kohle *f*; *carry* ~s *to Newcastle* Eulen nach Athen tragen; 2. ♣ (be)kohlen.

coalesce [kouə'les] zs.-wachsen; sich vereinigen.

coalition [kouə'liʃən] Verbindung *f*; Bund *m*, Koalition *f*.

coal-pit ['koulpit] Kohlengrube *f*.

coarse □ [kɔːs] grob; ungeschliffen.

coast [koust] 1. Küste *f*; *bsd. Am.* Rodelbahn *f*; 2. die Küste entlangfahren; im Freilauf fahren; rodeln; ~er ['koustə] *Am.* Rodelschlitten; ♣ Küstenfahrer *m*.

coat [kout] 1. Jackett *m*, Jacke *f*, Rock *m*; Mantel *m*; Pelz *m*, Gefieder *n*; Überzug *m*; ~ *of arms* Wappen(schild *m*, *n*) *n*; 2. überziehen; anstreichen; ~hanger ['kouthæŋə] Kleiderbügel *m*; ~ing ['koutiŋ] Überzug *m*; Anstrich *m*; Mantelstoff *m*.

coax [kouks] schmeicheln (*dat.*); beschwatzen (*into* zu).

cob [kəb] kleines starkes Pferd; Schwan *m*; *Am.* Maiskolben *m*.

cobbler ['kəblə] Schuhmacher *m*; Stümper *m*.

cobweb ['kəbweb] Spinn(en)gewebe *n*.

cock [kək] 1. Hahn *m*; Anführer *m*; Heuhaufen *m*; 2. *a.* ~ *up* aufrichten; *Gewehrhahn* spannen.

cockade [kə'keid] Kokarde *f*.

cockatoo [kəkə'tu:] Kakadu *m*.

cockboat ♣ ['kəkbout] Jolle *f*.

cockchafer ['kəktʃeifə] Maikäfer *m*.

cock|-eyed *sl.* ['kəkaid] schieläugig; *Am.* blau (*betrunken*); ~horse Steckenpferd *n*.

cockney ['kəkni] waschechter Londoner.

cockpit ['kəkpit] Kampfplatz *m* für Hähne; ♣ Raumdeck *n*; ✈ Führerraum *m*, Kanzel *f*.

cockroach *zo.* ['kəkroutʃ] Schabe *f*.

cock|sure F ['kək'ʃuə] absolut sicher; überheblich; ~tail Cocktail *m*; ~y □ F ['kəki] selbstbewußt; frech.

coco ['koukou] Kokospalme *f*.

cocoa ['koukou] Kakao *m*.

coco-nut ['koukənʌt] Kokosnuß *f*.

cocoon [kə'kun] *Seiden*-Kokon *m*.

cod [kəd] Kabeljau *m*.

coddle ['kədl] verhätscheln.

code [koud] 1. Gesetzbuch *n*; Kodex *m*; *Telegramm*-, *Signal*-Schlüssel *m*; 2. chiffrieren.

codger F ['kədʒə] komischer Kauz.

cod-liver ['kədlivə]: ~ *oil* Lebertran *m*.

co-ed *Am.* F ['kou'ed] Schülerin *f* e-r Koedukationsschule, *allg.* Studentin *f*.

coerc|e [kou'ə:s] (er)zwingen; ~ion [kou'ə:ʃən] Zwang *m*.

coeval □ [kou'i:vəl] gleichzeitig; gleichalt(e)rig.

coexist ['kouig'zist] gleichzeitig bestehen.

coffee ['kɔfi] Kaffee *m*; ~-pot Kaffeekanne *f*; ~-room Speisesaal *m* e-s Hotels; ~-set Kaffeeservice *n*.

coffer ['kɔfə] (Geld)Kasten *m*.

coffin ['kɔfin] Sarg *m*.

cogent □ ['koudʒənt] zwingend.

cogitate [ˈkɔdʒiteit] *v/i.* nachdenken; *v/t.* (er)sinnen.

cognate ['kɔgneit] verwandt.

cognition [kɔg'niʃən] Erkenntnis *f*.

cognizable ['kɔgnizəbl] erkennbar.

coheir ['kou'ɛə] Miterbe *m*.

coheren|ce [kou'hiərəns] Zs.-hang *m*; ~t □ [~nt] zs.-hängend.

cohesi|on [kou'hi:ʒən] Kohäsion *f*; ~ve [~i:siv] (fest) zs.-hängend.

coiff|eur [kwa:'fə:] Friseur *m*; ~ure [~'fjuə] Frisur *f*.

coil [kɔil] 1. *a.* ~ up aufwickeln; (sich) zs.-rollen; 2. Rolle *f*, Spirale *f*; Wicklung *f*; ⚡ Spule *f*; Windung *f*; ⊕ (Rohr)Schlange *f*.

coin [kɔin] 1. Münze *f*; 2. prägen (*a. fig.*); münzen; ~age ['kɔinidʒ] Prägung *f*; Geld *n*, Münze *f*.

coincide [kouin'said] zs.-treffen; übereinstimmen; ~nce [kou'insidəns] Zs.-treffen *n*; *fig.* Übereinstimmung *f*.

coke [kouk] Koks *m* (*a. sl.* = Kokain); *Am.* F Coca-Cola *n, f*.

cold [kould] 1. □ kalt; 2. Kälte *f*, Frost *m*; Erkältung *f*; ~ness ['kouldnis] Kälte *f*.

coleslaw *Am.* ['koulslɔ:] Krautsalat *m*.

colic ✗ ['kɔlik] Kolik *f*.

collaborat|e [kə'læbəreit] zs.-arbeiten; ~ion [kəlæbə'reiʃən] Zs.-, Mitarbeit *f*; in ~ gemeinsam.

collaps|e [kə'læps] 1. zs.-, einfallen; zs.-brechen; 2. Zs.-bruch *m*; ~ible [~səbl] zs.-klappbar.

collar ['kɔlə] 1. Kragen *m*; Halsband *n*; Kum(me)t *n*; ⊕ Lager *n*; 2. beim Kragen packen; Fleisch zs.-rollen; ~bone Schlüsselbein *n*; ~stud Kragenknopf *m*.

collate [kɔ'leit] *Texte* vergleichen.

collateral [kɔ'lætərəl] 1. □ parallel laufend; Seiten..., Neben...; indirekt; 2. Seitenverwandte(r *m*) *f*.

colleague ['kɔli:g] Kolleg|e *m*, -in *f*.

collect 1. *eccl.* ['kɔlekt] Kollekte *f*; 2. *v/t.* [kə'lekt] (ein)sammeln; *Gedanken etc.* sammeln; einkassieren; abholen; *v/i.* sich (ver)sammeln; ~ed □ *fig.* gefaßt; ~ion [~kʃən] Sammlung *f*; Einziehung *f*; ~ive [~ktiv] gesammelt; Sammel...; ~

bargaining Tarifverhandlungen *f/pl.*; ~ively [~vli] insgesamt; zs.-fassend; ~or [~tə] Sammler *m*; Steuereinnehmer *m*; 🚋 Fahrkartenabnehmer *m*; ⚡ Stromabnehmer *m*.

college ['kɔlidʒ] College *n* (*Teil e-r Universität*); höhere Schule *od.* Lehranstalt *f*; Hochschule *f*; Akademie *f*; Kollegium *n*.

collide [kə'laid] zs.-stoßen.

collie ['kɔli] Collie *m*, schottischer Schäferhund.

collier ['kɔliə] Bergmann *m*; ⚓ Kohlenschiff *n*; ~y ['kɔljəri] Kohlengrube *f*.

collision [kə'liʒən] Zs.-stoß *m*.

colloquial □ [kə'loukwiəl] umgangssprachlich, familiär.

colloquy ['kɔləkwi] Gespräch *n*.

colon *typ.* ['koulən] Doppelpunkt *m*.

colonel ✗ ['kə:nl] Oberst *m*.

coloni|al [kə'lounjəl] Kolonial...; ~alism *pol.* [~lizəm] Kolonialismus *m*; ~ze ['kɔlənaiz] kolonisieren; (sich) ansiedeln; besiedeln.

colony ['kɔləni] Kolonie *f*; Siedlung *f*.

colossal □ [kə'lɔsl] kolossal.

colo(u)r ['kʌlə] 1. Farbe *f*; *fig.* Färbung *f*; Anschein *m*; Vorwand *m*; ~s *pl.* ✗ Fahne *f*, Flagge *f*; 2. *v/t.* färben; anstreichen; *fig.* beschönigen; *v/i.* sich (ver)färben; erröten; ~-bar Rassenschranke *f*; ~ed gefärbt, farbig; ~ man Farbige(r) *m*; ~ful [~əful] farbenreich, -freudig; lebhaft; ~ing [~əriŋ] Färbung *f*; Farbton *m*; *fig.* Beschönigung *f*; ~less □ [~əlis] farblos; ~ line *bsd. Am.* Rassenschranke *f*.

colt [koult] Hengstfüllen *n*; *fig.* Neuling *m*.

column ['kɔləm] Säule *f*; *typ.* Spalte *f*; ✗ Kolonne *f*; ~ist *Am.* [~mnist] Kolumnist *m*.

comb [koum] 1. Kamm *m*; ⊕ Hechel *f*; 2. *v/t.* kämmen; striegeln; *Flachs* hecheln.

combat ['kɔmbət] 1. Kampf *m*; single ~ Zweikampf *m*; 2. (be-)kämpfen; ~ant [~tənt] Kämpfer *m*.

combin|ation [kɔmbi'neiʃən] Verbindung *f*; *mst* ~s *pl.* Hemdhose *f*; ~e [kəm'bain] (sich) verbinden, vereinigen.

combust|ible [kəm'bʌstəbl] 1. brennbar; 2. ~s *pl.* Brennmaterial *n*; *mot.* Betriebsstoff *m*; ~ion [~tʃən] Verbrennung *f*.

come [kʌm] [*irr.*] kommen; to ~ künftig, kommend; ~ about geschehen; ~ across auf *j. od. et.* stoßen; ~ at erreichen; ~ by vorbeikommen; zu *et.* kommen; ~ down heruntercome (*a. fig.*); *Am.* F erkranken (with *an dat.*); ~ for abholen; ~ off davonkommen; losgehen (*Knopf*), ausfallen (*Haare etc.*); stattfinden;

~ *round* vorbeikommen (*bsd. zu Besuch*); wiederkehren; F zu sich kommen; *fig.* einlenken; ~ *to adv.* dazukommen; ⚓ beidrehen; *prp.* betragen; ~ *up to* entsprechen (*dat.*); es *j-m* gleichtun; *Stand, Maß* erreichen; **~back** ['kʌmbæk] Wiederkehr *f*, Comeback *n*; *Am. sl.* schlagfertige Antwort.

comedian [kə'miːdjən] Schauspieler(in); Komiker(in); Lustspieldichter *m*.

comedy ['kɔmidi] Lustspiel *n*.

comeliness ['kʌmlinis] Anmut *f*.

comfort ['kʌmfət] **1.** Bequemlichkeit *f*; Behaglichkeit *f*; Trost *m*; *fig.* Beistand *m*; Erquickung *f*; **2.** trösten; erquicken; beleben; **~able** □ [˷təbl] behaglich; bequem; tröstlich; **~er** [˷tə] Tröster *m*; *fig.* wollenes Halstuch; Schnuller *m*; *Am.* Steppdecke *f*; **~less** □ [˷tlis] unbehaglich; trostlos; **~ station** *Am.* Bedürfnisanstalt *f*.

comic(al □) ['kɔmik(əl)] komisch; lustig, drollig.

coming ['kʌmiŋ] **1.** kommend; künftig; **2.** Kommen *n*.

comma ['kɔmə] Komma *n*.

command [kə'mɑːnd] **1.** Herrschaft *f*, Beherrschung *f* (*a. fig.*); Befehl *m*; ✕ Kommando *n*; *be* (*have*) *at* ~ zur Verfügung stehen (haben); **2.** befehlen; ✕ kommandieren; verfügen über (*acc.*); beherrschen; **~er** [˷də] Kommandeur *m*, Befehlshaber *m*; ⚓ Fregattenkapitän *m*; **~er-in-chief** [˷ərin-'tʃiːf] Oberbefehlshaber *m*; **~ment** [˷dmənt] Gebot *n*.

commemorat|e [kə'meməreit] gedenken (*gen.*), feiern; **~ion** [kəmemə'reiʃən] Gedächtnisfeier *f*.

commence [kə'mens] anfangen, beginnen; **~ment** [˷smənt] Anfang *m*. [loben; anvertrauen.]

commend [kə'mend] empfehlen;

commensurable □ [kə'menʃərəbl] vergleichbar (*with, to* mit).

comment ['kɔment] **1.** Kommentar *m*; Erläuterung *f*; An-, Bemerkung *f*; **2.** (*upon*) erläutern (*acc.*); sich auslassen (über *acc.*); **~ary** ['kɔməntəri] Kommentar *m*; **~ator** ['kɔmenteitə] Kommentator *m*; *Radio*: Berichterstatter *m*.

commerc|e ['kɔmə(ː)s] Handel *m*; Verkehr *m*; **~ial** □ [kə'məːʃəl] **1.** kaufmännisch; Handels...; Geschäfts...; gewerbsmäßig; ~ *traveller* Handlungsreisende(r) *m*; **2.** *bsd. Am. Radio, Fernsehen*: kommerzielle (Werbe)Sendung.

commiseration [kəmizə'reiʃən] Mitleid *n* (*for* mit).

commissary ['kɔmisəri] Kommissar *m*; ✕ Intendanturbeamte(r) *m*.

commission [kə'miʃən] **1.** Auftrag *m*; Übertragung *f von Macht etc.*;

Begehung *f e-s Verbrechens*; Provision *f*; Kommission *f*; (Offiziers-) Patent *n*; **2.** beauftragen; bevollmächtigen; ✕ bestallen; ⚓ in Dienst stellen; **~er** [˷ʃnə] Bevollmächtigte(r *m*) *f*; Kommissar *m*.

commit [kə'mit] anvertrauen; übergeben, überweisen; *Tat* begehen; bloßstellen; ~ (*o.s. sich*) verpflichten; ~ (*to prison*) in Untersuchungshaft nehmen; **~ment** [˷tmənt], **~tal** [˷tl] Überweisung *f*; Verpflichtung *f*; Verübung *f*; **~tee** [˷ti] Ausschuß *m*, Komitee *n*.

commodity [kə'mɔditi] Ware *f* (*mst pl.*), Gebrauchsartikel *m*.

common [kə'mən] **1.** □ (all)gemein; gewöhnlich; gemeinschaftlich; öffentlich; gemein (*niedrig*); ♀ *Council* Gemeinderat *m*; **2.** Gemeindewiese *f*; *in* ~ gemeinsam; *in* ~ *with fig.* genau wie; **~er** [˷nə] Bürger *m*, Gemeine(r) *m*; Mitglied *n* des Unterhauses; ~ *law* Gewohnheitsrecht *n*; ♀ **Market** Gemeinsamer Markt; **~place 1.** Gemeinplatz *m*; **2.** gewöhnlich; F abgedroschen; **~s** *pl.* das gemeine Volk; Gemeinschaftsverpflegung *f*; (*mst House of*) ♀ Unterhaus *n*; ~ *sense* gesunder Menschenverstand; **~ wealth** [˷nwelθ] Gemeinwesen *n*, Staat *m*; *bsd.* Republik *f*; *the British* ♀ das Commonwealth.

commotion [kə'mouʃən] Erschütterung *f*; Aufruhr *m*; Aufregung *f*.

communal □ ['kɔmjunl] gemeinschaftlich; Gemeinde...

commune 1. [kə'mjuːn] sich vertraulich besprechen; **2.** ['kɔmjuːn] Gemeinde *f*.

communicat|e [kə'mjuːnikeit] *v/t.* mitteilen; *v/i.* das Abendmahl nehmen, kommunizieren; in Verbindung stehen; **~ion** [kəmjuːni'keiʃən] Mitteilung *f*; Verbindung *f*; **~ive** [kə'mjuːnikətiv] gesprächig.

communion [kə'mjuːnjən] Gemeinschaft *f*; *eccl.* Kommunion *f*, Abendmahl *n*.

communis|m ['kɔmjunizəm] Kommunismus *m*; **~t** [˷ist] **1.** Kommunist(in); **2.** kommunistisch.

community [kə'mjuːniti] Gemeinschaft *f*; Gemeinde *f*; Staat *m*.

commut|ation [kɔmju(ː)'teiʃən] Vertauschung *f*; Umwandlung *f*; Ablösung *f*; Strafmilderung *f*; ~ *ticket Am.* Zeitkarte *f*; **~e** [kə'mjuːt] ablösen; Strafe (mildernd) umwandeln; *Am.* pendeln *im Arbeitsverkehr.*

compact 1. ['kɔmpækt] Vertrag *m*; **2.** [kəm'pækt] *adj.* dicht, fest; knapp, bündig; *v/t.* fest verbinden.

companion [kəm'pænjən] Gefährt|e *m*, -in *f*; Gesellschafter(in); **~able** [˷nəbl] gesellig; **~ship** [˷ʃip] Gesellschaft *f*.

company ['kʌmpəni] Gesellschaft f; Kompanie f; Handelsgesellschaft f; Genossenschaft f; ⚓ Mannschaft f; thea. Truppe f; have ~ Gäste haben; keep ~ with verkehren mit.

compar|able □ ['kɔmpərəbl] vergleichbar; **~ative** [kəm'pærətiv] **1.** □ vergleichend; verhältnismäßig; **2.** a. ~ degree gr. Komparativ m; **~e** [ˌ'peə] **1.**: beyond ~, without ~, past ~ unvergleichlich; **2.** v/t. vergleichen; gleichstellen (to mit); v/i. sich vergleichen (lassen); **~ison** [ˌ'pærisn] Vergleich(ung f) m.

compartment [kəm'pɑːtmənt] Abteilung f; ⚓ Fach n; ⚒ Abteil n.

compass ['kʌmpəs] **1.** Bereich m; ♪ Umfang m; Kompaß m; oft pair of ~es pl. Zirkel m; **2.** herumgehen um; einschließen; erreichen; planen.

compassion [kəm'pæʃən] Mitleid n; **~ate** □ [ˌ'nit] mitleidig.

compatible □ [kəm'pætəbl] vereinbar, verträglich; schicklich.

compatriot [kəm'pætriət] Landsmann m.

compel [kəm'pel] (er)zwingen.

compensat|e ['kɔmpenseit] j-n entschädigen; et. ersetzen; ausgleichen; **~ion** [kɔmpen'seiʃən] Ersatz m; Ausgleich(ung f) m; Entschädigung f; Am. Vergütung f (Gehalt).

compère ['kɔmpeə] **1.** Conférencier m; **2.** ansagen (bei).

compete [kəm'piːt] sich mitbewerben (for um); konkurrieren.

competen|ce, **~cy** ['kɔmpitəns, ˌsi] Befugnis f, Zuständigkeit f; Auskommen n; **~t** □ [ˌnt] hinreichend; (leistungs)fähig; fachkundig; berechtigt, zuständig.

competit|ion [kɔmpi'tiʃən] Mitbewerbung f; Wettbewerb m; ♥ Konkurrenz f; **~ive** [kəm'petitiv] wetteifernd; **~or** [ˌtə] Mitbewerber (-in); Konkurrent(in).

compile [kəm'pail] zs.-tragen, zs.-stellen (from aus); sammeln.

complacen|ce, **~cy** [kəm'pleisns, ˌsi] Selbstzufriedenheit f.

complain [kəm'plein] (sich be-)klagen; **~ant** [ˌnənt] Kläger(in); **~t** □ [ˌnt] Klage f, Beschwerde f; ⚕ Leiden n.

complaisan|ce [kəm'pleizəns] Gefälligkeit f; Entgegenkommen n; **~t** □ [ˌnt] gefällig; entgegenkommend.

complement 1. ['kɔmplimənt] Ergänzung f; volle Anzahl; **2.** [ˌment] ergänzen.

complet|e [kəm'pliːt] **1.** □ vollständig, ganz; vollkommen; **2.** vervollständigen; vervollkommnen; abschließen; **~ion** [ˌiːʃən] Vervollständigung f; Abschluß m; Erfüllung f.

complex ['kɔmpleks] **1.** □ zs.-gesetzt; fig. kompliziert; **2.** Gesamtheit f, Komplex m; **~ion** [kəm'plekʃən] Aussehen n; Charakter m, Zug m; Gesichtsfarbe f, Teint m; **~ity** [ˌksiti] Kompliziertheit f.

complian|ce [kəm'plaiəns] Einwilligung f; Einverständnis n; in ~ with gemäß; **~t** □ [ˌnt] gefällig.

complicate ['kɔmplikeit] komplizieren, erschweren.

complicity [kəm'plisiti] Mitschuld f (in an dat.).

compliment 1. ['kɔmplimənt] Kompliment n; Schmeichelei f; Gruß m; **2.** [ˌment] v/t. (on) beglückwünschen (zu); j-m Komplimente machen (über acc.); **~ary** [kɔmpli'mentəri] höflich.

comply [kəm'plai] sich fügen; nachkommen, entsprechen (with dat.).

component [kəm'pounənt] **1.** Bestandteil m; **2.** zs.-setzend.

compos|e [kəm'pouz] zs.-setzen; komponieren, verfassen; ordnen; beruhigen; typ. setzen; **~ed** □ ruhig, gesetzt; **~er** [ˌzə] Komponist(in); Verfasser(in); **~ition** [kɔmpə'ziʃən] Zs.-setzung f; Abfassung f; Komposition f; (Schrift-) Satz m; Aufsatz m; ♀ Vergleich m; **~t** ['kɔmpɔst] Kompost m; **~ure** [kəm'pouʒə] Fassung f, Gemütsruhe f.

compound 1. ['kɔmpaund] zs.-gesetzt; ~ interest Zinseszinsen m/pl.; **2.** Zs.-setzung f, Verbindung f; **3.** [kəm'paund] v/t. zs.-setzen; Streit beilegen; v/i. sich einigen.

comprehend [kɔmpri'hend] umfassen; begreifen, verstehen.

comprehen|sible □ [kɔmpri'hensəbl] verständlich; **~sion** [ˌnʃən] Verständnis n; Fassungskraft f; Umfang m; **~sive** □ [ˌnsiv] umfassend.

compress [kəm'pres] zs.-drücken; **~ed air** Druckluft f; **~ion** [ˌeʃən] phys. Verdichtung f; ⊕ Druck m.

comprise [kəm'praiz] in sich fassen, einschließen, enthalten.

compromise ['kɔmprəmaiz] **1.** Kompromiß m, n; **2.** v/t. Streit beilegen; bloßstellen; v/i. e-n Kompromiß schließen.

compuls|ion [kəm'pʌlʃən] Zwang m; **~ory** [ˌsəri] obligatorisch; Zwangs...; Pflicht...

compunction [kəm'pʌŋkʃən] Gewissensbisse m/pl.; Reue f; Bedenken n.

comput|ation [kɔmpju(ː)'teiʃən] (Be)Rechnung f; **~e** [kəm'pjuːt] (be-, er)rechnen; schätzen; **~er** [ˌtə] Computer m.

comrade ['kɔmrid] Kamerad m.

con¹ abbr. [kɔn] = contra.

con² *Am. sl.* [~] 1.: ~ man = confidence man; 2. 'reinlegen (*betrügen*).

conceal [kən'si:l] verbergen; *fig.* verhehlen, verheimlichen, verschweigen.

concede [kən'si:d] zugestehen; einräumen; gewähren, nachgeben.

conceit [kən'si:t] Einbildung *f*; spitzfindiger Gedanke; übertriebenes sprachliches Bild; ~ed □ eingebildet (*of* auf *acc.*).

conceiv|able □ [kən'si:vəbl] denkbar; begreiflich; ~e [kən'si:v] *v/i.* empfangen (*schwanger werden*); sich denken (*of acc.*); *v/t.* Kind empfangen; sich denken; aussinnen.

concentrate ['kɔnsentreit] (sich) zs.-ziehen, (sich) konzentrieren.

conception [kən'sepʃən] Begreifen *n*; Vorstellung *f*, Begriff *m*, Idee *f*; *biol.* Empfängnis *f*.

concern [kən'sɔ:n] 1. Angelegenheit *f*; Interesse *n*; Sorge *f*; Beziehung *f* (*with* zu); † Geschäft *n*, (industrielles) Unternehmen; 2. betreffen, angehen, interessieren; ~ o.s. *about od. for* sich kümmern um; *be* ~ed in Betracht kommen; ~ed □ interessiert, beteiligt (*in* an *dat.*); bekümmert; ~ing *prp.* [~niŋ] betreffend, über, wegen, hinsichtlich.

concert 1. ['kɔnsət] Konzert *n*; 2. [~sə(:)t] Einverständnis *n*; 3. [kən'sɔ:t] sich einigen, verabreden; ~ed gemeinsam; ♪ mehrstimmig.

concession [kən'seʃən] Zugeständnis *n*; Erlaubnis *f*. [räumend.\

concessive □ [kən'sesiv] ein-/

conciliat|e [kən'silieit] aus-, versöhnen; ausgleichen; ~or [~tə] Vermittler *m*; ~ory [~iətəri] versöhnlich, vermittelnd.

concise □ [kən'sais] kurz, bündig, knapp; ~ness [~snis] Kürze *f*.

conclude [kən'klu:d] schließen, beschließen; abschließen; folgern; sich entscheiden; *to be* ~d Schluß folgt.

conclusi|on [kən'klu:ʒən] Schluß *m*, Ende *n*; Abschluß *m*; Folgerung *f*; Beschluß *m*; ~ve □ [~u:siv] schlüssig; endgültig.

concoct [kən'kɔkt] zs.-brauen; *fig.* aussinnen; ~ion [~kʃən] Gebräu *n*; *fig.* Erfindung *f*.

concord ['kɔŋkɔ:d] Eintracht *f*; Übereinstimmung *f* (*a. gr.*); ♪ Harmonie *f*; ~ant □ [kən'kɔ:dənt] übereinstimmend; einstimmig; ♪ harmonisch.

concourse ['kɔŋkɔ:s] Zusammen-, Auflauf *m*; Menge *f*; *Am.* Bahnhofs-, Schalterhalle *f*.

concrete 1. ['kɔnkri:t] konkret; Beton...; 2. [~] Beton *m*; 3. [kən'kri:t] *zu e-r Masse* verbinden; ['kɔnkri:t] betonieren.

concur [kən'kɔ:] zs.-treffen, zs.-wirken; übereinstimmen; ~rence [~'kʌrəns] Zusammentreffen *n*; Übereinstimmung *f*; Mitwirkung *f*.

concussion [kən'kʌʃən] ~ *of the brain* Gehirnerschütterung *f*.

condemn [kən'dem] verdammen; verurteilen; verwerfen; *Kranke* aufgeben; beschlagnahmen; ~ation [kɔndem'neiʃən] Verurteilung *f*; Verdammung *f*; Verwerfung *f*.

condens|ation [kɔnden'seiʃən] Verdichtung *f*; ~e [kən'dens] (sich) verdichten; ⊕ kondensieren; zs.-drängen; ~er [~sə] ⊕ Kondensator *m*.

condescen|d [kɔndi'send] sich herablassen; geruhen; ~sion [~ʃən] Herablassung *f*.

condiment ['kɔndimənt] Würze *f*.

condition [kən'diʃən] 1. Zustand *m*, Stand *m*; Stellung *f*, Bedingung *f*; ~s *pl.* Verhältnisse *n/pl.*; 2. bedingen; in e-n bestimmten Zustand bringen; ~al □ [~nl] bedingt (*on, upon* durch); Bedingungs...; ~ clause *gr.* Bedingungssatz *m*; ~ mood *gr.* Konditional *m*.

condol|e [kən'doul] kondolieren (*with dat.*); ~ence [~ləns] Beileid *n*.

conduc|e [kən'dju:s] führen, dienen; ~ive [~siv] dienlich, förderlich.

conduct 1. ['kɔndʌkt] Führung *f*; Verhalten *n*, Betragen *n*; 2. [kən'dʌkt] führen; ♪ dirigieren; ~ion [~kʃən] Leitung *f*; ~or [~ktə] Führer *m*; Leiter *m*; Schaffner *m*; ♪ Dirigent *m*; ⚡ Blitzableiter *m*.

conduit ['kɔndit] (Leitungs-) Röhre *f*.

cone [koun] Kegel *m*; ♣ Zapfen *m*.

confabulation [kɔnfæbju'leiʃən] Plauderei *f*.

confection [kən'fekʃən] Konfekt *n*; ~er [~ʃnə] Konditor *m*; ~ery [~əri] Konfekt *n*; Konditorei *f*; *bsd. Am.* Süßwarengeschäft *n*.

confedera|cy [kən'fedərəsi] Bündnis *n*; *the* 2 *bsd. Am.* die 11 Südstaaten *bei der Sezession 1860—61*; ~te 1. [~rit] verbündet; 2. [~] Bundesgenosse *m*; 3. [~reit] (sich) verbünden; ~tion [kɔnfedə'reiʃən] Bund *m*, Bündnis *n*; *the* 2 *bsd. Am.* die Staatenkonföderation *f* von 1781—1789.

confer [kən'fə:] *v/t.* übertragen, verleihen; *v/i.* sich besprechen; ~ence [~'kɔnfərəns] Konferenz *f*.

confess [kən'fes] bekennen, gestehen; beichten; ~ion [~eʃən] Geständnis *n*; Bekenntnis *n*; Beichte *f*; ~ional [~nl] Beichtstuhl *m*; ~or [~esə] Bekenner *m*; Beichtvater *m*.

confide [kən'faid] *v/t.* anvertrauen; *v/i.* vertrauen (*in* auf *acc.*); ~nce ['kɔnfidəns] Vertrauen *n*; Zuversicht *f*; ~nce man Schwindler *m*;

Hochstapler *m*; ~ce trick Bauern-fängerei *f*; ~nt □ [~nt] vertrauend; zuversichtlich; ~ntial □ [konfi-'denʃəl] vertraulich.

confine [kən'fain] begrenzen; be-schränken; einsperren; be ~d niederkommen (of mit); be ~d to bed das Bett hüten müssen; ~ment [~nmənt] Haft *f*; Beschränkung *f*; Entbindung *f*.

confirm [kən'fə:m] (be)kräftigen; bestätigen; konfirmieren; firmen; ~ation [konfə'meiʃən] Bestätigung *f*; eccl. Konfirmation *f*; eccl. Firmung *f*.

confiscat|e ['konfiskeit] beschlag-nahmen; ~ion [konfis'keiʃən] Be-schlagnahme *f*.

conflagration [konflə'greiʃən] gro-ßer Brand.

conflict 1. ['konflikt] Konflikt *m*; **2.** [kən'flikt] im Konflikt stehen.

conflu|ence ['konfluəns], ~x [~lʌks] Zs.-fluß *m*; Auflauf *m*; ~ent [~luənt] **1.** zs.-fließend, zs.-laufend; **2.** Zu-, Nebenfluß *m*.

conform [kən'fɔ:m] (sich) an-passen; ~able □ [~məbl] (to) über-einstimmen (mit); entsprechend (dat.); nachgiebig (gegen); ~ity [~miti] Übereinstimmung *f*.

confound [kən'faund] vermengen; verwechseln; *j-n* verwirren; ~ it! F verdammt!; ~ed □ F verdammt.

confront [kən'frʌnt] gegenüber-stellen; entgegentreten (dat.).

confuse [kən'fju:z] verwechseln; verwirren; ~ion [~u:ʒən] Ver-wirrung *f*; Verwechs(e)lung *f*.

confut|ation [konfju'teiʃən] Wider-legung *f*; ~e [kən'fju:t] widerlegen.

congeal [kən'dʒi:l] erstarren (las-sen); gerinnen (lassen).

congenial □ [kən'dʒi:njəl] (geistes-)verwandt (with dat.); zusagend.

congenital [kən'dʒenitl] angeboren.

congestion [kən'dʒestʃən] (Blut-)Andrang *m*; Stauung *f*; traffic ~ Verkehrsstockung *f*.

conglomeration [kənglɔmə'reiʃən] Anhäufung *f*; Konglomerat *n*.

congratulat|e [kən'grætjuleit] be-glückwünschen; *j-m* gratulieren; ~ion [kəngrætju'leiʃən] Glück-wunsch *m*.

congregat|e ['kɔngrigeit] (sich) (ver)sammeln; ~ion [kɔngri'geiʃən] Versammlung *f*; eccl. Gemeinde *f*.

congress ['kɔngres] Kongreß *m*; ♀ Kongreß *m*, gesetzgebende Körper-schaft der USA; ♀man, ♀woman Am. pol. Mitglied *n* des Repräsen-tantenhauses.

congruous □ ['kɔngruəs] ange-messen (to für); übereinstimmend; folgerichtig.

conifer ['kounifə] Nadelholzbaum *m*.

conjecture [kən'dʒektʃə] **1.** Mut-maßung *f*; **2.** mutmaßen.

conjoin [kən'dʒɔin] (sich) ver-binden; ~t ['kɔndʒɔint] verbunden.

conjugal □ ['kɔndʒugəl] ehelich.

conjugat|e gr. ['kɔndʒugeit] kon-jugieren, beugen; ~ion gr. [kɔndʒu-'geiʃən] Konjugation *f*, Beugung *f*.

conjunction [kən'dʒʌŋkʃən] Ver-bindung *f*; Zs.-treffen *n*; gr. Kon-junktion *f*.

conjunctivitis [kəndʒʌŋkti'vaitis] Bindehautentzündung *f*.

conjure[1] [kən'dʒuə] beschwören, inständig bitten.

conjur|e[2] ['kʌndʒə] *v/t.* beschwö-ren; et. wohin zaubern; *v/i.* zaubern; ~er [~ərə] Zauberer *m*, -in *f*; Taschenspieler(in); ~ing-trick [~riŋtrik] Zauberkunststück *n*; ~or [~rə] = conjurer.

connect [kə'nekt] (sich) verbinden; ⚡ schalten; ~ed □ verbunden; zs.-hängend (Rede etc.); be ~ with in Verbindung stehen mit *j-m*; ~ion [~kʃən] = connexion.

connexion [kə'nekʃən] Verbindung *f*; ⚡ Schaltung *f*; Anschluß *m* (a. 🚌, ✈); Zs.-hang *m*; Verwandtschaft *f*.

connive [kə'naiv]: ~ at ein Auge zu-drücken bei.

connoisseur [kɔni'sə:] Kenner(in).

connubial □ [kə'nju:bjəl] ehelich.

conquer ['kɔŋkə] erobern; (be)sie-gen; ~or [~ərə] Eroberer *m*; Sieger *m*.

conquest ['kɔŋkwest] Eroberung *f*; Errungenschaft *f*; Sieg *m*.

conscience ['kɔnʃəns] Gewissen *n*.

conscientious □ [kɔnʃi'enʃəs] ge-wissenhaft; Gewissens...; ~ objector Kriegsdienstverweigerer *m* aus Überzeugung; ~ness [~snis] Ge-wissenhaftigkeit *f*.

conscious □ ['kɔnʃəs] bewußt; be ~ of sich bewußt sein (gen.); ~ness [~snis] Bewußtsein *n*.

conscript ✗ ['kɔnskript] Wehr-pflichtige(r) *m*; ~ion ✗ [kən'skrip-ʃən] Einberufung *f*.

consecrat|e ['kɔnsikreit] weihen, einsegnen; heiligen; widmen; ~ion [kɔnsi'kreiʃən] Weihung *f*, Ein-segnung *f*; Heiligung *f*.

consecutive □ [kən'sekjutiv] auf-ea.-folgend; fortlaufend.

consent [kən'sent] **1.** Zustimmung *f*; **2.** einwilligen, zustimmen (dat.).

consequen|ce ['kɔnsikwəns] (to) Folge *f*, Konsequenz *f* (für); Wir-kung *f*, Einfluß *m* (auf); Be-deutung *f* (für); ~t [~nt] **1.** folgend; **2.** Folge(rung) *f*; ~tial □ [kɔnsi-'kwenʃəl] sich ergebend (on aus); folgerichtig; wichtigtuerisch; ~tly ['kɔnsikwəntli] folglich, daher.

conserv|ation [kɔnsə(:)'veiʃən] Er-haltung *f*; ~ative □ [kən'sə:vətiv] **1.** erhaltend (of acc.); konservativ; vorsichtig; **2.** Konservative(r) *m*;

~atory [kɔn'sɔːvətri] Treib-, Gewächshaus n; ♩ Konservatorium n; **~e** [kɔn'sɔːv] erhalten.

consider [kɔn'sidə] v/t. betrachten; erwägen; überlegen; in Betracht ziehen; berücksichtigen; meinen, glauben; v/i. überlegen; *all things* **~ed** wenn man alles in Betracht zieht; **~able** □ [.ərəbl] ansehnlich, beträchtlich; **~ably** [.li] bedeutend, ziemlich, (sehr) viel; **~ate** □ [.rit] rücksichtsvoll; **~ation** [kɔnsidə'reiʃən] Betrachtung f, Erwägung f; Überlegung f; Rücksicht f; Wichtigkeit f; Entschädigung f; Entgelt n; *be under ~* erwogen werden; *in Betracht kommen; on no ~* unter keinen Umständen; **~ing** [kɔn'sidəriŋ] 1. *prp.* in Anbetracht (gen.); 2. F *adv.* den Umständen entsprechend.

consign [kɔn'sain] übergeben, überliefern; anvertrauen; ✝ konsignieren; **~ment** ✝ [.nmənt] Übersendung f; Konsignation f.

consist [kɔn'sist] bestehen (of aus); in Einklang stehen (with mit); **~ence, ~ency** [.təns, .si] Festigkeit(sgrad m) f; Übereinstimmung f; Konsequenz f; **~ent** [.nt] fest; übereinstimmend, vereinbar (with mit); konsequent.

consol|ation [kɔnsə'leiʃən] Trost m; **~e** [kɔn'soul] trösten.

consolidate [kɔn'sɔlideit] festigen; *fig.* vereinigen; zs.-legen.

consonan|ce [kɔnsənəns] Konsonanz f; Übereinstimmung f; **~t** [.nt] 1. □ übereinstimmend; 2. *gr.* Konsonant m, Mitlaut m.

consort [kɔn'sɔːt] Gemahl(in); ⚓ Geleitschiff n.

conspicuous □ [kɔn'spikjuəs] sichtbar; auffallend; hervorragend; *make o.s. ~* sich auffällig benehmen.

conspir|acy [kɔn'spirəsi] Verschwörung f; **~ator** [.ətə] Verschwörer m; **~e** [.'spaiə] sich verschwören.

constab|le ['kʌnstəbl] Polizist m; Schutzmann m; **~ulary** [kɔn-'stæbjuləri] Polizei(truppe) f.

constan|cy [kɔn'stənsi] Standhaftigkeit f; Beständigkeit f; **~t** □ [.nt] beständig, fest; unveränderlich; treu.

consternation [kɔnstə(:)'neiʃən] Bestürzung f.

constipation ⚕ [kɔnsti'peiʃən] Verstopfung f.

constituen|cy [kɔn'stitjuənsi] Wählerschaft f; Wahlkreis m; **~t** [.nt] 1. wesentlich; Grund..., Bestand...; konstituierend; 2. wesentlicher Bestandteil; Wähler m.

constitut|e ['kɔnstitjuːt] ein-, errichten; ernennen; bilden, ausmachen; **~ion** [kɔnsti'tjuːʃən] Ein-, Errichtung f; Bildung f; Körper-

bau m; Verfassung f; **~ional** □ [.nl] konstitutionell; natürlich; verfassungsmäßig.

constrain [kɔn'strein] zwingen; *et.* erzwingen; **~t** [.nt] Zwang m.

constrict [kɔn'strikt] zs.-ziehen; **~ion** [.kʃən] Zs.-ziehung f.

constringent [kɔn'strindʒənt] zs.-ziehend.

construct [kɔn'strʌkt] bauen, errichten; *fig.* bilden; **~ion** [.kʃən] Konstruktion f; Bau m; Auslegung f; **~ive** [.ktiv] aufbauend, schöpferisch, konstruktiv, positiv; Bau...; **~or** [.tə] Erbauer m, Konstrukteur m.

construe [kɔn'struː] *gr.* konstruieren; auslegen, auffassen; übersetzen.

consul ['kɔnsəl] Konsul m; **~-general** Generalkonsul m; **~ate** [.sjulit] Konsulat n (a. Gebäude).

consult [kɔn'sʌlt] v/t. konsultieren, um Rat fragen; *in e-m Buch* nachschlagen; v/i. sich beraten; **~ation** [kɔnsəl'teiʃən] Konsultation f, Beratung f; Rücksprache f; *~ hour* Sprechstunde f; **~ative** [kɔn'sʌltətiv] beratend.

consume [kɔn'sjuːm] v/t. verzehren; verbrauchen; vergeuden; **~r** [.mə] Verbraucher m; Abnehmer m.

consummate 1. □ [kɔn'sʌmit] vollendet; 2. ['kɔnsʌmeit] vollenden.

consumpti|on [kɔn'sʌmpʃən] Verbrauch m; ⚕ Schwindsucht f; **~ve** □ [.ptiv] verzehrend; ⚕ schwindsüchtig.

contact 1. ['kɔntækt] Berührung f; Kontakt m; *~ lenses pl.* Haft-, Kontaktschalen f/pl.; 2. [kɔn'tækt] Fühlung nehmen mit.

contagi|on ⚕ [kɔn'teidʒən] Ansteckung f; Verseuchung f; Seuche f; **~ous** □ [.əs] ansteckend.

contain [kɔn'tein] (ent)halten, (um-)fassen; *~ o.s.* an sich halten; **~er** [.nə] Behälter m; Großbehälter m (im Frachtverkehr).

contaminat|e [kɔn'tæmineit] verunreinigen; *fig.* anstecken, vergiften; verseuchen; **~ion** [kɔntæmi-'neiʃən] Verunreinigung f; (radioaktive) Verseuchung.

contemplat|e ['kɔntempleit] *fig.* betrachten; beabsichtigen; **~ion** [kɔntəm'pleiʃən] Betrachtung f; Nachsinnen n; **~ive** □ ['kɔntempleitiv] nachdenklich; [kɔn'templətiv] beschaulich.

contempora|neous □ [kɔntempə-'reinjəs] gleichzeitig; **~ry** [kɔn-'tempərəri] 1. zeitgenössisch; gleichzeitig; 2. Zeitgenosse m, -in f.

contempt [kɔn'tempt] Verachtung f; **~ible** □ [.təbl] verachtenswert; **~uous** □ [.tjuəs] geringschätzig (of gegen); verächtlich.

contend [kən'tend] v/i. streiten, ringen (for um); v/t. behaupten.
content [kən'tent] 1. zufrieden; 2. befriedigen; ~ o.s. sich begnügen; 3. Zufriedenheit f; to one's heart's ~ nach Herzenslust; ['kɔntent] Umfang m; Gehalt m; ~s pl. stofflicher Inhalt; ~ed □ [kən'tentid] zufrieden; genügsam.
contention [kən'tenʃən] (Wort-)Streit m; Wetteifer m.
contentment [kən'tentmənt] Zufriedenheit f, Genügsamkeit f.
contest 1. ['kɔntest] Streit m; Wettkampf m; 2. [kən'test] (be)streiten; anfechten; um et. streiten. [m.\
context ['kɔntekst] Zusammenhang]
contiguous □ [kən'tigjuəs] anstoßend (to an acc.); benachbart.
continent ['kɔntinənt] 1. □ enthaltsam; mäßig; 2. Kontinent m, Erdteil m; Festland n; ~al [kɔnti'nentl] 1. □ kontinental; Kontinental...; 2. Kontinentaleuropäer(in).
contingen|cy [kən'tindʒənsi] Zufälligkeit f; Zufall m; Möglichkeit f; ~t [~nt] 1. □ zufällig; möglich (to bei); 2. ⚔ Kontingent n.
continu|al □ [kən'tinjuəl] fortwährend, unaufhörlich; ~ance [~əns] (Fort)Dauer f; ~ation [kən tinju-'eiʃən] Fortsetzung f; Fortdauer f; ~ school Fortbildungsschule f; ~e [kən'tinju(:)] v/t. fortsetzen; beibehalten; to be ~d Fortsetzung folgt; v/i. fortdauern; fortfahren; ~ity [kɔnti'nju(:)iti] Kontinuität f; Film: Drehbuch n; Radio: verbindende Worte; ~ girl Skriptgirl n; ~ous □ [kən'tinjuəs] ununterbrochen.
contort [kən'tɔːt] verdrehen; verzerren; ~ion [~ɔːʃən] Verdrehung f; Verzerrung f.
contour ['kɔntuə] Umriß m.
contra ['kɔntrə] wider.
contraband ['kɔntrəbænd] Schmuggelware f; Schleichhandel m; attr. Schmuggel...
contraceptive [kɔntrə'septiv] 1. empfängnisverhütend; 2. empfängnisverhütendes Mittel.
contract 1. [kən'trækt] v/t. zs.-ziehen; sich et. zuziehen; Schulden machen; Heirat etc. (ab)schließen; v/i. einschrumpfen; e-n Vertrag schließen; sich verpflichten; 2. ['kɔntrækt] Kontrakt m, Vertrag m; ~ion [kən'trækʃən] Zs.-ziehung f; gr. Kurzform f; ~or [~ktə] Unternehmer m; Lieferant m.
contradict [kɔntrə'dikt] widersprechen (dat.); ~ion [~kʃən] Widerspruch m; ~ory □ [~ktəri] (sich) widersprechend.
contrar|iety [kɔntrə'raiəti] Widerspruch m; Widrigkeit f; ~y ['kɔntrəri] 1. entgegengesetzt; widrig; ~ to zuwider (dat.); gegen; 2. Gegenteil n; on the ~ im Gegenteil.

24*

contrast 1. ['kɔntraːst] Gegensatz m; 2. [kən'traːst] v/t. gegenüberstellen; vergleichen; v/i. sich unterscheiden, abstechen (with von).
contribut|e [kən'tribju(:)t] beitragen, beisteuern; ~ion [kɔntri'bju:ʃən] Beitrag m; ~or [kən'tribjutə] Beitragende(r m) f; Mitarbeiter(in) an e-r Zeitung; ~ory [~əri] beitragend.
contrit|e □ ['kɔntrait] reuevoll; ~ion [kən'triʃən] Zerknirschung f.
contriv|ance [kən'traivəns] Erfindung f; Plan m; Vorrichtung f; Kunstgriff m; Scharfsinn m; ~e [kən'traiv] v/t. ersinnen; planen; zuwegebringen; v/i. es fertig bringen (to inf. zu inf.); ~er [~və] Erfinder(in).
control [kən'troul] 1. Kontrolle f, Aufsicht f; Befehl m; Zwang m; Gewalt f; Zwangswirtschaft f; Kontrollvorrichtung f; Steuerung f; ~ board ⊕ Schaltbrett n; 2. einbeschränken; kontrollieren; beaufsichtigen, überwachen; beherrschen; (nach)prüfen; bewirtschaften; regeln; ⚓ steuern (a. fig. dat.); ~ler [~lə] Kontrolleur m, Aufseher m; Leiter m; Rechnungsprüfer m.
controver|sial □ [kɔntrə'vəːʃəl] umstritten; streitsüchtig; ~sy ['kɔntrəvəːsi] Streit(frage f) m; ~t [~əːt] bestreiten.
contumacious □ [kɔntju(:)'meiʃəs] widerspenstig; ⚖ ungehorsam.
contumely ['kɔntju(:)mli] Beschimpfung f; Schmach f.
contuse ⚕ [kən'tjuːz] quetschen.
convalesce [kɔnvə'les] genesen; ~nce [~sns] Genesung f; ~nt [~nt] 1. □ genesend; 2. Genesende(r m) f.
convene [kən'viːn] (sich) versammeln; zs.-rufen; ⚖ vorladen.
convenien|ce [kən'viːnjəns] Bequemlichkeit f; Angemessenheit f; Vorteil m; Klosett n; at your earliest ~ möglichst bald; ~t □ [~nt] bequem; passend; brauchbar.
convent ['kɔnvənt] (Nonnen)Kloster n; ~ion [kən'venʃən] Versammlung f; Konvention f, Übereinkommen n, Vertrag m; Herkommen n; ~ional [~nl] vertraglich; herkömmlich, konventionell.
converge [kən'vəːdʒ] konvergieren, zs.-laufen (lassen).
convers|ant [kən'vəːsənt] vertraut; ~ation [kɔnvə'seiʃən] Gespräch n, Unterhaltung f; ~ational [~nl] Unterhaltungs...; umgangssprachlich; ~e 1. □ ['kɔnvəːs] umgekehrt; 2. [kən'vəːs] sich unterhalten; ~ion [~əːʃən] Um-, Verwandlung f; ⊕, ⚡ Umformung f; eccl. Bekehrung f; pol. Meinungswechsel m, Übertritt m; ✝ Konvertierung f; Umstellung f e-r Währung etc.

convert 1. ['kɔnvə:t] Bekehrte(r *m*) *f*, Konvertit *m*; **2.** [kən'və:t] (sich) um-, verwandeln; ⊕, ⚡ umformen; *eccl.* bekehren; ✝ konvertieren; *Währung etc.* umstellen; **~er** ⊕, ⚡ [~tə] Umformer *m*; **~ible 1.** □ [~təbl] um-, verwandelbar; ✝ konvertierbar; **2.** *mot.* Kabrio(lett) *n*.

convey [kən'vei] befördern, bringen, schaffen; übermitteln; mitteilen; ausdrücken; übertragen; **~ance** [~eiəns] Beförderung *f*; ✝ Spedition *f*; Übermittlung *f*; Verkehrsmittel *n*; Fuhrwerk *n*; Übertragung *f*; **~er**, **~or** ⊕ [~eiə] *a*. **~ belt** Förderband *n*.

convict 1. ['kɔnvikt] Sträfling *m*; **2.** [kən'vikt] *j-n* überführen; **~ion** [~kʃən] ɑ̈ Überführung *f*; Überzeugung *f* (of von).

convince [kən'vins] überzeugen.

convivial □ [kən'viviəl] festlich, gesellig.

convocation [kɔnvə'keiʃən] Einberufung *f*; Versammlung *f*.

convoke [kən'vouk] einberufen.

convoy ['kɔnvoi] **1.** Geleit *n*; Geleitzug *m*; (Geleit)Schutz *m*; **2.** geleiten.

convuls|ion [kən'vʌlʃən] Zuckung *f*, Krampf *m*; **~ive** □ [~lsiv] krampfhaft, -artig, konvulsiv.

coo [ku:] girren, gurren.

cook [kuk] **1.** Koch *m*; Köchin *f*; **2.** kochen; *Bericht etc.* frisieren; **~book** *Am.* ['kukbuk] Kochbuch *n*; **~ery** ['kukəri] Kochen *n*; Kochkunst *f*; **~ie** *Am.* ['kuki] Plätzchen *n*; **~ing** [~iŋ] Küche *f* (*Kochweise*); **~y** *Am.* ['kuki] = *cookie*.

cool [ku:l] **1.** □ kühl; *fig.* kaltblütig, gelassen; unverfroren; **2.** Kühle *f*; **3.** (sich) abkühlen.

coolness ['ku:lnis] Kühle *f* (*a. fig.*); Kaltblütigkeit *f*.

coon *Am.* F [ku:n] *zo.* Waschbär *m*; Neger *m*; (schlauer) Bursche *m*.

coop [ku:p] **1.** Hühnerkorb *m*; **2. ~ up** *od. in* einsperren.

co-op F [kou'ɔp] = *co-operative* (*store*).

cooper ['ku:pə] Böttcher *m*, Küfer *m*.

co(-)operat|e [kou'ɔpəreit] mitwirken; zs.-arbeiten; **~ion** [kouɔpə-'reiʃən] Mitwirkung *f*; Zs.-arbeit *f*; **~ive** [kou'ɔpərətiv] zs.-wirkend; **~ society** Konsumverein *m*; **~ store** Konsum(vereinsladen) *m*; **~or** [~reitə] Mitarbeiter *m*.

co-ordinat|e 1. □ [kou'ɔ:dnit] gleichgeordnet; **2.** [~dineit] koordinieren, gleichordnen; auf-ea. einstellen; **~ion** [kouɔ:di'neiʃən] Gleichordnung *f*, -schaltung *f*.

copartner ['kou'pa:tnə] Teilhaber *m*.

cope [koup]: **~ with** sich messen mit, fertig werden mit.

copious □ ['koupjəs] reich(lich); weitschweifig; **~ness** [~snis] Fülle *f*.

copper¹ ['kɔpə] **1.** Kupfer *n*; Kupfermünze *f*; **2.** kupfern; Kupfer...

copper² *sl.* [~] Polyp *m* (*Polizist*).

coppice, copse ['kɔpis, kɔps] Unterholz *n*, Dickicht *n*.

copy ['kɔpi] **1.** Kopie *f*; Nachbildung *f*; Abschrift *f*; Durchschlag *m*; Muster *n*; Exemplar *n* e-s Buches; Zeitungs-Nummer *f*; druckfertiges Manuskript; *fair od. clean* **~** Reinschrift *f*; **2.** kopieren; abschreiben; nachbilden, nachahmen; **~-book** Schreibheft *n*; **~ing** [~iiŋ] Kopier...; **~ist** [~ist] Abschreiber *m*; Nachahmer *m*; **~right** Verlagsrecht *n*, Copyright *n*.

coral ['kɔrəl] Koralle *f*.

cord [kɔ:d] **1.** Schnur *f*, Strick *m*; *anat.* Strang *m*; **2.** (zu)schnüren, binden; **~ed** ['kɔ:did] gerippt.

cordial ['kɔ:djəl] **1.** □ herzlich; herzstärkend; **2.** (Magen)Likör *m*; **~ity** [kɔ:di'æliti] Herzlichkeit *f*.

cordon ['kɔ:dn] **1.** Postenkette *f*; **2. ~ off** abriegeln, absperren.

corduroy ['kɔ:dərɔi] Kord *m*; **~s** *pl.* Kordhosen *f/pl.*; **~ road** Knüppeldamm *m*.

core [kɔ:] **1.** Kerngehäuse *n*; *fig.* Herz *n*; Kern *m*; **2.** entkernen.

cork [kɔ:k] **1.** Kork *m*; **2.** (ver)korken; **~ing** *Am.* F ['kɔ:kiŋ] fabelhaft, prima; **~-jacket** Schwimmweste *f*; **~screw** Kork(en)zieher *m*.

corn [kɔ:n] **1.** Korn *n*; Getreide *n*; *a. Indian* **~** *Am.* Mais *m*; ✂ Hühnerauge *n*; **2.** einpökeln.

corner ['kɔ:nə] **1.** Ecke *f*, Winkel *m*; Kurve *f*; *fig.* Enge *f*; ✝ *Aufkäufer*-Ring *m*; **2.** Eck...; **3.** in die Ecke (*fig.* Enge) treiben; ✝ aufkaufen; **~ed** ...eckig.

cornet ♪ [kɔ:nit] (kleines) Horn.

cornice △ ['kɔ:nis] Gesims *n*.

corn|-juice *Am. sl.* ['kɔ:ndʒu:s] Maisschnaps *m*; **~ pone** *Am.* ['kɔ:npoun] Maisbrot *n*; **~stalk** Getreidehalm *m*; *Am.* Maisstengel *m*; **~starch** *Am.* Maisstärke *f*.

coron|ation [kɔrə'neiʃən] Krönung *f*; **~er** ['kɔrənə] Leichenbeschauer *m*; **~et** [~nit] Adelskrone *f*.

corpor|al ['kɔ:pərəl] **1.** □ körperlich; **2.** ✂ Korporal *m*; **~ation** [kɔ:pə'reiʃən] Körperschaft *f*, Innung *f*, Zunft *f*; Stadtverwaltung *f*; *Am.* Aktiengesellschaft *f*.

corpse [kɔ:ps] Leichnam *m*.

corpulen|ce, **~cy** ['kɔ:pjuləns, ~si] Beleibtheit *f*; **~t** [~nt] beleibt.

corral *Am.* [kɔ:'ra:l] **1.** Einzäunung *f*; **2.** zs.-pferchen, einsperren.

correct [kə'rekt] **1.** *adj.* □ korrekt, richtig; **2.** *v/t.* korrigieren; zurechtweisen; strafen; **~ion** [~kʃən] Berichtigung *f*; Verweis *m*; Strafe *f*;

Korrektur *f*; *house of* ~ Besserungsanstalt *f*.
correlate ['kɔrileit] in Wechselbeziehung stehen *od.* bringen.
correspond [kɔris'pɔnd] entsprechen (*with, to dat.*); korrespondieren; **~ence** [~dəns] Übereinstimmung *f*; Briefwechsel *m*; **~ent** [~nt] 1. □ entsprechend; 2. Briefschreiber(in); Korrespondent(in).
corridor ['kɔridɔ:] Korridor *m*; Gang *m*; ~ *train* D-Zug *m*.
corrigible □ ['kɔridʒəbl] verbesserlich; zu verbessern(d).
corroborate [kə'rɔbəreit] stärken; bestätigen.
corro|de [kə'roud] zerfressen; wegätzen; **~sion** [~ʒən] Ätzen *n*, Zerfressen *n*; ⊕ Korrosion *f*; Rost *m*; **~sive** [~ousiv] 1. □ zerfressend, ätzend; 2. Ätzmittel *n*.
corrugate ['kɔrugeit] runzeln; ⊕ riefen; **~d iron** Wellblech *n*.
corrupt [kə'rʌpt] 1. □ verdorben; verderbt; bestechlich; 2. *v/t.* verderben; bestechen; anstecken; *v/i.* (ver)faulen, verderben; **~ible** □ [~təbl] verderblich; bestechlich; **~ion** [~pʃən] Verderbnis *f*, Verdorbenheit *f*; Fäulnis *f*; Bestechung *f*.
corsage [kɔ:'sɑ:ʒ] Taille *f*, Mieder *n*; *Am.* Ansteckblume(*n pl.*) *f*.
corset ['kɔ:sit] Korsett *n*.
coruscate ['kɔrəskeit] funkeln.
co-signatory ['kou'signətəri] 1. mitunterzeichnend; 2. Mitunterzeichner *m*.
cosmetic [kɔz'metik] 1. kosmetisch; 2. Schönheitsmittel *n*; Kosmetik *f*; **~ian** [kɔzme'tiʃən] Kosmetiker(in).
cosmonaut ['kɔzmənɔ:t] Kosmonaut *m*, Weltraumfahrer *m*.
cosmopolit|an [kɔzmə'pɔlitən], **~e** [kɔz'mɔpəlait] 1. kosmopolitisch; 2. Weltbürger(in).
cost [kɔst] 1. Preis *m*; Kosten *pl.*; Schaden *m*; *first od. prime* ~ Anschaffungskosten *pl.*; 2. [*irr.*] kosten.
cost|iness ['kɔstlinis] Kostbarkeit *f*; **~y** ['kɔstli] kostbar; kostspielig.
costume ['kɔstju:m] Kostüm *n*; Kleidung *f*; Tracht *f*.
cosy ['kouzi] 1. □ behaglich, gemütlich; 2. = *tea-cosy*.
cot [kɔt] Feldbett *n*; ⚓ Hängematte *f* mit Rahmen, Koje *f*; Kinderbett *n*.
cottage ['kɔtidʒ] Hütte *f*; kleines Landhaus, Sommerhaus *n*; ~ *cheese Am.* Quark(käse) *m*; ~ *piano* Pianino *n*; **~r** [~dʒə] Häusler *m*; Hüttenbewohner *m*; *Am.* Sommergast *m*.
cotton ['kɔtn] 1. Baumwolle *f*; ♀ Kattun *m*; *Näh*-Garn *n*; 2. baumwollen; Baumwoll...; ~ *wool* Watte *f*; 3. ⸙ sich vertragen; sich anschließen; **~-wood** ♀ *e-e* amerikanische Pappel.

couch [kautʃ] 1. Lager *n*; Couch *f*, Sofa *n*, Liege *f*; Schicht *f*; 2. *v/t. Meinung etc.* ausdrücken; *Schriftsatz etc.* abfassen; ✒ *Star* stechen; *v/i.* sich (nieder)legen; versteckt liegen; kauern.
cough [kɔf] 1. Husten *m*; 2. husten.
could [kud] *pret. von can*[1].
coulee *Am.* ['ku:li] (trockenes) Bachbett.
council ['kaunsl] Rat(sversammlung *f*) *m*; **~(l)or** [~silə] Ratsmitglied *n*, Stadtrat *m*.
counsel ['kaunsəl] 1. Beratung *f*; Rat(schlag) *m*; ⚖ Anwalt *m*; ~ *for the defense* Verteidiger *m*; ~ *for the prosecution* Anklagevertreter *m*; 2. *j-n* beraten; *j-m* raten; **~(l)or** [~silə] Ratgeber(in); Anwalt *m*; *Am.* Rechtsbeistand *m*.
count[1] [kaunt] 1. Rechnung *f*; Zahl *f*; ⚖ Anklagepunkt *m*; 2. *v/t.* zählen; rechnen; dazurechnen; *fig.* halten für; *v/i.* zählen; rechnen; gelten (*for little* wenig).
count[2] [~] *nichtbritischer* Graf.
count-down ['kauntdaun] Countdown *m*, *n*, Startzählung *f* (*beim Raketenstart*).
countenance ['kauntinəns] 1. Gesicht *n*; Fassung *f*; Unterstützung *f*; 2. begünstigen, unterstützen.
counter[1] ['kauntə] Zähler *m*, Zählapparat *m*; Spielmarke *f*; Zahlpfennig *m*; Ladentisch *m*; Schalter *m*.
counter[2] [~] 1. entgegen, zuwider (*to dat.*); Gegen...; 2. Gegenschlag *m*; 3. Gegenmaßnahmen treffen.
counteract [kauntə'rækt] zuwiderhandeln (*dat.*).
counterbalance 1. ['kauntəbæləns] Gegengewicht *n*; 2. [kauntə'bæləns] aufwiegen; † ausgleichen.
counter-espionage ['kauntər'espiəna:ʒ] Spionageabwehr *f*.
counterfeit ['kauntəfit] 1. □ nachgemacht; falsch, unecht; 2. Nachahmung *f*; Fälschung *f*; Falschgeld *n*; 3. nachmachen; fälschen; heucheln.
counterfoil ['kauntəfɔil] Kontrollabschnitt *m*.
countermand [kauntə'ma:nd] 1. Gegenbefehl *m*; Widerruf *m*; 2. widerrufen; abbestellen.
counter-move *fig.* ['kauntəmu:v] Gegenzug *m*, -maßnahme *f*.
counterpane ['kauntəpein] Bettdecke *f*.
counterpart ['kauntəpa:t] Gegenstück *n*.
counterpoise ['kauntəpɔiz] 1. Gegengewicht *n*; 2. das Gleichgewicht halten (*dat.*) (*a. fig.*), ausbalancieren.
countersign ['kauntəsain] 1. Gegenzeichen *n*; ✗ Losung(swort *n*) *f*; 2. gegenzeichnen.

countervail ['kauntəveil] aufwiegen.

countess ['kauntis] Gräfin f.

counting-house ['kauntiŋhaus] Kontor n.

countless ['kauntlis] zahllos.

countrified ['kʌntrifaid] ländlich; bäurisch.

country ['kʌntri] 1. Land n; Gegend f; Heimatland n; 2. Land(s)..., ländlich; **~man** Landmann m (Bauer); Landsmann m; **~side** Gegend f; Land(bevölkerung f) n.

county ['kaunti] Grafschaft f, Kreis m; **~ seat** Am. = **~ town** Kreisstadt f.

coup [ku:] Schlag m, Streich m.

couple ['kʌpl] 1. Paar n; Koppel f; 2. (ver)koppeln; ⊕ kuppeln; (sich) paaren; **~r** [~ə] Radio: Koppler m.

coupling ['kʌpliŋ] Kupplung f; Radio: Kopplung f; attr. Kupplungs...

coupon ['ku:pɔn] Abschnitt m.

courage ['kʌridʒ] Mut m; **~ous** □ [kə'reidʒəs] mutig, beherzt.

courier ['kuriə] Kurier m, Eilbote m; Reiseführer m.

course [kɔ:s] 1. Lauf m, Gang m; Weg m, ♨, fig. Kurs m; Rennbahn f; Gang m (Speisen); Kursus m; univ. Vorlesung f; Ordnung f, Folge f; of **~** selbstverständlich; 2. v/t. hetzen; jagen; v/i. rennen.

court [kɔ:t] 1. Hof m; Hofgesellschaft f; Gericht(shof m) n; General ♀ Am. gesetzgebende Versammlung; pay (one's) **~** to j-m den Hof machen; 2. j-m den Hof machen; werben um; **~day** ['kɔ:tdei] Gerichtstag m; **~eous** □ ['kə:tjəs] höflich; **~esy** ['kə:tisi] Höflichkeit f; Gefälligkeit f; **~house** ['kɔ:thaus] Gerichtsgebäude n; Am. a. Amtshaus n e-s Kreises; **~ier** ['kɔ:tjə] Höfling m; **~ly** ['kɔ:tli] höfisch; höflich; **~martial** ⚔ Kriegs-, Militärgericht n; **~-martial** ⚔ ['kɔ:t'ma:ʃəl] vor ein Kriegs- od. Militärgericht stellen; **~ room** Gerichtssaal m; **~ship** ['kɔ:tʃip] Werbung f; **~yard** Hof m.

cousin ['kʌzn] Vetter m; Base f.

cove [kouv] 1. Bucht f; fig. Obdach n.

covenant ['kʌvinənt] 1. Vertrag m; Bund m; 2. v/t. geloben; v/i. übereinkommen.

cover ['kʌvə] 1. Decke f; Deckel m; Umschlag m; Hülle f; Deckung f; Schutz m; Dickicht n; Deckmantel m; Decke f, Mantel m (Bereifung); 2. (be-, zu)decken; einschlagen; einwickeln; verbergen, verdecken; schützen; Weg zurücklegen; ✝ decken; mit e-r Schußwaffe zielen nach; ⚔ Gelände bestreichen; umfassen; fig. erfassen; Zeitung: berichten über (acc.); **~age** [~əridʒ]

Berichterstattung f (of über acc.); **~ing** [~riŋ] Decke f; Bett-Bezug m; Überzug m; Bekleidung f; Bedachung f.

covert 1. □ ['kʌvət] heimlich, versteckt; 2. ['kʌvə] Schutz m; Versteck n; Dickicht n.

covet ['kʌvit] begehren; **~ous** □ [~təs] (be)gierig; habsüchtig.

cow[1] [kau] Kuh f.

cow[2] [~] einschüchtern, ducken.

coward ['kauəd] 1. □ feig; 2. Feigling m; **~ice** [~dis] Feigheit f; **~ly** [~dli] feig(e).

cow|boy ['kauboi] Cowboy m (berittener Rinderhirt); **~catcher** Am. ⚙ Schienenräumer m.

cower ['kauə] kauern; sich ducken.

cow|herd ['kauhə:d] Kuhhirt m; **~hide** 1. Rind(s)leder n; 2. peitschen; **~house** Kuhstall m.

cowl [kaul] Mönchskutte f; Kapuze f; Schornsteinkappe f.

cow|man ['kaumən] Melker m; Am. Viehzüchter m; **~puncher** Am. F ['kaupʌntʃə] Rinderhirt m; **~shed** Kuhstall m; **~slip** ♀ Schlüsselblume f; Am. Sumpfdotterblume f.

coxcomb ['kɔkskoum] Geck m.

coxswain ['kɔkswein, ♨ mst 'kɔksn] Bootsführer m; Steuermann m.

coy □ [kɔi] schüchtern; spröde.

crab [kræb] Krabbe f, Taschenkrebs m; ⊕ Winde f; F Querkopf m.

crab-louse ['kræblaus] Filzlaus f.

crack [kræk] 1. Krach m; Riß m, Sprung m; F derber Schlag; Versuch m; Witz m; 2. F erstklassig; 3. v/t. (zer)sprengen; knallen mit et.; (auf)knacken; **~ a joke** e-n Witz reißen; v/i. platzen, springen; knallen; umschlagen (Stimme); **~ed** geborsten; F verdreht; **~er** ['krækə] Knallbonbon m, n; Schwärmer m; Am. Keks m (ungesüßt); **~le** [~kl] knattern, knistern; **~-up** Zs.-stoß m; 💥 Bruchlandung f.

cradle ['kreidl] 1. Wiege f; Kindheit f (a. fig.); 2. (ein)wiegen.

craft [kra:ft] Handwerk n, Gewerbe n; Schiff(e pl.) n; Gerissenheit f; **~sman** ['kra:ftsmən](Kunst)Handwerker m; **~y** □ ['kra:fti] gerissen, raffiniert.

crag [kræg] Klippe f, Felsspitze f.

cram [kræm] (voll)stopfen; nudeln, mästen; F (ein)pauken.

cramp [kræmp] 1. Krampf m; ⊕ Klammer f; fig. Fessel f; 2. verkrampfen; einengen, hemmen.

cranberry ['krænbəri] Preiselbeere f.

crane [krein] 1. Kranich m; ⊕ Kran m; 2. (den Hals) recken; **~fly** zo. ['kreinflai] Schnake f.

crank [kræŋk] 1. Kurbel f; Schwengel m; Wortspiel n; Schrulle f; komischer Kauz; fixe Idee; 2. (an)kurbeln; **~-shaft** ⊕ ['kræŋkʃa:ft]

Kurbelwelle *f*; ～y [～ki] wacklig; launisch; verschroben.

cranny ['kræni] Riß *m*, Ritze *f*.

crape [kreip] Krepp *m*, Flor *m*.

craps *Am.* [kræps] *pl. Würfelspiel.*

crash [kræʃ] 1. Krach *m* (*a.* ✝); ✈ Absturz *m*; 2. *v/i.* krachen; einstürzen; ✈ abstürzen; *mot.* zs.-stoßen; fahren, fliegen, stürzen (*into* in, auf *acc.*); *v/t.* zerschmettern; 3. *Am.* F blitzschnell ausgeführt; ～**helmet** ['kræʃhelmit] Sturzhelm *m*; ～**landing** Bruchlandung *f*.

crate [kreit] Lattenkiste *f*.

crater ['kreitə] Krater *m*; Trichter *m*.

crave [kreiv] *v/t.* dringend bitten *od.* flehen um; *v/i.* sich sehnen.

craven ['kreivən] feig.

crawfish ['krɔːfiʃ] 1. Krebs *m*; 2. *Am.* F sich drücken.

crawl [krɔːl] 1. Kriechen *n*; 2. kriechen; schleichen; wimmeln; kribbeln; *Schwimmen:* kraulen; *it makes one's flesh* ～ man bekommt e-e Gänsehaut davon.

crayfish ['kreifiʃ] Flußkrebs *m*.

crayon ['kreiən] Zeichenstift *m*, *bsd.* Pastellstift *m*; Pastell(gemälde) *n*.

craz|e [kreiz] Verrücktheit *f*; F Fimmel *m*; *be the* ～ Mode sein; ～y [kreizi] baufällig; verrückt (*for, about* nach).

creak [kriːk] knarren.

cream [kriːm] 1. Rahm *m*, Sahne *f*; Creme *f*; Auslese *f*; *das Beste*; 2. den Rahm abschöpfen; ～ery ['kriːməri] Molkerei *f*; Milchgeschäft *n*; ～y □ [～mi] sahnig.

crease [kriːs] 1. (Bügel)Falte *f*; 2. (sich) kniffen, (sich) falten.

creat|e [kri(ː)'eit] (er)schaffen; *thea.* *e-e Rolle* gestalten; verursachen; erzeugen; ernennen; ～**ion** [～'eiʃən] Schöpfung *f*; Ernennung *f*; ～**ive** [～'eitiv] schöpferisch; ～**or** [～tə] Schöpfer *m*; ～**ure** ['kriːtʃə] Geschöpf *n*; Kreatur *f*.

creden|ce ['kriːdəns] Glaube *m*; ～**tials** [kri'denʃəlz] *pl.* Beglaubigungsschreiben *n*; Unterlagen *f/pl.*

credible └ ['kredəbl] glaubwürdig; glaubhaft.

credit ['kredit] 1. Glaube(n) *m*; Ruf *m*, Ansehen *n*; Guthaben *n*; ✝ Kredit *m*; ✝ Kredit *m*; Einfluß *m*; Verdienst *n*, Ehre *f*; *Am. Schule:* (Anrechnungs)Punkt *m*; 2. *j-m* glauben; *j-m* trauen; ✝ gutschreiben; ～ *s.o. with s.th.* j-m et. zutrauen; ～**able** └ [～təbl] achtbar; ehrenvoll (*to* für); ～**or** [～tə] Gläubiger *m*.

credulous □ ['kredjuləs] leichtgläubig.

creed [kriːd] Glaubensbekenntnis *n*.

creek [kriːk] Bucht *f*; *Am.* Bach *m*.

creel [kriːl] Fischkorb *m*.

creep [kriːp] [*irr.*] kriechen; *fig.* (sich ein)schleichen; kribbeln; *it makes my flesh* ～ ich bekomme e-e Gänsehaut davon; ～er ['kriːpə] Kriecher(in); Kletterpflanze *f*.

cremator|ium [kremə'tɔːriəm], *bsd. Am.* ～y ['kremətəri] Krematorium *n*.

crept [krept] *pret. u. p.p. von* creep.

crescent ['kresnt] 1. zunehmend; halbmondförmig; 2. Halbmond *m*; 2 *City Am.* New Orleans.

cress ✿ [kres] Kresse *f*.

crest [krest] *Hahnen-, Berg- etc.* Kamm *m*; Mähne *f*; Federbusch *m*; *Heraldik:* family ～ Familienwappen *n*; ～**fallen** ['krestfɔːlən] niedergeschlagen.

crevasse [kri'væs] (Gletscher)Spalte *f*; *Am.* Deichbruch *m*.

crevice ['krevis] Riß *m*, Spalte *f*.

crew[1] [kruː] Schar *f*; ⚓, ✈ Mannschaft *f*.

crew[2] [～] *pret. von* crow 2.

crib [krib] 1. Krippe *f*; Kinderbett (-stelle *f*) *n*; F *Schule:* Klatsche *f*; *bsd. Am.* Behälter *m*; 2. einsperren; F mausen; F abschreiben.

crick [krik] Krampf *m*; ～ *in the neck* steifer Hals.

cricket ['krikit] *zo.* Grille *f*; *Sport:* Kricket *n*; *not* ～ F nicht fair.

crime [kraim] Verbrechen *n*.

criminal ['kriminl] 1. verbrecherisch; Kriminal…, Straf…; 2. Verbrecher(in); ～**ity** [krimi'næliti] Strafbarkeit *f*; Verbrechertum *n*.

crimp [krimp] kräuseln.

crimson ['krimzn] karmesin(rot).

cringe [krindʒ] sich ducken.

crinkle ['krinkl] 1. Windung *f*; Falte *f*; 2. (sich) winden; (sich) kräuseln.

cripple ['kripl] 1. Krüppel *m*; Lahme(r *m*) *f*; 2. verkrüppeln; *fig.* lähmen.

cris|is ['kraisis], *pl.* ～es [～siːz] Krisis *f*, Krise *f*, Wende-, Höhepunkt *m*.

crisp [krisp] 1. kraus; knusperig; frisch; klar; steif; 2. (sich) kräuseln; knusperig machen *od.* werden; 3. ～ *pl., a. potato* ～s *pl.* Kartoffelchips *pl.*

criss-cross ['kriskrɔs] 1. Kreuzzeichen *n*; 2. (durch)kreuzen.

criterion [krai'tiəriən], *pl.* ～a [～riə] Kennzeichen *n*, Prüfstein *m*.

criti|c ['kritik] Kritiker(in); ～**cal** □ [～kəl] kritisch; bedenklich; ～**cism** [～isizəm] Kritik *f* (*of an dat.*); ～**cize** [～saiz] kritisieren; beurteilen; tadeln; ～**que** [kri'tiːk] kritischer Essay; *die* Kritik.

croak [krouk] krächzen; quaken.

crochet ['krouʃei] 1. Häkelei *f*; 2. häkeln.

crock [krɔk] irdener Topf; **~ery** ['krɔkəri] Töpferware f.

crocodile zo. ['krɔkədail] Krokodil n.

crone F [kroun] altes Weib.

crony F ['krouni] alter Freund.

crook [kruk] **1.** Krümmung f; Haken m; Hirtenstab m; sl. Gauner m; **2.** (sich) krümmen; (sich) (ver)biegen; **~ed** ['krukid] krumm; bucklig; unehrlich; [krukt] Krück...

croon [kru:n] schmalzig singen; summen; **~er** ['kru:nə] Schnulzensänger m.

crop [krɔp] **1.** Kropf m; Peitschenstiel m; Reitpeitsche f; Ernte f; kurzer Haarschnitt; **2.** (ab-, be-) schneiden; (ab)ernten; Acker bebauen; **~ up** fig. auftauchen.

cross [krɔs] **1.** Kreuz n (a. fig. Leiden); Kreuzung f; **2.** □ sich kreuzend; quer (liegend, laufend etc.); ärgerlich, verdrießlich; entgegengesetzt; Kreuz..., Quer...; **3.** v/t. kreuzen; durchstreichen; fig. durchkreuzen; überqueren; in den Weg kommen (dat.); **~ o.s.** sich bekreuzigen; keep one's fingers **~ed** den Daumen halten; v/i. sich kreuzen; **~bar** ['krɔsbɑ:] Fußball: Torlatte f; **~breed** (Rassen)Kreuzung f; **~country** querfeldein; **~examination** Kreuzverhör n; **~eyed** schieläugig; **~ing** [~siŋ] Kreuzung f; Übergang m; -fahrt f; **~road** Querstraße f; **~roads** pl. od. sg. Kreuzweg m; **~section** Querschnitt m; **~wise** kreuzweise; **~word** (puzzle) Kreuzworträtsel n.

crotchet ['krɔtʃit] Haken m; ♪ Viertelnote f; wunderlicher Einfall.

crouch [krautʃ] **1.** sich ducken; **2.** Hockstellung f.

crow [krou] **1.** Krähe f; Krähen n; eat ~ Am. F zu Kreuze kriechen; **2.** [irr.] krähen; triumphieren; **~bar** ['kroubɑ:] Brecheisen n.

crowd [kraud] **1.** Haufen m, Menge f; Gedränge n; F Bande f; **2.** (sich) drängen; (über)füllen; wimmeln.

crown [kraun] **1.** Krone f; Kranz m; Gipfel m; Scheitel m; **2.** krönen; Zahn überkronen; to ~ all zu guter Letzt, zu allem Überfluß.

cruci|al □ ['kru:ʃjəl] entscheidend; kritisch; **~ble** ['kru:sibl] Schmelztiegel m; **~fixion** [kru:si'fikʃən] Kreuzigung f; **~fy** ['kru:sifai] kreuzigen.

crude □ [kru:d] roh; unfertig; unreif; unfein; grob; Roh...; grell.

cruel □ ['kruəl] grausam; hart; fig. blutig; **~ty** [~lti] Grausamkeit f.

cruet ['kru:(:)it] (Essig-, Öl)Fläschchen n.

cruise ♣ [kru:z] **1.** Kreuzfahrt f, Seereise f; **2.** kreuzen; **~r** ['kru:zə]

♣ Kreuzer m; Jacht f; Am. Funkstreifenwagen m.

crumb [krʌm] **1.** Krume f; Brocken m; **2.** panieren; zerkrümeln; **~le** ['krʌmbl] (zer)bröckeln; fig. zugrunde gehen.

crumple ['krʌmpl] v/t. zerknittern; fig. vernichten; v/i. (sich) knüllen.

crunch [krʌntʃ] (zer)kauen; zermalmen; knirschen.

crusade [kru:'seid] Kreuzzug m (a. fig.); **~r** [~də] Kreuzfahrer m.

crush [krʌʃ] **1.** Druck m; Gedränge n; (Frucht)Saft m; Am. sl. Schwarm m; have a ~ on s.o. in j-n verliebt od. verschossen sein; **2.** v/t. (zer-, aus)quetschen; zermalmen; fig. vernichten; (sich) drängen; ~ barrier ['krʌʃbæriə] Absperrgitter n.

crust [krʌst] **1.** Kruste f; Rinde f; Am. sl. Frechheit f; **2.** (sich) be-, überkrusten, verharschen; **~y** □ ['krʌsti] krustig; fig. mürrisch.

crutch [krʌtʃ] Krücke f.

cry [krai] **1.** Schrei m; Geschrei n; Ruf m; Weinen n; Gebell n; **2.** schreien; (aus)rufen; weinen; ~ for verlangen nach.

crypt [kript] Gruft f; **~ic** ['kriptik] verborgen, geheim.

crystal ['kristl] Kristall m, n; Am. Uhrglas n; **~line** [~təlain] kristallen; **~lize** [~aiz] kristallisieren.

cub [kʌb] **1.** Junge(s) n; Flegel m; Anfänger m; **2.** (Junge) werfen.

cub|e ♣ [kju:b] Würfel m; Kubikzahl f; ~ root Kubikwurzel f; **~ic(al** □) ['kju:bik(əl)] würfelförmig; kubisch; Kubik...

cuckoo ['kuku:] Kuckuck m.

cucumber ['kju:kʌmbə] Gurke f; as cool as a ~ fig. eiskalt, gelassen.

cud [kʌd] wiedergekäutes Futter; chew the ~ wiederkäuen; fig. überlegen.

cuddle ['kʌdl] v/t. (ver)hätscheln.

cudgel ['kʌdʒəl] **1.** Knüttel m; **2.** (ver)prügeln.

cue [kju:] Billard-Queue n; Stichwort n; Wink m.

cuff [kʌf] **1.** Manschette f; Handschelle f; (Ärmel-, Am. a. Hosen-) Aufschlag m; Faust-Schlag m; **2.** puffen, schlagen.

cuisine [kwi:(')'zi:n] Küche f (Art zu kochen).

culminate ['kʌlmineit] gipfeln.

culpable □ ['kʌlpəbl] strafbar.

culprit ['kʌlprit] Angeklagte(r m) f; Schuldige(r m) f, Missetäter(in).

cultivat|e ['kʌltiveit] kultivieren; an-, bebauen; ausbilden; pflegen; **~ion** [kʌlti'veiʃən] (An-, Acker)Bau m; Ausbildung f; Pflege f, Zucht f; **~or** ['kʌltiveitə] Landwirt m; Züchter m; ✗ Kultivator m (Maschine).

cultural □ ['kʌltʃərəl] kulturell.
culture ['kʌltʃə] Kultur *f*; Pflege *f*; Zucht *f*; ~d kultiviert.
cumb|er ['kʌmbə] überladen; belasten; ~ersome [~əsəm], ~rous □ [~brəs] lästig; schwerfällig.
cumulative □ ['kju:mjulətiv] (an-, auf)häufend; Zusatz...
cunning ['kʌniŋ] **1.** □ schlau, listig; geschickt; *Am.* reizend; **2.** List *f*, Schlauheit *f*; Geschicklichkeit *f*.
cup [kʌp] Becher *m*, Schale *f*, Tasse *f*; Kelch *m*; *Sport*: Pokal *m*; ~board ['kʌbəd] (Speise- *etc.*)Schrank *m*.
cupidity [kju(:)'piditi] Habgier *f*.
cupola ['kju:pələ] Kuppel *f*.
cur [kə:] Köter *m*; Schurke *m*, Halunke *m*.
curable ['kjuərəbl] heilbar.
curate ['kjuərit] Hilfsgeistliche(r) *m*.
curb [kə:b] **1.** Kinnkette *f*; Kandare *f* (*a. fig.*); *a.* ~stone ['kə:bstoun] Bordschwelle *f*; **2.** an die Kandare nehmen (*a. fig.*); *fig.* zügeln; ~market *Am. Börse:* Freiverkehr *m*; ~roof Mansardendach *n*.
curd [kə:d] **1.** Quark *m*; **2.** (*mst* ~le ['kə:dl]) gerinnen (lassen).
cure [kjuə] **1.** Kur *f*; Heilmittel *n*; Seelsorge *f*; Pfarre *f*; **2.** heilen; pökeln; räuchern; trocknen.
curfew ['kə:fju:] Abendglocke *f*; *pol.* Ausgehverbot *n*; ~bell Abendglocke *f*.
curio ['kjuəriou] Rarität *f*; ~sity [kjuəri'ositi] Neugier *f*; Rarität *f*; ~us □ ['kjuəriəs] neugierig; genau; seltsam, merkwürdig.
curl [kə:l] **1.** Locke *f*; **2.** (sich) kräuseln; (sich) locken; (sich) ringeln; ~y ['kə:li] gekräuselt; lockig.
currant ['kʌrənt] Johannisbeere *f*; *a.* dried ~ Korinthe *f*.
curren|cy ['kʌrənsi] Umlauf *m*; ↑ Lauffrist *f*; Kurs *m*, Währung *f*; ~t [~nt] **1.** □ umlaufend; ↑ kursierend (*Geld*); allgemein (bekannt); laufend (*Jahr etc.*); **2.** Strom *m* (*a. ⚡*); Strömung *f* (*a. fig.*); Luft-Zug *m*.
curricul|um [kə'rikjuləm], *pl.* ~a [~lə] Lehr-, Stundenplan *m*; ~um vitae [~əm'vaiti:] Lebenslauf *m*.
curry[1] ['kʌri] Curry *m*, *n*.
curry[2] [~] *Leder* zurichten; *Pferd* striegeln.
curse [kə:s] **1.** Fluch *m*; **2.** (ver)fluchen; strafen; ~d □ ['kə:sid] verflucht.
curt □ [kə:t] kurz; knapp; barsch.
curtail [kə:'teil] beschneiden; *fig.* beschränken; kürzen (of um).
curtain ['kə:tn] **1.** Vorhang *m*; Gardine *f*; **2.** verhängen, verschleiern; ~lecture F Gardinenpredigt *f*.
curts(e)y ['kə:tsi] **1.** Knicks *m*; *m*; **2.** knicksen (to vor).

curvature ['kə:vətʃə] (Ver)Krümmung *f*.
curve [kə:v] **1.** Kurve *f*; Krümmung *f*; **2.** (sich) krümmen; (sich) biegen.
cushion ['kuʃən] **1.** Kissen *n*; Polster *n*; *Billard*-Bande *f*; **2.** polstern.
cuss *Am.* F [kʌs] **1.** Nichtsnutz *m*; **2.** fluchen.
custody ['kʌstədi] Haft *f*; (Ob)Hut *f*.
custom ['kʌstəm] Gewohnheit *f*, Brauch *m*; Sitte *f*; Kundschaft *f*; ~s *pl.* Zoll *m*; ~ary □ [~məri] gewöhnlich, üblich; ~er [~mə] Kund|e *m*, -in *f*; F Bursche *m*; ~house Zollamt *n*; ~made *Am.* maßgearbeitet.
cut [kʌt] **1.** Schnitt *m*; Hieb *m*; Stich *m*; (Schnitt)Wunde *f*; Einschnitt *m*; Graben *m*; Kürzung *f*; Ausschnitt *m*; Wegabkürzung *f* (*mst* short-~); *Holz*-Schnitt *m*; *Kupfer*-Stich *m*; Schliff *m*; Schnitte *f*, Scheibe *f*; *Karten*-Abheben *n*; *Küche:* cold ~s *pl.* Aufschnitt *m*; give s.o. the ~ (direct) F j. schneiden; **2.** [*irr.*] *v/t.* schneiden; schnitzen; gravieren; ab-, an-, auf-, aus-, be-, durch-, zer-, zuschneiden; *Edelstein etc.* schleifen; *Karten* abheben; *j. beim Begegnen* schneiden; ~ teeth zahnen; ~ short *j.* unterbrechen; ~ back einschränken; ~ down fällen; mähen; beschneiden; *Preis* drücken; ~ out ausschneiden; *Am. Vieh* aussondern *aus der Herde*; *fig. j.* ausstechen; ⚡ ausschalten; be ~ out for das Zeug zu e-r S. haben; *v/i.* ~ in sich einschieben; **3.** *adj.* geschnitten *etc.*, *s.* cut 2.
cute □ F [kju:t] schlau; *Am.* reizend.
cuticle ['kju:tikl] Oberhaut *f*; ~ scissors *pl.* Hautschere *f*.
cutlery ['kʌtləri] Messerschmiedearbeit *f*; Stahlwaren *f/pl.*; Bestecke *n/pl.*
cutlet ['kʌtlit] Kotelett *n*; Schnitzel *n*.
cut|-off *Am.* ['kʌtɔ:f] Abkürzung *f* (*Straße, Weg*); ~out *mot.* Auspuffklappe *f*; ⚡ Sicherung *f*; Ausschalter *m*; *Am.* Ausschneidebogen *m*, -bild *n*; ~purse Taschendieb *m*; ~ter ['kʌtə] Schneidende(r *m*) *f*; Schnitzer *m*; Zuschneider(in); *Film:* Cutter *m*; ⊕ Schneidezeug *n*, -maschine *f*; ♣ Kutter *m*; *Am.* leichter Schlitten; ~throat Halsabschneider *m*; Meuchelmörder *m*; ~ting ['kʌtiŋ] **1.** □ schneidend; scharf; ⊕ Schneid..., Fräs...; **2.** Schneiden *n*; ⛏ *etc.* Einschnitt *m*; ⚘ Steckling *m*; *Zeitungs*-Ausschnitt *m*; ~s *pl.* Schnipsel *m*, *n/pl.*; ⊕ Späne *m/pl.*
cycl|e ['saikl] **1.** Zyklus *m*; Kreis (-lauf) *m*; Periode *f*; ⊕ Arbeitsgang

m; Fahrrad *n*; 2. radfahren; ~ist [~list] Radfahrer(in).

cyclone ['saikloun] Wirbelsturm *m*.

cylinder ['silində] Zylinder *m*, Walze *f*; ⊕ Trommel *f*.

cymbal ♪ ['simbəl] Becken *n*.

cynic ['sinik] 1. *a*. ~al □ [~kəl] zynisch; 2. Zyniker *m*.

cypress ♀ ['saipris] Zypresse *f*.

cyst ✻ [sist] Blase *f*; Sackgeschwulst *f*; ~itis ✻ [sis'taitis] Blasenentzündung *f*.

Czech [tʃek] 1. Tschech|e *m*, -in *f*; 2. tschechisch.

Czechoslovak ['tʃekou'slouvæk] 1. Tschechoslowak|e *m*, -in *f*; 2. tschechoslowakisch.

D

dab [dæb] 1. Klaps *m*; Tupf(en) *m*, Klecks *m*; 2. klapsen; (be)tupfen.

dabble ['dæbl] bespritzen; plätschern; (hinein)pfuschen.

dad F [dæd], ~dy F ['dædi] Papa *m*.

daddy-longlegs F *zo.* ['dædi'lɔŋlegz] Schnake *f*; *Am.* Weberknecht *m*.

daffodil ♀ ['dæfədil] gelbe Narzisse.

daft F [dɑːft] blöde, doof.

dagger ['dægə] Dolch *m*; *be at ~s drawn fig.* auf Kriegsfuß stehen.

dago *Am. sl.* ['deigou] *contp. für Spanier, Portugiese, mst Italiener.*

daily ['deili] 1. täglich; 2. Tageszeitung *f*.

dainty ['deinti] 1. □ lecker; zart, fein; wählerisch; 2. Leckerei *f*.

dairy ['dɛəri] Molkerei *f*, Milchwirtschaft *f*; Milchgeschäft *n*; ~cattle Milchvieh *n*; ~man Milchhändler *m*.

daisy ♀ ['deizi] Gänseblümchen *n*.

dale [deil] Tal *n*.

dall|iance ['dæliəns] Trödelei *f*; Liebelei *f*; ~y ['dæli] vertrödeln; schäkern.

dam [dæm] 1. Mutter *f von Tieren*; Deich *m*, Damm *m*; 2. (ab)dämmen.

damage ['dæmidʒ] 1. Schaden *m*; ~s *pl.* ⚖ Schadenersatz *m*; 2. (be-)schädigen.

damask ['dæməsk] Damast *m*.

dame [deim] Dame *f*; *sl.* Weib *n*.

damn [dæm] verdammen; verurteilen; ~ation [dæm'neiʃən] Verdammung *f*.

damp [dæmp] 1. feucht, dunstig; 2. Feuchtigkeit *f*, Dunst *m*; Gedrücktheit *f*; 3. *a.* ~en ['dæmpən] anfeuchten; dämpfen; niederdrükken; ~er [~pə] Dämpfer *m*.

danc|e [dɑːns] 1. Tanz *m*; Ball *m*; 2. tanzen (lassen); ~er [dɑːnsə] Tänzer(in); ~ing [~siŋ] Tanzen *n*; *attr.* Tanz … [zahn *m*.\

dandelion ♀ ['dændilaiən] Löwen-\

dandle *sl.* ['dændl] wiegen, schaukeln.

dandruff ['dændrəf] (Kopf)Schuppen *f/pl.*

dandy ['dændi] 1. Stutzer *m*; F erstklassige Sache; 2. *Am.* F prima.

Dane [dein] Dän|e *m*, -in *f*.

danger ['deindʒə] Gefahr *f*; ~ous □ [~dʒrəs] gefährlich; ~-signal ✠ Notsignal *n*.

dangle ['dæŋgl] baumeln (lassen); schlenkern (mit); *fig.* schwanken.

Danish ['deiniʃ] dänisch.

dank [dæŋk] dunstig, feucht.

Danubian [dæ'njuːbjən] Donau…

dapper □ F ['dæpə] nett; behend.

dapple ['dæpl] sprenkeln; ~d scheckig; ~grey Apfelschimmel *m*.

dar|e [dɛə] *v/i.* es wagen; *v/t. et.* wagen; *j-n* herausfordern; *j-m* trotzen; ~e-devil ['dɛədevl] Draufgänger *m*; ~ing ['dɛəriŋ] 1. verwegen; 2. Verwegenheit *f*.

dark [dɑːk] 1. □ dunkel; brünett; schwerverständlich; geheim(nisvoll); trüb(selig); 2. Dunkel(heit *f*) *n*; *before (after)* ~ vor (nach) Einbruch der Dunkelheit; 2 **Ages** *pl. das* frühe Mittelalter; ~en ['dɑːkən] (sich) (ver)dunkeln; (sich) verfinstern; ~ness ['dɑːknis] Dunkelheit *f*, Finsternis *f*; ~y F ['dɑːki] Schwarze(r *m*) *f*.

darling ['dɑːliŋ] 1. Liebling *m*; 2. Lieblings…; geliebt.

darn [dɑːn] stopfen; ausbessern.

dart [dɑːt] 1. Wurfspieß *m*; Wurfpfeil *m*; Sprung *m*, Satz *m*; ~s *pl.* Wurfpfeilspiel *n*; 2. *v/t.* schleudern; *v/i. fig.* schießen, (sich) stürzen.

dash [dæʃ] 1. Schlag *m*, (Zs.-)Stoß *m*; Klatschen *n*; Schwung *m*; Ansturm *m*; *fig.* Anflug *m*; Prise *f*; Schuß *m Rum etc* ; *Feder*-Strich *m*; Gedankenstrich *m*; 2. *v/t.* schlagen, werfen, schleudern; zerschmettern; vernichten; (be)spritzen; vermengen; verwirren; *v/i.* stoßen, schlagen; stürzen; sturmen; jagen; ~board *mot.* ['dæʃbɔːd] Armaturenbrett *m*; ~ing ['dæʃiŋ] schneidig, forsch; flott, F fesch.

dastardly ['dæstədli] heimtückisch; feig.

data ['deitə] *pl.*, *Am. a. sg.* Angaben

f|pl.; Tatsachen *f|pl.*; Unterlagen *f|pl.*; Daten *pl.*

date [deit] 1. ♀ Dattel *f*; Datum *n*; Zeit *f*; Termin *m*; *Am.* F Verabredung *f*; Freund(in); *out of ~* veraltet, unmodern; *up to ~* zeitgemäß, modern; *auf dem laufenden*; 2. datieren; *Am.* F sich verabreden.

dative *gr.* ['deitiv] *a. ~ case* Dativ *m*.

daub [dɔːb] (be)schmieren; (be-)klecksen.

daughter ['dɔːtə] Tochter *f*; **~-in-law** [ˌɔːrinlɔ:] Schwiegertochter *f*.

daunt [dɔːnt] entmutigen; **~less** ['dɔːntlis] furchtlos, unerschrocken.

daw *orn.* [dɔː] Dohle *f*.

dawdle F ['dɔːdl] (ver)trödeln.

dawn [dɔːn] 1. Dämmerung *f*; *fig.* Morgenrot *n*; 2. dämmern, tagen; *it ~ed upon him fig.* es wurde ihm langsam klar.

day [dei] Tag *m*; *oft ~s pl.* (Lebens-)Zeit *f*; *~ off dienst*-freier Tag; *carry od. win the ~* den Sieg davontragen; *the other ~* neulich; *this ~ week* heute in einer Woche; heute vor einer Woche; *let's call it a ~* machen wir Schluß für heute; **~break** ['deibreik] Tagesanbruch *m*; **~-labo(u)rer** Tagelöhner *m*; **~-star** Morgenstern *m*.

daze [deiz] blenden; betäuben.

dazzle ['dæzl] blenden; ♣ tarnen.

dead [ded] 1. tot; unempfindlich (*to* für); matt (*Farbe etc.*); blind (*Fenster etc.*); erloschen (*Feuer*); schal (*Getränk*); tief (*Schlaf*); † tot (*Kapital etc.*); *~ bargain* Spottpreis *m*; *~ letter* unzustellbarer Brief; *~ loss* Totalverlust *m*; *a ~ shot ein* Meisterschütze; *~ wall* blinde Mauer; *~ wood* Reisig *n*; *Am.* Plunder *m*; 2. *adv.* gänzlich, völlig, total; durchaus, genau, (haar)scharf; *~ against* gerade *od.* ganz und gar (ent)gegen; 3. *the ~* der Tote; die Toten *pl.*; *Totenstille f*; *in the ~ of winter* im tiefsten Winter; *in the ~ of night* mitten in der Nacht; **~en** ['dedn] abstumpfen; dämpfen; (ab)schwächen; **~-end** Sackgasse *f* (*a. fig.*); **~-line** *Am.* Sperrlinie *f* im *Gefängnis*; Schlußtermin *m*; Stichtag *m*; **~-lock** Stockung *f*; *fig.* toter Punkt; **~ly** [ˌli] tödlich.

deaf □ [def] taub; **~en** ['defn] taub machen; betäuben.

deal [diːl] 1. Teil *m*; Menge *f*; Kartengeben *n*; F Geschäft *n*; Abmachung *f*; *a good ~* ziemlich viel; *a great ~* sehr viel; 2. [*irr.*] *v/t.* (aus-, ver-, zu)teilen; *Karten* geben; *e-n Schlag* versetzen; *v/i.* handeln (*in mit e-r Ware*); verkehren; *~ with* sich befassen mit, behandeln; **~er** ['diːlə] Händler *m*; Kartengeber *m*; **~ing** ['diːliŋ] mst

~s pl. Handlungsweise *f*; Verfahren *n*; Verkehr *m*; **~t** [delt] *pret. u p.p. von* deal 2.

dean [diːn] Dekan *m*.

dear [diə] 1. □ teuer; lieb; 2. Liebling *m*; herziges Geschöpf; 3. *o(h) ~!, ~ me!* F du liebe Zeit!; ach herrje!

death [deθ] Tod *m*; Todesfall *m*; **~-bed** ['deθbed] Sterbebett *n*; **~-duty** Erbschaftssteuer *f*; **~less** ['deθlis] unsterblich; **~ly** [ˌli] tödlich; **~-rate** Sterblichkeitsziffer *f*; **~-warrant** Todesurteil *n*.

debar [di'baː] ausschließen; hindern.

debarkation [diːbaːˈkeiʃən] Ausschiffung *f*.

debase [di'beis] verschlechtern; erniedrigen; verfälschen.

debat|able □ [di'beitəbl] strittig; umstritten; **~e** [di'beit] 1. Debatte *f*; 2. debattieren; erörtern; überlegen.

debauch [di'bɔːtʃ] 1. Ausschweifung *f*; 2. verderben; verführen.

debilitate [di'biliteit] schwächen.

debit † ['debit] 1. Debet *n*, Schuld *f*; 2. *j-n* belasten; debitieren.

debris ['debriː] Trümmer *pl.*

debt [det] Schuld *f*; **~or** ['detə] Schuldner(in).

debunk ['diːˈbʌŋk] den Nimbus nehmen (*dat.*).

début ['deibuː] Debüt *n*.

decade ['dekeid] Jahrzehnt *n*.

decadence ['dekədəns] Verfall *m*.

decamp [di'kæmp] aufbrechen; ausreißen; **~ment** [ˌpmənt] Aufbruch *m*.

decant [di'kænt] abgießen; umfüllen; **~er** [ˌtə] Karaffe *f*.

decapitate [di'kæpiteit] enthaupten; *Am.* F *fig.* absägen (*entlassen*).

decay [di'kei] 1. Verfall *m*; Fäulnis *f*; 2. verfallen; (ver)faulen.

decease *bsd.* ½½ [di'siːs] 1. Ableben *n*; 2. sterben.

deceit [di'siːt] Täuschung *f*; Betrug *m*; **~ful** □ [ˌtful] (be)trügerisch.

deceive [di'siːv] betrügen; täuschen; verleiten; **~r** [ˌvə] Betrüger(in).

December [di'sembə] Dezember *m*.

decen|cy ['diːsnsi] Anstand *m*; **~t** □ [ˌnt] anständig; F annehmbar, nett.

deception [di'sepʃən] Täuschung *f*.

decide [di'said] (sich) entscheiden; bestimmen; **~d** □ entschieden; bestimmt; entschlossen.

decimal ['desiməl] Dezimalbruch *m*; *attr.* Dezimal...

decipher [di'saifə] entziffern.

decisi|on [di'siʒən] Entscheidung *f*; ½½ Urteil *n*; Entschluß *m*; Entschlossenheit *f*; **~ve** □ [di'saisiv] entscheidend; entschieden.

deck [dek] 1. ♣ Deck n; Am. Pack m Spielkarten; on ~ Am. F da(bei), bereit; 2. rhet. schmücken; ~**chair** ['dek'tʃeə] Liegestuhl m.

declaim [di'kleim] vortragen; (sich er)eifern.

declar|able [di'kleərəbl] steuer-, zollpflichtig; ~**ation** [deklə'reiʃən] Erklärung f; Zoll-Deklaration f; ~**e** [di'kleə] (sich) erklären; behaupten; deklarieren.

declension [di'klenʃən] Abfall m (Neigung); Verfall m; gr. Deklination f.

declin|ation [dekli'neiʃər] Neigung f; Abweichung f; ~**e** [di'klain] 1. Abnahme f; Niedergang m; Verfall m; 2. v/t. neigen, biegen; gr. deklinieren; ablehnen; v/i. sich neigen; abnehmen; verfallen.

declivity [di'kliviti] Abhang m.

declutch mot. ['di:'klʌtʃ] auskuppeln.

decode tel. ['di:'koud] entschlüsseln.

decompose [di:kəm'pouz] zerlegen; (sich) zersetzen; verwesen.

decontrol ['di:kən'troul] Waren, Handel freigeben.

decorat|e ['dekəreit] (ver)zieren; schmücken; ~**ion** [dekə'reiʃən] Verzierung f; Schmuck m; Orden(sauszeichnung f) m; ♀ Day Am. Heldengedenktag m; ~**ive** ['dekərətiv] dekorativ; Zier...; ~**or** [‿reitə] Dekorateur m, Maler m.

decor|ous □ ['dekərəs] anständig; ~**um** [di'kɔ:rəm] Anstand m.

decoy [di'kɔi] 1. Lockvogel m (a. fig.); Köder m; 2. ködern; locken.

decrease 1. ['di:kri:s] Abnahme f; 2. [di:'kri:s] (sich) vermindern.

decree [di'kri:] 1. Dekret n, Verordnung f, Erlaß m; ⚖ Entscheid m; 2. beschließen; verordnen, verfügen.

decrepit [di'krepit] altersschwach.

decry [di'krai] in Verruf bringen.

dedicat|e ['dedikeit] widmen; ~**ion** [dedi'keiʃən] Widmung f.

deduce [di'dju:s] ableiten; folgern.

deduct [di'dʌkt] abziehen; ~**ion** [‿kʃən] Abzug m; ✝ Rabatt m; Schlußfolgerung f.

deed [di:d] 1. Tat f; Heldentat f; Urkunde f; 2. Am. urkundlich übertragen (to auf acc.).

deem [di:m] v/t. halten für; v/i. denken, urteilen (of über acc.).

deep [di:p] 1. □ tief; gründlich; schlau; vertieft; dunkel (a. fig.); verborgen; 2. Tiefe f; poet. Meer n; ~**en** ['di:pən] (sich) vertiefen; (sich) verstärken; ~**freeze** 1. tiefkühlen; 2. Tiefkühlfach n, -truhe f; ~**ness** ['di:pnis] Tiefe f.

deer [diə] Rotwild n; Hirsch m.

deface [di'feis] entstellen; unkenntlich machen; ausstreichen.

defalcation [di:fæl'keiʃən] Unterschlagung f.

defam|ation [defə'meiʃən] Verleumdung f; ~**e** [di'feim] verleumden; verunglimpfen.

default [di'fɔ:lt] 1. Nichterscheinen n vor Gericht; Säumigkeit f; Verzug m; in ~ of which widrigenfalls; 2. s-n etc. Verbindlichkeiten nicht nachkommen.

defeat [di'fi:t] 1. Niederlage f; Besiegung f; Vereitelung f; 2. ✗ besiegen; vereiteln; vernichten.

defect [di'fekt] Mangel m; Fehler m; ~**ive** □ [‿tiv] mangelhaft; unvollständig; fehlerhaft.

defen|ce, Am. ~**se** [di'fens] Verteidigung f; Schutzmaßnahme f; witness for the ~ Entlastungszeuge m; ~**celess**, Am. ~**seless** [‿slis] schutzlos, wehrlos.

defend [di'fend] verteidigen; schützen (from vor dat.); ~**ant** [‿dənt] Angeklagte(r m) f; Beklagte(r m) f; ~**er** [‿də] Verteidiger(in).

defensive [di'fensiv] Defensive f; attr. Verteidigungs...

defer [di'fə:] auf-, verschieben; Am. ✗ zurückstellen; sich fügen; nachgeben; payment on ~**red terms** Ratenzahlung f; ~**ence** [‿defərəns] Ehrerbietung f; Nachgiebigkeit f; ~**ential** □ [defə'renʃəl] ehrerbietig.

defian|ce [di'faiəns] Herausforderung f; Trotz m; ~**t** □ [‿nt] herausfordernd; trotzig.

deficien|cy [di'fiʃənsi] Unzulänglichkeit f; Mangel m; = deficit; ~**t** [‿nt] mangelhaft; unzureichend.

deficit ['defisit] Fehlbetrag m.

defile 1. ['di:fail] Engpaß m; 2. [di-'fail] v/i. vorbeiziehen; v/t. beflecken; schänden.

defin|e [di'fain] definieren; erklären; genau bestimmen; ~**ite** □ ['definit] bestimmt; deutlich; genau; ~**ition** [defi'niʃən] (Begriffs-)Bestimmung f; Erklärung f; ~**itive** □ [di'finitiv] bestimmt; entscheidend; endgültig.

deflect [di'flekt] ablenken; abweichen.

deform [di'fɔ:m] entstellen; verunstalten; ~**ed** verwachsen; ~**ity** [‿miti] Unförmigkeit f; Mißgestalt f.

defraud [di'frɔ:d] betrügen (of um).

defray [di'frei] Kosten bestreiten.

defroster mot. [di:'frɔstə] Entfroster m.

deft □ [deft] gewandt, flink.

defunct [di'fʌŋkt] verstorben.

defy [di'fai] herausfordern; trotzen.

degenerate 1. [di'dʒenəreit] entarten; 2. [‿rit] entartet.

degrad|ation [degrə'deiʃən] Absetzung f; ~**e** [di'greid] v/t. absetzen; erniedrigen; demütigen.

degree [di'gri:] Grad m; fig. Stufe f,

Schritt *m*; Rang *m*, Stand *m*; *by* ~s allmählich; *in no* ~ in keiner Weise; *in some* ~ einigermaßen; *take one's* ~ sein Abschlußexamen machen.
dehydrated [di:'haidreitid] Trocken...
deify ['di:ifai] vergöttern; vergöttlichen.
deign [dein] geruhen; gewähren.
deity ['di:iti] Gottheit *f*.
deject [di'dʒekt] entmutigen; ~ed □ niedergeschlagen; ~ion [~kʃən] Niedergeschlagenheit *f*.
delay [di'lei] 1. Aufschub *m*; Verzögerung *f*; 2. *v/t.* aufschieben; verzögern; *v/i.* zögern; trödeln.
delega|te 1. ['deligeit] abordnen; übertragen; 2. [~git] Abgeordnete(r *m*) *f*; ~tion [deli'geiʃən] Abordnung *f*; *Am. parl. die* Kongreßabgeordneten *m/pl. e-s* Staates.
deliberat|e 1. [di'libəreit] *v/t.* überlegen, erwägen; *v/i.* nachdenken; beraten; 2. □ [~rit] bedachtsam; wohlüberlegt; vorsätzlich; ~ion [dilibə'reiʃən] Überlegung *f*; Beratung *f*; Bedächtigkeit *f*.
delica|cy ['delikəsi] Wohlgeschmack *m*; Leckerbissen *m*, Zartheit *f*; Schwächlichkeit *f*; Feinfühligkeit *f*; ~te [~kit] schmackhaft; lecker; zart; fein; schwach; heikel; empfindlich; feinfühlig; wählerisch; ~tessen [delikə'tesn] Feinkost(geschäft *n*) *f*.
delicious [di'liʃəs] köstlich.
delight [di'lait] 1. Lust *f*, Freude *f*, Wonne *f*; 2. entzücken; (sich) erfreuen (*in an dat.*); ~ *to inf.* Freude daran finden, zu *inf.*; ~ful □ [~tful] entzückend; [schildern.\
delineate [di'linieit] entwerfen;/
delinquen|cy [di'liŋkwənsi] Vergehen *n*; Kriminalität *f*; Pflichtvergessenheit *f*; ~t [~nt] 1. straffällig; pflichtvergessen; 2. Verbrecher(in).
deliri|ous □ [di'liriəs] wahnsinnig; ~um [~iəm] Fieberwahn *m*.
deliver [di'livə] befreien; über-, aus-, abliefern; *Botschaft* ausrichten; äußern; *Rede etc.* vortragen, halten; ⚡ entbinden; *Schlag* führen; werfen; ~ance [~ərəns] Befreiung *f*; (Meinungs)Äußerung *f*; ~er [~ə] Befreier(in); Überbringer(in); ~y [~ri] ⚡ Entbindung *f*; (Ab)Lieferung *f*; ⚖ Zustellung *f*; Übergabe *f*; Vortrag *m*; Wurf *m*; *special* ~ Lieferung *f* durch Eilboten; ~y-truck, ~y-van Lieferwagen *m*.
dell [del] kleines Tal.
delude [di'lu:d] täuschen; verleiten.
deluge ['delju:dʒ] 1. Überschwemmung *f*; 2. überschwemmen.
delus|ion [di'lu:ʒən] Täuschung *f*, Verblendung *f*; Wahn *m*; ~ive □ [~u:siv] (be)trügerisch; täuschend.

demand [di'mɑ:nd] 1. Verlangen *n*; Forderung *f*; Bedarf *m*; ✝ Nachfrage *f*; ⚖ Rechtsanspruch *m*; 2. verlangen, fordern; fragen (nach).
demean [di'mi:n]: ~ *o.s.* sich benehmen; sich erniedrigen; ~o(u)r [~nə] Benehmen *n*.
demented [di'mentid] wahnsinnig.
demerit [di:'merit] Fehler *m*.
demesne [di'mein] Besitz *m*.
demi... ['demi] Halb..., halb...
demijohn ['demidʒɔn] große Korbflasche, Glasballon *m*.
demilitarize ['di:'militəraiz] entmilitarisieren.
demise [di'maiz] 1. Ableben *n*; 2. vermachen.
demobilize [di:'moubilaiz] demobilisieren.
democra|cy [di'mɔkrəsi] Demokratie *f*; ~t ['deməkræt] Demokrat(in); ~tic(al □) [demə'krætik(əl)] demokratisch.
demolish [di'mɔliʃ] nieder-, abreißen; zerstören.
demon ['di:mən] Dämon *m*; Teufel *m*.
demonstrat|e ['demənstreit] anschaulich darstellen; beweisen; demonstrieren; ~ion [demən'streiʃən] Demonstration *f*; anschauliche Darstellung; Beweis *m*; (Gefühls-)Äußerung *f*; ~ive □ [di'mɔnstrətiv] überzeugend; demonstrativ; ausdrucksvoll; auffällig, überschwenglich.
demote [di:'mouⁿ] degradieren.
demur [di'mə:] 1. Einwendung *f*; 2. Einwendungen erheben.
demure □ [di'mjuə] ernst; prüde.
den [den] Höhle *f*; Grube *f*; *sl.* Bude *f*.
denial [di'naiəl] Leugnen *n*; Verneinung *f*; abschlägige Antwort.
denizen ['denizn] Bewohner *m*.
denominat|e [di'nɔmineit] (be-) nennen; ~ion [dinɔmi'neiʃən] Benennung *f*; Klasse *f*; Sekte *f*, Konfession *f*.
denote [di'nout] bezeichnen; bedeuten.
denounce [di'nauns] anzeigen; brandmarken; *Vertrag* kündigen.
dens|e □ [dens] dicht, dick (*Nebel*); beschränkt; ~ity ['densiti] Dichte *f*; Dichtigkeit *f*.
dent [dent] 1. Kerbe *f*; Beule *f*; 2. ver-, einbeulen.
dent|al ['dentl] Zahn...; ~ *surgeon* Zahnarzt *m*; ~ist [~tist] Zahnarzt *m*.
denunciat|ion [dinʌnsi'eiʃən] Anzeige *f*; Kündigung *f*; ~or [di'nʌnsieitə] Denunziant *m*.
deny [di'nai] verleugnen; verweigern, abschlagen; *j-n* abweisen.
depart [di'pɑːt] *v/i.* abreisen, abfahren; abstehen, (ab)weichen;

verscheiden; **~ment** [ˌtmənt] Abteilung f; Bezirk m; ✝ Branche f; *Am.* Ministerium n; State ♀ *Am.* Außenministerium n; **~ store** Warenhaus n; **~ure** [ˌtʃə] Abreise f, ⑤, ⚓ Abfahrt f; Abweichung f.

depend [di'pend]: **~** (*up*)*on* abhängen von; angewiesen sein auf (*acc.*); sich verlassen auf (*acc.*); **it ~s** F es kommt (ganz) darauf an; **~able** [ˌdəbl] zuverlässig; **~ant** [ˌənt] Abhängige(r m) f; Angehörige(r m) f; **~ence** [ˌdəns] Abhängigkeit f; Vertrauen n; **~ency** [ˌsi] Schutzgebiet n; **~ent** [ˌnt] **1.** □ (*on*) abhängig (von); angewiesen (auf *acc.*); **2.** *Am.* = dependant.

depict [di'pikt] darstellen; schildern.

deplete [di'pliːt] (ent)leeren; *fig.* erschöpfen.

deplor|able □ [di'plɔːrəbl] beklagenswert; kläglich; jämmerlich; **~e** [di'plɔː] beklagen, bedauern.

deponent ⚖ [di'pounənt] vereidigter Zeuge.   [(entvölkern.)

depopulate [di'pɔpjuleit] (sich)/

deport [di'pɔːt] verlachen, abschieben; verbannen; **~ o.s.** sich benehmen; **~ment** [ˌtmənt] Benehmen n.

depose [di'pouz] absetzen; ⚖ (eidlich) aussagen.

deposit [di'pozit] **1.** Ablagerung f; Lager n; ✝ Depot n; *Bank*-Einlage f; Pfand n; Hinterlegung f; **2.** (nieder-, ab-, hin)legen; *Geld* einlegen, einzahlen; hinterlegen; (sich) ablagern; **~ion** [depəˈziʃən] Ablagerung f; eidliche Zeugenaussage; Absetzung f; **~or** [di'pozitə] Hinterleger m, Einzahler m; Kontoinhaber m.

depot ['depou] Depot n; Lagerhaus n; *Am.* Bahnhof m.

deprave [di'preiv] *sittlich* verderben.

deprecate ['deprikeit] ablehnen.

depreciate [di'priːʃieit] herabsetzen; geringschätzen; entwerten.

depredation [depri'deiʃən] Plünderung f.

depress [di'pres] niederdrücken; *Preise etc.* senken, drücken; bedrücken; **~ed** *fig.* niedergeschlagen; **~ion** [ˌeʃən] Senkung f; Niedergeschlagenheit f; ✝ Flaute f, Wirtschaftskrise f; ♀ Schwäche f; Sinken n.

deprive [di'praiv] berauben; entziehen; ausschließen (of von).

depth [depθ] Tiefe f; *attr.* Tiefen...

deput|ation [depju(:)'teiʃən] Abordnung f; **~e** [di'pjuːt] abordnen; **~y** ['depjuti] Abgeordnete(r m) f; Stellvertreter m, Beauftragte(r) m.

derail ⑤ [di'reil] v/i. entgleisen; v/t. zum Entgleisen bringen.

derange [di'reindʒ] in Unordnung bringen; stören; zerrütten; (*mentally*) **~d** geistesgestört; **a ~d stomach** eine Magenverstimmung.

derelict ['derilikt] **1.** verlassen; *bsd. Am.* nachlässig; **2.** herrenloses Gut; Wrack n; **~ion** [deri'likʃən] Verlassen n; Vernachlässigung f.

deri|de [di'raid] verlachen, verspotten; **~sion** [di'riʒən] Verspottung f; **~sive** □ [di'raisiv] spöttisch.

deriv|ation [deri'veiʃən] Ableitung f; Herkunft f; **~e** [di'raiv] herleiten; *Nutzen etc.* ziehen (from aus).

derogat|e ['derəgeit] schmälern (from *acc.*); **~ion** [derəˈgeiʃən] Beeinträchtigung f; Herabwürdigung f; **~ory** □ [di'rɔgətəri] (to) nachteilig (*dat.*, für); herabwürdigend.

derrick ['derik] ⊕ Drehkran m; ⚓ Ladebaum m; ⚒ Bohrturm m.

descend [di'send] (her-, hin)absteigen, herabkommen; sinken; ♀ niedergehen; **~** (*up*)*on* herfallen über (*acc.*); einfallen in (*acc.*); (ab)stammen; **~ant** [ˌənt] Nachkomme m.

descent [di'sent] Herabsteigen n; Abstieg m; Sinken n; Gefälle n; feindlicher Einfall; Landung f; Abstammung f; Abhang m.

describe [dis'kraib] beschreiben.

description [dis'kripʃən] Beschreibung f, Schilderung f; F Art f.

descry [dis'krai] wahrnehmen.

desecrate ['desikreit] entweihen.

desegregate *Am.* [di'segrigeit] die Rassentrennung aufheben in (*dat.*).

desert[1] ['dezət] **1.** verlassen; wüst, öde; Wüsten...; **2.** Wüste f.

desert[2] [di'zəːt] v/t. verlassen; v/i. ausreißen; desertieren.

desert[3] [di'zəːt] Verdienst n.

desert|er [di'zəːtə] Fahnenflüchtige(r) m; **~ion** [ˌʃən] Verlassen n; Fahnenflucht f.

deserv|e [di'zəːv] verdienen; sich verdient machen (of um); **~ing** [ˌviŋ] würdig (of gen.); verdienstvoll.

design [di'zain] **1.** Plan m; Entwurf m; Vorhaben n, Absicht f; Zeichnung f, Muster n; **2.** ersinnen; zeichnen, entwerfen; planen; bestimmen.

designat|e ['dezigneit] bezeichnen; ernennnen, bestimmen; **~ion** [dezig'neiʃən] Bezeichnung f; Bestimmung f, Ernennung f.

designer [di'zainə] (Muster)Zeichner(in); Konstrukteur m.

desir|able □ [di'zaiərəbl] wünschenswert; angenehm; **~e** [di'zaiə] **1.** Wunsch m; Verlangen n; **2.** verlangen, wünschen; **~ous** □ [ˌərəs] begierig.

desist [di'zist] abstehen, ablassen.

desk [desk] Pult n; Schreibtisch m.

desolat|e 1. ['desəleit] verwüsten; **2.** □ [ˌlit] einsam; verlassen; öde; **~ion** [desə'leiʃən] Verwüstung f; Einöde f; Einsamkeit f.

despair [dis'pɛə] **1.** Verzweiflung f;

2. verzweifeln (of an *dat.*); ~ing □ [~ərin] verzweifelt.

despatch [dis'pætʃ] = *dispatch*.

desperat|e *adj.* □ ['despərit] verzweifelt; hoffnungslos; F schrecklich; ~ion [despə'reiʃən] Verzweiflung *f*; Raserei *f*.

despicable □ ['despikəbl] verächtlich.

despise [dis'paiz] verachten.

despite [dis'pait] 1. Verachtung *f*; Trotz *m*; Bosheit *f*; in ~ of zum Trotz, trotz; 2. *prp. a.* ~ of trotz.

despoil [dis'pɔil] berauben (of *gen.*).

despond [dis'pɔnd] verzagen, verzweifeln; ~ency [~dənsi] Verzagtheit *f*; ~ent □ [~nt] verzagt.

despot ['despɔt] Despot *m*, Tyrann *m*; ~ism [~pɔtizəm] Despotismus *m*.

dessert [di'zə:t] Nachtisch *m*, Dessert *n*; *Am.* Süßspeise *f*.

destin|ation [desti'neiʃən] Bestimmung(sort *m*) *f*; ~e ['destin] bestimmen; ~y [~ni] Schicksal *n*.

destitute □ ['destitju:t] mittellos, notleidend; entblößt (of von).

destroy [dis'trɔi] zerstören, vernichten; töten; unschädlich machen; ~er [~ɔiə] Zerstörer(in).

destruct|ion [dis'trʌkʃən] Zerstörung *f*; Tötung *f*; ~ive □ [~ktiv] zerstörend; vernichtend (of, to *acc.*); ~or [~tə] (Müll)Verbrennungsofen *m*.

desultory □ ['desəltəri] unstet; planlos; oberflächlich.

detach [di'tætʃ] losmachen, (ab-)lösen; absondern; ✗ (ab)kommandieren; ~ed einzeln (stehend); unbeeinflußt; ~ment [~ʃmənt] Loslösung *f*; Trennung *f*; ✗ Abteilung *f*.

detail ['di:teil] 1. Einzelheit *f*; eingehende Darstellung; ✗ Kommando *n*; in ~ ausführlich; 2. genau schildern; ✗ abkommandieren.

detain [di'tein] zurück-, auf-, abhalten; *j-n* in Haft behalten.

detect [di'tekt] entdecken; (auf-)finden; ~ion [~kʃən] Entdeckung *f*; ~ive [~ktiv] Detektiv *m*; ~ story, ~ novel Kriminalroman *m*.

detention [di'tenʃən] Vorenthaltung *f*; Zurück-, Abhaltung *f*; Haft *f*.

deter [di'tə:] abschrecken (from)

detergent [di'tə:dʒənt] 1. reinigend; 2. Reinigungsmittel *n*.

deteriorat|e [di'tiəriəreit] (sich) verschlechtern; entarten; ~ion [ditiəriə'reiʃən] Verschlechterung *f*.

determin|ation [ditə:mi'neiʃən] Bestimmung *f*; Entschlossenheit *f*; Entscheidung *f*; Entschluß *m*; ~e [di'tə:min] *v/t.* bestimmen; entscheiden; veranlassen; *Strafe* festsetzen; beendigen; *v/i.* sich entschließen; ~ed entschlossen.

deterrent [di'terənt] 1. abschreckend; 2. Abschreckungsmittel *n*; *nuclear* ~ *pol.* atomare Abschreckung.

detest [di'test] verabscheuen; ~able □ [~təbl] abscheulich; ~ation [di:tes'teiʃən] Abscheu *m*.

dethrone [di'θroun] entthronen.

detonate ['detouneit] explodieren (lassen).

detour, détour ['deituə] 1. Umweg *m*; Umleitung *f*; 2. e-n Umweg machen.

detract [di'trækt]: ~ from *s.th.* et. beeinträchtigen, schmälern; ~ion [~kʃən] Verleumdung *f*; Herabsetzung *f*.

detriment ['detrimənt] Schaden *m*.

deuce [dju:s] Zwei *f* *im Spiel*; *Tennis:* Einstand *m*; F Teufel *m*; the ~! zum Teufel!

devalu|ation [di:vælju'eiʃən] Abwertung *f*; ~e [di:'vælju:] abwerten.

devastat|e ['devəsteit] verwüsten; ~ion [devəs'teiʃən] Verwüstung *f*.

develop [di'veləp] (sich) entwickeln; (sich) entfalten; (sich) erweitern; *Gelände* erschließen; ausbauen; *Am.* (sich) zeigen; ~ment [~pmənt] Entwicklung *f*, Entfaltung *f*; Erweiterung *f*; Ausbau *m*.

deviat|e ['di:vieit] abweichen; ~ion [di:vi'eiʃən] Abweichung *f*.

device [di'vais] Plan *m*; Kniff *m*; Erfindung *f*; Vorrichtung *f*; Muster *n*; Wahlspruch *m*; leave *s.o.* to his own ~s j. sich selbst überlassen.

devil ['devl] 1. Teufel *m* (*a. fig.*); ♊️ Hilfsanwalt *m*; Laufbursche *m*; 2. *v/t. Gericht* stark pfeffern; *Am.* plagen, quälen; ~ish □ [~liʃ] teuflisch; ~(t)ry [~l(t)ri] Teufelei *f*.

devious □ ['di:vjəs] abwegig.

devise [di'vaiz] 1. ♊️ Vermachen *n*; Vermächtnis *n*; 2. ersinnen; ♊️ vermachen.

devoid [di'vɔid] ~ of bar (*gen.*), ohne.

devot|e [di'vout] weihen, widmen; ~ed □ ergeben; zärtlich; ~ion [di'vouʃən] Ergebenheit *f*; Hingebung *f*; Frömmigkeit *f*; ~s *pl.* Andacht *f*.

devour [di'vauə] verschlingen.

devout □ [di'vaut] andächtig, fromm; innig.

dew [dju:] 1. Tau *m*; 2. tauen; ~y ['dju:i] betaut; taufrisch.

dexter|ity [deks'teriti] Gewandtheit *f*; ~ous □ ['dekstərəs] gewandt.

diabolic(al □) [daiə'bɔlik(əl)] teuflisch.

diagnose ['daiəgnouz] diagnostizieren, erkennen.

diagram ['daiəgræm] graphische Darstellung; Schema *n*, Plan *m*.

dial ['daiəl] 1. Sonnenuhr *f*; Zifferblatt *n*; *teleph.* Wähl(er)scheibe *f*; *Radio:* Skala *f*; 2. *teleph.* wählen.

dialect ['daiəlekt] Mundart *f*.

dialo|gue, *Am. a.* ~g ['daiələɔg]
Dialog *m*, Gespräch *n*.

dial-tone *teleph.* ['daiəltoun] Amts-
zeichen *n*.

diameter [dai'æmitə] Durchmesser
m.

diamond ['daiəmənd] Diamant *m*;
Rhombus *m*; *Am.* Baseball: Spielfeld *n*; *Karten:* Karo *n*.

diaper ['daiəpə] 1. Windel *f*; 2. *Am.*
Baby trockenlegen, wickeln.

diaphragm ['daiəfræm] Zwerch-
fell *n*; *opt.* Blende *f*; *teleph.* Mem-
bran(e) *f*.

diarrh(o)ea ♪ [daiə'riə] Durchfall
m.

diary ['daiəri] Tagebuch *n*.

dice [dais] 1. *pl. von* die²; 2. würfeln;
~-box ['daisbɔks] Würfelbecher *m*.

dick *Am. sl.* [dik] Detektiv *m*.

dicker *Am.* F ['dikə] (ver)schachern.

dick(e)y ['diki] 1. *sl.* schlecht,
schlimm; 2. F Notsitz *m*; Hemden-
brust *f*; *a.* ~*-bird* Piepvögelchen *n*.

dictat|e 1. ['dikteit] Diktat *n*, Vor-
schrift *f*; Gebot *n*; 2. [dik'teit] dik-
tieren; *fig.* vorschreiben; ~ion
[~eifən] Diktat *n*; Vorschrift *f*;
~orship [~eitəfip] Diktatur *f*.

diction ['dikfən] Ausdruck(sweise *f*)
m, Stil *m*; ~ary [~nri] Wörterbuch *n*.

did [did] *pret. von* do.

die¹ [dai] sterben, umkommen;
untergehen; absterben; F verschmach-
ten; ~ *away* ersterben; verhallen
(*Ton*); sich verlieren (*Farbe*); ver-
löschen (*Licht*); ~ *down* hinsiechen;
(dahin)schwinden; erlöschen.

die² [~], *pl.* dice [dais] Würfel *m*;
pl. dies [daiz] ⊕ Preßform *f*;
Münz-Stempel *m*; *lower* ~ Matrize *f*.

die-hard ['daiha:d] Reaktionär *m*.

diet ['daiət] 1. Diät *f*; Nahrung *f*,
Kost *f*; Landtag *m*; 2. *v/t.* Diät vorschreiben; beköstigen; *v/i.* diät
leben.

differ ['difə] sich unterscheiden;
anderer Meinung sein (*with, from*
als); abweichen; ~ence ['difrəns]
Unterschied *m*; Å, ✝ Differenz *f*;
Meinungsverschiedenheit *f*; ~ent
□ [~nt] verschieden; anders, ande-
re(r, -s) (*from* als); ~entiate [difə-
'renfieit] (sich) unterscheiden.

difficult □ ['difikəlt] schwierig; ~y
[~ti] Schwierigkeit *f*.

diffiden|ce ['difidəns] Schüchtern-
heit *f*; ~t □ [~nt] schüchtern.

diffus|e 1. *fig.* [di'fju:z] verbreiten;
2. □ [~u:s] weitverbreitet, zerstreut
(*bsd. Licht*); weitschweifig; ~ion
[~u:ʒən] Verbreitung *f*.

dig [dig] 1. [*irr.*] (um-, aus)graben;
wühlen (*in* in *dat.*); 2. (Aus)Gra-
bung(sstelle) *f*; ~s *pl.* F Bude *f*,
Einzelzimmer *n*; F Stoß *m*, Puff *m*.

digest 1. [di'dʒest] *v/t.* ordnen; verdauen (*a. fig.* = überdenken; *ver-
winden*); *v/i.* verdaut werden;

2. ['daidʒest] Abriß *m*; Auslese *f*,
Auswahl *f*; ☆☆ Gesetzsammlung *f*;
~ible [di'dʒestəbl] verdaulich; ~ion
[~tfən] Verdauung *f*; ~ive [~tiv]
Verdauungsmittel *n*.

digg|er ['digə] (*bsd.* Gold)Gräber
m; *sl.* Australier *m*; ~ings F ['diginz]
pl. Bude *f* (*Wohnung*); *Am.* Gold-
mine(n *pl.*) *f*.

dignif|ied □ ['dignifaid] würdevoll;
würdig; ~y [~fai] Würde verleihen
(*dat.*); (be)ehren; *fig.* adeln.

dignit|ary ['dignitari] Würden-
träger *m*; ~y [~ti] Würde *f*.

digress [dai'gres] abschweifen.

dike [daik] 1. Deich *m*; Damm *m*;
Graben *m*; 2. eindeichen; eindämmen. [(lassen).\]

dilapidate [di'læpideit] verfallen/

dilat|e [dai'leit] (sich) ausdehnen;
Augen weit öffnen; ~ory □ ['dilətə-
ri] aufschiebend; saumselig.

diligen|ce ['dilidʒəns] Fleiß *m*; ~t
□ [~nt] fleißig, emsig.

dilute [dai'lju:t] 1. verdünnen; verwässern; 2. verdünnt.

dim [dim] 1. □ trüb; dunkel; matt;
2. (sich) verdunkeln; abblenden;
(sich) trüben; matt werden.

dime *Am.* [daim] Zehncentstück *n*.

dimension [di'menfən] Abmessung
f; ~s *pl. a.* Ausmaß *n*.

dimin|ish [di'minif] (sich) vermin-
dern; abnehmen; ~ution [dimi-
'nju:fən] Verminderung *f*; Abnahme *f*; ~utive □ [di'minjutiv]
winzig.

dimple ['dimpl] 1. Grübchen *n*;
2. Grübchen bekommen.

din [din] Getöse *n*, Lärm *m*.

dine [dain] (zu Mittag) speisen; bewirten; ~r ['dainə] Speisende(r *m*)
f; (Mittags)Gast *m*; 🚃 *bsd. Am.*
Speisewagen *m*; *Am.* Restaurant *n*.

dingle ['dingl] Waldschlucht *f*.

dingy □ ['dindʒi] schmutzig.

dining|-car 🚃 ['dainiŋka:] Speise-
wagen *m*; ~-room Speisezimmer *n*.

dinner ['dinə] (Mittag-, Abend-)
Essen *n*; Festessen *n*; ~-jacket
Smoking *m*; ~-pail *Am.* Essen-
träger *m* (*Gerät*); ~-party Tisch-
gesellschaft *f*; ~-service, ~-set
Tafelgeschirr *n*.

dint [dint] 1. Beule *f*; *by* ~ *of* kraft,
vermöge (*gen.*); 2. ver-, einbeulen.

dip [dip] 1. *v/t.* (ein)tauchen; senken; schöpfen; abblenden; *v/i.*
(unter)tauchen, untersinken; sich
neigen; sich senken; 2. Eintauchen
n; F kurzes Bad; Senkung *f*, Neigung *f*. [rie *f*.\]

diphtheria ♪ [dif'θiəriə] Diphthe-/

diploma [di'ploumə] Diplom *n*;
~cy [~əsi] Diplomatie *f*; ~tic(al □)
[diplə'mætik(əl)] diplomatisch;
~tist [di'ploumətist] Diplomat(in).

dipper ['dipə] Schöpfkelle *f*; *Am.*
Great *od.* Big ♌ *ast. der* Große Bär.

dire ['daiə] gräßlich, schrecklich.
direct [di'rekt] 1. □ direkt; gerade; unmittelbar; offen, aufrichtig; deutlich; ~ current ⚡ Gleichstrom m; ~ train durchgehender Zug; 2. adv. geradeswegs; = ~ly 3. richten; lenken, steuern; leiten; anordnen; j-n (an)weisen; Brief adressieren; ~ion [~kʃən] Richtung f; Gegend f; Leitung f; Anordnung f; Adresse f; Vorstand m; ~ion-finder [~nfaində] Radio: (Funk)Peiler m; Peil-(funk)empfänger m; ~ion-indicator mot. Fahrtrichtungsanzeiger m; ⚡ Kursweiser m; ~ive [~ktiv] richtungweisend; leitend; ~ly [~tli] 1. adv. sofort; 2. cj. sobald, als.
director [di'rektə] Direktor m; Film: Regisseur m; board of ~s Aufsichtsrat m; ~ate [~ərit] Direktion f; ~y Adreßbuch n; telephone ~ Telephonbuch n.
dirge [də:dʒ] Klage(lied n) f.
dirigible ['diridʒəbl] 1. lenkbar; 2. lenkbares Luftschiff.
dirt [də:t] Schmutz m; (lockere) Erde; ~-cheap F ['də:t'tʃi:p] spottbillig; ~y ['də:ti] 1. □ schmutzig (a. fig.); 2. beschmutzen; besudeln.
disability [disə'biliti] Unfähigkeit f.
disable [dis'eibl] (dienst-, kampf-)unfähig machen; ~d dienst-, kampfunfähig; körperbehindert; kriegsbeschädigt.
disabuse [disə'bju:z] e-s Besseren belehren (of über acc.).
disadvantage [disəd'va:ntidʒ] Nachteil m; Schaden m; ~ous [disædvɑːn'teidʒəs] nachteilig, ungünstig.
disagree [disə'gri:] nicht übereinstimmen; uneinig sein; nicht bekommen (with s.o. j-m); ~able □ [~riəbl] unangenehm; ~ment [~ri:mənt] Verschiedenheit f; Unstimmigkeit f; Meinungsverschiedenheit f.
disappear [disə'piə] verschwinden; ~ance [~ərəns] Verschwinden n.
disappoint [disə'point] enttäuschen; vereiteln; j. im Stich lassen; ~ment [~tmənt] Enttäuschung f; Vereitelung f. [Mißbilligung f.]
disapprobation [disæprou'beiʃən]
disapprov|al [disə'pru:vəl] Mißbilligung f; ~e ['disə'pru:v] mißbilligen (of et.).
disarm [dis'ɑ:m] v/t. entwaffnen (a. fig.); v/i. abrüsten; ~ament [~məmənt] Entwaffnung f; Abrüstung f.
disarrange ['disə'reindʒ] in Unordnung bringen, verwirren.
disarray ['disə'rei] 1. Unordnung f; 2. in Unordnung bringen.
disast|er [di'zɑ:stə] Unglück(sfall m) n, Katastrophe f; ~rous □ [~trəs] unheilvoll; katastrophal.

disband [dis'bænd] entlassen; auflösen.
disbelieve ['disbi'li:v] nicht glauben.
disburse [dis'bə:s] auszahlen.
disc [disk] = disk.
discard 1. [dis'kɑːd] Karten, Kleid etc. ablegen; entlassen; 2. ['diskɑːd] Karten: Abwerfen n; bsd. Am. Abfall(haufen) m.
discern [di'sə:n] unterscheiden; erkennen; beurteilen; ~ing □ [~niŋ] kritisch, scharfsichtig; ~ment [~nmənt] Einsicht f; Scharfsinn m.
discharge [dis'tʃɑːdʒ] 1. v/t. ent-, ab-, ausladen; entlassen, entbinden; abfeuern; Flüssigkeit absondern; Amt versehen; Pflicht etc. erfüllen; Zorn etc. auslassen (on an dat.); Schuld tilgen; quittieren; Wechsel einlösen; entlassen; freisprechen; v/i. sich entladen; eitern; 2. Entladung f; Abfeuern n; Ausströmen n; Ausfluß m, Eiter(ung f) m; Entlassung f; Entlastung f; Bezahlung f; Quittung f; Erfüllung f e-r Pflicht.
disciple [di'saipl] Schüler m; Jünger m.
discipline ['disiplin] 1. Disziplin f, Zucht f; Erziehung f; Züchtigung f; 2. erziehen; schulen; bestrafen.
disclaim [dis'kleim] (ab)leugnen; ablehnen; verzichten auf (acc.).
disclose [dis'klouz] aufdecken; erschließen, offenbaren, enthüllen.
discolo(u)r [dis'kʌlə] (sich) verfärben.
discomfiture [dis'kʌmfitʃə] Niederlage f; Verwirrung f; Vereitelung f.
discomfort [dis'kʌmfət] 1. Unbehagen n; 2. j-m Unbehagen verursachen.
discompose [diskəm'pouz] beunruhigen.
disconcert [diskən'sə:t] außer Fassung bringen; vereiteln.
disconnect ['diskə'nekt] trennen (a. ⚡); ⊕ auskuppeln; ⚡ ab-, ausschalten; ~ed □ zs.-hanglos.
disconsolate □ [dis'kɔnsəlit] trostlos.
discontent ['diskən'tent] Unzufriedenheit f; ~ed □ mißvergnügt, unzufrieden.
discontinue ['diskən'tinju(:)] aufgeben, aufhören mit; unterbrechen.
discord ['diskɔ:d], ~ance [dis'kɔːdəns] Uneinigkeit f; ♪ Mißklang m.
discount ['diskaunt] 1. ✝ Diskont m; Abzug m, Rabatt m; 2. ✝ diskontieren; abrechnen; fig. absehen von; Nachricht mit Vorsicht aufnehmen; beeinträchtigen; ~enance [dis'kauntinəns] mißbilligen; entmutigen.
discourage [dis'kʌridʒ] entmutigen;

abschrecken; ~ment [~dʒmənt] Entmutigung f; Schwierigkeit f.

discourse [dis'kɔːs] **1.** Rede f; Abhandlung f; Predigt f; **2.** reden, sprechen; e-n Vortrag halten.

discourte|ous □ [dis'kəːtjəs] unhöflich; ~sy f [Ltisi] Unhöflichkeit f.

discover [dis'kʌvə] entdecken; ausfindig machen; ~y [Ləri] Entdeckung f.

discredit [dis'kredit] **1.** schlechter Ruf; Unglaubwürdigkeit f; **2.** nicht glauben; in Mißkredit bringen.

discreet □ [dis'kriːt] besonnen, vorsichtig; klug; verschwiegen.

discrepancy [dis'krepənsi] Widerspruch m; Unstimmigkeit f.

discretion [dis'kreʃən] Besonnenheit f, Klugheit f; Takt m; Verschwiegenheit f; Belieben n; age (od. years) of ~ Strafmündigkeit f (14 Jahre); surrender at ~ sich auf Gnade und Ungnade ergeben.

discriminat|e [dis'krimineit] unterscheiden; ~ against benachteiligen; ~ing □ [Ltin] unterscheidend; scharfsinnig; urteilsfähig; ~ion [diskrimi'neiʃən] Unterscheidung f; unterschiedliche (bsd. nachteilige) Behandlung; Urteilskraft f.

discuss [dis'kʌs] erörtern, besprechen; ~ion [Lʃən] Erörterung f.

disdain [dis'dein] **1.** Verachtung f; **2.** geringschätzen, verachten; verschmähen.

disease [di'ziːz] Krankheit f; ~d krank.

disembark ['disim'baːk] v/t. ausschiffen; v/i. landen, an Land gehen.

disengage ['disin'geidʒ] (sich) freimachen, (sich) lösen; ⊕ loskuppeln.

disentangle ['disin'tæŋgl] entwirren; fig. freimachen (from von).

disfavo(u)r ['dis'feivə] **1.** Mißfallen n, Ungnade f; **2.** nicht mögen.

disfigure [dis'figə] entstellen.

disgorge [dis'gɔːdʒ] ausspeien.

disgrace [dis'greis] **1.** Ungnade f; Schande f; **2.** in Ungnade fallen lassen; j-n entehren; ~ful □ [Lsful] schimpflich.

disguise [dis'gaiz] **1.** verkleiden; Stimme verstellen; verhehlen; **2.** Verkleidung f; Verstellung f; Maske f.

disgust [dis'gʌst] **1.** Ekel m; **2.** anekeln; ~ing □ [Ltiŋ] ekelhaft.

dish [diʃ] **1.** Schüssel f, Platte f; Gericht n (Speise); the ~es das Geschirr; **2.** anrichten; mst ~ up auftischen; ~-cloth ['diʃklɔθ] Geschirrspültuch n.

dishearten [dis'haːtn] entmutigen.

dishevel(l)ed [di'ʃevəld] zerzaust.

dishonest □ [dis'ɔnist] unehrlich, unredlich; ~y [Lti] Unredlichkeit f.

dishono(u)r [dis'ɔnə] **1.** Unehre f,

Schande f; **2.** entehren; schänden; Wechsel nicht honorieren; ~able □ [Lərəbl] entehrend; ehrlos.

dish|-pan Am. ['diʃpæn] Spülschüssel f; ~rag = dish-cloth; ~-water Spülwasser n.

disillusion [disi'luːʒən] **1.** Ernüchterung f, Enttäuschung f; **2.** ernüchtern, enttäuschen.

disinclined ['disin'klaind] abgeneigt.

disinfect [disin'fekt] desinfizieren; ~ant [Ltənt] Desinfektionsmittel n.

disintegrate [dis'intigreit] (sich) auflösen; (sich) zersetzen.

disinterested □ [dis'intristid] uneigennützig, selbstlos.

disk [disk] Scheibe f; Platte f; Schallplatte f; ~ brake mot. Scheibenbremse f; ~ jockey Ansager m e-r Schallplattensendung.

dislike [dis'laik] **1.** Abneigung f; Widerwille m; **2.** nicht mögen.

dislocate ['disləkeit] aus den Fugen bringen; verrenken; verlagern.

dislodge [dis'lɔdʒ] vertreiben, verjagen; umquartieren.

disloyal □ ['dis'lɔiəl] treulos.

dismal □ ['dizməl] trüb(selig); öde; trostlos, elend.

dismantl|e [dis'mæntl] abbrechen, niederreißen; ⚓ abtakeln; ⊕ demontieren; ~ing [Liŋ] Demontage f.

dismay [dis'mei] **1.** Schrecken m; Bestürzung f; **2.** v/t. erschrecken.

dismember [dis'membə] zerstükkeln.

dismiss [dis'mis] v/t. entlassen, wegschicken; ablehnen; Thema etc. fallen lassen; t͡z abweisen; ~al [Lsəl] Entlassung f; Aufgabe f; t͡z Abweichung f.

dismount ['dis'maunt] v/t. aus dem Sattel werfen; demontieren; ⊕ aus-ea.-nehmen; v/i. absteigen.

disobedien|ce [disə'biːdjəns] Ungehorsam m; ~t □ [Lnt] ungehorsam.

disobey ['disə'bei] ungehorsam sein.

disoblige ['disə'blaidʒ] ungefällig sein gegen; kränken.

disorder [dis'ɔːdə] **1.** Unordnung f; Aufruhr m; s͟ Störung f; **2.** in Unordnung bringen; stören; zerrütten; ~ly [Lli] unordentlich; ordnungswidrig; unruhig; aufrührerisch.

disorganize [dis'ɔːgənaiz] zerrütten.

disown [dis'oun] nicht anerkennen, verleugnen; ablehnen.

disparage [dis'pæridʒ] verächtlich machen, herabsetzen.

disparity [dis'pæriti] Ungleichheit f.

dispassionate □ [dis'pæʃnit] leidenschaftslos; unparteiisch.

dispatch [dis'pætʃ] **1.** (schnelle) Erledigung; (schnelle) Absendung; Abfertigung *f*; Eile *f*; Depesche *f*; **2.** (schnell) abmachen, erledigen (*a. fig.* = *töten*); abfertigen; (eilig) absenden.

dispel [dis'pel] vertreiben, zerstreuen.

dispensa|ble [dis'pensǝbl] entbehrlich; **~ry** [.ǝri] Apotheke *f*; **~tion** [dispen'seiʃǝn] Austeilung *f*; Befreiung *f* (*with* von); *göttliche* Fügung.

dispense [dis'pens] *v/t.* austeilen; *Gesetze* handhaben; *Arzneien* anfertigen und ausgeben; befreien.

disperse [dis'pǝːs] (sich) zerstreuen; auseinandergehen.

dispirit [di'spirit] entmutigen.

displace [dis'pleis] verschieben; absetzen; ersetzen; verdrängen.

display [dis'plei] **1.** Entfaltung *f*; Aufwand *m*; Schaustellung *f*; *Schaufenster*-Auslage *f*; **2.** entfalten; zur Schau stellen; zeigen.

displeas|e [dis'pliːz] *j-m* mißfallen; **~ed** ungehalten; **~ure** [.leʒǝ] Mißfallen *n*; Verdruß *m*.

dispos|al [dis'pouzǝl] Anordnung *f*; Verfügung(srecht *n*) *f*; Beseitigung *f*; Veräußerung *f*; Übergabe *f*; **~e** [.ouz] *v/t.* (an)ordnen, einrichten; geneigt machen, veranlassen; *v/i.* **~ of** verfügen über (*acc.*); erledigen; verwenden; veräußern; unterbringen; beseitigen; **~ed** geneigt; ...gesinnt; **~ition** [dispǝ'ziʃǝn] Disposition *f*; Anordnung *f*; Neigung *f*; Sinnesart *f*; Verfügung *f*.

dispossess [dispǝ'zes] (*of*) vertreiben (aus *od.* von); berauben (*gen.*).

dispraise [dis'preiz] tadeln.

disproof ['dis'pruːf] Widerlegung *f*.

disproportionate [disprǝ'pɔːʃnit] unverhältnismäßig.

disprove ['dis'pruːv] widerlegen.

dispute [dis'pjuːt] **1.** Streit(igkeit *f*) *m*; Rechtsstreit *m*; *beyond* (*all*) **~**, *past* **~** zweifellos; **2.** (be)streiten.

disqualify [dis'kwɔlifai] unfähig *od.* untauglich machen; für untauglich erklären.

disquiet [dis'kwaiǝt] beunruhigen.

disregard ['disri'gɑːd] **1.** Nicht(be)achtung *f*; **2.** unbeachtet lassen.

disreput|able [dis'repjutǝbl] schimpflich; verrufen; **~e** ['disri'pjuːt] übler Ruf; Schande *f*.

disrespect ['disris'pekt] Nichtachtung *f*; Respektlosigkeit *f*; **~ful** [.tful] respektlos; unhöflich.

disroot [dis'ruːt] entwurzeln.

disrupt [dis'rʌpt] zerreißen; spalten.

dissatis|faction ['dissætis'fækʃǝn] Unzufriedenheit *f*; **~factory** [.ktǝri] unbefriedigend; **~fy** ['dis'sætisfai] nicht befriedigen; *j-m* mißfallen.

dissect [di'sekt] zerlegen; zergliedern.

dissemble [di'sembl] *v/t.* verhehlen; *v/i.* sich verstellen, heucheln.

dissen|sion [di'senʃǝn] Zwietracht *f*, Streit *m*, Uneinigkeit *f*; **~t** [.nt] **1.** abweichende Meinung; Nichtzugehörigkeit *f* zur Staatskirche; **2.** andrer Meinung sein (*from* als).

dissimilar ['di'similǝ] (*to*) unähnlich (*dat.*); verschieden (von).

dissimulation [disimju'leiʃǝn] Verstellung *f*, Heuchelei *f*.

dissipat|e ['disipeit] (sich) zerstreuen; verschwenden; **~ion** [disi'peiʃǝn] Zerstreuung *f*; Verschwendung *f*; ausschweifendes Leben.

dissociate [di'souʃieit] trennen; **~ o.s.** sich distanzieren, abrücken.

dissoluble [di'sɔljubl] (auf)lösbar.

dissolut|e ['disǝluːt] liederlich, ausschweifend; **~ion** [disǝ'luːʃǝn] Auflösung *f*; Zerstörung *f*; Tod *m*.

dissolve [di'zɔlv] *v/t.* (auf)lösen; schmelzen; *v/i.* sich auflösen; vergehen.

dissonant ['disǝnǝnt] ♪ mißtönend; abweichend; uneinig.

dissuade [di'sweid] *j-m* abraten.

distan|ce ['distǝns] **1.** Abstand *m*, Entfernung *f*; Ferne *f*; Strecke *f*; Zurückhaltung *f*; *at a* **~** von weitem; *in e-r gewissen Entfernung*; weit weg; *keep s.o. at a* **~** *j-m* gegenüber reserviert sein; **2.** hinter sich lassen; **~t** [.nt] entfernt; fern; zurückhaltend; Fern...; **~ control** Fernsteuerung *f*.

distaste [dis'teist] Widerwille *m*; Abneigung *f*; **~ful** [.tful] widerwärtig; ärgerlich.

distemper [dis'tempǝ] Krankheit *f* (*bsd. von Tieren*); (Hunde)Staupe *f*.

distend [dis'tend] (sich) ausdehnen; (auf)blähen; (sich) weiten.

distil [dis'til] herabtröpfeln (lassen); ♣ destillieren; **~lery** [.lǝri] Branntweinbrennerei *f*.

distinct ['dis'tiŋkt] verschieden; getrennt; deutlich, klar; **~ion** [.kʃǝn] Unterscheidung *f*; Unterschied *m*; Auszeichnung *f*; Rang *m*; **~ive** ['.ktiv] unterscheidend; apart; kennzeichnend, bezeichnend.

distinguish [dis'tiŋgwiʃ] unterscheiden; auszeichnen; **~ed** berühmt, ausgezeichnet; vornehm.

distort [dis'tɔːt] verdrehen; verzerren.

distract ['dis'trækt] ablenken, zerstreuen; beunruhigen; verwirren; verrückt machen; **~ion** [.kʃǝn] Zerstreutheit *f*; Verwirrung *f*; Wahnsinn *m*; Zerstreuung *f*.

distraught [dis'trɔːt] verwirrt, bestürzt.

distress [dis'tres] **1.** Qual *f*; Elend *n*, Not *f*; Erschöpfung *f*; **2. in** Not bringen; quälen; erschöpfen; **~ed** in Not befindlich; bekümmert; **~ area** Notstandsgebiet *n*.

distribut|e [dis'tribju(:)t] verteilen; einteilen; verbreiten; **~ion** [distri'bju:ʃən] Verteilung *f*; *Film*-Verleih *m*; Verbreitung *f*; Einteilung *f*.

district ['distrikt] Bezirk *m*; Gegend *f*.

distrust [dis'trʌst] 1. Mißtrauen *n*; 2. mißtrauen (*dat.*); **~ful** □ [~tful] mißtrauisch; **~** (of o.s.) schüchtern.

disturb [dis'tə:b] beunruhigen; stören; **~ance** [~bəns] Störung *f*; Unruhe *f*; Aufruhr *m*; **~ of the peace** ≹ öffentliche Ruhestörung; **~er** [~bə] Störenfried *m*, Unruhestifter *m*.

disunite ['disju:'nait] (sich) trennen.

disuse ['dis'ju:z] nicht mehr gebrauchen.

ditch [ditʃ] Graben *m*.

ditto ['ditou] dito, desgleichen.

divan [di'væn] Diwan *m*; **~-bed** [*oft* 'daivænbed] Bettcouch *f*, Liege *f*.

dive [daiv] 1. (unter)tauchen; *vom Sprungbrett* springen; e-n Sturzflug machen; eindringen in (*acc.*); 2. *Schwimmen:* Springen *m*; (Kopf-) Sprung *m*; Sturzflug *m*; Kellerlokal *n*; *Am.* F Kaschemme *f*; **~r** ['daivə] Taucher *m*.

diverge [dai'və:dʒ] aus-ea.-laufen; abweichen; **~nce** [~dʒəns] Abweichung *f*; **~nt** □ [~nt] (von-ea.-)abweichend.

divers ['daivə(:)z] mehrere.

divers|e □ [dai'və:s] verschieden; mannigfaltig; **~ion** [~ʃən] Ablenkung *f*; Zeitvertreib *m*; **~ity** [~siti] Verschiedenheit *f*; Mannigfaltigkeit *f*.

divert [dai'və:t] ablenken; *j-n* zerstreuen; unterhalten; *Verkehr* umleiten.

divest [dai'vest] entkleiden (*a.fig.*).

divid|e [di'vaid] 1. *v/t.* teilen; trennen; einteilen; ♈ dividieren (*by* durch); *v/i.* sich teilen; zerfallen; ♈ aufgehen; sich trennen *od.* auflösen; 2. Wasserscheide *f*; **~end** ['dividend] Dividende *f*.

divine [di'vain] 1. □ göttlich; **~ service** Gottesdienst *m*; 2. Geistliche(r) *m*; 3. weissagen; ahnen.

diving ['daiviŋ] Kunstspringen *n*; *attr.* Taucher...

divinity [di'viniti] Gottheit *f*; Göttlichkeit *f*; Theologie *f*.

divis|ible □ [di'vizəbl] teilbar; **~ion** [~ʒən] Teilung *f*; Trennung *f*; Abteilung *f*; ✕, ♈ Division *f*.

divorce [di'vɔ:s] 1. (Ehe)Scheidung *f*; 2. *Ehe* scheiden; sich scheiden lassen.

divulge [dai'vʌldʒ] ausplaudern; verbreiten; bekanntmachen.

dixie ✕ *sl.* ['diksi] Kochgeschirr *n*;

Feldkessel *m*; ♀ *Am.* die Südstaaten *pl.*; ♀crat *Am. pol.* opponierender Südstaatendemokrat.

dizz|iness ['dizinis] Schwindel *m*; **~y** □ ['dizi] schwind(e)lig.

do [du:] [*irr.*] *v/t.* tun; machen; (zu)bereiten; *Rolle, Stück* spielen; **~ London** *sl.* London besichtigen; **have done reading** fertig sein mit Lesen; **~ in** F um die Ecke bringen; **~ into** übersetzen in; **~ over** überstreifen, -ziehen; **~ up** instand setzen; einpacken; *v/i.* tun; handeln; sich benehmen; sich befinden; genügen; **that will ~** das genügt; **how ~ you ~?** guten Tag!, Wie geht's?; **~ well** s-e Sache gut machen; gute Geschäfte machen; **~ away with ~** weg-, abschaffen; **I could ~ with ...** ich könnte ... brauchen *od.* vertragen; **~ without** fertig werden ohne; **~ be quick** beeile dich doch; **~ you like London? — I ~** gefällt Ihnen London? — Ja.

docil|e ['dousail] gelehrig; fügsam; **~ity** [dou'siliti] Gelehrigkeit *f*.

dock[1] [dɔk] stutzen; *fig.* kürzen.

dock[2] [~] 1. ♣ Dock *n*; *bsd. Am.* Kai *m*, Pier *m*; ≹ Anklagebank *f*; 2. ♣ docken.

dockyard ['dɔkja:d] Werft *f*.

doctor ['dɔktə] 1. Doktor *m*; Arzt *m*; 2.F verarzten; F*fig.* (ver)fälschen.

doctrine ['dɔktrin] Lehre *f*; Dogma *n*.

document 1. ['dɔkjumənt] Urkunde *f*; 2. [~ment] beurkunden.

dodge [dɔdʒ] 1. Seitensprung *m*; Kniff *m*, Winkelzug *m*; 2. *fig.* irreführen; ausweichen; Winkelzüge machen; **~r** ['dɔdʒə] Schieber(in); *Am.* Hand-, Reklamezettel *m*; *Am.* Maisbrot *n*, -kuchen *m*.

doe [dou] Hirschkuh *f*; Reh *n*; Häsin *f*.

dog [dɔg] 1. Hund *m*; Haken *m*, Klammer *f*; 2. nachspüren (*dat.*).

dogged □ ['dɔgid] verbissen.

dogma ['dɔgmə] Dogma *n*; Glaubenslehre *f*; **~tic(al** □) [dɔg'mæt-ik(əl)] dogmatisch; bestimmt; **~tism** ['dɔgmətizəm] Selbstherrlichkeit *f*.

dog's-ear F ['dɔgziə] Eselsohr *n im Buch*.

dog-tired F ['dɔg'taiəd] hundemüde.

doings ['du(:)iŋz] *pl.* Dinge *n/pl.*; Begebenheiten *f/pl.*; Treiben *n*; Betragen *n*.

dole [doul] 1. Spende *f*; F Erwerbslosenunterstützung *f*; 2. verteilen.

doleful □ ['doulful] trübselig.

doll [dɔl] Puppe *f*.

dollar ['dɔlə] Dollar *m*.

dolly ['dɔli] Püppchen *n*.

dolorous ['dɔlərəs] schmerzhaft; traurig.

dolphin ['dɔlfin] Delphin *m*.

dolt [doult] Tölpel *m*.

domain [də'mein] Domäne *f*; *fig.* Gebiet *n*; Bereich *m*.

dome [doum] Kuppel *f*; ⊕ Haube *f*; ~d gewölbt.

Domesday Book ['du:mzdei'buk] Reichsgrundbuch *n Englands.*

domestic [də'mestik] **1.** (~ally) häuslich; inländisch; einheimisch; zahm; ~ *animal* Haustier *n*; **2.** Dienstbote *m*; ~s *pl.* Haushaltsartikel *m/pl.*; ~ate [~keit] zähmen; domicile ['dɔmisail] Wohnsitz *m*; ~d wohnhaft.

domin|ant ['dɔminənt] (vor)herrschend; ~ate [~neit] (be)herrschen; ~ation [dɔmi'neiʃən] Herrschaft *f*; ~eer [~'niə] (despotisch) herrschen; ~eering [~'ɔriŋ] herrisch, tyrannisch; überheblich.

dominion [də'minjən] Herrschaft *f*; Gebiet *n*; ♀ Dominion *n* (*im Brt. Commonwealth*).

don [dɔn] anziehen; *Hut* aufsetzen.

donat|e *Am.* [dou'neit] schenken; stiften; ~ion [~eiʃən] Schenkung *f*.

done [dʌn] **1.** *p.p. von* do; **2.** *adj.* abgemacht; fertig; gar *gekocht.*

donkey ['dɔŋki] *zo.* Esel *m*; *attr.* Hilfs...

donor ['dounə] (⚛ *Blut*)Spender *m*.

doom [du:m] **1.** Schicksal *n*, Verhängnis *n*; **2.** verurteilen, verdammen.

door [dɔ:] Tür *f*, Tor *n*; next ~ nebenan; ~-handle ['dɔ:hændl] Türgriff *m*; ~-keeper, *Am.* ~man Pförtner *m*; Portier *m*; ~-way Türöffnung *f*; Torweg *m*; ~yard *Am.* Vorhof *m*, Vorgarten *m*.

dope [doup] **1.** Schmiere *f*; *bsd.* ✈ Lack *m*; Aufputschmittel *n*; Rauschgift *n*; *Am. sl.* Geheimtip *m*; **2.** lackieren; *sl.* betäuben; aufpulvern; *Am. sl.* herauskriegen.

dormant *mst fig.* ['dɔ:mənt] schlafend, ruhend; unbenutzt; † tot.

dormer(-window) ['dɔ:mə('window)] Dachfenster *n*.

dormitory [dɔ:mitri] Schlafsaal *m*; *bsd. Am.* Studenten(wohn)heim *n*.

dose [dous] **1.** Dosis *f*, Portion *f*; **2.** *j-m* e-e Medizin geben.

dot [dɔt] **1.** Punkt *m*, Fleck *m*; **2.** punktieren, tüpfeln; *fig.* verstreuen.

dot|e [dout]: ~ (*up*)*on* vernarrt sein in (*acc.*); ~ing ['doutiŋ] vernarrt.

double □ ['dʌbl] **1.** doppelt; zu zweien; gekrümmt; zweideutig; **2.** Doppelte(s) *n*; Doppelgänger(in) *f*; *Tennis*: Doppel(spiel) *n*; **3.** *v/t.* verdoppeln; *a.* ~ *up* zs.-legen; *v/t.* umfahren, umsegeln; ~d *up* zs.-gekrümmt; *v/i.* sich verdoppeln; *a.* ~ *back* e-n Haken schlagen (*Hase*); ~breasted zweireihig (*Jackett*); ~cross *sl.* Partner betrügen; ~dealing Doppelzüngigkeit *f*; ~edged zweischneidig; ~entry doppelte Buchführung;

~feature *Am.* Doppelprogramm *n im Kino*; ~header *Am. Baseball*: Doppelspiel *n*; ~park *Am.* verboten in zweiter Reihe parken.

doubt [daut] **1.** *v/i.* zweifeln; *v/t.* bezweifeln; mißtrauen (*dat.*); **2.** Zweifel *m*; no ~ ohne Zweifel; ~ful □ ['dautful] zweifelhaft; ~fulness [~lnis] Zweifelhaftigkeit *f*; ~less ['dautlis] ohne Zweifel.

douche [du:ʃ] **1.** Dusche *f*; Irrigator *m*; **2.** duschen; spülen.

dough [dou] Teig *m*; *sl.* ~boy *Am.* F ['doubɔi] Landser *m*; ~nut *Schmalzgebackenes.*

dove [dʌv] Taube *f*; *fig.* Täubchen *n*.

dowel ⊕ ['dauəl] Dübel *m*.

down¹ [daun] Daune *f*; Flaum *m*; Düne *f*; ~s *pl.* Höhenrücken *m*.

down² [~] **1.** *adv.* nieder; her-, hinunter, ab; abwärts; unten; *be* ~ *upon* F über *j-n* herfallen; **2.** *prp.* herab, hinab, her-, hinunter; ~ *the river* flußabwärts; **3.** *adj.* nach unten gerichtet; ~ *platform* Abfahrtsbahnsteig *m* (*London*); ~ *train* Zug *m* von London (fort); **4.** *v/t.* niederwerfen; herunterholen; ~cast ['daunka:st] niedergeschlagen; ~ *easter Am.* Neuengländer *m bsd. von Maine*; ~fall Fall *m*, Sturz *m*; Verfall *m*; ~hearted niedergeschlagen; ~hill bergab; ~pour Regenguß *m*; ~right □ **1.** *adv.* geradezu, durchaus; völlig; **2.** *adj.* ehrlich; plump (*Benehmen*); richtig, glatt (*Lüge etc.*); ~stairs die Treppe hinunter; (nach) unten; ~stream stromabwärts; ~town *bsd. Am.* Hauptgeschäftsviertel *n*; ~ward(s) ['daunwəd(z)] abwärts (gerichtet).

downy ['dauni] flaumig; *sl.* gerissen.

dowry ['dauəri] Mitgift *f* (*a. fig.*).

doze [douz] **1.** dösen; **2.** Schläfchen *n*.

dozen ['dʌzn] Dutzend *n*.

drab [dræb] gelblichgrau; eintönig.

draft [dra:ft] **1.** Entwurf *m*; † Tratte *f*; Abhebung *f*; ✕ (Sonder-)Kommando *n*; Einberufung *f*; = draught; **2.** entwerfen; aufsetzen; ✕ abkommandieren; *Am.* einziehen; ~ee *Am.* ✕ [~'ti:] Dienstpflichtige(r) *m*; ~sman ['dra:ftsmən] (technischer) Zeichner; Verfasser *m*, Entwerfer *m*.

drag [dræg] **1.** Schleppnetz *n*; Schleife *f für Lasten*; Egge *f*; **2.** *v/t.* schleppen, ziehen; *v/i.* (sich)schleppen, schleifen; (mit e-m Schleppnetz) fischen. [Libelle *f.*]

dragon ['drægən] Drache *m*; ~fly]

drain [drein] **1.** Abfluß(graben *m*, -rohr *n*) *m*; F Schluck *m*; **2.** *v/t.* entwässern; *Glas* leeren; *a.* ~ *off* abziehen; verzehren; *v/i.* ablaufen; ~age ['dreinidʒ] Abfluß *m*; Entwässerung(sanlage) *f.*

drake [dreik] Enterich *m.*

dram [dræm] Schluck *m; fig.* Schnaps *m.*

drama ['drɑːmə] Drama *n;* **~tic** [drə'mætik] (**~ally**) dramatisch; **~tist** ['dræmətist] Dramatiker *m;* **~tize** [**~**taiz] dramatisieren.

drank [dræŋk] *pret. von* drink 2.

drape [dreip] 1. drapieren; in Falten legen; 2. *mst* **~s** *pl.* Vorhänge *m/pl.;* **~ry** ['dreipəri] Tuchhandel *m;* Tuchwaren *f/pl.;* Faltenwurf *m.*

drastic ['dræstik] (**~ally**) drastisch.

draught [drɑːft] Zug *m* (*Ziehen; Fischzug; Zugluft; Schluck*); ⚓ Tiefgang *m;* **~s** *pl.* Damespiel *n; s. draft;* **~ beer** Faßbier *n;* **~horse** ['drɑːfthɔːs] Zugpferd *n;* **~sman** [**~**tsmən] Damestein *m;* = draftsman; **~y** [**~**ti] zugig.

draw [drɔː] 1. [*irr.*] ziehen; an-, auf-, ein-, zuziehen; (sich) zs.-ziehen; in die Länge ziehen; dehnen; herausziehen, herauslocken; entnehmen; *Geld* abheben; anlocken, anziehen; abzapfen; ausfischen; *Geflügel* ausnehmen; zeichnen; entwerfen; *Urkunde* abfassen; unentschieden spielen; *Luft* schöpfen; **~ near** heranrücken; **~ out** in die Länge ziehen; **~ up** ab-, verfassen; **~ (up)on** ↑ (e-n Wechsel) ziehen auf (*acc.*); *fig.* in Anspruch nehmen; 2. Zug *m* (*Ziehen*); *Lotterie:* Ziehung *f;* Los *n; Sport:* unentschiedenes Spiel; F Zugstück *n,* -artikel *m;* **~back** ['drɔːbæk] Nachteil *m;* Hindernis *n;* ✝ Rückzoll *m; Am.* Rückzahlung *f;* **~er** ['drɔːə] Ziehende(r *m*) *f;* Zeichner *m;* ✝ Aussteller *m,* Trassant *m;* [drɔː] Schublade *f;* (*a pair of*) **~s** *pl.* (eine) Unterhose; (ein) Schlüpfer *m; mst* chest of **~s** Kommode *f.*

drawing ['drɔːiŋ] Ziehen *n;* Zeichnen *n;* Zeichnung *f;* **~account** Girokonto *n;* **~board** Reißbrett *n;* **~room** Gesellschaftszimmer *n.*

drawn [drɔːn] 1. *p.p. von* draw 1; 2. *adj.* unentschieden; verzerrt.

dread [dred] 1. Furcht *f;* Schrecken *m;* 2. (sich) fürchten; **~ful** □ ['dredful] schrecklich; furchtbar.

dream [driːm] 1. Traum *m;* 2. [*irr.*] träumen; **~er** ['driːmə] Träumer (-in); **~t** [dremt] *pret. u. p.p. von* dream 2; **~y** □ ['driːmi] träumerisch; verträumt.

dreary □ ['driəri] traurig; öde.

dredge [dredʒ] 1. Schleppnetz *n;* Bagger(maschine *f*) *m;* 2. (aus-) baggern.

dregs [dregz] *pl.* Bodensatz *m,* Hefe *f.*

drench [drentʃ] 1. (Regen)Guß *m;* 2. durchnässen; *fig.* baden.

dress [dres] 1. Anzug *m;* Kleidung *f;* Kleid *n;* 2. an-, ein-, zurichten; ✕ (sich) richten; zurechtmachen; (sich) ankleiden; putzen; ✂ verbinden; frisieren; **~circle** *thea.* ['dres'səːkl] erster Rang; **~er** [**~**sə] Anrichte *f; Am.* Frisiertoilette *f.*

dressing ['dresiŋ] An-, Zurichten *n;* Ankleiden *n;* Verband *m;* Appretur *f; Küche:* Soße *f;* Füllung *f;* **~s** *pl.* ✂ Verbandzeug *n;* **~ down** Standpauke *f;* **~gown** Morgenrock *m;* **~table** Frisiertisch *m.*

dress|maker ['dresmeikə] Schneiderin *f;* **~parade** Modenschau *f.*

drew ['druː] *pret. von* draw 1.

dribble ['dribl] tröpfeln, träufeln (lassen); geifern; *Fußball:* dribbeln.

dried [draid] getrocknet; Dörr...

drift [drift] 1. (Dahin)Treiben *n; fig.* Lauf *m; fig.* Hang *m;* Zweck *m;* (Schnee-, Sand)Wehe *f;* 2. *v/t.* (zs.-)treiben, (zs.-)wehen; *v/i.* (dahin)treiben; sich anhäufen.

drill [dril] 1. Drillbohrer *m;* Furche *f;* ✔ Drill-, Sämaschine *f;* ✕ Exerzieren *n* (*a. fig.*); 2. bohren; ✕ (ein)exerzieren (*a. fig.*).

drink [driŋk] 1. Trunk *m;* (geistiges) Getränk; 2. [*irr.*] trinken.

drip [drip] 1. Tröpfeln *n;* Traufe *f;* 2. tröpfeln (lassen); triefen; **~dry shirt** ['drip'drai ʃəːt] bügelfreies Hemd; **~ping** [**~**piŋ] Bratenfett *n.*

drive [draiv] 1. (Spazier-)Fahrt *f;* Auffahrt *f,* Fahrweg *m;* ⊕ Antrieb *m; fig.* (Auf)Trieb *m;* Drang *m;* Unternehmen *n,* Feldzug *m; Am.* Sammelaktion *f;* 2. [*irr.*] *v/t.* (an-, ein)treiben; *Geschäft* betreiben; fahren; lenken; zwingen; vertreiben; *v/i.* treiben; fahren; **~ at** hinzielen auf.

drive-in *Am.* ['draiv'in] 1. *mst attr.* Auto...; **~ cinema** Autokino *n;* 2. Autokino *n;* Autorestaurant *n.*

drivel ['drivl] 1. geifern; faseln; 2. Geifer *m;* Faselei *f.*

driven ['drivn] *p.p. von* drive 2.

driver ['draivə] Treiber *m; mot.* Fahrer *m,* Chauffeur *m;* 🚋 Führer *m.*

driving| licence ['draiviŋ laisəns] Führerschein *m;* **~ school** Fahrschule *f.*

drizzle ['drizl] 1. Sprühregen *m;* 2. sprühen, nieseln.

drone [droun] 1. *zo.* Drohne *f; fig.* Faulenzer *m;* 2. summen; dröhnen.

droop [druːp] *v/t.* sinken lassen; *v/i.* schlaff niederhängen; den Kopf hängen lassen; (ver)welken; schwinden.

drop [drɔp] 1. Tropfen *m;* Fruchtbonbon *m, n;* Fall *m;* Falltür *f; thea.* Vorhang *m;* get (have) the **~ on** *Am.* F zuvorkommen; 2. *v/t.* tropfen (lassen); niederlassen; fallen lassen; *Brief* einwerfen; *Fahrgast* absetzen; senken; **~ s.o. a few lines** *pl.* j-m ein paar Zeilen schreiben; v/i. tropfen; (herab)fallen; um-, hinsinken; ~ in unerwartet kommen.

dropsy ✻ ['drɔpsi] Wassersucht f.

drought [draut], **drouth** [drauθ] Trockenheit f, Dürre f.

drove [drouv] **1.** Trift f Rinder; Herde f (a. fig.); **2.** pret. von drive 2.

drown [draun] v/t. ertränken; überschwemmen; fig. übertäuben; übertönen; v/i. ertrinken.

drows|e [drauz] schlummern, schläfrig sein od. machen; **~y** ['drauzi] schläfrig; einschläfernd.

drudge [drʌdʒ] **1.** fig. Sklave m, Packesel m, Kuli m; **2.** sich (ab-)placken.

drug [drʌg] **1.** Droge f, Arzneiware f; Rauschgift n; unverkäufliche Ware; **2.** mit (schädlichen) Zutaten versetzen; Arznei od. Rauschgift geben (dat.) od. nehmen; **~gist** ['drʌgist] Drogist m; Apotheker m; **~store** Am. Drugstore m.

drum [drʌm] **1.** Trommel f; Trommelfell n; **2.** trommeln; **~mer** ['drʌmə] Trommler m; bsd. Am. F Vertreter m.

drunk [drʌŋk] **1.** p.p. von drink 2; **2.** adj. (be)trunken; get ~ sich betrinken; **~ard** ['drʌŋkəd] Trinker m, Säufer m; **~en** adj. [~kən] (be-) trunken.

dry [drai] **1.** ▢ trocken; herb (Wein); F durstig; F antialkoholisch; ~ goods pl. Am. F Kurzwaren f/pl.; **2.** Am. F Alkoholgegner m; **3.** trocknen; dörren; ~ up austrocknen; verdunsten; **~-clean** ['drai'kli:n] chemisch reinigen; **~-nurse** Kinderfrau f.

dual ▢ ['dju(:)əl] doppelt; Doppel...

dubious ▢ ['dju:bjəs] zweifelhaft.

duchess ['dʌtʃis] Herzogin f.

duck [dʌk] **1.** zo. Ente f; Am. sl. Kerl m; Verbeugung f; Ducken n; (Segel)Leinen n; F Liebling m; **2.** (unter)tauchen; (sich) ducken; Am. j-m ausweichen.

duckling ['dʌkliŋ] Entchen n.

dude Am. [dju:d] Geck m; ~ ranch Am. Vergnügungsfarm f.

dudgeon ['dʌdʒən] Groll m.

due [dju:] **1.** schuldig; gebührend; gehörig; fällig; in ~ time zur rechten Zeit; be ~ to j-m gebühren; herrühren od kommen von; be ~ to inf. sollen, müssen; Am. im Begriff sein zu; **2.** adv. ⊕ gerade; genau; **3.** Schuldigkeit f; Recht n, Anspruch m; Lohn m; mst ~s pl. Abgabe(n pl.) f, Gebühr(en pl.) f; Beitrag m.   **2.** sich duellieren.

duel ['dju(:)əl] **1.** Zweikampf m;

dug [dʌg] pret. u. p.p. von dig 1.

duke [dju:k] Herzog m; **~dom** ['dju:kdəm] Herzogtum n; Herzogswürde f.

dull [dʌl] **1.** ▢ dumm; träge; schwerfällig; stumpf(sinnig); matt (Auge etc.); schwach (Gehör); langweilig; teilnahmslos; dumpf; trüb; ✝ flau; **2.** stumpf machen; fig. abstumpfen; (sich) trüben; **~ness** ['dʌlnis] Stumpfsinn m; Dummheit f; Schwerfälligkeit f; Mattheit f; Langweiligkeit f; Teilnahmslosigkeit f; Trübheit f; Flauheit f.

duly adv. ['dju:li] gehörig; richtig.

dumb ▢ [dʌm] stumm; sprachlos; Am. F doof, blöd; **~founded** [dʌm'faundid] sprachlos; **~waiter** ['dʌm'weitə] Drehtisch m; Am. Speiseaufzug m.

dummy ['dʌmi] Attrappe f; Schein m, Schwindel m; fig. Strohmann m; Statist m; attr. Schein...; Schwindel...

dump [dʌmp] **1.** v/t. auskippen; Schutt etc. abladen; Waren zu Schleuderpreisen ausführen; v/i. hinplumpsen; **2.** Klumpen m; Plumps m; Schuttabladestelle f; ✗ Munitionslager n; **~ing** ✝ ['dʌmpiŋ] Schleuderausfuhr f; **~s** pl.: (down) in the ~ F niedergeschlagen.

dun [dʌn] mahnen, drängen.

dunce [dʌns] Dummkopf m.

dune [dju:n] Düne f.

dung [dʌŋ] **1.** Dung m; **2.** düngen.

dungeon ['dʌndʒən] Kerker m.

dunk Am. F [dʌŋk] (ein)tunken.

dupe [dju:p] anführen, täuschen.

duplex ⊕ ['dju:pleks] attr. Doppel...; Am. Zweifamilienhaus n.

duplic|ate 1. ['dju:plikit] doppelt; **2.** [~] Duplikat n; **3.** [~keit] doppelt ausfertigen; **~ity** [dju:(')plisiti] Doppelzüngigkeit f.

dura|ble ['djuərəbl] dauerhaft; **~tion** [djuə'reiʃən] Dauer f.

duress(e) [djuə'res] Zwang m.

during prp. ['djuəriŋ] während.

dusk [dʌsk] Halbdunkel n, Dämmerung f; **~y** ['dʌski] dämmerig, düster (a. fig.); schwärzlich.

dust [dʌst] **1.** Staub m; **2.** abstauben; bestreuen; **~bin** ['dʌstbin] Mülleimer m; **~ bowl** Am. Sandstaubu. Dürregebiet n im Westen der USA; **~cart** Müllwagen m; **~er** [~tə] Staublappen m, -wedel m; Am. Staubmantel m; **~-jacket** Am. Schutzumschlag m e-s Buches; **~man** Müllabfuhrmann m; **~y** ▢ [~ti] staubig.

Dutch [dʌtʃ] **1.** holländisch; ~ treat Am. F getrennte Rechnung; **2.** Holländisch n; the ~ die Holländer pl.

duty ['dju:ti] Pflicht f; Ehrerbietung f; Abgabe f, Zoll m; Dienst m; off ~ dienstfrei; **~-free** zollfrei.

dwarf [dwɔ:f] **1.** Zwerg m; **2.** in der Entwicklung hindern; verkleinern.

dwell [dwel] [irr.] wohnen; verweilen (on, upon bei); ~ (up)on bestehen auf (acc.); **~ing** ['dweliŋ] Wohnung f.

dwelt [dwelt] *pret. u. p.p. von* dwell.
dwindle ['dwindl] (dahin)schwinden, abnehmen; (herab)sinken.
dye [dai] 1. Farbe *f*; *of deepest ~ fig.* schlimmster Art; 2. färben.
dying ['daiiŋ] 1. □ sterbend; Sterbe...; 2. Sterben *n*.

dynam|ic [dai'næmik] dynamisch, kraftgeladen; **~ics** [~ks] *mst sg.* Dynamik *f*; **~ite** ['dainəmait] 1. Dynamit *n*; 2. mit Dynamit sprengen.
dysentery ~ ['disntri] Ruhr *f*.
dyspepsia ~ [dis'pepsiə] Verdauungsstörung *f*.

E

each [i:tʃ] jede(r, -s); *~ other* einander, sich.
eager □ ['i:gə] (be)gierig; eifrig; **~ness** ['i:gənis] Begierde *f*; Eifer *m*.
eagle ['i:gl] Adler *m*; *Am.* Zehndollarstück *n*; **~-eyed** scharfsichtig.
ear [iə] Ähre *f*; Ohr *n*; Öhr *n*, Henkel *m*; *keep an ~ to the ground bsd. Am.* aufpassen, was die Leute sagen *od.* denken; **~drum** ['iədrəm] Trommelfell *n*.
earl [ə:l] *englischer* Graf.
early ['ə:li] früh; Früh...; Anfangs...; erst; bald(ig); *as ~ as* schon in (*dat.*). [nen.\
ear-mark ['iəmɑ:k] (kenn)zeich-\
earn [ə:n] verdienen; einbringen.
earnest ['ə:nist] 1. □ ernst(lich, -haft); ernstgemeint; 2. Ernst *m*.
earnings ['ə:niŋz] Einkommen *n*.
ear|piece *teleph.* ['iəpi:s] Hörmuschel *f*; **~shot** Hörweite *f*.
earth [ə:θ] 1. Erde *f*; Land *n*; 2. *v/t.* ⚡ erden; **~en** ['ə:θən] irden; **~enware** [~nweə] 1. Töpferware *f*; Steingut *n*; 2. irden; **~ing** ⚡ ['ə:θiŋ] Erdung *f*; **~ly** ['ə:θli] irdisch; **~quake** Erdbeben *n*; **~worm** Regenwurm *m*.
ease [i:z] 1. Bequemlichkeit *f*, Behagen *n*; Ruhe *f*; Ungezwungenheit *f*; Leichtigkeit *f*; *at ~* bequem, behaglich; 2. *v/t.* erleichtern; lindern; beruhigen; bequem(er) machen; *v/i.* sich entspannen (*Lage*).
easel ['i:zl] Staffelei *f*.
easiness ['i:zinis] = ease 1.
east [i:st] 1. Ost(en *m*); Orient *m*; *the* ⚹ *Am.* die Oststaaten *der USA*; 2. Ost...; östlich; ostwärts.
Easter ['i:stə] Ostern *n*; *attr.* Oster...
easter|ly ['i:stəli] östlich; Ost...; nach Osten; **~n** [~ən] *= easterly*; orientalisch; **~ner** [~nə] Ostländer (-in); Oriental|e *m*, -in *f*; ⚹ *Am.* Oststaatler(in).
eastward(s) ['i:stwəd(z)] ostwärts.
easy ['i:zi] □ leicht; bequem; frei von Schmerzen; ruhig; willig; ungezwungen; *in ~ circumstances* wohlhabend; *on ~ street Am.* in guten Verhältnissen; *take it ~!* immer mit der Ruhe!; **~ chair** Klubsessel *m*; **~-going** *fig.* bequem.

eat [i:t] 1. [*irr.*] essen; (zer)fressen; 2. **~s** *pl. Am. sl.* Essen *n*, Eßwaren *f/pl.*; **~ables** ['i:təblz] *pl.* Eßwaren *f/pl.*; **~en** ['i:tn] *p.p. von* eat 1.
eaves [i:vz] *pl.* Dachrinne *f*, Traufe *f*; **~drop** ['i:vzdrɔp] (er)lauschen; horchen.
ebb [eb] 1. Ebbe *f*; *fig.* Abnahme *f*; Verfall *m*; 2. verebben; *fig.* abnehmen, sinken; **~-tide** ['eb'taid] Ebbe *f*.
ebony ['ebəni] Ebenholz *n*.
ebullition [ebə'liʃən] Überschäumen *n*; Aufbrausen *n*.
eccentric [ik'sentrik] 1. exzentrisch; *fig.* überspannt; 2. Sonderling *m*.
ecclesiastic [ikli:zi'æstik] Geistliche(r) *m*; **~al** □ [~kəl] geistlich, kirchlich.
echo ['ekou] 1. Echo *n*; 2. widerhallen; *fig.* echoen, nachsprechen.
eclipse [i'klips] 1. Finsternis *f*; 2. (sich) verfinstern, verdunkeln.
econom|ic(al □) [i:kə'nɔmik(əl)] haushälterisch; wirtschaftlich; Wirtschafts...; **~ics** [~ks] *sg.* Volkswirtschaft(slehre) *f*; **~ist** [i(:)'kɔnəmist] Volkswirt *m*; **~ize** [~maiz] sparsam wirtschaften (mit); **~y** [~mi] Wirtschaft *f*; Wirtschaftlichkeit *f*; Einsparung *f*; *political ~* Volkswirtschaft(slehre) *f*.
ecsta|sy ['ekstəsi] Ekstase *f*, Verzückung *f*; **~tic** [eks'tætik] (~ally) verzückt.
eddy ['edi] 1. Wirbel *m*; 2. wirbeln.
edge [edʒ] 1. Schneide *f*; Schärfe *f*; Rand *m*; Kante *f*; Tisch-Ecke *f*; *be on ~* nervös sein; *have the ~ on s.o. bsd. Am.* F j-m über sein; 2. schärfen; (um)säumen; (sich) drängen; **~ways**, **~wise** ['edʒweiz, 'edʒwaiz] seitwärts; von der Seite.
edging ['edʒiŋ] Einfassung *f*; Rand *m*.
edgy ['edʒi] scharf; F nervös. [*m*.\
edible ['edibl] eßbar.
edict ['i:dikt] Edikt *n*.
edifice ['edifis] Gebäude *n*.
edifying □ ['edifaiiŋ] erbaulich.
edit ['edit] *Text* herausgeben, redigieren; *Zeitung* als Herausgeber leiten; **~ion** [i'diʃən] *Buch*-Ausgabe *f*; Auflage *f*; **~or** ['editə] Herausgeber *m*; Redakteur *m*; **~orial**

[edi'tɔ:riəl] Leitartikel m; attr. Redaktions...; **~orship** ['editəʃip] Schriftleitung f, Redaktion f.

educat|e ['edju(:)keit] erziehen; unterrichten; **~ion** [edju(:)'keiʃən] Erziehung f; (Aus)Bildung f; Erziehungs-, Schulwesen n; Ministry of ♀ Unterrichtsministerium n; **~ional** □ [~nl] erzieherisch; Erziehungs...; Bildungs...; **~or** ['edju:keitə] Erzieher m.

eel [i:l] Aal m.

efface [i'feis] auslöschen; fig. tilgen.

effect [i'fekt] 1. Wirkung f; Folge f; ⊕ Leistung f; **~s** pl. Effekten pl.; Habseligkeiten f/pl.; be of ~ Wirkung haben; take ~ in Kraft treten; in ~ in der Tat; to the ~ des Inhalts; 2. bewirken, ausführen; **~ive** □ [~tiv] wirkend; wirksam; eindrucksvoll; wirklich vorhanden; ⊕ nutzbar; ~ date Tag m des Inkrafttretens; **~ual** □ [~tjuəl] wirksam, kräftig.

effeminate □ [i'feminit] verweichlicht; weibisch.

effervesce [efə'ves] (auf)brausen; **~nt** [~snt] sprudelnd, schäumend.

effete [e'fi:t] verbraucht; entkräftet.

efficacy ['efikəsi] Wirksamkeit f, Kraft f.

efficien|cy [i'fiʃənsi] Leistung(s-fähigkeit) f; **~ expert** Am. Rationalisierungsfachmann m; **~t** □ [~nt] wirksam; leistungsfähig; tüchtig.

efflorescence [əflɔ:'resns] Blütezeit f; ⚕ Beschlag m.

effluence ['efluəns] Ausfluß m.

effort ['efət] Anstrengung f, Bemühung f (at um); Mühe f.

effrontery [e'frʌntəri] Frechheit f.

effulgent □ [e'fʌldʒənt] glänzend.

effus|ion [i'fju:ʒən] Erguß m; **~ive** □ [~:usiv] überschwenglich.

egg[1] [eg] mst ~ on aufreizen.

egg[2] □ Ei n; put all one's ~s in one basket alles auf eine Karte setzen; as sure as ~s is ~s F todsicher; **~-cup** ['egkʌp] Eierbecher m; **~head** Am. sl. Intellektuelle(r) m.

egotism ['egoutizm] Selbstgefälligkeit f.

egregious iro. □ [i'gri:dʒəs] ungeheuer.

egress ['i:grəs] Ausgang m; Ausweg m.

Egyptian [i'dʒipʃən] 1. ägyptisch; 2. Ägypter(in).

eider ['aidə]: **~ down** Eiderdaunen f/pl.; Daunendecke f.

eight [eit] 1. acht; 2. Acht f; behind the ~ ball Am. in der (die) Klemme; **~een** ['ei'ti:n] achtzehn; **~eenth** [~nθ] achtzehnt; **~fold** ['eitfould] achtfach; **~h** [eit] 1. achte(r, -s); 2. Achtel n; **~hly** ['eitθli] achtens; **~ieth** [eitiiθ] achtzigste(r, -s); **~y** ['eiti] achtzig.

either ['aiðə] 1. adj. u. pron. einer

von beiden; beide; 2. cj. ~ ... or entweder ... oder; not (...) ~ auch nicht.

ejaculate [i'dʒækjuleit] Worte, Flüssigkeit ausstoßen.

eject [i(:)'dʒekt] ausstoßen; vertreiben, ausweisen; entsetzen (e-s Am tes).

eke [i:k]: ~ out ergänzen; verlängern; sich mit et. durchhelfen.

el Am. F [el] = elevated railroad.

elaborat|e 1. □ [i'læbərit] sorgfältig ausgearbeitet; kompliziert; 2. [~reit] sorgfältig ausarbeiten; **~eness** [~ritnis], **~ion** [ilæbə'reiʃən] sorgfältige Ausarbeitung.

elapse [i'læps] verfließen, verstreichen.

elastic [i'læstik] 1. (~ally) dehnbar; spannkräftig; 2. Gummiband n; **~ity** [elæs'tisiti] Elastizität f, Dehnbarkeit f; Spannkraft f.

elate [i'leit] (er)heben, ermutigen, froh erregen; stolz machen; **~d** in gehobener Stimmung, freudig erregt (at über acc.; with durch).

elbow ['elbou] 1. Ellbogen m; Biegung f; ⊕ Knie n; at one's ~ nahe, bei der Hand; out at ~s fig. heruntergekommen; 2. mit dem Ellbogen (weg)stoßen; ~ out verdrängen; **~ grease** F Armschmalz n (Kraftanstrengung).

elder ['eldə] 1. älter; 2. der, die Ältere; (Kirchen)Älteste(r) m; ♀ Holunder m; **~ly** [~əli] ältlich.

eldest ['eldist] älteste(r, -s).

elect [i'lekt] 1. (aus)gewählt; 2. (aus-, er)wählen; **~ion** [~kʃən] Wahl f; **~ive** [~ktiv] 1. □ wählend; gewählt; Wahl...; Am. fakultativ; 2. Am. Wahlfach n; **~or** [~tə] Wähler m; Am. Wahlmann m; Kurfürst m; **~oral** [~ərəl] Wahl..., Wähler...; ~ college Am. Wahlmänner m/pl.; **~orate** [~it] Wählerschaft f) m/pl.

electric|(al □) [i'lektrik(əl)] elektrisch; Elektro...; fig. faszinierend; **~al engineer** Elektrotechniker m; **~ blue** stahlblau; **~ chair** elektrischer Stuhl; **~ian** [ilek'triʃən] Elektriker m; **~ity** [~isiti] Elektrizität f.

electri|fy [i'lektrifai], **~ze** [~raiz] elektrifizieren; elektrisieren.

electro|cute [i'lektrəkju:t] auf dem elektrischen Stuhl hinrichten; durch elektrischen Strom töten; **~metallurgy** Elektrometallurgie f.

electron [i'lektrɔn] Elektron n; **~-ray tube** magisches Auge.

electro|plate [i'lektroupleit] galvanisch versilbern; **~type** galvanischer Druck; Galvano n.

elegan|ce ['eligəns] Eleganz f; Anmut f; **~t** □ [~nt] elegant; geschmackvoll; Am. erstklassig.

element ['elimənt] Element n; Urstoff m; (Grund)Bestandteil m; **~s** pl. Anfangsgründe m/pl.; **~al** □

[eli'mentl] elementar; wesentlich; **~ary** [~təri] 1. □ elementar; Anfangs...; ~ **school** Volks-, Grundschule f; 2. **elementaries** pl. Anfangsgründe m/pl.

elephant ['elifənt] Elefant m.

elevat|e ['eliveit] erhöhen; fig. erheben; ~ed erhaben; ~ (railroad) Am. Hochbahn f; ~**ion** [eli'veiʃən] Erhebung f, Erhöhung f; Höhe f; Erhabenheit f; ~**or** ⊕ ['eliveitə] Aufzug m; Am. Fahrstuhl m; ✕ Höhenruder n; (grain) ~ Am. Getreidespeicher m.

eleven [i'levn] 1. elf; 2. Elf f; ~**th** [~nθ] elfte(r, -s).

elf [elf] Elf(e f) m, Kobold m; Zwerg m.

elicit [i'lisit] hervorlocken, herausholen.

eligible □ ['elidʒəbl] geeignet, annehmbar; passend.

eliminat|e [i'limineit] aussondern, ausscheiden; ausmerzen; ~**ion** [ilimi'neiʃən] Aussonderung f; Ausscheidung f.

élite [ei'li:t] Elite f; Auslese f.

elk zo. [elk] Elch m.

ellipse Å [i'lips] Ellipse f.

elm ♀ [elm] Ulme f, Rüster f.

elocution [elə'kju:ʃən] Vortrag(skunst, -sweise f) m.

elongate ['i:lɔŋgeit] verlängern.

elope [i'loup] entlaufen, durchgehen.

eloquen|ce ['eləkwəns] Beredsamkeit f; ~**t** □ [~nt] beredt.

else [els] sonst, andere(r, -s); weiter; ~**where** ['elswEə] anderswo(hin).

elucidat|e [i'lu:sideit] erläutern; ~**ion** [ilu:si'deiʃən] Aufklärung f.

elude [i'lu:d] geschickt umgehen; ausweichen, sich entziehen (dat.).

elus|ive [i'lu:siv] schwer faßbar; ~**ory** [~səri] trügerisch.

emaciate [i'meiʃieit] abzehren, ausmergeln.

emanat|e ['eməneit] ausströmen; ausgehen (from von); ~**ion** [emə-'neiʃən] Ausströmen n; fig. Ausstrahlung f.

emancipat|e [i'mænsipeit] emanzipieren, befreien; ~**ion** [imænsi-'peiʃən] Emanzipation f; Befreiung f.

embalm [im'ba:m] (ein)balsamieren; be ~ed in fortleben in (dat.).

embankment [im'bæŋkmənt] Eindämmung f; Deich m; (Bahn-)Damm m; Uferstraße f, Kai m.

embargo [em'ba:gou] (Hafen-, Handels)Sperre f, Beschlagnahme f.

embark [im'ba:k] (sich) einschiffen (for nach); Geld anlegen; sich einlassen (in, on, upon in, auf acc.).

embarrass [im'bærəs] (be)hindern; verwirren; in (Geld)Verlegenheit bringen; verwickeln; ~**ing** □ [~siŋ]

unangenehm; unbequem; ~**ment** [~smənt] (Geld)Verlegenheit f; Schwierigkeit f.

embassy ['embəsi] Botschaft f; Gesandtschaft f.

embed [im'bed] (ein)betten, lagern.

embellish [im'beliʃ] verschönern; ausschmücken. [Asche.]

embers ['embəz] pl. glühende}

embezzle [im'bezl] unterschlagen; ~**ment** [~lmənt] Unterschlagung f.

embitter [im'bitə] verbittern.

emblazon [im'bleizən] mit e-m Wappenbild bemalen; fig. verherrlichen.

emblem ['embləm] Sinnbild n; Wahrzeichen n.

embody [im'bɔdi] verkörpern; vereinigen; einverleiben (in dat.).

embolden [im'bouldən] ermutigen.

embolism ✗ ['embəlizəm] Embolie f.

embosom [im'buzəm] ins Herz schließen; ~ed with umgeben von.

emboss [im'bɔs] bossieren; mit dem Hammer treiben.

embrace [im'breis] 1. (sich) umarmen; umfassen; Beruf etc. ergreifen; Angebot annehmen; 2. Umarmung f.

embroider [im'brɔidə] sticken; ausschmücken; ~**y** [~əri] Stickerei f.

embroil [im'brɔil] (in Streit) verwickeln; verwirren.

emendation [i:men'deiʃən] Verbesserung f.

emerald ['emərəld] Smaragd m.

emerge [i'mə:dʒ] auftauchen; hervorgehen; sich erheben; sich zeigen; ~**ncy** [~dʒənsi] unerwartetes Ereignis; Notfall m; attr. Not...; ~ **brake** Notbremse f; ~ **call** Notruf m; ~ **exit** Notausgang m; ~ **man** Sport: Ersatzmann m; ~**nt** [~nt] auftauchend, entstehend; ~ **countries** Entwicklungsländer n/pl.

emersion [i(:)'mə:ʃən] Auftauchen n.

emigra|nt ['emigrənt] 1. auswandernd; 2. Auswanderer m; ~**te** [~reit] auswandern; ~**tion** [emi-'greiʃən] Auswanderung f.

eminen|ce ['eminəns] (An)Höhe f; Auszeichnung f; hohe Stellung; Eminenz f (Titel); ~**t** □ [~nt] fig. ausgezeichnet, hervorragend; ~**tly** [~tli] ganz besonders.

emissary ['emisəri] Emissär m.

emit [i'mit] von sich geben; aussenden, ausströmen; † ausgeben.

emolument [i'mɔljumənt] Vergütung f; ~**s** pl. Einkünfte pl.

emotion [i'mouʃən] (Gemüts-)Bewegung f; Gefühl(sregung f) n; Rührung f; ~**al** □ [~nl] gefühlsmäßig; gefühlvoll, gefühlsbetont; ~**less** [~nlis] gefühllos, kühl.

emperor ['empərə] Kaiser m.

empha|sis ['emfəsis] Nachdruck *m*; **~size** [~saiz] nachdrücklich betonen; **~tic** [im'fætik] (~ally) nachdrücklich; ausgesprochen.

empire ['empaiə] (Kaiser)Reich *n*; Herrschaft *f*; *the British* ♀ das britische Weltreich.

empirical □ [em'pirikəl] erfahrungsgemäß.

employ [im'plɔi] 1. beschäftigen, anstellen; an-, verwenden, gebrauchen; 2. Beschäftigung *f*; *in the ~ of* angestellt bei; **~ee** [emplɔi'i:] Angestellte(r *m*) *f*; Arbeitnehmer(in); **~er** [im'plɔiə] Arbeitgeber *m*; ✝ Auftraggeber *m*; **~ment** [~imənt] Beschäftigung *f*; Arbeit *f*; **~ agency** Stellenvermittlungsbüro *n*; ♀ *Exchange* Arbeitsamt *n*.

empower [im'pauə] ermächtigen; befähigen.

empress ['empris] Kaiserin *f*.

empt|iness ['emptinis] Leere *f*; Hohlheit *f*; **~y** □ ['empti] 1. leer; *fig.* hohl; 2. (sich) (aus-, ent)leeren.

emul|ate ['emjuleit] wetteifern mit; nacheifern, es gleichtun (*dat.*); **~ation** [emju'leiʃən] Wetteifer *m*.

enable [i'neibl] befähigen, es *j-m* ermöglichen; ermächtigen.

enact [i'nækt] verfügen, verordnen; *Gesetz* erlassen; *thea.* spielen.

enamel [i'næməl] 1. Email(le *f*) *n*, (Zahn)Schmelz *m*; Glasur *f*; Lack *m*; 2. emaillieren; glasieren.

enamo(u)r [i'næmə] verliebt machen; **~ed of** verliebt in.

encamp ✗ [in'kæmp] (sich) lagern.

encase [in'keis] einschließen.

enchain [in'tʃein] anketten; fesseln.

enchant [in'tʃɑ:nt] bezaubern; **~ment** [~tmənt] Bezauberung *f*; Zauber *m*; **~ress** [~tris] Zauberin *f*.

encircle [in'sə:kl] einkreisen.

enclos|e [in'klouz] einzäunen; einschließen; beifügen; **~ure** [~ouʒə] Einzäunung *f*; eingehegtes Grundstück; Bei-, Anlage *f zu e-m Brief.*

encompass [in'kʌmpəs] umgeben.

encore *thea.* [ɔŋ'kɔ:] 1. um e-e Zugabe bitten; 2. Zugabe *f*.

encounter [in'kauntə] 1. Begegnung *f*; Gefecht *n*; 2. begegnen (*dat.*); auf *Schwierigkeiten etc.* stoßen; mit *j-m* zs.-stoßen.

encourage [in'kʌridʒ] ermutigen; fördern; **~ment** [~dʒmənt] Ermutigung *f*; Unterstützung *f*.

encroach [in'krəutʃ] (*on, upon*) eingreifen, eindringen (in *acc.*); beschränken (*acc.*); mißbrauchen (*acc.*); **~ment** [~ʃmənt] Ein-, Übergriff *m*.

encumb|er [in'kʌmbə] belasten; (be)hindern; **~rance** [~brəns] Last *f*; *fig.* Hindernis *n*; Schuldenlast *f*; *without ~* ohne (*Familien)Anhang.*

encyclop(a)edia [ensaiklou'pi:djə] Enzyklopädie *f*, Konversationslexikon *n*.

end [end] 1. Ende *n*; Ziel *n*, Zweck *m*; *no ~ of* unendlich viel(e), unzählige; *in the ~* am Ende, auf die Dauer; *on ~* aufrecht; *stand on ~* zu Berge stehen; *to no ~* vergebens; *go off the deep ~ fig.* in die Luft gehen; *make both ~s meet* gerade auskommen; 2. enden, beend(ig)en.

endanger [in'deindʒə] gefährden.

endear [in'diə] teuer machen; **~ment** [~mənt] Liebkosung *f*, Zärtlichkeit *f*.

endeavo(u)r [in'devə] 1. Bestreben *n*, Bemühung *f*; 2. sich bemühen.

end|ing ['endiŋ] Ende *n*; Schluß *m*; *gr.* Endung *f*; **~less** □ ['endlis] endlos, unendlich; ⊕ ohne Ende.

endorse [in'dɔ:s] ✝ indossieren; *et.* vermerken (*on auf der Rückseite e-r Urkunde*); gutheißen; **~ment** [~smənt] Aufschrift *f*; ✝ Indossament *n*.

endow [in'dau] ausstatten; **~ment** [~aumənt] Ausstattung *f*; Stiftung *f*.

endue *fig.* [in'dju:] (be)kleiden.

endur|ance [in'djuərəns] (Aus-)Dauer *f*; Ertragen *n*; **~e** [in'djuə] (aus)dauern; ertragen.

enema ✗ ['enimə] Klistier(spritze *f*) *n*.

enemy ['enimi] 1. Feind *m*; *the* ♀ der Teufel; 2. feindlich.

energ|etic [enə'dʒetik] (~ally) energisch; **~y** ['enədʒi] Energie *f*.

enervate ['enə:veit] entnerven.

enfeeble [in'fi:bl] schwächen.

enfold [in'fould] einhüllen; umfassen.

enforce [in'fɔ:s] erzwingen; aufzwingen (*upon dat.*); bestehen auf (*dat.*); durchführen; **~ment** [~smənt] Erzwingung *f*; Geltendmachung *f*; Durchführung *f*.

enfranchise [in'fræntʃaiz] das Wahlrecht verleihen (*dat.*); *Sklaven* befreien.

engage [in'geidʒ] *v/t.* anstellen; verpflichten; mieten; in Anspruch nehmen; ✗ angreifen; *be ~d* verlobt sein (*to mit*); beschäftigt sein (*in mit*); besetzt sein; *~ the clutch* einkuppeln; *v/i.* sich verpflichten, versprechen, garantieren; sich beschäftigen (*in mit*); ✗ angreifen; ⊕ greifen (*Zahnräder*); **~ment** [~dʒmənt] Verpflichtung *f*; Verlobung *f*; Verabredung *f*; Beschäftigung *f*; ✗ Gefecht *n*; Einrücken *n e-s Ganges etc.*

engaging □ [in'geidʒiŋ] einnehmend.

engender *fig.* [in'dʒendə] erzeugen.

engine ['endʒin] Maschine *f*, Motor *m*; 🚂 Lokomotive *f*; **~-driver** Lokomotivführer *m*.

engineer [endʒi'niə] 1. Ingenieur *m*,

Techniker *m*; Maschinist *m*; *Am.* Lokomotivführer *m*; ✕ Pionier *m*; **2.** Ingenieur sein; bauen; **~ing** [~ərɪŋ] **1.** Maschinenbau *m*; Ingenieurwesen *n*; **2.** technisch; Ingenieur...

English ['ɪŋglɪʃ] **1.** englisch; **2.** English *n*; the ~ *pl.* die Engländer *pl.*; in plain ~ *fig.* unverblümt; **~man** Engländer *m*.

engrav|e [ɪn'greɪv] gravieren, stechen; *fig.* einprägen; **~er** [~və] Graveur *m*; **~ing** [~vɪŋ] (Kupfer-, Stahl)Stich *m*; Holzschnitt *m*.

engross [ɪn'grəʊs] an sich ziehen; ganz in Anspruch nehmen.

engulf *fig.* [ɪn'gʌlf] verschlingen.

enhance [ɪn'hɑːns] erhöhen.

enigma [ɪ'nɪgmə] Rätsel *n*; **~tic(al** □) [enɪg'mætɪk(əl)] rätselhaft.

enjoin [ɪn'dʒɔɪn] auferlegen (on *j-m*).

enjoy [ɪn'dʒɔɪ] sich erfreuen an (*dat.*); genießen; did you ~ it? hat es Ihnen gefallen?; ~ o.s. sich amüsieren; I ~ my dinner es schmeckt mir; **~able** [~ɔɪəbl] genußreich, erfreulich; **~ment** [~ɔɪmənt] Genuß *m*, Freude *f*.

enlarge [ɪn'lɑːdʒ] (sich) erweitern, ausdehnen; vergrößern, erweitern [~dʒmənt] Erweiterung *f*; Vergrößerung *f*.

enlighten [ɪn'laɪtn] *fig.* erleuchten; *j-n* aufklären; **~ment** [~nmənt] Aufklärung *f*.

enlist [ɪn'lɪst] *v/t.* ✕ anwerben; gewinnen; **~ed men** *pl. Am.* ✕ Unteroffiziere *pl.* und Mannschaften *pl.*; *v/i.* sich freiwillig melden.

enliven [ɪn'laɪvn] beleben.

enmity ['enmɪtɪ] Feindschaft *f*.

ennoble [ɪ'nəʊbl] adeln; veredeln.

enorm|ity [ɪ'nɔːmɪtɪ] Ungeheuerlichkeit *f*; **~ous** □ [~məs] ungeheuer.

enough [ɪ'nʌf] genug.

enquire [ɪn'kwaɪə] = inquire.

enrage [ɪn'reɪdʒ] wütend machen; **~d** wütend (at über *acc.*).

enrapture [ɪn'ræptʃə] entzücken.

enrich [ɪn'rɪtʃ] be~, anreichern.

enrol(l) [ɪn'rəʊl] in e-e Liste eintragen; ✕ anwerben; aufnehmen; **~ment** [~lmənt] Eintragung *f*; bsd. ✕ Anwerbung *f*, Einstellung *f*; Aufnahme *f*; Verzeichnis *n*; Schüler-, Studenten-, Teilnehmerzahl *f*.

ensign ['ensaɪn] Fahne *f*; Flagge *f*; Abzeichen *n*; ♪ *Am.* ['ensn] Leutnant *m* zur See.

enslave [ɪn'sleɪv] versklaven; **~ment** [~vmənt] Versklavung *f*.

ensnare *fig.* [ɪn'snɛə] verführen.

ensue [ɪn'sjuː] folgen, sich ergeben.

ensure [ɪn'ʃʊə] sichern.

entail [ɪn'teɪl] **1.** zur Folge haben; als unveräußerliches Gut vererben; **2.** (Übertragung *f* als) unveräußerliches Gut.

entangle [ɪn'tæŋgl] verwickeln; **~ment** [~lmənt] Verwicklung *f*; ✕ Draht-Verhau *m*.

enter ['entə] *v/t.* (ein)treten in (*acc.*); betreten; einsteigen, einfahren *etc.* in (*acc.*); eindringen in (*acc.*); eintragen, ✝ buchen; *Protest* einbringen; aufnehmen; melden; ~ s.o. at school *j-n* zur Schule anmelden; *v/i.* eintreten; sich einschreiben; *Sport*: sich melden; aufgenommen werden; ~ into *fig.* eingehen auf (*acc.*); ~ (up)on *Amt etc.* antreten; sich einlassen auf (*acc.*).

enterpris|e ['entəpraɪz] Unternehmen *n*; Unternehmungslust *f*; **~ing** □ [~zɪŋ] unternehmungslustig.

entertain [entə'teɪn] unterhalten; bewirten; in Erwägung ziehen; *Meinung etc.* hegen; **~er** [~nə] Gastgeber *m*; Unterhaltungskünstler *m*; **~ment** [~nmənt] Unterhaltung *f*; Bewirtung *f*; Fest *n*, Gesellschaft *f*.

enthral(l) *fig.* [ɪn'θrɔːl] bezaubern.

enthrone [ɪn'θrəʊn] auf den Thron setzen.

enthusias|m [ɪn'θjuːzɪæzəm] Begeisterung *f*; **~t** [~æst] Schwärmer (-in); **~tic** [ɪnθjuːzɪ'æstɪk] (~ally) begeistert (at, about von).

entice [ɪn'taɪs] (ver)locken; **~ment** [~smənt] Verlockung *f*, Reiz *m*.

entire □ [ɪn'taɪə] ganz; vollständig; ungeteilt; **~ly** [~əlɪ] völlig; lediglich; **~ty** [~ətɪ] Gesamtheit *f*.

entitle [ɪn'taɪtl] betiteln; berechtigen.

entity ['entɪtɪ] Wesen *n*; Dasein *n*.

entrails ['entreɪlz] *pl.* Eingeweide *n/pl.*; Innere(s) *n*.

entrance ['entrəns] Ein-, Zutritt *m*; Einfahrt *f*, Eingang *m*; Einlaß *m*.

entrap [ɪn'træp] (ein)fangen; verleiten.

entreat [ɪn'triːt] bitten, ersuchen; *et.* erbitten; **~y** [~tɪ] Bitte *f*, Gesuch *n*.

entrench ✕ [ɪn'trentʃ] (mit *od.* in Gräben) verschanzen.

entrust [ɪn'trʌst] anvertrauen (s. th. to s.o. *j-m* et.); betrauen.

entry ['entrɪ] Eintritt *m*; Eingang *m*; ♀ Besitzantritt *m* (on, upon gen.); Eintragung *f*; *Sport*: Meldung *f*; ~ permit Einreisegenehmigung *f*; book-keeping by double (single) ~ doppelte (einfache) Buchführung.

enumerate [ɪ'njuːməreɪt] aufzählen.

enunciate [ɪ'nʌnsɪeɪt] verkünden; *Lehrsatz* aufstellen; aussprechen.

envelop [ɪn'veləp] einhüllen; einwickeln; umgeben; ✕ einkreisen; **~e** ['enviləʊp] Briefumschlag *m*; **~ment** [ɪn'veləpmənt] Umhüllung *f*.

envi|able □ ['envɪəbl] beneidenswert; **~ous** □ [~ɪəs] neidisch.

environ [in'vaiərən] umgeben; ~ment [‿nmənt] Umgebung f e-r Person; ~s ['environz] pl. Umgebung f e-r Stadt.

envisage [in'vizidʒ] sich et. vorstellen.

envoy ['envoi] Gesandte(r) m; Bote m.

envy ['envi] 1. Neid m; 2. beneiden.

epic ['epik] 1. episch; 2. Epos n.

epicure ['epikjuə] Feinschmecker m.

epidemic [epi'demik] 1. (~ally) seuchenartig; ~ disease = 2. Seuche f.

epidermis [epi'də:mis] Oberhaut f.

epilepsy ['epilepsi] Epilepsie f.

epilogue ['epiləg] Nachwort n.

episcopa|cy [i'piskəpəsi] bischöfliche Verfassung; ~l [‿əl] bischöflich; ~te [‿pit] Bischofswürde f; Bistum n.

epist|le [i'pisl] Epistel f; ~olary [‿stələri] brieflich; Brief...

epitaph ['epitɑ:f] Grabschrift f.

epitome [i'pitəmi] Auszug m, Abriß m.

epoch ['i:pɔk] Epoche f.

equable □ ['ekwəbl] gleichförmig, gleichmäßig; fig. gleichmütig.

equal ['i:kwəl] 1. □ gleich, gleichmäßig; ~ to fig. gewachsen (dat.); 2. Gleiche(r m) f; 3. gleichen (dat.); ~ity [i(:)'kwɔliti] Gleichheit f; ~ization [i:kwəlai'zeiʃən] Gleichstellung f; Ausgleich m; ~ize [‿i:kwəlaiz] gleichmachen, gleichstellen; ausgleichen.

equanimity [i:kwə'nimiti] Gleichmut m.

equat|ion [i'kweiʃən] Ausgleich m; ⚛ Gleichung f; ~or [‿eitə] Äquator m.

equestrian [i'kwestriən] Reiter m.

equilibrium [i:kwi'libriəm] Gleichgewicht n; Ausgleich m.

equip [i'kwip] ausrüsten; ~ment [‿pmənt] Ausrüstung f; Einrichtung f.

equipoise ['ekwipɔiz] Gleichgewicht n; Gegengewicht n.

equity ['ekwiti] Billigkeit f; equities pl. ✝ Aktien f/pl.

equivalent [i'kwivələnt] 1. gleichwertig; gleichbedeutend (to mit); 2. Äquivalent n, Gegenwert m.

equivoca|l □ [i'kwivəkəl] zweideutig, zweifelhaft; ~te [‿keit] zweideutig reden.

era ['iərə] Zeitrechnung f; -alter n.

eradicate [i'rædikeit] ausrotten.

eras|e [i'reiz] ausradieren, ausstreichen; auslöschen; ~er [‿zə] Radiergummi m; ~ure [i'reiʒə] Ausradieren n; radierte Stelle.

ere [eə] 1. cj. ehe, bevor; 2. prp. vor.

erect [i'rekt] 1. □ aufrecht; 2. aufrichten; Denkmal etc. errichten; aufstellen; ~ion [‿kʃən] Auf-, Errichtung f; Gebäude n.

eremite ['erimait] Einsiedler m.

ermine zo. ['ə:min] Hermelin n.

erosion [i'rouʒən] Zerfressen n; Auswaschung f.

erotic [i'rɔtik] 1. erotisch; 2. erotisches Gedicht; ~ism [‿isizəm] Erotik f.

err [ə:] (sich) irren; fehlen, sündigen.

errand ['erənd] Botengang m, Auftrag m; ~boy Laufbursche m.

errant □ ['erənt] (umher)irrend.

errat|ic [i'rætik] (~ally) wandernd; unberechenbar; ~um [e'rɑ:təm], pl. ~a [‿tə] Druckfehler m.

erroneous □ [i'rounjəs] irrig.

error ['erə] Irrtum m, Fehler m; ~s excepted Irrtümer vorbehalten.

erudit|e □ ['eru(:)dait] gelehrt; ~ion [eru(:)'diʃən] Gelehrsamkeit f.

erupt [i'rʌpt] ausbrechen (Vulkan); durchbrechen (Zähne); ~ion [‿pʃən] Vulkan-Ausbruch m; ✗ Hautausschlag m.

escalat|ion [eskə'leiʃən] Eskalation f (stufenweise Steigerung); ~or ['eskəleitə] Rolltreppe f.

escap|ade [eskə'peid] toller Streich; ~e [is'keip] 1. entschlüpfen, entgehen; entkommen, entrinnen; entweichen; j-m entfallen; 2. Entrinnen n; Entweichen n; Flucht f.

eschew [is'tʃu:] (ver)meiden.

escort 1. ['eskɔ:t] Eskorte f; Geleit n; 2. [is'kɔ:t] eskortieren, geleiten.

escutcheon [is'kʌtʃən] Wappenschild m, n; Namensschild n.

especial [is'peʃəl] besonder; vorzüglich; ~ly [‿li] besonders.

espionage [espiə'nɑ:ʒ] Spionage f.

espresso [es'presou] Espresso m (Kaffee); ~ bar, ~ café Espressobar f.

espy [is'pai] erspähen.

esquire [is'kwaiə] Landedelmann m, Gutsbesitzer m; auf Briefen: John Smith Esq. Herrn J. S.

essay 1. [e'sei] versuchen; probieren; 2. ['esei] Versuch m; Aufsatz m, kurze Abhandlung, Essay m, n.

essen|ce ['esns] Wesen n e-r Sache; Extrakt m; Essenz f; ~tial [i'senʃəl] 1. □ (to für) wesentlich; wichtig; 2. Wesentliche(s) n.

establish [is'tæbliʃ] festsetzen; errichten, gründen; einrichten; einsetzen; ~ o.s. sich niederlassen; ⚑ed Church Staatskirche f; ~ment [‿ʃmənt] Festsetzung f; Gründung f; Er-, Einrichtung f; (bsd. großer) Haushalt; Anstalt f; Firma f.

estate [is'teit] Grundstück n; Grundbesitz m, Gut n; Besitz m; (Konkurs)Masse f, Nachlaß m; Stand m; real ~ Liegenschaften pl.; housing ~ Wohnsiedlung f; ~ agent Grundstücksmakler m; ~ car Kombiwagen m; ~ duty Nachlaßsteuer f.

esteem [is'ti:m] 1. Achtung f, Ansehen n (with bei); 2. (hoch)achten, (hoch)schätzen; erachten für.

estimable ['estiməbl] schätzenswert.

estimat|e 1. ['estimeit] (ab)schätzen; veranschlagen; 2. [-mit] Schätzung f; (Vor)Anschlag m; **.ion** [esti'meiʃən] Schätzung f; Meinung f; Achtung f.

estrange [is'treindʒ] entfremden.

estuary ['estjuəri] (den Gezeiten ausgesetzte) weite Flußmündung.

etch [etʃ] ätzen, radieren.

etern|al □ [i(:)'tə:nl] immerwährend, ewig; **.ity** [-niti] Ewigkeit f.

ether ['i:θə] Äther m; **.eal** [i(:)'θiəriəl] ätherisch (a. fig.).

ethic|al □ ['eθikəl] sittlich, ethisch; **.s** [-ks] sg. Sittenlehre f, Ethik f.

etiquette [eti'ket] Etikette f.

etymology [eti'mɔlədʒi] Etymologie f, Wortableitung f.

Eucharist ['ju:kərist] Abendmahl n.

euphemism ['ju:fimizəm] beschönigender Ausdruck.

European [juərə'pi(:)ən] 1. europäisch; 2. Europäer(in).

evacuate [i'vækjueit] entleeren; evakuieren; Land etc. räumen.

evade [i'veid] (geschickt) ausweichen (dat.); umgehen.

evaluate [i'væljueit] zahlenmäßig bestimmen, auswerten; berechnen.

evanescent [i:və'nesnt] (ver)schwindend. [evangelisch.)

evangelic|al □) [i:væn'dʒelik(əl)]]

evaporat|e [i'væpəreit] verdunsten, verdampfen (lassen); **.ion** [i'væpə-'reiʃən] Verdunstung f, Verdampfung f.

evasi|on [i'veiʒən] Umgehung f; Ausflucht f; **.ve** □ [i'veisiv] ausweichend; be **~** ausweichen.

eve [i:v] Vorabend m; Vortag m; on the **~** of unmittelbar vor (dat.), am Vorabend (gen.).

even ['i:vən] 1. adj. □ eben, gleich; gleichmäßig; ausgeglichen; glatt; gerade (Zahl); unparteiisch; get **~** with s.o. fig. mit j-m abrechnen; 2. adv. selbst, sogar, auch; not **~** nicht einmal; **~** though, **~** if wenn auch; 3. ebnen, glätten; gleichstellen; **.handed** unparteiisch.

evening ['i:vniŋ] Abend m; **~** dress Gesellschaftsanzug m; Frack m, Smoking m; Abendkleid n.

evenness ['i:vənnis] Ebenheit f; Geradheit f; Gleichmäßigkeit f; Unparteilichkeit f; Seelenruhe f.

evensong ['i:vənsɔŋ] Abendgottesdienst m.

event [i'vent] Ereignis n; Vorfall m; fig. Ausgang m; sportliche Veranstaltung; athletic **~s** pl. Leichtathletikwettkämpfe m/pl.; at all **~s** auf alle Fälle; in the **~** of im Falle (gen.); **.ful** [-tful] ereignisreich.

eventual □ [i'ventjuəl] etwaig, möglich; schließlich; **.ly** am Ende; im Laufe der Zeit; gegebenenfalls.

ever ['evə] je, jemals; immer; **~** so noch so (sehr); as soon as **~** I can sobald ich nur irgend kann; **~** after, **~** since von der Zeit an; **~** and anon von Zeit zu Zeit; for **~** für immer, auf ewig; Briefschluß: yours **~** stets Dein ...; **.glade** Am. Sumpfsteppe f; **.green** 1. immergrün; 2. immergrüne Pflanze; **.lasting** □ [evə-'la:stiŋ] ewig; dauerhaft; **.more** ['evə'mɔ:] immerfort.

every ['evri] jede(r, -s); alle(s); **~** now and then dann und wann; **~** one of them jeder von ihnen; **~** other day einen Tag um den anderen, jeden zweiten Tag; **.body** jeder (-mann); **.day** Alltags...; **.one** jeder(mann); **.thing** alles; **.where** überall.

evict [i(:)'vikt] exmittieren; ausweisen.

eviden|ce ['evidəns] 1. Beweis(material n) m; ⚖ Zeugnis n; Zeuge m; in **~** als Beweis; deutlich sichtbar; 2. beweisen; **.t** □ [-nt] augenscheinlich, offenbar, klar.

evil ['i:vl] 1. □ übel, schlimm, böse; the ♀ One der Böse (Teufel); 2. Übel n, Böse(s) n; **.minded** ['i:vl'maindid] übelgesinnt, boshaft.

evince [i'vins] zeigen, bekunden.

evoke [i'vouk] (herauf)beschwören.

evolution [i:və'lu:ʃən] Entwicklung f; ⚔ Entfaltung f e-r Formation.

evolve [i'vɔlv] (sich) entwickeln.

ewe [ju:] Mutterschaf n.

ex [eks] prp. ✝ ab Fabrik etc.; Börse: ohne; aus.

ex-... [-] ehemalig, früher.

exact [ig'zækt] 1. □ genau; pünktlich; 2. Zahlung eintreiben; fordern; **.ing** [-tiŋ] streng, genau; **.itude** [-itju:d], **.ness** [-tnis] Genauigkeit f; Pünktlichkeit f.

exaggerate [ig'zædʒəreit] übertreiben.

exalt [ig'zɔ:lt] erhöhen, erheben; verherrlichen; **.ation** [egzɔ:l'teiʃən] Erhöhung f, Erhebung f; Höhe f; Verzückung f.

exam Schul-sl. [ig'zæm] Examen n.

examin|ation [igzæmi'neiʃən] Examen n, Prüfung f; Untersuchung f; Vernehmung f; **.e** [ig'zæmin] untersuchen; prüfen, verhören.

example [ig'za:mpl] Beispiel n; Vorbild n, Muster n; for **~** zum Beispiel.

exasperate [ig'za:spəreit] erbittern; ärgern; verschlimmern.

excavate ['ekskəveit] ausgraben, ausheben, aushöhlen.

exceed [ik'si:d] überschreiten; übertreffen; zu weit gehen; **.ing** □ [-diŋ] übermäßig; **.ingly** [-ŋli] außerordentlich, überaus.

excel [ik'sel] v/t. übertreffen; v/i. sich auszeichnen; ~lence ['eksələns] Vortrefflichkeit f; hervorragende Leistung; Vorzug m; ~lency [~si] Exzellenz f; ~lent □ [~nt] vortrefflich.

except [ik'sept] 1. ausnehmen, et. einwenden; 2. prp. ausgenommen, außer; ~ for abgesehen von; ~ing prp. [~tiŋ] ausgenommen; ~ion [~pʃən] Ausnahme f; Einwendung f (to gegen); by way of ~ ausnahmsweise; take ~ to Anstoß nehmen an (dat.); ~ional [~l] außergewöhnlich; ~ionally [~ʃnəli] un-, außergewöhnlich.

excerpt ['eksə:pt] Auszug m.

excess [ik'ses] Übermaß n; Überschuß m; Ausschweifung f; attr. Mehr...; ~ fare Zuschlag m; ~ luggage Übergewicht n (Gepäck); ~ postage Nachgebühr f; ~ive □ [~siv] übermäßig, übertrieben.

exchange [iks'tʃeindʒ] 1. (aus-, ein-, um)tauschen (for gegen); wechseln; 2. (Aus-, Um)Tausch m; (bsd. Geld)Wechsel m; a. bill of ~ Wechsel m; a. ⌕ Börse f; Fernsprechamt n; foreign ~(s pl.) Devisen f/pl.; (rate of) ~ Wechselkurs m.

exchequer [iks'tʃekə] Schatzamt n; Staatskasse f; Chancellor of the ⌕ (britischer) Schatzkanzler, Finanzminister m.

excise[1] [ek'saiz] indirekte Steuer; Verbrauchssteuer f.

excise[2] [~] (her)ausschneiden.

excit|able [ik'saitəbl] reizbar; ~e [ik'sait] er-, anregen; reizen; ~ement [~tmənt] Auf-, Erregung f; Reizung f; ~ing [~tiŋ] erregend.

exclaim [iks'kleim] ausrufen; eifern.

exclamation [eksklə'meiʃən] Ausruf(ung f) m; ~s pl. Geschrei n; note of ~, point of ~, ~ mark Ausrufezeichen n.

exclude [iks'klu:d] ausschließen.

exclusi|on [iks'klu:ʒən] Ausschließung f, Ausschluß m; ~ve □ [~:siv] ausschließlich; sich abschließend; ~ of abgesehen von, ohne.

excommunicat|e [ekskə'mju:nikeit] exkommunizieren; ~ion ['ekskəmju:ni'keiʃən] Kirchenbann m.

excrement ['ekskrimənt] Kot m.

excrete [eks'kri:t] ausscheiden.

excruciat|e [iks'kru:ʃieit] martern; ~ing □ [~tiŋ] qualvoll.

exculpate ['ekskʌlpeit] entschuldigen; rechtfertigen; freisprechen (from von).

excursion [iks'kə:ʃən] Ausflug m; Abstecher m.

excursive □ [eks'kə:siv] abschweifend.

excus|able □ [iks'kju:zəbl] entschuldbar; ~e 1. [iks'kju:z] entschuldigen; ~ s.o. s.th. j-m et. erlassen; 2. [~u:s] Entschuldigung f.

exeat ['eksiæt] Schule etc.: Urlaub m.

execra|ble □ ['eksikrəbl] abscheulich; ~te ['eksikreit] verwünschen.

execut|e ['eksikju:t] ausführen; vollziehen; ♪ vortragen; hinrichten; Testament vollstrecken; ~ion [eksi-'kju:ʃən] Ausführung f; Vollziehung f; (Zwangs)Vollstreckung f; Hinrichtung f; ♪ Vortrag m; put od. carry a plan into ~ e-n Plan ausführen od. verwirklichen; ~ioner [~ʃnə] Scharfrichter m; ~ive [ig-'zekjutiv] 1. □ vollziehend; ~ committee Vorstand m; 2. vollziehende Gewalt; Am. Staats-Präsident m; ✝ Geschäftsführer m; ~or [~tə] (Testaments)Vollstrecker m.

exemplary [ig'zempləri] vorbildlich.

exemplify [ig'zemplifai] durch Beispiele belegen; veranschaulichen.

exempt [ig'zempt] 1. befreit, frei; 2. ausnehmen, befreien.

exercise ['eksəsaiz] 1. Übung f; Ausübung f; Schule: Übungsarbeit f; Leibesübung f; take ~ sich Bewegung machen; Am. ~s pl. Feierlichkeit(en pl.) f; ✗ Manöver n; 2. üben; ausüben; (sich) Bewegung machen; exerzieren.

exert [ig'zə:t] Einfluß etc. ausüben; ~ o.s. sich anstrengen od. bemühen; ~ion [~ə:ʃən] Ausübung f etc.

exhale [eks'heil] ausdünsten, ausatmen; aushauchen; Gefühlen Luft machen.

exhaust [ig'zɔ:st] 1. erschöpfen; entleeren; auspumpen; 2. ⊕ Abgas n, Abdampf m; Auspuff m; ~ box Auspufftopf m; ~ pipe Auspuffrohr n; ~ed erschöpft (a. fig.); vergriffen (Auflage); ~ion [~tʃən] Erschöpfung f; ~ive □ [~tiv] erschöpfend.

exhibit [ig'zibit] 1. ausstellen; zeigen, darlegen; aufweisen; 2. Ausstellungsstück n; Beweisstück n; ~ion [eksi'biʃən] Ausstellung f; Darlegung f; Zurschaustellung f; Stipendium n.

exhilarate [ig'ziləreit] erheitern.

exhort [ig'zɔ:t] ermahnen.

exigen|ce, -cy ['eksidʒəns, ~si] dringende Not; Erfordernis n; ~t [~nt] dringlich; anspruchsvoll.

exile ['eksail] 1. Verbannung f, Exil n; Verbannte(r m) f; 2. verbannen.

exist [ig'zist] existieren, vorhanden sein; leben; ~ence [~təns] Existenz f, Dasein n, Vorhandensein n; Leben n; in ~ = ~ent [~nt] vorhanden.

exit ['eksit] 1. Abgang m; Tod m; Ausgang m; 2. thea. (geht) ab.

exodus ['eksədəs] Auszug m.

exonerate [ig'zɔnəreit] fig. entlasten, entbinden, befreien; rechtfertigen.

exorbitant □ [ig'zɔːbitənt] maßlos, übermäßig.

exorci|se, **~ze** ['eksɔːsaiz] *Geister* beschwören, austreiben (*from* aus); befreien (*of* von).

exotic [eg'zɔtik] ausländisch, exotisch; fremdländisch.

expan|d [iks'pænd] (sich) ausbreiten; (sich) ausdehnen; (sich) erweitern; *Abkürzungen* (voll) ausschreiben; freundlich *od.* heiter werden; **~se** [~ns], **~sion** [~nʃən] Ausdehnung *f*; Weite *f*; Breite *f*; **~sive** □ [~nsiv] ausdehnungsfähig; ausgedehnt, weit; *fig.* mitteilsam.

expatiate [eks'peiʃieit] sich weitläufig auslassen (*on* über *acc.*).

expatriate [eks'pætrieit] ausbürgern.

expect [iks'pekt] erwarten; F annehmen; *be* **~ing** ein Kind erwarten; **~ant** [~tənt] **1.** erwartend (*of acc.*); **~** *mother* werdende Mutter; **2.** Anwärter *m*; **~ation** [ekspek'teiʃən] Erwartung *f*; Aussicht *f*.

expectorate [eks'pektəreit] *Schleim etc.* aushusten, auswerfen.

expedi|ent [iks'piːdjənt] **1.** □ zweckmäßig; berechnend; **2.** Mittel *n*; (Not)Behelf *m*; **~tion** [ekspi'diʃən] Eile *f*; ✕ Feldzug *m*; (Forschungs)Reise *f*; **~tious** □ [~ʃəs] schnell, eilig, flink.

expel [iks'pel] (hin)ausstoßen; vertreiben, verjagen; ausschließen.

expen|d [iks'pend] *Geld* ausgeben; aufwenden; verbrauchen; **~diture** [~ditʃə] Ausgabe *f*; Aufwand *m*; **~se** [iks'pens] Ausgabe *f*; Kosten *pl.*; **~s** *pl.* Unkosten *pl.*; Auslagen *f/pl.*; *at the* **~** *of* auf Kosten (*gen.*); *at any* **~** um jeden Preis; *go to the* **~** *of* Geld ausgeben für; **~se account** Spesenrechnung *f*; **~sive** □ [~siv] kostspielig, teuer.

experience [iks'piəriəns] **1.** Erfahrung *f*; Erlebnis *n*; **2.** erfahren, erleben; **~d** erfahren.

experiment **1.** [iks'perimənt] Versuch *m*; **2.** [~iment] experimentieren; **~al** □ [eksperi'mentl] Versuchs...; erfahrungsmäßig.

expert ['ekspəːt] **1.** □ [*pred.* eks'pəːt] erfahren, geschickt; fachmännisch; **2.** Fachmann *m*; Sachverständige(r *m*) *f*.

expiate ['ekspieit] büßen, sühnen.

expir|ation [ekspai'reiʃən] Ausatmung *f*; Ablauf *m*, Ende *n*; **~e** [iks'paiə] ausatmen; verscheiden; ablaufen; † verfallen; erlöschen.

explain [iks'plein] erklären, erläutern; *Gründe* auseinandersetzen; **~** *away* wegdiskutieren.

explanat|ion [eksplə'neiʃən] Erklärung *f*; Erläuterung *f*; **~ory** □ [iks'plænətəri] erklärend.

explicable ['eksplikəbl] erklärlich.

explicit □ [iks'plisit] deutlich.

explode [iks'ploud] explodieren (lassen); ausbrechen; platzen (*with* vor).

exploit 1. ['eksplɔit] Heldentat *f*; **2.** [iks'plɔit] ausbeuten; **~ation** [eksplɔi'teiʃən] Ausbeutung *f*.

explor|ation [eksplɔː'reiʃən] Erforschung *f*; **~e** [iks'plɔː] erforschen; **~er** [~ɔːrə] (Er)Forscher *m*; Forschungsreisende(r) *m*.

explosi|on [iks'plouʒən] Explosion *f*; Ausbruch *m*; **~ve** [~ousiv] **1.** □ explosiv; **2.** Sprengstoff *m*.

exponent [eks'pounənt] Exponent *m*; Vertreter *m*.

export 1. [eks'pɔːt] ausführen; **2.** ['ekspɔːt] Ausfuhr(artikel *m*) *f*; **~ation** [ekspɔː'teiʃən] Ausfuhr *f*.

expos|e [iks'pouz] aussetzen; *phot.* belichten; ausstellen; entlarven; bloßstellen; **~ition** [ekspə'ziʃən] Ausstellung *f*; Erklärung *f*.

expostulate [iks'postjuleit] protestieren; **~** *with j-m* Vorhaltungen machen.

exposure [iks'pouʒə] Aussetzen *n*; Ausgesetztsein *n*; Aufdeckung *f*; Enthüllung *f*, Entlarvung *f*; *phot.* Belichtung *f*; Bild *n*; Lage *f* *e-s Hauses*; **~** *meter* Belichtungsmesser *m*.

expound [iks'paund] erklären, auslegen.

express [iks'pres] **1.** □ ausdrücklich, deutlich; Expreß..., Eil...; **~** *company Am.* Transportfirma *f*; **~** *highway* Schnellverkehrsstraße *f*; **2.** Eilbote *m*; *a.* **~** *train* Schnellzug *m*; *by* **~** = **3.** *adv.* durch Eilboten; als Eilgut *n*; **4.** äußern, ausdrücken; auspressen; **~ion** [~eʃən] Ausdruck *m*; **~ive** □ [~esiv] ausdrückend (*of acc.*); ausdrucksvoll; **~ly** [~sli] ausdrücklich, eigens; **~way** *Am.* Autobahn *f*.

expropriate [eks'prouprieit] enteignen.

expulsi|on [iks'pʌlʃən] Vertreibung *f*; **~ve** [~lsiv] (aus)treibend.

expunge [eks'pʌndʒ] streichen.

expurgate ['ekspəːgeit] säubern.

exquisite □ ['ekskwizit] auserlesen, vorzüglich; fein; heftig, scharf.

extant [eks'tænt] (noch) vorhanden.

extempor|aneous □ [ekstempə'reinjəs], **~ary** [iks'tempərəri], **~e** [eks'tempəri] aus dem Stegreif (vorgetragen).

extend [iks'tend] *v/t.* ausdehnen; ausstrecken; erweitern; verlängern; *Gunst etc.* erweisen; ✕ (aus)schwärmen lassen; *v/i.* sich erstrecken.

extensi|on [iks'tenʃən] Ausdehnung *f*; Erweiterung *f*; Verlängerung *f*; Aus-, Anbau *m*; *teleph.* Nebenanschluß *m*; **~** *cord* ⚡ Verlängerungsschnur *f*; *University* ♀ Volkshochschule *f*; **~ve** □ [~nsiv] ausgedehnt, umfassend.

extent [iks'tent] Ausdehnung *f*, Weite *f*, Größe *f*, Umfang *m*; Grad *m*; to the ~ of bis zum Betrage von; to some ~ einigermaßen.

extenuate [eks'tenjueit] abschwächen, mildern, beschönigen.

exterior [eks'tiəriə] 1. äußerlich; Außen...; außerhalb; 2. Äußere(s) *n*; *Film* Außenaufnahme *f*.

exterminate [eks'tə:mineit] ausrotten, vertilgen.

external [eks'tə:nl] 1. □ äußere(r, -s), äußerlich; Außen...; 2. ~s *pl.* Äußere(s) *n*; *fig.* Äußerlichkeiten *f/pl.*

extinct [iks'tiŋkt] erloschen; ausgestorben.

extinguish [iks'tiŋgwiʃ] (aus)löschen; vernichten.

extirpate ['ekstə:peit] ausrotten; ✺ *Organ etc.* entfernen.

extol [iks'tɔl] erheben, preisen.

extort [iks'tɔ:t] erpressen; abnötigen (*from dat.*); ~ion [~'ɔ:ʃən] Erpressung *f*.

extra ['ekstrə] 1. Extra...; außer...; Neben...; Sonder...; ~ pay Zulage *f*; 2. *adv.* besonders; außerdem; 3. *et.* Zusätzliches; Zuschlag *m*; Extrablatt *n*; *thea.*, *Film:* Statist(in).

extract 1. ['ekstrækt] Auszug *m*; 2. [iks'trækt] (heraus)ziehen; herauslocken; ab-, herleiten; ~ion [~kʃən] (Heraus)Ziehen *n*; Herkunft *f*.

extradit|e ['ekstrədait] *Verbrecher* ausliefern (lassen); ~ion [ekstrə'diʃən] Auslieferung *f*.

extraordinary □ [iks'trɔ:dnri]

außerordentlich; Extra...; ungewöhnlich; *envoy* ~ außerordentlicher Gesandter.

extra student ['ekstrə'stju:dənt] Gasthörer(in).

extravagan|ce [iks'trævigəns] Übertriebenheit *f*; Überspanntheit *f*; Verschwendung *f*, Extravaganz *f*; ~t □ [~nt] übertrieben, überspannt; verschwenderisch; extravagant.

extrem|e [iks'tri:m] 1. □ äußerst, größt, höchst; sehr streng; außergewöhnlich; 2. Äußerste(s) *n*; Extrem *n*; höchster Grad; ~ity [~remiti] Äußerste(s) *n*; höchste Not; äußerste Maßnahme; extremities *pl.* Gliedmaßen *pl.*

extricate ['ekstrikeit] herauswinden, herausziehen; befreien; ♈ entwickeln.

extrude [eks'tru:d] ausstoßen.

exuberan|ce [ig'zju:bərəns] Überfluß *m*; Überschwenglichkeit *f*; ~t □ [~nt] reichlich; üppig; überschwenglich.

exult [ig'zʌlt] frohlocken.

eye [ai] 1. Auge *n*; Blick *m*; Öhr *n*; Öse *f*; up to the ~s in work bis über die Ohren in Arbeit; with an ~ to mit Rücksicht auf (*acc.*); mit der Absicht zu; 2. ansehen; mustern; ~ball ['aibɔ:l] Augapfel *m*; ~brow Augenbraue *f*; ~d ...äugig; ~glass Augenglas *n*; (a pair of) ~es *pl.* (ein) Kneifer; (e-e) Brille; ~lash Augenwimper *f*; ~lid Augenlid *n*; ~sight Augen(licht *n*) *pl.*; Sehkraft *f*; ~witness Augenzeug|e *m*, -in *f*.

F

fable ['feibl] Fabel *f*; Mythen *pl.*, Legenden *pl.*; Lüge *f*.

fabric ['fæbrik] Bau *m*, Gebäude *n*; Struktur *f*; Gewebe *n*, Stoff *m*; ~ate [~keit] fabrizieren (*mst fig.* = erdichten, fälschen).

fabulous □ ['fæbjuləs] legendär; sagen-, fabelhaft.

façade △ [fə'sɑ:d] Fassade *f*.

face [feis] 1. Gesicht *n*; Anblick *m*; *fig.* Stirn *f*, Unverschämtheit *f*; (Ober)Fläche *f*; Vorderseite *f*; Zifferblatt *n*; ~ to ~ with Auge in Auge mit; save one's ~ das Gesicht wahren; on the ~ of it auf den ersten Blick; set one's ~ against sich gegen *et.* stemmen; 2. *v/t.* ansehen; gegenüberstehen (*dat.*); (hinaus)gehen auf (*acc.*); die Stirn bieten (*dat.*); einfassen; △ bekleiden; *v/i.* ~ about sich umdrehen; ~cloth ['feisklɔθ] Waschlappen *m*.

facetious □ [fə'si:ʃəs] witzig.

facil|e ['fæsail] leicht; gewandt; ~itate [fə'siliteit] erleichtern; ~ity [~ti] Leichtigkeit *f*; Gewandtheit *f*; *mst facilities pl.* Erleichterung(en *pl.*) *f*, Möglichkeit(en *pl.*) *f*, Gelegenheit(en *pl.*) *f*.

facing ['feisin] ⊕ Verkleidung *f*; ~s *pl. Schneiderei:* Besatz *m*.

fact [fækt] Tatsache *f*; Wirklichkeit *f*; Wahrheit *f*; Tat *f*... [keit *f*.]

faction ['fækʃən] Partei *f*; Uneinig-}

factitious □ [fæk'tiʃəs] künstlich.

factor ['fæktə] *fig.* Umstand *m*, Moment *n*, Faktor *m*; Agent *m*; Verwalter *m*; ~y [~əri] Fabrik *f*.

faculty ['fækəlti] Fähigkeit *f*; Kraft *f*; *fig.* Gabe *f*; *univ.* Fakultät *f*.

fad F *fig.* [fæd] Steckenpferd *n*.

fade [feid] (ver)welken (lassen), verblassen; schwinden; *Radio:* ~ in einblenden.

fag F [fæg] *v/i.* sich placken; *v/t.* erschöpfen, mürbe machen.

fail [feil] 1. *v/i* versagen, mißlingen, fehlschlagen; versäumen; versiegen; nachlassen; Bankrott machen; durchfallen (*Kandidat*); he ~ed to do es mißlang ihm zu tun; he cannot ~ to er muß (einfach); *v/t.* im Stich lassen, verlassen; versäumen; 2. *without* ~ unfehlbar; ~ing ['feiliŋ] Fehler *m*, Schwäche *f*; ~ure [~ljə] Fehlen *n*; Ausbleiben *n*; Fehlschlag *m*; Mißerfolg *m*; Verfall *m*; Versäumnis *n*; Bankrott *m*; Versager *m* (*P.*).

faint [feint] 1. □ schwach, matt; 2. schwach werden; in Ohnmacht fallen (*with* vor); 3. Ohnmacht *f*; ~-hearted □ ['feint'hɑ:tid] verzagt.

fair[1] [feə] 1. *adj.* gerecht, ehrlich, anständig, fair; ordentlich; schön (*Wetter*), günstig (*Wind*), reichlich; blond; hellhäutig; freundlich; sauber, in Reinschrift; schön (*Frau*); 2. *adv.* gerecht, ehrlich, anständig, fair; in Reinschrift; direkt.

fair[2] [~] (Jahr)Markt *m*, Messe *f*.

fair|**ly** ['fɛəli] ziemlich; völlig; ~ness ['fɛənis] Schönheit *f*; Blondheit *f*; Gerechtigkeit *f*; Redlichkeit *f*; Billigkeit *f*; ~way ♣ Fahrwasser *n*.

fairy ['fɛəri] Fee *f*; Zauberin *f*; Elf(e *f*) *m*; 2land Feen-, Märchenland *n*; ~tale Märchen *n*.

faith [feiθ] Glaube *m*; Vertrauen *n*; Treue *f*; ~ful □ ['feiθful] treu; ehrlich; *yours* ~ly Ihr ergebener; ~less □ ['feiθlis] treulos; ungläubig.

fake *sl.* [feik] 1. Schwindel *m*; Fälschung *f*; Schwindler *m*; 2. *a.* ~ up fälschen.

falcon ['fɔ:lkən] Falke *m*.

fall [fɔ:l] 1. Fall(en *n*) *m*; Sturz *m*; Verfall *m*; Einsturz *m*; *Am.* Herbst *m*; Sinken *n der Preise etc.*; Fällen *n*; Wasserfall *m* (*mst pl.*); Senkung *f*, Abhang *m*; 2. [*irr.*] fallen; ab-, einfallen, sinken; sich legen (*Wind*); *in* ~*n Zustand* verfallen; ~ back zurückweichen; ~ back (*up*)*on* zurückkommen auf; ~ *ill od.* sick krank werden; ~ *in love with* sich verlieben in (*acc.*); ~ out sich entzweien; sich zutragen; ~ short knapp werden (*of an dat.*); ~ short of zurückbleiben hinter (*dat.*); ~ to sich machen an (*acc.*).

fallacious □ [fə'leiʃəs] trügerisch.

fallacy ['fæləsi] Täuschung *f*.

fallen ['fɔ:lən] *p.p. von fall* 2.

fall guy *Am. sl.* ['fɔ:l'gai] *der* Lackierte, *der* Dumme.

fallible □ ['fæləbl] fehlbar.

falling ['fɔ:liŋ] Fallen *n*; ~ **sickness**

Fallsucht *f*; ~ **star** Sternschnuppe *f*.

fallow ['fælou] *zo.* falb; ✗ brach (-liegend).

false □ [fɔ:ls] falsch; ~hood ['fɔ:lshud], ~ness [~snis] Falschheit *f*.

falsi|**fication** ['fɔ:lsifi'keiʃən] (Ver-) Fälschung *f*; ~fy ['fɔ:lsifai] (ver-) fälschen; ~ty [~iti] Falschheit *f*.

falter ['fɔ:ltə] schwanken; stocken (*Stimme*); stammeln; *fig.* zaudern.

fame [feim] Ruf *m*, Ruhm *m*; ~d [~md] berühmt (*for wegen*).

familiar [fə'miljə] 1. □ vertraut; gewohnt; familiär; 2. Vertraute(r *m*) *f*; ~ity [fəmili'æriti] Vertrautheit *f*; (plumpe) Vertraulichkeit; ~ize [fə'miljəraiz] vertraut machen.

family ['fæmili] 1. Familie *f*; 2. Familien...; Haus...; *in the* ~ *way* in anderen Umständen; ~ *allowance* Kinderzulage *f*; ~ *tree* Stammbaum *m*.

fami|**ne** ['fæmin] Hungersnot *f*; Mangel *m* (*of an dat.*); ~sh [~iʃ] (aus-, ver)hungern.

famous □ ['feiməs] berühmt.

fan[1] [fæn] 1. Fächer *m*; Ventilator *m*; 2. (an)fächeln; an-, *fig.* entfachen.

fan[2] F [~] *Sport- etc.* Fanatiker *m*, Liebhaber *m*; *Radio:* Bastler *m*; ...narr *m*, ...fex *m*.

fanatic [fə'nætik] 1. *a.* ~al □ [~kəl] fanatisch; 2. Fanatiker(in).

fanciful □ ['fænsiful] phantastisch.

fancy ['fænsi] 1. Phantasie *f*; Einbildung(skraft) *f*; Schrulle *f*; Vorliebe *f*; Liebhaberei *f*; 2. Phantasie...; Liebhaber...; Luxus...; Mode...; ~ *ball* Maskenball *m*; ~ *goods pl.* Modewaren *f/pl.*; 3. sich einbilden; Gefallen finden an (*dat.*); *just* ~! denken Sie nur!; ~work feine Handarbeit, Stickerei *f*.

fang [fæŋ] Fangzahn *m*; Giftzahn *m*.

fantas|**tic** [fæn'tæstik] (~ally) phantastisch; ~y ['fæntəsi] Phantasie *f*.

far [fɑ:] 1. *adj.* fern, entfernt; weit; 2. *adv.* fern; weit; (sehr) viel; *as* ~ *as* bis; *in so* ~ *as* insofern als; ~away ['fɑ:rəwei] weit entfernt.

fare [fɛə] 1. Fahrgeld *n*; Fahrgast *m*; Verpflegung *f*, Kost *f*; 2. *gut* leben; he ~*d well* es (er)ging ihm gut; ~*well* [fɛə'wel] 1. lebe(n Sie) wohl!; 2. Abschied *m*, Lebewohl *n*.

far|-**fetched** *fig.* ['fɑ:'fetʃt] weit hergeholt, gesucht; ~ **gone** F fertig (*todkrank, betrunken etc.*).

farm [fɑ:m] 1. Bauernhof *m*, -gut *n*; Gehöft *n*, Farm *f*; Züchterei *f*; *chicken* ~ Hühnerfarm *f*; 2. (ver-) pachten; *Land* bewirtschaften; ~er ['fɑ:mə] Landwirt *m*; Pächter *m*; ~hand Landarbeiter(in); ~house Bauern-, Gutshaus *n*; ~ing ['fɑ:miŋ]

1. Acker...; landwirtschaftlich;
2. Landwirtschaft *f*; ~**stead** Gehöft *n*; ~**yard** Wirtschaftshof *m e-s Bauernguts*.

far-off ['fɑːɔːf] entfernt, fern; ~**sighted** *fig.* weitblickend.

farthe|r ['fɑːðə] *comp. von far*; ~**st** ['fɑːðist] *sup. von far*.

fascinat|e ['fæsineit] bezaubern; ~**ion** [fæsi'neiʃən] Zauber *m*, Reiz *m*.

fashion ['fæʃən] Mode *f*; Art *f*; feine Lebensart; Form *f*; Schnitt *m*; *in (out of)* ~ (un)modern; **2.** gestalten; *Kleid* machen; ~**able** □ ['fæʃnəbl] modern, elegant.

fast¹ [fɑːst] schnell; fest; treu; waschecht; flott; *be* ~ *vorgehen (Uhr)*.

fast² [~] **1.** Fasten *n*; **2.** fasten.

fasten ['fɑːsn] *v/t.* befestigen; anheften; fest (zu)machen; zubinden; *Augen etc.* heften (*on, upon* auf *acc.*); *v/i.* schließen (*Tür*); ~ *upon fig.* sich klammern an (*acc.*); ~**er** [~nə] Verschluß *m*; Klammer *f*.

fastidious □ [fæs'tidiəs] anspruchsvoll, heikel, wählerisch, verwöhnt.

fat [fæt] **1.** □ fett; dick; fettig; **2.** Fett *n*; **3.** fett machen *od.* werden; mästen.

fatal □ ['feitl] verhängnisvoll (*to* für); Schicksals...; tödlich; ~**ity** [fə'tæliti] Verhängnis *n*; Unglücks-, Todesfall *m*; Todesopfer *n*.

fate [feit] Schicksal *n*; Verhängnis *n*.

father ['fɑːðə] **1.** Vater *m*; **2.** der Urheber sein von; ~**hood** [~əhud] Vaterschaft *f*; ~**-in-law** [~ərinlɔː] Schwiegervater *m*; ~**less** [~əlis] vaterlos; ~**ly** [~li] väterlich.

fathom ['fæðəm] **1.** Klafter *f (Maß)*; ⏚ Faden *m*; **2.** ⏚ loten; *fig.* ergründen; ~**less** [~mlis] unergründlich.

fatigue [fə'tiːg] **1.** Ermüdung *f*; Strapaze *f*; **2.** ermüden; strapazieren.

fat|ness ['fætnis] Fettigkeit *f*; Fettheit *f*; ~**ten** ['fætn] fett machen *od.* werden; mästen; *Boden* düngen.

fatuous □ ['fætjuəs] albern.

faucet *Am.* ['fɔːsit] (Zapf)Hahn *m*.

fault [fɔːlt] Fehler *m*; Defekt *m*; Schuld *f*; *find* ~ *with et.* auszusetzen haben an (*dat.*); *be at* ~ *auf falscher Fährte sein*; ~**finder** ['fɔːltfaində] Nörgler *m*; ~**less** □ [~lis] fehlerfrei, tadellos; ~**y** □ [~ti] mangelhaft.

favo(u)r ['feivə] **1.** Gunst(bezeigung) *f*; Gefallen *m*; Begünstigung *f*; *in* ~ *of* zugunsten von jdm. gen.; *do s.o. a* ~ *j-m e-n Gefallen tun*; **2.** begünstigen; beehren; ~**able** □ [~ərəbl] günstig; ~**ite** [~rit] Günstling *m*; Liebling *m*; *Sport:* Favorit *m*; *attr.* Lieblings...

fawn¹ [fɔːn] **1.** *zo.* (Dam)Kitz *n*; Rehbraun *n*; **2.** (Kitze) setzen.

fawn² [~] schwänzeln (*Hund*); kriechen (*upon* vor).

faze *bsd. Am.* F [feiz] durcheinanderbringen.

fear [fiə] **1.** Furcht *f* (*of* vor *dat.*); Befürchtung *f*; Angst *f*; **2.** (be-)fürchten; sich fürchten vor (*dat.*); ~**ful** □ ['fiəful] furchtsam; furchtbar; ~**less** □ ['fiəlis] furchtlos.

feasible ['fiːzəbl] ausführbar.

feast [fiːst] **1.** Fest *n*; Feiertag *m*; Festmahl *n*, Schmaus *m*; **2.** *v/t.* festlich bewirten; *v/i.* sich ergötzen; schmausen. [stück *n*.]

feat [fiːt] (Helden)Tat *f*; Kunst-]

feather ['feðə] **1.** Feder *f*; *a.* ~**s** Gefieder *n*; *show the white* ~ F sich feige zeigen; *in high* ~ in gehobener Stimmung; **2.** mit Federn schmücken; ~**bed 1.** *Feder*-Unterbett *n*; **2.** verwöhnen; ~**brained**, ~**headed** unbesonnen; albern; ~**ed** be-, gefiedert; ~**y** [~ori] feder(art)ig.

feature ['fiːtʃə] **1.** (Gesichts-, Grund-, Haupt-, Charakter)Zug *m*; (charakteristisches) Merkmal; *Radio:* Feature *n*; *Am.* Bericht *m*, Artikel *m*; ~**s** *pl.* Gesicht *n*; Charakter *m*; **2.** kennzeichnen; sich auszeichnen durch; groß aufziehen; *Film:* in der Hauptrolle zeigen; ~ **film** Haupt-, Spielfilm *m*.

February ['februəri] Februar *m*.

fecund ['fiːkənd] fruchtbar.

fed [fed] *pret. u. p.p. von feed* **2.**

federa|l ['fedərəl] Bundes...; ~**lize** [~laiz] (sich) verbünden; ~**tion** [fedə'reiʃən] Staatenbund *m*; Vereinigung *f*; Verband *m*.

fee [fiː] **1.** Gebühr *f*; Honorar *n*; Trinkgeld *n*; **2.** bezahlen.

feeble □ ['fiːbl] schwach.

feed [fiːd] **1.** Futter *n*; Nahrung *f*; Fütterung *f*; ⊕ Zuführung *f*, Speisung *f*; **2.** [*irr.*] *v/t.* füttern; speisen (*a.* ⊕), nähren; weiden; *Material etc.* zuführen; *be fed up with et. od. j-n* satt haben; *well fed* wohlgenährt; *v/i.* (fr)essen; sich nähren; ~**er** ['fiːdə] Fütterer *m*; *Am.* Viehmäster *m*; Esser(in) *m*; ~**er road** Zubringer(straße *f*) *m*; ~**ing-bottle** ['fiːdiŋbɔtl] Saugflasche *f*.

feel [fiːl] **1.** [*irr.*] (sich) fühlen; befühlen; empfinden; sich anfühlen; *I* ~ *like doing ich* möchte am liebsten tun; **2.** Gefühl *n*; Empfindung *f*; ~**er** ['fiːlə] Fühler *m*; ~**ing** ['fiːliŋ] **1.** □ (mit)fühlend; gefühlvoll; **2.** Gefühl *n*; Meinung *f*.

feet [fiːt] *pl. von foot* **1.**

feign [fein] heucheln; vorgeben.

feint [feint] Verstellung *f*; Finte *f*.

felicit|ate [fi'lisiteit] beglückwünschen; ~**ous** □ [~təs] glücklich; ~**y** [~ti] Glück(seligkeit *f*) *n*.

fell [fel] **1.** *pret. von fall* **2**; **2.** niederschlagen; fällen.

felloe ['felou] (Rad)Felge f.

fellow ['felou] Gefährt|e m, -in f, Kamerad(in); Gleiche(r, -s); Gegenstück n; univ. Fellow m, Mitglied n e-s College; Bursche m, Mensch m; attr. Mit...; old ~ F alter Junge; the ~ of a glove der andere Handschuh; **~country-man** Landsmann m; **~ship** [~ouʃip] Gemeinschaft f; Kameradschaft f; Mitgliedschaft f.

felly ['feli] (Rad)Felge f.

felon ɡʒ ['felən] Verbrecher m; **~y** [~ni] Kapitalverbrechen n.

felt[1] [felt] pret. u. p.p. von feel 1.

felt[2] [~] 1. Filz m; 2. (be)filzen.

female ['fi:meil] 1. weiblich; 2. Weib n; zo. Weibchen n.

feminine ☐ ['feminin] weiblich; weibisch.

fen [fen] Fenn n, Moor n; Marsch f.

fence [fens] 1. Zaun m; Fechtkunst f; sl. Hehler(nest n) m; sit on the ~ abwarten; 2. v/t. a. ~ in ein-, umzäunen; schützen; v/i. fechten; sl. hehlen.

fencing ['fensiŋ] Einfriedung f; Fechten n; attr. Fecht...

fend [fend]: ~ off abwehren; **~er** ['fendə] Schutzvorrichtung f; Schutzblech n; Kamingitter n, -vorsetzer m; Stoßfänger m.

fennel ♣ ['fenl] Fenchel m.

ferment 1. ['fə:ment] Ferment n; Gärung f; 2. [fə(:)'ment] gären (lassen); **~ation** [fə:men'teiʃən] Gärung f.

fern ♣ [fə:n] Farn(kraut n) m.

ferocious ☐ [fə'rouʃəs] wild; grausam; **~ty** [fə'rɔsiti] Wildheit f.

ferret ['ferit] 1. zo. Frettchen n; fig. Spürhund m; 2. v/t. (umher)stöbern; ~ out aufstöbern.

ferry ['feri] 1. Fähre f; 2. übersetzen; **~boat** Fährboot n, Fähre f; **~man** Fährmann m.

fertil|e ☐ ['fə:tail] fruchtbar; reich (of, in an dat.); **~ity** [fə:'tiliti] Fruchtbarkeit f (a. fig.); **~ize** ['fə:tilaiz] fruchtbar machen; befruchten; düngen; **~izer** [~zə] Düngemittel n.

ferven|cy ['fə:vənsi] Glut f; Inbrunst f; **~t** ☐ [~nt] heiß; inbrünstig, glühend; leidenschaftlich.

fervo(u)r ['fə:və] Glut f; Inbrunst f.

festal ☐ ['festl] festlich.

fester ['festə] eitern; verfaulen.

festiv|al ['festəvəl] Fest n; Feier f; Festspiele n/pl.; **~e** ☐ [~tiv] festlich; **~ity** [fes'tiviti] Festlichkeit f.

festoon [fes'tu:n] Girlande f.

fetch [fetʃ] holen; Preis erzielen; Seufzer ausstoßen; **~ing** ☐ F ['fetʃiŋ] reizend.

fetid ☐ ['fetid] stinkend.

fetter ['fetə] 1. Fessel f; 2. fesseln.

feud [fju:d] Fehde f; Leh(e)n n;

~al ☐ ['fju:dl] lehnbar; Lehns...;

~alism [~dəlizəm] Lehnswesen n.

fever ['fi:və] Fieber n; **~ish** ☐ [~əriʃ] fieb(e)rig; fig. fieberhaft.

few [fju:] wenige; a ~ ein paar; quite a ~, a good ~ e-e ganze Menge.

fiancé [fi'ã:nsei] Verlobte(r) m; **~e** [~] Verlobte f.

fiat ['faiæt] Befehl m; ~ money Am. Papiergeld n (ohne Deckung).

fib F [fib] 1. Flunkerei f, Schwindelei f; 2. schwindeln, flunkern.

fib|re, Am. **~er** ['faibə] Faser f; Charakter m; **~rous** ☐ ['faibrəs] faserig.

fickle ['fikl] wankelmütig; unbeständig; **~ness** [~nis] Wankelmut m.

fiction ['fikʃən] Erfindung f; Roman-, Unterhaltungsliteratur f; **~al** ☐ [~nl] erdichtet; Roman...

fictitious ☐ [fik'tiʃəs] erfunden.

fiddle F ['fidl] 1. Geige f, Fiedel f; 2. fiedeln; tändeln; **~r** [~lə] Geiger (-in); **~stick** Fiedelbogen m; **~s!** fig. dummes Zeug!

fidelity [fi'deliti] Treue f; Genauigkeit f.

fidget F ['fidʒit] 1. nervöse Unruhe; 2. nervös machen od. sein; **~y** [~ti] nervös.

fie [fai] pfui! [kribbelig.

field [fi:ld] Feld n; (Spiel)Platz m; Arbeitsfeld n; Gebiet n; Bereich m; hold the ~ das Feld behaupten; **~day** ['fi:lddei] ✕ Felddienstübung f; Parade f; fig. großer Tag; Am. (Schul)Sportfest n; Am. Exkursionstag m; **~events** pl. Sport: Sprung- u. Wurfwettkämpfe m/pl.; **~glass**(es pl.) Feldstecher m; **~officer** Stabsoffizier m; **~sports** pl. Jagen n u. Fischen n.

fiend [fi:nd] böser Feind, Teufel m; **~ish** ☐ ['fi:ndiʃ] teuflisch, boshaft.

fierce ☐ [fiəs] wild; grimmig; **~ness** ['fiəsnis] Wildheit f; Grimm m.

fiery ☐ ['faiəri] feurig; hitzig.

fif|teen ['fif'ti:n] fünfzehn; **~teenth** [~nθ] fünfzehnte(r, -s); **~th** [fifθ] 1. fünfte(r, -s); 2. Fünftel n; **~thly** ['fifθli] fünftens; **~tieth** ['fiftiiθ] fünfzigste(r, -s); **~ty** [~ti] fünfzig; **~ty-fifty** F halb und halb.

fig [fig] Feige f; F Zustand m.

fight [fait] 1. Kampf m; Kampflust f; show ~ sich zur Wehr setzen; 2. [irr.] v/t. bekämpfen; erkämpfen; v/i. kämpfen, sich schlagen; **~er** ['faitə] Kämpfer m, Streiter m; ✕ Jagdflugzeug n; **~ing** ['faitiŋ] Kampf m.

figurative ☐ ['figjurətiv] bildlich.

figure ['figə] 1. Figur f; Gestalt f; Ziffer f; Preis m; be good at ~s gut im Rechnen sein; 2. v/t. abbilden; darstellen; sich et. vorstellen; beziffern; ~ up ab. out berechnen; v/i. erscheinen; e-e Rolle spielen (as) als); ~ on *Am. et.* überdenken; ~skating [~əskeitiŋ] Eiskunstlauf *m.*

filament ['filəmənt] Faden *m*, Faser *f*; ⚥ Staubfaden *m*; ⚡ Glüh-, Heizfaden *m.*

filbert ⚥ ['filbə(:)t] Haselnuß *f.*

filch [filtʃ] stibitzen (*from dat.*).

file¹ [fail] 1. Akte *f*, Ordner *m*; Ablage *f*; Reihe *f*; ⚔ Rotte *f*; on ~ bei den Akten; 2. *v/t.* aufreihen; *Briefe etc.* einordnen; ablegen; einreichen; *v/i.* hinter-ea. marschieren.

file² [~] 1. Feile *f*; 2. feilen.

filial □ ['filjəl] kindlich, Kindes...

filibuster ['filibʌstə] 1. *Am.* Obstruktion(spolitiker *m*) *f*; 2. *Am.* Obstruktion treiben.

fill [fil] 1. (sich) füllen; an-, aus-, erfüllen; *Am. Auftrag* ausführen; ~ in *Formular* ausfüllen; 2. Fülle *f*, Genüge *f*; Füllung *f.*

fillet ['filit] Haarband *n*; Lendenbraten *m*; Roulade *f*; *bsd.* ⚓ Band *n.*

filling ['filiŋ] Füllung *f*; ~ station *Am.* Tankstelle *f.*

fillip ['filip] Nasenstüber *m.*

filly ['fili] (Stuten)Füllen *n*; *fig.* wilde Hummel.

film [film] 1. Häutchen *n*; Membran(e) *f*; Film *m*; Trübung *f des Auges*; Nebelschleier *m*; *take od.* shoot a ~ e-n Film drehen; 2. (sich) verschleiern; (ver)filmen.

filter ['filtə] 1. Filter *m*; 2. filtern.

filth [filθ] Schmutz *m*; ~y □ ['filθi] schmutzig; *fig.* unflätig.

filtrate ['filtreit] filtrieren.

fin [fin] Flosse *f* (*a. sl.* = Hand).

final ['fainl] 1. □ letzte(r, -s); endlich; schließlich; End...; endgültig; 2. Schlußprüfung *f*; *Sport:* Schlußrunde *f*, Endspiel *n.*

financ|e [fai'næns] 1. Finanzwesen *n*; ~s *pl.* Finanzen *pl.*; 2. *v/t.* finanzieren; *v/i.* Geldgeschäfte machen; ~ial □ [~nʃəl] finanziell; ~ier [~nsiə] Finanzmann *m*; Geldgeber *m.*

finch *orn.* [fintʃ] Fink *m.*

find [faind] 1. (*irr.*) finden; (an-) treffen; auf-, herausfinden; *schuldig etc.* befinden; beschaffen; versorgen; *all found* freie Station; 2. Fund *m*; ~ings ['faindiŋz] *pl.* Befund *m*; Urteil *n.*

fine¹ □ [fain] 1. schön; fein; verfeinert; rein; spitz, dünn, scharf; geziert; vornehm; 2. *adv.* gut, bestens.

fine² [~] 1. Geldstrafe *f*; 2. zu e-r Geldstrafe verurteilen.

fineness ['fainnis] Fein-, Zart-, Schönheit *f*, Eleganz *f*; Genauigkeit *f.*

finery ['fainəri] Glanz *m*; Putz *m*; Staat *m.*

finger ['fiŋgə] 1. Finger *m*; 2. betasten, (herum)fingern an (*dat.*);

~-language Zeichensprache *f*; ~-nail Fingernagel *m*; ~-print Fingerabdruck *m.*

fini|cal ['finikəl], ~cking [~kiŋ], ~kin [~in] geziert; wählerisch.

finish ['finiʃ] 1. *v/t.* beenden, vollenden; fertigstellen; abschließen; vervollkommnen; erledigen; *v/i.* enden; 2. Vollendung *f*, letzter Schliff (*a. fig.*); Schluß *m.*

finite □ ['fainait] endlich, begrenzt.

fink *Am. sl.* [fiŋk] Streikbrecher *m.*

Finn [fin] Finn|e *m*, -in *f*; ~ish ['finiʃ] finnisch.

fir [fə:] (Weiß)Tanne *f*; Fichte *f*; ~-cone ['fə:koun] Tannenzapfen *m.*

fire ['faiə] 1. Feuer *n*; on ~ in Brand, in Flammen; 2. *v/t.* an-, entzünden; *fig.* anfeuern; abfeuern; *Ziegel etc.* brennen; F 'rausschmeißen (*entlassen*); heizen; *v/i.* Feuer fangen (*a. fig.*); feuern; ~-alarm ['faiərəla:m] Feuermelder *m*; ~-brigade Feuerwehr *f*; ~-bug *Am.* F Brandstifter *m*; ~-cracker Frosch *m* (*Feuerwerkskörper*); ~ department *Am.* Feuerwehr *f*; ~-engine ['faiərendʒin] (Feuer)Spritze *f*; ~-escape [~riskeip] Rettungsgerät *n*; Nottreppe *f*; ~-extinguisher [~rikstiŋwiʃə] Feuerlöscher *m*; ~-man Feuerwehrmann *m*; Heizer *m*; ~-place Herd *m*; Kamin *m*; ~-plug Hydrant *m*; ~-proof feuerfest; ~-screen Ofenschirm *m*; ~ side Herd *m*; Kamin *m*; ~-station Feuerwache *f*; ~-wood Brennholz *n*; ~-works *pl.* Feuerwerk *n.*

firing ['faiəriŋ] Heizung *f*; Feuerung *f.*

firm [fə:m] 1. □ fest; derb; standhaft; 2. Firma *f*; ~ness ['fə:mnis] Festigkeit *f.*

first [fə:st] 1. *adj.* erste(r, -s) beste(r, -s); 2. *adv.* erstens; zuerst; ~ of all an erster Stelle; zu allererst; 3. Erste(r, -s) ~ of exchange ✝ Primawechsel *m*; *at* ~ zuerst, anfangs; *from the* ~ von Anfang an; ~-born ['fə:stbo:n] erstgeboren; ~ class 1. Klasse (*e-s Verkehrsmittels*); ~-class erstklassig; ~ly [~tli] erstlich; erstens; ~ name Vorname *m*; Beiname *m*; ~ papers *Am.* vorläufige Einbürgerungspapiere; ~-rate ersten Ranges; erstklassig.

firth [fə:θ] Förde *f*; (Flut)Mündung *f.*

fish [fiʃ] 1. Fisch(e *pl.*) *m*; F Kerl *m*; 2. fischen, angeln; haschen; ~-bone ['fiʃboun] Gräte *f.*

fisher ['fiʃə], ~man Fischer *m*; ~y [~əri] Fischerei *f.*

fishing ['fiʃiŋ] Fischen *n*; ~-line Angelschnur *f*; ~-tackle Angelgerät *n.*   [händler *m.*]

fishmonger ['fiʃmʌŋgə] Fisch-

fiss|ion ⚛ ['fiʃən] Spaltung *f*; ~ure ['fiʃə] Spalt *m*; Riß *m.*

fist [fist] Faust *f*; F Klaue *f*;
~icuffs ['fistikʌfs] *pl.* Faustschläge
m/pl.

fit¹ [fit] **1.** □ geeignet, passend;
tauglich; *Sport*: in (guter) Form;
bereit; **2.** *v/t.* passen für *od. dat.*;
anpassen, passend machen; befä-
higen; geeignet machen (*for, to* für,
zu); *a. ~ on* anprobieren; ausstatten;
~ out ausrüsten; **~ up** einrichten;
montieren; *v/i.* passen; sich schik-
ken; sitzen (*Kleid*); **3.** Sitz *m*
(*Kleid*).

fit² [~] Anfall *m*; ♂ Ausbruch *m*;
Anwandlung *f*; *by ~s and starts*
ruckweise; *give s.o. a ~* j-n hochbringen; j-m e-n Schock versetzen.

fit|ful □ ['fitful] ruckartig; *fig.* un-
stet; **~ness** ['fitnis] Schicklichkeit *f*;
Tauglichkeit *f*; **~ter** ['fitə] Mon-
teur *m*; Installateur *m*; **~ting** ['fitiŋ]
1. passend; **2.** Montage *f*; Anprobe
f; **~s** *pl.* Einrichtung *f*; Armaturen
f/pl.

five [faiv] **1.** fünf; **2.** Fünf *f*.

fix [fiks] **1.** *v/t.* befestigen, anheften;
fixieren; *Augen etc.* heften, richten;
fesseln; aufstellen; bestimmen,
festsetzen; *bsd. Am.* richten, *Bett
etc.* machen; *~ o.s.* sich niederlassen; **~ up** in Ordnung bringen, arrangie-
ren; *v/i.* fest werden; **~ on** sich entschließen für; **2.** F Klemme *f*; *Am.*
Zustand *m*; **~ed** fest; bestimmt;
starr; **~ing** ['fiksiŋ] Befestigen *n*;
Instandsetzen *n*; Fixieren *n*; Aufstellen *n*, Montieren *n*; Besatz *m*,
Versteifung *f*; *Am.* **~s** *pl.* Zubehör
n, Extraausrüstung *f*; **~ture** [~stʃə]
fest angebrachtes Zubehörteil, feste
Anlage; Inventarstück *n*; *lighting ~*
Beleuchtungskörper *m*.

fizz [fiz] **1.** zischen, sprudeln; **2.** Zischen *n*; F Schampus *m* (*Sekt*).

flabbergast F ['flæbəgɑːst] verblüffen; be **~ed** baff *od.* platt sein.

flabby □ ['flæbi] schlaff, schlapp.

flag [flæg] **1.** Flagge *f*, Fahne *f*;
Fliese *f*; Schwertlilie *f*; **2.** beflag-
gen; durch Flaggen signalisieren;
mit Fliesen belegen; ermatten,
mutlos werden; **~day** ['flægdei]
Opfertag *m*; *Flag Day Am.* Tag *m*
des Sternenbanners (*14. Juni*).

flagitious □ [flə'dʒiʃəs] schändlich.

flagrant □ ['fleigrənt] abscheulich;
berüchtigt; offenkundig.

flag|staff ['flægstɑːf] Fahnenstange
f; **~stone** Fliese *f*.

flair [flɛə] Spürsinn *m*, feine Nase.

flake [fleik] **1.** Flocke *f*; Schicht *f*;
2. (sich) flocken; abblättern.

flame [fleim] **1.** Flamme *f*, Feuer *n*;
fig. Hitze *f*; **2.** flammen, lodern.

flank [flæŋk] **1.** Flanke *f*, Weiche *f*
der Tiere; **2.** flankieren.

flannel ['flænl] Flanell *m*; Waschlappen *m*; **~s** *pl.* Flanellhose *f*.

flap [flæp] **1.** (Ohr)Läppchen *n*;

Rockschoß *m*; *Hut*-Krempe *f*;
Klappe *f*; Klaps *m*; (Flügel)Schlag
m; **2.** *v/t.* klatschen(d schlagen); *v/i.*
lose herabhängen; flattern.

flare [flɛə] **1.** flackern; sich nach
außen erweitern, sich bauschen;
~ up aufflammen; *fig.* aufbrausen;
2. flackerndes Licht; Lichtsignal *n*.

flash [flæʃ] **1.** aufgedonnert; unecht; Gauner...; **2.** Blitz *m*; *fig.*
Aufblitzen *n*; *bsd. Am. Zeitung*:
kurze Meldung; *in a ~* im Nu; *~ of
wit* Geistesblitz *m*; **3.** (auf)blitzen;
auflodern (lassen); *Blick etc.* werfen; flitzen; funken, telegraphieren;
it ~ed on me mir kam plötzlich der
Gedanke; **~back** ['flæʃbæk] *Film*:
Rückblende *f*; **~light** *phot.* Blitz-
licht *n*; Blinklicht *n*; Taschenlampe
f; **~y** □ [~ʃi] auffallend.

flask [flɑːsk] Taschen-, Reiseflasche
f.

flat [flæt] **1.** □ flach, platt; schal;
† flau; klar; glatt; ♪ um e-n halben
Ton erniedrigt; **~ price** Einheits-
preis *m*; **2.** *adv.* glatt; völlig; *fall ~*
danebengehen; *sing ~* zu tief sin-
gen; **3.** Fläche *f*, Ebene *f*; Flach-
land *n*; Untiefe *f*; (Miet)Wohnung
f; ♪ B *n*; F Simpel *m*; *mot. sl.* Plattfuß *m*; **~foot** ['flætfut] Plattfuß *m*;
Am. sl. Polyp *m* (*Polizist*); **~footed**
plattfüßig; *Am.* F *fig.* stur, eisern;
~iron Plätteisen *n*; **~ness** [~tnis]
Flachheit *f*; Plattheit *f*; † Flauheit
f; **~ten** [~tn] (sich) ab-, verflachen.

flatter ['flætə] schmeicheln (*dat.*);
~er [~ərə] Schmeichler(in); **~y**
[~ri] Schmeichelei *f*.

flavo(u)r ['fleivə] **1.** Geschmack *m*;
Aroma *n*; Blume *f* (*Wein*); *fig.* Beigeschmack *m*; Würze *f*; **2.** würzen;
~less [~əlis] geschmacklos, fad.

flaw [flɔː] **1.** Sprung *m*, Riß *m*;
Fehler *m*; ⚓ Bö *f*; **2.** zerbrechen;
beschädigen; **~less** □ ['flɔːlis] fehlerlos.

flax ♀ [flæks] Flachs *m*, Lein *m*.

flay [flei] die Haut abziehen (*dat.*).

flea [fliː] Floh *m*.

fled [fled] *pret. u. p.p. von* flee.

fledg|e [fledʒ] *v/i.* flügge werden;
v/t. befiedern; **~(e)ling** ['fledʒliŋ]
Küken *n* (*a. fig.*); Grünschnabel *m*.

flee [fliː] (*irr.*) fliehen; meiden.

fleec|e [fliːs] **1.** Vlies *n*; **2.** scheren;
prellen; **~y** ['fliːsi] wollig.

fleer [fliə] höhnen (*at über acc.*).

fleet [fliːt] **1.** □ schnell; **2.** Flotte *f*;
♀ *Street* die (Londoner) Presse.

flesh [fleʃ] **1.** *lebendiges* Fleisch; *fig.*
Fleisch(eslust *f*) *n*; *2. hunt.* Blut
kosten lassen; **~ly** ['fleʃli] fleisch-
lich; irdisch; **~y** [~ʃi] fleischig; fett.

flew [fluː] *pret. von* fly **2.**

flexib|ility [fleksə'biliti] Biegsam-
keit *f*; **~le** □ ['fleksəbl] flexibel,
biegsam; *fig.* anpassungsfähig.

flick [flik] schnippen; schnellen.

flicker ['flikə] 1. flackern; flattern; flimmern; 2. Flackern n, Flimmern n; Flattern n; Am. Buntspecht m.

flier ['flaiə] = flyer.

flight [flait] Flucht f; Flug m (a. fig.); Schwarm m; ⚔, ⚔ Kette f; (~ of stairs Treppen)Flucht f; put to ~ in die Flucht schlagen; ~y □ ['flaiti] flüchtig; leichtsinnig.

flimsy ['flimzi] dünn, locker; schwach; fig. fadenscheinig.

finch [flintʃ] zurückweichen; zukken.

fling [fliŋ] 1. Wurf m; Schlag m; have one's ~ sich austoben; 2. [irr.] v/i. eilen; ausschlagen (Pferd); fig. toben; v/t. werfen, schleudern; ~ o.s. sich stürzen; ~ open aufreißen.

flint [flint] Kiesel m; Feuerstein m.

flip [flip] 1. Klaps m; Ruck m; 2. schnippen; klapsen; (umher-) flitzen.

flippan|cy ['flipənsi] Leichtfertigkeit f; ~t □ [~nt] leichtfertig; vorlaut.

flirt [flə:t] 1. Kokette f; Weiberheld m; 2. flirten, kokettieren; = flip 2; ~ation [flə:'teiʃən] Flirt m.

flit [flit] flitzen; wandern; umziehen.

flivver Am. sl. ['flivə] 1. Nuckelpinne f (billiges Auto); 2. mißlingen.

float [flout] 1. Schwimmer m; Floß n; Plattformwagen m; 2. v/t. überfluten; flößen; tragen (Wasser); ⚓ flott machen, fig. in Gang bringen; † gründen; verbreiten; v/i. schwimmen, treiben; schweben; umlaufen.

flock [flɔk] 1. Herde f (a. fig.); Schar f; 2. sich scharen; zs.-strömen.

floe [flou] (treibende) Eisscholle.

flog [flɔg] peitschen; prügeln.

flood [flʌd] 1. a. ~-tide Flut f; Überschwemmung f; 2. überfluten, überschwemmen; ~gate ['flʌdgeit] Schleusentor n; ~light ⚡ Flutlicht n.

floor [flɔ:] 1. Fußboden m; Stock (-werk n) m; ⚔ Tenne f; ~ leader Am. Fraktionsvorsitzende(r) m; ~ show Nachtklubvorstellung f; take the ~ das Wort ergreifen; 2. dielen; zu Boden schlagen; verblüffen; ~cloth ['flɔ:klɔθ] Putzlappen m; ~ing ['flɔ:riŋ] Dielung f; Fußboden m; ~lamp Stehlampe f; ~walker Am. ['flɔ:wɔ:kə] = shopwalker.

flop [flɔp] 1. schlagen, flattern; (hin)plumpsen (lassen); Am. versagen; 2. Plumps m; Versager m; ~house Am. F Penne f.

florid □ ['flɔrid] blühend.

florin ['flɔrin] Zweischillingstück n.

florist ['flɔrist] Blumenhändler m.

floss [flɔs] Florettseide f.

flounce[1] [flauns] Volant m.

flounce[2] [~] stürzen; zappeln.

flounder[1] ichth. ['flaundə] Flunder f.

flounder[2] [~] sich (ab)mühen.

flour ['flauə] (feines) Mehl.

flourish ['flʌriʃ] 1. Schnörkel m; Schwingen n; ♪ Tusch m; 2. v/i. blühen, gedeihen; v/t. schwingen.

flout [flaut] (ver)spotten.

flow [flou] 1. Fluß m; Flut f; 2. fließen, fluten; wallen.

flower ['flauə] 1. Blume f; Blüte f (a. fig.); Zierde f; 2. blühen; ~pot Blumentopf m; ~y [~ɔri] blumig.

flown [floun] p.p. von fly 2.

flubdub Am. sl. ['flʌbdʌb] Geschwätz n.

fluctuat|e ['flʌktjueit] schwanken; ~ion [flʌktju'eiʃən] Schwankung f.

flu(e) F [flu:] = influenza.

flue [flu:] Kaminrohr n; Heizrohr n.

fluen|cy fig. ['flu(:)ənsi] Fluß m; ~t □ [~nt] fließend, geläufig (Rede).

fluff [flʌf] 1. Flaum f; Flocke f; fig. Schnitzer m; 2. Kissen aufschütteln; Federn aufplustern (Vogel); ~y [flʌfi] flaumig; flockig.

fluid ['flu(:)id] 1. flüssig; 2. Flüssigkeit f.

flung [flʌŋ] pret. u. p.p. von fling 2.

flunk Am. F fig.[flʌŋk] durchfallen (lassen).

flunk(e)y ['flʌŋki] Lakai m.

fluorescent [fluə'resnt] fluoreszierend.

flurry ['flʌri] Nervosität f; Bö f; Am. a. (Regen)Schauer m; Schneegestöber n.

flush [flʌʃ] 1. ⊕ in gleicher Ebene; reichlich; (über)voll; 2. Erröten n; Übermut m; Fülle f; Wachstum n; fig. Blüte f; Spülung f; Karten: Flöte f; 3. über-, durchfließen; (aus)spülen; strömen; sprießen (lassen); erröten (machen); übermütig machen; aufjagen.

fluster ['flʌstə] 1. Aufregung f; 2. v/t. aufregen.

flute [flu:t] 1. ♪ Flöte f; Falte f; 2. (auf der) Flöte spielen; riefeln; fälteln.

flutter ['flʌtə] 1. Geflatter n; Erregung f; F Spekulation f; 2. v/t. aufregen; v/i. flattern.

flux [flʌks] fig. Fluß m; ⚕ Ausfluß m.

fly [flai] 1. zo. Fliege f; Flug m; Am. Baseball: hochgeschlagener Ball; Droschke f; 2. [irr.] (a. fig.) fliegen (lassen); entfliehen (Zeit); ⚔ führen; Flagge hissen; fliehen; ⚔ überfliegen; ~ at herfallen über; ~ into a passion od. rage in Zorn geraten.

flyer ['flaiə] Flieger m; Renner m; take a ~ Am. F Vermögen riskieren.

fly-flap ['flaiflæp] Fliegenklatsche f.

flying ['flaiiŋ] fliegend; Flug...; ~ squad Überfallkommando n.

fly|-over ['flaiouvə] (Straßen)Überführung f; ~weight Boxen: Fliegengewicht n; **~-wheel** Schwungrad n.

foal [foul] 1. Fohlen n; 2. fohlen.

foam [foum] 1. Schaum m; 2. schäumen; **~y** ['foumi] schaumig.

focus ['foukəs] 1. Brennpunkt m; 2. (sich) im Brennpunkt vereinigen; opt. einstellen (a. fig.); konzentrieren.

fodder ['fɔdə] (Trocken)Futter n.

foe poet. [fou] Feind m, Gegner m.

fog [fɔg] 1. (dichter) Nebel; fig. Umnebelung f; phot. Schleier m; 2. mst fig. umnebeln; phot. verschleiern.

fogey F ['fougi]: old ~ komischer alter Kauz.

foggy ⌐ ['fɔgi] neb(e)lig; fig. nebelhaft.

fogy Am. ['fougi] = fogey.

foible fig. ['fɔibl] Schwäche f.

foil[1] [fɔil] Folie f; Hintergrund m.

foil[2] [~] 1. vereiteln; 2. Florett n.

fold[1] [fould] 1. Schafhürde f; fig. Herde f; 2. einpferchen.

fold[2] [~] 1. Falte f; Falz m; 2. ...fach, ...fältig; 3. v/t. falten; falzen; Arme kreuzen; ~ (up) einwickeln; v/i. sich falten; Am. F eingehen; **~er** ['fouldə] Mappe f, Schnellhefter m; Faltprospekt m.

folding ['fouldiŋ] zs.-legbar; Klapp...; **~-bed** Feldbett n; **~-boat** Faltboot n; **~-door(s** pl.) Flügeltür f; **~-screen** spanische Wand; **~-seat** Klappsitz m.

foliage ['fouliidʒ] Laub(werk) n.

folk [fouk] pl. Leute pl; **~s** pl. Leute pl. (F a. Angehörige); **~lore** ['fouk-lɔ:] Volkskunde f; Volkssagen f/pl.; **~-song** Volkslied n.

follow ['fɔlou] folgen (dat.); folgen auf (acc.); be-, verfolgen; s-m Beruf etc. nachgehen; **~er** [~ouə] Nachfolger(in); Verfolger(in); Anhänger(in); **~ing** [~ouiŋ] Anhängerschaft f, Gefolge n.

folly ['fɔli] Torheit f; Narrheit f.

foment [fou'ment] j-m warme Umschläge machen; Unruhe stiften.

fond [fɔnd] zärtlich; vernarrt (of in acc.); be ~ of gern haben, lieben; **~le** ['fɔndl] liebkosen; streicheln; (ver)hätscheln; **~ness** [~dnis] Zärtlichkeit f; Vorliebe f.

font [fɔnt] Taufstein m; Am. Quelle f.

food [fu:d] Speise f, Nahrung f; Futter n; Lebensmittel n/pl.; **~-stuff** ['fu:dstʌf] Nahrungsmittel n.

fool [fu:l] 1. Narr m, Tor m; Hanswurst m; make a ~ of s.o. j-n zum Narren halten; make a ~ of o.s. sich lächerlich machen; 2. Am. F närrisch, dumm; 3. v/t narren; prellen (out of um et.); ~ away vertrödeln; v/i. albern, (herum)spielen; ~ (a)round bsd. Am. Zeit vertrödeln.

fool|ery ['fu:ləri] Torheit f; **~hardy**

⌐ ['fu:lhɑ:di] tollkühn; **~ish** ⌐ ['fu:liʃ] töricht; **~ishness** [~ʃnis] Torheit f; **~-proof** kinderleicht.

foot [fut] 1. pl. feet [fi:t] Fuß m (a. Maß); Fußende n; ⚔ Infanterie f; on ~ zu Fuß; im Gange, in Gang; 2. v/t. mst ~ up addieren; ~ the bill F die Rechnung bezahlen; v/i. ~ it zu Fuß gehen; **~board** ['futbɔ:d] Trittbrett n; **~boy** Page m; **~fall** Tritt m, Schritt m; **~-gear** Schuhwerk n; **~hold** fester Stand; fig. Halt m.

footing ['futiŋ] Halt m, Stand m; Grundlage f, Basis f; Stellung f; fester Fuß; Verhältnis n; ⚔ Zustand m; Endsumme f; be on a friendly ~ with s.o. ein gutes Verhältnis zu j-m haben; lose one's ~ ausgleiten.

foot|lights thea. ['futlaits] pl. Rampenlicht(er pl.) n; Bühne f; **~man** Diener m; **~-passenger** Fußgänger (-in); **~-path** Fußpfad m; **~-print** Fußstapfe f, -spur f; **~-sore** fußkrank; step Fußstapfe f, Spur f; **~-stool** Fußbank f; **~-wear** = footgear.

fop [fɔp] Geck m, Fatzke m.

for [fɔ:, fɔr, fə] 1. prp. mst für; Zweck, Ziel, Richtung: zu; nach; warten, hoffen etc. auf (acc.); sich sehnen etc. nach; Grund, Anlaß: aus, vor (dat.), wegen; Zeitdauer: ~ three days drei Tage (lang); seit drei Tagen; Austausch: (an-)statt; in der Eigenschaft als; I ~ one ich zum Beispiel; ~ sure sicher!; gewiß!; 2. cj. denn.

forage ['fɔridʒ] 1. Futter n; 2. (nach Futter) suchen.

foray ['fɔrei] räuberischer Einfall m.

forbear[1] [fɔ:'bɛə] [irr. (bear)] v/t. unterlassen; v/i. sich enthalten (from gen.); Geduld haben.

forbear[2] ['fɔ:bɛə] Vorfahr m.

forbid [fə'bid] [irr. (bid)] verbieten; hindern; **~ding** ⌐ [~diŋ] abstoßend.

force [fɔ:s] 1. mst Kraft f, Gewalt f; Nachdruck m; Zwang m; Heer m; Streitmacht f; the ~ die Polizei; armed ~s pl. Streitkräfte f/pl.; come (put) in ~ in Kraft treten (setzen); 2. zwingen, nötigen; erzwingen; aufzwingen; Gewalt antun (dat.); beschleunigen; aufbrechen; künstlich reif machen; ~ open aufbrechen; **~d**: ~ landing Notlandung f; ~ loan Zwangsanleihe f; ~ march Bismarsch m; **~ful** ⌐ ['fɔ:s-ful] kräftig; eindringlich.

forceps ⚕ ['fɔ:seps] Zange f.

forcible ⌐ ['fɔ:səbl] gewaltsam; Zwangs...; eindringlich; wirksam.

ford [fɔ:d] 1. Furt f; 2. durchwaten.

fore [fɔ:] 1. adv. vorn; 2. Vorderteil m, n; bring (come) to the ~ zum

Vorschein bringen (kommen); **3.** *adj.* vorder; Vorder...; ~**bode** [fɔ:-ˈboud] vorhersagen; ahnen; ~**boding** [~diŋ] (böses) Vorzeichen; Ahnung *f*; ~**cast** [ˈfɔ:kɑ:st] **1.** Vorhersage *f*; **2.** *(irr. (cast))* vorhersehen; voraussagen; ~**father** Vorfahr *m*; ~**finger** Zeigefinger *m*; ~**foot** Vorderfuß *m*; ~**go** [fɔ:ˈgou] *[irr. (go)]* vorangehen; ~**gone** [fɔ:-ˈgɔn, *adj.* ˈfɔ:gɔn] von vornherein feststehend; ~ *conclusion* Selbstverständlichkeit *f*; ~**ground** Vordergrund *m*; ~**head** [ˈfɔrid] Stirn *f*.

foreign [ˈfɔrin] fremd; ausländisch; auswärtig; ~**er** [~nə] Ausländer(in), Fremde(r *m*) *f*; ♀ *Office* Außenministerium *n*; ~ *policy* Außenpolitik *f*; ~ *trade* Außenhandel *m*.

fore|knowledge [ˈfɔ:ˈnɔlidʒ] Vorherwissen *n*; ~**leg** [ˈfɔ:leg] Vorderbein *n*; ~**lock** Stirnhaar *n*; *fig.* Schopf *m*; ~**man** ♣ Obmann *m*; Vorarbeiter *m*, (Werk)Meister *m*; ♀ Steiger *m*; ~**most** vorderst, erst; ~**name** Vorname *m*; ~**noon** Vormittag *m*; ~**runner** Vorläufer *m*, Vorbote *m*, ~**see** [fɔ:ˈsi:] *[irr. (see)]* vorhersehen; ~**shadow** ankündigen; ~**sight** [ˈfɔ:sait] Voraussicht *f*; Vorsorge *f*.

forest [ˈfɔrist] **1.** Wald *m* (*a. fig.*), Forst *m*; **2.** aufforsten.

forestall [fɔ:ˈstɔ:l] *et.* vereiteln; *j-m* zuvorkommen.

forest|er [ˈfɔristə] Förster *m*; Waldarbeiter *m*; ~**ry** [~tri] Forstwirtschaft *f*; Waldgebiet *n*.

fore|taste [ˈfɔ:teist] Vorgeschmack *m*; ~**tell** [fɔ:ˈtel] *[irr. (tell)]* vorhersagen; vorbedeuten; ~**thought** [ˈfɔ:θɔ:t] Vorbedacht *m*; ~**woman** Aufseherin *f*; Vorarbeiterin *f*; ~**word** Vorwort *n*.

forfeit [ˈfɔ:fit] **1.** Verwirkung *f*; Strafe *f*; Pfand *n*; **2.** verwirken; einbüßen; ~**able** [~təbl] verwirkbar.

forge¹ [fɔ:dʒ] *mst* ~ *ahead* sich vor(wärts)arbeiten.

forge² [~] **1.** Schmiede *f*; **2.** schmieden (*fig. ersinnen*); fälschen; ~**ry** [ˈfɔ:dʒəri] Fälschung *f*.

forget [fəˈget] *[irr.]* vergessen; ~**ful** □ [~tful] vergeßlich; ~**me-not** ♀ Vergißmeinnicht *n*.

forgiv|e [fəˈgiv] *[irr. (give)]* vergeben, verzeihen; *Schuld* erlassen; ~**eness** [~vnis] Verzeihung *f*; ~**ing** □ [~viŋ] versöhnlich; nachsichtig.

forgo [fɔ:ˈgou] *[irr. (go)]* verzichten auf (*acc.*); aufgeben.

forgot [fəˈgɔt] *pret. von* forget; ~**ten** [~tn] *p.p. von* forget.

fork [fɔ:k] **1.** Gabel *f*; **2.** (sich) gabeln; ~**lift** [ˈfɔ:klift] Gabelstapler *m*.

forlorn [fəˈlɔ:n] verloren, verlassen.

form [fɔ:m] **1.** Form *f*; Gestalt *f*; Formalität *f*; Formular *n*; (Schul-) Bank *f*; *Schul-*Klasse *f*; Kondition

f; geistige Verfassung; **2.** (sich) formen, (sich) bilden, gestalten; ✗ (sich) aufstellen.

formal □ [ˈfɔ:məl] förmlich; formell; äußerlich; ~**ity** [fɔ:ˈmæliti] Förmlichkeit *f*, Formalität *f*.

formati|on [fɔ:ˈmeiʃən] Bildung *f*; ~**ve** [ˈfɔ:mətiv] bildend; gestaltend; ~ *years pl.* Entwicklungsjahre *n/pl.*

former [ˈfɔ:mə] vorig, früher; ehemalig, vergangen; erstere(r, -s); jene(r, -s); ~**ly** [~əli] ehemals, früher.

formidable □ [ˈfɔ:midəbl] furchtbar, schrecklich; ungeheuer.

formula [ˈfɔ:mjulə] Formel *f*; ♣ Rezept *n*; ~**te** [~leit] formulieren.

forsake [fəˈseik] *[irr.]* aufgeben; verlassen; ~**n** [~kən] *p.p. von* forsake.

forsook [fəˈsuk] *pret. von* forsake.

forsooth *iro.* [fəˈsu:θ] wahrlich.

forswear [fɔ:ˈswεə] *[irr. (swear)]* abschwören. [werk *n*) *f*.]

fort ✗ [fɔ:t] Fort *n*, Festungs-)

forth [fɔ:θ] vor(wärts), voran; heraus, hinaus, hervor; weiter, fort(an); ~**coming** [fɔ:θˈkamiŋ] erscheinend; bereit; bevorstehend; F entgegenkommend; ~**with** [ˈfɔ:θˈwiθ] sogleich.

fortieth [ˈfɔ:tiiθ] **1.** vierzigste(r, -s); Vierzigstel *n*.

forti|fication [fɔ:tifiˈkeiʃən] Befestigung *f*; ~**fy** [ˈfɔ:tifai] ✗ befestigen; *fig.* (ver)stärken; ~**tude** [~itjud] Seelenstärke *f*; Tapferkeit *f*.

fortnight [ˈfɔ:tnait] vierzehn Tage.

fortress [ˈfɔ:tris] Festung *f*.

fortuitous □ [fɔ:ˈtju(:)itəs] zufällig.

fortunate [ˈfɔ:tʃnit] glücklich; ~**ly** [~tli] glücklicherweise.

fortune [ˈfɔ:tʃən] Glück *n*; Schicksal *n*; Zufall *m*; Vermögen *n*; ~**teller** Wahrsager(in).

forty [ˈfɔ:ti] **1.** vierzig; ~**niner** *Am.* kalifornischer Goldsucher *von 1849*; ~ *winks pl.* F Nickerchen *n*; **2.** Vierzig *f*.

forward [ˈfɔ:wəd] **1.** *adj.* vorder; bereit(willig); fortschrittlich; vorwitzig, keck; **2.** *adv.* vor(wärts); **3.** *Fußball:* Stürmer *m*; **4.** (be)fördern; (ab~, ver)senden.

forwarding-agent [ˈfɔ:wədiŋeidʒənt] Spediteur *m*.

foster [ˈfɔstə] **1.** *fig.* nähren, pflegen; ~ *up* aufziehen; **2.** Pflege...

fought [fɔ:t] *pret. u. p.p. von* fight.

foul [faul] **1.** □ widerwärtig; schmutzig (*a. fig.*); unehrlich, regelwidrig; übelriechend; faul, verdorben; widrig; schlecht (*Wetter*); *fall* ~ *of* mit *dem Gesetz* in Konflikt kommen; **2.** Zs.-stoß *m*; *Sport:* regelwidriges Spiel; *through fair and* ~ durch dick und dünn; **3.** be-, verschmutzen; (sich) verwickeln.

found [faund] 1. *pret. u. p.p. von* find 1; 2. (be)gründen; stiften; ⊕ gießen.

foundation [faun'deiʃən] Gründung *f*; Stiftung *f*; Fundament *n*.

founder ['faundə] 1. (Be)Gründer (-in), Stifter(in); Gießer *m*; 2. *v/i.* scheitern; lahmen.

foundling ['faundliŋ] Findling *m*.

foundry ⊕ ['faundri] Gießerei *f*.

fountain ['fauntin] Quelle *f*; Springbrunnen *m*; **~pen** Füllfederhalter *m*.

four [fɔː] 1. vier; 2. Vier *f*; *Sport:* Vierer *m*; **~flusher** *Am. sl.* ['fɔː-'flʌʃə] Hochstapler *m*; **~square** viereckig; *fig.* unerschütterlich; **~stroke** *mot.* Viertakt...; **~teen** ['fɔː'tin] vierzehn; **~teenth** [ˌnθ] vierzehnte(r, -s); **~th** [fɔːθ] 1. vierte(r, -s); 2. Viertel *n*; **~thly** ['fɔːθli] viertens.

fowl [faul] Geflügel *n*; Huhn *n*; Vogel *m*; **~ing-piece** ['fauliŋpiːs] Vogelflinte *f*.

fox [fɔks] 1. Fuchs *m*; 2. überlisten; **~glove** ♀ ['fɔksglʌv] Fingerhut *m*; **~y** ['fɔksi] fuchsartig; schlau.

fraction ['frækʃən] Bruch(teil) *m*.

fracture ['fræktʃə] 1. (*bsd.* Knochen)Bruch *m*; 2. brechen.

fragile ['frædʒail] zerbrechlich.

fragment ['frægmənt] Bruchstück *n*.

fragran|ce ['freigrəns] Wohlgeruch *m*, Duft *m*; **~t** □ [ˌnt] wohlriechend.

frail □ [freil] ge-, zerbrechlich; schwach; **~ty** *fig.* ['freilti] Schwäche *f*.

frame [freim] 1. Rahmen *m*; Gerippe *n*; Gerüst *n*; (Brillen)Gestell *n*; Körper *m*; (An)Ordnung *f*; *phot.* (Einzel)Bild *n*; ♪ Frühbeetkasten *m*; **~ of mind** Gemütsverfassung *f*; 2. bilden, formen, bauen; entwerfen; (ein)rahmen; sich entwickeln; **~house** ['freimhaus] Holzhaus *n*; **~up** *bsd. Am.* F abgekartetes Spiel; **~work** ⊕ Gerippe *n*; Rahmen *m*; *fig.* Bau *m*.

franchise ⁊⁷⁄₂ ['fræntʃaiz] Wahlrecht *n*; Bürgerrecht *n*; *bsd. Am.* Konzession *f*.

frank [fræŋk] 1. □ frei(mütig), offen; 2. *Brief* maschinell frankieren.

frankfurter ['fræŋkfətə] Frankfurter Würstchen.

frankness ['fræŋknis] Offenheit *f*.

frantic ['fræntik] (~ally) wahnsinnig.

fratern|al □ [frə'təːnl] brüderlich; **~ity** [ˌniti] Brüderlichkeit *f*; Brüderschaft *f*; *Am. univ.* Verbindung *f*.

fraud [frɔːd] Betrug *m*; F Schwindel *m*; **~ulent** □ ['frɔːdjulənt] betrügerisch.

fray [frei] 1. (sich) abnutzen; (sich) durchscheuern; 2. Schlägerei *f*.

frazzle *bsd. Am.* F ['fræzl] 1. Fetzen *m/pl.*; 2. zerfetzen.

freak [friːk] Einfall *m*, Laune *f*.

freckle ['frekl] Sommersprosse *f*.

free [friː] 1. □ *allg.* frei; freigebig (of mit); freiwillig; he is ~ to inf. es steht ihm frei, zu *inf.*; ~ and easy zwanglos; sorglos; make ~ sich Freiheiten erlauben; set ~ freilassen; 2. befreien; freilassen, *et.* freimachen; **~booter** ['friːbuːtə] Freibeuter *m*; **~dom** ['friːdəm] Freiheit *f*; freie Benutzung; Offenheit *f*; Zwanglosigkeit *f*; (plumpe) Vertraulichkeit; ~ of a city (Ehren-) Bürgerrecht *n*; **~holder** Grundeigentümer *m*; **~man** freier Mann; Vollbürger *m*; **~mason** Freimaurer *m*; **~wheel** Freilauf *m*.

freez|e [friːz] (*irr.*) *v/i.* (ge)frieren; erstarren; *v/t.* gefrieren lassen; **~er** ['friːzə] Eismaschine *f*; Gefriermaschine *f*; Gefriertruhe *f*; **~ing** □ [ˌziŋ] eisig; **~point** Gefrierpunkt *m*.

freight [freit] 1. Fracht(geld *n*) *f*; *attr. Am.* Güter...; 2. be-, verfrachten; **~car** *Am.* ♙ ['freitkaː] Güterwagen *m*; **~train** *Am.* Güterzug *m*.

French [frentʃ] 1. französisch; take ~ leave heimlich weggehen; ~ window Balkon-, Verandatür *f*; 2. Französisch *n*; the ~ *pl.* die Franzosen *pl.*; **~man** ['frentʃmən] Franzose *m*.

frenz|ied ['frenzid] wahnsinnig; **~y** [ˌzi] Wahnsinn *m*.

frequen|cy ['friːkwənsi] Häufigkeit *f*; ⚡ Frequenz *f*; **~t** 1. □ [ˌnt] häufig; 2. [fri'kwent] (oft) besuchen.

fresh [freʃ] frisch; neu; unerfahren; *Am.* F frech; ~ water Süßwasser *n*; **~en** ['freʃn] frisch machen *od.* werden; **~et** [ˌʃit] Hochwasser *n*; *fig.* Flut *f*; **~man** *univ.* Student *m* im ersten Jahr; **~ness** [ˌʃnis] Frische *f*; Neuheit *f*; Unerfahrenheit *f*; **~water** Süßwasser...; ~ college *Am.* drittrangiges College.

fret [fret] 1. Aufregung *f*; Ärger *m*; ♪ Bund *m*, Griffleiste *f*; 2. zerfressen; (sich) ärgern; (sich) grämen; ~ away, ~ out aufreiben.

fretful □ ['fretful] ärgerlich.

fret-saw ['fretsɔː] Laubsäge *f*.

fretwork ['fretwəːk] (geschnitztes) Gitterwerk; Laubsägearbeit *f*.

friar ['fraiə] Mönch *m*.

friction ['frikʃən] Reibung *f* (*a. fig.*).

Friday ['fraidi] Freitag *m*.

fridge F [fridʒ] Kühlschrank *m*.

friend [frend] Freund(in); Bekannte(r *m*) *f*; **~ly** ['frendli] freund(schaft)lich; **~ship** [ˌdʃip] Freundschaft *f*.

frigate ⚓ ['frigit] Fregatte *f*.

frig(e) F [fridʒ] = *fridge*.

fright [frait] Schreck(en) m; fig. Vogelscheuche f; ~en ['fraitn] erschrecken; ~ed at od. of bange vor (dat.); ~ful □ [~tful] schrecklich.

frigid □ ['fridʒid] kalt, frostig.

frill [fril] Krause f, Rüsche f.

fringe [frindʒ] 1. Franse f; Rand m; a. ~s pl. Ponyfrisur f; 2. mit Fransen besetzen.

frippery ['fripəri] Flitterkram m. **Frisian** ['friziən] friesisch.

frisk [frisk] 1. Luftsprung m; 2. hüpfen; sl. nach Waffen etc. durchsuchen; ~y □ ['friski] munter.

fritter ['fritə] 1. Pfannkuchen m, Krapfen m; 2.: ~ away verzetteln.

frivol|ity [fri'vɔliti] Frivolität f, Leichtfertigkeit f; ~ous □ ['frivələs] nichtig; leichtfertig.

frizzle ['frizl] a. ~ up (sich) kräuseln; Küche: brutzeln.

fro [frou]: to and ~ hin und her.

frock [frɔk] Kutte f; Frauen-Kleid n; Kittel m; Gehrock m.

frog [frɔg] Frosch m.

frolic ['frɔlik] 1. Fröhlichkeit f; Scherz m; 2. scherzen, spaßen; ~some □ [~ksəm] lustig, fröhlich.

from [frɔm; frəm] von; aus, von ... her; von ... (an); aus, vor, wegen; nach, gemäß; defend ~ schützen vor (dat.); ~ amidst mitten aus.

front [frʌnt] 1. Stirn f; Vorderseite f; ✕ Front f; Hemdbrust f; Strandpromenade f; Kühnheit f, Frechheit f; in ~ vorn; in ~ of räumlich vor; 2. Vorder...; 3. a. ~ on, ~ towards die Front haben nach; gegenüberstehen, gegenübertreten (dat.); ~al ['frʌntl] Stirn...; Front-...; Vorder...; ~ door Haustür f; ~ier [~'tjə] Grenze f, bsd. Am. hist. Grenze zum Wilden Westen; attr. Grenz...; ~iersman [~əzmən] Grenzbewohner m; fig. Pionier m; ~ispiece [~tispi:s] ⚙ Vorderseite f; typ. Titelbild n; ~ man fig. Aushängefigur f; ~-page Zeitung: Titelseite f; ~-wheel drive mot. Vorderradantrieb m.

frost [frɔst] 1. Frost m; a. hoar ~ white ~ Reif m; 2. (mit Zucker) bestreuen; glasieren; mattieren; ~ed glass Milchglas n; ~-bite ❄ ['frɔstbait] Erfrierung f; ~y □ [~ti] frostig; bereift.

froth [frɔθ] 1. Schaum m; 2. schäumen; zu Schaum schlagen; ~y □ ['frɔθi] schaumig; fig. seicht.

frown [fraun] 1. Stirnrunzeln n; finsterer Blick; 2. v/i. die Stirn runzeln; finster blicken.

frow|sty □ ['frausti], ~zy ['frauzi] moderig; schlampig.

froze [frouz] pret. von freeze; ~n ['frouzn] 1. p.p. von freeze; 2. adj. (eis)kalt; (ein)gefroren.

frugal □ ['fru:gəl] mäßig, sparsam.

fruit [fru:t] 1. Frucht f; Früchte pl.; Obst n; 2. Frucht tragen; ~erer ['fru:tərə] Obsthändler m; ~ful □ [~tful] fruchtbar; ~less □ [~tlis] unfruchtbar.

frustrat|e [frʌs'treit] vereiteln; enttäuschen; ~ion [~'eiʃən] Vereitelung f; Enttäuschung f.

fry [frai] 1. Gebratene(s) n; Fischbrut f; 2. braten, backen; ~ing-pan ['fraiiŋpæn] Bratpfanne f.

fuchsia ⚘ ['fju:ʃə] Fuchsie f.

fudge [fʌdʒ] 1. F zurechtpfuschen; 2. Unsinn m; Weichkaramelle f.

fuel [fjuəl] 1. Brennmaterial n; Betriebs-, mot. Kraftstoff m; 2. mot. tanken.

fugitive ['fju:dʒitiv] 1. flüchtig (a. fig.); 2. Flüchtling m.

fulfil(l) [ful'fil] erfüllen; vollziehen; ~ment [~lmənt] Erfüllung f.

full [ful] 1. □ allg. voll; Voll...; vollständig, völlig; reichlich; ausführlich; of ~ age volljährig; 2. adv. völlig, ganz; genau; 3. Ganze(s) n; Höhepunkt m; in ~ völlig; ausführlich; to the ~ vollständig; ~-blooded ['ful'blʌdid] vollblütig; kräftig; reinrassig; ~ dress Gesellschaftsanzug m; ~-dress [~'fuldres] formell, Gala...; Am. ausführlich; ~-fledged ['ful'fledʒd] flügge; voll ausgewachsen; ~ stop Punkt m.

ful(l)ness ['fulnis] Fülle f.

full-time ['fultaim] vollbeschäftigt; Voll...

fulminate fig. ['fʌlmineit] wettern.

fumble ['fʌmbl] tasten; fummeln.

fume [fju:m] 1. Dunst m, Dampf m; 2. rauchen; aufgebracht sein.

fumigate ['fju:migeit] ausräuchern, desinfizieren.

fun [fʌn] Scherz m, Spaß m; make ~ of sich lustig machen über (acc.).

function ['fʌŋkʃən] 1. Funktion f; Beruf m; Tätigkeit f; Aufgabe f; Feierlichkeit f; 2. funktionieren; ~ary [~ʃnəri] Beamte(r) m; Funktionär m.

fund [fʌnd] 1. Fonds m; ~s pl. Staatspapiere n/pl.; Geld(mittel n/pl.) n; Vorrat m; 2. Schuld fundieren; Geld anlegen.

fundamental □ [fʌndə'mentl] 1. grundlegend; Grund...; 2. ~s pl. Grundlage f, -züge m/pl., -begriffe m/pl.

funer|al ['fju:nərəl] Beerdigung f; attr. Trauer...; Begräbnis...; ~eal □ [fju:(:)'niəriəl] traurig, düster.

fun-fair ['fʌnfeə] Rummelplatz m.

funicular [fju:(:)'nikjulə] 1. Seil...; 2. a. ~ railway (Draht)Seilbahn f.

funnel ['fʌnl] Trichter m; Rauchfang m; ⚓, 🚂 Schornstein m.

funnies Am. ['fʌniz] pl. Comics pl. (primitive Bildserien).

funny □ ['fʌni] spaßig, komisch.

fur [fə:] 1. Pelz *m*; Belag *m der Zunge*; Kesselstein *m*; ~s *pl.* Pelzwaren *pl.*; 2. mit Pelz besetzen *od.* füttern.

furbish ['fə:biʃ] putzen, polieren.

furious □ ['fjuəriəs] wütend; wild.

furl [fə:l] zs.-rollen; zs.-klappen.

furlough ✗ ['fə:lou] Urlaub *m*.

furnace ['fə:nis] Schmelz-, Hochofen *m*; (Heiz)Kessel *m*; Feuerung *f*.

furnish ['fə:niʃ] versehen (*with* mit); *et.* liefern; möblieren; ausstatten.

furniture ['fə:nitʃə] Möbel *pl.*, Einrichtung *f*; Ausstattung *f*; sectional ~ Anbaumöbel *pl.*

furrier ['fʌriə] Kürschner *m*.

furrow ['fʌrou] 1. Furche *f*; 2. furchen.

further ['fə:ðə] 1. *adj. u. adv.* ferner, weiter; 2. fördern; ~ance [~ərəns] Förderung *f*; ~more [~ə'mɔ:] ferner, überdies; ~most [~əmoust] weitest.

furthest ['fə:ðist] = furthermost.

furtive □ ['fə:tiv] verstohlen.

fury ['fjuəri] Raserei *f*, Wut *f*; Furie *f*.

fuse [fju:z] 1. (ver)schmelzen; ⚡ durchbrennen; ausgehen (*Licht*); ✗ mit Zünder versehen; 2. ⚡ (Schmelz)Sicherung *f*; ✗ Zünder *m*.

fuselage ['fju:zilɑ:ʒ] (Flugzeug-) Rumpf *m*.

fusion ['fju:ʒən] Schmelzen *n*; Verschmelzung *f*, Fusion *f*; ~ bomb ✗ Wasserstoffbombe *f*.

fuss F [fʌs] 1. Lärm *m*; Wesen *n*, Getue *n*; 2. viel Aufhebens machen (*about* um, von); (sich) aufregen.

fusty ['fʌsti] muffig; *fig.* verstaubt.

futile ['fju:tail] nutzlos, nichtig.

future ['fju:tʃə] 1. (zu)künftig; 2. Zukunft *f*; *gr.* Futur *n*, Zukunft *f*; ~s *pl.* † Termingeschäfte *n/pl.*

fuzz [fʌz] 1. feiner Flaum; Fussel *f*; 2. fusseln, (zer)fasern.

G

gab F [gæb] Geschwätz *n*; *the gift of the* ~ ein gutes Mundwerk.

gabardine ['gæbədi:n] Gabardine *m* (*Wollstoff*).

gabble ['gæbl] 1. Geschnatter *n*, Geschwätz *n*; 2. schnattern, schwatzen.

gaberdine ['gæbədi:n] Kaftan *m*; = gabardine.

gable ['geibl] Giebel *m*.

gad F [gæd]: ~ *about* sich herumtreiben.

gadfly *zo.* ['gædflai] Bremse *f*.

gadget *sl.* ['gædʒit] Dings *n*, Apparat *m*; Kniff *m*, Pfiff *m*.

gag [gæg] 1. Knebel *m*; Witz *m*; 2. knebeln; *pol.* mundtot machen.

gage¹ [geidʒ] Pfand *n*.

gage² [~] = gauge.

gaiety ['geiəti] Fröhlichkeit *f*.

gaily ['geili] *adv. von* gay.

gain [gein] 1. Gewinn *m*; Vorteil *m*; 2. *v/t.* gewinnen; erreichen; bekommen; *v/i.* vorgehen (*Uhr*); ~ in zunehmen an (*acc.*); ~ful □ ['geinful] einträglich.

gait [geit] Gang(art *f*) *m*; Schritt *m*.

gaiter ['geitə] Gamasche *f*.

gal *Am. sl.* [gæl] Mädel *n*.

gale [geil] Sturm *m*; steife Brise.

gall [gɔ:l] 1. Galle *f*; ✗ Wolf *m*; Pein *f*; *bsd. Am. sl.* Frechheit *f*; 2. wundreiben; ärgern.

gallant ['gælənt] 1. □ stattlich; tapfer, galant; höflich; 2. Kavalier *m*; 3. galant sein; ~ry [~tri] Tapferkeit *f*; Galanterie *f*.

gallery ['gæləri] Galerie *f*; Empore *f*.

galley ['gæli] ⚓ Galeere *f*; ⚓ Kombüse *f*; ~proof Korrekturfahne *f*.

gallon ['gælən] Gallone *f* (*4,54 Liter, Am. 3,78 Liter*).

gallop ['gæləp] 1. Galopp *m*; 2. galoppieren (lassen).

gallows ['gælouz] *sg.* Galgen *m*.

galore [gə'lɔ:] in Menge.

gamble ['gæmbl] (um Geld) spielen; 2. F Glücksspiel *n*; ~r [~lə] Spieler(in).

gambol ['gæmbəl] 1. Luftsprung *m*; 2. (fröhlich) hüpfen, tanzen.

game [geim] 1. Spiel *n*; Scherz *m*; Wild *n*; 2. F entschlossen; furchtlos; 3. spielen; ~keeper ['geimki:pə] Wildhüter *m*; ~licence Jagdschein *m*; ~ster ['geimstə] Spieler(in).

gander ['gændə] Gänserich *m*.

gang [gæŋ] 1. Trupp *m*; Bande *f*; 2. ~ *up* sich zs.-rotten *od.* zs.-tun; ~board ⚓ ['gæŋbɔ:d] Laufplanke *f*.

gangster *Am.* ['gæŋstə] Gangster *m*.

gangway ['gæŋwei] (Durch)Gang *m*; ⚓ Fallreep *n*; ⚓ Laufplanke *f*.

gaol [dʒeil], ~bird ['dʒeilbə:d], ~er ['dʒeilə] s. jail *etc.*

gap [gæp] Lücke *f*; Kluft *f*; Spalte *f*.

gape [geip] gähnen; klaffen; gaffen.

garage ['gærɑ:ʒ] 1. Garage *f*; Autowerkstatt *f*; 2. Auto einstellen.

garb [gɑ:b] Gewand *n*, Tracht *f*.

garbage ['gɑ:bidʒ] Abfall *m*;

Schund *m*; ~ *can Am.* Mülltonne *f*; ~ *pail* Mülleimer *m*.

garden ['gɑːdn] **1.** Garten *m*; **2.** Gartenbau treiben; ~**er** [~nə] Gärtner(in); ~**ing** [~niŋ] Gartenarbeit *f*.

gargle ['gɑːgl] **1.** gurgeln; **2.** Gurgelwasser *n*.

garish □ ['gɛəriʃ] grell, auffallend.

garland ['gɑːlənd] Girlande *f*.

garlic ♃ ['gɑːlik] Knoblauch *m*.

garment ['gɑːmənt] Gewand *n*.

garnish ['gɑːniʃ] garnieren; zieren.

garret ['gærət] Dachstube *f*.

garrison ⚔ ['gærisn] **1.** Besatzung *f*; Garnison *f*; **2.** mit e-r Besatzung belegen. [haft.\]

garrulous □ ['gæruləs] schwatz-

garter ['gɑːtə] Strumpfband *n*; *Am.* Socken-, Strumpfhalter *m*.

gas [gæs] **1.** Gas *n*; *Am.* = *gasoline*; **2.** *v/t.* vergasen; *v/i.* F faseln; ~**eous** ['geizjəs] gasförmig.

gash [gæʃ] **1.** klaffende Wunde; Hieb *m*; Riß *m*; **2.** tief (ein)schneiden in (*acc.*).

gas|-light ['gæslait] Gasbeleuchtung *f*; ~**-meter** Gasuhr *f*; ~**o-lene**, ~**oline** *Am. mot.* ['gæsəli:n] Benzin *n*.

gasp [gɑːsp] **1.** Keuchen *n*; **2.** keuchen; nach Luft schnappen.

gas|sed [gæst] gasvergiftet; ~**-stove** ['gæs'stouv] Gasofen *m*, -herd *m*; ~**works** ['gæswəːks] *sg.* Gaswerk *n*, -anstalt *f*.

gat *Am. sl.* [gæt] Revolver *m*.

gate [geit] Tor *n*; Pforte *f*; Sperre *f*; ~**man** ☞ ['geitmən] Schrankenwärter *m*; ~**way** Tor(weg *m*) *n*, Einfahrt *f*.

gather ['gæðə] **1.** *v/t.* (ein-, ver-) sammeln; ernten; pflücken; schließen (*from* aus); zs.-ziehen; kräuseln; ~ *speed* schneller werden; *v/i.* sich (ver)sammeln; sich vergrößern; ✚ *u. fig.* reifen; **2.** Falte *f*; ~**ing** [~əriŋ] Versammlung *f*; Zs.-kunft *f*.

gaudy □ ['gɔːdi] grell; protzig.

gauge [geidʒ] **1.** (Normal)Maß *n*; Maßstab *m*; ⊕ Lehre *f*; ☞ Spurweite *f*; Meßgerät *n*; **2.** eichen; (aus)messen; *fig.* abschätzen.

gaunt □ [gɔːnt] hager; finster.

gauntlet ['gɔːntlit] *fig.* Fehdehandschuh *m*; *run the* ~ Spießruten laufen.

gauze [gɔːz] Gaze *f*.

gave [geiv] *pret. von* give.

gavel *Am.* ['gævl] Hammer *m des Versammlungsleiters od. Auktionators*.

gawk F [gɔːk] Tölpel *m*; ~**y** [gɔːki] tölpisch.

gay □ [gei] lustig, heiter; bunt, lebhaft, glänzend.

gaze [geiz] **1.** starrer *od.* aufmerksamer Blick; **2.** starren.

gazette [gə'zet] **1.** Amtsblatt *n*; **2.** amtlich bekanntgeben.

gear [giə] **1.** ⊕ Getriebe *n*; *mot.* Gang *m*; Mechanismus *m*; Gerät *n*; *in* ~ mit eingelegtem Gang; *in* Betrieb; *out of* ~ im Leerlauf; außer Betrieb; *landing* ~ ✈ Fahrgestell *n*; *steering* ~ ⚓ Ruderanlage *f*; *mot.* Lenkung *f*; **2.** einschalten; ⊕ greifen; ~**ing** ['giəriŋ] (Zahnrad-) Getriebe *n*; Übersetzung *f*; ~**lever**, *bsd. Am.* ~**shift** Schalthebel *m*.

gee [dʒiː] **1.** *Kindersprache*: Hottehü *n* (*Pferd*); **2.** *Fuhrmannsruf*: hü! hott!; *Am.* nanu!, so was!

geese [giːs] *pl. von* goose.

gem [dʒem] Edelstein *m*; Gemme *f*; *fig.* Glanzstück *n*.

gender *gr.* ['dʒendə] Genus *n*, Geschlecht *n*.

general ['dʒenərəl] **1.** □ allgemein; gewöhnlich; Haupt..., General...; ~ *election* allgemeine Wahlen; **2.** ⚔ General *m*; Feldherr *m*; ~**ity** [dʒenə'ræliti] Allgemeinheit *f*; *die* große Masse; ~**ize** ['dʒenərəlaiz] verallgemeinern; ~**ly** [~li] im allgemeinen, überhaupt; gewöhnlich.

generat|e ['dʒenəreit] erzeugen; ~**ion** [dʒenə'reiʃən] (Er)Zeugung *f*; Generation *f*; Menschenalter *n*; ~**or** ['dʒenəreitə] Erzeuger *m*; ⊕ Generator *m*; *bsd. Am. mot.* Lichtmaschine *f*.

gener|osity [dʒenə'rɔsiti] Großmut *f*; Großzügigkeit *f*; ~**ous** □ ['dʒenərəs] großmütig, großzügig.

genial □ ['dʒiːnjəl] freundlich; anregend; gemütlich (*Person*); heiter.

genitive *gr.* ['dʒenitiv] *a.* ~ *case* Genitiv *m*.

genius ['dʒiːnjəs] Geist *m*; Genie *n*.

gent F [dʒent] Herr *m*.

genteel □ [dʒen'tiːl] vornehm; elegant.

gentile ['dʒentail] **1.** heidnisch, nichtjüdisch; **2.** Heid|e *m*, -in *f*.

gentle □ ['dʒentl] sanft, mild; zahm; leise, sacht; vornehm; ~**man** Herr *m*; Gentleman *m*; ~**manlike**, ~**manly** [~li] gebildet; vornehm; ~**ness** [~lnis] Sanftheit *f*; Milde *f*, Güte *f*, Sanftmut *f*.

gentry ['dʒentri] niederer Adel; gebildete Stände *m/pl.*

genuine □ ['dʒenjuin] echt; aufrichtig.

geography [dʒi'ɔgrəfi] Geographie *f*.

geology [dʒi'ɔlədʒi] Geologie *f*.

geometry [dʒi'ɔmitri] Geometrie *f*.

germ [dʒəːm] **1.** Keim *m*; **2.** keimen.

German[1] ['dʒəːmən] **1.** deutsch; **2.** Deutsche(r *m*) *f*; Deutsch *n*.

german[2] [~] *brother* ~ leiblicher Bruder; ~**e** [dʒəː'mein] (*to*) verwandt (mit); entsprechend (*dat.*).

germinate ['dʒəːmineit] keimen.

gesticulat|e [dʒes'tikjuleit] gestikulieren; **~ion** [dʒestikju'leiʃən] Gebärdenspiel n.
gesture ['dʒestʃə] Geste f, Gebärde f.
get [get] [irr.] v/t. erhalten, bekommen, F kriegen; besorgen; holen; bringen; erwerben; verdienen; ergreifen, fassen; (veran)lassen; mit adv. mst bringen, machen; have got haben; ~ one's hair cut sich das Haar schneiden lassen; ~ by heart auswendig lernen; v/i. gelangen, geraten, kommen; gehen; werden; ~ ready sich fertig machen; ~ about auf den Beinen sein; ~ abroad bekannt werden; ~ ahead vorwärtskommen; ~ at (heran)kommen an ... (acc.); zu et. kommen; ~ away wegkommen; sich fortmachen; ~ in einsteigen; ~ on with s.o. mit j-m auskommen; ~ out aussteigen; ~ to hear (know, learn) erfahren; ~ up aufstehen; **~-up** ['getʌp] Aufmachung f; Am. F Unternehmungsgeist m.
ghastly ['gɑːstli] gräßlich; schrecklich; (toten)bleich; gespenstisch.
gherkin ['gəːkin] Gewürzgurke f.
ghost [goust] Geist m, Gespenst n; fig. Spur f; **~like** ['goustlaik], **~ly** [~li] geisterhaft.
giant ['dʒaiənt] 1. riesig; 2. Riese m.
gibber ['dʒibə] kauderwelschen; **~ish** ['gibəriʃ] Kauderwelsch n.
gibbet ['dʒibit] 1. Galgen m; 2. hängen.
gibe [dʒaib] verspotten, aufziehen.
giblets ['dʒiblits] pl. Gänseklein n.
gidd|iness ['gidinis] ✠ Schwindel m; Unbeständigkeit f; Leichtsinn m; **~y** □ ['gidi] schwind(e)lig; leichtfertig; unbeständig; albern.
gift [gift] Gabe f; Geschenk n; Talent n; **~ed** ['giftid] begabt.
gigantic [dʒai'gæntik] (~ally) riesenhaft, riesig, gigantisch.
giggle ['gigl] 1. kichern; 2. Gekicher n.
gild [gild] [irr.] vergolden; verschönen; **~ed youth** Jeunesse f dorée.
gill [gil] ichth. Kieme f; ♀ Lamelle f.
gilt [gilt] 1. pret. u. p.p. von gild; 2. Vergoldung f.
gimmick Am. sl. ['gimik] Trick m.
gin [dʒin] Gin m (Wacholderschnaps); Schlinge f; ⊕ Entkörnungsmaschine f.
ginger ['dʒindʒə] 1. Ingwer m; Lebhaftigkeit f; 2. ~ up in Schwung bringen; 3. hellrot, rötlich-gelb; **~bread** Pfefferkuchen m; **~ly** [~əli] zimperlich; sachte.
gipsy ['dʒipsi] Zigeuner(in).
gird [gəːd] sticheln; [irr.] (um)gürten; umgeben.
girder ⊕ ['gəːdə] Tragbalken m.

girdle ['gəːdl] 1. Gürtel m; Hüfthalter m, -gürtel m; 2. umgürten.
girl [gəːl] Mädchen n; ♀ Guide ['gəːlgaid] Pfadfinderin f; **~hood** ['gəːlhud] Mädchenzeit f; Mädchenjahre n/pl.; **~ish** □ ['gəːliʃ] mädchenhaft; **~y** Am. F ['gəːli] mit spärlich bekleideten Mädchen (Magazin, Varieté etc.).
girt [gəːt] pret. u. p.p. von gird.
girth [gəːθ] (Sattel)Gurt m; Umfang m.
gist [dʒist] das Wesentliche.
give [giv] [irr.] v/t. geben; ab-, übergeben; her-, hingeben; überlassen; zum besten geben; schenken; gewähren; von sich geben; ergeben; ~ birth to zur Welt bringen; ~ away verschenken; F verraten; ~ forth von sich geben; herausgeben; ~ in einreichen; ~ up Geschäft etc. aufgeben; j-n ausliefern; v/i. mst ~ in nachgeben; weichen; ~ into, ~ (up)on hinausgeben auf (acc.) (Fenster etc.); ~ out aufhören; versagen; **~ and take** [givən'teik] (Meinungs)Austausch m; Kompromiß m, n; **~away** Preisgabe f; ~ show od. program bsd. Am. Radio, Fernsehen: öffentliches Preisraten; **~n** ['givn] 1. p.p. von give; 2. ~ to ergeben (dat.).
glaci|al □ ['gleisjəl] eisig; Eis...; Gletscher...; **~er** ['glæsjə] Gletscher m.
glad □ [glæd] froh, erfreut; erfreulich; **~ly** gern; **~den** ['glædn] erfreuen.
glade [gleid] Lichtung f; Am. sumpfige Niederung.
gladness ['glædnis] Freude f.
glair [glɛə] Eiweiß n.
glamo|rous ['glæmərəs] bezaubernd; **~(u)r** ['glæmə] 1. Zauber m, Glanz m, Reiz m; 2. bezaubern.
glance [glɑːns] 1. Schimmer m, Blitz m; flüchtiger Blick; 2. hinweggleiten; mst ~ off abprallen; blitzen; glänzen; ~ at flüchtig ansehen; anspielen auf (acc.).
gland anat. [glænd] Drüse f.
glare [glɛə] 1. grelles Licht; wilder, starrer Blick; 2. grell leuchten; wild blicken; (at an)starren.
glass [glɑːs] 1. Glas n; Spiegel m; Opern-, Fernglas n; Barometer n; (a pair of) ~es pl. (eine) Brille; 2. gläsern; Glas...; 3. verglasen; **~case** ['glɑːskeis] Vitrine f; Schaukasten m; **~house** Treibhaus n; ✗ sl. Bau m; **~y** [~si] gläsern; glasig.
glaz|e [gleiz] 1. Glasur f; 2. v/t. verglasen; glasieren; polieren; v/i. trüb(e) od. glasig werden (Auge); **~ier** ['gleizjə] Glaser m.
gleam [gliːm] 1. Schimmer m, Schein m; 2. schimmern.

glean [gli:n] v/t. sammeln; v/i. Ähren lesen.

glee [gli:] Fröhlichkeit f; mehrstimmiges Lied; ~ club Gesangverein m.

glen [glen] Bergschlucht f.

glib □ [glib] glatt, zungenfertig.

glid|e [glaid] 1. Gleiten n; ⚓ Gleitflug m; 2. (dahin)gleiten (lassen); e-n Gleitflug machen; ~er ['glaidə] Segelflugzeug n.

glimmer ['glimə] 1. Schimmer m; min. Glimmer m; 2. schimmern.

glimpse [glimps] 1. flüchtiger Blick (of auf acc.); Schimmer m; flüchtiger Eindruck; 2. flüchtig (er)blicken.

glint [glint] 1. blitzen, glitzern; 2. Lichtschein m.

glisten ['glisn], **glitter** ['glitə] glitzern, glänzen.

gloat [glout]: ~ (up)on od. over sich weiden an (dat.).

globe [gloub] (Erd)Kugel f; Globus m.

gloom [glu:m], ~iness ['glu:minis] Düsterkeit f, Dunkelheit f; Schwermut f; ~y □ ['glu:mi] dunkel, düster; schwermütig; verdrießlich.

glori|fy ['glɔːrifai] verherrlichen; ~ous □ [~iəs] herrlich; glorreich.

glory ['glɔːri] 1. Ruhm m; Herrlichkeit f, Pracht f; Glorienschein m; 2. frohlocken; stolz sein.

gloss [glɔs] 1. Glosse f, Bemerkung f; Glanz m; 2. Glossen machen (zu); Glanz geben (dat.); ~ over beschönigen.

glossary ['glɔsəri] Wörterverzeichnis n.

glossy □ ['glɔsi] glänzend, blank.

glove [glʌv] Handschuh m.

glow [glou] 1. Glühen n; Glut f; 2. glühen.

glower ['glauə] finster blicken.

glow-worm ['glouwə:m] Glühwürmchen n.

glucose ['glu:kous] Traubenzucker m.

glue [glu:] 1. Leim m; 2. leimen.

glum □ [glʌm] mürrisch.

glut [glʌt] überfüllen.

glutinous □ ['glu:tinəs] klebrig.

glutton ['glʌtn] Unersättliche(r m) f; Vielfraß m; ~ous □ [~nəs] gefräßig; ~y [~ni] Gefräßigkeit f.

G-man Am. F ['dʒiːmæn] FBI-Agent m.

gnarl [nɑːl] Knorren m, Ast m.

gnash [næʃ] knirschen (mit).

gnat [næt] (Stech)Mücke f.

gnaw [nɔː] (zer)nagen; (zer)fressen.

gnome [noum] Erdgeist m, Gnom m.

go [gou] 1. [irr.] allg. gehen, fahren; vergehen (Zeit); werden; führen (to nach); sich wenden (to an); funktionieren, arbeiten; passen; kaputtgehen; let ~ loslassen; ~

shares teilen; ~ to od. and see besuchen; ~ at losgehen auf (acc.); ~ between vermitteln (zwischen); ~ by sich richten nach; ~ for gehen nach, holen; ~ for a walk, etc. einen Spaziergang etc. machen; ~ in for an examination e-e Prüfung machen; ~ on weitergehen; fortfahren; ~ through durchgehen; durchmachen; ~ without sich behelfen ohne; 2. F Mode f; Schwung m, Schneid m; on the ~ auf den Beinen; im Gange; it is no ~ es geht nicht; in one ~ auf Anhieb; have a ~ at es versuchen mit.

goad [goud] 1. Stachelstock m; fig. Ansporn m; 2. fig. anstacheln.

go-ahead F ['gouəhed] 1. zielstrebig; unternehmungslustig; 2. bsd. Am. F Erlaubnis f zum Weitermachen.

goal [goul] Mal n; Ziel n; Fußball: Tor n; ~keeper ['goulki:pə] Torwart m.

goat [gout] Ziege f, Geiß f.

gob [gɔb] ∨ Schleimklumpen m; F Maul n; Am. F Blaujacke f (Matrose).

gobble ['gɔbl] gierig verschlingen; ~dygook Am. sl. [~ldiguk] Amts-, Berufsjargon m; Geschwafel n; ~r [~lə] Vielfraß m; Truthahn m.

go-between ['goubitwiːn] Vermittler(in).

goblet ['gɔblit] Kelchglas n; Pokal m.

goblin ['gɔblin] Kobold m, Gnom m.

god, eccl. ♀ [gɔd] Gott m; fig. Abgott m; ~child ['gɔdtʃaild] Patenkind n; ~dess [~dis] Göttin f; ~father Pate m; ~head Gottheit f; ~less ['gɔdlis] gottlos; ~like gottähnlich; göttlich; ~ly [~li] gottesfürchtig; fromm; ~mother Patin f.

go-getter Am. sl. ['gou'getə] Draufgänger m.

goggle ['gɔgl] 1. glotzen; 2. ~s pl. Schutzbrille f.

going ['gouiŋ] 1. gehend; im Gange (befindlich); be ~ to inf. im Begriff sein zu inf., gleich tun wollen od. werden; 2. Gehen n; Vorwärtskommen n; Straßenzustand m; Geschwindigkeit f, Leistung f; ~s-on F [~ŋz'ɔn] pl. Treiben n.

gold [gould] 1. Gold n; 2. golden; ~digger Am. F ['goulddigə] Goldgräber m; ~en mst fig. [~dən] golden, goldgelb; ~finch zo. Stieglitz m; ~smith Goldschmied m.

golf [gɔlf] 1. Golf(spiel) n; 2. Golf spielen; ~course ['gɔlfkɔːs], ~ links pl. Golfplatz m.

gondola ['gɔndələ] Gondel f.

gone [gɔn] 1. p.p. von go 1; 2. adj. fort; F futsch; vergangen; tot; F hoffnungslos.

good [gud] 1. allg. gut; artig; gütig;

† zahlungsfähig; gründlich; ~ *at* geschickt in (*dat.*); **2.** Gute(s) *n*; Wohl *n*, Beste(s) *n*; ~s *pl.* Waren *f*/*pl.*; Güter *n*/*pl.*; *that's no* ~ das nützt nichts; *for* ~ für immer; **~by(e) 1.** [gud'bai] Lebewohl *n*; **2.** ['gud'bai] (auf) Wiedersehen!; ♀ **Friday** Karfreitag *m*; **~ly** ['gudli] anmutig, hübsch; *fig.* ansehnlich; **~natured** gutmütig; **~ness** [~nis] Güte *f*; *das Beste*; *thank* ~! Gott sei Dank!; **~will** Wohlwollen *n*; † Kundschaft *f*; † Firmenwert *m*.

goody ['gudi] Bonbon *m*, *n*.

goon *Am. sl.* [gu:n] bestellter Schläger *bsd. für Streik*; Dummkopf *m*.

goose [gu:s], *pl.* **geese** [gi:s] Gans *f* (*a. fig.*); Bügeleisen *n*.

gooseberry ['guzbəri] Stachelbeere *f*.

goose|-flesh ['gu:sfleʃ], *Am.* **~pimples** *pl. fig.* Gänsehaut *f*.

gopher *bsd. Am.* ['goufə] Erdeichhörnchen *n*.

gore [gɔ:] **1.** (geronnenes) Blut; *Schneiderei*: Keil *m*; **2.** durchbohren, aufspießen.

gorge [gɔ:dʒ] **1.** Kehle *f*, Schlund *m*; enge (Fels)Schlucht *f*; **2.** (ver-)schlingen; (sich) vollstopfen.

gorgeous □ ['gɔ:dʒəs] prächtig.

gory □ ['gɔ:ri] blutig.

gospel ['gɔspəl] Evangelium *n*.

gossip ['gɔsip] **1.** Geschwätz *n*; Klatschbase *f*; **2.** schwatzen.

got [gɔt] *pret. u. p.p. von* **get**.

Gothic ['gɔθik] gotisch; *fig.* barbarisch.

gotten *Am.* ['gɔtn] *p.p. von* **get**.

gouge [gaudʒ] **1.** ⊕ Hohlmeißel *m*; **2.** ausmeißeln; *Am.* F betrügen.

gourd ♀ [guəd] Kürbis *m*.

gout ♂ [gaut] Gicht *f*.

govern ['gʌvən] *v/t.* regieren, beherrschen; lenken, leiten; *v/i.* herrschen; **~ess** [~nis] Erzieherin *f*; **~ment** ['gʌvnmənt] Regierung(s-form) *f*; Leitung *f*; Herrschaft *f* (*of* über *acc.*); Ministerium *n*; Statthalterschaft *f*; *attr.* Staats...; **~mental** [gʌvən'mentl] Regierungs...; **~or** ['gʌvənə] Gouverneur *m*; Direktor *m*, Präsident *m*; F Alte(r) *m* (*Vater, Chef*).

gown [gaun] **1.** (Frauen)Kleid *n*; Robe *f*, Talar *m*; **2.** kleiden.

grab F [græb] **1.** grapsen; an sich reißen, packen; **2.** plötzlich(er) Griff; ⊕ Greifer *m*; **~bag** *bsd. Am.* Glückstopf *m*.

grace [greis] **1.** Gnade *f*; Gunst *f*; (Gnaden)Frist *f*; Grazie *f*, Anmut *f*; Anstand *m*; Zier(de) *f*; Reiz *m*; Tischgebet *n*; *Your* ♀ Euer Gnaden; **2.** zieren, schmücken; begünstigen, auszeichnen; **~ful** [~greisful] anmutig; **~fulness** [~nis] Anmut *f*.

gracious □ ['greiʃəs] gnädig.

gradation [grə'deiʃən] Abstufung *f*.

grade [greid] **1.** Grad *m*, Rang *m*; Stufe *f*; Qualität *f*; *bsd. Am.* = *gradient*; *Am. Schule*: Klasse *f*, Note *f*; *make the* ~ *Am.* Erfolg haben; ~ *crossing bsd. Am.* schienengleicher Bahnübergang; **~(d)** *school bsd. Am.* Grundschule *f*; **2.** abstufen; einstufen; ⊕ planieren.

gradient 🜨 *etc.* ['greidjənt] Steigung *f*.

gradua|l □ ['grædjuəl] stufenweise, allmählich; **~te 1.** [~ueit] graduieren; (sich) abstufen; die Abschlußprüfung machen; promovieren; **2.** *univ.* [~uit] Graduierte(r) *m*) *f*; **~tion** [grædju'eiʃən] Gradeinteilung *f*; Abschlußprüfung *f*; Promotion *f*.

graft [grɑ:ft] **1.** ♐ Pfropfreis *n*; *Am.* Schiebung *f*; **2.** ♐ pfropfen; ♐ verpflanzen; *Am. fig.* schieben.

grain [grein] (Samen)Korn *n*; Getreide *n*; Gefüge *n*; *fig.* Natur *f*; Gran *n* (*Gewicht*).

gram [græm] = *gramme*.

gramma|r ['græmə] Grammatik *f*; **~r-school** höhere Schule, Gymnasium *n*; *Am. a.* Mittelschule *f*; **~tical** □ [grə'mætikəl] grammati(kali)sch.

gramme [græm] Gramm *n*.

granary ['grænəri] Kornspeicher *m*.

grand □ [grænd] **1.** *fig.* großartig; erhaben; groß; Groß..., Haupt...; ♀ *Old Party Am.* Republikanische Partei; ~ *stand Sport*: (Haupt-)Tribüne *f*; **2.** ♪ *a.* ~ *piano* Flügel *m*; *Am. sl.* tausend Dollar *pl.*; **~child** ['græntʃaild] Enkel(in); **~eur** [~ndʒə] Größe *f*, Hoheit *f*; Erhabenheit *f*; **~father** Großvater *m*.

grandiose □ ['grændious] großartig.

grand|mother ['grænmʌðə] Großmutter *f*; **~parents** [~npeərənts] *pl.* Großeltern *pl.*

grange [greindʒ] Gehöft *n*; Gut *n*; *Am.* Name für Farmerorganisation *f*.

granny F ['græni] Oma *f*.

grant [grɑ:nt] **1.** Gewährung *f*; Unterstützung *f*; Stipendium *n*; **2.** gewähren; bewilligen; verleihen; zugestehen; ⚖ übertragen; *take for* ~ed als selbstverständlich annehmen.

granul|ate ['grænjuleit] (sich) körnen; **~e** [~ju:l] Körnchen *n*.

grape [greip] Weinbeere *f*, -traube *f*; **~fruit** ♀ ['greipfru:t] Pampelmuse *f*.

graph [græf] graphische Darstellung; **~ic(al** □) ['græfik(əl)] graphisch; anschaulich; *graphic arts pl.* Graphik *f*; **~ite** *min.* [~fait] Graphit *m*.

grapple ['græpl] entern; packen; ringen.

grasp [grɑːsp] **1.** Griff *m*; Bereich *m*; Beherrschung *f*; Fassungskraft *f*; **2.** (er)greifen, packen; begreifen.

grass [grɑːs] Gras *n*; Rasen *m*; **send to ~** auf die Weide schicken; **~hopper** ['grɑːshɔpə] Heuschrecke *f*; **~ roots** *pl. Am. pol. die* landwirtschaftlichen Bezirke, *die* Landbevölkerung; **~widow(er)** F Strohwitwe(r *m*) *f*; **~y** [~si] grasig; Gras...

grate [greit] **1.** (Kamin)Gitter *n*; (Feuer)Rost *m*; **2.** (zer)reiben; mit *et.* knirschen; *fig.* verletzen.

grateful □ ['greitful] dankbar.

grater ['greitə] Reibeisen *n*.

grati|fication [grætifi'keiʃən] Befriedigung *f*; Freude *f*; **~fy** ['grætifai] erfreuen; befriedigen.

grating ['greitiŋ] **1.** □ schrill; unangenehm; **2.** Gitter(werk) *n*.

gratitude ['grætitjuːd] Dankbarkeit *f*.

gratuit|ous □ [grə'tjuː(:)itəs] unentgeltlich; freiwillig; **~y** [~ti] Abfindung *f*; Gratifikation *f*; Trinkgeld *n*.

grave [greiv] **1.** □ ernst; (ge)wichtig; gemessen; **2.** Grab *n*; **3.** [*irr.*] *mst fig.* (ein)graben; **~-digger** ['greivdigə] Totengräber *m*.

gravel ['grævəl] **1.** Kies *m*; Harngrieß *m*; **2.** mit Kies bedecken.

graven ['greivən] *p.p. von* grave 3.

graveyard ['greivjɑːd] Kirchhof *m*.

gravitation [grævi'teiʃən] Schwerkraft *f*; *fig.* Hang *m*.

gravity ['græviti] Schwere *f*; Wichtigkeit *f*; Ernst *m*; Schwerkraft *f*.

gravy ['greivi] Fleischsaft *m*, Bratensoße *f*.

gray *bsd. Am.* [grei] *= grey*.

graze [greiz] (ab)weiden; (ab)grasen; streifen, schrammen.

grease 1. [griːs] Fett *n*; Schmiere *f*; **2.** [griːz] (be)schmieren.

greasy □ ['griːzi] fettig; schmierig.

great [greit] *allg.* groß; Groß...; F großartig; **~coat** ['greit'kout] Überzieher *m*; **~-grandchild** Urenkel(in); **~-grandfather** Urgroßvater *m*; **~ly** [~tli] sehr; **~ness** [~tnis] Größe *f*; Stärke *f*.

greed [griːd] Gier *f*; **~y** □ ['griːdi] (be)gierig (of, for nach); habgierig.

Greek [griːk] **1.** griechisch; **2.** Griech|e *m*, -in *f*; Griechisch *n*.

green [griːn] **1.** □ grün (a. fig.); frisch (Fisch etc.); neu; Grün...; **2.** Grün *n*; Rasen *m*; Wiese *f*; **~s** *pl.* frisches Gemüse; **~back** *Am.* ['griːnbæk] Dollarnote *f*; **~grocer** Gemüsehändler(in); **~grocery** Gemüsehandlung *f*; **~horn** Grünschnabel *m*; **~house** Gewächshaus *n*; **~ish** [~niʃ] grünlich; **~sickness** Bleichsucht *f*.

greet [griːt] (be)grüßen; **~ing** ['griːtiŋ] Begrüßung *f*; Gruß *m*.

grenade ✗ [gri'neid] Granate *f*.

grew [gruː] *pret. von* grow.

grey [grei] **1.** □ grau; **2.** Grau *n*; **3.** grau machen *od.* werden; **~hound** ['greihaund] Windhund *m*.

grid [grid] Gitter *n*; Netz *n*; *Am. Fußball:* Spielfeld *n*; **~iron** ['gridaiən] (Brat)Rost *m*.

grief [griːf] Gram *m*, Kummer *m*; **come to ~** zu Schaden kommen.

griev|ance ['griːvəns] Beschwerde *f*; Mißstand *m*; **~e** [griːv] kränken; (sich) grämen; **~ous** □ ['griːvəs] kränkend, schmerzlich; schlimm.

grill [gril] **1.** grillen; braten (a. fig.); **2.** Bratrost *m*, Grill *m*; gegrilltes Fleisch; a. **~-room** Grillroom *m*.

grim □ [grim] grimmig; schrecklich.

grimace [gri'meis] **1.** Fratze *f*, Grimasse *f*; **2.** Grimassen schneiden.

grim|e [graim] Schmutz *m*; Ruß *m*; **~y** □ ['graimi] schmutzig; rußig.

grin [grin] **1.** Grinsen *n*; **2.** grinsen.

grind [graind] **1.** [*irr.*] (zer)reiben; mahlen; schleifen; *Leierkasten etc.* drehen; *fig.* schinden; mit *den* Zähnen knirschen; **2.** Schinderei *f*; **~stone** ['graindstoun] Schleif-, Mühlstein *m*.

grip [grip] **1.** packen, fassen (a. fig.); **2.** Griff *m*; Gewalt *f*; Herrschaft *f*; *Am. = gripsack.*

gripe [graip] Griff *m*; **~s** *pl.* Kolik *f*; *bsd. Am.* Beschwerden *f*/*pl.*

gripsack *Am.* ['gripsæk] Handtasche *f*, -köfferchen *n*.

grisly □ ['grizli] gräßlich, schrecklich.

gristle ['grisl] Knorpel *m*.

grit [grit] **1.** Kies *m*; Sand(stein) *m*; *fig.* Mut *m*; **2.** knirschen (mit).

grizzly ['grizli] **1.** grau; **2.** Graubär *m*.

groan [groun] seufzen, stöhnen.

grocer ['grousə] Lebensmittelhändler *m*; **~ies** [~əriz] *pl.* Lebensmittel *n*/*pl.*; **~y** [~ri] Lebensmittelgeschäft *n*.

groceteria *Am.* [grousi'tiəriə] Selbstbedienungsladen *m*.

groggy ['grɔgi] taumelig; wackelig.

groin *anat.* [grɔin] Leistengegend *f*.

groom [grum] **1.** Reit-, Stallknecht *m*; Bräutigam *m*; **2.** pflegen; *Am. pol.* Kandidaten lancieren.

groove [gruːv] **1.** Rinne *f*, Nut *f*; *fig.* Gewohnheit *f*; **2.** nuten, falzen.

grope [group] (be)tasten, tappen.

gross [grous] **1.** □ dick; grob; derb; ✝ Brutto...; **2.** Gros *n* (12 Dutzend); **in the ~** im ganzen.

grotto ['grɔtou] Grotte *f*.

grouch *Am.* F [grautʃ] **1.** quengeln, meckern; **2.** Griesgram *m*; schlechte Laune; **~y** ['grautʃi] quenglig.

ground[1] [graund] **1.** *pret. u. p.p. von* **grind** 1; **2.** ~ *glass* Mattglas *n.*

ground[2] [graund] **1.** *mst* Grund *m*; Boden *m*; Gebiet *n*; *Spiel- etc.* Platz *m*; *Beweg- etc.* Grund *m*; ⚡ Erde *f*; ~s *pl.* Grundstück *n*, Park(s *pl.*) *m*, Gärten *m/pl.*; Kaffee-Satz *m*; *on the* ~(s) *of* auf Grund (*gen.*); *stand od. hold od. keep one's* ~ sich behaupten; **2.** niederlegen; (be)gründen; *j-m die* Anfangs-gründe beibringen; ⚡ erden; ~ **floor** ['graund'flɔ:] Erdgeschoß *n*; ~-**hog** [~dhɔg] *bsd. Am.* Murmel-tier *n*; ~**less** □ [~dlis] grundlos; ~-**staff** ✈ Bodenpersonal *n*; ~-**work** Grundlage *f.*

group [gru:p] **1.** Gruppe *f*; **2.** (sich) gruppieren.

grove [grouv] Hain *m*; Gehölz *n.*

grovel *mst fig.* ['grɔvl] kriechen.

grow [grou] [*irr.*] *v/i.* wachsen; werden; *v/t.* ⚘ anpflanzen, an-bauen; ~**er** ['grouə] Bauer *m*, Züchter *m.*

growl [graul] knurren, brummen; ~**er** ['graulə] *fig.* Brummbär *m*; *Am. sl.* Bierkrug *m.*

grow|n [groun] **1.** *p.p. von* grow; **2.** *adj.* erwachsen; bewachsen; ~**n-up** ['grounʌp] **1.** erwachsen; **2.** Erwachsene(r *m*) *f*; ~**th** [grouθ] Wachstum *n*; (An)Wachsen *n*; Ent-wicklung *f*; Wuchs *m*; Gewächs *n*, Erzeugnis *n.*

grub [grʌb] **1.** Raupe *f*, Larve *f*, Made *f*; *contp.* Prolet *m*; **2.** graben; sich abmühen; ~**by** ['grʌbi] schmie-rig.

grudge [grʌdʒ] **1.** Groll *m*; **2.** miß-gönnen; ungern geben *od.* tun *etc.*

gruel [gruəl] Haferschleim *m.*

gruff □ [grʌf] grob, schroff, barsch.

grumble ['grʌmbl] murren; (g)rol-len; ~**r** *fig.* [~lə] Brummbär *m.*

grunt [grʌnt] grunzen.

guarant|ee [gærən'ti:] **1.** Bürge *m*; = guaranty; **2.** bürgen für; ~**or** [~'tɔ:] Bürge *m*; ~**y** ['gærənti] Bürg-schaft *f*, Garantie *f*; Gewähr *f.*

guard [gɑ:d] **1.** Wacht *f*; ⚔ Wache *f*; Wächter *m*, Wärter *m*; 🚂 Schaffner *m*; Schutz(vorrichtung *f*) *m*; ⚔s *pl.* Garde *f*; *be on (off) one's* ~ (nicht) auf der Hut sein; **2.** *v/t.* bewachen, (be)schützen (*from* vor *dat.*); *v/i.* sich hüten (*against* vor *dat.*); ~**ian** ['gɑ:djən] Hüter *m*, Wächter *m*; 🏛 Vormund *m*; *attr.* Schutz...; ~**ianship** [~nʃip] Obhut *f*; Vor-mundschaft *f.*

guess [ges] **1.** Vermutung *f*; **2.** ver-muten; (er)raten; *Am.* denken.

guest [gest] Gast *m*; ~-**house** ['gesthaus] (Hotel)Pension *f*, Frem-denheim *n*; ~-**room** Gast-, Frem-denzimmer *n.*

guffaw [gʌ'fɔ:] schallendes Ge-lächter.

guidance ['gaidəns] Führung *f*; (An)Leitung *f.*

guide [gaid] **1.** Führer *m*; ⊕ Füh-rung *f*; *attr.* Führungs...; **2.** leiten; führen; lenken; ~-**book** ['gaidbuk] Reiseführer *m*; ~-**post** Wegweiser *m.*

guild [gild] Gilde *f*, Innung *f*; ♀**hall** ['gild'hɔ:l] Rathaus *n* (*Lon-don*).

guile [gail] Arglist *f*; ~**ful** □ ['gailful] arglistig; ~**less** □ ['gaillis] arglos.

guilt [gilt] Schuld *f*; Strafbarkeit *f*; ~**less** □ ['giltlis] schuldlos; un-kundig; ~**y** □ [~ti] schuldig; straf-bar.

guinea ['gini] Guinee *f* (*21 Schil-ling*); ~-**pig** Meerschweinchen *n.*

guise [gaiz] Erscheinung *f*, Gestalt *f*; Maske *f.*

guitar 🎵 [gi'tɑ:] Gitarre *f.*

gulch *Am.* [gʌlʃ] tiefe Schlucht.

gulf [gʌlf] Meerbusen *m*, Golf *m*; Abgrund *m*; Strudel *m.*

gull [gʌl] **1.** Möwe *f*; Tölpel *m*; **2.** übertölpeln; verleiten (*into* zu).

gullet ['gʌlit] Speiseröhre *f*; Gur-gel *f.*

gulp [gʌlp] Schluck *m*; Schlucken *n.*

gum [gʌm] **1.** *a.* ~s *pl.* Zahnfleisch *n*; Gummi *n*; Klebstoff *m*; ~s *pl. Am.* Gummischuhe *m/pl.*; **2.** gummie-ren; zukleben.

gun [gʌn] **1.** Gewehr *n*; Flinte *f*; Geschütz *n*, Kanone *f*; *Am.* Re-volver *m*; *big* ~ F *fig.* hohes Tier; **2.** *Am.* auf die Jagd gehen; ~-**boat** ['gʌnbout] Kanonenboot *n*; ~-**licence** Waffenschein *m*; ~-**man** *Am.* Gangster *m*; ~-**ner** ⚔, ⚓ ['gʌnə] Kanonier *m*; ~-**powder** Schießpulver *n*; ~-**smith** Büchsen-macher *m.*

gurgle ['gə:gl] gluckern, gur-geln.

gush [gʌʃ] **1.** Guß *m*; *fig.* Erguß *m*; **2.** (sich) ergießen, schießen (*from* aus); *fig.* schwärmen; ~-**er** ['gʌʃə] *fig.* Schwärmer(in); Ölquelle *f.*

gust [gʌst] Windstoß *m*, Bö *f.*

gut [gʌt] Darm *m*; 🎵 Darmsaite *f*; ~s *pl.* Eingeweide *n/pl.*; *das* In-nere; *fig.* Mut *m.*

gutter ['gʌtə] Dachrinne *f*; Gosse *f* (*a. fig.*), Rinnstein *m.*

guy [gai] **1.** Halteseil *n*; F Vogel-scheuche *f*; *Am.* F Kerl *m*; **2.** ver-ulken.

guzzle ['gʌzl] saufen; fressen.

gymnas|ium [dʒim'neizjəm] Turn-halle *f*, -platz *m*; ~**tics** [~'næstiks] *pl.* Turnen *n*; Gymnastik *f.*

gypsy *bsd. Am.* ['dʒipsi] = gipsy.

gyrate [dʒaiə'reit] kreisen; wir-beln.

gyroplane ['dʒaiərəplein] Hub-schrauber *m.*

H

haberdasher ['hæbədæʃə] Kurz-
warenhändler m; Am. Herrenarti-
kelhändler m; ~y [~əri] Kurzwaren
(-geschäft n) f/pl.; Am. Herren-
artikel m/pl.

habit ['hæbit] 1. (An)Gewohnheit
f; Verfassung f; Kleid(ung f) n;
fall od. get into bad ~s schlechte
Gewohnheiten annehmen; 2. (an-)
kleiden; ~able [~təbl] bewohnbar;
~ation [hæbi'teiʃən] Wohnung f.

habitual ☐ [hə'bitjuəl] gewohnt,
gewöhnlich; Gewohnheits...

hack [hæk] 1. Hieb m; Einkerbung
f; Miet-, Arbeitspferd n (a. fig.);
a. ~ writer literarischer Lohn-
schreiber m; 2. (zer)hacken.

hackneyed fig. ['hæknid] abgedroschen.

had [hæd] pret. u. p.p. von have.

haddock ['hædək] Schellfisch m.

h(a)emorrhage☼ ['heməridʒ] Blut-
sturz m.

hag [hæg] (mst fig. alte) Hexe.

haggard ☐ ['hægəd] verstört; hager.

haggle ['hægl] feilschen, schachern.

hail [heil] 1. Hagel m; Anruf m;
2. (nieder)hageln (lassen); anrufen;
(be)grüßen; ~ from stammen aus;
~stone ['heilstoun] Hagelkorn n;
~storm Hagelschauer m.

hair [heə] Haar n; ~breadth
['heəbredθ] Haaresbreite f; ~cut
Haarschnitt m; ~do Am. Frisur f;
~dresser (bsd. Damen)Friseur m;
~drier [~draiə] Trockenhaube f;
Fön m; ~less ['heəlis] ohne Haare,
kahl; ~pin Haarnadel f; ~raising
['heəreiziŋ] haarsträubend; ~split-
ting Haarspalterei f; ~y ['heəri]
haarig.

hale [heil] gesund, frisch, rüstig.

half [hɑːf] 1. pl. halves [hɑːvz]
Hälfte f; by halves nur halb; go
halves halbpart ' machen, teilen
2. halb; ~ a crown eine halbe
Krone; ~back ['hɑːfbæk] Fußball: Läufer m; ~breed ['hɑːf-
briːd] Halbblut n; ~caste Halbblut n; ~hearted ☐ ['hɑːf'hɑːtid]
lustlos, lau; ~length Brustbild n;
~penny ['heipni] halber Penny;
~time Sport: Halb-
zeit f; ~way halbwegs; ~witted
einfältig, idiotisch.

halibut ichth. ['hælibət] Heilbutt m.

hall [hɔːl] Halle f; Saal m; Vorraum
m; Flur m; Diele f; Herren-, Gutshaus n; univ. Speisesaal m; ~ of
residence Studentenwohnheim n.

halloo [hə'luː] (hallo) rufen.

hallow ['hælou] heiligen, weihen;
☐mas [~ouməs] Allerheiligenfest n.

halo ['heilou] ast. Hof m; Heiligenschein m.

halt [hɔːlt] 1. Halt(estelle f) m;
Stillstand m; 2. (an)halten; mst fig.
hinken; schwanken.

halter ['hɔːltə] Halfter f; Strick m.

halve [hɑːv] halbieren; ~s [hɑːvz]
pl. von half 1.

ham [hæm] Schenkel m; Schinken
m.

hamburger Am. ['hæmbəːgə] Frikadelle f; mit Frikadelle belegtes
Brötchen.

hamlet ['hæmlit] Weiler m.

hammer ['hæmə] 1. Hammer m;
2. (be)hämmern.

hammock ['hæmək] Hängematte f.

hamper ['hæmpə] 1. Geschenk-,
Eßkorb m; 2. verstricken; behin-
dern.

hamster zo. ['hæmstə] Hamster m.

hand [hænd] 1. Hand f (a. fig.);
Handschrift f; Handbreite f;
(Uhr)Zeiger m; Mann m, Arbeiter
m; Karten: Blatt n; at ~ bei der
Hand; nahe bevorstehend; at first ~
aus erster Hand; a good (poor) ~ at
(un)geschickt in (dat.); ~ and glove
ein Herz und eine Seele; change ~s
den Besitzer wechseln; lend a ~
(mit) anfassen; off ~ aus dem Handgelenk od. Stegreif; on ~ † vorrätig, auf Lager; bsd. Am. zur
Stelle, bereit; on one's ~s auf dem
Halse; on the one ~ einerseits; on
the other ~ andererseits; ~ to ~
Mann gegen Mann; come to ~
sich bieten; einlaufen (Briefe); 2.
reichen; ~ about herumreichen; ~
down vererben; ~ in einhändigen;
einreichen; ~ over aushändigen;
~bag ['hændbæg] Handtasche f;
~bill Hand-, Reklamezettel m;
~brake ⊕ Handbremse f; ~cuff
Handfessel f; ~ful [~dful] Hand-
voll f; F Plage f; ~glass Hand-
spiegel m; Leselupe f.

handicap ['hændikæp] 1. Handikap
n; Vorgaberennen n, Vorgabespiel
n; (Extra)Belastung f; 2. (extra)
belasten; beeinträchtigen.

handi|craft ['hændikrɑːft] Hand-
werk n; Handfertigkeit f; ~crafts-
man Handwerker m; ~work Handarbeit f; Werk n.

handkerchief ['hæŋkətʃi(ː)f] Taschentuch n; Halstuch n.

handle ['hændl] 1. Griff m; Stiel m;
Henkel m; Pumpen- etc. Schwengel
m; fig. Handhabe f; fly off the ~ F
platzen vor Wut; 2. anfassen; handhaben; behandeln; ~bar Lenk-
stange f e-s Fahrrades.

hand|-luggage ['hændlʌgidʒ]
Handgepäck n; ~made handgear-
beitet; ~me-downs Am. F pl. Fer-
tigkleidung f; getragene Kleider pl.;
~rail Geländer n; ~shake Hände-

druck m; ~some □ ['hænsəm] ansehnlich; hübsch; anständig; ~work Handarbeit f; ~writing Handschrift f; ~y □ ['hændi] geschickt; handlich; zur Hand.

hang [hæŋ] 1. [irr.] v/t. hängen; auf-, einhängen; verhängen; (pret. u. p.p. mst ~ed) (er)hängen; hängen lassen; Tapete ankleben; v/i. hängen; schweben; sich neigen; ~ about (Am. around) herumlungern; sich an j-n hängen; ~ back sich zurückhalten; ~ on sich klammern an (acc.); fig. hängen an (dat.); 2. Hang m; Fall m e-r Gardine etc.; F Wesen n; F fig. Kniff m; Dreh m.

hangar ['hæŋə] Flugzeughalle f.

hang-dog ['hændog] Armesünder...

hanger ['hæŋə] Aufhänger m; Hirschfänger m; ~-on fig. [ˌær'ɔn] Klette f.

hanging ['hæŋiŋ] 1. Hänge...; 2. ~s pl. Behang m; Tapeten f/pl.

hangman ['hæŋmən] Henker m.

hang-nail ['hæŋneil] Niednagel m.

hang-over sl. ['hæŋouvə] Katzenjammer m, Kater m.

hanker ['hæŋkə] sich sehnen.

hap|hazard ['hæp'hæzəd] 1. Zufall m; at ~ aufs Geratewohl; 2. zufällig; ~less □ ['hæplis] unglücklich.

happen ['hæpən] sich ereignen, geschehen; he ~ed to be at home er war zufällig zu Hause; ~ (up)on zufällig treffen auf (acc.); ~ in Am. F hereinschneien; ~ing ['hæpniŋ] Ereignis n.

happi|ly ['hæpili] glücklicherweise; ~ness [ˌinis] Glück(seligkeit f) n.

happy □ ['hæpi] allg. glücklich; beglückt; erfreut; erfreulich; geschickt; treffend; F angeheitert; ~-go-lucky F unbekümmert.

harangue [hə'ræŋ] 1. Ansprache f, Rede f; 2. v/t. feierlich anreden.

harass ['hærəs] belästigen, quälen.

harbo(u)r ['haːbə] 1. Hafen m; Zufluchtsort m; 2. (be)herbergen; Rache etc. hegen; ankern; ~age [ˌəridʒ] Herberge f; Zuflucht f.

hard [haːd] 1. adj. allg. hart; schwer; mühselig; streng; ausdauernd; fleißig; heftig; Am. stark (Spirituosen); ~ of hearing schwerhörig; 2. adv. stark; tüchtig; mit Mühe; ~ by nahe bei; ~ up in Not; ~-boiled ['haːd'boild] hartgesotten; Am. gerissen; ~ cash Bargeld n; klingende Münze; ~en ['haːdn] härten; hart machen od. werden; (sich) abhärten; fig. (sich) verhärten; ✝ sich festigen (Preise); ~-headed nüchtern denkend; ~-hearted □ hartherzig; ~ihood ['haːdihud] Kühnheit f; ~iness [ˌinis] Widerstandsfähigkeit f, Härte f; ~ly ['haːdli] kaum; streng;

mit Mühe; ~ness ['haːdnis] Härte f; Schwierigkeit f; Not f; ~pan Am. harter Boden, fig. Grundlage f; ~ship ['haːdʃip] Bedrängnis f, Not f; Härte f; ~ware Eisenwaren f/pl.; ~y □ ['haːdi] kühn; widerstandsfähig, hart; abgehärtet; winterfest (Pflanze).

hare [hɛə] Hase m; ~bell ♀ ['hɛəbel] Glockenblume f; ~-brained zerfahren; ~lip anat. ['hɛə'lip] Hasenscharte f.

hark [haːk] horchen (to auf acc.).

harlot ['haːlət] Hure f.

harm [haːm] 1. Schaden m; Unrecht n, Böse(s) n; 2. beschädigen, verletzen; schaden, Leid zufügen (dat.); ~ful □ ['haːmful] schädlich; ~less □ ['haːmlis] harmlos, unschädlich.

harmon|ic [haː'mɔnik] (~ally), ~ious □ [haː'mounjəs] harmonisch; ~ize ['haːmənaiz] v/t. in Einklang bringen; v/i. harmonieren; ~y [ˌni] Harmonie f.

harness ['haːnis] 1. Harnisch m; Zug-Geschirr n; die in ~ in den Sielen sterben; 2. anschirren; bändigen; Wasserkraft nutzbar machen.

harp [haːp] 1. Harfe f; 2. Harfe spielen; ~ (up)on herumreiten auf (dat.).

harpoon [haː'puːn] 1. Harpune f; 2. harpunieren.

harrow ✗ ['hærou] 1. Egge f; 2. eggen; fig. quälen, martern.

harry ['hæri] plündern; quälen.

harsh □ [haːʃ] rauh; herb; grell; streng; schroff; barsch.

hart zo. [haːt] Hirsch m.

harvest ['haːvist] 1. Ernte(zeit) f; Ertrag m; 2. ernten; einbringen.

has [hæz] 3. sg. pres. von have.

hash [hæʃ] 1. gehacktes Fleisch; Am. F Essen n, Fraß m; fig. Mischmasch m; 2. (zer)hacken.

hast|e [heist] Eile f; Hast f; make ~ (sich be)eilen; ~en ['heisn] (sich be)eilen; j-n antreiben; et. beschleunigen; ~y □ ['heisti] (vor-)eilig; hastig; hitzig, heftig.

hat [hæt] Hut m.

hatch [hætʃ] 1. Brut f, Hecke f; ⊕, ✗ Luke f; serving ~ Durchreiche f; 2. (aus)brüten (a. fig.).

hatchet ['hætʃit] Beil n.

hatchway ⊕ ['hætʃwei] Luke f.

hat|e [heit] 1. Haß m; 2. hassen; ~ful □ ['heitful] verhaßt; abscheulich; ~red ['heitrid] Haß m.

haught|iness ['hɔːtinis] Stolz m; Hochmut m; ~y □ ['hɔːti] stolz; hochmütig.

haul [hɔːl] 1. Ziehen n (Fisch-)Zug m; Am. Transport(weg) m; 2. ziehen; schleppen; transportieren; ✗ fördern; ⊕ abdrehen; ~ down one's flag die Flagge streichen; fig. sich geschlagen geben.

haunch [hɔːntʃ] Hüfte *f*; Keule *f* *von Wild.*

haunt [hɔːnt] **1.** Aufenthaltsort *m*; Schlupfwinkel *m*; **2.** oft besuchen; heimsuchen; verfolgen; spuken in (*dat.*).

have [hæv] [*irr.*] *v/t.* haben; bekommen; *Mahlzeit* einnehmen; lassen; ~ to do tun müssen; *I* ~ *my hair cut* ich lasse mir das Haar schneiden; *he will* ~ *it that* ... er behauptet, daß ...; *I had better go* es wäre besser, wenn ich ginge; *I had rather go* ich möchte lieber gehen; ~ *about one* bei *od.* an sich haben; ~ *on* anhaben; ~ *it out with* sich auseinandersetzen mit; *v/aux.* haben; *bei v/i.* oft sein; ~ *come* gekommen sein.

haven ['heivn] Hafen *m* (*a. fig.*).

havoc ['hævək] Verwüstung *f*; *make* ~ *of*, *play* ~ *with od. among* verwüsten; übel zurichten.

haw ♀ [hɔː] Hagebutte *f*.

Hawaiian [hɑːˈwaiiən] **1.** hawaiisch; **2.** Hawaiier(in).

hawk [hɔːk] **1.** Habicht *m*; Falke *m*; **2.** sich räuspern; hausieren mit.

hawthorn ♀ ['hɔːθɔːn] Weißdorn *m*.

hay [hei] **1.** Heu *n*; **2.** heuen; ~**cock** ['heikɔk] Heuhaufen *m*; ~**fever** Heuschnupfen *m*; ~**loft** Heuboden *m*; ~**maker** *bsd. Am.* K.o.-Schlag *m*; ~**rick** = haycock; ~**seed** *bsd. Am.* F Bauerntölpel *m*; ~**stack** = haycock.

hazard ['hæzəd] **1.** Zufall *m*; Gefahr *f*, Wagnis *n*; Hasard(spiel) *n*; **2.** wagen; ~**ous** □ [~dəs] gewagt.

haze [heiz] **1.** Dunst *m*; **2.** ♣ *u. Am.* schinden; F schurigeln.

hazel ['heizl] **1.** ♀ Hasel(staude) *f*; **2.** nußbraun; ~**nut** Haselnuß *f*.

hazy □ ['heizi] dunstig; *fig.* unklar.

H-bomb ⚔ ['eitʃbɔm] H-Bombe *f*, Wasserstoffbombe *f*.

he [hiː] **1.** er; ~ *who* derjenige, welcher; **2.** Mann *m*; *zo.* Männchen *n*; **3.** *adj. in Zssgn:* männlich, ...männchen *n*; ~**goat** Ziegenbock *m*.

head [hed] **1.** *allg.* Kopf *m* (*a. fig.*); Haupt *n* (*a. fig.*); *nach Zahlwort:* Mann *m* (*a. pl.*); Stück *n* (*a. pl.*); Leiter(in); Chef *m*; Kopfende *n e-s Bettes etc.*; Kopfseite *f e-r Münze*; Gipfel *m*; Quelle *f*; *Schiffs*-Vorderteil *n*; Hauptpunkt *m*, Abschnitt *m*; Überschrift *f*; *come to a* ~ eitern (*Geschwür*); *fig.* sich zuspitzen, zur Entscheidung kommen; *get it into one's* ~ *that* ... es sich in den Kopf setzen, daß; ~ *over heels* Hals über Kopf; **2.** erst; Ober...; Haupt...; **3.** *v/t.* (an)führen; an der Spitze von *et.* stehen; vorausgehen (*dat.*); mit e-r Überschrift versehen; ~ *off* ablenken; *v/i.* ♣ zusteuern (*for auf acc.*); *Am.* entspringen (*Fluß*); ~**ache** ['hedeik] Kopfweh *n*; ~

dress Kopfputz *m*; Frisur *f*; ~**gear** Kopfbedeckung *f*; Zaumzeug *n*; ~**ing** ['hediŋ] Brief-, Titelkopf *m*, Rubrik *f*; Überschrift *f*, Titel *m*; *Sport:* Kopfball *m*; ~**land** ['hedlənd] Vorgebirge *n*; ~**light** *mot.* Scheinwerfer(licht *n*) *m*; ~**line** Überschrift *f*; Schlagzeile *f*; ~*s pl.* *Radio: das* Wichtigste in Kürze; ~**long 1.** *adj.* ungestüm; **2.** *adv.* kopfüber; ~**master** Direktor *m e-r Schule*; ~**phone** *Radio:* Kopfhörer *m*; ~**quarters** *pl.* ⚔ Hauptquartier *n*; Zentral(stell)e *f*; ~**strong** halsstarrig; ~**waters** *pl.* Quellgebiet *n*; ~**way** Fortschritt(e *pl.*) *m*; *make* ~ vorwärtskommen; ~**word** Stichwort *n e-s Wörterbuchs*; ~**y** □ ['hedi] ungestüm; voreilig; zu Kopfe steigend.

heal [hiːl] heilen; ~ *up* zuheilen.

health [helθ] Gesundheit *f*; ~**ful** □ ['helθful] gesund; heilsam; ~**resort** Kurort *m*; ~**y** □ ['helθi] gesund.

heap [hiːp] **1.** Haufe(n) *m*; **2.** *a.* ~ *up* (auf)häufen; überhäufen.

hear [hiə] [*irr.*] hören; erfahren; anhören, *j-m* zuhören; erhören; *Zeugen* vernehmen; *Lektion* abhören; ~**d** [hɔːd] *pret. u. p.p. von hear*; ~**er** ['hiərə] (Zu)Hörer(in); ~**ing** [~riŋ] Gehör *n*; Audienz *f*; ½ Verhör *n*; Hörweite *f*; ~**say** Hörensagen *n*.

hearse [hɔːs] Leichenwagen *m*.

heart [hɑːt] *allg.* Herz *n* (*a. fig.*); Innere(s) *n*; Kern *m*; *fig.* Schatz *m*; *by* ~ auswendig; *out of* ~ mutlos; *lay to* ~ sich zu Herzen nehmen; *lose* ~ den Mut verlieren; *take* ~ sich ein Herz fassen; ~**ache** ['hɑːteik] Kummer *m*; ~**break** Herzeleid *n*; ~**breaking** □ [~kiŋ] herzzerbrechend; ~**broken** gebrochenen Herzens; ~**burn** Sodbrennen *n*; ~**en** ['hɑːtn] ermutigen; ~**failure** ⚕ Herzversagen *n*; ~**felt** innig, tief empfunden.

hearth [hɑːθ] Herd *m* (*a. fig.*).

heart|less □ ['hɑːtlis] herzlos; ~**rending** ['hɑːtrendiŋ] herzzerreißend; ~ **transplant** Herzverpflanzung *f*; ~**y** ['hɑːti] □ herzlich; aufrichtig; gesund; herzhaft.

heat [hiːt] **1.** *allg.* Hitze *f*; Wärme *f*; Eifer *m*; *Sport:* Gang *m*, einzelner Lauf *m*; *zo.* Läufigkeit *f*; **2.** heizen; (sich) erhitzen (*a. fig.*); ~**er** ⊕ ['hiːtə] Erhitzer *m*; Ofen *m*.

heath [hiːθ] Heide *f*; ♀ Heidekraut *n*.

heathen ['hiːðən] **1.** Heid|e *m*, -in *f*; **2.** heidnisch.

heather ♀ ['heðə] Heide(kraut *n*) *f*.

heat|ing ['hiːtiŋ] Heizung *f*; *attr.* Heiz...; ~ **lightning** *Am.* Wetterleuchten *n*.

heave [hiːv] **1.** Heben *n*; Übelkeit *f*;

2. [irr.] v/t. heben; schwellen; *Seufzer* ausstoßen; *Anker* lichten; v/i. sich heben, wogen, schwellen.

heaven ['hevn] Himmel m; ~ly [~nli] himmlisch.

heaviness ['hevinis] Schwere f, Druck m; Schwerfälligkeit f; Schwermut f.

heavy □ ['hevi] allg. schwer; schwermütig; schwerfällig; trüb; drückend; heftig (*Regen etc.*); unwegsam (*Straße*) Schwer...; ~ current ⚡ Starkstrom m; ~-handed ungeschickt; ~-hearted niedergeschlagen; ~-weight *Boxen:* Schwergewicht n.

heckle ['hekl] durch Zwischenfragen in die Enge treiben.

hectic ♣ ['hektik] hektisch (*auszehrend; sl. fieberhaft erregt*).

hedge [hedʒ] 1. Hecke f; 2. v/t. einhegen, einzäunen; umgeben; ~ up sperren; v/i. sich decken; sich nicht festlegen; ~hog zo. ['hedʒhɔg] Igel m; Am. Stachelschwein n; ~row Hecke f.

heed [hi:d] 1. Beachtung f, Aufmerksamkeit f; take ~ of, give od. pay ~ to achtgeben auf (acc.), beachten; 2. beachten, achten auf (acc.); ~less □ ['hi:dlis] unachtsam; unbekümmert (of um).

heel [hi:l] 1. Ferse f; Absatz m; Am. sl. Lump m; head over ~s Hals über Kopf; down at ~ mit schiefen Absätzen; fig. abgerissen; schlampig; 2. mit e-m Absatz versehen; ~ed Am. F finanzstark; ~er Am. sl. pol. ['hi:lə] Befehlsempfänger m.

heft [heft] Gewicht n; Am. F Hauptteil m.

heifer ['hefə] Färse f (*junge Kuh*).

height [hait] Höhe f; Höhepunkt m; ~en ['haitn] erhöhen; vergrößern.

heinous □ ['heinəs] abscheulich.

heir [ɛə] Erbe m; ~ apparent rechtmäßiger Erbe; ~ess ['ɛəris] Erbin f; ~loom ['ɛəlu:m] Erbstück n.

held [held] pret. u. p.p. von hold 2.

helibus Am. F ['helibəs] Lufttaxi n.

helicopter ✈ ['helikɔptə] Hubschrauber m.

hell [hel] Hölle f; attr. Höllen...; what the ~ ...? F was zum Teufel ...?; raise ~ Krach machen; ~bent ['helbent] Am. sl. unweigerlich entschlossen; ~ish □ ['heliʃ] höllisch.

hello ['he'lou] hallo!

helm ⚓ [helm] (Steuer)Ruder n.

helmet ['helmit] Helm m.

helmsman ⚓ ['helmzmən] Steuermann m.

help [help] 1. allg. Hilfe f; (Hilfs-)Mittel n; (Dienst)Mädchen n; 2. v/t. (ab)helfen (dat.); unterlassen; bei Tisch geben, reichen;

~ o.s. sich bedienen, zulangen; I could not ~ laughing ich konnte nicht umhin zu lachen; v/i. helfen, dienen; ~er ['helpə] Helfer(in), Gehilf|e m, -in f; ~ful □ [~pful] hilfreich; nützlich; ~ing [~piŋ] Portion f; ~less □ [~plis] hilflos; ~lessness [~snis] Hilflosigkeit f; ~mate, ~meet Gehilf|e m, -in f; Gattin f.

helter-skelter ['heltə'skeltə] holterdiepolter.

helve [helv] Stiel m, Griff m.

Helvetian [hel'vi:ʃən] Helvetier (-in); attr. Schweizer...

hem [hem] 1. Saum m; 2. v/t. säumen; ~ in einschließen; v/i. sich räuspern.

hemisphere ['hemisfiə] Halbkugel f.

hem-line ['hemlain] Kleid: Saum m.

hemlock ♣ ['hemlɔk] Schierling m; ~-tree Schierlingstanne f.

hemp [hemp] Hanf m.

hemstitch ['hemstitʃ] Hohlsaum m.

hen [hen] Henne f; Vogel-Weibchen n.

hence [hens] weg; hieraus; daher; von jetzt an; a year ~ heute übers Jahr; ~forth ['hens'fɔ:θ], ~forward [~ɔ:'wəd] von nun an.

hen|-coop ['henku:p] Hühnerstall m; ~pecked unter dem Pantoffel (stehend).

hep Am. sl. [hep]: to be ~ to kennen; ~cat Am. sl. ['hepkæt] Eingeweihte(r m) f; Jazzfanatiker(in).

her [hə:, hə] sie; ihr; ihr(e).

herald ['herəld] 1. Herold m; 2. (sich) ankündigen; ~ in einführen; ~ry [~dri] Wappenkunde f, Heraldik f.

herb [hə:b] Kraut n; ~age ['hə:bidʒ] Gras n; Weide f; ~ivorous [~'bivərəs] pflanzenfressend.

herd [hə:d] 1. Herde f (a. fig.); 2. v/t. Vieh hüten; v/i. a. ~ together in e-r Herde leben; zs.-hausen; ~er ['hə:də], ~sman ['hə:dzmən] Hirt m.

here [hiə] hier; hierher; ~'s to ...! auf das Wohl von ...!

here|after [hiər'a:ftə] 1. künftig; 2. Zukunft f; ~by ['hiə'bai] hierdurch.

heredit|ary [hi'reditəri] erblich; Erb...; ~y [~ti] Erblichkeit f.

here|in ['hiər'in] hierin; ~of [hiər-'ɔv] hiervon.

heresy ['herəsi] Ketzerei f.

heretic ['herətik] Ketzer(in).

here|tofore ['hiətu'fɔ:] bis jetzt; ehemals; ~upon ['hiərə'pɔn] hierauf; ~with hiermit.

heritage ['heritidʒ] Erbschaft f.

hermit ['hə:mit] Einsiedler m.

hero ['hiərou] Held m; ~ic(al □) [hi'rouik(əl)] heroisch; heldenhaft;

Helden...; **~ine** ['herouin] Heldin
f; **~ism** [~izəm] Heldenmut *m*,
-tum *n*.

heron *zo.* ['herən] Reiher *m*.

herring *ichth.* ['heriŋ] Hering *m*.

hers [hə:z] der (die, das) ihrige;
ihr.

herself [hə:'self] (sie, ihr, sich)
selbst; sich; *of* ~ von selbst; *by* ~
allein.

hesitat|e ['heziteit] zögern, un-
schlüssig sein; Bedenken tragen;
~ion [hezi'teiʃən] Zögern *n*; Un-
schlüssigkeit *f*; Bedenken *n*.

hew [hju:] [*irr.*] hauen, hacken; **~n**
[hju:n] *p.p. von* hew.

hey [hei] ei!; hei!; he!, heda!

heyday ['heidei] **1.** heisa!; oho!;
2. *fig.* Höhepunkt *m*, Blüte *f*.

hi [hai] he!, heda!; hallo!

hicc|ough, ~up ['hikʌp] **1** Schluk-
ken *m*; **2.** schlucken; den Schluk-
ken haben.

hid [hid] *pret. u. p.p. von* hide 2;
~den ['hidn] *p.p. von* hide 2.

hide [haid] **1.** Haut *f*; **2.** [*irr.*] (sich)
verbergen, verstecken; **~-and-seek**
['haidənd'si:k] Versteckspiel *n*.

hidebound *fig.* ['haidbaund] engherzig.

hideous ☐ ['hidiəs] scheußlich.

hiding ['haidiŋ] F Tracht *f* Prügel;
Verbergen *n*; **~-place** Versteck *n*.

hi-fi *Am.* ['hai'fai] = high-fidelity.

high [hai] **1.** *adj.* ☐ *allg.* hoch; vornehm; gut, edel (*Charakter*); stolz;
hochtrabend; angegangen (*Fleisch*);
extrem; stark; üppig, flott (*Leben*);
Hoch...; Ober...; *with a* ~ *hand*
arrogant, anmaßend; *in* ~ *spirits* in
gehobener Stimmung, guter Lau-
ne; ~ *life die* vornehme Welt; ~
time höchste Zeit; ~ *words* heftige
Worte; **2.** *meteor.* Hoch *n*; *bsd. Am.*
für Zssgn wie high school, etc.; **3.**
adv. hoch; sehr, mächtig; ~*ball*
Am. ['haibɔːl] Whisky *m* mit Soda;
~-bred vornehm erzogen; ~**brow**
F **1.** Intellektuelle(r *m*) *f*; **2.** betont
intellektuell; **~-class** erstklassig;
~-fidelity mit höchster Wieder-
gabetreue, Hi-Fi; ~**grade** hoch-
wertig; ~**handed** anmaßend; ~
land [hailənd] Hochland *n*; ~
lights *pl. fig.* Höhepunkte *m/pl.*;
~ly ['haili] hoch; sehr; *speak* ~ *of*
s.o. j-n loben; ~**minded** hochher-
zig; ~**ness** ['hainis] Höhe *f*; *fig.*
Hoheit *f*; ~**pitched** schrill (*Ton*);
steil (*Dach*); ~**power**: ~ *station*
Großkraftwerk *n*; ~**road** Landstraße *f*; ~ **school** höhere Schule;
~**strung** überempfindlich; ~ *tea*
frühes Abendessen *mit Tee u.*
Fleisch etc.; ~**water** Hochwasser
n; ~**way** Landstraße *f*; *fig.* Weg *m*;
~ *code* Straßenverkehrsordnung *f*;
~**wayman** Straßenräuber *m*.

hike F [haik] **1.** wandern; **2.** Wan-

derung *f*; *bsd. Am.* F Erhöhung *f*
(*Preis etc.*); ~**r** ['haikə] Wanderer *m*.

hilarious [hi'lɛəriəs] ausgelassen.

hill [hil] Hügel *m*, Berg *m*; ~**billy**
Am. F ['hilbili] Hinterwäldler *m*;
~**ock** ['hilək] kleiner Hügel; ~**side**
['hil'said] Hang *m*; ~**y** ['hili] hüge-
lig.

hilt [hilt] Griff *m* (*bsd. am Degen*).

him [him] ihn; ihm; den, dem(je-
nigen); ~**self** [him'self] (er, ihm,
ihn, sich) selbst; sich; *of* ~ von
selbst; *by* ~ allein.

hind[1] *zo.* [haind] Hirschkuh *f*.

hind[2] [~] Hinter..; ~**er 1.** ['haində]
hintere(r, -s); Hinter...; **2.** ['hində]
v/t. hindern (*from an dat.*); hemmen; ~**most** ['haindmoust] hinterst, letzt.

hindrance ['hindrəns] Hindernis *n*.

hinge [hindʒ] **1.** Türangel *f*; Scharnier *n*; *fig.* Angelpunkt *m*; **2.** ~
upon fig. abhängen von.

hint [hint] **1.** Wink *m*; Anspielung *f*;
2. andeuten, anspielen (*at auf acc.*).

hinterland ['hintəlænd] Hinterland
n.   [butte *f.*]

hip [hip] *anat.* Hüfte *f*; ♀ Hage-]

hippopotamus *zo.* [hipə'potəməs]
Flußpferd *n*.

hire ['haiə] **1.** Miete *f*; Entgelt *m*, *n*,
Lohn *m*; **2.** mieten; *j-n* anstellen;
~ *out* vermieten.

his [hiz] sein(e); der (die, das) sei-
nige.

hiss [his] *v/i.* zischen; zischeln; *v/t.*
a. ~ *off* auszischen, auspfeifen.

histor|ian [his'tɔ:riən] Historiker
m; ~**ic(al** [his'tɔrik(əl)] histo-
risch, geschichtlich; Geschichts...;
~**y** ['histəri] Geschichte *f*.

hit [hit] **1.** Schlag *m*, Stoß *m*; *fig.*
(Seiten)Hieb *m*; (Glücks)Treffer
m; *thea.*, ♪ Schlager *m*; **2.** [*irr.*]
schlagen, stoßen; treffen; auf *et.*
stoßen; *Am* F eintreffen in (*dat.*)
~ *s.o. a blow* j-m e-n Schlag versetzen; ~ *it off with* F sich vertragen
mit; ~ (*up*)*on* (zufällig) kommen *od.*
stoßen *od.* verfallen auf (*acc.*).

hitch [hitʃ] **1.** Ruck *m*; ♣ Knoten *m*;
fig. Haken *m*, Hindernis *n*; **2** rük-
ken; (sich) festmachen, festhaken;
hängenbleiben; rutschen; ~**hike**
F ['hitʃhaik] per Anhalter fahren.

hither *lit.* ['hiðə] hierher; ~**to** bisher.

hive [haiv] **1.** Bienenstock *m*;
Bienenschwarm *m*; *fig.* Schwarm
m; **2.** ~ *up* aufspeichern; zs.-woh-
nen.

hoard [hɔ:d] **1.** Vorrat *m*, Schatz *m*;
2. *a.* ~ *up* aufhäufen; horten.

hoarfrost [hɔ:'frɔst] (Rauh)Reif *m*.

hoarse [hɔ:s] heiser, rauh.

hoary ['hɔ:ri] (alters)grau.

hoax [houks] **1.** Täuschung *f*;
Falschmeldung *f*; **2.** foppen.

hob [hɔb] = hobgoblin; *raise* ~ *bsd.*
Am. F Krach schlagen.

hobble ['hɔbl] **1.** Hinken n, Humpeln n; F Klemme f, Patsche f; **2.** v/i. humpeln, hinken (a. fig.); v/t. an den Füßen fesseln.

hobby ['hɔbi] fig Steckenpferd n, Hobby n; **~-horse** Steckenpferd n; Schaukelpferd n

hobgoblin ['hɔbgɔblin] Kobold m.

hobo Am. sl. ['houbou] Landstreicher m.

hock¹ [hɔk] Rheinwein m.

hock² zo [␣] Sprunggelenk n.

hod [hɔd] Mörteltrog m.

hoe ✗ [hou] **1.** Hacke f; **2.** hacken.

hog [hɔg] **1.** Schwein n (a. fig.); **2.** Mähne stutzen; mot. drauflos rasen; **~gish** ['hɔgiʃ] schweinisch; gefräßig.

hoist [hɔist] **1.** Aufzug m; **2.** hochziehen, hissen.

hokum sl ['houkəm] Mätzchen n/pl.; Kitsch m; Humbug m.

hold [hould] **1.** Halten n; Halt m, Griff m; Gewalt f, Einfluß m; ⊕ Lade-, Frachtraum m, catch (od. get, lay, take, seize) ␣ of erfassen, ergreifen; sich aneignen; keep ␣ of festhalten; **2.** [irr.] v/t. allg. halten; fest-, aufhalten; enthalten; fig. behalten; Versammlung etc. abhalten; (inne)haben; Ansicht vertreten; Gedanken etc hegen; halten für, glauben; behaupten; ␣ one's ground, ␣ one's own sich behaupten; ␣ the line teleph. am Apparat bleiben; ␣ on et (an s-m Platz fest)halten; ␣ over aufschieben; ␣ up aufrecht halten, (unter-)stützen; aufhalten; (räuberisch) überfallen, v/i (test)halten; gelten; sich bewähren; standhalten; ␣ forth Reden halten; ␣ good od. true gelten, sich bestätigen; ␣ off sich fernhalten; ␣ on ausharren; fortdauern, sich festhalten; teleph. am Apparat bleiben; ␣ to festhalten an (dat.); ␣ up sich (aufrecht) halten; **~er** ['houldə] Pächter m; Halter m (Gerät), Inhaber(in) (bsd. ✝); **~ing** [␣diŋ] Halten n; Halt m; Pachtgut n, Besitz m; ␣ company Dachgesellschaft f; **~-over** Am. Rest m; **~-up** Raubüberfall m; Stauung f, Stockung f.

hole [houl] **1.** Loch n; Höhle f; F fig. Klemme f, pick ␣ s in bekritteln; **2.** aushöhlen, durchlöchern.

holiday ['hɔlədi] Feiertag m; freier Tag; ␣s pl Ferien pl., Urlaub m; **~maker** Urlauber(in).

holler Am f ['hɔlə] laut rufen.

hollow ['hɔlou] **1.** hohl; leer; falsch, f; **2.** Höhle f, (Aus)Höhlung f; Land-Senke f; **3.** aushöhlen.

holly ♀ ['hɔli] Stechpalme f.

holster ['houlstə] Pistolentasche f.

holy ['houli] heilig; ♀ Thursday Gründonnerstag m; ␣ water Weihwasser n; ♀ Week Karwoche f.

homage ['hɔmidʒ] Huldigung f; do od. pay od. render ␣ huldigen (to dat.).

home [houm] **1.** Heim n; Haus n, Wohnung f; Heimat f; Mal n; at ␣ zu Hause; **2.** adj. (ein)heimisch, inländisch; wirkungsvoll; tüchtig (Schlag etc.); ♀ Office Innenministerium n; ␣ rule Selbstregierung f; ♀ Secretary Innenminister m; ␣ trade Binnenhandel m; **3.** adv. heim, nach Hause; an die richtige Stelle; gründlich; hit od. strike ␣ den rechten Fleck treffen; ♀ Counties die Grafschaften um London; **~economics** Am. Hauswirtschaftslehre f; **~felt** ['houmfelt] tief empfunden; **~less** ['houmlis] heimatlos; **~like** [␣laik] heimelig, gemütlich; fig. hausbacken; schlicht; anspruchslos; reizlos; **~made** selbstgemacht, Hausmacher...; **~sickness** Heimweh n; **~stead** Anwesen n; ␣ team Sport Gastgeber m/pl.; **~ward(s)** ['houmwəd(z)] heimwärts (gerichtet); Heim...; **~work** Hausaufgabe(n pl.) f, Schularbeiten f/pl.

homicide ['hɔmisaid] Totschlag m; Mord m; Totschläger(in).

homogeneous □ [hɔmə'dʒiːnjəs] homogen, gleichartig.

hone ⊕ [houn] **1.** Abziehstein m; **2.** Rasiermesser abziehen.

honest □ ['ɔnist] ehrlich, rechtschaffen; aufrichtig; echt; **~y** [␣ti] Ehrlichkeit f, Rechtschaffenheit f; Aufrichtigkeit f.

honey ['hʌni] Honig m; fig. Liebling m; **~comb** [␣koum] (Honig-)Wabe f; **~ed** ['hʌnid] honigsüß; **~moon 1.** Flitterwochen f/pl.; **2.** die Flitterwochen verleben.

honk mot. [hɔŋk] hupen, tuten.

honky-tonk Am. sl. ['hɔŋkitɔŋk] Spelunke f.

honorary ['ɔnərəri] Ehren...; ehrenamtlich.

hono(u)r ['ɔnə] **1.** Ehre f; Achtung f; Würde f; fig. Zierde f; Your ♀ Euer Gnaden; **2.** (be)ehren; ✝ honorieren; **~able** □ ['ɔnərəbl] ehrenvoll; redlich; ehrbar; ehrenwert.

hood [hud] **1.** Kapuze f; mot. Verdeck n; Am. (Motor)Haube f; ⊕ Kappe f; **2.** mit e-r Kappe etc. bekleiden; ein-, verhüllen.

hoodlum Am. F ['huːdləm] Strolch m.

hoodoo bsd. Am. ['huːduː] Unglücksbringer m; Pech n (Unglück).

hoodwink ['hudwiŋk] täuschen.

hooey Am. sl. ['huːi] Quatsch m.

hoof [huːf] Huf m; Klaue f.

hook [huk] **1.** (bsd. Angel)Haken m; Sichel f; by ␣ or by crook so oder so;

2. (sich) (zu-, fest)haken; angeln
(a. fig.); ~y ['huki] **1.** hakig; **2.:** play
~ Am. sl. (die Schule) schwänzen.

hoop [hu:p] **1.** Faß- etc. Reif(en)
m; ⊕ Ring m; **2.** Fässer binden.

hooping-cough ❦ ['hu:piŋkɔf]
Keuchhusten m.

hoot [hu:t] **1.** Geschrei n; **2.** v/i.
heulen; johlen; mot. hupen; v/t.
auspfeifen, auszischen.

Hoover ['hu:və] **1.** Staubsauger m;
2. (mit e-m Staubsauger) saugen.

hop [hɔp] **1.** ♣ Hopfen m; Sprung
m; F Tanzerei f; **2.** hüpfen, springen (über acc.).

hope [houp] **1.** Hoffnung f; **2.** hoffen (for auf acc.); ~ in vertrauen auf
(acc.); ~ful ['houpful] hoffnungs-
voll; ~less ['houplis] hoffnungslos; verzweifelt.

horde [hɔ:d] Horde f.

horizon [hə'raizn] Horizont m.

horn [hɔ:n] Horn n; Schalltrichter
m; mot. Hupe f; ~s pl. Geweih n;
~ of plenty Füllhorn n.

hornet zo. ['hɔ:nit] Hornisse f.

horn|swoggle Am. sl. ['hɔ:nswɔgl]
j-n ²reinlegen; ~y ['hɔ:ni] hornig;
schwielig.

horr|ible ['hɔrəbl] entsetzlich;
scheußlich; ~id ['hɔrid] gräßlich, abscheulich; schrecklich; ~ify
[~ifai] erschrecken; entsetzen; ~or
['hɔrə] Entsetzen n, Schauder m;
Schrecken m; Greuel m.

horse [hɔ:s] zo. Pferd n; Reiterei f;
Bock m, Gestell n; ~back ['hɔ:s-
bæk]: on ~ zu Pferde; ~hair Roß-
haar n; ~laugh F wieherndes
Lachen; ~man Reiter m; ~man-
ship [~nʃip] Reitkunst f; ~ opera
Am. drittklassiger Wildwestfilm;
~power Pferdestärke f; ~radish
Meerrettich m; ~shoe Hufeisen n.

horticulture ['hɔ:tikʌltʃə] Gartenbau m.

hose [houz] Schlauch m; Strumpf-
hose f; coll Strümpfe m/pl.

hosiery ['houʒəri]Strumpfwaren f/pl.

hospitable ['hɔspitəbl] gastfrei.

hospital ['hɔspitl] Krankenhaus n;
✕ Lazarett m; ~ity [hɔspi'tæliti]
Gastfreundschaft f, Gastlichkeit f.

host [houst] Wirt m; Gastgeber m;
Gastwirt m; fig. Heer n; Schwarm
m; eccl. Hostie f.

hostage ['hɔstidʒ] Geisel m, f.

hostel ['hɔstəl] Herberge f; univ.
Studenten(wohn)heim n.

hostess ['houstis] Wirtin f; Gast-
geberin f; ~ air ~.

hostil|e ['hɔstail] feindlich (ge-
sinnt); ~ity [hɔs'tiliti] Feindseligkeit f (to gegen).

hot [hɔt] heiß; scharf; beißend;
hitzig, heftig; eifrig; warm (Speise,
Fährte); Am. sl. falsch (Scheck);
gestohlen; radioaktiv; ~bed ['hɔt-
bed] Mistbeet n; fig. Brutstätte f.

hotchpotch ['hɔtʃpɔtʃ] Mischmasch
m; Gemüsesuppe f.   [chen.\

hot dog F ['hɔt 'dɔg] heißes Würst-\

hotel [hou'tel] Hotel n.

hot|head ['hɔthed] Hitzkopf m;
~house Treibhaus n; ~pot Irish
Stew n; ~ rod Am. sl. mot. frisiertes
altes Auto; ~spur Hitzkopf m.

hound [haund] **1.** Jagd-, Spürhund
m; fig. Hund m; **2.** jagen, hetzen.

hour ['auə] Stunde f; Zeit f, Uhr f;
~ly ['auəli] stündlich.

house 1. [haus] allg. Haus n; the ⟂
das Unterhaus; die Börse; **2.** [hauz]
v/t. unterbringen; v/i. hausen;
~agent ['hauseidʒənt] Häuser-
makler m; ~breaker ['hausbreikə]
Abbrucharbeiter m; ~hold Haushalt m; attr. Haushalts...; Haus...;
~holder Hausherr m; ~keeper
Haushälterin f; ~keeping Haus-
haltung f; ~maid Hausmädchen
n; ~warming ['hauswɔ:miŋ] Ein-
zugsfeier f; ~wife ['hauswaif]
Hausfrau f; ['hʌzif] Nähtäschchen
n; ~wifery ['hauswifəri] Haushal-
tung f; ~work Haus(halts)arbeit
f/pl.

housing ['hauziŋ] Unterbringung f;
Wohnung f; ~ estate Wohnsiedlung f.

hove [houv] pret. u. p.p. von heave **2.**

hovel ['hɔvəl] Schuppen m; Hütte f.

hover ['hɔvə] schweben; lungern;
fig. schwanken; ~craft Luftkissen-
fahrzeug n.

how [hau] wie; ~ do you do? Begrü-
ßungsformel bei der Vorstellung;
~ about ...? wie steht's mit ...?
~ever [hau'evə] **1.** adv. wie auch
(immer); wenn auch noch so ...;
2. cj. jedoch.

howl [haul] **1.** heulen, brüllen;
2. Geheul n; ~er ['haulə] Heuler
m; sl. grober Fehler.

hub [hʌb] (Rad)Nabe f; fig. Mittel-,
Angelpunkt m.

hubbub ['hʌbʌb]   Tumult   m,
Lärm m.

hub(by) F ['hʌb(i)] (Ehe)Mann m.

huckleberry ♣ ['hʌklberi] amerikanische Heidelbeere.

huckster ['hʌkstə] Hausierer(in).

huddle ['hʌdl] **1.** ~ together (sich)
zs.-drängen, zs.-pressen; ~ (o.s.) up
sich zs.-kauern; **2.** Gewirr n, Wirrwarr m.   [cry Zetergeschrei n.\

hue [hju:] Farbe f; Hetze f; ~ and\

huff [hʌf] **1.** üble Laune; **2.** v/t.
grob anfahren; beleidigen; v/i.
wütend werden; schmollen.

hug [hʌg] **1.** Umarmung f; **2.** an
sich drücken, umarmen; fig. festhalten an (dat.); sich dicht am
Weg etc. halten.

huge □ [hju:dʒ] ungeheuer, riesig;
~ness   ['hju:dʒnis]   ungeheure
Größe.

hulk fig. [hʌlk] Klotz m.

hull ['hʌl] 1. ⚓ Schale f; Hülse f; ⚓ Rumpf m; 2. enthülsen; schälen.

hullabaloo [hʌləbə'luː] Lärm m.

hullo ['hʌ'lou] hallo (bsd. teleph.).

hum [hʌm] summen; brumme(l)n; make things ∼ F Schwung in die Sache bringen.

human ['hjuːmən] 1. ☐ menschlich; ∼ly nach menschlichem Ermessen; 2. F Mensch m; ∼e ☐ [hju(ː)'mein] human, menschenfreundlich; ∼itarian [hju(ː)mæni'teəriən] 1. Menschenfreund m; 2. menschenfreundlich; ∼ity [hju(ː)'mæniti] menschliche Natur; Menschheit f; Humanität f; ∼kind ['hjuːmən'kaind] Menschengeschlecht n.

humble ['hʌmbl] 1. ☐ demütig; bescheiden; 2. erniedrigen; demütigen.

humble-bee ['hʌmblbiː] Hummel f.

humbleness ['hʌmblnis] Demut f.

humbug ['hʌmbʌg] 1. (be)schwindeln; 2. Schwindel m.

humdinger Am. sl. [hʌm'diŋə] Mordskerl m, -sache f.

humdrum ['hʌmdrʌm] eintönig.

humid ['hjuːmid] feucht, naß; ∼ity [hju(ː)'miditi] Feuchtigkeit f.

humiliat|e [hju(ː)'milieit] erniedrigen, demütigen; ∼ion [hju(ː)mili'eiʃən] Erniedrigung f, Demütigung f.

humility [hju(ː)'militi] Demut f.

humming F ['hʌmiŋ] mächtig, gewaltig; ∼bird zo. Kolibri m.

humorous ☐ ['hjuːmərəs] humoristisch, humorvoll; spaßig.

humo(u)r ['hjuːmə] 1. Laune f, Stimmung f; Humor m; das Spaßige; ⚕ hist. Körpersaft m; out of ∼ schlecht gelaunt; 2. j-m s-n Willen lassen; eingehen auf (acc.).

hump [hʌmp] 1. Höcker m, Buckel m; 2. krümmen; ärgern, verdrießen; ∼ o.s. Am. sl. sich dranhalten; ∼back ['hʌmpbæk] = hunchback.

hunch [hʌntʃ] 1. Höcker m; großes Stück; Am. F Ahnung f; 2. a. ∼ out, ∼ up krümmen; ∼back ['hʌntʃbæk] Bucklige(r m) f.

hundred ['hʌndrəd] 1. hundert; 2. Hundert n; ∼th [∼dθ] 1. hundertste; 2. Hundertstel n; ∼weight englischer Zentner (50,8 kg).

hung [hʌŋ] 1. pret. u. p.p. von hang 1; 2. adj. abgehangen (Fleisch).

Hungarian [hʌŋ'gɛəriən] 1. ungarisch; 2. Ungar(in); Ungarisch n.

hunger ['hʌŋgə] 1. Hunger m (a. fig.; for nach); 2. v/i. hungern (for, after nach); v/t. durch Hunger zwingen (into zu).

hungry ☐ ['hʌŋgri] hungrig.

hunk F [hʌŋk] dickes Stück.

hunt [hʌnt] 1. Jagd f (for nach); Jagd(revier n) f; Jagd(gesellschaft) f; 2. jagen; Revier bejagen; hetzen; ∼ out od. up aufspüren; ∼ for, ∼ after

Jagd machen auf (acc.); ∼er ['hʌntə] Jäger m; Jagdpferd n; ∼ing [∼tiŋ] Jagen n; Verfolgung f; attr. Jagd...; ∼ing-ground Jagdrevier n; ∼sman [∼tsmən] Jäger m; Rüdemann m (Meutenführer).

hurdle ['həːdl] Hürde f (a. fig.); ∼r [∼lə] Hürdenläufer(in); ∼-race Hürdenrennen n.

hurl [həːl] 1. Schleudern n; 2. schleudern; Worte ausstoßen.

hurricane ['hʌrikən] Orkan m.

hurried ☐ ['hʌrid] eilig; übereilt.

hurry ['hʌri] 1. (große) Eile, Hast f; be in a ∼ es eilig haben; not ... in a ∼ F nicht so bald, nicht so leicht; 2. v/t. (an)treiben; drängen; et. beschleunigen; eilig schicken od. bringen; v/i. eilen, hasten; ∼ up sich beeilen.

hurt [həːt] 1. Verletzung f; Schaden m; 2. [irr.] verletzen (a. fig.); weh tun (dat.); schaden (dat.).

husband ['hʌzbənd] 1. (Ehe)Mann m; 2. haushalten mit; verwalten; ∼man Landwirt m; ∼ry [∼dri] Landwirtschaft f, Ackerbau m.

hush [hʌʃ] 1. still!; 2. Stille f; 3. v/t. zum Schweigen bringen; beruhigen; Stimme dämpfen; ∼ up vertuschen; v/i. still sein; ∼-money ['hʌʃmani] Schweigegeld n.

husk [hʌsk] 1. ⚓ Hülse f, Schote f; Schale f (a. fig.); 2. enthülsen; ∼y ['hʌski] 1. ☐ hülsig; trocken; heiser; F stramm, stämmig; 2. F stämmiger Kerl.

hussy ['hʌsi] Flittchen n; Range f.

hustle ['hʌsl] 1. v/t. (an)rempeln; stoßen; drängen; v/i. (sich) drängen; eilen; bsd. Am. mit Hochdruck arbeiten; 2. Hochbetrieb m; Rührigkeit f; ∼ and bustle Gedränge und Gehetze n.

hut [hʌt] Hütte f; ⚔ Baracke f.

hutch [hʌtʃ] Kasten m; bsd. Kaninchen-Stall m (a. fig.); Trog m.

hyacinth ⚓ ['haiəsinθ] Hyazinthe f.

hyaena zo. [hai'iːnə] Hyäne f.

hybrid Ⓤ ['haibrid] Bastard m, Mischling m; Kreuzung f; attr. Bastard...; Zwitter...; ∼ize [∼daiz] kreuzen.

hydrant ['haidrənt] Hydrant m.

hydro|... Ⓤ ['haidrou] Wasser...; ∼carbon Kohlenwasserstoff m; ∼chloric acid [∼rə'klɔrikæsid] Salzsäure f; ∼gen [∼ridʒən] Wasserstoff m; ∼gen bomb Wasserstoffbombe f; ∼pathy [hai'drɔpəθi] Wasserheilkunde f, Wasserkur f; ∼phobia [haidrə'foubjə] Wasserscheu f; ⚕ Tollwut f; ∼plane ['haidrouplein] Wasserflugzeug n; (Motor)Gleitboot n, Rennboot n.

hyena zo. [hai'iːnə] Hyäne f.

hygiene ['haidʒiːn] Hygiene f.

hymn [him] 1. Hymne f; Lobgesang m; Kirchenlied n; 2. preisen.

hyphen ['haifən] **1.** Bindestrich *m*;
2. mit Bindestrich schreiben *od.*
verbinden; **~ated** [~neitid] mit
Bindestrich geschrieben; **~** *Americans pl.* Halb-Amerikaner *m/pl.*
(*z. B. German-Americans*). [ren.]
hypnotize ['hipnətaiz] hypnotisie-⌐
hypo|chondriac [haipou'kɔndriæk]
Hypochonder *m*; **~crisy** [hi'pɔ-

krəsi] Heuchelei *f*; **~crite** ['hipə-
krit] Heuchler(in); Scheinheilige(r
m) *f*; **~critical** □ [hipə'kritikəl]
heuchlerisch; **~thesis** [hai'pɔθisis]
Hypothese *f*.
hyster|ia 🗙 [his'tiəriə] Hysterie *f*;
~ical □ [~'terikəl] hysterisch; **~ics**
[~ks] *pl.* hysterischer Anfall; *go
into ~* hysterisch werden.

I

I [ai] ich.
ice [ais] **1.** Eis *n*; **2.** gefrieren lassen;
a. ~ up vereisen; *Kuchen* mit Zuk-
kerguß überziehen; in Eis kühlen;
~age ['aiseidʒ] Eiszeit *f*; **~berg**
['aisbə:g] Eisberg *m* (*a. fig.*); **~bound** eingefroren; **~box** Am.
Eisschrank *m*; *Am. a.* Kühlschrank *m*;
~cream Speiseeis *n*; **~floe** Eisscholle *f*.
icicle ['aisikl] Eiszapfen *m*.
icing ['aisiŋ] Zuckerguß *m*; Ver-
eisung *f*.
icy □ ['aisi] eisig (*a. fig.*); vereist.
idea [ai'diə] Idee *f*; Begriff *m*;
Vorstellung *f*; Gedanke *m*; Meinung *f*; Ahnung *f*; Plan *m*; **~l** [~əl]
1. □ ideell; eingebildet; ideal;
2. Ideal *n*.
identi|cal □ [ai'dentikəl] identisch,
gleich(bedeutend); **~fication**
[aidentifi'keiʃən] Identifizierung *f*;
Ausweis *m*; **~fy** [ai'dentifai] identifizieren; ausweisen; erkennen; **~ty**
[~iti] Identität *f*; Persönlichkeit *f*,
Eigenart *f*; **~ card** Personalaus-
weis *m*, Kennkarte *f*; **~ disk** 🗙 Er-
kennungsmarke *f*.
ideological □ [aidiə'lɔdʒikəl] ideo-
logisch.
idiom ['idiəm] Idiom *n*; Mundart *f*;
Redewendung *f*.
idiot ['idiət] Idiot(in), Schwach-
sinnige(r *m*) *f*; **~ic** [idi'ɔtik] (*~ally*)
blödsinnig.
idle ['aidl] **1.** □ müßig, untätig; träg,
faul; unnütz; nichtig; *~ hours pl.*
Mußestunden *f/pl.*; **2.** *v/t. mst ~
away* vertrödeln; *v/i.* faulenzen; ⊕
leer laufen; **~ness** ['aidlnis] Muße
f; Trägheit *f*; Nichtigkeit *f*; **~r**
['aidlə] Müßiggänger(in).
idol ['aidl] Idol *n*, Götzenbild *n*;
fig. Abgott *m*; **~atrous** □ [ai'dɔlə-
trəs] abgöttisch; **~atry** [~ri] Ab-
götterei *f*; Vergötterung *f*; **~ize**
['aidəlaiz] vergöttern.
dyl(l) ['idil] Idyll(e *f*) *n*.
if [if] **1.** wenn, falls; ob; **2.** Wenn *n*;
~fy *Am.* F ['ifi] zweifelhaft.
ignite [ig'nait] (sich) entzünden;
zünden; **~ion** [ig'niʃən] 🔩 Entzündung *f*; *mot.* Zündung *f*.

ignoble □ [ig'noubl] unedel;
niedrig, gemein.
ignominious □ [ignə'miniəs]
schändlich, schimpflich.
ignor|ance ['ignərəns] Unwissen-
heit *f*; **~ant** [~nt] unwissend; un-
kundig; **~e** [ig'nɔ:] ignorieren,
nicht beachten; 🔩 verwerfen.
ill [il] **1.** *adj. u. adv.* übel, böse;
schlimm, schlecht; krank; *adv.*
kaum; *fall ~, be taken ~* krank werden; **2.** Übel *n*; Üble(s) *n*, Böse(s) *n*.
ill|-advised □ ['iləd'vaizd] schlecht
beraten; unbesonnen, unklug;
~bred ungebildet, ungezogen;
~ breeding schlechtes Benehmen.
illegal □ [i'li:gəl] ungesetzlich.
illegible □ [i'ledʒəbl] unleserlich.
illegitimate □ [ili'dʒitimit] illegitim; unrechtmäßig; unehelich.
ill|-favo(u)red ['il'feivəd] häßlich;
~humo(u)red übellaunig.
illiberal □ [i'libərəl] engstirnig;
intolerant; knauserig.
illicit □ [i'lisit] unerlaubt.
illiterate □ [i'litərit] **1.** ungelehrt,
ungebildet; **2.** Analphabet(in).
ill|-judged ['il'dʒʌdʒd] unklug, un-
vernünftig; **~mannered** ungezogen; mit schlechten Umgangs-
formen; **~natured** □ boshaft, bösartig.
illness ['ilnis] Krankheit *f*.
illogical □ [i'lɔdʒikəl] unlogisch.
ill|-starred ['il'stɑ:d] unglücklich;
~tempered schlecht gelaunt;
~timed ungelegen; **~treat** mißhandeln.
illuminat|e [i'lju:mineit] be-, er-
leuchten (*a. fig.*); erläutern; aufklären; **~ing** [~iŋ] Leucht...; *fig.*
aufschlußreich; **~ion** [ilju:mi'nei-
ʃən] Er-, Beleuchtung *f*; Erläuterung *f*; Aufklärung *f*.
ill-use ['il'ju:z] mißhandeln.
illus|ion [i'lu:ʒən] Illusion *f*, Täu-
schung *f*; **~ive** [i'lu:siv], **~ory** □
[~səri] illusorisch, täuschend.
illustrat|e ['iləstreit] illustrieren;
erläutern; bebildern; **~ion** ['iləs-
'treiʃən] Erläuterung *f*; Illustration *f*; **~ive** □ ['iləstreitiv] erläu-
ternd.

illustrious □ [i'lʌstriəs] berühmt.
ill will ['il'wil] Feindschaft *f*.
image ['imidʒ] Bild *n*; Standbild *n*; Ebenbild *n*; Vorstellung *f*; ~ry [.dʒəri] Bilder *n/pl*.; Bildersprache *f*, Metaphorik *f*.
imagin|able □ [i'mædʒinəbl] denkbar; ~ary [.əri] eingebildet; ~ation [imædʒi'neiʃən] Einbildung(skraft) *f*; ~ative □ [i'mædʒinətiv] ideen-, einfallsreich; ~e [i'mædʒin] sich *et*. einbilden *od*. vorstellen *od*. denken.
imbecile □ ['imbisi:l] **1.** geistesschwach; **2.** Schwachsinnige(r *m*) *f*.
imbibe [im'baib] einsaugen; *fig*. sich zu eigen machen.
imbue [im'bju:] (durch)tränken; tief färben; *fig*. erfüllen.
imitat|e ['imiteit] nachahmen; imitieren; ~ion [imi'teiʃən] **1.** Nachahmung *f*; **2.** künstlich, Kunst...
immaculate □ [i'mækjulit] unbefleckt, rein; fehlerlos.
immaterial □ [imə'tiəriəl] unkörperlich; unwesentlich (*to* für).
immature [imə'tjuə] unreif.
immeasurable □ [i'meʒərəbl] unermeßlich.
immediate □ [i'mi:djət] unmittelbar; unverzüglich, sofortig; ~ly [.tli] **1.** *adv*. sofort; **2.** *cj*. gleich nachdem.
immense □ [i'mens] ungeheuer.
immerse [i'mə:s] (ein-, unter)tauchen; *fig*. ~ o.s. in sich versenken *od*. vertiefen in (*acc*.).
immigra|nt ['imigrənt] Einwanderer(in); ~te [.greit] *v/i*. einwandern; *v/t*. ansiedeln (*into* in *dat*.); ~tion [imi'greiʃən] Einwanderung *f*.
imminent □ ['iminənt] bevorstehend, drohend.
immobile [i'moubail] unbeweglich.
immoderate □ [i'mɔdərit] maßlos.
immodest □ [i'mɔdist] unbescheiden; unanständig.
immoral □ [i'mɔrəl] unmoralisch.
immortal [i'mɔ:tl] **1.** □ unsterblich; **2.** Unsterbliche(r *m*) *f*; ~ity [imɔ:'tæliti] Unsterblichkeit *f*.
immovable □ [i'mu:vəbl] **1.** □ unbeweglich; unerschütterlich; **2.** ~s *pl*. Immobilien *pl*.
immun|e [i'mju:n] immun, gefeit (*from* gegen); ~ity [.niti] Immunität *f*, Freiheit *f* (*from* von); Unempfänglichkeit *f* (für).
immutable □ [i'mju:təbl] unveränderlich.
imp [imp] Teufelchen *n*; Schelm *m*.
impact ['impækt] (Zs.-)Stoß *m*; Anprall *m*; Einwirkung *f*.
impair [im'pɛə] schwächen; (ver)mindern; beeinträchtigen.
impart [im'pɑ:t] verleihen; weitergeben.
impartial [im'pɑ:ʃəl] unparteiisch; ~ity [impa:ʃi'æliti] Unparteilichkeit *f*, Objektivität *f*.

impassable □ [im'pɑ:səbl] ungangbar, unpassierbar.
impassible □ [im'pæsibl] unempfindlich; gefühllos (*to* gegen).
impassioned [im'pæʃənd] leidenschaftlich.
impassive □ [im'pæsiv] unempfindlich; teilnahmslos; heiter.
impatien|ce [im'peiʃəns] Ungeduld *f*; ~t □ [.nt] ungeduldig.
impeach [im'pi:tʃ] anklagen (*of*, *with gen*.); anfechten, anzweifeln.
impeccable □ [im'pekəbl] sündlos; makellos, einwandfrei.
impede [im'pi:d] (ver)hindern.
impediment [im'pedimənt] Hindernis *n*.
impel [im'pel] (an)treiben.
impend [im'pend] hängen, schweben; bevorstehen, drohen.
impenetrable □ [im'penitrəbl] undurchdringlich; *fig*. unergründlich; *fig*. unzugänglich (*to dat*.).
impenitent □ [im'penitənt] unbußfertig, verstockt.
imperative [im'perətiv] **1.** □ notwendig, dringend, unbedingt erforderlich; befehlend; gebieterisch; *gr*. imperativisch; **2.** Befehl *m*; *a*. ~ mood *gr*. Imperativ *m*, Befehlsform *f*.   [unmerklich.\
imperceptible □ [impə'septəbl]
imperfect [im'pə:fikt] **1.** □ unvollkommen; unvollendet; **2.** *a*. ~ tense *gr*. Imperfekt *n*.
imperial □ [im'piəriəl] kaiserlich; Reichs...; majestätisch; großartig; ~ism [.lizəm] Imperialismus *m*, Weltmachtpolitik *f*.
imperil [im'peril] gefährden.
imperious □ [im'piəriəs] gebieterisch, anmaßend; dringend.
imperishable □ [im'periʃəbl] unvergänglich.
impermeable □ [im'pə:mjəbl] undurchdringlich, undurchlässig.
impersonal □ [im'pə:snl] unpersönlich.
impersonate [im'pə:səneit] verkörpern; *thea*. darstellen.
impertinen|ce [im'pə:tinəns] Unverschämtheit *f*; Nebensächlichkeit *f*; ~t □ [.nt] unverschämt; ungehörig; nebensächlich.
imperturbable □ [impə(:)'tə:bəbl] unerschütterlich.
impervious □ [im'pə:vjəs] unzugänglich (*to* für); undurchlässig.
impetu|ous □ [im'petjuəs] ungestüm, heftig; ~s ['impitəs] Antrieb *m*.
impiety [im'paiəti] Gottlosigkeit *f*.
impinge [im'pindʒ] *v/i*. (ver)stoßen (*on*, *upon*, *against* gegen).
impious □ ['impiəs] gottlos; pietätlos; frevelhaft.
implacable □ [im'plækəbl] unversöhnlich, unerbittlich.
implant [im'plɑ:nt] einpflanzen.

implement 1. ['implimənt] Werkzeug *n*; Gerät *n*; 2. [⁓iment] ausführen.

implicat|e ['implikeit] verwickeln; in sich schließen; ⁓ion [impli'keiʃən] Verwick(e)lung *f*; Folgerung *f*.

implicit ☐ [im'plisit] mit eingeschlossen; blind (*Glaube etc.*).

implore [im'plɔ:] (an-, er)flehen.

imply [im'plai] mit einbegreifen, enthalten; bedeuten; andeuten.

impolite ☐ [impə'lait] unhöflich.

impolitic ☐ [im'pɔlitik] unklug.

import 1. ['impɔ:t] Bedeutung *f*; Wichtigkeit *f*; Einfuhr *f*; ⁓s *pl.* Einfuhrwaren *f/pl.*; 2. [im'pɔ:t] einführen; bedeuten; ⁓ance [⁓təns] Wichtigkeit *f*; ⁓ant ☐ [⁓nt] wichtig; wichtigtuerisch; ⁓ation [impɔ:-'teiʃən] Einfuhr(waren *f/pl.*) *f*.

importun|ate ☐ [im'pɔ:tjunit] lästig; zudringlich; ⁓e [im'pɔ:tju:n] dringend bitten; belästigen.

impos|e [im'pouz] *v/t.* auf(er)legen, aufbürden (*on, upon dat.*); *v/i.* ⁓ upon *j-m* imponieren; *j-n* täuschen; ⁓ition [impə'ziʃən] Auf(er)legung *f*; Steuer *f*; Straferlaß *f*; Betrügerei *f*.

impossib|ility [impɔsə'biliti] Unmöglichkeit *f*; ⁓le ☐ [im'pɔsəbl] unmöglich.

impost|or [im'pɔstə] Betrüger *m*; ⁓ure [⁓tʃə] Betrug *m*.

impoten|ce ['impətəns] Unfähigkeit *f*; Machtlosigkeit *f*; ⁓t [⁓nt] unvermögend, machtlos, schwach.

impoverish [im'pɔvəriʃ] arm machen; Boden auslaugen.

impracticable ☐ [im'præktikəbl] undurchführbar; unwegsam.

impractical [im'præktikəl] unpraktisch; theoretisch; unnütz.

imprecate ['imprikeit] Böses herabwünschen (*upon auf acc.*).

impregn|able ☐ [im'pregnəbl] uneinnehmbar; unüberwindlich; ⁓ate ['impregneit] schwängern; 🜛 sättigen; ⊕ imprägnieren.

impress 1. ['impres] (Ab-, Ein-)Druck *m*; *fig.* Stempel *m*; 2. [im-'pres] eindrücken, prägen; Kraft *etc.* übertragen; Gedanken *etc.* einprägen (*on dat.*); *j-n* beeindrucken; *j-n mit et.* erfüllen; ⁓ion [⁓eʃən] Eindruck *m*; *typ.* Abzug *m*; Auflage *f*; be under the ⁓ that den Eindruck haben, daß; ⁓ive ☐ [⁓esiv] eindrucksvoll.

imprint 1. [im'print] aufdrücken, prägen; *fig.* einprägen (*on, in dat.*); 2. ['imprint] Eindruck *m*; Stempel *m* (*a. fig.*); *typ.* Druckvermerk *m*.

imprison [im'prizn] inhaftieren; ⁓ment [⁓nment] Haft *f*; Gefängnis (-strafe *f*) *n*.

improbable ☐ [im'prɔbəbl] unwahrscheinlich.

improper ☐ [im'prɔpə] ungeeignet, unpassend; falsch; unanständig.

impropriety [imprə'praiəti] Ungehörigkeit *f*; Unanständigkeit *f*.

improve [im'pru:v] *v/t.* verbessern; veredeln; aus-, benutzen; *v/i.* sich (ver)bessern; ⁓ upon vervollkommnen; ⁓ment [⁓vmənt] Verbesserung *f*, Vervollkommnung *f*; Fortschritt *m* (*on, upon gegenüber dat.*).

improvise ['imprəvaiz] improvisieren.

imprudent ☐ [im'pru:dənt] unklug.

impuden|ce ['impjudəns] Unverschämtheit *f*, Frechheit *f*; ⁓t ☐ [⁓nt] unverschämt, frech.

impuls|e ['impʌls], ⁓ion [im'pʌl-ʃən] Impuls *m*, (An)Stoß *m*; *fig.* (An)Trieb *m*; ⁓ive ☐ [⁓lsiv] (an-)treibend; *fig.* impulsiv; rasch (handelnd).

impunity [im'pju:niti] Straflosigkeit *f*; with ⁓ ungestraft.

impure ☐ [im'pjuə] unrein (*a. fig.*); unkeusch.

imput|ation [impju(:)'teiʃən] Beschuldigung *f*; ⁓e [im'pju:t] zurechnen, beimessen; zur Last legen.

in [in] 1. *prp. allg.* in (*dat.*); *engS.:* (⁓ the morning, ⁓ number, ⁓ itself, professor ⁓ the university) an (*dat.*); (⁓ the street, ⁓ English) auf (*dat.*); (⁓ this manner) an (*acc.*); (coat ⁓ velvet) aus; (⁓ Shakespeare, ⁓ the daytime, ⁓ crossing the road) bei; (engaged ⁓ reading, ⁓ a word) mit; (⁓ my opinion) nach; (rejoice ⁓ s.th.) über (*acc.*); (⁓ the circumstances, ⁓ the reign of, one ⁓ ten) unter (*dat.*); (cry out ⁓ alarm) vor (*dat.*); (grouped ⁓ tens, speak ⁓ reply, ⁓ excuse, ⁓ honour of) zu; ⁓ 1949 im Jahre 1949; ⁓ that ... insofern als, weil; 2. *adv.* drin(nen); herein; hinein; be ⁓ for et. zu erwarten haben; e-e Prüfung etc. vor sich haben; F be well ⁓ with sich gut mit *j-m* stehen; 3. *adj.* hereinkommend; Innen...

inability [inə'biliti] Unfähigkeit *f*.

inaccessible ☐ [inæk'sesəbl] unzugänglich.   [unrichtig.|

inaccurate ☐ [in'ækjurit] ungenau;

inactiv|e ☐ [in'æktiv] untätig, ✝ lustlos; 🜛 unwirksam; ⁓ity [inæk-'tiviti] Untätig-, Lustlosigkeit *f*.

inadequate ☐ [in'ædikwit] unangemessen; unzulänglich.

inadmissible ☐ [inəd'misəbl] unzulässig.

inadvertent ☐ [inəd'və:tənt] unachtsam; unbeabsichtigt, versehentlich.

inalienable ☐ [in'eiljənəbl] unveräußerlich.

inane ☐ [i'nein] *fig.* leer; albern.

inanimate ☐ [in'ænimit] leblos; *fig.* unbelebt; geistlos, langweilig.

inapproachable [inə'proutʃəbl] unnahbar, unzugänglich.

inappropriate ☐ [inə'proupriit] unangebracht, unpassend.

inapt ☐ [in'æpt] ungeeignet, untauglich; ungeschickt; unpassend.

inarticulate ☐ [inɑː'tikjulit] undeutlich; schwer zu verstehen(d); undeutlich sprechend.

inasmuch [inəz'mʌtʃ]: ~ *as* insofern als. [merksam.]

inattentive ☐ [inə'tentiv] unaufl

inaudible ☐ [in'ɔːdəbl] unhörbar.

inaugura|l [i'nɔːgjurəl] Antrittsrede *f*; *attr.* Antritts...; **~te** [~reit] (feierlich) einführen, einweihen; beginnen; **~tion** [inɔːgju'reiʃən] Einführung *f*, Einweihung *f*; ♀ *Day Am.* Amtseinführung *f* des neugewählten Präsidenten der USA.

inborn ['in'bɔːn] angeboren.

incalculable ☐ [in'kælkjuləbl] unberechenbar; unzählig.

incandescent [inkæn'desnt] weiß glühend; Glüh...

incapa|ble ☐ [in'keipəbl] unfähig, ungeeignet (*of* zu); **~citate** [inkə'pæsiteit] unfähig machen; **~city** [~ti] Unfähigkeit *f*.

incarnate [in'kɑːnit] Fleisch geworden; *fig.* verkörpert.

incautious ☐ [in'kɔːʃəs] unvorsichtig.

incendiary [in'sendjəri] **1.** brandstifterisch; *fig.* aufwieglerisch; **2.** Brandstifter *m*; Aufwiegler *m*.

incense¹ ['insens] Weihrauch *m*.

incense² [in'sens] in Wut bringen.

incentive [in'sentiv] Antrieb *m*.

incessant ☐ [in'sesnt] unaufhörlich.

incest ['insest] Blutschande *f*.

inch [intʃ] Zoll *m* (2,54 *cm*); *fig.* ein bißchen; *by* ~es allmählich; *every* ~ ganz (u. gar).

inciden|ce ['insidəns] Vorkommen *n*; Wirkung *f*; **~t** [~nt] **1.** (*to*) vorkommend (bei), eigen (*dat.*); **2.** Zu-, Vor-, Zwischenfall *m*; Nebenumstand *m*; **~tal** ☐ [insi'dentl] zufällig, gelegentlich; Neben...; *be ~ to* gehören zu; **~ly** nebenbei.

incinerate [in'sinəreit] einäschern; Müll verbrennen.

incis|e [in'saiz] einschneiden; **~ion** [in'siʒən] Einschnitt *m*; **~ive** [in'saisiv] (ein)schneidend, scharf; **~or** [~aizə] Schneidezahn *m*.

incite [in'sait] anspornen, anregen, anstiften; **~ment** [~tmənt] Anregung *f*; Ansporn *m*; Anstiftung *f*.

inclement [in'klemənt] rauh.

inclin|ation [inkli'neiʃən] Neigung *f* (*a. fig.*); **~e** [in'klain] **1.** *v/i.* sich neigen (*a. fig.*); *~ to fig.* zu *et.* neigen; *v/t.* neigen; geneigt machen; **2.** Neigung *f*, Abhang *m*.

inclos|e [in'klouz], **~ure** [~ouʒə] *s.* enclose, enclosure.

inclu|de [in'kluːd] einschließen; enthalten; **~sive** ☐ [~uːsiv] einschließlich; alles einbegriffen; *be ~ of* einschließen; **~** *terms pl.* Pauschalpreis *m*.

incoheren|ce, **~cy** [inkou'hiərəns, ~si] Zs.-hangslosigkeit *f*; Inkonsequenz *f*; **~t** ☐ [~nt] unzs.-hängend; inkonsequent.

income ['inkəm] Einkommen *n*; **~tax** Einkommensteuer *f*.

incommode [inkə'moud] belästigen.

incommunica|do *bsd. Am.* [inkəmjuːni'kɑːdou] ohne Verbindung mit der Außenwelt; **~tive** ☐ [inkə'mjuːnikətiv] nicht mitteilsam, verschlossen.

incomparable ☐ [in'kɔmpərəbl] unvergleichlich.

incompatible ☐ [inkəm'pætəbl] unvereinbar; unverträglich.

incompetent ☐ [in'kɔmpitənt] unfähig; unzuständig, unbefugt.

incomplete ☐ [inkəm'pliːt] unvollständig; unvollkommen.

incomprehensible ☐ [inkɔmpri-'hensəbl] unbegreiflich.

inconceivable ☐ [inkən'siːvəbl] unbegreiflich, unfaßbar.

incongruous ☐ [in'kɔngruəs] nicht übereinstimmend; unpassend.

inconsequent ☐ [in'kɔnsikwənt] inkonsequent, folgewidrig; **~ial** [inkɔnsi'kwenʃəl] unbedeutend; = *inconsequent.*

inconsidera|ble ☐ [inkən'sidərəbl] unbedeutend; **~te** ☐ [~rit] unüberlegt; rücksichtslos.

inconsisten|cy [inkən'sistənsi] Unvereinbarkeit *f*; Inkonsequenz *f*; **~t** ☐ [~nt] unvereinbar; widerspruchsvoll; inkonsequent.

inconsolable ☐ [inkən'souləbl] untröstlich.

inconstant ☐ [in'kɔnstənt] unbeständig; veränderlich.

incontinent ☐ [in'kɔntinənt] unmäßig; ausschweifend.

inconvenien|ce [inkən'viːnjəns] **1.** Unbequemlichkeit *f*; Unannehmlichkeit *f*; **2.** belästigen; **~t** ☐ [~nt] unbequem; unpassend; lästig.

incorporat|e **1.** [in'kɔːpəreit] einverleiben (*into dat.*); (sich) vereinigen; *als Mitglied* aufnehmen; *♀ als Körperschaft* eintragen; **2.** [~rit] einverleibt; vereinigt; **~ed** (amtlich) eingetragen; **~ion** [inkɔːpə'reiʃən] Einverleibung *f*; Verbindung *f*. [fehlerhaft; unehörig.\]

incorrect ☐ [inkə'rekt] unrichtig;

incorrigible ☐ [in'kɔridʒəbl] unverbesserlich.

increas|e **1.** [in'kriːs] *v/i.* zunehmen; sich vergrößern *od.* vermehren; *v/t.* vermehren, vergrößern; erhöhen; **2.** ['inkriːs] Zunahme *f*; Vergrößerung *f*; Zuwachs *m*; **~ingly** [in'kriːsiŋli] zunehmend, immer (*mit folgendem comp.*); **~** *difficult* immer schwieriger.

incredible ☐ [in'kredəbl] unglaublich.

incredul|ity [inkri'dju:liti] Unglaube m; ~ous □ [in'kredjuləs] ungläubig, skeptisch.

incriminate [in'krimineit] beschuldigen; belasten.

incrustation [inkrʌs'teiʃən] Verkrustung f; Kruste f; ⊕ Belag m.

incub|ate ['inkjubeit] (aus)brüten; ~ator [˷tə] Brutapparat m.

inculcate ['inkʌlkeit] einschärfen (upon dat.).

incumbent [in'kʌmbənt] obliegend; be ~ on s.o. j-m obliegen.

incur [in'kə:] sich et. zuziehen; geraten in (acc.); Verpflichtung eingehen; Verlust erleiden.

incurable [in'kjuərəbl] 1. □ unheilbar; 2. Unheilbare(r m) f.

incurious □ [in'kjuəriəs] gleichgültig, uninteressiert.

incursion [in'kə:ʃən] feindlicher Einfall.

indebted [in'detid] verschuldet; fig. (zu Dank) verpflichtet.

indecen|cy [in'di:snsi] Unanständigkeit f; ~t □ [˷nt] unanständig.

indecisi|on [indi'siʒən] Unentschlossenheit f; ~ve □ [˷'saisiv] nicht entscheidend; unbestimmt.

indecorous □ [in'dekərəs] unpassend; ungehörig.

indeed [in'di:d] 1. adv. in der Tat, tatsächlich; wirklich; allerdings; 2. int. so?; nicht möglich!

indefatigable □ [indi'fætigəbl] unermüdlich.

indefensible □ [indi'fensəbl] unhaltbar.

indefinite □ [in'definit] unbestimmt; unbeschränkt; ungenau.

indelible □ [in'delibl] untilgbar.

indelicate □ [in'delikit] unfein; taktlos.

indemni|fy [in'demnifai] sicherstellen; j-m Straflosigkeit zusichern; entschädigen; ~ty [˷iti] Sicherstellung f; Straflosigkeit f; Entschädigung f.

indent 1. [in'dent] einkerben, auszacken; eindrücken; 🐾 Vertrag mit Doppel ausfertigen; ~ upon s.o. for s.th. ✝ et. bei j-m bestellen; 2. ['indent] Kerbe f; Vertiefung f; ✝ Auslandsauftrag m; = indenture. ~ation [inden'teiʃən] Einkerbung f; Einschnitt m; ~ure [in'dentʃə] 1. Vertrag m; Lehrbrief m; 2. vertraglich verpflichten.

independen|ce [indi'pendəns] Unabhängigkeit f; Selbständigkeit f; Auskommen n; ♀ Day Am. Unabhängigkeitstag m (4. Juli); ~t □ [˷nt] unabhängig; selbständig.

indescribable □ [indis'kraibəbl] unbeschreiblich.

indestructible □ [indis'trʌktəbl] unzerstörbar.

indeterminate □ [indi'tə:minit] unbestimmt.

index ['indeks] 1. (An)Zeiger m; Anzeichen n; Zeigefinger m; Index m; (Inhalts-, Namen-, Sach)Verzeichnis n; 2. Buch mit e-m Index versehen.

Indian ['indjən] 1. indisch; indianisch; 2. Inder(in); a. Red ~ Indianer(in); ~ corn Mais m; ~ file: in ~ im Gänsemarsch; ~ pudding Am. Maismehlpudding m; ~ summer Altweiber-, Nachsommer m.

Indiarubber ['indjə'rʌbə] Radiergummi m.

indicat|e ['indikeit] (an)zeigen; hinweisen auf (acc.); andeuten; ~ion [indi'keiʃən] Anzeige f; Anzeichen n; Andeutung f; ~ive [in'dikətiv] a. ~ mood gr. Indikativ m; ~or ['indikeitə] Anzeiger m (a. ⊕); mot. Blinker m.

indict [in'dait] anklagen (for wegen); ~ment [˷mənt] Anklage f.

indifferen|ce [in'difrəns] Gleichgültigkeit f; ~t □ [˷nt] gleichgültig (to gegen); unparteiisch; (nur) mäßig; unwesentlich; unbedeutend.

indigenous □ [in'didʒinəs] eingeboren, einheimisch.

indigent □ ['indidʒənt] arm.

indigest|ible □ [indi'dʒestəbl] unverdaulich; ~ion [˷tʃən] Verdauungsstörung f, Magenverstimmung f.

indign|ant □ [in'dignənt] entrüstet, empört, ungehalten; ~ation [indig'neiʃən] Entrüstung f; ~ity [in'digniti] Beleidigung f.

indirect □ [indi'rekt] indirekt; nicht direkt; gr. a. abhängig.

indiscre|et □ [indis'kri:t] unbesonnen; unachtsam; indiskret; ~tion [˷'reʃən] Unachtsamkeit f; Unbesonnenheit f; Indiskretion f.

indiscriminate □ [indis'kriminit] unterschiedslos, wahllos.

indispensable □ [indis'pensəbl] unentbehrlich, unerläßlich.

indispos|ed [indis'pouzd] unpäßlich; abgeneigt; ~ition [indispə'ziʃən] Abneigung f (to gegen); Unpäßlichkeit f.

indisputable □ [indis'pju:təbl] unbestreitbar, unstreitig.

indistinct □ [indis'tiŋkt] undeutlich; unklar.

indistinguishable □ [indis'tiŋgwiʃəbl] nicht zu unterscheiden(d).

indite [in'dait] ab-, verfassen.

individual [indi'vidjuəl] 1. persönlich, individuell; besondere(r, -s); einzeln; Einzel...; 2. Individuum n; ~ism [˷lizəm] Individualismus m; ~ist [˷ist] Individualist m; ~ity [individju'æliti] Individualität f.

indivisible □ [indi'vizəbl] unteilbar.

indolen|ce ['indələns] Trägheit f;

~t □ [~nt] indolent, träge, lässig; ~ schmerzlos.
indomitable □ [in'dɔmitəbl] unbezähmbar.
indoor ['indɔ:] im Hause (befindlich); Haus..., Zimmer..., *Sport:* Hallen...; ~s ['in'dɔ:z] zu Hause; im *od.* ins Haus.
indorse [in'dɔ:s] = *endorse etc.*
induce [in'dju:s] veranlassen; ~ment [~smənt] Anlaß *m*, Antrieb *m*.
induct [in'dʌkt] einführen; ~ion [~kʃən] Einführung *f*, Einsetzung *f* in *Amt, Pfründe*; ⚡ Induktion *f*.
indulge [in'dʌldʒ] nachsichtig sein gegen *j-n*; *j-m* nachgeben; ~ with *j-n* erfreuen mit; ~ (*o.s.*) in *s.th.* sich et. gönnen; sich e-r S. hin- *od.* ergeben; ~nce [~dʒəns] Nachsicht *f*; Nachgiebigkeit *f*; Sichgehenlassen *n*; Vergünstigung *f*; ~nt □ [~nt] nachsichtig.
industri|al □ [in'dʌstriəl] gewerbetreibend, gewerblich; industriell; Gewerbe...; ~ Industrie...; ~ area Industriebezirk *m*; ~ estate Industriegebiet *n* e-r *Stadt*; ~ school Gewerbeschule *f*; ~alist [~list] Industrielle(r) *m*; ~alize [~laiz] industrialisieren; ~ous □ [~iəs] fleißig.
industry ['indəstri] Fleiß *m*; Gewerbe *n*; Industrie *f*.
inebriate 1. [i'ni:brieit] betrunken machen; 2. [~iit] Trunkenbold *m*.
ineffable □ [in'efəbl] unaussprechlich.
ineffect|ive [ini'fektiv], ~ual □ [~tjuəl] unwirksam, fruchtlos.
inefficient □ [ini'fiʃənt] wirkungslos; (leistungs)unfähig.
inelegant □ [in'eligənt] unelegant, geschmacklos.
ineligible □ [in'elidʒəbl] nicht wählbar; ungeeignet; *bsd.* ⚔ untauglich.
inept □ [i'nept] unpassend; albern.
inequality [ini(:)'kwɔliti] Ungleichheit *f*; Ungleichmäßigkeit *f*; Unebenheit *f*.
inequitable [in'ekwitəbl] unbillig.
inert □ [i'nə:t] träge; ~ia [i'nə:ʃjə], ~ness [i'nə:tnis] Trägheit *f*.
inescapable [inis'keipəbl] unentrinnbar.
inessential ['ini'senʃəl] unwesentlich (*to* für).
inestimable □ [in'estiməbl] unschätzbar.
inevitab|le □ [in'evitəbl] unvermeidlich; ~ly [~li] unweigerlich.
inexact □ [inig'zækt] ungenau.
inexcusable □ [iniks'kju:zəbl] unentschuldbar.
inexhaustible □ [inig'zɔ:stəbl] unerschöpflich; unermüdlich.
inexorable □ [in'eksərəbl] unerbittlich.

inexpedient □ [iniks'pi:djənt] unzweckmäßig, unpassend.
inexpensive □ [iniks'pensiv] nicht teuer, billig, preiswert.
inexperience [iniks'piəriəns] Unerfahrenheit *f*; ~d [~d] unerfahren.
inexpert □ [ineks'pə:t] unerfahren.
inexplicable □ [in'eksplikəbl] unerklärlich.
inexpressi|ble □ [iniks'presəbl] unaussprechlich; ~ve [~siv] ausdruckslos.
inextinguishable □ [iniks'tiŋgwiʃəbl] unauslöschlich.
inextricable □ [in'ekstrikəbl] unentwirrbar.
infallible □ [in'fæləbl] unfehlbar.
infam|ous □ ['infəməs] ehrlos; schändlich; verrufen; ~y [~mi] Ehrlosigkeit *f*; Schande *f*; Niedertracht *f*.
infan|cy ['infənsi] Kindheit *f*; ⚖ Minderjährigkeit *f*; ~t [~nt] Säugling *m*; (kleines) Kind; Minderjährige(r *m*) *f*.
infanti|le ['infəntail], ~ne [~ain] kindlich; Kindes..., Kinder...; kindisch.
infantry ⚔ ['infəntri] Infanterie *f*.
infatuate [in'fætjueit] betören; ~d vernarrt (*with* in *acc.*).
infect [in'fekt] anstecken (*a. fig.*); infizieren, verseuchen, verpesten; ~ion [~kʃən] Ansteckung *f*; ~ious □ [~ʃəs], ~ive [~ktiv] ansteckend; Ansteckungs...
infer [in'fə:] folgern, schließen; ~ence ['infərəns] Folgerung *f*.
inferior [in'fiəriə] 1. untere(r, -s); minderwertig; ~ to niedriger *od.* geringer als; untergeordnet (*dat.*); unterlegen (*dat.*); 2. Geringere(r *m*) *f*; Untergebene(r *m*) *f*; ~ity [infiəri'ɔriti] geringerer Wert *od.* Stand; Unterlegenheit *f*; Minderwertigkeit *f*.
infern|al □ [in'fə:nl] höllisch; ~o [~nou] Inferno *n*, Hölle *f*.
infertile [in'fə:tail] unfruchtbar.
infest [in'fest] heimsuchen; verseuchen; *fig.* überschwemmen.
infidelity [infi'deliti] Unglaube *m*; Untreue *f* (*to* gegen).
infiltrate [infiltreit] *v/t.* durchdringen; *v/i.* durchsickern, eindringen.
infinite □ ['infinit] unendlich.
infinitive [in'finitiv] *a.* ~ mood gr. Infinitiv *m*, Nennform *f*.
infinity [in'finiti] Unendlichkeit *f*.
infirm □ [in'fə:m] kraftlos, schwach; ~ary [~məri] Krankenhaus *n*; ~ity [~miti] Schwäche *f* (*a. fig.*); Gebrechen *n*.
inflame [in'fleim] entflammen (*mst fig.*); (sich) entzünden (*a. fig. u.* ⚡).
inflamma|ble □ [in'flæmabl] entzündlich; feuergefährlich; ~tion [inflə'meiʃən] Entzündung *f*; ~tory

[in'flæmətəri] entzündlich; *fig.* aufrührerisch; hetzerisch; Hetz...

inflat|e [in'fleit] aufblasen, aufblähen (*a. fig.*); **~ion** [~'eifən] Aufblähung *f*; † Inflation *f*; *fig.* Aufgeblasenheit *f*.

inflect [in'flekt] biegen; *gr.* flektieren, beugen.

inflexi|ble □ [in'fleksəbl] unbiegsam; *fig.* unbeugsam; **~on** [~kfən] Biegung *f*; *gr.* Flexion *f*, Beugung *f*; Modulation *f*.

inflict [in'flikt] auferlegen; zufügen; *Hieb* versetzen; *Strafe* verhängen; **~ion** [~kfən] Auferlegung *f*; Zufügung *f*; Plage *f*.

influen|ce [in'fluəns] **1.** Einfluß *m*; **2.** beeinflussen; **~tial** □ [influ'enfəl] einflußreich.

influenza ♂ [influ'enzə] Grippe *f*.

influx [in'flaks] Einströmen *n*; *fig.* Zufluß *m*, (Zu)Strom *m*.

inform [in'fɔ:m] *v/t.* benachrichtigen, unterrichten (*of* von); *v/i.* anzeigen (*against s.o.* j.); **~al** □ [~ml] formlos, zwanglos; **~ality** [infɔ:'mæliti] Formlosigkeit *f*; Formfehler *m*; **~ation** [infə'meifən] Auskunft *f*; Nachricht *f*, Information *f*; **~ative** [in'fɔ:mətiv] informatorisch; lehrreich; mitteilsam; **~er** [in'fɔ:mə] Denunziant *m*; Spitzel *m*.

infrequent [in'fri:kwənt] selten.

infringe [in'frindʒ] *a.* **~ upon** *Vertrag etc.* verletzen; übertreten.

infuriate [in'fjuərieit] wütend machen.

infuse [in'fju:z] einflößen; aufgießen.

ingen|ious □ [in'dʒi:njəs] geistsinnreich; erfinderisch; raffiniert; genial; **~uity** [indʒi'nju(:)iti] Genialität *f*; **~uous** □ [in'dʒenjuəs] freimütig; unbefangen, naiv.

ingot [ingət] *Gold- etc.* Barren *m*.

ingrati|ate [in'greifieit]: **~** *o.s.* sich beliebt machen (*with* bei); **~tude** [~rætitju:d] Undankbarkeit *f*.

ingredient [in'gri:djənt] Bestandteil *m*.

ingrowing [ingrouiŋ] nach innen wachsend; eingewachsen.

inhabit [in'hæbit] bewohnen; **~able** [~təbl] bewohnbar; **~ant** [~ənt] Bewohner(in), Einwohner(in).

inhal|ation [inhə'leifən] Einatmung *f*; **~e** [in'heil] einatmen.

inherent □ [in'hiərənt] anhaftend; innewohnend, angeboren (*in dat.*).

inherit [in'herit] (er)erben; **~ance** [~təns] Erbteil *n*, Erbe *n*; Erbschaft *f*; *biol.* Vererbung *f*.

inhibit [in'hibit] (ver)hindern; verbieten; zurückhalten; **~ion** [inhi'bifən] Hemmung *f*; Verbot *n*.

inhospitable □ [in'hɔ✓pitəbl] ungastlich, unwirtlich.

inhuman □ [in'hju:mən] unmenschlich.

inimical □ [i'nimikəl] feindlich; schädlich.

inimitable □ [i'nimitəbl] unnachahmlich.

iniquity [i'nikwiti] Ungerechtigkeit *f*; Schlechtigkeit *f*.

initia|l [i'nifəl] **1.** □ Anfangs...; anfänglich; **2.** Anfangsbuchstabe *m*; **~te 1.** [~fiit] Eingeweihte(r *m*) *f*; **2.** [~fieit] beginnen; anbahnen; einführen, einweihen; **~tion** [inifi'eifən] Einleitung *f*; Einführung *f*, Einweihung *f*; **~ fee** *bsd. Am.* Aufnahmegebühr *f* (*Vereinigung*); **~tive** [i'nifiətiv] Initiative *f*; einleitender Schritt; Entschlußkraft *f*; Unternehmungsgeist *m*; Volksbegehren *n*; **~tor** [~ieitə] Initiator *m*, Urheber *m*.

inject [in'dʒekt] einspritzen; **~ion** [~kfən] Injektion *f*, Spritze *f*.

injudicious □ [indʒu(:)'difəs] unverständig, unklug, unüberlegt.

injunction [in'dʒʌŋkfən] gerichtliche Verfügung; ausdrücklicher Befehl.

injur|e [indʒə] (be)schädigen; schaden (*dat.*); verletzen; beleidigen; **~ious** [in'dʒuəriəs] schädlich; ungerecht; beleidigend; **~y** [indʒəri] Unrecht *n*; Schaden *m*; Verletzung *f*; Beleidigung *f*.

injustice [in'dʒʌstis] Ungerechtigkeit *f*; Unrecht *n*.

ink [iŋk] **1.** Tinte *f*; *mst printer's* **~** Druckerschwärze *f*; *attr.* Tinten...; **2.** (mit Tinte) schwärzen; beklecksen.

inkling [inkliŋ] Andeutung *f*; dunkle *od.* leise Ahnung.

ink|pot [inkpɔt] Tintenfaß *n*; **~stand** Schreibzeug *n*; **~y** [inki] tintig; Tinten...; tintenschwarz.

inland 1. [inlənd] inländisch; Binnen...; **2.** [~] Landesinnere(s) *n*, Binnenland *n*; **3.** [in'lænd] landeinwärts.

inlay 1. [in'lei] [*irr.* (*lay*)] einlegen; **2.** [inlei] Einlage *f*; Einlegearbeit *f*.

inlet [inlet] Bucht *f*; Einlaß *m*.

inmate [inmeit] Insass|e *m*, -in *f*; Hausgenoss|e *m*, -in *f*.

inmost [inmoust] innerst.

inn [in] Gasthof *m*, Wirtshaus *n*.

innate □ [i'neit] angeboren.

inner [inə] inner, inwendig; geheim; **~most** innerst; geheimst.

innervate [inə:veit] Nervenkraft geben (*dat.*); kräftigen.

innings [iniŋz] *Sport:* Dransein *n*.

innkeeper [inki:pə] Gastwirt(in).

inno⌒n|ce [inəsns] Unschuld *f*; Harmlosigkeit *f*; Einfalt *f*; **~t** [~nt] **1.** □ unschuldig; harmlos; **2.** Unschuldige(r *m*) *f*; Einfältige(r *m*) *f*.

innocuous □ [i'nɔkjuəs] harmlos.

innovation [inou'veifən] Neuerung *f*.

innoxious □ [i'nɔkfəs] unschädlich.

innuendo [inju(:)'endou] Andeutung *f*.

innumerable □ [i'nju:mərəbl] unzählbar, unzählig.

inoccupation ['inɔkju'peiʃən] Beschäftigungslosigkeit *f*.

inoculate [i'nɔkjuleit] (ein)impfen.

inoffensive [inə'fensiv] harmlos.

inofficial [inə'fiʃəl] inoffiziell.

inoperative [in'ɔpərətiv] unwirksam.

inopportune □ [in'ɔpətju:n] unangebracht, zur Unzeit.

inordinate □ [i'nɔ:dinit] unmäßig.

in-patient ['inpeiʃənt] Krankenhauspatient *m*, stationärer Patient.

inquest ſ⅛ ['inkwest] Untersuchung *f*; *coroner's* ~ Leichenschau *f*.

inquir|e [in'kwaiə] fragen, sich erkundigen (*of* bei *j-m*); ~ *into* untersuchen; **~ing** □ [~riŋ] forschend; **~y** [~ri] Erkundigung *f*, Nachfrage *f*; Untersuchung *f*; Ermittlung *f*.

inquisit|ion [inkwi'ziʃən] Untersuchung *f*; **~ive** □ [in'kwizitiv] neugierig; wißbegierig.

inroad ['inroud] *feindlicher* Einfall; Ein-, Übergriff *m*.

insan|e □ [in'sein] wahnsinnig; **~ity** [in'sæniti] Wahnsinn *m*.

insatia|ble □ [in'seiʃjəbl], **~te** [~ʃiit] unersättlich (*of* nach).

inscribe [in'skraib] ein-, auf-, beschreiben; beschriften; *fig.* einprägen (*in*, *on dat.*); *Buch* widmen.

inscription [in'skripʃən] In-, Aufschrift *f*; ✝ Eintragung *f*.

inscrutable □ [in'skru:təbl] unerforschlich, unergründlich.

insect ['insekt] Insekt *n*; **~icide** [in'sektisaid] Insektengift *n*.

insecure □ [insi'kjuə] unsicher.

insens|ate [in'senseit] gefühllos; unvernünftig; **~ible** □ [~səbl] unempfindlich; bewußtlos; unmerklich; gleichgültig; **~itive** [~sitiv] unempfindlich.

inseparable □ [in'sepərəbl] untrennbar; unzertrennlich.

insert 1. [in'sɔ:t] einsetzen, einschalten, einfügen; (hinein)stecken; *Münze* einwerfen; inserieren; 2. ['insə:t] Bei-, Einlage *f*; **~ion** [in'sə:ʃən] Einsetzung *f*, Einfügung *f*, Eintragung *f*; Einwurf *m* *e-r Münze*; Anzeige *f*, Inserat *n*.

inshore ⚓ ['in'ʃɔ:] an *od.* nahe der Küste (befindlich); Küsten...

inside [in'said] 1. Innenseite *f*; Innere(s) *n*; *turn* ~ *out* umkrempeln; *auf den Kopf stellen*; 2. *adj.* inner, inwendig; Innen...; 3. *adv.* im Innern; 4. *prp.* innerhalb.

insidious □ [in'sidiəs] heimtückisch.

insight ['insait] Einsicht *f*, Einblick *m*.

insignia [in'signiə] *pl.* Abzeichen *n/pl.*, Insignien *pl.*

insignificant [insig'nifikənt] bedeutungslos; unbedeutend.

insincere □ [insin'siə] unaufrichtig.

insinuat|e [in'sinjueit] unbemerkt hineinbringen; zu verstehen geben; andeuten; **~ion** [insinju'eiʃən] Einschmeichelung *f*; Anspielung *f*, Andeutung *f*; Wink *m*.

insipid [in'sipid] geschmacklos, fad.

insist [in'sist]: ~ (*up*)*on* bestehen auf (*dat.*); dringen auf (*acc.*); **~ence** [~təns] Bestehen *n*; Beharrlichkeit *f*; Drängen *n*; **~ent** □ [~nt] beharrlich; eindringlich.

insolent □ ['insələnt] unverschämt.

insoluble □ [in'sɔljubl] unlöslich.

insolvent [in'sɔlvənt] zahlungsunfähig. [keit *f*.]

insomnia [in'sɔmniə] Schlaflosig-ſ

insomuch [insou'mʌtʃ]: ~ *that* dermaßen *od.* so sehr, daß.

inspect [in'spekt] untersuchen, prüfen, nachsehen; **~ion** [~kʃən] Prüfung *f*, Untersuchung *f*; Inspektion *f*; **~or** [~ktə] Aufsichtsbeamte(r) *m*.

inspir|ation [inspə'reiʃən] Einatmung *f*; Eingebung *f*; Begeisterung *f*; **~e** [in'spaiə] einatmen; *fig.* eingeben, erfüllen; *j-n* begeistern.

install [in'stɔ:l] einsetzen; (sich) niederlassen; ⊕ installieren; **~ation** [instə'leiʃən] Einsetzung *f*; Installation *f*, Einrichtung *f*; ⚡ *etc.* Anlage *f*.

instal(l)ment [in'stɔ:lmənt] Rate *f*; Teil-, Ratenzahlung *f*; (Teil)Lieferung *f*; Fortsetzung *f*.

instance ['instəns] Ersuchen *n*; Beispiel *n*; (besonderer) Fall; ſ⅛ Instanz *f*; *for* ~ zum Beispiel.

instant □ ['instənt] 1. dringend; sofortig; *on the 10th* ~ am 10. dieses Monats; 2. Augenblick *m*; **~aneous** □ [instən'teinjəs] augenblicklich; Moment...; **~ly** ['instəntli] sogleich.

instead [in'sted] dafür; ~ *of* anstatt.

instep ['instep] Spann *m*.

instigat|e [in'stigeit] anstiften; aufhetzen; **~or** [~tə] Anstifter *m*, Hetzer *m*.

instil(l) [in'stil] einträufeln; *fig.* einflößen (*into dat.*).

instinct ['instiŋkt] Instinkt *m*; **~ive** □ [in'stiŋktiv] instinktiv.

institut|e ['institju:t] 1. Institut *n*; 2. einsetzen, stiften, einrichten; an-, verordnen; **~ion** [insti'tju:ʃən] Einsetzung *f*, Einrichtung *f*; An-, Verordnung *f*; Satzung *f*; Institut(ion *f*) *n*; Gesellschaft *f*; Anstalt *f*; **~ional** [~nl] Instituts..., Anstalts...

instruct [in'strʌkt] unterrichten; belehren; *j-n* anweisen; **~ion** [~kʃən] Vorschrift *f*; Unterweisung *f*; Anweisung *f*; **~ive** □ [~ktiv] lehrreich; **~or** [~tə] Lehrer *m*; Ausbilder *m*; *Am. univ.* Dozent *m*.

instrument ['instrumənt] Instrument n, Werkzeug n (a. fig.); ғ̃ᵗ Urkunde f; ~al □ [instru'mentl] als Werkzeug dienend; dienlich; ♪ Instrumental...; ~ality [instrumen'tæliti] Mitwirkung f, Mittel n.

insubordinat|e [insə'bɔ:dnit] aufsässig; ~ion ['insəbɔ:di'neiʃən] Auflehnung f.

insubstantial [insəb'stænʃəl] unwirklich; gebrechlich.

insufferable □ [in'sʌfərəbl] unerträglich, unausstehlich.

insufficient □ [insə'fiʃənt] unzulänglich, ungenügend.

insula|r □ ['insjulə] Insel...; fig. engstirnig; ~te [~leit] isolieren; ~tion [insju'leiʃən] Isolierung f.

insult 1. ['insʌlt] Beleidigung f; 2. [in'sʌlt] beleidigen.

insupportable □ [insə'pɔ:təbl] unerträglich, unausstehlich.

insur|ance [in'ʃuərəns] Versicherung f; attr. Versicherungs...; ~ance policy Versicherungspolice f, -schein m; ~e [in'ʃuə] versichern.

insurgent [in'sə:dʒənt] 1. aufrührerisch; 2. Aufrührer m.

insurmountable □ [insə(:)'mauntəbl] unübersteigbar, fig. unüberwindlich.

insurrection [insə'rekʃən] Aufstand m, Empörung f.

intact [in'tækt] unberührt; unversehrt.

intangible □ [in'tændʒəbl] unfühlbar; unfaßbar; unantastbar.

integ|ral □ ['intigrəl] ganz, vollständig; wesentlich; ~rate [~reit] ergänzen; zs.-tun; einfügen; ~rity [in'tegriti] Vollständigkeit f; Redlichkeit f, Integrität f.

intellect ['intilekt] Verstand m; konkr. die Intelligenz; ~ual [inti'lektjuəl] 1. □ intellektuell; Verstandes...; geistig; verständig; 2. Intellektuelle(r m) f.

intelligence [in'telidʒəns] Intelligenz f; Verstand m; Verständnis n; Nachricht f, Auskunft f; ~ department Nachrichtendienst m.

intellig|ent □ [in'telidʒənt] intelligent; klug; ~ible [~dʒəbl] verständlich (to für).

intempera|nce [in'tempərəns] Unmäßigkeit f; Trunksucht f; ~te □ [~rit] unmäßig; zügellos; unbeherrscht; trunksüchtig.

intend [in'tend] beabsichtigen, wollen; ~ for bestimmen für od. zu; ~ed 1. absichtlich; beabsichtigt, a. zukünftig; 2. F Verlobte(r m) f.

intense □ [in'tens] intensiv; angestrengt; heftig; kräftig (Farbe).

intensify [in'tensifai] (sich) verstärken od. steigern.

intensity [in'tensiti] Intensität f.

intent [in'tent] 1. □ gespannt; bedacht; beschäftigt (on mit); 2. Absicht f; Vorhaben n; to all ~s and purposes in jeder Hinsicht; ~ion [~nʃən] Absicht f; Zweck m; ~ional □ [~nl] absichtlich; ~ness [~ntnis] gespannte Aufmerksamkeit; Eifer m.

inter [in'tə:] beerdigen, begraben.

inter... ['intə(:)] zwischen; Zwischen...; gegenseitig, einander.

interact [intər'ækt] sich gegenseitig beeinflussen.

intercede [intə(:)'si:d] vermitteln.

intercept [intə(:)'sept] ab-, auffangen; abhören; aufhalten; unterbrechen; ~ion [~pʃən] Ab-, Auffangen n; Ab-, Mithören n; Unterbrechung f; Aufhalten n.

intercess|ion [intə'seʃən] Fürbitte f; ~or [~esə] Fürsprecher m.

interchange 1. [intə(:)'tʃeindʒ] v/t. austauschen, auswechseln; v/i. abwechseln; 2. ['intə(:)'tʃeindʒ] Austausch m; Abwechs(e)lung f.

intercourse ['intə(:)kɔ:s] Verkehr m.

interdict 1. [intə(:)'dikt] untersagen, verbieten (s.th. to s.o. j-m et.; s.o. from doing j-m zu tun); 2. ['intə(:)-dikt], ~ion [intə(:)'dikʃən] Verbot n; Interdikt n.

interest ['intrist] 1. Interesse n; Anziehungskraft f; Bedeutung f; Nutzen m; ✝ Anteil m, Beteiligung f, Kapital n; Zins(en pl.) m; ~s pl. Interessenten m/pl., Kreise m/pl.; take an ~ in sich interessieren für; return a blow with ~ noch heftiger zurückschlagen; banking ~s pl. Bankkreise m/pl.; 2. allg. interessieren (in für et.); ~ing [~tiŋ] interessant.

interfere [intə'fiə] sich einmischen (with in acc.); vermitteln; (ea.) stören; ~nce [~ərəns] Einmischung f; Beeinträchtigung f; Störung f.

interim ['intərim] 1. Zwischenzeit f; 2. vorläufig; Interims...

interior [in'tiəriə] 1. □ inner; innerlich; Innen...; ~ decorator Innenarchitekt m; Maler m, Tapezierer m; 2. Innere(s) n; Interieur n; pol. innere Angelegenheiten; Department of the ♀ Am. Innenministerium n.

interjection [intə(:)'dʒekʃən] Ausruf m.

interlace [intə(:)'leis] v/t. durchflechten, -weben; v/i. sich kreuzen.

interlock [intə(:)'lɔk] in-ea.-greifen; in-ea.-schlingen; in-ea.-haken.

interlocut|ion [intə(:)lou'kju:ʃən] Unterredung f; ~or [~ə(:)'lɔkjutə] Gesprächspartner m.

interlope [intə(:)'loup] sich eindrängen; ~r ['intə(:)loupə] Eindringling m.

interlude ['intə(:)lu:d] Zwischenspiel n; Zwischenzeit f; ~s of bright weather zeitweilig schön.

intermarriage [intə(:)'mæridʒ] Mischehe f.

intermeddle [intə(:)'medl] sich einmischen (with, in in acc.).

intermedia|ry [intə(:)'mi:djəri]
1. = intermediate; vermittelnd;
2. Vermittler m; ~te □ [~ət] in der
Mitte liegend; Mittel..., Zwischen...; ~range ballistic missile
Mittelstreckenrakete f; ~ school
Am. Mittelschule f.

interment [in'tə:mənt] Beerdigung f.

interminable □ [in'tə:minəbl] endlos, unendlich.

intermingle [intə(:)'miŋgl] (sich)
vermischen.

intermission [intə(:)'miʃən] Aussetzen n, Unterbrechung f; Pause f.

intermit [intə(:)'mit] unterbrechen,
aussetzen; ~tent □ [~tənt] aussetzend; ~ fever ✳ Wechselfieber
n.

intermix [intə(:)'miks] (sich) vermischen.

intern¹ [in'tə:n] internieren.

intern² ['intə:n] Assistenzarzt m.

internal □ [in'tə:nl] inner(lich);
inländisch.

international □ [intə(:)'næʃənl]
international; ~ law Völkerrecht n.

interphone ['intəfoun] Haustelephon n; Am. 🖂 Bordsprechanlage
f.

interpolate [in'tə:pouleit] einschieben.

interpose [intə(:)'pouz] v/t. Veto
einlegen; Wort einwerfen; v/i.
dazwischentreten; vermitteln.

interpret [in'tə:prit] auslegen, erklären, interpretieren; (ver)dolmetschen; darstellen; ~ation [intə:-
pri'teiʃən] Auslegung f; Darstellung f; ~er [in'tə:pritə] Ausleger
(-in); Dolmetscher(in); Interpret
(-in).

interrogat|e [in'terəgeit] (be-, aus-)
fragen; verhören; ~ion [intərə-
'geiʃən] (Be-, Aus)Fragen n, Verhör(en) n; Frage f; note od. mark
od. point of ~ Fragezeichen n; ~ive
□ [intə'rɔgətiv] fragend; Frage...

interrupt [intə'rʌpt] unterbrechen;
~ion [~pʃən] Unterbrechung f.

intersect [intə(:)'sekt] (sich) schneiden; ~ion [~kʃən] Durchschnitt m;
Schnittpunkt m; Straßen- etc.
Kreuzung f.

intersperse [intə(:)'spə:s] einstreuen; untermengen, durchsetzen.

interstate Am. [intə(:)'steit] zwischenstaatlich.

intertwine [intə(:)'twain] verflechten.

interval ['intəvəl] Zwischenraum m;
Pause f; (Zeit)Abstand m.

interven|e [intə(:)'vi:n] dazwischenkommen; sich einmischen; einschreiten; dazwischenliegen; ~tion
[~'venʃən] Dazwischenkommen n;
Einmischung f; Vermitt(e)lung f.

interview ['intəvju:] 1. Zusammenkunft f, Unterredung f; Interview
n; 2. interviewen.

intestine [in'testin] 1. inner; 2.
Darm m; ~s pl. Eingeweide n/pl.

intima|cy ['intiməsi] Intimität f,
Vertraulichkeit f; ~te 1. [~meit]
bekanntgeben; zu verstehen geben;
2. □ [~mit] intim; 3. [~] Vertraute(r m) f; ~tion [inti'meiʃən] Andeutung f, Wink m; Ankündigung f.

intimidate [in'timideit] einschüchtern.

into prp. ['intu, vor Konsonant 'intə]
in (acc.), in ... hinein.

intolera|ble □ [in'tɔlərəbl] unerträglich; ~nt □ [~ənt] unduldsam,
intolerant.

intonation [intou'neiʃən] Anstimmen n; gr. Intonation f, Tonfall m.

intoxica|nt [in'tɔksikənt] 1. berauschend; 2. berauschendes Getränk;
~te [~keit] berauschen (a. fig.);
~tion [intɔksi'keiʃən] Rausch m (a.
fig.).

intractable □ [in'træktəbl] unlenksam, störrisch; schwer zu bändigen(d).

intransitive □ gr. [in'trænsitiv]
intransitiv.

intrastate Am. [intrə'steit] innerstaatlich.

intrench [in'trentʃ] = entrench.

intrepid [in'trepid] unerschrocken.

intricate □ ['intrikit] verwickelt.

intrigue [in'tri:g] 1. Ränkespiel n,
Intrige f; (Liebes)Verhältnis n;
2. v/i. Ränke schmieden, intrigieren; ein (Liebes)Verhältnis haben;
v/t. neugierig machen; ~r [~gə]
Intrigant(in).

intrinsic(al □) [in'trinsik(əl)] inner(lich); wirklich, wahr.

introduc|e [intrə'dju:s] einführen
(a. fig.); bekannt machen (to mit),
vorstellen (to j-m); einleiten; ~tion
[~'dʌkʃən] Einführung f; Einleitung f; Vorstellung f; letter of ~
Empfehlungsschreiben n; ~tory
[~ktəri] einleitend, einführend.

introspection [introu'spekʃən]
Selbstprüfung f; Selbstbetrachtung f.

introvert 1. [introu'və:t] einwärtskehren; 2. psych. ['introuvə:t] nach
innen gekehrter Mensch.

intru|de [in'tru:d] hineinzwängen;
(sich) ein- od. aufdrängen; ~der
[~də] Eindringling m; ~sion [~u:-
ʒən] Eindringen n; Auf-, Zudringlichkeit f; ~sive □ [~u:siv] zudringlich.

intrust [in'trʌst] = entrust.

intuition [intju(:)'iʃən] unmittelbare Erkenntnis, Intuition f.

inundate ['inʌndeit] überschwemmen.

inure [i'njuə] gewöhnen (to an acc.).

invade [in'veid] eindringen in, ein-

fallen in (acc.); fig. befallen; ~r [~də] Angreifer m; Eindringling m.
invalid[1] ['invəli:d] 1. dienstunfähig; kränklich; 2. Invalide m.
invalid[2] [in'vælid] (rechts)ungültig; ~ate [~deit] entkräften; ~ ungültig machen. [schätzbar.)
invaluable □ [in'væljuəbl] un-)
invariab|le □ [in'veəriəbl] unveränderlich; ~ly [~li] ausnahmslos.
invasion [in'veiʒən] Einfall m, Angriff m, Invasion f; Eingriff m; ⚕ Anfall m.
invective [in'vektiv] Schmähung f, Schimpfrede f, Schimpfwort n.
inveigh [in'vei] schimpfen (against über, auf acc.).
inveigle [in'vi:gl] verleiten.
invent [in'vent] erfinden; ~ion [~nʃən] Erfindung(sgabe) f; ~ive □ [~ntiv] erfinderisch; ~or [~tə] Erfinder(in); ~ory ['invəntri] 1. Inventar n; Inventur f; 2. inventarisieren.
invers|e □ ['in'və:s] umgekehrt; ~ion [in'və:ʃən] Umkehrung f; gr. Inversion f.
invert [in'və:t] umkehren; umstellen; ~ed commas pl. Anführungszeichen n/pl.
invest [in'vest] investieren, anlegen; bekleiden; ausstatten; umgeben (with von); ✕ belagern.
investigat|e [in'vestigeit] erforschen; untersuchen; nachforschen; ~ion [investi'geiʃən] Erforschung f; Untersuchung f; Nachforschung f; ~or [in'vestigeitə] Untersuchende(r m) f.
invest|ment † [in'vestmənt] Kapitalanlage f; Investition f; ~or [~tə] Geldgeber m.
inveterate □ [in'vetərit] eingewurzelt.
invidious □ [in'vidiəs] verhaßt; gehässig; beneidenswert.
invigorate [in'vigəreit] kräftigen.
invincible □ [in'vinsəbl] unbesiegbar; unüberwindlich.
inviola|ble □ [in'vaiələbl] unverletzlich; ~te [~lit] unverletzt.
invisible [in'vizəbl] unsichtbar.
invit|ation [invi'teiʃən] Einladung f, Aufforderung f; ~e [in'vait] einladen; auffordern; (an)locken.
invoice † ['invɔis] Faktura f, Warenrechnung f.
invoke [in'vouk] anrufen; zu Hilfe rufen (acc.); sich berufen auf (acc.); Geist heraufbeschwören.
involuntary □ [in'vɔləntəri] unfreiwillig; unwillkürlich.
involve [in'vɔlv] verwickeln, hineinziehen; in sich schließen, enthalten; mit sich bringen; ~ment [~vmənt] Verwicklung f; (bsd. Geld)Schwierigkeit f.
invulnerable □ [in'vʌlnərəbl] unverwundbar; fig. unanfechtbar.

inward ['inwəd] 1. □ inner(lich); 2. adv. mst ~s einwärts; nach innen; 3. ~s pl. Eingeweide n/pl.
iodine ['aiədi:n] Jod n.
IOU ['aiou'ju:] (= I owe you) Schuldschein m.
irascible □ [i'ræsibl] jähzornig.
irate [ai'reit] zornig, wütend.
iridescent [iri'desnt] schillernd.
iris ['aiəris] anat. Regenbogenhaut f, Iris f; ♀ Schwertlilie f.
Irish ['aiəriʃ] 1. irisch; 2. Irisch n; the ~ pl. die Iren pl.; ~man Ire m.
irksome ['ə:ksəm] lästig, ermüdend.
iron ['aiən] 1. Eisen n; a. flat-~ Bügeleisen n; ~s pl. Fesseln f/pl.; strike while the ~ is hot fig. das Eisen schmieden, solange es heiß ist; 2. eisern (a. fig.); Eisen...; 3. bügeln; in Eisen legen; ~-bound eisenbeschlagen; felsig; unbeugsam; ~clad 1. gepanzert; 2. Panzerschiff n; ~ curtain pol. eiserner Vorhang; ~-hearted fig. hartherzig.
ironic(al □) [ai'rɔnik(əl)] ironisch, spöttisch.
iron|ing ['aiəniŋ] Plätten n, Bügeln n; attr. Plätt..., Bügel...; ~ lung ⚕ eiserne Lunge; ~-monger Eisenhändler m; ~mongery [~əri] Eisenwaren f/pl.; ~mo(u)ld Rostfleck m; ~work schmiedeeiserne Arbeit; ~works mst ⚠ Eisenhütte f.
irony[1] ['aiəni] eisenartig, -haltig.
irony[2] ['aiərəni] Ironie f.
irradiant [i'reidjənt] strahlend (with vor Freude etc.).
irradiate [i'reidieit] bestrahlen (a. ✖); fig. aufklären; strahlen lassen.
irrational [i'ræʃənl] unvernünftig.
irreclaimable □ [iri'kleiməbl] unverbesserlich.
irrecognizable □ [i'rekəgnaizəbl] nicht (wieder)erkennbar.
irreconcilable □ [i'rekənsailəbl] unversöhnlich; unvereinbar.
irrecoverable □ [iri'kʌvərəbl] unersetzlich; unwiederbringlich.
irredeemable □ [iri'di:məbl] unkündbar; nicht einlösbar; unersetzlich.
irrefutable □ [i'refjutəbl] unwiderleglich, unwiderlegbar.
irregular □ [i'regjulə] unregelmäßig, regelwidrig; ungleichmäßig.
irrelevant □ [i'relivənt] nicht zur Sache gehörig; unzutreffend; unerheblich, belanglos (to für).
irreligious □ [iri'lidʒəs] gottlos.
irremediable □ [iri'mi:djəbl] unheilbar; unersetzlich.
irremovable □ [iri'mu:vəbl] nicht entfernbar; unabsetzbar.
irreparable □ [i'repərəbl] nicht wieder gutzumachen(d).
irreplaceable [iri'pleisəbl] unersetzlich.
irrepressible □ [iri'presəbl] ununterdrückbar; unbezähmbar.

irreproachable □ [iri'proutʃəbl] einwandfrei, untadelig.
irresistible □ [iri'zistəbl] unwiderstehlich.
irresolute □ [i'rezəlu:t] unentschlossen.
irrespective □ [iris'pektiv] (*of*) rücksichtslos (gegen); ohne Rücksicht (auf *acc.*); unabhängig (von).
irresponsible □ [iris'pɔnsəbl] unverantwortlich; verantwortungslos.
irretrievable □ [iri'tri:vəbl] unwiederbringlich, unersetzlich; nicht wieder gutzumachen(d).
irreverent □ [i'revərənt] respektlos, ehrfurchtslos.
irrevocable □ [i'revəkəbl] unwiderruflich; unabänderlich, endgültig.
irrigate ['irigeit] bewässern.
irrita|ble □ ['iritəbl] reizbar; **~nt** [~ənt] Reizmittel *n*; **~te** [~teit] reizen; ärgern; **~ting** □ [~tiŋ] aufreizend; ärgerlich (*Sache*); **~tion** [iri'teiʃən] Reizung *f*; Gereiztheit *f*, Ärger *m*.
irrupt|ion [i'rʌpʃən] Einbruch *m* (*mst fig.*); **~ive** [~ptiv] (her)einbrechend.
is [iz] *3. sg. pres. von* be.
island ['ailənd] Insel *f*; Verkehrsinsel *f*; **~er** [~də] Inselbewohner(in).
isle [ail] Insel *f*; **~t** ['ailit] Inselchen *n*.
isolat|e ['aisəleit] absondern; isolieren; **~ed** abgeschieden; **~ion** [aisə'leiʃən] Isolierung *f*, Absonderung *f*; **~ ward** *⚕* Isolierstation *f*; **~ionist** *Am. pol.* [~ʃnist] Isolationist *m*.
issue ['isju:, *Am.* 'iʃu:] **1.** Heraus-

kommen *n*, Herausfließen *n*; Abfluß *m*; Ausgang *m*; Nachkommen (-schaft *f*) *m*/*pl.*; *fig.* Ausgang *m*, Ergebnis *n*; Streitfrage *f*; Ausgabe *f* *v. Material etc.*, Erlaß *m* *v. Befehlen*; Ausgabe *f*, Exemplar *n*; Nummer *f* *e-r Zeitung*; **~** *in law* Rechtsfrage *f*; *be at* **~** uneinig sein; *point at* **~** strittiger Punkt; **2.** *v*/*i.* herauskommen; herkommen, entspringen; endigen (*in in acc.*); *v*/*t.* von sich geben; *Material etc.* ausgeben; *Befehl* erlassen; *Buch* herausgeben.
isthmus ['isməs] Landenge *f*.
it [it] **1.** es; *nach prp.* da... (*z.B. by* **~** dadurch; *for* **~** dafür); **2.** das gewisse Etwas.
Italian [i'tæljən] **1.** italienisch; **2.** Italiener(in); Italienisch *n*.
italics *typ.* [i'tæliks] Kursivschrift *f*.
itch [itʃ] **1.** *𝓈* Krätze *f*; Jucken *n*; Verlangen *n*; **2.** jucken; *be ~ing to inf.* darauf brennen, zu *inf.*; *have an ~ing palm* raffgierig sein; **~ing** ['itʃiŋ] Jucken *n*; *fig.* Gelüste *n*.
item ['aitem] **1.** desgleichen; **2.** Einzelheit *f*, Punkt *m*; Posten *m*; (Zeitungs)Artikel *m*; **~ize** [~maiz] einzeln angeben *od.* aufführen.
iterate ['itəreit] wiederholen.
itiner|ant □ [i'tinərənt] reisend; umherziehend; Reise...; **~ary** [ai-'tinərəri] Reiseroute *f*, -plan *m*; Reisebericht *m*; *attr.* Reise...
its [its] sein(e); dessen, deren.
itself [it'self] (es, sich) selbst; sich; *of* **~** von selbst; *in* **~** in sich, an sich; *by* **~** für sich allein, besonders.
ivory ['aivəri] Elfenbein *n*.
ivy *♇* ['aivi] Efeu *m*.

J

jab F [dʒæb] **1.** stechen; stoßen; **2.** Stich *m*, Stoß *m*.
jabber ['dʒæbə] plappern.
jack [dʒæk] **1.** Hebevorrichtung *f*, *bsd.* Wagenheber *m*; Malkugel *f* *beim Bowlspiel*; *⚓* Gösch *f*, kleine Flagge; *Karten:* Bube *m*; **2.** *a.* **~** *up* aufbocken. [Handlanger *m.*]
jackal ['dʒækɔ:l] *zo.* Schakal *m*; *fig.*]
jack|ass ['dʒækæs] Esel *m* (*a. fig.*); **~boots** Reitstiefel *m*/*pl.*; hohe Wasserstiefel *m*/*pl.*; **~daw** *orn.* Dohle *f*.
jacket ['dʒækit] Jacke *f*; *⊕* Mantel *m*; Schutzumschlag *m* *e-s Buches.*
jack|-knife ['dʒæknaif] (großes) Klappmesser *n*; **♀** *of all trades* Hansdampf in allen Gassen; **♀** *of all work* Faktotum *n*; **~pot** *Poker:* Einsatz *m*; *hit the* **~** *Am.* F großes Glück haben.
jade [dʒeid] (Schind)Mähre *f*, Klepper *m*; *contp.* Frauenzimmer *n*.

jag [dʒæg] Zacken *m*; *sl.* Sauferei *f*; **~ged** ['dʒægid] zackig; gekerbt; *bsd. Am. sl.* voll (*betrunken*).
jaguar *zo.* ['dʒægjuə] Jaguar *m*.
jail [dʒeil] **1.** Kerker *m*; **2.** einkerkern; **~bird** ['dʒeilbə:d] F Knastbruder *m*; Galgenvogel *m*; **~er** ['dʒeilə] Kerkermeister *m*.
jalop(p)y *bsd. Am.* F *mot.*, *✈* [dʒə-'lɔpi] Kiste *f*.
jam¹ [dʒæm] Marmelade *f*.
jam² [~] **1.** Gedränge *n*; *⊕* Hemmung *f*; *Radio:* Störung *f*; *traffic* **~** Verkehrsstockung *f*; *be in a* **~** *sl.* in der Klemme sein; **2.** (sich) (fest-, ver)klemmen; pressen, quetschen; versperren; *Radio:* stören; **~** *the brakes* mit aller Kraft bremsen.
jamboree [dʒæmbə'ri:] *der* Pfadfinder)Treffen *n*; *sl.* Vergnügen *n*, Fez *m*.

jangle ['dʒæŋgl] schrillen (lassen); laut streiten, keifen.

janitor ['dʒænitə] Portier m.

January ['dʒænjuəri] Januar m.

Japanese [dʒæpə'niːz] 1. japanisch; 2. Japaner(in); Japanisch n; the ~ pl. die Japaner pl.

jar [dʒɑː] 1. Krug m; Topf m; Glas n; Knarren n, Mißton m; Streit m; mißliche Lage; 2. knarren; unangenehm berühren; erzittern (lassen); streiten.

jaundice ♈ ['dʒɔːndis] Gelbsucht f; ~d [~st] ♈ gelbsüchtig; fig. neidisch.

jaunt [dʒɔːnt] 1. Ausflug m, Spritztour f; 2. e-n Ausflug machen; ~y □ ['dʒɔːnti] munter; flott.

javelin ['dʒævlin] Wurfspeer m.

jaw [dʒɔː] Kinnbacken m, Kiefer m; ~s pl. Rachen m; Maul n; Schlund m; ⊕ Backen f/pl.; ~-bone ['dʒɔːboun] Kieferknochen m.

jay orn. [dʒei] Eichelhäher m; ~walker Am. F ['dʒeiwɔːkə] achtlos die Straße überquerender Fußgänger.

jazz [dʒæz] 1. Jazz m; 2. F grell.

jealous □ ['dʒeləs] eifersüchtig; besorgt (of um); neidisch; ~y [~si] Eifersucht f; Neid m.

jeans [dʒiːnz] pl. Jeans pl., Niet(en)hose f.

jeep [dʒiːp] Jeep m.

jeer [dʒiə] 1. Spott m, Spötterei f; 2. spotten (at über acc.); (ver)höhnen.

jejune □ [dʒi'dʒuːn] nüchtern, fad.

jelly ['dʒeli] 1. Gallert(e f) n; Gelee n; 2. gelieren; ~fish zo. Qualle f.

jeopardize ['dʒepədaiz] gefährden.

jerk [dʒəːk] 1. Ruck m; (Muskel-)Krampf m; 2. rucken od. zerren (an dat.); schnellen; schleudern; ~water Am. ['dʒəːkwɔːtə] 1. ⚙ Nebenbahn f; 2. F klein, unbedeutend; ~y ['dʒəːki] 1. □ ruckartig; holperig; 2. Am. luftgetrocknetes Rindfleisch.

jersey ['dʒəːzi] Wollpullover m; wollenes Unterhemd.

jest [dʒest] 1. Spaß m; 2. scherzen; ~er ['dʒestə] Spaßmacher m.

jet [dʒet] 1. (Wasser-, Gas)Strahl m; Strahlrohr n; ⊕ Düse f; Düsenflugzeug n; Düsenmotor m; 2. hervorsprudeln; ~-propelled ['dʒetprəpeld] mit Düsenantrieb.

jetty ⚓ ['dʒeti] Mole f; Pier m.

Jew [dʒuː] Jude m; attr. Juden...

jewel ['dʒuːəl] Juwel m, n; ~(l)er [~lə] Juwelier m; ~(le)ry [~lri] Juwelen pl., Schmuck m.

Jew|ess ['dʒu(ː)is] Jüdin f; ~ish ['dʒu(ː)iʃ] jüdisch.

jib ⚓ [dʒib] Klüver m.

jibe [dʒaib] F [dʒaib] zustimmen.

jiffy F ['dʒifi] Augenblick m.

jig-saw ['dʒigsɔː] Laubsägema-

schine f; ~ puzzle Zusammensetzspiel n.

jilt [dʒilt] 1. Kokette f; 2. Liebhaber versetzen.

Jim [dʒim]: ~ Crow Am. Neger m; Am. Rassentrennung f.

jingle ['dʒiŋgl] 1. Geklingel n; 2. klingeln, klimpern (mit).

jitney Am. sl. ['dʒitni] 5-Cent-Stück n; billiger Omnibus.

jive Am. sl. [dʒaiv] heiße Jazzmusik; Jazzjargon m.

job [dʒɔb] 1. (Stück n) Arbeit f; Sache f, Aufgabe f; Beruf m; Stellung f; by the ~ stückweise; im Akkord; ~ lot F Ramschware f; ~work Akkordarbeit f; 2. v/t. Pferd etc. (ver)mieten; ⊕ vermitteln; v/i. im Akkord arbeiten; Maklergeschäfte machen; ~ber ['dʒɔbə] Akkordarbeiter m; Makler m; Schieber m.

jockey ['dʒɔki] 1. Jockei m; 2. prellen.

jocose □ [dʒə'kous] scherzhaft, spaßig.

jocular □ ['dʒɔkjulə] lustig; spaßig.

jocund □ ['dʒɔkənd] lustig, fröhlich.

jog [dʒɔg] 1. Stoß(en n) m; Rütteln n; Trott m; 2. v/t. (an)stoßen, (auf)rütteln; v/i. mst ~ along, ~ on dahintrotten, dahinschlendern.

John [dʒɔn]: ~ Bull John Bull (der Engländer); ~ Hancock Am. ♭ F Friedrich Wilhelm m (Unterschrift).

join [dʒɔin] 1. v/t. verbinden, zs.-fügen (to mit); sich vereinigen mit, sich gesellen zu; eintreten in (acc.); ~ battle den Kampf beginnen; ~ hands die Hände falten; sich die Hände reichen (a. fig.); v/i. sich verbinden, sich vereinigen; ~ in mitmachen bei; ~ up Soldat werden; 2. Verbindung(sstelle) f.

joiner ['dʒɔinə] Tischler m; ~y [~əri] Tischlerhandwerk n; Tischlerarbeit f.

joint [dʒɔint] 1. Verbindung(sstelle) f; Scharnier n; anat. Gelenk n; ♭ Knoten m; Braten m; Am. sl. Spelunke f; put out of ~ verrenken; 2. □ gemeinsam; Mit...; ~ heir Miterbe m; ~ stock ♭ Aktienkapital n; 3. zs.-fügen; zerlegen; ~ed ['dʒɔintid] gegliedert; Glieder...; ~-stock ♭ Aktien...; ~ company Aktiengesellschaft f.

jok|e [dʒouk] 1. Scherz m, Spaß m; practical ~ Streich m; 2. v/i. scherzen; schäkern; v/t. necken (about mit); ~er ['dʒoukə] Spaßvogel m; Karten: Joker m; Am. versteckte Klausel; ~y □ ['dʒouki] spaßig.

jolly ['dʒɔli] lustig, fidel; F nett.

jolt [dʒoult] 1. stoßen, rütteln; holpern; 2. Stoß m; Rütteln n.

Jonathan ['dʒɔnəθən]: Brother ~ der Amerikaner.

josh *Am. sl.* [dʒɔʃ] **1.** Ulk *m*; **2.** aufziehen, auf die Schippe nehmen.

jostle ['dʒɔsl] **1.** anrennen; zs.-stoßen; **2.** Stoß *m*; Zs.-Stoß *m*.

jot [dʒɔt] **1.** Jota *n*, Pünktchen *n*; **2.** ~ *down* notieren.

journal ['dʒə:nl] Journal *n*; Tagebuch *n*; Tageszeitung *f*; Zeitschrift *f*; ⊕ Wellenzapfen *m*; ~ism ['dʒə:-nəlizəm] Journalismus *m*.

journey ['dʒə:ni] **1.** Reise *f*; Fahrt *f*; **2.** reisen; ~man Geselle *m*.

jovial □ ['dʒouvjəl] heiter; gemütlich.

joy [dʒɔi] Freude *f*; Fröhlichkeit *f*; ~ful □ ['dʒɔiful] freudig; erfreut; fröhlich; ~less □ ['dʒɔilis] freudlos; unerfreulich; ~ous □ ['dʒɔiəs] freudig, fröhlich.

jubil|ant ['dʒu:bilənt] jubilierend, frohlockend; ~ate [~leit] jubeln; ~ee [~li:] Jubiläum *n*.

judge [dʒʌdʒ] **1.** Richter *m*; Schiedsrichter *m*; Beurteiler(in), Kenner(in); **2.** *v/i.* urteilen (*of* über *acc.*); *v/t.* richten; aburteilen; beurteilen (*by* nach); ansehen als.

judg(e)ment ['dʒʌdʒmənt] Urteil *n*; Urteilsspruch *m*; Urteilskraft *f*; Einsicht *f*; Meinung *f*; *göttliches* (Straf)Gericht; *Day of* ⊙, ⊙ *Day* Jüngstes Gericht.

judicature ['dʒu:dikətʃə] Gerichtshof *m*; Rechtspflege *f*.

judicial □ ['dʒu:(:)'diʃəl] gerichtlich; Gerichts...; kritisch; unparteiisch.

judicious □ [dʒu:(:)'diʃəs] verständig, klug; ~ness [~snis] Einsicht *f*.

jug [dʒʌg] Krug *m*, Kanne *f*.

juggle ['dʒʌgl] **1.** Trick *m*; Schwindel *m*; **2.** jonglieren (*a. fig.*); verfälschen; betrügen; ~r [~lə] Jongleur *m*; Taschenspieler(in).

Jugoslav ['ju:gou'slɑ:v] **1.** Jugoslaw|e *m*, -in *f*; **2.** jugoslawisch.

juic|e [dʒu:s] Saft *m*; *sl. mot.* Sprit *m*, Gas *n*; ~y □ ['dʒu:si] saftig; F interessant;   [sikautomat *m.*)

juke-box *Am.* F ['dʒu:kbɔks] Mu-ɟ

julep ['dʒu:lep] *süßes* (Arznei)Getränk; *bsd. Am. alkoholisches* Eisgetränk.

July [dʒu:(:)'lai] Juli *m*.

jumble ['dʒʌmbl] **1.** Durcheinander *n*; **2.** *v/t.* durch-ea.-werfen; ~sale Wohltätigkeitsbasar *m*.

jump [dʒʌmp] **1.** Sprung *m*; ~s *pl.*

nervöses Zs.-fahren; *high (long)* ~ Hoch- (Weit)Sprung *m*; *get (have) the* ~ *on Am.* F zuvorkommen; **2.** *v/i.* (auf)springen; ~ *at* sich stürzen auf (*acc.*); ~ *to conclusions* übereilte Schlüsse ziehen; *v/t.* hinwegspringen über (*acc.*); überspringen; springen lassen; ~er ['dʒʌmpə] Springer *m*; Jumper *m*; ~y [~pi] nervös.

junct|ion ['dʒʌŋkʃən] Verbindung *f*; Kreuzung *f*; 🚂 Knotenpunkt *m*; ~ure [~ktʃə] Verbindungspunkt *m*, -stelle *f*; (kritischer) Zeitpunkt; *at this* ~ bei diesem Stand der Dinge.

June [dʒu:n] Juni *m*.

jungle ['dʒʌŋgl] Dschungel *m*, *n*, *f*.

junior ['dʒu:njə] **1.** jünger (*to* als); *Am. univ.* der Unterstufe (angehörend); ~ *high school Am.* Oberschule *f* mit Klassen 7, 8, 9; **2.** Jüngere(r *m*) *f*; *Am.* (Ober)Schüler *m od.* Student *m* im 3. Jahr; F Kleine(r) *m*.

junk [dʒʌŋk] ⚓ Dschunke *f*; Plunder *m*, alter Kram.

junket ['dʒʌŋkit] Quarkspeise *f*; *Am.* Party *f*; Vergnügungsfahrt *f*.

juris|diction [dʒuəris'dikʃən] Rechtsprechung *f*; Gerichtsbarkeit *f*; Gerichtsbezirk *m*; ~pru-dence ['dʒuərispru:dəns] Rechtswissenschaft *f*.

juror ['dʒuərə] Geschworene(r) *m*.

jury ['dʒuəri] *die* Geschworenen *pl.*; Jury *f*, Preisgericht *n*; ~man Geschworene(r) *m*.

just □ [dʒʌst] **1.** *adj.* gerecht; rechtschaffen; **2.** *adv.* richtig; genau; (so)eben; nur; ~ *now* eben *od.* gerade jetzt.

justice ['dʒʌstis] Gerechtigkeit *f*; Richter *m*; Recht *n*; Rechtsverfahren *n*; *court of* ~ Gericht(shof *m*) *n*.

justification [dʒʌstifi'keiʃən] Rechtfertigung *f*.

justify ['dʒʌstifai] rechtfertigen.

justly ['dʒʌstli] mit Recht.

justness ['dʒʌstnis] Gerechtigkeit *f*, Billigkeit *f*; Rechtmäßigkeit *f*; Richtigkeit *f*.

jut [dʒʌt] *a.* ~ *out* hervorragen.

juvenile ['dʒu:vinail] **1.** jung, jugendlich; Jugend...; **2.** junger Mensch.

K

kale [keil] (*bsd.* Kraus-, Grün)Kohl *m*; *Am. sl.* Moos *n* (*Geld*).

kangaroo [kæŋgə'ruː] Känguruh *n*.

keel ⏚ [kiːl] 1. Kiel *m*; 2. ~ over kiel-oben legen *od.* liegen; umschlagen.

keen □ [kiːn] scharf (*a. fig.*); eifrig, heftig; stark, groß (*Appetit etc.*); ~ on F scharf *od.* erpicht auf *acc.*; be ~ on hunting ein leidenschaftlicher Jäger sein; ~edged ['kiːnedʒd] scharfgeschliffen; ~ness ['kiːnnis] Schärfe *f*; Heftigkeit *f*; Scharfsinn *m*.

keep [kiːp] 1. (Lebens)Unterhalt *m*; for ~s F für immer; 2. [*irr.*] *v/t. allg.* halten; behalten; unterhalten; (er-)halten; einhalten; (ab)halten; *Buch, Ware etc.* führen; *Bett etc.* hüten; fest-, aufhalten; (bei)behalten; (auf)bewahren; ~ s.o. company j-m Gesellschaft leisten; ~ company with verkehren mit; ~ one's temper sich beherrschen; ~ time richtig gehen (*Uhr*); ♩, ✗ Takt, Schritt halten; ~ s.o. waiting j-n warten lassen; ~ away fernhalten; ~ s.th. from s.o. j-m et. vorenthalten; ~ in zurückhalten; *Schüler* nachsitzen lassen; ~ on *Kleid* anbehalten, *Hut* aufbehalten; ~ up aufrechterhalten; (*Mut*) bewahren; in Ordnung halten; hindern, zu Bett zu gehen; aufbleiben lassen; ~ it up (es) durchhalten; *v/i.* sich halten, bleiben; F sich aufhalten; ~ doing immer wieder tun; ~ away sich fernhalten; ~ from sich enthalten (*gen.*); ~ off sich fernhalten; ~ on talking fortfahren zu sprechen; ~ to sich halten an (*acc.*); ~ up sich aufrecht halten; sich aufrechterhalten; ~ up with *Schritt* halten mit; ~ up with the Joneses es den Nachbarn gleichtun.

keep|er ['kiːpə] Wärter *m*, Wächter *m*, Aufseher *m*; Verwalter *m*; Inhaber *m*; ~ing ['kiːpiŋ] Verwahrung *f*; Obhut *f*; Gewahrsam *m*, *n*; Unterhalt *m*; be in (out of) ~ with ... (nicht) übereinstimmen mit ...; ~sake ['kiːpseik] Andenken *n*.

keg [keg] Fäßchen *n*.

kennel ['kenl] Gosse *f*, Rinnstein *m*; Hundehütte *f*, -zwinger *m*.

kept [kept] *pret. u. p.p. von* keep 2.

kerb [kəːb], ~stone ['kəːbstoun] = curb *etc.*

kerchief ['kəːtʃif] (Kopf)Tuch *n*.

kernel ['kəːnl] Kern *m* (*a. fig.*); Hafer-, Mais- *etc.* Korn *n*.

kettle ['ketl] Kessel *m*; ~drum ♩ Kesselpauke *f*.

key [kiː] 1. Schlüssel *m* (*a. fig.*); ♩ Schlußstein *m*; ⊕ Keil *m*; Schraubenschlüssel *m*; *Klavier-etc.* Taste *f*; ⌨ Taste *f*, Druck-knopf *m*; ♩ Tonart *f*; *fig.* Ton *m*; 2. ~ up ♩ stimmen; erhöhen; *fig.* in erhöhte Spannung versetzen; ~board ['kiːbɔːd] Klaviatur *f*, Tastatur *f*; ~hole Schlüsselloch *n*; ~man Schlüsselfigur *f*; ~money Ablösung *f* (*für e-e Wohnung*); ~note ♩ Grundton *m*; ~stone Schlußstein *m*; *fig.* Grundlage *f*.

kibitzer *Am.* F ['kibitsə] Kiebitz *m*, Besserwisser *m*.

kick [kik] 1. (Fuß)Tritt *m*; Stoß *m*; Schwung *m*; F Nervenkitzel *m*; get a ~ out of F Spaß finden an (*dat.*); 2. *v/t.* (mit dem Fuß) stoßen *od.* treten; *Fußball:* schießen; ~ out F hinauswerfen; *v/i.* (hinten) ausschlagen; stoßen (*Gewehr*); sich auflehnen; ~ in with *Am. sl.* Geld 'reinbuttern; ~ off *Fußball:* anstoßen; ~back *bsd. Am.* F ['kikbæk] Rückzahlung *f*; ~er ['kikə] Fußballspieler *m*.

kid [kid] 1. Zicklein *n*; *sl.* Kind *n*; Ziegenleder *n*; 2. *sl.* foppen; ~dy *sl.* ['kidi] Kind *n*; ~ glove Glacéhandschuh *m* (*a. fig.*); ~-glove sanft, zart.

kidnap ['kidnæp] entführen; ~(p)er [~pə] Kindesentführer *m*, Kidnapper *m*.

kidney ['kidni] *anat.* Niere *f*; F Art *f*; ~ bean ♀ weiße Bohne.

kill [kil] 1. töten (*a. fig.*); *fig.* vernichten; *parl.* zu Fall bringen; ~ off abschlachten; ~ time die Zeit totschlagen; 2. Tötung *f*; Jagdbeute *f*; ~er ['kilə] Totschläger *m*; ~ing ['kiliŋ] 1. ⌐ mörderisch; F komisch; 2. *Am.* F *finanzieller* Volltreffer.

kiln [kiln] Brenn-, Darrofen *m*.

kilo|gram(me) ['kiləgræm] Kilogramm *n*; ~metre, *Am.* ~meter Kilometer *m*.

kilt [kilt] Kilt *m*, Schottenrock *m*.

kin [kin] (Bluts)Verwandtschaft *f*.

kind [kaind] 1. ⌐ gütig, freundlich; 2. Art *f*, Gattung *f*, Geschlecht *n*; Art und Weise *f*; pay in ~ in Naturalien zahlen; *fig.* mit gleicher Münze heimzahlen.

kindergarten ['kindəgɑːtn] Kindergarten *m*.

kind-hearted ['kaind'hɑːtid] gütig.

kindle ['kindl] anzünden; (sich) entzünden (*a. fig.*).

kindling ['kindliŋ] Kleinholz *n*.

kind|ly [kaindli] freundlich; günstig; ~ness [~dnis] Güte *f*, Freundlichkeit *f*; Gefälligkeit *f*.

kindred [kindrid] 1. verwandt, gleichartig; 2. Verwandtschaft *f*.

king [kiŋ] König *m* (*a. fig. u. Schach, Kartenspiel*); ~dom [~dəm] Königreich *n*; *bsd.* ♀, *zo.* Reich *n*, Gebiet *n*; *eccl.* Reich *n* Gottes; ~like

['kiŋlaik], **~ly** [~li] königlich; **~size**
F ['kiŋsaiz] überlang, übergroß.
kink [kiŋk] Schlinge f, Knoten m;
fig. Schrulle f, Fimmel m.
kin|ship ['kiŋʃip] Verwandtschaft f;
~sman ['kinzmən] Verwandte(r) m.
kipper ['kipə] Räucherhering m
Bückling m; *sl.* Kerl m.
kiss [kis] 1. Kuß m; 2. (sich) küssen.
kit [kit] Ausrüstung f (a. ⚔ u.
Sport); Handwerkszeug n; Werkzeug n; **~bag** ['kitbæg] ⚔ Tornister m; Seesack m; Reisetasche f.
kitchen ['kitʃin] Küche f; **~ette**
[kitʃi'net] Kochnische f; **~garden**
['kitʃin'gɑːdn] Gemüsegarten m.
kite [kait] *Papier*-Drachen m.
kitten ['kitn] Kätzchen n.
Klan *Am.* [klæn] Ku-Klux-Klan m;
~sman ['klænzmən] Mitglied n des
Ku-Klux-Klan.
knack [næk] Kniff m, Dreh m; Geschicklichkeit f. [Rucksack m.\
knapsack ['næpsæk] Tornister m;\
knave [neiv] Schurke m; *Kartenspiel:* Bube m; **~ry** ['neivəri] Gaunerei f.
knead [niːd] kneten; massieren.
knee [niː] Knie n; ⊕ Kniestück n;
~cap ['niːkæp] Kniescheibe f; **~
deep** bis an die Knie (reichend);
~joint Kniegelenk n; **~l** [niːl] [*irr.*]
knien (to vor *dat.*).
knell [nel] Totenglocke f.
knelt [nelt] *pret. u. p.p. von* kneel.
knew [njuː] *pret. von* know.
knicker|bockers ['nikəbɔkəz] *pl.*
Knickerbocker *pl.*, Kniehosen f/pl.;
~s F ['nikəz] *pl.* Schlüpfer m; =
knickerbockers.
knick-knack ['niknæk] Spielerei f;
Nippsache f.
knife [naif] 1. *pl.* **knives** [naivz]
Messer n; 2. schneiden; (er)ste-
chen.
knight [nait] 1. Ritter m; Springer m
im Schach; 2. zum Ritter schlagen;
~errant ['nait'erənt] fahrender
Ritter; **~hood** ['naithud] Ritter-
tum n; Ritterschaft f; **~ly** ['naitli]
ritterlich.
knit [nit] [*irr.*] stricken; (ver)knüp-

fen; (sich) eng verbinden; **~ the
brows** die Stirn runzeln; **~ting**
['nitiŋ] Stricken n; Strickzeug n;
attr. Strick...
knives [naivz] *pl. von* knife 1.
knob [nɔb] Knopf m; Buckel m;
Brocken m.
knock [nɔk] 1. Schlag m; Anklopfen
n; *mot.* Klopfen n; 2. v/i. klopfen;
pochen; stoßen; schlagen; **~ about**
F sich herumtreiben; v/t. klopfen,
stoßen, schlagen; *Am. sl.* bekritteln, schlechtmachen; **~ about** her-
umstoßen, übel zurichten; **~ down**
niederschlagen; *Auktion:* zuschlagen; ⊕ aus-ea.-nehmen; be **~ed
down** überfahren werden; **~ off** aufhören mit; F zs.-hauen (*schnell erledigen*); *Summe* abziehen; **~ out**
Boxen: k.o. schlagen; **~er** ['nɔk]
Klopfende(r) m; Türklopfer m; *Am.
sl.* Kritikaster m; **~kneed** ['nɔk-
niːd] x-beinig; *fig.* hinkend; **~out**
Boxen: Knockout m, K.o. m; *sl.*
tolle Sache *od.* Person.
knoll[1] [noul] kleiner Erdhügel.
knoll[2] [~] (*bsd. zu Grabe*) läuten.
knot [nɔt] 1. Knoten m; Knorren m;
Seemeile f; Schleife f; Band n (a.
fig.); Schwierigkeit f; 2. (ver)kno-
ten, (ver)knüpfen (a. *fig.*); *Stirn*
runzeln; verwickeln; **~ty** ['nɔti]
knotig; knorrig; *fig.* verwickelt.
know [nou] [*irr.*] wissen; (er)ken-
nen; erfahren; **~ French** Französisch
können; come to **~** erfahren; get to
~ kennenlernen; **~** one's business,
~ the ropes, **~** a thing or two, **~** what's
what sich auskennen, Erfahrung
haben; you **~** (*am Ende des Satzes*)
nämlich; **~ing** □ ['nouiŋ] erfahren;
klug; schlau; verständnisvoll; wissentlich; **~ledge** ['nɔlidʒ] Kennt-
nis(se *pl.*) f; Wissen n; to my **~**
meines Wissens; **~n** [noun] *p.p. von*
know; come to be **~** bekannt werden;
make **~** bekanntmachen.
knuckle ['nʌkl] 1. Knöchel m; 2. **~
down**, **~ under** nachgeben.
Kremlin ['kremlin] der Kreml.
Ku-Klux-Klan *Am.* ['kjuːklʌks-
'klæn] *Geheimbund in den USA.*

L

label ['leibl] 1. Zettel m, Etikett n;
Aufschrift f; Schildchen n; Bezeichnung f; 2. etikettieren, beschriften; *fig.* abstempeln (*as*
als).
laboratory [lə'bɔrətəri] Laboratorium n; **~** *assistant* Laborant(in).
laborious □ [lə'bɔːriəs] mühsam;
arbeitsam; schwerfällig (*Stil*).
labo(u)r ['leibə] 1. Arbeit f; Mühe

f; (Geburts)Wehen f/pl.; Arbeiter
m/pl.; *Ministry of* ⚥ Arbeitsministe-
rium n; *hard* **~** Zwangsarbeit f; 2.
Arbeiter...; Arbeits...; 3. v/i. arbeiten; sich abmühen; **~** *under* leiden
unter (*dat.*), zu kämpfen haben mit;
v/t. ausarbeiten; **~ed** schwerfällig
(*Stil*); mühsam (*Atem etc.*); **~er**
[~ərə] ungelernter Arbeiter; ⚥ **Exchange** Arbeitsamt n; **Labour**

Party *pol.* Labour Party *f*; **labor union** *Am.* Gewerkschaft *f*.

lace [leis] **1.** Spitze *f*; Borte *f*; Schnur *f*; **2.** (zu)schnüren; mit Spitze *etc.* besetzen; *Schnur* durch-, einziehen; ~ (*into*) s.o. j-n verprügeln.

lacerate ['læsəreit] zerreißen; *fig.* quälen.

lack [læk] **1.** Fehlen *n*, Mangel *m*; **2.** *v/t.* ermangeln (*gen.*); he ~s money es fehlt ihm an Geld; *v/i.* be ~ing fehlen, mangeln; ~**lustre** ['læklʌstə] glanzlos, matt.

laconic [lə'kɔnik] (~ally) lakonisch, wortkarg, kurz und prägnant.

lacquer ['lækə] **1.** Lack *m*; **2.** lackieren.

lad [læd] Bursche *m*, Junge *m*.

ladder ['lædə] Leiter *f*; Laufmasche *f*; ~**proof** maschenfest (*Strumpf etc.*).

laden ['leidn] beladen.

lading ['leidiŋ] Ladung *f*, Fracht *f*.

ladle ['leidl] **1.** Schöpflöffel *m*, Kelle *f*; **2.** ~ out Suppe austeilen.

lady ['leidi] Dame *f*; Lady *f*; Herrin *f*; ~ *doctor* Ärztin *f*; ~**bird** Marienkäfer *m*; ~**like** damenhaft; ~**love** Geliebte *f*; ~**ship** [~iʃip]: her ~ die gnädige Frau; Your Q gnädige Frau, Euer Gnaden.

lag [læg] **1.** zögern; *a.* ~ behind zurückbleiben; **2.** Verzögerung *f*.

lager (beer) ['lɑːgə(biə)] Lagerbier *n*.

laggard ['lægəd] Nachzügler *m*.

lagoon [lə'guːn] Lagune *f*.

laid [leid] *pret. u. p.p. von* lay³ **2;** ~ up bettlägerig (*with mit, wegen*).

lain [lein] *p.p. von* lie² 2.

lair [lɛə] Lager *n* e-s *wilden Tieres.*

laity ['leiiti] Laien *m/pl.*

lake [leik] See *m*; rote Pigmentfarbe.

lamb [læm] **1.** Lamm *n*; **2.** lammen.

lambent ['læmbənt] leckend; züngelnd (*Flamme*); funkelnd.

lamb|kin ['læmkin] Lämmchen *n*; ~**like** lammfromm.

lame [leim] **1.** □ lahm (*a. fig.* = *mangelhaft*); **2.** lähmen.

lament [lə'ment] **1.** Wehklage *f*; **2.** (be)klagen; trauern; ~**able** □ ['læməntəbl] beklagenswert; kläglich; ~**ation** [læmən'teiʃən] Wehklage *f*.

lamp [læmp] Lampe *f*; *fig.* Leuchte *f*.

lampoon [læm'puːn] **1.** Schmähschrift *f*; **2.** schmähen.

lamp-post ['læmppoust] Laternenpfahl *m*.

lampshade ['læmpʃeid] Lampenschirm *m*.

lance [lɑːns] **1.** Lanze *f*; Speer *m*; **2.** ✄ aufschneiden; ~**corporal** ⚔ ['lɑːns'kɔːpərəl] Gefreite(r) *m*.

land [lænd] **1.** Land *n*; Grundstück *n*; *by* ~ auf dem Landweg; ~*s pl.*

Ländereien *f/pl.*; **2.** landen; ⚓ löschen; *Preis* gewinnen; ~**agent** ['lændeidʒənt] Grundstücksmakler *m*; Gutsverwalter *m*; ~**ed** grundbesitzend; Land..., Grund...; ~**holder** Grundbesitzer(in).

landing ['lændiŋ] Landung *f*; Treppenabsatz *m*; Anlegestelle *f*; ~**field** ✈ Landebahn *f*; ~**gear** Fahrgestell *n*; ~**stage** Landungsbrücke *f*.

land|lady ['lænleidi] Vermieterin *f*, Wirtin *f*; ~**lord** [~lɔːd] Vermieter *m*; Wirt *m*; Haus-, Grundbesitzer *m*; ~**lubber** ⚓ *contp.* Landratte *f*; ~**mark** Grenz-, Markstein *m* (*a fig.*); Wahrzeichen *n*; ~**owner** Grundbesitzer(in); ~**scape** [~skeip] Landschaft *f*; ~**slide** Erdrutsch *m* (*a. pol.*); *a Democratic* ~ ein Erdrutsch zugunsten der Demokraten; ~**slip** *konkr.* Erdrutsch *m*.

lane [lein] Feldweg *m*; Gasse *f*; Spalier *n*; *mot.* Fahrbahn *f*, Spur *f*.

language ['læŋgwidʒ] Sprache *f*; *strong* ~ Kraftausdrücke *m/pl.*

languid □ ['læŋgwid] matt; träg.

languish ['læŋgwiʃ] matt werden; schmachten; dahinsiechen.

languor ['læŋgə] Mattigkeit *f*; Schmachten *n*; Stille *f*.

lank □ [læŋk] schmächtig, dünn; schlicht; ~**y** □ ['læŋki] schlaksig.

lantern ['læntən] Laterne *f*; ~**slide** Dia(positiv) *n*, Lichtbild *n*.

lap [læp] **1.** Schoß *m*; ⊕ Vorstoß *m*; Runde *f*; **2.** über-ea.-legen; (ein-)hüllen; auflecken; schlürfen; plätschern (gegen) (*Wellen*).

lapel [lə'pel] Aufschlag *m* am Rock.

lapse [læps] **1.** Verlauf *m* der Zeit; Verfallen *n*; Versehen *n*; **2.** (ver-)fallen; verfließen; fehlen.

larceny ⚖ ['lɑːsni] Diebstahl *m*.

larch ♣ [lɑːtʃ] Lärche *f*.

lard [lɑːd] **1.** (Schweine)Schmalz *n*; **2.** spicken (*a. fig.*); ~**er** ['lɑːdə] Speisekammer *f*.

large □ [lɑːdʒ] groß; weit; reichlich; weitherzig; flott; Groß...; *at* ~ auf freiem Fuß; ausführlich; als Ganzes; ~**ly** ['lɑːdʒli] zum großen Teil, weitgehend; ~**minded** weitherzig; ~**ness** ['lɑːdʒnis] Größe *f*; Weite *f*; ~**sized** groß(formatig).

lariat *Am.* ['læriət] Lasso *n*, *m*.

lark [lɑːk] *orn.* Lerche *f*; *fig.* Streich *m*.

larkspur ♣ ['lɑːkspəː] Rittersporn *m*.

larva *zo.* ['lɑːvə] Larve *f*, Puppe *f*.

larynx *anat.* ['læriŋks] Kehlkopf *m*.

lascivious □ [lə'siviəs] lüstern.

lash [læʃ] **1.** Peitsche(nschnur) *f*; Hieb *m*; Wimper *f*; **2.** peitschen; *fig.* geißeln; schlagen; anbinden.

lass, ~ie [læs, 'læsi] Mädchen *n*.

lassitude ['læsitjuːd] Mattigkeit *f*, Abgespanntheit *f*; Desinteresse *n*.

last¹ [lɑːst] 1. adj. letzt; vorig; äußerst; geringst; ~ but one vorletzt; ~ night gestern abend; 2. Letzte(r m, -s n) f; Ende n; at ~ zuletzt, endlich; 3. adv. zuletzt; ~, but not least nicht zuletzt.

last² [~] dauern; halten (Farbe); ausreichen; ausdauern.

last³ [~] (Schuhmacher)Leisten m.

lasting □ ['lɑːstiŋ] dauerhaft; beständig.

lastly ['lɑːstli] zuletzt, schließlich.

latch [lætʃ] 1. Klinke f, Drücker m; Druckschloß n; 2. ein-, zuklinken.

late [leit] spät; (kürzlich) verstorben; ehemalig; jüngst; at (the) ~st spätestens; as ~ as noch (in dat.); of ~ letzthin; ~r on später; be ~ (zu) spät kommen; ~ly ['leitli] kürzlich.

latent □ ['leitənt] verborgen, latent; gebunden (Wärme etc.).

lateral □ ['lætərəl] seitlich; Seiten...

lath [lɑːθ] 1. Latte f; 2. belatten.

lathe ⊕ [leið] Drehbank f; Lade f.

lather ['lɑːðə] 1. (Seifen)Schaum m; 2. v/t. einseifen; v/i. schäumen.

Latin ['lætin] 1. lateinisch; 2. Latein n.

latitude ['lætitjuːd] Breite f; fig. Umfang m, Weite f; Spielraum m.

latter ['lætə] neuer; der (die, das) letztere; ~ly ['~əli] neuerdings.

lattice ['lætis] a. ~work Gitter n.

laud [lɔːd] loben, preisen; ~able □ ['lɔːdəbl] lobenswert, löblich.

laugh [lɑːf] 1. Gelächter n, Lachen n; 2. lachen; ~ at j-n auslachen; he ~s best who ~s last wer zuletzt lacht, lacht am besten; ~able □ ['lɑːfəbl] lächerlich; ~ter ['lɑːftə] Gelächter n, Lachen n.

launch [lɔːntʃ] 1. ⊕ Stapellauf m; Barkasse f; 2. vom Stapel laufen lassen; Boot aussetzen; schleudern (a. fig.); Schläge versetzen; Rakete starten, abschießen; fig. in Gang bringen; ~ing-pad ['lɔːntʃiŋpæd] (Raketen)Abschußrampe f.

launderette [lɔːndə'ret] Selbstbedienungswaschsalon m.

laund|ress ['lɔːndris] Wäscherin f; ~ry [~ri] Waschanstalt f; Wäsche f.

laurel ♀ ['lɔrəl] Lorbeer m (a. fig.).

lavatory ['lævətəri] Waschraum m; Toilette f; public ~ Bedürfnisanstalt f.

lavender ♀ ['lævində] Lavendel m.

lavish ['læviʃ] 1. □ freigebig, verschwenderisch; 2. verschwenden.

law [lɔː] Gesetz n; (Spiel)Regel f; Recht(swissenschaft f) n; Gericht(sverfahren) n; go to ~ vor Gericht gehen; lay down the ~ den Ton angeben; ~-abiding ['lɔːəbaidiŋ] friedlich; ~-court Gericht(shof m) n; ~ful □ ['lɔːful] gesetzlich; gültig; ~less □ ['lɔːlis] gesetzlos; ungesetzlich; zügellos.

lawn [lɔːn] Rasen(platz) m; Batist m.

law|suit ['lɔːsjuːt] Prozeß m; ~yer ['lɔːjə] Jurist m; (Rechts)Anwalt m.

lax □ [læks] locker; schlaff (a. fig.); lasch; ~ative ⚕ ['læksətiv] 1. abführend; 2. Abführmittel n.

lay¹ [lei] pret. von lie² 2.

lay² [~] weltlich; Laien...

lay³ [~] 1. Lage f, Richtung f; 2. [irr.] v/t. legen; umlegen; Plan etc. ersinnen; stellen, setzen; Tisch decken; lindern; besänftigen; auferlegen; Summe wetten; ~ before s.o. j-m vorlegen; ~ in einlagern, sich eindecken mit; ~ low niederwerfen; ~ open darlegen; ~ out auslegen; Garten etc. anlegen; ~ up Vorräte hinlegen, sammeln; be laid up ans Bett gefesselt sein; ~ with belegen mit; v/i. (Eier) legen; a. ~ a wager wetten.

lay-by ['leibai] Park-, Rastplatz m an e-r Fernstraße.

layer ['leiə] Lage f, Schicht f.

layman ['leimən] Laie m.

lay|off ['leiɔːf] Arbeitsunterbrechung f; ~out Anlage f; Plan m.

lazy □ ['leizi] faul.

lead¹ [led] Blei n; ⊕ Lot n, Senkblei n; typ. Durchschuß m.

lead² [liːd] 1. Führung f; Leitung f; Beispiel n; thea. Hauptrolle f; Kartenspiel: Vorhand f; ⚡ Leitung f; Hunde-Leine f; 2. [irr.] v/t. (an-)führen, leiten; bewegen (to zu); Karte ausspielen; ~ on (ver)locken; v/i. vorangehen; ~ off den Anfang machen; ~ up to überleiten zu.

leaden ['ledn] bleiern (a. fig.); Blei...

leader ['liːdə] (An)Führer(in), Leiter(in); Erste(r) m; Leitartikel m; ~ship [~ʃip] Führerschaft f.

leading ['liːdiŋ] 1. leitend; Leit...; Haupt...; 2. Leitung f, Führung f.

leaf [liːf], pl. leaves [liːvz] Blatt n; Tür- etc. Flügel m; Tisch-Platte f; ~let ['liːflit] Blättchen n; Flug-Merkblatt n; ~y ['liːfi] belaubt.

league [liːg] 1. Liga f (a. hist. u. Sport); Bund m; mst poet. Meile f; 2. (sich) verbünden.

leak [liːk] 1. Leck n; 2. leck sein; tropfen; ~ out durchsickern; ~age ['liːkidʒ] Lecken n; ⚡ Leckage f; Verlust m (a. fig.), Schwund m; Durchsickern n; ~y ['liːki] leck; undicht.

lean [liːn] 1. [irr.] (sich) (an)lehnen; (sich) stützen; (sich) (hin)neigen; 2. mager; 3. mageres Fleisch.

leant [lent] pret. u. p.p. von lean 1.

leap [liːp] 1. Sprung m; 2. [irr.] (über)springen; ~t [lept] pret. u. p.p. von leap 2; ~year ['liːpjəː] Schaltjahr n.

learn [ləːn] [irr.] lernen; erfahren, hören; ~ from ersehen aus; ~ed [ləːnid] gelehrt; ~er ['ləːnə] Anfänger(in); ~ing ['lɔ:niŋ] Lernen n; Gelehrsamkeit f; ~t [lɛ:nt] pret. u. p.p. von learn.

lease [li:s] 1. Verpachtung f, Vermietung f; Pacht f, Miete f; Pacht-, Mietvertrag m; 2. (ver-)pachten, (ver)mieten.

leash [li:ʃ] 1. Koppelleine f; Koppel f (3 Hunde etc.); 2. koppeln.

least [li:st] 1. adj. kleinst, geringst; wenigst, mindest; 2. adv. a. ~ of all am wenigsten; at ~ wenigstens; 3. das Mindeste, das Wenigste; to say the ~ gelinde gesagt.

leather ['leðə] 1. Leder n (fig.Haut); 2. a. ~n ledern; Leder...

leave [li:v] 1. Erlaubnis f; a. ~ of absence Urlaub m; Abschied m; 2. [irr.] v/t. (ver)lassen; zurück-, hinterlassen; übriglassen; überlassen; ~ off aufhören (mit); Kleid ablegen; v/i. ablassen; weggehen, abreisen (for nach).

leaven ['levn] Sauerteig m; Hefe f.

leaves [li:vz] pl. von leaf; Laub n.

leavings ['li:viŋz] pl. Überbleibsel n/pl.

lecherous ['letʃərəs] wollüstig.

lecture ['lektʃə] 1. Vorlesung f, Vortrag m; Strafpredigt f; 2. v/i. Vorlesungen od. Vorträge halten; v/t. abkanzeln; ~r [~ərə] Vortragende(r m) f; univ. Dozent(in).

led [led] pret. u. p.p. von lead² 2.

ledge [ledʒ] Leiste f; Sims m, n; Riff n.

ledger † ['ledʒə] Hauptbuch n.

leech zo. [li:tʃ] Blutegel m; fig. Schmarotzer m.

leek ♀ [li:k] Lauch m, Porree m.

leer [liə] 1. (lüsterner od. finsterer) Seitenblick; 2. schielen (at nach).

lees [li:z] pl. Bodensatz m, Hefe f.

lee|**ward** ⚓ ['li:wəd] leewärts; ~way ['li:wei] ⚓ Abtrift f; make up ~ fig. Versäumtes nachholen.

left¹ [left] pret. u. p.p. von leave 2.

left² [~] 1. link(s); 2. Linke f; ~-handed ['left'hændid] linkshändig; linkisch.

left-luggage office ['left'lʌgidʒ-ɔfis] Gepäckaufbewahrung(sstelle) f; ~overs pl. Speisereste m/pl.

leg [leg] Bein n; Keule f; (Stiefel-) Schaft m; ⚓ Schenkel m; pull s.o.'s ~j-n auf den Arm nehmen (hänseln).

legacy ['legəsi] Vermächtnis n.

legal ◻ ['li:gəl] gesetzlich; rechtsgültig; juristisch; Rechts...; ~ize [~laiz] rechtskräftig machen; beurkunden.

legation [li'geiʃən] Gesandtschaft f.

legend ['ledʒənd] Legende f; ~ary [~dəri] legendär, sagenhaft.

leggings ['legiŋz] pl. Gamaschen f/pl.

legible ◻ ['ledʒəbl] leserlich.

legionary ['li:dʒənəri] Legionär m.

legislat|**ion** [ledʒis'leiʃən] Gesetz-

gebung f; ~ive ['ledʒislətiv] gesetzgebend; ~or [~leitə] Gesetzgeber m.

legitima|**cy** [li'dʒitiməsi] Rechtmäßigkeit f; ~te 1. [~meit] legitimieren; 2. [~mit] rechtmäßig.

leisure ['leʒə] Muße f; at your ~ wenn es Ihnen paßt; ~ly [~əli] gemächlich.

lemon ['lemən] Zitrone f; ~ade [lemə'neid] Limonade f; ~ squash Zitronenwasser n.

lend [lend] [irr.] (ver-, aus)leihen; Hilfe leisten, gewähren.

length [leŋθ] Länge f; Strecke f; (Zeit)Dauer f; at ~ endlich, zuletzt; go all ~s aufs Ganze gehen; ~en ['leŋθən] (sich) verlängern, (sich) ausdehnen; ~wise ['~θwaiz] der Länge nach; ~y ◻ [~θi] sehr lang.

lenient ◻ ['li:njənt] mild, nachsichtig.

lens opt. [lenz] Linse f.

lent¹ [lent] pret. u. p.p. von lend.

Lent² [~] Fasten pl., Fastenzeit f.

leopard ['lepəd] Leopard m.

lepr|**osy** ♀ ['leprəsi] Aussatz m, Lepra f; ~ous [~əs] aussätzig.

less [les] 1. adj. u. adv. kleiner, geringer; weniger; 2. prp. minus.

lessen ['lesn] v/t. vermindern, schmälern; v/i. abnehmen.

lesser ['lesə] kleiner; geringer.

lesson ['lesn] Lektion f; Aufgabe f; (Unterrichts)Stunde f; Lehre f; ~s pl. Unterricht m.

lest [lest] damit nicht, daß nicht.

let [let] [irr.] lassen; vermieten, verpachten; ~ alone in Ruhe lassen; geschweige denn; ~ down j-n im Stich lassen; ~ go loslassen; ~ into einweihen in (acc.); ~ off abschießen; j-n laufen lassen; ~ out hinauslassen; ausplaudern; vermieten; ~ up aufhören.

lethal ◻ ['li:θəl] tödlich; Todes...

lethargy ['leθədʒi] Lethargie f.

letter ['letə] 1. Buchstabe m; Type f; Brief m; ~s pl. Literatur f, Wissenschaft f; attr. Brief...; to the ~ buchstäblich; 2. beschriften, betiteln; ~box Briefkasten m; ~card Kartenbrief m; ~carrier Am. Briefträger m; ~case Brieftasche f; ~cover Briefumschlag m; ~ed (literarisch) gebildet; ~file Briefordner m; ~ing [~əriŋ] Beschriftung f; ~press Kopierpresse f.

lettuce ♀ ['letis] Lattich m, Salat m.

leuk(a)emia ♀ [lju:'ki:miə] Leukämie f.

levee¹ ['levi] Morgenempfang m.

levee² [~] Am. Uferdamm m.

level ['levl] 1. waag(e)recht, eben; gleich; ausgeglichen; my ~ best mein möglichstes; ~ crossing 🚃 schienengleicher Übergang; 2. ebene Fläche; (gleiche) Höhe, Niveau n, Stand m; fig. Maßstab m; Wasserwaage f; sea ~ Meeresspiegel m; on the ~ F offen, aufrichtig; 3. v/t. gleichmachen, ebnen; fig. anpassen; richten, zielen mit; ~ up erhöhen; v/i. ~ at, against zielen auf (acc.); ~-headed vernünftig, nüchtern.

lever ['li:və] Hebel m; Hebestange f; ~age [_ərɪdʒ] Hebelkraft f.

levity ['levɪtɪ] Leichtfertigkeit f.

levy ['levɪ] 1. Erhebung f von Steuern; ✗ Aushebung f; Aufgebot n; 2. Steuern erheben; ✗ ausheben.

lewd □ [lu:d] liederlich, unzüchtig.

liability [laɪə'bɪlɪtɪ] Verantwortlichkeit f; ✿t Haftpflicht f; Verpflichtung f; fig. Hang m; liabilities pl. Verbindlichkeiten f/pl., ✝ Passiva pl.

liable □ ['laɪəbl] verantwortlich; haftpflichtig; verpflichtet; ausgesetzt (to dat.); be ~ to neigen zu.

liar ['laɪə] Lügner(in).

libel ['laɪbəl] 1. Schmähschrift f; Verleumdung f; 2. schmähen; verunglimpfen.

liberal ['lɪbərəl] 1. □ liberal (a. pol.); freigebig; reichlich; freisinnig; 2. Liberale(r) m; ~ity [lɪbə'rælɪtɪ] Freigebigkeit f; Freisinnigkeit f.

liberat|e ['lɪbəreɪt] befreien; freilassen; ~ion [lɪbə'reɪʃən] Befreiung f; ~or ['lɪbəreɪtə] Befreier m.

libertine ['lɪbə(:)taɪn] Wüstling m.

liberty ['lɪbətɪ] Freiheit f; take liberties sich Freiheiten erlauben; be at ~ frei sein.

librar|ian [laɪ'brɛərɪən] Bibliothekar(in); ~y ['laɪbrərɪ] Bibliothek f.

lice [laɪs] pl. von louse.

licen|ce, Am. ~se ['laɪsəns] 1. Lizenz f; Erlaubnis f; Konzession f; Freiheit f; Zügellosigkeit f; driving ~ Führerschein m; 2. lizenzieren, berechtigen; et. genehmigen; ~see [laɪsən'si:] Lizenznehmer m.

licentious □ [laɪ'senʃəs] unzüchtig; ausschweifend.

lichen ♀, ✿ ['laɪkən] Flechte f.

lick [lɪk] 1. Lecken n; Salzlecke f; F Schlag m; 2. (be)lecken; F verdreschen; übertreffen; ~ the dust im Staub kriechen; fallen; geschlagen werden; ~ into shape zurechtstutzen.

licorice ['lɪkərɪs] Lakritze f.

lid [lɪd] Deckel m; (Augen)Lid n.

lie¹ [laɪ] 1. Lüge f; give s.o. the ~ j-n Lügen strafen; 2. lügen.

lie² [~] 1. Lage f; 2. [irr.] liegen; ~ by still-, brachliegen; ~ down sich niederlegen; ~ in wait for j-m auflauern; let sleeping dogs ~ fig. daran rühren wir lieber nicht; ~-down [laɪ'daun] Nickerchen n; ~-in: have a ~ sich gründlich ausschlafen.

lien ✿t ['lɪən] Pfandrecht n.

lieu [lju:]: in ~ of (an)statt.

lieutenant [lef'tenənt; ✿ le'tenənt; Am. lu:'tenənt] Leutnant m; Statthalter m; ~-commander ✿ Korvettenkapitän m.

life [laɪf], pl. lives [laɪvz] Leben n; Menschenleben n; Lebensbeschreibung f; for ~ auf Lebenszeit; for one's ~ for dear ~ ums (liebe) Leben; to the ~ naturgetreu; ~ sentence lebenslängliche Zuchthausstrafe; ~ assurance Lebensversicherung f; ~belt ['laɪfbelt] Rettungsgürtel m; ~boat Rettungsboot n; ~guard Leibwache f; Badewärter m am Strand; ~insurance Lebensversicherung f; ~jacket ✿ Schwimmweste f; ~less □ ['laɪflɪs] leblos; matt (a. fig.); ~like lebenswahr; ~long lebenslänglich; ~preserver Am. ['laɪfprɪzə:və] Schwimmgürtel m; Totschläger m (Stock mit Bleikopf); ~time Lebenszeit f.

lift [lɪft] 1. Heben n; phys., ✈ Auftrieb m; fig. Erhebung f; Fahrstuhl m; give s.o. a ~ j-m helfen; j-n (im Auto) mitnehmen; 2. v/t. (auf)heben; erheben; beseitigen; sl. klauen, stehlen; v/i. sich heben.

ligature ['lɪgətʃuə] Binde f; ✿ Verband m.

light¹ [laɪt] 1. Licht n (a. fig.); Fenster n; Aspekt m, Gesichtspunkt m; Feuer n; Glanz m; fig. Leuchte f; ~s pl. Fähigkeiten f/pl.; will you give me a ~ darf ich Sie um Feuer bitten; put a ~ to anzünden; 2. licht, hell; blond; 3. [irr.] v/t. oft ~ up be-, erleuchten; anzünden; v/i. mst ~ up aufleuchten; ~ out Am. sl. schnell losziehen, abhauen.

light² [~] 1. adj. □ u. adv. leicht (a. fig.); ~ current ✿ Schwachstrom m; make ~ of et. leicht nehmen; 2. ~ (up)on stoßen od. fallen auf (acc.), geraten an (acc.); sich niederlassen auf (dat.).

lighten ['laɪtn] blitzen; (sich) erhellen; leichter machen; (sich) erleichtern.

lighter ['laɪtə] Anzünder m; (Taschen)Feuerzeug n; ✿ L(e)ichter m.

light|-headed ['laɪt'hedɪd] wirr im Kopf, irr; ~hearted □ [~'hɑ:tɪd] leichtherzig; fröhlich; ~house ['laɪthaus] Leuchtturm m.

lighting ['laɪtɪŋ] Beleuchtung f; Anzünden n.

light|-minded ['laɪt'maɪndɪd] leichtsinnig; ~ness ['laɪtnɪs] Leichtigkeit f; Leichtsinn m.

lightning ['laɪtnɪŋ] Blitz m; ~ bug Am. zo. Leuchtkäfer m; ~-conductor, ~-rod ⚡ Blitzableiter m.

light-weight ['laɪtweɪt] Sport: Leichtgewicht n.

like [laɪk] 1. gleich; ähnlich; wie; such ~ dergleichen; feel ~ F sich aufgelegt fühlen zu *et.*; ~ *that* so; *what is he* ~? wie sieht er aus? wie ist er?; **2.** Gleiche *m, f, n*; ~*s pl.* Neigungen *f/pl.*; *his* ~ seinesgleichen; *the* ~ der-, desgleichen; **3.** mögen, gern haben; *how do you* ~ *London?* wie gefällt Ihnen L.?; *I should* ~ *to know* ich möchte wissen.

like|lihood ['laiklihud] Wahrscheinlichkeit *f*; ~**ly** ['laikli] wahrscheinlich; geeignet; *he is* ~ *to die* er wird wahrscheinlich sterben.

like|n ['laikən] vergleichen (*to* mit); ~**ness** ['laiknis] Ähnlichkeit *f*; (Ab-) Bild *n*; Gestalt *f*; ~**wise** ['laikwaiz] gleich-, ebenfalls.

liking ['laikiŋ] (*for*) Neigung *f* (für, zu), Gefallen *n* (an *dat.*).

lilac ['lailək] **1.** lila; **2.** ♀ Flieder *m*.

lily ♀ ['lili] Lilie *f*; ~ *of the valley* Maiglöckchen *n*; ~**white** schneeweiß.

limb [lim] *Körper-Glied n*; Ast *m*.

limber ['limbə] **1.** biegsam, geschmeidig; **2.**: ~ *up* (sich) lockern.

lime [laim] Kalk *m*; Vogelleim *m*; ♀ Limone *f*; ♀ Linde *f*; ~**light** ['laimlait] Kalklicht *n*; *thea.* Scheinwerfer(licht *n*) *m*; *fig.* Mittelpunkt *m* des öffentlichen Interesses.

limit ['limit] **1.** Grenze *f*; *in* (*off*) ~*s* Zutritt gestattet (verboten) (*to* für); *that is the* ~! F das ist der Gipfel!; das ist (doch) die Höhe!; *go the* ~ *Am.* F bis zum Äußersten gehen; **2.** begrenzen; beschränken (*to* auf *acc.*); ~**ation** [limi'teiʃən] Begrenzung *f*, Beschränkung *f*; *fig.* Grenze *f*; ⚖ Verjährung *f*; ~**ed**: ~ (*liability*) *company* Gesellschaft *f* mit beschränkter Haftung; ~ *in time* befristet; ~**less** (~*tlis*) grenzenlos.

limp [limp] **1.** hinken; **2.** Hinken *n*; **3.** schlaff; weich.

limpid □ ['limpid] klar, durchsichtig.

line [lain] **1.** Linie *f*; Reihe *f*, Zeile *f*; Vers *m*; Strich *m*; Falte *f*, Furche *f*; (Menschen)Schlange *f*; Folge *f*; Verkehrsgesellschaft *f*; Eisenbahnlinie *f*; Strecke *f*; *tel.* Leitung *f*; Branche *f*, Fach *n*; Leine *f*, Schnur *f*; Äquator *m*; Richtung *f*; ✗ Linie(ntruppe) *f*; Front *f*; ~*s pl.* Richtlinien *f/pl.*; Grundlage *f*; ~ *of conduct* Lebensweise *f*; *hard* ~*s pl.* hartes Los, Pech *n*; *in* ~ *with* in Übereinstimmung mit; *stand in* ~ Schlange stehen; *draw the* ~ *fig.* nicht mehr mitmachen; *hold the* ~ *teleph.* am Apparat bleiben; **2.** *v/t.* liniieren; aufstellen; *Weg etc.* säumen, einfassen; *Kleid* füttern; ~ *out* entwerfen; *v/i.* ~ *up* sich auf-, anstellen.

linea|ge ['liniidʒ] Abstammung *f*; Familie *f*; Stammbaum *m*; ~**l** □ [~jəl] gerade, direkt (*Nachkomme*

etc.); ~**ment** [~əmənt] (Gesichts-) Zug *m*; ~**r** ['liniə] geradlinig.

linen ['linin] **1.** Leinen *n*, Leinwand *f*; Wäsche *f*; **2.** leinen; ~**closet**, ~**cupboard** Wäscheschrank *m*; ~**draper** [~ndreipə] Weißwarenhändler *m*, Wäschegeschäft *n*.

liner ['lainə] Linienschiff *n*, Passagierdampfer *m*; Verkehrsflugzeug *n*.

linger ['liŋgə] zögern; (ver)weilen; sich aufhalten; sich hinziehen; dahinsiechen; ~ *at*, ~ *about* sich herumdrücken an *od.* bei (*dat.*).

lingerie ['lɛ̃ːnʒəri] Damenunterwäsche *f*. [Einreibemittel *n*.]

liniment ♂ ['linimənt] Liniment *n*.)

lining ['lainiŋ] *Kleider- etc.* Futter *n*; Besatz *m*; ⊕ Verkleidung *f*.

link [liŋk] **1.** *Ketten-*Glied *n*, Gelenk *n*; Manschettenknopf *m*; *fig.* Bindeglied *n*; **2.** (sich) verbinden.

links [liŋks] *pl.* Dünen *f/pl.*; *a.* golf-~ Golf(spiel)platz *m*.

linseed ['linsi:d] Leinsame(n) *m*; ~ *oil* Leinöl *n*.

lion ['laiən] Löwe *m*; *fig.* Größe *f*, Berühmtheit *f*; ~**ess** [~nis] Löwin *f*.

lip [lip] Lippe *f*; Rand *m*; *sl.* Unverschämtheit *f*; ~**stick** ['lipstik] Lippenstift *m*.

liquefy ['likwifai] schmelzen.

liquid ['likwid] **1.** flüssig; ♐ liquid; klar (*Luft etc.*); **2.** Flüssigkeit *f*.

liquidat|e ['likwideit] ♐ liquidieren; bezahlen; ~**ion** [likwi'deiʃən] Abwicklung *f*, Liquidation *f*.

liquor ['likə] Flüssigkeit *f*; Alkohol *m*, alkoholisches Getränk.

liquorice ['likəris] Lakritze *f*.

lisp [lisp] **1.** Lispeln *n*; **2.** lispeln.

list [list] **1.** Liste *f*, Verzeichnis *n*; Leiste *f*; Webkante *f*; **2.** (in e-e Liste) eintragen; verzeichnen.

listen ['lisn] (*to*) lauschen, horchen (auf *acc.*); anhören (*acc.*), zuhören (*dat.*); hören (auf *acc.*); ~ *in teleph.*, *Radio:* (mit)hören (*to* auc.); ~**er** [~nə] Zuhörer(in); *a.* ~*in* (Rundfunk)Hörer(in).

listless □ ['listlis] gleichgültig; lustlos.

lists [lists] *pl.* Schranken *f/pl.*

lit [lit] *pret. u. p.p. von* light[1] 3.

literal □ ['litərəl] buchstäblich; am Buchstaben klebend; wörtlich.

litera|ry □ ['litərəri] literarisch; Literatur...; Schrift...; ~**ture** [~ritʃə] Literatur *f*.

lithe [laið] geschmeidig, wendig.

lithography [li'θɔgrəfi] Lithographie *f*, Steindruck *m*.

litigation [liti'geiʃən] Prozeß *m*.

lit|re, *Am.* ~**er** ['li:tə] Liter *n, m*.

litter ['litə] **1.** Sänfte *f*; Tragbahre *f*; Streu *f*; Abfall *m*; Unordnung *f*; *Wurf m junger Tiere*; **2.** ~ *down* mit Streu versehen; ~ *up* in Unordnung bringen; *Junge* werfen; ~**basket**, ~**bin** Abfallkorb *m*.

little ['litl] 1. *adj.* klein; gering(fügig); wenig; a ~ one ein Kleines (*Kind*); 2. *adv.* wenig; 3. Kleinigkeit *f*; a ~ ein bißchen; ~ *by* ~ nach und nach; *not a* ~ nicht wenig.

live 1. [liv] *allg.* leben; wohnen; ~ *to see* erleben; ~ *s.th. down* et. durch guten Lebenswandel vergessen machen; ~ *through* durchmachen, durchstehen, überleben; ~ *up to s-m Ruf* gerecht werden, *s-n Grundsätzen* gemäß leben; *Versprechen* halten; 2. [laiv] lebendig; richtig; aktuell; glühend; ✗ scharf (*Munition*); ⚡ stromführend; *Radio:* Direkt..., Original...; **~lihood** ['laivlihud] Unterhalt *m*; **~liness** ['~inis] Lebhaftigkeit *f*; **~ly** ['laivli] lebhaft; lebendig; aufregend; schnell; bewegt.

liver *anat.* ['livə] Leber *f*.

livery ['livəri] Livree *f*; (Amts-)Tracht *f*; *at* ~ in Futter (*stehen etc.*).

live|s [laivz] *pl. von life*; **~stock** ['laivstɔk] Vieh(bestand *m*) *n*.

livid ['livid] bläulich; fahl; F wild.

living ['liviŋ] 1. ⌑ lebend(ig); *the* ~ *image of* das genaue Ebenbild *gen.*; 2. Leben *n*; Lebensweise *f*; Lebensunterhalt *m*; *eccl.* Pfründe *f*; **~-room** Wohnzimmer *n*.

lizard *zo.* ['lizəd] Eidechse *f*.

load [loud] 1. Last *f*; Ladung *f*; 2. (be)laden; *fig.* überhäufen; überladen; **~ing** ['loudiŋ] Laden *n*; Ladung *f*, Fracht *f*; *attr.* Lade...

loaf [louf] 1. *pl.* loaves [louvz] Brot-Laib *m*; (Zucker)Hut *m*; 2. herumlungern.

loafer ['loufə] Bummler *m*.

loam [loum] Lehm *m*, Ackerkrume *f*.

loan [loun] 1. Anleihe *f*, Darlehen *n*; Leihen *n*; Leihgabe *f*; *on* ~ leihweise; 2. *bsd. Am.* ausleihen.

loath ⌑ [louθ] abgeneigt; **~e** [louð] sich ekeln vor (*dat.*); verabscheuen; **~ing** ['louðiŋ] Ekel *m*; **~some** ⌑ ['louðsəm] ekelhaft; verhaßt.

loaves [louvz] *pl. von loaf* 1.

lobby ['lɔbi] 1. Vorhalle *f*; *parl.* Wandelgang *m*; *thea.* Foyer *n*; 2. *parl.* s-n Einfluß geltend machen.

lobe *anat.*, ♀ [loub] Lappen *m*.

lobster ['lɔbstə] Hummer *m*.

local ⌑ ['loukəl] 1. örtlich; Orts...; lokal; ~ *government* Gemeindeverwaltung *f*; 2. *Zeitung:* Lokalnachricht *f*; 👘 *a.* ~ *train* Vorortzug *m*; F Wirtshaus *n* (am Ort); **~ity** [lou'kæliti] Örtlichkeit *f*; Lage *f*; **~ize** ['loukəlaiz] lokalisieren.

locat|e [lou'keit] *v/t.* versetzen, verlegen, unterbringen; ausfindig machen; *Am.* an-, festlegen; be ~d gelegen sein; wohnen; *v/i.* sich niederlassen; **~ion** [~'eiʃən] Lage *f*; Niederlassung *f*; *Am.* Anweisung *f* von Land; angewiesenes Land; Ort

m; *Film:* Gelände *n* für Außenaufnahmen.

loch *schott.* [lɔk] See *m*; Bucht *f*.

lock [lɔk] 1. Tür-, Gewehr- etc. Schloß *n*; Schleuse(nkammer) *f*; ⊕ Sperrvorrichtung *f*; Stauung *f*; Locke *f*; Wollflocke *f*; 2. (ver-)schließen (*a. fig.*), absperren; sich verschließen lassen; ⊕ blockieren, sperren, greifen; umschließen; ~ *s.o. in* j-n einsperren; ~ *up* wegschließen; abschließen; einsperren; *Geld* fest anlegen.

lock|er ['lɔkə] Schrank *m*, Kasten *m*; **~et** ['lɔkit] Medaillon *n*; **~out** Aussperrung *f von Arbeitern*; **~smith** Schlosser *m*; **~up** 1. Haftzelle *f*; ✝ zinslose Kapitalanlage *f*; 2. verschließbar.

loco *Am. sl.* ['loukou] verrückt.

locomot|ion [loukə'mouʃən] Fortbewegung(sfähigkeit) *f*; **~ive** ['loukəmoutiv] 1. sich fortbewegend; beweglich; 2. *a.* ~ *engine* Lokomotive *f*.

locust ['loukəst] *zo.* Heuschrecke *f*; ♀ unechte Akazie.

lode|star ['loudsta:] Leitstern *m* (*a. fig.*); **~stone** Magnet(eisenstein) *m*.

lodg|e [lɔdʒ] 1. Häus-chen *n*; (Forst-, Park-, Pförtner)Haus *n*; Portierloge *f*; Freimaurer-Loge *f*; 2. *v/t.* beherbergen, aufnehmen; *Geld* hinterlegen; *Klage* einreichen; *Hieb* versetzen; *v/i.* (*bsd. zur Miete*) wohnen; logieren; **~er** ['lɔdʒə] (Unter)Mieter(in); **~ing** ['lɔdʒiŋ] Unterkunft *f*; **~s** *pl.* möbliertes Zimmer; Wohnung *f*.

loft [lɔ:ft] (Dach)Boden *m*; Empore *f*; **~y** ⌑ ['lɔ:fti] hoch; erhaben; stolz.

log [lɔg] Klotz *m*; Block *m*; gefällter Baumstamm; ♧ Log *n*; **~-cabin** ['lɔgkæbin] Blockhaus *n*; **~gerhead** ['lɔgəhed]: be at ~s sich in den Haaren liegen; **~house**, **~hut** Blockhaus *n*.

logic ['lɔdʒik] Logik *f*; **~al** ⌑ [~kəl] logisch.

logroll *bsd. Am. pol.* ['lɔgroul] (sich gegenseitig) in die Hände arbeiten.

loin [lɔin] Lende(nstück *n*) *f*.

loiter ['lɔitə] trödeln, schlendern.

loll [lɔl] (sich) strecken; (sich) rekeln; ~ *about* herumlungern.

lone|liness ['lounlinis] Einsamkeit *f*; **~ly** ⌑ ['lounli], **~some** ⌑ ['lounsəm] einsam.

long[1] [lɔŋ] 1. Länge *f*; *before* ~ binnen kurzem; *for* ~ lange; *take* ~ lange brauchen *od.* dauern; 2. *adj.* lang; langfristig; langsam; *in the* ~ *run* am Ende; *auf die Dauer*; be ~ lange dauern *od.* brauchen; 3. *adv.* lang(e); *so* ~! bis dann! (*auf Wiedersehen*); (no) ~er (nicht) länger *od.* mehr.

long² [~] sich sehnen (for nach).
long|-distance['lɒŋ'distəns]Fern...,
Weit...; ~evity [lɔn'dʒeviti] Lang-
lebigkeit f; langes Leben, f;
['lɒŋhænd] Langschrift f.
longing ['lɒŋiŋ] 1. □ sehnsüchtig;
2. Sehnsucht f; Verlangen n.
longitude geogr. ['lɒndʒitjuːd] Länge f.
long|-shore-man ['lɒŋʃɔːmən] Ha-
fenarbeiterm;~-sighted['lɒŋ'saitid]
weitsichtig; ~-standing seit langer
Zeit bestehend, alt; ~-suffering 1.
langmütig; 2. Langmut f; ~-term
['lɒŋtɜːm] langfristig; ~-winded □
['lɒŋ'windid] langatmig.
look [luk] 1. Blick m; Anblick m;
oft ~s pl. Aussehen n; have a ~ at
s.th. sich et. ansehen; I don't like
the ~ of it es gefällt mir nicht; 2. v/i.
sehen, blicken (at, on auf acc.,
nach); zusehen, daß od. wie...; nachsehen, wer etc. ...; krank etc. aussehen; nach e-r Richtung liegen;
~ after sehen nach, sich kümmern
um; versorgen; nachsehen, nachblicken (dat.); ~ at ansehen; ~ for
erwarten; suchen; ~ forward to sich
freuen auf (acc.); ~ in als Besucher
hereinschauen (on bei); ~ into prüfen; erforschen; ~ on zuschauen
(dat.); betrachten (as als); liegen zu,
gehen auf (acc.) (Fenster); ~ out
vorsehen; ~ (up)on fig. ansehen (as
als); v/t. ~ disdain verächtlich
blicken; ~ over et. durchsehen; j-n
mustern; ~ up et. nachschlagen.
looker-on ['lukər'ɒn] Zuschauer(in).
looking-glass ['lukiŋglɑːs] Spiegel
m.
look-out ['luk'aut] Ausguck m,
Ausblick m, Aussicht f (a. fig.);
that is my ~ F das ist meine Sache.
loom [luːm] 1. Webstuhl m; 2. undeutlich zu sehen sein, sich ab-
zeichnen.
loop [luːp] 1. Schlinge f, Schleife f,
Öse f; 2. v/t. in Schleifen legen;
schlingen; v/i. e-e Schleife machen;
sich winden; ~-hole ['luːphoul]
Guck-, Schlupfloch n; ⚔ Schieß-
scharte f.
loose [luːs] 1. □ allg. lose, locker;
schlaff; weit; frei; un-zs.-hängend;
ungenau; liederlich; 2. lösen; aufbinden; lockern; ~n ['luːsn] (sich)
lösen, (sich) lockern.
loot [luːt] 1. plündern; 2. Beute f.
lop [lɒp] Baum beschneiden, stutzen; schlaff herunterhängen (lassen); ~-sided ['lɒp'saidid] schief,
einseitig.
loquacious □ [lou'kweiʃəs] geschwätzig.
lord [lɔːd] Herr m; Gebieter m;
Magnat m; Lord m; the ♀ der Herr
(Gott); my ~ [mi'lɔːd] Mylord,
Euer Gnaden; the ♀'s Prayer das
Vaterunser; the ♀'s Supper das

Abendmahl; ~ly ['lɔːdli] vornehm,
edel; großartig; hochmütig; ~ship
['lɔːdʃip] Lordschaft f (Titel).
lore [lɔː] Lehre f, Kunde f.
lorry ['lɔri] Last(kraft)wagen m,
LKW m; 🚋 Lore f.
lose [luːz] [irr.] v/t. verlieren; vergeuden; verpassen; abnehmen; ~
o.s. sich verirren; v/i. verlieren;
nachgehen (Uhr).
loss [lɒs] Verlust m; Schaden m;
at a ~ in Verlegenheit; außerstande.
lost [lɒst] pret. u. p.p. von lose; be ~
verlorengehen; verschwunden sein;
fig. versunken sein; ~-property office
Fundbüro n.
lot [lɒt] Los n (a. fig.); Anteil m;
✝ Partie f; Posten m; F Menge f;
Parzelle f; Am. Film: Atelierge-
lände n; a ~ of people F eine Menge
Leute; draw ~s losen; fall to s.o.'s ~
j-m zufallen.
loth □ [louθ] s. loath.
lotion ['louʃən] (Haut)Wasser n.
lottery ['lɒtəri] Lotterie f.
loud □ [laud] laut (a. adv.); fig.
schreiend, grell; ~-speaker ['laud-
'spiːkə] Lautsprecher m.
lounge [laundʒ] 1. sich rekeln; faulenzen; 2. Bummel m; Wohnzimmer n, -diele f; Gesellschaftsraum
m e-s Hotels; thea. Foyer n; Chaiselongue f; ~-chair ['laundʒ'tʃeə]
Klubsessel m; ~-suit Straßenanzug
m.
lour ['lauə] finster blicken od. aussehen; die Stirn runzeln.
lous|e [laus], pl. lice [lais] Laus f;
~y ['lauzi] verlaust; lausig; Lause...
lout [laut] Tölpel m, Lümmel m.
lovable □ ['lʌvəbl] liebenswürdig,
liebenswert.
love [lʌv] 1. Liebe f (of, a. for, to,
towards zu); Liebschaft f; Ange-
betete f; Liebling m (als Anrede);
liebe Grüße m/pl.; Sport: nichts, null;
attr. Liebes...; give od. send one's
~ to s.o. j-n freundlichst grüßen
(lassen); in ~ with verliebt in (acc.);
fall in ~ with sich verlieben in (acc.);
make ~ to werben um; 2. lieben;
gern haben; ~ to do gern tun;
~-affair ['lʌvəfeə] Liebschaft f;
~ly ['lʌvli] lieblich; entzückend,
reizend; ~r ['lʌvə] Liebhaber m;
fig. Verehrer(in), Liebhaber(in).
loving □ ['lʌviŋ] liebevoll.
low¹ [lou] 1. niedrig; tief; gering;
leise; fig. niedergeschlagen;
schwach; gemein; ~est bid Min-
destgebot n; 2. meteor. Tief(druck-
gebiet) n; bsd. Am. Tiefstand m,
-punkt m.
low² [~] brüllen, muhen (Rind).
low-brow F ['loubrau] 1. geistig anspruchslos, spießig; 2. Spießer m,
Banause m.
lower¹ ['louə] 1. niedriger; tiefer;
geringer; leiser; untere(r, -s); Un-

ter...; 2. v/t. nieder-, herunterlassen; senken; erniedrigen; abschwächen; Preis etc. herabsetzen; v/i. fallen, sinken.

lower² ['lauə] s. lour.

low|land ['loulənd] Tiefland n; **~liness** ['loulinis] Demut f; **~ly** ['louli] demütig; bescheiden; **~necked** (tief) ausgeschnitten (Kleid); **~spirited** niedergeschlagen. [Treue f.\

loyal □ ['lɔiəl] treu; **~ty** [~lti/] lozenge ['lɔzindʒ] Pastille f.

lubber ['lʌbə] Tölpel m, Stoffel m.

lubric|ant ['lu:brikənt] Schmiermittel n; **~ate** [~keit] schmieren; **~ation** [lu:bri'keiʃən] Schmieren n, ⊕ Ölung f.

lucid □ ['lu:sid] leuchtend, klar.

luck [lʌk] Glück(sfall m) n; Geschick n; good ~ Glück n; bad ~, hard ~, ill ~ Unglück n, Pech n; worse ~ unglücklicherweise; **~ily** ['lʌkili] glücklicherweise, zum Glück; **~y** □ ['lʌki] glücklich; Glücks...; be ~ Glück haben.

lucr|ative □ ['lu:krətiv] einträglich; **~e** ['lu:kə] Gewinn(sucht f) m.

ludicrous □ ['lu:dikrəs] lächerlich.

lug [lʌg] zerren, schleppen.

luge [lu:ʒ] 1. Rodelschlitten m; 2. rodeln.

luggage ['lʌgidʒ] Gepäck n; **~carrier** Gepäckträger m am Fahrrad; **~office** 🚂 Gepäckschalter m; **~rack** Gepäcknetz n; **~ticket** Gepäckschein m.

lugubrious □ [lu:'gju:briəs] traurig.

lukewarm ['lu:kwɔ:m] lau (a. fig.).

lull [lʌl] 1. einlullen; (sich) beruhigen; 2. (Wind)Stille f; Ruhepause f.

lullaby ['lʌləbai] Wiegenlied n.

lumbago 🩺 [lʌm'beigou] Hexenschuß m.

lumber ['lʌmbə] 1. Bau-, Nutzholz n; Gerümpel n; 2. v/t. a. ~ up vollstopfen; v/i. rumpeln, poltern; sich (dahin)schleppen; **~er** [~ərə], **~jack**, **~man** Holzfäller m, -arbeiter m; **~mill** Sägewerk n; **~room** Rumpelkammer f; **~yard** Holzplatz m, -lager n.

lumin|ary ['lu:minəri] Himmelskörper m; Leuchtkörper m; fig. Leuchte f; **~ous** □ [~nəs] leuchtend; Licht...; Leucht...; fig. lichtvoll.

lump [lʌmp] 1. Klumpen m; fig. Klotz m; Beule f; Stück n Zucker etc.; in the ~ in Bausch und Bogen; ~ sugar Würfelzucker m; ~ sum

Pauschalsumme f; 2. v/t. zs.-werfen, zs.-fassen; v/i. Klumpen bilden; **~ish** ['lʌmpiʃ] schwerfällig; **~y** □ [~pi] klumpig.

lunacy ['lu:nəsi] Wahnsinn m.

lunar ['lu:nə] Mond...

lunatic ['lu:nətik] 1. irr-, wahnsinnig; 2. Irre(r m) f; Wahnsinnige(r m) f; Geistesgestörte(r m) f; ~ asylum Irrenhaus n, -anstalt f.

lunch|(eon) [lʌntʃ, 'lʌntʃən] 1. Lunch m, Mittagessen n; zweites Frühstück; 2. zu Mittag essen; j-m ein Mittagessen geben; **~hour** Mittagszeit f, -pause f.

lung anat. [lʌŋ] Lunge(nflügel m) f; the ~s pl. die Lunge.

lunge [lʌndʒ] 1. Fechten: Ausfall m; 2. v/i. ausfallen (at gegen); (dahin)stürmen; v/t. stoßen.

lupin(e) ♀ ['lu:pin] Lupine f.

lurch [lə:tʃ] 1. taumeln, torkeln; 2.: leave in the ~ im Stich lassen.

lure [ljuə] 1. Köder m; fig. Lockung f; 2. ködern, (an)locken.

lurid ['ljuərid] unheimlich; erschreckend, schockierend; düster, finster.

lurk [lə:k] lauern; versteckt liegen.

luscious □ ['lʌʃəs] köstlich; üppig; süß(lich), widerlich.

lust [lʌst] (sinnliche) Begierde; fig. Gier f, Sucht f.

lust|re, Am. **~er** ['lʌstə] Glanz m; Kronleuchter m; **~rous** □ [~trəs] glänzend.

lusty □ ['lʌsti] rüstig; fig. lebhaft, kräftig.

lute¹ ♪ [lu:t] Laute f.

lute² [~] 1. Kitt m; 2. (ver)kitten.

Lutheran ['lu:θərən] lutherisch.

luxate 🩺 ['lʌkseit] verrenken.

luxur|iant □ [lʌg'zjuəriənt] üppig; **~ious** □ [~iəs] luxuriös, üppig; **~y** ['lʌkʃəri] Luxus m, Üppigkeit f; Luxusartikel m; Genußmittel n.

lyceum [lai'siəm] Vortragsraum m; bsd. Am. Volkshochschule f.

lye [lai] Lauge f.

lying ['laiiŋ] 1. p.pr. von lie¹ 2 u. lie² 2; 2. adj. lügnerisch; **~in** [~ŋ'in] Wochenbett n; ~ hospital Entbindungsheim n.

lymph 🩺 [limf] Lymphe f.

lynch [lintʃ] lynchen; **~law** ['lintʃlɔ:] Lynchjustiz f.

lynx zo. [liŋks] Luchs m.

lyric ['lirik] 1. lyrisch; 2. lyrisches Gedicht; **~s** pl. (Lied)Text m (bsd. e-s Musicals); Lyrik f; **~al** □ [~kəl] lyrisch, gefühlvoll; schwärmerisch, begeistert.

M

ma'am [mæm] Majestät f (Anrede für die Königin); Hoheit f (Anrede für Prinzessinnen); F [məm] gnä' Frau f (von Dienstboten verwendete Anrede).

macaroni [mækə'rouni] Makkaroni pl.

macaroon [mækə'ru:n] Makrone f.

machin|ation [mæki'neiʃən] Anschlag m; ~s pl. Ränke pl.; ~e [mə'ʃi:n] 1. Maschine f; Mechanismus m (a. fig.); 2. maschinell herstellen od. (be)arbeiten; ~e-made maschinell hergestellt; ~ery [~nəri] Maschinen f/pl.; Maschinerie f; ~ist [~nist] Maschinist m; Maschinennäherin f.

mackerel ichth. ['mækrəl] Makrele f.

mackinow Am. ['mækinɔ:] Stutzer m (Kleidungsstück).

mackintosh ['mækintɔʃ] Regenmantel m.

mad □ [mæd] wahnsinnig; toll (-wütig); fig. wild; F wütend; go ~ verrückt werden; drive ~ verrückt machen.

madam ['mædəm] gnädige Frau, gnädiges Fräulein (Anrede).

mad|cap ['mædkæp] 1. toll; 2. Tollkopf m; Wildfang m; ~den ['mædn] toll od. rasend machen.

made [meid] pret. u. p.p. von make 1.

made-up ['meid'ʌp] zurechtgemacht; erfunden; fertig; ~ clothes pl. Konfektion f.

mad|house ['mædhaus] Irrenhaus n; ~man Wahnsinnige(r) m; ~ness ['mædnis] Wahnsinn m; (Toll)Wut f.

magazine [mægə'zi:n] Magazin n; (Munitions)Lager n; Zeitschrift f.

maggot zo. ['mægət] Made f.

magic ['mædʒik] 1. a. ~al □ [~kəl] magisch; Zauber...; 2. Zauberei f; fig. Zauber m; ~ian [me'dʒiʃən] Zauberer m.

magistra|cy ['mædʒistrəsi] Richteramt n; die Richter m/pl.; ~te [~rit] (Polizei-, Friedens)Richter m.

magnanimous □ [mæg'næniməs] großmütig.

magnet ['mægnit] Magnet m; ~ic [mæg'netik] (~ally) magnetisch.

magni|ficence [mæg'nifisns] Pracht f, Herrlichkeit f; ~ficent □ [~nt] prächtig, herrlich; ~fy ['mægnifai] vergrößern; ~tude [~itju:d] Größe f, Wichtigkeit f.

magpie orn. ['mægpai] Elster f.

mahagony [mə'hɔgəni] Mahagoni (-holz) n.

maid [meid] lit. Mädchen n; (Dienst)Mädchen n; old ~ alte Jungfer; ~ of all work Mädchen n für alles; ~ of honour Ehren-, Hofdame f.

maiden ['meidn] 1. = maid; 2. jungfräulich; unverheiratet; fig. Jungfern..., Erstlings...; ~ name Mädchenname m e-r Frau; ~head Jungfräulichkeit f; ~hood [~hud] Mädchenjahre n/pl.; ~ly [~nli] jungfräulich, mädchenhaft.

mail¹ [meil] (Ketten)Panzer m.

mail² [~] 1. Post(dienst m) f; Post(sendung) f; 2. Am. mit der Post schicken, aufgeben; ~able Am. ['meiləbl] postversandfähig; ~bag Briefträger-, Posttasche f; Postsack m; ~box bsd. Am. Briefkasten m; ~ carrier Am. Briefträger m; ~man Am. Briefträger m; ~order firm, bsd. Am. ~order house (Post)Versandgeschäft n.

maim [meim] verstümmeln.

main [mein] 1. Haupt..., hauptsächlich; by ~ force mit voller Kraft; 2. Hauptrohr n, -leitung f; ~s pl. ⚡ (Strom)Netz n; in the ~ in der Hauptsache, im wesentlichen; ~land ['meinlənd] Festland n; ~ly [~li] hauptsächlich; ~spring Uhrfeder f; fig. Haupttriebfeder f; ~stay ⚓ Großtag n; fig. Hauptstütze f ⚓ Street Am. Hauptstraße f; ⚓ Streeter Am. Kleinstadtbewohner m.

maintain [men'tein] (aufrecht)erhalten; beibehalten; (unter)stützen; unterhalten; behaupten.

maintenance ['meintinəns] Erhaltung f; Unterhalt m; ⊕ Wartung f.

maize ♀ [meiz] Mais m.

majest|ic [mə'dʒestik] (~ally) majestätisch; ~y ['mædʒisti] Majestät f; Würde f, Hoheit f.

major ['meidʒə] 1. größer; wichtig(er); mündig; ♪ Dur n; ~ key Dur-Tonart f; ~ league Am. Baseball: Oberliga f; 2. ✕ Major m; Mündige(r m) f; Am. univ. Hauptfach n; ~-general ✕ Generalmajor m; ~ity [mə'dʒɔriti] Mehrheit f; Mündigkeit f; Majorsrang m.

make [meik] 1. [irr.] v/t. allg. machen; verfertigen, fabrizieren; bilden; (aus)machen; ergeben; (veran)lassen; gewinnen, verdienen; sich erweisen als, abgeben; Regel etc. aufstellen; Frieden etc. schließen; e-e Rede halten; ~ good wieder gutmachen; wahr machen; do you ~ one of us? machen Sie mit?; ~ port ♂ den Hafen anlaufen; ~ way vorwärtskommen; ~ into verarbeiten zu; ~ out ausfindig machen; erkennen; verstehen; entziffern; Rechnung etc. ausstellen; ~ over übertragen; ~ up ergänzen; vervoll-

ständigen; zs.-stellen; bilden, ausmachen; *Streit* beilegen; zurechtmachen, schminken; = ~ *up for
(v/i.)*; ~ *up one's mind* sich entschließen; *v/i.* sich begeben;
gehen; ~ *away with* beseitigen;
Geld vertun; ~ *for* zugehen auf
(acc.); sich aufmachen nach; ~ *off*
sich fortmachen; ~ *up* sich zurechtmachen; sich schminken; ~ *up for*
nach-, aufholen; für *et.* entschädigen; 2. Mach-, Bauart *f*; Bau *m des
Körpers*; Form *f*; Fabrikat *n*, Erzeugnis *n*; **~believe** ['meikbili:v]
Schein *m*, Vorwand *m*, Verstellung
f; **~r** ['meikə] Hersteller *m*; ☊
Schöpfer *m* (*Gott*); **~shift** ☐ 1. Notbehelf *m*; 2. behelfsmäßig; **~up**
typ. Umbruch *m*; *fig.* Charakter *m*;
Schminke *f*, Make-up *n*.
maladjustment ['mælə'dʒʌstmənt]
mangelhafte Anpassung.
maladministration ['mælədmi-
nis'treiʃən] schlechte Verwaltung.
malady ['mælədi] Krankheit *f*.
malcontent ['mælkəntent] 1. unzufrieden; 2. Unzufriedene(r) *m*.
male [meil] 1. männlich; 2. Mann
m; *zo.* Männchen *n*.
malediction [mæli'dikʃən] Fluch
m.
malefactor ['mælifæktə] Übeltäter
m.
malevolen|ce [mə'levələns] Bös-
willigkeit *f*; **~t** ☐ [~nt] böswillig.
malice ['mælis] Bosheit *f*; Groll *m*.
malicious [mə'liʃəs] boshaft;
böswillig; **~ness** [~snis] Bosheit *f*.
malign [mə'lain] 1. ☐ schädlich;
2. verleumden; **~ant** ☐ [mə-
'lignənt] böswillig; ✞ bösartig;
~ity [~niti] Bosheit *f*; Schadenfreude *f*; *bsd.* ✞ Bösartigkeit *f*.
malleable ['mæliəbl] hämmerbar;
fig. geschmeidig.
mallet ['mælit] Schlegel *m*.
malnutrition ['mælnju(:)'triʃən]
Unterernährung *f*.
malodorous ☐ [mæ'loudərəs] übelriechend.
malpractice ['mæl'præktis] Übel-
tat *f*; ✞ falsche Behandlung.
malt [mɔ:lt] Malz *n*.
maltreat [mæl'tri:t] schlecht behandeln; mißhandeln.
mam(m)a [mə'mɑ:] Mama *f*.
mammal ['mæməl] Säugetier *n*.
mammoth ['mæməθ] riesig.
mammy F ['mæmi] Mami *f*; *Am.*
farbiges Kindermädchen.
man [mæn, *in Zssgn* ...mən] 1. *pl.*
men [men] Mann *m*; Mensch(en
pl.) *m*; Menschheit *f*; Diener *m*;
Schach: Figur *f*; Damestein *m*;
2. männlich; 3. ✕, ✞ bemannen;
~ *o.s.* sich ermannen.
manage ['mænidʒ] *v/t.* handhaben;
verwalten, leiten; *Menschen, Tiere*
lenken; mit *j-m* fertig werden; *et.*

fertigbringen; ~ *to inf.* es fertigbringen, zu *inf.*; *v/i.* die Aufsicht
haben, die Geschäfte führen; auskommen; F es schaffen; **~able** ☐
[~dʒəbl] handlich; lenksam; **~ment**
[~dʒmənt] Verwaltung *f*, Leitung *f*,
Direktion *f*, Geschäftsführung *f*;
geschickte Behandlung; **~r** [~dʒə]
Leiter *m*, Direktor *m*; Regisseur *m*;
Manager *m*; **~ress** [~ərəs] Leiterin
f, Direktorin *f*.
managing ['mænidʒiŋ] geschäfts-
führend; Betriebs...; ~ *clerk* Ge-
schäftsführer *m*, Prokurist *m*.
mandat|e ['mændeit] Mandat *n*;
Befehl *m*; Auftrag *m*; Vollmacht *f*;
~ory [~dətəri] befehlend.
mane [mein] Mähne *f*.
maneuver [mə'nu:və] = *manoeuvre*.
manful ☐ ['mænful] mannhaft.
mange *vet.* [meindʒ] Räude *f*.
manger ['meindʒə] Krippe *f*.
mangle ['mæŋgl] 1. Wringmaschine
f; Wäschemangel *f*; 2. mangeln;
wringen; zerstückeln; *fig.* verstümmeln.
mangy ['meindʒi] räudig; *fig.*
schäbig.
manhood ['mænhud] Mannesalter
n; Männlichkeit *f*; die Männer *m/pl.*
mania ['meinjə] Wahnsinn *m*;
Sucht *f*, Manie *f*; **~c** ['meiniæk]
1. Wahnsinnige(r *m*) *f*; 2. wahnsinnig.
manicure ['mænikjuə] 1. Maniküre
f; 2. maniküren.
manifest ['mænifest] 1. ☐ offenbar;
2. ⚓ Ladungsverzeichnis *n*; 3. *v/t.*
offenbaren; kundtun; **~ation**
[mænifes'teiʃən] Offenbarung *f*;
Kundgebung *f*; **~o** [mæni'festou]
Manifest *n*.
manifold ☐ ['mænifould] 1. mannigfaltig; 2. vervielfältigen.
manipulat|e [mə'nipjuleit] (ge-
schickt) handhaben; **~ion** [məni-
pju'leiʃən] Handhabung *f*, Behandlung *f*, Verfahren *n*; Kniff *m*.
man|kind [mæn'kaind] die Mensch-
heit; ['mænkaind] die Männer *pl.*,
~ly ['mænli] männlich; mannhaft.
manner ['mænə] Art *f*, Weise *f*;
Stil(art *f*) *m*; Manier *f*; *s pl.* Manieren *f/pl.*; Sitten *f/pl.*; *in a* ~
gewissermaßen; *of* [~d] ...gear-
tet; gekünstelt; **~ly** [~əli] manier-
lich, gesittet.
manoeuvre, *Am. a.* **maneuver**
[mə'nu:və] 1. Manöver *n* (*a. fig.*);
2. manövrieren (lassen).
man-of-war ⚓ ['mænəv'wɔ:]
Kriegsschiff *n*.
manor ['mænə] Rittergut *n*; *lord of
the* ~ Gutsherr *m*; **~house** Herr-
schaftshaus *n*, Herrensitz *m*; Schloß
n.
manpower ['mænpauə] Men-
schenpotential *n*; Arbeitskräfte *f/pl.*

man-servant ['mænsə:vənt] Diener *m*.

mansion ['mænʃən] (herrschaftliches) Wohnhaus.

manslaughter *g̃* ['mænslɔːtə] Totschlag *m*, fahrlässige Tötung.

mantel|piece ['mæntlpi:s], **~shelf** Kaminsims *m*, -platte *f*.

mantle ['mæntl] 1. Mantel *m*; *fig*. Hülle *f*; Glühstrumpf *m*; 2. *v/t*. verhüllen; *v/i*. sich röten (*Gesicht*).

manual ['mænjuəl] 1. □ Hand...; mit der Hand (gemacht); 2. Handbuch *n*. [brik *f*.\

manufactory [mænju'fæktəri] Fa-)

manufactur|e [mænju'fæktʃə] 1. Fabrikation *f*; Fabrikat *n*; 2. fabrizieren; verarbeiten; **~er** [~ərə] Fabrikant *m*; **~ing** [~riŋ] Fabrik...; Gewerbe...; Industrie...

manure [mə'njuə] 1. Dünger *m*; 2. düngen.

manuscript ['mænjuskript] Manuskript *n*; Handschrift *f*.

many ['meni] 1. viele; **~** *a manche*(r, -s); *be one too ~ for s.o.* j-m überlegen sein; 2. Menge *f*; *a good ~, a great ~* ziemlich viele, sehr viele.

map [mæp] 1. (Land)Karte *f*; 2. aufzeichnen; **~ out** planen; einteilen.

maple 💠 ['meipl] Ahorn *m*.

mar [mɑ:] schädigen; verderben.

maraud [mə'rɔːd] plündern.

marble ['mɑ:bl] 1. Marmor *m*; Murmel *f*; 2. marmorn.

March¹ [mɑ:tʃ] März *m*.

march² [~] 1. Marsch *m*; Fortschritt *m*; Gang *m der Ereignisse etc.*; 2. marschieren (lassen); *fig*. vorwärtsschreiten.

marchioness ['mɑ:ʃənis] Marquise *f*.

mare [meə] Stute *f*; **~'s** *nest fig*. Schwindel *m*; (Zeitungs)Ente *f*.

marg|arine [mɑːdʒə'riːn], *a*. **~e** F [mɑ:dʒ] Margarine *f*.

margin ['mɑ:dʒin] Rand *m*; Grenze *f*; Spielraum *m*; Verdienst-, Gewinn-, Handelsspanne *f*; **~al** □ [~nl] am Rande (befindlich); Rand...; **~** *note* Randbemerkung *f*.

marine [mə'ri:n] Marineinfanterist *m*; Marine *f*; *paint*. Seestück *n*; *attr*. See...; Marine...; Schiffs...; **~r** ['mærinə] Seemann *m*.

marital □ ['mæritl] ehelich, Ehe...

maritime ['mæritaim] an der See liegend *od.* lebend; See...; Küsten...; Schiffahrt(s)...

mark¹ [mɑːk] Mark *f* (*Geldstück*).

mark² [~] 1. Marke *f*, Merkmal *n*, Zeichen *n*; ✝ Preiszettel *m*; Fabrik-, Schutzmarke *f*; (Körper)Mal *n*; Norm *f*; *Schule*: Zensur *f*, Note *f*, Punkt *m*; *Sport*: Startlinie *f*; Ziel *n*; *a man of ~* ein Mann von Bedeutung; *fig. up to the ~* auf der Höhe;

beside the ~, wide of the **~** den Kern der Sache verfehlend; unrichtig; 2. *v/t*. (be)zeichnen, markieren; *Sport*: anschreiben; kennzeichnen; be(ob)achten; sich *et.* merken; **~** *off* abtrennen; **~** *out* bezeichnen; abstecken; **~** *time* auf der Stelle treten; *v/i*. achtgeben; **~ed** □ auffallend; merklich; ausgeprägt.

market ['mɑ:kit] 1. Markt(platz) *m*; Handel *m*; ✝ Absatz *m*; *in the ~* auf dem Markt; *play the ~ Am. sl.* an der Börse spekulieren; 2. *v/t*. auf den Markt bringen, verkaufen; *v/i*. einkaufen gehen; **~able** □ [~təbl] marktfähig, -gängig; **~ing** [~tiŋ] ✝ Marketing *n*, Absatzpolitik *f*; Marktbesuch *m*.

marksman ['mɑ:ksmən] (guter) Schütze.

marmalade ['mɑ:məleid] Orangenmarmelade *f*.

maroon [mə'ru:n] 1. kastanienbraun; 2. *auf e-r einsamen Insel* aussetzen; 3. Leuchtrakete *f*.

marquee [mɑ:'ki] (großes) Zelt.

marquis ['mɑ:kwis] Marquis *m*.

marriage ['mæridʒ] Heirat *f*, Ehe (-stand *m*) *f*; Hochzeit *f*; *civil ~* standesamtliche Trauung; **~able** [~dʒəbl] heiratsfähig; **~ articles** *pl*. Ehevertrag *m*; **~ lines** *pl*. Trauschein *m*; **~ portion** Mitgift *f*.

married ['mærid] verheiratet; ehelich; Ehe...; **~** *couple* Ehepaar *n*.

marrow ['mærou] Mark *n*; *fig*. Kern *m*, Beste(s) *n*; **~y** [~oui] markig.

marry ['mæri] *v/t*. (ver)heiraten; *eccl*. trauen; *v/i*. (sich ver)heiraten.

marsh [mɑ:ʃ] Sumpf *m*, Morast *m*.

marshal ['mɑ:ʃəl] 1. Marschall *m*; *hist*. Hofmarschall *m*; Zeremonienmeister *m*; *Am*. Bezirkspolizeichef *m*; Leiter *m* der Feuerwehr; 2. ordnen; führen; zs.-stellen.

marshy ['mɑ:ʃi] sumpfig.

mart [mɑ:t] Markt *m*; Auktionsraum *m*.

marten zo. ['mɑ:tin] Marder *m*.

martial □ ['mɑ:ʃəl] kriegerisch; Kriegs...; **~** *law* Stand-, Kriegsrecht *n*.

martyr ['mɑ:tə] 1. Märtyrer(in) (*to gen*.); 2. (zu Tode) martern.

marvel ['mɑ:vel] 1. Wunder *n*; 2. sich wundern; **~lous** □ ['mɑ:viləs] wunderbar, erstaunlich.

mascot ['mæskət] Maskottchen *n*.

masculine ['mɑ:skjulin] männlich.

mash [mæʃ] 1. Gemisch *n*; Maische *f*; Mengfutter *n*; 2. mischen; zerdrücken; (ein)maischen; **~ed** *potatoes* *pl*. Kartoffelbrei *m*.

mask [mɑ:sk] 1. Maske *f*; 2. maskieren; *fig*. verbergen; tarnen; **~ed**: **~** *ball* Maskenball *m*.

mason ['meisn] Steinmetz *m*; Maurer *m*; Freimaurer *m*; **~ry** [~nri] Mauerwerk *n*.

masque [mɑːsk] Maskenspiel n.
masquerade [mæskə'reid] 1. Maskenball m; Verkleidung f; 2. fig. sich maskieren.
mass [mæs] 1. eccl. Messe f; Masse f; Menge f; ~ meeting Massenversammlung f; 2. (sich) (an)sammeln.
massacre ['mæsəkə] 1. Blutbad n; 2. niedermetzeln.
massage ['mæsɑːʒ] 1. Massage f; 2. massieren.
massif ['mæsiːf] (Gebirgs)Massiv n.
massive ['mæsiv] massiv; schwer.
mast ⚓ [mɑːst] Mast m.
master ['mɑːstə] 1. Meister m; Herr m (a. fig.); Gebieter m; Lehrer m; Kapitän m e-s Handelsschiffs; Anrede: (junger) Herr; univ. Rektor m e-s College; 2 of Arts Magister m Artium; 2 of Ceremonies Conférencier m; 2. Meister...; fig. führend; 3. Herr sein od. werden über (acc.); Sprache etc. meistern, beherrschen; ~builder Baumeister m; ~ful □ [~ful] herrisch; meisterhaft; ~key Hauptschlüssel f; ~ly [~li] meisterhaft; ~piece Meisterstück n; ~ship [~ʃip] Meisterschaft f; Herrschaft f; Lehramt n; ~y [~əri] Herrschaft f; Vorrang m; Oberhand f; Meisterschaft f; Beherrschung f.
masticate ['mæstikeit] kauen.
mastiff ['mæstif] englische Dogge.
mat [mæt] 1. Matte f; Deckchen n; Unterlage f; 2. fig. bedecken; (sich) verflechten; 3. mattiert, matt.
match¹ [mætʃ] Streichholz n.
match² [~] 1. Gleiche(r m, -s n) f; Partie f; Wettspiel n, -kampf m; Heirat f; be a ~ for j-m gewachsen sein; meet one's ~ s-n Meister finden; 2. v/t. anpassen; passen zu; et. Passendes finden od. geben zu; es aufnehmen mit; verheiraten; well ~ed zs.-passend; v/i. zs.-passen; to ~ dazu passend; ~less □ ['mætʃlis] unvergleichlich, ohnegleichen; ~maker Ehestifter(in).
mate¹ [meit] Schach: matt (setzen).
mate² [~] 1. Gefährt|e m, -in f; Kamerad(in); Gatt|e m, -in f; Männchen n, Weibchen n von Tieren; Gehilf|e m, -in f; ⚓ Maat m; 2. (sich) verheiraten; (sich) paaren.
material □ [mə'tiəriəl] 1. materiell; körperlich; materialistisch; wesentlich; 2. Material n, Stoff m; Werkstoff m; writing ~s pl. Schreibmaterial(ien pl.) n.
matern|al □ [mə'təːnl] mütterlich; Mutter...; mütterlicherseits; ~ity [~niti] Mutterschaft f; Mütterlichkeit f; mst ~ hospital Entbindungsanstalt f.
mathematic|ian [mæθimə'tiʃən] Mathematiker m; ~s [~'mætiks] mst sg. Mathematik f.

matriculate [mə'trikjuleit] (sich) immatrikulieren (lassen).
matrimon|ial □ [mætri'mounjəl] ehelich; Ehe...; ~y ['mætriməni] Ehe(stand m) f.
matrix ['meitriks] Matrize f.
matron ['meitrən] Matrone f; Hausmutter f; Oberin f.
matter ['mætə] 1. Materie f, Stoff m; 🎖 Eiter m; Gegenstand m; Ursache f; Sache f; Angelegenheit f; Geschäft n; printed ~ 🖂 Drucksache f; what's the ~? was gibt es?; what's the ~ with you? was fehlt Ihnen?; no ~ es hat nichts zu sagen; no ~ who gleichgültig wer; ~ of course Selbstverständlichkeit f; for that ~, for the ~ of that was dies betrifft; ~ of fact Tatsache f; 2. von Bedeutung sein; it does not ~ es macht nichts; ~-of-fact tatsächlich; sachlich.
mattress ['mætris] Matratze f.
matur|e [mə'tjuə] 1. □ reif; reiflich; ✝ fällig; 2. reifen; zur Reife bringen; ✝ fällig werden; ~ity [~əriti] Reife f; ✝ Fälligkeit f.
maudlin □ ['mɔːdlin] rührselig.
maul [mɔːl] beschädigen; fig. heruntermachen; roh umgehen mit.
Maundy Thursday eccl. ['mɔːndi 'θəːzdi] Gründonnerstag m.
mauve [mouv] 1. Malvenfarbe f; 2. hellviolett.
maw [mɔː] Tier-Magen m; Rachen m.
mawkish □ ['mɔːkiʃ] rührselig, sentimental.
maxim ['mæksim] Grundsatz m; ~um [~məm] Höchstmaß n, -stand m, -betrag m; attr. Höchst...
May¹ [mei] Mai m.
may² [~] [irr.] mag, kann, darf.
maybe Am. ['meibi] vielleicht.
may|-beetle zo. ['meibiːtl], ~-bug Maikäfer m.
May Day ['meidei] der 1. Mai.
mayor [mɛə] Bürgermeister m.
maypole ['meipoul] Maibaum m.
maz|e [meiz] Irrgarten m, Labyrinth n; fig. Wirrnis f; in a ~ = ~ed [meizd] bestürzt, verwirrt; ~y □ ['meizi] labyrinthisch; wirr.
me [miː, mi] mich; mir; F ich.
mead [miːd] Met m; poet. = meadow.
meadow ['medou] Wiese f.
meag|re, Am. ~er □ ['miːgə] mager, dürr; dürftig.
meal [miːl] Mahl(zeit f) n; Mehl n.
mean¹ □ [miːn] gemein, niedrig, gering; armselig; knauserig.
mean² [~] 1. mittler, mittelmäßig; Durchschnitts...; in the ~ time inzwischen; 2. Mitte f; ~s pl. (Geld-)Mittel n/pl.; (a. sg.) Mittel n; by all ~s jedenfalls; by no ~s keineswegs; by ~s of mittels (gen.).
mean³ [~] [irr.] meinen; beabsich-

tigen; bestimmen; bedeuten; ~ well (ill) es gut (schlecht) meinen.

meaning ['mi:niŋ] 1. □ bedeutsam; 2. Sinn m, Bedeutung f; ~less [~nlis] bedeutungslos; sinnlos.

meant [ment] pret. u. p.p. von mean³.

mean|time ['mi:n'taim], ~while mittlerweile, inzwischen.

measles ♀ ['mi:zlz] sg. Masern pl.

measure ['meʒə] 1. Maß n; ♪ Takt m; Maßregel f; ~ of capacity Hohlmaß n; beyond ~ über alle Maßen; in a great ~ großenteils; made to ~ nach Maß gemacht; 2. (ab-, aus-, ver)messen; j-m Maß nehmen; ~ up Am. heranreichen; ~less □ [~əlis] unermeßlich; ~ment [~əmənt] Messung f; Maß n.

meat [mi:t] Fleisch n; fig. Gehalt m; ~ tea frühes Abendessen mit Tee; ~y ['mi:ti] fleischig; fig. gehaltvoll.

mechanic [mi'kænik] Handwerker m; Mechaniker m; ~al □ [~kəl] mechanisch; Maschinen...; ~ian [mekə'niʃən] Mechaniker m; ~s [mi'kæniks] mst sg. Mechanik f.

mechan|ism ['mekənizəm] Mechanismus m; ~ize [~naiz] mechanisieren; ✕ motorisieren.

medal ['medl] Medaille f; Orden m.

meddle ['medl] sich einmischen (with, in in acc.); ~some [~lsəm] zu-, aufdringlich.

mediaeval □ [medi'i:vəl] mittelalterlich.

media|l □ ['mi:djəl], ~n [~ən] Mittel..., in der Mitte (befindlich).

mediat|e ['mi:dieit] vermitteln; ~ion [mi:di'eiʃən] Vermittlung f; ~or ['mi:dieitə] Vermittler m.

medical □ ['medikəl] medizinisch, ärztlich; ~ certificate Krankenschein m, Attest n; ~ evidence ärztliches Gutachten; ~ man Arzt m, Mediziner m; ~ supervision ärztliche Aufsicht.

medicate ['medikeit] medizinisch behandeln; mit Arzneistoff versehen; ~d bath medizinisches Bad.

medicin|al □ [me'disinl] medizinisch; heilend, heilsam; ~e ['medsin] Medizin f.

medieval □ [medi'i:vəl] = mediaeval.

mediocre ['mi:dioukə] mittelmäßig.

meditat|e ['mediteit] v/i. nachdenken, überlegen; v/t. sinnen auf (acc.); erwägen; ~ion [medi'teiʃən] Nachdenken n; innere Betrachtung; ~ive □ ['meditətiv] nachdenklich, meditativ.

Mediterranean [meditə'reinjən] Mittelmeer n; attr. Mittelmeer...

medium ['mi:djəm] 1. Mitte f; Mittel n; Vermittlung f; Medium n; Lebens-Element n; 2. mittler; Mittel..., Durchschnitts...

medley ['medli] Gemisch n; ♪ Potpourri n.

meek □ [mi:k] sanft-, demütig; ~ness ['mi:knis] Sanft-, Demut f.

meerschaum ['miəʃəm] Meerschaum(pfeife f) m.

meet¹ [mi:t] passend; schicklich.

meet² [~] [irr.] v/t. treffen; begegnen (dat.); abholen; stoßen auf den Gegner; Wunsch etc. befriedigen; e-r Verpflichtung nachkommen; Am. j-m vorgestellt werden; go to ~ s.o. j-m entgegengehen; v/i. sich treffen; zs.-stoßen; sich versammeln; ~ with stoßen auf (acc.); erleiden; ~ing [~tiŋ] Begegnung f; (Zs.-)Treffen n, Versammlung f; Tagung f.

melancholy ['melənkəli] 1. Schwermut f; 2. melancholisch.

meliorate ['mi:ljəreit] (sich) verbessern.

mellow ['melou] 1. □ mürbe; reif; weich; mild; 2. reifen (lassen); weich machen od. werden; (sich) mildern.

melo|dious □ [mi'loudjəs] melodisch; ~dramatic [melʌudrə'mætik] melodramatisch; ~dy ['melədi] Melodie f; Lied n.

melon ♀ ['melən] Melone f.

melt [melt] (zer)schmelzen; fig. zerfließen; Gefühl erweichen.

member ['membə] (Mit)Glied n; parl. Abgeordnete(r m) f; ~ship [~ʃip] Mitgliedschaft f; Mitgliederzahl f.

membrane ['membrein] Membran(e) f, Häutchen n. [n.\

memento [mi'mentou] Andenken n.

memo ['mi:mou] = memorandum.

memoir ['memwa:] Denkschrift f; ~s pl. Memoiren pl.

memorable □ ['memərəbl] denkwürdig.

memorandum [memə'rændəm] Notiz f; pol. Note f; Schriftsatz m.

memorial [mi'mɔ:riəl] Denkmal n; Gedenkzeichen n; Denkschrift f, Eingabe f; attr. Gedächtnis..., Gedenk...

memorize ['meməraiz] auswendig lernen, memorieren.

memory ['meməri] Gedächtnis n; Erinnerung f; Andenken n; commit to ~ dem Gedächtnis einprägen; in ~ of zum Andenken an (acc.).

men [men] pl. von man 1; Mannschaft f.

menace ['menəs] 1. (be)drohen; 2. Gefahr f; Drohung f.

mend [mend] 1. v/t. (ver)bessern; ausbessern, flicken; besser machen; ~ one's ways sich bessern; v/i. sich bessern; 2. Flicken m; on the ~ auf dem Wege der Besserung.

mendacious □ [men'deiʃəs] lügnerisch, verlogen.

mendicant ['mendikənt] 1. bet-

telnd; Bettel...; 2. Bettler m; Bettel-
mönch m.
menial contp. ['mi:njəl] 1. □ knech-
tisch; niedrig; 2. Knecht m; Lakai m.
meningitis ⚕ [menin'dʒaitis] Hirn-
hautentzündung f, Meningitis f.
mental □ ['mentl] geistig; Geistes...; ~ arithmetic Kopfrechnen n;
~ity [men'tæliti] Mentalität f.
mention ['menʃən] 1. Erwähnung f;
2. erwähnen; don't ~ it! bitte!
menu ['menju:] Speisenfolge f,
Menü n; Speisekarte f.
mercantile ['mə:kəntail] kaufmännisch; Handels...
mercenary ['mə:sinəri] 1. □ feil,
käuflich; gedungen; gewinnsüch-
tig; 2. ✕ Söldner m.
mercer ['mə:sə] Seidenwaren-,
Stoffhändler m.
merchandise ['mə:tʃəndaiz] Wa-
re(n pl.) f.
merchant ['mə:tʃənt] 1. Kaufmann
m; Am. (Klein)Händler m; 2. Handels..., Kaufmanns...; law ~ Han-
delsrecht n; ~man Handelsschiff n.
merci|ful □ ['mə:siful] barmher-
zig; ~less □ [~ilis] unbarmherzig.
mercury ['mə:kjuri] Quecksilber n.
mercy ['mə:si] Barmherzigkeit f;
Gnade f; be at s.o.'s ~ in j-s Gewalt sein.
mere [miə] rein, lauter; bloß;
~ly ['miəli] bloß, lediglich, allein.
meretricious □ [meri'triʃəs] aufdringlich; kitschig.
merge [mə:dʒ] verschmelzen (in
mit); ~r ['mə:dʒə] Verschmelzung f.
meridian [mə'ridiən] geogr. Meridian m; fig. Gipfel m; attr. Mittags...
merit ['merit] 1. Verdienst n; Wert
m; Vorzug m; bsd. ⚖ ~s pl. Haupt-
punkte m/pl., Wesen n e-r Sache;
make a ~ of als Verdienst ansehen;
2. fig. verdienen; ~orious □
[meri'tɔ:riəs] verdienstvoll.
mermaid ['mə:meid] Nixe f.
merriment ['merimənt] Lustigkeit
f; Belustigung f.
merry □ ['meri] lustig, fröhlich;
make ~ lustig sein; ~ andrew
Hanswurst m; ~-go-round Karussell n; ~-making ['~imeikiŋ] Lustbarkeit f.
mesh [meʃ] 1. Masche f; fig. oft ~es
pl. Netz n; be in ~ ⊕ (in-ea.-)grei-
fen; 2. in e-m Netz fangen.
mess¹ [mes] 1. Unordnung f;
Schmutz m, F Schweinerei f; F Patsche f; make a ~ of verpfuschen; 2.
v/t. in Unordnung bringen; verpfuschen; v/i. ~about F herummurksen.
mess² [~.] Kasino n, Messe f.
message ['mesidʒ] Botschaft f; go
on a ~ e-e Besorgung machen.
messenger ['mesindʒə] Bote m.
Messieurs, mst Messrs. ['mesəz]
(die) Herren m/pl.; Firma f.

met [met] pret. u. p.p. von meet².
metal ['metl] 1. Metall n; Schotter
m; 2. beschottern; ~lic [mi'tælik]
(~ally) metallisch; Metall...; ~lurgy
[me'tælədʒi] Hüttenkunde f.
metamorphose [metə'mɔ:fouz] verwandeln, umgestalten.
metaphor ['metəfə] Metapher f.
meteor ['mi:tjə] Meteor m (a. fig.);
~ology [mi:tjə'rɔlədʒi] Meteorologie f, Wetterkunde f.
meter ['mi:tə] Messer m, Zähler m;
Am. = metre.
methinks † [mi'θiŋks] mich dünkt.
method ['meθəd] Methode f; Art
u. Weise f; Verfahren n; Ordnung
f, System n; ~ic(al □) [mi'θɔ-
dik(əl)] methodisch.
methought [mi'θɔ:t] pret. von
methinks.
meticulous □ [mi'tikjuləs] peinlich
genau.
met|re, Am. ~er ['mi:tə] Meter n,
m; Versmaß n.
metric ['metrik] (~ally) metrisch;
~ system Dezimalsystem n.
metropoli|s [mi'trɔpəlis] Haupt-
stadt f, Metropole f; ~tan [metrə-
'pɔlitən] hauptstädtisch.
mettle ['metl] Feuereifer m, Mut m;
be on one's~ sein Bestes tun.
mews [mju:z] Stallung f; daraus
entstandene Garagen f/pl. od. Wohn-
häuser n/pl.
Mexican ['meksikən] 1. mexika-
nisch; 2. Mexikaner(in).
miaow [mi(:)'au] miauen; mauzen.
mice [mais] pl. von mouse.
Michaelmas ['miklməs] Michaelis
(-tag m) n (29. September).
micro... ['maikrou] klein..., Klein...
micro|phone ['maikrəfoun] Mikro-
phon n; ~scope Mikroskop n.
mid [mid] mittler; Mitt(el)...; in ~
air mitten in der Luft; in ~ winter
mitten im Winter; ~day ['middei]
1. Mittag m; 2. mittägig; Mittags...
middle ['midl] 1. Mitte f; Hüften
f/pl.; 2. mittler; Mittel...; 2 Ages
pl. Mittelalter n; ~-aged von mittlerem Alter; ~-class Mittelstands-
...; ~ class(es pl.) Mittelstand m;
~man Mittelsmann m; ~ name
zweiter Vorname m; ~-sized mittel-
groß; ~-weight Boxen: Mittelge-
wicht n.
middling ['midliŋ] mittelmäßig;
leidlich; Mittel...
middy F ['midi] = midshipman.
midge [midʒ] Mücke f; ~t ['midʒit]
Zwerg m, Knirps m.
mid|land ['midlənd] 1. binnenlän-
disch; 2. the 2s pl. Mittelengland n;
~most mittelste(r, -s); ~night
Mitternacht f; ~riff ['midrif]
Zwerchfell n; ~shipman Leutnant
m zur See; Am. Oberfähnrich m
zur See; ~st [midst] Mitte f; in the
~ of inmitten (gen.); ~summer

Sommersonnenwende *f*; Hochsommer *m*; **~way** 1. halber Weg; *Am.* Schaubudenstraße *f*; 2. *adj.* in der Mitte befindlich; 3. *adv.* auf halbem Wege; **~wife** Hebamme *f*; **~wifery** ['midwifəri] Geburtshilfe *f*; **~winter** Wintersonnenwende *f*; Mitte *f* des Winters.

mien [mi:n] Miene *f*.

might [mait] 1. Macht *f*, Gewalt *f*, Kraft *f*; *with ~ and main* mit aller Gewalt; 2. *pret. von* may²; **~y** □ ['maiti] mächtig, gewaltig.

migrat|e [mai'greit] (aus)wandern; **~ion** [~eiʃən] Wanderung *f*; **~ory** ['maigrətəri] wandernd; Zug...

mild □ [maild] mild, sanft; gelind.

mildew ♀ ['mildju:] Mehltau *m*.

mildness ['maildnis] Milde *f*.

mile [mail] Meile *f* (1609.33 m).

mil(e)age ['mailidʒ] Laufzeit *f in Meilen*, Meilenstand *m e-s Autos*; Kilometergeld *n*.

milestone ['mailstoun] Meilenstein *m*.

milit|ary ['militəri] 1. □ militärisch; Kriegs...; ♀ *Government* Militärregierung *f*; 2. *das Militär*; **~ia** [mi'liʃə] Land-, Bürgerwehr *f*.

milk [milk] 1. Milch *f*; *it's no use crying over spilt ~* geschehen ist geschehen; 2. *v/t.* melken; *v/i.* Milch geben; **~maid** ['milkmeid] Melkerin *f*; Milchmädchen *n*; **~man** Milchmann *m*; **~powder** Milchpulver *n*; **~shake** Milchmischgetränk *n*; **~sop** Weichling *m*; **~y** ['milki] milchig; Milch...; ♀ *Way* Milchstraße *f*.

mill¹ [mil] 1. Mühle *f*; Fabrik *f*, Spinnerei *f*; 2. mahlen; ⊕ fräsen; *Geld* prägen; *Münze* rändeln.

mill² *Am.* [~] ¹/₁₀₀₀ Dollar *m*.

millepede *zo.* ['milipi:d] Tausendfüß(l)er *m*.

miller ['milə] Müller *m*; ⊕ Fräsmaschine *f*.

millet ♀ ['milit] Hirse *f*.

milliner ['milinə] Putzmacherin *f*, Modistin *f*; **~y** [~əri] Putz-, Modewaren(geschäft *n*) *pl.*

million ['miljən] Million *f*; **~aire** [miljə'nɛə] Millionär(in); **~th** ['miljənθ] 1. millionste(r, -s); 2. Millionstel *n*.

mill|-pond ['milpɔnd] Mühlteich *m*; **~stone** Mühlstein *m*.

milt [milt] Milch *f der Fische*.

mimic ['mimik] 1. mimisch; Schein...; 2. Mime *m*; 3. nachahmen, nachäffen; **~ry** [~kri] Nachahmung *f*; *zo.* Angleichung *f*.

mince [mins] 1. *v/t.* zerhacken; *he does not ~ matters* er nimmt kein Blatt vor den Mund; *v/i.* sich zieren; 2. *a.* **~d meat** Hackfleisch *n*; **~meat** ['minsmi:t] *e-e* Tortenfüllung; **~pie** Torte *f* aus *mincemeat*; **~r** [~sə] Fleischwolf *m*.

mincing-machine ['minsiŋməʃi:n] = *mincer*.

mind [maind] 1. Sinn *m*, Gemüt *n*; Geist *m*, Verstand *m*; Meinung *f*; Absicht *f*; Neigung *f*, Lust *f*; Gedächtnis *n*; Sorge *f*; *to my ~* meiner Ansicht nach; *out of one's ~*, not *in one's right ~* von Sinnen; *change one's ~* sich anders besinnen; *bear s.th. in ~* (immer) an et. denken; *have (half) a ~ to* (beinahe) Lust haben zu; *have s.th. on one's ~* et. auf dem Herzen haben; *make up one's ~* sich entschließen; 2. merken *od.* achten auf (*acc.*); sich kümmern um; etwas (einzuwenden) haben gegen; *~! gib acht!*; *never ~! macht nichts!*; *~ the step! Achtung, Stufe!*; *I don't ~* (it) ich habe nichts dagegen; *do you ~ if I smoke?* stört es Sie, wenn ich rauche?; *would you ~ taking off your hat?* würden Sie bitte den Hut abnehmen?; *~ your own business! kümmern Sie sich um Ihre Angelegenheiten!*; **~ful** □ ['maindful] (*of*) eingedenk (*gen.*); achtsam (auf *acc.*).

mine¹ [main] 1. der (die, das) meinige; mein; 2. die Mein(ig)en *pl.*

mine² [~] 1. Bergwerk *n*, Grube *f*; *fig.* Fundgrube *f*; ✕ Mine *f*; 2. *v/i.* graben, minieren; *v/t.* graben; ✕ fördern; ✕ unterminieren; ✕ verminen; **~r** [mainə] Bergmann *m*.

mineral ['minərəl] 1. Mineral *n*; **~s** *pl.* Mineralwasser *n*; 2. mineralisch.

mingle ['miŋgl] (ver)mischen; sich mischen *od.* mengen (*with unter*).

miniature ['minjətʃə] 1. Miniatur (-gemälde *n*) *f*; 2. in Miniatur; Miniatur...; Klein...; *~ camera* Kleinbildkamera *f*.

minikin ['minikin] 1. winzig; geziert; 2. Knirps *m*.

minim|ize ['minimaiz] möglichst klein machen; *fig.* verringern; **~um** [~məm] Minimum *n*; Mindestmaß *n*; Mindestbetrag *m*; *attr.* Mindest...

mining ['mainiŋ] Bergbau *m*; *attr.* Berg(bau)...; Gruben...

minion ['minjən] Günstling *m*; *fig.* Lakai *m*.

miniskirt ['miniskə:t] Minirock *m*.

minister ['ministə] 1. Diener *m*; *fig.* Werkzeug *n*; Geistliche(r) *m*; Minister *m*; Gesandte(r) *m*; 2. *v/t.* darreichen; *v/i.* dienen; Gottesdienst halten.

ministry ['ministri] geistliches Amt; Ministerium *n*; Regierung *f*.

mink *zo.* [miŋk] Nerz *m*.

minor ['mainə] 1. kleiner, geringer, weniger bedeutend; ♪ Moll *n*; *A ~* A-moll *n*; 2. Minderjährige(r *m*) *f*; *Am. univ.* Nebenfach *n*; **~ity** [mai'nɔriti] Minderheit *f*; Unmündigkeit *f*.

minster ['minstə] Münster *n*.

minstrel ['minstrəl] Minnesänger m; ~s pl. Negersänger m/pl.

mint [mint] 1. ♀ Minze f; Münze f; fig. Goldgrube f; a ~ of money e-e Menge Geld; 2. münzen, prägen.

minuet ♪ [minju'et] Menuett n.

minus ['mainəs] 1. prp. weniger; F ohne; 2. adj. negativ.

minute 1. □ [mai'njuːt] sehr klein, winzig; unbedeutend; sehr genau; 2. ['minit] Minute f; Augenblick m; ~s pl. Protokoll n; ~ness [mai-'njuːtnis] Kleinheit f; Genauigkeit f.

mirac|le ['mirəkl] Wunder n; ~ulous □ [mi'rækjuləs] wunderbar.

mirage ['miraːʒ] Luftspiegelung f.

mire ['maiə] 1. Sumpf m; Kot m, Schlamm m; 2. mit Schlamm od. Schmutz bedecken.

mirror ['mirə] 1. Spiegel m; 2. (wider)spiegeln (a. fig.).

mirth [məːθ] Fröhlichkeit f; ~ful □ ['məːθful] fröhlich; ~less □ ['məːθlis] freudlos.

miry ['maiəri] kotig.

mis... [mis] miß..., übel, falsch.

misadventure ['misəd'ventʃə] Mißgeschick n, Unfall m.

misanthrop|e ['mizənθroup], ~ist [mi'zænθrəpist] Menschenfeind m.

misapply ['misə'plai] falsch anwenden; [mißverstehen.]

misapprehend ['misæpri'hend]

misappropriate ['misə'prouprieit] unterschlagen, veruntreuen.

misbehave ['misbi'heiv] sich schlecht benehmen.

misbelief ['misbi'liːf] Irrglaube m.

miscalculate ['miskælkjuleit] falsch (be)rechnen.

miscarr|iage ['mis'kæridʒ] Mißlingen n; Verlust m v. Briefen; Fehlgeburt f; ~ of justice Fehlspruch m; ~y [~ri] mißlingen; verlorengehen (Brief); fehlgebären.

miscellan|eous □ ['misi'leinjəs] ge-, vermischt; vielseitig; ~y [mi-'seləni] Gemisch n; Sammelband m.

mischief ['mistʃif] Schaden m, Unfug m; Mutwille m, Übermut m; ~-maker Unheilstifter(in).

mischievous □ ['mistʃivəs] schädlich; boshaft, mutwillig.

misconceive ['miskən'siːv] falsch auffassen od. verstehen.

misconduct 1. [mis'kɔndəkt] schlechtes Benehmen; Ehebruch m; schlechte Verwaltung; 2. ['miskən-'dʌkt] schlecht verwalten; ~ o.s. sich schlecht benehmen; e-n Fehltritt begehen.

misconstrue ['miskən'struː] mißdeuten.

miscreant ['miskriənt] Schurke m.

misdeed ['mis'diːd] Missetat f.

misdemeano(u)r ⚖ [misdi'miːnə] Vergehen n.

misdirect ['misdi'rekt] irreleiten; an die falsche Adresse richten.

misdoing ['misdu(ː)iŋ] Vergehen n (mst pl.).

mise en scène thea. ['miːzãːn'sein] Inszenierung f.

miser ['maizə] Geizhals m.

miserable □ ['mizərəbl] elend; unglücklich, erbärmlich.

miserly ['maizəli] geizig, filzig.

misery ['mizəri] Elend n, Not f.

misfit ['misfit] schlecht passendes Stück (Kleid, Stiefel etc.); Einzelgänger m, Eigenbrötler m.

misfortune [mis'fɔːtʃən] Unglück(sfall m) n; Mißgeschick n.

misgiving [mis'giviŋ] böse Ahnung, Befürchtung f.

misguide ['mis'gaid] irreleiten.

mishap ['mishæp] Unfall m; mot. Panne f.

misinform ['misin'fɔːm] falsch unterrichten. [deuten.]

misinterpret ['misin'təːprit] miß-]

mislay [mis'lei] irr. (lay) verlegen.

mislead [mis'liːd] irr. (lead) irreführen; verleiten.

mismanage ['mis'mænidʒ] schlecht verwalten.

misplace ['mis'pleis] falsch stellen, verstellen; verlegen; falsch anbringen.

misprint 1. [mis'print] verdrucken; 2. ['mis'print] Druckfehler m.

misread ['mis'riːd] irr. (read) falsch lesen od. deuten.

misrepresent['misrepri'zent]falsch darstellen, verdrehen.

miss¹ [mis] mst ♀ Fräulein n.

miss² [~] 1. Verlust m; Fehlschuß m, -stoß m, -wurf m; 2. v/t. (ver)missen; verfehlen; verpassen; auslassen; übersehen; überhören; v/i. fehlen (nicht treffen); fehlgehen.

misshapen ['mis'ʃeipən] verunstaltet; mißgestaltet.

missile ['misail] (Wurf)Geschoß n; Rakete f.

missing ['misiŋ] fehlend; ⚔ vermißt; be ~ fehlen; vermißt werden.

mission ['miʃən] Sendung f; Auftrag m; Berufung f, Lebensziel n; Gesandtschaft f; eccl., pol. Mission f; ~ary ['miʃnəri] Missionar m; attr. Missions...

missive ['misiv] Sendschreiben n.

mis-spell ['mis'spel] irr. (spell) falsch buchstabieren od. schreiben.

mis-spend ['mis'spend] irr. (spend)] falsch verwenden; vergeuden.

mist [mist] 1. Nebel m; 2. (um)nebeln; sich trüben; beschlagen.

mistake [mis'teik] 1. irr. (take) sich irren in (dat.), verkennen; mißverstehen; verwechseln (for mit); be ~n sich irren; 2. Irrtum m; Versehen n; Fehler m; ~n □ [~kən] irrig, falsch (verstanden).

mister ['mistə] Herr *m* (*abbr.* **Mr.**).
mistletoe ❦ ['misltou] Mistel *f*.
mistress ['mistris] Herrin *f*; Hausfrau *f*; Lehrerin *f*; Geliebte *f*; Meisterin *f*.
mistrust ['mis'trʌst] **1.** mißtrauen (*dat.*); **2.** Mißtrauen *n*; ~**ful** □ [~tful] mißtrauisch.
misty] ['misti] neb(e)lig; unklar.
misunderstand ['misʌndə'stænd] [*irr.* (*stand*)] mißverstehen; ~**ing** [~diŋ] Mißverständnis *n*.
misus|age [mis'ju:zidʒ] Mißbrauch *m*; Mißhandlung *f*; ~**e 1.** ['mis'ju:z] mißbrauchen, mißhandeln; **2.** [~u:s] Mißbrauch *m*.
mite [mait] *zo.* Milbe *f*; Heller *m*; *fig.* Scherflein *n*; Knirps *m*.
mitigate ['mitigeit] mildern, lindern (*a. fig.*).
mit|re, *Am.* ~**er** ['maitə] Bischofsmütze *f*.
mitt [mit] *Baseball*-Handschuh *m*; F Boxhandschuh *m*; = **mitten.**
mitten ['mitn] Fausthandschuh *m*; Halbhandschuh *m* (*ohne Finger*); *Am. sl.* Tatze *f* (*Hand*).
mix [miks] (sich) (ver)mischen; verkehren (*with mit*); ~**ed** gemischt; *fig.* zweifelhaft; ~ *up* durch-ea.-bringen; *be* ~*ed up with in e-e S.* verwickelt sein; ~**ture** ['mikstʃə] Mischung *f*.
moan [moun] **1.** Stöhnen *n*; **2.** stöhnen.
moat [mout] Burg-, Stadtgraben *m*.
mob [mɔb] **1.** Pöbel *m*; **2.** anpöbeln.
mobil|e ['moubail] beweglich; ✕ mobil; ~**ization** ✕ [moubilai'zeiʃən] Mobilmachung *f*; ~**ize** ✕ ['moubilaiz] mobil machen.
moccasin ['mɔkəsin] weiches Leder; Mokassin *m* (*Schuh*).
mock [mɔk] **1.** Spott *m*; **2.** Schein...; falsch, nachgemacht; **3.** *v/t.* verspotten; nachmachen; täuschen; *v/i.* spotten (*at über acc.*); ~**ery** ['mɔkəri] Spötterei *f*, Gespött *n*; Äfferei *f*.
mocking-bird *orn.* ['mɔkiŋbə:d] Spottdrossel *f*.
mode [moud] Art und Weise *f*; (Erscheinungs)Form *f*; Sitte *f*, Mode *f*.
model ['mɔdl] **1.** Modell *n*; Muster *n*; *fig.* Vorbild *n*; Vorführdame *f*; *attr.* Muster...; **2.** modellieren; (ab)formen; *fig.* modeln, bilden.
moderat|e 1. □ ['mɔdərit] (mittel-)mäßig; **2.** [~reit] (sich) mäßigen; ~**ion** [mɔdə'reiʃən] Mäßigung *f*; Mäßigkeit *f*.
modern ['mɔdən] modern, neu; ~**ize** [~ə(:)naiz] (sich) modernisieren.
modest □ ['mɔdist] bescheiden, anständig; ~**y** [~ti] Bescheidenheit *f*.
modi|fication [mɔdifi'keiʃən] Ab-,

Veränderung *f*; Einschränkung *f*; ~**fy** ['mɔdifai] (ab)ändern; mildern.
mods [mɔdz] *pl.* Halbstarke *m/pl.*
modulate ['mɔdjuleit] modulieren.
moiety ['mɔiəti] Hälfte *f*; Teil *m*.
moist [mɔist] feucht, naß; ~**en** ['mɔisn] be-, anfeuchten; ~**ure** ['mɔistʃə] Feuchtigkeit *f*.
molar ['moulə] Backenzahn *m*.
molasses [mə'læsiz] Melasse *f*; Sirup *m*.
mole[1] *zo.* [moul] Maulwurf *m*.
mole[2] [~] Muttermal *n*.
mole[3] [~] Mole *f*, Hafendamm *m*.
molecule ['mɔlikju:l] Molekül *n*.
molehill ['moulhil] Maulwurfshügel *m*; *make a mountain out of a* ~ aus e-r Mücke e-n Elefanten machen.
molest [mou'lest] belästigen.
mollify ['mɔlifai] besänftigen.
mollycoddle ['mɔlikɔdl] **1.** Weichling *m*, Muttersöhnchen *n*; **2.** verzärteln.
molten ['moultən] geschmolzen.
moment ['moumənt] Augenblick *m*; Bedeutung *f*; = *momentum*; ~**ary** □ [~təri] augenblicklich; vorübergehend; ~**ous** □ [mou'mentəs] (ge)wichtig, bedeutend; ~**um** *phys.* [~təm] Moment *n*; Triebkraft *f*.
monarch ['mɔnək] Monarch(in); ~**y** [~ki] Monarchie *f*.
monastery ['mɔnəstəri] (Mönchs-) Kloster *n*.
Monday ['mʌndi] Montag *m*.
monetary ['mʌnitəri] Geld...
money ['mʌni] Geld *n*; *ready* ~ Bargeld *n*; ~**-box** Sparbüchse *f*; ~**-changer** [~tʃeindʒə] (Geld-) Wechsler *m*; ~**-order** Postanweisung *f*.
monger ['mʌŋgə] ...händler *m*, ...krämer *m*.
mongrel ['mʌŋgrəl] Mischling *m*, Bastard *m*; *attr.* Bastard...
monitor ['mɔnitə] ⊕ Monitor *m*; (Klassen)Ordner *m*.
monk [mʌŋk] Mönch *m*.
monkey ['mʌŋki] **1.** *zo.* Affe *m* (*a. fig.*); ⊕ Rammblock *m*; *put s.o.'s* ~ *up* F j-n auf die Palme bringen; ~ *business Am. sl.* fauler Zauber; **2.** F (herum)albern; ~ *with* herummurksen an (*dat.*); ~**-wrench** ⊕ Engländer *m* (*Schraubenschlüssel*); *throw a* ~ *in s.th. Am. sl.* et. über den Haufen werfen.
monkish ['mʌŋkiʃ] mönchisch.
mono|... ['mɔnou] ein(fach)...; ~**cle** ['mɔnɔkl] Monokel *n*; ~**gamy** [mɔ'nɔgəmi] Einehe *f*; ~**logue,** *Am. a.* ~**log** ['mɔnələg] Monolog *m*; ~**polist** [mə'nɔpəlist] Monopolist *m*; ~**polize** [~laiz] monopolisieren; *fig.* an sich reißen; ~**poly** [~li] Monopol *n* (*of auf acc.*); ~**tonous** □ [~'ɔtnəs] monoton, eintönig; ~**tony** [~ni] Monotonie *f*.

monsoon [mɔn'suːn] Monsun *m*.

monster ['mɔnstə] Ungeheuer *n* (*a. fig.*); Monstrum *n*; *attr.* Riesen...

monstro|sity [mɔns'trɔsiti] Ungeheuer(lichkeit *f*) *n*; ~us □ ['mɔnstrəs] ungeheuer(lich); gräßlich.

month [mʌnθ] Monat *m*; *this day* ~ heute in e-m Monat; ~ly ['mʌnθli] 1. monatlich; Monats...; 2. Monatsschrift *f*.

monument ['mɔnjumənt] Denkmal *n*; ~al □ [mɔnju'mentl] monumental; Gedenk...; großartig.

mood [muːd] Stimmung *f*, Laune *f*; ~y □ ['muːdi] launisch; schwermütig; übellaunig.

moon [muːn] 1. Mond *m*; *once in a blue* ~ F alle Jubeljahre einmal; 2. *mst* ~ *about* F herumdösen; ~light ['muːnlait] Mondlicht *n*, -schein *m*; ~lit mondhell; ~struck mondsüchtig.

Moor[1] [muə] Maure *m*; Mohr *m*.

moor[2] [~] Ödland *n*, Heideland *n*.

moor[3] ⚓ [~] (sich) vertäuen; ~ings ⚓ ['muəriŋz] *pl.* Vertäuungen *f/pl.*

moose *zo.* [muːz] *a.* ~*deer amerikanischer* Elch.

moot [muːt]: ~ *point* Streitpunkt *m*.

mop [mɔp] 1. Mop *m*; (Haar)Wust *m*; 2. auf-, abwischen.

mope [moup] den Kopf hängen lassen.

moral ['mɔrəl] 1. □ Moral...; moralisch; 2. Moral *f*; Nutzanwendung *f*; ~s *pl.* Sitten *f/pl.*; ~e [mɔ'rɑːl] *bsd.* ✗ Moral *f*, Haltung *f*; ~ity [mɔ'ræliti] Moralität *f*; Sittlichkeit *f*, Moral *f*; ~ize ['mɔrəlaiz] moralisieren.

morass [mɔ'ræs] Morast *m*, Sumpf *m*.

morbid □ ['mɔːbid] krankhaft.

more [mɔː] mehr; *once* ~ noch einmal, wieder; *so much od. all the* ~ um so mehr; *no* ~ nicht mehr.

morel ⚕ [mɔ'rel] Morchel *f*.

moreover [mɔː'rouvə] überdies, weiter, ferner.

morgue [mɔːg] Leichenschauhaus *n*; Archiv *n*.

moribund ['mɔribʌnd] im Sterben (liegend), dem Tode geweiht.

morning ['mɔːniŋ] Morgen *m*; Vormittag *m*; *tomorrow* ~ morgen früh; ~ dress Tagesgesellschaftsanzug *m*.   [*m*] *f*.\

moron ['mɔːrɔn] Schwachsinnige(r)

morose □ [mɔ'rous] mürrisch.

morph|ia ['mɔːfjə], ~ine ['mɔːfiːn] Morphium *n*.

morsel ['mɔːsəl] Bissen *m*; Stückchen *n*, *das* bißchen.

mortal ['mɔːtl] 1. □ sterblich; tödlich; Tod(es)...; 2. Sterbliche(r *m*) *f*; ~ity [mɔː'tæliti] Sterblichkeit *f*.

mortar ['mɔːtə] Mörser *m*; Mörtel *m*.

mortgag|e ['mɔːgidʒ] 1. Pfandgut *n*; Hypothek *f*; 2. verpfänden; ~ee [mɔːgə'dʒiː] Hypothekengläubiger *m*; ~er ['mɔːgidʒə], ~or [mɔːgə'dʒɔː] Hypothekenschuldner *m*.

mortician *Am.* [mɔː'tiʃən] Leichenbestatter *m*.

morti|fication [mɔːtifi'keiʃən] Kasteiung *f*; Kränkung *f*; ~fy ['mɔːtifai] kasteien; kränken.

morti|se, ~ce ⊕ ['mɔːtis] Zapfenloch *n*.

mortuary ['mɔːtjuəri] Leichenhalle *f*.

mosaic [mə'zeiik] Mosaik *n*.

mosque [mɔsk] Moschee *f*.

mosquito *zo.* [məs'kiːtou] Moskito *m*.   [moosig.\

moss [mɔs] Moos *n*; ~y ['mɔsi]

most [moust] 1. *adj.* □ meist; 2. *adv.* meist, am meisten; höchst; 3. das meiste; die meisten; Höchste(s) *n*; *at* (*the*) ~ höchstens; *make the* ~ *of* möglichst ausnutzen; ~ly ['moustli] meistens.

moth [mɔθ] Motte *f*; ~-eaten ['mɔθiːtn] mottenzerfressen.

mother ['mʌðə] 1. Mutter *f*; 2. bemuttern; ~ country Vaterland *n*; Mutterland *n*; ~hood [~hud] Mutterschaft *f*; ~-in-law [~rinlɔ:] Schwiegermutter *f*; ~ly [~li] mütterlich; ~-of-pearl [~rəv'pəːl] Perlmutter *f*; ~-tongue Muttersprache *f*.

motif [mou'tiːf] (Leit)Motiv *n*.

motion ['mouʃən] 1. Bewegung *f*; Gang *m* (*a.* ⊕); *parl.* Antrag *m*; 2. *v/t.* durch Gebärden auffordern *od.* andeuten; *v/i.* winken; ~less [~nlis] bewegungslos; ~ picture Film *m*.

motivate ['moutiveit] motivieren, begründen.

motive ['moutiv] 1. bewegend; 2. Motiv *n*, Beweggrund *m*; 3. veranlassen; ~less [~vlis] grundlos.

motley ['mɔtli] (bunt)scheckig.

motor ['moutə] 1. Motor *m*; treibende Kraft; Automobil *n*; ✗ Muskel *m*; 2. motorisch, bewegend; Motor...; Kraft...; Auto...; 3. (im) Auto fahren; ~-assisted [~ɔːs-'sistid] mit Hilfsmotor; ~ bicycle, ~bike = *motor cycle*; ~ boat Motorboot *n*; ~ bus Autobus *m*; ~cade *Am.* [~keid] Autokolonne *f*; ~-car Auto(mobil) *n*; ~ coach Reisebus *m*; ~ cycle Motorrad *n*; ~ing [~əriŋ] Autofahren *n*; ~ist [~rist] Kraftfahrer(in); ~ize [~raiz] motorisieren; ~ launch Motorbarkasse *f*; ~-road, ~way Autobahn *f*.

mottled ['mɔtld] gefleckt.

mo(u)ld [mould] 1. Gartenerde *f*; Schimmel *m*, Moder *m*; (Guß-)Form *f* (*a. fig.*); Abdruck *m*; Art *f*; 2. formen, gießen (*on, upon* nach).

mo(u)lder ['mouldə] zerfallen.
mo(u)lding △ ['mouldiŋ] Fries m.
mo(u)ldy ['mouldi] schimm(e)lig, dumpfig, mod(e)rig.
mo(u)lt [moult] (fig. sich) mausern.
mound [maund] Erdhügel m, -wall m.
mount [maunt] 1. Berg m; Reitpferd n; 2. v/i. (empor)steigen; aufsteigen (Reiter); v/t. be-, ersteigen; beritten machen; montieren; aufziehen, aufkleben; Edelstein fassen.
mountain ['mauntin] 1. Berg m; ~s pl. Gebirge n; 2. Berg..., Gebirgs...; ~eer [maunti'niə] Bergbewohner(in); Bergsteiger(in); ~ous ['mauntinəs] bergig, gebirgig.
mountebank ['mauntibæŋk]Marktschreier m, Scharlatan m.
mourn [mɔ:n] (be)trauern; ~er ['mɔ:nə] Leidtragende(r m) f; ~ful □ ['mɔ:nful] Trauer...; traurig; ~ing ['mɔ:niŋ] Trauer f; attr. Trauer... [Maus f.\
mouse [maus], pl. mice [mais]
moustache [məs'ta:ʃ] Schnurrbart m.
mouth [mauθ], pl. ~s [mauðz]Mund m; Maul n; Mündung f; Öffnung f; ~ful ['mauθful] Mundvoll m; ~organ Mundharmonika f; ~piece Mundstück n; fig. Sprachrohr n.
move [mu:v] 1. v/t. allg. bewegen; in Bewegung setzen; (weg)rücken; (an)treiben; Leidenschaft erregen; seelisch rühren; beantragen; ~ heaven and earth Himmel und Hölle in Bewegung setzen; v/i. sich (fort)bewegen; sich rühren; Schach: ziehen; (um)ziehen (Mieter); ~ for s.th. et. beantragen; ~ in einziehen; ~ on weitergehen; ~ out ausziehen; 2. Bewegung f; Schach: Zug m; fig. Schritt m; on the ~ in Bewegung; make a ~ die Tafel aufheben; ~ment ['mu:vmənt] Bewegung f; ♪ Tempo n; ♪ Satz m; ⊕ (Geh-) Werk n.
movies F ['mu:viz] pl. Kino n.
moving □ ['mu:viŋ] bewegend; beweglich; ~ staircase Rolltreppe f.
mow [mou] [irr.] mähen; ~er['mouə] Mäher(in); Mähmaschine f; ~ing machine ['mouiŋməʃi:n] Mähmaschine f; ~n [moun] p.p. von mow.
much [mʌtʃ] 1. adj. viel; 2. adv. sehr; viel; bei weitem; fast; ~ as I would like so gern ich möchte; I thought as ~ das dachte ich mir; make ~ of viel Wesens machen von; I am not ~ of a dancer ich bin kein großer Tänzer.
muck [mʌk] Mist m (F a. fig.); ~rake ['mʌkreik] 1. Mistgabel f; = ~r; 2. im Schmutz wühlen; ~raker [~kə] Am. Korruptionsschnüffler m.
mucus ['mju:kəs] (Nasen)Schleim m.

mud [mʌd] Schlamm m; Kot m; ~dle ['mʌdl] 1. v/t. verwirren; a. ~ up, ~ together durcheinanderbringen; F benebeln; v/i. stümpern; ~ through F sich durchwursteln; 2. Wirrwarr m; F Wurstelei f; ~dy ['mʌdi] schlammig; trüb; ~guard Kotflügel m.
muff [mʌf] Muff m.
muffin ['mʌfin] Muffin n (heißes Teegebäck).
muffle ['mʌfl] oft ~ up ein-, umhüllen, umwickeln; Stimme etc. dämpfen; ~r [~lə] Halstuch n; Boxhandschuh m; mot. Auspufftopf m.
mug [mʌg] Krug m; Becher m.
muggy ['mʌgi] schwül.
mugwump Am. iro. ['mʌgwʌmp] großes Tier (Person); pol. Unabhängige(r) m.
mulatto [mju(:)'lætou] Mulatt|e m, -in f.
mulberry ['mʌlbəri] Maulbeere f.
mule [mju:l] Maultier n, -esel m; störrischer Mensch; ~teer [mju:li-'tiə] Maultiertreiber m.
mull¹ [mʌl] Mull m.
mull² [~.]: ~ over überdenken.
mulled [mʌld]: ~ wine Glühwein m.
mulligan Am. F ['mʌligən] Eintopf m aus Resten.
mullion ['mʌliən] Fensterpfosten m.
multi|farious □ [mʌlti'fɛəriəs] mannigfaltig; ~form ['mʌltifɔ:m] vielförmig; ~ple [~ipl] 1. vielfach; 2. Vielfache(s) n; ~plication [mʌltipli'keiʃən] Vervielfältigung f, Vermehrung f; Multiplikation f; compound (simple) ~ Großes (Kleines) Einmaleins; ~ table Einmaleins n; ~plicity [~i'plisiti] Vielfalt f; ~ply ['mʌltiplai] (sich) vervielfältigen; multiplizieren; ~tude [~itju:d] Vielheit f, Menge f; ~tudinous [mʌlti-'tju:dinəs] zahlreich.
mum [mʌm] still.
mumble ['mʌmbl] murmeln, nuscheln; mummeln (mühsam essen).
mummery contp. ['mʌməri] Mummenschanz m.
mummify ['mʌmifai] mumifizieren.
mummy¹ ['mʌmi] Mumie f.
mummy² F [~] Mami f, Mutti f.
mumps ♂ [mʌmps] sg. Ziegenpeter m, Mumps m.
munch [mʌntʃ] mit vollen Backen (fr)essen, mampfen.
mundane □ ['mʌndein] weltlich.
municipal □ [mju(:)'nisipəl] städtisch, Gemeinde..., Stadt...; ~ity [mju(:)nisi'pæliti] Stadtbezirk m; Stadtverwaltung f.
munificen|ce [mju(:)'nifisns] Freigebigkeit f; ~t [~nt] freigebig.
munitions [mju(:)'niʃənz] pl. Munition f.
mural ['mjuərəl] Mauer...
murder ['mə:də] 1. Mord m; 2. (er-)

morden; *fig.* verhunzen; **~er** [~ərə]
Mörder *m*; **~ess** [~ris] Mörderin *f*;
~ous □ [~rəs] mörderisch.
murky □ ['mə:ki] dunkel, finster.
murmur ['mə:mə] 1. Gemurmel *n*;
Murren *n*; 2. murmeln; murren.
murrain ['mʌrin] Viehseuche *f*.
musc|le ['mʌsl] 1. Muskel *m*; 2. **~** *in*
Am. sl. sich rücksichtslos eindrängen; **~le-bound** mit Muskelkater;
be **~** Muskelkater haben; **~ular**
['mʌskjulə] Muskel...; muskulös.
Muse[1] [mju:z] Muse *f*.
muse[2] [~] (nach)sinnen, grübeln.
museum [mju:(:)'ziəm] Museum *n*.
mush [mʌʃ] Brei *m*, Mus *n*; *Am.*
Polenta *f*, Maisbrei *m*.
mushroom ['mʌʃrum] 1. Pilz *m*,
bsd. Champignon *m*; 2. rasch wachsen; **~** *up* in die Höhe schießen.
music ['mju:zik] Musik *f*; Musik-
stück *n*; Noten *f/pl.*; set to **~** ver-
tonen; **~al** □ [~kəl] musikalisch;
Musik...; wohlklingend; **~** *box*
Spieldose *f*; **~ box** *Am.* Spieldose *f*;
~-hall Varieté(theater) *n*; **~ian**
[mju:(:)'ziʃən] Musiker(in); **~-stand**
Notenständer *m*; **~-stool** Klavier-
stuhl *m*.
musk [mʌsk] Moschus *m*, Bisam *m*;
~-deer *zo.* ['mʌsk'diə] Moschus-
tier *n*.
musket ['mʌskit] Muskete *f*.
musk-rat *zo.* ['mʌskræt] Bisamratte *f*.
muslin ['mʌzlin] Musselin *m*.
musquash ['mʌskwɔʃ] Bisamratte *f*;
Bisampelz *m*.
muss *bsd. Am.* F [mʌs] Durcheinander *n*.
mussel ['mʌsl] (Mies)Muschel *f*.
must[1] [mʌst] 1. muß(te); darf;
durfte; *I* **~** *not* ich darf nicht; 2.
Muß *n*.
must[2] [~] Schimmel *m*, Moder *m*.

must[3] [~] Most *m*.
mustach|e *Am.* [məs'tæʃ], **~io** *Am.*
[məs'ta:ʃou] = *moustache*.
mustard ['mʌstəd] Senf *m*.
muster ['mʌstə] 1. ✗ Musterung *f*;
fig. Heerschau *f*; 2. ✗ mustern;
aufbieten, aufbringen.
musty ['mʌsti] mod(e)rig, muffig.
muta|ble □ ['mju:təbl] veränder-
lich; wankelmütig; **~tion** [mju:(:)-
'teiʃən] Veränderung *f*.
mute [mju:t] 1. □ stumm; 2. Stum-
me(*r m*) *f*; Statist(in); 3. dämpfen.
mutilate ['mju:tileit] verstümmeln.
mutin|eer [mju:ti'niə] Meuterer *m*;
~ous □ ['mju:tinəs] meuterisch;
~y [~ni] 1. Meuterei *f*; 2. meu-
tern.
mutter ['mʌtə] 1. Gemurmel *n*;
Gemurre *n*; 2. murmeln; murren.
mutton ['mʌtn] Hammelfleisch *n*;
leg of **~** Hammelkeule *f*; **~ chop**
Hammelkotelett *n*.
mutual □ ['mju:tjuəl] gegenseitig;
gemeinsam.
muzzle ['mʌzl] 1. Maul *n*, Schnauze
f; Mündung *f e-r Feuerwaffe*;
Maulkorb *m*; 2. e-n Maulkorb anlegen (*dat.*); *fig.* den Mund stopfen
(*dat.*).
my [mai] mein(e).
myrrh ♀ [mə:] Myrrhe *f*.
myrtle ♀ ['mə:tl] Myrte *f*.
myself [mai'self] (ich) selbst; mir;
mich; *by* **~** allein.
myster|ious □ [mis'tiəriəs] ge-
heimnisvoll, mysteriös; **~y** ['mistəri]
Mysterium *n*; Geheimnis *n*; Rätsel
n.
mysti|c ['mistik] 1. *a.* **~cal** □
[~kəl] mystisch, geheimnisvoll; 2.
Mystiker *m*; **~fy** [~ifai] mystifizie-
ren, täuschen.
myth [miθ] Mythe *f*, Mythos *m*,
Sage *f*.

N

nab *sl.* [næb] schnappen, erwischen.
nacre ['neikə] Perlmutter *f*.
nadir ['neidiə] *ast.* Nadir *m* (*Fuß-
punkt*); *fig.* tiefster Stand.
nag [næg] 1. F Klepper *m*; 2. *v/i.*
nörgeln, quengeln; *v/t.* bekritteln.
nail [neil] 1. (Finger-, Zehen)Nagel
m; ⊕ Nagel *m*; *zo.* Kralle *f*, Klaue
f; 2. (an-, fest)nageln; *Augen etc.*
heften (*to auf acc.*); **~-scissors**
['neilsizəz] *pl.* Nagelschere *f*; **~-
varnish** Nagellack *m*.
naïve □ [nɑ:'i:v], **naive** □ [neiv]
naiv; ungekünstelt.
naked □ ['neikid] nackt, bloß; kahl;
fig. unverhüllt; *poet.* schutzlos;

~ness [~dnis] Nacktheit *f*, Blöße *f*;
Kahlheit *f*; Schutzlosigkeit *f*; *fig.*
Unverhülltheit *f*.
name [neim] 1. Name *m*; Ruf *m*;
of od. by the **~** *of* ... namens ...;
call s.o. **~s** j-n beschimpfen; 2. (be-)
nennen; erwähnen; ernennen; **~
less** □ ['neimlis] namenlos; unbekannt; **~ly** [~li] nämlich; **~plate**
Namens-, Tür-, Firmenschild *n*;
~sake ['neimseik] Namensvetter *m*.
nanny ['næni] Kindermädchen *n*;
~-goat Ziege *f*.
nap [næp] 1. *Tuch*-Noppe *f*; Schläfchen *n*; *have od. take a* **~** ein
Nickerchen machen; 2. schlummern.

nape [neip] *mst* ~ *of the neck* Genick *n.*
nap|kin ['næpkin] Serviette *f*; Win-
del *f*; *mst sanitary* ~ *Am.* Monats-
binde *f*; ~**py** F ['næpi] Windel *f.*
narcosis ✶ [nɑː'kousis] Narkose *f.*
narcotic [nɑː'kɔtik] **1.** (~*ally*) narko-
tisch; **2.** Betäubungsmittel *n.*
narrat|e [næ'reit] erzählen; ~**ion**
[~'eiʃən] Erzählung *f*; ~**ive** ['nærə-
tiv] **1.** □ erzählend; **2.** Erzählung *f*;
~**or** [næ'reitə] Erzähler *m.*
narrow ['nærou] **1.** eng, schmal;
beschränkt; knapp (*Mehrheit, Entkommen*); engherzig; **2.** ~**s** *pl.* Engpaß *m*; Meerenge *f*; **3.** (sich) ver-
engen; beschränken; einengen; *Ma-
schen* abnehmen; ~**chested** schmal-
brüstig; ~**minded** □ engherzig;
~**ness** [~ounis] Enge *f*; Beschränkt-
heit *f* (*a. fig.*); Engherzigkeit *f.*
nary *Am.* F ['nɛəri] kein.
nasal □ ['neizəl] nasal; Nasen...
nasty □ ['nɑːsti] schmutzig; garstig;
eklig, widerlich; häßlich; unflätig;
ungemütlich.
natal ['neitl] Geburts...
nation ['neiʃən] Nation *f*, Volk *n.*
national ['næʃənl] **1.** □ national;
Volks..., Staats...; **2.** Staatsange-
hörige(r *m*) *f*; ~**ity** [næʃə'næliti] Na-
tionalität *f*; ~**ize** ['næʃnəlaiz] naturalisieren, einbürgern; verstaatlichen.
nation-wide ['neiʃənwaid] die ganze
Nation umfassend.
native ['neitiv] **1.** □ angeboren;
heimatlich, Heimat...; eingeboren;
einheimisch; ~ *language* Muttersprache *f*; **2.** Eingeborene(r *m*) *f*;
~**born** (im Lande) geboren, einheimisch.
nativity [nə'tiviti] Geburt *f.*
natter F ['nætə] plaudern.
natural □ ['nætʃrəl] natürlich;
engS.: angeboren; ungezwungen;
unehelich (*Kind*); ~ *science* Natur-
wissenschaft *f*; ~**ist** [~list] Natura-
list *m*; Naturforscher *m*; Tierhänd-
ler *m*; ~**ize** [~laiz] einbürgern; ~**ness**
[~lnis] Natürlichkeit *f.*
nature ['neitʃə] Natur *f.*
naught [nɔːt] Null *f*; *set at* ~ für
nichts achten; ~**y** □ ['nɔːti] un-
artig.
nause|a ['nɔːsjə] Übelkeit *f*; Ekel *m*;
~**ate** ['nɔːsieit] *v/i.* Ekel empfinden;
v/t. verabscheuen; *be* ~*d* sich ekeln;
~**ous** □ ['nɔːsjəs] ekelhaft.
nautical ['nɔːtikəl] nautisch; See...
naval ⚓ ['neivəl] See..., Marine...;
~ *base* Flottenstützpunkt *m.*
nave[1] ⚓ [neiv] (Kirchen)Schiff *n.*
nave[2] [~] Rad-Nabe *f.*
navel ['neivəl] Nabel *m*; Mitte *f.*
naviga|ble □ ['nævigəbl] schiffbar;
fahrbar; lenkbar; ~**te** [~geit] *v/i.*
schiffen, fahren; *v/t. See etc.* befahren; steuern; ~**tion** [nævi'geiʃən]

Schiffahrt *f*; Navigation *f*; ~**tor**
['nævigeitə] Seefahrer *m.*
navy ['neivi] (Kriegs)Marine *f.*
nay † [nei] nein; nein vielmehr.
near [niə] **1.** *adj.* nahe; gerade
(*Weg*); nahe verwandt; verwandt;
vertraut; genau; knapp; knauserig;
~ *at hand* dicht dabei; **2.** *adv.* nahe;
3. *prp.* nahe (*dat.*), nahe bei *od.*
an; **4.** sich nähern (*dat.*); ~**by**
['niəbai] in der Nähe (gelegen);
nah; ~**ly** ['niəli] nahe; fast, beinahe;
genau; ~**ness** ['niənis] Nähe *f*;
~**sighted** kurzsichtig.
neat □ [niːt] nett; niedlich; geschickt; ordentlich; sauber; rein;
~**ness** ['niːtnis] Nettigkeit *f*; Sau-
berkeit *f*; Zierlichkeit *f.*
nebulous □ ['nebjuləs] neblig.
necess|ary □ ['nesisəri] **1.** notwen-
dig; unvermeidlich; **2.** *mst necessaries pl.* Bedürfnisse *n/pl.*; ~**itate**
[ni'sesiteit] *et.* erfordern; zwingen;
~**ity** [~ti] Notwendigkeit *f*; Zwang
m; Not *f.*
neck [nek] **1.** (*a. Flaschen*)Hals *m*;
Nacken *m*, Genick *n*; Ausschnitt *m*
(*Kleid*); ~ *and* ~ Kopf an Kopf;
~ *or nothing* F alles oder nichts;
2. *sl.* sich abknutschen; ~**band**
['nekbænd] Halsbund *m*; ~**erchief**
['nekətʃif] Halstuch *n*; ~**lace** ['nek-
lis], ~**let** [~lit] Halskette *f*; ~**tie**
Krawatte *f.*
necromancy ['nekroumænsi] Zauberei *f.*
née [nei] *bei Frauennamen*: geborene.
need [niːd] **1.** Not *f*; Notwendigkeit
f; Bedürfnis *n*; Mangel *m*, Bedarf
m; *be od. stand in* ~ *of* brauchen;
2. nötig haben, brauchen; bedürfen
(*gen.*); müssen; ~**ful** ['niːdful] notwendig.
needle ['niːdl] **1.** Nadel *f*; Zeiger *m*;
2. nähen; *bsd. Am.* irritieren; anstacheln.
needless □ ['niːdlis] unnötig.
needle|woman ['niːdlwumən] Nä-
herin *f*; ~**work** Handarbeit *f.*
needy □ ['niːdi] bedürftig, arm.
nefarious □ [ni'fɛəriəs] schändlich.
negat|e [ni'geit] verneinen; ~**ion**
[~eiʃən] Verneinung *f*; Nichts *n*;
~**ive** ['negətiv] **1.** □ negativ; ver-
neinend; **2.** Verneinung *f*; *phot.*
Negativ *n*; **3.** ablehnen.
neglect [ni'glekt] **1.** Vernachlässigung *f*; Nachlässigkeit *f*; **2.** ver-
nachlässigen; ~**ful** □ [~tful] nachlässig.
negligen|ce ['neglidʒəns] Nachläs-
sigkeit *f*; ~**t** □ [~nt] nachlässig.
negligible □ ['neglidʒəbl] nebensächlich; unbedeutend.
negotia|te [ni'gouʃieit] verhandeln
(über *acc.*); zustande bringen; bewältigen; *Wechsel* begeben; ~**tion**
[nigouʃi'eiʃən] Begebung *f* *e-s
Wechsels etc.*; Ver-, Unterhandlung

f; Bewältigung *f*; **~tor** [ni'gouʃieitə] Unterhändler *m*.

negr|ess ['ni:gris] Negerin *f*; **~o** [~rou], *pl.* **~oes** Neger *m*.

neigh [nei] 1. Wiehern *n*; 2. wiehern.

neighbo(u)r ['neibə] Nachbar(in); Nächste(r *m*) *f*; **~hood** [~əhud] Nachbarschaft *f*; **~ing** [~əriŋ] benachbart; **~ly** [~əli] nachbarlich, freundlich; **~ship** [~əʃip] Nachbarschaft *f*.

neither ['naiðə] 1. keiner (von beiden); 2. **~** ... **nor** ... weder ... noch ...; **not** ... **~** auch nicht.

nephew ['nevju(:)] Neffe *m*.

nerve [nə:v] 1. Nerv *m*; Sehne *f*; *Blatt-*Rippe *f*, Kraft *f*, Mut *m*; Dreistigkeit *f*; **get on one's ~s** e-m auf die Nerven gehen; 2. kräftigen; ermutigen; **~less** □ ['nə:vlis] kraftlos.

nervous □ ['nə:vəs] Nerven...; nervig, kräftig, nervös; **~ness** [~snis] Nervigkeit *f*; Nervosität *f*.

nest [nest] 1. Nest *n* (*a. fig.*); 2. nisten; **~le** ['nesl] *v/i.* sich (an-)nisten; sich (an)schmiegen; *v/t.* schmiegen.

net[1] [net] 1. Netz *n*; 2. mit e-m Netz fangen *od.* umgeben.

net[2] [~] 1. netto; Rein...; 2. netto einbringen.

nether ['neðə] nieder; Unter...

nettle ['netl] 1. ♀ Nessel *f*; 2. ärgern.

network ['netwə:k] (Straßen-, Kanal- *etc.*)Netz *n*; Sendergruppe *f*.

neurosis *f* [njuə'rousis] Neurose *f*.

neuter ['nju:tə] 1. geschlechtslos; 2. geschlechtsloses Tier; *gr.* Neutrum *n*.

neutral ['nju:trəl] 1. neutral; unparteiisch; 2. Neutrale(r *m*) *f*; Null(punkt *m*) *f*; Leerlauf(stellung *f*) *m*; **~ity** [nju:(:)'træliti] Neutralität *f*; **~ize** ['nju:trəlaiz] neutralisieren.

neutron *phys.* ['nju:trɔn] Neutron *n*.

never ['nevə] nie(mals); gar nicht; **~more** [~'mɔ:] nie wieder; **~theless** [nevəðə'les] nichtsdestoweniger.

new [nju:] neu; frisch; unerfahren; **~comer** ['nju:kʌmə] Ankömmling *m*; **~ly** ['nju:li] neulich; neu.

news [nju:z] *mst. sg.* Neuigkeit(en *pl.*) *f*, Nachricht(en *pl.*) *f*; **~agent** ['nju:zeidʒənt] Zeitungshändler *m*; **~boy** Zeitungsausträger *m*; **~butcher** *Am. sl.* Zeitungsverkäufer *m*; **~cast** *Radio:* Nachrichten *f/pl.*; **~monger** Neuigkeitskrämer *m*; **~paper** Zeitung *f*; *attr.* Zeitungs...; **~print** Zeitungspapier *n*; **~reel** *Film:* Wochenschau *f*; **~room** Lesezimmer *n*; *Am. Zeitung:* Nachrichtenredaktion *f*; **~stall**, *Am.* **~stand** Zeitungskiosk *m*.

new year ['nju:'jə:] *das* neue Jahr; *New Year's Day* Neujahr(stag *m*) *n*; *New Year's Eve* Silvester *n*.

next [nekst] 1. *adj.* nächst; **~** *but one* der übernächste; **~** *door to fig.* beinahe; **~** *to* nächst (*dat.*); 2. *adv.* zunächst, gleich darauf; nächstens.

nibble ['nibl] *v/t.* knabbern an (*dat.*); *v/i.* **~** *at* nagen *od.* knabbern an (*dat.*); (herum)krritteln an (*dat.*).

nice [|] [nais] fein; wählerisch; peinlich (genau); heikel; nett; niedlich; hübsch; **~ly** ['naisli] F (sehr) gut; **~ty** ['naisiti] Feinheit *f*; Genauigkeit *f*; Spitzfindigkeit *f*.

niche [nitʃ] Nische *f*.

nick [nik] 1. Kerbe *f*; *in the ~ of time* gerade zur rechten Zeit; 2. (ein)kerben; *sl.* j-n schnappen.

nickel ['nikl] 1. *min.* Nickel *m* (*Am. a. Fünfcentstück*); 2. vernickeln.

nick-nack ['niknæk] = *knicknack*.

nickname ['nikneim] 1. Spitzname *m*; 2. e-n Spitznamen geben (*dat.*).

niece [ni:s] Nichte *f*.

nifty *Am. sl.* ['nifti] elegant, stinkend.

niggard ['nigəd] Geizhals *m*; **~ly** [~dli] geizig, knauserig; karg.

nigger F *mst contp.* ['nigə] Nigger *m* (*Neger*); **~** *in the woodpile Am. sl.* der Haken an der Sache.

night [nait] Nacht *f*; Abend *m*; *by ~*, *in the ~*, *at ~* nachts; **~cap** ['naitkæp] Nachtmütze *f*; Nachttrunk *m*; **~club** Nachtlokal *n*; **~dress** (Damen)Nachthemd *n*; **~fall** Einbruch *m* der Nacht; **~gown** = *night-dress*; **~ingale** *orn.* ['naitiŋgeil] Nachtigall *f*; **~ly** ['naitli] nächtlich; jede Nacht; **~mare** Alptraum *m*; **~shirt** (Herren)Nachthemd *n*; **~spot** *Am.* Nachtlokal *n*; **~y** ['naiti] F(Damen- *od.* Kinder)Nachthemd *n*.

nil [nil] *bsd. Sport:* nichts, null.

nimble □ ['nimbl] flink, behend.

nimbus ['nimbəs] Nimbus *m*, Heiligenschein *m*; Regenwolke *f*.

nine [nain] 1. neun; 2. Neun *f*; **~pins** ['nainpinz] *pl.* Kegel(spiel *n*) *m/pl.*; **~teen** ['nain'ti:n] neunzehn; **~ty** ['nainti] neunzig.

ninny F ['nini] Dummkopf *m*.

ninth [nainθ] 1. neunte(r, -s) 2. Neuntel *n*; **~ly** ['nainθli] neuntens.

nip [nip] 1. Kniff *m*; scharfer Frost; Schlückchen *n*; 2. zwicken; schneiden (*Kälte*); *sl.* flitzen; nippen; **~ in the bud** im Keime ersticken.

nipper ['nipə] Krebsschere *f*; (*a pair of*) **~s** *pl.* (eine) (Kneif)Zange.

nipple ['nipl] Brustwarze *f*.

Nisei *Am.* ['ni:'sei] (*a. pl.*) Japaner *m*, *geboren in den USA.*

nit|re, *Am.* **~er** 🜍 ['naitə] Salpeter *m*.

nitrogen ['naitridʒən] Stickstoff *m*.

no [nou] 1. *adj.* kein; *in ~ time* im Nu; *~ one* keiner; 2. *adv.* nein; nicht; 3. Nein *n*.

nobility [nou'biliti] Adel *m* (*a. fig.*).

noble ['noubl] 1. □ adlig; edel, vornehm; vortrefflich; 2. Adlige(r *m*) *f*; **~man** Adlige(r) *m*; **~minded** edelmütig; **~ness** [⁔nis] Adel *m*; Würde *f*.

nobody ['noubədi] niemand.

nocturnal [nɔk'tə:nl] Nacht...

nod [nɔd] 1. nicken; schlafen; (sich) neigen; *~ding acquaintance* oberflächliche Bekanntschaft; 2. Nicken *n*; Wink *m*.

node [noud] Knoten *m* (*a. ♀ u. ast.*); ⚕ Überbein *n*.

noise [nɔiz] 1. Lärm *m*; Geräusch *n*; Geschrei *n*; *big ~ bsd. Am.* F großes Tier (*Person*); 2. *~ abroad* ausschreien; **~less** □ ['nɔizlis] geräuschlos.

noisome ['nɔisəm] schädlich; widerlich.

noisy □ ['nɔizi] geräuschvoll, lärmend; aufdringlich (*Farbe*).

nomin|al □ ['nɔminl] nominell; (nur) dem Namen nach (vorhanden); namentlich; *~ value* Nennwert *m*; **~ate** [⁔neit] ernennen; zur Wahl vorschlagen; **~ation** [⁔'neiʃən] Ernennung *f*; Vorschlagsrecht *n*.

nominative ['nɔminətiv] *a. ~ case* gr. Nominativ *m*.

non [nɔn] *in Zssgn*: nicht, un..., Nicht...

nonage ['nounidʒ] Minderjährigkeit *f*.

non-alcoholic ['nɔnælkə'hɔlik] alkoholfrei.

nonce [nɔns]: *for the ~* nur für diesen Fall.

non-commissioned ['nɔnkə'miʃənd] nicht bevollmächtigt; *~ officer* ⚔ Unteroffizier *m*.

non-committal ['nɔnkə'mitl] unverbindlich.

non-compliance ['nɔnkəm'plaiəns] Zuwiderhandlung *f*, Verstoß *m*.

non-conductor ⚡ ['nɔnkəndʌktə] Nichtleiter *m*.

nonconformist ['nɔnkən'fɔ:mist] Dissident(in), Freikirchler(in).

nondescript ['nɔndiskript] unbestimmbar; schwer zu beschreiben(d).

none [nʌn] 1. keine(r, -s); nichts; 2. keineswegs, gar nicht; *~ the less* nichtsdestoweniger.

nonentity [nɔ'nentiti] Nichtsein *n*; Unding *n*; Nichts *n*; *fig.* Null *f*.

non-existence ['nɔnig'zistəns] Nicht(da)sein *n*.

non-fiction ['nɔn'fikʃən] Sachbücher *n/pl.*

nonpareil ['nɔnpərəl] Unvergleichliche(r *m*, -s *n*) *f*.

non-party ['nɔn'pɑ:ti] parteilos.

non-performance ⚜ ['nɔnpə-'fɔ:məns] Nichterfüllung *f*.

nonplus ['nɔn'plʌs] 1. Verlegenheit *f*; 2. in Verlegenheit bringen.

non-resident ['nɔn'rezidənt] nicht im Haus *od* am Ort wohnend.

nonsens|e ['nɔnsəns] Unsinn *m*; **~ical** [nɔn'sensikəl] unsinnig.

non-skid ['nɔn'skid] rutschfest.

non-smoker ['nɔn'smoukə] Nichtraucher *m*.

non-stop ⚞, ✈ ['nɔn'stɔp] durchgehend; Ohnehalt...

non-union ['nɔn'ju:njən] nicht organisiert (*Arbeiter*).

non-violence ['nɔn'vaiələns] (Politik *f* der) Gewaltlosigkeit *f*.

noodle ['nu:dl] Nudel *f*.

nook [nuk] Ecke *f*, Winkel *m*.

noon [nu:n] Mittag *m*; *attr.* Mittags...; **~day** ['nu:ndei], **~tide**, **~time** = *noon.*

noose [nu:s] 1. Schlinge *f*; 2. (mit der Schlinge) fangen; schlingen.

nope *Am.* F [noup] nein.

nor [nɔ:] noch; auch nicht.

norm [nɔ:m] Norm *f*, Regel *f*; Muster *n*; Maßstab *m*; **~al** □ ['nɔ:məl] normal; **~alize** [⁔laiz] normalisieren; normen.

north [nɔ:θ] 1. Nord(en *m*); 2. nördlich; Nord...; **~-east** ['nɔ:θ'i:st] 1. Nordost *m*; 2. *a.* **~-eastern** [⁔tən] nordöstlich; **~erly** ['nɔ:ðəli], **~ern** [⁔ən] nördlich; Nord...; **~erner** [⁔nə] Nordländer(in); *Am.* ♀ Nordstaatler(in); **~ward(s)** ['nɔ:θwəd(z)] *adv.* nördlich; nordwärts; **~west** ['nɔ:θ'west] 1. Nordwest *m*; 2. *a.* **~western** [⁔tən] nordwestlich.

Norwegian [nɔ:'wi:dʒən] 1. norwegisch; 2. Norweger(in); Norwegisch *n*.

nose [nouz] 1. Nase *f*; Spitze *f*; Schnauze *f*; 2. *v/t.* riechen; *~ one's way* vorsichtig fahren; *v/i.* schnüffeln; **~-dive** ✈ ['nouzdaiv] Sturzflug *m*; **~gay** ['nouzgei] Blumenstrauß *m*.

nostalgia [nɔs'tældʒiə] Heimweh *n*, Sehnsucht *f*.

nostril ['nɔstril] Nasenloch *n*, Nüster *f*.

nostrum ['nɔstrəm] Geheimmittel *n*; Patentlösung *f*.

nosy F ['nouzi] neugierig.

not [nɔt] nicht.

notable ['noutəbl] 1. □ bemerkenswert; 2. angesehene Person.

notary ['noutəri] *oft ~ public* Notar *m*. [*f*.]

notation [nou'teiʃən] Bezeichnung|

notch [nɔtʃ] 1. Kerbe *f*, Einschnitt *m*; Scharte *f*; *Am.* Engpaß *m*, Hohlweg *m*; 2. einkerben.

note [nout] 1. Zeichen *n*; Notiz *f*; Anmerkung *f*; Briefchen *n*; (*bsd.* Schuld)Schein *m*; Note *f*; Ton *m*; Ruf *m*; Beachtung *f*; *take ~s* sich

Notizen machen; 2. be(ob)achten; besonders erwähnen; *a. ~ down* notieren; mit Anmerkungen versehen; ~book ['noutbuk] Notizbuch *n*; ~d bekannt; berüchtigt; ~paper Briefpapier *n*; ~worthy beachtenswert.

nothing ['nʌθiŋ] **1.** nichts; **2.** Nichts *n*; Null *f*; *for ~* umsonst; *good for ~* untauglich; *bring (come) to ~* zunichte machen (werden).

notice ['noutis] **1.** Notiz *f*; Nachricht *f*, Bekanntmachung *f*; Kündigung *f*; Warnung *f*; Beachtung *f*; *at short ~* kurzfristig; *give ~ that* bekanntgeben, daß; *give a week's ~* acht Tage vorher kündigen; *take ~ of* Notiz nehmen von; *without ~* fristlos; **2.** bemerken; beachten; ~able □ [~səbl] wahrnehmbar; bemerkenswert.

noti|fication [noutifi'keiʃən] Anzeige *f*; Meldung *f*; Bekanntmachung *f*; ~fy ['noutifai] *et.* anzeigen, melden; bekanntmachen.

notion ['nouʃən] Begriff *m*, Vorstellung *f*; Absicht *f*; ~s *pl. Am.* Kurzwaren *f/pl.*

notorious □ [nou'tɔːriəs] all-, weltbekannt; notorisch; berüchtigt.

notwithstanding *prp.* [nɔtwiθ-'stændiŋ] ungeachtet, trotz (*gen.*).

nought [nɔːt] Null *f*, Nichts *n*.

noun *gr.* [naun] Hauptwort *n*.

nourish ['nʌriʃ] (er)nähren; *fig.* hegen; ~ing [~ʃiŋ] nahrhaft; ~ment [~ʃmənt] Nahrung(smittel *n*) *f*.

novel ['nɔvəl] **1.** neu; ungewöhnlich; **2.** Roman *m*; ~ist [~list] Romanschriftsteller(in), Romancier *m*; ~ty [~lti] Neuheit *f*.

November [nou'vembə] November *m*.

novice ['nɔvis] Neuling *m*; *eccl.* Novize *m*, *f*.

now [nau] **1.** nun, jetzt; eben; *just ~* soeben; *~ and again od. then* dann u. wann; **2.** *cj. a. ~ that* nun da.

nowadays ['nauədeiz] heutzutage.

nowhere ['nouwɛə] nirgends.

noxious □ ['nɔkʃəs] schädlich.

nozzle ['nɔzl] ⊕ Düse *f*; Tülle *f*.

nuance [nju(:)'ãːns] Nuance *f*, Schattierung *f*.

nub [nʌb] Knubbe(n *m*) *f*; *Am.* F springender Punkt in *e-r* Sache.

nucle|ar ['njuːkliə] Kern...; ~ *reactor* Kernreaktor *m*; ~ *research* (Atom-)Kernforschung *f*; ~us [~iəs] Kern *m*.

nude [njuːd] **1.** nackt; **2.** *paint.* Akt *m*.

nudge F [nʌdʒ] **1.** *j-n* heimlich anstoßen; **2.** Rippenstoß *m*.

nugget ['nʌgit] (*bsd.* Gold)Klumpen *m*.

nuisance ['njuːsns] Mißstand *m*;

Ärgernis *n*; Unfug *m*; *fig.* Plage *f*; *what a ~!* wie ärgerlich!; *make o.s. od. be a ~* lästig fallen.

null [nʌl] nichtig; nichtssagend; *~ and void* null u. nichtig; ~ify ['nʌlifai] zunichte machen; aufheben, ungültig machen; ~ity [~iti] Nichtigkeit *f*, Ungültigkeit *f*.

numb [nʌm] **1.** starr; taub (*empfindungslos*); **2.** starr *od.* taub machen; ~ed erstarrt.

number ['nʌmbə] **1.** Nummer *f*; (An)Zahl *f*; Heft *n*, Lieferung *f*, Nummer *f* *e-s Werkes*; *without ~* zahllos; *in ~* an der Zahl; **2.** zählen; numerieren; ~less [~lis] zahllos; ~-plate *mot.* Nummernschild *n*.

numera|l ['njuːmərəl] **1.** Zahl...; **2.** Ziffer *f*; ~tion [njuːmə'reiʃən] Zählung *f*; Numerierung *f*.

numerical □ [njuːˈ)'merikəl] zahlenmäßig; Zahl...

numerous □ ['njuːmərəs] zahlreich.

numskull F ['nʌmskʌl] Dummkopf *m*.

nun [nʌn] Nonne *f*; *orn.* Blaumeise *f*.

nunnery ['nʌnəri] Nonnenkloster *n*.

nuptial ['nʌpʃəl] **1.** Hochzeits..., Ehe...; **2.** ~s *pl.* Hochzeit *f*.

nurse [nəːs] **1.** Kindermädchen *n*, Säuglingsschwester *f*; *a. wet-Amme f*; (Kranken)Pflegerin *f*, (Kranken)Schwester *f*; *at ~* in Pflege; *put out to ~* in Pflege geben; **2.** stillen, nähren; großziehen; pflegen; hätscheln; ~ling ['nəːsliŋ] Säugling *m*; Pflegling *m*; ~maid ['nəːsmeid] Kindermädchen *n*; ~ry ['nəːsri] Kinderzimmer *n*; ♪ Pflanzschule *f*; ~ *rhymes pl.* Kinderlieder *n/pl.*, -reime *m/pl.*; ~ *school* Kindergarten *m*; ~ *slopes pl.* Ski: Idiotenhügel *m/pl.*

nursing ['nəːsiŋ] Stillen *n*; (Kranken)Pflege *f*; ~ *bottle* Saugflasche *f*; ~ *home* Privatklinik *f*.

nursling ['nəːsliŋ] = *nurseling*.

nurture ['nəːtʃə] **1.** Pflege *f*; Erziehung *f*; **2.** aufziehen; nähren.

nut [nʌt] Nuß *f*; ⊕ (Schrauben-)Mutter *f*; *sl.* verrückter Kerl; ~s *pl.* Nußkohle *f*; ~cracker ['nʌtkrækə] Nußknacker *m*; ~meg ['nʌtmeg] Muskatnuß *f*.

nutriment ['njuːtrimənt] Nahrung *f*.

nutri|tion [njuː(:)'triʃən] Ernährung *f*; Nahrung *f*; ~tious [~əs], ~tive □ ['njuːtritiv] nahrhaft; Ernährungs...

nut|shell ['nʌtʃel] Nußschale *f*; *in a ~* in aller Kürze; ~ty [~i] nußreich; nußartig; *sl.* verrückt.

nylon ['nailən] Nylon *n*; ~s *pl.* Nylonstrümpfe *m/pl.*

nymph [nimf] Nymphe *f*.

O

o [ou] 1. oh!; ach!; 2. (in Telefonnummern) Null f.

oaf [ouf] Dummkopf m; Tölpel m.

oak [ouk] Eiche f.

oar [ɔ:] 1. Ruder n; 2. rudern; ~sman ['ɔ:zmən] Ruderer m.

oas|is [ou'eisis], pl. ~es [ou'eisi:z] Oase f (a. fig.).

oat [out] mst ~s pl. Hafer m; feel one's ~s Am. F groß in Form sein; sich wichtig vorkommen; sow one's wild ~s sich austoben.

oath [ouθ], pl. ~s [ouðz] Eid m; Schwur m; Fluch m; take (make, swear) an ~ e-n Eid leisten, schwören.

oatmeal ['outmi:l] Haferflocken f/pl.

obdurate □ ['ɔbdjurit] verstockt.

obedien|ce [ə'bi:djəns] Gehorsam m; ~t □ [~nt] gehorsam.

obeisance [ou'beisəns] Ehrerbietung f; Verbeugung f; do ~ huldigen.

obesity [ou'bi:siti] Fettleibigkeit f.

obey [ə'bei] gehorchen (dat.); Befehl etc. befolgen, Folge leisten (dat.).

obituary [ə'bitjuəri] Totenliste f; Todesanzeige f; Nachruf m; attr. Todes..., Toten...

object 1. ['ɔbdʒikt] Gegenstand m; Ziel n, fig. Zweck m; Objekt n (a. gr.); 2. [ɔb'dʒekt] v/t. einwenden (to gegen) v/i. et. dagegen haben (to ger. daß).

objection [ɔb'dʒekʃən] Einwand m; ~able □ [~ʃnəbl] nicht einwandfrei; unangenehm.

objective [ɔb'dʒektiv] 1. □ objektiv, sachlich; 2. ✕ Ziel n.

object-lens opt. ['ɔbdʒiktlenz] Objektiv n.

obligat|ion [ɔbli'geiʃən] Verpflichtung f; ✝ Schuldverschreibung f; be under (an) ~ to s.o. j-m zu Dank verpflichtet sein; be under ~ to inf. die Verpflichtung haben, zu inf.; ~ory □ [ɔ'bligətəri] verpflichtend; verbindlich.

oblig|e [ə'blaidʒ] (zu Dank) verpflichten; nötigen; ~ s.o. j-m e-n Gefallen tun; much ~d sehr verbunden; danke bestens; ~ing □ [~dʒiŋ] verbindlich, hilfsbereit, gefällig.

oblique □ [ə'bli:k] schief, schräg.

obliterate [ə'blitəreit] auslöschen, tilgen (a. fig.); Schrift ausstreichen; Briefmarken entwerten.

oblivi|on [ə'bliviən] Vergessen(heit f) n; ~ous □ [~iəs] vergeßlich.

oblong ['ɔblɔŋ] länglich; rechteckig.

obnoxious □ [ɔb'nɔkʃəs] anstößig; widerwärtig, verhaßt.

obscene □ [ɔb'si:n] unanständig.

obscur|e □ [əb'skjuə] 1. □ dunkel (a. fig.); unbekannt; 2. verdunkeln; ~ity [~əriti] Dunkelheit f (a. fig.); Unbekanntheit f; Niedrigkeit f der Geburt.

obsequies ['ɔbsikwiz] pl. Leichenbegängnis n, Trauerfeier f.

obsequious □ [əb'si:kwiəs] unterwürfig (to gegen).

observ|able □ [əb'zə:vəbl] bemerkbar; bemerkenswert; ~ance [~əns] Befolgung f; Brauch m; ~ant □ [~nt] beobachtend; achtsam; ~ation [ɔbzə(:)'veiʃən] Beobachtung f; Bemerkung f; attr. Beobachtungs...; Aussichts...; ~atory [əb'zə:vətri] Sternwarte f; ~e [əb'zə:v] v/t. be(ob)achten; acht(geb)en auf (acc.); bemerken; v/i. sich äußern.

obsess [əb'ses] heimsuchen, quälen; ~ed by od. with besessen von; ~ion [~eʃən] Besessenheit f.

obsolete ['ɔbsəli:t] veraltet.

obstacle ['ɔbstəkl] Hindernis n.

obstina|cy ['ɔbstinəsi] Hartnäckigkeit f; ~te □ [~nit] halsstarrig; eigensinnig; hartnäckig.

obstruct [əb'strʌkt] verstopfen, versperren; hindern; ~ion [~kʃən] Verstopfung f; Hemmung f; Hindernis n; ~ive □ [~ktiv] hinderlich.

obtain [əb'tein] v/t. erlangen, erhalten, erreichen, bekommen; v/i. sich erhalten (haben); ~able ✝ [~nəbl] erhältlich.

obtru|de [əb'tru:d] (sich) aufdrängen (on dat.); ~sive □ [~u:siv] aufdringlich.   [schwerfällig.]

obtuse □ [əb'tju:s] stumpf(sinnig);]

obviate ['ɔbvieit] vorbeugen (dat.).

obvious □ ['ɔbviəs] offensichtlich, augenfällig, einleuchtend.

occasion [ə'keiʒən] 1. Gelegenheit f; Anlaß m; Veranlassung f; F (festliches) Ereignis; on the ~ of anläßlich (gen.); 2. veranlassen; ~al □ [~nl] gelegentlich; Gelegenheits...

occident ['ɔksidənt] Westen m; Okzident m, Abendland n; ~al □ [ɔksi'dentl] abendländisch, westlich.

occult □ [ɔ'kʌlt] geheim, verborgen; magisch, okkult.

occup|ant ['ɔkjupənt] Besitzergreifer(in); Bewohner(in); ~ation [ɔkju'peiʃən] Besitz(ergreifung f) m; ✕ Besetzung f; Beruf m; Beschäftigung f; ~y ['ɔkjupai] einnehmen, in Besitz nehmen, ✕ besetzen; besitzen; innehaben; in Anspruch nehmen; beschäftigen.

occur [ə'kə:] vorkommen; sich ereignen; it ~red to me es fiel mir ein; ~rence [ə'kʌrəns] Vorkommen n; Vorfall m, Ereignis n.

ocean ['ouʃən] Ozean *m*, Meer *n*.

o'clock [ə'klɔk] Uhr (*bei Zeitangaben*); *five ~* fünf Uhr.

October [ɔk'toubə] Oktober *m*.

ocul|ar □ ['ɔkjulə] Augen...; **~ist** [~list] Augenarzt *m*.

odd □ [ɔd] ungerade (*Zahl*); einzeln; *und einige od.* etwas darüber; überzählig; gelegentlich, sonderbar, merkwürdig; **~ity** ['ɔditi] Seltsamkeit *f*; **~s** [ɔdz] *oft sg.* (Gewinn)Chancen *f/pl.*; Wahrscheinlichkeit *f*; Vorteil *m*; Vorgabe *f*, Handikap *n*; Verschiedenheit *f*; Unterschied *m*; Streit *m*; *be at ~ with s.o.* mit j-m im Streit sein; nicht übereinstimmen mit j-m; *~ and ends* Reste *m/pl.*; Krimskrams *m*.

ode [oud] Ode *f* (*Gedicht*).

odious □ ['oudjəs] verhaßt; ekelhaft.

odo(u)r ['oudə] Geruch *m*; Duft *m*.

of *prp.* [ɔv, əv] *allg.* von; *Ort*: bei (*the battle ~ Quebec*); um (*cheat s.o. ~ s.th.*); aus (*~ charity*); vor (*dat.*) (*afraid ~*); auf (*acc.*) (*proud ~*); über (*acc.*) (*ashamed ~*); nach (*smell ~ roses; desirous ~*); an (*acc.*) (*think ~ s.th.*); *nimble ~ foot* leichtfüßig.

off [ɔ:f, ɔf] **1.** *adv.* weg; ab; herunter; aus (*vorbei*); *Zeit*: hin (*3 months ~*); *~ and on* ab und an; hin und her; *be ~* fort sein, weg sein; *engS.*: (weg)gehen; zu sein (*Hahn etc.*); aus sein; *well etc. ~* gut *etc.* daran; **2.** *prp.* von ... (weg, ab, herunter); frei von, ohne; unweit (*gen.*); neben; ⏚ auf der Höhe von; **3.** *adj.* entfernt(er); abseitsliegend; Neben...; arbeits-, dienstfrei; ✝ *~ shade* Fehlfarbe *f*; **4.** *int.* weg!, fort!, raus!

offal ['ɔfəl] Abfall *m*; Schund *m*; *~s pl.* Fleischerei: Innereien *f/pl.*

offen|ce, *Am.* **~se** [ə'fens] Angriff *m*; Beleidigung *f*, Kränkung *f*; Ärgernis *n*, Anstoß *m*; Vergehen *n*.

offend [ə'fend] *v/t.* beleidigen, verletzen; ärgern; *v/i.* sich vergehen; **~er** [~də] Übel-, Missetäter(in); Straffällige(r *m*) *f*; *first ~* noch nicht Vorbestrafte(r *m*) *f*.

offensive [ə'fensiv] **1.** □ beleidigend; anstößig; ekelhaft; Offensiv..., Angriffs...; **2.** Offensive *f*.

offer ['ɔfə] **1.** Angebot *n*, Anerbieten *n*; *~ of marriage* Heiratsantrag *m*; **2.** *v/t.* anbieten; Preis, Möglichkeit *etc.* bieten; Gebet, Opfer darbringen; versuchen; zeigen; *Widerstand* leisten; *v/i.* sich bieten; **~ing** ['ɔfəriŋ] Opfer *n*; Anerbieten *n*, Angebot *n*.

off-hand ['ɔ:f'hænd] aus dem Handgelenk *od.* Stegreif, unvorbereitet; ungezwungen, frei.

office ['ɔfis] Büro *n*; Geschäftsstelle

f; Ministerium *n*; Amt *n*, Pflicht *f*; *~s pl.* Hilfe *f*; *booking-~* Schalter *m*; *box-~* (Theater- *etc.*)Kasse *f*; *Divine* ⚪ Gottesdienst *m*; *~r* [~sə] Beamt|e(r) *m*, *-in f*; ✗ Offizier *m*.

official [ə'fiʃəl] **1.** □ offiziell, amtlich; Amts...; **2.** Beamte(r) *m*.

officiate [ə'fiʃieit] amtieren.

officious □ [ə'fiʃəs] aufdringlich, übereifrig; offiziös, halbamtlich.

off|-licence ['ɔ:flaisəns] Schankrecht *n* über die Straße; **~print** Sonderdruck *m*; **~set** ausgleichen; **~shoot** Sproß *m*; Ausläufer *m*; **~side** ['ɔ:f'said] *Sport*: abseits; **~spring** ['ɔ:fspriŋ] Nachkomme(n-schaft *f*) *m*; Ergebnis *n*.

often ['ɔ:fn] oft(mals), häufig.

ogle ['ougl] liebäugeln (mit).

ogre ['ougə] Menschenfresser *m*.

oh [ou] oh!; ach!

oil [ɔil] **1.** Öl *n*; Erdöl *n*, Petroleum *n*; **2.** ölen; (*a. fig.*) schmieren; **~cloth** ['ɔilklɔθ] Wachstuch *n*; **~skin** Ölleinwand *f*; *~s pl.* Ölzeug *n*; **~y** □ ['ɔili] ölig (*a. fig.*); fettig; schmierig (*a. fig.*).

ointment ['ɔintmənt] Salbe *f*.

O.K., okay F ['ou'kei] **1.** richtig, stimmt!; gut, in Ordnung; **2.** annehmen, gutheißen.

old [ould] alt; altbekannt; althergebracht; erfahren; *~ age* (das) Alter; *days of~* alte Zeiten *f/pl.*; **~age** ['ouldeidʒ] Alters...; **~-fashioned** ['ould'fæʃənd] altmodisch; altväterlich; ⚪ *Glory* Sternenbanner *n*; **~ish** ['ouldiʃ] ältlich.

olfactory *anat.* [ɔl'fæktəri] Geruchs...

olive ['ɔliv] ♀ Olive *f*; Olivgrün *n*.

Olympic Games [ou'limpik 'geimz] Olympische Spiele *pl.*

ominous □ ['ɔminəs] unheilvoll.

omission [ou'miʃən] Unterlassung *f*; Auslassung *f*.

omit [ou'mit] unterlassen; auslassen.

omnipoten|ce [ɔm'nipətəns] Allmacht *f*; **~t** □ [~nt] allmächtig.

omniscient □ [ɔm'nisiənt] allwissend.

on [ɔn] **1.** *prp. mst* auf; *engS.*: an (*~ the wall, ~ the Thames*); auf ... (los), nach ... (hin) (*march ~ London*); auf ... (hin) (*~ his authority*); *Zeit*: an (*~ the 1st of April*); (gleich) nach, bei (*~ his arrival*); über (*acc.*) (*talk ~ a subject*); nach (*~ this model*); *get ~ a train* bsd. *Am.* in e-n Zug einsteigen; *~ hearing* it als ich *etc.* es hörte; **2.** *adv.* darauf; auf (*keep one's hat ~*), an (*have a coat ~*); voraus, vorwärts; weiter (*and so ~*); *be ~* im Gange sein; an sein (*Hahn etc.*); an sein (*Licht etc.*); **3.** *int.* drauf!, an!

once [wʌns] **1.** *adv.* einmal; einst (-mals); *at ~* (so)gleich, sofort; zugleich; ~ for all ein für allemal; ~ in a while dann und wann; this ~ dieses eine Mal; 2. cj. a. ~ that so-bald.

one [wʌn] 1. ein; einzig; eine(r), ein; eins; man; ~ day eines Tages; 2. Eine(r) m; Eins f; the little ~s pl. die Kleinen pl.; ~ another ein-ander; at ~ einig; ~ by ~ einzeln; I for ~ ich für meinen Teil.

onerous □ ['ɔnərəs] lästig.

one|self [wʌn'self] (man) selbst, sich; ~-sided □ ['wʌn'saidid] ein-seitig; ~-way ['wʌnwei]: ~ street Einbahnstraße f.

onion ['ʌnjən] Zwiebel f.

onlooker ['ɔnlukə] Zuschauer(in).

only ['ounli] 1. adj. einzig; 2. adv. nur; bloß; erst; ~ yesterday erst gestern; 3. cj. ~ (that) nur daß.

onrush ['ɔnrʌʃ] Ansturm m.

onset ['ɔnset], **onslaught** ['ɔnslɔ:t] Angriff m; bsd. fig. Anfall m; An-fang m.

onward ['ɔnwəd] 1. adj. fortschrei-tend; 2. a. ~s adv. vorwärts, weiter.

ooze [u:z] 1. Schlamm m; 2. v/i. (durch)sickern; ~ away schwinden; v/t. ausströmen, ausschwitzen.

opaque □ [ou'peik] undurchsichtig.

open ['oupən] 1. □ allg. offen; ge-öffnet, auf; frei (Feld etc.); öffent-lich; offenstehend, unentschieden; aufrichtig; zugänglich (to dat.); auf-geschlossen (to gegenüber); mild (Wetter); 2. in the ~ (air) im Freien; come out into the ~ fig. an die Öffent-lichkeit treten; 3. v/t. öffnen; er-öffnen (a. fig.); v/i. (sich) öffnen; anfangen; ~ into führen in (acc.) (Tür etc.); ~ on to hinausgehen auf (acc.) (Fenster etc.); ~ out sich aus-breiten; ~-air ['oupn'eə] im Freien (stattfindend), Freilicht..., Frei-(luft)...; ~-armed ['oupn'ɑ:md] herzlich, warm; ~er ['oupnə] (Er-)Öffner(in); (Dosen)Öffner m; ~-eyed ['oupn'aid] wach; mit offenen Augen; aufmerksam; ~-handed ['oupn'hændid] freigebig, groß-zügig; ~-hearted ['oupn'hɑ:tid] offen(herzig), aufrichtig; ~ing ['oupniŋ] (Er)Öffnung f; Gele-genheit f; attr. Eröffnungs...; ~-minded ['oupn'maindid] auf-geschlossen. [pl.] Opernglas n.\

opera ['ɔpərə] Oper f; ~-glass(se)

operat|e ['ɔpəreit] v/t. ℱ operieren; bsd. Am. in Gang bringen; Maschine bedienen; Unternehmen leiten; v/i. (ein)wirken; sich auswirken; arbei-ten; ♥, ♣, ✕ operieren; ~ion [ɔpə-'reiʃən] Wirkung f; Tätigkeit f; ℱ, ✕, ✝ Operation f; be in ~ in Betrieb sein; in Kraft sein; ~ive ['ɔpərətiv] 1. □ wirksam, tätig; praktisch; ℱ operativ; 2. Arbeiter m; ~or [~reitə] Operateur m; Telephonist(in); ⊕ Maschinist m.

opin|e [ou'pain] meinen; ~ion [ə'pinjən] Meinung f; Ansicht f; Stellungnahme f; Gutachten n; in my ~ meines Brachtens.

opponent [ə'pounənt] Gegner m.

opportun|e □ ['ɔpətju:n] passend; rechtzeitig; günstig; ~ity [ɔpə'tju:-niti] (günstige) Gelegenheit.

oppos|e [ə'pouz] entgegen-, gegen-überstellen; bekämpfen; ~ed ent-gegengesetzt; be ~ to gegen ... sein; ~ite ['ɔpəzit] 1. □ gegenüberlie-gend; entgegengesetzt; 2. prp. u. adv. gegenüber; 3. Gegenteil n; ~ition [ɔpə'ziʃən] Gegenüberste-hen n; Widerstand m; Gegensatz m; Widerspruch m, -streit m; ✝ Kon-kurrenz f; Opposition f.

oppress [ə'pres] be-, unterdrücken; ~ion [~eʃən] Unterdrückung f; Druck m; Bedrängnis f; Bedrückt-heit f; ~ive □ [~esiv] (be)drückend; gewaltsam.

optic ['ɔptik] Augen..., Seh...; = ~al □ [~kəl] optisch; ~ian [ɔp'tiʃən] Optiker m.

optimism ['ɔptimizəm] Optimis-mus m.

option ['ɔpʃən] Wahl(freiheit) f; ✝ Vorkaufsrecht n, Option f; ~al □ [~nl] freigestellt, wahlfrei.

opulence ['ɔpjuləns] Reichtum m.

or [ɔ:] oder; ~ else sonst, wo nicht.

oracular □ [ɔ'rækjulə] orakelhaft.

oral □ ['ɔ:rəl] mündlich; Mund...

orange ['ɔrindʒ] 1. Orange(farbe) f; Apfelsine f; 2. orangefarben; ~ade ['ɔrindʒ'eid] Orangenlimonade f.

orat|ion [ɔ:'reiʃən] Rede f; ~or ['ɔrətə] Redner m; ~ory [~əri] Re-dekunst f, Rhetorik f; Kapelle f.

orb [ɔ:b] Ball m; fig. Himmelskörper m; poet. Augapfel m; ~it ['ɔ:bit] 1. Planetenbahn f; Kreis-, Umlauf-bahn f; Auge(nhöhle f) n; 2. sich in e-r Umlaufbahn bewegen.

orchard ['ɔ:tʃəd] Obstgarten m.

orchestra ♪ ['ɔ:kistrə] Orchester n.

orchid ♀ ['ɔ:kid] Orchidee f.

ordain [ɔ:'dein] an-, verordnen; be-stimmen; Priester ordinieren.

ordeal fig. [ɔ:'di:l] schwere Prüfung.

order ['ɔ:də] 1. Ordnung f; An-ordnung f; Befehl m; Regel f; ✝ Auftrag m; Zahlungsanweisung f; Klasse f, Rang m; Orden m (a. eccl.); take (holy) ~s in den geist-lichen Stand treten; in ~ to inf. um zu inf.; in ~ that damit; make to ~ auf Bestellung anfertigen; stand-ing ~s pl. parl. Geschäftsordnung f; 2. (an)ordnen; befehlen; ✝ bestel-len; j-n beordern; ~ly ['ɔ:dəli] 1. ordentlich; ruhig; regelmäßig; 2. ✕ Ordonnanz f; ✕ Bursche m; Krankenpfleger m.

ordinal ['ɔ:dinl] 1. Ordnungs...; 2. a. ~ number Ordnungszahl f.

ordinance ['ɔ:dinəns] Verordnung f.

ordinary □ ['ɔːdnri] gewöhnlich.
ordnance ✕, ⚓ ['ɔːdnəns] Artillerie f, Geschütze n/pl.; Feldzeugwesen n.
ordure ['ɔːdjuə] Kot m, Schmutz m.
ore [ɔː] Erz n.
organ ['ɔːgən] ♪ Orgel f; Organ n; **~grinder** [~ngraində] Leierkastenmann m; **~ic** [ɔː'gænik] (~ally) organisch; **~ization** [ɔːgənai'zeiʃən] Organisation f; **~ize** ['ɔːgənaiz] organisieren; **~izer** [~zə] Organisator(in).
orgy ['ɔːdʒi] Ausschweifung f.
orient ['ɔːrient] 1. Osten m; Orient m, Morgenland n; 2. orientieren; **~al** [ɔːri'entl] 1. □ östlich; orientalisch; 2. Orientale m, -in f; **~ate** ['ɔːrienteit] orientieren.
orifice ['ɔrifis] Mündung f; Öffnung f.
origin ['ɔridʒin] Ursprung m; Anfang m; Herkunft f.
original [ə'ridʒən] 1. □ ursprünglich; originell; Original...; ♂ Stamm...; 2. Original n; **~ity** [əridʒi'næliti] Originalität f; **~ly** [ə'ridʒnəli] originell; ursprünglich, zuerst, anfangs, anfänglich.
originat|e [ə'ridʒineit] v/t. hervorbringen, schaffen; v/i. entstehen; **~or** [~tə] Urheber m.
ornament 1. ['ɔːnəmənt] Verzierung f; fig. Zierde f; 2. [~ment] verzieren; schmücken; **~al** □ [ɔːnə'mentl] zierend; schmückend.
ornate □ [ɔː'neit] reich verziert; überladen.
orphan ['ɔːfən] 1. Waise f; 2. a. **~ed** verwaist; **~age** [~nidʒ] Waisenhaus n.
orthodox □ ['ɔːθədɔks] rechtgläubig; üblich; anerkannt.
oscillate ['ɔsileit] schwingen; fig. schwanken.
osier ⚘ ['ouʒə] Korbweide f.
osprey orn. ['ɔspri] Fischadler m.
ossify ['ɔsifai] verknöchern.
ostensible □ [ɔs'tensəbl] angeblich.
ostentatio|n [ɔstən'teiʃən] Zurschaustellung f; Protzerei f; **~us** □ [~ʃəs] prahlend, prahlerisch.
ostler ['ɔslə] Stallknecht m.
ostracize ['ɔstrəsaiz] verbannen; ächten.
ostrich orn. ['ɔstritʃ] Strauß m.
other ['ʌðə] andere(r, -s); the ~ day neulich; the ~ morning neulich morgens; every ~ day einen Tag um den anderen, jeden zweiten Tag; **~wise** ['ʌðəwaiz] anders; sonst.
otter zo. ['ɔtə] Otter(pelz) m.
ought [ɔːt] sollte; you ~ to have done it Sie hätten es tun sollen.
ounce [auns] Unze f (= 28,35 g).
our ['auə] unser; **~s** ['auəz] der (die, das) unsrige; unsere(r, -s); pred. unser; **~selves** [auə'selvz] wir selbst; uns (selbst).

oust [aust] verdrängen, vertreiben, hinauswerfen; e-s Amtes entheben.
out [aut] 1. adv. aus; hinaus, heraus; draußen; außerhalb; (bis) zu Ende; be ~ with böse sein mit; ~ and ~ durch und durch; ~ and about wieder auf den Beinen; way ~ Ausgang m; 2. Am. F Ausweg m; the ~s pl. parl. die Opposition; 3. ✝ übernormal, Über... (Größe); 4. prp. ~ of aus, aus ... heraus; außerhalb; außer; aus, von.
out|balance [aut'bæləns] schwerer wiegen als; **~bid** [~'bid] (irr. (bid)) überbieten; **~board** ['autbɔːd] Außenbord...; **~break** [~breik] Ausbruch m; **~building** [~bildiŋ] Nebengebäude n; **~burst** [~bəːst] Ausbruch m; **~cast** [~kɑːst] 1. ausgestoßen; 2. Ausgestoßene(r m) f; **~come** [~kʌm] Ergebnis n; **~cry** [~krai] Aufschrei m, Schrei m der Entrüstung; **~dated** [aut'deitid] zeitlich überholt; **~distance** [~'distəns] überholen; **~do** [~'du:] (do)] übertreffen; **~door** adj. ['autdɔː], **~doors** adv. [~'dɔːz] Außen...; draußen, dem Hause; im Freien.
outer ['autə] äußer; Außen...; **~most** ['autəmoust] äußerst.
out|fit ['autfit] Ausrüstung f, Ausstattung f; Am. Haufen m, Trupp m, (Arbeits)Gruppe f; **~going** [~gouiŋ] 1. weg-, abgehend; 2. Ausgehen n; **~s** pl. Ausgaben f/pl.; **~grow** [aut'grou] (irr. (grow)] herauswachsen aus; hinauswachsen über (acc.); **~house** ['authaus] Nebengebäude n; Am. Außenabort m.
outing ['autiŋ] Ausflug m, Tour f.
out|last [aut'lɑːst] überdauern; **~law** ['autlɔː] 1. Geächtete(r m) f; 2. ächten; **~lay** [~lei] Geld-Auslage(n pl.) f; **~let** [~let] Auslaß m; Ausgang m; Abfluß m; **~line** [~lain] 1. Umriß m; Überblick m; Skizze f; 2. umreißen; skizzieren; **~live** [aut'liv] überleben; **~look** ['autluk] Ausblick m (a. fig.); Auffassung f; **~lying** [~laiiŋ] entlegen; **~match** [aut'mætʃ] weit übertreffen; **~number** [~'nʌmbə] an Zahl übertreffen; **~patient** ⚕ ['autpeiʃənt] ambulanter Patient; **~post** [~poust] Vorposten m; **~pouring** [~pɔːriŋ] Erguß m (a. fig.); **~put** [~put] Produktion f, Ertrag m.
outrage ['autreidʒ] 1. Gewalttätigkeit f; Attentat n; Beleidigung f; 2. gröblich verletzen; Gewalt antun (dat.); **~ous** [aut'reidʒəs] abscheulich; empörend; gewalttätig.
out|reach [aut'riːtʃ] weiter reichen als; **~right** [adj. 'autrait, adv. aut'rait] gerade heraus; völlig; **~run** [~'rʌn] [irr. (run)] schneller laufen als; hinausgehen über (acc.); **~set**

['autset] Anfang *m*; Aufbruch *m*; ~shine [aut'∫ain] [*irr.* (*shine*)] überstrahlen; ~side ['aut'said] 1. Außenseite *f*; *fig.* Außerste(s) *n*; *at the* ~ höchstens; 2. Außen...; außenstehend; äußerst (*Preis*); 3. (nach) (dr)außen; 4. *prp.* außerhalb; ~sider [~də] Außenseiter(in), ~stehende(r *m*) *f*; ~size [~saiz] Übergröße *f*; ~skirts [~skə:ts] *pl.* Außenbezirke *m/pl.*, (Stadt)Rand *m*; ~smart *Am.* F [aut'smɑ:t] übervorteilen; ~spoken [~'spoukən] freimütig; ~spread ['aut'spred] ausgestreckt, ausgebreitet; ~standing [aut'stændiŋ] hervorragend (*a. fig.*); ausstehend (*Schuld*); offenstehend (*Frage*); ~stretched ['autstret∫t] = outspread; ~strip [aut'strip] überholen (*a. fig.*).

out|ward ['autwəd] 1. äußer(lich); nach (dr)außen gerichtet; 2. *adv. mst* ~s auswärts, nach (dr)außen; ~ly [~dli] äußerlich; an der Oberfläche.

out|weigh [aut'wei] überwiegen; ~wit [~'wit] überlisten; ~worn ['autwo:n] erschöpft; *fig.* abgegriffen; überholt.

oval ['ouvəl] 1. oval; 2. Oval *n*.

oven ['ʌvn] Backofen *m*.

over ['ouvə] 1. *adv.* über; hin-, herüber; drüben; vorbei; übermäßig; darüber; von Anfang bis zu Ende; noch einmal; ~ *and above* neben, zusätzlich zu; (*all*) ~ *again* noch einmal (von vorn); ~ *against* gegenüber (*dat.*); *all* ~ ganz und gar; ~ *and* ~ *again* immer wieder; *read* ~ durchlesen; 2. *prp.* über; *all* ~ *the town* durch die ganze *od.* in der ganzen Stadt.

over|act ['ouvər'ækt] übertreiben; ~all [~ro:l] 1. Arbeitsanzug *m*, -kittel *m*; Kittel(schürze *f*) *m*; 2. gesamt, Gesamt...; ~awe [ouvər'ɔ:] einschüchtern; ~balance [ouvə'bæləns] 1. Übergewicht *n*; 2. umkippen; überwiegen; ~bearing □ [~'bɛəriŋ] anmaßend; ~board ['ouvəbɔ:d] über Bord; ~cast [~kɑ:st] bewölkt; ~charge [~'t∫ɑ:dʒ] 1. überladen; überfordern; 2. Überladung *f*; Überforderung *f*; ~coat [~kout] Mantel *m*; ~come [ouvə'kʌm][*irr.*(*come*)] überwinden, überwältigen; ~crowd [~'kraud] überfüllen; ~do [~'du:] [*irr.* (*do*)] zu viel tun; übertreiben; zu sehr kochen; überanstrengen; ~draw ['ouvə'drɔ:] [*irr.* (*draw*)] übertreiben; ✝ *Konto* überziehen; ~dress [~'dres] (sich) übertrieben anziehen; ~due [~'dju:] (über)fällig; ~eat [~'i:t] [*irr.* (*eat*)]: ~ *o.s.* sich überessen; ~flow 1. [ouvə'flou] [*irr.* (*flow*)] *v/t.* überfluten; *v/i.* überfließen; 2.['ouvəflou] Überschwemmung *f*; Überfüllung *f*; ~grow

[~'grou] [*irr.* (*grow*)] *v/t.* überwuchern; *v/i.* zu sehr wachsen; ~hang 1. [~'hæŋ] [*irr.* (*hang*)] *v/t.* über (*acc.*) hängen; *v/i.* überhängen; 2. [~hæŋ] Überhang *m*; ~haul [ouvə'hɔ:l] überholen; ~head 1. *adv.* ['ouvə'hed] (Über)ben; 2. *adj.* [~hed] Über...; ↑ allgemein (*Unkosten*); 3. ~s *pl.* ↑ allgemeine Unkosten *pl.*; ~hear [ouvə'hiə] [*irr.* (*hear*)] belauschen; ~joyed [~'dʒɔid] überglücklich; ~lap [~'læp] *v/t.* übergreifen auf (*acc.*); überschneiden; *v/i.* ineinandergreifen, überlappen; ~lay [~'lei] [*irr.* (*lay*)] über lagern; ~leaf ['ouvə'li:f] umseitig; ~load [~'loud] überladen; ~look [ouvə'luk] übersehen; beaufsichtigen; ~master [~'mɑ:stə] überwältigen; ~much ['ouvə'mʌt∫] zu viel; ~night [~'nait] 1. am Vorabend; über Nacht; 2. Nacht...; nächtlich; Übernachtungs...; ~pay [~'pei] [*irr.* (*pay*)] zu viel bezahlen für; ~peopled [ouvə'pi:pld] übervölkert; ~plus ['ouvəplʌs] Überschuß *m*; ~power [ouvə'pauə] überwältigen; ~rate ['ouvə'reit] überschätzen; ~reach [ouvə'ri:t∫] übervorteilen; ~ *o.s.* sich übernehmen; ~ride *fig.* [~'raid] [*irr.* (*ride*)] sich hinwegsetzen über (*acc.*); umstoßen; ~rule [~'ru:l] überstimmen; ᵼᵼ verwerfen; ~run [~'rʌn] [*irr.* (*run*)] überrennen; überziehen; überlaufen; bedecken; ~sea ['ouvə'si:] 1. *a.* ~s überseeisch; Übersee...; 2. ~s *in od.* nach Übersee; ~see [~'si:] [*irr.* (*see*)] beaufsichtigen; ~seer [~siə] Aufseher *m*; ~shadow [ouvə'∫ædou] überschatten; ~sight ['ouvəsait] Versehen *n*; ~sleep [~'sli:p] [*irr.* (*sleep*)] verschlafen; ~state [~'steit] übertreiben; ~statement [~tmənt] Übertreibung *f*; ~strain 1. [~'strein] (sich) überanstrengen; *fig.* übertreiben; 2. [~strein] Überanstrengung *f*.

overt ['ouvə:t] offen(kundig).

over|take [ouvə'teik] [*irr.* (*take*)] einholen; *j-n* überraschen; ~tax ['ouvə'tæks] zu hoch besteuern; *fig.* überschätzen; übermäßig in Anspruch nehmen; ~throw 1. [ouvə-'θrou] [*irr.* (*throw*)] (um)stürzen (*a. fig.*); vernichten; 2. ['ouvəθrou] Sturz *m*; Vernichtung *f*; ~time [~taim] Überstunden *f/pl.*

overture ['ouvətjuə] ♪ Ouvertüre *f*; Vorspiel *n*; Vorschlag *m*, Antrag *m*.

over|turn [ouvə'tə:n] (um)stürzen; ~value ['ouvə'vælju:] zu hoch einschätzen; ~weening [~'wi:niŋ] eingebildet; ~weight ['ouvəweit] Übergewicht *n*; ~whelm [ouvə-'welm] überschütten (*a. fig.*); überwältigen; ~work ['ouvə'wə:k] 1.

Überarbeitung f; 2. [irr. (work)] sich überarbeiten; ~wrought [~-'rɔːt] überarbeitet; überreizt.

owe [ou] Geld, Dank etc. schulden, schuldig sein; verdanken.

owing ['ouiŋ] schuldig; ~ to infolge.

owl orn. [aul] Eule f.

own [oun] 1. eigen; richtig; einzig, innig geliebt; 2. my ~ mein Eigentum; a house of one's ~ ein eigenes Haus; hold one's ~ standhalten;

3. besitzen; zugeben; anerkennen; sich bekennen (to zu).

owner['ounə] Eigentümer(in); ~ship ['ounəʃip] Eigentum(srecht) n.

ox [ɔks], pl. oxen ['ɔksən] Ochse m; Rind n.

oxid|ation ⚗ [ɔksi'deiʃən] Oxydation f, Oxydierung f; ~e ['ɔksaid] Oxyd n; ~ize ['ɔksidaiz] oxydieren.

oxygen ⚗ ['ɔksidʒən] Sauerstoff m.

oyster ['ɔistə] Auster f.

ozone ⚗ ['ouzoun] Ozon n.

P

pace [peis] 1. Schritt m; Gang m; Tempo n; 2. v/t. abschreiten; v/i. (einher)schreiten; (im) Paß gehen.

pacific [pə'sifik] (~ally) friedlich; the ♀ (Ocean) der Pazifik, der Pazifische od. Stille Ozean; ~ation [pæsifi'keiʃən] Beruhigung f.

pacify ['pæsifai] beruhigen.

pack [pæk] 1. Pack(en) m; Paket n; Ballen m; Spiel n Karten; Meute f; Rotte f, Bande f; Packung f; v/t. oft ~ up (zs.-, ver-, ein)packen; a. ~ off fortjagen; Am. F (bei sich) tragen (als Gepäck etc.); bepacken, vollstopfen; ⊕ dichten; v/i. oft ~ up packen; sich packen (lassen); ~age ['pækidʒ] Pack m, Ballen m; bsd. Am. Paket n; Packung f; Frachtstück n; ~er ['pækə] Pakker(in); Am. Konservenfabrikant m; ~et ['pækit] Paket n; Päckchen n; a. ~-boat Postschiff n.

packing ['pækiŋ] Packen n; Verpackung f; ~ house Am. (bsd. Fleisch)Konservenfabrik f.

packthread ['pækθred] Bindfaden m.

pact [pækt] Vertrag m, Pakt m.

pad [pæd] 1. Polster n; Sport: Beinschutz m; Schreibblock m; Stempelkissen n; (Abschuß)Rampe f; 2. (aus)polstern; ~ding ['pædiŋ] Polsterung f; fig. Lückenbüßer m.

paddle ['pædl] 1. Paddel(ruder) n; ⚓ (Rad)Schaufel f; 2. paddeln; planschen; ~-wheel Schaufelrad n.

paddock ['pædək] (Pferde)Koppel f; Sport: Sattelplatz m.

padlock ['pædlɔk] Vorhängeschloß n.

pagan ['peigən] 1. heidnisch; 2. Heide m, -in f; Heidin f.

page[1] [peidʒ] 1. Buch-Seite f; fig. Buch n; 2. paginieren.

page[2] [~] 1. (Hotel)Page m; Am. Amtsdiener m; 2. Am. (durch e-n Pagen) holen lassen.

pageant ['pædʒənt] historisches Festspiel; festlicher Umzug.

paid [peid] pret. u. p.p. von pay 2.

pail [peil] Eimer m.

pain [pein] 1. Pein f, Schmerz m; Strafe f; ~s pl. Leiden n/pl.; Mühe f; on od. under ~ of death bei Todesstrafe; be in ~ leiden; take ~s sich Mühe geben; 2. j-m weh tun; ~ful □ ['peinful] schmerzhaft, schmerzlich; peinlich; mühevoll; ~less □ ['peinlis] schmerzlos; ~staking □ ['peinzteikiŋ] fleißig.

paint [peint] 1. Farbe f; Schminke f; Anstrich m; 2. (be)malen; anstreichen; (sich) schminken; ~-brush ['peintbrʌʃ] Malerpinsel m; ~er [~tə] Maler(in); ~ing [~tiŋ] Malen n; Malerei f; Gemälde n.

pair [pɛə] 1. Paar n; a ~ of scissors eine Schere; 2. (sich) paaren; zs.passen; a. ~ off paarweise weggehen.

pal sl. [pæl] Kumpel m, Kamerad m.

palace ['pælis] Palast m.

palatable □ ['pælətəbl] schmackhaft. [schmack m (a. fig.).\

palate ['pælit] Gaumen m; Ge-\

pale[1] [peil] 1. □ blaß, bleich; fahl; ~ ale helles Bier; 2. (er)bleichen.

pale[2] [~] Pfahl m; fig. Grenzen f/pl.

paleness ['peilnis] Blässe f.

palisade [pæli'seid] 1. Palisade f, Staket n; ~s pl. Am. Steilufer n; 2. umpfählen.

pall [pɔːl] schal werden; ~ (up)on j-n langweilen.

pallet ['pælit] Strohsack m.

palliat|e ['pælieit] bemänteln; lindern; ~ive [~iətiv] Linderungsmittel n.

pall|id □ ['pælid] blaß; ~idness [~dnis], ~or ['pælə] Blässe f.

palm [pɑːm] 1. Handfläche f; ♀ Palme f; 2. in der Hand verbergen; ~ s.th. off upon s.o. j-m et. andrehen; ~-tree ['pɑːmtriː] Palme f.

palpable □ ['pælpəbl] fühlbar; fig. handgreiflich, klar, eindeutig.

palpitat|e ['pælpiteit] klopfen (Herz); ~ion [pælpi'teiʃən] Herzklopfen n.

palsy ['pɔːlzi] 1. Lähmung f; fig. Ohnmacht f; 2. fig. lähmen.

palter ['pɔːltə] sein Spiel treiben.

paltry □ ['pɔːltri] erbärmlich.

pamper ['pæmpə] verzärteln.

pamphlet ['pæmflit] Flugschrift f.

pan [pæn] Pfanne f; Tiegel m.

pan... [~] all..., gesamt...; pan..., Pan...

panacea [pænə'siə] Allheilmittel n.

pancake ['pænkeik] Pfannkuchen m; ~ landing ✈ Bumslandung f.

pandemonium fig. [pændi'mounjəm] Hölle(nlärm m) f.

pander ['pændə] 1. Vorschub leisten (to dat.); kuppeln; 2. Kuppler m.

pane [pein] (Fenster)Scheibe f.

panegyric [pæni'dʒirik] Lobrede f.

panel ['pænl] 1. ⚠ Fach n; Tür-Füllung f; ⚖ Geschworenen(liste f) m/pl.; Diskussionsteilnehmer m/pl.; Kassenarztliste f; 2. täfeln.

pang [pæŋ] plötzlicher Schmerz, Weh n; fig. Angst f, Qual f.

panhandle ['pænhændl] 1. Pfannenstiel m; Am. schmaler Fortsatz e-s Staatsgebiets; 2. Am. F betteln.

panic ['pænik] 1. panisch; 2. Panik f.

pansy ♀ ['pænzi] Stiefmütterchen n.

pant [pænt] nach Luft schnappen; keuchen; klopfen (Herz); lechzen (for, after nach).

panther zo. ['pænθə] Panther m.

panties F ['pæntiz] (Damen)Schlüpfer m; (Kinder)Hös-chen n.

pantry ['pæntri] Vorratskammer f.

pants [pænts] pl. Hose f; ⚓ lange Unterhose.

pap [pæp] Brei m. [Unterhose.]

papa [pə'pɑː] Papa m.

papal □ ['peipəl] päpstlich.

paper ['peipə] 1. Papier n; Zeitung f; Prüfungsaufgabe f; Vortrag m, Aufsatz m; ~s pl. (Ausweis)Papiere n/pl.; 2. tapezieren; ~back Taschenbuch n, Paperback n; ~bag Tüte f; ~clip Büroklammer f; ~fastener Musterklammer f; ~hanger Tapezierer m; ~mill Papierfabrik f; ~weight Briefbeschwerer m.

pappy ['pæpi] breiig.

par [pɑː] ⚓ Nennwert m, Pari n; at ~ zum Nennwert; be on a ~ with gleich od. ebenbürtig sein (dat.).

parable ['pærəbl] Gleichnis n.

parachut|e ['pærəʃuːt] Fallschirm m; ~ist [~tist] Fallschirmspringer(in).

parade [pə'reid] 1. ✕ (Truppen-)Parade f; Zurschaustellung f; Promenade f; (Um)Zug m; programme ~ Radio: Programmvorschau f; make a ~ of et. zur Schau stellen; 2. ✕ antreten (lassen); ✕ vorbeimarschieren (lassen); zur Schau stellen; ~ground ✕ Exerzier-, Paradeplatz m.

paradise ['pærədais] Paradies n.

paragon ['pærəgən] Vorbild n; Muster n.

paragraph ['pærəgrɑːf] Absatz m; Paragraph(zeichen n) m; kurze Zeitungsnotiz.

parallel ['pærəlel] 1. parallel; 2. Parallele f (a. fig.); Gegenstück n; Vergleich m; without (a) ~ ohnegleichen; 3. vergleichen; entsprechen; gleichen; parallel laufen (mit).

paraly|se ['pærəlaiz] lähmen; fig. unwirksam machen; ~sis ✎ [pə-'rælisis] Paralyse f, Lähmung f.

paramount ['pærəmaunt] oberst, höchst, hervorragend; größer, höher stehend (to als).

parapet ['pærəpit] ✕ Brustwehr f; Brüstung f; Geländer n.

paraphernalia [pærəfə'neiljə] pl. Ausrüstung f; Zubehör n, m.

parasite ['pærəsait] Schmarotzer m.

parasol ['pærə'sɔl] Sonnenschirm m.

paratroops ✕ ['pærətruːps] Luftlandetruppen f/pl.

parboil ['pɑːbɔil] ankochen.

parcel ['pɑːsl] 1. Paket n; Parzelle f; 2. ~ out aus-, aufteilen.

parch [pɑːtʃ] rösten, (aus)dörren.

parchment ['pɑːtʃmənt] Pergament n.

pard Am. sl. [pɑːd] Partner m.

pardon ['pɑːdn] 1. Verzeihung f; ⚖ Begnadigung f; 2. verzeihen; j. begnadigen; ~able □ [~nəbl] verzeihlich.

pare [pɛə] (be)schneiden (a. fig.); schälen.

parent ['pɛərənt] Vater m, Mutter f; fig. Ursache f; ~s pl. Eltern pl.; ~age [~tidʒ] Herkunft f; ~al [pə'rentl] elterlich.

parenthe|sis [pə'renθisis], pl. ~ses [~siːz] Einschaltung f; typ. (runde) Klammer.

paring ['pɛəriŋ] Schälen n, Abschneiden n; ~s pl. Schalen f/pl., Schnipsel m/pl.

parish ['pæriʃ] 1. Kirchspiel n, Gemeinde f; 2. Pfarr...; Gemeinde...; ~ council Gemeinderat m; ~ioner [pə'riʃənə] Pfarrkind n, Gemeindemitglied n.

parity ['pæriti] Gleichheit f.

park [pɑːk] 1. Park m, Anlagen f/pl.; Naturschutzgebiet n; mst car-~ Parkplatz m; 2. mot. parken; ~ing mot. ['pɑːkiŋ] Parken n; ~ing lot Parkplatz m; ~ing meter Parkuhr f.

parlance ['pɑːləns] Ausdrucksweise f.

parley ['pɑːli] 1. Unterhandlung f; 2. unterhandeln; sich besprechen.

parliament ['pɑːləmənt] Parlament n; ~arian [pɑːləmen'tɛəriən] Parlamentarier(in); ~ary □ [pɑːlə'mentəri] parlamentarisch; Parlaments...

parlo(u)r ['pɑːlə] Wohnzimmer n; Empfangs-, Sprechzimmer n; beauty ~ bsd. Am. Schönheitssalon m; ~ car ⚏ Am. Salonwagen m; ~maid Stubenmädchen n.

parochial □ [pə'roukjəl] Pfarr...; Gemeinde...; fig. engstirnig, beschränkt.

parole [pə'roul] 1. ✟✟ mündlich; 2. ✕ Parole f; Ehrenwort n; put on ~ = 3. ✟✟ bsd. Am. bedingt freilassen.

parquet ['pɑːkei] Parkett(fußboden m) n; Am. thea. Parkett n.

parrot ['pærət] 1. orn. Papagei m (a. fig.); 2. (nach)plappern.

parry ['pæri] abwehren, parieren.

parsimonious □ [pɑːsi'mounjəs] sparsam, karg; knauserig.

parsley ♧ ['pɑːsli] Petersilie f.

parson ['pɑːsn] Pfarrer m; ~age [~nidʒ] Pfarrei f; Pfarrhaus n.

part [pɑːt] 1. Teil m; Anteil m; Partei f; thea., fig. Rolle f; ♪ Einzel-Stimme f; Gegend f; a man of ~s ein fähiger Mensch; take ~ in s.th. an e-r Sache teilnehmen; take in good (bad) ~ gut (übel) aufnehmen; for my (own) ~ meinerseits; in ~ teilweise; on the ~ of von seiten (gen.); on my ~ meinerseits; 2. adv. teils; 3. v/t. (ab-, ein-, zer)teilen; Haar scheiteln; ~ company sich trennen (with von); v/i. sich trennen (with von); scheiden.

partake [pɑː'teik] (irr. (take)) teilnehmen, teilhaben; ~ of Mahlzeit einnehmen; grenzen an (acc.).

partial □ ['pɑːʃəl] Teil...; teilweise; partiell; parteiisch; eingenommen (to von, für); ~ity [pɑːʃi'æliti] Parteilichkeit f; Vorliebe f.

particip|ant [pɑː'tisipənt] Teilnehmer(in); ~ate [~peit] teilnehmen; ~ation [pɑːtisi'peiʃən] Teilnahme f.

participle gr. ['pɑːtsipl] Partizip n, Mittelwort n.

particle ['pɑːtikl] Teilchen n.

particular [pə'tikjulə] 1. □ mst besonder; einzeln; Sonder...; genau; eigen; wählerisch; 2. Einzelheit f; Umstand m; in ~ insbesondere; ~ity [pətikju'læriti] Besonderheit f; Ausführlichkeit f; Eigenheit f; ~ly [pə'tikjuləli] besonders.

parting ['pɑːtiŋ] 1. Trennung f; Teilung f; Abschied m; Haar-Scheitel m; ~ of the ways bsd. fig. Scheideweg m; 2. Abschieds...

partisan [pɑːti'zæn] Parteigänger (-in); ✕ Partisan m; attr. Partei...

partition [pɑː'tiʃən] 1. Teilung f; Scheidewand f; Verschlag m, Fach n; 2. mst ~ off (ab)teilen.

partly ['pɑːtli] teilweise, zum Teil.

partner ['pɑːtnə] 1. Partner(in); 2. (sich) zs.-tun mit, zs.-arbeiten mit; ~ship [~əʃip] Teilhaber-, Part-

nerschaft f; ✟ Handelsgesellschaft f.

part-owner ['pɑːtounə] Miteigentümer(in).

partridge orn. ['pɑːtridʒ] Rebhuhn n.

part-time ['pɑːttaim] 1. adj. Teilzeit..., Halbtags...; 2. adv. halbtags.

party ['pɑːti] Partei f; ✕ Trupp m, Kommando n; Party f, Gesellschaft f; Beteiligte(r) m; co. Type f, Individuum n; ~ line pol. Parteilinie f, -direktive f.

pass [pɑːs] 1. Paß m, Ausweis m; Passierschein m; Bestehen n e-s Examens; univ. gewöhnlicher Grad; (kritische) Lage; Fußball: Paß m; Bestreichung f, Strich m; (Gebirgs-) Paß m, Durchgang m; Karten: Passen n; free ~ Freikarte f; 2. v/i. passieren, geschehen; hingenommen werden; Karten: passen; (vorbei)gehen, (vorbei)kommen, (vorbei)fahren; vergehen (Zeit); sich verwandeln; angenommen werden (Banknoten); bekannt sein; vergehen; aussterben; a. ~ away sterben; durchkommen (Gesetz; Prüfling); ~ for gelten als; ~ off vonstatten gehen; ~ out F ohnmächtig werden; come to ~ geschehen; bring to ~ bewirken; v/t. vorbeigehen od. vorbeikommen od. vorbeifahren an (dat.); passieren; kommen od. fahren durch; verbringen; reichen, geben; Bemerkung machen, von sich geben; Banknoten in Umlauf bringen; Gesetz durchbringen, annehmen; Prüfling durchkommen lassen; Prüfung bestehen; (hinaus-) gehen über (acc.); Urteil abgeben; Meinung äußern; bewegen; streichen mit; Ball zuspielen; Truppen vorbeimaschieren lassen; ~able □ ['pɑːsəbl] passierbar; gangbar, gültig (Geld); leidlich.

passage ['pæsidʒ] Durchgang m, Durchfahrt f; Überfahrt f; Durchreise f; Korridor m, Gang m; Weg m; Annahme f e-s Gesetzes; ♪ Passage f; Text-Stelle f; bird of ~ Zugvogel m.

passbook ✟ ['pɑːsbuk] Sparbuch n.

passenger ['pæsindʒə] Passagier m, Fahr-, Fluggast m, Reisende(r m) f.

passer-by ['pɑːsə'bai] Vorübergehende(r m) f, Passant(in).

passion ['pæʃən] Leidenschaft f; (Gefühls)Ausbruch m; Zorn m; ☿ eccl. Passion f; be in a ~ zornig sein; in ~ ✟✟ im Affekt; ☿ Week eccl. Karwoche f; ~ate □ [~nit] leidenschaftlich.

passive □ ['pæsiv] passiv (a. gr.); teilnahmslos; untätig.

passport ['pɑːspɔːt] (Reise)Paß m.

password ✕ ['pɑːswəːd] Losung f.

past [pɑːst] 1. adj. vergangen; gr. Vergangenheits...; früher; for some time ~ seit einiger Zeit; ~ tense gr. Vergangenheit f; 2. adv. vorbei; 3. prp. nach, über; über ... (acc.) hinaus; an ... (dat.) vorbei; half ~ two halb drei; ~ endurance unerträglich; ~ hope hoffnungslos; 4. Vergangenheit f (a. gr.).

paste [peist] 1. Teig m; Kleister m; Paste f; 2. (be)kleben; **board** ['peistbɔːd] Pappe f; attr. Papp...

pastel ['pæstel] Pastell(bild) n.

pasteurize ['pæstəraiz] pasteurisieren, keimfrei machen.

pastime ['pɑːstaim] Zeitvertreib m.

pastor ['pɑːstə] Pastor m; Seelsorger m; **al** □ [.ərəl] Hirten...; pastoral.

pastry ['peistri] Tortengebäck n, Konditorwaren f/pl.; Pasteten f/pl.; **cook** Pastetenbäcker m, Konditor m.

pasture ['pɑːstʃə] 1. Vieh-Weide f; Futter n; 2. (ab)weiden.

pat [pæt] 1. Klaps m; Portion f Butter; 2. tätscheln; klopfen; 3. gelegen, gerade recht; bereit.

patch [pætʃ] 1. Fleck m; Flicken m; Stück n Land; **∗** Pflaster n; 2. flikken; **work** ['pætʃwəːk] Flickwerk n.

pate F [peit] Schädel m.

patent ['peitənt, Am. 'pætənt] 1. offenkundig; patentiert; Patent...; letters ~ ['pætənt] pl. Freibrief m; ~ leather Lackleder n; 2. Patent n; Privileg n, Freibrief m; ~ agent Patentanwalt m; 3. patentieren; **ee** [peitən'tiː] Patentinhaber m.

patern|al □ [pə'təːnl] väterlich; **ity** [.niti] Vaterschaft f.

path [pɑːθ], pl. **s** [pɑːðz] Pfad m; Weg m.

pathetic [pə'θetik] (**ally**) pathetisch; rührend, ergreifend.

pathos ['peiθɔs] Pathos n.

patien|ce ['peiʃəns] Geduld f; Ausdauer f; Patience f (Kartenspiel); **t** [.nt] 1. □ geduldig; 2. Patient(in).

patio Am. ['pætiou] Innenhof m, Patio m.

patrimony ['pætriməni] väterliches Erbteil.

patriot ['peitriət] Patriot(in).

patrol ✕ [pə'troul] 1. Patrouille f, Streife f; ~ wagon Am. Polizeigefangenenwagen m; 2. (ab)patrouillieren; **man** [.lmæn] patrouillierender Polizist; Pannenhelfer m e-s Automobilclubs.

patron ['peitrən] (Schutz)Patron m; Gönner m; Kunde m; **age** ['pætrənidʒ] Gönnerschaft f; Kundschaft f; Schutz m; **ize** [.naiz] beschützen; begünstigen; Kunde sein bei; gönnerhaft behandeln.

patter ['pætə] v/i. platschen; trappeln; v/t. (her)plappern.

pattern ['pætən] 1. Muster n (a.

fig.); Modell n; 2. formen (after, on nach).

paunch ['pɔːntʃ] Wanst m.

pauper ['pɔːpə] Fürsorgeempfänger(in), **ize** [.əraiz] arm machen.

pause [pɔːz] 1. Pause f; 2. pausieren.

pave [peiv] pflastern; fig. Weg bahnen; **ment** ['peivmənt] Bürgersteig m, Gehweg m; Pflaster n.

paw [pɔː] 1. Pfote f, Tatze f; 2. scharren; F befingern; rauh behandeln.

pawn [pɔːn] 1. Bauer m im Schach; Pfand n; in od. at ~ verpfändet; 2. verpfänden; **broker** ['pɔːnbroukə] Pfandleiher m; **shop** Leihhaus n.

pay [pei] 1. (Be)Zahlung f; Sold m, Lohn m; 2. [irr.] v/t. (be)zahlen; (be)lohnen; sich lohnen für; Ehre etc. erweisen; Besuch abstatten; ~ attention od. heed to achtgeben auf (acc.); ~ down bar bezahlen; ~ off j-n bezahlen u. entlassen; j-n voll auszahlen; v/i. zahlen; sich lohnen; ~ for (für) et. bezahlen; **able** ['peiəbl] zahlbar; fällig; **day** Zahltag m; **ee** **†** [pei'iː] Zahlungsempfänger m; **ing** ['peiiŋ] lohnend; **master** Zahlmeister m; **ment** ['peimənt] (Be)Zahlung f; Lohn m, Sold m; **off** Abrechnung f (a. fig.); Am. F Höhepunkt m; **roll** Lohnliste f.

pea **♀** [piː] Erbse f.

peace [piːs] Frieden m, Ruhe f; at ~ friedlich; **able** □ ['piːsəbl] friedliebend, friedlich; **ful** □ ['piːsful] friedlich; **maker** Friedensstifter(in).

peach **♀** [piːtʃ] Pfirsich(baum) m.

pea|cock orn. ['piːkɔk] Pfau(hahn) m; **hen** orn. ['piːhen] Pfauhenne f.

peak [piːk] Spitze f; Gipfel m; Mützen-Schirm m; attr. Spitzen..., Höchst...; **ed** [piːkt] spitz.

peal [piːl] 1. Geläut n; Glockenspiel n; Dröhnen n; **s** of laughter dröhnendes Gelächter; 2. erschallen (lassen); laut verkünden; dröhnen.

peanut ['piːnʌt] Erdnuß f.

pear **♀** [pεə] Birne f.

pearl [pəːl] 1. Perle f (a. fig.); attr. Perl(en)...; 2. tropfen, perlen; **y** ['pəːli] perlenartig.

peasant ['pezənt] 1. Bauer m; 2. bäuerlich; **ry** [.tri] Landvolk n.

peat [piːt] Torf m.

pebble ['pebl] Kiesel(stein) m.

peck [pek] 1. Viertelscheffel m (9,087 Liter); fig. Menge f; 2. pikken, hacken (at nach).

peculate ['pekjuleit] unterschlagen.

peculiar □ [pi'kjuːljə] eigen(tümlich); besonder; seltsam; **ity** [pikjuːli'æriti] Eigenheit f; Eigentümlichkeit f.

pecuniary [pi'kjuːnjəri] Geld...

pedagog|ics [pedə'gɔdʒiks] mst sg.

Pädagogik f; ~ue ['pedəgɔg] Pädagoge m; Lehrer m.

pedal ['pedl] 1. Pedal n; 2. Fuß...; 3. *Radfahren*: fahren, treten.

pedantic [pi'dæntik] (~ally) pedantisch.

peddle ['pedl] hausieren (mit); ~r *Am.* [~ə] = *pedlar.*

pedestal ['pedistl] Sockel m (*a. fig.*).

pedestrian [pi'destriən] 1. zu Fuß; nüchtern; 2. Fußgänger(in); ~ crossing Fußgängerübergang m.

pedigree ['pedigri:] Stammbaum m.

pedlar ['pedlə] Hausierer m.

peek [pi:k] 1. spähen, gucken, lugen; 2. flüchtiger Blick.

peel [pi:l] 1. Schale f; Rinde f; 2. a. ~ off v/t. (ab)schälen; *Kleid* abstreifen; v/i. sich (ab)schälen.

peep [pi:p] 1. verstohlener Blick, Piepen n; 2. (verstohlen) gucken; a. ~ out (hervor)gucken (*a. fig.*); piepen; ~hole ['pi:phoul] Guckloch n.

peer [piə] 1. spähen, lugen; ~ at angucken; 2. Gleiche(r m) f; *Pair* m; ~less □ ['piəlis] unvergleichlich.

peevish □ ['pi:viʃ] verdrießlich.

peg [peg] 1. Stöpsel m, Dübel m, Pflock m; *Kleider*-Haken m; ♪ Wirbel m; *Wäsche*-Klammer f; *fig.* Aufhänger m; take s.o. down a ~ or two j-n demütigen; 2. festpflöcken; *Grenze* abstecken; ~ away od. along F darauflosarbeiten; ~top ['pegtɔp] Kreisel m.

pelican *orn.* ['pelikən] Pelikan m.

pellet ['pelit] Kügelchen n; Pille f; Schrotkorn n.

pell-mell ['pel'mel] durcheinander.

pelt [pelt] 1. Fell n; † rohe Haut; 2. v/t. bewerfen; v/i. niederprasseln.

pelvis *anat.* ['pelvis] Becken n.

pen [pen] 1. (Schreib)Feder f; Hürde f; 2. schreiben; [*irr.*] einpferchen.

penal ['pi:nl] Straf...; strafbar; ~ code Strafgesetzbuch n; ~ servitude Zuchthausstrafe f; [pi:'nɔlaiz] bestrafen; ~ty ['penlti] Strafe f; *Sport*: Strafpunkt m; ~ area *Fußball*: Strafraum m; ~ kick *Fußball*: Freistoß m.

penance ['penəns] Buße f.

pence [pens] pl. von penny.

pencil ['pensl] 1. Bleistift m; 2. zeichnen; (mit Bleistift) anzeichnen od. anstreichen; *Augenbrauen* nachziehen; ~sharpener Bleistiftspitzer m.

pendant ['pendənt] Anhänger m.

pending ['pendiŋ] 1. ♫ schwebend; 2. prp. während; bis zu.

pendulum ['pendjuləm] Pendel n.

penetra|ble □ ['penitrəbl] durchdringbar; ~te [~reit] durchdringen; ergründen; eindringen (in *acc.*); vordringen (to bis zu); ~tion [peni-

'treiʃən] Durch-, Eindringen n; Scharfsinn m; ~tive □ ['penitrətiv] durchdringend (*a. fig.*); eindringlich; scharfsinnig.

pen-friend ['penfrend] Brieffreund (-in).

penguin *orn.* ['peŋgwin] Pinguin m.

penholder ['penhouldə] Federhalter m.

peninsula [pi'ninsjulə] Halbinsel f.

peniten|ce ['penitəns] Buße f, Reue f; ~t 1. □ reuig, bußfertig; 2. Büßer(in); ~tiary [peni'tenʃəri] Besserungsanstalt f; *Am.* Zuchthaus n.

pen|knife ['pennaif] Taschenmesser n; ~man Schönschreiber m; Schriftsteller m; ~name Schriftstellername m, Pseudonym n.

pennant ⚓ ['penənt] Wimpel m.

penniless □ ['penilis] ohne Geld.

penny ['peni], pl. mst pence [pens] (englischer) Penny (¹/₁₂ *Schilling*); *Am.* Cent m; Kleinigkeit f; ~weight *englisches* Pennygewicht (1¹/₂ *Gramm*).

pension ['penʃən] 1. Pension f, Ruhegehalt n; 2. oft ~ off pensionieren; ~er [~nəri, ~nə] Pensionär(in).

pensive □ ['pensiv] gedankenvoll.

pent [pent] pret. u. p.p. von pen 2; ~up aufgestaut (*Zorn etc.*).

Pentecost ['pentikɔst] Pfingsten n.

penthouse ['penthaus] Schutzdach n; Dachwohnung f auf e-m Hochhaus.

penu|rious □ [pi'njuəriəs] geizig; ~ry ['penjuri] Armut f; Mangel m.

people ['pi:pl] 1. Volk n, Nation f; coll. die Leute pl.; man; 2. bevölkern.

pepper ['pepə] 1. Pfeffer m; 2. pfeffern; ~mint ♣ Pfefferminze f; ~y □ [~əri] pfefferig; *fig.* hitzig.

per [pə:] per, durch, für; laut; je.

perambulat|e [pə'ræmbjuleit] (durch)wandern; bereisen; ~or ['præmbjuleitə] Kinderwagen m.

perceive [pə'si:v] (be)merken, wahrnehmen; empfinden; erkennen.

per cent [pə'sent] Prozent n.

percentage [pə'sentidʒ] Prozentsatz m; Prozente n/pl.; *fig.* Teil m.

percept|ible □ [pə'septəbl] wahrnehmbar; ~ion [pə'sepʃən] Wahrnehmung(svermögen n) f; Erkenntnis f; Auffassung(skraft) f.

perch [pə:tʃ] 1. *ichth.* Barsch m; Rute f (5,029 m); (Sitz)Stange f *für Vögel*; 2. (sich) setzen; sitzen.

perchance [pə'tʃɑ:ns] zufällig; vielleicht.

percolate ['pə:kəleit] durchtropfen, durchsickern (lassen); sickern.

percussion [pə:'kʌʃən] Schlag m; Erschütterung f; ⚕ Abklopfen n.

perdition [pə:'diʃən] Verderben n.

peregrination [perigri'neiʃən] Wanderschaft f; Wanderung f.

peremptory □ [pə'remptəri] bestimmt; zwingend; rechthaberisch.
perennial □ [pə'renjəl] dauernd; immerwährend; ⚇ perennierend.
perfect 1. ['pə:fikt] □ vollkommen; vollendet; gänzlich, völlig; 2. [~] a. ~ tense gr. Perfekt n; 3. [pə-'fekt] vervollkommnen; vollenden; ~ion [~kʃən] Vollendung f; Vollkommenheit f; fig. Gipfel m.
perfidious [pə:'fidiəs] treulos (to gegen), verräterisch.
perfidy ['pə:fidi] Treulosigkeit f.
perforate ['pə:fəreit] durchlöchern.
perforce [pə'fɔ:s] notgedrungen.
perform [pə'fɔ:m] verrichten; ausführen; tun; Pflicht etc. erfüllen; thea., ♪ aufführen, spielen, vortragen (a. v/i.); ~ance [~məns] Verrichtung f; thea. Aufführung f; Vortrag m; Leistung f; ~er [~mə] Vortragende(r m) f.
perfume 1. ['pə:fju:m] Wohlgeruch m; Parfüm n; 2. [pə'fju:m] parfümieren; ~ry [~məri] Parfümerie(n pl.) f.
perfunctory □ [pə'fʌŋktəri] mechanisch; oberflächlich.
perhaps [pə'hæps, præps] vielleicht.
peril ['peril] 1. Gefahr f; 2. gefährden; ~ous □ [~ləs] gefährlich.
period ['piəriəd] Periode f; Zeitraum m; gr. Punkt m; Satz m; (Unterrichts)Stunde f; mst ~s pl. ⚇ Periode f; ~ic [~piəri'ɔdik] periodisch; ~ical [~kəl] 1. □ periodisch; 2. Zeitschrift f.
perish ['periʃ] umkommen, zugrunde gehen; ~able □ [~ʃəbl] vergänglich; leicht verderblich; ~ing □ [~ʃiŋ] vernichtend, tödlich.
periwig ['periwig] Perücke f.
perjur|e ['pə:dʒə] v/i. ~ o.s. falsch schwören; ~y [~əri] Meineid m.
perk F [pə:k] v/i. mst ~ up selbstbewußt auftreten; sich wieder erholen; v/t. recken; ~ o.s. (up) sich putzen.
perky □ ['pə:ki] keck, dreist; flott.
perm F [pə:m] 1. Dauerwelle f; 2. j-m Dauerwellen machen.
permanen|ce ['pə:mənəns] Dauer f; ~t □ [~nt] dauernd, ständig; dauerhaft; Dauer...; ~ wave Dauerwelle f.
permea|ble □ ['pə:mjəbl] durchlässig; ~te ['pə:mieit] durchdringen; eindringen.
permissi|ble □ [pə'misəbl] zulässig; ~on [~ʃən] Erlaubnis f.
permit 1. [pə'mit] erlauben, gestatten; 2. ['pə:mit] Erlaubnis f, Genehmigung f; Passierschein m.
pernicious □ [pə:'niʃəs] verderblich; ⚇ bösartig.
perpendicular □ [pə:pən'dikjulə] senkrecht; aufrecht; steil.
perpetrate ['pə:pitreit] verüben.
perpetu|al □ [pə'petjuəl] fort-

während, ewig; ~ate [~ueit] verewigen.
perplex [pə'pleks] verwirren; ~ity [~siti] Verwirrung f.
perquisites ['pə:kwizits] pl. Nebeneinkünfte pl.
persecut|e ['pə:sikju:t] verfolgen; ~ion [pə:si'kju:ʃən] Verfolgung f; ~or ['pə:sikju:tə] Verfolger m.
persever|ance [pə:si'viərəns] Beharrlichkeit f, Ausdauer f; ~e [pə:-si'viə] beharren; aushalten.
persist [pə'sist] beharren (in auf dat.); ~ence, ~ency [~təns, ~si] Beharrlichkeit f; ~ent □ [~nt] beharrlich.
person ['pə:sn] Person f (a. gr.); Persönlichkeit f; thea. Rolle f; ~age [~nidʒ] Persönlichkeit f; thea. Charakter m; ~al □ [~nl] persönlich (a. gr.); attr. Personal...; Privat...; eigen; ~ality [pə:sə'næliti] Persönlichkeit f; personalities pl. persönliche Bemerkungen f/pl.; ~ate ['pə:səneit] darstellen; sich ausgeben für; ~ify [pə:'sɔnifai] verkörpern; ~nel [pə:sə'nel] Personal n.
perspective [pə'spektiv] Perspektive f; Ausblick m, Fernsicht f.
perspex ['pə:speks] Plexiglas n.
perspicuous □ [pə'spikjuəs] klar.
perspir|ation [pə:spə'reiʃən] Schwitzen n; Schweiß m; ~e [pəs-'paiə] (aus)schwitzen.
persua|de [pə'sweid] überreden; überzeugen; ~sion [~eiʒən] Überredung f; Überzeugung f; Glaube m; ~sive □ [~eisiv] überredend, überzeugend.   [weis.)
pert □ [pə:t] keck, vorlaut, nase-)
pertain [pə:'tein] (to) gehören (dat. od. zu); betreffen (acc.).
pertinacious □ [pə:ti'neiʃəs] hartnäckig, zäh.
pertinent □ ['pə:tinənt] sachdienlich, -gemäß; zur Sache gehörig.
perturb [pə'tə:b] beunruhigen; stören.
perus|al [pə'ru:zəl] sorgfältige Durchsicht; ~e [~u:z] durchlesen; prüfen.
pervade [pə'veid] durchdringen.
pervers|e □ [pə'və:s] verkehrt; ⚇ pervers; eigensinnig; vertrackt (Sache); ~ion [~ə:ʃən] Verdrehung f; Abkehr f; ~ity [~ə:siti] Verkehrtheit f; ⚇ Perversität f; Eigensinn m.
pervert 1. [pə'və:t] verdrehen; verführen; 2. ⚇ ['pə:və:t] perverser Mensch.
pessimism ['pesimizəm] Pessimismus m.
pest [pest] Pest f; Plage f; Schädling m; ~er ['pestə] belästigen.
pesti|ferous □ [pes'tifərəs] krankheiterregend; ~lence ['pestiləns] Seuche f, bsd. Pest f; ~lent [~nt] gefährlich; co. verdammt; ~lential

□ [pesti'lenʃəl] pestartig; verder-
benbringend.
pet [pet] 1. üble Laune; zahmes
Tier; Liebling m; 2. Lieblings...;
~ dog Schoßhund m; ~ name Kosename m; 3. (ver)hätscheln; knut-
schen.
petal ♀ ['petl] Blütenblatt n.
petition [pi'tiʃən] 1. Bitte f; Bitt-
schrift f, Eingabe f; 2. bitten, ersuchen; e-e Eingabe machen.
petrify ['petrifai] versteinern.
petrol mot. ['petrəl] Benzin n; ~
station Tankstelle f.
petticoat ['petikout] Unterrock m.
pettish □ ['petiʃ] launisch.
petty □ ['peti] klein, geringfügig.
petulant ['petjulənt] gereizt.
pew [pju:] Kirchensitz m, -bank f.
pewter ['pju:tə] Zinn(gefäße n/pl.) n.
phantasm ['fæntæzəm] Trugbild n.
phantom ['fæntəm] Phantom n,
Trugbild n; Gespenst n.
Pharisee ['færisi:] Pharisäer m.
pharmacy ['fɑːməsi] Pharmazie f;
Apotheke f.   [Phasen.)
phase [feiz] Phase f; ~d [feizd] in)
pheasant orn. ['feznt] Fasan m.
phenomen|on [fi'nɔminən], pl. ~a
[~nə] Phänomen n, Erscheinung f.
phial ['faiəl] Phiole f, Fläschchen n.
philander [fi'lændə] flirten.
philanthrop|ist   [fi'lænθrəpist]
Menschenfreund(in).
philolog|ist [fi'lɔlədʒist] Philolog|e
m, -in f; ~y [~dʒi] Philologie f.
philosoph|er [fi'lɔsəfə] Philosoph
m; ~ize [~faiz] philosophieren; ~y
[~fi] Philosophie f.
phlegm [flem] Schleim m; Phlegma n.
phone F [foun] s. telephone.
phonetics [fou'netiks] pl. Phonetik
f, Lautbildungslehre f.
phon(e)y Am. sl. ['founi] 1. Fälschung f; Schwindler m; 2. unecht.
phosphorus ['fɔsfərəs] Phosphor m.
photograph ['foutəgrɑːf] 1. Photographie f (Bild); 2. photographie-
ren; ~er [fə'tɔgrəfə] Photograph
(-in) m; ~y [~fi] Photographie f.
phrase [freiz] 1. (Rede)Wendung f,
Redensart f, Ausdruck m; 2. ausdrücken.
physic|al □ ['fizikəl] physisch; kör-
perlich; physikalisch; ~ education,
~ training Leibeserziehung f; ~ian
[fi'ziʃən] Arzt m; ~ist ['fizisist]
Physiker m; ~s [~iks] sg. Physik f.
physique [fi'zi:k] Körperbau m.
piano ['pjænou] Klavier n.
piazza [pi'ætsə] Piazza f, (Markt-)
Platz m; Am. große Veranda.
pick [pik] Auswahl f; = pickaxe;
2. auf-, wegnehmen; pflücken;
(herum)stochern; in der Nase bohren; abnagen; Schloß knacken;
Streit suchen; auswählen; (auf-)
picken; bestehlen; ~ out auswählen;

heraussuchen; ~ up aufreißen, aufbrechen; aufnehmen, auflesen;
sich e-e Fremdsprache aneignen; erfassen; (im Auto) mitnehmen, abholen; Täter ergreifen; gesund
werden; ~a-back ['pikəbæk]
huckepack; ~axe Spitzhacke f.
picket ['pikit] 1. Pfahl m; ✕ Feld-
wache f; Streikposten m; 2. ein-
pfählen; an e-n Pfahl binden; mit
Streikposten besetzen.
picking ['pikiŋ] Picken n, Pflücken
n; Abfall m; mst ~s pl. Nebenge-
winn m.
pickle ['pikl] 1. Pökel m; Einge-
pökelte(s) n, Pickles pl.; F mißliche
Lage; 2. (ein)pökeln; ~d herring
Salzhering m.
pick|lock ['piklɔk] Dietrich m;
~pocket Taschendieb m; ~up
Ansteigen n; Tonabnehmer m;
Kleinlieferwagen m; sl. Straßen-
bekanntschaft f.
picnic ['piknik] Picknick n.
pictorial [pik'tɔːriəl] 1. □ malerisch;
illustriert; 2. Illustrierte f.
picture ['piktʃə] 1. Bild n, Gemälde
n; et. Bildschönes; ~s pl. Kino n;
attr. Bilder...; put s.o. in the ~ j. ins
Bild setzen, j. informieren; 2. (aus-)
malen; sich et. ausmalen; ~ postcard Ansichtskarte f; ~sque
[piktʃə'resk] malerisch.
pie [pai] Pastete f; Obsttorte f.
piebald ['paibɔːld] (bunt)scheckig.
piece [pi:s] 1. Stück n; Geschütz n;
Gewehr n; Teil n e-s Services;
Schach- etc. Figur f; a ~ of advice
ein Rat; a ~ of news e-e Neuigkeit;
of a ~ gleichmäßig; give s.o. a ~ of
one's mind j-m gründlich die Meinung sagen; take to ~s zerlegen;
2. a. ~ up flicken, ausbessern; ~ together zs.-stellen, -setzen, -stücken,
-flicken; ~ out ausfüllen; ~meal
['pi:smi:l] stückweise; ~work Akkordarbeit f.
pieplant Am. ['paiplɑːnt] Rhabarber m.
pier [piə] Pfeiler m; Wellenbrecher
m; Pier m, f, Hafendamm m, Mole
f, Landungsbrücke f.
piety ['paiəti] Frömmigkeit f;
Pietät f.
pig [pig] Ferkel n; Schwein n.
pigeon ['pidʒin] Taube f; ~hole
1. Fach n; 2. in ein Fach legen.
pig|headed ['pig'hedid] dickköpfig;
~iron ['pigaiən] Roheisen n; ~skin
Schweinsleder n; ~sty Schweinestall m; ~tail (Haar)Zopf m.
pike [paik] ✕ Pike f, Spitze f;
ichth. Hecht m; Schlagbaum m;
gebührenpflichtige Straße.
pile [pail] 1. (Scheiter)Haufen m;
Stoß m (Holz); großes Gebäude;
⚡ Batterie f; Pfahl m; Haar n;

Noppe f; ~s pl. ✻ Hämorrhoiden f|pl.; (atomic) ~ phys. Atommeiler m, Reaktor m; 2. oft ~ up, ~ on auf-, anhäufen, aufschichten.

pilfer ['pilfə] mausen, stibitzen.

pilgrim ['pilgrim] Pilger m; ~age [~midʒ] Pilgerfahrt f.

pill [pil] Pille f.

pillage ['pilidʒ] 1. Plünderung f; 2. plündern.

pillar ['pilə] Pfeiler m, Ständer m; Säule f; ~box Briefkasten m.

pillion mot. ['piljən] Soziussitz m.

pillory ['piləri] 1. Pranger m; 2. an den Pranger stellen; anprangern.

pillow ['pilou] (Kopf)Kissen n; ~case, ~slip (Kissen)Bezug m.

pilot ['pailət] 1. ✈ Pilot m; ⚓ Lotse m; fig. Führer m; 2. lotsen, steuern; ~balloon Versuchsballon m.

pimp [pimp] 1. Kuppler(in); 2. kuppeln.

pin [pin] 1. (Steck-, Krawatten-, Hut- etc.)Nadel f; Reißnagel m; Pflock m; ⚙ Wirbel m; Kegel m; 2. (an)heften; befestigen; fig. festnageln.

pinafore ['pinəfɔ:] Schürze f.

pincers ['pinsəz] pl. Kneifzange f.

pinch [pintʃ] 1. Kniff m; Prise f (Tabak etc.); Druck m, Not f; 2. v/t. kneifen, zwicken; F klauen; v/i. drücken; in Not sein; knausern.

pinch-hit Am. ['pintʃhit] einspringen (for für).

pincushion ['pinkuʃin] Nadelkissen n.

pine [pain] 1. ♣ Kiefer f, Föhre f; 2. sich abhärmen; sich sehnen, schmachten; ~apple ♣ ['painæpl] Ananas f; ~cone Kiefernzapfen m.

pinion ['pinjən] 1. Flügel(spitze f) m; Schwungfeder f; ⊕ Ritzel n (Antriebsrad); 2. die Flügel beschneiden (dat.); fig. fesseln.

pink [piŋk] 1. ♣ Nelke f; Rosa n; fig. Gipfel m; 2. rosa(farben).

pin-money ['pinmʌni] Nadelgeld n.

pinnacle ['pinəkl] △ Zinne f, Spitztürmchen n; (Berg)Spitze f; fig. Gipfel m.

pint [paint] Pinte f (0,57 od. Am. 0,47 Liter).

pioneer [paiə'niə] 1. Pionier m (a. ✗); 2. den Weg bahnen (für).

pious □ ['paiəs] fromm, religiös; pflichtgetreu.

pip [pip] vet. Pips m; sl. miese Laune; Obstkern m; Auge n auf Würfeln etc.; ✗ Stern m (Rangabzeichen).

pipe [paip] 1. Rohr n, Röhre f; Pfeife f (a. ♪); Flöte f; Lied n e-s Vogels; Luftröhre f; Pipe f (Weinfaß = 477,3 Liter); 2. pfeifen; quieken; ~layer ['paipleiə] Rohrleger m; Am. pol. Drahtzieher m.

~line Ölleitung f, Pipeline f; ~r ['paipə] Pfeifer m.

piping ['paipiŋ] 1. pfeifend; schrill (Stimme); ~ hot siedend heiß; 2. Rohrnetz n; Schneiderei: Paspel f.

piquant □ ['pi:kənt] pikant.

pique [pi:k] 1. Groll m; 2. j-n reizen; ~ o.s. on sich brüsten mit.

pira|cy ['paiərəsi] Seeräuberei f; Raubdruck m von Büchern; ~te [~rit] 1. Seeräuber(schiff n) m; Raubdrucker m; 2. unerlaubt nachdrucken.

pistol ['pistl] Pistole f.

piston ⊕ ['pistən] Kolben m; ~rod Kolbenstange f; ~stroke Kolbenhub m.

pit [pit] 1. Grube f (a. ✗, anat.); ♪ Miete f; thea. Parterre n; Pockennarbe f; (Tier)Falle f; Am. Börse: Maklerstand m; Am. Obst-Stein m; 2. ♪ einmieten; mit Narben bedecken.

pitch [pitʃ] 1. Pech n; Stand(platz) m; Tonhöhe f; Grad m, Stufe f; Steigung f, Neigung f; Wurf m; ⚓ Stampfen n; 2. v/t. werfen; schleudern; Zelt etc. aufschlagen; ♪ stimmen (a. fig.); ~ too high fig. Ziel etc. zu hoch stecken; v/i. ✗ (sich) lagern; fallen; ⚓ stampfen; ~ into F herfallen über (acc.).

pitcher ['pitʃə] Krug m.

pitchfork ['pitʃfɔ:k] Heu-, Mistgabel f; ♪ Stimmgabel f.

piteous □ ['pitiəs] kläglich.

pitfall ['pitfɔ:l] Fallgrube f, Falle f.

pith [piθ] Mark n; fig. Kern m; Kraft f; ~y □ ['piθi] markig, kernig.

pitiable □ ['pitiəbl] erbärmlich.

pitiful □ ['pitiful] mitleidig; erbärmlich, jämmerlich (a. contp.).

pitiless □ ['pitilis] unbarmherzig.

pittance ['pitəns] Hungerlohn m.

pity ['piti] 1. Mitleid n (on mit); it is a ~ es ist schade; 2. bemitleiden.

pivot ['pivət] 1. ⊕ Zapfen m; (Tür-)Angel f; fig. Drehpunkt m; 2. sich drehen (on, upon um). [verrückt.]

pixilated Am. F ['piksileitid] leicht

placable □ ['plækəbl] versöhnlich.

placard ['plæka:d] 1. Plakat n; 2. anschlagen; mit e-m Plakat bekleben.

place [pleis] 1. Platz m; Ort m; Stadt f; Stelle f; Stätte f; Stellung f; Aufgabe f; Anwesen n, Haus n, Wohnung f; ~ of delivery ✝ Erfüllungsort m; give ~ to j-m Platz machen; in ~ of an Stelle (gen.); out of ~ fehl am Platz; 2. stellen, legen, setzen; j-n anstellen; Auftrag erteilen; I can't place him fig. ich weiß nicht, wo ich ihn hintun soll (identifizieren).

placid □ ['plæsid] sanft; ruhig.

plagiar|ism ['pleidʒjərizəm] Plagiat n; ~ize [~raiz] abschreiben.

plague [pleig] 1. Plage *f*; Seuche *f*; Pest *f*; 2. plagen, quälen.

plaice *ichth.* [pleis] Scholle *f*.

plaid [plæd] *schottisches* Plaid.

plain [plein] 1. □ flach, eben; klar; deutlich; rein; einfach, schlicht; unscheinbar; offen, ehrlich; einfarbig; 2. *adv.* klar, deutlich; 3. Ebene *f*, Fläche *f*; *bsd. Am.* Prärie *f*; ~clothes man ['plein-klouðʒ mən] Geheimpolizist *m*; ~ dealing ehrliche Handlungsweise; ~dealing ehrlich.

plainsman ['pleinzmən] Flachlandbewohner *m*; *Am.* Präriebewohner *m*.

plaint|iff ⚖ ['pleintif] Kläger(in); ~ive □ [~iv] traurig, klagend.

plait [plæt, *Am.* pleit] 1. *Haar- etc.* Flechte *f*; Zopf *m*; 2. flechten.

plan [plæn] 1. Plan *m*; 2. e-n Plan machen von *od.* zu; *fig.* planen.

plane [plein] 1. flach, eben; 2. Ebene *f*, Fläche *f*; ✈ Tragfläche *f*; Flugzeug *n*; *fig.* Stufe *f*; ⊕ Hobel *m*; 3. ebnen; (ab)hobeln; ✈ fliegen.

plank [plæŋk] 1. Planke *f*, Bohle *f*, Diele *f*; *Am. pol.* Programmpunkt *m*; 2. dielen; verschalen; ~ down *sl., Am.* F Geld auf den Tisch legen.

plant [plɑːnt] 1. Pflanze *f*; ⊕ Anlage *f*; Fabrik *f*; 2. (an-, ein)pflanzen (*a. fig.*); (auf)stellen; anlegen; *Schlag* verpassen; bepflanzen; besiedeln; ~ation [plæn'teiʃən] Pflanzung *f* (*a. fig.*); Plantage *f*; Besiedelung *f*; ~er ['plɑːntə] Pflanzer *m*.

plaque [plɑːk] Platte *f*; Gedenktafel *f*.

plash [plæʃ] platschen.

plaster ['plɑːstə] 1. *pharm.* Pflaster *n*; ⊕ Putz *m*; *mst* ~ of Paris Gips *m*, Stuck *m*; 2. bepflastern; verputzen.

plastic ['plæstik] 1. (~ally) plastisch; Plastik...; 2. *oft* ~s *pl.* Plastik(material) *n*, Kunststoff *m*.

plat [plæt] *s. plait; s. plot* 1.

plate [pleit] 1. *allg.* Platte *f*; Bild-Tafel *f*; Schild *n*; *Kupfer-*Stich *m*; Tafelsilber *n*; Teller *m*; *Am. Baseball:* (Schlag)Mal *n*; ⊕ Grobblech *n*; 2. plattieren; ⚔, ⚓ panzern.

platform ['plætfɔːm] Plattform *f*; *geogr.* Hochebene *f*; ⬛ Bahnsteig *m*; *Am. bsd.* Plattform *f am Wagenende*; Rednerbühne *f*; *pol.* Parteiprogramm *n*; *bsd. Am. pol.* Aktionsprogramm *n im Wahlkampf.*

platinum *min.* ['plætinəm] Platin *n*.

platitude *fig.* ['plætitjuːd] Plattheit *f*.

platoon ⚔ [plə'tuːn] Zug *m*.

plat(t)en ['plætən] (Schreibmaschinen)Walze *f*.

platter ['plætə] (Servier)Platte *f*.

plaudit ['plɔːdit] Beifall *m*.

plausible □ ['plɔːzəbl] glaubhaft.

play [plei] 1. Spiel *n*; Schauspiel *n*; ⊕ Spiel *n*, Gang *m*; Spielraum *m*; 2. spielen; ⊕ laufen; ~ upon einwirken auf (*acc.*); ~ off *fig.* ausspielen (*against* gegen); ~ed out erledigt; ~bill ['pleibil] Theaterzettel *m*; ~book *thea.* Textbuch *n*; ~boy Playboy *m*; ~er ['pleiə] (Schau)Spieler(in); ~piano elektrisches Klavier; ~fellow Spielgefährt|e *m*, -in *f*; ~ful □ [~ful] spielerisch, scherzhaft; ~goer ['pleigouə] Theaterbesucher(in); ~ground Spielplatz *m*; Schulhof *m*; ~house Schauspielhaus *n*; *Am.* Miniaturhaus *n für Kinder*; ~mate *s. playfellow*; ~thing Spielzeug *n*; ~wright Bühnenautor *m*, Dramatiker *m*.

plea [pliː] ⚖ Einspruch *m*; Ausrede *f*; Gesuch *n*; *on the* ~ of *od. that* unter dem Vorwand (*gen.*) *od.* daß.

plead [pliːd] *v/i.* plädieren; ~ for für *j-n* sprechen; sich einsetzen für; ~ guilty sich schuldig bekennen; *v/t. Sache* vertreten; als Beweis anführen; ~er ⚖ ['pliːdə] Verteidiger *m*; ~ing ⚖ [~diŋ] Schriftsatz *m*.

pleasant □ ['plezənt] angenehm; erfreulich; ~ry [~tri] Scherz *m*, Spaß *m*.

please [pliːz] *v/i.* gefallen; belieben; *if you* ~ *iro.* stellen Sie sich vor; ~ come in! bitte, treten Sie ein!; *v/t. j-m* gefallen, angenehm sein; befriedigen; ~ yourself tun Sie, was Ihnen gefällt; be ~d to *od. e.t.* gerne tun; be ~d with Vergnügen haben an (*dat.*); ~d erfreut; zufrieden.

pleasing □ ['pliːziŋ] angenehm.

pleasure ['pleʒə] Vergnügen *n*, Freude *f*; Belieben *n*; *attr.* Vergnügungs...; *at* ~ nach Belieben; ~-ground (Vergnügungs)Park *m*.

pleat [pliːt] 1. (Plissee-)Falte *f*; 2. fälteln, plissieren.

pledge [pledʒ] 1. Pfand *n*; Zutrinken *n*; Gelöbnis *n*; 2. verpfänden; *j-m* zutrinken; he ~d himself er gelobte.

plenary ['pliːnəri] Voll...

plenipotentiary [plenipə'tenʃəri] Bevollmächtigte(r *m*) *f*. [reichlich.\

plenteous □ *poet.* ['plentjəs] voll,\

plentiful □ ['plentiful] reichlich.

plenty ['plenti] 1. Fülle *f*, Überfluß *m*; ~ of reichlich; 2. F reichlich.

pliable □ ['plaiəbl] biegsam; *fig.* geschmeidig, nachgiebig.

pliancy ['plaiənsi] Biegsamkeit *f*.

pliers ['plaiəz] *pl.* (*a pair of* ~ *pl.* eine) (Draht-, Kombi)Zange.

plight [plait] 1. *Ehre, Wort* verpfänden; verloben; 2. Gelöbnis *n*; Zustand *m*, (Not)Lage *f*.

plod [plɔd] *a.* ~ along, ~ on sich dahinschleppen; sich plagen, schuften.

plot [plɔt] **1.** Platz *m*; Parzelle *f*; Plan *m*; Komplott *n*, Anschlag *m*; Intrige *f*; Handlung *f e-s Dramas etc.*; **2.** *v/t.* aufzeichnen; planen, anzetteln; *v/i.* intrigieren.

plough, *Am. mst.* **plow** [plau] **1.** Pflug *m*; **2.** pflügen; (*a. fig.*) furchen; **~man** ['plaumən] Pflüger *m*; **~share** ['plauʃɛə] Pflugschar *f*.

pluck [plʌk] **1.** Mut *m*, Schneid *m*, *f*; Innereien *f/pl.*; Zug *m*, Ruck *m*; **2.** pflücken; *Vogel* rupfen (*a. fig.*); reißen; **~** *at* zerren an; **~** *up courage* Mut fassen; **~y** F □ ['plʌki] mutig.

plug [plʌg] **1.** Pflock *m*; Dübel *m*; Stöpsel *m*; ⚡ Stecker *m*; Zahn-Plombe *f*; Priem *m* (*Tabak*); *Am. Radio:* Reklamehinweis *m*; alter Gaul; **~** *socket* Steckdose *f*; **2.** *v/t.* zu-, verstopfen; *Zahn* plombieren; stöpseln; *Am.* F *im Rundfunk etc.* Reklame machen für *et.*

plum [plʌm] Pflaume *f*; Rosine *f* (*a. fig.*).

plumage ['plu:midʒ] Gefieder *n*.

plumb [plʌm] **1.** lotrecht; gerade; richtig; **2.** (Blei)Lot *n*; **3.** *v/t.* lotrecht machen; loten; sondieren (*a. fig.*); F Wasser- od. Gasleitungen legen in; *v/i.* F als Rohrleger arbeiten; **~er** ['plʌmə] Klempner *m*, Installateur *m*; **~ing** [‚miŋ] Klempnerarbeit *f*; Rohrleitungen *f/pl.*

plume [plu:m] **1.** Feder *f*; Federbusch *m*; **2.** mit Federn schmücken; *die Federn* putzen; **~** *o.s. on* sich brüsten mit.

plummet ['plʌmit] Senkblei *n*.

plump [plʌmp] **1.** *adj.* drall, prall, mollig; F □ glatt (*Absage etc.*); **2.**(hin)plumpsen (lassen); **3.**Plumps *m*; **4.** F *adv.* geradewegs.

plum pudding ['plʌm'pudiŋ] Plumpudding *m*.

plunder ['plʌndə] **1.** Plünderung *f*; Raub *m*, Beute *f*; **2.** plündern.

plunge [plʌndʒ] **1.** (Unter)Tauchen *n*; (Kopf)Sprung *m*; Sturz *m*; *make od. take the* **~** den entscheidenden Schritt tun; **2.** (unter-) tauchen; (sich) stürzen (*into* in *acc.*); *Schwert etc.* stoßen; ⚓ stampfen.

plunk [plʌŋk] *v/t. Saite* zupfen; *et.* hinplumpsen lassen, hinwerfen; *v/i.* (hin)plumpsen, fallen.

pluperfect *gr.* ['plu:'pə:fikt] Plusquamperfekt *n*.

plural *gr.* ['pluərəl] Plural *m*, Mehrzahl *f*; **~ity** [plua'ræliti] Vielheit *f*, Mehrheit *f*; Mehrzahl *f*.

plus [plʌs] **1.** *prp.* plus; **2.** *adj.* positiv; **3.** Plus *n*; Mehr *n*.

plush [plʌʃ] Plüsch *m*.

ply [plai] **1.** Lage *f Tuch etc.*; Strähne *f*; *fig.* Neigung *f*; **2.** *v/t.* fleißig anwenden; *j-m* zusetzen, *j-n* überhäufen; *v/i. regelmäßig* fahren; **~wood** ['plaiwud] Sperrholz *n*.

pneumatic [nju(:)'mætik] **1.** (**~ally**) Luft...; pneumatisch; **2.** Luftreifen *m*.

pneumonia ❦ [nju(:)'mounjə] Lungenentzündung *f*.

poach [poutʃ] wildern; *Erde* zertreten; **~ed eggs** *pl.* verlorene Eier *n/pl.*

poacher ['poutʃə] Wilddieb *m*.

pock ❦ [pɔk] Pocke *f*, Blatter *f*.

pocket ['pɔkit] **1.** Tasche *f*; ⚒ Luft-Loch *n*; **2.** einstecken (*a. fig.*); *Am. pol. Gesetzesvorlage* nicht unterschreiben; *Gefühl* unterdrücken; **3.** Taschen...; **~book** Notizbuch *n*; Brieftasche *f*; *Am.* Geldbeutel *m*; Taschenbuch *n*.

pod ♀ [pɔd] Hülse *f*, Schale *f*, Schote *f*.

poem ['pouim] Gedicht *n*.

poet ['pouit] Dichter *m*; **~ess** [‚tis] Dichterin *f*; **~ic(al)** □ [pou'etik(əl)] dichterisch; **~ics** [‚ks] *sg.* Poetik *f*; **~ry** ['pouitri] Dichtkunst *f*; Dichtung *f*, *coll.* Dichtungen *f/pl.*

poignan|cy ['pɔinənsi] Schärfe *f*; **~t** [‚nt] scharf; *fig.* eindringlich.

point [pɔint] **1.** Spitze *f*; Pointe *f*; Landspitze *f*; *gr.*, ⅍, *phys. etc.* Punkt *m*; Fleck *m*, Stelle *f*; ⚓ Kompaßstrich *m*; Auge *n auf Karten etc.*; Grad *m*; (springender) Punkt; Zweck *m*; *fig.* Eigenschaft *f*; **~s** *pl.* ⬤ Weichen *f/pl.*; **~** *of view* Stand-, Gesichtspunkt *m*; *the* **~** *is that ...* die Sache ist die, daß ...; *make a* **~** *of s.th.* auf *et.* bestehen; *in* **~** *of* in Hinsicht auf (*acc.*); *off od. beside the* **~** nicht zur Sache (gehörig); *on the* **~** *of ger.* im Begriff zu *inf.*; *win on* **~s** nach Punkten siegen; *to the* **~** zur Sache (gehörig); **2.** *v/t.* (zu)spitzen; *oft* **~** *out* zeigen, hinweisen auf (*acc.*); punktieren; **~** *at Waffe etc.* richten auf (*acc.*); *v/i.* **~** *at* weisen auf (*acc.*); **~** *to* nach *e-r Richtung* weisen; **~ed** □ ['pɔintid] spitz(ig), Spitz...; *fig.* scharf; **~er** [‚tə] Zeiger *m*; Zeigestock *m*; Hühnerhund *m*; **~less** [‚tlis] stumpf; witzlos; zwecklos.

poise [pɔiz] **1.** Gleichgewicht *n*; Haltung *f*; **2.** *v/t.* im Gleichgewicht erhalten; *Kopf etc.* tragen, halten; *v/i.* schweben.

poison ['pɔizn] **1.** Gift *n*; **2.** vergiften; **~ous** □ [‚nəs] giftig (*a. fig.*).

poke [pouk] **1.** Stoß *m*, Puff *m*; **2.** *v/t.* stoßen; schüren; *Nase etc. in et.* stecken; *~ fun at* sich über *j-n* lustig machen; *v/i.* stoßen; stochern.

poker ['poukə] Feuerhaken *m*.

poky ['pouki] eng; schäbig; erbärmlich. [*bär.*]

polar ['poulə] polar; **~** *bear* Eisbär

Pole¹ [poul] Pole *m*, Polin *f*.

pole² [‚] Pol *m*; Stange *f*, Mast *m*; Deichsel *f*; (Sprung)Stab *m*.

polecat zo. ['poulkæt] Iltis m; Am. Skunk m.

polemic [pɔ'lemik], a. **~al** □ [~kəl] polemisch; feindselig.

pole-star ['poulstɑ:] Polarstern m; fig. Leitstern m.

police [pɔ'li:s] 1. Polizei f; 2. überwachen; **~man** Polizist m; **~office** Polizeipräsidium n; **~officer** Polizeibeamte(r) m, Polizist m; **~station** Polizeiwache f.

policy ['pɔlisi] Politik f; (Welt-) Klugheit f; Police f; Am. Zahlenlotto n.

polio(myelitis) ♋ ['pouliou(maiɔ-'laitis)] spinale Kinderlähmung.

Polish¹ ['pouliʃ] polnisch.

polish² ['pɔliʃ] 1. Politur f; fig. Schliff m; 2. polieren; fig. verfeinern.

polite □ [pɔ'lait] artig, höflich; fein; **~ness** [~tnis] Höflichkeit f.

politic □ ['pɔlitik] politisch; schlau; **~al** □ [pɔ'litikəl] politisch; staatlich; Staats..; **~ian** [pɔli'tiʃən] Politiker m; **~s** ['pɔlitiks] oft sg. Staatswissenschaft f, Politik f.

polka ['pɔlkə] Polka f; **~ dot** Am. Punktmuster n auf Stoff.

poll [poul] 1. Wählerliste f; Stimmenzählung f; Wahl f; Stimmenzahl f; Umfrage f; co. Kopf m; 2. v/t. Stimmen erhalten; v/i. wählen; **~book** ['poulbuk] Wählerliste f.

pollen ['pɔlin] Blütenstaub m.

polling-district ['pouliŋdistrikt] Wahlbezirk m.

poll-tax ['poultæks] Kopfsteuer f.

pollute [pɔ'lu:t] beschmutzen, beflecken; entweihen.

polyp(e) zo. ['pɔlip], **~us** ♋ [~pəs] Polyp m.

pommel ['pʌml] 1. Degen-, Sattel-Knopf m; 2. knuffen, schlagen.

pomp [pɔmp] Pomp m, Gepränge n.

pompous □ ['pɔmpəs] prunkvoll; hochtrabend; pompös.

pond [pɔnd] Teich m, Weiher m.

ponder ['pɔndə] v/t. erwägen; v/i. nachdenken; **~able** [~ərəbl] wägbar; **~ous** □ [~rəs] schwer(fällig).

pontiff ['pɔntif] Hohepriester m; Papst m.

pontoon ⚓ [pɔn'tu:n] Ponton m; **~bridge** Schiffsbrücke f.

pony ['pouni] Pony n, Pferdchen n.

poodle ['pu:dl] Pudel m.

pool [pu:l] 1. Teich m; Pfütze f, Lache f; (Schwimm)Becken n; (Spiel)Einsatz m; † Ring m, Kartell n; **~ room** Am. Billardspielhalle f; Wettannahmestelle f; 2. † zu e-m Ring vereinigen; Gelder zs.-werfen.

poop ⚓ [pu:p] Heck n; Achterhütte f.

poor □ [puə] arm(selig); dürftig; schlecht; **~house** ['puəhaus] Armenhaus n; **~law** ᵗ⸝ᵗ Armenrecht

n; **~ly** [~li] 1. adj. unpäßlich; 2. adv. dürftig; **~ness** ['puənis] Armut f.

pop¹ [pɔp] 1. Knall m; F Sprudel m; F Schampus m; 2. v/t. knallen lassen; Am. Mais rösten; schnell wohin tun, stecken; v/i. puffen, knallen; mit adv. huschen; **~ in** hereinplatzen.

pop² F [~] 1. populär, beliebt; 2. Schlager m; volkstümliche Musik.

pop³ Am. F [~] Papa m, alter Herr.

popcorn Am. ['pɔpkɔ:n] Puffmais m.

pope [poup] Papst m.

poplar ♀ ['pɔplə] Pappel f.

poppy ♀ ['pɔpi] Mohn m; **~cock** Am. F Quatsch m.

popu|lace ['pɔpjuləs] Pöbel m; **~lar** □ [~lə] Volks...; volkstümlich, populär; **~larity** [pɔpju'læriti] Popularität f.

populat|e ['pɔpjuleit] bevölkern; **~ion** [pɔpju'leiʃən] Bevölkerung f.

populous □ ['pɔpjuləs] volkreich.

porcelain ['pɔ:slin] Porzellan n.

porch [pɔ:tʃ] Vorhalle f, Portal n; Am. Veranda f.

porcupine zo. ['pɔ:kjupain] Stachelschwein n.

pore [pɔ:] 1. Pore f; 2. fig. brüten.

pork [pɔ:k] Schweinefleisch n; **~barrel** Am. sl. ['pɔ:kbærəl] politisch berechnete Geldzuwendung der Regierung; **~y** F ['pɔ:ki] 1. fett, dick; 2. Am. = porcupine.

porous □ ['pɔ:rəs] porös.

porpoise ichth. ['pɔ:pəs] Tümmler m.

porridge ['pɔridʒ] Haferbrei m.

port [pɔ:t] 1. Hafen m; ⚓ (Pfort-, Lade)Luke f; ⚓ Backbord n; Portwein m; 2. ⚓ das Ruder nach der Backbordseite umlegen.

portable ['pɔ:təbl] transportabel.

portal ['pɔ:tl] Portal n, Tor n.

portend [pɔ:'tend] vorbedeuten.

portent ['pɔ:tent] (bsd. üble) Vorbedeutung; Wunder n; **~ous** □ [pɔ:'tentəs] unheilvoll; wunderbar.

porter ['pɔ:tə] Pförtner m; (Gepäck)Träger m; Porterbier n.

portion ['pɔ:ʃən] 1. (An)Teil m; Portion f Essen; Erbteil n; Aussteuer f; fig. Los n; 2. teilen; ausstatten.

portly ['pɔ:tli] stattlich.

portmanteau [pɔ:t'mæntou] Handkoffer m. [nis n.]

portrait ['pɔ:trit] Porträt n, Bild-)

portray [pɔ:'trei] (ab)malen, porträtieren; schildern; **~al** [~eiəl] Porträtieren n; Schilderung f.

pose [pouz] 1. Pose f; 2. (sich) in Positur setzen; F sich hinstellen (as als); Frage aufwerfen.

posh sl. [pɔʃ] schick, erstklassig.

position [pɔ'ziʃən] Lage f, Stellung f (a. fig.); Stand m; fig. Standpunkt m.

positive ['pozɔtiv] 1. ☐ bestimmt, ausdrücklich; feststehend, sicher; unbedingt; positiv; überzeugt; rechthaberisch; 2. *das* Bestimmte; *gr.* Positiv *m*; *phot.* Positiv *n*.

possess [pə'zes] besitzen; beherrschen; *fig.* erfüllen; ~ *o.s. of et.* in Besitz nehmen; ~ed besessen; ~ion [~eʃən] Besitz *m*; *fig.* Besessenheit *f*; ~ive *gr.* [~esiv] 1. ☐ besitzanzeigend; ~ *case* Genitiv *m*; 2. Possessivpronomen *n*, besitzanzeigendes Fürwort; Genitiv *m*; ~or [~sə] Besitzer *m*.

possib|ility [posə'biliti] Möglichkeit *f*; ~le ['posəbl] möglich; ~ly [~li] möglicherweise, vielleicht; *if I* ~ *can* wenn ich irgend kann.

post [poust] 1. Pfosten *m*; Posten *m*; Stelle *f*, Amt *n*; Post *f*; ~ *exchange Am.* ✕ Einkaufsstelle *f*; 2. *v/t.* Plakat *etc.* anschlagen; postieren; eintragen; zur Post geben; per Post senden; ~ *up j-n* informieren; *v/i.* (dahin)eilen.

postage ['poustidʒ] Porto *n*; ~ **stamp** Briefmarke *f*.

postal ☐ ['poustəl] 1. postalisch; Post...; ~ *order* Postanweisung *f*; 2. *a.* ~ **card** *Am.* Postkarte *f*.

postcard ['poustka:d] Postkarte *f*.

poster ['poustə] Plakat *n*, Anschlag *m*.

posterior [pos'tiəriə] 1. ☐ später (*to* als); hinter; 2. Hinterteil *n*.

posterity [pos'teriti] Nachwelt *f*; Nachkommenschaft *f*.

post-free ['poust'fri:] portofrei.

post-graduate ['poust'grædjuit] 1. nach beendigter Studienzeit; 2. Doktorand *m*.

post-haste ['poust'heist] eilig(st).

posthumous ☐ ['postjuməs] nachgeboren; hinterlassen.

post|man ['poustmən] Briefträger *m*; ~**mark** 1. Poststempel *m*; 2. abstempeln; ~**master** Postamtsvorsteher *m*.

post-mortem ['poust'mɔ:tem] 1. nach dem Tode; 2. Leichenschau *f*.

post|(-)office ['poustofis] Postamt *n*; ~ *box* Post(schließ)fach *n*; ~ **paid** frankiert.

postpone [poust'poun] ver-, aufschieben; ~**ment** [~nmənt] Aufschub *m*. [tum *n.*]

postscript ['poustskript] Postskrip-/

postulate 1. ['postjulit] Forderung *f*; 2. [~leit] fordern; (als gegeben) voraussetzen.

posture ['postʃə] 1. Stellung *f*, Haltung *f des Körpers*; 2. (sich) zurechtstellen; posieren.

post-war ['poust'wɔ:] Nachkriegs...

posy ['pouzi] Blumenstrauß *m*.

pot [pot] 1. Topf *m*; Kanne *f*; Tiegel *m*; 2. in e-n Topf tun; einlegen.

potation [pou'teiʃən] *mst* ~*spl.* Trinken *n*, Zecherei *f*; Trunk *m*.

potato [pə'teitou], *pl.* ~**es** Kartoffel *f*.

pot-belly ['potbeli] Schmerbauch *m*.

poten|cy ['poutənsi] Macht *f*; Stärke *f*; ~**t** [~nt] mächtig; stark; ~**tial** [po'tenʃəl] 1. potentiell; möglich; 2. Leistungsfähigkeit *f*.

pother ['poðə] Aufregung *f*.

pot|-herb ['pothə:b] Küchenkraut *n*; ~**-house** Kneipe *f*.

potion ['pouʃən] (Arznei)Trank *m*.

potter[1] ['potə]: ~ *about* herumwerkeln.

potter[2] [~] Töpfer *m*; ~**y** [~əri] Töpferei *f*; Töpferware(n *pl.*) *f*.

pouch [pautʃ] 1. Tasche *f*; Beutel *m*; 2. einstecken; (sich) beuteln.

poulterer ['poultərə] Geflügelhändler *m*.

poultice ☞ ['poultis] Packung *f*.

poultry ['poultri] Geflügel *n*.

pounce [pauns] 1. Stoß *m*, Sprung *m*; 2. sich stürzen (*on, upon* auf *acc.*).

pound [paund] 1. Pfund *n*; ~ (*sterling*) Pfund *n* Sterling (*abbr.* £ = 20 *shillings*); Pfandstall *m*; Tierasyl *n*; 2. (zer)stoßen; stampfen; schlagen.

pounder ['paundə] ...pfünder *m*.

pour [pɔ:] *v/t.* gießen, schütten; ~ *out Getränk* eingießen; *v/i.* sich ergießen, strömen; *it never rains but it* ~*s fig.* ein Unglück kommt selten allein.

pout [paut] 1. Schmollen *n*; 2. *v/t.* Lippen aufwerfen; *v/i.* schmollen.

poverty ['povəti] Armut *f*.

powder ['paudə] 1. Pulver *n*; Puder *m*; 2. pulverisieren; (sich) pudern; bestreuen; ~**-box** Puderdose *f*.

power ['pauə] Kraft *f*; Macht *f*, Gewalt *f*; ⚡ Vollmacht *f*; ⚖ Potenz *f*; *in* ~ an der Macht, im Amt; ~**-current** Starkstrom *m*; ~**ful** ☐ ['pauəful] mächtig, kräftig; wirksam; ~**less** ['pauəlis] macht-, kraftlos; ~**plant** *s. power-station*; **politics** *oft sg.* Machtpolitik *f*; ~**station** Kraftwerk *n*.

powwow ['pauwau] Medizinmann *m*; *Am.* F Versammlung *f*.

practica|ble ☐ ['præktikəbl] ausführbar; gangbar (*Weg*); brauchbar; ~**l** ☐ [~əl] praktisch; tatsächlich; eigentlich; sachlich; ~ *joke* Schabernack *m*; ~**lly** [~li] so gut wie.

practice ['præktis] 1. Praxis *f*; Übung *f*; Gewohnheit *f*; Brauch *m*; Praktik *f*; *put into* ~ in die Praxis umsetzen; 2. *Am.* = **practise**.

practise [~] *v/t.* in die Praxis umsetzen; ausüben; betreiben; üben; *v/i.* (sich) üben; praktizieren; ~ *upon j-s Schwäche* ausnutzen; ~**d** geübt (*P.*).

practitioner [præk'tiʃnə] a. general ~ praktischer Arzt; Rechtsanwalt m.

prairie Am. ['prɛəri] Grasebene f; Prärie f; ~-schooner Am. Planwagen m.

praise [preiz] 1. Preis m, Lob n; 2. loben, preisen.

praiseworthy □ ['preizwɔːði] lobenswert.

pram F [præm] Kinderwagen m.

prance [prɑːns] sich bäumen; paradieren; einherstolzieren.

prank [præŋk] Possen m, Streich m.

prate [preit] 1. Geschwätz n; 2. schwatzen, plappern.

prattle ['prætl] s. prate.

pray [prei] beten; (er)bitten; bitte!

prayer [prɛə] Gebet n; Bitte f; oft ~s pl. Andacht f; Lord's ♀ Vaterunser n; ~-book ['prɛəbuk] Gebetbuch n.

pre... [priː; pri] vor(her)...; Vor...; früher.

preach [priːtʃ] predigen; ~er ['priːtʃə] Prediger(in).

preamble [priː'æmbl] Einleitung f.

precarious □ [pri'kɛəriəs] unsicher.

precaution [pri'kɔːʃən] Vorsicht(smaßregel) f; ~ary [~ʃnəri] vorbeugend.

precede [priː'siːd] voraus-, vorangehen (dat.); ~nce, ~ncy [~dəns, ~si] Vortritt m, Vorrang m; ~nt ['presidənt] Präzedenzfall m.

precept ['priːsept] Vorschrift f, Regel f; ~or [pri'septə] Lehrer m.

precinct ['priːsiŋkt] Bezirk m, bsd. Am. Wahlbezirk m, -kreis m; ~s pl. Umgebung f; Bereich m; Grenze f; pedestrian ~ Fußgängerzone f.

precious ['preʃəs] 1. □ kostbar; edel; F arg, gewaltig, schön; 2. F adv. recht, äußerst.

precipi|ce ['presipis] Abgrund m; ~tate 1. [pri'sipiteit] (hinab)stürzen; ⚕ fällen; überstürzen; 2. □ [~tit] übereilt, hastig, 3. [~] ⚕ Niederschlag m; ~tation [prisipi-'teiʃən] Sturz m; Überstürzung f, Hast f; ⚕ Niederschlag(en n) m; ~tous □ [pri'sipitəs] steil, jäh.

précis ['preisiː] gedrängte Übersicht, Zs.-fassung f.

precis|e □ [pri'sais] genau; ~ion [~'siʒən] Genauigkeit f; Präzision f.

preclude [pri'kluːd] ausschließen; vorbeugen (dat.); j-n hindern.

precocious □ [pri'kouʃəs] frühreif; altklug.

preconceive ['priːkən'siːv] vorher ausdenken; ~d vorgefaßt (Meinung).

preconception ['priːkən'sepʃən] vorgefaßte Meinung. [m.)

precursor [pri(:)'kəːsə] Vorläufer)

predatory ['predətəri] räuberisch.

predecessor ['priːdisesə] Vorgänger m.

predestin|ate [pri(:)'destineit] vorherbestimmen; ~ed [~nd] auserkoren.

predetermine ['priːdi'təːmin] vorher festsetzen; vorherbestimmen.

predicament [pri'dikəmənt] (mißliche) Lage.

predicate 1. ['predikeit] aussagen; 2. gr. [~kit] Prädikat n, Satzaussage f.

predict [pri'dikt] vorhersagen; ~ion [~kʃən] Prophezeiung f.

predilection [priːdi'lekʃən] Vorliebe f.

predispos|e ['priːdis'pouz] vorher geneigt od. empfänglich machen (to für); ~ition [~spə'ziʃən] Geneigtheit f; bsd. ⚕ Anfälligkeit f (to für).

predomina|nce[pri'dɔminəns]Vorherrschaft f; Übergewicht n; Vormacht(stellung) f; ~nt □ [~nt] vorherrschend; ~te [~neit] die Oberhand haben; vorherrschen.

pre-eminent □ [priː(')'eminənt] hervorragend.

pre-emption [priː(')'empʃən] Vorkauf(srecht n) m.

pre-exist ['priːig'zist] vorher dasein.

prefabricate ['priː'fæbrikeit] vorfabrizieren.

preface ['prefis] 1. Vorrede f, Vorwort n, Einleitung f; 2. einleiten.

prefect ['priːfekt] Präfekt m; Schule: Vertrauensschüler m, Klassensprecher m.

prefer [pri'fəː] vorziehen; Gesuch etc. vorbringen; Klage einreichen; befördern; ~able □ ['prefərəbl] (to) vorzuziehen(d) (dat.); vorzüglicher (als); ~ably [~li] vorzugsweise; besser; ~ence [~rəns] Vorliebe f; Vorzug m; ~ential □ [prefə'renʃəl] bevorzugt; Vorzugs-...; ~ment [pri'fəːmənt] Beförderung f.

prefix ['priːfiks] Präfix n, Vorsilbe f.

pregnan|cy ['pregnənsi] Schwangerschaft f; fig. Fruchtbarkeit f; Bedeutungsreichtum m; ~t □ [~nt] schwanger; fig. fruchtbar, inhaltsvoll.

prejud|ge ['priː'dʒʌdʒ] vorher (ver-)urteilen; ~ice ['predʒudis] 1. Voreingenommenheit f; Vorurteil n; Schaden m; 2. voreinnehmen; benachteiligen; e-r S. Abbruch tun; ~d (vor)eingenommen; ~icial □ [predʒu'diʃəl] nachteilig.

prelate ['prelit] Prälat m.

preliminary [pri'liminəri] 1. □ vorläufig; einleitend; Vor...; 2. Einleitung f.

prelude ♪ ['preljuːd] Vorspiel n.

premature □ [premə'tjuə] fig. frühreif, vorzeitig; vorschnell.

premeditat|e [priː'mediteit] vorher überlegen; ~ion [priː(:)medi-'teiʃən] Vorbedacht m.

premier ['premjə] **1.** erst; **2.** Premierminister *m.*

premises ['premisiz] *pl.* (Gebäude *pl.* mit) Grundstück *n*, Anwesen *n*; Lokal *n.*

premium ['pri:mjəm] Prämie *f*; Anzahlung *f*; † Agio *n*; Versicherungsprämie *f*; Lehrgeld *n*; *at a* ~ über pari; sehr gesucht.

premonition [pri:mə'niʃən] Warnung *f*; (Vor)Ahnung *f.*

preoccup|ied [pri(:)'ɔkjupaid] in Gedanken verloren; ~**y** [~pai] vorher in Besitz nehmen; ausschließlich beschäftigen; in Anspruch nehmen.

prep F [prep] = *preparation*, *preparatory school.*

preparat|ion [prepə'reiʃən] Vorbereitung *f*; Zubereitung *f*; ~**ory** □ [pri'pærətəri] vorbereitend; ~ (*school*) Vorschule *f.*

prepare [pri'pɛə] *v/t.* vorbereiten; zurechtmachen; (zu)bereiten; (aus-)rüsten; *v/i.* sich vorbereiten; sich anschicken; ~**d** □ bereit.

prepay ['pri:'pei] (*irr. (pay)*) vorausbezahlen; frankieren.

prepondera|nce [pri'pɔndərəns] Übergewicht *n*; ~**nt** □ [~nt] überwiegend; ~**te** [~reit] überwiegen.

preposition *gr.* [prepə'ziʃən] Präposition *f*, Verhältniswort *n.*

prepossess [pri:pə'zes] günstig stimmen; ~**ing** □ [~siŋ] einnehmend.

preposterous [pri'pɔstərəs] widersinnig, albern; grotesk.

prerequisite ['pri:'rekwizit] Vorbedingung *f*, Voraussetzung *f.*

prerogative [pri'rɔgətiv] Vorrecht *n.*

presage [presidʒ] **1.** Vorbedeutung *f*; Ahnung *f*; **2.** vorbedeuten; ahnen; prophezeien.

prescribe [pris'kraib] vorschreiben; ⚕ verschreiben.

prescription [pris'kripʃən] Vorschrift *f*, Verordnung *f*; ⚕ Rezept *n.*

presence ['prezns] Gegenwart *f*; Anwesenheit *f*; Erscheinung *f*; ~ *of mind* Geistesgegenwart *f.*

present[1] ['preznt] **1.** □ gegenwärtig; anwesend, vorhanden; jetzig; laufend (*Jahr etc.*); vorliegend (*Fall etc.*); ~ *tense gr.* Präsens *n*; **2.** Gegenwart *f*, *gr. a.* Präsens *n*; Geschenk *n*; *at* ~ jetzt; *for the* ~ einstweilen.

present[2] [pri'zent] präsentieren; (dar)bieten; (vor)zeigen; *j-n* vorstellen; vorschlagen; (über)reichen; (be)schenken.

presentation [prezen'teiʃən] Darstellung *f*; Vorstellung *f*; Ein-, Überreichung *f*; Schenkung *f*; Vorzeigen *n*, Vorlage *f.*

presentiment [pri'zentimənt] Vorgefühl *n*, Ahnung *f.*

presently ['prezntli] sogleich, bald (darauf), alsbald; *Am.* zur Zeit.

preservati|on [prezə(:)'veiʃən] Bewahrung *f*, Erhaltung *f*; ~**ve** [pri-'zə:vətiv] **1.** bewahrend; **2.** Schutz-, Konservierungsmittel *n.*

preserve [pri'zə:v] **1.** bewahren, behüten; erhalten; einmachen; *Wild* hegen; **2.** *hunt.* Gehege *n* (*a. fig.*); *mst* ~**s** *pl.* Eingemachte(s) *n.* [ren (over bei).\]

preside [pri'zaid] den Vorsitz füh-

presiden|cy ['prezidənsi] Vorsitz *m*; Präsidentschaft *f*; ~**t** [~nt] Präsident *m*, Vorsitzende(r) *m*; *Am.* † Direktor *m.*

press [pres] **1.** Druck *m der Hand*; (Wein- *etc.*)Presse *f*; *die* Presse (*Zeitungen*); Druckerei *f*; Verlag *m*; Druck(en *n*) *m*; *a. printing-*~ Druckerpresse *f*; Menge *f*; *fig.* Druck *m*, Last *f*, Andrang *m*; Schrank *m*; **2.** *v/t.* (aus)pressen; drücken; lasten auf (*dat.*); (be)drängen; dringen auf (*acc.*); aufdrängen (*on dat.*); bügeln; *be* ~*ed for time* es eilig haben; *v/i.* drücken; (sich) drängen; ~ *for* sich eifrig bemühen um; ~ *on* weitereilen; ~ (*up*)*on* eindringen auf (*acc.*); ~ **agency** Nachrichtenbüro *n*; ~ **agent** Reklameagent *m*; ~ **button** Druckknopf *m*; ~**ing** □ ['presiŋ] dringend; ~**ure** [ˈpreʃə] Druck *m* (*a. fig.*); Drang(sal *f*) *m.*

prestige [pres'ti:ʒ] Prestige *n.*

presum|able □ [pri'zju:məbl] vermutlich; ~**e** [pri'zju:m] *v/t.* annehmen; vermuten; voraussetzen; *v/i.* vermuten; sich erdreisten; anmaßend sein; ~ (*up*)*on* pochen auf (*acc.*); ausnutzen, mißbrauchen.

presumpt|ion [pri'zʌmpʃən] Mutmaßung *f*; Wahrscheinlichkeit *f*; Anmaßung *f*; ~**ive** □ [~ptiv] mutmaßlich; ~**uous** □ [~tjuəs] überheblich; vermessen.

presuppos|e [pri:sə'pouz] voraussetzen; ~**ition** [pri:sʌpə'ziʃən] Voraussetzung *f.*

preten|ce, *Am.* ~**se** [pri'tens] Vortäuschung *f*; Vorwand *m*; Schein *m*, Verstellung *f.*

pretend [pri'tend] vorgeben; vortäuschen; heucheln; Anspruch erheben (*to auf acc.*); ~**ed** □ angeblich.

pretension [pri'tenʃən] Anspruch *m* (*to auf acc.*); Anmaßung *f.*

preterit(e) *gr.* ['preterit] Präteritum *n*, Vergangenheitsform *f.*

pretext ['pri:tekst] Vorwand *m.*

pretty ['priti] **1.** □ hübsch, niedlich; nett; **2.** *adv.* ziemlich.

prevail [pri'veil] die Oberhand haben *od.* gewinnen; (vor)herrschen; maßgebend *od.* ausschlaggebend sein; ~ (*up*)*on s.o.* *j-n* dazu bewegen, *et.* zu tun; ~**ing** □ [~liŋ] (vor)herrschend.

prevalent □ ['prevələnt] vorherrschend, weit verbreitet.

prevaricate [pri'værikeit] Ausflüchte machen.

prevent [pri'vent] verhüten, *e-r S.* vorbeugen; *j-n* hindern; ~ion [~n-∫ən] Verhinderung *f;* Verhütung *f;* ~ive [~ntiv] **1.** □ vorbeugend; **2.** Schutzmittel *n.*

preview ['pri:'vju:] Vorschau *f;* Vorbesichtigung *f.*

previous □ ['pri:vjəs] vorhergehend; vorläufig; Vor...; ~ **to** vor *(dat.)*; ~**ly** [~sli] vorher, früher.

pre-war ['pri:'wo:] Vorkriegs...

prey [prei] **1.** Raub *m,* Beute *f; beast of* ~ Raubtier *n; bird of* ~ Raubvogel *m; be a* ~ *to* geplagt werden von; **2.** ~ *(up)on* rauben, plündern; fressen; *fig.* nagen an *(dat.).*

price [prais] **1.** Preis *m;* Lohn *m;* **2.** *Waren* auszeichnen; die Preise festsetzen für; (ab)schätzen; ~**less** ['praislis] unschätzbar; unbezahlbar.

prick [prik] **1.** Stich *m;* Stachel *m (a. fig.);* **2.** *v/t.* (durch)stechen; *fig.* peinigen; *a.* ~ *out Muster* punktieren; ~ *up one's ears* die Ohren spitzen; *v/i.* stechen; ~**le** ['prikl] Stachel *m,* Dorn *m;* ~**ly** [~li] stachelig.

pride [praid] **1.** Stolz *m;* Hochmut *m; take* ~ *in* stolz sein auf *(acc.);* **2.** ~ *o.s.* sich brüsten *(on, upon* mit).

priest [pri:st] Priester *m.*

prig [prig] Tugendbold *m,* selbstgerechter Mensch; Pedant *m.*

prim □ [prim] steif; zimperlich.

prima|cy ['praiməsi] Vorrang *m;* ~**rily** [~ərili] in erster Linie; ~**ry** □ [~ri] **1.** ursprünglich; hauptsächlich; Ur..., Anfangs..., Haupt...; Elementar...; höchst; ✝, ⚡ Primär...; **2.** *a.* ~ *meeting Am.* Wahlversammlung *f;* ~**ry school** Elementar-, Grundschule *f.*

prime [praim] **1.** □ erst; wichtigst; Haupt...; vorzüglich(st); ~ *cost* ✝ Selbstkosten *pl.;* ~ *minister* Ministerpräsident *m;* ~ *number* Primzahl *f;* **2.** *fig.* Blüte(zeit) *f;* Beste(s) *n;* höchste Vollkommenheit; **3.** *v/t.* vorbereiten; *Pumpe* anlassen; instruieren; F vollaufen lassen *(betrunken machen); paint.* grundieren.

primer ['praimə] Fibel *f,* Elementarbuch *n.* _____ [lich; Ur...]

primeval [prai'mi:vəl] uranfäng-/

primitive ['primitiv] **1.** □ erst, ursprünglich; Stamm...; primitiv; **2.** *gr.* Stammwort *n.*

primrose ❦ ['primrouz] Primel *f.*

prince [prins] Fürst *m;* Prinz *m;* ~**ss** [prin'ses, *vor npr.* 'prinses] Fürstin *f;* Prinzessin *f.*

principal ['prinsəpəl] **1.** □ erst, hauptsächlich(st); Haupt...; ~ *parts pl. gr.* Stammformen *f/pl. des vb.;*

2. Hauptperson *f;* Vorsteher *m; bsd. Am.* (Schul)Direktor *m,* Rektor *m;* ✝ Chef *m;* ⚖ Hauptschuldige(r) *m;* ✝ Kapital *n;* ~**ity** [prinsi'pæliti] Fürstentum *n.*

principle ['prinsəpl] Prinzip *n;* Grund(satz) *m;* Ursprung *m; on* ~ grundsätzlich, aus Prinzip.

print [print] **1.** Druck *m;* (Finger-*etc.*)Abdruck *m;* bedruckter Kattun, Druckstoff *m;* Stich *m; phot.* Abzug *m; Am.* Zeitungsdrucksache *f; out of* ~ vergriffen; **2.** (ab-, auf-, be)drucken; *phot.* kopieren; *fig.* einprägen *(on dat.);* in Druckbuchstaben schreiben; ~**er** ['printə] (Buch)Drucker *m.*

printing ['printiŋ] Druck *m;* Drucken *n; phot.* Abziehen *n,* Kopieren *n;* ~**ink** Druckerschwärze *f;* ~**office** (Buch)Druckerei *f;* ~**press** Druckerpresse *f.*

prior ['praiə] **1.** früher, älter *(to* als); **2.** *adv.* ~ *to* vor *(dat.);* **3.** *eccl.* Prior *m;* ~**ity** [prai'oriti] Priorität *f;* Vorrang *m;* Vorfahrtsrecht *n.*

prism ['prizəm] Prisma *n.*

prison ['prizn] Gefängnis *n;* ~**er** [~nə] Gefangene(r *m) f;* Häftling *m; take s.o.* ~ j-n gefangennehmen.

privacy ['praivəsi] Zurückgezogenheit *f;* Geheimhaltung *f.*

private ['praivit] **1.** □ privat; Privat...; persönlich; vertraulich; geheim; **2.** ✕ (gewöhnlicher) Soldat; *in* ~ privatim; im geheimen.

privation [prai'vei∫ən] Mangel *m,* Entbehrung *f.*

privilege ['privilid3] **1.** Privileg *n;* Vorrecht *n;* **2.** bevorrechten.

privy ['privi] **1.** □ ~ *to* eingeweiht in *(acc.);* ♀ *Council* Staatsrat *m;* ♀ *Councillor* Geheimer Rat; ♀ *Seal* Geheimsiegel *n;* **2.** ⚖ Mitinteressent *m (to an dat.);* Abort *m.*

prize [praiz] **1.** Preis *m,* Prämie *f;* ⚓ Beute *f;* (Lotterie)Gewinn *m;* **2.** preisgekrönt, Preis...; **3.** (hoch-) schätzen; aufbrechen *(öffnen);* ~**fighter** ['praizfaitə] Berufsboxer *m.*

pro [prou] für.

probab|ility [prɔbə'biliti] Wahrscheinlichkeit *f;* ~**le** □ ['prɔbəbl] wahrscheinlich.

probation [prə'bei∫ən] Probe *f,* Probezeit *f;* ⚖ Bewährungsfrist *f;* ~ *officer* Bewährungshelfer *m.*

probe [proub] **1.** ⚕ Sonde *f; fig.* Untersuchung *f; lunar* ~ Mondsonde *f;* **2.** *a.* ~ *into* sondieren; untersuchen.

probity ['proubiti] Redlichkeit *f.*

problem ['prɔbləm] Problem *n;* Å Aufgabe *f;* ~**atic(al** □) [prɔbli-'mætik(əl)] problematisch, zweifelhaft. _____ [*n;* Handlungsweise *f.*]

procedure [prə'si:d3ə] Verfahren/

proceed [prə'si:d] weitergehen; fortfahren; vor sich gehen; vorgehen; *univ.* promovieren; ~ *from von od.* aus *et.* kommen; ausgehen von; ~ *to* zu *et.* übergehen; **~ing** [.diŋ] Vorgehen *n*; Handlung *f*; **~s** *pl.* 貰荳 Verfahren *n*; Verhandlungen *f/pl.*, (Tätigkeits)Bericht *m*; **~s** ['prousi:dz] *pl.* Ertrag *m*, Gewinn *m*.

process ['prouses] **1.** Fortschreiten *n*, Fortgang *m*; Vorgang *m*; Verlauf *m der Zeit*; Prozeß *m*, Verfahren *n*; *in* ~ im Gange; *in* ~ *of construction* im Bau (befindlich); **2.** gerichtlich belangen; ⊕ bearbeiten; **~ion** [prə'seʃən] Prozession *f*.

proclaim [prə'kleim] proklamieren; erklären; ausrufen.

proclamation [prɔklə'meiʃən] Proklamation *f*; Bekanntmachung *f*; Erklärung *f*.

proclivity [prə'kliviti] Neigung *f*.

procrastinate [prou'kræstineit] zaudern.

procreate ['proukrieit] (er)zeugen.

procurat|ion [prɔkjuə'reiʃən] Vollmacht *f*; † Prokura *f*; **~or** ['prɔkjuəreitə] Bevollmächtigte(r) *m*.

procure [prə'kjuə] *v/t.* be-, verschaffen; *v/i.* Kuppelei treiben.

prod [prɔd] **1.** Stich *m*; Stoß *m*; *fig.* Ansporn *m*; **2.** stechen; stoßen; *fig.* anstacheln.

prodigal ['prɔdigəl] **1.** □ verschwenderisch; *the* ~ *son* der verlorene Sohn; **2.** Verschwender(in).

prodig|ious □ [prə'didʒəs] erstaunlich, ungeheuer; **~y** ['prɔdidʒi] Wunder *n* (*a. fig.*); Ungeheuer *n*; *oft infant* ~ Wunderkind *n*.

produce 1. [prə'dju:s] vorbringen, vorführen, vorlegen; beibringen; hervorbringen; produzieren, erzeugen; *Zinsen etc.* (ein)bringen; ↯ verlängern; *Film etc.* herausbringen; **2.** ['prɔdju:s] (Natur)Erzeugnis(se *pl.*) *n*, Produkt *n*; Ertrag *m*; **~r** [prə'dju:sə] Erzeuger *m*, Hersteller *m*; *Film:* Produzent *m*; *thea.* Regisseur *m*.

product ['prɔdəkt] Produkt *n*, Erzeugnis *n*; **~ion** [prə'dʌkʃən] Hervorbringung *f*; Vorlegung *f*, Beibringung *f*; Produktion *f*, Erzeugung *f*; *thea.* Herausbringen *n*; Erzeugnis *n*; **~ive** □ [.ktiv] schöpferisch, produktiv, erzeugend; ertragreich; fruchtbar; **~iveness** [.vnis], **~ivity** [prɔdʌk'tiviti] Produktivität *f*.

prof *Am.* F [prɔf] Professor *m*.

profan|ation [prɔfə'neiʃən] Entweihung *f*; **~e** [prə'fein] **1.** □ profan; weltlich; uneingeweiht; gottlos; **2.** entweihen; **~ity** [.'fæniti] Gottlosigkeit *f*; Fluchen *n*.

profess [prə'fes] (sich) bekennen (zu); erklären; *Reue etc.* bekunden; *Beruf* ausüben; lehren; **~ed** □ erklärt; angeblich; Berufs...; **~ion**

[.eʃən] Bekenntnis *n*; Erklärung *f*; Beruf *m*; **~ional** [..nl] **1.** □ Berufs...; Amts...; berufsmäßig; freiberuflich; ~ *men* Akademiker *m/pl.*; **2.** Fachmann *m*; *Sport:* Berufsspieler *m*; Berufskünstler *m*; **~or** [.esə] Professor *m*.

proffer ['prɔfə] **1.** anbieten; **2.** Anerbieten *n*.

proficien|cy [prə'fiʃənsi] Tüchtigkeit *f*; **~t** [.nt] **1.** □ tüchtig; bewandert; **2.** Meister *m*.

profile ['proufail] Profil *n*.

profit ['prɔfit] **1.** Vorteil *m*, Nutzen *m*, Gewinn *m*; **2.** *v/t.* j-m Nutzen bringen; *v/i.* ~ *by* Nutzen ziehen aus; ausnutzen; **~able** □ [.təbl] nützlich, vorteilhaft, einträglich; **~eer** [prɔfi'tiə] **1.** Schiebergeschäfte machen; **2.** Profitmacher *m*, Schieber *m*; **~sharing** ['prɔfitʃeəriŋ] Gewinnbeteiligung *f*.

profligate ['prɔfligit] **1.** □ liederlich; **2.** liederlicher Mensch.

profound] [prə'faund] tief; tiefgründig; gründlich; *fig.* dunkel.

profundity [prə'fanditi] Tiefe *f*.

profus|e □ [prə'fju:s] verschwenderisch; übermäßig, überreich; **~ion** *fig.* [.u:ʒən] Überfluß *m*.

progen|itor [prou'dʒenitə] Vorfahr *m*, Ahn *m*; **~y** ['prɔdʒini] Nachkommen(schaft *f*) *m/pl.*; Brut *f*.

prognos|is ⚕ [prɔg'nousis], *pl.* **~es** [.siz] Prognose *f*.

prognostication [prəgnɔsti'keiʃən] Vorhersage *f*.

program(me) ['prougræm] Programm *n*.

progress 1. ['prougres] Fortschritt(e *pl.*) *m*; Vorrücken *n* (*a.* ✕); Fortgang *m*; *in* ~ im Gange; **2.** [prə'gres] fortschreiten; **~ion** [prə'greʃən] Fortschreiten *n*; ↯ Reihe *f*; **~ive** [.esiv] **1.** □ fortschreitend; fortschrittlich; **2.** *pol.* Fortschrittler *m*.

prohibit [prə'hibit] verbieten; verhindern; **~ion** [proui'biʃən] Verbot *n*; Prohibition *f*; **~ionist** [.ʃnist] *bsd. Am* Prohibitionist *m*; **~ive** □ [prə'hibitiv] verbietend; Sperr...; unerschwinglich.

project 1. ['prɔdʒekt] Projekt *n*; Vorhaben *n*, Plan *m*; **2.** [prə'dʒekt] *v/t.* planen; (ent)werfen; ↯ projizieren; *v/i.* vorspringen; ↯ **~ile** ['prɔdʒektail] Projektil *n*, Geschoß *n*; **~ion** [prə'dʒekʃən] Werfen *n*; Entwurf *m*; Vorsprung *m*; ↯, *ast.*, *phot.* Projektion *f*; **~or** [.ktə] † Gründer *m*; *opt.* Projektor *m*.

proletarian [proule'teəriən] **1.** proletarisch; **2.** Proletarier(in).

prolific [prə'lifik] (.ally) fruchtbar.

prolix □ ['prouliks] weitschweifig.

prolo|gue, *Am. a.* **~g** ['prouləg] Prolog *m*.

prolong [prə'lɔŋ] verlängern.

promenade [prɔmi'nɑ:d] **1.** Promenade f; **2.** promenieren.

prominent □ ['prɔminənt] hervorragend (a. fig.); fig. prominent.

promiscuous □ [prə'miskjuəs] unordentlich, verworren; gemeinsam; unterschiedslos.

promis|e ['prɔmis] **1.** Versprechen n; fig. Aussicht f; **2.** versprechen; ~ing [,~siŋ] vielversprechend; ~sory [,~səri] versprechend; ~ note ✝ Eigenwechsel m.

promontory ['prɔmɔntri] Vorgebirge n.

promot|e [prə'mout] et. fördern; j-n befördern; bsd. Am. Schule: versetzen; parl. unterstützen; ✝ gründen; bsd. Am. Verkauf durch Werbung steigern; ~ion [,~ou∫ən] Förderung f; Beförderung f; ✝ Gründung f.

prompt [prɔmpt] **1.** □ schnell; bereit(willig); sofortig; pünktlich; **2.** j-n veranlassen; Gedanken eingeben; j-m vorsagen, souffliieren; ~er ['prɔmptə] Souffleu|r m, -se f; ~ness [,~tnis] Schnelligkeit f; Bereitschaft f.

promulgate ['prɔmʌlgeit] verkünden, verbreiten.

prone [' [proun] mit dem Gesicht nach unten (liegend); hingestreckt; ~ to fig. geneigt od. neigend zu.

prong [prɔŋ] Zinke f; Spitze f.

pronoun gr. ['prounaun] Pronomen n, Fürwort n.

pronounce [prə'nauns] aussprechen; verkünden; erklären (für).

pronto Am. F ['prɔntou] sofort.

pronunciation [prənʌnsi'ei∫ən] Aussprache f.

proof [pru:f] **1.** Beweis m; Probe f, Versuch m; typ. Korrekturbogen m; typ., phot. Probeabzug m; **2.** fest; in Zssgn. ...fest, ...dicht, ...sicher; ~reader typ. ['pru:fri:də] Korrektor m.

prop [prɔp] **1.** Stütze f (a. fig.); **2.** a. ~ up (unter)stützen.

propaga|te ['prɔpəgeit] (sich) fortpflanzen; verbreiten; ~tion [prɔpə'gei∫ən] Fortpflanzung f; Verbreitung f.

propel [prə'pel] (vorwärts-, an-)treiben; ~ler [,~lə] Propeller m, (Schiffs-, Luft)Schraube f.

propensity [prə'pensiti] Neigung f.

proper ['prɔpə] eigen(tümlich); eigentlich; passend, richtig; anständig; ~ty [,~ti] Eigentum n, Besitz m, Vermögen n; Eigenschaft f.

prophe|cy ['prɔfisi] Prophezeiung f; ~sy [,~sai] prophezeien.

prophet ['prɔfit] Prophet m.

propi|tiate [prə'pi∫ieit] günstig stimmen, versöhnen; ~tious □ [,~∫əs] gnädig; günstig.

proportion [prə'pɔ:∫ən] **1.** Verhältnis n; Gleichmaß n; (An)Teil m; ~s pl. (Aus)Maße n/pl.; **2.** in ein Verhältnis bringen; ~al □ [,~nl] im Verhältnis (to zu); ~ate □ [,~∫nit] angemessen.

propos|al [prə'pouzəl] Vorschlag m, (a. Heirats)Antrag m; Angebot n; Plan m; ~e [,~ouz] v/t. vorschlagen; e-n Toast ausbringen auf (acc.); ~ to o.s. sich vornehmen; v/i. beabsichtigen; anhalten (to um); ~ition [prɔpə'zi∫ən] Vorschlag m, Antrag m; Behauptung f; Problem n.

propound [prə'paund] Frage etc. vorlegen; vorschlagen.

propriet|ary [prə'praiətəri] Eigentümer..., Eigentums...; Besitz(er)...; gesetzlich geschützt (bsd. Arzneimittel); ~or [,~tə] Eigentümer m; ~y [,~ti] Richtigkeit f; Schicklichkeit f; the proprieties pl. die Anstandsformen f/pl. [m.]

propulsion ⊕ [prə'pʌl∫ən] Antrieb

prorate Am. [prou'reit] anteilmäßig verteilen.

prosaic [prou'zeiik] (~ally) fig. prosaisch (nüchtern, trocken).

proscribe [prous'kraib] ächten.

proscription [prous'krip∫ən] Achtung f; Acht f; Verbannung f.

prose [prouz] **1.** Prosa f; **2.** prosaisch.

prosecut|e ['prɔsikju:t] (a. gerichtlich) verfolgen; Gewerbe etc. betreiben; verklagen; ~ion [prɔsi'kju:∫ən] Verfolgung f e-s Plans etc.; Betreiben n e-s Gewerbes etc.; gerichtliche Verfolgung; ~or ɡ'ʒ ['prɔsikju:tə] Kläger m; Anklagevertreter m; public ~ Staatsanwalt m.

prospect 1. ['prɔspekt] Aussicht f (a. fig.); Anblick m; ✝ Interessent m; **2.** [prəs'pekt] ⚒ schürfen, bohren (for nach Öl); ~ive □ [,~tiv] vorausblickend; voraussichtlich; ~us [,~təs] (Werbe)Prospekt m.

prosper ['prɔspə] v/i. Erfolg haben, gedeihen, blühen; v/t. begünstigen, segnen; ~ity [prɔs'periti] Gedeihen n; Wohlstand m; Glück n; fig. Blüte f; ~ous □ ['prɔspərəs] glücklich, gedeihlich; fig. blühend; günstig.

prostitute ['prɔstitju:t] **1.** Dirne f; **2.** zur Dirne machen; (der Schande) preisgeben, feilbieten (a. fig.).

prostrat|e 1. ['prɔstreit] hingestreckt; erschöpft; daniederliegend; demütig; gebrochen; **2.** [prɔs'treit] niederwerfen; fig. niederschmettern; entkräften; ~ion [,~ei∫ən] Niederwerfung f; Fußfall m; fig. Demütigung f; Entkräftung f.

prosy fig. ['prouzi] prosaisch; langweilig.

protagonist [prou'tægɔnist] thea. Hauptfigur f; fig. Vorkämpfer(in).

protect [prə'tekt] (be)schützen; ~ion [,~k∫ən] Schutz m; Wirtschaftsschutz m, Schutzzoll m; ~ive

[~ktiv] schützend; Schutz...; ~ duty Schutzzoll m; ~or [~tə] (Be)Schützer m; Schutz-, Schirmherr m; ~orate [~ərit] Protektorat n.

protest 1. ['proutest] Protest m; Einspruch m; **2.** [prə'test] beteuern; protestieren; reklamieren.

Protestant ['prɔtistənt] **1.** protestantisch; **2.** Protestant(in).

protestation [proutes'teiʃən] Beteuerung f; Verwahrung f.

protocol ['proutəkɔl] **1.** Protokoll n; **2.** protokollieren.

prototype ['proutətaip] Urbild n; Prototyp m, Modell n.

protract [prə'trækt] in die Länge ziehen, hinziehen.

protru|de [prə'tru:d] (sich) (her)-vorstrecken; (her)vorstehen, (her)-vortreten (lassen); ~sion [~u:ʒən] Vorstrecken n; (Her)Vorstehen n, (Her)Vortreten n.

protuberance [prə'tju:bərəns] Hervortreten n; Auswuchs m, Höcker m.

proud □ [praud] stolz (of auf acc.).

prove [pru:v] v/t. be-, er-, nachweisen; prüfen; erleben, erfahren; v/i. sich herausstellen od. erweisen (als); ausfallen; ~n ['pru:vən] erwiesen; bewährt.

provenance ['prɔvinəns] Herkunft f.

provender ['prɔvində] Futter n.

proverb ['prɔvəb] Sprichwort n.

provide [prə'vaid] v/t. besorgen, beschaffen, liefern; bereitstellen; versehen, versorgen; ⚹ vorsehen, festsetzen; v/i. (vor)sorgen; ~d (that) vorausgesetzt, daß; sofern.

providen|ce ['prɔvidəns] Vorsehung f; Voraussicht f; Vorsorge f; ~t □ [~nt] vorausblickend; vorsorglich; haushälterisch; ~tial [prɔvi'den-ʃəl] durch die *göttliche* Vorsehung bewirkt; glücklich.

provider [prə'vaidə] Ernährer m der Familie; Lieferant m.

provinc|e ['prɔvins] Provinz f; fig. Gebiet n; Aufgabe f; ~ial [prə'vin-ʃəl] **1.** provinziell; kleinstädtisch; **2.** Provinzbewohner(in).

provision [prə'viʒən] Beschaffung f; Vorsorge f; ⚹ Bestimmung f; Vorkehrung f, Maßnahme f; Vorrat m; ~s pl. Proviant m, Lebensmittel pl.; ~al □ [~nl] provisorisch.

proviso [prə'vaizou] Vorbehalt m.

provocat|ion [prɔvə'keiʃən] Herausforderung f; ~ive [prə'vɔkətiv] herausfordernd; (auf)reizend.

provoke [prə'vouk] auf-, anreizen; herausfordern.

provost ['prɔvəst] Leiter m e-s College; schott. Bürgermeister m; ⚔ [prə'vou]: ~ marshal Kommandeur m der Militärpolizei.

prow ⚓ [prau] Bug m, Vorschiff n.

prowess ['prauis] Tapferkeit f.

prowl [praul] **1.** v/i. umherstreifen; v/t. durchstreifen; **2.** Umherstreifen n; ~ car Am. ['praulka:] Streifenwagen m der Polizei.

proximity [prɔk'simiti] Nähe f.

proxy ['prɔksi] Stellvertreter m; Stellvertretung f; Vollmacht f; by ~ in Vertretung.

prude [pru:d] Prüde f, Spröde f; Zimperliese f.

pruden|ce ['pru:dəns] Klugheit f, Vorsicht f; ~t □ [~nt] klug, vorsichtig.

prud|ery ['pru:dəri] Prüderie f, Sprödigkeit f, Zimperlichkeit f; ~ish □ [~diʃ] prüde, zimperlich, spröde.

prune [pru:n] **1.** Backpflaume f; **2.** ✂ beschneiden (a. fig.); a. ~ away, ~ off wegschneiden.

prurient □ ['pruəriənt] geil, lüstern.

pry [prai] **1.** neugierig gucken; ~ into s-e Nase stecken in (acc.); ~ open aufbrechen; ~ up hochheben; **2.** Hebel(bewegung f) m.

psalm [sɑːm] Psalm m.

pseudo|... ['psju:dou] Pseudo..., falsch; ~nym [~dənim] Deckname m.

psychiatr|ist [sai'kaiətrist] Psychiater m (*Nervenarzt*); ~y [~ri] Psychiatrie f.

psychic(al □) ['saikik(əl)] psychisch, seelisch.

psycholog|ical □ [saikə'lɔdʒikəl] psychologisch; ~ist [sai'kɔlədʒist] Psychologe m, -in f; ~y [~dʒi] Psychologie f (*Seelenkunde*).

pub F [pʌb] Kneipe f, Wirtschaft f.

puberty ['pju:bəti] Pubertät f.

public ['pʌblik] **1.** □ öffentlich; staatlich, Staats...; allbekannt; ~ spirit Gemeinsinn m; **2.** Publikum n; Öffentlichkeit f; ~an [~kən] Gastwirt m; ~ation [pʌbli'keiʃən] Bekanntmachung f; Veröffentlichung f; Verlagswerk n; monthly ~ Monatsschrift f; ~ house Wirtshaus n; ~ity [pʌb'lisiti] Öffentlichkeit f; Propaganda f, Reklame f, Werbung f; ~ library Volksbücherei f; ~ relations pl. Verhältnis n zur Öffentlichkeit; Public Relations pl.; ~ school Public School f, Internatsschule f.

publish ['pʌbliʃ] bekanntmachen, veröffentlichen; Buch etc. herausgeben, verlegen; ~ing house Verlag m; ~er [~ʃə] Herausgeber m, Verleger m; ~s pl. Verlag(sanstalt f) m.

pucker ['pʌkə] **1.** Falte f; **2.** falten; Falten werfen; runzeln.

pudding ['pudiŋ] Pudding m; Süßspeise f; Auflauf m; Wurst f; black ~ Blutwurst f.

puddle ['pʌdl] Pfütze f.

pudent ['pju:dənt] verschämt.

puerile □ ['pjuərail] kindisch.

puff [pʌf] **1.** Hauch m; Zug m beim

Rauchen; (Dampf-, Rauch)Wölkchen *n*; Puderquaste *f*; (aufdringliche) Reklame; 2. *v/t.* (auf)blasen, pusten; paffen; anpreisen; ~ *out* sich (auf)blähen; ~ *up Preise* hochtreiben; ~*ed up fig.* aufgeblasen; ~*ed eyes* geschwollene Augen; *v/i.* paffen; pusten; ~**paste** ['pʌfpeist] Blätterteig *m*; ~**y** ['pʌfi] böig; kurzatmig; geschwollen; dick; bauschig.

pug [pʌg], ~**dog** ['pʌgdɔg] Mops *m.*

pugnacious [pʌg'neiʃəs] kämpferisch; kampflustig; streitsüchtig.

pug-nose ['pʌgnouz] Stupsnase *f.*

puissant ['pjuː(ː)isnt] mächtig.

puke [pjuːk] (sich) erbrechen.

pull [pul] 1. Zug *m*; Ruck *m*; *typ.* Abzug *m*; Ruderpartie *f*; Griff *m*; Vorteil *m*; 2. ziehen; zerren; reißen; zupfen; pflücken; rudern; ~ *about* hin- u. herzerren; ~ *down* niederreißen; ~ *in* einfahren (*Zug*); ~ *off* zustande bringen; *Preis* erringen; ~ *out* heraus-, hinausfahren; ausscheren; ~ *round* wiederherstellen; ~ *through j-n* durchbringen; ~ *o.s. together* sich zs.-nehmen; ~ *up Wagen* anhalten; halten; ~ *up with*, ~ *up* to einholen.

pulley ⊕ ['puli] Rolle *f*; Flaschenzug *m*; Riemenscheibe *f.*

pull|**-over** ['pulouvə] Pullover *m*; ~**-up** Halteplatz *m*, Raststätte *f.*

pulp [pʌlp] Brei *m*; *Frucht-, Zahn*Mark *n*; ⊕ Papierbrei *m*; *a.* ~ *magazine Am.* Schundillustrierte *f.*

pulpit ['pulpit] Kanzel *f.*

pulpy □ ['pʌlpi] breiig; fleischig.

puls|**ate** ['pʌlseit] pulsieren; schlagen; ~**e** [pʌls] Puls(schlag) *m.*

pulverize ['pʌlvəraiz] *v/t.* pulverisieren; *v/i.* zu Staub werden.

pumice ['pʌmis] Bimsstein *m.*

pump [pʌmp] 1. Pumpe *f*; Pumps *m*; 2. pumpen; F *j-n* aushorchen.

pumpkin ♀ ['pʌmpkin] Kürbis *m.*

pun [pʌn] 1. Wortspiel *n*; 2. ein Wortspiel machen.

Punch[1] [pʌntʃ] Kasperle *m, n.*

punch[2] [~] 1. ⊕ Punze(n *m*) *f*, Locheisen *n*, Locher *m*; Lochzange *f*; (Faust)Schlag *m*; Punsch *m*; 2. punzen, durchbohren; lochen; knuffen, puffen; *Am.* Vieh treiben, hüten.

puncher ['pʌntʃə] Locheisen *n*; Locher *m*; F Schläger *m*; *Am.* Cowboy *m.*

punctilious [pʌŋk'tiliəs] peinlich (genau), spitzfindig; förmlich.

punctual □ ['pʌŋktjuəl] pünktlich; ~**ity** [pʌŋktjuˈæliti] Pünktlichkeit *f.*

punctuat|**e** ['pʌŋktjueit] (inter-)punktieren; *fig.* unterbrechen; ~**ion** *gr.* [pʌŋktjuˈeiʃən] Interpunktion *f.*

puncture ['pʌŋktʃə] 1. Punktur *f*,

Stich *m*; Reifenpanne *f*; 2. (durch-)stechen; platzen (*Luftreifen*).

pungen|**cy** ['pʌndʒənsi] Schärfe *f*; ~**t** [~nt] stechend, beißend, scharf.

punish ['pʌniʃ] (be)strafen; ~**able** □ [~ʃəbl] strafbar; ~**ment** [~ʃmənt] Strafe *f*, Bestrafung *f.*

punk *Am.* [pʌŋk] Zunderholz *n*; Zündmasse *f*; F *fig.* Mist *m*, Käse *m.*

puny □ ['pjuːni] winzig; schwächlich.

pupa *zo.* ['pjuːpə] Puppe *f.*

pupil ['pjuːpl] *anat.* Pupille *f*; Schüler(in); Mündel *m, n.*

puppet ['pʌpit] Marionette *f (a. fig.)*; ~**-show** Puppenspiel *n.*

pup(**py**) [pʌp, 'pʌpi] Welpe *m*, junger Hund; *fig.* Laffe *m*, Schnösel *m.*

purchase ['pəːtʃəs] 1. (An-, Ein-)Kauf *m*; Erwerb(ung *f*) *m*; Anschaffung *f*; ⊕ Hebevorrichtung *f*; *fig.* Ansatzpunkt *m*; *make* ~*s* Einkäufe machen; 2. kaufen; *fig.* erkaufen; anschaffen; ⊕ aufwinden; ~**r** [~sə] Käufer(in).

pure □ [pjuə] *allg.* rein; *engS.*: lauter; echt; gediegen; theoretisch; ~**bred** *Am.* ['pjuəbred] reinrassig.

purgat|**ive** & ['pəːgətiv] 1. abführend; 2. Abführmittel *n*; ~**ory** [~təri] Fegefeuer *n.*

purge [pəːdʒ] 1. & Abführmittel *n*; *pol.* Säuberung *f*; 2. *mst fig.* reinigen; *pol.* säubern; & abführen.

purify ['pjuərifai] reinigen; läutern.

Puritan ['pjuəritən] 1. Puritaner (-in); 2. puritanisch.

purity ['pjuəriti] Reinheit *f (a. fig.).*

purl [pəːl] murmeln (*Bach*).

purlieus ['pəːljuːz] *pl.* Umgebung *f.*

purloin [pəːˈlɔin] entwenden.

purple ['pəːpl] 1. purpurn, purpurrot; 2. Purpur *m*; 3. (sich) purpurn färben.

purport ['pəːpət] 1. Sinn *m*; Inhalt *m*; 2. besagen; beabsichtigen; vorgeben.

purpose ['pəːpəs] 1. Vorsatz *m*; Absicht *f*, Zweck *m*; Entschlußkraft *f*; *for the* ~ *of ger.* um zu *inf.*; *on* ~ absichtlich; *to the* ~ zweckdienlich; *to no* ~ vergebens; 2. vorhaben, bezwecken; ~**ful** □ [~sful] zweckmäßig; absichtlich; zielbewußt; ~**less** □ [~slis] zwecklos; ziellos; ~**ly** [~li] vorsätzlich.

purr [pəː] schnurren (*Katze*).

purse [pəːs] 1. Börse *f*, Geldbeutel *m*; Geld(preis *m*) *n*; *public* ~ Staatssäckel *m*; 2. *oft* ~ *up Mund* spitzen; *Stirn* runzeln; *Augen* zs.-kneifen.

pursuan|**ce** [pəˈsjuː(ː)əns] Verfolgung *f*; *in* ~ *of* zufolge (*dat.*); *at* □ [~nt]: ~ *to* zufolge, gemäß, entsprechend (*dat.*).

pursu|**e** [pəˈsjuː] verfolgen (*a. fig.*); streben nach; *e-m Beruf etc.* nachgehen; fortsetzen, fortfahren; ~**er**

[~ju(:)ə] Verfolger(in); **~it** [~ju:t] Verfolgung *f*; *mst* ~*s pl.* Beschäftigung *f*.

purvey [pə'vei] *Lebensmittel* liefern; **~or** [~eiə] Lieferant *m*.

pus [pʌs] Eiter *m*.

push [puʃ] 1. (An-, Vor)Stoß *m*; Schub *m*; Druck *m*; Notfall *m*; Energie *f*; Unternehmungsgeist *m*; Elan *m*; 2. stoßen; schieben; drängen; *Knopf* drücken; (an)treiben; *a.* ~ through durchführen; *Anspruch etc.* durchdrücken; ~ s.th. on *s.o.* j-m et. aufdrängen; ~ one's way sich durch- *od.* vordrängen; ~ along, ~ on, ~ forward weitermachen, -gehen, -fahren *etc.*; **~button** ⚡ ['puʃbʌtn] Druckknopf *m*; **~over** *Am. fig.* Kinderspiel *n*; leicht zu beeinflussender Mensch.

pusillanimous □ [pju:si'læniməs] kleinmütig.

puss [pus] Kätzchen *n*, Katze *f* (*a. fig.* = *Mädchen*); **~y** ['pusi], *a.* **~cat** Mieze *f*, Kätzchen *n*; **~yfoot** *Am.* F leisetreten, sich zurückhalten.

put [put] (*irr.*) *v/t.* setzen, legen, stellen, stecken, tun, machen; *Frage* stellen, vorlegen; werfen; ausdrücken, sagen; ~ about *Gerüchte etc.* verbreiten; ⚓ wenden; ~ across *sl.* drehen, schaukeln; ~ back zurückstellen; ~ by *Geld* zurücklegen; ~ down niederlegen, -setzen, -werfen; aussteigen lassen; notieren; zuschreiben (to *dat.*); unterdrücken; ~ forth *Kräfte* aufbieten; *Knospen etc.* treiben; ~ forward *Meinung etc.* vorbringen; ~ o.s. forward sich hervortun; ~ in hinein-, hereint(r)ecken; *Anspruch* erheben; *Gesuch* einreichen; *Urkunde* vorlegen; anstellen; ~ off auf-, verschieben; vertrösten; abbringen; hindern; *fig.* ablegen; ~ on *Kleid* anziehen, *Hut* aufsetzen; *fig.* annehmen; an-, einschalten;

vergrößern; ~ on airs sich aufspielen; ~ on weight zunehmen; ~ out ausmachen, (aus)löschen; verrenken; (her)ausstrecken; verwirren; j-m Ungelegenheiten bereiten; *Kraft* aufbieten; *Geld* ausleihen; ~ right in Ordnung bringen; ~ through *teleph.* verbinden (to mit); ~ to hinzufügen; ~ to death hinrichten; ~ to the rack *od.* torture auf die Folter spannen; ~ up aufstellen *etc.*; errichten, bauen; *Waren* anbieten; *Miete* erhöhen; ver-, wegpacken; *Widerstand* leisten; *Kampf* liefern; *Gäste* unterbringen; *Bekanntmachung* anschlagen; *v/i.* ~ off, ~ out, ~ to sea ⚓ auslaufen; ~ in ⚓ einlaufen; ~ up at einkehren *od.* absteigen in (*dat.*); ~ up for sich bewerben um; ~ up with sich gefallen lassen; sich abfinden mit.

putrefy ['pju:trifai] (ver)faulen.

putrid □ ['pju:trid] faul, verdorben; *sl.* scheußlich, saumäßig; **~ity** [pju:'triditi] Fäulnis *f*.

putty ['pʌti] 1. Kitt *m*; 2. kitten.

puzzle ['pʌzl] 1. schwierige Aufgabe, Rätsel *n*; Verwirrung *f*; Geduldspiel *n*; 2. *v/t.* irremachen; j-m Kopfzerbrechen machen; ~ out austüfteln; *v/i.* sich den Kopf zerbrechen; **~-headed** konfus.

pygm|(a)ean [pig'mi:ən] zwerghaft; **~y** ['pigmi] Zwerg *m*; *attr.* zwerghaft.

pyjamas [pə'dʒɑ:məz] *pl.* Schlafanzug *m*.

pyramid ['pirəmid] Pyramide *f*; **~al** □ [pi'ræmidl] pyramidal.

pyre ['paiə] Scheiterhaufen *m*.

pyrotechnic|(al □) [pairou'teknik(əl)] pyrotechnisch, Feuerwerks...; **~s** *pl.* Feuerwerk *n* (*a. fig.*).

Pythagorean [paiθægə'ri(:)ən] 1. pythagoreisch; 2. Pythagoreer *m*.

pyx *eccl.* [piks] Monstranz *f*.

Q

quack [kwæk] 1. Quaken *n*; Scharlatan *m*; Quacksalber *m*, Kurpfuscher *m*; Marktschreier *m*; 2. quacksalberisch; 3. quaken; quacksalbern (an *dat.*); **~ery** ['kwækəri] Quacksalberei *f*.

quadrangle ['kwɔdræŋgl] Viereck *n*; Innenhof *m* e-s College.

quadrennial □ [kwɔ'dreniəl] vierjährig; vierjährlich.

quadru|ped ['kwɔdruped] Vierfüßer *m*; **~ple** [~pl] 1. □ vierfach; 2. (sich) vervierfachen; **~plets** [~lits] *pl.* Vierlinge *m/pl.*

quagmire ['kwægmaiə] Sumpf (-land *n*) *m*, Moor *n*.

quail¹ *orn.* [kweil] Wachtel *f*.

quail² [~] verzagen; beben.

quaint □ [kweint] anheimelnd, malerisch; putzig; seltsam.

quake [kweik] 1. beben, zittern (with, for vor *dat.*); 2. Erdbeben *n*.

Quaker ['kweikə] Quäker *m*.

quali|fication [kwɔlifi'keiʃən] (erforderliche) Befähigung; Einschränkung *f*; *gr.* nähere Bestimmung; **~fy** ['kwɔlifai] *v/t.* befähigen; (be-) nennen; *gr.* näher bestimmen; einschränken, mäßigen; mildern; *v/i.* seine Befähigung nachweisen; **~ty** [~iti] Eigenschaft *f*, Beschaffenheit *f*; ⚓ Qualität *f*; vornehmer Stand.

qualm [kwɔːm] plötzliche Übelkeit; Zweifel *m*; Bedenken *n*.

quandary ['kwɔndəri] verzwickte Lage, Verlegenheit *f*.

quantity ['kwɔntiti] Quantität *f*, Menge *f*; großer Teil.

quantum ['kwɔntəm] Menge *f*, Größe *f*, Quantum *n*; Anteil *m*.

quarantine ['kwɔrəntiːn] **1.** Quarantäne *f*; **2.** unter Quarantäne stellen.

quarrel ['kwɔrəl] **1.** Zank *m*, Streit *m*; **2.** (sich) zanken, streiten; **~some** □ [~ləsm] zänkisch; streitsüchtig.

quarry ['kwɔri] **1.** Steinbruch *m*; *fig.* Fundgrube *f*; (Jagd)Beute *f*; **2.** *Steine* brechen; *fig.* stöbern.

quart [kwɔːt] Quart *n* (*1,136 l*).

quarter ['kwɔːtə] **1.** Viertel *n*, vierter Teil; *bsd.* Viertelstunde *f*; Vierteljahr *n*, Quartal *n*; Viertelzentner *m*; *Am.* 25 Cent; Keule *f*, Viertel *n* *e-s geschlachteten Tieres*; Stadtviertel *n*; (Himmels)Richtung *f*, Gegend *f*; ✕ Gnade *f*, Pardon *m*; **~s** *pl.* Quartier *n* (*a.* ✕), Unterkunft *f*; *fig.* Kreise *m/pl.*; *live in close ~s* beengt wohnen; *at close ~s* dicht aufeinander; *come to close ~s* handgemein werden; **2.** vierteln, vierteilen; beherbergen; ✕ einquartieren; **~back** *Am. Sport:* Abwehrspieler *m*; **~day** Quartalstag *m*; **~deck** Achterdeck *n*; **~ly** [~əli] **1.** vierteljährlich; **2.** Vierteljahresschrift *f*; **~master** ✕ Quartiermeister *m*. [*n.*]

quartet(te) ♪ [kwɔː'tet] Quartett

quarto ['kwɔːtou] Quart(format) *n.*

quash ⚖ [kwɔʃ] aufheben, verwerfen; unterdrücken.

quasi ['kwɑːziː(ː)] gleichsam, sozusagen; Quasi..., Schein...

quaver ['kweivə] **1.** Zittern *n*; ♪ Triller *m*; **2.** mit zitternder Stimme sprechen *od.* singen; trillern.

quay [kiː] Kai *m*; Uferstraße *f*.

queasy □ ['kwiːzi] empfindlich (*Magen, Gewissen*); heikel, mäkelig; ekelhaft.

queen [kwiːn] Königin *f*; **~ bee** Bienenkönigin *f*; **~like** ['kwiːnlaik], **~ly** [~li] wie eine Königin, königlich.

queer [kwiə] sonderbar, seltsam; wunderlich; komisch; homosexuell.

quench [kwentʃ] *fig. Durst etc.* löschen, stillen; kühlen; *Aufruhr* unterdrücken.

querulous □ ['kwerʊləs] quengelig, mürrisch, verdrossen.

query ['kwiəri] **1.** Frage(zeichen *n*) *f*; **2.** (be)fragen; (be-, an)zweifeln.

quest [kwest] **1.** Suche(n *n*) *f*, Nachforschen *n*; **2.** suchen, forschen.

question ['kwestʃən] **1.** Frage *f*; Problem *n*; Untersuchung *f*; Streitfrage *f*; Zweifel *m*; Sache *f*, Angelegenheit *f*; *beyond* (*all*) *~* ohne Frage; *in ~* fraglich; *call in ~* anzweifeln; *that is out of the ~* das steht außer *od.* kommt nicht in Frage; **2.** befragen; bezweifeln; **~able** □ [~nəbl] fraglich; fragwürdig; **~er** [~nə] Fragende(r *m*) *f*; **~mark** Fragezeichen *n*; **~naire** [kwestiə'neə] Fragebogen *m.*

queue [kjuː] **1.** Reihe *f* *v. Personen etc.*, Schlange *f*; Zopf *m*; **2.** *mst ~ up* (in e-r Reihe) anstehen, Schlange stehen.

quibble ['kwibl] **1.** Wortspiel *n*; Spitzfindigkeit *f*; Ausflucht *f*; **2.** *fig.* ausweichen; witzeln.

quick [kwik] **1.** schnell, rasch; voreilig; lebhaft; gescheit; beweglich; lebendig; scharf (*Gehör etc.*); **2.** lebendes Fleisch; *the ~* die Lebenden; *to the ~* (bis) ins Fleisch; *fig.* (bis) ins Herz, tief; *cut s.o. to the ~* j-n aufs empfindlichste kränken; **~en** ['kwikən] *v/t.* beleben; beschleunigen; *v/i.* aufleben; sich regen; **~ly** [~kli] schnell, rasch; **~ness** [~knis] Lebhaftigkeit *f*; Schnelligkeit *f*; Voreiligkeit *f*; Schärfe *f* *des Verstandes etc.*; **~sand** Triebsand *m*; **~set** ✔ Setzling *m*, *bsd.* Hagedorn *m*; *a. ~ hedge* lebende Hecke; **~sighted** scharfsichtig; **~silver** *min.* Quecksilber *n*; **~witted** schlagfertig.

quid¹ [kwid] Priem *m* (*Kautabak*).

quid² *sl.* [~] Pfund *n* Sterling.

quiescen|ce [kwai'esns] Ruhe *f*, Stille *f*; **~t** □ [~nt] ruhend; *fig.* ruhig, still.

quiet ['kwaiət] **1.** □ ruhig, still; **2.** Ruhe *f*; *on the ~* (*sl. on the q.t.*) unter der Hand, im stillen; **3.** *a. ~ down* (sich) beruhigen; **~ness** [~tnis], **~ude** ['kwaiitjuːd] Ruhe *f*, Stille *f*.

quill [kwil] **1.** Federkiel *m*; *fig.* Feder *f*; Stachel *m* *des Igels etc.*; **2.** rund fälteln; **~ing** [~wilin] Rüsche *f*, Krause *f*; **~pen** Gänsefeder *f* *zum Schreiben*.

quilt [kwilt] **1.** Steppdecke *f*; **2.** steppen; wattieren.

quince ✔ [kwins] Quitte *f*.

quinine *pharm.* [kwi'niːn, *Am.* 'kwainain] Chinin *n.*

quinquennial □ [kwiŋ'kweniəl] fünfjährig; fünfjährlich.

quinsy ⚕ ['kwinzi] Mandelentzündung *f.*

quintal ['kwintl] (Doppel)Zentner *m.*

quintessence [kwin'tesns] Quintessenz *f*, Kern *m*, Inbegriff *m.*

quintuple ['kwintjupl] **1.** □ fünffach; 2. (sich) verfünffachen; ~ts [~lits] pl. Fünflinge m/pl.

quip [kwip] Stich(elei f) m; Witz (-wort n) m; Spitzfindigkeit f.

quirk [kwəːk] Spitzfindigkeit f; Witz(elei f) m; Kniff m; Schnörkel m; Eigentümlichkeit f; △ Hohlkehle f.

quisling ['kwizliŋ] Quisling m, Kollaborateur m.

quit [kwit] 1. v/t. verlassen; aufgeben; Am. aufhören (mit); vergelten; Schuld tilgen; v/i. aufhören; ausziehen (Mieter); give notice to ~ kündigen; 2. quitt; frei, los.

quite [kwait] ganz, gänzlich; recht; durchaus; ~ a hero ein wirklicher Held; ~ (so)!, ~ that! ganz recht; ~ the thing F große Mode.

quittance ['kwitəns] Quittung f.

quitter ['kwitə] Am. F Drückeberger m.

quiver¹ ['kwivə] zittern, beben.

quiver² [~] Köcher m.

quiz [kwiz] 1. Prüfung f, Test m; Quiz n; belustigter Blick; 2. (aus-) fragen; prüfen; necken, foppen; anstarren, beäugen; ~zical □ ['kwizikəl] spöttisch; komisch.

quoit [kɔit] Wurfring m; ~s pl. Wurfringspiel n.

Quonset Am. ['kwɔnsit] a. ~ hut Wellblechbaracke f.

quorum parl. ['kwɔːrəm] beschlußfähige Mitgliederzahl.

quota ['kwoutə] Quote f, Anteil m, Kontingent n.

quotation [kwou'teiʃən] Anführung f, Zitat n; ✝ Preisnotierung f; Kostenvoranschlag m; ~marks pl. Anführungszeichen n/pl.

quote [kwout] anführen, zitieren; ✝ berechnen, notieren (at mit).

quotient ⅄ ['kwouʃənt] Quotient m.

quoth † [kwouθ]: ~ I sagte ich; ~ he sagte er.

quotidian [kwɔ'tidiən] (all)täglich.

R

rabbi ['ræbai] Rabbiner m.

rabbit ['ræbit] Kaninchen n.

rabble ['ræbl] Pöbel(haufen) m.

rabid □ ['ræbid] tollwütig (Tier); fig. wild, wütend.

rabies vet. ['reibiːz] Tollwut f.

raccoon [rə'kuːn] = racoon.

race [reis] 1. Geschlecht n, Stamm m; Rasse f, Schlag m; Lauf m (a. fig.); Wettrennen n; Strömung f; ~s pl. Pferderennen n; 2. rennen; rasen; um die Wette laufen (mit); ⊕ leer laufen; ~course ['reiskɔːs] Rennbahn f, -strecke f; ~horse Rennpferd n; ~r ['reisə] Rennpferd n; Rennboot n; Rennwagen m.

racial ['reiʃəl] Rassen... [m.]

racing ['reisiŋ] Rennsport m; attr. Renn...

rack [ræk] 1. Gestell n; Kleiderständer m; Gepäcknetz n; Raufe f, Futtergestell n; Folter(bank) f; go to ~ and ruin völlig zugrunde gehen; 2. strecken; foltern, quälen (a. fig.); ~ one's brains sich den Kopf zermartern.

racket ['rækit] 1. Tennis-Schläger m; Lärm m; Trubel m; Am. F Schwindel(geschäft n) m; Strapaze f; 2. lärmen; sich amüsieren; ~eer Am. [ræki'tiə] Erpresser m; ~eering Am. [~əriŋ] Erpresserwesen n; ~y ['rækiti] ausgelassen.

racoon zo. [rə'kuːn] Waschbär m.

racy □ ['reisi] kraftvoll, lebendig; stark; würzig; urwüchsig.

radar ['reidə] Radar(gerät) n.

radian|ce, ~cy ['reidjəns, ~si]

Strahlen n; ~t □ [~nt] strahlend, leuchtend.

radiat|e ['reidieit] (aus)strahlen; strahlenförmig ausgehen; ~ion [reidi'eiʃən] (Aus)Strahlung f; ~or ['reidieitə] Heizkörper m; mot. Kühler m.

radical ['rædikəl] 1. □ Wurzel..., Grund...; gründlich; eingewurzelt; pol. radikal; 2. pol. Radikale(r m) f.

radio ['reidiou] 1. Radio n; Funk (-spruch) m; ~ drama, ~ play Hörspiel n; ~ set Radiogerät n; 2. funken; ~(-)active radioaktiv; ~graph [~ougrɑːf] 1. Röntgenbild n; 2. ein Röntgenbild machen von; ~telegram Funktelegramm n; ~therapy Strahlen-, Röntgentherapie f.

radish ♀ ['rædiʃ] Rettich m; (red) ~ Radieschen n.

radius ['reidjəs] Radius m.

raffle ['ræfl] 1. Tombola f, Verlosung f; 2. verlosen.

raft [rɑːft] 1. Floß n; 2. flößen; ~er ['rɑːftə] ⊕ (Dach)Sparren m.

rag¹ [ræg] Lumpen m; Fetzen m; Lappen m.

rag² sl. [~] 1. Unfug m; Radau m; 2. Unfug treiben (mit); j-n aufziehen; j-n beschimpfen; herumtollen, Radau machen.

ragamuffin ['rægəmʌfin] Lumpenkerl m; Gassenjunge m.

rage [reidʒ] 1. Wut f, Zorn m, Raserei f; Sucht f, Gier f (for nach); Manie f; Ekstase f; it is all the ~ es ist allgemein Mode; 2. wüten, rasen.

rag-fair ['rægfɛə] Trödelmarkt m.
ragged □ ['rægid] rauh; zottig; zackig; zerlumpt.
ragman ['rægmən] Lumpensammler m.
raid [reid] 1. (feindlicher) Überfall, Streifzug m; (Luft)Angriff m; Razzia f; 2. einbrechen in (acc.); überfallen.
rail¹ [reil] schimpfen.
rail² [~] 1. Geländer n; Stange f; 🚋 Schiene f; off the ~s entgleist; fig. in Unordnung; by ~ per Bahn; 2. a. ~ in, ~ off mit e-m Geländer umgeben.
railing ['reiliŋ], a. ~s pl. Geländer n; Staket n.
raillery ['reiləri] Spötterei f.
railroad Am. ['reilroud] Eisenbahn f. [~man Eisenbahner m.]
railway ['reilwei] Eisenbahn f;)
rain [rein] 1. Regen m; 2. regnen; ~bow ['reinbou] Regenbogen m; ~coat Regenmantel m; ~fall Regenmenge f; ~proof 1. regendicht; 2. Regenmantel m; ~y □ ['reini] regnerisch; Regen...; a ~ day fig. Notzeiten f/pl.
raise [reiz] oft ~ up heben; (oft fig.) erheben; errichten; erhöhen (a. fig.); Geld etc. aufbringen; Anleihe aufnehmen; verursachen; fig. erwecken; anstiften; züchten, ziehen; Belagerung etc. aufheben.
raisin ['reizn] Rosine f.
rake [reik] 1. Rechen m, Harke f; Wüstling m; Lebemann m; 2. v/t (zs.-)harken; zs.-scharren; fig. (durch)stöbern; ~-off Am. sl. ['reikɔ:f] Schwindelprofit m.
rakish □ ['reikiʃ] schnittig; liederlich, ausschweifend; verwegen; salopp.
rally ['ræli] 1. Sammeln n; Treffen n; Am. Massenversammlung f; Erholung f; mot. Rallye f; 2. (sich ver)sammeln; sich erholen; necken.
ram [ræm] 1. zo., ast. Widder m; ⊕, ⚓ Ramme f; 2. (fest)rammen; ⚓ rammen.
ramble ['ræmbl] 1. Streifzug m; 2. umherstreifen; abschweifen; ~er [~lə] Wanderer m; ♀ Kletterrose f; ~ing [~liŋ] weitläufig.
ramify ['ræmifai] (sich) verzweigen.
ramp [ræmp] Rampe f; ~ant □ ['ræmpənt] wuchernd; fig. zügellos.
rampart ['ræmpɑ:t] Wall m.
ramshackle ['ræmʃækl] wack(e)lig.
ran [ræn] pret. von run 1.
ranch [rɑːntʃ, Am. ræntʃ] Ranch f, Vieharm f; ~er [~ə, Am. 'ræntʃə], ~man Rancher m, Viehzüchter m; Farmer m.
rancid □ ['rænsid] ranzig.
ranco(u)r ['ræŋkə] Groll m, Haß m.
random ['rændəm] 1. at ~ aufs Geratewohl, blindlings; 2. ziel-, wahllos; zufällig.

rang [ræŋ] pret. von ring 2.
range [reindʒ] 1. Reihe f; (Berg-) Kette f; ↑ Kollektion f, Sortiment n; Herd m; Raum m; Umfang m, Bereich m; Reichweite f; Schußweite f; (ausgedehnte) Fläche; Schießstand m; 2. v/t. (ein)reihen, ordnen; Gebiet etc. durchstreifen; ⚓ längs et. fahren; v/i. in e-r Reihe od. Linie stehen; (umher-) streifen; sich erstrecken, reichen; ~r ['reindʒə] Förster m; Aufseher m e-s Parks; Am. Förster m; ⚔ Nahkampfspezialist m.
rank [ræŋk] 1. Reihe f, Linie f; ⚔ Glied n; Klasse f; Rang m, Stand m; the ~s pl., the ~ and file die Mannschaften f/pl.; fig. die große Masse; 2. v/t. (ein)reihen, (ein-) ordnen; v/i. sich reihen, sich ordnen; gehören (with zu); e-e Stelle einnehmen (above über dat.); ~ as gelten als; 3. üppig; ranzig; stinkend.
rankle fig. ['ræŋkl] nagen.
ransack ['rænsæk] durchwühlen, durchstöbern, durchsuchen; ausrauben.
ransom ['rænsəm] 1. Lösegeld n; Auslösung f; 2. loskaufen; erlösen.
rant [rænt] 1. Schwulst m; 2. Phrasen dreschen; mit Pathos vortragen.
rap [ræp] 1. Klaps m; Klopfen n; fig. Heller m; 2. schlagen, klopfen.
rapacious [rə'peiʃəs] raubgierig; ~ty [rə'pæsiti] Raubgier f.
rape [reip] 1. Raub m; Entführung f; Notzucht f, Vergewaltigung f; ♀ Raps m; 2. rauben; vergewaltigen.
rapid ['ræpid] 1. □ schnell, reißend, rapid(e); steil; 2. ~s pl. Stromschnelle(n pl.) f; ~ity [rə'piditi] Schnelligkeit f.
rapprochement pol. [ræ'prɔʃmɑ̃:ŋ] Wiederannäherung f.
rapt [ræpt] entzückt; versunken; ~ure ['ræptʃə] Entzücken n; go into ~s in Entzücken geraten.
rare □ [rɛə] selten; phys. dünn.
rarebit ['rɛəbit]: Welsh ~ geröstete Käseschnitte.
rarefy ['rɛərifai] (sich) verdünnen.
rarity ['rɛəriti] Seltenheit f; Dünnheit f.
rascal ['rɑːskəl] Schuft m; co. Gauner m; ~ity [rɑːs'kæliti] Schurkerei f; ~ly ['rɑːskəli] schuftig; erbärmlich.
rash¹ □ [ræʃ] hastig, vorschnell; übereilt; unbesonnen; waghalsig.
rash² 🌸 [~] Hautausschlag m.
rasher ['ræʃə] Speckschnitte f.
rasp [rɑːsp] 1. Raspel f; 2. raspeln; j-m weh(e) tun; kratzen; krächzen.
raspberry ['rɑːzbəri] Himbeere f.
rat [ræt] zo. Ratte f; pol. Überläufer m; smell a ~ Lunte od. den Braten riechen; ~s! Quatsch!
rate [reit] 1. Verhältnis n, Maß n,

Satz m; Rate f; Preis m, Gebühr f; Taxe f; (Gemeinde)Abgabe f; Steuer f; Grad m, Rang m; bsd. ♣ Klasse f; Geschwindigkeit f; at any ~ auf jeden Fall; ~ of exchange (Umrechnungs)Kurs m; ~ of interest Zinsfuß m; 2. (ein)schätzen; besteuern; ~ among rechnen, zählen zu (dat.); ausschelten.

rather ['rɑ:ðə] eher, lieber; vielmehr; besser gesagt; ziemlich; ~! F und ob!; I had ~ would ~ do ich möchte lieber tun.

ratify ['rætifai] ratifizieren.

rating ['reitiŋ] Schätzung f; Steuersatz m; ♣ Dienstgrad m; ♣ (Segel-) Klasse f; Matrose m; Schelte(n) f.

ratio Å etc. ['reiʃiou] Verhältnis n.

ration ['ræʃən] 1. Ration f, Zuteilung f; 2. rationieren.

rational □ ['ræʃənl] vernunftgemäß; vernünftig, (a. Å) rational; **~ity** [ræʃə'næliti] Vernunft(mäßigkeit) f; **~ize** ['ræʃnəlaiz] rationalisieren; wirtschaftlich gestalten.

rat race ['ræt 'reis] sinnlose Hetze; rücksichtsloses Aufstiegsstreben.

ratten ['rætn] sabotieren.

rattle ['rætl] 1. Gerassel n; Geklapper n; Geplapper n; Klapper f; (Todes)Röcheln n; 2. rasseln (mit); klappern; plappern; röcheln; ~ off herunterrasseln; **~brain**, **~pate** Hohl-, Wirrkopf m; **~snake** Klapperschlange f; **~trap** fig. Klapperkasten m (Fahrzeug).

rattling ['rætliŋ] 1. adj. rasselnd; fig. scharf (Tempo); 2. adv. sehr, äußerst.

raucous □ ['rɔ:kəs] heiser, rauh.

ravage ['rævidʒ] 1. Verwüstung f; 2. verwüsten; plündern.

rave [reiv] rasen, toben; schwärmen (about, of von).

ravel ['rævəl] v/t. verwickeln; ~ (out) auftrennen; fig. entwirren; v/i. a. ~ out ausfasern, aufgehen.

raven orn. ['reivn] Rabe m.

raven|ing ['rævniŋ], **~ous** ['rævinəs] gefräßig; heißhungrig; raubgierig.

ravine [rə'vi:n] Hohlweg m; Schlucht f.

ravings ['reiviŋz] pl. Delirien n/pl.

ravish ['ræviʃ] entzücken; vergewaltigen; rauben; **~ing** □ [~ʃiŋ] hinreißend, entzückend; **~ment** [~ʃmənt] Schändung f; Entzücken n.

raw □ [rɔ:] roh, Roh...; wund; rauh (Wetter); ungeübt, unerfahren; **~boned** ['rɔ:bound] knochig, hager; ~ hide Rohleder n.

ray [rei] Strahl m; fig. Schimmer m.

rayon ['reiɔn] Kunstseide f.

raze [reiz] Haus etc. abreißen; Festung schleifen; tilgen.

razor ['reizə] Rasiermesser n; Ra-

sierapparat m; **~blade** Rasierklinge f; **~edge** fig. des Messers Schneide f, kritische Lage.

razz Am. sl. [ræz] aufziehen.

re... [ri:] wieder...; zurück...; neu...; um...

reach [ri:tʃ] 1. Ausstrecken n; Griff m; Reichweite f; Fassungskraft f, Horizont m; Flußstrecke f; beyond ~, out of ~ unerreichbar; within easy ~ leicht erreichbar; 2. v/i. reichen; langen, greifen; sich erstrecken; v/t. (hin-, her)reichen, (hin-, her)langen; ausstrecken; erreichen.

react [ri(:)'ækt] reagieren (to auf acc.); (ein)wirken (on, upon auf acc.); sich auflehnen (against gegen).

reaction [ri(:)'ækʃən] Reaktion f (a. pol.); **~ary** [~ʃnəri] 1. reaktionär; 2. Reaktionär(in).

reactor phys. [ri(:)'æktə] Reaktor m.

read 1. [ri:d] [irr.] lesen; deuten; (an)zeigen (Thermometer); studieren; sich gut etc. lesen; lauten; ~ to s.o. j-m vorlesen; 2. [red] pret. u. p.p. von † ; 3. [..] adj. belesen; **~able** □ ['ri:dəbl] lesbar; leserlich; lesenswert; **~er** ['ri:də] (Vor)Leser(in); typ. Korrektor m; Lektor m; univ. Dozent m; Lesebuch n.

readi|ly ['redili] adv. gleich, leicht; gern; **~ness** [~inis] Bereitschaft f; Bereitwilligkeit f; Schnelligkeit f.

reading ['ri:diŋ] Lesen n; Lesung f (a. parl.); Stand m des Thermometers; Belesenheit f; Lektüre f; Lesart f; Auffassung f; attr. Lese...

readjust ['ri:ə'dʒʌst] wieder in Ordnung bringen; wieder anpassen; **~ment** [~tmənt] Wiederanpassung f; Neuordnung f.

ready □ ['redi] bereit, fertig; bereitwillig; im Begriff (to do zu tun); schnell; gewandt; leicht; zur Hand; † bar; ~ for use gebrauchsfertig; make od. get ~ (sich) fertig machen; **~made** fertig, Konfektions...

reagent Å [ri(:)'eidʒənt] Reagens n.

real □ [riəl] wirklich, tatsächlich, real; echt; ~ estate Grundbesitz m, Immobilien pl.; **~ism** ['riəlizəm] Realismus m; **~istic** [riə'listik] (~ally) realistisch; sachlich; wirklichkeitsnah; **~ity** [ri(:)'æliti] Wirklichkeit f; **~ization** [riəlai'zeiʃən] Verwirklichung f; Erkenntnis f; † Realisierung f; **~ize** ['riəlaiz] sich klarmachen; erkennen; verwirklichen; realisieren, zu Geld machen; **~ly** [~li] wirklich, in der Tat.

realm [relm] Königreich n; Reich n.

realt|or Am. ['riəltə] Grundstücksmakler m; **~y** ‡‡ [~ti] Grundeigentum n.

reap [ri:p] Korn schneiden; Feld

mähen; *fig.* ernten; ~er ['ri:pə] Schnitter(in); Mähmaschine *f.*

reappear ['ri:ə'piə] wieder erscheinen.

rear [riə] 1. *v/t.* auf-, großziehen; züchten; *v/i.* sich aufrichten; 2. Rück-, Hinterseite *f; mot.,* ⊕ Heck *n;* ✕ Nachhut *f; at the ~ of, in (the)* ~ *of* hinter *(dat.);* 3. Hinter..., Nach...; ~ *wheel drive* Hinterradantrieb *m;* ~**admiral** ⊕ ['riə'ædmərəl] Konteradmiral *m;* ~**guard** ✕ Nachhut *f;* ~**lamp** *mot.* Schlußlicht *n.*

rearm ['ri:'ɑ:m] (wieder)aufrüsten; ~**ament** [,məmənt] Aufrüstung *f.*

rearmost ['riəmoust] hinterst.

rearward ['riəwəd] 1. *adj.* rückwärtig; 2. *adv. a.* ~s rückwärts.

reason ['ri:zn] 1. Vernunft *f;* Verstand *m;* Recht *n,* Billigkeit *f;* Ursache *f,* Grund *m; by ~ of* wegen; *for this* ~ aus diesem Grund; *listen to* ~ Vernunft annehmen; *it stands to* ~ *that* es leuchtet ein, daß; 2. *v/i.* vernünftig denken; schließen; urteilen; argumentieren; *v/t. a.* ~ *out* durchdenken; ~ *away* fortdisputieren; ~ *s.o. into (out of)* *s.th.* j-m et. ein- (aus)reden; ~**able** □ [,nəbl] vernünftig; billig; angemessen; leidlich.

reassure [ri:ə'ʃuə] wieder versichern; (wieder) beruhigen.

rebate ['ri:beit] ✝ Rabatt *m,* Abzug *m;* Rückzahlung *f.*

rebel 1. ['rebl] Rebell *m;* Aufrührer *m;* 2. [,] rebellisch; 3. [ri'bel] sich auflehnen; ~**lion** [,ljən] Empörung *f;* ~**lious** [,jəs] = *rebel* 2.

rebirth ['ri:'bə:θ] Wiedergeburt *f.*

rebound [ri'baund] 1. zurückprallen; 2. Rückprall *m,* Rückschlag *m.*

rebuff [ri'bʌf] 1. Zurück-, Abweisung *f;* 2. zurück-, abweisen.

rebuild ['ri:'bild] *[irr. (build)]* wieder (auf)bauen.

rebuke [ri'bju:k] 1. Tadel *m;* 2. tadeln.

rebut [ri'bʌt] zurückweisen.

recall [ri'kɔ:l] 1. Zurückrufung *f;* Abberufung *f;* Widerruf *m; beyond* ~ *past* ~ unwiderruflich; 2. zurückrufen; ab(be)rufen; (sich) erinnern an *(acc.);* widerrufen; ✝ *Kapital* kündigen.

recapitulate [ri:kə'pitjuleit] kurz wiederholen; zs.-fassen.

recapture ['ri:'kæptʃə] wieder (gefangen)nehmen; ✕ zurückerobern.

recast ['ri:'kɑ:st] *[irr. (cast)]* ⊕ umgießen; umformen, neu gestalten.

recede [ri(:)'si:d] zurücktreten.

receipt [ri'si:t] 1. Empfang *m;* Eingang *m v. Waren;* Quittung *f;* (Koch)Rezept *n;* ~*s pl.* Einnahmen *f/pl.;* 2. quittieren.

receiv|able [ri'si:vəbl] annehmbar; ✝ noch zu fordern(d), ausstehend;

~e [ri'si:v] empfangen; erhalten; bekommen; aufnehmen; annehmen; anerkennen; ~ed anerkannt; ~er [,və] Empfänger *m;* teleph. Hörer *m;* Hehler *m; Steuer- etc.* Einnehmer *m; official* ~ *zʒz* Masseverwalter *m.*

recent □ ['ri:snt] neu; frisch; modern; ~ *events pl. die* jüngsten Ereignisse *n/pl.;* ~**ly** [,tli] neulich, vor kurzem.

receptacle [ri'septəkl] Behälter *m.*

reception [ri'sepʃən] Aufnahme *f* (a. fig.), (a. Radio)Empfang *m;* Annahme *f;* ~**ist** [,nist] Empfangsdame *f,* -herr *m;* ~**room** Empfangszimmer *n.*

receptive □ [ri'septiv] empfänglich, aufnahmefähig (of für).

recess [ri'ses] Pause *f; bsd. parl.* Ferien *pl.;* (entlegener) Winkel; Nische *f;* ~es *pl. fig.* Tiefe(n *pl.*) *f;* ~**ion** [,eʃən] Zurückziehen *n,* Zurücktreten *n;* ✝ Konjunkturrückgang *m,* rückläufige Bewegung.

recipe ['resipi] Rezept *n.*

recipient [ri'sipiənt] Empfänger(in).

reciproc|al [ri'siprəkəl] wechselgegenseitig; ~**ate** [,keit] *v/i.* sich erkenntlich zeigen; ⊕ sich hin- und herbewegen; *v/t. Glückwünsche etc.* erwidern; ~**ity** [resi'prositi] Gegenseitigkeit *f.*

recit|al [ri'saitl] Bericht *m;* Erzählung *f;* ♪ (Solo)Vortrag *m,* Konzert *n;* ~**ation** [resi'teiʃən] Hersagen *n;* Vortrag *m;* ~e [ri'sait] vortragen; aufsagen; berichten.

reckless □ ['reklis] unbekümmert; rücksichtslos; leichtsinnig.

reckon ['rekən] *v/t.* rechnen; *a.* ~ *for,* ~ *as* schätzen als, halten für; ~ *up* zs.-zählen; *v/i.* rechnen; denken, vermuten; ~ *(up)on* sich verlassen auf *(acc.);* ~**ing** ['rekniŋ] Rechnen *n;* (Ab-, Be)Rechnung *f.*

reclaim [ri'kleim] wiedergewinnen; *j-n* bessern; zivilisieren; *urbar* machen.

recline [ri'klain] (sich) (zurück-) lehnen; ~ *upon fig.* sich stützen auf.

recluse [ri'klu:s] Einsiedler(in).

recogni|tion [rekəg'niʃən] Anerkennung *f;* Wiedererkennen *n;* ~**ze** ['rekəgnaiz] anerkennen; (wieder-) erkennen.

recoil [ri'kɔil] 1. zurückprallen; 2. Rückstoß *m,* -lauf *m.*

recollect[1] [rekə'lekt] sich erinnern an *(acc.).*

re-collect[2] ['ri:kə'lekt] wieder sammeln; ~ *o.s.* sich fassen.

recollection [rekə'lekʃən] Erinnerung *f* (of an *acc.*); Gedächtnis *n.*

recommend [rekə'mend] empfehlen; ~**ation** [rekəmən'deiʃən] Empfehlung *f;* Vorschlag *m.*

recompense ['rekəmpens] 1. Belohnung *f,* Vergeltung *f;* Ersatz *m;*

2. belohnen, vergelten; entschädigen; ersetzen.

reconcil|e ['rekənsail] aus-, versöhnen; in Einklang bringen; schlichten; **~iation** [rekənsili'eiʃən] Ver-, Aussöhnung f.

recondition ['ri:kən'diʃən] wieder herrichten; ⊕ überholen.

reconn|aissance ✗ [ri'kɔnisəns] Aufklärung f, Erkundung f; fig. Übersicht f; **~oitre**, Am. **~oiter** [rekə'nɔitə] erkunden, auskundschaften.

reconsider ['ri:kən'sidə] wieder erwägen; nochmals überlegen.

reconstitute ['ri:'kɔnstitjut] wiederherstellen.

reconstruct ['ri:kəns'trʌkt] wiederaufbauen; **~ion** [ˌ~kʃən] Wiederaufbau m, Wiederherstellung f.

reconvert ['ri:kən'və:t] umstellen.

record 1. ['rekɔ:d] Aufzeichnung f, 👫 Protokoll n; schriftlicher Bericht; Ruf m, Leumund m; Wiedergabe f; Schallplatte f; Sport: Rekord m; place on ~ schriftlich niederlegen; ♀ Office Staatsarchiv n; off the ~ Am. inoffiziell; 2. [ri'kɔ:d] auf-, verzeichnen; auf Schallplatte etc. aufnehmen; **~er** [ˌ~də] Registrator m; Stadtrichter m; Aufnahmegerät n, bsd. Tonbandgerät n; ♪ Blockflöte f; **~ing** [ˌ~diŋ] Radio: Aufzeichnung f, Aufnahme f; **~-player** Plattenspieler m.

recount [ri'kaunt] erzählen.

recoup [ri'ku:p] j-n entschädigen (for für); et. wieder einbringen.

recourse [ri'kɔ:s] Zuflucht f; have ~ to s-e Zuflucht nehmen zu.

recover [ri'kʌvə] v/t. wiedererlangen, wiederfinden; wieder einbringen, wiedergutmachen; Schulden etc. eintreiben; be ~ed wiederhergestellt sein; v/i. sich erholen; genesen; **~y** [ˌ~əri] Wiedererlangung f; Wiederherstellung f; Genesung f; Erholung f.

recreat|e [ri'rekrieit] v/t. erfrischen; v/i. a. ~ o.s. sich erholen; **~ion** [rekri'eiʃən] Erholung(spause) f.

recrimination [rikrimi'neiʃən] Gegenbeschuldigung f; Gegenklage f.

recruit [ri'kru:t] 1. Rekrut m; fig. Neuling m; 2. erneuern, ergänzen; Truppe rekrutieren; ✗ Rekruten ausheben; sich erholen.

rectangle ['rektæŋgl] Rechteck n.

recti|fy ['rektifai] berichtigen; verbessern; ⚡, Radio: gleichrichten; **~tude** [ˌ~tju:d] Geradheit f.

rector ['rektə] Pfarrer m; Rektor m; **~y** [ˌ~əri] Pfarre(i) f; Pfarrhaus n.

recumbent □ [ri'kʌmbənt] liegend.

recuperate [ri'kju:pəreit] wiederherstellen; sich erholen.

recur [ri'kə:] zurück-, wiederkehren (to zu), zurückkommen (to auf acc.); ~ to j-m wieder einfallen; **~rence**

[ri'kʌrəns] Wieder-, Rückkehr f; **~rent** □ [ˌ~nt] wiederkehrend.

red [red] 1. rot; ~ heat Rotglut f; ~ herring Bückling m; ~ tape Amtsschimmel m; 2. Rot n; (bsd. pol.) Rote(r m) f; be in the ~ Am. F in Schulden stecken.

red|breast ['redbrest] a. robin ~ Rotkehlchen n; **~cap** Militärpolizist m; Am. Gepäckträger m; **~den** ['redn] (sich) röten; erröten; **~dish** ['rediʃ] rötlich.

redecorate ['ri:'dekəreit] Zimmer renovieren (lassen).

redeem [ri'di:m] zurück-, loskaufen; ablösen; Versprechen einlösen; büßen; entschädigen für; erlösen; 😀er eccl. [ˌ~mə] Erlöser m, Heiland m.

redemption [ri'dempʃən] Rückkauf m; Auslösung f; Erlösung f.

red|-handed ['red'hændid]: catch od. take s.o. ~ j-n auf frischer Tat ertappen; **~head** Rotschopf m; Hitzkopf m; **~-headed** rothaarig; **~hot** rotglühend; fig. hitzig; 😀 **Indian** Indianer(in); **~-letter day** Festtag m; fig. Freuden-, Glückstag m; **~ness** ['rednis] Röte f.

redolent ['redoulənt] duftend.

redouble [ri'dʌbl] (sich) verdoppeln.

redoubt ✗ [ri'daut] Redoute f; **~able** rhet. [ˌ~təbl] fürchterlich.

redound [ri'daund]: ~ to beitragen od. gereichen od. führen zu.

redress [ri'dres] 1. Abhilfe f; Wiedergutmachung f; 👫 Entschädigung f; 2. abhelfen (dat.); wiedergutmachen.

red|-tapism ['red'teipizəm] Bürokratismus m; **~tapist** [ˌ~ist] Bürokrat m.

reduc|e [ri'dju:s] fig. zurückführen, bringen (to auf, in acc., zu); verwandeln (to in acc.); verringern, vermindern; einschränken; Preise herabsetzen; (be)zwingen; 👫, 🩺 reduzieren; 🔪 einrenken; ~ to writing schriftlich niederlegen; **~tion** [ri'dʌkʃən] Reduktion f; Verwandlung f; Herabsetzung f; (Preis)Nachlaß m, Rabatt m; Verminderung f; Verkleinerung f; 🔪 Einrenkung f.

redundant □ [ri'dʌndənt] überflüssig; übermäßig; weitschweifig.

reed [ri:d] Schilfrohr n; Rohrflöte f.

re-education ['ri:edju(:)'keiʃən] Umschulung f, Umerziehung f.

reef [ri:f] (Felsen)Riff n; ⚓ Reff n.

reefer ['ri:fə] Seemannsjacke f; Am. sl. Marihuana-Zigarette f.

reek [ri:k] 1. Rauch m, Dampf m; Dunst m; 2. rauchen, dampfen (with von); unangenehm riechen.

reel [ri:l] 1. Haspel f; (Garn-, Film)Rolle f, Spule f; 2. v/t. haspeln; wickeln, spulen; v/i. wirbeln, schwanken; taumeln.

re-elect ['ri:i'lekt] wiederwählen.
re-enter [ri:'entə] wieder eintreten
(in *acc.*).
re-establish ['ri:is'tæbliʃ] wiederherstellen.
refection [ri'fekʃən] Erfrischung *f.*
refer [ri'fə:]: ~ to ver-, überweisen
an (*acc.*); sich beziehen auf (*acc.*);
erwähnen (*acc.*); zuordnen (*dat.*);
befragen (*acc.*), nachschlagen in
(*dat.*); zurückführen auf (*acc.*), zuschreiben (*dat.*); ~ee [refə'ri:]
Schiedsrichter *m*; *Boxen*: Ring-
richter *m*; ~ence ['refrəns] Refe-
renz *f*, Empfehlung *f*, Zeugnis *n*;
Verweisung *f*; Bezugnahme *f*; Anspielung *f*; Beziehung *f*; Auskunft
(-geber *m*) *f*; *in od. with* ~ to in betreff (*gen.*), in bezug auf (*acc.*); ~
book Nachschlagewerk *n*; ~ *library*
Handbibliothek *f*; ~ *number* Akten-
zeichen *n*; *make* ~ to *et.* erwähnen.
referendum [refə'rendəm] Volks-
entscheid *m.*
refill 1. ['ri:fil] Nachfüllung *f*;
Ersatzfüllung *f*; 2. ['ri:'fil] (sich)
wieder füllen, auffüllen.
refine [ri'fain] (sich) verfeinern *od.*
veredeln; ⊕ raffinieren; (sich) läutern (*a. fig.*); klügeln; ~ (*up*)*on et.*
verfeinern, verbessern; ~ment
[~nmənt] Verfeinerung *f*, Vered(e)-
lung *f*; Läuterung *f*; Feinheit *f*,
Bildung *f*; Spitzfindigkeit *f*; ~ry
[~nəri] ⊕ Raffinerie *f*; *metall.*
(Eisen)Hütte *f.*
refit ⚓ ['ri:'fit] *v/t.* ausbessern; neu
ausrüsten; *v/i.* ausgebessert werden.
reflect [ri'flekt] *v/t.* zurückwerfen,
reflektieren; zurückstrahlen, wider-
spiegeln (*a. fig.*); zum Ausdruck
bringen; *v/i.* ~ (*up*)*on* nachdenken
über (*acc.*); sich abfällig äußern
über (*acc.*); ein schlechtes Licht
werfen auf (*acc.*); ~ion [~kʃən] Zu-
rückstrahlung *f*, Widerspiegelung
f; Reflex *m*; Spiegelbild *n*; Überlegung *f*; Gedanke *m*; abfällige
Bemerkung *f*; Makel *m*; ~ive
[~ktiv] zurückstrahlend; nachdenklich.
reflex ['ri:fleks] 1. Reflex...; 2.Wi-
derschein *m*, Reflex *m* (*a. physiol.*).
reflexive □ [ri'fleksiv] zurückwir-
kend; *gr.* reflexiv, rückbezüglich.
reforest ['ri:'fɔrist] aufforsten.
reform[1] [ri'fɔ:m] 1. Verbesserung *f*,
Reform *f*; 2. verbessern, reformie-
ren; (sich) bessern.
re-form[2] ['ri:'fɔ:m] (sich) neu bilden; ⚔ sich wieder formieren.
reform|ation [refə'meiʃən] Um-
gestaltung *f*; Besserung *f*; *eccl.* ⚥
Reformation *f*; ~atory [ri'fɔ:mə-
təri] 1. bessernd; 2. Besserungsanstalt *f*; ~er [ri'fɔ:mə] *eccl.* Refor-
mator *m*; *bsd. pol.* Reformer *m.*

refract|ion [ri'frækʃən] Strahlen-
brechung *f*; ~ory □ [~ktəri] widerspenstig; hartnäckig; ⊕ feuerfest.
refrain [ri'frein] 1. sich enthalten
(*from gen.*), unterlassen (*from acc.*);
2. Kehrreim *m*, Refrain *m.*
refresh [ri'freʃ] (sich) erfrischen;
auffrischen; ~ment [~ʃmənt] Erfrischung *f* (*a. Getränk etc.*).
refrigerat|e [ri'fridʒəreit] kühlen;
~or [~tə] ⊕ Kühlschrank *m*, -raum *m*;
~ *car* Kühlwagen *m.*
refuel ['ri:'fjuəl] tanken.
refuge ['refju:dʒ] Zuflucht(sstätte)
f; *a. street-*~ Verkehrsinsel *f*; ~e
[refju:(')'dʒi:] Flüchtling *m*; ~ *camp*
Flüchtlingslager *n.*
refulgent □ [ri'fʌldʒənt] strahlend.
refund [ri:'fʌnd] zurückzahlen.
refurbish ['ri:'fə:biʃ] aufpolieren.
refusal [ri'fju:zəl] abschlägige Antwort; (Ver)Weigerung *f*; Vorkaufsrecht *n* (*of auf acc.*).
refuse[1] [ri'fju:z] *v/t.* verweigern;
abweisen, ablehnen; scheuen vor
(*dat.*); *v/i.* sich weigern; scheuen
(*Pferd*). [fall *m*, Müll *m.*]
refuse[2] ['refju:s] Ausschuß *m*; Ab-⎰
refute [ri'fju:t] widerlegen.
regain [ri'gein] wiedergewinnen.
regal □ ['ri:gəl] königlich; Königs...
regale [ri'geil] *v/t.* festlich bewirten; *v/i.* schwelgen (*on* in *dat.*).
regard [ri'gɑ:d] 1. *fester* Blick;
(Hoch)Achtung *f*, Rücksicht *f*;
Beziehung *f*; *with* ~ to im Hinblick
auf (*acc.*); *kind* ~s herzliche Grüße;
2. ansehen; (be)achten; betrachten;
betreffen; *as* ~s ... was ... anbe-
trifft; ~ing □ [~diŋ] hinsichtlich
(*gen.*); ~less □ [~dlis]: ~ *of* ohne
Rücksicht auf (*acc.*).
regenerate 1. [ri'dʒenəreit] (sich)
erneuern; (sich) regenerieren; (sich)
neu bilden; 2. [~rit] wiedergeboren.
regent ['ri:dʒənt] 1. herrschend;
2. Regent *m.*
regiment ⚔ ['redʒimənt] 1. Regiment *n*; 2. [~ment] organisieren;
~als ⚔ [redʒi'mentlz] *pl.* Uniform*f.*
region ['ri:dʒən] Gegend *f*, Gebiet
n; *fig.* Bereich *m*; ~al □ [~nl] örtlich; Orts...
register ['redʒistə] 1. Register *n*,
Verzeichnis *n*; ⊕ Schieber *m*, Ventil *n*; ♪ Register *n*; Zählwerk *n*;
cash ~ Registrierkasse *f*; 2. registrieren *od.* eintragen (lassen); (an-)
zeigen, auf-, verzeichnen; *Postsache*
einschreiben (lassen), *Gepäck* aufgeben; sich *polizeilich* melden.
registr|ar [redʒis'trɑ:] Registrator
m; Standesbeamte(r) *m*; ~ation
[~reiʃən] Eintragung *f*; ~ *fee* An-
meldegebühr *f*; ~y ['redʒistri] Eintragung *f*; Registratur *f*; Register
n; ~ *office* Standesamt *n.*
regress, ~ion ['ri:gres, ri'greʃən]
Rückkehr *f*; *fig.* Rückgang *m.*

regret [ri'gret] **1.** Bedauern *n*; Schmerz *m*; **2.** bedauern; *Verlust* beklagen; **~ful** □ [.tful] bedauernd; **~fully** [.li] mit Bedauern; **~table** □ [.təbl] bedauerlich.

regular □ ['regjulə] regelmäßig; regelrecht, richtig; ordentlich; pünktlich; ✗ regulär; **~ity** [regju-'læriti] Regelmäßigkeit *f*; Richtigkeit *f*, Ordnung *f*.

regulat|e ['regjuleit] regeln, ordnen; regulieren; **~ion** [regju'leiʃən] **1.** Regulierung *f*; Vorschrift *f*, Bestimmung *f*; **2.** vorschriftsmäßig.

rehash *fig.* ['ri:'hæʃ] **1.** wieder durchkauen *od.* aufwärmen; **2.** Aufguß *m*.

rehears|al [ri'hɔ:səl] *thea.*, ♪ Probe *f*; Wiederholung *f*; **~e** [ri'hə:s] *thea.* proben; wiederholen; aufsagen.

reign [rein] **1.** Regierung *f*; *fig.* Herrschaft *f*; **2.** herrschen, regieren.

reimburse [ri:im'bə:s] *j-n* entschädigen; *Kosten* wiedererstatten.

rein [rein] **1.** Zügel *m*; **2.** zügeln.

reindeer *zo.* ['reindiə] Ren(tier)*n*.

reinforce [ri:in'fɔ:s] verstärken; **~ment** [.smənt] Verstärkung *f*.

reinstate [ri:in'steit] wieder einsetzen; wieder instand setzen.

reinsure ['ri:in'ʃuə] rückversichern.

reiterate [ri:'itəreit] (dauernd) wiederholen.

reject [ri'dʒekt] ver-, wegwerfen; ablehnen, ausschlagen; zurückweisen; **~ion** [.kʃən] Verwerfung *f*; Ablehnung *f*; Zurückweisung *f*.

rejoic|e [ri'dʒɔis] *v/t.* erfreuen; *v/i.* sich freuen (*at*, *in* über *acc.*); **~ing** [.siŋ] **1.** □ freudig; **2.** *oft* **~s** *pl.* Freude(nfest *n*) *f*.

rejoin ['ri:'dʒɔin] (sich) wieder vereinigen (mit); wieder zurückkehren zu; [ri'dʒɔin] erwidern.

rejuvenate [ri'dʒu:vineit] verjüngen. [entzünden.]

rekindle ['ri:'kindl] (sich) wieder]

relapse [ri'læps] **1.** Rückfall *m*; **2.** zurückfallen, rückfällig werden.

relate [ri'leit] *v/t.* erzählen; in Beziehung bringen; *v/i.* sich beziehen (*to auf acc.*); **~d** verwandt (*to* mit).

relation [ri'leiʃən] Erzählung *f*; Beziehung *f*; Verhältnis *n*; Verwandtschaft *f*; Verwandte(r *m*) *f*; *in* **~** *to* in bezug auf (*acc.*); **~ship** [.nʃip] Verwandtschaft *f*; Beziehung *f*.

relative ['relətiv] **1.** □ bezüglich (*to gen.*); *gr.* relativ; verhältnismäßig; entsprechend; **2.** *gr.* Relativpronomen *n*; Verwandte(r *m*) *f*.

relax [ri'læks] (sich) lockern; mildern; nachlassen (in *dat.*); (sich) entspannen, ausspannen; milder werden; **~ation** [ri:læk'seiʃən] Lockerung *f*; Nachlassen *n*; Entspannung *f*, Erholung *f*.

relay[1] **1.** [ri'lei] frisches Gespann; Ablösung *f*; ['ri:'lei] ∮ Relais *n*; *Radio:* Übertragung *f*; **2.** [.] *Radio:* übertragen.

re-lay[2] ['ri:'lei] *Kabel etc.* neu verlegen.

relay-race ['ri:leireis] *Sport:* Staffellauf *m*.

release [ri'li:s] **1.** Freilassung *f*; *fig.* Befreiung *f*; Freigabe *f*; *Film: oft first* **~** Uraufführung *f*; ⊕, *phot.* Auslöser *m*; **2.** freilassen; erlösen; freigeben; *Recht* aufgeben, übertragen; *Film* uraufführen; ⊕ auslösen.

relegate ['religeit] verbannen; verweisen (*to an acc.*).

relent [ri'lent] sich erweichen lassen; **~less** □ [.tlis] unbarmherzig.

relevant ['relivənt] sachdienlich; zutreffend; wichtig, erheblich.

reliab|ility [rilaiə'biliti] Zuverlässigkeit *f*; **~le** □ [ri'laiəbl] zuverlässig.

reliance [ri'laiəns] Ver-, Zutrauen *n*; Verlaß *m*.

relic ['relik] Überrest *m*; Reliquie *f*; **~t** [.kt] Witwe *f*.

relief [ri'li:f] Erleichterung *f*; (angenehme) Unterbrechung; Unterstützung *f*; ✗ Ablösung *f*; ✗ Entsatz *m*; Hilfe *f*; ⊕ Relief *n*; **~** *works pl.* Notstandsarbeiten *f/pl.*

relieve [ri'li:v] erleichtern; mildern, lindern; *Arme etc.* unterstützen; ✗ ablösen; ✗ entsetzen; ⚕ (ab)helfen (*dat.*); befreien; hervortreten lassen; (angenehm) unterbrechen.

religion [ri'lidʒən] Religion *f*; Ordensleben *n*; *fig.* Ehrensache *f*.

religious □ [ri'lidʒəs] Religions...; religiös; *eccl.* Ordens...; gewissenhaft.

relinquish [ri'liŋkwiʃ] aufgeben; verzichten auf (*acc.*); loslassen.

relish ['reliʃ] **1.** (Bei)Geschmack *m*; Würze *f*; Genuß *m*; **2.** gern essen; Geschmack finden an (*dat.*); schmackhaft machen.

reluctan|ce [ri'lʌktəns] Widerstreben *n*; *bsd. phys.* Widerstand *m*; **~t** □ [.nt] widerstrebend, widerwillig.

rely [ri'lai] **~** *on* (*up*)*on* sich verlassen (auf *acc.*), bauen auf (*acc.*).

remain [ri'mein] **1.** (ver)bleiben; übrigbleiben; **2.** **~s** *pl.* Überbleibsel *n/pl.*, Überreste *m/pl.*; sterbliche Reste *m/pl.*; **~der** [.ndə] Rest *m*.

remand [ri'mɑ:nd] **1.** (⚖ in die Untersuchungshaft) zurückschicken; **2.** (Zurücksendung *f* in die) Untersuchungshaft *f*; *prisoner on* **~** Untersuchungsgefangene(r *m*) *f*; **~** *home* Jugendstrafanstalt *f*.

remark [ri'mɑ:k] **1.** Beachtung *f*; Bemerkung *f*; **2.** *v/t.* bemerken; *v/i.* sich äußern; **~able** □ [.kəbl] bemerkenswert; merkwürdig.

remedy ['remidi] 1. (Heil-, Hilfs-, Gegen-, Rechts)Mittel *n*; (Ab-)Hilfe *f*; 2. heilen; abhelfen (*dat.*).

rememb|er [ri'membə] sich erinnern an (*acc.*); denken an (*acc.*); beherzigen; ~ me to her grüße sie von mir; ~rance [~brəns] Erinnerung *f*; Gedächtnis *n*; Andenken *n*; ~s *pl.* Empfehlungen *f/pl.*, Grüße *m/pl.*

remind [ri'maind] erinnern (*of* an *acc.*); ~er [~də] Mahnung *f*.

reminiscen|ce [remi'nisns] Erinnerung *f*; ~t □ [~nt] (sich) erinnernd.

remiss □ [ri'mis] schlaff, (nach-)lässig; ~ion [~ʃən] *Sünden*-Vergebung *f*; Erlassung *f* v. *Strafe etc.*; Nachlassen *n*.

remit [ri'mit] *Sünden* vergeben; *Schuld etc.* erlassen; nachlassen in (*dat.*); überweisen; ~tance [~təns] (Geld)Sendung *f*; ✝ Rimesse *f*.

remnant ['remnənt] (Über)Rest *m*.

remodel ['ri:'mɔdl] umbilden.

remonstra|nce [ri'mɔnstrəns] Vorstellung *f*, Einwendung *f*; ~te [~treit] Vorstellungen machen (*on* über *acc.*; *with* s.o. *j*-m); einwenden.

remorse [ri'mɔːs] Gewissensbisse *m/pl.*; ~less □ [~slis] hart(herzig).

remote □ [ri'mout] entfernt, entlegen; ~ness [~tnis] Entfernung *f*.

remov|al [ri'mu:vəl] Entfernen *n*; Beseitigung *f*; Umzug *m*; Entlassung *f*; ~ van Möbelwagen *m*; ~e [~u:v] 1. *v/t.* entfernen; wegräumen, wegrücken; beseitigen; entlassen; *v/i.* (aus-, um-, ver)ziehen; 2. Entfernung *f*; Grad *m*; *Schule*: Versetzung *f*; Abteilung *f* e-r *Klasse*; ~er [~və] (Möbel)Spediteur *m*.

remunerat|e [ri'mju:nəreit] (be-)lohnen; entschädigen; ~ive □ [~rətiv] lohnend.

Renaissance [rə'neisəns] Renaissance *f*.

renascen|ce [ri'næsns] Wiedergeburt *f*; Renaissance *f*; ~t [~nt] wieder wachsend.

rend [rend] (*irr.*) (zer)reißen.

render ['rendə] wieder-, zurückgeben; *Dienst etc.* leisten; *Ehre etc.* erweisen; *Dank* abstatten; übersetzen; ♪ vortragen; darstellen, interpretieren; *Grund* angeben; ✝ *Rechnung* überreichen; übergeben; machen (zu); *Fett* auslassen; ~ing [~əriŋ] Wiedergabe *f*; Interpretation *f*; Übersetzung *f*, Wiedergabe *f*; △ Rohbewurf *m*.

rendition [ren'diʃən] Wiedergabe *f*.

renegade ['renigeid] Abtrünnige(r *m*) *f*.

renew [ri'nju:] erneuern; ~al [~u:(:)əl] Erneuerung *f*.

renounce [ri'nauns] entsagen (*dat.*); verzichten auf (*acc.*); verleugnen.

renovate ['renouveit] erneuern.

renown [ri'naun] Ruhm *m*, Ansehen *n*; ~ed [~nd] berühmt, namhaft.

rent[1] [rent] 1. *pret. u. p.p.* von *rend*; 2. Riß *m*; Spalte *f*.

rent[2] [~] 1. Miete *f*; Pacht *f*; 2. (ver)mieten, (ver)pachten; ~al ['rentl] (Einkommen *n* aus) Miete *f* *od.* Pacht *f*.

renunciation [rinʌnsi'eiʃən] Entsagung *f*; Verzicht *m* (*of* auf *acc.*).

repair[1] [ri'peə] 1. Ausbesserung *f*, Reparatur *f*; ~s *pl.* Instandsetzungsarbeiten *f/pl.*; ~ shop Reparaturwerkstatt *f*; *in good* ~ in gutem (baulichen) Zustand, gut erhalten; *out of* ~ baufällig; 2. reparieren, ausbessern; erneuern; wiedergutmachen.

repair[2] [~] : ~ *to* sich begeben nach.

reparation [repə'reiʃən] Ersatz *m*; Entschädigung *f*; *make* ~s *pol.* Reparationen leisten.

repartee [repɑː'tiː] schlagfertige Antwort; Schlagfertigkeit *f*.

repast [ri'pɑːst] Mahl(zeit *f*) *n*.

repay [ri:'pei] (*irr.* (pay)) *et.* zurückzahlen; *fig.* erwidern; *et.* vergelten; *j-n* entschädigen; ~ment [~mənt] Rückzahlung *f*.

repeal [ri'piːl] 1. Aufhebung *f* von *Gesetzen*; 2. aufheben, widerrufen.

repeat [ri'piːt] 1. (sich) wiederholen; aufsagen; nachliefern; aufstoßen (*Essen*); 2. Wiederholung *f*; *oft* ~ *order* Nachbestellung *f*; ♪ Wiederholungszeichen *n*.

repel [ri'pel] zurückstoßen, zurücktreiben, zurückweisen; *fig.* abstoßen.

repent [ri'pent] bereuen; ~ance [~təns] Reue *f*; ~ant □ [~nt] reuig.

repercussion [ri:pəˈkʌʃən] Rückprall *m*; *fig.* Rückwirkung *f*.

repertory ['repətəri] *thea.* Repertoire *n*; *fig.* Fundgrube *f*.

repetition [repi'tiʃən] Wiederholung *f*; Aufsagen *n*; Nachbildung *f*.

replace [ri'pleis] wieder hinstellen *od.* einsetzen; ersetzen; *an j-s* Stelle treten; ~ment [~smənt] Ersatz *m*.

replant ['riːˈplɑːnt] umpflanzen.

replenish [ri'pleniʃ] wieder auffüllen; ~ment [~mənt] Auffüllung *f*; Ergänzung *f*.

replete [ri'pliːt] angefüllt, voll.

replica ['replikə] Nachbildung *f*.

reply [ri'plai] 1. antworten, erwidern (*to* auf *acc.*); 2. Erwiderung *f*, Antwort *f*.

report [ri'pɔːt] 1. Bericht *m*; Gerücht *n*; *guter* Ruf; Knall *m*; *school* ~ (Schul)Zeugnis *n*; 2. berichten (*über* *acc.*); (sich) melden; anzeigen; ~er [~tə] Berichterstatter(in).

repos|e [ri'pouz] 1. *allg.* Ruhe *f*; 2. *v/t.* ausruhen; (aus)ruhen lassen; ~ *trust etc. in* Vertrauen *etc.* setzen auf (acc.); v/i. a. ~ o.s. (sich) ausruhen; ruhen; beruhen (on auf dat.); ~itory [ri'pozitəri] Verwahrungsort m; Warenlager n; fig. Fundgrube f.

reprehend [repri'hend] tadeln.

represent [repri'zent] darstellen; verkörpern; thea. aufführen; schildern; bezeichnen (as als); vertreten; ~ation [reprizən'teiʃən] Darstellung f; thea. Aufführung f; Vorstellung f; Vertretung f; ~ative □ [repri'zentətiv] 1. dar-, vorstellend (of acc.); vorbildlich; (stell)vertretend; parl. repräsentativ; typisch; 2. Vertreter(in); House of ~s Am. parl. Repräsentantenhaus n.

repress [ri'pres] unterdrücken; ~ion [~eʃən] Unterdrückung f.

reprieve [ri'priːv] 1. (Gnaden)Frist f; Aufschub m; 2. j-m Aufschub od. eine Gnadenfrist gewähren.

reprimand ['reprimɑːnd] 1. Verweis m; 2. j-m e-n Verweis geben.

reprisal [ri'praizəl] Repressalie f.

reproach [ri'prout∫] 1. Vorwurf m; Schande f; 2. vorwerfen (s.o. with s.th. j-m et.); Vorwürfe machen; ~ful □ [~sful] vorwurfsvoll.

reprobate ['reproubeit] 1. verkommen, verderbt; 2. verkommenes Subjekt; 3. mißbilligen; verdammen.

reproduc|e [riːprə'djuːs] wiedererzeugen; (sich) fortpflanzen; wiedergeben, reproduzieren; ~tion [~'dʌkʃən] Wiedererzeugung f; Fortpflanzung f; Reproduktion f.

reproof [ri'pruːf] Vorwurf m, Tadel m.

reprov|al [ri'pruːvəl] Tadel m, Rüge f; ~e [~uːv] tadeln, rügen.

reptile zo. ['reptail] Reptil n.

republic [ri'pʌblik] Republik f; ~an [~kən] 1. republikanisch; 2. Republikaner(in).

repudiate [ri'pjuːdieit] nicht anerkennen; ab-, zurückweisen.

repugnan|ce [ri'pʌgnəns] Abneigung f, Widerwille m; ~t □ [~nt] abstoßend; widerwärtig.

repuls|e [ri'pʌls] 1. Zurück-, Abweisung f; 2. zurück-, abweisen; ~ive □ [~siv] abstoßend; widerwärtig.

reput|able □ ['repjutəbl] achtbar, ehrbar, anständig; ~ation [repju(:)-'teiʃən] (bsd. guter) Ruf, Ansehen n; ~e [ri'pjuːt] 1. Ruf m; 2. halten für; ~ed vermeintlich; angeblich.

request [ri'kwest] 1. Gesuch n, Bitte f; Ersuchen n; ✝ Nachfrage f; by ~, on ~ auf Wunsch; in (great) ~ (sehr) gesucht, begehrt; ~ stop Bedarfshaltestelle f; 2. um et. bitten od. ersuchen; j-n bitten; et. erbitten.

require [ri'kwaiə] verlangen, fordern; brauchen, erfordern; ~d er-

forderlich; ~ment [~əmənt] (An-) Forderung f; Erfordernis n.

requisit|e ['rekwizit] 1. erforderlich; 2. Erfordernis n; Bedarfs-, Gebrauchsartikel m; toilet ~s pl. Toilettenartikel m/pl.; ~ion [rekwi-'ziʃən] 1. Anforderung f; ✕ Requisition f; 2. anfordern; ✕ requirieren.

requital [ri'kwaitl] Vergeltung f.

requite [ri'kwait] j-m et. vergelten.

rescind [ri'sind] aufheben.

rescission [ri'siʒən] Aufhebung f.

rescue ['reskjuː] 1. Rettung f; (a⁝⁝ gewaltsame) Befreiung; 2. retten; (a⁝⁝ gewaltsam) befreien.

research [ri'səːtʃ] Forschung f; Untersuchung f; Nachforschung f; ~er [~ʃə] Forscher m.

resembl|ance [ri'zembləns] Ähnlichkeit f (to mit); ~e [ri'zembl] gleichen, ähnlich sein (dat.).

resent [ri'zent] übelnehmen; ~ful □ [~tful] übelnehmerisch; ärgerlich; ~ment [~tmənt] Ärger m; Groll m.

reservation [rezə'veiʃən] Vorbehalt m; Am. Indianerreservation f; Vorbestellung f von Zimmern etc.

reserve [ri'zəːv] 1. Vorrat m; ✝ Rücklage f; Reserve f (a. fig., ✕); Zurückhaltung f, Verschlossenheit f; Vorsicht f; Vorbehalt m; Sport: Ersatzmann m; 2. aufbewahren, aufsparen; vorbehalten; zurücklegen; Platz etc. reservieren; ~d □ fig. zurückhaltend, reserviert.

reservoir ['rezəvwɑː] Behälter m für Wasser etc.; Sammel-, Staubekken n; fig. Reservoir n.

reside [ri'zaid] wohnen; (orts)ansässig sein; ~ in innewohnen (dat.); ~nce ['rezidəns] Wohnen n; Ortsansässigkeit f; (Wohn)Sitz m; Residenz f; ~ permit Aufenthaltsgenehmigung f; ~nt [~nt] 1. wohnhaft; ortsansässig; 2. Ortsansässige(r m) f, Einwohner(in).

residu|al [ri'zidjuəl] übrigbleibend; ~e ['rezidju] Rest m; Rückstand m; ✝⁝ Reinnachlaß m.

resign [ri'zain] v/t. aufgeben; Amt niederlegen; überlassen; ~ o.s. to sich ergeben in (acc.), sich abfinden mit; v/i. zurücktreten; ~ation [rezig'neiʃən] Rücktritt m; Ergebung f; Entlassungsgesuch n; ~ed □ ergeben, resigniert.

resilien|ce [ri'ziliəns] Elastizität f; ~t [~nt] elastisch, fig. spannkräftig.

resin ['rezin] 1. Harz n; 2. harzen.

resist [ri'zist] widerstehen (dat.); sich widersetzen (dat.); ~ance [~təns] Widerstand m; attr. Widerstands...; line of least ~ Weg m des geringsten Widerstands; ~ant [~nt] widerstehend; widerstandsfähig.

resolut|e □ ['rezəluːt] entschlossen; ~ion [rezə'luːʃən] (Auf)Lösung f;

Entschluß *m*; **Entschlossenheit** *f*; **Resolution** *f*.

resolve [ri'zɔlv] **1.** *v/t.* auflösen; *fig.* lösen; *Zweifel etc.* beheben; entscheiden; *v/i. a.* ~ *o.s.* sich auflösen; beschließen; ~ (*up*)*on* sich entschließen zu; **2.** **Entschluß** *m*; *Am.* **Beschluß** *m*; ~**d** ☐ entschlossen.

resonan|ce ['reznəns] **Resonanz** *f*; ~**t** ☐ [~nt] nach-, widerhallend.

resort [ri'zɔ:t] **1.** **Zuflucht** *f*; **Besuch** *m*; **Aufenthalt**(sort) *m*; **Erholungsort** *m*; *health* ~ **Kurort** *m*; *seaside* ~ **Seebad** *n*; *summer* ~ **Sommerfrische** *f*; **2.** ~ *to* oft besuchen; seine Zuflucht nehmen zu. [sen).|

resound [ri'zaund] widerhallen(las-|

resource [ri'sɔ:s] *natürlicher* **Reichtum**; **Hilfsquelle** *f*, **-mittel** *n*; **Zuflucht** *f*; **Findigkeit** *f*; **Zeitvertreib** *m*, **Entspannung** *f*; ~**ful** ☐ [~sful] findig.

respect [ris'pekt] **1.** **Rücksicht** *f* (*to*, *of* auf *acc.*); **Beziehung** *f*; **Achtung** *f*; ~*s pl.* **Empfehlungen** *f*/*pl.*; **2.** *v/t.* (hoch)achten; **Rücksicht** nehmen auf (*acc.*); betreffen; ~**able** ☐ [~təbl] achtbar; ansehnlich, anständig; *bsd.* † solid; ~**ful** ☐ [~tful] ehrerbietig; *yours* ~*ly* hochachtungsvoll; ~**ing** [~tiŋ] hinsichtlich (*gen.*); ~**ive** ☐ [~iv] jeweilig; *we went to our* ~ *places* wir gingen jeder an seinen Platz; ~**ively** [~vli] beziehungsweise; je.

respirat|ion [respə'reiʃən] **Atmen** *n*; **Atemzug** *m*; ~**or** ['respəreitə] **Atemfilter** *m*; ⚕ **Atemgerät** *n*; **Gasmaske** *f*.

respire [ris'paiə] atmen; aufatmen.

respite ['respait] **Frist** *f*; **Stundung** *f*.

resplendent ☐ [ris'plendənt] glänzend.

respond [ris'pɔnd] antworten, erwidern; ~ *to* reagieren auf (*acc.*).

response [ris'pɔns] **Antwort** *f*, **Erwiderung** *f*; *fig.* **Reaktion** *f*.

responsi|bility [rispɔnsə'biliti] **Verantwortlichkeit** *f*; **Verantwortung** *f*; † **Zahlungsfähigkeit** *f*; ~**ble** [ris'pɔnsəbl] verantwortlich; verantwortungsvoll; † zahlungsfähig.

rest [rest] **1.** **Rest** *m*; **Ruhe** *f*; **Rast** *f*; **Schlaf** *m*; *fig.* **Tod** *m*; **Stütze** *f*; **Pause** *f*; **2.** *v/i.* ruhen; rasten; schlafen; (sich) lehnen, sich stützen (*on* auf *acc.*); ~ (*up*)*on fig.* beruhen auf (*dat.*); *in* ~ *em Zustand* bleiben; *v/t.* (aus)ruhen lassen; stützen.

restaurant ['restərɔ̃:ŋ, ~rɔnt] **Gaststätte** *f*.

rest-cure ⚕ ['restkjuə] **Liegekur** *f*.

restful ['restful] ruhig, geruhsam.

resting-place ['restiŋpleis] **Ruheplatz** *m*, **-stätte** *f*.

restitution [resti'tju:ʃən] **Wiederherstellung** *f*; **Rückerstattung** *f*.

restive ☐ ['restiv] widerspenstig.

restless ['restlis] ruhelos; rastlos; unruhig; ~**ness** [~snis] **Ruhelosigkeit** *f*; **Rastlosigkeit** *f*; **Unruhe** *f*.

restorat|ion [restə'reiʃən] **Wiederherstellung** *f*; **Wiedereinsetzung** *f*; **Rekonstruktion** *f*, **Nachbildung** *f*; ~**ive** [ris'tɔrətiv] **1.** stärkend; **2.** **Stärkungsmittel** *n*.

restore [ris'tɔ:] wiederherstellen; wiedereinsetzen (*to in acc.*); wiedergeben; ~ *to health* wieder gesund machen.

restrain [ris'trein] zurückhalten (*from* von); in **Schranken** halten; unterdrücken; einsperren; ~**t** [~nt] **Zurückhaltung** *f*; **Beschränkung** *f*, **Zwang** *m*; **Zwanghaft** *f*.

restrict [ris'trikt] be-, einschränken; ~**ion** [~kʃən] **Be-**, **Einschränkung** *f*; **Vorbehalt** *m*.

result [ri'zʌlt] **1.** **Ergebnis** *n*, **Folge** *f*, **Resultat** *n*; **2.** folgen, sich ergeben (*from* aus); ~ *in* hinauslaufen auf (*acc.*), zur **Folge** haben.

resum|e [ri'zju:m] wiedernehmen, -erlangen; wiederaufnehmen; zs.-fassen; ~**ption** [ri'zʌmpʃən] **Zurücknahme** *f*; **Wiederaufnahme** *f*.

resurgent [ri'sə:dʒənt] sich wiedererhebend, wieder aufkommend.

resurrection [rezə'rekʃən] **Wiederaufleben** *n*; ⚭ *eccl.* (Wieder)**Auferstehung** *f*.

resuscitate [ri'sʌsiteit] wiedererwecken, wiederbeleben.

retail 1. ['ri:teil] **Einzelhandel** *m*; *by* ~ im **Einzelverkauf**; **2.** [~] **Einzelhandels...**, **Detail...**; **3.** [ri:'teil] im kleinen verkaufen; ~**er** [~lə] **Einzelhändler(in)**.

retain [ri'tein] behalten (*a. fig.*); zurück-, festhalten; beibehalten; *Anwalt* nehmen.

retaliat|e [ri'tælieit] *v/t.* **Unrecht** vergelten; *v/i.* sich rächen; ~**ion** [ritæli'eiʃən] **Vergeltung** *f*.

retard [ri'tɑ:d] verzögern; aufhalten; verspäten.

retention [ri'tenʃən] **Zurück-**, **Behalten** *n*; **Beibehaltung** *f*.

reticent ['retisənt] verschwiegen; schweigsam; zurückhaltend.

retinue ['retinju:] **Gefolge** *n*.

retir|e [ri'taiə] *v/t.* zurückziehen; pensionieren; *v/i.* sich zurückziehen; zurück-, abtreten; in den **Ruhestand** treten; ~**ed** ☐ zurückgezogen; im **Ruhestand** (lebend); entlegen; ~ *pay* **Pension** *f*; ~**ement** [~əmənt] **Sichzurückziehen** *n*; **Aus-**, **Rücktritt** *m*; **Ruhestand** *m*; **Zurückgezogenheit** *f*; ~**ing** [~əriŋ] zurückhaltend; schüchtern; ~ *pension* **Ruhegehalt** *n*.

retort [ri'tɔ:t] **1.** **Erwiderung** *f*; 🝪 **Retorte** *f*; **2.** erwidern.

retouch ['ri:'tʌtʃ] *et.* überarbeiten; *phot.* retuschieren.

retrace [ri'treis] zurückverfolgen; ∼ one's steps zurückgehen.

retract [ri'trækt] (sich) zurückziehen; ⊕ einziehen; widerrufen.

retread ['ri:tred] 1. Reifen runderneuern; 2. runderneuerter Reifen.

retreat [ri'tri:t] 1. Rückzug m; Zurückgezogenheit f; Zuflucht(sort m) f; ✕ Zapfenstreich m; beat a ∼ a. fig. es aufgeben; 2. sich zurückziehen; fig. zurücktreten.

retrench [ri'trentʃ] (sich) einschränken; kürzen; Wort etc. streichen; ✕ verschanzen.

retribution [retri'bju:ʃən] Vergeltung f.

retrieve [ri'tri:v] wiederbekommen; wiederherstellen; wiedergutmachen; hunt. apportieren.

retro|... ['retrou] (zu)rück...; ∼active [retrou'æktiv] rückwirkend; ∼grade ['retrougreid] 1. rückläufig; 2. zurückgehen; ∼gression [retrou'greʃən] Rück-, Niedergang m; ∼spect ['retrouspekt] Rückblick m; ∼spective □ [retrou'spektiv] zurückblickend; rückwirkend.

retry ⚖ ['ri:'trai] Prozeß wiederaufnehmen.

return [ri'tə:n] 1. Rückkehr f; Wiederkehr f; parl. Wiederwahl f; oft ∼s pl. ✚ Gewinn m, Ertrag m; Umsatz m; ⚕ Rückfall m; Rückgabe f, Rückzahlung f; Vergeltung f; Erwiderung f; Gegenleistung f; Dank m; amtlicher Bericht; Wahlergebnis n; Steuererklärung f; F Rückfahrkarte f; attr. Rück...; many happy ∼s of the day herzliche Glückwünsche zum Geburtstag; in ∼ dafür; als Ersatz (for für); by ∼ (of post) postwendend; ∼ ticket Rückfahrkarte f; 2. v/i. zurückkehren, wiederkehren; v/t. zurückgeben; zurücktun; zurückzahlen; zurücksenden; Dank abstatten; erwidern; berichten, angeben; parl. wählen; Gewinn abwerfen.

reunification pol. ['ri:ju:nifi'keiʃən] Wiedervereinigung f.

reunion ['ri:'ju:njən] Wiedervereinigung f; Treffen n, Zs.-kunft f.

reval|**orization** ✝ [ri:vælərai'zeiʃən] Aufwertung f; ∼**uation** [‿lju:'eiʃən] Neubewertung f.

revamp ⊕ ['ri:'væmp] vorschuhen; Am. F aufmöbeln; erneuern.

reveal [ri'vi:l] enthüllen; offenbaren; ∼**ing** [‿liŋ] aufschlußreich.

revel ['revl] 1. Lustbarkeit f; Gelage n; 2. ausgelassen sein; schwelgen; zechen.

revelation [revi'leiʃən] Enthüllung f; Offenbarung f.

revel|**l)er** ['revlə] Feiernde(r m) f; Zecher m; ∼**ry** [‿lri] Gelage n; Lustbarkeit f, Rummel m; Orgie f.

revenge [ri'vendʒ] 1. Rache f;

Sport: Revanche f; 2. rächen; ∼**ful** □ [‿dʒful] rachsüchtig; ∼**r** [‿dʒə] Rächer(in).

revenue ['revinju:] Einkommen n; ∼s pl. Einkünfte pl.; ∼ board, ∼ office Finanzamt n.

reverberate [ri'və:bəreit] zurückwerfen; zurückstrahlen; widerhallen.

revere [ri'viə] (ver)ehren; ∼**nce** ['revərəns] 1. Verehrung f; Ehrfurcht f; 2. (ver)ehren; ∼**nd** [‿nd] 1. ehrwürdig; 2. Geistliche(r) m.

reverent(ial) □ ['revərənt, revə'renʃəl] ehrerbietig, ehrfurchtsvoll.

reverie ['revəri] Träumerei f.

revers|**al** [ri'və:səl] Umkehrung f; Umschwung m; ⚖ Umstoßung f; ⊕ Umsteuerung f; ∼**e** [‿ə:s] 1. Gegenteil n; Kehrseite f; Rückschlag m; 2. □ umgekehrt; Rück(wärts)...; ∼ (gear) mot. Rückwärtsgang m; ∼ side linke Stoff-Seite; 3. umkehren, umdrehen; Urteil umstoßen; ⊕ umsteuern; ∼**ion** [‿ə:ʃən] Umkehrung f; Rückkehr f; ⚖ Heimfall m; biol. Rückartung f.

revert [ri'və:t] um-, zurückkehren; biol. zurückarten; Blick wenden.

review [ri'vju:] 1. Nachprüfung f; ⚖ Revision f; ✕, ⚓ Parade f; Rückblick m; Überblick m; Rezension f; Zeitschrift f; pass s.th. in ∼ et. Revue passieren lassen; 2. (über-, nach)prüfen; zurückblicken auf (acc.); überblicken; ✕, ⚓ besichtigen; rezensieren; ∼**er** [‿u(:)ə] Rezensent m. [fen.\

revile [ri'vail] schmähen, beschimp-\

revis|**e** [ri'vaiz] überarbeiten, durchsehen, revidieren; ∼**ion** [ri'viʒən] Revision f; Überarbeitung f.

reviv|**al** [ri'vaivəl] Wiederbelebung f; Wiederaufleben n, Wiederaufblühen n; Erneuerung f; fig. Erweckung f; ∼**e** [‿aiv] wiederbeleben; wieder aufleben (lassen); erneuern; wieder aufblühen.

revocation [revə'keiʃən] Widerruf m; Aufhebung f.

revoke [ri'vouk] v/t. widerrufen; v/i. Karten: nicht bedienen.

revolt [ri'voult] 1. Revolte f, Empörung f, Aufruhr m; 2. v/i. sich empören; abfallen; v/t. fig. abstoßen.

revolution [revə'lu:ʃən] Umwälzung f, Umdrehung f; pol. Revolution f; ∼**ary** [‿ʃnəri] 1. revolutionär; 2. a. ∼**ist** [‿ʃnist] Revolutionär(in); ∼**ize** [‿ʃnaiz] aufwiegeln; umgestalten.

revolv|**e** [ri'vɔlv] v/i. sich drehen (about, round um); v/t. umdrehen; fig. erwägen; ∼**ing** [‿viŋ] sich drehend; Dreh...

revue thea. [ri'vju:] Revue f; Kabarett n.

revulsion [ri'vʌlʃən] fig. Umschwung m; ⚕ Ableitung f.

reward [ri'wɔːd] **1.** Belohnung *f*; Vergeltung *f*; **2.** belohnen; vergelten.

rewrite ['riː'rait] [*irr. (write)*] neu (*od.* um)schreiben.

rhapsody ['ræpsədi] Rhapsodie *f*; *fig.* Schwärmerei *f*; Wortschwall *m*.

rhetoric ['retərik] Rhetorik *f*.

rheumatism ⚕ ['ruːmətizəm] Rheumatismus *m*.

rhubarb ⚘ ['ruːbɑːb] Rhabarber *m*.

rhyme [raim] **1.** Reim *m* (*to* auf *acc.*); Vers *m*; *without ~ or reason* ohne Sinn u. Verstand; **2.** (sich) reimen.

rhythm ['riðəm] Rhythmus *m*; **~ic(al** □) ['riðmik(əl)] rhythmisch.

Rialto *Am.* [ri'æltou] Theaterviertel *n e-r Stadt, bsd. in New York.*

rib [rib] **1.** Rippe *f*; **2.** rippen; *sl.* aufziehen, necken.

ribald ['ribəld] lästerlich; unflätig; **~ry** [ˌdri] Zoten *f/pl.*; derbe Späße *m/pl.*

ribbon ['ribən] Band *n*; Streifen *m*; **~s** *pl.* Fetzen *m/pl.*; Zügel *m/pl.*; *~ building, ~ development* Reihenbau *m*.

rice [rais] Reis *m*.

rich □ [ritʃ] reich (*in* an *dat.*); reichlich; prächtig, kostbar; ergiebig, fruchtbar; voll (*Ton*); schwer (*Speise, Wein, Duft*); satt (*Farbe*); **~es** ['ritʃiz] *pl.* Reichtum *m*, Reichtümer *m/pl.*; **~ness** [ˌnis] Reichtum *m*; Fülle *f*.

rick ⚘ [rik] (Heu)Schober *m*.

ricket|s ⚕ ['rikits] *sg. od. pl.* Rachitis *f*; **~y** [ˌti] rachitisch; wack(e)lig (*Möbel*).

rid [rid] [*irr.*] befreien, frei machen (*of* von); *get ~ of* loswerden.

ridden ['ridn] **1.** *p.p. von* ride 2; **2.** *in Zssgn:* bedrückt *od.* geplagt von ...

riddle ['ridl] **1.** Rätsel *n*; grobes Sieb; **2.** sieben; durchlöchern.

ride [raid] **1.** Ritt *m*; Fahrt *f*; Reitweg *m*; **2.** [*irr.*] *v/i.* reiten; rittlings sitzen; fahren; treiben; schweben; liegen; *v/t.* Pferd *etc.* reiten; *Land* durchreiten; **~r** ['raidə] Reiter(in) *f*; Fahrende(r *m*) *f*.

ridge [ridʒ] **1.** (Gebirgs)Kamm *m*, Grat *m*; ▲ First *m*; ⚘ Rain *m*; **2.** (sich) furchen.

ridicul|e ['ridikjuːl] **1.** Hohn *m*, Spott *m*; **2.** lächerlich machen; **~ous** □ [ri'dikjuləs] lächerlich.

riding ['raidiŋ] Reiten *n*; *attr.* Reit... [*~ with* voll von.]

rife □ [raif] häufig; vorherrschend;}

riff-raff ['rifræf] Gesindel *n*.

rifle ['raifl] **1.** Gewehr *n*; **2.** (aus-) plündern; **~man** ⚔ Schütze *m*.

rift [rift] Riß *m*, Sprung *m*; Spalte *f*.

rig[1] [rig] **1.** Markt *etc.* manipulieren; **2.** Schwindelmanöver *n*.

rig[2] [ˌ] **1.** ⚓ Takelung *f*; F Aufma-chung *f*; **2.** auftakeln; *~ s.o. out* j-n versorgen *od.* ausrüsten; *j-n herausputzen od.* herrichten; **~ging** ⚓ ['rigiŋ] Takelage *f*.

right [rait] **1.** □ recht; richtig; recht (*Ggs. left*); *be ~* recht haben; *all ~!* alles in Ordnung!; ganz recht!; *put od. set ~* in Ordnung bringen; berichtigen; **2.** *adv.* recht, richtig; gerade; direkt; ganz (und gar); *~ away* sogleich; *~ on* geradeaus; **3.** Recht *n*; Rechte *f*, rechte Seite *od.* Hand; *the ~ and wrongs* der wahre Sachverhalt; *by ~ of* auf Grund (*gen.*); *on od. to the ~* rechts; *~ of way* Wegerecht *n*; Vorfahrt(srecht *n*) *f*; **4.** *j-m* Recht verschaffen; *et. in* Ordnung bringen; ⚓ (sich) aufrichten; **~-down** ['rait'daun] regelrecht, ausgemacht; wirklich; **~eous** □ ['raitʃəs] rechtschaffen; **~ful** □ ['raitful] recht(mäßig); gerecht.

rigid □ ['ridʒid] starr; *fig. a.* streng, hart; **~ity** [ri'dʒiditi] Starrheit *f*; Strenge *f*, Härte *f*.

rigmarole ['rigməroul] Geschwätz *n*.

rigor ⚕ ['raigɔː] Fieberfrost *m*.

rigo(u)r ['rigə] Strenge *f*, Härte *f*. **rigorous** □ ['rigərəs] streng, rigoros.

rim [rim] **1.** Felge *f*; Radkranz *m*; Rand *m*; **2.** rändern; einfassen.

rime [raim] Reim *m*; Rauhreif *m*.

rind [raind] Rinde *f*, Schale *f*; *Speck*-Schwarte *f*.

ring[1] [riŋ] **1.** Klang *m*; Geläut(e) *n*; Klingeln *n*; Rufzeichen *n*; Anruf *m*; *give s.o. a ~* j-n anrufen; **2.** [*irr.*] läuten; klingen (lassen); erschallen (*with* von); *~ again* widerhallen; *~ off teleph.* das Gespräch beenden; *~ the bell* klingeln; *~ s.o. up* j-n *od.* bei j-m anrufen.

ring[2] [ˌ] **1.** Ring *m*; Kreis *m*; **2.** beringen; *mst ~ in, ~ round, ~ about* umringen; **~leader** ['riŋliːdə] Rädelsführer *m*; **~let** [ˌlit] (Ringel)Locke *f*.

rink [riŋk] Eisbahn *f*; Rollschuhbahn *f*.

rinse [rins] *oft ~ out* (aus)spülen.

riot ['raiət] **1.** Tumult *m*; Aufruhr *m*; Orgie *f* (*a. fig.*); *run ~* durchgehen; (sich aus)toben; **2.** Krawall machen, im Aufruhr sein; toben; schwelgen; **~er** [ˌtə] Aufrührer(in); Randalierer *m*; **~ous** □ [ˌtəs] aufrührerisch; lärmend; liederlich (*Leben*).

rip [rip] **1.** Riß *m*; **2.** (auf)trennen; (auf-, zer)reißen; (dahin)sausen.

ripe □ [raip] reif; *~n* ['raipən] reifen; **~ness** ['raipnis] Reife *f*.

ripple ['ripl] **1.** kleine Welle; Kräuselung *f*; Geriesel *n*; **2.** (sich) kräuseln; rieseln.

rise [raiz] **1.** (An-, Auf)Steigen *n*;

Anschwellen *n*; (Preis-, Gehalts-) Erhöhung *f*; *fig.* Aufstieg *m*; Steigung *f*; Anhöhe *f*; Ursprung *m*; take (one's) ~ entstehen; entspringen; **2.** [*irr.*] sich erheben, aufstehen; die Sitzung schließen; steigen; aufsteigen (*a. fig.*); auferstehen; aufgehen (*Sonne, Samen*); anschwellen; sich empören; entspringen (*Fluß*); ~ to sich e-r Lage gewachsen zeigen; **~n** ['rizn] *p.p. von* rise **2**; **~r** ['raizə]: early ~ Frühaufsteher(in).

rising ['raiziŋ] **1.** (Auf)Steigen *n*; Steigung *f*; *ast.* Aufgang *m*; Aufstand *m*; **2.** heranwachsend (*Generation*).

risk [risk] **1.** Gefahr *f*, Wagnis *n*; ✝ Risiko *n*; run the ~ Gefahr laufen; **2.** wagen, riskieren; **~y** □ ['riski] gefährlich, gewagt.

rit|e [rait] Ritus *m*, Brauch *m*; **~ual** ['ritjuəl] **1.** rituell; **2.** Ritual *n*.

rival ['raivəl] **1.** Nebenbuhler(in); Rivale *m*; **2.** rivalisierend; ✝ Konkurrenz...; **3.** wetteifern (mit); **~ry** [.lri] Rivalität *f*; Wetteifer *m*.

rive [raiv] [*irr.*] (sich) spalten; **~n** ['rivən] *p.p. von* rive.

river ['rivə] Fluß *m*; Strom *m* (*a. fig.*); **~side 1.** Flußufer *n*; **2.** am Wasser (gelegen).

rivet ['rivit] **1.** ⊕ Niet(e *f*) *m*; **2.** (ver)nieten; *fig.* heften (to an *acc.*; on, upon auf *acc.*); fesseln.

rivulet ['rivjulit] Bach *m*, Flüßchen *n*.

road [roud] Straße *f* (*a. fig.*), Weg *m*; *Am.* railroad; *mst* **~s** *pl.* ⚓ Reede *f*; **~stead** ⚓ ['roudsted] Reede *f*; **~ster** [.tə] Roadster *m*, offener Sportwagen; **~way** Fahrbahn *f*.

roam [roum] *v/i.* umherstreifen, wandern; *v/t.* durchstreifen.

roar [rɔː] **1.** brüllen; brausen, tosen, donnern; **2.** Gebrüll *n*; Brausen *n*; Krachen *n*, Getöse *n*; brüllendes Gelächter.

roast [roust] **1.** rösten, braten; **2.** geröstet; gebraten; ~ meat Braten *m*.

rob [rɔb] (be)rauben; **~ber** ['rɔbə] Räuber *m*; **~bery** [.əri] Raub (-überfall) *m*; Räuberei *f*.

robe [roub] (Amts)Robe *f*, Talar *m*; (Staats)Kleid *n*; *Am.* Morgenrock *m*.

robin *orn.* ['rɔbin] Rotkehlchen *n*.

robust □ [rə'bʌst] robust, kräftig.

rock [rɔk] **1.** Felsen *m*; Klippe *f*; Gestein *n*; Zuckerstange *f*; ~ crystal Bergkristall *m*; **2.** schaukeln; (ein)wiegen.

rocker ['rɔkə] Kufe *f*; *Am.* Schaukelstuhl *m*; Rocker *m*, Halbstarke(r) *m*.

rocket ['rɔkit] Rakete *f*; *attr.* Ra-

keten...; **~powered** mit Raketenantrieb; **~ry** [.tri] Raketentechnik*f*.

rocking-chair ['rɔkiŋtʃeə] Schaukelstuhl *m*.

rocky ['rɔki] felsig; Felsen...

rod [rɔd] Rute *f*; Stab *m*; ⊕ Stange *f*; Meßrute *f* (5½ *yards*); *Am. sl.* Pistole *f*.

rode [roud] *pret. von* ride **2**.

rodent ['roudənt] Nagetier *n*.

rodeo *Am.* [rou'deiou] Rodeo *m*; Zusammentreiben *n*; Cowboyturnier *n*.

roe¹ [rou] Reh *n*.

roe² *ichth.* [.] *a.* hard ~ Rogen *m*; soft ~ Milch *f*.

rogu|e [roug] Schurke *m*; Schelm *m*; **~ish** ['rougiʃ] schurkisch; schelmisch.

roister ['rɔistə] krakeelen.

role, rôle *thea.* [roul] Rolle *f* (*a. fig.*).

roll [roul] **1.** Rolle *f*; ⊕ Walze *f*; Brötchen *n*, Semmel *f*; Verzeichnis *n*; Urkunde *f*; (Donner)Rollen *n*; (Trommel)Wirbel *m*; ⚓ Schlingern *n*; **2.** *v/t.* rollen; wälzen; walzen; *Zigarette* drehen; ~ up zusammenrollen; einwickeln; *v/i.* rollen; sich wälzen; wirbeln (*Trommel*); ⚓ schlingern; **~call** ✕ ['roulkɔːl] Appell *m*; **~er** ['roulə] Rolle *f*, Walze *f*; Sturzwelle *f*; ~ coaster *Am.* Achterbahn *f*; ~ skate Rollschuh *m*.

rolliking ['rɔlikiŋ] übermütig.

rolling ['rouliŋ] rollend; Roll..., Walz...; ~ mill ⊕ Walzwerk *n*.

Roman ['roumən] **1.** römisch; **2.** Römer(in); *mst* ♀ *typ.* Antiqua *f*.

romance¹ [rə'mæns] **1.** (Ritter-, Vers)Roman *m*; Abenteuer-, Liebesroman *m*; Romanze *f* (*a. fig.*); *fig.* Märchen *n*; Romantik *f*; **2.** *fig.* aufschneiden.

Romance² *ling.* [.]: ~ languages romanische Sprachen *f/pl.*

romancer [rə'mænsə] Romanschreiber(in); Aufschneider(in).

Romanesque [roumə'nesk] **1.** romanisch; **2.** romanischer Baustil.

romantic [rə'mæntik] (~ally) romantisch; **~ism** [.isizəm] Romantik *f*; **~ist** [.ist] Romantiker(in).

romp [rɔmp] **1.** Range *f*, Wildfang *m*; Balgerei *f*; **2.** sich balgen, toben; **~er(s)** ['rɔmpə(z)] Spielanzug *m*.

rood [ruːd] Kruzifix *n*; Viertelmorgen *m* (10,117 *Ar*).

roof [ruːf] **1.** Dach *n*; ~ of the mouth Gaumen *m*; **2.** *a.* ~ over überdachen; **~ing** ['ruːfiŋ] **1.** Bedachung *f*; **2.** Dach...; ~ felt Dachpappe *f*.

rook [ruk] **1.** *Schach:* Turm *m*; *fig.* Gauner *m*; *orn.* Saatkrähe *f*; **2.** betrügen.

room [rum] **1.** Raum *m*; Platz *m*; Zimmer *n*; Möglichkeit *f*; **~s** *pl.* Wohnung *f*; in my ~ an meiner Stelle; **2.** *Am.* wohnen; **~er** ['rumə]

bsd. *Am.* Untermieter(in); ~ing-
house ['ruminhaus] *bsd. Am.*
Miets-, Logierhaus *n*; ~mate Stu-
benkamerad *m*; ~y □ ['rumi] geräumig.

roost [ru:st] **1.** Schlafplatz *m e-s
Vogels*; Hühnerstange *f*; Hühner-
stall *m*; **2.** sich (zum Schlaf) nieder-
hocken; *fig.* übernachten; ~er
['ru:stə] Haushahn *m*.

root [ru:t] **1.** Wurzel *f*; **2.** (ein)wur-
zeln; (auf)wühlen; ~ *for Am. sl.*
Stimmung machen für; ~ out
ausrotten; ~ *od.* up ausgraben;
~ed ['ru:tid] eingewurzelt; ~er *Am.
sl.* ['ru:tə] Fanatiker *m für et.*

rope [roup] **1.** Tau *n*, Seil *n*; Strick
m; Schnur *f Perlen etc.*; *be at the
end of one's* ~ F mit s-m Latein zu
Ende sein; *know the* ~s sich auskennen; **2.** mit e-m Seil befestigen
od. (*mst* ~ *in od. off od. out*) absperren; anseilen; ~way ['roupwei]
Seilbahn *f*.

ropy ['roupi] klebrig, zähflüssig.

rosary *eccl.* ['rouzəri] Rosenkranz
m.

rose[1] [rouz] ⚥ Rose *f*; (Gießkan-
nen)Brause *f*; Rosenrot *n*.

rose[2] [~] *pret. von* rise 2.

rosebud ['rouzbʌd] Rosenknospe *f*;
Am. hübsches Mädchen; Debü-
tantin *f*.

rosin ['rɔzin] (Geigen)Harz *n*.

rostrum ['rɔstrəm] Rednertribüne *f*.

rosy □ ['rouzi] rosig.

rot [rɔt] **1.** Fäulnis *f*; *sl.* Quatsch *m*;
2. *v/t.* faulen lassen; Quatsch
machen mit *j-m*; *v/i.* verfaulen,
vermodern.

rota|ry ['routəri] drehend; Rota-
tions...; ~te [rou'teit] (sich) drehen,
(ab)wechseln; ~tion [~'eiʃən] Umdrehung *f*; Kreislauf *m*; Ab-
wechs(e)lung *f*; ~tory ['routətəri]
s. rotary; abwechselnd.

rote [rout]: *by* ~ auswendig.

rotten □ ['rɔtn] verfault, faul(ig);
mod(e)rig; morsch (*alle a. fig.*); *sl.*
saumäßig, dreckig.

rotund □ [rou'tʌnd] rund; voll
(*Stimme*); hochtrabend.

rouge [ru:ʒ] **1.** Rouge *n*; Silberputz-
mittel *n*; **2.** Rouge auflegen (auf
acc.).

rough [rʌf] **1.** □ rauh; roh; grob;
fig. ungehobelt; ungefähr (*Schätzung*); ~ *and ready* grob (gearbeitet);
Not..., Behelfs...; ~ *copy* roher Entwurf; **2.** Rauhe *n*, Grobe *n*; Lümmel *m*; **3.** (an-, auf)rauhen; ~ *it*
sich mühsam durchschlagen; ~cast
['rʌfka:st] **1.** ⊕ Rohputz *m*; **2.** unfertig; **3.** ⊕ roh verputzen; roh entwerfen; ~en ['rʌfən] rauh machen
od. werden; ~neck *Am. sl.* Rabau-
ke *m*; ~ness [~nis] Rauheit *f*; Roheit *f*; Grobheit *f*; ~shod: *ride* ~
over rücksichtslos behandeln.

round [raund] **1.** □ rund; voll
(*Stimme etc.*); flott (*Gangart*); ab-
gerundet (*Stil*); unverblümt; ~
game Gesellschaftsspiel *n*; ~ *trip*
Rundreise *f*; **2.** *adv.* rund-, rings-
um(her); *a.* ~ *about in der Runde;
all* ~ ringsum; *fig.* ohne Unterschied; *all the year* ~ das ganze Jahr
hindurch; **3.** *prp.* um ... herum;
4. Rund *n*, Kreis *m*; Runde *f*;
Kreislauf *m*; (Leiter)Sprosse *f*;
Rundgesang *m*; *Lach- etc.*Salve *f*;
100 ~s ⚔ 100 Schuß; **5.** *v/t.* runden;
herumgehen *od.* herumfahren um;
~ *off* abrunden; ~ *up* einkreisen; *v/i.*
sich runden; sich umdrehen; ~
about ['raundəbaut] **1.** umschwei-
fig; **2.** Umweg *m*; Karussell *n*;
Kreisverkehr *m*; ~ish [~diʃ] rundlich; ~up Einkreisung *f*; Razzia *f*.

rous|e [rauz] *v/t.* wecken; ermun-
tern; aufjagen; (auf)reizen; ~ *o.s.*
sich aufraffen (*mst* Hafen)Arbeiter.

roustabout *Am.* ['raustəbaut] ungelernter (*mst* Hafen)Arbeiter.

rout [raut] **1.** Rotte *f*; wilde Flucht;
a. put to ~ vernichtend schlagen;
2. aufwühlen.

route [ru:t, ⚔ *a.* raut] Weg *m*; ⚔
Marschroute *f*.

routine [ru:'ti:n] **1.** Routine *f*;
2. üblich; Routine...

rove [rouv] umherstreifen, umherwandern.

row[1] [rou] **1.** Reihe *f*; Ruderfahrt *f*;
2. rudern.

row[2] F [rau] **1.** Spektakel *m*; Krach
m; Schlägerei *f*; **2.** ausschimpfen.

row-boat ['roubout] Ruderboot *n*.

rower ['rouə] Ruder|er *m*, -in *f*.

royal □ ['rɔiəl] königlich; prächtig;
~ty [~lti] Königtum *n*, -reich *n*;
Königswürde *f*; königliche Persönlichkeit; Tantieme *f*.

rub [rʌb] **1.** Reiben *n*; Schwierigkeit *f*; *fig.* Stichelei *f*; Unannehmlichkeit *f*; **2.** *v/t.* reiben; (ab)wischen;
(wund)scheuern; schleifen; ~ *down*
abreiben; ~ *in* einreiben; *fig.* betonen; ~ *off* abreiben; ~ *out* auslöschen; ~ *up* auffrischen; verreiben;
v/i. sich reiben; *fig.* ~ *along od.
on od. through* sich durchschlagen.

rubber ['rʌbə] **1.** Gummi *n*, *m*; Radiergummi *m*; Masseur *m*; Wisch-
tuch *n*; *Whist:* Robber *m*; ~s *pl.
Am.* Gummischuhe *m/pl.*; **2.**
Gummi...; ~ *check Am. sl.* geplatz-
ter Scheck; ~neck *Am. sl.* **1.** Gaf-
fer(in); **2.** sich den Hals verrenken; mithören; ~ *stamp* Gummi-
stempel *m*; *Am.* F *fig.* Nachbeter
m; ~stamp automatisch gutheißen.

rubbish ['rʌbiʃ] Schutt *m*; Abfall *m*;
Kehricht *m*; *fig.* Schund *m*; Unsinn *m*.

rubble ['rʌbl] Schutt *m*.

rube *Am.sl.* [ru:b] Bauernlümmel *m.*
ruby ['ru:bi] Rubin(rot *n*) *m.*
rucksack ['ruksæk] Rucksack *m.*
rudder ['rʌdə] ⏚ (Steuer)Ruder *n*; ⚓ Seitenruder *n.*
rudd|iness ['rʌdinis] Röte *f*; ~y ['rʌdi] rot; rotbäckig.
rude □ [ru:d] unhöflich; unanständig; heftig, unsanft; ungebildet; einfach, kunstlos; robust; roh.
rudiment *biol.* ['ru:dimənt] Ansatz *m*; ~s *pl.* Anfangsgründe *m/pl.*
rueful □ ['ru:ful] reuig; traurig.
ruff [rʌf] Halskrause *f.*
ruffian ['rʌfjən] Rohling *m*; Raufbold *m*; Schurke *m.*
ruffle ['rʌfl] 1. Krause *f*, Rüsche *f*; Kräuseln *n*; *fig.* Unruhe *f*; 2. kräuseln; zerdrücken; zerknüllen; *fig.* aus der Ruhe bringen; stören.
rug [rʌg] (Reise-, Woll)Decke *f*; Vorleger *m*, Brücke *f*; ~ged □ ['rʌgid] rauh (*a. fig.*); uneben; gefurcht.
ruin [ruin] 1. Ruin *m*, Zs.-bruch *m*; Untergang *m*; *mst* ~s *pl.* Ruine(n *pl.*) *f*, Trümmer *f/pl.*; 2. ruinieren; zugrunde richten; zerstören; verderben; ~ous □ ['ruinəs] ruinenhaft, verfallen; verderblich, ruinös.
rul|e [ru:l] 1. Regel *f*; Vorschrift *f*; Ordnung *f*; Satzung *f*; Herrschaft *f*; Lineal *n*; *as a* ~ in der Regel; ~(s) *of the road* Straßenverkehrsordnung *f*; 2. *v/t.* regeln; leiten; beherrschen; verfügen; liniieren; ~ *out* ausschließen; *v/i.* herrschen; ~er *f* [ru:lə] Herrscher(in); Lineal *n.*
rum [rʌm] Rum *m*; *Am.* Alkohol *m.*
Rumanian [ru(:)'meinjən] 1. rumänisch; 2. Rumän|e *m*, -in *f*; Rumänisch *n.*
rumble ['rʌmbl] 1. Rumpeln *n*; *a.* ~seat *Am. mot.* Notsitz *m*; *Am.* F Fehde *f* zwischen Gangsterbanden; 2. rumpeln, rasseln; grollen (*Donner*).
rumina|nt ['ru:minənt] 1. wiederkäuend; 2. Wiederkäuer *m*; ~te [~neit] wiederkäuen; *fig.* nachsinnen.
rummage ['rʌmidʒ] 1. Durchsuchung *f*; Ramsch *m*, Restwaren *f/pl.*; 2. *v/t.* durchsuchen, durchstöbern, durchwühlen; *v/i.* wühlen.
rumo(u)r ['ru:mə] 1. Gerücht *n*; 2. (als Gerücht) verbreiten; *it is* ~ed es geht das Gerücht.   [*m.*\
rump *anat.* [rʌmp] Steiß *m*; Rumpf/
rumple ['rʌmpl] zerknittern; zerren, (zer)zausen.
rum-runner *Am.* ['rʌmrʌnə] Alkoholschmuggler *m.*
run [rʌn] 1. [*irr.*] *v/i. allg.* laufen; rennen, (*Maschine, Tier*); eilen; zerlaufen (*Farbe etc.*); umgehen (*Gerücht etc.*); lauten (*Text*); gehen (*Melodie*); † sich stellen (*Preis*); ~ *across s.o.* j-m in die Arme laufen;

~ *away* davonlaufen; ~ *down* ablaufen (*Uhr etc.*); *fig.* herunterkommen; ~ *dry* aus-, vertrocknen; ~ *for parl.* kandidieren für; ~ *into* geraten in (*acc.*); werden zu; *j-m* in die Arme laufen; ~ *low* zur Neige gehen; ~ *mad* verrückt werden; ~ *off* weglaufen; ~ *on* fortfahren; ~ *out*, ~ *short* zu Ende gehen; ~ *through* durchmachen; durchlesen; ~ *to* sich belaufen auf (*acc.*); sich entwickeln zu; ~ *up to* sich belaufen auf (*acc.*); *v/t.* Strecke durchlaufen; Weg einschlagen; laufen lassen; Hand etc. gleiten lassen; stecken, stoßen; transportieren; *Flut* ergießen; *Geschäft* betreiben, leiten; *hunt.* verfolgen, hetzen; um die Wette rennen mit; schmuggeln; heften; ~ *the blockade* die Blockade brechen; ~ *down* umrennen; zur Strecke bringen; *fig.* schlecht machen; herunterwirtschaften; *be* ~ *down* abgearbeitet sein; ~ *errands* Botengänge machen; ~ *in mot.* einfahren; F *Verbrecher* einbuchten; ~ *off* ablaufen lassen; ~ *out* hinausjagen; ~ *over* überfahren; *Text* überfliegen; ~ *s.o. through* j-n durchbohren; ~ *up* Preis, Neubau etc. emportreiben; *Rechnung etc.* auflaufen lassen; 2. Laufen *n*, Rennen *n*, Lauf *m*; Verlauf *m*; Fahrt *f e-s Schiffes*; Reihe *f*; Folge *f*; Serie *f*; Reise *f*, Ausflug *m*; † Andrang *m*; Ansturm *m*; *Am.* Bach *m*; *Am.* Laufmasche *f*; Vieh-Trift *f*; freie Benutzung; Art *f*, Schlag *m*; *the common* ~ die große Masse; *have a* ~ *of 20 nights thea.* 20mal nacheinander gegeben werden; *in the long* ~ auf die Dauer, am Ende; *in the short* ~ fürs nächste.
run|about *mot.* ['rʌnəbaut] kleiner (Sport)Wagen *m*; ~away Ausreißer *m.*
rune [ru:n] Rune *f.*
rung[1] [rʌŋ] *p.p. von* ring 2.
rung[2] [~] (Leiter)Sprosse *f* (*a. fig.*).
run-in ['rʌn'in] *Sport:* Einlauf *m*; *Am.* F Krach *m*, Zs.-stoß *m* (*Streit*).
run|let ['rʌnlit], ~nel ['rʌnl] Rinnsal *n*; Rinnstein *m.*
runner ['rʌnə] Läufer *m*; Bote *m*; (Schlitten)Kufe *f*; Schieber *m am Schirm*; ⚘ Ausläufer *m*; ~up [~ər'ʌp] *Sport:* Zweitbeste(r *m*) *f*; Zweite(r *m*) *f.*
running ['rʌniŋ] 1. laufend; *two days* ~ zwei Tage nacheinander; ~ *hand* Kurrentschrift *f*; 2. Rennen *n*; ~board Trittbrett *n.*
runt [rʌnt] *zo.* Zwergrind *n*; *fig.* Zwerg *m*; *attr.* Zwerg...
runway ['rʌnwei] ⚓ Rollbahn *f*; *hunt.* Wechsel *m*; Holzrutsche *f*; ~ *watching* Ansitzjagd *f.*
rupture ['rʌptʃə] 1. Bruch *m* (*a. ⚕*); 2. brechen; sprengen.
rural □ ['ruərəl] ländlich; Land...

ruse [ruːz] List *f*, Kniff *m*.

rush [rʌʃ] **1.** ♀ Binse *f*; Jagen *n*, Hetzen *n*, Stürmen *n*; (An)Sturm *m*; Andrang *m*; ~ stürmische Nachfrage; ~ hour(s *pl*.) Hauptverkehrszeit *f*; **2.** *v/i.* stürzen, jagen, hetzen, stürmen; ~ at sich stürzen auf (*acc*.); ~ into print *et*. überstürzt veröffentlichen; *v/t*. jagen, hetzen; drängen; ⚔ *a. fig.* stürmen; *sl.* neppen.

russet ['rʌsit] braunrot; grob.

Russian ['rʌʃən] **1.** russisch; **2.** Russ|e *m*, -in *f*; Russisch *n*.

rust [rʌst] **1.** Rost *m*; **2.** (ver-, ein-) rosten (lassen) (*a. fig.*).

rustic ['rʌstik] **1.** (~ally) ländlich; bäurisch; Bauern...; **2.** Bauer *m*.

rustle ['rʌsl] **1.** rascheln (mit *od.* in *dat.*); rauschen; *Am*. F sich ranhalten; *Vieh* stehlen; **2.** Rascheln *n*.

rust|less ['rʌstlis] rostfrei; ~y [~ti] rostig; eingerostet (*a. fig.*); verschossen (*Stoff*); rostfarben.

rut [rʌt] Wagenspur *f*; *bsd. fig.* ausgefahrenes Geleise; *hunt.* Brunst *f*, Brunft *f*.

ruthless □ ['ruːθlis] unbarmherzig; rücksichts-, skrupellos.

rutted ['rʌtid] ausgefahren (*Weg*).

rutty ['rʌti] ausgefahren (*Weg*).

rye ♀ [rai] Roggen *m*.

S

sable ['seibl] Zobel(pelz) *m*; Schwarz *n*.   [**2.** sabotieren.)

sabotage ['sæbətɑːʒ] **1.** Sabotage *f*;)

sabre ['seibə] Säbel *m*.

sack [sæk] **1.** Plünderung *f*; Sack *m*; *Am*. Tüte *f*; Sackkleid *n*; Sakko *m*, *n*; give (get) the ~ F entlassen (werden); den Laufpaß geben (bekommen); **2.** plündern; einsacken; F rausschmeißen; *j-m* den Laufpaß geben; ~cloth [~kləθ], ~ing ['sækiŋ] Sackleinwand *f*.

sacrament *eccl.* ['sækrəmənt] Sakrament *n*.

sacred □ ['seikrid] heilig; geistlich.

sacrifice ['sækrifais] **1.** Opfer *n*; at a ~ ✝ mit Verlust; **2.** opfern; ✝ mit Verlust verkaufen.

sacrileg|e ['sækrilidʒ] Kirchenraub *m*, -schändung *f*; Sakrileg *n*; ~ious □ [sækri'lidʒəs] frevelhaft.

sad □ [sæd] traurig; jämmerlich, kläglich; schlimm, arg; dunkel.

sadden ['sædn] (sich) betrüben.

saddle ['sædl] **1.** Sattel *m*; **2.** satteln; *fig.* belasten; ~r [~lə] Sattler *m*.

sadism ['sædizəm] Sadismus *m*.

sadness ['sædnis] Traurigkeit *f*, Trauer *f*, Schwermut *f*.

safe [seif] **1.** □ *allg.* sicher; unversehrt; zuverlässig; **2.** Safe *m*, *n*, Geldschrank *m*; Speiseschrank *m*; ~-blower *Am*. ['seifblouə] Geldschrankknacker *m*; ~ conduct freies Geleit; Geleitbrief *m*; ~ guard **1.** Schutz *m*; **2.** sichern, schützen.

safety ['seifti] Sicherheit *f*; ~-belt *mot.* Sicherheitsgurt *m*; ~ island Verkehrsinsel *f*; ~-lock Sicherheitsschloß *n*; ~-pin Sicherheitsnadel *f*; ~ razor Rasierapparat *m*.

saffron ['sæfrən] Safran(gelb *n*) *m*.

sag [sæg] durchsacken; ⊕ durchhängen; ⚓ (ab)sacken (*a. fig.*).

sagaci|ous □ [sə'geiʃəs] scharfsinnig; ~ty [sə'gæsiti] Scharfsinn *m*.

sage [seidʒ] **1.** □ klug, weise; **2.** Weise(r) *m*; ♀ Salbei *m*, *f*.

said [sed] *pret. u. p.p. von* say **1.**

sail [seil] **1.** Segel *n*; Fahrt *f*; Windmühlenflügel *m*; (Segel-) Schiff(e *pl.*) *n*; set ~ in See stechen; **2.** *v/i.* (ab)segeln, fahren; *fig.* schweben; *v/t.* befahren; *Schiff* führen; ~-boat *Am*. ['seilbout] Segelboot *n*; ~er ['seilə] Segler *m* (*Schiff*); ~ing-ship ['seiliŋʃip], ~ing-vessel [~ŋvesl] Segelschiff *n*; ~or ['seilə] Seemann *m*, Matrose *m*; be a good (bad) ~ (nicht) seefest sein; ~plane Segelflugzeug *n*.

saint [seint] **1.** Heilige(r *m*) *f*; [*vor npr.* snt] Sankt...; **2.** heiligsprechen; ~ly ['seintli] *adj.* heilig, fromm.

saith ✝ *od. poet.* [seθ] *3. sg. pres. von* say **1.**

sake [seik]: for the ~ of um ... (*gen*.) willen; for my ~ meinetwegen; for God's ~ um Gottes willen.

salad ['sæləd] Salat *m*.

salary ['sæləri] **1.** Besoldung *f*; Gehalt *n*; **2.** besolden; ~-earner [~iəːnə] Gehaltsempfänger(in).

sale [seil] (Aus)Verkauf *m*; Absatz *m*; Auktion *f*; for ~, on ~ zum Verkauf, zu verkaufen, verkäuflich.

sal(e)able ['seiləbl] verkäuflich.

sales|man ['seilzmən] Verkäufer *m*; ~woman Verkäuferin *f*.

salient □ ['seiljənt] vorspringend; *fig.* hervorragend, hervortretend; Haupt...

saline ['seilain] salzig; Salz...

saliva [sə'laivə] Speichel *m*.

sallow ['sælou] blaß; gelblich.

sally ['sæli] **1.** ⚔ Ausbruch *m*; witziger Einfall; **2.** *a.* ~ out ⚔ ausbrechen; ~ forth, ~ out sich aufmachen.

salmon *ichth.* ['sæmən] Lachs *m*, Salm *m*.

saloon [sə'luːn] Salon *m*; (Gesellschafts)Saal *m*; erste Klasse *auf Schiffen*; *Am.* Kneipe *f*.

salt [sɔːlt] 1. Salz *n*; *fig.* Würze *f*; *old* ~ alter Seebär; 2. salzig; gesalzen; Salz...; Pökel...; 3. (ein)salzen; pökeln; ~cellar ['sɔːltselə] Salzfäßchen *n*; ~petre, *Am.* ~peter [ˌtpiːtə] Salpeter *m*; ~water Salzwasser...; ~y [ˌti] salzig.

salubrious □ [sə'luːbriəs], **salutary** □ ['sæljutəri] heilsam, gesund.

salut|ation [sælju(ː)'teiʃən] Gruß *m*, Begrüßung *f*; Anrede *f*; ~e [sə'luːt] 1. Gruß *m*; *co.* Kuß *m*; ✕ Salut *m*; 2. (be)grüßen; ✕ salutieren.

salvage ['sælvidʒ] 1. Bergung(sgut *n*) *f*; Bergegeld *n*; 2. bergen.

salvation [sæl'veiʃən] Erlösung *f*; (Seelen)Heil *n*; *fig.* Rettung *f*; ♀ Army Heilsarmee *f*.

salve¹ [sælv] retten, bergen.

salve² [sɑːv] 1. Salbe *f*; *fig.* Balsam *m*; 2. *mst fig.* (ein)salben; beruhigen.

salvo ['sælvou] Vorbehalt *m*; ✕ Salve *f* (*fig.* Beifall).

same [seim]: the ~ der-, die-, dasselbe; *all the* ~ trotzdem; *it is all the* ~ *to me* es ist mir (ganz) gleich.

samp *Am.* [sæmp] grobgemahlener Mais.

sample ['sɑːmpl] 1. Probe *f*, Muster *n*; 2. bemustern; (aus)probieren.

sanatorium [sænə'tɔːriəm] (*bsd.* Lungen)Sanatorium *n*; Luftkurort *m*.

sanct|ify ['sæŋktifai] heiligen; weihen; ~imonious □ [sæŋkti'mounjəs] scheinheilig; ~ion ['sæŋkʃən] 1. Sanktion *f*; Bestätigung *f*; Genehmigung *f*; Zwangsmaßnahme *f*; 2. bestätigen, genehmigen; ~ity [ˌktiti] Heiligkeit *f*; ~uary [ˌtjuəri] Heiligtum *n*; *das* Allerheiligste; Asyl *n*, Freistätte *f*.

sand [sænd] 1. Sand *m*; ~s *pl.* Sand (-massen *f*/*pl.*) *m*; Sandwüste *f*; Sandbank *f*; 2. mit Sand bestreuen.

sandal ['sændl] Sandale *f*.

sand|-glass ['sændglɑːs] Sanduhr*f*; ~-hill Sanddüne *f*; ~-piper *orn.* Flußuferläufer *m*.

sandwich ['sænwidʒ] 1. Sandwich *n*; 2. *a.* ~ *in* einlegen, einklemmen.

sandy ['sændi] sandig; sandfarben.

sane [sein] geistig gesund; vernünftig (*Antwort etc.*).

sang [sæŋ] *pret. von* sing.

sanguin|ary □ ['sæŋgwinəri] blutdürstig; blutig; ~e [ˌwin] leichtblütig; zuversichtlich; vollblütig.

sanitarium *Am.* [sæni'tɛəriəm] = sanatorium.

sanitary □ ['sænitəri] Gesundheits...; gesundheitlich; ⊕ Sanitär...; ~ *towel* Damenbinde *f*.

sanit|ation [sæni'teiʃən] Gesundheitspflege *f*; sanitäre Einrichtung; ~y ['sæniti] gesunder Verstand.

sank [sæŋk] *pret. von* sink 1.

Santa Claus [sæntə'klɔːz] Nikolaus *m*.

sap [sæp] 1. ♀ Saft *m*; *fig.* Lebenskraft *f*; ✕ Sappe *f*; 2. untergraben (*a. fig.*); *sl.* büffeln; ~less ['sæplis] saft-, kraftlos; ~ling [ˌliŋ] junger Baum; *fig.* Grünschnabel *m*.

sapphire *min.* ['sæfaiə] Saphir *m*.

sappy ['sæpi] saftig; *fig.* kraftvoll.

sarcasm ['sɑːkæzəm] bitterer Spott.

sardine *ichth.* [sɑː'diːn] Sardine *f*.

sash [sæʃ] Schärpe *f*; Fensterrahmen *m*. [befenster *n*.]

sash-window ['sæʃwindou] Schie-}

sat [sæt] *pret. u. p.p. von* sit.

Satan ['seitən] Satan *m*.

satchel ['sætʃəl] Schulmappe *f*.

sate [seit] (über)sättigen.

sateen [sæ'tiːn] Satin *m*.

satellite ['sætəlait] Satellit(enstaat) *m*.

satiate ['seiʃieit] (über)sättigen.

satin ['sætin] Seidensatin *m*.

satir|e ['sætaiə] Satire *f*; ~ist ['sætərist] Satiriker *m*; ~ize [ˌraiz] verspotten.

satisfaction [sætis'fækʃən] Befriedigung *f*; Genugtuung *f*; Zufriedenheit *f*; Sühne *f*; Gewißheit *f*.

satisfactory □ [sætis'fæktəri] befriedigend, zufriedenstellend.

satisfy ['sætisfai] befriedigen; genügen (*dat.*); zufriedenstellen; überzeugen; *Zweifel* beheben.

saturate [ˌ u. *fig.* ['sætʃəreit] sättigen.

Saturday ['sætədi] Sonnabend *m*, Samstag *m*.

saturnine ['sætənain] düster, finster.

sauce [sɔːs] 1. (*oft kalte*) Soße; *Am.* Kompott *n*; *fig.* Würze *f*; F Frechheit *f*; 2. würzen; F frech werden zu *j-m*; ~boat ['sɔːsbout] Soßenschüssel *f*; ~pan Kochtopf *m*; Kasserolle *f*; ~r ['sɔːsə] Untertasse *f*.

saucy □ F ['sɔːsi] frech; dreist.

saunter ['sɔːntə] 1. Schlendern *n*; Bummel *m*; 2. (umher)schlendern; bummeln.

sausage ['sɔsidʒ] Wurst *f*.

savage ['sævidʒ] 1. □ wild; roh, grausam; 2. Wilde(r *m*) *f*; *fig.* Barbar *m*; ~ry [ˌdʒəri] Wildheit *f*; Barbarei *f*.

savant ['sævənt] Gelehrte(r) *m*.

save [seiv] 1. retten; erlösen; bewahren; (er)sparen; schonen; 2. *rhet. prp. u. cj.* außer; ~ *for* bis auf (*acc.*); ~ *that* nur daß.

saver ['seivə] Retter(in); Sparer(in).

saving ['seiviŋ] 1. □ sparsam; 2. Rettung *f*; ~s *pl.* Ersparnisse*f*/*pl.*

savings|-bank ['seiviŋzbæŋk] Sparkasse *f*; ~deposit Spareinlage *f*.

savio(u)r ['seivjə] Retter *m*; *Saviour eccl.* Heiland *m*.

savo(u)r ['seivə] 1. Geschmack *m*; *fig.* Beigeschmack *m*; 2. *fig.* schmecken, riechen (*of* nach).

savo(u)ry¹ □ ['seivəri] schmackhaft; appetitlich; pikant.

savo(u)ry² ♀ [∼] Bohnenkraut *n*.

saw¹ [sɔ:] *pret. von* see.

saw² [∼] Spruch *m*.

saw³ [∼] 1. [*irr.*] sägen; 2. Säge *f*; ∼dust ['sɔ:dʌst] Sägespäne *m/pl.*; ∼mill Sägewerk *n*; ∼n [sɔ:n] *p.p. von* saw³ 1.

Saxon ['sæksn] 1. sächsisch; *ling. oft* germanisch; 2. Sachse *m*, Sächsin *f*.

say [sei] 1. [*irr.*] sagen; hersagen; berichten; ∼ grace das Tischgebet sprechen; *that is to* ∼ das heißt; *you don't* ∼ *so!* was Sie nicht sagen!; *I* ∼ sag(en Sie) mal; ich muß schon sagen; *he is said to be* ... er soll ... sein; *no sooner said than done* gesagt, getan; 2. Rede *f*, Wort *n*; *it is my* ∼ *now* jetzt ist die Reihe zu reden an mir; *have a* od. *some* (no) ∼ *in s.th.* et. (nichts) zu sagen haben bei et.; ∼ing ['seiiŋ] Rede *f*; Redensart *f*; Ausspruch *m*; *it goes without* ∼ es versteht sich von selbst.

scab [skæb] ♀, ♀ Schorf *m*; *vet.* Räude *f*; *sl.* Streikbrecher *m*.

scabbard ['skæbəd] *Säbel*-Scheide*f*.

scabrous ['skeibrəs] heikel.

scaffold ['skæfəld] (Bau)Gerüst *n*; Schafott *n*; ∼ing [∼diŋ] (Bau)Gerüst *n*.

scald [skɔ:ld] 1. Verbrühung *f*; 2. verbrühen; *Milch* abkochen.

scale¹ [skeil] 1. Schuppe *f*; Kesselstein *m*; ♀ Zahnstein *m*; Waagschale *f*; (*a pair of*) ∼s *pl.* (eine) Waage; 2. (sich) abschuppen, ablösen; ⊕ *Kesselstein* abklopfen; ♀ Zähne vom Zahnstein reinigen; wiegen.

scale² [∼] 1. Stufenleiter *f*; ♪ Tonleiter *f*; Skala *f*; Maßstab *m*; *fig.* Ausmaß *n*; 2. ersteigen; ∼ *up* (*down*) maßstabsgetreu vergrößern (verkleinern).

scallop ['skɔləp] 1. *zo.* Kammuschel *f*; ⊕ Langette *f*; 2. ausbogen.

scalp [skælp] 1. Kopfhaut *f*; Skalp *m*; 2. skalpieren.

scaly ['skeili] schuppig; voll Kesselstein.

scamp [skæmp] 1. Taugenichts *m*; 2. pfuschen; ∼er ['skæmpə] 1. (umher)tollen; hetzen; 2.*fig.* Hetzjagd*f*.

scan [skæn] *Verse* skandieren; absuchen; *fig.* überfliegen.

scandal ['skændl] Skandal *m*; Ärgernis *n*; Schande *f*; Klatsch *m*; ∼ize ['∼dəlaiz] Anstoß erregen bei *j-m*; ∼ous □ [∼ləs] skandalös, anstößig; schimpflich; klatschhaft.

Scandinavian [skændi'neivjən]

1. skandinavisch; 2. Skandinavier (-in).

scant *lit.* [skænt] 1. knapp, kärglich; 2. knausern mit, sparen an (*dat.*); ∼y □ ['skænti] knapp, spärlich, kärglich, dürftig.

scape|goat ['skeipgout] Sündenbock *m*; ∼grace [∼greis] Taugenichts *m*.

scar [ska:] 1. Narbe *f*; *fig.* (Schand-) Fleck *m*, Makel *m*; Klippe *f*; 2. *v/t.* schrammen; *v/i.* vernarben.

scarc|e [skɛəs] knapp; rar; selten; ∼ely ['skɛəsli] kaum; ∼ity [∼siti] Mangel *m*; Knappheit *f*; Teuerung *f*.

scare [skɛə] 1. er-, aufschrecken; verscheuchen; ∼d verstört; ängstlich; 2. Panik *f*; ∼crow ['skɛəkrou] Vogelscheuche *f* (*a. fig.*); ∼head (-ing) Riesenschlagzeile *f*.

scarf [ska:f], *pl.* ∼s, **scarves** [∼fs, ska:vz] Schal *m*; Hals-, Kopftuch *n*; Krawatte *f*; ✂ Schärpe *f*.

scarlet ['ska:lit] 1. Scharlach(rot *n*) *m*; 2. scharlachrot; ∼ *fever* ♀ Scharlach *m*; ∼ *runner* ♀ Feuerbohne *f*.

scarred [ska:d] narbig.

scarves [ska:vz] *pl. von* scarf.

scathing *fig.* ['skeiðiŋ] vernichtend.

scatter ['skætə] (sich) zerstreuen; aus-, verstreuen; (sich) verbreiten.

scavenger ['skævindʒə] Straßenkehrer *m*.

scenario [si'na:riou] *Film:* Drehbuch *n*.

scene [si:n] Szene *f*; Bühne(nbild *n*) *f*; Schauplatz *m*; ∼s *pl.* Kulissen *f/pl.*; ∼ry ['si:nəri] Szenerie *f*; Bühnenausstattung *f*; Landschaft*f*.

scent [sent] 1. (Wohl)Geruch *m*; Duft *m*; Parfüm *n*; *hunt.* Witterung(svermögen *n*) *f*; Fährte *f*; 2. wittern; parfümieren; ∼less ['sentlis] geruchlos.

sceptic ['skeptik] Skeptiker(in); ∼al □ [∼kəl] skeptisch.

scept|re, *Am.* ∼**er** ['septə] Zepter *n*.

schedule ['ʃedju:l, *Am.* 'skedju:l] 1. Verzeichnis *n*; Tabelle *f*; *Am.* Fahrplan *m*; *on* ∼ fahrplanmäßig; 2. auf-, verzeichnen; festsetzen.

scheme [ski:m] 1. Schema *n*; Zs.-stellung *f*; Plan *m*; 2. *v/t.* planen; *v/i.* Pläne machen; Ränke schmieden.

schism ['sizəm] (Kirchen)Spaltung *f*.

scholar ['skɔlə] Gelehrte(r) *m*; *univ.* Stipendiat *m*; † Schüler(in); ∼ly *adj.* [∼li] gelehrt; ∼ship [∼ʃip] Gelehrsamkeit *f*; Wissenschaftlichkeit *f*; *univ.* Stipendium *n*.

scholastic [skə'læstik] 1. (∼ally) *phls.* scholastisch; schulmäßig; Schul...; 2. *phls.* Scholastiker *m*.

school [sku:l] 1. Schwarm *m*; Schule *f* (*a. fig.*); *univ.* Fakultät *f*;

Disziplin f; Hochschule f; at ~ auf od. in der Schule; 2. schulen, erziehen; ~boy ['sku:lbɔi] Schüler m; ~fellow Mitschüler(in); ~girl Schülerin f; ~ing [~liŋ] (Schul-) Ausbildung f; ~master Lehrer m (bsd. e-r höheren Schule); ~mate Mitschüler(in); ~mistress Lehrerin f (bsd. e-r höheren Schule); ~teacher (bsd. Volksschul)Lehrer (-in).

schooner ['sku:nə] ⚓ Schoner m; Am. großes Bierglas; = prairie-schooner.

science ['saiəns] Wissenschaft f; Naturwissenschaft(en pl.) f; Technik f.

scientific [saiən'tifik] (~ally) (engS. natur)wissenschaftlich; kunstgerecht.

scientist ['saiəntist] (bsd. Natur-) Wissenschaftler m.

scintillate ['sintileit] funkeln.

scion ['saiən] Sproß m, Sprößling m.

scissors ['sizəz] pl. (a pair of ~ pl. eine) Schere.

scoff [skɔf] 1. Spott m; 2. spotten.

scold [skould] 1. zänkisches Weib; 2. (aus)schelten, schimpfen.

scon(e) [skɔn] weiches Teegebäck.

scoop [sku:p] 1. Schaufel f, Schippe f; Schöpfeimer m, -kelle f; F Coup m, gutes Geschäft; F Exklusivmeldung f; 2. (aus)schaufeln; einscheffeln.

scooter ['sku:tə] (Kinder)Roller m; Motorroller m.

scope [skoup] Bereich m; geistiger Gesichtskreis; Spielraum m.

scorch [skɔːtʃ] v/t. versengen, verbrennen; v/i. F (dahin)rasen.

score [skɔː] 1. Kerbe f; Zeche f, Rechnung f; 20 Stück; Sport: Punktzahl f; (Tor)Stand m; Grund m; ♩ Partitur f; ~s of viele; four ~ achtzig; run up ~s Schulden machen; on the ~ of wegen (gen.); 2. (ein)kerben; anschreiben; Sport: (Punkte) machen; Fußball: ein Tor schießen; gewinnen; instrumentieren; Am. F scharfe Kritik üben an (dat.).

scorn [skɔːn] 1. Verachtung f; Spott m; 2. verachten; verschmähen; ~ful □ ['skɔːnful] verächtlich.

Scotch [skɔtʃ] 1.schottisch; 2.Schottisch n; the ~ die Schotten pl.; ~man ['skɔtʃmən] Schotte m.

scot-free ['skɔt'friː] straflos.

Scots [skɔts], ~man ['skɔtsmən] = Scotch(man).

scoundrel ['skaundrəl] Schurke m.

scour ['skauə] v/t. scheuern; reinigen; durchstreifen, absuchen; v/i. eilen.

scourge [skəːdʒ] 1. Geißel f; 2. geißeln.

scout [skaut] 1. Späher m, Kundschafter m; ⚓ Aufklärungsfahrzeug n; ✈ Aufklärer m; mot. Mitglied n der Straßenwacht; (Boy) ♀ Pfadfinder m; ~ party ⚔ Spähtrupp m; 2. (aus)kundschaften, spähen; verächtlich zurückweisen.

scowl [skaul] 1. finsteres Gesicht; 2. finster blicken.

scrabble ['skræbl] (be)kritzeln; scharren; krabbeln.

scrag fig. [skræg] Gerippe n (dürrer Mensch etc.).

scramble ['skræmbl] 1. klettern; sich balgen (for um); ~d eggs pl. Rührei n; 2. Kletterei f; Balgerei f.

scrap [skræp] 1. Stückchen n; (Zeitungs)Ausschnitt m, Bild n zum Einkleben; Altmaterial n; Schrott m; ~s pl. Reste m/pl.; 2. ausrangieren; verschrotten; ~book ['skræpbuk] Sammelalbum n.

scrap|e [skreip] 1. Kratzen n, Scharren n; Kratzfuß m; Not f, Klemme f; 2. schrap(p)en; (ab-) schaben; (ab)kratzen; scharren; (entlang)streifen; ~er ['skreipə] Kratzeisen n.

scrap|-heap ['skræphiːp] Abfall-, Schrotthaufen m; ~-iron Alteisen n, Schrott m.

scratch [skrætʃ] 1. Schramme f; Sport: Startlinie f; 2. zs.-gewürfelt; Zufalls...; Sport: ohne Vorgabe; 3. (zer)kratzen; (zer)schrammen; parl. u. Sport: streichen; ~ out ausstreichen.

scrawl [skrɔːl] 1. kritzeln; 2. Gekritzel n.

scrawny Am. F ['skrɔːni] dürr.

scream [skriːm] 1. Schrei m; Gekreisch n; he is a ~ F er ist zum Schreien komisch; 2. schreien, kreischen.

screech [skriːtʃ] s. scream; ~owl orn. ['skriːtʃaul] Käuzchen n.

screen [skriːn] 1. Wand-, Ofen-, Schutzschirm m; fig. Schleier m; (Film)Leinwand f; der Film; Sandsieb n; (Fliegen)Gitter n; 2. (ab-) schirmen; (be)schützen; ⚔ tarnen; auf der Leinwand zeigen; verfilmen; (durch)sieben; ~ play Drehbuch n; Fernsehfilm m.

screw [skruː] 1. Schraube f; ⚓ Propeller m; 2. (fest)schrauben; fig. bedrängen; ver-, umdrehen; ~ up festschrauben; ~ up one's courage Mut fassen; ~ball Am. sl. ['skruːbɔːl] komischer Kauz; ~driver Schraubenzieher m; ~jack Wagenheber m; ~propeller Schiffs-, Flugzeugschraube f.

scribble ['skribl] 1. Gekritzel n; 2. kritzeln. [skimp etc.]

scrimp [skrimp], ~y ['skrimpi] =]

scrip ✝ [skrip] Interimsschein(e pl.) m.

script [skript] Schrift f; Schreibschrift f; Manuskript n; Film: Drehbuch n.

Scripture ['skriptʃə] *mst the Holy* ∼*s pl.* die Heilige Schrift.

scroll [skroul] Schriftrolle *f*, Liste *f*; ⚙ Schnecke *f*; Schnörkel *m*.

scrub [skrʌb] **1.** Gestrüpp *n*; Zwerg *m*; *Am. Sport*: zweite (Spieler-) Garnitur; **2.** schrubben, scheuern.

scrubby ['skrʌbi] struppig; schäbig.

scrup|le ['skruːpl] **1.** Skrupel *m*, Zweifel *m*, Bedenken *n*; **2.** Bedenken haben; ∼**ulous** □ [∼pjuləs] (allzu) bedenklich; gewissenhaft; ängstlich.

scrutin|ize ['skruːtinaiz] (genau) prüfen; ∼**y** [∼ni] forschender Blick; genaue (*bsd.* Wahl)Prüfung.

scud [skʌd] **1.** (Dahin)Jagen *n*; (da- hintreibende) Wolkenfetzen *m/pl.*; Bö *f*; **2.** eilen, jagen; gleiten.

scuff [skʌf] schlurfen, schlorren.

scuffle ['skʌfl] **1.** Balgerei *f*, Raufe- rei *f*; **2.** sich balgen, raufen.

scull ⚓ [skʌl] **1.** kurzes Ruder; **2.** rudern, skullen.

scullery ['skʌləri] Spülküche *f*.

sculptor ['skʌlptə] Bildhauer *m*.

sculpture ['skʌlptʃə] **1.** Plastik *f*; Bildhauerkunst *f*, Skulptur *f*; **2.** (heraus)meißeln, formen.

scum *fig.* [skʌm] (Ab)Schaum *m*.

scurf [skəːf] (Haut)Schuppen *f/pl.*

scurrilous ['skʌriləs] gemein.

scurry ['skʌri] hasten, rennen.

scurvy[1] ⚕ ['skəːvi] Skorbut *m*.

scurvy[2] [∼] (hunds)gemein.

scuttle [skʌtl] **1.** Kohlenbehälter *m*; **2.** eilen; *fig.* sich drücken.

scythe ⚋ [saið] Sense *f*.

sea [siː] See *f*, Meer *n* (*a. fig.*); hohe Welle; *at* ∼ auf See; *fig.* rat- los; ∼**board** ['siːbɔːd] Küste(nge- biet *n*) *f*; ∼**coast** Küste *f*; ∼**faring** ['siːfɛəriŋ] seefahrend; ∼**food** eß- bare Seefische *m/pl.*; Meeresfrüchte *pl.*; ∼**going** Hochsee...; ∼**gull** (See)Möwe *f*.

seal[siːl] **1.** *zo.* Seehund *m*, Robbe *f*; Siegel *n*; Stempel *m*; Bestätigung *f*; **2.** versiegeln; *fig.* besiegeln; ∼ *up* (fest) verschließen; ⊕ abdichten.

sea-level ['siːlevl] Meeresspiegel *m*.

sealing-wax ['siːliŋwæks] Siegel- lack *m*.

seam [siːm] **1.** Saum *m*; (*a.* ⊕) Naht *f*; ⊕ Fuge *f*; *geol.* Flöz *n*; Narbe *f*; **2.** schrammen; furchen.

seaman ['siːmən] Seemann *m*, Matrose *m*.

seamstress ['semstris] Näherin *f*.

sea|-plane ['siːplein] Wasserflug- zeug *n*; ∼**power** Seemacht *f*.

sear [siə] **1.** dürr, welk; **2.** aus- trocknen, versengen; ⚕ brennen; *fig.* verhärten.

search [səːtʃ] **1.** Suchen *n*, Forschen *n*; Unter-, Durchsuchung *f*; *in* ∼ *of* auf der Suche nach; **2.** *v/t.* durch-, untersuchen; ∼ sondieren; erfor-

schen; durchdringen; *v/i.* suchen, forschen (*for* nach); ∼ *into* ergrün- den; ∼**ing** □ ['səːtʃiŋ] forschend, prüfend; eingehend (*Prüfung etc.*); ∼**-light** (Such)Scheinwerfer *m*; ∼**-warrant** ⚖ Haussuchungsbe- fehl *m*.

sea|-shore ['siːʃɔː] Seeküste *f*; ∼**sick** seekrank; ∼**side** Strand *m*, Küste *f*; ∼ *place*, ∼ *resort* Seebad *n*; *go to the* ∼ an die See gehen.

season ['siːzn] **1.** Jahreszeit *f*; (rechte) Zeit; Saison *f*; F *für* ∼**-ticket**: *cherries are in* ∼ jetzt ist Kirschenzeit; *out of* ∼ zur Unzeit; *with the compliments of the* ∼ mit den besten Wünschen zum Fest; **2.** *v/t.* reifen (lassen); wür- zen; abhärten (*to* gegen); *v/i.* ab- lagern; ∼**able** □ [∼nəbl] zeitgemäß; rechtzeitig; ∼**al** □ ['siːzənl] Saison...; periodisch; ∼**ing** ['siːzniŋ] Würze *f*; ∼**-ticket** ⚙ Zeitkarte *f*; *thea.* Abon- nement *n*.

seat [siːt] **1.** Sitz *m* (*a. fig.*); Sessel *m*, Stuhl *m*, Bank *f*; (Sitz)Platz *m*; Landsitz *m*; Gesäß *n*; Schauplatz *m*; **2.** (hin)setzen; e-n Hosenboden einsetzen in (*acc.*); fassen, Sitz- plätze haben für; ∼**ed** sitzend; ...*sitzig*; *be* ∼**ed** sitzen; sich setzen; ∼**-belt** ⚙ ['siːtbelt] Sicherheits- gurt *m*.

sea|-urchin *zo.* ['siːəːtʃin] Seeigel *m*; ∼**ward** ['siːwəd] **1.** *adj.* seewärts gerichtet; **2.** *adv. a.* ∼**s** seewärts; ∼**weed** ⚓ (See)Tang *m*; ∼**worthy** seetüchtig.

secede [siˈsiːd] sich trennen.

secession [siˈseʃən] Lossagung *f*; Abfall *m*; ∼**ist** [∼ʃnist] Abtrünni- ge(r *m*) *f*.

seclu|de [siˈkluːd] abschließen, ab- sondern; ∼**ded** einsam; zurückge- zogen; abgelegen; ∼**sion** [∼ːʒən] Abgeschlossen-, Abgeschieden- heit *f*.

second ['sekənd] **1.** □ zweite(r, -s) nächste(r, -s); geringer (*to* als); *on* ∼ *thoughts* bei genauerer Überle- gung; **2.** Zweite(r, -s); Sekundant *m*; Beistand *m*; Sekunde *f*; ∼*s pl.* Waren *pl.* zweiter Wahl; **3.** sekun- dieren (*dat.*); unterstützen; ∼**ary** □ [∼dəri] sekundär; untergeordnet; Neben...; Hilfs...; Sekundär...; ∼**ary school** höhere Schule; wei- terführende Schule; ∼**-hand** aus zweiter Hand; gebraucht; antiqua- risch; ∼**ly** [∼dli] zweitens; ∼**-rate** zweiten Ranges; zweitklassig.

secre|cy ['siːkrisi] Heimlichkeit *f*; Verschwiegenheit *f*; ∼**t** [∼it] **1.** □ geheim; Geheim...; verschwiegen; verborgen; **2.** Geheimnis *n*; *in* ∼ insgeheim; *be in the* ∼, *be taken into the* ∼ eingeweiht sein.

secretary ['sekrətri] Schriftführer *m*; Sekretär(in); ♀ *of State* Staatssekretär m, Minister m; Am. Außenminister m.

secret|e [si'kri:t] verbergen; absondern; ~ion [~'i:ʃən] Absonderung f; ~ive [~i:tiv] fig. verschlossen; geheimtuerisch.

section ['sekʃən] ⚓ Sektion f; (Durch)Schnitt m; Teil m; Abschnitt m, Paragraph m; typ. Absatz m; Abteilung f; Gruppe f.

secular □ ['sekjulə] weltlich.

secur|e [si'kjuə] 1. □ sicher; 2. (sich et.) sichern; schützen; festmachen; ~ity [~riti] Sicherheit f; Sorglosigkeit f; Gewißheit f; Schutz m; Kaution f; securities pl. Wertpapiere n/pl.

sedan [si'dæn] Limousine f; a. ~-chair Sänfte f.

sedate □ [si'deit] gesetzt; ruhig.

sedative mst ⚕ ['sedətiv] 1. beruhigend; 2. Beruhigungsmittel n.

sedentary □ ['sedntəri] sitzend; seßhaft.

sediment ['sedimənt] (Boden)Satz m; geol. Ablagerung f.

sediti|on [si'diʃən] Aufruhr m; ~ous □ [~ʃəs] aufrührerisch.

seduc|e [si'dju:s] verführen; ~tion [si'dakʃən] Verführung f; ~tive □ [~ktiv] verführerisch.

sedulous □ ['sedjuləs] emsig.

see¹ [si:] [irr.] v/i. sehen; fig. einsehen; ~ ich verstehe; ~ about s.th. sich um et. kümmern; ~ through s.o. od. s.th. j-n od. et. durchschauen; ~ to achten auf (acc.); v/t. sehen; beobachten; einsehen; sorgen (daß et. geschieht); besuchen; Arzt aufsuchen; ~ s.o. home j-n nach Hause begleiten; ~ off Besuch etc. wegbringen; ~ out Besuch hinausbegleiten; et. zu Ende erleben; ~ s.th. through et. durchhalten; ~ s.o. through j-m durchhelfen; live to ~ erleben.

see² [~] (erz)bischöflicher Stuhl.

seed [si:d] 1. Same(n) m, Saat(gut n) f; (Obst)Kern m; Keim m (a. fig.); go od. run to ~ in Samen schießen; fig. herunterkommen. 2. v/t. (be-)säen; entkernen; v/i. in Samen schießen; ~less [~dlis] kernlos (Obst); ~ling ⚘ [~liŋ] Sämling m; ~y ['si:di] schäbig; F elend.

seek [si:k] [irr.] suchen (nach); begehren; trachten nach.

seem [si:m] (er)scheinen; ~ing □ ['si:miŋ] anscheinend; scheinbar; ~ly ['si:mli] schicklich.

seen [si:n] p.p. von see¹.

seep [si:p] durchsickern, tropfen.

seer ['si:(ə] Seher(in), Prophet(in).

seesaw ['si:sɔ:] 1. Wippen n; Wippe f, Wippschaukel f; 2. wippen; fig. schwanken.

seethe [si:ð] sieden, kochen.

segment ['segmənt] Abschnitt m.

segregat|e ['segrigeit] absondern, trennen; ~ion [segri'geiʃən] Absonderung f; Rassentrennung f.

seiz|e [si:z] ergreifen, fassen; mit Beschlag belegen; fig. erfassen; a. ~ upon sich e-r S. od. j-s bemächtigen; ~ure ['si:ʒə] Ergreifung f; ⚖ Beschlagnahme f; ⚕ plötzlicher Anfall.

seldom adv. ['seldəm] selten.

select [si'lekt] 1. auswählen, auslesen, aussuchen; 2. auserwählt; erlesen; exklusiv; ~ion [si'lekʃən] Auswahl f, Auslese f; ~man Am. Stadtrat m in den Neuenglandstaaten.

self [self] 1. pl. selves [selvz] Selbst n, Ich n; Persönlichkeit f; 2. pron. selbst; † od. F = myself etc.; 3. adj. ⚘ einfarbig; ~-centered ['self-'sentəd] egozentrisch; ~-command Selbstbeherrschung f; ~-conceit Eigendünkel m; ~-conceited dünkelhaft; ~-confidence Selbstvertrauen n; ~-conscious befangen, gehemmt; ~-contained (in sich) abgeschlossen; fig. verschlossen; ~-control Selbstbeherrschung f; ~-defence, Am. ~-defense Selbstverteidigung f; in ~ in (der) Notwehr; ~-denial Selbstverleugnung f; ~-employed selbständig (Handwerker etc.); ~-evident selbstverständlich; ~-government Selbstverwaltung f, Autonomie f; ~-indulgent bequem; zügellos; ~-interest Eigennutz m; ~-ish □ [~fiʃ] selbstsüchtig; ~-possession Selbstbeherrschung f; ~-reliant [~fri'laiənt] selbstsicher; ~-righteous selbstgerecht; ~-seeking [~f'si:kiŋ] eigennützig; ~-willed eigenwillig.

sell [sel] [irr.] v/t. verkaufen (a. fig.); Am. aufschwatzen; v/i. handeln; gehen (Ware); ~ off, ~ out † ausverkaufen; ~er ['selə] Verkäufer m; good etc. ~ † gut etc. gehende Ware.

selves [selvz] pl. von self 1.

semblance ['sembləns] Anschein m; Gestalt f.

semi|... ['semi] halb...; Halb...; ~colon Strichpunkt m; ~detached house Doppelhaus(hälfte f) n; ~final Sport: Vorschlußrunde f.

seminary ['seminəri] (Priester)Seminar n; fig. Schule f.

sempstress ['sempstris] Näherin f.

senate ['senit] Senat m.

senator ['senətə] Senator m.

send [send] [irr.] senden, schicken; (mit adj. od. p.pr.) machen; ~ for kommen lassen, holen (lassen); ~ forth aussenden; veröffentlichen; ~ in einsenden; einreichen; ~ up in die Höhe treiben; ~ word mitteilen.

senil|e ['si:nail] greisenhaft, senil; ~ity [si'niliti] Greisenalter n.

senior ['si:njə] 1. älter; dienstälter; Ober...; ~ partner † Chef m; 2. Ältere(r) m; Dienstältere(r) m;

Senior m; he is my ~ by a year er ist ein Jahr älter als ich; ~ity [si:ni-'oriti] höheres Alter od. Dienstalter.

sensation [sen'seiʃən] (Sinnes-) Empfindung f, Gefühl n; Eindruck m; Sensation f; ~al □ [~nl] Empfindungs...; sensationell.

sense [sens] 1. allg. Sinn m (of für); Empfindung f, Gefühl n; Verstand m; Bedeutung f; Ansicht f; in (out of) one's ~s bei (von) Sinnen; bring s.o. to his ~s j-n zur Vernunft bringen; make ~ Sinn haben (S.); talk ~ vernünftig reden; 2. spüren.

senseless □ ['senslis] sinnlos; bewußtlos; gefühllos; ~ness [~snis] Sinnlosigkeit f; Bewußt-, Gefühllosigkeit f.

sensibility [sensi'biliti] Sensibilität f, Empfindungsvermögen n; Empfindlichkeit f; sensibilities pl. Empfindsamkeit f, Zartgefühl n.

sensible □ ['sensəbl] verständig, vernünftig; empfänglich (of für); fühlbar; be ~ of sich e-r S. bewußt sein; et. empfinden.

sensitiv|e □ ['sensitiv] empfindlich (to für); Empfindungs...; feinfühlig; ~eness [~vnis], ~ity [sensi-'tiviti] Empfindlichkeit f (to für).

sensual □ ['sensjuəl] sinnlich.

sensuous □ ['sensjuəs] sinnlich; Sinnes...; sinnenfreudig.

sent [sent] pret. u. p.p. von send.

sentence ['sentəns] 1. ᵗⁱ Urteil n; gr. Satz m; serve one's ~ s-e Strafe absitzen; 2. verurteilen.

sententious □ [sen'tenʃəs] sentenziös; salbungsvoll; salbaderisch.

sentient ['senʃənt] empfindend.

sentiment ['sentimənt] (seelische) Empfindung, Gefühl n; Meinung f; s. sentimentality; ~al □ [senti'mentl] empfindsam; sentimental; ~ality [sentimen'tæliti] Sentimentalität f.

sent|inel ⚔ ['sentinl], ~ry ⚔ [~tri] Schildwache f, Posten m.

separa|ble □ ['sepərəbl] trennbar; ~te 1. □ ['seprit] (ab)getrennt, gesondert, besonder, separat, für sich; 2. ['sepəreit] (sich) trennen; (sich) absondern; (sich) scheiden; ~tion [sepə'reiʃən] Trennung f, Scheidung f.

sepsis ⚕ ['sepsis] Sepsis f, Blutvergiftung f. [m.]

September [səp'tembə] September

septic ⚕ ['septik] septisch.

sepul|chral [si'pʌlkrəl] Grab...; Toten...; fig. düster; ~chre ['sepəlkə] Grab(stätte f) n; ~ture [~ltʃə] Begräbnis n.

sequel ['si:kwəl] Folge f; Nachspiel n; (Roman)Fortsetzung f.

sequen|ce ['si:kwəns] Aufeinander-, Reihenfolge f; Film: Szene f; ~ of tenses gr. Zeitenfolge f; ~t [~nt] aufeinanderfolgend.

sequestrate ᵗⁱ [si'kwestreit] Eigentum einziehen; beschlagnahmen.

serenade [seri'neid] 1. ♪ Serenade f, Ständchen n; 2. j-m ein Ständchen bringen.

seren|e □ [si'ri:n] klar, heiter; ruhig; ~ity [si'reniti] Heiterkeit f; Ruhe f.

serf [sə:f] Leibeigene(r m) f, Hörige(r m) f; fig. Sklave m.

sergeant ['sa:dʒənt] ⚔ Feldwebel m, Wachtmeister m; (Polizei)Wachtmeister m.

serial □ ['siəriəl] 1. fortlaufend, reihenweise, Serien...; Fortsetzungs...; 2. Fortsetzungsroman m.

series ['siəriz] sg. u. pl. Reihe f; Serie f; Folge f; biol. Gruppe f.

serious □ ['siəriəs] allg. ernst; ernsthaft, ernstlich; be ~ es im Ernst meinen; ~ness [~snis] Ernst (-haftigkeit f) m.

sermon ['sə:mən] (iro. Straf)Predigt f.

serpent ['sə:pənt] Schlange f; ~ine [~tain] schlangengleich, -förmig; Serpentinen...

serum ['siərəm] Serum n.

servant ['sə:vənt] Diener(in); a. domestic ~ Dienstbote m, Bedienstete(r m) f; Dienstmädchen n.

serve [sə:v] 1. v/t. dienen (dat.); Zeit abdienen; bedienen; Speisen reichen; Speisen auftragen; behandeln; nützen, dienlich sein (dat.); Zweck erfüllen; Tennis: angeben; (it) ~s him right (das) geschieht ihm recht; s. sentence; ~ out: austeilen; v/i. dienen (a. ⚔; as, for als, zu); bedienen; nützen, zweckmäßig sein; ~ at table servieren; 2. Tennis: Aufschlag m.

service ['sə:vis] 1. Dienst m; Bedienung f; Gefälligkeit f; a. divine ~ Gottesdienst m; Betrieb m; Verkehr m; Nutzen m; Gang m von Speisen; Service n; ᵗⁱ Zustellung f; Tennis: Aufschlag m; be at s.o.'s ~ j-m zu Diensten stehen; 2. ⊕ warten, pflegen; ~able □ [~səbl] dienlich, nützlich; benutzbar; strapazierfähig; ~ station Tankstelle f; Werkstatt f.

servile □ ['sə:vail] sklavisch (a. fig.); unterwürfig; kriecherisch; ~ity [sə:'viliti] Unterwürfigkeit f, Kriecherei f.

serving ['sə:viŋ] Portion f.

servitude ['sə:vitju:d] Knechtschaft f; Sklaverei f.

session ['seʃən] (a. Gerichts)Sitzung f; be in ~ tagen.

set [set] 1. irr.] v/t. setzen; stellen; legen; zurechtstellen; (ein)richten, ordnen; Aufgabe, Wecker stellen; Messer abziehen; Edelstein fassen; festsetzen; erstarren lassen; Haar legen; ⚕ Knochenbruch einrichten; ~ s.o. laughing j-n zum Lachen

bringen; ~ *an example* ein Beispiel
geben; ~ *sail* Segel setzen; ~ *one's
teeth* die Zähne zs.-beißen; ~ *aside*
beiseite stellen *od.* legen; *fig.* verwerfen; ~ *at ease* beruhigen; ~ *at
rest* beruhigen; *Frage* entscheiden;
~ *store by* Wert legen auf (*acc.*); ~
forth darlegen; ~ *off* hervorheben;
anrechnen; ~ *up* auf-, er-, einrichten; aufstellen; *j-n* etablieren; *v/i.
ast.* untergehen; gerinnen, fest
werden; laufen (*Flut etc.*); sitzen
(*Kleid etc.*); ~ *about s.th.* sich an et.
machen; ~ *about s.o.* F über j-n
herfallen; ~ *forth* aufbrechen; ~
off aufbrechen; ~ (*up*)*on* anfangen;
angreifen; ~ *out* aufbrechen; ~ *to*
sich daran machen; ~ *up* sich niederlassen; ~ *up for* sich ausspielen
als; 2. fest; starr; festgesetzt, bestimmt; vorgeschrieben; ~ (*up*)*on*
versessen auf (*acc.*); ~ *with* besetzt
mit; *Barometer:* ~ *fair* beständig;
hard ~ in großer Not; ~ *speech*
wohlüberlegte Rede; 3. Reihe *f*,
Folge *f*, Serie *f*, Sammlung *f*, Satz
m; Garnitur *f*; Service *n*; *Radio-*
Gerät *n*; ✝ Kollektion *f*; Gesellschaft *f*; Sippschaft *f*; ✞ Setzling
m; *Tennis:* Satz *m*; Neigung *f*;
Richtung *f*; Sitz *m e-s Kleides etc.*;
poet. Untergang *m der Sonne*; *thea.*
Bühnenausstattung *f*.
set|-back ['setbæk] *fig.* Rückschlag
m; **~-down** *fig.* Dämpfer *m*; **~-off**
Kontrast *m*; *fig.* Ausgleich *m*.
settee [se'ti:] *kleines* Sofa.
setting ['setiŋ] Setzen *n*; Einrichten
n; Fassung *f e-s Edelsteins*; Lage *f*;
Schauplatz *m*; Umgebung *f*; *thea.*
Ausstattung *f*; *fig.* Umrahmung *f*;
♪ Komposition *f*; (*Sonnen- etc.*)
Untergang *m*; ⊕ Einstellung *f*.
settle ['setl] 1. Sitzbank *f*; 2. *v/t.*
(*fest*)setzen; *Kind etc.* versorgen,
ausstatten; *j-n* etablieren; regeln;
Geschäft abschließen, abmachen,
erledigen; *Frage* entscheiden; *Rechnung* begleichen; ordnen; beruhigen; *Streit* beilegen; *Rente* aussetzen; ansiedeln; *Land* besiedeln;
v/i. sich senken (*Haus*); oft ~ *down*
sich niederlassen; *a.* ~ *in* sich einrichten; sich legen (*Wut etc.*);
beständig werden (*Wetter*); sich
entschließen; ~ *down to* sich widmen (*dat.*); **~d** fest; beständig;
auf Rechnungen: bezahlt; **~ment**
[.mənt] Erledigung *f*; Übereinkunft *f*; (Be)Siedlung *f*; ⚖ (Eigen-
tums)Übertragung *f*; **~r** [.lə]
Siedler *m*.
set|-to F ['set'tu:] Kampf *m*; Schlä-
gerei *f*; **~up** F Aufbau *m*; *Am. sl.*
abgekartete Sache.
seven ['sevn] 1. sieben; 2. Sieben *f*;
~teen(th) [.n'ti:n(θ)] siebzehn
(-te[r, -s]); **~th** [.nθ] 1. ☐ sieb(en)-
te(r, -s); 2. Sieb(en)tel *n*; **~thly**

[.θli] sieb(en)tens; **~tieth** [.ntiiθ]
siebzigste(r, -s); **~ty** [.ti] 1. siebzig;
2. Siebzig *f*.
sever ['sevə] (sich) trennen; (auf-)
lösen; zerreißen.
several ☐ ['sevrəl] mehrere, verschiedene; einige; einzeln; besonder; getrennt; **~ly** [.li] besonders,
einzeln.
severance ['sevərəns] Trennung *f*.
sever|e ☐ [si'viə] streng; rauh
(*Wetter*); hart (*Winter*); scharf
(*Tadel*); ernst (*Mühe*); heftig
(*Schmerz etc.*); schlimm, schwer
(*Unfall etc.*); **~ity** [si'veriti] Strenge
f, Härte *f*; Schwere *f*; Ernst *m*.
sew [sou] [*irr.*] nähen; heften.
sewage ['sju:(:)idʒ] Abwasser *n*.
sewer[1] ['souə] Näherin *f*.
sewer[2] ['sjuə] Abwasserkanal *m*;
~age [.ridʒ] Kanalisation *f*.
sew|ing ['souiŋ] Nähen *n*; Nähe-
rei *f*; *attr.* Näh...; **~n** [soun] *p.p.
von* sew.
sex [seks] Geschlecht *n*.
sexton ['sekstən] Küster *m*, Totengräber *m*.
sexual ☐ ['seksjuəl] geschlechtlich;
Geschlechts...; sexuell; Sexual...
shabby ☐ ['ʃæbi] schäbig; gemein.
shack *Am.* [ʃæk] Hütte *f*, Bude *f*.
shackle ['ʃækl] 1. Fessel *f* (*fig. mst
pl.*); 2. fesseln.
shade [ʃeid] 1. Schatten *m*, Dunkel
n (*a. fig.*); *Lampen- etc.* Schirm *m*;
Schattierung *f*; *Am.* Rouleau *n*;
fig. Spur *f*, Kleinigkeit *f*; 2. beschatten; verdunkeln (*a. fig.*); ab-
schirmen; schützen; schattieren; ~
away, ~ *off* allmählich übergehen
(lassen) (*into* in *acc.*).
shadow ['ʃædou] 1. Schatten *m* (*a.
fig.*); Phantom *n*; Spur *f*, Kleinigkeit *f*; 2. beschatten; *mst ~ forth
od. out*) andeuten; versinnbildlichen;
j-n beschatten, überwachen; **~y**
[.oui] schattig, dunkel; schatten-
haft; wesenlos.
shady ['ʃeidi] schattenspendend;
schattig; dunkel; F zweifelhaft.
shaft [ʃɑːft] Schaft *m*; Stiel *m*;
Pfeil *m* (*a. fig.*); *poet.* Strahl *m*; ⊕
Welle *f*; Deichsel *f*; ⚒ Schacht *m*.
shaggy ['ʃægi] zottig.
shake [ʃeik] 1. [*irr.*] *v/t.* schütteln,
rütteln; erschüttern; ~ *down* her-
unterschütteln; *Stroh etc.* hin-
schütten; ~ *hands* sich die Hände
geben *od.* schütteln; ~ *up Bett* aufschütteln; *fig.* aufrütteln; *v/i.* zittern, beben, wackeln, wanken (*with*
vor *dat.*); ♪ trillern; 2. Schütteln *n*;
Erschütterung *f*; Beben *n*; ♪ Triller *m*; **~down** ['ʃeik'daun] 1. Not-
lager *n*; *Am. sl.* Erpressung *f*; 2.
adj.: ~ *cruise* ⚓ Probefahrt *f*;
~hands *pl.* Händedruck *m*; **~n**
['ʃeikən] 1. *p.p. von* shake 1; 2. *adj.*
erschüttert.

shaky □ ['ʃeiki] wack(e)lig (a. fig.); (sch)wankend; zitternd, zitterig.

shall [ʃæl] [irr.] v/aux. soll; werde.

shallow ['ʃælou] 1. seicht; flach; fig. oberflächlich; 2. Untiefe f; 3. (sich) verflachen.

sham [ʃæm] 1. falsch; Schein...; 2. Trug m; Täuschung f; Schwindler(in); 3. v/t. vortäuschen; v/i. sich verstellen; simulieren; ~ ill (-ness) sich krank stellen.

shamble ['ʃæmbl] watscheln; ~s pl. od. sg. Schlachthaus n; fig. Schlachtfeld n.

shame [ʃeim] 1. Scham f; Schande f; for ~!, ~ on you! pfuil, schäm dich!; put to ~ beschämen; 2. beschämen; j-m Schande machen; ~faced □ ['ʃeimfeist] schamhaft, schüchtern; ~ful □ [~ful] schändlich, beschämend; ~less □ ['ʃeimlis] schamlos.

shampoo [ʃæm'puː] 1. Shampoo n; Haarwäsche f; 2. Haare waschen.

shamrock ['ʃæmrɔk] Kleeblatt n.

shank [ʃæŋk] (Unter)Schenkel m; ⚓ Stiel m; (⚓ Anker)Schaft m.

shanty ['ʃænti] Hütte f, Bude f.

shape [ʃeip] 1. Gestalt f, Form f (a. fig.); Art f; 2. v/t. gestalten, formen, bilden; anpassen (to dat.); v/i. sich entwickeln; ~d ...förmig; ~less ['ʃeiplis] formlos; ~ly [~li] wohlgestaltet.

share [ʃɛə] 1. (An)Teil m; Beitrag m; ✝ Aktie f; ⚒ Kux m; have a ~ in teilhaben an (dat.); go ~s teilen; 2. v/t. teilen; v/i. teilhaben (in an dat.); ~cropper Am. ['ʃɛəkrɔpə] kleiner Farmpächter; ~holder ✝ Aktionär(in).

shark [ʃɑːk] ichth. Hai(fisch) m; Gauner m; Am. sl. Kanone f (Experte).

sharp [ʃɑːp] 1. □ allg. scharf (a. fig.); spitz; schneidend, stechend; schrill; hitzig; schnell; pfiffig, schlau; gerissen; C ♪ Cis n; 2. adv. ♪ zu hoch; F pünktlich; look ~! (mach) schnell!; 3. ♪ Kreuz n; durch ein Kreuz erhöhte Note; F Gauner m; ~en ['ʃɑːpən] (ver-)schärfen; spitzen; ~ener ['ʃɑːpnə] Messer-Schärfer m; Bleistift-Spitzer m; ~er ['ʃɑːpə] Gauner m; ~ness ['ʃɑːpnis] Schärfe f (a. fig.); ~set ['ʃɑːp'set] hungrig; erpicht; ~sighted scharfsichtig; ~witted scharfsinnig.

shatter ['ʃætə] zerschmettern, zerschlagen; Nerven etc. zerrütten.

shave [ʃeiv] 1. [irr.] (sich) rasieren; (ab)schälen; haarscharf vorbeigehen od. vorbeifahren od. vorbeikommen an (dat.); 2. Rasieren n, Rasur f; have a ~ sich rasieren (lassen); a close ~ ein Entkommen mit knapper Not; ~n ['ʃeivn] p.p. von shave 1.

shaving ['ʃeiviŋ] 1. Rasieren n; ~s pl. (bsd. Hobel)Späne m/pl.; 2. Rasier...

shawl [ʃɔːl] Schal m, Kopftuch n.

she [ʃiː] 1. sie; 2. Sie f; zo. Weibchen n; 3. adj. in Zssgn: weiblich, ...weibchen n; ~dog Hündin f.

sheaf [ʃiːf], pl. sheaves [ʃiːvz] Garbe f; Bündel n.

shear [ʃiə] 1. [irr.] scheren; fig. rupfen; 2. ~s pl. große Schere.

sheath [ʃiːθ] Scheide f; ~e [ʃiːð] (in die Scheide) stecken; einhüllen; ⊕ bekleiden, beschlagen.

sheaves [ʃiːvz] pl. von sheaf.

shebang Am. sl. [ʃə'bæŋ] Bude f, Laden m.

shed¹ [ʃed] [irr.] aus~, vergießen; verbreiten; Blätter etc. abwerfen.

shed² [~] Schuppen m (bsd. Stoff).

sheen [ʃiːn] Glanz m (bsd. Stoff).

sheep [ʃiːp] Schaf(e pl.) n; Schafleder n; ~cot ['ʃiːpkɔt] = sheepfold; ~dog Schäferhund m; ~fold Schafhürde f; ~ish □ ['ʃiːpiʃ] blöd(e), einfältig; ~man Am. Schafzüchter m; ~skin Schaffell n; Schafleder n; F Diplom n.

sheer [ʃiə] rein; glatt; Am. hauchdünn; steil; senkrecht; direkt.

sheet [ʃiːt] Bett-, Leintuch n, Laken n; (Glas- etc.)Platte f; ⊕ ...blech n; Blatt n, Bogen m Papier; weite Fläche (Wasser etc.); ⚓ Schot(e) f; the rain came down in ~s es regnete in Strömen; ~ iron Eisenblech n; ~ lightning ['ʃiːtlaitniŋ] Wetterleuchten n.

shelf [ʃelf], pl. shelves [ʃelvz] Brett n, Regal n, Fach n; Riff n; on the ~ fig. ausrangiert.

shell [ʃel] 1. Schale f, Hülse f, Muschel f; Gehäuse n; Gerippe n e-s Hauses; ✗ Granate f; 2. schälen, enthülsen; ✗ bombardieren; ~fire ['ʃelfaiə] Granatfeuer n; ~fish zo. Schalentier n; ~proof bombensicher.

shelter ['ʃeltə] 1. Schuppen m; Schutz-, Obdach n; fig. Schutz m, Schirm m; 2. v/t. (be)schützen; (be)schirmen; Zuflucht gewähren (dat.); v/i. a. take ~ Schutz suchen.

shelve [ʃelv] mit Brettern od. Regalen versehen; auf ein Brett stellen; fig. zu den Akten legen; fig. beiseite legen; sich allmählich neigen.

shelves [ʃelvz] pl. von shelf.

shenanigan Am. F [ʃi'næniɡən] Gaunerei f; Humbug m.

shepherd ['ʃepəd] 1. Schäfer m, Hirt m; 2. (be)hüten; leiten.

sherbet ['ʃɔːbət] Brauselimonade f; (Art) (Speise)Eis n.

shield [ʃiːld] 1. (Schutz)Schild m; Wappenschild m; 2. (be)schirmen (from vor dat., gegen).

shift [ʃift] 1. Veränderung f, Verschiebung f, Wechsel m; Notbehelf m; List f, Kniff m; Ausflucht f; (Arbeits)Schicht f; make ~ es möglich machen (to inf. zu inf.); sich behelfen; sich durchschlagen; 2. v/t. (ver-, weg)schieben; (ab)wechseln; verändern; Platz, Szene verlegen, verlagern; v/i. wechseln; sich verlagern; sich behelfen; ~ for o.s. sich selbst helfen; ~less □ ['ʃiftlis] hilflos; faul; ~y □ [~ti] fig. gerissen; unzuverlässig.

shilling ['ʃiliŋ] englischer Schilling.

shin [ʃin] 1. a. ~bone Schienbein n; 2. ~ up hinaufklettern.

shine [ʃain] 1. Schein m; Glanz m; 2. [irr.] v/i. scheinen; leuchten; fig. glänzen, strahlen; v/t. blank putzen.

shingle ['ʃiŋl] Schindel f; Am. F (Aushänge)Schild n; Strandkiesel m/pl.; ~s pl. ⚕ Gürtelrose f.

shiny □ ['ʃaini] blank, glänzend.

ship [ʃip] 1. Schiff n; Am. F Flugzeug n; 2. an Bord nehmen od. bringen; verschiffen, versenden; ⚓ heuern; ~board ['ʃipbɔ:d]: on ~ ⚓ an Bord; ~ment ['ʃipmənt] Verschiffung f; Versand m; Schiffsladung f; ~owner Reeder m; ~ping ['ʃipiŋ] Verschiffung f; Schiffe n/pl., Flotte f; attr. Schiffs...; Verschiffungs..., Verlade..., ~wreck 1. Schiffbruch m; 2. scheitern (lassen); ~wrecked schiffbrüchig; ~yard Schiffswerft f. [schaft f.)

shire ['ʃaiə, in Zssgn ...ʃiə] Graf-)

shirk [ʃə:k] sich drücken (um et.); ~er ['ʃə:kə] Drückeberger m.

shirt [ʃə:t] Herrenhemd n; a. ~ waist Am. Hemdbluse f; ~sleeve ['ʃə:tsli:v] 1. Hemdsärmel m; 2. hemdsärmelig; informell; ~ diplomacy bsd. Am. offene Diplomatie.

shiver ['ʃivə] 1. Splitter m; Schauer m; 2. zersplittern; schau(d)ern; (er)zittern; frösteln; ~y [~əri] fröstelnd.

shoal [ʃoul] 1. Schwarm m, Schar f; Untiefe f; 2. flacher werden; 3. seicht.

shock [ʃɔk] 1. Garbenhaufen m; (Haar)Schopf m; Stoß m; Anstoß m; Erschütterung f, Schlag m; ⚡ (Nerven)Schock m; 2. fig. verletzen; empören, Anstoß erregen bei; erschüttern; ~ing □ ['ʃɔkiŋ] anstößig; empörend; haarsträubend.

shod [ʃɔd] pret. u. p.p. von shoe 2.

shoddy ['ʃɔdi] 1. Reißwolle f; fig. Schund m; Am. Protz m; 2. falsch; minderwertig; Am. protzig.

shoe [ʃu:] 1. Schuh m; Hufeisen n; 2. [irr.] beschuhen; beschlagen; ~black ['ʃu:blæk] Schuhputzer m; ~blacking Schuhwichse f; ~horn Schuhanzieher m; ~lace Schnürsenkel m; ~maker Schuhmacher m; ~string Schnürsenkel m.

shone [ʃɔn] pret. u. p.p. von shine 2.

shook [ʃuk] pret. von shake 1.

shoot [ʃu:t] 1. fig. Schuß m; ⚘ Schößling m; 2. [irr.] v/t. (ab-)schießen; erschießen; werfen, stoßen; Film aufnehmen, drehen; fig. unter e-r Brücke etc. hindurchschießen, über et. hinwegschießen; ⚘ treiben; ⚕ (ein)spritzen; v/i. schießen; stechen (Schmerz); daherschießen; stürzen; a. ~ forth ⚘ ausschlagen; ~ ahead vorwärtsschießen; ~er ['ʃu:tə] Schütze m.

shooting ['ʃu:tiŋ] 1. Schießen n; Schießerei f; Jagd f; Film: Dreharbeiten f/pl.; 2. stechend (Schmerz); ~gallery Schießstand m, -bude f; ~range Schießplatz m; ~ star Sternschnuppe f.

shop [ʃɔp] 1. Laden m, Geschäft n; Werkstatt f, Betrieb m; talk ~ fachsimpeln; 2. mst go ~ping einkaufen gehen; ~assistant ['ʃɔpəsistənt] Verkäufer(in); ~keeper Ladeninhaber(in); ~lifter ['ʃɔpliftə] Ladendieb m; ~man Ladengehilfe m; ~per ['ʃɔpə] Käufer(in); ~ping ['ʃɔpiŋ] Einkaufen n; attr. Einkaufs...; ~ centre Einkaufszentrum n; ~steward Betriebsrat m; ~walker ['ʃɔpwɔ:kə] Aufsichtsherr m, -dame f; ~window Schaufenster n.

shore [ʃɔ:] 1. Küste f, Ufer n; Strand m; Stütze f; on ~ an Land; 2. ~ up abstützen.

shorn [ʃɔ:n] p.p. von shear 1.

short [ʃɔ:t] 1. adj. kurz (a. fig.); klein; knapp; mürbe (Gebäck); wortkarg; in ~ kurz(um); ~ of knapp an (dat.); 2. adv. ~ of abgesehen von; come od. fall ~ of et. nicht erreichen; cut ~ plötzlich unterbrechen; run ~ (of) ausgehen (Vorräte); stop ~ of zurückschrecken vor (dat.); ~age ['ʃɔ:tidʒ] Fehlbetrag m; Gewichtsverlust m; Knappheit f; ~coming Unzulänglichkeit f; Fehler m; Mangel m; ~cut Abkürzungsweg m; ~dated † auf kurze Sicht; ~en ['ʃɔ:tn] v/t. ab-, verkürzen; v/i. kürzer werden; ~ening [~niŋ] Backfett m; ~hand Kurzschrift f; ~ typist Stenotypistin f; ~ly adv. kurz; bald; ~ness ['ʃɔ:tnis] Kürze f; Mangel m; ~sighted kurzsichtig; ~term kurzfristig; ~winded kurzatmig.

shot [ʃɔt] 1. pret. u. p.p. von shoot 2; 2. Schuß m; Geschoß n, Kugel f; Schrot(korn) n; Schußweite f; Schütze m; Sport: Stoß m, Schlag m, Wurf m; phot., Film: Aufnahme f; ⚕ Spritze f; have a ~ at et. versuchen; not by a long ~ F noch lange nicht; big ~ F großes Tier; ~gun ['ʃɔtgʌn] Schrotflinte f; ~ marriage Am. F Mußheirat f.

should [ʃud, ʃəd] pret. von shall.

shoulder ['∫ouldə] **1.** Schulter f (a. v. Tieren; fig. Vorsprung); Achsel f; **2.** auf die Schulter od. fig. auf sich nehmen; ✗ schultern; drängen; **~blade** anat. Schulterblatt n; **~strap** Träger m am Kleid; ✗ Schulter-, Achselstück n.

shout [∫aut] **1.** lauter Schrei od. Ruf; Geschrei n; **2.** laut schreien.

shove [∫ʌv] **1.** Schub m, Stoß m; **2.** schieben, stoßen.

shovel ['∫ʌvl] **1.** Schaufel f; **2.** schaufeln.

show [∫ou] **1.** [irr.] v/t. zeigen; ausstellen; erweisen; beweisen; **~ in** hereinführen; **~ off** zur Geltung bringen; **~ out** hinausgeleiten; **~ round** herumführen; **~ up** hinaufführen; entlarven; v/i. a. **~ up** sich zeigen; zu sehen sein; **~ off** angeben, prahlen, sich aufspielen; **2.** Schau(stellung) f; Ausstellung f; Auf-, Vorführung f; Anschein m; **on ~** zu besichtigen; **~ business** ['∫oubiznis] Unterhaltungsindustrie f; Schaugeschäft n; **~-case** Schaukasten m, Vitrine f; **~-down** Aufdecken n der Karten (bsd. Am. a. fig.); fig. Kraftprobe f.

shower ['∫auə] **1.** (Regen)Schauer m; Dusche f; fig. Fülle f; **2.** v/t. herabschütten (a. fig.); überschütten; v/i. sich ergießen; **~y** ['∫auəri] regnerisch.

show|n [∫oun] p.p. von show **1**; **~room** ['∫ourum] Ausstellungsraum m; **~-window** Schaufenster n; **~y** □ ['∫oui] prächtig; protzig.

shrank [∫ræŋk] pret. von shrink.

shred [∫red] **1.** Stückchen n; Schnitz(el n) m; Fetzen m (a. fig.); **2.** [irr.] (zer)schnitzeln; zerfetzen.

shrew [∫ru:] zänkisches Weib.

shrewd □ [∫ru:d] scharfsinnig; schlau.

shriek [∫ri:k] **1.** (Angst)Schrei m; Gekreisch n; **2.** kreischen, schreien.

shrill [∫ril] **1.** □ schrill, gellend; **2.** schrillen, gellen; schreien.

shrimp [∫rimp] zo. Krabbe f; fig. Knirps m. [m.]

shrine [∫rain] Schrein m; Altar]

shrink [∫riŋk] [irr.] (ein-, zs.-) schrumpfen (lassen); einlaufen; sich zurückziehen; zurückschrecken (from, at vor dat.); **~age** ['∫riŋkidʒ] Einlaufen n, Zs.-schrumpfen n; Schrumpfung f; fig. Verminderung f.

shrivel ['∫rivl] einschrumpfen (lassen).

shroud [∫raud] **1.** Leichentuch n; fig. Gewand n; **2.** in ein Leichentuch einhüllen; fig. hüllen.

Shrove|tide ['∫rouvtaid] Fastnachtszeit f; **~ Tuesday** Fastnachtsdienstag m.

shrub [∫rʌb] Strauch m; Busch m; **~bery** ['∫rʌbəri] Gebüsch n.

shrug [∫rʌg] **1.** (die Achseln) zucken; **2.** Achselzucken n.

shrunk [∫rʌŋk] p.p. von shrink; **~en** ['∫rʌŋkən] adj. (ein)geschrumpft.

shuck bsd. Am. [∫ʌk] **1.** Hülse f, Schote f; **~s!** F Quatsch!; **2.** enthülsen.

shudder ['∫ʌdə] **1.** schaudern; (er-) beben; **2.** Schauder m.

shuffle ['∫ʌfl] **1.** schieben; Karten: mischen; schlurfen; Ausflüchte machen; **~ off** von sich schieben; abstreifen; **2.** Schieben n; Mischen n; Schlurfen n; Ausflucht f; Schiebung f.

shun [∫ʌn] (ver)meiden.

shunt [∫ʌnt] **1.** 🚂 Rangieren n; 🚂 Weiche f; ⚡ Nebenschluß m; **2.** 🚂 rangieren; ⚡ nebenschließen; fig. verschieben.

shut [∫ʌt] [irr.] (sich) schließen; zumachen; **~ down** Betrieb schließen; **~ up** ein-, verschließen; einsperren; **~ up!** F halt den Mund!; **~ter** ['∫ʌtə] Fensterladen m; phot. Verschluß m.

shuttle ['∫ʌtl] **1.** ⊕ Schiffchen n; Pendelverkehr m; **2.** pendeln.

shy [∫ai] **1.** □ scheu; schüchtern; **2.** (zurück)scheuen (at vor dat.).

shyness ['∫ainis] Schüchternheit f; Scheu f.

shyster sl., bsd. Am. ['∫aistə] gerissener Kerl; Winkeladvokat m.

Siberian [sai'biəriən] **1.** sibirisch; **2.** Sibirier(in).

sick [sik] krank (of an dat.; with vor dat.); übel; überdrüssig; **be ~ for** sich sehnen nach; **be ~ of** genug haben von; **go ~** report □ sich krank melden; **~-benefit** ['sik-benifit] Krankengeld n; **~en** ['sikn] v/i. krank werden; kränkeln; **~ at** sich ekeln vor (dat.); v/t. krank machen; anekeln.

sickle ['sikl] Sichel f.

sick|-leave ['sikli:v] Krankheitsurlaub m; **~ly** [~li] kränklich; schwächlich; bleich, blaß; ungesund (Klima); ekelhaft; matt (Lächeln); **~ness** ['siknis] Krankheit f; Übelkeit f.

side [said] **1.** allg. Seite f; **~ by Seite** an Seite; **take ~ with** Partei ergreifen für; **2.** Seiten...; Neben...; **3.** Partei ergreifen (with für); **~board** ['saidbɔ:d] Anrichte(tisch m) f, Sideboard n; **~-car** mot. Beiwagen m; **~d** ...seitig; **~-light** Streiflicht n; **~long 1.** adv. seitwärts; **2.** adj. seitlich; Seiten...; **~-stroke** Seitenschwimmen n; **~-track 1.** 🚂 Nebengleis n; **2.** auf ein Nebengleis schieben; bsd. Am fig. aufschieben; beiseite schieben; **~walk** bsd. Am. Bürgersteig m; **~ward(s)** [~wəd(z)], **~ways** seitlich; seitwärts.

siding 🚂 ['saidiŋ] Nebengleis n.

sidle ['saidl] seitwärts gehen.

siege [si:dʒ] Belagerung f; lay ~ to belagern.

sieve [siv] 1. Sieb n; 2. (durch-) sieben.

sift [sift] sieben; fig. sichten; prüfen.

sigh [sai] 1. Seufzer m; 2. seufzen; sich sehnen (after, for nach).

sight [sait] 1. Sehvermögen n, Sehkraft f; fig. Auge n; Anblick m; Visier n; Sicht f; ~s pl. Sehenswürdigkeiten f/pl.; at ~ a. on ~ beim Anblick; ♪ vom Blatt; ♦ nach Sicht; catch ~ of erblicken, zu Gesicht bekommen; lose ~ of aus den Augen verlieren; within ~ in Sicht; know by ~ vom Sehen kennen; 2. sichten; (an)visieren; ~ed ['saitid] ...sichtig; ~ly ['saitli] ansehnlich, stattlich; ~seeing ['saitsi:iŋ] Besichtigung f von Sehenswürdigkeiten; bloß. ~seer Tourist(in).

sign [sain] 1. Zeichen n; Wink m; Schild n; in ~ of zum Zeichen (gen.); 2. v/i. winken, Zeichen geben; v/t. (unter)zeichnen, unterschreiben.

signal ['signl] 1. Signal n; Zeichen n; 2. ☐ bemerkenswert, außerordentlich; 3. signalisieren; ~ize [~nəlaiz] auszeichnen; ~ signal 3.

signat|ory ['signətəri] 1. Unterzeichner m; 2. unterzeichnend; ~powers pl. Signatarmächte f/pl.; ~ure [~nitʃə] Signatur f; Unterschrift f; ~ tune Radio: Kennmelodie f.

sign|board ['sainbɔːd] (Aushänge-) Schild n; ~er ['sainə] Unterzeichner(in).

signet ['signit] Siegel n.

signific|ance [sig'nifikəns] Bedeutung f; ~ant ☐ [~nt] bedeutsam; bezeichnend (of für); ~ation [signifi'keiʃən] Bedeutung f.

signify ['signifai] bezeichnen, andeuten; kundgeben; bedeuten.

signpost ['sainpoust] Wegweiser m.

silence ['sailəns] 1. (Still)Schweigen n; Stille f, Ruhe f; ~! Ruhe! put od. reduce to ~ = 2. zum Schweigen bringen; ~r [~sə] ⊕ Schalldämpfer m; mot. Auspufftopf m.

silent ☐ ['sailənt] still; schweigend; schweigsam; stumm; ~ partner ♦ stiller Teilhaber.

silk [silk] Seide f; attr. Seiden...; ~en ☐ ['silkən] seiden; ~stocking Am. vornehm; ~worm Seidenraupe f; ~y ☐ [~ki] seid(en)artig.

sill [sil] Schwelle f; Fensterbrett n.

silly ☐ ['sili] albern, töricht.

silt [silt] 1. Schlamm m; 2. mst ~ up verschlammen.

silver ['silvə] 1. Silber n; 2. silbern; Silber...; 3. versilbern; silberig od. silberweiß werden (lassen); ~ware Am. Tafelsilber n; ~y [~əri] silberglänzend; silberhell.

similar ☐ ['similə] ähnlich, gleich; ~ity [simi'læriti] Ähnlichkeit f.

simile ['simili] Gleichnis n.

similitude [si'militjuːd] Gestalt f; Ebenbild n; Gleichnis n.

simmer ['simə] sieden od. brodeln (lassen); fig. kochen, gären (Gefühl, Aufstand); ~ down ruhig(er) werden.

simper ['simpə] 1. einfältiges Lächeln; 2. einfältig lächeln.

simple ☐ ['simpl] einfach; schlicht; einfältig; arglos; ~-hearted, ~-minded arglos, naiv; ~ton [~ltən] Einfaltspinsel m.

simpli|city [sim'plisiti] Einfachheit f; Klarheit f; Schlichtheit f; Einfalt f; ~fication [simplifi'keiʃən] Vereinfachung f; ~fy ['simplifai] vereinfachen.

simply ['simpli] einfach; bloß.

simulate ['simjuleit] vortäuschen; (er)heucheln; sich tarnen als.

simultaneous ☐ [siməl'teinjəs] gleichzeitig.

sin [sin] 1. Sünde f; 2. sündigen.

since [sins] 1. prp. seit; 2. adv. seitdem; 3. cj. seit(dem); da (ja).

sincer|e ☐ [sin'siə] aufrichtig; Yours ~ly Ihr ergebener; ~ity [~'seriti] Aufrichtigkeit f.

sinew ['sinjuː] Sehne f; fig. mst. ~s pl. Nerven(kraft f) m/pl., Seele f; ~y [~ju(ː)i] sehnig; nervig, stark.

sinful ☐ ['sinful] sündig, sündhaft, böse.

sing [siŋ] (irr.) singen; besingen; ~ to s.o. j-m vorsingen.

singe [sindʒ] (ver)sengen.

singer ['siŋə] Sänger(in).

singing ['siŋiŋ] Gesang m, Singen n; ~ bird Singvogel m.

single ['siŋgl] 1. ☐ einzig; einzeln; Einzel...; einfach; ledig, unverheiratet; book-keeping by ~ entry einfache Buchführung; ~ file Gänsemarsch m; 2. einfache Fahrkarte; mst ~s sg. Tennis: Einzel n; 3. ~ out auswählen, aussuchen; ~breasted einreihig (Jacke etc.); ~-engined ☀ einmotorig; ~-handed eigenhändig, allein; ~-hearted ☐, ~-minded ☐ aufrichtig; zielstrebig; ~t [~lit] Unterhemd n; ~-track eingleisig.

singular ['siŋgjulə] 1. ☐ einzigartig; eigenartig; sonderbar; 2. a. ~ number gr. Singular m, Einzahl f; ~ity [siŋgju'læriti] Einzigartigkeit f; Sonderbarkeit f.

sinister ☐ ['sinistə] unheilvoll; böse.

sink [siŋk] 1. (irr.) v/i. sinken; niede-, unter-, versinken; sich senken; eindringen; erliegen; v/t. (ver)senken; Brunnen bohren; Geld festlegen; Namen etc. aufgeben; 2. Ausguß m; ~ing ['siŋkiŋ] (Ver-) Sinken n; Versenken n; ☀ Schwäche(gefühl n) f; Senkung f; ♦

Tilgung f; ~ **fund** (Schulden)Tilgungsfonds m.

sinless ['sinlis] sündenlos, -frei.

sinner ['sinə] Sünder(in).

sinuous □ ['sinjuəs] gewunden.

sip [sip] 1. Schlückchen n; 2. schlürfen; nippen; langsam trinken.

sir [sə:] Herr m; ♀ Sir (Titel).

sire ['saiə] mst poet. Vater m; Vorfahr m; zo. Vater(tier n) m.

siren ['saiərin] Sirene f.

sirloin ['sə:lɔin] Lendenstück n.

sissy Am. ['sisi] Weichling m.

sister ['sistə] (a. Ordens-, Ober-) Schwester f; ~**hood** [~əhud] Schwesternschaft f; ~**in-law** [~ərinlɔ:] Schwägerin f; ~**ly** [~əli] schwesterlich.

sit [sit] (irr.) v/i. sitzen; Sitzung halten, tagen; fig. liegen; ~ **down** sich setzen; ~ **up** aufrecht sitzen; aufbleiben; v/t. setzen; sitzen auf (dat.).

site [sait] Lage f; (Bau)Platz m.

sitting ['sitiŋ] Sitzung f; ~**room** Wohnzimmer n.

situat|ed ['sitjueitid] gelegen; be ~ liegen, gelegen sein; ~**ion** [sitju'eiʃən] Lage f; Stellung f.

six [siks] 1. sechs; 2. Sechs f; ~**teen** ['siks'ti:n] sechzehn; ~**teenth** [~nθ] 1. sechzehnte(r, -s); 2. Sechzehntel n; ~**th** [siksθ] 1. sechste(r, -s); 2. Sechstel n; ~**thly** ['siksθli] sechstens; ~**tieth** [~stiiθ] sechzigste(r, -s); ~**ty** [~ti] 1. sechzig; 2. Sechzig f.

size [saiz] 1. Größe f; Format n; 2. nach der Größe ordnen; ~ **up** F j-n abschätzen; ~**d** von ... Größe.

siz(e)able □ ['saizəbl] ziemlich groß.

sizzle ['sizl] zischen, knistern; brutzeln; sizzling hot glühend heiß.

skat|e [skeit] 1. Schlittschuh m; roller-~, Rollschuh m; 2. Schlittod. Rollschuh laufen; ~**er** ['skeitə] Schlittschuh- Rollschuhläufer(in).

skedaddle F [ski'dædl] abhauen.

skeesicks Am. F ['ski:ziks] Nichtsnutz m.

skein [skein] Strähne f, Docke f.

skeleton ['skelitn] Skelett n; Gerippe n; Gestell n; attr. Skelett...; ⚔ Stamm...; ~**key** Nachschlüssel m.

skeptic ['skeptik] s. sceptic.

sketch [sketʃ] 1. Skizze f; Entwurf m; Umriß m; 2. skizzieren, entwerfen.

ski [ski:] 1. pl. a. ski Schi m, Ski m; 2. Schi od. Ski laufen.

skid [skid] 1. Hemmschuh m, Bremsklotz m; ✈ (Gleit)Kufe f; Rutschen n; mot. Schleudern n; 2. v/t. hemmen; v/i. (aus)rutschen.

skiddoo Am. sl. [ski'du:] abhauen.

ski|er ['ski:ə] Schi-, Skiläufer(in); ~**ing** ['ski:iŋ] Schi-, Skilauf(en n) m.

skilful □ ['skilful] geschickt; kundig.

skill [skil] Geschicklichkeit f, Fertigkeit f; ~**ed** [skild] geschickt; gelernt; ~ **worker** Facharbeiter m.

skilful Am. ['skilful] s. skilful.

skim [skim] 1. abschöpfen; abrahmen; dahingleiten über (acc.); Buch überfliegen; ~ **through** durchblättern; 2. ~ **milk** Magermilch f.

skimp [skimp] j-n knapp halten; sparen (mit et.); ~**y** □ ['skimpi] knapp, dürftig.

skin [skin] 1. Haut f; Fell n; Schale f; 2. v/t. (ent)häuten; abbalgen; schälen; ~ **off** F abstreifen; v/i. a. ~ **over** zuheilen; ~**deep** ['skin'di:p] (nur) oberflächlich; ~**flint** Knicker m; ~**ny** [~ni] mager.

skip [skip] 1. Sprung m; 2. v/i. hüpfen, springen; seilhüpfen; v/t. überspringen.

skipper ['skipə] ⚓ Schiffer m; ✈, ⚔, Sport: Kapitän m.

skirmish ['skə:miʃ] 1. ⚔ Scharmützel n; 2. plänkeln.

skirt [skə:t] 1. (Damen)Rock m; (Rock)Schoß m; oft ~**s** pl. Rand m, Saum m; 2. umsäumen; (sich) entlangziehen (an dat.); entlangfahren; ~**ing-board** ['skə:tiŋbɔ:d] Scheuerleiste f.

skit [skit] Stichelei f; Satire f; ~**tish** □ ['skiti] ungebärdig.

skittle ['skitl] Kegel m; play (at) ~**s** Kegel schieben; ~**alley** Kegelbahn f. [Gemeinheit f.)

skulduggery Am. F [skʌl'dʌgəri]

skulk [skʌlk] schleichen; sich verstecken; lauern; sich drücken; ~**er** ['skʌlkə] Drückeberger m.

skull [skʌl] Schädel m.

sky [skai] oft skies pl. Himmel m; ~**lark** ['skaila:k] 1. orn. Feldlerche f; 2. Ulk treiben; ~**light** Oberlicht n; Dachfenster n; ~**line** Horizont m; Silhouette f; ~**rocket** F emporschnellen; ~**scraper** Wolkenkratzer m; ~**ward(s)** ['skaiwəd(z)] himmelwärts.

slab [slæb] Platte f; Scheibe f; Fliese f.

slack [slæk] 1. schlaff; locker; (nach)lässig; ✈ flau; 2. ⚓ Lose n (loses Tauende); ✈ Flaute f; Kohlengrus m; 3. = slacken; = slake; ~**en** ['slækən] schlaff machen od. werden; verringern; nachlassen; (sich) lockern; (sich) entspannen; (sich) verlangsamen; ~**s** pl. (lange) Hose.

slag [slæg] Schlacke f.

slain [slein] p.p. von slay.

slake [sleik] Durst, Kalk löschen; fig. stillen.

slam [slæm] 1. Zuschlagen n; Knall m; 2. Tür etc. zuschlagen, zuknallen; et. auf den Tisch etc. knallen.

slander ['sla:ndə] 1. Verleumdung f; 2. verleumden; ~**ous** □ [~ərəs] verleumderisch.

slang [slæŋ] 1. Slang m; Berufssprache f; lässige Umgangssprache; 2. j-n wüst beschimpfen.

slant [slɑːnt] 1. schräge Fläche; Abhang m; Neigung f; Am. Standpunkt m; 2. schräg legen od. liegen; sich neigen; **~ing** adj., □ ['slɑːntiŋ], **~wise** adv. [**~twaiz**] schief, schräg.

slap [slæp] 1. Klaps m, Schlag m; 2. klapsen; schlagen; klatschen; **~jack** Am. ['slæpdʒæk] Art Pfannkuchen m; **~stick** (Narren)Pritsche f; a. ~ comedy thea. Posse f, Burleske f.

slash [slæʃ] 1. Hieb m; Schnitt m; Schlitz m; 2. (auf)schlitzen; schlagen, hauen; verreißen (Kritiker).

slate [sleit] 1. Schiefer m; Schiefertafel f; bsd. Am. Kandidatenliste f; 2. mit Schiefer decken; heftig kritisieren; Am. F für e-n Posten vorschlagen; **~pencil** ['sleit'pensl] Griffel m.

slattern ['slæta(ː)n] Schlampe f.

slaughter ['slɔːtə] 1. Schlachten n; Gemetzel n; 2. schlachten; niedermetzeln; **~house** Schlachthaus n.

Slav [slɑːv] 1. Slaw|e m, -in f; 2. slawisch.

slave [sleiv] 1. Sklav|e m, -in f (a. fig.); 2. F sich placken, schuften.

slaver ['slævə] 1. Geifer m, Sabber m; 2. (be)geifern, F (be)sabbern.

slav|ery ['sleivəri] Sklaverei f; F Plackerei f; **~ish** □ [**~viʃ**] sklavisch.

slay rhet. [slei] [irr.] erschlagen; töten.

sled [sled] = sledge 1.

sledge[1] [sledʒ] 1. Schlitten m; 2. Schlitten fahren.

sledge[2] [**~**] a. **~hammer** Schmiedehammer m.

sleek [sliːk] 1. □ glatt, geschmeidig; 2. glätten; **~ness** ['sliːknis] Glätte f.

sleep [sliːp] 1. [irr.] v/i. schlafen; ~ (up)on od. over et. beschlafen; v/t. j-n für die Nacht unterbringen; ~ away Zeit verschlafen; 2. Schlaf m; go to ~ einschlafen; **~er** ['sliːpə] Schläfer(in); ⑄ Schwelle f; Schlafwagen m; **~ing** [**~piŋ**] schlafend; Schlaf...; ⑄ing Beauty Dornröschen n; **~ing-car(riage)** ⑄ Schlafwagen m; **~ing partner** † stiller Teilhaber; **~less** □ [**~plis**] schlaflos; **~walker** Schlafwandler(in); **~y** □ [**~pi**] schläfrig; verschlafen.

sleet [sliːt] 1. Graupelregen m; 2. graupeln; **~y** ['sliːti] graupelig.

sleeve [sliːv] Ärmel m; ⊕ Muffe f; **~link** ['sliːvliŋk] Manschettenknopf m.

sleigh [slei] 1. (bsd. Pferde)Schlitten m; 2. (im) Schlitten fahren.

sleight [slait]: **~of-hand** Taschenspielerei f; Kunststück n.

slender □ ['slendə] schlank; schmächtig; schwach; dürftig.

slept [slept] pret. u. p.p. von sleep 1.

sleuth [sluːθ], **~hound** ['sluːθhaund] Blut-, Spürhund m (a. fig.).

slew [sluː] pret. von slay.

slice [slais] 1. Schnitte f, Scheibe f, Stück n; Teil m, n; 2. (in) Scheiben schneiden; aufschneiden.

slick F [slik] 1. adj. glatt; fig. raffiniert; 2. adv. direkt; 3. a. ~ paper Am. sl. vornehme Zeitschrift; **~er** Am. F ['slikə] Regenmantel m; gerissener Kerl.

slid [slid] pret. u. p.p. von slide 1.

slide [slaid] 1. [irr.] gleiten (lassen); rutschen; schlittern; ausgleiten; geraten (into in acc.); let things ~ die Dinge laufen lassen; 2. Gleiten n; Rutsche f; ⊕ Schieber m; Diapositiv n; a. land~ Erdrutsch m; **~rule** ['slaidruːl] Rechenschieber m.

slight [slait] 1. □ schmächtig; schwach; gering, unbedeutend; 2. Geringschätzung f; 3. geringschätzig behandeln; unbeachtet lassen.

slim [slim] 1. □ schlank; dünn; schmächtig; dürftig; sl. schlau, gerissen; 2. e-e Schlankheitskur machen.

slim|e [slaim] Schlamm m; Schleim m; **~y** ['slaimi] schlammig; schleimig.

sling [sliŋ] 1. Schleuder f; Tragriemen m; ✠ Schlinge f, Binde f; Wurf m; 2. [irr.] schleudern; aufumhängen; a. ~ up hochziehen.

slink [sliŋk] [irr.] schleichen.

slip [slip] 1. [irr.] v/i. schlüpfen, gleiten, rutschen; ausgleiten; ausrutschen; oft ~ away entschlüpfen; sich versehen; v/t. schlüpfen od. gleiten lassen; loslassen; entschlüpfen; into hineinstecken od. hineinschieben in (acc.); ~ on (off) Kleid über-, (ab)streifen; have **~ped** s.o.'s memory j-m entfallen sein; 2. (Aus)Gleiten n; Fehltritt m (a. fig.); Versehen n; (Flüchtigkeits)Fehler m; Verstoß m; Streifen m; Zettel m; Unterkleid n; a. **~way** ♨ Helling f; (Kissen)Überzug m; **~s** pl. Badehose f; give s.o. the ~ j-m entwischen; **~per** ['slipə] Pantoffel m, Hausschuh m; **~pery** □ [**~pəri**] schlüpfrig; **~shod** [**~ʃɔd**] schlampig, nachlässig; **~t** [slipt] pret. u. p.p. von slip 1.

slit [slit] 1. Schlitz m; Spalte f; 2. [irr.] (auf-, zer)schlitzen.

sliver ['slivə] Splitter m.

slobber ['slɔbə] 1. Sabber m; Gesabber n; 2. F (be)sabbern.

slogan ['slougən] Schlagwort n, Losung f; (Werbe)Slogan m.

sloop ♨ [sluːp] Schaluppe f.

slop [slɔp] 1. Pfütze *f*; ~*s pl.* Spül-, Schmutzwasser *n*; Krankenspeise *f*; 2. *v/t.* verschütten; *v/i.* überlaufen.

slope [sloup] 1. (Ab)Hang *m*; Neigung *f*; 2. schräg legen; ⊕ abschrägen; abfallen; schräg verlaufen; (sich) neigen.

sloppy □ ['slɔpi] naß, schmutzig; schlampig; F labb(e)rig; rührselig.

slops [slɔps] *pl.* billige Konfektionskleidung, ⚓ Kleidung *f* u. Bettzeug *n*.

slot [slɔt] Schlitz *m*.

sloth [slouθ] Faulheit *f*; *zo.* Faultier *n*.

slot-machine ['slɔtməʃiːn] (Warenod. Spiel)Automat *m*.

slouch [slautʃ] 1. faul herumhängen; F herumlatschen; 2. schlaffe Haltung; ~ *hat* Schlapphut *m*.

slough[1] [slau] Sumpf(loch *n*) *m*.

slough[2] [slʌf] *Haut* abwerfen.

sloven ['slʌvn] unordentlicher Mensch; F Schlampe *f*; ~**ly** [~nli] liederlich.

slow [slou] 1. □ langsam (*of in dat.*); schwerfällig; lässig; *be* ~ nachgehen (*Uhr*); 2. *adv.* langsam; 3. *oft* ~ *down od. up od. off v/t.* verlangsamen; *v/i.* langsam(er) werden *od.* gehen *od.* fahren; ~**coach** ['sloukoutʃ] Langweiler *m*; altmodischer Mensch; ~**motion picture** Zeitlupenaufnahme *f*; ~**worm** *zo.* Blindschleiche *f*.

sludge [slʌdʒ] Schlamm *m*; Matsch *m*.

slug [slʌg] 1. Stück *n* Rohmetall; *zo.* Wegschnecke *f*; *Am.* F (Faust-) Schlag *m*; 2. *Am.* F hauen.

slugg|ard ['slʌgəd] Faulenzer(in); ~**ish** □ [~giʃ] träge, faul.

sluice [sluːs] 1. Schleuse *f*; 2. ausströmen (lassen); ausspülen; waschen.

slum [slʌm] schmutzige Gasse; ~*s pl.* Elendsviertel *n*, Slums *pl.*

slumber ['slʌmbə] 1. *a.* ~*s pl.* Schlummer *m*; 2. schlummern.

slump [slʌmp] *Börse:* 1. fallen, stürzen; 2. (Kurs-, Preis)Sturz *m*.

slung [slʌŋ] *pret. u. p.p. von sling* 2.

slunk [slʌŋk] *pret. u. p.p. von slink.*

slur [sləː] 1. Fleck *m*; *fig.* Tadel *m*; ♩ Bindebogen *m*; 2. *v/t. oft* ~ *over* übergehen; ♩ *Töne* binden.

slush [slʌʃ] Schlamm *m*; Matsch *m*; F Kitsch *m*.

slut [slʌt] F Schlampe *f*; Nutte *f*.

sly [] [slai] schlau, verschmitzt; hinterlistig; *on the* ~ heimlich.

smack [smæk] 1. (Bei)Geschmack *m*; Prise *f Salz etc.*; *fig.* Spur *f*; Schmatz *m*; Schlag *m*, Klatsch *m*, Klaps *m*; 2. schmecken (*of nach*); e-n Beigeschmack haben; klatschen, knallen (mit); schmatzen (mit); *j-m* e-n Klaps geben.

small [smɔːl] 1. *allg.* klein; unbe-

deutend; *fig.* kleinlich; niedrig; wenig; *feel* ~, *look* ~ sich gedemütigt fühlen; *the* ~ *hours* die frühen Morgenstunden *f/pl.*; *in a* ~ *way* bescheiden; 2. dünner Teil; ~*s pl.* F Leibwäsche *f*; ~ *of the back anat.* Kreuz *n*; ~**arms** ['smɔːlɑːmz] *pl.* Handfeuerwaffen *f/pl.*; ~ **change** Kleingeld *n*; *fig.* triviale Bemerkungen *f/pl.*; ~**ish** [~liʃ] ziemlich klein; ~**pox** *💊* [~pɔks] Pocken *f/pl.*; ~ **talk** Plauderei *f*; ~**time** *Am.* F unbedeutend.

smart [smɑːt] 1. □ scharf; gewandt; geschickt; gescheit; gerissen; schmuck, elegant, adrett; forsch; ~ *aleck Am.* F Neunmalkluge(r) *m*; 2. Schmerz *m*; 3. schmerzen; leiden; ~**money** ['smɑːtmʌni] Schmerzensgeld *n*; ~**ness** [~tnis] Klugheit *f*; Schärfe *f*; Gewandtheit *f*; Gerissenheit *f*; Eleganz *f*.

smash [smæʃ] 1. *v/t.* zertrümmern; *fig.* vernichten; (zer)schmettern; *v/i.* zerschellen; zs.-stoßen; *fig.* zs.-brechen; 2. Zerschmettern *n*; Krach *m*; Zs.-bruch *m* (*a.* †); *Tennis:* Schmetterball *m*; ~**up** ['smæʃʌp] Zs.-stoß *m*; Zs.-bruch *m*.

smattering ['smætəriŋ] oberflächliche Kenntnis.

smear [smiə] 1. (be)schmieren; *fig.* beschmutzen; 2. Schmiere *f*; Fleck *m*.

smell [smel] 1. Geruch *m*; 2. [*irr.*] riechen (*of nach et.*); *a.* ~ *at* riechen an (*dat.*); ~**y** ['smeli] übelriechend.

smelt[1] [smelt] *pret. u. p.p. von smell* 2.

smelt[2] [~] schmelzen.

smile [smail] 1. Lächeln *n*; 2. lächeln.

smirch [sməːtʃ] besudeln.

smirk [sməːk] grinsen.

smite [smait] [*irr.*] schlagen; heimsuchen; *schwer* treffen; quälen.

smith [smiθ] Schmied *m*.

smithereens ['smiðə'riːnz] *pl.* Stücke *n/pl.*, Splitter *m/pl*, Fetzen *m/pl.*

smithy ['smiði] Schmiede *f*.

smitten ['smitn] 1. *p.p. von smite*; 2. *adj.* ergriffen; betroffen; *fig.* hingerissen (*with* von).

smock [smɔk] 1. fälteln; 2. Kittel *m*; ~**frock** ['smɔk'frɔk] Bauernkittel *m*.

smog [smɔg] Smog *m*, Gemisch *n* von Nebel und Rauch.

smoke [smouk] 1. Rauch *m*; *have a* ~ (eine) rauchen; 2. rauchen; dampfen; (an)räuchern; ~**dried** ['smoukdraid] geräuchert; ~**r** [~kə] Raucher *m*; 🚃 F Raucherwagen *m*, -abteil *n*; ~**stack** *🚂* ⚓ Schornstein *m*.

smoking ['smoukiŋ] Rauchen *n*; *attr.* Rauch(er)...; ~**compartment** 🚃 Raucherabteil *n*.

smoky □ ['smouki] rauchig; verräuchert. [der.)

smolder *Am.* ['smouldə] = *smoul-)*

smooth [smu:ð] **1.** □ glatt; *fig.* fließend; mild; schmeichlerisch; **2.** glätten; ebnen (*a. fig.*); plätten; mildern; *a.* ~ over, ~ away *fig.* wegräumen; ~ness ['smu:ðnis] Glätte *f.*

smote [smout] *pret. von* smite.

smother ['smʌðə] ersticken.

smoulder ['smouldə] schwelen.

smudge [smʌdʒ] **1.** (be)schmutzen; (be)schmieren; **2.** Schmutzfleck *m.*

smug [smʌg] selbstzufrieden.

smuggle ['smʌgl] schmuggeln; ~r [,.Jə] Schmuggler(in).

smut [smʌt] Schmutz *m*; Ruß(fleck) *m*; Zoten *f/pl.*; **2.** beschmutzen.

smutty □ ['smʌti] schmutzig.

snack [snæk] Imbiß *m*; ~bar ['snækba:], ~counter Snackbar *f*, Imbißstube *f.*

snaffle ['snæfl] Trense *f.*

snag [snæg] (Ast-, Zahn)Stumpf *m*; *fig.* Haken *m*; *Am.* Baumstumpf *m* (*bsd. unter Wasser*).

snail *zo.* [sneil] Schnecke *f.*

snake *zo.* [sneik] Schlange *f.*

snap [snæp] **1.** Schnappen *n*, Biß *m*; Knack(s) *m*; Knall *m*; *fig.* Schwung *m*, Schmiß *m*; Schnappschloß *n*; *phot.* Schnappschuß *m*; *cold* ~ Kältewelle *f*; **2.** *v/i.* schnappen (*at* nach); zuschnappen (*Schloß*); krachen; knacken; (zer)brechen; knallen; schnauzen; ~ *at s.o.* j-n anschnauzen; ~ *into it! Am. sl.* mach schnell!, Tempo! ~ *out of it! Am. sl.* hör auf damit!; komm, komm!; *v/t.* (er)schnappen; (zu)schnappen lassen; *phot.* knipsen; zerbrechen; ~ *out Wort* hervorstoßen; ~ *up* wegschnappen; ~fastener ['snæpfɑːsnə] Druckknopf *m*; ~pish □ [,.piʃ] bissig; schnippisch; ~py [,.pi] bissig; F flott; ~shot Schnappschuß *m*, Photo *n*, Momentaufnahme *f.*

snare [snɛə] **1.** Schlinge *f*; **2.** fangen; *fig.* umgarnen.

snarl [snɑːl] **1.** knurren; murren; **2.** Knurren *n*; Gewirr *n.*

snatch [snætʃ] **1.** schneller Griff; Ruck *m*; Stückchen *n*; **2.** schnappen; ergreifen; an sich reißen; nehmen; ~ *at* greifen nach.

sneak [sni:k] **1.** *v/i.* schleichen; F petzen; *v/t.* F stibitzen; **2.** Schleicher *m*; F Petzer *m*; ~ers ['sni:kəz] *pl.* F leichte Segeltuchschuhe *m/pl.*

sneer [sniə] **1.** Hohnlächeln *n*; Spott *m*; **2.** hohnlächeln; spotten; spötteln.

sneeze [sni:z] **1.** niesen; **2.** Niesen *n.*

snicker ['snikə] kichern; wiehern.

sniff [snif] schnüffeln, schnuppern; riechen; die Nase rümpfen.

snigger ['snigə] kichern.

snip [snip] **1.** Schnitt *m*; Schnipsel

m, *n*; **2.** schnippeln, schnipseln; knipsen.

snipe [snaip] **1.** *orn.* (Sumpf-) Schnepfe *f*; **2.** ✕ aus dem Hinterhalt (ab)schießen; ~r ✕ ['snaipə] Scharf-, Heckenschütze *m.*

snivel ['snivl] schniefen; schluchzen; plärren.

snob [snɔb] Großtuer *m*; Snob *m*; ~bish □ ['snɔbiʃ] snobistisch.

snoop *Am.* [snu:p] **1.** *fig.* (herum-)schnüffeln; **2.** Schnüffler(in).

snooze F [snu:z] **1.** Schläfchen *n*; **2.** dösen.

snore [snɔ:] schnarchen.

snort [snɔ:t] schnauben, schnaufen.

snout [snaut] Schnauze *f*; Rüssel *m.*

snow [snou] **1.** Schnee *m*; **2.** (be-) schneien; *be* ~*ed under fig.* erdrückt werden; ~bound ['snoubaund] eingeschneit; ~capped, ~clad, ~covered schneebedeckt; ~drift Schneewehe *f*; ~drop ♀ Schneeglöckchen *n*; ~y □ ['snoui] schneeig; schneebedeckt, verschneit; schneeweiß.

snub [snʌb] **1.** schelten, anfahren; **2.** Verweis *m*; ~nosed ['snʌbnouzd] stupsnasig.

snuff [snʌf] **1.** Schnuppe *f e-r Kerze*; Schnupftabak *m*; **2.** *a.* take ~ schnupfen; *Licht* putzen; ~le ['snʌfl] schnüffeln; näseln.

snug □ [snʌg] geborgen; behaglich; eng anliegend; ~gle ['snʌgl] (sich) schmiegen *od.* kuscheln (*to* an *acc.*).

so [sou] so; deshalb; also; *I hope* ~ ich hoffe es; *are you tired?* ~ *I am* bist du müde? Ja; *you are tired,* ~ *am I* du bist müde, ich auch; ~ *far* bisher.

soak [souk] *v/t.* einweichen; durchnässen; (durch)tränken; auf-, einsaugen; *v/i.* weichen; durchsickern.

soap [soup] **1.** Seife *f*; *soft* ~ Schmierseife *f*; **2.** (ein)seifen; ~box ['soupbɔks] Seifenkiste *f*; improvisierte Rednertribüne; ~y □ ['soupi] seifig; *fig.* unterwürfig.

soar [sɔ:] sich erheben, sich aufschwingen; schweben; ✈ segelfliegen.

sob [sɔb] **1.** Schluchzen *n*; **2.** schluchzen.

sober ['soubə] **1.** □ nüchtern; **2.** (sich) ernüchtern; ~ness [,.ənis] *f*, **sobriety** [sou'braiəti] Nüchternheit *f.*

so-called ['sou'kɔ:ld] sogenannt.

soccer F ['sɔkə] (Verbands)Fußball *m* (*Spiel*).

sociable ['souʃəbl] **1.** □ gesellig; gemütlich; **2.** geselliges Beisammensein.

social ['souʃəl] **1.** □ gesellschaftlich; gesellig; sozial(istisch), Sozial...; ~ *insurance* Sozialversicherung *f*; ~ *services* *pl.* Sozialeinrichtungen *f/pl.*; **2.** geselliges Beisammensein;

~ism [ˌ~lizəm] Sozialismus *m*; **~ist** [ˌ~ist] **1.** Sozialist(in); **2.** *a.* **~istic** [souʃə'listik] (**~ally**) sozialistisch; **~ize** ['souʃəlaiz] sozialisieren; verstaatlichen.

society [sə'saiəti] Gesellschaft *f*; Verein *m*, Klub *m*.

sociology [sousi'ɔlədʒi] Sozialwissenschaft *f*.

sock [sɔk] Socke *f*; Einlegesohle *f*.

socket ['sɔkit] (Augen-, Zahn)Höhle *f*; (Gelenk)Pfanne *f*; ⊕ Muffe *f*; ⚡ Fassung *f*; ⚡ Steckdose *f*.

sod [sɔd] **1.** Grasnarbe *f*; Rasen (-stück *n*) *m*; **2.** mit Rasen bedecken.

soda ['soudə] Soda *f, n*; **~-fountain** Siphon *m*; *Am.* Erfrischungshalle *f*, Eisdiele *f*.

sodden ['sɔdn] durchweicht; teigig.

soft [sɔft] **1.** □ *allg.* weich; *engS.*: mild; sanft; sacht, leise; zart, zärtlich; weichlich; F einfältig; **~ drink** F alkoholfreies Getränk; **2.** *adv.* weich; **3.** F Trottel *m*; **~en** ['sɔfn] weich machen; (sich) erweichen; mildern; **~headed** schwachsinnig; **~hearted** gutmütig.

soggy ['sɔgi] durchnäßt; feucht.

soil [sɔil] **1.** Boden *m*, Erde *f*; Fleck *m*; Schmutz *m*; **2.** (be)schmutzen; beflecken.

sojourn ['sɔdʒəːn] **1.** Aufenthalt *m*; **2.** sich aufhalten.

solace ['sɔləs] **1.** Trost *m*; **2.** trösten.

solar ['soulə] Sonnen...

sold [sould] *pret. u. p.p. von* sell.

solder ['sɔldə] **1.** Lot *n*; **2.** löten.

soldier ['souldʒə] Soldat *m*; **~like**, **~ly** [ˌ~li] soldatisch; **~y** [ˌ~əri] Militär *n*.

sole[1] □ [soul] alleinig, einzig; **~ agent** Alleinvertreter *m*.

sole[2] [ˌ~] **1.** Sohle *f*; **2.** besohlen.

solemn □ ['sɔləm] feierlich; ernst; **~ity** [sə'lemniti] Feierlichkeit *f*; Steifheit *f*; **~ize** ['sɔləmnaiz] feiern; feierlich vollziehen.

solicit [sə'lisit] (dringend) bitten; ansprechen, belästigen; **~ation** [sɔlisi'teiʃən] dringende Bitte; **~or** [sə'lisitə] ⚖ Anwalt *m*; *Am.* Agent *m*, Werber *m*; **~ous** □ [ˌ~təs] besorgt; **~ of** begierig nach; **~ to** *inf.* bestrebt zu *inf.*; **~ude** [ˌ~tjuːd] Sorge *f*, Besorgnis *f*; Bemühung *f*.

solid ['sɔlid] **1.** □ fest; dauerhaft, haltbar; derb; massiv; A körperlich, Raum...; *fig.* gediegen; solid; triftig; solidarisch; **a ~ hour** e-e volle Stunde; **2.** (fester) Körper *m*; **~arity** [sɔli'dæriti] Solidarität *f*; **~ify** [sə'lidifai] (sich) verdichten; **~ity** [ˌ~iti] Solidität *f*; Gediegenheit *f*.

soliloquy [sə'liləkwi] Selbstgespräch *n*, Monolog *m*.

solit|**ary** □ ['sɔlitəri] einsam; einzeln; einsiedlerisch; **~ude** [ˌ~tjuːd] Einsamkeit *f*; Verlassenheit *f*; Öde *f*.

solo ['soulou] Solo *n*; ✈ Alleinflug *m*; **~ist** [ˌ~ouist] Solist(in).

solu|**ble** ['sɔljubl] löslich; (auf)lösbar; *Am.* **~tion** [sə'luːʃən] (Auf)Lösung *f*; ⊕ Gummilösung *f*.

solve [sɔlv] lösen; **~nt** ['sɔlvənt] **1.** (auf)lösend; ✝ zahlungsfähig; **2.** Lösungsmittel *n*.

somb|**re**, *Am.* **~er** □ ['sɔmbə] düster.

some [sʌm, səm] irgendein; etwas; einige, manche *pl.*; *Am.* F prima; **~ 20 miles** etwa 20 Meilen; *in* **~ degree**, *to* **~ extent** einigermaßen; **~body** ['sʌmbədi] jemand; **~ day** eines Tages; **~how** irgendwie; **~ or other** so oder so; **~one** jemand.

somersault ['sʌməsɔːlt] Salto *m*; Rolle *f*, Purzelbaum *m*; **turn a ~** e-n Purzelbaum schlagen.

some|**thing** ['sʌmθiŋ] (irgend) etwas; **~ like** so etwas wie, so ungefähr; **~time** **1.** einmal, dereinst; **2.** ehemalig; **~times** manchmal; **~what** etwas, ziemlich; **~where** irgendwo(hin).

somniferous □ [sɔm'nifərəs] einschläfernd.

son [sʌn] Sohn *m*.

song [sɔŋ] Gesang *m*; Lied *n*; Gedicht *n*; **for a mere** *od. an old* **~** für e-n Pappenstiel; **~bird** ['sɔŋbəːd] Singvogel *m*; **~ster** ['sɔŋstə] Singvogel *m*; Sänger *m*.

sonic ['sɔnik] Schall...

son-in-law ['sʌninlɔː] Schwiegersohn *m*.

sonnet ['sɔnit] Sonett *n*.

sonorous □ [sə'nɔːrəs] klangvoll.

soon [suːn] bald; früh; gern; *as od. so* **~** *as* sobald als *od.* wie; **~er** ['suːnə] eher; früher; lieber; *no* **~** *... than* kaum ... als; *no* **~** *said than done* gesagt, getan.

soot [sut] **1.** Ruß *m*; **2.** verrußen.

sooth [suːθ] *in* **~** in Wahrheit, fürwahr; **~e** [suːð] beruhigen; mildern; **~sayer** ['suːθseiə] Wahrsager(in).

sooty □ ['suti] rußig.

sop [sɔp] **1.** eingeweichter Brocken; *fig.* Bestechung *f*; **2.** eintunken.

sophist|**icate** [sə'fistikeit] verdrehen; verfälschen; **~icated** kultiviert, raffiniert; intellektuell; blasiert; hochentwickelt, kompliziert; **~ry** ['sɔfistri] Spitzfindigkeit *f*.

sophomore *Am.* ['sɔfəmɔː] Student *m* im zweiten Jahr.

soporific [soupə'rifik] **1.** (**~ally**) einschläfernd; **2.** Schlafmittel *n*.

sorcer|**er** ['sɔːsərə] Zauberer *m*; **~ess** [ˌ~ris] Zauberin *f*; Hexe *f*; **~y** [ˌ~ri] Zauberei *f*.

sordid □ ['sɔːdid] schmutzig, schäbig (*bsd. fig.*).

sore [sɔː] **1.** □ schlimm, entzündet;

wund; weh; empfindlich; ~ throat
Halsweh n; 2. wunde Stelle; ~head
Am. F ['soːhed] 1. mürrischer
Mensch; 2. enttäuscht.

sorrel ['sorəl] 1. rötlichbraun (bsd.
Pferd); 2. Fuchs m (Pferd).

sorrow ['sorou] 1. Sorge f; Kummer m, Leid n; Trauer f; 2. trauern; sich grämen; ~ful □ ['sorəful]
traurig, betrübt; elend.

sorry □ ['sori] betrübt, bekümmert;
traurig; (I am) (so) ~! es tut mir
(sehr) leid; Verzeihung!; I am ~
for him er tut mir leid; we are ~ to
say wir müssen leider sagen.

sort [soːt] 1. Sorte f, Art f; what ~
of was für; of a ~, of ~s F so was
wie; ~ of F gewissermaßen; out of
~s F unpäßlich; verdrießlich; 2.
sortieren; ~ out (aus)sondern.

sot [sot] Trunkenbold m.

sough [sau] 1. Sausen n; 2. rauschen.

sought [soːt] pret. u. p.p. von seek.

soul [soul] Seele f (a. fig.).

sound [saund] 1. □ allg. gesund;
ganz; vernünftig; gründlich; fest;
♰ sicher; ⚯ gültig; 2. Ton m,
Schall m, Laut m, Klang m; ⚓
Sonde f; Meerenge f; Fischblase f;
3. (er)tönen, (er)klingen; erschallen
(lassen); sich gut etc. anhören; sondieren; ⚓ loten; ⚕ abhorchen;
~film ['saundfilm] Tonfilm m;
~ing ⚓ [~diŋ] Lotung f; ~s pl.
lotbare Wassertiefe; ~less □ [~dlis]
lautlos; ~ness [~dnis] Gesundheit
f; ~proof schalldicht; ~track
Film: Tonspur f; ~wave Schallwelle f.

soup¹ [suːp] Suppe f.

soup² Am. sl. mot. [~] 1. Stärke f;
2. ~ up Motor frisieren.

sour ['sauə] 1. □ sauer; fig. bitter;
mürrisch; 2. v/t. säuern; fig. vererbittern; v/i. sauer (fig. bitter)
werden.

source [soːs] Quelle f; Ursprung m.

sour|ish □ ['sauəriʃ] säuerlich; ~
ness ['sauənis] Säure f; fig. Bitterkeit f.

souse [saus] eintauchen; (mit Wasser) begießen; Fisch etc. einlegen,
einpökeln.

south [sauθ] 1. Süd(en m); 2. Süd...;
südlich; ~east ['sauθ'iːst] 1. Südosten m; 2. a. ~eastern [sauθ-
'iːstən] südöstlich.

souther|ly ['sʌðəli], ~n [~ən] südlich; Süd...; ~ner [~nə] Südländer(in), Am. Südstaatler(in).

southernmost ['sʌðənmoust] südlichst.

southpaw Am. ['sauθpɔː] Baseball:
Linkshänder m.

southward(s) adv. ['sauθwəd(z)]
südwärts, nach Süden.

south|-west ['sauθ'west] 1. Südwesten m; 2. südwestlich; ~
wester [sauθ'westə] Südwestwind

m; ⚓ Südwester m; ~westerly,
~western südwestlich.

souvenir ['suːvəniə] Andenken n.

sovereign ['sovrin] 1. □ höchst;
unübertrefflich; unumschränkt;
2. Herrscher(in); Sovereign m (20-
Schilling-Stück); ~ty [~rənti] Oberherrschaft f, Landeshoheit f.

soviet ['souviet] Sowjet m; attr.
Sowjet...

sow¹ [sau] zo. Sau f, (Mutter-)
Schwein n; ⊕ Sau f, Massel f.

sow² [sou] [irr.] (aus)säen, ausstreuen; besäen; ~n [soun] p.p. von
sow².

spa [spaː] Heilbad n; Kurort m.

space [speis] 1. (Welt)Raum m;
Zwischenraum m; Zeitraum m;
2. typ. sperren; ~craft f'speis-
kraːft], ~ship Raumschiff n; ~
suit Raumanzug m.

spacious □ ['speiʃəs] geräumig;
weit, umfassend.

spade [speid] Spaten m; Kartenspiel: Pik n.

span¹ [spæn] 1. Spanne f; Spannweite f; Am. Gespann n; 2. (um-,
über)spannen; (aus)messen.

span² [~] pret. von spin 1.

spangle ['spæŋgl] 1. Flitter m;
2. (mit Flitter) besetzen; fig. übersäen.

Spaniard ['spænjəd] Spanier(in).

Spanish ['spæniʃ] 1. spanisch; 2.
Spanisch n.

spank F [spæŋk] 1. verhauen;
2. Klaps m; ~ing ['spæŋkiŋ] 1. □
schnell, scharf; 2. F Haue f, Tracht
f Prügel.

spanner ⊕ ['spænə] Schraubenschlüssel m.

spar [spaː] 1. ⚓ Spiere f; ⚒ Holm
m; 2. boxen; fig. sich streiten.

spare [spεə] 1. □ spärlich, sparsam;
mager; überzählig; überschüssig;
Ersatz...; Reserve...; ~ hours Mußestunden f/pl.; ~ room Gastzimmer
n; ~ time Freizeit f; 2. ⊕ Ersatzteil m, n; 3. (ver)schonen; erübrigen; entbehren; (übrig)haben für;
(er)sparen; sparen mit.

sparing □ ['spεəriŋ] sparsam.

spark [spaːk] 1. Funke(n) m; fig.
flotter Kerl; Galan m; 2. Funken
sprühen; ~(ing)-plug mot. ['spaːk-
(iŋ)plʌg] Zündkerze f.

sparkle ['spaːkl] 1. Funke(n) m;
Funkeln n; fig. sprühendes Wesen;
2. funkeln; blitzen; schäumen;
sparkling wine Schaumwein m.

sparrow orn. ['spærou] Sperling m,
Spatz m; ~hawk orn. Sperber m.

sparse □ [spaːs] spärlich, dünn.

spasm ⚕ ['spæzəm] Krampf m;
~odic(al □) [spæz'modik(əl)]
krampfhaft, -artig; fig. sprunghaft.

spat¹ [spæt] (Schuh)Gamasche f.

spat² [~] pret. u. p.p. von spit² 2.

spatter ['spætə] (be)spritzen.

spawn [spɔːn] **1.** Laich *m*; *fig. contp.* Brut *f*; **2.** laichen; *fig.* aushecken.

speak [spiːk] [*irr.*] *v/i.* sprechen; reden; ~ out, ~ up laut sprechen; offen reden; ~ to *j-n* od. mit *j-m* sprechen; *v/t.* (aus)sprechen; äußern; ~-easy *Am. sl.* ['spiːkizi] Flüsterkneipe *f* (*ohne Konzession*); ~er [.kə] Sprecher(in), Redner(in); *parl.* Vorsitzende(r) *m*; ~ing-trumpet [.kiŋtrʌmpit] Sprachrohr *n*.

spear [spiə] **1.** Speer *m*, Spieß *m*; Lanze *f*; **2.** (auf)spießen.

special ['speʃəl] **1.** □ besonder; Sonder...; speziell; Spezial...; **2.** Hilfspolizist *m*; Sonderausgabe *f*; Sonderzug *m*; *Am.* Sonderangebot *n*; *Am.* (Tages)Spezialität *f*; ~ist [.list] Spezialist *m*; ~ity [speʃi'æliti] Besonderheit *f*; Spezialfach *n*; ~ Spezialität *f*; ~ize ['speʃəlaiz] besonders anführen; (sich) spezialisieren; ~ty [.lti] *s.* speciality.

specie ['spiːʃi] Metall-, Hartgeld *n*; ~s [.iːz] *pl. u. sg.* Art *f*, Spezies *f*.

speci|fic [spi'sifik] (~ally) spezifisch; besonder; bestimmt; ~fy ['spesifai] spezifizieren, einzeln angeben; ~men [.imin] Probe *f*, Exemplar *n*.

specious □ ['spiːʃəs] blendend, bestechend; trügerisch; Schein...

speck [spek] **1.** Fleck *m*; Stückchen *n*; **2.** flecken; ~le ['spekl] **1.** Fleckchen *n*; **2.** flecken, sprenkeln.

spectacle ['spektəkl] Schauspiel *n*; Anblick *m*; (*a pair of*) ~s *pl.* (eine) Brille.

spectacular [spek'tækjulə] **1.** □ eindrucksvoll; auffallend, spektakulär; **2.** *Am.* F Galarevue *f*.

spectator [spek'teitə] Zuschauer *m*.

spect|ral □ ['spektrəl] gespenstisch; ~re, *Am.* ~er [.tə] Gespenst *n*.

speculat|e ['spekjuleit] grübeln, nachsinnen; † spekulieren; ~ion [spekju'leiʃən] theoretische Betrachtung; Grübelei *f*; † Spekulation *f*; ~ive □ ['spekjulətiv] grüblerisch; theoretisch; † spekulierend; ~or [.leitə] Denker *m*; † Spekulant *m*.

sped [sped] *pret. u. p.p. von* speed 2.

speech [spiːtʃ] Sprache *f*; Rede *f*, Ansprache *f*; make a ~ e-e Rede halten; ~ ['spiːtʃdei] *Schule:* (Jahres)Schlußfeier *f*; ~less [.flis] sprachlos.

speed [spiːd] **1.** Geschwindigkeit *f*; Schnelligkeit *f*; Eile *f*; ⊕ Drehzahl *f*; **2.** [*irr.*] *v/i.* schnell fahren, rasen; ~ up (*pret. u. p.p.* ~ed) die Geschwindigkeit erhöhen; *v/t.* ~ up Glück verleihen; befördern; ~ up (*pret. u. p.p.* ~ed) beschleunigen; ~-limit ['spiːdlimit] Geschwindigkeitsbegrenzung *f*; ~ometer *mot.*

[spi'dɔmitə] Geschwindigkeitsmesser *m*, Tachometer *n*; ~way Motorradrennbahn *f*; *bsd. Am.* Schnellstraße *f*; ~y □ [.di] schnell.

spell [spel] **1.** (Arbeits)Zeit *f*, ⊕ Schicht *f*; Weilchen *n*; Zauber (-spruch) *m*; **2.** abwechseln mit *j-m*; [*irr.*] buchstabieren; richtig schreiben; bedeuten; ~binder *Am.* ['spelbaində] fesselnder Redner; ~bound *fig.* (fest)gebannt; ~er *bsd. Am.* [.lə] Fibel *f*; ~ing [.liŋ] Rechtschreibung *f*; ~ing-book Fibel *f*.

spelt [spelt] *pret. u. p.p. von* spell 2.

spend [spend] [*irr.*] verwenden; (*Geld*) ausgeben; verbrauchen; verschwenden; verbringen; ~ o.s. sich erschöpfen; ~thrift ['spendθrift] Verschwender *m*.

spent [spent] **1.** *pret. u. p.p. von* spend; **2.** *adj.* erschöpft, matt.

sperm [spəːm] Same(n) *m*.

spher|e [sfiə] Kugel *f*; Erd-, Himmelskugel *f*; *fig.* Sphäre *f*; (Wirkungs)Kreis *m*; Bereich *m*; *fig.* Gebiet *n*; ~ical □ ['sferikəl] sphärisch; kugelförmig.

spice [spais] **1.** Gewürz(e *pl.*) *n*; *fig.* Würze *f*; Anflug *m*; **2.** würzen.

spick and span ['spikən'spæn] frisch u. sauber; schmuck; funkelnagelneu.

spicy □ ['spaisi] würzig; pikant.

spider *zo.* ['spaidə] Spinne *f*.

spiel *Am. sl.* [spiːl] Gequassel *n*.

spigot ['spigət] (Faß)Zapfen *m*.

spike [spaik] **1.** Stift *m*; Spitze *f*; Dorn *m*; Stachel *m*; *Sport:* Laufdorn *m*; *mot.* Spike *m*; ♀ Ähre *f*; **2.** festnageln; mit *eisernen* Stacheln versehen.

spill [spil] **1.** [*irr.*] *v/t.* verschütten; vergießen; F *Reiter etc.* abwerfen; schleudern; *v/i.* überlaufen; **2.** F Sturz *m*.

spilt [spilt] *pret. u. p.p. von* spill 1; cry over ~ milk über et. jammern, was doch nicht zu ändern ist.

spin [spin] **1.** [*irr.*] spinnen (*a.fig.*); wirbeln; sich drehen; *Münze* hochwerfen; sich *et.* ausdenken; erzählen; ⚓ trudeln; ~ along dahinsausen; ~ s.th. out et. in die Länge ziehen; **2.** Drehung *f*; Spritztour *f*; ⚓ Trudeln *n*.

spinach ♀ ['spinidʒ] Spinat *m*.

spinal *anat.* ['spainl] Rückgrat...; ~ column Wirbelsäule *f*; ~ cord, ~ marrow Rückenmark *n*.

spindle ['spindl] Spindel *f*.

spin-drier ['spindraiə] Wäscheschleuder *f*.

spine [spain] *anat.* Rückgrat *n*; Dorn *m*; (Gebirgs)Grat *m*; (Buch-) Rücken *m*.

spinning|-mill ['spiniŋmil] Spinnerei *f*; ~-wheel Spinnrad *n*.

spinster ['spinstə] unverheiratete Frau; (alte) Jungfer.

spiny ['spaini] dornig.

spiral ['spaiərəl] 1. □ spiralig; ~ staircase Wendeltreppe *f*; 2. Spirale *f*; *fig.* Wirbel *m*.

spire ['spaiə] Turm-, Berg- *etc.* Spitze *f*; Kirchturm(spitze *f*) *m*.

spirit ['spirit] 1. *allg.* Geist *m*; Sinn *m*; Temperament *n*, Leben *n*; Mut *m*; Gesinnung *f*; Spiritus *m*; Sprit *m*, Benzin *n*; ~s *pl.* Spirituosen *pl.*; high (low) ~s *pl.* gehobene (gedrückte) Stimmung; 2. ~ away *od.* off wegzaubern; ~ed □ geistvoll; temperamentvoll; mutig; ~less □ [~tlis] geistlos; temperamentlos; mutlos.

spiritual □ ['spiritjuəl] geistig; geistlich; geistvoll; ~ism [~lizəm] Spiritismus *m*.

spirituous ['spiritjuəs] alkoholisch.

spirt [spə:t] (hervor)spritzen.

spit[1] [spit] 1. Bratspieß *m*; Landzunge *f*; 2. aufspießen.

spit[2] [~] 1. Speichel *m*; F Ebenbild *n*; 2. [*irr.*] (aus)spucken; fauchen; sprühen (*fein regnen*).

spite [spait] 1. Bosheit *f*; Groll *m*; in ~ of trotz (*gen.*); 2. ärgern; kränken; ~ful □ ['spaitful] boshaft, gehässig.

spitfire ['spitfaiə] Hitzkopf *m*.

spittle ['spitl] Speichel *m*, Spucke *f*.

spittoon [spi'tu:n] Spucknapf *m*.

splash [splæʃ] 1. Spritzfleck *m*; P(l)atschen *n*; 2. (be)spritzen; p(l)atschen; planschen; (hin)klecksen.

splay [splei] 1. Ausschrägung *f*; 2. auswärts gebogen; 3. *v/t.* ausschrägen; *v/i.* ausgeschrägt sein; ~foot ['spleifut] Spreizfuß *m*.

spleen [spli:n] *anat.* Milz *f*; üble Laune, Ärger *m*.

splend|id □ ['splendid] glänzend, prächtig, herrlich; ~o(u)r [~də] Glanz *m*, Pracht *f*, Herrlichkeit *f*.

splice [splais] (ver)spleißen.

splint [splint] 1. Schiene *f*; 2. schienen; ~er ['splintə] 1. Splitter *m*; 2. (zer)splittern.

split [split] 1. Spalt *m*, Riß *m*; *fig.* Spaltung *f*; 2. gespalten; 3. [*irr.*] *v/t.* (zer)spalten; zerreißen; (sich) *et.* teilen; ~ hairs Haarspalterei treiben; ~ one's sides with laughter sich totlachen; *v/i.* sich spalten; platzen; ~ting ['spliting] heftig, rasend (*Kopfschmerz*).

splutter ['splʌtə] *s.* sputter.

spoil [spoil] 1. *oft* ~s *pl.* Beute *f*, Raub *m*; *fig.* Ausbeute *f*; Schutt *m*; ~s *pl. pol. bsd. Am.* Futterkrippe *f*; 2. [*irr.*] (be)rauben; plündern; verderben; verwöhnen; *Kind* verziehen; ~sman *Am. pol.* ['spoilzmən] Postenjäger *m*; ~sport Spielver-

derber(in); ~s system *Am. pol.* Futterkrippensystem *n*.

spoilt [spoilt] *pret. u. p.p. von* spoil 2.

spoke [spouk] 1. *pret. von* speak; 2. Speiche *f*; (Leiter)Sprosse *f*; ~n ['spoukən] *p.p. von* speak; ~sman [~ksmən] Wortführer *m*.

sponge [spʌndʒ] 1. Schwamm *m*; 2. *v/t.* mit e-m Schwamm (ab)wischen; ~ up aufsaugen; *v/i.* schmarotzen; ~cake ['spʌndʒ'keik] Biskuitkuchen *m*; ~r F *fig.* [~dʒə] Schmarotzer(in).

spongy ['spʌndʒi] schwammig.

sponsor ['sponsə] 1. Pate *m*; Bürge *m*; Förderer *m*; Auftraggeber *m* für Werbesendungen; 2. Pate stehen bei; fördern; ~ship [~əʃip] Paten-, Gönnerschaft *f*.

spontane|ity [spontə'ni:iti] Freiwilligkeit *f*; eigener Antrieb; ~ous □ [spon'teinjəs] freiwillig, von selbst (entstanden); Selbst...; spontan; unwillkürlich; unvermittelt.

spook [spu:k] Spuk *m*; ~y ['spu:ki] geisterhaft, Spuk...

spool [spu:l] 1. Spule *f*; 2. spulen.

spoon [spu:n] 1. Löffel *m*; 2. löffeln; ~ful ['spu:nful] Löffelvoll *m*.

sporadic [spə'rædik] (~ally) sporadisch, verstreut.

spore ♀ [spɔ:] Spore *f*, Keimkorn *n*.

sport [spɔ:t] 1. Sport *m*; Spiel *n*; *fig.* Spielball *m*; Scherz *m*; *sl.* feiner Kerl; ~s *pl. allg.* Sport *m*; Sportfest *n*; 2. *v/i.* sich belustigen; spielen; *v/t.* F protzen mit; ~ive □ ['spɔ:tiv] lustig; scherzhaft; ~sman [~tsmən] Sportler *m*.

spot [spot] 1. *allg.* Fleck *m*; Tupfen *m*; Makel *m*; Stelle *f*; ☞ Leberfleck *m*; ☞ Pickel *m*; Tropfen *m*; a ~ of F etwas; on the ~ auf der Stelle; sofort; 2. sofort liefer- *od.* zahlbar; 3. (be)flecken; ausfindig machen; erkennen; ~less □ ['spotlis] fleckenlos; ~light *thea.* Scheinwerfer (-licht *n*) *m*; ~ter [~tə] Beobachter *m*; *Am.* Kontrolleur *m*; ~ty [~ti] fleckig.

spouse [spauz] Gatte *m*; Gattin *f*.

spout [spaut] 1. Tülle *f*; Strahlrohr *n*; (Wasser)Strahl *m*; 2. (aus)spritzen; F salbadern.

sprain ☞ [sprein] 1. Verstauchung *f*; 2. verstauchen.

sprang [spræŋ] *pret. von* spring 2.

sprat *ichth.* [spræt] Sprotte *f*.

sprawl [sprɔ:l] sich rekeln, ausgestreckt daliegen; ♀ wuchern.

spray [sprei] 1. zerstäubte Flüssigkeit; Sprühregen *m*; Gischt *m*; Spray *m*, *n*; = sprayer; 2. zerstäuben; *et.* besprühen; ~er ['spreiə] Zerstäuber *m*.

spread [spred] 1. [*irr.*] *v/t.* a. ~ out ausbreiten; (aus)dehnen; verbreiten; belegen; *Butter etc.* aufstreichen; *Brot etc.* bestreichen; ~ the *table* den Tisch decken; *v/i.* sich aus- *od.* verbreiten; 2. Aus-, Verbreitung *f;* Spannweite *f;* Fläche *f; Am. Bett-* etc. Decke *f;* Brot-Aufstrich *m;* F Festschmaus *m.*

spree F [spri:] Spaß *m*, Jux *m;* Zechgelage *n;* Orgie *f; Kauf-* etc. Welle *f.*

sprig [sprig] Sproß *m*, Reis *n* (*a. fig.*); ⊕ Zwecke *f*, Stift *m.*

sprightly ['spraitli] lebhaft, munter.

spring [spriŋ] 1. Sprung *m*, Satz *m;* (Sprung)Feder *f*, Federkraft *f*, Elastizität *f;* Triebfeder *f;* Quelle *f; fig.* Ursprung *m;* Frühling *m;* 2. [*irr.*] *v/t.* springen lassen; (zer-)sprengen; *Wild* aufjagen; ~ *a leak* ♣ leck werden; ~ *a surprise on s.o.* j-n überraschen; *v/i.* springen; entspringen; ♀ aufkommen (*Ideen* etc.); **~board** ['spriŋbɔ:d] Sprungbrett *n;* ~ **tide** Springflut *f;* ~**tide**, ~**time** Frühling(szeit *f*) *m;* ~**y** □ [~ŋi] federnd.

sprinkl|e ['spriŋkl] (be)streuen; (be)sprengen; ~**er** [~lə] Berieselungsanlage *f;* Rasensprenger *m;* ~**ing** [~liŋ] Sprühregen *m; a* ~ *of* ein wenig, ein paar.

sprint [sprint] *Sport:* 1. sprinten; spurten; 2. Sprint *m;* Kurzstreckenlauf *m;* Endspurt *m;* ~**er** ['sprintə] Sprinter *m*, Kurzstreckenläufer *m.*

sprite [sprait] Geist *m*, Kobold *m.*

sprout [spraut] 1. sprießen, wachsen (lassen); 2. ♀ Sproß *m; (Brussels)* ~**s** *pl.* Rosenkohl *m.*

spruce[1] ['spru:s] schmuck, nett.

spruce[2] ♀ [~] *a.* ~ *fir* Fichte *f*, Rottanne *f.*

sprung [sprʌŋ] *pret.* (<) *u. p.p. von* spring 2.

spry [sprai] munter, flink.

spun [spʌn] *pret. u. p.p. von* spin 1.

spur [spə:] 1. Sporn *m* (*a. zo.*, ♀); *fig.* Ansporn *m;* Vorsprung *m*, Ausläufer *m e-s Berges; on the* ~ *of the moment* der Eingebung des Augenblicks folgend; spornstreichs; 2. (an)spornen.

spurious □ ['spjuəriəs] unecht, gefälscht.

spurn [spə:n] verschmähen, verächtlich zurückweisen.

spurt [spə:t] 1. alle s-e Kräfte zs.-nehmen; *Sport:* spurten; *s. spirt;* 2. plötzliche Anstrengung, Ruck *m; Sport:* Spurt *m.*

sputter ['spʌtə] 1. Gesprudel *n;* 2. (hervor)sprudeln; spritzen.

spy [spai] 1. Späher(in); Spion(in); 2. (er)spähen; erblicken; spionieren; ~**glass** ['spaiglɑ:s] Fernglas *n;* ~**hole** Guckloch *n.*

squabble ['skwɔbl] 1. Zank *m*, Kabbelei *f;* 2. (sich) zanken.

squad [skwɔd] Rotte *f*, Trupp *m;* ~**ron** ['skwɔdrən] ⚔ Schwadron *f;* ✈ Staffel *f;* ♣ Geschwader *n.*

squalid □ ['skwɔlid] schmutzig, armselig.

squall [skwɔ:l] 1. ♣ Bö *f;* Schrei *m;* ~**s** *pl.* Geschrei *n;* 2. schreien.

squalor ['skwɔlə] Schmutz *m.*

squander ['skwɔndə] verschwenden.

square [skwɛə] 1. □ viereckig; quadratisch; rechtwinklig; eckig; passend, stimmend; in Ordnung; direkt; quitt, gleich; ehrlich, offen; F altmodisch, spießig; ~ *measure* Flächenmaß *n;* ~ *mile* Quadratmeile *f;* 2. Quadrat *n;* Viereck *n; Schach-* Feld *n; öffentlicher* Platz; Winkelmaß *n;* F altmodischer Spießer; 3. *v/t.* viereckig machen; einrichten (*with nach*), anpassen (*dat.*); † be-, ausgleichen; *v/i.* passen (*with zu*); übereinstimmen; ~**built** ['skwɛə'bilt] vierschrötig; ~ *dance* Quadrille *f;* ~**toes** *sg.* F Pedant *m.*

squash[1] [skwɔʃ] 1. Gedränge *n;* Fruchtsaft *m;* Platsch(en *n*) *m;* Rakettspiel *n;* 2. (zer-, zs.-)quetschen; drücken.

squash[2] ♀ [~] Kürbis *m.*

squat [skwɔt] 1. kauernd; untersetzt; 2. hocken, kauern; ~**ter** ['skwɔtə] *Am.* Schwarzsiedler *m; Australien:* Schafzüchter *m.*

squawk [skwɔ:k] 1. kreischen, schreien; 2. Gekreisch *n*, Geschrei *n.*

squeak [skwi:k] quieken, quietschen.

squeal [skwi:l] quäken; gell schreien; quieken.

squeamish □ ['skwi:miʃ] empfindlich; mäkelig; heikel; penibel.

squeeze [skwi:z] 1. (sich) drücken, (sich) quetschen; auspressen; *fig.* (be)drängen; 2. Druck *m;* Gedränge *n;* ~**r** ['skwi:zə] Presse *f.*

squelch F [skweltʃ] zermalmen.

squid *zo.* [skwid] Tintenfisch *m.*

squint [skwint] schielen; blinzeln.

squire ['skwaiə] 1. Gutsbesitzer *m;* (Land)Junker *m; Am.* F (Friedens-)Richter *m;* 2. *e-e* Dame begleiten.

squirm F [skwə:m] sich winden.

squirrel *zo.* ['skwirəl, *Am.* 'skwə:rəl] Eichhörnchen *n.*

squirt [skwə:t] 1. Spritze *f;* Strahl *m;* F Wichtigtuer *m;* 2. spritzen.

stab [stæb] 1. Stich *m;* 2. *v/t.* (er-)stechen; *v/i.* stechen (*at nach*).

stabili|ty [stə'biliti] Stabilität *f;* Standfestig-, Beständigkeit *f;* ~**ze** ['steibilaiz] stabilisieren (*a.* ✈).

stable[1] □ ['steibl] stabil, fest.

stable[2] [~] 1. Stall *m;* 2. einstallen.

stack [stæk] 1. ✿ (Heu-, Stroh-, Getreide)Schober *m;* Stapel *m;* Schornstein(reihe *f*) *m;* Regal *n;* ~**s** *pl. Am.* Hauptmagazin *n e-r*

Bibliothek; F Haufen *m*; 2. auf-stapeln.

stadium ['steidjəm] *Sport*: Stadion *n*, Sportplatz *m*, Kampfbahn *f*.

staff [sta:f] 1. Stab *m* (*a.* ✕), Stock *m*; Stütze *f*; ♪ Notensystem *n*; Personal *n*; Belegschaft *f*; Beamten-, Lehrkörper *m*; 2. (mit Personal, Beamten *od.* Lehrern) besetzen.

stag *zo.* [stæg] Hirsch *m*.

stage [steidʒ] 1. Bühne *f*, Theater *n*; *fig.* Schauplatz *m*; Stufe *f*, Stadium *n*; Teilstrecke *f*, Etappe *f*; Haltestelle *f*; Gerüst *n*, Gestell *n*; 2. inszenieren; **~-coach** ['steidʒkoutʃ] Postkutsche *f*; **~craft** dramatisches Talent; Theatererfahrung *f*; **~ direction** Bühnenanweisung *f*; **~ fright** Lampenfieber *n*; **~ manager** Regisseur *m*.

stagger ['stægə] 1. *v/i.* (sch)wanken, taumeln; *fig.* stutzen; *v/t.* ins Wanken bringen; staffeln; 2. Schwanken *n*; Staffelung *f*.

stagna|nt □ ['stægnənt] stehend (*Wasser*); stagnierend; stockend; träg; ✝ still; **~te** [~neit] stocken.

staid □ [steid] gesetzt, ruhig.

stain [stein] 1. Fleck(en) *m* (*a. fig.*); Beize *f*; 2. fleckig machen; *fig.* beflecken; beizen, färben; **~ed glass** buntes Glas; **~less** □ ['steinlis] ungefleckt; *fig.* fleckenlos; rostfrei.

stair [steə] Stufe *f*; **~s** *pl.* Treppe *f*, Stiege *f*; **~case** f ['steəkeis], **~way** Treppe(nhaus *n*) *f*.

stake [steik] 1. Pfahl *m*; Marterpfahl *m*; (Spiel)Einsatz *m* (*a. fig.*); **~s** *pl.* Pferderennen: Preis *m*; Rennen *n*; *pull up* **~** *Am.* F abhauen; *be at* **~** auf dem Spiel stehen; 2. (um)pfählen; aufs Spiel setzen; **~ out**, **~ off** abstecken.

stale □ [steil] alt; schal, abgestanden; verbraucht (*Luft*); fad.

stalk [stɔ:k] 1. Stengel *m*, Stiel *m*; Halm *m*; *hunt.* Pirsch *f*; 2. *v/i.* einherstolzieren; heranschleichen; *hunt.* pirschen; *v/t.* beschleichen.

stall [stɔ:l] 1. (Pferde)Box *f* (Verkaufs)Stand *m*, Marktbude *f*; *thea.* Sperrsitz *m*; 2. *v/t.* einstallen; *Motor* abwürgen; *v/i. mot.* aussetzen.

stallion ['stæljən] Hengst *m*.

stalwart □ ['stɔ:lwət] stramm, stark.

stamina ['stæminə] Ausdauer *f*.

stammer ['stæmə] 1. stottern, stammeln; 2. Stottern *n*.

stamp [stæmp] 1. (Auf)Stampfen *n*; ⊕ Stampfe(r *m*) *f*; Stempel *m* (*a. fig.*); (Brief)Marke *f*; Gepräge *n*; Art *f*; 2. (auf)stampfen; prägen; stanzen; (ab)stempeln (*a. fig.*); frankieren.

stampede [stæm'pi:d] 1. Panik *f*, wilde Flucht; 2. *v/i.* durchgehen; *v/t.* in Panik versetzen.

stanch [sta:ntʃ] 1. hemmen; stillen; 2. □ fest; zuverlässig; treu.

stand [stænd] 1. [*irr.*] *v/i. allg.* stehen; sich befinden; beharren; *mst* **~** *still* stillstehen, stehenbleiben; bestehen (bleiben); **~** *against j-m* widerstehen; **~** *aside* beiseite treten; **~** *back* zurücktreten; **~** *by* dabeistehen; *fig.* (fest) stehen zu; helfen; bereitstehen; **~** *for* kandidieren für; bedeuten; eintreten für; F sich *et.* gefallen lassen; **~** *in* einspringen; **~** *in with* sich gut stellen mit; **~** *off* zurücktreten (von); **~** *off!* weg da!; **~** *on* (*fig.* be)stehen auf; **~** *out* hervorstehen; sich abheben (*against* gegen); standhalten (*dat.*); **~** *over* stehen *od.* liegen bleiben; **~** *pat Am.* F stur bleiben; **~** *to* bleiben bei; **~** *up* aufstehen; sich erheben; **~** *up for* eintreten für; **~** *up to* sich zur Wehr setzen gegen; standhalten (*dat.*); **~** *upon* (*fig.* be)stehen auf (*dat.*); *v/t.* (hin)stellen; aushalten, (v)ertragen; über sich ergehen lassen; F spendieren; 2. Stand *m*; Standplatz *m*; Bude *f*; Standpunkt *m*; Stillstand *m*; Ständer *m*; Tribüne *f*; *bsd. Am.* Zeugenstand *m*; *make a od. one's* **~** *against* standhalten (*dat.*).

standard ['stændəd] 1. Standarte *f*, Fahne *f*; Standard *m*, Norm *f*, Regel *f*, Maßstab *m*; Niveau *n*; Stufe *f*; Münzfuß *m*; Währung *f*; Ständer *m*, Mast *m*; 2. maßgebend; Normal...; **~ize** [~daiz] norm(ier)en.

stand-by ['stændbai] Beistand *m*.

standee [stæn'di:] Stehende(r) *m*; *Am.* Stehplatzinhaber *m*.

standing ['stændiŋ] 1. □ stehend; fest; (be)ständig; **~** *orders pl. parl.* Geschäftsordnung *f*; 2. Stellung *f*, Rang *m*, Ruf *m*; Dauer *f*; *of long* **~** alt; **~-room** Stehplatz *m*.

stand|off *Am.* ['stænd:ɔf] Unentschieden *n*; Dünkel *m*; **~offish** [~d'ɔ:fiʃ] zurückhaltend; **~patter** *Am. pol.* [stænd'pætə] sturer Konservativer; **~point** ['stændpɔint] Standpunkt *m*; **~still** Stillstand *m*; **~-up:** **~** *collar* Stehkragen *m*.

stank [stæŋk] *pret. von* **stink** 2.

stanza ['stænzə] Stanze *f*; Strophe *f*.

staple[1] ['steipl] Haupterzeugnis *n*; Hauptgegenstand *m*; *attr.* Haupt...

staple[2] [~] Krampe *f*; Heftklammer *f*.

star [sta:] 1. Stern *m*; *thea.* Star *m*; *♀s and Stripes pl. Am.* Sternenbanner *n*; 2. mit Sternen schmücken; *thea.*, *fig.* die Hauptrolle spielen.

starboard ⚓ ['sta:bəd] 1. Steuerbord *n*; 2. *Ruder* steuerbord legen.

starch [sta:tʃ] 1. (Wäsche)Stärke *f*; *fig.* Steifheit *f*; 2. stärken.

stare [steə] 1. Starren *n*; Staunen *n*; starrer Blick; 2. starren, staunen.

stark [stɑːk] **1.** *adj.* starr; bar, völlig (*Unsinn*); **2.** *adv.* völlig.

starlight ['stɑːlait] Sternenlicht *n.*

starling *orn.* ['stɑːliŋ] Star *m.*

starlit ['stɑːlit] sternenklar.

star|ry ['stɑːri] Stern(en)...; gestirnt; **~-spangled** ['stɑːspæŋgld] sternenbesät; ♀ *Banner Am.* Sternenbanner *n.*

start [stɑːt] **1.** Auffahren *n*, Stutzen *n*; Ruck *m*; *Sport*: Start *m*; Aufbruch *m*; Anfang *m*; *fig.* Vorsprung *m*; *get the ~ of s.o.* j-m zuvorkommen; **2.** *v/i.* aufspringen, auffahren; stutzen; *Sport*: starten; abfahren; aufbrechen; *mot.* anspringen; anfangen (*on mit*; *doing* zu tun); *v/t.* in Gang bringen; *mot.* anlassen; *Sport*: starten (lassen); aufjagen; *fig.* anfangen; veranlassen (*doing* zu tun); **~er** ['stɑːtə] *Sport* Starter *m*; Läufer *m*; *mot.* Anlasser *m.*

startl|e ['stɑːtl] (er-, auf)schrecken; **~ing** [~liŋ] bestürzend, überraschend, aufsehenerregend.

starv|ation [stɑːˈveiʃən] (Ver)Hungern *n*, Hungertod *m*; *attr.* Hunger...; **~e** [stɑːv] verhungern (lassen); *fig.* verkümmern (lassen).

state [steit] **1.** Zustand *m*; Stand *m*; Staat *m*; *pol. mst* ♀ Staat *m*; *attr.* Staats...; *in ~* feierlich; **2.** angeben; darlegen, darstellen; feststellen; melden; *Regel etc.* aufstellen; ♀ **Department** *Am. pol.* Außenministerium *n*; **~ly** ['steitli] stattlich; würdevoll; erhaben; **~ment** [~tmənt] Angabe *f*; Aussage *f*; Darstellung *f*; Feststellung *f*; Aufstellung *f*; ♱ (*~ of account* Konto-) Auszug *m*; **~room** Staatszimmer *n*; ♣ Einzelkabine *f*; **~side** *Am.* F **1.** *adj.* USA-..., Heimat...; **2.** *adv.*: *go ~* heimkehren; **~sman** [~smən] Staatsmann *m.*

static ['stætik] statisch, Ruhe...

station ['steiʃən] **1.** Stand(ort) *m*; Stelle *f*; Stellung *f*; ⚔, ♣, ⚓ Station *f*; Bahnhof *m*; Rang *m*, Stand *m*; **2.** aufstellen, postieren, stationieren; **~ary** □ [~ʃnəri] stillstehend; feststehend; **~ery** [~] Schreibwaren *f/pl.*; **~-master** ⚓ Stationsvorsteher *m*; **~ wagon** *Am. mot.* Kombiwagen *m.*

statistics [stəˈtistiks] *pl.* Statistik *f.*

statu|ary ['stætjuəri] Bildhauer (-kunst *f*) *m*; **~e** [~ju:] Standbild *n*, Plastik *f*, Statue *f.*

stature ['stætʃə] Statur *f*, Wuchs *m.*

status ['steitəs] Zustand *m*; Stand *m.*

statute ['stætjuːt] Statut *n*, Satzung *f*; (Landes)Gesetz *n.*

staunch [stɔːntʃ] *s.* stanch.

stave [steiv] **1.** Faßdaube *f*; Strophe *f*; **2.** [*irr.*] *mst ~ in* ein Loch schlagen in (*acc.*); **~ off** abwehren.

stay [stei] **1.** ♣ Stag *n*; ⊕ Strebe *f*; Stütze *f*; Aufschub *m*; Aufenthalt *m*; **~s** *pl.* Korsett *n*; **2.** bleiben; wohnen; (sich) aufhalten; Ausdauer haben; hemmen; aufschieben; *Hunger* vorläufig stillen; stützen; **~er** ['steiə] *Sport*: Steher *m.*

stead [sted] Stelle *f*, Statt *f*; **~fast** □ ['stedfəst] fest, unerschütterlich; standhaft; unverwandt (*Blick*).

steady ['stedi] **1.** □ (be)ständig; stetig; sicher; fest; ruhig; gleichmäßig; unerschütterlich; zuverlässig; **2.** stetig *od.* sicher machen *od.* werden; (sich) festigen; stützen; (sich) beruhigen; **3.** *Am.* F feste Freundin, fester Freund.

steal [stiːl] **1.** [*irr.*] *v/t.* stehlen (*a. fig.*); *v/i.* sich stehlen *od.* schleichen; **2.** *Am.* Diebstahl *m.*

stealth [stelθ] Heimlichkeit *f*; *by ~* heimlich; **~y** □ ['stelθi] verstohlen.

steam [stiːm] **1.** Dampf *m*; Dunst *m*; *attr.* Dampf...; **2.** *v/i.* dampfen; *~ up* beschlagen (*Glas*); *v/t.* ausdünsten; dämpfen; **~er** ♣ ['stiːmə] Dampfer *m*; **~y** □ [~mi] dampfig; dampfend; dunstig.

steel [stiːl] **1.** Stahl *m*; **2.** stählern; Stahl...; **3.** (ver)stählen.

steep [stiːp] **1.** steil, jäh; F toll; **2.** einweichen; einlegen; eintauchen; tränken; *fig.* versenken.

steeple ['stiːpl] Kirchturm *m*; **~-chase** *Sport*: Hindernisrennen *n.*

steer[1] [stiə] junger Ochse.

steer[2] [~] steuern; *age* ♣ ['stiəridʒ] Steuerung *f*; Zwischendeck *n*; **~ing-wheel** [~riŋwiːl] Steuerrad *n*; *mot.* Lenkrad *n*; **~sman** ♣ [~zmən] Rudergänger *m.*

stem [stem] **1.** (Baum-, Wort-) Stamm *m*; Stiel *m*; Stengel *m*; ♣ Vordersteven *m*; **2.** *Am.* (ab)stammen (*from von*); sich stemmen gegen, ankämpfen gegen.

stench [stentʃ] Gestank *m.*

stencil ['stensl] Schablone *f*; *typ.* Matrize *f.* [graph(in).]

stenographer [steˈnɔgrəfə] Steno-]

step[1] [step] **1.** Schritt *m*, Tritt *m*; *fig.* Strecke *f*; Fußstapfe *f*; (Treppen)Stufe *f*; Trittbrett *n*; *~s pl.* Trittleiter *f*; **2.** *v/i.* schreiten; treten, gehen; *~ out* ausschreiten; *v/t.* *~ off*, *~ out* abschreiten; *~ up* ankurbeln.

step[2] [~] *in Zssgn* Stief...; **~father** ['stepfɑːðə] Stiefvater *m*; **~mother** Stiefmutter *f.*

steppe [step] Steppe *f.*

stepping-stone *fig.* ['stepiŋstoun] Sprungbrett *n.*

steril|e ['sterail] unfruchtbar; steril; **~ity** [steˈriliti] Sterilität *f*; **~ize** ['sterilaiz] sterilisieren.

sterling ['stəːliŋ] vollwertig, echt; gediegen; ♱ Sterling *m* (*Währung*).

stern [stəːn] **1.** □ ernst; finster, streng, hart; **2.** ♣ Heck *n*; **~ness**

['stə:nnis] Ernst *m*; Strenge *f*; ~post ⚓ Hintersteven *m*.

stevedore ⚓ ['sti:vidɔ:] Stauer *m*.

stew [stju:] 1. schmoren, dämpfen; 2. Schmorgericht *n*; F Aufregung *f*.

steward [stjuəd] Verwalter *m*; ⚓, ⚓ Steward *m*; (Fest)Ordner *m*; ~ess ⚓, ⚓ ['stjuədis] Stewardeß *f*.

stick [stik] 1. Stock *m*; Stecken *m*; Stab *m*; (Besen- *etc.*)Stiel *m*; Stange *f*; F Klotz *m* (*unbeholfener Mensch*); ~s *pl.* Kleinholz *n*; the ~s *pl.* Am. F die hinterste Provinz; 2. [*irr.*] *v/i.* stecken (bleiben); haften; kleben (to an *dat.*); ~ at nothing vor nichts zurückscheuen; ~ out, ~ up hervorstehen; F standhalten; ~ to bleiben bei; *v/t.* (ab)stechen; (an)stecken, (an)heften; (an)kleben; F ertragen; ~ing-plaster ['stikiŋplɑ:stə] Heftpflaster *n*.

sticky ☐ ['stiki] kleb(e)rig; zäh.

stiff ☐ [stif] steif; starr; hart; fest; mühsam; stark (*Getränk*); be bored ~ F zu Tode gelangweilt sein; keep a ~ upper lip die Ohren steifhalten; ~en ['stifn] (sich) (ver)steifen; ~-necked [~nekt] halsstarrig.

stifle ['staifl] ersticken (*a. fig.*).

stigma ['stigmə] (Brand-, Schand-) Mal *n*; Stigma *n*; ~tize [~ətaiz] brandmarken.

stile [stail] Zauntritt *m*, Zaunübergang *m*.

still [stil] 1. *adj.* still; 2. *adv.* noch (immer); 3. *cj.* doch, dennoch; 4. stillen; beruhigen; 5. Destillierapparat *m*; ~-born ['stilbɔ:n] totgeboren; ~ life Stilleben *n*; ~ness Stille *f*, Ruhe *f*.

stilt [stilt] Stelze *f*; ~ed ['stiltid] gespreizt, hochtrabend, geschraubt.

stimul|ant ['stimjulənt] 1. ⚗ stimulierend; 2. ⚗ Reizmittel *n*; Genußmittel *n*; Anreiz *m*; ~ate [~leit] (an)reizen; anregen; ~ation [stimju-'leiʃən] Reizung *f*, Antrieb *m*; ~us ['stimjuləs] Antrieb *m*; Reizmittel *n*.

sting [stiŋ] 1. Stachel *m*; Stich *m*, Biß *m*; *fig.* Schärfe *f*; Antrieb *m*; 2. [*irr.*] stechen; brennen; schmerzen; (an)treiben.

sting|iness ['stindʒinis] Geiz *m*; ~y ☐ ['stindʒi] geizig; knapp, karg.

stink [stiŋk] 1. Gestank *m*; 2. [*irr.*] *v/i.* stinken; *v/t.* verstänkern.

stint [stint] 1. Einschränkung *f*; Arbeit *f*; 2. knausern mit; einschränken; *j-n* knapp halten.

stipend ['staipend] Gehalt *n*.

stipulat|e ['stipjuleit] *a.* ~ for ausbedingen, ausmachen, vereinbaren; ~ion [stipju'leiʃən] Abmachung *f*; Klausel *f*, Bedingung *f*.

stir [stə:] 1. Regung *f*; Bewegung *f*; Rühren *n*; Aufregung *f*; Aufsehen *n*; 2. (sich) rühren; umrühren, bewegen; aufregen; ~ up aufrühren; aufrütteln.

34*

stirrup ['stirəp] Steigbügel *m*.

stitch [stitʃ] 1. Stich *m*; Masche *f*; Seitenstechen *n*; 2. nähen; heften.

stock [stɔk] 1. (Baum)Strunk *m*; Pfropfunterlage *f*; Griff *m*, Kolben *m* *e-s Gewehrs*; Stamm *m*, Herkunft *f*; Rohstoff *m*; (Fleisch-, Gemüse)Brühe *f*; Vorrat *m*, (Waren)Lager *n*; (Wissens)Schatz *m*; *a.* live~ Vieh(bestand *m*) *n*; † Stammkapital *n*; Anleihekapital *n*; ~s *pl.* Effekten *pl.*; Aktien *f/pl.*; Staatspapiere *n/pl.*; ~s *pl.* ⚓ Stapel *m*; in (out of) ~ (nicht) vorrätig; take ~ † Inventur machen; take ~ of *fig.* sich klarwerden über (*acc.*); 2. vorrätig; ständig; gängig; Standard...; 3. versorgen; *Waren* führen; † vorrätig haben.

stockade [stɔ'keid] Staket *n*.

stock|-breeder ['stɔkbri:də] Viehzüchter *m*; ~broker † Börsenmakler *m*; ~ exchange † Börse *f*; ~farmer Viehzüchter *m*; ~holder † Aktionär(in).

stockinet [stɔki'net] Trikot *n*.

stocking ['stɔkiŋ] Strumpf *m*.

stock|jobber † ['stɔkdʒɔbə] Börsenmakler *m*; ~market † Börse *f*; ~still unbeweglich; ~taking Inventur *f*; ~y ['stɔki] stämmig.

stog|ie, ~y Am. ['stougi] billige Zigarre.

stoic ['stouik] 1. stoisch; 2. Stoiker *m*.

stoker ['stoukə] Heizer *m*.

stole [stoul] *pret. von* steal 1; ~n ['stoulən] *p.p. von* steal 1.

stolid ☐ ['stɔlid] schwerfällig; gleichmütig; stur.

stomach ['stʌmək] 1. Magen *m*; Leib *m*, Bauch *m*; *fig.* Lust *f*; 2. verdauen, vertragen; *fig.* ertragen.

stomp Am. [stɔmp] (auf)stampfen.

stone [stoun] 1. Stein *m*; (Obst-) Kern *m*; *Gewichtseinheit von 6,35 kg*; 2. steinern; Stein...; 3. steinigen; entsteinen; ~-blind ['stoun'blaind] stockblind; ~dead mausetot; ~ware [~nwɛə] Steingut *n*.

stony ['stouni] steinig; *fig.* steinern.

stood [stud] *pret. u. p.p. von* stand 1.

stool [stu:l] Schemel *m*; ⚗ Stuhlgang *m*; ~-pigeon Am. ['stu:l-pidʒin] Lockvogel *m*; Spitzel *m*.

stoop [stu:p] 1. *v/i.* sich bücken; sich erniedrigen *od.* herablassen; krumm gehen; *v/t.* neigen; 2. gebeugte Haltung; Am. Veranda *f*.

stop [stɔp] 1. *v/t.* anhalten; hindern; aufhören; *a.* ~ up (ver)stopfen; *Zahn* plombieren; (ver)sperren; *Zahlung* einstellen; *Lohn* einbehalten; *v/i.* stehenbleiben; aufhören; halten; F bleiben; ~ dead, ~ short plötzlich anhalten; ~ over haltmachen; 2. (Ein)Halt *m*; Pause *f*; Hemmung *f*; ⊕ Anschlag *m*; Aufhören *n*, Ende *n*; Haltestelle *f*; *mst full* ~ *gr.* Punkt *m*; **~gap** ['stɔpgæp] Notbehelf *m*; **~page** [~pidʒ] Verstopfung *f*; (Zahlungs- *etc.*)Einstellung *f*; Sperrung *f*; (Lohn)Abzug *m*; Aufenthalt *m*; ⊕ Hemmung *f*; Betriebsstörung *f*; (Verkehrs-) Stockung *f*; **~per** [~pə] Stöpsel *m*; **~ping** ⚓ [~piŋ] Plombe *f*.

storage ['stɔːridʒ] Lagerung *f*, Aufbewahrung *f*; Lagergeld *n*.

store [stɔː] 1. Vorrat *m*; *fig.* Fülle *f*; Lagerhaus *n*; *Am.* Laden *m*; **~s** *pl.* Kauf-, Warenhaus *n*; *in* ~ vorrätig, auf Lager; 2. *a.* ~ *up* (auf)speichern; (ein)lagern; versorgen; **~house** Lagerhaus *n*; *fig.* Schatzkammer *f*; **~keeper** Lagerverwalter *m*; *Am.* Ladenbesitzer *m*.

stor(e)y ['stɔːri] Stock(werk *n*) *m*.

storeyed ['stɔːrid] mit ... Stockwerken, ...stöckig.

storied [~] *s.* storeyed.

stork [stɔːk] Storch *m*.

storm [stɔːm] 1. Sturm *m*; Gewitter *n*; 2. stürmen; toben; **~y** ['stɔːmi] stürmisch.

story ['stɔːri] Geschichte *f*; Erzählung *f*; Märchen *n*; *thea.* Handlung *f*; F Lüge *f*; *short* ~ Kurzgeschichte *f*.

stout [staut] 1. □ stark, kräftig; derb; dick; tapfer; 2. Starkbier *n*.

stove [stouv] 1. Ofen *m*; Herd *m*; 2. *pret. u. p.p. von* stave 2.

stow [stou] (ver)stauen, packen; **~away** ⚓ ['stouəwei] blinder Passagier.

straddle ['strædl] (die Beine) spreizen; rittlings sitzen auf (*dat.*); *Am. fig.* es mit beiden Parteien halten; schwanken.

straggl|e ['strægl] verstreut *od.* einzeln liegen; umherstreifen; bummeln; *fig.* abschweifen; ⚘ wuchern; **~ing** □ [~liŋ] weitläufig, lose.

straight [streit] 1. *adj.* gerade; *fig.* aufrichtig, ehrlich; glatt (Haar); *Am.* pur, unverdünnt; *Am. pol.* hundertprozentig; *put* ~ in Ordnung bringen; 2. *adv.* gerade(wegs); geradeaus; direkt; sofort; ~ *away* sofort; ~ *out* rundheraus; **~en** ['streitn] gerade machen *od.* werden; ~ *out* in Ordnung bringen; **~forward** □ [streit'fɔːwəd] gerade; ehrlich, redlich.

strain [strein] 1. Abstammung *f*; Art *f*; ⊕ Spannung *f*; (Über)Anstrengung *f*; starke Inanspruchnahme (*on gen.*); Druck *m*; ♪ Zerrung *f*; Ton *m*; *mst* ~s *pl.* ♪ Weise *f*; Hang *m* (*of zu*); 2. *v/t.* (an)spannen; (über)anstrengen; überspannen; ⊕ beanspruchen; ♪ zerren; durchseihen; *v/i.* sich spannen; sich anstrengen; sich abmühen (*after um*); zerren (*at an dat.*); **~er** ['streinə] Durchschlag *m*; Filter *m*; Sieb *n*.

strait [streit] (*in Eigennamen* ~s *pl.*) Meerenge *f*, Straße *f*; **~s** *pl.* Not (-lage) *f*; ~ *jacket* Zwangsjacke *f*; **~ened** ['streitnd] dürftig; in Not.

strand [strænd] 1. Strand *m*; Strähne *f* (*a. fig.*); 2. auf den Strand setzen; *fig.* stranden (lassen).

strange □ [streindʒ] fremd (*a. fig.*); seltsam; **~r** ['streindʒə] Fremde(r) *m*.

strangle ['stræŋgl] erwürgen.

strap [stræp] 1. Riemen *m*; Gurt *m*; Band *n*; 2. an-, festschnallen; mit Riemen peitschen. [List *f.*]

stratagem ['strætidʒəm] (Kriegs-)]

strateg|ic [strə'tiːdʒik] (~ally) strategisch; **~y** ['strætidʒi] Kriegskunst *f*, Strategie *f*.

strat|um *geol.* ['strɑːtəm], *pl* **~a** [~tə] Schicht *f* (*a. fig.*), Lage *f*.

straw [strɔː] 1. Stroh(halm *m*) *n*; 2. Stroh...; ~ *vote Am.* Probeabstimmung *f*; **~berry** ['strɔːbəri] Erdbeere *f*.

stray [strei] 1. irregehen; sich verirren; abirren; umherschweifen; 2. *a.* ~*ed* verirrt; vereinzelt; 3. verirrtes Tier.

streak [striːk] 1. Strich *m*, Streifen *m*; *fig.* Ader *f*, Spur *f*; kurze Periode; ~ *of lightning* Blitzstrahl *m*; 2. streifen; jagen, F flitzen.

stream [striːm] 1. Bach *m*; Strom *m*; Strömung *f*; 2. *v/i.* strömen; triefen; flattern; *v/t.* strömen lassen; ausströmen; **~er** ['striːmə] Wimpel *m*; (fliegendes) Band; Lichtstrahl *m*; *typ.* Schlagzeile *f*.

street [striːt] Straße *f*; **~-car** *Am.* ['striːtkɑː] Straßenbahn(wagen *m*) *f*.

strength [streŋθ] Stärke *f*, Kraft *f*; *on the* ~ *of auf* ... hin, auf Grund (*gen.*); **~en** ['streŋθən] *v/t.* stärken, kräftigen; bestärken; *v/i.* erstarken.

strenuous □ ['strenjuəs] rührig, emsig; eifrig; anstrengend.

stress [stres] 1. Druck *m*; Nachdruck *m*; Betonung *f* (*a. gr.*); *fig.* Schwergewicht *n*; Ton *m*; *psych.* Stress *m*; 2. betonen.

stretch [stretʃ] 1. *v/t.* strecken; (aus)dehnen; *mst* ~ *out* ausstrecken; (an)spannen; *fig.* überspannen; *Gesetz* zu weit auslegen; *v/i.* sich (er-) strecken; sich dehnen (lassen); 2. Strecken *n*; Dehnung *f*; (An-) Spannung *f*; Übertreibung *f*, Überschreitung *f*; Strecke *f*, Fläche *f*; **~er** ['stretʃə] Tragbahre *f*; Streckvorrichtung *f*.

strew [struː] [*irr.*] (be)streuen; **~n** [~uːn] *p.p. von* strew.

stricken ['strikən] 1. *p.p. von* strike 2; 2. *adj.* ge~, betroffen.

strict [strikt] streng; genau; **~ly** *speaking* strenggenommen; **~ness** ['striktnis] Genauigkeit *f*; Strenge *f*.

stridden ['stridn] *p.p. von* stride 1.

stride [straid] 1. [*irr.*] *v/t.* über-, durchschreiten. 2. (weiter) Schritt.

strident □ ['straidnt] kreischend.
strife [straif] Streit *m*, Hader *m*.
strike [straik] **1.** Streik *m*; (Öl-, Erz)Fund *m*; *fig.* Treffer *m*; ✕ (Luft)Angriff *m auf ein Einzelziel*; *Am. Baseball*: Verlustpunkt *m*; be on ~ streiken; **2.** [*irr.*] *v/t.* treffen, stoßen; schlagen; gegen *od.* auf (*acc.*) schlagen *od.* stoßen; stoßen *od.* treffen auf (*acc.*); *Flagge etc.* streichen; *Ton* anschlagen; auffallen (*dat.*); ergreifen; *Handel* abschließen; *Streichholz, Licht* anzünden; *Wurzel* schlagen; *Pose* annehmen; *Bilanz* ziehen; ~ up ♩ anstimmen; *Freundschaft* schließen; *v/i.* schlagen; ⚓ auf Grund stoßen; streiken; ~ home (richtig) treffen; **~r** ['straikə] Streikende(r) *m*.
striking □ ['straikiŋ] Schlag...; auffallend; eindrucksvoll; treffend.
string [striŋ] **1.** Schnur *f*; Bindfaden *m*; Band *n*; *Am.* F Bedingung *f*; (Bogen)Sehne *f*; ♩ Faser *f*; ♩ Saite *f*, Reihe *f*, Kette *f*; ~s *pl.* ♩ Saiteninstrumente *n/pl.*, Streicher *m/pl.*; *pull the* ~s *der Drahtzieher sein*; **2.** [*irr.*] spannen; aufreihen; besaiten (*a. fig.*), bespannen; (ver-, zu)schnüren; *Bohnen* abziehen; *Am. sl. j-n* verkohlen; *be strung up* angespannt *od.* erregt sein; **~band♩** ['striŋbænd] Streichorchester *n*.
stringent □ ['strindʒənt] streng, scharf; bindend, zwingend; knapp.
stringy ['striŋi] faserig; zäh.
strip [strip] **1.** entkleiden (*a. fig.*); (sich) ausziehen; abziehen; *fig.* entblößen, berauben; ⊕ auseinandernehmen; ⚓ abtakeln; *a.* ~ *off* ausziehen, abstreifen; **2.** Streifen *m*.
stripe [straip] Streifen *m*; ✕ Tresse *f*.
stripling ['stripliŋ] Bürschchen *n*.
strive [straiv] [*irr.*] streben; sich bemühen; ringen (*for* um); **~n** ['strivn] *p.p. von* strive.
strode [stroud] *pret. von* stride 1.
stroke [strouk] **1.** Schlag *m* (*a.* 🕰); Streich *m*; Stoß *m*; Strich *m*; ~ *of luck* Glücksfall *m*; **2.** streiche(l)n.
stroll [stroul] **1.** schlendern; umherziehen; **2.** Bummel *m*; Spaziergang *m*; **~er** ['stroulə] Bummler(in), Spaziergänger(in); *Am.* (Falt)Sportwagen *m*.
strong □ [strɔŋ] *allg.* stark; kräftig; energisch, eifrig; fest; schwer (*Speise etc.*); **~box** ['strɔŋbɔks] Stahlkassette *f*; **~hold** Festung *f*; *fig.* Bollwerk *n*; **~room** Stahlkammer *f*; **~willed** eigenwillig.
strop [strɔp] **1.** Streichriemen *m*; **2.** Messer abziehen.
strove [strouv] *pret. von* strive.
struck [strʌk] *pret. u. p.p. von* strike 2.
structure ['strʌktʃə] Bau(werk *n*) *m*; Struktur *f*, Gefüge *n*; Gebilde *n*.

struggle ['strʌgl] **1.** sich (ab)mühen; kämpfen, ringen; sich sträuben; **2.** Kampf *m*; Ringen *n*; Anstrengung *f*.
strung [strʌŋ] *pret. u. p.p. von* string 2.
strut [strʌt] **1.** *v/i.* stolzieren; *v/t.* ⊕ abstützen; **2.** Stolzieren *n*; ⊕ Strebe(balken *m*) *f*; Stütze *f*.
stub [stʌb] **1.** (Baum)Stumpf *m*; Stummel *m*; *Am.* Kontrollabschnitt *m*; **2.** (aus)roden; sich *den Fuß* stoßen.
stubble ['stʌbl] Stoppel(n *pl.*) *f*.
stubborn □ ['stʌbən] eigensinnig; widerspenstig; stur; hartnäckig.
stuck [stʌk] *pret. u. p.p. von* stick 2; **~up** ['stʌk'ʌp] F hochnäsig.
stud [stʌd] **1.** (Wand)Pfosten *m*; Ziernagel *m*; Knauf *m*; Manschetten-, Kragenknopf *m*; Gestüt *n*; **2.** beschlagen; besetzen; **~book** ['stʌdbuk] Gestütbuch *n*.
student ['stju:dənt] Student(in).
studied □ ['stʌdid] einstudiert; gesucht; gewollt.
studio ['stju:diou] Atelier *n*; Studio *n*; *Radio*: Aufnahme-, Senderaum *m*.
studious □ ['stju:djəs] fleißig; bedacht; bemüht; geflissentlich.
study ['stʌdi] **1.** Studium *n*; Studier-, Arbeitszimmer *n*; *paint. etc.* Studie *f*; *be in a brown* ~ versunken sein; **2.** (ein)studieren; sich *et.* genau ansehen; sich bemühen um.
stuff [stʌf] **1.** Stoff *m*; Zeug *n*; *fig.* Unsinn *m*; **2.** *v/t.* (voll-, aus)stopfen; **~ed shirt** *Am. sl.* Fatzke *m*; *v/i.* sich vollstopfen; **~ing** ['stʌfiŋ] Füllung *f*; **~y** □ [‿fi] dumpf(ig), muffig, stickig; *fig.* verärgert.
stultify ['stʌltifai] lächerlich machen, blamieren; *et.* hinfällig machen.
stumble ['stʌmbl] **1.** Stolpern *n*; Fehltritt *m*; **2.** stolpern; straucheln; ~ *upon* stoßen auf (*acc.*).
stump [stʌmp] **1.** Stumpf *m*, Stummel *m*; **2.** *v/t.* F verblüffen; *Am.* F herausfordern; ~ *the country* als Wahlredner im Land umherziehen; *v/i.* (daher)stapfen; **~y** □ ['stʌmpi] gedrungen; plump.
stun [stʌn] betäuben (*a. fig.*).
stung [stʌŋ] *pret. u. p.p. von* sting 2.
stunk [stʌŋk] *pret. u. p.p. von* stink 2.
stunning □ F ['stʌniŋ] toll, famos.
stunt[1] F [stʌnt] Kraft-, Kunststück *n*; (Reklame)Trick *m*; Sensation *f*.
stunt[2] [‿] im Wachstum hindern; **~ed** ['stʌntid] verkümmert.
stup|efy ['stju:pifai] *fig.* betäuben; verblüffen; verdummen; **~endous** □ [stju:(:)'pendəs] erstaunlich; **~id** □ ['stju:pid] dumm, einfältig, stumpfsinnig; blöd; **~idity** [stju:(:)-'piditi] Dummheit *f*; Stumpfsinn *m*; **~or** ['stju:(:)pə] Erstarrung *f*, Betäubung *f*.

sturdy ['stɔːdi] derb, kräftig, stark; stämmig; stramm; handfest.

stutter ['stʌtə] 1. stottern; 2. Stottern n.

sty¹ [stai] Schweinestall m, Koben m.

sty², **stye** 𝄞 [~] Gerstenkorn n am Auge.

style [stail] 1. Stil m; Mode f; Betitelung f; 2. (be)nennen, betiteln.

stylish □ ['stailiʃ] stilvoll; elegant; **~ness** [~ʃnis] Eleganz f.

stylo F ['stailou], **~graph** [~ləgrɑːf] Tintenkuli m.

suave □ [swɑːv] verbindlich; mild.

sub... [sʌb] mst Unter..., unter...; Neben...; Hilfs...; fast ...

subdeb Am. F ['sʌb'deb] Backfisch m, junges Mädchen.

subdivision ['sʌbdiviʒən] Unterteilung f; Unterabteilung f.

subdue [səb'djuː] unterwerfen; bezwingen; bändigen; unterdrücken, verdrängen; dämpfen.

subject ['sʌbdʒikt] 1. unterworfen; untergeben, abhängig; untertan; unterliegend (to dat.); be ~ to neigen zu; 2. adv. ~ to vorbehaltlich (gen.); 3. Untertan m, Staatsangehörige(r m) f; phls., gr. Subjekt n; a. ~ matter Thema n, Gegenstand m; 4. [səb'dʒekt] unterwerfen; fig. aussetzen; **~ion** [~kʃən] Unterwerfung f. [chen.]

subjugate ['sʌbdʒugeit] unterjo-]

subjunctive gr. [səb'dʒʌŋktiv] a. ~ mood Konjunktiv m.

sub|lease ['sʌb'liːs], **~let** [irr. (let)] untervermieten.

sublime □ [sə'blaim] erhaben.

submachine-gun ['sʌbmə'ʃiːngʌn] Maschinenpistole f.

submarine ['sʌbməriːn] 1. unterseeisch; 2. 🚢 Unterseeboot n.

submerge [səb'mɔːdʒ] untertauchen; überschwemmen.

submiss|ion [səb'miʃən] Unterwerfung f; Unterbreitung f; **~ive** □ [~isiv] unterwürfig.

submit [səb'mit] (sich) unterwerfen; anheimstellen; unterbreiten, einreichen; fig. sich fügen od. ergeben (to in acc.).

subordinate 1. □ [sə'bɔːdnit] untergeordnet; untergeben; ~ clause gr. Nebensatz m; 2. [~] Untergebene(r m) f; 3. [~dineit] unterordnen.

suborn ⚖ [sʌ'bɔːn] verleiten.

subscribe [səb'skraib] v/t. Geld stiften (to für); Summe zeichnen; s-n Namen setzen (to unter acc.); unterschreiben mit; v/i. ~ to Zeitung etc. abonnieren; e-r Meinung zustimmen, et. unterschreiben; **~r** [~bə] (Unter)Zeichner(in); Abonnent(in); teleph. Teilnehmer(in).

subscription [səb'skripʃən] (Unter-)Zeichnung f; Abonnement n.

subsequent □ ['sʌbsikwent] folgend; später; **~ly** hinterher.

subservient □ [səb'sɔːvjənt] dienlich; dienstbar; unterwürfig.

subsid|e [səb'said] sinken, sich senken; fig. sich setzen; sich legen (Wind); ~ into verfallen in (acc.); **~iary** [~'sidjəri] 1. □ Hilfs...; Neben...; untergeordnet; 2. Tochtergesellschaft f; Filiale f; **~ize** ['sʌbsidaiz] mit Geld unterstützen; subventionieren; **~y** [~di] Beihilfe f; Subvention f.

subsist [səb'sist] bestehen; leben (on, by von); **~ence** [~təns] Dasein n; (Lebens)Unterhalt m.

substance ['sʌbstəns] Substanz f; Wesen n; fig. Hauptsache f; Inhalt m; Wirklichkeit f; Vermögen n.

substantial □ [səb'stænʃəl] wesentlich; wirklich; kräftig; stark; solid; vermögend; namhaft (Summe).

substantiate [səb'stænʃieit] beweisen, begründen, dartun.

substantive gr. ['sʌbstəntiv] Substantiv n, Hauptwort n.

substitut|e ['sʌbstitjuːt] 1. an die Stelle setzen od. treten (for von); unterschieben (for statt); 2. Stellvertreter m; Ersatz m; **~ion** ['sʌbsti'tjuːʃən] Stellvertretung f; Ersatz m.

subterfuge ['sʌbtəfjuːdʒ] Ausflucht f.

subterranean □ [sʌbtə'reinjən] unterirdisch.

sub-title ['sʌbtaitl] Untertitel m.

subtle □ ['sʌtl] fein(sinnig); subtil; spitzfindig; **~ty** [~lti] Feinheit f.

subtract 🇦 [səb'trækt] abziehen, subtrahieren.

subtropical ['sʌb'trɔpikəl] subtropisch.

suburb ['sʌbəːb] Vorstadt f, Vorort m; **~an** [sə'bɔːbən] vorstädtisch.

subvention [səb'venʃən] 1. Subvention f; 2. subventionieren.

subver|sion [sʌb'vɔːʃən] Umsturz m; **~sive** [~ɔːsiv] zerstörend (of acc.); subversiv; **~t** [~ɔːt] (um-)stürzen; untergraben.

subway ['sʌbwei] (bsd. Fußgänger-) Unterführung f; Am. Untergrundbahn f.

succeed [sək'siːd] Erfolg haben; glücken, gelingen; (nach)folgen (dat.); ~ to übernehmen; erben.

success [sək'ses] Erfolg m; **~ful** □ [~sful] erfolgreich; **~ion** [~eʃən] (Nach-, Erb-, Reihen)Folge f; Nachkommenschaft f; in ~ nacheinander; **~ive** □ [~esiv] aufeinanderfolgend; **~or** [~sə] Nachfolger(in). [fen.]

succo(u)r ['sʌkə] 1. Hilfe f; 2. hel-]

succulent □ ['sʌkjulənt] saftig.

succumb [sə'kʌm] unter-, erliegen.

such [sʌtʃ] solch(er, -e, -es); derartig; so groß; ~ a man ein solcher Mann; ~ as die, welche.

suck [sʌk] **1.** (ein)saugen; saugen an (*dat.*); aussaugen; lutschen; **2.** Saugen *n*; ~er ['sʌkə] Saugorgan *n*; ♀ Wurzelsproß *m*; *Am.* Einfaltspinsel *m*; ~le ['sʌkl] säugen, stillen; ~ling [~liŋ] Säugling *m*.

suction ['sʌkʃən] (An)Saugen *n*; Sog *m*; *attr.* Saug...

sudden □ ['sʌdn] plötzlich; *all of a* ~ ganz plötzlich.

suds [sʌdz] *pl.* Seifenlauge *f*; Seifenschaum *m*; ~y *Am.* ['sʌdzi] schaumig, seifig.

sue [sjuː] *v/t.* verklagen; ~ *out* erwirken; *v/i.* nachsuchen (*for* um); klagen.

suède [sweid] (feines) Wildleder.

suet [sjuit] Nierenfett *n*; Talg *m*.

suffer ['sʌfə] *v/i.* leiden (*from* an *dat.*); *v/t.* erleiden, erdulden, (zu-)lassen; ~ance [~ərəns] Duldung *f*; ~er [~rə] Leidende(r *m*) *f*; Dulder(in); ~ing [~riŋ] Leiden *n*.

suffice [sə'fais] genügen; ~ *it to say* es sei nur gesagt.

sufficien|cy [sə'fiʃənsi] genügende Menge; Auskommen *n*; ~t [~nt] genügend, ausreichend.

suffix *gr.* ['sʌfiks] **1.** anhängen; **2.** Nachsilbe *f*, Suffix *n*.

suffocate ['sʌfəkeit] ersticken.

suffrage ['sʌfridʒ] (Wahl)Stimme *f*; Wahl-, Stimmrecht *n*.

suffuse [sə'fjuːz] übergießen; überziehen.

sugar ['ʃugə] **1.** Zucker *m*; **2.** zukkern; ~basin, *Am.* ~bowl Zuckerdose *f*; ~cane ♀ Zuckerrohr *n*; ~coat überzuckern, versüßen; ~y [~əri] zuckerig; zuckersüß.

suggest [sə'dʒest] vorschlagen, anregen; nahelegen; vorbringen; *Gedanken* eingeben; andeuten; denken lassen an (*acc.*); ~ion [~tʃən] Anregung *f*; Rat *m*, Vorschlag *m*; Suggestion *f*; Eingebung *f*; Andeutung *f*; ~ive [~tiv] anregend; andeutend (*of acc.*); gehaltvoll; zweideutig.

suicide ['sjuisaid] **1.** Selbstmord *m*; Selbstmörder(in); **2.** *Am.* Selbstmord begehen.

suit [sjuit] **1.** (Herren)Anzug *m*; (Damen)Kostüm *n*; Anliegen *n*; (Heirats)Antrag *m*; *Karten:* Farbe *f*; ✠ Prozeß *m*; **2.** *v/t.* j-m passen, zusagen, bekommen; j-n kleiden, j-m stehen, passen zu (*Kleidungsstück etc.*); ~ *oneself* tun, was e-m beliebt; ~ *s.th. to et.* anpassen (*dat.*); *be* ~*ed* geeignet sein (*for* für), passen (*to* zu); *v/i.* passen; ~able □ ['sjuitəbl] passend, geeignet; entsprechend; ~case (Hand)Koffer *m*; ~e [swiːt] Gefolge *n*; (Reihen)Folge *f*; ♩ Suite *f*; *a.* ~ *of rooms* Zimmerflucht *f*; Garnitur *f*, (Zimmer)Einrichtung *f*; ~or ['sjuitə] Freier *m*; ✠ Kläger(in).

sulk [sʌlk] schmollen, bocken; ~iness ['sʌlkinis] üble Laune; ~s *pl.* = sulkiness; ~y ['sʌlki] **1.** verdrießlich; launisch; schmollend; **2.** *Sport:* Traberwagen *m*, Sulky *n*.

sullen □ ['sʌlən] verdrossen; mürrisch.

sully ['sʌli] *mst fig.* beflecken.

sulphur ♔ ['sʌlfə] Schwefel *m*; ~ic [sʌl'fjuərik] Schwefel...

sultriness ['sʌltrinis] Schwüle *f*.

sultry □ ['sʌltri] schwül; *fig.* heftig, hitzig.

sum [sʌm] **1.** Summe *f*; Betrag *m*; *fig.* Inbegriff *m*, Inhalt *m*; Rechenaufgabe *f*; *do* ~*s* rechnen; **2.** *mst* ~ *up* zs.-rechnen; zs.-fassen.

summar|ize ['sʌməraiz] (kurz) zs.-fassen; ~y [~ri] **1.** □ kurz (zs.-gefaßt); ✠ Schnell...; **2.** (kurze) Inhaltsangabe, Auszug *m*.

summer ['sʌmə] Sommer *m*; ~ *resort* Sommerfrische *f*; ~ *school* Ferienkurs *m*; ~ly [~əli], ~y [~əri] sommerlich.

summit ['sʌmit] Gipfel *m* (*a. fig.*).

summon ['sʌmən] auffordern; (be-)rufen; ✠ vorladen; *Mut etc.* aufbieten; ~s Aufforderung *f*; ✠ Vorladung *f*.

sumptuous □ ['sʌmptjuəs] kostbar.

sun [sʌn] **1.** Sonne *f*; *attr.* Sonnen...; **2.** (sich) sonnen; ~bath ['sʌnbɑːθ] Sonnenbad *n*; ~beam Sonnenstrahl *m*; ~burn Sonnenbräune *f*; Sonnenbrand *m*.

Sunday ['sʌndi] Sonntag *m*.

sun|-dial ['sʌndaiəl] Sonnenuhr *f*; ~down Sonnenuntergang *m*.

sundr|ies ['sʌndriz] *pl. bsd.* ✝ Verschiedene(s) *n*; Extraausgaben *f/pl.*; ~y [~ri] verschiedene.

sung [sʌŋ] *pret. u. p.p. von* sing.

sun-glasses ['sʌnglɑːsiz] *pl.* (*a pair of* ~ *pl.* eine) Sonnenbrille *f*.

sunk [sʌŋk] *pret. u. p.p. von* sink **1.**

sunken ['sʌŋkən] **1.** *p.p. von* sink **1**; **2.** *adj.* versunken; *fig.* eingefallen.

sun|ny □ ['sʌni] sonnig; ~rise Sonnenaufgang *m*; ~set Sonnenuntergang *m*; ~shade Sonnenschirm *m*; ~shine Sonnenschein *m*; ~stroke ✦ Sonnenstich *m*.

sup [sʌp] zu Abend essen.

super *F* ['sjuːpə] erstklassig, prima, super.

super|... ['sjuːpə] Über..., über...; Ober..., ober...; Groß...; ~abundant □ [sjuːpərə'bʌndənt] überreichlich; überschwenglich; ~annuate [~'rænjueit] pensionieren; ~d ausgedient; veraltet (*S.*).

superb □ [sjuː(ː)'pəːb] prächtig; herrlich.

super|charger *mot.* ['sjuːpətʃɑːdʒə] Kompressor *m*; ~cilious [sjuːpə-

'siliəs] hochmütig; ~ficial □ [~ə'fiʃəl] oberflächlich; ~fine ['sjuːpə'fain] extrafein; ~fluity [sjuːpə-flu(ː)iti] Überfluß m; ~fluous □ [sju(ː)'pɔːfluəs] überflüssig; ~heat ⊕ [sjuːpə'hiːt] überhitzen; ~human □ [~'hjuːmən] übermenschlich; ~impose ['sjuːpərim'pouz] darauf-, darüberlegen; ~induce [~rin'djuːs] noch hinzufügen; ~intend [sjuːprin'tend] die Oberaufsicht haben über (acc.); überwachen; ~intendent [~dənt] 1. Leiter m, Direktor m; (Ober)Aufseher m, Inspektor m; 2. aufsichtführend.

superior [sjuːˈpiəriə] 1. □ ober; höher(stehend); vorgesetzt; besser, hochwertiger; überlegen (to dat.); vorzüglich; 2. Höherstehende(r m) f, bsd. Vorgesetzte(r m) f; eccl. Obere(r) m; mst Lady ⚲, Mother ⚲ eccl. Oberin f; ~ity [sjuː(ː)piəriˈɔriti] Überlegenheit f.

superlative [sju(ː)'pəːlətiv] 1. □ höchst; überragend; 2. a. ~ degree gr. Superlativ m; ~market Supermarkt m; ~natural [[sjuːpə'nætʃ-rəl] übernatürlich; ~numerary [~'njuːmərəri] 1. überzählig; 2. Überzählige(r m) f; thea. Statist (-in); ~scription [~ə'skripʃən] Über-, Aufschrift f; ~sede [~'siːd] ersetzen; verdrängen; absetzen; fig. überholen; ~sonic phys. ['sjuː-pə'sɔnik] Überschall...; ~stition [sjuːpə'stiʃən] Aberglaube m; ~stitious □ [~ʃəs] abergläubisch; ~vene [~ə'viːn] noch hinzukommen; unerwartet eintreten; ~vise ['sjuːpəvaiz] beaufsichtigen, überwachen; ~vision [sjuːpə'viʒən] (Ober)Aufsicht f; Beaufsichtigung f; ~visor ['sjuːpəvaizə] Aufseher m, Inspektor m.

supper ['sʌpə] Abendessen n; the (Lord's) ⚲ das Heilige Abendmahl.

supplant [sə'plɑːnt] verdrängen.

supple ['sʌpl] geschmeidig (machen).

supplement 1. ['sʌplimənt] Ergänzung f; Nachtrag m; (Zeitungsetc.)Beilage f; 2. [~ment] ergänzen; ~al □ [sʌpli'mentl], ~ary [~təri] Ergänzungs...; nachträglich; Nachtrags...

suppliant ['sʌpliənt] 1. □ demütig bittend, flehend; 2. Bittsteller(in).

supplicat|e ['sʌplikeit] demütig bitten, anflehen; ~ion [sʌpli'keiʃən] demütige Bitte.

supplier [sə'plaiə] Lieferant(in).

supply [sə'plai] 1. liefern; e-m Mangel abhelfen; e-e Stelle ausfüllen; vertreten; ausstatten, versorgen; ergänzen; 2. Lieferung f; Versorgung f; Zufuhr f; Vorrat m; Bedarf m; Angebot n; (Stell)Vertretung f; mst supplies pl. parl. Etat m.

support [sə'pɔːt] 1. Stütze f; Hilfe f; ⊕ Träger m; Unterstützung f; Lebensunterhalt m; 2. (unter)stützen; unterhalten, sorgen für (Familie etc.); aufrechterhalten; (v)ertragen.

suppose [sə'pouz] annehmen; voraussetzen; vermuten; he is ~d to do er soll tun; ~ we go gehen wir; wie wär's, wenn wir gingen.

supposed □ [sə'pouzd] vermeintlich; ~ly [~zidli] vermutlich.

supposition [sʌpə'ziʃən] Voraussetzung f; Annahme f; Vermutung f.

suppress [sə'pres] unterdrücken; ~ion [~eʃən] Unterdrückung f.

suppurate ['sʌpjuəreit] eitern.

suprem|acy [sju'preməsi] Oberhoheit f; Vorherrschaft f; Überlegenheit f; Vorrang m; ~e □ [sjuː(ː)'priːm] höchst; oberst; Ober...; größt.

surcharge [səː'tʃɑːdʒ] 1. überladen; Zuschlag od. Nachgebühr erheben von j-m; 2. ['səːtʃɑːdʒ] Überladung f; (Straf)Zuschlag m; Nachgebühr f; Überdruck m auf Briefmarken.

sure □ [ʃuə] allg. sicher; to be ~!, ~ enough!, Am. ~! F sicher(lich)!; ~ly ['ʃuəli] sicherlich; ~ty ['ʃuəti] Bürge m.

surf [səːf] Brandung f.

surface ['səːfis] 1. (Ober)Fläche f; ✕ Tragfläche f; 2. ⚓ auftauchen (U-Boot).

surf|-board ['səːfbɔːd] Wellenreiterbrett n; ~-boat Brandungsboot n.

surfeit ['səːfit] 1. Übersättigung f; Ekel m; 2. (sich) überladen.

surf-riding ['səːfraidiŋ] Sport: Wellenreiten n.

surge [səːdʒ] 1. Woge f; 2. wogen.

surg|eon ['səːdʒən] Chirurg m; ~ery [~əri] Chirurgie f; Sprechzimmer n; ~ hours pl. Sprechstunde(n pl.) f.

surgical □ ['səːdʒikəl] chirurgisch.

surly □ ['səːli] mürrisch; grob.

surmise 1. ['səːmaiz] Vermutung f; Argwohn m; 2. [səː'maiz] vermuten; argwöhnen.

surmount [səː'maunt] übersteigen; überragen; fig. überwinden.

surname ['səːneim] Zu-, Nachname m.

surpass fig. [səː'pɑːs] übersteigen, übertreffen; ~ing [~siŋ] überragend.

surplus ['səːpləs] 1. Überschuß m, Mehr n; 2. überschüssig; Über...

surprise [sə'praiz] 1. Überraschung f; ✕ Überrump(e)lung f; 2. überraschen; ✕ überrumpeln.

surrender [sə'rendə] 1. Übergabe f, Ergebung f; Kapitulation f; Aufgeben n; 2. v/t. übergeben; aufgeben; v/i. a. ~ o.s. sich ergeben.

surround [sə'raund] umgeben; ✕

umzingeln; ~ing [~diŋ] umliegend; ~ings pl. Umgebung f.

surtax ['sɔːtæks] Steuerzuschlag m.

survey 1. [sə'vei] überblicken; mustern; begutachten; surv. vermessen; 2. ['sə'vei] Überblick m (a. fig.); Besichtigung f; Gutachten n; surv. Vermessung f; ~or [sə(:)-'veiə] Land-, Feldmesser m.

surviv|al [sə'vaivəl] Über-, Fortleben n; Überbleibsel n; ~e [~aiv] überleben; noch leben; fortleben; am Leben bleiben; bestehen bleiben; ~or [~və] Überlebende(r m) f.

suscept|ible □ [sə'septəbl], ~ive [~tiv] empfänglich (of, to für); empfindlich (gegen); be ~ of et. zulassen.

suspect 1. [səs'pekt] (be)argwöhnen; in Verdacht haben, verdächtigen; vermuten, befürchten; 2. ['sʌspekt] Verdächtige(r m) f; 3. [~] = ~ed [səs'pektid] verdächtig.

suspend [səs'pend] (auf)hängen; aufschieben; in der Schwebe lassen; Zahlung einstellen; aussetzen; suspendieren, sperren; ~ed schwebend; ~er [~də] Strumpf-, Sockenhalter m; ~s pl. Am. Hosenträger m/pl.

suspens|e [səs'pens] Ungewißheit f; Unentschiedenheit f; Spannung f; ~ion [~nʃən] Aufhängung f; Aufschub m; Einstellung f; Suspendierung f, Amtsenthebung f; Sperre f; ~ion bridge Hängebrücke f; ~ive □ [~nsiv] aufschiebend.

suspici|on [səs'piʃən] Verdacht m; Argwohn m; fig. Spur f; ~ous □ [~ʃəs] argwöhnisch; verdächtig.

sustain [səs'tein] stützen; fig. aufrechterhalten; aushalten; erleiden; ♫ anerkennen; ~ed anhaltend; ununterbrochen.

sustenance ['sʌstinəns] (Lebens-) Unterhalt m; Nahrung f.

svelte [svelt] schlank (Frau).

swab [swɔb] 1. Aufwischmop m; ♣ Tupfer m; ♣ Abstrich m; 2. aufwischen.

swaddl|e ['swɔdl] Baby wickeln; ~ing-clothes mst fig. [~liŋklouðz] pl. Windeln f/pl.

swagger ['swægə] 1. stolzieren; prahlen, renommieren; 2. F elegant.

swale Am. [sweil] Mulde f, Niederung f.

swallow ['swɔlou] 1. orn. Schwalbe f; Schlund m; Schluck m; 2. (hinunter-, ver)schlucken; fig. Ansicht etc. begierig aufnehmen.

swam [swæm] pret. von swim 1.

swamp [swɔmp] 1. Sumpf m; 2. überschwemmen (a. fig.); versenken; ~y ['swɔmpi] sumpfig.

swan [swɔn] Schwan m.

swank sl. [swæŋk] 1. Angabe f,

Protzerei f; 2. angeben, protzen; ~y ['swæŋki] protzig, angeberisch.

swap F [swɔp] 1. Tausch m; 2. (ver-, aus)tauschen.

sward [swɔːd] Rasen m.

swarm [swɔːm] 1. Schwarm m; Haufe(n) m, Gewimmel n; 2. schwärmen; wimmeln (with von).

swarthy □ ['swɔːði] dunkelfarbig.

swash [swɔʃ] plan(t)schen.

swat [swɔt] Fliege klatschen.

swath ✗ [swɔːθ] Schwade(n m) f.

swathe [sweið] (ein)wickeln.

sway [swei] 1. Schaukeln n; Einfluß m; Herrschaft f; 2. schaukeln; beeinflussen; beherrschen.

swear [swεə] [irr.] (be)schwören; fluchen; ~ s.o. in j-n vereidigen.

sweat [swet] 1. Schweiß m; by the ~ of one's brow im Schweiße seines Angesichts; all of a ~ F in Schweiß gebadet (a. fig.); 2. [irr.] v/i. schwitzen; v/t. (aus)schwitzen; in Schweiß bringen; Arbeiter ausbeuten; ~er ['swetə] Sweater m, Pullover m; Trainingsjacke f; fig. Ausbeuter m; ~y ['~ti] schweißig; verschwitzt.

Swede [swiːd] Schwed|e m, -in f.

Swedish ['swiːdiʃ] 1. schwedisch; 2. Schwedisch n.

sweep [swiːp] 1. [irr.] fegen (a.fig.), kehren; fig. streifen; bestreichen (a. ✗); (majestätisch) (dahin)rauschen; 2. (fig. Dahin)Fegen n; Kehren n; Schwung m; Biegung f; Spielraum m; Bereich m; Schornsteinfeger m; make a clean ~ reinen Tisch machen (of mit); ~er ['swiːpə] (Straßen)Feger m; Kehrmaschine f; ~ing □ [~piŋ] weitgehend; schwungvoll; ~ings pl. Kehricht m, Müll m.

sweet [swiːt] 1. □ süß; lieblich; freundlich; frisch; duftend; have a ~ tooth ein Leckermaul sein; 2. Liebling m; Süßigkeit f, Bonbon m, n; Nachtisch m; ~en ['swiːtn] (ver)süßen; ~heart Liebling m, Liebste(r m) f; ~ish [~tiʃ] süßlich; ~meat Bonbon m, n; kandierte Frucht; ~ness [~tnis] Süßigkeit f; Lieblichkeit f; ~ pea ♣ Gartenwicke f.

swell [swel] 1. [irr.] v/i. (an)schwellen; sich blähen; sich (auf)bauchen; v/t. (an)schwellen lassen; aufblähen; 2. F fein; sl. prima; 3. Anschwellen n; Schwellung f; ♪ Dünung f; F feiner Herr; ~ing ['sweliŋ] Geschwulst f.

swelter ['sweltə] vor Hitze umkommen.

swept [swept] pret. u. p.p. von sweep 1.

swerve [swɔːv] 1. (plötzlich) abbiegen; 2. (plötzliche) Wendung f.

swift □ [swift] schnell, eilig, flink; ~ness ['swiftnis] Schnelligkeit f.

swill [swil] 1. Spülicht n; Schweine-
trank m; 2. spülen; saufen.
swim [swim] 1. [irr.] (durch-)
schwimmen; schweben; my head
~s mir schwindelt; 2. Schwimmen
n; be in the ~ auf dem laufenden
sein; ~ming ['swimiŋ] 1. Schwimmen n; 2. Schwimm...; ~bath
(bsd. Hallen)Schwimmbad n; ~pool
Schwimmbecken n; ~suit Badeanzug m.
swindle ['swindl] 1. (be)schwin-
deln; 2. Schwindel m.
swine [swain] Schwein(e pl.) n.
swing [swiŋ] 1. [irr.] schwingen,
schwanken; F baumeln; (sich)
schaukeln; schwenken; sich drehen;
2. Schwingen n; Schwung m;
Schaukel f; Spielraum m; in full ~
in vollem Gange; ~door ['swiŋdɔ:]
Drehtür f.
swinish □ ['swainiʃ] schweinisch.
swipe [swaip] 1. aus vollem Arm
schlagen; 2. starker Schlag.
swirl [swə:l] 1. (herum)wirbeln,
strudeln; 2. Wirbel m, Strudel m.
Swiss [swis] 1. schweizerisch,
Schweizer...; 2. Schweizer(in); the
~ pl. die Schweizer m/pl.
switch [switʃ] 1. Gerte f; 🌣 Weiche
f; ⚡ Schalter m; falscher Zopf;
2. peitschen; 🌣 rangieren; ⚡ (um-)
schalten; fig. wechseln, überleiten;
~ on (off) ⚡ ein- (aus)schalten; ~
board ⚡ ['switʃbɔ:d] Schaltbrett n,
-tafel f.
swivel ⊕ ['swivl] Drehring m; attr.
Dreh...
swollen ['swoulən] p.p. von swell 1.
swoon [swu:n] 1. Ohnmacht f;
2. in Ohnmacht fallen.
swoop [swu:p] 1. ~ down on od. upon
(herab)stoßen auf (acc.) (Raubvogel); überfallen; 2. Stoß m.
swop [swɔp] s. swap.
sword [sɔ:d] Schwert n, Degen
m.
swordsman ['sɔ:dzmən] Fechter m.

swore [swɔ:] pret. von swear.
sworn [swɔ:n] p.p. von swear.
swum [swʌm] p.p. von swim 1.
swung [swʌŋ] pret. u. p.p. von
swing 1.
sycamore 💠 ['sikəmɔ:] Bergahorn
m; Am. Platane f.
sycophant ['sikəfənt] Kriecher m.
syllable ['siləbl] Silbe f.
syllabus ['siləbəs] (bsd. Vorlesungs-)
Verzeichnis n; (bsd. Lehr)Plan m.
sylvan ['silvən] waldig, Wald...
symbol ['simbəl] Symbol n, Sinnbild n; ~ic(al □) [sim'bɔlik(əl)]
sinnbildlich; ~ism ['simbəlizəm]
Symbolik f.
symmetr|ical □ [si'metrikəl] eben-
mäßig; ~y ['simitri] Ebenmaß n.
sympath|etic [simpə'θetik] (~ally)
mitfühlend; sympathisch; ~ strike
Sympathiestreik m; ~ize ['sim-
pəθaiz] sympathisieren, mitfühlen;
~y [~θi] Sympathie f, Mitgefühl n.
symphony ♪ ['simfəni] Symphonie f.
symptom ['simptəm] Symptom n.
synchron|ize ['siŋkrənaiz] v/i.
gleichzeitig sein; v/t. als gleichzeitig
zs.-stellen; Uhren auf-ea. abstimmen; Tonfilm: synchronisieren;
~ous □ [~nəs] gleichzeitig.
syndicate 1. ['sindikit] Syndikat n;
2. [~keit] zu e-m Syndikat verbinden.
synonym ['sinənim] Synonym n;
~ous | [si'nɔniməs] sinnverwandt.
synop|sis [si'nɔpsis], pl. ~ses [~si:z]
zs.-fassende Übersicht.
syntax gr. ['sintæks] Syntax f.
synthe|sis ['sinθisis], pl. ~ses [~si:z]
Synthese f, Verbindung f; ~tic(al
□) [sin'θetik(əl)] synthetisch.
syringe ['sirindʒ] 1. Spritze f;
2. (be-, ein-, aus)spritzen.
syrup ['sirəp] Sirup m.
system ['sistim] System n; Organismus m, Körper m; Plan m, Ordnung f; ~atic [sisti'mætik] (~ally)
systematisch.

T

tab [tæb] Streifen m; Schildchen n;
Anhänger m; Schlaufe f, Aufhänger
m; F Rechnung f, Konto n.
table ['teibl] 1. Tisch m, Tafel f;
Tisch-, Tafelrunde f; Tabelle f,
Verzeichnis n; Bibel: Gesetzestafel
f; s. ~land; at ~ bei Tisch; turn
the ~s den Spieß umdrehen (on
gegen); 2. auf den Tisch legen;
tabellarisch anordnen.
tableau ['tæblou], pl. ~x [~ouz]
lebendes Bild.
table|-cloth ['teiblklɔθ] Tischtuch
n; ~land Tafelland n, Plateau n,

Hochebene f; ~linen Tisch-
wäsche f; ~spoon Eßlöffel m.
tablet ['tæblit] Täfelchen n; (Gedenk)Tafel f; (Schreib- etc.)Block
m; Stück n Seife; Tablette f.
table-top ['teibltɔp] Tischplatte f.
taboo [tə'bu:] 1. tabu, unantastbar;
verboten; 2. Tabu n; Verbot n;
3. verbieten.
tabulate ['tæbjuleit] tabellarisch
ordnen.
tacit □ ['tæsit] stillschweigend;
~urn □ [~tə:n] schweigsam.
tack [tæk] 1. Stift m, Zwecke f;

Heftstich *m*; ⚓ Halse *f*; ⚓ Gang *m* beim Lavieren; *fig.* Weg *m*; **2.** *v/t.* (an)heften; *fig.* (an)hängen; *v/i.* ⚓ wenden; *fig.* lavieren.

tackle ['tækl] **1.** Gerät *n*; ⚓ Takel-, Tauwerk *n*; ⊕ Flaschenzug *m*; **2.** (an)packen; in Angriff nehmen; fertig werden mit; *j-n* angehen (*for* um).

tacky ['tæki] klebrig; *Am.* F schäbig.

tact [tækt] Takt *m*, Feingefühl *n*; **~ful** □ ['tæktful] taktvoll.

tactics ['tæktiks] Taktik *f*.

tactless □ ['tæktlis] taktlos.

tadpole *zo.* ['tædpoul] Kaulquappe*f*.

taffeta ['tæfitə] Taft *m*.

taffy *Am.* ['tæfi] = **toffee**; F Schmus *m*, Schmeichelei *f*.

tag [tæg] **1.** (Schnürsenkel)Stift *m*; Schildchen *n*, Etikett *n*; Redensart *f*, Zitat *n*; Zusatz *m*; loses Ende; Fangen *n* (*Kinderspiel*); **2.** etikettieren, auszeichnen; anhängen (*to*, *onto* an *acc.*); ~ *after* herlaufen hinter (*dat.*); ~ *together* an-ea.-reihen.

tail [teil] **1.** Schwanz *m*; Schweif *m*; hinteres Ende, Schluß *m*; ~*s pl.* Rückseite *f* e-r Münze; F Frack *m*; *turn* ~ davonlaufen; ~*s up* in Hochstimmung; **2.** ~ *after s.o.* j-m nachlaufen; ~ *s.o. Am.* j-n beschatten; ~ *away*, ~ *off* abflauen, sich verlieren; zögernd enden; **~coat** ['teil'kout] Frack *m*; **~light** *mot. etc.* ['teillait] Rück-, Schlußlicht *n*.

tailor ['teilə] **1.** Schneider *m*; **2.** schneidern; **~-made** Schneider..., Maß...

taint [teint] **1.** Flecken *m*, Makel *m*; ✳ Ansteckung *f*; *fig. krankhafter* Zug; Verderbnis *f*; **2.** beflecken; verderben; ✳ anstecken.

take [teik] **1.** [*irr.*] *v/t.* nehmen; an-, ab-, auf-, ein-, fest-, hin-, wegnehmen; (weg)bringen; *Speise* (zu sich) nehmen; *Maßnahme, Gelegenheit* ergreifen; *Eid, Gelübde, Examen* ablegen; *phot.* aufnehmen; *et. gut etc.* aufnehmen; *Beleidigung* hinnehmen; fassen, ergreifen; fangen; *fig.* fesseln; sich *e-e Krankheit* holen; erfordern; brauchen; *Zeit* dauern; auffassen; halten, ansehen (*for* für); *I* ~ *it that* ich nehme an, daß; ~ *breath* verschnaufen; ~ *comfort* sich trösten; ~ *compassion on* Mitleid empfinden mit; sich erbarmen (*gen.*); ~ *counsel* beraten; ~ *a drive* e-e Fahrt machen; ~ *fire* Feuer fangen; ~ *in hand* unternehmen; ~ *hold of* ergreifen; ~ *pity on* Mitleid haben mit; ~ *place* stattfinden; spielen (*Handlung*); ~ *a seat* Platz nehmen; ~ *a walk* e-n Spaziergang machen; ~ *my word for it* verlaß dich drauf; ~ *about* herumführen; ~ *along* mitnehmen; ~ *down* herunternehmen; notieren; ~ *for* halten für; ~ *from j-m* wegnehmen;

abziehen von; ~ *in* enger machen; *Zeitung* halten; aufnehmen (*als Gast etc.*); einschließen; verstehen; erfassen; F *j-n* reinlegen; ~ *off* ab-, wegnehmen; *Kleid* ausziehen, *Hut* abnehmen; ~ *on* an-, übernehmen; *Arbeiter etc.* einstellen; *Fahrgäste* zusteigen lassen; ~ *out* heraus-, entnehmen; *Fleck* entfernen; *j-n* ausführen; *Versicherung* abschließen; ~ *to pieces* auseinandernehmen; ~ *up* aufnehmen; sich *e-r S.* annehmen; *Raum, Zeit* in Anspruch nehmen; *v/i.* wirken, ein-, anschlagen; gefallen, ziehen; ~ *after j-m* nachschlagen; ~ *off* abspringen; 🐦 aufsteigen, starten; ~ *on* F Anklang finden; ~ *over* die Amtsgewalt übernehmen; ~ *to liebgewinnen*; *fig.* sich verlegen auf (*acc.*); *Zuflucht* nehmen zu; sich ergeben (*dat.*); ~ *up* F sich bessern (*Wetter*); ~ *up with* sich anfreunden mit; *that won't* ~ *with me* das verfängt bei mir nicht; **2.** Fang *m*; *Geld*-Einnahme *f*; *Film:* Szene(naufnahme) *f*; **~-in** F ['teik'in] Reinfall *m*; **~n** ['teikən] *p.p. von* take 1; *be* ~ *besetzt sein; be* ~ *with entzückt sein von; be* ~ *ill* krank werden; **~-off** ['teikɔ:f] Karikatur *f*; Absprung *m*; 🐦 Start *m*.

taking ['teikiŋ] **1.** □ F anziehend, fesselnd, einnehmend; ansteckend; **2.** (An-, Ab-, Auf-, Ein-, Ent-, Hin-, Weg- *etc.*)Nehmen *n*; Inbesitznahme *f*; ✕ Einnahme *f*; F Aufregung *f*; ~*s pl.* 🞠 Einnahmen *f/pl.*

tale [teil] Erzählung *f*, Geschichte *f*; Märchen *n*, Sage *f*; *it tells its own* ~ es spricht für sich selbst; **~-bearer** ['teilbɛərə] Zuträger(in).

talent ['tælənt] Talent *n*, Begabung *f*, Anlage *f*; **~ed** [~tid] talentvoll, begabt.

talk [tɔ:k] **1.** Gespräch *n*; Unterredung *f*; Plauderei *f*; Vortrag *m*; Geschwätz *n*; **2.** sprechen, reden (*von et.*); plaudern; **~ative** □ ['tɔ:kətiv] gesprächig, geschwätzig; **~er** ['tɔ:kə] Schwätzer(in); Sprechende(r *m*) *f*.

tall [tɔ:l] groß, lang, hoch; F übertrieben, unglaublich; *that's a* ~ *order* F das ist ein bißchen viel verlangt.

tallow ['tælou] ausgelassener Talg.

tally ['tæli] **1.** Kerbholz *n*; Gegenstück *n* (*of zu*); Kennzeichen *n*; **2.** übereinstimmen.

talon *orn.* ['tælən] Kralle *f*, Klaue *f*.

tame [teim] **1.** □ zahm; folgsam; harmlos; lahm, fad(e); **2.** (be)zähmen, bändigen.

Tammany *Am.* ['tæməni] New Yorker Demokraten-Vereinigung.

tamper ['tæmpə]: ~ *with* sich (unbefugt) zu schaffen machen mit;

j-n zu bestechen suchen; *Urkunde* fälschen.

tan [tæn] **1.** Lohe *f*; Lohfarbe *f*; (Sonnen)Bräune *f*; **2.** lohfarben; **3.** gerben; bräunen.

tang [tæŋ] Beigeschmack *m*; *scharfer* Klang; & Seetang *m*.

tangent ['tændʒənt] ᴀ Tangente *f*; *fly od.* go off *at a ~* vom Gegenstand abspringen.

tangerine & [tændʒəˈriːn] Mandarine *f*.

tangible □ ['tændʒəbl] fühlbar, greifbar (*a. fig.*); klar.

tangle ['tæŋgl] **1.** Gewirr *n*; Verwicklung *f*; **2.** (sich) verwirren, verwickeln.

tank [tæŋk] **1.** Zisterne *f*, Wasserbehälter *m*; ⊕, ✕ Tank *m*; **2.** tanken. [(Bier)Krug *m.*\]

tankard ['tæŋkəd] Kanne *f*, *bsd.*)

tanner ['tænə] Gerber *m*; ~y [~əri] Gerberei *f*.

tantalize ['tæntəlaiz] quälen.

tantamount ['tæntəmaunt] gleichbedeutend (mit).

tantrum F ['tæntrəm] Koller *m*.

tap [tæp] **1.** leichtes Klopfen; (Wasser-, Gas-, Zapf)Hahn *m*; Zapfen *m*; Schankstube *f*; F Sorte *f*; ~s *pl. Am.* ✕ Zapfenstreich *m*; **2.** pochen, klopfen, tippen (*auf, an, gegen acc.*); an-, abzapfen; ~**dance** ['tæpdɑːns] Stepptanz *m*.

tape [teip] schmales Band; *Sport*: Zielband *n*; *tel.* Papierstreifen *m*; Tonband *n*; *red ~* Bürokratismus *m*; ~**measure** ['teipmeʒə] Bandmaß *n*.

taper ['teipə] **1.** dünne Wachskerze; **2.** *adj.* spitz (zulaufend); schlank; **3.** *v/i.* spitz zulaufen; *v/t.* zuspitzen.

tape| **recorder** ['teiprikɔːdə] Tonbandgerät *n*; ~ **recording** Tonbandaufnahme *f*.

tapestry ['tæpistri] Gobelin *m*.

tapeworm ['teipwəːm] Bandwurm *m*.

tap-room ['tæprum] Schankstube *f*.

tar [tɑː] **1.** Teer *m*; **2.** teeren.

tardy □ ['tɑːdi] langsam; spät.

tare † [tɛə] Tara *f*.

target ['tɑːgit] (Schieß)Scheibe *f*; *fig.* Ziel(scheibe *f*) *n*; Ziel(leistung *f*) *n*; Soll *n*; ~ *practice* Scheibenschießen *n*.

tariff ['tærif] (*bsd.* Zoll)Tarif *m*.

tarnish ['tɑːniʃ] **1.** *v/t.* ⊕ trüb *od.* blind machen; *fig.* trüben; *v/i.* trüb werden, anlaufen; **2.** Trübung *f*; Belag *m*.

tarry[1] *lit.* ['tæri] säumen, zögern; verweilen.

tarry[2] ['tɑːri] teerig.

tart [tɑːt] **1.** □ sauer, herb; *fig.* scharf, schroff; **2.** (Obst)Torte *f*; *sl.* Dirne *f*.

tartan ['tɑːtən] Tartan *m*; Schottentuch *n*; Schottenmuster *n*.

task [tɑːsk] **1.** Aufgabe *f*; Arbeit *f*; *take to ~* zur Rede stellen; **2.** beschäftigen; in Anspruch nehmen.

tassel ['tæsəl] Troddel *f*, Quaste *f*.

taste [teist] **1.** Geschmack *m*; (Kost)Probe *f*; Lust *f* (*for* zu); **2.** kosten, schmecken; versuchen; genießen; ~**ful** □ ['teistful] geschmackvoll; ~**less** □ [~tlis] geschmacklos.

tasty □ F ['teisti] schmackhaft.

ta-ta ['tæˈtɑː] *auf* Wiedersehen!

tatter ['tætə] **1.** zerfetzen; **2.** ~*s pl.* Fetzen *m/pl.*

tattle ['tætl] **1.** schwatzen; tratschen; **2.** Geschwätz *n*; Tratsch *m*.

tattoo [təˈtuː] **1.** ✕ Zapfenstreich *m*; Tätowierung *f*; *fig.* trommeln; tätowieren.

taught [tɔːt] *pret. u. p.p. von* teach.

taunt [tɔːnt] **1.** Stichelei *f*, Spott *m*; **2.** verhöhnen, verspotten.

taut ⚓ [tɔːt] steif, straff; schmuck.

tavern ['tævən] Schenke *f*.

tawdry □ ['tɔːdri] billig; kitschig.

tawny ['tɔːni] lohfarben.

tax [tæks] **1.** Steuer *f*, Abgabe *f*; *fig.* Inanspruchnahme *f* (*on, upon gen.*); **2.** besteuern; *fig.* stark in Anspruch nehmen; ⅌ *Kosten* schätzen; auf e-e harte Probe stellen; *j-n* zur Rede stellen; ~ *s.o.* *with s.th.* j-n e-r S. beschuldigen; ~**ation** [tækˈseiʃən] Besteuerung *f*; Steuer(n *pl.*) *f*; *bsd.* ⅌ Schätzung *f*.

taxi F ['tæksi] **1.** = ~*cab*; **2.** mit e-m Taxi fahren; ✈ rollen; ~**cab** Taxi *n*, (Auto)Droschke *f*.

taxpayer ['tækspeiə] Steuerzahler *m*.

tea [tiː] Tee *m*; *high ~*, *meat ~* frühes Abendbrot mit Tee.

teach [tiːtʃ] [*irr.*] lehren, unterrichten, *j-m et.* beibringen; ~**able** □ ['tiːtʃəbl] gelehrig; lehrbar; ~**er** [~tʃə] Lehrer(in); ~**in** [~ʃˈin] (politische) Diskussion *als Großveranstaltung.*

tea|**-cosy** ['tiːkouzi] Teewärmer *m*; ~**cup** Teetasse *f*; *storm in a ~ fig.* Sturm *m* im Wasserglas; ~**-kettle** Wasserkessel *m*.

team [tiːm] Team *n*, Arbeitsgruppe *f*; Gespann *n*; *bsd. Sport*: Mannschaft *f*; ~**ster** ['tiːmstə] Gespannführer *m*; *Am.* LKW-Fahrer *m*; ~**work** Zusammenarbeit *f*, Teamwork *n*; Zusammenspiel *n*.

teapot ['tiːpɔt] Teekanne *f*.

tear[1] [tɛə] **1.** [*irr.*] zerren, (zer)reißen; rasen, stürmen; **2.** Riß *m*.

tear[2] [tiə] Träne *f*.

tearful □ ['tiəful] tränenreich.

tea-room ['tiːrum] Tearoom *m*. Teestube *f*, Café *n*.

tease [tiːz] **1.** necken, hänseln; quälen; **2.** Necker *m*; Quälgeist *m*.

teat [tiːt] Zitze *f*; Brustwarze *f*; (Gummi)Sauger *m*.

technic|al □ ['teknikəl] technisch; gewerblich, Gewerbe...; fachlich, Fach...; **~ality** [tekni'kæliti] technische Eigentümlichkeit *od.* Einzelheit; Fachausdruck *m*; **~ian** [tek-'niʃən] Techniker(in).

technique [tek'ni:k] Technik *f*, Verfahren *n*.

technology [tek'nɔlədʒi] Gewerbekunde *f*; *school of ~* Technische Hochschule.

teddy boy F ['tediboi] Halbstarke(r) *m*.

tedious □ ['ti:djəs] langweilig, ermüdend; weitschweifig.

tee [ti:] *Sport:* Mal *n*, Ziel *n*; *Golf:* Abschlagmal *n*.

teem [ti:m] wimmeln, strotzen (*with* von).

teens [ti:nz] *pl.* Lebensjahre *n/pl.* von 13—19.

teeny F ['ti:ni] winzig.

teeth [ti:θ] *pl. von* tooth; **~e** [ti:ð] zahnen.

teetotal(l)er [ti:'toutlə] Abstinenzler(in).

telecast ['telika:st] **1.** Fernsehsendung *f*; **2.** (*irr.* (*cast*)) im Fernsehen übertragen.

telecourse *Am.* F ['telikɔ:s] Fernsehlehrgang *m*.

telegram ['teligræm] Telegramm *n*.

telegraph ['teligra:f] **1.** Telegraph *m*; **2.** Telegraphen...; **3.** telegraphieren; **~ic** [teli'græfik] (**~ally**) telegraphisch; telegrammäßig (*Stil*); **~y** [ti'legrəfi] Telegraphie *f*.

telephon|e ['telifoun] **1.** Telephon *n*, Fernsprecher *m*; **2.** telephonieren; anrufen; **~e booth** Telephonzelle *f*; **~ic** [teli'fɔnik] (**~ally**) telephonisch; **~y** [ti'lefəni] Fernsprechwesen *n*.

telephoto *phot.* ['teli'foutou] *a. ~ lens* Teleobjektiv *n*.

teleprinter ['teliprintə] Fernschreiber *m*.

telescope ['teliskoup] **1.** *opt.* Fernrohr *n*; **2.** (sich) ineinanderschieben.

teletype ['telitaip] Fernschreiber *m*.

televis|e ['telivaiz] im Fernsehen übertragen; **~ion** [~viʒən] Fernsehen *n*; *watch ~* fernsehen; **~ion set**, **~or** [~vaizə] Fernsehapparat *m*.

tell [tel] (*irr.*) *v/t.* zählen; sagen, erzählen; erkennen; **~** *s.o. to do s.th.* j-m sagen, er solle et. tun; **~** *off* abzählen; auswählen; F abkanzeln; *v/i.* erzählen (*of*, *about* von); (aus)plaudern; sich auswirken; sitzen (*Hieb etc.*); **~er** ['telə] (Er)Zähler *m*; **~ing** □ ['teliŋ] wirkungsvoll; **~tale** ['telteil] **1.** Klatschbase *f*; ⊕ Anzeiger *m*; **2.** *fig.* verräterisch.

temerity [ti'meriti] Unbesonnenheit *f*, Verwegenheit *f*.

temper ['tempə] **1.** mäßigen, mildern; *Kalk etc.* anrühren; *Stahl* anlassen; **2.** ⊕ Härte(grad *m*) *f*;

(Gemüts)Ruhe *f*, Gleichmut *m*; Temperament *n*, Wesen *n*; Stimmung *f*; Wut *f*; *lose one's ~* in Wut geraten; **~ament** [~rəmənt] Temperament *n*; **~amental** □ [temprə'mentl] anlagebedingt; launisch; **~ance** ['tempərəns] Mäßigkeit *f*; Enthaltsamkeit *f*; **~ate** □ [~rit] gemäßigt; zurückhaltend; maßvoll; mäßig; **~ature** [~pritʃə] Temperatur *f*.

tempest ['tempist] Sturm *m*; Gewitter *n*; **~uous** □ [tem'pestjəs] stürmisch; ungestüm.

temple ['templ] Tempel *m*; *anat.* Schläfe *f*.

tempor|al □ ['tempərəl] zeitlich; weltlich; **~ary** □ [~əri] zeitweilig; vorläufig; vorübergehend; Not..., (Aus)Hilfs..., Behelfs...; **~ize** [~raiz] Zeit zu gewinnen suchen.

tempt [tempt] *j-n* versuchen; verleiten; verlocken; **~ation** [temp'teiʃən] Versuchung *f*; Reiz *m*; **~ing** □ ['temptiŋ] verführerisch.

ten [ten] **1.** zehn; **2.** Zehn *f*.

tenable ['tenəbl] haltbar (*Theorie etc.*); verliehen (*Amt*).

tenaci|ous □ [ti'neiʃəs] zäh; festhaltend (*of an dat.*); gut (*Gedächtnis*); **~ty** [ti'næsiti] Zähigkeit *f*; Festhalten *n*; Verläßlichkeit *f des Gedächtnisses*.

tenant ['tenənt] Pächter *m*; Mieter *m*.

tend [tend] *v/i.* (*to*) gerichtet sein (auf *acc.*); hinstreben (zu); abzielen (auf *acc.*); neigen (zu); *v/t.* pflegen; hüten; ⊕ bedienen; **~ance** ['tendəns] Pflege *f*; Bedienung *f*; **~ency** [~si] Richtung *f*; Neigung *f*; Zweck *m*.

tender ['tendə] **1.** □ zart; weich; empfindlich; heikel (*Thema*); zärtlich; **2.** Angebot *n*; Kostenanschlag *m*; 🚂, ⚓ Tender *m*; *legal ~* gesetzliches Zahlungsmittel; **3.** anbieten; *Entlassung* einreichen; **~foot** *Am.* F Neuling *m*, Anfänger *m*; **~loin** *bsd. Am.* Filet *n*; *Am.* berüchtigtes Viertel; **~ness** [~nis] Zartheit *f*; Zärtlichkeit *f*.

tendon *anat.* ['tendən] Sehne *f*.

tendril ♀ ['tendril] Ranke *f*.

tenement ['tenimənt] Wohnhaus *n*; (*bsd.* Miet)Wohnung *f*; *~ house* Mietshaus *n*.

tennis ['tenis] Tennis(spiel) *n*; **~court** Tennisplatz *m*.

tenor ['tenə] Fortgang *m*, Verlauf *m*; Inhalt *m*; ♪ Tenor *m*.

tens|e [tens] **1.** *gr.* Zeit(form) *f*, Tempus *n*; **2.** □ gespannt (*a. fig.*); straff; **~ion** ['tenʃən] Spannung *f*.

tent [tent] **1.** Zelt *n*; **2.** zelten.

tentacle *zo.* ['tentəkl] Fühler *m*; Fangarm *m e-s Polypen*.

tentative □ ['tentətiv] versuchend; Versuchs...; **~ly** versuchsweise.

tenth [tenθ] 1. zehnte(r, -s);
2. Zehntel n; ~ly ['tenθli] zehntens.

tenuous □ ['tenjuəs] dünn; zart,
fein; dürftig.

tenure ['tenjuə] Besitz(art f, -dauer
f) m.

tepid □ ['tepid] lau(warm).

term [təːm] 1. (bestimmte) Zeit,
Frist f, Termin m; Zahltag m;
Amtszeit f; ⚖ Sitzungsperiode f;
Semester n, Quartal n, Trimester n,
Tertial n; Åᵣ, phls. Glied n; (Fach-)
Ausdruck m, Wort n, Bezeichnung
f; Begriff m; ~s pl. Bedingungen
f/pl.; Beziehungen f/pl.; be on good
(bad) ~s with gut (schlecht) stehen
mit; come to ~s, make ~s sich einigen; 2. (be)nennen; bezeichnen
(als).

termagant ['təːməgənt] 1. □ zank-
süchtig; 2. Zankteufel m (Weib).

termina|l ['təːminl] 1. □ End...;
letzt; ~ly terminweise; 2. Endstück
n; ⚡ Pol m; Am. 🚌 Endstation f;
~te [~neit] begrenzen; (be)endigen;
~tion [təːmi'neiʃən] Beendigung f;
Ende n; gr. Endung f.

terminus ['təːminəs] Endstation f.

terrace ['terəs] Terrasse f; Häuser-
reihe f; ~-house Reihenhaus n; ~d
[~st] terrassenförmig.

terrestrial □ [ti'restriəl] irdisch;
Erd...; bsd. zo., ⚘ Land...

terrible □ ['terəbl] schrecklich.

terri|fic [tə'rifik] (~ally) fürchter-
lich, schrecklich; F ungeheuer,
großartig; ~fy ['terifai] v/t. erschrecken.

territor|ial [teri'tɔːriəl] 1. □ terri-
torial; Land...; Bezirks...; ⚔ Army,
⚔ Force Territorialarmee f; ⚔ 💂
Angehörige(r) m der Territorialarmee; ~y ['teritəri] Territorium
n, (Hoheits-, Staats)Gebiet n.

terror ['terə] Schrecken m, Entsetzen n; ~ize [~əraiz] terrorisieren.

terse □ [təːs] knapp; kurz u.
bündig.

test [test] 1. Probe f; Untersuchung
f; (Eignungs)Prüfung f; Test m;
🧪 Reagens n; 2. probieren, prüfen,
testen.

testament ['testəmənt] Testament
n.

testicle anat. ['testikl] Hode(n m)
[m, f.

testify ['testifai] (be)zeugen; (als
Zeuge) aussagen (on über acc.).

testimon|ial [testi'mounjəl] (Füh-
rungs)Zeugnis n; Zeichen n der An-
erkennung; ~y ['testiməni] Zeugnis
n; Beweis m.

test-tube 🧪 ['testtjuːb] Reagenz-
glas n.

testy □ ['testi] reizbar, kribbelig.

tether ['teðə] 1. Haltestrick m; fig.
Spielraum m; at the end of one's ~
fig. am Ende s-r Kraft; 2. anbinden.

text [tekst] Text m; Bibelstelle f;

~book ['tekstbuk] Leitfaden m,
Lehrbuch n.

textile ['tekstail] 1. Textil..., Web...;
2. ~s pl. Webwaren f/pl., Textilien
pl.

texture ['tekstʃə] Gewebe n; Gefüge n.

than [ðæn, ðən] als.

thank [θæŋk] 1. danken (dat.); ~
you, bei Ablehnung no, ~ you danke;
2. ~s pl. Dank m; ~s! vielen Dank!;
danke (schön)!; ~s to dank (dat.);
~ful □ ['θæŋkful] dankbar; ~less
□ [~klis] undankbar; ~sgiving
[~ksgiviŋ] Danksagung f; Dankfest
n; ♀ (Day) bsd. Am. (Ernte)Dank-
fest n.

that [ðæt, ðət] 1. pl. those [ðouz]
pron. jene(r, -s); der, die, das; der-
die-, das(jenige); welche(r, -s); 2.
cj. daß; damit.

thatch [θætʃ] 1. Dachstroh n;
Strohdach n; 2. mit Stroh decken.

thaw [θɔː] 1. Tauwetter n; (Auf-)
Tauen n; 2. (auf)tauen.

the [ði:; vor Vokalen ði; vor Konsonanten ðə] 1. art. der, die, das; 2.
adv. desto, um so; ~ ... ~ ... je ...
desto ...

theat|re, Am. ~er ['θiətə] Theater
n; fig. (Kriegs)Schauplatz m;
~ric(al □) [θi'ætrik(əl)] Theater...;
theatralisch.

thee Bibel, poet. [ði:] dich; dir.

theft [θeft] Diebstahl m.

their [ðeə] ihr(e); ~s [~z] der (die,
das) ihrige od. ihre.

them [ðem, ðəm] sie (acc. pl.);
ihnen.

theme [θiːm] Thema n; Aufgabe f.

themselves [ðem'selvz] sie (acc. pl.)
selbst; sich selbst.

then [ðen] 1. adv. dann; damals;
da; by ~ bis dahin; inzwischen;
every now and ~ alle Augenblicke;
there and ~ sogleich; now ~ nun
denn; 2. cj. denn, also, folglich;
3. adj. damalig.

thence lit. [ðens] daher; von da.

theolog|ian [θiə'loudʒən] Theologe
m; ~y [θi'ɔlədʒi] Theologie f.

theor|etic(al □) [θiə'retik(əl)] theo-
retisch; ~ist ['θiərist] Theoretiker
m; ~y [~ri] Theorie f.

therap|eutic [θerə'pjuːtik] 1. (~ally)
therapeutisch; 2. ~s mst. sg. Thera-
peutik f; ~y ['θerəpi] Therapie f,
Heilbehandlung f.

there [ðeə] da, dort; darin; dort-
hin; na!; ~ is, ~ are es gibt, es ist,
es sind; ~about(s) ['ðeərəbaut(s)]
da herum; so ungefähr ...; ~after
[θeər'aːftə] danach; ~by ['ðeəbai]
dadurch, damit; ~fore ['ðeəfɔː]
darum, deswegen; deshalb, daher;
~upon ['ðeərə'pɔn] darauf(hin);
~with [ðeə'wiθ] damit.

thermal ['θəːməl] 1. □ Thermal...;
phys. Wärme...; 2. Aufwind m.

thermo|meter [θə'mɔmitə] Thermometer *n*; 2s [θə:məs] *a.* ~ flask, ~ bottle Thermosflasche *f*.

these [ði:z] *pl. von* this.

thes|is ['θi:sis], *pl.* ~es ['θi:si:z] These *f*; Dissertation *f*.

they [ðei] sie (*pl.*).

thick [θik] 1. □ *allg.* dick; dicht; trüb; legiert (*Suppe*); heiser; dumm; *pred.* F dick befreundet; ~ with dicht besetzt mit; 2. dickster Teil; *fig.* Brennpunkt *m*; *in the* ~ *of* mitten in (*dat.*); ~en ['θikən] (sich) verdicken; (sich) verstärken; legieren; (sich) verdichten; ~et ['θikit] Dickicht *n*; ~-headed dumm; ~ness ['θiknis] Dicke *f*, Stärke *f*; Dichte *f*; ~-set dicht (gepflanzt); untersetzt; ~-skinned *fig.* dickfellig.

thief [θi:f], *pl.* thieves [θi:vz] Dieb(in); thieve [θi:v] stehlen.

thigh [θai] (Ober)Schenkel *m*.

thimble ['θimbl] Fingerhut *m*.

thin [θin] 1. □ *allg.* dünn; leicht; mager; spärlich, dürftig; schwach; fadenscheinig (*bsd. fig.*); 2. verdünnen; (sich) lichten; abnehmen.

thine *Bibel, poet.* [ðain] dein; der (die, das) deinige *od.* deine.

thing [θiŋ] Ding *n*; Sache *f*; Geschöpf *n*; ~s *pl.* Sachen *f/pl.*; die Dinge *n/pl.* (*Umstände*); the ~ F das Richtige; richtig; die Hauptsache; ~s are going better es geht jetzt besser.

think [θiŋk] [*irr.*] *v/i.* denken (*of* an *acc.*); nachdenken; sich besinnen; meinen, glauben; gedenken (*to inf.* zu *inf.*); *v/t.* (sich) et. denken; halten für; ~ much etc. of viel etc. halten von; ~ s.th. over (sich) et. überlegen, über et. nachdenken.

third [θə:d] 1. dritte(r, -s); 2. Drittel *n*; ~ly ['θə:dli] drittens; ~-rate ['θə:d'reit] drittklassig.

thirst [θə:st] 1. Durst *m*; 2. dürsten; ~y □ ['θə:sti] durstig; dürr (*Boden*).

thirt|een ['θə:'ti:n] dreizehn; ~eenth [~nθ] dreizehnte(r, -s); ~ieth ['θə:tiiθ] dreißigste(r, -s); ~y ['θə:ti] dreißig.

this [ðis], *pl.* these [ði:z] diese(r, -s); ~ morning heute morgen.

thistle ♀ ['θisl] Distel *f*.

thong [θɔŋ] (Leder-, Peitschen-) Riemen *m*.

thorn [θɔ:n] Dorn *m*; ~y ['θɔ:ni] dornig, stach(e)lig; beschwerlich.

thorough □ ['θʌrə] vollkommen; vollständig; vollendet; gründlich; ~ly *a.* durchaus; ~bred Vollblüter *m*; *attr.* Vollblut...; ~fare Durchgang *m*, Durchfahrt *f*; Hauptverkehrsstraße *f*; ~going gründlich; tatkräftig.

those [ðouz] *pl. von* that 1.

thou *Bibel, poet.* [ðau] du.

though [ðou] obgleich, obwohl, wenn auch; zwar; aber, doch; freilich; *as* ~ als ob.

thought [θɔ:t] 1. *pret. u. p.p. von* think; 2. Gedanke *m*; (Nach)Denken *n*; *on second* ~s nach nochmaliger Überlegung; ~ful □ ['θɔ:tful] gedankenvoll, nachdenklich; rücksichtsvoll (*of* gegen); ~less □ ['θɔ:tlis] gedankenlos; unbesonnen; rücksichtslos (*of* gegen).

thousand ['θauzənd] 1. tausend; 2. Tausend *n*; ~th [~ntθ] 1. tausendste(r, -s); 2. Tausendstel *n*.

thrash [θræʃ] (ver)dreschen, (ver-) prügeln; (hin und her) schlagen; *s. thresh*; ~ing ['θræʃiŋ] Dresche *f*, Tracht *f* Prügel; *s. threshing*.

thread [θred] 1. Faden *m* (*a. fig.*); Zwirn *m*, Garn *n*; ⊕ (Schrauben-) Gewinde *n*; 2. einfädeln; sich durchwinden (durch); durchziehen; ~bare ['θredbɛə] fadenscheinig.

threat [θret] Drohung *f*; ~en ['θretn] (be-, an)drohen; ~ening [~niŋ] bedrohlich.

three [θri:] 1. drei; 2. Drei *f*; ~fold ['θri:fould] dreifach; ~pence ['θrepəns] Dreipence(stück *n*) *m/pl.*; ~score ['θri:'skɔ:] sechzig.

thresh [θreʃ] ✗ (aus)dreschen; *s. thrash*; ~ out *fig.* durchdreschen; ~er ['θreʃə] Drescher *m*; Dreschmaschine *f*; ~ing [~ʃiŋ] Dreschen *n*; ~ing-machine Dreschmaschine *f*.

threshold ['θreʃhould] Schwelle *f*.

threw [θru:] *pret. von* throw 1.

thrice [θrais] dreimal.

thrift [θrift] Sparsamkeit *f*, Wirtschaftlichkeit *f*; ~less □ ['θriftlis] verschwenderisch; ~y □ [~ti] sparsam; *poet.* gedeihend.

thrill [θril] 1. *v/t.* durchdringen, durchschauern; *fig.* packen, aufwühlen; aufregen; *v/i.* (er)beben; 2. Schauer *m*; Beben *n*; aufregendes Erlebnis; Sensation *f*; ~er F ['θrilə] Reißer *m*, Thriller *m*, Schauerroman *m*, Schauerstück *n*; ~ing [~liŋ] spannend.

thrive [θraiv] [*irr.*] gedeihen; *fig.* blühen; Glück haben; ~n ['θrivn] *p.p. von* thrive.

throat [θrout] Kehle *f*; Hals *m*; Gurgel *f*; Schlund *m*; *clear one's* ~ sich räuspern.

throb [θrɔb] 1. pochen, klopfen, schlagen; pulsieren; 2. Pochen *n*; Schlagen *n*; Pulsschlag *m*.

throes [θrouz] *pl.* Geburtswehen *f/pl.* [Thrombose *f*.]

thrombosis ❀ [θrɔm'bousis]

throne [θroun] Thron *m*.

throng [θrɔŋ] 1. Gedränge *n*; Menge *f*, Schar *f*; 2. sich drängen (in *dat.*); anfüllen mit.

throstle *orn.* ['θrɔsl] Drossel *f*.

throttle ['θrɔtl] 1. erdrosseln; ⊕ (ab)drosseln; 2. ⊕ Drosselklappe *f*.

through [θruː] 1. durch; 2. Durch-gangs...; durchgehend; ~out [θru(ː)'aut] 1. *prp.* überall in (*dat.*); 2. *adv.* durch u. durch, ganz und gar, durchweg.

throve [θrouv] *pret. von* thrive.

throw [θrou] 1. [*irr.*] (ab)werfen, schleudern; *Am.* F *Wettkampf etc.* betrügerisch verlieren; würfeln; ⊕ schalten; ~ *off* (die Jagd) beginnen; ~ *over* aufgeben; ~ *up* in die Höhe werfen; erbrechen; *fig.* hinwerfen; 2. Wurf *m*; ~**n** [θroun] *p.p. von* throw 1.

thru *Am.* [θruː] = through.

thrum [θrʌm] klimpern (auf *dat.*).

thrush *orn.* [θrʌʃ] Drossel *f.*

thrust [θrʌst] 1. Stoß *m*; Vorstoß *m*; ⊕ Druck *m*, Schub *m*; 2. [*irr.*] stoßen; ~ *o.s. into* sich drängen in (*acc.*); ~ *upon s.o.* j-m aufdrängen.

thud [θʌd] 1. dumpf aufschlagen, F bumsen; 2. dumpfer (Auf)Schlag, F Bums *m.*

thug [θʌg] Strolch *m.*

thumb [θʌm] 1. Daumen *m*; Tom ♀ Däumling *m im Märchen*; 2. *Buch etc.* abgreifen; ~ *a lift* per Anhalter fahren; ~**tack** *Am.* ['θʌmtæk] Reißzwecke *f.*

thump [θʌmp] 1. F Bums *m*; F Puff *m*; 2. *v/t.* F bumsen *od.* pochen auf (*acc.*) *od.* gegen; F knuffen, puffen; *v/i.* F (auf)bumsen.

thunder ['θʌndə] 1. Donner *m*; 2. donnern; ~**bolt** Blitz *m* (u. Donner *m*); ~**clap** Donnerschlag *m*; ~**ous** □ [.ərəs] donnernd; ~**storm** Gewitter *n*; ~**struck** wie vom Donner gerührt.

Thursday ['θəːzdi] Donnerstag *m.*

thus [ðʌs] so; also, somit.

thwart [θwɔːt] 1. durchkreuzen; hintertreiben; 2. Ruderbank *f.*

thy *Bibel, poet.* [ðai] dein(e).

tick[1] *zo.* [tik] Zecke *f.*

tick[2] [.] 1. Ticken *n* (Vermerk-) Häkchen *n*; 2. *v/i.* ticken; *v/t.* an-haken; ~ *off* abhaken.

tick[3] [.] Inlett *n*; Matratzenbezug *m.*

ticket ['tikit] 1. Fahrkarte *f*, ~schein *m*; Flugkarte *f*; Eintrittskarte *f*; (Straf)Zettel *m*; (Preis- *etc.*)Schild-chen *n*; *pol.* (Wahl-, Kandidaten-) Liste *f*; 2. etikettieren, *Ware* aus-zeichnen; ~**machine** Fahrkarten-automat *m*; ~ *office*, ~ *window bsd. Am.* Fahrkartenschalter *m.*

tickl|e ['tikl] kitzeln (*a. fig.*); ~**ish** □ [.liʃ] kitzlig; heikel.

tidal [*taidl*] *fig.* Strom *m*: ~ *wave* Flutwelle *f.*

tide [taid] 1. Gezeit(en *pl.*) *f*; Ebbe *f* und Flut *f*; *fig.* Strom *m*, Flut *f*; *in Zssgn: rechte* Zeit; *high* ~ Flut *f*; *low* ~ Ebbe *f*; 2. ~ *over fig.* hinweg-kommen *od. j-m* hinweghelfen über (*acc.*).

tidings ['taidiŋz] *pl. od. sg.* Neuig-keiten *f/pl.*, Nachrichten *f/pl.*

tidy ['taidi] 1. ordentlich, sauber, reinlich; F ganz schön, beträchtlich (*Summe*); 2. Behälter *m*; Abfallkorb *m*; 3. *a.* ~ *up* zurechtmachen; ord-nen; aufräumen.

tie [tai] 1. Band *n* (*a. fig.*); Schleife *f*; Krawatte *f*, Schlips *m*; Bindung *f*; *fig.* Fessel *f*, Verpflichtung *f*; *Sport*: Punkt-, *parl.* Stimmengleichheit *f*; *Sport*: Entscheidungsspiel *n*; ☒ *Am.* Schwelle *f*; 2. *v/t.* (ver)binden; ~ *down fig.* binden (to an *acc.*); ~ *up* zu-, an-, ver-, zs.-binden; *v/i. Sport*: punktgleich sein.

tier [tiə] Reihe *f*; Rang *m.*

tie-up ['taiʌp] (Ver)Bindung *f*; ⯗ Fusion *f*; Stockung *f*; *bsd. Am.* Streik *m.*

tiffin ['tifin] Mittagessen *n.*

tiger ['taigə] *zo.* Tiger *m*; *Am.* F Beifallsgebrüll *n.*

tight [tait] 1. □ dicht; fest; eng; knapp (sitzend); straff, prall; knapp; F beschwipst; *be in a* ~ *place od. corner* F in der Klemme sein; 2. *adv.* fest; *hold* ~ festhalten; ~**en** ['taitn] *a.* ~ *up* (sich) zs.-ziehen; *Gürtel* enger schnallen; ~**fisted** knick(e)rig; ~**ness** ['taitnis] Festig-keit *f*, Dichtigkeit *f*; Straffheit *f*; Knappheit *f*; Enge *f*; Geiz *m*; ~**s** [taits] *pl.* Trikot *n.*

tigress ['taigris] Tigerin *f.*

tile [tail] 1. (Dach)Ziegel *m*; Kachel *f*; Fliese *f*; 2. mit Ziegeln *etc.* decken; kacheln; fliesen.

till[1] [til] Laden(tisch)kasse *f.*

till[2] [.] 1. *prp.* bis (zu); 2. *cj.* bis.

till[3] ✍ [.] bestellen, bebauen; ~**age** ['tilidʒ] (Land)Bestellung *f*; Acker-bau *m*; Ackerland *n.*

tilt [tilt] 1. Plane *f*; Neigung *f*, Kippe *f*; Stoß *m*; Lanzenbrechen *n* (*a. fig.*); 2. kippen; ~ *against* an-rennen gegen.

timber ['timbə] 1. (Bau-, Nutz-) Holz *n*; Balken *m*; Baumbestand *m*, Bäume *m/pl.*; 2. zimmern.

time [taim] 1. Zeit *f*; Mal *n*; Takt *m*; Tempo *n*; ~ *and again* immer wieder; *at a* ~ zugleich; *for the* ~ *being* einstweilen; *have a good* ~ es gut haben; sich amüsieren; *in* ~, *on* ~ zur rechten Zeit, recht-zeitig; 2. zeitlich festsetzen; zeit-lich abpassen; die Zeitdauer mes-sen; ~**hono(u)red** ['taimɒnəd] alt-ehrwürdig; ~**ly** ['taimli] (recht)zei-tig; ~**piece** Uhr *f*; ~**sheet** An-wesenheitsliste *f*; ~**table** Termin-kalender *m*; Fahr-, Stundenplan *m.*

tim|id □ ['timid], ~**orous** □ ['ti-mərəs] furchtsam; schüchtern.

tin [tin] 1. Zinn *n*; Weißblech *n*; (Konserven)Büchse *f*; 2. verzinnen; in Büchsen einmachen, eindosen.

tincture ['tiŋktʃə] 1. Farbe *f*; Tink-tur *f*; *fig.* Anstrich *m*; 2. färben.

tinfoil ['tin'fɔil] Stanniol *n.*

tinge [tindʒ] 1. Färbung f; fig. Anflug m, Spur f; 2. färben; fig. e-n Anstrich geben (dat.).

tingle ['tiŋgl] klingen; prickeln.

tinker ['tiŋkə] basteln (at an dat.).

tinkle ['tiŋkl] klingeln (mit).

tin|-opener ['tinoupnə] Dosenöffner m; ~plate Weißblech n.

tinsel ['tinsəl] Flitter(werk n) m; Lametta n.

tin-smith ['tinsmiθ] Klempner m.

tint [tint] 1. Farbe f; fig. Schattierung f; 2. färben; (ab-)tönen.

tiny ['taini] winzig, klein.

tip [tip] 1. Spitze f; Mundstück n; Trinkgeld n; Tip m, Wink m; leichter Stoß m; Schuttabladeplatz m; 2. mit e-r Spitze versehen; (um-)kippen; j-m ein Trinkgeld geben; a. ~ off j-m ein Wink geben.

tipple ['tipl] zechen, picheln.

tipsy ['tipsi] angeheitert.

tiptoe ['tiptou] 1. auf Zehenspitzen gehen; 2. on ~ auf Zehenspitzen.

tire¹ ['taiə] (Rad-, Auto)Reifen m.

tire² [~] ermüden, müde machen od. werden; ~d □ müde; ~less □ ['taiəlis] unermüdlich; ~some □ ['taiəsəm] ermüdend; lästig.

tiro ['taiərou] Anfänger m.

tissue ['tisju:, Am. 'tiʃu:] Gewebe n; ~paper Seidenpapier n.

tit¹ [tit] = teat.

tit² orn. [~] Meise f.

titbit ['titbit] Leckerbissen m.

titillate ['titileit] kitzeln.

title ['taitl] 1. (Buch-, Ehren)Titel m; Überschrift f; fig. Anspruch m; 2. betiteln; ~d bsd. ad(e)lig.

titmouse orn. ['titmaus] Meise f.

titter ['titə] 1. kichern; 2. Kichern n.

tittle ['titl] Pünktchen n; fig. Tütelchen n; ~tattle [~ˌtætl] Schnickschnack m.

to [tu:, tu, tə] prp. zu (a. adv.); gegen, nach, an, in, auf; bis zu, bis an (acc.); um zu; für; ~ me etc. mir etc.; I weep ~ think of it ich weine, wenn ich daran denke; here's ~ you! auf Ihr Wohl!, Prosit!

toad zo. [toud] Kröte f; ~stool ['toudstu:l] (größerer Blätter)Pilz; Giftpilz m; ~y ['toudi] 1. Speichellecker m; 2. fig. vor j-m kriechen.

toast [toust] 1. Toast m, geröstetes Brot; Trinkspruch m; 2. toasten, rösten; fig. wärmen; trinken auf (acc.).

tobacco [tə'bækou] Tabak m; ~nist [~kənist] Tabakhändler m.

toboggan [tə'bɔgən] 1. Toboggan m; Rodelschlitten m; 2. rodeln.

today [tə'dei] heute.   [teln.⟩

toddle ['tɔdl] unsicher gehen; zot-⟩

toddy ['tɔdi] Art Grog m.

to-do F [tə'du:] Lärm m, Aufheben n.

toe [tou] 1. Zehe f; Spitze f; 2. mit den Zehen berühren.

toff|ee, ~y ['tɔfi] Sahnebonbon m, n, Toffee m.

together [tə'geðə] zusammen; zugleich; nacheinander.

toil [tɔil] 1. schwere Arbeit; Mühe f, F Plackerei f; 2. sich plagen.

toilet ['tɔilit] Toilette f; ~paper Toilettenpapier n; ~table Frisiertoilette f.   [n.⟩

toils [tɔilz] pl. Schlingen f/pl., Netz⟩

toilsome □ ['tɔilsəm] mühsam.

token ['toukən] Zeichen n; Andenken n, Geschenk n; ~ money Notgeld n; in ~ of zum Zeichen (gen.).

told [tould] pret. u. p.p. von tell.

tolera|ble □ ['tɔlərəbl] erträglich; ~nce [~əns] Duldsamkeit f; ~nt □ [~nt] duldsam (of gegen); ~te [~reit] dulden; ertragen; ~tion [tɔlə'reiʃən] Duldung f.

toll [toul] 1. Zoll m (a. fig.); Wege-, Brücken-, Marktgeld n; fig. Tribut m; ~ of the road die Verkehrsopfer n/pl.; 2. läuten; ~bar ['toulba:], ~gate Schlagbaum m.

tomato ♀ [tə'ma:tou, Am. tə'meitou], pl. ~es Tomate f.

tomb [tu:m] Grab(mal) n.

tomboy ['tɔmbɔi] Range f.

tombstone ['tu:mstoun] Grabstein m.

tom-cat ['tɔm'kæt] Kater m.

tomfool ['tɔm'fu:l] Hansnarr m.

tomorrow [tə'mɔrou] morgen.

ton [tʌn] Tonne f (Gewichtseinheit).

tone [toun] 1. Ton m; Klang m; Laut m; out of ~ verstimmt; 2. e-n Ton geben (dat.); stimmen; paint. abtönen; ~ down (sich) abschwächen, mildern.

tongs [tɔŋz] pl. (a pair of ~ pl. eine) Zange.

tongue [tʌŋ] Zunge f; Sprache f; Landzunge f; (Schuh)Lasche f; hold one's ~ den Mund halten; ~tied ['tʌŋtaid] sprachlos; schweigsam; stumm.

tonic ['tɔnik] 1. (~ally) tonisch; ⚕ stärkend; 2. ♪ Grundton m; ⚕ Stärkungsmittel n, Tonikum n.

tonight [tə'nait] heute abend od. nacht.

tonnage ⚓ ['tʌnidʒ] Tonnengehalt m; Lastigkeit f; Tonnengeld n.

tonsil anat. ['tɔnsl] Mandel f; ~litis ⚕ [tɔnsi'laitis] Mandelentzündung f.

too [tu:] zu, allzu; auch, noch dazu.

took [tuk] pret. von take.

tool [tu:l] Werkzeug n, Gerät n; ~bag ['tu:lbæg], ~kit Werkzeugtasche f.

toot [tu:t] 1. blasen, tuten; 2. Tuten n.

tooth [tu:θ] pl. teeth [ti:θ] Zahn m; ~ache ['tu:θeik] Zahnschmerzen pl. ~brush Zahnbürste f; ~less □

['tu:θlis] zahnlos; **~-paste** Zahnpasta *f;* **~pick** Zahnstocher *m;* **~some** □ ['tu:θsəm] schmackhaft.

top [tɔp] 1. oberstes Ende; Oberteil *n;* Gipfel *m (a. fig.);* Wipfel *m;* Kopf *m e-r Seite; mot. Am.* Verdeck *n; fig.* Haupt *n,* Erste(r) *m; Stiefel*-Stulpe *f;* Kreisel *m; at the ~ of one's voice* aus voller Kehle; *on ~* obenauf; obendrein; 2. ober(er, -e, -es); oberst; höchst; 3. oben bedecken; *fig.* überragen; vorangehen in *(dat.);* als erste(r) stehen auf *e-r Liste;* **~-boots** ['tɔp'bu:ts] *pl.* Stulpenstiefel *m/pl.*

toper ['toupə] Zecher *m.*

tophat F ['tɔp'hæt] Zylinderhut *m.*

topic ['tɔpik] Gegenstand *m,* Thema *n;* **~al** □ [~kəl] lokal; aktuell.

topmost ['tɔpmoust] höchst, oberst.

topple ['tɔpl] (um)kippen.

topsyturvy □ ['tɔpsi'tə:vi] auf den Kopf gestellt; das Oberste zuunterst; drunter und drüber.

torch [tɔ:tʃ] Fackel *f; electric ~* Taschenlampe *f;* **~light** ['tɔ:tʃlait] Fackelschein *m; ~ procession* Fakkelzug *m.*

tore [tɔ:] *pret. von* tear[1][1].

torment 1. [tɔ:ment] Qual *f,* Marter *f;* 2. [tɔ:'ment] martern, quälen.

torn [tɔ:n] *p.p. von* tear[1] 1.

tornado [tɔ:'neidou], *pl.* **~es** Wirbelsturm *m,* Tornado *m.*

torpedo [tɔ:'pi:dou], *pl.* **~es** 1. Torpedo *m;* 2. ⚓ torpedieren *(a. fig.).*

torp|id □ ['tɔ:pid] starr; apathisch; träg; **~idity** [tɔ:'piditi], **~or** ['tɔ:pə] Erstarrung *f,* Betäubung *f.*

torrent ['tɔrənt] Sturz-, Gießbach *m;* (reißender) Strom; **~ial** □ [tɔ'renʃəl] gießbachartig; strömend; *fig.* ungestüm.

torrid ['tɔrid] brennend heiß.

tortoise *zo.* ['tɔ:təs] Schildkröte *f.*

tortuous □ ['tɔ:tjuəs] gewunden.

torture ['tɔ:tʃə] 1. Folter *f,* Marter *f,* Tortur *f;* 2. foltern, martern.

toss [tɔs] 1. Werfen *n,* Wurf *m;* Zurückwerfen *n (Kopf);* 2. *a. ~ about* (sich) hin und her werfen; schütteln; *(mit adv.)* werfen; *a. ~ up* hochwerfen; *~ off* Getränk hinunterstürzen; *Arbeit* hinhauen; *a. ~ up* losen *(für was);* **~-up** ['tɔsʌp] Losen *f; fig.* etwas Zweifelhaftes.

tot F [tɔt] Knirps *m (kleines Kind).*

total ['toutl] 1. □ ganz, gänzlich; total; gesamt; 2. Gesamtbetrag *m;* 3. sich belaufen auf *(acc.);* summieren; **~itarian** [toutæli'tɛəriən] totalitär; **~ity** [tou'tæliti] Gesamtheit *f.*

totter ['tɔtə] wanken, wackeln.

touch [tʌtʃ] 1. (sich) berühren; anrühren, anfassen; stoßen an *(acc.);* betreffen; *fig.* rühren; erreichen; ♪ anschlagen; *a bit ~ed fig.* ein biß-

chen verrückt; *~ at* ⚓ anlegen in *(dat.);* *~ up* auffrischen; retuschieren; 2. Berührung *f;* Gefühl(ssinn *m) n;* Anflug *m,* Zug *m;* Fertigkeit *f;* ♪ Anschlag *m;* (Pinsel-) Strich *m;* **~-and-go** ['tʌtʃən'gou] gewagte Sache; *it is ~* es steht auf des Messers Schneide; **~ing** [~ʃiŋ] rührend; **~stone** Prüfstein *m;* **~y** [~ʃi] empfindlich; heikel.

tough [tʌf] zäh *(a. fig.);* schwer, hart; grob, brutal, übel; **~en** ['tʌfn] zäh machen *od.* werden; **~ness** [~nis] Zähigkeit *f.*

tour [tuə] 1. (Rund)Reise *f,* Tour (-nee) *f; conducted ~* Führung *f;* Gesellschaftsreise *f;* 2. (be)reisen; **~ist** ['tuərist] Tourist(in); *~ agency;* *~ bureau, ~ office* Reisebüro *n; ~ season* Reisezeit *f.* [*n.*\
tournament ['tuənəmənt] Turnier|

tousle ['tauzl] (zer)zausen.

tow [tou] 1. Schleppen *n; take in ~* ins Schlepptau nehmen; 2. (ab-) schleppen; treideln; ziehen.

toward(s) [tə'wɔ:d(z)] gegen; nach ... zu, auf ... *(acc.)* zu; (als Beitrag) zu.

towel ['tauəl] 1. Handtuch *n;* 2. abreiben; **~-rack** Handtuchhalter *m.*

tower ['tauə] 1. Turm *m; fig.* Hort *m,* Bollwerk *n;* 2. sich erheben; **~ing** □ ['tauəriŋ] (turm)hoch; rasend *(Wut).*

town [taun] 1. Stadt *f;* 2. Stadt...; städtisch; *~ clerk* Stadtsyndikus *m;* *~ council* Stadtrat *m (Versammlung);* *~ councillor* Stadtrat *m (Person);* *~ hall* Rathaus *n;* **~sfolk** ['taunzfouk] *pl.* Städter *pl.;* **~ship** ['taunʃip] Stadtgemeinde *f;* Stadtgebiet *n;* **~sman** ['taunzmən] (Mit)Bürger *m;* **~speople** [~zpi:pl] *pl. = townsfolk.*

toxi|c|al □ ['tɔksik(əl)] giftig; Gift...; *~n* [~in] Giftstoff *m.*

toy [tɔi] 1. Spielzeug *n;* Tand *m;* **~s** *pl.* Spielwaren *f/pl.;* 2. Spiel- (zeug)...; Miniatur...; Zwerg...; 3. spielen; **~-book** ['tɔibuk] Bilderbuch *n.*

trace [treis] 1. Spur *f (a. fig.);* Strang *m;* 2. nachspüren *(dat.); fig.* verfolgen; herausfinden; (auf-) zeichnen; (durch)pausen.

tracing ['treisiŋ] Pauszeichnung *f.*

track [træk] 1. Spur *f; Sport:* Bahn *f;* Rennstrecke *f;* Pfad *m;* Gleis *n; ~ events pl.* Laufdisziplinen *f/pl.;* 2. nachspüren *(dat.);* verfolgen; *~ down, ~ out* aufspüren.

tract [trækt] Fläche *f,* Strecke *f,* Gegend *f;* Traktat *n,* Abhandlung *f.*

tractable □ ['træktəbl] lenk-, fügsam.

tract|ion ['trækʃən] Ziehen *n,* Zug *m; ~ engine* Zugmaschine *f;* **~or** ⊕ [~ktə] Trecker *m,* Traktor *m.*

trade [treid] **1.** Handel *m*; Gewerbe *n*; Handwerk *n*; *Am.* Kompensationsgeschäft *n*; **2.** Handel treiben; handeln; ~ on ausnutzen; ~ **mark** ✝ Warenzeichen *n*, Schutzmarke *f*; ~ **price** Händlerpreis *m*; ~**r** ['treidə] Händler *m*; ~**sman** [~dzmən] Geschäftsmann *m*; ~ **union** Gewerkschaft *f*; ~ **wind** ⚓ Passatwind *m*.

tradition [trə'diʃən] Tradition *f*, Überlieferung *f*; ~**al** □ [~nl] traditionell.

traffic ['træfik] **1.** Verkehr *m*; Handel *m*; **2.** handeln (*in* mit); ~ **jam** Verkehrsstauung *f*; ~ **light** Verkehrsampel *f*.

traged|ian [trə'dʒi:djən] Tragiker *m*; *thea.* Tragöd|e *m*, -in *f*; ~**y** ['trædʒidi] Tragödie *f*.

tragic(al □) ['trædʒik(əl)] tragisch.

trail [treil] **1.** *fig.* Schweif *m*; Schleppe *f*; Spur *f*; Pfad *m*; **2.** *v/t.* hinter sich (her)ziehen; verfolgen; *v/i.* (sich) schleppen; ♀ kriechen; ~ **blazer** *Am.* Bahnbrecher *m*; ~**er** ['treilə] (Wohnwagen)Anhänger *m*; ♀ Kriechpflanze *f*; *Film:* Vorschau *f*.

train [trein] **1.** (Eisenbahn)Zug *m*; *allg.* Zug *m*; Gefolge *n*; Reihe *f*, Folge *f*, Kette *f*; Schleppe *f am Kleid*; **2.** erziehen; schulen; abrichten; ausbilden; trainieren; (sich) üben; ~**ee** [trei'ni:] in der Ausbildung Begriffene(r) *m*; ~**er** ['treinə] Ausbilder *m*; Trainer *m*.

trait [trei] (Charakter)Zug *m*.

traitor ['treitə] Verräter *m*.

tram [træm] *s.* ~**car**, ~**way**; ~**car** ['træmkɑː] Straßenbahnwagen *m*.

tramp [træmp] **1.** Getrampel *n*; Wanderung *f*; Tramp *m*, Landstreicher *m*; **2.** trampeln, treten; (durch)wandern; ~**le** ['træmpl] (zer)trampeln.

tramway ['træmwei] Straßenbahn *f*.

trance [trɑːns] Trance *f*.

tranquil □ ['træŋkwil] ruhig; gelassen; ~(**l**)**ity** [træŋ'kwiliti] Ruhe *f*; Gelassenheit *f*; ~(**l**)**ize** ['træŋkwilaiz] beruhigen; ~(**l**)**izer** [~zə] Beruhigungsmittel *n*.

transact [træn'zækt] abwickeln, abmachen; ~**ion** [~kʃən] Verrichtung *f*; Geschäft *n*, Transaktion *f*; ~**s** *pl.* (Tätigkeits)Bericht(e *pl.*) *m*.

transalpine ['trænz'ælpain] transalpin(isch).

transatlantic ['trænzət'læntik] transatlantisch, Transatlantik...

transcend [træn'send] überschreiten, übertreffen; hinausgehen über (*acc.*); ~**ence**, ~**ency** [~dəns, ~si] Überlegenheit *f*; *phls.* Transzendenz *f*.

transcribe [træns'kraib] abschreiben; *Kurzschrift* übertragen.

transcript ['trænskript], ~**ion** [træns'kripʃən] Abschrift *f*; Umschrift *f*.

transfer 1. [træns'fəː] *v/t.* übertragen; versetzen, verlegen; *v/i.* übertreten; *Am.* umsteigen; **2.** ['trænsfə(ː)] Übertragung *f*; ✝ Transfer *m*; Versetzung *f*, Verlegung *f*; *Am.* Umsteigefahrschein *m*; ~**able** [træns'fəːrəbl] übertragbar.

transfigure [træns'figə] umgestalten; verklären.

transfix [træns'fiks] durchstechen; ~**ed** *fig.* versteinert, starr (*with* vor *dat.*).

transform [træns'fɔːm] umformen; um-, verwandeln; ~**ation** [trænsfə'meiʃən] Umformung *f*; Um-, Verwandlung *f*.

transfus|e [træns'fjuːz] ⚕ *Blut etc.* übertragen; *fig.* einflößen; *fig.* durchtränken; ~**ion** [~uːʒən] (*bsd.* ⚕ Blut)Übertragung *f*, Transfusion *f*.

transgress [træns'gres] *v/t.* überschreiten; übertreten, verletzen; *v/i.* sich vergehen; ~**ion** [~eʃən] Überschreitung *f*; Übertretung *f*; Vergehen *n*; ~**or** [~esə] Übertreter *m*.

transient ['trænziənt] **1.** = *transitory*; **2.** *Am.* Durchreisende(r *m*) *f*.

transit ['trænsit] Durchgang *m*; Durchgangsverkehr *m*.

transition [træn'siʒən] Übergang *m*.

transitive □ *gr.* ['trænsitiv] transitiv.

transitory □ ['trænsitəri] vorübergehend; vergänglich, flüchtig.

translat|e [træns'leit] übersetzen, übertragen; überführen; *fig.* umsetzen; ~**ion** [~eiʃən] Übersetzung *f*, Übertragung *f*; *fig.* Auslegung *f*; ~**or** [~eitə] Übersetzer(in).

translucent [trænz'luːsnt] durchscheinend; *fig.* hell.

transmigration [trænzmai'greiʃən] (Aus)Wanderung *f*; Seelenwanderung *f*.

transmission [trænz'miʃən] Übermittlung *f*; *biol.* Vererbung *f*; *phys.* Fortpflanzung *f*; *mot.* Getriebe *n*; *Radio:* Sendung *f*.

transmit [trænz'mit] übermitteln, übersenden; übertragen; senden; *biol.* vererben; *phys.* fortpflanzen; ~**ter** [~tə] Übermittler(in); *tel. etc.* Sender *m*.

transmute [trænz'mjuːt] um-, verwandeln.

transparent □ [træns'pɛərənt] durchsichtig (*a. fig.*).

transpire [træns'paiə] ausdünsten, ausschwitzen; *fig.* durchsickern.

transplant [træns'plɑːnt] um-, verpflanzen; ~**ation** [trænsplɑːn'teiʃən] Verpflanzung *f*.

transport 1. [træns'pɔːt] fortschaffen, befördern, transportieren; *fig.* hinreißen; **2.** ['trænspɔːt] Fortschaffen *n*; Beförderung *f*; Transport *m*; Verkehr *m*; Beförderungsmittel *n*; Transportschiff *n*; Verzückung *f*; *be in ~s* außer sich sein; **~ation** [trænspɔ:ˈteiʃən] Beförderung *f*, Transport *m*.

transpose [trænsˈpouz] versetzen, umstellen; ♪ transponieren.

transverse □ [ˈtrænzvə:s] quer laufend; Quer...

trap [træp] 1. Falle *f* (*a. fig.*); Klappe *f*; 2. (in e-r Falle) fangen, in die Falle locken; *fig.* ertappen; **~door** [ˈtræpdɔ:] Falltür *f*; *thea.* Versenkung *f*.

trapeze [trəˈpi:z] *Zirkus:* Trapez *n*.

trapper [ˈtræpə] Trapper *m*, Fallensteller *m*, Pelzjäger *m*.

trappings *fig.* [ˈtræpiŋz] *pl.* Schmuck *m*, Putz *m*.

traps F [træps] *pl.* Siebensachen *pl.*

trash [træʃ] Abfall *m*; *fig.* Plunder *m*; Unsinn *m*, F Blech *n*; Kitsch *m*; **~y** [ˈtræʃi] wertlos, kitschig.

travel [ˈtrævl] 1. *v/i.* reisen; sich bewegen; wandern; *v/t.* bereisen; 2. das Reisen; ⊕ Lauf *m*; *~s pl.* Reisen *f/pl.*; **~(l)er** [ˌlə] Reisende(r) *m*; *~'s cheque* (*Am.* check) Reisescheck *m*.

traverse [ˈtrævə(:)s] 1. Durchquerung *f*; 2. (über)queren; durchqueren; *fig.* durchkreuzen.

travesty [ˈtrævisti] 1. Travestie *f*; Karikatur *f*; 2. travestieren; verulken.

trawl [trɔ:l] 1. (Grund)Schleppnetz *n*; 2. mit dem Schleppnetz fischen; **~er** [ˈtrɔ:lə] Trawler *m*.

tray [trei] (Servier)Brett *n*, Tablett *n*; Ablage *f*; *pen~* Federschale *f*.

treacher|ous □ [ˈtretʃərəs] verräterisch, treulos; (heim)tückisch; trügerisch; **~y** [ˌri] Verrat *m*, Verräterei *f*, Treulosigkeit *f*; Tücke *f*.

treacle [ˈtri:kl] Sirup *m*.

tread [tred] 1. *[irr.]* treten; schreiten; 2. Tritt *m*, Schritt *m*; Lauffläche *f*; **~le** [ˈtredl] Pedal *n*; Tritt *m*; **~mill** Tretmühle *f*.

treason [ˈtri:zn] Verrat *m*; **~able** □ [ˌnəbl] verräterisch.

treasure [ˈtreʒə] 1. Schatz *m*, Reichtum *m*; *~ trove* Schatzfund *m*; 2. *Schätze* sammeln, aufhäufen; **~r** [ˌərə] Schatzmeister *m*, Kassenwart *m*.

treasury [ˈtreʒəri] Schatzkammer *f*; (*bsd.* Staats)Schatz *m*; ♀ **Bench** *parl.* Ministerbank *f*; ♀ **Board**, *Am.* ♀ **Department** Finanzministerium *n*.

treat [tri:t] 1. *v/t.* behandeln; betrachten; *~ s.o. to s.th.* j-m et. spendieren; *v/i.* *~ of* handeln von; *~ with* unterhandeln mit; 2. Vergnügen *n*; *school ~* Schulausflug *m*; *it is my ~* F es geht auf meine Rechnung; **~ise** [ˈtri:tiz] Abhandlung *f*;

~ment [ˌtmənt] Behandlung *f*; ♣ Kur *f*; *follow-up ~* ♣ Nachkur *f*; **~y** [ˌti] Vertrag *m*.

treble [ˈtrebl] 1. □ dreifach; 2. Dreifache(s) *n*; ♪ Diskant *m*, Sopran *m*; 3. (sich) verdreifachen.

tree [tri:] Baum *m*.

trefoil ♀ [ˈtrefɔil] Klee *m*.

trellis [ˈtrelis] 1. ↗ Spalier *n*; 2. vergittern; ↗ am Spalier ziehen.

tremble [ˈtrembl] zittern.

tremendous □ [triˈmendəs] schrecklich, furchtbar; F kolossal, riesig.

tremor [ˈtremə] Zittern *n*, Beben *n*.

tremulous □ [ˈtremjuləs] zitternd, bebend.

trench [trentʃ] 1. (Schützen)Graben *m*; Furche *f*; 2. *v/t.* mit Gräben durchziehen; ⊕ umgraben; *~ (up)on* eingreifen in (*acc.*); **~ant** □ [ˈtrentʃənt] scharf.

trend [trend] 1. Richtung *f*; *fig.* Lauf *m*; *fig.* Strömung *f*; Tendenz *f*; 2. sich erstrecken, laufen.

trepidation [trepiˈdeiʃən] Zittern *n*, Beben *n*; Bestürzung *f*.

trespass [ˈtrespəs] 1. Übertretung *f*; 2. unbefugt eindringen (*on, upon* in *acc.*); über Gebühr in Anspruch nehmen; **~er** ⅓ [ˌsə] Rechtsverletzer *m*; Unbefugte(r *m*) *f*.

tress [tres] Haarlocke *f*, -flechte *f*.

trestle [ˈtresl] Gestell *n*, Bock *m*.

trial [ˈtraiəl] Versuch *m*; Probe *f*, Prüfung *f* (*a. fig.*); Plage *f*; ⅓ Verhandlung *f*, Prozeß *m*; *on ~* auf Probe; vor Gericht; *give s.o. a ~* es mit j-m versuchen; *~ run* Probefahrt *f*.

triang|le [ˈtraiæŋgl] Dreieck *n*; **~ular** □ [traiˈæŋgjulə] dreieckig.

tribe [traib] Stamm *m*; Geschlecht *n*; *contp.* Sippe *f*; ♀, *zo.* Klasse *f*.

tribun|al [traiˈbju:nl] Richterstuhl *m*; Gericht(shof *m*) *n*; **~e** [ˈtribju:n] Tribun *m*; Tribüne *f*.

tribut|ary [ˈtribjutəri] 1. □ zinspflichtig; *fig.* helfend; Neben...; 2. Nebenfluß *m*; **~e** [ˌju:t] Tribut *m* (*a. fig.*), Zins *m*; Anerkennung *f*.

trice [trais]: *in a ~* im Nu.

trick [trik] 1. Kniff *m*, List *f*, Trick *m*; Kunstgriff *m*, -stück *n*; Streich *m*; Eigenheit *f*; 2. betrügen; herausputzen; **~ery** [ˈtrikəri] Betrügerei *f*.

trickle [ˈtrikl] tröpfeln, rieseln.

trick|ster [ˈtrikstə] Gauner *m*; **~y** □ [ˌki] verschlagen; F heikel; verzwickt, verwickelt, schwierig.

tricycle [ˈtraisikl] Dreirad *n*.

trident [ˈtraidənt] Dreizack *m*.

trifl|e [ˈtraifl] 1. Kleinigkeit *f*; Lappalie *f*; *a ~* ein bißchen, ein wenig, etwas; 2. *v/i.* spielen, spaßen; *v/t.* *~ away* verschwenden; **~ing** □ [ˌliŋ] geringfügig; unbedeutend.

trig [trig] 1. hemmen; 2. schmuck.

trigger ['trigə] Abzug *m am Gewehr*; *phot.* Auslöser *m*.

trill [tril] 1. Triller *m*; gerolltes R; 2. trillern; *bsd.* das R rollen.

trillion ['triljən] Trillion *f*; *Am.* Billion *f*.

trim [trim] 1. □ ordentlich; schmuck; gepflegt; 2. (richtiger) Zustand; Ordnung *f*; 3. zurechtmachen; (~ up aus)putzen, schmükken; besetzen; stutzen; beschneiden; ⚓, ⚓ trimmen; ~ming ['trimiŋ] *mst* ~*s pl.* Besatz *m*, Garnierung *f*.

Trinity *eccl.* ['triniti] Dreieinigkeit *f*.

trinket ['triŋkit] wertloses Schmuckstück; ~*s pl.* F Kinkerlitzchen *pl.*

trip [trip] 1. Reise *f*, Fahrt *f*; Ausflug *m*, Spritztour *f*; Stolpern *n*, Fallen *n*; Fehltritt *m* (*a. fig.*); *fig.* Versehen *n*, Fehler *m*; 2. *v/i.* trippeln; stolpern; e-n Fehltritt tun (*a. fig.*); *fig.* e-n Fehler machen; *v/t. a.* ~ up *j-m* ein Bein stellen (*a. fig.*).

tripartite ['trai'pɑːtait] dreiteilig.

tripe [traip] Kaldaunen *f/pl.*

triple □ ['tripl] dreifach; ~ts [~lits] *pl.* Drillinge *m/pl.*

triplicate 1. ['triplikit] dreifach; 2. [~keit] verdreifachen.

tripod ['traipɔd] Dreifuß *m*; *phot.* Stativ *n*.

tripper F ['tripə] Ausflügler(in).

trite □ [trait] abgedroschen, platt.

triturate ['tritjureit] zerreiben.

triumph ['traiəmf] 1. Triumph *m*, Sieg *m*; 2. triumphieren; ~al [trai-'ʌmfəl] Sieges..., Triumph...; ~ant □ [~ənt] triumphierend.

trivial □ ['triviəl] bedeutungslos; unbedeutend; trivial; alltäglich.

trod [trɔd] *pret. von* tread 1; ~den ['trɔdn] *p.p. von* tread 1.

troll [troul] (vor sich hin)trällern.

troll(e)y ['trɔli] Karren *m*; Draisine *f*; Servierwagen *m*; ✠ Kontaktrolle *f* *e-s Oberleitungsfahrzeugs*; *Am.* Straßenbahnwagen *m*; ~bus ⊙(Oberleitungs)bus *m*.   [Hure *f*.\

trollop ['trɔləp] F Schlampe *f*.\

trombone ♩ [trɔm'boun] Posaune *f*.

troop [truːp] 1. Truppe *f*; Schar *f*; ✗ (Reiter)Zug *m*; 2. sich scharen, sich sammeln; ~ away, ~ off abziehen; ~ing the colour(s) ✗ Fahnenparade *f*; ~er ✗ ['truːpə] Kavallerist *m*.

trophy ['troufi] Trophäe *f*.

tropic ['trɔpik] Wendekreis *m*; ~s *pl.* Tropen *pl.*; ~(al □) [~k(ə)l)] tropisch.

trot [trɔt] 1. Trott *m*, Trab *m*; 2. traben (lassen).

trouble ['trʌbl] 1. Unruhe *f*; Störung *f*; Kummer *m*, Not *f*; Mühe *f*; Plage *f*; Unannehmlichkeiten *f/pl.*; ask *od.* look for ~ sich (selbst) Schwierigkeiten machen; das

Schicksal herausfordern; take (the) ~ sich (die) Mühe machen; 2. stören, beunruhigen, belästigen; quälen, plagen; Mühe machen (*dat.*); (sich) bemühen; ~ *s.o.* for *j-n* bemühen um; ~man, ~shooter *Am.* F Störungssucher *m*; ~some □ [~lsəm] beschwerlich, lästig.

trough [trɔf] (Futter)Trog *m*; Backtrog *m*, Mulde *f*.

trounce F [trauns] *j-n* verhauen.

troupe *thea.* [truːp] Truppe *f*.

trousers ['trauzəz] *pl.* (a pair of ~ *pl.* eine) (lange) Hose; Hosen *f/pl.*

trousseau ['truːsou] Aussteuer *f*.

trout *ichth.* [traut] Forelle(n *pl.*) *f*.

trowel ['trauəl] Maurerkelle *f*.

truant ['truː(:)ənt] 1. müßig; 2. Schulschwänzer *m*; *fig.* Bummler *m*.

truce [truːs] Waffenstillstand *m*.

truck [trʌk] 1. (offener) Güterwagen; Last(kraft)wagen *m*, Lkw *m*; Transportkarren *m*; Tausch (-handel) *m*; Verkehr *m*; Naturallohnsystem *n*; *Am.* Gemüse *n*; 2. (ver)tauschen; ~farm *Am.* ['trʌkfɑːm] Gemüsegärtnerei *f*.

truckle ['trʌkl] zu Kreuze kriechen.

truculent □ ['trʌkjulənt] wild, roh.

trudge [trʌdʒ] wandern; sich (dahin)schleppen, mühsam gehen.

true [truː] wahr; echt, wirklich; treu; genau; richtig; *it is ~* gewiß, freilich, zwar; *come ~* sich bewahrheiten; in Erfüllung gehen; ~ *to nature* naturgetreu.

truism ['truː(:)izəm] Binsenwahrheit *f*.

truly ['truːli] wirklich; wahrhaft; aufrichtig; genau; treu; *Yours ~* Hochachtungsvoll.

trump [trʌmp] 1. Trumpf *m*; 2. (über)trumpfen; ~ up erdichten; ~ery ['trʌmpəri] Plunder *m*.

trumpet ['trʌmpit] 1. Trompete *f*; 2. trompeten; *fig.* ausposaunen.

truncheon ['trʌntʃən] (Polizei-) Knüppel *m*; Kommandostab *m*.

trundle ['trʌndl] rollen.

trunk [trʌŋk] (Baum)Stamm *m*; Rumpf *m*; Rüssel *m*; *großer* Koffer; ~call *teleph.* [trʌŋkɔːl] Ferngespräch *n*; ~exchange *teleph.* Fernamt *n*; ~line ⊙ Hauptlinie *f*; *teleph.* Fernleitung *f*; ~s [trʌŋks] *pl.* Turnhose *f*; Badehose *f*; Herrenunterhose *f*.

trunnion ⊕ ['trʌnjən] Zapfen *m*.

truss [trʌs] 1. Bündel *n*, Bund *n*; ✗ Bruchband *n*; △ Binder *m*, Gerüst *n*; 2. (zs.-)binden; △ stützen.

trust [trʌst] 1. Vertrauen *n*; Glaube *m*; Kredit *m*; Pfand *n*; Verwahrung *f*; ✠ Treuhand *f*; ✠ Ring *m*, Trust *m*; ~ company Treuhandgesellschaft *f*; in ~ zu treuen Händen; 2. *v/t.* (ver)trauen (*dat.*); anvertrauen, übergeben (*s.o. with s.th., s.th. to s.o.* j-m et.); zuversichtlich hoffen;

v/i. vertrauen (*in, to* auf *acc.*); ~ee [trʌsˈtiː] Sach-, Verwalter *m*; ⚓ Treuhänder *m*; ~ful □ [ˈtrʌstful], ~ing □ [ˌtiŋ] vertrauensvoll; ~worthy [ˌtwɔːði] vertrauenswürdig; zuverlässig.

truth [truːθ], *pl.* ~s [truːðz] Wahrheit *f*; Wirklichkeit *f*; Wahrhaftigkeit *f*; Genauigkeit *f*; ~ful □ [ˈtruːθful] wahrhaft(ig).

try [trai] **1.** versuchen; probieren; prüfen; ⚓ verhandeln über *et. od.* gegen *j-n*; vor Gericht stellen; aburteilen; *die Augen etc.* angreifen; sich bemühen *od.* bewerben; ~ *on Kleid* anprobieren; **2.** Versuch *m*; ~ing □ [ˈtraiiŋ] anstrengend; kritisch.

Tsar [zɑː] Zar *m*.

T-shirt [ˈtiːʃɔːt] kurzärmeliges Sporthemd.

tub [tʌb] **1.** Faß *n*, Zuber *m*; Kübel *m*; Badewanne *f*; F (Wannen)Bad *n*.

tube [tjuːb] Rohr *n*; (*Am. bsd.* Radio)Röhre *f*; Tube *f*; (Luft-) Schlauch *m*; Tunnel *m*; F (Londoner) Untergrundbahn *f*.

tuber ♀ [ˈtjuːbə] Knolle *f*; ~culosis [tju(ː)bəːkjuˈlousis] Tuberkulose *f*.

tubular □ [ˈtjuːbjulə] röhrenförmig.

tuck [tʌk] **1.** Falte *f*; Abnäher *m*; **2.** ab-, aufnähen; packen, stecken; ~ *up* hochschürzen, aufkrempeln; *in e-e Decke etc.* einwickeln.

Tuesday [ˈtjuːzdi] Dienstag *m*.

tuft [tʌft] Büschel *n*, Busch *m*; (Haar)Schopf *m*.

tug [tʌg] **1.** Zug *m*, Ruck *m*; ⚓ Schlepper (*m*); *fig.* Anstrengung *f*; **2.** ziehen, zerren; ⚓ schleppen; sich mühen.

tuition [tju(ː)ˈiʃən] Unterricht *m*; Schulgeld *n*.

tulip ♀ [ˈtjuːlip] Tulpe *f*.

tumble [ˈtʌmbl] **1.** *v/i.* fallen, purzeln; taumeln; sich wälzen; *v/t.* werfen; zerknüllen; **2.** Sturz *m*; Wirrwarr *m*; ~down baufällig; ~r [ˌlə] Becher *m*; *orn.* Tümmler *m*.

tumid □ [ˈtjuːmid] geschwollen.

tummy F [ˈtʌmi] Bäuchlein *n*, Magen *m*.

tumo(u)r ➤ [ˈtjuːmə] Tumor *m*.

tumult [ˈtjuːmʌlt] Tumult *m*; ~uous □ [tju(ː)ˈmʌltjuəs] stürmisch.

tun [tʌn] Tonne *f*, Faß *n*.

tuna *ichth.* [ˈtuːnə] Thunfisch *m*.

tune [tjuːn] **1.** Melodie *f*, Weise *f*; ♪ Stimmung *f* (*a. fig.*); in ~ (gut-) gestimmt; *out of* ~ verstimmt; **2.** stimmen (*a. fig.*); ~ *in Radio:* einstellen; ~ *out Radio:* ausschalten; ~ *up* die Instrumente stimmen; *fig. Befinden etc.* heben; *mot.* die Leistung erhöhen; ~ful □ [ˈtjuːnful] melodisch; ~less □ [ˌnlis] unmelodisch.

tunnel [ˈtʌnl] **1.** Tunnel *m*; ⚒

Stollen *m*; **2.** e-n Tunnel bohren (durch).

tunny *ichth.* [ˈtʌni] Thunfisch *m*.

turbid [ˈtɔːbid] trüb; dick.

turb|ine ⊕ [ˈtɔːbin] Turbine *f*; ~o-jet [ˈtɔːbouˈdʒet] Strahlturbine *f*; ~o-prop [ˌouˈprɔp] Propellerturbine *f*.

turbot *ichth.* [ˈtɔːbət] Steinbutt *m*.

turbulent □ [ˈtɔːbjulənt] unruhig; ungestüm; stürmisch, turbulent.

tureen [təˈriːn] Terrine *f*.

turf [tɔːf] **1.** Rasen *m*; Torf *m*; Rennbahn *f*; Rennsport *m*; **2.** mit Rasen bedecken; ~y [ˈtɔːfi] rasenbedeckt.

turgid □ [ˈtɔːdʒid] geschwollen.

Turk [tɔːk] Türk|e *m*, -in *f*.

turkey [ˈtɔːki] *orn.* Truthahn *m*, -henne *f*, Pute(r *m*) *f*; *Am. sl. thea., Film:* Pleite *f*, Versager *m*.

Turkish [ˈtɔːkiʃ] türkisch.

turmoil [ˈtɔːmɔil] Aufruhr *m*, Unruhe *f*; Durcheinander *n*.

turn [tɔːn] **1.** *v/t.* drehen; (um)wenden, umkehren; lenken; verwandeln; abbringen; abwehren; übertragen; bilden; drechseln; verrückt machen; ~ *a corner* um die Ecke biegen; ~ *s.o. against* j-n aufhetzen gegen; ~ *aside* abwenden; ~ *away* abwenden; abweisen; ~ *down* umbiegen; *Gas etc.* kleinstellen; *Decke etc.* zurückschlagen; ablehnen; ~ *off* ableiten (*a. fig.*); hinauswerfen; wegjagen; ~ *off (on)* ab- (an)drehen, ab- (ein)schalten; ~ *out* hinauswerfen; *Fabrikat* herausbringen; *Gas etc.* ausdrehen; ~ *over* umwenden; *fig.* übertragen; ✝ umsetzen; überlegen; ~ *up* nach oben richten; hochklappen; umwenden; *Hose etc.* auf-, umschlagen; *Gas etc.* aufdrehen; *v/i.* sich (um)drehen; sich wenden; sich verwandeln; umschlagen (*Wetter etc.*); *Christ, grau etc.* werden; *a.* ~ *sour* sauer werden (*Milch*); ~ *about* sich umdrehen; ✕ kehrtmachen; ~ *back* zurückkehren; ~ *in* einkehren; F zu Bett gehen; ~ *off* abbiegen; ~ *on* sich drehen um; ~ *out* ausfallen, ausgehen; sich herausstellen als; ~ *to* sich zuwenden (*dat.*), sich wenden an (*acc.*); werden zu; ~ *up* auftauchen; ~ *upon* sich wenden gegen; **2.** (Um)Drehung *f*; Biegung *f*; Wendung *f*; Neigung *f*; Wechsel *m*; Gestalt *f*, Form *f*; Spaziergang *m*; Reihe(nfolge) *f*; Dienst(leistung *f*) *m*; F Schreck *m*; *at every* ~ auf Schritt und Tritt; *by od. in* ~s der Reihe nach, abwechselnd; *it is my* ~ ich bin an der Reihe; *take* ~s mit-ea. abwechseln; *does it serve your* ~? entspricht das Ihren Zwecken?; ~coat [ˈtɔːnkout] Abtrünnige(r) *m*; ~er [ˈtɔːnə] Drechsler *m*; ~ery [~əri] Drechslerei *f*; Drechslerarbeit *f*.

turning ['tə:niŋ] Drechseln *n*; Wendung *f*; Biegung *f*; Straßenecke *f*; (Weg)Abzweigung *f*; Querstraße *f*; ~point *fig*. Wendepunkt *m*.

turnip ♀ ['tə:nip] (*bsd*. weiße) Rübe.

turn|key ['tə:nki:] Schließer *m*; ~out ['tə:n'aut] Ausstaffierung *f*; Arbeitseinstellung *f*; ✝ Gesamtproduktion *f*; ~over ['tə:nouvə] ✝ Umsatz *m*; Verschiebung *f*; ~pike Schlagbaum *m*; (gebührenpflichtige) Schnellstraße *f*; ~stile Drehkreuz *n*. [pentin *n*.]

turpentine ⌐ ['tə:pəntin] Ter-⌐ **turpitude** ['tə:pitju:d] Schändlichkeit *f*.

turret ['tʌrit] Türmchen *n*; ✕, ⚓ Panzerturm *m*; ✈ Kanzel *f*.

turtle ['tə:tl] *zo*. Schildkröte *f*; *orn*. *mst* ~dove Turteltaube *f*.

tusk [tʌsk] Fangzahn *m*; Stoßzahn *m*; Hauer *m*.

tussle ['tʌsl] 1. Rauferei *f*, Balgerei *f*; 2. raufen, sich balgen.

tussock ['tʌsək] Büschel *n*.

tut [tʌt] ach was!; Unsinn!

tutelage ['tju:tilidʒ] ⚖ Vormundschaft *f*; Bevormundung *f*.

tutor ['tju:tə] 1. (Privat-, Haus-) Lehrer *m*; *univ*. Tutor *m*; *Am.univ.* Assistent *m mit Lehrauftrag*; ⚖ Vormund *m*; 2. unterrichten, schulen, erziehen; *fig*. beherrschen; ~ial [tju(:)'tɔ:riəl] *univ*. Unterrichtsstunde *f e-s Tutors*; *attr*. Lehrer...; Tutoren...

tuxedo *Am*. [tʌk'si:dou] Smoking *m*.

TV ['ti:'vi:] Fernsehen *n*; Fernsehapparat *m*; *attr*. Fernseh...

twaddle ['twɔdl] 1. Geschwätz *n*; 2. schwatzen, quatschen.

twang [twæŋ] 1. Schwirren *n*; *mst nasal* ~ näselnde Aussprache; 2. schwirren (lassen); klimpern; näseln.

tweak [twi:k] zwicken.

tweet [twi:t] zwitschern.

tweezers ['twi:zəz] *pl*. (*a pair of* ~ *pl*. eine) Pinzette.

twelfth [twelfθ] 1. zwölfte(r, -s); 2. Zwölftel *n*; ⌐-night ['twelfθnait] Dreikönigsabend *m*.

twelve [twelv] zwölf.

twent|ieth ['twentiiθ] 1. zwanzigste(r, -s); 2. Zwanzigstel *n*; ~y [~ti] zwanzig.

twice [twais] zweimal.

twiddle ['twidl] (sich) drehen; mit *et*. spielen.

twig [twig] Zweig *m*, Rute *f*.

twilight ['twailait] Zwielicht *n*; Dämmerung *f* (*a. fig*.).

twin [twin] 1. Zwillings...; doppelt; 2. Zwilling *m*; ~engined ✈ ['twinendʒind] zweimotorig.

twine [twain] 1. Bindfaden *m*,

Schnur *f*; Zwirn *m*; 2. zs.-drehen; verflechten; (sich) schlingen *od*. winden; umschlingen, umranken.

twinge [twindʒ] Zwicken *n*; Stich *m*; bohrender Schmerz.

twinkle ['twiŋkl] 1. funkeln, blitzen; huschen; zwinkern; 2. Funkeln *n*, Blitzen *n*; (Augen)Zwinkern *n*, Blinzeln *n*.

twirl [twə:l] 1. Wirbel *m*; 2. wirbeln.

twist [twist] 1. Drehung *f*; Windung *f*; Verdrehung *f*; Verdrehtheit *f*; Neigung *f*; (Gesichts)Verzerrung *f*; Garn *n*; Kringel *m*, Zopf *m* (*Backwaren*); 2. (sich) drehen *od*. winden; zs.-drehen; verdrehen, verziehen, verzerren.

twit *fig*. [twit] *j-n* aufziehen.

twitch [twitʃ] 1. zupfen (an *dat*.); zucken; 2. Zupfen *n*; Zuckung *f*.

twitter ['twitə] 1. zwitschern; 2. Gezwitscher *n*; *be in a* ~ zittern.

two [tu:] 1. zwei; *in* ~ entzwei; *put* ~ *and* ~ *together* sich et. zs.-reimen; 2. Zwei *f*; *in* ~*s* zu zweien; ~bit *Am*. F ['tu:bit] 25-Cent...; *fig*. unbedeutend, Klein...; ~edged ['tu:'edʒd] zweischneidig; ~fold ['tu:fould] zweifach; ~pence ['tʌpəns] zwei Pence; ~penny ['tʌpni] zwei Pence wert; ~piece ['tu:pi:s] zweiteilig; ~seater *mot*. ['tu:'si:tə] Zweisitzer *m*; ~storey ['tu:stɔ:ri], ~storied zweistöckig; ~stroke *mot*. Zweitakt...; ~way Doppel...; ~ *adapter* ⚡ Doppelstecker *m*; ~ *traffic* Gegenverkehr *m*.

tycoon *Am*. F ['tai'ku:n] Industriekapitän *m*, Industriemagnat *m*.

tyke [taik] Köter *m*; Kerl *m*.

type [taip] Typ *m*; Urbild *n*; Vorbild *n*; Muster *n*; Art *f*; Sinnbild *n*; *typ*. Type *f*, Buchstabe *m*; *true to* ~ artecht; *set in* ~ setzen; ~write ['taiprait] [*irr*. (*write*)] (mit der) Schreibmaschine schreiben; ~writer Schreibmaschine *f*; ~ribbon Farbband *n*.

typhoid 🔬 ['taifoid] 1. typhös; ~ *fever* = 2. (Unterleibs)Typhus *m*.

typhoon [tai'fu:n] Taifun *m*.

typhus 🔬 ['taifəs] Flecktyphus *m*.

typi|cal ⌐ ['tipikəl] typisch; richtig; bezeichnend, kennzeichnend; ~fy [~ifai] typisch sein für; versinnbildlichen; ~st ['taipist] *a. shorthand* ~ Stenotypistin *f*.

tyrann|ic(al ⌐) [ti'rænik(əl)] tyrannisch; ~ize ['tirənaiz] tyrannisieren; ~y [~ni] Tyrannei *f*.

tyrant ['taiərənt] Tyrann(in).

tyre ['taiə] *s*. tire.

tyro ['taiərou] *s*. tiro.

Tyrolese [tirə'li:z] 1. Tiroler(in); 2. tirolisch, Tiroler...

Tzar [za:] Zar *m*.

U

ubiquitous □ [ju(:)'bikwitəs] allgegenwärtig, überall zu finden(d).

udder ['ʌdə] Euter *n*.

ugly □ ['ʌgli] häßlich; schlimm.

ulcer ✶ ['ʌlsə] Geschwür *n*; (Eiter-) Beule *f*; **~ate** ✶ [~ʌreit] eitern (lassen); **~ous** ✶ [~rəs] geschwürig.

ulterior □ [ʌl'tiəriə] jenseitig; *fig.* weiter; tiefer liegend, versteckt.

ultimate □ ['ʌltimit] letzt; endlich; End...; **~ly** [~tli] zu guter Letzt.

ultimat|um [ʌlti'meitəm], *pl. a.* **~a** [~tə] Ultimatum *n*.

ultimo † ['ʌltimou] vorigen Monats.

ultra ['ʌltrə] übermäßig; Ultra..., ultra...; **~fashionable** ['ʌltrə'fæʃə-nəbl] hypermodern; **~modern** hypermodern.

umbel ✤ ['ʌmbəl] Dolde *f*.

umbrage ['ʌmbridʒ] Anstoß *m* (Ärger); Schatten *m*.

umbrella [ʌm'brelə] Regenschirm *m*; *fig.* Schirm *m*, Schutz *m*; ✗ Abschirmung *f*.

umpire ['ʌmpaiə] **1.** Schiedsrichter *m*; **2.** Schiedsrichter sein.

un... [ʌn] un...; Un...; ent...; nicht...

unabashed ['ʌnə'bæʃt] unverfroren; unerschrocken.

unabated ['ʌnə'beitid] unvermindert. [stande.)

unable ['ʌn'eibl] unfähig, außer-)

unaccommodating ['ʌnə'kɔmədei-tiŋ] unnachgiebig.

unaccountable □ ['ʌnə'kauntəbl] unerklärlich; seltsam; nicht zur Rechenschaft verpflichtet.

unaccustomed ['ʌnə'kʌstəmd] ungewohnt; ungewöhnlich.

unacquainted ['ʌnə'kweintid]: **~ with** unbekannt mit, e-r S unkundig.

unadvised □ ['ʌnəd'vaizd] unbedacht; unberaten.

unaffected □ ['ʌnə'fektid] unberührt; ungerührt; ungekünstelt.

unaided ['ʌn'eidid] ohne Unterstützung; (ganz) allein; bloß (Auge).

unalter|able □ [ʌn'ɔːltərəbl] unveränderlich; **~ed** [ʌn'ɔːltəd] unverändert.

unanim|ity [juːnə'nimiti] Einmütigkeit *f*; **~ous** □ [juː(ː)'næniməs] einmütig, einstimmig.

unanswer|able □ [ʌn'ɑːnsərəbl] unwiderleglich; **~ed** [ʌn'ɑːnsəd] unbeantwortet.

unapproachable □ [ʌnə'proutʃəbl] unzugänglich.

unapt □ [ʌn'æpt] ungeeignet.

unashamed □ ['ʌnə'ʃeimd] schamlos.

unasked ['ʌn'ɑːskt] unverlangt; ungebeten.

unassisted □ ['ʌnə'sistid] ohne Hilfe *od.* Unterstützung.

unassuming □ ['ʌnə'sjuːmiŋ] anspruchslos, bescheiden.

unattached ['ʌnə'tætʃt] nicht gebunden; ungebunden, ledig, frei.

unattractive □ [ʌnə'træktiv] wenig anziehend, reizlos; uninteressant.

unauthorized ['ʌn'ɔːθəraizd] unberechtigt, unbefugt.

unavail|able ['ʌnə'veiləbl] nicht verfügbar; **~ing** [~liŋ] vergeblich.

unavoidable □ [ʌnə'vɔidəbl] unvermeidlich.

unaware ['ʌnə'wɛə] ohne Kenntnis; be **~** of et. nicht merken; **~s** [~ɛəz] unversehens, unvermutet; versehentlich.

unbacked ['ʌn'bækt] ohne Unterstützung; ungedeckt (Scheck).

unbag ['ʌn'bæg] aus dem Sack holen *od.* lassen.

unbalanced ['ʌn'bælənst] nicht im Gleichgewicht befindlich; unausgeglichen; geistesgestört.

unbearable □ [ʌn'bɛərəbl] unerträglich.

unbeaten ['ʌn'biːtn] ungeschlagen; unbetreten (Weg).

unbecoming □ ['ʌnbi'kʌmiŋ] unkleidsam; unziemlich, unschicklich.

unbeknown F ['ʌnbi'noun] unbekannt.

unbelie|f ['ʌnbi'liːf] Unglaube *m*; **~vable** □ [ʌnbi'liːvəbl] unglaublich; **~ving** □ ['ʌnbi'liːviŋ] ungläubig.

unbend ['ʌn'bend] [irr. (bend)] (sich) entspannen; freundlich werden, auftauen; **~ing** □ [~diŋ] unbiegsam; *fig.* unbeugsam.

unbias(s)ed □ [ʌn'baiəst] vorurteilsfrei, unbefangen, unbeeinflußt.

unbid(den) [ʌn'bid(n)] ungeheißen, unaufgefordert; ungebeten.

unbind ['ʌn'baind] [irr. (bind)] losbinden, befreien; lösen.

unblushing □ [ʌn'blʌʃiŋ] schamlos. [boren.)

unborn ['ʌn'bɔːn] (noch) unge-)

unbosom [ʌn'buzəm] offenbaren.

unbounded [ʌn'baundid] unbegrenzt; schrankenlos.

unbroken □ ['ʌn'broukən] ungebrochen; unversehrt; ununterbrochen.

unbutton ['ʌn'bʌtn] aufknöpfen.

uncalled-for [ʌn'kɔːldfɔː] ungerufen; unverlangt (S.); unpassend.

uncanny □ [ʌn'kæni] unheimlich.

uncared-for ['ʌn'kɛədfɔː] unbeachtet, vernachlässigt.

unceasing □ [ʌn'siːsiŋ] unaufhörlich.

unceremonious □ ['ʌnseri'mou-njəs] ungezwungen; formlos.

uncertain □ [ʌn'səːtn] unsicher; ungewiß; unbestimmt; unzuverlässig; ~ty [~nti] Unsicherheit f.

unchallenged ['ʌn'tʃælindʒd] unangefochten.

unchang|eable □ [ʌn'tʃeindʒəbl] unveränderlich, unwandelbar; ~ed ['ʌn'tʃeindʒd] unverändert; ~ing □ [ʌn'tʃeindʒiŋ] unveränderlich.

uncharitable □ [ʌn'tʃæritəbl] lieblos; unbarmherzig; unfreundlich.

unchecked ['ʌn'tʃekt] ungehindert.

uncivil □ ['ʌn'sivl] unhöflich; ~ized [~vilaizd] unzivilisiert.

unclaimed ['ʌn'kleimd] nicht beansprucht; unzustellbar (bsd. Brief).

unclasp ['ʌn'klɑːsp] auf-, loshaken, auf-, losschnallen; aufmachen.

uncle ['ʌŋkl] Onkel m.

unclean [ˈʌn'kliːn] unrein.

unclose ['ʌn'klouz] (sich) öffnen.

uncomely ['ʌn'kʌmli] reizlos; unpassend.

uncomfortable □ [ʌn'kʌmfətəbl] unbehaglich, ungemütlich; unangenehm.

uncommon □ [ʌn'kɔmən] ungewöhnlich.

uncommunicative □ ['ʌnkə'mjuːnikətiv] wortkarg, schweigsam.

uncomplaining □ ['ʌnkəm'pleiniŋ] klaglos; ohne Murren; geduldig.

uncompromising □ [ʌn'kɔmprəmaiziŋ] kompromißlos.

unconcern ['ʌnkən'səːn] Unbekümmertheit f; Gleichgültigkeit f; ~ed □ [~nd] unbekümmert; unbeteiligt.

unconditional □ ['ʌnkən'diʃənl] unbedingt; bedingungslos.

unconfirmed ['ʌnkən'fəːmd] unbestätigt; eccl. nicht konfirmiert.

unconnected □ ['ʌnkə'nektid] unverbunden.

unconquer|able □ [ʌn'kɔŋkərəbl] unüberwindlich; ~ed [ʌn'kɔŋkəd] unbesiegt.

unconscionable □ [ʌn'kɔnʃnəbl] gewissenlos; F unverschämt, übermäßig.

unconscious □ [ʌn'kɔnʃəs] unbewußt; bewußtlos; ~ness [~snis] Bewußtlosigkeit f.

unconstitutional □ ['ʌnkɔnsti'tjuːʃnl] verfassungswidrig.

uncontroll|able □ [ʌnkən'troulbl] unkontrollierbar; unbändig; ~ed ['ʌnkən'trould] unbeaufsichtigt; fig. unbeherrscht.

unconventional □ ['ʌnkən'venʃənl] unkonventionell; ungezwungen.

unconvinc|ed ['ʌnkən'vinst] nicht überzeugt; ~ing [~siŋ] nicht überzeugend.

uncork ['ʌn'kɔːk] entkorken.

uncount|able ['ʌn'kauntəbl] unzählbar; ~ed [~tid] ungezählt.

uncouple ['ʌn'kʌpl] loskoppeln.

uncouth □ [ʌn'kuːθ] ungeschlacht.

uncover [ʌn'kʌvə] aufdecken, freilegen; entblößen.

unct|ion ['ʌŋkʃən] Salbung f (a. fig.); Salbe f; ~uous □ ['ʌŋktjuəs] fettig, ölig; fig. salbungsvoll.

uncult|ivated ['ʌn'kʌltiveitid], ~ured [~tʃəd] unkultiviert.

undamaged ['ʌn'dæmidʒd] unbeschädigt.

undaunted □ [ʌn'dɔːntid] unerschrocken.

undeceive ['ʌndi'siːv] j-n aufklären.

undecided □ ['ʌndi'saidid] unentschieden; unentschlossen.

undefined □ ['ʌndi'faind] unbestimmt; unbegrenzt.

undemonstrative □ ['ʌndi'mɔnstrətiv] zurückhaltend.

undeniable □ ['ʌndi'naiəbl] unleugbar; unbestreitbar.

under ['ʌndə] 1. adv. unten; darunter; 2. prp. unter; 3. adj. unter; in Zssgn: unter...; Unter...; mangelhaft ...; ~bid [~'bid] [irr. (bid)] unterbieten; ~brush [~brʌʃ] Unterholz n; ~carriage ✈ (Flugzeug)Fahrwerk n; mot. Fahrgestell n; ~clothes, ~clothing Unterkleidung f, Unterwäsche f; ~cut [~'kʌt] Preise unterbieten; ~dog [~dɔg] Unterlegene(r) m; Unterdrückte(r) m; ~done [~'dʌn] nicht gar; ~estimate [~r'estimeit] unterschätzen; ~fed [~'fed] unterernährt; ~go [ʌndə'gou] [irr. (go)] erdulden; sich unterziehen (dat.); ~graduate [~'grædjuit] Student (-in); ~ground ['ʌndəgraund] 1. unterirdisch; Untergrund...; 2. Untergrundbahn f; ~growth Unterholz n; ~hand unter der Hand; heimlich; ~lie [ʌndə'lai] [irr. (lie)] zugrunde liegen (dat.); ~line [~'lain] unterstreichen; ~ling ['ʌndəliŋ] Untergeordnete(r) m; ~mine [ʌndə'main] unterminieren; fig. untergraben; schwächen; ~most ['ʌndəmoust] unterst; ~neath [ʌndə'niːθ] 1. prp. unter (-halb); 2. adv. unten; darunter; ~pin [~'pin] untermauern; ~plot ['ʌndəplɔt] Nebenhandlung f; ~privileged [~'privilidʒd] benachteiligt; ~rate [ʌndə'reit] unterschätzen; ~secretary ['ʌndə'sekrətəri] Unterstaatssekretär m; ~sell ✝ [~'sel] [irr. (sell)] j-n unterbieten; Ware verschleudern; ~signed [~saind] Unterzeichnete(r) m; ~sized [~'saizd] zu klein; ~staffed [~'stɑːft] unterbesetzt; ~stand [~'stænd] [irr. (stand)] allg. verstehen; sich verstehen auf (acc.); (als sicher) annehmen; auffassen; (sinngemäß) ergänzen; make o.s. understood sich verständlich machen; an understood thing e-e abgemachte Sache; ~standable [~dəbl] verständlich; ~standing [~diŋ]

Verstand *m*; Einvernehmen *n*; Verständigung *f*; Abmachung *f*; Voraussetzung *f*; ~state ['ʌndə'steit] zu gering angeben; abschwächen; ~statement Unterbewertung *f*; Understatement *n*, Untertreibung *f*; ~take [ʌndə'teik] [*irr.* (*take*)] unternehmen; übernehmen; sich verpflichten; ~taker ['ʌndəteikə] Bestattungsinstitut *n*; ~taking [ʌndə'teikiŋ] Unternehmung *f*; Verpflichtung *f*; ['ʌndəteikiŋ] Leichenbestattung *f*; ~tone leiser Ton; ~value [,'vælju:] unterschätzen; ~wear [,~weə] Unterkleidung *f*, Unterwäsche *f*; ~wood Unterholz *n*; ~write [*irr.* (*write*)] Versicherung abschließen; ~writer Versicherer *m*.

undeserv|ed □ ['ʌndi'zə:vd] unverdient; ~ing [,~viŋ] unwürdig.

undesigned □ ['ʌndi'zaind] unbeabsichtigt, absichtslos.

undesirable ['ʌndi'zairəbl] 1. □ unerwünscht; 2. unerwünschte Person.

undeviating □ [ʌn'di:vieitiŋ] unentwegt.

undignified □ [ʌn'dignifaid] würdelos.

undisciplined [ʌn'disiplind] zuchtlos, undiszipliniert; ungeschult.

undisguised □ ['ʌndis'gaizd] unverkleidet; unverhohlen.

undisputed □ ['ʌndis'pju:tid] unbestritten.

undo ['ʌn'du:] [*irr.* (*do*)] aufmachen; (auf)lösen; ungeschehen machen, aufheben; vernichten; ~ing [,~u(:)iŋ] Aufmachen *n*; Ungeschehenmachen *n*; Vernichtung *f*; Verderben *n*; ~ne ['ʌn'dʌn] erledigt, vernichtet.

undoubted □ [ʌn'dautid] unzweifelhaft, zweifellos.

undreamt [ʌn'dremt]: ~of ungeahnt.

undress ['ʌn'dres] 1. (sich) entkleiden *od.* ausziehen; 2. Hauskleid *n*; ~ed unbekleidet; unangezogen; nicht zurechtgemacht.

undue □ ['ʌn'dju:] ungebührlich; übermäßig; † noch nicht fällig.

undulat|e ['ʌndjuleit] wogen; wallen; wellig sein; ~ion [ʌndju'leiʃən] wellenförmige Bewegung.

undutiful □ ['ʌn'dju:tiful] ungehorsam, pflichtvergessen.

unearth ['ʌn'ə:θ] ausgraben; *fig.* aufstöbern; ~ly [ʌn'ə:θli] überirdisch.

uneas|iness [ʌn'i:zinis] Unruhe *f*; Unbehagen *n*; ~y □ [ʌn'i:zi] unbehaglich; unruhig; unsicher.

uneducated ['ʌn'edjukeitid] unerzogen; ungebildet.

unemotional □ ['ʌni'mouʃənl] leidenschaftslos; passiv; nüchtern.

unemploy|ed ['ʌnim'plɔid] 1. unbeschäftigt; arbeitslos; unbenutzt; 2.: *the* ~ *pl.* die Arbeitslosen *pl.*; ~ment [,~mənt] Arbeitslosigkeit *f*.

unending □ [ʌn'endiŋ] endlos.

unendurable □ ['ʌnin'djuərəbl] unerträglich.

unengaged ['ʌnin'geidʒd] frei.

unequal □ ['ʌn'i:kwəl] ungleich; nicht gewachsen (*to dat.*); ~(l)ed [,~ld] unvergleichlich, unerreicht.

unerring □ ['ʌn'ə:riŋ] unfehlbar.

unessential □ ['ʌni'senʃəl] unwesentlich, unwichtig (*to* für).

uneven □ ['ʌn'i:vən] uneben; ungleich(mäßig); ungerade (*Zahl*).

uneventful □ ['ʌni'ventful] ereignislos; ohne Zwischenfälle.

unexampled [ʌnig'za:mpld] beispiellos.

unexceptionable □ [ʌnik'sepʃnəbl] untadelig; einwandfrei.

unexpected □ ['ʌniks'pektid] unerwartet.

unexplained ['ʌniks'pleind] unerklärt.

unfading □ [ʌn'feidiŋ] nicht welkend; unvergänglich; echt (*Farbe*).

unfailing □ [ʌn'feiliŋ] unfehlbar; nie versagend; unerschöpflich; *fig.* treu.

unfair □ ['ʌn'feə] unehrlich; unfair; ungerecht.

unfaithful □ ['ʌn'feiθful] un(ge)treu, treulos; nicht wortgetreu.

unfamiliar ['ʌnfə'miljə] unbekannt; ungewohnt.

unfasten ['ʌn'fɑ:sn] aufmachen; lösen; ~ed unbefestigt, lose.

unfathomable □ [ʌn'fæðəməbl] unergründlich.

unfavo(u)rable □ ['ʌn'feivərəbl] ungünstig.

unfeeling □ [ʌn'fi:liŋ] gefühllos.

unfilial □ ['ʌn'filjəl] respektlos, pflichtvergessen (*Kind*).

unfinished ['ʌn'finiʃt] unvollendet; unfertig.

unfit 1. □ ['ʌn'fit] ungeeignet, unpassend; 2. ['ʌn'fit] untauglich machen.

unfix ['ʌn'fiks] losmachen, lösen.

unfledged ['ʌn'fledʒd] ungefiedert; (noch) nicht flügge; *fig.* unreif.

unflinching □ [ʌn'flintʃiŋ] fest entschlossen, unnachgiebig.

unfold ['ʌn'fould] (sich) entfalten *od.* öffnen; [ʌn'fould] klarlegen; enthüllen.

unforced □ ['ʌn'fɔ:st] ungezwungen.

unforeseen ['ʌnfɔ:'si:n] unvorhergesehen.

unforgettable □ ['ʌnfə'getəbl] unvergeßlich.

unforgiving ['ʌnfə'giviŋ] unversöhnlich.

unforgotten ['ʌnfə'gɔtn] unvergessen.

unfortunate [ʌn'fɔ:tʃnit] 1. □ unglücklich; 2. Unglückliche(r *m*) *f*; **~ly** [~tli] unglücklicherweise, leider.

unfounded □ ['ʌn'faundid] unbegründet; grundlos.

unfriendly ['ʌn'frendli] unfreundlich; ungünstig.

unfurl [ʌn'fəːl] entfalten, aufrollen.

unfurnished ['ʌn'fəːniʃt] unmöbliert.

ungainly [ʌn'geinli] unbeholfen, plump.

ungenerous □ ['ʌn'dʒenərəs] unedelmütig; nicht freigebig.

ungentle □ ['ʌn'dʒentl] unsanft.

ungodly □ ['ʌn'gɔdli] gottlos.

ungovernable □ [ʌn'gʌvənəbl] unlenksam; zügellos, unbändig.

ungraceful □ ['ʌn'greisful] ungraziös, ohne Anmut; unbeholfen.

ungracious □ ['ʌn'greiʃəs] ungnädig; unfreundlich.

ungrateful □ [ʌn'greitful] undankbar.

unguarded □ ['ʌn'gɑːdid] unbewacht; unvorsichtig; ungeschützt.

unguent ['ʌŋgwənt] Salbe *f*.

unhampered ['ʌn'hæmpəd] ungehindert. [schön.]

unhandsome □ [ʌn'hænsəm] un-]

unhandy □ [ʌn'hændi] unhandlich; ungeschickt; unbeholfen.

unhappy □ [ʌn'hæpi] unglücklich.

unharmed ['ʌn'hɑːmd] unversehrt.

unhealthy □ [ʌn'helθi] ungesund.

unheard-of [ʌn'həːdɔv] unerhört.

unheed|ed [ʌn'hiːdid] unbeachtet, unbewacht; **~ing** [~diŋ] sorglos.

unhesitating □ [ʌn'heziteitiŋ] ohne Zögern; unbedenklich.

unholy [ʌn'houli] unheilig; gottlos.

unhono(u)red ['ʌn'ɔnəd] ungeehrt; uneingelöst (*Pfand*, *Scheck*).

unhook ['ʌn'huk] auf-, aushaken.

unhoped-for [ʌn'houptfɔː] unverhofft.

unhurt ['ʌn'həːt] unverletzt.

unicorn ['juːnikɔːn] Einhorn *n*.

unification [juːnifi'keiʃən] Vereinigung *f*; Vereinheitlichung *f*.

uniform ['juːnifɔːm] **1.** □ gleichförmig, gleichmäßig; einheitlich; **2.** Dienstkleidung *f*; Uniform *f*; **3.** uniformieren; **~ity** [juːni'fɔːmiti] Gleichförmigkeit *f*, Gleichmäßigkeit *f*.

unify ['juːnifai] verein(ig)en; vereinheitlichen.

unilateral □ ['juːni'lætərəl] einseitig.

unimagina|ble □ [ʌni'mædʒinəbl] undenkbar; **~tive** □ ['ʌni'mædʒinətiv] einfallslos.

unimportant □ ['ʌnim'pɔːtənt] unwichtig.

unimproved ['ʌnim'pruːvd] nicht kultiviert, unbebaut (*Land*); unverbessert.

uninformed ['ʌnin'fɔːmd] nicht unterrichtet.

uninhabit|able ['ʌnin'hæbitəbl] unbewohnbar; **~ed** [~tid] unbewohnt.

uninjured ['ʌn'indʒəd] unbeschädigt, unverletzt.

unintelligible □ ['ʌnin'telidʒəbl] unverständlich.

unintentional □ ['ʌnin'tenʃənl] unabsichtlich.

uninteresting □ ['ʌn'intristiŋ] uninteressant.

uninterrupted □ ['ʌnintə'rʌptid] ununterbrochen.

union ['juːnjən] Vereinigung *f*; Verbindung *f*; Union *f*, Verband *m*; Einigung *f*; Einigkeit *f*; Verein *m*, Bund *m*; *univ.* (Debattier)Klub *m*; Gewerkschaft *f*; **~ist** [~nist] Gewerkschaftler *m*; ♀ **2** Jack Union Jack *m* (*britische Nationalflagge*); **~ suit** *Am.* Hemdhose *f*.

unique □ [juː'niːk] einzigartig, einmalig.

unison ♪ *u. fig.* ['juːnizn] Einklang *m*.

unit ['juːnit] Einheit *f*; ⚔ Einer *m*; **~e** [juː'nait] (sich) vereinigen, verbinden; sich vereinigt, vereint; **~y** ['juːniti] Einheit *f*; Einigkeit *f*.

univers|al □ [juːni'vəːsəl] allgemein; allumfassend; Universal...; Welt...; **~ality** [juːnivəː'sæliti] Allgemeinheit *f*; umfassende Bildung, Vielseitigkeit *f*; **~e** ['juːnivəːs] Weltall *n*, Universum *n*; **~ity** [juːni'vəːsiti] Universität *f*.

unjust □ ['ʌn'dʒʌst] ungerecht; **~ifiable** □ [ʌn'dʒʌstifaiəbl] nicht zu rechtfertigen(d), unverantwortlich.

unkempt ['ʌn'kempt] ungepflegt.

unkind □ [ʌn'kaind] unfreundlich.

unknow|ing □ ['ʌn'nouiŋ] unwissend; unbewußt; **~n** [~oun] **1.** unbekannt; unbewußt; **~ to me** ohne mein Wissen; **2.** Unbekannte(r *m*, -s *n*) *f*.

unlace ['ʌn'leis] aufschnüren.

unlatch ['ʌn'lætʃ] aufklinken.

unlawful □ ['ʌn'lɔːful] ungesetzlich; *weitS.* unrechtmäßig.

unlearn ['ʌn'ləːn] [*irr.* (*learn*)] verlernen.

unless [ən'les] wenn nicht, außer wenn; es sei denn, daß.

unlike ['ʌn'laik] **1.** *adj.* □ ungleich; **2.** *prp.* anders als; **~ly** [ʌn'laikli] unwahrscheinlich.

unlimited [ʌn'limitid] unbegrenzt.

unload ['ʌn'loud] ent-, ab-, ausladen; *Ladung* löschen.

unlock ['ʌn'lɔk] aufschließen; *Waffe* entsichern; **~ed** unverschlossen.

unlooked-for [ʌn'luktfɔː] unerwartet.

unloose , **~n** ['ʌn'luːs, ʌn'luːsn] lösen, losmachen.

unlov|ely ['ʌn'lʌvli] reizlos, unschön; **~ing** □ [~viŋ] lieblos.

unlucky □ [ʌn'lʌki] unglücklich.

unmake ['ʌn'meik] [irr. (make)] vernichten; rückgängig machen; umbilden; Herrscher absetzen.

unman ['ʌn'mæn] entmannen.

unmanageable □ [ʌn'mænidʒəbl] unlenksam, widerspenstig.

unmarried ['ʌn'mærid] unverheiratet, ledig.

unmask ['ʌn'mɑːsk] (sich) demaskieren; fig. entlarven.

unmatched ['ʌn'mætʃt] unerreicht; unvergleichlich.

unmeaning □ [ʌn'miːniŋ] nichtssagend.

unmeasured [ʌn'meʒəd] ungemessen; unermeßlich.

unmeet ['ʌn'miːt] ungeeignet.

unmentionable □ [ʌn'menʃnəbl] nicht zu erwähnen(d), unnennbar.

unmerited ['ʌn'meritid] unverdient.

unmindful □ [ʌn'maindful] unbedacht; sorglos; ohne Rücksicht.

unmistakable □ ['ʌnmis'teikəbl] unverkennbar; unmißverständlich.

unmitigated [ʌn'mitigeitid] ungemildert; richtig; fig. Erz...

unmolested ['ʌnmou'lestid] unbelästigt.

unmounted ['ʌn'mauntid] unberitten; nicht gefaßt (Stein); unaufgezogen (Bild); unmontiert.

unmoved ['ʌn'muːvd] unbewegt, ungerührt.

unnamed ['ʌn'neimd] ungenannt.

unnatural □ [ʌn'nætʃrəl] unnatürlich. [nötig.\]

unnecessary □ [ʌn'nesisəri] un-\
unneighbo(u)rly ['ʌn'neibəli] nicht gutnachbarlich.

unnerve ['ʌn'nəːv] entnerven.

unnoticed ['ʌn'noutist] unbemerkt.

unobjectionable □ ['ʌnəb'dʒekʃnəbl] einwandfrei.

unobserv|ant □ ['ʌnəb'zəːvənt] unachtsam; ~ed □ [~vd] unbemerkt.

unobtainable ['ʌnəb'teinəbl] unerreichbar.

unobtrusive □ ['ʌnəb'truːsiv] unaufdringlich, bescheiden.

unoccupied ['ʌn'ɔkjupaid] unbesetzt; unbewohnt; unbeschäftigt.

unoffending ['ʌnə'fendiŋ] harmlos.

unofficial □ ['ʌnə'fiʃəl] nichtamtlich, inoffiziell.

unopposed ['ʌnə'pouzd] ungehindert.

unostentatious □ ['ʌnɔstən'teiʃəs] anspruchslos; unauffällig; schlicht.

unowned ['ʌn'ound] herrenlos.

unpack ['ʌn'pæk] auspacken.

unpaid ['ʌn'peid] unbezahlt; unbelohnt; & unfrankiert.

unparalleled [ʌn'pærəleld] beispiellos, ohnegleichen.

unperceived ['ʌnpə'siːvd] unbemerkt.

unperturbed ['ʌnpə(ː)'təːbd] ruhig, gelassen.

unpleasant □ [ʌn'pleznt] unangenehm; unerfreulich; ~ness [~tnis] Unannehmlichkeit f.

unpolished ['ʌn'pɔliʃt] unpoliert; fig. ungebildet.

unpolluted ['ʌnpə'luːtid] unbefleckt.

unpopular ['ʌn'pɔpjulə] unpopulär, unbeliebt; ~ity ['ʌnpɔpju-'læriti] Unbeliebtheit f.

unpracti|cal □ ['ʌn'præktikəl] unpraktisch; ~sed, Am. ~ced [ʌn'præktist] ungeübt.

unprecedented □ [ʌn'presidəntid] beispiellos; noch nie dagewesen.

unprejudiced □ [ʌn'predʒudist] unbefangen, unvoreingenommen.

unpremeditated □ ['ʌnpri'mediteitid] unbeabsichtigt.

unprepared □ ['ʌnpri'peəd] unvorbereitet.

unpreten|ding □ ['ʌnpri'tendiŋ], ~tious □ [~nʃəs] anspruchslos.

unprincipled [ʌn'prinsəpld] ohne Grundsätze; gewissenlos.

unprivileged [ʌn'privilidʒd] sozial benachteiligt; arm.

unprofitable □ [ʌn'prɔfitəbl] unnütz.

unproved ['ʌn'pruːvd] unerwiesen.

unprovided ['ʌnprə'vaidid] nicht versehen (with mit); ~ for unversorgt, mittellos.

unprovoked □ ['ʌnprə'voukt] ohne Grund.

unqualified □ ['ʌn'kwɔlifaid] ungeeignet; unberechtigt; [ʌn'kwɔlifaid] unbeschränkt.

unquestion|able□[ʌn'kwestʃənəbl] unzweifelhaft, fraglos; ~ed [~nd] ungefragt; unbestritten.

unquote ['ʌn'kwout] Zitat beenden.

unravel [ʌn'rævəl] (sich) entwirren; enträtseln.

unready □ ['ʌn'redi] nicht bereit od. fertig; unlustig, zögernd.

unreal □ ['ʌn'riəl] unwirklich; ~istic['ʌnriə'listik] (~ally) wirklichkeitsfremd, unrealistisch.

unreasonable □ [ʌn'riːznəbl] unvernünftig; grundlos; unmäßig.

unrecognizable □ ['ʌn'rekəgnaizəbl] nicht wiederzuerkennen(d).

unredeemed □ ['ʌnri'diːmd] unerlöst; uneingelöst; ungemildert.

unrefined ['ʌnri'faind] ungeläutert; fig. ungebildet. [dankenlos.\]

unreflecting □['ʌnri'flektiŋ] ge-\
unregarded ['ʌnri'gɑːdid] unbeachtet; unberücksichtigt.

unrelated ['ʌnri'leitid] ohne Beziehung (to zu).

unrelenting □ ['ʌnri'lentiŋ] erbarmungslos; unerbittlich.

unreliable ['ʌnri'laiəbl] unzuverlässig.

unrelieved □ [ʌnri'li:vd] ungelindert; ununterbrochen.

unremitting □ [ʌnri'mitiŋ] unablässig, unaufhörlich; unermüdlich.

unrepining □ [ʌnri'painiŋ] klaglos; unverdrossen.

unrequited □ [ʌnri'kwaitid] unerwidert; unbelohnt.

unreserved □ [ʌnri'zə:vd] rückhaltlos; unbeschränkt; ohne Vorbehalt.

unresisting □ [ʌnri'zistiŋ] widerstandslos.

unresponsive [ʌnris'pɔnsiv] unempfänglich (to für).

unrest ['ʌn'rest] Unruhe f.

unrestrained □ [ʌnris'treind] ungehemmt; unbeschränkt.

unrestricted □ [ʌnris'triktid] uneingeschränkt.

unriddle ['ʌn'ridl] enträtseln.

unrighteous □ ['ʌn'raitʃəs] ungerecht; unredlich.

unripe ['ʌn'raip] unreif.

unrival(l)ed [ʌn'raivəld] unvergleichlich, unerreicht, einzigartig.

unroll ['ʌn'roul] ent-, aufrollen.

unruffled ['ʌn'rʌfld] glatt; ruhig.

unruly [ʌn'ru:li] ungebärdig.

unsafe □ ['ʌn'seif] unsicher.

unsal(e)able ['ʌn'seiləbl] unverkäuflich.

unsanitary ['ʌn'sænitəri] unhygienisch.

unsatisf|actory □ ['ʌnsætis'fæktəri] unbefriedigend; unzulänglich; ~ied ['ʌn'sætisfaid] unbefriedigt; ~ying [~aiiŋ] = unsatisfactory.

unsavo(u)ry □ ['ʌn'seivəri] unappetitlich (a. fig.), widerwärtig.

unsay ['ʌn'sei] [irr. (say)] zurücknehmen, widerrufen.

unscathed ['ʌn'skeiðd] unversehrt.

unschooled ['ʌn'sku:ld] ungeschult; unverbildet.

unscrew ['ʌn'skru:] v/t. ab-, losaufschrauben; v/i. sich abschrauben lassen.

unscrupulous □ [ʌn'skru:pjuləs] bedenkenlos; gewissenlos; skrupellos.

unsearchable □ [ʌn'sə:tʃəbl] unerforschlich; unergründlich.

unseason|able □ [ʌn'si:znəbl] unzeitig; fig. ungelegen; ~ed ['ʌn'si:znd] nicht abgelagert (Holz); fig. nicht abgehärtet; ungewürzt.

unseat ['ʌn'si:t] des Amtes entheben; abwerfen.

unseemly [ʌn'si:mli] unziemlich.

unseen ['ʌn'si:n] ungesehen; unsichtbar.

unselfish □ ['ʌn'selfiʃ] selbstlos, uneigennützig; ~ness [~nis] Selbstlosigkeit f.

unsettle ['ʌn'setl] in Unordnung bringen; verwirren; erschüttern; ~d nicht festgesetzt; unbeständig; † unbezahlt; unerledigt; ohne festen Wohnsitz; unbesiedelt.

unshaken ['ʌn'ʃeikən] unerschüttert; unerschütterlich.

unshaven ['ʌn'ʃeivn] unrasiert.

unship ['ʌn'ʃip] ausschiffen.

unshrink|able ['ʌn'ʃriŋkəbl] nicht einlaufend (Stoff); ~ing □ [ʌn'ʃriŋkiŋ] unverzagt.

unsightly [ʌn'saitli] häßlich.

unskil|(l)ful □ ['ʌn'skilful] ungeschickt; ~led [~ld] ungelernt.

unsoci|able [ʌn'souʃəbl] ungesellig; ~al [~əl] ungesellig; unsozial.

unsolder ['ʌn'sɔldə] los-, ablöten.

unsolicited ['ʌnsə'lisitid] nicht gefragt (S.); unaufgefordert (P.).

unsolv|able [ʌn'sɔlvəbl] unlösbar; ~ed [~vd] ungelöst.

unsophisticated ['ʌnsə'fistikeitid] unverfälscht; ungekünstelt; unverdorben, unverbildet.

unsound □ ['ʌn'saund] ungesund; verdorben; wurmstichig; morsch; nicht stichhaltig (Beweis); verkehrt.

unsparing □ [ʌn'speəriŋ] freigebig; schonungslos, unbarmherzig.

unspeakable □ [ʌn'spi:kəbl] unsagbar; unsäglich.

unspent ['ʌn'spent] unverbraucht; unerschöpft.

unspoil|ed, ~t ['ʌn'spɔilt] unverdorben; unbeschädigt; nicht verzogen (Kind).

unspoken ['ʌn'spoukən] ungesagt; ~of unerwähnt.

unstable □ ['ʌn'steibl] nicht (stand)fest; unbeständig; unstet(ig); labil.

unsteady □ ['ʌn'stedi] unstet(ig), unsicher; schwankend; unbeständig; unsolid; unregelmäßig.

unstrained ['ʌn'streind] unfiltriert; fig. ungezwungen.

unstrap ['ʌn'stræp] los-, abschnallen.

unstressed ['ʌn'strest] unbetont.

unstring ['ʌn'striŋ] [irr. (string)] Saite entspannen.

unstudied ['ʌn'stʌdid] ungesucht, ungekünstelt, natürlich.

unsubstantial □ ['ʌnsəb'stænʃəl] wesenlos; gegenstandslos; inhaltlos; gehaltlos; dürftig.

unsuccessful □ ['ʌnsək'sesful] erfolglos, ohne Erfolg.

unsuitable □ ['ʌn'sju:təbl] unpassend; unangemessen.

unsurpassed ['ʌnsə(:)'pɑ:st] unübertroffen.

unsuspect|ed ['ʌnsəs'pektid] unverdächtig; unvermutet; ~ing [~tiŋ] nichts ahnend; arglos.

unsuspicious □ ['ʌnsəs'piʃəs] nicht argwöhnisch, arglos.

unswerving □ [ʌn'swəːviŋ] unentwegt.

untangle ['ʌn'tæŋgl] entwirren.

untarnished ['ʌn'tɑːniʃt] unbefleckt; ungetrübt.

unteachable ['ʌn'tiːtʃəbl] unbelehrbar (P.); unlehrbar (S.).

untenanted ['ʌn'tənəntid] unvermietet, unbewohnt.

unthankful □ ['ʌn'θæŋkful] undankbar.

unthink|able [ʌn'θiŋkəbl] undenkbar; **~ing** □ ['ʌn'θiŋkiŋ] gedankenlos.

unthought ['ʌn'θɔːt] unbedacht; **~of** unvermutet.

unthrifty □ ['ʌn'θrifti] verschwenderisch; nicht gedeihend.

untidy □ [ʌn'taidi] unordentlich.

untie ['ʌn'tai] aufbinden, aufknüpfen; *Knoten etc.* lösen; *j-n* losbinden.

until [ən'til] 1. *prp.* bis; 2. *cj.* bis (daß); *not* ~ erst wenn *od.* als.

untimely [ʌn'taimli] unzeitig; vorzeitig; ungelegen. (lich.)

untiring □ [ʌn'taiəriŋ] unermüd-⌡

unto ['ʌntu] = *to*.

untold ['ʌn'tould] unerzählt; ungezählt; unermeßlich, unsäglich.

untouched ['ʌn'tʌtʃt] unberührt; *fig.* ungerührt; *phot.* unretuschiert.

untried ['ʌn'traid] unversucht; unerprobt; *ɪtɪ* noch nicht verhört.

untrod, ~den ['ʌn'trɔd, ~dn] unbetreten.

untroubled ['ʌn'trʌbld] ungestört.

untrue ['ʌn'truː] unwahr; untreu.

untrustworthy □ ['ʌn'trʌstwəːði] unzuverlässig, nicht vertrauenswürdig.

unus|ed ['ʌn'juːzd] ungebraucht; [~uːst] nicht gewöhnt (*to an acc.*; zu *inf.*); **~ual** □ [ʌn'juːʒuəl] ungewöhnlich; ungewohnt.

unutterable □ [ʌn'ʌtərəbl] unaussprechlich.

unvarnished *fig.* ['ʌn'vɑːniʃt] ungeschminkt.

unvarying □ [ʌn'vɛəriiŋ] unveränderlich.

unveil [ʌn'veil] entschleiern, enthüllen.

unversed ['ʌn'vəːst] unbewandert, unerfahren (*in* in *dat.*).

unvouched ['ʌn'vautʃt] *a.* **~-for** unverbürgt, unbezeugt.

unwanted ['ʌn'wɔntid] unerwünscht.

unwarrant|able □ [ʌn'wɔrəntəbl] unverantwortlich; **~ed** [~tid] unberechtigt; ['ʌn'wɔrəntid] unverbürgt.

unwary □ [ʌn'wɛəri] unbedachtsam.

unwelcome [ʌn'welkəm] unwillkommen.

unwholesome ['ʌn'houlsəm] ungesund; schädlich.

unwieldy □ [ʌn'wiːldi] unhandlich; ungefüge, sperrig.

unwilling □ ['ʌn'wiliŋ] un-, widerwillig, abgeneigt.

unwind ['ʌn'waind] [*irr. (wind)*] auf-, loswickeln; (sich) abwickeln.

unwise □ ['ʌn'waiz] unklug.

unwitting □ [ʌn'witiŋ] unwissentlich; unbeabsichtigt.

unworkable ['ʌn'wəːkəbl] undurchführbar; ⊕ nicht betriebsfähig.

unworthy □ [ʌn'wəːði] unwürdig.

unwrap ['ʌn'ræp] auswickeln, auspacken, aufwickeln.

unwrought ['ʌn'rɔːt] unbearbeitet; roh; Roh...

unyielding □ [ʌn'jiːldiŋ] unnachgiebig.

up [ʌp] 1. *adv.* (her-, hin)auf; aufwärts, empor; oben; auf(gestanden); aufgegangen (*Sonne*); hoch; abgelaufen, um (*Zeit*); *Am. Baseball:* am Schlag; ~ *and about* wieder auf den Beinen; *be hard* ~ in Geldschwierigkeiten sein; ~ *against a task* e-r Aufgabe gegenüber; ~ *to* bis (zu); *it is* ~ *to me to do* es ist an mir, zu tun; *what are you* ~ *there?* was macht ihr da? *what's* ~? *sl.* was ist los? 2. *prp.* hinauf; ~ *the river* flußaufwärts; 3. *adj.:* ~ *train* Zug *m* nach der Stadt; 4.: *the* ~*s and downs* das Auf und Ab, die Höhen und Tiefen *des Lebens*; 5. F (sich) erheben; hochfahren; hochtreiben.

up|-and-coming *Am.* F ['ʌpən-'kʌmiŋ] unternehmungslustig; **~braid** [ʌp'breid] schelten; **~bringing** ['ʌpbriŋiŋ] Erziehung *f*; **~country** ['ʌp'kʌntri] landeinwärts (gelegen); **~heaval** [ʌp'hiːvl] Umbruch *m*; **~hill** ['ʌp'hil] bergan; mühsam; **~hold** [ʌp'hould] [*irr. (hold)*] aufrecht(er)halten; stützen; **~holster** [~lstə] *Möbel* (auf)polstern; *Zimmer* dekorieren; **~holsterer** [~ərə] Tapezierer *m*, Dekorateur *m*, Polsterer *m*; **~holstery** [~ri] Polstermöbel *n/pl.*; Möbelstoffe *m/pl.*; Tapeziererarbeit *f*.

up|keep ['ʌpkiːp] Instandhaltung(skosten *pl.*) *f*; Unterhalt *m*; **~land** ['ʌplənd] Hoch-, Oberland *n*; **~lift 1.** [ʌp'lift] (empor-, er)heben; 2. ['ʌplift] Erhebung *f*; *fig.* Aufschwung *m*.

upon [ə'pɔn] = *on*.

upper ['ʌpə] ober; Ober...; **~most** oberst, höchst.

up|raise [ʌp'reiz] erheben; **~rear** [ʌp'riə] aufrichten; **~right 1.** □ ['ʌp'rait] aufrecht; ~ *piano* ♪ Klavier *n*; *fig.* ['ʌprait] rechtschaffen; 2. Pfosten *m*; Ständer *m*; **~rising** [ʌp'raiziŋ] Erhebung *f*, Aufstand *m*.

uproar ['ʌprɔː] Aufruhr *m*; **~ious** □ [ʌp'rɔːriəs] tobend; tosend.

up|root [ʌp'ruːt] entwurzeln; (her-) ausreißen; **set** [ʌp'set] [*irr.* (set)] umwerfen; (um)stürzen; außer Fassung *od.* in Unordnung bringen; stören; verwirren; *be* ~ außer sich sein; **shot** ['ʌpʃɔt] Ausgang *m*; **side** ['ʌpsaid] *adv.*: ~ *down* das Oberste zuunterst; verkehrt; **stairs** ['ʌp'stɛəz] die Treppe hinauf, (nach) oben; **start** ['ʌpstɑːt] Emporkömmling *m*; **state** *Am.* ['ʌp'steit] Hinterland *n e-s Staates*; **stream** ['ʌp'striːm] fluß-, stromaufwärts; **~-to-date** ['ʌptə'deit] modern, neuzeitlich; **town** ['ʌp'taun] im *od.* in den oberen Stadtteil; *Am.* im Wohn- *od.* Villenviertel; **turn** [ʌp'tɜːn] nach oben kehren; **ward**(s) ['ʌpwəd(z)] aufwärts (gerichtet).

uranium ⚗ [juə'reinjəm] Uran *n*.

urban ['ɜːbən] städtisch; Stadt...; **~e** □ [əː'bein] höflich; gebildet.

urchin ['əːtʃin] Bengel *m*.

urge [əːdʒ] 1. *oft* ~ *on j-n* drängen, (an)treiben; dringen in *j-n*; dringen auf *et.*; *Recht* geltend machen; 2. Drang *m*; **~ncy** ['əːdʒənsi] Dringlichkeit *f*; Drängen *n*; **~nt** □ [~nt] dringend; dringlich; eilig.

urin|al ['juərinl] Harnglas *n*; Bedürfnisanstalt *f*; **~ate** [~neit] urinieren; **~e** [~in] Urin *m*, Harn *m*.

urn [əːn] Urne *f*; Tee- *etc.* Maschine *f*.

us [ʌs, əs] uns; *of* ~ unser.

usage ['juːzidʒ] Brauch *m*, Gepflogenheit *f*; Sprachgebrauch *m*; Behandlung *f*, Verwendung *f*, Gebrauch *m*.

usance † ['juːzəns] Wechselfrist *f*.

use 1. [juːs] Gebrauch *m*; Benutzung *f*; Verwendung *f*; Gewohnheit *f*, Übung *f*; Brauch *m*; Nutzen *m*; (*of*) *no* ~ unnütz, zwecklos; *have no* ~ *for* keine Verwendung haben

für; *Am.* F nicht mögen; 2. [juːz] gebrauchen; benutzen, ver-, anwenden; behandeln; ~ *up* ver-, aufbrauchen; *I* ~*d to do* ich pflegte zu tun, früher tat ich; **~d** [juːzd] gewöhnt (*to an acc.*); gewohnt (*to zu od. acc.*); **~ful** □ ['juːsful] brauchbar; nützlich; Nutz...; **~less** □ ['juːslis] nutz-, zwecklos, unnütz.

usher ['ʌʃə] 1. Türhüter *m*, Pförtner *m*; Gerichtsdiener *m*; Platzanweiser *m*; 2. *mst.* ~ *in* (hin)einführen, anmelden; **~ette** [ʌʃə'ret] Platzanweiserin *f*.

usual □ ['juːʒuəl] gewöhnlich; üblich; gebräuchlich.

usurer ['juːʒərə] Wucherer *m*.

usurp [juː'zəːp] sich *et.* widerrechtlich aneignen, an sich reißen; **~er** [~pə] Usurpator *m*.

usury ['juːʒuri] Wucher(zinsen *pl.*) *m*.

utensil [juː(ː)'tensl] Gerät *n*; Geschirr *n*.

uterus *anat.* ['juːtərəs] Gebärmutter *f*.

utility [juː(ː)'tiliti] 1. Nützlichkeit *f*, Nutzen *m*; *public* ~ öffentlicher Versorgungsbetrieb; 2. Gebrauchs..., Einheits...

utiliz|ation [juːtilai'zeiʃən] Nutzbarmachung *f*; Nutzanwendung *f*; **~e** ['juːtilaiz] sich *et.* zunutze machen.

utmost ['ʌtmoust] äußerst.

Utopian [juː'toupjən] 1. utopisch; 2. Utopist(in), Schwärmer(in).

utter ['ʌtə] 1. □ *fig.* äußerst; völlig, gänzlich; 2. äußern; *Seufzer etc.* ausstoßen, von sich geben; *Falschgeld etc.* in Umlauf setzen; **~ance** ['ʌtərəns] Äußerung *f*, Ausdruck *m*; Aussprache *f*; **~most** ['ʌtəmoust] äußerst.

uvula *anat.* ['juːvjulə] Zäpfchen *n*.

V

vacan|cy ['veikənsi] Leere *f*; leerer *od.* freier Platz; Lücke *f*; offene Stelle; **~t** □ [~nt] leer (*a. fig.*); frei (*Zeit, Zimmer*); offen (*Stelle*); unbesetzt, vakant (*Amt*).

vacat|e [və'keit, *Am.* 'veikeit] räumen; *Stelle* aufgeben, aus *e-m Amt* scheiden; **~ion** [və'keiʃən, *Am.* vei'keiʃən] 1. (Schul)Ferien *pl.*; *bsd. Am.* Urlaub *m*; Räumung *f*; Niederlegung *f e-s Amtes*; 2. *Am.* Urlaub machen; **~ionist** *Am.* [~nist] Ferienreisende(r *m*) *f*.

vaccin|ate ['væksineit] impfen;

~ation [væksi'neiʃən] Impfung *f*; **~e** ['væksiːn] Impfstoff *m*.

vacillate ['væsileit] schwanken.

vacu|ous □ ['vækjuəs] *fig.* leer, geistlos; **~um** *phys.* [~uəm] Vakuum *n*; ~ *cleaner* Staubsauger *m*; ~ *flask*, ~ *bottle* Thermosflasche *f*.

vagabond ['vægəbɔnd] 1. vagabundierend; 2. Landstreicher *m*.

vagary ['veigəri] wunderlicher Einfall, Laune *f*, Schrulle *f*.

vagrant ['veigrənt] 1. wandernd; *fig.* unstet; 2. Landstreicher *m*, Vagabund *m*; Strolch *m*.

vague □ [veig] unbestimmt; unklar.

vain □ [vein] eitel, eingebildet; leer; nichtig; vergeblich; *in ~* vergebens, umsonst; **~glorious** □ [vein'glɔːriəs] prahlerisch.

vale [veil] *poet. od. in Namen:* Tal *n.*

valediction [væli'dikʃən] Abschied(sworte *n/pl.*) *m.*

valentine ['vælǝntain] Valentinsschatz *m*, -gruß *m* (*am Valentinstag, 14. Februar, erwählt, gesandt.*).

valerian ♀ [vǝ'liǝriǝn] Baldrian *m.*

valet ['vælit] **1.** (Kammer)Diener *m*; **2.** Diener sein bei *j-m*; *j-n* bedienen.

valetudinarian ['vælitjuːdi'nεǝriǝn] **1.** kränklich; **2.** kränklicher Mensch; Hypochonder *m.*

valiant □ ['væljǝnt] tapfer.

valid □ ['vælid] triftig, richtig, stichhaltig; (rechts)gültig; *be ~* gelten; **~ity** [vǝ'liditi] Gültigkeit *f*; Triftig-, Richtigkeit *f.*

valise [vǝ'liːz] Reisetasche *f*; ✕ Tornister *m.*

valley ['væli] Tal *n.*

valo(u)r ['vælǝ] Tapferkeit *f.*

valuable □ ['væljuǝbl] **1.** □ wertvoll; **2.** *~s pl.* Wertsachen *f/pl.*

valuation [vælju'eiʃən] Abschätzung *f*; Taxwert *m.*

value ['væljuː] **1.** Wert *m*; Währung *f*; *give (get) good ~* (*for one's money*) ✝ reell bedienen (bedient werden); **2.** (ab)schätzen; *fig.* schätzen; **~less** [~julis] wertlos.

valve [vælv] Klappe *f*; Ventil *n*; *Radio:* Röhre *f.*

vamoose *Am. sl.* [vǝ'muːs] *v/i.* abhauen; *v/t.* räumen (*verlassen*).

vamp F [væmp] **1.** Vamp *m* (*verführerische Frau*); **2.** neppen.

vampire ['væmpaiǝ] Vampir *m.*

van [væn] Möbelwagen *m*; Lieferwagen *m*; ⊞ Pack-, Güterwagen *m*; ✕ Vorhut *f.*

vane [vein] Wetterfahne *f*; (Windmühlen-, Propeller)Flügel *m.*

vanguard ✕ ['vænɡɑːd] Vorhut *f.*

vanilla ♀ [vǝ'nilǝ] Vanille *f.*

vanish ['væniʃ] (ver)schwinden.

vanity ['væniti] Eitelkeit *f*, Einbildung *f*; Nichtigkeit *f*; *~ bag* Kosmetiktäschchen *n.*

vanquish ['væŋkwiʃ] besiegen.

vantage ['vɑːntidʒ] *Tennis:* Vorteil *m*; **~-ground** günstige Stellung.

vapid □ ['væpid] schal; fad(e).

vapor|ize ['veipǝraiz] verdampfen, verdunsten (lassen); **~ous** □ [~rǝs] dunstig; nebelhaft.

vapo(u)r ['veipǝ] Dunst *m*; Dampf *m.*

varia|ble □ ['vεǝriǝbl] veränderlich; **~nce** [~ǝns] Veränderung *f*; Uneinigkeit *f*; *be at ~* uneinig sein; (sich) widersprechen; *set at ~* entzweien; **~nt** [~nt] **1.** abweichend; **2.** Variante *f*; **~tion** [vεǝri'eiʃǝn]

Abänderung *f*; Schwankung *f*; Abweichung *f*; ♪ Variation *f.*

varicose ✿ ['værikous] Krampfader(n)...; *~ vein* Krampfader *f.*

varie|d □ ['vεǝrid] verschieden, geändert, mannigfaltig; **~gate** [~igeit] bunt gestalten; **~ty** [vǝ'raiǝti] Mannigfaltigkeit *f*, Vielzahl *f*; *biol.* Abart *f*; ✝ Auswahl *f*; Menge *f*; *~ show* Varietévorstellung *f*; *~ theatre* Varieté(theater) *n.*

various □ ['vεǝriǝs] verschiedene, mehrere; mannigfaltig; verschiedenartig.   [Racker.\]

varmint *sl.* ['vɑːmint] *kleiner*

varnish ['vɑːniʃ] **1.** Firnis *m*, Lack *m*; *fig.* (äußerer) Anstrich; **2.** firnissen, lackieren; *fig.* beschönigen.

vary ['vεǝri] (sich) (ver)ändern; wechseln (mit *et.*); abweichen.

vase [vɑːz] Vase *f.*

vassal ['væsǝl] Vasall *m*; *attr.* Vasallen...

vast □ [vɑːst] ungeheuer, gewaltig, riesig, umfassend, weit.

vat [væt] Faß *n*; Bottich *m*; Kufe *f.*

vaudeville *Am.* ['voudǝvil] Varieté *n.*

vault [vɔːlt] **1.** Gewölbe *n*; Wölbung *f*; Stahlkammer *f*; Gruft *f*; *bsd. Sport:* Sprung *m*; *wine-* Weinkeller *m*; **2.** (über)wölben; *bsd. Sport:* springen (über *acc.*).

vaulting-horse ['vɔːltiŋhɔːs] Turnen: Pferd *n.*

vaunt *lit.* [vɔːnt] (sich) rühmen.

veal [viːl] Kalbfleisch *n*; *roast ~* Kalbsbraten *m.*

veer [viǝ] (sich) drehen.

vegeta|ble ['vedʒitǝbl] **1.** Pflanzen..., pflanzlich; **2.** Pflanze *f*; *mst ~s pl.* Gemüse *n*; **~rian** [vedʒi'tεǝriǝn] **1.** Vegetarier(in); **2.** vegetarisch; **~te** ['vedʒiteit] vegetieren; **~tive** □ [~tǝtiv] vegetativ; wachstumfördernd.

vehemen|ce ['viːimǝns] Heftigkeit *f*; Gewalt *f*; **~t** □ [~nt] heftig; ungestüm.

vehicle ['viːikl] Fahrzeug *n*, Beförderungsmittel *n*; *fig.* Vermittler *m*, Träger *m*; Ausdrucksmittel *n.*

veil [veil] **1.** Schleier *m*; Hülle *f*; **2.** (sich) verschleiern (*a. fig.*).

vein [vein] Ader *f* (*a. fig.*); Anlage *f*; Neigung *f*; Stimmung *f.*

velocipede [vi'lɔsipiːd] *Am.* (Kinder)Dreirad *n*; *hist.* Veloziped *n.*

velocity [vi'lɔsiti] Geschwindigkeit *f.*

velvet ['velvit] **1.** Samt *m*; *hunt.* Bast *m*; **2.** Samt...; samten; **~y** [~ti] samtig.

venal ['viːnl] käuflich, feil.

vend [vend] verkaufen; **~er**, **~or** ['vendǝ, ~dɔː] Verkäufer *m*, Händler *m.*

veneer [vi'niǝ] **1.** Furnier *n*; **2.** furnieren; *fig.* bemänteln.

venera|ble □ ['venərəbl] ehrwürdig; **~te** [.reit] (ver)ehren; **~tion** [venə'reiʃən] Verehrung *f*.

venereal [vi'niəriəl] Geschlechts...

Venetian [vi'ni:ʃən] 1. venetianisch; **~ blind** (Stab)Jalousie *f*; 2. Venetianer(in).

vengeance ['vendʒəns] Rache *f*; **with a ~** F und wie, ganz gehörig.

venial □ ['vi:njəl] verzeihlich.

venison ['venzn] Wildbret *n*.

venom ['venəm] (*bsd.* Schlangen-) Gift *n*; *fig.* Gift *n*; Gehässigkeit *f*; **~ous** [.məs] giftig.

venous ['vi:nəs] Venen...; venös.

vent [vent] 1. Öffnung *f*; Luft-, Spundloch *n*; Auslaß *m*; Schlitz *m*; **give ~ to** s-m Zorn *etc.* Luft machen; 2. *fig.* Luft machen (*dat.*).

ventilat|e ['ventileit] ventilieren, (be-, ent-, durch)lüften; *fig.* erörtern; **~ion** [venti'leiʃən] Ventilation *f*, Lüftung *f*; *fig.* Erörterung *f*; **~or** ['ventileitə] Ventilator *m*.

ventral *anat.* ['ventrəl] Bauch...

ventriloquist [ven'triləkwist] Bauchredner *m*.

ventur|e ['ventʃə] 1. Wagnis *n*; Risiko *n*; Abenteuer *n*; Spekulation *f*; **at a ~** auf gut Glück; 2. (sich) wagen; riskieren; **~esome** □ [.əsəm], **~ous** □ [.ərəs] verwegen, kühn.

veracious [ve'reiʃəs] wahrhaft.

verb *gr.* [və:b] Verb(um) *n*, Zeitwort *n*; **~al** □ ['və:bəl] wörtlich; mündlich; **~iage** ['və:biidʒ] Wortschwall *m*; **~ose** □ [və:'bous] wortreich. [reif.]

verdant □ ['və:dənt] grün; *fig.* un-]

verdict ['və:dikt] ½⅔ (Urteils-) Spruch *m der Geschworenen*; *fig.* Urteil *n*; **bring in** *od.* **return a ~ of** guilty auf schuldig erkennen.

verdigris ['və:digris] Grünspan *m*.

verdure ['və:dʒə] Grün *n*.

verge [və:dʒ] 1. Rand *m*, Grenze *f*; **on the ~ of** am Rande (*gen.*); dicht vor (*dat.*); 2. sich (hin)neigen; **~ (up)on** grenzen an (*acc.*).

veri|fy ['verifai] (nach)prüfen; beweisen; bestätigen; **~similitude** [verisi'militju:d] Wahrscheinlichkeit *f*; **~table** □ ['veritəbl] wahr (-haftig).

vermic|elli [və:mi'seli] Fadennudeln *f/pl.*; **~ular** [və:'mikjulə] wurmartig.

vermilion [və'miljən] 1. Zinnoberrot *n*; 2. zinnoberrot.

vermin ['və:min] Ungeziefer *n*; *hunt.* Raubzeug *n*; *fig.* Gesindel *n*; **~ous** [.nəs] voller Ungeziefer.

vernacular [və'nækjulə] 1. □ einheimisch; Volks...; 2. Landes-, Muttersprache *f*; Jargon *m*.

versatile □ ['və:sətail] wendig.

verse [və:s] Vers(e *pl.*) *m*; Strophe *f*; Dichtung *f*; **~d** □ [və:st] bewandert.

versify ['və:sifai] *v/t.* in Verse bringen; *v/i.* Verse machen.

version ['və:ʃən] Übersetzung *f*; Fassung *f*, Darstellung *f*; Lesart *f*.

versus *bsd.* ½⅔ ['və:səs] gegen.

vertebra *anat.* ['və:tibrə], *pl.* **~e** [.ri:] Wirbel *m*.

vertical □ ['və:tikəl] vertikal, senkrecht.

vertig|inous □ [və:'tidʒinəs] schwindlig; schwindelnd (*Höhe*); **~o** ['və:tigou] Schwindel(anfall) *m*.

verve [veəv] Schwung *m*, Verve *f*.

very ['veri] 1. *adv.* sehr; **the ~ best** das allerbeste; 2. *adj.* wirklich; eben; bloß; **the ~ same** ebenderselbe; **in the ~ act** auf frischer Tat; gerade dabei; **the ~ thing** gerade das; **the ~ thought** der bloße Gedanke; **the ~ stones** sogar die Steine; **the veriest rascal** der größte Schuft.

vesicle ['vesikl] Bläs-chen *n*.

vessel ['vesl] Gefäß *n* (*a. anat.*, ⚕, *fig.*); ♣ Fahrzeug *n*, Schiff *n*.

vest [vest] 1. Unterhemd *n*; Weste *f*; 2. *v/t.* bekleiden (with mit); *j-n* einsetzen (in in *acc.*); *et.* übertragen (in s.o. j-m); *v/i.* verliehen werden.

vestibule ['vestibju:l] Vorhof *m* (*a. anat.*); Vorhalle *f*; Hausflur *m*; *bsd. Am.* ⚙ Korridor *m zwischen zwei D-Zug-Wagen*; **~ train** D-Zug *m*.

vestige ['vestidʒ] Spur *f*.

vestment ['vestmənt] Gewand *n*.

vestry ['vestri] *eccl.* Sakristei *f*; Gemeindevertretung *f*; Gemeindesaal *m*; **~man** Gemeindevertreter *m*.

vet F [vet] 1. Tierarzt *m*; *Am.* ⚔ Veteran *m*; 2. *co.* verarzten; gründlich prüfen.

veteran ['vetərən] 1. ausgedient; erfahren; 2. Veteran *m*.

veterinary ['vetərinəri] 1. tierärztlich; 2. *a.* **~ surgeon** Tierarzt *m*.

veto ['vi:tou] 1. *pl.* **~es** Veto *n*; 2. sein Veto einlegen gegen.

vex [veks] ärgern; schikanieren; **~ation** [vek'seiʃən] Verdruß *m*; Ärger(nis *n*) *m*; **~atious** [.ʃəs] ärgerlich.

via [vaiə] über, via.

viaduct ['vaiədʌkt] Viadukt *m*, Überführung *f*.

vial ['vaiəl] Phiole *f*, Fläschchen *n*.

viand ['vaiənd] *mst.* **~s** *pl.* Lebensmittel *n/pl.*

vibrat|e [vai'breit] vibrieren; zittern; **~ion** [.ʃən] Schwingung *f*, Zittern *n*, Vibrieren *n*, Erschütterung *f*.

vicar *eccl.* ['vikə] Vikar *m*; **~age** [.əridʒ] Pfarrhaus *n*.

vice[1] [vais] Laster *n*; Fehler *m*; Unart *f*; ⊕ Schraubstock *m*.

vice[2] *prp.* [vais] an Stelle von.

vice[3] [vais] F Stellvertreter *m*; *attr.* Vize..., Unter...; **~roy** ['vaisrɔi] Vizekönig *m*.

vice versa ['vaisi'vɔ:sə] umgekehrt.
vicinity [vi'siniti] Nachbarschaft f; Nähe f.
vicious □ ['viʃəs] lasterhaft; bösartig; boshaft; fehlerhaft.
vicissitude [vi'sisitju:d] Wandel m, Wechsel m; ~s pl. Wechselfälle m/pl.
victim ['viktim] Opfer n; ~ize [~maiz] (hin)opfern; fig. j-n hereinlegen.
victor ['viktə] Sieger m; ♀ian hist. [vik'tɔ:riən] Viktorianisch; ~ious □ [~iəs] siegreich; Sieges...; ~y ['viktəri] Sieg m.
victual ['vitl] 1. (sich) verpflegen od. verproviantieren; 2. mst ~s pl. Lebensmittel n/pl., Proviant m; ~(l)er [~lə] Lebensmittellieferant m.
video ['vidiou] Fernseh...
vie [vai] wetteifern.
Viennese [vie'ni:z] 1. Wiener(in); 2. Wiener..., wienerisch.
view [vju:] 1. Sicht f, Blick m; Besichtigung f; Aussicht f (of auf acc.); Anblick m; Ansicht f (a. fig.); Absicht f; at first ~ auf den ersten Blick; in ~ sichtbar, zu sehen; in ~ of im Hinblick auf (acc.); fig. angesichts (gen.); on ~ zu besichtigen; with a ~ to inf. od. of ger. in der Absicht zu inf.; have (keep) in ~ im Auge haben (behalten); 2. ansehen, besichtigen; fig. betrachten; ~er ['vju:ə] Betrachter(in), Zuschauer (-in); ~less ['vju:lis] ohne eigene Meinung; poet. unsichtbar; ~point Gesichts-, Standpunkt m.
vigil ['vidʒil] Nachtwache f; ~ance [~ləns] Wachsamkeit f; ~ant □ [~nt] wachsam.
vigo|rous □ ['vigərəs] kräftig; energisch; nachdrücklich; ~(u)r ['vigə] Kraft f; Vitalität f; Nachdruck m.
viking ['vaikin] 1. Wiking(er) m; 2. wikingisch, Wikinger...
vile □ [vail] gemein; abscheulich.
vilify ['vilifai] verunglimpfen.
village ['vilidʒ] Dorf n; ~ green Dorfanger m, -wiese f; ~r [~dʒə] Dorfbewohner(in).
villain ['vilən] Schurke m, Schuft m, Bösewicht m; ~ous □ [~nəs] schurkisch; F scheußlich; ~y [~ni] Schurkerei f.
vim F [vim] Schwung m, Schneid m.
vindicat|e ['vindikeit] rechtfertigen (from gegen); verteidigen; ~ion [vindi'keiʃən] Rechtfertigung f.
vindictive □ [vin'diktiv] rachsüchtig.
vine ♀ [vain] Wein(stock) m, Rebe f; ~gar ['vinigə] (Wein)Essig m; ~growing ['vaingrouin] Weinbau m; ~yard ['vinjəd] Weinberg m.
vintage ['vintidʒ] 1. Weinlese f; (Wein)Jahrgang m; 2. klassisch; erlesen; altmodisch; ~ car mot. Veteran m; ~r [~dʒə] Winzer m.

viola ♪ [vi'oulə] Bratsche f.
violat|e ['vaiəleit] verletzen; Eid etc. brechen; vergewaltigen, schänden; ~ion [vaiə'leiʃən] Verletzung f; (Eid- etc.)Bruch m; Vergewaltigung f, Schändung f.
violen|ce ['vaiələns] Gewalt(samkeit, -tätigkeit) f; Heftigkeit f; ~t □ [~nt] gewaltsam; gewalttätig; heftig.
violet ♀ ['vaiəlit] Veilchen n.
violin ♪ [vaiə'lin] Violine f, Geige f.
V.I.P., VIP ['vi:ai'pi:] F hohes Tier.
viper zo. ['vaipə] Viper f, Natter f.
virago [vi'rɑ:gou] Zankteufel m.
virgin ['və:dʒin] 1. Jungfrau f; 2. a. ~al □ [~nl] jungfräulich; Jungfern...; ~ity [və:'dʒiniti] Jungfräulichkeit f.
viril|e ['virail] männlich; Mannes...; ~ity [vi'riliti] Männlichkeit f.
virtu [və:'tu:]: article of ~ Kunstgegenstand m; ~al □ ['və:tjuəl] eigentlich; ~ally [~li] praktisch; ~e ['və:tju:] Tugend f; Wirksamkeit f; Vorzug m, Wert m; in od. by ~ of kraft, vermöge (gen.); make a ~ of necessity aus der Not e-e Tugend machen; ~osity [və:tju'ɔsiti] Virtuosität f; ~ous □ ['və:tjuəs] tugendhaft.
virulent □ ['virulənt] giftig; ⚕ virulent; fig. bösartig.
virus ⚕ ['vaiərəs] Virus n; fig. Gift n.
visa ['vi:zə] Visum n, Sichtvermerk m; ~ed [~əd] mit e-m Sichtvermerk od. Visum versehen.
viscose ⚗ ['viskous] Viskose f; ~ silk Zellstoffseide f.
viscount ['vaikaunt] Vicomte m; ~ess [~tis] Vicomtesse f.
viscous □ ['viskəs] zähflüssig.
vise Am. [vais] Schraubstock m.
visé ['vi:zei] = visa.
visib|ility [vizi'biliti] Sichtbarkeit f; Sichtweite f; ~le □ ['vizəbl] sichtbar; fig. (er)sichtlich; pred. zu sehen (S.); zu sprechen (P.).
vision ['viʒən] Sehvermögen n, Sehkraft f; fig. Scherblick m; Vision f, Erscheinung f; ~ary ['viʒənəri] 1. phantastisch; 2. Geisterseher(in); Phantast(in).
visit ['vizit] 1. v/t. besuchen; besichtigen; fig. heimsuchen; et. vergelten, v/i. Besuche machen; Am. sich unterhalten, plaudern (with mit); 2. Besuch m; ~ation [vizi'teiʃən] Besuch m; Besichtigung f; fig. Heimsuchung f; ~or ['vizitə] Besucher(in), Gast m; Inspektor m.
vista ['vistə] Durchblick m; Rückod. Ausblick m.
visual □ ['vizjuəl] Seh...; Gesichts-...; ~ize [~laiz] (sich) vor Augen stellen, sich ein Bild machen von.
vital □ ['vaitl] 1. Lebens...; lebenswichtig, wesentlich; lebensgefähr-

lich; ~ parts pl. = 2. ~s pl. lebenswichtige Organe n/pl.; edle Teile m/pl.; ~ity [vai'tæliti] Lebenskraft f; Vitalität f; ~ize ['vaitəlaiz] beleben.

vitamin(e) ['vitəmin] Vitamin n.

vitiate ['viʃieit] verderben; beeinträchtigen; hinfällig (zɮ ungültig) machen.

vitreous □ ['vitriəs] Glas...; gläsern.

vituperate [vi'tju:pəreit] schelten; schmähen, beschimpfen.

vivaci|ous □ [vi'veiʃəs] lebhaft; ~ty [vi'væsiti] Lebhaftigkeit f.

vivid □ ['vivid] lebhaft, lebendig.

vivify ['vivifai] (sich) beleben.

vixen ['viksn] Füchsin f; zänkisches Weib.

vocabulary [və'kæbjuləri] Wörterverzeichnis n; Wortschatz m.

vocal □ ['voukəl] stimmlich; Stimm...; gesprochen; laut; ♪ Vokal..., Gesang...; klingend; gr. stimmhaft; ~ist [~list] Sänger(in); ~ize [~laiz] (gr. stimmhaft) aussprechen; singen.

vocation [vou'keiʃən] Berufung f; Beruf m; ~al [~nl] beruflich; Berufs...

vociferate [vou'sifəreit] schreien.

vogue [voug] Beliebtheit f; Mode f.

voice [vɔis] 1. Stimme f; active (passive) ~ gr. Aktiv n (Passiv n); give ~ to Ausdruck geben (dat.); 2. äußern, ausdrücken; gr. stimmhaft aussprechen.

void [vɔid] 1. leer; zɮ ungültig; ~ of frei von; arm an (dat.); ohne; 2. Leere f; Lücke f; 3. entleeren; ungültig machen, aufheben.

volatile ['vɔlətail] 🜍 flüchtig (a. fig.); flatterhaft.

volcano [vɔl'keinou] pl. ~es Vulkan m.

volition [vou'liʃən] Wollen n; Wille(nskraft f) m.

volley ['vɔli] 1. Salve f; (Geschoßetc.)Hagel m; fig. Schwall m; Tennis: Flugball m; 2. mst ~ out e-n Schwall von Worten etc. von sich geben; Salven abgeben; fig. hageln; dröhnen; ~-ball Sport: Volleyball m, Flugball m.

volt ⚡ [voult] Volt n; ~age ⚡ ['voultidʒ] Spannung f; ~meter ⚡ Volt-, Spannungsmesser m.

volub|ility [vɔlju'biliti] Redegewandtheit f; ~le □ ['vɔljubl] (rede-) gewandt.

volum|e ['vɔljum] Band m e-s Buches; Volumen n; fig. Masse f,

große Menge; (bsd. Stimm)Umfang m; ~ of sound Radio: Lautstärke f; ~inous □ [və'lju:minəs] vielbändig; umfangreich, voluminös.

volunt|ary □ ['vɔləntəri] freiwillig; willkürlich; ~eer [vɔlən'tiə] 1. Freiwillige(r m) f; attr. Freiwilligen...; 2. v/i. freiwillig dienen; sich freiwillig melden; sich erbieten; v/t. anbieten; sich e-e Bemerkung erlauben.

voluptu|ary [və'lʌptjuəri] Wolllüstling m; ~ous □ [~uəs] wolllüstig; üppig.

vomit ['vɔmit] 1. (sich) erbrechen; fig. (aus)speien, ausstoßen; 2. Erbrochene(s) n; Erbrechen n.

voraci|ous □ [və'reiʃəs] gefräßig; gierig; ~ty [və'ræsiti] Gefräßigkeit f; Gier f.

vort|ex ['vɔ:teks], pl. mst ~ices ['vɔ:tisi:z] Wirbel m, Strudel m (mst fig.).

vote [vout] 1. (Wahl)Stimme f; Abstimmung f; Stimmrecht n; Beschluß m, Votum n; ~ of no confidence Mißtrauensvotum n; cast a ~ (s)eine Stimme abgeben; take a ~ on s.th. über et. abstimmen; 2. v/t. stimmen für; v/i. (ab)stimmen; wählen; ~ for stimmen für; F für et. sein; et. vorschlagen; ~r ['voutə] Wähler(in).

voting ['voutiŋ] Abstimmung f; attr. Wahl...; ~ machine Stimmenzählmaschine f; ~-paper Stimmzettel m; ~-power Stimmrecht n.

vouch [vautʃ] verbürgen; ~ for bürgen für; ~er ['vautʃə] Beleg m, Unterlage f; Gutschein m; Zeuge m; ~safe [vautʃ'seif] gewähren; geruhen.

vow [vau] 1. Gelübde n; (Treu-) Schwur m; 2. v/t. geloben.

vowel gr. ['vauəl] Vokal m, Selbstlaut m.

voyage ['vɔidʒ] 1. längere (See-, Flug)Reise; 2. reisen, fahren; ~r ['vɔidʒə] (See)Reisende(r m) f.

vulgar ['vʌlgə] 1. □ gewöhnlich, gemein, vulgär, pöbelhaft; ~ tongue Volkssprache f; 2.: the ~ der Pöbel; ~ism [~rizəm] vulgärer Ausdruck; ~ity [vʌl'gæriti] Gemeinheit f; ~ize ['vʌlgəraiz] gemein machen; erniedrigen; populär machen.

vulnerable □ ['vʌlnərəbl] verwundbar; fig. angreifbar.

vulpine ['vʌlpain] Fuchs...; fuchsartig; schlau, listig.

vulture orn. ['vʌltʃə] Geier m.

vying ['vaiiŋ] wetteifernd.

W

wacky *Am. sl.* ['wæki] verrückt.
wad [wɔd] **1.** (Watte)Bausch *m*; Polster *n*; Pfropf(en) *m*; Banknotenbündel *n*; **2.** wattieren; polstern; zs.-pressen; zustopfen; **~ding** ['wɔdiŋ] Wattierung *f*; Watte *f*.
waddle ['wɔdl] watscheln, wackeln.
wade [weiː] *v/i.* waten; *fig.* sich hindurcharbeiten; *v/t.* durchwaten.
wafer ['weifə] Waffel *f*; Oblate *f*; *eccl.* Hostie *f*.
waffle ['wɔfl] **1.** Waffel *f*; **2.** F quasseln.
waft [wɑːft] **1.** wehen, tragen; **2.** Hauch *m*.
wag [wæg] **1.** wackeln (mit); wedeln (mit); **2.** Schütteln *n*; Wedeln *n*; Spaßvogel *m*.
wage¹ [weidʒ] *Krieg* führen.
wage² [⌐] *mst* **~s** *pl.* Lohn *m*; **~-earner** ['weidʒəːnə] Lohnempfänger *m*.
wager ['weidʒə] **1.** Wette *f*; **2.** wetten.
waggish □ ['wægiʃ] schelmisch.
waggle F ['wægl] wackeln (mit).
wag(g)on ['wægən] (Roll-, Güter-) Wagen *m*; **~er** [⌐nə] Fuhrmann *m*.
wagtail *orn.* ['wægteil] Bachstelze *f*.
waif [weif] herrenloses Gut; Strandgut *n*; Heimatlose(r *m*) *f*.
wail [weil] **1.** (Weh)Klagen *n*; **2.** (weh)klagen.
wainscot ['weinskət] (Holz)Täfelung *f*.
waist [weist] Taille *f*; schmalste Stelle; ♨ Mitteldeck *n*; **~coat** ['weiskout] Weste *f*; **~-line** ['weistlain] *Schneiderei*: Taille *f*.
wait [weit] **1.** *v/i.* warten (*for auf acc.*); *a.* **~** at (*Am. on*) *table* bedienen, servieren; **~** (*up*)*on j-n* bedienen; *j-n* besuchen; **~** *and see* abwarten; *v/t.* abwarten; mit *dem Essen* warten (*for auf j-n*); **2.** Warten *n*, Aufenthalt *m*; *lie in* **~** *for s.o.* j-m auflauern; **~er** ['weitə] Kellner *m*; Tablett *n*.
waiting ['weitiŋ] Warten *n*; Dienst *m*; *in* **~** diensttuend; **~-room** Wartezimmer *n*; 🚃 *etc.* Wartesaal *m*.
waitress ['weitris] Kellnerin *f*.
waive [weiv] verzichten auf (*acc.*), aufgeben; **~r** 🕮 ['weivə] Verzicht *m*.
wake [weik] **1.** ♨ Kielwasser *n* (*a. fig.*); Totenwache *f*; Kirmes *f*; **2.** [*irr.*] *v/i. a.* **~** *up* aufwachen; *v/t. a.* **~** *up* (auf)wecken; erwecken; *fig.* wachrufen; **~ful** □ ['weikful] wachsam; schlaflos; **~n** ['weikən] *s.* wake 2.
wale *bsd. Am.* [weil] Strieme *f*.
walk [wɔːk] **1.** *v/i.* (zu Fuß) gehen; spazierengehen; wandern; Schritt gehen; **~** *out* F streiken; **~** *out on sl.*

im Stich lassen; *v/t.* führen; *Pferd* Schritt gehen lassen; begleiten; (durch)wandern; umhergehen auf *od.* in (*dat.*); **2.** (Spazier)Gang *m*; Spazierweg *m*; **~** *of life* Lebensstellung *f*, Beruf *m*; **~er** ['wɔːkə] Fuß-, Spaziergänger(in).
walkie-talkie ⚔ ['wɔːki'tɔːki] tragbares Sprechfunkgerät.
walking ['wɔːkiŋ] Spazierengehen *n*, Wandern *n*; *attr.* Spazier...; Wander...; **~** *papers pl. Am.* F Entlassung(spapiere *n/pl.*) *f*; Laufpaß *m*; **~-stick** Spazierstock *m*; **~-tour** (Fuß)Wanderung *f*.
walk|-out *Am.* ['wɔːkaut] Ausstand *m*; **~over** Kinderspiel *n*, leichter Sieg.
wall [wɔːl] **1.** Wand *f*; Mauer *f*; **2.** mit Mauern umgeben; **~** *up* zumauern.
wallet ['wɔlit] Ränzel *n*; Brieftasche *f*.
wallflower *fig.* ['wɔːlflauə] Mauerblümchen *n*.
wallop F ['wɔləp] *j-n* verdreschen.
wallow ['wɔlou] sich wälzen.
wall|-paper ['wɔːlpeipə] Tapete *f*; **~socket** ⚡ Steckdose *f*.
walnut ♦ ['wɔːlnət] Walnuß(baum *m*) *f*.
walrus *zo.* ['wɔːlrəs] Walroß *n*.
waltz [wɔːls] **1.** Walzer *m*; **2.** Walzer tanzen.
wan □ [wɔn] blaß, bleich, fahl.
wand [wɔnd] (Zauber)Stab *m*.
wander ['wɔndə] wandern; umherschweifen, umherwandern; *fig.* abschweifen; irregehen; phantasieren.
wane [wein] **1.** abnehmen (*Mond*); *fig.* schwinden; **2.** Abnehmen *n*.
wangle *sl.* ['wæŋgl] *v/t.* deichseln, hinkriegen; *v/i.* mogeln.
want [wɔnt] **1.** Mangel *m* (*of an dat.*); Bedürfnis *n*; Not *f*; **2.** *v/i.*: *be* **~ing** fehlen; es fehlen lassen (*in an dat.*); unzulänglich sein; **~** *for* Not leiden an (*dat.*); *it* **~s** *of* es fehlt an (*dat.*); *v/t.* bedürfen (*gen.*), brauchen; nicht haben; wünschen, (haben) wollen; *it* **~s** *s.th.* es fehlt an et. (*dat.*); *he* **~s** *energy* es fehlt ihm an Energie; **~ed** gesucht; **~-ad** F ['wɔntæd] Kleinanzeige *f*; Stellenangebot *n*, -gesuch *n*.
wanton ['wɔntən] **1.** □ geil; üppig; mutwillig; **2.** Dirne *f*; **3.** umhertollen.
war [wɔː] **1.** Krieg *m*; *attr.* Kriegs...; *make* **~** Krieg führen (*upon gegen*); **2.** (ea. wider)streiten.
warble ['wɔːbl] trillern; singen.
ward [wɔːd] **1.** Gewahrsam *m*; Vormundschaft *f*; Mündel *n*; Schützling *m*; Gefängniszelle *f*; Abteilung *f*, Station *f*, Krankenzimmer *n*;

(Stadt)Bezirk *m*; ⊕ Einschnitt *m im Schlüsselbart*; 2. ~ *off* abwehren; **~en** ['wɔːdn] Aufseher *m*; (Luftschutz)Wart *m*; *univ.* Rektor *m*; **~er** ['wɔːdə] (Gefangenen)Wärter *m*; **~robe** ['wɔːdroub] Garderobe *f*; Kleiderschrank *m*; ~ *trunk* Schrankkoffer *m*.

ware [wɛə] Ware *f*; Geschirr *n*.

warehouse 1. ['wɛəhaus] (Waren-) Lager *n*; Speicher *m*; 2. [..auz] auf Lager bringen, einlagern.

war|fare ['wɔːfɛə] Krieg(führung *f*) *m*; **~head** ⚔ Sprengkopf *m* e-r *Rakete etc.*

wariness ['wɛərinis] Vorsicht *f*.

warlike ['wɔːlaik] kriegerisch.

warm [wɔːm] 1. □ warm (*a. fig.*); heiß; *fig.* hitzig; 2. F Erwärmung *f*; 3. *v/t. a.* ~ *up* (auf-, an-, er)wärmen; *v/i. a.* ~ *up* warm werden, sich erwärmen; **~th** [wɔːmθ] Wärme *f*.

warn [wɔːn] warnen (*of, against* vor *dat.*); verwarnen; ermahnen; verständigen; **~ing** ['wɔːniŋ] (Ver-) Warnung *f*; Mahnung *f*; Kündigung *f*.

warp [wɔːp] *v/i.* sich verziehen (*Holz*); *v/t. fig.* verdrehen, verzerren; beeinflussen; *j-n* abbringen (*from* von).

warrant ['wɔrənt] 1. Vollmacht *f*; Rechtfertigung *f*; Berechtigung *f*; ⚖ (Vollziehungs)Befehl *m*; Berechtigungsschein *m*; ~ *of arrest* ⚖ Haftbefehl *m*; 2. bevollmächtigen; *j-n* berechtigen; *et.* rechtfertigen; verbürgen; † garantieren; **~y** [..ti] Garantie *f*; Berechtigung *f*.

warrior ['wɔriə] Krieger *m*.

wart [wɔːt] Warze *f*; Auswuchs *m*.

wary □ ['wɛəri] vorsichtig, behutsam; wachsam.

was [wɔz, wəz] 1. *und* 3. *sg. pret. von* be; *pret. pass. von* be; *he* ~ *to have come* er hätte kommen sollen.

wash [wɔʃ] 1. *v/t.* waschen; (um-) spülen; ~ *up* abwaschen, spülen; *v/i.* sich waschen (lassen); waschecht sein (*a. fig.*); spülen, schlagen (*Wellen*); 2. Waschen *n*; Wäsche *f*; Wellenschlag *m*; Spülwasser *n*; *contp.* Gewäsch *n*; *mouth-*~ Mundwasser *n*; **~able** ['wɔʃəbl] waschbar; **~basin** Waschbecken *n*; **~cloth** Waschlappen *m*; **~er** ['wɔʃə] Wäscherin *f*; Waschmaschine *f*; ⊕ Unterlagscheibe *f*; **~erwoman** Waschfrau *f*; **~ing** ['wɔʃiŋ] 1. Waschen *n*; Wäsche *f*; ~s *pl.* Spülicht *n*; 2. Wasch...; **~ing-up** Abwaschen *n*; **~rag** *bsd. Am.* Waschlappen *m*; **~y** ['wɔʃi] wässerig.

wasp [wɔsp] Wespe *f*.

wastage ['weistidʒ] Abgang *m*, Verlust *m*; Vergeudung *f*.

waste [weist] 1. wüst, öde; unbebaut; überflüssig; Abfall...; *lay* ~ verwüsten; ~ *paper* Altpapier *n*;

2. Verschwendung *f*, Vergeudung *f*; Abfall *m*; Einöde *f*, Wüste *f*; 3. *v/t.* verwüsten; verschwenden; verzehren; *v/i.* verschwendet werden; **~ful** □ ['weistful] verschwenderisch; **~-paper-basket** [weist'peipəbɑːskit] Papierkorb *m*; **~-pipe** ['weistpaip] Abflußrohr *n*.

watch [wɔtʃ] 1. Wache *f*; Taschenuhr *f*; 2. *v/i.* wachen; ~ *for* warten auf (*acc.*); ~ *out* F aufpassen; *v/t.* bewachen; beobachten; achtgeben auf (*acc.*); *Gelegenheit* abwarten; **~dog** ['wɔtʃdɔg] Wachhund *m*; **~ful** □ [..ful] wachsam, achtsam; **~maker** Uhrmacher *m*; **~man** (Nacht)Wächter *m*; **~word** Losung *f*.

water ['wɔːtə] 1. Wasser *n*; Gewässer *n*; *drink the* ~s Brunnen trinken; 2. *v/t.* bewässern; (be-) sprengen; (be)gießen; mit Wasser versorgen; tränken; verwässern (*a. fig.*); *v/i.* wässern (*Mund*) tränen (*Augen*); Wasser einnehmen; **~-closet** (Wasser)Klosett *n*; **~-colou(u)r** Aquarell(malerei *f*) *n*; **~course** Wasserlauf *m*; **~cress** ♣ Brunnenkresse *f*; **~fall** Wasserfall *m*; **~front** Ufer *n*, *bsd. Am. städtisches* Hafengebiet; **~ga(u)ge** ⊕ Wasserstands(an)zeiger *m*; Pegel *m*.

watering ['wɔːtəriŋ]: **~can** Gießkanne *f*; **~place** Wasserloch *n*; Tränke *f*; Bad(eort *m*) *n*; Seebad *n*; **~pot** Gießkanne *f*.

water|-level ['wɔːtəlevl] Wasserspiegel *m*; Wasserstand(slinie *f*) *m*; ⊕ Wasserwaage *f*; **~man** Fährmann *m*; Bootsführer *m*; Ruderer *m*; **~proof** 1. wasserdicht; 2. Regenmantel *m*; 3. imprägnieren; **~shed** Wasserscheide *f*; Stromgebiet *n*; **~side** 1. Fluß-, Seeufer *n*; 2. am Wasser (gelegen); **~tight** wasserdicht; *fig.* unangreifbar; **~way** Wasserstraße *f*; **~works** *oft sg.* Wasserwerk *n*; **~y** [..əri] wässerig.

watt ⚡ [wɔt] Watt *n*.

wattle ['wɔtl] 1. Flechtwerk *n*; 2. aus Flechtwerk herstellen.

wave [weiv] 1. Welle *f*; Woge *f*; Winken *n*; 2. *v/t.* wellig machen, wellen; schwingen; schwenken; ~ *s.o. aside* *j-n* beiseite winken; *v/i.* wogen, wehen, flattern; winken; **~-length** *phys.* ['weivleŋθ] Wellenlänge *f*.

waver ['weivə] (sch)wanken; flakkern.

wavy ['weivi] wellig; wogend.

wax¹ [wæks] 1. Wachs *n*; Siegellack *m*; Ohrenschmalz *n*; 2. wachsen; bohnern.

wax² [..] [*irr.*] zunehmen (*Mond*).

wax|en *fig.* ['wæksən] wächsern; **~y** □ [..si] wachsartig; weich.

way [wei] 1. *mst* Weg *m*; Straße *f*;

Art u. Weise *f; eigene* Art; Strecke *f;* Richtung *f;* F Gegend *f;* ⚓ Fahrt *f; fig.* Hinsicht *f;* Zustand *m;* ⚓ Helling *f;* ~ in Eingang *m;* ~ out Ausgang *m; fig.* Ausweg *m; right of* ~ gȴ Wegerecht *n; bsd. mot.* Vorfahrt(srecht *n*) *f; this* ~ hierher, hier entlang; *by the* ~ übrigens; *by* ~ *of* durch; *on the* ~, *on one's* ~ unterwegs; *out of the* ~ ungewöhnlich; *under* ~ in Fahrt; *give* ~ zurückgehen; *mot.* die Vorfahrt lassen (*to dat.*); nachgeben; abgelöst werden (*to von*); sich hingeben (*to dat.*); *have one's* ~ s-n Willen haben; *lead the* ~ vorangehen; **2.** *adv.* weit; ~-**bill** ['weibil] Frachtbrief *m;* ~**farer** ['weifєərə] Wanderer *m;* ~**lay** ['wei'lei] [*irr.* (*lay*)] j-m auflauern; ~**side 1.** Wegrand *m;* **2.** am Wege; ~ **station** *Am.* Zwischenstation *f;* ~ **train** *Am.* Bummelzug *m;* ~**ward** ☐ ['weiwəd] starrköpfig, eigensinnig.

we [wi:, wi] wir.

weak ☐ [wi:k] schwach; schwächlich; dünn (*Getränk*); ~**en** ['wi:kən] *v/t.* schwächen; *v/i.* schwach werden; ~**ling** ['wi:kliŋ] Schwächling *m;* ~**ly** [ᴸᴸi] schwächlich; ~-**minded** ['wi:k'maindid] schwachsinnig; ~**ness** ['wi:knis] Schwäche *f.*

weal [wi:l] Wohl *n;* Strieme *f.*

wealth [welθ] Wohlstand *m;* Reichtum *m; fig.* Fülle *f;* ~**y** ☐ ['welθi] reich; wohlhabend.

wean [wi:n] entwöhnen; ~ *s.o. from s.th.* j-m et. abgewöhnen.

weapon ['wepən] Waffe *f.*

wear [wɛə] **1.** [*irr.*] *v/t.* am Körper tragen; zur Schau tragen; *a.* ~ *away,* ~ *down,* ~ *off,* ~ *out* abnutzen, abtragen, verbrauchen; erschöpfen; ermüden; zermürben; *v/i.* sich *gut etc.* tragen *od.* halten; *a.* ~ *off od. out* sich abnutzen *od.* abtragen; *fig.* sich verlieren; ~ *on* vergehen; **2.** Tragen *n;* (Be)Kleidung *f;* Abnutzung *f; for hard* ~ strapazierfähig; *the worse for* ~ abgetragen; ~ *and tear* Verschleiß *m.*

wear|iness ['wiərinis] Müdigkeit *f;* Ermüdung *f; fig.* Überdruß *m;* ~**some** [ᴸisəm] ermüdend; langweilig; ~**y** ['wiəri] **1.** ☐ müde; *fig.* überdrüssig; ermüdend; anstrengend; **2.** ermüden.

weasel *zo.* ['wi:zl] Wiesel *n.*

weather ['weðə] **1.** Wetter *n,* Witterung *f;* **2.** *v/t.* dem Wetter aussetzen; ⚓ *Sturm* abwettern; *fig.* überstehen; *v/i.* verwittern; ~**beaten** vom Wetter mitgenommen; ~**bureau** Wetteramt *n;* ~**chart** Wetterkarte *f;* ~**forecast** Wetterbericht *m,* -vorhersage *f;* ~**worn** verwittert.

weav|e [wi:v] [*irr.*] weben; wirken; flechten; *fig.* ersinnen, erfinden;

sich schlängeln; ~**er** ['wi:və] Weber *m.*

weazen ['wi:zn] verhutzelt.

web [web] Gewebe *n; orn.* Schwimmhaut *f;* ~**bing** ['webiŋ] Gurtband *n.*

wed [wed] heiraten; *fig.* verbinden (*to* mit); ~**ding** ['wediŋ] **1.** Hochzeit *f;* **2.** Hochzeits...; Braut...; Trau...; ~**ring** Ehe-, Trauring *m.*

wedge [wedʒ] **1.** Keil *m;* **2.** (ver)keilen; *a.* ~ *in* (hin)einzwängen.

wedlock ['wedlɔk] Ehe *f.*

Wednesday ['wenzdi] Mittwoch *m.*

wee [wi:] klein, winzig; *a* ~ *bit* ein klein wenig.

weed [wi:d] **1.** Unkraut *n;* **2.** jäten; säubern (*of* von); ~ *out* ausmerzen; ~-**killer** ['wi:dkilə] Unkrautvertilgungsmittel *n;* ~**s** *pl. mst widow's* ~ Witwenkleidung *f;* ~**y** ['wi:di] voll Unkraut, verkrautet; *fig.* lang aufgeschossen.

week [wi:k] Woche *f; this day* ~ heute in *od.* vor e-r Woche; ~-**day** ['wi:kdei] Wochentag *m;* ~-**end** ['wi:k'end] Wochenende *n;* ~**ly** ['wi:kli] **1.** wöchentlich; **2.** *a.* ~ *paper* Wochenblatt *n,* Wochen(zeit)-schrift *f.*

weep [wi:p] [*irr.*] weinen; tropfen; ~**ing** ['wi:piŋ] Trauer...; ~ *willow* ♀ Trauerweide *f.*

weigh [wei] *v/t.* (ab)wiegen, *fig.* ab-, erwägen; ~ *anchor* ⚓ den Anker lichten; ~*ed down* niedergebeugt; *v/i.* wiegen (*a. fig.*); ausschlaggebend sein; ~ (*up*)*on* lasten auf (*dat.*).

weight [weit] **1.** Gewicht *n* (*a. fig.*); Last *f* (*a. fig.*); *fig.* Bedeutung *f;* Wucht *f;* **2.** beschweren; *fig.* belasten; ~**y** ☐ ['weiti] (ge)wichtig; wuchtig.

weir [wiə] Wehr *n;* Fischreuse *f.*

weird [wiəd] Schicksals...; unheimlich; F sonderbar, seltsam.

welcome ['welkəm] **1.** willkommen; *you are* ~ *to inf.* es steht Ihnen frei, zu *inf.;* (*you are*) ~! gern geschehen!, bitte sehr!; **2.** Willkomm(en *n*) *m;* **3.** willkommen heißen; *fig.* begrüßen.

weld ⊕ [weld] (zs.-)schweißen.

welfare ['welfɛə] Wohlfahrt *f;* ~ **centre** Fürsorgeamt *n;* ~ **state** Wohlfahrtsstaat *m;* ~ **work** Fürsorge *f,* Wohlfahrtspflege *f;* ~ **worker** Fürsorger(in).

well[1] [wel] **1.** Brunnen *m; fig.* Quelle *f;* ⊕ Bohrloch *n;* Treppen-, Aufzugs-, Licht-, Luftschacht *m;* **2.** quellen.

well[2] [ᴸ] **1.** wohl; gut; ordentlich, gründlich; gesund; ~ *off* in guten Verhältnissen, wohlhabend; *I am not* ~ mir ist nicht wohl; **2.** *int.* nun!, F na!; ~-**being** ['wel'bi:iŋ] Wohl(sein) *n;* ~-**born** von guter

Herkunft; **~-bred** wohlerzogen; **~-defined** deutlich, klar umrissen; **~-favo(u)red** gut aussehend; **~-intentioned** wohlmeinend; gut gemeint; **~ known**, **~-known** bekannt; **~-mannered** mit guten Manieren; **~-nigh** ['welnai] beinahe; **~ timed** rechtzeitig; **~-to-do** ['weltə'du:] wohlhabend; **~-wisher** Gönner *m*, Freund *m*; **~-worn** abgetragen; *fig.* abgedroschen.

Welsh [welʃ] **1.** walisisch; **2.** Walisisch *n*; *the* ~ *pl.* die Waliser *pl.*; ~ **rabbit** überbackene Käseschnitte.

welt [welt] ⊕ Rahmen *m*, *Schuh*-Rahmen *m*; Einfassung *f*; Strieme *f*.

welter ['weltə] **1.** rollen, sich wälzen; **2.** Wirrwarr *m*, Durcheinander *n*.

wench [wentʃ] Mädchen *n*; Dirne *f*.

went [went] *pret. von* go 1.

wept [wept] *pret. u. p.p. von* weep.

were [wɔ:, wə] **1.** *pret. pl. u. 2. sg. von* be; **2.** *pret. pass. von* be; **3.** *subj. pret. von* be.

west [west] **1.** West(en *m*); **2.** West...; westlich; westwärts; **~erly** ['westəli], **~ern** [ˌɔn] westlich; **~erner** [ˌnə] *Am.* Weststaatler(in); Abendländer(in); **~ward(s)** [ˌtwəd(z)] westwärts.

wet [wet] **1.** naß, feucht; *Am.* den Alkoholhandel gestattend; **2.** Nässe *f*; Feuchtigkeit *f*; **3.** [*irr.*] naß machen, anfeuchten.

wetback *Am. sl.* ['wetbæk] illegaler Einwanderer *aus Mexiko*.

wether ['weðə] Hammel *m*.

wet-nurse ['wetnə:s] Amme *f*.

whack F [wæk] **1.** verhauen; **2.** Hieb *m*.

whale [weil] Wal *m*; **~bone** ['weilboun] Fischbein *n*; **~-oil** Tran *m*; **~r** ['weilə] Walfischfänger *m*.

whaling ['weiliŋ] Walfischfang *m*.

wharf [wɔ:f], *pl. a.* **wharves** [wɔ:vz] Kai *m*, Anlegeplatz *m*.

what [wɔt] **1.** was; das, was; *know* ~'s ~ Bescheid wissen; **2.** was?; wie?; wieviel?; welch(er, -e, -es)?; was für ein(e)?; ~ *about* ...? wie steht's mit ...?; ~ *for*? wozu?; ~ *of it*? was ist denn dabei?; ~ *next*? was sonst noch?; *iro.* was denn noch alles?; ~ *a blessing!* was für ein Segen!; **3.** ~ *with* ... ~ *with* ... teils durch ... teils durch ...; **~-(so)ever** [wɔt(sou)'evə] was *od.* welcher auch (immer).

wheat ♧ [wi:t] Weizen *m*.

wheedle ['wi:dl] beschwatzen; ~ *s.th. out of s.o.* j-m et. abschwatzen.

wheel [wi:l] **1.** Rad *n*; Steuer *n*; *bsd. Am.* F Fahrrad *n*; Töpferscheibe *f*; Drehung *f*; ⚔ Schwenkung *f*; **2.** rollen, fahren, schieben; sich drehen; sich umwenden; ⚔ schwenken; F radeln; **~barrow**

['wi:lbærou] Schubkarren *m*; ~ **chair** Rollstuhl *m*; **~ed** mit Rädern; fahrbar; ...räd(e)rig.

wheeze [wi:z] schnaufen, keuchen.

whelp [welp] **1.** *zo.* Welpe *m*; *allg.* Junge(s) *n*; F Balg *m*, *n* (*ungezogenes Kind*); **2.** (Junge) werfen.

when [wen] **1.** wann?; **2.** wenn; als; während *od.* da doch; und da.

whence [wens] woher, von wo.

when(so)ever [wen(sou)'evə] immer *od.* jedesmal wenn; sooft (als).

where [wɛə] wo; wohin; **~about(s) 1.** ['wɛərə'bauts] wo herum; **2.** [ˌəbauts] Aufenthalt *m*; **~as** [ˌr'æz] wohingegen, während (doch); **~at** [ˌ'æt] wobei, worüber, worauf; **~by** [wɛə'bai] wodurch; **~fore** ['wɛəfɔ:] weshalb; **~in** [wɛər'in] worin; **~of** [ˌr'ɔv] wovon; **~upon** [ˌrə'pɔn] worauf(hin); **~ver** [ˌr'evə] wo(hin) (auch) immer; **~withal** ['wɛəwiðɔ:l] Erforderliche(s) *n*; Mittel *n/pl.*

whet [wet] wetzen, schärfen; anstacheln.

whether ['weðə] ob; ~ *or no* so oder so.

whetstone ['wetstoun] Schleifstein *m*.

whey [wei] Molke *f*.

which [witʃ] **1.** welche(r, -s)?; **2.** der, die, das; was; **~ever** [ˌʃ'evə] welche(r, -s) (auch) immer.

whiff [wif] **1.** Hauch *m*; Zug *m beim Rauchen*; Zigarillo *n*; **2.** paffen.

while [wail] **1.** Weile *f*; Zeit *f*; *for a* ~ e-e Zeitlang; *worth* ~ der Mühe wert; **2.** *mst* ~ *away* Zeit verbringen; **3.** *a.* **whilst** [wailst] während.

whim [wim] Schrulle *f*, Laune *f*.

whimper ['wimpə] wimmern.

whim|sical ⬚ ['wimzikəl] wunderlich; **~sy** ['wimzi] Grille *f*, Laune *f*.

whine [wain] winseln; wimmern.

whinny ['wini] wiehern.

whip [wip] **1.** *v/t.* peitschen; geißeln (*a. fig.*); *j-n* verprügeln; schlagen (F *a. fig.*); umsäumen; werfen; reißen; ~ *in parl.* zs.-trommeln; ~ *on Kleidungsstück* überwerfen; ~ *up* antreiben; aufraffen; *v/i.* springen, flitzen; **2.** Peitsche *f*; Geißel *f*.

whippet *zo.* ['wipit] Whippet *m* (*kleiner englischer Rennhund*).

whipping ['wipiŋ] Prügel *pl.*; **~-top** Kreisel *m*.

whippoorwill *orn.* ['wippuəwil] Ziegenmelker *m*.

whirl [wə:l] **1.** wirbeln; (sich) drehen; **2.** Wirbel *m*, Strudel *m*; **~pool** ['wə:lpu:l] Strudel *m*; **~wind** Wirbelwind *m*.

whir(r) [wə:] schwirren.

whisk [wisk] **1.** Wisch *m*; Staubwedel *m*; *Küche*: Schneebesen *m*; Schwung *m*; **2.** *v/t.* (ab-, weg)wischen, (ab-, weg)fegen; wirbeln (mit); schlagen; *v/i.* huschen, flitzen; **~er** ['wiskə] Barthaar *n*; *mst* **~s** *pl.* Backenbart *m.*

whisper ['wispə] **1.** flüstern; **2.** Geflüster *n.*

whistle ['wisl] **1.** pfeifen; **2.** Pfeife *f*; Pfiff *m*; F Kehle *f*; **~-stop** *Am.* 🏛 Haltepunkt *m*; *fig.* Kaff *n*; *pol.* kurzes Auftreten *e-s* Kandidaten im *Wahlkampf.*

Whit [wit] *in Zssgn:* Pfingst...

white [wait] **1.** *allg.* weiß; rein; F anständig; Weiß...; **2.** Weiß(e) *n*; Weiße(r *m*) *f* (*Rasse*); **~-collar** ['wait'kolə] geistig, Kopf..., Büro...; **~ workers** *pl.* Angestellte *pl.*; **~ heat** Weißglut *f*; **~ lie** fromme Lüge; **~n** ['waitn] weiß machen *od.* werden; bleichen; **~ness** [~nis] Weiße *f*; Blässe *f*; *fig.* Weiß *n*; **~wash 1.** *mst* **~** Tünche *f*; **2.** weißen; *fig.* rein waschen.

whither *lit.* ['wiðə] wohin.

whitish ['waitiʃ] weißlich.

Whitsun ['witsn] Pfingst...; **~tide** Pfingsten *pl.*

whittle ['witl] schnitze(l)n; **~ away** verkleinern, schwächen.

whiz(z) [wiz] zischen, sausen.

who [hu:, hu] **1.** welche(r, -s); der, die, das; **2.** wer?

whodun(n)it *sl.* [hu:'dʌnit] Krimi (-nalroman, -nalfilm) *m.*

whoever [hu(:)'evə] wer auch immer.

whole [houl] **1.** □ ganz; heil, unversehrt; *made out of* **~** *cloth Am.* F frei erfunden; **2.** Ganze(s) *n*; (*up*)on the **~** im ganzen; im allgemeinen; **~-hearted** □ ['houl'ha:tid] aufrichtig; **~-meal bread** ['houmi:l bred] Vollkorn-, Schrotbrot *n*; **~sale 1.** *mst* **~ trade** Großhandel *m*; **2.** Großhandels...; Engros...; *fig.* Massen...; **~ dealer** = **~saler** [~lə] Großhändler *m*; **~some** □ [~səm] gesund.

wholly *adv.* ['houlli] ganz, gänzlich.

whom [hu:m, hum] *acc. von* who.

whoop [hu:p] **1.** Schrei *m*, Geschrei *n*; **2.** laut schreien; **~ it up** *Am. sl.* laut feiern; **~ee** *Am.* F ['wupi:] Freudenfest *n*; *make* **~** *auf die Pauke hauen; **~ing-cough** 🏛 ['hu:piŋkɔf] Keuchhusten *m.*

whore [hɔ:] Hure *f.*

whose [hu:z] *gen. von* who.

why [wai] **1.** warum, weshalb; **~ so?** wieso?; **2.** ei!, ja!; (je) nun.

wick [wik] Docht *m.*

wicked □ ['wikid] *moralisch* böse, schlimm; **~ness** [~dnis] Bosheit *f.*

wicker ['wikə] aus Weide geflochten; Weiden...; Korb...; **~ basket** Weidenkorb *m*; **~ chair** Korbstuhl *m.*

wicket ['wikit] Pförtchen *n*; *Kricket:* Dreistab *m*, Tor *n*; **~-keeper** Torhüter *m.*

wide [waid] *a.* □ *u. adv.* weit; ausgedehnt; weitgehend; großzügig;

breit; weitab; **~ awake** völlig (*od.* hellwach); aufgeweckt (*schlau*); *3 feet* **~ 3** Fuß breit; **~n** ['waidn] (sich) erweitern; **~-open** ['waid'oupən] weit geöffnet; *Am. sl.* großzügig *in der Gesetzesdurchführung*; **~-spread** weitverbreitet, ausgedehnt.

widow ['widou] Witwe *f*; *attr.* Witwen...; **~er** [~ouə] Witwer *m.*

width [widθ] Breite *f*, Weite *f.*

wield *lit.* [wi:ld] handhaben.

wife [waif], *pl.* **wives** [waivz] (Ehe-) Frau *f*; Gattin *f*; Weib *n*; **~ly** ['waifli] fraulich.

wig [wig] Perücke *f.*

wigging F ['wigiŋ] Schelte *f.*

wild [waild] **1.** □ wild; toll; unbändig; abenteuerlich; planlos; *run* **~** wild (auf)wachsen; *talk* **~** (wild) drauflos reden; **~ for** *od.* *about* (ganz) verrückt nach; **2.** *mst* **~s** *pl.* Wildnis *f*; **~cat** ['waildkæt] **1.** *zo.* Wildkatze *f*; *Am.* Schwindelunternehmen *n*; *bsd. Am.* wilde Ölbohrung; **2.** wild (*Streik*); Schwindel...; **~erness** ['wildənis] Wildnis *f*, Wüste*f*; Einöde*f*; **~fire**: *like* **~** wie ein Lauffeuer.

wile [wail] List *f*; *mst* **~s** *pl.* Tücke*f.*

wil(l)ful □ ['wilful] eigensinnig; vorsätzlich.

will [wil] **1.** Wille *m*; Wunsch *m*; Testament *n*; *of one's own free* **~** aus freien Stücken; **2.** [*irr.*] *v/aux.*: *he* **~** *come* er wird kommen; *er kommt gewöhnlich; I* **~** *do it* ich will es tun; **3.** wollen; durch Willenskraft zwingen; entscheiden; 🏛 vermachen.

willing □ ['wiliŋ] willig, bereit (-willig); *pred.* gewillt (*to inf.* zu); **~ness** [~nis] (Bereit)Willigkeit *f.*

will-o'-the-wisp ['wiləðwisp] Irrlicht *n.*

willow 🎵 ['wilou] Weide *f.*

willy-nilly ['wili'nili] wohl oder übel.

wilt [wilt] (ver)welken.

wily □ ['waili] schlau, verschmitzt.

win [win] **1.** [*irr.*] *v/t.* gewinnen; erringen; erlangen, erreichen; *j-n* dazu bringen (*to do* zu tun); **~ s.o.** *over j-n für sich gewinnen; *v/i.* gewinnen; siegen; **2.** *Sport:* Sieg *m.*

wince [wins] (zs.-)zucken.

winch [wintʃ] Winde *f*; Kurbel *f.*

wind¹ [wind, *poet./a.* waind] **1.** Wind *m*; Atem *m*, Luft *f*; 🎵 Blähung *f*; 🎵 Blasinstrumente *n/pl.*; **2.** wittern; außer Atem bringen; verschnaufen lassen.

wind² [waind] [*irr.*] *v/t.* winden; wickeln; *Horn* blasen; **~ up** *Uhr* aufziehen; *Geschäft* abwickeln; 🏛 liquidieren; *v/i.* sich winden; sich schlängeln.

wind|bag ['windbæg] Schwätzer *m*; **~fall** Fallobst *n*; Glücksfall *m.*

winding ['waindiŋ] 1. Windung f; 2. □ sich windend; ~ stairs pl. Wendeltreppe f; ~sheet Leichentuch n.

wind-instrument ♪ ['windinstrumənt] Blasinstrument n.

windlass ⊕ ['windləs] Winde f.

windmill ['winmil] Windmühle f.

window ['windou] Fenster n; Schaufenster n; ~dressing Schaufensterdekoration f; fig. Aufmachung f, Mache f; ~shade Am. Rouleau n; ~shopping Schaufensterbummel m.

wind|pipe ['windpaip] Luftröhre f; ~screen, Am. ~shield mot. Windschutzscheibe f; ~ wiper Scheibenwischer m.

windy □ ['windi] windig (a. fig. inhaltlos); geschwätzig.

wine [wain] Wein m; ~press ['wainpres] Kelter f.

wing [wiŋ] 1. Flügel m (a. ✗ u. ♙); Schwinge f; ✗ co. Arm m; mot. Kotflügel m; ✗ Tragfläche f; ✗, ✗ Geschwader n; ~s pl. Kulissen f/pl.; take ~ weg-, auffliegen; on the ~ im Fluge; 2. fig. beflügeln; fliegen.

wink [wiŋk] 1. Blinzeln n, Zwinkern n; not get a ~ of sleep kein Auge zutun; s. forty; 2. blinzeln, zwinkern (mit); ~ at ein Auge zudrücken bei et.; j-m zublinzeln.

winn|er ['winə] Gewinner(in); Sieger(in); ~ing ['winiŋ] 1. □ einnehmend, gewinnend; 2. ~s pl. Gewinn m.

winsome ['winsəm] gefällig, einnehmend.

wint|er ['wintə] 1. Winter m; 2. überwintern; ~ry ['wintri] winterlich; fig. frostig.

wipe [waip] (ab-, auf)wischen; reinigen; (ab)trocknen; ~ out wegwischen; (aus)löschen; fig. vernichten; tilgen.

wire ['waiə] 1. Draht m; Leitung f; F Telegramm n; pull the ~s der Drahtzieher sein; s-e Beziehungen spielen lassen; 2. (ver)drahten; telegraphieren; ~drawn ['waiədrɔ:n] spitzfindig; ~less ['waiəlis] 1. □ drahtlos; Funk...; 2. a. ~ set Radio (-apparat m) n; on the ~ im Rundfunk; 3. funken; ~netting ['waiə'netiŋ] Drahtgeflecht n.

wiry □ ['waiəri] drahtig, sehnig.

wisdom ['wizdəm] Weisheit f; Klugheit f; ~ tooth Weisheitszahn m.

wise [waiz] 1. □ weise, verständig; klug; erfahren; ~ guy Am. sl. Schlauberger m; 2. Weise f, Art f.

wise-crack F ['waizkræk] 1. witzige Bemerkung; 2. witzeln.

wish [wiʃ] 1. wünschen; wollen; ~ for (sich) et. wünschen; ~ well (ill) wohl- (übel)wollen; 2. Wunsch m;

~ful □ ['wiʃful] sehnsüchtig; ~ thinking Wunschdenken n.

wisp [wisp] Wisch m; Strähne f.

wistful □ ['wistful] sehnsüchtig.

wit [wit] 1. Witz m; a. ~s pl. Verstand m; witziger Kopf; be at one's ~'s end mit s-r Weisheit zu Ende sein; keep one's ~s about one e-n klaren Kopf behalten; 2.: to ~ nämlich, das heißt.

witch [witʃ] Hexe f, Zauberin f; ~craft ['witʃkra:ft], ~ery [ʃəri] Hexerei f; ~hunt pol. Hexenjagd f (Verfolgung politisch verdächtiger Personen).

with [wið] mit; nebst; bei; von; durch; vor (dat.); ~ it sl. schwer auf der Höhe.

withdraw [wið'drɔ:] [irr. (draw)] v/t. ab-, ent-, zurückziehen; zurücknehmen; Geld abheben; v/i. sich zurückziehen; abtreten; ~al [~ɔ:əl] Zurückziehung f; Rückzug m.

wither ['wiðə] v/i. (ver)welken; verdorren; austrocknen; v/t. welk machen.

with|hold [wið'hould] [irr. (hold)] zurückhalten; et. vorenthalten; ~in [wi'ðin] 1. adv. lit. im Innern, drin(nen); zu Hause; 2. prp. in(nerhalb); ~ doors im Hause; ~ call in Rufweite; ~out [wi'ðaut] 1. adv. lit. (dr)außen; äußerlich; 2. prp. ohne; lit. außerhalb; ~stand [wið'stænd] [irr. (stand)] widerstehen (dat.).

witness ['witnis] 1. Zeug|e m, -in f; bear ~ Zeugnis ablegen (to für; of von); in ~ of zum Zeugnis (gen.); 2. (be)zeugen; Zeuge sein von et.; ~box, Am. ~ stand Zeugenstand m.

wit|ticism ['witisizəm] Witz m; ~ty □ ['witi] witzig; geistreich.

wives [waivz] pl. von wife.

wiz Am. sl. [wiz] Genie n; ~ard ['wizəd] Zauberer m; Genie n.

wizen(ed) ['wizn(d)] schrump(e)lig.

wobble ['wɔbl] schwanken; wackeln.

woe [wou] Weh n, Leid n; ~ is me! wehe mir! ~begone ['woubigɔn] jammervoll; ~ful □ ['wouful] jammervoll, traurig, elend.

woke [wouk] pret. u. p.p. von wake 2; ~n ['woukən] p.p. von wake 2.

wold [would] (hügeliges) Heideland.

wolf [wulf] 1. zo. pl. wolves [wulvz] Wolf m; 2. verschlingen; ~ish □ ['wulfiʃ] wölfisch; Wolfs...

woman ['wumən], pl. women ['wimin] 1. Frau f; Weib n; 2. weiblich; ~ doctor Ärztin f; ~ student Studentin f; ~hood [~nhud] die Frauen f/pl.; Weiblichkeit f; ~ish □ [~niʃ] weibisch; ~kind [~n-'kaind] Frauen(welt f) f/pl.; ~like [~nlaik] fraulich; ~ly [~li] weiblich.

womb [wu:m] anat. Gebärmutter f; Mutterleib m; fig. Schoß m.

women ['wimin] *pl. von* woman; **~folk(s)**, **~kind** die Frauen *f/pl.*; F Weibervolk *n*.

won [wʌn] *pret. u. p.p. von* win 1.

wonder ['wʌndə] **1.** Wunder *n*; Verwunderung *f*; **2.** sich wundern; gern wissen mögen, sich fragen; **~ful** □ [~əful] wunderbar, -voll; **~ing** □ [~əriŋ] staunend, verwundert.

won't [wount] = *will not*.

wont [~] **1.** *pred.* gewohnt; be ~ to *inf.* pflegen zu *inf.*; **2.** Gewohnheit *f*; **~ed** ['wountid] gewohnt.

woo [wu:] werben um; locken.

wood [wud] Wald *m*, Gehölz *n*; Holz *n*; Faß *n*; ♪ Holzblasinstrument (-e *pl.*) *n*; *touch* ~! unberufen!; **~-chuck** *zo.* ['wudtʃʌk] Waldmurmeltier *n*; **~cut** Holzschnitt *m*; **~cutter** Holzfäller *m*; *Kunst*: Holzschneider *m*; **~ed** ['wudid] bewaldet; **~en** ['wudn] hölzern (*a. fig.*); Holz...; **~man** Förster *m*; Holzfäller *m*; **~pecker** *orn.* ['wudpekə] Specht *m*; **~sman** ['wudzmən] *s. woodman*; **~wind** ♪ Holzblasinstrument *n*; *oft* **~s** *pl.* ♪ Holzbläser *m/pl.*; **~work** Holzwerk *n*; **~y** ['wudi] waldig; holzig.

wool [wul] Wolle *f*; **~-gathering** ['wulgæðəriŋ] Geistesabwesenheit *f*; **~(l)en** ['wulin] **1.** wollen; Woll...; **2.** **~s** *pl.* Wollsachen *f/pl.*; **~(l)y** ['wuli] **1.** wollig; Woll...; belegt (*Stimme*); verschwommen; **2.** woollies *pl.* F Wollsachen *f/pl.*

word [wɔːd] **1.** *mst* Wort *n*; *engS.*: Vokabel *f*; Nachricht *f*; ⚔ Losung(swort *n*) *f*; Versprechen *n*; Befehl *m*; Spruch *m*; **~s** *pl.* Wörter *n/pl.*; Worte *n/pl.*; *fig.* Wortwechsel *m*; Text *m e-s Liedes*; *have a* ~ *with* mit *j-m* sprechen; **2.** (in Worten) ausdrücken, (ab-) fassen; **~ing** ['wɔːdiŋ] Wortlaut *m*, Fassung *f*; **~-splitting** Wortklauberei *f*.

wordy □ ['wɔːdi] wortreich; Wort...

wore [wɔː] *pret. von* wear 1.

work [wɔːk] **1.** Arbeit *f*; Werk *n*; *attr.* Arbeits...; **~s** *pl.* ⊕ (Uhr-, Feder)Werk *n*; ⚔ Befestigungen *pl.*; **~s** *sg.* Werk *n*, Fabrik *f*; ~ *of art* Kunstwerk *n*; *at* ~ bei der Arbeit; *be in* ~ Arbeit haben; *be out of* ~ arbeitslos sein; *set to* ~, *set od. go about one's* ~ an die Arbeit gehen; **~s council** Betriebsrat *m*; **2.** [*a. irr.*] *v/i.* arbeiten (*a. fig.*); wirken; gären; sich *hindurch- etc.* arbeiten; ~ *at* arbeiten an (*dat.*); ~ *out* herauskommen (*Summe*); *v/t.* (be)arbeiten; arbeiten lassen; betreiben; *Maschine etc.* bedienen; (be)wirken; ausrechnen, *Aufgabe* lösen; ~ *one's way* sich durcharbeiten; ~ *off* abarbeiten; *Gefühl* abreagieren; ✝ abstoßen; ~ *out* ausarbeiten; lösen;

ausrechnen; ~ *up* hochbringen; aufregen; verarbeiten (*into zu*).

work|able □ ['wɔːkəbl] bearbeitungs-, betriebsfähig; ausführbar; **~aday** [~ədei] Alltags...; **~day** Werktag *m*; **~er** ['wɔːkə] Arbeiter (-in); **~house** Armenhaus *n*; *Am.* Besserungsanstalt *f*, Arbeitshaus *n*.

working ['wɔːkiŋ] **1.** Bergwerk *n*; Steinbruch *m*; Arbeits-, Wirkungsweise *f*; **2.** arbeitend; Arbeits...; Betriebs...; **~class** Arbeiter...; **~-day** Werk-, Arbeitstag *m*; **~hours** *pl.* Arbeitszeit *f*.

workman ['wɔːkmən] Arbeiter *m*; Handwerker *m*; **~like** [~nlaik] kunstgerecht; **~ship** [~nʃip] Kunstfertigkeit *f*.

work|out *Am.* F ['wɔːkaut] *mst Sport*: (Konditions)Training *n*; Erprobung *f*; **~shop** Werkstatt *f*; **~woman** Arbeiterin *f*.

world [wɔːld] *allg.* Welt *f*; *a* ~ *of* e-e Unmenge (von); *bring (come) into the* ~ zur Welt bringen (kommen); *think the* ~ *of* alles halten von; **~ling** [~ldliŋ] Weltkind *n*.

worldly ['wɔːldli] weltlich; Welt...; **~-wise** [~'waiz] weltklug.

world|-power *pol.* ['wɔːldpauə] Weltmacht *f*; **~-wide** weltweit; weltumspannend; Welt...

worm [wɔːm] **1.** Wurm *m* (*a. fig.*); **2.** *ein Geheimnis* entlocken (*out of dat.*); ~ *o.s.* sich schlängeln; *fig.* sich einschleichen (*into in acc.*); **~-eaten** ['wɔːmiːtn] wurmstichig.

worn [wɔːn] *p.p. von* wear 1; **~-out** ['wɔːn'aut] abgenutzt; abgetragen; verbraucht (*a. fig.*); müde, erschöpft; abgezehrt; verhärmt.

worry ['wʌri] **1.** (sich) beunruhigen; (sich) ärgern; sich sorgen; sich aufregen; bedrücken; zerren, (ab-) würgen; plagen, quälen; **2.** Unruhe *f*; Sorge *f*; Ärger *m*; Qual *f*, Plage *f*; Quälgeist *m*.

worse [wɔːs] schlechter; schlimmer; ~ *luck!* leider!; um so schlimmer!; *from bad to* ~ vom Regen in die Traufe; **~n** ['wɔːsn] (sich) verschlechtern.

worship ['wɔːʃip] **1.** Verehrung *f*; Gottesdienst *m*; Kult *m*; **2.** verehren; anbeten; den Gottesdienst besuchen; **~(p)er** [~pə] Verehrer (-in); Kirchgänger(in).

worst [wɔːst] **1.** schlechtest; ärgst; schlimmst; **2.** überwältigen.

worsted ['wustid] Kammgarn *n*.

worth [wɔːθ] **1.** wert; ~ *reading* lesenswert; **2.** Wert *m*; Würde *f*; **~less** [] ['wɔːθlis] wertlos; unwürdig; **~-while** ['wɔː'wail] der Mühe wert; **~y** □ ['wɔːði] würdig.

would [wud] [*pret. von* will 2] wollte; würde, möchte; pflegte; **~-be** ['wudbiː] angeblich, sogenannt; möglich, potentiell; Pseudo...

wound[1] [wu:nd] **1.** Wunde *f*, Verwundung *f*, Verletzung *f*; *fig.* Kränkung *f*; **2.** verwunden, verletzen (*a. fig.*).

wound[2] [waund] *pret. u. p.p. von* wind 2.

wove [wouv] *pret. von* weave; **~n** ['wouvən] *p.p. von* weave.

wow *Am.* [wau] **1.** *int.* Mensch!; toll!; **2.** *sl.* Bombenerfolg *m*.

wrangle ['ræŋgl] **1.** streiten, (sich) zanken; **2.** Streit *m*, Zank *m*.

wrap [ræp] **1.** *v/t.* (ein)wickeln; *fig.* einhüllen; *be* **~***ped up in* gehüllt sein in (*acc.*); ganz aufgehen in (*dat.*); *v/i.* **~** *up* sich einhüllen; **2.** Hülle *f*; *engS.:* Decke *f*; Schal *m*; Mantel *m*; **~per** ['ræpə] Hülle *f*, Umschlag *m*; *a. postal* **~** Streifband *n*; **~ping** ['ræpiŋ] Verpackung *f*.

wrath *lit.* [rɔ:θ] Zorn *m*, Grimm *m*.

wreak [ri:k] *Rache* üben, *Zorn* auslassen (*upon an j-m*).

wreath [ri:θ], *pl.* **~s** [ri:ðz] (Blumen)Gewinde *n*; Kranz *m*; Girlande *f*; Ring *m*, Kreis *m*; Schneewehe *f*; **~e** [ri:ð] [*irr.*] *v/t.* (um-) winden; *v/i.* sich ringeln.

wreck [rek] **1.** ⚓ Wrack *n*; Trümmer *pl.*; Schiffbruch *m*; *fig.* Untergang *m*; **2.** zum Scheitern (🚂 Entgleisen) bringen; zertrümmern; vernichten; *be* **~***ed* ⚓ scheitern; Schiffbruch erleiden; **~age** ['rekidʒ] Trümmer *pl.*; Wrackteile *n/pl.*; **~ed** schiffbrüchig; ruiniert; **~er** ['rekə] ⚓ Bergungsschiff *n*, -arbeiter *m*; Strandräuber *m*; Abbrucharbeiter *m*; *Am. mot.* Abschleppwagen *m*; **~ing** ['rekiŋ] Strandraub *m*; **~** *company Am.* Abbruchfirma *f*; **~** *service Am. mot.* Abschlepp-, Hilfsdienst *m*.

wren *orn.* [ren] Zaunkönig *m*.

wrench [rentʃ] **1.** drehen; reißen; entwinden (*from s.o.* j-m); verdrehen (*a. fig.*); verrenken; **~** *open* aufreißen; **2.** Ruck *m*; Verrenkung *f*; *fig.* Schmerz *m*; ⊕ Schraubenschlüssel *m*.

wrest [rest] reißen; verdrehen; entreißen; **~le** ['resl] ringen (mit); **~ling** ['resliŋ] Ringkampf *m*, Ringen *n*.

wretch [retʃ] Elende(r *m*) *f*; Kerl *m*.

wretched ☐ ['retʃid] elend.

wriggle ['rigl] sich winden *od.* schlängeln; **~** *out of* sich drücken von *et.*

wright [rait] ...macher *m*, ...bauer *m*.

wring [riŋ] [*irr.*] *Hände* ringen; (aus)wringen; pressen; *Hals* umdrehen; abringen (*from s.o.* j-m); **~** *s.o.'s heart* j-m zu Herzen gehen.

wrinkle ['riŋkl] **1.** Runzel *f*; Falte *f*; Wink *m*; Trick *m*; **2.** (sich) runzeln.

wrist [rist] Handgelenk *n*; **~** *watch* Armbanduhr *f*; **~band** ['ristbænd] Bündchen *n*, (Hemd)Manschette *f*.

writ [rit] Erlaß *m*; (gerichtlicher) Befehl; *Holy* ♀ Heilige Schrift.

write [rait] [*irr.*] schreiben; **~** *down* auf-, niederschreiben; ausarbeiten; hervorheben; **~r** ['raitə] Schreiber (-in) *f*; Verfasser(in); Schriftsteller (-in).

writhe [raið] sich krümmen.

writing ['raitiŋ] Schreiben *n*; Aufsatz *m*; Werk *n*; Schrift *f*; Schriftstück *n*; Urkunde *f*; Stil *m*; *attr.* Schreib...; *in* **~** schriftlich; **~case** Schreibmappe *f*; **~desk** Schreibtisch *m*; **~paper** Schreibpapier *n*.

written ['ritn] **1.** *p.p. von* write; **2.** *adj.* schriftlich.

wrong [rɔŋ] **1.** ☐ unrecht; verkehrt, falsch; *be* **~** unrecht haben; in Unordnung sein; falsch gehen (*Uhr*); *go* **~** schiefgehen; *on the* **~** *side of sixty* über die 60 hinaus; **2.** Unrecht *n*; Beleidigung *f*; **3.** unrecht tun (*dat.*); ungerecht behandeln; **~doer** ['rɔŋ'duə] Übeltäter(in); **~ful** ☐ ['rɔŋful] ungerecht; unrechtmäßig.

wrote [rout] *pret. von* write.

wrought [rɔ:t] *pret. u. p.p. von* work 2; **~** *iron* Schmiedeeisen *n*; **~-iron** ['rɔ:t'aiən] schmiedeeisern; **~-up** erregt.

wrung [rʌŋ] *pret. u. p.p. von* wring.

wry ☐ [rai] schief, krumm, verzerrt.

X, Y

Xmas ['krismǝs] = *Christmas*.

X-ray ['eks'rei] **1.** **~***s pl.* Röntgenstrahlen *m/pl.*; **2.** Röntgen...; **3.** durchleuchten, röntgen.

xylophone ♪ ['zailəfoun] Xylophon *n*.

yacht ⚓ [jɔt] **1.** (Motor)Jacht *f*; Segelboot *n*; **2.** auf e-r Jacht fahren; segeln; **~club** ['jɔtklʌb] Segel-, Jachtklub *m*; **~ing** ['jɔtiŋ] Segelsport *m*; *attr.* Segel...

Yankee F ['jænki] Yankee *m* (*Amerikaner, bsd. der Nordstaaten*).

yap [jæp] kläffen; F quasseln.

yard [jɑ:d] Yard *n*, *englische* Elle (= *0,914 m*); ⚓ Rah(e) *f*; Hof *m*; (Bau-, Stapel)Platz *m*; *Am.* Garten *m* (*um das Haus*); **~measure**

['jɑːdmeзə], ⁓stick Yardstock *m*,
-maß *n*.

yarn [jɑːn] **1.** Garn *n*; F Seemanns-
garn *n*; abenteuerliche Geschichte;
2. F erzählen.

yawl ⚓ [jɔːl] Jolle *f*.

yawn [jɔːn] **1.** gähnen; **2.** Gähnen *n*.

ye †, *poet.*, *co.* [jiː] ihr.

yea †, *prov.* [jei] **1.** ja; **2.** Ja *n*.

year [jəː] Jahr *n*; ⁓**ly** ['jəːli] jährlich.

yearn [jəːn] sich sehnen, verlangen;
⁓**ing** ['jəːniŋ] **1.** Sehnen *n*, Sehnsucht *f*; **2.** □ sehnsüchtig.

yeast [jiːst] Hefe *f*; Schaum *m*.

yegg(man) *Am. sl.* ['jeg(mən)]
Stromer *m*; Einbrecher *m*.

yell [jel] **1.** (gellend) schreien; auf-
schreien; **2.** (gellender) Schrei; an-
feuernder Ruf.

yellow ['jelou] **1.** gelb; F hasen-
füßig (*feig*); Sensations...; Hetz...;
2. Gelb *n*; **3.** (sich) gelb färben;
⁓**ed** vergilbt; ~ **fever** ⚕ Gelb-
fieber *n*; ⁓**ish** [⁓ouiʃ] gelblich.

yelp [jelp] **1.** Gekläff *n*; **2.** kläffen.

yen *Am. sl.* [jen] brennendes Verlangen.

yeoman ['joumən] freier Bauer.

yep *Am.* F [jep] ja.

yes [jes] **1.** ja; doch; **2.** Ja *n*.

yesterday ['jestədi] gestern.

yet [jet] **1.** *adv.* noch; bis jetzt;
schon; sogar; *as* ~ bis jetzt; *not* ~
noch nicht; **2.** *cj.* (je)doch, dennoch, trotzdem.

yew ♦ [juː] Eibe *f*, Taxus *m*.

yield [jiːld] **1.** *v/t.* hervorbringen,
liefern; ergeben; *Gewinn* (ein)brin-
gen; gewähren; übergeben; zugestehen; *v/i.* ⚲ tragen; sich fügen;
nachgeben; **2.** Ertrag *m*; ⁓**ing** □
['jiːldiŋ] nachgebend; *fig.* nachgiebig.

yip *Am.* F [jip] jaulen.

yod|el, ⁓**le** ['joudl] **1.** Jodler *m*;
2. jodeln.

yoke [jouk] **1.** Joch *n* (*a. fig.*); Paar
n (Ochsen); Schultertrage *f*; **2.** an-,
zs.-spannen; *fig.* paaren (to mit).

yolk [jouk] (Ei)Dotter *m*, *n*, Eigelb *n*.

yon [jɔn], ⁓**der** *lit.* ['jɔndə] **1.** je-
ne(r, -s); jenseitig; **2.** dort drüben.

yore [jɔː]: of ~ ehemals, ehedem.

you [juː, ju] ihr; du, Sie; man.

young [jʌŋ] **1.** □ jung; *von Kindern*
a. klein; **2.** (Tier)Junge(s) *n*;
(Tier)Junge *pl.*; *with* ~ trächtig;
⁓**ster** ['jʌŋstə] Junge *m*.

your [jɔː] euer(e); dein(e), Ihr(e);
⁓**s** [jɔːz] der (die, das) eurige, deinige, Ihrige; euer; dein, Ihr;
⁓**self** [jɔːˈself], *pl.* ⁓**selves** [⁓lvz]
(du, ihr, Sie) selbst; dich, euch,
Sie (selbst), sich (selbst); *by* ~
allein.

youth [juːθ], *pl.* ⁓**s** [juːðz] Jugend *f*;
Jüngling *m*; ~ **hostel** Jugendher-
berge *f*; ⁓**ful** □ ['juːθful] jugendlich.

yule *lit.* [juːl] Weihnacht *f*.

Z

zeal [ziːl] Eifer *m*; ⁓**ot** ['zelət]
Eiferer *m*; ⁓**ous** □ [⁓əs] eifrig;
eifrig bedacht (*for* auf *acc.*); innig,
heiß.

zebra *zo.* ['ziːbrə] Zebra *n*; ~ **cross-**
ing Fußgängerüberweg *m*.

zenith ['zeniθ] Zenit *m*; *fig.* Höhepunkt *m*.

zero ['ziərou] Null *f*; Nullpunkt *m*.

zest [zest] **1.** Würze *f* (*a. fig.*); Lust
f, Freude *f*; Genuß *m*; **2.** würzen.

zigzag ['zigzæg] Zickzack *m*.

zinc [ziŋk] **1.** *min.* Zink *n*; **2.** ver-
zinken.

zip [zip] Schwirren *n*; F Schwung *m*;
⁓**-fastener** ['zipfɑːsnə], ⁓**per** ['zipə]
Reißverschluß *m*.

zodiac *ast.* ['zoudiæk] Tierkreis *m*.

zone [zoun] Zone *f*; *fig.* Gebiet *n*.

Zoo F [zuː] Zoo *m*.

zoolog|ical □ [zouəˈlɔdʒikəl] zoo-
logisch; ⁓**y** [zouˈɔlədʒi] Zoologie *f*.

Alphabetical List of the German Irregular Verbs

Infinitive — Preterite — Past Participle

backen - backte (buk) - gebacken
bedingen - bedang (bedingte) - bedungen (*conditional*: bedingt)
befehlen - befahl - befohlen
beginnen - begann - begonnen
beißen - biß - gebissen
bergen - barg - geborgen
bersten - barst - geborsten
bewegen - bewog - bewogen
biegen - bog - gebogen
bieten - bot - geboten
binden - band - gebunden
bitten - bat - gebeten
blasen - blies - geblasen
bleiben - blieb - geblieben
bleichen - blich - geblichen
braten - briet - gebraten
brauchen - brauchte - gebraucht (*v/aux.* brauchen)
brechen - brach - gebrochen
brennen - brannte - gebrannt
bringen - brachte - gebracht
denken - dachte - gedacht
dreschen - drosch - gedroschen
dringen - drang - gedrungen
dürfen - durfte - gedurft (*v/aux.* dürfen)
empfehlen - empfahl - empfohlen
erlöschen - erlosch - erloschen
erschrecken - erschrak - erschrocken
essen - aß - gegessen
fahren - fuhr - gefahren
fallen - fiel - gefallen
fangen - fing - gefangen
fechten - focht - gefochten
finden - fand - gefunden
flechten - flocht - geflochten
fliegen - flog - geflogen
fliehen - floh - geflohen
fließen - floß - geflossen
fressen - fraß - gefressen
frieren - fror - gefroren
gären - gor (*esp. fig.* gärte) - gegoren (*esp. fig.* gegärt)
gebären - gebar - geboren
geben - gab - gegeben
gedeihen - gedieh - gediehen
gehen - ging - gegangen
gelingen - gelang - gelungen
gelten - galt - gegolten
genesen - genas - genesen
genießen - genoß - genossen
geschehen - geschah - geschehen
gewinnen - gewann - gewonnen

gießen - goß - gegossen
gleichen - glich - geglichen
gleiten - glitt - geglitten
glimmen - glomm - geglommen
graben - grub - gegraben
greifen - griff - gegriffen
haben - hatte - gehabt
halten - hielt - gehalten
hängen - hing - gehangen
hauen - haute (hieb) - gehauen
heben - hob - gehoben
heißen - hieß - geheißen
helfen - half - geholfen
kennen - kannte - gekannt
klingen - klang - geklungen
kneifen - kniff - gekniffen
kommen - kam - gekommen
können - konnte - gekonnt (*v/aux.* können)
kriechen - kroch - gekrochen
laden - lud - geladen
lassen - ließ - gelassen (*v/aux.* lassen)
laufen - lief - gelaufen
leiden - litt - gelitten
leihen - lieh - geliehen
lesen - las - gelesen
liegen - lag - gelegen
lügen - log - gelogen
mahlen - mahlte - gemahlen
meiden - mied - gemieden
melken - melkte (molk) - gemolken (gemelkt)
messen - maß - gemessen
mißlingen - mißlang - mißlungen
mögen - mochte - gemocht (*v/aux.* mögen)
müssen - mußte - gemußt (*v/aux.* müssen)
nehmen - nahm - genommen
nennen - nannte - genannt
pfeifen - pfiff - gepfiffen
preisen - pries - gepriesen
quellen - quoll - gequollen
raten - riet - geraten
reiben - rieb - gerieben
reißen - riß - gerissen
reiten - ritt - geritten
rennen - rannte - gerannt
riechen - roch - gerochen
ringen - rang - gerungen
rinnen - rann - geronnen
rufen - rief - gerufen
salzen - salzte - gesalzen (gesalzt)
saufen - soff - gesoffen

saugen - sog - gesogen
schaffen - schuf - geschaffen
schallen - schallte (scholl) - geschallt (*for erschallen a.* erschollen)
scheiden - schied - geschieden
scheinen - schien - geschienen
schelten - schalt - gescholten
scheren - schor - geschoren
schieben - schob - geschoben
schießen - schoß - geschossen
schinden - schund - geschunden
schlafen - schlief - geschlafen
schlagen - schlug - geschlagen
schleichen - schlich - geschlichen
schleifen - schliff - geschliffen
schließen - schloß - geschlossen
schlingen - schlang - geschlungen
schmeißen - schmiß - geschmissen
schmelzen - schmolz - geschmolzen
schneiden - schnitt - geschnitten
schrecken - schrak - † geschrocken
schreiben - schrieb - geschrieben
schreien - schrie - geschrie(e)n
schreiten - schritt - geschritten
schweigen - schwieg - geschwiegen
schwellen - schwoll - geschwollen
schwimmen - schwamm - geschwommen
schwinden - schwand - geschwunden
schwingen - schwang - geschwungen
schwören - schwor - geschworen
sehen - sah - gesehen
sein - war - gewesen
senden - sandte - gesandt
sieden - sott - gesotten
singen - sang - gesungen
sinken - sank - gesunken
sinnen - sann - gesonnen
sitzen - saß - gesessen
sollen - sollte - gesollt (*v/aux.* sollen)
spalten - spaltete - gespalten (gespaltet)
speien - spie - gespie(e)n
spinnen - spann - gesponnen
sprechen - sprach - gesprochen

sprießen - sproß - gesprossen
springen - sprang - gesprungen
stechen - stach - gestochen
stecken - steckte (stak) - gesteckt
stehen - stand - gestanden
stehlen - stahl - gestohlen
steigen - stieg - gestiegen
sterben - starb - gestorben
stieben - stob - gestoben
stinken - stank - gestunken
stoßen - stieß - gestoßen
streichen - strich - gestrichen
streiten - stritt - gestritten
tragen - trug - getragen
treffen - traf - getroffen
treiben - trieb - getrieben
treten - trat - getreten
triefen - triefte (troff) - getrieft
trinken - trank - getrunken
trügen - trog - getrogen
tun - tat - getan
verderben - verdarb - verdorben
verdrießen - verdroß - verdrossen
vergessen - vergaß - vergessen
verlieren - verlor - verloren
verschleißen - verschliß - verschlissen
verzeihen - verzieh - verziehen
wachsen - wuchs - gewachsen
wägen - wog (✎ wägte) - gewogen (✎ gewägt)
waschen - wusch - gewaschen
weben - wob - gewoben
weichen - wich - gewichen
weisen - wies - gewiesen
wenden - wandte - gewandt
werben - warb - geworben
werden - wurde - geworden (worden*)
werfen - warf - geworfen
wiegen - wog - gewogen
winden - wand - gewunden
wissen - wußte - gewußt
wollen - wollte - gewollt (*v/aux.* wollen)
wringen - wrang -gewrungen
ziehen - zog - gezogen
zwingen - zwang - gezwungen

* only in connexion with the past participles of other verbs, *e.g.* er *ist gesehen worden* he has been seen.

Alphabetical List of the English Irregular Verbs

Infinitive — Preterite — Past Participle

Irregular forms marked with asterisks (*) can be exchanged for the regular forms.

abide (*bleiben*) - abode* - abode*
arise (*sich erheben*) - arose - arisen
awake (*erwachen*) - awoke - awoke*
be (*sein*) - was - been
bear (*tragen; gebären*) - bore - getragen: borne - geboren: born
beat (*schlagen*) - beat - beat(en)
become (*werden*) - became - become
beget (*zeugen*) - begot - begotten
begin (*anfangen*) - began - begun
bend (*beugen*) - bent - bent
bereave (*berauben*) - bereft* - bereft*
beseech (*ersuchen*) - besought - besought
bet (*wetten*) - bet* - bet*
bid ([*ge*]*bieten*) - bade, bid - bid(den)
bide (*abwarten*) - bode* - bided
bind (*binden*) - bound - bound
bite (*beißen*) - bit - bitten
bleed (*bluten*) - bled - bled
blend (*mischen*) - blent* - blent*
blow (*blasen; blühen*) - blew - blown
break (*brechen*) - broke - broken
breed (*aufziehen*) - bred - bred
bring (*bringen*) - brought - brought
build (*bauen*) - built - built
burn (*brennen*) - burnt* - burnt*
burst (*bersten*) - burst - burst
buy (*kaufen*) - bought - bought
cast (*werfen*) - cast - cast
catch (*fangen*) - caught - caught
chide (*schelten*) - chid - chid(den)*
choose (*wählen*) - chose - chosen
cleave ([*sich*] *spalten*) cleft, clove* - cleft, cloven*
cling (*sich [an]klammern*) - clung - clung
clothe ([*an-, be*]*kleiden*) - clad* - clad*
come (*kommen*) - came - come
cost (*kosten*) - cost - cost
creep (*kriechen*) - crept - crept
crow (*krähen*) - crew* - crowed
cut (*schneiden*) - cut - cut
deal (*handeln*) - dealt - dealt
dig (*graben*) - dug - dug
do (*tun*) - did - done
draw (*ziehen*) - drew - drawn
dream (*träumen*) - dreamt* - dreamt*
drink (*trinken*) - drank - drunk
drive (*treiben; fahren*) - drove - driven
dwell (*wohnen*) - dwelt - dwelt

eat (*essen*) - ate, eat - eaten
fall (*fallen*) - fell - fallen
feed (*füttern*) - fed - fed
feel (*fühlen*) - felt - felt
fight (*kämpfen*) - fought - fought
find (*finden*) - found - found
flee (*fliehen*) - fled - fled
fling (*schleudern*) - flung - flung
fly (*fliegen*) - flew - flown
forbid (*verbieten*) - forbade - forbidden
forget (*vergessen*) - forgot - forgotten
forsake (*aufgeben; verlassen*) - forsook - forsaken
freeze ([*ge*]*frieren*) - froze - frozen
get (*bekommen*) - got - got, Am. gotten
gild (*vergolden*) - gilt* - gilt*
gird ([*um*]*gürten*) - girt* - girt*
give (*geben*) - gave - given
go (*gehen*) - went - gone
grave ([*ein*]*graben*) - graved - graven*
grind (*mahlen*) - ground - ground
grow (*wachsen*) - grew - grown
hang (*hängen*) - hung - hung
have (*haben*) - had - had
hear (*hören*) - heard - heard
heave (*heben*) - hove* - hove*
hew (*hauen, hacken*) - hewed - hewn*
hide (*verbergen*) - hid - hid(den)
hit (*treffen*) - hit - hit
hold (*halten*) - held - held
hurt (*verletzen*) - hurt - hurt
keep (*halten*) - kept - kept
kneel (*knien*) - knelt* - knelt*
knit (*stricken*) - knit* - knit*
know (*wissen*) - knew - known
lay (*legen*) - laid - laid
lead (*führen*) - led - led
lean ([*sich*] [*an*]*lehnen*) - leant* - leant*
leap ([*über*]*springen*) - leapt* - leapt*
learn (*lernen*) - learnt* - learnt*
leave (*verlassen*) - left - left
lend (*leihen*) - lent - lent
let (*lassen*) - let - let
lie (*liegen*) - lay - lain
light (*anzünden*) - lit* - lit*
lose (*verlieren*) - lost - lost
make (*machen*) - made - made
mean (*meinen*) - meant - meant
meet (*begegnen*) - met - met
mow (*mähen*) - mowed - mown*

pay (*zahlen*) - paid - paid
pen (*einpferchen*) - pent - pent
put (*setzen, stellen*) - put - put
read (*lesen*) - read - read
rend ([*zer*]*reißen*) - rent - rent
rid (*befreien*) - rid* - rid*
ride (*reiten*) - rode - ridden
ring (*läuten*) - rang - rung
rise (*aufstehen*) - rose - risen
rive ([*sich*] *spalten*) - rived - riven*
run (*laufen*) - ran - run
saw (*sägen*) - sawed - sawn*
say (*sagen*) - said - said
see (*sehen*) - saw - seen
seek (*suchen*) - sought - sought
sell (*verkaufen*) - sold - sold
send (*senden*) - sent - sent
set (*setzen*) - set - set
sew (*nähen*) - sewed - sewn*
shake (*schütteln*) - shook - shaken
shave ([*sich*] *rasieren*) - shaved - shaven*
shear (*scheren*) - sheared - shorn
shed (*ausgießen*) - shed - shed
shine (*scheinen*) - shone - shone
shoe (*beschuhen*) - shod - shod
shoot (*schießen*) - shot - shot
show (*zeigen*) - showed - shown*
shred ([*zer*]*schnitzeln, zerfetzen*) - shred* - shred*
shrink (*einschrumpfen*) - shrank - shrunk
shut (*schließen*) - shut - shut
sing (*singen*) - sang - sung
sink (*sinken*) - sank - sunk
sit (*sitzen*) - sat - sat
slay (*erschlagen*) - slew - slain
sleep (*schlafen*) - slept - slept
slide (*gleiten*) - slid - slid
sling (*schleudern*) - slung - slung
slink (*schleichen*) - slunk - slunk
slip (*schlüpfen, gleiten*) - slipt* - slipt*
slit (*schlitzen*) - slit - slit
smell (*riechen*) - smelt* - smelt*
smite (*schlagen*) - smote - smitten, smote
sow ([*aus*]*säen*) - sowed - sown*
speak (*sprechen*) - spoke - spoken
speed (*eilen*) - sped* - sped*
spell (*buchstabieren*) - spelt* - spelt*
spend (*ausgeben*) - spent - spent

spill (*verschütten*) - spilt* - spilt*
spin (*spinnen*) - spun - spun
spit ([*aus*]*spucken*) - spat - spat
split (*spalten*) - split - split
spoil (*verderben*) - spoilt* - spoilt*
spread (*verbreiten*) - spread - spread
spring (*springen*) - sprang - sprung
stand (*stehen*) - stood - stood
stave (*den Boden einschlagen*) - stove* - stove*
steal (*stehlen*) - stole - stolen
stick (*stecken*) - stuck - stuck
sting (*stechen*) - stung - stung
stink (*stinken*) - stank - stunk
strew ([*be*]*streuen*) - strewed - strewn*
stride (*über-, durchschreiten*) - strode - stridden
strike (*schlagen*) - struck - struck
string (*spannen*) - strung - strung
strive (*streben*) - strove - striven
swear (*schwören*) - swore - sworn
sweat (*schwitzen*) - sweat* - sweat*
sweep (*fegen*) - swept - swept
swell ([*an*]*schwellen*) - swelled - swollen
swim (*schwimmen*) - swam - swum
swing (*schwingen*) - swung - swung
take (*nehmen*) - took - taken
teach (*lehren*) - taught - taught
tear (*ziehen*) - tore - torn
tell (*sagen*) - told - told
think (*denken*) - thought - thought
thrive (*gedeihen*) - throve* - thriven*
throw (*werfen*) - threw - thrown
thrust (*stoßen*) - thrust - thrust
tread (*treten*) - trod - trodden
wake (*wachen*) - woke* - woke(n)*
wax (*zunehmen*) - waxed - waxen*
wear ([*Kleider*] *tragen*) - wore - worn
weave (*weben*) - wove - woven
weep (*weinen*) - wept - wept
wet (*nässen*) - wet* - wet*
win (*gewinnen*) - won - won
wind (*winden*) - wound - wound
work (*arbeiten*) - wrought* - wrought*
wreathe ([*um*]*winden*) - wreathed - wreathen*
wring ([*aus*]*wringen*) - wrung - wrung
write (*schreiben*) - wrote - written

German Proper Names

Aachen ['ɑːxən] n Aachen, Aix-la-Chapelle.

Adenauer ['ɑːdənauər] first chancellor of the German Federal Republic.

Adler ['ɑːdlər] Austrian psychologist.

Adria ['ɑːdria] f Adriatic Sea.

Afrika ['ɑːfrika] n Africa.

Ägypten [ɛ'gyptən] n Egypt.

Albanien [al'bɑːnjən] n Albania.

Algerien [al'geːrjən] n Algeria.

Algier ['alʒiːr] n Algiers.

Allgäu ['algɔy] n Al(l)gäu (region of Bavaria).

Alpen ['alpən] pl. Alps pl.

Amerika [a'meːrika] n America.

Anden ['andən] pl. the Andes pl.

Antillen [an'tilən] f/pl. Antilles pl.

Antwerpen [ant'verpən] n Antwerp.

Apenninen [ape'niːnən] m/pl. the Apennines pl.

Argentinien [argɛn'tiːnjən] n Argentina, the Argentine.

Ärmelkanal ['ɛrməlkanɑːl] m English Channel.

Asien ['ɑːzjən] n Asia.

Athen [a'teːn] n Athens.

Äthiopien [ɛti'oːpjən] Ethiopia.

Atlantik [at'lantik] m Atlantic.

Australien [au'strɑːljən] n Australia.

Bach [bax] German composer.

Baden-Württemberg ['bɑːdən-'vyrtəmberk] n Land of the German Federal Republic.

Barlach ['barlax] German sculptor.

Basel ['bɑːzəl] n Bâle, Basle.

Bayern ['baiərn] n Bavaria (Land of the German Federal Republic).

Becher ['beçər] German poet.

Beckmann ['bɛkman] German painter.

Beethoven ['beːthoːfən] German composer.

Belgien ['bɛlgjən] n Belgium.

Belgrad ['bɛlgrɑːt] n Belgrade.

Berg [berk] Austrian composer.

Berlin [ber'liːn] n Berlin.

Bermuda-Inseln [ber'muːdaʔinzəln] f/pl. Bermudas pl.

Bern [bern] n Bern(e).

Bismarck ['bismark] German statesman.

Bloch [blɔx] German philosopher.

Böcklin ['bœkliːn] German painter.

Bodensee ['boːdənzeː] m Lake of Constance.

Böhm [bøːm] Austrian conductor.

Böhmen ['bøːmən] n Bohemia.

Böll [bœl] German author.

Bonn [bɔn] n capital of the German Federal Republic.

Brahms [brɑːms] German composer.

Brandt [brant] German politician.

Brasilien [bra'ziːljən] n Brazil.

Braunschweig ['braunʃvaik] n Brunswick.

Brecht [brɛçt] German dramatist.

Bremen ['breːmən] n Land of the German Federal Republic.

Bruckner ['bruknər] Austrian composer.

Brüssel ['brysəl] n Brussels.

Budapest ['buːdapest] n Budapest.

Bukarest ['buːkarest] n Bucharest.

Bulgarien [bul'gɑːrjən] n Bulgaria.

Calais [ka'lɛ] n: Straße von ~ Straits of Dover.

Calvin [kal'viːn] Swiss religious reformer.

Chile ['tʃiːlə] n Chile.

China ['çiːna] n China.

Christus ['kristus] m Christ.

Daimler ['daimlər] German inventor.

Dänemark ['dɛːnəmark] n Denmark.

Deutschland ['dɔytʃlant] n Germany.

Diesel ['diːzəl] German inventor.

Döblin [dø'bliːn] German author.

Dolomiten [dolo'miːtən] pl. the Dolomites pl.

Donau ['doːnau] f Danube.

Dortmund ['dɔrtmunt] n industrial city in West Germany.

Dresden ['dreːsdən] n capital of Saxony.

Dublin ['dʌblin] n Dublin.

Dünkirchen ['dyːnkirçən] n Dunkirk.

Dürer ['dyːrər] German painter.

Dürrenmatt ['dyrənmat] Swiss dramatist.

Düsseldorf ['dysəldɔrf] n capital of North Rhine-Westphalia.

Ebert ['eːbərt] first president of the Weimar Republic.

Egk [ɛk] German composer.

Eichendorff ['aiçəndɔrf] German poet.

Eiger ['aigər] Swiss mountain.

Einstein ['ainʃtain] German physicist.

Elbe ['ɛlbə] f German river.

Elsaß ['ɛlzas] n Alsace.

Engels ['ɛŋəls] German philosopher.

England ['ɛŋlant] *n* England.
Essen ['esən] *n industrial city in West Germany*.
Europa [ɔʏ'ro:pa] *n* Europe.

Feldberg ['fɛltbɛrk] *German mountain*.
Finnland ['finlant] *n* Finland.
Florenz [flo'rɛnts] *n* Florence.
Fontane [fɔn'ta:nə] *German author*.
Franken ['fraŋkən] *n* Franconia.
Frankfurt ['fraŋkfurt] *n* Frankfort.
Frankreich ['fraŋkraɪç] *n* France.
Freud [frɔʏt] *Austrian psychologist*.
Frisch [friʃ] *Swiss author*.

Garmisch ['garmiʃ] *n health resort in Bavaria*.
Genf [gɛnf] *n* Geneva; ~er See *m* Lake of Geneva.
Genua ['ge:nua] *n* Genoa.
Gibraltar [gi'braltar] *n* Gibraltar.
Goethe ['gø:tə] *German poet*.
Grass [gras] *German author*.
Graubünden [grau'byndən] *n* the Grisons.
Griechenland ['gri:çənlant] *n* Greece.
Grillparzer ['grilpartsər] *Austrian dramatist*.
Grönland ['grø:nlant] *n* Greenland.
Gropius ['gro:pjus] *German architect*. [Great Britain.\
Großbritannien [gro:sbri'tanjən] *n*\
Großglockner [gro:s'glɔknər] *Austrian mountain*.
Grünewald ['gry:nəvalt] *German painter*.

Haag [ha:k]: Den ~ The Hague.
Habsburg *hist.* ['ha:psburk] *n* Hapsburg (*German dynasty*).
Hahn [ha:n] *German chemist*.
Hamburg ['hamburk] *n Land of the German Federal Republic*.
Händel ['hɛndəl] Handel (*German composer*).
Hannover [ha'no:fər] *n* Hanover (*capital of Lower Saxony*).
Hartmann ['hartman] *German composer*.
Harz [ha:rts] *m* Harz Mountains *pl*.
Hauptmann ['hauptman] *German dramatist*.
Haydn ['haɪdən] *Austrian composer*.
Hegel ['he:gəl] *German philosopher*.
Heidegger ['haɪdɛgər] *German philosopher*.
Heidelberg ['haɪdəlbɛrk] *n university town in West Germany*.
Heine ['haɪnə] *German poet*.
Heinemann ['haɪnəman] *president of the German Federal Republic*.
Heisenberg ['haɪzənbɛrk] *German physicist*.
Heißenbüttel ['haɪsənbytəl] *German poet*.
Helgoland ['hɛlgolant] *n* Heligoland.

Helsinki ['hɛlziŋki] *n* Helsinki.
Henze ['hɛntsə] *German composer*.
Hesse ['hesə] *German poet*.
Hessen ['hesən] *n* Hesse (*Land of the German Federal Republic*).
Heuß [hɔʏs] *first president of the German Federal Republic*.
Hindemith ['hindəmit] *German composer*.
Hohenzollern *hist.* [ho:ən'tsɔlərn] *n German dynasty*.
Hölderlin ['hœldərli:n] *German poet*.
Holland ['hɔlant] *n* Holland.

Indien ['indjən] *n* India.
Inn [in] *m affluent of the Danube*.
Innsbruck ['insbruk] *n capital of the Tyrol*.
Irak [i'ra:k] *m* Iraq, *a.* Irak.
Irland ['irlant] *n* Ireland.
Island ['i:slant] *n* Iceland.
Israel ['israel] *n* Israel.
Italien [i'ta:ljən] *n* Italy.

Japan ['ja:pan] *n* Japan.
Jaspers ['jaspərs] *German philosopher*.
Jesus ['je:zus] *m* Jesus.
Jordanien [jɔr'da:njən] *n* Jordan.
Jugoslawien [jugo'sla:vjən] *n* Yugoslavia.
Jung [juŋ] *Swiss psychologist*.
Jungfrau ['juŋfrau] *f Swiss mountain*.

Kafka ['kafka] *Czech poet*.
Kanada ['kanada] *n* Canada.
Kant [kant] *German philosopher*.
Karajan ['ka:rajan] *Austrian conductor*.
Karlsruhe [karls'ru:ə] *n city in South-Western Germany*.
Kärnten ['kɛrntən] *n* Carinthia.
Kassel ['kasəl] *n* Cassel.
Kästner ['kɛstnər] *German author*.
Kiel [ki:l] *n capital of Schleswig-Holstein*.
Kiesinger ['ki:ziŋər] *German politician*.
Klee [kle:] *German painter*.
Kleist [klaɪst] *German poet*.
Klemperer ['klɛmpərər] *German conductor*.
Koblenz ['ko:blɛnts] *n* Coblenz, Koblenz.
Kokoschka [ko'kɔʃka] *German painter*.
Köln [kœln] *n* Cologne.
Kolumbien [ko'lumbjən] *n* Columbia.
Kolumbus [ko'lumbus] *m* Columbus.
Königsberg ['kø:niçsbɛrk] *n capital of East Prussia*.
Konstanz ['kɔnstants] *n* Constance.
Kopenhagen [kopən'ha:gən] *n* Copenhagen.
Kordilleren [kɔrdil'je:rən] *f/pl. the* Cordilleras *pl*.

Kreml ['kre:məl] *m the* Kremlin.

Leibniz ['laɪbnɪts] *German philosopher.*

Leipzig ['laɪptsɪç] *n* Leipsic.

Lessing ['lesɪŋ] *German poet.*

Libanon ['li:banɔn] *m* Lebanon.

Liebig ['li:bɪç] *German chemist.*

Lissabon ['lisabɔn] *n* Lisbon.

London ['lɔndɔn] *n* London.

Lothringen ['lo:trɪŋən] *n* Lorraine.

Lübeck ['ly:bɛk] *n city in West Germany.*

Luther ['lutər] *German religious reformer.*

Luxemburg ['luksəmburk] *n* Luxemb(o)urg.

Luzern [lu'tsɛrn] *n* Lucerne.

Maas [mɑ:s] *f* Meuse.

Madrid [ma'drɪt] *n* Madrid.

Mahler ['mɑ:lər] *Austrian composer.*

Mailand ['maɪlant] *n* Milan.

Main [maɪn] *m German river.*

Mainz [maɪnts] *n* Mayence (*capital of Rhineland-Palatinate*).

Mann [man] *name of three German authors.*

Marokko [ma'rɔko] *n* Morocco.

Marx [marks] *German philosopher.*

Matterhorn ['matərhɔrn] *Swiss mountain.*

Meißen ['maɪsən] *n* Meissen.

Meitner ['maɪtnər] *German female physicist.*

Memel ['me:məl] *f frontier river in East Prussia.*

Menzel ['mɛntsəl] *German painter.*

Mexiko ['mɛksiko] *n* Mexico.

Mies van der Rohe ['mi:sfandər-'ro:ə] *German architect.*

Mittelamerika ['mɪtəlʔa'me:rika] *n* Central America.

Mitteleuropa ['mɪtəlʔɔʏ'ro:pa] *n* Central Europe.

Mittelmeer ['mɪtəlme:r] *n* Mediterranean (Sea).

Moldau ['mɔldau] *f Bohemian river.*

Mörike ['mø:rikə] *German poet.*

Mosel ['mo:zəl] *f* Moselle.

Mössbauer ['mœsbauər] *German physicist.*

Moskau ['mɔskau] *n* Moscow.

Mozart ['mo:tsart] *Austrian composer.*

München ['mynçən] *n* Munich (*capital of Bavaria*).

Neapel [ne'a:pəl] *n* Naples.

Neisse ['naɪsə] *f German river.*

Neufundland [nɔʏ'funtlant] *n* Newfoundland.

Neuseeland [nɔʏ'ze:lant] *n* New Zealand.

Niederlande ['ni:dərlandə] *n/pl. the* Netherlands *pl.*

Niedersachsen ['ni:dərzaksən] *n* Lower Saxony (*Land of the German Federal Republic*).

Nietzsche ['ni:tʃə] *German philosopher.*

Nil [ni:l] *m* Nile.

Nordamerika ['nɔrtʔa'me:rika] *n* North America.

Nordrhein-Westfalen ['nɔrtraɪn-vest'fa:lən] *n* North Rhine-Westphalia (*Land of the German Federal Republic*).

Nordsee ['nɔrtze:] *f* German Ocean, North Sea.

Norwegen ['nɔrve:gən] *n* Norway.

Nürnberg ['nyrnbɛrk] *n* Nuremberg.

Oder ['o:dər] *f German river.*

Orff [ɔrf] *German composer.*

Oslo ['ɔslo] *n* Oslo.

Ostasien ['ɔst'a:zjən] *n* Eastern Asia.

Ostende [ɔst'ɛndə] *n* Ostend.

Österreich ['ø:stəraɪç] *n* Austria.

Ostsee ['ɔstze:] *f* Baltic.

Palästina [palɛ'sti:na] *n* Palestine.

Paris [pa'ri:s] *n* Paris.

Persien ['perzjən] *n* Persia.

Pfalz [pfalts] *f* Palatinate.

Philippinen [fili'pi:nən] *f/pl.* Philippines *pl.,* Philippine Islands *pl.*

Planck [plaŋk] *German physicist.*

Polen ['po:lən] *n* Poland.

Pommern ['pɔmərn] *n* Pomerania.

Portugal ['portugal] *n* Portugal.

Prag [prɑ:g] *n* Prague.

Preußen *hist.* ['prɔʏsən] *n* Prussia.

Pyrenäen [pyre'nɛ:ən] *pl.* Pyrenees *pl.*

Regensburg ['re:gənsburk] *n* Ratisbon.

Reykjavik ['raɪkjavi:k] *n* Reykjavik.

Rhein [ram] *m* Rhine.

Rheinland-Pfalz ['raɪnlant'pfalts] *n* Rhineland-Palatinate (*Land of the German Federal Republic*).

Rilke ['rɪlkə] *Austrian poet.*

Rom [ro:m] *n* Rome.

Röntgen ['rœntgən] *German physicist.*

Ruhr [ru:r] *f German river;* **Ruhrgebiet** ['ru:rgəbi:t] *n industrial centre of West Germany.*

Rumänien [ru'mɛ:njən] *n* Ro(u)mania.

Rußland ['ruslant] *n* Russia.

Saale ['za:lə] *f German river.*

Saar [za:r] *f affluent of the Moselle;* **Saarbrücken** [za:r'brykən] *n capital of the Saar;* **Saarland** ['za:rlant] *n* Saar (*Land of the German Federal Republic*).

Sachsen ['zaksən] *n* Saxony.

Scherchen ['ʃerçən] *Swiss conductor.*

Schiller ['ʃilər] *German poet.*

Schlesien ['ʃle:zjən] *n* Silesia.

Schleswig-Holstein ['ʃle:svɪç'hɔlʃtaɪn] n Land of the German Federal Republic.

Schönberg [ˈʃøːnbɛrk] Austrian composer.

Schottland [ˈʃɔtlant] n Scotland.

Schubert [ˈʃuːbərt] Austrian composer.

Schumann [ˈʃuːman] German composer.

Schwaben [ˈʃvaːbən] n Swabia.

Schwarzwald [ˈʃvartsvalt] m Black Forest.

Schweden [ˈʃveːdən] n Sweden.

Schweiz [ʃvaɪts] f: die ~ Switzerland.

Sibirien [ziˈbiːrjən] n Siberia.

Siemens [ˈziːməns] German inventor.

Sizilien [ziˈtsiːljən] n Sicily.

Skandinavien [skandiˈnaːvjən] n Scandinavia.

Sofia [ˈzɔfja] n Sofia.

Sowjetunion [zɔˈvjetʔunjoːn] f the Soviet Union.

Spanien [ˈʃpaːnjən] n Spain.

Spitzweg [ˈʃpɪtsveːk] German painter.

Spranger [ˈʃpraŋər] German philosopher.

Steiermark [ˈʃtaɪərmark] f Styria.

Stifter [ˈʃtɪftər] Austrian author.

Stockholm [ˈʃtɔkhɔlm] n Stockholm.

Storm [ʃtɔrm] German poet.

Strauß [ʃtraʊs] Austrian composer.

Strauss [ʃtraʊs] German composer.

Stresemann [ˈʃtreːzəman] German statesman.

Stuttgart [ˈʃtutgart] n capital of Baden-Württemberg.

Südamerika [ˈzyːtʔaˈmeːrika] n South America.

Sudan [zuˈdaːn] m S(o)udan.

Syrien [ˈzyːrjən] n Syria.

Themse [ˈtɛmzə] f Thames.

Thoma [ˈtoːma] German author.

Thüringen [ˈtyːrɪŋən] n Thuringia.

Tirana [tiˈraːna] n Tirana.

Tirol [tiˈroːl] n the Tyrol.

Trakl [ˈtraːkəl] Austrian poet.

Tschechoslowakei [tʃɛçoslovaˈkaɪ] f: die ~ Czechoslovakia.

Türkei [tyrˈkaɪ] f: die ~ Turkey.

Ungarn [ˈungarn] n Hungary.

Ural [uˈraːl] m Ural (Mountains pl.).

Vatikan [vatiˈkaːn] m the Vatican.

Venedig [veˈneːdiç] n Venice.

Vereinigte Staaten [vərˈaɪnɪçtə ˈʃtaːtən] m/pl. the United States pl.

Vierwaldstätter See [fiːrˈvaltʃtɛtər ˈzeː] m Lake of Lucerne.

Wagner [ˈvaːgnər] German composer.

Wankel [ˈvaŋkəl] German inventor.

Warschau [ˈvarʃaʊ] n Warsaw.

Weichsel [ˈvaɪksəl] f Vistula.

Weiß [vaɪs] German dramatist.

Weizsäcker [ˈvaɪtszɛkər] German physicist.

Werfel [ˈvɛrfəl] Austrian author.

Weser [ˈveːzər] f German river.

Westdeutschland pol. [ˈvɛstdɔytʃlant] n West Germany.

Wien [viːn] n Vienna.

Wiesbaden [ˈviːsbaːdən] n capital of Hesse.

Zeppelin [ˈtsɛpəliːn] German inventor.

Zuckmayer [ˈtsukmaɪər] German dramatist.

Zweig [tsvaɪg] Austrian author.

Zürich [ˈtsyːriç] n Zurich.

Zypern [ˈtsyːpərn] n Cyprus.

German Abbreviations

a. a. O. *am angeführten Ort* in the place cited, *abbr.* loc. cit., l. c.

Abb. *Abbildung* illustration.

Abf. *Abfahrt* departure, *abbr.* dep.

Abg. *Abgeordnete* Member of Parliament, *etc.*

Abk. *Abkürzung* abbreviation.

Abs. *Absatz* paragraph; *Absender* sender.

Abschn. *Abschnitt* paragraph, chapter. [dept.]

Abt. *Abteilung* department, *abbr.*

a. D. *außer Dienst* retired.

Adr. *Adresse* address.

AG *Aktiengesellschaft* joint-stock company, *Am.* (stock) corporation.

allg. *allgemein* general.

a. M. *am Main* on the Main.

Ank. *Ankunft* arrival.

Anm. *Anmerkung* note.

a. O. *an der Oder* on the Oder.

a. Rh. *am Rhein* on the Rhine.

Art. *Artikel* article.

atü *Atmosphärenüberdruck* atmospheric excess pressure.

Aufl. *Auflage* edition.

b. *bei* at; with; *with place names*: near, *abbr.* nr; care of, *abbr.* c/o.

Bd. *Band* volume, *abbr.* vol.; **Bde.** *Bände* volumes, *abbr.* vols.

beil. *beiliegend* enclosed.

Bem. *Bemerkung* note, comment, observation.

bes. *besonders* especially.

betr. *betreffend, betrifft, betreffs* concerning, respecting, regarding.

Betr. *Betreff, betrifft letter*: subject, re. [reference to.]

bez. *bezahlt* paid; *bezüglich* with

Bez. *Bezirk* district.

Bhf. *Bahnhof* station.

bisw. *bisweilen* sometimes, occasionally.

BIZ *Bank für Internationalen Zahlungsausgleich* Bank for International Settlements.

Bln. *Berlin* Berlin.

BRD *Bundesrepublik Deutschland* Federal Republic of Germany.

BRT *Bruttoregistertonnen* gross register tons.

b. w. *bitte wenden* please turn over, *abbr.* P.T.O.

bzw. *beziehungsweise* respectively.

C *Celsius* Celsius, *abbr.* C.

ca. *circa, ungefähr, etwa* about, approximately, *abbr.* c.

cbm *Kubikmeter* cubic met|re, *Am.* -er.

ccm *Kubikzentimeter* cubic centimet|re, *Am.* -er, *abbr.* c.c.

CDU *Christlich-Demokratische Union* Christian Democratic Union.

cm *Zentimeter* centimet|re, *Am.* -er.

Co. *Kompagnon* partner; *Kompanie* Company.

CSU *Christlich-Soziale Union* Christian Social Union.

d. Ä. *der Ältere* senior, *abbr.* sen.

DB *Deutsche Bundesbahn* German Federal Railway.

DDR *Deutsche Demokratische Republik* German Democratic Republic.

DGB *Deutscher Gewerkschaftsbund* Federation of German Trade Unions.

dgl. *dergleichen, desgleichen* the like.

d. Gr. *der Große* the Great.

d. h. *das heißt* that is, *abbr.* i. e.

d. i. *das ist* that is, *abbr.* i. e.

DIN, Din *Deutsche Industrie-Norm* (*-en*) German Industrial Standards.

Dipl. *Diplom* diploma.

d. J. *dieses Jahres* of this year; *der Jüngere* junior, *abbr.* jr, jun.

DM *Deutsche Mark* German Mark.

d. M. *dieses Monats* instant, *abbr.* inst.

do. *dito* ditto, *abbr.* do.

d. O. *der (die, das) Obige* the above-mentioned.

dpa, DPA *Deutsche Presse-Agentur* German Press Agency.

Dr. *Doktor* Doctor, *abbr.* Dr; ~ **jur.** *Doktor der Rechte* Doctor of Laws (LL.D.); ~ **med.** *Doktor der Medizin* Doctor of Medicine (M.D.); ~ **phil.** *Doktor der Philosophie* Doctor of Philosophy (D. ph[il]., Ph. D.); ~ **theol.** *Doktor der Theologie* Doctor of Divinity (D. D.).

DRK *Deutsches Rotes Kreuz* German Red Cross.

dt(sch). *deutsch* German.

Dtz., Dtzd. *Dutzend* dozen.

d. Verf. *der Verfasser* the author.

ebd. *ebenda* in the same place.

ed. *edidit* = *hat (es) herausgegeben*.

eig., eigtl. *eigentlich* properly.

einschl. *einschließlich* including, inclusive, *abbr.* incl.

entspr. *entsprechend* corresponding.

Erl. *Erläuterung* explanation, (explanatory) note.

ev. *evangelisch* Protestant.

e. V. *eingetragener Verein* registered association, incorporated, *abbr.* inc.

evtl. *eventuell* perhaps, possibly.
EWG *Europäische Wirtschaftsgemeinschaft* European Economic Community, *abbr.* EEC.
exkl. *exklusive* except(ed), not included.
Expl. *Exemplar* copy.

Fa. *Firma* firm; *letter*: Messrs.
FDGB *Freier Deutscher Gewerkschaftsbund* Free Federation of German Trade Unions.
FDP *Freie Demokratische Partei* Liberal Democratic Party.
FD(-Zug) *Fernschnellzug* long-distance express.
ff. *sehr fein* extra fine; *folgende Seiten* following pages.
Forts. *Fortsetzung* continuation.
Fr. *Frau* Mrs.
frdl. *freundlich* kind.
Frl. *Fräulein* Miss.

g *Gramm* gram(me).
geb. *geboren* born; *geborene ...* née; *gebunden* bound.
Gebr. *Gebrüder* Brothers.
gef. *gefällig(st)* kind(ly).
gegr. *gegründet* founded.
geh. *geheftet* stitched.
gek. *gekürzt* abbreviated.
Ges. *Gesellschaft* association, company; society.   [registered.)
ges. gesch. *gesetzlich geschützt)*
gest. *gestorben* deceased.
gez. *gezeichnet* signed, *abbr.* sgd.
GmbH *Gesellschaft mit beschränkter Haftung* limited liability company, *abbr.* Ltd., *Am.* closed corporation under German law.

ha *Hektar* hectare.
Hbf. *Hauptbahnhof* central *or* main station.
Hbg. *Hamburg* Hamburg.
h.c. *honoris causa* = *ehrenhalber academic title*: honorary.
Hr., Hrn. *Herr(n)* Mr.
hrsg. *herausgegeben* edited, *abbr.* ed.
Hrsg. *Herausgeber* editor, *abbr.* ed.

i. *im, in* in.
i. A. *im Auftrage* for, by order, under instruction.
i. allg. *im allgemeinen* in general, generally speaking.
i. Durchschn. *im Durchschnitt* on an average.
inkl. *inklusive, einschließlich* inclusive.
i. J. *im Jahre* in the year.
Ing. *Ingenieur* engineer.
Inh. *Inhaber* proprietor.
'Interpol *Internationale Kriminalpolizei-Kommission* International Criminal Police Commission, *abbr.* ICPC.
i. V. *in Vertretung* by proxy, as a substitute.

Jb. *Jahrbuch* annual.
jr., jun. *junior, der Jüngere* junior *abbr.* jr, jun.

Kap. *Kapitel* chapter.
kath. *katholisch* Catholic.
Kfm. *Kaufmann* merchant.
kfm. *kaufmännisch* commercial.
Kfz. *Kraftfahrzeug* motor vehicle.
kg *Kilogramm* kilogram(me).
KG *Kommanditgesellschaft* limited partnership.
Kl. *Klasse* class; *school*: form.
km *Kilometer* kilomet|re, *Am.* -er.
'Kripo *Kriminalpolizei* Criminal Investigation Depártment, *abbr.* CID.
Kto. *Konto* account, *abbr.* a/c.
kW *Kilowatt* kilowatt, *abbr.* kw.
kWh *Kilowattstunde* kilowatt hour.

l *Liter* lit|re, *Am.* -er.
LDP *Liberal-Demokratische Partei* Liberal Democratic Party.
lfd. *laufend* current, running.
lfde. Nr. *laufende Nummer* consecutive number.
Lfg., Lfrg. *Lieferung* delivery; instalment, part.
Lit. *Literatur* literature.
Lkw. *Lastkraftwagen* lorry, truck.
lt. *laut* according to.

m *Meter* met|re, *Am,* -er.
m. A. n. *meiner Ansicht nach* in my opinion.
M. d. B. *Mitglied des Bundestages* Member of the Bundestag.
m. E. *meines Erachtens* in my opinion.
MEZ *mitteleuropäische Zeit* Central European Time.
mg *Milligramm* milligram(me[s]), *abbr.* mg.
Mill. *Million(en)* million(s).
mm *Millimeter* millimet|re, *Am.* -er.
möbl. *möbliert* furnished.
MP *Militärpolizei* Military Police.
mtl. *monatlich* monthly.
m. W. *meines Wissens* as far as I know.

N *Nord(en)* north.
nachm. *nachmittags* in the afternoon, *abbr.* p. m.
n. Chr. *nach Christus* after Christ, *abbr.* A. D.
n. J. *nächsten Jahres* of next year.
n. M. *nächsten Monats* of next month.
No., Nr. *Numero, Nummer* number, *abbr.* N°.
NS *Nachschrift* postscript, *abbr.* P. S.

O *Ost(en)* east.
o. B. *ohne Befund* ♂ without findings.
od. *oder* or.

OEZ *osteuropäische Zeit* time of the East European zone.

OHG *Offene Handelsgesellschaft* ordinary partnership.

o. J. *ohne Jahr* no date.

p. Adr. *per Adresse* care of, *abbr.* c/o.

Pf *Pfennig German coin:* pfennig.

Pfd. *Pfund German weight:* pound.

PKW, Pkw. *Personenkraftwagen* (motor) car.

P. P. *praemissis praemittendis* omitting titles, to whom it may concern.

p.p., p.pa., ppa. *per procura* per proxy, *abbr.* per pro.

Prof. *Professor* professor.

PS *Pferdestärke(n)* horse-power, *abbr.* H.P., h.p.; *postscriptum, Nachschrift* postscript, *abbr.* P.S.

qkm *Quadratkilometer* square kilomet|re, *Am.* -er. [*Am.* -er.⎫
qm *Quadratmeter* square met|re,⎭

Reg. Bez. *Regierungsbezirk* administrative district.

Rel. *Religion* religion.

resp. *respektive* respectively.

S *Süd(en)* south.

S. *Seite* page.

s. *siehe* see, *abbr.* v., vid. (= vide).

s. a. *siehe auch* see also.

Sa. *Summa, Summe* sum, total.

s. d. *siehe dies* see this.

SED *Sozialistische Einheitspartei Deutschlands* United Socialist Party of Germany.

sen. *senior, der Ältere* senior.

sm *Seemeile* nautical mile.

s. o. *siehe oben* see above.

sog. *sogenannt* so-called.

SPD *Sozialdemokratische Partei Deutschlands* Social Democratic Party of Germany.

St. *Stück* piece; *Sankt* Saint.

St(d)., Stde. *Stunde* hour, *abbr.* h.

Str. *Straße* street, *abbr.* St.

s. u. *siehe unten* see below.

s. Z. *seinerzeit* at that time.

t *Tonne* ton.

tägl. *täglich* daily, per day.

Tel. *Telephon* telephone; *Telegramm* wire, cable.

TH *Technische Hochschule* technical university *or* college.

u. *und* and.

u. a. *und andere(s)* and others; *unter anderem or anderen* among other things, inter alia.

u. ä. *und ähnliche(s)* and the like.

U.A.w.g. *Um Antwort wird gebeten* an answer is requested, *répondez s'il vous plait, abbr.* R.S.V.P.

u. dgl. (m.) *und dergleichen (mehr)* and the like.

u. d. M. *unter dem Meeresspiegel* below sea level; **ü. d. M.** *über dem Meeresspiegel* above sea level.

UdSSR *Union der Sozialistischen Sowjetrepubliken* Union of Soviet Socialist Republics.

u. E. *unseres Erachtens* in our opinion. [following.⎫

u. f., u. ff. *und folgende* and the⎭

UKW *Ultrakurzwelle* ultra-short wave, very high frequency, *abbr.* VHF.

U/min. *Umdrehungen in der Minute* revolutions per minute, *abbr.* r.p.m.

urspr. *ursprünglich* original(ly).

US(A) *Vereinigte Staaten (von Amerika)* United States (of America).

usw. *und so weiter* and so on, *abbr.* etc. [stances permitting.⎫

u. U. *unter Umständen* circum-⎭

v. *von, vom* of; from; by.

V *Volt* volt; *Volumen* volume.

V. *Vers* line, verse.

v. Chr. *vor Christus* before Christ, *abbr.* B. C.

VEB *Volkseigener Betrieb* People's Own Undertaking.

Verf., Vf. *Verfasser* author.

Verl. *Verlag* publishing firm; *Verleger* publisher.

vgl. *vergleiche* confer, *abbr.* cf.

v.g.u. *vorgelesen, genehmigt, unterschrieben* read, confirmed, signed.

v. H. *vom Hundert* per cent.

v. J. *vorigen Jahres* of last year.

v. M. *vorigen Monats* of last month.

vorm. *vormittags* in the morning, *abbr.* a. m.; *vormals* formerly.

Vors. *Vorsitzender* chairman.

v. T. *vom Tausend* per thousand.

VW *Volkswagen* Volkswagen, People's Car.

W *West(en)* west; *Watt* watt(s).

WE *Wärmeeinheit* thermal unit.

WEZ *westeuropäische Zeit* Western European time (Greenwich time).

WGB *Weltgewerkschaftsbund* World Federation of Trade Unions, *abbr.* WFTU.

Wwe. *Witwe* widow.

Z. *Zahl* number; *Zeile* line.

z. zu, zum, zur at; to.

z. B. *zum Beispiel* for instance, *abbr.* e. g.

z. H(d). *zu Händen* attention of, to be delivered to, care of, *abbr.* c/o.

z. S. *zur See* of the navy.

z. T. *zum Teil* partly.

Ztg. *Zeitung* newspaper.

Ztr. *Zentner* centner.

Ztschr. *Zeitschrift* periodical.

zus. *zusammen* together.

zw. *zwischen* between; among.

z. Z(t). *zur Zeit* at the time, at present, for the time being.

American and British Proper Names

Aberdeen [æbə'di:n] *Stadt in Schottland.*
Africa ['æfrikə] Afrika *n.* [U.S.A.]
Alabama [ælə'bæmə] *Staat der* U.S.A.
Alaska [ə'læskə] *Staat der U.S.A.*
Albania [æl'beinjə] Albanien *n.*
Alberta [æl'bə:tə] *Provinz in Kanada.* [U.S.A.]
Alleghany ['ælige ni] *Gebirge in* U.S.A.
Alsace ['ælsæs] Elsaß *n.*
America [ə'merikə] Amerika *n.*
Antilles [æn'ti'li:z] *die* Antillen.
Appalachians [æpə'leitʃjənz] *die* Appalachen (*Gebirge in U.S.A.*).
Arizona [æri'zounə] *Staat der* U.S.A. [U.S.A.]
Arkansas ['a:kənsɔ:] *Staat der* U.S.A.
Arlington ['a:liŋtən] *Nationalfriedhof bei Washington.*
Ascot ['æskət] *Stadt in England.*
Asia ['eifə] Asien *n.*
Athens ['æθinz] Athen *n.*
Australia [ɔs'treiljə] Australien *n.*
Austria ['ɔstriə] Österreich *n.*
Avon ['eivən] *Fluß in England.*
Azores [ə'zɔ:z] *die* Azoren.

Bacon ['beikən] *engl. Philosoph.*
Bahamas [bə'ha:məz] *die* Bahamainseln.
Balmoral [bæl'mɔrəl] *Königsschloß in Schottland.*
Bedford(shire) ['bedfəd(ʃiə)] *Grafschaft in England.*
Belfast [bel'fa:st] *Hauptstadt von Nordirland.*
Belgium ['beldʒəm] Belgien *n.*
Belgrade [bel'greid] Belgrad *n.*
Ben Nevis [ben'nevis] *höchster Berg in Großbritannien.*
Berkshire ['ba:kʃiə] *Grafschaft in England.*
Bermudas [bə:'mju:dəz] *die* Bermudainseln.
Bern(e) [bə:n] Bern *n.*
Birmingham ['bə:miŋəm] *Industriestadt in England* [Biskaya.]
Biscay ['biskei] *Bay of ~* Golf *m* von
Boston ['bɔstən] *Stadt in U.S.A.*
Bournemouth ['bɔ:nməθ] *Seebad in England.*
Brighton ['braitn] *Seebad in England.* [land.]
Bristol ['bristl] *Hafenstadt in England.*
Britten ['britn] *engl. Komponist.*
Brooklyn ['bruklin] *Stadtteil von New York.*
Brussels ['brʌslz] Brüssel *n.*
Bucharest ['bju:kərest] Bukarest *n.*
Buckingham(shire) ['bʌkiŋəm(ʃiə)] *Grafschaft in England.*

Budapest ['bju:də'pest] Budapest *n.*
Bulgaria [bʌl'gɛəriə] Bulgarien *n.*
Burns [bə:nz] *schott. Dichter.*
Byron ['baiərən] *engl. Dichter.*

California [kæli'fɔ.njə] Kalifornien *n (Staat der U.S.A.).*
Cambridge ['keimbridʒ] *engl. Universitätsstadt; Stadt in U.S.A.; a.* ~**shire** ['-ʃiə] *Grafschaft in England.*
Canada ['kænədə] Kanada *n.*
Canary Islands [kə'nɛəri 'ailəndz] *die* Kanarischen Inseln.
Canberra ['kænbərə] *Hauptstadt von Australien.* [England.]
Canterbury ['kæntəbəri] *Stadt in*
Capetown ['keiptaun] Kapstadt *n.*
Cardiff ['ka:dif] *Hauptstadt von Wales.*
Carinthia [kə'rinθiə] Kärnten *n.*
Carlyle [ka:'lail] *engl. Autor.*
Carolina [kærə'lainə]: *North ~* Nordkarolina *n (Staat der U.S.A.); South ~* Südkarolina *n (Staat der U.S.A.).*
Ceylon [si'lɔn] Ceylon *n.*
Chamberlain ['tʃeimbəlin, ~lein] *Name mehrerer brit. Staatsmänner.*
Cheshire ['tʃeʃə] *Grafschaft in England.*
Chicago [ʃi'ka:gou, *Am.* ʃi'kɔ:gou] *Industriestadt in U.S.A.*
China ['tʃainə] China *n.* [mann.]
Churchill ['tʃə:tʃil] *brit. Staats-*
Cleveland ['kli:vlənd] *Industrieund Hafenstadt in U.S.A.*
Clyde [klaid] *Fluß in Schottland.*
Coleridge ['koulridʒ] *engl. Dichter.*
Colorado [kɔlə'ra:dou] *Staat der* U.S.A.
Columbia [kə'lʌmbiə] *Fluß in U.S.A.; Bundesdistrikt der U.S.A.*
Connecticut [kə'netikət] *Staat der* U.S.A.
Constance ['kɔnstəns]: *Lake of ~* Bodensee *m.*
Cooper ['ku:pə] *amer. Autor.*
Copenhagen [koupn'heigən] Kopenhagen *n.* [dilleren.]
Cordilleras [kɔ:di'ljeərəz] *die* Kor-
Cornwall ['kɔ:nwəl] *Grafschaft in England.*
Coventry ['kɔvəntri] *Industriestadt in England.* [mann.]
Cromwell ['krɔmwəl] *engl. Staats-*
Cumberland ['kʌmbələnd] *Grafschaft in England.*
Cyprus ['saiprəs] Zypern *n.*
Czecho-Slovakia ['tʃekouslou'væ-kiə] *die* Tschechoslowakei.

Dakota [də'koutə]: *North ~ Norddakota n (Staat der U.S.A.); South ~ Süddakota n (Staat der U.S.A.).*

Defoe [də'fou] *engl. Autor.*

Delaware ['deləwɛə] *Staat der U.S.A.*

Denmark ['denmɑːk] *Dänemark n.*

Derby(shire) ['dɑːbi(ʃə)] *Grafschaft in England.*

Detroit [də'trɔit] *Industriestadt in U.S.A.*

Devon(shire) ['devn(ʃiə)] *Grafschaft in England.*

Dickens ['dikinz] *engl. Autor.*

Dorset(shire) ['dɔːsit(ʃiə)] *Grafschaft in England.* [land.\

Dover ['douvə] *Hafenstadt in Eng-\

Downing Street ['dauniŋ 'striːt] *Straße in London mit der Amtswohnung des Prime Minister.*

Dublin ['dʌblin] *Hauptstadt von Irland.*

Dunkirk [dʌn'kəːk] *Dünkirchen n.*

Durham ['dʌrəm] *Grafschaft in England.*

Edinburgh ['edinbərə] *Edinburg n.*

Edison ['edisn] *amer. Erfinder.*

Egypt ['iːdʒipt] *Ägypten n.*

Eire ['ɛərə] *Republik Irland.*

Eisenhower ['aizənhauə] *Präsident der U.S.A.*

Eliot ['eljət] *engl. Dichter.*

Emerson ['eməsn] *amer. Philosoph.*

England ['iŋglənd] *England n.*

Epsom ['epsəm] *Stadt in England.*

Erie ['iəri]: *Lake ~ Eriesee m.*

Essex ['esiks] *Grafschaft in England.*

Eton ['iːtn] *berühmte Public School.*

Europe ['juərəp] *Europa n.*

Falkland Islands ['fɔːlklənd 'ailəndz] *die Falklandinseln.*

Faulkner ['fɔːknə] *amer. Autor.*

Finland ['finlənd] *Finnland n.*

Florida ['flɔridə] *Staat der U.S.A.*

Flushing ['flʌʃiŋ] *Vlissingen n.*

France [frɑːns] *Frankreich n.*

Franklin ['fræŋklin] *amer. Staatsmann und Physiker.*

Galsworthy ['gɔːlzwəːði] *engl. Autor.*

Geneva [dʒi'niːvə] *Genf n; Lake of ~ Genfer See m.*

Georgia ['dʒɔːdʒiə] *Staat der U.S.A.*

Germany ['dʒəːməni] *Deutschland n.* [nist.\

Gershwin ['gəːʃwin] *amer. Kompo-\

Gibraltar [dʒi'brɔːltə] *Gibraltar n.*

Glasgow ['glɑːsgou] *Hafenstadt in Schottland.*

Gloucester ['glɔstə] *Stadt in England; a. ~shire* ['~ʃiə] *Grafschaft in England.*

Great Britain ['greit 'britn] *Großbritannien n.*

Greece [griːs] *Griechenland n.*

Greene [griːn] *engl. Autor.*

Greenland ['griːnlənd] *Grönland n.*

Greenwich ['grinidʒ] *Vorort von London.*

Guernsey ['gəːnzi] *Kanalinsel.*

Hague [heig]: *The ~ Den Haag.*

Hampshire ['hæmpʃiə] *Grafschaft in England.*

Harlem ['hɑːlem] *Stadtteil von New York.*

Harrow ['hærou] *berühmte Public School.*

Harvard University ['hɑːvəd juːni'vəːsiti] *amer. Universität.*

Harwich ['hæridʒ] *Hafenstadt in England.*

Hawaii [hɑː'waiiː] *Staat der U.S.A.*

Hebrides ['hebridiːz] *die Hebriden.*

Helsinki ['helsiŋki] *Helsinki n.*

Hemingway ['hemiŋwei] *amer. Autor.*

Hereford(shire) ['herifəd(ʃiə)] *Grafschaft in England.*

Hertford(shire) ['hɑːfəd(ʃiə)] *Grafschaft in England.*

Hollywood ['hɔliwud] *Filmstadt in Kalifornien, U.S.A.*

Houston ['juːstən] *Stadt in U.S.A.*

Hudson ['hʌdsn] *Fluß in U.S.A.*

Hull [hʌl] *Hafenstadt in England.*

Hume [hjuːm] *engl. Philosoph.*

Hungary ['hʌŋgəri] *Ungarn n.*

Huntingdon(shire) ['hʌntiŋdən (-ʃiə)] *Grafschaft in England.* [m.\

Huron ['hjuərən]: *Lake ~ Huronsee\

Huxley ['hʌksli] *engl. Autor.*

Iceland ['aislənd] *Island n.*

Idaho ['aidəhou] *Staat der U.S.A.*

Illinois [ili'nɔi] *Staat der U.S.A.*

India ['indjə] *Indien n.*

Indiana [indi'ænə] *Staat der U.S.A.*

Iowa ['aiouə] *Staat der U.S.A.*

Irak, Iraq [i'rɑːk] *Irak m.*

Iran [i'rɑːn] *Iran m.*

Ireland ['aiələnd] *Irland n.*

Irving ['əːviŋ] *amer. Autor.*

Italy ['itəli] *Italien n.*

Jefferson ['dʒefəsn] *Präsident der U.S.A., Verfasser der Unabhängigkeitserklärung von 1776.*

Johnson ['dʒɔnsn] **1.** *engl. Autor;* **2.** *Präsident der U.S.A.*

Kansas ['kænzəs] *Staat der U.S.A.*

Kashmir [kæʃ'miə] *Kaschmir n.*

Keats [kiːts] *engl. Dichter.*

Kennedy ['kenidi] *Präsident der U.S.A.; ~ Airport Flughafen von New York.*

Kent [kent] *Grafschaft in England.*

Kentucky [ken'tʌki] *Staat der U.S.A.*

Kipling ['kipliŋ] *engl. Dichter.*

Klondike ['klɔndaik] *Fluß und Landschaft in Kanada und Alaska.*

Kremlin ['kremlin] *der Kreml.*

Labrador ['læbrədɔ:] *Halbinsel Nordamerikas.*

Lancashire ['læŋkəʃiə] *Grafschaft in England.*

Lancaster ['læŋkəstə] *Name zweier Städte in England und U.S.A.; s. Lancashire.* [land.\

Leeds [li:dz] *Industriestadt in Eng-\

Leicester ['lestə] *Stadt in England; a. ~shire* ['~ʃiə] *Grafschaft in England.*

Lincoln ['liŋkən] **1.** *Präsident der U.S.A.;* **2.** *a. ~shire* ['~ʃiə] *Grafschaft in England.*

Lisbon ['lizbən] *Lissabon n.*

Liverpool ['livəpu:l] *Hafen- und Industriestadt in England.*

Locke [lɔk] *engl. Philosoph.*

London ['lʌndən] *London n.*

Los Angeles [lɔs 'ændʒili:z] *Stadt in U.S.A.* [U.S.A.\

Louisiana [lu:izi'ænə] *Staat der\

Lucerne [lu:'sə:n] *Lake of ~ Vierwaldstätter See m.*

Luxemburg ['lʌksəmbə:g] *Luxemburg n.*

Madrid [mə'drid] *Madrid n.*

Maine [mein] *Staat der U.S.A.*

Malta ['mɔ:ltə] *Malta n.*

Manchester ['mæntʃistə] *Industriestadt in England.*

Manhattan [mæn'hætən] *Stadtteil von New York.* [Kanada.\

Manitoba [mæni'toubə] *Provinz in\

Maryland ['mɛərilənd, Am.* 'merilənd] *Staat der U.S.A.*

Massachusetts [mæsə'tʃu:sits] *Staat der U.S.A.*

Melbourne ['mɛlbən] *Stadt in Australien.*

Miami [mai'æmi] *Badeort in Florida, U.S.A.*

Michigan ['miʃigən] *Staat der U.S.A.; Lake ~ Michigansee m.*

Middlesex ['midlseks] *Grafschaft in England.*

Miller ['milə] *amer. Dramatiker.*

Milton ['miltən] *engl. Dichter.*

Milwaukee [mil'wɔ:ki:] *Stadt in U.S.A.*

Minneapolis [mini'æpəlis] *Stadt in U.S.A.* [U.S.A.\

Minnesota [mini'soutə] *Staat der\

Mississippi [misi'sipi] *Strom und Staat der U.S.A.*

Missouri [mi'zuəri] *Fluß und Staat der U.S.A.*

Monmouth(shire) ['mɔnməθ(ʃiə)] *Grafschaft in England.*

Monroe [mən'rou] *Präsident der U.S.A.* [U.S.A.\

Montana [mɔn'tænə] *Staat der\

Montgomery [mənt'gɔməri] *brit. Feldmarschall.*

Montreal [mɔntri'ɔ:l] *Stadt in Kanada.*

Moore [muə] *engl. Bildhauer.*

Moscow ['mɔskou] *Moskau n.*

Nebraska [ni'bræskə] *Staat der U.S.A.*

Nelson ['nelsn] *engl. Admiral.*

Netherlands ['neðələndz] *die Niederlande.*

Nevada [ne'va:də] *Staat der U.S.A.*

New Brunswick [nju: 'brʌnzwik] *Provinz in Kanada.*

Newcastle ['nju:ka:sl] *Hafenstadt in England.* [von Indien.\

New Delhi [nju: 'deli] *Hauptstadt)

New England [nju: 'iŋglənd] *Neuengland n.* [Neufundland n.\

Newfoundland [nju:fənd'lænd]

New Hampshire [nju: 'hæmpʃiə] *Staat der U.S.A.*

New Jersey [nju: 'dʒə:si] *Staat der U.S.A.*

New Mexico [nju: 'meksikou] *Neumexiko n (Staat der U.S.A.).*

New Orleans [nju: 'ɔ:liəns] *Hafenstadt in U.S.A.*

Newton ['nju:tn] *engl. Physiker.*

New York ['nju: 'jɔ:k] *Stadt und Staat der U.S.A.*

New Zealand [nju: 'zi:lənd] *Neuseeland n.*

Niagara [nai'ægərə] *Niagara m.*

Nixon ['niksn] *Präsident der U.S.A.*

Norfolk ['nɔ:fək] *Grafschaft in England.*

Northampton [nɔ:'θæmptən] *Stadt in England; a. ~shire* ['~ʃiə] *Grafschaft in England.*

Northumberland [nɔ:'θʌmbələnd] *Grafschaft in England.*

Norway ['nɔ:wei] *Norwegen n.*

Nottingham ['nɔtiŋəm] *Stadt in England; a. ~shire* ['~ʃiə] *Grafschaft in England.*

Nova Scotia ['nouvə 'skouʃə] *Provinz in Kanada.*

Ohio [ou'haiou] *Staat der U.S.A.*

O'Neill [ou'ni:l] *amer. Dramatiker.*

Ontario [ɔn'tɛəriou] *Provinz in Kanada; Lake ~ Ontariosee m.*

Oregon ['ɔrigən] *Staat der U.S.A.*

Orkney Islands ['ɔ:kni 'ailəndz] *die Orkneyinseln.*

Osborne ['ɔzbən] *engl. Dramatiker.*

Oslo ['ɔzlou] *Oslo n.*

Ostend [ɔs'tend] *Ostende n.*

Ottawa ['ɔtəwə] *Hauptstadt von Kanada.*

Oxford ['ɔksfəd] *engl. Universitätsstadt; a. ~shire* ['~ʃiə] *Grafschaft in England.*

Pakistan [pa:kis'ta:n] *Pakistan n.*

Paris ['pæris] *Paris n.*

Pearl Harbour ['pə:l 'ha:bə] *Hafenstadt auf Hawaii.*

Pennsylvania [pensil'veinjə] *Pennsylvanien n (Staat der U.S.A.).*

Philadelphia [filə'delfjə] *Stadt in U.S.A.*

Philippines ['filipi:nz] *die Philippinen.*

Pittsburg(h) ['pitsbə:g] *Stadt in U.S.A.*

Plymouth ['pliməθ] *Hafenstadt in England.*

Poe [pou] *amer. Autor.*

Poland ['pouland] Polen *n.*

Portsmouth ['pɔ:tsməθ] *Hafenstadt in England.*

Portugal ['pɔ:tjugəl] Portugal *n.*

Prague [prɑːg] Prag *n.*

Purcell ['pɔ:sl] *engl. Komponist.*

Quebec [kwi'bek] *Provinz und Stadt in Kanada.*

Reykjavik ['reikjəvi:k] Reykjavik *n.*

Rhode Island [roud 'ailənd] *Staat der U.S.A.*

Rocky Mountains ['rɔki 'mauntinz] *Gebirge in U.S.A.*

Rome [roum] Rom *n.*

Roosevelt ['rouzəvelt] *Name zweier Präsidenten der U.S.A.* [School.\

Rugby ['rʌgbi] *berühmte Public\

Rumania [ru:'meinjə] Rumänien *n.*

Russell ['rʌsl] *engl. Philosoph.*

Russia ['rʌʃə] Rußland *n.*

Rutland(shire) ['rʌtlənd(ʃiə)] *Grafschaft in England.*

San Francisco [sænfrən'siskou] *Hafenstadt in U.S.A.*

Saskatchewan [səs'kætʃiwən] *Provinz von Kanada.*

Scandinavia [skændi'neivjə] *Skandinavien n.*

Scotland ['skɔtlənd] Schottland *n.*

Shakespeare ['ʃeikspiə] *engl. Dichter.*

Shaw [ʃɔ:] *engl. Dramatiker.*

Shelley ['ʃeli] *engl. Dichter.*

Shetland Islands ['ʃetlənd 'ailəndz] *die Shetlandinseln.*

Shropshire ['ʃrɔpʃiə] *Grafschaft in England.*

Snowdon ['snoudn] *Berg in Wales.*

Sofia ['soufjə] Sofia *n.*

Somerset(shire) ['sʌməsit(ʃiə)] *Grafschaft in England.*

Southhampton [sauθ'æmptən] *Hafenstadt in England.*

Spain [spein] Spanien *n.*

Stafford(shire) ['stæfəd(ʃiə)] *Grafschaft in England.*

Stevenson ['sti:vnsn] *engl. Autor.*

St. Lawrence [snt'lɔrəns] *der St. Lorenz-Strom.*

St. Louis [snt'luis] *Industriestadt in U.S.A.* [n.\

Stockholm ['stɔkhoum] Stockholm\

Stratford ['strætfəd]: ~-on-Avon *Geburtsort Shakespeares.*

Suffolk ['sʌfək] *Grafschaft in England.* [rer See m.\

Superior [sju:'piəriə]: Lake ~ *Obe-\

Surrey ['sʌri] *Grafschaft in England.*

Sussex ['sʌsiks] *Grafschaft in England.*

Sweden ['swi:dn] Schweden *n.*

Swift [swift] *engl. Autor.*

Switzerland ['switsələnd] *die Schweiz.* [tralien.\

Sydney ['sidni] *Hafenstadt in Aus-\

Tennessee [tene'si] *Staat der U.S.A.*

Tennyson ['tenisn] *engl. Dichter.*

Texas ['teksəs] *Staat der U.S.A.*

Thackeray ['θækəri] *engl. Autor.*

Thames [temz] Themse *f.*

Tirana [ti'rɑːnə] Tirana *n.* [nada.\

Toronto [tə'rɔntou] *Stadt in Ka-\

Toynbee ['tɔinbi] *engl. Historiker.*

Trafalgar [trə'fælgə] *Vorgebirge bei Gibraltar.* [U.S.A.\

Truman ['tru:mən] *Präsident der\

Turkey ['tə:ki] *die Türkei.*

Twain [twein] *amer. Autor.*

Tyrol ['tirəl] Tirol *n.*

United States of America [ju:'naitid 'steitsəvə'merikə] *die Vereinigten Staaten von Amerika.*

Utah ['ju:tɑ:] *Staat der U.S.A.*

Vancouver [væn'ku:və] *Stadt in Kanada.*

Vermont [və:'mɔnt] *Staat der\

Vienna [vi'enə] Wien *n.* [U.S.A.\

Virginia [və'dʒinjə] Virginien *n (Staat der U.S.A.);* West ~ *Staat der U.S.A.*

Wales [weilz] Wales *n.*

Warsaw ['wɔ:sɔ:] Warschau *n.*

Warwick(shire) ['wɔrik(ʃiə)] *Grafschaft in England.*

Washington ['wɔʃiŋtən] 1. *Präsident der U.S.A.;* 2. *Staat der U.S.A.;* 3. *Bundeshauptstadt der U.S.A.*

Wellington ['weliŋtən] *Hauptstadt von Neuseeland.*

Westmoreland ['westmələnd] *Grafschaft in England.*

White House ['wait 'haus] *das Weiße Haus.*

Whitman ['witmən] *amer. Dichter.*

Wilson ['wilsn] 1. *Präsident der U.S.A.;* 2. *brit. Premier.*

Wiltshire ['wiltʃiə] *Grafschaft in England.*

Wimbledon ['wimbldən] *Vorort von London.* [Kanada.\

Winnipeg ['winipeg] *Stadt in\

Wisconsin [wis'kɔnsin] *Staat der U.S.A.*

Worcester ['wustə] *Industriestadt in England;* a. ~shire ['_ʃiə] *Grafschaft in England.*

Wordsworth ['wə:dzwə:θ] *engl. Dichter.*

Yale University ['jeil ju:ni'və:siti] *amer. Universität.*

York [jɔ:k] *Stadt in England;* a. ~shire ['_ʃiə] *Grafschaft in England.*

Yugoslavia ['ju:gou'slɑ:vjə] Jugoslawien *n.*

American and British Abbreviations

abbr. *abbreviated* abgekürzt; *abbreviation* Abk., Abkürzung f.

A.B.C. *American Broadcasting Company* Amer. Rundfunkgesellschaft f. [strom m.]

A.C. *alternating current* Wechsel-}

A.E.C. *Atomic Energy Commission* Atomenergie-Kommission f.

AFL–CIO *American Federation of Labor & Congress of Industrial Organizations* (größter amer. Gewerkschaftsverband).

A.F.N. *American Forces Network* (Rundfunkanstalt der amer. Streit-}

Ala. *Alabama.* [kräfte).}

Alas. *Alaska.*

a.m. *ante meridiem* (lateinisch = before noon) vormittags.

A.P. *Associated Press* (amer. Nachrichtenbüro). [Rotes Kreuz.}

A.R.C. *American Red Cross* Amer.}

Ariz. *Arizona.*

Ark. *Arkansas.*

arr. *arrival* Ank., Ankunft f.

B.A. *Bachelor of Arts* Bakkalaureus m der Philosophie.

B.B.C. *British Broadcasting Corporation* Brit. Rundfunkgesellschaft f.

B.E.A. *British European Airways* Brit.-Europäische Luftfahrtge-}

Beds. *Bedfordshire.* [sellschaft.}

Benelux *Belgium, Netherlands, Luxemburg* (Zollunion).

Berks. *Berkshire.*

B.F.N. *British Forces Network* (Sender der brit. Streitkräfte in Deutschland). [m des Rechts.}

B.L. *Bachelor of Law* Bakkalaureus}

B.M. *Bachelor of Medicine* Bakkalaureus m der Medizin.

B.O.A.C. *British Overseas Airways Corporation* Brit. Übersee-Luftfahrtgesellschaft f.

B.R. *British Railways.*

Br(it). *Britain* Großbritannien n; *British* britisch.

B.S. *Bachelor of Science* Bakkalaureus m der Naturwissenschaften.

Bucks. *Buckinghamshire.*

C. *Celsius, centigrade.*

c. *cent(s)* Cent m; *circa* ca., ungefähr, zirka; *cubic* Kubik...

Cal(if). *California.*

Cambs. *Cambridgeshire.*

Can. *Canada* Kanada n; *Canadian* kanadisch.

cf. *confer* vgl., vergleiche.

Ches. *Cheshire.*

C.I.C. *Counter Intelligence Corps* (Spionageabwehrdienst der U.S.A.).

C.I.D. *Criminal Investigation Department* (brit. Kriminalpolizei).

Co. *Company* Gesellschaft f; *County* Grafschaft f, Kreis m.

c/o *care of* p.A., per Adresse, bei.

Col(o). *Colorado.*

Conn. *Connecticut.*

cp. *compare* vgl., vergleiche.

Cumb. *Cumberland.* [ner m.}

cwt. *hundredweight* (etwa 1) Zent-}

d. *penny, pence.*

D.C. *direct current* Gleichstrom m; *District of Columbia* (mit der amer. Hauptstadt Washington).

Del. *Delaware.*

dep. *departure* Abf., Abfahrt f.

Dept. *Department* Abt., Abteilung f.

Derby. *Derbyshire.*

Devon. *Devonshire.*

Dors. *Dorsetshire.*

Dur(h). *Durham.*

dz. *dozen* Dutzend n od. pl.

E. *east* Ost(en m); *eastern* östlich; *English* englisch.

E.C. *East Central* (London) Mitte-Ost (Postbezirk).

ECOSOC *Economic and Social Council* Wirtschafts- und Sozialrat m (U.N.).

Ed., ed. *edition* Auflage f; *edited* hrsg., herausgegeben; *editor* Hrsg., Herausgeber m.

E.E.C. *European Economic Community* EWG, Europäische Wirtschaftsgemeinschaft.

E.F.T.A. *European Free Trade Association* EFTA, Europäische Freihandelsgemeinschaft od. -zone.

e.g. *exempli gratia* (lateinisch = for instance) z.B., zum Beispiel.

Enc. *enclosure(s)* Anlage(n pl.) f.

Ess. *Essex.*

F. *Fahrenheit.*

f. *fathom(s)* Faden m, Klafter f, m, n; *feminine* weiblich; *foot, pl. feet* Fuß m od. pl.; *following* folgend.

F.A.O. *Food and Agricultural Organization* Organisation f für Ernährung und Landwirtschaft (U.N.).

FBI *Federal Bureau of Investigation* (Bundeskriminalamt der U.S.A.).

fig. *figure(s)* Abb., Abbildung(en Fla. Florida. [pl.) f.}

F.O. *Foreign Office* brit. Auswärtiges

fr. *franc(s)* Frank(en pl.) m. [Amt.}

ft. *foot, pl. feet* Fuß m od. pl.

German Weights and Measures

I. Linear Measure

1 mm — *Millimeter* millimet|re, *Am.* -er = 0.039 inch

1 cm — *Zentimeter* centimet|re, *Am.* -er = 10 mm = 0.394 inch

1 m — *Meter* met|re, *Am.* -er = 100 cm = 1.094 yards = 3.281 feet

1 km — *Kilometer* kilomet|re, *Am.* -er = 1000 m = 0.621 mile

1 sm — *Seemeile* nautical mile = 1852 m

II. Square Measure

1 mm² — *Quadratmillimeter* square millimet|re, *Am.* -er = 0.002 square inch

1 cm² — *Quadratzentimeter* square centimet|re, *Am.* -er = 100 mm² = 0.155 square inch

1 m² — *Quadratmeter* square met|re, *Am.* -er = 10 000 cm² = 1.196 square yards = 10.764 square feet

1 a — *Ar* are = 100 m² = 119.599 square yards

1 ha — *Hektar* hectare = 100 a = 2.471 acres

1 km² — *Quadratkilometer* square kilomet|re, *Am.* -er = 100 ha = 247.11 acres = 0.386 square mile

III. Cubic Measure

1 cm³ — *Kubikzentimeter* cubic centimet|re, *Am.* -er = 1000 mm³ = 0.061 cubic inch

1 m³ — *Kubikmeter* cubic met|re, *Am.* -er = 1000 000 cm³ = 35.315 cubic feet = 1.308 cubic yards

1 RT — *Registertonne* register ton = 2,832 m³ = 100 cubic feet

IV. Measure of Capacity

1 l — *Liter* lit|re, *Am.* -er = 1.760 pints = *U.S.* 1.057 liquid quarts *or* 0.906 dry quart

1 hl — *Hektoliter* hectolit|re, *Am.* -er = 100 l = 2.75 bushels = *U.S.* 26.418 gallons

V. Weight

1 g — *Gramm* gram(me) = 15.432 grains

1 Pfd. — *Pfund* pound (German) = 500 g = 1.102 pounds avdp.

1 kg — *Kilogramm* kilogram(me) = 1000 g = 2.205 pounds avdp. = 2.679 pounds troy

1 Ztr. — *Zentner* centner = 100 Pfd. = 0.984 hundredweight = 1.102 *U.S.* hundredweights

1 dz — *Doppelzentner* = 100 kg = 1.968 hundredweights = 2.204 *U.S.* hundredweights

1 t — *Tonne* ton = 1000 kg = 0.984 long ton = *U.S.* 1.102 short tons

American and British Weights and Measures

1. Linear Measure

1 inch (in.) = 2,54 cm
1 foot (ft)
= 12 inches = 30,48 cm
1 yard (yd)
= 3 feet = 91,439 cm
1 perch (p.)
= 5 1/2 yards = 5,029 m
1 mile (m.)
= 1,760 yards = 1,609 km

2. Nautical Measure

1 fathom (f., fm)
= 6 feet = 1,829 m
1 nautical mile
= 6,080 feet = 1853,18 m

3. Square Measure

1 square inch (sq. in.)
= 6,452 cm²
1 square foot (sq. ft)
= 144 square inches
= 929,029 cm²
1 square yard (sq. yd)
= 9 square feet = 8361,26 cm²
1 square perch (sq. p.)
= 30 1/4 square yards = 25,293m²
1 rood
= 40 square perches = 10,117 a
1 acre (a.) = 4 roods = 40,47 a
1 square mile
= 640 acres = 258,998 ha

4. Cubic Measure

1 cubic inch (cu. in.)
= 16,387 cm³
1 cubic foot (cu. ft)
= 1,728 cubic inches = 0,028 m³
1 cubic yard (cu. yd)
= 27 cubic feet = 0,765 m³
1 register ton (reg. ton)
= 100 cubic feet = 2,832 m³

5. Measure of Capacity
Dry and Liquid Measure

1 British *or* imperial gill (gl, gi.)
= 0,142 l
1 British *or* imperial pint (pt)
= 4 gills = 0,568 l
1 British *or* imperial quart (qt)
= 2 pints = 1,136 l
1British*or*imp. gallon(imp. gal.)
= 4 imperial quarts = 4,546 l

Dry Measure

1 British *or* imperial peck (pk)
= 2 imperial gallons = 9,092 l
1 Brit. *or* imp. bushel (bu., bus.)
= 8 imperial gallons = 36,366 l

1 Brit. *or* imp. quarter (qr)
= 8 imperial bushels = 290,935 l

Liquid Measure

1 Brit. *or* imp. barrel (bbl, bl)
= 36 imperial gallons = 163,656 l

*

1 U.S. dry pint = 0,551 l
1 U.S. dry quart
= 2 dry pints = 1,101 l
1 U.S. dry gallon
= 4 dry quarts = 4,405 l
1 U.S. peck
= 2 dry gallons = 8,809 l
1 U.S. bushel
= 8 dry gallons = 35,238 l
1 U.S. gill = 0,118 l
1 U.S. liquid pint
= 4 gills = 0,473 l
1 U.S. liquid quart
= 2 liquid pints = 0,946 l
1 U.S. liquid gallon
= 8 liquid pints = 3,785 l
1 U.S. barrel
= 3 1/8 liquid gallons = 119,228 l
1 U.S. barrel petroleum
= 42 liquid gallons = 158,97 l

6. Avoirdupois Weight

1 grain (gr.) = 0,065 g
1 dram (dr.)
= 27.344 grains = 1,772 g
1 ounce (oz.)
= 16 drams = 28,35 g
1 pound (lb.)
= 16 ounces = 453,592 g
1 quarter (qr)
= 28 pounds = 12,701 kg
(*U.S.A.* 25 pounds
= 11,339 kg)
1 hundredweight (cwt.)
= 112 pounds
= 50,802 kg (*U.S.A.* 100 pounds
= 45,359 kg)
1 ton (t.)
(*a.* long ton) = 20 hundredweights = 1016,05 kg (*U.S.A.*,
a. short ton, = 907,185 kg)
1 stone (st.) = 14 pounds = 6,35 kg

7. Troy Weight

1 grain = 0,065 g
1 pennyweight (dwt.)
= 24 grains = 1,555 g
1 ounce
= 20 pennyweights = 31,103 g
1 pound = 12 ounces = 373,242 g

g. gramme g, Gramm n; guinea Guinee f (21 Schilling).

Ga. Georgia.

gal. gallon Gallone f.

G.A.T.T. General Agreement on Tariffs and Trade Allgemeines Zoll- und Handelsabkommen.

G.B. Great Britain Großbritannien n.

G.I. government issue von der Regierung ausgegeben; Staatseigentum n; fig. der amer. Soldat.

Glos. Gloucestershire.

G.P.O. General Post Office Hauptpostamt n.

gr. gross brutto.

Gt.Br. Great Britain Großbritannien n.

h. hour(s) Std., Stunde(n pl.) f.

Hants. Hampshire.

H.C. House of Commons Unterhaus n.

Heref. Herefordshire.

Herts. Hertfordshire.

hf. half halb.

H.I. Hawaiian Islands.

H.L. House of Lords Oberhaus n.

H.M. His (Her) Majesty Seine (Ihre) Majestät.

H.M.S. His (Her) Majesty's Service Dienst m, & Dienstsache f; His (Her) Majesty's Ship Seiner (Ihrer) Majestät Schiff n.

H.O. Home Office brit. Innenministerium n. [stärke f.]

H.P., h.p. horse-power PS, Pferdestärke f.

H.Q., Hq. Headquarters Stab(squartier n) m, Hauptquartier n.

H.R. House of Representatives Repräsentantenhaus n (der U.S.A.).

H.R.H. His (Her) Royal Highness Seine (Ihre) Königliche Hoheit f.

Hunts. Huntingdonshire.

Ia. Iowa.

I.C.B.M. intercontinental ballistic missile interkontinentaler ballistischer Flugkörper.

I.D. Intelligence Department Nachrichtenamt n.

Id(a). Idaho. [d.h., das heißt.]

i.e. id est (lateinisch = that is to say))

Ill. Illinois.

I.M.F. International Monetary Fund Weltwährungsfonds m.

in. inch(es) Zoll m od. pl. [gen.]

Inc. Incorporated (amtlich) eingetragen)

Ind. Indiana.

I.O.C. International Olympic Committee Internationales Olympisches Komitee.

Ir. Ireland Irland n; Irish irisch.

I.R.C. International Red Cross Internationales Rotes Kreuz.

J.P. Justice of the Peace Friedensrichter m.

Kan(s). Kansas.

k.o. knock(ed) out Boxen: k.o. (ge-) schlagen; fig. erledigen (erledigt).

Ky. Kentucky.

£ pound sterling Pfund n Sterling.

La. Louisiana.

Lancs. Lancashire. [wicht).]

lb. pound(s) Pfund n od. pl. (Ge-)

L.C. letter of credit Kreditbrief)

Leics. Leicestershire. [m.]

Lincs. Lincolnshire.

LP long-playing Langspiel...(Platte).

L.P. Labour Party (brit. Arbeiterpartei). [tung.]

Ltd. limited mit beschränkter Haf-)

m. male männlich; metre m, Meter n, m; mile Meile f; minute Min., Minute f. [Philosophie.]

M.A. Master of Arts Magister m der)

Mass. Massachusetts.

M.D. Medicinae Doctor (lateinisch = Doctor of Medicine) Dr. med., Doktor m der Medizin.

Md. Maryland.

Me. Maine.

mi. mile Meile f.

Mich. Michigan.

Middx. Middlesex.

Minn. Minnesota.

Miss. Mississippi.

Mo. Missouri.

M.O. money order Postanweisung f.

Mon. Monmouthshire.

Mont. Montana.

MP, M.P. Member of Parliament Parlamentsabgeordnete m; Military Police Militärpolizei f.

m.p.h. miles per hour Stundenmei-)

Mr Mister Herr m. [len pl.]

Mrs Mistress Frau f.

Mt. Mount Berg m.

N. north Nord(en m); northern nörd-)

n. noon Mittag m. lich.)

NASA National Aeronautics and Space Administration (amer. Luftfahrt- und Raumforschungsbehörde).

NATO North Atlantic Treaty Organization Nordatlantikpakt-Organisation f.

N.C. North Carolina.

N.D(ak). North Dakota.

Neb(r). Nebraska.

Nev. Nevada.

N.H. New Hampshire.

N.H.S. National Health Service Nationaler Gesundheitsdienst (brit. Krankenversicherung).

N.J. New Jersey.

N.M(ex). New Mexico.

Norf. Norfolk.

Northants. Northamptonshire.

Northumb. Northumberland.

Notts. Nottinghamshire.

nt. net netto.

N.Y. New York. [York.]

N.Y.C. New York City Stadt f New)

O. Ohio; order Auftrag m.

O.A.S. Organization of American States Organisation f amerikanischer Staaten.

O.E.E.C. *Organization of European Economic Co-operation* Organisation *f* für europäische wirtschaftliche Zusammenarbeit.
Okla. *Oklahoma.*
Ore(g). *Oregon.*
Oxon. *Oxfordshire.*

Pa. *Pennsylvania.*
P.A.A. *Pan-American Airways* Pan-amer. Luftfahrtgesellschaft *f.*
P.C. *police constable* Schutzmann *m.*
p.c. *per cent* %, Prozent *n od. pl.*
pd. *paid* bezahlt.
P.E.N., *mst* **PEN Club** *Poets, Playwrights, Editors, Essayists, and Novelists* Pen-Club *m*, *(Internationale Vereinigung von Dichtern, Dramatikern, Redakteuren, Essayisten und Romanschriftstellern).*
Penn(a). *Pennsylvania.*
Ph.D. *Philosophiae Doctor (lateinisch = Doctor of Philosophy)* Dr. phil., Doktor *m* der Philosophie.
p.m. *post meridiem (lateinisch = after noon)* nachmittags, abends.
P.O. *Post Office* Postamt *n*; *postal order* Postanweisung *f.*
P.O.B. *Post Office Box* Postschließfach *n.*
P.S. *Postscript* P.S., Nachschrift *f.*
P.T.O., p.t.o. *please turn over* b.w., bitte wenden.
PX *Post Exchange (Verkaufsläden der amer. Streitkräfte).*

R.A.F. *Royal Air Force* Königlich-Brit. Luftwaffe *f.*
Rd. *Road* Straße *f.*
ref(c). *(In) reference (to) (in)* Bezug *m* (auf); Empfehlung *f.*
regd. *registered* eingetragen; ⸺ eingeschrieben. [tonne *f.*⸜
reg. tn. *register ton* RT, Register-⸜
resp. *respective(ly)* bzw., beziehungsweise.
ret. *retired* i.R., im Ruhestand.
Rev. *Reverend* Ehrwürden.
R.I. *Rhode Island.* Marine *f.*⸜
R.N. *Royal Navy* Königlich-Brit.⸜
R.R. *Railroad Am.* Eisenbahn *f.*
Rutland. *Rutlandshire.*
Ry. *Railway* Eisenbahn *f.*

S. *south* Süd(en *m*); *southern* südlich.
s. *second(s)* Sek., Sekunde(n *pl.*) *f*; *shilling(s)* Schilling *m od. pl.*
$ *dollar* Dollar *m.*
S.A. *South Africa* Südafrika *n*; *South America* Südamerika *n.*
Salop *Shropshire.*
S.C. *South Carolina; Security Council* Sicherheitsrat *m (U.N.).*
S.D(ak). *South Dakota.*
SEATO *South East Asia Treaty Organization* Südostasienpakt-Organisation *f.*
sh. *shilling(s)* Schilling *m od. pl.*
Soc. *society* Gesellschaft *f*; Verein *m.*

Som. *Somersetshire.*
Sq. *Square* Platz *m.*
sq. *square* ... Quadrat...
Staffs. *Staffordshire.*
St(.) *Saint* ... Sankt ...; *Station* Bahnhof *m*; *Street* Straße *f.*
Suff. *Suffolk.*
suppl. *supplement* Nachtrag *m.*
Sur. *Surrey.*
Suss. *Sussex.*

t. *ton(s)* Tonne(n *pl.*) *f.*
Tenn. *Tennessee.*
Tex. *Texas.*
T.M.O. *telegraph money order* telegraphische Geldanweisung.
T.O. *Telegraph (Telephone) Office* Telegraphen- (Fernsprech)amt *n*
T.U. *Trade(s) Union(s)* Gewerkschaft(en *pl.*) *f.*
T.U.C. *Trade(s) Union Congress brit.* Gewerkschaftsverband *m.*

U.K. *United Kingdom* Vereinigtes Königreich *(England, Schottland, Wales und Nordirland).*
U.N. *United Nations* Vereinte Nationen *pl.*
UNESCO *United Nations Educational, Scientific, and Cultural Organization* Organisation *f* der Vereinten Nationen für Wissenschaft, Erziehung und Kultur.
U.N.S.C. *United Nations Security Council* Sicherheitsrat *m* der Vereinten Nationen.
U.P.I. *United Press International (amer. Nachrichtenagentur).*
U.S.(A.) *United States (of America)* Vereinigte Staaten *pl.* (von Ame-⸝
Ut. *Utah.* [rika.)⸝

Va. *Virginia.*
vol(s). *volume(s)* Band *m* (Bände⸝
Vt. *Vermont.* [*pl.*).⸝
V.T.O.(L.) *vertical take-off (and landing) (aircraft)* Senkrechtstart(er) *m.*

W. *west* West(en *m*); *western* west-⸝
War. *Warwickshire.* [lich.⸝
Wash. *Washington.*
W.C. *West Central (London)* Mitte-West *(Postbezirk).*
W.F.T.U. *World Federation of Trade Unions* Weltgewerkschaftsbund *m.*
W.H.O. *World Health Organization* Weltgesundheitsorganisation *f (U.N.).*
W.I. *West Indies* Westindien *n.*
Wilts. *Wiltshire.*
Wis. *Wisconsin.*
Worcs. *Worcestershire.*
wt. *weight* Gewicht *n.*
W.Va. *West Virginia.*
Wyo. *Wyoming.*

yd. *yard(s)* Elle(n *pl.*) *f.*
Yorks. *Yorkshire.*